Schroeder's
ANTIQUES
Price Guide

COLLECTOR BOOKS

A Division of Schroeder Publishing Co., Inc.

COLLECTOR BOOKS
P.O. Box 3009
Paducah, Kentucky 42002-3009

www.collectorbooks.com

The current values in this book should be used only as a guide. They are not
intended to set prices, which vary from one section of the country to another.
Auction prices as well as dealer prices vary greatly and are affected by condition
as well as demand. Neither the editors nor the publisher assumes responsibility
for any losses that might be incurred as a result of consulting this guide.

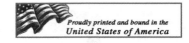

Proudly printed and bound in the
United States of America

Schroeder's: Satisfying the Collecting Bug

by Donald-Brian Johnson

collect: /kə'lekt/ v. to acquire, accumulate, gather together.
collector: n. one who collects.

There's no doubt about it; becoming a collector is as easy as one, two, three:

ONE: Buy a knickknack.

TWO: Buy a second. Now you have a matched pair.

THREE: Buy a third. Now you have a collection. (Or at least the start of one.)

The collecting bug bites at an early age — and once bitten, there's no cure. A boy who spends his formative years pawing through the latest Superman comics, until the corners crease and the staples give way, may one day grow up to collect. . .well, Superman comics. The girl who played with her Barbie dolls until their hair frizzed and their heads bobbled can, as an adult, keep that curvaceous collection going, since newly minted Barbie dolls continue to join the statuesque lineup.

As grownups though, we often let the joy leach out of our collecting habit. Nowadays, those prized Superman comics, with nary a bent edge among them, are securely stored in acid-free, archival sleeves. Only occasionally are they taken out and admired by a lint-free, white-gloved hand. As for Barbie, playtime is over. Her fate is life on a display shelf, nestled among the rows of her designer-gowned sisterhood, each serenely suffocating in the original cardboard and plastic packaging.

Hmmm. Acid-free sleeves. White gloves. Unopened boxes. That doesn't sound like much fun, does it?

The secret to being a contented collector is to not only enjoy collecting — but also to enjoy what you collect! If your treasures remain forever under guard, under wraps, and off-limits, they might as well remain where you first found them. Acquisition is only the first step. Appreciation (and sharing that appreciation) is the next — and the most important.

That's where *Schroeder's* comes in.

Now in its 29th edition, *Schroeder's Antiques Price Guide* is key to developing and nurturing an appreciation of the collecting experience. Since its inception, *Schroeder's* has provided collectors, and collectors-to-be, with the informational building blocks necessary to grow a collection. Long before the days of the omnipresent internet, with information (valid or not), just a mouse-click away, *Schroeder's* was there, offering clear, concise, and up-to-the-minute commentaries on every item imaginable, from 'A' ('ABC Plates') to 'Z' ('Zsolnay') — a veritable cornucopia of collecting topics.

What makes paging through the guide such fun is that you never can be sure what treasure (or would-be treasure) awaits you on the next page. It could be something you've heard about or something totally new on your personal collecting horizon (many categories are unique to this publication). Chances are, while thumbing through the latest edition in search of subjects nearest and dearest to your heart, you've often found yourself happily sidetracked: 'Wow! Mustache Cups! My granddad had one of those!' Before you know it, another collection is born.

If an antique was manufactured in any discernible quantity, you can be sure that nowadays there's someone, somewhere, who collects it. And that means that, sooner or later, it will be starring in the pages of *Schroeder's*. While not every listing will appeal to your individual collecting taste, one and all are certainly enjoyable to read about. And, best of all, these are the sort of things that actually turn up at antique shops and shows, at garage sales and flea markets. In other words, what you read about in *Schroeder's* is actually within reach. Maybe not today or tomorrow. But someday.

What makes *Schroeder's* so special?

- *Multiple categories, compiled by multiple expert advisors.* Each edition offers in the neighborhood of 750 categories — and 38,000 price listings! The information is provided by advisors well-versed in their specific areas of expertise, guaranteeing both accuracy and in-depth knowledge of the subject. Succinct intros provide helpful histories, while annually updated single-line price listings, with readily understandable abbreviations, reflect current, reliable market values. And, should more details be needed, a 'by state' Directory of advisors paves the way for additional contact (and possible shops to visit on your next antiquing jaunt.)

- *Color photos.* Gone are the days when antiquers had to make a purchase, cross their fingers, and hope for the best. The crisp color photos accompanying each *Schroeder's* category offer a clear depiction of what to look for. No more 'pigs in a poke.' When riffling through *Schroeder's* at a show or sale, it's easy to locate a visual representation of the item you're considering for purchase (even if you're not exactly sure what it's called). Handy color reference photos save shoppers time — and money.

- *Clubs and contacts.* Captivated by Ceramic Arts Studio? Fond of Fenton? Daffy for Dragonware? A comprehensive all-in-one-place listing of clubs, newsletters, and websites makes it easy to connect with those who share your collecting interests. There's also a comprehensive checklist of auction houses nationwide, including their areas of specialization, so you know at a glance where to go to buy (or sell).

- *A format that's easy to follow.* Here's a major *Schroeder's* advantage: the index listings are all alphabetical and complete. Now this may seem a given, but in many reference guides, it isn't. If, while rummaging about in a dusty antique shop, you stumble across a potential 'find,' you want to know all about it — and right away, too. Perhaps it's a lamp by a specific manufacturer or of a specific type. With *Schroeder's* straight-up organization, you head directly to the index, look up the manufacturer or product name, and, in a snap, locate the correct page in the Lamps section. (There's cross-referencing too, especially helpful with items that fall into more than one category.) For those who've experienced the frustration of references equipped with 'general' indexes. . .or 'partial' indexes. . .or, worst of all, *no* indexes. . .the *Schroeder's* thoroughness proves as refreshing as a spring rain.

- *A healthy helping of no-nonsense common sense.* When just starting out as a collector (and later, as a writer), I found *Schroeder's* to be a treasure trove of rock-solid, down-to-earth advice on 'the basics' of the collecting experience. I still do. Each year's edition makes a point of stressing those collecting basics — and each year, they bear repeating:

     'Since *Schroeder's* cannot provide all available information on antiques and collectibles, there are other sources available that you may want to pursue. The local library is always a good place to start; check their section on reference books. Museums are public facilities that are willing and able to help you establish the origin, and possibly even the value of your particular treasure. A more recent source of information is the world of e-commerce, where many websites provide pertinent, up-to-date information. Another alternative: the 'yellow pages' of your phone book; phone books from other cities are available from your library or the telephone company office. The 'Antique Dealers' heading in the yellow pages is a good place to start. Look for qualified appraisers (this may be mentioned in their advertisement). Always remember that a dealer interested in buying your merchandise will set a price low enough that he will be able to make a reasonable profit when the item is sold.

'Unless you are able to visit a dealer or an appraiser directly, you'll need to take photographs. Don't send photos that are under- or over-exposed, out of focus, or shot against a background that detracts from important details. It's almost impossible to provide a value judgment based on photos of poor quality. Shoot the front, top, and the bottom, describe any marks and number (or send a pencil rubbing), give accurate measurements, and explain how and when you acquired the article, along with any further background information that may be helpful. Appraisers and auction houses make their living at providing this information; expect to pay a reasonable fee for their services and expertise. You are, of course, never under an obligation to sell or consign an item (especially if you disagree with the appraised value).

'Each up and down of the economy presents opportunities for both buyers and sellers. Location and demand will always affect pricing. Our best advice: buy what you like, and buy the best you can afford.'

Now those are words to the wise that each and every collector can (and should) take to heart.

Collectors. There are young ones, old ones, and in-between ones. There are collectors who can't wait for the next high-end antiques show, and collectors who can't wait for the next neighborhood garage sale. There are a great many more who can't wait for either.

But, whether just starting out on the hunt or looking back on a lifetime of accumulating treasures, each and every collector shares two things in common: a passion for what they collect and a passionate desire to learn everything they can about it.

For 29 years, *Schroeder's* has both satisfied and stoked the collecting urge. This essential reference provides much more than the answers to 'what's this?' and 'what's it worth?' (although, don't get me wrong—those elements are important, too!). The knowledge *Schroeder's* imparts helps give a collection its foundation. After all, without its back story, a collection, no matter how elegant or exotic, is just another pile of 'stuff.' By celebrating the past, *Schroeder's Antiques Price Guide* builds interest for the future. That ongoing interest offers readers (and writers, too) the invaluable opportunity to explore new and varied vistas. It keeps the collecting bug biting.

Now, take those comics out of their acid-free sleeves. Release Barbie from her packaging. Read. Remember. And *enjoy!*

Donald-Brian Johnson is the co-author of numerous books on collectibles, including *Postwar Pop*; *Deco Décor*; *Higgins: Adventures in Glass*; *Higgins: Poetry in Glass*; *Moss Lamps: Lighting the '50s*; *Specs Appeal*; *Whiting & Davis Purses: The Perfect Mesh*; *Popular Purses: It's In the Bag!*; *Ceramic Arts Studio: The Legacy of Betty Harrington*; and a four-book series on the Chase Brass & Copper Co. Mr. Johnson's syndicated column, 'Smack Dab in the Middle: Design Trends of the Mid-Twentieth Century,' runs monthly in antique papers nationwide. He also writes frequently for such publications as *Antiques & Collecting Magazine*, *The Old Times*, *Antiques & Auction News*, *Collectors News*, *Modernism*, and *Paper & Advertising Collectors' Marketplace*. Please address inquiries to: donaldbrian@msn.com

Editorial Staff

Managing Editor
Amy Sullivan

Scanning & Digital Image Technician
Donna Ballard

Copy Editor
Laurie Swick

Layout and Cover Design
Terri Hunter

On the Cover

Front cover: **American Indian Art, pipe, Catlinite, egg-shaped bowl clutched in eagle talons, bowl: 2x3", $1,000.00** (Photo courtesy James D. Julia Inc.). **Knife, Case, XX USA, 5172, Bulldog, India stag handle, $125.00** (Photo courtesy Ron Stewart and Roy Ritchie). **Doll, Gebruder Heubach, #8971, character child, pink bisque throughout, mohair wig, fully articulated composition body, 15", $1,440.00** (Photo courtesy Skinner Auctioneers and Appraisers of Antiques and Fine Art). **Libbey Glass, compote, 12-ribbed morning glory form, circular logo, 8", $875.00** (Photo courtesy Cincinnati Art Galleries, LLC on LiveAuctioneers.com). **Lamp, reverse painted, Moe Bridges, black enamel base, 24", $6,000.00** (Photo courtesy David Rago Auctions). **Jewelry, costume, earrings, clip, light blue moonstone cabochon stones, baguette rhinestones, Jomaz, 1952 – 1955, 1", $75.00 to $100.00** (Photo courtesy Julia C. Carroll, Costume Jewelry 202, 2nd Edition). **Bank, mechanical, Bad Accident, N-1150, cast iron, EX, $3,500.00** (Photo courtesy Morphy Auctions on LiveAuctioneers.com). **Royal Copley, planter, deer and fawn, 9¼", $32.00** (Photo courtesy T & S Auction Company on LiveAuctioneers.com). **Carnival glass, Grape and Cable (Northwood), bowl, amethyst, 8" – 9", $55.00** (Photo courtesy Mike Carwile). **Stickley, L. & J.G., table, #516, unsigned, 29x27x27", VG, $8,400.00** (Photo courtey Treadway Gallery, Inc. on LiveAuctioneers.com). **Hummel, #471, Harmony in Four Parts, TMK-6: Goebel West Germany, 1989, 9¾", $1,440.00** (Photo courtesy Jackson's International Auctioneers & Appraisers of Fine Art & Antiques). **Paperweight, Rick Ayotte, Blueberry Morning, 4", $1,680.00** (Photo courtesy San Rafael Auction Gallery on LiveAuctioneers.com). **Morton Pottery, Midwest Potteries, Inc. sunfish, hand airbrushed decoration, 11", $30.00** (Photo courtesy Doris and Burdell Hall). Back cover: **Webb, Cameo, bowl, blue and white on cobalt, Gem mark, 3¾", $11,400.00** (Photo courtesy Skinner Auctioneers and Appraisers of Antiques and Fine Art on LiveAuctioneers.com).

On the Title Page

Knife, Case, XX USA, 5172, Bulldog, India stag handle, $125.00 (Photo courtesy Ron Stewart and Roy Ritchie). **German porcelain, plaque, Alpenfee (after Bernard), signed Sontag, museum mounted, 27x25", $660.00** (Photo courtesy Burchard Galleries on LiveAuctioneers.com). **Boehm, Gyr Falcon #10178, Rusticlos, limited edition, circa 1990, 34x32", $1,560.00** (Photo courtesy Dallas Auction Gallery on LiveAuctioneers.com). **Roseville, Wisteria, vase, #682, tan, 9", $500.00 to $550.00** (Photo courtesy Cincinnati Art Galleries, LLC on LiveAuctioneers.com). **Jewelry, costume, brooches, Juliana, butterflies, each $195.00** (Photo courtesy Marcia 'Sparkles' Brown).

Listing of Standard Abbreviations

The following is a list of abbreviations that have been used throughout this book in order to provide you with the most detailed descriptions possible in the limited space available. No periods are used after initials or abbreviations. When two dimensions are given, height is noted first. If only one dimension is listed, it will be height, except in the case of bowls, dishes, plates, or platters, when it will be diameter. The standard two-letter state abbreviations apply.

For glassware, if no color is noted, the glass is clear. Hyphenated colors, for example blue-green, olive-amber, etc., describe a single color tone; colors divided by a slash mark indicate two or more colors, i.e. blue/white. Biscuit jars, teapots, sugar bowls, and butter dishes are assumed to be 'with cover.' Condition is extremely important in determining market value. Common sense suggests that art pottery, china, and glassware values would be given for examples in pristine, mint condition, while suggested prices for utility wares such as redware, mocha, and blue and white stoneware, for example, reflect the probability that since such items were subjected to everyday use in the home they may show minor wear (which is acceptable) but no notable damage. Values for other categories reflect the best average condition in which the particular collectible is apt to be offered for sale without the dealer feeling it necessary to mention wear or damage. A basic rule of thumb is that an item listed as VG (very good) will bring 40% to 60% of its mint price — a first-hand, personal evaluation will enable you to make the final judgement; EX (excellent) is a condition midway between mint and very good, and values would correspond.

AD............after dinner	Fed............Federal	Pat............patented
alum............aluminum	fr............frame, framed	pc(s)............piece(s)
Am............American	Fr............French	ped............pedestal
appl............applied	ft, ftd............foot, feet, footed	pg(s)............page(s)
att............attributed to	G............good	pk............pink
bbl............barrel	gr............green	pkg............package
bk............back	grad............graduated	pnt............paint(ed), painting
bkgrnd............background	grnd............ground	poly............polychrome
bl............blue	grpt............grain painted	pr............pair
blk............black	H............high, height	porc............porcelain
b/o............battery operated	Hplwht............Hepplewhite	Pro............Productions
brd............board	hdl(s), hdld............handle(s), handled	prof............professional
brn............brown	HP............hand painted	pwt............paperweight
bsk............bisque	illus............illustration, illustrated by	QA............Queen Anne
bulb............bulbous	imp............impressed	re............regarding
b3m............blown 3-mold	ind............individual	rect............rectangle, rectangular
C............century	int............interior	rfn............refinished
c............copyright	Invt T'print............Inverted Thumbprint	rnd............round
ca............circa	irid............iridescent	rpl............replaced
cb............cardboard	jtd............jointed	rpr............repaired
Chpndl............Chippendale	L............length, long	rpt............repainted
CI............cast iron	lav............lavender	rstr............restored
Co............Company	ldgl............leaded glass	rtcl............reticulated
compo............composition	lg............large	rvpt............reverse painted
cr/sug............creamer and sugar	litho............lithograph	s&p............salt and pepper
c/s............cup and saucer	lt............light	sgn............signed
cvd............carved	ltd............limited	sm............small
cvg............carving	M............mint	SP............silverplated
dbl............double	mahog............mahogany	sq............square
dc............die cut	mc............multicolor(ed)	std............standard
decor............decorated, decoration	mfg............manufacturing/manufacturer	str............straight
demi............demitasse	mg............milk glass	sz............size
dia............diameter	MIB............mint in box	trn............turned, turning
dk............dark	MIG............Made in Germany	turq............turquoise
dmn............diamond	MIJ............Made in Japan	unmk............unmarked
Dmn Quilt............Diamond Quilted	min............minimum value	uphl............upholstered
drw............drawer	MIP............mint in package	VG............very good
dtd............dated	mk............mark	Vict............Victorian
dvtl............dovetail	MOC............mint on card	vnr............veneer
ea............each	mono............monochrome	W............width
ed............edition	MOP............mother-of-pearl	WDE............Walt Disney Enterprises
emb............embossed, embossing	mt, mtd............mount, mounted	wht............white
embr............embroidered	NE............New England	w/............with
Emp............Empire	NM............near mint	w/o............without
eng............engraved, engraving	NRFB............never removed from box	X, Xd............cross, crossed
EPNS............electroplated nickel silver	NP............nickel plated	x............times (i.e. 4x)
EX............excellent	opal............opalescent	yr(s)............year(s)
EXIB............excellent in box	orig............original	yel............yellow
EXOC............excellent on card	o/l............overlay	(+)............has been reproduced
ext............exterior	o/w............otherwise	

ABC Plates

Children's china featuring the alphabet as part of the design has been made from the late eighteenth century up to the present day. The earliest creamware items, plates, and mugs were often decorated with embossed or printed letters and prim, moralistic verses or illustrations and were made in Staffordshire, England. In later years they were made by American potters as well, and varied pictures of animals, events, famous people, and childhood activities became popular design themes. All were decorated by the transfer method, and many had colors brushed on for added interest.

Be sure to inspect these plates carefully for damage, since condition is a key price-assessing factor, and aside from obvious chips and hairlines, even wear can substantially reduce their values. Another problem for collectors is the fact that there are current reproductions of glass and tin plates, particularly the glass plate referred to as Emma (child's face in center) and a tin plate showing children with hoops. These plates are so common as to be worthless as collectibles. Our advisor for this category is Dr. Joan George; she is listed in the Directory under New Jersey.

Ceramic

Abraham Lincoln, red transfer, unmk, 7½"................................500.00
Aesop's Fables, crow & the pitcher, Pountney & Allies, 1816-35, 6½"..175.00
Aesop's Fables, lion & the mouse, unmk, 7"................................230.00
Aesop's Fables, man & boy carrying donkey, red transfer, 7"........135.00
Animated Conundrums, red outline, unmk Staffordshire, 5".......225.00
April, unmk Staffordshire, 6¾"................................150.00

Arrival of General McClellan, unmarked Staffordshire, 6", EX+, $350.00. (Photo courtesy Heritage Auctions on LiveAuctioneers.com)

B, Boat, Bat, Ball, unmk Staffordshire, 5"................................225.00
Bear w/Cubs, Wild Animals series, mc transfer, Brownhills Pottery, 1872-96, 7½"..250.00
Candle Fish (The), Indians in canoe, CA & Sons, England, blk transfer, 6½"..160.00
Cats shaking hands, blk transfer, red outline, H Aynsley & Co, Longton England, 6"..275.00
Chinese Amusement — My Pretty Pheasant, red transfer, unmk, 5"..130.00
Crusoe Making a Boat, bl transfer, England Rd No 69963, Brownhills Pottery Co, 6"..175.00
Dr Franklin's Maxims, By diligence & perseverance..., bl transfer, unmk, 7"..150.00
F Is for the Fowls..., red transfer, 7"................................150.00
Finding of Moses (The), blk transfer, HC Edmiston, England, saucer, 4¾"..125.00
Franklin's Proverbs, Dost Though Love Life..., unmk Staffordshire, 7".165.00
Frolics of Youth — Don't I Look Like Papa, unmk Staffordshire, 7"...175.00
Garden Flower (The), mc transfer, 8"................................145.00
Girls playing music & tambourine, Edge Malkin & Co, England, 8¼"..150.00
In a Soft Place, 2 cats in basket, Adams, 7"................................125.00
Machinery Hall, World's Fair Chicago, red transfer, Brownhills Pottery, unmk, 6¼"..135.00
Nursery Rhymes, Goosey Goosey Gander, mc transfer, unmk, 8½"..230.00
Nursery Tales, Cinderella, Brownhills Pottery, RD No 75,500, 7¼".275.00
Pretty Child on Tiptoe Stands to Reach the Piano with Her Hands (The), 7¼".175.00
Punch & Judy, blk transfer, CA & Sons, England, 6¾"................140.00
Rugby, brn transfer, CA & Sons England, 6¾"................................160.00
Snuffing, unmk Staffordshire, 5"................................275.00
Tired of Play, Staffordshire, 5"................................150.00
Zebra, blk transfer, bl outline, Powell & Bishop, 1876-78, 6".......150.00

Glass

Clock, ABCs, Roman & std numerals, scalloped rim, vaseline, 7"...75.00
Dog's head etched in clear, emb rim, Higbee, 6½" (+)....................75.00
Emma (child's face), ABC rim, vaseline, Clay's Crystal Works, 8"...35.00
Months, days, clock face & scalloped ABC rim, unmk, 7"............60.00
President Garfield, ABC rim, clear & frosted................................80.00
Rooster, smooth rim, unmk, 6", $65 to................................75.00
Sancho Panza & Dapple center, unmk, 6", $50 to........................75.00
Stork among rushes, clear & frosted, 6", NM................................85.00
Stork, marigold carnival, 7½"................................95.00

Tin

George Washington, 13 stars, 5⅝", VG................................75.00
Geometric center, emb ABC rim, 2¼"................................55.00
Lion, emb ABC rim, ca 1860s, 2¾"................................125.00
Victorian girl on swing, mc litho, Ohio Art, early 1900s, 8"..........65.00
Who Killed Cock Robin?, unmk, 7¾"................................55.00

Abingdon

From 1934 until 1950, the Abingdon Pottery Co. of Abingdon, Illinois, made a line of art pottery with a white vitrified body decorated with various types of glazes in many lovely colors. Novelties, cookie jars, utility ware, and lamps were made in addition to several lines of simple yet striking art ware. Fern Leaf, introduced in 1937, featured molded vertical feathering. La Fleur, in 1939, consisted of flowerpots and flower-arranger bowls with rows of vertical ribbing. Classic, 1939 – 1940, was a line of vases, many with evidence of Chinese influence. Several marks were used, most of which employed the company name. In 1950 the company reverted to the manufacture of sanitary ware that had been their mainstay before the artware division was formed.

Highly decorated examples and those with black, bronze, or red glaze usually command at least 25% higher prices.

For further information we recommend *Abingdon Pottery Artware 1934 – 1950, Stepchild of the Great Depression*, by Joe Paradis (Schiffer).

#30, vase, Chan, bronze................................225.00
#84, vase, What Not, 5"................................60.00
#101, vase, Alpha, 10"................................25.00

#104, vase, Delta, 10", $45.00.

#113, water jug................................95.00
#116, vase, Classic, 10"................................27.50
#149, flowerpot, La Fleur, 3"................................15.00
#158, candleholder, La Fleur, 2x3½", ea................................12.50
#258, lamp base, fluted shaft, 23"................................75.00
#305, bookends, Sea Gull, 6"................................85.00
#308D, jar, Coolie, 11"................................90.00
#322, goblet, Swedish, 6½"................................60.00
#324, vase, Rope, 6¼"................................20.00

#336, bowl, sq, 9" 35.00
#360, candleholders, Quatrain, sq, 3", pr 40.00
#365, jar, Dart Candy, 6" dia 65.00
#377, wall pocket, Morning Glory, 7½" 32.50
#412, floor vase, Volute, 15" 55.00
#424, bowl, Fern Leaf, 8½" 75.00
#426, flower boat, Fern Leaf, 4x13" 90.00
#432, fruit boat, Fern Leaf, 6½x15" 15.00
#463, vase, Star, 7½", $20 to 25.00
#513, vase, Double Cornucopia, 8" 32.00
#539, urn, Regency, 7" 22.00
#542, vase, Bali, 9" 75.00
#550, vase, Fluted, 11" 25.00
#568, mint compote, pk, 6" dia 25.00
#591, vase, Pleat, 10" 28.00
#610, bowl, Shell, deep, 9" 42.50
#615, ashtray, Chic, 4" dia 22.50

#616D, vase, Cactus with Sleeping Mexican, 6½x7", $55.00.

#672, planter, Fawn, 5" 38.00
#690D, range set, Daisy, 3-pc 45.00
#705, vase, Modern, 8" 20.00
Cookie jar, #471, Old Lady, plaid apron, min 400.00
Cookie jar, #495, Fat Boy, $250 to 300.00
Cookie jar, #549, Hippo, decor, 1942, $250 to 300.00
Cookie jar, #588, Money Bag, $45 to 50.00
Cookie jar, #602, Hobby Horse, $200 to 250.00
Cookie jar, #611, Jack-in-the-Box, $300 to 325.00
Cookie jar, #622, Miss Muffet 200.00
Cookie jar, #651, Choo Choo (Locomotive), blk/yel decor 145.00
Cookie jar, #653, Clock, 1949, $65 to 75.00
Cookie jar, #663, Humpty Dumpty, decor 200.00
Cookie jar, #664, Pineapple 65.00
Cookie jar, #665, Wigwam 200.00
Cookie jar, #674, Pumpkin, 1949, min 300.00
Cookie jar, #677, Daisy, 1949, $35 to 45.00
Cookie jar, #678, Windmill, $125 to 150.00
Cookie jar, #692, Witch, min 1,000.00
Cookie jar, #693, Little Girl, $80 to 95.00
Cookie jar, #694, Bo Peep (must have serial # & ink stamp) 300.00
Cookie jar, #695, Mother Goose 295.00
Cookie jar, #696, Three Bears, $90 to 115.00

Matthew Adams

In the 1950s a trading post in Alaska contacted Sascha Brastoff to design a line of porcelain with scenes of Eskimos, Alaskan motifs, and animals indigenous to that area. These items were to be sold in Alaska to the tourist trade.

Brastoff selected Matthew Adams, born in April 1915, to decorate the Alaska series. Pieces from the line have the Sascha B mark on the front; some have a pattern number on the reverse. They did not have the rooster back-stamp. (See the Sascha Brastoff category for information on this mark.)

After the Alaska series was introduced and proved to be successful, Matthew Adams left the employment of Sascha Brastoff (working three years there in all) and opened his own studio. Pieces made in his studio are signed Matthew Adams or Matt Adams in script and may have the word Alaska on the front.

Our advisor for this category is Steve Conti; he is listed in the Directory under California. He welcomes new information on this subject.

Ashtray, cabin on stilts, biomorphic shape, 8½" 25.00
Ashtray, Eskimo girl, 13" 75.00
Ashtray, hooded, walrus on brn bkgrnd, 5" 45.00
Bowl, caribou on forest gr bkgrnd, 11½" 95.00
Bowl, grizzly bear, freeform 6½" 40.00

Bowl, moose, gold trim, #190b, 8½x10", $50.00 to $60.00. (Photo courtesy Chuck Samus, eBay seller gc13)

Bowl, seal cub face, 9" 55.00
Box, glacier on bl, 12" 100.00
Box, 2 polar bears on wht grnd, 2¼x6" 65.00
Charger, caribou & cabin on stilts, 18" 160.00
Charger, walrus, 18" 160.00
Cigarette lighter, male Eskimo face, 6" 35.00
Creamer/sugar, seals, 5x5" 38.00
Ginger jar w/lid, walrus on turq bkgrnd, 6" 68.00
Lamp w/custom period shade, Eskimo & dogsled, 22" 120.00
Pitcher, grizzly bear, 11", w/six 4" tumblers 225.00
Plate, Eskimo mother & child, 10½" 60.00
Platter, rustic cabin, 12" 45.00
Shakers, rams on gr, 4", pr 35.00
Tile, mtn & glacier on blk, 10x8½" 90.00
Tray, polar bear on iceberg, #910, 13x9¾" 85.00
Vase, mtn & glacier on blk, #114, 12" 90.00
Vase, reindeer, 5" 45.00
Vase, walrus, 10" 100.00

Advertising

The advertising world has always been a fiercely competitive field. In an effort to present their product to the customer, every imaginable gimmick was put into play. Colorful and artfully decorated signs and posters, thermometers, tape measures, fans, hand mirrors, and attractive tin containers (all with catchy slogans, familiar logos, and often-bogus claims) are only a few of the many examples of early advertising memorabilia that are of interest to today's collectors.

Porcelain signs were made as early as 1890 and are highly prized for their artistic portrayal of life as it was then… often allowing amusing insights into the tastes, humor, and way of life of a bygone era. As a general rule, older signs are made from a heavier gauge metal. Those with three or more fired-on colors are especially desirable.

Tin containers were used to package consumer goods ranging from crackers and coffee to tobacco and talcum. After 1880 can companies began to decorate their containers by the method of lithography. Though colors were still subdued, intricate designs were used to attract the eye of the consumer. False labeling and unfounded claims were curtailed by the Pure Food and Drug Administration in 1906, and the name of the manufacturer as well as the brand name of the product had to be printed on the label. By 1910 color was rampant with more than a dozen hues printed on the tin or on paper labels. The tins themselves were often designed with a second use in mind, such as canisters, lunch boxes, even toy trains. As a general rule, tobacco-related tins are the most desirable, though personal preference may direct the interest of the collector to peanut butter pails with illustrations of children or talcum tins with irresistible babies or beautiful ladies. Coffee tins are popular, as are those made to contain a particularly successful or well-known product.

Perhaps the most visual of the early advertising gimmicks were the character logos, the Fairbank Company's Gold Dust Twins, the goose trademark of the Red Goose Shoe Company, Nabisco's ZuZu Clown and Uneeda Kid, the Campbell Kids, the RCA dog Nipper, and Mr. Peanut, to name only a few. Many early examples of these bring high prices on the market today.

Our listings are alphabetized by product name or, in lieu of that information, by word content or other pertinent description. Items are evaluated according to condition as stated in the line descriptions. When no condition code is present, assume items are in at least near mint condition. Remember that condition greatly affects value (especially true for tin items). For instance, a sign in excellent to near mint condition may bring twice as much as the same one in only very good condition, sometimes even more. On today's market, items in good to very good condition are slow to sell unless they are extremely rare.

Our advisor for advertising is B. J. Summers (see Directory, Kentucky); see specific subheads for other advisors. For further information we recommend *Hake's Price Guide to Character Toys* by Ted Hake; and *Antique & Contemporary Advertising Memorabilia, Collectible Soda Pop Memorabilia,* and *Value Guide to Gas Station Memorabilia,* all by B.J. Summers. *Garage Sale & Flea Market* is another good reference. See also Advertising Cards; Automobilia; Banks; Black Americana; Calendars; Coca-Cola; Cookbooks; Dolls, Advertising; Paperweights; Posters; Sewing Items; Thermometers.

Key:
cl — celluloid   sf — self-framed

Buster Brown

Buster Brown was the creation of cartoonist Richard Felton Outcault; his comic strip first appeared in the *New York Herald* on May 4, 1902. Since then Buster and his dog Tige (short for Tiger) have adorned sundry commercial products but are probably best known as the trademark for the Brown Shoe Company established early in the twentieth century. Today hundreds of Buster Brown premiums, store articles, and advertising items bring substantial prices from many serious collectors.

Key:
BB — Buster Brown

Display, tin, good restoration, 12x7x4", display condition: NM, $275.00 to $325.00. (Photo courtesy Dan Morphy Auctions, LLC on LiveAuctioneers.com)

Air tank inflator, fits on air/helium tank, 20x21x24", EX............. 150.00
Balloon blower, Fiberglas head w/orig pnt, 1960s, 24x21", EX, $350 to.400.00
Bank, pnt CI, BB & Tige, 5¼", EX... 480.00
Bank, pnt CI, horse/horseshoe w/BB & Tige, gold & blk, 4¼", EX, $240 to.275.00
Bank, pnt plaster, BB & Tige, 5x5x3", EX, $300 to 350.00

Banner, cloth, BB Shoes, BB & Tige, fringed bottom, 1900s, 12x9", EX.200.00
Bowl, porc, BB running w/Tige transfer on wht, Elkins NY, EX... 125.00
Clock, metal w/glass cover & face, lt-up, BB & Tige, Pam Clock Co, 15" dia, P...500.00
Comic book, BB's Antics, full color, Outcault, 1906, G 100.00
Cup, china, BB & Tige decal on wht, ca 1910, $45 to.................... 75.00
Door plate, blk & brass, BB & Tige above text, 5½x11¼", EX..... 150.00
Hobby horse, pnt wood, BB & Tige decal on pnt saddle, EX 300.00
Humidor, bsk, BB, bag mk Good Luck, pnt, mk JM C3505, 1920s, 8½".160.00
Mug, silver, emb BB & Tige/sunburst, mk Sterling, 3¼", VG....... 325.00
Pennant, felt, BB Guaranteed Hosiery, BB & Tige w/sock, 29", EX.240.00
Plaque, plaster, emb, BB & Tige, 12x12", EX................................. 275.00
Poster, BB & Tige, Felton/Outcault/Selchow & Righter, 24x18", EX. 1,325.00
Rocking chair, pnt wood, BB Shoes on bk rail, slat seat, 22", VG . 80.00
Rug, throw, rnd, shoe store w/BB & Tige on face, 54" dia, EX 315.00
Sign, neon, BB & Tige, Tige winks, Krin Signs, St Louis, 54x54x10", VG..4,200.00
Sign, rvpt in wood fr, BB Shoes, lights up, 10½x24½", VG.......... 210.00
Statuette, pnt chalkware, BB & Tige, dtd 1972, 19x11", VG....... 100.00
Target, litho paper on wood beanbag toss, BB graphics, 24" W, VG+... 540.00
Toy, CI, Tige pulls BB in cart, EX pnt, 7" L 210.00
Waffle press, CI, Buster Waffles, BB & Tige, Pat 1906, 14", EX ... 225.00

Dr. Pepper

A young pharmacist, Charles C. Alderton, was hired by W.B. Morrison, owner of Morrison's Old Corner Drug Store in Waco, Texas, around 1884. Alderton, an observant sort, noticed that the drugstore's patrons could never quite make up their minds as to which flavor of extract to order. He concocted a formula that combined many flavors, and Dr. Pepper was born. The name was chosen by Morrison in honor of a beautiful young girl with whom he had once been in love. The girl's father, a Virginia doctor by the name of Pepper, had discouraged the relationship due to their youth, but Morrison had never forgotten her. On December 1, 1885, a U.S. patent was issued to the creators of Dr. Pepper. Our advisor for this category is Craig Stifter; he is listed in the Directory under Colorado. See also Soda Fountain Collectibles.

Sign, die-cut cardboard, designed to sit on counter with arm and skirt hanging over edge, circa 1940s, 16x18x2", EX, $800.00. (Photo courtesy Dan Morphy Auctions, LLC on LiveAuctioneers.com)

Bottle, Baylor, Cotton Bowl Champs, unopened............................ 42.50
Calendar, lady w/glass, full pad, 1937, 32x15¼", EX, $180 to 200.00
Can, red/wht/bl cone top, Dallas TX, 6-oz, 4½", EX..................... 450.00
Clock, convex glass front, 10-2-4, dmn shape, Pam, 15½", EX 250.00
Clock, Dr Pepper in red banner, 10-2-4 in red, GE, electric, rnd, VG 200.00
Clock, glass front, Drink a Bite To Eat, 1950s, 15" dia, EX 550.00
Clock, mc numbers on wht face, lights up, sq, 1960s, 15¾", EX .. 220.00
Clock, neon-lit, octagonal, chrome bezel, 18", VG 525.00
Clock, oak, mirrored glass w/logo, pendulum, Roman numerals, 35x15" ..325.00
Clock, printed paper dial, Telechron, electric, gr fr, 14" dia, EX .. 375.00
Clock, rvpt Drink Dr P...Thanks Call Again, EX........................3,600.00
Cooler, alum ice chest, w/decal, EX 75.00
Menu sign, chalkboard, logo at top, 1960s, 27x19", EX, $55 to 80.00
Seltzer bottle, pk glass, Dr Pepper spigot top, Czech, 1920s, 12".. 425.00
Sign, cb, girl w/bottle, The Friendly Pepper-Upper, fr, 17x27", EX .225.00
Sign, cb, Smart Lift, blond lady, 1940s-50s, fr, 21x33½", VG....... 225.00

Sign, flange, metal dc, bottle at right, 1939, 15x24", EX 1,200.00
Sign, flange, tin, Dr Pepper on brick ground, 10-2-4 below, 16x24", VG. 480.00
Sign, metal bottlecap, 10-2-4, red & wht, unknown age, EX 45.00
Sign, paper litho, girl w/fishing gear, wood fr, 1940s, 28x34", VG. 155.00
Sign, porc, Dr Pepper Bottling Co, red/wht, triangular, 23x18", EX. 1,080.00
Sign, porc, Dr Pepper on brick design, 10½x26¼", EX, $275 to... 350.00
Sign, porc, Drink...Good for Life, Texlite/Dallas, 10½x26", EX ... 325.00
Sign, tin litho, bottle, 10-2-4 on yel, 54x18¼", VG 240.00
Thermometer, bubble glass front, Pam, 12" dia, VG.................... 145.00
Thermometer, tin, bottle on yel, 1940s, 25x10", EX.................... 360.00
Thermometer, tin, bottle on yel, faded/weathered, 1940s, 17½", G. 95.00
Thermometer, tin, Drink DP, Good for Life, ca 1940s, 17", EX, $325 to .. 350.00
Thermometer, tin litho, Drink...Frosty Cold, 1950s, 26x9", VG.. 215.00
Tray, tin litho, Free From Caffeine..., Shonk, 13½x16½", EX....... 900.00

Hires

Charles E. Hires, a drugstore owner in Philadelphia, became interested in natural teas. He began experimenting with roots and herbs and soon developed his own special formula. Hires introduced his product to his own patrons and began selling concentrated syrup to other soda fountains and grocery stores. Samples of his 'root beer' were offered for the public's approval at the 1876 Philadelphia Centennial. Today's collectors are often able to date their advertising items by observing the Hires boy on the logo. From 1891 to 1906, he wore a dress. From 1906 until 1914, he was shown in a bathrobe; and from 1915 until 1926, he was depicted in a dinner jacket. The apostrophe may or may not appear in the Hires name; this seems to have no bearing on dating an item. Our advisor for this category is Craig Stifter; he is listed in the Directory under Colorado. See also Soda Fountain Collectibles.

Banner, Enjoy Hires Float/Only 50¢, 32x42" 125.00
Bottle, rvpt label, alum top, sm ding/clouding, 12", EX............... 150.00
Clock, glass face, Drink..., red/wht/bl, 15" dia, EX.................... 215.00
Cooler, metal, Hires emb on wht (2 sides), 1940s, 10x19x16", VG ... 135.00
Dispenser, Drink It's Pure, ceramic, orig pump, Germany 1,200.00
Dispenser, hourglass shape, w/spigot & pump, EX 1,300.00
Dispenser, marble base, Munimaker #8049, 35x16", EX............. 7,900.00
Dispenser, wht Vitrolite base, rnd mg ball top, 23", EX, $4,800 to. 6,000.00
Dispenser, wooden bbl, metal bands, 1930s, 27", EX 660.00
Mug, ceramic, bbl form, Hires boy, Mettlach.............................. 225.00
Mug, ceramic, Hires boy pointing, Cauldon Ware, England, 4"... 125.00
Mug, stoneware, bl & gray, bark hdl, 5½", EX.............................. 300.00
Mug, stoneware, Hires on hourglass form, 6", $30 to...................... 40.00
Pocketknife, enamel on silver-tone, boy pointing, ca 1915, EX... 425.00
Sign, cb, Drink Hires in Bottles, ca mid-teens, 14¾x20¾", G...... 600.00
Sign, cb standup, lady w/Hires ribbon & tray, 1910-15, 58", VG. 200.00
Sign, cb, lady in yel dress by sign, rpl easel bk, 1940s, 12x7", G... 175.00
Sign, glass front, lt-up bubble in metal fr, 16" dia, EX 800.00

Sign, metal, circa 1940s, 66", $150.00 to $225.00. (Photo courtesy Dan Morphy Auctions, LLC on LiveAuctioneers.com)

Sign, metal over cb, brunette in evening gown, 1920s, 9x6½", EX .325.00
Sign, paper, dc foaming glass, ca 1910-15, 11x5½" 600.00
Sign, porc, Drink...It Is Pure, blk on yel, 1908, 15x36", EX.......... 400.00
Sign, porc, Hires boy as cop, Stop!..., ca 1900, 3x15", G, $180 to. 250.00
Sign, tin bottle cap, Drink...in Bottles, 1950s, 35" dia, EX........... 240.00
Sign, tin, Enjoy...Helpful & Delicious, 9½x27½", VG................. 840.00
Sign, tin, Have a...& Refresh, mc, 9x18", G 155.00
Sign, tin, Hires Delicious in Bottles, 1948, 11½x35½", EX.......... 120.00
Sign, tin, Hires in Bottles & bottle, 1930s, 9¾x27½", EX............ 480.00
Sign, tin, Hires Milkshake a Frosted Delight, 6x9", VG.............. 240.00
Sign, tin, Hires R-J Root Beer, 24" dia, VG................................. 170.00
Straw dispenser, CI, Hires on 4 panels, dtd 1911, 5½x10", EX.. 3,600.00
Thermometer, dc tin bottle, 29x8", EX+....................................... 130.00
Tray, tin litho, 2 ladies w/glasses, much rstr, 19½x23½", $180 to . 225.00

Moxie

The Moxie Company was organized in 1884 by George Archer of Boston, Massachusetts. It was at first touted as a 'nerve food' to improve the appetite, promote restful sleep, and in general to make one 'feel better'! Emphasis was soon shifted, however, to the good taste of the brew, and extensive advertising campaigns rivaling those of such giant competitors as Coca-Cola and Hires resulted in successful marketing through the 1930s. Today the term Moxie has become synonymous with courage and audacity, traits displayed by the company who dared compete with such well-established rivals. Our advisor for this category is Craig Stifter; he is listed in the Directory under Colorado. See also Soda Fountain Collectibles.

Blackboard, sf tin, It's Always a Pleasure..., 28", VG 125.00
Fan, hand, cb, Francis Prichard w/glass, 1916, EX, $85 to............ 110.00
Fan, hand, cl, folding, ca 1900-10, 6½" (closed), VG, $85 to 100.00
Shade, ldgl, Moxie lettering, 14x16" dia, $150 to....................... 175.00
Sign, cb, mc man delivering case of bottles, 7x3".......................... 180.00
Sign, cb, Try Our Soda Syrups 5¢, fr under glass, 18x13", EX 900.00
Sign, flange, tin, Moxie in red oval, 2-sided, 9x18", VG 685.00

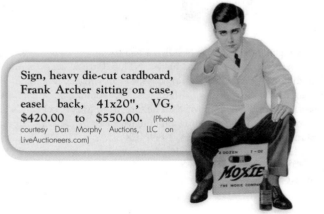

Sign, heavy die-cut cardboard, Frank Archer sitting on case, easel back, 41x20", VG, $420.00 to $550.00. (Photo courtesy Dan Morphy Auctions, LLC on LiveAuctioneers.com)

Sign, rvpt, lady w/glass, easel bk, minor flaking, 10x8", G............ 360.00
Sign, sf tin, Drink... & bottle cap, red & wht, Donaldson, 20x17", EX. 395.00
Sign, sf tin, man pointing, 1930-40s, 41½x15", EX 660.00
Sign, tin, Drink Moxie & Soda Syrups, listing products, 19x13", VG.. 1,325.00
Sign, tin, Drink Moxie in oval, rolled edge, 19x27", EX 325.00
Sign, tin, lady on horse in Moxiemobile, 19x27"+wood fr, VG ... 850.00
Sign, tin, Yes! We Sell..., oval, Kaufmann & Strauss, 28x10", VG... 425.00
Thermometer, tin, man pointing, early, 25x10", VG..................... 900.00
Tip tray, lady w/glass on flower bkgrnd, 1906, 6"........................... 425.00
Tip tray, Moxie among flowers, 6" dia, G 215.00
Tray, girl w/Moxie glass, red ribbon in hair, 9", VG 780.00

Old Crow

Old Crow Whiskey items have become popular with collectors primarily because of the dapper crow dressed in a tuxedo and top hat that was used by the company for promotional purposes during the 1940s through the 1960s. However, there is a vast variety of Old Crow collectibles, some of which carry only the whiskey's name. In the 1970s ceramic decanters shaped like chess pieces were available; these carried nothing more than a paper label and a presentation box to identify them. In 1985, the 150th anniversary of Old Crow, the realistic crow that had been extensively used prior to 1950, re-emerged.

Very little Old Crow memorabilia has been issued since National Distillers Products Corporation, the parent company since 1933, was purchased by Jim Beam Brands in 1987. No reproductions have surfaced, although a few fantasies have been found where the character crow was borrowed for private use. Note that with the increased popularity of Old Crow memorabilia, many items have surfaced, especially the more common ones, thus their values have decreased.

Ashtray, Bakelite, 3" dia, NM.. 25.00
Bank, wooden bbl, 1985, 6", EX... 25.00
Counter display, plastic crow, Advertising Novelty & Sign Co, Phila 23 Pa, 31"..140.00
Decanter, figural, orange vest, Royal Doulton, 12", MIB, $100 to.125.00
Dice, I Buy, You Buy, crow on 1 side, ½", set of 2, M, $45 to.......... 75.00
Display, backbar, compo figural, 3½x11½", EX, $95 to 125.00
Figure, plastic, Advertising Novelty & Sign Co, 32", EX............. 200.00
Label, paper, gold w/Hermitage Distillery bbls, ca 1903, 4x4+", NM ...25.00
Money clip, chromed metal, emb disk w/crow on 2" clip, EX 35.00
Pitcher, ceramic, 'broken leg' graphics, NM.................................. 100.00

Pitcher, ceramic with embossed crow, 7", $45.00 to $85.00. (Photo courtesy Carol Lochman, www.BonbonsOnEbay.com)

Pitcher, glass w/metal ring & hdl, 5", $25 to 45.00
Pocketknife, pearlized hdls, 2 blades, NM, $20 to 40.00
Punch bowl, porc, w/8 matching cups, 8x13", EX......................... 360.00
Radio, figural, 8-transistor, MIB 300.00
Sign, plastic bbl form w/crow & The Orig Sour Mash, 3x15", EX . 50.00
Stirrer, plastic, full-figure crow on end, M, $1 to 3.00
Thermometer, rnd dial, 1950s, 13x9", EX 150.00
Tray, Hedi Schoop Orig, 11x7½" 150.00

Pepsi-Cola

Pepsi-Cola was first served in the early 1890s to customers of Caleb D. Bradham, a young pharmacist who touted his concoction to be medicinal as well as delicious. It was first called 'Brad's Drink' but was renamed Pepsi-Cola in 1898. Various logos have been registered over the years. The familiar oval was first used in the early 1940s. At about the same time, the two 'dots' (indicated in our listings by '=') between the words Pepsi and Cola became one, though more recent items may carry the double-dot logo as well, especially when they're designed to be reminiscent of the old ones. The bottle-cap logo came along in 1943 and with variations was used through the early 1960s. Our advisor for this category is Craig Stifter; he is listed in the Directory under Colorado. See also Soda Fountain Collectibles.

Beach towel, red/wht/bl terrycloth, 57x34", EX............................. 12.50
Bottle opener, cast brass, old patina, 5¼" 48.00
Bottles, 6-pack, 12 oz ea, 9" T, $40 to 50.00
Cap, tin, emb bottle & cap, 48x18", EX... 300.00
Carrier, tin, worn pnt, holds 8 bottles, G, $24 to............................ 35.00
Cigarette lighter, Drink... on chrome, Wind Master, EX, $13 to.... 18.00
Clock, bk-lit bubble, Be Sociable, Have a ..., 16" dia, EX 375.00
Clock, bubble glass front, lights up, bottle cap on yel, 16" dia, EX..375.00
Cooler, alum, red lettering on wht, ca 1940-50s, 18" H, EX......... 150.00
Cooler, metal chest, wht lettering on bl enamel, G, $85 to.......... 125.00
Cooler, metal, red lettering on gray enamel, 19x17½", EX............ 300.00
Fan, hand, cb, Drink P=C, red/wht/bl, fading, VG, $15 to 20.00
Miniature, carton & 6 bottles, 2½x2½"... 30.00
Sign, cl on cb button, P=C, ca 1945, 9", EX.................................... 175.00
Sign, emb metal, Drink 5¢ Pepsi=Cola, 1940s, 10x30", EX+....... 595.00
Sign, tin, Drink P=C 5¢ Bigger-Better, 3-color, 22x40", EX......... 425.00

Sign with hanging message, reverse glass, single dot, 18x15½", $480.00 to $600.00. (Photo courtesy Showtime Auction Services on LiveAuctioneers.com)

Syrup drum, metal, P=C logo, red & wht, 18x16" dia, VG, $85 to .95.00
Tip tray, lady w/glass on gr, oval, 6", VG+..................................... 825.00
Toy boxing gloves, Everlast, Diet Pepsi on red, NMIB, $30 to....... 40.00
Toy truck, metal, w/accessories, Nylint #5500, 16", MIB 600.00
Vending machine, logo on bl enameling, 10¢ bottle, VG 1,800.00

Planters Peanuts

The Planters Peanut Company was founded in 1906. Mr. Peanut, the dashing peanut man with top hat, spats, monocle, and cane, has represented Planters since 1916. He took on his modern-day appearance after the company was purchased by Standard Brands in November 1960. He remains perhaps the most highly recognized logo of any company in the world. Mr. Peanut has promoted the company's products by appearing in ads; on product packaging; on or as store displays, novelties, and premiums; and even in character at promotional events (thanks to a special Mr. Peanut costume).

Among the favorite items of collectors today are the glass display jars which were sent to retailers nationwide to stimulate 'point-of-sale' trade. They come in a variety of shapes and styles. The first, distributed in the early 1920s, was a large universal candy jar (round covered bowl on a pedestal) with only a narrow paper label affixed at the neck to identify it as 'Planters.' In 1924 an octagonal jar was produced, all eight sides embossed, with Mr. Peanut on the narrow corner panels. On a second octagon jar, only seven sides were embossed, leaving one of the large panels blank to accommodate a paper label.

In late 1929 a fishbowl jar was introduced, and in 1932 a beautiful jar with a blown-out peanut on each of the four corners was issued. The football shape was also made in the 1930s, as were the square jar, the large barrel jar, and the hexagon jar with yellow fired-on designs alternating on each of the six sides. All of these early jars had glass lids which after 1930 had peanut finials.

In 1937 jars with lithographed tin lids were introduced. The first of these was the slant-front streamline jar, which is also found with screened yellow lettering. Next was a squat version, the clipper jar, then the upright rectangular 1940 leap year jar, and last, another upright rectangular jar with a screened, fired-on design similar to the red, white, and blue design on the cellophane 5¢ bags of peanuts of the period. This last jar was issued again after WWII with a plain red tin lid.

In 1959 Planters first used a stock Anchor Hocking one-gallon round jar with a 'customer-special' decoration in red. As the design was not plainly evident when the jar was full, the decoration was modified with a white under-panel. The two jars we've just described are perhaps the rarest of them all due to their limited production. After Standard Brands purchased Planters, they changed the red-on-white panel to show their more modern Mr. Peanut and in 1963 introduced this most plentiful, thus very common, Planters jar. In 1966 the last counter display jar was distributed: the Anchor Hocking jar with a fired-on large four-color design such as that which appeared on peanut bags of the period. Prior to this, a plain jar with a transfer decal in an almost identical but smaller design was used.

Some Planters jars have been reproduced: the octagon jar (with only seven of the sides embossed), a small version of the barrel jar, and the four peanut corner jar. Some of the first were made in clear glass with 'Made in Italy' embossed on the bottom, but most have been made in Asia, many in various colors of glass (a dead giveaway) as well as clear, and carrying only small paper stickers, easily removed, identifying the country of origin. At least two reproductions of the Anchor Hocking jar with a four-color design have been made, one circa 1978, the other in 1989. Both, using the stock jar, are difficult to detect, but there are small differences between them and the original that will enable you to make an accurate identification. With the exception of several of the earliest and the Anchor Hocking, all authentic Planters jars have 'Made in USA' embossed on the bottom, and all, without exception, are clear glass. Unfortunately, several paper labels have also been reproduced, no doubt due to the fact that an original label or decal will greatly increase the value of an original jar. Jar prices continue to remain stable in today's market.

In the late 1920s, the first premiums were introduced in the form of story and paint books. Late in the 1930s, the tin nut set (which was still available into the 1960s) was distributed. A wood jointed doll was available from Planters Peanuts stores at that time. Many post-WWII items were made of plastic: banks, salt and pepper shakers, cups, cookie cutters, small cars and trucks, charms, whistles, various pens and mechanical pencils, and almost any other item imaginable. Since 1981 the company, as a division of Nabisco (NGH) has continued to distribute a wide variety of novelties. In late 2000 NGH was sold to Philip Morris Cos. and Nabisco was combined with its Kraft Foods unit. With the increased popularity of Mr. Peanut memorabilia, more items surface, and the value of common items decrease.

Note that there are many unauthorized Planters/Mr. Peanut items. Although several are reproductions or 'copycats,' most are fantasies and fakes. Our advisors for this category are Anthony Scola (See Directory, Pennsylvania), and John Buchner (see Directory, Florida).

Key: MrP — Mr. Peanut

Jar, Streamline, original label, 10", $3,000.00. (Photo courtesy Dan Morphy Auctions, LLC on LiveAuctioneers.com)

Ball, Kick 'n Throw, orange, 1970s, 6½", VG 35.00
Box, wooden, dvtl, Clean Crisp Peanut Bars, 1918 .... 100.00

Chocolate mold, dbl cavity...2,000.00
Container, peanut, figural, MrP, papier mache, ½-lb, 1930s 225.00
Cup, bowl & dinner plate set, plastic, child's, 1970s 30.00
Hand puppet, rubber, 1940s...600.00
Jar, pickle, glass, tin screw lid, wooden bale hdl, 10¼", VG 850.00
Key chain/flashlight combo, MrP, wht plastic w/flip top, 1950s, EX.1,200.00
Lunch box, cb, yel, Canadian...350.00
Megaphone, MrP, cb, 1940s, 12", VG 500.00
Paint book, famous men, unpnt, 1935, EX 15.00
Pitcher, ceramic, Miyaya Ware, Made in Japan, MrP, 1930s, 8", VG.3,000.00
Pocket tin, 1923, 3½x2¾x¾", EX..4,000.00
Pop gun, paper, bl hdl, 1940s, 6½", EX...650.00
Puppet, hand, rubber, 1940s, 6½", EX..650.00
Safety marker, street crosswalk 125.00
Scoop, tin, 1-45/100-oz...65.00
Statue, fiberglass, MrP, Canadian, 1940s, EX..................................9,000.00
Thermometer, key shaped, red or bl plastic, 8", 1940s, ea 325.00
Tin, Hi-Hat Peanut Oil, full, 1-pt 60.00
Tin, Sal-in-Shell peanut, 10-lb, 1930s-40s................................3,200.00

Truck, toy, carousel revolves when truck is pushed forward, Acme Plastics, 1950s, 4" long, $500.00 to $600.00. (Photo courtesy Dan Morphy Auctions, LLC on LiveAuctioneers.com)

Vending machine, Dan, Canadian, 1960s....................................350.00
Wastebasket, MrP, bl, metal, 1970s, 13", VG...............................15.00
Whistles, plastic, navy bl, yel, pk, gold, or silver, 2¼", 1950s, ea ...30.00

RCA Victor

Nipper, the RCA Victor trademark, was the creation of Francis Barraud, an English artist. His pet's intense fascination with the music of the phonograph seemed to him a worthy subject for his canvas. Although he failed to find a publishing house who would buy his work, the Gramophone Co. in England saw its potential and adopted Nipper to advertise their product. The painting was later acquired and trademarked in the United States by the Victor Talking Machine Co., which was purchased by RCA in 1929. The trademark is owned today by EMI in England and by General Electric in the U.S. Nipper's image appeared on packages, accessories, ads, brochures, and in three-dimensional form. You may find a life-size statue of him, but all are not old. They have been manufactured for the owner throughout RCA history and are marketed currently by licensees, BMG Inc. and Thomson Consumer Electronics (dba RCA). Except for the years between 1968 and 1976, Nipper has seen active duty, and with his image spruced up only a bit for the present day, the ageless symbol for RCA still listens intently to 'His Master's Voice.' Many of the items have been reproduced in recent years. Exercise care before you buy. The true Nipper collectible is one which has been authorized by either Victor or RCA Victor as an advertising aid. This includes items used in showrooms, billboards, window dressings, and customer give-aways. The showroom items included three-dimensional Nippers first in papier-maché, later in spun rubber, and finally in plastic. Some were made in chalk. Throughout the years these items were manufactured largely by one company, Old King Cole, but often were marketed through others who added their names to the product. The key to collecting Nipper is to look for those items which were authorized and to overlook those items that were copied or made without permission of the copyright/trademark owner. Some of the newer but unauthorized items, however, are quite good and have become collectible notwithstanding their lack of authenticity.

The phenomenon of internet auctions has played havoc with prices paid for Victor and RCA Victor collectibles. Often prices paid for online sales bear little resemblance to the true value of the item. Reproductions are often sold as old on the internet and bring prices accordingly. Auction prices, more often than not, are inflated over sales made through traditional sales outlets. The internet has exacerbated the situation by focusing a very large number of buyers and sellers through the narrow portal of a modem. The prices here are intended to reflect what one might expect to pay through traditional sales.

Armchair, chrome, vinyl & wood, blk stenciled logo, 33", EX.....175.00
Bank, pot metal covered by felt, Nipper, 6", NM..........................185.00
Clock, RCA Victor Radio, bk-lit bubble, PAM, 19½" dia, EX.....350.00
Clock, RCA Victor Television, bk-lit bubble, 16" dia, EX...........325.00
Bank, Nipper, pot metal, flocked, VG, $75 to.............................100.00
Figure, Nipper, chalkware, 4", EX, $45 to....................................50.00
Figure, Nipper, chalkware, 14", VG+, $165 to.............................195.00

Figure, Nipper, older plaster version, 15", VG, $780.00 to $900.00. (Photo courtesy Rich Penn Auctions on LiveAuctioneers.com)

Figure, Nipper, papier-maché, 11", VG 200.00
Figure, Nipper, papier-maché, 14", VG 300.00
Figure, Nipper, papier-maché, 18" 300.00
Figure, Nipper, papier-maché, 36" 600.00
Figure, Nipper, plastic, 11" 75.00
Figure, Nipper, plastic, 36" 350.00
Figure, Nipper, Visco...125.00
Figure, Nipper, zinc, glass eyes, studded collar, pnt touchups, 18"..3,600.00
Oleograph, Victor Records, His Master's Voice, fr, 30x24", EX....650.00
Placemat, Nipper, w/Donald Duck logo, G 35.00
Shakers, Nipper, ceramic, 4", pr 85.00
Sign, glass, rvpt, Tubest Tested Free..., EX 145.00
Sign, porc, His Master's Voice, Nipper & player, 4-color, 12", VG+..515.00
Sign, porc, His Master's Voice, Nipper & player, oval, 26" L, EX.375.00
Sign, porc, vertical, Radio, HMV..800.00
Stickpin, cl, VG...100.00
Thermometer, porc, bl, wht, & yel, 39", EX..................................450.00
Tray, Nipper, mixed wood inlay, glass covered, 8-sided, 1930s, 18" dia.125.00
Watch fob, sterling silver, Nipper at the horn, 1⅜x1½", EX.........135.00

Red Goose Shoes

Realizing that his last name was difficult to pronounce, Herman Giesceke, a shoe company owner, resolved to give the public a modified, shortened version that would be better suited to the business world. The results suggested the use of the goose trademark with the last two letters, 'ke,' represented by the key that this early goose held in his mouth. Upon observing an employee casually coloring in the goose trademark with a red pencil, Giesceke saw new advertising potential and renamed the company Red Goose Shoes. Although the company has changed hands down through the years, the Red Goose emblem has remained. Collectors of this desirable fowl increase in number yearly, as do prices. Beware of reproductions; new chalkware figures are prevalent.

Bank, CI goose figural, 3¾", EX, $400 to 450.00
Bank, CI goose, squatty version, orig pnt, rare, EX+ 1,925.00
Bank, NP goose, 3¾"...1,300.00
Bench, pnt wood, red goose stencil ea end, 72", VG, $360 to......400.00
Carpet, store entry, 2 Red Goose images, Half the Fun of Having Feet, 27x59", G...525.00
Clock, goose on face (lg), lights up, electric, 14" dia....................725.00
Clock, goose on face, glass front, 8-sided, windup, EX 400.00
Clock, goose on face, Kohnop's Shoes, rpl #s, windup alarm, EX.325.00
Clock, goose on face, plastic & wood, lt-up, 19½x18", VG..........195.00
Display, chalkware goose w/neck extended, 10½x16x5½", EX 150.00
Display, compo, goose shape, 11½x5½", VG................................285.00
Marbles, yel clay & 1 steelie, EX, in yel cloth pouch w/red goose..60.00
Poster, cb, easel-bk, 11x13", EX..65.00
Sign, porc, neon, dc, 20x36", VG..450.00
Sign, porc, red goose, red neon, 1940s, 36", $1,925 to.............2,600.00
Sign, tin, goose on yel, 13x9", EX 155.00

String holder, cast iron, circa 1920s – 1930s, VG, 15x11", $1,200.00 to $1,500.00. (Photo courtesy Dan Morphy Auctions, LLC on LiveAuctioneers.com)

String holder, metal, dc, logo goose w/string holder underneath, 18x36", VG..1,500.00
Thermometer, tin, red goose on yel, 13x4", EX 25.00

Roly Poly

The Roly Poly tobacco tins were patented on November 5, 1912, by Washington Tuttle and produced by Tindeco of Baltimore, Maryland. These tins did not exhibit typical tobacco tin shapes; they had round bodies with lift-off heads, each clothed in a decorative lithographed costume. Each tin held approximately one pound of tobacco. There were six characters in all: Dutchman, Mammy, Satisfied Customer, Scotland Yard (aka The Inspector), Singing Waiter, and Storekeeper. Four brands of tobacco (Dixie Queen, Mayo's, Red Indian, and U.S. Marine) were packaged in selected characters. The brand of tobacco the Roly Poly contained was displayed on its reverse side, and, in the case of Mammy and Dutchman, also on the front (Mammy has a tiny tin with the tobacco company name in her front pocket). Mayo's and Dixie Queen Tobacco were packed in all six; Red Indian and U.S. Marine Tobacco in only Mammy, Singing Waiter, and Storekeeper. Of the set, Scotland Yard is considered the rarest, and in near mint condition may fetch more than $1,000.00 on today's market. These tins are very rare and should not be confused with the reproductions offered in the 1980s by Bristol Ware.

Dutchman, red neckscarf, wht belt, Mayo's, VG, $300 to 350.00
Mammy, Mayo's Cut Plug Tobacco Co, M 850.00
Satisfied Customer, man w/pipe, tooth on watch chain, Mayo's, EX..420.00
Scotland Yard (Inspector), cane in hand, tan outfit, smoking pipe, Mayo's, VG.1,000.00
Singing Waiter, Dixie Queen Cut Plug, song sheet in hands, 7x6", EX..450.00
Singing Waiter, Mayo's, song sheet in hands, VG+ 425.00
Storekeeper, bald man, smoking pipe, Mayo's, G..........................300.00

Seven-Up

The Howdy Company of St. Louis, Missouri, was founded in 1920 by Charles L. Grigg. His first creation was an orange drink called Howdy. In the late 1920s Howdy's popularity began to wane, so in 1929 Grigg invented a lemon-lime soda called Seven-Up as an alternative to colas.

Grigg's Seven-Up became a widely accepted favorite. Our advisor for this category is Craig Stifter; he is listed in the Directory under Colorado. See also Soda Fountain Collectibles.

Clock, 7-Up on red in center, sq gold fr, EX, $150 to 175.00
Cooler, metal, logo on wht, Progress Refr Co..., 1955, 19x16x13", EX. 200.00
Door push, porc, 7-Up in red sq on wht, 34½", EX, $125 to 150.00
Figure, squeeze toy, Fresh Up Freddie, vinyl, logo on shirt, 1959, EX. 130.00
Sign, cl button, 7-Up & bubbles, 9" dia 180.00
Sign, tin, 7Up (no hyphen) & bubbles on red, 13x11", EX.......... 135.00
Sign, tin, Fresh Up & bottle, on yel, 54x18", VG, $120 to 175.00
Sign, tin, Fresh Up, hand holds bottle on gr, wood fr, 59x35", EX .. 525.00
Sign, tin, hand holds bottle on wht, 42x13", EX 240.00
Sign, tin, Nothing Does It Like..., red/wht/gr, 18¾x13", EX, $50 to. 75.00
Thermometer, rising sun, Made in USA, 12¼" dia, EX, $70 to...... 95.00
Thermometer, tin, 7-Up on blk, 20x5", EX.................................... 90.00

Miscellaneous

Airline Flexible Flyer, sled, wood & metal, salesman's sample, 23x9", EX. 750.00
Alabama Brewing Co, serving tray, metal, woman dressed in red, EX .. 450.00
Am Express Co, sign, tin w/emb, Est 1841, Money Orders..., 1913, 27x20", EX.. 900.00
Arden Dairy, sign, porc, delivery boy holding milk bottle, 14x24", NM. 1,900.00
Aunt Jemima, display, cb, dc, string-climbing, 1905, EX........... 2,000.00
Aunt Jemima, sign, porc, curved, Burdick, Chicago, NM 7,500.00

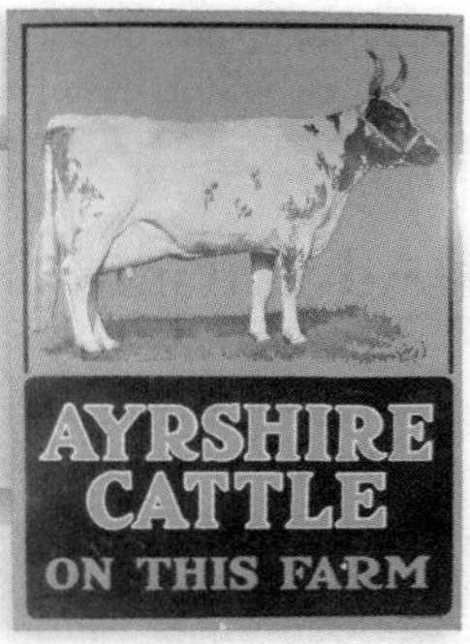

Ayrshire Cattle on This Farm, tin sign, embossed, 19½x28", EX, $650.00. (Photo courtesy Showtime Auction Services on LiveAuctioneers.com)

Badger Mutual Fire Insurance, pwt, CI, badger shape, 1937, EX.... 95.00
Bagdad Coffee, pail, metal, 5-lb, EX.. 145.00
Bancroft Tennis Racquets, sign, cl over cb, Whitehead & Hoag, 6x9", EX 400.00
Bartholomay's Brewing Co, Yel Kid match holder, yel & blk, 5¼x2¼". 400.00
Baugh's Fertilizers, thermometer, wood, cow at top of scale, 12", VG .. 95.00
BHL Black Indian, cigar store Indian, cvd wood, 20x20x73", G. 13,500.00
Big Ben, tobacco tin, horse on front, Brn Williamson Tobacco Co, 1-lb, VG. 100.00
Champion Spark Plugs, sign, tin, emb, Cost Less, More Power, 14¾x5⅝", NM .. 600.00
Chiclets, container, tin, countertop, litho, Help Yourself, EX...... 115.00
Chiclets, sign, tin, dc, monkey, 1910s, EX 1,100.00
Clemax Razor, sign, porc, flange, man feeling his smooth shave, 12x12", EDX .. 800.00
Clicquot Club Soda, calendar, paper, metal strips on top & bottom, full pad, 1942, NM.. 225.00
Climax Peanut Butter, pail, metal w/press lid & bail hdl, 16-oz, EX... 135.00
Colgan's Orange Gum, display cabinet, wood & etched glass, 17½", G.. 1,000.00
Colt Arms, ad, paper, Texas Ranger, 1920s, 20x32", EX........... 2,500.00
Creamsicle (Buck Rogers for), paper sign, 8x20", 1930, EX 1,100.00
Diamond D Coffee, container, cb, Dwinell-Wright, NY, 1-lb, EX . 35.00
Donald Duck Beverages, sign, metal, sf, 28x20", EX.................... 365.00
Dr Bell's Pine Tar Honey, bottle, 1900-10s, 2¼x7¼x1¼", EX......... 35.00
Dr Warner's Health Corset, statue, chalkware, 1880s, 28", EX . 5,500.00
Du Pont Smokeless, pin-bk, cl, Champion's Powder, 1¼ dia, NM . 95.00
Du Pont, poster, Du Pont Sporting Powders, 17x25⅜", EX 850.00
Dutch Boy White Lead Paint, display, papier mache, 12x30", G . 750.00
Dutch Master Cigar, can, metal, Dutchmen seated around table, 5¼x5¼", VG.. 45.00
Edison Phonography, sign, litho, woman listening, 20¾x28", EX . 3,100.00
Edison-Mazda, service station counter display box, Name Your Car..., EX... 695.00
Edward Heuer Bottler, calendar, paper, 12x19", EX.................. 1,000.00
Elephant Salted Peanuts, container, tin, elephant on lid, 4x4x2", EX .. 325.00
Elgin Watches, sign, glass, rvpt, fr, Full Ruby Jeweled, 23x29½", VG ... 475.00
Ellwood Whiskey, ad, oil on wood, Louisville KY, 1909, 26¼x32⅛", VG. 575.00
Evinrude Detachable Motor, pennant, cloth, company logo, 29" L, EX. 175.00
Fairbank's Gold Dust Scouring Cleanser, sign, paper, 20x11", EX. 450.00
Finck's Detroit Special Overalls, mirror, metal/glass, 2¾", VG 135.00
Folger's Coffee, container, cb, holds free puzzle, 2¾x3½", NM....... 45.00
Ford, sign, porc, bl script, bl bckgrd, 39x25", EX 1,500.00
Fry's Chocolate, sign, porc, single-sided, young boy crying, 36x30", VG.. 840.00
Fun-to-Wash Washing Powder, box, unopened, Mammy on front, EX.. 85.00
Gene Autry World's Greatest Cowboy..., cb standup, 59x31", EX .. 450.00
Gillette Safety Razor, pock mirror, No Stropping, No Honing, 2⅛" dia, 1913, EX. 140.00
Gold Medal Flour, poster, paper, litho, wheat kernel, 28x42", EX. 150.00
Gold Medal, watch fob, cl & metal, 1½" dia, VG........................ 100.00
Golden Pheasant Coffee, tin, litho w/bird on bl bkgrnd, 1-lb, EX.. 1,500.00
Great Northwestern Railroad, calendar, Indian in headdress, 1944, 15½x33", EX. 305.00

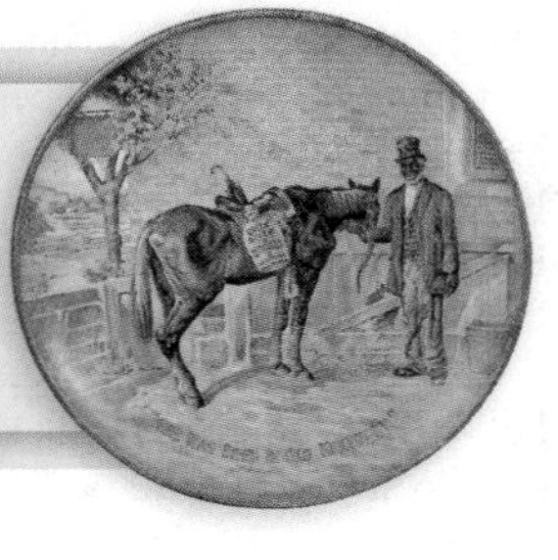

Green River Whiskey, charger, tin, minor rust to edge, 24" diameter, $650.00. (Photo courtesy Showtime Auction Services on LiveAuctioneers.com)

Green River Whiskey, sign, metal, 45x33", EX......................... 1,500.00
Grisdale Coffee, container, screw-top, 4x6", VG 45.00
Gulf Gasoline, blotter, paperboard, There Is More Power..., 6x4", VG.. 75.00
Gyspy Hosiery, tip tray, metal, Owensville MO, 6" dia, EX.......... 225.00
Hatchway Union Suits, box, cb, 1915, 10x15x1½", EX 35.00
Heinz 57 Varieties, string holder, dc, dbl-sided, rare, 17x14x7", EX. 5,400.00
Heinz, delivery truck, tin litho, working lights, orig box, 12x3½x5", EX.. 550.00
Hercules Gunpowder, poster, paper, 1924, 13½x19", VG 110.00
Hickman's Silver Birch Chewing Gum, display, cb, 6¼x5¼x4¼", EX.. 1,200.00
Honey-Fruit Gum, sign, tin litho over cb, 9⅛x6¼", EX............. 2,500.00
Horlick's Malted Milk, pocket mirror, young girl w/ calf, 2" dia, EX... 125.00
Huyler's Candies, sign, porc, flange, dbl-sided, made to eat..., 20¼x7", VG. 235.00
Hyroler Whiskey, tip tray, metal, Louis J Adler & Co, 4¼" dia, EX . 95.00
Indian Motorcycles, match holder, metal, emb Indian face, 1½x2", VG . 600.00
Indianapolis Speedway, checkered flag, silk, 17x17", EX 175.00
Ingersol Watches, sign, porc, dbl-sided, dc, pocket watch shape, 8x12", EX.. 475.00
Jackie Coogan Kid Candy, pail, metal w/slip lid, Jackie Coogan, 7 oz, EX. 825.00
Joe Anderson Havana Cigars, match dispenser, 14½x9" dia, VG.. 800.00
Juicy Fruit, match holder, metal, image of the founder, VG 250.00
Just Born Nuts Brazil & Almonds, display case, 7¼x7½x11", VG. 175.00
Kellogg's, ceral box, cb, Corn Flakes, Yogi Bear, unopened, 1962, EX... 350.00
Kentucky Fried Chicken, sign, molded plastic, the Colonel, 3½x36", F. 50.00
Key West Extras, cigar box label, paper, cigar production, 4½x4½", EX. 50.00
Knox Sparkling Gelatin, sign, cb, dc, 10x15x16", VG 2,200.00
LaAzora Cigars, charger, metal, 24" dia, EX................................ 385.00
Laddies Short Smokes, sign, cb, 21x33", EX 250.00
Lady Hellen Coffee, container, cb, metal top & bottom, 1-lb, EX. 90.00
Lava Soap, fan pull, cb, dbl-sided, product in center, 11" sq, EX ... 95.00
Lear & Olver Ice Cream, menu board, cb, wood fr, 20", G 50.00
Lee, banner, cloth, authentic western wear, EX.......................... 145.00
Levi's, poster, cowboy lore, 1933, 25x36½", EX 355.00
Log Cabin Syrup, store counter display, cb, 31½x21¾x2", VG . 1,500.00
Lorillard Indian Snuff, bottle, glass, complete contents, unbroken seal, 1898, NM. 65.00
Lucky Strike, fan, cb, dc, tobacco leaf shape, Frank Sinatra, EX.. 250.00
Luxury Tobacco, counter sign, cb, easel bk, man enjoying pipe, 9x11", EX. 325.00

Mail Pouch Tobacco, string holder, metal, 1908, 15x20", G 2,350.00
Majestic Batteries, sign, tin, pnt, Sales and Service, 19½x26", NM ...350.00
Mangus Root Beer, dispenser, ceramic, bbl shape, VG 500.00
Manhattan Gasoline, sign, porc, dbl-sided, 30" dia, EX 1,775.00
Mascot Tobacco, tip tray, metal, animals at water, 5" L, EX............ 75.00
McLaughlin's Coffee, store bin, slant top, c/s, 16¾x13x19¼", EX. 275.00
Meadow Gold Milk, sign, wood & masonite, 13x12", G 115.00
Meiers Ice Cream, sign, porc, dbl-sided, We Serve..., 35¾x24", VG... 325.00
Metlox Dog Food, sign, porc, dog on large ball, 18x26", EX 875.00
Military Brand, cigar box label, paper, campsite scene of sliders, EX ..250.00
Missouri Smoking Pipes, blister pack from country store w/full sheet of pipes, EX...65.00
Munyon's Homeopathic Home Remedy, store cabinet, tin litho, salesman on top, EX.505.00
Nash Auto, playing cards, vinyl coated, Nash automobiles, EXIB . 65.00
Nation's Choice Whiskey, flask, glass, paper label, Parker-Davis, VG. 525.00
National Biscuit Co, display rack, metal & wood, 55½", EX........ 600.00
National Oats Co, box, cb, paper label w/Donald Duck, 3-lb, VG... 275.00
Nuvana Cigar, door push, alum, emb lettering, 2x6", VG 135.00
Nylotis Baby Powder, container, tin litho, 3 babies in front, unopened, NM.170.00
Oconto Brewing Co, tip tray, metal, Compliments of courtesy panel, 1908, EX.. 165.00
Old Judge Rye, statue, cvd wood, yarn hair, 9½x12x47½", VG. 1,000.00
Paige Sales & Service, globe, mg, Sales & Service, 1920s, EX .. 1,100.00
Parker Bros AA Pigeon Gun, sign, 1 of 2 known, 7x26", EX 7,000.00
Pear's Soap, ad, paper, 1912, 10x14", EX.. 95.00
Peter Rabbit Peanut Butter, pail, tin litho, wire side-mtd hdls, 1-lb, EX.485.00
Peters Big Game Ammunition, sign, paper, moose, company logo, 18x29", VG. 700.00
Police Foot Powder, Purity Laboratories, early, 4¾", EX+.......... 1,200.00
Poll-Parrot Shoes, sidewalk sign, wooden, dbl-sided, 46", G 375.00
Quadroom Smoking Tobacco, pouch, cloth w/paper label, 4-oz, VG ... 225.00
Quaker Oats, sign, porc, titled box of oats, Eat..., In Packages Only, 24x42", EX... 750.00
Quincy Mutual Fire Insurance, calendar, cb, 1889, 7x10", EX .. 5,750.00
Rajah Motor Oil, sign, metal, Dbl Milage..., 20x28", EX 1,400.00
Red Belt, pocket tin, vertical, belt & buckle from John J Bagley & Co, 3x3x1", EX... 90.00
Red Dot Cigars, fan pull, cb, dbl-sided, 6½x8½", EX..................... 100.00
Reliance Baking Powder, matchholder, tin litho, 5¾", G 425.00
Rex Flintkote Roofing, match holder, tin litho, barn w/message on roof, 5", G ...350.00
Rexall, McFarlin, sign, porc, dbl-sided, arm-hung, 72x30x4¼", EX. 1,000.00
Royal Club Cut Plug, container, metal, company name & emb lion & crown, EX.250.00
Royal Tailors (The), sign, tin, dc, pnt, stand-up, 19½x9", EX...... 550.00
Ryzon, The Perfect Baking Powder, sign, tin, 1940s, 12x16", EX. 475.00
Sanford's Ink and Mucilage, sign, metal, Faultness, 20x14", VG. 2,450.00
Schmidt's Bl Ribbon Bread, door push, metal, bread loaf shape, 19" W, VG...160.00
Schroeder's Honey Top Whiskey, sign, metal, 23x33", EX 1,500.00
Scott's Emulsion, trolley sign, cb, 1920s, 24x11", VG 250.00
Scott's Emulson, trolley sign, cb, boy & girl playing marbles, 1920s, 24x11", VG.250.00
Scull's Coffeee, store bin, tin, stenciled, litho, 21½", VG.............. 800.00
Sealtest, menu brd, metal fr w/cb inserts for flavors & prices, 10x22", EX.. 95.00
Sharples Tubular Cream Separator, pot scraper, 1909, EX............. 280.00
Shell, badge, metal in shape of company logo w/red inlaid cloissone, 2x2", EX...450.00
Sheridan Sugar Co, pocket mirror, cl, factory, 2¾x1¾", EX.............. 95.00
Shipmate Cigarettes, pocket mirror, 2 sailors on front, 2" dia, VG... 185.00
Sinclair Shamrock Lubricant, can, metal, rnd, w/cone lid, 3-lb, EX...400.00
Southern Rose Hair Dressing, calendar, 1950, 17x35", EX........... 110.00
Sparkle Soda, bottle topper, cb, elf & 5¢, EX.................................. 65.00

Sunbeam Bread, tin sign, A. A. W. 8-53, 27½x19½", EX, $575.00. (Photo courtesy Burley Auction Group on LiveAuctioneers.com)

Sun Flower Brand Steel Cut Coffee, tin litho, pry-type lid, 1-lb, 5¼x3¾", EX ..1,000.00
Tasty Food Ltd, cb sign w/free toy train offer, 1920s, VG 630.00

Teddy Brand Peanuts, tin, label on both sides, red, 1-lb, EX 75.00
Texaco, pin-bk badge, metal, Texaco Scotties, 3¼x3¼", EX 525.00
Times Sq Smoking Tobacco, pocket tin, skyline at night, flip-lid, EX .. 2,255.00
Tomahawk Scrap Tobacco, sign, tin litho, orig oak frm, 9¼x12", EX.. 500.00
UMC Cartridges, Shooting Gallery, tin litho sign, bull's head shape, 18½x26¾" ..4,000.00
Uncle John's Syrup, display, window, 45x50", NM 875.00
Vanderbilt Premium Tread, clock, rnd, lt-up, center logo, 1958, 14½" dia, EX.175.00
Velvet Tobacco, watch fob, cloisonne, pocket tin shape, 1x2", EX .. 155.00
Victor Duck Decoys, store pc, papier mache, HP, 6x6x4½", EX... 575.00
Victory Brand Pure Lard, can, metal, rnd wire hdls, 25-lb, G......... 50.00
Wake-Em-Up Coffee, pail, metal, bail hdl, slip lid, Indian, 9½x9", EX ..335.00
Wales-Goodyear Rubbers, cb sign, image: 30x20", VG 3,000.00

Whistle Soda, clock, 24x24", VG, $650.00. (Photo courtesy Ferrell Auction Co., Inc. on LiveAuctioneers.com)

White House Coffee, sign, tin, litho, dc, flange, 13½x8¾", EX .2,500.00
White Rock, tip tray, fairy looking at reflection in water, 4¼" dia, VG. 180.00
White Rock Water, pastel on canvas, 1910s, 42x62", EX..........4,500.00
Wrigley's Soap, tip tray, tin litho, cat on soap bars on yel, EX...... 330.00

Advertising Cards

Advertising trade cards enjoyed great popularity during the last quarter of the nineteenth century when the chromolithography printing process was refined and put into common use. The purpose of the trade card was to acquaint the public with a business, product, service, or event. Most trade cards range in size from 2" x 3" to 4" x 6"; however, many are found in both smaller and larger sizes.

There are two classifications of trade cards: 'private design' and 'stock.' Private design cards were used by a single company or individual; the images on the cards were designed for only that company. Stock cards were generics that any individual or company could purchase from a printer's inventory. These cards usually had a blank space on the front for the company to overprint with their own name and product information.

Four categories of particular interest to collectors are:

Mechanical — a card which achieves movement through the use of a pull tab, fold-out side, or movable part.

Hold-to-light — a card that reveals its design only when viewed before a strong light.

Die-cut — a card in the form of something like a box, a piece of clothing, etc.

Metamorphic — a card that by folding down a flap shows a transformed image, such as a white beard turning black after use of a product.

For a more thorough study of the subject, we recommend *Reflections 1* and *Reflections 2* by our advisor, Kit Barry; his address can be found in the Directory under Vermont. Values are given for cards in near-mint condition.

Alden Vinegar, watermelon & other fruit on table......................... 12.00
American Ball Bl (laundry), juggler on ball 18.00
Atmore's Mince Meat, man serving plum pudding 7.00

Aultman, Miller farm machinery, circa 1885, $35.00. (Photo courtesy Kit Barry Ephemera, Brattleboro, Vermont)

Birdsall farm machinery, girl holding birds nest 18.00
Bradley plows, man & 3 women playing Blind Man's Bluff 20.00
Bucher plows, farmer w/ft on plow, 'I tell you sir' 25.00
Bullard hay tedder, man & wht horse w/tedder 35.00
Button's Raven Gloss shoe dressing, cupid & giant box 12.00
Carter's Backache Plasters, 'Oh! My poor back' 6.00
Carter's Iron Pills, woman w/parasol, 'I declare!' 6.00
Carter's Little Nerve Pills, 2 boys playing horn & drum 6.00
Cox & Bros, shoes, violin player & wedding party 9.00
Day & Martin shoe blacking, 3 men & 4 ladies in store 10.00
Deering farm machinery, 2 girls w/sheaves, factory 35.00
Deering farm machinery, 'After the harvest w/Deering' 35.00
Deering farm machinery, lame injured horse w/farmer 25.00
Deering farm machinery, 'The Deering in 1890' 35.00
Deuscher farm machinery, 6 inserts of machines 35.00
Diamond Dye, 'Class in Economy' 8.00
Domestic Sewing Machine, 'Jersey Cow Rarity' 7.00
Fidelity & Casualty Co, H-wheel bicycle accident 20.00
Household sewing machine, 2 sailboats on beach 5.00
Household sewing machine, 3 children w/apple basket 6.00
Household sewing machine, lady sewing, child & 3 cats 5.00
Hoyt's German Cologne, lady holding baby in fountain 5.00
Jayne's medicines, 'Faith, Hope, & Charity' 6.00
Jayne's medicines, 'Seasonable Suggestions' 6.00
Jayne's medicines, 'The Morning Prayer' 6.00
Jayne's medicines, 'Words of Comfort' 6.00
JP Coats thread, 3 children pulling spool, 1 child driving 6.00
JP Coats thread, flying bird w/spool around neck 6.00
JP Coats thread, girl w/3 dogs standing on hind legs 6.00
JP Coats thread, ship towing Cleopatra's Needle 7.00
Kirk soap, 2 natives w/baby elephant 6.00
Lavine soap, child riding swan on water 6.00
Margaret Mather, actress, her portrait image, side view 8.00
Muzzy corn starch, 2 clowns & a pudding 8.00
New Home sewing machine, 'In the Far West' 6.00
Pearline soap, boy w/crayfish, dog, cat 6.00
Pettijohn cereal, 2 babies w/cereal bowls & kitten 18.00
Pinkham's Vegetable Compound, blk & wht, Brooklyn Bridge 8.00
Prudential Insurance, 1 thin & 2 fat men, 'Great Features' 8.00
Remington Sewing Machine, man & 2 women w/machine 9.00
Rex breakfast cereal, boy & girl holding boxes in field 18.00
Royal Milling Co, girl & boy on flour sacks in field 25.00
Sea Foam baking powder, man & lady at table w/lamp 8.00
Singer Sewing Machine, Spain - Seville 6.00
Soapine, magician, lady & night stars saying 'Soapine' 6.00
Soapine, sailor on ship's rigging daydreaming of home 6.00
Stoddard & Co Tiger Rake, man on horse-drawn rake 35.00
Street's Perfection Buckwheat, blk & wht, girl & box, 'I eat...' 12.00
Venable Red Tag tobacco, 'Idol Worshipping' 35.00
Wheat Bitters, 3 cupids w/dog wagon & giant bottle 9.00
Wheat Bitters, boy w/giant bottle & sick man in chair 9.00
Wheat Bitters, man, woman & bottle in rowboat 9.00
Wheeler & Wilson sewing machine, lady, sleeping girl 7.00
White Sewing Machine, crying boy & girl w/snow sleds 7.00
Willimantic thread, cat lowering kittens out window 8.00

Wilson's beef, blk & wht, man w/ax eating w/girl 12.00
Wilson's beef, blk & wht, woman sleeping 12.00

Agata Glass

Agata is New England peachblow (the factory called it 'Wild Rose') with an applied metallic stain which produces gold tracery and dark blue mottling. The stain is subject to wear, and the amount of remaining stain greatly affects the value. It is especially valuable (and rare) on satin-finish items when found on peachblow of intense color. Caution! Be sure to use only gentle cleaning methods.

Currently rare types of art glass have been realizing erratic prices at auction; until they stabilize, we can only suggest an average range of values. In the listings that follow, examples are glossy unless noted otherwise. A condition rating of 'EX' indicates that the stain shows a moderate amount of wear. To evaluate an item with very worn stain, deduct from 60% to 75% from these prices. When 'color' is included in the condition assessment, it will refer to the intensity of the glass itself. For more information, we recommend *The Collector's Encyclopedia of American Art Glass* by John A. Shuman III.

Bowl, sauce, G color & stain 350.00
Bowl, tricorner, G overall stain, 2x5" 500.00
Celery, EX stain, 6⅜" 750.00
Cruet, alabaster stopper & hdl, EX color & stain, 6" 1,300.00

Pitcher, exceptional color and stain, very rare, 8", $5,500.00 to $6,000.00. (Photo courtesy Brunk Auctions on LiveAuctioneers.com)

Pitcher, reeded hdl, EX color & stain, water sz, 7" 4,000.00
Pitcher, sq mouth, reed hdl, lt stain, 6½" 2,500.00
Punch cup, EX stain, 2" 495.00
Shaker, pillar form, EX color & stain, 4", ea 2,070.00
Toothpick holder, crimped top, 2½" 425.00
Toothpick holder, sq rim, Tufts SP stand w/Kate Greenaway boy, 3¼" . 700.00
Tumbler, EX stain, 3" 400.00
Tumbler, lemonade, w/hdl, EX stain, 5" 1,750.00
Vase, lily, 3-fold rim, VG stain, 10½" 1,100.00
Vase, lily, EX color & stain, 8" 1,500.00
Vase, lily, in Cattail & Reed Tufts fr, 11" 1,500.00
Vase, much gold tracery, petal top, thin walls, 4½" 800.00
Vase, satin (rare), 3-fold rim, emb ring at neck, dk stain, 3¾" ... 1,750.00
Vase, slightly shouldered, tight crimped rim, EX color & stain, 6x4" .. 850.00

Agate Ware

Clays of various natural or artificially dyed colors were combined to produce agate ware, a procedure similar to the methods used by Niloak in potting their Mission Ware. It was made by many Staffordshire potteries from about 1740 until about 1825.

Bowl, ivory/mocha swirl, scalloped rim, 5¾" 850.00
Canister, tea, brn/cream/rust w/gr band, silver lid/neck, 5" 1,400.00

Cheese dish, Copeland & Garrett, 1840s, 11¾" T...................1,920.00
Cup/saucer, bls & brns, 2⅜", 4½"...1,995.00
Jardiniere, pearlware, brn tones/off-wht rim, Wedgwood, 3¾x5", EX .480.00
Sauceboat, 2-spout, Whieldon style, missing pc of rim, 7" L.....1,600.00
Tankard, buff/iron red, 8-sided, 1760, 7" 7,650.00
Teapot, brn/bl, shell form, foo lion finial, serpent hdl, 5" 7,650.00
Teapot, brn/buff/rust w/gr trim, globular, early, 4" 4,115.00
Teapot, griffin knob, 5¼", EX 3,000.00
Teapot, scalloped shell form, griffin finial, 5", EX 3,000.00
Vase, gilt laurel hdls w/mask heads, w/lid, Wedgwood & Bentley, 12".. 2,700.00
Vase, mc speckles, porphyry type, Ralph Wood, 9¼" 700.00
Vase, mc w/gilt-to-cream bird-form hdls & swags, Neale, w/lid, 13" .1,000.00
Vase, mc w/portrait/florets, gilt/cream hdls, bl plinth, 9" 700.00

Akro Agate Glass

The Akro Agate Company operated in Clarksburg, West Virginia, from 1914 until 1951. In addition to their famous marbles, they also produced children's dishes and a general line consisting of vases, planters, and flowerpots in the garden line. They made ashtrays, bathroom fixtures, lamps, powder jars, bells, baskets, and candlesticks as well. Akro made a number of novelty items which were distributed in 5 & 10¢ stores such as Woolworth. Though many pieces are not marked, you will find some that bear their distinctive logo: a crow flying through the letter 'A' holding an Aggie in its beak and one in each claw. Some novelty items may instead carry one of these trademarks: 'J.V. Co., Inc.,' 'Braun & Corwin,' 'N.Y.C. Vogue Merc Co. U.S.A.,' 'Hamilton Match Co.,' and 'Mexicali Pickwick Cosmetic Corp.'

Color is a very important worth-assessing factor. Some pieces may be common in one color but rare in others. Occasionally an item will have exceptionally good colors, and this would make it more valuable than an example with only average color. When buying either marbles or juvenile tea sets in original boxes, be sure the box contains its original contents.

Note: Original written information has discounted the generally accepted attribution of the Chiquita and J.P. patterns to the Akro company, proving instead that they were made by the Alley Agate Company.

Due to the influence of eBay and other online auctions, the prices of children's dishes have fallen considerably over the past few years, with only the rare boxed sets retaining their higher values.

For more information we recommend *The Complete Line of the Akro Agate Co.* by our advisors, Roger and Claudia Hardy (available from the authors); they are listed in the Directory under West Virginia. Our advisor for miscellaneous Akro Agate is Albert Morin, who is listed in the Directory under Massachusetts. See also Marbles.

Children's Dishes

Concentric Rib, bl teapot w/wht lid, 2¼" dia..................................14.00
Concentric Rib, creamer, gr & wht 4.00
Concentric Rib, creamer, transparent bl 28.00
Concentric Rib, c/s, gr opaque 6.00
Concentric Rib, cup, transparent bl, 1¼" 12.00
Concentric Rib, teapot w/lid, bl opaque 16.00
Interior Panel, cup, gr opaque, 1¼" 5.00
Interior Panel, cup, pumpkin, 1¼" 12.00
Interior Panel, plate, gr & wht 6.00
Interior Panel, plate, maroon & wht..9.00
Interior Panel, teapot w/lid, gr & wht 24.00
Interior Panel, teapot w/lid, transparent gr 14.00
Octagonal Band, teapot w/lid, gr opaque 18.00
Octagonal, cr/sug, sm, yel opaque..32.00
Octagonal, creamer, sm, pumpkin 14.00
Octagonal, plate, pk opaque...6.00

Raised Daisy, creamer, yel opaque 21.00
Raised Daisy, cup, bl opaque...14.00
Stippled Band, teapot w/domed lid, transparent topaz.....................18.00

Children's Tea Sets

American Maid, lemonade & oxblood, 9-pc, orig box 400.00
Little Am Maid, mixed colors, #355, orig box 120.00
Little Am Maid, mixed gr, yel & bl opaque, #355, orig box 85.00
Play-Time, mixed colors, 8-pc, orig box 95.00

Play-Time, Raised Daisy, 19-piece, mixed colors, MIB, $225.00. (Photo courtesy Randy Inman Auctions Inc. on LiveAuctioneers.com)

Play-Time, topaz, 16-pc, orig box 190.00
Stippled Band, transparent topaz, 8-pc: teapot w/lid, 2 ea plate, c/s, no box...35.00

Flowerpots, Vases, and Planters

Planter, Lily, marbleized wht, red & gr, #657, 5½" 10.00
Planter, solid bl opaque, oval, #6546..12.00
Planter, solid pumpkin opaque, oval, #6546...............................10.00
Planter, solid yel opaque, rect, w/ribs, #653, 8" 16.00
Pot, ivory, grad dart, Grandaddy, #308, 6½" 170.00
Pot, marbleized gr & wht, Stacked Disk, 5" 20.00
Pot, opaque gr, grad dart, #297, mk, smooth top...........................15.00
Pot, orange & wht, Rib top, mini, #290, 1¼".................................30.00
Pot, pumpkin, combination rib top & banded dart, #295, 5" 210.00
Pot, solid bl & wht, Ribs & Flutes, scalloped top, #296, 3" 24.00
Pot, solid bl opaque, grad dart, #297, mk, smooth top, 3"...............15.00
Pot, solid bl opque, Ribs & Flutes, scalloped top, #296, 3"............10.00
Pot, solid gr opaque, Ribs & Flutes, scalloped top, #296, 3" 10.00
Pot, wht & bl, grad dart, #297, mk, scalloped top, 3" 24.00
Vase, cream, grad dart, ftd, #321, mk 45.00
Vase, Lily, gr & wht, #658 ....12.00
Vase, Lily, gr, wht & orange, #658 ....10.00
Vase, Lily, ivory, #658 ....15.00
Vase, pumpkin, narrow ledge, #314, 4½"......................................60.00

Smoking Items

Ashtray, slag bl, wht & oxblood, rect, 2 rests, #249........................55.00
Ashtray, slag wht & oxblood, shell, #246......................................8.00
Ashtray, transparent gr, 3 rests, w/matchholder, triangular.............50.00
Ashtray, wht & bl, rect, 2 rests, #249 ....10.00
Ashtray, wht & gr, rect, 2 rests, #249 ....8.00
Ashtray, wht & oxblood, rect, 2 rests, #249 ....40.00
Cigarette holder, wht & oxblood, 8-sided, 2¾"..............................30.00
Cigarette jar, orange & wht, w/ashtray, sombrero lid, #803............18.00

Tableware

Bowl, bl opaque, grad dart, scalloped, 3-toed, 5¼".........................15.00
Bowl, yel, ftd, 8"...250.00
Cup/saucer, demi, gr & wht...12.00

Cup/saucer, demi, pumpkin, rare 400.00
Sugar bowl, crystal w/bl fired-on color, hinged metal lid, 5" 35.00

Miscellaneous

Bell, bl opaque, #725 .... 45.00
Jar, powder, bl opaque, Scottie dog, w/lid 70.00
Jar, powder, wht, Colonial lady, 2-pc, #647 .... 45.00
Jar, powder, wht, Scottie dog, w/lid 55.00
Lamp, electric boudoir, orange & wht, marbleized, 3-part 70.00
Mortar & pestle jar, wht, w/lid 10.00

Alexandrite Glass

Alexandrite is a type of art glass introduced around the turn of the twentieth century by Thomas Webb and Sons of England. It is recognized by its characteristic shading, pale yellow to rose and blue at the edge of the item. Although other companies (Moser, for example) produced glass they called Alexandrite, only examples made by Webb possess all the described characteristics and command premium prices. Amount and intensity of blue determines value. Our prices are for items with good average intensity, unless otherwise noted.

Bowl, slightly ruffled edge, shallow, 5" 400.00
Compote, Honeycomb, petal rim, wide amber ft, 5½" dia 1,650.00
Compote, Honeycomb (rare pattern), Webb, 2x5½" 1,650.00
Compote, Honeycomb, scalloped, 4½" dia 1,150.00
Cordial, bl rim to amber bowl, stem & ft, lt ribbing, 3" 635.00

Finger bowl and plate, peacock feather pattern, bowl: 1½x3⅜", $1,200.00 to $1,500.00. (Photo courtesy Cincinnati Art Galleries, LLC on LiveAuctioneers.com)

Hat, deep bl rim shading to amber at bottom, grnd pontil, 2¾" . 1,265.00
Punch cup, 2¾" 600.00
Vase, cylindrical w/ruffled top, 2½" 1,095.00
Vase, Dmn Quilt, petal rim, 3" 2,500.00
Vase, Honeycomb, ovoid w/6-sided rim, 2¾" 1,200.00
Wine, amber stem & ft, 4½" 2,000.00

Almanacs

The earliest evidence indicates that almanacs were used as long ago as ancient Egypt. Throughout the Dark Ages they were circulated in great volume and were referred to by more people than any other book except the Bible. *The Old Farmer's Almanac* first appeared in 1793 and has been issued annually since that time. Usually more of a pamphlet than a book (only a few have hard covers), the almanac provided planting and harvesting information to farmers, weather forecasts for seamen, medical advice, household hints, mathematical tutoring, postal rates, railroad schedules, weights and measures, 'receipts,' and jokes. Before 1800 the information was unscientific and based entirely on astrology and folklore. The first almanac in America was printed in 1639 by William Pierce Mariner; it contained data of this nature. One of the best-known editions, Ben Franklin's

Poor Richard's Almanac, was introduced in 1732 and continued to be printed for 25 years.

By the nineteenth century, merchants saw the advertising potential in a publication so widely distributed, and the advertising almanac evolved. These were distributed free of charge by drugstores and mercantiles and were usually somewhat lacking in information, containing simply a calendar, a few jokes, and a variety of ads for quick remedies and quack cures.

Today their concept and informative, often amusing text make almanacs popular collectibles that may usually be had at reasonable prices. Because they were printed in such large numbers and often saved from year to year, their prices are still low. Most fall within a range of $4.00 to $15.00. Very common examples may be virtually worthless; those printed before 1860 are especially collectible. Quite rare and highly prized are the Kate Greenaway 'Almanacks,' printed in London from 1883 to 1897. These are illustrated with her drawings of children, one for each calendar month. See also Kate Greenaway.

1839, The American Anti-Slavery Almanac for 1839, Vol 1 No. 4; 48 pages, published by S. W. Benedict, New York, many engravings showing injustices to slaves, string binding, VG, 7¼x4⅝", $235.00. (Photo courtesy Scott J. Winslow Associates, Inc. on LiveAuctioneers.com)

1829, Almanach de Gotha, G 50.00
1840, Harrison Almanac, JP Giffing, G- 45.00
1841, NE Anti-Slavery Almanac, JA Collins, VG 55.00
1845, Whig Almanac & United States Register, Greeley & McElrath, VG ..115.00
1846, Boston Almanac, VG 48.00
1847, General Taylor Old Rough & Ready Almanac, G 32.00
1849, Agricultural & Family Almanac, EX 30.00
1850, VB Palmer's Business-Men's Almanac, EX 48.00
1884, Ayer's Am Almanac, Dr JC Ayer & Co, 7½x5", G 130.00
1892, Warner's Safe Cure Almanac, EX 25.00
1898, Seven Barks Almanac, EX 75.00
1908, Gr's Almanac/August Flower & German Syrup, EX 35.00
1912, IHC Almanac & Encyclopedia, about 100 pgs, VG 90.00
1913, Swamp Root, Dr Kilmer & Co, Binghampton, NY 15.00
1917, Cirencester Almanac & Directory, VG 50.00
1941, Wilkes-Barre Record Almanac & Yearbook, VG 85.00
1966, Drag World...Drag Racing Almanac, EX 45.00

Aluminum

Aluminum, though being the most abundant metal in the earth's crust, always occurs in combination with other elements. Before a practical method for its refinement was developed in the late nineteenth century, articles made of aluminum were very expensive. After the process for commercial smelting was perfected in 1916, it became profitable to adapt the ductile, nontarnishing material to many uses.

By the late '30s, novelties, trays, pitchers, and many other tableware items were being produced. They were often handcrafted with elaborate decoration. Russel Wright designed a line of lovely pieces such as lamps, vases, and desk accessories that are becoming very collectible. Many who crafted the ware marked it with their company logo, and these signed pieces are attracting the most interest. Wendell August Forge (Grove City,

Pennsylvania) is a mark to watch for; this firm was the first to produce hammered aluminum (it is still made there today), and some of their examples are particularly nice. Upwardly mobile market values reflect their popularity with today's collectors. In general, 'spun' aluminum is from the '30s or early '40s, and 'hammered' aluminum is from the '30s to the '60s.

Basket, palm leaves, rnd w/flat-sided grip inserted on hdl, Everlast . 10.00
Basket, rnd hammered bowl w/beaded rim, dbl hdl w/twists, Buenilum .. 5.00
Basket, sq w/rolled-up rims, finger-wave hdl, Continental, 6x8" 35.00
Bookends, appl horseshoes, horses' heads in relief 85.00
Bowl, deep w/plain flat flared rim, no decor, Kensington, 7x11" 15.00
Bowl, dogwood pattern, plain fluted rim, Wendell A Forge, 2x7" .. 45.00
Buffet server/bun warmer, 3-ftd w/tulip inserts, II Farberware, 9" ... 25.00
Butter dish, bamboo design w/bamboo finial, Everlast, 4x4x7" L ... 10.00
Cake stand, band of shields decor, serrated, ped ft, Wilson, 8x12" . 15.00
Candy dish, 2 leaves w/looped stems, serrated, Buenilum, 6" 10.00
Candy dish, fruits, rnd w/3 indents, fluted rim, scrolled hdl, 9" dia ... 5.00
Casserole, bamboo w/bamboo finial & hdls, Everlast, 7" dia 10.00
Cigarette box, 4 pine cones on hammered hinged lid, Town, 5x3x2" .. 75.00
Coaster set, bamboo, 4 in ftd trivet-type folder, Everlast 20.00
Coaster set, mnt lion/duck/2 turkeys, Wendell A Forge, 3", w/cb box . 45.00
Compote, deep hammered bowl, short flared ped ft, unmk, 5x6" ... 10.00
Creamer/sugar, hammered, elbow hdls, flower finial, World Hand Forged .. 5.00
Creamer/sugar/tray, plain/beaded rims, scrolled hdl/finial, Buenilum . 15.00
Gravy boat, hammered w/mums, long hdl, w/tray, Continental 25.00
Ice bucket, hammered int, beaded rim, twisted hdl, Buenilum, 6" . 10.00
Lazy Susan, fruits/flowers, 2-tiered, upturned rims, 13" H, Cromwell . 10.00
Matchbox covers, pine cone or bittersweet, Wendell A Forge, ea . 65.00
Mint dish, dogwood, flat rim, 3-part glass insert, Wendell Forge, 12" ... 45.00
Pitcher, acorn & leaf, bulb, coiled hdl, Continental, 8" 25.00
Pitcher, bamboo, rolled rim w/ice lip, Everlast, 8" 35.00
Relish tray, flying geese in 4 compartments, tab hdls, A Armour, 5x16" .. 75.00
Tray, bar, ducks in flight & cattail, tab hdls, unmk, 9x16" 30.00
Tray, bread, tulips, appl tulip & ribbon hdls, R Kent, 8x13" 25.00
Tray, bread, wild rose, tab hdls, serrated, Continental, 6x13" 15.00

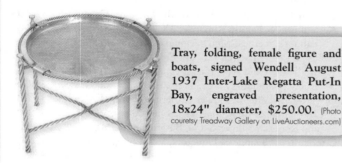

Tray, folding, female figure and boats, signed Wendell August 1937 Inter-Lake Regatta Put-In Bay, engraved presentation, 18x24" diameter, $250.00. (Photo couretsy Treadway Gallery on LiveAuctioneers.com)

Tray, sandwich, crane/bamboo, rnd w/appl hdls, Hand Forged, 9" . 35.00
Tray, serving, hammered w/deer/geese, appl hdls, Continental, 12x16" . 75.00

AMACO, American Art Clay Co.

AMACO is the logo of the American Art Clay Co. Inc., founded in Indianapolis, Indiana, in 1919, by Ted O. Philpot. They produced a line of art pottery from 1931 through 1938. The company is still in business but now produces only supplies, implements, and tools for the ceramic trade.

Values for AMACO have risen sharply, especially those for figurals, items with Art Deco styling, and pieces with uncommon shapes.

Bust, woman's head, hair drawn at nape, ivory gloss, 7" 395.00
Bust, woman's head, long str hair, bl gloss, paper label, 7" 395.00
Sculpture, woman's head, hair pulled bk, ivory gloss, 7" 390.00

Vase, bl mottle, incurvate rim, 4" 40.00
Vase, bl w/uneven texture, bulb, 4" 15.00
Vase, stylized trees, bl on red, sgn EA, #31, 7", EX 150.00
Vase, trees scenic, blk/bl on red, shouldered, #31, 7", EX 150.00
Vase, yel matt, organic form w/4 sides, 13¼" 360.00

Amberina Glass

Amberina, one of the earliest types of art glass, was developed in 1883 by Joseph Locke of the New England Glass Company. The trademark was registered by W.L. Libbey, who often signed his name in script within the pontil.

Amberina was made by adding gold powder to the batch, which produced glass in the basic amber hue. Part of the item, usually the top, was simply reheated to develop the characteristic deep red or fuchsia shading. Early amberina was mold blown, but cut and pressed amberina was also produced. The rarest type is plated amberina, made by New England for a short time after 1886. It has been estimated that less than 2,000 pieces were ever produced. Other companies, among them Hobbs, Brockunier; Mt. Washington Glass Company; and Sowerby's Ellison Glassworks of England, made their own versions, being careful to change the name of their product to avoid infringing on Libbey's patent. Prices realized at auction seem to be erratic, to say the least, and dealers appear to be 'testing the waters' with prices that start out very high only to be reduced later if the item does not sell at the original asking price. Lots of amberina glassware is of a more recent vintage — look for evidence of an early production, since the later wares are worth much less than glassware that can be attributed to the older makers. Generic amberina with hand-painted flowers will bring lower prices as well. Our values are taken from auction results and dealer lists, omitting the extremely high and low ends of the range.

Basket, swirled w/rigaree rim, thorny hdl w/raspberry prunts, 7" 450.00
Bowl, centerpiece, enamel & gold florals, 16" L, NM 2,525.00
Bowl, Dmn Quilt, ovoid w/inverted scalloped rim, 8" 225.00
Celery vase, Dmn Optic, cylinder w/crimped sq rim, NE, 6½" 225.00
Celery vase, Dmn Quilt, cylinder w/tight ruffled rim, NE, 4½" ... 175.00
Condiment set, cruet/2 shakers/mustard, Coinspot, Pairpoint caddy .. 600.00
Epergne, 1-lily, crimped everted rim, ruffled base, Mt WA, 9" ... 2,600.00
Punch cup, Dmn Quilt & thorn pattern, amber reed hdl, 2½" 75.00

Salt and pepper shakers in silver-plated holder signed James W. Tufts, 7¼x5", $180.00. (Photo courtesy Ferrell Auction Co., Inc. on LiveAuctioneers.com)

Spittoon, Dmn Quilt, rose ruffled rim, Mt WA, 5" dia 225.00
Toothpick holder, cylindrical cup in swan-hdld Tufts holder, 3½" ... 550.00
Vase, diagonal swirls, bulb urn, amber rigaree rim, Harach, 10" ... 250.00
Vase, jack-in-pulpit, optic ribs, fuchsia rim, Libbey, 5" 450.00
Vase, jack-in-pulpit, ruby rim, amber stem w/ruby ft, NE, 10" 275.00
Vase, optic ribs, ft lily form w/trifold rim, Libbey, 9" 350.00
Vase, swirl ribbed trumpet form w/amber ruffled rim & ft, 20" 515.00
Vinegar jar, Coinspot, fuchsia around top, metal spout, NE, 4" ... 425.00

Plated Amberina

Bowl, 6-pinch rim, minor mfg anomalies, 3¼x8" 9,000.00
Bowl, bulb w/inverted rim, 3x5" 7,800.00
Creamer, wide spout, amber hdl, minor mfg anomalies, 2½" ... 10,800.00
Cruet, swirled/ribbed neck, amber stopper/hdl, 7", EX 10,800.00
Cup, bulb, amber hdl, 2½" 4,500.00
Mug, slightly incurvate sides, amber ring hdl, 2⅝" 225.00
Pitcher, tankard, 8¾" 17,000.00
Pitcher, tankard, amber ear hdl, 5½" 18,000.00
Shaker, pillar form, strong color, 4" 4,500.00
Sugar bowl, 2 appl amber hdls, 3¾x5¾" 15,600.00
Toothpick holder, hexagonal rim, star pontil, minor rim wear, 2½". 10,800.00
Tumbler, 3¾", $2,100 to 2,900.00
Tumbler, lemonade, appl hdl, 5" 4,000.00
Vase, 4 lg dents to body, flared/crimped rim, minor mfg flaws, 4¾".19,200.00

American Indian Art

That time when the American Indian was free to practice the crafts and culture that was his heritage has always held a fascination for many. They were a people who appreciated beauty of design and colorful decoration in their furnishings and clothing; and because instruction in their crafts was a routine part of their rearing, they were well accomplished. Several tribes developed areas in which they excelled. The Navajo were weavers and silversmiths, the Zuni, lapidaries. Examples of their craftsmanship are very valuable. Today even the work of contemporary Indian artists — weavers, silversmiths, carvers, and others — is highly collectible. Unless otherwise noted, values are for items with no obvious damage or excessive wear (EX/NM). For more information we recommend *Ornamental Indian Artifacts; Rare & Unusual Indian Artifacts; Antler, Bone & Shell Artifacts;* and *Indian Trade Relics,* all by Lar Hothem. Our advisor for this section is Larry Garvin of Back to Earth; he is listed in the Directory under Ohio.

Key:
bw — beadwork   p-h — prehistoric
COA — Certificate of Authenticity   s-s — sinew sewn

Apparel and Accessories

Before the white traders brought the Indian women cloth from which to sew their garments and beads to use for decorating them, clothing was made from skins sewn together with sinew, usually made of animal tendon. Porcupine quills were dyed bright colors and woven into bags and armbands and used to decorate clothing and moccasins. Examples of early quillwork are scarce today and highly collectible.

Early in the nineteenth century, beads were being transported via pony pack trains. These 'pony' beads were irregular shapes of opaque glass imported from Venice. Nearly always blue or white, they were twice as large as the later 'seed' beads. By 1870 translucent beads in many sizes and colors had been made available, and Indian beadwork had become commercialized. Each tribe developed its own distinctive methods and preferred decorations, making it possible for collectors today to determine the origin of many items. Soon after the turn of the twentieth century, the craft of beadworking began to diminish.

Bandolier, Chippewa, floral bw on wht, early 1900s, 40x16" 1,400.00
Belt, Chippewa, bw on satin w/red tradecloth trim, 1900s, 42x10"..1,900.00
Cuffs, Chippewa, floral bw w/cloth trim, 1900s, 7x6"+9" fringe... 250.00
Cuffs, Sioux, geometric bw, s-s buckskin, 1900s, 5x5"+5" fringe.. 275.00
Dress, Cheyenne child's, s-s bw on buckskin w/shells/tin cones, 1880s. 5,000.00

Leggings, Blackfoot, striped buckskin, bw/horsehair trim, 1950s, 40" ...350.00
Moccasins, Cheyenne, s-s ochered buffalo hide, 1880s, 11" 3,250.00
Moccasins, Potowatomi, deer hide, quills, bw, silk ribbon, 7¼x3". 600.00
Moccasins, Seneca child's, bw tops & cuffs on buckskin, 1890s, 9"..1,800.00
Moccasins, s-s beads, leather, rawhide soles, 1940, 11½" L........... 650.00
Vest, Sioux child's, geometrics, s-s, 15x16" 2,000.00
Yoke, Plateau child's, mc bw stars & cowry shells, early 1900s, 12x15"...650.00

Bags and Cases

The Indians used bags for many purposes, and most display excellent form and workmanship. Of the types listed below, many collectors consider the pipe bag to be the most desirable form. Pipe bags were long, narrow, leather and bead or quillwork creations made to hold tobacco in a compartment at the bottom and the pipe, with the bowl removed from the stem, in the top. Long buckskin fringe was used as trim and complemented the quilled and beaded design to make the bag a masterpiece of Indian art.

Sioux, quill and beaded dance/tobacco bag, 1890, 9¼", $985.00.
(Photo courtesy Jackson's International Auctioneers and Appraisers of Fine Art and Antiques)

Apache, flap pouch, silver Navajo-made button, ca 1880-90s, 12x6½"..4,500.00
Cheyenne, tobacco, bl & wht pony bw w/tin cones, fringe, ca 1790-1830s, 20".6,000.00
Comanche, coin purse, brass & seed beads, thong tie, ca 1890s...400.00
Great Lakes, change purse, 5 kinds of beads, some cloth deterioriation, 3¾".55.00
Great Lakes, flat, beads, red cloth edging, early 1900s, 7⅝x7⅝"... 100.00
Iroquois, lady's purse, Great Lakes region, early 1900s, 6¾" 175.00
Lakota Sioux, woman's, buffalo bull design in beading, beaded hdl, 17".4,500.00
Lakota, pouch, geometric design in red/wht/bl/gr, fringe, 7x7" .4,500.00
Menomonee, friendship, seed beads, edging, yarn & thread, 11½x6" ...450.00
Northern Plains/Prairie, personal, bw outline, hawk bells, 12x4" .550.00
Plains, strike-a-lite, buckskin, tin cone attachments, beaded, ca 1950s ..350.00
Winnebago, woman's, bw on leather w/cloth lining, 1925, 14" L .475.00

Baskets

In the following listings, examples are coil built unless noted otherwise.

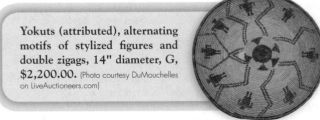

Yokuts (attributed), alternating motifs of stylized figures and double zigags, 14" diameter, G, $2,200.00. (Photo courtesy DuMouchelles on LiveAuctioneers.com)

Cherokee, split river cane, hdld, 6⅛x6⅛" 50.00
Hopi, Second Mesa, grass/split yucca, 1940s, 16x14" 3,200.00
Hopi, tray, wicker, Siwi warp, Sivaapi weft, eagle design, 1980, 14"...225.00
Jicarilla Apache, berry, willow/aniline dyes, 1940s, 5½x15¼" 750.00
Jicarilla Apache, tray, willow/aniline dyes, 1993, 4½x19".............. 850.00
Micmac, lidded, thistle design sides, periwinkle design top, ca 1920s, 7¾x10½".350.00
Navajo, wedding, natural & dyed yucca, ca 1875, 2¾x11¼" 325.00

Pomo, gift, sage root/bulrush/willow, flying geese design, unused, ca 1920s, 3x6" .. 750.00
Yokuts, sedge root, redbud, fern root, ca 1900s, 6¼x12" 3,500.00

Blades and Points

Relics of this type usually display characteristics of a general area, time period, or a particular location. With study, those made by the Plains Indians are easily discerned from those of the West Coast. Because modern man has imitated the art of the Indian by reproducing these artifacts through modern means, use caution before investing your money in 'too good to be authentic' specimens. For a more thorough study we recommend *Authenticating Ancient Indian Artifacts: How to Recognize Reproduction and Altered Artifacts; Ancient Indian Artifacts, Volume I, Introduction to Collecting;* and *Ancient Indian Artifacts, Volume 2, Collecting Flint Weapons & Tools*, by Jim Bennett; and *Indian Artifacts: The Best of the Midwest; Paleo-Indian Artifacts; and Arrowheads & Projectile Points;* by Lar Hothem; and *Indian Bannerstones & Related Artifacts*, by Lar Hothem and James R. Bennett.

Agate Basin, mottle bl Upper Mercer, 3⅞" 2,500.00
Alamance, weathered silicified shale, deeply incurvate baseline, Late Paleo, 2½" ... 275.00
Beaver Lake, gray hornstone, COA, Late Paleo, 1x2⅞" 450.00
Birch Creek, reddish-brn jasper w/basal color line, ½x2³⁄₁₆" 235.00
Browns Valley, Niobrara chert, Late Paleo, 1⅞" 75.00
Clovis, translucent, obverse fluted, COA, Knife River, 2¹¹⁄₁₆" ... 2,500.00
Coshocton, flint, diagonal lightning line, COA, 1⅛x3½" 4,000.00
Dalton, serrated, Crowley's Ridge chert, 2½" 150.00
Golondrina, salvaged as an end-scraper, rstrs ear, 2⅜" 350.00
Hell Gap, orange-amber flint, resharpened sz, 1¾" 250.00
Holcombe, cream/bl Upper Mercer, thin, fluted faces, 2" 500.00
Lanceolate, tan, high shoulders, Late Paleo, 3⅛" 400.00
Lanceolate, patinated tan-cream Flint Ridge, Late Paleo, 3¼" 150.00
Paleo, patinated preform, Burlington chert, COA, 2x5¾" 2,000.00
Plainview, wht flint trn cherry-yel w/age, 1x3" 250.00
Prismatic, honey-colored translucent Flint Ridge, sm shaft-scraper & graver tips. 20.00
Quad, gray hornstone, base sides ground, COA, Late Paleo, 2" ... 400.00
Scottsbluff, slight shouldering & ground stem edges, Late Paleo, 3⅛" . 475.00
Stemmed lanceolate, gray & tan Nellie chert, Stringtown, Late Paleo, 2⅝" . 35.00

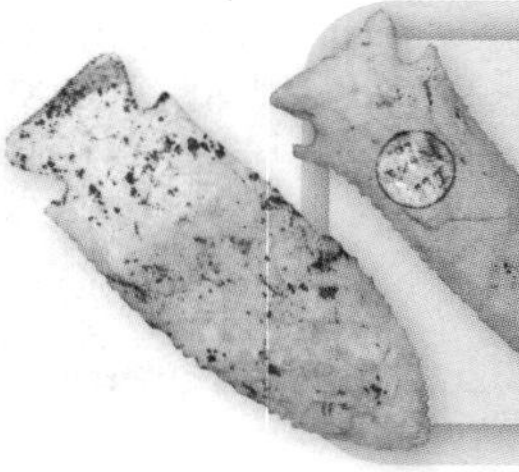

Stilwell, numerous ground deposits, Archaic, Illinois, 4⅛", $400.00 to $425.00; Stilwell, serrated blade edges, Archaic, Illinois, 3⅞", $350.00 to $375.00. (Photo courtesy Back to Earth/Larry Garvin)

Stringtown lance, patinated, basal spurs, 3 sm fire pops, Flint Ridge, 3¼" .. 950.00
Uniface, Coastal Plains chert, heavy dk amber patina, partly translucent, 3¾" ... 150.00

Ceremonial Items

Dance cuffs, harness leather covered w/sm shells, 1930s, 9x3" 110.00
Dance moccasins, Cheyenee, bw on hide, V design/flying geese, ca 1880s, 10" L ... 900.00
Dance roach, Plains, porcupine hair w/mc ornaments, 1950s, 15" .. 225.00
Dance roach, Prairie, porcupine & deer hair, 11" woven base, 1900s.. 550.00
Dance wand, Sioux, hide bound, wrapped w/2 mtd buffalo horns, 9x22" .. 190.00
Drum, Pueblo, rawhide on cottonwood, mc pnt, mid-1900s, 7x11" ... 325.00
Headdress, Hopi, 2 corrugated cb layers, earth pigments, 1950s, 13x12" .. 325.00
Mask, Mexican, hand cvd & colored, early 1900s, 10x6" 60.00
Medicine necklace, Crow, dog teeth/trade beads, attached bag, 19th C .. 450.00
Rattle, Plains, rawhide w/wood hdl, s-s, X on face, 1870s, 10x5" . 500.00
Rattle, Sioux, rawhide 'doughnut,' wrapped bw hdl, 1930s, 10x5"+fringe. 800.00
Spoon, NW Coast, wrought silver w/human figural hdl, 1950s, 12" .. 140.00
Spoon, Ojibway, cvd w/eagle effigy hdl, late 1800s, 14x5" 325.00
Staff, Peyote, cvd wood w/3 2" beaded bands, ca 1910, 43" 225.00
Staff, speaker's, owl effigy, cvd from branch, dk patina, 1900s, 34" ... 250.00
War club, steatite/wood/feathers, horsehair hdl, early 1900s, 20" L, 8½" drop. 450.00

Dolls

Female with molded leather head and arms, painted features, beaded costume, moccasins and headdress, early twentieth century, 15", VG, $210.00. (Photo courtesy Skinner Auctioneers and Appraisers of Antiques and Fine Art on LiveAuctioneers.com)

Hopi, kachina, cottonwood/cloth, ca 1970s, 12¼" 225.00
Hopi, kachina, Eagle Dancer, R Allison, 1990, 14" 250.00
Hopi, kachina, OTA Skirt Man, dtd 1937, 10" 800.00
Hopi, kachina, Payik'ala or Three-horn, 1980, 10¾" 250.00
Hopi, kachina, Road Runner, 1950s, 11" 425.00
Hopi, kachina, Shalako Mana, EX cvg & detail, 1950s, 11" 110.00
Hopi, kachina, Shalako, 1-pc, 1980s, 20" 225.00
Sioux, buckskin & cloth, human hair, fringed leggings, 1950s, 12" .. 650.00
Ute, stuffed calico w/beaded leggings & ft, 1900, 11" 300.00

Domestics

Blanket, Navajo chief, 2nd Phase, stripes/steps/dmns, 1900s, 60x51" ... 7,000.00
Cradle cover, bw on buckskin, s-s, early heavy muslin, 1890s, 27x8" . 4,250.00
Cradleboard, Menominee, pine w/bentwood sunshade, plain, 1900s, 17" . 550.00
Saddle, Cheyenne, buffalo rawhide w/wooden sides/horn trees, 19th C .. 900.00
Spoon, Ojibway, cvd wood, stepped neck, bird effigy finial, 1890s, 9" . 275.00

Jewelry and Adornments

As early as 500 A.D., Indians in the southwest drilled turquoise nuggets and strung them on cords made of sinew or braided hair. The Spanish introduced them to coral, and it became a popular item of jewelry; abalone and clamshells were favored by the Coastal Indians. Not until the last half of the nineteenth century did the Indians learn to work with silver. Each tribe developed its own distinctive style and preferred design, which until about 1920 made it possible to determine tribal origin with some degree of accuracy. Since that time, because of modern means of communication and travel, motifs have become less distinct.

Quality Indian silver jewelry may be antique or contemporary. Age, though certainly to be considered, is not as important a factor as fine workmanship and good stones. Pre-1910 silver will show evidence of hammer marks, and designs are usually simple. Beads have sometimes been shaped from coins. Stones tend to be small; when silver wire was used, it is usually square. To insure your investment, choose a reputable dealer.

Belt, Navajo, 8 silver conchos ea w/natural turq cabochon, 3x39" ... 325.00
Belt, Navajo, 9 silver & turq conchos & buckle on blk leather, 1970s . 550.00
Bolo, Navajo, eagle dancer figural, silver/turq/coral, 1980s, 7" 275.00
Bolo, Zuni, chanel inlay Sun Face, jet/MOP/coral, matching tips, 21" . 160.00
Bolo, Zuni, inlay eagle, jet/turq/MOP, sgn, 1970s, 18" 425.00
Bracelet, Navajo, coral cabochons set in silver, late 1900s, ⅝" W . 275.00
Bracelet, Navajo, wrought silver w/lg turq stone, 1980s, 3" W 110.00
Bracelet, Zuni, wrought silver w/3 rows of turq, 1980s, 1" W 200.00

Breast collar, Sioux, 4" hairpipe bone beads/trade beads, 1950s, 54" ..275.00
Earrings, Navajo, wrought silver & turq cluster, late 1900s, 1" 120.00
Hair ties, Sioux, quilled, tin cones, 19th C, 11", pr 300.00
Hat band, Navajo, silver w/turq cabochons, narrow, 1940s, 26" .. 140.00
Necklace, Comanche, beads & cvd bone elk teeth, 1900s, 12".... 275.00
Necklace, Navajo, silver w/cross pendant, top-shaped beads, historic .. 300.00
Necklace, Navajo, sterling silver beads, 1930, 20", $300 to 500.00
Necklace, shell beads, stone pendant, Late Horizon, 22", $200 to ..300.00
Pendant, Navajo, Kings Manassa turq, silver leaf decor, hallmark, 2x1" .130.00
Squash blossom, Navajo, silver, 12-segment/lg turq stone, 3" naja, 24" ..350.00
Watch bracelet, Navajo, 6 lt turq stones, 2" W 130.00

Pipes

Pipe bowls were usually carved from soft stone, such as catlinite or red pipestone, an argilaceous sedimentary rock composed mainly of hardened clay. Steatite was also used. Some ceremonial pipes were simply styled, while others were intricately designed naturalistic figurals, sometimes in bird or frog forms called effigies. Their stems, made of wood and often covered with leather, were sometimes nearly a yard in length.

Bird effigy, steatite, incised wings, polished surface, 4" L 2,500.00
Catlinite, decorative stem flange, security hole, 1⅜x2¼" 350.00

Catlinite, effigy with egg-shaped bowl clutched in eagle talons, carved wooden stem, bowl: 2x3", $1,000.00. (Photo courtesy James D. Julia Inc.)

Catlinite, extended prow & angled bowl, 1¾x2⅝" 300.00
Catlinite, lead/pewter inlay on bowl & stem, 1⅞x3¼" 425.00
Catlinite, ring decor, dot embellishment on rim, 1⅞x3¼" 375.00
Coffee bean, blk polished steatite, rare, 2⅜" L 1,250.00
Effigy, Copena-type hawk, Middle Woodland, 8" L, VG 2,000.00
Effigy, gray steatite, otter holding fish in front paws, 3½" 450.00
Elbow type, catlinite, protohistoric, 1x1" 300.00
Elbow, Cherokee, polished steatite, 1¼x¹¹⁄₁₆x2⅝" 300.00
Elbow, gray steatite, pecked & ground to shape, 4¼" L 100.00
Elbow, sq bowl & stem, gray steatite, 3¼x4¹⁄₁₆" 750.00
Micmac, catlinite, early historic, 1⅝x⅞", $700 to 800.00
Plains style, catlinite, t-shaped, 3¹³⁄₁₆x6¹³⁄₁₆" 1,000.00
Plains type, catlinite head, wooden stem, heavy patina, 17¼" ..1,800.00
Sun-disc, red pipestone, prothistoric, 3¾" L 1,500.00
T-shaped, dk gr polished steatite, 2⅛x5¾" 1,500.00
Wichita, catlinite, 6 dimples on stem & bowl, early historic, 1⅞x1⅝", $500 to ...600.00

Pottery

Indian pottery is nearly always decorated in such a manner as to indicate the tribe that produced it or the pueblo in which it was made. For instance, the designs of Cochiti potters were usually scattered forms from nature or sacred symbols. The Zuni preferred an ornate repetitive decoration of a closer configuration. They often used stylized deer and bird forms, sometimes in dimensional applications.

Acoma, jar, birds w/in arched frames, sq prayer boxes, 1890s, 10x14" .. 3,500.00
Acoma, olla w/charcoal stepped designs, reddish int & base bands, 11x13" ..1,950.00
Acoma, olla, ca 1930s, 11¼" dia.. 800.00
Acoma, olla, curvilinear forms, concave base, 1920s, 10x11" 800.00
Anasazi, bowl, blk-on-wht w/geometrics, p-h, as found, 3x8" 450.00

Anasazi, bowl, Salado Gila deer w/geometrics, p-h, rpr, 7x13"..... 475.00
Anasazi, jar, olla form w/busy geometrics, rstr, 12x18"...............1,600.00
Anasazi, ladle, blk on wht curvilinear decor, p-h, rstr, 3x11x6" ... 500.00
Anasazi, pitcher, blk-on-wht geometrics, crude hdl, p-h, rstr, 9x6" ..450.00
Anasazi, pitcher, blk-on-wht geometrics, p-h, rstr, 5x5" 225.00
Casas Grandes, effigy pot, rabbits/lines, lizard on top, Quesada, 10"...2,500.00
Hopi, jar, effigy, full face, necklace/earrings/brow band, 1900s, 6x5" ... 1,800.00
Hopi, jar, mc bird-tail decor at shoulder, mid-1900s, 2x5" 110.00
Hopi, jar, stylized avian/geometric forms, buff slip, Frog Woman, 4x6"...275.00
Hopi, wedding vase, polished blkware, swirl form, Komalestawa, 6" ..650.00
Matsaki, bowl, birds/feathers, mc, p-h, rstr/over-pnt, 5x12" 275.00

Mississippian, bottle, red on buff, painted swastika swirl, neck with stairstep temple design, perforated base, 1200 – 1650 A.D., 9¾x7", $1,800.00 to $2,000.00. (Photo courtesy Back to Earth/Larry Garvin)

Santa Clara, basket, Yei figures/bugs, mc, Margaret & Luther, 7".425.00
Santa Clara, bowl, redware w/cvd motif revealing buff core, 4x8".. 1,100.00
Santa Clara, jar, blackware, repeating feathers/serpents, 1970s, 9x10"..600.00
Santa Clara, jar, blackware, serpents, M Tafoya, w/lid, 7x8" 3,000.00
Santa Clara, jar, blackware, stylized kachina/chief heads, Tafoya, 8x10" ..900.00
Santa Clara, vase, blackware, serpents, Margaret (Tafoya), 14x11"..7,500.00
Zia/Acoma, olla, pnt vessel w/concave base, ca 1915, 11½" dia 1,800.00
Zuni, jar, birds/foliage/classic figures, 1890s, 8x11"....................1,700.00
Zuni, jar, X-hatched bands/geometrics/etc, 1890s, 8x12" 6,000.00

Pottery, San Ildefonso

The pottery of the San Ildefonso pueblo is especially sought after by collectors today. Under the leadership of Maria Martinez and her husband Julian, experiments began about 1918 which led to the development of the 'black-on-black' design achieved through exacting methods of firing the ware. They discovered that by smothering the fire at a specified temperature, the carbon in the smoke that ensued caused the pottery to blacken. Maria signed her work (often 'Marie') from the late teens to the sixties; she died in 1980. Today examples with her signature may bring prices in the $500.00 to $4,500.00 range.

Bowl, blackware, birds along rim, Marie & Julian, ca 1954, 4x8", NM...2,040.00
Jar, blackware/gunmetal finish, no decor, long neck, Maria, 9x9"..6,000.00
Jar, blackware, curvilinear designs in 4 panels, Marie & Julian, 7x10".. 3,250.00
Jar, blackware, feathers, early 1900s, 7x6" 300.00
Jar, blackware, traditional/non-traditional forms, C Dunlap, '78, 11x16".2,750.00
Jar, high polish, raindrop lip, Maria Poveka, mid-1900s, 8x9"....7,500.00
Plate, blackware, lg 10-leg serpent, Rose, 1977, 11" 5,000.00
Plate, buff & red slip, feathers, Blue Corn, 1974, 4" 950.00
Seed jar, sgraffito zoomorphic figure on marbleized slip, Sanchez, 5"..650.00

Rugs, Navajo

Classic geometrics, blk/red/wht/gray, 1950s, 51x84" 850.00
Dmn eye dazzler w/serrated bands, 3-color border, 1940s, 84x52" .1,600.00
Diamonds (3) & fancy zigzags, 1940s, 63x40" 1,100.00
Diamonds, 4 swastika & 4 sm dmns, brn/wht/red/wht, 1940s, 60x40"..600.00
Ganado area, dmns & zigzag bands, red/blk/gray/wht, G age, 92x64". 1,500.00
Ganado area, terraced dmns, gray/blk/red/brn, 1920s, 96x55"...1,100.00

Klagetoh classic, natural & vegetal dyes, 1960s, 57x35"............... 550.00
Pictorial, 3 Yei figures/cornstalk/rainbow, 1950s, 46x36".............. 350.00
Stepped deisgn w/centeral lozenge, red/gray/blk, 1930s, 64x40" .. 900.00
Two Gray Hills, central dbl dmn, 3-color border, 1980s, 36x25".. 400.00
Valero stars/dmns/stepped sqs on cream, 1930s, 60x37" 600.00

Shaped Stone Artifacts

Bannerstone, green banded slate pick, excellent banding, Ohio, 3¾", $700.00 to $800.00. (Photo courtesy Larry Garvin/Back to Earth)

Bannerstone, banded slate, dbl-notched butterfly type, 4½" W, $400 to.. 500.00
Bannerstone, pick, gr banded slate, COA, 3¼x1⁵⁄₁₆" 450.00
Bannerstone, yel & wht quartzite, 3⅝x2" 2,000.00
Discoidal, quartzite, lg cup, Mississippian, 2⅛" dia 350.00
Discoidal, rose quartz, cupped, Mississippian, 1⅝x2½" dia 500.00
Discoidal, translucent gold quartzite, biscuit type, 3" 1,000.00
Gamestone, egg-shaped, polished, Woodland, brn quartz, 2⁷⁄₁₆x1¾" .. 50.00
Plummet, grooved-top, dk quartz, Archaic-Woodland, 2¼x1⅛", $175 to. 200.00
Plummet, wht quartzite, 1⅛x3⅜"..................................... 100.00

Tools

Awl, needle, bone splinter w/EX patina/polish, OH, 2".................. 30.00
Awl, needle, split bird bone, Late Woodland, 3" 200.00
Awl, split deer bone, tip has abrupt taper, OH, 3" 30.00
Awl, trigger, raccoon bone, 3".. 45.00
Axe, ¾-groove w/facial effigy on heel, p-h, 4x6".......................325.00
Fishhook, deer bone, U-shape, Midwest, ¹⁵⁄₁₆" 100.00
Gouge, beaver tooth w/wood hdl, leather wrap, 1x3" 175.00
Needle, split bird bone, glossy, Woodland, OH, 4" 75.00

Spatulate/spud, drilled Southern style, Georgia, 5⁹⁄₁₆x4½", $1,000.00 to $1,500.00. (Photo courtesy Back to Earth/ Larry Garvin)

Weapons

Bow, Apache, yel ochred hardwood, buckskin hdl, 1900s, 37".....400.00
Bow, Hupa, str w/pnt int, red ext, traditional type, 1950s, 33".....350.00
Bow & arrow, Sioux, cvd wood, 19th C, 47", +arrow w/sinew-bound point. 400.00
Tomahawk/pipe, brass tack hdl decor, 1890-1900, 21" L 1,800.00
War club, Catlinite, lead insets, horsehair wrap, 1900, 2¼x5½" ..635.00
War club, Cheyenne, stone head, rawhide-wrapped hdl, 19th C, 15" ..650.00
War club, Great Lakes, hardwood head w/cvd otter effigy, 1900s, 26" ..300.00
War club, horn head, Plains, 1860-90, 17½x9", $600 to 800.00
War club, stone w/pewter inlay, bw hdl, late 1800s, 23" 800.00

Miscellaneous

Aquatint, Wahktageli Yankton Sioux, K Bodmer, mid-1900s, 17x12"+fr...700.00

Multi-media art, Navajo landscape w/hogan, R Draper, 10x24"+fr.. 225.00
Peace medal, JQ Adams, silver, on ornate presentation collar, 1825..425.00
Peace medal, Millard Fillmore, S Ellis hallmark, 1859, 3" 400.00
Silkscreen, Navajo on horse lights cigarette, Chee, 1959, 13x18"+fr.. 325.00
Tempera pnt, Long Journey, figures in robes, D O'leary, 22x30"+fr .. 300.00
Watercolor, 2 horses & lg Ponderosa pine, Tahoma, '45, 17x13"+fr .3,000.00
Watercolor, Horse Tail Dancers, JE Pena, 1950s, 10x11"+fr 375.00
Watercolor, mtn lion in tree waiting for deer, Tahoma, '45, 26x20"+fr...3,750.00
Watercolor, Navajo dancer w/lg torches, Tahoma, 1941, 6x4"+fr .. 1,400.00
Watercolor, Navajo, Yeibeichai figure, R Chee, ca 1970, 14x11"+fr..550.00

American Painted Porcelain

    The American china-painting movement can be traced back to an extracurricular class attended by art students at the McMicken School of Design in Cincinnati. These students, who were the wives and daughters of the city's financial elite, managed to successfully paint numerous porcelains for display in the Woman's Pavilion of the 1876 United States Centennial Exposition held in Philadelphia — an amazing feat considering the high technical skill required for proficiency, as well as the length of time and multiple firings necessary to finish the ware. From then until 1917 when the United States entered World War I, china painting was a profession as well as a popular amateur pursuit for many people, particularly women. In fact, over 25,000 people were involved in this art form at the turn of the last century.

    Collectors and antique dealers have discovered American hand-painted porcelain, and they have become aware of its history, beauty, and potential value. For more information on this subject, *Antique Trader's Comprehensive Guide to American Painted Porcelain* and *Painted Porcelain Jewelry and Buttons: Collector's Identification & Value Guide* by our advisor, Dorothy Kamm (see Directory, Florida) are the culmination of a decade of research; we recommend them highly for further study.

    Though American pieces are of high quality and commensurate with their European counterparts, they are much less costly today. Generally, you will pay as little as $20.00 for a 6" plate and less than $75.00 for many other items. Values are based on aesthetic appeal, quality of the workmanship, size, rarity of the piece and of the subject matter, and condition. Age is the least important factor, because most American painted porcelains are not dated. (Factory backstamps are helpful in establishing the approximate time period an item was decorated, but they aren't totally reliable.)

Bar pin, brass-plated bezel, 1½" W, $25 to 55.00
Bowl, 4¾", $50 to.. 75.00
Bowl, fruit/currants, Hutschenreuther, Selb, 1880-1910, 10½" L. 105.00
Brooch, gold-plated bezel, 1½" dia, $35 to 55.00
Cake plate, $35 to 75.00
Celery tray, $35 to 75.00
Cup/saucer.. 45.00
Cup/saucer, bouillon, $35 to.. 55.00
Gravy boat, $55 to 75.00
Mug, $40 to... 75.00
Mugs, juice, apple branches, Bavaria, 1900-15, 3", set of 4, $60 to.80.00
Pin tray, $30 to.. 50.00
Plate, 6", $10 to... 35.00
Plate, 8", $45 to... 75.00
Plate, blank: C.T. Altwasser, Germany, 1875, $25 to 50.00
Ring stand, forget-me-nots, gold rim & hdl, Fr, 1900-41, 5⅞" L ... 65.00
Salt cellar, $20 to 40.00
Scarf pin, medallion, brass-plated bezel & shank, 1¼", $35 to 65.00
Shakers, pr, $25 to 40.00
Shirtwaist button, 1" dia, $20 to.. 40.00

Tray, oval, pink roses on light blue band, double handled, unmarked, signed Elaswot, slight wear to gold edge, circa 1900 – 1925, 16½x11", $75.00. (Photo courtesy Dorothy Kamm)

Amphora

The Amphora Porcelain Works in the Teplitz-Turn area of Bohemia produced Art Nouveau-styled vases and figurines during the latter part of the 1800s through the first few decades of the twentieth century. They marked their wares with various stamps, some incorporating the name and location of the pottery with a crown or a shield. Because Bohemia was part of the Austro-Hungarian empire prior to WWI, some examples are marked Austria; items marked with the Czechoslovakia designation were made after the war.

Teplitz was a town where most of the Austrian pottery was made. There are four major contributors to this pottery. One was Amphora, also known as RStK (Reissner, Stellmacher & Kessel). This company was the originator of the Amphora line. Edward Stellmacher, who was a founding member, went out on his own, working from 1905 until 1910. During this same time, Ernst Wahliss often used Amphora molds for his wares. He did similar work and was associated with the Amphora line. Turn Teplitz was never a pottery line. It was a stamp used to signify the towns where the wares were made. There were four lines: Amphora, Paul Dachsel, Edward Stellmacher, and Ernst Wahliss. More information can be found by referring to *Monsters and Maidens, Amphora Pottery of the Art Nouveau Era*, by Byron Vreeland, and *The House of Amphora* by Richard L. Scott. All decoration described in the listings that follow is hand painted unless otherwise indicated.

Our advisor for this category is Kevin Cobabe; he is listed in the Directory under California.

Amphora

Vase, appl flower heads, 4 upswept scrolled supports, #3581, 14x6" . 295.00
Vase, floral panels w/gold, gourd shape, #G3730, ca 1900, 16½", NM . 3,600.00
Vase, frog (3D) on lily pads on rim, mc, sm rstr, #4099/52, 10x7" .. 7,200.00
Vase, lady in landscape w/gold, RStK, 8½x5½" 6,600.00
Vase, lady's emb profile, 3D flowers, mc swirls/pk, #0607, 17x12" .. 1,650.00
Vase, lady's portrait, gold hdls, w/lid, #321, 7x5½", EX 6,600.00
Vase, lady's portrait in landscape, #464, RStK, ca 1900, 15x6" . 3,350.00
Vase, lady's portrait/moth/thistles, shouldered, RStK, 12x5" 6,600.00
Vase, lady's portrait, waisted neck/wide base, RStK, 5¾x5½" 5,150.00
Vase, lady's portrait/water/sun setting, ovoid, RStK, 8½x4½" 6,600.00
Vase, lady's portrait (great detail) w/much gold, #468, 10x6" .. 14,500.00
Vase, lady's portrait w/much gold, bottle form, #525, 6¾", NM.. 4,250.00
Vase, maiden w/flowers in long hair, cylindrical, RStK, 9¾x5¾". 5,500.00
Vase, moth/flowers/garlands w/gold, slim, ftd, RStK, 15⅜"........ 3,000.00
Vase, tiger/flowers/leaves w/gold (VG), RStK, drilled, 10" 950.00

Paul Dachsel

Jug, mushrooms w/red caps/forest scene w/lustre, #1110 6, 6⅝", NM. 850.00
Vase, artichoke form w/faux jewels, #103/10, 6" 1,950.00
Vase, elk in landscape, circle borders w/gold, 17½" 1,550.00
Vase, invt fern fronds in relief, bl, ca 1907, 6½" 2,350.00
Vase, mushrooms at base, blk trees in bkgrnd, slight irid, 15¼".. 2,100.00
Vase, mushrooms w/pearlescent stems/birch trees, 15¾", NM.26,500.00
Vase, pines w/appl red pine cones, 6" 1,175.00
Vase, tree trunks/leaves/berries, bl/tan/gold, cylindrical, 6", EX... 775.00
Water jug, roses/foliage/gold, 2-spout, arched hdls, #1165, 8⅛". 2,150.00

Edward Stellmacher

Bust, lady w/ribboned hat, gold trim, sm chips, 20x16" 2,400.00
Vase, Bedouin on horseback, mc on blk, 4 sm loop hdls, 10½" 150.00
Vase, cactus form w/ornate hdls/blossoms, ftd, 18" 1,550.00
Vase, female warrior w/eagle helmet, squeeze-bag, 12x7" 7,200.00
Vase, maiden w/poppy crown, tube-line & enameling, 8½x7½". 5,700.00
Vase, roses, mc on mottle, 4 sm loop hdls, 10½" 120.00

Ernst Wahliss

Centerpiece, 2 cherubs kissing on curled leaf form, NM 1,450.00
Plaque, Nouveau lady, leafy border, oval, 19x16" 1,325.00
Vase, birches/3 blk birds/snow w/gold, #5530II/9028, 9½" 480.00
Vase, classical lady on blk, #113, ca 1900-10, 7½" 480.00

Vase, colorful overlapping leaves, marked, #9487, 5x6", $1,200.00. (Photo courtesy Treadway Gallery on LiveAuctioneers.com)

Vase, corset form w/rtcl rim, floral w/unfired gold, 6", pr 235.00
Vase, Pergamon, florals/clouds, #5639/24194, 9" 500.00

Animal Dishes with Covers

Animal covered dishes have been produced for over 150 years in both glass and ceramic media with the preponderance of the forms being made in pressed glass starting both in the U.S. and abroad around 1850. Prior to this time, beginning in the 1700s, tureens with the covers made to resemble the contents were made for the luxurious tables of the rich. From 1740 to 1796, the manufacture of earthenware in animal forms was done in Germany, France, Scandinavia, and England. After 1850, the dishes in both glass and ceramic reflected the naturalistic movement in art. It was not until the advent of the mechanical press for pressing glass that the forms could be made in glass with fine details. Vallerysthal/Portieux, in France, produced a great many covered dishes with a variety of animals, but the hen is the most commonly seen.

For more information, we recommend *The Milk Glass Book* by Frank Chiarenza and James Slater. We also suggest *Collector's Encyclopedia of Milk Glass* by Betty and Bill Newbound; *Westmoreland, The Popular Years*, by Lorraine Kovar; and *Glass Hen on Nest Covered Dishes* by our advisor, Shirley Smith (see Directory, West Virginia), all of which are published by Collector Books.

Ceramic

Ceramic animal dishes have been made by many companies in Europe, the U.S., and Asia, but the hen covered dishes made by many manufacturers in the Staffordshire area of England are particularly desirable. Beware of copies made in the 1990s. These would not be marked. Beware also of 'Made in England,' 'Genuine Staffordshire,' and 'Ye Olde Staffordshire.' Other companies who made ceramic animal covered dishes include Portmerion, Quimper, McCoy, Hull, Fitz & Floyd, and Metlox. L.G. Wright also made Staffordshire copies in the 1990s; these would not be marked. See also Hull; Lefton; Majolica; McCoy; Metlox; Quimper; Staffordshire. Refer to www.staffordshires.com/fake.html.

Burleigh, Ironstone, hen on nest 130.00
Dresden, egg server, HP, 15" L 600.00
Fitz & Floyd, Gallo de Oro, hen w/chick, 11½" L 67.00
Hull, hen, brn, mk, 13½" L 41.00
McCoy, hen, cookie jar 33.00
Portugal, Majolica, hen on nest 25.00
Staffordshire, dove, tureen, 8" L, pr 2,750.00
Staffordshire, duck & duckling, tureen 2,000.00
Staffordshire, hen, 10" L 250.00
Staffordshire, hen, Bantam, 7" L 350.00

Pig, mg, split rib base, McKee, sgn, 5½" L 1,700.00
Pointer, mg, Flaccus, mk, 6¾" L 400.00
Rabbit, mg, Atterbury, 10" L 110.00
Rabbit, purple slag, lacy base, Imperial, 7¾" L 400.00
Rooster, cobalt, box, Imperial, 7" W 102.00
Steer head, mg, Challinor & Taylor, 7½" L 1,400.00
Swan, bl opaque, Christmas tree base, Challinor & Taylor 650.00
Turkey, amber, standing, Cambridge, 8" 550.00
Turkey, jadeite, lacy base, Mosser 65.00

Staffordshire, hen on nest, 6½" long, $235.00. (Photo courtesy Shirley Smith)

Water Buffalo with Rider, Vallerysthal, 10" long, $1,200.00. (Photo courtesy Shirley Smith, from the collection of Carol Howell)

Glass

Glass animal covered dishes, all of which are pressed glass, have been produced for over 150 years and are as varied as their manufacturers. Following the design precedent set in Europe and continued by immigrant glass workers in America, they were made to grace the Victorian table in many types of glass (slag, clear, colored, and milk glass). On decorative bases of baskets and sometimes the bottom half of the animal itself, you will find any creature that runs, crawls, swims, or flies. Beware of mismatched tops and bottoms! Except for Atterbury's patent marks and McKee's logo, few were marked before 1950. Some of the smaller versions were made by McKee, Indiana Tumbler and Goblet Company (Greentown), Flaccus, and Westmoreland Specialty Glass. These were sold by the box-car load to food-processing companies who attached their own paper labels and filled them with condiments.

Many of the glass versions produced during the latter part of the nineteenth and early twentieth centuries have been reproduced from original molds by several companies including Kemple Glass Company (McKee bases), Summit Art Glass (Westmoreland/Tiffin, Imperial, Cambridge), Rosso Wholesale Glass (Westmoreland), and Fenton (Wright/McKee and Westmoreland). Many original molds have been used by several succeeding companies such as Westmoreland molds with original markings intact that have gone through Summit, Plum, Levay, and Rosso. Other companies such as L.G. Wright and various Asian glass companies have created their own original molds which copy earlier items. Color and type of glass are the best clues for differentiating reproductions. See also Atterbury & Company; Milk Glass; Vallerysthal.

Bear, clear w/blk pnt, JC Dowd, 8" L 650.00
Camel, opaque custard, sgn, Vallerysthal, 7½" L 425.00
Cat, vaseline, lacy base, sgn, Westmoreland 450.00
Chick on sleigh, emerging from egg, mg, Dithridge, early 1900s, 4¾". $75.00
Cocks, fighting, chocolate, Greentown, 5½" L 4,250.00
Cow, purple slag, butter, Greener & Co, 7¾" L 500.00
Duck, mg, HP, Challinor & Taylor, 8" L 160.00
Eagle, mother, mg, Challinor & Taylor, 7½" 400.00
Easter chicks, mg, in rect basket, 4⅓" L 350.00
Fox, chocolate, Westmoreland, 7½" L 475.00
Hen, frosted potpourri slag, salt, Boyd, 2" 183.00
Hen on nest, bl carnival, Sowerby 65.00
Hen on nest, cobalt, Sandwich, 8" L 2,300.00
Lovebirds, bl opaque, von Streit, 7" L 550.00
Mouse on Toadstool, opaque cream, Vallerystahl, 6" W 550.00

Appliances, Electric

Antique electric appliances represent a diverse field and are always being sought after by collectors. There were over 100 different companies manufacturing electric appliances in the first half of the twentieth century; some were making over ten different models under several different names at any given time in all fields: coffeepots, toasters, waffle irons, etc., while others were making only one or two models for extended periods of time. Today collectors and decorators alike are seeking those items to add to a collection or to use as accent pieces in a period kitchen. Refer to *Toasters and Small Kitchen Appliances* published by L-W Book Sales for more information.

Always check the cord before use and make sure the appliance is in good condition, free of rust and pitting. Unless noted otherwise, our values are for appliances in excellent condition. Prices may vary around the country.

Broiler, Farberware Open Hearth #4550 Smokeless, stainless steel ..90.00
Coffee urn, Farberware, chrome w/red-stained wood hdls, ca 1933 ..30.00
Coffeepot, Farberware Superfast, chrome/blk Bakelite, 12-cup 32.50
Coffeepot, General Electric #A3P15, chrome w/glass finial, 11½". 40.00
Coffeepot, Sunbeam Vacuum Drip #C30A, chrome, 1939-44, 12x6" .80.00
Fan, Century S3 #15, 4-blade, 5-speed, Pat Dec 20 1914, 20½" 385.00
Fan, Emerson #2010, 6 brass blades & cage, 1908 .... 750.00
Fan, Emerson #29646, 4 Parker blades, 1922-1925, rstr, 12" dia ..615.00
Fan, General Electric #C106576, 4-blade, oscillates, ca 1915, 12" dia..315.00
Fan, General Electric, 4-blade pancake model, 5-speed, 1905, 12" dia.375.00
Fan, General Electric, 4-blade, CI base, 1903, 12" dia 645.00
Griddle, Farberware #260, cast alum, immersible, 12x18" 95.00
Kettle, General Electric #4002-12, chrome, Deco styling, NMIB .. 45.00
Kettle, General Electric, stainless w/cream-pnt metal hdl, 1940s, 9" ...25.00
Mixer, KitchenAid Model G, brn, 1929 .... 435.00
Percolator, Royal Robeston Rochester Royalite, birds/flowers, +cr/sug ..95.00
Percolator, Universal #E9637, chrome w/blk hdl & glass lid, 1920s, 10".. 50.00
Skillet, Farberware #344, stainless, domed lid, 12" dia 75.00
Skillet, Miracle Maid Lektro, alum w/blk hdls & base 175.00
Toaster oven, General Electric, Deco, chrome w/blk hdls, 10x12x7". 50.00
Toaster, Delta Pop-Down Automatic, red w/chrome sides 85.00
Toaster, Hot Point, chrome, side drops, July 28 1914 .... 57.50
Toaster, Samson Trimatic, chrome & Bakelite, 3-slot 150.00
Toaster, Toast-O-Lator Model J, Deco style, blk base & hdls 150.00
Toaster, Universal #9410, 2 side buttons, needs replated, 1920s ..235.00
Vacuum cleaner, Electrolux Silverado, gray canister, +accessories ..265.00
Vacuum cleaner, General Electric, Deco-style upright, 2-speed ...125.00

Vacuum cleaner, Vaquette, Scott & Fetzer CO...OH, upright...... 215.00
Waffle iron, chrome w/Bakelite hdls, 5x13x11" 100.00
Waffle iron, Dominion #1208A, w/griddles, thermometer in lid.... 65.00

Arequipa

Following the example of the Marblehead sanatorium and pottery, the director of the Arequipa sanatorium turned to the craft of pottery as a curative occupation for his patients. In 1911 Dr. Philip K. Brown asked Frederick Hurten Rhead and his wife Agnes to move to Fairfax, California, to organize such a department. Rhead had by then an impressive resume, having worked at Vance/Avon, Weller, Roseville, Jervis, and University City. The Rheads' stay at Arequipa was short-lived, and by 1913 they were replaced by Albert Solon, another artist from a renowned pottery family. That same year, the pottery was incorporated as a separate entity from the sanatorium and greatly expanded in the following few years. It distinguished itself with two medals at the Pan-Pacific Exposition in 1915. A third Englishman, Frederick H. Wilde, replaced Solon in 1916 and remained at the helm of the pottery until its closing in 1918.

The finest pieces produced at Arequipa were done during the Rhead years, decorated in squeeze-bag or slip-trail. Others were embossed with floral patterns and covered in single-color glazes. Early vases are marked with a hand-painted Arequipa in blue on applied white glaze or incised in the clay. Our advisors for this category are Suzanne Perrault and David Rago; they are listed in the Directory under New Jersey.

Bowl, medallion emb, wht on plum matt, #37, 1912, rstr, 2¾x7". 900.00
Vase, cinquefoils cvd under dk gr crystalline, CH 11 77 16, 4x6"..2,400.00
Vase, floral band cvd under bl-gray frothy matt, MMKW 1624, 3½".960.00
Vase, Greek Key/quatrefoils cvd under gr matt, 5x3½" 1,450.00
Vase, leaves (squeeze-bag), yel on gr, ca 1912, glaze bubbles, 8x4" . 9,600.00
Vase, quatrefoils/leaves cvd under gr/brn lustre, 3x4¼", NM 1,300.00
Vase, spade leaves in slip trails, brn/gr/dk gr, 1912, 2½x5½"......2,525.00
Vase, squeeze-bag chain of leaves, wht & brn on gr matt, 6¼", NM ..6,000.00
Vase, squeeze-bag, wht on cobalt & gr, rim hairlines, 6x3¼".....4,200.00
Vase, stylized blossoms HP in brn on gray-brn, 3½x3"................1,200.00

G. Argy-Rousseau

Gabriel Argy-Rousseau produced both fine art glass and quality commercial ware in Paris, France, in 1918. He favored Art Nouveau as well as Art Deco and in the '20s produced a line of vases in the Egyptian manner, made popular by the discovery of King Tut's tomb. One of the most important types of glass he made was pate-de-verre. Most of his work is signed. Items listed below are pate-de-verre unless noted otherwise.

Atomizer, poppy band, pear shape, orange/brn/ivory, 6" 3,680.00
Box, hydrangea, purple w/wht & blk centers, 3¾" dia 5,750.00
Box, mask (laughing) orange red on mc geometrics, 6" dia 7,000.00
Lamp, grotesque masks, zigzag-band panels, egg, ftd base, 6".....8,400.00

Lamp, leaves and geometrics in orange and brown, shade signed and marked France, wrought iron base marked #406 France, 9x5", $4,800.00. (Photo courtesy Treadway Gallery on LiveAuctioneers.com)

Lamp shade, Veilleuse, moths on shade, ftd metal base, 5½"...15,800.00
Lamp shade, Veilleuse, lg roses, bl/purples, 6x3¼" 5,000.00
Lamp shade, Veilleuse, spade leaves, rose garlands, 6x3¼" 5,700.00
Pendant, butterfly, burgundy, sq, 2¼", on gold silk cord.............1,900.00
Pendant, cicada, purple & red, 2¼x1¾", on purple silk cord 1,700.00
Pendant, dogwood blossoms, 2½" dia, on bl silk cord 1,450.00
Pendant, moth, purple & fuchsia on frost w/lav, 2½" L 1,435.00
Pendant, peony blossom, 2½" dia, on ivory silk cord 1,550.00
Pendant, thistle-like blossom, red/gr, 2½" dia, on red silk cord .1,150.00
Vase, 2 male masks/ivy, 4x2¾"..3,250.00
Vase, bud, eagles, clear w/raspberry on purple ft, 5¼" 4,000.00
Vase, Deco panels & floral medallions, 9¾" 7,200.00

Art Glass Baskets

Popular novelty and gift items from 1880 to 1900 and some as late as 1930, these one-of-a-kind works of art were produced in just about any type of art glass in use at that time. Few were signed, thus attribution is usally very difficult. Many were not true production pieces but 'whimsies' made by glassworkers to relieve the tedium of the long work day. Some were made as special gifts. The more decorative and imaginative the design, the more valuable the basket. Many were mold blown, thus they display ribbed, swirled, diamond, and Hobnail patterns. Most baskets have ruffled and crimped tops; rarely will you find examples with four or more applied feet. No two are ever found to be identical, and this fact alone makes them well worth acquiring. Do not confuse the art glass basket with the bride's basket; the art glass basket is constructed entirely of glass, possibly two or three different kinds, always possessing a handle, and serving as a separate entity. The bride's basket is always constructed of fine glass in the shape of a bowl, usually ten or more inches in diameter, and always sits in a metal holder. For more information we recommend *The Collector's Encyclopedia of American Art Glass* (Collector Books) by our advisor, John A. Shuman III. Mr. Shuman is listed in the Directory under Pennsylvania.

Note: Prices on art glass baskets have softened due to the influence of the internet which has made them much more accessible.

Tomato with yellow overlay, clear crimping and thorn handle, Sandwich, 6½x6½", $200.00.
(Photo courtesy Mark Mussio, Cincinnati Art Galleries, LLC/John A. Shuman III)

Cranberry threading, crystal, pulled drape, appl flowers/leaves 725.00
Lime Gr, shades to wht opal, emb florals, scalloped rim, clear braided hdl, 7¾"...135.00
Opaline swirls, cased, oxblood/Aventurine, gold enameling, crystal appl hdl, 7½"..325.00
Pink & wht swirl, bulb, wht int, twisted thorn hdl, 8" 200.00
Pink opal, Dmn Quilt, vaseline leaves, ruffled rim, thorn hdl 300.00
Spangle, bl/silver mica flecks, wht int, clear appl ft, twisted thorn hdl.. 310.00
Spatter, maroon/yel/pk ext, ruffled rim, bulb shape, clear appl hdl, 6½" .175.00
Yellow, emb Dmn Quilt, crimped rim, star shaped, clear appl hdl .100.00

Arts and Crafts

The Arts and Crafts movement began in England during the last quarter of the nineteenth century, and its influence was soon felt in this country. Among its proponents in America were Elbert Hubbard (see Roycroft) and Gustav Stickley (see Stickley). They rebelled against the mechanized mass production of the Industrial Revolution and against the cumulative influence of hundreds of years of man's changing taste. They subscribed to a theory of purification of style: that designs be geared strictly to necessity. At the same time they sought to elevate these basic ideals to the level of accepted 'art.' Simplicity was their virtue; to their critics it was a fault.

The type of furniture they promoted was squarely built, usually of heavy oak, and so simple was its appearance that as a result many began to copy the style which became known as 'Mission.' Soon various manufacturers' factories had geared production toward making cheap copies of the designs. In 1915 Stickley's own operation failed, a victim of changing styles and tastes. Hubbard lost his life that same year on the ill-fated *Lusitania*. By the end of the decade the style had lost its popularity.

Metalware was produced by numerous crafts people, from experts such as Dirk van Erp and Albert Berry to unknown novices. Metal items or hardware should not be scrubbed or scoured; to do so could remove or damage the rich, dark patina typical of this period. Collectors have become increasingly fussy, rejecting outright pieces with damage or alteration to their original condition (such as refinishing, patina loss, repairs, and replacements). As is true for other categories of antiques and collectibles, premium prices have been paid for objects in mint original and untouched condition. Our advisor for this category is Bruce A. Austin; he is listed in the Directory under New York. See also Heintz Art Metal Shop; Jewelry; Limbert; Roycroft; Silver; Stickley; Dirk van Erp; specific manufacturers.

Note: When no condition is noted within the description lines, assume that values are given for examples in excellent condition. That is, metal items retain their original patina and wooden items are still in their original finish. Values for examples in conditions other than excellent will be indicated in the descriptions with appropriate condition codes.

Key: h/cp — hammered copper

Armchair, Cortland, 3 vertical slats at bk/under arms, rfn, 35" 450.00
Armchair, Old Hickory, caned seat & bk, 44x29x25", +caned footstool . 1,200.00
Bookcase, 2 door w/divided glass at top, recoated finish, 55x42x14" .. 1,300.00
Bookcase, Paine, 2 12-pane doors w/sq copper knobs, rfn, 45x48", VG .. 2,400.00
Box, E Burton, copper, abalone inserts, hinged clasp, 2x6¾x4" .. 3,500.00
Box, G Twichell (att), h/cp & enamel, maiden/deer, 2x4¾x3¾" .. 10,800.00
Box, Rohlfs, cvd wood, h/cp hinges, velvet lined, 1901, 9" L.. 23,000.00

Box, stamp, Jarvie, bronze, designed by Elmslie, signed Made by Robert Jarvie, Union Stockyards, Chicago, 2x4x", $1,320.00. (Photo courtesy Treadway Gallery on LiveAuctioneers.com)

Brooch, Harry Dixon, hammered sterling w/citrine, #9259, 1933, 1x2" . 500.00
Buttons, Liberty, Cymric silver, emb ship/orange sky, 1", 6 in box .. 2,000.00
Cabinet, Lifetime, Puritan Line, 2-shelf, panel door, 28x13x21" .. 1,200.00
Candelabra, Jarvie, brass w/2 riveted coils, no bobeches, 10½" . 4,800.00
Candle snuffer, Kalo, hammered silver, Sterling mk, 2¼x10" 1,000.00
Candlesticks, C Fridell, sterling, hammered, 4 tapered sides, 7", pr.. 1,400.00
Candlesticks, Jarvie, Beta, bronze, rpl bobeches, new patina, 12", pr. 1,500.00
Candlesticks, Kalo, silver gilt, elongated teardrop stems, 12", pr 5,100.00
Candlesticks, Liberty, SP, leaves/berries, #0530, 11x9½", VG ... 2,650.00
Chair, Morris, Lifetime, reuphl w/brn leather, slat sides, 41x32x36" .. 2,650.00
Chair, Morris, Shop of Crafters, leather uphl, label, 38¼" 9,600.00
Chair, side, Shop of Crafters, geometric inlay bk/leather seat, 43" ... 1,200.00
Chairs, dining, Lifetime, #116, T-bk, reuphl seat, 5 side+1 arm . 1,200.00
Chalice, Bruckmann, silver w/hardstone cabochons, gilt int, 11¼x7".. 2,500.00
Chandelier, ldgl panels w/stylized flowers, orig cap, 14x25" dia.. 2,200.00
Chandelier, wrought-iron geometric shade over gr & yel slag, 15x19x18"... 500.00

China cabinet, Lifetime, 1-pane door/sides, 3-shelf, Paine, 56x32x16" .. 960.00
China cabinet, Michigan Chair Co, 1-pane doors, glass sides, 56x44x16"... 850.00
China cabinet, Prairie School style, 1-pane doors, glass sides, 60x52" .. 1,000.00
Chocolate pot, KF Leinonen, swollen form w/ebony hdl, 10" 560.00
Clock, Liberty, pewter w/enameled face, #0721, 4¾x3¼x2½" ... 4,200.00
Compote, Joseph Heinrichs, hammered silver, petal rim/column std, 14". 750.00
Costumer, Barber Bros, dbl posts, iron hooks, missing drip pan, 67" .. 475.00
Desk, Lifetime, Puritan Line drop-front, slatted sides, 43x32x16" .. 1,550.00
Desk, partners, McHugh (att), 2 blind drw ea side, shelf, 72" ... 1,100.00
Etching, WM Rice, CA Foothills, 6¾x8¼"+mat & fr.................. 800.00
Footstool, Lakeside Crafters, cutouts, leather seat, 16x22x16".. 1,000.00
Frame, Rohlfs, eagle shape, rustic, branded R, 1904, 11x9¾" 1,100.00
Lamp, floor; Yellin, wrought-iron twisted tripod, 19" mica shade, 60".. 4,800.00
Lamp, twisted iron base & chain, gr glass shade, 19x15x15"........ 325.00
Lantern, ldgl pk blossoms on caramel slag, 25x10½" 1,325.00
Lantern, pierced brass w/mc jewels, hanging, 14x8x11" 350.00
Linen press, English, dbl doors, 4-shelf/3-drw int, 49x43x20"... 2,150.00
Magazine stand, Lakeside, inv't V crest rail/sides w/sq cutouts, 47".. 1,200.00
Mirror, hall, dmn-shape in sq fr, thru-tenons, iron hooks, rfn, 27x27" 375.00
Mirror, hall, paneled splayed sides, pyramidal caps, hooks, 26x37" .. 250.00
Nightstand, Lifetime (att), shelf inside, 27½x14x14" 1,300.00
Painting, Toothaker, mtn scene, watercolor/gouache/ink, 7¼x3"+fr .. 1,440.00
Pastel on paper, PJ de Lemos, Castle de Lemos...Spain, 1934, 13x10"+fr. 1,325.00
Plate stand, Rohlfs, ebonized, branded R, 1901, 9x6x5"............ 1,800.00
Plate, Linossier, h/cp w/silver inlay, 6" 200.00
Poker, Yellin, wrought iron/brass, 41"............................2,500.00
Rocker, Plail, slatted bbl form, reuphl seat, 32x25x32" 900.00
Rug, poppy/scrolling vines, wool, Wm Morris style, 210x140".. 1,200.00
Rug, Wm Morris style, delicate floral, rust/amber tones, 108x72" . 600.00
Rug, Wm Morris style, leafy patterns, gold/dk red, 96x61"........ 1,440.00
Rug, Wm Morris style, leaves, cinnamon on blk, 142x111" 850.00
Server, gallery over 2 open shelves divided by 2 drw, 41x46x21"... 1,100.00
Settee & armchair, Old Hickory, caned bks/seats, curved arms, child's.. 1,200.00
Settee, Lifetime, 5 wide bk slats, open drop arms, 64" L, VG.... 1,800.00
Shaker, Guild of Handicrafts, hammered sterling, jade cabochons, 3" . 1,300.00
Spratling, fruit bowl, incised bands, 3 curved/beaded hdls, 10".5,760.00
Stool, folding, Rose Valley, cvd rosettes, 25x25x17" 6,000.00

Table, dining, oak, marked Watertown Table-Slide Company Patent June 30, 1889, Wisconsin, 29x55", $750.00. (Photo courtesy Kamelot Auctions on LiveAuctioneers.com)

Table, library, 3-drw, overhang top, rpl hdw/rfn, 30x90x36" 960.00
Table, library, Lifetime #909, 1 drw, thru-tenons, 44" L, VG 720.00
Table, Lifetime, Puritan, gate-leg extension, rfn, label, 31x48" . 1,675.00
Table, octagonal 19" brass top, 4-post base w/inlay & ball ft, Austria . 1,680.00
Tray, unmk, h/cp w/tooled florals/leaves, 10½"............................. 300.00
Vase, Harry Dixon, h/cp, med patina, incurvate rim, 7¾x4½"...2,400.00
Vase, Tudric, hammered pewter, organic hdls, 9¾" 600.00
Woodblock print, G Baumann, 3 Pines, 10½x9¼"+mat & fr 9,000.00
Woodblock print, JB Judson, Gorge of Genesee River..., 6x8"+mat & fr. 2,000.00
Woodblock print, pr of swans in park pond, sgn/#d, 9x9", +mat & fr ... 660.00

Asian Antiques

The art of the Orient is an area of collecting currently enjoying strong collector interest, not only in those examples that are truly 'antique' but in the twentieth-century items as well. Because of the many aspects involved in a study of Asian Antiques, we can only try through brief comments to acquaint the reader with some of the more readily available examples. We suggest you refer to specialized reference sources for more detailed information. See also specific categories.

Key:
Ch — Chinese	hdwd — hardwood
Dy — Dynasty	Jp — Japan
E — export	Ko — Korean
FR — Famille Rose	lcq — lacquer
FV — Famille Verte	mdl — medallion
gb — guard border	tkwd — teakwood

Blanc de Chine

Bowl, flowering prunus branch, thick stem & ft, 18th C, 12½". 1,350.00
Figurine, Buddha stands w/smiling face, 20th C, 12" 480.00
Figurine, Dehua, Guayin, 28" 3,300.00
Figurine, Kuan Yan on throne w/servant, Te Hua, 18th C, 8½". 2,150.00
Figurine, lady w/vase & monkey w/peach, Ch'ien Lung, 18th C, 7¼".. 850.00
Figurine, monk seated w/arms folded, ca 1920, 12", +teak base ... 900.00
Figurine, Quan Yan standing on wave sphere, 19th C, 19x6" 950.00

Blue and White Porcelain

Beaker, warrior above lotus band, cylindrical, 17th C, 14" 7,200.00
Bowl, floral, ftd, Arita Ware, Jp, 19th C, 6x8¾" 800.00
Bowl, stylized floral scrolls, Ch, 1821-51, sm rpr, 6" 525.00

Cachepot, lotus and vines, Chinese, eighteenth century, 9" diameter, $3,300.00. (Photo courtesy Sloans & Kenyon on LiveAuctioneers.com)

Charger, birds/peonies/chrysanthemums, scalloped, 1572-1620, 14¼". 3,300.00
Figurine, riders on elephants, Ch, late Qing Dy, 9¼", pr 1,950.00
Jar, precious objects, w/lid, Kangxi Dy, 6", pr 3,300.00
Jar, prunus blossoms, baluster, domed lid, Ch, Kangxi Dy, 17½". 2,750.00
Kendi, elephant form, Ch, Wanli Dy, ca 1600, rstr, 8¾" 8,400.00
Vase, dragon & foliage, cylindrical, Ch, ca 1650, 15" 5,250.00
Vase, dragon among clouds, baluster, Ko, Yi/Choson Dy, 11½". 2,350.00
Vase, dragon pursues flaming pearl/flowers/etc, Ch, Yuan/Ming Dy, 7".. 6,600.00
Vase, Ku form w/Hua decor at mouth & ft, Immortals, 17th C, 14" .. 3,800.00
Vase, riverscape baluster, w/lid, Ch, Kangxi Dy, 16" 8,400.00

Bronze

Figure, elephant w/trunk raised, pnt details, blk patina, 13x13"..... 85.00
Figure, foo dog w/pierced sphere, 14¼x19" 1,265.00
Figure, peasant man w/yoke & 2 baskets, marble base, 12x11"....... 90.00
Figure, warrior on horseback, much detail, 40" 1,080.00
Incense burner, birds/flowers in relief, dragon hdls, ftd, 8" 180.00
Incense burner, cast designs on base w/4 mask legs, rtcl lid, 17x15" . 750.00
Incense burner, foo dog, hinged lid & open mouth 1,100.00
Urn, mtn scene, gold hdls & trim, 12" 120.00
Vase, dragon in relief, cylindrical neck, 9" 150.00
Vase, elephant heads & tusks in relief, old rpr, 12½x8½" 1,550.00

Celadon

Bowl, petal rim, Ming Dy, 5" 450.00
Charger, emb ribs, Ming Dy, 12" 950.00
Incense burner, foo dog form, 19th C, 7½", VG 960.00
Vase, crackle glaze on ribbed body, sq, 10" 135.00
Vase, crackle glaze, domed lid w/foo dog finial, Ch, 21", pr 465.00
Vase, incised floral, bottle neck, Ch, 8" 145.00

Furniture

Cabinet on fr, blk lcq w/HP landscape, 2 doors/3 drws, 31x32x21".. 300.00
Cabinet, blk lcq, gold/appl figures, 3 glass doors on base w/drws, 84" . 700.00
Cabinet, lacquer & gilt decor in Rococo style, 20th C, 63½x41x21".840.00
Cabinet, red lcq, mortised, 2 blind doors, shelved int, 2 drws, 73x45".. 180.00
Cabinet, sliding panels & drws, bentwood shelf, glass doors, 38x30x11". 975.00
Chest, apothecary, 37-drw, brass ring pulls, mortised, Ch, 47x27x19".. 315.00
Plant stand, tkwd, pk marble top, pierced/cvd legs & shelf, 19x14x14"..725.00
Press, red lcq w/gold decor, dbl doors, Shan Xi province, 70x52x24".. 1,150.00
Screen, coromandel, blk lcq w/MOP inlay, appl stones, 6-panel, 72".. 600.00
Screen, cvd wood fr, silk panel w/embr shrimp, 40x38" 235.00

Screen, four-panel, rosewood with foliate-carved latticework over embroidered silk, circa 1900, 67½", each panel 20" wide, VG, $10,680.00. (Photo courtesy Leland Little Auction & Estate Sales Ltd. on LiveAuctioneers.com)

Screen, semiprecious stones/lcq landscape, wood fr in base, 36x40"...1,500.00
Server, elm, scalloped returns/apron, 3-drw, 30x83x10" 525.00
Stand, hdwd, 2-tier, pierced aprons, mid-1800s, 31x20x12" 315.00
Table, alter, teak w/pierced/cvd cloud-band frieze, 1950s, 33x45x17". 600.00

Hardstones

Amethyst, bottle, cvd lotus plants, 2" 300.00
Amethyst, cvg, Quan Yin, Ch, 7" 90.00
Jade, belt buckle, wht, dragons cvg, 1¾x4¼" 4,250.00
Jade, brush holder, celadon w/russet areas, birds/trees cvgs, 5" ..7,800.00
Jade, cigarette holder, gr, silver mts mk Lebkuecher & Co, ca 1900.2,650.00
Jade, cvg, celadon, Shoulao w/staff & peach, ca 1900, 13"........7,800.00
Jade, cvg, gr & brn, animals & fruit, rect, early 20th C, 6".......2,500.00
Jade, cvg, wht, carp leaping, lg age crack, 15x10½" 5,100.00
Jade, cvg, wht, sheep (3) in huddle, 1½"+stand 4,450.00
Jade, rouge box, wht, cvd Ju'i knots/dragon, K'ang Hsi, 3½" dia...13,250.00
Jade, scholar's pwt, wht, foliate cvg, wire inlay stand, 2" 5,250.00
Malachite, robed figure, 20th C, 11½" 575.00
Nephrite jade, cvg, Buddha holding Ch scepter, 8⅛" 115.00
Rose quartz, cvgs, phoenix bird, Ch, 13x19"+stand, pr 3,000.00
Rose quartz, table lamp, cvd florals, brass mts, 16" urn form, 38"...4,800.00
Rose quartz, vase, shield form w/foliage, foo lion finial, 10"+stand. 2,750.00

Inro

Bone, finely cvd figure of man in boat/Senin, 19th C, 2¼" 425.00
Gold lcq w/emb flowering trees, 4-part, Sagemono, 19th C, w/netsuke . 780.00

Gold lcq w/emb tigers by waterfall, 19th C.................................... 840.00
Gold lcq w/maki-e of sparrows/bamboo, 4-compartment, 19th C, 3¼" ..1,200.00
Ivory w/lcq & ryusa, Sagemono, late 19th C, w/katydid netsuke . 400.00
Lcq w/pearl/coral/MOP inlay insects & flowers, 5-compartment, 19th C. 600.00

Lacquerware

Lacquerware is found in several colors, but the one most likely to be encountered is cinnabar. It is often intricately carved, sometimes involving hundreds of layers built one at a time on a metal or wooden base. Later pieces remain red, while older examples tend to darken.

Box, cricket, cvd dragon & clouds, red on ebonized base, ftd, 21x10" .. 350.00
Box, sewing, E, gold mums on blk, 8-sided, Ch, 19th C 400.00
Box, travel, red w/dragons/pearls/etc, 18th C, 19x15x12"+stand ..1,750.00
Cabinet, Mt Fuji-shape top, tooled gilt panels/bronze hdw, 1920s, 20"...325.00
Cigar case, dk cinnabar, little cvg, Jp, ca 1833, 4¾" 60.00
Pen case, blk w/yel hunt scenes, Persia, 19th C, 8"...................... 175.00
Water bucket, lcq on metal, Jp, ca 1945-53, 9x3" 200.00

Netsukes

A netsuke is a miniature Japanese carving made with two holes called the Himitoshi, either channeled or within the carved design. As kimonos (the outer garment of the time) had no pockets, the Japanese man hung his pipe, tobacco pouch, or other daily necessities from his waist sash. The most highly valued accessory was a nest of little drawers called an Inro, in which they carried snuff or sometimes opium. The netsuke was the toggle that secured them. Although most are of ivory, others were made of bone, wood, metal, porcelain, or semiprecious stones. Some were inlaid or lacquered. They are found in many forms — figurals the most common, mythological beasts the most desirable. They range in size from 1" up to 3", which was the maximum size allowed by law. Many netsukes represented the owner's profession, religion, or hobbies. Scenes from the daily life of Japan at that time were often depicted in the tiny carvings. The more detailed the carving, the greater the value.

Careful study is required to recognize the quality of the netsuke. Many have been made in Hong Kong in recent years; and even though some are very well carved, these are considered copies and avoided by the serious collector. There are many books that will help you learn to recognize quality netsukes, and most reputable dealers are glad to assist you. Use your magnifying glass to check for repairs. In the listings that follow, netsukes are ivory unless noted otherwise; 'stain' indicates a color wash.

Costumed boy wearing a foo dog mask with hinged lower jaw, standing on drum with inset ebony dots, brown ink detail, signed Seisho, 1⅞", $575.00. (Photo courtesy Garth's Auction, Inc. on LiveAuctioneers.com)

Badger hiding under lotus, boxwood, ca 1800, 1¾" 500.00
Dog w/2 puppies, boxwood, EX patina, 19th C, 2" 4,250.00
Figure w/silver clapper in hands, mc stain, 1½" 1,150.00
Fisherman w/oversz pufferfish, inlaid eyes, 19th C, 2" 660.00
Foreigner w/trumpet, inlaid eyes, Issan, ca 1800, 1½".................... 950.00
Horse w/inlaid eyes, att Tanatoshi, 20th C, 2" 1,325.00
Hotei sleeping w/bag of wealth, boxwood w/ivory inlay, Tokasai, 1800s...1,800.00
Hotei standing on bag of wealth, 18th C, 2"................................. 475.00

Man holding mask, mc stain, 1¼" 480.00
Marine life surrounds clamshell, Iwami school, late 1700s, 2¾". 8,400.00
Quail w/millet plant, rich brn stain, Okatomo, 1½" 1,150.00
Rabbit w/red inset eyes, Gyokuzan, 19th C, 1¼x2" 1,200.00
Sage holding loquat over shoulder, late 18th C, 2¾" 850.00
Toad on worn-out sandal, boxwood, EX patina, Masanao, 18th C...5,000.00
Two tigers, ivory w/inlaid eyes, Hakuryu, 19th C, 1½" 1,800.00

Porcelain

Chinese export ware was designed to appeal to Western tastes and was often made to order. During the eighteenth century, vast amounts were shipped to Europe and on westward. Much of this fine porcelain consisted of dinnerware lines that were given specific pattern names. Rose Mandarin, Fitzhugh, Armorial, Rose Medallion, and Canton are but a few of the more familiar.

Bowl, punch, E, FV, floral vignettes, Ch, 18th C, 5½x12" 800.00
Bowl, vegetable, Rose Canton, mc w/gold, w/lid, Ch, 1890s, 6½x10x8"..3,325.00
Cup, E, flower tree w/orange border, strap hdl, dome lid, 1800s, 7 for... 980.00
Food warmer, E, Fitzhugh, bl, domed lid w/fruit finial, 1850s, 13" L...750.00
Jar, E, FV, figures w/horse, w/lid, mtd as lamp, 22x6¾" 480.00
Jug, cider, armorial/floral sprigs, bl/mc on wht, twist hdl, 8x7"..1,880.00
Mug, E, FR, maritime scene w/Am ship, 19th C, 5½", NM.......... 925.00
Plate, arms of Mills & Webber, shipping scenes/castle, ca 1800, 9".. 550.00
Plate, E, FR, court scene reserve, floral border, 19th C, 11" 615.00
Platter, E, FR, floral sprays/gilt borders 1700s, 13x10" 825.00
Platter, E, FR, mandarin scene, EX gold, 15¼x12" 1,500.00
Platter, FR, E, central mdl, quilted border, 17¼x14".................... 285.00
Punch bowl, E, FR, sm banded/diapered decor w/in & w/o, 1800s, 4x10" ...925.00
Spittoon, E, FR, birds/butterflies/bugs/flowers, 1850s, 7¼x8" 700.00
Teapot, butterfly frieze, gilt, squat oval form, 1900, 5x6".............. 370.00

Temple jar, Chinese export, hunters and warriors on horseback, foo dog on lid, 41", $1,320.00. (Photo courtesy Great Gatsby's Antiques and Auctions on LiveAuctioneers.com)

Tray, warming, E, Fitzhugh, bl, mid-1800s, 2¾x15¾x11" 575.00
Tureen, E, flower finial, rabbit head hdls, 18th C, rprs, 14½" L ... 3,840.00
Tureen, Rose Canton, mc w/gold, w/lid, Ch, 1890s, 11x13½", EX..450.00
Vase, 3 rows of elaborately robed figures, mc on wht, hdls, 1800s, 17"..850.00
Vase, E, children at play, appl children figures, 12½", pr.............. 575.00
Vase, E, FR, floral sprays, gilt dragons/butterflies, 24", pr.......... 1,150.00
Vase, E, FR, floral, foo dog hdls, flared rim, 18", NM.................... 300.00
Vase, E, Mandarin, lion & ring gilt hdls, prof rstr, 1850s, 24x8½" .. 2,300.00
Vases, E, Mandarin & FR decor, ruffled, appl dragons, 14", pr ..9,775.00

Rugs

The Eastern rug market has enjoyed a renewal of interest as collectors have become aware of the fact that some of the semi-antique rugs (those 60 to 100 years old) may be had at a price within the range of the average buyer. Unless noted otherwise, values are for rugs in excellent or better condition.

Afshar, dk bl abrash, burgundy/dk bl borders, 96x63"................ 1,150.00
Afshar, ornate floral, fringe, 1920s, 89x58" 700.00

Afshar, red spandrels on bl, flat woven ends, 105x59" 750.00
Armenian Shirvan, bright mdls on salmon, ivory/bl borders, 111x46"...635.00
Bahktiari, dk bl w/wide ivory border, 246x81" 2,415.00
Caucasian Kazak, indigo & madder red, ca 1930, 103x68" 1,700.00

Ferghan Sarouk, navy blue medallions on red field with vines and foliate scrolls, circa 1890, 58x40", $3,360.00. (Photo courtesy Jackson's Auction on LiveAuctioneers.com)

Hamadan, floral, bl border on brick red, lt wear/losses, 70x60" . 1,400.00
Heriz, dk bl border, ivory spandrels on red, 208x116" 2,875.00
Heriz, floral, wide bl borders/ivory spandrels on red, 151x113" . 1,850.00
Indo-Serape, camel spandrels/bl border on salmon, 114x96" 500.00
Kars Karaba, dk bl w/red & ivory borders, 67x50" 700.00
Kashan, lt plum w/dk bl borders, lt wear, 215x109" 3,450.00
Kashan, red w/lg mdl, 7 gb, late 20th C, 156x112" 750.00
Kazak, geometric borders w/bl mdl on red, lt wear, 56x44" 1,495.00
Kermin, lg red mdl, outer portion w/allover pattern, 150x110", VG... 635.00
NW Persia, geometric dmns, ca 1925, 61x32" 850.00
NW Persia, gr spandrels on rust w/ivory border, 129x44" 700.00
Persian Heriz, center mdl, red tones, ca 1970, 146x99" 900.00
Persian Qashqai, serrated/floral mdls on red/bl, 98x60" 1,000.00
Peshawar Serapi, geometric floral, rust colors, 120x98" 1,600.00
S Persia, stylized flowers on red & bl, ca 1920, 84x60" 850.00
Sarouk, burgundy border on dk bl, lt wear, fringe, 78x49" 550.00
Sarouk, burgundy w/wide bl border, 256x118" 1,150.00
Serapi, bl mdl w/ivory spandrels on red w/red border, 144x115"... 18,400.00
Shiraz, dk bl spandrels/mc borders on brn, 84x74" 500.00
Shirvan prayer, dk bl w/geometric borders, bright mc, 76x46" 575.00
Tabriz, dk bl w/wide pale pk border, 154x110" 1,150.00

Snuff Bottles

The Chinese were introduced to snuff in the seventeenth century, and their carved and painted snuff bottles typify their exquisite taste and workmanship. These small bottles, seldom measuring over 2½", were made of amber, jade, ivory, and cinnabar; tiny spoons were often attached to their stoppers. By the eighteenth century, some were being made of porcelain, others were of glass with delicate interior designs tediously re-verse painted with minuscule brushes sometimes containing a single hair. Copper and brass were used but to no great extent.

Amber, well hollowed, Ch, 19th C, 2½" 2,400.00
Amethyst, vasiform w/cvd flowers, w/stopper, Ch, 3" 250.00
Banded agate w/tourmaline stopper, 19th C, 2¾" 3,890.00
Bronze, cicada clutches cvd jade floret, coral stopper, 19th C, 2¾" .. 600.00
Ceramic, cabbage shape, gr to wht, coral stopper, Ch, ca 1900, 2⅝"... 725.00
Cloisonné lotus blossoms on turq, gilt metal rims, 2½" 1,450.00
Fluorite, dull gr, cvd masks/ram's head hdls, Ch, 1⅞" 660.00
Fossiliferous limestone, carnelian stopper w/ivory collar, 20th C, 2" .. 550.00
Jade, dk yel w/lotus branch cvg, ovoid, Qing Dy 1,100.00
Jade, pebble form, lav w/gr streaks, 2" 1,325.00
Jade, spinach nephrite, lobed melon, 1890s, 2⅜" 2,400.00
Jade, wht, 2 cvd figures, coral stopper, 19th C, 2¼" 6,000.00

MOP, gourd form w/pod, coral stopper, Ch, late 19th C, 2½" 660.00
Nephrite, gray to wht, globular, late 19th C, 2" 780.00
Opal, robed man w/flower bundle figural, coral stopper, 1890s, 2"...950.00
Porc, dragon chasing pearl, bl/wht, cylinder, red stopper, 19th C, 5"... 550.00
Porc, HP landscapes, Ch, early 20th C, 2¾" 1,950.00
Ruby glass, 8 horses cvg, coral stopper, Ch, Qing Dy, 3¾" 1,650.00

Textiles

Kimono, vertical stripes on silk, Jp, ca 1900 .... 120.00
Kimono, wedding, embr gold/wht flowers on wht silk, Jp, mid-1900s . 300.00
Obi, brocade silk w/flowering prunus blossoms, Jp, 1940s............. 200.00
Panel, river landscape & immortals woven in silk, Ch, 19th C, 81x40" .5,500.00
Panel, warriors on horseback, woven silk, gold threads, Quing Dy, 90x61".6,500.00
Robe, bl silk kesi w/floral embr, Ch, 18th C.............................. 5,700.00
Robe, dragon/Buddhist emblems in gold & bl embr on silk, Ch. 5,150.00
Robe, dragons & gold threads embr on bl silk, Ch, 19th C, 59" L.. 3,150.00
Robe, dragons/bats/etc embr on bl silk, Ch, 19th C 5,500.00
Robe, dragons chasing pearl w/gold, lishui stripes, Qing Dy 7,200.00
Robe, Imperial court, silk w/embr symbols of authority, ca 1900 .. 12,000.00
Tapestry, cranes in marsh, silk on linen, late 19th C, 67x45" 850.00

Woodblock Prints

Framed prints are of less value than those not framed, since it is impossible to inspect their condition or determine whether or not they have borders or have been trimmed. Our values are for unframed prints unless otherwise noted.

Goyo, Hashiguchi; Woman Holding Towel, 1920, 17¼x11" 2,400.00
Harunobu, Suzuki; Girl in Bathhouse, 18th C, 7½x10¼"..........2,400.00
Hashiguchi, Goyo; Woman Holding Tray, 1920, 15⅛x10"........6,000.00
Hoshi, Joichi; Red Tree, 1973, 16½x22" 4,750.00
Kiyoshi, Kobayakawa; Dance (Odori), 1931, 16⅝x11⅞" 2,150.00
Kogan, Tobari; Profile of School Girl, 1920s, 15x9¾" 3,450.00
Kotondo, Torii; Snow (Yuki), seated geisha, 1929, 16⅛x10⅜"..3,600.00
Lum, Bertha; Theatre Street Scene, 1905, 8⅞x4⅜" 6,000.00
Nakayama, I Wish To Fly Too, 1971, 29½x21½" 4,350.00
Yoshida, Hiroshi; Moraine Lake, 1925, 14½x9¾" 3,600.00
Yoshida, Hiroshi; Night in Kyoto, 1933, 14¾x9⅝" 2,700.00

Atterbury & Company

Atterbury & Company (1859 – 1893) was founded in Pittsburgh, Pennsylvania, by James Seaman Atterbury and Thomas Atterbury, among others. Although called the White House factory due to its considerable production of milk glass (opal), the company produced glass in clear transparent, translucent amber, blue, green, canary, and opaque colors of blue, lavender, black, and green as well as marble (slag) in blue, red/orange, green, and marvered (dappled) colors of yellow, blue, red/orange, and a mixture of colors. Starting out with lamps, the Atterbury factory produced a full range of tableware, barware, bottles, and novelties. The Atterbury brothers patented over 100 inventions (from a glass hand grenade to spun glass cloth) and designs including: nine animal covered dishes (rabbit, duck, lion, fox, cat, chick in eggpile, hand and dove, bull's head mustard, and entwined fish), a unique duck bottle, boat pickle dish, Fern (aka Crossed Fern, Crossed Ferns with Ball and Claw), and Lily (aka Sunflower). Other patterns used included Bird and Wheat, Double Hands, Basket Weave, Rib and Bow, Rib and Scallop, Zipper Side, Woven Panel, Plain Melon, Melon with Leaf (aka Paneled Fern), Melon with Net, Prism, Reeded, and Medallion (aka Ceres, Cameo, Goddess of Liberty). Some patterns have been reproduced such as Crossed Fern, Basket Weave, and Medallion.

There is no evidence of what became of the Atterbury molds, but many patterns and designs, especially the animal covered dishes, have been reproduced (perhaps from original molds) or copied (from new molds) by Westmoreland, Imperial, Kemple, L.G. Wright, and other companies. See also Milk Glass; Opaque Glass; Pattern Glass. For further information consult *American Pressed Glass & Figure Bottles* by Albert Christian Revi; *Yesterday's Milk Glass Today* by Regis and Mary Ferson; and *Glass Patents and Patterns* by Arthur Peterson.

Our advisor for Atterbury is Shirley Smith; she is listed in the Directory under West Virginia.

Sugar, Melon with Leaf, milk glass, 5¾", $56.00. (Photo courtesy www.dnf-antiques.com)

Covered dish, boar's head, mg, 9" L 1,125.00
Covered dish, Chick on Eggpile, mg, Pat date, 7½" W 260.00
Covered dish, entwined fish, mg, 6" W 286.00
Covered dish, frog on rocks, mg, 5½" 5,700.00
Covered dish, hand & dove, mg, 5" 60.00
Covered dish, hen, bl marble, 7" 203.00
Covered dish, hen, mg w/bl head, 7" 100.00
Covered dish, rabbit, mg, 6" 215.00
Jar, owl, mg, 6¾" 75.00
Lamp base, swan, mg, 5" 149.00
Mug, child's, bird & wheat, blk, 2" 30.00
Mustard, bull's head, mg, 4¼" 69.00
Oil lamp, Ribbed Loop, mg, 8½" 52.00
Platter, Rock of Ages, crystal, 12½" 60.00

Austrian Glass

Many examples of fine art glass were produced in Austria during the times of Loetz and Moser that cannot be attributed to any glasshouse in particular, though much of it bears striking similarities to the products of both artists.

Vase, bl & gold irid, pleated rim, ca 1905, 8¼" 215.00
Vase, bl w/mc irid, shaped rim, long stem, disk ft, 10½" 120.00
Vase, bl w/oilspot irid, Nouveau flared cylinder w/flared ft, 11¾". 275.00
Vase, brn mottle, incurvate rim, bulb body, flared ft, 7" 280.00

Vase, cameo-cut florals, textured and frosted, three fold-down tendrils, 5½x5", $960.00. (Photo courtesy Dirk Soulis Auctions on LiveAuctioneers.com)

Vase, cobalt w/copper o/l, scattered mica at rim & throughout, 8"... 425.00
Vase, deep amethyst w/irridescent lines, 10", NM 180.00
Vase, gold w/mc irid, Nouveau shape, brass mts, ca 1904, 13¼". 1,675.00
Vase, gold-bl satin, rnd w/short neck, appl 'worm' under hdls, WMT, 5".450.00

Vase, gr irid w/platinum tendrils, vertical ribs, ruffled rim, 5½".... 115.00
Vase, gr/purple lustre, swollen stick neck, fancy pewter sgn/#d mt, 7"... 585.00
Vase, irid purple tones, Heliosine, 6" 275.00
Vase, irid w/random vines, in hdld bronze Nouveau shoulder mt, 11x3"... 540.00
Vase, peachblow, gold pheasant, cup-top stick neck, #1122 V429, 10" ..385.00
Vase, purple w/threading, ruffled rim, 6½" 540.00
Vase, ruby w/floral o/l, gourd shape w/3 twisted hdls, 9" 2,300.00
Vase, wine irid, notched rim/folded-bk hdls, 9" 265.00

Autographs

Autographs can be as simple as signatures on cards or album pages, signed photos, signed documents, or letters, but they can also be signed balls, bats, T-shirts, books, and a variety of other items.

Simple signatures are the most common form and thus are usually of lesser value than signed photos, letters, or anything else. But as with any type of collectible, the condition of the autograph is paramount to value. If the signature is in pencil, value drops automatically by one-half or more. If the item signed is torn, creased, stained, laminated, or is a menu, bus ticket, magazine page, or something unusual, many collectors will avoid buying these because they are less desirable than a nice dark ink signature on an undamaged card or autograph album page.

When pricing signed photos, many variables come into play. Size is important (all things being equal, the larger the photo, the more it's worth), as is condition (wrinkles, tape stains, tears, or fading will all have a negative impact). If the signature is signed over a dark area, making it difficult to see, the photo's value can drop by 90%. Finally, the age of the signed photo will cause the value to increase or decrease. Generally speaking, if the photo is signed when the celebrity was young and not well known, it will be worth more than those signed in later years. For example, the photos signed by Shirley Temple as a child are worth hundreds of dollars, whereas her adult-signed photos can be purchased for as little as $20.00.

The savvy autograph buyer or antique/collectibles dealer needs to know that since the 1950s, many U.S. presidents, politicians, and astronauts commonly used (and still do) a machine known as the 'autopen,' a mechanical device that 'signs' photos and letters for fans requesting an autograph through the mail. The tip-off to an autopenned signature is that each one will be identical.

Autopens aren't so common with movie and television stars, however. If you were to write to a famous entertainer asking for a signed photo, the chances are extremely high you'll either receive a photo signed by a secretary or one bearing a 'machine-imprinted' signature which will appear as real ink on the photo.

Yes, there are authentic and valuable autographs out there, but make sure you are buying from a reputable autograph dealer or from a seller who has convincing evidence that his offering is genuine. The internet is full of autograph auction sites that sell forgeries, so always beware of a deal with a price that's too good to be true — you might be getting conned!

Most reputable autograph dealers belong to one of several autograph organizations: the UACC (The Universal Autograph Collectors Club) or The Manuscript Society. If you buy from a dealer, make sure the autograph has a lifetime guarantee of authenticity. If you buy from a private party, then as the old saying goes, '...let the buyer beware!' Just because the autograph listed for sale says it comes with a 'COA' (certificate of authenticity) doesn't mean it's authentic if the seller is a forger or unscrupulous dealer. Our advisor for autographs is Tim Anderson; he is listed in the Directory under Utah.

Key:
ALS — handwritten letter   sig — signature
DS — document signed   SP — signed photo
ISP — inscribed signed photo

Ali, Muhammad; SP, color, 8x10" 145.00
Aniston, Jennifer; SP, topless portrait, color, 8x10", +COA 40.00
Armstrong, Neil; sig (bold) on cover of Apollo 11, 20th Anniv program. 1,200.00
Astaire, Fred; sig on clipped pg, matted w/blk & wht 9x7" photo.215.00
Berlin, Irving; sig on clipped paper, w/blk & wht picture 36.00
Bush, George; sig on baseball 150.00
Cagney, James; sig on pg, matted w/early blk & wht photo 95.00
Carol, Sue; SP postcard, blk & wht, bl ink, 1920s, COA 60.00
Carpenter, Richard; ISP, blk & wht, 1995, 8x10" 95.00
Carter, Jimmy; typed thank-you card 75.00
Churchill, Winston; ALS, varied subjects, 4 pgs, 1905, 5x8"....4,000.00
Coolidge, Grace; sig (4" L) on clipped paper, 2½x4½" 55.00
Cummings, Bob; sig on trimmed album pg, 2x5" 38.00
Day, Doris; SP, color, 8x10", +mat & fr 120.00
Disney, Walt; album leaf, Mickey drawing, ink/pencil, 1930s ..3,700.00
Eastwood, Clint; SP, as Dirty Harry, 8x10"................................ 45.00
Ellington, Duke; SP, blk & wht, 8x10" 120.00
Esposito, Phil; sig on Espo Line poster 120.00
Eysler, Edmund; ISP postcard, dedication w/cord, 1948, 4x6", COA...62.00
Franchi, Sergio; sig on wht 3x5" card, dtd 1963........................... 39.00
Gable, Clark; SP, sepia, 11x14" 2,500.00
Goldwater, Barry; SP, blk & wht, 8x10" 45.00
Griffith, Andy; SP, blk & wht, 7x9" 25.00
Harpo (Marx), ins sig on Harpo Speaks! 1st ed book 480.00
Hepburn, Katharine; sig on playbill from Colonial........................ 50.00
Hodges, Gil; sig on baseball, 1966 .... 30.00
Hoover, Herbert; bold sig on Waldorf-Astoria stationery, 1956 ..... 75.00
Jenner, Alexander; SP, blk & wht, 1969, 4x6" 68.00
Johnson, London B; SP (not autopen), blk & wht, 8x10"............. 750.00
Jones, Catherine Zeta; SP, color, 8x10", +COA 37.50
Leigh, Janet; SP, 11x14".. 125.00
Leslie, Joan; ISP, blk & wht, 1941, 4x6", COA 20.00
Lincoln, Abraham; sig on alum pg 4,000.00
Loren, Sophia; SP, early postcard, bl ink, 4x5", COA 25.00
Loy, Myrna; SP, color, w/COA 30.00
Mahone, William; sig on business-sz card, ca 1880s 125.00

Mantle, Mickey; black and white photo signed in blue sharpie, 8x10", framed and matted under glass, $540.00. (Photo courtesy DuMouchelles on LiveAuctioneers.com)

Mantle, Mickey; sig on baseball cap.. 275.00
March, Hal; ISP, blk & wht, 1950s, 8x10" 25.00
Nicholson, Jack; SP, from The Shining, color, 8x10", +COA........ 40.00
Nixon, Richard; ins & bold sig inside Six Crises book, 1st ed, 1962 ..395.00
Page, Ruth; ISP, sepia, early in career, 7x9" 59.00
Pauling, Linus; Pauling stationery, 1985, 1-pg 125.00
Polk, James K; sig on postal frank, as president........................2,500.00
Ride, Sally; SP, in bl NASA shirt, color, 8x10", +COA................. 36.00
Rutherford, Ann; SP, from Gone w/Wind, blk & wht 8x10", +COA..35.00
Scott, Fred; SP, blk & wht, 1988, 8x10"................................ 44.00
Shaw, Robert; ISP, sepia, 4x6" 123.00
Shirley, Anne; ISP, sepia, closeup, 1930s, 8x10" 40.00
Skelton, Red; bold sig on card w/name & 8/18/64 at top, 3x5"...... 20.00
Smith, Joseph; DS, 1840...1,850.00
Strasberg, Susan; sig on wht 3x5" card, dtd 1961........................ 39.00

Warren, Earl; sig on lg sheet of wht paper..................................... 75.00
Wayne, John; True Grit program card w/sig, 7x10"...................... 515.00
Werner, Hans; ISP, blk & wht, 1950s, 4x6", COA 85.00
Westmoreland, General William C; sig on banquet program......... 24.00
Wood, Natalie; ISP, blk & wht, as child, 8x10" 150.00
Woods, Tiger; SP, golf action, color, 8x10", +COA 65.00
Wray, Fay; SP, blk & wht, bold sig, 4x6", +COA............................ 50.00

Automobilia

While some automobilia buffs are primarily concerned with restoring vintage cars, others concentrate on only one area of collecting. For instance, hood ornaments were often quite spectacular. Made of chrome or nickel plate on brass or bronze, they were designed to represent the 'winged maiden' Victory, flying bats, sleek greyhounds, soaring eagles, and a host of other creatures. Today they often bring prices in the $75.00 to $200.00 range. R. Lalique glass ornaments go much higher.

Horns, radios, clocks, gear shift knobs, and key chains with company emblems are other areas of interest. Generally, items pertaining to the classics of the '30s are most in demand. Paper advertising material, manuals, and catalogs in excellent condition are also collectible.

License plate collectors search for the early porcelain-on-cast-iron examples. First year plates (e.g., Massachusetts, 1903; Wisconsin, 1905; Indiana, 1913) are especially valuable. The last of the states to issue regulation plates were South Carolina and Texas in 1917, and Florida in 1918. While many northeastern states had registered hundreds of thousands of vehicles by the 1920s making these plates relatively common, those from the southern and western states of that period are considered rare. Naturally, condition is important. While a pair in mint condition might sell for as much as $100.00 to $125.00, a pair with chipped or otherwise damaged porcelain may sometimes be had for as little as $25.00 to $30.00. Unless noted otherwise our values are for examples in excellent to near mint condition. Our advisor for this category is Leonard Needham; he is listed in the Directory under California. See also Gas Globes and Panels.

Badge, chauffeur's, NY, screw-type bk, 1926-27, VG...................... 35.00
Badge, hat, Yellow Cab, enamel over nickel silver, 2½" 60.00
Book, Buick Facts 1946, red/wht/bl cover, 114-pg, 6½x5".............. 95.00
Book, Chevrolet America's Most Popular Car, for showroom, 1947, 29-pg..155.00
Book, instruction, Ford V-8, 1932, 62-pg, VG 120.00
Booklet, Chevrolet, covers models from 1911 to 1954, 36-pg, VG ..24.00
Booklet, Dodge Brothers Brief History of Great Achievement, 1928 ..50.00
Booklet, Studebaker a Story of Contests, 1909, 7¾x9¾" 45.00
Brochure, Autocar, 1950s-60s, 4-pg, 8½x11", VG 12.00
Brochure, Buick, full-pg views of 1934 models, 50+pgs, 10x14" 90.00
Brochure, Cadillac El Dorado, 1953, unfolds to 24x21" 65.00
Brochure, Chevrolet, 1946-47, G...................................... 15.00
Brochure, Chevrolet, 1958 models, opens to 14½x20½" 15.00
Brochure, Edsel, 1958 models in color, opens to 50x24" 32.00
Brochure, Oldsmobile 6 & 8, Prices - Terms..., 1934, unfolds: 12x8", M..45.00
Brochure, Plymouth, Deco cover, 1936, 16-pg, 10x6", G 45.00
Cap, radiator, LaSalle 50.00
Catalog, Chevrolet Truck Parts, 1955-65, 804-pg, G..................... 20.00
Catalog, Edsel Master Parts, 1958-60, 931-pg............................ 235.00
Catalog, Lil' 500 America's No 1 Kart & Scooter Line, 1960s, G.. 25.00
Catalog, Mr Bug Street & Off Road Parts, illus, 1980, 122-pg 40.00
Catalog, Reading Standard Motorcycles, illustrated, 1916, 12-pg, 10x7".130.00
Catalog, White Steam Car, Models K&L, 1908, 26-pg, 6x9", VG...... 120.00
Catalog, Western Auto Supply Co, 1928 Auto Owner's Supply Book ..20.00
Catalog, World Car 1970, 439-pg...................................... 40.00
Clock, Chrysler, glass bubble face, lights up, Telechron 535.00
Coin, Ford Thunderbird 35th ltd ed, silver, w/holder & booklet, M .. 65.00
Emblem, Hupmobile w/in H, faded enameling, 2" dia.................... 35.00

Emblem, Oldsmobile 88 Rocket, chrome.................................. 35.00
Emblem, Oldsmobile Hydra-Matic Drive, enamel on chrome, 15" L, VG ..30.00
Emblem, radiator, Chevrolet, cloisonnè, 1931, 3x3", VG+ 60.00
Game, Test Driver at the Chrysler Corp, brd game, 1956, EXIB.... 35.00
Gauge, tire pressure; Studebaker, US Gauge Co 120.00
Gauge, tire, Buick models 28-58 pressures listed on front, +pouch ..55.00
Grill pc, Studebaker Bullet Nose, 1950, VG................................. 165.00
Handbook, Hand Book of Gasoline Automobiles 1912, 200+pgs, VG .65.00
Hood ornament, Cadillac emblem, chrome w/mc enameling 32.50
Hood ornament, Chevrolet, gazelle, gold pnt, ca 1951, 14½" L ... 170.00
Hood ornament, Chrysler Imperial, eagle w/in circle, early 1960s . 25.00
Hood ornament, Chrysler, gazelle, cast metal, 1932, 2½x5" 235.00
Hood ornament, Pierce Arrow, nude man, chromed, Franklin Mint, 1987 ..95.00
Horn, Model T Ford (script), rpt blk finish, 9½x4½"dia+bracket . 145.00
Key holder, Hupmobile, emb metal, scarce 70.00
Lapel pin, Studebaker Star Honor Club, red enamel on silver..... 125.00
License plate topper, Pontiac & Cadillac emblems, 1930s-40s, 4x5" ...25.00
Manual, Ford, Lincoln, Mercury & Edsel Special Tools, 1958 .... 25.00
Manual, owner's, Buick, 1948, 32-pg, VG..................................... 45.00
Manual, owner's, Chrysler Imperial, 1962................................... 35.00
Manual, owner's, Corvair, 1969, VG.. 20.00
Manual, owner's, Corvette, 1969... 40.00
Manual, owner's, Jaguar 4.2 Litre E-type Series 2, 1960s?, G......... 30.00
Manual, owner's, Packard Six, brn cover, 1939, VG....................... 30.00
Manual, shop, Ford Thunderbird, 1961, 300-pg, 8½x11", G 40.00
Manual, shop, Kaiser-Frazer Hydra-Matic, 1950, 160-pg, 8x11", VG ..30.00
Mirror, side, Buick, 1950s, 6½x5" 37.50
Motometer, Buick, Boyce, missing glass lens, 5x3⅞" dia 40.00
Pennant, Buick 1916 in bl on gr & pk felt, 9x28"........................... 75.00
Pennant, Dort, red, Own a Dort You Will Like It, 1915-24, 5½x2" ..88.00
Pin, Studebaker Master Mechanic, emb metal, ¾" dia 210.00
Pin-back, Chevrolet, Watch the Leader, band leader, ¾" 20.00
Pin-back, Chrysler Desoto 2 for 1 in '41, red/yel/bl, 2½" 37.50
Pin-back, Yellow Cab, orange cello, Maier Lavaty, 2¼".................. 50.00
Pocket mirror, Chevrolet, celluloid, 1920s Maine dealership, 2x3"....230.00
Postcard, 16 HP Decauville w/Fred Terry & J Neilson photo, 1906, VG ..9.00
Postcard, Rambler Super Cross Country Station Wagon photo, 1960, NM ..6.50
Poster, Maxwell Truck, Be Cold Blooded..., 1920, 23x17", G 85.00
Promo record, Ford the Going Thing, 1969, 33⅓ LP 75.00
Promotional car, Buick Roadmaster, pnt metal, Brooklin, 1994, MIB ...58.00
Promotional car, Buick Skylark 1954 convertible, red/cream, 8½" ...55.00
Promotional car, Cadillac Eldorado, olive gr, Johan, 1968 .... 165.00
Promotional car, Cadillac Eldorado Brougham 1957, Franklin Mint, MIB ..62.50
Promotional car, Chevrolet 1956 Convertible, Franklin Mint, MIB . 60.00
Promotional car, Chevrolet Camaro SS, bright orange, 1969 .... 90.00
Promotional car, Edsel, bl & wht, friction drive, 1958 .... 75.00
Promotional car, Ford Fairlane 300, Hubley, 1960s, VG 100.00
Promotional car, Ford Thunderbird convertible, AMT, 1960s..... 125.00
Promotional car, Mercury Monterey convertible, silver & wht, 1961....70.00
Promotional car, Mercury sedan, dk red, AMT, 1962, VG 165.00
Promotional car, Oldsmobile Cutlass, Cypress Gr, Jo-Han, 1974, MIB .. 50.00
Promotional car, Yellow Cab, tin litho, friction, Japan, 1950s, 6" .. 80.00

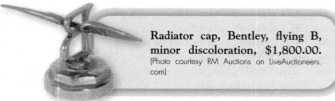

Radiator cap, Bentley, flying B, minor discoloration, $1,800.00. (Photo courtesy RM Auctions on LiveAuctioneers.com)

Radiator cap, Ford Model A, flying quail, chrome, 4", VG 100.00
Shift knob, Dodge Brothers, butterscotch Bakelite & NP brass ... 225.00
Sign, Chevrolet Super Service, tin litho, 60x56", G 525.00

Sign, dealer's, 1955 Studebaker President V-8 4-door sedan, 19x24" . 90.00
Sign, GM Chevrolet Genuine Parts, tin litho, 1950s-60s, 23x18" ..535.00
Sign, Studebaker...Service, pnt porc, 31½x48", G 850.00
Speedometer, Ford Special, Stewart-Warner Co, magnetic type, ca 1914. 90.00
Step plate, rumble-seat rear-ft, LaSalle, 1937-38 .... 60.00
Thermometer, Buick Motor Cars, 28x7", VG, (+) 200.00
Thermometer, Cadillac, Weld It, NP, 3" dia 130.00
Tool box, Model T Ford running brd type, Yale lock, 10x24x12".. 135.00
Wrench, hubcap, Hudson, 13", G 12.00
Wrench, hubcap, Kissel, 12", G.. 130.00
Wrench, hubcap, Moon, 10", VG 60.00

Autumn Leaf

In 1933 the Hall China Company designed a line of dinnerware for the Jewel Tea Company, who offered it to their customers as premiums. Although you may hear the ware referred to as 'Jewel Tea,' it was officially named 'Autumn Leaf' in the 1940s. In addition to the dinnerware, frosted Libbey glass tumblers, stemware, and a melmac service with the orange and gold bittersweet pod were available over the years, as were tablecloths, plastic covers for bowls and mixers, and metal items such as cake safes, hot pads, coasters, wastebaskets, and canisters. Even shelf paper and playing cards were made to coordinate. In 1958 the International Silver Company designed silver-plated flatware in a pattern called 'Autumn' which was to be used with dishes in the Autumn Leaf pattern. A year later, a line of stainless flatware was introduced. These accessory lines are prized by collectors today.

One of the most fascinating aspects of collecting the Autumn Leaf pattern has been the wonderful discoveries of previously unlisted pieces. Among these items are two different bud-ray lid one-pound butter dishes; most recently a one-pound butter dish in the 'Zephyr' or 'Bingo' style; a miniature set of the 'Casper' salt and pepper shakers; coffee, tea, and sugar canisters; a pair of candlesticks; an experimental condiment jar; and a covered candy dish. All of these china pieces are attributed to the Hall China Company. Other unusual items have turned up in the accessory lines as well and include a Libbey frosted tumbler in a pilsner shape, a wooden serving bowl, and an apron made from the oilcloth (plastic) material that was used in the 1950s tablecloth. These latter items appear to be professionally done, and we can only speculate as to their origin. Collectors believe that the Hall items were sample pieces that were never meant to be distributed.

Hall discontinued the Autumn Leaf line in 1978. At that time the date was added to the backstamp to mark ware still in stock in the Hall warehouse. A special promotion by Jewel saw the reintroduction of basic dinnerware and serving pieces with the 1978 backstamp. These pieces have made their way into many collections. Additionally, in 1979 Jewel released a line of enamel-clad cookware and a Vellux blanket made by Martex which were decorated with the Autumn Leaf pattern. They continued to offer these items for a few years only, then all distribution of Autumn Leaf items was discontinued.

It should be noted that the Hall China Company has produced several limited edition items for the National Autumn Leaf Collectors' Club (NALCC): a New York-style teapot (1984); an Edgewater vase (1987, different than the original shape); candlesticks (1988); a Philadelphia-style teapot, creamer, and sugar set (1990); a tea-for-two set and a Solo tea set (1991); a donut jug; and a large oval casserole. Later came the small ball jug, one-cup French teapot, and a set of four chocolate mugs. Other special items over the past few years made for them by Hall China include a sugar packet holder, a chamberstick, and an oyster cocktail. Additional items are scheduled for production. All of these are plainly marked as having been made for the NALCC and are appropriately dated. A few other pieces have been made by Hall as limited editions for China Specialties, but these are easily identified: the Airflow teapot and the Norris refrigerator pitcher (neither of which was previously decorated with the Autumn

Leaf decal), a square-handled beverage mug, and the new-style Irish mug. A production problem with the square-handled mugs halted their production. Additional items available now are a covered onion soup, tall bud vase, china kitchen memo board, canisters, and egg drop-style salt and pepper shakers with a mustard pot. They have also issued a deck of playing cards and Libbey tumblers. See *Garage Sale & Flea Market* (Collector Books) for suggested values for club pieces. For more information we recommend *Collector's Encyclopedia of Hall China* by Margaret and Kenn Whitmyer. For information on the NALCC refer to the Clubs, Newsletters, and Websites section. Our advisor for this category is Gwynneth Harrison; she is listed in the Directory under California.

Bottle, Jim Beam, w/stand 130.00
Bowl cover set, plastic, 8-pc, 7 assorted covers in pouch 100.00
Bowl, cereal, 6", $8 to 12.00
Bowl, cream soup, hdls 40.00
Bowl, fruit, 5½", $3 to 6.00
Bowl, Royal Glas-Bake, set of 4, $300 to 450.00
Bowl, vegetable, divided, oval 125.00
Bowl, vegetable, oval, Melmac, $40 to 50.00
Butter dish, 1-lb, regular, ruffled top, $400 to 500.00
Cake safe, metal, motif on top or sides, 5", ea 50.00
Calendar, 1920s-30s, $100 to 200.00
Candlesticks, metal, Douglas, pr $70 to 100.00
Canister, brn & gold, wht plastic lid 30.00
Canisters, sq, 4-pc set, $295 to 350.00
Casserole, Heatflow, Dunbar, clear, w/lid, rnd, 1½-qt, $50 to 75.00
Casserole, Heatflow, rnd, w/lid, 2-qt 85.00
Casserole, rnd, w/lid, 2-qt, $30 to 45.00
Casserole, Royal Glas-Bake, milk wht w/clear glass lid, rnd 90.00
Coaster, metal, 3⅛" 8.00
Coffee percolator, electric, all china, 4-pc, $325 to 400.00
Coffeepot, all china, 4-pc, $275 to 350.00
Coffeepot, Rayed, 8-cup 45.00
Cookware, New Metal, 7-pc set, $450 to 700.00
Creamer/sugar bowl, Nautilus 75.00
Custard cup, Heatflow clear glass, Mary Dunbar, $40 to 60.00
Custard cup, Radiance 10.00
Flatware, SP, ea 35.00
Flatware, stainless steel, serving pc, ea $90 to 130.00

Flour sifter, metal, 6¼", $275.00. (Photo courtesy Jackson's Auction on LiveAuctioneers.com)

Gravy boat w/underplate (pickle dish) 55.00
Hurricane lamps, Douglas, w/metal base, pr, min 500.00
Loaf pan, Mary Dunbar, $90 to 125.00
Marmalade, 3-pc, $100 to 125.00
Mug, conic, $50 to 65.00
Mustard, 3-pc, $100 to 120.00
Pie plate, 9½" 35.00
Plate, 6", $5 to 8.00
Plate, 7¼", $5 to 10.00
Pressure cooker, Mary Dunbar, metal 225.00
Saucepan, metal, w/lid, 2-qt 100.00
Saucer, regular, Ruffled D 3.00
Tablecloth, cotton sailcloth w/gold stripe, 54x72" 140.00

Teapot, Newport, dtd 1978, $200 to 250.00
Teapot, Rayed, long spout, 1978, rare, $800 to 1,600.00
Teapot, Solo, club pc, 1,400 made, 1991 .... 100.00
Tidbit tray, 3-tier 100.00
Tin, fruitcake, wht or tan 10.00
Towel, tea, cotton, 16x33" 60.00
Toy, Jewel Truck, gr, $350 to 425.00
Toy, Jewel Van, brn, Buddy L, $400 to 650.00
Tray, metal, oval 100.00
Tumbler, Brockway, 9-oz, 13-oz or 16-oz, ea 45.00
Tumbler, Libbey, gold frost etched, flat or ftd, 10-oz, ea 65.00
Warmer, oval, $150 to 225.00

Aviation

Aviation buffs are interested in any phase of flying, from early developments with gliders, balloons, airships, and flying machines to more modern innovations. Books, catalogs, photos, patents, lithographs, ad cards, and posters are among the paper ephemera they treasure alongside models of unlikely flying contraptions, propellers and rudders, insignia and equipment from WWI and WWII, and memorabilia from the flights of the Wright Brothers, Lindbergh, Earhart, and the Zeppelins. See also Militaria. Our advisor for this category is John R. Joiner; he is listed in the Directory under Georgia. Our values are for examples in near mint to mint condition unless noted otherwise.

Badge, hat, South African Airways pilot, type 1, 2½" W 160.00
Badge, hat, Transcontinental & Western captain, brass chief's head .250.00
Badge, Pan Am Deputy Sheriff, eng Indian scene on silver, 2" 365.00
Bank, United Airlines, plastic Menehune (Hawaiian male) figure, 9" .265.00
Book, ABC of Aviation Aircraft, Victor Page, 1942, 598-pg, EX... 75.00
Book, Ozark Air Lines Contrails, pictorial history, hardbound, 1983 .. 215.00
Brochure, Air-India 40 Yrs, 12-pg 35.00
Brochure, Continental Airlines, aircraft fleet, ca 1973, 30 mc pgs. 25.00
Brochure, TWA Disneyland map, 1955, open: 15x8", EX 55.00
Cachet, Graf Zeppelin First Flight, US – Germany, Oct 1928, VG .90.00
Calendar, Alaska Northern..., Yard Antarctica, 1932, 20x13¼" 165.00
Cap & goggles, Alex Taylor & Co, leather, pre-WWII, VG 145.00
Cap, Braniff Airlines pilot, bl w/gold braid & badge, 1960s 200.00
Clock, travel alarm, Pan Am, windup, Sloan, 1950s, 3x3" 70.00
Coffee mug, Eastern Airlines, bl logo (both sides) on wht 10.00
Dispenser/coffee thermos, TWA Arrow, stainless steel, 1930s-40s, 17" ..185.00
Flatware, Air France Concorde, Art Moderne, 1965, 12-pc 85.00
Hat, Eastern Airlines stewardess', w/wings pin, w/1966 certificate ..100.00
Hat, Pan Am attendant, navy wool, Escrello, 1980s 85.00
Hat, TWA pilot's, w/Indian head hat badge, 1930s, EX 400.00
Headset, David Clark Model H10-13.4 .... 200.00
Ice bucket, Pan Am, International Silver Co, 8" 60.00
Label, Capital Airlines, red & wht, 1950s, 2x3", EX 5.00
Luggage label, Am Airlines, Airship Hindenburg, mc, 5¼" L 55.00
Luggage label, Pennsylvania Airlines, tri-motor plain, 1938, 3x4½" .65.00
Manual, Eastern Airlines, Lockheed Constellation plane, 1950 ..115.00
Manual, TWA Boeing 727 flight handbook, 1980s, 12x11½" 85.00
Menu, Pan Am Airways System, 1935, unfolds to: 12x19", VG ..260.00
Model, Airbus A-330, resin, removable wings, chrome stand, 1:50 scale ..750.00
Model, Boeing 747 SP, PacMin, 1:100 scale, MIB 650.00
Model, Boeing Model 314 Dixie Clipper Flying Boat, alum, 32" W ..550.00
Model, Pan Am Boeing B-377 Stratocruiser, plastic, 1950s, 11" wingspan ..85.00
Model, Republic F-105/FH-105 Thunderchief Fighter/bomber jet, alum ..495.00
Model, TWA Boeing 707-320, pnt mahog, 1:100 scale, MIB 70.00
Navigation compass, Bendix WWII vintage, EX 75.00
Pennant, Goodyear Zeppelin, Akron OH, felt, 30" 65.00
Photo, Boeing B-314 Pan Am Clipper, blk & wht, 1939, 8x10" 60.00

Pin, Braniff flight attendant's wings, gold-filled, 1970s, MOC, pr . 115.00
Pin, Delta Jr Captain, gold-tone metal w/old bl logo, 2" L 10.00
Pin, lapel, Hughes Aircraft 25 Yr Service, 10k gold & dmn.......... 80.00
Pin, Zeppelin airship form, silver, mk Sterling, 1x3½".................... 75.00
Platter, Graf Zeppelin, Heinrich & Co, Bavaria, 1928, 12x9"...2,000.00

Program from San Diego, California's Third Annual Meet, Glenn H. Curtiss on cover, 1912, four pages, rare, $1,000.00. (Photo courtesy Philip Weiss Auctions on LiveAuctioneers.com)

Sign, Taylorcraft America's Most..., porc on steel, 1946, 14x10" . 200.00
Stainless flatware, Am Airlines, AA Stainless, 18-pc set 50.00
Tickets, Northern Consolidated Airlines, 1963, EX, pr.................5.00
Timetable, Aloha Airlines, columnar format, trifold, 1959 .... 55.00
Timetable, Northwest Airlines, showing Boeing 720B jet, 1961.... 35.00
Timetable, Northwest Airways, columnar format, 1932 .... 100.00
Timetable, Northwest, tin, red/wht/bl, 1946, 7", VG 30.00
Tumbler, Delta Airlines, SS w/logo, mk #3759, 3¾"....................... 60.00
Validation plate, Alaska Airlines, emb metal 85.00
Wings, cap, Piedmont Airline pilot's, screw-bk, 1974-89, 3"........ 230.00
Wings, Capital pilot's, mc enamel, Blackington Hallmark, 3" 160.00
Wings, Darr Aero Tech Military Flight Commander, silver/enamel, 1940s..275.00
Wings, TWA stewardess', red/wht enamel, gold-tone metal, 1960s, 2" ..180.00

Baccarat Glass

The Baccarat Glass company was founded in 1765 near Luneville, France, and continues to this day to produce quality crystal tableware, vases, perfume bottles, and figurines. The firm became famous for the high-quality millefiori and caned paperweights produced there from 1845 until about 1860. Examples of these range from $300.00 to as much as several thousand. Since 1953 they have resumed the production of paperweights on a limited edition basis. Our advisors for this category are Randall Monsen and Rod Baer; their address is listed in the Directory under Virginia. See also Bottles and Flasks, Commercial Perfume Bottles; Paperweights.

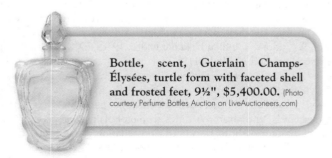

Bottle, scent, Guerlain Champs-Élysées, turtle form with faceted shell and frosted feet, 9½", $5,400.00. (Photo courtesy Perfume Bottles Auction on LiveAuctioneers.com)

Bottle, scent, bronze doré cherubs/scrolls, prism stopper, 7x2" sq.. 750.00
Bottle, scent, yel w/silver lattice o/l, silver screw-on lid, 3"........ 200.00
Bowl, 6 melon ribs, ftd, medallion mk, 1970s, 3x6"......................... 48.00
Box, cut crystal w/starburst base, brass mts, 4½x5x3½" 360.00
Candelabra, 5-light, crystal/bronze w/winged figures/swans, 23", pr .2,400.00
Candlesticks, swirled crystal, 9", pr 360.00
Champagne, Vence, 4", 12 for... 135.00
Chandelier, crystal/silver, 10 candle lights, ca 1860, 57x36" ...12,000.00
Chandelier, draped/cascading prisms, 26" doré ceiling mt, 72x40"..30,000.00

Chandelier, foliate cast candle arms, 12-light, prisms, 32x28" ..4,000.00
Chandelier, Louis XV, w/gilt fr, 8-light, crystal drops, 27x28" 2,300.00
Chandelier, tiered vasiform, rope-twist supports, 10-light, 36"..3,200.00
Cornucopias, cut crystal, bronze doré/marble bases, 11x7½", pr.6,600.00
Decanter set, 6" decanter+5 cordials in glass/gilt-mtd 12" box..1,200.00
Decanter, cut crystal, paneled sides, faceted stopper, +12 wines ..425.00
Decanter, cut crystal, sq w/flattened stopper, 9½x4" 350.00
Decanter, flowers & hearts eng, bell shape, made for Rocher Freres. 110.00
Decanter, Louis XIII Remi Martin, crystal fleur-de-lis, 11x7"....... 300.00
Figurine, boxer dog standing, 5x5x2" 155.00
Figurine, eagle resting on boulder, 10x4x4", $185 to 215.00
Figurine, eagle w/wings wide, 7x9½", MIB................................ 360.00
Figurine, hippo standing, 3x5¾", MIB 275.00
Figurine, jaguar crouching, 3½x10", MIB................................... 360.00
Figurine, leopard sitting, blk, 6¼", MIB 300.00
Figurine, owl, 4" 50.00
Ice bucket, crystal w/gold hdls, box-pleat design, 9x8" 425.00
Ice bucket, cut crystal w/gold rim, bail hdl, 6x9" dia, +tongs 395.00
Inkwell, swirled crystal, Gorham silver cap, 6x4½" 480.00
Obelisk, crystal, 18" 780.00
Punch bowl, cut crystal w/bronze dorè acanthus leaves/mts, 1860, 17"...5,500.00
Rose bowl, sunflower cuttings, 8½x8" 350.00
Stem, cordial, Carcassone, 3x1" 15.00
Stem, sherry, Lafayette, 4" 35.00
Vase, cut crystal w/gilt bronze mts & rim, 21¼" 1,800.00
Vase, Diane, thick cut crystal, 10x6" 500.00
Vase, opal crystal w/HP flowers, etched Baccarat in script, 8x8" .. 150.00
Vase, smoked glass w/etched/gilt swallows, bronze ft, 9½", pr....3,600.00
Vase, spiral cuttings, swollen cylinder, 9¾" 360.00

Badges

The breast badge came into general usage in this country about 1840. Since most are not marked and styles have changed very little to the present day, they are often difficult to date. The most reliable clue is the pin and catch. One of the earliest types, used primarily before the turn of the century, involved a 't-pin' and a 'shell' catch. In a second style, the pin was hinged with a small square of sheet metal, and the clasp was cylindrical. From the late 1800s until about 1940, the pin and clasp were made from one continuous piece of thin metal wire. The same type, with the addition of a flat back plate, was used a little later. There are exceptions to these findings, and other types of clasps were also used. Hallmarks and inscriptions may also help pinpoint an approximate age.

Badges have been made from a variety of materials, usually brass or nickel silver; but even solid silver and gold were used for special orders. They are found in many basic shapes and variations — stars with five to seven points, shields, disks, ovals, and octagonals being most often encountered. Of prime importance to collectors, however, is that the title and/or location appear on the badge. Those with designations of positions no longer existing (city constable, for example) and names of early western states and towns are most valuable.

Badges are among the most commonly reproduced (and faked) types of antiques on the market. At any flea market, 10 fakes can be found for every authentic example. Genuine law badges start at $30.00 to $40.00 for recent examples (1950 – 1970); earlier pieces (1910 – 1930) usually bring $50.00 to $90.00. Pre-1900 badges often sell for more than $100.00. Authentic gold badges are usually priced at a minimum of scrap value (karat, weight, spot price for gold); fine gold badges from before 1900 can sell for $400.00 to $800.00, and a few will bring even more. A fire badge is usually valued at about half the price of a law badge of the same era and material. Our values have been gleaned from internet auctions and are actual selling prices.

Alturas Police, NP 6-point star, early 1900s, 2½" 515.00
Boston Special Police, scallops at edge of oval, 1930s, 1½x2¼" ... 195.00
CA State Brd of Health Engineer, brass, bl enamel, Shreve, 2¾x2"...725.00
Chicago Police, 6-point star w/red enamel, Meyer & Wenth, early 1900s...500.00
Chicago Police, NP/enamel, 2nd issue, SD Childs, ca 1899, 3x2¼".865.00
City of New York Police Detective, shield w/eagle above, ca 1898, 3x2".690.00
Deputy Sheriff Clark Co Nev, Aero Squadron, 7-point star......... 510.00
Deputy Sheriff Franklin Co OH, eagle on shield, gold plate, 1890s. 160.00
Deputy Sheriff, 5-point star in shield, nickel, hallmark, 1900s, 2". 160.00
Deputy Sheriff, Boston MA, NP shield, SM Spencer Mfg, 1900, 2¾".... 275.00
Deputy Sheriff, Sacramento CA, NP 6-point star, HE Sleeper, 1950s..240.00
Deputy Sheriff, star in circle, brass, Pannier Bro, 1900s, 2" 110.00
Deputy Warden, CT, State Brd of Fisheries..., NP shield, 1⅞" 260.00
Director of Public Safety Toledo OH, gold metal, 1910, 2" 850.00
Forest Fire Warden, CT, emb shield, Whitehead & Hoag, 1¾x2".230.00
LI (Long Island) City FD #3, early 1900s, NP brass, 2" dia 150.00

Montana Bureau of Indian Affairs, gold-tone, unissued, $850.00. (Photo courtesy Old West Auction Office on LiveAuctioneers.com)

NYC Police Inspector, bl enamel on bronze, 1910, 1¾x1¾" 900.00
Park Saddle Horse Co #93, Glacier Park Mont, NP brass, 1" dia. 800.00
Reserve Captain Police Dept of NY, eagle on shield, gold-tone, 3"....300.00
Special Deputy Sheriff New Haven CT, shield, nickel, 2".............. 60.00
US Special Police, Inauguration of President, gold & bl shield, 1985. 215.00
William Penn Hose #18, ca 1830-1870, shield shape, 1x1".......... 365.00

Banks

It is apparent that, by and large, mechanical banks have held up well against other collectibles and have withstood the trend of declining values as a result of economic downturn. It is only natural that in some areas of the field there would be an impact. This is most prevalent where the condition of a bank is diminished, especially with more common examples of mechanical banks.

In the very upper echelon of condition (e.g., banks which were sold in the Steckbeck Sale in late 2007 and noted in *Schroeder's, 27th Edition, 2009*), prices have been unaffected. Those examples are the 'creme de le creme,' and collectors seeking to acquire the best are still very competitive about owning the most outstanding examples they can find, and they are willing to pay whatever it takes to obtain a mechanical bank in that category. Having said that, values have not increased in this area either, and we will have to see what happens with the economy in the coming year to determine its impact on valuation.

As a bank declines in condition, it is safe to say that the value will decline exponentially greater than in previous years. For example, banks in the 90% paint condition area have been reduced by a factor of say 5% – 10%, whereas those in the 80% paint condition area have been reduced by approximately 20% for some examples. Those figures may be even higher for banks in 60% – 80% paint condition. This is not an exact science, and on any given day at any given auction, competition could surface which would shatter this hypothesis. Remember, examples of the same bank can have a wide range of value depending on condition, sometimes resulting in 10 – 20 times the value factor. At the end of the day, the price established will be what a buyer is willing to pay a seller.

Mechanical banks should be sought after for their art form, as opposed to investment opportunities. However, it cannot be overlooked that acquiring mechanical banks has proven to be profitable over the long haul, and many people consider it to be a 'safe haven,' especially during economic turmoil. In order to make wise decisions and investments in mechanical banks, dealers and collectors alike must learn to carefully determine overall condition by assessing the amount and strength (depth) of paint, and by checking for breaks, repairs, and replaced parts. Variations in castings and paint color are other factors which influence price. Black lights and high-powered magnifying glasses along with careful measurements are some of the tools used by seasoned collectors and legitimate, reputable dealers. It is not enough to 'use' these tools. One must also know how to read them. Those skills only come with time and experience, so for the majority of collectors, and especially prospective collectors, making purchases from those who are knowledgeable and experienced in the field might provide a substantial comfort level even though you may pay a little bit more. Buying a defective bank inexpensively is not necessarily a bargain — especially if you are not aware of the defect!

For those not familiar with mechanical banks, a brief history is in order. Mechanical banks have always been at the pinnacle of the toy collecting field. They typically are the most sought after and consequently the most expensive collectible in the field. They are recognized as among the most successful of the mass-produced goods of the nineteenth century. The earliest mechanical banks were made of wood and lead. In 1869 John Hall introduced 'Hall's Excelsior' bank, made of cast iron. It was an immediate success. The J. & E. Stevens Company produced the bank for Hall and, as a result, soon began making their own designs. Several companies followed suit, most of which were already in the hardware business. They used newly developed iron casting techniques to produce novelty savings devices for an emerging toy market. The social mores and customs of the times, political attitudes, racial and ethnic biases, the excitement of the circus, and humorous everyday events all served as inspiration for the creation of hundreds of banks. Designers made the most of simple mechanics to produce models with captivating actions that served to amuse, and encouraged the concept of saving to children. The quality and detail of the castings were remarkable as was the 'action' in many banks. The majority of collectible banks were made from 1870 to 1910, and, in limited amounts, until World War II, the cutoff point for most collectors. The most prolific manufacturers were J. & E. Stevens Co., Keyser and Rex, and the Shepard Hardware Company. They all made still banks as well.

Still banks are widely collected. Various materials were used in their construction, and each material represents a sub-field in still bank collections. Nobody knows exactly how many different still banks were made, but upwards of 5,000 pre-WWII examples have been identified in the various books published on this subject. Cast iron examples still dominate the market, but lead banks from Europe have recently increased significantly in value. Tin and pottery banks also draw quite a substantial amount of interest.

Both mechanical and still banks have been reproduced. One way to detect a reproduction is by measuring. The dimensions of a reproduced bank will always be fractionally smaller, since the original bank was cast from a pattern, while the reproduction was made from a casting of the original bank. As both values and interest continue to rise, it becomes increasingly important to educate ourselves to the fullest extent possible. The following are recommended books on the subject: *The Bank Book* by Norman, *The Dictionary of Still Banks* by Long and Pitman, *The Penny Bank Book* by Moore, *Penny Banks around the World* by Duer, *Registering Banks* by Robert L. McCumber, and *Penny Lane* by Davidson, which contains a cross-reference listing of all other publications on mechanical banks.

Unlike mechanical banks, the preponderance of still banks are sold in many different venues, e.g., flea markets, estate sales, antique shows, toy shows, eBay, online dealer sales, auctions, etc. Prices seem to vary so much that it is hard to get a handle on valuations. Often it is difficult to examine the banks; consequently we cannot say with any certainty the condition of those examples which sold. It is safe to say that the better condition still banks in the 92%+ condition have maintained value, while anything below that has probably declined slightly. There is more forgiveness for lack of paint as the bank becomes more rare.

'Banthrico Banks' (giveaway banks from institutions and souvenir banks from the 1940s to 1980s) are quite collectible and more information can be acquired by reading *Coin Banks by Banthrico*, written by author and collector James L. Redwine.

Given the foregoing, this year we will concentrate on those mechanical banks in the 90% paint condition area, since these seem to have provided the most consistent maintenance of value in the 'affordable' range (relatively speaking). We will use some of the same banks as last year for comparative purposes in addition to new listings. It should be noted that when traps are an integral part of the body of the bank, such as the key lock trap for the 'Uncle Sam' bank, lack of same results in a significant reduction in the value of that bank. When the trap is underneath the bank (typically a twist trap, as in 'Eagle and Eaglets'), reduction in value is minimal.

Our advisor for mechanical and still banks is Clive Devenish, who is listed in the Directory under California.

To most accurately represent current market values, we have used condition codes in some of our listings that correspond with guidelines developed by today's bank collectors.

NM — 98% paint	VG — 80% paint
EX — 90% paint	G — 70% paint

Key:
M — Andy Moore Book: RM — Robert McCumber Book:
The Penny Bank Book   *Registering Banks*
N — Bill Norman Book: SM — sheet metal
The Bank Book   WM — white metal

Mechanical

In order to compare all mechanical banks one against another, we will consider them to be in 90% paint and in all-original, excellent condition. Deductions will have to be taken by the collector or dealer for replaced parts, touch-up paint, or any other restoration.

Acrobat, N-1010, CI	12,000.00
Always Did 'Spise a Mule (Bench), N-2940, CI	3,800.00
Bad Accident, N-1150, CI	3,500.00
Boy on Trapeze, N-1350, CI	4,600.00
Boys Stealing Watermelons, N-1380, CI	3,700.00
Bulldog – Standing, N-1450, CI	1,100.00
Bulldog (coin on nose), N-1430, CI	3,300.00
Cabin Bank, N-1610, CI	850.00
Cat & Mouse (cat balancing), N-1700, CI	4,800.00
Chief Big Moon, N-1740, CI	8,000.00
Clown & Dog, N-1850, tin	2,000.00
Cowboy w/Tray, N-1990, tin	1,700.00
Creedmor, N-2000, CI	700.00
Dinah, N-2150, CI	1,200.00
Eagle & Eaglets, N-2230, CI	1,850.00
Girl Skipping Rope, N-2680, CI	35,000.00
Guessing Bank, N-2680, CI	4,200.00
Hen & Chick (wht hen), N-2790, CI	4,800.00
Home Bank, N-2840, tin	300.00

Home Bank, N-2860, CI, no dormers	4,000.00
Humpty Dumpty, N-2900, CI	5,000.00
Indian & Bear, N-2980, CI	4,800.00
Jonah & the Whale, N-3490, CI	5,400.00
Leap Frog, N-3590, CI	6,000.00
Lighthouse, N-3620, CI	5,500.00
Lucky Wheel Money Box, N-3710, CI	700.00
Monkey & Parrot, N-3950, tin	650.00
Monkey Bank, N-3960, CI	600.00
Mule Entering Barn, N-4030, CI	2,500.00
Novelty, N-4260, CI	3,000.00
Organ Bank (boy & girl), N-4310, CI	3,200.00
Organ Bank (mini), N-4340, CI	1,400.00
Organ Grinder & Performing Bear, N-4350, CI	9,000.00
Owl, slot in book, N-4360, CI	500.00
Owl Turns Head, N-4380, CI	950.00
Paddy & The Pig, N-4400, CI	4,800.00
Pelican, N-4490, CI	3,900.00
Pig in a High Chair, N-4570, CI	1,600.00
Presto (building), N-4650, CI	650.00
Punch & Judy, N-4740, CI	5,000.00
Rabbit in Cabbage, N-4790, CI	1,100.00
Rooster, N-4920, CI	1,200.00
Speaking Dog – Red Dress, N-5170, CI	4,500.00
Stump Speaker, N-5370, CI	3,800.00
Tammany, N-5420, CI	1,250.00
Teddy & The Bear, N-5460, CI	3,800.00
Trick Dog (6-part base), N-5620, CI	3,000.00
Trick Dog, Hubley, bl, N-5630, CI	600.00
Uncle Remus, N-5730, CI	9,000.00
Uncle Sam, N-5740, CI, rpl trap	5,000.00
Weeden's Plantation, N-5910, wood & tin	3,500.00
William Tell, N-5940, CI	3,000.00
Wireless Bank, N-5980, wood	300.00
World's Fair Bank, N-6040, CI	1,000.00
Zoo, N-6070, CI	3,000.00

Registering

Time Is Money, EX, $1,680.00. (Photo courtesy Dan Morphy Auctions, LLC on LiveAuctioneers.com)

Captain Marvel's Magic Dime Saver (pocket), tin, RM-223, EX.	150.00
Clock Face, 2 hands registering dollars & cents, ornate CI, VG	1,450.00
Clown & Monkey Daily Dime (pocket), RM-224, tin, EX	60.00
Coin Registering Bank, mid-Eastern building, Kayser & Rex, 1890s, NM	8,050.00
Dime a Day Thrifty Elf (pocket), RM-229, tin, EX	100.00
Donald Duck Clock Vault, tin, Spanish sayings on drum, EX	140.00
Dopey Dime Register (pocket), RM-218, tin, EX	180.00
Gem Registering, w/orig paper label, J&E Stevens, ca 1893, NM	4,500.00
George Washington Bank, RM-67, tin, EX	150.00
Imperial 3 Coin Bank, RM-16, bronze, EX	400.00
Jackie Robinson (pocket), tin, RM-234, EX	450.00
Keep 'Em Sailing Dime Register (pocket), RM-220, tin, EX	250.00
Little Orphan Annie (pocket), RM-213, tin, EX	225.00
Mickey Mouse Dime Register, litho tin, 2½" sq, VG+	450.00

National Recording Bank, dime register, CI, Pat Apr 7, 1891 ..... 265.00
New York World's Fair Daily Dime Register, RMS Sales, litho tin box, NMOC. 70.00
Penny Register (Pail), K&R, bail hdl, 3", EX................ 175.00
Popeye Daily Dime Register, M-1573, silver pnt on tin, 2½", MIP 150.00
Prince Valiant (pocket), tin, RM-231, EX.................... 125.00
Recording Dime Bank, NP CI, registering window in front, 6½", EX. 200.00
Spar-Uhr, Germany, litho tin, registering clock on front, 5¾", EX+ ..300.00
Time Clock, NPCI, Ives, Blakeslee & Williams, ca 1893, EX ...2,750.00
Uncle Sam's Nickel Register Bank, RM-79, SM cash register, EX ..125.00
Vacation Daily Dime, tin litho, Kalon Mfg, 2⅝", NM................... 90.00
Woven Basket Dime Bank, RM-28, CI, EX....................... 200.00

Still

$100,000 Money Bag, M-1262, CI, 3⅝", EX...................... 440.00
1882 Villa, M-959, CI, 5⅞", VG............................ 880.00
1889 Tower, Kyser & Rex, 6⅞", VG......................... 990.00
1890 Tower Bank, M-1198, CI, 6⅞", EX...................... 1,320.00
1893 World's Fair Administration Building, M-1072, CI, 6", EX. 715.00
Airplane Spirit of St Louis, M-1423, steel, EX................ 600.00
Amherst Buffalo, M-556, CI, 5¼", EX........................ 525.00
Andy Gump, M-217, CI, EX................................ 1,380.00
Apple on Leafy Twig, K&R, ca 1882, 3x5", EX................ 1,725.00
Arcade Steamboat, M-1460, CI, 2⅜" H, EX................... 500.00
Baby in Egg (blk), M-261, lead, 7¼", EX.................... 495.00
Baby in Cradle, M-51, NPCI, EX........................... 1,840.00
Baseball Player, M-18, CI, 5¾", VG........................ 160.00
Baseball Player, M-19, CI, 5¾", NM....................... 1,090.00
Battleship Maine, M-1439, CI, 6", EX...................... 4,950.00
Battleship Oregon, M-1439, CI, EX........................ 3,800.00
Bear Stealing Pig, M-693, CI, rpl screw, 5½", G............ 650.00
Bear w/Honey Pot, M-717, CI, 6½", EX..................... 195.00
Begging Rabbit, M-566, CI, 5⅛", EX....................... 250.00
Billiken Bank, M-74, CI, EX............................... 85.00
Billy Bounce (Give Billy a Penny), M-15, CI, 4¾", VG.............. 385.00
Bird on Stump (Songbird), M-664, CI, EX................... 400.00
Blackpool Tower, M-984, CI, partial rpt, rpl screw, 7⅜" 400.00
Boston Bull Terrier, M-421, CI, 5¼", EX................... 220.00
Boy Scout, M-45, CI, EX.................................. 150.00
Buffalo, M-560, CI w/gold pnt, 3⅛", EX.................... 145.00
Bugs Bunny (bbl), M-270, WM, EX.......................... 175.00
Bugs Bunny by the Tree, M-278, CI, 5½", EX................ 140.00
Building w/Eagle Finial, M-1134, CI, 9¾", EX............... 935.00
Bulldog (seated), M-396, CI, 3⅞", NM..................... 440.00
Bulldog w/Sailor Cap, M-363, lead, 4⅜", EX 440.00
Buster Brown & Tige, M-241, CI, gold & red pnt, 5½", VG........ 175.00
Buster Brown & Tige, M-242 variant, CI, 5½", NM............ 935.00
Cadet, M-8, CI, crack at slot, 5¾", VG..................... 165.00
Camel (kneeling), M-770, CI, 2½", EX 825.00
Camel (Oriental), M-769, CI, EX.......................... 1,800.00
Campbell Kids, M-163, CI, gold pnt, 3¾", EX............... 330.00
Cat on Tub, M-358, CI, 4⅛", EX........................... 195.00
Cat on Tub, M-358, CI, gold pnt, 4⅛", EX.................. 175.00
Cat w/Ball, M-352, CI, EX................................ 225.00
Charles Russell, M-247, WM, gold pnt, 6¼", EX............. 55.00
Charlie McCarthy on Trunk, M-207, compo, 5¼", M 475.00
City Bank w/Teller, M-1097, CI, 5¾", NM.................. 315.00
Clown, bl costume, M-211, CI, EX......................... 325.00
Colonial House, M-992, CI, 4", EX........................ 140.00
Columbia Bank, M-1070, CI, 5¾", EX...................... 615.00
Crystal Bank, M-926, CI & glass, EX...................... 70.00
Cupola, M-1146, CI, 4⅛", EX............................. 375.00
Deer (lg), M-737, CI, EX.................................. 200.00
Deer (sm), M-736, CI, EX................................. 100.00

Dime Bank, M-1183, CI, 4¾", EX........................... 140.00
Dog (Cutie), M-414, CI, EX................................ 250.00
Dog (Scottie), M-419, CI, EX.............................. 275.00
Dog (Scottie standing), M-435, CI, 3¾", VG................ 155.00
Dog (Spaniel), M-418, CI, EX.............................. 225.00
Dog on Tub, M-359, CI, 4¹⁄₁₆", EX......................... 195.00
Dolphin, M-33, CI, gold pnt, 4½", EX...................... 880.00

Dreadnaught Bank, cast iron, Sydenham and McOustra (British), circa 1915, pristine, $1,560.00. (Photo courtesy The RSL Auction Co. on LiveAuctioneers.com)

Duck, M-624, CI, 4¾", EX................................. 330.00
Duck on Tub, M-616, CI, 5⅜", EX.......................... 220.00
Dutch Boy, M-180, CI, EX................................. 150.00
Dutch Girl w/Flowers, M-181, CI, 5¼", EX................. 120.00
Elmer at Barrel, M-306, WM, EX........................... 150.00
Eureka Trust & Savings Safe, CI, 5¾", EX.................. 470.00
Every Copper Helps, M-71, CI, EX......................... 900.00
Feed My Sheep (lamb), M-596, lead, gold pnt, 2¾", VG 155.00
Fidelity Trust Vault, M-903, CI, EX....................... 650.00
Fido, M-417, CI, 5", EX................................... 140.00
Flat Iron Building, M-1159, CI, 8¼", EX................... 2,640.00
Flat Iron Building, M-1160, CI, no trap, 5¾", EX........... 410.00
Football Player, M-11, CI, 5⅞", EX........................ 460.00
Forlorn Dog, M-408, WM, 4¾", G........................... 85.00
Fortune Ship, M-1457, CI, 4⅛", NM....................... 1,760.00
Foxy Grandpa, M-320, CI, 5½", EX......................... 375.00
Foxy Grandpa, M-320, CI, 5½", G.......................... 215.00
Frowning Face, M-12, CI, 5⅝", EX......................... 1,815.00
Gas Pump, M-1485, CI, EX................................. 250.00
General Butler, M-54, CI, 6½", EX......................... 3,960.00
General Grant, M-115 variant, CI, Harper, 5⅝", EX........... 3,740.00
Give Me a Penny, M-166, CI, EX........................... 300.00
Globe on Arc, M-789, CI, 5¼", G.......................... 140.00
Globe on Arc, M-789, CI, red pnt, 5¼", EX................. 420.00
Globe Savings Fund, M-1199, CI, 7⅛", EX.................. 3,300.00
Golliwog, M-85, CI, 6¼", EX.............................. 400.00
Graf Zeppelin, M-1428, CI, 1¾" H, EX..................... 245.00
Grizzly Bear, M-703, lead, pnt worn in bk, 2¾" 110.00
Hansel & Gretel, M-1016, tin, 2¼", EX.................... 140.00
Hen on Nest, M-546, CI, EX............................... 1,600.00
High Rise, M-1217, CI w/japanning, 5½", EX............... 330.00
High Rise, M-1219, CI, 4⅝", EX........................... 430.00
Home Savings, M-1126, CI, 5⅞", EX....................... 320.00
Horse on Wheels, M-512, CI, 5", EX....................... 470.00
Horse Prancing, M-517, CI, EX............................ 85.00
Horse Tally Ho, M-535, CI, EX............................ 275.00
Horseshoe 'Good Luck,' M-508, CI, EX..................... 300.00
Horseshoe Wire Mesh, M-524, CI/tin, G- Arcade label, 3¼", VG... 110.00
Independence Hall, M-1244, CI, 8⅞", EX................... 660.00
Indian w/Tomahawk, M-228, CI, EX........................ 460.00
Iron Master's Cabin, M-1027, CI, 4¼", EX................. 3,630.00
Jimmy Durante, M-259, WM, 6¾", EX....................... 220.00
Key, M-1616, CI, EX...................................... 800.00
King Midas, M-13, CI, EX................................. 1,200.00
Labrador Retriever, M-412, CI, 4½", EX................... 295.00
Lamb, M-595, CI, EX...................................... 150.00

Liberty Bell (Harper), M-780, CI, EX 300.00
Lindy Bank, M-124, AL, 6½", EX 200.00
Lion (sm, tail right), M-755, CI, 4", EX 85.00
Lion on Tub, M-747, CI, 4⅛", EX 165.00
Lion, M-765, CI, sm, 4", EX 110.00
Litchfield Cathedral, M-968, CI, 6⅝", EX 495.00
Main Street Trolley (no people), M-1469, CI, gold pnt, 3", EX ... 330.00
Maine (sm battleship), M-1440, CI, 4⅝", EX 375.00
Mammy w/Hands on Hips, M-176, CI, 5¼", EX 200.00
Man on Bale of Cotton, M-37, CI, 4⅞", EX 3,960.00
Mary & Lamb, M-164, CI, 4¾", VG 770.00
Mascot Bank, M-3, CI, NM 3,800.00
Metropolitan Safe, CI, 5⅞", NM 2,420.00
Mickey Mouse Post Office, tin, cylindrical, 6", NM 155.00
Middy, M-36, CI, w/clapper, 5¼", G 150.00
Model T (2nd version), M-1483, CI, 4", NM 1,155.00
Monkey w/Removable Hat, M-740, brass, 3⅞", EX 990.00
Mule 'I Made St Louis Famous,' M-489, CI, Harper, 4¾", EX ...2,145.00
Mulligan, M-177, CI, 5¾", EX 175.00
Mutt & Jeff, M-157, CI, gold pnt, 4¼", EX 165.00
Newfoundland (dog), M-440, CI, 3⅝", EX 330.00
Ocean Liner, M-1444, lead, 2¾" H, VG 155.00
Oregon (battleship), M-1452, CI, rpl turn pin, VG 440.00
Oriental Boy on a Pillow (conversion), M-186, CI, 5½", EX 275.00

Owl, painted lead, 4½", NM, $425.00. (Photo courtesy Dan Morphy Auctions, LLC on LiveAuctioneers.com)

Owl on Stump, M-598, CI, EX...225.00
Pass Round the Hat (derby), M-1381, CI, 1⅝", EX 220.00
Peaceful Bill/Harper Smiling Jim, M-109, CI, 4", EX 2,640.00
Pearl Street Building, M-1096, worn gold overpnt, 4¼" 420.00
Pelican, M-679, CI, EX 1,400.00
Pet Safe, M-866, CI, 4½", EX 250.00
Pig 'I Made Chicago Famous,' M-629, CI, Harper, 2⅛", EX 400.00
Pig 'I Made Chicago Famous,' M-631, CI, EX 175.00
Pig (standing), M-478, CI, 3", EX 265.00
Pocahontas Bust, M-226, lead, 3⅛", EX 195.00
Policeman, M-182, CI, Arcade, 5½", EX 1,200.00
Polish Rooster, M-541, CI, 5½", EX 1,375.00
Porky Pig (bbl), M-265, WM, EX 150.00
Porky Pig, M-264, CI, 6", EX+ 440.00
Porky Pig, M-264, CI, 6", VG 195.00
Possum, M-561, CI, EX..400.00
Potato Bank, M-1663, CI, EX 900.00
Professor Pug Frog, M-311, CI, 3¼", EX 365.00
Puppo, M-416, CI, 4⅞", VG 170.00
Quilted Lion, M-758, CI, 3¾", EX 330.00
Rabbit Begging, M-566, CI, EX 150.00
Radio (Crosley), M-819, CI, 5⅛", EX 745.00
Radio (sm Crosley), M-820, CI, EX 175.00
Reindeer, M-376, CI, 6¼", NM 310.00
Retriever w/a Pack, M-436, CI, 4¹¹⁄₁₆", EX 165.00
Rhino, M-721, CI, 2⅝", NM 1,155.00
Rhino, M-721, CI, EX 400.00

Roller Safe, M-880, CI, 3¹¹⁄₁₆", EX...250.00
Roof Bank Building, M-1122, CI, 5¼", G 330.00
Rooster, M-548, CI, 4¾", EX 145.00
Rumplestiltskin, M-27, CI, 6", VG 220.00
Sailor, M-27, CI, 5¼", G 95.00
Sailor, M-28, CI, 5½", G 140.00
Santa Claus w/Tree, M-61, CI, EX 1,120.00
Santa Claus, Ive's, M-56, CI, 7¼", EX 770.00
Save & Smile, M-1641, CI, 4¼", EX 415.00
Saving Sam, M-158, alum, 5¼", EX 935.00
Scotties (6 in basket), M-427, WM, 4½", EX 85.00
Seal on Rock, M-732, CI, ½", EX 660.00
Seated Rabbit, M-368, CI, 3⅝", EX 165.00
Sharecropper, M-173, CI, 5½", EX 305.00
Shell Out, M-1622, CI, EX 500.00
Skyscraper (6 posts), M-1241, CI, 6½", EX 330.00
Skyscraper, M-1239, CI, 4⅜", EX 150.00
Squirrel w/Nut, M-660, CI, 4⅛", VG 515.00
State Bank, M-1078, CI, w/key, 8", NM 1,485.00
State Bank, M-1083, CI, 4", EX 275.00
State Bank, M-1085, CI, 3", EX 330.00
Statue of Liberty (lg), M-1166, CI, EX 850.00
Statue of Liberty (sm), M-1164, CI, EX 150.00
Stop Sign, M-1479, CI, 4½", G 240.00
Tank Bank USA 1918 (lg), M-1435, CI, 3", EX 300.00
Tank Bank USA 1918 (sm), M-1437, CI, 2⅜", EX 250.00
Tank, M-1436, lead, 3", VG 800.00
Teddy Roosevelt, M-120, CI, EX 350.00
Temple Bar Building, M-1163, CI, 4", EX 660.00
Tower Bank, M-1208, CI, 9¼", EX 440.00
Transvaal Money Box, M-1, CI, recast pipe, 6¼", VG 3,500.00
Trust Bank, The; M-154, CI, 7¼", EX 4,950.00
Turkey (lg), M-585, CI, 4¼", EX 495.00
Turkey (sm), M-587, CI, 3⅜", EX 165.00
Two Kids (goats), M-594, CI, EX 900.00
Two-Faced Black Boy (lg), M-83, CI, EX 330.00
Two-Faced Black Boy (sm), M-84, CI, 3⅛", EX 220.00
Two-Faced Devil, M-31, CI, 4¼", EX 770.00
US Army/Navy Safe, electroplated CI, 6⅛", EX 1,320.00
US Mail Mailbox w/Eagle, M-850, CI, 4⅛", EX 135.00
USA Mail Mailbox w/Eagle, M-851, CI, 4⅛", EX 85.00
Villa Bank, M-1179, CI, EX 850.00
Watch Me Grow, M-279 variant, tin, 5¾", EX 75.00
Westminster Abbey, M-973, CI, old gold pnt, 6¼" 275.00
White City Barrel on Cart, M-907, CI, 4", EX 580.00
Woolworth Building (lg), M-1041, CI, 7⅞", EX 330.00
Woolworth Building (sm), M-1042, CI, 5¾", EX 195.00
Yellow Cab, M-1493, CI, 4¼", EX 2,000.00
Young Negro, M-170, CI, 4½", EX 275.00

Book of Knowledge

Book of Knowledge banks were produced by John Wright (Pennsylvania) from circa 1950 until 1975. Of the 30 models they made during those years, a few continued to be made in very limited numbers until the late 1980s; these they referred to as the 'Medallion' series. (Today the Medallion banks command the same prices as the earlier Book of Knowledge series.) Each bank was a handcrafted, hand-painted duplicate of an original that was found in the collection of The Book of Knowledge, the first children's encyclopedia in this country. Because the antique banks are often priced out of the range of today's collectors, these banks are being sought out as affordable substitutes for their very expensive counterparts. It should also be noted that China has reproduced banks with the Book of Knowledge inscription on them. These copies are flooding the market, causing authentic Book of Knowledge banks to decline in value. Buyers should take extra caution when investing in Book of Knowledge banks and purchase them through a reputable dealer who offers a satisfaction guarantee as well as a guarantee that the bank is authentic. Our advisor for Book of Knowledge banks is Dan Iannotti; he is listed in the Directory under Michigan.

Always Did 'Spise a Mule, Boy on Bench, M.................................. 150.00
Artillery Bank, NM 135.00
Boy on Trapeze, M 225.00
Butting Buffalo, M 135.00
Cat & Mouse, NM 150.00
Cow (Kicking), NM 175.00
Creedmore Bank, M... 175.00
Dentist Bank, EX 110.00
Eagle & Eaglets, M.. 175.00
Humpty Dumpty, M.. 150.00

Indian and Bear, M, $195.00. (Photo courtesy B.S. Slosberg, Inc. Auctioneers on LiveAuctioneers.com)

Jonah & the Whale, M.. 150.00
Leap Frog, NM 175.00
Magician, MIB 150.00
Organ Bank (Boy & Girl), NM 125.00
Owl (Turns Head), NM 150.00
Paddy & Pig, NM 175.00
Punch & Judy, NM 150.00
Teddy & the Bear, NM 125.00
Uncle Remus, M... 150.00
US & Spain, M... 150.00
William Tell, M.. 175.00

Barbershop Collectibles

Even for the stranger in town, the local barbershop was easy to find, its location vividly marked with the traditional red and white striped barber pole that for centuries identified such establishments. As far back as the twelfth century, the barber has had a place in recorded history. At one time he not only groomed the beards and cut the hair of his gentlemen clients but was known as the 'blood-letter' as well, hence the red stripe for blood and the white for the bandages. Many early barbers even pulled teeth! Later, laws were enacted that divided the practices of barbering and surgery.

The Victorian barbershop reflected the charm of that era with fancy barber chairs upholstered in rich wine-colored velvet; rows of bottles made from colored art glass held hair tonics and shaving lotion. Backbars of richly carved oak with beveled mirrors lined the wall behind the barber's station. During the late nineteenth century, the barber pole with a blue stripe added to the standard red and white as a patriotic gesture came into vogue.

Today the barbershop has all but disappeared from the American scene, replaced by modern unisex salons. Collectors search for the barber poles, the fancy chairs, and the tonic bottles of an era gone but not forgotten. See also Bottles and Flasks, Barber Bottles; Razors; Shaving Mugs.

Antiseptor, wht porc, 1940s, 3½x3½x1½", M 30.00
Brush, hair removal, trn wood hdl, 4" bristles, 5" 20.00
Brush, Syroco German shepherd (head) figural hdl, pnt eyes, 1900s, 7". 38.00
Brush/duster, wooden soldier hdl, mc pnt 18.00
Cabinet, chestnut/walnut/poplar, dvtl drw amid 16 slots, OH, 14x10x7" 600.00
Cabinet, drw over 2-pane door, 1 w/Wildroot decal, 25x11x12", VG ..185.00
Chair pc, solid alum horse head, bolts to chair, 19"...................... 155.00
Chair, Kochs, stainless steel/porc/leather, Pats 1909 & 1910, NM ...850.00
Chair, Koken, CI & porc w/brass footrests, blk leather, operating hydraulics, NM..1,150.00
Chair, porc, blk leather & NP, 50", VG 250.00
Display, Bakelite, model of shaving brush, Culmak Senior, '40s, 9"...100.00
Finger bowl, amethyst, emb ribs, mc floral, 2⅝", M 140.00
Heater, hot water, CI, Hoffman 45, early 1900s, 30x18" dia 125.00
Jar, Burma Shave emb on clear glass, bl/yel tin lid, ½-lb sz............. 27.50
Machine, Campbell Hot Lather, shiny chrome, 115 volts, 1950s?, EX. 145.00
Mirror, Burma Shave, pnt poles/foamy mug/etc on face, wood fr, 22x15".. 90.00
Pole, glass red/wht/bl stripes, lights up, Wm Marvy #55, 26x10" . 465.00

Pole, Kline, wall mount, restored, 42", $900.00. (Photo courtesy Rich Penn Auctions on LiveAuctioneers.com)

Pole, rnd top spins as does glass-encased pole, Marvy #188, working.450.00
Pole, tapered wood w/acorn finial, red/bl/wht pnt, metal stand, 70"...1,100.00
Pole, trn wood, red/wht/bl rpt w/gold ball finials, ca 1950, 85", VG...460.00
Pole, trn wood, red/wht/bl stripes, cone/ball finial, 1890s, 68" 900.00
Sign, Barber Shop between 2 poles pnt on tin, 2-sided, 21x32" ...265.00
Sign, glass w/tin trim & bk, Barber Shop over arrow, 6x19", EX.. 120.00
Sign, Member Assoc Master Barbers of Am, tin on cb, 6x15", VG..75.00
Sterilizer, razor/comb, chrome over brass w/glass front, w/key 115.00
Sterilizer, wood cabinet w/glass shelf, Deco style, 12½x12½x8" ... 145.00
Strop, brn leather, Genuine Shell #356 Lakeside, EX 30.00

Barometers

Barometers are instruments designed to measure the weight or pressure of the atmosphere in order to anticipate approaching weather changes. They have a glorious history. Some of the foremost thinkers of the seventeenth century developed the mercury barometer, as the discovery of the natural laws of the universe progressed. Working in 1644 from experiments by Galileo, Evangelista Torrecelli used a glass tube and a jar of mercury to create a vacuum and therefore prove that air has weight. Four years later, Rene Descartes added a paper scale to the top of Torrecelli's mercury tube and created the basic barometer. Blaise Pascal, working with Descartes, used it to determine the heights of mountains; only later was the correlation between changes in air pressure and changes in the weather observed and the term 'weather-glass' applied. Robert Boyle introduced it to England, and Robert Hook modified the form and designed the wheel barometer.

The most common type of barometer is the wheel or banjo, followed by the stick type. Modifications of the plain stick are the marine gimballed type and the laboratory, Kew, or Fortin type. Another style is the Admiral Fitzroy of which there are 12 or more variations. The above all have mercury contained either in glass tubing or wood box cisterns.

The aneroid is a variety of barometer that works on atmospheric pressure changes. These come in all sizes ranging from 1" in diameter to 12" or larger. They may be in metal or wood cases. There is also a barograph which records on a graph that rotates around a drum powered by a seven-day clock mechanism. Pocket barometers (altimeters) vary in sizes from 1" in diameter up to 6". One final type of barometer is the symphisometer, a modification of the stick barometer; these were used for a limited time as they were not as accurate as the conventional marine barometer. Our advisor for this category is Dr. Robert Elsner; he is listed in the Directory under Florida. Prices are subject to condition of wood, tube, etc.; number of functions; and whether or not they are signed.

American Stick Barometers

Chas Wilder, Peterboro NH 1,250.00
DE Lent, Rochester NY 1,250.00
EO Spooner, Storm King, Boston MA 1,450.00
FD McKay Jr, Elmira MA 3,100.00
Simmons & Sons, Fulton NY 1,250.00

English Barometers

Admiral Fitzory, various kinds, ea $500 to 4,500.00
Fortin type (Kew or Laboratory), metal on brd w/mg, $750 to..1,250.00
Marine gimballed, sgn Walker, London 4,000.00
Oak aneroid, 37x12" 4,200.00
P Brambano, Evesham, inlaid mahog, two dials, 39" 1,530.00
Right angle, sgn John Whitehurst, ca 1790 ....20,000.00
Stick, mahog bowfront w/urn-shaped cistern, S Mason, Dublin, 1824-30...5,000.00
Stick, rosewood w/ivory scale, sgn Adie, dbl vernier, ca 1840...3,500.00
Stick, rosewood, sgn L Casella, London 1,950.00
Symphisometer, sgn Adie 3,950.00
Wheel, 6", sgn Stanley, Peterborough 1,500.00
Wheel, 8", sgn F Molten, Norwich...1,450.00
Wheel, 10", mahog, J Smith Royal Exchange...Optican...Prince of Wales..1,950.00
Wheel, 10", MOP, sgn Spelizini, London....................................1,950.00

Other Types

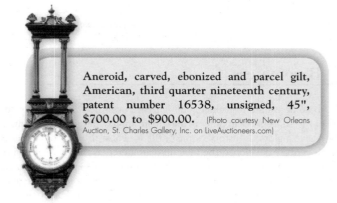

Aneroid, carved, ebonized and parcel gilt, American, third quarter nineteenth century, patent number 16538, unsigned, 45", $700.00 to $900.00. (Photo courtesy New Orleans Auction, St. Charles Gallery, Inc. on LiveAuctioneers.com)

Aneroid, 4-6" dia in brass case w/half-rnd thermometer, $200 to..350.00
Mahog barograph (recording type), sgn Negretti & Zambra 950.00
Pocket barometer (altimeter), w/case, $200 to 400.00
Swiss, castle w/fox greeting ducks, ca 1890, 18x13"....................1,250.00

Barware

Back in the '30s when social soirees were very elegant affairs thanks to the influence of Hollywood in all its glamour and mystique, cocktails were often served up in shakers styled as miniature airplanes, zeppelins, skyscrapers, lady's legs, penguins, roosters, bowling pins, etc. Some were by top designers such as Norman Bel Geddes and Russel Wright. They were made of silver plate, glass, and chrome, often trimmed with colorful Bakelite handles. Today these are hot collectibles, and even the more common Deco-styled chrome cylinders are often priced at $25.00 and up. Ice buckets, trays, and other bar accessories are also included in this area of collecting.

For further information we recommend *Vintage Bar Ware* by Stephen Visakay, our advisor for this category; he is listed in the Directory under New York. See also Bottle Openers.

Book, Authentic & Hilarious Bar Guide, True Magazine, 1950s ... 45.00
Book, Old Mr Boston...Bartender's Guide, hardbk, 1951 later ed .. 20.00
Coaster, Queen's Surf, girl on surfboard, 1950s, 3½".....................32.50
Cocktail glass, amber w/pierced chrome holder, Farber Bros, 3½".. 30.00
Cocktail glasses, conical top w/orange ball base, 1960s, 4⅝", 4 for. 48.00
Ice bucket, chrome w/porc lining, Bakelite trim, Keystone Ware, 11" ...75.00
Ice bucket, musical pigs (3) in orange pyro on clear glass...............45.00
Ice bucket, rabbit form, Arthur Court Alum, 18½" 1,100.00
Napkins (36), paper, in orig box, 1950s, M, $10 to 12.00
Napkins, linen, pk elephants, 1930s, set of 8, $50 to...................... 60.00
Napkins, linen, rooster holding cocktail glass, set of 8, $45 to....... 65.00
Pick set, bellhop w/suitcase of picks, Bakelite, $65 to.................... 75.00
Pick set, sword swallower, Japan, $30 to...................................... 40.00
Pick set, wonder bar, $40 to... 60.00
Picks, silver, fruit finial, mk Sterling, 3", set of 12, NMIB 68.00
Pitcher, brass w/rattan woven hdl, thermos lined, M Phillip, 11" ... 95.00
Pitcher, chrome-plated w/red Bakelite hdl, blk-pnt stripes, 1930s . 45.00
Pitcher, polka dots w/gold fleur-de-lis on clear, slim, 11x3" 45.00
Pitcher, rainbow-colored rings on clear glass, 72-oz 45.00
Shaker, brushed alum w/red Bakelite trim, West Bend, 10"..........140.00
Shaker, chrome bell shape, wood hdl removes, 1920s-30s............ 40.00
Shaker, chrome w/blk metal top, Soda King Syphon, 1938, 10" ..100.00
Shaker, chrome w/butterscotch Bakelite, Farber Bros, 12½" 115.00
Shaker, chrome, Froman Bros, $75 to..125.00
Shaker, chrome, Krome Kraft/Farber Bros, 11x7½"+6 5" stems...... 60.00
Shaker, Deco figures wave flags, red/bl on clear glass, SP lid 75.00
Shaker, extinguisher form, red glass, Thirst Extinguisher, 1940s-50s.. 68.00
Shaker, glass, 3-pc, Heisey, plain, $65 to...................................... 85.00
Shaker, glass, 3-pc, rooster head, Heisey, $125 to 135.00
Shaker, NP, hammered & plain, Expressware, 17½" 200.00

Shaker, silver plate, designed by Silvia Stave for Hallbergs AB, Stockholm, circa 1950s, 6", $8,400.00. (Photo courtesy Sotheby's on LiveAuctioneers.com)

Shaker, SP, LCGC NY 1923 eng on top, 8" 195.00
Shaker, SP, penguin, Towle, 1997, MIB 50.00
Shaker, silver rooster, $1,500 to..2,000.00
Shaker, stainless steel, rocket shape, 1930s-40s, 11½" 65.00
Stopper, silver w/emb decor, orig cork, Silver 800 mk, 3x1⅜"........ 25.00
Swizzle stick, Trader Vic, canoe paddle shape, $6 to.......................8.00
Swizzle stick, Trader Vic, Tiki god hdl, $3 to 6.00
Traveling barn, NP shaker form, 9-pc, mk Germany, ca 1928, 8" .. 85.00
Tray, rvpt Deco design in rosewood fr, Fr, 1930s, 16½x11"..........100.00
Tumbler, circus elephants on clear, ftd, Libbey, 5¼" 20.00
Tumblers, Manhattans w/backgammon decor on clear, Cassini, 6 for..65.00

Baskets

Basket weaving is a craft as old as ancient history. Baskets have been used to harvest crops, for domestic chores, and to contain the catch of fishermen. Materials at hand were utilized, and baskets from a specific region are often distinguishable simply by analyzing the natural fibers used in their construction. Early Indian baskets were made of corn husks or woven grasses. Willow splint, straw, rope, and paper were also used. Until the invention of the veneering machine in the late 1800s, splint was made by water-soaking a split log until the fibers were softened and flexible. Long strips were pulled out by hand and, while still wet and pliable, woven into baskets in either a cross-hatch or hexagonal weave.

Most handcrafted baskets on the market today were made between 1860 and the early 1900s. Factory baskets with a thick, wide splint cut by machine are of little interest to collectors. The more popular baskets are those designed for a specific purpose, rather than the more commonly found utility baskets that had multiple uses. Among the most costly forms are the Nantucket Lighthouse baskets, which were basically copied from those made there for centuries by aboriginal Indians. They were designed in the style of whale-oil barrels and named for the South Shoal Nantucket Lightship where many were made during the last half of the nineteenth century. Cheese baskets (used to separate curds from whey), herb-gathering baskets, and finely woven Shaker miniatures are other highly prized examples of the basket-weaver's art.

In the listings that follow, assume that each has a center bentwood handle (unless handles of another type are noted) that is not included in the height. Unless another type of material is indicated, assume that each is made of splint. Prices are subjective and hinge on several factors: construction, age, color, and general appearance. Baskets rated very good (VG) will have minor losses and damage. See also American Indian Art, Baskets; Eskimo Artifacts; Sewing Items; Shaker Items.

Round with deep concave bottom, circa 1840, 14x16", $570.00. (Photo courtesy TW Conroy, LLC on LiveAuctioneers.com)

Baby, willow, wrapped rim, early 20th C, 30" L, VG 60.00
Buttocks, 18-rib, splint hdl, 6x16x12"... 115.00
Buttocks, minor splits, 8x16" 120.00
Buttocks, red pnt, cvd upright hdl, losses/breaks, 19th C, 13½" ... 175.00
Buttocks, tight weave, varnished, 4½x9" 150.00
Feather or tow, w/lid, ca 1860, 17x13" 40.00
Gathering, orig dk surface, kicked-up base, 14x12", EX 350.00
Gathering, rect, no hdl, 12x37x31".. 360.00
Gathering, shallow, 1890s, 7¼x12¼" dia...................................... 175.00
Gathering, tight weave, 27x18".. 100.00
Half-buttocks, bl-gr tinted bands, 7x8", EX 100.00
Half-buttocks, old dk red pnt, minor damage, 4x8½" 200.00
Market, rect, 15x14½" 100.00
Melon, tight weave, 34-rib, EX patina, sm break, 16x18" 325.00
Mini, 18 melon ribs, varnished, 3" 175.00
Mini, tight weave, 3x5" 270.00
Nantucket, curly maple bottom, branded 4¼x19" 725.00
Nantucket, paper label, Ferdinand Sylvaro, 4x10¼"..................... 975.00
Nantucket, purse, ivory whale on lid, JF Reyes, 1950s, 7x11" dia... 4,115.00

Nantucket, purse, oval w/ivory shells on lid, 1973, 7x10½" 3,300.00
Nantucket, rattan/splint, cvd swing hdl & ears, wood base, 7x9⅜"....1,900.00
Nantucket, rattan, rnd maple base, swing hdl, losses, ca 1900, 6x14" ...765.00
Nantucket, swing hdl, 1940s, 9" dia 660.00
Oval w/sq bottom, 2 rim hdls, thick red pnt, 1900s, 3x8x7", VG.. 120.00
Oval, radiating ribs, wrapped rim, ca 1900, 10x10" 550.00
Oval, wide splint, dk red pnt, lt wear, 13½" 375.00
Painted woven splint, 19th C, 9½x9¾x11", EX..........................6,500.00
Produce, raised bottom, 2 hdls, ca 1900, 13x23¼" 175.00
Rectangular, bl/gr/red stripes, cvd hdls, minor rim loss, 5x14x12".460.00
Rectangular, wide splint, 9½x11" 125.00
Round, ash splint, swing hdl, fine & tight weave, natural, NY, 8x12" ..660.00
Round, dk ash splint, dbl hdls, 13" 155.00
Round, orig gr pnt, 8x15", VG 325.00
Round, ribbed, fine/thin splints, cvd upright hdl, 1890s, 5½" 230.00
Round w/domed base, ash, swing hdl, NY, 11x14"...................... 345.00
Round w/domed center, tin reinforcement, HH Harris, 15x18"...265.00
Round w/flat bottom, wrapped rim, 8x12" 60.00
Round w/wrapped ft, ash w/mixed wood hdl, 14x11" 200.00
Utility, 16x16" 110.00

Batchelder

Ernest A. Batchelder was a leading exponent of the Arts and Crafts movement in the United States. His influential book, *Design in Theory and Practice,* was originally published in 1910. He is best known, however, for his artistic tiles which he first produced in Pasadena, California, from 1909 to 1916. In 1916 the business was relocated to Los Angeles where it continued until 1932, closing because of the Depression.

In 1938 Batchelder resumed production in Pasadena under the name of 'Kinneola Kiln.' Output of the new pottery consisted of delicately cast bowls and vases in an Oriental style. This business closed in 1951. Tiles carry a die-stamped mark; vases and bowls are hand incised. For more information we recommend *Collector's Encyclopedia of California Pottery* by Jack Chipman (Collector Books) and *American Art Tiles,* in four volumes by Norman Karlson (Schiffer). Our advisors for this category are Suzanne Perrault and David Rago; they are listed in the Directory under New Jersey.

Bookends, monk, engobe patina, ca 1923, 4½", pr 800.00
Chest, daffodils on pyrography panel, 18½x30½x17½" 3,180.00
Corbels, medieval musicians (trumpet, lute, cymbals, singer), 6" sq, set of 4 ..2,160.00
Jardiniere, engobe, 12x13" 1,000.00
Tile, Dutch girl by bed of roses in front of village, 11¾" sq........1,000.00
Tile fountain, Moorish-shaped, peacocks/mosaics, 14x24½" 1,000.00
Tile frieze (3), cattle drive w/ox carts through Southwestern desert, 7¾x54".2,400.00
Tile, grapevine, patina glazed, 3" 200.00
Tile, landscape w/oak tree, engobe, 7¾" 700.00
Tile, Medieval hunting scene, ca 1928, 4" 450.00

Tile panel, embossed with angel playing tambourine, 12¾x8¼", $1,100.00. (Photo courtesy Rago Arts and Auction Center)

Tile, peacock, engobe, imp mk, 6" 750.00
Tile, stylized rose in foliage w/bl engobe, #1674, minor edge chips, 8¾".425.00

Battersea

Battersea is a term that refers to enameling on copper or other metal. Though originally produced at Battersea, England, in the mid-eighteenth century, the craft was later practiced throughout the Staffordshire district. Boxes are the most common examples. Some are figurals, and many bear an inscription. Unless a condition is noted in the description, values are given for examples with only minimal damage, which is normal. Please note that items with printed Bilston labels are new.

Salt cellar, landscape reserve, pad feet, minor interior cracks, 1¼x2½", **$150.00.** (Photo courtesy Stefek's, Ltd. on LiveAuctioneers.com)

Box, courting couple/mtn scene, 2x2¾" dia, +Cartier gift box..... 660.00
Box, Fair Words Are Always... on seafoam gr, 1⅛x2", EX 235.00
Box, May the Enemies of Liberty Feel..., 1775, ⅝x⅞" dia........... 1,500.00
Box, peach form & color, stem finial, 1¾x1½" dia.....................2,500.00
Box, scenic reserves on pk w/gold, no-hinge lid, late 1700s, 3½" .. 900.00
Box, snuff, wrestling scene, 1¾" 270.00
Box, W/Grateful Heart This Trifle...Content, mc on lav enamel, sm, EX. 210.00
Candlesticks, floral on wht, petal bobeche removes, 1750s, 10¾", pr . 2,350.00
Candlesticks, flowers & birds, ca 1770, 9", pr 3,000.00

Bauer

The Bauer Pottery Company is one of the best known of the California pottery companies, noted for both its artware and its dinnerware. In the past 10 years, Bauer has become particularly collectible, and prices have risen accordingly, although prices have fallen off for many items. The pottery actually started in Paducah, Kentucky, in 1885. It moved to Los Angeles in 1910 where it remained in operation until 1962. The company produced several successful dinnerware lines, including La Linda, Monterey, and Brusche Al Fresco. Most popular and most significant was the Ringware line introduced in 1932 which preceded Fiesta as a popular solid-color everyday dinnerware. The earliest pieces are unmarked, although to collectors they are unmistakable, partly due to their distinctive glazes which have an almost primitive charm due to their drips, misses, and color variations.

Another dinnerware line favored by collectors is Speckleware, its name derived from the 1950s-era speckled glaze Bauer used on various products, including vases, flowerpots, kitchenware items, and dinnerware. Though not as popular as Ringware, Speckleware holds its value and is usually available at much lower prices than Ringware. Keep an eye out for other flowerpots and mixing bowls as well.

Artware by Bauer is not so easy to find now, but it is worth seeking out because of its high values. So-called oil jars sell for upwards of $1,500.00, and Rebekah vases routinely fetch $400.00 or more. Matt Carlton is one of the most desirable designers of handmade ware.

After WWII a flood of foreign imports and loss of key employees drastically curtailed their sales, and the pottery began a steady decline that ended in failure in 1962. Prices listed below reflect the California market. For more information we recommend *California Pottery Scrapbook* and *Collector's Encyclopedia of California Pottery*, both by Jack Chipman (Collector Books).

In the lines of Ringware and Plainware, pricing depends to some extent on color. Low-end colors include light brown, Chinese yellow, orange-red, Jade green, red-brown, olive green, light blue, turquoise, and gray; the high-end colors are Delph blue, ivory, dusty burgundy, co-

balt, chartreuse, papaya, and burgundy. In the following listings, when no specific color is mentioned, use this information to interpret the ranges. Black is highly collectible in all of these lines; to evaluate black, add at least 100% to an item's value in any other color. White Ringware is even more rare and prized because it was a 'special order only' color. An in-depth study of colors may be found in the books referenced above. Our advisor for this category is Jack Chipman; he is listed in the Directory under California.

Ringware

Baking dish, blk, covered, 4" 80.00
Bowl, berry, wht... 80.00
Bowl, cereal, ivory.. 75.00

Bowl, mixing, orange-red, 14½", $125.00. (Photo courtesy Clars Auction Gallery on LiveAuctioneers.com)

Bowls, mixing, std colors, in-mold mks, nesting set of 6.............. 750.00
Cigarette jar, royal bl 600.00
Cookie jar, orange-red.. 600.00
Goblet, Delph bl 200.00
Jug, ball 375.00
Jug, water, covered, w/6 tumblers (6-oz), in metal caddy, complete..2,000.00
Mug, beer, ca 1933 .... 250.00
Mustard jar, orange-red.. 650.00
Pitcher, beer, ca 1933... 800.00
Plate, bread & butter, Delph bl, 5"... 60.00
Plate, bread & butter, royal bl, 6"... 20.00
Plate, dinner, Chinese yel, 9" 30.00
Plate, soup, burgundy, 7½" 80.00
Refrigerator stack set (3 jars), turq/orange-red/Chinese yel, /w/rack, 7½" .. 400.00
Salt & pepper, orange-red.. 50.00
Soup, lug, orange-red, w/cover, 5½" 375.00
Spice jar, orange-red, #3 .... 375.00
Tumbler w/metal hdl, 4½", $40 to 50.00

Miscellaneous

Art pottery, oil jar, orange-red, #122, 20" 1,500.00
Art pottery, vase, matt gr, Carnation, ca 1915, unmk, 24½" 1,500.00
Art pottery, vase, matt gr, Rebekah, ca 1915, unmk, 24½"........2,500.00
Cal-Art, candleholder, turq bl, single, oval, 2½x6" 40.00
Cal-Art, ewer, 10".. 100.00
Cal-Art, figurine, Madonna, matt wht, 8"................................... 150.00
Cal-Art, vase, matt wht, Rotary Club Los Angeles, rare, 8"....................200.00
Cal-Art, figurine, Scottie, matt glaze.. 375.00
Cal-Art, vase pitcher, matt gr, Ray Murray, 5½x7" 75.00
Cal-Art, vase, midget, rare burgundy glaze, 4" 100.00
Cal-Art, vase, turq, Ray Murray, 8".. 100.00
Florist ware, bowl, oval, Chinese yel, 10½" L.............................. 85.00
Florist ware, hanging basket, orange-red, 8".............................200.00
Florist ware, jar, cactus, gr, 8-cup, handmade, 6x12" 300.00
Florist ware, pinnacle pot, olive gr, 10"...................................... 85.00
Florist ware, strawberry pot, burgundy, 8-cup, 9" 200.00
Florist ware, vase, #506, 8" 50.00
Florist ware, vase, #678, 13" 175.00
Florist ware, vase, Chinese yel, ruffled, Matt Carlton, 7½"........... 200.00
Florist ware, vase, Delph bl, Matt Carlton, 9½".......................... 500.00
Florist ware, vase, royal bl, Matt Carlton, hdld, 17" 1,000.00

Plainware, ashtray, orange-red, sq, 3", $60 to.................................... 75.00
Plainware, bean pot, ind, Chinese yel, $100 to............................ 150.00
Plainware, coffee server, dk bl, wood hdl, 8", $50 to....................... 65.00
Plainware, Dutch pitcher, Jade, 12", $300 to 450.00

Marc Bellaire

Born in Toledo in 1925, Marc Bellaire (Donald Fleischman) studied at the Chicago Academy of Art and Chicago Art Institute, before moving to California in 1950 and beginning his association with ceramics artist Sascha Brastoff. The object shapes and placement of decoration on many Bellaire pieces show the Brastoff influence. A curved-edge central image is often the focal point of a design, echoing the curved edges of the object itself — whether an ashtray, bowl, or rounded platter. Bold, contrasting color combinations were favored by both designers, as well as metallic color accents. Themes, however, show a much greater variance: Brastoff's images are often romanticized and ethereal. Bellaire's fierce 'Jungle Dancers,' slyly smiling 'Cotillion' women, and blank-faced 'Mardi Gras' celebrants are darker, more knowing, and more exotic.

In the early 1950s Bellaire branched out on his own, opening the Marc Bellaire Ceramics Studio in Culver City, California. While he produced artware in the Brastoff vein — platters, planters, and the like — the stylistic touch became distinctly Bellaire. Brastoff's figures, though often whimsical, generally retain normal proportions. Bellaire's, with arms and legs of exaggerated length and bizarre or rudimentary features, at times resemble aliens or stick figures.

Although not as universally recognized as the heavily promoted Brastoff, Marc Bellaire's design influence was equally long-lasting. In fact, many amateur ceramists of the 1950s and 1960s owe their entire technique to Bellaire. After achieving his own success, he wrote numerous 'how-to' articles for *Popular Ceramics*, allowing the general public to try their hand at bowls, vases, and other vessels featuring his characteristic elongated figures and colorful glazes. Bellaire's later designs, until his death in 1994, focused on pots and vases in the Southwestern style with little reference to his earlier work. His pieces can be identified by a full or partial signature on the object surface or reverse.

Our advisor for this category is Donald-Brian Johnson, an author specializing in mid-twentieth century design. His latest book, *Postwar Pop* (Schiffer Publishing, Ltd.), includes more information on Marc Bellaire. Mr. Johnson can be found in the Directory under Nebraska.

Ashtray, Beachcomber, triangular, 11¾" L, $125 to 150.00
Ashtray, Oriental, single-fold, 9½" L, $75 to .... 100 .00
Ashtray, Pastorale, 14½" L, $125 to 150.00
Bowl, Green Bird, 6½", $50 to 75.00
Candleholders, Balinese, 7¾", pr $250 to 275.00
Decanter, Greek figures, 13", $325 to 350.00
Dish, Beachcomber, 17¾" L, $225 to 250.00
Dish, Bird Isle, boomerang-shape, covered, 11½" L, $175 to 200.00
Dish, Native Women, freeform, 14" L, $225 to 250.00
Dish, Park Avenue Primitive, oblong, 15" L, $225 to 250.00
Dish, Root Heads, triangular, 15½" L, $250 to 275.00
Figurine, horse, gray/gr/brn, 8x7"... 140.00
Figurine, Mardi Gras, man standing, 11¼", $400 to 425.00

Lamp, Birdcage, Rembrandt Mfg, 13½", $500 to 600.00
Pitcher, Butterfly, 13", $175 to 200.00
Plate, Lion, scalloped edge, 12½", $125 to 150.00
Platter, Cotillion, lady holding bird, freeform, 12", $175 to 200.00
Platter, Jungle Dancer, 18", $300 to 325.00
Server, Balinese, dbl w/hdl, 9", $125 to 150.00
Vase, Grecian Woman, 11", $275 to 300.00
Vase, Green Bird, 7¼", $175 to 200.00
Vase, Jamaica, 3-ftd, 8", $125 to.. 150.00
Vase, Mardi Gras, pillow-style, 7¼", $275 to 300.00
Vase, Oriental, 15¾", $250 to 275.00
Vase, Polynesian Star, sq bottle style, 7½", $150 to 175.00

Belleek, American

From 1883 until 1930, several American potteries located in New Jersey and Ohio manufactured a type of china similar to the famous Irish Belleek soft-paste porcelain. The American manufacturers identified their porcelain by using 'Belleek' or 'Beleek' in their marks. American Belleek is considered the highest achievement of the American porcelain industry. Production centered around artistic cabinet pieces and luxury tablewares. Many examples emulated Irish shapes and decor with marine themes and other naturalistic styles. While all are highly collectible, some companies' products are rarer than others. The best-known manufacturers are The Ceramic Art Company (CAC), Lenox, Ott and Brewer, and Willets. You will find more detailed information in those specific categories. Our advisor for this category is Mary Frank Gaston.

Key:
AAC — American Art China   CAP — Columbian Art Pottery

Vase, cherub musicians and flowers, signed S. E. Waterbury, 11½", $1,200.00. (Photo courtesy Point Pleasant Galleries on LiveAuctioneers.com)

Bowl, tiny flowers w/in & w/o, gold rim, AAC, 2½x5"................ 425.00
Cup/saucer, floral reserves in red border, Morgan.......................... 250.00
Cup/saucer, floral, bl & orange, mk Coxon Belleek...................... 200.00
Cup/saucer, morning glories, Morgan.. 175.00
Demitasse set, Lenox, 1st quarter 20th C, pot: 11", 3-pc set 1,650.00
Ewer, cranes, ivory w/gold trim, branch hdl, mk 2,700.00
Mug, monk playing violin, CAP, 5" 150.00
Salt cellar, sponged gold, scalloped, pk int, AAC, 2½" 145.00
Shell dish, pk lustre int, AAC, 4x5".. 150.00
Vase, floral on wht, gold emb hdls, AAC, 12" 1,200.00

Belleek, Irish

Belleek is a very thin translucent porcelain that takes its name from the village in Ireland where it originated in 1859. The glaze is a creamy ivory color with a pearl-like lustre. The tablewares, baskets, figurines, and vases that have always been made there are being crafted yet today. Shamrock, Tridacna, Echinus, and Thorn are but a few of the many patterns of tableware which have been made during some periods of the pottery's history. Throughout the years, their most popular pattern has been Shamrock.

It is possible to date an example to within 20 to 30 years of crafting by the mark. Pieces with an early stamp often bring prices nearly triple that of a similar but current item. With some variation, the marks have always incorporated the Irish wolfhound, Celtic round tower, harp, and shamrocks. The first three marks (usually in black) were used from 1863 to 1946. A series of green marks identified the pottery's offerings from 1946 until the seventh mark (in gold/brown) was introduced in 1980 (it was discontinued in 1992). The eighth mark was blue and closely resembled the gold mark. It was used from 1993 to 1996. The ninth, tenth, and eleventh marks went back to the simplicity of the first mark with only the registry mark (an R encased in a circle) to distinguish them from the original. The ninth mark, which was used from 1997 to 1999, was blue. A special black version of that mark was introduced for the year 2000 and a Millennium 2000 banner was added. The tenth or Millennium mark was retired at the end of 2000, and the current green mark was introduced as the eleventh mark. Belleek Collector's International Society limited edition pieces are designated with a special mark in red. In the listings below, numbers designated with the prefix 'D' relate to the book *Belleek, The Complete Collector's Guide and Illustrated Reference,* by Richard K. Degenhardt (published by Wallace-Homestead Book Company, One Chilton Way, Radnor, PA 19098-0230). The numbers designated with the prefix 'B' are current production numbers used by the pottery. Our advisor for this category is Liz Stillwell; she is listed in the Directory under California.

Key:
A — plain (glazed only)
B — cob lustre
C — hand tinted
D — hand painted
E — hand-painted shamrocks
F — hand gilted
G — hand tinted and gilted
H — hand-painted shamrocks
    and gilted
J — mother-of-pearl
K — hand painted and gilted
L — bisque and plain
M — decalcomania
N — special hand-painted decoration
T — transfer design

I — 1863 – 1890
II — 1891 – 1926
III — 1926 – 1946
IV — 1946 – 1955
V — 1955 – 1965
VI — 1965 – 3/31/1980
VII — 4/1/1980 – 1992
VIII —1/4/1993 – 1996
IX — 1997 – 1999
X — 2000 only
XI — 2001 – current

Further information concerning Periods of Crafting (Baskets):
1 — 1865 – 1890, BELLEEK (three-strand)
2 — 1865 – 1890, BELLEEK CO. FERMANAGH (three-strand)
3 — 1891 – 1920, BELLEEK CO. FERMANAGH IRELAND (three-strand)
4 — 1921 – 1954, BELLEEK CO. FERMANAGH IRELAND (four-strand)
5 — 1955 – 1979, BELLEEK® CO. FERMANAGH IRELAND (four-strand)
6 — 1980 – 1985, BELLEEK® IRELAND (four-strand)
7 — 1985 – 1989, BELLEEK® IRELAND 'ID NUMBER' (four-strand)
8 – 12 — 1990 to present (Refer to *Belleek, The Complete Collector's Guide and Illustrated Reference, 2nd Edition,* Chapter 5)

Aberdeen Tea Ware Tea & Saucer, D489-II, B	575.00
Artichoke Tea Ware Teapot, D710-I, F	800.00
Basket Compote, D30-I, A	950.00
Bird's Nest Basket, D123-II, J	700.00
Boat ashtray, D229-VI, B	55.00
Bust of Queen of the Hops, D1130-III, L&B, 11½"	4,000.00
Cane Spill, D165-1, C, lg, 11"	700.00
Celtic Design Tea Ware Coffee & Saucer, D1428 & 1430-III, K	300.00
Cherry Blossom Plate, 3 Strand, Flowered, D1685-6, D	650.00
Chinese Tea Ware Teapot, D484-I, K	1,500.00
Cleary Mug, D218-II, B, 2½"	150.00
Cone flowerpot, D224-VI, B, sm, 3½"	50.00
Convolvulus basket, 3-color, 2 pad marks, Belleek (and) Ireland, 9"	600.00
Dairy cr/sug, D251-III, D	300.00
Diamond Biscuit Jar, D600-IV, D	400.00
Dragonfly Collection trinket box, D1914-VII, D	175.00
Earthenware Jelly Mould, D883-II, A, 9"	175.00
Earthenware platter, D903-I, T, 20"	850.00
Echinus Footed Bowl, D1521-VI, G	600.00
Egg Frame & 6 cups, D621-VI, G	300.00
Egyptian Napkin Ring, D1551-I, F	600.00
Fan Brush tray, D317-I, K	325.00
Finner Tea Ware tea & saucer, D669-XI, D	70.00
Forget-Me-Not Box, D111-II, A, 2"	650.00
Gospel Plates (4), D1811-VI, D1813-VII, D1815-VII, D1817-VII, M&F	650.00
Grass Mug, D214-III, B	190.00
Grass Tea Ware Teapot, D733-II, D, med	650.00
Harebell Vase, D180-V, K	105.00
Harp Shamrock Tea Ware tray, D528-II, E	1,200.00
Harp w/Applied Shamrocks, D1640-II, K	550.00
Hexagon Tea Ware kettle, D409-II, C, lg	850.00
Irish Bunny egg box, B2826-XI, C/E	35.00
Irish Harp, D77-V, E, sm	280.00
Irish pot & cream, D232-III, A, sz 2	175.00
Irish Squirrel Wall Bracket, D1803-I, A	4,750.00
Ivy Sugar & Cream, D237-I & D238-I, B, lg	325.00
Ivy Tea Ware Bread Plate, D1410-III, B	325.00

Jardiniere, applied flowers and three full-figured birds, third black mark, 1926 – 1946, 8", $450.00. (Photo courtesy Jackson's Auction on LiveAuctioneers.com)

Killarney Candlestick, D1982-VII, D, ea	85.00
Lily of the Valley Frame, D1720-I, J, sm	1,700.00
Mask Tea Ware Cream, tall, D1483-III, B, lg	195.00
Milk Maid lithophane, B2436-XI, L&B, 9¼x11⅛"	175.00
Neptune Tea Ware Kettle, D431-VII, B, lg	275.00
Neptune Tea Ware Tea & Saucer, D414-III, C	150.00
New Shell Tea Ware tea & saucer, D1385 & 1386-V, B	80.00
Oak flowerpot, ftd, D46-II, J	2,700.00
Pierced Spill, Flowered, D49-III, A, lg	350.00
Pierced Spill, Flowered, D1179-II, A, sm	250.00
Plain Heart Shape Basket, D1284-4, A	525.00
Prince Arthur Vase, D73-II, J	800.00
Rock Spill, D162-II, C, med	300.00
Rope Handle Mug, D215-II, B	250.00
Shamrock flowerpot, D98-II, H, 8"	850.00
Shamrock Mug, D216-II, E	150.00
Shamrock Tea Ware Covered Muffin Dish, D388-III, E	525.00
Shamrock Tea Ware Tea & Saucer, D366-III, E, low	200.00
Shamrock Ware TV Set, D2017-VII, E	110.00
Single Hippiritus, D146-I, B, 7"	850.00
Sydney Tea Ware Tea & Saucer, D607-II, C	425.00
Table Centre, D56-IV, D	1,200.00
Thorn Tea Ware Bread Plate, D767-II, K, 9" L	1,200.00
Tridacna Tea Ware Covered Muffin Dish, D479-II, A	425.00

Victoria Shell, D128-II, B......550.00
Victoria Tea Ware Tea & Saucer, D593-II, G 550.00
Wild Irish Rose, thimble, D2110-VII, D......30.00

Bells

Some areas of interest represented in the study of bells are history, religion, and geography. Since Biblical times, bells have announced morning church services, vespers, deaths, christenings, school hours, fires, and community events. Countries have used them en masse to peal out the good news of Christmas, New Year's, and the endings of World Wars I and II. They've been rung in times of great sorrow, such as the death of Abraham Lincoln.

For further information, we recommend *World of Bells* by Dorothy Malone Anthony (a series of 10 books). All have over 200 colored pictures covering many bell categories. See also Nodders; Schoolhouse Collectibles.

Brass hotel type on CI base, 4½" 85.00
Brass lady figural, hands folded, legs as clapper, 19th C, 4¼"......48.00
Brass sleigh, 8 on leather strap......55.00
Brass sleigh, varied szs, 16 on leather strap......120.00
Brass w/CI parrot figural hdl, mc pnt, 4⅞"......120.00
Brass, boxing ring type, Bevin, 8" dia......180.00
Brass, Chiantel Fondeur Saicnelecier 1878 emb, 4½x4½"......95.00
Brass, Flemish royal woman w/headdress/cape/brocade gown, 4" .115.00
Brass, Kewpie figural hdl, 5x2"......165.00
Brass, Qui Me Tangit Vocem..., detailed frieze, 19th C, 8x5" 135.00
Brass, simple casting, 12" 110.00
Brass, wood hdl, ca 1880/1900, 2x3", EX 150.00
Bronze, cat w/bowtie as hdl, England, 6½"......120.00
Bronze, dragon hdl, EX patina, Japan, 7½x4⅞"......450.00
Cast iron hotel type, Atlas supporting world figural, 1860s, 7".....275.00
Cast iron, lady in hooped skirt, mc pnt, 3"......170.00
Ceramic, Aunt Agnes (mate to Uncle Toby), rare, 3"......50.00
Glass, Happy Birthday, clear & frosted, Goebel, 6x3" 50.00
Metal lady figural, nodder head, Renaissance dress, EB, 4¾"......235.00
Metal, cowbell type, orig clapper, 4x5" 38.00
Nickel-plated CI, knight in armor figural, hotel type, GES #103, 7x4½x2", EX+...160.00

Silver cowbell, Goldsmiths & Silversmiths Co. Ltd., England, circa 1900, 9.27 troy ounces, 3¾", $340.00. (Photo courtesy Leslie Hindman Auctioneers on LiveAuctioneers.com)

Silver on bronze, Catherine the Great, Gorham, 5" 150.00
Silver, repoussé hdl, Kirk Stieff......80.00
Silver, repoussé w/Neoclassical figures, Cupid hdl, 5" 300.00
Silverplated, 3 ladies' faces, hotel twist type, Meriden, ca 1887, 4" dia.160.00
Sleigh, 51 on 14' strap ranging in sz 1" to 3" dia......225.00

John Bennett

Bringing with him the knowledge and experience he had gained at the Doulton (Lambeth) Pottery in England, John Bennett opened a studio in New York City around 1877, where he continued his methods of decorating faience under the glaze. Early wares utilized imported English biscuit, though subsequently local clays (both white and cream colored) were also used. His first kiln was on Lexington Avenue; he built another on East Twenty-Fourth Street. Pieces are usually signed 'J. Bennett, N.Y.,' often with the street address and date. Later examples may be marked 'West Orange, N.J.,' where he retired. The pottery was in operation approximately six years in New York. Pieces signed with other initials are usually worth less. Our advisor for this category is Robert Tuggle; he is listed in the Directory under New York.

Vase, brown-eyed Susans on black and green ground, signed J. Bennett N. Y. R. (1881), small firing chip to base, 7x4¾", $4,800.00. (Photo courtesy Rago Arts and Auction Center)

Bottle, chrysanthemums, cobalt/cadmium yel, rstr, 13½x6½" ...5,400.00
Bottle, nasturtiums/leaves, rosewater sprinkler, nicks, 10¼x5"..2,400.00
Charger, bird on branch, 1877, sgn #1077, 12¾", EX 3,890.00
Jar, dogwood & roses, mc on blk, floral inner lid, 1881, 15½".66,000.00
Spittoon, flint enamel, 4½x8"......60.00
Vase, baluster, brn-eyed Susans on blk & gr, 1881, 7x4¾"......4,800.00
Vase, chrysanthemums, mc on dk, bulb, rare red clay, 11x7" 3,600.00

Bennington

Although the term has become a generic one for the mottled brown ware produced there, Bennington is not a type of pottery, but rather a town in Vermont where two important potteries were located. The Norton Company, founded in 1793, produced mainly redware and salt-glazed stoneware; only during a brief partnership with Fenton (1845 – 1847) was any Rockingham attempted. The Norton Company endured until 1894, operated by succeeding generations of the Norton family. Fenton organized his own pottery in 1847. There he manufactured not only redware and stoneware, but more artistic types as well — graniteware, scroddled ware, flint enamel, a fine parian, and vast amounts of their famous Rockingham. Though from an esthetic standpoint his work rated highly among the country's finest ceramic achievements, he was economically unsuccessful. His pottery closed in 1858.

It is estimated that only one in five Fenton pieces were marked; and although it has become a common practice to link any fine piece of Rockingham to this area, careful study is vital in order to be able to distinguish Bennington's from the similar wares of many other American and Staffordshire potteries. Although the practice was without the permission of the proprietor, it was nevertheless a common occurrence for a potter to take his molds with him when moving from one pottery to the next, so particularly well-received designs were often reproduced at several locations. Of eight known Fenton marks, four are variations of the '1849' impressed stamp: 'Lyman Fenton Co., Fenton's Enamel Patented 1849, Bennington, Vermont.' These are generally found on examples of Rockingham and flint enamel. A raised, rectangular scroll with 'Fenton's Works, Bennington, Vermont,' was used on early examples of porcelain. From 1852 to 1858, the company operated under the title of the United States Pottery Company. Three marks — the ribbon mark with the initials USP, the oval with a scrollwork border and the name in full, and the plain oval with the name in full — were used during that period.

Among the more sought-after examples are the bird and animal figurines, novelty pitchers, figural bottles, and all of the more finely modeled items. Recumbent deer, cows, standing lions with one forepaw on a ball, and opposing pairs of poodles with baskets in their mouths and 'coleslaw' fur were made in Rockingham, flint enamel, and occasionally in parian.

Numbers in the listings below refer to the book *Bennington Pottery and Porcelain* by Barret. Our advisors for Bennington (except for parian and stoneware) are Barbara and Charles Adams; they are listed in the Directory under Massachusetts.

Book flask, Departed Spirits, flint enamel, 5¾x4x2" 795.00
Bottle, coachman, Rockingham, att Fenton Pottery, ca 1849, 10" ... 1,000.00
Candlestick, flint enamel, 9", ea 875.00
Candlestick, flint enamel, ca 1849, 7", ea 695.00
Coffee urn, flint enamel, paneled form on ped ft, 20", EX 8,000.00
Cuspidor, flint enamel, sm flake, 4x8" 150.00
Figurine, dog on base, sitting, 10½", EX 600.00
Figurine, poodle w/basket, Rockingham w/coleslaw fur, 9x11", pr.. 6,500.00
Kettle, croup, Rockingham, w/lid, ca 1850, 6½", NM 245.00
Pitcher, paneled, Rockingham, ca 1850s, 12" 465.00
Snuff jar, male figure sitting, flint enamel, hat lid, 1849 mk, 4¼". 795.00

Stoneware

Cooler, #4/dotted leaf, E&LP Norton, bbl form, ca 1880, 13½" ... 600.00
Cream pot, #2/flower, c/s, Norton & Fenton, 1840s, stain/lines, 7" 440.00
Cream pot, #2/flower, J&E Norton, ca 1880, prof rstr lines, 11" .. 250.00
Cream pot, bird on twig, J&E Norton, ca 1855, staining, 8½" .1,155.00
Crock, #2/flower (triple), c/s, Norton & Fenton, 1840s, 10" 475.00
Crock, #2/ribbed leaf, J Norton & Co, sm flakes, 11x9" 635.00

Crock, #4, floral decoration, E. & L. P. Norton, Bennington, Vermont, 11", $400.00. (Photo courtesy Garth's Auction Inc. on LiveAuctioneers.com)

Crock, #5/floral spray (lg), E&LP Norton, ca 1880, chip, 13" ... 1,045.00
Crock, #6/bird on stump, E&LP Norton, ca 1880, crack, 13½" .1,925.00
Crock, lg-tailed rooster, minor age spiders, 2-gal, 9" 800.00
Jar, #3/bird (dbl), J Norton & Co, ca 1861, prof rstr, 13" 1,200.00
Jar, preserve, #1/flower (Benny Bl), J&E Norton, ca 1855, 11" 385.00
Jug, #1/bird on twig, J Norton & Bennington, ca 1861, 10½" 850.00
Jug, #1/bird on twig, J Norton & Co, ca 1861, 11" 635.00
Jug, #1/bud, Julius Norton, ca 1848, ping, 13" 2,200.00
Jug, #2 & accents, c/s, L Norton & Son, stain, ca 1835, 13" 360.00
Jug, #2/flower, Julius Norton, ca 1848, sm chip, 14" 775.00
Jug, #2/pheasant on stump, J&E Norton, ca 1855, lt stain, 14".2,650.00
Jug, #2/pheasant on stump, J&E Norton, ca 1855, rstr lines, 14"...1,540.00
Jug, #3/flower, c/s, E&LP Norton, ca 1880, separation, 16" 275.00
Jug, #4/flower basket, J&E Norton, ca 1855, 16" 1,650.00
Jug, bird on branch, c/s, J&E Bennington, lt wear, ca 1855, 11" .. 715.00

Beswick

In the early 1890s, James Wright Beswick operated a pottery in Longston, England, where he produced fine dinnerware as well as ornamental ceramics. Today's collectors are most interested in the figurines made since 1936 by a later generation Beswick firm, John Beswick, Ltd. They specialize in reproducing accurately detailed bone china models of authentic breeds of animals. Their Fireside Series includes dogs, cats, elephants, horses, the Huntsman, and an Indian figure, which measure up to 14" in height. The Connoisseur line is modeled after the likenesses of fa-

mous racing horses. Beatrix Potter's characters and some of Walt Disney's are charmingly re-created and appeal to children and adults alike. Other items, such as character Tobys, have also been produced. The Beswick name is stamped on each piece. The firm was absorbed by the Doulton group in 1973.

Animaland, Loopy Hare, c GB – Animation Ltd Beswick..., 4⅛". 325.00
Beatrix Potter, Ginger, BP-3B, c 1976, 3¾", MIB 255.00
Beatrix Potter, Head Gardener, BP11A 295.00
Beatrix Potter, Miss Moppet, 3B 80.00
Beatrix Potter, Mr Jackson, gr version, BP-3, 2¾" 225.00
Beatrix Potter, Pig-Wig, blk version, 1972, 4" 200.00
Beatrix Potter, Pigling Bland, gold mk, 4½" 150.00
Beatrix Potter, Sir Isaac Newton, c 1973, 1981 ed, MIB 140.00
Bird, Dove, #1614, blk circle mk, 6" 475.00
Bird, Pheasants (cock & hen), #2078, 6¾" 425.00
Butterfly, Purple Emperor, 1957-63, 4x6" 260.00
Cow, Brahma Bull Champion of Champions, #3095, ca 1910, 7¾" L.175.00
Cow, Friesian bull, #1439A, 1985-89 .... 285.00
Cow, Hereford, brn & wht gloss, #1360, 6¾" L 340.00
Fish, Lg Mouthed Black Bass, 1952-68, 5x8" 625.00

Fox, #2348, designed by Graham Tongue, issued 1970 – 1984, large, $960.00. (Photo courtesy Burchard Galleries Inc. on LiveAuctioneers.com)

Horse, Black Beauty foal, blk, 1976-89, #2536, 3" 30.00
Horse, Cardigan Bay, #2340, 1st version w/bk leg free from base . 755.00
Horse, Mare, chestnut gloss, #1812, red label, 1962-67, 5¾" 875.00
Horse, Shire mare, rocking-horse gray, Gredington, 1940-62.... 1,200.00
Horse, Welsh Cob stallion, blk w/wht socks, #A270 .... 415.00
Kitty MacBride, Racegoer, #2528, 1975-83, 3" 55.00
Wild Animal, Tiger, attacking elephant, #1720, 12x16½" 750.00

Bicycle Collectibles

Bicycles and related ephemera and memorabilia have been collected since the end of the nineteenth century, but for the last 20 years, they have been regarded as bonafide collectibles. Today they are prized not only for their charm and appearance, but for historical impact as well. Many wonderful items are now being offered through live and internet auctions, rare book sites, etc.

Hobby horse/draisienne bicycles were handmade between circa 1818 and 1821. If found today, one of these would almost certainly be 'as found.' (Be suspect of any that look to be restored or are brightly painted; it would be very doubtful that it was authentic.)

Bicycle collectors are generally split as specializing in pre- and post-1920. Those specializing in pre-1920 might want only items from the hobby horse era (1816 – 1821), velocipede and manumotive era (1830 – 1872), high-wheel and hard-tired safety era (1873 – 1890), or the pneumatic safety era (post 1890). With the introduction of the pneumatic tire, the field was impacted both socially and technically. From this point, collector interest relates to social, sport, fashion, manufacturing, urbanization, financial, and technical history. Post 1920 collectors tend to be drawn to Art Deco and aerodynamic design, which forge prices. Many seek not only cycles but signage, prints and posters, watches, medals, photographs, porcelains, toys, and various other types of ephemera and memorabilia. Some prefer to specialize in items relating to military cycling, certain factories, racing, country of origin, type of bike, etc. All radiate from a common interest.

The bicycle has played an important role in the rapid developement of the twentieth century and onwards, impacting the airplane, motorcycle, and automobile, also the manufacture of drawn tubing, differentials, and spoked wheels. It has affected advertising, urbanization, women's lib, and the vote. There are still many treasures to be discovered.

Cleveland Deluxe Roadmaster, boy's, prewar, 24", EX 375.00
Colson Bullnose, boy's, 1939, front lt, EX rstr 1,800.00
Columbia Air-Rider, boy's, 1940-42, EX 800.00
Elgin Robin, boy's, 1937, G 1,600.00
High-wheeler, 1890s, leather seat, rpl #9 lamp, 60" w/54" front wheel. 2,415.00
JC Higgins Murray, boy's, 1948, rstr, $150 to 200.00
JC Higgins, boy's, Wonderide Spring Fork, EX, $800 to 900.00
Murray Fire Cat, boy's, 1977, VG 250.00
Raleigh Chopper, boy's, 1970s, EX, $150 to 250.00
Schwinn Sting Ray Tornado, boy's, 1970s, NM, $150 to 250.00
Schwinn, poster, Chicago IL, fr, 20x24", EX 400.00
Swiss Army, boy's, 1941, VG, $700 to 1,000.00

Campagnolo

Founded by Tullio Campagnolo, this company began manufacturing in 1933 in the small town of Vicenza, Italy. The company soon expanded, focusing on the three fundamental concepts that would also characterize its future — performance, technological innovation, and quality of its products. The founder was an accomplished bicycle racer in Italy of the 1920s and he conceived of several innovative ideas while racing, which later turned into such revolutionary fundamental cycling products as the quick-release mechanism for bicycle wheels, derailleurs, and the patented 'rod' gear for gear changing. Campagnolo has equipped most of the greatest names in cycling and winners of the Tour de France such as Eddy Merckx. By the 1970s, Campagnolo cycling components had become the gold standard; however, by the early 1980s Campagnolo was losing sales to its competitors due to the outdated designs of both Nouvo and Super Record groups. On February 3, 1983, Campagnolo was dealt another loss when founder Tullio Campagnolo died just after the introduction of the Gruppo del Cinquantenario (50th anniversary Campagnolo group set). In 1984 with his son Vallentino at the helm, Campagnolo introduced its first group since Tullio's passing, the 180 Record Corsa Group. Its sculpted and aerodynamic lines were a major departure from the dated but much celebrated Super Record group. From 1984 till 1994 the Record Corsa Group or, C-Record as it is also known, was refined and well known for their sleek triangular shaped Delta brakes, and during this time synchronized shifting was introduced. In 1987 Campagnolo ended production of the venerable Super Record Road Group, which debuted in 1974. This was a blow to many cyclists as it seemed to be the final end to the components made great by the late Tullio Campagnolo. Now seen for their beauty and old world craftsmanship, these components are collected for display or for vintage bicycle restoration.

Collectors are advised to diversify, but the C Record era has become the most important and sought after decades of Campagnolo. NOS (new old stock) and rare items such as components in Century finish will continue to be very sought after and values are expected to rise. Campagnolo does not have a museum or give tours of the factory, so it is up to private collectors worldwide to preserve Campagnolo history. All prices are for NOS unless otherwise stated. Our advisor for this category is David Weddington; he is listed in the Directory under Tennessee.

50th anniversary group set, w/case & bag 3,500.00
C-Record Chainwheel set, Century finish, 172.5mm 41/52 .... 695.00
C-Record Cobalto brakeset, w/levers & cables, +box 525.00

C-Record Delta brakeset, NOS with levers in Century Finish, $950.00. (Photo courtesy David Weddington)

C-Record front derailleur brake on, early model in catalog, 18bis... 189.00
C-Record headset, Century finish 550.00
C-Record PISTA lg flanges, hubs NJS Keirin approved, 36/36 .... 700.00
C-Record PISTA small flange hubs 32/32 hole 650.00
C-Record, sm flange q/r hubs 36/36, rear 130mm, OLN Century finish. 475.00
Croce d'Aune, 1st generation front/rear derailleurs, w/box 250.00
CdA brakeset, graphite finish, Powergrade aero brake levers, blk hoods, pr.. 675.00
NR sm flange q/r hubs 32/32 126.5mm, FLAT skewers, w/box 250.00
Nuovo Record Hi-Lo hub set, 36-hole, front & rear, w/box 450.00
Nuovo Record front derailleur, band on, 3 cutouts in cage face ... 125.00
Nuovo Record rear derailleur 210.00
Record/NR Down tube band on dbl levers 75.00
Record/NR seat post, 2-bolt, 27.2x130mm 198.00
Regina ORO 5-speed freewheel 14-20, 14-22, 14-24, 15-19, 15-23.50.00
Regina Record ORO drilled chain 75.00
Regina TITANIO 5-speed freewheel, 5 titanium sprockets 14-22 .. 250.00
Regina TITALL 7-speed freewheel 2/3/4 Ti/Alloy sprockets relative to ratios, 12-18.300.00
SR Alloy freewheel, 7-speed 12-21, 12-23, 12-27 .... 325.00
SR Alloy head set, Italian thread 225.00
SR front derailleur, band on 105.00
SR Pista unfluted cranks w/dust caps, 170mm, late production.... 423.00
SR rear derailleur, 1977 .... 435.00
SR seat post, 2nd generation, 1-bolt, 27.2x180mm 255.00
SR Strada chain set, 170mm 39/52 unfluted cranks, eng blk logo. 400.00
Strada Superleggeri pedals, alloy body, blk alloy fr 250.00

Big Little Books

The first Big Little Book was published in 1933 and copyrighted in 1932 by the Whitman Publishing Company of Racine, Wisconsin. Its hero was Dick Tracy. The concept was so well accepted that others soon followed Whitman's example; and though the 'Big Little Book' phrase became a trademark of the Whitman Company, the formats of his competitors (Saalfield, Goldsmith, Van Wiseman, Lynn, and World Syndicate) were exact copies. Today's Big Little Book buffs collect them all.

These hand-sized sagas of adventure were illustrated with full-page cartoons on the right-hand page and the story narration on the left. Colorful cardboard covers contained hundreds of pages, usually totaling over an inch in thickness. Big Little Books originally sold for 10¢ at the dime store; as late as the mid-1950s when the popularity of comic books caused sales to decline, signaling an end to production, their price had risen to a mere 20¢. Their appeal was directed toward the pre-teens who bought, traded, and hoarded Big Little Books. Because so many were stored in attics and closets, many have survived. Among the super heroes are G-Men, Flash Gordon, Tarzan, the Lone Ranger, and Red Ryder; in a lighter vein, you'll find such lovable characters as Blondie and Dagwood, Mickey Mouse, Little Orphan Annie, and Felix the Cat.

In the early to mid-'30s, Whitman published several Big Little Books as advertising premiums for the Coco Malt Company, who packed them in boxes of their cereal. These are highly prized by today's collectors, as are Disney stories and super-hero adventures.

At the present time, the market for these books is fairly stable — values for common examples are actually dropping. Only the rare, character-related titles and any mint condition examples are increasing somewhat. Values listed are for books in mint condition unless otherwise noted. For more information we recommend *Encyclopedia of Collectible Children's Books* by Diane McClure Jones and Rosemary Jones (Collector Books), and *Big Little Books* by our advisor, Larry Jacobs; he is listed in the Directory under New Hampshire.

The Shadow and the Living Death, 1940, M, $250.00.
(Photo courtesy Larry Jacobs)

Ace Drumond, #1177 .... 35.00
Alice in Wonderland, #759 .... 55.00
Andy Panda & the Pirate Ghosts, #1459 .... 40.00
Apple Mary & Dennie Foil the Swindlers, #1130 .... 35.00
Blondie, Papa Knows Best, #1490 .... 45.00
Bobby Benson on the H-Bar-O Ranch, #1108 .... 40.00
Brenda Starr & the Masked Imposter, #1427 .... 45.00
Buck Rogers 25th C AD, #742 .... 150.00
Captain Midnight & the Moon Woman, #1452 .... 75.00
Charlie Chan, #1478 .... 60.00
Charlie McCarthy & Edgar Bergen, The Story, #1456 ...... 30.00
Chester Gump in the City of Gold, #1146 .... 40.00
Clyde Beatty Daredevil Lion & Tiger Tamer, #1410 ...... 45.00
Coach Bernie Bierman's Brick Barton & the Winning Eleven, #1480 ... 25.00
David Copperfield, #1148 .... 35.00
Desert Eagle Rides Again, #1458 .... 25.00
Dick Tracy on the Trail of Larceny Lu, #1170 .... 75.00
Donald Duck Gets Fed Up, #1462 .... 70.00
Donald Duck in Volcano Valley, #1457 .... 65.00
Donald Duck Is Here Again, #1484 .... 65.00
Ellery Queen the Adventure of the Last Man Club, #1406 ...... 60.00
Frank Buck Presents Ted Towers Animal Master, #1175 ...... 30.00
Freckles & the Lost Diamond Mine, #1164 .... 35.00
G-Man vs the Fifth Column, #1470 .... 35.00
G-Men on the Job, #1168 .... 30.00
Hall of Fame of the Air, #1159 .... 25.00
Jimmie Allen in the Air Mail Robbery, #1143 .... 30.00
Jungle Jim & the Vampire Woman, #1139 .... 70.00
Kazan in Revenge of the North, #1105 .... 30.00
Lone Ranger & the Red Renegades, #1489 .... 50.00
Mandrake the Magician & the Midnight Monster, #1431 ...... 55.00
Mickey Mouse & the Sacred Jewel, #1187 .... 80.00
Nancy & Sluggo, #1400 .... 75.00
Our Gang Adventures, #1456 .... 50.00
Perry Winkle & the Rinkeydinks, #1199 .... 40.00
Popeye in a Sock for Susan's Sake, #1485 .... 50.00
Powder Smoke Range, #1176 .... 40.00
Red Ryder & Circus Luck, #1466 .... 45.00
Roy Rogers King of the Cowboys, #1476 .... 45.00
Scrappy, #1122 .... 70.00
Smilin' Jack & the Escape from Deatch Rock, #1445 ...... 55.00

Terry & the Pirates, #1156 .... 55.00
Tiny Tim & the Mechanical Men, #1172 .... 65.00
Tom Mix & Tony Jr in Terror Trails, #762 .... 70.00
Uncle Ray's Story of the United States, #722 .... 45.00
Wash Tubbs, #751 .... 50.00
World War in Photographs, #779 .... 35.00
Zane Gray's King of the Royal Mounted, #1103 .... 45.00

Bing and Grondahl

In 1853 brothers M.H. and J.H. Bing formed a partnership with Frederick Vilhelm Grondahl in Copenhagen, Denmark. Their early wares were porcelain plaques and figurines designed by the noted sculptor Thorvaldsen of Denmark. Dinnerware production began in 1863, and by 1889 their underglaze color 'Copenhagen Blue' had earned them worldwide acclaim. They are perhaps most famous today for their Christmas plates, the first of which was made in 1895. See also Limited Edition Plates.

Note: Prices for all figurines are auction values plus buyer's premium.

Blue Traditional, creamer, 8-oz 60.00
Blue Traditional, plate, bread & butter, 6¼", $15 to 18.00
Buel Traditional, plate, dinner, 10" 60.00
Christmas Rose, bowl, vegetable, rnd, w/lid 195.00
Christmas Rose, coffeepot 115.00
Christmas Rose, creamer, 4" 30.00
Christmas Rose, c/s 30.00
Christmas Rose, plate, dinner, 9½" 50.00
Christmas Rose, plate, luncheon, 8½" 30.00
Christmas Rose, platter, 10" L 75.00
Figurine, baker holds tray w/lg pretzel, #2223, 11" 300.00
Figurine, ballerina kneeling, #2284, 8x9½" 325.00
Figurine, bison, sgn KN, #7054, 1980 ltd ed, 19" L, $900 to 1,050.00
Figurine, boy & girl reading, #1567, 4x4" 50.00
Figurine, boy sitting on book, #1742, 6x5½x2½" 165.00
Figurine, calf, recumbent, #2168/10, ca 1901-04, 3¾" L 70.00
Figurine, cat lying on side, gray w/blk stripes, #2236, 1915, 7" L . 470.00
Figurine, children on bench, #2176, 5" 225.00
Figurine, Children Playing, child in girl's lap, #1568, 4¾" 95.00
Figurine, Emperor's New Clothes, 1950s, 10½" 625.00
Figurine, First Kiss, #2162P, 7½" 175.00
Figurine, fox, #1719, 1950, 12" L 235.00
Figurine, girl seated, holding flowers, #2298, 6" 75.00
Figurine, Hans Christian Andersen, #2037, 9⅛x5¾" 225.00
Figurine, Japanese Chin, S Madsen, #2114, 1950s, 6" L 300.00
Figurine, lady w/guitar, #1684, 10x6" 165.00
Figurine, lion (male) on rock, L Jensen, #2057, 1955, 7¾" 385.00
Figurine, lion cub seated, #1923, 6x6" 225.00
Figurine, lioness & cub, #2268, 6x12" 545.00
Figurine, Mary, girl holding doll, #1721, 1970-83, 7", $110 to 145.00
Figurine, milkmaid w/cow & cat, #2017, 7" 565.00
Figurine, nude male w/pitcher holds bowl for eagle, wht, 8½x10". 720.00
Figurine, orangutan pr cuddling, K Kyhn, #1454/721, 1925, 3½" .. 525.00
Figurine, Padding About, barefoot boy, #1757, 8" 60.00
Figurine, perch fish, #23174, ca 1902-04, 3¾" L 70.00
Figurine, polar bear, #2218, 2¼", $75 to 90.00
Figurine, Sealyham terrier, #2017, 2½x4" 150.00
Figurine, tiger, Laurits Jensen, #2056, 1975, 9" 825.00
Seagull, bowl, rimmed soup, 9¾", $25 to 30.00
Seagull, bowl, vegetable, 9½" 90.00
Seagull, coffeepot 100.00
Seagull, creamer, 3", $30 to 35.00
Seagull, c/s 30.00

Seagull, egg cup, #57, 2" 22.00
Seagull, pitcher, 16-oz, 5", $75 to 90.00
Seagull, plate, salad, #618, 7" 30.00
Seagull, sandwich tray, 10½" 60.00
Seagull, shakers, 3", pr 55.00
Seagull, vase, 5½", $60 to 75.00
Seagull, vase, bud, 2" 27.50
Tray, 2 mice at side, tails wrap circumference, #1562, 3x5" 325.00
Vase, lg flower, bl tones on wht, sgn, #681, ca 1960s, 5" 120.00
Vase, mahog mottle, bulb top w/sm opening, A Jorgensen, 24" .. 2,000.00
Vase, tree along river, sgn BS, 1950s, 9" 95.00

Binoculars

There are several types of binoculars, and the terminology used to refer to them is not consistent or precise. Generally, 'field glasses' refer to simple Galilean optics, where the lens next to the eye (the ocular) is concave and dished away from the eye. By looking through the large lens (the objective), it is easy to see that the light goes straight through the two lenses. These are lower power, have a very small field of view, and do not work nearly as well as prism binoculars. In a smaller size, they are opera glasses, and their price increases if they are covered with mother-of-pearl (fairly common but very attractive), abalone shell (more colorful), ivory (quite scarce), or other exotic materials. Field glasses are not valuable unless very unusual or by the best makers, such as Zeiss or Leitz. Prism binoculars have the objective lens offset from the eyepiece and give a much better view. This is the standard binocular form, called Porro prisms, and dates from around 1900. Another type of prism binocular is the roof prism, which at first resembles the straight-through field glasses, with two simple cylinders or cones, here containing very small prisms. These can be distinguished by the high quality views they give and by a thin diagonal line that can be seen when looking backwards through the objective. In general, German binoculars are the most desirable, followed by American, English, and finally French, which can be of good quality but are very common unless of unusual configuration. Japanese optics of WWII or before are often of very high quality. 'Made in Occupied Japan' binoculars are very common, but collectors prize those by Nippon Kogaku (Nikon). Some binoculars are center focus (CF), with one central wheel that focuses both sides at once. These are much easier to use but more difficult to seal against dirt and moisture. Individual focus (IF) binoculars are adjusted by rotating each eyepiece and tend to be cleaner inside in older optics. Each type is preferred by different collectors. Very large binoculars are always of great interest. All binoculars are numbered according to their magnifying power and the diameter of the objective in millimeters. Optics of 6x30 magnify six times and have 30 millimeter objectives.

Prisms are easily knocked out of alignment, requiring an expensive and difficult repair. If severe, this misalignment is immediately noticeable on use by the double-image scene. Minor damage can be seen by focusing on a small object and slowly moving the binoculars away from the eye, which will cause the images to appear to separate. Overall cleanliness should be checked by looking backwards (through the objective) at a light or the sky, when any film or dirt on the lenses or prisms can easily be seen. Pristine binoculars are worth far more than when dirty or misaligned, and broken or cracked optics lower the value far more. Cases help keep binoculars clean but do not add materially to the value.

As of 2008, any significant changes in value are due to internet sales. Some of the prices listed here are lower than would be reached at an online auction. Revisions of these values would be inappropriate at this point for these reasons: First, values are fluctuating wildly on the internet; 'auction fever' is extreme. Second, some common instruments can fetch a high price at an internet sale, and it is clear that the price will not be supported as more of them are placed at auction. In fact, an overlooked collectible like the binocular will be subject to a great increase in supply as they are retrieved from closets in response to the values people see at an online auction. Third, sellers who have access to these internet auctions can use them for price guides if they wish, but the values in this listing have to reflect what can be obtained at an average large antique show. The following listings assume a very good overall condition, with generally clean and aligned optics. Our advisor for this category is Jack Kelly; he is listed in the Directory under Washington.

Field Glasses

Fernglas 08, German WWI, 6x39, military gr, many makers 50.00
Folding or telescoping, no bbls, old 125.00
Folding, modern, hinged flat case, oculars outside 10.00
Ivory covered, various sm szs & makers 200.00
LeMaire, bl leather/brass, various szs, other Fr same 25.00
Metal, emb hunting scene, various sm szs & makers 45.00
Pearl covered, various sm szs & makers 90.00
Porc covered, delicate pnt, various sm szs & makers 200.00
US Naval Gun Factory Optical Shop 6x30 .... 75.00
Zeiss 'Galan' 2.5x34, modern design look, early 1920s 170.00
Zeiss, 8x56 Dialyt, SN 1543413, W Germany, orig case, M 1,265.00

Prism Binoculars (Porro)

Barr & Stroud, 7x50, Porro II prisms, IF, WWII 120.00
Bausch & Lomb Zephyr, 7x35 & other, CF 160.00
Bausch & Lomb, 6x30, IF, WWI, Signal Corps 50.00
Bausch & Lomb, 7x50, IF, WWII, other makers same 140.00
Bausch & Lomb/Zeiss, 8x17, CF, Pat 1897 .... 140.00
Crown Optical, 6x30, IF, WWI, filters 50.00
France, various makers & szs, if not unusual 30.00
German WWII 6x30, 3-letter code for various makers 60.00

German WWII, 10x50, in hard black leather case stamped with a 'Waffen' mark and dated 1943, $360.00. (Photo courtesy Mohawk Arms Inc. on LiveAuctioneers.com)

German WWII 10x80, eyepieces at 45 degrees 500.00
Goertz Trieder Binocle, various szs, unusual adjustment 110.00
Huet, Paris 7x22, other sm szs, unusual shapes 80.00
Leitz 6x30 Dienstglas, IF, G optics 75.00
Leitz 8x30 Binuxit, CF, outstanding optics 150.00
M19, US military 7x50, ca 1980 .... 180.00
Nikon 9x35, 7x35, CF, 1950s-70s 140.00
Nippon Kogaku, 7x50, IF, Made in Occupied Japan 150.00
Ross 6x30, std British WWI issue 50.00
Ross Stepnada, 7x30, CF, wide angle, 1930s 250.00
Sard, 6x42, IF, very wide angle, WWII 900.00
Toko (Tokyo Opt Co) 7x50, IF, Made in Occupied Japan 45.00
Universal Camera 6x30, IF, WWII, other makers same 50.00
US Naval Gun Factory Optical 10x45, IF, WWI 200.00
US Naval Gun Factory Optical Shop 6x30, IF, filters, WWI 70.00
US Navy, 20x120, various makers, WWII & later 2,200.00
Warner & Swasey (important maker) 8x20, CF, 1902 .... 200.00
Wollensak 6x30, ca 1940 .... 50.00

Zeiss 15x60, CF or IF, various models...700.00
Zeiss 8x40 Delactis, CF or IF, 1930s...230.00
Zeiss Deltrintem 8x30, CF, 1930s..95.00
Zeiss DF 95, 6x18, sq shoulder, very early..................................160.00
Zeiss Starmorbi 12/24/42x60, turret eyepcs, 1920s...................2,500.00
Zeiss Teleater 3x13, CF, bl leather...120.00

Roof Prism Binoculars

Hensoldt Dialyt, various szs, 1930s-80s.......................................140.00
Hensoldt Universal Dialyt, 6x26, 3.5x26, 1920s..........................120.00
Leitz Trinovid, 7x42 & other, CF, 1960s-80s, EX........................500.00
Zeiss Dialyt, 8x30, CF, 1960s...400.00

Bisque

Bisque is a term referring to unglazed earthenware or porcelain that has been fired only once. During the Victorian era, bisque figurines became very popular. Most were highly decorated in pastels and gilt and demonstrated a fine degree of workmanship in the quality of their modeling. Few were marked. See also Dolls, Heubach; Nodders; Piano Babies.

Two women holding shell, 9x10", $120.00. (Photo courtesy Apple Tree Auction Center on LiveAuctioneers.com)

18th-C lady w/1 hand raised, fine details, 16"................................215.00
Black boy on chair, humidor, 10"...1,200.00
Black man playing accordion, seated on plinth, 11".....................215.00
Black man playing banjo, fine attire, 6"...215.00
Boy w/glasses sits astride column, 16", NM................................225.00
Bust, shy young girl in floral dress, hat, pastels/gilt, 17"..............210.00
Bust, young maid in hat, scarf about neck, mc, on socle, 1870, 24"....2,350.00
Child holding leaves, intaglio eyes, unmk, 12".............................150.00
Child seated, hands holding sm cup, Germany, ca 1900, 14".......600.00
Group, pr w/arms about ea other hold hands of child, rstr, 26"....780.00
Male in feathered hat, wide gold necklace, gr anchor mk, 27", VG...390.00
Mother & father, ea w/child on shoulder, floral attire, 20", EX, pr...360.00
Nude blond w/bird in perched on hand, lying on side, Germany, 6"...275.00

Black Americana

Black memorabilia is without a doubt a field that encompasses the most widely exploited ethnic group in our history. But within this field there are many levels of interest: arts and achievements such as folk music and literature, caricatures in advertising, souvenirs, toys, fine art, and legitimate research into the days of their enslavement and enduring struggle for equality. The list is endless.

In the listings below are some with a derogatory connotation. Thankfully, these are from a bygone era and represent the mores of a culture that existed nearly a century ago. They are included only to convey the fact that they are a part of this growing area of collecting interest. Black Americana catalogs featuring a wide variety of items for sale are available; see Clubs, Newsletters, and Websites for more information. We

also recommend *Collectible African American Dolls* by Yvonne H. Ellis. See also Cookie Jars; Postcards; Posters; Salt Shakers; Sheet Music.

Ad, 4-flour flavor of Aunt Jemima pancakes, 1955, 13x10", EX.....18.00
Ad, Cream of Wheat/A Dainty Breakfast, 1915, 15x12" w/fr, EX..40.00
Ashes/Cigarettes/Matches holder, mc bsk washday motif, 4", EX..85.00
Ashtray/match holder, boy on bk w/lg bare ft, ceramic, 4", EX......50.00
Bank, baby seated w/mc fruit, nodder head, Kenmar, 7", NM........65.00
Bank, boy seated w/melon, chalkware, GMB, 1940s, 12", NM+..125.00
Bank, minstrel playing banjo, litho tin cylinder, red lid, prewar, 4", NM.175.00
Book, Andy's Exciting Day, England, 1930, EX............................125.00
Book, Further Adventures of Wongabilla, Australian, hardcover, 50 pgs, EX.300.00
Book, Little Black Sambo, Bannerman, 5 mechanical pgs, 1949, 9x18", NM+...150.00
Book, Little Brown Koko, Blanch Hunt, pgs to color, EX..............95.00
Book, Watermelon Pete & Other Stories, E Gordon, 1937 ed, VG...115.00
Book, Well Done Noddy!, Enid Blyton, EX......................................30.00
Bottle opener, native head, silver trim, rhinestone eyes, 5", EX.....30.00
Card, birthday, I's Got an Idea, girl among flowers, 1930s, 4", EX..25.00
Card, Christmas, Greetings Frum Me To You, Hallmark, 4x3", EX..20.00
Celluloid novelty, boy rolling dice on base, Japan, 1920s, 3", EX+..90.00
Charm, Sam & Lew outhouse, 14k gold, 2 enameled figures, EX...90.00
Clock, alarm, De Tar Baby, rnd, 3-ftd, Disney, 6", VG.................300.00
Clock, alarm, Little Brown Koko image, blk sq case, Spur, EX........90.00
Clock, bell atop rnd 3-ftd chrome case, man ion face w/blk numbers, 6", EX.850.00
Coloring book, Little Brown Koko, 1941, 22 pgs, unused, EX......125.00
Cookbook, The Savannah Cook Book, HR Colquitt, 1933, EX....65.00
Cookie Jar, Uncle Mose figure, ceramic, Japan, 1930s, 7", VG...200.00
Creamer/sugar, yel, Aunt Jemima & Uncle Mose hdls, F&F, EX..225.00
Display, cb, Aunt Jemima, dc, string-climbing pc, 1905, VG....1,300.00
Doll, Dream Baby, Armand Marseille, compo/bsk, wht gown, 1920s, 10", EX.275.00
Doll, girl, G Heubach, 7670-4", bsk, orig dress, 10", EX.............1,200.00
Doll, Kewpie, nude, compo, jtd shoulders, 12", VG.....................125.00
Doll, Little Red Riding Hood (2-face), Bartenstein, 18", VG...1,000.00
Doll, Mammy, stuffed blk stockinette, 1900-10, 20", EX.............475.00
Fan, man's head in top hat, cb, wood hdl, Darkie Toothpaste, EX..100.00
Figurine set, 4 choir boys, wht robes w/gold trim, ceramic, 5½", NM....200.00
Figurine set, kissing couple, ceramic, 5", NM..............................100.00
Figurine, island girl w/tin cymbal, Art Deco, papier mache, 12", VG....90.00
Figurine, Sambo dancing, pnt CI, Hubley, 1920s, 2¼", EX..........150.00
Game, Chuck Target Game, litho cb, Ottman/USA, 1890s, rare, EXIB.350.00
Game, Joll Darky Target, McLoughlin Bros, EX+IB....................500.00
Game, Pickaninny Bowling, Bavaria, mini version, 1920s, EXIB.275.00
Game, Zoo Hoo, USA, 1920s, complete, NMIB..........................125.00
Hand puppet, mammy, pnt wood head, cloth outfit, 12", EX........125.00
Head vase, turbaned head, gold earrings, 3-strand pearls, 6", EX...50.00

Humidor, ceramic, no mark, 4", $275.00. (Photo courtesy Burley Auction Group on LiveAuctioneers.com)

Jack-in-the-box, compo man's head, pnt features, cloth outfit, 5".125.00
Jigsaw puzzle, Amos/Andy hotel scene, Pepsodent, 8x10", EX.......75.00
Key holder, nodder-head couple atop 4-key rack, mc wood, 8", EX.75.00
Knife holder, wood, 3-holder wall mt w/appl chef's head, 12", EX.50.00
Lamp, lawn jockey on ped base, mc pnt metal, 12", EX.................65.00
Lighter, on base w/slim Art Deco-style metal figure, VG...............75.00
Marionette, Golliwog (Jumpelles), Pelham, 9", NMIB.................175.00

Marionette, minstrel w/banjo, Pelham, 13", MIB 200.00
Nodder, lady w/hand on hip, cvd pnt wood, lg ft on sq base, 12", EX . 4,000.00
Notepad/pencil holder, mammy figure, chalkware, wall mt, 9", EX..90.00
Paper dolls, Oh Susanna! Musical Pack O' Fun, complete, unused, EX ... 50.00
Paperclip, Johnny Griffin bust, brass, 4x2½", EX 550.00
Pencil sharpener, pot metal caricature head, blade in mouth, VG ..150.00
Pickle jar, mammy head, wide-eyed, ceramic, Japan, 1950s, 6½", VG....150.00
Pie bird, mammy half-figure w/bowl, ceramic, 4½", EX 30.00
Postcard, crying baby w/bare bottom, Curteich, 1930s-40s, VG 15.00
Program, Michael Todd's Hot Mikado, NY World's Fair, 1939, EX..32.00
Pull toy, Sambo, Velo, wood, 12", VG................................... 85.00
Puzzle, Darktown Fire Brigade, jigsaw, Parker Bros, EXIB 425.00
Recipe box, plastic, molded mammy head, Fosta, 1950s, 4x5x3", NM...200.00
Sand pail, litho tin, beach/2 Golliwogs, England, 1920s, 7", EX..200.00
Shakers, Aunt Jemima/Uncle Mose figures, plastic, F&F, 5", NM, pr ..85.00
Sign, porc, Aunt Jemima Flour, Burdick, Chicago, NM 7,500.00
Souvenir novelty, lady w/cotton bale on head, wood/cloth dress, 7", VG.. 15.00
Spice set, 6 ceramic chefs/wood box-like rack, 1940s, 3" chefs, EX....275.00
Spice set, 6 plastic Aunt Jemimas, metal MS Queen rack, F&F, EX+...750.00
Spoon, sterling/enameled bowl/beaded rim, It's the Real Thing, 4", EX ..400.00
Squeeze toy, Golliwog figure, pnt rubber, England, 1930s, 6", NM...75.00
Tablecloth, figures w/melons & banjos, mc, Pennicraft, 1950s, 53" sq, M.175.00
Teapot, mammy half figure, ceramic, Maruhan Ware/Japan, 7", NM.. 250.00
Tin, biscuit, rnd, yel, w/image of goose chasing boy, 3½x6" dia, VG+...100.00
Tobacco jar, child's head in brimmed hat, chalkware, 1930s, 5", EX+..95.00
Towel bar, dc wood mammy bust, arms hold rod, wall mt, 12", EX ..45.00
Toy, acrobat on trapeze, Kobe, wood, 5", EX.......................... 375.00
Toy, banjo, litho tin w/various images, Chad Valley, 1950s, 19", EX... 175.00
Vase, girl figure w/basket (vase) on bk, ceramic, 1940s-50s, 6", NM .. 60.00
Ventriloquist doll, Sammy, plaid clothes, 37", EX (poor box) 500.00
Wall pocket, chef on stove, wht w/brn & bl trim, ceramic, EX...... 75.00
Wall pocket, chef's head, wht hat/shoulders, ceramic, 6", NM 100.00

Black Glass

Black glass, which is also called black amethyst, has been made in the U.S. since the beginning of the nineteenth century. England was first to isolate nickel as a coloring agent for black glass, but later varying amounts of manganese were used in its manufacture. Black is a combination of all colors, so black glass that is transilluminated will show purple or dark ruby. Even though satinizing it in the late 1800s increased demand, it was never very popular. A different formula for producing a black glass, Ferraline, was used from about 1881 to 1885. It is very rare and is marked with the company name.

Many American companies made items in black glass. Tiffin made their bulldog doorstop and Chessie cat. Cambridge made swans in Ebony (1928). Imperial made black items in their Cathay line. Heisey, which made their black glass over cobalt, never made it for commercial production, but some rare items were made for personal gifts. L.E. Smith produced much black glass including dog and swan figurines, horse bookends, and particularly their Mt. Pleasant tableware pattern. Westmoreland also produced a lot of black glass, including their 5" hen covered dish in 1924 and their raised wing swan in the 1950s. Akro Agate (Westite) produced a small amount of black glass in their novelty items. Beware of reproductions such as Fenton's Thumbprint pattern.

For more information we recommend A Collector's Guide to Black Glass, books 1 and 2, by Marlena Toohey. Our advisor for black glass is Shirley Smith; she is listed in the Directory under West Virginia.

Bookends, Black Feather, Fostoria, 8½" 77.00
Bowl, #400/74N, Candlewick, ft, 5¾" W 256.00
Bowl, mixing, McKee, mk, 7¼" W 35.00
Bowl, Murano, gold flecks, 8½" L 120.00

Cake plate, Mt Pleasant, LE Smith, 10½" W 41.00
Cake stand, Hobnail, ASP2004, 5" 163.00
Candlesticks, #725, Northwood, 10"... 31.00
Covered jar, Chessie, satin, 8" 110.00
Figurine, alley cat, Fenton, HP, 11" 82.00
Figurine, panther, Daum, pate-de-verre, mk, 6"............................... 600.00
Figurine, swan, Duncan & Miller 30.00
Humidor, Cambridge, 5" W... 330.00
Perfume, Baccarat, sgn, 3" W.. 560.00
Vase, Black Forest etched, Paden City, 6½" 42.00

Vase, 'Confetti Ware,' L.E. Smith, $45.00. (Photo courtesy Shirley Smith)

Vase, Peacock & Rose, Paden City, 11⅞"...................................... 96.00
Vase, Poppy, Tiffin, 9" 51.00
Vase, Westmoreland, HP, 8¼" 109.00
Vase, #463, Lalique, sgn, Tanzania, 8"..3,000.00

Blown Glass

Blown glass is rather difficult to date; eighteenth- and nineteenth-century examples vary little as to technique or style. It ranges from the primitive to the sophisticated, but the metallic content of very early glass caused tiny imperfections that are obvious upon examination, and these are often indicative of age.

In America, Stiegel introduced the English technique of using a patterned, part-size mold, a practice which was generally followed by many glasshouses after the Revolution. From 1820 to about 1850, glass was blown into full-size three-part molds. In the listings below, glass is assumed clear unless color is mentioned. Our advisor for this category is Mark Vuono; he is listed in the Directory under Connecticut. See also Bottles; Lamps, Whale Oil Burning Fluid; specific manufacturers.

Bottle, amber, 24 swirled ribs, ovoid, att Kent, broken blister, 7".. 260.00
Bottle, aqua, club shape w/24 broken-swirl ribs, blisters, 8" 250.00
Bowl, aquamarine, on short std & rnd ft, NY, 6x6" 1,200.00
Bowl, dk amber, pontil, rolled rim/tooled spout, 1850-70, 3½x9½"..550.00
Bowl, pale amethyst, 16 dainty ribs, folded rim, 2x5"....................235.00
Canister, clear w/3 cobalt rings, cobalt wafer finial, 9¾x4" 575.00
Canister, str sides, domed lid, folded base, Am, 1850s, 15x7½"....235.00

Creamer, amethyst with heavy striations, 16-rib, 4¼", $1,200.00. (Photo courtesy Pook & Pook, Inc. on LiveAuctioneers.com)

Creamer, cobalt, 14 horizontal ribs, pontil, 1850-70, 3⅛" 1,200.00
Creamer, cobalt, 20-dmn, appl ft, solid hdl, Pittsburgh, 4⅛"........450.00

Creamer, cobalt, 20-rib, flared rim/spout, solid hdl, ftd, 4" 400.00
Dish, lt amethyst, faint 15-Dmn Quilt, folded rim, ftd, 2½x4" 350.00
Jar, apothecary, appl ft, tooled rim, orig lid, pontil, 14¼" 150.00
Jar, aquamarine, sheared/tooled mouth, pontil scar, Am, 6x5" 550.00
Jar, lt yel olive, cylinder, tooled flared mouth, pontil, NE, 12" 700.00
Jar, yel amber, sheared mouth w/rim, pontil, burst bubble, NE, 7"...850.00
Pan, cobalt, flared/folded rim, domed base, 2¼x8¼" 65.00
Pitcher, 12 swirl ribs, flint, Pittsburgh, 8¼" 435.00
Pitcher, 8-Pillar mold, sheared rim, solid hdl, Pittsburgh area, 9".. 375.00
Pitcher, appl hdl & 4 rings, flint, 8½" 175.00
Pitcher, aquamarine, Lily Pad, bulb, solid hdl, NY, 6" 2,100.00
Rolling pin, clear w/red & bl spots, plaster cased, knob hdls, 16".. 220.00
Rolling pin, fiery opal, knob hdls, pontil, late 19th C, 15" 150.00
Salt cellar, yel olive, ogee bowl, short stem, flared ft, 1820-50, 3" .1,700.00
Snuff jar, bright gr, rect w/chamfered corners, 4½" 600.00
Tumbler, gr aquamarine, left-swirl ribs, Midwest, 1820-40, 4¾" 1,500.00
Tumbler, smoky yel gr, 6 arched panels, pontil, 3⅝" 300.00
Vase, med purple amethyst, Hyacinth, pontil, tooled lip, 7⅛" 130.00

Blown Three-Mold Glass

A popular collectible in the 1920s, 1930s, and 1940s, blown three-mold glass has again gained the attention of many. Produced from approximately 1815 to 1840 in various New York, New England, and Midwestern glasshouses, it was a cheaper alternative to the expensive imported Irish cut glass.

Distinguishing features of blown three-mold glass are the three distinct mold marks and the concave-convex appearance of the glass. For every indentation on the inner surface of the ware, there will be a corresponding protuberance on the outside. Blown three-mold glass is most often clear with the exception of inkwells and a few known decanters. Any colored three-mold glass commands a premium price.

The numbers in the listings that follow refer to the book *American Glass* by George and Helen McKearin. Our advisor for this category is Mark Vuono; he is listed in the Directory under Connecticut.

Creamer, milky med gr (nearly opaque), solid hdl, smooth base, 5" ...300.00
Decanter, GI-27, half-post pinch bottle w/etch castle, 12½" 300.00
Decanter, GI-29, dk cobalt, tooled mouth, pontil, tam stopper, 5½".900.00

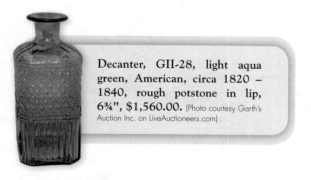

Decanter, GII-28, light aqua green, American, circa 1820 – 1840, rough potstone in lip, 6¾", $1,560.00. (Photo courtesy Garth's Auction Inc. on LiveAuctioneers.com)

Decanter, GIII-09, faint aqua, tooled mouth, pontil, w/stopper, 5⅜".350.00
Decanter, GIII-16, olive w/amber tone, 7¼" 300.00
Inkwell, Dmn Quilt, dk amber, mid-19th C, Am, 2x2⅞" dia 275.00
Inkwell, GIII-29, olive amber, 1½x2¼" 300.00
Salt cellar, GII-21, 16-dmn, dk amethyst, flared mouth, Keene, 1". 10,000.00
Sugar bowl, GII-18, clear w/lt bl tint, Sandwich, 6½", $5,000 to ... 6,000.00

Blue and White Stoneware

'Salt glaze' (slang term) or molded stoneware was most commonly produced in a blue and white coloration, much of which was also deco-

rated with numerous 'in-mold' designs (some 150 plus patterns). It was made by practically every American pottery from the turn of the century until the mid-1930s. Crocks, pitchers, wash sets, rolling pins, and other household wares are only a few of the items that may be found in this type of 'country' pottery, now one of today's popular collectibles.

Logan, Brush-McCoy, Uhl Co., and Burley-Winter were among those who produced it, but very few pieces were ever signed. Research and the availability of some manufacturers' sales catalogs has enabled collectors to attribute certain pattern lines to some companies. Naturally condition must be a prime consideration, especially if one is buying for resale; pieces with good, strong color and fully molded patterns bring premium prices. Be mindful that very good reproductions are on the market and are often misrepresented as the real thing. Normal wear and signs of age are to be expected, since this was utility ware and received heavy use in busy households.

In the listings that follow, crocks, salts, and butter crocks are assumed to be without lids unless noted otherwise. Items are in near-mint condition unless noted otherwise. Though common pieces seem to have softened to some degree, scarce items and those in outstanding mint condition are stronger than ever. Nationwide internet sales such as eBay have stabilized and standardized prices that once fluctuated from region to region. They have also helped to determine what is really rare and what isn't. See also specific manufacturers. For information on the Blue & White Pottery Club, see the Clubs, Newsletters, and Websites section or visit their website at: www.blueandwhitepottery.org.

Bean pot, Wildflower, no lid 178.00
Bowl, Apricot, common 80.00
Bowl, Daisy on Lattice, 10¾" 115.00
Bowl, mixing, Flying Bird, 4x6" 200.00
Bowl, Wedding Ring, 6 szs, $150 ea, or set of 6 for 1,000.00
Butter crock, Apricot, appl wood & wire hdl, w/lid, 4x7" 275.00
Butter crock, Butterfly, w/lid & bail, 6½" 225.00
Butter crock, Daisy & Waffle, 4x8" 175.00
Butter crock, Eagle, in rarely found perfect condition 1,000.00
Butter crock, Peacock, w/lid, 6x6" 600.00
Butter jar, Wildflower, appl wood & wire hdl, 5x7" 275.00
Canister, Basketweave, Crackers, w/lid 740.00
Canister, Basketweave, Put Your Fist In, w/lid, 7½" 760.00
Chamberpot, Peacock, att Brush-McCoy, 9¾"............................. 1,250.00
Chamberpot, Wildflower & Fishscale, w/lid 400.00
Coffeepot, Peacock, w/lid & insides 5,900.00
Coffeepot, Swirl, w/lid & metal base plate 900.00
Cooler, water, Cupid, brass spigot, patterned lid, 15x12" 700.00
Cooler, water, Polar Bear, Ice Water, w/lid, hairlines, 6-gal, 15" .. 900.00
Cuspidor, Basketweave & Morning Glory, 5x2½" 125.00
Jardiniere ped, Tulip pattern.. 183.00
Jardiniere, Tulips, hairline, 7x⅞" (complete w/stand & crock) .1,625.00
Mug, Basketweave & Flower, 5x3" 150.00
Mug, beer, advertising, Diffused Bl, sq hdl 150.00
Mug, Dainty Fruit, 5x3" 800.00
Mug, Flying Bird, 5x3".. 130.00
Pitcher, Acorns, stenciled, 8x6" 175.00
Pitcher, Barrel, +6 mugs.. 395.00
Pitcher, Bluebird, 9x7".. 450.00
Pitcher, Cattails, stenciled design, bulb, 7" 225.00
Pitcher, Cherry Band, w/advertising, 9¼" 1,600.00
Pitcher, Cherry Cluster, scarce, 7½" 450.00
Pitcher, Dutch Boy & Girl by Windmill, 9"....................................... 200.00
Pitcher, Eagle w/Shield & Arrows, rare, 8" 750.00
Pitcher, Girl & Dog, regular bl, 9"... 800.00
Pitcher, Grazing Cows, 6" (scarce sz) 500.00
Pitcher, Leaping Deer in 1 oval, Swan in other (mfg error), 8".2,424.00
Pitcher, Leaping Deer, 8½" 375.00
Pitcher, Lovebird, arc bands, deep color, 8½", EX............................. 500.00

Pitcher, Lovebird, pale color, 8½".................................300.00
Pitcher, Pine Cone, scarce, 9½".............................1,500.00
Pitcher, Scroll & Leaf, Trade at IGA Store, Deshler, NE Phone 193, 8"..1,290.00
Pitcher, Shield, prof rpr, 8"....................................200.00
Pitcher, Swan, in oval, deep color, 8½", EX...............400.00
Pitcher, Wildflowers/Cosmos, w/advertising................2,100.00
Pitcher, Windmills, common, 7¼", EX......................175.00
Pitcher, Windy City (Fannie Flagg), Robinson Clay, 8½"........450.00
Rolling pin, orange band w/advertising & dtd 1916.........756.00
Rolling pin, Swirl, orig wooden hdls, 13"..................1,500.00

Salt crock, Butterfly, missing lid, few minor chips, 6" diameter, $90.00. (Photo courtesy Grand View Antiques & Auction on LiveAuctioneers.com)

Salt crock, Butterfly, w/lid..................................350.00
Salt crock, Eagle, w/lid.......................................800.00
Salt crock, Peacock, w/lid..................................1,000.00
Soap dish, Indian in War Bonnet (+).......................250.00
Washboard, sponged...400.00
Washbowl & pitcher, Wildflower & Fishscale...............500.00
Water bottle, Diffused Bl Swirl, stopper w/cork, 10x5"......800.00

Bluebird China

Bluebird china continues to charm the U.S. population simply because bluebirds are such special little creatures — epitomizing such virtues as hope, innocence, sweetness, and fortitude. And, because they are indigenous only to North America, they are ingrained in our culture and folklore. But our love of bluebirds is only part of the story. The industrious, optimistic, and enterprising potters who emigrated from England at the end of the eighteenth and beginning of the nineteenth centuries to settle in the Ohio River Valley and establish America as a leading producer of stoneware, dinneware, and art pottery is another captivating aspect of this saga. Potteries such as Homer Laughlin, Knowles Taylor Knowles (KT & K), W.S. George, Hopewell, Elpco, Carrollton, French, Pope-Gosser, and about 300 others amazed the world with their innovations, design, and art.

Every year examples of bluebird china become harder and harder to find as the number of collectors continues to grow faster than the recirculating supply. The best source for bluebird china continues to be eBay, but, even in that market, quality pieces are offered less and less frequently. Our advisor for this category is Kenna Rosen, author of *Bluebird China* (Schiffer); she is listed in the Directory under Texas.

Bone dish, Empress, Homer Laughlin......................125.00
Bowl, berry, Cleveland, ind....................................20.00
Bowl, gravy, Hopewell China, w/saucer......................100.00
Bowl, oatmeal, Newell pattern, Homer Laughlin............50.00
Butter dish, Empress, Homer Laughlin......................150.00
Butter dish, Salem China.......................................150.00
Butter dish, sq, Carrollton, 6¼"...............................75.00
Butter dish, Steubenville, 4½" holder w/in 7" dish........150.00
Canister set, rnd, unmk, 6½x5", 6 for........................300.00
Casserole, Pope Gosser, w/lid, 10½x10½"....................100.00
Casserole, SPI Clinchfield China, w/lid.......................75.00
Casserole, Taylor, Smith & Taylor, w/lid, 11x7½"............75.00

Casserole, Vodrey China, early 1900s, w/lid, 12x6"..........75.00
Chamber pot, unmk, w/lid, late 1890s......................150.00
Chocolate cup, ftd, no mk, 3"..................................85.00
Chocolate pot, KT&K...200.00
Creamer/sug bowl, SP Co, w/lid...............................85.00
Creamer, unmk, 4"...25.00
Cup, 2 hdls, unmk...40.00
Custard cup, KT&K, 3½"...35.00
Egg cup, Buffalo China, very rare, 2½".........................75.00

Egg cup, 4½", $60.00. (Photo courtesy eBay seller mikem3310)

Pitcher, wash, Bennett China................................400.00
Pitcher, water, Crown Pottery Co............................200.00
Pitcher, water, DE McNicol..................................150.00
Pitcher, water, Empress, Homer Laughlin...................250.00
Pitcher, water, National China..............................200.00
Plate, KT&K, 9¾"...40.00
Plate, Steubenville, 9"...40.00
Plate, Wilmer Ware...20.00
Platter, 10 bluebirds, gold trim at rim, DE McNichol, 15x11"......75.00
Platter, Edwin M Knowles, 14½x11".........................60.00
Platter, H Wiley Co, 13"..50.00
Platter, Hopewell China, 13x10".............................60.00
Platter, Pope Gosser, 17x13"..................................75.00
Platter, Thompson Glenwood, 13x10".........................50.00
Platter, West End Pottery Co, 15½x11".......................60.00
Shakers, Art Deco styling, tall, unmk, rare, pr, $250 to......400.00
Shaving mug, The Potters Co-Op..............................65.00
Sugar bowl, Illinois China Co, w/lid, 7x6"....................50.00
Teacup, unmk..15.00
Teapot, Carrollton...250.00
Teapot, ELP Co, 8½x8½"..250.00
Teapot, Homer Laughlin.......................................500.00
Teapot, KT&K, 3½x7¼"..250.00
Teapot, West Virginia Pottery Co, sm........................150.00
Tea set, child's, CPCo, 21-pc..................................400.00
Tea set, child's, Summit China Co............................500.00

Blue Ridge

Blue Ridge dinnerware was produced by Southern Potteries of Erwin, Tennessee, from the late 1930s until 1956 in 12 basic styles and 2,000 different patterns, all of which were hand decorated under the glaze. Vivid colors lit up floral arrangements of seemingly endless variation, fruit of every sort from simple clusters to lush assortments, barnyard fowl, peasant figures, and unpretentious textured patterns. Although it is these dinnerware lines for which they are best known, collectors prize the artist-signed plates from the '40s and the limited line of character jugs made during the '50s most highly. Examples of the French Peasant pattern are valued at double the prices listed below; very simple patterns will bring 25% to 50% less.

Betty and Bill Newbound have compiled four books, all published by Collector Books, with beautiful color illustrations: *Blue Ridge*

Dinnerware; The Collector's Encyclopedia of Blue Ridge, Volumes I and II; and *Best of Blue Ridge.* For information concerning the Blue Ridge Collector Club, see the Clubs, Newsletters, and Websites section.

Ashtray, ind... 20.00
Baking dish, plain, 8x13".. 25.00
Basket, alum edge, $25 to 30.00
Bonbon, Charm House, china, $150 to...................... 175.00
Bonbon, divided, center hdl, china, $85 to................. 95.00
Bonbon, flat shell, china.. 75.00
Bonbon, Verna, $75 to (pattern has bearing on values) 90.00
Bowl, flat soup, Premium, $25 to 35.00
Bowl, mixing, med 25.00
Bowl, mixing, sm, $15 to 20.00
Box, cigarette, sq... 90.00
Box, Mallard Duck... 700.00
Breakfast set.. 500.00
Butter dish, $35 to 45.00
Cake lifter, $25 to 30.00
Celery, Fox Grape, leaf shape, china, $40 to............... 50.00
Celery, Skyline 40.00
Child's cereal bowl, $125 to 160.00
Child's feeding dish, divided, $125 to 150.00
Chocolate pot 225.00
Coffeepot, Rose Marie, Ovoid shape, $110 to............. 125.00
Creamer, Fifties shape, $15 to..................................... 20.00
Creamer, lg, Colonial, open, $18 to 25.00
Cup/saucer, demi, earthenware, $25 to 30.00
Cup/saucer, tea, HP strawberries 65.00
Cup/saucer, Turkey & Acorn, $75 to.......................... 100.00
Egg cup, Premium 60.00
Gravy boat, Premium, $35 to 55.00
Jug, character, Daniel Boone, $400 to......................... 500.00
Jug, character, Indian, $600 to.................................... 700.00
Lamp, china, $125 to 150.00
Lazy Susan, side pcs... 75.00
Pitcher, Abby, china, $175 to 200.00
Pitcher, Betsy, gold decor, $250 to 300.00

**Pitcher, Easter Parade, 8",
$120.00.** (Photo courtesy Brunk Auctions
on LiveAuctioneers.com)

Pitcher, Sally, china 250.00
Pitcher, Virginia, china, 6", $125 to 150.00
Plate, advertising, lg... 325.00
Plate, artist sgn, 10", $325 to 450.00
Plate, dinner, Premium, 9", $25 to 35.00
Plate, Still Life, 8" 30.00
Platter, artist sgn, 15", $1,200 to................................ 1,500.00
Ramekin, w/lid, 7½", $35 to 45.00
Relish, Anniversary Song, heart shape, china, $90 to 125.00
Shakers, Apple, 1", pr 45.00
Shakers, Good Housekeeping, pr $125 to 150.00
Shakers, Mallards, pr $400 to 450.00
Spoon, salad, china 50.00

Sugar bowl, Colonial, eared, $15 to 20.00
Sugar bowl, ped ft, china 65.00
Teapot, Charm House.. 350.00
Teapot, Mini Ball, china.. 250.00
Teapot, Snub Nose, china, $175 to 200.00
Tidbit, 2-tier, $30 to.. 40.00
Toast, Premium, w/lid 250.00
Tray, cake, Maple Leaf, china 75.00
Tray, chocolate 500.00
Tray, demi, Colonial, 5½x7", $150 to.......................... 175.00
Tumbler, glass, $15 to 20.00
Vase w/hdls, china.. 100.00
Vase, boot, 8"... 95.00
Vase, bud, $225 to.. 250.00
Vase, ruffled top, china, 9½", $95 to 125.00
Wall sconce, $70 to... 75.00

Blue Willow

Blue Willow, inspired no doubt by the numerous patterns of the blue and white Nanking imports, has been popular since the late eighteenth century and has been made in as many variations as there were manufacturers. English transfer wares by such notable firms as Allerton and Ridgway are the most sought after and the most expensive. Japanese potters have been producing Willow-patterned dinnerware since the late 1800s, and American manufacturers have followed suit. Although blue is the color most commonly used, mauve and black lines have also been made. For further study we recommend *Gaston's Blue Willow*, with full-color photos and current prices, by Mary Frank Gaston, our advisor for this category. In the listings, if no manufacturer is noted, the ware is unmarked. See also Buffalo Pottery.

Ashtray, Schweppes Table Waters, English, $50 to........... 65.00
Biscuit jar, cane hdl, octagonal, Gibson, 1912-30, 6½", $250 to .. 275.00
Bonbon, divided, center hdl, $85 to............................ 95.00
Bonbon, flat shell, $55 to.. 65.00
Bowl & pitcher, Wedgwood.. 1,200.00
Bowl, cream soup, w/saucer, Ridgways, ca 1927 & after, $75 to ... 100.00
Bowl, lug soup, Homer Laughlin, $25 to...................... 30.00
Bowl, rice, Pountney & Co, 1930s, $30 to 45.00
Bowl, vegetable, int pattern, w/lid, Grimwades...Hanley..., 1900s. 185.00
Bowl, vegetable, scalloped, Allerton, 1890-1912, 8" 110.00
Bowl, vegetable, undecorated ext, WR Midwinter mk, ca 1933, $80 to .. 85.00
Butter dish, scalloped, Allerton, 1903-12, 7", $250 to... 275.00
Butter dish, w/drainer, Ridgways, 1927 & after, $300 to.... 350.00
Candleholder, ship's lt, brass w/ceramic backplate, $80 to........ 100.00
Canisters, sq, tin, set of 4, $400 to............................... 500.00
Carafe, w/warmer, Japan, $250 to................................ 300.00
Chamber pot, flow bl, Doulton, 1891-1902, $350 to 400.00
Charger/chop plate, 13", Allerton & Sons, $75 to 90.00
Children's butter dish, china, Edge, Malkin & Co, 1873-1903, 5½", $225 to. 250.00
Cigar lighter, metal stand & fittings, metal mk B & Co London, $500 to. 600.00
Coaster, ceramic dish in wooden holder, English, $55 to 65.00
Coffee jar, for instant coffee, Japan, $75 to 85.00
Creamer, cow, English, $1,400 to 1,500.00
Creamer, demi, china, $75 to 85.00
Creamer, hotel ware, Am, Buffalo China, 1922, $45 to 55.00
Cup, chili, Japan, 3x4".. 50.00
Cup, chili, w/liner plate, Japan.................................... 75.00
Cup, cream soup, John Maddock, ca 1961, $30 to........ 35.00
Cup/saucer, Barlow, $40 to 50.00
Cup/saucer, demi, Johnson Bros, $40 to 50.00
Cup/saucer, jumbo, $75 to 100.00

Cup/saucer, Meakin for Nieman-Marcus, 1970s 30.00
Egg cup, reverse traditional pattern, Wood & Sons, ca early 1900s, $35 to..45.00
Gravy boat, Homer Laughlin, $20 to 25.00
Gravy boat, Wood & Sons, ca 1971, $55 to..................................... 65.00
Honey dish, WR Midwinter, 1946 & after, 4" dia, $40 to 45.00
Inkwells, dbl style, Booths mk, early 1900s, 8½", $550 to 650.00
Jardiniere, John Tams Ltd, after 1930, $300 to 350.00
Lamp, kerosene, ceramic shade, Japan, 11½", $125 to.................. 150.00
Leaf dish, unmk English, 6" 175.00
Match safe, Shenango, $75 to 85.00
Mug, shaving, Am, Buffalo Pottery, 1911, $125 to 150.00
Mustard pot, Shenango, $75 to 85.00
Napkin ring, unmk, $80 to 100.00
Pitcher, Staffordshire, late 19th C, 7" 125.00
Pitcher, Traditional center, Wedgwood, 11¼"............................... 150.00
Pitcher, triangular, Doulton, 1891-1902, 6", $250 to.................... 275.00
Plate, dessert, sq, Traditional pattern, Washington Pottery, $15 to..18.00
Plate, dinner, Johnson Bros, after 1912, $25 to.............................. 35.00
Plate, grill, Booth's center pattern, Bowknot border, 10¾" 35.00
Plate, grill, MIJ, 10", $35 to 45.00
Plate, grill, Made in Poland, 10", $25 to 35.00
Platter, fish, gold trim, Minton, 1880, 10½x11½", $800 to........ 1,000.00
Platter, oval, James Kent, ca 1950s, 14x11", $100 to 125.00

Platter, well and tree, nineteenth century, 22", EX, $325.00. (Photo courtesy Kaminski Auctions on LiveAuctioneers.com)

Punch bowl, 7x9¼", $300 to.. 400.00
Relish tray, Booth's center pattern, Bowknot border, Wood & Sons, 9"... 30.00
Relish, sq, Doulton, in nickel silver fr mk Beresford EPNS, 1891-1902..285.00
Soap pad holder, mk Japan, $60 to 70.00
Spice set, in wooden holder, 5 shakers, 2 ceramic drws, Japanese, $175 to.225.00
Spoon rest, dbl rests, Japan, 9", $40 to 50.00
Tea jar, Jappa, 8-sided, Gibson, 1912-30, 7", $225 to 250.00
Teapot, Doulton, 1882-90, $250 to 300.00
Teapot, gold finial & trim, Sadler & Sons, ca 1947, 2-cup, $70 to. 80.00
Teapot, Mintons, England, early 1900s, $300 to 350.00
Teapot, North Staffordshire Pottery Co, 4-cup, ca 1940s, $70 to... 85.00
Teapot, unmk Homer Laughlin, $60 to 70.00
Toast rack, Grimwades, 1930, $120 to 140.00
Toothbrush holder, Made in England, Doulton mk, ca 1930, $150 to..175.00
Tumbler, juice, glass, Jeannette, 3" 12.00
Tureen, soup, Traditional center, Ridgways, 1912-27 mk, 7¾x11".. 45.00
Washbowl/pitcher, Flow Blue, Doulton, 1891-1902, $1,800 to.2,000.00

Boch Freres

Founded in the early 1840s in La Louviere, Boch Freres Keramis became the foremost producer of art pottery in Belgium. Though primarily they served a localized market, in 1844 they earned worldwide recognition for some of their sculptural works on display at the International Exposition in Paris.

In 1907 Charles Catteau of France was appointed head of the art department. Before that time, the firm had concentrated on developing glazes and perfecting elegant forms. The style they pursued was traditional, favoring the re-creation of established eighteenth-century ceramics.

Catteau brought with him to Boch Freres the New Wave (or Art Nouveau) influence in form and decoration. His designs won him international acclaim at the Exhibition d'Art Decoratif in Paris in 1925, and it is for his work that Boch Freres is so highly regarded today. He occasionally signed his work as well as that of others who under his direct supervision carried out his preconceived designs. He was associated with the company until 1950 and lived the remainder of his life in Nice, France, where he died in 1966. The Boch Freres Keramis factory continues to operate today, producing bathroom fixtures and other utilitarian wares. A variety of marks have been used, most incorporating some combination of 'Boch Freres,' 'Keramis,' 'BFK,' or 'Ch Catteau.' A shield topped by a crown and flanked by a 'B' and an 'F' was used as well.

Bowl, bird of paradise/flower int, rstr to ft, 5x14".......................1,900.00
Box, Deco floral, mc on blk & gr stripes, La Louviere, 2⅞x4⅝"... 300.00
Box, floral on wht crackle, petals on lid, ormolu, La Louviere, 4x6" ... 175.00
Box, floral-on-blk stripes alternate w/gr, La Louviere, 3x4" 300.00
Charger, horse-drawn sleigh w/riders, Delft style, 15" 125.00
Lamp base, Deco floral, mc on tan crackle, Catteau, 6½"............. 165.00
Stein, seated robed man in Gothic arch, brn/tan pottery, 8", EX. 165.00
Tiles, set of 44, all mk Boch Freres Maubeuce, 6¾", NM........... 1,000.00
Vase, antelopes on ivory crackle, ovoid, Catteau, #D943, ca 1925, 10" ..1,175.00
Vase, birds (stylized) in panels, brn/cream crackle, Catteau/#931, 11".. 9,000.00
Vase, birds on branches form band on brn, Catteau, #1348, rstr, 7" ...1,200.00
Vase, birds on branches, mc on wht crackle, D1322, 12x7" 1,025.00
Vase, blk sphere w/fired-on parallel silver lines, #894, 9⅛" 600.00
Vase, Deco floral band atop vertical stripes, Catteau, 10½".......1,450.00
Vase, Deco floral on tan pebbled ground, #889, 8⅜" 240.00
Vase, Deco floral, 3-color, Catteau, La Louviere, #898C, 11".....2,400.00
Vase, deer in cuerda seca, turq/indigo on wht crackle, 9x8½" 800.00
Vase, deer in relief, fired-on silver accents on blk, #1221, 9½"..... 660.00
Vase, elk (stylized) leaping, brn tones, Catteau, #1291, 9⅛" 6,000.00
Vase, floral on copper lustre, floral neck band, 8" 400.00
Vase, floral stripes on wht crackle, ovoid, Fabrication Belge, 20x11".5,250.00
Vase, floral, mc on blk & yel stripes, brass rim, #D681, 10x5"...... 350.00

Vase, incised grazing deer on both sides, cracked ground accented in cobalt blue and turquoise, #D-943, incised #1291, Catteau design, 9½", $790.00. (Photo courtesy DuMouchelles on LiveAuctioneers.com)

Vase, Nouveau floral on gr shading to bl, bulb, 7" 265.00
Vase, penguins in cuerda seca, blk/M/wht, #976, 14½x13½".....9,600.00
Vase, rows of lappets, bl/wht/blk/tan, Catteau, La Louviere, #986, 11". 5,750.00
Vase, squirrel reserves (3), blk & gold, #2237, 8¾", NM.............. 360.00

Boehm

Boehm sculptures were the creation of Edward Marshall Boehm, a ceramic artist who coupled his love of the art with his love of nature to produce figurines of birds, animals, and flowers in lovely background settings accurate to the smallest detail. Sculptures of historical figures and those representing the fine arts were also made and along with many of the bird figurines, have established secondary-market values many times their original prices. His first pieces were made in the very early 1950s in Trenton, New Jersey, under the name of Osso Ceramics. Mr. Boehm died in 1969, and the firm has since been managed by his wife. Today known as Edward Marshall Boehm, Inc., the private family-held corporation produces not only porcelain sculptures but collector plates as well. Both limited and non-limited editions of their works have been issued. Examples are marked with various backstamps, all of which have incorporated the Boehm name since 1951. 'Osso Ceramics' in upper case lettering was used in 1950 and 1951. Our advisor for this category is Leon Reimert; he is listed in the Directory under Pennsylvania.

American Redstarts, #447V, 11½" 325.00
Arctic Tern, #78, 19x22" 750.00
Bird of Paradise, Helen Boehm/FJ Cansentins, #58, 15x11x10". 1,025.00
Blue Grosbeak, #489, 11" 215.00
Catbird among hyacinths, #483, 14" 480.00
Chickadee (chick) on pine branch, #461Y, 1962-72, 3" 150.00
Chipmunk, #514-01, 3" 150.00
Deer Mouse, #400-89, 3¾x7½" 95.00
Great Egret, Helen Boehm, #867/40221, 12x17" 660.00

Gyr Falcon #10178, Rusticlos, limited edition, circa 1990, 34x32", $1,560.00. (Photo courtesy Dallas Auction Gallery on LiveAuctioneers.com)

Hooded Merganser (male) on hollow log w/fish in beak, #4966, 10".. 700.00
Lesser Prairie Chickens, #464G, 10", NM.................................... 150.00
Mockingbirds, #439, 12" 335.00
Mountain Bluebirds, #470, 12" 1,800.00
Mourning Doves on stump, #443, 14" 425.00
Nuthatch on branch w/ivy, #469U, 10" 240.00
Osprey in flight along cattails, 26" 1,100.00
Owl, winter plumage, #40122, 5" 150.00
Parula Warblers, #484, 16" 600.00
Puffin (chick), #RPC-514-01, ca 1973, 5" 150.00
Robin beside daffodil, #472, 15" 900.00
Robin beside nest w/eggs, #143, 9" 840.00
Rufus Hummingbirds among lg yel flower, #487, 14"................ 1,400.00
Schnauzer, #40144, 5x5" 185.00
Sweet Pea, shell w/flowers, #25010, 6" 250.00
Tree Sparrow on log, #468, 8".. 110.00
Trumpeter Swan, #112, 14½x18½".. 425.00
Tufted Titmice, #482P, 13½".. 425.00
Tutenkhamen Sacred Cow, #513, 12" 135.00
Woodcock, oval base, #413, 10½" 300.00
Yellow-Throated Warbler, #481, 9" 300.00
Young Am Bald Eagle, #498, mid-20th C, 10" 300.00

Bohemian Glass

The term 'Bohemian glass' has come to refer to a type of glass developed in Bohemia in the late sixteenth century at the Imperial Court of Rudolf II, the Hapsburg Emperor. The popular artistic pursuit of the day was stone carving, and it naturally followed to transfer familiar procedures to the glassmaking industry. During the next century, a formula was discovered that produced a glass with a fine crystal appearance which lent itself well to deep, intricate engraving, and the art was further advanced.

Although many other kinds of art glass were made there, we are using the term 'Bohemian glass' to indicate glass overlaid or stained with color

through which a design is cut or etched. (Unless otherwise described, the items in the listing that follows are of this type.) Red or yellow on clear glass is common, but other colors may also be found. Another type of Bohemian glass involves cutting through and exposing two layers of color in patterns that are often very intricate. Items such as these are sometimes further decorated with enamel and/or gilt work.

Vase, red stain, woodland scene with stag, 8¾", $175.00. (Photo courtesy Bill Hood & Sons Art & Antiques Auctions on LiveAuctioneers.com)

Beaker, amber, Rheinstein Castle scene, 1860s, 5" 175.00
Beaker, red stain, cut circles, 1900, 5½" 65.00
Beaker, red, hunting dogs & birds, ca 1870, 6" 225.00
Beaker, ruby o/l, cameo cut knight w/sword, ca 1850-60, rare, 6" ... 2,000.00
Beaker, wht o/l, HP floral, stained/cut panels, 1860, 5" 250.00
Bowl, red, gilt/enamel scrolls, scalloped, ftd, 20th C, 8" dia.......... 75.00
Decanter, red, stag/scrolls/castle, slim neck, 20th C, 10" 75.00
Pitcher, red stain, woodland scene, late 19th C, 6" 225.00
Pokal, red stain, woodland deer, ca 1900, 11½", pr...................... 700.00
Pokal, ruby o/l, stags/trees, bk: reducing lens, facet lid, 1860, 14" ... 1,725.00
Pokal, ruby, o/l, stags in forest, fluted/faceted lid, 1850-60, 16".. 3,750.00
Powder box, cranberry opaline w/HP foliage & gold, 19th C, 2¼x4" . 250.00
Tumbler, bl stain, hunting dogs/trees, ca 1890, 4" 150.00
Vase, amber, floral/deer/castle, ca 1900, 14" 135.00
Vase, gr stain, deer & castle, ca 1930, 12" 100.00
Vase, red stain, hunting scenes, ca 1900, 13", pr.......................... 600.00

Bookends

Though a few were produced before 1880, bookends became a necessary library accessory and a popular commodity after the printing industry was revolutionized by Mergenthaler's invention, the linotype. Books became abundantly available at such affordable prices that almost every home suddenly had need for bookends. They were carved from wood; cast in iron, bronze, or brass; or cut from stone. Chalkware and glass were used as well. Today's collectors may find such designs as ships, animals, flowers, and children. Patriotic themes, art reproductions, and those with Art Nouveau and Art Deco styling provide a basis for a diverse and interesting collection.

Currently, figural cast-iron pieces are in demand, especially examples with good original polychrome paint. This has driven the value of painted cast-iron bookends up considerably.

For further information we recommend Collector's Encyclopedia of Bookends by Louis Kuritzky and Charles De Costa (Collector Books). Mr. Kuritzky is our advisor for this category; he is listed in the Directory under Florida. See also Arts and Crafts; Bradley and Hubbard.

Airedales, Gorham, bronze, EB Parsons, mk, ca 1920, 5½" 1,900.00
Alden & Priscilla, poly, Bradley & Hubbard, 5¾" 195.00
Angelfish, gray metal on polished stone base,attr JB Hirsch, ca 1930, 6".120.00
Bass, alum, Bruce Fox, mk, ca 1950, 7" 175.00
Belly Dancer, gray metal, ca 1930, 6¾" 300.00
Bird Takes a Bow, bronze, ca 1925, 7½" 350.00
Bonnet Lady, bronze, Armor Bronze, mk, ca 1924, 9" 450.00
Bull & Bear, bronze, Gorham, mk, ca 1920, 5¼" 2,700.00
Butterfly Girl, CI, ca 1925, 5⅞"... 295.00

Campfire Girls of America, Kathodion Bronze Works, mk, ca 1925, 7½". 400.00
Childhood Au Natural, gray metal base, AMG, ca 1925, 9" 750.00
Classic Minstrel, brass, Judd, expandable, ca 1925, 6" 125.00
Classic Polar Bear, gray metal, Ronson, ca 1930, 6½" 325.00
Colonial Couple, bronze, ca 1925, 6" 375.00
Country Dogs, bronze, Made in Austria, ca 1920, 5" 475.00
Drinking Flamingo, bronze, Made in Austria, ca 1920, 7" 650.00
Gazelle, glass, Steuben, ca 1935, 6½" 750.00
Gnome in Library, CI base, metal, Bradley & Hubbard, 1924, 5". 195.00
Great Moment (A), CI, ca 1925, 5" 125.00
Griffin, gray metal, K&O, Yellowstone Park, poly, mk, ca 1932, 5¾".. 275.00
Hall's Bookcase, SW Hall, bakelite, mk, ca 1928, 5¾" 350.00
Hunters, bronze, Laboy Trauy, mk, 1930, 8¾" 1,000.00
James Whitcomb Riley, CI, Bradley & Hubbard, ca 1925, 5½" 75.00
Jaybird, pottery, Rookwood, mk #2829, XXIX, 1929, 5½" 550.00
Kingfisher, bronze in marble enclosure, Made in Austria, ca 1928, 5¾".250.00
Kneeling Nude, gray metal, ca 1933, 5" 110.00
Lincoln Profile, CI, CT Foundry, mk, 1930 .... 110.00
Little Goas, Gorham, bronze, ca 1904, 4½" 1,200.00
Longhorn Gazelle, gray metal, Crescent Metal Works, 1932, 7¼" ..160.00
Mantarani's Dante, Galvano Bronze, ca 1925, 6" 175.00
Mr Winkle's First Shot, bronze, mk, England, 1953, 4¾" 150.00
Nouveau Girls, gray metal, Judd, ca 1920, 5" 110.00
Pennsylvania State Police, brass, CJR Steward, mk, 1946, 6¼" ... 125.00
Perched Peacock, CI, mk, Bradley & Hubbard, ca 1925, 6½" 135.00
Pig, bronze, ca 1930, 8½" 110.00
Platinum Girls, gray metal, att Greist Inc, ca 1927, 7" 300.00
Playful Terriers, bronze, Zoppo Foundry, mk, 1914, 7" 1,200.00
Poetry & Thought, bronze, attr Roman Bronze Works, I Konti, mk, 1911, 9"..3,800.00
Pontiac, alum, Bruce Fox, mk, paper tag, 1983, 6" 65.00
Puppy Triplets, gray metal, Ronson, company paper tag, ca 1925, 6".. 175.00
Queen of the Nile, Ronson, ca 1924 .... 375.00

Raggedy Ann and Andy, painted cast iron, P. F. Volland and Co., copyright 1931, rare, 6", $1,920.00.
(Photo courtesy Dan Morphy Auctions, LLC on LiveAuctioneers.com)

Rhinoceros, bronze, Gorham, AV Hyatt, mk, 6½" 3,000.00
Russian Wolfhound, CI, CT Foundry, mk, #933, ca 1929, 5¼" 125.00
Sailor Boy & Dog, gray metal, Frankart, mk, ca 1934, 6¾" 175.00
Sowing Farmer, bronze, HMH (Austria), ca 1920, 4¼" 850.00
Thorn Boy, Galvano Bronze, ca 1925, 5½" 400.00
Toddlers, bronze, Griffoul, A Eberle, 1911, 6½" 1,200.00
Viking Spirit, CI, ca 1928, 5¼" 110.00
Warbler, gray metal, Nuart, mk, a 1930 .... 225.00
White Elephants, gray metal, ca 1930, 4¾" 75.00
Wisdom Well, CI, Littco, a 1929, 5½" 75.00
Woodpecker, gray metal, marble base, Franjou, mk, ca 1930, 7" .. 175.00
Working for Peanuts, CI, ca 1925, 4½" 75.00

Bootjacks and Bootscrapers

Bootjacks were made from metal or wood. Some were fancy figural shapes, others strictly business. Their purpose was to facilitate the otherwise awkward process of removing one's boots. Bootscrapers were handy gadgets that provided an effective way to clean the soles of mud and such.

Bootjacks

Aluminum, bull's head, Ricardo, worn pnt 55.00
Brass, Longhorn steer, brass, 10" 15.00
Brass, sunflower, Musselman's Plug advertising 150.00
Cast iron American Bull Dog, pistol shape, blk pnt, 8" 90.00
Cast iron & wood, lever action, EX 150.00
Cast iron, beetle-shaped jaws, no pnt, ca 1880 .... 50.00
Cast iron, Boss emb on shaft, lacy, 15" L...................................... 135.00
Cast iron, cat silhouette, blk pnt, 10½x10" 295.00
Cast iron, cricket, Harvester Bros & Co, Reading PA, 11x4¾".... 110.00
Cast iron, Labrador retriever, 3x10x4¾" 15.00
Cast iron, moose, 11x8" 15.00
Cast iron, Naughty Nellie, nudy lady on bk, no pnt, 9½".............. 75.00
Wood w/brass hinges, unfolds, att military, 19th C, 10¼x2" 1,200.00
Wood, fish (stylized), cvd wood, worn finish, 22" L..................... 115.00
Wrought iron, scrolled top, granite base, early............................. 280.00

Bootscrapers

Brass, Scottie dogs (2) sit between wall (scraper), 4x10½" 85.00
Cast iron, 2 figures at log holding crosscut saw, ca 1900, 5x16x2". 560.00
Cast iron, beetle form, orig pnt 85.00
Cast iron, black man sits above base, rust/soiling, 13x10", EX 225.00
Cast iron, black shoeshine boy atop, oval base, 13", VG.............. 140.00

Cast iron, cat with incised whiskers and long tail, black paint, 17½" long, $1,200.00.
(Photo courtesy Cowan's Auctions, Inc. on LiveAuctioneers.com)

Cast iron, cat w/long tail sticking up, 10x15" 35.00
Cast iron, dachshund, blk rpt, 5x5x13"... 50.00
Cast iron, dachshund, no pnt, tail forms ring, 10½x7½x7" 185.00
Cast iron, duck, full body, 14" L 350.00
Cast iron, horseshoe mtd on rimmed base, 9x11x9" 2,500.00
Cast iron, pan base w/flared rim & emb decor, pitting, 17x13x16" ..195.00
Cast iron, Scottie dog in fr, ca 1940s, 7x4x7", $100 to................. 150.00
Wrought iron, ram's-horn scrolls, marble block 150.00
Wrought iron, scrolled finial (detailed), 21x24" 500.00

Antonio Borsato

Borsato was a remarkable artist/sculptor who produced some of the most intricately modeled and executed figurines ever made. He was born in Italy and at an early age enjoyed modeling wildlife from clay he dug from the river banks near his home. At age 11, he became an apprentice of Guido Cacciapuotti of Milan, who helped him develop his skills. During the late '20s and '30s, he continued to concentrate on wildlife studies. Because of his resistance to the fascist government, he was interred at Sardinia from 1940 until the end of the war, after which he returned to Milan where he focused his attention on religious subjects. He entered the export market in 1948 and began to design pieces featuring children and more romantic themes. By the 1960s his work had become very popular in this country. His talent for creating lifelike figures has seldom been rivaled. He contributed much of his success to the fact that each of his figures, though built from the same molded pieces, had its own personality, due the unique way he would tilt a head or position an arm. All had eyelashes, fingernails, and defined musculature; and each piece was painted by hand with antiquated colors and signed 'A. Borsato.' He made over 600 different models, with some of his groups requiring more than 160 components and several months of work to reach completion. Various pieces were made in two mediums, gres and porcelain, with porcelain being double the cost of gres. Borsato died in 1982. Today, some of his work is displayed in the Vatican Museum as well as in private collections.

Antique Dealer (The), 11½x16", $850.00 to $900.00. (Photo courtesy Gulfcoast Coin & Jewelry on LiveAuctioneers.com)

Boulevardier, man seated on rustic bench, 6x5"	1,350.00
Bullfighter, man on rearing horse charges bull, 13½x18½"	18,000.00
Chestnuts & Tales, girl on box by stove w/old man, 10½"	1,400.00
Child's Prayer, child on lady's lap w/hands folded, 8x6x9"	1,925.00
Cobbler's Dilemma, man & boy at bench, 10½x7½x8½"	2,900.00
Coffee Counter, 3 figures surrounding coffee urn, 10x9"	4,000.00
Columbine, lady in costume from comedy opera, 6⅛"	475.00
Comfort & Love, lady & dog in interior, 12x22"	13,600.00
Cowboy w/guitar, man seated on saddle w/instrument, 6¼"	500.00
Dog Trainer, man working w/upright poodle, 6x9½"	1,600.00
Expresso Vendors, 2 men & 1 woman at coffee stand, 8x11x7"	2,450.00
Fiddler's Revelry, man seated/playing fiddle, 6x10"	2,140.00
Golden Years, 9"	225.00
Grandma's Well, lady/child/goose at well, 10x12"	5,125.00
Lover's Lane, figures in horse-drawn carriage on base, 11x24"	8,775.00
Man w/pipe, head of old man w/eyes closed smoking pipe, 7½"	250.00
Miss Fragrance, lady seated in chair w/legs crossed, 6½"	550.00
Mother & Child, mother wrapping baby in blanket, 6½x6"	650.00
Musketeer (bust of) in plumed hat, 9x12"	375.00
Psyche & Eros, classical couple on base, 7¾x8"	1,575.00
Rescue, man on horse lifting woman up by waist, 12x15"	6,800.00
Sailor & Old Lady, aged couple seated on rocks, 7¾x7"	775.00
Serenity, lady by sm tree w/birds, butterfly on finger, 9½"	3,000.00
Siesta's Price, fruit cart, peddler asleep, case drw being robbed	3,200.00
Spring Song, 2 birds on branch, 6"	485.00

Bossons Artware

The late William Henry Bossons (W. H. Bossons) founded Bossons in 1946. It was under his direction and artistic genius that most of the numerous ever-popular Floral plaques were produced. When he died in 1951, his son, W. Ray Bossons (WRB) took charge and in 1958 oversaw the designing of the first 'character wall masks' (called wall 'heads'). Ray inherited and applied exceptional artistic abilities to Bossons, and as a photographer, he designed and produced the colorful advertisements and brochures that helped expose Bossons to the entire world.

Though over the years he employed many freelance sculptors and painters (Stefan Czarnota, Patricia Easterbrook Roberts, Colin Melbourne, Basil Ede, Kay Nixon Blundell, and Doris Condliffe, to name a few), WRB had many loyal employees that worked their entire adult lives at Bossons. Principal sculptors/modelers of Bossons were Fred Wright (1957 – 1972, deceased), Alice Wilde Brindley (1952 and 1971 – 1995), and Ray Bossons (1951 – 1993, deceased), who oversaw all Bossons creations and made sure that they met the highest standards of excellence.

It is extremely important to note that there are a limited number of rare, collectible Bossons products that are made of fired pottery. In some cases, the Bossons pottery products have limited ('Made in England' or 'Bossons England') or no copyright markings or incisions. Deemed experimental by Bossons, they include The Jazz Figures, Modern Dance Figures, Pooch and Patch Dogs, Garden Figures (pottery gnomes), National Head Vases, Miniature African Masks, Bookends, Sets of Birds, Aboriginal Plaques, Scenic Plaques with ornate frames, and many table lamps of various sizes and shapes including the TV Night Lights depicting water and windmills.

The closing of all operations in December 1996 has caused a rise in values for most Bossons. The authenticity of Bossons's products has been troublesome for several reasons: production records were only kept for one or two years; the company produced a large number of experimental models; and there are many variations in material substance, mold structure, color, and in copyrights. Gypsum-plaster products made by Bossons continue to be copied and fraudulently molded, principally on the internet. Amateur touchups in color and intentionally changing and defacing the original Bossons colorings are very serious violations found on the internet. Legend products are not Bossons. Except for a very few known examples (see the larger version of the 1959 Red Setter Dog or the Series B Smuggler Mask), plaster 'heads/faces' that are simply incised with 'Made in England' are not Bossons. One of the easiest ways to recognize an authentic Bossons is by viewing the reverse/back side. The back is most often silver, and the hanging mechanism may be protruding or recessed, a factor that is sometimes helpful in determining production dates. Though the mark has changed slightly over the years, an authentic Bossons will have the following copyright incision on the back: BOSSONS Congleton England World Copyright Reserved. Regardless of when they were produced or released, most Bossons had their own copyright date. The release and production dates (not the same as the copyright) were most often one to two years later.

Though scarcity is a prime worth-assessing factor, condition is enormously important in determining value. 'Mint' in box examples can command several hundred dollars, though the original cardboard boxes for the most early dated and valuable Bossons have been discarded. Popular Bossons produced in mid-1960 to early 1990 are found in great numbers. Many can be readily purchased for under $100.00. But condition is critical! With only a few facial blemishes, plentiful Bossons are not worth more than $10.00 to $20.00. Especially when new products are available for reasonable prices and unless for sentimental reasons, professional restorations of these common Bossons are impractical due to the time involved and resultant cost. As a general rule, early editions, those produced from 1957 to 1959, and from the early '60s sell for the highest prices. Literature by Bossons such as large descriptive, color brochures and the miniature folders that they published nearly every year is also collectible.

Our values are for items that are in new condition, in their original boxes. (Where dates are given they are release dates, not copyright dates.) For more information on the *Bossons Briefs* newsletter, refer to the Clubs, Newsletters, and Websites section. Our advisor for Bossons is Donald Hardisty; you can find him in the Directory under New Mexico.

Abduhl, 1961-89, $85 to	125.00
Aruj Barbarossa (Redbeard), Seafarer collection, Series B, 1996, 5", $225 to	285.00
Betsey Trotwood, w/bl collar, 1964-82, $125 to	150.00
Betsey Trotwood, w/pk collar, 1982-96, $65 to	85.00
Birds & Sunflowers, 1969-70, $475 to	750.00
Blackbeard, 1993-96, $145 to	175.00
Boatman, $85 to	125.00
Captain Pierre Le Grand, $150 to	225.00
Carnival Annie, 1961-63, $600 to	900.00
Carnival Joe, 1961-63, $500 to	900.00
Cheyenne w/red coat, 1970-92, $165 to	200.00

Cheyenne, bare arm, no coat, 1970-71, $6,500 to 7,500.00
Churchill, Winston, gilded, 1 issue, 1966, $750 to 1,200.00
Clipper Captain, $165 to 185.00
Coolie, 1964-70, $150 to 165.00
Cossack, Russian Guard, 1996, $200 to 275.00
Dickens Characters, 1964-96, $85 to 145.00

Espana, 1959, 9", $6,500.00 to $7,500.00. (Photo courtesy Donald Hardisty)

Evzon, $185 to 275.00
Floral Plaque, circular, Autumn Gold, 1982-96, 14", $185 to 250.00
Fly-Fisherman, $175 to 200.00
Golfer, $150 to 185.00
Highwayman, 1966-69, $225 to 350.00
Indian Chief, 1961-64, $350 to 500.00
Jolly Tar, 1988-96, $135 to 175.00
Karim, 1967-69, $145 to 165.00
King Henry VIII, 1986-94, $175 to 250.00
Kurd, 1964-96, $45 to 65.00
Lifeboatman, 1966-96, $85 to 145.00
Military Masks, w/o eyes, ea $350 to 500.00
Nigerian Woman, 1961-62, $900 to 1,450.00
Nuvolari, 1996, $185 to 250.00
Paddy, 1969-96, $75 to 85.00
Paddy, blk hair, 1959, $125 to 145.00
Paddy, issued for IBCS, must have sgn certificate, $185 to 200.00
Parson, $145 to 165.00
Persian, $45 to 85.00
Rawhide, 1968-96, $85 to 145.00
Rob Roy, 1995-96, $175 to 200.00
Santa Claus, 1995-96, $175 to 250.00
Shepherd, 1995-96, $150 to 175.00
Sherlock Holmes, 1984-96, $150 to 175.00
Sinbad, $250 to 325.00
Smuggler, $45 to 65.00
Squire, $125 to 165.00
Syrian, 1960-96, $50 to 85.00
Tecumseh, 1962-96, $165 to 185.00
Tulip Time, 1994-96, $175 to 225.00
White Swan, Fraser-Art (PVC), 1970-71, $750 to 900.00

Bottle Openers

At the beginning of the nineteenth century, manufacturers began to seal bottles with a metal cap that required a new type of bottle opener. Now the screw cap and the flip top have made bottle openers nearly obsolete. There are many variations, some in combination with other tools. Many openers were used as means of advertising a product. Various materials were used, including silver and brass.

A figural bottle opener is defined as a figure designed for the sole purpose of lifting a bottlecap. The actual opener must be an integral part of the figure itself. A base-plate opener is one where the lifter is a separate metal piece attached to the underside of the figure. The major producers

of iron figurals were Wilton Products, John Wright Inc., Gadzik Sales, and L & L Favors. Openers may be free standing and three dimensional, wall hung or flat. They can be made of cast iron (often painted), brass, bronze, or aluminum.

Numbers within the listings refer to a reference book printed by the FBOC (Figural Bottle Opener Collectors) organization. The items below are all in excellent original condition unless noted otherwise. For information on the Just for Openers club, see the Clubs, Newsletters, and Websites section. Our advisor for this category is Barbara Rosen; she is listed in the Directory under New Jersey.

4-eyed woman w/lg front teeth, CI, worn mc pnt 45.00
Alligator & Black Boy, souvenir Tybart Dam, F-133, 3x4½" 400.00
Billy goat, brass, Made in Canada, 4x2½" 38.00
Boy winking, CI, worn pnt, Wilton...70.00
Caddy, black, NPCI & mc pnt, #F44, 5" 275.00
Clown, CI, mc pnt, 3 holes for wall mt, 4½x4", VG 60.00
Cockatoo, CI, mc pnt, John Wright, #F121 ....120.00
Cocker spaniel, John Wright, 3¾" L 150.00
Drunken man hanging on to palm tree, CI, mc pnt, 4x2", NM 55.00
Elephant seated w/trunk up, CI, pnt traces, 3¾" 48.00
Elephant walking, trunk up, pnt CI, Wilton, 3¼" L 75.00
False Teeth, Wilton, F-420, 2½x3½" 230.00

Fish, painted cast iron, 5" long, $180.00. (Photo courtesy Randy Inman Auctions Inc. on LiveAuctioneers.com)

Foundry man, CI, mc pnt, John Wright, #F-29 ....65.00
German shepherd, Syroco 70.00
Goose, CI, mc pnt, Scott Products, 5¼x2¾x1½" 45.00
Greek lady, enamel on brass, Enamel Work on Solid Brass..., 5"....25.00
Hockey player, Molson Ice, place bottle in mouth, cap tray at chest..230.00
Hula girls & shaking palm tree, copper on metal w/mc enamel, 2x4¼"..45.00
Kansas Jayhawk, CI, mc pnt, 4x1¾" 75.00
Mallard duck, CI, mc pnt, John Wright, 1940s-50s, 2½" 58.00
Man at lamppost, Moosehead ME, CI, mc pnt, 4", NM 48.00
Modernist dog, Hagenauer style, shiny metal, Austria, 3x4½" 95.00
Nude lady, brass, Lions Illinois 1954, 5" 60.00
Parrot on tall perch, CI, mc pnt 150.00
Pelican on base, CI, mc pnt, 3¼" 60.00
Pirate face, N-622, CI, EX 230.00
Pointer hunting dog, CI, blk & wht pnt 2½x4⅜" 50.00
Rooster, CI, mc pnt, #F100..235.00
Seagull on stump, CI, mc pnt, 3¼" 48.00
Skunk, CI, mc pnt, 1940s, 2¼x3", NM 125.00
Squirrel, brass, 2x2¾" 45.00
Timberjack on base, metal, 3"..75.00

Bottles and Flasks

As far back as the first century B.C., the Romans preferred blown glass containers for their pills and potions. American business firms preferred glass bottles in which to package their commercial products and used them extensively from the late eighteenth century on. Bitters bottles contained 'medicine' (actually herb-flavored alcohol). Because of a heavy tax imposed on the sale of liquor in seventeenth-century

England by King George, who hoped to curtail alcohol abuse among his subjects, bottlers simply added 'curative' herbs to their brew and thus avoided taxation. Since gin was taxed in America as well, the practice continued in this country. Scores of brands were sold; among the most popular were Dr. H.S. Flint & Co. Quaker Bitters, Dr. Kaufman's Anti-Cholera Bitters, and Dr. J. Hostetter's Stomach Bitters. Most bitters bottles were made in shades of amber, brown, and aquamarine. Clear glass was used to a lesser extent, as were green tones. Blue, amethyst, red-brown, and milk glass examples are rare. Color is a strong factor when pricing bottles.

Perfume or scent bottles were produced by companies all over Europe from the late sixteenth century on. Perfume making became such a prolific trade that as a result beautifully decorated bottles were fashionable. In America they were produced in great quantities by Stiegel in 1770 and by Boston and Sandwich in the early nineteenth century. Cologne bottles were first made in about 1830 and toilet-water bottles in the 1880s. Rene Lalique produced fine scent bottles from as early as the turn of the century. The first were one-of-a-kind creations done in the cire perdue method. He later designed bottles for the Coty Perfume Company with a different style for each Coty fragrance. (See Lalique.)

Spirit flasks from the nineteenth century were blown in specially designed molds with varied motifs including political subjects, railroad trains, and symbolic devices. The most commonly used colors were amber, dark brown, and green.

Pitkin flasks were the creation of the Pitkin Glass Works which operated in East Manchester, Connecticut, from 1783 to 1830. However, other glasshouses in New England and the Midwest copied the Pitkin flask style. All are known as Pitkins.

From the twentieth century, early pop and beer bottles are very collectible as is nearly every extinct commercial container. Dairy bottles are also desirable; look for round bottles in good condition with both city and state as well as a nice graphic relating to the farm or the dairy.

Bottles may be dated by the methods used in their production. For instance, a rough pontil indicates a date before 1845. After the bottle was blown, a pontil rod was attached to the bottom, a glob of molten glass acting as the 'glue.' This allowed the glassblower to continue to manipulate the extremely hot bottle until it was finished. From about 1845 until approximately 1860, the molten glass 'glue' was omitted. The rod was simply heated to a temperature high enough to cause it to afix itself to the bottle. When the rod was snapped off, a metallic residue was left on the base of the bottle; this is called an 'iron pontil.' (The presence of a pontil scar thus indicates early manufacture and increases the value of a bottle.) A seam that reaches from base to lip marks a machine-made bottle from after 1903, while an applied or hand-finished lip points to an early mold-blown bottle. The Industrial Revolution saw keen competition between manufacturers, and as a result, scores of patents were issued. Many concentrated on various types of closures; the crown bottle cap, for instance, was patented in 1892. If a manufacturer's name is present, consulting a book on marks may help you date your bottle. For more information we recommend *Bottle Pricing Guide* by Hugh Cleveland.

Among our advisors for this category are Madeleine France (see Directory, Florida), Mark Vuono (see Directory, Connecticut), and Monsen and Baer (see Directory, Virginia). Values suggested below reflect hammer prices (plus buyer's premium) of bottles that were sold through cataloged auctions. See also Advertising, various companies; Blown Glass; Blown Three-Mold Glass; California Perfume Company; Czechoslovakia Collectibles; De Vilbiss; Firefighting Collectibles; Lalique; Steuben; Zanesville Glass.

Key:
am — applied mouth	bt — blob top
b3m — blown 3-mold	cm — collared mouth
bbl — barrel	fm — flared mouth

gm — ground mouth	rm — rolled mouth
grd — ground pontil	sb — smooth base
GW — Glass Works	shm — sheared mouth
ip — iron pontil	sl — sloping
op — open pontil	tm — tooled mouth
ps — pontil scar	

Barber Bottles

Amethyst, mc geometric floral, rm, ps, mallet form, 7⅝" 80.00
Blue-gr, Mary Gregory girl w/twig, rm, ps, 8" 275.00

Blue opaque with hand-painted hunting scene and Bay Rum, rare, 8¾", $900.00. (Photo courtesy Rich Penn Auctions on LiveAuctioneers.com)

Canary yel opal, Hobnail, rm, ps, 6¾", EX 50.00
Clear frost, palm tree in gr & wht, tm, sb, 8⅛" 1,100.00
Clear w/red flashing, yel & silver floral, ribs, ps, 7⅞" 375.00
Clear w/ruby flashed int, Hobnail, rm, ps, 7½", EX 70.00
Clear, floral, mc on pk, tm, ps, 8" 375.00
Cranberry opal, wht swirl, tm, ps, 7⅛" 450.00
Dark amethyst, Bay Rum/grist mill, ribs, ps, 7" 325.00
Dark amethyst, geometric mc floral, rm, 8" 100.00
Dark amethyst, Mary Gregory girl sitting, rm, ps, haze, 8" 110.00
Dark cobalt w/emb ribs, red/wht/gold enamel, ps, tm, 7¾" 80.00
Milk glass, Bay Rum & mc roses, tm, ps, 10⅜" 250.00
Milk glass, cherubs & roses, HP, 8" 310.00
Milk glass, cranes in mc, WT&Co on sb, tm, 9¼" 425.00
Milk glass, running horse in mc, sb, pewter cap, 9½" 425.00
Milk glass w/enamel cherubs on bl & yel, ca 1890-1925, 7¾" 350.00
Purple amethyst, fleur-de-lis in yel, tm, ps, 7½" 175.00
Turquoise, Hobnail, rm, ps, 6⅞" 125.00
Turquoise opal, wht swirl, tm, ps, 6⅞" 375.00
Turquoise w/gold & wht floral, emb ribs, tm, ps, 8" 325.00
White opal, Bay Rum in red, twisted swirl, tm, sb, 8¼" 200.00
White opal, Coinspot, rm, sb, 7⅛" 160.00
White opal, Hair Tonic in blk, mc tulips, rm, sb, 8⅝" 160.00
White opal, Sea Foam/swallows/roses, mc, tm, ps, 10⅜" 250.00
White opal, Stars & Stripes, rm, ps, 7⅛" 300.00
White opal, Swirl, tm, ps, 6¾" 300.00
White opal, Toilet Water/mc tulips, rm, sb, 8⅝" 100.00
Yellow amber, Hobnail, rm, ps, 6⅞", NM 110.00
Yellow gr, Mary Gregory girl w/twig, emb ribs, rm, ps, 8" 120.00

Bitters Bottles

1834 John Root's...Buffalo NY, aqua, tapered cm, sb, 10⅜" 600.00
African Stomach..., yel amber, tapered cm, sb, 9⅝" 160.00
Baker's Orange Grove, B-9, dk yel amber, sb, 9" 800.00
Big Bill Best... (2 sides), amber, tm, sb, NM label, 12¼" 425.00
Bissell's Tonic...1868...Peoria Ill, med amber to yel amber, sb, 9". 300.00
Bitters Wild Cherry...Reading PA, med amber, am, semi-cabin, 10"..400.00
Bourbon Whiskey Bitters, pk puce, sb, am, bbl, chips, 9" 275.00
Brown's Celebrated Indian Herb...1867, dk amber, sb, 12¼" 500.00

Brown's Celebrated Indian..., yel amber, sb, princess, 12¼" 1,700.00
Burdock Blood...Buffalo NY, aqua sample, tm, sb, open bubble, 4⅛".140.00
California Fig...San Francisco Cal, med amber, tm, sb, 9¾" 50.00
Congress/Congress, C-217, bl aqua, sb, sl cm, semi-cabin, 10"..... 200.00
Cooley's Anti-Dispeptic or Jaundice..., bl aqua, 8-panel roof, 6¼" . 1,400.00
Crookess Stomach, C-253, olive gr, sb, am, lady's leg, 10" 1,800.00
Dr CW Roback's Stomach..., yel olive, sl cm, sb, bbl, 1860-80, 9". 1,500.00
Dr CW Roback's...Cincinnati, amber, tapered cm, sb, bbl, 9⅜"... 275.00
Dr CW Roback's...Cincinnati O, yel amber, sb, stain, 9½" 300.00
Dr CW Roback's...Cincinnati O, yel olive amber, bbl, 9¼" 600.00
Dr Geo Pierce's Indian Restorative..., bl aqua, am, op, 7⅝" 350.00
Dr Henley's Wild Grape Root..., bl aqua, sb, am, crude, 12¼" 200.00
Dr J Hostetter's Stomach..., med to dk olive gr, cm, sb, crude, 9½". 250.00
Dr Loew's Celebrated...Cleveland O, med yel lime gr, sb, 3⅞" 220.00
Dr Loew's Celebrated...Cleveland O, med yel lime gr, sb, 9½" 400.00
Dr Stephen Jewett's..., J-37, gr aqua, red ip, am, EX label, 7" 450.00
Dr XX Lovegood's Family..., deep amber, sb, cabin, 9⅜"............. 1,000.00
Drake's Plantation...Pat 1862, D-102, dk cherry puce (blk), 10".. 550.00
Drake's Plantation...Pat 1862, D-103, med copper puce, sb, 6-log, 10".425.00
Drake's Plantation...Pat 1862, D-105, med yel olive, 6-log cabin, 10".. 2,750.00
Drake's Plantation...Pat 1862, D-106, cherry puce, sb, 6-log, 10".. 325.00
Drake's Plantation...Pat 1862, D-108, pk strawberry puce, 6-log, 10".. 550.00
Drake's Plantation...Pat 1862, D-109, med yel amber, 5-log, 9" ... 325.00
Drake's Plantation...Pat 1862, D-110, amber, sb, 4-log cabin, 10". 150.00
Drake's Plantation...Pat 1862, dk copper puce, sb, 6-log cabin, 10" . 180.00
Drake's Plantation...Pat 1862, dk strawberry puce, 6-log, D-105, 8". 220.00
Drake's Plantation...Pat 1862, med strawberry puce, 6-log cabin, 10". 750.00
Drake's Plantation...Pat 1862, yel amber w/olive tone, 4-log, 10" . 475.00
Edw Wilder...(building)...Patented, amethyst tint, semi-cabin, 10½".. 325.00
Established 1845 Schroeder's..., amber, lady's leg, 11⅜".................... 1,900.00
Great Tonic Caldwell's Herb, amber, am, ip, 12½" 300.00
Greeley's Bourbon Bitters, G-101, med chartreuse, sb, bbl, 9" ..2,750.00
Greeley's Bourbon Bitters, G-101, smoky copper topaz, sb, bbl, 9"... 425.00
Greeley's Bourbon Whiskey..., med apricot puce, bbl, sb, 9⅛" 700.00
Greeley's Bourbon, G-101, med olive gr, sb, bbl, prof rpr, 9"........ 350.00
Hall's...Est 1842, H-10, med amber, sb, am, NM label, 9" 550.00
Hall's...Est 1842, H-10, med yel amber, sg, G whittle, bbl, 9" 325.00
Hall's/EE Hall New Haven...1842, golden yel amber, sb, bbl, 9" .. 130.00
Holtzermann's Pat Stomach, H-154, med amber, 4-roof cabin, 9" ..800.00
Holtzermann's Pat Stomach, H-155, amber, sb, 2-roof cabin, 9" . 1,800.00

Hops & Malt..., med amber, sl cm, sb, semi-cabin, 9½" 400.00
Kelly's Old Cabin...1863, dk tobacco amber, sb, 2-story cabin, 9" .2,750.00
Keystone..., orange amber, cm, sb, bbl, 9¾" 750.00
Khoosh..., yel olive, dbl cm, sb, 8¼"... 100.00
Koehler & Hinrich's Red Star...Minn, yel amber, tm, sb, 11½".... 600.00
Lediard's Celebrated Stomach..., bl gr, sl dbl cm, sb, 10⅛" 1,700.00
Litthauer Stomach...Berlin, mg, gin form, sb, 9½" 100.00
Malabac...M Cziner Chemist, yel amber, semi lady's leg, 11¾" 700.00
Mckeever's Army..., med amber, cm, sb, cannonballs/drum, 10⅝" ...2,750.00
Mishler's Herb...Graduation, yel olive, cm, sb, stain, 9¼" 275.00

Moulton's Olorosa...Trade (pineapple) Mark, bl aqua, sb, 11¼"... 300.00
National, N-8, med amber, Pat 1867 on sb, ear of corn, 12¾" 300.00
Old Sachem...& Wigwam Tonic, med copper puce, am, sb, 9½"..600.00
Old Sachem...Wigwam Tonic, O-46, golden yel amber, sb, bbl, 9" ..550.00
Old Sachem...Wigwam Tonic, O-46, med copper topaz, sb, bbl, 9" .850.00
Pat'd 1884 Dr Petzold's...Incpt 1862, yel amber, sb, semi-cabin, 8" .300.00

Black Glass Bottles

Horse Hoof onion, med yel olive amber, sm w/appl string lip, 8". 165.00
Mallet, med yel olive gr, sm, ps, blown in dip mold, 7¼x4⅝"....... 325.00
Onion, emerald gr, ps, sm w/appl string lip, scuffs, 1720-50, 5" 90.00
Onion, med bl emerald gr, tm w/appl string lip, op, 1720-50, 7½" . 90.00
Onion, med bl gr, sm w/appl string lip, op, 1720-1750, 6½x5⅝".. 150.00
Onion, emerald gr, sm w/appl string lip, op, 1720-50, 6⅜x5⅝".... 130.00
Onion, med olive gr, sm w/appl string lip, op, haze, 7⅜x5¾" 100.00
Onion, med yel olive gr, sm w/appl string lip, op, 7¼x5½" 120.00
Onion, med yel olive w/amber tone, sm w/appl string lip, op, 7½"...80.00
Onion, yel gr, appl string lip, op, Dutch, chip, 5⅝x4⅝" 375.00
Seal: IC Hoffman, med olive gr, ps, dbl cm, cylinder, 8⅜".........3,325.00
Seal: Superfine Olive Oil...Clarified, med olive gr, op, 11".......... 180.00
Seal: V Led Giraudeao (snake/tree) Paris, yel olive gr, ps, 8⅜" ..1,300.00
Wine/ale, dk olive amber, IV on shoulder, am, ps, 9".................... 475.00

Blown Glass Bottles and Flasks

Chestnut flask, dk teal gr, appl lip & hdl, 6⅜" 125.00
Chestnut flask, med cobalt w/purple tone, 22 broken ribs, ps, tm, 5".375.00
Chestnut flask, med emerald gr, am, op, crude/bubbles, 5¾" 1,100.00
Globular, golden amber, tooled outward rm, ps, Midwest, mini, 3" ..1,200.00
Globular, yel amber w/16 ribs, att Mantua, blisters/bruise, 5".......840.00
Pitkin flask, bright yel gr, 16 right-swirl ribs, sm, ps, Midwest, 7".850.00
Pitkin flask, sea gr, 32 left-swirl ribs, sm, ps, Midwest, 6½"........... 500.00
Pitkin flask, yel root beer amber, 36 broken left-swirl ribs, 6".......950.00
Pocket flask, dk amber, 24 left-swirl ribs, sm, ps, Midwest, 4¾"....750.00
Teardrop, med emerald gr, outward rm, ps, pebble mks, 9¾" 110.00

Cologne, Perfume, and Toilet Water Bottles

Atomizer, bl cut to clear pinwheels, unmk, 5½" 60.00
Blown, lady's hand w/wedding ring, unmk, 5¼" L......................... 40.00
Cobalt, 12-sided w/sloped shoulders, ps, rm, 6"............................ 325.00
Corseted, 8-sided, cobalt, inward rm, ps, Sandwich, 6x2" 850.00
Crown top, Asian lady's head, pnt porc, Germany, 3" 250.00
Crown top, lady head, pk hat, pnt porc, Germany, #8051, 2¼".... 200.00
Crown top, lady's head, L earring, pnt porc, Germany, 2½" 150.00
Crown top, pirate's head, bl hat, pnt porc, Germany, #8057, 2⅜". 200.00
Cut o/l, red/crystal geometric pyramidal form, Saks 5th Ave, 5½" ..175.00
Dark grape amethyst, 12-sided w/sl shoulders, sb, rm, 4⅛" 145.00
Lundberg Studios, wht blossoms in dk bl, long dauber, 7¼" 195.00
Medium pk amethyst, 12-sided, sb, rm, 6½"................................. 115.00
Rectangular, powder bl, bulb neck, fm, ps, 1830-60, 5" 950.00

Sunburst, pontil scar, Am, ca 1810-30, deep cobalt bl, 18 beads ea side, 2" .525.00
Sunburst, pontil scar, Am, ca 1810-30, med teal gr (rare color), 2" ..2,750.00

Commercial Perfume Bottles

One of the most popular and growing areas of perfume bottle collecting is the 'commercial' perfume bottle. They are called commercial because they were sold with perfume in them — in a sense one pays for the perfume and the bottle is free. Collectors especially value bottles that retain their original label and box, called a perfume presentation. If the bottle is unopened, so much the better. Rare fragrances and those from the 1920s are highly prized. Our advisors are Randall Monsen and Rod Baer; they are listed in the Directory under Virginia. For more information we recommend *The Wonderful World of Collecting Perfume Bottles* by Jane Flanagan (Collector Books).

Ybry Femme de Paris, green cased crystal with enameled metal cap, with stopper, Baccarat, 1925, 2¾", original box, $600.00. (Photo courtesy Perfume Bottles Auction on LiveAuctioneers.com)

Annette, airplane w/bird pilot, blown, Germany, 1920s, 4⅜" 350.00
Bichara, Chypre, clear w/gold, paneled, wigged man's-head dauber, 6" ...1,000.00
Caron, Infini, plastic stopper w/mirror image of bottle, 4⅜", MIB...100.00
Caron, Royal Bain de Champagne, wine bottle form, 10½", MIB. 200.00
Chu Chin Chow, Asian figure seated, mc, Bryenne, 1918, 2½" .1,675.00
Corday, Orchidee Bleue, flower form, Baccarat, 3" 300.00
Coty, Le Vertige, clear w/gold cap, gold label, 2¼", MIB.............. 100.00
D'Orsay, Bel de Jour, wht satin, emb ribbon, 3" 300.00
D'Orsay, Muguet, gold label, faceted ball stopper, 4", MIB........... 600.00
Elizabeth Arden, Cyclamen, wht & clear fan shape w/gold, Baccarat, 6" .. 1,750.00
Elizabeth Arden, My Love, clear, plume dauber, 3", +box w/Lucite front.. 425.00
Fabergé, Woodhue, blk lettering, wooden cap, mini, 2½", +bag, MIB.45.00
Gai Montmartre, windmill, red w/pnt brass lid, 1926, to roof: 4¾" ..2,350.00
Gilbert Orcel, Coup de Chapeau, mg lady w/gold, 5" 300.00
H Rubinstein, Town, canteen form w/blk enameling, 3⅜", MIB.. 250.00
Houbigant, Chantilly, gold 17th-C figures, Baccarat, 7", MIB 500.00
J Patou, Amour Amour, gold & bl labels, Baccarat, 1924, 3½", MIB.. 450.00
L Lelong, Murmure, rect stopper, gold/wht label, 2", +box base... 200.00
L Lelong, Parfum J, 4-sided, gold stopper, 2½", +atomizer, MIB... 200.00
Lentheric, Ambre-Mousse, clear w/gr o/l, lady on whale, Baccarat, 5" .450.00
Lentheric, Babana, rect, gold/wht label, 2¼", MIB......................... 50.00
Lentheric, Pink Party, clear w/gold cap, yel label, 2⅜", MIB.......... 50.00
Mary Chess, White Lilac, chess castle form, 3", MIB 150.00
Ming Toy, Asian figure seated w/fan, mc, Baccarat, 1923, 4⅜"..3,250.00
Richard Hudnut, Extreme Violet, mc label, sealed, 4", +floral/eagle box.300.00
Rochambeau, cat figural, clear frost, Rochambeau, ca 1924, 3".... 600.00
Schiaparelli, Shocking Body Radiance, Dali art front, 5¼" 400.00
Schiaparelli, Snuff, pipe form w/amber stopper (stem), 5⅜", MIB.... 450.00
Silka, Ombre du Soir, rect, leather cover, Baccarat, 3" 1,875.00
Vando, Julius Casear head, wht pottery, 5¼", NM.......................... 30.00

Dairy Bottles

Assoc Dairies Malvern Pty Ltd, Clotted Cream, emb letters, 1920s...115.00
Biltmore Dairy Farms, Asheville NC, blk pyro, rnd qt 230.00
Byron Pepper & Sons, Georgetown DE, emb lettering, rnd pt..... 120.00
Clark Dairy, West Haven CT, orange pyro front & bk, cream sz, 2"... 82.50

Creole Dairy Co, Ste. Genevieve MO, red pyro, rnd ½-gal.......... 115.00
Crown Dairy, Chelsea MA, orange pyro, rnd qt 85.00
Cueman's Dairy Farm, Hackettstown NJ, cow, blk pyro, dmn rim, rnd qt.285.00
Dari-Maid Batavia Dairy Co, lady & windmill, orange pyro, gal.. 175.00
Exclusive Briggs Dairy Service, red pyro, cream top, 1940s, rnd qt ..65.00
Fairview Jersey Farm, Jackson MI, orange pyro, 1944, tall rnd qt... 75.00
Herlihy's Dairy Products, purple pyro, cream top, rnd qt, +spoon.. 60.00
Jones Dairy Grade A Milk, Thomasville NC, emb letters, rnd qt . 250.00
Keep 'Em Flying, aviator, red pyro, Pat Nov 22 27, rnd qt 135.00
Kona Dairy, Keauhou HI, red pyro, rnd qt 145.00
Maple City Dairy, Monmouth IL, Keep 'em Flying..., red pyro, rnd qt..100.00
Munger's Dairy, Cassopolis MI, red & bl pyro, rnd qt 215.00
Pet Milk, orange pyro, wire hdl, Duraglas, gal.............................. 75.00
Prairie Farms Dairy...3 in 1 Concentrate, red pyro, sq qt 58.00
Purdue University Creamery, Lafayette IN, emb letters, rnd ½-pt . 70.00
Purity Dairy, blk pyro, Baby Face, rnd pnt.................................. 110.00
Sanitary Creamery, Tonopah NV, orange pyro, Owens, 1948, rnd qt.125.00
Sibley Farms, Disney graphics (Mickey, Clarabelle), red pyro, '30s, pt.. 155.00
Sunshine Goat Milk, emb letters & goat, rnd ½-pt 55.00
Thatcher Dairy, Martinsburg WV, nursery rhyme, red pyro, sq qt . 110.00
Vern Tex Dairy, Keep 'Em Flying..., airplane, red pyro, rnd qt, EX... 160.00
Wht Thorn Dairy Farm, New Alexandria PA, bl pyro, rnd qt........ 63.00
WS Dunn Dairy, Acton Mass, maroon pyro, rnd qt........................ 20.00

Flasks

Baltimore Monument/Corn for the World, GVI-4, Prussian Bl, sb, qt. 1,300.00
Eagle/Cornucopia, GII-46, aqua, sm w/tooled lip, op, flake, ½-pt . 240.00
Eagle/Eagle, GII-101, yel olive gr, ringed cm, sb, flake, qt 375.00
Eagle/Eagle, GII-106, dk olive gr, ringed am, sb, pt 350.00
Eagle/Eagle, GII-81, yel amber, tm, op, pt...................................... 300.00
Eagle/Louisville..., GII-33, med amber, am, sb, dullness, ½-pt...... 200.00
Eagle/Man w/Bag, GII-140, pt, ringed am, sb, rare, pt.............1,200.00
Flag w/13 Stars/Granite GW..., GX-027, yel amber, sm, ps, rpr, pt . 1,100.00
Great Western Trapper/Deer, GX-30, aqua, am, C on sb, pt 550.00
Liberty/Willington..., GII-61, dk root beer, dbl cm, sb, potstone, qt...325.00
M'Carty & Torreyson/Sunburst, GIX-48, bl aqua, sm, ip, pebbly, pt..2,500.00
Masonic Arch/Eagle, GIV-18, yel olive amber, sm, op, chip, pt.... 160.00
Masonic/Eagle, GIV-32, golden amber w/reddish tone, sm, ps, pt. 800.00
Masonic/Eagle, GIV-7a, bright med gr w/yel tone, sm, ps, Keene, pt, EX ..650.00
Pitkin, bright med gr, 16-rib, sm, ps, Midwest or NJ, 5" 1,000.00
Railroad/Horse & Cart/Lowell-Eagle, GV-10, amber, ps, ½-pt..... 425.00

Scroll, amber, pontil scar to base, slightly cloudy, 7x5", $720.00. (Photo courtesy Dirk Soulis Auctions on LiveAuctioneers.com)

Scroll, GIX-30 variant, aqua, fleur-de-lis only, sm, ps, 2-qt 600.00
Scroll, GIX-34a, med yel gr, sm, ps, stress crack, ½-pt.................. 275.00
Sunburst, GVIII-1, bright gr w/bluish tone, sm, ps, flake, pt 950.00
Sunburst, GVIII-16, lt yel olive, sm, ps, 1815-30, ½-pt 750.00
Sunburst, GVIII-18, yel olive, sm, ps, 1815-30, ½-pt.................... 950.00
Sunburst, GVIII-29, lt bl gr, melon ribs, ps, ½-pt......................... 450.00
Sunburst/Keen-P&W, GVIII-10, olive gr w/amber tone, ps, ½-pt....... 750.00
Traveler's Star Companion/Sheaf of Grain, GXIV-1, yel amber, sb, qt...400.00
Union/Eagle, GXII-25, med olive yel, ringed cm, sb, pt.............3,500.00
W Ihmsens/Agriculture, GII-10, pale yel gr, sm, ps, pt 600.00

Washington/Wheat Sheaf, GI-59, cobalt, sm, ps, flakes, ½-pt ... 13,000.00
Washington/Taylor, GI-24, aqua, tm, ps, faint stain, pt 190.00
Washington/Taylor, GI-54, med to dk pk amethyst, tm, op, bold emb, qt. 4,750.00

Food Bottles and Jars

Demi-john storage, yel 'old' amber, cm, ps, crude, bubbles, 12½" .. 70.00
Demi-john, med yel 'old' amber, sl cm, ps, bubbles, 12¼x6½" 120.00
Pickle, golden amber, 6-sided w/simple arches, fm, sb, 13" 1,500.00

Pickle, medium emerald green with four paneled Gothic arched sides, hand-tooled folded lip, press molded, circa 1865 – 1875, 11½x3¼", $720.00. (Photo courtesy Cowan's Auctions, Inc. on LiveAuctioneers.com)

Pickle, Wells Miller & Provost, bl gr, sq cm, ip, chip, 11" 375.00
Pickles, CP Sanborn & Son Union..., yel olive, sm, sb, 5" 110.00
Storage, dk yel olive, sm w/flared-out lip, ps, 12½" 600.00
Storage, med bl gr, cm, ps, stain, 1850-70, 20½" 325.00
Storage, med bl gr, dbl ringed mouth, ps w/kick-up, bubbles, 12¾". 475.00
Storage, med yel olive amber, sl cm, ps, 1770-80, 14" 250.00
Utility, dk tobacco amber, 2" tm w/appl string lip, ps, 10½" 350.00
Utility, med olive amber, 3" W tm w/appl string lip, ps, 14¾" 325.00
Utility, yel olive gr, wide flared tm, ps, chip, 12⅛" 80.00

Ink Bottles

6-sided, Carter, ruby red, 2½x2" 15.00
Cathedral, Carter, cobalt, 9¾", NM 55.00
Cone w/rope twist, amber, 2¾x2⅞" 90.00
Cone, Carter (on base), dk teal, crude, lt haze, 2" 60.00
Cone, Carter's #77, dk amber, 2x2" 20.00
Cone, Carter's Made in USA, dk emerald gr, 2x2" 55.00
Conical, Carter's, bl aqua, tm, sb, whittled, 2⅜" 350.00
Cylinder, Harrison's Columbian, cobalt, am, op, flake, 5¾" 1,900.00
Geometric, GIII-29, med amber, ps, 1½" 240.00
Globe, J Raynald, The World, aqua, sb, 2¼" 135.00
Igloo, gr, J&IEM, chip, 1½" 125.00
Igloo, Harrison's Columbian, aqua, 1¾x2⅛" 265.00
Igloo, Kirkland's Ink W&H, aqua, sm, 2x2¼" 25.00
Igloo, pk puce w/vertical ribs, gm, sb, 1870-90, 2x2" 950.00

Medicine Bottles

Arthur's Elixer of Sulphur...Catarrh, bl aqua, oval w/panel, 8⅜".. 210.00
Baker's Vegetable Blood & Liver...Tenn, med red amber, sb, 9⅝". 450.00
Boston Lung Institute, wide mouth w/rm, ps, 2⅝" 270.00
Brown's Blood Cure Philadelphia, lime gr, tm, sb, stain, 6¼" 140.00
Bryant's Indian Pulmonary Balsam, lt gr aqua, 8-sided, op, 6" 120.00
Butler & Son London...Toronto, bl aqua, am, op, bubbles, 5¾" 450.00
Chloride Calcium St Catharine's..., aqua, tapered cm, op, 5⅝" 275.00
Cod Liver Oil, fish form, amber 110.00
Dr Craig's Kidney Cure, med red amber, dbl cm, sb, 9⅝" 2,000.00
Dr Craig's Cough/Consumption Cure, yel amber, dbl cm, sb, 7⅞" ... 4,000.00
Dr FS Hutchinson Co...Paralysis Cure, aqua, dbl cm, sb, 8½" 250.00

Dr Goers's Chaulmoogra East India...MD, red amber, tm, sb, 6" .. 180.00
Dr Ham's Aromatic Invigorating..., gr aqua, ip, sq cm, 8" 300.00
Dr JA Sherman's Rupture Curative..., med amber, am, sb, 8⅜".... 350.00
Dr Kelling's Per Herb..., aqua, cylinder, am, op, 6⅜" 150.00
Dr MM Fenner's People's Remedies...1872-1898, yel amber, tm, sb, 10" ... 200.00
Dr Seelye's Magic Cough & Consumption...Kansas, aqua, dbl cm, sb, 9".. 600.00
Dr Seelye's Magic Cough...Chemists, aqua, dbl cm, sb, stain, 7⅛". 400.00
Frog Pond Chill & Fever Cure, amber, tm, sb, 7" 425.00
Genuine Swaim's Panacea..., lt aqua, op, sl cm, wear, 7" 850.00
Gibbs Bone Liniment, med olive gr, 6-sided, tapered cm, op, 6⅜" . 1,900.00
GW Merchant Chemist...NY, bl gr, tapered cm, sb, flake, 7" 200.00
Hampton's V Tincture...Balto, dk copper puce, oval, sb, 6¼" 300.00

Hartman's Celery and Damiana Compound, ribbed neck, hobnail collar, original label (with toning, losses), embossed Hartman, Schuylkill Haven, Penna., with nude, flakes and fleabites to rim, 11½", $25.00. (Photo courtesy Cordier Antiques & Fine Art on LiveAuctioneers.com)

Juniper Berry Gin Diuretic Cures...KY, bl aqua, tm, sb, 9¾" 160.00
LQC Wishart's Pine Tree Tar..., emerald gr, crude am, sb, 9¾"..... 230.00
LQC Wishart's Pine Tree Tar..., teal, tm, sb, 10" 230.00
LQC Wishart's Pine Tree...1859, med bl gr, sb, sl cm, stain, 7" 150.00
Lucien Pratte Kidney & Ronova Liver...Conn, med amber, tm, sb, 9½"..300.00
Masta's Indian Pulmonic Balsam..., bl aqua, op, dbl cm, 5" 275.00
Mizpah Cure for Weak Lungs...PA USA, tm, sb, lt haze, 10⅛" 300.00
Mrs Dr Secor Boston Mass, dk cobalt (vivid), tm, sb, 9½" 150.00
National Kidney & Liver Cure, red amber, tm, sb, 9¼" 90.00
Parks Liver & Kidney Cure..., amber to yel amber, tm, sb, 9⅝".... 250.00
Parks Liver & Kidney Cure...NY, aqua, tm, sb, 9⅝" 110.00
Rohrer's Expectoral Wild Cherry..., root beer amber, ip, 10", EX. 350.00
SparkS Kidney & Liver Cure...NJ, med yel amber, tm, sb, 9"....1,300.00
Warner's Safe Cure (safe) Frankfort A/Main, red amber, sb, 9½". 400.00
Warner's Safe Cure (safe) London, yel olive gr, am, sb, 11", NM ..1,900.00
Warner's Safe Nervine (safe) London, med yel topaz, bt, sb, chip, 9" ... 100.00
Winans Bros...Indian Cure, bl aqua, tm, sb, 9" 450.00
Wm Johnson's Pure Herb...Malarial Diseases, yel amber, sb, 8¾". 375.00

Mineral Water, Beer, and Soda Bottles

AG Van Norstrano...Bunker Hill..., med amber, tm, sb, 9⅝" 110.00
August Reinig 2107...Philada..., yel w/olive tone, 1A on sb, 9½" .. 80.00
August Stoehr...Manchester NH...Sold, med yel olive, No 2 on sb, 9".130.00
C Andrae Port Huron...C&CO 2, med cobalt hutch, sb, chips, 6⅝".120.00
Central Bottling...C&CO Lim No 5, cobalt hutch, JJG on sb, chips, 7" .100.00
City Bottling...Louisville..., cobalt hutch, MIK on sb, 6⅝" 750.00
Claussen...Charleston SC, yel amber w/olive tone hutch, 6⅝" .2,100.00
Distilled Soda Water Co...SB&C, aqua hutch, 10-panel, flake, 7½"... 800.00
E Wagner Trade W...Not Sold, med yel amber, tm, sb, 9⅜"............ 60.00
E Wagner Trade W...Not Sold, yel w/olive tone, tm, sb, 9⅛" 140.00
F Jacob Jockers 803-...12 oz, lt to med cobalt, porc stopper, 9".....275.00
FJ Kastner Newark NJ..., med golden yel w/amber tone, 9⅜"....... 140.00
Geo Schmuck's Ginger Ale...Lim, yel amber hutch, 12-sided, sb, 7" ..275.00
Gleason & Cole Pittsb..., yel olive, 10-sided, ip, chip, 7¾" 500.00
Guyette & Co...C&CO Lim No 5, cobalt hutch, G on sb, 6⅞" ... 110.00
GW Erandt Carlisle (in slug plate), emerald gr, ip, 7⅜" 400.00

H Clausen & Son Brewing...Phoenix..., olive gr, tm, sb, 9⅛"....... 550.00
H Koehler & Co Fidelio...NY, dk amber, tm, sb, porc stopper, 8⅝" .40.00
Hayes Bros...Chicago Ill MCC, cobalt hutch, 10-panel, sb, 7⅜".. 140.00
J Gahm Trade (mug) Mark...Lager Beer, yel amber, tm, sb, 9⅜".......30.00
J Weilerbacher Pittsburgh PA...DCC 149, yel amber hutch, sb, 7⅝" .300.00
JG Bolton Lement Ills A&DHC, cobalt hutch, sb, ding, 6¾"...... 325.00
Lohrberg Bros's Bud Bell Ill, lt to med apple gr hutch, sb, 6¾"..... 400.00
Lynch Bros Plymouth PA...Sold, med citron, tm, sb, w/closure, 9¼"..230.00
MJ McNerney (in slug plate), bl gr, squat, dbl cm, ip, 6⅞".......... 150.00
Moriarity & Caroll...Conn, dk amber hutch, 10-panel, tm, sb, 7⅜". 375.00
Pensacola Bottling...Fla, dk bl aqua hutch, tm, sb, 6¾"................. 80.00
Phillips Bros Champion...Baltimore..., amber, tm, sb, chip, 9⅛".... 60.00
Registered C Norris...C&CO Lim, cobalt hutch, CN&CO on sb, 6¾"......100.00
Registered WH Cawley Co...Flemington..., lt gr, C on sb, bruise, 9".. 40.00
S Smith...Water, med cobalt, 10-sided, b3m, ip, 7⅜" 600.00
Standard Bottling...SABCO, dk amber hutch, HR on sb, 6⅞"..... 140.00

Poison Bottles

Dr Oreste Sinanide's..., dk cobalt, tm, sb, orig stopper, 4⅝" 275.00
Dr Oreste Sinanide's..., mg, tm, sb, orig stopper, 4½" 350.00
Not To Be Taken, cobalt, hexagonal, NM label, 4 on sb, 5½"...... 160.00
Poison Bowman's Drug..., cobalt, hexagonal, GLG & Co... on sb, 7½".1,200.00
Poison, amber, hexagonal, EB& CO LO/5000 on sb, flake, 8⅜" .. 200.00
Poison, cobalt, HBCO on sb, scarce, 5⅝" 90.00
Poison, dk cobalt coffin, Crystal on sb, tm, NM label, 3" 3,750.00

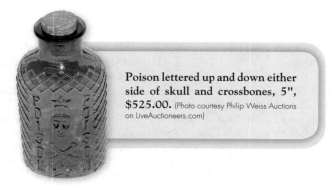

Poison lettered up and down either side of skull and crossbones, 5", $525.00. (Photo courtesy Philip Weiss Auctions on LiveAuctioneers.com)

Skeleton (draped), porc, mk Shofu, MIJ, 7"................................... 180.00
USPHS on sb, cobalt, wide tm, 5⅜".. 230.00

Sarsaparilla Bottles

BF Williams Syrup of...& Iodid...TN, bl aqua, sl cm, ps, 9½"....... 950.00
Carl's...& Celery Comp Aurora IL, yel amber, tm, sb, 9⅛"........... 475.00
Catlin's...For Blood St Louis, med amber, tm, sb, stain, 8¼" 210.00
Chas Cable & Son Po'Keepsie...Soda, med bl gr, bt, ps, 7"........... 475.00
Compound Syrup of...Cures Rheumatism...VA, gr aqua, tm, sb, 9½" . 3,500.00
Currier's..., lt aqua hutch, tm, sb, 6¾" 240.00
Custer's Extract..., lt aqua, tm, MCC on sb, 9" 200.00
Dana's... For the Blood Liver & Kidneys, bl aqua, tm, sb, 6⅝" 60.00
De Witt's...Chicago, lt aqua, tm, sb, 8⅞".. 50.00
Dr AP Sawyer's (eclipsed sun) Eclipse..., bl aqua, tm, sb, stain, 9" ..180.00
Dr Clarke's..., dk olive gr, tm, sb, open bubble, 8½"....................... 375.00
Dr Foster's Jamaica..., gr aqua, tm, sb, 9¾" 120.00
Dr Guysott's Compound Extract..., bl aqua, sb, dbl am, sb, 9½"... 375.00
Dr Guysott's Yel Dock..., bl aqua, ps, am, bold emb, 10" 1,300.00
Dr Guysott's Yel Dock...Cincinnati O, med gr aqua, oval, ip, 9⅝"..400.00
Dr Morley's...& Iod Potas St Louis, tm, sb, EX label, 9⅜" 150.00
Dr Townsend's...NY, dk yel olive, sq w/beveled corners, ps, 9½"... 240.00
Dr Townsend's...NY, med bl gr, sb, sl dbl cm, 9" 130.00
Dr Townsend's...NY, med gr aqua, lacks 'Old' emb, ip, 9⅞".......... 400.00

Dr Townsend's...NY, olive gr, sl cm, ps, flake, 9" 275.00
Dr Weiley's..., gr aqua, tapered cm, sb, whittled, 9" 240.00
Dr White's...Adrian Paradis...NY, bl aqua, am, sb, 8⅜" 130.00
Indian Vegetable &...Bitters...Goodwin Boston, aqua, ps, dbl cm, 8" . 1,000.00
Kennedy's...& Celery Compound, tm, sb, VG label, bruise, 9¾" . 175.00
McBride Medicine Co..., tm, sb, 7¾" 50.00
Miner's...Henry a Miner Pharmacist..., bl aqua, dbl cm, sb, 9⅜" .. 750.00
Moroney's...Moroney Medicine...Indianapolis Ind, bl aqua, sb, chip, 9" .250.00
Old Dr J Townsend's...NY, med yel gr, sb, tm, 10¼" 140.00
Old Dr Townsend's, Sarsaparilla NY, bl gr, sb, cm, 9" 140.00
SB Goff...& Blood Purifier Camden NJ, tm, sb, NM label, 6¾" ... 215.00
Tyler's Indian, bl aqua, tm, sb, stress crack, 9"............................... 200.00
Vickery's...Dover NH, bl aqua, WT&Co on sb, 9⅝"....................... 200.00
Walker's Vegetable..., aqua, tm, WT&Co USA on sb, haze, 9½". 160.00

Spirits Bottles

Batter Up Rye & Bourbon, graphic baseball label, heavily embossed glass, 12x4", $125.00. (Photo courtesy Philip Weiss Auctions on LiveAuctioneers.com)

AM Binninger...NY, med yel amber, tm, sb, cannon, 12⅝".......1,100.00
Bininnger's Travelers' Guide...NY, med yel amber, sb, teardrop, 6⅞" .700.00
Bouquet Pure Rye Whiskey, rvpt, ground stopper, 10"...............2,000.00
Chestnut Grove (sm crown) Whiskey CW, dk tobacco amber, ps, 8¾".275.00
Chestnut Grove (sm crown) Whiskey CW, yel amber, op, 8⅝" 250.00
EG Booz's Old Cabin...Philadelphia, yel amber, cm, sb, 7⅝"......... 450.00
Griffith Hyatt & Co Baltimore, dk yel amber w/olive tone, op, 7"..650.00
Hopatkong Whiskey...Phila, dk cobalt, 12 fluted panels, sb, 10¼" . 3,750.00
Horse hoof onion, med yel olive amber, sm, op, 8⅜x5⅞"........... 160.00
Jacob A Wolford Chicago..., yel amber, am, sb, bbl, 8⅝"............... 475.00
JT Gayen Altona, red amber, bt, cannon, bubbles, crude, 13⅝".. 1,700.00
M Schwartzkopf Liquors...PA, bright yel olive, strap-sided, 9¾".. 1,100.00
Star Whiskey NY WB Crowell Jr, yel w/amber tone, ribs/hdl, ps, 8"..1,000.00
Wharton's...1850 Chestnut Grove, cobalt, am, sb, teardrop, 5¼" . 325.00

Boxes

Boxes have been used by civilized man since ancient Egypt and Rome. Down through the centuries, specifically designed containers have been made from every conceivable material. Precious metals, papier maché, Battersea, Oriental lacquer, and wood have held riches from the treasuries of kings, snuff for the fashionable set of the last century, China tea, and countless other commodities. In the following descriptions, when only one dimension is given, it is length. For more information we recommend *Antique Porcelain Boxes* by Jim and Susan Harran (Collector Books). See also Toleware; specific manufacturers.

Bride's, bentwood w/laced seams, floral decor on ivory, 5½x15"... 460.00
Bride's, bentwood w/laced seams, HP flowers/couple, 6½x17"...... 700.00
Bride's, pnt pine/maple, cvd pinwheels/etc on domed lid, PA, 8x18x10".5,450.00
Candle, bl pnt pine w/chamfered sliding lid, 8x27x10" 1,050.00
Candle, curly maple, dvtl & chip cvd, sq nails, rfn, 4¾x13x6½".. 865.00
Candle, pine, slide lid w/thumb notch, old grpt, nailed, 6x16x7" . 175.00

Desk, cvd oak, slant front, butterfly hinges, 12x25x16"............. 435.00
Dome top, dvtl pine w/sq nails, red grpt, iron bail hdls, 13x24x12". 250.00
Dome top, patterned putty pnt w/compass flower, 19th C, 16x17x17"...1,525.00
Dome top, pine/poplar w/blk & red grpt, lt wear, 7x15x7"........... 175.00
Dome top, poplar, dvtl/appl molding, old pnt, 6¾x14x10"........... 460.00
Knife, mahog Hplwht style w/inlay, slip lid, 14⅞x8⅜"................ 700.00
Knife, mahog w/dvtl canted sides, scalloped edges, heart cutout, 17" L, VG..1,150.00
Pantry, dk bl pnt, copper tacks, 2⅛x5½x4"..................................... 485.00
Pantry, pine top/bottom, bent ash lapped sides, rosehead nails, 8x11"..645.00
Rosewood & maple w/inlaid dmns, bone escutcheon, 19th C, 5x10x6"..500.00
Round w/lapped seams, pnt medallion on red, PA, 5x15½" dia .2,100.00
Spice, walnut, lift-lid, heart-shaped cutout on crest, 7x14x8"...... 460.00
Wall, pine, peaked crest/lift-lid & 2 open compartments, rfn, 24x13x6" .345.00
Writing, mahog w/bow-tie inlay, fitted int, dvtl drw, 18th C, 7x19x10"...975.00

Bradley and Hubbard

The Bradley and Hubbard Mfg. Company produced metal accessories for the home. They operated from about 1860 until the early part of this century, and their products reflected both the Arts and Crafts and Art Nouveau influence. Their logo was a device with a triangular arrangement of the company name containing a smaller triangle and an Aladdin lamp. Our advisor is Bruce A. Austin; he is listed in the Directory under New York.

Lamps

Angle, dbl, clear globes, mg shades, blk rpt, 35x22"..................... 350.00
Banquet, floral ball shade; brass std w/wht metal foliage, 36½".... 600.00
Piano, 7" ruby-to clear ruffled globe w/chimney; brass base, 30¼" 475.00
Student, 2 12" mg shades; center stem w/loop finial, 21½"........... 950.00
Student, 2 5x6" faceted gr slag shades; mk gilt base, 16x15½" ..2,350.00

Table, 12" four-sided mosaic type slag-glass shade with dragonflies and lily pads, unmarked, 22", $2,760.00.
(Photo courtesy Rago Arts and Auction Center)

Table, 15" red on cream/caramel shade w/o/l (floral); #261 std 450.00
Table, 16" rvpt 6-panel shade; bronzed #302B std, 21"............. 1,400.00
Table, 17" slag 8-panel shade w/floral o/l; bronzed metal std, 21". 750.00
Table, 18" ldgl floral shade; 4-socket std w/brass wash, 24"........ 1,200.00
Table, 18" slag 6-panel shade w/geometric o/l; bronzed std, 22" ... 600.00
Table, 18" slag 8-panel shade w/metal o/l; stick std, 22½" 1,375.00
Table, 20" slag 6-panel shade w/o/l (leaves), foliate CI std, 25".. 1,550.00

Miscellaneous

Andirons, backs swivel, #5950, wear & rust, 16x8x22½" 400.00
Andirons, dolphin form, CI, 14½x17" 235.00
Bookends, Boston terrier, pnt CI, 4⅞x5¼", EX............................. 250.00
Bookends, Egyptian masks/temple design, pnt CI, ca 1920, 6x4¾", EX. 240.00
Bookends, Lincoln Memorial, CI, ca 1925, 3⅝" 150.00
Bookends, Nouveau draped nude/dolphin, pnt metal, 1890-1900, 6½"...400.00
Candlesticks, chrome socket/copper capital/brass std, sq base, 9", pr... 150.00
Clock, John Bull, man figural, blinking eyes, 1857, 14", NM.... 1,100.00

Clock, lion with blinking eyes, painted cast iron, circa 1879, very rare, $6,000.00.
(Photo courtesy The RSL Auction Co. on LiveAuctioneers.com)

Desk set, brass, sq-in-sq motif, letter holder/calendar/tray/blotter. 240.00
Desk set, Tree of Life, 2 blotters/wells+tray+knife+box+calendar+rack...525.00
Doorstop, Boston terrier, pnt CI, 9⅝x12", EX 650.00
Doorstop, boy in waders stands w/pipe, pnt CI, #7903, 8½", EX 1,200.00
Doorstop, Old Woman, Vict lady w/flower basket/parasol, 11x7", EX ..900.00
Doorstop, owl on ped, pnt CI, #7797, 15⅝x5", NM.................. 3,000.00
Doorstop, rabbit sitting, pnt CI, #7800, 15¼x8¼", NM 2,400.00
Doorstop, squirrel on log w/nut, EX pnt/details, 11½x9⅞" 4,000.00
Humidor, brass w/hammered/appl decor, wood lined, 3½x9½"....... 50.00
Inkwell, stag scene, brass w/2 brass wells, ca 1910-15 .... 300.00
Letter holder, elk & chasing dogs, cast brass, #3549 & #7030........ 85.00
Parade lantern clock, pierced brass w/glass inserts, 30-hr, 13" 900.00
Plaques, lady w/flowers emb, bronzed w/mc pnt, #1810/#1811, 8", pr. 350.00

Brass

Brass is an alloy consisting essentially of copper and zinc in variable proportions. It is a medium that has been used for both utilitarian items and objects of artistic merit. Today, with the inflated price of copper and the popular use of plastics, almost anything made of brass is collectible, though right now, at least, there is little interest in items made after 1950. Our advisor, Mary Frank Gaston, has compiled a lovely book, *Antique Brass & Copper,* with full-color photos.

Ash can, lion mask hdls, domed lid w/orb-shaped finial, 19x13" . 315.00
Bucket, wrought-iron swing hdl, 8x13"... 98.00
Desk accessory, inkwell/pen holders, ftd, wall mt, English, 8x8" .. 650.00
Kettle stand, pierced design at top & front apron, 4-leg, hdls, 12x18"....485.00
Lighter, street lamp; ball-shaped font, trn wood hdl, 27½"........... 115.00
Stand, music, lyre-shaped rest, 40", EX... 40.00
Standish, sander/ink/cup w/candle socket on base, 5x9", VG 920.00
Statue, satyr by tree trunk holding child, bronze patina, 24".....1,375.00

Sascha Brastoff

Sascha Brastoff was born Samuel Brostofsky in Cleveland, Ohio, in 1918. By 1938, an early aptitude for art led him to The Clay Club in New York City, where Sascha made his living designing window displays for the famed Macy's Department Store. In 1941, his first one-man show featured 37 original hand-sculpted and highly detailed terra cotta figures he dubbed 'Whimsys.' While serving his patriotic duty during WWII, Sascha spent much of his time designing war bond posters and illustrating army newsletters, along with conducting private art lessons for kids of the top brass. Post war, Sascha settled at 20th Century Fox Studios in Los Angeles as a costume designer. By 1947, and with the help of financier and mentor Winthrop Rockefeller, he began creating commercial ceramics. Eventually, they built a state-of-the-art studio factory which opened on November 18, 1953, in West Los Angeles. He left his factory sometime in mid-1962 and entered into a period of reflection, personal reevaluation, and reinvention, concentrating on pastel and oil painting and enamelwork. The years 1964 to 1966 brought experimentation in freeform magnesium sculpture and other arc welded metalwork. More pastel painting sustained Sascha in 1967, when he was commissioned to create the 13 foot by 7 foot gold-plated crucifix (and altar pieces) for St. Augustine By-The-Sea Episcopal Church, Santa Monica, California. His next endeavor was 'Esplanade,' a rare upscale retail venue. The early to mid-1970s exposed Sascha to the world of product endorsement (or, lending his name and reputation to designing for other companies). Among these were 24K gold-plated costume jewelry for Merle Norman Cosmetics, decorative lighting switchplates and bathroom accessories for Melard, Inc. and, arguably his best co-venture, designing the six-piece sterling 'Silver Circus' in conjunction with Franklin Mint. Custom fine jewelry in the mid to late 1970s, retailed from California Jewelsmiths of Beverly Hills (and eventually Sascha's home), brought him into the early '80s, when poor health prevented him from keeping up the usual pace and creative output. Sascha passed away on February 4, 1993, leaving a 45+ year legacy forged in all media except glass.

Items hand signed in full and not merely backstamped 'Sascha Brastoff' were personally crafted by him and command a much higher value than those decorated by his staff and signed 'Sascha B.' Although resin animals and votive candleholders are signed in part or in full, they were actually purchased by Sascha's ex-company in his absence (they retained the right to use his name through the early 1970s) and simply sold through Sascha Brastoff Products, Inc.

In the listings that follow, items are ceramic and signed 'Sascha B.' unless 'full signature' or another medium is indicated. All pieces signed 'Sascha' or 'SASCHA' are originals. 'Sascha B' and 'Sascha B.' generally denote staff decorated pieces, although there are rare exceptions. Our advisor for this section is Steve Conti, co-author of *Collector's Encyclopedia of Sascha Brastoff*. He is listed in the Directory under California.

Sculpture, Whimsy, 'Tumblers,' signed Sascha, only one known (close-up shown), 1939, 6", $3,750.00. (Photo courtesy Zhe Zhang)

Ashtray, Celadon, humanoid figures outlined in gold, F8, 17" 160.00
Ashtray, Mosaic, fish shape, M14, 17" 145.00
Box, Mosaic, w/lid, animal figure hdl, M5B, 8" sq 85.00
Chalice compote, fish/seaweed, porc, O618, ⅜x8½", dtd '60, rare ..650.00
Cross, bronze, handmade, sgn Sascha, 2¼x1⅝" 145.00
Dish, Fiesta Pools, advertising, F42, 10" 125.00
Egg, Abstract Originals, O44C, largest of 3 available szs, 13" 150.00
Egg, Celadon, leaf motif, O44B, 10" 110.00
Egg, Lucite, tooled in flower design, sgn Sascha '72, rare, 9x6" 295.00
Fabric, dancers, mk Sascha Brastoff-Roomaker, 10 sq yards, NOS ..400.00
Figurine, hippo, resin, not designed or sgn by Brastoff, 10" 285.00
Figurine, Percheron horse, antique crackle glaze, S12, 13½" 1,250.00
Hologram, Sunburst in 24K gold-plated bezel, Sascha B, 2" 175.00
Lamp, Rooster, LM-7, w/orig Matchsticks shade, 27" 300.00
Lamp, Temple Dog, L-29, w/o Matchsticks shade, 36" 275.00
Lighter, Americana, L1A, 3½" 30.00
Painting on ceramic, floral & fruit in still life, CP1, 23x19" unfr. 425.00
Painting on ceramic, Star Steed, CP5, 13x11+fr 165.00
Pastel, 'Black Jesus,' full sgn, dtd 1965, only 1 known, 24x18 ...1,850.00
Pastel on paper, MerBaby, full sgn, dtd 1965, 24x18" 525.00
Pendant, butterfly w/nude, 24K gold plated, sgn Sascha B 125.00

Pendant, scorpion, heavy 14K gold, initialed SB.......................... 750.00
Plate, chop, Vanity Fair, O53, 17" 195.00
Plate, dessert, floral design w/glaze notes, porc, sgn Sascha, 7"....125.00
Plate, dinner, Jade Tree, porc, 11⅛" 43.00
Plate, mythical dragon, sgn & dtd, 10½"...................................... 475.00
Plate, rooster, sgn Sascha, 10½" 350.00
Print, gold foil, Star Steed head, 14⅛x11⅜", F 20.00
Scratchboard, mythical dragon, some smudging & wear, sgn, 12". 175.00
Sculpture, seahorse, 24K plated lead, marble w/stamped sgn, 5" ..155.00
Sculpture, Whimsy, 'Mermaid,' plaque, sgn Sascha, 1 known, 1939, 14x10" ..3,750.00
Silver Circus, 8-pc sterling/24K plated, orig boxes/COA's, Franklin Mint ..1,200.00
Tile, Temple Towers, CP3, fr by Earl's of Brentwood, 21".............. 250.00
Wall pocket, Abstract Originals, O31, 20" 175.00

Brayton Laguna

A few short years after Durlin Brayton married Ellen Webster Grieve, his small pottery, which he had opened in 1927, became highly successful. Extensive lines were created and all of them flourished. Hand-turned pieces were done in the early years; today these are the most difficult to find. Durlin Brayton hand incised ashtrays, vases, and dinnerware (plates in assorted sizes, pitchers, cups and saucers, and creamers and sugar bowls). These early items were marked 'Laguna Pottery,' incised on unglazed bases.

Brayton's children's series is highly collected today as is the Walt Disney line. Also popular are the Circus line, Calasia (art pottery decorated with stylized feathers and circles), Webton ware, the Blackamoor series, and the Gay Nineties line. Each seemed to prove more profitable than the lines before it. Both white and pink clays were utilized in production. At its peak, the pottery employed more than 150 people. After World War II when imports began to flood the market, Brayton Laguna was one of the companies that managed to hold their own. By 1968, however, it was necessary to cease production.

For more information on this as well as many other potteries in the state, we recommend *Collector's Encyclopedia of California Pottery* and *California Pottery Scrapbook*, both by Jack Chipman; he is listed in the Directory under California.

Candy jar, Coachman (Pinnochio), Disney line, ca 1939, unmk ..3,100.00
Candy jar, hen.. 200.00
Chamberstick, orange, tri-cornered base rim, w/hdl, early, 3¼" ... 165.00
Chess pc, castle, from lg-scale set designed by Peter Ganine, 1946, 10½"..275.00
Cookie jar, Christina, Swedish maid, ca 1941, 11" 500.00
Cookie jar, Grannie Smith, #40-85, $350 to................................ 400.00
Cookie jar, hen, 10" 375.00
Figurine, abstract, torso, wht crackle, 1950s 225.00

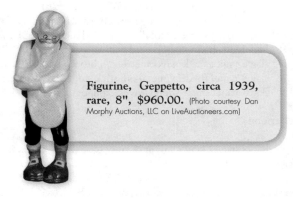

Figurine, Geppetto, circa 1939, rare, 8", $960.00. (Photo courtesy Dan Morphy Auctions, LLC on LiveAuctioneers.com)

Figurine, Lovers in Cab, Gay Nineties series, ca 1941, 7½x11"....550.00
Figurine, Mexican man, A Anderson, 9" 275.00
Figurine, mule, A Anderson, 7¼x10"... 225.00
Figurine, Pedro, Childhood series, 6½" 225.00

Figurine, Pluto howling, Disney line, 6"........................150.00
Figurine, Rosita, Chidhood series, 5½".........................125.00
Figurine, St Bernard, A Anderson, late 1930s 175.00
Figurine, toucan, woodtone w/high glaze, 1950s-60s, 9"..............135.00
Figurines, Fighting Pirates, C Safholm, ca 1956, 9", pr..............775.00
Figurines, Hillbilly Shotgun Wedding set, A Anderson, ca 1938, tallest man 9".1,100.00
Flower holder, Swedish peasant woman, ca 1939, rare, 11½".......300.00
Flowerpot, blk 300.00
Head vase, gypsy woman, ca 1939, 9"...........................325.00
Lamp base, little girl holding doll, early 1940s...............375.00
Sculpture, head & shoulders, matt blk, 12x13"...............375.00
Tile, blk cats on mc roof, ca 1928, 4½"...........................550.00
Tile, man in sombrero sleeping under cactus, HP, ca 1929, 6"......650.00
Tile, wht/yel mushrooms on lt bl, 4½"...........................450.00
Vase, bud, turq bl, entwined snake, 8"...........................550.00

Bread Plates and Trays

Bread plates and trays have been produced not only in many types of glass but in metal and pottery as well. Those considered most collectible were made during the last quarter of the nineteenth century from pressed glass with well-detailed embossed designs, many of them portraying a particularly significant historical event. A great number of these plates were sold at the 1876 Philadelphia Centennial Exposition by various glass manufacturers who exhibited their wares on the grounds. Among the themes depicted are the Declaration of Independence, the Constitution, McKinley's memorial 'It Is God's Way,' Remembrance of Three Presidents, the Purchase of Alaska, and various presidential campaigns, to mention only a few.

'L' numbers correspond with a reference book by Lindsey. Our advisor for this category is Darlene Yohe; she is listed in the Directory under Arkansas.

Actress, HMS Pinafore, oval, La Belle, 1880s, 11" 100.00
Banner Baking Powder, shield center, 11".........................85.00
Barley (Cable Edge & Stippled) 65.00
Be Industrious, oval 80.00
Beaded Grape 25.00
Bishop, L-201..200.00
Bunker Hill, L-44, 13x9"..75.00
Cleopatra, rect 95.00
Continental (Memorial Hall), hand & bar hdls, 12¾".........60.00
Daisy & Button (Hobbs) 25.00
Deer & Pine Tree, bl...65.00

Do Unto Others As You Would Have Them Do Unto You, $65.00.

Eagle, Constitution, motto, oval 60.00
Fleur-de-lis w/Pan Am (Buffalo) Exposition center............17.50
Flower Pot, We Trust in God.......................................75.00
Frosted Lion, Give Us This Day, 12½x9" 175.00
Gladstone, 9"...45.00
Good Luck, dbl horseshoe hdls.....................................120.00
In Remembrance, 3 Presidents, frosted 60.00

It Is Pleasant To Labor, grapes & leaf center, 12" dia.........55.00
Jeweled Band (Scalloped Tape) 25.00
Let Us Have Peace, amber...65.00
Liberty Bell Signers..95.00
Memorial Hall...65.00
Mormon Tabernacle, stippled border, rare 425.00
National, shield shape, rare 85.00
Nelly Bly, L-136, 12"..200.00
Niagara Falls, L-489...95.00
Pope Leo XIII, L-240, 10"...35.00
Statuette, Ruth the Gleaner, frosted, 1876 Phila Expo, Gillinder.175.00
Teddy Roosevelt, platter..185.00
Three Graces, Pat dtd 1865 ....65.00
Volunteer, emerald gr, L-101.......................................575.00
Washington, First War/First Peace, L2-7, 12x8½"...............100.00
William J Bryan, mg..45.00

Bretby

Bretby art pottery was made by Tooth & Co., at Woodville, near Burton-on-Trent, Derbyshire, from as early in 1884 until well into the twentieth century. Marks containing the 'Made in England' designation indicate twentieth-century examples.

Vase, hand-painted irises, artist signed, #53H, 2-12-11-91, late nineteenth century, 27x7", $1,320.00. (Photo courtesy Neal Auction Company on LiveAuctioneers.com)

Bookends, lions on box w/ball, lime gr............................70.00
Bust, boy smiling, bronzed look, blk sockle, 20¾".............425.00
Bust, Neapolitan fisherboy, bronzed earthenware, 20th C, 21" 400.00
Figurine, barn owl, wht w/brn wash, #1317, ca 1890, 12".....625.00
Jar, apple form, gr w/touches of yel & red, #847, 3½" 100.00
Jug, bl-gr drip over red, red rope-twist hdl, #113, 7" 100.00
Lamp base, bronzed look w/appl designs/stones, unmk, 32x12".1,800.00
Ligna vessel, cvd/pnt, appl insects, hdl, #1517, very slim, 16"......600.00
Mug, Edward VII commemorative, cream, 4½" 50.00
Pitcher, sgraffito sailboats, gr, #359, 7" 24.00
Tankard, Japanese scene, bronzed-look base, 10" 180.00
Vase, bl heron by bamboo stalks, #917, 11½"...................150.00
Vase, brn/gr/yel mottle, slim neck, bulb body, #2455H, 10" 70.00
Vase, bronzed look w/appl stones, invt cone w/hdls, #1588E, 9", NM ..600.00
Vase, bronzed look w/enameled stones, hdls, Solon, #1669, 12¼".1,050.00
Vase, Clanta, appl enameled stones, designed by Louis Solon, #1588E, 8½"...600.00
Vase, Clanta, sailboats/appl stones, hdls, Solon, #1811, 13¼", EX ..480.00
Vase, hammered bronze look, 3 tear-shaped cabochons, 3-hdl, 9". 100.00

Bride's Baskets and Bowls

Victorian brides were showered with gifts, as brides have always been; one of the most popular gift items was the bride's basket. Art glass inserts from both European and American glasshouses, some in lovely transparent hues with dainty enameled florals, others of Peachblow, Vasa Murrhina, satin, or cased glass, were cradled in complementary silver-plated holders. While many of these holders were simply engraved or delicately embossed, others (such as those from Pairpoint and Wilcox) were wonderfully ornate, often with figurals of cherubs or animals or birds. The bride's basket was no longer in fashion after the turn of the century.

Watch for 'marriages' of bowls and frames. To warrant the best price, the two pieces should be the original pairing. If you can't be certain of this, at least check to see that the bowl fits snugly into the frame. Beware of later-made bowls (such as Fenton's) in Victorian holders and new frames being produced in Taiwan. In the listings that follow, if no frame is described, the price is for a bowl only.

Blue cased, HP floral, dbl-crimp rim w/clear edge; SP fr, 12x12".. 240.00
Blue Coin Dot, dbl crimped w/wht edge, SP fr, 12x12" 215.00
Blue satin cased, HP floral, ruffled; Meriden SP fr, 1880s, 17x16". 660.00
Blue w/HP floral, ruffled/crimped rim; unmk SP fr, 13x11½" 175.00
Burmese, mums, ruffled/crimped, Mt WA; SP Pairpoint fr, rope hdls, 11". 3,750.00
Chartreuse pk cased, enamel floral, SP Wilcox holder, 10" dia . 3,000.00
Cranberry to wht w/HP floral, ruffles/pleats; SP fr, 14½x14" 240.00
Custard w/floral, tooled rim, Meriden #01532 fr, rtcl cherub hdls, 7".... 875.00
Gold satin w/birds & floral, clear ruffle, 13", mk fr 495.00
Milk glass shaded to bl, ruffled/pleated rim; SP fr, 9x7" 150.00
Opal-cased dk rose w/florals w/in & w/out, Mt WA, Aurora #1823 fr .. 525.00
Peach to vaseline opal, Rib Optic, Adelphi SP fr, 10" 950.00
Pink cased w/clear edge, ruffled/pleated; SP fr, 11x10x10¼" 135.00
Pink cased w/clear ruffle, HP floral; SP basket fr, 12x11" 335.00
Pink cased w/floral, 7-crimp rim; SP Pairpoint #2175 fr, 10x10" 360.00
Pink cased, HP floral, ruffled; SP fr, ca 1870, 11½x12½" 335.00
Pink cased, ruffled rim; simple SP fr, 12x11" 150.00

Pink overlay with amber-edged crimped and tooled rim, in Webster & Son Quadruple plate stand, 9x11", $650.00. (Photo courtesy Northgate Gallery, Inc. on LiveAuctioneers.com)

Red to clear cased, HP floral, ruffled rim; SP fr, 12x11" 300.00
Rose w/wht o/l, florals, crenelated rim, Tufts #2270 fr, 16x13" 375.00
White opal w/bl opaque rim, ruffled/crimped, SP fr, 9x7" 150.00
White opal w/HP floral, ruffled/crimped; SP fr, 12x10" 165.00
White w/pk ruffled edge, HP floral; SP fr, ca 1870, 11½x12½" 325.00

Bristol Glass

Bristol is a type of semi-opaque opaline glass whose name was derived from the area in England where it was first produced. Similar glass was made in France, Germany, and Italy. In this country, it was made by the New England Glass Company and to a lesser extent by its contemporaries. During the eighteenth and nineteenth centuries, Bristol glass was imported in large amounts and sold cheaply, thereby contributing to the demise of the earlier glasshouses here in America. It is very difficult to distinguish the English Bristol from other opaline types. Style, design, and decoration serve as clues to its origin; but often only those well versed in the field can spot these subtle variations.

Bottle, wht, floral, slender neck, flower stopper, 11", pr 80.00
Cheese dish, wht w/bl & gold Nouveau decor, gold finial, 6" 75.00
Epergne, bl w/floral, bronze ft, single lily, 11½" 80.00
Jar, wht w/floral & gold, flower finial, 9" 70.00
Vase, lt bl, allover floral/scrolls, EX art, U300-3, ftd, 8" 275.00
Vase, wht w/gold floral, slim, flared ft, 12", pr 85.00
Vase, wht, boy (& girl) in outdoor scene, ftd, 12", pr 120.00
Vase, wht, landscape & bl foliage, ftd, trumpet neck, 8¼", pr 85.00
Vase, wht, stork/lg flowers, ovoid w/cupped neck, 12x6" 60.00
Vases, pk w/HP birds & foliage, gilt trim, England, 19th C, 13", pr....250.00

British Royalty Commemoratives

Royalty commemoratives have been issued for royal events since Edward VI's 1547 coronation through modern-day occasions, so it's possible to start collecting at any period of history. Many collectors begin with Queen Victoria's reign, collecting examples for each succeeding monarch and continuing through modern events.

Some collectors identify with a particular royal personage and limit their collecting to that era, i.e., Queen Elizabeth's life and reign. Other collectors look to the future, expanding their collection to include the heirs apparent Prince Charles and his first-born son, Prince William.

Royalty commemorative collecting is often further refined around a particular type of collectible. Nearly any item with room for a portrait and a description has been manufactured as a souvenir. Thus royalty commemoratives are available in glass, ceramic, metal, fabric, plastic, and paper. This wide variety of material lends itself to any pocketbook. The range covers expensive limited edition ceramics to inexpensive souvenir key chains, puzzles, matchbooks, etc.

Many recent royalty headline events have been commemorated in a variety of souvenirs. Buying some of these modern commemoratives at the moderate issue prices could be a good investment. After all, today's events are tomorrow's history.

For further study we recommend *British Royal Commemoratives* by our advisor for this category, Audrey Zeder; she is listed in the Directory under Washington.

Key:
C/D — Charles and Diana   Pr — prince
cor — coronation   Prs — princess
inscr — inscription, inscribed   QM — queen mother
jub — jubilee   wed — wedding
LE — limited edition

Album, Royal Family, 1983, 3-ring binder, 200 pictures................. 85.00
Baby dish, Geo VI, mc portrait, Baby Plate on rim, inscr............. 125.00
Beaker, C/D betrothal, mc portrait/decor, Caverswall 155.00
Beaker, Elizabeth II jub, mc, lion-head hdls, Caverswall 80.00
Beaker, Victoria 1897 jub, enamel w/portrait, 3¾" 195.00
Book, Elizabeth II cor, Her Majesty Queen..., child's book.......... 25.00
Book, Royal Souvenirs by Geoffrey Warren, hardback, 1977......... 45.00
Book, Victoria 1897, Queen's Resolve, some wear.......................... 65.00
Booklet, Elizabeth II cor, Our Queen & Her Consort, Pitkins 15.00
Booklet, His Royal Highness Pr of Wales, Pitkins, 1958 .... 25.00
Booklet, Prs Margaret's Betrothal, Pitkins, 1960............................ 20.00
Bowl, Edward VIII 1937, mc portrait w/crown, Grindley, 1x5" 55.00
Bowl, Victoria 1887 jub, brn portrait w/mc decor, 1x8½" 175.00
Child's toy dish, Victoria 1858, chidren w/cart, Prattware, 4"...... 295.00
Compact, Elizabeth II cor, mc portrait, unused in orig folder......... 55.00
Compact, Geo V jub, mc portrait, cor robes, hinged, 2"................. 80.00
Doll, Pr Phillip, vinyl, bl uniform, Nisbit, ca 1950, 8½" 150.00
Doll, Pr Wm birth, cloth, Nottingham lace gown, 3", MIB 50.00

Doll, Victoria, plastic, blk dress, modern mfg, 7½" 25.00
Egg cup, Geo VI cor, shaded portrait, gold rim, ftd...................... 35.00
Ephemera, Duchess of Windsor, unused letter paper/envelope....... 65.00
Ephemera, Geo V 1935 visit, invitation to watch procession 15.00
Glass, Edward VII 1937, beaker, frosted wht portrait, 4½".............. 30.00
Glass, George VI 1937 cor, basket, clear w/emb portrait/decor, 10" ...165.00
Horse brass, Elizabeth II jub, brass w/emb crown 20.00
ILN Record No, Elizabeth II jub, bl cover/silver decor, 14x10"...... 55.00
ILN Record No, George V cor, rnd cover/gold decor, 16x11" 175.00
Jewelry, Elizabeth II cor, crown earrings, MOC 25.00
Jewelry, Elizabeth II pin, mc portrait on MOP, 2" 45.00
Jewelry, Geo VI stickpin, cut-out profile, brass 20.00
Jug, George III, emb portrait, Westerwald, late 18th C 425.00
Loving cup, C/D wed, bl portrait, Adams, 3½x5¾"......................... 50.00

Loving cup, Elizabeth II coronation, two gold lion handles, Paragon, circa 1953, $65.00. (Photo courtesy Jim & Susan Harran)

Loving cup, Geo V cor 1911 & Mary Ascension 1910..............2,000.00
Magazine, Country Life Royal Wed Number, November 28, 1947 ..35.00
Magazine, Daily Mail, Prs Diana memorial, 9-6-97 .... 30.00
Magazine, Geo V jub, ILN, May 4, 1935... 35.00
Magazine, Geo VI cor, Weekly Illustrated Cor Souvenir................ 25.00
Magazine, Hello, Charles/Harry in S Africa, 11/15/97 .... 12.00
Magazine, Sphere, Funeral of King Geo V, February 1, 1936.......... 45.00
Magazine, Star Weekly, Toronto, Geo VI Canada visit, 1939 .... 25.00
Matchbox, Geo V jub, blk & wht portrait, inscr, unused 25.00
Medallion, Victoria/Albert 1858 visit w/Napoleon, brass, ⅞" 75.00
Miniature, photo album, of 1982 Royal Family, 1¼x2".................. 35.00
Miniature, Pr Wm 1st birthday plate, mc w/Diana, 2¼" 35.00
Mug, C/D engagement, blk line portrait, Carlton.......................... 75.00
Mug, C/D wed, mg, mc portrait/decor.. 25.00
Mug, Elizabeth II cor, pk w/emb portrait & floral decor, 4¼" 40.00
Mug, Geo V cor, mc portrait in robes, presentation pc.................. 150.00
Mug, Pr Wm 25 birthday, LE 30, Chown... 20.00
Mug, Prs Diana '95 Argentina visit, mc decor, Chown, LE 50 ..... 125.00
Newspaper, QM 100 birthday, Daily Express, Tribute, July 19, 2000.. 15.00
Newspaper, The Queen, Edward VII funeral, 5-21-1910 .... 30.00
Novelty, Edward VII cor letter opener, emb figure, ivory color 60.00
Novelty, Elizabeth II 1977 jub bedwarmer, copper w/ceramic insert .. 25.00
Novelty, Pr Albert document clip, relief portrait, 1860, 5x2" 55.00
Photo, sgn on photograher's mat, 'Diana,' 5½x7" 4,200.00
Picture, Elizabeth II jub needlepoint, in wooden fr, 15x13" 60.00
Pin-back, Edward VII cor, mc figure on bl w/copper lustre, 6"...... 360.00
Pitcher, Edward VII cor, mc portrait, pk lustre, 6" 150.00
Pitcher, Victoria 1897 jub, Queen/Pr Edward, Balmoral, 4" 270.00
Plate, C/D wed, mc portrait, emb design on rim, 9"........................ 65.00
Plate, Edward VIII '37, mc portrait in cor robe, Royal Winston, 9" ..90.00
Plate, Prs Anne 1973 wed, bl jasper, Wedgwood, 4½" 60.00
Plate, Prs Margaret 1930 birth, bird design, Paragon, 7"............... 120.00
Playing cards, C/D wed, mc portrait/etc, 2-pack, unused................ 55.00
Playing cards, Edward VII cor, mc portrait/decor, full deck 95.00
Postcard, Edward VII memorial, blk/wht inscr, blk border, Rotary. 25.00
Postcard, Geo V at front, WWI, mc, Daily Mail, unused 15.00
Postcard, QM 100 birthday, set of 5 picturing royal postage stamps .. 20.00
Puzzle, Royal Family, comic version, dbl-sided, Buffalo 75.00
Sheet music, Pr of Wales 1863 wed, mc wed scene, for piano 50.00
Sheet music, When the King Goes Riding By, 1937....................... 35.00

Spoon, Geo VI cor, annointing featured SP, 4½" 35.00
Teapot stand, Geo V jub, mc portrait/decor, silver rim, 6" 95.00
Teapot, Edward VII cor, mc portrait in red uniform, Doulton, 2-cup .210.00
Textile, Elizabeth II jub place mat, hand embr, 19x13" 25.00
Thimble, C/D/Wm '83 New Zealand visit, mc, Caverswall........... 45.00
Thimble, Pr William '83 1st birthday, mc portrait/decor, Fenton... 35.00
Tin, Edward VII cor, mc portrait on purple, angular.................... 195.00
Tin, Elizabeth II cor, standing portrait in formal gown, 6x4x2"...... 45.00
Toby mug, Victoria, HP, L&S, 3"... 55.00

Broadmoor

In October of 1933, the Broadmoor Art Pottery was formed and space rented at 217 East Pikes Peak Avenue, Colorado Springs, Colorado. Most of the pottery they produced would not be considered elaborate, and only a handful was decorated. Many pieces were signed by P.H. Genter, J.B. Hunt, Eric Hellman, and Cecil Jones. It is reported that this plant closed in 1936, and Genter moved his operations to Denver.

Broadmoor pottery is marked in several ways: a Greek or Egyptian-type label depicting two potters (one at the wheel and one at a tile-pressing machine) and the word Broadmoor; an ink-stamped 'Broadmoor Pottery, Colorado Springs (or Denver), Colorado'; and an incised version of the latter.

The bottoms of all pieces are always white and can be either glazed or unglazed. Glaze colors are turquoise, green, yellow, cobalt blue, light blue, white, pink, pink with blue, maroon red, black, and copper lustre. Both matt and high gloss finishes were used.

The company produced many advertising tiles, novelty items, coasters, ashtrays, and vases for local establishments around Denver and as far away as Wyoming. An Indian head was incised into many of the advertising items, which also often bear a company or a product name. A series of small animals (horses, dogs, elephants, lambs, squirrels, a toucan bird, and a hippo), each about 2" high, are easily recognized by the style of their modeling and glaze treatments, though all are unmarked.

Ashtray, bl w/wht puppy in center, 5⅜" dia..................................... 50.00
Ashtray, pirate ship in nautical surround, matchbook slot, orange, 7" .. 175.00
Bust of lady, 1 shoulder raised, looking upward, turq gloss, 5" 420.00

Scarab, impressed maker's mark, circa 1930s, 3¼x2½", $130.00. (Photo courtesy John Coker, Ltd. on LiveAuctioneers.com)

Theatrical masks, sgn HW Schwartz, 14½", ea 200.00
Tile, bird & foliage, mc faience, flakes, 5¾x5¾" 285.00
Tray, 3-leaf form w/centered swirl knob, turq, 11" dia 35.00
Vase, orange-red, incurvate rim, PH Genter, 4½x5½" 35.00
Vase, spherical, dk bl, w/paper label, 5"... 45.00

Bronzes

Thomas Ball, George Bessell, and Leonard Volk were some of the earliest American sculptors who produced figures in bronze for home decor during the 1840s. Pieces of historical significance were the most popular, but by the 1880s a more fanciful type of artwork took hold. Some of the fine sculptors of the day were Daniel Chester French, Augustus St.

Gaudens, and John Quincy Adams Ward. Bronzes reached the height of their popularity at the turn of the century. The American West was portrayed to its fullest by Remington, Russell, James Frazier, Hermon Mac-Neil, and Solon Borglum. Animals of every species were modeled by A.P. Proctor, Paul Bartlett, and Albert Laellele, to name but a few.

Art Nouveau and Art Deco influenced the medium during the '20s, evidenced by the works of Allen Clark, Harriet Frismuth, E.F. Sanford, and Bessie P. Vonnoh.

Be aware that recasts abound. While often aesthetically satisfactory, they are not original and should be priced accordingly. In much the same manner as prints are evaluated, the original castings made under the direction of the artist are the most valuable. Later castings from the original mold are worth less. A recast is not made from the original mold. Instead, a rubber-like substance is applied to the bronze, peeled away, and filled with wax. Then, using the same 'lost wax' procedure as the artist uses on completion of his original wax model, a clay-like substance is formed around the wax figure and the whole fired to vitrify the clay. The wax, of course, melts away, hence the term 'lost wax.' Recast bronzes lose detail and are somewhat smaller than the original due to the shrinkage of the clay mold. Values in the listings that follow are prices realized at auction.

Aichele, Paul; nude female dancer on carpet, marble ped, 11½"..650.00
Alonzo, D; mother w/basket holds daughter's hand, 18"..............600.00
Alonzo, D; Rose Peddler, ivory head/arms, w/red rose, 9¼"........2,875.00
Austrian, cat/mouse & shoe, Geschutzt, 3" L..................................635.00
Barye, AL; & Guillemin, E; Arabian huntsman w/gazelle & goose, 30"+ped.1,725.00
Barye, AL; bear raiding bird's nest, 4½x6"+base 5,600.00
Barye, AL; lion stands w/curved tail/open mouth, 5½"...............2,875.00
Belvedere, Apollo (after); classical male figure on ovoid base, 5".. 325.00
Boisseau, E; lute player, color-tinted patina, 31"........................1,100.00
Bourron, Marie-Josephe; nude on stomach, ca 1967, 4½x10¾"..1,200.00
Canova, Venus a la Pomme, 20th-C replica, 45½".........................975.00
Cassel, S; man w/guitar, gilt & cold pnt, ca 1900, 13".............14,500.00

Chiparus, Demetre H.; Favorite, Art Deco dancer, gold patina, marble and bronze base, #1708, 14½" (without stand), $5,750.00. (Photo courtesy Dallas Auction Gallery on LiveAuctioneers.com)

Chiparus, Friends Forever, Deco maid w/2 whippets, ivory/enamel, 25"..26,450.00
Chiurazzi Naples, fawn bound to gnarled tree, gilt surface, 26".2,650.00
Choppin, Paul-Francois; Call to Arms, soldier w/rifle, 35"......10,600.00
Colinet, CL JR; dancing nude, parrot on ea arm, marble ped, 11"..920.00
Dallin, E; Appeal to the Great Spirits, chief on horseback, 9x9x6".2,500.00
Dubucand, Alfred; Alert Stag, 19th C, 16¼x11½x4"..................1,000.00
Erte, Summer Breeze, pnt surface, ltd ed, 1987, 23"..................1,525.00
Falconet, Etienne-Maurice; woman bather, brn patina, 1757, 23"..700.00
Fatori, Deco lady dancer, ivory inlay, marble base, 1920s, 12"..18,000.00
Fayral, nude w/gazelle, verdigris, stone base, 8½x11"..................1,550.00
Fratin, lion standing on base, detailed mane, 22" L...................3,850.00
Fremiet, E; Credo, knight in chain mail w/banner, 16¼x12¼"..1,375.00
Fremiet, E; horse w/military saddle/accessories, 12x13".............2,550.00
Gardet, G; lioness attacking snake, 2 dead cubs, 12x29"...........4,700.00
Gauguie, H; hunter w/lion, ca 1885, 20"...................................1,960.00
Landowski, PM; nude male on plinth, orig brn patina, 27¾"....4,600.00

Lemon, David; Applejack Pete, mountain man, late 1900s, 11¼" ..200.00
Lorenzl, Deco maiden spreading cape, silvered/HP, 16¼"...........3,600.00
Lorenzl, lady dancer w/leg kicked bk, silvered, gr onyx base, 10"...1,950.00
Madrassi, Luca; Tree Nymph, sits on stump w/hands above head, 27".3,165.00
Moigniez, J; pheasant on rocky plinth, 14x14"...........................3,165.00
Omerth, G; Madeleon, lady w/pitcher & jug, ivory inlay, 1920s, 10".2,200.00
Pilanos, C; nude torso of woman, gr patina, 1979, 36¾"...........1,650.00
Quinto (?), hunter w/bow on plinth, late 1800s, 30¼".............4,200.00
Remington, F; Bronco Buster, man on horse, restrike, 22½"...........1,600.00
Remington, F; Cheyenne, hunter w/spear on horse, restrike, 16x19".2,300.00
Remington, F; Rattlesnake, cowboy on horse, restrike, 23¾"...........1,600.00
Russell, CM; Double Buffalo Hunt, ltd ed, 1906, 17x28x21"....1,300.00
Unmk, boxer fallen & sprawling on 1 knee, verdigris, 20th C, 9x12x9"..1,950.00
Unmk, fox prowling, pk marble base, 7½" L................................115.00
Unmk, lion roaring, dk brn patina, red marble base, 8" L.............285.00
Varenne, HF; 18th-C lady w/arm extended behind her, 7⅛".......175.00
Vienna, Arab man praying on rug, cold pnt, 4"............................725.00
Vienna, Banana Seller, cold pnt/brn patina, 19th C, 2¾x4x4".1,450.00
Vienna, Bavarian peasant dancers, cold pnt, 19th C, 7½"............660.00
Vienna, horse, cold pnt, articulated reins/stirrups, 5½x6½"..........850.00
Vienna, parrot w/extended tail, cold pnt, onyx base, 6¼x12"......600.00
Vienna, rabbit seated w/ears bk, brn patina, 6¼x8x3½"............1,450.00

Brouwer

Theophilis A. Brouwer operated a one-man studio on Middle Lane in East Hampton, Long Island, from 1894 until 1903, when he relocated to West Hampton. He threw rather thin vessels of light, porous white clay which he fired at a relatively low temperature. He then glazed them and fired them in an open-flame kiln, where he manipulated them with a technique he later patented as 'flame painting.' This resulted in lustered glazes, mostly in the orange and amber family, with organic, free-form patterns. Because of the type of clay he used and the low firing, the wares are brittle and often found with damage. This deficiency has kept them undervalued in the art pottery market.

Brouwer turned to sculpture around 1911. His pottery often carries the 'whalebone' mark, M-shaped for the Middle Lane Pottery, and reminiscent of the genuine whalebones Brouwer purportedly found on his property. Other pieces are marked 'Flame' or 'Brouwer.' Our advisors for this category are Suzanne Perrault and David Rago; they are listed in the Directory under New Jersey.

Vase, bulbous, with flame glaze, incised 'FLAME,' with flame, 6½x6", $2,400.00. (Photo courtesy Rago Arts and Auction Center)

Vase, baluster, lustered glaze, Brouwer w/whalebone, 7x3¾" 1,200.00
Vase, flame-pnt bronze, Chinese melon shape, 3¾x4½"............1,200.00
Vase, flame-pnt copper tones, flat shoulder, 4x4"......................950.00
Vase, flame-pnt gold & burgundy, 5x5½" 1,100.00
Vase, flame-pnt lustered gold & amber, whalebone mk & 'Brouwer,' 4x4¾".1,325.00
Vase, flame-pnt orange & yel lustre, paper label, 4x4"...............1,325.00
Vase, flame-pnt yel & amber, flat shoulder, 4x4¾" 1,325.00
Vase, flame-pnt yel/amber/gunmetal, flakes, 9¾x5¼"...............1,500.00
Vase, modeled snake around rim, w/whalebone, 4½x4¼" 5,800.00
Vessel, Aladdin lamp w/lotus leaf (stem hdl), gold/brn, 3½x6½"...2,800.00

Brownies by Palmer Cox

Created by Palmer Cox in 1883, the Brownies charmed children through the pages of books and magazines, as dolls, on their dinnerware, in advertising material, and on souvenirs. Each had his own personality, among them The Dude, The Cadet, The Policeman, and The Chairman. They represented many nations; one national character was Uncle Sam. But the oversized, triangular face with the startled expression, the protruding tummy, and the spindle legs were characteristics of them all. They were inspired by the Scottish legends related to Cox as a child by his parents, who were of English descent. His introduction of the Brownies to the world was accomplished by a poem called *The Brownies Ride*. Books followed in rapid succession, 13 in the series, all written as well as illustrated by Palmer Cox.

By the late 1890s, the Brownies were active in advertising. They promoted such products as games, coffee, toys, patent medicines, and rubber boots. 'Greenies' were the Brownies' first cousins, created by Cox to charm and to woo through the pages of the advertising almanacs of the G.G. Green Company of New Jersey. The Kodak Brownie camera became so popular and sold in such volume that the term became synonymous with this type of camera. (However, it was not endorsed by Cox. George Eastman named the camera but avoided royalty payment to Palmer Cox by doing his own version of them.)

Since the late 1970s a biography on Palmer Cox has been written, a major rock band had their concert T-shirts adorned with his Brownies, and a reproduction of the Uncle Sam candlestick is known to exist. Because of the resurging interest in Cox's Brownies, beware of other possible reproductions. Unless noted otherwise, our values are for items in at least near mint condition.

Book, Another Brownie Book, NY, 1890, 1st ed, w/dust jacket, VG .250.00
Book, Brownies & Other Stories, 1918, EX 40.00
Book, Comic Yarns in Verse, Prose & Picture, 1898, 7x5", VG 25.00
Book, Little Goody Two Shoes, 1903, EX 40.00
Bottle, soda, emb Brownies, M 30.00

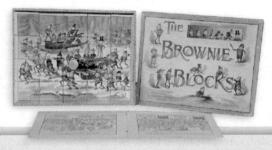

Brownie Blocks, McLoughlin Brothers, lithographed paper on wood, six different illustrations, original guide book and box, 13½" long, EX, $1,920.00. (Photo courtesy Dan Morphy Auctions, LLC on LiveAuctioneers.com)

Brownie Tower, min 950.00
Camera, Eastman-Kodak Brownie 2A, EXIB (not endorsed by Cox) ..145.00
Candy dish, 15 Brownies, ball ft, Tufts SP, 7x5½" 265.00
Comic book, The Brownies, Dell Four-Color, #398, 1952, VG 20.00
Creamer, Little Boy Blue verse & 4 Brownies, gold trim, china 95.00
Creamer, Scottsman head, Majolica, 3¼" 125.00
Cup, SP w/9 enameled Brownies, Middletown Plate Co, 3" 195.00
Figures, papier-maché w/stick legs, jtd arms, 1900s, 5", EX, 4 for...1,500.00
Fruit crate label, harvesting orange juice, 1930s, 10x11", EX 20.00
Game, Nine Pins, litho-on-wood bowling, McLoughlin, EXIB.2,000.00
Humidor, Policeman (Bobby) head, Majolica, 6" 350.00
Ice cream bag, Cox illus, 5¢ orig value, 1930s, M 35.00

Magazine pg, Ladies' Home Journal, Cox illus, ca 1890 .... 15.00
Match holder, Brownie on striker, majolica 235.00
Needle book, Brownies, 1892 World's Fair, rare 75.00
Paperweight, Brownie figural, SP 145.00
Pitcher, china, Brownies playing golf on tan, 6½" 150.00
Plate, SP, Brownies on rim, 8" 85.00
Print, Brownies fishing, matted, 1895, 13½x15½" 55.00
Rubber stamp, set of 12 .... 120.00
Shaker, opal glass w/Brownie, ovoid, Mt WA, 2⅝" 275.00
Sheet music, Dance of the Brownies 35.00
Sign, emb Brownies on tin, Howell's Root Beer, EX 185.00
Sign, If You Like Chocolate Soda Drink Brownie, MCA Co, 59x21", G .230.00
Table set, brass, emb Brownies, 3-pc (knife/fork/spoon), no box.... 85.00
Table set, brass, emb Brownies, 6", in orig box 95.00
Toy, Movie Top, litho tin w/3 windows, ca 1927, 1⅞x4¾" dia 150.00
Trade card, Mitchell, Lewis & Stave Co, 3x5", VG 25.00
Trade card, Sheriff's Sale Segars, Brownies & product, 5x3" 25.00

Brush-McCoy, Brush

George Brush began his career in the pottery industry in 1901 working for the J.B. Owens Pottery Co. in Zanesville, Ohio. He left the company in 1907 to go into business for himself, only to have fire completely destroy his pottery less than one year after it was founded. In 1909 he became associated with J.W. McCoy, who had operated a pottery of his own in Roseville, Ohio, since 1899. The two men formed the Brush-McCoy Pottery in 1911, locating their headquarters in Zanesville. After the merger, the company expanded and produced not only staple commercial wares but also fine artware. Lines of the highest quality such as Navarre, Venetian, Oriental, and Sylvan were equal to that of their larger competitors. Because very little of the ware was marked, it is often mistaken for Weller, Roseville, or Peters and Reed.

In 1918 after a fire in Zanesville had destroyed the manufacturing portion of that plant, all production was contained in their Roseville (Ohio) plant #2. A stoneware type of clay was used there, and as a result the artware lines of Jewel, Zuniart, King Tut, Florastone, Jetwood, Krakle-Kraft, and Panelart are so distinctive that they are more easily recognizable. Examples of these lines are unique and very beautiful, also quite rare and highly prized!

After McCoy died, the family withdrew their interests, and in 1925 the name of the firm was changed to The Brush Pottery. The era of hand-decorated art pottery production had passed for the most part, having been almost completely replaced by commercial lines. The Brush-Barnett family retained their interest in the pottery until 1981 when it was purchased by the Dearborn Company.

For more information we recommend *The Collector's Encyclopedia of Brush-McCoy Pottery* by Sharon and Bob Huxford; and *Sanford's Guide to Brush-McCoy Pottery, Books I* and *II*, written by Martha and Steve Sanford, our advisors for this category, and edited by David P. Sanford. They are listed in the Directory under California.

Of all the wares bearing the later Brush script mark, their figural cookie jars are the most collectible, and several have been reproduced. Information on Brush cookie jars (as well as confusing reproductions) can be found in *The Ultimate Collector's Encyclopedia of Cookie Jars* by Fred and Joyce Roerig; they are listed in the Directory under South Carolina. Beware! Cookie jars marked Brush-McCoy are not authentic.

Cookie Jars

Antique Touring Car, $850 to 1,000.00
Boy & balloons, min 800.00
Cherry Jar, #H5, $40 to 50.00

Chick & Nest, #W38 (+), $275 to	375.00
Cinderella Pumpkin, #W32	200.00
Clown bust, #W49, unmk, 1970, 10¾", $200 to	250.00
Clown, red pants, #W22, $175 to	200.00
Clown, yel, bl, or pk pants, #W22, $275 to	300.00
Cookie House, #W31, $60 to	75.00
Cow w/cat on back, brn, #W10 (+), $100 to	125.00
Cow w/cat on back, purple, rare, min, (+)	900.00
Cylinder w/tulips, Brush-137 USA, $50 to	60.00
Cylinder, pk crock, w/little girl praying finial, #K26, $40 to	50.00
Cylinder, wood grain or pk crock, w/cat finial, #K26, $40 to	50.00
Cylinder, wood grain or pk crock, w/duck finial, #K26, $40 to	50.00
Dog w/basket, #W54, $250 to	275.00
Donkey & cart, ears down, gray, #W33, $300 to	400.00
Donkey & cart, ears up, #W33	700.00
Elephant w/monkey on back, rare	4,500.00
Elephant, wearing baby hat, #W8 (+)	450.00
Formal Pig, gold trim, #W7 Brush USA (+), $350 to	400.00
Granny, pk apron, bl dots on skirt, #019, $200 to	250.00
Granny, plain skirt, $250 to	275.00

Happy Bunny, 13", $100.00 to $125.00. (Photo courtesy Desert West Auction Service on LiveAuctioneers.com)

Hen on Basket, unmk, $75 to	100.00
Hillbilly Frog, $3,000 to	3,500.00
Hobby Horse, #W55, unmk, 1971, rare, $1,150 to	1,250.00
Humpty Dumpty, w/beany & bowtie #W18, (+), $175 to	200.00
Humpty Dumpty, w/peaked hat & shoes, #W29	200.00
Lantern, #K1, $50 to	60.00
Laughing Hippo, #W27 (+), $650 to	750.00
Little Angel (+), $650 to	700.00
Little Boy Blue, gold trim, #K25D, sm, $650 to	750.00
Little Girl, #017 (+), $450 to	500.00
Little Red Riding Hood, gold trim, mk, lg, (+) min	800.00
Little Red Riding Hood, no gold, #K24, sm, $425 to	475.00
Nite Owl, #W40, $70 to	80.00
Old Clock, #W20, $75 to	100.00
Old Shoe, #W23 (+), $65 to	85.00
Panda, #W21 (+), $175 to	200.00
Peter Pan, gold trim, lg (+), $725 to	775.00
Peter Pan, no gold, sm, $425 to	475.00
Pumpkin (Peter, Peter Pumpkin Eater), #W24, $200 to	250.00
Puppy Police, #W39 (+), $450 to	500.00
Sitting Hippo, #W45, unmk, 1969, $450 to	475.00
Sitting Piggy, #W37 (+) $325 to	375.00
Smiling Bear, #W46 (+), $225 to	275.00
Squirrel on Log, #W26, $60 to	80.00
Squirrel w/top hat, blk coat & hat, #W15, $225 to	300.00
Stylized Owl, #W42, $250 to	300.00
Teddy Bear, ft apart, #W14, $175 to	225.00
Teddy Bear, ft together, #014 USA, $125 to	175.00
Three Bears, #K2, $75 to	95.00
Treasure Chest, #W28, $100 to	125.00

Miscellaneous

Vase, Water Carrier from Pompeian line, red clay with green wash, unmarked, 20½", NM, $425.00. (Photo courtesy Tom Harris Auctions on LiveAuctioneers.com)

Bank, frog, 1916, 3½", $75 to	100.00
Bookends, Venetian, Indian chief, Ivotint, 1929, 5x5"	300.00
Bowl, Jewell, #055, 1923, 2½", $300 to	400.00
Bowl, Moss Gr, #01, 6", $20 to	30.00
Butter crock, Corn, w/lid, #60, $300 to	350.00
Candlestick, Vogue, blk geometrics on wht, 12", ea	325.00
Candlestick, Zuniart, #032, 1923, 10", pr $700 to	1,000.00
Casserole, Grape Ware, w/lid, #178, 1913, $150 to	200.00
Clock, Flapper, Onyx (gr), #336, 1926, 4½", $75 to	150.00
Decanter, Onyx (bl), 7", $100 to	150.00
Flower arranger, Princess Line, #560, 5½-6½", ea $30 to	40.00
Garden ornament, squirrel, #482, 8x8", $100 to	125.00
Garden ornament, turtle, gr or brn, #487D, 6½", $75 to	100.00
Hanging pot, #168, 1962, 8", $24 to	40.00
Jardiniere, Egyptian, bl, 1923, 5½"	200.00
Jardiniere, Fancy Blended, #202, 1910, 10½", $150 to	175.00
Jardiniere, Florastone, 6¾"	425.00
Jardiniere, Jetwood, 1923, 9", $700 to	800.00
Jardiniere, Modern Kolorkraft, #260, 1929, 10", $125 to	175.00
Jardiniere, Woodland, #2230, 7", +7½" ped, $300 to	400.00
Jug, Decorated Ivory, #131, 1915, 2-qt, $150 to	175.00
Jug, Florastone, 1924, 10", $1,000 to	1,200.00
Lamp base, Kolorkraft, 1920s, 10½", $125 to	175.00
Oil lamp, Ivotint, 1929, 8x4", $550 to	700.00
Ornament, birdbath, wht, 2 frogs (standing/sitting), 7½"	200.00
Pitcher, Nurock, #351, 1916, 5-pt, 8½", $165 to	200.00
Pitcher, Peacock, Bristol, #351, $900 to	1,500.00
Planter, frog, 1920s-1930s, 3", $40 to	50.00
Planter, penguin, #332A, $30 to	40.00
Planter, rooster, 1956, $40 to	55.00
Radio bug, 1927, 9½x3", $500 to	950.00
Tray, divided, w/hdl, Mt Pelee, 1902, 7x2", $600 to	700.00
Umbrella stand, Liberty, #73, 1912, $600 to	800.00
Urn, Onyx (gr), #699, 11½", $125 to	175.00
Vase, Bronze Line, palette mk USA 720, 8", $2,500 to	40.00
Vase, Cleo, #042, 11¾", $750 to	900.00
Vase, ftd, Princess Line, mid-1960s, 5", $40 to	50.00
Vase, Onyx (brn), shouldered, 4"	45.00
Vase, Vestal, #729, 10½", $250 to	300.00
Wall plaques, African Masks, mk USA, 10", pr	300.00

Buffalo Pottery

The founding of the Buffalo Pottery in Buffalo, New York, in 1901, was a direct result of the success achieved by John Larkin through his innovative methods of marketing 'Sweet Home Soap.' Choosing to omit 'middle-man' profits, Larkin preferred to deal directly with the consumer and offered premiums as an enticement for sales. The pottery soon proved a success in its own right and began producing advertising and commemorative items for other companies, as well as commercial tableware. In 1905 they introduced their Blue Willow line after extensive experimentation resulted in the development of the first successful underglaze cobalt achieved by an American company. Between 1905 and 1909, a line of pitchers and jugs were hand decorated in historical, literary, floral, and outdoor themes. Twenty-nine styles are known to have been made.

Their most famous line was Deldare Ware, the bulk of which was made from 1908 to 1909. It was hand decorated after illustrations by Cecil Aldin. Views of English life were portrayed in detail through unusual use of color against the natural olive green cast of the body of the ware. Today the 'Fallowfield Hunt' scenes are more difficult to locate than 'Scenes of Village Life in Ye Olden Days.' The line was revived in 1923 and dropped again in 1925. Every piece was marked 'Made at Ye Buffalo Pottery, Deldare Ware Underglaze.' Most are dated, though date has little bearing on the value. Emerald Deldare was made on the same olive body and on standard Deldare Ware shapes and featured historical scenes and Art Nouveau decorations. Most pieces are found with a 1911 date stamp. Production was very limited due to the intricate, time-consuming detail. Needless to say, it is very rare and extremely desirable.

Abino Ware, most of which was made in 1912, also used standard Deldare shapes, but its colors were earthy and the decorations more delicately applied. Sailboats, windmills, and country scenes were favored motifs. These designs were achieved by overpainting transfer prints and were often signed by the artist. The ware is marked 'Abino' in hand-printed block letters. Production was limited; and as a result, examples of this line are scarce today.

Commercial or institutional ware was another of Buffalo Pottery's crowning achievements. In 1917 vitrified china production began, and the firm produced for major U.S. railroads, steamships, hotels, and smaller accounts. Much of today's sought-after Buffalo China commercial collectibles are from the 1917 – 1950s period. After 1956 all commercial ware bore the name Buffalo China. In the early 1980s, the Oneida Company purchased Buffalo China and continued production of commercial and institutional ware. However, in 2004, Oneida divested itself of Buffalo China.

All items listed below are in excellent to mint condition unless otherwise noted. See also Bluebird China.

Key:
BC — Buffalo China	SL — side logo
BC-Oneida — Buffalo China after 1983	SM — side mark
BL — bottom logo	TL — top logo
BS — bottom stamp	TM — top mark
comm — commemorative	

Abino

Tankard, sailboats, 1912, 6⅞", $720.00. (Photo courtesy Dargate Auction Galleries on LiveAuctioneers.com)

Matchbox holder w/attached ashtray, windmill scene, 3¾" 1,180.00
Pitcher, windmill, harbor scene w/sm sailboats, Harris, 9" 710.00
Plate, seascape w/sailing ships, Harris, 9½" 268.00
Sugar bowl, sailing ships on choppy water, hdls, 3½" 440.00

Commercial China

All items listed below are of the heavy 'restaurant' weight china.

Bone dish, Blue Willow, oval, scalloped, 1922, 4½x6½" 12.00
Bowl, cereal, children's ware w/mc circus animals, 1926, 5" 22.00
Bowl, cereal, Natural Wood Design, 5½" 78.00
Bowl, cereal, US Forest Service, 1926, 5¾", $38 to 59.00
Bowl, cereal, US Forest Service, BC-Onieda, 5½", $11 to 25.00
Bowl, serving, Buffalo Athletic Club, TL, ftd, 2½x7½" 26.00
Bowl, vegetable, Indian Tree, flared base, 8½" 49.00
Bowl, vegetable, Natural Wood Design, 8" 135.00
Butter pat, Blue Willow, 3½", $9 to 26.00
Butter pat, Cecil's San Diego Calif, w/stylized cocktail glass, TL ... 49.00
Butter pat, golf balls & trees, TM, 3½" 45.00
Butter pat, Henry Ford Hospital, HFM in dmn, TM, 3¼" 49.00
Butter pat, pine trees & pine cones TM, 3¼" 29.00
Butter pat, stylized rooster silhouette, blk pinstripe, 3¼" 42.00
Butter pat, TCC TL in script w/acorn border, 3¼" 62.00

Creamer, Blue Willow, 4½", $65.00. (Photo courtesy Apple Tree Auction Center on LiveAuctioneers.com)

Creamer, ind, X golf clubs, FCC, SL, no hdl, 3¼" 44.00
Creamer, ind, desert scene w/MCC, SL, hdl, 3¼" 28.00
Creamer, ind, Gr Willow, hdl, 3¼" 10.00
Creamer, ind, Laramie (WY) Golf Club, SL Indian w/Golf Club, hdl, 3" 66.00
Creamer, ind, mc band w/sailing ship, Hotel Commodore, hdl, BS, 3" .. 18.00
Creamer, ind, Trocadero Hotel, SL, hdl, 3" 44.00
Cup, 1939 NY World's Fair, Trylon & Perisphere SL, teacup style. 56.00
Cup/saucer, Airport Café, Akron OH, SL & TM of plane 110.00
Cup/saucer, Blue Willow, demi 31.00
Cup/saucer, demi, Ritz-Carlton, BL, demi 15.00
Cup/saucer, Mallard Seeds w/images of soaring mallard, SL, 1960s.. 18.00
Gravy boat, Multifleure Lamelle, 3½x6½" 98.00
Match holder (sm), Commonwealth Poultry, Boston, 3½x6½" 20.00
Match holder (sm), detailed lighthouse image, Lighthouse Inn, SL..... 46.00
Matchbox holder (sm) w/attached ashtray, Buffalo Trap & Field SL, 4" .. 46.00
Mug, gr stripe, heavy base, 1926, 3⅛" 12.00
Mug, US Army Medical Dept, SL, 3½" 14.00
Mustard pot, ivory w/gr bands, hdl, 1924, 3½" 18.00
Mustard pot, Patio Risoli, helmet & arrow SM, Rouge Ware, 3½" ..29.00
Pitcher, Ahwahnee, Yosemite Park & Curry Co, BS, 1926, 6½" .. 100.00
Pitcher, detailed Am Indian image, Plains, 5¾" 101.00
Pitcher, pelican in blk & wht SL, 7½" 120.00
Plate, Ahwahnee, Yosemite Park & Curry Co, BS, 1927, 10½" 49.00
Plate, Automobile Club of (buffalo image), TL, 1915, 9" 125.00
Plate, Benny's Bistro, Gardena, smiling man w/moustache TL, 1925, 10". 39.00
Plate, bl sailing ship/waves/moon, Gandy's, Made Especially BM, 7"... 12.00
Plate, Bluebird Inn, bluebird TL, 7½" 32.00
Plate, Country Gardens, bl, 10¾" 12.00
Plate, grill, Blue Willow, w/4 sections, 1926, 10¼" 56.00
Plate, Howard Johnson's Pie Man, fluted edge, TL, 6½" 10.00
Plate, mallard soaring, Mallard Seeds, 1960s, 9½" 16.00
Plate, Masonic Temple, Orlando FL, TL, 1926, 9½" 15.00
Plate, Multifleure, 5½" 58.00
Plate, stylized grand piano w/musical notes, blk pinstripes, 10½" ... 95.00

Plate, Tahoe Tavern, TL, 1922, 5¾" 250.00
Plate, USSB (US Bureau of Fisheries), TL, 1926, 8¼" 68.00
Platter, Radcliffe pattern, WCC, 1925, 8x11" 272.00
Platter, USSB (US Bureau of Fisheries), TL, 1926, 8x11½" 155.00
Relish dish, floral border, Charlie's Café, Springfield OR, TL, 4x8" .48.00
Relish dish, gold decor, shell shape, 5½x7½" 26.00
Spittoon, Edgemoor in script w/striping, SL, 1915, 7¾" 55.00
Teapot, Roycroft, BC-Oneida, 3½", $26 to 65.00
Teapot, US Forest Service, BC-Oneida, SL, 3½" 88.00
Tray, pin, LAAC, Los Angeles Athletic Club, TL, 1928, 5x 3½" .. 27.00

Deldare

Ashtray/matchholder, Fallowfield Hunt, A Lang, 3½x6" 790.00
Bowl, fruit, Ye Village Tavern, EB, 3¾x9", $280 to 325.00
Bowl, nut, Ye Lion Inn, inward rolled rim, 3¼x8", $380 to 550.00
Calendar plate, 1910, by Evan Horn, 9¼" 1,430.00
Candleholder/matchholder, untitled Village Scene, unmk, 5½" .. 489.00
Candlesticks, Ye Village Scene, drilled, 9", pr 650.00
Chamberstick, Emerald Ware, sgn MB, 6¾" 3,600.00
Chamberstick, Fallowfield scenes, finger ring, 5¾" dia, ea 778.00
Chocolate pot, Ye Village Street, 6-sided, 9¼" 955.00
Creamer, Emerald Ware, Dr Syntax w/the Dairymaid, 3" 355.00
Cup/saucer, chocolate, Ye Village Street 409.00
Cup/saucer, Emerald Ware, Dr Syntax & Bookseller 339.00
Cup/saucer, Fallowfield Hunt 285.00
Egg cup, untitled Fallowfield scene, no horses, 4" 485.00
Hair receiver, Ye Village Street, w/lid, 4¼" 310.00
Humidor, Emerald Ware, Dr Syntax, lid vented for sponge, 7" .1,100.00
Humidor, There Was an Old Sailor..., vented lid, 8" 880.00
Humidor, Ye Village Tavern, 7" 400.00
Mug, Scenes of Village Life in Ye Olden Days, 1924, 2½" 160.00
Mug, The Fallowfield Hunt, M Gerhardt, 2½" 350.00
Mug, The Fallowfield Hunt, M Gerhardt, 4½" 295.00
Mug, Ye Lion Inn, M Gerhardt, 4½" 185.00
Mustard pot, Scenes of Village Life..., N Sheehan, 1908, 3⅞" ..1,150.00
Pitcher, Emerald Ware, Dr Syntax Setting Out to the Lakes, Stuart, 9" .1,160.00
Pitcher, Fallowfield Hunt, The Return, 8-sided, W Foster, 8" 765.00
Pitcher, Robin Hood (on Deldare body), 8¼" 955.00
Pitcher, To Advise Me in a Whisper..., 8-sided, 7" 415.00
Plate, bread & butter, Ye Olden Days, 6" 75.00
Plate, chop, Emerald Ware, Dr Syntax Sell's Grizzle, A Sauter, 13" .1,360.00
Plate, Emerald Ware, Dr Sytax Soliloquising, J Gerhardt, 7½" 795.00
Plate, Fallowfield Hunt, The Death, 1909, 8½" 180.00
Plate, Fallowfield Hunt, The Death, 1908, 9½" 265.00
Plate, Hand Painted Deldare, salesman sample, 6" 925.00
Plate, rim soup, Fallowfield Hunt, Breaking Cover, 9" 310.00
Plate, rim soup, Fallowfield Hunt, The Start, 6¼" 80.00
Powder jar, Ye Village Street, 4¼" 362.00
Punch bowl, Fallowfield Hunt, various scenes, ped ft, 9x14½" ..5,420.00
Relish tray, Ye Olden Times, W Foster, 6½x12" 305.00
Sugar bowl, Fallowfield Hunt, 6-sided, open, 3½" 388.00
Sugar bowl, Scenes of Village Life in Ye Olden Days, 3¼" 195.00
Sugar bowl, Scenes of Village Life, 6-sided, open, 3¼" 260.00
Tankard, The Great Controversy, Steiner, 12½" 800.00
Tea tile, Fallowfield Hunt, Breaking Cover, 6" 435.00
Teapot, Scenes of Village Life in Ye Olden Days, 3¾" 390.00
Teapot, Scenes of Village Life in Ye Olden Days, 5¾" 485.00
Tray, calling card, Emerald Ware, Dr Syntax Robbed..., tab hdls, 7" ..500.00
Tray, calling card, Fallowfield Hunt, Breakfast, Sauter, tab hdls, 8" ..380.00
Tray, dresser, Dancing Ye Minuet, 9x12" 398.00
Tray, pin, Ye Olden Days, 6½x3½", $105 to 200.00
Tray, relish, Fallowfield Hunt, The Dash, A Lang, 6½x12" 795.00
Tray, tea, Emerald Ware, Dr Syntax Mistakes a..., M Ramlin, 10x13½" .1,389.00

Vase, Emerald Ware, signed M.,
8½x6½", $3,840.00. (Photo courtesy
Treadway Gallery on LiveAuctioneers.com)

Vase, untitled Village scene, fashionable man, 7" 218.00
Vase, untitled Village scene, fashionable man, 9" 410.00

Miscellaneous

In this section all items are marked Buffalo Pottery unless noted. It does not include any commerical (restaurant type) china or items marked Deldare.

Bowl, mixing, Geranium, metal rim, ped ft, 10½" 144.00
Bowl, vegetable, Bonrea, gr/bl floral & swags border, 9½" 17.00
Butter dish, Beverly, pk roses, gold trim, w/ice ring, domed lid, 6" .67.00
Butter dish, Bluebird, w/ice ring, w/knob, rnd, 8" 110.00
Butter pat, Blue Willow, 3¼", $12 to 38.00
Butter pat, Bluebird, 3" 45.00
Butter pat, Bonrea, ornate bl/gr scroll border w/gold, 3" 12.00
Butter tub, Bluebird, mk BC, w/ice ring, tab hdls 86.00
Canister, Cinnamon, bl floral on ivory, bbl shape, 4x2¾" 48.00
Canisters, Flour, Sugar, Coffee, Tea, roses on gingham band, 8¼" .. 56.00
Chocolate pot, floral bouquet on gr shading w/gold, ornate hdl, 11" .. 88.00
Coaster, BlueWillow, 1913, 3½" 23.00
Creamer, Children's Ware, Dutch children, 4½" 39.00
Creamer/sugar bowl, Bluebird, w/lid 85.00
Creamer, Vienna, Art Nouveau decor on cobalt w/gold, 3" 28.00
Cup/saucer, Vienna, Art Nouveau decor on cobalt w/gold 55.00
Egg cup, Bluebird, very rare, 2½" 75.00
Feeding dish, Roosevelt Bears w/Model T, gold trim, 1½x7½" 260.00
Fruit set, natural fruit decor, bowl (8")+4 bowls (4½") 67.00
Gravy/sauceboat, Princess, gr floral w/gold 10.00
Mug, advertising, Bing & Nathan, mc monk image, 4½" 39.00
Mug, Anticipation, Celebration, Fascination...series, 4½", $32 to . 87.00
Pitcher, Blue Willow, rnd, 1905, 4½" 67.00
Pitcher, Geraniums, gr, 4¼" 43.00
Pitcher, Geraniums, mc w/gold accents, 4¼" 130.00
Pitcher, Geraniums, mc w/gold accents, 8" 265.00
Pitcher, John Paul Jones, battle scene, bl & wht, crazing, 9½" 389.00
Pitcher, Roosevelt Bears, 8" 1,800.00
Pitcher, water, Bluebird 100.00
Plate, advertising, stork image, Compliments...Home Furniture, 7" ... 88.00
Plate, Automobiling, early car image, mc pnt, 9½" 675.00
Plate, Christmas, Ebenezer Scrooge reformed state of mind, 1957, 10" ... 66.00
Plate, Christmas, Master Peter Cratchit, mc, 1959, 10" 12.00
Plate, comm, Natatorium, Broadwater Hotel, Helena MT, 7½" 46.00
Plate, comm, White House, bl/gr border, Washington DC, 8" 54.00
Plate, Dr Syntax Disputing...Landlady, flow bl transfer, 1909, 9¼" ..125.00
Plate, Gaudy Willow, cobalt, brick red & gold, scalloped rim, 10" .66.00
Plate, Historical Mt Vernon, bl/gr floral border, 10" 35.00
Plate, historical, White House, bl floral border, Washington DC, 10" .65.00
Plate, Maple Leaf, pk floral, gr maple leaf border w/gold, 9½" 32.00
Plate, Roosevelt Bears, 5 lg & 5 sm scenes, scalloped edge, 10¼" .310.00
Plate, Two Roosevelt Bears Had a Home..., scalloped gold rim, 7½" ..255.00
Plate, Wild Turkey (from fowl set), gold edge, 9½" 83.00
Platter, Blue Willow, 11x14" 92.00
Platter, Bonrea, ornate bl & gr scroll border w/gold, 11x14" 125.00

Platter, Buffalo Hunt, teal gr, scalloped edge, 14x11" 110.00
Relish dish, lg rose clusters on gr/bl border, gold rim, open hdls 95.00
Salt box, Salt in blk block letters, hanging, hinged wood lid, 6".... 62.00
Slop jar, Cairo w/pk & yel roses, w/lid, 10" 161.00
Sugar bowl, Blue Willow, 8-sided, hdls, 6x5x6", $66 to................ 119.00
Sugar bowl, Bluebird, hdls 76.00
Tea & toast set, Lucerne, underplate (10½x6")+cup 47.00
Tea set, Baby Bunting, pot+cr/sug w/lid+2 plates (7"), child sz.... 188.00
Teapot, Argyle, bl on wht, vitreous body, w/orig infusor 88.00
Teapot, Blue Willow, sq, 1911, 4½x6¼" 101.00
Teapot, Blue Willow, sq, 1911, 6x9" 194.00
Teapot, child's, Bluebird 500.00
Tureen, vegetable, forget-me-not border, gold trim, 7½x9½" 119.00
Tureen, vegetable, pk floral w/gr leaves, gold trim, hdls, 7½x9½". 119.00
Vase, Geraniums, mc, rose bowl shape, 3¾" 89.00
Vase, roses & violets w/gold, low ped, ornate hdls, 10½"............... 48.00
Warming dish, Bluebird, metal fr w/hdls, 8½" 152.00

Burley-Winter

Located in Crooksville, Ohio, this family venture had its roots in a company started in 1872 by William Newton Burley and Wilson Winter. From 1885 it operated under the name of Burley, Winter and Brown, reverting back to Burley & Winter after Mr. Brown left the company in 1892. They merged with the Keystone Pottery about 1900 (its founders were brothers Z.W. Burley and S.V. Burley), and merged again in 1912 with the John G. Burley Pottery. This company was dissolved in the early 1930s. A variety of marks were used.

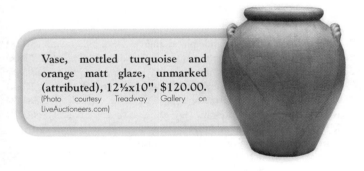

Vase, mottled turquoise and orange matt glaze, unmarked (attributed), 12½x10", $120.00.
(Photo courtesy Treadway Gallery on LiveAuctioneers.com)

Ash receiver, frog figural, orange & gr mottle, 3¾" 28.00
Vase, drip glaze on wht clay, 20"... 1,840.00
Vase, foliage at neck, rim-to-hip hdls, ftd, bl & wht mottle, 9"...... 50.00
Vase, geometrics at rim, rim-to-hip hdls, gr/brn/purple mottle, 20".. 350.00
Vase, geometrics at shoulder, bulb, pk/gr/cream mottle, chips, 9" .. 32.00
Vase, lion-head medallions on olive/turq/ivory mottle, 18x14" ... 480.00
Vase, yel, purple & gr mottle, flared rim, hdls, 7" 50.00

Burmese Glass

Burmese glass was patented in 1885 by the Mount Washington Glass Co. It is typically shaded from canary yellow to a rosy salmon color. The yellow is produced by the addition of uranium oxide to the mix. The salmon color comes from the addition of gold salts and is achieved by reheating the object (partially) in the furnace. It is thus called 'heat sensitive' glass. Thomas Webb of England was licensed to produce Burmese and often added more gold, giving an almost fuchsia tinge to the salmon in some cases. They called their glass 'Queen's Burmese,' and this is sometimes etched on the base of the object. This is not to be confused with Mount Washington's 'Queen's Design,' which refers to the design painted on the object. Both companies added decoration to many pieces.

Mount Washington-Pairpoint produced some Burmese in the late 1920s and Gundersen and Bryden in the 1950s and 1970s, but the color and shapes are different. In the listings that follow, examples are assumed to have the satin finish unless noted 'shiny.'

For more information we recommend *Mt. Washington Art Glass* by Betty B. Sisk (Collector Books). See also Lamps, Fairy.

Bottle, perfume, Webb, sterling lid, gold gingko decor, 5" 700.00
Bowl, Gunderson, 3 wishbone ft, 7" 55.00
Candlestick, Pairpoint, ft, 6½" 35.00
Celery, Mt WA, shiny, bulb, long neck, crimped 300.00
Condiment, Mt WA, 4-pc, w/2 stoppers, in metal fr 1,800.00
Cup/saucer, Mt WA, acid finish, undecorated.............................. 155.00
Cup/saucer, Mt WA, glossy, undecorated 250.00

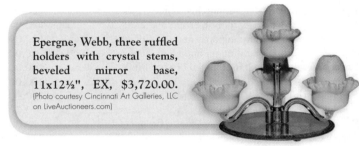

Epergne, Webb, three ruffled holders with crystal stems, beveled mirror base, 11x12½", EX, $3,720.00.
(Photo courtesy Cincinnati Art Galleries, LLC on LiveAuctioneers.com)

Jar, biscuit, Mt WA, SP lid, beaded enamel floral decor, 5" 800.00
Jar, biscuit, Webb, SP lid, red butterfly & floral decor, 5" 600.00
Lamp, fairy, 3-pc, 2 fluted rims, crystal candle cup, 12" 1,200.00
Lamp, fairy, Mt WA, 2-pc, crystal base... 180.00
Lamp, floral decor, HP, int of base mk S Clarke Patent Trade Mark Fairy, 5". 1,100.00
Pitcher, Mt WA, floral decor w/Thomas Hood poem, 4½" 1,300.00
Rose bowl, Mt WA, fall colors, Prunis decor, 2½"........................ 250.00
Rose bowl, Mt WA, quad-ra-fold rim, orange & wht floral decor. 220.00
Toothpick holder, Mt WA, Dmn Quilt, acid, sq top, 2¾"............. 140.00
Toothpick holder, Mt WA, glossy sq top, undecorated 225.00
Toothpick holder, Mt WA, hat form, wht floral decor.................. 475.00
Tumbler, Dmn Optic, undecorated.. 125.00
Tumbler, Mt WA, fern 410.00
Tumbler, Mt WA, violets 480.00
Vase, Egyptian bottle form, ftd, 2-hdld, undecorated, 10½" 1,500.00
Vase, Mt WA, 2-hdld, acid finish, floral enamel decor, 12" 2,200.00
Vase, Mt WA, bulb, long neck, stylized gold floral decor, 9½"...... 750.00
Vase, Mt WA, dbl gourd, acid finish, 7" 350.00
Vase, Mt WA, jack-in-pulpit, crimped, acid, 12" 240.00
Vase, Mt WA, jack-in-pulpit, crimped, acid, 18" 350.00
Vase, Mt WA, jack-in-pulpit, crimped, glossy, 8"......................... 180.00
Vase, Pairpoint, bl Burmese, trumpet, tri-cornered, crimp, sgn, 7¾" .. 75.00
Vase, Webb, Queen's ware, bl & wht floral, 3¼" 90.00
Vase, Webb, Queen's ware, crimped ft & rim, red berries & fall leaves, 4" ...250.00
Vase, Webb, Queen's ware, mk, ovoid body, flared top, leaf & nut decor, 7½" ..800.00

Butter Molds and Stamps

The art of decorating butter began in Europe during the reign of Charles II. This practice was continued in America by the farmer's wife who sold her homemade butter at the weekly market to earn extra money during hard times. A mold or stamp with a special design, hand carved either by her husband or a local craftsman, not only made her product more attractive but also helped identify it as hers. The pattern became the trademark of Mrs. Smith, and all who saw it knew that this was her butter. It was usually the rule that no two farms used the same mold within a certain area, thus the many variations and patterns available to the collector today. The most valuable are those which have animals, birds, or odd shapes. The most sought-after motifs are the eagle, cow, fish, and rooster. These works of early folk art are quickly disappearing from the market.

Molds

Anchor w/rope border, tight hairline, ca 1860, 3½" 90.00
Cow grazing w/branch on her bk, notched border, 1880s, 1⅞" 180.00
Donkey standing in grass, minor chip, 1850s, 3¾" 1,800.00
Eagle & olive branch, rope border, 19th C, 4½" 215.00
Eagle facing left holds shield, worn hdl, 3½" 150.00
Fish (5) in folky style, EX details, notched border, 1840s, 3" 1,200.00
Fish over 3 fern leaves & seaweed, notched border, hairline, 3¼". 270.00
Flower (stylized), cvd border, rect, 19th C, 2x8x4" 235.00
Maple leaf thistle, dbl-sided, ca 1850, 4⅛x3¼" 1,980.00
Maple leaf, realistic details, notched border, 1880s, 3½" 120.00
Pheasant among foliage, rpl hdl, crack, 3¼" 120.00
Rooster crowing & standing on branches, chips, 1960s, 4⅝" 150.00
Rooster crowing & standing on branches, hairline, 1860s, 4⅛" ... 180.00
Sheep in grass, facing left, notched border, 1860s, 2" 480.00
Strawberry, scrubbed, 1" 200.00
Sunflower (lg), single line border, 1860s, 4⅜" 240.00
Sunflower center, line border, 4⅜" 200.00
Swan in rough water among reeds, rpl hdl, sm crack, 4" 300.00
Turkey standing in grass, notched/sawtooth borders, EX patina, 4"..1,325.00
UNION letters, geometric design, notched border, ca 1864, 4¼" 480.00

Stamps

Acorn (stylized), dk patina, w/hdl, 4½" 120.00
Basket of mixed flowers, worm holes/scrubbed, 3" 285.00
Compass star w/X-hatched bkgrnd, trn poplar, aged patina, 4½".240.00
Cow facing left, branch over bk, scalloped edge, 1-pc hdl, 4¾" ... 120.00
Eagle (stylized), curly maple w/EX figure, lollipop form, rfn, 4"....600.00
Eagle among grasses, sm snowflake at shoulder, coggled rim, 4⅛" . 360.00

Fish (5), with carved eye details, notched borders, circa 1840s, 3", NM, $1,200.00. (Photo courtesy Morphy Auctions on LiveAuctioneers.com)

Heart & leaves, semicircular, 6¾x4½" 1,025.00
Heart & star on oval block, EX detail & cvg, 5½x3¼" 1,650.00
Horse/2 partridges, dbl-sided, dry patina, 1840s, 3¼" 725.00
Lyre, deep cvg, notched border, 1840s, EX patina, 5" 1,200.00
Quatrefoil flowers/ribbed leaves, dbl-sided, scrubbed, 3½x4½".....270.00
Radish w/wreath for border, rare subject, ca 1880, 3" 1,450.00
Sheaves of wheat, checked wood, 3½" 48.00
Swirls/stars, dbl-sided lollipop, butternut wood, 1800s, 4½".......3,000.00
Tulip (stylized), serrated border, aged patina, flat, 3¾" 360.00

Buttonhooks

The earliest known written reference to buttonhooks (shoe hooks, glove hooks, or collar buttoners) is dated 1611. They became a necessary implement in the 1850s when tight-fitting high-button shoes became fashionable. Later in the nineteenth century, ladies' button gloves and men's button-on collars and cuffs dictated specific types of buttoners, some with a closed wire loop instead of a hook end. Both shoes and gloves used as many as 24 buttons each. Usage began to wane in the late 1920s following a fashion change to low-cut laced shoes and the invention of the zipper. There was a brief resurgence of use following the 1948 movie *High Button Shoes*. For a simple, needed utilitarian device, buttonhook handles were made from a surprising variety of materials: natural wood, bone, ivory, agate, and mother-of-pearl to plain steel, celluloid, aluminum, iron, lead and pewter, artistic copper, brass, silver, gold, and many other materials in lengths that varied from under 2" to over 20". Many designs folded or retracted, and buttonhooks were often combined with shoehorns and other useful implements. Stamped steel buttonhooks often came free with the purchase of shoes, gloves, or collars. Material, design, workmanship, condition, and relative scarcity are the primary market value factors. Prices range from $1.00 to over $500.00, with most being in the $10.00 to $100.00 range. Buttonhooks are fairly easy to find, and they are interesting to display.

See the Buttonhook Society in the Clubs, Newsletters, and Websites section.

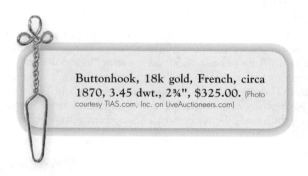

Buttonhook, 18k gold, French, circa 1870, 3.45 dwt., 2¾", $325.00. (Photo courtesy TIAS.com, Inc. on LiveAuctioneers.com)

Buttonhook/penknife, ivory side plates, man's.................................. 50.00
Buttonhooks, brass, folding type... 27.00
Buttonhooks, sterling silver 30.00
Collar buttoner, stamped steel, advertising, closed end, 3"............. 20.00
Glove hook, gold-plated, retractable, 3" 90.00
Glove hook, loop end, agate hdl, 2½" 60.00
Shoe hook, colored celluloid hdl, 8" 15.00
Shoe hook, lathe-trn hardwood hdl, dk finish, 8" 15.00
Shoe hook, SP w/blade, repousse hdl, Pat Jan 5 1892, 5" 40.00
Shoe hook, stamped steel, advertising, 5" 8.00
Shoe hook, sterling, floral & geometrics, 8" 55.00
Shoe hook, sterling, Nouveau lady's face, 6½" 75.00
Shoe hook, sterling, W w/arrow, hammered Florentine decor, mk. 55.00
Shoe hook/shoehorn, combination, steel & celluloid, 9" 35.00

Bybee

The Bybee Pottery was founded in 1845 in the small town of Bybee, Kentucky, by the Cornelison family. Their earliest wares were primarily stoneware churns and jars. Today the work is carried on by sixth-generation Cornelison potters who still use the same facilities and production methods to make a more diversified line of pottery. From a fine white clay mined only a few miles from the potting shed itself, the shop produces vases, jugs, dinnerware, and banks in a variety of colors, some of which are shipped to the larger cities to be sold in department stores and specialty shops. The bulk of their wares, however, is sold to the thousands of tourists who are attracted to the pottery each year.

Bowl, bl, fluted & scalloped rim, 7½" 24.00
Jar, orange (uranium oxide) on stoneware, 3-hdl, 17½" 450.00

Mug, gr crystalline, sgn Cornelison, 3½" 25.00
Vase, cattails on purple and bl matt, 11" 180.00
Vase, gr matt, Genuine Bybee sticker, 4¾x3½" 135.00
Vase, mauve matt over molded grasses, #512, 10½" 275.00

Cabat

From its inception in New York City around 1940, through various types of clays, designs, and glazes, the Rose Cabat 'Feelie' evolved into present forms and glazes in the late 1950s, after a relocation to Arizona. Rose was aided and encouraged through the years by her late husband Erni. Their small 'weed pots' are readily recognizable by their light weight, tiny necks, and soft glazes. Pieces are marked with a hand-incised 'Cabat' on the bottom. Our advisor for this category is Suzanne Perrault; she is listed in the Directory under New Jersey.

Bottle, brn matt w/crystalline inclusions, sm chip, 6" 1,680.00
Vase, bl w/gr runs, #841 47, 4¼x1⅞" 600.00
Vase, butterscotch w/brn drips/spatters, onion form, #384, 3¼x2" .. 400.00
Vase, cobalt, pear shape, #841 43, 3¾x2¼" 600.00

Vase, Feelie, teal over cobalt vellum glazes, incised CABAT, 6½x4", $1,920.00. (Photo courtesy Rago Arts and Auction Center)

Vase, gr w/brn streaks on brn clay, bulb, 3x3" 480.00
Vase, gr w/gray streaks, #380, 4x1½" 630.00
Vase, gunmetal gray & turq matt on stoneware, bulb, 5x3¾" 780.00
Vase, lemon yel/gr/tan, 3½x2¾" 500.00
Vase, lime gr & celadon, 5¼x4" 780.00
Vase, streaky brn, onion form, 3x2¼" 330.00
Vase, turq to olive gr, spherical, 3⅞" 840.00
Vase, turq w/tan drips on brn clay, gourd form, 5x3" 725.00

Calendar Plates

Calendar plates were advertising giveaways most popular from about 1906 until the late 1920s. They were decorated with colorful underglaze decals of lovely ladies, flowers, animals, birds and, of course, the 12 months of the year of their issue. During the 1950s they came into vogue again but never to the extent they were originally. Those with exceptional detailing or those with scenes of a particular activity are most desirable, so are any from before 1906.

1895, months in center w/floral & swirl border, 8" 270.00
1904, Happy New Year, Cupid & bell, 8" 50.00
1904, months surrounded by berries 65.00
1907, lady drinking from fountain of Roman god Pan 75.00
1908, lg red rose w/leaves, MC Kittle, Bell Vernon PA, 9" 40.00
1908, pk rose border 30.00
1909, cherries & strawberry blossoms, Imperial, 7½" 60.00
1909, Gibson Girl, scalloped edge, 9¼", $60 to 70.00
1909, monks drinking wine, 9" 55.00
1909, roses in center w/months around border w/flowers, Wedgwood . 50.00
1909, William Jennings Bryan sepia-tone portrait, 9¼" 90.00

1910, dog (upright) holds months suspended from stick in mouth ... 60.00
1910, holly berries on 3 sides w/Hauri Bros Grocery ad, 7¼" 45.00
1910, Indian chief, months on feathers of headdress, 7½" 65.00
1910, lady w/horse in center w/months surrounding, Princeton on border .. 68.00
1910, sailing scene, months w/pk & gr floral along rim, TB Colby, 9" . 42.00
1910, Washington's Old Home at Mt Vernon, 9⅛" 50.00
1910, winter church scene & summer lakeside home, months in 3 groups .. 48.00
1911, Abraham Lincoln portrait, 9" 150.00
1911, cherub & advertising in center, Kingburg Departmant Store, 8" .. 56.00
1911, Niagara Falls scene, gold trim, 9¼" 65.00
1911, ocean scene w/months & roses, emb/scalloped edge, 8¼", $45 to .. 55.00
1911, Salem Evangelical Church, w/floral & months border, 8¼" 45.00
1911, time-zone clocks & flowers, 8⅛" 50.00
1912, airplane/scenic view, fruit & flower border, 8½", EX 65.00

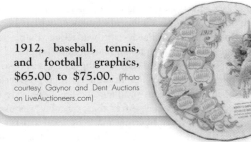

1912, baseball, tennis, and football graphics, $65.00 to $75.00. (Photo courtesy Gaynor and Dent Auctions on LiveAuctioneers.com)

1912, floral w/months & cherubs border, Old Plantation Distilling, 8" .. 40.00
1912, mixed fruits, cherubs & months along border, gold trim, 8" . 90.00
1913, Rainbow Falls, Yosemite Valley, 9⅜" 75.00
1914, Plymouth Rock center w/months at border, mk Carnation .. 35.00
1915, floral w/butterflies & months, scalloped rim, AC Lubenow, 8" ... 32.00
1916, yel roses, months separated by bluebirds in border, 8¼" 35.00
1918, Am flag center, months & birds along rim, DE McNicol, 8" .. 60.00
1922, hunting dogs & game, 9¼" 45.00
1945, English Setter, months along rim, Walter's Auction Gallery, 10" . 55.00
1954, Indian chief in full headdress, months along rim 35.00
1973, Bountiful Butterfly theme, Wedgwood 55.00

Calendars

Calendars are collected for their colorful prints, often attributed to a well recognized artist of the period. Advertising calendars from the turn of the century often have a double appeal when representing a company whose tins, signs, store displays, etc., are also collectible. See also Maxfield Parrish; Railroadiana; Winchester.

1893, S Allen's Sons, military man & horse, full pad, 16x11", EX . 90.00
1895, Nordeck 10¢ Cigars, dc, blond lady, full pad, 11x8", EX 130.00
1896, Norton Bros Cans..., folding pocket type, 3", EX+ 375.00
1904, Devers Golden West, girl w/basket, 7x3½", EX+ 300.00
1905, DeLaval Cream Separator, full date pad, NM 1,100.00
1907, Harrington & Richardson Arms, figure on snowshoes, 27x14", NM .. 3,100.00
1909, Metropolitan Life Ins, Vict lady & child, 21x12", NM 275.00
1910, Kis-Me Chewing Gum, lady in oval on faux leather cb, 11x6", VG .. 150.00
1910, Western Dressed Beef, wood fr, complete, vertical, NM 615.00
1912, Wrigley's Spearmint Pepsin Gum, children w/dog, 9x5", EX . 140.00
1915, Answering the Call, moose scene, full pad, 37x18", EX+ ... 425.00
1918, Lehigh Nat'l Cement, lady w/hat, bow on shoulder, 15x9", EX ... 70.00
1919, North Ferguson & Co, Eager for the Hunt, dogs, 25x16", EX . 210.00
1920, Conradi's Pharmacy, man on horse in water, Goodwin, 16x8", EX+ .. 60.00
1922, Peters Cartridges, Lest We Forget, Forbes, 31½x12", NM.. 1,050.00
1928, US Shell Shots, boy w/mother dog & pups, 33x16", EX .. 1,200.00
1929, Am Stores, children in landscape, full pad, 26x12", NM ... 100.00

1929, US Cartridge Co, man & dog in winter scene, 35x16", EX. 975.00
1930, Western Ammunition, Veteran, canoe scene, Parsons, 27x14", EX+.625.00
1933, Rett Bros...Taxidermists, Scouting for Game, Russeau, 22x14", VG ..70.00
1938, Walt Disney's Silly Symphony, Brn & Bigelow, 17x9", NM ..525.00
1942, PA Railroad, Partners in Nat'l Defence, G Teller, 28x20", EX+...75.00
1943, Hercules Powder, Not This Trip Old Pal, Fuller, 30x13", EX+ .350.00
1948, Hercules Powder, Veterans, Cronwell, full pad, 30x13", EX. 90.00
1949, Burns Tool Co, Vision of Beauty, Elvgren nude, 46x22", EX.375.00
1953, Famous Mint, Who Killed the Bear, Russell, 14x18½", EX+..60.00

California Faience

California Faience was founded in 1913 as 'The Tile Shop' by Chauncey R. Thomas in Berkeley, California. He was joined by William V. Bragdon in 1915 who became sole owner in 1938. The product line was apparently always marked 'California Faience,' which became the company's legal name in 1924. Production was reduced after 1933, but the firm stayed in business as a studio and factory until it closed in 1959. Products consisted of hand-pressed tiles and slip-cast vases, bowls, flower frogs, and occasional figures. They are notable for high production quality and aesthetic simplicity. Items produced before 1934 were made of dark brown or reddish brown clay. After that, tan clay was used. Later production consisted mainly of figurines made by local artists. The firm made many of the tiles at Hearst Castle, San Simeon, California. From 1928 to 1930 a line marked 'California Porcelain' was produced in white porcelain at West Coast Porcelain Manufacturers in Millbrae.

The multicolored art tiles are especially popular with collectors. Generally speaking, matt glazes were in use mostly before 1921 and are rare. Prices continue to be weak, reflecting the overall depressed art pottery market. Collectors are quite fussy about condition; impaired pieces sell for very low prices. Almost all known pieces are marked on the bottom. Shape numbers are from a salesman's catalog and do not appear on the pieces. Unmarked pieces in a pale creamy clay were made from cast off West Coast Porcelain molds by Potlatch pottery in Seattle, Washington, from 1934 to 1941. Unmarked tiles were made until recently from original molds by Deer Creek Pottery, Grass Valley, California. They can be distinguished from the old tiles as they are thinner and there is a repetition of the raised designs on their backs. Our advisor for this category is Dr. Kirby William Brown; he is listed in the Directory under California. He is currently researching a book on this topic and welcomes input from collectors.

Tile, bisque, Chicago 1933 Expo logo, 6½x4⅝", $1,100.00. (Photo courtesy Dr. Kirby William Brown)

Ashtray, mottled orange matt, dog facing backward, 5½" 130.00
Bowl, brn matt & yel gloss, flared rim, #60, 6" dia........................... 80.00
Bowl, dk bl & turq gloss, flared rim, #58, 7¾" dia 90.00
Bowl, grn gloss, porc, Pueblo Indian, incurved rim, 5" dia 140.00
Bowl, oxblood gloss, Pueblo Indian, raised rim, #22, 5½" dia....... 134.00
Bowl, turq gloss, flared rim, flower petal form, #101, 6" dia............ 50.00
Candlestick, dk bl matt, flared base, no rings, #63, 4¼" 56.00
Figurine, Art Deco semi-nude, turq gloss, M Geisendorfer, 10" ... 300.00
Flower frog, turq gloss, rnd, 16 holes, #5, 4⅜" dia........................... 21.00
Jar, plum gloss, acorn shape jar, #45, lid missing, 3" 70.00
Lamp, dk bl gloss, cylindrical, 12-sided, stepped, Art Deco, 12" .. 750.00

Planter box, turq gloss w/yel rim, rect, 7x4" 58.00
Temple jar, turq gloss, broad ovoid, flat top lid, #71, 9½" 220.00
Tile, mc gloss, flying cranes, Persian design, mc gloss, sq, 8" 1,400.00
Tile, mc gloss, stylized lotus, Hearst Castle, 4x6" 400.00
Tile, plain field, grn matt, sq, 6" 60.00
Trivet, grn matt rim, mc matt, Yucca in desert, 5¼" dia 460.00
Trivet, turq gloss rim, mc matt, stylized peacock, 5¼" dia 270.00
Trivet, yel gloss rim, mc matt, Carmel Mission, 5⅜" dia............... 290.00
Vase, dk bl & rust matt, squat tapered, moth in relief, 5" 840.00
Vase, rose gloss, Pueblo Indian olla, #24, 3" 190.00
Vase, turq gloss, ovoid, no lip, 5".. 50.00
Vase, turq gloss, wide flared trumpet, decagonal, #97, 4" 40.00
Vase, yel matt, porc, tapered bumpy gourd, 10" 1,080.00

California Perfume Company

In 1886, Mr. David Hall McConnell, Sr. and his wife Lucy (Hays) started the California Perfume Company out of a single room at 126 Chamber's Street, New York. McConnell was a bookseller working for the Union Publishing House in New York. As McConnell worked his door-to-door sales, he found that he primarily dealt with the lady of the house. In an attempt to gain entry, as well as secure the sales of his books, McConnell presented his prospective customers a complimentary bottle of inexpensive perfume. Upon determining that customers were more interested in the perfumes than his books, McConnell decided that the manufacture of perfumes and other consumables would be more lucrative. He bottled toiletries and household products under the banner of the California Perfume Company. In 1923, McConnell introduced a line of household products called Perfection; in 1928 the name 'Avon' appeared on the label of five products; and by 1939 all production bore the name Avon and the C.P.C. name was entirely removed. The phenomenal success of the company is attributed to two foundational elements: 1) the door-to-door sales approach, and 2) the money-back guarantee offered by his first Depot Agent, Mrs. P. F. E. Albee, acknowledged as the 'Mother of the California Perfume Company.'

Along with the myriad of CPC collectibles, the seasoned CPC collectors also search for items that are closely, or even loosely, associated with the California Perfume Company. In 1896 McConnell secured the help of one of New York's finest perfumers, Mr. Adolph Goetting, to run his growing laboratory in Suffern, New York. Goetting was in business from 1870 to 1896. That acquisition required McConnell to buy out Goetting's entire inventory and concern — a move that proved fruitful in that McConnell continued Goetting & Co. until at least 1918. Goetting collectibles are labeled: Goetting & Co., New York; Goetting's; Savoi Et Cie, Paris; or Savoi Et Cie, New York. Another business was initiated by McConnell and CPC treasurer, Mr. Alexander Henderson, in 1897 and continued well into the early 1900s: the Mutual Mfg. Company of New York. This endeavor sold perfumes, silverware, household items, and more. Items discovered thus far mirror the CPC packaging/labeling. Other McConnell businesses include South American Silver company, D. H. McConnell company, and Mecca Oil. Because very little is known about these companies and since only a few examples of their product containers and advertising material have been found, market values for such items have not yet been established. Extremely rare items sought by the seasoned collector include products marked Marvel Electric Silver Cleaner, Easy Day Automatic Clothes Washer, the 1915 Automassage Shaving Brush, 1896 – 1899 California Cough Syrup, pre-1900 CPC Catalogs, and 1926 Calopad Sanitary Napkins, to name just a few.

Inquiries concerning California Perfume Company items and the companies or items mentioned in the previous paragraphs should be directed toward our advisor, Russell Mills, whose address is in the Directory under Pennsylvania. (Please send a large SASE and be sure to request clearly the information you are seeking.) For more information on products and pricing, we recommend *Bud Hastin's Avon Collector's Encyclopedia*. For more information on the history of the California Perfume Company and associated concerns, we recommend the California Perfume Company website, www.californiaperfumecompany.net.

Note: Our values are for items in mint condition unless otherwise noted. A very rare item or one in super mint condition might go for 10% more. Damage, wear, missing parts, etc., must be considered; items judged to be in only good to very good condition should be priced at up to 50% of listed values, with fair to good at 25% and excellent at 75%. Parts (labels, stoppers, caps, etc.) might be evaluated at 10% of these prices.

5 Ring Circus Soap Set, 1st figural soap set, 1939, MIB	400.00
American Ideal Set, 1918-20, MIB	600.00
Ariel Perfume, triangular, bl & silver label, 1-oz, 1930, MIB	135.00
Baby Set w/Baby Powder, Baby Soap, & Toilet Water, 1923-25, MIB	375.00
Bay Rum Bottle, blk/wht label, glass stopper, 8-oz, 1914-16, MIB	200.00
California Shampoo Cream, glass, zinc lid, 4-oz, 1894-97, MIB	225.00
Calopad, box of 12 feminine napkins, 1925-28, MIB	500.00
Color Plate Catalog, color litho, 1915-29	180.00
CP Tooth Powder, brn & cream label, 1915	190.00
Daphne Lipstick, metal case, 1919, MIB	85.00
Depilatory, glass bottle, 1914-15, 1-oz, MIB	75.00
Depot Manager's ID pin, emb w/CPC, gold finish, 1910-25	125.00
Easy Cleaner Soap, 2½-lb soap bars & instruction card, 1925, MIB	140.00
Elite Foot Powder, bl can, 1923-31, 4-oz, MIB	40.00
Flavoring Extract, cork stopper, variety of flavors, 64-oz, 1899	500.00
Florida Water, crown glass stopper, 1½-oz, 1905, MIB	275.00
Food Flavoring Demonstrator Kit, woven reed case, holds 20 bottles, 1915	1,600.00
Juvenile Set, 1913-15	700.00

Lavendar Salts, green bottle with flower design glass stopper, 1898 – 1899, MIB, $325.00. (Photo courtesy Russell Mills)

Lotus Cream, rnd glass stopper, 12-oz, 1917, MIB	250.00
Mission Garden Perfume, Bohemian glass bottle, 1½-oz, 1922-25, MIB	600.00
Narcissus Perfume Falconette, glass stopper, dk bl box, ½-oz, 1925-30, MIB	135.00
Natoma Talcum Powder, orange tin w/portrait of Indian Maiden, 3½-oz, MIB	575.00
Shoe White, colorful graphics on box, sack of powder, 5-oz, 1915-18, MIB	300.00
Stephanotis Perfume, blk & wht label w/red Eureka Trademark, 1-oz, 1904, MIB	160.00
Trailing Arbutus Toilet Water, 2-oz, 1915, MIB	140.00
Vegetable Coloring, various colors, 2-oz, 1898-1901, MIB	160.00
Vernafleur Ardent Face Powder, 1925-30, MIB	40.00
Violet Perfume, rnd glass stopper, 1-oz, 1905-07, MIB	225.00
Witch Hazel, blk & wht label, cork stopper, 4-oz, 1914-19, MIB	145.00

Camark

The Camden Art and Tile Company (commonly known as Camark) of Camden, Arkansas, was organized in the fall of 1926 by Samuel J. 'Jack' Carnes. Using clays from Arkansas, John Lessell, who had been hired as art director by Carnes, produced the initial lustre and iridescent Lessell wares for Camark ('CAM'den, 'ARK'ansas) before his death in Decem-

ber 1926. Before the plant opened in the spring of 1927, Carnes brought John's wife, Jeanne, and stepdaughter, Billie, to oversee the art department's manufacture of Le-Camark. Production by the Lessell family included variations of J.B. Owens' Soudanese and Opalesce and Weller's Marengo and Lamar. Camark's version of Marengo was called Old English. They also made wares identical to Weller's LaSa. Pieces made by John Lessell back in Ohio were signed 'Lessell,' while those made by Jeanne and Billie in Arkansas during 1927 were signed 'Le-Camark.' By 1928 Camark's production centered on traditional glazes. Drip glazes similar to Muncie Pottery were produced, in particular the green drip over pink. In the 1930s commercial castware with simple glossy and matt finishes became the primary focus and would continue so until Camark closed in the early 1960s. Between the 1960s and 1980s the company operated mainly as a retail store selling existing inventory, but some limited production occurred. In 1986 the company was purchased by the Ashcroft family of Camden, but no pottery has yet been made at the factory.

Our advisor for this category is Tony Freyaldenhoven; he is listed in the Directory under Arkansas.

Ashtray, Orange-Gr Overflow, 1st block letter mk, 3½", $60 to	80.00
Basket, ivory scratch ware, bl/gr int, hdl, unmk, 9"	60.00
Bowl, console, gray & bl mottled, w/frog, Arkansas sticker, unmk, 3x15", $250 to	300.00
Bowl, Ivory Crackle Bright, Gus Blass Co sticker, unmk, 10¼x3¼", $250 to	300.00
Bowl, Orange-Gr Overflow, Arkansas sticker, 12¼x5¾", $140 to	160.00
Bowl, Rose Pk, HP tulip, scalloped edge, hdls, ftd, unmk, 13"	250.00
Canoe, bl & wht stipple, 1st block letter mk, 11x3¼", $100 to	120.00
Charger, bl & wht stipple, 1st block letter mk, 13¼"	250.00
Figurine, elephant, Sea Gr, unmk, 5x3½", $140 to	160.00
Figurine, frog, Olive Gr, Lt Overflow, 1st block letter mk, 4x3", $80 to	100.00
Fish bowl, bird, Frosted Gr, Arkansas sticker, $100 to	120.00
Flower frog, Rose-Gr Overflow, 1st block letter mk, ¾x3"	30.00
Ginger jar, Ivory Crackle Matt, gold ink stamp, 9"	350.00
Humidor, Delphinium Bl, 1st block letter mk, 6½", $80 to	100.00
Humidor, Mirror Blk, 1st block letter, Arkansas sitcker, 5½", $120 to	140.00
Lamp base, Aztec Red mottle, Arkansas sticker, 8", $600 to	800.00
Lamp base, palm trees on lustre, Lessell, 13"	1,200.00
Pig bottle, orange, 1st block letter mk, 3x9"	250.00
Pitcher, Celestial Bl, waffle batter, parrot hdl, Arkansas stamp, 6½", $160 to	180.00
Pitcher, Sea Gr, Barcelona/Spano ware, unmk, 8⅓", $180 to	200.00
Planter, Frosted Gr, ruffled rim, Arkansas sticker, 4"	60.00
Planter, Rose-Gr Overflow, unmk, 13½x5¼x8½", $300 to	350.00
Shot glass, Orange-Gr Overflow, unmk, 2", $20 to	30.00
Vase, Autumn, flower form, 1st block letter mk, 10"	100.00
Vase, Azurite Bl, 1st block letter mk, 8", $100 to	120.00
Vase, bl matt w/yel drip, paper label, 6½"	360.00
Vase, brn stipple, baluster, unmk, 3"	30.00
Vase, Emerald Gr, integral hdls, USA Camark N #40, 14"	80.00
Vase, fan, Yel-Gr Overflow, 1st block letter mk, 6", $60 to	80.00

Vase, Forest Green crackle, gold stamp, 9", $425.00. (Photo courtesy Belhorn Auction Services LLC on LiveAuctioneers.com)

Vase, LeCamark Venetian Jonquil on blk lustre, Arkansas stamp, 8", $800 to	900.00
Vase, Mulberry w/lt overflow, Deco shape, #405, 6¾"	120.00
Vase, Old English Ivory, shouldered, Camark, 8"	700.00

Vase, Old English Rose, Lessell, cylindrical, 11¾" 1,000.00
Vase, Oxford w/silver lustre, LeCamark, 8" 1,000.00
Vase, Pastel Bl-Gr Overflow, 1st block letter mk, 7" 140.00
Vase, Rose-Gr Overflow, Deco, unmk, 8", $200 to 250.00
Vase, turq matt, fan shape, unmk, 5" 60.00
Vase, Yel Crackle Bright, modernistic, Arkansas stamp & sticker, 16¼", $1,100 to .1,300.00
Vase, yel, Nouveau floral, hdl, #800-R, bl/gold Arkansas sticker, 14" 225.00

Cambridge Glass

The Cambridge Glass Company began operations in 1901 in Cambridge, Ohio. Primarily they made crystal dinnerware and well-designed accessory pieces until the 1920s when they introduced the concept of color that was to become so popular on the American dinnerware market. Always maintaining high standards of quality and elegance, they produced many lines that became bestsellers; through the '20s and '30s they were recognized as the largest manufacturer of this type of glassware in the world.

Of the various marks the company used, the 'C in triangle' is the most familiar. Production stopped in 1958. For a more thorough study of the subject, we recommend *Colors in Cambridge Glass* by the National Cambridge Collectors, Inc., who may be found in the Clubs, Newsletters, and Websites section. See also Carnival Glass; Glass Animals and Figurines.

Achilles, crystal, bowl, #3900/62, 4-toed, flared, 12" 75.00
Achilles, crystal, cake plate, 2-hdl, #3900/35, 13½" 85.00
Achilles, crystal, candy box, w/cover, #3900/165 .... 65.00
Achilles, crystal, celery/relish, #3900/126, 3-part, 12" 65.00
Achilles, crystal, cocktail icer, #968, w/liner 75.00
Achilles, crystal, cocktail, #3121, 3-oz 25.00
Achilles, crystal, compote, #3900, 5½" 60.00
Achilles, crystal, creamer, #3900/41 .... 22.00
Achilles, crystal, floor vase, #1336, 18" 995.00
Achilles, crystal, mayonnaise, #3900/11, 2-part 35.00
Achilles, crystal, pitcher, #3400/38, ball jug, 80-oz 265.00
Achilles, crystal, plate, #3900/166, rolled edge, 14" 75.00
Achilles, crystal, stem, wine, #3121, 3½-oz 50.00
Achilles, crystal, tumbler, water, #3121, ftd, 10-oz 33.00
Adonis, crystal, bonbon, #3900/130, ftd, w/hdls, 7" 40.00
Adonis, crystal, candy dish, #3900/165, w/lid 145.00
Adonis, crystal, compote, #3500, w/hdls, 8" 110.00
Adonis, crystal, decanter, #1321, 28-oz 295.00
Adonis, crystal, plate, cake, 2-hdld, #3900/35, 13½" 85.00
Adonis, crystal, plate, luncheon, #3500, 8" 14.00
Adonis, crystal, relish, 2-hdl, 2-pt 75.00
Adonis, crystal, shakers, pr 75.00
Adonis, crystal, tumbler, juice, #3500, ftd, 5-oz 28.00
Apple Blossom, amber or yel, bowl, console, 12" 75.00
Apple Blossom, amber or yel, bowl, low ft, 11" 100.00
Apple Blossom, amber or yel, cordial, #3130, 1-oz 75.00
Apple Blossom, amber or yel, cup, #3400/75 .... 22.00
Apple Blossom, amber or yel, vase, rippled sides, 6" 145.00
Apple Blossom, crystal, bowl, cereal, 6" 25.00
Apple Blossom, crystal, cabinet flask, #3400/46, 12-oz 110.00
Apple Blossom, crystal, plate, dinner, 9" 35.00
Apple Blossom, crystal, relish tray, w/hdls, 7" 25.00
Apple Blossom, gr or pk, ashtray, heavy, 6" 125.00
Apple Blossom, gr or pk, bowl, cereal, 6" 50.00
Apple Blossom, gr or pk, candlestick, 2-lt, keyhole, ea 45.00
Apple Blossom, gr or pk, candy box w/cover, 4 ft 195.00
Apple Blossom, gr or pk, plate, dinner, 9" 80.00
Candlelight, crystal, bowl, #3400/48, 4-ftd, fancy edge, 11" 85.00

Candlelight, crystal, cake plate, #3900/35, w/hdls, 13" 75.00
Candlelight, crystal, candlestick, #3900/74, 3-lt, 6", ea 85.00
Candlelight, crystal, candy jar, #3500/41, 10" 185.00
Candlelight, crystal, cocktail, #3776, 3-oz 28.00
Candlelight, crystal, cup, #3900/17 .... 28.00
Candlelight, crystal, keyhole base #1237, 12" 175.00
Candlelight, crystal, mayonnaise, #3900/19, ftd, 2-pc 65.00
Candlelight, crystal, saucer, #3900/17 .... 7.00
Candlelight, crystal, tumbler, iced tea, #3114, ftd, 12-oz 40.00
Candlelight, crystal, vase, bud, #274, 10" 95.00
Candlelight, crystal, vase, globe #1309, 5" 75.00
Candlelight, crystal, vase, keyhole base, #1237, 9" 125.00
Caprice, bl or pk, bonbon, #133, sq, ftd, 6" 35.00
Caprice, bl or pk, bowl, #49, 4-ftd, 8" 95.00
Caprice, bl or pk, bowl, salad, #84, shallow, 15" 150.00
Caprice, bl or pk, cigarette box, #208, w/lid, 4x3" 45.00
Caprice, bl or pk, nut dish, divided, #94, 2" 35.00
Caprice, bl or pk, plate, salad, #23, 7" 18.00
Caprice, bl or pk, tray, #42, oval, 9" 35.00
Caprice, bl or pk, tumbler, iced tea, #310, flat, 12-oz 90.00
Caprice, bl or pk, vase, #338, crimped top, 6" 195.00
Caprice, bl or pk, vase, ball, #239, 8½" 275.00
Caprice, bl or pk, vase, ftd rose bowl, 6" 110.00
Caprice, crystal, ashtray, #216, 5" 6.00
Caprice, crystal, bowl, #52, crimped, 4-ftd, 9" 40.00
Caprice, crystal, bowl, almond, #95, 4-ftd, 2" 15.00
Caprice, crystal, cake plate, #36, ftd, 13" 125.00
Caprice, crystal, candlestick, #1338, 3-lt, ea 35.00
Caprice, crystal, candy dish, #165, 3-ftd, w/lid, 6" 40.00
Caprice, crystal, marmalade, #89, w/lid, 6-oz 60.00
Caprice, crystal, plate, luncheon, #22, 8½" 9.00
Caprice, crystal, shakers, #91, ball, pr 35.00
Caprice, crystal, tumbler, water, stem ft, #300, blown, 9-oz 15.00
Caprice, crystal, tumbler, whiskey, #300, 2½-oz 35.00

Caprice, crystal, two-part salad dressing server, $175.00. (Photo courtesy Hewletts Antiques on LiveAuctioneers.com)

Caprice, crystal, vase, ivy bowl #232, 5" 70.00
Chantilly, crystal, bowl, ftd, tab hdls, 11" 40.00
Chantilly, crystal, butter dish, rnd 150.00
Chantilly, crystal, candy dish, ftd, w/lid 65.00
Chantilly, crystal, marmalade, w/lid 50.00
Chantilly, crystal, plate, dinner, 10½" 50.00
Chantilly, crystal, plate, salad, 8" 10.00
Chantilly, crystal, sherbet, #3600, 7-oz 14.00
Chantilly, crystal, tumbler, juice, #3775, ftd, 5-oz 15.00
Chantilly, crystal, tumbler, water, stem ft, #3779, 9-oz 24.00
Chantilly, crystal, vase, bud, 10" 95.00
Chantilly, crystal, vase, flower, ftd, 11" 95.00
Chantilly, crystal, vase, high ft, flower, 6" 45.00
Chantilly, crystal, vase, keyhole base, 9" 60.00
Cleo, amber, gr, pk or yel, bowl, cranberry, 3" 40.00
Cleo, amber, gr, pk or yel, bowl, vegetable, w/lid, 9" 295.00
Cleo, amber, gr, pk or yel, compote, #877, 12" 75.00
Cleo, amber, gr, pk or yel, platter, 12" 95.00

Cleo, amber, gr, pk or yel, tumbler, #3007, ftd, 5-oz......................18.00
Cleo, amber, gr, pk or yel, tumbler, water, stem ft, #3115, 9-oz......22.00
Cleo, bl, bowl, 8½"...75.00
Cleo, bl, bowl, cranberry, 3"..60.00
Cleo, bl, bowl, oval, 11½"..110.00
Cleo, bl, candlestick, 3-lt, ea..130.00
Cleo, bl, humidor...450.00
Cleo, bl, ice bucket, #394..185.00
Cleo, bl, sugar sifter, ftd, 6¾"...750.00
Cleo, bl, toast & cover, rnd...400.00
Cleo, bl, tumbler, #3077, ftd, 5-oz...50.00
Cleo, bl, gravy boat, w/ liner plate, Decagon, #1091......................500.00
Daffodil, crystal, bonbon, #1181...28.00
Daffodil, crystal, cake plate, #1495, 11½"......................................70.00
Daffodil, crystal, candlestick, #628, 3", ea.....................................35.00
Daffodil, crystal, compote, #533, ftd, 5"...40.00
Daffodil, crystal, jug, #3400/140...275.00
Daffodil, crystal, relish, #214, 3-part, 10"......................................55.00
Daffodil, crystal, shakers, #360, squatty, pr....................................50.00
Daffodil, crystal, sugar bowl, #254..20.00
Daffodil, crystal, tumbler, water, stem ft, #3779, 9-oz......................33.00
Decagon, bl, bowl, berry, #1087, 10"..45.00
Decagon, bl, bowl, fruit, #1009, flat rim, 5".....................................20.00
Decagon, bl, plate, dinner, 9"..50.00
Decagon, bl, tray, #1078, oval, 12"...40.00
Decagon, bl, tumbler, #3077, ftd, 12-oz...30.00
Decagon, pastels, bowl, cranberry, flat rim, 3".................................16.00
Decagon, pastels, bowl, vegetable, #1085, rnd, 9"............................30.00
Decagon, pastels, celery tray, #1083, 11"..28.00
Decagon, pastels, compote, #877, 9"..35.00
Decagon, pastels, ice pail, #851...35.00
Decagon, pastels, plate, grill, #1200, 10"...30.00
Decagon, pastels, shakers, #396, pr..30.00
Diane, amber, gold encrusted, bowl, 4 ft, flared, 12".........................85.00
Diane, crystal, bitters...175.00
Diane, crystal, bowl, 4-ftd, flared, 12"..70.00
Diane, crystal, bowl, cereal, 6"...30.00
Diane, crystal, butter, rnd...145.00
Diane, crystal, candlestick, 5", ea..25.00
Diane, crystal, compote, 5"...35.00
Diane, crystal, creamer, #3400, scroll hdl..18.00
Diane, crystal, goblet, water, #3122, 9-oz..24.00
Diane, crystal, pitcher, martini..695.00
Diane, crystal, plate, dinner, #3900/24, 10"....................................60.00
Diane, crystal, platter, 13½"...90.00
Diane, crystal, saucer..4.00
Diane, crystal, sugar bowl, #3400, scroll hdl...................................18.00
Diane, crystal, tumbler, water, #1066, 9-oz.....................................18.00
Diane, crystal, vase, bud, 10"...60.00
Diane, crystal, vase, flower, 11"..115.00
Diane, crystal, vase, ftd, #1301, 10"...75.00
Diane, crystal, vase, keyhole base, 9"..75.00
Elaine, crystal, bonbon, ftd, tab hdl, 7"..32.00
Elaine, crystal, cabaret plate, #1397, 13½"......................................50.00
Elaine, crystal, candlestick, 3-lt, 6", ea...40.00
Elaine, crystal, candy dish, #306, 6"...95.00
Elaine, crystal, creamer, various styles, ea.......................................18.00
Elaine, crystal, goblet, #3104, 9-oz...195.00
Elaine, crystal, hurricane lamp, candlestick base.............................175.00
Elaine, crystal, hurricane lamp, keyhole base w/prisms....................225.00
Elaine, crystal, ice bucket, chrome hdl..80.00
Elaine, crystal, pickle/relish dish, 7"..28.00
Elaine, crystal, pitcher, ball, 80-oz...195.00
Elaine, crystal, plate, bread & butter, 6"...8.00

Elaine, crystal, plate, dinner, 10"...55.00
Elaine, crystal, plate, torte, 4-ftd, 13"...50.00
Elaine, crystal, shakers, flat or ftd, pr..33.00
Elaine, crystal, sherbet, #1402...14.00
Elaine, crystal, tumbler, water, #3500, ftd, 10-oz.............................24.00
Elaine, crystal, vase, ftd, 8"...85.00
Gloria, crystal, bowl, cranberry, 3"..30.00
Gloria, crystal, bowl, oval, 4-ftd, 12"..65.00
Gloria, crystal, butter dish, hdls, w/lid..160.00
Gloria, crystal, candy dish, tab hdls, 4-ftd, w/lid............................100.00
Gloria, crystal, compote, 4-ftd, 6"..26.00
Gloria, crystal, cordial, #3130, 1-oz...45.00
Gloria, crystal, cup, sq, 4-ftd...30.00
Gloria, crystal, pitcher, w/lid, 64-oz...275.00
Gloria, crystal, plate, salad, #3400/62, 8"..12.00
Gloria, crystal, plate, torte, 11"..65.00
Gloria, crystal, shakers, short, pr..38.00
Gloria, crystal, sugar bowl, #3400/16..17.00
Gloria, crystal, tumbler, #3130, ftd, 12-oz.......................................24.00
Gloria, crystal, vase, #1308, 6"..50.00
Gloria, gr, pk or yel, bowl, cereal, rnd, 6"...45.00
Gloria, gr, pk or yel, butter dish, hdls, w/lid...................................325.00
Gloria, gr, vase, #407, 12"...250.00
Imperial Hunt Scene, colors, plate, #224, 10"...................................40.00
Imperial Hunt Scene, crystal, bowl, 8"...35.00
Imperial Hunt Scene, crystal, plate, #244, 10"..................................25.00
Marjorie, crystal, cup...50.00
Marjorie, crystal, jug, #93, 3-pt..195.00
Mt Vernon, amber or crystal, ashtray, #63, 3".....................................6.00
Mt Vernon, amber or crystal, candelabrum, #38, 13", ea..................130.00
No 704 Windows Border, colors, cup, #933.....................................10.00
No 704 Windows Border, colors, plate, dinner, 9"..............................40.00
No 704 Windows Border, colors, tumbler, #3060, 10-oz.....................16.00
No 704 Windows Border, gr, cigarette box, #430..............................40.00
No 704 Windows Border, gr, claret, #3075, 4-oz...............................26.00
No 704 Windows Border, gr, sugar bowl, #137/#942/#943/#944, flat, ea..15.00
Nude Stem, Amber, compote, #3011/27, 5" dia...............................350.00
Nude Stem, Crown Tuscan, candlestick, #3011, 9", ea......................150.00
Nude Stem, Royal Bl, wine, #3011/12, 3-oz....................................275.00
Portia, crystal, candy box, w/cover, ram's head, #3500/78, 6"...........175.00
Portia, crystal, candy dish, rnd, w/lid..110.00
Rosalie, bl, gr or pk, tray, center hdl, 11"...35.00
Rosalie, bl, gr or pk, vase, ftd, 6"..125.00
Rose Point, crystal, bowl, rimmed soup, #361, 8"............................200.00
Rose Point, crystal, cheese dish, #980, w/lid, 5".............................525.00

Rose Point, crystal, decanter, #1321, 11", $395.00. (Photo courtesy B.S. Slosberg Inc. Auctioneers on LiveAuctioneers.com)

Rose Point, crystal, ice bucket, #3900/671, chrome lid................145.00
Rose Point, crystal, plate, luncheon, #3400/63, 9"..........................24.00
Rose Point, crystal, tumbler, #498, str sides, 12-oz..........................65.00
Tally Ho, amber or crystal, bowl, 8"..25.00
Wildflower, crystal, plate, dinner, #3900/24, 10"..............................55.00

Wildflower, crystal, vase, flower, ftd, #278, 11" 100.00
Wildflower, crystal, vase, flower, ftd, #279, 13" 195.00
Wildflower, crystal, vase, keyhole ft, #1238, 12" 110.00

Cameo Glass

The technique of glass carving was perfected 2,000 years ago in ancient Rome and Greece. The most famous ancient example of cameo glass is the Portland Vase, made in Rome around 100 A.D. After glass blowing was developed, glassmakers devised a method of casing several layers of colored glass together, often with a light color over a darker base, to enhance the design. Skilled carvers meticulously worked the fragile glass to produce incredibly detailed classic scenes. In the eighteenth and nineteenth centuries, Oriental and Near-Eastern artisans used the technique more extensively. European glassmakers revived the art during the last quarter of the nineteenth century. In France, Galle and Daum produced some of the finest examples of modern times, using as many as five layers of glass to develop their designs, usually scenics or subjects from nature. Hand carving was supplemented by the use of a copper engraving wheel, and acid was used to cut away the layers more quickly.

In England, Thomas Webb and Sons used modern machinery and technology to eliminate many of the problems that plagued early glass carvers. One of Webb's best-known carvers, George Woodall, is credited with producing over 400 pieces. Woodall was trained in the art by John Northwood, famous for reproducing the Portland Vase in 1876. Cameo glass became very popular during the late 1800s, resulting in a market that demanded more than could be produced due to the tedious procedures involved. In an effort to produce greater volume, less elaborate pieces with simple floral or geometric designs were made, often entirely acid etched with little or no hand carving. While very little cameo glass was made in this country, a few pieces were produced by James Gillinder, Tiffany, and the Libbey Glass Company. Though some continued to be made on a limited scale into the 1900s (and until about 1920 in France), for the most part, inferior products caused a marked reduction in its manufacture by the turn of the century. Beware of new 'French' cameo glass from Romania and Taiwan. Some of it is very good and may be signed with 'old' signatures. Know your dealer! Our advisor for this category is Don Williams; he is listed in the Directory under Missouri. See also Daum Nancy Glass; De Vez Glass; Galle; Mont Joye; Muller Frers Glass; Peking Cameo Glass; Richard.

English

Bottle, scent, daffodils, wht on bl, lay down, silver lid, 3½" L ... 1,000.00
Bottle, scent, floral, wht on red to yel, silver lid, lay down, 3¾" . 1,600.00
Bottle, scent, floral, wht opal on citrine, silver lid, lay down, 4" .. 850.00
Bottle, scent, flowers, butterfly on bk, wht on red, missing stopper, 3½". 900.00
Pitcher, floral, wht on bl, appl bl hdl, 6½" 2,500.00
Vase, apple blossoms, wht on turq w/gray ft, 7¼" 1,500.00
Vase, berries & leaves, wht on lav, short neck, 9¾" 2,450.00
Vase, floral vines, wht on citron, bulb, 5½" 480.00
Vase, floral, wht on bl, stick neck, 11" 2,000.00
Vase, floral, wht on citron, baluster, 4¾" 650.00
Vase, floral, wht on red, bowling-pin shape, 12" 2,000.00
Vase, lilies, wht on cranberry, shouldered, 6", NM 1,000.00
Vase, morning glories, wht on chartreuse, slim neck, #519/5, 9" ... 1,200.00
Vase, morning glories, wht on red, bulb, 5½" 950.00
Vase, oak leaves & acorns, wht on red, 4½" 600.00
Vase, peach branch, wht on citron, 5¾" 500.00

French

Atomizer, berried branches, amethyst on wht, Raspiller, 7" 450.00
Vase, bud, roses, rose red on lt gray frost, stick neck, Vessisere, 7"... 300.00

Vase, floral, celery gr on frost, slim, Mercier, 13¾" 425.00
Vase, floral, gr on pale pk frost w/gold, hdls, att St Louis, 3⅛" 235.00
Vase, floral, peach/gr on pk to wht frost, Arsall, 10" 725.00

Vase, floral, red with gilt highlights on finely etched translucent green, circa 1900, attributed to Cristallerie de Pantin, light wear to gilt, 10½", $3,200.00. (Photo courtesy Kodner Galleries Inc. on LiveAuctioneers.com)

Vase, foliage, aqua/beige on frost, Cristallerie de Pantin, 4½" 335.00
Vase, grapes/leaves, brn & rust on orange, slim, ftd, Arsall, 12¼". 600.00
Vase, irises, violet on frost w/gold, Cristallerie de Pantin, 14"...... 450.00
Vase, leaves, brn/peach on frost, Degue, 19x8" 360.00
Vase, lotus/butterfly, bl on yel, flared body, Camila, 6" 270.00
Vase, thistle flowers/quote, purple to wht, Vessiere Nancy, 5x2½"... 270.00
Vase, trees/lake/birds, brn on orange, slim neck, Michel, 6¼" 515.00

Canary Ware

Canary ware was produced from the late 1700s until about the mid-nineteenth century in the Staffordshire district of England. It was potted of yellow clay and the overglaze was yellow as well. More often than not, copper or silver lustre trim was added. Decorations were usually black-printed transfers, though occasionally hand-painted polychrome designs were also used.

Cup and saucer, minor loss to paint on rim, saucer: 5⅝", $660.00. (Photo courtesy Alderfer Auction Company on LiveAuctioneers.com)

Cup/saucer, woman & child playing harp, blk transfer, 2¾", 5" ... 350.00
Inkwell, shoe form w/mc pattern, 3½" L..................................... 2,000.00
Mug, LaFayette/Washington/eagle/stars, rust transfer, 2⅜" 1,175.00
Pitcher, eagle, bk: roses, roses at incurvate neck, ftd, 6x8" 1,900.00
Pitcher, floral, grape decor, w/brn bands, figure of man on spout, 5¼". 750.00
Pitcher, gaudy floral, mask spout, emb grapevines, mc w/brn bands, 5" .. 900.00
Pitcher, Peace & Plenty, blk transfer, silver lustre trim, 6½" 1,450.00
Plate, floral at rim, red/gr, brn edge, underside chip, 8¾" 1,320.00
Teabowl & saucer, roses, red/gr w/brn rim, strong colors, NM...... 660.00

Candleholders

The earliest type of candlestick, called a pricket, was constructed with a sharp point on which the candle was impaled. The socket type, first used in the sixteenth century, consisted of the socket and a short stem with a wide drip pan and base. These were made from sheets of silver or other metal; not until late in the seventeenth century were candlesticks made by casting. By the 1700s, styles began to vary from the traditional fluted column or baluster form and became more elaborate. A Rococo style with scrolls, shellwork, and naturalistic leaves and flowers came into vogue that afforded the individual silversmith the opportunity to exhibit his skill and artistry. The last half of the eighteenth century brought a return to fluted columns with neoclassic motifs. Because they were made of thin sheet silver, weighted bases were used to add stability. The Rococo styles of the Regency period were heavily encrusted with applied figures and flowers. Candelabra with six to nine branches became popular. By the Victorian era when lamps came into general use, there was less innovation and more adaptation of the earlier styles. For more information, we recommend *Glass Candlesticks of the Depression Era, Vol. 1* and *2*, by Gene and Cathy Florence and *The Glass Candlestick Book, Vols. 1, 2,* and *3*, by Tom Felt and Elaine and Rich Stoer (Collector Books). Unless noted 'pair,' values are for single candleholders. See also Silver; Tinware; specific manufacturers.

Brass pricket, Gothic revival, bl/wht enamel/turq-studded finials, 20"..555.00
Brass, chamberstick w/scissor & cone snuffers, sq base, 5x7x5".... 200.00
Brass, domed base w/6 lg/6 sm scallops, side pushup, 7½", pr.....1,265.00
Brass, gilt/pnt swags, domed leafy base, Emp style, 1850s, 11", pr..2,465.00
Brass, hollow baluster stem on sq base w/gallery rim, 5¼x5¼" 285.00
Brass, hollow knobbed column, sq base w/4 ft, 6½" 200.00
Brass, open spiral sticks, threaded posts, rnd bases, 12", pr........... 230.00
Brass, scalloped base, hollow stem w/pushup, 8½" 375.00
Bronze dore, Fr Emp, core cast/seamed, removable bobeches, 10", pr. 1,050.00
Bronze dore, pricket, elaborate std, busts at base, paw ft, 34", pr....2,760.00
Bronze dore, putto rests on oval base, scroll brackets, 13", pr....... 470.00
Bronze dore/lapis lazuli, 3-arm, ornate castings, 13x9", pr.........4,400.00
Bronze, Gothic style w/hexagonal drip pan, arched base, 34", pr...1,400.00
Candelabra, alabaster w/gilt bronze mts, rose branches/cups, 12", pr... 150.00
Candelabra, bronze w/gilt, Napoleon III, 6-arm, scrolls/swags, 28", pr..2,350.00
Candelabra, SP, 7-arm, std w/3 scroll supports, Fr, 1880s, 32x20", pr.4,200.00
Gilt gesso, trn post on tringular base w/3 cvd ft, early, 31", G 100.00
Gilt metal, Art Nouveau, 5-candle, #89, 19x14" 2,880.00
Giltwood w/cream enamel, Italian classical style, 38", pr.......... 1,500.00
Glass, amber, twist stem, Cambridge, $25 to................................... 30.00
Glass, amethyst w/silver o/l, trumpet shape, Dmn, 9x4⅜" 45.00
Glass, burgundy, Fostoria #4113, 1936-44, 5⅝x3¼", $40 to 50.00
Glass, crystal, Chaucer (No 1504 Line), Paden City, 6½x4⅞" 30.00
Glass, emerald, 3-lt, Cambridge #824, 4⅜x9⅛x3¾" 35.00
Glass, Florentine No 2, gr, Hazel-Atlas, 2½x4¼", $25 to............... 30.00
Glass, Heirloom candle-vase, yel opal, Fostoria #2730/319, 6" 200.00
Glass, Loop & Pillar, crystal, US Glass #15077, 6x3½", $60 to...... 75.00
Glass, Moongleam, swan hdls, Heisey #133, 1929-36, 6" 325.00
Glass, Willow, gr, 2-light, Indiana, 5½x4¾x2¾", $20 to................ 30.00
Maple, trn columnar std on sq base, pewter cup, 1800s, 32"........ 235.00
Pewter, Queen Ann, oval base, early, 4½x4", pr 175.00
Pewter, rnd base w/trumpet shaft, Reed & Barton I, 9" 230.00
Silver, shaped ovals w/floral vines, Silver City, 1900, 10", pr 175.00
SP, Corinthian columns w/stepped bases, Sheffield style, 12", pr . 320.00

Tin hogscraper w/seamed brass wedding band, Shaw's Birm on pushup, 7" .430.00
Tin hogscraper, brass wedding ring above pushup stamped Fisher, 7".. 525.00
Tin, rnd column on cone-shape weighted base, pushup, 1820s, 10", pr..865.00
Wood w/dk gr & gilt over gesso, acanthus leaves, 14", VG, pr..1,700.00
Wrought iron, spiral, twisted iron strip adjusts, wood base, 8" 235.00

Candlewick

Candlewick crystal was made by the Imperial Glass Corporation, a division of Lenox Inc., Bellaire, Ohio. It was introduced in 1936, and though never marked except for paper labels, it is easily recognized by the beaded crystal rims, stems, and handles inspired by the tufted needlework called candlewicking, practiced by our pioneer women. During its production, more than 741 items were designed and produced. In September 1982 when Imperial closed its doors, 34 pieces were still being made.

Identification numbers and mold numbers used by the company help collectors recognize the various styles and shapes. Most of the pieces are from the #400 series, though other series numbers were also used. Stemware was made in eight styles — five from the #400 series made from 1941 to 1962, one from #3400 series made in 1937, another from #3800 series made in 1941, and the eighth style from the #4000 series made in 1947. In the listings that follow, some #400 items lack the mold number because that information was not found in the company files.

A few pieces have been made in color or with a gold wash. At least two lines, Valley Lily and Floral, utilized Candlewick with floral patterns cut into the crystal. These are scarce today. Other rare items include gifts such as the desk calendar made by the company for its employees and customers; the dresser set comprised of a mirror, clock, puff jar, and cologne; and the chip and dip set.

Ashtray, 3-pc nesting, sq, #400/650... 90.00
Ashtray, rnd, #400/19, 2½" 7.00
Ashtray, sq, #400/653, 5½" 30.00
Basket, hdls, #400/73/0, 11"..200.00
Bell, #400/108, 5"... 78.00
Bell, #400/179, 4"... 75.00
Bottle, cologne, #400/117, 4 beads... 60.00
Bowl, baked apple, rolled edge, #400/53X, 6" 32.00
Bowl, bouillon, w/hdls, #400/126 .... 45.00
Bowl, cupped edge, #400/75F, 10" 40.00
Bowl, finger, #3800 .... 30.00
Bowl, finger, ftd, #3400 .... 30.00
Bowl, fruit, #400/3F, 6" 10.00
Bowl, salad, #400/75B, 10½".. 37.00
Bowl, shallow, #400/17F, 12" 42.00
Bowl, vegetable, #400/65/1, w/lid, 8" 360.00
Butter & jam set, #400/204, 5-pc 465.00
Butter, #400/276, no beads, CA 120.00
Cake stand, low ft, #400/67D, 10" 60.00
Calendar, desk, 1947...250.00
Candleholder urn, #400/129R, 4½"...100.00
Candleholder, #400/81, w/finger hold, 3½" 50.00
Candleholder, 2-way, beaded base, #400/115, ea 125.00
Candleholder, 3-bead stem, #400/224, 5½", ea 125.00
Candleholder, 3-toed, #400/207, 4½" 95.00
Candleholder, flat, #400/2880, 3½" 35.00
Candy dish, w/lid, #400/259 ....125.00
Celery boat, oval, #400/46, 11" 50.00
Celery, oval, w/hdls, #400/105, 13½"... 35.00
Claret, #3400, 5-oz.. 40.00
Cocktail, #400/190, 4-oz... 18.00
Compote, beaded stem, #400/220, 5" 80.00
Cordial, #400/190, 1-oz.. 75.00
Creamer, domed ft, #400/18 .... 90.00

Cup, coffee, #400/37 ....6.00
Egg cup, #400/19 .... 50.00
Goblet, #4000, 11-oz 26.00
Goblet, water, #3800, 9-oz 30.00
Ice tub, w/hdls, #400/168, 7" 195.00
Ladle, mayonnaise, #400/135, 6½" 10.00
Marmalade, w/spoon & lid, #400/79 .... 42.00
Mint dish, w/hdl, #400/51F, 6" 20.00
Nappy, 4-ftd, #400/74B, 8½" 65.00
Oil bottle, #400/177, 4-oz 45.00
Parfait, #3400, 6-oz 50.00

Pitcher, beaded handle, #400/24, 80-ounce, $125.00.
(Photo courtesy Strawser Auction Group on LiveAuctioneers.com)

Pitcher, flat, #400/16, 16-oz 160.00
Pitcher, juice/cocktail, #400/19, 40-oz 195.00
Plate, cracker, #400/145, 13½" 40.00
Plate, cupped edge, #400/20V, 17" 95.00
Plate, dinner, #400/10D, 10½" 35.00
Plate, oval, #400/124, 12½" 80.00
Plate, oval, #400/169, 8" 22.00
Plate, salad, #400/3D, 7" 6.00
Plate, service, #400/92D, 14" 50.00
Puff box, #E409 .... 65.00
Punch set, bowl on 18" plate, 12 cups & ladle, #400/102 .... 250.00
Relish, 2-part, #400/85, 6½" 22.00
Relish, 5-part, #400/102, 13" 65.00
Relish, 5-part, 5 hdls, #400/56 .... 65.00
Salt & pepper shakers, #400/190 .... 50.00
Sauceboat, #400/169 .... 90.00
Saucer, coffee or tea, #400/35 or #400/37, ea 2.00
Shakers, str-sided, beaded ft, chrome top, #400/247, pr 18.00
Sherbet, low stem, #3800 .... 22.00
Sugar bowl, flat, beaded hdl, #400/126 .... 28.00
Tidbit, 2-tier, cupped, #400/2701 .... 50.00
Tray, center hdl, #400/68D, 11½" 55.00
Tray, hdls, #400/113E, 14" 80.00
Tumbler, #400/19, 10-oz 10.00
Tumbler, #400/19, 12-oz 18.00
Tumbler, juice, #400/18, 5-oz 50.00
Tumbler, old-fashioned, #400/18, 7-oz 60.00
Vase, bud, #400/28C, 8½" 110.00
Vase, crimped edge, flat, #400/287C, 6" 40.00
Vase, pitcher, #400/227, 8½" 595.00
Vase, rose bowl, #400/142K, 7" 300.00

Candy Containers

Figural glass candy containers were first created in 1876 when ingenious candy manufacturers began to use them to package their products. Two of the first containers, the Liberty Bell and Independence Hall, were distributed for our country's centennial celebration. Children found these toys appealing, and an industry was launched that lasted into the mid-1960s.

Figural candy containers include animals, comic characters, guns, telephones, transportation vehicles, household appliances, and many other intriguing designs. The oldest (those made prior to 1920) were usually hand painted and often contained extra metal parts in addition to the metal strip or screw closures. During the 1950s these metal parts were replaced with plastic, a practice that continued until candy containers met their demise in the 1960s. While predominately clear, they are found in nearly all colors of glass including milk glass, green, amber, pink, emerald, cobalt, ruby flashed, and light blue. Usually the color was intentional, but leftover glass was used as well and resulted in unplanned colors. Various examples are found in light or ice blue, and new finds are always being discovered. Production of the glass portion of candy containers was centered around the western Pennsylvania city of Jeannette. Major producers include Westmoreland Glass, West Bros., Victory Glass, J.H. Millstein, J.C. Crosetti, L.E. Smith, Jack Stough, and T.H. Stough. While 90% of all glass candies were made in the Jeannette area, other companies such as Eagle Glass, Play Toy, and Geo. Borgfeldt Co. have a few to their credit as well.

Our advisor for glass containers is Jeff Bradfield; he is listed in the Directory under Virginia. You may contact him with questions, if you will include an SASE. See Clubs, Newsletters, and Websites for the address of the Candy Container Collectors of America. A bimonthly newsletter offers insight into new finds, reproductions, updates, and articles from over 400 collectors and members, including authors of books on candy containers. Dues are $25.00 yearly. The club holds an annual convention in June in Lancaster, Pennsylvania, for collectors of candy containers.

'L' numbers used in this guide refer to a standard reference series, *An Album of Candy Containers, Vols. I* and *II*, by Jennie Long. 'E&A' numbers correlate with *The Compleat American Glass Candy Containers Handbook* by Eikelberner and Agadjanian, revised by Adele Bowden. D&P numbers refer to *Collector's Guide to Candy Containers* by Doug Dezso and Leon and Rose Poirier (out of print).

Buyer beware! Many candy containers have been reproduced. Some, including the Camera and the Rabbit Pushing Wheelbarrow, come already painted from distributors. Others may have a slick or oily feel to the touch. The following list may also alert you to possible reproductions:

Amber Pistol, L #144 (first sold full in the 1970s, not listed in E&A)

Auto, D&P #173/E&A #33/L #377

Auto, D&P #163/E&A #60/L #356

Black and White Taxi, D&P #182/L #353 (Silk-screened metal roofs are being reproduced. They are different from originals in that the white section is more silvery in color than the original cream. These closures are put on original bases and often priced for hundreds of dollars. If the top is not original, the value of these candy containers is reduced by 80%.)

Camera, D&P #419/E&A #121/L #238 (original says 'Pat Apld For' on bottom, reproduction says 'B. Shakman' or is ground off)

Carpet Sweeper, D&P 296/E&A #133/L #243 (currently being sold with no metal parts)

Carpet Sweeper, E&A #132/L #242 (currently being sold with no metal parts)

Charlie Chaplin, D&P 195/E&A #137/L #83 (original has 'Geo. Borgfeldt' on base; reproduction comes in pink and blue)

Chicken on Nest, D&P #10/E&A #149/L #12

Display Case, D&P #422/E&A #177/L #246 (original should be painted silver and brown)

Dog, D&P #21/E&A #180/L #24 (clear and cobalt)

Drum Mug, D&P #431/E&A #543/L #255

Happifats on Drum, D&P #199/E&A #208/L #89 (no notches on repro for closure to hook into)

Fire Engine, D&P 258/E&A #213/L #386 (repros in green and blue glass)

Independence Hall, D&P #130/E&A #342/L #76 (original is rectangular; repro has offset base with red felt-lined closure)

Jackie Coogan, D&P #202/E&A #345/L #90 (marked inside 'B')

Kewpie, D&P #204/E&A #349/L #91 (must have Geo. Borgfeldt on base to be original)

Mailbox, D&P #216/E&A #521/L #254 (repro marked Taiwan)

Mantel Clock, D&P #483/E&A #162/L #114 (originally in ruby flashed, milk glass, clear, and frosted only)

Mule and Waterwagon, D&P #51/E&A #539/L #38 (original marked Jeannette, PA)

Naked Child, E&A 546/L #94

Owl, D&P #52/E&A #566/L #37 (original in clear only, often painted; repro found in clear, blue, green, and pink with a higher threaded base and less detail)

Peter Rabbit, D&P #60/E&A #618/L #55

Piano, D&P #460/E&A #577/L #289 (original in only clear and milk glass, both painted)

Rabbit Pushing Wheelbarrow, D&P #72/E&A #601/L #47 (eggs are speckled on the repro; solid on the original)

Rocking Horse, D&P #46/E&A #651/L #58 (original in clear only, repro marked 'Rocky')

Safe, D&P #311/E&A #661/L #268 (original in clear, ruby flashed, and milk glass only)

Santa, D&P 284/E&A #674/L #103 (original has plastic head; repro [1970s] is all glass and opens at bottom)

Santa's Boot, D&P #273/E&A #111/L #233

Scottie Dog, D&P #35/E&A #184/L #17 (repro has a ice-like color and is often slick and oily)

Station Wagon, D&P #178/E&A #56/L #378

Stough Rabbit, D&P #53/E&A #617/L #54

Uncle Sam's Hat, D&P #428/E&A #303/L #168

Wagon, U.S. Express D&P #530 (glass is being reproduced without any metal parts)

Others are possible. If in doubt, do not buy without a guarantee from the dealer and return privilege in writing. Also note that other reproductions are possible.

Airplane, Boyd, various colors, D&P 77 .... 28.00
Airplane, Patent 113053, tin propeller, D&P 81/E&A 4 .... 85.00
Airplane, Spirit of St Louis, amber body, D&P 85/E&A 9, $500 to...700.00
Airplane, Spirit of St Louis, gr body, slight wing damage, D&P 85/E&A 9 ..450.00
Barney Google by Barrel, King Features Syndicate, G pnt, D&P 188/E&A 71..1,500.00
Baseball Player by Barrel, G pnt, D&P 190/E&A 77/L 80 .... 800.00
Bell, Liberty w/Hanger, bl glass, wire bail, D&P 95/E&A 85 .... 60.00
Bird on Mound, no whistle, ca 1920, D&P 3/E&A 94 .... 600.00
Bottle, Apothecary-Lg, 5", D&P 113 .... 80.00
Bottle, Dolly's Milk, VG Co, D&P 109/E&A 527/L 66 .... 60.00
Bottle, Maude Muller Candies, 4 in cb crate, D&P 110 .... 250.00
Bus, Victory Stage, 8 side windows, D&P 157/E&A 118-1 .... 425.00
Candleabrum, 2 glass shakers in metal stand, D&P 317/E&A 174/L 202. 45.00
Cannon, US Defense Field Gun, tin bbl, D&P 387/E&A 128/L 142. 350.00
Car, Coupe-Long Hood w/Tin Wheels, D&P 160/E&A 50/L 357 ..175.00
Car, Hearse #2, open top, D&P 165/E&A 40/L 360 .... 140.00
Car, Little Touring, Stough, D&P 172/E&A 32 .... 30.00
Carpet Sweeper, Baby, wire hdl, orig parts, D&P 295/E&A 132/L 242 (+)..475.00
Cash Register, open bottom, tin closure, D&P 420/E&A 135/L 244.. 450.00
Chick in Shell Auto w/Balloon Tires, tin closure, D&P 9............ 900.00
Clarinet, red/wht striped tube as mouthpc, D&P 448/E&A 316/L 285.. 35.00
Clock Lynne Bank, 2-pc tin w/glass base, D&P 481/E&A 159 .... 600.00
Clock, Octagon, deep open base, paper dial, D&P 484/E&A 163 ..225.00
Condiment Set, Rainbow Candy, metal base, D&P 297/E&A 174/L 503 ..50.00
Dog w/Umbrella, wide opening, D&P 37/E&A 194-2/L 29 .... 50.00
Dog, Scottie, looking str ahead, D&P 35/E&A 184/L 17 (+) 25.00
Fire Engine, 1914 Stough, orig wheels, mk Pat Pending, D&P 262/E&A 223...175.00
Fire Engine, Ladder Truck, Victory, orig wheels, D&P 254/E&A 216/L 384 ..250.00
Gun, Grooved Barrel, X-hatching on grip, D&P 392 .... 35.00
Gun, Medium w/Hook Grip, screw head in grip, D&P 396/E&A 259 ..25.00
Horn, Musical Clarinet No 515a, whistle cap, D&P 452/E&A 315 ..175.00

Horn, Musical Clarinet No 55, cb tube/tin whistle cap, D&P 451/E&A 316..30.00
Jack o' Lantern, Big Str Eyes, bail hdl, D&P 264/E&A 347/L 160 ...275.00
Kiddie Kar Horse Cart, Avor 1oz & USA Measurements, D&P 430/E&A 360, 4½" L, EX..135.00
Lamp, Library, mk Pat Pending on metal base, D&P 334/E&A 372... 525.00
Lantern, Beaded #2, pnt clear or mg, D&P 348/E&A 405/L 180... 35.00
Lantern, Stough's All Glass, D&P 364/E&A 406 .... 25.00
Locomotive, Am Type 23, bl, 4-4-0 wheels/3 stacks, D&P 489/E&A 480..150.00
Locomotive, Man in Window 888, 4-4-0 wheels, D&P 497/E&A 486.400.00
Mail Box, Letters US Mail, tin closure, Westmoreland, D&P 216/E&A 521 ..250.00
Nurser, Lynne Doll, rubber nipple mk Hygeia, D&P 122/E&A 550 ....35.00
Oil Can, Independence Bell, w/oil-can spout, D&P 435/E&A 556...550.00
Parlor Car, arched windows, D&P 516/E&A 169 .... 325.00
Powder Horn, blown, mk Pat Appd For, D&P 411/E&A 589/L 265 ...65.00
Racer #12, 2-vent sides, disk wheels, D&P 476/E&A 642/L 432. 200.00
Racer, Plastic, clear w/gr wheels, D&P 472 .... 30.00
Racer, Stough's, wheels mtd on axles, D&P 473/E&A 640 .... 80.00
Racer, Stutz Bear Cat, 10-rib radiator, D&P 474/E&A 639 ......1,500.00
Rocking Horse w/Rider, pnt clown & horse, D&P 47/E&A 652. 200.00
Rooster, Crowing, Victory Glass, G pnt, D&P 73/E&A 151 .... 350.00
Safe, Dime, CD Kenny, D&P 312/E&A 661/L 268 .... 100.00

Safety First, D&P 266/E&A 668, VG, $300.00. (Photo courtesy Henry Peirce on LiveAuctioneers.com)

Santa Claus in Long Coat, gold-tone cap, REGDNO716934, D&P 279.300.00
Santa Claus Leaving Chimney, Victory Glass, G pnt, D&P 281/E&A 673/L 102 ..150.00
Settee, Rocking, gold edge/arms/risers, ruby flashed, D&P 313/E&A 653/L 134.650.00
Soldier, Doughboy, emb helmet/uniform, D&P 209/L 525 .... 200.00
Table, emb drw w/center knob, D&P 316/E&A 714/L 136 .... 850.00
Tank, 2 Cannons, D&P 413/E&A 723 .... 35.00
Tank, Man in Turret; emb treads/geared wheels, D&P 412/E&A 722.... 45.00
Telephone, Lynne-Sunken Dial, candlestick, complete, D&P 232/E&A 741.50.00
Telephone, Pewter Top #1, blown, blk wood receiver, D&P 236/E&A 756.90.00
Telephone, Stough's Musical Toy, ringed base, D&P 246/E&A 732/L 310..45.00
Tomahawk & Gun, wood hdl, cb head, glass gun, D&P 416.......... 50.00
Toonerville Trolley, Fontaine Fox, G pnt, D&P 214/E&A 767/L 111 ...800.00
Train, Coal Car/No Couplers, tin wheels, D&P 518 .... 600.00
Village Drug Store, w/insert, D&P 137/E&A 810 .... 135.00
Village School House, tin w/insert, D&P 143/E&A 808/L 76J 170.00
Wagon, US Express, metal wheels, wire hdl, D&P 530/E&A 821, (+) ...750.00
Watch, Eagle, w/eagle fob, D&P 486/E&A 823/L 122 .... 450.00
Wheelbarrow, Victory Glass, tin snap-on closure, D&P 531/E&A 832/L 273.90.00
Windmill, Candy Guaranteed, tin blades, D&P 533/E&A 840 .1,000.00
Windmill, Plastic Bank, D&P 536 .... 30.00
Windmill, TG Stough's 1915, D&P 538/E&A 842 .... 375.00

Miscellaneous

These types of candy containers are generally figural. Many are holiday related. Small sizes are common; larger sizes are in greater demand. Because of eBay's influence, prices have dropped and remain soft. Our prices reflect this trend. Our advisor for this category is Jenny Tarrant; she is listed in the Directory under Missouri. See also Christmas Collectibles; Easter; Halloween.

Key: pm — papier-maché

Baseball player, compo, w/wood bat, early, 7½", EX...................... 780.00
Baseball player, pm & wood, 9½", NM... 350.00
Bulldog, compo, cream w/orange hat Germany, 4", VG 130.00
Cat in shoe, compo & gesso w/mc pnt, rpr, 4" 175.00
Cat, pm w/gesso, mc pnt, glass eyes, red ribbon, rpt 6" 225.00
Cat, seated, pm w/gesso, worn flocking, glass eyes, rpt 4" 130.00
Doll, bsk open dome head, crepe-paper/cb cylinder body, Germany, 6" .120.00

Donkey sitting on his haunches, papier-mache, German, circa 1910, restorations, 7", $360.00. (Photo courtesy Skinner Auctioneers and Appraisers of Antiques and Fine Art)

Dove, compo w/gray pnt, pk-pnt metal fr, orange eyes, 4½x8" 100.00
Elephant, pm, porc tusks, Germany, ca 1885-1920, 6" 155.00
English Bobby, pm, EX pnt, Pat No 28063, 12" 160.00
George Washington bust, compo, bottom plug, 4-6" 150.00
George Washington w/tree stump, compo, Germany, 3-4"........... 150.00
George Washington w/tree stump, compo, Germany, 5-7"........... 225.00
George Washington, compo, stands on rnd box w/silk flag, Germany, 5".. 150.00
Hen, compo w/metal fr, yel/red/brn pnt, lt ft wear, 4½x4¾" 75.00
Horse, Dapple gray, compo w/leather ears & saddle, Germany, ca 1910, 7", VG .650.00
Peter the Pumpkin Bellhop, compo, Germany, 1920s-30s, 7" 375.00
Pigeon, comp w/metal fr, gray/wht/irid purple, 4½x6" 75.00
St Patrick's Day, Irishman bust, compo, w/plug, Germany, 3-4" 75.00
St Patrick's Day, pig, flocked gr, wood legs, plug in tummy, 3-5" 95.00
St Patrick's Day, potato, compo, Germany, 3-4" 45.00
Stork w/baby, spun cotton/paper, lifts legs, Germany, 1930s, 6½" .. 95.00
Turkey, compo w/metal ft, head removes, Germany, 10" 375.00
Watermelon w/face, molded cb w/celluloid body, Austria, 4¼".... 125.00

Canes

Fancy canes and walking sticks were once the mark of a gentleman. Hand-carved examples are collected and admired as folk art from the past. The glass canes that never could have been practical are unique whimseys of the glassblower's profession. Gadget and container sticks, which were produced in a wide variety, are highly desirable. Character, political, and novelty types are also sought after as are those with handles made of precious metals.

Our values reflect actual prices realized at auction. For more information we recommend *American Folk Art Canes, Personal Sculpture,* by George H. Meyer, Sandringham Press, 100 West Long Lake Rd., Suite 100, Bloomfield Hills, MI 48304. Other possible references are *Canes in the United States* by Catherine Dike and *Canes From the 17th – 20th Century* by Jeffrey Snyder. For information concerning the Cane Collectors Club, see the Clubs, Newsletters, and Websites section.

Bone hdl contains microscope/magnifier/spyglass/kaleidoscope, 1800s...2,000.00
Dagger w/in hardwood crook hdl, 8½" blade, wood shaft 215.00
Flashlight in L-shaped metal hdl (not working), hardwood shaft.. 120.00
Glass whimsey, mc spiral, knob hdl, hollow blown, silver tip, 45". 180.00
Gold-cap hdl, whalebone w/gold mts, gold eyelets, ca 1840...... 1,000.00
Horn hdl w/gold collar, blk wooden shaft, ca 1900...................... 360.00
Horn knob hdl, whalebone shaft, 19th C.................................... 425.00
Ivory bonneted child hdl, brass collar, rosewood shaft, 1890s 550.00
Ivory bulldog head hdl, quartz eyes, silver collar, wood shaft, 1880s. 1,000.00

Ivory eagle-head hdl w/mechanical eyes, cvd shaft, EX 780.00
Ivory grapevines/leaves hdl, cherrywood shaft, ivory ferrule, 1870s.. 700.00
Ivory lady w/flowing hair/hat hdl, partridgewood stepped shaft, 1900s....3,400.00
Ivory Mother Goose hdl, silver collar, snakewood shaft, 1880s.3,250.00
Ivory umbrella-like hdl, baleen separators, whalebone shaft, 1870s ...2,500.00
Ivory/wood Buddhist deity hdl, ivory collar, hardwood shaft, 1890s. 1,100.00
Leather-covered hdl w/gold hallmk matchsafe compartment, wood shaft ...360.00
Porcelain knob hdl w/HP Queen Victoria scene, hardwood shaft.240.00
Porcelain Royal Copenhagen hdl, w/2 chicks, ebony shaft, 1880 . 650.00
Quartz purple top, silver mt, ebony shaft, brass ferrule, ca 1900... 750.00
Rock crystal hdl w/jewels/gold snake w/jewel eye, ebony shaft, 1900s.. 7,000.00
Rock crystal hdl w/jewels/pearls, silver collar, horn ferrule, 1900s.1,400.00
Silver Art Nouveau lady w/pheasant headdress hdl, ebony shaft, 1900s..650.00
Silver emb knob hdl, rfn malacca shaft w/silver eyelets, 1770s .2,000.00
Silver pheasant w/glass eyes, bamboo shaft, w/brass ferrule, 1890s ..750.00
Silver swan's head hdl w/glass eyes, hardwood shaft 300.00
Silver/branch whistle hdl, mahog shaft, metal ferrule, Brigg London.... 350.00
Vertebrae, horn tip & end w/8 horn rings, curved hdl, 35" 220.00
Vertebrae, lg ivory knob top, horn tip, grad, 34".......................... 225.00

Wood, carved head of an African American man, smooth silver collar, twisted and carved shaft with brass ferrule, circa 1880, 39", $3,000.00. (Photo courtesy Cowan's Auctions, Inc. on LiveAuctioneers.com)

Wood, dog's head (2½" L) w/pull-down mouth, glass eyes, silver mts.460.00
Wood, dog's head hdl w/mechanical mouth to hold gloves, wood shaft.240.00
Wood, cvd Am flag/spiraling banner/acorns/etc, mc stain............ 350.00
Wood, cvd Vict lady w/book reclining on gr grass, minor damage, 34" ...3,600.00
Wood, cvd wood w/decoupage prints, varnish, JCS 1935............. 115.00

Canton

Canton is a blue and white porcelain that was first exported in the 1790s by clipper ships from China to the United States. Importation continued into the 1920s. Canton became very popular along the East Coast where the major ports were located. Its popularity was due to several factors: it was readily available, inexpensive, and due to the fact that it came in many different forms, appealing to homeowners.

The porcelain's blue and white color and simple motif (teahouse, trees, bridge, and a rain-cloud border) have made it a favorite of people who collect early American furniture and accessories. Buyers of Canton should shop at large outdoor shows and up-scale antique shows. Collections are regularly sold at auction and many examples may be found on eBay. However, be aware of reproductions and fantasy pieces being sold on eBay by sellers in Hong Kong and Shanghai. Collectors usually prefer a rich, deep tone rather than a lighter blue. Cracks, large chips, and major repairs will substantially affect values. Prices of Canton have escalated sharply over the last 20 years, and rare forms are highly sought after by advanced collectors. Our advisor for this category is Hobart D. Van Deusen; he is listed in the Directory under Connecticut.

Bowl, outside scenes and int bottom scene, 1800s, 9½" dia....... 1,200.00
Bowl, salad, notched corners, 19th C, 4¾x9¾"........................... 1,000.00

Bowl, vegetable, notched corners, scenic lid w/berry knop, 6x11x10"..650.00
Cider jug, mid-19th C, 8½" 2,500.00
Ginger jar, mid-19th C, 7", pr 500.00
Ginger jar, sm flat lid, 8x8" 400.00
Platter, canted corners, 14½x11¾" 300.00
Shrimp dish, 10½x10" 495.00
Teapot, cylindrical, 19th C, 7½".. 660.00
Teapot, G form, high dome lid, 9" 500.00
Teapot, strap hdl, lg orig lid, 19th C, 7½" 725.00
Tureen, boar's head hdls, w/lid, 8½x12¾"+15" platter...............1,440.00

Capodimonte

The relief style, highly colored and defined porcelain pieces in this listing are commonly called and identified in our current marketplace as Capodimonte. It was King Ferdinand IV, son of King Charles, who opened a factory in Naples in 1771 and began to use the mark of the blue crown N (BCN). When the factory closed in 1834, the Ginori family at Doccia near Florence, Italy, acquired what was left of the factory and continued using its mark. The factory operated until 1896 when it was then combined with Societa Ceramica Richard of Milan which continues today to manufacture fine porcelain pieces marked with a crest and wreaths under a blue crown with R. Capodimonte.

Boxes and steins are highly sought after as they are cross collectibles. Figurines, figure groupings, flowery vases, urns, and the like are also very collectible, but most items on the market today are of recent manufacture. In the past several years, Europeans have been attending U.S. antique shows and auctions in order to purchase Capodimonte items to take back home, since many pieces were destroyed during the two world wars. This has driven up prices of the older ware. Our advisor for this category is James R. Highfield; he is listed in the Directory under Indiana.

Box, banqueting scene lid, painted Chinese scene interior lid, BCN, bronze feet, 8½x5x4", $588.00. (Photo courtesy James R. Highfield)

Bowl, covered, musical cherubs in mts, Occupied Japan, 6" rnd 63.00
Box, Cupids w/musical instruments, BCN, 3x2x2" 165.00
Box, pr of Cupids w/musical horns, BCN, 2x3" 47.00
Box, pr of sheep pulling Apollo in chariot, BCN, 7x5x5" 316.00
Casket, faun, cherubs, wine bbl, BCN, 12x9x5" 450.00
Casket, frolicking cherubs, BCN France, 11x7x6" 370.00
Creamer, mustached face, woodlike hdl, BCN, 3½" 31.00
Cup, lion, eagle, bull, toga men, swan hdl, BCN, 4" 32.00
Cup/saucer, Napoleon & Josephine, crest, gold bee, BCN 35.00
Cup/saucer, sea scenes, SGK, Occupied Japan 21.00
Humidor, battle scene, BCN, rpr, 9½"...................................... 66.00
Inkwell, playful children surround, BCN, 4x3x3" 78.00
Jar w/lid, nude children in orchard, BCN, 8½" 86.00
Nut tray, B Altman & Co, Paris-New York, mk, 3½x2¾" 10.00
Snuff box, pr of winged cherubs, BCN, 2½x1½x1¾" 41.00
Stein, rams leading cherubs on wine bbl, BCN, 8½" 136.00
Stein, winged nude female hdl & Cupid finial, BCN, Fr, 10"........ 380.00
Tea caddy, dancing maidens w/lute & tambourine, BCN, 4½"..... 126.00
Urn w/lid, mythological scenes, gold CN, pressed 302 mk, 8"........ 60.00
Urn, Roman soldiers, dbl face hdls, BCN, 10" 76.00

Urns, lidded, sea chariot scene, BCN, 14", pr............................. 655.00
Vase, pr goddesses flaming offering scene, BCN, 10½" 225.00
Vases, 3 graces & adoration scene, BCN, 7", pr.......................... 150.00

Carlton

Carlton Ware was the product of Wiltshaw and Robinson, who operated in the Staffordshire district of England from about 1890. During the 1920s, they produced ornamental ware with enameled and gilded decorations such as flowers and birds, often on a black background. From 1935 until about 1961, in an effort to thwart the theft of their designs by Japanese potters, Carlton adapted the 'Registered Australian Design' mark, taking advantage of the South East Asia Treaty Organization which prohibited such piracy. In 1958 the firm was renamed Carlton Ware Ltd. Their trademark was a crown over a circular stamp with 'W & R, Stoke on Trent,' surrounding a swallow. 'Carlton Ware' was sometimes added by hand.

Bowl, Asian scene on yel, cartouches on blk w/gold rim, 1920s, 10"..150.00
Bowl, Hazelnut, brn & cream, script Australian mk, 2x9" 32.00
Bowl, pagoda scene on Rouge Royale, 2 lg gilt scrolls at rim, 12" L ...125.00
Bowl, spiderweb & dragonfly on Rouge Royale, 12x7" 100.00
Box, Oak Tree, 4x4"... 95.00
Candlestick, Deco flowers on bl w/gold, disk ft, 4x5¾" 165.00
Coffeepot, Lily of the Valley on Rouge Lustre w/gold, 6¾" 180.00
Compote, wisteria & heron on Rouge Royale, ped ft, 9" 110.00
Condiment set, 3 footballs & referee, 1920s-30s 150.00
Creamer/sugar bowl, Foxglove, pre-1959, 2½", 3" 150.00
Cruet, Walking, pk shoes, 4" 60.00
Cup/saucer, demi, heron/flowers/gold on Rouge Royale, 2¼" 132.00
Cup/saucer, Wild Duck on wht w/gilt, 2¼", 4¼" 230.00
Dish, butterfly & berries on Rouge Royale, gold hdls, 7x4¼" 48.00
Egg cup, Walking, Hawaiian decor, yel shoes............................. 80.00
Figurine, nude lady surrounded by hollyhocks, ltd ed, 11"............ 165.00
Ginger jar, Asian scenic on blk w/orange bands, 11", pr............... 525.00
Ginger jar, bird/butterfly/floral on Rouge Royale, 8½" 185.00
Ginger jar, dragonfly & floral on gr w/gold, 1952-62, 7¼" 220.00
Ginger jar, pagoda scenes, gold on cobalt, domed lid, 10¼", pr....425.00
Jam dish, Apple Blossom on gr, 4".. 20.00
Jug, Anemone on yel, scalloped rim, 5½".................................. 150.00
Jug, Foxglove on gr, brn stem hdl, 10½"................................... 380.00
Leaf dish, floral on wht, 1x5x4".. 40.00
Teapot, 2 golliwogs dancing, 1980, 9" 150.00
Teapot, Foxglove, brn stem hdl, pre-1958, 5½"..........................200.00
Teapot, Wild Rose on cream, brn hdl, 4½" 185.00
Vase, Asian scene on bl lustre w/gold, 1920s, 10x4" 150.00
Vase, Asian scene on yel, cylindrical neck, 10" 120.00
Vase, bird & floral, mc on bl w/gilt, bulb, ped ft, ca 1910, 7" 175.00
Vase, butterfly lustre, mottled ground, bulb base, 6" 135.00
Vase, Deco flowers on Rouge Royale, waist-to-hip hdls, ca 1930, 4½"..120.00
Vase, Deco flowers, blk/wht on red, hexagonal, ca 1935, w/lid, 12" ...335.00

Vase, Deco geometrics hand-painted, 8½", $480.00. (Photo courtesy Showplace Antique + Design Center on LiveAuctioneers.com)

Vase, Deco poppies & hollyhocks on wht, 5 mc rings, ovoid, 6¾" ..160.00
Vase, egrets in landscape on powder bl w/gold, w/lid, 7", pr 360.00
Vase, fairies & moon, orange & gold on blk, 8-sided rim, 1930, 9" ..300.00
Vase, floral on gray, flambé int, ovoid, #456, w/lid, 9¼", pr 1,500.00
Vase, Forest Tree on bl w/gold, domed lid, early 20th C, 11½" 150.00
Vase, hollyhocks on orange lustre, mushroom shape, ca 1935, 4¾".225.00
Vase, Kingfisher on Rouge Royale, w/sm gold hdls, 4½" 165.00
Vase, Medley, ftd, ca 1930, 7" 125.00
Vase, Oak Tree, limb hdls, 8½", pr 375.00
Vase, Rouge Royale w/gold ribbon-like hdls, 1930s, 5", pr 60.00
Vase, spider web/berries/foliage on bl/blk mottle, gold hdls, 4¾"...170.00
Vase, tropical birds/butterflies on orange lustre, 5¼", pr 1,325.00
Vase, weeping willows/gold prunus tree on Rouge Royale, hdls, 10" ..600.00
Vase, Worcester Birds, blk & gold on orange panels, trumpet shape, 8".160.00

Carnival Collectibles

Carnival items from the early part of this century represent the lighter side of an America that was alternately prospering and sophisticated or devastated by war and domestic conflict. But whatever the country's condition, the carnival's thrilling rides and shooting galleries were a sure way of letting it all go by — at least for an evening.

In the shooting gallery target listings below, items are rated for availability from 1, commonly found, to 10, rarely found (these numbers appear just before the size), and all are made of cast iron. Our advisors for shooting gallery targets are Richard and Valerie Tucker; their address is listed in the Directory under Colorado.

Chalkware Figures

Abe Lincoln bust, 1940-50, 12"...55.00
Army girl, mc pnt, 1946, 9", EX+..20.00
Bugs Bunny holding carrot, mc pnt, ca 1940, 14½" 240.00

Canes, each $25.00 to $50.00.
(Photo courtesy Kimball M. Sterling Inc. TFL-1915 on LiveAuctioneers.com)

Clarabelle (cow) sitting, wearing bonnet, Disney, 1945-50, 11" 65.00
Cowboy w/hat in left hand, gr shirt, red scarf, 1947, 8½", NM 30.00
Dale Evans, mc pnt, ca 1940s, 15"...120.00
Donald Duck, bl jacket, mc pnt, 1940s, 13½", $125 to.................150.00
Donald Duck holding coin aloft, mc pnt, 7" 60.00
Hopalong Cassidy, mc pnt, 1940s, 13" 275.00
Indian chief standing w/arms X, 1930-45, 19" 45.00
Kewpie-like black child w/hands raised, yel outfit, 12½", NM 45.00
Lone Ranger, 16"...85.00
Mickey Mouse, blk w/red shorts & shoes, 10" 100.00
Rabbit seated w/ears up, bank, mc pnt, 1940s, 12" 27.50
Snow White, bl dress w/glitter details, 15", NM............................175.00
Terrier dog seated, brn & yel w/red ribbon, 1948, 7x7x4¼", VG+ .30.00

Shooting Gallery Targets

Battleship, worn wht pnt, Mangels, 5, 6¼x11⅜", $200 to 300.00
Bull's-eye w/pop-up duck, old pnt, Quackenbush, 7, 12" dia, $500 to.600.00

Clown standing, bull's-eye, mc pnt, Evans or Hoffman, 10, 12", min. 1,000.00
Clown, worn red/wht/pnt, Mangels, 9, 19x19½"+movable arms 1,000.00
Dog running, worn wht pnt, Smith or Evans, 6, 6x11", $100 to ..200.00
Duck, detailed feathers, worn pnt, Evans, 4, 5½x8½", $100 to.....200.00
Eagle w/wings wide, mc pnt, Smith or Evans, 6, 14¾", $650 to ...750.00
Elephant, wht pnt, flakes, 9½" 250.00
Greyhound, bull's-eye, old patina, Parker, 8, 26" W, min 1,000.00
Indian chief, worn mc pnt, Hoffmann or Smith, 10, 20x15", min.. 1,000.00
Lion running, old wht pnt, 12½" L..220.00
Monkey standing, worn pnt, 10, 9¾x8½", $300 to 400.00
Mountain goat leaping, worn wht pnt, 8¾" 150.00
Owl, bull's-eye, wht traces, Evans, 6, 10¾x5⅛", $400 to 500.00
Pipe, old patina, Smith, 1, 5¾x1¾", value less than 50.00
Rabbit running, bull's-eye, old patina, Parker, 8, 12x25x1", min...1,000.00
Rabbit standing, worn pnt, Smith or Mueller, 8, 18x10", $900 to.. 1,000.00
Reindeer (elk), wht pnt (worn/rusty), 7, 10x9", $300 to 4,000.00
Saber-tooth tiger, old patina, Mangels, 7, 7¾x13", $300 to..........400.00
Soldier w/rifle, pnt traces/old patina, Mueller, 5, 9x5", $100 to ...200.00
Squirrel running, old patina, Smith, 4, 5⅛x9¾", $100 to.............200.00
Stag running, worn blk pnt, hooves missing, 9½" 220.00
Star spinner, dbl, worn mc pnt, Mangels, 6, 8x2¾", $200 to 300.00
Swan, worn pnt, Mueller, 7, 5¾x5", $100 to.................................200.00

Carnival Glass

Carnival glass is pressed glass that has been sprayed with a metallic salt solution and fired to give it an exterior lustre. First made in America in 1905, it was produced until the late 1920s and had great popularity in the average American household, for unlike the costly art glass produced by Tiffany, carnival glass could be mass produced at a small cost. Colors most found are marigold, green, blue, and purple; but others exist in lesser quantities and include white, clear, red, aqua opalescent, peach opalescent, ice blue, ice green, amber, lavender, and smoke.

Companies mainly responsible for its production in America include the Fenton Art Glass Company, Williamstown, West Virginia; the Northwood Glass Company, Wheeling, West Virginia; the Imperial Glass Company, Bellaire, Ohio; the Millersburg Glass Company, Millersburg, Ohio; and the Dugan Glass Company (Diamond Glass), Indiana, Pennsylvania. In addition to these major manufacturers, lesser producers included the U.S. Glass Company, the Cambridge Glass Company, the Westmoreland Glass Company, and the McKee Glass Company.

Carnival glass has been highly collectible since the 1950s and has been reproduced ever since. Several national and state collectors' organizations exist, and many fine books are available on old carnival glass, including *Standard Encyclopedia of Carnival Glass*, *Standard Encyclopedia of Carnival Glass Price Guide*, *Standard Companion to Carnival Glass*, and *Standard Companion to Non-American Carnival Glass*, all by our advisor, Mike Carwile (see Directory, Virginia).

Arcs (Imperial), bowl, amethyst, 8½", $60.00. (Photo courtesy Mike Carwile)

Acanthus, banana bowl, marigold..200.00
Acorn (Fenton), plate, wht 2,500.00
Adam's Rib (Dugan/Dmn), fan vase, Celeste bl.........................175.00

Apple Blossom (Diamond), bowl, amethyst, 6-7½" 55.00
Apple Tree (Fenton), pitcher, bl 1,100.00
Arcadia Lace (McKee), rose bowl, marigold 175.00
Argentina Blossom, inkwell, amber, very rare.....................3,000.00
Aurora Pearls, bowl in bride's basket, iridized moonstone 1,750.00
Aztec (McKee), sugar, clambroth.. 250.00
Banded Drape (Fenton), tumbler, gr 75.00
Banded Flute, compote, marigold, 4½".. 60.00
Barbella (Northwood), plate, teal 85.00
Basket of Roses, bonbon, amethyst... 550.00
Beaded Panels & Grapes (Jain), tumbler, marigold 275.00
Beaded Shell (Dugan), mug whimsey, wht................................. 700.00
Beaded Swirl (English), butter, bl... 85.00
Bells & Beads (Dugan), gravy boat, hdld, peach opal.................. 140.00
Big Basketweave (Dugan), vase, lav, 8-14"................................... 450.00
Big Thistle (Millersburg), punch bowl & base, amethyst, very rare ..15,000.00
Bird Galaxy, vase, very rare, wht, 10¼".....................................3,800.00
Bird of Paradise (Northwood), plate, advertising, amethyst.........450.00
Blackberry Rays (Northwood), compote, gr................................. 500.00
Blackberry Spray Variant (Fenton), hat shape, clambroth 125.00
Blazing Cornucopia (US Glass), spooner, marigold...................... 150.00
Blueberry (Fenton), pitcher, bl...2,000.00
Bo Peep (Westmoreland), ABC plate, scarce, marigold ... 550.00
Bow & Knot, perfume, marigold... 45.00
Bride's Vase, in metal stand, clear... 25.00
Brocaded Acorns (Fostoria), candleholder, lav 65.00
Brocaded Roses (Fostoria), covered box, ice gr........................... 185.00
Brocaded Summer Gardens, cake plate, center hdl, wht 85.00
Brooklyn, bottle, w/stopper, amethyst 95.00
Bubble Berry, shade, cranberry flash 75.00
Butterflies (Fenton), card tray, bl... 60.00
Butterfly (Jeannette), party set, orig box, teal 95.00
Buzz Saw (Cambridge), cruet, gr, 4" 575.00
Cameo (Fenton), vase, scarce, Celeste bl, 11-17" 250.00
Cane & Panels, tumble-up, marigold 350.00
Cannonball Variant, pitcher, bl... 285.00
Caroline, basket, scarce, lav opal 600.00
Cathedral Arches, compote, tall, rare, bl 700.00
Charlotte's Web, mirror, pk 200.00
Chatham (US Glass), candlesticks, marigold, pr 90.00
Checkers, ashtray, marigold.. 40.00
Cherries & Daisies (Fenton), banana boat, bl 1,000.00
Cherry (Dugan), chop plate, amethyst, rare, 11" 4,000.00
Cherry Blossoms, pitcher, bl 150.00
Cherub, lamp, clear, rare.. 150.00
Chrysanthemum Leaf, wine, tall stemmed, iridized chocolate glass, rare..1,200.00
Chyrsanthemum (Fenton), bowl, flat, teal, 9" 250.00
Circle Scroll (Dugan), butter, marigold 375.00
Colonial (Imperial), lemonade goblet, marigold.......................... 40.00
Columbia (Imperial), vase, smoke... 110.00
Concave Flute (Westmoreland), rose bowl, gr 100.00
Consolidated Shade, rare, marigold mg, 16" 500.00

Cornucopia (Fenton), candlesticks, ice bl, pr 195.00
Cornucopia (Jeannette), vase, marigold....................................... 40.00
Crab Claw (Imperial), bowl, amethyst, 5"................................... 35.00
Cut Stars, shot glass, marigold, 2" 50.00
Dahlia (Fenton), twist epergne, one lily, wht.............................. 325.00
Daisy (Fenton), bonbon, bl, scarce.. 200.00
Daisy & Plume Banded (Northwood), compote, stemmed, pastel horehound..125.00
Deco, vase, marigold... 275.00
Diagonal Band, tankard, marigold... 675.00
Diamond Cane, sugar box, marigold 165.00
Diamond Points (Northwood), basket, wht, rare.......................2,800.00
Diamond Thumbprint, mini oil lamp, marigold, 6½" 250.00
Diana, the Huntress, bowl, marigold, 8" 350.00
Dogwood Sprays (Dugan), bowl, bl opal, 9".............................. 325.00
Dot, vase, amethyst, rare, 5¼" 350.00
Drapery (Northwood), rose bowl, Renniger bl...........................3,000.00
Dugan Many Ribs, vase, peach opal 125.00
Egg & Dart, candlesticks, marigold, pr 90.00
Elks (Fenton), Detroit bowl, gr, scarce......................................1,100.00
Enameled Blossom Spray (Dugan), handgrip plate, decor, peach opal ...145.00
Enameled Grape Band, tumbler, marigold 50.00
English Hobnail (Westmoreland), toilet bottle, cranberry flash... 125.00
Euro Diamonds, berry bowl, lg, gr.. 45.00
Fanciful, plate, lav, 9".. 950.00
Feather & Heart (Millersburg), pitcher, vaseline, very rare.....14,500.00
Fenton Smooth Rays, bowl, tri-corner, ice gr, 6½"...................... 70.00
Fentonia Fruit (Fenton), bowl, ftd, bl, 10"................................. 175.00
File & Fan, compote, marigold mg.. 175.00
Fine Rib (Fenton), vase, sapphire bl, 2⅝" base 250.00
Fine Rib (Northwood), vase, aqua, 7-14".................................... 225.00
Fine Rib (Northwood), vase, aqua opal, 8-14"............................ 500.00
Flashed Diamonds, shakers, marigold, pr..................................... 50.00
Fluted Rib, jelly jar, marigold 50.00
Foxhunt, decanter, marigold... 275.00
Garden Mums (Fenton), plate, regular or handgrip, amethyst, 7". 450.00
Gibson Girl, toothpick holder, marigold..................................... 60.00
Good Luck, plate, amethyst, 9¼" 600.00
Gothic Arches (Imperial), vase, smoke, rare, 9-17"..................... 400.00

Grape & Cable (Northwood), bowl, ruffled, amethyst, 8"–9", $55.00.
(Photo courtesy Mike Carwile)

Greek Key (Northwood), pitcher, gr, rare 1,800.00
Heavy Grape (Dugan), bowl, peach opal, scarce, 10" 435.00
Hexagon Square, child's breakfast set, lav, complete 60.00
Hobstar (Imperial), pickle castor, marigold, complete................. 750.00
Honeycomb & Clover (Fenton), spooner, amber, rare 200.00
Humpty-Dumpty, mustard jar, marigold...................................... 75.00
Indiana Statehouse (Fenton), plate, bl, rare 16,000.00
Interior Flute, creamer, marigold.. 50.00
Inverted Strawberry (Cambridge), lady's spittoon, gr, rare 1,800.00
Jester's Cap (Dugan/Diamond), vase, peach opal......................... 100.00
Jeweled Butterflies (Indiana), bowl, sq, marigold, rare................. 225.00
Kittens (Fenton), ruffled bowl, aqua, scarce................................ 285.00
Laco, oil bottle, marigold, 9¼" 80.00

Corn (Northwood), vase, husk base, green, 6½", $700.00. (Photo courtesy Classic Edge Auctions on LiveAuctioneers.com)

Liberty Bell, bank, marigold 20.00
Lotus Land (Northwood), bon bon, marigold, rare.................... 1,500.00
Lovebirds, bottle, w/stopper, marigold............................... 575.00
Maize (Libbey), syrup/cruet, clear, rare 235.00
Marilyn (Millersburg), tumbler, gr, rare............................. 350.00
Melon Rib, powder jar, w/lid, marigold 35.00
Mirrored Lotus (Fenton), plate, Celeste bl, rare, 7½" 4,900.00
Morning Glory, vase, squat, gr, 4-7" 120.00
Napoleon, bottle, clear 85.00
Night Stars (Millersburg), card tray, gr, rare...................... 1,200.00
Northwood Wide Panel, vase, vaseline 335.00
Octagon (Imperial), milk pitcher, clambroth, scarce................. 150.00
Olympus (Northwood), bowl, bl, rare 12,000.00
Orange Peel (Westmoreland), custard cup, marigold, scarce.......... 25.00
Palm Beach (US Glass), sugar, lime gr.............................. 125.00
Paneled Tree Trunk (Dugan), vase, amethyst, rare, 7-12" 5,250.00
Paperchain, candlesticks, marigold, pr 80.00
Peacock & Urn (Fenton), plate, Beaded Berry ext pattern, marigold. 425.00
Peacock & Urn (Northwood), bowl, ice cream, gr, 10" 2,600.00
Peacock Tail (Fenton), chop plate, marigold, rare, 11" 2,200.00
Petals (Dugan), banana bowl, peach opal 100.00
Pineapple & Fan, wine set, 8 pcs, marigold, complete................ 575.00
Plums & Cherries (Northwood), spooner, bl, rare 1,800.00
Prayer Rug (Fenton), plate, iridized custard, rare, 7" 7,000.00
Radiance (New Martinsville), vase, marigold, rare, 12" 400.00
Ribbon Swirl, cake stand, amber, scarce............................ 425.00
Roly Poly, jar, w/lid, marigold.................................... 30.00
Rosalind (Millersburg), compote, jelly, bl, rare, 9" 15,000.00
Royalty (Imperial), fruit bowl, w/stand, smoke 100.00
S-Repeat (Dugan), punch bowl, w/base, amethyst, rare 4,800.00
Satin Swirl, atomizer, clear 75.00
Scroll Embossed (Imperial), dessert, stemmed, amethyst.............. 110.00
Shasta Daisy, pitcher, ice gr...................................... 425.00
Small Thumbprint, toothpick holder, marigold 70.00
Spiral (Imperial), candlesticks, amethyst 185.00
Star Medallion (Imperial), celery, hdld, smoke..................... 65.00
Swirl Hobnail (Millersburg), spittoon, gr, scarce.................. 4,000.00
Threaded Butterflies (US Glass), plate, ftd, aqua, rare 6,500.00
Three Roll, tumble-up, marigold, complete 90.00
Tiger Lily (Imperial), tumbler, olive gr........................... 100.00
Tree of Life Base (Northwood), compote, iridized custard, rare, 6" .. 550.00
Tulip (Millersburg), compote, amethyst, rare, 9" 1,500.00

Tulip Scroll (Millersburg), vase, amethyst, $750.00. (Photo courtesy Mike Carwile)

US Regal, sherbet, stemmed, w/hdl, marigold........................ 125.00
Vintage (Fenton), spittoon whimsey, marigold...................... 6,500.00
Vintage (Millersburg), bowl, gr, rare, 5" 1,100.00
Waffle Block (Imperial), sherbet, clambroth........................ 35.00
Water Lily & Cattails (Northwood), pitcher, bl 6,000.00
Wide Rib (Dugan), vase, squat, amethyst, 4-6" 100.00
Woodpecker & Ivy, vase, vaseline, rare............................. 7,500.00
Wreath of Roses (Fenton), punch bowl, w/base, peach opal 2,200.00
Zig Zag (Millersburg), bowl, ice cream shape, gr, 10" 1,200.00
Zipper Variant, sugar, marigold.................................... 35.00

Carousel Figures

For generations of Americans, visions of carousel horses revolving majestically around lively band organs rekindle wonderful childhood experiences. These memories are the legacy of the creative talent from a dozen carving shops that created America's carousel art. Skilled craftsmen brought their trade from Europe and American carvers took the carousel animal from a folk art creation to a true art form. The golden age of carousel art lasted from 1880 to 1929.

There are two basic types of American carousels. The largest and most impressive is the 'park style' carousel built for permanent installation in major amusement centers. These were created in Philadelphia by Gustav and William Dentzel, Muller Brothers, and E. Joy Morris who became the Philadelphia Toboggan Company in 1902. A more flamboyant group of carousel animals was carved in Coney Island, New York, by Charles Looff, Marcus Illions, Charles Carmel, and Stein & Goldstein's Artistic Carousel Company. These park-style carousels were typically three, four, and even five rows with 45 to 68 animals on a platform. Collectors often pay a premium for the carvings by these men. The outside row animals are larger and more ornate and command higher prices. The horses on the inside rows are smaller, less decorated, and of lesser value.

The most popular style of carousel art is the 'country fair style.' These carousels were portable affairs created for mobility. The horses are smaller and less ornate with leg and head positions that allow for stacking and easy loading. These were built primarily for North Tonawanda, New York, near Niagara Falls, by Armitage Herschell Company, Herschell Spillman Company, Spillman Engineering Company, and Allen Herschell. Charles W. Parker was also well known for his portable merry-go-rounds. He was based in Leavenworth, Kansas. Parker and Herschell Spillman both created a few large park-style carousels as well, but they are better known for their portable models.

Horses are by far the most common figure found, but there are two dozen other animals that were created for the carousel platform. Carousel animals, unlike most other antiques, are oftentimes worth more in a restored condition. Figures found with original factory paint are extraordinarily rare and bring premium amounts. Typically, carousel horses are found in garish, poorly applied 'park paint' and are often missing legs or ears. Carousel horses are hollow. They were glued up from several blocks for greater strength and lighter weight. Bass and poplar woods were used extensively.

If you have an antique carousel animal you would like to have identified, send a clear photograph and description along with a SASE to our advisor, William Manns, who is listed in the Directory under New Mexico. Mr. Manns is the author of *Painted Ponies*, containing many full-color photographs, guides, charts, and directories for the collector.

Key:
IR — inside row   OR — outside row
MR — middle row   PTC — Philadelphia Toboggan
                                              Company

Coney Island-Style Horses

Looff, rope tail, glass eyes, circa 1890, 48x58", VG, $4,700.00. (Photo courtesy Philip Weiss Auctions on LiveAuctioneers.com)

Carmel, IR jumper, unrstr......................................4,500.00
Carmel, MR jumper, unrstr......................................7,300.00
Carmel, OR jumper w/cherub, rstr.........................16,000.00
Illions, IR jumper, rstr...4,500.00
Illions, MR stander, rstr...7,800.00
Looff, IR jumper unrstr...4,500.00
Looff, OR jumper, unrstr.......................................14,000.00
Stein & Goldstein, IR jumper, unrstr........................4,700.00
Stein & Goldstein, MR jumper, rstr..........................8,000.00
Stein & Goldstein, OR stander w/bells, unrstr.........20,000.00

European Horses

Anderson, English, unrstr..3,500.00
Bayol, Fr, unrstr..2,500.00
Heyn, German, unrstr...3,200.00
Hubner, Belgian, unrstr..2,000.00
Savage, English, unrstr...2,500.00

Menagerie Animals (Non-Horses)

Dentzel, bear, unrstr...20,000.00
Dentzel, cat, unrstr...22,000.00
Dentzel, deer, unrstr...16,000.00
Dentzel, lion, unrstr..30,000.00
Dentzel, pig, unrstr...9,500.00
Dentzel, rabbit, ca 1905, losses to tail & ear, 78x50x20".........63,000.00
E Joy Morris, deer, unrstr......................................10,000.00
Herschell Spillman, cat, unrstr...............................11,000.00
Herschell Spillman, chicken, portable, unrstr..............5,500.00
Herschell Spillman, dog, portable, unrstr...................6,500.00
Herschell Spillman, frog, unrstr.............................18,000.00
Looff, camel, unrstr...9,000.00
Looff, goat, rstr...13,500.00
Muller, tiger, rstr...32,000.00
Parker, cat w/Am flag, jumper, restr, missing pole/base, 24x62"..1,600.00

Philadelphia-Style Horses

Dentzel, IR 'topknot' jumper, unrstr.........................5,500.00
Dentzel, MR jumper, unrstr......................................7,800.00
Dentzel, OR stander, female cvg on shoulder, rstr......20,000.00
Dentzel, prancer, rstr..8,000.00
Morris, IR prancer, rstr...4,500.00
Morris, MR stander, unrstr.......................................7,000.00
Morris, OR stander, rstr...17,000.00
Muller, IR jumper, rstr...5,000.00
Muller, MR jumper, rstr...7,500.00
Muller, OR stander w/military trappings...................27,000.00
Muller, OR stander, rstr...23,000.00
PTC, chariot (bench-like seat), rstr...........................7,500.00
PTC, IR jumper, rstr...4,000.00
PTC, MR jumper, rstr..8,500.00
PTC, OR stander, armored, rstr..............................25,000.00
PTC, OR stander, unrstr...17,000.00

Portable Carousel Horses

Allan Herschell, all alum, ca 1950..............................500.00
Allan Herschell, half & half, wood & alum head.........1,100.00
Allan Herschell, IR Indian pony, unrstr.....................2,000.00
Allan Herschell, OR Trojan-style jumper, rstr............3,500.00
Armitage Herschell, track-machine jumper..................2,800.00
Dare, jumper, unrstr..3,000.00

Herschell Spillman, chariot (bench-like seat).............3,800.00
Herschell Spillman, IR jumper, unrstr.......................2,400.00
Herschell Spillman, MR jumper, unrstr......................2,900.00
Herschell Spillman, OR, eagle decor..........................4,300.00
Herschell Spillman, OR, park machine........................7,500.00
Parker, MR jumper, unrstr.......................................4,200.00
Parker, OR jumper, park machine, unrstr....................6,500.00
Parker, OR jumper, rstr...5,800.00

Cartoon Art

Collectors of cartoon art are interested in many forms of original art — animation cels, sports, political or editorial cartoons, syndicated comic strip panels, and caricature. To produce even a short animated cartoon strip, hundreds of original drawings are required, each showing the characters in slightly advancing positions. Called 'cels' because those made prior to the 1950s were made from a celluloid material, collectors often pay hundreds of dollars for a frame from a favorite movie. Prices of Disney cels with backgrounds vary widely. Background paintings, model sheets, storyboards, and preliminary sketches are also collectible — so are comic book drawings executed in India ink and signed by the artist. Daily 'funnies' originals, especially the earlier ones portraying super heroes, and Sunday comic strips, the early as well as the later ones, are collected. Cartoon art has become recognized and valued as a novel yet valid form of contemporary art. In the listings below all cels are untrimmed, full size, and in excellent condition unless noted otherwise.

Model sheet, Cinderella, 15 various poses, 14x11", VG, $85.00. (Photo courtesy Philip Weiss Auctions on LiveAuctioneers.com)

Cartoon, War Gardens, watercolor, 6 scenes, S Slippers, 14x22"+fr..215.00
Cel, Bambi's mother/Bambi, Courvoisier, Disney, 1942, 5x6"...1,265.00
Cel, Black Cauldron, Tara/Horned King, Disney, 1985, 11x14"...250.00
Cel, Briar Rose (Sleeping Beauty), full bkgrnd, Disney, 6x10"..1,900.00
Cel, Cinderella, Fairy Godmother on yel bkgrnd, Disney, 1950s.460.00
Cel, Daffy Duck/Porky Pig, sgn, ltd ed 200, 1987, 9x12"............350.00
Cel, Elmer Fudd, profile view, sgn Chuck Jones, Warner Bros, 1980, 4x6"..115.00
Cel, Fantasia, Courvoisier, Cupid/Pegasus, Disney, 1940s, 8x7".1,735.00
Cel, Flower (skunk/Bambi), Courvoisier bkgrnd, Disney, 1937, 7x7⅞".......900.00
Cel, Little Mermaid, 5-cel setup, Disney, fr, 10x14", NM.........4,600.00
Cel, Maleficent & Diablo w/bkgrnd, Disney, 5½x8"..................3,000.00
Cel, Mickey Mouse, Bandleader Mickey, Disney, 1955, 11x14"...690.00
Cel, Nine to Five, pnt bkgrd, fr, 11x15" (visible), NM.............300.00
Cel, Pink Panther, Clouseau, DePatatie-Freleng, 10x14"............140.00
Cel, Pinocchio & Figaro, Courvoisier, Disney, 5½x6½"............1,800.00
Cel, Robin Hood, 1973, 12x15"...2,750.00
Cel, Sleeping Beauty, Maleficent, Disney, 1959, 10x13"...........2,070.00
Cel, Super Chicken & Fred in desert, Jay Ward, 9x7".................515.00
Cel, The Practical Pig, Courvoisier, Disney, 1939, 9x17", VG..2,750.00
Cel, Tramp (dog) walking, Disney, 5x4".....................................800.00
Cel, Who Framed Roger Rabbit?, Jessica/Valient, Disney, 10x15"..230.00
Concept art, Donald w/paintbrush, Darren Hunt, Disney, 7x8".....60.00
Concept art, Great Mouse Detective int, mc, Disney/Peraza, 11x14".1,450.00
Concept art, Minnie Mouse, Alex Maher, Disney, 6x8"................65.00
Drawing, Breakers Ahead, boat, pen/ink, T Brown, 1940, 9x17".......48.00
Drawing, Centaurette, waist up, Disney, 7x2" image, 10x12".......275.00

Drawing, Country Mouse, pencil, unsgn, 6x6" 195.00
Drawing, Kotik (seal) from White Seal, Chuck Jones, 1975, 8½x11" . 55.00
Drawing, lady w/sign, charcoal/pencil, W Darrow Jr/New Yorker, 14x10" ... 215.00
Drawing, Mama Bear, bl pencil, Engel, Disney, 1940s, 9½x7½" ... 360.00
Drawing, Minnie Mouse w/hat, full figure, 2x3" image, stain 275.00
Drawing, Red Riding Hood as nightclub singer, Blair, 1943, 8x4" .. 215.00
Drawing, Uncle Sam/Mateo Cagasta play chess, pen/ink, Corey, 1898.. 120.00
Model sheet, Sneezy/Bashful in varied poses, Disney, 10½x12½" .. 1,000.00
Sericel, Gift for Olive Oyl, Popeye & Olive Oyl, 1999, 16x13" 85.00
Sericel, Lion King's Simba & Nala as cubs, Disney, 5½x9" 180.00
Sericel, Mr Duck Steps Out, Donald & Daisy, Disney 400.00
Sericel, Superman, 'Clark Kent's Secret Secret,' 1 of 350, 1997, fr 23x40" ... 725.00
Sericel, Yogi Bear, 'Do or Diet,' 1 of 2,500, 1996, fr 19x17", M 235.00
Sunday pg, Hagar the Horrible, D Browne, 1977, 11½x16" 600.00
Sunday pg, Mandrake the Magician, Falk & Davis, 1952, full pg .. 1,080.00

Cast Iron

In the mid-1800s, the cast-iron industry was raging in the United States. It was recognized as a medium extremely adaptable for uses ranging from ornamental architectural filigree to actual building construction. It could be cast from a mold into any conceivable design that could be reproduced over and over at a relatively small cost. It could be painted to give an entirely versatile appearance. Furniture with openwork designs of grapevines and leaves and intricate lacy scrollwork was cast for gardens as well as inside use. Figural doorstops of every sort, bootjacks, trivets, and a host of other useful and decorative items were made before the 'ferromania' had run its course. For more information, we recommend *Antique Iron* by Kathryn McNerney (Collector Books). See also Kitchen Collectibles, Cast-Iron Kitchen Ware; and other specific categories. Values in the listings that follow are for items in excellent original condition unless noted otherwise.

Architectural ornament, eagle w/wings spread on orb, 18x47" . 1,295.00
Bench, serpentine crest rail forms dbl bk, pierced supports, 30x40" ... 975.00
Bracket, grapevines, late 19th C, 20x33½" 230.00
Figure, Geo Washington w/scroll, mc pnt, Design Pat Aug 26 1843, 47" . 18,115.00
Figure, lion, After A Canova, old ochre pnt, 1850s, 19x39x16", pr ... 9,695.00
Finials, pineapple in urn w/petal rim, pnt traces, 22", pr 400.00
Garden gate, archet top w/acanthus crest, rocaille elements, 48x47" .. 1,000.00
Hitching post finial, bridled horse w/acanthus-leaf base, rpt, 13". 200.00
Hitching post, jockey, right arm extended, mc, 1800s, 24", VG .. 240.00
Jardiniere, floral panels, loose ring hdls/ftd, oval, 1800s, 35" L, pr .. 3,290.00
Kettle, sugar, flared rim, LA, 27x72" 6,400.00
Lawn jockey, red & bl jacket, wht pants, blk boots, 46" 1,450.00
Lawn sprinkler, alligator facing upward, sprinkler head in mouth, 10" ... 145.00
Lawn sprinkler, arrow on base, WD Allen Chicago emb on feathers, 11". 690.00
Lawn sprinkler, frog facing upward, sprinkler head in mouth, 4" . 200.00
Lawn sprinkler, mallard duck w/sprinkler atop head, mc rpt, 13". 975.00
Lawn sprinkler, mermaid, 14x7" 3,000.00
Lawn sprinkler, turtle w/sprinkler head in mouth, blk & red, 9" L ... 800.00
Mirror, rtcl oval, hoop-skirted lady ea side, flag at base, 21" 1,680.00
Paperweight, Black Sambo w/cigar, mc pnt, Hubley, 3x1" 335.00
Paperweight, chicken, Whitmoyer Feed Myerstown, 2x2½", NM ... 450.00
Paperweight, quail pr, grassy base, Fred Everett/Hubley, 2x2" 345.00
Settee & 2 armchairs, scrolled fern bks, openwork seats, old pnt, 3-pc. 1,250.00
Settee, grape clusters, set-in grill seat, wht pnt, 33x44", pr 345.00
Settee, Urn of Blossoms pattern, C&S Scrolls, old wht pnt, 42x46"..3,525.00
Urn, campagna form on ped, scrolled foliage, 31x22½", pr 1,800.00

Castor Sets

Castor sets became popular during the early years of the eighteenth century and continued to be used through the late Victorian era. Their purpose was to hold various condiments for table use. The most common type was a circular arrangement with a center handle on a revolving pedestal base that held three, four, five, or six bottles. A few were equipped with a bell for calling the servant. Frames were made of silverplate, glass, or pewter. Though most bottles were of pressed glass, some of the designs were cut, and on rare occasion, colored glass with enameled decorations was used as well. To maintain authenticity and value, castor sets should have matching bottles. Prices listed below are for those with matching bottles and in frames with plating that is in excellent condition (unless noted otherwise). Note: Watch for new frames and bottles in clear, cranberry, cobalt, and vaseline Inverted Thumbprint as well as reproductions of Czechoslovakian cut glass bottles. These have recently been appearing on the market. Our advisor for this category is Barbara Aaronson; she is listed in the Directory under California.

3-bottle, Am Shield, pewter fr w/eagle, mini, child sz 165.00
3-bottle, amberina Invt T'print, Hartford #0204, NE Glass, s&p .. 1,000.00
3-bottle, Burmese, #740, Mt WA, SP Pairpoint fr 1,800.00
3-bottle, paneled cylinder, mk fr w/loop hdl & triangle base 100.00
4-bottle, 2 rose amber Invt T'print w/stoppers, s&p, Mt WA 2,000.00
4-bottle, 2 w/stoppers+2 s&p shakers, Crown Milano, Mt WA, SP fr.. 7,000.00
4-bottle, Bellflower, single vine, pewter fr 400.00

Four-bottle, green glass, in matching stand, VG, $325.00.
(Photo courtesy John McInnis Auctioneers on LiveAuctioneers.com)

4-bottle, King's Crown ruby stain, Adams, matching glass fr, NM .. 575.00
4-bottle, Log & Star, amber; orig ped-base fr 145.00
4-bottle, mg w/HP insects, 8" dia glass stand w/metal hdl, NM 125.00
4-bottle, navette-shaped rtcl stand w/center loop hdl, 9½x7¾" ... 700.00
5-bottle, Bristol glass, floral on pk, cherub SP fr, 15x5" 975.00
5-bottle, etched amberina, cut amberina stoppers, gilt fr 2,200.00
5-bottle, etched floral w/cutting, much decor, Meriden ft 450.00
5-bottle, pressed glass, rstr Meriden fr w/cherub hdl revolves 525.00
6-bottle, amber w/etched trees/deer, Rogers fr #116 (VG plating) .. 636.00
6-bottle, etched, NP fr w/bell, ftd, 17" 175.00
6-bottle, pressed, 18" Simpson-Hall-Miller fr 550.00

Catalina Island

Catalina Island pottery was made on the island of the same name, which is about 26 miles off the coast of Los Angeles. The pottery was started in 1927 at Pebble Beach, by Wm. Wrigley, Jr., who was instrumental in developing and using the native clays. Its principal products were brick and tile to be used for construction on the island. Garden pieces were first produced, then vases, bookends, lamps, ashtrays, novelty items, and finally dinnerware. The ware became very popular and was soon being shipped to the mainland as well.

Some of the pottery was hand thrown; some was made in molds. Most pieces are marked Catalina Island or Catalina with a printed incised stamp or handwritten with a pointed tool. Cast items were sometimes marked in the mold, a few have an ink stamp, and a paper label was also used. The most favored colors in tableware and accessories are 1) black (rare), 2) Seafoam and Monterey Brown (uncommon), 3) matt blue and green, 4) Toyon Red (orange), 5) other brights, and 6) pastels with a matt finish.

The color of the clay can help to identify approximately when a piece was made: 1927 to 1932, brown to red (Island) clay (very popular with collectors, tends to increase values); 1931 to 1932, an experimental period with various colors; 1932 to 1937, mainly white clay, though tan to brown clays were also used on occasion.

Items marked Catalina Pottery are listed in Gladding-McBean. For further information we recommend *Catalina Island Pottery Collectors Guide* by Steven and Aisha Hoefs, and *Collector's Encyclopedia of California Pottery* and *California Pottery Scrapbook*, both by Jack Chipman (Collector Books).

Ashtray, bl, goat, 4"	575.00
Ashtray, brn bear, 3¼x5½"	775.00
Ashtray, Toyon red, sombrero-style, unmk, 2½x4"	575.00
Bookend, monk, Descanso gr, ca 1932, 5x4"	825.00
Bowl, mixing, orange-red, Catalina, 11"	375.00
Candleabra, gr, seals, 5x10½"	575.00
Cigarette box, bl, horse's head on lid	350.00
Creamer, powder bl matt, Rope design, ca 1936	40.00
Cup, demi, pearly wht	35.00
Pitcher, Toyon red	275.00
Planter, cactus, Cat-lina, Descanso gr, Santa Catalina, 1936	600.00
Plate, 11"	700.00
Plate, decorative, orange-red/wht/lt bl, Moorish design, ca 1932, 11"	750.00
Plate, decorative, Submarine Garden, 14"	1,600.00
Plate, HP old Mexico scene, ca 1932, 11½"	825.00
Refrigerator jar, w/cover, unmk, 2¾"	200.00
Sugar, powder bl matt, Rope design, ca 1936	50.00
Tumbler, Monterey brn	75.00
Vase, 2 hdls, 9"	500.00
Vase, bl, #325, 5"	325.00
Vase, fluted, Catalina bl, 6"	300.00

Vase, sage green matt glaze, circa 1927 – 1937, marked Catalina, 18", $2,400.00. (Photo courtesy O'Gallerie on LiveAuctioneers.com)

Vase, step, Monterey brn, Catalina	500.00
Wall pocket, turq, seashell	350.00

Catalogs

Catalogs are not only intriguing to collect on their own merit, but for the collector with a specific interest, they are often the only remaining source of background information available, and as such they offer a wealth of otherwise unrecorded data. The mail-order industry can be traced as far back as the mid-1800s. Even before Aaron Montgomery Ward began his career in 1872, Laacke and Joys of Wisconsin and the Orvis Company of Vermont, both dealers in sporting goods, had been well established for many years. The E.C. Allen Company sold household necessities and novelties by mail on a broad scale in the 1870s. By the end of the Civil War, sewing machines, garden seed, musical instru-

ments, even medicine, were available from catalogs. In the 1880s Macy's of New York issued a 127-page catalog; Sears and Spiegel followed suit in about 1890. Craft and art supply catalogs were first available about 1880 and covered such varied fields as china painting, stenciling, wood burning, brass embossing, hair weaving, and shellcraft. Today some collectors confine their interests not only to craft catalogs in general but often to just one subject. There are several factors besides rarity which make a catalog valuable: age, condition, profuse illustrations, how collectible the field is that it deals with, the amount of color used in its printing, its size (format and number of pages), and whether it is a manufacturer's catalog verses a jobber's catalog (the former being the most desirable).

Abbott's Magic Novelty Co Catalogue No 2, 64 pgs, EX	90.00
American Flyer Trains Erector & Other Gilbert Toys, 1953, EX+	22.00
American Printing Equipment, 1968, 264 pgs, VG+	32.00
Atwater Kent Radio, 1928, 30 pgs, 9x6", EX	35.00
Bennett Bros 1956 Bl Book of Quality Merchandise, hardbound, VG	95.00
Billy & Ruth Go A-Christmas Shopping! big-name toys, 1931, 16 pgs, EX	105.00
Britains Ltd, lead toy soldiers, 1954, 125+ pgs, VG	75.00
Buddy L Catalog of Steel Toys for 1935, EX	450.00
Caterpillar Line Condensed Catalog, 1936, 43 pgs, EX	80.00
Charles Williams Stores, New York Styles, Fall/Winter 1917, 515 pgs, G	15.00
Coleman Happier Vacations, camping equipment, 1965, EX	12.00
Crest Wedding Cake Ornaments, blk & wht illus, 1920s, 24+ pgs, VG	70.00
DeMoulin Bros & Co, burlesque/props/costumes, 1924, 200-pg, 6x9", EX	80.00
Dinky Toys, 1950s, 20 pgs, 6", EX	50.00
Dress Goods Silks & General Yard Goods, Spring/Summer 1916, 66 pgs, VG	175.00
Epiphone Recording Banjos, 1928, 22 pgs, EX	15.00
Estes Model Rocketry Catalog, 1975, w/Star Trek models, EX	15.00
Evinrude Outboard Motors, 1941, w/price list, EX	40.00
Excelsior Stove & MFG Co, 1912, 8 pgs, G+	10.00
Fairmount Tools, 1940s, 25 pgs, EX	60.00
Firestone Extra Value Merchandise, car parts/toys.., 1947, 96 pgs, VG	15.00
Gimbels Schuster, Christmas 1966, general, 91 pgs, EX	18.00
Griswold, Palmer & Co, clothing, 1893, G+	88.00
Guitars for Moderns by Gretsch, 1955, 16 pgs, EX	150.00
Harley-Davidson Accessories, 1940, 32 pgs, EX	65.00
Hawkes & Son Cornets, 20 pgs, G	110.00
His Master's Voice 1957-1958 Recording Entertainment, 704 pgs, VG	20.00
Hobbies for Family Fun, 1960, 24 pgs, EX	15.00
Howdy Doody Merchandise Catalogue, 1955, VG	250.00
International Harvester 1958 Farmer's Catalogue, 48 pgs, EX	55.00

Ives Miniature Railway System (The), circa 1906 – 1907, VG, $385.00. (Photo courtesy New England Toy Train Exchange on LiveAuctioneers.com)

JC Penney, Spring/Summer or Fall/Winter 1985, both EX, ea	35.00
John Deere Model 'T' General Purpose Tractor, 1940, 32 pgs, EX	95.00
Joliet Mfg Co, farming, 1918, 32 pgs, G	41.00
Kem-Tone, pnt, 1944, 8 pgs, G	7.00
Lane Bryant Tall Girls Summer Fashion Sale, 1958, VG	100.00
Lionel 1941 Price List Catalog, M	250.00
Lionel, 1957, New 'O' Super Track, VG	25.00
Lone Star Carefreedom Line for '59, 32 pgs of boats, EX	45.00
Louie Miller Wholesale Millinery Jobber, 1951, VG	80.00

Ludwig Quality Percussion (Ludwig 64), 72 full-color pgs, rare, VG.. 80.00
Magnavox Annual Sale, Save Up to $100, radios, etc, 1960s, 23 pgs, EX . 18.00
Marshall Field & Co Chicago Holiday Goods No 203, 1912, 288 pgs, VG . 105.00
Martin Guitar Catalogue, 1960s, 24 pgs, EX..................................... 15.00
Mattel Toys, 1968, for distributors and stores only, EX+ 395.00
Mobile Life, mobile homes, 1955, 125 pgs, 11x8½", VG............... 21.00
Montgomery Ward Spring & Summer 1938, general, 832 pgs, VG . 30.00
Napa Tractor Parts, 1943, 256 pgs, EX 15.00
Neiman Marcus, Christmas 1966, VG 12.00
Nicholas Beazley Airplane Co Inc, airplanes, parts & misc materials, 1928.. 125.00
Peck & Hills, furniture, 1942, 224 pgs, VG 65.00
Proto Tools/Plomb Tool Co, No 5023, 1950, 64 pgs, VG 21.00
Radolek 1931 Catalog of Radio & Electrical Bargains, 98 pgs, VG . 12.00
Randall Made Knives, 1950s, 20 pgs, EX 150.00
Rogers Drums w/Memriloc Hardware '76/'77, 8 pgs, EX.............. 35.00
Rumely Cream Separators Instructions for Size 14, 33 pgs, G...... 160.00
S&H Gr Stamp Idea Book, 1960-61, 98 pgs, EX 25.00
Samuel Kirk & Son Sterling Silver, 1940, 48 pgs, 6½x9", VG....... 20.00
Schlage Locks, 1936, binder cover, EX... 105.00
Schoenhut's Humpty Dumpty Circus, 1918, VG........................... 150.00
Schwinn Hornet...(The Popular), various bike photos, 1940s-50s, EX.. 50.00
Sears 1960 Christmas Book, 482 pgs, VG 95.00
Sears Roebuck & Co Chicago Catalog No 122, 1911, 1,265 pgs, VG .. 7.50
Sheaffer's Writing Instruments Featuring the Snorkel, 1950s, EX.. 80.00
Snap-On Bl Point/Snap-On Tools Inc, 1935, 96 pgs, VG 140.00
Spiegel The Golden Christmas Book, 1959, 403 pgs, EX 55.00
Stanley Tools No 34, July 1, 1927, 192 pgs, w/Sweetheart logo, EX... 38.00
Storrs & Harrison Co (Seed Catalog), Spring 1899, 168 pgs, VG .. 145.00
Studebaker Motors, automobiles, 1936, 8 pgs, G+........................ 16.00
Swimaster New for 1960, 8 pgs, VG... 75.00
Topper Toys, ...Here Comes Johnny Express, insert booklet, 1965, EX... 20.00
Vogue Pattern Catalog, 1959, EX 18.00
Wagner Fans, 1937, 18 pgs, G+ 35.00
York Gas Engine, For Sale by Flinchbaugh Mfg Co York PA, VG... 175.00

Caughley Ware

The Caughley Coalport Porcelain Manufactory operated from about 1775 until 1799 in Caughley, near Salop, Shropshire, in England. The owner was Thomas Turner, who gained his potting experience from his association with the Worcester Pottery Company. The wares he manufactured in Caughley are referred to as 'Salopian.' He is most famous for his blue-printed earthenwares, particularly the Blue Willow pattern, designed for him by Thomas Minton. For a more detailed history, see Coalport.

Cup and saucer, Chinoiserie Landscape, blue on white, marked with a crescent, circa 1775, $150.00. (Photo courtesy New Orleans Auction, St. Charles Gallery, Inc. on LiveAuctioneers.com)

Jug, floral w/emb cabbage leaves, mask spout, ca 1785, 8½" 500.00
Mug, Chinese scenic vignettes, 7"... 800.00
Strainer, fisherman, S mk, ca 1780, 3"... 375.00
Sugar bowl, Willow w/gold, acorn finial, late 18th C 100.00
Tea bowl & saucer, birds on branches, 18th C.............................. 175.00
Tea canister, fence pattern, bbl form, 18th C, rpl wooden lid, 4½"... 180.00
Teapot, transfer cottage in landscape, Salopian, ca 1825, spout repair, 10¾" ... 425.00
Teapot, wht w/gold band, ear hdl on reeded bbl form, 1785, 6", NM.. 265.00

Cauldon

Formerly Brown-Westhead, Moore & Co., Cauldon Ltd. was a Staffordshire pottery that operated under that name from 1905 until 1920, producing dinnerware that was most often transfer decorated. The company operated under the title Cauldon Potteries Ltd. from 1920 until 1962.

Pitcher, milk, Candia, bl on wht w/gold, 5¾"................................. 60.00
Plate, blk w/tan devices, Tiffany Co/Brn Westhead Moore, 10", 18 for... 1,800.00

Plate, fox hunt scene, black mark, 11", $180.00. (Photo courtesy Mid-Hudson Auction Galleries on LiveAuctioneers.com)

Plate, lady w/fan, Maurice, bl & gold rim, blk mk, 10⅛" 190.00
Plates, Fern, bl on wht, scalloped, 9¾", 10 for.............................. 275.00
Plates, morning glories on wht w/gold, scalloped, 8¾", 12 for 240.00
Platter, Sylvan, bl on wht, 17¾x14½", NM.................................... 50.00
Platter, turkey scene, bl on wht, rect, 22x18½"............................. 725.00
Platter, vining border, turkey in center, bl on wht, 1890s, 20" L.. 275.00
Tureen, flowers & butterflies, w/lid, sm, w/underplate 60.00
Vase, Cairo Ware, flowering foliage, baluster, Royal Couldon, 14"... 150.00

Celluloid

Celluloid, the world's first commercially successful plastic, was invented in 1869 by Albany, New York, printer John Wesley Hyatt. Initially intended as an imitative material for ivory billiard balls, it soon found applications in dentures, as waterproof linen for detachable cuffs and collars, as imitation tortoiseshell in ornamental hair combs and frames for eyeglasses, and as an imitation for amber, coral, and jet in jewelry items. The introduction of sheet celluloid in the 1880s found this material being used for colorful pin-back buttons, advertising premiums, and fanciful photograph albums and storage boxes. Some of the most collectible celluloid objects are dolls and toys that were manufactured between 1898 and 1930. Celluloid found a unique identity as photography and cinema film, but due to its flammable nature was phased out by the 1930s. Japanese manufacturers continued to make and import toys of celluloid during the Occupation years of 1945 – 1952. Between 1881 and 1901 several American manufacturers were making celluloid-type plastics with tradenames like Zylonite, Pyralin, Fiberloid, and Viscoloid.

Collectors should take care with celluloid objects. The high nitric acid content used in its manufacture rendered it highly flammable. Celluloid is still being manufactured today for use in ping pong balls, instrument binding, and guitar picks.

Our Celluloid advisor is Julie P. Robinson; you will find her in our Directory under New York.

Action figures, baseball or football, Occupied Japan, 6¼", ea......... 35.00
Action figures, soldiers, various uniforms, MIJ, house in circle mk, 5" tall, ea .. 35.00
Animals, Am Viscoloid, 4-7", ea $12 to... 25.00
Back comb, Deco, channel set rhinestones, 6x4"........................... 200.00
Billiard Balls, Hyatt Vitalite Pocket, orig gr box, ca 1930, set...... 250.00
Bookmark, dc, butterfly, The First Psalm, Westminster Press, 4".... 22.00
Box, collar, lined w/pk satin, couple playing instruments, 6x8" .. 225.00

Box, jewelry, piano, imitation ivory grained celluloid with pink velour lining, 3x5", $65.00. (Photo courtesy Julie P. Robinson)

Box, necktie, oblong, courting couple, red & gr floral, 3x14x4"...175.00
Bracelet, hinged, cream w/metal decorations resembling pique ...125.00
Brooch, Grecian woman cameo, gold filigree fr, C-clasp 45.00
Collar/cuffs, waterproof, Fiberloid, Litholin, fake linen, ea set.......15.00
Doll, boy, brn hair, glass eyes, German, Schildkrot, ca 1936, 18".250.00
Doll, Boopie, gold hair, feather skirt, earrings, hat/cane, 11" 75.00
Doll, Parsons Jackson, bald, molded shoes, Stork, unclothed, 10" .85.00
Doll, Viscoloid, Made in USA, 7" 55.00
Dresser set, ivory Pyralin, DuBarry, 13 pcs, ca 1925.....................155.00
Fan, Brise, gold neoclassical design, 2 women medallion, HP, 10" .75.00
Fraternal pin, bow shaped, WCTU, C-clasp, ca 1874 ....65.00
Hair comb, imitation tortoise w/filigree leaf swags, ca 1910, 3x3"..45.00
Hatpin holder, ivory grained, sq w/sq pyramid base, ca 1910, 6" 55.00
Hatpin, Magnificant, 5" elephant head ornament, ca 1900, 17" ..225.00
Manicure box, rect, house in snow, lined w/bl satin, 5x7x2"........125.00
Mirror, pocket, Mifflin County Jewelry, Lewistown PA, 2" dia.......35.00
Necklace, Cameo profile, Art Nouveau faux ivory pendant.........110.00
Photographic brooch, sepia photo, Gibson Girl, twisted metal trim, 2" ...65.00
Play food on rnd or oval platters, Viscoloid USA 125.00
Shoehorn, lady's slipper red/blk laminate, rhinestones at heel, 6"..35.00
Stickpin/cufflinks, lever closure backs, octagonal framework, set...45.00
Toy, car, Easter, bk full of eggs, VCO (Viscoloid), 3" L.................175.00
Toy, Halloween, blk cat, balancing on orange ring, VCO 150.00

Central Glass Company

The Central Glass Company (1863 – 1893) was formed in Wheeling, West Virginia. It burned in 1888 and was rebuilt. In 1891 it joined the U.S. Glass combine as Factory O. Central produced tableware, lamps, clocks, novelties, stemware, and barware in clear, amber, blue, and canary. It is not known if they produced milk glass. They produced many patterns, some of them patented by one of the founders, John Oesterling. Among their patterns were Silver Age (aka Coin), Rose (aka Cabbage Rose), Wheat in Shield, Cord and Tassel, Mountain Laurel, Master Argus, Ripple, Paneled Diamond & Flowers, Stippled Swag, Flat Diamond, Oak Wreath, Prism and Diamond Band, and Log Cabin (#748, reproduced by Mosser Glass Company in 1982). Do not confuse this manufacturer with Central Glass Works (1898 – 1939), which was a new company formed by new owners. It is not firmly established whether this new company got back the original Central molds from U.S. Glass. For further information, consult Albert Christian Revi's *American Pressed Glass and Figure Bottles*, Marilyn R. Hallock's *Central Glass Company, The First Thirty Years, 1863 – 1893*, and http://centralglassconnection.com/gallery.htm.

Our advisor for Central Glass is Shirley Smith; she is listed in the Directory under West Virginia.

Cake salver, Coin, high ped...425.00
Compote, covered, Coin, low ped 400.00
Finger lamp, Cabbage Rose, 3¼" 58.00
Goblet, clear, Loop, 6⅛" 27.00
Jug, syrup, Coin..270.00

Lamp, Coin, 8"...316.00
Lamp, Hobnail w/Tudor base, bl, 8¼" 88.00
Lamp, kerosene, Coin..1,000.00
Lamp, mini, Dew Drop #821, 4⅝"..58.00
Open salt, vaseline, 1⅞" W 14.00
Platter, clear, 10¼"...95.00
Sauce dish, clear, Cabbage Rose, 4⅛"...11.00
Toothpick, Coin, 3" 13.00

Ceramic Art Company

Johnathan Coxon, Sr., and Walter Scott Lenox established the Ceramic Art Company in 1889 in Trenton, New Jersey, where they introduced fine belleek porcelain. Both were experienced in its production, having previously worked for Ott and Brewer. They hired artists to hand paint their wares with portraits, scenes, and lovely florals. Today artist-signed examples bring the highest prices. Several marks were used, three of which contain the 'CAC' monogram. A green wreath surrounding the company name in full was used on special-order wares, but these are not often encountered. Coxon eventually left the company, and it was later reorganized under the Lenox name. Lenox beleek items are included in this listing. Our advisor for this category is Mary Frank Gaston.

Creamer, gold floral, hdl & trim, mk 3"...135.00
Demitasse pot, couple reserve w/gold & turq trim, CAC mk, 8½" ..165.00
Jug, portrait of man, silver o/l, artist sgn, gr CAC logo, minor scratches, 6½".1,450.00
Jug, Rye, brn & gr w/silver o/l, palette mk 200.00
Loving cup, commemorative w/initials, much gold, 8x6"...........225.00
Mug, drunken taverners w/pk lustre, sgn EMS '04, 4½" 120.00
Mustache cup, floral w/gold, CAC palette mk, 1900s, 4" 180.00
Mustache mug, roses w/gold, 4x4x3" 180.00
Pitcher, grape clusters/vines w/gold, slender, 14½" 390.00
Pitcher, monk drinking/grapes, earth tones, gr CAC mk, 1901, 14½" ..240.00
Pitcher, strawberries & leaves w/gold, sgn Lenox, 6" 400.00
Vase, blueberries/autumn foliage, sgn AFS, Lenox, 1916, 9½" 165.00
Vase, bluebirds on stump, cylindrical, 16".....................................250.00
Vase, chrysanthemums, bulb, sgn, 7"..725.00
Vase, chrysanthemums, gold rim, WH Morley, bulb, 12x8½"....1,200.00
Vase, lg roses w/multi-tone gr leaves, uptrn hdls, 13" 540.00
Vase, peacocks, mc on gold, Lenox, #402, drilled, 14⅝" 515.00

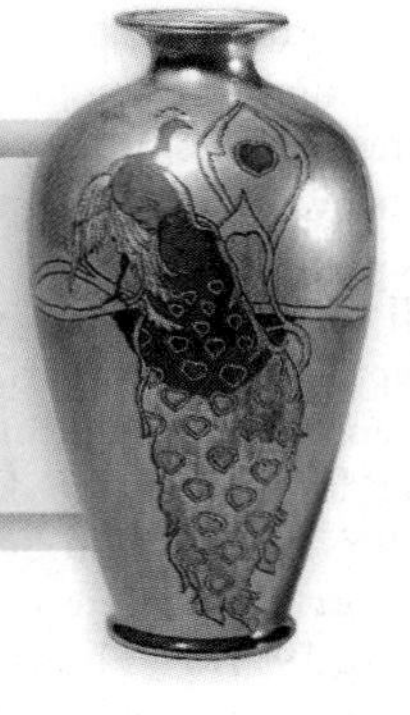

Vase, peacocks (three repeats), hearts, and vines, artist signed, #403, drilled, 14½", $510.00. (Photo courtesy Cincinnati Art Galleries, LLC on LiveAuctioneers.com)

Vase, Queen Louise reserve, shouldered, CAC mk, 1889-1906, 13", NM..240.00
Vase, semi-nude w/Aladdin's lamp, w/gold, amphora shape, CAC mk, 15"..1,250.00
Vase, vines & leaves, gold on wht, rtcl neck & hdls, CAC mk, 9¼"..425.00
Vase, wht gloss w/cherub hdls, Lenox, 12" 240.00

Ceramic Arts Studio, Madison, Wisconsin

Although most figural ceramic firms of the 1940s and 1950s were located on the West Coast, one of the most popular had its base of operations in Madison, Wisconsin. Ceramic Arts Studio was founded in 1940 as a collaboration between entrepreneur Reuben Sand and potter Lawrence Rabbitt. Early ware consisted of hand-thrown pots by Rabbitt, but CAS came into its own with the 1941 arrival of Betty Harrington. A self-taught artist, Harrington served as the studio's principal designer until it closed in 1955. Her imagination and skill quickly brought Ceramic Arts Studio to the forefront of firms specializing in decorative ceramics. During its peak production period in the late 1940s, CAS turned out more than 500,000 figurines annually.

Harrington's themes were wide-ranging, from ethnic and theatrical subjects, to fantasy characters, animals, and even figural representations of such abstractions as fire and water. While the majority of the studio's designs were by Harrington, CAS also released a limited line of realistic and modernistic animal figures designed by 'Rebus' (Ulle Cohen). In addition to traditional figurines, the studio responded to market demand with such innovations as salt-and-pepper pairs, head vases, banks, bells, shelf sitters, and candleholders. Metal display shelves for CAS pieces were produced by Jon-San Creations, a nearby Reuben Sand operation. Most Jon-San designs were by Ceramic Arts Studio's head decorator Zona Liberace, stepmother of the famed pianist.

Betty Harrington carved her own master molds, so the finished products are remarkably similar to her initial sketches. CAS figurines are prized for their vivid colors, characteristic high-gloss glaze, lifelike poses, detailed decoration, and skill of execution. Unlike many ceramics of the period, CAS pieces today show little evidence of crazing.

Most Ceramic Arts Studio pieces are marked, although in pairs only one piece may have a marking. While there are variants, including early paper stickers, one common base stamp reads 'Ceramic Arts Studio, Madison, Wis.' (The initials 'BH' which appear on many pieces do not indicate that the piece was personally decorated by Betty Harrington. This is simply a designer indicator.)

In the absence of a base stamp, a sure indicator of a CAS piece is the decorator 'color marking' found at the drain hole on the base. Each studio decorator had a separate color code for identification purposes, and almost any authentic CAS piece will display these tick marks.

Following the Madison studio's closing in 1955, Reuben Sand briefly moved his base of operations to Japan. While perhaps a dozen master molds from Madison were also utilized in Japan, most of the Japanese designs were original ones and do not correlate to those produced in Madison. Additionally, about 20 master molds and copyrights were sold to Mahana Imports, which created its own CAS variations, and a number of molds and copyrights were sold to Coventry Ware for a line of home hobbyware. Pieces produced by these companies have their own individual stampings or labels. While these may incorporate the Ceramic Arts Studio name, the vastly different stylings and skill of execution are readily apparent to even the most casual observer, easily differentiating them from authentic Madison products. When the CAS building was demolished in 1959, all remaining molds were destroyed. Betty Harrington's artistic career continued after the studio's demise, and her later works, including a series of nudes and abstract figurals, are especially prized by collectors. Mrs. Harrington died in 1997. Her last assignment, the limited-edition M'amselle series was commissioned for the Ceramic Arts Studio Collectors Association Convention in 1996.

Our advisors for this category are BA Wellman (his address can be found in the Directory under Massachusetts) and Donald-Brian Johnson (see Directory, Nebraska). Both encourage collectors to email them with any new information concerning company history and/or production. Mr. Johnson, in association with Timothy J. Holthaus and James E. Petzold, is the co-author of *Ceramic Arts Studio: The Legacy of Betty Harrington* (Schiffer). See CAS Collectors in the Clubs, Newsletters, and Websites section for more information.

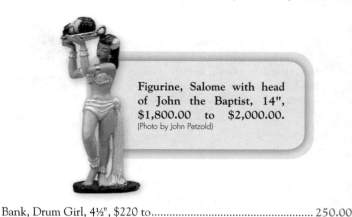

Figurine, Salome with head of John the Baptist, 14", $1,800.00 to $2,000.00.
(Photo by John Petzold)

Bank, Drum Girl, 4½", $220 to	250.00
Bank, Honey Spaniel, 5¾", $300 to	350.00
Bank, Skunky, 4", $260 to	280.00
Bank, Tony the Barber (blade bank), 4¾", $75 to	100.00
Bell, Lillibelle, 6½", $75 to	85.00
Bell, Summer Belle, 5¼", $100 to	120.00
Bell, Winter Belle, 5¼", $75 to	85.00
Bowl, Bonita, 3¾", $30 to	45.00
Candleholders, Triad Girls, left & right, 7", center, 5", $250 to	340.00
Figurine, Adonis & Aphrodite, gr/gray, 9", 7", pr $500 to	700.00
Figurine, Al the Hunter & Kirby the English Setter, 7½", 2", pr $275 to	350.00
Figurine, Alice & March Hare (Wht Rabbit), 4½", 6", pr, $350 to	450.00
Figurine, All Children's Orchestra, 5" boys/4½" girls, 5-pc, $700 to	800.00
Figurine, Ancient Cat & Kitten, 4½", 2½", pr $150 to	190.00
Figurine, Annie (baby elephant) & Benny, 3¼", 3¾", pr, $115 to	160.00
Figurine, Bear Mother & Cub, realistic, 3¼", 2¼", pr, $320 to	380.00
Figurine, Betty & Benny Running Bunnies, 3", 2¼", pr $260 to	300.00
Figurine, Bird of Paradise, A&B, 3", pr $360 to	440.00
Figurine, Blythe & Pensive, 6½", 6", pr $300 to	350.00
Figurine, Bride & Groom, 4¾", 5", pr $250 to	300.00
Figurine, Bruce & Beth, 6½", 5", pr $80 to	100.00
Figurine, Butch & Billy (boxer dogs), snugglers, 3", pr $120 to	160.00
Figurine, Carmen & Carmelita, 7¼", 4¼", pr $300 to	350.00
Figurine, Chinese Girl w/umbrella, very rare, 5½", $400 to	500.00
Figurine, Chivalry Suite, St Geo/Lady Rowena/dragon, 3-pc, $465 to	550.00
Figurine, Chubby St Francis, 9", $180 to	200.00
Figurine, Colonial Boy & Girl, 5½", 5", pr $200 to	250.00
Figurine, Colonial Man & Woman, 6½", pr $130 to	170.00
Figurine, Dachshund, 3½" L, $85 to	100.00
Figurine, Dawn, sandstone, 6½", $175 to	200.00
Figurine, Donkey Mother & Young Donkey, 3¼", 3", pr $320 to	380.00
Figurine, Duck Mother & Duckling, 3¼", 2¼", pr $80 to	125.00
Figurine, Dutch Dance Boy & Girl, 7½", pr $400 to	500.00
Figurine, Farmer Boy & Girl Fishing, 4¾", pr $70 to	90.00
Figurine, Fifi/Fufu poodles, stand/crouch, 3", 2½", pr, $180 to	240.00
Figurine, Fire Man & Woman, 11¼", pr $400 to	500.00
Figurine, Frisky & Balky Colts, 3¾", pr $200 to	250.00
Figurine, Gay '90s #1, Harry & Lillibeth, 6½", 6", pr $90 to	110.00
Figurine, Giraffes, 5½", 4", pr $150 to	200.00
Figurine, Guitar Man on stool, rare, 6½", $500 to	600.00
Figurine, Gypsy Man & Woman, 6½", 7", pr $80 to	100.00
Figurine, Harem Trio, Sultan & 2 harem girls, $320 to	395.00
Figurine, Isaac & Rebekah, 10", pr $140 to	200.00
Figurine, King's Flutist & Lutist Jesters, 11½", 12", pr, $250 to	350.00
Figurine, Leopards A&B, fighting, 3½", 6¼" L, pr $180 to	250.00
Figurine, Lion & Lioness, 7¼", 5½" L, pr $340 to	380.00
Figurine, Little Boy Bl, 4½" L, $30 to	40.00
Figurine, Little Miss Muffet #1, 4½", $50 to	75.00
Figurine, Love Trio, Lover Boy, Willing & Bashful girls, 3-pc, $300 to	375.00
Figurine, Madonna w/Bible, 9½", $235 to	350.00
Figurine, Mermaid Trio, 4" mother, 3" & 2½" babies, 3-pc, $475 to	550.00

Figurine, Minnehaha & Hiawatha, 6½", 4½", pr $480 to 540.00
Figurine, Modern Doe & Fawn, 3¾", 2", pr $175 to 225.00
Figurine, Modern Fox, sandstone, 6½" L, $120 to 150.00
Figurine, Mother Horse & Spring Colt, 4¼", 3½", pr $425 to...... 475.00
Figurine, Musical Trio, Accordion & Harmonica Boys/Banjo Girl, $420 to.480.00
Figurine, Our Lady of Fatima, 9", $260 to 285.00
Figurine, Peek-a-Boo Pixie, 2½", $40 to 50.00
Figurine, Peter Pan & Wendy, 5¼", pr $220 to 270.00
Figurine, Petrov & Petrushka, 5½", 5", pr $120 to 150.00
Figurine, Pied Piper Set, piper+running boy/girl+praying girl, $380 to... 465.00
Figurine, Polish Boy & Girl, 6¾", 6", pr $60 to 80.00
Figurine, Rhumba Man & Woman, 7¼", 7", pr $80 to 120.00
Figurine, Saucy Squirrel w/Jacket, 2¼", $175 to 200.00
Figurine, Sitting Elf & Toadstool, 2½", 3", pr $55 to 70.00
Figurine, Smi-Li & Mo-Pi, chubby man & woman, 6", pr $60 to .. 80.00
Figurine, St Agnes w/Lamb, 6", $260 to 285.00
Figurine, Tall Ballerina, 11", $350 to.. 400.00
Figurine, Tembo Elephant & Tembino Baby, 6½", 2½", pr, $345 to. 415.00
Figurine, Thai & Thai Thai Siamese, snugglers, 4½"/5½" L, $70 to... 90.00
Figurine, Tom Cat standing, 5", $75 to 95.00
Figurine, Water Man & Woman, 11½", pr $350 to 400.00
Figurine, Wee Eskimo Boy & Girl, 3¼", 3", pr $50 to 70.00
Figurine, Wee Swede Boy & Girl, 3¼", 3", pr $100 to 130.00
Figurine, Wing-Sang & Lu-Tang, 6", pr $90 to 110.00
Figurine, Winter Willie, 4", $90 to 120.00
Head vase, Manchu & Lotus, head vase plaques, 8½", pr $400 to. 450.00
Head vase, Mei-Ling, 5", $150 to 175.00
Lamp, Fire Man (on base), very scarce, Moss Mfg, 19½", $350 to. 375.00
Lamp, Water Man & Woman, Moss Mfg, 2'4", $450 to 475.00
Miniature, Adam & Eve Autumn Pitcher, 3", $40 to 50.00
Miniature, Aladdin's Lamp Server, 2" L, $65 to 85.00
Miniature, Toby Mug, 3¼", $75 to 95.00
Mug, Barbershop Quartet (1949), 3½", $650 to 750.00
Planter, Lorelei on Shell, 6", $250 to 300.00
Plaque, Attitude & Arabesque, 9½", 9¼", pr $70 to 100.00
Plaque, Dutch Boy & Girl, 8½", 8", pr $120 to 150.00
Plaque, Goosey Gander, scarce, 4½", $140 to 160.00
Plaque, Jack Be Nimble, 5", $400 to 450.00
Plaque, Zor & Zorina, 9", pr $120 to 180.00
Shakers, bear & cub, snuggle, 4¼", 2¼", pr $40 to 60.00
Shakers, Calico Cat & Gingham Dog, 3", 2¾", pr $90 to 100.00
Shakers, Chirp & Twirp Parakeets on Branches, 4", pr $200 to ... 250.00
Shakers, Covered Wagon & Ox, 3" L, pr $100 to.......................... 135.00
Shakers, Fish Up on Tail, 4", pr $40 to 70.00
Shakers, Sambo & Tiger, 3½", 5" L, $500 to 575.00
Shakers, Santa Claus & Evergreen, 2¼", 2½", pr $325 to 375.00
Shakers, Wee Scotch Boy & Girl, 3¼", 3", pr $70 to..................... 80.00
Shelf sitter, collie mother, 5", $75 to 100.00
Shelf sitters, Budgie & Pudgie Parakeets, 6", pr $100 to 120.00
Shelf sitters, Canaries, sleeping/singing, 5", pr $300 to 350.00
Shelf sitters, Jack & Jill, 4¾", 5", pr $90 to 120.00
Shelf sitters, Young Love Couple (kissing boy & girl), 4½", $90 to.100.00
Snuggle pr, Circus Clown & Dog, 3¾", 2½", pr $150 to 190.00
Teapot, appl swan, mini, 3", $60 to 75.00
Vase, Bamboo, 6", $55 to 75.00
Vase, Flying Duck, rnd, 2½", $75 to 85.00

Metal Accessories

Arched Window for religious figure, 6½", $125 to 150.00
Artist palette w/shelves, left & right, 12" W, pr $200 to 250.00
Circle Bench w/Crescent Planter, 8¾" dia, $200 to 245.00
Corner Spider Web for Miss Muffet, flat bk, 4", $175 to 225.00
Diamond shape, 15x13", $45 to.. 55.00

Garden shelf for Mary Contrary, 4x12", $100 to.......................... 120.00
Heart shape w/shelf, 11½", $100 to 120.00
Ladder for Jack, rare, 13", $125 to 150.00
Musical score, flat bk, 14x12", $85 to 100.00
Parakeet Cage, 13", $125 to... 150.00
Rainbow Arch w/Shelf, blk, 13½x19", $100 to 120.00
Sofa for Maurice & Michelle, 7½" L, $250 to 275.00
Stairway to the Stars, 18½", $100 to 120.00
Star for Angel, flat bk, 9¾", $65 to.. 75.00
Triple Ring, left or right, w/shelf, 15", $110 to............................. 130.00

Chalkware

Chalkware was popular from 1860 until 1890. It was made from gypsum or plaster of Paris formed in a mold and then hand painted in oils or watercolors. Items such as animals and birds, figures, banks, toys, and religious ornaments modeled after more expensive Staffordshire wares were often sold door to door. Their origin is attributed to Italian immigrants. Today regarded as a form of folk art, nineteenth-century American pieces bring prices in the hundreds of dollars. Carnival chalkware from this century is also collectible, especially figures that are personality related. For those, see Carnival Collectibles.

Squirrel, original paint and smoke decoration (some wear), nineteenth century, 5⅝", $570.00. (Photo courtesy Pook & Pook, Inc. on LiveAuctioneers.com)

Bouquet, mc pnt, rstr, late 19th C, 13¾" 150.00
Carrier pigeon on rock, mc pnt, glass eyes, 13" 335.00
Cat seated on base, mc details, fine form, ca 1900, 6¼"............. 3,800.00
Cat, recumbent w/tail curled around body, gray pnt, hollow, 7x15", VG... 100.00
Dove on rock, mc pnt, ca 1900, 9½", VG 180.00
Dove on stump, mc, worn beak, 10" 230.00
Fruit garniture, mc pnt, wht plinth, 19th C, 13"........................ 3,000.00
Garniture, fruit on flowered base, orig pnt, lt fading & wear, 1850s, 10½". 4,250.00
Garniture, fruit/foliage on ped base, strong colors, wear, 11"........ 545.00
Horse on rocky base, yel & blk pnt, hollow body, 10¼x8½"......... 195.00
Lamb reclining on book, mc pnt, detailed fleece, 19th C, 9x10½". 1,450.00
Mother & Child, mc pnt, late 19th C, 16½", VG 515.00
Owl, brn tones, inset eyes, 14", NM 900.00
Pug dog, free-standing, tan w/blk details, 7"................................. 300.00
Rooster, bright mc, 19th C, 6¾", NM 2,275.00
Rooster, pronounced tail feathers, mc pnt, 7", EX 200.00
Spaniel seated, mc pnt, Staffordshire style, rprs, 8¾".................... 170.00

Challinor & Taylor Company

Challinor & Taylor Company (1864 – 1891, Pittsburgh, Pennsylvania; Tarentum, Pennsylvania) went through a number of name changes until it became a part of U.S. Glass Company in 1891 as Plant C. The plant burned down shortly after joining the combine, but many of the old molds were utilized for many years by U.S. Glass. Challinor & Taylor is most noted for its patented (1886) slag glass, which it called

Mosaic. Although purple slag was used the most, the company also made brown and green slag. Other items were made in milk glass, turquoise opaque, green (olive) opaque, black, and jade green. Besides production of dishes, plates, vases, bowls, and novelties, it, like Atterbury & Company, was well-known for its many distinctive covered dishes in animal forms: Mother Eagle, Block Swan, Wavy Base Duck, Open Block Fish Pickle, Steer's Head, Swan on Water, Dog, and Owl pitcher and creamer. Colors of its ware included clear amber, clear (crystal), opaque blue, milk white, rose, and yellow, any of which could have fired-on enamel or gilding. Patterns included Paneled Flower #23, Oval Medallion #28, Daisy #313, Tree of Life #313, Forget Me Not #20, Scroll, Clio, Fan & Star #304, Oval Panel #28, Flower & Panel #23, Hobnail with Bars #307, Double Fan #305, Opaque Scroll, Flying Swan, Blockade #309, Ear of Corn pitcher (two sizes), and Fluted #13.

For further information refer to *American Pressed Glass & Figure Bottles* by Albert Christian Revi and *Yesterday's Milk Glass Today* by Regis & Mary Ferson. Our advisor for this category is Shirley Smith; she can be found in the Directory under West Virginia. See also Milk Glass; Slag Glass.

Covered dish, Dominecker, hen on nest, mg, pnt, 7" L 150.00
Covered dish, duck, gr opaque, 8" L 2,070.00
Covered dish, flying swan, slag, 5¾" 258.00
Covered dish, mother eagle, mg, 7" L 460.00
Covered dish, rooster, mg, pnt, 7" L 240.00
Covered dish, steer's head, mg, 7¾" L 3,000.00
Covered dish, swan, Christmas base, bl opaque, 7" L 700.00
Covered dish, turkey, standing, mg, pnt, 8" 747.00
Covered dish, Walking Fish, mg, 8¾" L 98.00
Creamer, Waffle, gr opaque 47.00
Pitcher, owl, mg, 7¼" 53.00
Plate, Dogwood, HP, mg, 10½" 40.00
Plate, lacy rim, bl opaque, 8" 20.00
Platter, owl, mg 67.00
Shaker, pnt, mg, 3" 25.00
Spooner, Flying Swan, mg, 4½" 24.00
Sugar shaker, forget-me-not, butterscotch slag, 4" 316.00
Syrup, Tree of Life, bl opaque, 7" 135.00
Tumbler, Scroll, mg, 3⅞" 15.00

Champlevé

Champlevé, enameling on brass or other metal, differs from cloisonné in that the design is depressed or incised into the metal, rather than being built in with wire dividers as in the cloisonné procedure. The cells, or depressions, are filled in with color, and the piece is then fired.

Bowl, centerpiece, onyx & gilt bronze w/cherub hdls, 16" W .10,000.00
Casket, gilt brass and mc enamels, Fr, nineteenth C, 7x6x4" 3,000.00

Clock, mantel, W. W. Wattles & Sons, Pittsburgh, first quarter twentieth century, 12½x13x5", $1,925.00. (Photo courtesy New Orleans Auction, St. Charles Gallery, Inc. on LiveAuctioneers.com)

Planter, floral bands w/foliage, shouldered, 9x12" 120.00
Vase, dragons on moon form, dragon hdls, 19th C, 13" 275.00

Vase, dragons, mc on gr, shouldered, bottle neck, 6", pr, NM 90.00
Vase, floral bands, shouldered, 10x6" 85.00
Vase, floral tendrils on turq, melon ribs, late 19th C, 14" 390.00
Vase, long neck, ped ft on sq base, stone center (body), 5" 150.00

Chase Brass & Copper Company

Chase introduced this logo in 1928. The company was incorporated in 1876 as the Waterbury Manufacturing Company and was located in Waterbury, Connecticut. This location remained Chase's principal fabrication plant, and it was here that the 'Specialties' were made.

In 1900 the company chose the name Chase Companies Inc., in honor of their founder, Augustus Sabin Chase. The name encompassed Chase's many factories. Only the New York City sales division was called Chase Brass and Copper Co., but from 1936 on, that name was used exclusively.

In 1930 the sales division invited people to visit their new Specialties Sales Showroom in New York City 'where an interesting assortment of decorative and utilitarian pieces in brass and copper in a variety of designs and treatments are offered for your consideration.' Like several other large companies, Chase hired well-known designers such as Walter Von Nessen, Lurelle Guild, the Gerths, Russel Wright, and Dr. A Reimann. Harry Laylon, an in-house designer, created much of the new line.

From 1930 to 1942 Chase offered lamps, smoking accessories, and housewares similar to those Americans were seeing on the Hollywood screen — generally at prices the average person could afford.

Besides chromium, Chase manufactured many products in a variety of finishes, some even in silver plate. Many objects were of polished or satin-finished brass and/or copper; other pieces were chromium plated.

After World War II Chase no longer made the Specialties line. It had represented only a tiny fraction of this huge company's production. Instead they concentrated on a variety of fabricated mill items. Some dedicated Chase collectors even have shower heads, faucet aerators, gutter pipe, and metal samples. Is anyone using Chase window screening?

Chase products are marked either on the item itself or on a screw or rivet. Because Chase sold screws, rivets, nails, etc. (all with their logo), not all items having these Chase-marked components were actually made at Chase. It should also be noted that during the 1930s, China produced good quality chromium copies; so when you're not absolutely positive an item is Chase, buy it because you like it, understanding that its authenticity may be in question. Remember that if a magnet sticks to it, it's not Chase. Brass and copper are not magnetic, and Chase did not use steel.

Prior to 1933 Chase made smoking accessories for the Park Sherman Co. Some are marked 'Park Sherman, Chicago, Illinois, Made of Chase Brass.' Others carry a Park Sherman logo. It is believed that the 'heraldic emblem' was also used during this period. Many items are identical or very similar to Chase-marked pieces. Produced in the 1950s, National Silver's 'Emerald Glo' wares look very similar to Chase pieces, but Chase did not make them. It is very possible that National purchased Chase tooling after the Chase Specialties line was discontinued.

Although Chase designer pieces and rarer items are still commanding good prices, the market has softened on the more common wares. This year's price guide will reflect this trend. The availability of Chase on the internet has helped the collector, but has also contributed to the leveling off of values.

For further study we recommend *Chase Complete*, *Chase Catalogs 1934 & 1935*, *1930s Lighting — Deco & Traditional by Chase*, and *The Chase Era, 1933 and 1942 Catalogs of the Chase Brass & Copper Co.*, all by Donald-Brian Johnson and Leslie Piña (Schiffer); *Art Deco Chrome, The Chase Era*, by Richard Kilbride; and *Art Deco Chrome* by James Linz (Schiffer). Our advisors for this category are Donna and John Thorpe; they are listed in the Directory under Wisconsin.

Antelope ash receiver, frosted glass w/chrome trim, #881, 4"....... 115.00
Ashtray, Globe, chromium, #17068, $50 to 60.00
Band box, chromium, red plastic hdl, 3-compartment, #852, 7⅛" L. 85.00
Bell, Ming, chromium, #13007, $40 to 5000
Bookends, Davy Jones, wheel, brass/walnut/Bakelite, #90142........ 50.00
Bookends, Horse, very stylized, polished brass, #17044, 6", $650 to. 700.00
Bookends, Moderne, brass/copper, rivets/panels, #11246, 6½", G. 950.00
Bookends, stylized soldier/brass ball, red jacket/blk helmet, 7", $250 to.. 350.00
Box, occasional, chromium w/plastic hearts, glass insert, #90144, $35 to .. 40.00
Brittany bell, brass, #13002 .... 75.00
Canape plate, #27001, $15 to.. 20.00
Candlesticks, Bubble, copper/orange Catalin, #17063, 1935, 2½", pr, $60 to. 70.00
Carefree set, chromium, #8003, 4 cup holders+tray 95.00
Cigarette box, Bacchus, RK, bronze, #847 .... 700.00
Cigarette lighter, Automatic Table; chromium, #825, 3¼", $40 to. 45.00
Circlet tray, chromium & ivory compo, #90060, 7" 175.00
Cocktail set, Doric, chrome, 12½" shaker+6 3" cups+12" tray 350.00
Cocktail shakers, Gaiety, chrome w/blk rings #90034, $40 to 45.00
Coffee set, Continental, chrome/Bakelite, VN, #17052, 3-pc...... 250.00
Colonel & Colonel's Lady lamps, red/wht/blk figures, LG, 8", pr .. 300.00
Continental sugar bowl, chrome w/blk, VN, #17052 .... 25.00
Crumber set, Tidy, moon shape, chromium, plastic hdls, #90092... 35.00
Devonshire pitcher, polished copper or chromium, RW, #90025, $50 to... 60.00
Dish, Tulip, polished chromium, scroll hdl, #90095 .... 35.00
Doric cocktail set, chrome, 12" shaker +6 3" cups+tray 350.00
Flower bowl, Diana, chromium on plastic base, #15005, 10" 65.00
Glow lamp, #01001, copper & brass, cone shade, 8", M................. 50.00
Ice bowl, chromium, w/tongs, #28002, $65 to 75.00
Informal tray, copper, #09012 .... 70.00
Jubilee Globe mustard, copper or chrome w/wht, #90070, 4", $45 to .. 55.00
Lamp, binnacle, wired, 1933-34 Chicago Expo, #25002, $75 to 95.00
Lamp, desk, chrome w/pivoting socket, ribbed O shaft, 13½x12" 50.00
Manchu table bell, chrome/Catalin, #13006, 1936, $45 to 50.00
Marionette ashtray, #304 .... 30.00
Meridian tray, chromium w/wht hdls, #17078, 7⅞", $35 to........... 40.00
Newspaper rack, English bronze or brass & copper, #27027, $35 to... 45.00
Nob-Top ashtray, chromium w/colored knob center, #810, 6½" dia... 40.00
Nut Cracker Big 'n Small, copper or brass, HL, #90150, $45 to..... 50.00
Pelican smokers' stand, English bronze, VN, #17056, 21x8¼" 375.00
Piccadilly cigarette box, chromium-plate & wht, #867, ½x8x3", $70 to.. 90.00

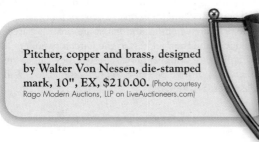

Pitcher, copper and brass, designed by Walter Von Nessen, die-stamped mark, 10", EX, $210.00. (Photo courtesy Rago Modern Auctions, LLP on LiveAuctioneers.com)

Savoy creamer & sugar bowl, w/tray, #26008, 1936, $45 to............. 50.00
Smokeless ashtray, polished brass w/mc enameling, #537, $40 to .. 50.00
Sparta water pitcher, chromium, wht plastic hdl, #90055, 8", $60 to... 70.00
Spiral bookends, blk & satin nickel, #17018, 1933, $200 to 250.00
Stratosphere smoking stand, chrome, VN, 1937, #17076, $350 to... 400.00
Sugar Sphere, chromium, RW, #90078, 2⅞x2⅝", $45 to 50.00
Sunday Supper candleholders, blk nickel, #24002, 4 for 50.00
Sunshine watering can, brass & copper, Ge, #5003, 5x8", $30 to 40.00
Tarpon fishbowl, amber bronze, HD, #90125, 8"........................... 80.00
Taurex candlesticks, chrome or copper, VN, #24003, 7", pr, $125 to.. 150.00
Three-layer candy box, apple/ leaves on lid, chromium, #90104, 5⅝".... 60.00

Tripod ashtray, copper & brass, 3-leg, VN, #301...................... 40.00
Watering can, Waterbury, Connecticut, centaur mk, 7½", M 95.00

Chelsea Dinnerware

Made from about 1830 to 1880 in the Staffordshire district of England, this white dinnerware is decorated with lustre embossings in the grape, thistle, sprig, or fruit and cornucopia patterns. The relief designs vary from lavender to blue, and the body of the ware may be porcelain, ironstone, or earthenware. Because it was not produced in Chelsea as the name would suggest, dealers often prefer to call it 'Grandmother's Ware.' For more information we recommend *English China Patterns & Pieces* by Mary Frank Gaston, our advisor for this category.

Grape, bowl, 8" 35.00
Grape, cake plate, emb ribs, 10", $30 to 40.00
Grape, cake plate, enameled pattern, unmk, ca 1830s, $30 to 40.00
Grape, cake plate, w/copper lustre, sq, 10", $25 to 30.00
Grape, coffeepot, stick hdl, 2-cup, 7" 75.00
Grape, coffeepot, w/copper lustre, unmk, att Edward Walley, 1845-56. 225.00
Grape, creamer, 5½"... 55.00
Grape, c/s, $25 to 35.00
Grape, c/s, w/copper lustre, unmk, ca 1830, $35 to........................ 45.00
Grape, egg cup, 2¼", $35 to 50.00
Grape, pitcher, milk, 40-oz 60.00

Grape, pitcher, water, $60.00 to $75.00. (Photo courtesy Jackson's Auction on LiveAuctioneers.com)

Grape, plate, 6", $12 to... 15.00
Grape, plate, 7" 18.00
Grape, plate, 8", $22 to.. 25.00
Grape, plate, 9½"... 22.50
Grape, sugar bowl w/lid, Edward Walley, 8", $150 to..................... 175.00
Grape, teapot, 2-cup 75.00
Grape, teapot, octagonal, 8½", $125 to................................ 150.00
Grape, teapot, octagonal, 10" 165.00
Grape, waste bowl.. 40.00
Sprig, cake plate, 9" 40.00
Sprig, c/s.. 40.00
Sprig, pitcher, milk 60.00
Sprig, plate, 7".. 18.00
Sprig, plate, dinner 25.00
Thistle, butter pat 15.00
Thistle, cake plate, 8¾", $25 to 30.00
Thistle, c/s, $30 to 35.00
Thistle, plate, 6", $6 to 8.00
Thistle, plate, 7".. 15.00
Thistle, sugar bowl, 8-sided, w/lid, 7½" 45.00

Chelsea Keramic Art Works

In 1866 fifth-generation Scottish potter Alexander Robertson started a pottery in Chelsea, Massachusetts, where his brother Hugh joined him the following year. Their father James left the firm he partnered to help his sons in 1872, teaching them techniques and pressing decorative tiles, an extreme rarity at that early date. Their early production consisted mainly of classical Grecian and Asian shapes in redware and stoneware, several imitating metal vessels. They then betrayed influences from Europe's most important potteries, such as Royal Doulton and Limoges, in underglaze and barbotine or Haviland painting. Hugh's visit to the Philadelphia Centennial Exposition introduced him to the elusive sang-de-boeuf or oxblood glaze featured on Ming porcelain, which he would strive to achieve for well over a decade at tremendous costs.

James passed away in 1880, and Alexander moved to California in 1884, leaving Hugh in charge of the pottery and his oxblood glaze experiments. The time and energy spent doing research were taken away from producing saleable artwares. Out of funds, Hugh closed the pottery in 1889.

Wealthy patrons supported the founding of a new company, the short-lived Chelsea Pottery U.S., where the emphasis became the production of Chinese-inspired crackleware, vases, and tableware underglaze-painted in blue with simplified or stylized designs. The commercially viable pottery found a new home in Dedham, Massachusetts, in 1896, whose name it adopted. Hugh died in 1908, and the production of crackleware continued until 1943.

The ware is usually stamped CKAW within a diamond or Chelsea Keramic Art Works/Robertson & Sons. Our advisors for this category are Suzanne Perrault and David Rago; they are listed in the Directory under New Jersey. See also Dedham Pottery.

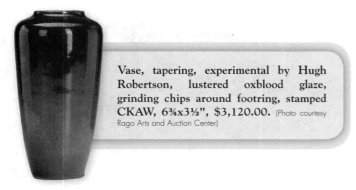

Vase, tapering, experimental by Hugh Robertson, lustered oxblood glaze, grinding chips around footring, stamped CKAW, 6¾x3½", $3,120.00. (Photo courtesy Rago Arts and Auction Center)

Ewer, cvd geometrics & scrolls, gr gloss, CKAW, ca 1885, 11" .. 1,650.00
Plate, 8 wedges of experimental colors, 1870-80, 5½" 3,100.00
Plate, glaze samples, Chelsea Keramic Art Works, Robertson & Sons, 6". 2,920.00
Plate, Lotus border w/rare gr leaves on crackleware, 1895, 10", ex ... 3,000.00
Vase, appl floral vines/masks, burnished clay, sgn WFG, 17" 3,800.00
Vase, brn & gr mottle, pinched rim, CKAW, 3¼x4" 120.00
Vase, brn & oxblood lustre, 3x3" 850.00
Vase, brn-gr luster & oxblood, experimental, 3¼x3¼" . 850.00
Vase, bud, dk gr gloss, CKAW, 5x2½" 1,175.00
Vase, gr-brn & oxblood, ring hdls, att Robertson, CKAW, 5" 250.00
Vase, orange-peel oxblood, experimental, Robertson, 6¼x4" 1,800.00
Vase, oxblood, experimental, Robertson, CKAW, 6¾x3½" 3,120.00
Vase, streaky brn & gr, 5-lobed ruffled rim, CKAW, 6⅝x5⅝" 350.00
Vase, wht crackle w/ash from firing, swollen body, 1880-99, 8¾". 550.00

Chicago Crucible

For only a few years during the 1920s, the Chicago (Illinois) Crucible Company made a limited amount of decorative pottery in addition to their regular line of architectural wares. Examples are very scarce today; they carry a variety of marks, all with the company name and location. Our advisors for this category are Suzanne Perrault and David Rago; they are listed in the Directory under New Jersey.

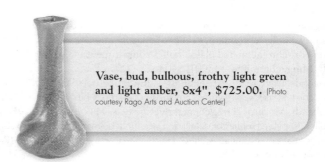

Vase, bud, bulbous, frothy light green and light amber, 8x4", $725.00. (Photo courtesy Rago Arts and Auction Center)

Vase, frothy gr, angle hdls, ca 1900, 7" 1,325.00
Vase, frothy gr, twisted body, unmk, 8x4" 500.00
Vase, gr mottled matt, twisted bulb form, stamped, 8" 650.00
Vase, grapevines emb, gr bottle form w/scalloped rim, 10½x6" . 1,100.00
Vase, stylized floral, pk on dk gr, shouldered, 8¾" 725.00

Children's Things

Nearly every item devised for adult furnishings has been reduced to child size — furniture, dishes, sporting goods, even some tools. All are very collectible. During the later seventeenth and early eighteenth centuries, miniature china dinnerware sets were made both in China and in England. They were not intended primarily as children's playthings, however, but instead were made to furnish miniature rooms and cabinets that provided a popular diversion for the adults of that period. By the nineteenth century, the emphasis had shifted, and most of the small-scaled dinnerware and tea sets were made for children's play.

Late in the nineteenth century and well into the twentieth, toy pressed glass dishes were made, many in the same patterns. Today these toy dishes often fetch prices in the same range or above those for the 'grown-ups'!

Children's books, especially those from the Victorian era, are charming collectibles. Colorful lithographic illustrations that once delighted little boys in long curls and tiny girls in long stockings and lots of ribbons and lace have lost none of their appeal. Some collectors limit themselves to a specific subject, while others may be far more interested in the illustrations. First editions are more valuable than later issues, and condition and rarity are very important factors to consider before making your purchase. For further information we recommend *Encyclopedia of Collectible Children's Books* by Diane McClure Jones and Rosemary Jones.

Our advisors for children's china and glassware are Margaret and Kenn Whitmyer; you will find their address in the Directory under Ohio.

In the following listings, unless otherwise noted, our values are for examples in excellent condition. See also ABC Plates; Blue Willow; Clothing and Accessories; Stickley.

Key:
ds — doll size   HM — Houghton Mifflin
dj — dust jacket   OUP — Oxford University Press
ed — edition   RH — Random House
hc — hardcover

Books

13 Clocks, J Thurber, Simon & Schuster, 1957, 1st ed, w/dj 100.00
Adventures of Huckleberry Finn, M Twain, Harper & Bros, 1940, w/dj .. 45.00
Babar's Castle, L de Brunhoff, RH, 1962, 1st ed, w/dj 100.00
Berenstain Bears' Vacation, S & J Berenstain, 1968, 1st ed, w/dj... 30.00
Big Ball of String, M Holland, RH, 1958, hc, 1st ed, w/dj 80.00
Big Book of Fables, Aesop, Blackie, London, 1912, oversz wht hc, 1st ed.. 1,000.00
Biggest Bear, L Ward, HM, 1952, 1st ed, w/dj 50.00

Call of the Wild, J London, MacMillan, 1903, 1st ed, w/dj, min.... 4,500.00
Cat in the Hat, Dr Seuss, RH, 1957, oversz hc, 1st ed, w/dj 7,000.00
Charlie & the Great Glass Elevator, R Dahl, 1972, hc, 1st ed, w/dj...300.00
Chaucer for Children, Mrs HR Haweis, Chatto, 1882, oversz........ 90.00
Child's Book of Manners, F Maschler, Jonathan Cape, 1978, hc ... 40.00
Corduroy, D Freeman, Viking Press, 1968, hc, 1st ed 30.00
Cricket in Times Square, G Selden, 1960, Farrar, hc, 2st ed, w/dj . 50.00
Down the Mississippi, CR Bulla, Crowell, 1954, 1st ed, w/dj 40.00
Eloise, K Thompson, 1955, 1st ed, w/dj 300.00
Fairy-Tales from France, T Larned, Volland, 1920........................... 50.00
Father Goose: His Book, L Frank Baum, Bobbs Merrill, 1903, hc . 200.00
Felix on Television, P Sullivan, flip-it book, 1956, Treasure Books..30.00
God's Frozen Child, H McCracken, Doubleday, 1930 .... 50.00
Grimm Fairy Tales, J Grimm, McLoughlin Bros, ca 1897, hc....... 150.00
Gus Was a Friendly Ghost, J Thayer, William Morrow, 1962, 1st ed, w/dj...30.00
Hotel Cat, E Averill, Harper & Row, 1969, 1st ed, w/dj............... 80.00
I Can Write! A Book by Me, Myself, T LeSieg, 1971, 1st ed 500.00
I Met a Man, J Ciardi, HM, 1961, 1st ed, w/dj............................. 40.00
Jock the Scot, AG Rosman, Cassell, 1951 .... 80.00
Joseph's Yard, C Keeping, OUP, 1969, 1st ed, w/dj 90.00
Katy & the Big Snow, VL Burton, HM, 1943, oblong, 1st ed, w/dj..200.00
Last of the Mohicans, JF Cooper, Scribner, 1919, 1st ed 200.00
Little Witch, AE Bennett, Lippincott, 1953, hc, 1st ed, w/dj 50.00
Magical Land of Noom, J Gruelle, Volland, 1922, w/dj 250.00
Man Elephant, a Book of African Fairy Tales, J Hartwell, Altemus, 1906. 35.00
Man Who Lost His Head, CH Bishop, Viking Press, 1942, oblong, 1st ed, w/dj..120.00
Mike Mulligan & His Steam Shovel, VL Burton, HM, 1939, 1st ed.. 100.00
Millions of Cats, W Gag, Coward-McCann, 1928, oblong, 1st ed, w/dj..600.00
Miss Pooky Peckinpaugh, K Thompson, Harper, 1970, 1st ed, w/dj. 100.00
Mother's Hero, EC Dow, Stern, 1910.. 60.00
National Velvet, E Bagnold, Morrow, 1935, 1st US ed, w/dj........ 500.00
Old Yeller, F Gipson, Harper, 1956, 1st ed, w/dj 200.00
Open Gate, K Seredy, Viking Press, 1943, 1st ed, w/dj 90.00
Pedro, the Angel of Olvera Street, L Politi, Scribner, 1946, 1st ed, w/dj .. 80.00
Pilgrim's Progress, J Bunyan, Stokes, 1939, 1st ed..................... 50.00
Poems of Childhood, E Field, Charles Scribner's Sons, 1904 ed, 1st ed, w/dj ..300.00
Rabbit Hill, R Lawson, Viking Press, 1944, 1st ed, w/dj 250.00

Railway Pictures, A Panorama Book for Children; Sheila Braine, Ernest Lister & New York: E.P. Dutton & Co., no date, first edition, unpaginated, four pop-up illustrations with additional illustrations in text, VG, $120.00. (Photo courtesy Heritage Auction Galleries on LiveAuctioneers.com)

Robin Hood, P Creswick, David McKay, 1917, hc 125.00
Story about Ping, M Flack, Viking Press, 1933, 1st ed, w/dj 300.00
Swiss Family Robinson, J Wyss, C Arthur Pearson, 1904, hc 30.00
Tales of Little Dogs, C Jacobs-Bond, Volland, 1921 .... 70.00
True Story of Smokey the Bear, JW Watson, Big Golden Book, 1955, hc ..40.0
Visitors from Oz, J Kellogg, 1960, Reilley & Lee, oversz hc, w/dj. 250.00
Watership Down, R Adams, Macmillan, 1974, 1st Am ed, w/dj .. 300.00
Where is Yonkela?, M Hirsh, Crown, 1969, tall, early ed 150.00
Where the Sidewalk Ends, S Silverstein, 1974, Harper, hc, 1st ed, w/dj... 40.00
Why Mosquitoes Buzz in People's Ears, V Aardema, Dial, 1975, 1st ed, w/dj..50.00
Wind in the Willows, K Grahame, 1928, w/dj 65.00
Wizard of Oz, J Wehr, Baum adaptation, Saalfield, 1944, 1st ed, w/dj... 300.00
Wump World, B Peet, HM, 1970, 1st ed, w/dj........................... 40.00
Yama Yama Land, GD Boylan, Reilly & Britton, 1909................. 150.00

China, Pottery, and Stoneware

Winnie the Pooh, dish, party scene with text around trim, Bavaria, Schumann, rampant lion mark, 6¼" long, $180.00. (Photo courtesy Dargate Auction Galleries on LiveAuctioneers.com)

Acorn, creamer, brn & wht, Cork Edge & Malkin, 2"..................... 22.50
Angel w/Shining Star, creamer, Germany, 3" 37.00
Athens, gravy boat, bl & wht, Davenport, mid-1800s, 1¾".............. 38.00
Athens, tureen underplate, 4", $12 to...................................... 15.00
Barnyard Animals, plate, mc transfer, Germany, 5½"........................8.00
Barnyard Animals, sugar bowl, w/lid, Germany, 4" 22.50
Basket, plate, Salem China, 6"...7.00
Blue Acorn, casserole, England, 5".. 35.00
Blue Banded Ironstone, bowl, soup, England, 4", $10 to 12.00
Blue Banded, teapot, Dimmock, 3".. 90.00
Bluebird, plate, Choisy & Roi, 3", $9 to.................................. 11.00
Bluebird, platter, mc on wht, Noritake, 7⅛"............................. 27.50
Blue Marble, bowl, oval, England, 4" 55.00
Blue Marble, gravy boat, England, 1", $54 to 65.00
Blue Willow, bowl, England, 2" 42.50
Blue Willow, cup, Occupied Japan, $9 to................................. 10.00
Blue Willow, gravy boat, Japan... 30.00
Brundage Girls, creamer, Germany, 4" 32.00
Buster Brown, sugar bowl, mc transfer, Germany, w/lid, 3¾".......... 75.00
Calico, tureen, brn on cream, 3" 60.00
Children w/Toy Animals, creamer, mc transfer, Germany, 3¼"...... 20.00
Dimity, tray, gr & cream, rect, England, 5¾"............................. 21.50
Father Christmas & the Children, plate, Germany, 5" 25.00
Flow Blue Dogwood, bowl, oval, Minton, 4⅜" 60.00
Forget-Me-Not, casserole, bl & wht, England, 4¾" 110.00
Forget-Me-Not, platter, bl & wht, England, 4" 95.00
Forget-Me-Not, tureen, bl & wht, England, 7⅞" 150.00
Friends, sugar bowl, mc transfer, Germany, w/lid, 3⅝"................. 28.00
Gaudy Floral, vegetable bowl, England, 4"................................ 55.00
Gaudy Ironstone, creamer, mc on wht, England, 2⅜"" 48.00
Gaudy Ironstone, waste bowl, England, 2"............................... 120.00
Gold Floral, casserole, England, 5".. 55.00
Greek Key, gravy boat, brn & wht, England, 4" 32.00
Gumdrop Tree, c/s, Southern Potteries, 2", 4"........................... 32.00
Holly, sugar bowl, mc on wht, Germany, w/lid............................ 42.50
Kite Fliers, plate, England, 3½" 48.00
Lady Standing by Urn, teapot, purple & wht, England, 4"........... 160.00
Livesley Fern & Floral, tureen w/stand, gr floral, 1885, 5½"........... 72.50
Mandarin Willow, cup, Copeland, late 1800s, $80 to.................. 100.00
Mandarin Willow, saucer, Copeland, late 1800s, $80 to............... 100.00
Mandarin Willow, sugar, Copeland, late 1800s, $80 to................. 100.00
Mary Had a Little Lamb, teapot, mc on wht, England, 3½" 65.00
May, plate, brn transfer w/lustre border, att Allerton, 1880s, $125 to .150.00
May w/Dog, plate, brn transfer, 1887, $125 to 150.00
May w/Pets, plate, brn transfer, 1884, $125 to 150.00
Myrtle Wreath, gravy boat, JM&S, 2", $32 to 36.00
Myrtle Wreath, tureen, JM&S, 4", $60 to.................................. 85.00
Old Curiosity Shop, bowl, Ridgways, early 1900s, $60 to............... 75.00
Orient, sugar bowl, w/lid, 3", $34 to...................................... 40.00
Pembroke, casserole, bl & wht, Bistro, England, 5¼" 55.00
Pembroke, tureen, red floral, Bistro, England, 6½" 78.00
Pink Lustre, pitcher, England, 3"... 48.00

Pink Open Rose, c/s, mc on wht, England, 2", 3⅞" 12.00
Playful Cats, sugar bowl, w/lid, Germany, 2" 45.00
Playful Zoo Animals, creamer, Edwin M Knowles, 2" 15.00
Punch & Judy, cup, England, 1", $30 to 36.00
Ralston Purina, bowl, 6", $42 to 54.00
Roman Chariots, creamer, bl & wht, Cauldon England, 2" 40.00
Roman Chariots, c/s, bl on wht, Cauldon England 40.00
Scenes From England, plate, bl & wht, England, 3" 35.00
Scenes From England, bowl, vegetable, bl & wht, w/lid, England, 4" . 135.00
Silhouette Children, creamer, Victoria/Czechoslovakia, 2¼" 14.50
Silhouette Children, plate, Victoria/Czechoslovakia, $6 to 8.00
Simplified Willow, platter, Edge, Malkin & Co, 1872-1903, $120 to. 140.00
Snow White, teapot, Disney, MIJ, ca 1937, 3¼" 70.00
St Nicholas, plate, mc on wht, Germany, 5⅛" 15.00
St Nicholas, sugar bowl, mc on wht, Germany, 3" 48.00
Standing Pony, teapot, mc transfer w/gr lustre, Germany, 6" 78.00
Stick Spatter, teapot, Staffordshire, 5" 80.00
Sunset, sugar bowl, w/lid, MIJ, 3" 13.00
Tan Lustre, creamer, mc dots, MIJ 3.50
Twin Flower, bowl, flow bl, England, 4" 80.00
Twin Flower, casserole, flow bl, 4", $95 to 105.00
Twin Flower, plate, flow bl, England, 3" 25.00
Water Hen, waste bowl, bl & wht, England, 2" 60.00
Wheel, waste bowl, Flow Blue/copper lustre, HP, unmk, 1800s.... 125.00
Willow, covered vegetable dish & underplate, Ridgways, 1927, $180 to . 250.00
Willow, gravy boat & underplate, Ridgways, 1927, $100 to 120.00
Willow, plate, dinner, Ridgways, 1927, $40 to 50.00
Willow, platter, Ridgways, 1927, $80 to 100.00

Furniture

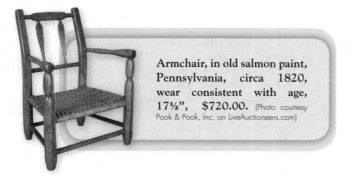

Armchair, in old salmon paint, Pennsylvania, circa 1820, wear consistent with age, 17½", $720.00. (Photo courtesy Pook & Pook, Inc. on LiveAuctioneers.com)

Armchair, 3-slat ladder-bk w/tulip & ball finials, rush seat, rpt, 26" . 700.00
Armchair, maple, 2-slat bk, trn handholds, rfn, 21" 475.00
Baby tender, pnt pine, canted sides w/rails/extending tray, 22x18x11" . 700.00
Bed, mahog tall post w/canopy, acorn finials, 36x33x18" 400.00
Blanket chest, pine, flowers on salmon pnt, European, ca 1893, 16x23" .. 285.00
Chair, 3-slat ladder-bk w/mushroom finials, string seat, 25" 100.00
Chair, mixed woods, trn stiles/legs/stretchers, cane seat, pnt, 15" . 300.00
Chair, pnt decor, spool trn, from PA 1,450.00
Chair, pnt peaches on curved crest & splat, gold stripes, rpr, 21" . 285.00
Chair, side, Windsor pnt fan-bk w/serpentine crest, 18th C, 34" . 2,600.00
Chest, cherry Sheraton, 3 grad drw w/inlay/paneled ends, 16x16x10" . 2,415.00
Chest, cherry/poplar Sheraton, 4 dvtl drws, 38x25x16" 1,200.00
Chest, pnt pine, 6-brd, hinged lid, cut-out ends, NE, 1790s, 16x31x13" .. 3,300.00
Chest, walnut/poplar, 4 dvtl drws, trn legs, old rfn, 31x22x12" 800.00
Cradle, hanging, mustard pnt/bl int/red knobs, NE, 1800s, 34" L . 500.00
Cradle, pine w/floral decor, rprs, 24x35x25" 150.00
Cradle, pine w/HP decor on red pnt, sq nails, ds, 10x16x14" 115.00
Cradle, pine, orig gr/mustard pnt w/foliate borders, NH, 26x44x22" .. 700.00
Cradle, redware w/molded lattice work, mc glaze, ds, 9x12" 115.00
Cradle, shallow hood w/scallops, pine w/worn bl pnt, 38x36x14" . 460.00
Dry sink, pnt poplar, china knobs, side drw/door, 17x20x10" 1,150.00
Highchair, 3-slat ladder-bk, trn arms/post, old bl pnt, 36" 200.00
Highchair, blk & red grpt w/yel striping, stencil on crest, PA, 34" .. 550.00
Highchair, mixed woods/curly maple legs, captain's style, rfn, 38" .. 115.00
Highchair, Windsor rod-bk, maple, NE, 1810, rfn/rpr, 37" 500.00
Rocker, 2-slat bk, trn posts, woven seat, old gr pnt, ds, 14" 175.00
Rocker, serpentine crest, banister bk, spindle arms, rush seat, 25" .. 600.00
Rocker, trn arms, cloth seat & bk, gold gr pnt over salmon, 22" . 1,000.00

Glass

Acorn, creamer, 3⅜" 110.00
Acorn, spooner, frosted, 3" 200.00
Acorn, table set, frosted, 4-pc, $1,000 to 1,100.00
Arched Panel, pitcher, amber, 3¼" 96.00
Austrian No 200, butter dish, canary, Greentown, 2¼" 350.00
Baby Thumbprint, cake stand, tall, US Glass, 3" 110.00
Bead & Scroll, butter dish, dk gr or bl, 4" 300.00
Bead & Scroll, creamer, 3", $84 to 96.00
Beaded Swirl, creamer, amber or cobalt, 2¼" 90.00
Beaded Swirl, sugar bowl, w/lid, 3¼" 42.00
Betty Jane, casserole, w/lid, #209, McKee Glass, $36 to 40.00
Betty Jane, set, 6-pc, McKee Glass, $90 to 100.00

Birds and trees motif, mug, amber, 3¼", $35.00. (Photo courtesy Dirk Soulis Auctions on LiveAuctioneers.com)

Block, spooner, 3", $96 to 120.00
Braided Belt, butter dish, amber or lt gr, 2¼", $365 to 385.00
Braided Belt, creamer, 2⅝", $80 to 90.00
Braided Belt, creamer, amber or lt gr, 2⅝" 140.00
Bucket (aka Wooden Pail), creamer, 2½" 60.00
Button Panel No 44 (w/gold trim), butter dish, 4" 125.00
Button Panel No 44 (w/gold trim), creamer, 2½" 60.00
Button Panel No 44 (w/gold trim), spooner, 2⅝" 70.00
Button Panel No 44 (w/gold trim), sugar bowl w/lid, 4⅝" 100.00
Buzz Saw No 2697, butter dish, 2⅜" 35.00
Cherry Blossom, cup, pk, 1½", $30 to 34.00
Cherry Blossom, saucer, Delphite, 4½" 5.00
Chimo, butter dish, 2⅜" 125.00
Chimo, cup, punch, 1 7/16" 15.00
Colonial Flute, pitcher, 3¼" 22.00
Colonial Flute, punch set, 7-pc, $140 to 150.00
D&M No 42, butter dish, George Duncan & Sons, 4", $160 to... 180.00
Diamond Ridge/D&M No 48, spooner, 2¾" 110.00
Doric & Pansy, plate, pk, Jeannette Glass Co, 5⅞" 8.00
Doyle No 500, mug, amber, 2" 37.00
Doyle No 500, spooner, Doyle & Co, 2¼", $48 to 55.00
Drum, sugar bowl, w/lid, 3¼", $110 to 120.00
Dutch Boudoir, bowl, mg, 1 3/16" 90.00
Dutch Boudoir, candlestick, bl opaque, 3", ea 125.00
Dutch Boudoir, tray, mg, 3x6", $150 to 160.00
Flattened Dmn & Sunburst, creamer, Westmoreland, 2¼" 20.00
Grape Stein, tankard, Fed Glass Co, $160 to 185.00
Grapevine w/Ovals, mug, amber, bl or yel, McKee, 1⅞" 50.00
Hawaiian Lei, sugar bowl, w/lid, JB Higbee, 3", $32 to 36.00
Hobnail w/Thumbprint Base No 150, butter dish, bl or amber, 2" .. 120.00
Homespun, saucer, pk, Jeannette Glass Co, 3¼" 5.00

Homespun, tea set, 12-pc, Jeannette Glass Co	175.00
Horizontal Threads, butter dish, 1⅞"	90.00
Horizontal Threads, table set, 4-pc, $250 to	265.00
Inverted Strawberry, berry set, Cambridge Glass, $190 to	210.00
Kidibake, ramekin, clear opal, Fry Glass Co, #1923, 2¼", $24 to	27.00
Kittens, bowl, cereal, marigold, Fenton, 3½", $110 to	125.00
Kittens, cup, marigold, Fenton, 2", $100 to	110.00
Lacy Daisy, berry set, 7-pc, EX	75.00
Lamb, butter dish, 3", $180 to	210.00
Laurel, creamer, Scottie decal, McKee Glass Co, 2⅝", $175 to	200.00
Lion, creamer, frosted, Gillinder & Sons, 3", $90 to	96.00
Michigan, stein set, 7-pc, US Glass, $85 to	100.00
Monk, tankard, 4", $85 to	95.00
Nearcut, tumbler, Cambridge, 2"	6.50
Nursery Rhyme, punch bowl, bl opaque, US Glass, 3", $360 to	400.00
Nursery Rhyme, table set, 4-pc, US Glass, $295 to	345.00
Nursery Rhyme, water set, 7-pc, $250 to	275.00
Oval Star No 300, pitcher, Indiana Glass, 4", $65 to	70.00
Palm Leaf Fan, banana stand	72.00
Pattee Cross, bowl, master berry, US Glass, 1¾"	40.00
Pattee Cross, tumbler, US Glass, 1¾", $14 to	16.00
Peacock Feather, creamer, US Glass, 2", $50 to	55.00
Pert, butter dish, 2¾", $145 to	150.00
Plain Pattern No 13, table set, King, 4-pc, $325 to	350.00
Pointed Jewel 'Long Dmn' No 15006, butter dish, US Glass, 2"	170.00
Pointed Jewel 'Long Dmn' No 15006, spooner, US Glass, 2½"	100.00
Pyrexette, bakeware, boxed set, $180 to	210.00
Rooster No 140, butter dish, King, 2¾", $210 to	240.00
Rooster No 140, creamer, King, 3¼", $125 to	140.00
Sandwich Ivy, creamer, amethyst, 2⅜", $130 to	150.00
Sawtooth Band No 1225, spooner, Heisey, 2¾", $70 to	80.00
Sawtooth, butter dish, 3", $50 to	60.00
Stippled Vines & Beads, butter dish, teal or amber, 2⅜"	140.00
Stippled Vines & Beads, sugar bowl, w/lid, 3"	85.00
Sunbeam No 15139 (aka Twin Snowshoes), spooner, US Glass, 2"	110.00
Twist, butter dish, bl opal, Albany, 3⅝"	200.00
Two Band, butter dish, 2", $70 to	80.00
Wheat Sheaf No 500, bowl, master berry, 2¼"	45.00
Whirlgig No 1501, butter dish, US Glass, 2½"	28.00
Wild Rose, candlesticks, Greentown, 4", ea	125.00
Wild Rose, table set, mg, Greentown, 4-pc, $240 to	275.00

Miscellaneous

Sled, wooden with original paint and stenciling, cast iron swan pulls, minor wear, 39x16½x14", $840.00. (Photo courtesy Showtime Auction Services on LiveAuctioneers.com)

Carriage, brn wicker w/wicker hood, spring steel chassis & wood wheels	120.00
Carriage, gr pnt w/red & yel decor, oak/iron, faux leather seat, 36"	500.00
Horse, wood w/old pnt on gesso, rpl bridle & tail, 30x40", VG	350.00
Noah's ark, HP & stenciled wood, 7 wooden animals, mini, 2x7"	200.00
Noah's ark, mc pnt wood, early, 13" +116 animals, people & bugs	1,100.00
Noah's ark, mc pnt wood, Germany, ca 1900, 20x40", +42 animals	4,560.00
Noah's ark, pnt pine w/2 figures+72 cvd animals, Germany, 1890s, 24" L	2,350.00
Noah's ark, pnt pine w/HP dove on roof, 28 cvd/HP animals, 23" L	1,200.00
Rocking horse, felt-covered w/hair, glass eyes/felt harness, 37"	1,380.00
Rocking horse, wood, horsehair mane/tail, leather saddle, 27x46"	1,300.00

Sled, G Welch 1889 in banner & horses on dk gr pnt, 4-person, 14x70"	1,000.00
Sled, pine brd w/red pnt & nautical scene, 22" L, VG	320.00
Sled, reindeer in gold script on wood, pnt deer on gr, 19x32"	8,400.00
Sled, wooden w/iron runners, litho bee & clover, Wagner, 31" L	650.00
Teapot, tin litho, boy/dog/old lady/cat, AMS C USA, 3½"	110.00

Chintz Dinnerware

'Chintz' is the generic name for English china with an allover floral transfer design. This eye-catching china is reminiscent of chintz dress fabric. It is colorful, bright, and cheery with its many floral designs and reminds one of an English garden in full bloom. It was produced in England during the first half of this century and stands out among other styles of china. Pattern names often found with the manufacturer's name on the bottom of pieces include Florence, Blue Chintz, English Roses, Delphinium, June Roses, Hazel, Eversham, Royalty, Sweet Pea, Summertime, and Welbeck, among others.

The older patterns tend to be composed of larger flowers, while the later, more popular lines can be quite intricate in design. And while the first collectors preferred the earthenware lines, many are now searching for the bone china dinnerware made by such firms as Shelley. You can concentrate on reassembling a favorite pattern, or you can mix two or more designs together for a charming, eclectic look. Another choice may be to limit your collection to teapots (the stacking ones are especially nice), breakfast sets, or cups and saucers.

Though the Chintz market remains very active, prices for some pieces have been significantly compromised due to their having been reproduced. For further information we recommend *Charlton Book of Chintz, I, II,* and *II,* by Susan Scott. Our advisor for Chintz is Mary Jane Hastings; she is listed in the Directory under Illinois. See also Shelley.

Apple Blossom, c/s, Dmn, James Kent	45.00
Apple Blossom, nut dish, James Kent, 6½x6½"	65.00
Apple Blossom, plate, 8-sided, James Kent, 9"	95.00
Bedale, plate, Ascot, sq, Royal Winton, 6"	45.00
Beeston, milk jug, Countess, Royal Winton, 3"	250.00
Beeston, mustard jar, Ascot, Royal Winton, 2⅛"	235.00
Beeston, tennis set, Royal Winton, 2-pc	195.00
Blue Chintz, plate, Crown Ducal, 8"	60.00
Cheadle, c/s, Raleigh shape, Royal Winton	95.00
Cheadle, plate, Athena shape, Royal Winton, 7"	65.00
Dorset, plate, Royal Winton, 8"	60.00
DuBarry, creamer, Granvilel shape, James Kent, 3"	75.00
DuBarry, creamer, James Kent, 2½"	40.00
DuBarry, jug, James Kent, 4½"	150.00

DuBarry, teapot, James Kent, 7½", $450.00. (Photo courtesy Richard D. Hatch & Associates on LiveAuctioneers.com)

Eleanor, coffeepot, Albans, Royal Winton	750.00
Eleanor, c/s, Royal Winton, 2x3½", 5"	75.00
Eleanor, pin dish, Royal Winton, 4⅜x3½"	48.00
Eleanor, teapot, Albans, Royal Winton, 4-cup	350.00
English Rose, bowl, dessert, Royal Winton	70.00
English Rose, sandwich tray, 12x6"	175.00
English Rose, sugar bowl, Royal Winton, 1x3"	125.00

English Rose, toast rack, Queen shape, 5-bar, Royal Winton 395.00
Evesham, milk jug, Globe, Royal Winton, 3¾" 275.00
Evesham, teapot, stacking, Royal Winton, 3-pc set 500.00
Floral Feast, milk jug, Dutch, Royal Winton, 3¾" 350.00
Floral Feast, sugar bowl, w/hdls & lid, Royal Winton 75.00
Florita, shell bowl, wavy edge, James Kent, 8x6" 120.00
Hazel, shell dish, Royal Winton, 5x4" 75.00
Hazel, sugar shaker & underplate, Fife, Royal Winton, 4⅛" 675.00
Hazel, vase, bud, Clywd, Royal Winton 275.00
Hazel, water jug, Sexta, Royal Winton, w/lid, 7" 950.00
Julia, coffeepot, Albans, Royal Winton 725.00
Julia, plate, Ascot, sq, Royal Winton, 6" 150.00
Julia, relish tray, 2-compartment, Royal Winton, 9⅛x5¼" 500.00
Majestic, plate, Athena, 6" 60.00
Majestic, plate, serving, 5-section, Royal Winton, 12x10¾" 255.00
Marguerite, bonbon dish, center hdl, Royal Winton, 5½x9¼" 75.00
Marguerite, tray, Seville, bl trim, Royal Winton, 10x9" 145.00
Marina, cake plate, Lord Nelson, 10" 175.00
Marina, jug, Lord Nelson, 4⅞" 195.00
Marina, trio, Lord Nelson, c/s+7½" plate 125.00
Nantwich, creamer, for stacking set, Royal Winton 110.00
Nantwich, mustard jar, Royal Winton, 2⅜" 200.00
Old Cottage, breakfast set, Countess, Royal Winton, 5-pc 450.00
Old Cottage, milk jug, Dutch, Royal Winton, 3¾" 200.00
Old Cottage, mustard jar, Royal Winton, 2¼" 165.00
Old Cottage, plate, Ascot, sq, Royal Winton, 6" 35.00
Old Cottage, trivet, Royal Winton, 8¼x6¾" 65.00
Pansy, candy dish, shell shape, Royal Albert, 5x5¼" 38.00
Pansy, plate, Art Deco, hdld, Crown Ducal, 8" 55.00
Pansy, trio, Lord Nelson 95.00
Peony, plate, Crown Ducal, sq, 7" 85.00
Primula, c/s, Royal Albert 35.00
Primula, oval dish, Crown Ducal, 9x8" 100.00
Queen Anne, compote, Royal Winton, 2½x7x5¾" 125.00
Queen Anne, plate, Royal Winton, 9" 40.00
Rapture, pin dish, James Kent, 3¼x3¼" 25.00
Rapture, sugar bowl, James Kent 45.00
Richmond, M sauce w/undertray, Era, Royal Winton 260.00
Rosalynde, teapot, James Kent, Granville #24, 6½x10" 125.00
Rosalynde, toast rack, 4-slice, James Kent, rare 500.00
Rosetime, jug, Lord Nelson, 5" 150.00
Royal Anne, tray, 3-lobe, Gem, Royal Winton 125.00
Royal Brocade, c/s, Royal Nelson, 2¾x3", 5¾" 60.00
Royal Brocade, cup, jumbo, Lord Nelson, 4x4⅛" 20.00
Royalty, hot water jug, Countess, w/lid, Royal Winton, 7" 775.00
Royalty, milk jug, Globe, Royal Winton, 4" 300.00
Somerset, dish, Seville shape, Royal Winton, 4x4" 90.00
Spring Glory, breakfast set, Countess, 5-pc 500.00
Stratford, butter dish, Royal Winton 235.00
Summertime, compote, Royal Winton, 2¼x6¼" 85.00
Summertime, c/s, Royal Winton 100.00
Summertime, dish, 3-section, Royal Winton, 9½" 110.00
Summertime, milk jug, Dutch, Royal Winton, 4½" 350.00
Summertime, nut dish, Royal Winton, sm 75.00
Summertime, plate, Royal Winton, 9¾" 95.00
Summertime, teapot, stacking, Royal Winton, 3-pc 725.00
Summertime, tray, Royal Winton, 8x5" 495.00
Sunshine, bud vase, Royal Winton, 3" 10.00
Sunshine, compote, allover pattern, Lily, Royal Winton, 3x6" 175.00
Sunshine, cup, Countess, Royal Winton 45.00
Sweet Pea, bowl, rimmed soup, Royal Winton, 8" 85.00
Sweet Pea, candy dish, Royal Winton 150.00
Sweet Pea, compote, Royal Winton, 7x6" 155.00
Sweet Pea, mustard jar, Ascot, Royal Winton, 2⅛" 245.00

Sweet Pea, plate, Ascot, sq, Royal Winton, 6" 90.00
Sweet Pea, rimmed soup, Royal Winton, 8" 160.00
Sweet Pea, toast rack, 5-bar, Royal Winton 450.00
Victoria, creamer, Royal Cauldon, w/lid 20.00
Victorian Rose, nut dish, Ascot, Royal Winton, ind 95.00
Welbeck, jam jar, Rosebud, w/lid, Royal Winton 225.00
Welbeck, plate, Ascot, sq, Royal Winton, 6" 150.00
White Crocus, teapot, Albans, Royal Winton, 2-cup 300.00

Chocolate Glass

Jacob Rosenthal developed chocolate glass, a rich shaded opaque brown sometimes referred to as caramel slag, in 1900 at the Indiana Tumbler and Goblet Company of Greentown, Indiana. Later, other companies produced similar ware. Only the latter is listed here. Our advisor for this category is Sandi Garrett; she is listed in the Directory under Indiana. See also Greentown Glass.

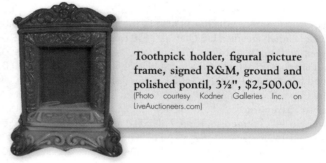

Toothpick holder, figural picture frame, signed R&M, ground and polished pontil, 3½", $2,500.00. (Photo courtesy Kodner Galleries Inc. on LiveAuctioneers.com)

Bowl, Aldine, oval, w/lid 1,650.00
Bowl, Beaded Triangle, 4⅜" 350.00
Bowl, Geneva, McKee, oval, 10½" 250.00
Bowl, Shield w/Daisy & Button, 8⅜" 1,300.00
Butter dish, Fleur-de-Lis, Royal 850.00
Butter dish, Water Lily & Cattails, Fenton 1,200.00
Butter dish, White Oak, McKee 5,000.00
Compote, Chrysanthemum Leaf, 4½" dia 325.00
Compote, jelly, Majestic, McKee 650.00
Compote, Melrose, Royal, 7¼" 175.00
Cracker jar, Chrysanthemum Leaf, w/lid 3,000.00
Creamer, Rose Garland 1,350.00
Creamer, Wild Rose w/ Bowknot, McKee & Brothers, 4¼" 225.00
Dish, Honeycomb, rect, Royal, 6¾x4" 300.00
Hatpin holder, Orange Tree, Fenton 450.00
Jewel box, Venetian, McKee 400.00
Lamp, Cloverleaf 1,250.00
Mug, Swirl 600.00
Pickle dish, Aurora, violin shape, Royal 100.00
Pitcher, Fleur-de-Lis, Royal 1,250.00
Pitcher, Rose Garland 5,000.00
Plate, Serenade, 6¼" 125.00
Salt dip, master, Honeycomb, 3½" dia 650.00
Sauce dish, Waffle 450.00
Shaker, Big Rib 500.00
Shaker, Geneva 375.00
Smoking set, McKee, 3-pc 1,100.00
Spooner, Fleur-de-Lis, Royal 225.00
Spooner, Geneva, McKee 150.00
Spooner, Touching Squares 1,500.00
Sugar bowl, Water Lily & Cattails, w/lid, Fenton 650.00
Toothpick holder, Chrysanthemum Leaf 900.00
Toothpick holder, Kingfisher 4,000.00

Tumbler, File, Royal Glass 750.00
Tumbler, Water Lily & Cattails, Fenton 200.00
Vase, #400, Fenton, 6" 600.00
Vase, Beaded Triangle, 6¼" 200.00
Vase, Masonic, McKee, 6" 475.00

Christmas Collectibles

Christmas past... lovely mementos from long ago attest to the ostentatious Victorian celebrations of the season.

St. Nicholas, better known as Santa, has changed much since 300 A.D. when the good Bishop Nicholas showered needy children with gifts and kindnesses. During the early eighteenth century, Santa was portrayed as the kind gift-giver to well-behaved children and the stern switch-bearing disciplinarian to those who were bad. In 1822 Clement Clark Moore, a New York poet, wrote his famous *Night Before Christmas*, and the Santa he described was jolly and jovial — a lovable old elf who was stern with no one. Early Santas wore robes of yellow, brown, blue, green, red, white, or even purple. But Thomas Nast, who worked as an illustrator for *Harper's Weekly*, was the first to depict Santa in a red suit instead of the traditional robe and to locate him the entire year at the North Pole headquarters.

Today's collectors prize early Santa figures, especially those in robes of fur or mohair or those dressed in an unusual color. Some early examples of Christmas memorabilia are the ornaments from Dresden, Germany. These cardboard figures — angels, gondolas, umbrellas, dirigibles, and countless others — sparkled with gold and silver trim. Late in the 1870s, blown glass ornaments were imported from Germany. There were over 6,000 recorded designs. From 1890 through 1910, blown glass spheres were often decorated with beads, tassels, and tinsel rope. The golden age of figural glass ornaments was between the two World Wars (1917 – 1937).

Christmas lights, made by Sandwich and some of their contemporaries, were either pressed or mold-blown glass shaped into a form similar to a water tumbler. They were filled with water and then hung from the tree by a wire handle; oil floating on the surface of the water served as fuel for the lighted wick.

Kugels are glass ornaments that were made as early as 1820 and as late as 1890. Ball-shaped examples are more common than the fruit and vegetable forms and have been found in sizes ranging from 1" to 14" in diameter. They were made of thick colored glass with heavy brass caps, in cobalt, green, gold, silver, red, and occasionally in amethyst.

Although experiments involving the use of electric light bulbs for the Christmas tree occurred before 1900, it was 1903 before the first manufactured socket set was marketed. These were very expensive and often proved a safety hazard. In 1921 safety regulations were established, and products were guaranteed safety approved. The early bulbs were smaller replicas of Edison's household bulb. By 1910 G.E. bulbs were rounded with a pointed end, and until 1919 all bulbs were hand blown. The first figural bulbs were made around 1910 in Austria. Japan soon followed, but their product was never of the high quality of the Austrian wares. American manufacturers produced their first machine-made figurals after 1919. Today figural bulbs (especially character-related examples) are very popular collectibles. Bubble lights were popular from about 1945 to 1960 when miniature lights were introduced. These tiny lamps dampened the public's enthusiasm for the bubblers, and manufacturers stopped providing replacement bulbs.

Feather trees were made from 1850 to 1950. All are collectible. Watch for newly manufactured feather trees that have been reintroduced. For further information concerning Christmas collectibles, we recommend *Pictorial Guide to Christmas Ornaments and Collectibles* by our advisor, George Johnson (see Directory, Ohio) and *Antique Santa Claus Collectibles* by David Longest, available from Collector Books or your local bookstore.

Note: Values are given for bulbs that are in good paint, with no breaks or cracks, and in working order. Assume that values are for examples in excellent to near mint condition except paper items; those should be assumed near mint to mint.

Bulbs

Boy boxer, mg, 3", $100 to 125.00
Cat in an evening gown, mg, Japan, ca 1950, 3", $150 to 175.00
Crystal Spire Light, purple glass, ca 1935, Japan, 2½", $40 to 50.00
Dog (frowning) in basket, mg, Japan, 2¾", $30 to 40.00
Elephant sitting on ball, mg, 2¾", $30 to 40.00
Hippo w/raised arms, clear glass, Japan, 2", $125 to 150.00
Jack-o'-lantern w/leaves, mg, ca 1950, 1¾", $45 to 55.00
Lion reclining, clear glass, Germany, 2¼", $250 to 275.00
Monkey w/stick, clear glass, 2¼", $75 to 100.00
Mushroom, tan glass, Austria, ca 1920 .... 25.00
Pineapple, clear glass, Japan, ca 1950, 2", $70 to 80.00
Rabbit sitting w/paws on hips, mg, 2½", $75 to 85.00
Rooster playing golf, mg, ca 1950, 2¾", $25 to 30.00

Santa, Edison, 9½", MIB, $225.00. (Photo courtesy Premier Auction Center on LiveAuctioneers.com)

Tadpole, clear glass, Japan, ca 1950, 2½", $90 to 100.00
Turkey by house, mg, Germany, 3", $300 to 375.00

Candy Containers

Bedroll, fabric-covered paper, 4", $225 to 250.00
Canteen, paper w/cord trim & hdl, 4¾", $200 to 225.00
Clock, printed paper, Russian, 4", $110 to 125.00
Drum, emb silver paper, 3", $110 to 135.00
Ear of corn, paper, 4¾", $100 to 125.00
Globe, printed paper on cb, 3", $150 to 175.00
Hot-air balloon, paper, Dresden, 3", $450 to 500.00
Liberty shield, fabric covered cb, 3", $90 to 110.00
Man's hat box, pnt cb w/leather accents, 2", $110 to 115.00

Ornament, with small feather tree on top, cotton batting, 6½", $165.00. (Photo courtesy Cornestoga Auction Company on LiveAuctioneers.com)

Pine cone, pnt paper, w/sm red bow, ca 1948, 7", $35 to 50.00
Santa on dmn-shaped box, ca 1930, $60 to 70.00
Slipper, Dresden-like, netting on top holds candy, 7½", $75 to 100.00

Novelty Lighting

Bells, Raylite, plastic, 6-socket, ca 1950.. 30.00
Boxed set, Illuminated Yule Birds, plastic, Glolite, 1950, $90 to . 120.00
Bubble-Lites, Deer Brand #1207, snap-over set, 12-socket, Hong Kong.. 300.00
Bubble-Lites, mini, Glolite #840, 10-socket replacements, 1957 ... 60.00
Bubble-Lites, mini, Noma #3108, USA, 8-socket, 1961.............. 175.00
Bubble-Lites, mini, Noma #421, USA, 10-socket, 1949................. 55.00

Bubble-Lites, Noma, MIB, $180.00. (Photo courtesy Morphy Auctions on LiveAuctioneers.com)

Bubble-Lites, Pifco #1261, 7-tube snap-over set, ca 1950............. 225.00
Candelabra, Noma #520, 10-socket, ca 1958................................. 60.00
Candelabra, Raylite, #340K, 7-socket, ca 1948............................ 300.00
Candelabra, Royal Electric #782, 8-socket, ca 1954, mini 65.00
Fairy Tales, Noma of Canada #105, images on 8 plastic bells, 1940.10.00
Lantern cover, Santa figure, Dresden, ca 1928, sm 350.00
Socket replacement, mini, Noma #C-151, Mexico, ca 1960.......... 15.00
Socket set, Japan #485, 10 pk candles, ca 1960 .... 15.00
Socket set, Lighted Ice, Raylite #556K, Japan, 7-socket, ca 1960 .. 25.00
Socket set, mini, Krystal Snow, Raylite #330K, 1947................... 450.00
Socket set, mini, Raylite #1330K, 8-socket, ca 1949 .... 125.00
Socket set, Royalite, Royal Electric #8408, ca 1958 .... 60.00
Socket set, St Nick, Hy-G #B68, 8-socket, ca 1960...................... 100.00
Socket set, Twinkling Star, Noma #3148, 8 stars & 48 lights, 1961 .. 85.00
Socket set, Wonder Star, Matchless #2000, 8-socket, ca 1935 ..... 450.00
Table topper, Angel Candelite, Majestic Electric #6720, ca 1950.. 20.00
Tree, Glolite #560, prewired, 9-socket, w/base, 1956, 16" 150.00
Tree, Raylite, prewired, 1-socket, w/base, ca 1950, 9".................. 25.00
Tree, Royal Electric #980, prewired, 11 mini sockets, ca 1949, 22" .. 150.00
Tree topper, Elite Angel, Noma #700, 1941................................. 35.00
Tree topper, Star of Bethlehem, Noma #124, ca 1935 .... 20.00
Tubelites, 8-tube set, ca 1955 .... 400.00
Wall hanger, Santa's Coming to Town, Royal Electric #906, 1955, 15" ... 60.00
Wall hanger, wht chenille X, Raylite #181M, 8-socket, 1936 .... 75.00
Wall sconce, M Propp #300, 8 mini sockets, ca 1927 .... 100.00
Wreath, Noma #1508, 9-socket, 1935.. 75.00
Wreath, Raylite #6A, plastic Santa face in chenille wreath, ca 1950. 30.00

Ornaments

4th of July boy, cotton, Cynthia Jones, 5¼", $60 to...................... 90.00
American flags X on ball, emb glass, 1950s, 2", $50 to 75.00
Angel w/decorated tree, paper w/tinsel, 6½", $50 to..................... 65.00
Basket, glass, pk w/clear hdl, fabric flowers inside, 5", $100 to 125.00
Basket, woven wire, 1920-30, 1½", $15 to 20.00
Bear w/trainer, glass, Dresden, 2x3", $600 to.............................. 625.00
Bell, molded glass, stars around middle, ca 1930-40, $5 to 10.00
Bust of lady w/flowers, glass, Germany, 1970s, $150 to................. 175.00
Carousel w/rnd top, emb glass, 3¼", $50 to 75.00
Carrot, cotton, 4", $25 to 30.00
Cello, wire-wrapped glass, 6½", $50 to... 60.00
Champagne bottle, cotton, 3", $50 to 75.00
Civil War soldier, flat metal, Dresden, 4", $90 to........................... 110.00
Duck in egg, glass, Germany, 3¼", $225 to 250.00

Dutch couple kissing, emb windmill on bk, rare, 3¼"................... 525.00
Girl on skis, cotton girl, glass skis, 4½x6", $400 to 450.00
Girl w/roses, paper & cloth, 1910, 20", $175 to............................ 200.00
Goat mother, cotton w/pnt face, 6¼", $250 to............................... 275.00
Horse prancing, glass, Dresden, 2¼", $160 to 180.00
Knight, flat metal, Dresden, 10¼", $175 to 225.00
Man in derby hat, glass, 3", $200 to 250.00
Nativity scene in wreath, plastic, ca 1940-50s, $10 to.................... 15.00
Parrot on branch w/leaves, flat glass, Dresden, 7¾", $110 to........ 125.00
Sailboat w/sails, glass, D Blumchen, 6½", $40 to 50.00
Santa head on cb star w/tinsel, 7¼", $15 to 20.00
Snow angel w/nest of birds, paper, Heymann & Schmidt, 10½" 70.00
Snow children (5) w/toys, paper w/tinsel, 7¾", $100 to 125.00
Stork, fabric, 4½", $85 to.. 95.00

Miscellaneous

Tree, feather, white with berries, 36", VG, $500.00. (Photo courtesy Morphy Auctions on LiveAuctioneers.com)

Bank, Rudolph, recumbent, battery, ca 1960, 5¼" 35.00
Belsnickle Santa, 7", $300 to... 400.00
Belsnickle Santa, high collar, 9¼", $850 to.................................. 950.00
Chain, glass berry beads, Blumchen & Co, $35 to 45.00
Fireplace, cb w/bubble lt, battery, Japan, ca 1960 .... 40.00
Lantern, snowman, Amico #59861, Japan, ca 1960........................ 35.00
Lapel pin, Santa in chimney, battery, USA, ca 1956 .... 20.00
Plaque, church in snow scene, A Merry Christmas, oval, 1945, 12½". 40.00
Santa, doll, posable fabric arms & legs, Germany, ca 1925, 10" ... 450.00
Santa, doll, straw-stuffed, ca 1920s-30s, 25½", $200 to 275.00
Santa on nodder donkey, fabric on compo, 8x6", $600 to 700.00
Santa, roly-poly, Germany, 6", $300 to 400.00
Santa, waving, papier-maché, ca 1920-30, 9", $85 to 95.00
Santa, wind-up drummer, celluloid/cloth, Japan, 10½", $310 to .. 350.00
Socket clips, gr enamel on metal, Malex Mfg, 20 clips, ca 1920 .... 20.00
Tester, lamp & fuse, Royal Electric #910, ca 1949 .... 45.00

Cleminsons

The home-based enterprising business, Cleminson Clay, was started by George and Betty Cleminson of Monterey Park, California, in 1941. The business started with the highly demanded cute rooster pie birds Raphael and Patrick, and oval wall hangings. They used a special technique of slip decorating. This process of hand painting the unfired pottery with colored slip liquefied clay. Demand grew beyond expectation and soon many of the neighbors helped hand paint the pieces, leading to the building of a large factory, renamed Cleminsons of California Pottery Company, in the 1940s in El Monte, California, which employed over 150 people. They produced whimsical items for everyday home use, including canisters, cookie jars, decorative cups and saucers, dinnerware, egg cups, planters, pottery figurines, razor banks, salt and pepper shakers, sock darners, souvenir pieces, vases, wall pockets, and many more pieces. During the early 1960s the company hired famous potters Hedi Schoop and Millisen Drews to increase designs and keep the business growing. Finally, in 1963 the company decided to close due to the increase of the foreign import market and their unwillingness to cut quality to compete with the market, thus, the end of a 20+ year famous California Pottery company. Many of these wonderful old pottery pieces are in high demand by the kitsch and American pottery collectible market. For more information we recommend *Collector's Encyclopedia of California Pottery* by Jack Chipman (Collector Books). Our advisor for this section is Richard Robar. He is listed in the Directory under Michigan.

Ashtrays, rose flower in center, w/bl flowers, set of 3, 5½", 6¼", 7"...45.00
Bobby pin holder, w/cover, 'Bobbie Guard,' officer, 4½" 40.00
Butter, Distlefink, bird form lid, Butter Bird, 6½x4½" 40.00
Button holder, figural girl w/lift-off head, Button Bonnie, 6¾"....... 50.00
Cleanser shakers, Katrina & Fritz, girl & boy figural, 6¼", pr......... 95.00
Clothes sprinkler bottle, Chinaman, Cholly style, 8½" 85.00
Clothes sprinkler bottle, Mary Poppins style, 8½" 125.00
Cookie canister, Gala Gray, octagonal, gray & red design, 9¾"...... 90.00
Cookie jar, heart shape, 'Mother's Best,' pr birds finial, 9¼" 375.00

Cookie jar, stylized rooster, rare, 12¾", $1,200.00 to $1,500.00. (Photo courtesy Richard Robar)

Egg cup, bride and groom figural, 4", pr.............................. 40.00
Grease jar, Patriotic Pig, sitting upright, w/bib & chef hat, 7" 125.00
Jar, covered, Chinese man, stamped mk.............................. 60.00
Mug, hangover w/ice bag lid, no ice cube tag.......................... 15.00
Mug, hangover w/ice bag lid, w/orig ice cube tag...................... 45.00
Napkin ring, hen or rooster stylized, 3½", 5¾", ea 75.00
Pie bird, Patrick, Raphael, price varies w/colors & styles, $50 to . 250.00
Pincushion, porcupine, pk, w/flowers, 2x4"............................ 75.00
Plate, dk brn w/Zodiac sign, 9¼" 75.00
Razor bank, dome shape, man shaving raised on front, 3½" 35.00
Shakers, s&p, artist w/palatte, 6¼", pr................................ 45.00
Shakers, s&p, Colonel Shoes, 2¼x2¾".................................. 100.00
Sock darner, Darn It, Sailor Boy, 5" 65.00
String holder, puffed heart shape w/You'll Always Have a Pull w/Me, gr.. 40.00
Toothpick holder, butler figural, Parker, 4½"......................... 40.00
Tray, bird bread, Distlefink, 12½" L 15.00
Wall pocket, kettle, ...the kitchen is the Heart of the Home, 7¼". 20.00
Wall pocket, key, Welcome Guest, 7¼" 60.00
Wall pocket, stylized hen & rooster, 5½", 9", pr...................... 175.00
Wall pocket, teapot w/wire bail hdl, 6¼x7½"........................... 20.00

Clewell

Charles Walter Clewell was a metal worker who perfected the technique of plating an entire ceramic vessel with a thin layer of copper or bronze treated with an oxidizing agent to produce a natural deterioration of the surface. Through trial and error, he was able to control the degree of patina achieved. In the early stages, the metal darkened and if

allowed to develop further formed a natural turquoise-blue or green corrosion. He worked alone in his small Akron, Ohio, studio from about 1906, buying undecorated pottery from several Ohio firms, among them Weller, Owens, and Cambridge. His work is usually marked. Clewell died in 1965, having never revealed his secret process to others.

Prices for Clewell have advanced rapidly during the past few years along with the Arts and Crafts market in general. Right now, good examples are bringing whatever the traffic will bear.

Our advisors for this category are Suzanne Perrault and David Rago; they are listed in the Directory under New Jersey.

Bowl, strong patina, #384-2-6, 4x9½", EX 1,080.00
Jar, floral panels, Weller Claywood blank, unmk, 6x5¼" 1,000.00
Vase, brn patina w/hints of gr, #351-258, ovoid w/flared rim, 8" .. 800.00
Vase, brn to bright gr patina, #417-206, 4½" 475.00
Vase, bronze patina, w/hdls, #505-21, 7¼x7" 450.00
Vase, bud, copper patina, #361-2-6, 10x4½" 1,025.00
Vase, copper clad, bottle, bronze patina, #367-4, 6¾x2¾".......... 200.00
Vase, copper clad, bulb, fine verdigris patina, #4-40-4, 5½x6" 500.00
Vase, copper clad, ovoid, bl to red patina, 14¼x6¾".................... 3,900.00

Vase, copper clad with bronze and verdigris patina, #303-2-9, 13¾x7", $850.00. (Photo courtesy Rago Arts and Auction Center)

Vase, copper patina to strong gr at base, ftd, #424-26, 8" 500.00
Vase, copper w/strong gr at base, ovoid, #317, 7"..................... 900.00
Vase, deep gr verdigris, shouldered w/sm neck, #365-2-7, 6x4" 720.00
Vase, hammered copper look, 4 buttress ft, #4098/#1088-12, 20x7", NM. 8,400.00
Vase, landscape emb, orig patina, sm splits to copper, #X2, 13½"....3,900.00
Vase, mythological motif, Weller Burntwood, #257-01, 8¼", NM..........1,300.00
Vase, over Vance-Avon blank, emb w/lilies, stamped, 9½x7" 750.00
Vase, slender ovoid, #313-2-1, 13", VG 1,175.00
Vase, verdigris, few lines/worn spots, #442-29, 9¾x9" 1,600.00
Vase, VG patina, #314-26, drilled, 12x7".............................. 470.00

Clarice Cliff

Between 1928 and 1935 in Burslem, England, as the director and part owner of Wilkinson and Newport Pottery Companies, Clarice Cliff, along with her 'paintresses,' created a body of hand-painted pottery that is still influential today.

The name for the oeuvre was Bizarre Ware, and the predominant sensibility, style, and appearance was Deco. Almost all pieces are signed. There were over 160 patterns and more than 400 shapes, all of which are illustrated in *A Bizarre Affair — The Life and Work of Clarice Cliff*, published by Harry N. Abrams, Inc., written by Len Griffen and Susan and Louis Meisel.

Note: Non-hand-painted work (transfer printed) was produced after World War II and into the 1950s. Some of the most common names are 'Tonquin' and 'Charlotte.' These items, while attractive and enjoyable to own, have little value in the collector market.

Beaker, Pine Grove, blk band at base, 5".................................. 300.00
Biscuit jar, Nuage, mc floral, 5" 400.00
Bowl, Delecia, 5x11"... 360.00

Bowl, Inspiration Fruit, rpr, 5x10"...................................350.00
Bowl, Inspiration Lily, stepped sides, sq.........................850.00
Bowl, Inspiration Odilon, conical, ftd, 4⅛"...................240.00
Bowl, Latona (tree), ca 1930, 16".............................1,650.00
Charger, Killarney, geometrics, wide rim, 17"...........1,115.00
Clog, Coral Firs, 5½" L...375.00
Cup/saucer, demi, Cabbage Flower, 3"......................400.00
Cup/saucer, demi, Capri, 3".......................................350.00
Jardiniere, water lily form, 1940s, 5x7"......................175.00
Jug, Celtic Harvest, ca 1930, 11x7"...........................95.00
Jug, Crocus, flared ft, 6"...250.00
Jug, Isis, Latona tree, 9½".......................................4,200.00
Jug, Lotus, Football, 12"..5,500.00
Jug, Lotus, Geometric, 12"..5,500.00
Jug, Lotus, Latona floral, 12"....................................6,000.00
Jug, Lotus, Pebbles, 12"..5,500.00
Jug, milk, Oranges Cafe-Au-Lait, 3½"........................300.00
Jug, milk, Pebbles, squat, 4"......................................425.00
Jug, My Garden, twig hdls w/leaves at base, 9"...........200.00
Jug, triangles & dmns, Athens shape, 6".....................585.00
Planter, Sungold, yel/orange/brn/wht, 6¾x7½"..........515.00
Plate, Autumn Pastel, mc bands form border, smooth rim, 10"....725.00
Plate, Gibralter, rainbow-like border, 6".....................300.00
Plate, Leaf Tree on speckled orange, gr border, 7½".....480.00
Plate, Pink Pearls, pastel floral, smooth rim, 6"............11.00
Plate, Secrets, tree to left of landscape, 6"..................135.00
Plate, Summerhouse, yel border, 10"..........................550.00
Plate, Sunrise, smooth rim, 8¾"..................................660.00
Plate, Woodland, Deco style & colors, 9"....................395.00
Preserves pot, Forest Glen, beehive form, 4"................395.00
Preserves pot, Moonflower, beehive form, 3½".............300.00
Preserves pot, Trees & House, cylindrical, 3½".............565.00
Sandwich set, Floreat, canted corners, 6 5" plates+11" platter.....700.00
Shaker, Nasturtium, conical, 5"...................................700.00
Sugar sifter, Coral Firs, autumn tones, 5"....................660.00
Sugar sifter, Hononulu, landscape, conical, 5½".........1,450.00
Teacup & saucer, Gr Cowslip, 6-sided..........................360.00
Teapot, Crocus, gr & wht lid, 5"..................................200.00
Teapot, early geometric pattern, cream/bl/orange, 4½"..........360.00
Vase, Caprice, flared cylinder, 7"................................900.00
Vase, Fantasque floral band on orange, flared rim, 7"...1,880.00
Vase, foliate design, #353, 7"....................................885.00
Vase, Goldstone, jug-like w/hdl...................................240.00

Vase, Honolulu, Bizarre Ware inkstamp, #602-48, 9", $1,800.00. (Photo courtesy Cincinnati Art Galleries, LLC on LiveAuctioneers.com)

Vase, Liberty, mc bands on wht, 3½"...........................300.00
Vase, Nasturtium, triangular, 7½"...............................300.00
Vase, Patina Country, mc on cream, ca 1930, 9".......1,300.00
Vase, Patina Tree, slightly bulb, ring-trn base, 8¼"......600.00
Vase, Poplar, simple floral w/orange & red-orange bands, 12"...1,150.00

Clifton

Clifton Art Pottery of Clifton, New Jersey, was organized around

1903. Until 1911 when they turned to the production of wall and floor tile, they made artware of several varieties. The founders were Fred Tschirner and William A. Long. Long had developed the method for underglaze slip painting that had been used at the Lonhuda Pottery in Steubenville, Ohio, in the 1890s. Crystal Patina, the first artware made by the small company, utilized a fine white body and flowing, blended colors, the earliest a green crystalline. Indian Ware, copied from the pottery of the American Indians, was usually decorated in black geometric designs on red clay. (On the occasions when white was used in addition to the black, the ware was often not as well executed; so even though two-color decoration is very rare, it is normally not as desirable to the collector.) Robin's Egg Blue, pale blue on the white body, and Tirrube, a slip-decorated matt ware, were also produced.

Bowl vase, #240, Pueblo Viejo, Upper Gila Valley AZ, 7¾x12½" ..645.00
Jardiniere, Indian Ware, buff/brn/blk, 4 Mile Ruin AZ, 8x11".....500.00
Vase, Crystal Patina, celadon w/yel & gr drips, w/hdls, #116, 4½" ..300.00
Vase, Crystal Patina, dk gr, hexagonal, squat, 1905, 4" dia...........420.00

Vase, Crystal Patina, green, #150, designer's mark, dated 1906, 7", $250.00 to $300.00. (Photo courtesy Belhorn Auction Services, LLC on LiveAuctioneers.com)

Vase, Crystal Patina, gr, cylindrical neck, #115, 5¼"...................400.00
Vase, Crystal Patina, gr, deeply cvd fish, #180, 1906, 3½x3½".....500.00
Vase, Crystal Patina, gr, integral rim-to-shoulder hdls, 1906, 7x8"...570.00
Vase, Crystal Patina, tan to gr, sq trumpet neck, 1905, 7¼x5¼"..275.00
Vase, Crystal Patina, yel/buff mottle, 4-sided flared neck, 7"........275.00
Vase, Indian Ware, blk & tan incised on red clay, #241, 10x13"..480.00
Vase, Indian Ware, blk & tan on red clay, #205, 6½x6¼"............300.00
Vase, Indian Ware, blk on red clay, #218, 1906, 2"......................200.00
Vase, Indian Ware, blk, tan & gray on red clay, #219, 3¼x6".......120.00
Vase, Tirrube, floral, gray & wht on terra cotta, stick neck, 12"...850.00

Clocks

In the early days of our country's history, clock makers were influenced by styles imported from Europe. They copied the Europeans' cabinets and reconstructed their movements — needed materials were in short supply; modifications had to be made. Of necessity was born mainspring motive power and spring clocks. Wooden movements were made on a mass-production basis as early as 1808. Before the middle of the century, brass movements had been developed.

Today's collectors prefer clocks from the eighteenth and nineteenth centuries with pendulum-regulated movements. Bracket clocks made during this period utilized the shorter pendulum improvised in 1658 by Fromentiel, a prominent English clock maker. These smaller square-face clocks usually were made with a dome top fitted with a handle or a decorative finial. The case was usually walnut or ebony and was sometimes decorated with pierced brass mountings. Brackets were often mounted on the wall to accommodate the clock, hence the name. The banjo clock was patented in 1802 by Simon Willard. It derived its descriptive name from its banjo-like shape. A similar but more elaborate style was called the lyre clock.

The first electric novelty clocks were developed in the 1940s. Lux, who was the major producer, had been in business since 1912, making wind-up novelties during the '20s and '30s. Another company, Mastercrafter Novelty Clocks, first obtained a patent to produce these clocks in the late 1940s. Other manufacturers were Keebler, Westclox, and Columbia Time. The cases were made of china, Syroco, wood, and plastic; most were animated and some had pendulettes. Prices vary according to condition and rarity. Unless noted otherwise, values are given for clocks in excellent condition. Clocks that have been altered, damaged, or have had parts replaced are worth considerably less. Our advisor is Bruce A. Austin; he is listed in the Directory under New York.

Key:
br — brass
dl — dial
esc — escapement
hr — hour
mvt — movement
pnd — pendulum

reg — regulator
rswd — rosewood
T — time
S — strike
wt — weight

Calendar Clocks

Davis Clock Co, simple calendar, rswd, 8-day TS, 1890, 25" 400.00
E Ingraham, Dew Drop, simple, rswd grain pnt, 1900 .... 275.00

Ithaca #1 Double Dial Calendar Clock (aka eight-day hanging weight-driven bank clock), two 12" dials, walnut case with shelf, 26" long pendulum rod, both dials with staining and damage, 49", $6,600.00. (Photo courtesy Tom Harris Auctions on LiveAuctioneers.com)

Ithaca, #3½ Parlor, perpetual, walnut, 1885, 20" 2,500.00
New Haven, Fashion #9, simple, walnut, 1890s, 32" 1,100.00
Seth Thomas, #1 Office, perpetual, rswd, 1890, 40" 1,500.00
Seth Thomas, Emp style, dbl dl, rswd, 1890, 30" 1,200.00
W Gilbert, Observatory reg, simple, oak, 1920, 36" 250.00
W Gilbert, schoolhouse style, simple, oak, 1920, 32" 350.00
Welch, #4, perpetual, rswd, 1890, 31" 1,250.00

Novelty Clocks

Bird in cage, gilt metal, German?, mk GESCH #204, 19th C, 3¾" .395.00
Cowboy on bucking bronco, copper pnt on wht metal, Sessions, 14x11" .135.00
Knight's helmet, Camerden & Forster, 1880s, 11½", VG 1,200.00
Liberty Bell, wood front, Lux, 5" 200.00
Lighthouse, lantern top revolves, 2" dl, New Haven, 12½", VG. 1,200.00
Rotating sphere w/pnd held by 3 br pillars, US Clock Co, 10½"..240.00
Sambo w/banjo, blinking eyes, 34-hr, partial rpt, 15½" 1,800.00
Stacked Arms (named Army), triangular base/gilt flag, Ansonia.900.00
Tick Tack, Nouveau lady beside clock, Syrian bronze look, Ansonia, 10".250.00
Winged cherub stands beside clock on pillar, gilt bronze, New Haven.395.00

Shelf Clocks

Ansonia, Crystal Palace, walnut, 8-day TS, glass dome, 1900, 19"...575.00
Ansonia, Crystal Reg, gilt metal w/beveled glass sides, 1915, 17"...1,800.00
Ansonia, porc, LaLorne, Royal Bonn case, 8-day TS, 1900, 12"..225.00
Candle night timepiece, metal case w/mg dl, 30-hr T-only, 1890, 12"..325.00

Connecticut Clock Co, MOP & stenciled case, 8-day TS, 1860, 16" ..625.00
Dutch mini br bracket clock, 8-day fusee T & alarm, 1890, 7" .2,600.00
E Ingraham, Forestville, ripple front beehive, 8-day TS, 1850, 19" ..975.00
E Manross, steeple on steeple, 8-day TS fusee mvt, 1860, 23"...1,100.00
EN Welch, mini Patti #2, rswd, 8-day TS, 1890, 11" 2,200.00
English skeleton, 8-day fusee T-only, glass dome, 1890, 19" 1,800.00
French porc, onyx base, br eagle, 1890, 9" 400.00
French slate & bronze w/calendar, 8-day TS, open esc, 1900, 18". 700.00
French, carriage clock, mini, 30-hr TS, 1890, 3¼" 100.00
French, La Beaute, swinging, patinated metal, 8-day T-only, 1900, 25"..875.00
Italian bracket clock, ebonized wood case w/drw br finials, 1900, 25". 3,900.00
J Ives mirror clock, mahog, rev pnt tablets, 8-day TS spring, 1830, 54" ..1,650.00
Japy Freres, china HP decor, TS, 1900, 12"................................... 325.00
JC Brn, acorn, rvpt tablets, 8-day fusee TS, mahog, 1870, 24"..8,500.00
Jerome & Darrow, transitional, mahog, stenciled columns, 30-hr TS, 1830, 28" .625.00
Jerome & Darrow, triple decker w/paw ft, 30-hr TS wood works, 1870, 32"..2,300.00
M Leavenworth, mahog, 30-hr TS wood works, 1850, 28" 1,300.00
New Haven, Vercel, 30-hr, eagle finial, 1905, 7" 125.00
Olcott Cheney, pillar & scroll, mahog, 30-hr TS wood works, 1830, 19"..650.00
Sessions, tambour, 8-day TS, mahog, 1920, 10x15"......................... 75.00
Seth Thomas, 8-bell Sonora chime, mahog, 1920, 14"............... 1,500.00
Seth Thomas, pillar & scroll, 30-hr, wt, rstr, 1820, 32" 1,100.00
Terry Clock Co, candlestick, mg under glass dome, 1890, 11" 250.00
W Gilbert, Mitra, walnut, 8-day TS, 1890, 23" 125.00
W Gilbert, steeple, mahog, 8-day TS, rvpt tablet, 1890, 20"........ 175.00

Tall Case Clocks

Chandler, pnt dol, rolling moon/calendar, mahog, 1820, 90"....5,000.00
D Blasdell, red pnt pine w/raised panel door, mvt not orig, 1790, 91". 3,200.00
D Burnap, CT, cherry, fretwork crest, 8-day TS wt, 1810, 87" ..8,700.00
J Hill, NJ, mahog, pnt iron dl, 8-day wt TS, moon phase, 1820, 97"..9,000.00
Pennsylvania country Sheraton, 30-hr wt, cherry, 1790, 92" 1,600.00
Pennsylvania inlaid cherry, 8-day wt TS, 1825, 92" 2,200.00
R Whiting, grain pnt pine, flat top, 30-hr wood works, 1850, 85"...900.00
S Hoadley, grain pnt pine, trn finals, wood dl, 1820s, 90" 1,900.00
Seth Thomas, #14 floor reg, burl mahog, 8-day wt, mercury pnd, 1890, 100"...14,000.00

Wall Clocks

Aaron Williard, Jr, banjo, iron dl, 8-day wt, mahog, 1835, 33" .3,100.00
Ansonia Brass & Copper, rswd schoolhouse-style, 8-day T-only, 1900, 26"...325.00
Ansonia, Capitol, 30-day T-only, 1900, 55".............................. 1,200.00

Ansonia General, oak case (loss), eight-day, two-weight, movement and dial signed, circa 1915, replaced weights and bottom glass, 68", EX, $2,280.00. (Photo courtesy Cowan's Auctions, Inc. on LiveAuctioneers.com)

Asa Munger, lg Emp-style, mahog, 8-day TS, 1860, 40" 1,900.00
Bundy, time recorder, cvd oak case, 1900, 56" 950.00
D Williams, gilt front presentation banjo, rvpt tablets, 1820, 41" .2,200.00
Dutch hooded, oak, pnt dl, metal figures, 8-day TS, 1885, 48" 950.00

E Stennes, late 20th C repro banjo, 8-day wt, rvpt tablets, 1975, 41". 2,500.00
EN Welch, Vict style, walnut, 8-day TS, advertising pnd, 1890, 30".. 750.00
English, gallery, fusee 8-day time only, 19900, 15"........................ 225.00
Howard & Davis, #1 banjo, 8-day T-only, wt, 1870, 50" 4,250.00
Lyre front banjo, mahog w/rvpt tablets, 1830, 40" 1,600.00
New Hampshire, mirror, rvpt tablet, 8-day wt driven, 1830, 30". 2,600.00
Seth Thomas, #2 reg, mahog, 8-day T-only, wt, 1900, 36" 1,000.00
Seth Thomas, gallery, 30-day T-only, mahog, 1900, 18"............... 535.00
Seth Thomas, schoolhouse style, oak, 8-day TS, 1900, 24"......... 225.00
Seth Thomas, ship's bell, 8-day TS, br bell, 1900, 11".................. 475.00
Simon Willard & Son, presentation banjo, mahog, rvpt tablets, 1815, 41".. 12,500.00
Vienna 3-wt reg, walnut, porc dl, 1880, 48".............................. 1,000.00
Waltham, banjo, mahog, rvpt tablets, 1910, 41"........................ 2,600.00
Waterbury Study #3, oak, 8-day pull-up wt TS, 1900, 22"............ 375.00

Cloisonné

Cloisonné is defined as 'enamel ware in which the surface decoration is formed by different colors of enamel separated by thin strips of metal.' In the early original process, precious and semi-precious stones were crushed and their colors placed into the thin wire cells (cloisons) in selected artistic designs. Though a French word, cloisonné was first made in tenth-century Egypt. To achieve the original result, many processes may be used. There are are also several styles and variations of this art form. Standard cloisonné involves only one style, using opaque enamel within cloison borders. Besides metal, cloisonné is also worked into and on ceramics, glass, gold, porcelain, silver, and wood. Pliqué a jour is a style in which the transparent enamel is used between cloisons that are not anchored to a base material. In wireless cloisonné, the wires (cloisons) are pulled from the workmanship before the enamel is ever fired. Household items, decorative items, and ceremonial pieces made for royalty have been decorated with cloisonné. It has been made for both export and domestic use.

General cloisonné varies in workmanship as well as color, depending on the country of origin. In later years some cloisonné was made in molds, almost by assembly line. Examples of Chinese cloisonné made in the past 100 years or so seem to have brighter colors, as does the newer Taiwan cloisonné. In most of the Japanese ware, the maker actually studies his subject in nature before transfering his art into cloisonné form.

Cloisonné is a medium that demands careful attention to detail; please consult a professional for restoration. Our advisor for this category is Jeffery M. Person. Mr. Person has been a collector and dealer for 40 years. He is a speaker, writer, and appraiser on the subject of cloisonné. He is listed in the Directory under Florida.

Chinese

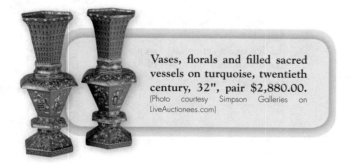

Vases, florals and filled sacred vessels on turquoise, twentieth century, 32", pair $2,880.00. (Photo courtesy Simpson Galleries on LiveAuctionees.com)

Basin, horses & waves, int w/foo dogs, Ming period, 18" 7,650.00
Box, foo dogs & qilin circle rim, bat/peach reserve, 4½x9x8" 600.00
Censor, tripod ft, Buddhist lion finial, 19th C, 8" 900.00
Figure, seated Quan Yin, bronze face/bib/hands/ft, 23" 820.00

Plate, foo dog surrounded w/5 red floral-design petals on turq, 12"... 115.00
Table, rosewood w/floral insert top, 20th C, 24x14" dia 120.00
Teapot, elephant form, bronze tusks at spout, dbl hdl, ca 1900, 1½x2". 540.00
Teapot/wine server, foo lions on bl, rpl wire hdl, 1800s, 5½x7".... 135.00
Vase, floral, mc on iron red, baluster, 1900-30, 9½x4½" 180.00
Vase, mc patterns, acorn form w/4 lg bronze buttresses, 1900, 14" ..525.00
Vase, peonies, bl on geometric wht, tassel rim, stick neck, 15x7" . 960.00

Japanese

Tray, rooster, chicken, and hen, signed Teizan, Kinzan seal, late nineteenth century, wear, pitting and enamel loss, 10¾x10¾", VG, $4,800.00. (Photo courtesy Susanin's Auctions on LiveAuctioneers.com)

Charger, flying crane on bl, 19th C, 14¼" 350.00
Vase, birds & wisteria on dk bl, silver wire type, 1900s, 10", pr. 1,295.00
Vase, birds in reserves on blk w/lav bands, 7" 550.00
Vase, bl reserve w/lg bird & roses, bk: 2nd bird/floral reserve, 18" .4,000.00
Vase, finches & pk blossoms on gr, sm bruise, 12", pr 500.00
Vase, flowering tree/bird/rooster/hen on blk, 7½", pr................. 1,560.00
Vase, lg rooster, bk: hen, ovoid w/L neck, 6", pr 3,000.00
Vase, orchid flowers on pale apricot, ca 1900, 9" 585.00
Vase, pheasants/quail/sparrows/etc, gilt silver mts, 19th C, 9", pr ... 3,300.00
Vase, roosters/flowers/banana trees on yel, Meijo period, 27", pr. 2,825.00

Clothing and Accessories

Antique and vintage fashions from the eighteenth to nineteenth centuries offer high-quality, ornate, and simple pieces for day and evening wear. Antique and vintage fashions of any age with ornate designs or unusual appearance, of superior condition and distinctive design, and of the highest quality construction are most desirable by collectors. Fashions crafted from beautiful fabrics or displaying fanciful ornaments will usually command a higher price for any time period compared to lesser examples. Fashions made by top designers are highly coveted. Collectors also value the beautiful but unmarked antique and vintage fashions as they are stunning examples and testaments to their creators. Provenance and accurate historical documentation of original ownership is important and can increase the value of any antique or vintage fashion item. Women's clothing is more prevalent than children's and men's fashions. As earlier fashions are rarer, pieces not in pristine condition are still considerably valuable. Collectors should date their items down to a specific year or tight date range in order to properly identify, value, and organize their collections. Be wary of modern reproductions or pieces that have been altered as they are less desirable than artifacts in their original and unadulterated condition.

Collectors must rely on an extensively researched pictorial fashion reference book with research documenting annual fashion trends to facilitate dating. For further information we recommend *Ladies' Vintage Accessories* by LaRee Johnson Bruton; *Vintage Hats & Bonnets, 1770 – 1970*, by Susan Langley; *Antique & Vintage Clothing: A Guide to Dating and Valuation of Women's Clothing, 1850 – 1940*, by our advisor, Diane Snyder-Haug (see Directory, Florida); and *Antique & Vintage Fashions, 1745 to 1979*, by our other advisor, Barbara Johnson, Ph.D. (see Directory, New York). Our values are for items of ladies' clothing unless noted man's or child's. Assume them to be in mint condition unless otherwise described. Please note that prices for vintage clothing do vary from one section of the country to another.

Apron, silk, chenille embroidery, ca 1745-60s 1,750.00
Apron, silk, pnt ornament, ca late 1870s-early 1880s 425.00
Bathing suit, middy bloomers, ca 1886 .... 200.00
Bathing suit, navy wool, 2-pc, ca 1900 .... 165.00
Bellbottom pants outfit, bolero style top, ca 1977 .... 105.00
Belt, cut steel, ornate links, chatelaine loop, ca 1890s 700.00
Blouse, sheer orange & yel print, label: Vera, ca 1966-68 .... 90.00
Blouse, taupe silk, embr, abstract Arts & Crafts style, ca 1923 ..... 100.00
Bodice, apple gr taffeta, gauze ruffles on cuffs, ca 1871 .... 925.00
Bodice, ball gown, electric bl silk, str neckline, silk lace, ca 1841 . 850.00
Bodice, brocaded silk, embr flowers, bow epaulettes, ca 1887 ...... 750.00
Bodice, child's silk, pk & blk checkered, fringe trim, ca 1854 ...... 150.00
Bodice, child's, ecru muslin, embr polka dots, ca 1824 .... 575.00
Bodice, child's, muslin, empire waist, ca 1813 .... 325.00
Bodice, evening gown, off the shoulder neckline, ca 1854 .... 200.00
Bodice, lace, pigeon pouter waist, H collar, ca 1898-99 .... 300.00
Bodice, Polonaise cotton, brocaded fabric, pearl buttons, ca 1879 .. 375.00
Bodice, Polonaise style, voided velvet, chenille fringe, ca 1885 ... 325.00
Bodice, rust voided velvet & silk, ornamental buttons, ca 1883 .. 325.00
Bodice, watered silk, tape tie closure, ca 1825 .... 575.00
Bodice, woven plaid, ruffled cuffs, ca 1881 .... 425.00
Bodice, yel silk chiffon, pointed sleeves, ca 1831 .... 575.00
Bonnet, calash bonnet, caned supports, ca 1770-1800 .... 725.00
Bonnet, chipped straw, silk flowers, ca 1891 .... 125.00
Bonnet, pk crinoline, silk flowers, ribbon, ca 1840 .... 800.00
Bonnet, red silk & velvet, ca late 19th C 135.00
Bonnet, silk shirred, caned, brocaded silk ribbon, ca 1833 .... 400.00
Bonnet, spoon, child's, shirred lt gray silk, silk flowers, ca 1865 ... 425.00
Bonnet, spoon, gray shirred silk, floral & feather trim, ca 1865 ... 425.00

Bonnet, straw, light green silk ribbon tied into rosettes, circa 1805 – 1807, $1,000.00.
(Photo courtesy Barbara Johnson, Ph.D.)

Bonnet, straw, olive gr silk trim, bow, ca 1822-23 .... 950.00
Bonnet, straw, high wide brim, tall crown, ca 1818 .... 400.00
Bonnet, striped brn silk coal scuttle shape, ca 1849 .... 800.00
Bonnet, woven straw, ca 1842 .... 800.00
Buckles, crystal paste, gilded metal, ca late 19th C, ea 250.00
Buckles, shoe, eng, raised designs, ca 1775-90 .... 400.00
Caftan, bl, gr, plum & yel print, ca 1972-73 .... 55.00
Camisole cover, wht lace, Vict 15.00
Cap, day, high muslin, ca 1830-33 .... 400.00
Cape, blk silk faille, embr lace at sleeves, ca 1893-94 .... 325.00
Coat dress, mod knit, blk & wht polyester, ca 1967-69 .... 150.00
Coat, bustle, voided velvet, rabbit fur cuffs & collar, ca 1886 ... 1,000.00
Coat, mod, bl, gr & lime gr stripes, ca 1960s 40.00
Collar, embr organza bib front, ca 1931 .... 35.00
Collar, gold beaded & embr net, ca 1910-12 .... 60.00
Corset, boning and lacing, Paris Label, Vict 800.00
Dress, A-line shift, burlap psychedelic floral print, ca 1967-68 .... 120.00
Dress, batiste, pnt flowers & ruffles, Valenciennes lace, ca 1903 .. 465.00
Dress, bustle, pinstripe taffeta, basque waist, ca 1878-83 .... 1,450.00
Dress, centennial, plaid cotton, red, wht & bl trimming, ca 1876 . 650.00
Dress, chiffon, gr, velvet zigzags, silk flower, ca 1925 .... 275.00
Dress, child's jumper, velvet, sailor collar, ca 1922-23 .... 70.00
Dress, child's, abstract roller print, drawstring waistline, ca 1811-13 .. 650.00

Dress, cocktail, plum taffeta, asymmetrical, pointed wings, ca 1956-57 .. 145.00
Dress, cotton checkered, eyelet trim, sq neck, ca 1944-45 .... 60.00
Dress, day, brn cotton, ornamental waist buttons, ca 1955 .... 115.00
Dress, electric bl taffeta, sq collar, ca 1951 .... 110.00
Dress, gigot sleeves, roller printed cotton, ca 1834 .... 2,600.00
Dress, girl's, pinstripe gray taffeta silk, 2 rows of skirt pleats, ca 1867 ... 700.00
Dress, girl's, striped wool, velvet panels, ca 1890 .... 400.00
Dress, halter, mustard velvet, winged collar, ca 1953 .... 145.00
Dress, housecoat, pique, stripe print, ca 1946-48 .... 200.00
Dress, lilac silk brocade, shirring, smocking, ca 1843 .... 1,700.00
Dress, maxi, purple & lav floral chiffon, puffed sleeves, ca 1973 .. 225.00
Dress, mini, gray faux silk shantung, pearls, bugle beads, bow belt, ca 1968 . 300.00
Dress, peasant, gauze floral print, ca 1971 .... 120.00
Dress, prairie, flannel, floral print, label: Vicky Vaughn, ca 1976 ... 80.00
Dress, purple plaid silk, fringe yoke collar, peplum, ca 1856 .... 900.00
Dress, rayon, cut work, fabric scrolls, belt, gathered waist, ca 1945 .. 245.00
Dress, satin & brocade bodice, irid bead strands at waist, ca 1893 .. 1,000.00
Dress, silk plaid, princess lines, military cuffs, apron effect, ca 1882 . 975.00
Dress, silk taffeta, red plaid, fabric buttons, purple fringe, ca 1867 .. 1,150.00
Dress, watered taffeta, split skirt, puffed sleeves, ca 1837 .... 1,850.00
Dress, wedding, satin, hip panniers, lace, flower corsage, ca 1923 ... 3,000.00
Dress, wht cotton eyelet, scrolled pattern, embr, ca 1910 .... 275.00
Dress, woven rayon, chiffon collar & cuffs, ca 1939 .... 165.00
Fan, blk lacquer, gilded, pnt, outdoor scene, ca 1850s-60s 150.00
Fan, feathers, peacock & turkey, cvd sandalwood sticks, ca 1885 .. 75.00
Fan, Jenny Lind brisé, spangles, pierced ivory sticks, ca 1847-52 ... 45.00
Fan, paper, Asian influenced design, bamboo sticks, ca 1883 .... 80.00
Fan, point de gaze lace, MOP gilded sticks, late 19th C 150.00
Fur cape, mink stole, ca 1950s 65.00
Gown, ball, lt pk, sleeveless bodice, draped netting, train, ca 1890 .. 950.00
Gown, brn floral silk chiffon, bell sleeves, ca 1854 .... 1,700.00
Gown, bustle, bright robin egg bl damask, embr, ca 1884 .... 1,600.00
Gown, bustle, velvet, spun glass & pearl beads, ball fringe, ca 1883 . 1,550.00
Gown, Chantilly lace, satin, pearl & rhinestone ornaments, ca 1910-11 .. 3,000.00
Gown, christening, pleating, embr, long, ca 1870s 75.00
Gown, coffee colored silk taffeta, leg o'mutton sleeves, lace collar, ca 1893 . 675.00
Gown, cornflower bl liquid satin, lace yoke, peplum, ca 1945 ...... 400.00
Gown, dressing, raspberry satin, central metal zipper, ca 1938-40 . 225.00
Gown, evening, dk rose, bl-gray cotton, organdy neck ruffles, ca 1935 . 850.00
Gown, evening, satin & tulle, halter, spaghetti straps, Ceil Chapman, ca 1941 ... 2,000.00
Gown, evening, violet strapless, ribbon embr, ca 1937 .... 300.00
Gown, hot pk silk, lg puffs on rear hip sides, ca late 1864 .... 1,150.00
Gown, ivory net tulle, ribbon flowers, silver embr, ca 1916 .... 2,500.00
Gown, mustard crepe covered w/gold metal sequins, ca 1906 ...... 850.00
Gown, pistachio gr organza, ruffles, posy centers, ca 1953 .... 300.00
Gown, pk wool, sequined berries & leaves on shoulder & waist, ca 1946 . 325.00

Gown, robin's egg blue damask silk, plain bodice ornamented with embroidery, openwork on apron and cuffs, original crystal centered buttons, circa 1884, $1,800.00. (Photo courtesy Barbara Johnson, Ph.D.)

Gown, satin, satin piping swirls, bloused sleeves, tight cuff, ca 1935 .. 2,000.00
Gown, silk brocade, Chantilly lace, fringe, ca 1852-55 .... 1,325.00

Gown, silk, empire waistline, ruffled collar, ca 1795-1800 ....2,000.00
Gown, wedding, ivory satin, chiffon ruffles, ca 1900 ....575.00
Gown, wedding, ivory silk, asymmetrical drapery, beading ca 1911 .1,500.00
Gown, wedding, ivory silk, leg o'mutton sleeves, train, ca 1896.. 2,500.00
Gown, wedding, ivory silk, portrait neckline, embr, ca 1839 ....1,850.00
Gown, wht muslin, shirred bodice, ca 1823-24........................1,900.00
Hat, bl satin, wine velvet, jet trim, ruffled ornament, ca 1885 .....100.00
Hat, blk woven horsehair, chipped straw, flowers, ca 1902 ....225.00
Hat, child's, cloche, navy bl straw, ribbon, buckle, ca 1924..........100.00
Hat, cloche, netting, silk flower, leaves, rhinestones, ca 1926......180.00
Hat, cloche, tan straw, gr feather embr, ca 1924 ....150.00
Hat, cone, blk, orange cording, red tassel, ca 1936 ....70.00
Hat, flat topped blk Chantilly lace, purple flowers, ca 1867 ....400.00
Hat, fluffy wht marabou feathers, ca 1964.......................................55.00
Hat, picture, musketeer style, ostrich feather, jet ornament, ca 1911.200.00
Hat, plaited straw hat, Greek Key straw top pc, ca 1867 ....400.00
Hat, red, pointed top, feathers, ca 1955 ....50.00
Hat, sailor hat, lady's navy wool, pompoms, ca 1922-23.................100.00
Hat, skullcap, plastic red & gr currants, ca 1957............................90.00
Hat, straw, high telescopic crown, ca 1880 ....1,500.00
Hat, toque, velvet bows & trim, rhinestones, lace, ca 1898-99 ....200.00
Hat, toy, tilted, blk straw, veil, hatpin, ca 1947 ....100.00
Hat, turban, chartreuse & olive, 1940-41 ....120.00
Headdress, blk net & red chenille, blk beads, ca 1850s-60s............60.00
Headpiece, bandeau, satin, beads, pearls, ostrich feather, ca 1911...200.00
Headpiece, bridal, wax floral & taffeta, tulle, ca 1938 ....55.00
Headpiece, lace, lappets, ca early-mid 19th C 175.00
Headpiece, pearls, seed beads, Cleopatra style, gold netting, ca 1917 .450.00
Headpiece, rhinestone, oval designs, ca 1920-29...........................575.00
Hood, quilted silk, long points, chin ties, ca 1842 ....400.00
Hot pants, brn suede, lace closure, ca 1971....................................70.00
Jacket, mod, red, wht & bl hounds tooth, ca 1960s 60.00
Jacket, Spencer, brn silk satin, floral embr, ca 1803-05...............1,800.00
Jeans, heart pockets, label: Clouds, ca 1979....................................45.00
Jumpsuit, psychedelic paisley, halter collar, wide legs, ca 1973.......95.00
Muff, fur, handbag combination, ca 1940s 20.00
Necktie, HP, tropical theme, ca 1940s 70.00
Nightgown, ivory satin, ca 1930s...20.00
Outfit, yel cotton, bare midriff, ruffled top, narrow pants, ca 1965 ..150.00
Pajamas, Japanese silk, ca 1950s...50.00
Pantaloons, wht, lace trim, ca 19th C 30.00
Pants, plaid, ca 1970s...5.00
Pantsuit, pk abstract polyester print, cape, ca 1971 ....55.00
Parasol, blk Chantilly lace, cvd ivory hdl, monogram, ca 1875.1,650.00
Parasol, brn, corded brn floral lace, wooden hdl, ca 1886...............85.00

Parasol, chantilly lace and ivory silk, carved ivory handle with monogram, circa 1875, $1,650.00.
(Photo courtesy Barbara Johnson, Ph.D.)

Parasol, cvd ivory, lace hinged hdl, ca 1830s-70s.......................1,650.00
Peignoir, chiffon & lace set, ca 1960s..40.00
Petticoat, tulle & crinoline, ca 1950s..10.00
Pocket case, Spitafields silk, ca 1760 mid-late 18th C.............1,260.00
Pocketbook, Flame stitch, purple silk satin int, ca 1740s-90s....2,500.00
Purse, beaded, Art Deco style, filigree clasp, ca 1920s 200.00
Purse, linen, bl beadwork, metal sequins, fringe, ca 1810s-50s 950.00
Purse, reticule, beaded, drawstring, floral motif, ca 1800s-30s 750.00

Purse, tapestry, metallic embr, enamel closures, ca 1915-25 ....100.00
Reticule purse, silk, embr birds & blossoms, ca 1883...................100.00
Robe, mod quilted hostess road, psychedelic pattern, ca 1960s......25.00
Shawl, paisley, ivory grnd, red paisley border design, ca 1860s.....500.00
Shawl, blk Chantilly lace, ca 1860s...200.00
Shirt, polyester, abstract print, ca 1970s..15.00
Shoes, Edwardian satin, ca 1910s 125.00
Shoes, gr silk shoes, gold embr, ca 1790s...................................2,800.00
Shoes, ivory silk wedding, cut steel buckles, ruffled ornament, ca late 1861 ..425.00
Shoes, lady's, ivory silk embr, ca 1772-85.................................3,000.00
Shoes, lady's, silk embr, 1764..3,000.00
Shoes, Mary Jane, chunky heels, gold & silver brocade, ca 1970 ...35.00
Shoes, platform, peep toe, gr leather, ca 1940s 65.00
Shoes, silk satin, button closure, ca 1920s......................................85.00
Shoes, silk str slipper shoes, ankle ribbons, ca 1827-40s, pr..........650.00
Shoes, sling bk, gr, flower on front, ca 1960s..................................30.00
Shoes, Turkish inspired, metallic embr, side laces, ca 1854-56.....450.00
Shorts set, vest, striped cotton, ca 1957-58 ....60.00
Skirt, circle, HP, Mexican design, roses, sequins, ca 1953-58.......160.00
Suit, apricot wool 2 pc, cowl collar, necktie, ca 1966 ....110.00
Suit, gray wool, shirred shoulders & wrists, ca 1947 ....325.00
Suit, wool check, wht collar, cuffs, neck bow, ca 1959 ....125.00
Sunbonnet, woven straw, blk cotton, mid-late 19th C...................225.00
Sundress, hot pk, triangular hip cutouts, ca 1968 ....115.00
Sweater, cashmere, embr, ca 1950s...45.00
Sweater, rainbow striped crocheted, fold-down collar, ca 1975-77. 40.00
Tiara, bridal coronet, buckram cutwork, wht glass beads, ca 1935. 115.00
Under sleeve, blk Chantilly lace pagoda shaped, ca 1850s-60s 75.00
Veil, bonnet, mourning, blk lace, ca 1820s 115.00
Vest, men's Centennial, ivory satin, gold braiding & buttons, ca 1876. 375.00
Vest, men's wedding, ivory silk brocade, ca 1850s........................150.00
Waistcoat, man's disassembled, embr vines & flowers, ca 1760-85. 1,250.00

Vintage Denim

Condition is very important in evaluating vintage denims. Unless otherwise described, assume our values are for items in Number 1 grade. To qualify as a Number 1 grade, there must be no holes larger than a pinhole. A missing belt loop is permissible as long as it has not resulted in a hole. Only a few very light stains and minor fading may be present, the crotch seam must be strong with no holes, and the item must not have been altered. Be sure to access the condition of the garment you are dealing with objectively, then adjust our prices up or down as your assessment dictates. The term 'deadstock' refers to a top-grade item that has never been worn or washed and still has its original tags. 'Hedge' indicates the faded fold lines that develop on the front of denim jeans from sitting.

Coveralls, denim, ca 1930s 500.00
Coveralls, denim, ca 1940s 120.00
Jacket, Burlington, denim, railroad style, ca 1940s 190.00
Jacket, denim, indigo, ca 1950s...125.00
Jacket, denim, railroad, ca 1930s...260.00
Jacket, denim, western style, ca 1950s...160.00
Jacket, Lee, denim, ca 1950s..110.00
Jacket, Levis, 506XX, ca 1940s..1,150.00
Jacket, Levis, 507, big E, ca 1950s 1,000.00
Jacket, Levis 507XX, big E, ca 1950s...325.00
Jacket, Oshkosh denim, railroad style, ca 1940s 160.00
Jacket, railroad, ca 1930s...240.00
Jacket, railroad, indigo denim, ca 1940s...140.00
Jacket, Wards, railroad, ca 1950s..100.00
Jeans, indigo denim, ca 1940s...70.00
Jeans, Lee, carpenter pants, ca 1940s 125.00
Jeans, Levis 501XX big E, ca 1950s..1,250.00

Jeans, Levis, ca 1950s	130.00
Overalls, denim, ca 1930s-40s	240.00
Overalls, denim, ca 1950s	100.00
Overalls, Liberty, ca 1940s	185.00
Overalls, Sears, denim, ca 1950s	35.00
Pants, carpenter, denim, ca 1940s	125.00
Pants, work, denim, ca 1950s	100.00

Cluthra

The name cluthra is derived from the Scottish word 'clutha,' meaning cloudy. Glassware by this name was first produced by J. Couper and Sons, England. Frederick Carder developed cluthra while at the Steuben Glass Works, and similar types of glassware were also made by Durand and Kimble. It is found in both solid and shaded colors and is characterized by a spotty appearance resulting from small air pockets trapped between its two layers. For more information, we recommend *The Collector's Encyclopedia of American Art Glass* by John A. Shuman III. See also specific manufacturers.

Vase, orange with crystal foot marked K 2011-8 Dec 7, Kimball, 8½", $240.00. (Photo courtesy Cincinnati Art Galleries, LLC on LiveAuctioneers.com)

Urn, vase, 'M' pk & wht on crystal w/dbl opal hdls, Steuben sgn, #6795, 10½"	2,200.00
Urn, vase, 'M' wht on crystal w/dbl opal hdls, Steuben sgn, #6795, 10½"	850.00
Vase, bl & wht on crystal, bulb to shoulder, Steuben #2683, 10½"	1,300.00
Vase, bl & wht on crystal, bulb to shoulder, Steuben #2683, 6½"	400.00
Vase, blk & crystal, ovoid, Steuben sgn #6883	550.00
Vase, blk-olive & crystal, wide mouth tapering to ft, Kimble, #1970-8K, 8"	250.00
Vase, gr to wht, 3-step, Steuben #6192, 12"	700.00
Vase, gr w/ribs, Kimble, #30177-6 dec 9, 6"	280.00
Vase, gr, brn & rose, Steuben sgn #7007, 14"	5,600.00
Vase, gr, Steuben sgn #7412, 16"	2,800.00
Vase, pk, wht & crystal, bulb to shoulder, lg bubbles, Steuben #2683, 8½"	900.00

Coalport

In 1745 in Caughley, England, Squire Brown began a modest business fashioning crude pots and jugs from clay mined in his own fields. Tom Turner, a young potter who had apprenticed his trade at Worcester, was hired in 1772 to plan and oversee the construction of a 'proper' factory. Three years later he bought the business, which he named Caughley Coalport Porcelain Manufactory. Though the dinnerware he produced was meant to be only everyday china, the hand-painted florals, birds, and landscapes used to decorate the ware were done in exquisite detail and in a wide range of colors. In 1780 Turner introduced the Willow pattern which he produced using a newly perfected method of transfer printing. (Wares from the period between 1775 and 1799 are termed 'Caughley' or 'Salopian.') John Rose purchased the Caughley factory from Thomas Turner in 1799, adding that holding to his own pottery which he had built two years before in Coalport. (It is from this point that the pottery's history that the wares are termed 'Coalport.') The porcelain produced there before 1814 was unmarked with very few exceptions. After 1820 some examples were marked with a '2' with an oversize top loop. The term 'Coalbrookdale' refers to a fine type of porcelain decorated in floral bas relief, similar to the work of Dresden.

After 1835 highly decorated ware with rich ground colors imitated the work of Sevres and Chelsea, even going so far as to copy their marks. From about 1895 until the 1920s, the mark in use was 'Coalport' over a crown with 'England A.D. 1750' indicating the date claimed as the founding, not the date of manufacture. From the 1920s until 1945, 'Made in England' over a crown and 'Coalport' below was used. Later the mark was 'Coalport' over a smaller crown with 'Made in England' in a curve below.

Each of the major English porcelain companies excelled in certain areas of manufacture. Coalport produced the finest 'jeweled' porcelain, made by picking up a heavy mixture of slip and color and dropping it onto the surface of the ware. These 'jewels' are perfectly spaced and are often graduated in size with the smaller 'jewels' at the neck or base of the vase. Some ware was decorated with very large 'jewels' resembling black opals or other polished stones. Such pieces are in demand by the advanced collector.

It is common to find considerable crazing in old Coalport, since the glaze was thinly applied to increase the brilliance of the colors. Many early vases had covers; look for a flat surface that would have supported a lid (just because it is gilded does not mean the vase never had one). Pieces whose lids are missing are worth about 40% less. Most lids had finials which have been broken and restored. You should deduct about 10% for a professional restoration on a finial.

In 1926 the Coalport Company moved to Shelton in Staffordshire and today belongs to a group headed by the Wedgwood Company. See also Indian Tree.

Vase, lady's portrait on front, enameled starbursts on back, allover jeweling, black paint highlights, retailed by Bailey, Banks & Biddle, Philadelphia, 8", $3,600.00. (Photo courtesy Alex Cooper Auctioneers, Inc. on LiveAuctioneers.com)

Bowl, dessert, Rock & Tree, oval, ca 1805, 11¼" L	1,100.00
Bowl, flowers & insects, floral finial, hdls, ca 1830, 8½", EX	500.00
Bowl, moth/insects reserve on bl w/gold, shell shape, ca 1810, 8¼"	2,000.00
Bowl, vegetable, Ming Rose, w/lid, 10"	295.00
Figurine, Emma Hamilton, ltd ed, 8"	150.00
Goblet, landscape reserves w/gold on cobalt, H Percy, 3-hdl, 1900s, 8"	1,750.00
Ice pail, floral on wht w/gr & gold bands, ca 1820, 14", pr	4,485.00
Plaque, mixed flowers in vase, S Lawrance, oval, 1824, 14"	9,600.00
Plate, cake, floral sprays, pierced hdls, 1891-1920s, 10x9"	125.00
Plate, Hong Kong, #7708, ca 1800-30, 10"	130.00
Plate, plain wht center, pk rim w/gold scrolls, 8¾", 8 for	660.00
Platter, Ming Rose, 14"	125.00
Platter, Rock & Tree, Imari colors, oval, ca 1805, 18"	2,280.00
Tea canister w/inner & outer lid, gold w/turq enamel jewels, printed mk, 5¾"	2,300.00
Teapot, flowers/fruited vines, pk on wht w/gold, ca 1825, 7"	400.00
Teapot, fluted body w/gold foliage on cobalt bands, 9⅞"	300.00
Vase, Dragons in Compartments/landscape panel, 1840s, mtd as lamp, 24"	2,700.00
Vase, floral band w/butterflies on cream, amphora form, 1895, 4"	300.00
Vase, pk w/raised gold foliage, 1890s, 6", pr	850.00

Coca-Cola

J.S. Pemberton, creator of Coca-Cola, originated his world-famous drink in 1886. From its inception the Coca-Cola Company began an incredible advertising campaign which has proven to be one of the most successful promotions in history. The quantity and diversity of advertising material put out by Coca-Cola in the last 100 years is literally mind-boggling. From the beginning, the company has projected an image of wholesomeness and Americana. Beautiful women in Victorian costumes, teenagers and schoolchildren, blue- and white-collar workers, the men and women of the Armed Forces, even Santa Claus, have appeared in advertisements with a Coke in their hands. Some of the earliest collectibles include trays, syrup dispensers, gum jars, pocket mirrors, and calendars. Many of these items fetch prices in the thousands of dollars. Later examples include radios, signs, lighters, thermometers, playing cards, clocks, and toys — particularly toy trucks.

In 1970 the Coca-Cola Company initialed a multimillion-dollar 'image-refurbishing campaign' which introduced the new 'Dynamic Contour' logo, a twisting white ribbon under the Coca-Cola and Coke trademarks. The new logo often serves as a cut-off point to the purist collector. Newer and very ardent collectors, however, relish the myriad of items marketed since that date, as they often cannot afford the high prices that the vintage pieces command. For more information we recommend *Petretti's Coca-Cola Collectibles Price Guide*; and *B.J. Summers' Guide to Coca-Cola, B.J. Summers' Pocket Guide to Coca-Cola*, and *Collectible Soda Pop Memorabilia*, all by B.J. Summers. Our advisors for this category are Craig Stifter (Colorado) and B.J. Summers (Kentucky).

Key:
CC — Coca-Cola   sf — self-framed

Reproductions and Fantasies

Beware of reproductions! Warning! The 1924, 1925, and 1935 calendars have been reproduced. They are identical in almost every way; only a professional can tell them apart. These are *very* deceiving! Watch for frauds: genuinely old celluloid items, including combs, mirrors, knives, forks, and doorknobs, that have been recently etched with a new double-lined trademark. Still another area of concern deals with reproduction and fantasy items. A fantasy item is a novelty made to appear authentic with inscriptions such as 'Tiffany Studios,' 'Trans Pan Expo,' 'World's Fair,' etc. In reality, these items never existed as originals. For instance, don't be fooled by a Coca-Cola cash register; no originals are known to exist! Large mirrors for bars are being reproduced and are often selling for $10.00 to $50.00.

Of the hundreds of reproductions (designated 'R' in the following examples) and fantasies (designated 'F') on the market today, these are the most deceiving.

Belt buckle, no originals thought to exist (F), up to 8.00
Bottle, dk amber, w/arrows, heavy, narrow spout (R)..................... 18.00
Bottle carrier, wood, yel w/red logo, holds 6 bottles (R)................ 20.00
Clock, Gilbert, regulator, b/o, ¾-sz, NM+ (R) 125.00
Cooler, Glascock Jr, made by Coca-Cola USA (R) 250.00
Doorknob, glass etched w/tm (F)...5.00
Knife, bottle shape, 1970s, many variations (F), ea 8.00
Knife, fork or spoon w/celluloid hdl, newly etched tm (F) 5.00
Letter opener, stamped metal, Coca-Cola for 5¢ (F) 5.00
Pocket watch, often old watch w/new face (R)............................ 15.00
Pocketknife, yel & red, 1933 World's Fair (F)................................3.00
Sign, cb, lady w/fur, dtd 1911, 9x11" (F)..................................... 25.00
Soda fountain glass holder, (R) 3.00
Thermometer, bottle form, DONASCO, 17" (R)......................... 25.00
Trade card, copy of 1905 'Bathtub' foldout, emb 1978 (R)............ 20.00

The following items have been reproduced and are among the most deceptive of all:
Pocket mirrors from 1905, 1906, 1908, 1909, 1910, 1911, 1916, and 1920
Trays from 1899, 1910, 1913, 1914, 1917, 1920, 1923, 1925, 1926, 1934, and 1937

Tip trays from 1907, 1909, 1910, 1913, 1914, 1917, and 1920
Knives: many versions of the German brass model
Cartons: wood versions, yellow with logo
Calendars: 1924, 1925, and 1935
These items have been marketed:
Brass thermometer, bottle shape, Taiwan, 24"
Cast-iron toys (none ever made)
Cast-iron door pull, bottle shape, made to look old
Poster, Yes Girl (R)
Button sign, has one round hole while original has four slots, most have bottle logo, 12", 16", 20" (R)
Bullet trash receptacles (old cans with decals)
Paperweight, rectangular, with Pepsin Gum insert
1930 Bakelite radio, 24" tall, repro is lighter in weight than the original, of poor quality, and cheaply made
1949 cooler radio (reproduced with tape deck)
Tin bottle sign, 40"
Fishtail die-cut tin sign, 20" long
Straw holders (no originals exist)
Coca-Cola bicycle with cooler, fantasy item: the piece has been totally made-up, no such original exists
1914 calendar top, reproduction, 11¼x23¾", printed on smooth-finish heavy ivory paper
Countless trays — most unauthorized (must read 'American Artworks; Coshocton, OH.')

Centennial Items

The Coca-Cola Company celebrated its 100th birthday in 1986, and amidst all the fanfare came many new collectible items, all sporting the 100th-anniversary logo. These items are destined to become an important part of the total Coca-Cola collectible spectrum. The following pieces are among the most popular centennial items.

Bottle, gold-dipped, in velvet sleeve, 6½-oz....................................... 75.00
Bottle, Hutchinson, amber, Root Co, ½-oz, 3 in case 375.00
Bottle, International, set of 9 in plexiglas case 300.00
Bottle, leaded crystal, 100th logo, 6½-oz, MIB 175.00
Medallion, bronze, 3" dia, w/box 100.00
Pin set, wood fr, 101 pins.. 350.00
Scarf, silk, 30x30".. 50.00
Thermometer, glass cover, 14" dia 35.00

Coca-Cola Originals

Ad, newspaper, full pg, opening of new bottling plant, 1939, G..................100.00
Ad, paper, Santa, toy train/helicopter, 1962, 10x7", VG, $8 to 12.00
Ashtray, desk, ceramic, Partners...CC, 1950s, 7¼" sq, EX 85.00
Ashtray, tabletop, Bakelite/metal, 1940s, EX, $1,500 to...........2,300.00
Ashtray, tabletop, ceramic/plastic, mini bottle on edge, 1950s 250.00
Ashtray, tabletop, glass, CC Bottling Co, Dickson, TN, 4 grooves, EX.. 25.00
Bandana, Kit Carson, red, Coke logos in corners, 1950s, 20x22", EX... 100.00
Bank, dispenser form, red w/single glass, EX+............................... 325.00
Bank, vendor, plastic, Drink CC..., 1950s, EX, $145 to................ 195.00
Banner, canvas, Bergen w/McCarthy, truck mtd, 1950s, 60x42", EX.. 1,250.00
Banner, King Size, paper, 1958, 36x20", NM............................... 110.00
Blotter, cb, Drink CC in Bottles...Good!, Sprite Boy, 7¼x3½", EX..40.00
Blotter, cb, Good w/ food...Try it, 1930s, NM, $75 to 85.00
Bookmark, celluloid, 1900s, 2x2¼", EX 800.00
Bottle, hobbleskirt, glass, no return, full, 10-oz, 1965, EX, $12 to.. 15.00
Bottle, hobbleskirt, glass, reissue of orig 1915 bottle, 5,000 made, 1965, EX..495.00
Bottle, hobbleskirt, glass, wht letters, screw top, Canadian, 40-oz. 40.00
Bottle, seltzer, CC Bottling Co Bradford PA, EX, $285 to............. 325.00
Bottle, str-sided, arrow, Cincinnati OH, amber, 6-oz, 1910s, EX.. 300.00

Bottles, mini wooden case w/24 bottles, Louisville KY, 1930s, VG .. 1,100.00
Bowl, Vernonware, Drink CC emb on gr ceramic, 1930s, 4x10", EX.. 230.00
Bumper sticker, Don't Say the 'P' Word/Max Headroom, 1980s, EX ... 15.00
Calendar, 1905, Lillian Nordica, 7x15", EX 5,400.00
Calendar, 1906, Drink CC Delicious Refreshing, 15x7", EX 5,300.00
Calendar, 1908, Drink CC...Relieves Fatigue, 7x4", EX 7,200.00
Calendar, 1919, Marian Davis, matted & fr, 10½x6", EX 3,300.00
Calendar, 1920s, bamboo, Drink CC in Bottles..., VG 400.00
Calendar, 1922, girl, baseball, matted & framed, 32x12", NM.. 2,200.00
Calendar, 1931, fishing boy w/sandwich & Coke, 24x12", M.... 1,200.00
Calendar, 1940, girl in red dress, matted & fr, 24x12", VG 650.00
Calendar, 1942, snowman w/boy & girl, dbl-month display, VG . 375.00
Calendar, 1954, Santa, Me, too!, full monthly sheets, VG, $150 to... 195.00
Calendar, 1961, Santa, A Merry Christmas calls for Coke, M, $45 to ... 55.00
Calendar top, paper, girl sitting on ben drinking Coke, 1913, 16x24", G. 4,500.00
Can, dynamic wave, waxed paper, CC, prototype, 12-oz, EX 175.00
Canvas, orig oil, soda fountain server, 1940s, 22½x17¼", VG .. 8,050.00
Carrier, alum, 6-pack, Drink CC...King Size, wire hdl, 1950s, EX... 125.00
Carton insert, Take Home This Handy..., 1936, EX 200.00
Chest, wood/zinc, Help Yourself...Deposit in Box 5¢, 1920s, VG.. 350.00
Clock, boudoir, leather, gold letters, 1910, 3x8", VG. $2,000 to. 3,000.00
Clock, counter, metal & glass, 1950s, 19¼x9x5", EX, $1,200 to. 1,500.00
Clock, light-up countertop, Serve Yourself, 1940s-50s, EX, $750 to .800.00
Clock, light-up, ca 1930s-40s, VG 4,500.00
Clock, wall, metal & glass, 1940-50s, EX 650.00
Clock, wall, metal & plastic, 1950s, 25x55", EX 500.00
Coasters, ceramic, Sprite Boy, 1950s, EX, set of 4 .... 144.00
Coin purse, ...CC Bottling Co, Memphis TN, 1910-20s, VG 200.00
Cooler, picnic, metal, bottle-in-hand decal, 1940s-50s, 8x13x12", EX. 450.00
Cooler, store, metal & zinc, made by Icy-O, 1928, rare, 26x24x24".. 14,950.00
Cooler, store, metal, Westinghouse salesman's sample, EX 3,000.00
Creamer, Drink CC, red on wht, 1930s, VG, $350 to 400.00
Cufflinks, bottle form, gold, mk 1/10, 10k, ¾", NM, pr 50.00
Decal, Drink CC Ice Cold, 1960, G 35.00
Dispenser, countertop, porc & glass, red base, 1920s, NM 6,200.00
Dispenser, syrup, ceramic, CC, soda fountain, 1896, VG 5,500.00
Display, 3-D dc cb, button/soda jerk/patrons at counter, 1955, EX... 500.00
Display, cb, clown balancing, 1950s, EX, $1,000 to 1,400.00
Display, cb, Friends for Life, fishing boy, Rockwell, 1935, 36", VG .. 2,200.00
Display, cb, Santa in dc 3-D rocketship, 1950s, 33", VG, $325 to. 375.00
Display, cb, Santa, Things Go Better With Coke, 1960s, 36", EX . 80.00

Display, cast iron, stand-up policeman, reverse: Drink Coca-Cola, touched-up front, repainted back, 63", G, $1,800.00. (Photo courtesy Richard Opfer Auctioneering, Inc. on LiveAuctioneers.com)

Display, celluloid, CC, rnd disk w/bottle, 1950s, 9" dia, EX 295.00
Display, window, cb diecut, 3-D, 1950s, 36x24", EX 400.00
Display rack, 6-Pack/25¢ red sign atop 3 wire tiers, 1940s-50s, 47", EX.. 225.00
Display rack, metal/wire, Take Some CC Home Today, EX 325.00
Doll, Buddy Lee, comp, CC uniform & patches, 1950s, 12", EX.. 650.00
Dominos, wood, orig cb box, 1940-50s, EX, $65 to 95.00

Door push, flat plate, porc, Come in! Have a CC, Canadian, 4x11½", NM... 320.00
Door push, porc w/CC push plate, bright colors, 1940s-50s, 8x4". 450.00
Fan, cb, Have a Coke, Sprite Boy, on wooden stick, 1950s, EX, $85 to.. 100.00
Fan, Quality Carries On, bottle in hand, 1950, EX 65.00
Festoon, Autumn Girl, 5-pc, 1927, NM 3,500.00
Festoon, cb, Drink CC Delicious & Refreshing, 3 ladies w/umbrellas, EX. 3,750.00
Flange, porc, Drink CC Here, 1940s, NM, $850 to 950.00
Game, flip, cb, fr & under glass, 1910-20, VG, $875 to 1,000.00
Glass, bell, Drink CC 5¢, acid-etched arrow & syrup line, 1912-13, EX.. 875.00
Hat, cowboy, cloth, Enjoy CC, employee award, never worn, NMIB, $150 to.. 185.00
Ice pick, sq hdl, Ice-Coal...Phone 87, 1930-40s, EX 35.00
Ice pick, wood & metal, bulb hdl w/CC in blk, 1920s, VG 65.00
Jug, stoneware, ½-gal, CC, w/paper label, 1910, VG 4,300.00
Key chain, w/customer appreciation card, VGIB 125.00

Lamp, hanging, leaded glass shade, Property of Coca-Cola To Be Returned on Demand lettered on top rim, working, EX, 19" diameter, $3,500.00 to $4,500.00. (Photo courtesy Rich Penn Auctions on LiveAuctioneers.com)

Lamp shade, mg, Drink CC, w/hardware, 1930s, 9½" dia, NM, $800 to.. 1,200.00
License plate attachment, metal, Aloysius Purple Flashes, 11x4", EX... 450.00
Lighter, pocket, metal, Drink CC, musical when lit, 1970s, EX, $225 to. 250.00
Menu, table, plastic holder w/paper insert for specials, 1950s, NM.. 35.00
Menu board, chrome fr, Sprite Boy, 13x28" 300.00
Menu board, wall hung, cb, Have a Coke, 1940s, VG 250.00
Milage meter, plastic/masonite, Travel Refreshed, 1950s, VG, $935 to. 1,050.00
Mirror, pocket, celluloid, Drink CC, Elaine, 1916, 1¾x2¾", G, $225 to. 300.00
Mirror, wall, glass & wood, 1920-30s, 8x17½", G 600.00
Money clip, metal, Nashville TN, EX, $85 to 100.00
Music box, 1950s cooler, rotating girl, NM 4,200.00
Napkin holder, metal, foreign, 1940s 300.00
No-drip protector, paper, 1930-40s, 6½x3¾", EX 15.00
No-drip protector dispenser, metal w/2 orig sleeves & box, unmk, 6½x5", EX.. 225.00
Notepad, leather cover, 1905, 4x2", EX 225.00
Opener, handheld, 50th Anniversary, Nashville TN, 1952, EX... 105.00
Opener, handheld, metal, Drink Bottled CC, saber shape, 1920s, EX.. 200.00
Plate, art, metal, Western CC Bottling Co, 1908-12, 9⅞" dia, EX.. 475.00
Plate, ...Refresh Yourself, Knowles China, 1931, 8¼", NM 825.00
Playing cards, plastic, Drink CC, military nurse, 1943, M, $145 to. 185.00
Playing cards, plastic, lady w/dog, unopened, 1943 .... 240.00
Pocketknife, Drink CC in bottles, blade & corkscrew, 1930s, EX, $145 to.. 165.00
Postcard, CC girl, 1910, NM+ 775.00
Postcard, Weldmech truck, 1930, EX 30.00
Poster, cb, Cooling lift, red-headed beauty in pool w/Coke bottle, 1958, EX... 500.00
Pretzel bowl, alum w/3 cast CC bottle supports, 1930s, 4x9", VG. 175.00
Radio, bottle, Bakelite, Crosley, Cincinnati, 1931-34, 7½" dia, 24", EX... 3,000.00
Radio, can w/dynamic wave, 1970s, EX 45.00
Radio, cooler, CC Refreshes You Best, airline-type, 1950s, G ... 3,800.00
Roller skates, metal & leather, 1914, VG 900.00
Score card, St Louis Cardinals stadium vendor, Ice-Cold CC, EX, $30 to.... 40.00
Service pin, 15 yrs, EX 100.00
Sheet music, The Coca-Cola Girl, fr, 1927, EX 395.00
Sign, bk bar, cb, swans, 1930s, EX 1,500.00
Sign, cb, string hanger w/Santa, Canadian, 1949, 10½x18½", EX... 900.00
Sign, cb, Refreshed Through 70 Years, 2-sided, 1955, 28x56", EX. 300.00
Sign, display, cb, cherub holding tray w/glass, dc, matted & fr, rare, 1908, VG .. 4,000.00
Sign, flat mt, Drink CC, couple w/bottle, sf, 1940s, 35x11", EX.......... 600.00
Sign, hanging, metal, Rx Drug Rx...CC...Store, EX, $1,500 to. 1,800.00

Sign, metal, flat mt, Drink CC, wood fr, 1920s, 39x13", VG 2,150.00
Sign, porc, 2-sided lollipop, Drink CC Refresh!, CI base, 65x30" dia, EX .2,000.00
Sign, porc, Come In! Have a CC, yel & wht, 1940s, 54", NM..1,200.00
Sign, sidewalk, metal, fishtail/bottle, wht/gr stripes, 1960s, 33", EX.500.00
Sign, sidewalk, porc, Drink CC...Stop Here, 1941, 27x46", VG, $850 to.950.00
Sign, tin flange, Grocery/fishtail logo/Refreshes You Best, 15x18", EX...275.00
Sign, tin, dc ribbon, Sign of Good Taste, 1957, 36", NM............. 275.00
Sign, tin, Drink..on red/bottle on wht, gr rim, 1934, 12x36", EX.. 235.00
Sign, tin, str-sided bottle emb, Shonk litho, 1914, 20x27", VG. 1,920.00
Sign, wood, Welcome Friend..., dc, Sprite Boy, 1940, 32x14", EX, $650 to.750.00
Straws, cb box, 1960s, EX.. 225.00
String holder, metal, Take Home CC in Cartons, 1930s, 14x16", EX.. 1,000.00
Syrup jug, Drink CC in wreath (frosted), metal cap, 1910, 13", EX...500.00
Syrup jug, paper label w/Coke glass, 1950s, EX.................... 20.00
Thermometer, desk, metal, Drink CC, 1940s, VG, $55 to 75.00
Thermometer, metal/glass, rnd dial, 1950s, 12", EX, $250 to 285.00
Thermometer, tin, dbl bottles/wheat detail/Drink CC, 1940s, 16x7", EX. 375.00
Thermometer, wood, Drink CC/D&R, 1905, 21", EX 500.00
Toy truck, Buddy L, metal, Enjoy CC, w/hand dolly, 1970s, EX, $100 to.. 130.00
Toy truck, German, #426-20, wind-up, 1949, EX 2,600.00
Toy truck, Marx #991, metal, Sprite Boy, 1951, NM 625.00
Toy truck, Metalcraft, metal, rubber tires, 1930s, G 375.00
Toy truck, Smith-Miller, metal, w/cases & bottles, 1953, 13", EX, $865 to.975.00
Train, Lionel, plastic/metal, 1970s, EXIB, $425 to 500.00
Wallet, leather, blk w/emb gold lettering, 1907, EX 100.00
Wallet, tri-fold, plastic, Enjoy CC in gold lettering, 1960s, EX, $15 to... 20.00
Writing tablet, landmarks of the USA, 1960s, EX......................... 10.00

Trays

All 10½x13½" original serving trays produced from 1910 to 1942 are marked with a date, Made in USA, and the American Artworks Inc., Coshocton, Ohio. All original trays of this format (1910 – 1940) had REG TM in the tail of the C.

The 1934 Weismuller and O'Sullivan tray has been reproduced at least three times. To be original, it will have a black back and must say 'American Artworks, Coshocton, Ohio.' It was not reproduced by Coca-Cola in the 1950s.

1928, Bobbed Hair, 13½x10½", EX-, $920.00.
(Photo courtesy Dan Morphy Auctions, LLC on LiveAuctioneers.com)

1897, Vict Lady, 9¼" dia, VG..15,000.00
1899, Change Receiver, ceramic, The Ideal Brain Tonic..., rare, EX .6,200.00
1899, Hilda Clark, 9¼" dia, EX 11,000.00
1900, Change Receiver, metal, 8½" dia, EX..............................4,500.00
1903, Bottle tilted w/paper label, Drink a Bottle of...5¢, 9¼" dia, EX .6,700.00
1903, Hilda Clark, oval, 18x15", EX 5,750.00
1905, Lillian Russell, glass or bottle, 10½x13½", EX 3,500.00
1906, Juanita, glass or bottle, oval, 10½x13½", EX....................2,000.00
1907, Change Receiver, glass, Drink Coca-Cola 5¢, 7" dia, EX .2,000.00
1907, Relieves Fatigue, 13x16", EX.................................3,400.00
1909, St Louis Fair, 10½x13½", EX 1,500.00
1910, Coca-Cola Girl, Hamilton King, 10½x13½", EX+ 950.00
1914, Betty, 10½x13½", EX+... 500.00

1920, Garden Girl, oval, 10½x13½", EX+ 750.00
1921, White Fox Fur, 10½x13½", EX 650.00
1922, Summer Girl, 10½x13½", NM...............................1,100.00
1923, Flapper Girl, 10½x13½", NM 500.00
1924, Smiling Girl, brn rim, 10½x13½", NM 600.00
1924, Smiling Girl, maroon rim, 10½x13½", EX+ 950.00
1925, Autumn Girl, also on the 1922 calendar, 10½x13½", EX.1,200.00
1926, Golfers, 10½x13½", EX+ 700.00
1927, Curbside Service, 10½x13½", EX, $750 to 850.00
1929, Girl in Swimsuit w/Glass, 10½x13½", EX+ 500.00
1930, Swimmer, 10½x13½", EX 400.00
1931, Boy w/Sandwich & Dog, 10½x13½", EX...................900.00
1932, Girl in Swimsuit on Beach, Hayden, 10½x13½", EX+ 600.00
1933, Francis Dee, 10½x13½", NM, $800 to 900.00
1935, Madge Evans, 10½x13½", NM 600.00
1936, Hostess, 10½x13½", NM......................................650.00
1937, Running Girl, 10½x13½", NM 430.00
1938, Girl in the Afternoon, 10½x13½", NM 275.00
1939, Springboard Girl, 10½x13½", NM 375.00
1940, Sailor Girl, 10½x13½", NM..................................395.00
1941, Ice Skater, 10½x13½", NM...................................395.00
1942, Roadster, 10½x13½", NM+ 475.00
1950s, Girl w/umbrella & bottle of Coke, Fr version, 10½x13½", G..185.00
1950s, Girl w/wind in hair, screen bkgrnd, 10½x13½", M 95.00
1950s, Girl w/wind in hair, solid bkgrnd, 10½x13½", NM............200.00
1955, Menu Girl, 10½x13½", M......................................75.00
1956, Food, 18¼x13½", EX 20.00
1957, Birdhouse, 10½x13½", NM....................................110.00
1957, Rooster, 10½x13½", NM..150.00
1957, Umbrella Girl, 10½x13½", M.................................300.00
1961, Pansy Garden, 10½x13½", NM 25.00
1968, Lillian Nordica, 10½x13½", EX...............................85.00

Vendors

Though interest in Coca-Cola machines of the 1949 – 1959 era rose dramatiacally over the last decade, values currently seem to have leveled off. The major manufacturers of these curved-top, 5¢ and 10¢ machines were Vendo (V), Vendorlator (VMC), Cavalier (C or CS), and Jacobs. Prices are for machines as noted in the description. A mint restored model will bring approximately twice as much as the same model in excellent condition.

Cavalier, model #C27, EX orig....................................1,000.00
Cavalier, model #C51, EX orig....................................1,000.00
Cavalier, model #CS72, M rstr.....................................2,850.00
Jacobs, model #26, EX orig 950.00
Vendo, model #23, EX orig, $1,700 to 2,300.00

Vendo, model #39, restored, $1,000.00 to $1,500.00.
(Photo courtesy Showtime Auction Services on LiveAuctioneers.com)

Vendo, model #44, EX orig..3,100.00
Vendo, model #56, EX orig..1,200.00

Vendo, model #80, EX orig, $650 to 750.00
Vendo, model #81, EX orig 1,250.00
Vendo, model #HA56-B, EX orig 795.00
Vendorlator, model #27, EX orig 1,150.00
Vendorlator, model #27A, EX orig 800.00
Vendorlator, model #33, EX orig 1,100.00
Vendorlator, model #44, EX orig 1,500.00
Vendorlator, model #72, EX orig 1,800.00
Westinghouse, model #42T, EX orig 2,295.00

Enterprise #2, all original, 12", EX, $660.00. (Photo courtesy Dan Morphy Auctions, LLC on LiveAuctioneers.com)

Coffee Grinders

Coffee mills or grinders continue to fascinate and draw new collectors to the hobby each year. These wonderful, utilitarian devices recall times past and are interesting due to both their appearance and mechanical nature. Hundreds of coffee mill patents have been issued in the U.S. and many coffee mills can be found which bear some part of the patent information. Some patented mills or particular patented features were never marked as such, so lack of information does not mean the mill wasn't patented. Be aware, however, if you limit yourself to only patented mills you are missing out on hundreds of mills which did not receive patents. Although many collectors prefer their mills in unrestored condition, replacement parts can be found, so restoration to a near original appearance is possible. New, previously undocumented mills continue to enter the market and are highly prized. While most casual antique collectors recognize the name Enterprise, you should be aware this company was one of the most prolific producers, so while desirable to collect, few are considered rare. Be aware that many mills pulled double duty and while not specifically for grinding coffee, could have been used to do so. Some mills appearing on internet auction sites are grist mills or spice mills and, though generally less valuable, can also be found in the collections of coffee mill enthusiasts. We recommend joining online collector clubs, seeking information from coffee mill websites, and collector organizations to learn more. (See Association of Coffee Mill Enthusiasts/ ACME listed in the Clubs, Newsletters, and Websites section.) Our advisor for this category is Shane Branchcomb; he is listed in the Directory under Virginia.

American Duplex Big Pot, Elec, resembles coffeepot, EX 750.00
Arcade Crystal #3, glass hopper, CI, orig lid, wall mt, EX 160.00
Arcade Crystal #4, glass hopper, CI, orig lid, wall mt, EX 175.00
Arcade Crystal #9010, Art Deco, orig lid & cup, NM 300.00
Arcade Favorite #17, med version of #7, CI, wall mt, EX 145.00
Arcade Favorite #27, largest in series, CI, wall mt, EX 165.00
Arcade Imperial #999, box mill, orig label, NM 160.00
Arcade Telephone, CI front, nickel plated, VG 450.00
Arcade Telephone, fancy CI front, later version, EX 600.00
Arcade Telephone, wood front, CI, brass tag, early, EX 850.00
Arcade, Jewel, mkd glass hopper, NM 375.00
Belmont Hardware, #2870 Improved, wood box, orig label, EX ... 175.00
Belmont Hardware, King No 22, CI, tin hopper, EX 195.00
Belmont Hardware, Lightning No 23, tin canister, CI, EX 275.00
Bronson & Walton, 'Old Glory,' flags, cavalry officer, tin litho, NM .. 700.00
Bronson & Walton, Aroma No 9, CI, tin hopper, VG 135.00
Bronson & Walton, Ever Ready No 2, tin canister, w/cup EX 250.00
Carrington's, CI, side mt, brass tag, EX 325.00
Cavanaugh Bros, wood box, front fill, 1-lb, EX 325.00
Coles Mfg Co, No 00, CI, w/CI cup, wall mt, EX 375.00
Coles Mfg No 7, counter, CI, Pat 1887, 16" wheels, 28", EX ... 1,100.00
CPCo (Parker) No 1350, CI, w/CI lid, wall mt, EX 125.00
Crescent #3, CI, Rutland VT, orig pnt, 12" wheels, VG 750.00
Crescent #7, CI, Rutland VT, orig pnt, 20" wheels, EX 1,300.00
Enterprise #00, CI, w/CI cup, wall mt, NM 180.00

Enterprise #3, 10" wheels, CI, pat 1898, EX 1,050.00
Enterprise #4, CI, nickel hopper, 10" wheels, EX 1,100.00
Enterprise #6, brass hopper, rstr, 12" wheels, NM 1,650.00
Enterprise #8, CI, nickel hopper, 15" wheels, EX 1,300.00
Enterprise #9, brass eagle, Pat 1898, 20" wheels, 28", VG 895.00
Enterprise #350, wall mt, CI w/CI cup, EX 475.00
Enterprise #450, CI, w/CI lid, clamps on, 20", VG 425.00
Enterprise Boss, floor, nickel hopper, 1873, 39" wheels, EX 3,750.00
Fairbanks Morse, floor, brass hopper, 2 wheels, EX 2,750.00
Golden Rule, ornate CI front, wall mt, by Arcade, NM 350.00
Grand Union Tea Co, CI box, made by Griswold, NM 600.00
Griswold, CI box, same as Grand Union Tea Co, NM .... 1,200 .00
Hamilton Beach, 1st home electric coffee mill, ca 1915, NM 450.00
Henry Hart, CI, side mt, mkd on bk, Detroit, NM 155.00
Hoffmann's Old Time, by Arcade, like Telephone, VG 650.00
J Fisher Warranted, mkd on front, lap, dvtl walnut, VG 275.00
Landers, Frary & Clark, #11, CI, w/CI lid, single crank, EX 190.00
Landers, Frary & Clark, #20, CI, 9" wheels, VG 700.00
Landers, Frary & Clark, Universal No 110, table, tin box, EX 90.00
Lane Bros, Swift, #12, tin receiver, single 9" wheel, VG 400.00
Lane Bros, Swift, #14, tin receiver, 15" wheels, EX 850.00
Little Tot (toy), CI hopper & drw front, wood box, decal, mini .. 110.00
Logan & Strobridge, Franco Am, wood box, EX 125.00
Logan & Strobridge, Queen, mkd glass hopper, NM 425.00
Luther, CI, tin hopper, brass plate, Pat 1843 .... 475.00
MJB, CI, tin canister, wall mt, VG 155.00
National Specialty #0, CI w/CI lid, clamps to table, EX 375.00
National Specialty #1, CI w/CI lid, 8-sided hopper, EX 625.00
National Specialty #7, CI, orig drw, 16½" wheels, EX 1,400.00
NCRA, rect, glass window, wall mt, 1915, EX 130.00
None-Such, tin box mill, Mirroscope Co, orig label, NM 165.00
Old 74, CI, parts mkd 71,72,73,74, ca 1840, NM 165.00
Olde Thompson, redwood, lap, 1960s-70s, EX 70.00
Parker & Wht, CI, side, brass tag, ca 1832, NM 700.00
Parker No 200, counter, CI, orig decals, 9" wheels, NM 1,700.00
Parker No 350, ornate, CI, w/CI lid, on wood bk, NM 225.00
Parker No 444, mkd on lid, tin hopper, w/cup, VG 175.00
Parker No 446, wall mt 185.00
Parker No 470, CI, wall mt, no cup, EX 275.00
Parker No 1200, CI orig pnt, 25½" wheels, EX 3,000.00
Parker No 5000, counter, CI Pat 1897, 12" wheels, 17" H, EX . 1,200.00
Parker Victor No 535, table, wood box, tin hopper, hdl, EX 150.00
Peck, Stow & Wilcox, (PS&W) 3600, CI, NM 275.00
Queen (toy), CI hopper & drw front, wood box, label, mini 130.00
Royal Bl, Supplee Hardware, CI, tin hopper, EX 350.00
RU Richmond, side, CI, Chatham CT (2 szs made), EX, ea 550.00
Russell & Erwin Iron Box Mill #90, hourglass shape, NM 800.00
Russell & Erwin, Dmn, CI box, bronze finish, EX 475.00
Selsor, Cook & Co, lap, name on hdl, Pat 1859 .... 250.00
Simmons Hardware, KK #13, 11" wheels, NM 2,300.00
Simmons, Defiance, label, CI fill lid, 1-lb box, EX 165.00
Simplex No 6, by Steinfeld, nickel hopper, 10½" wheels, EX ... 1,000.00

Star No 7, counter, CI w/catch pan, 2 wheels, VG 750.00
Star No 10, CI red & bl pnt, Pat May 26 1885, 22½" wheels.......650.00
Star No 12, CI brass hopper, 2 wheels, rstr, EX 2,500.00
Steinfeld No 10, CI, glass hopper, EX 165.00
Steinfeld No 11, CI, glass hopper, EX 170.00

Henry Stuttle #2, patent 2/20/1877, EX, $650.00. (Photo courtesy Shane Branchcomb)

Stuttle, Pat Feb 20, 1877 on mt, orig rnd tin hopper, EX 650.00
Sun #1080, 1-lb challenge fast grinder, label, NM 155.00
Sun Success #25, rnd wood box, EX 375.00
Tillmann's Hawaiian Coffee, CI, wall mt, EX 275.00
Vandegrift, CI, side, hinged, brass tag, ca 1870, EX 475.00
Waddell A-17, CI, Sunflower design, wall mt, EX 350.00
Wardway, CI, glass hopper, wall mt, pinch adjust, EX 225.00
Woodruff & Edwards Elgin National, 12" wheels, EX 850.00
Wrightsville Hardware Co, Peerless #200, glass hopper, EX.........165.00
WW Weaver, PA box mill, hand dvtls, EX 250.00

Coin-Operated Machines

Coin-operated machines may be the fastest-growing area of collector interest in today's market. Many machines are bought, restored, and used for home entertainment. Older examples from the turn of the twentieth century and those with especially elaborate decoration and innovative features are most desirable.

The www.GameRoomAntiques.com website is an excellent source of information for those interested in coin-operated machines. Another source available is the Coin-Operated Collector's Association (www.coinopclub.org). See the Clubs, Newsletters, and Websites section for publishing information. Ken and Jackie Durham are our advisors; they are listed in the Directory under the District of Columbia.

Arcade Machines

Baby Jacks by Fields, pressed alum, EX 1,850.00
Baseball, gumball, w/penny return, 1950s, 16x9x8", rstr 495.00
Benedict Happy Home, fortune teller, ca 1905, rstr, 66" 3,850.00
Chicago Coin Goalee, hockey game, 1954, EX 3,450.00
Drop card machine, electric, EX..700.00
Egyptian Seeress 5¢, fortune teller, pnt plywood, 27", EX 700.00
Fortune, penny drop, rpt wood case, 1930s-40s, EX.....................675.00
Hi-Ball, ball flip, 1940s-50s, rstr 2,250.00
International Mutoscope, hand crank, metal trellis base, 53", +1 reel.. 2,250.00
Jr Deputy Sheriff Pistol Range, 1940s-50s, 62", EX....................1,250.00
Mercury Strength Tester, works 3 ways, rstr...............................1,850.00
Panama Digger, cast-alum marquee, 65", EX..............................4,675.00
Seeburg Coon Hunt, Ray-O-Lite shooting game, rstr.................3,900.00
Slezek 1¢ Scale, 1920-30, 81", EX 1,875.00
Swami 1¢ Fortune Teller, w/napkin dispenser, no cards, 9x9", EX orig.275.00
Williams Deluxe Batting Champ, pitch & bat, 1961, rstr 4,550.00
Williams Gridiron Football, 1968, rstr 2,995.00

Jukeboxes

The coin-operated phonograph of the early 1900s paved the way for the jukeboxes of the '20s. Seeburg was first on the market with an automatic eight-tune phonograph. By the 1930s Wurlitzer was the top name in the industry with dealerships all over the country. As a result of the growing ranks of competitors, the '40s produced the most beautiful machines made. Wurlitzers from this era are probably the most popularly sought-after models on the market today. The model #1015 of 1946 is considered the all-time classic and often brings prices in excess of $9,000.00.

AMI Rowe Tropicana JBM-200, 45 rpm, 1964, EX 1,995.00
Seeburg #147, 78 rpm, EX 2,995.00
Seeburg #161, 1958, rstr 7,295.00
Seeburg #201, 1958, rstr 7,295.00
Seeburg #222, 1959, rstr 6,800.00
Seeburg B, 1951, rstr..5,995.00
Seeburg C, Art Deco case, 1953, rstr...6,800.00
Seeburg R, Art Deco, 1954, rstr 7,995.00
Seeburg W, 1953, rstr...6,595.00
Speaker, Wurlitzer #4000 Star, 24" dia, VG 1,450.00
Wurlitzer #750, rstr..4,950.00
Wurlitzer #1015, 78 rpm, rstr..14,995.00
Wurlitzer #1100, holds 24 78 rpms, late 1940s, rstr 8,450.00

Pinball Machines

Bally Fireball, rstr...4,995.00
Bally Twilight Zone, rstr 4,995.00
Criss Cross, floor model, G 330.00
Farfalla 25¢, floor model, colorful graphics, EX............................300.00

Play Ball, 1 cent, plywood and steel with glass front, 16x12x5", NM, $850.00. (Photo courtesy Cowan's Auctions, Inc. on LiveAuctioneers.com)

Sega Independence Day, 1996, EX 3,595.00
Star 35¢ Sit Down Pinball, wooden case, 29", VG 360.00
United 10¢ Emp Bowling, 97x34", VG.......................................1,550.00
Williams Perky, rvpt bk glass scoreboard, ca 1950s, EX 875.00

Slot Machines

Many people enjoy the fun of playing a slot machine in their home. Antique slots have become very collectible. The legality of owning a slot machine is different in each state. Also beware of reproduction or re-manufactured slot machines.

Bally #809 5 Coin Play, fruit reels, 1968, rstr.............................2,500.00
Bally #856 25¢, 5-coin multiplier, 1974-75, rstr 2,000.00
Bally #873, criss-X fruit reels, 5-line, 1970, rstr 2,995.00
Bally #1091 Dollar, 3-coin multiplier, 1973, rstr.........................1,500.00
Bally #8000, 5-line play, 1980s, rstr...2,795.00
Bally Star Special (742 Money Honey) 25¢, 1964, rstr 2,500.00
Bally Stars & Bars, converted to free play, rstr.............................1,495.00
Jennings Deluxe Chief Silver Dollar w/Chinese front, 1947-48, rstr .. 7,495.00
Jennings Golden Nugget Standard Chief 25¢, 1945, rstr 6,595.00
Jennings Hunting, hunting scene w/2 Indians, late 1930s, rstr..4,495.00

Jennings Little Duke 1¢, w/side vendor, 1933, rstr.....................3,495.00
Jennings Little Duke 5¢, rare, rstr 4,495.00
Jennings Sportsman Golf Ball, rstr 12,995.00
Jennings Super Chief 25¢, orig pnt, 1937, EX 2,995.00
Mills Admiral Dewey Upright, ca 1899, rstr............................12,000.00
Mills Black Cherry 50¢, fish mouth coin entry, 1948, rstr 6,495.00
Mills Bonus 25¢, working marque, 1949, rstr...........................4,495.00
Mills Bursting Cherry 5¢, EX..2,495.00
Mills Brown Front Bursting Cherry 25¢, 1938-42, rstr.............. 2,995.00
Mills Castle Front 25¢, dbl jackpot, 1930s, rstr.......................2,595.00
Mills Castle Front 50¢ w/fish mouse coin entry, ca 1938, rstr....6,495.00
Mills Futurity, rstr 5,900.00
Mills Golden Nugget 25¢, blk or wht, rstr..............................2,495.00
Mills Golden Nugget 50¢, 1947, rstr.......................................2,995.00
Mills High Top 25¢, authentic-made rpl wood case/bk bonnet, rstr.2,495.00
Mills Operator Bell 5¢, quartersawn oak case w/alum face, VG .2,295.00
Mills Vest Pocket 5¢, hidden reel strips, 8" cube, rstr 650.00
Watling Rol-A-Top 5¢, ca 1936, rstr..6,995.00
Watling Rol-A-Top Checkerboard 5¢, 1947-51, rstr 6,495.00
Watling Treasury 5¢, M vendor front, 1934-35, rstr 8,595.00

Trade Stimulators

Banker 1¢, penny drop, EX..3,995.00
Baseball Atlas Indicator, penny drop, mahog case, w/score card, EX .1,850.00
Buckley Groetchen Cent-A-Pack, cigarette reel strips, 1935, EX rstr . 895.00
Cowber Cracker Jacks, 1898-1911, rstr w/new base...................4,750.00
Daval Cent-A-Smoke, cast alum case, ca 1936, VG orig 750.00
Daval Penny Pack, cigarette reel strips, 1939, EX rstr 795.00
Drobish Star Advertiser, cigar vendor oak case, ca 1897, rstr....2,450.00
Field's 5 Jacks 1¢, penny drop, oak case, 19", EX 1,450.00
Gem 1¢ by Garden City Novelty, lg gumball window, rpt, 1937.. 395.00
Griswald Star Wheel of Fortune, 5¢ drop, cigar vendor, 1902, EX. 1,350.00
Groetchen Ball Gum, fruit reel strips, 1930s, EX rstr 895.00
Hit the Target, gumball vendor, all metal, 1960s, rstr.................. 450.00
Mills Jumbo Success, ca 1900, rstr...7,850.00
Pace Cardinal, slot type, 1936, 12", EX....................................1,250.00
Puritan Bell, cash register shape, 1930s, VG orig......................1,650.00
Spino, 1¢ drop, winner every time, 1940s-50s, EX rstr 495.00
Wiz Ball, pnt steel & CI w/wooden base, marquee, 17", EX......... 600.00

Vendors

Vending machines sold a product or a service. They were already in common usage by 1900 selling gum, cigars, matches, and a host of other commodities. Peanut and gumball machines are especially popular today. Older machines made of cast iron are especially desirable, while those with plastic globes have little collector value. When buying unrestored peanut machines, beware of salt damage.

4-in-1, peanuts/candy, Deco style, 4-compartment, chrome, 1930s, EX .2,450.00
Adam's Tuti-Fruiti Gum, quartersawn case, 32", EX..................3,300.00
Advance 1¢, gumball, glass globe, 1920s, 14", rstr......................... 495.00
Advance Big Mouth 1¢, peanuts/candy, oval glass globe, ca 1920, rstr...495.00
Atlas Bantam 5¢, peanuts, tray base, 1940s, 11x10x8", rstr.......... 485.00
Baby Grand, all purpose, Project-OpView windows, ca 1951, 12", EX .195.00
Baseball 1¢, gumball, penny return feature, 1950s, 16x9x8", rstr . 575.00
Bluebird 1¢, gumball, rare penny return feature, 1920s, EX 875.00
Columbus A 1¢, hourglass shape, glass globe, 1920s, 16", rstr...... 675.00
Columbus M, glass globe, 1920s, 14", rstr 450.00
Dietz 5¢, gum packets, 1940s, 14x9x5", EX................................. 450.00
Ford 1¢, gumball, glass globe, alum base, 1930s-60s, 12", rstr....... 125.00
Freeport, Owl, CI w/wood base, 1910, 17", EX 4,950.00
Hawkeye 1¢, glass globe, 1940s, rstr.. 550.00

JH Moore, gumball, quartersawn oak case, 24", VG 4,125.00
Lions International 1¢, 2 glass globes, alum base w/decal, 1930s, rstr....650.00
Master, gumball, porc & cast alum, w/key, G............................ 295.00
Masters 1¢/5¢, emb casting, 15x8x8", rstr................................. 875.00
Northwestern #33, gumball, ca 1933, 15x6" dia, rstr.................. 495.00
Northwestern 1¢, peanuts, porc base, Deco style, 1930s, 15", EX . 495.00
Price Collar Buttons, CI & glass, 11", EX 1,450.00
Pulver Spearmint, gum, 1-column w/tab, 1950s, 26", rstr.......... 475.00
Pulver Yellow Kid 1¢, tab gum vendor, 1920s-30s, 21", EX...........1,475.00
Regal, polished alum, 1940s, rstr 195.00
Silver King 1¢, peanuts/candy, glass globe, 1940s, 11", rstr 295.00
Silver King Hot Nut 5¢, red hobnail glass top lights up, 1947, rstr .485.00
Vendor-Bar Lil' Abner, pnt steel w/litho, 24", EX....................1,045.00
Victor Topper 1¢, glass globe, 1940s-50s, 11", rstr 195.00
Victor V, metal globe, ca 1940, rstr 195.00
William Michaels Nat'l, gumball, 1910, 11", rstr........................ 875.00

A. R. Cole

A second generation North Carolina potter, Arthur Ray Cole opened his own shop in 1926, operating under the name Rainbow Pottery until 1941 when he adopted his own name for the title of his business. He remained active until he died in 1974. He was skilled in modeling the pottery and highly recognized for his fine glazes.

Vases, floor, each with two round openings resembling staring eyes (these are known as owl vases), earth tones with black interior, applied handle to the rear, unsigned, 19", pair $540.00. (Photo courtesy Leland Little Auction & Estate Sales Ltd. on LiveAuctioneers.com)

Ashtray, blk drips on brn, ca 1930, 4" dia 50.00
Basket, turq/bl/gr mottle w/sm drips, scalloped rim, twist hdl, 9½" ..75.00
Jar, apothecary, royal bl, lg split hdls, 1930s, 9" 130.00
Pitcher, cobalt/violet/gr/aqua/gr/wht splashes, #244, 11 1/4x5½".275.00
Teapot, turq satin, late 1950-62, 7" 40.00
Vase, brn mottle, lt bl ring at bottom, barrel shape, 5" 56.00
Vase, multi-toned matt, hairline/rim bruises, 17½", $250 to 350.00
Vase, rose gloss, neck-to-hip hdls, #276, 12¾" 130.00

Compacts

The use of cosmetics before WWI was looked upon with disdain. After the war women became liberated, entered the work force, and started to use makeup. The compact, a portable container for cosmetics, became a necessity. The basic compact contains a mirror and a powder puff.

Vintage compacts were fashioned in a myriad of shapes, styles, materials, and motifs. They were made of precious metals, fabrics, plastics, and in almost any other conceivable medium. Commemorative, premium, patriotic, figural, Art Deco, plastic, and gadgetry compacts are just a few of the most sought-after types available today. Those that are combined with other accessories (music/compact, watch/compact, cane/compact) are also very much in demand. Vintage compacts are an especially desirable collectible since the workmanship, design, techniques, and materials used in their execution would be very expensive and virtually impossible to duplicate today.

For more information we recommend *Ladies' Compacts of the 19th and 20th Centuries*; *Vintage Vanity Bags & Purses*; *Vintage and Contemporary Purse Accessories*; *Vintage Ladies' Compacts*; *Vintage & Vogue Ladies' Compacts*; and *The Estée Lauder Solid Perfume Compact Collection*, all by Roselyn Gerson. She is listed in the Directory under New York. Another excellent reference is *Mueller's Overview of American Compacts and Vanity Cases* by Laura M. Mueller. See Clubs, Newsletters, and Websites for information concerning the Compact Collectors' Club and their periodical publication, *Powder Puff*.

Agme, gold/silver-tone, dials on sides move center Paris scenes, 2x3" .. 150.00
Antonin of France, blk celluloid, eng/enamel lady's face, rnd, 3" .. 150.00
Atomette, brushed gold-tone w/crystal poodle, rnd, 2¾" 100.00
Cornucopia, gold-tone w/emb leaves, mirror/sifter/puff, 2x4" 425.00
DBF Co, bl enamel w/windmill scene, w/finger ring, chain & key, 2x3" ..200.00
DF Briggs, silver/gold-tone, gypsy w/crystal ball in center, 2x2¾" .. 85.00
Dorset, gold-tone, valentine w/I Love You script border, rnd, 2½". 70.00
Eisenberg Orig, gold-tone w/mc marquise & rnd stones, sq, 3" 150.00
Elgin Am, brn on gold-tone, Greek Key border, shield shape, 3x2" .60.00
Elgin Am, gold/silver-tone w/3 running deer, rect, 2¼x3" 55.00
Elgin Am, teardrop, gr enamel w/3-color lightning bolt, 3" 90.00
Estée Lauder, gold-tone, turq stone in lt & dk bl bull's-eye, 1½" 25.00

Estée Lauder, Lucidity, part of Dr. Albert Eschen's Mice collection, $225.00. (Photo courtesy Cruce Kodner Galleries on LiveAuctioneers.com)

Evans, silver-tone & blk enamel panels, pentagonal, w/chain, 2x2" ..120.00
Evans, silver-tone starburst design w/rhinestones in center, sq, 3" . 60.00
France, gr irid Lucite w/enamel lady on swing, rnd, 2½" 180.00
Germaine Monteil, gold-tone w/mobe pearl amid turq stones, rnd, 2" ..45.00
Italy, silver w/enameled ladies in a garden, mk 800, 3¼x3½" 540.00
KIGU, gold-plate w/mc bouquet on purple enamel, scalloped rim, rnd, 3" ..65.00
La Mode, silver-tone w/military wings on gold-tone sq, 1¾x2¾" ... 60.00
Lampl, blk enamel, gold-tone fr, slide-out comb, sq, 3" 160.00
Paul Flato, blk enamel/gold-tone/rhinestones, lipstick tube, 2½x2" .60.00
Rectangle, aqua enamel w/silver-tone gazelle, mirror, Evans, 3" .. 150.00
Rectangle, gold-tone w/rhinestone pave bar opener, Bonita, 3" 65.00
Rectangle, wht metal w/emb oval flowerpot, 2 mirrors, Lachere, 2".100.00
Roger & Gallet, gold-tone w/sunburst medallion, rnd, 3" 60.00
Square, gold-tone/gr enamel, snowflake/roses, La Mode, 2" 90.00
Square, tortoise enamel lid on silver-tone, thin, Bliss Bros, 2" 75.00
Stratton, gold-plate w/mc butterfly on lt bl enamel, thin, rnd, 3" .. 50.00
Stratton, gold-tone w/mc enamel Zodiac images on wht, rnd, 3" ... 65.00
Stratton, portrait of lady in '50s nightclub attire on gold-tone, rnd....100.00
Unmarked, amber Bakelite base w/red lid, rnd, ca 1940-50s, 3" 80.00
Unmarked, celluloid/Bakelite, ballerina in orange tutu on blk/wht, rnd, 2".400.00
Unmarked, Deco-style chrome w/blk & gold enamel, w/chain, 1920s, 3x1" ..265.00
Unmarked, gold-tone w/silver confetti Lucite, snake chain, 3x5x1" .70.00
Unmarked, silver-tone w/enamel pk & bl flowers on yel, w/chain, sq. 125.00
Unmarked, silver w/guilloche turq enamel, pk roses/ bl bows, rnd, 1½" .250.00
Volupté, gold-tone w/blk geometric Deco enamel, swing hdl, sq, 3" .. 55.00
Volupté, sterling silver w/raised flowers, vase & swirls, sq, 2½" 100.00

Consolidated Lamp and Glass

The Consolidated Lamp and Glass Company of Coraopolis, Pennsylvania, was incorporated in 1894. For many years their pri-

mary business was the manufacture of lighting glass such as oil lamps and shades for both gas and electric lighting. The popular 'Cosmos' line of lamps and tableware was produced from 1894 to 1915. (See also Cosmos.) In 1926 Consolidated introduced their Martele line, a type of 'sculptured' ware closely resembling Lalique glassware of France. (Compare Consolidated's 'Lovebirds' vase with the Lalique 'Perruches' vase.) It is this line of vases, lamps, and tableware which is often mistaken for a very similar type of glassware produced by the Phoenix Glass Company, located nearby in Monaca, Pennsylvania. For example, the so-called Phoenix 'Grasshopper' vases are actually Consolidated's 'Katydid' vases.

Items in the Martele line were produced in blue, pink, green, crystal, white, or custard glass decorated with various fired-on color treatments or a satin finish. For the most part, their colors were distinctively different from those used by Phoenix. Although not foolproof, one of the ways of distinguishing Consolidated's wares from those of Phoenix is that most of the time Consolidated applied color to the raised portion of the design, leaving the background plain, while Phoenix usually applied color to the background, leaving the raised surfaces undecorated. This is particularly true of those pieces in white or custard glass.

In 1928 Consolidated introduced their Ruba Rombic line, which was their Art Deco or Art Moderne line of glassware. It was only produced from 1928 to 1932 and is quite scarce. Today it is highly sought after by both Consolidated and Art Deco collectors.

Consolidated closed its doors for good in 1964. Subsequently a few of the molds passed into the hands of other glass companies that later reproduced certain patterns; one such reissue is the 'Chickadee' vase, found in avocado green, satin-finish custard, or milk glass. For further information we recommend *Phoenix and Consolidated Art Glass, 1926 – 1980*, by Jack D. Wilson. Our advisors for this category are Bruce Mueller and Gary Wickland; see Directory, Illinois.

Bird of Paradise, fan vase, gr wash, 6"... 165.00
Bird of Paradise, fan vase, pk wash, 10".. 475.00
Bittersweet, vase, bl-gr & orange on mg, 9½" 185.00
Bittersweet, vase, purple cased, 9½" 350.00
Bittersweet, vase, ruby stain on crystal, 9½" 150.00
Blackberry, umbrella vase, russet wash, rare, 18"........................... 900.00
Catalonian, candlestick (Spanish knobs), yel, ea 75.00
Catalonian, vase, amethyst, triangular top, 4" 36.00
Chickadee, vase, bl on mg, 6½" 85.00
Chickadee, vase, gr wash on crystal, 6½" 125.00
Chrysanthemum, vase, dk red, 12".. 450.00
Chrysanthemum, vase, gold on mg, 12" 125.00
Chrysanthemum, vase, ruby stain on crystal, metal surmount...... 200.00
Con-Cora, cookie jar, violets on mg, orig label, 9" 145.00
Dancing Nymph, lamp base, dk red, 20½" 725.00
Dancing Nymph, palace platter, clear/frosted, 16"........................ 900.00
Dancing Nymph, plate, frosted, 8¼" 100.00
Dancing Nymph, plate, reverse ruby stain, rare, 8¼" 250.00
Dancing Nymph, vase, bl on satin mg, 11½" 350.00
Dancing Nymph, vase, caramel on custard, w/label, 11½" 450.00
Dogwood, lamp, 3-color on satin mg.. 125.00
Dogwood, vase, gold highlights on glossy mg, 10½" 125.00
Dogwood, vase, yel cased, 10½".. 395.00
Dragon Fly, vase, gr & brn on satin mg, 6"..................................... 85.00
Dragon Fly, vase, gr cased, orig Martele label, 6" 225.00
Dragon Fly, vase, purple cased on 6" 250.00
Five Fruits, tumbler, gr wash, ftd.. 30.00
Floral, vase, bl & gr on mg, 9" 95.00
Floral, vase, ruby stain on crystal... 125.00
Hummingbird, powder jar, amethyst, 3" dia....................................225.00
Hummingbird, powder jar, purple wash, 5" 150.00
Hummingbird, vase, 3-color on satin custard, 5½" 135.00

Iris, jug, sepia wash.. 425.00
Katydid, vase, bl on satin mg, ovoid, 7" 165.00
Katydid, vase, gr & brn on mg, ovoid, 7" 180.00
Katydid, vase, gr & brn on satin custard, cylindrical, paper label, 8"..180.00
Line 700, bowl, fruit, Coronation Blue, 10" 225.00
Line 700, vase, dk red, 10" 695.00
Line 700, vase, gold on custard, 10" 300.00
Lovebird, banana boat, Reuben Blue reverse highlights on crystal, 14½".. 575.00
Lovebird, vase, bl on mg, 10½" 250.00
Olive, bowl, reverse bl highlighting (rare color), 8" 225.00
Olive, vase, gold highlights on glossy mg, 4" 125.00
Olive, vase, purple & gr on satin custard, 4" 125.00
Pine Cone, vase, purple cased, 6½" 295.00
Pine Cone, vase, reverse rose highlights on glossy custard 225.00
Poppy, vase, irid red & gold on glossy custard, rare, 10½" 375.00
Poppy, vase, purple cased 495.00
Regent Line, cookie jar (Florette), ash-rose pk on wht opal......... 195.00
Ruba Rombic, candleholder, lilac, ea 325.00
Ruba Rombic, finger bowl, lilac 225.00
Ruba Rombic, plate, salad, jade, 8" 245.00

Ruba Rombic, vase, green with overall opalescence, 6½", $1,100.00. (Photo courtesy Treadway Gallery on LiveAuctioneers.com)

Ruba Rombic, vase, Jade Gr, 9½" 2,400.00
Ruba Rombic, vase, smoky topaz, 9½" 1,600.00
Ruba Rombic, whiskey glass, jungle gr 225.00
Screech Owl, vase, sepia cased, 5¾" 250.00
Seagull, vase, orange highlights on satin custard, 11" 325.00
Seagulls, vase, reverse bl highlighting on mg, 11"........ 375.00
Tropical Fish, tray, ruby stain reverse highlights on crystal, 10" ... 395.00
Tropical Fish, vase, straw opal, 9"........................... 350.00

Conta & Boehme

The Conta & Boehme company was in business for 117 years in the quaint town of Poessneck, Germany (Thuringer district). Hand-painted dishes and pipe heads were their main products. However, in 1840, when the owner's two young sons took over the company, production changed drastically from dishes to porcelain items of almost every imaginable type.

For their logo, the brothers chose an arm holding a dagger inside a shield. This mark was either impressed or ink stamped onto the porcelain. Another mark they used is called the 'scissor brand' which looks just like it sounds, a pair of scissors in a blue or green ink stamp. Not all pieces were marked, many were simply given a model number or left completely unmarked.

England and the U.S. were the largest buyers, and as a result the porcelain ended up at fairs, gift shops, and department stores throughout both countries. Today their fairings are highly collectible. Fairings are small, brightly colored nineteenth-century hard-paste porcelain objects, largely figural groups and boxes. Most portray amusing if not risqué scenes of courting couples, marital woes, and political satire complete with an appropriate caption on the base. For more information we recommend *Victorian Trinket Boxes* by Janice and Richard Vogel, and their latest book, *Conta & Boehme Porcelain*, accompanied by a reprint of the original company product catalog dated 1912 – 1917, published by the authors.

Conta & Boehme often produced their porcelain items in several different sizes (sometimes as many as nine). When ranges are used in our listings, it is to accomodate these different sizes (unless a specific size is given). Values are for items with no chips, cracks, or repairs. Our advisors for this category are Richard and Janice Vogel; they are listed in the Directory under South Carolina.

Candleholders

Apple pickers, 7½", pr, $75 to 100.00
Black man on elephant, 2 lights, #8325, $150 to........... 175.00
Lady w/lute & man, Conta shield, #697, pr, $75 to 100.00
Man playing violin, girl dancing, #8306, pr, $100 to...... 125.00
Man w/nodding bird on shoulder, $75 to 100.00
Tree climbers, 7½", pr, $100 to 150.00

Cigar Holders

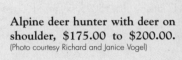

Alpine deer hunter with deer on shoulder, $175.00 to $200.00. (Photo courtesy Richard and Janice Vogel)

Frogs, singing, 1 playing piano, $100 to 125.00
Horse w/saddle, $75 to.. 100.00
Prince Otto von Bismarck & Napoleon III, $200 to.......... 300.00
Scottish lad sitting, holding sword, $175 to 250.00

Dresser Boxes

Lady holding layered skirt, $75 to 100.00
Lady holding purse, $75 to....................................... 100.00
Lady w/fan to her shoulder, $75 to 100.00
Lamp, $35 to 50.00

Fairings, Figurals

Attack, 2 children climbing cabinet for cookies, $125 to........ 200.00
Broken Hoop (The), blacksmith, boy, donkey, $150 to......... 200.00
Children's Meeting, 3 little girls, $125 to.................. 200.00
Courtship & Marriage, 2 cats (before & after), ea 400.00
Don't Awake the Baby, mother, daughter & baby, $300 to.......... 400.00
Sarah's Young Man, man hiding under table, $100 to 150.00

Figurines

Lady carrying lamb, lamb on ground, 10¼", $125 to 150.00
Lady riding horse sidesaddle, $200 to 250.00
Lovers w/umbrella, #1457, 8", $100 to 150.00
Lovers walking together, #1465, 7½", $100 TO........... 125.00
Rocking chair w/2 cats & girl sitting on rockers, $125 to.......... 150.00
Two boys pulling girl on a cart, $100 to 125.00

Figurines, Hanging

Cherub sitting on rim of boat w/oar, $50 to 75.00
Lady on swing, 8½", $500 to...................................... 600.00

Lady riding tricycle, #6342, 5¼", $50 to.................................... 75.00
Man sitting on half-moon shape hammock, $50 to 100.00
Sailor boy & girl w/fish, nets & baskets, pr, $75 to 125.00

Inkwells

Boys (2) fighting, $125 to 200.00
Child sitting on bed, putting on socks, $125 to 150.00
Inkwell, dog & cat on pillow, unmk 95.00
Erst Beten (first pray), mother & child at table, 7½", $300 to...... 400.00
Girl peering into mirror, c/s, #3221, $100 to 125.00
Girls (2) sitting, bird's nest on lap, $200 to.............................. 300.00
Table set for tea, ink pots in front, #3202, $75 to 100.00

Jardinieres

Boy falling off broken branch trying to feed birds, $175 to........... 200.00
Boy offering hand to sitting girl, #5095, 6", $75 to 125.00
Children (2) pulling egg-shaped cart, $125 to 150.00
Lady pushing lg basket on wooden dolly, $100 to 150.00
Lady sitting on shell cart pulled by 2 horses, 12½" L, $300 to...... 400.00
Man/lady standing beside well, sitting girl, #5095, 6", pr, $100 to .150.00

Matchstrikers

Boy & girl filling water containers from well, #4238, $125 to...... 150.00
Boy & girl playing w/hoops, #4192, pr, $125 to 150.00
Boy & girl w/dog, toys & basket (washday), pr, $150 to 200.00
Boy & girl w/roosters & feeding bucket, pr, $75 to 100.00
Boy & girl w/water pail & shovel, #4200, $75 to 100.00
Taking a Walk, dog dressed in hat & shawl w/purse, $100 to 150.00

Menu Holders

Boy carrying flag for menu, $125 to... 150.00
Boy holding & pointing to menu, #5216, $125 to......................... 150.00

Boy with a covered dish sitting next to menu, $125.00 to $150.00. (Photo courtesy Richard and Janice Vogel)

Frogs singing, 1 playing piano, $100 to 125.00
Girl standing w/fan & holding menu, #5207, $150 to 175.00

Napkin Rings and Placecard Holders

Napkin ring, child w/loincloth holding a glass, #5402, $75 to 100.00
Napkin ring, clown w/holder on his bk, #5401, $125 to............... 150.00
Napkin ring, simple ribbon tied w/bow on top, #5403, $35 to 75.00
Placecard, Asian couple holding fans, #3452/3453, $75 to 100.00
Placecard, cat on bk holding card holder, $125 to........................ 150.00
Placecard, child sitting holding lg fan, #3482, $75 to................... 100.00

Nodders

Card players, 2 men, 2 ladies, $400 to.. 500.00
Cat w/glass eyes, 6½" L, $250 to... 300.00

Chess players, man & lady, $200 to... 300.00
Lady juggling ball, head & hands nod, 9", $500 to 600.00
Man & woman, Asian, head/tongue/hands nod, #5380, 6¼", pr, $500 to...600.00

Salt Cellars

Clowns (3), s&p & mustard, #6241, $100 to............................... 150.00
Donkey pulling cart, s&p, #5778, $75 to 100.00
Girl sitting in wheelbarrow w/shovel, #5752, $50 to 100.00
Man, 3-legged, s&p & mustard, $75 to 100.00
Shell w/sea coral base, #2423, Conta shield, $75 to 100.00

Tobacco Boxes

Bulldog head, #2584, 5¼", $250 to... 300.00
Child sitting on chamber pot crying, #2572, 9", $600 to............. 700.00
Lady inside wine bbl filled w/grapes, #2552, 7", $150 to............. 200.00
Man & lady kneeling, Asian, #2395, 9¼", pr, $500 to................. 800.00
Owl w/glass eyes, #6009, 8", min...1,000.00

Trinket Boxes

Baby in highchair w/rattle, #2196, $75 to 100.00
Cat & dog playing, #2998, $75 to 100.00
Cherubs (2) on toe of shoe, kissing, #2986, $100 to 125.00
Child sitting in chair holding bowl, #2187, $75 to 100.00
Girl playing w/jack-in-the-box, #3673, $100 to........................... 125.00
Little Turk (A), boy w/water pipe, #3679, $150 to 175.00

Vases

Boy & girl reading books, #6688, pr, $75 to................................ 100.00
Boy/girl holding cone-shaped holder (vase), #6505/6, pr, $100 to...125.00

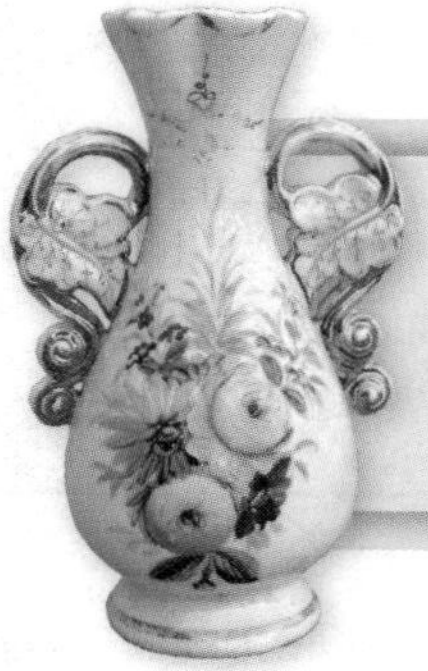

Flowers, hand painted, #1141, on two-handled vase, Conta shield, 6¼", $50.00 to $75.00. (Photo courtesy Richard and Janice Vogel)

Lady playing coffee grinder & bootjack man, 8", pr $150 to 200.00
Man & lady artists w/easels, #1174, 6½", pr, $125 to.................... 150.00
Man & lady, Art Nouveau, lg, ea, $250 to 300.00

Watch Stands

Blacksmith w/hammer & anvil, #2721, 5¼", $175 to 200.00
Cherubs (2) on toe of shoe, kissing, #2734, $125 to 150.00
Hand, lady's, holding watch holder, #2720, 6¾", $100 to............. 150.00
Horse w/saddle, #2716, 5½", $125 to.. 150.00
Joan of Arc (Columbia), shield, sword & crown, $300 to 400.00

Cookbooks

Cookbooks from the nineteenth century, though often hard to find, are a delight to today's collectors both for their quaint formats and printing methods as well as for their outmoded, often humorous views on nutrition. Recipes required a 'pinch' of salt, butter 'the size of an egg' or a 'walnut,' or a 'handful' of flour. Collectors sometimes specialize in cookbooks issued as advertising premiums. Especially desirable are the figurals that were shaped like a jar, a slice of bread, or some other form relative to the product. Others with unique features such as illustrations by well-known artists or references to famous people or places are priced in accordance. Cookbooks written earlier than 1874 are the most valuable and when found command prices as high as $200.00; figurals usually sell in the $10.00 to $15.00 range.

Our listings are for examples in near-mint condition. As is true with all other books, if the original dust jacket is present and in nice condition, a cookbook's value goes up by at least $5.00. Right now, books on Italian cooking from before circa 1940 are in demand, and bread-baking is important this year. Our advisor for this category is Charlotte Safir; she is listed in the Directory under New York.

Key:
CB — Cookbook
dj — dust jacket
hb — hardback/hardbound
pb — paperbound/paperback

Agate Iron Ware CB, L&G Mfg Co, pb, 1880, 36 pgs 80.00
All-Ways Preferable CB, Malleable Steel Range Mfg, pb, 1898, 96 pgs . 75.00
American Frugal Housewife, Mrs Childs, hb, 1836, 130 pgs, G ... 145.00
American Practical Cookery Book, JE Potter, hb, 1859, 319 pgs . 200.00
American Pure Food CB, M Hill Co, pb, 1899, 508 pgs, G............. 35.00
Appledore CB, Maria Parloa, Graves Locke & Co, hb, 1872....... 200.00
Ballet CB, Tanaquil Le Clercq, Stein & Day, hb w/dj, 1966, 416 pgs ... 175.00
Baron's CB, Paroutand & Watson, pb, 1900, 96 pgs 100.00
Bettina's Cakes & Cookies, LB Weaver & HC LeCron, hb, 1924 . 90.00
Betty Crocker's CB, Golden Press, hb in red cloth, 1972, 480 pgs . 55.00
Betty Crocker's Picture CB, hb, 1956, 472 pgs................................ 35.00
Buckeye Cookery & Practical Housekeeping, Wilcox, hb, 1877, 462 pgs. 150.00
Catering for Special Occasions, Fannie M Farmer, hb, 1911, 249 pgs....60.00
Common Sense in the Household, M Harland, Scribner, hb, 1881, 546 pgs..100.00
Culinary Gems: A Collection of Choice Recipes, E Squire, hb, 1884 .. 100.00
Dessert Lovers' Handbook, Eagle Brand, pb, 1973, 31 pgs.............. 10.00
Dr Price CB, Royal Baking Powder, pb, 1929 .... 15.00
Fall & Winter Menus & Recipes for 2 or 4 or 6, pb, 1935, 31 pgs.....6.00
Family & Householder's Guide, EG Storke, Auburn, hb, 1859, 288 pgs..250.00

Good Housekeeping Cook Book, Farrar & Rinehart Inc., Seventh Edition, 1942 – 1944, broken binding, $10.00 to $20.00. (Photo courtesy The Auction House on LiveAuctioneers.com)

Good Housekeeping International CB, Official World's Fair..., hb, 1964. 37.50
Jell-O Pudding Idea Book, General Foods, pb, 1968, 44 pgs.............. 3.00
Larkin Housewives' CB, Larkin Co, hb, 1923................................. 25.00
Let's Start Cooking, Garel Clark, illus K Elgin, spb, 1951 .... 34.00
Lucky CB for Boys & Girls, Scholastic, oversized pb, 1969, 48 pgs..18.00
McNess Recipes From Around the World CB, Furst-McNess, ca 1930, 64 pgs... 16.00
New New Can Opener CB, Poppy Cannon, hb, 1968, 314 pgs 14.00
Pyrex Prize Recipes, Corning Glass Works, hb, 1953, 128 pgs 20.00
Quantity Cookery, Lenore Richards & Nola Treat, hb, 1925, 200 pgs... 8.00
Ralston Mother Goose Recipe Book, Ralston Purina Co, pb, 1919, 16 pgs .45.00
Reader's Service Bureau CB, R Berolzheimer, hb, 1941, 816 pgs ... 15.00
Recipes From the Old South, Martha L Meade, hb w/dj, 1961 ...... 24.00

Savannah CB, Harriet Ross Colquitt, 1961, spiral hb, 186 pgs 35.00
Treasury of Great Recipes, Mary & Vincent Price, hb, 1965........ 125.00
US Navy CB, Division of Naval Militia Affairs, pb, 1908, 62 pgs . 20.00
Women's Favorite CB, Annie E Gregory, hb, 1902, 610 pgs 55.00
Young Wife's Own CB, Mrs Jane Warren, Grand Union Tea Co, hb, 1890 .40.00

Cookie Cutters

Interest in collecting cookie cutters has steadily risen over the last few years and tinsmiths are pumping out cutters of all shapes and sizes to meet the demands of collectors and catalog companies. Purchase prices are rising right along with the demand. People collect cutters for different reasons, sometimes for the shape or color, or because 'Grandma used to have one of those.'

In Europe the carved mold was used to press an intricate design into dough to make the first 'cakes,' more commonly known in America as 'cookies.' Molds began appearing with metal inserts outlining the carved mold, which cut and pressed a design into the dough. This led to a metal outline which cut only. In America the most widely used implement for shaping cookies is the cookie cutter. Early cutters were made of scrap metal by tinkers traveling in wagons among the farms. The lady of the home had cutters designed to a specified shape of their liking, often birds, horses, dogs, rabbits, flowers, or other common shapes. This would make her cookies unique from the other ladies in the area. American metal outline cutters were made with flat metal backs and sometimes handles. These cutters have crude spot soldering to join the metal. In the nineteenth century the backs changed to the outline of the cutter manufactured and cut by machine. Some cutters are 2½" to 3" deep. The Dover Company is one of the oldest known manufacturers, dating from around 1869. Other later names were Davis Baking Powder, Fries, and Kreamer.

Cutters were issued as advertising premiums which were made by a manufacturer for a specific company. The company name was often printed on the cutter and made in a particular shape. These are highly sought after by collectors. Cutters with the name of the maker only are not considered premium cutters; however, cutters with a manufacturer name on them are also valuable. In the 1920s the aluminum cutters became popular and are still being made today. Colored aluminum and wooden handles also came at this time.

In the 1940s plastic cutters emerged. After World War II molding technology made it possible to make a variety of shapes and colors. Because during wartime the red plastic was sometimes hard to obtain, cutters were made in other colors. Some manufacturers that made only red cutters were forced to make their cutters in other colors for a short period of time. These were limited and thus highly collectible. Values for cutters with irregular colors are much higher than the same shape and manufacturer in a red color. Therefore, it is wise to know the makers of only one color of cutter versus the manufacturer of multiple colors. Occasionally, one-of-a-kind cutters appear on the market that are mistakes, with mixed colors or without handles. These are known as Maverick cutters. There is also renewed interest in hand-crafted cookie cutters with and without backs, handles, or braces. These are of a variety of metals. Some are replicas of the early American cutters.

Setting a value on a cookie cutter requires being able to tell its approximate age and whether it was manufactured or hand crafted, and taking into account the design, condition, scarcity, and desirability of the cutter. The material is also important: cooper, tin, aluminum, or plastic. In addition, having original packaging will also increase the value. Collectors will pay a high price for a children's bake set with cutters in the original box. Sometimes cutters are worth more individually than in sets. A few older cutters are still manufactured today, so the older may not be the more valuable. Metal cutters with intricate interior designs carry high prices. Campaign cutters are very collectible, especially with original boxes. Hand-crafted cutters are often marked with the maker's mark such as their initials or name; however, if that maker sells to a catalog the maker's name may change to the seller's name. Hand-crafted replica cutters (copied from early American cutters) will have a much smoother solder and a better quality of metal. Most cutters sell from $3.00 to $30.00 with unusual or intricate designs bringing $40.00 to $150.00. Warriors on horses and intricate figures can go much higher. We have noticed a change to lower prices this year, perhaps due to a slower economy. However, the demand and the number of collectors are still rising.

For information about the Cookie Cutter Collectors Club, see the Clubs, Newsletters, and Websites section in the back of the book. Our advisor for Cookie Cutters is Connie Teeters; she is listed in the Directory under Florida.

Metal

Card shapes, spade, club, heart, dmn, 2", set.................................... 25.00
Card shapes, spade, club, heart, dmn, alum, wooden hdls, orig box, set.... 10.00
Chick, children's cutter, self hdls, late 1920s, ea $5, set 25.00
Chimney sweep, 8x6" 650.00
Christmas, reindeer/Santa/tree/etc, alum, Chilton Ware 15.00
Comicooky cutter, A to F set, Pillsbury... 25.00
Figure w/weapon, on horse 75.00
For All Party Occasions, orig box, set of 12 .... 50.00
Hansel & Gretel, Educational Products Co, 1947, set of 5............. 25.00

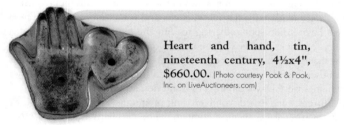

Heart and hand, tin, nineteenth century, 4½x4", $660.00. (Photo courtesy Pook & Pook, Inc. on LiveAuctioneers.com)

Man & woman, backs, metal bent arms, Pflatzgraff 150.00
Rabbit, Formay shortening, Swift & Co, 6x3", 1930s..................... 15.00
Round cutter, Egg Baking Powder, egg form hdl 150.00
Rumford, biscuit or cookie cutter, emb, closed pipe-type hdls........ 20.00
Seagram's 7 in oval, advertising.. 15.00
Troll, advertising premium, Wrigley Gum, alum, self hdl, Mirro, 1965... 25.00
Women, bird & fish, alum, riveted hdls, ea...5.00

Plastic

Angel/heart/rocking, Stanley Products, 1971, set of 7 .... 20.00
Boy & girl twins, bl, Avon, 1965...6.00
Gingerbread boy, gr, Betty Crocker 4.00
Gingerbread boy, Miller Co, w/orig pat number 10.00
Mickey Mouse characters, Loma, Ft Worth TX, set of 4 .... 35.00

Cookie Jars

The appeal of the cookie jar is universal; folks of all ages, both male and female, love to collect 'em! The early '30s' heavy stoneware jars of a rather nondescript nature quickly gave way to figurals of every type imaginable. Those from the mid to late '30s were often decorated over the glaze with 'cold paint,' but by the early '40s underglaze decorating resulted in cheerful, bright, permanent colors and cookie jars that still have a new look 50 years later.

Stimulated by the high prices commanded by desirable cookie jars, a broad spectrum of 'new' cookie jars are flooding the marketplace in three categories: 1) Manufacturers have expanded their lines with exciting new designs specifically geared toward attracting the collector market. 2) Limited editions and artist-designed jars have proliferated. 3) Reproductions, signed and unsigned, have pervaded the market, creating uncertainty among new collectors and inexperienced dealers. One of the most troublesome reproductions is the Little Red Riding Hood jar marked McCoy. Several Brush jars are being reproduced, and because the old molds are being used, these are especially deceptive. In addition to these reproductions, we've also been alerted to watch for cookie jars marked Brush-McCoy made from molds that Brush never used. Remember that none of Brush's cookie jars were marked Brush-McCoy, so any bearing the compound name is fraudulent. For more information on cookie jars and reproductions, we recommend *The Ultimate Collector's Encyclopedia of Cookie Jars* by Fred and Joyce Roerig, our advisors for this category; they are listed in the Directory under South Carolina.

Albert Apple, Pitman-Dreitzer & Co, $50 to 75.00
Alpo Dan the Dog, USA, $50 to.. 60.00
Baby Elephant, unmk, Am Bisque, $125 to 150.00
Baseball, Omnibus Collections International, $30 to..................... 35.00
Big Bird, Newcor, $35 to... 45.00
Bluebird Love Nest, Lefton #7525, 11", $150 to 175.00
Bossie Cow, Lefton, #6594, $125 to 150.00
Bud, Army man, brn, RRPCo, 1942-43, 12", $375 to.................. 400.00
Cat w/Bell, yel w/wht spots, OCI Omnibus Korea label, $25 to..... 35.00
Clown, Maurice of California, $150 to 175.00
Coke Six-pack, mk Coca-Cola c 1996, Enesco, $35 to................... 40.00
Cookie Crock, brn w/wht decor, mk Hull Ovenproof USA, $20 to.. 25.00
Cookie Thief, Fitz & Floyd, 1976, $50 to....................................... 60.00
Corn, yel & gr, Terrace Ceramics USA #4299, $35 to 45.00
Country Sunflower Hampshire Hog, FF Taiwan label, Fitz & Floyd, $30 to....40.00
Covered Wagon, Marcia of California, $20 to 25.00
Cow on Moon, Doranne of California, $275 to 325.00
Dog, tongue out, mk 458, California Originals, $30 to................... 35.00
Dorothy & Toto, Star Jars, $325 to 375.00
Duck, William H Hirsch Mfg Co, 1961, $125 to 150.00
Elephant, ABCO, bank in lid, USA, $175 to 200.00
Elephant, Sierra Vista, $125 to... 150.00
Elsie, unmk Pottery Guild (+) 400.00
Ernie & Bert Fine Cookies, California Originals, #977, 1978, $350 to... 375.00
Fred Flintstone, Vandor c 1989, $125 to 150.00
French Girl, Lefton, #1174, 9", $225 to 250.00
Garfield on Stack of Cookies, Enesco, 1978, $250 to 275.00
Gingham Dog, Brayton Laguna, unmk, $375 to 400.00
Gnome, Holiday Designs 40.00
Grandfather Clock, Treasure Craft, Made in USA, $35 to............. 45.00
Halo Boy, DeForest of California, 1956, $700 to 725.00
Harley-Davidson Gas Tank, Taiwan, $75 to 85.00
Hen & Chick, Hull, #968, 1940 11½", $375 to 425.00
Hi Diddle Diddle, Robinson-Ransbottom, gold-trimmed, #317, $325 to.. 375.00
Jack-'O-Lantern w/Bat, Exclusively for Lotus, 1989, $40 to........... 50.00
Joe Carioca (Three Caballeros), Walt Disney USA, Leeds China, $400 to .425.00
Katy the Korn Top Pig, Haeger, $100 to 125.00

Lion with Gold Mane, California Originals, $45.00. (Photo courtesy Fred and Joyce Roerig)

Little Angel, Brush, 1956, 11¾", (+), $675 to 750.00
Little Boy Blue, Hull, #968, 1940, 12½", min 1,500.00
Majorette, Am Bisque, USA, $350 to 375.00
Mammy, Brayton Laguna, 13", (+), min 900.00
Mary Poppins, Walt Disney Pro, min 1,000.00
Michael Jordan & Bugs Bunny Space Jam, TM & c 1996 WB, $100 to... 125.00
Mickey Mouse Car, Disney, Japan, 1978, $400 to 425.00
Mohawk Indian, Am Bisque, unmk, Mohawk Carpet, (+), min 1,000.00
Mother Goose, Doranne of California, 1960s, $225 to 250.00
Mushrooms, Sierra Vista Ceramics...USA c 1957 .... 40.00
Nick at Night Television, Treasure Craft for Nickelodeon, $350 to...400.00
Panda Bear, Goebel, gr lid, $70 to 80.00
Peasant Woman, Department 56, $60 to 75.00
Pelican, Fitz & Floyd, 1980, $50 to 60.00
Peter Pan, Brush, gold trim, USA, 1956, rare, $750 to 800.00
Peter, Peter, Pumpkin Eater, Robinson-Ransbottom, #1502, $250 to . 275.00
Pig Goody Bank, DeForest of California, 1965, $375 to 400.00
Pig w/Straw Hat, Am Bisque, USA, (+), $125 to 150.00
Pinocchio, William H Hirsch Mfg Co, 1960, $275 to 300.00
Plaid Teddy, w/Christmas Tree, FF label, Fitz & Floyd, 1991, $50 to.60.00
Puppy, Treasure Craft, USA, $35 to 45.00
Rabbit in Hat, brn w/mc details, DeForest of California c USA, $35 to. 40.00
Ricky Raccoon, Cookie Bandit (Shirttales), Hallmark Cards, Inc, 1981, $75 to.95.00
Road Hog, pig on red motorcycle, mk Clay Art..., 1995, $45 to 55.00
Rocking Horse, Lane 125.00
Rosa Rabbit, Treasure Craft, Made in Mexico, $30 to 40.00
Snoopy Doghouse, Benjamin & Medwin c '58 '66 UFS, Taiwan, $35 to. 45.00
Snow White, California Originals, #866, Walt Disney Prod, min. 1,500.00
Snowman, Los Angeles Pottery, #10H, $85 to 95.00
Stagecoach, mk Sierra Vista Ceramics Pasadena Calif..., 1956, $150 to.175.00
Strawberry Shortcake, Am Greetings Corp, MCML XXXIII, $250 to. 275.00
Sweet Pickles Alligator, Enesco, 1981, $75 to 95.00
Sylvester Head w/Tweety, Applause 95.00
Telephone, Cardinal, #311, $50 to 60.00
Train, smiling face, Sierra Vista California, $50 to 60.00
Vegetable House, mk Dept 56 1990, $50 to 60.00
Woody, Am Roadside, Omnibus Collections International, 1993, $55 to...65.00

Susie Cooper

A twentieth-century ceramic designer whose works are now attracting the attention of collectors, Susie Cooper was first affiliated with the A.E. Gray Pottery in Henley, England, in 1922, where she designed in lustres and painted items with her own ideas as well. (Examples of Gray's lustreware is rare and costly.) By 1930 she and her brother-in-law, Jack Beeson, had established a family business. Her pottery soon became a success, and she was subsequently offered space at Crown Works, Burslem. In 1940 she received the honorary title of Royal Designer for Industry, the only such distinction ever awarded by the Royal Society of Arts solely for pottery design. Miss Cooper received the Order of the British Empire in the New Year's Honors List of 1979. She was the chief designer for the Wedgwood group from 1966 until she resigned in 1972. After 1980 she worked on a free-lance basis until her death in July 1995.

Key:
CW — Crown Works   GP — Gray's Pottery

Bowl, cereal, Patricia Rose, 6" 22.50
Bowl, serving, White Flute, w/lid, ca 1950, lg................................ 45.00
Bowl, soup, Autumn Leaf, 8" 35.00
Bowl, vegetable, Endon, 9" 50.00
Bowl, vegetable, Whispering Grass, 9".. 40.00

Coffeepot, White Flute, unmk, ca 1950, 8"................................... 50.00
Coffee/tea set, architectural view w/pillars/arches, 8" pot+cr/sug. 485.00
Creamer, White Flute, ca 1950.. 20.00
Creamer, Wild Strawberry, 8-oz.. 28.00
Cup/saucer, coffee, Persian Bird, can form, ca 1929..................... 150.00
Cup/saucer, demi, fruit (various), 2", 5", set of 6.......................... 90.00
Cup/saucer, Endon 28.00
Cup/saucer, Whispering Grass 25.00
Cup/saucer, Wild Strawberry, flat 25.00
Jug, bird reserve w/silver o/l, bulb, GP, 5".................................... 95.00
Jug, Cubist pattern, Paris shape, 4¼"... 280.00
Jug, Gloria Lustre, HP foliage, GP, 4"... 145.00
Jug, mc bands on wht, GP, 8"... 40.00
Jug, Moon & Mountains, GP, 4"... 400.00
Lamp base, Nosegay, yel trim, CW, 8".. 130.00
Mustache cup & saucer, barber theme, CW, 2x4", 6"..................... 235.00
Plate, dinner, Dresden Spray #1005 .... 25.00
Plate, dinner, Patricia Rose, 10" 35.00
Plate, luncheon, Endon, 9".. 20.00
Plate, luncheon, Patricia Rose, 9".. 22.00
Plate, salad, Autumn Leaf, 8" 18.00
Plates, dinner, swirling foliate design, CW, 11", 15 for 125.00
Sandwich set, flowers/foxglove, red rim, GP, 1928, tray+6 plates. 350.00
Teacup, gray w/pk abstracts, pk rim, CW 65.00
Teapot, Glen Mist 35.00
Teapot, White Flute, squat, ca 1950, 5" 45.00

Tea set, including pot, creamer and sugar bowl, underplate, and four cups and saucers, $780.00. (Photo courtesy DuMouchelles on LiveAuctioneers.com)

Vase, bl-lined trumpet flowers & gr leaves on cream, 6½" 200.00
Vase, dbl band of grooved decor on cream, ca 1935, 8".............. 270.00
Vase, Jazz Age design, HP, 7½" 380.00
Vase, squirrels in branches on yel ochre, ovoid, 11" 325.00

Coors Rosebud

The firm that became known as Coors Porcelain Company in 1920 was founded in 1908 by John J. Herold, originally of the Roseville Pottery in Zanesville, Ohio. Though still in business today, they are best known for their artware vases and Rosebud dinnerware produced before 1939.

Coors vases produced before the late '30s were made in a matt finish; by the latter years of the decade, high-gloss glazes were also being used. Nearly 50 shapes were in production, and some of the more common forms were made in three sizes. Typical colors in matt are white, orange, blue, green, yellow, and tan. Yellow, blue, maroon, pink, and green are found in high gloss. All vases are marked with a triangular arrangement of the words 'Coors Colorado Pottery' enclosing the word 'Golden.' You may find vases (usually 6" to 6½") marked with the Colorado State Fair stamp and dated 1939.

Please note: Prices for Coors, like many other collectibles, have taken a downward turn. Our prices here reflect those adjustments for today's current market. Listings below are for Rosebud dinnerware. Our advisor for this category is Rick Spencer; he is listed in the Directory under Utah.

Apple baker, w/lid 45.00
Ashtray 185.00
Baker, lg 40.00
Baker, tab hdls, 7" 20.00
Bean pot, hdls, lg, 5x7" 70.00
Bean pot, sm 65.00
Bowl, batter, lg 65.00
Bowl, batter, sm 45.00
Bowl, cream soup, 4" 22.00
Bowl, fruit, lg 45.00
Bowl, mixing, 3-pt 35.00
Bowl, mixing, 6-pt 50.00
Bowl, mixing, hdls, 1½-pt 40.00
Bowl, oatmeal 22.00
Bowl, pudding, 2-pt 40.00
Bowl, pudding, 7-pt 75.00
Cake knife 85.00
Cake plate, 11" 30.00
Casserole, 9", min 100.00
Casserole, Dutch, w/lid, 1¾-pt 50.00
Casserole, Dutch, w/lid, 3¾-pt 72.00
Casserole, Fr, w/lid, 3¾-pt 45.00
Casserole, triple service, w/lid, lg, 7-pt 55.00
Cup/saucer 50.00
Egg cup 55.00
Honey pot, w/lid & spoon 300.00
Honey pot, w/lid, no spoon 80.00
Loaf pan 40.00
Muffin set, w/lid, rare 200.00
Pitcher, water, w/stopper 120.00

Pitcher, with lid, 5", $125.00. (Photo courtesy Eirik N. Huset)

Plate, 7¼" 10.00
Plate, 9¼" 23.00
Platter, 12x9" 38.00
Ramekin 45.00
Saucer, 5½" 5.00
Shakers, either syle, sm or lg, pr 50.00
Shirred egg dish 25.00
Sugar bowl, w/lid 40.00
Sugar shaker 60.00
Teapot, 2-cup, rare 150.00
Teapot, 6-cup 125.00
Tumbler, ftd 125.00
Water server, cork stopper, 6-cup 120.00

Copper

Handcrafted copper was made in America from early in the eighteenth century until about 1850, with the center of its production in Pennsylvania. Examples have been found signed by such notable coppersmiths as Kidd, Buchanan, Babb, Bently, and Harbeson. Of the many utilitarian items made, teakettles are the most desirable. Early examples from the eighteenth century were made with a dovetailed joint which was hammered and smoothed to a uniform thickness. Pots from the nineteenth century were seamed. Coffeepots were made in many shapes and sizes and, along with mugs, kettles, warming pans, and measures, are easiest to find. Stills ranging in sizes of up to 50-gallon are popular with collectors today. Mary Frank Gaston, our advisor, has compiled a lovely book, *Antique Brass & Copper*, with many full-color photos which we recommend for more information. See also Arts and Crafts; Roycroft; Stickley; and other specific categories.

Bathtub, EX patina, full sz 1,950.00
Birdbath, 26x16" dia 72.50
Boiler, 2 hdls, oval, polished, 12x25" 30.00
Bowl, brass hdl, polished, no mk, 4½x8¼" 36.00
Cauldron, EX patina, 19th C, 15x24" 185.00
Firewood bucket, hammered, EX patina, Townshends Ld, 13x16" .. 480.00
Fish steamer, appl hdls, w/lid, 19th C, 2x9x4" 42.50
Jardiniere, appl brass hdls, 19x25" dia 395.00
Kettle, gooseneck spout, appl hdl, polished, lg 215.00
Olla, hand formed w/peened finish, swing hdl, EX patina, 1940s, 5x10" . 215.00
Pitcher, tin lined, unmk, 17x11" 36.00
Plates, hammered, EX patina, 10", 6 for 65.00
Pot, bulb, EX patina, 24x27½" dia 120.00
Pot, hand-hammered, tin lined, riveted hdls, Gallard Paris, 18x24" dia . 500.00
Soup pot, hammered, 2 loop hdls, tinned int, ca 1860, 8x9", G .. 475.00
Teakettle, dvtl seams, brass lid, swing hdl, 8x13½" 180.00
Teakettle, dvtl, swing hdl, brass finial, dents, A&I Sheriff, 7" 485.00

Teakettle, gooseneck spout, C-handle, dome lid with brass finial, canted dovetailed seams, minor dents, stamped John Getz, 12½x14x10", $2,500.00. (Photo courtesy Conestoga Auction Company on LiveAuctioneers.com)

Tray, geometric silver inlay, 15½" 55.00
Washtub, hdls, polished, 20" dia 240.00
Washtub, rect, 2 appl hdls, 7x25x16" 215.00
Watering can, emb rings, strap hdl 36.00

Coralene Glass

Coralene is a unique type of art glass easily recognized by the tiny grains of glass that form its decoration. Lacy allover patterns of seaweed, geometrics, and florals were used, as well as solid forms such as fish, plants, and single blossoms. (Seaweed is most commonly found and not as valuable as the other types of decoration.) It was made by several glasshouses both here and abroad. Values are based to a considerable extent on the amount of beading that remains. Our readers should know that recent coralene has raised bead decoration that is at least 10 millimeters thick. For more information, we recommend *The Collector's Encyclopedia of American Art Glass* by John A. Shuman III. See also Mt. Washington Glass.

Bowl, dk bl w/wht floral & geometric pattern, ca 1900, 6½" 275.00
Bowl, peachblow w/yel seaweed, dk red int, everted cut rim, 7" ... 400.00
Cup, pk to wht w/yel seaweed, wht hdl, 3¾x3" 60.00
Vase, bl & wht vertical bands w/yel seaweed, waisted neck, 9" 360.00
Vase, lemon-cased w/wildflowers/butterfly, ruffled rim, 8" 325.00
Vase, peachblow w/yel seaweed, flared neck, 8¼x4" 235.00

Vase, red to wht herringbone MOP, seaweed pattern, mk Patent, 8¾" . 780.00
Vase, rose pk to wht w/yel seaweed, sq top, ca 1910, 2¾" 240.00
Vase, seaweed coralene, Webb, bl, 7" 450.00
Vase, seaweed coralene, Webb, pk, 5" 400.00
Vase, shaded pk w/yel seaweed, bulb base, 9" 250.00
Vase, yel to wht w/yel seaweed, bulb w/flared neck, 7" 180.00

Cordey

The Cordey China Company was founded in 1942 in Trenton, New Jersey, by Boleslaw Cybis. The operation was small with less than a dozen workers. They produced figurines, vases, lamps, and similar wares, much of which was marketed through gift shops both nationwide and abroad. Though the earlier wares were made of plaster, Cybis soon developed his own formula for a porcelain composition which he called 'Papka.' Cordey figurines and busts were characterized by old-world charm, Rococo scrolls, delicate floral appliqués, ruffles, and real lace which was dipped in liquefied clay to add dimension to the work.

Although on rare occasions some items were not numbered or signed, the 'basic' figure was cast both with numbers and the Cordey signature. The molded pieces were then individually decorated and each marked with its own impressed identification number as well as a mark to indicate the artist-decorator. Their numbering system began with 200 and in later years progressed into the 8000s. As can best be established, Cordey continued production until sometime in the mid-1950s. Boleslaw Cybis died in 1957, his wife in 1958.

Due to the increased availability of Cordey on the internet over the last few years, values of the more common pieces have fallen off. All items in our listings are considered to be in mint condition unless noted otherwise. Our advisor for this category is Sharon A. Payne; she is listed in the Directory under Washington.

Union solider on drum base, 13", $95.00. (Photo courtesy Sharon A. Payne)

#155, lamp, little girl figure.. 95.00
#300/#301, man & lady, 16", pr $125 to 175.00
#303, man, plumed hat, ff, 16" 95.00
#304/#305, Grape Harvesters, 15", pr $125 to 175.00
#312, bust of lady in pk shawl w/flowers exposed, mk MB Cybis, 8" .. 75.00
#313, bust of lady, sgn MB Cybis.. 75.00
#324R, mallard, 1940s, 14" 100.00
#325, Chinese wood duck, intricate base, EX colors, rare 175.00
#326, Chinese duck, 13" 145.00
#339, rooster, vibrant colors, 14½" 175.00
#504, lady, gray & bl dress, w/basket of grapes, 16" 95.00
#624, c/s, appl pk roses, leaves on cup 35.00
#852, wall decor, nosegay, experimental................................. 65.00
#861, wall sconces w/roses, pr 85.00
#909, clock, bird on roses at top, scrolled, 14" 95.00
#1027, centerpiece planter, lg swan..................................... 150.00
#1047, vase, rtcl top w/appl flower band, 12", EX 60.00

#1949, bust of lady, drilled for lamp, 7" 60.00
#4027, lady w/parasol, 8" 90.00
#4034, lady in lt bl dress w/pk roses, matching hat, ff, 8" 85.00
#4049-P, lady, 10"... 85.00
#4074, gentleman, lace shirt neck & cuffs, 13" 125.00
#4128, lady in lacy gown, curls, dbl bustle, 10½" 95.00
#5002, bust of lady in pk w/roses at base & in hair, 5" 45.00
#5005, bust of lady in pk w/bl roses at base & in hair, 6" 40.00
#5009, bust of lady, bl Fedora-style hat, 6" 40.00
#5011, bust of lady in wht w/lg collar, gold rose at base & hair, 6". 45.00
#5014, bust of lady, 6" 40.00
#5020, bust of man in pk w/lg wht curls, 2 roses at base, 6"........... 60.00
#5025, bust of lady w/lace shawl, 6" 45.00
#5027, bust of lady w/bow on hat, rose on dress, 7", NM................ 40.00
#5028, lady, ff, blond ringlets, Jr Colonial group, 6¾" 40.00
#5034, Raleigh, bust of man, gr shirt, blk vest, 8"..................... 70.00
#5036, bust of lady in silver gown, bl hat w/pk roses, 8½" 65.00
#5042, Vict man, bl coat & pk breeches, 11"............................. 75.00
#5045, girl w/water jug, 10" 65.00
#5047/#5048, man & lady, she w/grapes/jar, he w/flowers, 11", pr. 125.00
#5051, bust of lady in cream dress, bl ribbon at neck, bl hat w/roses 75.00
#5054, bust of lady in wht w/roses at base & in hair, 9" 75.00
#5059, bust of Vict lady (3/4), 9½" 75.00
#5077, woman praying, 13" 90.00
#5084, Madame DuBarry in bl & pk, 11" 95.00
#5091, man holds coattail wide as if to bow, 10½" 55.00
#5138, bust of lady w/bl bow on dress & bl Fedora hat, Papka curls, 6" .. 40.00
#6037, box w/roses and cherubs.. 110.00
#6046, ashtray 10.00
#7028, wall shelf, Art Nouveau nude w/cornucopia, 8x6½" 85.00
#7032, candlesticks, pk roses, 7½", pr................................. 75.00
#7033, vase, wide mouth, 9"... 35.00
Candlesticks, appl flowers at base, 7¼", M, pr......................... 85.00
Confederate soldier on drum base, 13".................................. 95.00
Dish, Cupid among bed of roses w/lav shawl, gold trim, 8½x6".... 110.00
Lamp, lady in kimono, 11¼" figure, 24" overall 90.00
Lamps, ladies' high-button shoe, appl flowers, brass base, 30", pr. 125.00

Corkscrews

The history of the corkscrew dates back to the mid-1600s, when wine makers concluded that the best-aged wine was that stored in smaller containers, either stoneware or glass. Since plugs left unsealed were often damaged by rodents, corks were cut off flush with the bottle top and sealed with wax or a metal cover. Removing the cork cleanly with none left to grasp became a problem. The task was found to be relatively simple using the worm on the end of a flintlock gun rod. So the corkscrew evolved. Endless patents have been issued for mechanized models. Handles range from carved wood, ivory, and bone to porcelain and repoussé silver. Exotic materials such as agate, mother-of-pearl, and gold plate were also used on occasion. Celluloid ladies' legs are popular.

For further information, we recommend *The Ultimate Corkscrew Book* and *Bull's Pocket Guide to Corkscrews* by Donald Bull, our advisor for this category. He is listed in the Directory under Virginia. For information on the Just for Openers club, see the Clubs, Newsletters, and Websites section. In the following descriptions, values are for examples in excellent condition, unless noted otherwise.

2-finger celluloid ivory hdl, mid sz (3-4½"), $50 to...................... 60.00
3-finger pull (eyebrow hdl spanning 2¼-3¼"), unmk, $5 to 25.00
Abyssinian type w/threaded tube, dbl hdls................................ 78.00
Advertising, beer, Nifty, $10 to 50.00

Barrel (closed), continually trn hdl, chrome, Italy, $30 to 40.00
Barrel, chromed, closed, hdl mk Italy, $20 to................................. 34.00
Barrel, perpetual type, mk Dico Wakefield Mass Pat Pend, $250 to . 400.00
Bow, folding type w/corkscrew & foil cutter, $75 to 150.00
Can opener combination, mini, 3", $35 to..................................... 50.00
Carter's Ink, folding, Pat 1894.. 18.00
Clough's 1876 Pat, mk Williamson's on wire wrap, 3" hdl, $25 to . 35.00
Clough's 1899 oak hdl, wire terminates in button above worm, $40 to .50.00
Codd type, boxwood hdl, J&W Roper of Birmingham, $100 to... 150.00
Columbus, metal hdl mk Langbein Germany, $75 to 90.00
Double-action, wood, Copex Made in France, $10 to 20.00
Double-lever, 1880 English Pat by Wm Baker, England, $1,000 to. 1,200.00
England, 4-finger pull, w/button, ca 1895 .... 27.50
England, ebonized wood hdl, thick disk, 1880s............................. 50.00
England, polished steel peg & worm, ca 1810, 4½" 130.00
Figural, anchor, friction-fit sheath covers worm, HMS Victory, $20 to..30.00
Figural, Bar Bum, pnt alum or bronze, $40 to 50.00

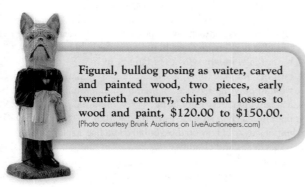

Figural, bulldog posing as waiter, carved and painted wood, two pieces, early twentieth century, chips and losses to wood and paint, $120.00 to $150.00.
(Photo courtesy Brunk Auctions on LiveAuctioneers.com)

Figural, Mannekin Pis, holding worm w/1 or 2 hands, ea $10 to.... 50.00
Figural, monk's head lifts to expose corkscrew, $30 to 60.00
Flynut fixed to fr, J Perille Depose Paris/Helice JHP Depose, $50 to .. 80.00
Flynut, brass colored, hourglass bbl, Spain, $50 to........................ 60.00
Flynut, brass, Edwin Jay Made in Italy, $10 to 20.00
Frame, ivory or bone hdl, unmk, mini, $100 to 300.00
Frame, Ornate cast metal w/spring & wood hdl, $200 to 300.00
Frame, rococo design w/locking roll-over hdl, $300 to 500.00
Germany, spring over shaft, ca 1895, VG, $20 to 80.00
Happy Face, ca 1935, 10".. 75.00
Italy, swivel-collar type, NP brass, VG 15.00
London Rack, rack & pinion actions, unmk English, 1800s, $150 to . 250.00
Mini, folding bow, plain, folded: ¾-1¾", $20 to 40.00
Mini, fr type w/ivory or bone hdl, $100 to 300.00
Perfume, tiger head, Birmingham 1896, $400 to........................... 500.00
Picnic, wood sheath, rare, $200 to 300.00
Pocket folder, So-Ezy, Made in USA Pat Pend, $40 to 50.00
Pocket, silver w/various hdls, English or Dutch, 19th C, $600 to... 2,500.00
Prong puller, Magic Cork Extractor, Pats 1879 & 1892, $700 to...1,000.00
Rack & pinion, Four Poster, King's Screw, bone-top, hdl, $800 to. 1,200.00
Rosewood hdl w/brass shank, English, early 19th C, 6x5" 120.00
Roundlet, machined & eng NP w/threaded case, $150 to 250.00
Roundlet, silver threaded case slides apart & forms hdl, $150 to . 350.00
Sardine key, w/folding fork, $150 to... 200.00
Single-lever, Lund & Hipkins, single worm, 1854, $100 to.......... 250.00
Single-lever, Tucker, Pat 1878, $1,800 to....................................3,000.00
Slide-out worm, German or Fr version of Jansen Pat, $150 to 250.00
Spring, Richard Recknagel's 1899 German Pat, diagonal guide, $250 to. 300.00
Staghorn hdl, mk sterling cap, 7½" 85.00
T-hdl, bone, ivory, or brass, direct pull, mini, 1-2", $30 to 200.00
T-hdl, metal, fancy design w/cork-gripping teeth, $150 to 250.00
T-hdl w/button, wood, $75 to... 200.00
US Hollweg 1891 Pat, Pabst Milwaukee advertising 150.00

US Williamson 1897 Pat Bullet, copper finish, early..................... 80.00
US, brass band & boar's tooth hdl, 6" 85.00
Waiter's friend, Davis Pat w/knife blade on top of hdl, $150 to ... 200.00
Waiter's friend, Liftmaster, chrome body, $15 to........................... 25.00
Waiter's friend, Universal, 1906 Am Pat by H Noyes, $30 to 50.00
Weir's Pat 12804 25, Sept 1884, VG bronze finish 125.00
Williamson's Don't Swear, Catalin sheath, $25 to.......................... 50.00

Cosmos Glass

Cosmos, sometimes called Stemless Daisy, is a patterned glass tableware produced from 1894 through 1915 by Consolidated Lamp and Glass Company. Relief-molded flowers on a finely crosscut background were painted in soft colors of pink, blue, and yellow. Though nearly all were made of milk glass, a few items may be found in clear glass with the designs painted on. In addition to the tableware, lamps were also made.

All prices are for pieces in very good condition. Some roughness or 'fleabites' around the edges of most pieces (e.g. lamp globes, top of the covered butter dish) are acceptable, except for the tumblers where they severely reduce their value. Any cracks or significant chips reduce the values considerably. These are average 'selling' prices; some dealers may ask as much as 20% to 30% more but will often come down to close a sale. Our advisors for this category are Michael A. and Valarie Bozarth (info@BeauxArtsUSA.com). They are listed in the Directory under New York.

Bottle, cologne, w/stopper, rare, 4¾" 275.00
Butter dish, 5x8" 180.00
Butter dish, underplate only 45.00

Condiment set, salt, pepper, and mustard on glass stand, 7x6", $325.00 to $400.00. (Photo courtesy Forsythes' Auctions, LLC on LiveAuctioneers.com)

Creamer, 5" 90.00
Lamp, base only, 7" 105.00
Lamp, mini, 7" 290.00
Lamp, mini, base only, 3½".. 65.00
Lamp, w/globe, 16".. 425.00
Pickle castor, fr mk Toronto, rare 690.00
Pitcher, milk, 5" 250.00
Pitcher, water, 9".. 190.00
Shakers, w/orig lids, 2½", pr... 130.00
Spooner, 4" 95.00
Sugar bowl, open.. 90.00
Sugar bowl, w/lid... 165.00
Sugar shaker, rare 350.00
Syrup pitcher, rare, 6½" 325.00
Tumbler, 3¾" 55.00
Water set, pitcher (9") w/6 tumblers...525.00

Cottageware

You'll find a varied assortment of novelty dinnerware items, all styled as cozy little English cottages or huts with cone-shaped roofs; some may have a waterwheel or a windmill. Marks will vary. English-made Price Brothers or Beswick pieces are valued in the same range as those marked Occupied Japan, while items marked simply Japan are considerably less pricey. All of the following examples are Price Brothers/Kensington unless noted otherwise.

Bank, dbl slot, 4½x3x5" 80.00
Bell, min 60.00

Biscuit jar, wicker handle, 9½" to top of handle, base: 6x5", $45.00 to $60.00. (Photo courtesy Premier Auction Center on LiveAuctioneers.com)

Bowl, salad 50.00
Butter dish, $50 to 65.00
Butter dish, cottage int (fireplace), Japan, 6¾x5", $65 to 80.00
Butter dish, oval, Burlington Ware, 6" 60.00
Butter dish, rnd, Beswick, England, w/lid, 3½x6" 75.00
Butter pat, emb cottage, rect, Occupied Japan 20.00
Chocolate pot, 9½", $85 to 135.00
Condiment set, 3-part cottage on shaped tray w/appl bush, 4½" 75.00
Condiment set, mustard, 2½" s&p on 5" hdld leaf tray 75.00
Condiment set, mustard pot, s&p, tray, row arrangement, 6" 45.00
Condiment set, mustard pot, s&p, tray, row arrangement, 7¾" 45.00
Cookie jar, pk/brn/gr, sq, Japan, 8½x5½" 60.00
Cookie jar, wicker hdl, Maruhon Ware, Occupied Japan, 6½" 80.00
Cookie jar, windmill, wicker hdl, $145 to 165.00
Cookie jar/canister, cylindrical, 8½x5", $85 to 125.00
Cookie/biscuit jar, Occupied Japan, 6½" 80.00
Covered dish, Occupied Japan, sm 35.00
Creamer, windmill, Occupied Japan, 2⅝" 25.00
Creamer/sugar bowl, 2½x4½" 40.00
Cup/saucer, 2½", 4½" 35.00
Cup/saucer, chocolate, str-sided cup, 3½x2¾", 5½" 35.00
Demitasse pot, 6x6¼", $80 to 110.00
Egg cup set, 4 (single) on 6" sq tray 65.00
Gravy boat & tray, rare, $250 to 275.00
Hot water pot, Westminster England, 8½x4" 50.00
Marmalade, 4" 45.00
Marmalade & jelly, 2 conjoined houses, 5x7" 75.00
Mug, 3⅞" 55.00
Pin tray, 4" dia 22.00
Pitcher, lg flower on hdl 100.00
Pitcher, tankard, rnd, 7 windows on front, $80 to 120.00
Platter, oval, 11¾x7½" 60.00
Reamer, windmill, Japan 150.00
Sugar box/butterdish, roof as lid, 6½" L 50.00
Teapot, 6½", $60 to 65.00
Teapot, Keele Street, w/cr/sug bowl 65.00
Teapot, Occupied Japan, 6½" 45.00
Teapot, Ye Olde Fireside, Occupied Japan, 9x5", $70 to 85.00
Tea set, Japan, child's, serves 4 .... 165.00
Toast rack, 3-slot, 3½" 75.00
Toast rack, 4-slot, 5½" 75.00
Tumbler, Occupied Japan, 3½", set of 6 .... 65.00

Coverlets

The Jacquard attachment for hand looms represented a culmination of weaving developments made in France. Introduced to America by the early 1820s, it gave professional weavers the ability to easily create complex patterns with curved lines. Those who could afford the new loom adaptation could now use hole-punched pasteboard cards to weave floral patterns that before could only be achieved with intense labor on a draw-loom.

Before the Jacquard mechanism, most weavers made their coverlets in geometric patterns. Use of indigo-blue and brightly colored wools often livened the twills and overshot patterns available to the small-loom home weaver. Those who had larger multiple-harness looms could produce warm double-woven, twill-block, or summer-and-winter designs.

While the new floral and pictorial patterns' popularity had displaced the geometrics in urban areas, the mid-Atlantic, and the Midwest by the 1840s, even factory production of the Jacquard coverlets was disrupted by cotton and wool shortages during the Civil War. A revived production in the 1870s saw a style change to a center-medallion motif, but a new fad for white 'Marseilles' spreads soon halted sales of Jacquard-woven coverlets. Production of Jacquard carpets continued to the turn of the century.

Even earlier, German weavers in the eighteenth century made double-weave coverlets in a style of weaving called Beiderwand that produced a two-layer fabric from a single set of warp threads with patterns created by selecting threads at specific intervals that tied the layers together. Most are quite colorful, and patterns were often very elaborate.

Rural and frontier weavers continued to make geometric-design coverlets through the nineteenth century, and local craft revivals have continued the tradition through this century. All-cotton overshots were factory produced in Kentucky from the 1940s, and factories and professional weavers made cotton-and-wool overshots during the past decade. Many Beiderwand and Jacquard-woven coverlets have dates and names of places and people (often the intended owner — not the weaver) woven into corners or borders.

Note: In the listings that follow, examples are blue and white and in excellent condition unless noted otherwise. When dates are given, they actually appear on the coverlet itself as part of the woven design.

Key: mdl — medallion

Jacquard

Beiderwand, bird/swag border, Mathias Klein, 1846, OH, 82x97" .950.00
Beiderwand, birds w/young, Christian & Heathen border, 1-pc, 86x82" .715.00
Beiderwand, eagle/branches/foliage/roses, red/bl/wht, 2-pc, 90x74" ...400.00
Beiderwand, floral mdls w/trees/crowned lions/swords border, 76x86" .. 3,725.00
Beiderwand, floral mdls/grapevine borders, 4-color, 2-pc, 1859, 86x78" .925.00
Beiderwand, floral/dmn mdls/bird/foliage, 4-color, sgn/1854, 71x84" .. 2,350.00
Beiderwand, mdls/grapevines, red/bl/aqua/cream, 2-pc, sgn/1859, 78x86" ...960.00
Beiderwand, roses/baskets/birds, red/bl/tan, 2-pc, OH/1850, 90x76" ... 400.00
Beiderwand, roses/rosettes/grapevines, 4-color, 2-pc, 92x76"+fringe... 575.00
Beiderwand, roses/stars/fruit baskets, red/gr/gray/natural, 91x86" ..1,300.00
Beiderwand, stars/mdls, birds & tree border, Peace & Plenty, 2-pc 490.00
Birds/flowers/triple border, 4-color, single weave/2-pc, 92x89" 175.00
Capitol buildings/monuments/foliage, gr/rust, 2-pc, OH, 84x87", VG.. 200.00
Eagles/stars/borders, 2-pc, sgn/1849, 88x82"+fringe 460.00
Floral mdl amid strawberry vines, bl/gr/red, dbl weave, sgn/1850, 75". 1,100.00
Floral mdl, floral/foliate borders, 2-pc, dbl-weave, 90x80" 475.00
Floral mdls (12 lg+6 sm), 2-pc, Delhi 1839, 93x74" 600.00
Flowers/foliage/leaves, 2-pc/dbl weave, IN/1845, 84x77" 300.00
Geometric floral on stripes, turq/gr/red/bl, sgn/1840, 96x84", VG.1,560.00
Geometric floral, eagle & shield corners, dbl weave, sgn/1834, 80x91" ..1,680.00
Geometrics/trees, wool/cotton, 2-pc, early 1800s, 94x76" 300.00
Rose mdl, bird border, red/bl/natural, 2-pc, PA/1834, 85x62" 635.00

Overshot

Diamonds & triangles, red/navy bl/olive-amber/natural, 2-pc, 91x77" . 500.00
Geometric floral w/Pine Tree border, bl/natural, reversible, 92x68" . 360.00
Geometric floral, dk gr/cream, J Brosney/D Ginrich, 1840, 95x73". 450.00
Geometric grid, navy/gold/natural, 2-pc, EX color rstr at top, 92x90" .. 425.00
Geometric, dk gr/wht, 2-pc, VA, 96x72" 425.00
Monk's Belt variant, red/bl/natural, 2-pc, fringe, 92x77" 435.00
Optical, dk & lt bl, 2-pc, fringe on 3 sides, 86x70" 300.00
Stars w/a Table, blk/natural, 2-pc, fringe, 90x68" 180.00
Sunrise, dk bl/cream, 2-pc, lt wear, 92x72" 300.00

Cowan

R. Guy Cowan opened a pottery near Cleveland, Ohio, in 1913, where he made tile and artware on a small scale from the natural red clay available in the area. He developed distinctive glazes, necessary to cover the dark red clay body. After WWI and a temporary halt in production, Cowan moved his pottery to Rocky River just west of Cleveland where he made a commercial line of artware utilizing highly fired white clay porcelain. Although he acquiesced to the necessity of mass production, every effort was made to ensure a product of highest quality and artistic design. Fine artists, among them Waylande Gregory, Thelma Frazier, A. Drexel Jacobson, and Viktor Schreckengost, designed pieces which were often produced in limited editions of 500, 100, 50, 25, and some as few as 10 pieces. Most all of the pieces were marked 'Cowan' or 'RG Cowan' with impressed stamps, but some — mainly lamps — also had applied foil or paper labels. Later in 1930, a secondary production line called Lakeware was produced for florist shops. From original Cowan Pottery catalog pages most all pieces were assigned shape numbers (see shape # when known in listings below) but rarely were those numbers ever placed on the pieces themselves. Many of the pottery's finest works were produced in the final year of production as the designers and artists were free to create unique pieces and sculptures outside the normal production items, many of which today sell for well into the thousands of dollars. Falling under the pressures of the Great Depression, the pottery closed its doors in 1931.

For more information, we recommend *The Collector's Encyclopedia of Cowan Pottery*, by our advisors, Tim and Jamie Saloff. They are listed in the Directory under Pennsylvania.

Bookends, boy & girl, arts/crafts style, ivory, Wilcox, 6½", pr 350.00
Bookends, elephants sitting upright deco/angular, ivory, Postgate, 6½", pr... 1,000.00
Bookends, elephants, push/pull deco/angular, caramel/tan, Postgate, 4¾", pr.. 650.00
Bookends, elephants, rounded on stepped base, Oriental Red, Postgate, 7", pr. 1,500.00
Bookends, fish, Oriental Red, 4⅝", pr 550.00
Bookends, horse kicking, matt blk, Gregory, 9", pr 1,500.00
Bookends, king/queen, matt blk w/gold trim, Gregory, 10", pr.. 1,000.00
Bookends, monks, sitting x-legged reading open book, matt gr, 6½", pr. 750.00
Bookends, polar bears, eating fish, ivory, Postgate, 6", pr 1,500.00
Bookends, rams/goats butting heads, ivory, Gregory, 7½", pr........ 850.00
Bookends, rams/goats butting heads, matt blk, Gregory, 7½", pr . 1,500.00
Bookends, Sunbonnet girls, arts/crafts style, antique gr, 7½", pr .. 350.00
Bookends, toucan/pelican, #E564, matt blk/bronze, Jacobson, 8½", pr... 3,800.00
Bookends, unicorn/deer, foliage, Gregory, 7", pr 750.00
Bowl, console, #763, ivory w/pk int, 3x16½x9" 75.00
Bowl, low console, #B4, Oriental Red, Gregory, 3x11x15" 150.00
Bowl, low console, waves design, antique gr, Gregory, 2¾x17x9" . 250.00
Bowl, mini cabinet, #514, orange lustre, 2x3½" 60.00
Bowl, molded rnd, imitates hand mold, #B827, 2-tone blues, 3x11".......... 275.00
Bowl, octagon, #B5B, hand decor, brn/yel/bl, 3x8" 300.00
Bowl, rnd flared lip, bl pearlized swirling glaze, 2¼x10¼" 150.00
Bowl, rnd, #B12, Egyptian bl crackle, 2½x10" 75.00

Bowl, scalloped rim, sit or stand-up design, #689, antique g, 3x8½x8".. 120.00
Bowl, tiered pyramid design, matt gr & blk 2-tone, Baggs, 5¼x8".1,800.00
Candlesticks, Byzantine, 3 angels, #746, salmon crackle, 9¼", single 350.00
Candlesticks, circular wave design, #751, ivory, 4¾", pr................ 85.00
Candlesticks, low flared design, #692, ivory, 2¼", pr 35.00
Candlesticks, marlins/sea serpents, antique gr, Gregory, 8", pr ..1,200.00
Candlesticks, nude entwined in vines, #745, ivory, Cowan, 9½", pr... 1,250.00
Candlesticks, Rowfant Club, groundhog shape, matt gr, Wilcox, single, 9".1,600.00
Candlesticks, unicorn/deer, caramel glaze, Gregory, 6x6", pr 350.00
Candlesticks, Viking ship prow design, #777, gr, 4", pr 50.00
Charger/plaque, Arabesque, #X10B, guava & blk, Cowan, 11¼"........... 800.00
Charger/plaque, Atlanta, #778, bl/cream/sienna, Gregory, 13".............. 1,750.00
Charger/plaque, Seascape, pearlized bl, Frazier, 11½" 780.00
Charger/plaque, sports plate, golfer, hand decoratd, Schreckengost, 11¼".1,200.00
Charger/plaque, Thunderbird, #739, Egyptian bl crackle, Blazys, 15½"..750.00
Decanter, king, standing, #X13, ivory, Gregory, 12" 675.00
Figurine, flamingo, shelf/mantel base, #D2, azure bl, Gregory, 11" 650.00
Figurine, flamingo, shelf/mantel base, #D2, ivory, Gregory, 11" 550.00
Figurine, Pierette, #792, ivory, Anderson, 8¼" 650.00
Figurine, Pierette, #792, russet/salmon crackle, Anderson, 8¼" ... 850.00
Figurine, Spanish dancer, female, #793, hand decor, Anderson, 8½".. 950.00
Figurine, Spanish dancer, female, #793, ivory, Anderson, 8½" 750.00
Figurine, Spanish dancer, male, #794, ivory, Anderson, 8¾" 750.00
Flower frog, deer w/antlers, #903, poly glaze, Gregory, 11"............. 1,250.00
Flower frog, deer, caramel, Gregory, 8¾" 750.00
Flower frog, deer, #F905, ivory, Gregory, 8¼" 550.00
Flower frog, deer, Wildwood stag, #926, ivory, Gregory, 13½"............. 1,750.00
Flower frog, flamingo, #D2F, Oriental Red, Gregory, 11¾" 800.00
Flower frog, nude bending backwards, #709, ivory, Cowan, 7½"........... 700.00
Flower frog, nude diver, #683, ivory, Cowan, 8" 1,000.00
Flower frog, nude marching girl, #680, ivory, Cowan, 8" 350.00
Flower frog, nude repose, #712, ivory, Cowan, 6½" 390.00
Flower frog, nude scarf dancer, #686, ivory, Cowan, 7" 350.00
Flower frog, nude w/arm stretched to sky, #F812X, ivory, Cowan, 10½"............. 850.00

Flower frog, nude with arm stretched to sky, #F812, ivory, Cowan, 14½", $1,850.00. (Photo courtesy Tim & Jamie Saloff Collection/tim.saloff@verizon.net)

Flower frog, nude w/wreath, #721, ivory, Cowan, 10" 600.00
Flower frog, Oriental Lotus Girl, Cowan, 11" 1,200.00
Flower frog, Pan on toadstool, #F9, ivory, Gregory, 9" 900.00
Flower frog, swan, #F7, ivory, Gregory, 11½" 1,500.00
Flower frog, swirl dancer, #720, ivory, Cowan, 10" 1,500.00
Flower frog, twin entwined dbl nudes, #685, ivory, Cowan, 7½" 500.00
Lamp base, Art Deco cvd designs, #821, gr, pottery portion 8⅜"............. 180.00
Lamp base, Aztec man warrior, foliage, Gregory, pottery portion 13" . 1,500.00
Lamp base, Aztec man warrior, ivory, Gregory, pottery portion 13" .1,200.00
Lamp base, cat, deco/angular, ivory, Gregory, pottery portion 13". 480.00
Lamp base, king, sitting, ivory, Gregory, pottery portion 9½".......550.00
Lamp base, moth on both sides, bl luster, pottery portion 13" 350.00
Nut dish/compote, Pierrot, #788, various colors, Anderson, 3" 125.00
Pwt, elephant, rounded on sq base, #D3, ivory, Postgate, 4¾" 350.00
Pwt, elephant, rounded on sq base, #D3, Oriental Red, Postgate, 4¾"............. 500.00

Sculpture, Antinea, matt blk, Jacobson, 14" 7,200.00
Sculpture, bird on wave, #749A, Egyptian bl crackle, Blazys, 12" .. 1,500.00
Sculpture, Chinese horse, Egyptian bl crackle, Ralph Cowan, 9"..1,800.00
Sculpture, Guilia, matt blk, Jacobson, 10" 4,800.00
Sculpture, head of girl, ivory, Gregory, 16"............................... 3,000.00
Sculpture, head of girl, matt blk, Gregory, 16" 3,750.00

Sculpture, horse, Egyptian blue crackle, Schreckengost, 7¾", $6,000.00. (Photo courtesy Tim & Jamie Saloff Collection/tim.saloff@verizon.net)

Sculpture, Introspection, bird, Maltese falcon-like, matt blk, Jacobson, 8¼" .2,500.00
Sculpture, LaReveuse, matt blk, Jacobson, 12" 10,000.00
Sculpture, Mary, terra cotta, Postgate, 10¼x14½" 6,000.00
Sculpture, Nautch dancer, silver, Gregory, 17½" 5,500.00
Sculpture, Nautch dancer, wht/blk shadows, Gregory, 17½" 5,500.00
Sculpture, Persephone, #D6, ivory, Gregory, 15" 3,000.00
Sculpture, Russian dancer/accordian, #757-760, ivory crackle, Blazys, 8½"..850.00
Sculpture, Russian dancer/tambourine, #757-760, ivory crackle, Blazys, 9"..850.00
Sculpture, torso of a nude, terra cotta, Gregory, 17"..................3,500.00
Sculpture, winged women, orig, ivory, Blazys, 27¼" 5,000.00
Sculpture, woman's head, orig, terra cotta, Martin, 13½"..........8,000.00
Sculpture, Woodland Nymph, ivory, Gregory, 14"....................3,000.00
Statue, Congo Head by Waylande Gregory, blk & bronze, sgn & mk, 14¾" ..4,600.00
Tea tile/trivet, girl's head, Flemish bl, 6" 150.00
Tea tile/trivet, vines & flowers, ivory, 6½" 150.00
Vase, Amazon, nudes, hand decor, #V78, brn & tan, Frazier, 10"..2,800.00
Vase, bulb pot, #V99, Egyptian bl crackle, Schreckengost, 6½"............. 400.00
Vase, bulb pot, #V38, Egyptian bl & blk, Atchley, 6½"................1,200.00
Vase, Chinese bird, #V747, Egyptian gr crackle, Cowan, 11¼" 750.00
Vase, flared lip, #V932, Feu Rouge, 8"................................... 225.00
Vase, flared lip, variegated red/orange/brn/yel, 6" 300.00
Vase, Grecian urn, #V47, crystalline gr, Baggs, 12¼"................2,900.00
Vase, hdld form, Egyptian gr crackle, Schreckengost, 5½" 450.00
Vase, Lake Erie/waves & boats, turq, 10" 360.00
Vase, Logan award, #649B, antique gr, Cowan, 8¼" 175.00
Vase, Logan award, #649B, Egyptian bl crackle, Cowan, 8¼" 220.00
Vase, Michelin Man/ringed design, antique gr, Cowan, 5".......... 275.00
Vase, seahorse, #715A, mottled pk, 7" 65.00
Vase, squirrel, #V19, April gr, Gregory, 8½" 960.00
Vase, squirrel, #V19, pearlized bl, Gregory, 8½" 1,500.00
Vase, star/leaf, #V32, foliage, Gregory, 10½"........................... 420.00
Vase, traditional form, jet gloss blk, 4" 150.00
Vase, traditional form, Oriental Red, 8" 240.00
Vase, waterfall, #V77, hand decor in maroons, Bogatay, 4¾".............. 650.00

Cracker Jack

Kids have been buying Cracker Jack since it was first introduced in the 1890s. By 1912 it was packaged with a free toy inside. Before the first kernel was crunched, eager fingers had retrieved the surprise from the depth of the box — actually no easy task, considering the care required to keep the contents so swiftly displaced from spilling over the side! Though a little older, perhaps, many of those same kids still are looking — just as eagerly — for the Cracker Jack prizes. Point of sale, company collectibles, and the prizes as well have over the years reflected America's changing culture. Grocer sales and incentives from around the turn of the twentieth century — paper dolls, postcards, and song books — were often marked Rueckheim Brothers (the inventors of Cracker Jack) or Reliable Confections. Over the years the company made some changes, leaving a trail of clues that often helps collectors date their items. The company's name changed in 1922 from Rueckheim Brothers & Eckstein (who had been made a partner for inventing a method for keeping the caramelized kernels from sticking together) to The Cracker Jack Company. Their Brooklyn office was open from 1914 until it closed in 1923. The first time the sailor Jack logo was used on their packaging was in 1919. The sailor image of a Rueckheim child (with red, white, and blue colors) was introduced by these German immigrants in an attempt to show support for America during the time of heightened patriotism after WW I. For packages and 'point of sale' dating, note that the word 'prize' was used from 1912 to 1925, 'novelty' from 1925 to 1932, and 'toy' from 1933 on.

The first loose-packed prizes were toys made of wood, clay, tin, metal, and lithographed paper (the reason some early prizes are stained). Plastic toys were introduced in 1946. Paper wrapped for safety purposes in 1948, subjects echo the 'hype' of the day — yo-yos, tops, whistles, and sports cards in the simple, peaceful days of our country, propaganda and war toys in the '40s, games in the '50s, and space toys in the '60s. Few of the estimated 15 billion prizes were marked. Advertising items from Angelus Marshmallows, their second bestselling product, are also collectible. Checkers Popcorn Confection turned out to be stiff competition for the Cracker Jack Co., and to solve the problem they purchased the popcorn division in August 1926 and sold both Cracker Jack and Checkers until about 1950. When no condition is indicated, the items listed below are assumed to be in excellent to mint condition. 'CJ' indicates that the item is marked. Note: An often-asked question concerns the tin Toonerville Trolley called 'CJ.' No data has been found in the factory archives to authenticate this item; it is assumed that the 'CJ' merely refers to its small size. For further information see *Cracker Jack Toys, The Complete, Unofficial Guide for Collectors*, by Larry White. Our advisor for this category is Harriet Joyce; she is listed in the Directory under under Florida. Also look for the Cracker Jack Collector's Association listed in the Clubs, Newsletters, and Websites section.

Key: CJ — Cracker Jack

Dealer Incentives and Premiums

Badge, pin-bk, celluloid, lady w/CJ label on bk, 1905, 1¼" 75.00
Blotter, CJ Angelus Marshmallows & Checkers Popcorn, early 1920s, 2x6" .125.00
Blotter, CJ question mk box, yel, 7¾x3¾"................................. 185.00
Book, pocket, riddle/sailor boy/dog on cover, RWB, CJ, 1919........ 14.00
Book, Uncle Sam Song Book, CJ, 1911, ea............................. 18.00
Business card, lg, Rueckheim, 3x5" 25.00
Corkscrew/opener, metal plated, CJ/Angelus, 3¾" tube case.......... 22.00
Jigsaw puzzle, CJ or Checkers, 1 of 4, 7x10", in envelope.............. 35.00
Mask, Halloween, paper, CJ, series, 10" or 12", ea.................... 28.00
Mirror, oval, Angelus (redhead or blond) on box 50.00
Pen, ink, w/nib, tin litho bbl, CJ 300.00
Pencil top clip, metal/celluloid, tube shape w/pkg........................ 220.00
Puzzle, metal, CJ/Checkers, 1 of 15, 1934, in envelope, ea............. 10.00
Tablet, school, CJ, 1929, 8x10" 195.00
Thimble, alum, CJ Co/Angelus, red pnt, rare, ea........................... 90.00
Wings, Air Corps type, silver or blk, stud-bk, CJ, 1930s, 3", ea...... 22.00

Prizes, Cast Metal

Badge, 6-point star, mc CJ Police, silver, 1931, 1¼" 35.00
Button, stud bk, Xd bats & ball, CJ pitcher/etc series, 1928......... 130.00
Coins, Presidents, 31 series, CJ, mk cancelled on bk, 1933, ea 18.00

Dollhouse items, lantern, mug, candlestick, etc, unmk, ea...............5.00
Pistol, soft lead, inked, CJ on bbl, early, rare, 2⅛" 180.00
Rocking horse, no rider, 3-D, inked, early, 1⅛"................................ 15.00
Spinner, early pkg in center, More You Eat..., CJ, rare 295.00

Prizes, Paper

Book, Animals (or Birds) to Color, Makatoy, unmk, 1949, mini ... 35.00
Book, Birds We Know, CJ, 1928, mini 90.00
Book, Chaplin flip book, CJ, 1920s, ea.. 85.00
Book, Twigg & Sprigg, CJ, 1930, mini.. 30.00
Card, Mov-I-Graff, Man of a Thousand Faces, 1922, 6¼x3½" 300.00
Decal, cartoon or nursery rhyme figure, 1947-49, CJ 12.00
Disguise, ears, red (still in carrier), CJ, 1950, pr 22.00
Disguise, glasses, hinged, w/eyeballs, unmk, 1933 ....6.00
Fortune Teller, boy/dog on film in envelope, CJ, 1920s, 1¾x2½" ... 65.00
Game spinner, ...baseball at home, unmk, 1946, 1" dia 60.00
Game, Midget Auto Race, wheel spins, CJ, 1949, 3⅜" 12.00
Hat, Indian headdress, CJ, 1910-20, 5⅜" 275.00
Hat, Me for CJ, early, ea 120.00

Indian headdress, orange and blue, purple tissue-like paper over top, one-piece, very early and rare, $300.00. (Photo courtesy Harriet Joyce)

Movie, Goofy Zoo, trn wheel(s) to change animals, unmk, 1939 .. 25.00
Movie, pull tab for 2nd picture, yel, early, 3", in envelope 125.00
Paint Set, Mysticolor, w/pnt & paper brush, 1970s..........................3.00
Puzzle, punch-out, cb, letters C, E, H or M, 2x3" card.................... 45.00
Sand toys, tilt picture, sand moves, 1960, ea................................... 45.00
Standups, animals & buildings, cb, most mk Germany, set 25.00
Top, string, Rainbow Spinner, 2-pc, cb, different designs, ea 45.00
Whistle, Blow for More, CJ/Angelus pkgs, 1928, '31 or '33, ea...... 45.00

Prizes, Plastic

Baseball players, 3-D, bl or gray team, 1948, 1½", ea.........................4.00
Disk, emb fish plaque, oval, series of 10, 1956, unmk, ea............... 30.00
Fob, alphabet letter w/loop on top, 1 of 26, 1954, 1½" 2.00
Palm puzzle, ball(s) roll into holes, dome or rnd, from 1966, ea........6.00
Picture fr, Statue of Liberty, House on Hill, etc, series 1392, late 1970s, ea....4.00
Pocket Peepers, ea..1.50
Rollers, oval, boy, monkey, or muscle man inside, ea..........................4.00
Ships in a bottle, 6 different, unmk, 1960, ea 4.00
Spring toys, serpentine springs, giraffe, dachshund, or clown, ea 5.00
Tags, hole at top to attach string, 4-leaf clover, eagle, horse head, emb, ea..2.00
WWII C Cloud punch-out war vehicles, CJ, series of 10, ea.......... 30.00

Prizes, Tin

Badge, boy & dog dc, complete w/bend-over tab, CJ.................... 125.00
Bank, 3-D book form, red/gr/or blk, CJ Bank, early, 2" 120.00
Brooch or pin, various designs on card, CJ/logo, early, ea.............. 85.00
Car, Ford, 1 of 2 XL prizes made, CJ on roof twice, 1½x2¼" 300.00
Cat w/spring tail, early... 65.00
Clicker, Noisy CJ Snapper, pear shape, alum, 1949 .... 12.00
Doll dishes, tin plated, CJ, 1931, 1¾", 1⅞", & 2⅛" dia, ea 35.00
Helicopter, yel propeller, wood stick, unmk, 1937, 2⅝"................... 27.00

Horse & wagon, litho dc, CJ & Angelus, 2⅛" 45.00
Horse & wagon, litho dc, gray/red mks, CJ, 1914-23, 3⅛" 350.00
Pocketwatch, silver or gold, CJ as numerals, 1931, 1½" 18.00
Small box shape, electric stove litho, unmk, 1⅛" 60.00
Small box shape, garage litho, unmk, 1⅛" 60.00
Soldier, litho, dc standup, officer/private/etc, unmk, ea................. 17.00
Spinner, wood stick, 2 Toppers, red/wht/bl, Angelus/Jack, 1½"....... 55.00
Spinner, wood stick, Fortune Teller Game, red/wht/bl, CJ, 1½"..... 65.00
Standup, oval Am Flag, series of 4, unmk, 1940-49, ea 12.00
Tall box shape, Frozen Foods locker freezer, unmk, 1947, 1¾" 75.00
Tall box shape, grandfather clock, unmk, 1947, 1¾" 65.00
Train, engine & tender, litho, CJ Line/512 .... 75.00
Train, litho engine only, red, unmk, 1941 .... 10.00
Train, Lone Eagle Flyer engine, unmk.. 60.00
Truck, litho, RWB, CJ/Angelus, 1931, ea....................................... 45.00

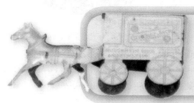

Wagon, horse-drawn, tin litho, one of only two prizes made in this larger size, pre-1922, 1½x3", $300.00. (Photo courtesy Harriet Joyce)

Wagon shape: CJ Shows, yel circus wagon, series of 5, ea 125.00
Wagon shape: Tank Corps No 57, gr & blk, 1941 .... 20.00
Wheelbarrow, tin plated, bk leg in place, CJ, 1931, 2½" L............. 22.00

Miscellaneous

Ad, Saturday Evening Post, mc, CJ, 1919, 11x14" 18.00
Lunch box, tin emb, CJ, 1970s, 4x7x9".. 30.00
Medal, CJ salesman award, brass, 1939, scarce............................. 125.00
Poster, trolley card, early 1910s, 10½x20½" 400.00
Sign, bathing beauty, 5-color cb, CJ, early, 17x22" 250.00
Sign, Santa & prizes, mc cb, Angelus, early, lg 220.00
Sign, Santa & prizes, mc cb, CJ, early, lg 265.00
Toy, train car, cast metal, 1920s, 1" 25.00
Toy, truck, originally sold w/box of CJ for 10¢, mid-1930s, 8" L.....300.00

Crackle Glass

Though this type of glassware was introduced as early as the 1880s (by the New England Glass Co.), it was made primarily from 1930 until about 1980. It was produced by more than 500 companies here (by Blenko, Rainbow, and Kanawha, among others) and abroad (by such renown companies as Moser, for example), and its name is descriptive. The surface looks as though the glass has been heated then plunged into cold water, thus producing a network of tight cracks. It was made in a variety of colors; among the more expensive today are ruby red, amberina, cobalt, cranberry, and gray. For more information we recommend *Crackle Glass from Around the World* by Stan and Arlene Weitman, our advisors for this category; they are listed in the Directory under North Carolina. See also Moser Glass.

Apple, red w/gr stem & leaf, Blenko, 1950s-60s, $100 to 125.00
Ashtray, amberina, Viking, 1944-70, 7¼", $45 to 65.00
Basket, red w/clear twisted hdl, Hamon/Kanawha, 1960s-70s, 5", $75 to.. 100.00
Beaker, clear w/sea gr leaves, Blenko, 1940s-50s, 7", $110 to....... 150.00
Bonbon, red heart shape w/yel hdl, 1950s-60s, 3¼", $85 to.......... 110.00
Bottle, bl, flat-sided, unkown maker, 8", $80 to 90.00
Candlesticks, bl, Rainbow, 1940s-50s, 6", pr $150 to 175.00
Candy dish, dk topaz/clear ribbed pan hdl, Hamon, 5½", 100 to .. 125.00
Candy dish, ruby, Bischoff, 1940-63, 4½x5" dia, $85 to 115.00

Compote, tangerine, Blenko, 1950s, 6", $100 to 125.00
Creamer, bl, drop-over hdl, unknown maker & date, 3⅛", $50 to . 75.00
Cruet, bl, pulled-bk hdl, Pilgrim, 1949-69, $75 to 100.00
Cup, amberina, drop-over hdl, Kanawha, 1957-87, 2½", $40 to 50.00
Decanter, amber w/ship, unknown mfg, early 1900s, 8", $350 to . 450.00
Decanter, clear ball/pnt flowers, bl stopper/hdl, Czech, 1920s, 10"... 650.00
Decanter, clear, pointed stopper, Pilgrim, 1949-69, 11", $100 to . 125.00
Decanter, gr pitcher w/ball stopper, Bischoff, 1950s, $125 to 150.00
Decanter, smoke gray, teardrop stopper, Pilgrim, 1950s, 11", $175 to.. 250.00
Decanter, topaz, lg ball stopper, Rainbow, 1953, 11", $150 to...... 175.00
Fish wine bottle, topaz, unknown maker, 1960s, 9x21", $160 to.. 185.00
Hat, turq, Blenko, 1950s-60s, 3", $50 to 75.00
Mug, amber, bulb w/drop-over hdl, 1950s-60s, 6¼", $30 to............ 35.00
Perfume bottle, rose crystal, w/rnd stopper, unknown mfg, 6" 125.00
Pitcher, amethyst, pulled-bk hdl, Hamon, 1940s-66, 5", $70 to..... 80.00
Pitcher, bl w/clear pulled-bk hdl, Pilgrim, 1940-69, 7", $80 to....... 90.00
Pitcher, bl, pulled-bk hdl, scalloped, Kanawha, 1957-87, 4", $45 to .. 55.00
Pitcher, clear w/amber drop-over hdl, Hamon, 1960s, 5¼", $50 to ..55.00
Pitcher, gr, pulled-bk hdl, Pilgrim, 1949-69, 4", $45 to................. 50.00
Pitcher, mini, amberina, drop-over hdl, Pilgrim, 1949-69, 4", $50 to. 55.00
Pitcher, olive gr, pulled-bk hdl, ruffled rim, Blenko, 1960s, 8" 125.00
Pitcher, tangerine w/clear drop-over hdl, Blenko, 1960s, 11", $110 to.. 150.00

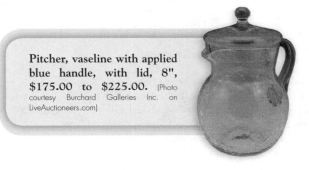

Pitcher, vaseline with applied blue handle, with lid, 8", $175.00 to $225.00. (Photo courtesy Burchard Galleries Inc. on LiveAuctioneers.com)

Pitcher, yel, drop-over hdl, Rainbow, 1940s-60s, 9", $90 to 100.00
Punch cup, clear, Germany, 2½", $50 to 75.00
Rose bowl, bl w/inverted fluting, Blenko, 1950s, 8", $110 to 135.00
Vase, bl, Bischoff, 1940-63, 10", $135 to...................................... 175.00
Vase, clear goblet w/sea gr stem, Blenko, 1940s-50s, 8", $100 to.. 125.00
Vase, lemon-lime tumbler form, Viking, 1944-60, 7", $100 to 125.00
Vase, sea gr jug w/sm neck, Blenko, 1960s, 7¾", $110 to.............. 130.00
Vase, sea gr, pinched, Blenko, 1940s-50s, 3½", $75 to 95.00

Cranberry Glass

Cranberry glass is named for its resemblance to the color of cranberry juice. It was made by many companies both here and abroad, becoming popular in America soon after the Civil War. It was made in free-blown ware as well as mold-blown. Today cranberry glass is being reproduced, and it is sometimes difficult to distinguish the old from the new. Ask a reputable dealer if you are unsure. For further information we recommend *American Art Glass* by our advisor, John A. Shuman III (see Directory, Pennsylvania), available from Collector Books or your local bookstore. See also Cruets; Salts, Open; Sugar Shakers; Syrups.

Bottle, cologne, wht enameled flowers/leaves, w/stopper.............. 235.00
Box, rnd, enameled leaves & strawberries, lift-off lid, 2¼" 195.00
Cracker jar, sq, gold floral & leaves, SP cover & hdl, 7¼"............. 325.00
Creamer, Invt T'print, sq mouth, bulb, clear hdl, 4¾" 150.00
Cruet, gr leaves, lav thistle, gold trim, ovoid body, bubble stopper, 8¼" ...225.00
Epergne, single lily, threaded snake, wide bowl dish, appl ped ft.. 350.00
Finger bowl, Zipper, mk Rd 55693, crimped rim........................... 140.00

Pitcher, ovoid, cylindrical neck, pinched spout, clear appl angled hdl, 4¾". 125.00
Rose bowl, appl vaseline matsu-no-ke florals & branches, squat & bulb, 2½". 575.00
Shaker, salt, Honeycomb, orig top... 75.00
Shaker, sugar, Venicia, orig top.. 275.00

Straw holder, Thumbprint, NM, 13", $1,200.00. (Photo courtesy Rich Penn Auctions on LiveAuctioneers.com)

Tumbler, Invt T'print, enameled flowers 60.00
Vase, Dmn Quilt, short neck, bulb base, clear appl rigaree on rim, 4½" 150.00
Waer set, Invt T'print, tankard pitcher & 6 tumblers.................. 360.00

Creamware

Creamware was a type of earthenware developed by Wedgwood in the 1760s and produced by many other Staffordshire potteries, including Leeds. Since it could be potted cheaply and was light in weight, it became popular abroad as well as in England, due to the lower freight charges involved in its export. It was revived at Leeds in the late nineteenth century, and the type most often reproduced was heavily reticulated or molded in high relief. These later wares are easily distinguished from the originals since they are thicker and tend to craze heavily. See also Leeds; Wedgwood.

Basket, emb floral w/pk feather edge, Herculaneum, 10½"+undertray.. 575.00
Bowl, potpourri, rtcl form w/rose finial, twist hdls, 13"............. 1,950.00
Charger, flowers in urn, mc w/bl feather scalloped rim, 19th C, 13"...1,025.00
Jug, sparrow-beak spout, loop hdl, ca 1770, 3⅛", EX 60.00
Mug, pate-sur-pate, unmk, late 1700s, $150 to 175.00
Pitcher, acorns/oak leaves, trunk hdl, Charles Meigh, 1848, 8" ... 180.00
Plate, dinner, pierced rim w/emb swags/scallops, 18th C, 10", 12 for..6,000.00
Plate, rtcl border w/beaded edge, 1780-1800, 9", 4 for............... 1,450.00
Plate, rtcl border w/swags, sm scallops, 1800s, 11½" L 360.00
Plate, rtcl, molded basketweave pattern, imp mk, 1861, $175 to . 200.00
Platter, gr scalloped feather edge, Britain, ca 1800, 19"................ 560.00
Teapot, Aurora in chariot/angels among clouds, globular, 18th C, 5". 1,300.00

Crown Devon, Devon

Devon and Crown Devon were trade names of S. Fielding and Company, Ltd., an English firm founded after 1879. They produced majolica, earthenware mugs, vases, and kitchenware. In the 1930s they manufactured an exceptional line of Art Deco vases that have recently been much in demand.

Basket, floral w/gold on rouge lustre w/gold hdls, Fielding, 3⅜x7" . 60.00
Bowl, butterflies on bl lustre, C Howe, Fielding, 3½".................... 132.50
Bowl, floral w/gold, scalloped rim, Fielding, 8" +8½" underplate.... 85.00
Chamber pot, floral transfer w/gold, 6x9½" 75.00
Egg caddy, floral on cream w/gold hdl, w/6 cups, 4x9½x5½" 145.00
Figurine, Scottie dog, 10" 35.00
Jug, flower garlands w/gold, cylindrical, 6" 65.00
Jug, QA Wye, 6¾"... 45.00

Jug, Scotsman in tartan, bk: Auld Lang Syne verse, thistle hdl, 7x5" . 185.00
Jug, Widdicombe Fair, musical, Fielding, 7" 100.00
Mug, Daisy Bell, couple on bicycle, missing music box, 5" 50.00
Pitcher, Captain Cook, kangaroo hdl, ca 1930, 9" 65.00
Plate, grapevines on cream, sq, 8½" 25.00
Tray, sailing ship & gulls on bl lustre, 8x4¼" 48.00
Vase, Asian landscape on bl w/gold o/l, ca 1930, 7½x4" 55.00
Vase, Fairy Castle, ovoid, #2406, 4¼" 375.00
Vase, floral on rouge lustre, hdls, Fielding, #A148-9, 8x6¼" 90.00
Washbowl & pitcher, medallions/swags on cream, ca 1909, 13", 15" .435.00

Crown Ducal

The Crown Ducal mark was first used by the A.G. Richardson & Co. pottery of Tunstall, England, in 1925. The items collectors are taking a particular interest in were decorated by Charlotte Rhead, a contemporary of Susie Cooper and Clarice Cliff, and a member of the esteemed family of English pottery designers and artists. See also Chintz Dinnerware.

Key: tl — tube lined

Bowl, Bl Bristol, oval, 10x7", pr 225.00
Bowl, floral chintz, rose border on blk int, 8-sided, 1890s, 4x8" 48.00
Charger, Bl Peony, C Rhead, 12½" 425.00

Charger, dragon motif, signed C Rhead, 13", $210.00. (Photo courtesy Treadway Gallery on LiveAuctioneers.com)

Charger, floral, blk/gold on crackled ivory, C Rhead, 12¾" 425.00
Charger, Manchu (dragon) C Rhead, #4511, 1930s, 14½" 195.00
Coffeepot, Orange Tree, rare side hdl, 1930s, 6", NM 135.00
Compote, Orange Tree, ftd, 3½x8½" 32.50
Pitcher, Deco floral w/lustre, C Rhead, #146, ca 1920, 7" 90.00
Pitcher, geometric linear band on rust speckles, C Rhead, #186, 7⅝"..55.00
Plate, Florentine, fruit & flowers, 1900s, 9" 110.00
Plate, Monticello commemorative, red transfer 42.50
Teapot, Britannia Rose, lg 185.00
Vase, #121, Crown Ducal Ware England, 9" 95.00
Vase, butterflies on orange lustre, hexagonal trumpet shape, 7½" .. 95.00
Vase, daffodils on ivory, C Rhead, 8" 60.00
Vase, Deco flowers, tl, C Rhead, 8" 175.00
Vase, fish on orange lustre, Deco style, 11" 195.00
Vase, flowers & foliage, mc on cream, #121, 9" 60.00
Vase, fruit band, trumpet form, C Rhead, 6" 110.00
Vase, Hydrangea, sgn B (Violet Barber), #198, 7½" 180.00
Vase, Persian Rose, tl, C Rhead, #4318, ca 1936, 9" 325.00
Vase, Spectria Flambé, red/blk/gold, shouldered, 3⅞" 85.00
Vase, stylized floral w/lustre, C Rhead, 1920s, 6¾" 90.00

Crown Milano Glass

Crown Milano was a line of decorated milk glass (or opal ware) introduced by the Mt. Washington Glass Co. of New Bedford, Massachussetts,

in the early 1890s. It had previously been called Albertine Ware. Some pieces are marked with a 'CM,' and a few had paper labels. This ware is usually highly decorated and will most likely have a significant amount of gold trim. The shiny pieces were recently discovered to have been called 'Colonial Ware'; these were usually marked with a laurel wreath and a crown. This ware was well received in its day, and outstanding pieces bring high prices on today's market. For more information we recommend *The Collector's Encyclopedia of American Art Glass* by our advisor, John A. Shuman III (Collector Books); see Directory, Pennsylvania.

Bowl, tricorner, roses/pansies/forget-me-nots on yel-gr, sgn, 3¼" . 485.00
Box, dresser, swirl mold, covered, florals & scrolls, silver plated. 1,650.00
Cracker jar, lg florals, Burmese colors, bbl, mk, bail hdl, 7¼" 595.00
Creamer/sugar bowl, pk violets on satin cream, 3½", 4¼" 945.00
Jar, covered, roses & tulips, squatty & ftd, gold hdls, gilded trim, mk 1013, 5¾"...1,900.00

Jar, reeded curled handles and steepled top, delicate floral decoration, unmarked, 5¾", NM, $325.00. (Photo courtesy Green Valley Auctions on LiveAuctioneers.com)

Jardiniere, medallions/pansies, gold trim, bulb, sgn, 7" 825.00
Pitcher, syrup, florals/leaves, SP top, melon shaped, 7½" 1,300.00
Rose bowl, pansies, sphere, gold foliage, shaded w/bl purple, brn & wht, 5⅝".600.00
Spooner, Dmn Quilt, mums, gold trim 785.00
Syrup, bl to wht w/gold-washed wild rose vine, 5½" 1,000.00
Tumbler, garlands of flowers/bows/ribbons, mk, semi-glossy, 3⅝" . 575.00
Vase, enameled ivy leaves & vines, gr/brn, swirl cover design...2,400.00

Cruets

Cruets, containers made to hold oil or vinegar, are usually bulbous with tall, narrow throats, a handle, and a stopper. During the nineteenth century and for several years after, they were produced in abundance in virtually every type of glassware available. Those listed below are assumed to be with stopper and mint unless noted otherwise. See also specific manufacturers; Custard Glass; Opalescent Glass; other types of glass.

Ada #2577, TeePee body w/cut neck, Cambridge, ca 1903, 8-oz.... 60.00
Amazon, Bar-in-Hand stopper, ftd, 8" 185.00
Amberette 90.00
Amberina, Invt T'print, conical, amber hdl/faceted stopper, Hobbs, 9" .350.00
Apollo, rose, McKee 95.00
Arched Ovals 60.00
Argonaut Shell, wht opal 350.00
Artichoke 65.00
Basketweave, bl 90.00
Beaded Grape/California, gr, 6¾", NM.. 40.00
Beaded Medallion, gr 250.00
Beaded Ovals in Sand, gr opal 225.00
Beveled Dmn & Star, ruby stain.. 125.00
Bismark Star... 50.00
Brittanic 55.00
Broken Column 60.00
Cane Column.. 45.00

Cathedral 60.00
Cathedral, amethyst 125.00
Chrysanthemum Base Swirl, gr opal 675.00
Columbian Coin (US Coin) 70.00
Cord Drapery, amber 275.00
Criss-Cross, cranberry opal, ca 1893-94 ...... 1,375.00
Cupid & Venus 175.00
Daisy & Button, bulb, faceted stopper, 7½" ... 130.00
Daisy & Fern, bl opal, 7" 125.00
Daisy & Fern, wht opal, Northwood 225.00
Delaware, bl 225.00
Dewey 65.00
Diamond Quilted, bl satin MOP 210.00
Diamond Quilted, cranberry stain 110.00

Diamond Quilted, rainbow mother of pearl glass with frosted handle and stopper, 6¾", $350.00. (Photo courtesy Bloomington Auction on LiveAuctioneers.com)

Empress, gr w/gold, 7", $85 to 95.00
Faceted Flower (Swirl) 65.00
Fandango, 2 szs, $45 to 60.00
Guttate, glossy pk w/clear hdl & faceted stopper, Consolidated, 5¾" .125.00
Heisey #300 Colonial, made in 5 szs 85.00
Hildalgo, frosted 70.00
Homestead (#63), Duncan 50.00
Honeycomb w/Star 50.00
Indiana 45.00
Intaglio, vaseline opal 795.00
Invt T'print, Prussian Bl w/HP floral, 5" 80.00
Invt T'print, rubena verde, gr stopper/faceted hdl, 6" 225.00
Invt T'print, rubena verde teepee shape, Hobbs Brockunier, 7" ... 550.00
Jacob's Ladder 95.00
Masonic 45.00
Michigan 65.00
New Garland #284, amber, tall melon-ribbed stopper, Fostoria, 9" .. 300.00
New Jersey 50.00
Panelled 44 .... 50.00
Panelled Forget-Me-Not 55.00
Pennsylvania 45.00
Plume 40.00
Polka Dot, rubena verde, teepee form, Hobbs Brockunier, 7" 400.00
Polka-Dot #308, rubena verde, Hobbs Brockunier, 7", NM 350.00
Portland 65.00
Priscilla, Fostoria 75.00
Prize, gr 225.00
Reverse Cruet, vaseline opal 175.00
Ribbed Opal Lattice, cranberry opal 500.00
Rose Point, loop hdl, Cambridge, 5-oz 150.00
Royal Crystal, ruby stain 110.00
Scroll w/Acanthus, vaseline opal 325.00
Semitar #2647, Cambridge 70.00
Shuttle 45.00
Spangle, blk w/gold inclusions, blown stopper, Hobbs Brockunier, 6". 425.00
Spanish Lattice, wht opal 200.00
Spatter, gr w/emb leaves 200.00

Starburst, etched florals, notched neck, faceted top, 6½" 70.00
Stripe, wht opal 175.00
Swag w/Brackets, sapphire bl, Jefferson Glass, ca 1903, 7" 135.00
Swirl, amberina hdl/faceted stopper, bulb, 6" .. 330.00
Swirl, cased spatter w/MOP finish, ribbed spatter hdl, 8" .. 425.00
Teasel 65.00
Thousand Eye, apple gr 65.00
Tile (Optical Cube) 50.00
Tiny Optic, amethyst w/decor 125.00
Zipper 45.00

Cup Plates, Glass

Before the middle 1850s, it was socially acceptable to pour hot tea into a deep saucer to cool. The tea was sipped from the saucer rather than the cup, which frequently was handleless and too hot to hold. The cup plate served as a coaster for the cup. It is generally agreed that the first examples of pressed glass cup plates were made about 1826 at the Boston and Sandwich Glass Co. in Sandwich, Cape Cod, Massachusetts. Other glassworks in three major areas (New England, Philadelphia, and the Midwest, especially Pittsburgh) quickly followed suit.

Antique glass cup plates range in size from 2⅝" up to 4¼" in diameter. The earliest plates had simple designs inspired by cut glass patterns, but by 1829 they had become more complex. The span from then until about 1845 is known as the lacy period, when cup plate designs and pressing techniques were at their peak. They were made in a multitude of designs — some purely decorative, others commemorative. Subjects include the American eagle, hearts, sunbursts, log cabins, ships, George Washington, the political candidates Clay and Harrison, plows, and beehives.

Authenticity is most important. Collectors must be aware that contemporary plates which have no antique counterparts and fakes modeled after antique patterns have had wide distribution. Condition is also important, though it is the exceptional plate that does not have some rim roughness. More important considerations are scarcity of design and color.

The definitive book is *American Glass Cup Plates* by Ruth Webb Lee and James H. Rose. Numbers in the listings that follow refer to this volume. When attempting to evaluate a cup plate, remember that minor rim roughness is normal. See also Staffordshire; Pairpoint.

Note: Most of the values listed below are prices realized at auction. The more common varieties generally run between $10.00 and $75.00 in very good condition. Unless noted otherwise, our values are for examples in very good to excellent condition.

R-4-A, red & wht swirled latticinio, plain rim, mfg unknown. 4⅛" ... 690.00
R-13-C, cobalt bl, plain rim, NE or Philadelphia, rare 3½" 4,125.00
R-38, amethyst, 17 scallops, Boston & Sandwich, unique 3¾" .. 2,640.00
R-64-X, Parker White, 16 scallops, rope top rim, 3¼" 19,800.00
R-83, opaque powder bl w/plain rim, Boston & Sandwich?, 4" .2,200.00
R-90, opal to colorless rim, plain rope top & bottom, Boston & Sandwich, 3¾" . 80.00
R-127, dk amethyst, plain rope top rim, Pittsburgh?, 3" 1,725.00
R-132, colorless, bull's-eye scallops w/single point between, 3½" .. 80.00
R-135-A, bl, 36 bull's-eye scallops, midwestern, probably Pittsburgh, 3½" ..1,650.00
R-159, col R-4-A, red & wht swirled latticinio, plain rim, mfg unknown, 4⅛" .690.00
R-179, colorless, 10-scallop rope rim, top & bottom, Philadelphia area, 3½" .23.00
R-179, dk amethyst, 10-scallops, rope rim top & bottom, 3½" .1,760.00
R-253, bl-gr, 8 scallops w/single point between, 3½" 77.00
R-285, strong fiery opal, 12 scallops, Boston & Sandwich, 3½" .. 110.00
R-440-B, deep bl, 24 scallops, Boston & Sandwich, 3½" 150.00
R-531, yel gr, 34 bull's-eye scallops, Midwestern, 3½" 110.00
R-565-B, bl, 51 even scallops, scarce, Boston & Sandwich, 3½" . 100.00
R-586, colorless, Ringgold Palo Alto, 72 scallops, 3¼" 460.00
R-594, amber, 66 scallops, Boston & Sandwich, rare, 3¼" 700.00
R-615-A, colorless, 25 scallops w/single point between, 3¼" 120.00

R-631, dk emerald gr, Chancellor Livingston, 63 scallops, 3½" .2,100.00
R-658, emerald gr, 78 scallops, Boston & Sandwich, 3½" 1,100.00
R-680, bl, 44 scallops, probably Midwestern, 3" 650.00
R-685, colorless, New Patent Steam Coach, 3½" 3,300.00

Cups and Saucers

The earliest utensils for drinking were small porcelain and stone-ware bowls imported from China by the East Indian Company in the early seventeenth century. European and English tea bowls and saucers, imitating Chinese and Japanese originals, were produced from the early eighteenth century and often decorated with Chinese-type motifs. By about 1810, handles were fitted to the bowl to form the now familiar teacup, and this form became almost universal. Coffee in England and on the Continent was often served in a can — a straight-sided cylinder with a handle. After 1820 the coffee can gave way to the more fanciful form of the coffee cup.

An infinite variety of cups and saucers are available for both the new and experienced collector, and they can be found in all price ranges. There is probably no better way to thoroughly know and understand the various ceramic manufacturers than to study cups and saucers. Our advisors for this category, Susan and Jim Harran, have written a series entitled *Collectible Cups & Saucers, Identification & Values, Books I, II, III,* and *IV,* published by Collector Books. The Harrans are listed in the Directory under New Jersey.

Bouillon, cactus, gold flower bud hdls, Ott & Brewer, 1883-93, $150 to..175.00
Bouillon, covered, flower sprigs, Dresden, Lamm, 1887-90 ....325.00
Bouillon, pk flowers, gr foliage, Limoges, GDA, ca 1941, $40 to ... 45.00
Cafe-au-lait, lilies of the valley, Bourdois & Bloch, 1890-1920.... 300.00
Chocolate, floral, heavy gold leaves, Limoges, Lanternier, 1910.... 65.00
Chocolate, HP cherry blossoms, gold beading, Nippon, 1891-1921, $75 to..95.00
Chocolate, HP wht rose, Beyer & Bock, Royal Rudolstadt, 1905-31...65.00
Coffee, appl flowers on gold, Murano, 1930s, $200 to 225.00
Coffee, pk, HP leaves, 4 twig ft, ES Germany, 1890s, $250 to......300.00
Coffee, HP flowers, gilt, 16 panels, Meissen, 1850-1924, $200 to . 250.00
Coffee, pk forget-me-nots, Sansouci shape, Rosenthal, 1890s, $45 to....60.00
Demitasse, Art Deco ribbed engagement, all ivory, Lenox, 1930s, $60 to.. 75.00
Demitasse, courting scene, floral transfer, Royal Vienna style, 1920s, $45 to.60.00
Demitasse, glass, cranberry to clear, gold floral, Moser, 1895........275.00
Demitasse, gold paste/jewels, Amelia portrait, Dresden, Klemm, 1890s.525.00

Demitasse, Haviland, Limoges, $35.00. (Photo courtesy The Auction House on LiveAuctioneers.com)

Demitasse, HP gold scroll, enamel portrait, ruby red, Moser, 1895, $150 to..175.00
Demitasse, ivory w/heavy silver o/l, Koenigszelt Co, 1950-60s, $100 to.125.00
Demitasse, litho, HP bamboo trees, Japanese mk, $45 to 60.00
Demitasse, silver lace floral border, Hutschenreuther, 1914-38, $60 to..75.00
Demitasse, wht, HP flowers, gold swirls, Gardner, Russia, 1890s, $400 to..450.00
Mini tea, Court Dragon, yel, dragons/birds, Meissen, 1850-1924. 325.00
Mini tea, Crown Staffordshire, gr, rose inside cup, 1930-39, $75 to.......95.00
Mini tea, Royal Crown Derby, Imari, #2451, 1940, $200 to 250.00
Mustache, HP roses, raised gold, beads, Nippon, 1891-1921, $250 to. 300.00
Mustache, King George Coronation set, Aynsley, 1911, $250 to . 275.00
Mustache, pk roses & gr leaves, Alice shape, Rosenthal, 1898-1900 .165.00

Mustache, wht roses, H Ohme, Silesia, Germany, 1883-1900......145.00
Tea bowl, pk lusterware, bird on branch, English, unmk, 1850s, $50 to ... 75.00
Tea, amethyst glass, Moderntone, Depression, Hazel-Atlas, 1934-41, $20 to .25.00
Tea, blk, 8 lg wht & yel flowers, inscribed To the Bride, Paragon, 1939-49 .50.00
Tea, cobalt, ducks, gold decor, pearl jeweling, Shelley, 1945-66... 375.00
Tea, Cornflower, #2411, Richmond shape, Shelley, 1940-66, $50 to ...65.00
Tea, cup w/bamboo hdl, Rose Medallion, Made in China, 1930s, $75 to.. 95.00
Tea, fruit w/much gold, kicked loop hdl, Aynsley, sgn H Brunt, 1930s, $100 to..125.00
Tea, gold w/turq jewels, 5-point scalloped star, Coalport, 1890-1920, $700 to...800.00
Tea, hummingbird hdl, Franz, Taiwan, China, current, $60 to....... 75.00
Trio, pale peach, HP flowers, Nautilus, 1896-1913, $250 to......... 275.00
Trio, Rose Trellis, New Cambridge, Shelley, 1950s, $80 to 100.00
Trio, gold dragon, Kutani lithophane, 1930-50s, $60 to................. 75.00
Trio, Windsor shape, Spring Bouquet, Shelley, 1940-66, $90 to .. 115.00

Currier & Ives by Royal

Royal China was founded in 1934 by three entrepreneurs: Beatrice L. Miller, John 'Bert' Briggs, and William H. Habenstreit. They chose the former E.H. Sebring Building in Sebring, Ohio, as the location of their new company. During the brunt of the Great Depression, the company initially began with only $500.00 in cash, six months of free rent, and employees working without pay. In 1969 the company was sold to the Jeannette Glass Corporation. Jeannette continued to operate Royal from the building until fire destroyed the plant in 1970. After the fire, operations moved to the French Saxon China Company which Royal had previously purchased in 1964. In 1976 the Coca-Cola Bottling Company of New York bought the company and continued operations until 1981 when the Jeannette Corporation was sold to the 'J' Corporation, a private investment group. Three years later, Nordic Capital Corporation of New York bought the company. It is interesting to note that 1984 was the fiftieth anniversary of the Nordic Group and the slogan they adoped was 'A New Beginning.' Unfortunately, however, Jeannette filed bankruptcy early in 1996, and in March Royal China shut down completely. The building and its contents were sold during a bankruptcy auction in January of 1987. It is currently being used as a warehouse.

The number of shapes and patterns produced by Royal can boggle the mind of even the most advanced collector. The most popular line by far is Currier and Ives. Its familiar scrolled border was designed by Royal's art director, the late Gorden Parker. Our suggested values for this pattern reflect the worth of examples in the blue colorway. The line was also produced in limited quantities in the following colors: pink, brown, black, and green. To evaluate examples in these colors, double the prices for blue.

For further reading on Royal China, we recommend *Royal China Company, Sebring, Ohio,* by David J. Folckemer and Deborah G. Folckemer. Our advisor for this category is Mark J. Skrobis; he is listed in the Directory under Wisconsin.

Bowl, cream soup, tab hdl, 7" 55.00
Bowl, dessert, 5½" 5.00
Bowl, dip, from Hostess set, 4⅜"...125.00
Bowl, fruit nappy, 5½"...6.00
Bowl, soup, 8"...10.00
Bowl, vegetable, deep, 10¼" 30.00
Butter dish, winter or summer scene, ¼-lb, $35 to............................45.00
Cake plate, flat, 10"...45.00
Cake plate, from Hostess set, flat, 10" 35.00
Cake plate, ftd, 10" 200.00
Candle lamp, w/globe 375.00
Casserole, angle hdls, all wht lid 175.00
Casserole, angle hdls, w/lid..100.00
Casserole, tab hdls, w/lid 200.00
Clock, Charles Denning, 10" or 12"..1,000.00

Coffee mug, Express Train 35.00
Coffee mug, Fashionable Turnouts 20.00
Creamer, angle hdl 8.00
Cup/saucer, angle hdl 6.00
Gravy boat, tab hdls, w/liner (like 7" plate) 150.00

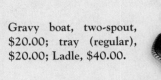

Gravy boat, two-spout, $20.00; tray (regular), $20.00; Ladle, $40.00.

Lamp, candle, w/globe 375.00
Mug, coffee, Express Train 35.00
Mug, coffee, Fashionable Turnouts 25.00
Pie baker, from Hostess set, 11" 60.00
Plate, calendar, 10" 20.00
Plate, chop, Getting Ice, 12½" 30.00
Plate, dinner, 10" 5.00
Plate, snack, w/scrolled hdl teacup, 9" 175.00
Platter, chop, rnd, 13" 125.00
Platter, Rocky Mountains, tab hdls, 10½" dia 20.00
Shakers, pr $30 to 35.00
Sugar bowl, no hdls, str sides, w/lid 35.00
Teacup, regular 3.00
Teacup, str sides 2.00
Teapot, 8 different decal & shape variations, $125 to 400.00
Tile & rack, 6x6" 150.00
Tray, deviled egg, from Hostess set 250.00
Tray, sugar bowl, flare top, w/lid 50.00
Tumbler, juice, 6-oz 15.00
Tumbler, juice, glass, 5-oz, 3½" 15.00
Tumbler, water, glass, 8-oz, 4¾" 15.00
Wall plaque, very scarce 1,000.00

Custard Glass

As early as the 1880s, custard glass was produced in England. Migrating glassmakers brought the formula for the creamy ivory ware to America. One of them was Harry Northwood, who in 1898 founded his company in Indiana, Pennsylvania, and introduced the glassware to the American market. Soon other companies were producing custard, among them Heisey, Tarentum, Fenton, and McKee. Not only dinnerware patterns but souvenir items were made. The formula for producing the luminous glass contains uranium salts which imparts the cream color to the batch and causes it to glow when it is examined under a black light.

Argonaut Shell, jelly compote, gr & gold decor 55.00
Beaded Swag, goblet, floral & gold 45.00
Cherry & Scales, berry, ind, nutmeg stain 25.00
Chrysanthemum Sprig, pitcher, water, gr & gold decor 150.00
Chrysanthemum Sprig, spooner, gold decor 40.00
Diamond w/Peg, creamer, ind, souvenir 24.00
Diamond w/Peg, spooner, w/gold 30.00
Diamond w/Peg, toothpick holder, souvenir 40.00
Everglades, tumbler, gr & gold decor 35.00
Everglades, water set, pitcher & 6 tumblers 500.00
Geneva, bowl, master berry, oval, ftd, floral decor 75.00
Grape & Cable, hatpin holder, nutmeg decor, 6½" 450.00
Inverted Fan & Feather, berry, ind, gold decor 30.00

Inverted Fan and Feather, butter dish, gold and decoration, $100.00. (Photo courtesy Green Valley Auctions on LiveAuctioneers.com)

Inverted Fan & Feather, master berry, sgn, gold decor 125.00
Inverted Fan & Feather, tumbler, gold decor 35.00
Inverted Fan & Feather, water set, pitcher & 6 tumblers, gold decor .. 280.00
Louis XV, creamer, gold decor 45.00
Louis XV, sugar, gold decor 80.00
Maple Leaf, tumbler, gr & gold decor 40.00
Prayer Rug, bonbon, red, gr & gold decor 24.00
Ring Band, butter, roses & gold decor 80.00
Ring Band, cruet, w/orig stopper 190.00
Winged Scroll, toothpick holder, gold decor 75.00
Winged Scroll, tumbler, gold decor 45.00

Cut Glass

The earliest documented evidence of commercial glass cutting in the United States was in 1810; the producers were Bakewell and Page of Pittsburgh. These first efforts resulted in simple patterns with only a moderate amount of cutting. By the middle of the century, glass cutters began experimenting with a thicker glass which enabled them to use deeper cuttings, though patterns remained much the same. This period is usually referred to as rich cut. Using three types of wheels — a flat edge, a mitered edge, and a convex edge — facets, miters, and depressions were combined to produce various designs. In the late 1870s, a curved miter was developed which greatly expanded design potential. Patterns became more elaborate, often covering the entire surface. The brilliant period of cut glass covered a span from about 1880 until 1915. Because of the pressure necessary to achieve the deeply cut patterns, only glass containing a high grade of metal could withstand the process. For this reason and the amount of handwork involved, cut glass has always been expensive. Bowls cut with pinwheels may be either foreign or of a newer vintage, beware! Identifiable patterns and signed pieces that are well cut and in excellent condition bring the higher prices on today's market. Refer to *Evers' Standard Cut Glass Value Guide* (Collector Books). See also Dorflinger Glass; Hawkes Glass; Libbey Glass; Tuthill; Val St. Lambert; other specific manufacturers.

Basket, Sunbeam, Pitkins & Brooks, 7", $275 to 325.00
Basket, Zesta, Pitkins & Brooks, P&B Grade, 7", $300 to 350.00
Bell, Premier, JD Bergen, 6", $200 to 225.00
Bonbon, Dmn, Averbeck, $60 to 75.00
Bonbon, Saratoga, Averbeck, $65 to 80.00
Bonbon/olive dish, Bedford, JD Bergen, 7", $60 to 75.00
Bonbon/olive dish, Hawthorne, JD Bergen, 5x9", $150 to 175.00
Bonbon/olive dish, Walter Scott, Higgins & Seiter, 4x8", $65 to .. 75.00
Bottle, cologne, Prism, JD Bergen, 9", $100 to 125.00
Bottle, cologne, Radium, Averbeck, 3½", $50 to 60.00
Bottle, cologne, St George, TB Clark & Co, sq, 12-oz, $125 to ... 140.00
Bowl, Arlington, Higgins & Seiter, 8", $70 to 80.00
Bowl, Cairo, Averbeck, 9", $200 to 250.00
Bowl, Desdemona, TB Clark & Co, 9", $200 to 225.00
Bowl, Goldenrod, JD Bergen, 10", $200 to 250.00
Bowl, Manhattan, TB Clark & Co, ftd, 9", $250 to 300.00
Bowl, Mars Fancy, Pitkins & Brooks, P&B grade, 9", $300 to 350.00

Bowl, Monarch, 8", $80 to 100.00
Bowl, Venus, TB Clark & Co, 10", $300 to 350.00
Butter plate, Ruby, JD Bergen, w/hdl, 5", $75 to 95.00
Candlestick, Oro, Pitkins & Brooks, P&B grade, 8", ea $200 to .. 250.00
Candlestick, Victoria, JD Bergen, 7", ea $125 to 150.00
Carafe, Daisy, Averbeck, qt, $150 to 200.00
Carafe, Dmn Fan, Higgins & Seiter, qt, $100 to 125.00
Carafe, Jewel, TB Clark, qt, $125 to 150.00
Carafe, Newport, JD Bergen, qt, $150 to 175.00
Carafe, Trixy, Averbeck, qt, $150 to 175.00
Carafe, Winola, TB Clark & Co, qt, $100 to 125.00
Celery dip, Pitkins & Brooks, 2", $8 to 10.00
Celery dish, Delhi, Higgins & Seiter, 4½x11¾", $75 to 100.00
Celery dish, Winola, TB Clark & Co, $75 to 100.00
Celery tray, Dmn, Averbeck, 12", $175 to 200.00
Celery tray, Empress, Averbeck, 11", $200 to 225.00
Celery tray, Liberty, Averbeck, 11¼", $175 to 200.00
Celery tray, Nordica, TB Clark & Co, $75 to 100.00
Celery tray, Rajah Fancy, Pitkins & Brooks, P&B grade, 11½" 250.00
Celery tray, TB Clark & Co, $50 to 75.00
Cheese dish, Glenwood, JD Bergen, 5", $150 to 175.00
Cigar jar, Majestic, Higgins & Seiter, 6½", $200 to 225.00
Comport, Crete, Pitkins & Brooks, 5", $175 to 200.00
Comport, Vienna, Averbeck, $250 to 300.00
Compote, Enterprise, JD Bergen, 8", $150 to 200.00
Compote, Manhattan, TB Clark & Co, 6", $100 to 150.00
Compote, Topaz, Pitkins & Brooks, P&B grade, 9x6", $300 to 350.00
Creamer, Emblem, JD Bergen, ½-pt, $50 to 70.00
Creamer, Grace, JD Bergen, ½-pt, $50 to 60.00
Cruet, Bermuda, Pitkins & Brooks, P&B grade, 8½", $175 to 200.00
Cruet, Strawberry Dmn & Fan, Higgins & Seiter, ½-pt, $75 to ... 100.00
Cruet, Viola, JD Bergen, ½-pt, $175 to 200.00
Cup, Edna, JD Bergen, $25 to 30.00
Cup, Mars, Pitkins & Brooks, P&B grade, $20 to 25.00
Cup, Occident, Averbeck, ftd, $40 to 45.00
Cup, Wabash, JD Bergen, $25 to 30.00
Decanter, Ashton, JD Bergen, 1-qt, $275 to 325.00
Decanter, Marie, JD Bergen, 1-qt, $350 to 400.00
Decanter, Savoy, JD Bergen, 1-pt, $150 to 200.00
Finger bowl, Georgia, Averbeck, $35 to 40.00
Finger bowl, Winola, TB Clark & Co, $35 to 40.00
Goblet, Florence, Higgins & Seiter, $65 to 75.00
Goblet, Venice, Pitkins & Brooks, $40 to 50.00
Hair Receiver, Larose, Pitkins & Brooks, P&B grade, 5", $200 to ... 250.00
Ice cream tray, Adonis, TB Clark & Co, $400 to 450.00
Ice tub, The Estelle, Higgins & Seiter, 4x4", $150 to 175.00
Ice tub, Webster, Higgins & Seiter, 4¾x4", $175 to 200.00
Knife rest, Pitkins & Brooks, 5", $25 to 30.00
Lamp, electric, ARC, Pitkins & Brooks, 12", $500 to 600.00
Nappy, Corsair Berry, Pitkins & Brooks, std grade, 7", $100 to 120.00
Nappy, Frisco, Averbeck, 6", $75 to 95.00
Nappy, Jewel, TB Clark & Co, 6", $55 to 70.00
Nappy, Monarch, Higgins & Seiter, 10", $150 to 175.00
Olive dish, Priscilla, Averbeck, 7¾", $125 to 150.00
Pin tray, Ruby, Averbeck, $50 to 70.00
Pitcher, Alabama, Averbeck, 1-qt, $225 to 250.00
Pitcher, Arbutus, TB Clark & Co, wide mouth, 3-pt, $175 to 250.00
Pitcher, Delta, JD Bergen, 1-qt, $175 to 200.00
Pitcher, Dewey, Higgins & Seiter, 1-qt, $150 to 175.00
Pitcher, Electric, JD Bergen, 1-qt, $200 to 225.00
Plate, Boston, Averbeck, 7", $70 to 80.00
Plate, Lowell, Averbeck, 7", $85 to 95.00
Punch bowl, Marlow, JD Bergen, low ft, 12", $900 to 1,200.00
Punch bowl, Rajah, Pitkins & Brooks, ftd, 10", $750 to 900.00

Punch bowl on stand, hobstars, hobnails, and cross-hatched mitres, early twentieth century, 12½x14½", $780.00. (Photo courtesy Jackson's Auction on LiveAuctioneers.com)

Salt dip, JD Bergen, rnd, 2¾", $10 to 12.00
Spooner, Prism, Averbeck, $75 to 95.00
Spooner, Saratoga, Averbeck, $125 to 150.00
Sugar bowl, Emblem, JD Bergen, $50 to 60.00
Sugar bowl, Golf, JD Bergen, $50 to 60.00
Tumbler, Coral, TB Clark & Co, $40 to 45.00
Tumbler, Goldenrod, JD Bergen, $30 to 35.00
Tumbler, Liberty, Averbeck, $22 to 25.00
Tumbler, Melba, Averbeck, $18 to 20.00
Vase, Amanda, Pitkins & Brooks, P&B grade, 10", $150 to 200.00
Vase, Creswick, sgn w/Egginton logo, 8x7", NM 525.00
Vase, Everett, Higgins & Seiter, 12", $125 to 150.00
Vase, Halle, Pitkins & Brooks, P&B grade, 14", $150 to ... 175.00
Vase, Orient, TB Clark & Co, 9", $175 to 200.00
Vase, Trophy, JD Bergen, 6", $30 to 40.00
Whipped cream bowl, Liberty, Averbeck, 7x4", $125 to 150.00

Cut Overlay Glass

Glassware with one or more overlying colors through which a design has been cut is called 'Cut Overlay.' It was made both here and abroad. Watch for new imitations!

Bottle, scent, cobalt/clear, oval/groove cuttings, Sandwich, 9" . 1,265.00
Bottle, scent, cobalt/clear, punty & loop, star-cut base, Sandwich, 6" ... 770.00
Bottle, scent, wht/gr opaque, scalloped panels w/gold, bbl form, 6" 115.00
Bowl, cobalt/clear, floral, serrated rim, 5x9" 55.00
Bowl, ruby/clear, grapevines at rim, ca 1900, 13" 95.00
Decanter, red/wht, geometric floral, cylindrical, clear hdl, 11½" .. 135.00
Egg cup, rose/wht/clear, flute cuttings, att Sandwich, 2" 80.00
Newel-post finial, red/clear, Quatrefoil & Loop, 7½ x3½" 1,200.00
Stem, cobalt/wht/clear, ovals/punties/etc, att Sandwich, 5" 50.00
Vase, hanging, powder bl/wht/clear, panel & punty cuttings, 6x4" 500.00
Vase, ruby/clear, geometric bands, scalloped top, clear ft, 15" 150.00
Wine, gr/clear, 6 windows w/gold tracery, optic stem, rnd ft, 6½" .. 60.00

Cut Velvet Glass

Cut Velvet glassware was made during the late 1800s. It is characterized by the effect achieved through the execution of relief-molded patterns, often ribbing or diamond quilting, which allows its white inner casing to show through the outer layer. For more information we recommend *The Collector's Encyclopedia of American Art Glass* by John A. Shuman III.

Cup, Dmn Quilt, pk 130.00
Finger bowl, Dmn Quilt, bl, 2½" 230.00
Ice bucket, Dmn Quilted, rose, SP mts, 6¼" 425.00
Lamp, Dmn Quilt, rose pk, opal glass ball shade, 17" 495.00
Pitcher, Dmn Quilt, deep sapphire bl, bl reeded hdl, 8x6" 400.00

Pitcher, Dmn Quilt, dk sapphire bl, bl reeded hdl, 8¾x6" 400.00
Pitcher, Dmn Quilt, pk, shouldered ewer form, 7½" 165.00
Pitcher, Dmn Quilt, rose to wht, ewer form, 11" 425.00

Rose bowl, Diamond Quilted, aqua, 3½", $135.00. (Photo courtesy Cincinnati Art Galleries, LLC on LiveAuctioneers.com)

Rose bowl, Ribbon (swirled), bl, 4" 235.00
Tumbler, Dmn Quilt, yel w/pk int, 4" 100.00
Vase, Dmn Quilt, dk to lt pk, ruffled 4-lobe top, Mt WA, 4¼x3". 225.00
Vase, Dmn Quilt, lt gold, dbl-gourd w/curved neck, 13½" 650.00
Vase, Dmn Quilt, pk, gold coralene, red jewels, 11½" 300.00
Vase, Herringbone, pk, bulb, 11" 335.00
Vase, vertical ribs, bl, crimped rim, 4¼" 70.00

Cybis

Boleslaw Cybis was a graduate of the Academy of Fine Arts in Warsaw, Poland, and was well recognized as a fine artist by the time he was commissioned by his government to paint murals in the Polish Pavilion's Hall of Honor at the 1939 World's Fair. Finding themselves stranded in America at the outbreak of WWII, the Cybises founded an artists' studio, first in Astoria, New York, and later in Trenton, New Jersey, where they made fine figurines and plaques with exacting artistry and craftsmanship entailing extensive handwork. The studio still operates today producing exquisite porcelains on a limited edition basis.

Asian lady in ornate costume w/hands away, MB Cybis, 22" 225.00
Attis (half man/half horse, companion of Cybele), #90, 10x8" 900.00
Ballerina w/sm crown stands on pointe, 1983, 9" 150.00
Bear cub, 1985, 4x6" 50.00
Beatrice, half-figure of lady w/flowers in hair, retired, 13" 480.00
Beaverhead Medicine Man, fine details, 1979, 18", NM 1,950.00
Betty Blue standing w/flowing bl ribbon on gown, 8½" 150.00
Bison standing, 3¼x5¾", NM 50.00
Brahma bull down on front legs, wht w/HP details, on base, 11x14" .. 250.00
Bunny Bisquet, rabbit baby sitting in daisies, 3½x4½" 75.00
Calla lily, ltd ed, 16x8x7" 350.00
Carousel Sugar Plum Pony, on base, 12" 750.00
Carousel tiger, 12x19x3" 575.00
Chantilly, cat w/bl ribbon, 4x8" 85.00
Cinderella at ball, in finery, 8" 125.00
Clara, ballerina from Nutcracker, 9x2" 180.00
Clarion Lily, 12x9" 325.00
Clown boy's head, ruffled collar, 2 bl balls on hat, 9" 155.00
Cynthia, ballerina, 9x3" 150.00
Deer mouse in clover, 3½" 60.00
Doves of Peace (2 wht doves), 11x11" 350.00
Eskimo boy's head, bust only, on wooden base, 10" 100.00
Felicity flower basket, blk-eyed susans/peach blossoms, 1976 .... 215.00
George Washington bust, wht bsk, 11" on 2" bsk base 265.00
George Washington standing by plinth, bl coat, 14" 515.00
Girl's head, short curls, butterfly in hair, 7"+blk base 265.00
Guinevere, ¾-figure, ltd ed, 12" 360.00
Harlequin standing w/hand on head, artist proof, 1980, 15¼x6" . 780.00

Horse head, ornate bridle & flowers, wht w/mc & gold, 12" 500.00
Horses (2) running, #837, 8x12" 600.00
Indian youth, single feather in hair, bust only, 10" 75.00
Juliet, half-figure of girl w/flower, 12x6" 480.00
Kestrel w/wings up, perched on log before walking stick, 16x9"... 480.00
King Richard the Lionheart, #69, 14⅞" 660.00
Lady Berengaira (King Richard's wife) w/falcon, #404, 15" 785.00
Lady Godiva on wht horse, 13x15" 1,200.00
Little Miss Muffet on tuffet w/spider, 1979, 7" 95.00
Madonna w/bird, 12" 100.00
Madonna w/Wreath of Roses bust, 11x4" 360.00
Magnolia flower & bud, 6x11", NM 120.00
Maximillan, dormouse on driftwood eating acorns, 6" 180.00
Mick the Melodious Cat, cat in vest playing concertina, 7" 150.00
Mr Fluffy Tail, squirrel w/tail up, 7½x3¾" 90.00
Nanook bust, Eskimo child, 10x6" 95.00
Pandora seated w/box, Children's Collection, 4½x4" 110.00
Phineas, circus elephant w/trunk up, 7x6" 425.00
Rabbit seated w/ears bk, wht w/pnt details, 3" 48.00
Raccoon eating berries on limb, 7" 100.00
Raffles, raccoon on base, 7" 240.00
Sandpiper, bird on grassy base, ltd ed, 5x8" 150.00
Storyteller, girl seated w/book, Children Series, 9x4" 215.00
Sugar Plum, carousel horse, on ebonized wooden stand, 13¼x9¼" . 300.00

Turtle Doves, 11½x11½x7½", $840.00. (Photo courtesy Ken's Antiques and Auction on LiveAuctioneers.com)

Wendy, girl stands w/doll in left hand, 6½" 60.00
Young Eskimo, #292 .... 350.00

Czechoslovakian Collectibles

Czechoslovakia came into being as a country in 1918. Located in the heart of Europe, it was a land with the natural resources necessary to support a glass industry that dated back to the mid-fourteenth century. The glass that was produced there has captured the attention of today's collectors, and for good reason. There are beautiful vases — cased, ruffled, applied with rigaree or silver overlay — fine enough to rival those of the best glasshouses. Czechoslovakian art glass baskets are quite as attractive as Victorian America's, and the elegant cut glass perfumes made in colors as well as crystal are unrivaled. There are also pressed glass perfumes, molded in lovely Deco shapes, of various types of art glass. Some are overlaid with gold filigree set with 'jewels.' Jewelry, lamps, porcelains, and fine art pottery are also included in the field.

More than 70 marks have been recorded, including those in the mold, ink stamped, acid etched, or on a small metal nameplate. The newer marks are incised, stamped 'Royal Dux Made in Czechoslovakia' (see Royal Dux), or printed on a paper label which reads 'Bohemian Glass Made in Czechoslovakia.' (Communist controlled from 1948, Czechoslovakia once again was made a free country in December 1989. Today it no longer exists; after 1993 it was divided to form two countries, the Czech Republic and the Slovak Republic.) For a more thorough study of the subject, we recommend the following books: *Czechoslovakian Glass & Collectibles*, Books 1 and 2, by Dale & Diane Barta (see Directory, Kansas) and Helen M. Rose; *Made in Czechoslovakia* and *Made in Czechoslovakia, Book 2*, by Ruth A. Forsythe; *Czechoslovakian Perfume Bottles and Boudoir Accessories* by Jacquelyne Y. Jones North; and *Czechoslovakian Pottery* by Bowers, Closser, and Ellis. In the listings that follow, when one dimension is given, it refers to height; decoration is enamel unless noted otherwise. See also Amphora; Erphila.

Glass

Bottle, blk w/random red threading, matching stopper, 6x3" 195.00
Bowl, orange-red w/blk at flared rim, blk ball ft, 5x10" 160.00
Candy dish, mc mottle, amber ft, pointed finial, 1920s-30s, 8x5" . 170.00
Cordial set, orange egg shape w/mc florals, holds 6 shots & decanter .. 50.00
Figurine, musician, Am Cut Crystal Corp, 8" 125.00
Flower frog, owl figural, dk amber, 8 holes in base, 1940s, 4" 20.00
Orange & red spatter w/red o/l, 3 emb ribs encircle body, 6x3" 60.00
Pink/gr/wht spatter, ruffled rim, 1950s, 5x4" 30.00
Vase, autumn mottle w/yel int, handkerchief rim, 13x12" 40.00
Vase, bud, orange w/dotted floral, blk trim, 1930s, 8" 80.00
Vase, cranberry w/controlled bubbles, flared rim w/blk, 1930s, 5" . 125.00
Vase, jack-in-pulpit, yel opaque w/blk trim at rim, 13" 50.00
Vase, orange cased in clear, slim w/flared ft, ruffled rim, 6" 35.00
Vase, orange opaque w/mc mottle at ft, stepped shape, 6x2" 52.50
Vase, orange w/blk swags, wht int, bulb body, 10x7" 100.00
Vase, orange w/mc spatter at bottom, ruffled rim, 6" 35.00
Vase, peach trumpet form w/3 buttressed low hdls, 1930s, 7x3" 95.00
Vase, pk to wht, wide rolled rim, block-letter mk, 3x6" 80.00
Vase, red w/blk mottle, 3 emb ribs encircle body, 1930s, 6x3" 40.00
Vase, red/gr/blk spider-web design, Kralik, 1920s, 7" 155.00
Vase, vaseline w/mottled bottom, 8", $65 to 70.00

Lamps

Basket, beaded, filled with glass fruits and nuts, 11", $1,900.00. (Photo courtesy Burchard Galleries Inc. on LiveAuctioneers.com)

Basket, beaded, filled w/mc glass flowers, metal ft, 12" 960.00
Basket, beaded, filled w/red berries, metal ft, 10" 525.00
Boudoir, lady figure, porc, glass flower skirt & bodice, 10¼" 1,200.00
Boudoir, stone bridge in woods HP on bl frost, Ruckl, 12½" 150.00
Cylinder orange shade w/blk silhouettes jumping rope, bronze ft, 10" .. 250.00
Lady (metal) on bk/arms behind head, balances 7" glass ball, 23", EX .. 360.00
Peacock, figural spelter bird, glass beadwork fanned tail, 13x9" ... 425.00
Perfume, wht floral on frosted egg shape, mk on base rim, 5", NM .. 85.00
Shade only: allover mc single grapes, dome: 3x6", EX 150.00
Shade only: spatter glass, bl/gr, globe w/angular protrusions, 7½" .200.00
Table, basket form, mc flowers/leaves in clear beaded metal fr, 12" ..800.00

Perfume Bottles

Amber arched shape w/clear figure stopper, 5" 250.00
Amethyst arched shape w/jewels, frosted floral stopper, 5" 360.00
Birth of Venus, amber, swirling fish, nude stopper, 7" 2,000.00

Black transparent w/jewels, matching plain stopper, 4" 750.00
Blue shouldered shape w/clear fan stopper, 4" 125.00
Crystal/frosted, nude ea side, 5¼" 650.00
Crystal, gr-cut-to clear floral stopper, 3" 160.00

Crystal, intaglio stopper with frosted courting couple, 7x6", $325.00. (Photo courtesy Richard D. Hatch & Associates on LiveAuctioneers.com)

Crystal shouldered w/abstract decor, red crystal stopper, 4¾" 300.00
Crystal shouldered w/floral intaglio stopper, 5" 75.00
Dark yel w/faceted sides, 4-ftd, intaglio floral stopper, 6" 300.00
Green waisted shape w/matching spear-like stopper, 5" 125.00
Green, pyriform ribbed base, disk stopper w/horn of plenty, 5x4" 45.00
Lavender, flat-sided w/undulating sides, Cupid in 4-lobe stopper, 4¾" ..120.00
Pink faceted base w/9 ft, nude holding world stopper, 7½" 4,500.00
Pink low-dome shape, frosted floral stopper, 6" 180.00
Pink, body resembling sun rays, kneeling nude stopper, 6" 5,000.00
Pink, shouldered, low, lg pk 16-petal cut stopper, 5" 200.00
Red shouldered form w/bottle neck, crystal stopper, 5" 450.00
Turquoise opaque, emb maid kneels/bk: deer, roses stopper, Ingrid...... 2,250.00
Yellow w/ornate geometric design, faceted stopper, 6" 250.00

Pottery and Porcelain

Basket, appl rose to front, bird perched on rim, mc, 7x6" 30.00
Bowl, mc Dresden-type floral on wht porc w/gold trim, 6", set of 6 ..35.00
Bowl, orange form w/lid, porc, mk PV, lt wear, 3x4", set of 6 .... 60.00
Bowl, shallow shell form, 3-D maid w/lyre seated on rim, 9x10" ..350.00
Creamer/sugar bowl, bl-gray luster w/orange trim, w/lid 28.00
Figure vase, heron standing, bill tucked to breast, wht/gr/brn 38.00
Figurine, nude seated on grass, leaning bk, 1 knee up, head trn, 9" ..120.00
Figurine, nude seated on sphere w/geometric star, P in circle mk, 12"...585.00
Flower frog, bird on arched branch on donut base, Czecho-Slovakia, 4"..30.00
Flower frog, bird on stump, mc, red mk, 1948, 5" 60.00
Flower frog/bud vase, yel bird on tree branch w/3 openings, #13-25, 5"..20.00
Pitcher, cat, tail hdl, Deco, red/blk on ivory, Ditmar-Urbach, 8" .420.00
Pitcher, figural cat hdl, pearl lustre w/lav rim, #31, 6½" 28.00
Pitcher, floral, brn/orange/wht airbrushing, #3586, 9" 75.00
Pitcher, floral, mc on ivory, red rim/hdl, tankard form, Urbach, 8" ..75.00
Pitcher, floral/fruit, bright colors on med bl, ftd, Urbach, 7½x6" ... 85.00
Pitcher, pelican figural, #5025, 6" 78.00
Pitcher, primitive blk rooster on ivory, Czecho-Slovakia, 3¾" 40.00
Pitcher, pussy willow branches/bl leafy twigs on wht, 7" 35.00
Pitcher, stylized fruit, strong colors on blk/yel, Ditmar-Urbach, 7" ...135.00
Planter, section of tree trunk w/bird on lower end, rnd mk 40.00
Plaque, classical figure scene, oval w/integral gold fr, 8½", pr 345.00
Plaque, stylized head/hand of lady w/flower, appl curls, FBS #157, 10" . 120.00
Vase, castle/bridge on yel w/lg bl stars, lg brn/yel hdls/ft, 8" 28.00
Vase, Deco floral on wht w/orange trim, fan form, #10852, 7x8" ... 32.00
Vase, Deco floral sprig, bright colors on lt bl, shouldered, 5x6" 80.00
Vase, floral on cream, teardrop shape w/shell hdls, gold trim, 8" 25.00
Vase, vertical blk finger-like panels on orange mottle, loop hdls, 10" ..120.00
Vase, wht w/3 lg handmade pastel floral stems appl to side, 6x5", EX ..50.00
Wall pocket, bird by birdhouse on forked branch, #55, 5x5" 22.00
Wall pocket, bird on pine cones, airbrushed mc, 7" 60.00
Wall pocket, bird w/lg tail feathers, opening in bk, #5952-A, 7" ... 50.00

D'Argental

D'Argental cameo glass was produced in France from the 1870s until about 1920 in the Art Nouveau style. Our advisor for this category is Don Williams; he is listed in the Directory under Missouri.

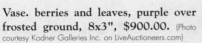

Vase, berries and leaves, purple over frosted ground, 8x3", $900.00. (Photo courtesy Kodner Galleries Inc. on LiveAuctioneers.com)

Box, lilies, brn on yel to amber, w/lid, 6¼" dia 960.00
Vase, cherries/leaves, bl on citron, swollen w/slim neck, 11½"..1,445.00
Vase, clematis vine, purple on bl, 5" 600.00
Vase, floral on leafy vine, brn on shaded amber & frost, slim, 11¾".1,025.00
Vase, floral, purple/brn on lt bl frost, shouldered, slim, 18" 1,200.00
Vase, floral/leaves, red on yel frost, shouldered, 4" 275.00
Vase, fronds, amber on gr, ca 1905, 4½" 775.00
Vase, rocky coast w/ships, orange/pk on yel frost, swollen, 3¾x4". 480.00
Vase, village landscape, brn/red/pk on yel frost, shouldered, 8".... 780.00
Vase, wild roses, amethyst on citron, bulb w/slim neck, 7" 900.00

Daum Nancy Glass

Daum was an important producer of French cameo glass, operating from the late 1800s until after the turn of the century. They used various techniques — acid cutting, wheel engraving, and handwork — to create beautiful scenic designs and nature subjects in the Art Nouveau manner. Virtually all examples are signed. Daum is still in production, producing many figural items. Our advisor for this category is Don Williams; he is listed in the Directory under Missouri.

Cameo

Basket, winter scene, cut/pnt on amber, amber hdl, 7" 15,000.00
Bottle, lily of the valley on amber, acid etched/gilded, ovoid, 7", NM......149.50
Bowl vase, winter scene w/windmills, cut/pnt, oval, 4½x5¾"....3,000.00
Bowl, exotic floral/foliage, dk gr on amethyst martele, 12 " L ...6,325.00
Bowl, grapes, purple/burgundy on orange/yel, appl snail, 6" 4,600.00
Bowl, underwater flora, orange/butterscotch/gr/brn on bl, 3x14¼".3,165.00
Box, Parlante, mistletoe springs, wht enamel berries, 4" dia......1,800.00
Creamer, winter trees/snow on mottled yel, 5½" L 2,588.00
Ewer, crocus/branches, cut/pnt, mc on textured frost, 9¾" 4,375.00
Inkwell, berries/leaves, bl/gr/brn on gr to frost, 3¼x5" 8,000.00
Lamp, leaves, gr on yel to cream, 3-arm matching std, 13½x7" .. 10,350.00
Lamp, trees/rain scene on hat-form shade & vasiform base, 13". 35,650.00
Lamp, winter scenic, cut/pnt on orange to yel, 14¾" 16,800.00
Perfume lamp, flowers & appl dragonflies, gr/yel on bl to wine, 6" ...8,000.00
Rose bowl, columbines, cut/pnt burnt yel to mauve, 2" 1,600.00
Rose bowl, trees/lake/sky, dk gr on orange mottle, sq sides, 2½"...865.00
Tumbler, berries/leaves, cut/pnt on yel mottle, 3¼" 1,265.00
Tumbler, poppies, cut/pnt on yel to orange mottle, gold ft, 5"...2,000.00

Vase, berried vines, cut/pnt on yel/opal mottle, 12" 3,500.00
Vase, berries/leaves, cut/pnt on orange to dk mauve, sq sides, 3¾". 1,150.00
Vase, berries/leaves, cut/pnt on orange to mauve, pyramidal, 10"..2,350.00
Vase, berries/leaves, cut/pnt on yel to purple, pillow form, 4¾"..2,875.00
Vase, blackbirds in winter, blk on bl & wht mottle, HP details, 6"..7,250.00
Vase, blk-eyed Susans, burnt salmon/olive gr on martelé frost, 8¾"..9,775.00
Vase, bud, wild orchids, burgundy/gr on yel/orange/mauve, 5"..2,100.00
Vase, crocus, red/wine on lav to gold martele, bulb base, 12"....7,500.00
Vase, Deco geometrics, yel/amber on brn mottle w/bubbles, 10¾". 1,150.00
Vase, floral, bl/gr on wht mottle, ftd, ca 1900, 9½" 6,600.00
Vase, floral, cut/pnt on lt bl to peach, slim, 19½" 9,200.00
Vase, floral, gr on martelé lt gr/apricot/frost/gr, 10½"...............10,925.00
Vase, floral, wht & chocolate on wht to bl, shouldered/slim, 7½"..8,000.00
Vase, fruit, orange/brn on raspberry to gr, slim, ftd, 15½"..........8,000.00
Vase, fruit/leaves, orange/gr on raspberry/citron, ftd, 15¼"......11,500.00
Vase, fuchsia, cut/pnt on wht to dk bl, freeform rim, 6¾"..........1,600.00
Vase, gulls/turtle/sun/waves, cut/pnt on clear to frost, 15½"....10,350.00
Vase, lake scene, cut/pnt en grisaille on lav to frost, 3¼x4¼"....1,150.00
Vase, leaves/cornflowers, cut/pnt on bl to mauve, egg form, 3" .7,000.00
Vase, marguerites, pk/wht w/appl cabochon centers on yel, 15" . 25,300.00
Vase, morning glories, cut/pnt on yel mottle, cylindrical, 13½".. 10,350.00
Vase, mushrooms, brn/red/gr on yel/orange/mauve, slim, 16"..17,250.00
Vase, rose hip berries/leaves, cut/pnt on yel-orange to purple, 3¼"...1,495.00
Vase, roses, pk on frost to yel, 5 appl cabochons/gold trim, 10¼"... 12,650.00
Vase, sailboats in harbor, purple/gr on mc mottle, ca 1900, 14"..2,400.00
Vase, spring scenic, cut/pnt on frost to purple to gr, pillow form, 4"..4,315.00
Vase, trees, cut/pnt on yel, bottle form, 2¼" 575.00
Vase, trees/lake, dk gr on orange to citron, bulb w/cup rim, 13" .5,530.00
Vase, trees/lake/sky, purple/bl on yel mottle, 7½".....................1,800.00
Vase, trees/sky, cut/pnt brn/gr on yel to frost, 4¾" 2,875.00
Vase, windblown trees, brn on cream/butterscotch, classic form, 17".. 4,430.00
Vase, winter scenic, cut/pnt on butterscotch, sm shoulder/slim, 10" .5,175.00
Vase, winter trees/blkbirds, cut/pnt on icy opal, ftd, 10"..........20,125.00
Vase, wooded landscape, dk gr on yel/red/purple mottle, ca 1900, 13" .5,000.00
Wall pocket, orchids/appl tendrils on gr to brn mottle, 5".........5,175.00

Enameled Glass

Bottle, thistles, mc w/gold on textured frost, metal lid, 4"............ 750.00
Bowl, Dutch windmills/ships on textured grnd, 4-lobe rim, 5"..1,250.00
Vase, berries/leaves, mc on orange mottle, slim, ftd, 12" 785.00
Vase, bleeding hearts on amber mottle, stick neck, 4"...............1,800.00

Vase, enameled daisies, signed in cameo with Croix de Lorraine, 18", $6,300.00. (Photo courtesy Neal Auction Company on LiveAuctioneers.com)

Vase, morning glories, mc on frost to amber mottle, 19½" 7,200.00
Vase, mushrooms/vegetation on orange/yel mottle, 5" 7,200.00
Vase, pk w/prairie flowers/trees, bottom half pnt as gr grass, 4¾"..12,650.00
Vase, winter landscape on orange/yel mottle, 4" 3,000.00
Vase, winter scene on gray, 11"...4,250.00
Vase, wisteria, mauve/gr on frosted orange/brn mottle, 7¼" 3,350.00

Miscellaneous

Bowl in wrought iron framework, sgn L Majorelle & Daum Nancy, 11¾" dia..3,600.00
Bowl, clear w/cut & etched geometrics, flared, 6¼x11" 780.00
Lamp, purple-bl ribs on gr to raspberry 9" shade; yel to bl std, 17". 13,800.00
Plaque, La Danse, lady in flowing shawl, pate-sur-pate, 11" L...... 660.00
Vase, controlled bubbles, lt bl, tapering body, 4½x4½" 180.00
Vase, purple ribs on powdered/shaded orange to gr, cylinder neck, 14"..2,300.00
Vase, ribbed & bubbled, clear bl, shoulderd, slim neck/flared rim, 14"....900.00
Vase, smoky w/cvd geometrics, ovoid, 10" 750.00

De Vez Glass

De Vez was a type of acid-cut French cameo glass produced by Cristal-lerie de Pantin in Paris around the turn of the century. Our advisor for this category is Don Williams; he is listed in the Directory under Missouri.

Bell, floral, red on amber, gilt-metal collar & hanger, 10" 1,950.00
Bowl, trumpet flowers/foliage, brn/salmon on yel, 3⅛x4¾", NM. 1,200.00
Box, sunset scene, brn/gray on rose-red, 2⅝x3¼" 360.00
Lamp, fisherman/boats, bl/pk on orange, brass ft, 1900s, 6½" 950.00
Lamp, leaves/rocks/water on base & globe, 2-color, 1920s, 12" 600.00
Vase, alpine scene, bl/yel on wht to pk, shouldered, 10½".........1,550.00
Vase, birch/lake scene, brn/gr on shaded bl, slim, fanned rim, 11" ..850.00
Vase, boats/water/branches, reds on lt gr, shouldered, 8" 850.00
Vase, castle scene, cobalt/terra cotta on lt yel, 7½" 950.00
Vase, eagle/nest/woods, brns on pk, 7½"................................... 850.00
Vase, fishing boats in harbor, purple/blk on rose pk, gourd form, 7x4".. 550.00
Vase, fishing boats/village scene, mauve/gr on yel to orange, 17" ..1,950.00
Vase, gondola/village, moonlit landscape, brn/red on lt yel, 10".. 1,560.00
Vase, lady/castle scene, gr/pk on wht, sm ft, 7" 785.00
Vase, landscape, cobalt on faded yel, 3½" 270.00
Vase, mtn goat/evergreens/mtns, bl/wht on pk sky, 10¼" 1,560.00
Vase, mtn lake/woods, gr/red on yel to wht, flared cylinder, 12¼" .. 1,500.00
Vase, mtn/cabin/stag, 2-color, slim, 9¾" 725.00
Vase, mtn/lake/trees, gr/dk bl on med to lt bl, 8¼" 850.00
Vase, Nouveau flowers, red/gr on yel, bulb, 7½"......................... 1,000.00
Vase, palm treess, bl on pk to yel, stick neck, 6" 375.00

Vase, poppies and butterflies, CP cameo monogram, 9½", $1,200.00. (Photo courtesy Clars Auction Gallery on LiveAuctioneers.com)

Vase, pyramids/palm trees/boats, russet on camphor, slim form, 9½"..420.00
Vase, swamp w/trees/plants/cockatoo, purples on pk, 8¼x4½" ..1,600.00
Vase, swans/mtns/branches, bl on yel to frost, slim, 7" 660.00
Vase, trees/water/village, gr/yel on frost, ca 1920, 14x4" 1,325.00
Vase, tropical scene, bl/gr/yel on amber opal, 10" 900.00

De Vilbiss

Perfume bottles, atomizers, and dresser accessories marketed by the De Vilbiss Company are appreciated by collectors today for the various types of lovely glassware used in their manufacture as well as for their pleasing shapes. Various companies provided the glass, while De Vilbiss made only the metal tops. They marketed their merchandise not only here but in Paris, England, Canada, and Havana as well. Their marks were acid stamped, ink stamped, in gold script, molded in, or on paper labels. One is no more significant than another. Our advisor for this category is Randall Monsen; he is listed in the Directory under Virginia.

Key:
A — atomizer   B — bulb

Bottles

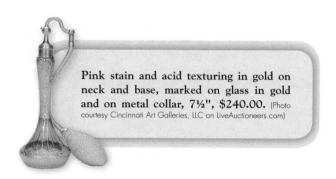

Pink stain and acid texturing in gold on neck and base, marked on glass in gold and on metal collar, 7½", $240.00. (Photo courtesy Cincinnati Art Galleries, LLC on LiveAuctioneers.com)

Blue Aurene, brass stopper, Steuben #6136, mk, slim/ftd, 6" 515.00
Blue irid, slender stem w/flared ft, A, rpl gold B w/tassel, 8"......... 450.00
Clear w/swirled feathers in relief, bulb, 3¾" 42.50
Clear/frosted floral cylinder, gold cap, orig sticker, 1920s, 5¼" 96.00
Cobalt w/Deco HP floral, Moser type, flared ft, 6½" 110.00
Cranberry w/cut patterns/bright gold, A, non-working B, 10", pr . 415.00
Crystal irid, 6-sided ft, A, rpl bulb, 6" 120.00
Gold to bl Aurene w/cut floral, cylinder w/flared ft, A/no B, 8½" . 600.00
Green w/bird figural stem, disk ft, A w/orig ball/tassel, 6⅜" 1,200.00
Green/gold/blk geometrics, purple int, A w/rpl B/tassel, 10" 1,500.00
Imperial, gold-encrusted custard shading to gray, NM...............1,650.00
Jade gr w/gold at lower body & disk ft, L dauber, 7" 275.00
Lavender, bulb top w/slim stem, disk ft, A, hard B, 6" 80.00
Marigold, shouldered, 6-sided ft, A, no bulb, 7½"...................... 110.00
Orange base, gold & blk top, Deco look, A, no bulb, 7".............. 240.00
Orange w/gold enamel, disk ft, gold stopper, 7" 350.00
Pearl lustre w/cameo bird & branches, much gold, A, G- B, 10¼"..415.00
Purple w/Deco dragonflies, gold stopper w/dauber, disk ft, 5⅞" 135.00

Miscellaneous

Cigarette box, gr w/HP gold bird & foliage, 3⅜x4⅜"................... 350.00
Ginger jar, amber w/gold pine needle design, w/A insert, 6½" 250.00
Perfume lamp, fairy silhouettes, sm rpr, 8x2½"............................ 475.00
Perfume lamp, monkey among leaves, Deco shape, 1920s, 8½" .1150.00
Powder jar, coral pk w/blk abstract decor lid, 4¾"......................... 65.00
Tray, enameled and gilded flowering vines, 7x10½"....................... 365.00

Decanters

Ceramic whiskey decanters were brought into prominence in 1955 by the James Beam Distilling Company. Few other companies besides Beam produced these decanters during the next 10 years or so; however, other companies did eventually follow suit. At its peak in 1975, at least 20 prominent companies and several on a lesser scale made these decanters. Beam stopped making decanters in mid-1992. Now only a couple of companies are still producing these collectibles.

Liquor dealers have told collectors for years that ceramic decanters are not as valuable, and in some cases worthless, if emptied or if the federal tax stamp has been broken. Nothing is further from the truth. Following are but a few of many reasons you should consider emptying ceramic decanters:

1) If the thin glaze on the inside ever cracks (and it does in a small percentage of decanters), the contents will push through to the outside. It is then referred to as a 'leaker' and worth a fraction of its original value.

2) A large number of decanters left full in one area of your house poses a fire hazard.

3) A burglar, after stealing jewelry and electronics, may make off with some of your decanters just to enjoy the contents. If they are empty, chances are they will not be bothered.

4) It is illegal in most states for collectors to sell a full decanter without a liquor license.

Unlike years ago, few collectors now collect all types of decanters. Most now specialize. For example, they may collect trains, cars, owls, Indians, clowns, or any number of different things that have been depicted on or as a decanter. They are finding exceptional quality available at reasonable prices, especially when compared with many other types of collectibles.

We have tried to list those brands that are the most popular with collectors. Likewise, individual decanters listed are the ones (or representative of the ones) most commonly found. The following listing is but a small fraction of the thousands of decanters that have been produced.

These decanters come from all over the world. While Jim Beam owned its own china factory in the U.S., some of the others have been imported from Mexico, Taiwan, Japan, and elsewhere. They vary in size from miniatures (approximately two-ounce) to gallons. Values range from a few dollars to more than $3,000.00 per decanter. Most collectors and dealers define a 'mint' decanter as one with no chips, no cracks, and label intact. A missing federal tax stamp or lack of contents has no bearing on value. All values are given for 'mint' decanters. A 'mini' behind a listing indicates a miniature. All others are fifth or 750 ml unless noted otherwise. Our advisor for this category is Roy Willis; he is listed in the Directory under Kentucky.

Aesthetic Specialties (ASI)

Automotive & Transportation, Cadillac (1903), bl or wht 65.00
Automotive & Transportation, Chevrolet (1914), blk, 1979 .... 65.00
Sports, Golf, Bing Crosby 38th, 1978 .... 50.00

Beam

Wheels Series, 1917 Mack Bulldog Fire Truck, 1982, $125.00. (Photo courtesy Leslie Hindman Auctioneers on LiveAuctioneers.com)

Casino Series, Golden Gate, 1970 .... 15.00
Casino Series, Harold's Club Pinwheel, 1965 .... 35.00
Casino Series, Reno Horseshoe, Prima Donna or Cal-Neva, 1969, ea...10.00
Centennial Series, Alaska Purchase, 1966 .... 9.00
Centennial Series, Key West, 1972 .... 8.00
Centennial Series, Lombard, 1969 .... 5.00
Centennial Series, Statue of Liberty, 1975 .... 16.00
Executive Series, Am Pitcher, 1982 .... 15.00
Executive Series, Caroler's Bell, 1984 .... 25.00
Executive Series, Mother of Pearl, 1979 .... 15.00
Executive Series, Partridge Bell, 1983 .... 35.00
Executive Series, Royal Filigree, 1981 .... 12.00
Foreign Series, Australia, Galah Bird, 1980 .... 20.00

Foreign Series, Australia, Kangaroo, 1977 .... 15.00
Foreign Series, Fiji Islands, 1971 .... 6.00
New Zealand, Kiwi Bird, 1974 .... 14.00
Organization Series, Ducks Unlimited #6, 1980 .... 40.00
Organization Series, Ducks Unlimited #7, 1981 .... 42.00
Organization Series, Ducks Unlimited #9, 1983 .... 55.00
Organization Series, Ducks Unlimited #10, 1984 .... 85.00
Organization Series, Elks, 1968 .... 5.00
Organization Series, Phi Sigma Kappa, 1973 .... 25.00
Organization Series, Shriner Raja Temple 24.00
Organization Series, VFW, 1971 .... 8.00
People Series, Cowboy, 1981 .... 20.00
People Series, Emmett Kelly, 1973 .... 35.00
People Series, George Washington, 1976 .... 20.00
People Series, Martha Washington, 1976 .... 12.00
State Series, Delaware, 1972 .... 10.00
State Series, Kentucky, blk head stopper, 1967 .... 25.00
State Series, Maine 9.00
State Series, Ohio 10.00
Wheels Series, '57 Chevy, turq & wht, 1991 .... 70.00
Wheels Series, Cable Car, 1968 .... 6.00
Wheels Series, Cable Car, 1983 .... 50.00
Wheels Series, Corvette, bl, 1954 .... 125.00
Wheels Series, Corvette, copper, 1955 .... 125.00
Wheels Series, Corvette, red, yelor wht, 1978, ea 75.00
Wheels Series, Ford 1913 Model T, blk or gr, 1974 .... 45.00
Wheels Series, Ford 1964 Mustang, blk, 1985 .... 130.00
Wheels Series, Ford 1964 Mustang, wht, 1985 .... 75.00
Wheels Series, Golf Car, 1985 .... 45.00
Wheels Series, Harold's Club Covered Wagon, 1974 .... 35.00
Wheels Series, Train, Caboose, gray, 1987 .... 90.00
Wheels Series, Train, Caboose, red, 1980 .... 75.00
Wheels Series, Train, Coal Tender for Grant, 1980 .... 65.00
Wheels Series, Train, Locomotive, Grant, 1980 .... 75.00
Wheels Series, Train, Locomotive, JB Turner, 1982 .... 125.00
Wheels Series, Train, Passenger Car, 1981 .... 50.00
Wheels Series, Train, Wood Tender for General, 1988 .... 130.00

Brooks

American Legion, Denver, 1971 .... 12.00
Amvets, 1974 .... 10.00
Automotive & Transportation, 1962 Corvette Mako Shark, 1979 ..30.00
Automotive & Transportation, Auburn Boattail, 1978 .... 28.00

Automotive and Transportation, Duesenberg, 1971, $35.00. (Photo courtesy Aurora on LiveAuctioneers.com)

Elk, 1972 .... 20.00
Fire Engine, 1971 .... 15.00
Indy Racer #21, 1970 .... 35.00
Keystone Kops, 1971 .... 60.00
Killer Whale, 1972 .... 20.00
Man O' War, 1969 .... 35.00
Phonograph, 1970 .... 18.00
Pistol, Dueling, 1968 .... 10.00
Setter, w/bird, 1970 .... 12.00
Ticker Tape, 1970 .... 9.00
Trail Bike, 1972 .... 20.00

Train, Iron Horse, 1969 .... 12.00
Vermont Skier, 1972 .... 10.00

J.W. Dant

American Legion, 1969 ....8.00
Field Birds, 8 different, 1969, ea 10.00
Indy 500, 1969 ....8.00

George Dickel

Golf Club, 1967 .... 10.00
Powderhorn, amber, qt 15.00
Powderhorn, dk, ⅘-qt 12.00

Famous Firsts

Coffee Mill, orange, 1971 .... 29.00
Roulette Wheel, 1972 .... 29.00
Scale, Lombardy, 1970 .... 29.00
Spirit of St Louis, midi 75.00
Spirit of St Louis, mini, 1972 .... 50.00

Hoffman

Automotive & Transportation, Race Car, AJ Foyt #2, 1972 .... 125.00
Cats, mini, 6 different, 1981, ea 15.00
College Series, helmet, Auburn, 1981 .... 40.00
College Series, helmet, Missouri, 1981 .... 40.00
College Series, mascot, Nevada Wolfpack, 1979 .... 45.00
Mr Lucky Series, Blacksmith, 1976 .... 35.00
Mr Lucky Series, Blacksmith, mini, 1976 .... 15.00
Mr Lucky Series, Fireman, mini, 1976 .... 25.00
Mr Lucky Series, Policeman, 1975 .... 48.00
Mr Lucky Series, Policeman, mini, 1975 .... 16.00
Sports Series, Big Red Machine, 1973 .... 60.00
Wildlife Series, Doe & Fawn, 1975 .... 45.00

Kontinental

Dentist, 1978 .... 35.00
Dock Worker, 1978 .... 32.00
Innkeeper, 1978 .... 28.00
Stephen Foster, 1975 .... 28.00
Surveyor, 1978 .... 35.00

Lionstone

Automotive & Transportation, Johnny Lightning #1, gold, 1972 . 100.00
Automotive & Transportation, Johnny Lightning #2, silver, 1973 ..90.00
Automotive & Transportation, Turbo Car, STP, red, 1972 .... 50.00
Bird Series, Canada Goose, w/base, 1980 .... 55.00
Bird Series, Meadowlark, 1969 .... 24.00
Clowns, 6 different, 1978, ea 35.00
Old West Series, Barber, 1976 .... 42.00
Old West Series, Barber, mini, 1976 .... 18.00
Old West Series, Camp Cook, 1969 .... 25.00
Old West Series, Camp Follower, 1969 .... 25.00
Old West Series, Chinese Laundry Man, 1969 .... 25.00
Old West Series, Country Doctor, 1969 .... 24.00
Old West Series, Photographer, 1976 .... 60.00
Old West Series, Photographer, mini, 1976 .... 24.00
Old West Series, Rain Maker, mini, 1976 .... 15.00
Old West Series, Riverboat Captain, 1969 .... 25.00

Old West Series, Sheepherder, 1969 .... 40.00
Old West Series, Telegrapher, 1969 .... 25.00
Sports Series, Backpacker, 1980 .... 30.00
Sports Series, Fisherman, 1980 .... 38.00
Sports Series, Football Players, 1974 .... 50.00

McCormick

Abe Lincoln, 1976 .... 40.00
Alexander Graham Bell, 1977 .... 28.00
Elvis, #1, wht, mini, music box plays 'Love Me Tender' 50.00
Elvis, #3, blk, mini, music box plays 'Can't Help Falling in Love' .. 45.00
Elvis, #3, blk, music box plays 'Can't Help Falling in Love' 75.00
Elvis, Designer #1, mini, silver, music box plays 'Are You Lonesome Tonight?' .. 175.00
Elvis, Designer #3, gold encore, music box plays 'It's Now or Never' .. 275.00
Elvis, gold tribute, mini, music box plays 'My Way' 140.00
Elvis, Teddy Bear, music box plays 'Let Me Be Your Teddy Bear' . 600.00
Hank Williams, Sr, 1980 .... 125.00
Iwo Jima, 1983 .... 150.00
Iwo Jima, mini, 1984 .... 75.00
Jimmy Durante, 1981 .... 65.00
King Arthur, 1979 .... 45.00
Marilyn Monroe, 1984 .... 500.00
Pony Express, 1978 .... 50.00
Robert Peary, 1977 .... 32.00
Shrine Dune Buggy, 1976 .... 40.00
Telephone Operator, 1982 .... 60.00

OBR

General Engine, 1974 .... 15.00
Guitar, Music City 18.00
WC Fields, Bank Dick, 1976 .... 50.00
WC Fields, Top Hat, 1976 .... 55.00

Old Bardstown

Foster Brooks, 1978 .... 25.00
Surface Miner, 1978 .... 25.00
Tiger, 1979 .... 30.00

Old Commonwealth

Coal Miner #1, w/shovel, 1975 .... 85.00
Coal Miner #1, w/shovel, mini, 1980 .... 25.00
Coal Miner #2, w/pick, 1976 .... 40.00
Firefighter, Fallen Comrade, 1983 .... 75.00
Firefighter, Fallen Comrade, mini, 1983 .... 28.00
Firefighter, Modern Hero #1, 1982 .... 65.00
Firefighter, Modern Hero #1, mini, 1982 .... 22.00
Firefighter, Nozzelman #2, 1983 .... 65.00

Old Fitzgerald

Irish Luck, 1972 .... 25.00
Irish Wish, 1975 .... 22.00
Irish, Blarney, 1970 .... 12.00
Irish, Leprechaun, Please God, 1968 .... 25.00
Rip Van Winkle, 1971 .... 28.00

Ski Country

Birds, Birth of Freedom, 1976 .... 100.00
Birds, Birth of Freedom, gal 1,750.00

Bob Cratchit, 1977 .... 60.00
Bob Cratchit, mini, 1977 .... 35.00
Cardinals, Holiday, 1991 .... 95.00
Deer, White Tail, 1982 .... 175.00
Ducks Unlimited, Pintail, 1978 .... 90.00
Ducks Unlimited, Pintail, 1978, ½-gal 180.00
Ducks Unlimited, Pintail, 1978, mini 30.00
Ducks Unlimited, Widgeon, 1979 .... 60.00
Ducks Unlimited, Widgeon, 1979, 1¾-liter 175.00
Eagle, Majestic, 1971 .... 275.00
Eagle, Majestic, gal, 1971 .... 1,600.00
Eagle, Majestic, mini, 1971 .... 125.00
Elk, 1980 .... 190.00

Indian, Ceremonial Dancer, Buffalo, 1979, $170.00. (Photo courtesy Desert West Auction Service on LiveAuctioneers.com)

Indian, Cigar Store, 1974 .... 40.00
Indian, Cigar Store, mini, 1975 .... 30.00
Indian, North Am, 1977, set of 6 .... 260.00
Indian, Southwest Dancers, mini, 1975, set of 6 ... 200.00
Jaguar, 1983 .... 175.00
Jaguar, mini, 1983 .... 50.00
Koala, 1973 .... 50.00
Owl, barred wall plaque 140.00
Owl, Great Gray, 1985 .... 90.00
Owl, Great Gray, mini, 1985 .... 50.00
Pelican, 1976 .... 65.00
Pelican, mini, 1976 .... 30.00
Pheasant, Standing, mini, 1984 .... 65.00
Phoenix Bird, 1981 .... 60.00
Ram, Big Horn, mini, 1980 .... 40.00
Rodeo, Barrel Racer, 1982 .... 95.00
Rodeo, Barrel Racer, mini, 1982 .... 40.00
Ruffed Grouse, 1981 .... 70.00
Ruffed Grouse, mini, 1981 .... 30.00
Skunk Family, 1978 .... 60.00
Skunk Family, mini, 1978 .... 30.00
Wild Turkey, 1976 .... 130.00

Wild Turkey

Series I, #1 .... 150.00
Series I, #1, #2, #3 or #4, mini, ea 22.00
Series I, #2 .... 95.00
Series I, #3 or #4, ea 45.00
Series I, #5, #6 or #7, ea 25.00
Series I, #5, #6, #7 & #8 mini, set of 4 .... 175.00
Series I, #8 .... 45.00
Series II, Lore #1 .... 20.00
Series II, Lore #2 .... 35.00
Series II, Lore #3 .... 45.00
Series II, Lore #4 .... 55.00

Series III, #1, In Flight 100.00
Series III, #1, In Flight, mini 45.00
Series III, #2, Turkey & Bobcat 125.00
Series III, #2, Turkey & Bobcat, mini 55.00
Series III, #3, Fighting Turkeys 130.00
Series III, #3, Fighting Turkeys, mini 60.00
Series III, #4, Turkey & Eagle 95.00
Series III, #4, Turkey & Eagle, mini 85.00
Series III, #5, Turkey & Raccoon 95.00
Series III, #5, Turkey & Raccoon, mini 45.00
Series III, #6, Turkey & Poults 95.00
Series III, #6, Turkey & Poults, mini 45.00
Series III, #7, Turkey & Red Fox 100.00
Series III, #7, Turkey & Red Fox, mini 60.00
Series III, #8, Turkey & Owl 100.00
Series III, #8, Turkey & Owl, mini 60.00
Series III, #9, Turkey & Bear Cubs 100.00
Series III, #9, Turkey & Bear Cubs, mini 60.00
Series III, #10, Turkey & Coyote 100.00
Series III, #10, Turkey & Coyote, mini 60.00
Series III, #11, Turkey & Falcon 100.00
Series III, #11, Turkey & Falcon, mini 60.00
Series III, #12, Turkey & Skunks 125.00
Series III, #12, Turkey & Skunks, mini 65.00

Decoys

American colonists learned the craft of decoy making from the Indians who used them to lure birds out of the sky as an important food source. Early models were carved from wood such as pine, cedar, and balsa, and a few were made of canvas or papier-maché. There are two basic types of decoys: water floaters and shorebirds (also called 'stick-ups'). Within each type are many different species, ducks being the most plentiful since they migrated along all four of America's great waterways. Market hunting became big business around 1880, resulting in large-scale commercial production of decoys which continued until about 1910 when such hunting was outlawed by the Migratory Bird Treaty.

Today decoys are one of the most collectible types of American folk art. The most valuable are those carved by such artists as Laing, Crowell, Ward, and Wheeler, to name only a few. Each area, such as Massachusetts, Connecticut, Maine, the Illinois River, and the Delaware River, produces decoys with distinctive regional characteristics. Examples of commercial decoys produced by well-known factories — among them Mason, Stevens, and Dodge — are also prized by collectors. Though mass produced, these nevertheless required a certain amount of hand carving and decorating. Well-carved examples, especially those of rare species, are appreciating rapidly, and those with original paint are more desirable. In the listings that follow, all decoys are solid-bodied unless noted hollow.

Key:
CG — Challenge Grade   ORP — old repaint
EDF — Evans Decory Factory   PDF — Peterson Decoy Factory
MDF — Mason's Decoy Factory   PG — Premier Grade
OP — original paint   WDF — Wildfowler Decoy Factory

Black duck, Ben Dye, ORP, neck crack/sm dents 750.00
Black duck, Ira Hudson, football body w/fluted tail, ORP ... 450.00
Black duck, John Blair, OP/ORP, crack in tail 6,250.00
Black duck, PDF, CG, OP, minor to moderate wear 5,000.00
Black duck, Sanford Gorsline, hollow, OP, minor wear ... 8,500.00
Black-bellied Plover, Harry V Shrouds, OP, minor wear ... 1,750.00
Bluebill drake, John Holly, ORP, few cracks/chips 600.00

Bluebill hen, JR Wells, hollow, orig comb pnt, cracks/dents/shot marks .2,800.00
Bluebill pr, Charlie Joiner, 1976, pnt eyes, NM 900.00
Bluewing Teal drake, EDF, OP, minor to moderate wear 1,200.00
Brant, Hurley Conklin, swimming, earlier style, OP, VG 425.00
Brant, Madison Mitchell, cork body, NM 350.00
Bufflehead drake, Hurley Conklin, hollow, EX 700.00
Bufflehead hen, Cigar Daisey, detailed feather cvg, EX 650.00
Canada goose, Cigar Daisey, 1971, cork body, OP, minor wear 900.00
Canada goose, Jasper Dodge, OP, sm dents 9,500.00
Canvasback drake, Leonard Pryor, preening, ORP, cracks/dents.. 800.00
Canvasback drake, Taylor Boyd, OP, few cracks 1,200.00
Canvasback drake, Tom Chambers, short bodied, hollow, G comb pnt.7,000.00
Curlew, Harry V Shrouds, OP, moderate wear 2,550.00
Dowitcher, MA, laminated 3-pc body, OP, moderate wear.......... 250.00
Dowitcher, MDF, glass eyes, fall plumage, ca 1900, OP, minor wear.2,200.00
Golden plover, MA, tack eyes, OP, sm dents 300.00
Goldeneye drake, Jess Urie, OP, sm neck crack, few dents 400.00
Goldeneye hen, Elmer Crowell, fluted tail, OP, minor wear...... 7,500.00
Goldeneye hen, John R Wells, JA & C brand, OP, sm crack/few dents..1,300.00
Goldeneye hen, Tom Schroeder, G cvd wing & tail detail, mini, 7" L. 1,000.00
Gull, Connecticut, 1940s, hollow, extended wing tips, OP, minor wear...5,000.00
Long-billed curlew, MDF, late 1890s, OP, moderate wear.......... 3,250.00
Magnum Bluebill drake, EDF, OP, few cracks............................ 1,300.00
Mallard drake, Charles Perdew, OP/sm dents/shot marks 2,500.00
Mallard drake, Charlie Joiner, sleeping, 1975, VG OP 1,050.00
Mallard drake, Heck Whittington, orig comb pnt 3,200.00
Mallard hen, Ned Burgess, OP, minor wear, very rare.............21,000.00
Merganser drake, Chincoteague VA, red-breasted, OP, moderate wear ... 350.00
Merganser drake, Doug Jester, short body style, OP, minor wear ...1,750.00
Merganser hen, WDF, worn OP, some chips 500.00
Owl, Leonard Doren, glass eyes, OP, moderate wear.................2,500.00
Pintail drake, Ed Phillips, lifted head/extended tail sprig, OP, EX. 10,500.00
Pintail drake, Ignatius Staichowiak, OP, sm neck crack/sm dents .1,600.00
Pintail drake, Joe Morgan, raised/appl primaries, hollow, ORP.... 200.00
Pintail hen, Dave Watson, worn OP, numerous dents 400.00
Pintail hen, MDF, glass eyes, OP, 2 bk cracks.........................9,000.00
Pintail hen, Xavier Bourg, relief wing cvg, OP, minor wear.......... 400.00
Pintail pr, Charlie Joiner, flat bottoms w/wooden keels, EX 3,250.00

Piping Plover, split tail, signed in ink: James Lapham, Dennisport, Mass., Cape Cod, excellent original condition, lifesize, **$600.00.** (Photo courtesy Decoys Unlimited, Inc. on LiveAuctioneers.com)

Redhead drake, Jim Currier, OP, NM... 500.00
Redhead drake, Ward Bros, 1940s, balsa/slightly trn cedar head, OP.2,200.00
Redhead pr, Charlie Joiner, 1985, pnt eyes, NM......................... 950.00
Robin snipe, Harry V Shrouds, spring plumage, OP, EX..........10,750.00
Shoveler drake, Davey W Nichol, unweighted, unused, M 2,100.00
Shoveler pr, Madison Mitchell, 1979, EX 1,200.00
Surf scoter drake, Gus Wilson, inlet head, cvd eyes/wings, ORP, chips...1,600.00
Swan, Jim Cockey, cvd eyes, ORP, age bk split/sm cracks 30,000.00
Swan, John Vickers, ORP, several cracks 800.00
Turkey, Sherman Jones & Lloyd Tyler, relief wing cvg, ⅔ sz, NM..2,750.00
Wht-wing scoter, Gus Wilson, extended head, raised wings, ORP ..2,500.00
Widgeon drake, Delbert Hudson, OP pnt by Ira Hudson, moderate wear... 1,000.00
Widgeon drake, MDF, glass eyes, EX OP, PG 55,000.00
Widgeon hen, DDF, ca 1890, OP, minor wear.............................. 950.00

Dedham Pottery

Originally founded in Chelsea, Massachusetts, as the Chelsea Keramic Works, the name was changed to Dedham Pottery in 1895 after the firm relocated in Dedham, near Boston, Massachusetts. The ware utilized a gray stoneware body with a crackle glaze and simple cobalt border designs of flowers, birds, and animals. Decorations were brushed on by hand using an ancient Chinese method which suspended the cobalt within the overall glaze. There were 13 standard patterns, among them Magnolia, Iris, Butterfly, Duck, Polar Bear, and Rabbit, the latter of which was chosen to represent the company on their logo. On the very early pieces, the rabbits face left; decorators soon found the reverse position easier to paint, and the rabbits were turned to the right. (Earlier examples are worth from 10% to 20% more than identical pieces manufactured in later years.) In addition to the standard patterns, other designs were produced for special orders. These and artist-signed pieces are highly valued by collectors today.

Though their primary product was the blue-printed, crackle-glazed dinnerware, two types of artware were also produced: crackle glaze and flambé. Their notable volcanic ware was a type of the latter. The mark is incised and often accompanies the cipher of Hugh Robertson. The firm was operated by succeeding generations of the Robertson family until it closed in 1943. Our advisor for this category is Dale MacLean; he is listed in the Directory under Massachusetts. See also Chelsea Keramic Art Works.

Ashtray, Rabbit, stamped/registered, 4".. 400.00
Bacon rasher, Magnolia, stamped/registered/imp, 1½x9¾" 475.00
Bacon rasher, Swan, stamped/registered, 1½x9½" 550.00
Bowl, Double Turtle, stamped, 3x6" 800.00
Bowl, Grape, stamped, 3½x7" 325.00
Bowl, lotus, Lotus Petal, stamped, 2½x5" 600.00
Bowl, nappy, Rabbit, stamped, 1½x5¼" 395.00
Bowl, Rabbit, stamped, 2½x10½" 450.00
Bowl, Rabbit, stamped/registered, sq, 8½" 350.00
Bowl, rice, Duck, stamped, 2x3½" 275.00
Bowl, Swan, #2, stamped/registered, 3½x8" 500.00
Candleholders, Rabbit, stamped/registered, 1¾", pr 500.00
Chamberstick, Rabbit, stamped, 2½x7" 700.00
Charger, Rabbit (clockwise), M Davenport, stamped/imp, 12¼" . 575.00
Coffeepot, Rabbit (clockwise), stamped, 7x9"................................ 950.00
Compote, Rabbit, faint stain, stamped, 3½x5½" 275.00
Creamer/sugar bowl, Lion Head, w/lid, stamped, 4½", 6½" 2,000.00
Cup/saucer, bouillon, Azalea, stamped/registered, 2x5½", 6"........ 250.00
Cup/saucer, Grape, stamped, 2¼", 5¾" 275.00
Cup/saucer, Rabbit, stamped registered, 3¼x5", 6¾" 275.00
Dish, child's, Cat, stamped/registered, 1⅛x7¾".............................5,000.00
Egg cup, Elephant & Baby, stamped /registered, 4¼x5" 800.00
Flower holder, turtle, stamped/registered, 3½" dia 500.00
Humidor, log cabin and farmhouse, incised, #13, 6¾" 3,000.00
Knife rest, rabbit crouching, stamped, rstr, 3x3½" 425.00
Medallion, Rabbit, slightly domed, sgn EM/2-36, 2" dia 325.00
Oyster dish, Rabbit, 4½" L.. 600.00

Pitcher, Night and Morning, rooster and owl, ink stamp, 5", **$550.00.** (Photo courtesy Cincinnati Art Galleries, LLC on LiveAuctioneers.com)

Pitcher, Rabbit, looped hdl, bulb, stamped, 6¾x7", NM 650.00
Plate, Clover, CPUS, 8½" 900.00
Plate, Crab, stamped/imp, 8½" 600.00
Plate, Day Lily, Hugh Robertson, stamped & mk, hairline, 8½" .. 935.00
Plate, Double Turtle, stamped/imp, 6" 800.00
Plate, Duck, stamped/imp, 9¾" 475.00
Plate, Elephant, stamped, 7¾" 675.00
Plate, Elephant, stamped/imp, 6½" 650.00
Plate, Fish, w/cobalt wave, stamped, 8½" 2,250.00
Plate, Fr Mushroom, Davenport, stamped/imp, 8½" 900.00
Plate, Grape, dbl stamped/imp, 8¾" 275.00
Plate, Grape, stamped/registered/imp, 7½" 225.00
Plate, Horse Chestnut, stamped, 6" 225.00
Plate, Iris, experimental pk, stamped/imp, 9¾" 275.00
Plate, Landscape & Boat, stamped, 6" 900.00
Plate, Lily Pond, peppering, stamped, 10½" 250.00
Plate, Lobster, stamped/imp, 8½" 675.00
Plate, Magnolia, stamped, 10" 350.00
Plate, Mushroom, stamped, imp rabbit mk, 8½" 645.00
Plate, Pineapple, CPUS, 8½" 750.00
Plate, Pineapple, CPUS/imp, flake, 10" 800.00
Plate, Pomegranate, #98/unidentified initials, 8½" 1,500.00
Plate, Pond Lily, registered/imp, 6" 250.00
Plate, poppy amid poppy pods, stamped/imp, rare, 6¼" 700.00
Plate, Rabbit, Single Ear, stamped, 8¼" 275.00
Plate, Rabbit, w/Fairbanks House, stamped/registered, 1931, 9½" .. 1,765.00
Plate, Scottie Dog Pr, stamped/registered/1931, hairline, 8½" 800.00
Plate, Snow Tree, stamped, 10½" 350.00
Plate, Tufted Duck, imp, 10¼" 400.00
Plate, Turkey, early stamp, 10" 500.00
Plate, Turtle, #2, stamped, chips to ft ring, 8½" 800.00
Plate, Turtle, stamped/imp, 6¼" 650.00
Plate, Water Lily, stamped, 6" 175.00
Salt cellar, Walnut on Leaf, sgn DP in bl, 3" 475.00
Shakers, Rabbit, bulb, long necks, mk DP, 3½", pr 450.00
Shakers, Rabbit, bulb, stamped, 2⅝", pr 400.00
Tea tile, Elephant & Baby, stamped/registered, rstr kiln pop, 5½" . 800.00
Tea tile, Rabbit, stamped, 6¼", EX 450.00
Teapot, Elephant, stamped, 6¾x8½" 1,500.00
Teapot, Rabbit, stamped, ca 1932, 4½" 900.00
Tureen, Rabbit, 2 rabbit bands, ftd/hdld, rabbit finial, 8x8x11", EX.1,950.00
Tureen, Rabbit, dome lid w/knob hdl, stamped, 4x7", NM 700.00

Miscellaneous

Vase, bubbly oxblood over wht & bl crackle, WA, hairlines, 5½x4"..1,700.00
Vase, clear gr drips over wht/bl crackle, H Robertson, flaw, 7x4" ..1,100.00
Vase, emerald gr opaque drips on wht orange peel, H Robertson, 6¼"....1,200.00
Vase, forest gr & bl mottle, H Robertson, experimental, 7¼x4¼" .1,000.00
Vase, khaki gr on bl & gr, H Robertson, 7¾x5" 1,000.00
Vase, mahog & oxblood flambé, H Robertson, HCR/DP24A, flaw, 8x6". 2,350.00
Vase, oxblood drip, experimental, H Robertson, 5½x4" 1,200.00

Vase, oxblood, two-tone, partly lustered, incised Dedham Pottery BW HCR #217, 8½", NM, $2,400.00. (Photo courtesy Rago Arts and Auction Center)

Vase, thick bl-gray & oxblood, H Robertson, experimental, 5x4".. 1,000.00
Vase, thick wht/beige drips on frothy gr, HCR/DP718, 8½x4½" . 2,200.00
Vase, volcanic amber/gr/brn mottle, experimental, HCR, ca 1900, 7¼" ..1,000.00
Vase, volcanic creamy buff, can neck, H Robertson, 10½x6" 1,200.00

Degenhart Glass

After many years of working at Cambridge Glass Co. and making paperweights, John Degenhart and his wife, Elizabeth, started their Crystal Art Glass (1947 – 1970) company in Cambridge, Ohio. By 1964, 24 novelty molds were being worked in about 12 colors. Hundreds of colors were produced over the years. Items were marked with a D or a D in a heart after 1972. Early colors included clear, sapphire, amber, amethyst, green, milk white, opaque blue, vaseline, and cobalt. When the company ceased operation and was sold to Bernard Boyd, ten molds were kept at the Degenhart Museum and never reproduced: Priscilla, Owl, Portrait plate, Ring for the top of the Bird toothpick, Daisy & Button salt, Daisy & Button sugar bowl, Daisy & Button creamer, Seal of Ohio cup plate, Portrait paperweight, and Mini Slipper.

For additional information, see Boyd Crystal Art Glass in *Garage Sale & Flea Market* (Collector Books). We also suggest Gene Florence's *Degenhart Glass & Paperweights*, and the website for the Degenhart Museum, www.degenhartglass.com.

Our advisor for Degenhart is Shirley Smith; she is located in the Directory under West Virginia.

Box, heart-shaped, mk, 4x4" 36.00
Covered dish, hen on nest, lemon custard, mk, 3¼" L.................... 28.00
Covered dish, hen on nest, orange satin, 3¼" L............................. 53.00
Doll, Priscilla, pk opal, mk, 5½" 20.00
Mug, stork, pk, mk, 2⅝" 20.00
Ornament, bl/brn, 3½" 41.00
Owl, #60, brn slag, mk 60.00
Paperweight, Charles Degenhart, 2¾" 350.00
Robin w/ Cherry, cobalt, mk, 5x6" 65.00
Salt, open, heart-shaped, ruby, mk, 1⅝" W 51.00

Salt and pepper, birds, milk glass, $35.00. (Photo courtesy Shirley Smith)

Shoe, cat head, orange slag, mk, 5½" L 18.00
Toothpick, heart-shaped, bl opaque, 2¾" 25.00
Toothpick bowl, cobalt, mk, 1½" W.. 22.00

Delatte

Delatte was a manufacturer of French cameo glass. Founded in 1921, their style reflected the influence of the Art Deco era with strong color contrasts and bold design. Our advisor for this category is Don Williams; he is listed in the Directory under Missouri.

Chandelier, grapevines, brn/orange, 18" bowl shade+3 pendant lilies.. 3,300.00
Vase, blackberries, reds on yel to wht, bulb, 5¾" 960.00
Vase, buckeye & foliage, brn on mottled pumpkin, 9½" 550.00
Vase, floral, brn on yel mottle, teardrop, 8" 775.00
Vase, floral, reds on pk to wht mottle, fp, gourd shape, 8" 900.00

Vase, fruit on branches, bl on wht w/citron & burgundy mottle, 4" . 515.00
Vase, fuchsia, lt & dk burgundy on frosted wht, 11" 1,000.00
Vase, lake scene, brn tones to frost, cylinder, metal base, 6" 600.00
Vase, orchids & leaves, purple/gr on pk, ovoid, 8x5" 1,765.00
Vase, thorny flowers, amethyst on citron, teardop, 7½" 550.00

Delft

Old Delftware, made as early as the sixteenth century, was originally a low-fired earthenware coated in a thin opaque tin glaze with painted-on blue or polychrome designs. It was not until the last half of the nineteenth century, however, that the ware became commonly referred to as Delft, acquiring the name from the Dutch village that had become the major center of its production. English, German, and French potters also produced Delft, though with noticeable differences both in shape and decorative theme.

In the early part of the eighteenth century, the German potter Bottger developed a formula for porcelain; in England, Wedgwood began producing creamware — both of which were much more durable. Unable to compete, one by one the Delft potteries failed. Soon only one remained. In 1876 De Porcelyne Fles reintroduced Delftware on a hard white body with blue and white decorative themes reflecting the Dutch countryside, windmills by the sea, and Dutch children. This manufacturer is the most well known of several operating today. Their products are now produced under the Royal Delft label.

For further information we recommend *Discovering Dutch Delftware, Modern Delft and Makkum Pottery* by Stephen J. Van Hook (Glen Park Press, Alexandria, Virginia). Examples listed here are blue on white unless noted otherwise. See also specific manufacturers.

Bowl, England, floral, 18th C, 10⅜" 480.00
Bowl, Holland, flower vase, floral rim, 18th C, 9", NM 260.00

Charger, Dutch, Adoration of the Magi, circa 1605, repaired cracks and rim chips, 15", $2,000.00. (Photo courtesy Rachel Davis Fine Arts on LiveAuctioneers.com)

Charger, England, chinoiserie, 18th C, 13⅝", EX 275.00
Charger, England, floral w/yel centers, 18th C, 1½3" 900.00
Charger, English, flower basket & flower borders, 18th C, 13" 785.00
Charger, Holland, exotic bird, flower & feather borders, rstr, 12" . 450.00
Charger, Holland, figures in landscape, scrolled border, 19th C, 16" ... 725.00
Charger, Holland, figures in sleigh, Maastricht, 18th C, 15½" 90.00
Charger, Holland, floral w/much bl, ca 1900, 15½" 240.00
Charger, Holland, floral, 3 reserves in border, 20th C, 14¼" 120.00
Charger, Holland, flower basket, floral rim, 18th C, 13½" 950.00
Charger, Holland, mixed flowers, vining border, 18th C, 12", NM .. 660.00
Charger, poly landscapes w/figures, David Kam, 1st quarter 18th C, 20" .. 5,600.00
Jar, wet drug, Holland, Rosar Sol, w/spout, mid-18th C, rpr, 9" ... 925.00
Lamp base, England, rampant lion figural, ca 1880-1890, 17" ... 1,200.00
Pitcher, Holland, windmill scene, integral hdl, Maastricht, 7x4¼" .. 135.00
Plaque, Holland, Mother & Child, OT Schwartz, 1850s, 17½x11"+fr... 780.00
Plate, England, bird & floral, mc, 18th C, 8⅞" 515.00
Plate, England, pagoda & flowers, WCA 1716 on rim, 8⅞" 1,675.00
Plate, England, Sarah Pearson Born 17th Agust (sic) 1734, 9⅛" ... 2,650.00
Plate, England, vase/figure/flag w/floral border, 18th C, 8½" 150.00
Vase, England, scenic reserve, urn form, bird finial, 18th C, 14", pr ... 1,975.00
Vase, Holland, floral, bulb body, 8-sided base, ca 1740, 9½" 900.00
Vase, Holland, teasel, HJ Sanders, shouldered, 5¾" 300.00

Denbac

The French pottery was founded in Vierzon in 1909 by René Denert. René Denert became known as Denbac in 1921 when René Louis Balichon became its financial manager (Denbac being a contraction of the partners' names). They became well known for producing not only Art Nouveau-style wares, Art Deco majolica and stoneware, but Arts and Crafts designs as well. Micro-crystalline glazes were their specialty. Operations halted temporarily during WWII but resumed again shortly thereafter. The company closed in 1952.

Box, sculpted beetle on lid, brown and green matt, #322, 2½x4", $250.00. (Photo courtesy Treadway Gallery on LiveAuctioneers.com)

Pitcher, multi-tone brn crystalline, gourd form, 8½" 150.00
Vase, 3 appl orange lobsters on bl & brn drip, 7x8" 510.00
Vase, dragonflies, bl/gr/brn crystalline, 8" W 200.00
Vase, gr/gray crystalline drip, gourd form, 9½" 375.00
Vase, leaves emb on brn matt, #15, 3¾" 210.00
Vase, multi-tone brn crystalline, twisted form, 8½" 200.00
Vase, organic design at shoulder, blk/brn crystalline, 11¼" 300.00
Vase, organic design, gr/bl/brn crystalline, 4 rim-to-hip hdls, 9¼". 225.00
Vase, organic designs, gr/brn crystalline, low integral hdls, 8" 300.00

Depression Glass

Depression glass is defined by Cathy and Gene Florence, authors of several bestselling books on the subject, as 'the inexpensive glassware made primarily during the Depression era in the colors of amber, green, pink, blue, red, yellow, white, and crystal.' This glass was mass produced, sold through five-and-dime stores and mail-order catalogs, and given away as premiums with gas and food products.

The listings in this book are far from complete. If you want a more thorough presentation of this glassware, we recommend *Collector's Encyclopedia of Depression Glass, Pocket Guide to Depression Glass & More, Elegant Glassware of the Depression Era, Glass Candlesticks of the Depression Era,* and *Florences' Glassware Pattern Identification Guides, I – IV,* all by Cathy and Gene Florence, whose address is listed in the Directory under Kentucky. See also McKee Glass; New Martinsville Glass.

Adam, pk, ashtray, 4½" 22.00
Adam's Rib, irid, comport, 6½" 60.00
Addie, blk, cream soup 20.00
Amelia, smoke, bowl, sq, fluted, 5½" 45.00
American Pioneer, crystal, whiskey, 2-oz, 2¼" 25.00
American Sweetheart, monax, lamp shade 495.00
Ardith, cobalt, candle, sq flattened top, 4⅝" 32.00
Artura, gr, creamer 10.00
Aunt Polly, bl, tumbler, 8-oz, 3⅝" 24.00
Aurora, cobalt, tumbler, 10-oz, 4¾" 22.00
Avocado, crystal, plate, cake, 2-hdld, 10¼" 14.00
Beaded Block, amber, stemmed jelly, 4½" 25.00

Berlin, crystal, basket ... 25.00
Block Optic, yel, candy jar & cover, 2¼" ... 75.00
Bowknot, gr, bowl, cereal, 5½" ... 22.00
Cameo, crystal w/platinum rim, decanter, w/stopper, 10" ... 300.00
Cherry Blossom, delphite, bowl, berry, 4¾" ... 16.00
Cherryberry, pk, comport, 5¾" ... 25.00

Cherry Blossom, pink, mug, seven-ounce, $400.00. (Photo courtesy Cathy and Gene Florence)

Chinex Classic, castle decal, butter ... 100.00
Circle, gr, pitcher, 60-oz ... 60.00
Cloverleaf, blk, ashtray, match holder in center, 4" ... 45.00
Colonial Fluted, gr, bowl, lg berry, 7½" ... 20.00
Colonial, gr, cheese dish ... 250.00
Columbia, pk, plate, luncheon, 9½" ... 26.00
Coronation, royal ruby, bowl, nappy, hdld, 6½" ... 18.00
Crackle, crystal, candy box, hexagonal lid ... 28.00
Cremax, bl, sugar, open ... 7.00
Crow's Foot, Ritz bl, bowl, Nasturtium, 3-ftd ... 125.00
Cube, pk, pitcher, 45-oz, 8¾" ... 210.00
Cupid, bl, bowl, fruit, 10¼" ... 350.00
Daisy & Button w/Narcissus, tray, 10⅜" ... 22.00
Della Robbia, crystal w/lustre colors, basket, 9" ... 135.00
Diamond Quilted, blk, sandwich server, center hdl ... 40.00
Diana, pk, s&p, pr ... 65.00
Dogwood, gr, tumbler, decor, 5-oz, 3½" ... 135.00
Doric & Pansy, ultramarine, butter ... 250.00
Doric, delphite, pitcher, flat, 32-oz, 5½" ... 1,500.00
Ellipse, crystal, jug, 61-oz, 7½" ... 60.00
English Hobnail, ice bl, bowl, hexagonal ftd, 2-hdld, 8" ... 165.00
Fancy Colonial, gr, vase, flat, bead base, ruffled rim, 12" ... 110.00
Floral & Dmn Band, pk, sugar, 5¼" ... 10.00
Floral, jadite, canister set: coffee, tea, cereal, sugar, 5¼", ea ... 135.00
Florentine No 1, yel, coaster/ashtray, 3¾" ... 20.00
Florentine No 2, cobalt bl, comport, ruffled, 3½" ... 50.00
Flower Garden w/Butterflies, plate, indent for 3" comport, 10" ... 32.00
Flute & Cane, crystal, celery, oval, 8½" ... 22.00
Fortune, pk, cup ... 8.00
Frances, bl, candlestick, 3½" ... 35.00
Fruits, pk, sherbet ... 12.00
Gem, bl, plate, bread, 6" ... 12.00
Georgian, gr, tumbler, flat, 2-oz, 5¼" ... 95.00
Glades, crystal, ice tub, 4x6⅜" ... 50.00
Glades, red, candle, dbl lt, 5" ... 53.00
Gothic Garden, amber, cake stand, ftd, sq, 10½" ... 90.00
Grape, s&p, pr ... 30.00
Hex Optic, pk, bucket reamer ... 65.00
Hobnail, pk, bowl, crimped, 9½" ... 75.00
Homespun, crystal, platter, closed hdls, 13" ... 16.00
Indiana Custard, Fr ivory, sherbet ... 60.00
Indiana Silver, crystal w/sterling silver o/l, cup, custard ... 8.00
Iris, irid, demi saucer ... 250.00
Jubilee, yel, candlestick, pr ... 100.00
Laced Edge, gr, vase, flower bowl ... 300.00
Laced Edge, opal, tidbit, 2-tiered, 8" & 10" plates ... 90.00
Lake Como, Vitrock w/bl scene, saucer, St Denis ... 6.00
Largo, bl, cigarette box, 4x3¼x1½ ... 55.00
Laurel, poudre bl, plate, dinner, 2 styles, 9⅛" ... 26.00
Lincoln Inn, red, sugar ... 20.00
Line #555, crystal, tray, center hdl, 11" ... 18.00
Little Jewel, wht, celery tray, 8½" ... 14.00
Lois, pk, mayonnaise or whipped cream w/ladle ... 40.00
Lorain, yel, bowl, deep berry, 8" ... 155.00
Lotus, bl, cologne, ½-oz ... 110.00
Lucy, royal bl, candlestick, dbl, 5⅛" ... 60.00
Madrid, gr, ashtray, sq, 6" ... 350.00
Manhattan, pk, relish tray, w/insert, 14" ... 70.00
Maya, crystal, cheese dish w/lid ... 60.00
Mayfair Fed, amber, creamer, ftd ... 10.00
Mayfair/Open Rose, pk, sugar bowl, ftd ... 2,750.00
Mayfair/Open Rose, yel, cookie jar & lid ... 895.00
Miss America, royal ruby, goblet, wine, 3-oz, 3¾" ... 325.00
Modernistic, wht, sugar lid ... 7.50
Moderntone, cobalt, platter, oval, 12" ... 50.00
Monticello, crystal, cuspidor ... 60.00
Moondrops, bl, bonbon, triangular, 3-ftd ... 35.00
Mt Pleasant, blk, bowl, sq, 2-hdld, 8" ... 22.00
Mt Vernon, crystal, spooner ... 20.00
New Century, amethyst, pitcher, w/ or w/o ice lip 60-oz, 7¾" ... 35.00
Newport, Hazel-Atlas, cobalt, tumbler, 9-oz, 4½" ... 40.00
Newport, New Martinsville, gr, saucer ... 3.00
No 610 Pyramid, gr, ice tub ... 165.00
No 612 Horseshoe, yel, pitcher, 64-oz, 8½" ... 350.00
No 616, Vernon, gr, plate, sandwich, 11½" ... 20.00
No 618 Pineapple & Floral, red, tumbler, 8-oz, 4¼" ... 20.00
Normandie, irid, bowl, oval vegetable, 10" ... 14.00
Old Cafe, royal ruby, lamp ... 100.00
Old Colony, pk, comport, 9" ... 995.00
Old English, pk, sandwich server, center hdl ... 40.00
Olive, emerald, bowl, bun or fruit tray, 9" ... 20.00
Orchid, blk, mayonnaise, 3-pc ... 135.00
Ovide, blk, candy dish & cover ... 40.00
Oyster & Pearl, crystal, bowl, ruffled edge, 10½" ... 75.00
Parrot, amber, butter dish top ... 1,300.00
Party Line, bl, cocktail shaker, w/lid, 18-oz ... 75.00
Patrician, gr, jam dish ... 25.00
Patrick, yel, tray, 2-hdld, 11" ... 50.00
Peacock & Wild Rose, lt bl, tumbler, 10-oz, 5¼" ... 100.00
Peacock Reverse, blk, creamer, flat, 2¾" ... 75.00
Peacock Reverse, gr, candy dish, rnd ... 175.00
Pebbled Rim, amber, candleholder ... 14.00

Penny Line, green, sherbet, low foot, $7.00. (Photo courtesy Cathy and Gene Florence)

Penny Line, Mulberry, stem, cocktail, 6-oz ... 10.00
Petalware, monax, saucer, cream soup liner ... 15.00
Pillar Optic, royal ruby, bowl, oval vegetable ... 150.00
Primo, yel, cake plate, 3-ftd, 10" ... 30.00
Princess, apricot, bowl, salad, octagonal, 9" ... 175.00
Queen Mary, pk, sherbet, ftd or flat ... 9.00
Radiance, ice bl, condiment set, 4-pc, w/tray ... 295.00

Raindrops, gr, cup 8.00
Reeded, tangerine, perfume w/triangle stop 50.00
Ribbon, gr, s&p, pr.. 45.00
Ring, crystal, vase, 8" 15.00
Rock Crystal, red, bowl, oblong, celery or relish, 12" 75.00
Romanesque, gr, powder jar 45.00
Rose Cameo, plate, salad, 7" 12.00
Rose Point Band, crystal, goblet, wine 15.00
Rosemary, amber, plate, grill...6.00
Roulette, pk, plate, sandwich, 12" 16.00
Round Robin, irid, plate, luncheon, 8" 4.00
Roxana, yel, tumbler, 9-oz, 4¼" 20.00
Royal Lace, gr, pitcher, str sides, 48-oz 105.00
Royal Ruby, ruby red, tumbler, juice, 3" 15.00
Sandwich, crystal, celery, 10½"... 12.00
Sharon, pk, bowl, cream soup, 5" 32.00
Ships, bl, cocktail shaker 40.00
Sierra, pk, platter, oval, 11" 35.00
Spiral, gr, ice or butter tub... 20.00
Springtime, stem, cocktail, 2½-oz 22.00
Square, ruby, plate, dessert, 6" 9.00
Starlight, crystal, creamer, oval 5.00
Strawberry, irid, comport, 5¾" 18.00
Sunburst, crystal, relish, 2-part 10.00
Sunflower, pk, ashtray, center design only, 5".................................9.00
Sunshine, gr, candle, hex ft, single 25.00
Swirl, ultramarine, pitcher, ftd, 48-oz......................................1,750.00
Tea Room, gr or pk, cr/sug bowl on tray 85.00
Tea Room, pk, marmalade, notched lid... 180.00
Thistle, gr, plate, heavy cake, 13" 145.00
Top Notch, cobalt, plate, serving tray 30.00

Tulip, amethyst, candleholder, 5¼" base, 3", $35.00. (Photo courtesy Cathy and Gene Florence)

Tulip, amethyst, decanter w/stopper.. 395.00
Twisted Optic, canary yel, powder jar w/lid.................................... 85.00
US Scroll, blk, saucer...3.00
US Swirl, gr, vase, 6½".. 25.00
Victory, bl, candlesticks, 3", pr 100.00
Vitrock, wht, plate, soup, 9" 16.00
Waterford, crystal, relish, 5-part, 13¾".. 18.00
White Band, crystal w/wht band & red stripes, cocktail shaker, 32-oz..22.00
Windsor, pk, tray, sq, w/hdl, 4" 8.00
Woolworth, crystal, plate, plain rim, 8⅝"...................................... 14.00

Derby

William Duesbury operated in Derby, England, from about 1755, purchasing a second establishment, The Chelsea Works, in 1769. During this period fine porcelains were produced which so impressed the King that in 1773 he issued the company the Crown Derby patent. In 1810, several years after Duesbury's death, the factory was bought by Robert Bloor. The quality of the ware suffered under the new management, and the main Derby pottery closed in 1848. Within a short time, the work was revived by a dedicated number of former employees who established their own works on King Street in Derby.

The earliest known Derby mark was the crown over a script 'D'; however, this mark is rarely found today. Soon after 1782, that mark was augmented with a device of crossed batons and six dots, usually applied in underglaze blue. During the Bloor period, the crown was centered within a ring containing the words 'Bloor' above and 'Derby' below the crown, or with a red printed stamp — the crowned Gothic 'D.' The King Street plant produced figurines that may be distinguished from their earlier counterparts by the presence of an 'S' and 'H' on either side of the crown and crossed batons.

In 1876 a new pottery was constructed in Derby, and the owners revived the earlier company's former standard of excellence. The Queen bestowed the firm the title Royal Crown Derby in 1890; it still operates under that name today. See also Royal Crown Derby.

Bowl, Imari-like floral, 19th C, 10" 60.00
Figurine, Britannia w/shield, much gold, late 18th C, 10⅜"......... 500.00

Figurine, Dr. Syntax, circa 1820, 5¼", $660.00. (Photo courtesy Skinner Auctioneers and Appraisers of Antiques and Fine Art)

Figurine, Dr Syntax on horseback, 19th C, 7½" 395.00
Figurine, Fame, draped angel blowing horn, rstr, late 18th C, 11"...240.00
Figurines, musketeer & lady in fine attire, red mk, 9¼", pr........... 350.00
Inkstand, floral w/gr bands, 4-compartment, 1840s, 5½x11½x7" . 480.00
Soup tureen, Japan pattern, ftd, w/hdls & lid, ca 1810, 13"........... 950.00
Vase, Japan pattern, gilt trim, mask hdls, ca 1810, EX..............4,200.00

Desert Sands

As early as the 1850s, the Evans family living in the Ozark Mountains of Missouri produced domestic clay products. Their small pot shop was passed on from one generation to the next. In the 1920s it was moved to North Las Vegas, Nevada, where the name Desert Sands was adopted. Succeeding generations of the family continued to relocate, taking the business with them. From 1937 to 1962 it operated in Boulder City, Nevada; then it was moved to Barstow, California, where it remained until it closed in the late 1970s.

Desert Sands pottery is similar to Mission Ware by Niloak. Various mineral oxides were blended to mimic the naturally occurring sand formations of the American West. A high-gloss glaze was applied to add intensity to the colorful striations that characterize the ware. Not all examples are marked, making it sometimes difficult to attribute. Marked items carry an ink stamp with the Desert Sands designation. Paper labels were also used.

Bowl, 2x7", $25 to.. 35.00
Bowl, 3x9".. 50.00
Bowl, flared rim, 2x4" 25.00
Bowl, nut, T'print pattern, early mk, 1¾x3½" 35.00
Compote, flared ft & rim, 7".. 150.00

Compote, flared ft, bell-like bowl, unmk, 4¾x5⅝".......................... 45.00
Compote, ftd, unmk, 4¾x5⅝".. 35.00

Compote, vibrant colors, 4¾x5⅝", $45.00. (Photo courtesy Belhorn Auction Services, LLC on LiveAuctioneers.com)

Shakers, slim waisted form, 5", pr... 30.00
Vase, 7⅝x3¾".. 40.00
Vase, flared cylinder, 2 paper labels, Hand Made by Ferrel on base, 7"...36.00

Documents

Although the word 'document' is defined in the general sense as 'anything printed or written, etc., relied upon to record or prove something...,' in the collectibles market, the term is more diversified with broadsides, billheads, checks, invoices, letters and letterheads, land grants, receipts, and waybills some of the most sought after. Some documents in demand are those related to a specific subject such as advertising, mining, railroads, military, politics, banking, slavery, nautical, or legal (deeds, mortgages, etc.). Other collectors look for examples representing a specific period of time such as colonial documents, Revolutionary or Civil War documents, early Western documents, or those from a specific region, state, or city.

Aside from supply and demand, there are five major factors which determine the collector-value of a document. These are:

1) Age — Documents from the eastern half of the country can be found that date back to the 1700s or earlier. Most documents sought by collectors usually date from 1700 to 1900. Those with twentieth-century dates are still abundant and not in demand unless of special significance or beauty.

2) Region of origin — Depending on age, documents from rural and less-populated areas are harder to find than those from major cities and heavily populated states. The colonization of the West and Midwest did not begin until after 1850, so while an 1870s billhead from New York or Chicago is common, one from Albuquerque or Phoenix is not, since most of the Southwest was still unsettled.

3) Attractiveness — Some documents are plain and unadorned, but collectors prefer colorful, profusely illustrated pieces. Additional artwork and engravings add to the value.

4) Historical content — Unusual or interesting content, such as a letter written by a Civil War soldier giving an eyewitness account of the Battle of Gettysburg or a western territorial billhead listing numerous animal hides purchased from a trapper, will sell for more than one with mundane information.

5) Condition — Through neglect or environmental conditions, over many decades paper articles can become stained, torn, or deteriorated. Heavily damaged or stained documents are generally avoided altogether. Those with minor problems are more acceptable, although their value will decrease anywhere from 20% to 50%, depending upon the extent of damage. Avoid attempting to repair tears with Scotch tape — sell 'as is' so that the collector can take proper steps toward restoration.

Foreign documents are plentiful; and though some are very attractive, resale may be difficult. The listings that follow are generalized; prices are variable depending entirely upon the five points noted above. Values here are based upon examples with no major damage. Common grade documents without significant content are found in abundance and generally have little collector value. These usually date from the late 1800s to mid-1900s. It should be noted that the items listed below are examples of those that meet the criteria for having collector value. There is little demand for documents worth less than $5.00. For more information we recommend *Owning Western History* by Warren Anderson. Cheryl Anderson is our advisor; her address may be found in the Directory under Utah.

Key:
pp — pre-printed   vgn — vignette

Account of items used by 52nd PA Volunteer, 1885, 10x15" 12.00
Account of Sales, 7th Cavalry, dtd 1878, sgn 15.00
Appointment of Commissioner of Deeds, CA, pp, w/gold seal, 1868 ..55.00

Broadside of the Declaration of Independence, copyright James D. McBride, engraved and printed (by the Continental Publishing Co., Philadelphia, PA), to celebrate the United States' centennial, facsimile signature by Secretary of the Interior certifying that this is a 'Fac.Simile of the original.' 19½x14½", $800.00. (Photo courtesy Early American on LiveAuctioneers.com)

Certificate, Airline Transport Pilot, pp, 1941 .... 12.00
Certificate, steamboat inspection, pp, vgn, 1950, +fr 30.00
Certificate, steamship inspection, pp, eagle vgn, 1844, 8x10" 48.00
Check, Carson NV, to Senator, $56 for a week's work, 1881.......... 25.00
Civil War claims, partially pp, sgn by Paymaster General, 1865, 1-pg ...48.00
Civil War discharge, IA, 1864, w/GAR medal, in shadowbox fr.. 132.50
Deed of release, property in PA, 1794, 28½x12" 30.00
Grand jury findings, GA, selling liquor to slave, 1853, 9x12½" pg... 110.00
Indenture, for land in VA, 1795, on vellum, 27x25" 48.00
Land grant, member of TX militia, emb seal, sgn Buchanan, 1859 .. 120.00
Land grant, Montgomery Co VA, sgn by Governor B Randolf, 1789, 13x14" ...230.00
Land transfer, MA, sgn/witnessed, 1716, 10x15" 270.00
Ledger page, itemized business receipts, 1830, 12½x8" 18.00
Letter, Civil War soldier, camp activities/etc, 1862, 4-pg 60.00
Letterhead, AG Spalding & Bros, w/logo, sgn/dtd 1929................. 12.00
Letterhead, Findlay Baseball Assoc, ca 1910.................................... 48.00
Letterhead, Philadelphia A's, sgn John D Shibe, 1932.................... 18.00
License to trade w/Sioux, partial pp, sgn JQ Smith, 1844, 1-pg ... 425.00
List of quartermaster's stores, Fort Snelling, 1865, 10¼x16"........ 135.00
Promise of payment, $3,000 amount, sgn/sealed/witnessed, 1865, 8x8".. 12.00
Receipt, Army shipment of hay bales via ship, 1864, +envelope ... 18.00
Receipt, bounty paid to serve 3 months in army, 1776, 1-pg........ 110.00
Receipt, for discharge pay/etc, NY Volunteer, 1863, 8x10" 18.00
Receipt, Moline Plow Co, pp, vgn, 1878 .... 36.00
Receipt, sale of 2 slaves, KY, 1817, 10x7½", VG 315.00
Receipt, to Sheriff of Frederick Co, taxes, pp, 1860, 2x6½" 12.00
Register of Revolutionary War warrants, 1928, folio, leather bound ..345.00
Slave document, TN, use of freed 8-yr old, 1867, +revenue stamp ..215.00
Substance account, Artillery Corps, Fort Constitution, 1813 .... 65.00
Telegram, Spanish-Am war plans for black infantry, 1898 .... 75.00

Dollhouses and Furnishings

Dollhouses were introduced commercially in this country late in the 1700s by Dutch craftsmen who settled in the east. By the mid-1800s, they had become meticulously detailed, divided into separate rooms, and lavishly furnished to reflect the opulence of the day. Originally intended for the amusement of adults of the household, by the late 1800s their status had changed to that of a child's toy. Though many early dollhouses were lovingly hand fashioned for a special little girl, those made commercially by such companies as Bliss and Schoenhut are highly valued.

Furniture and furnishings in the Biedermeier style featuring stenciled Victorian decorations often sell for several hundred dollars each. Other early pieces made of pewter, porcelain, or papier-maché are also quite valuable. Certainly less expensive but very collectible, nonetheless, is the quality, hallmarked plastic furniture produced during the '40s by Renwal and Acme, and the 1960s Petite Princess line produced by Ideal. For more information and suggested values for dollhouse furniture, see *Schroeder's Collectible Toys, Antique to Modern*, and *Garage Sale & Flea Market*, both published by Collector Books. Our advisor for this category is Barbara Rosen; she is listed in the Directory under New Jersey. See also Miniatures.

Key:
PLW — paper litograph on wood   PW — painted wood

Bliss, 1-story/3-room, PLW, porch/columns, 23x19x11", VG+..2,050.00
Bliss, 2-story Vict, 2 chimneys, 23x19", VG 1,750.00
Bliss, 2-story/2-room, PLW w/bl clapboards & yel shingles, 16x11", EX ..800.00
Bliss, 2-story/2-room, PLW, cut-out windows, 13x9x6", VG 600.00
Bliss, 2-story/4-room, PLW, 2nd story balcony, 23x20x11", VG...500.00
Christian Hacker, 2-story/2-room, red roof, 22x20x14", G........2,000.00
Christian Hacker, 2-story mansion, mansard roof, 30x28", VG.3,100.00
Christian Hacker, 2-story/4-room, German, 31x28", VG..........1,800.00
Christian Hacker, 2-story villa, 4 rooms, 28x18", G 2,750.00

English, Netta Villa 1899 lettered on front, original paint and some accessories, 33x26½x22", $840.00.
(Photo courtesy Wiederseim Associates, Inc. on LiveAuctioneers.com)

Gottschalk, 2-story mansion/attic, 2 chimneys, front opens, 37x31x20", VG...8,050.00
Gottschalk, 2-story/2-room, Vict, bay window, 15x10x7", VG 750.00
Gottschalk, 2-story/2-room, PLW, 'brick', bl roof, 16x7x10", VG .850.00
Gottschalk, 2-story/2-room, PLW, wht-pnt balcony, 14x6", VG+.425.00
Gottschalk, 2-story/4-room, 2 hallways, 32x28", G 3,500.00
Gottschalk, 3-story/6-room, elevator, wood, 23x18x13", G 3,500.00
Reed, 2-story Gutter Roof, PLW, 18x10x9", EX.........................1,500.00
Schoenhut, 2-story Colonial, 4 rooms & attic, 17x12x15", F.......150.00
Schoenhut, 2-story PA colonial style, 4 rooms, 17x17x12", EX...425.00
Schoenhut, cottage w/gray brick ext, red roof, 20x13x17", VG ...325.00
Tynietoy, 2-story Nantucket or Saltbox style, 4 rooms, wood, 25x29x25", G..600.00
Tynietoy, 2-story NE townhouse, furnished, 29x48x17", VG+..5,500.00
Unknown, 2-story 'gutter' house, 2-room, PLW, 11x5x8", G+.....325.00

Shops and Single Rooms

Barn, Bliss, PLW & heavy cb, take-apart style, 19x18", EX..........500.00
Bedroom, Marjorie Wentworth, Am colonial style, 13x22", VG .250.00
Butcher Shop, Fr, 2 cutout arched windows, 10x20x10", G 800.00

Confectionary Shop, Fr, 3 front openings, 20x29x7", EX..........5,500.00
General Store, Germany, PW, bk shelving, 8x17x11", G 425.00
Kitchen, 1870s, tin, 3-sided, tin chimney/hood, 12x22x9", VG.2,750.00
Kitchen, Fr, 1900-10, bl/wht, tin stove, 19x27x8", VG+...........1,100.00
Kitchen, PLW, metal stove, wooden table/chairs, 12x12x18", EX. 275.00
Parlor, Germany, box folds to form parlor, 8x14", VG 375.00
Stable, Christian Hacker, PW, 3 stalls, gates, 27x42x22", VG+.2,500.00
Stable, England, 1910s, 2 stalls w/hay bins & wooden bench, 12x21", VG.175.00
Store, Gottschalk, bk wall w/12 drawers, 13x23x10", VG+ 1,500.00
Store, Gottschalk, cvd clock on bk wall, drws, 16x29x14", G+.3,000.00

Dolls

To learn to invest your money wisely as you enjoy the hobby of doll collecting, you must become aware of defects which may devaluate a doll. In bisque, watch for eye chips, hairline cracks and chips, or breaks on any part of the head. Composition should be clean, not crazed or cracked. Vinyl and plastic should be clean with no pen or crayon marks. Though a quality replacement wig is acceptable for bisque dolls, composition and hard plastic dolls should have their originals in uncut condition. Although perfect examples of antique dolls will always bring the best values, it is easier to forgive slight surface wear or appropriately replaced costumes of nineteenth or early twentieth century dolls. Dolls from 1930 to the present must be in very good, all-original condition to achieve good value.

It is important to remember that prices are based on condition and rarity. When no condition is noted, either in the line listing or the subcategory narrative, dolls are assumed to be in excellent condition. In relation to bisque dolls, excellent means having no cracks, chips, or hairlines, wearing original or appropriate replacement clothing, being shoed, wigged, and ready to be placed into a collection. Some of our values are for dolls that are 'mint in box' or 'never removed from box.' As a general rule, a mint-in-the-box doll is worth twice as much (or there about) as one mint, no box. The same doll, played with and in only good condition, is worth half as much (or even less) than the mint-condition doll. Never-removed-from-box examples sell at a premium; allow an additional 10% to 20% over MIB prices for a doll in this pristine condition.

For a more thorough study of the subject, refer to *Doll Values* by our advisor Linda Edward; *Collector's Guide to Dolls of the 1960s and 1970s* by Cindy Sabulis; *Collector's Encyclopedia of American Composition Dolls, 1900 – 1950, Vols. 1* and *2*, by Ursula R. Mertz; *Horsman Dolls, The Vinyl Era*, by Don Jensen; and *Collectible African American Dolls* by Yvonne H. Ellis. All are published by Collector Books. Several other book are referenced throughout this category. Our advisor for this category is author Linda Edward; she is listed in the directory under Rhode Island.

Key:

bjtd — ball-jointed	o/c/m — open closed mouth
blb — bent limb body	o/m — open mouth
c/m — closed mouth	p/e — pierced ears
ge — glass eyes	RpC — replaced clothes
hh — human hair	ShHd — shoulder head
hp — hard plastic	ShPl — shoulder plate
ltd ed —limited edition	SkHd — socket head
OC — original clothes	sl — sleep eyes

Advertising Dolls

Whether your interest in advertising dolls is fueled by nostalgia or strictly because of their amusing, often clever advertising impact, there are several points that should be considered before making your purchases. Condition is of utmost importance; never pay book price for dolls in poor condition, whether they are cloth or of another material. Restoring fabric dolls is usually unsatisfactory and involves a good deal of work. Seams must be opened, stuffing removed, the doll washed and dried, and then reassembled. Washing old fabrics may prove to be disastrous. Colors may fade or run, and most stains are totally resistant to washing. It's usually best to leave the fabric doll as it is.

Watch for new dolls as they become available. Save related advertising literature, extra coupons, etc., and keep these along with the doll to further enhance your collection. Old dolls with no marks are sometimes challenging to identify. While some products may use the same familiar trademark figures for a number of years (the Jolly Green Giant, Pillsbury's Poppin' Fresh, and the Keebler Elf, for example) others appear on the market for a short time only and may be difficult to trace. Most libraries have reference books with trademarks and logos that might provide a clue in tracking down your doll's identity. Children see advertising figures on Saturday morning cartoons that are often unfamiliar to adults, or other ad doll collectors may have the information you seek.

Some advertising dolls are still easy to find and relatively inexpensive, ranging in cost from $1.00 to $100.00. The hard plastic and early composition dolls are bringing the higher prices. Advertising dolls are popular with children as well as adults. For a more thorough study of the subject, we recommend *Advertising Dolls with Values* by Myra Yellin Outwater (Schiffer).

Allied Van Lines, gr uniform & hat, Lion Uniform Inc, 14", MIB. 1,200.00
Bazooka Bubble Gum, Bazooka Joe, stuffed cloth, 19", 1970s, NM .27.00
Blue Bonnet Sue, cloth, Dakin, 1980s, 12", EX+............................ 25.00
Bonnie Blue Ribbon, Barbie type, 1960s, scarce, 17", MIB 200.00
Borden, Elsie the cow, plush w/vinyl head, makes 'moo' sound, 12", 1950s, EX.. 50.00
Burger Chef, hand puppet, flannel felt, vinyl head, early 1970s, 10".. 35.00
Campbell's Soup, boy, pirate, 10", Home Shopper, 1995, in soup can box, EX. 80.00

Campbell's Soup, girl, Scottish outfit, NM, $85.00. (Photo courtesy June Moon)

Cheer Girl, plastic w/cloth clothes, Cheer detergent, 1960, 10", NM ...20.00
Chester Cheetah, plush, Cheetos, 18" 20.00
Cream of Wheat, chef, stuffed cloth, holds bowl, 16", 1949, G ... 100.00
Dairy Queen, doll, Dairy Queen Kid, stuffed cloth, 1974, EX 12.00
Del Monte's Fluffy Lamb/Lushie Peach/Reddie Tomato, plush, 1980s, ea.. 20.00
Grapette Soda, Buddy Lee 200.00
Green Giant Girl, vinyl w/rooted hair, dress/hat, 1950s, 17", M.... 40.00
Harley-Davidson's 'Fat Bob,' stuffed, 1998, 7", EX+ 8.00
Hawaiian Punch's Punchy, stuffed cloth, 20", NM 65.00
McDonald's, Ronald, stuffed, Grimace in pocket, 20", M............... 50.00
Miss Curity, compo/cloth nurse's uniform & cap, 1940s, 21", VG+ ...275.00
Mobile Man, bl rubber, 5", EX.. 20.00
Nestlé, Little Hans, red hair & beard, brn pants, yel hat, ca 1969, 12½".. 60.00
Nexium Robot, purple bendable vinyl, digital clock face, 7", M.... 12.00
Oreo Girl, vinyl, Oreo hat/wht heart/OREO on red pinafore, 5", M.5.00
Seven-Up, Fresh-Up Freddie, pnt squeeze vinyl, 9", 1959, NM ...235.00
Snuggles Bear, plush hand puppet, Lever Bros, 1993, 15", NM 12.00
Tommy Tagamet, pk bendable vinyl on rnd base, 1988, 5", M 25.00
USDA Forest Service, Smokey Bear, plush, Knickerbocker, 1972, 6 ", MIB...55.00

American Character

For more information we recommend *American Character Dolls* by Judith Izen (Collector Books).

AC or Petite mk mama, compo & cloth, sleep eyes, hh wig, OC, 16, EX. 225.00
Baby Sue, vinyl, sl, says mama, OC, 1963, 21" 225.00
Baby, hp & vinyl, bottle, 12", MIB.. 250.00
Betsy McCall, vinyl, rooted hair, chemise, 1958, 14", MIB.......... 600.00
Chuckles, vinyl/cloth, rooted saran hair, OC, 19" 225.00

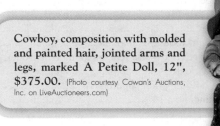

Cowboy, composition with molded and painted hair, jointed arms and legs, marked A Petite Doll, 12", $375.00. (Photo courtesy Cowan's Auctions, Inc. on LiveAuctioneers.com)

Freckles, face changes, OC, 1966, 13", EX...................................... 40.00
Hedda Get Bedda, 3-face w/knot on nightcap, OC, 1961, 23"..... 325.00
Little Girl Toodles, vinyl, Peek-a-Boo eyes, OC, 1960, 25", MIB . 550.00
Little Love (Newborn Babe), cloth body, Bye-Lo type, 1942, 20".350.00
Little Love, compo/cloth, o/m/2 teeth, sl, says mama, OC, 21" ... 300.00
Petite Baby Doll, compo ShPl, cloth body, crier, OC, 12½", MIB...225.00
Sally Says, plastic & vinyl, talker, 1965, OC, 19", EX.................... 70.00
Sweet Sue Sophisticate, vinyl walker, bl gown, 1957, 20", MIB.... 650.00
Sweet Sue, hp or hp & vinyl, 1953-61, OC, 15", EX.................... 200.00
Sweet Sue, hp walker, rooted hair, School Girl outfit, 15", MIB.. 350.00
Tiny Tears, hp w/rubber body, christening gown/jacket, 11½", MIB.500.00
Tiny Tears, hp w/rubber body, molded hair, romper, 1950s, 16" .. 325.00
Tiny Tears, vinyl, platinum hair w/bangs, romper, 1950s, 16" 250.00
Toni, vinyl head, rooted hair, ca 1958, OC, 10", EX 300.00
Toni, vinyl, rooted hair, sl, c/m, jtd, Country Club oufit, 14"....... 600.00
Toodles, vinyl, w/accessories & wardrobe, ca 1960, 11", MIB 500.00
Tressy, all vinyl, high heels, 1963-66, OC, 11", EX........................ 75.00
Tressy, vinyl, platinum blond, str legs, OC, 1964, 11½", MIB 150.00

Annalee

Barbara Annalee Davis began making her dolls in the 1950s. What began as a hobby, very soon turned into a commercial venture. Her whimsical creations range from tiny angels atop powder puff clouds to funky giant frogs, some 42" in height. In between there are dolls for every occasion (with Christmas being her specialty), all characterized by their unique construction methods (felt over flexible wire framework) and wonderful facial expressions. Naturally, some of the older dolls are the most valuable (though more recent examples are desirable as well, depending on scarcity and demand), and condition, as usual, is very important. To date your doll, look at the tag. If made before 1986, that date is only the copyright date. (Dolls made after 1986 do carry the manufacturing date.) Dolls from the '50s have a long white red-embroidered tag with no date. From 1959 to 1964, that same tag had a date in the upper right-hand corner. From 1965 until 1970, it was folded in half and sewn into the seam. In 1970, a satiny white tag with a date preceded by a copyright symbol in the upper right-hand corner was used. In '75, the tag was a long white cotton strip with a copyright date. This tag was folded over in 1982, making it shorter. Our advisor for Annalee dolls is Jane Holt; she is listed in the Directory under New Hampshire. Values are for dolls in at least excellent condition.

1957, boy building boat, 10" 250.00
1959, Santa, w/striped stocking, 12", rare 250.00
1962, monk, wht beard, blk hooded robe & skullcap, 10" 75.00
1964, monk, red or wht robe, 10", ea 75.00
1966, beach girl w/towel, 10" 275.00
1968, elephant, 10" 95.00
1970, choir boys (2) and girl, w/song sheets, 10", ea............... 60.00
1970, Country Cousin boy & girl mice, 7", pr 100.00
1970, monkey girl w/bow & muff, chartreuse, 10" 150.00
1970, yel bunny, 7" 65.00
1971, bunny girl, yel or wht w/polka-dot bandana, w/basket, 18" .. 75.00
1971+, Santa & Mrs Claus, w/cape, 7", pr (made several yrs)........ 30.00
1972-85, teacher mouse (male or female), 7", ea 35.00
1972, reindeer w/flat face (36") w/2 18" gnomes in red 375.00
1974, choir girl, 10" 40.00
1974, cowboy or cowgirl mouse, 7", ea 25.00
1974, Fireman mouse, red hat w/wht felt shield, missing ladder, 7"..25.00
1974, leprechaun w/sack, 10" 25.00
1975, Mrs Cratchet holding plum pudding, 18" 75.00
1976, colonial drummer boy, 18" 95.00
1976, elephant, 18" 150.00
1977, Mr Santa mouse holding brn bag, 7" 15.00
1977, scarecrow, 10" 35.00
1978, pilgrim couple, 18" & 16", pr 75.00
1979, jogger mouse, 7" 25.00
1980 only, disco mouse (boy or girl), 7" (made only 1 yr), ea........ 35.00
1980, clown, 18" 75.00
1981, Baby in Basket.. 35.00
1981, clown, 42" 350.00
1983, Easter Parade boy & girl bunnies, 29", pr ... 100.00
1983, snowman w/red & wht hat & broom, 7" 30.00
1983, witch mouse on broom, flying, 12" 65.00
1984-86, Valentine bunny, 7" 40.00
1985, Annie Oakley, Folk Hero, 10" 100.00
1985, Christmas panda bear, 18" 75.00
1985, downhill skier, 10" 35.00
1985, Happy Birthday boy or girl, 7", ea 25.00
1985, kid w/sled, 12" 35.00
1985, Milk & Cookies, Logo Kid (1st logo), w/pin, 7" 95.00
1985, ornament, Be Mine heart 5.00
1986, Logo Kid w/pin, 7" 75.00
1986, Valentine panda holding red heart, 10" (made only 2 yrs)... 50.00
1987-91, Ghost kid, carrying pumpkin, 7" 25.00
1988, reindeer w/gifts in pouches, 36"+antlers..................... 70.00
1991-92, spider, mobile, 12" 50.00
1991, country bunny, boy or girl, 10" 20.00
1991, reindeer, animated, w/saddlebags, 36" 175.00
1993, Indian boy mouse, 12" 50.00
1994, naughty angel w/blk eye holding slingshot, 7" 25.00

1997, Bathtime for Buddy, 7", $30.00. (Photo courtesy Jane Holt)

1997, Mrs Santa, Last Minute Wrapping, 30" 125.00
1998, wht reindeer, 18" 50.00

Armand Marseille

#225, character child, bsk SkHd, ge, teeth, jtd, RpC, 14" 3,200.00
#231, Fany, RpC, ca 1912, 17", EX................................10,000.00
#256, bsk SkHd, o/m, ge, wig, RpC, 12", EX 300.00
#259, Kiddiejoy, bsk solid-dome or wigged SkHd, ge, RpC, 12" 350.00
#310, Just Me, bsk SkHd, flirty eyes, wig, RpC, 1929, 9", EX....1,600.00
#341, My Dream Baby, toddler body, RpC, 28" 1,000.00
#345, Kiddiejoy, bsk SkHd, ge, cloth body, RpC, 1926, 16", EX 350.00
#351, My Dream Baby, bsk SkHd, cloth body, RpC, 12", EX 300.00
#360a, bsk SkHd, o/m, ge, blb, wig, RpC, 24", EX................. 800.00
#370, bsk ShHd, o/m, ge, kid body, RpC, 12" 100.00
#372, Kiddiejoy, ShHd, p/e, o/c/m, 2 teeth, kid body, RpC, 1925, 21" . 1,025.00
#449, c/m, pnt eyes, ca 1930, 18" 1,000.00
#500, intaglio eyes, bent-limb compo, RpC, 15"....................600.00
#600, ShHd, solid dome w/molded hair, c/m, intaglio eyes, 14" ...600.00
#690, SkHd, o/m, 18"..850.00
#992, Our Pet, compo bent-leg baby, o/m, ge, OC, 24"...........625.00
#1330, SkHd, o/m, ge, wig, bent-leg baby, RpC, 21" 600.00
#1890, bsk ShHd, ge, o/m/teeth, kid body, OC, 12" 225.00
#1894, bsk ShHd, ge, compo body, o/m/teeth, RpC, 8", EX 150.00
#1899, bsk ShHd, ge, o/m/teeth, wig, RpC, 26", EX.................500.00
Baby Betty mold, bsk ShHd, ge, wig, RpC, 16"....................325.00
Baby Betty, bent-leg baby body, RpC, 16" 500.00
Baby Gloria, solid dome, o/m, pnt hair, OC, 15" 500.00
No mold #, child, bsk SkHd, ge, 5-pc body, EX quality, RpC, 7"............250.00
No mold #, child, bsk SkHd, ge, 5-pc body, G quality, RpC, 12"............135.00
No mold #, child, bsk SkHd, o/m, ge, jtd compo, wig, 16" 300.00
No mold #, child, bsk SkHd, o/m, ge, jtd compo, wig, 36" 900.00
No mold #, child, bsk SkHd, o/m, ge, jtd compo, wig, RpC, 10"............275.00
Queen Louise or Rosebud mold, bsk SkHd, ge, wig, RpC, 13" 300.00

Barbie Dolls® and Related Dolls

Though her face and body sculpt have changed over the years, Barbie is still as popular today as she was when she was first introduced. Named after the young daughter of the first owner of the Mattel Company, the original Barbie had a white iris but no eye color. These dolls are nearly impossible to find, but there is a myriad of her successors and related collectibles just waiting to be found.

For further information we recommend *Barbie, The First 30 Years*, by Stefanie Deutsch and Bettina Dorfmann; *Collector's Encyclopedia of Barbie Doll Exclusives, Collector's Encyclopedia of Barbie Doll Collector's Editions, Barbie Doll Around the World*, and *Barbie Doll Photo Album*, all by J. Michael Augustyniak; *Barbie Doll Fashion, Vols. I, II,* and *III,* by Sarah Sink Eames; and *Schroeder's Toys, Antique to Modern*. All these are published by Collector Books.

Allan, 1965, bendable legs, MIB 300.00
Barbie, #1, brunette (or blond) hair, 1958-59, MIB, $6,000 to .6,500.00
Barbie, 1958-59, #1, blond or brunette, MIB, $5,000 to............5,250.00
Barbie, 1962, #6, any hair color, MIB, ea $375 to........................ 425.00
Barbie, Am Girl, 1966, Color-Magic, NRFB 3,000.00
Barbie, Antique Rose, 1996, NRFB................................... 190.00
Barbie, Blossom Beautiful, 1992, NRFB..............................225.00
Barbie, Bubble-Cut, 1962, blond or brunette, MIB, $175 to 200.00
Barbie, Career Girl, 1964, MIB 750.00
Barbie, Celebration, 1986, NRFB.................................... 65.00
Barbie, Day-to-Night, 1985, NRFB.................................. 45.00
Barbie, Dorothy (Wizard of Oz), 1994, Hollywood Legends Series, NRFB....350.00
Barbie, Fabulous Fur, 1986, NRFB................................... 65.00
Barbie, Glinda (Wizard of Oz), 2000, NRFB 40.00

Barbie, Knitting Pretty (pk), 1964, NRFB 1,265.00
Barbie, Pepsi Spirit, 1989, Toys R Us, NRFB 75.00
Barbie, Pink & Pretty, 1982, MIB 50.00
Barbie, Police Officer (wht or blk), 1993, Toys R Us, NRFB 75.00
Barbie, Queen of Hearts, 1994, Bob Mackie, NRFB 250.00
Barbie, Serenade in Satin, 1997, Barbie Couture Collection, MIB 100.00
Barbie, Standard, 1967, any hair color, MIB, ea 475.00
Barbie, Sun Valley, 1973, NRFB 125.00
Barbie, Swirl Ponytail, 1964, brunette, MIB 625.00
Barbie, That Girl, 2003, Pop Culture Collection, NRFB 35.00
Barbie, Theater Date, 1964, NRFB 660.00

Barbie, Twist 'n Turn, 1966, blond with long hair and bangs, $165.00; outfit, #1063 Hot Togs, 1972, very rare, $635.00. (Photo courtesy McMasters Harris Auction Co. on LiveAuctioneers.com)

Barbie, Twist 'n Turn, 1969, flip hairdo, blond or brunette, NRFB ... 475.00
Barbie, Winter Fantasy, 1990, FAO Schwarz, NRFB 200.00
Brad, 1970, darker skin, bendable legs, NRFB 200.00
Brad, Talking, 1970, NRFB 225.00
Cara, Free Moving, 1974, MIB 115.00
Casey, Twist 'n Turn, 1968, blond or brunette hair, NRFB 300.00
Chris, 1967, any hair color, MIB 200.00
Christie, Fashion Photo, 1978, MIB 95.00
Christie, Kissing, 1979, MIB 50.00
Christie, Talking, 1970, MIB 250.00
Christie, Twist 'n Turn, 1968, red hair, MIB 300.00
Francie, Growin' Pretty Hair, 1971, MIB 150.00
Francie, Malibu, 1971, NRFB 50.00
Ginger, Growing Up, 1977, MIB 115.00
Kelley, Quick Curl, 1972, NRFB 80.00
Kelley, Yellowstone, 1974, brunette hair, NRFB 575.00
Ken, 1961, flocked hair, blond or brunette, NRFB 150.00
Ken, Busy, 1972, NRFB 150.00
Ken, Crystal, 1984, NRFB 40.00
Ken, Free Moving, 1974, MIB 75.00
Ken, Live Action on Stage, 1971, NRFB 150.00
Ken, Malibu, 1976, NRFB 30.00
Ken, Mod Hair, 1973, NRFB 100.00
Ken, Rocker, 1986, MIB 30.00
Ken, Sport & Shave, 1980, MIB 40.00
Ken, Superstar, 1977, MIB 100.00
Ken, Talking, 1970, NRFB 115.00
Ken, Walk Lively, 1972, MIB 150.00
Midge, 30th Anniversary, 1992, porc, MIB, D2 .... 175.00
Midge, Cool Times, 1989, NRFB 15.00
PJ, Fashion Photo, 1978, MIB 75.00
PJ, Malibu (The Sun Set), 1971, blond hair, NRFP 100.00
Ricky, 1965, MIB 130.00
Scott, 1979, MIB 55.00
Skipper, 1965, bendable legs, any hair color, MIB 150.00
Skipper, Malibu, 1977, MIB 50.00
Skipper, Western, 1982, NRFB 40.00

Stacy, Twist 'n Turn, 1969, any hair color, NRFB 450.00
Teresa, Rappin' Rockin', 1992, NRFB 30.00
Tutti, 1967, any hair color, MIB 175.00
Whitney, Style Magic, 1989, NRFB 15.00

Barbie Doll® Accessories and Gift Sets

Case, Barbie Goes Travelin', 1965, EX+ 75.00
Case, Barbie in Party Date/Ken in Sat Night Date on blk, 1963, EX ... 50.00
Case, Barbie, All That Jazz, 1967, NM 40.00
Case, Barbie, Stacey, Francie & Skipper, pk hard plastic, rare, NM ... 100.00
Case, Easter Parade, 1961, EX+ 20.00
Case, Ken, gr vinyl w/lg image of Ken & 3 smaller Barbies, 1961, NM .. 35.00
Case, Midge wearing Movie Date, bl vinyl, 1963, NM 125.00
Case, Skipper & Scooter, 1965, NM 150.00
Furniture, Barbie & Midge Queen Size Chifferobe (Susy Goose), NM ... 100.00
Furniture, Barbie Dream House Bedroom, 1981, MIB 6.00
Furniture, Barbie Dream Kitchen-Dinette, #4095, 1964, MIB 600.00
Furniture, Barbie Fashion Living Room Set, #7404, 1984, NRFB .. 30.00
Furniture, Go-Together Chaise Lounge, MIB 75.00
Furniture, Skipper & Scooter Dbl Bunk Beds & Ladder, MIB 100.00
Furniture, Susy Goose Mod-A-Go-Go Bedroom, 1966, NRFB .2,300.00
Gift Set, Army Barbie & Ken, 1993, Stars 'n Stripes, MIB 60.00
Gift Set, Ballerina Barbie on Tour, 1976, MIB 175.00
Gift Set, Cinderella, 1992, NRFB 125.00
Gift Set, Dance Sensation Barbie, 1985, MIB 35.00
Gift Set, Golden Groove Barbie, Sears Exclusive, 1969, NRFB .. 2,000.00
Gift Set, Pretty Pairs 'n Fran, 1970, NRFB 250.00
Gift Set, Skipper Party Time, 1964, NRFB 500.00
Gift Set, Tutti & Todd Sundae Treat, 1966, NRFB 500.00
House, Barbie Dream House, 1st ed, 1961, complete, NM 85.00
House, Jamie's Penthouse, Sears Exclusive, 1971, MIB 475.00
House, Magical Mansion, 1989, MIB 125.00
House, Surprise House, 1972, MIB 100.00
House, Tuttie Playhouse, 1966, M 100.00
House, World of Barbie, 1966, MIB 175.00
Outfit, Barbie, After Five, #934, 1962, NRFP 300.00
Outfit, Barbie, Baby Doll Pinks, #3403, 1971, NRFP 100.00
Outfit, Barbie, Beautiful Bride, #1698, 1967, NRFP 2,100.00
Outfit, Barbie, Bouncy Flouncy, #1805, 1967, NRFP 300.00
Outfit, Barbie, Cinderella, #872, 1964, NRFB 475.00
Outfit, Barbie, Dog 'n Duds, #1613, 1964, NRFP 350.00
Outfit, Barbie, Fraternity Dance, #1638, NRFP 600.00
Outfit, Barbie, Fun Fakes, #3412, 1971, NRFP 100.00
Outfit, Barbie, Groovin' Gauchos, #1057, 1971, NRFP 300.00
Outfit, Barbie, Midnight Bl, #1617, NRFP 850.00
Outfit, Barbie, Movie Groovie, #1866, 1969, NRFP 125.00
Outfit, Barbie, Perfectly Pink, #4805, 1984, NRFP 10.00
Outfit, Barbie, Rare Pair, #1462, 1970, NRFP 125.00
Outfit, Barbie, Sugar Plum Fairy, #9326, 1976, NRFP 40.00
Outfit, Barbie, Walking Pretty Pak, 1971, NRFP 130.00
Outfit, Francie & Casey, Cool It! Fashion Pak, 1968, MIP 50.00
Outfit, Francie, Hip Knits, #1265, 1966, NRFB 225.00
Outfit, Holiday Dance, #1639, 1965, NRFP 625.00
Outfit, Ken, Army & Air Force, #797, 1963, NRFP 250.00
Outfit, Ken, Big Business, #1434, 1970, NRFP 75.00
Outfit, Ken, Date Night, #5651, 1983, NRFP 10.00
Outfit, Ken, Fun on Ice, #791, 1963, NRFP 125.00
Outfit, Ken, Mr Astronaut, #1415, 1965, NRFP 725.00
Outfit, Ken, Sea Scene, #1449, 1971, NRFP 60.00
Outfit, Skipper, Budding Beauty, #1731, 1970, NRFP 75.00
Outfit, Skipper, Chilly Chums, #1973, 1969, NRFP 125.00
Room, Barbie Cookin' Fun Kitchen, MIB 100.00
Room, Barbie's Full Country Kitchen, #7404, 1974, NRFB 100.00

Room, Barbie's Lively Livin' Room, MIB......................... 50.00
Room, Full Firelight Living Room, 1974, MIB 100.00
Shop, Barbie & the Rockers Dance Cafe, 1987, MIB.................. 50.00
Shop, Barbie Beauty Boutique, 1976, MIB............................ 40.00
Shop, Barbie Fashion Salon, Sears Exclusive, 1964, MIB............ 600.00
Shop, Barbie Unique Boutique, Sears Exclusive, 1971, MIB....... 185.00
Shop, Barbie's Beauty Boutique, 1976, MIB........................ 40.00
Shop, Superstar Barbie Beauty Salon, 1977, MIB.................... 55.00
Vehicle, 1957 Belair Chevy, 1989, 1st ed, aqua, MIB.............. 150.00
Vehicle, Barbie & Ken Dune Buggy, Irwin, pk, 1970, MIB 250.00
Vehicle, Ken's Dream 'Vette, 1981, dk bl, MIB 100.00
Vehicle, Ken's Hot Rod, Sears Exclusive, 1964, red, MIB......... 900.00
Vehicle, Snowmobile, Montgomery Ward, 1972, MIB.................. 65.00
Vehicle, Starlight Motorhome, 1982, MIB 50.00
Vehicle, Western Star Traveler Motorhome, 1982, MIB............... 50.00

Belton Type

French-type face, bsk, o/c/m or c/m, wig, RpC, 13" 1,900.00
French-type face, bsk, o/c/m or c/m, wig, RpC, 22" 3,000.00
German-type face, bsk, o/c/m or c/m, wig, 9", VG 800.00
German-type face, bsk, o/c/m or c/m, wig, 12", VG 900.00
German-type face, bsk, o/c/m or c/m, wig, 23", EX.................2,750.00
German-type face, bsk, o/c/m or c/m, wig, 25", VG.................2,250.00
German-type face, bsk, o/c/m or c/m, wig, RpC, 8" 850.00
German-type face, bsk, o/c/m or c/m, wig, RpC, 15" 1,600.00
German-type face, bsk, o/c/m or c/m, wig, RpC, 20" 2,200.00
Mold #137, 15½"..2,500.00

Betsy McCall

Am Character, hp, sleep eyes, jtd knees, 1957-63, undies only, 8" ..250.00
Am Character, Linda McCall (cousin), 1959, 36", EX................ 350.00
Am Character, vinyl w/jtd limbs & waist, 1961, 29", EX........ 300.00
Am Character, vinyl w/Patti Play Pal-style body, rooted hair, 1959, 36", EX...325.00
Am Character, vinyl w/swivel waist or 1-pc torso, rooted hair, 1958, 14", EX, ea.500.00
Am Character, vinyl, rooted hair, 1-pc torso, 1959, 19" or 20", EX, ea.500.00
Amsco, plastic, complete w/Pretty Pac accessories & booklet, 8", G ..325.00
Companion sz, vinyl, McCall Corp 1959 on head, OC, 34" 900.00
Horsman, rigid body w/vinyl head, w/extra hair & accessories, 1974, 12½", EX.50.00
Ideal, vinyl head, hp Tony body, saran wig, 1952-53, OC, 14"..... 300.00
Uneeda, rigid vinyl body, rooted hair, wore mod outfits, 1964, 11½", $125 to...225.00

Boudoir Dolls

Boudoir dolls, often called bed dolls, French dolls, or flapper dolls, were popular from the late teens through the 1940s. The era of the 1920s and 1930s was the golden age of boudoir dolls.

More common boudoir dolls are usually found with composition head, arms, and high-heeled feet. Clothes are nailed on (later ones have stapled-on clothes). Wigs are usually mohair, human hair, or silk floss. Smoking boudoir dolls were made in the late teens and early 1920s. More expensive boudoir dolls were made in France, Italy, and Germany, as well as the U.S. Usually they are all cloth with elaborate sewn or pinned-on costumes and silk, felt, or velvet painted faces. Sizes of boudoir dolls vary, but most are around 30". These dolls were made to adorn a lady's boudoir or sit on a bed. They were not meant as children's playthings. Our advisor for this category is Bonnie Groves; she is listed in the Directory under Texas.

Anita, compo & cloth, 1920s, OC, P.................................. 30.00
Anita, compo & cloth, pk floss hair, 1920s, EX 330.00
Anita, head only, compo, OC, 1920s 20.00
Anita, lobby doll, H color, compo & cloth, OC, 1920s, EX......... 180.00
Anita, OC, 27", VG 230.00

Anita, smoker, compo & cloth, 1920s, OC, 30", G 135.00
Anita, smoker, compo, 1925, OC, 27", VG 385.00
Anita, smoker, re-dressed, rpr, rpt, 30" 200.00
Anita, vinyl & plastic, OC, 1950s, 26", EX 68.00
Apache male, cloth, all orig, 26", VG, min.......................... 300.00
Bif face, compo & cloth, OC, 1920s, 34", EX......................... 625.00
Blossom, cloth, OC, tagged, 30", G 600.00
Blossom, Garbo face, OC, 20", EX, min............................1,000.00
Bucilla kit for making boudoir doll costume, EX, min.............. 600.00
Cloth, Gerling type, all orig, 1920s, 30", VG, min 300.00
Cloth, std quality, 1920s, OC, 32", EX, min 325.00
Compo, std quality, OC, 1930s, 28", EX, $125 to 175.00
Cubeb smoker, compo, jtd, all orig, 1925, 25", EX, min............. 900.00
Etta, cloth, OC, tagged, 1920s, EX...............................1,900.00

Etta court lady, original dress shattering a little, 1920s, 30", VG, $2,000.00.
(Photo courtesy Bonnie M. Groves)

French, cloth w/bsk arms & legs, 1920s, OC, 27", VG................ 455.00
French, cloth w/bsk arms & legs, tagged, 18", VG, pr................ 395.00
French, cloth, OC, 29", VG 355.00
French, harlequin, pierrot, compo & cloth, OC, 1920s, 30", VG.800.00
French, topsy-turvy, cloth w/bsk arms, 21", VG, min 395.00
Gerbs, cloth, FR, 1920s, OC, 25", EX, min.......................... 375.00
Gerbs, cloth, FR, 1920s, OC, 30", G, min 300.00
Gerling, cloth, OC, 1920s, 30", EX 900.00
German, Pierrot w/compo face, OC, 16", G 330.00
Halloween, std quality, OC, 27", min............................... 500.00
Lenci, Fadette, RpC, 26", VG 2,050.00
Lenci, Fadette, smoker, 25", VG, min.............................3,000.00
Lenci, salon lady, OC, 25", EX, min..............................3,000.00
Patriotic, std quality, 1940s, 25", G, min......................... 200.00
Ring lady, cloth, floss hair, OC, 1920s, 32", EX 699.00
Shoes, orig, 3", G 25.00
Smoker, cloth, 1920s, OC, 16", EX 500.00
Smoker, cloth, 1920s, OC, 25", EX 525.00
Smoker, cloth, OC, 1920s, 16", EX 300.00
Sterling, 1930, OC, 27", VG, min................................... 200.00
Sterling, Halloween, 1930s, OC, 28", G, min........................ 400.00
W-K-S, compo head & hands, cloth body, nude, 1920s, G 40.00
W-K-S, patriotic, compo & cloth, OC, 1930s, VG 75.00
W-K-S, Remember Pearl Harbor, compo/cloth, 1940s, OC, EX .. 350.00

Bru

Bebe Respirant (breathing/talking), torso mechanism, RpC, 24".. 12,000.00
Bebe Baiser (kiss-throwing), string mechanism, 1892, RpC, 15". 4,400.00
Bebe Marchant (walker), clockwork mechanism, RpC, 17", VG... 6,800.00
Bebe Modele, cvd wood body, 1880+, RpC, 18".....................40,000.00
Bru Jne R, bsk swivel head, pwt eyes, o/m/teeth, RpC, 20", VG.. 3,000.00
Bru Jne, bsk SkHd on ShPl, pwt eyes, c/m, mohair wig, RpC, 10" .. 30,000.00
Bru Jne, bsk swivel head, pwt eyes, o/c/m/teeth, RpC, 12", VG . 30,000.00
Bru Jne, bsk swivel head, pwt eyes, o/c/m/teeth, RpC, 14", VG . 35,000.00
Bru Jne, bsk swivel head, pwt eyes, o/c/m/teeth, RpC, 17", EX... 38,000.00
Bru Poupée, bsk SkHd on ShPl, ge, smiling, 12".....................4,000.00

Circle Dot Bebe, bsk swivel head, pwt eyes, o/c/m/teeth, RpC, 11", EX ..25,000.00
Circle Dot Bebe, bsk swivel head, pwt eyes, o/c/m/teeth, RpC, 26", VG .30,000.00
Circle dot or crescent mk, bsk swivel head, pwt eyes, hh wig, RpC, 13" ..18,000.00
Fashion lady, bsk SkHd w/spring, kid body, RpC, 13"...............4,200.00
Fashion lady, bsk SkHd w/spring, smiling c/m, kid body/arms, RpC, 11" .3,600.00
Fashion lady, bsk SkHd w/spring, wood lower arms, kid body, RpC, 17"..5,500.00
Fashion lady, bsk SkHd w/spring, wooden body, RpC, 18" 8,500.00
Fashion type (smiler), swivel head, ShPl, kid body, RpC, 13", EX............4,000.00
Nurser, o/m, screw key at bk of head, RpC, 13" 6,500.00

China

1840 style, boy, smiling, side-parted brn hair, RpC, 21", VG 3,450.00
1840 style, center part w/bun or coronet, pk tint, RpC, 13"......2,200.00
1840 style, center part w/sausage curls, pk tint, RpC, 14" 650.00
1840 style, center part w/sausage curls, pk tint, RpC, 7" 325.00
1840 style, Covered Wagon, center part w/sausage curls, RpC, 10", EX.500.00
1840 style, Covered Wagon, center part w/sausage curls, RpC, 25" 1,000.00
1850 style, bald head, hh or mohair wig, RpC, 12", VG...............475.00
1850 style, fashion lady, pnt eyes, kid body, wig, RpC, 12"........2,900.00

1850 style, flat-top black hair with center part with short curls, attributed to Kloster Veilsdorf, glazed porcelain shoulder head, cloth body with kid leather arms, painted black shoes, original clothes, 15½", $2,880.00. (Photo courtesy Skinner Auctioneers and Appraisers of Antiques and Fine Art on LiveAuctioneers.com)

1850 style, Greiner type, ge, varied hairdos, RpC, 15", EX.......... 4,000.00
1850 style, Greiner type, ge, varied hairdos, RpC, 21", EX................5,100.00
1850 style, high forehead, curls, rnd face, RpC, 13" 300.00
1850 style, high forehead, curls, rnd face, RpC, 15" 500.00
1850 style, lady w/morning glories molded in brn hair, RpC, 21"..8,000.00
1850 style, molded necklace, RpC, 21"..700.00
1850 style, young Queen Victoria, molded braids, RpC, 18".....3,500.00
1860 style, flat-top blk hair w/center part/curls, RpC, 24"............475.00
1860 style, flat-top blk hair, center part, swivel neck, RpC, 15" .1,400.00
1860 style, highbrow w/curls, rnd face, RpC, 19", EX...................700.00
1860 style, man w/curls, RpC, 17"...800.00
1860 style, Mary Todd Lincoln, blk hair, gold snood, RpC, 18" .1,100.00
1860 style, Mary Todd Lincoln, blk hair, gold snood, RpC, 21", EX ..850.00
1870 style, Adelina Patti, center part w/ringlets at bk, RpC, 15".600.00
1870 style, blk hair w/full bangs, RpC, 14" 400.00
1870 style, blond hair w/full bangs, RpC, 18" 550.00
1870 style, Jenny Lind, blk hair in bun or coronet, RpC, 15", VG. 1,150.00
1870 style, ShHd, blk or blond hair, pk facial details, RpC, 18", EX ... 325.00
1870 style, ShHd, fine pnt, pk tint, blk or blond hair, RpC, 16" ..400.00
1880 style, Bawo & Dotter, Pat 1880, RpC, 18" 225.00
1880 style, child, blk or blond curls, RpC, 16".............................425.00
1880 style, molded curls allover, fat cheeks, RpC, 27", EX...........675.00
1890 style, center-part wavy hairdo, jeweled necklace, RpC, 20".425.00
1890 style, center-part wavy hairdo, short forehead, RpC, 8" 125.00
1890 style, center-part wavy hairdo, short forehead, RpC, 10" 175.00
1899-1933, Agnes, Bertha, Daisy, etc, German mfg, RpC, 9" 100.00
1899-1933, Agness, Bertha, Daisy, etc, German mfg, RpC, 21", EX ..325.00

1910-20, Japan, mk or unmk, blk or blond hair, RpC, 10" 125.00
1950 style, Alice in Wonderland, snood/headband, RpC, 20" ..1,150.00
Dolly Madison, OC, 24", EX 950.00
Japanese, mk or unmk, blk or blond hair, RpC, 1910-20, 15", EX. 190.00
KPM, man or boy, ge, RpC, 17", EX..9,000.00
Swivel-neck, ShPl, flange type, 10", EX.......................................2,100.00

Cloth

A cloth doll in very good condition will display light wear and soiling, while one assessed as excellent will be clean and bright. Unless otherwise noted, our values are for dolls in excellent condition.

Alabama Indestructible, child, bobbed hair, 1900-25, 15" 1,800.00
Arnold Printworks, Brownie, 1892-1907, 7½", $75 to..................100.00
Arnold Printworks, Dolly Dear, Flaked Rice, etc, printed undies, 9".. 95.00
Art Fabric Mills, printed, 16" 125.00
Babyland Rag, Buster Brown, 1892-1928, 17"..............................550.00
Black, Mammy type, pnt or embr features, 1910-20s, 16"............285.00
Chad Valley, Grenadier Guard, ge, 1930s, OC, 21"..................1,000.00
Chad Valley, Princess Elizabeth, 16" 1,700.00
Dollywood Studios, Miss Catalina, pnt bl eyes, ca 1946, OC, 13" ..100.00
Drayton, Dolly Dingle, printed features, 1923, RpC, 11" 385.00
Foxy Grandpa, 18", $200 to...225.00
Georgene Averill, Dutch girl, mask face, yarn hair, 1930s-40s, 13"...75.00
Gorham, Taffy, Sweet Inspirations, molded face, brn curls, 1985, 19"....50.00
Gund, cloth mask face, pnt features, ca 1898, 19" 300.00
Improved Life Size Doll, printed undies, 1876+, 16-18", $125 to.150.00
JB Sheppard & Co, Philadelphia Baby, oil-pnt head, 1900, OC, 21" ... 2,200.00

Judy (of Punch and Judy), oil painted head and features, nineteenth century, 22", VG, $840.00. (Photo courtesy Skinner Auctioneers and Appraisers of Antiques and Fine Art on LiveAuctioneers.com)

Martha Chase baby, oil-pnt stockinette head, 1889+, 27".........1,600.00
Molly, Susette of France, mask face, blk yarn hair, 1940s, OC, 14"..75.00
Peck, Santa Claus, printed, Pat 1886, 14½" 275.00
Saalfield, Golden Locks Girl, litho on cloth, c 1908, 24" 165.00

Effanbee

Bernard Fleischaker and Hugo Baum became business partners in 1910, and after two difficult years of finding toys to buy, they decided to manufacture dolls and toys of their own. The Effanbee trademark is a blending of their names, Eff for Fleischaker and bee for Baum. The company still exists today. For more information we recommend *Collector's Encyclopedia of American Composition Dolls, 1900 – 1950*, by Ursula R. Mertz (Collector Books). Unless noted othewise, values are for early dolls in excellent condition.

Alyssa, vinyl/hp, sl, jtd body, walker, 1960-61, OC, 23", M 225.00
Ann Shirley, all compo, grown-up body style, 1936-40, OC, 15".. 275.00
Baby Bud, compo, pnt features, o/c/m, RpC, 1918+, 6"...............195.00
Baby Evelyn, compo/cloth, 1925, OC, 17", $250 to 275.00
Baby Grumpy Gladys, compo ShHd, cloth body, 1923, OC, 15" .350.00
Babyette, compo, eyes molded closed, 1943, OC, 13", $300 to....400.00
Barbara Lou, compo, o/m, separate fingers, OC, 1936-39+, 21" 900.00

Betty Bounce, compo w/tousel head, o/c/e, 1932+, OC, 19" 400.00
Bubbles, compo ShHd, o/c/m, pnt eyes, toddler, 1924+, OC, 18". 400.00
Bubbles, compo ShHd, o/c/m/teeth, heart necklace, RpC, 1924+, 16", VG...250.00
Button Nose, vinyl head, cloth body, 1968-71, OC, 18", M........... 35.00
Candy Kid, all compo, sl, toddler, 1946+, OC, 13" 500.00
Christina, all vinyl, jtd, rooted hair, 1984, OC, 15", M................ 110.00
Flower girl, all vinyl, 1984 only, OC, M.................................. 95.00
Fluffy, all vinyl, Girl Scout, 1954+, OC, 10"........................... 75.00
Grumpy Aunt Dinah, black, cloth body, stocking legs, RpC, 14" 375.00
Grumpykins, compo/cloth, RpC, 1927, 12"............................. 200.00
Harmonica Joe, cloth body, rubber ball for air, RpC, 1923, 15", VG..450.00
Historical replica, all compo, jtd body, hh wigs, 1939+, OC, 14".. 600.00

Honey, composition, closed mouth, human hair wig, with original outfit and tag, 21", $480.00. (Photo courtesy Dan Morphy Auctions LLC on LiveAuctioneers.com)

Honey Walker, hp, walker, 1952+, OC, 14" 275.00
Ice Queen, compo, o/m, 1937+, orig skater outfit, 17" 750.00
Johnny Tu-Face, compo w/face front & bk, RpC, 1912, 16" 400.00
Lamkin, compo/cloth, sl, o/m, curled fingers, 1930+, OC, 16"..... 425.00
Little Lady, compo, sleep eyes, wig, OC (formal), 1939+, 18" 375.00
Mae Starr, compo ShHd, cloth body, talker, 1928, OC, 29"......... 700.00
Mary Jane, bsk head, sleep eyes, compo w/wooden limbs, RpC, 20".........700.00
Miss Chips, vinyl, sl, fully jtd, rooted hair, 1966-81, OC, 17", M .. 45.00
Pat-a-Pat, compo/cloth, pnt eyes, claps hands, 1925+, OC, 15" .. 275.00
Patrica Joan, compo, sl, slim body, wig, 1935, OC, 16" 550.00
Patsy Ann, vinyl, sl, 1959 ltd ed, OC, 15", M........................... 265.00
Patsy Baby, compo w/molded hair, 1931, OC, 10-11".................... 300.00
Patsy Joan, compo, 1931, OC, 16" 475.00
Patsy Mae, compo ShHd, cloth body, sl, swing legs, 1934, OC, 29".1,600.00
Patsy, compo/cloth, o/m w/teeth, sl, hh wig, 1924, OC, 15"........ 350.00
Patsyette/Ann Shirley, compo, mk Effanbee Patsyette Doll, OC, 9"... 350.00
Polka Dottie, vinyl, molded pigtails on fabric body, OC, 1954, 21"..........165.00
Susie Sunshine, vinyl, sl, jtd, rooted hair, 1961-79, OC, 18", M.... 50.00
Suzette, compo, pnt eyes, c/m, fully jtd, wig, 1939, OC, 12" 275.00
WC Fields, compo ShHd, hinged mouth, 1929+, OC, 17½" 950.00

Half Dolls

Half dolls were never meant to be objects of play. Most were modeled after the likenesses of lovely ladies, though children and animals were represented as well. Most of the ladies were firmly sewn onto pincushion bases that were beautifully decorated and served as the skirts of their gowns. Other skirts were actually covers for items on milady's dressing table. Some were used as parasol or brush handles or as tops to candy containers or perfume bottles. Most popular from 1900 to about 1930, they will most often be found marked with the area of their origin, usually Bavaria, Germany, France, and Japan. You may also find some fine quality pieces marked Goebel, Dressel and Kester, KPM, and Heubach. Values are for dolls in undamaged, original condition.

Arms away, china or bsk, bald head w/wig, 4"................................. 140.00

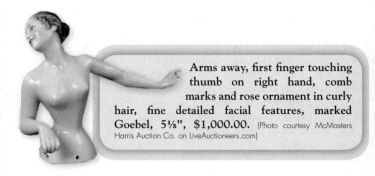

Arms away, first finger touching thumb on right hand, comb marks and rose ornament in curly hair, fine detailed facial features, marked Goebel, 5⅛", $1,000.00. (Photo courtesy McMasters Harris Auction Co. on LiveAuctioneers.com)

Arms away, flamenco dancer, pincushion, 6" 430.00
Arms away, holding item, 6", VG.. 200.00
Arms away, mk by maker or mold #, 12" 900.00
Arms in, close to figure, bald head w/wig, 4".............................. 80.00
Arms in, decor bodice, necklace, fancy hair or holding article, 3" ..125.00
Arms in, mk by maker or mold #, 5" 135.00
Arms in, w/legs, dressed, fancy decor, 5" 300.00
Jointed shoulders, china or bsk, molded hair, 5" 145.00
Jointed shoulders, china or bsk, molded hair, 7" 200.00
Jointed shoulders, solid dome, mohair wig, 4" 220.00
Jointed shoulders, solid dome, mohair wig, 6" 400.00
Man or child, 4" 120.00
Marked Germany, 4" 200.00
Marked Germany, 6" 400.00
Marked Japan, 3" 25.00
Marked Japan, 6" 50.00

Heinrich Handwerck

#69, child, bsk SkHd, o/m, sl or set eyes, wig, Rpc, 10" 550.00
#79, child, bsk SkHd, c/m, sl or set eyes, wig, RpC, 20" 2,200.00
#89, child, bsk ShHd, c/m, sl or set eyes, wig, RpC, 26" 3,000.00
#99, child, bsk SkHd, o/m, sl or set eyes, wig, RpC, 36" 1,300.00
#119, child, bsk SkHd, o/m, sl or set eyes, wig, RpC, 22" 550.00
#139 or no #, child, bsk ShHd, o/m, ge, kid body, RpC, 12" 125.00
#139 or no #, child, bsk ShHd, o/m, ge, kid body, RpC, 18" 200.00
#189, child, bsk SkHd, o/m, sl or set eyes, wig, RpC, 15" 750.00

Hertel, Schwab, and Company

#126, so-called Skippy, toddler body, RpC, 9" 875.00
#127, child, character face, dome w/molded hair, sl, RpC, 15" .1,350.00
#130, baby, bsk head, o/m or o/c/m w/teeth, sleep eyes, RpC, 12" ...275.00
#131, child, character face, solid dome, pnt c/m, ca 1912, RpC, 18"..1,100.00
#134, child, character face, sl, c/m, ca 1915, RpC, 15" 3,500.00
#140, child, character face, ge, laughing, ca 1912, RpC, 12"............3,400.00
#142, bsk head, o/m/teeth, sl or pnt eyes, RpC, 19"...................... 400.00
#150, baby, bsk head w/molded hair, sl, compo body, RpC, 22" ... 550.00
#152, bsk head, molded hair, o/m, toddler body, RpC, 20"........... 450.00

Ernst Heubach

#250, child, o/m, compo body, RpC, 8"................................... 200.00
#261, character child, bsk ShHd, pnt eyes, cloth body, RpC, 12" . 350.00
#275, child, ShHd, o/m, kid body, RpC, 16" 150.00
#300, baby, SkHd, o/m, ge, 5-pc body, RpC, 14"......................... 250.00
#320, SkHd, ge, o/m, 5-pc blb, RpC, 14", EX 250.00
#338, newborn baby, solid dome w/pnt hair, c/m, ge, RpC, 12" 400.00
#348, newborn, solid dome, ge, c/m, cloth body, RpC, 15", EX 500.00
#444, black newborn, solid dome, cloth body, RpC, 12", EX.............. 400.00
#1900, child, ShHd, o/m, ge, kid or cloth body, RpC, 12".............90.00
#1900, ShHd, o/m, ge, kid or cloth body, RpC, 26" 275.00

Gebruder Heubach

#5636, SkHd, ge, laughing o/c/m w/teeth, RpC, 15" 2,300.00
#5777, Dolly Dimple, SkHd, o/m, Hamburger & Co, RpC, 16".2,600.00
#6/0// (Heubach square mark), winker, compo 5-piece body, 7" ..925.00
#6688, character child, molded hair, intaglio eyes, RpC, 10".......625.00
#6811, SkHd, intaglio eyes, laughing o/c/m, ca 1912, RpC, 11" ..600.00
#764, SkHd, o/c/m w/2 teeth, ca 1912, RpC, 14" 6,200.00
#7759, character baby, intaglio eyes, c/m, RpC, 20" 1,000.00
#7852, character child, molded hair in braids, RpC, 16"..........2,200.00
#8381, Princess Juliana, molded hair, pnt eyes, c/m, RpC, 16".13,000.00
#8940, laughing girl, bl hair bow, RpC, 18" 7,200.00
No mold #, adult, o/m, ge, mk Heubach, RpC, 14" 4,500.00

Horsman

Baby Bumps, blk, compo, cloth body, cork stuffing, orig romper, 11".350.00
Baby Bumps, compo, cloth body, cork stuffing, orig romper, 11"..250.00
Baby Butterfly (Asian), compo head/hands, ca 1913, OC, 15" 400.00
Billiken, compo/cloth, molded hair, slanted eyes, OC, 12" 400.00
Body Twist, compo, jtd waist, OC, 11"....................................200.00
Campbell's Kid, all compo, 1930-40s, OC, 13" 250.00
Campbell's Kid, compo head/arms, cloth body/ft, 1910+, OC, 11".350.00
Can't Break 'Em character boy or girl, 1911+, OC, 11-13", ea $200 to....275.00
Can't Break 'Em character, Cotton Joe, Blk, OC, 13" 400.00

Early art doll #61x4289-NR, composition, original box, 20", $200.00. (Photo courtesy Tom Harris Auctions on LiveAuctioneers.com)

Ella Cinders, compo/cloth, o/c/m, pnt hair or wig, OC, 14".........450.00
Gene Carr Kid, Snowball, Blk, compo, o/c/m w/teeth, OC, 14"..500.00
Gold Metal Baby, compo head/limbs, 1911+, OC, 12"...............250.00
Peek-a-Boo, all compo, Grace Drayton design, OC, 8" 125.00
Tynie Baby, bsk head, cloth body, 1924-29, OC, 21".....................425.00

Ideal

Two of Ideal's most collectible lines of dolls are Crissy and Toni. Dolls listed are in excellent condition unless otherwise noted. For more information, refer to *Collector's Guide to Ideal Dolls* by Judith Izen (Collector Books).

Baby Pebbles, vinyl w/soft body, OC, 1963-64, 16", MIB.............265.00
Baby, compo/cloth, sleep eyes, pnt hair or wig, OC, 16" 250.00
Bonny Braids, toddler body, vinyl/rubber, o/m/tooth, OC, 11" 125.00
Buster Brown, compo/cloth, tin eyes, OC, 17" 375.00
Charlie McCarthy, hand puppet, compo/felt/cloth, Edgar Bergen's, 8".....60.00
Child or toddler, compo, pnt or sleep eyes, wig, OC, 1915+, 18" 200.00
Child/toddler, compo/cloth, sl, wig, OC, 15"..............................250.00
Cracker Jack boy, compo/cloth, sailor suit, 1917, 14" 375.00
Crissy, vinyl, brn grow hair, swivel waist, OC, 1971, 17"..............110.00
Deanna Durbin, all compo, brn sl, o/m/teeth, OC, 15" 700.00
Deanna Durbin, all compo, brn sl, o/m/teeth, wig, OC, 24"......1,200.00

Flossie Flirt, compo/cloth, crier, tin flirty eyes, OC, 14" 250.00
Flossie Flirt, compo/cloth, crier, tin flirty eyes, OC, 28" 400.00
Happy Hooligan, compo/cloth, 1910s, OC, 21" 525.00
Harmony, vinyl, battery-op, plays guitar, OC, 1972, 21" 150.00
Howdy Doody, hp head, ca 1953, 25".......................................75.00
Mama, compo, pnt or sleep eyes, crier, wig, 1921+, 24", min...........325.00
Naughty Marietta, Coquette type, compo/cloth, 1912, OC, 14"..150.00
Princess Beatrix, compo/cloth, flirty sl, OC, 16"........................400.00
Saucy Walker, hp, flirty eyes/crier, o/c/m/teeth, OC, 1951-55, 16".........125.00
Snoozie, compo/rubber/cloth, yawning o/m, OC, 14"..................200.00
Snow White, cloth mask face, cloth body, blk mohair wig, OC, 16".550.00
Snow White, compo, flirty eyes, o/m/teeth, wig, OC, 1938+, 22"......650.00
Soozie Smiles, compo head w/2 faces, cloth body, OC, 15"..........375.00
Sparkle Plenty, hp, Magic Skin body, yarn hair, all orig, 14"........250.00
Tickletoes, compo/rubber, squeaker, flirty eyes, o/m/teeth, 14".........250.00
Tickletoes, compo/rubber/cloth, flirty sl, o/m, OC, 20" 350.00
Uneeda Kid, compo/cloth, OC w/rain slicker & biscuit box, 16".. 475.00

Jumeau

The Jumeau factory manufactured dolls from 1842 on, but is perhaps best known for the dolls produced during 'the golden era' of French dolls from 1877 to 1890. Early dolls were works of art with closed mouths and paperweight eyes. When son Emile Jumeau took over, he patented sleep eyes with eyelids that drooped down over the eyes. This model also had flirty (eyes that move from side to side) eyes and is extremely rare. Over 98% of Jumeau dolls have paperweight eyes. The less-expensive German dolls were the downfall of the French doll manufacturers, and in 1899 the Jumeau company had to combine with several others to form SFBJ, in an effort to save the French doll industry from German competition.

#230, child, SkHd, ge, o/m, compo body, RpC, 12".....................600.00
BL Bebe, SkHd, pwt/e, c/m, p/e, wig, jtd body, RpC, 18" 4,200.00
Depose above E # J mk, bsk SkHd, pwt/e, p/e, wig, 16" 14,000.00
Depose Jumeau & sz #, poured bsk head, pwt/e, c/m, p/e, RpC, 20".9,000.00
EJ Bebe, # over initals, bsk SkHd, pwt/e, c/m, wig, RpC, 18"..13,000.00
Fashion type, #d swivel head, c/m, pwt/e, p/e, kid body, RpC, 13" .2,900.00
Fashion type, #d swivel head, c/m, pwt/e, p/e, kid body, RpC, 18" .5,000.00
Fashion type, #d swivel head, c/m, pwt/e, p/e, wood body, RpC, 14"..11,000.00
Fashion type, #d swivel head, portrait face, wood body, RpC, 21". 12,000.00
Long-face bebe, # only on head, pwt/e, c/m, p/e, mk body, RpC, 23".26,000.00
Phonograph in torso, bsk head, o/m, working, RpC, 25"...........8,000.00
Portrait child, almond pwt/e, c/m, p/e, wig, 1st series, RpC, 14½".30,000.00
Portrait, 2nd series, c/m, pwt eyes, p/e, wigged, compo, 15" 9,000.00
RR Bebe, pwt eyes, c/m, jtd compo body, wig, RpC, 23" 4,700.00
Tete Jumeau, bsk SkHd w/red stamp, ge, c/m, wig, RpC, 10".............9,000.00
Tete Jumeau, bsk SkHd w/red stamp, ge, c/m, p/e, RpC, 24"................7,000.00

Kammer & Reinhardt

#117, Mein Liebling, bisque socket head, sleep eyes, applied upper eyelashes, closed mouth, mohair wig, finest quality, 30", $3,800.00. (Photo courtesy Frasher's Doll Auction on LiveAuctioneers.com)

#100, character baby, solid dome, intaglio eyes, o/c/m, RpC, 14".. 475.00
#101, Peter or Marie, pnt eyes, c/m, jtd, OC, ca 1909, 15" 4,500.00
#102, Elsa or Walter, pnt eyes, molded hair, c/m, RpC, rare, 14", VG..24,000.00

#109, Elise, pnt eyes, c/m, OC, ca 1909, 14".............................18,000.00
#109, Elise, pnt eyes, c/m, RpC, 10"..8,000.00
#114, Groom, 18"...7,000.00
#115, solid dome, pnt hair, sl, c/m, toddler body, RpC, 12".......3,500.00
#115A, toddler, sl, c/m, jtd compo, wig, OC, 18".....................4,900.00
#117, Mein Liebling, ge, c/m, RpC, 14"..................................3,800.00
#121, baby, sl, o/m, RpC, ca 1912, EX.......................................900.00
#123, Max, flirty sl, laughing c/m, RpC, ca 1913, 16", VG......30,000.00
#128, sl, o/m, baby body, RpC, 10"..500.00
Lady, bsk SkHd, ge, o/m, compo body, OC, 16"......................1,300.00
No mold # or mold #191/#401/#402/#403, dolly face, 5-pc body, RpC, 7"..475.00
No mold #, child, dolly face, jtd compo body, RpC, 12"..............475.00
No mold #, child, ShHd, kid body, RpC, 22".............................475.00
Size # only, child, ShHd, ge, plaster pate, o/m, wig, OC, 22"...........500.00

Kestner

Johannes D. Kestner made buttons at a lathe in a Waltershausen factory in the early 1800s. When this line of work failed, he used the same lathe to turn doll bodies. Thus the Kestner company began. It was one of the few German manufacturers to make the complete doll. By 1860, with the purchase of a porcelain factory, Kestner made doll heads of china and bisque as well as wax, worked-in-leather, celluloid, and cardboard. In 1895 the Kestner trademark of a crown with streamers was registered in the U.S. and a year later in Germany. Kestner felt the mark was appropriate since he referred to himself as the 'king of German dollmakers.'

#142, child, bsk SkHd, ge, o/m, bjtd body, OC, 8"....................700.00
#143, character, SkHd, ge, o/m, jtd body, OC, 8".......................950.00
#146, child, bsk SkHd, ge, o/m, bjtd body, OC, 20"................1,100.00
#162, adult, bsk & compo, o/m, RpC, 1898, 18", EX..............1,525.00
#171, Klein Mammi (Little Mammy), dome, o/m, 15"..............3,500.00
#172, Gibson Girl, ShHd, ge, c/m, kid body, OC, 10"..............1,100.00
#192, bsk SkHd, sl, c/m, jtd compo body, RpC, 7"....................700.00
#192, child, bsk SkHd, sl, c/m, jtd compo body, RpC, 22"........2,400.00
#192, child, bsk SkHd, sl, o/m, jtd compo body, RpC, 18"........2,200.00
#208, character child, pnt eyes, RpC, 12", EX........................10,000.00
#210, character baby, ShHd, sl, o/c/m, RpC, ca 1912, 12", EX.....700.00
#210, character baby, SkHd, ge, o/m, bent legs, RpC, 8", EX.......300.00
#210, solid-dome ShHd, sl, o/c/m, OC, 12"...............................750.00
#214, ShHd, pnt eyes, c/m, muslin body, RpC, 15"..................3,000.00
#237, Hilda, sl, o/m, RpC, ca 1914, 13", EX............................1,900.00
#243, Asian baby, sl, o/m, RpC, ca 1914, 13", EX....................4,000.00
#263, character baby, SkHd, ge, o/m, bent legs, RpC, 26", EX..1,650.00

Lenci

Characteristics of Lenci dolls include steam-molded felt heads, quality clothing, childishly plump bodies, and painted eyes that glance to the side. Fine mohair wigs were used, and the middle and fourth fingers were sewn together. Look for the factory stamp on the foot, though paper labels were also used. Values are for dolls in excellent condition — no moth holes, very little fading. Dolls from the 1940s, 1950s, and beyond generally bring the lower prices; add for tags, boxes, and accessories. Mint dolls and rare examples bring higher prices. Dolls in only good condition are worth approximately 25% of one rated excellent.

Baby, OC, pre-1940s, 22", EX..3,200.00
Bali dancer, OC, pre-1940, 15", EX..1,500.00
Benedetta, 18", $1,000 to..1,100.00
Child, hard face, less ornate OC, 1940s-50s, 15", EX..................500.00
Child, softer face, ornate costume, 1920s-30s, 13", $1,300 to ...1,500.00
Child, softer scowling face (model #1500), ornate costume, 1920s, 17".2,200.00
Cupid, 17"...5,200.00

Eugenia, regional costume, 25"..1,100.00
Fadette, adult face, flapper type w/L limbs, OC, pre-1940s, 17" .1,050.00
Flirty ge, 15"..2,200.00
Golfer, ca 1930, 17", VG+...2,700.00
Madame Butterfly, ca 1926, 25"..4,800.00
Mascotte, regional costume, 9", $350 to....................................375.00
Mascotte, swing legs, OC, pre-1940, 8½"..................................325.00
Modern, 1979+, 13", $95 to..125.00
Modern, 1979+, 21", $150 to..200.00
Modern, OC, ca 1979+, 21"..200.00
Modern, OC, ca 1979+, 26", EX..250.00
Pan, hoofed ft, 8"...1,000.00
Spanish lady, ge, five-pc body, tagged outfit, 19".....................1,500.00
Tom Mix, 18"...3,500.00

Madame Alexander

Beatrice Alexander founded the Alexander Doll Company in 1923 by making an all-cloth, oil-painted face, Alice in Wonderland doll. With the help of her three sisters, the company prospered; and by the late 1950s there were over 600 employees making Madame Alexander dolls. The company still produces these lovely dolls today. For more information, refer to *Collector's Encyclopedia of Madame Alexander Dolls* and *Madame Alexander Collector's Dolls Price Guide* by Linda Crowsey. Both are published by Collector Books. In the listings that follow, values represent dolls in mint condition. To bring top prices, dolls made after 1972 must be mint and retain their original boxes. Alexander dolls in less than mint condition are worth one-half to one-third the value of mint examples.

Agatha, hp, red gown, Jacqueline, 1967, #2171, 21"....................650.00
Anna Ballerina, compo, Pavlova (Wendy Ann), 1940, 18", min.950.00
Arlene Dahl, hp, Maggie, red wig, lav gown, 1950-51, 18".......7,000.00
Baby Betty, compo, 1933-36, 10-12"..300.00
Baby Brother or Sister, cloth/vinyl, Mary Mine, 1977-79, 20", ea.125.00
Baby Lynn, compo/vinyl, 1973-76, 20".....................................125.00
Ballerina, hp, Wendy Ann, 1953, #354, 8"................................750.00
Blue Boy, cloth, 1930s, 16"..650.00
Bobby Q, cloth, 1940-42..750.00
Bonnie Walker, hp, skater, 1955, 15", min................................700.00
Bridesmaid, compo, Little Betty, 1937-39, 9".............................350.00
Caroline, vinyl, riding habit, 1961-62, 15"................................375.00
Carrot Top, cloth, 1967, 21"...125.00
Chatterbox, plastic/vinyl talker, 1961, 24"................................250.00
Coco, plastic/vinyl, sheath-style ballgown, 1966, 21"...............2,200.00
Country Cousins, cloth, 1940s, 26"...650.00
Danish, compo, Tiny Betty, 1937-41, 7"....................................325.00
Dude Ranch, hp, Wendy Ann, 1955, #449, 8", min....................750.00
Easter Sunday, hp, Am Series, 1993, #340 or #340-1, 8", ea..........65.00
Edith the Lonely Doll, plastic/vinyl, Mary-Bel, 1958-59, 16"......325.00
Estrella, hp, Maggie, lilac gown, 1953, 18"............................1,200.00
Fairy Princess, compo, Wendy Ann, 1939, 11"..........................425.00
Flower Child, Maggie, 1999, #17790, 8"................................— 60.00
Flower Girl, compo, Princess Elizabeth, 1939, 1944-47, 16-18" ...650.00
Flower Girl, hp, Margaret, 1954, 15", min...............................800.00
Get Well, hp, red striped outfit/vase of flowers, 1998-99, #21090, 8" ...65.00
Godey, compo, Wendy Ann, wht lace over pk satin, 1945-47, 21"..2,700.00
Grandma Jane, plastic/vinyl, Mary Ann, 1970-72, #1420, 14".....225.00
Happy, cloth/vinyl, 1970, 20"...200.00
Heidi, compo, Tiny Betty, 1938-39, 7".....................................325.00
Hiawatha, hp, Wendy Ann (Americana Series), 1967-69, #720, 8"..375.00
Hulda, hp, Margaret, lamb's wool wig, 1949, 18".....................1,900.00
Jacqueline, hp/vinyl, street dress or suit w/hat, 1961-62, 21".......950.00
Japanese Bride, in kimono, #28590, 10"...................................125.00
Juliet, compo, Wendy Ann, Portrait series, 1945-46, 21".........2,500.00

Karen Ballerina, compo, Margaret, 1946-49, 15", min 950.00
Kelly, hp, Lissy, 1959, 12" 500.00
Klondike Kate, hp, Cissette, 1963, 10" 1,500.00
Lady Lee, Storybook Series, 1988, #442, 8" 60.00
Laura Ingalls, Mary Ann (Classic Series), 1989-91, #1531, 14" 85.00
Little Bo Peep, compo, Little Betty/Wendy Ann, 1936-40, 9-11". 350.00
Melinda, plastic/vinyl, party dress, 22" 475.00
Mimi, hp, jtd, in formal, 1961, 30" 950.00
Mistress Mary, compo, Tiny Betty, 1937-41, 7" 375.00
Natasha, Jacqueline, 1989-90, brn & paisley brocade, #2255, 21" ..325.00
Nina Ballerina, compo, Little Betty, 1939-41, 9" 375.00
Oliver Twist, compo, Tiny Betty, 1935-36, 7" 300.00
Pamela, in window box, Lissy face, changeable wigs, 1962-63, 12"....1,300.00
Patty, plastic/vinyl, 1965, 18" 275.00
Persia, compo, Tiny Betty, 1936-38, 7" 300.00
Pitty Pat, cloth, 1950s, 16" 475.00
Red Riding Hood, compo, Tiny Betty, 7" 375.00
Rodeo, hp, Wendy Ann, 1955, #483, 8", min 850.00
Ruffles the Clown, 1954, 21" 425.00
Scarlett O'Hara, compo, Wendy Ann, 1941-43, 14-15" 800.00
So Lite Baby or Toddler, cloth, 1930s-40s, 20", ea min 375.00
South Am, compo, Little Betty, 1939-41, 9" 325.00
Tommy, hp, Lissy, 1962, 12" 800.00
Victoria, hp, Margaret, 1950-51, 14" 900.00
Virginia Dare, compo, Little Betty, 1940-41, 9" 450.00
Wendy Ann, compo, pnt eyes, 1936-40, 9" 375.00

Papier-Maché

French child, brighter coloring, wig, ethnic costume, 13" 125.00
French type (Germany), ShHd, ge, o/m, RpC, 14" 1,200.00
French type (Germany), ShHd, pnt eyes, pnt blk hair, RpC, 12".. 700.00
Milliner's type, 'Apollo' topknot, sm waist, kid body, RpC, 16" .3,000.00
Milliner's type, braided bun, sm waist, kid body, 11" 1,800.00
Milliner's type, coiled braids over ears, braided bun, RpC, 11" .1,000.00
Milliner's type, molded bonnet, kid body, wooden limbs, RpC, 15".1,700.00
Patent Washable, ShHd w/mohair wig, ge, G quality, RpC, 12" 800.00
Patent Washable, ShHd w/mohair wig, o/m or c/m, EX quality, RpC, 18"..650.00
Pre-Grenier type, ShHd, molded/pnt blk hair, ge, RpC, 22" 1,900.00

Shoulder head, black lady with set brown glass eyes, open/closed mouth with painted teeth, composition lower arms and legs, cloth upper torso, mohair wig, circa 1890, 15", $540.00. (Photo courtesy McMasters Harris Auction Co. on LiveAuctioneers.com)

ShHd, molded pnt hair, pnt eyes, wood limbs, RpC, 12" 675.00
ShHd, molded/pnt hair w/long curls, pnt eyes, wood limbs, RpC, 16"....1,550.00
ShHd, molded/pnt hair, ge, wood limbs, RpC, 24" 2,400.00

Parian

Alice in Wonderland, molded headband or comb, RpC, 10" 500.00
Alice in Wonderland, molded headband or comb, RpC, 16", EX . 800.00
Countess Dagmar, headband, curls on forehead, unmk, RpC, 21" ...1,400.00
Dolly Madison, RpC, 22", EX 1,000.00

Empress Eugenie, headpc snood, RpC, 25" 1,300.00
Lady w/molded hat, blond or blk pnt hair, pnt eyes, RpC, 19"..2,900.00
Lady, common hairdo, molded bodice, fancy trim, RpC, 17" 800.00
Lady, common hairdo, no decor, cloth body, RpC, 1850-90+, 15"...325.00
Lady, fancy hairdo, ge, p/e, RpC, 20" 2,700.00
Lady, fancy hairdo, pnt eyes, p/e, RpC, 1850-1900+, 22", EX ...1,700.00
Lady, fancy hairdo, swivel neck, ge, RpC, 15" 2,700.00

Lady, untinted bisque shoulder head, molded bodice with gold lustre trim, painted and molded features and hair, cloth body with kid arms and china feet, 12", VG, $660.00. (Photo courtesy Dan Morphy Auctions LLC on LiveAuctioneers.com)

Man or boy, ge, RpC, 16" 2,800.00
Man or boy, pnt eyes, decor shirt & tie, RpC, 13" 775.00
Man, ShHd, pnt bl eyes, c/m, glazed collar/tie, cloth, RpC, 27" .. 700.00

Schoenhut

 Albert Schoenhut left Germany in 1866 to go to Pennsylvania to work as a repairman for toy pianos. He eventually applied his skills to wooden toys and later designed an all-wood doll which he patented on January 17, 1911. These uniquely jointed dolls were painted with enamels and came with a metal stand. Some of the later dolls had stuffed bodies, voice boxes, and hollow heads. Due to the changing economy and fierce competition, the company closed in the mid-1930s.

#101, girl, cvd hair (bob w/bow), rnd eyes/smile, RpC, 16", VG ...3,200.00
#104, girl, fine cvd hair w/braids, RpC, ca 1911-12, 16", EX.....3,600.00
#109W (walker), toddler, sl, RpC, 1921-23, 14", EX................... 800.00
#300, girl, long curly wig, dimple in chin, RpC, 16", EX........... 1,200.00
#407, wigged boy, face of #310 girl, RpC, 1912-16, 21", EX.....4,000.00
Baby Boy, wig, pnt eyes, RpC, 12", EX...................................... 200.00
Baby Girl, pnt hair & eyes, bent arms & legs, RpC, 13", EX........ 300.00
Cartoon character, Moritz, cvd/pnt hair, cvd shoes, 8" 525.00
Character Boy, #309, wig, intaglio eyes, smiling, 16", VG 3,025.00
Character Girl, #16/306, wig, intaglio eyes, c/m, OC, 16" 4,125.00
Girl, cvd bobbed hair w/headband, intaglio eyes, OC, 17", EX.1,550.00
Girl, wig, intaglio eyes, OC, 14", VG.. 700.00
Girl, wig, intaglio eyes, RpC, 16", VG 600.00
Griziano Boy, cvd hair combed forward, intaglio eyes, OC, 16½", VG...1,980.00
Griziano Girl, human hair wig/middle part, intaglio eyes, OC, 16", EX..3,575.00
Miss Dolly, wig, pnt eyes, OC, 19½", VG 600.00
Nature Boy, pnt hair, spring-jtd, RpC, 12½", G 200.00
Toddler Boy, wig, pnt eyes, OC, 11", G+ 450.00
Toddler Girl, wig, intaglio eyes, RpC, 16", VG............................ 500.00
Walker Boy, wig, intaglio eyes, closed mouth, RpC, EX 350.00
Walker Girl, wig, intaglio eyes, OC, 16", VG............................... 500.00

SFBJ

 By 1895 Germany was producing dolls at much lower prices than the French dollmakers could, so to save the doll industry, several leading French manufacturers united to form one large company. Bru, Raberry and Delphieu, Pintel and Godshaux, Fleischman and Bodel, Jumeau, and many others united to form the company Société Francaise de Fabrication de Bebes et Jouets (SFBJ).

#60, child, bsk head, ge, o/m, p/e, RpC, 18".........................700.00
#226, character face, ge, c/m, rpC, 20"............................2,200.00
#227, bsk SkHd, compo body, o/m w/teeth, ge, 22".............3,100.00
#227, bsk SkHd, ge, o/m/teeth, RpC, 17".........................2,700.00
#227, bsk SkHd, jtd wood & compo body, set eyes, o/m, RpC, 14"....1,900.00
#230, character face, ge, o/m/teeth, RpC, 22"..................1,000.00
#238, character, bsk SkHd, sm o/m, wig, RpC, 18"..............2,000.00
#248, ge, lowered eyebrows, pouty c/m, ca 1912, 10".........7,500.00
#250, character face, o/m/teeth, RpC, 18"........................3,000.00

#252, character baby with closed pouty mouth, sleep eyes with mohair upper lashes, toddler body, replaced wig, 18", $7,500.00. (Photo courtesy Skinner Auctioneers and Appraisers of Antiques and Fine Art)

#301, bsk SkHd, o/m/teeth, ge, wig, RpC, 24", EX..................1,200.00
#301, child, bsk head, 5-pc body, RpC, 8"...........................300.00
Bluette, 301, bsk SkHd, o/m/teeth, ge, wig, OC, 10⅝".............3,300.00
Jumeau type, no mold #, o/m, ge, RpC, 28"......................2,100.00
Jumeau type, no mold #, o/m, RpC, 15".............................1,300.00
Kiss thrower, child, bsk head, ge, o/m, p/e, RpC, 24".................1,750.00

Shirley Temple

Prices are suggested for dolls in excellent to near mint condition, in complete original outfits, and made by the Ideal Toy Company unless noted otherwise.

Bisque, unlicensed Japanese, 6"....................................225.00
Celluloid, metal pate, sl, dimples, tagged Dutch OC, 1937+, 13". 350.00
Celluloid, unlicensed Japanese, 5"..................................125.00
Celluloid, unlicensed Japanese, Dutch girl, 1937+, 13".............320.00
Composition, wig, cowgirl outfit, felt hat, 17", VG 875.00
Composition, Baby Shirley, tagged OC, 1934+, 18"...............1,100.00
Composition, bl & wht pinafore, wig, 13", VGIB....................1,000.00
Composition, gr o/c eys, o/m/teeth, mohair wig, 1934-40s, 22".. 1,000.00
Composition, gr sl, o/m/teeth, mohair wig, 1934-40s, 16"...........850.00
Composition, Hawaiian Marama, blk yarn hair, OC, Ideal, 18"... 950.00
Composition, molded brn curls, pnt eyes, o/c/m, Japan, OC, 7" .. 225.00
Composition, o/e/c, o/m/teeth, mohair wig, OC, 1934+, 20".......900.00
Composition, sl, o/m/teeth, mohair wig, OC, 1934+, 11"...........950.00
Vinyl, Montgomery Ward's reissue, 17", MIB 225.00
Vinyl, jtd wrists, mk ST-35-38-2, 1960, 36".....................1,600.00
Vinyl, rooted hair, red & wht polka dot dress, 16"...................85.00
Vinyl, sl, rooted wig, o/c/m/teeth, mk ST//12 on head, 12".........225.00

Simon & Halbig

Simon & Halbig was one of the finest German makers to operate during the 1870s into the 1930s. Due to the high quality of this maker, the dolls still command large prices today. During the 1890s a few Simon & Halbig heads were used by a French maker, but these are extremely rare and well marked S&H.

#151, pnt eyes, laughing c/m, RpC, ca 1912, 15", EX.............15,000.00
#530, child, SkHd, ge, compo body, RpC, 22"......................575.00
#600, child, sl, o/m, RpC, 17"..800.00

#719, child, sl, c/m, p/e, compo/wood body, RpC, 18", EX........2,100.00
#749, SkHd, ge, wig, p/e, wood body, RpC, 21"....................2,700.00
#1009, sl, o/m/teeth, p/e, kid body, wig, RpC, ca 1889, 19", EX... 750.00
#1059, bsk SkHd, ge, p/e, o/m, compo/wood body, RpC, 34", EX.............800.00
#1078, ge, o/m, p/e, clockwork walker, RpC, 23", EX.............2,900.00
#1079, Ondine, swimming doll, RpC, 16", VG 1,600.00
#1159, Gibson Girl, ge, o/m, ca 1894, 20", EX....................2,600.00
#1160, lady, ShHd, ge, c/m, fancy wig, RpC, 14".................... 675.00
#1249, open mouth w/ teeth, rpr, 27"................................450.00
#1250, ShHd, ge, o/m, kid body, RpC, 19", EX.......................700.00
#1294, character face, pnt eyes, o/c/m, bent-leg baby, RpC, 16" .. 750.00
#1303, lady face, ge, c/m, RpC, 14".................................6,500.00
#1428, ge, o/c/m, toddler, RpC, 16", EX............................2,300.00
#1469, flapper adult, ge, c/m, RpC, ca 1920, 15", EX.............4,000.00
#1488, baby, ge, o/c/m, bent-leg body, RpC, 20"..................4,500.00
Fashion type, bsk SkHd, kid over wood body, c/m, RpC, 18"....2,700.00
S&H w/no mold #, child, ShHd, molded hair, c/m, RpC, 17"...1,200.00
S&H w/no mold #, child, ShHd, swivel neck, RpC, 12"............ 900.00
S&H w/no mold #, ShHd child, molded hair, RpC, 1870s, 19", EX ..1,400.00

Skookum

Representing real Indians of various tribes, stern-faced Skookum dolls were designed by Mary McAboy of Missoula, Montana, in the early 1900s. The earliest of McAboy's creations were made with air-dried apple faces that bore a resemblance to the neighboring Chinook Indian tribe. The name Skookum is derived from the Chinook/Siwash term for large or excellent (aka Bully Good) and appears as part of the oval paper labels often attached to the feet of the dolls. In 1913 McAboy applied for a patent that described her dolls in three styles: a female doll, a female doll with a baby, and a male doll. In 1916 George Borgman and Co. partnered with McAboy, registered the Skookum trademark, and manufactured these dolls which were distributed by the Arrow Novelty Co. of New York and the HH Tammen Co. of Denver. The Skookum (Apple) Packers Association of Washington state produced similar 'friendly faced' dolls as did Louis Ambery for the National Fruit exchange. The dried apple faces of the first dolls were replaced by those made of a composition material. Plastic faces were introduced in the 1940s, and these continued to be used until production ended in 1959. Skookum dolls were produced in a variety of styles, with the most collectible having stern, lined faces with small painted eyes glancing to the right, colorful Indian blankets pulled tightly across the straw- or paper-filled body to form hidden arms, felt pants or skirts over wooden legs, and wooden feet covered with decorated felt suede or masking tape. Skookums were produced in sizes ranging from a 2" souvenir mailer with a cardboard address tag to 36" novelty and advertising dolls. Collectors highly prize 21" to 26" dolls as well as dolls that glance to their left. Felt or suede feet predate the less desirable brown plastic feet of the late 1940s and 1950s. Unless noted otherwise, our values are for skookums in excellent condition. Our advisor for this category is Glen Rairigh; he is listed in the Directory under Michigan.

Baby mailer, 1¢ postcard attached, feather/ribbon binding, 4" 100.00
Baby, looks left, cradle brd, beaded body/head covering, 10" 1,100.00
Baby, mc blanket, leather headband w/pnt decor, 4" 30.00
Baby/child in loop basket, blanket wrap, necklace, 14"............. 200.00
Boy, brn ft w/pnt decor, Bully Good label, 6"....................... 100.00
Boy, brn suede ft w/decor, headband, 10" 150.00
Boy, mc blanket, felt pants, leather shoes, 6", VG 50.00
Chief w/headdress, paper tape shoes w/decor, 12"................. 250.00
Family, chief & female w/baby, clothes match, 15", 14" 600.00
Female, baby, wooden legs, paper label on moccasin, 12½"......... 210.00
Female, w/baby, w/blanket, purple felt/ft/skirt, necklace, 11"....... 200.00
Female, w/baby, w/blanket, worn paper tape ft, 12", VG 150.00
Girl, cotton-wrapped legs, beaded ft decor, headband, 9"............ 150.00

Girl, cotton-wrapped legs, pnt suede ft covers, Bully Good, 6" 100.00
Mailer, baby in bl & yel cotton, Grand Canyon, 10-1-52 .... 25.00
Mailer, baby in patterned cotton on yel cb 25.00
Mailer, baby in red bandana on yel cb.. 55.00

Steiner

Jules Nicholas Steiner established one of the earliest French manufacturing companies (making dishes and clocks) in 1855. He began with mechanical dolls with bisque heads and open mouths with two rows of bamboo teeth; his patents grew to include walking and talking dolls. In 1880 he registered a patent for a doll with sleep eyes. This doll could be put to sleep by turning a rod that operated a wire attached to its eyes.

Baby w/rnd face, bsk SkHd, pwt/e, o/m/teeth, p/e, wig, Rpc, 18"...6,800.00
Bébé le Parisien, SkHd w/cb pate, pwt eyes, wig, jtd, RpC, 10", EX.5,500.00
Bébé le Parisien, SkHd, pwt eyes, o/m, p/e, jtd compo, OC, 21" . 9,500.00
Bébé w/figure E, SkHd, ge, o/m, p/e, RpC, 27"........................36,000.00
Bébé w/rnd face, bsk SkHd, c/m, dimples, OC, 18" 11,500.00
Bébé, Series A or C, bsk SkHd, cb pate, pwt/e, p/e, wig, RpC, 10".12,000.00
Bébé, Series E or G, bsk SkHd, pwt eyes, RpC, 14", EX 18,000.00
Crying/kicking child, key-wind, solid dome/ge, teeth, RpC, 20".............2,200.00
Taufling-style baby, dome head, ge, c/m, wig, RpC, 20"................10,000.00
Taufling-style baby, dome head, ge, c/m, wig, RpC, 14", EX.................13,000.00
Unmk Bébé, SkHd, pwt eyes, o/m/teeth, p/e, wig, OC, 1870s, 18" ..6,800.00

Vogue

This company is perhaps best known for its Ginny dolls. Composition dolls such as Toodles were made during most of the 1940s, but by 1948, hard plastic dolls were being produced. Dolls of the late 1950s often had vinyl heads and hard plastic bodies, but the preferred material throughout the decade of the '60s was vinyl. An original mint-condition composition Toodles would be worth $400.00 to $450.00 on the market today (played-with, about $90.00 to $150.00). Another Vogue doll that is very collectible is Jill. For more information, we recommend *Collector's Encyclopedia of Vogue Dolls* by Judith Izen and Carol Stover. Our advisor for Jill dolls is Bonnie Groves; she is listed in the Directory under Texas.

Baby Dear, vinyl & cloth, pnt eyes, squeaker, OC, 1960-64, 18", M... 225.00
Dora Lee, compo, sl, c/m, 11", $375 to... 425.00
Ginny accessory, tablecloth, 1956-57, MIB 300.00
Ginny baby, vinyl, sleep eyes, jtd body, drinks/wets, 1959-82, 12". 40.00

Ginny, hard plastic, painted eyes, strung joints, molded hair with mohair wig, 1948 – 1950, 8", $375.00. (Photo courtesy Elaine Holda/Linda Edward)

Ginny outfit, 1948-53, $65 to.. 95.00
Ginny outfit, 1954-62, min... 40.00
Ginny outfit, Sugar 'n Spice, #1352, 1960, MIB............................ 75.00
Ginny, hp walker, sl, dynel wig, common dress, 1950-54, 8", $250 to... 300.00
Ginny, hp, bent-knee walker, sleep eyes, saran wig, 1957-62, 8".. 150.00
Ginny, hp, sleep eyes, 7-pc body, saran wig, 1954-56, 8", $195 to. 225.00

Ginny, hp, sleep eyes, strung joints, 1953, 8", $450 to.................. 550.00
Ginny, Queen of Hearts, hp/strung, sl, OC, 1950, 8", M, min 500.00
Ginny, soft vinyl & hp, sleep eyes, rooted hair, 1963-65, 8", $35 to... 50.00
Ginny, vinyl walker, bl sl, OC, 1960, 36", M, min........................ 250.00
Ginny, vinyl, resembles 1963-71 Ginny, Hong Kong, 1984-86, 8", $35 to...55.00
Ginny, vinyl, sleep eyes, non-walker, Hong Kong, 1977-82, 8", $25 to .. 35.00
Ginny, vinyl, sleep eyes, non-walker, rooted hair, 1965-72, 8", $35 to...50.00
Ginny, Wavette, hp/strung, sl, #80, OC, 1951, 8", M, min 400.00
Jan, vinyl head, 6-pc rigid vinyl body, 10", $125 to 125.00
Jan, vinyl, sl, str legs, swivel waist, OC, 1959-60, 10", M.............. 75.00
Jill, 7-pc teenage body, bend-knee walker/H heels, 10½", MIB, $250 to..800.00
Jill, Ginny, Jimmy, Jan booklet, 1958.. 20.00
Jill, hp, nude, 10", VG, min... 25.00
Jill, in basic leotard, VG 125.00
Jill, in leotard, hp, OC, 1957, 10½", EX.. 47.00
Jill, in red gown, scarce, EX 200.00
Jill, nude, G 30.00
Jill, poodle, felt purse, NM... 40.00
Jill, record hop outfit, #7406, EX 175.00
Jill, shoes & undies, MIB 11.00
Jill, Sweetheart, vinyl, rooted hair, H heels, OC, 1963, M............ 175.00
Jill, tagged dress, bl leather coat, OC, VG 155.00
Jill, vinyl hat box 10.00
Little Miss Ginny, vinyl, 1-pc hp body, 1965-71, 12", $30 to 40.00
Littlest Angel, vinyl head, sl, rooted hair, 1961-63, 10" 175.00
Miss Ginny, soft vinyl head, jtd arms/swivel waist, 1960s, 15-16".. 40.00
Toodles, compo, 1937-48, 8", $450 to.. 625.00

Wax, Poured Wax

Shoulder head, molded with painted features, pupil-less sleeping glass eyes attached to wire in torso, mohair wig, muslin body with wax arms, original clothing, 15", $1,680.00. (Photo courtesy Noel Barrett on LiveAuctioneers.com)

2-faced (laughing/crying), 1880-90s, RpC, 15"............................... 600.00
Over compo ShHd, child, ge, o/m or c/m, later, OC, 12"............. 800.00
Over compo ShHd, ge, molded hair, cloth body, OC, 15"............. 775.00
Over compo ShHd, ge, RpC, 18" 900.00
Over papier-maché, mechanical baby, ge, bellows, RpC, 18".............2,000.00
Over SkHd, child, ge, OC, 18"..1,500.00
Poured ShHd, pnt features, ge, c/m, cloth body, wig, OC, 25"............. 2,200.00
Poured ShHd, pnt features, ge, c/m, cloth body, wig, RpC, 18"............. 1,100.00

Door Knockers

Door knockers, those charming precursors of the doorbell, come in an intriguing array of shapes and styles. The very rare ones come from England. Cast-iron examples made in this country were often produced in forms similar to the more familiar doorstop figures. Beware: Many of the brass door knockers being offered on internet auctions are of recent vintage. Our values represent examples in excellent original condition unless otherwise noted. Those with mint paint will bring premium prices.

Basket of daffodils, bow at top, pnt CI, 4¼x2½" 300.00
Bat w/wings open on top, pnt CI, JM 75 mk, 1-lb 12-oz, 9⅜" L 75.00
Birdhouse, cream w/mc, pnt CI, Hubley #629, 3¾x8x2⅝" 525.00

Bluebirds at birdhouse, pnt CI, Hubley, 3¾x1¾" 335.00
Boy on fence, dog as knocker, pnt CI, 1930s, 3½x2", VG 300.00
Bulldog, brass, unmk, 3" dog on 5" backplate 75.00
Cardinal on twigs, pnt CI, rare, 5x3", M 350.00
Centurion on figurative base, blk CI, Iron Art JM 79, 4½x2" 155.00
Cherub faces amid ornate scrolls, pnt CI, 10x7" 90.00
Cottage in trees w/road & porch, pnt CI, rare, 4x2½", min 800.00
Dartmoor Pixie on mushroom base, pnt brass, ca 1900, 3¼" 100.00
Dog at entrance to doghouse, pnt CI, 4x3", $800 to..................... 850.00
Dove w/olive branch, pnt CI, detailed, rare, 4x3" 550.00
Dragon, tooled wrought iron, w/strike, 6½" 115.00
Eagle, talons holding ball, detailed, gold on bronze, ca 1900, 8½"...275.00
Elephant holding log in trunk (knocker), CI, EX detail, 7⅜"....... 335.00
Flower basket, pnt CI, Hubley #13, 4x2⅞", NM 175.00
Flower on ornate knocker, Kenrick & Sons #423, brass, ca 1880, 9" .. 200.00
Gargoyle, pnt CI, ca 1900, 4½" 100.00
Girl knocking & holding black doll, pnt CI, rare, 3¾x2¾" 1,000.00
Hand holding ball (detailed) on shield, wood, ca 1900, 11x6½", NM.... 985.00
Hand of Fatima, bronzed patina, #609, 6" 185.00
Hand w/hammer (knocker) on figural coin amid leaves, bronze, 7½x5" .. 165.00
Heart in hands, arms form ring, brass, 6¼" 60.00
Ivy pot, pnt CI, Hubley #123 .... 250.00
Kewpie, brass, ca 1920, 4¾" 80.00
Lion head w/beaded ring knocker, brass, England, 1920s, 9½x6x3½" ... 460.00
Lions & shields, Tudor style, w/peep hole, cast bronze, ca 1920, 9x6"... 300.00
Monks on Sherborne Abby base, bronze, 1911-12, 4x3" 120.00
Morning glory (knocker) on leaves, pnt CI, 1890-1910, 3½x3x1¼"... 250.00

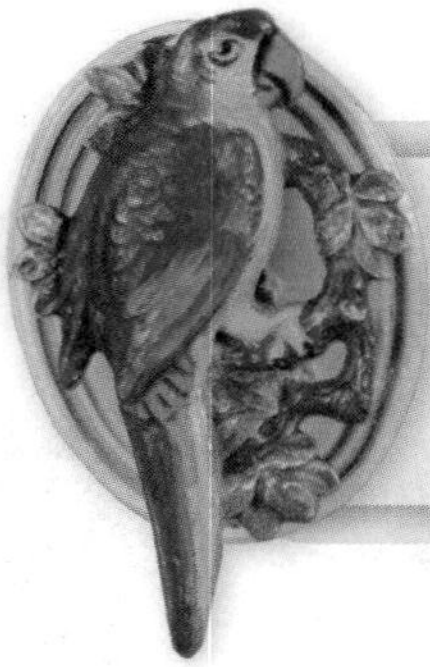

Parrot on branch, painted cast iron, Hubley, 3⅞x2⅞", NM, $250.00.
(Photo courtesy Dan Morphy Auctions LLC on LiveAuctioneers.com)

Parrot on leafy branch on oval, pnt CI, Hubley, ca 1900, 4¼x3" ... 65.00
Pear & emb flowers, pnt CI, Hubley, 3½x3" 445.00
Rooster (crowing) on branch, pnt CI, 4½x2⅞", NM 395.00
Russian eagle, dbl-headed, brass, 12¾x12¼" 105.00
Sarah W Symonds Cottage, pnt CI, Nichols House 1870... on base, 5½". 1,000.00
Spaniels (2), shell shape at top of base, brass, ca 1930, 3½x2¼" .. 100.00
Spider w/captured fly, pnt CI, rare, 3½x1¾" 450.00
Tulip, wide fr, alum, 8x5¼" 165.00
Zinnias, pnt CI, mk Pat Pend LVL, rare, 3¾x2½" 550.00

Doorstops

Although introduced in England in the mid-1800s, cast-iron doorstops were not made to any great extent in this country until after the Civil War. Once called 'door porters,' their function was to keep doors open to provide better ventilation. They have been produced in many shapes and sizes, both dimensional and flat-backed. Doorstops retained their usefulness and appeal well into the 1930s. In some areas of the country, it may be necessary to adjust prices down about 25%. Most of our listings describe examples in excellent original condition; all are made of cast iron. To evaluate a doorstop in only very good paint, deduct at least 35%. Values for examples in near-mint or better conditon sell at a premium, while prices for examples in poor to good paint drop dramatically. See also Bradley and Hubbard.

St. Bernard, Copyright U.S.A., 7x10", $2,400.00.
(Photo courtesy Dan Morphy Auctions LLC on LiveAuctioneers.com)

Airplane 'flying' over mountains, gold pnt, Pat Appld For LVL, 10" ..920.00
Apple blossoms in woven basket, Hubley #329, 7⅝x5⅜", $100 to .. 150.00
Bathing beauties, Deco style, Hubley #250, 10⅞x5½" 1,795.00
Bellhop, bl uniform, #1244, 8⅞x4⅝", $275 to 350.00
Boston terrier begging, 8¾x5", $300 to 375.00
Buddha, 8⅞x8⅛" 200.00
Castle on mountain w/road, 8x5¼", $350 to 425.00
Cat sleeping, 4½x13½x10¼", NM 925.00
Cat w/bell on braided rug, c Sarah W Symonds..., rare, 13x10", VG .2,300.00
Cavalier King Charles spaniel, 9¼x6⅞" 1,380.00
Clipper ship, National Foundry #3, 9½x12" 520.00
Clown, Hubley, 10½x4½" 975.00
Cockatoo (wht) on branch w/red blossoms, 11¼x9½" 5,175.00
Concertina player (Blk man), on base, mc pnt, 7" 1,380.00
Cosmos flower basket, National Foundry #42, 8⅜x7", G 115.00
Cottage doorway w/flowers, Leave Grouch Behind..., S Symonds, 6", NM...2,590.00
Cottage, Albany Foundry, 5¾x8¾" 290.00
Cottage, Hiram Powers, rare, 5½x11¾" 4,025.00
Daffodils & Mixed Flowers in Woven Basket, 11⅛x10¾" 850.00
Duck in bl bonnet, 6¼x4⅜", VG 345.00
Elephant, 10¾x9¾", VG 180.00
English bulldog, sitting, Hubley, 4⅞x4", G 800.00
English bulldog, standing, Hubley #220, 7x9" 520.00
Fence w/urn & shrubs, c Sarah W Symonds, 8x4⅞", VG 1,265.00
German Shepherd, Littco, 9x10¾" 200.00
German Shepherd, wedge, Germany & P inside dbl triangle, 12½"...225.00
Gladiolas in vase, Hubley #489, 10x8", VG 200.00
Goldenrod flowers, Hubley #268, 7⅛x5½" 575.00
Hessian soldier, 21x11¾", NM 700.00
Indian brave bust, Carmen, rare, 5½x7½", VG 560.00
Indian brave w/spear on rearing horse, oblong base, mc pnt, 9½" . 430.00
Jayhawk (KS University mascot), rare, 8⅜x6⅝" 675.00
Jungle boy kneeling, oblong base, leopard pelt around waist, mc, 13". 1,150.00
Milkmaid lady in apron, CJO #1242, 9x4¾" 200.00
Mill w/bridge & road, c 1926 Greenblatt...#3, 9¾x7¼" 2,070.00
Monkey & organ grinder, 10x6", NM 2,600.00
Mouse on wedge of cheese, mc pnt, 2¼" 2,000.00
Olive picker, Hubley #507, 7¾x7½", NM 800.00
Owl facing forward, 6¼x3½" 145.00
Peacock, tail closed, National Foundry #56, 15¼x7⅛", VG 173.00
Peacock, tail spread, 6x6" 230.00
Pelican on dock, Albany Foundry, 8x7" 690.00
Pheasant, Hubley #458, c Fred Everett, 8x7", NM 630.00
Pirate girl w/sword, 13x7" 200.00
Pirate w/pack on bk, 12x9", NM 2,875.00
Popeye, Hubley, c 1929 King Features Syn Made in USA, 9x4" . 6,900.00
Puppy w/Duck, c 1922 by AM Greenblatt Boston Mass, 9x8" .. 1,035.00
Rabbit in Top Hat & Tails, National Foundry #89, 10", VG 920.00
Rabbit in top hat & tails, National Foundry, 10x4", NM 1,725.00

Rabbit sitting, life-sz, 11x⅝x12", VG 275.00
Red Riding Hood w/Wolf, Nuydea #860, Pat Pending..., 7x9", NM..2,900.00
Roses w/flowers in ftd basket, 8x7" 230.00
Scotty, Hubley #412, 11x16" 16.00
Sealyham, natural pnt, Hubley #382, rare, 9x14" 4,025.00
Sheep, folky sheep facing left, mk Julia, 7x10" 1,380.00
Snooper detective, mk The Snooper, 13x4", NM 1,265.00
Spanish dancer w/fan, hand on hip, skirt flared up, Trade WS Mark, 10"....350.00
Squirrel w/nut, Emig #1382, 8x5" 345.00
St Bernard, natural lifelike pnt, scarce, 6x10" 3,450.00
Sunbonnet Girl w/lg bow, 9x5" 400.00
Wine Man, multiple bottles in ea hand, 9x7" 1,100.00

Dorchester Pottery

Taking its name from the town in Massachusetts where it was organized in 1895, the Dorchester Pottery Company made primarily utilitarian wares, though other types of items were made as well. By 1940 a line of decorative pottery was introduced, some of which was painted by hand with scrollwork or themes from nature. The buildings were destroyed by fire in the late 1970s, and the pottery was never rebuilt. In the listings that follow, the decorations described are all in cobalt unless otherwise noted. Our advisor for this category is Dale MacLean; he is listed in the Directory under Massachusetts.

Key:
CAH — Charles A. Hill   JM — Joseph McCune
EHH — Ethel Hill Henderson   NR — Nando Ricci
IM — in memory of   RT — Robert Trotter

Bedwarmer, stoneware, no decor, stamped, 5x11" 75.00
Bowl, cereal, scrollwork, CAH/IM EHH, 2x5¾" 75.00
Bowl, clown, CAH/NR, 1⅛x4" 110.00
Candleholder, cobalt scrollwork, CAH/NR/IM EHH, 6" dia, ea... 125.00
Casserole, Pine Cone, CAH, w/lid, 2¼x4½" 225.00

Chamberstick, Pine Cone, N. Ricci, VG, $85.00. (Photo courtesy MV Auctions on LiveAuctioneers.com)

Charger, Fruit, stamped, 12½" 400.00
Coffee set, Blueberry, CAH, pot+mug+sugar bowl 400.00
Creamer, Strawberry, CAH 100.00
Cup/saucer, Pine Cone, CAH, stamped, 3", 6¼" 100.00
Dish, Tear Drop, CAH, 4½x7½" 150.00
Mug, Anchor, stylized anchor & rope on ivory, stamped, 4½" 100.00
Mug, Apple, CAH, 3", set of 4 .... 250.00
Mug, Pine Cone & Blizzard, ...Blizzard of 1978, stamped, 4⅛" 225.00
Pitcher, Daffodil, CAH/NR, 5x5½" 250.00
Pitcher, Pilgrim, RT, stamped, 7½", EX 300.00
Pitcher, Pussy Willow, CAH/NR, stamped, 5½x4¼" 225.00
Plate, Blueberry, CAH/NR, 10" 225.00
Plate, Lily of the Valley, CAH/NR, 7½" 200.00
Plate, Lily of the Valley, NR/ CAH, 6", EX, $185 to 200.00
Sugar bowl, Blueberry, w/lid 150.00
Sugar bowl, Sacred Cod, CAH, stamped, w/lid, 4x4½" 150.00
Syrup, flowers, CAH/NR, w/lid, 5" 175.00
Syrup, Half Scroll, striped hdl, sgn, stamped, w/lid, 4¾" 175.00

Toby jug, Quaker Oats replica, early orig label, 8x7½" 350.00
Vase, 2-tone bl, 4-sided, crimped mouth, bulb, stamped, 4½x5" .. 125.00

Dorflinger Glass

C. Dorflinger was born in Alsace, France, and came to this country when he was 10 years old. When still very young, he obtained a job in a glass factory in New Jersey. As a young man, he started his own glassworks in Brooklyn, New York, opening new factories as profits permitted. During that time he made cut glass articles for many famous people including President and Mrs. Lincoln, for whom he produced a complete service of tableware with the United States Coat of Arms. In 1863 he sold the New York factories because of ill health and moved to his farm near White Mills, Pennsylvania. His health returned, and he started a plant near his home. It was there that he did much of his best work, making use of only the very finest materials. Christian died in 1915, and the plant was closed in 1921 by consent of the family. Dorflinger glass is rare and often hard to identify. Very few pieces were marked. Many only carried a small paper label which was quickly discarded; these are seldom found today. Identification is more accurately made through a study of the patterns, as colors may vary. For more information we recommend *The Collector's Encyclopedia of American Art Glass* by John A. Shuman III.

Cologne bottle, cranberry cut overlay, button and cane design, unsigned, chip to interior of stopper, 6", $780.00. (Photo courtesy Richard D. Hatch & Associates on LiveAuctioneers.com)

Bowl, Gravic Intaglio cut, 13½" 120.00
Comport, Kalana Rose etch, 8" 180.00
Finger bowl, Florida/tinted Kalana Poppy 120.00
Finger bowl, Kalana Poppy 45.00
Goblet, water, Kalana Hawthorn etch 65.00
Goblet, water, Kalana Lily etch 60.00
Goblet, wine, Marlboro, gr cut to clear, 4½" 1,700.00
Goblet, wine, Persian, gold cut to clear, 4½" 3,400.00
Jug, Kalana Forget-Me-Not etch 140.00
Napkin ring, cut #85 .... 55.00
Tumbler, Vict cut, colorless 90.00
Vase, Fine Dmn & Panels w/Kalana Poppy etch, 16" 1,200.00

Dragonware

Dragonware has always been fairly easy to find. Today, internet auctions have made it even more so. It is still being produced and is often marketed in areas with a strong Asian influence and in souvenir shops in major cities around the United States and abroad.

As the name suggests, this china features a slip-painted dragon. Behind and around the moriage dragon (often done in a whitish color) are swirling clouds (rain), lines of color (water), fire, and in the dragon's clutch, a pearl — the dragon's most prized possession. (Although most Dragonware is ceramic, on rare occasion, you may find some beautiful examples of Dragonware executed in slip on glassware as well.) Gray (varying tones of gray and black) is the most common background color; however, it may also be done in shades of green, blue, orange, yellow, pink, white, pearl, and red. Sometimes the slip decoration will be applied in a flatter, slicker manner, rather than in the more traditional raised moriage style. On these pieces the dragon may be any color, and often the colors will be brighter and crisper. This style of painting is newer, seen on pieces from the 1940s and later.

Sometimes a three-dimensional dragon may act as the spout of a teapot or may seem to 'fly off' a vase; items with this type of modeling are a form of (but not actually considered true) Dragonware.

A lithophane is made by varying the density of the china in order to create an image when viewed with light behind it. They are often found in the bottom of coffee, demitasse, and sake cups and in this ware typically represent a geisha girl portrayed from the shoulders up. On rare occasions you may find nude ladies, usually only one, though groups of two and three may be found as well. Some cups have actual pictures in the bottom instead of lithophanes; these are newer.

Dragonware is divided into three categories. Nippon or Nippon quality pieces are the most desirable. The dragon and its background are typically done in vibrant, bold colors, and the slip work is well defined. Translucent jewels are often used for the dragon's eyes instead of the blue slip found on the more commonplace items. These pieces are usually executed in the gray tones; however, other colors have also been used. Many pieces have a lustre interior. Nippon or Nippon-quality pieces with a recognizable Nippon mark command the highest prices.

Mid-century Dragonware was mass produced in the late 1930s, 1940s, and 1950s. Tea sets could be found in the local drug store. These sets would serve up to six people and became popular in the days of bridge club and tea parties. Colors vary in this era of Dragonware, and interiors are sometimes painted in a goldish peach lustre. The slip work is not as detailed as it is on the earlier ware, and the mass-prodution techniques are evident. Many of these sets do not carry a mark, signature, or paper label, as they were brought to the states by servicemen who had been stationed in Japan. Other sets may have had only one or two marked pieces. Mid-century Dragonware falls in the mid-price range, although many of the pieces most popular with collectors were made during this era.

Turn-of-the-century pieces made from the 1970s up to the present time are obviously mass produced; the dragon often falls flat, without detail or personality. Background colors are no longer vibrant but lacklustre with a shiny appearance. Pastel pink, teal, orange, and green are commonly seen. These pieces are usually marked; however, some carried a paper label which may have been lost or removed. Dealers sometimes mistake unmarked pieces for the older ware and often sell them as such. Typically these pieces, if identified and priced correctly, would represent the lower end of the price spectrum.

These three styles are in addition to the typical gray pattern seen and positively recognized as Dragonware. Swirl: All the colors, including the background are actually slipped on, giving the effect of color having been 'drizzled' onto the surface. These pieces are usually made with white china, though on the occasion when the china body is more nearly a shade lighter than the drizzled paint, a 'squiggled' design is achieved. Cloud: These pieces have backgrounds that have been airbrushed on, achieving a flowing, soft, unified cloud effect. Solid: This type is first painted in a solid color before the dragon is applied. There may be slip painting (to represent the clouds, water, and fire) or airbrushing. Pearlized painting as well as lustre painting would fall under this category, as both techniques are, in effect, one overall color.

At the present time, the older pieces in colors other than gray are commanding the higher prices; so are the more unusual items. As always, condition is a major price-assessing issue, so be sure to check for damage before buying or selling. Overall, prices have increased. Our advisor for this category is Suzi Hibbard; she is listed in the Directory under California. In the following listing, all pieces are in the typical Dragonware style and from the mid-century period unless noted otherwise.

Key:
lth — lithophane   NQ — Nippon Quality
MIJ — Made in Japan   TD — traditional
MIOJ — Made in Occupied Japan

Item	Price
Ashtray, blk, jewel eyes, HP Nippon, 3¾x5", $125 to	200.00
Bell, pk, souvenir of Niagara Falls, 5¾x3", $10 to	25.00
Candlestick, cylindrical, sq ft, unmk, Nippon, 10"	180.00
Cookie jar, blk swirl, glass eyes, Noritake, 8x5", $350 to	500.00
Creamer/sugar bowl, orange & wht, 3½", $25 to	40.00
Cup/saucer, demi, bl swirl, MIJ, $25 to	30.00
Cup/saucer, demi, dbl nude lth, Niknoiko China, $75 to	125.00
Cup/saucer, demi, google eyes, orange solid, $25 to	45.00
Cup/saucer, demi, gr w/blk rim, HP, Shafford, $30 to	45.00
Cup/saucer, demi, nude lth, gray TD, $45 to	75.00
Dutch shoe, gray TD, $15 to	30.00
Incense burner, gray, HP MIJ, 3½", $15 to	25.00
Lamp, gray TD, jewel eyes, NQ, 7¾", $150 to	225.00
Nappy, brn, HP MIJ, sq, 5½", $25 to	45.00
Pitcher, yel cloud, MIJ, mini, 2⅞", $15 to	25.00
Planter, orange solid, w/frog, MIJ, 5½", $30 to	75.00
Saki cups, red cloud, whistling, set of 6, $50 to	125.00
Saki set, bl cloud, geisha in plate center, Kutani, 8-pc, $75 to	150.00
Saki set, bl cloud, whistling, kitten on decanter/plate, 8-pc, $125 to	175.00
Saki set, wht pearlized, whistling, HP Japan, 5-pc, $50 to	125.00
Shakers, bl cloud, unmk, pr $10 to	30.00
Shakers, orange solid, pagoda style, Japan, 4", pr $15 to	40.00
Snack set, brn cloud, gold dragon, MIJ, 2-pc, $20 to	45.00
Table lighter, blk solid, $50 to	100.00
Tea set, demi, gray TD, Nippon bl circle mk, NQ, 17-pc, $225 to	350.00
Tea set, demi, gray, Nippon bl circle mk, NQ, 17-pc, $225 to	350.00
Tea set, demi, wht pearl, Japan, newer, 17-pc, $50 to	100.00
Tea set, gray w/gold, 7½", pot+cr/sug, $45 to	70.00
Tea set, gray, MIOJ, 7½" pot+cr/sug+4 c/s, $75 to	175.00
Tea set, stacking, blk, MIJ, 5x6", $45 to	75.00
Tea/coffee set, gr cloud, lth, dragon spout, 23-pc, $175 to	275.00
Teapot, gr cloud, 8x3", $35 to	60.00
Teapot, gray, 6-sided, 7x4", $45 to	60.00
Vase, bl cloud, wide mouth, 5", $30 to	50.00
Vase, gr swirl, unmk, 3¾", $10 to	25.00
Vase, gray, glass eyes/ftd, HP Nippon w/wreath, NQ, 4⅜", $125 to	275.00
Vase, gray, jewel eyes, gr HP Nippon M in wreath, 9¾", $500 to	1,500.00

Vase, Nippon, green M in wreath mark, circa 1920, 8", $335.00 to $365.00. (Photo courtesy Jackson's Auction on LiveAuctioneers.com)

Item	Price
Vase, orange, 4", $20 to	50.00
Vase, orange, MIJ, 7½", $30 to	75.00
Vase, yel swirl, MIJ, 5", $15 to	50.00
Wall pocket, bl/orange lustre, Japan flower mk, 7", $35 to	75.00
Watering can, gr solid, MIJ, 2½", $8 to	15.00

Dresden

The city of Dresden was a leading cultural center in the seventeenth century and in the eighteenth century became known as the Florence on the Elbe because of its magnificent baroque architecture and its outstanding museums. Artists, poets, musicians, philosophers, and porcelain artists took up residence in Dresden. In the late nineteenth century, there was a considerable demand among the middle classes for porcelain. This demand was met by Dresden porcelain painters. Between 1855 and 1944, more than 200 painting studios existed in the city. The studios bought porcelain white ware from manufacturers such as Meissen and Rosenthal for decorating, marketing, and reselling throughout the world. The largest of these studios include Donath & Co., Franziska Hirsch, Richard Klemm, Ambrosius Lamm, Carl Thieme, and Helena Wolfsohn.

Most of the Dresden studios produced work in imitation of Meissen and Royal Vienna. Flower painting enhanced with burnished gold, courting couples, landscapes, and cherubs were used as decorative motifs. As with other hand-painted porcelains, value is dependent upon the quality of the decoration. Sometimes the artwork equaled or even surpassed that of the Meissen factory.

Some of the most loved and eagerly collected of all Dresden porcelains are the beautiful and graceful lace figures. Many of the figures found in the maketplace today were not made in Dresden but in other areas of Germany. For more information, we recommend *Dresden Porcelain Studios* by Jim and Susan Harran, our advisors for this category. They are listed in the Directory under New Jersey.

Cake plate, HP flowers, rtcl, gilt, Thieme, 1920s, 9¾" 150.00
Cup, chocolate, HP flowers, gilt, sq hdl, Klemm, 1891-1914 .... 75.00
Cup, demi, raised gold flowers, bows, bird hdl, Klemm, ca 1891-1914...95.00
Cup, tea, royal bl, Hutschenreuther, 1918-45, $300 to................. 350.00
Cup/saucer, HP flowers & gilt, loop hdl, rtcl rim on saucer, Thieme, 1920-30s.80.00

Dish, triangular shaped, lovers in garden, purple ground, circa 1888 – 1916, each side 8", $175.00 to $200.00. (Photo courtesy Jim and Susan Harran)

Egg server, flowers, 6 oval recesses, Hirsch, 1893-1930s, $150 to . 175.00
Figure group, musical, lace costumes, Irish Dresden, ca 1960, 14x7½"..800.00
Figurine, ballerina, lace skirt, Peck, Kronach, 1945, 3½", $150 to ..175.00
Plate, HP flowers, gilt, H Wolfsohn, 1886-90, 8⅛", $60 to............. 75.00
Plate, HP flowers, gilt, rtcl border, Thieme, 1920s, 8¼", $125 to . 150.00
Plate, HP Hoopac birds, cobalt, raised gold, Lamm, ca 1890s, 9½", $300 to .350.00
Plate, oyster, wht w/gilt, Klemm, 1890-1910, 8¼", $250 to.......... 275.00
Plate, portrait of Cupid, quill & arrows, roses, Klemm, 1893-1916, 8⅞" ..300.00
Plate, portrait of Ruth, dk gr border, Klemm, 1890-1910, 9½", $900 to..1,000.00
Plates, dessert, HP flowers, gilt, Thieme, 1920-30s, 7½", set of 8 . 850.00
Tea set, pot & cr/sug, HP flowers, gilt, Donath & Co, 1890-1910, $400 to .500.00
Tureen, HP flowers, gilt, ruffled ft, Hirsch, 1901-30, 11 2/", $750 to ... 850.00
Vase, aqua Tiffany luster, putti, Klemm, 1891-1914, $600 to 700.00
Vase, Art Nouveau, HP lady in bl gown, hdl, Klemm, 1890s, $275 to .300.00
Vase, flowerpot, HP flowers, gilt, horizontal ribbing, Wolfsohn, 1886-91, $150 to..175.00
Vase, harbor/flowers, scrolled hdls, Wolfsohn, 1880-90, 5¾"........ 280.00
Vase, potpourri, rtcl, HP flowers, gilt, Thieme, 1910-20, $300 to.. 350.00

Dryden

World War II veteran, Jim Dryden founded Dryden Pottery in Ellsworth, Kansas, in 1946. Starting in a Quonset hut, Dryden created molded products which he sold at his father's hardware store in town. Using Kansas clay from the area and volcanic ash as a component, durable glossy glazes were created. Soon Dryden was selling pottery to Macy's of New York and the Fred Harvy Restaurants on the Santa Fe Railroad.

After 10 years, 600 stores stocked Dryden Pottery. However direct sales to the public from the pottery studio offered the most profit because of increasing competition from Japan and Europe. Using dental tools to make inscriptions, Dryden began to offer pottery with personalized messages and logos. This specialized work was appreciated by customers and is admired by collectors today.

In 1956 the interstate bypassed the pottery and Dryden decided to move to Hot Springs National Park to find a broader and larger tourist base. Again, local clays and quartz for the glazes were used. Later, in order to improve consistency, commercial clay (that fired bone white) and controlled glazes were used. Sometimes overlooked by collectors who favor the famous potteries of the past, Jim Dryden's son Kimbo, and grandsons Zach, Cheyenne, and Arrow, continue to develop new glazes and shapes in the studio in Hot Springs, Arkansas. Glazes comparable to those created by Fulper, Grueby, and Rookwood can be found on pottery for sale there. Dryden was the first to use two different glazes successfully at the same time.

In 2001 The Book Stops Here published the first catalog and history of Dryden pottery. The book shows the evolution of Dryden art pottery from molded ware to unique hand-thrown pieces; the studio illustrations show the durable and colorful glazes that make Dryden special. Visitors are always welcome at the Dryden Pottery, Hot Springs, Arkansas, studio where they can watch pottery being made by the talented Dryden family.

Kansas pieces have a golden tan clay base and were made between 1946 and 1956. Arkansas pieces made after 1956 were made from bone white clay. Dryden pottery has a wide range of values. Many collectors are interested in the early pieces while a fast-growing number search for wheel-thrown and hand-decorated pieces made within the past 20 years. One-of-a-kind specialty pieces can far exceed $500.00. Our advisor for this category is Ralph Winslow; he is listed in the Directory under Arizona.

Kansas Dryden (1946 – 1956)

Ashtray, Great Bend, 6"... 32.00
Boot, #90, Ellsworth 1867-1947, 5".. 68.00
Figurine, #9, 3 trailing elephants, 3" 118.00
Figurine, #10, elephant, 11"... 185.00
Figurine, #15, leopard, 18".. 240.00
Figurine, #Z, donkey on stand, 8"... 60.00
Figurine, buffalo, bl, repro, 4".. 39.00
Mug, #41, slouch, 6".. 20.00
Pitcher, #94, Souv Messiah Chorus, 6" 38.00
Pitcher, milk, #101, 5".. 23.00
Planter, #Y, rooster, Bridal Cave, 9".. 60.00
Shakers, #70, Carry Nation, 4"... 28.00
Shakers, #70B, dimple, 3".. 32.00
Tankard, #49, nude, 11".. 150.00
Vase, #95, 3-tiered, 10"... 21.00
Vase, #800, flared base, 10"... 50.00
Wall pocket, 4-H, 4"... 48.00

Arkansas Dryden (1956 – Present)

Bowl, mixing, drip glaze, 11" 43.00
Bowl, ped, JK Dryden '99, 9" 32.00
Mugs (5), faces, 4".. 63.00
Platter, fish, mc, 9".. 43.00
Stein, snake, JK Dryden, 5".. 35.00
Tankard, mc, 11".. 40.00
Vase, fish, 8½"... 35.00
Vase, JK Dryden Orig, 50th Anniversary, 15"................................. 125.00
Vase, mini, fish, 3".. 27.00

Vase, stippled, JK Dryden, 7" 38.00
Vase, twisted top, JK Dryden 95, 15" 125.00
Vase, U shape, 8" 20.00
Vase, wheel-trn, bulb, 50th Year, 7" 34.00
Vase, wheel-trn, JK Dryden '80, 12" 42.00
Vase, wheel-trn, JK Dryden '93, 11" 80.00
Vase, wheel-trn, Last Kiln '99, 7" 26.00
Vase, wheel-trn, Ozark Frontier, 9" 30.00

Duncan and Miller

The firm that became known as the Duncan and Miller Glass Company in 1900 was organized in 1874 in Pittsburgh, Pennsylvania, a partnership between George Duncan, his sons Harry and James, and his son-in-law Augustus Heisey. John Ernest Miller was hired as their designer. He is credited with creating the most famous of all Duncan's glassware lines, Three Face (see Pattern Glass). The George Duncan and Sons Glass Company, as it was titled, was one of 18 companies that merged in 1891 with U.S. Glass. Soon after the Pittsburgh factory burned in 1892, the association was dissolved, and Heisey left the firm to set up his own factory in Newark, Ohio. Duncan built his new plant in Washington, Pennsylvania, where he continued to make pressed glassware in such notable patterns as Bagware, Amberette, Duncan Flute, Button Arches, and Zippered Slash. The firm was eventually sold to U.S. Glass in Tiffin, Ohio, and unofficially closed in August 1955.

In addition to the early pressed dinnerware patterns, today's Duncan and Miller collectors enjoy searching for opalescent vases in many patterns and colors, frosted 'Satin Tone' glassware, acid-etched designs, and lovely stemware such as the Rock Crystal cuttings. Milk glass was made in limited quantity and is considered a good investment. Ruby glass, Ebony (a lovely opaque black glass popular during the '20s and '30s) and, of course, the glass animal and bird figurines are all highly valued examples of the art of Duncan and Miller.

Add approximately 40% to 50% to listed prices for opalescent items. Etchings, cuttings, and other decorations will increase values by about 50%. For further study we recommend *The Encyclopedia of Duncan Glass* by Gail Krause; she is listed in the Directory under Pennsylvania. Several Duncan and Miller lines are shown in *Elegant Glassware of the Depression Era* by Cathy and Gene Florence. Our advisor for this category is Roselle Schleifman; she is listed in the Directory under New York. See also Glass Animals and Figurines.

Canterbury, crystal, ashtray, 3" 5.00
Canterbury, crystal, basket, crimped, 3½" 35.00
Canterbury, crystal, bowl, 1-hdl, 5½x1¾" 7.00
Canterbury, crystal, bowl, sweetmeat, star shape, hdls, 6x2" 15.00
Canterbury, crystal, celery dish, hdls, 9x4x1¼" 22.50
Canterbury, crystal, cocktail, 3½-oz, 4¼" 12.00
Canterbury, crystal, compote, H stem, 6x5½" 20.00
Canterbury, crystal, creamer, ind, 3-oz, 2¾" 9.00
Canterbury, crystal, finger bowl, 4½x2" 12.00
Canterbury, crystal, pitcher, martini, 32-oz, 9¼" 80.00
Canterbury, crystal, plate, 11¼" 25.00
Canterbury, crystal, plate, cake, hdl, 13½" 40.00
Canterbury, crystal, relish, 5-part, 11x2" 33.00
Canterbury, crystal, saucer 3.00
Canterbury, crystal, tumbler, ice tea, 13-oz, 6¼" 18.00
Canterbury, crystal, tumbler, str sides, 9-oz, 4½" 14.00
Canterbury, crystal, tumbler, whiskey, 1-oz, 2½" 12.50
Canterbury, crystal, urn, 4½x4½" 15.00
Canterbury, crystal, vase, cloverleaf, 4" 17.50
Canterbury, crystal, vase, cloverleaf, 5" 25.00
Canterbury, crystal, vase, crimped, 3½" 15.00
Canterbury, crystal, vase, crimped, 5½" 20.00

Canterbury, crystal, vase, crimped, 7" 35.00
Caribbean, bl, bowl, punch, 6¼-qt, 10" 495.00
Caribbean, bl, finger bowl, 4½" 30.00
Caribbean, bl, plate, 8½" 30.00
Caribbean, bl, tumbler, ftd, 8½-oz, 5½" 55.00

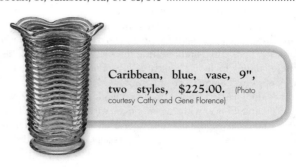

Caribbean, blue, vase, 9", two styles, $225.00. (Photo courtesy Cathy and Gene Florence)

Caribbean, crystal, bowl, vegetable, 9¼" 40.00
Caribbean, crystal, mustard, w/slotted lid, 4" 35.00
Caribbean, crystal, punch ladle 35.00
Caribbean, crystal, relish, oblong, 9½" 25.00
Caribbean, crystal, server, center hdl, 5¾" 13.00
Caribbean, crystal, vase, ruffled rim, ftd, 5¾" 22.00
First Love, crystal, ashtray, #30, 5x3¼" 20.00
First Love, crystal, bottle, oil, w/stopper, #5200, 8" 50.00
First Love, crystal, bowl, #6, 12x3½" 70.00
First Love, crystal, bowl, 3-part, ftd, #117, 7½x3" 35.00
First Love, crystal, candleholder, #115, low, 3", ea 25.00
First Love, crystal, cocktail, #115, 3-oz, 4¼" 16.00
First Love, crystal, compote, #111, 3½x4¾" 30.00
First Love, crystal, cornucopia, #117, 8x4¾" 65.00
First Love, crystal, cup, #115 .... 12.50
First Love, crystal, mayonnaise, #111, w/hdld tray, 5¾x3" 35.00
First Love, crystal, nappy, #115, hdl, 5x1¾" 18.00
First Love, crystal, plate, #111, sq, 6" 14.00
First Love, crystal, plate, #115, 11¼" 55.00
First Love, crystal, urn, #111, 4½x4½" 25.00
First Love, crystal, vase, flared rim, #115, 4" 25.00
First Love, crystal, wine, #5111½, 3-oz, 5¼" 25.00
Lily of the Valley, crystal, ashtray, 3" 25.00
Lily of the Valley, crystal, candy dish, w/lid 95.00
Lily of the Valley, crystal, cheese & cracker 75.00
Lily of the Valley, crystal, sherbet, high stem 25.00
Nautical, bl, cake plate, hdls, 6½" 35.00
Nautical, bl, cigarette jar 75.00
Nautical, bl, relish, 7-part, 12" 75.00
Nautical, bl, sugar bowl 45.00
Nautical, bl, tumbler, highball 33.00
Nautical, crystal, bowl, 10" L 60.00
Nautical, crystal, ice bucket 95.00
Nautical, crystal, plate, 8" 10.00
Nautical, crystal, tumbler, juice, ftd 15.00
Nautical, crystal, tumbler, water, ftd, 9-oz 15.00
Nautical, opal, compote, 7" 595.00
Plaza, amber or crystal, cocktail 10.00
Plaza, amber or crystal, mustard, w/slotted lid 17.50
Plaza, amber or crystal, parfait 12.00
Plaza, amber or crystal, plate, 6½" 3.00
Plaza, amber or crystal, tumbler, juice 6.00
Plaza, amber or crystal, vase, 8" 30.00
Plaza, amber or crystal, wine 14.00
Plaza, gr or pk, bottle, oil 60.00
Plaza, gr or pk, bowl, vegetable, deep, 10" 50.00
Plaza, gr or pk, candlestick, 2-lt, 4¾x7", ea 45.00

Plaza, gr or pk, plate, hdls, 10½" 35.00
Plaza, gr or pk, saucer 4.00
Plaza, gr or pk, sherbet, 3¾" 12.00
Plaza, gr or pk, tumbler, tea.................................... 20.00
Plaza, gr or pk, tumbler, whiskey 15.00
Puritan, all colors, bowl, 9¼" 55.00
Puritan, all colors, bowl, cream soup, hdls 20.00
Puritan, all colors, cup, demi 15.00
Puritan, all colors, goblet 20.00
Puritan, all colors, plate, 7½" 8.00
Puritan, all colors, saucer 2.00
Puritan, all colors, server, center hdl 35.00

Puritan, green, pitcher, $125.00. (Photo courtesy Cathy and Gene Florence)

Sandwich, crystal, ashtray, sq, 2¼" 7.00
Sandwich, crystal, bowl, hdls, 5½" 12.50
Sandwich, crystal, bowl, ice cream, ped ft, 5-oz, 4¼" 8.00
Sandwich, crystal, bowl, nut, cupped, 11" 50.00
Sandwich, crystal, bowl, salad, shallow, 12" 35.00
Sandwich, crystal, butter dish, w/lid,¼-lb 50.00
Sandwich, crystal, canape, 6" 10.00
Sandwich, crystal, candelabra, 3-lt, w/bobeche & prisms, 16", ea . 225.00
Sandwich, crystal, candleholder, 4" 25.00
Sandwich, crystal, candlestick, 3-lt, 5", ea 40.00
Sandwich, crystal, candy jar, ftd, w/lid, 8½" 75.00
Sandwich, crystal, coaster, 5" 9.00
Sandwich, crystal, compote, low ft, 5" 25.00
Sandwich, crystal, nappy, 2-part, 6" 14.00
Sandwich, crystal, pitcher, w/ice lip, 64-oz, 8½" 100.00
Sandwich, crystal, plate, cake, plain ped ft, 13" 75.00
Sandwich, crystal, plate, deviled egg, 12" 65.00
Sandwich, crystal, plate, service, hdls, 11½" 35.00
Sandwich, crystal, relish, 2-part, rnd, ring hdl, 6" 20.00
Sandwich, crystal, shakers, w/glass tops, 2½", pr 20.00
Sandwich, crystal, tray, M, rolled edge, w/ring hdl, 7" 22.00
Spiral Flutes, amber, gr or pk, bowl, mayonnaise, 4" ... 17.50
Spiral Flutes, amber, gr or pk, candlestick, 9½", ea 90.00
Spiral Flutes, amber, gr or pk, celery dish, 10¾x4¾" ... 17.50
Spiral Flutes, amber, gr or pk, chocolate jar, w/lid 195.00
Spiral Flutes, amber, gr or pk, compote, 6⅝" 17.50
Spiral Flutes, amber, gr or pk, nappy, 9" 27.50
Spiral Flutes, amber, gr or pk, nappy, hdls, 6" 20.00
Spiral Flutes, amber, gr or pk, plate, pie, 6" 3.00
Spiral Flutes, amber, gr or pk, platter, 13" 55.00
Spiral Flutes, amber, gr or pk, sherbet, low, 5-oz, 3¾" 7.00
Spiral Flutes, amber, gr or pk, wine, 3½-oz, 3¾" 15.00
Tear Drop, crystal, basket, candy, oval, hdls, 5½x7½" ... 85.00
Tear Drop, crystal, bottle, oil, 3-oz 18.00
Tear Drop, crystal, bowl, flower, flared, 11½" 32.50
Tear Drop, crystal, bowl, sq, 4-hdl, 12" 40.00
Tear Drop, crystal, canape set, 6" plate w/ring, 4-oz ftd, cocktail ... 30.00
Tear Drop, crystal, celery dish, hdls, 11" 20.00
Tear Drop, crystal, compote, low ft, hdl, 6" 15.00

Tear Drop, crystal, marmalade, w/lid, 4" 40.00
Tear Drop, crystal, olive dish, 2-part, 6" 15.00
Tear Drop, crystal, plate, hdls, 11" 27.50
Tear Drop, crystal, relish, 3-part, hdls, 11" 32.50
Tear Drop, crystal, shakers, 5", pr 25.00
Tear Drop, crystal, sugar bowl, 8-oz 8.00
Tear Drop, crystal, teacup, 6-oz 6.00
Tear Drop, crystal, tumbler, iced tea, ftd, 14-oz, 6" 18.00
Terrace, amber or crystal, ashtray, sq, 4¾" 20.00
Terrace, amber or crystal, bowl, ftd, 9x4½" 42.00
Terrace, amber or crystal, candy urn, w/lid 135.00
Terrace, amber or crystal, claret, #5111½, 4½-oz, 6" 45.00

Terrace, amber or crystal, comport, 3½x4¾", $26.00. (Photo courtesy Cathy and Gene Florence)

Terrace, amber or crystal, cup 15.00
Terrace, amber or crystal, plate, 6" 10.00
Terrace, amber or crystal, plate, lemon, hdls, 6" 12.00
Terrace, amber or crystal, plate, torte, rolled edge, 13" 37.50
Terrace, cobalt or red, cheese stand, 3x5¼" 40.00
Terrace, cobalt or red, creamer, 10-oz, 3" 35.00
Terrace, cobalt or red, finger bowl, #5111½, 4¼" 65.00
Terrace, cobalt or red, pitcher 995.00
Terrace, cobalt or red, plate, cracker, w/ring, hdls, 11" 100.00
Terrace, cobalt or red, saucer champagne, #5111½, 5-oz, 5" 50.00
Terrace, cobalt or red, urn, 10½x4½" 350.00

Durand Glass

Durand art glass was made by the Vineland Flint Glass Works of Vineland, New Jersey. Victor Durand Jr. was its proprietor. Hand-blown art glass in the style of Tiffany and Quezal was produced from 1924 to 1931 through a division called the 'Fancy Shop.' Durand hired owner Martin Bach Jr. along with his team of artisans from the failed Quezal Art Glass and Decorating Co. in Brooklyn, New York, to run this division. Much Durand art glass went unsigned; when it was, it was generally signed Durand in silver script within the polished pontil or across the top of a large letter V. The numbers that sometimes appear along with the signature indicate the shape and height of the object. Decorative names such as King Tut, Heart and Vine, Peacock Feather, and Egyptian Crackle became the company's trademarks. In 1926 Durand art glass was awarded a gold medal at the Sesquicentennial International Exposition in Philadelphia. Durand had by this time taken its place alongside other famous art glass manufacturers such as Tiffany, Steuben, and Quezal, which were regarded as the epitome of American art glass. Our advisor for this category is Edward J. Meschi, author of *Durand — The Man and His Glass* (Antique Publications); he is listed in the Directory under New Jersey.

Candy jar, Heart & Vine, gr on marigold, shouldered, dome lid, 9½" ... 3,450.00
Compote, King Tut, silver & gold on bl, oil lustre ft/finial, 10¼" ... 3,000.00
Ginger jar, King Tut, wht & gold on bl, #1964-6, 7½x5¾" 4,600.00
Lamps, King Tut, bl on marigold, bronze/glass base, 6" 350.00
Shade, Moorish Crackle, gold/wht/bl, scalloped rim, 8x6" 780.00
Vase, bl irid, flared cylinder w/incurvate rim, #1970, 6" 780.00
Vase, coil pattern, wht on gold, stick neck, bulb, #1974-15, 15" ... 2,525.00

Vase, gold w/opal coils, #1868-6, 6x4¼" 1,150.00
Vase, gold w/raised ribs, slightly bulb, 11" 780.00
Vase, gold, bulb w/trumpet neck, #20167, 14" 840.00
Vase, gr/wht/gold crackle, bulb, 10", NM 1,200.00
Vase, Heart & Vine, gr on marigold irid, #1968, 6" 1,800.00
Vase, Heart & Vine, wht on ambergris, cylindrical, 12¼" 565.00
Vase, Heart & Vine, wht on bl irid, shouldered, flared rim, 7¾".. 1,200.00
Vase, Heart & Vine, wht on bl, gold ft, 9" 3,600.00

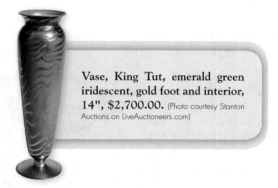

Vase, King Tut, emerald green iridescent, gold foot and interior, 14", $2,700.00. (Photo courtesy Stanton Auctions on LiveAuctioneers.com)

Vase, King Tut, gold on bl-gr, #1968-6V, 6" 900.00
Vase, King Tut, opal on bl irid, #1970, 8x8¼" 1,800.00
Vase, King Tut, opal on gold, 6x4¼" 1,150.00
Vase, King Tut, silver on bl irid, flared cylinder, wide rim, 6" 850.00
Vase, Lady Gay Rose, pk w/opal-tipped gold feathers, gold int, 10½" . 8,000.00
Vase, Lady Gay Rose, red optic ribs, gold int, 1977-10, 8x10" ..6,000.00
Vase, Moorish Crackle, emerald gr o/l on amber, 12" 3,400.00
Vase, Peacock Feather, red & wht (at base) on cranberry, #1907, 9¾". 1,150.00
Vase, threading on bl irid, #2028, 8½" 1,325.00
Vase, threading, bl on bl irid, #1968, 8x5¼" 1,200.00

Durant Kilns

The Durant Pottery Company operated in Bedford Village, New York, in the early 1900s. Its founder was Mrs. Clarence Rice; she was aided by L. Volkmar to whom she assigned the task of technical direction. (See also Volkmar.) The art and table wares they produced were simple in form and decoration. The creative aspects of the ware were carried on almost entirely by Volkmar himself, with only a minimal crew to help with production. After Mrs. Rice's death in 1919, the property was purchased by Volkmar, who chose to drop the Durant name by 1930. Prior to 1919 the ware was marked simply Durant and dated. After that time a stylized 'V' was added. Our advisors for this category are Suzanne Perrault and David Rago; they are listed in the Directory under New Jersey.

Bowl, aubergine flambé, geometrics, ftd, 1929, 3x9" 390.00
Bowl, band of modeled flowers, bl crackle w/oxblood int, 3x9", NM.. 450.00
Bowl, center, Persian Bl, flared rim, ftd, 1918, 3¾x10" 360.00
Bowl, volcanic Persian Bl w/finger ridges, wide/flared, '15, 15", EX.... 600.00
Candlesticks, upright dolphin stem, wht crackle, 1916, 7½", EX, pr..420.00
Jar, Sang de Boeuf, bulb w/lid, Leon, 1923, 4½" 1,100.00
Tiles, landscape, bl-gr, sgn V, 8" sq, set of 3 in fr 6,600.00
Vase, Apple Gr, Asian form, ca 1930, 7¾" 1,200.00
Vase, aubergine flambé, bulb, flared rim, ftd, 1924, 5¼x7" 570.00
Vase, geometrics, bl on clear, bulb, 6" 240.00
Vase, gr matt, bulb, V mk, chips around footring, 18½x8" 1,680.00
Vase, gray mottle w/brn speckles, slightly bulb, 1936, 10½", NM.. 660.00
Vase, indigo matt, sgn, 3-hdl, 7x6" 960.00
Vase, iron spot, bulb, recessed ft, 1919, 12" 1,200.00
Vase, Persian Bl, vasiform, ca 1920, 8¼" 850.00
Vase, volcanic wht curdling on sheer amber, bulb, 1923, 4x6½" ..650.00

Easter

In the early 1900s to the 1930s, Germany made the first composition candy containers in the shapes of Easter rabbits, ducks, and chicks. A few were also made of molded cardboard. In the 1940s West Germany made candy containers out of molded cardboard. Many of these had spring necks to give a nodding effect. From the 1930s and into the 1950s, United States manufacturers made Easter candy containers out of egg-carton material (pulp) or pressed cardboard. Ducks and chicks are not as high in demand as rabbits. Rabbits with painted-on clothes or attached fabric clothes bring more than the plain brown or white rabbits. When no condition is mentioned in the description, assume that values reflect excellent to near mint condition for all but paper items; those assume to be in near mint to mint condition. Our advisor for this category is Jenny Tarrant; she is listed in the Directory under Missouri.

Note: In the candy container section, measurements given for the rabbit and cart or rabbit and wagon containers indicate the distance to the tip of the rabbits' ears.

Key: hp — hard plastic

Candy Containers

Advertising dc for Bunte Chocolates, cb, 21", pr............................ 50.00
Duck on jet, w/wheels, hp, 1950s, 3".. 45.00
German, begging rabbit, brn w/glass eyes, compo, 1900-30s, 5" 75.00
German, begging rabbit, brn w/glass eyes, compo, 1900-30s, 7" 95.00
German, begging rabbit, brn w/glass eyes, compo, 1900-30s, 9" ... 125.00
German, begging rabbit, mohair covered, compo, 1900-30s, 4" ... 135.00
German, begging rabbit, mohair covered, compo, 1900-30s, 6" ... 195.00
German, duck or chick, pnt-on clothes, compo, 1900-30s, 3-4" 75.00
German, duck or chick, pnt-on clothes, compo, 1900-30s, 6"...... 125.00
German, duck or chick, pnt-on clothes, compo, 1900-30s, 7"...... 150.00
German, duck, yel w/glass eyes, compo, 1900-30s, 3" 75.00
German, duck, yel w/glass eyes, compo, 1900-30s, 5" 130.00
German, egg, molded cb, 1900-30, 3-7", $65 to.............................. 25.00
German, egg, molded cb, 1900-30, 8" 40.00
German, egg, tin, 1900-10, EX, 2-3" 55.00

German, lamb, cloth-covered composition with decoupage decoration and glass eyes, fur-covered chick and duckling riding on back, 9", $1,800.00. (Photo courtesy Dan Morphy Auctions LLC on LiveAuctioneers.com)

German, rabbit (dressed) in shoe, compo, 1900-30s, $250 to 275.00
German, rabbit (dressed) on egg, compo, 1900-30s, $250 to........ 250.00
German, rabbit pulling fancy wagon, brn compo, 1900-30s, 7".... 185.00
German, rabbit pulling wood cart, mohair covered, 1900-30s, 4" . 150.00
German, rabbit pulling wood cart, mohair covered, 1900-30s, 6" . 250.00
German, rabbit pulling wood wagon, brn compo, 1900-30s, 4".... 100.00
German, rabbit pulling wood wagon, brn compo, 1900-30s, 6".... 145.00
German, rabbit w/fabric clothes, compo, 1900-30s, 4" 250.00
German, rabbit w/fabric clothes, compo, 1900-30s, 6" 325.00
German, rabbit w/fabric clothes, compo, 1900-30s, 7", min......... 350.00
German, rabbit w/glass beading, compo, 1900-30s, 6" 150.00
German, rabbit w/pnt-on clothes, compo, 1900-30s, 5" 150.00
German, rabbit w/pnt-on clothes, compo, 1900-30s, 7" 190.00
German, sitting rabbit, brn w/glass eyes, compo, 1900-30s, 6" 90.00

German, sitting rabbit, mohair covered, compo, 1900-30s, 4" 125.00
German, sitting rabbit, mohair covered, compo, 1900-30s, 5" 140.00
German, sitting rabbit, mohair covered, compo, 1900-30s, 6" 150.00
German, standing rabbit (Ma or Pa), pnt-on clothes, compo, 10½" ..250.00
German, walking rabbit, brn w/glass eyes, compo, 1900-30s, 6"... 110.00
German, walking rabbit, brn w/glass eyes, compo, 1900-30s, 8"... 150.00
German, walking rabbit, mohair covered, compo, 1900-30s, 4"... 125.00
German, walking rabbit, mohair covered, compo, 1900-30s, 6"... 175.00
German, walking rabbit, mohair covered, compo, 1900-30s, 7"... 200.00
Rabbit bank, w/plug & glasses, Knickerbocker, hp, 1950s, 11"....... 45.00
Rabbit father w/son on bk, w/wheels, hp, 1950s, 6" 150.00
Rabbit in car pulled by lamb, hp, 1950s, 7".................................... 55.00
Rabbit in car pulled by rooster, hp, 1950s, 10"............................... 55.00
Rabbit in car, hp, 1950s, 6".. 95.00
Rabbit in jalopy car, hp, 1950s, 7".. 125.00
Rabbit on jet, w/wheels, hp, 1950s, 3"... 55.00
Rabbit on rocket, vertical, w/wheels, hp, 1950s, 3½" 55.00
Rabbit pushing wheelbarrow on wheels, hp, 1950s, 5½" 45.00
Rabbit pushing wheelbarrow, hp, 1950s, 5".................................. 35.00
Rabbit sitting, w/top hat, hp, 1950s, 3½", $25 to 35.00
Rabbit TV camera on wheels, hp, 1950s, 5" 55.00
Rabbit w/glasses, Knickerbocker, hp, 1950s, 6" 45.00
Rabbit w/hat, bank, hp, 1950s, 10"... 75.00
Rabbit, Knickerbocker, hp, 1950s, 4" 30.00
Rooster pushing wheelbarrow on wheels, hp, 1950s, 5½".............. 45.00
Rooster pushing wheelbarrow, hp, 1950s, 5" 35.00
US, begging rabbit, pulp, w/base, 1940-50 .... 55.00
US, sitting rabbit next to lg basket, pulp, 1930-50 .... 75.00
US, sitting rabbit w/basket on bk, pulp, 1940-50 .... 65.00
US, sitting rabbit, pulp, brn w/glass eyes, Burk Co, 1930 .... 85.00
W German/US Zone, dressed duck or chick, cb, spring neck, 1940-50.. 60.00
W German/US Zone, dressed rabbit, cb, spring neck, 1940-50...... 80.00
W German/US Zone, egg, molded cb, 1940-60, 3-8", $25 to 40.00
W German/US Zone, plain rabbit, cb, spring neck, 1940-50 .... 60.00
W German/US Zone, molded cb rabbit, 1940s-50s, 9" 65.00

Miscellaneous

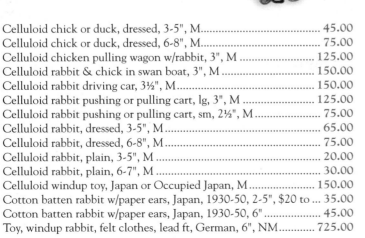

Toy, rabbit pushing stroller with umbrella that spins, tin litho and celluloid, Japan, 6x5", $90.00. (Photo courtesy Dirk Soulis Auctions on LiveAuctioneers.com)

Celluloid chick or duck, dressed, 3-5", M.. 45.00
Celluloid chick or duck, dressed, 6-8", M.. 75.00
Celluloid chicken pulling wagon w/rabbit, 3", M 125.00
Celluloid rabbit & chick in swan boat, 3", M 150.00
Celluloid rabbit driving car, 3½", M.. 150.00
Celluloid rabbit pushing or pulling cart, lg, 3", M 125.00
Celluloid rabbit pushing or pulling cart, sm, 2½", M 75.00
Celluloid rabbit, dressed, 3-5", M.. 65.00
Celluloid rabbit, dressed, 6-8", M.. 75.00
Celluloid rabbit, plain, 3-5", M 20.00
Celluloid rabbit, plain, 6-7", M 30.00
Celluloid windup toy, Japan or Occupied Japan, M...................... 150.00
Cotton batten rabbit w/paper ears, Japan, 1930-50, 2-5", $20 to ... 35.00
Cotton batten rabbit w/paper ears, Japan, 1930-50, 6" 45.00
Toy, windup rabbit, felt clothes, lead ft, German, 6", NM............ 725.00

Egg Cups

Egg cups, one of the fastest growing collectibles, have been traced back to the ruins of Pompeii. They have been made in almost every country and in almost every conceivable material (ceramics, glass, metal, papier maché, plastic, wood, ivory, even rubber, and straw). Popular categories include Art Deco, Black memorabilia, chintz, personalities, figurals, golliwoggs, railroadiana, steamship, and souvenir ware. Egg cups also come in a variety of shapes. A bucket egg cup is a single cup without a foot. A double is two sided with a small end for eating an egg in a shell and a large end for mixing an egg with toast and butter. A figural egg cup is actually molded into the shape of an animal, bird, car, or person, etc. A hoop is a single open cup with a waistline. A single is a goblet-shaped egg cup with a foot. A set consists of a tray or cruet (stand, frame, or basket) with two to eight cups.

Still being produced today, egg cups appeal to collectors on many levels. Prices range from the inexpensive to thousands of dollars. Those made prior to 1840 are scarce and sought after, as are the character/personality egg cups of the 1930s. For a more thorough study of egg cups we recommend *Egg Cups: An Illustrated History and Price Guide* (Antique Publications) by Brenda Blake, our advisor. You will find her address listed in the Directory under Maine.

American

Bucket, mustard, Paul Revere Pottery 90.00
Double, Autumn, mc fruit basket, Lenox.. 35.00
Double, Ballerina, khaki-gr, Universal.. 15.00
Double, Bride, Cleminson, 1940s 35.00
Double, Brittany, Homer Laughlin 19.00
Double, English Abbey, Taylor, Smith & Taylor 35.00
Double, Festival, Stangl... 24.00
Double, Homespun, plaid, Vernon Kilns, 1950s 32.00
Double, Juvenile, chick, Roseville, ca 1917 .... 270.00
Double, Magnolia, Stangl, 1950s 25.00
Double, Norma, Blue Ridge 35.00
Double, Rooster, Pennsbury.. 28.00
Double, woman in apron, Cleminson, 1940s 30.00
Single, Apple, Franciscan.. 32.00

Single, hand-painted china, signed and dated 1945, 2¾", $15.00. (Photo courtesy Homestead Auctions on LiveAuctioneers.com)

Single, Valencia, Louise Bauer, Shawnee, 1937 .... 22.00
Single, yel ware, no decor, ca 1880.. 325.00

Characters/Personalities

Bucket, Katzenjammer Kids, color illus, early 100.00
Bucket, Marilyn Monroe, transfer, 1993, rare 65.00
Bucket, Tonto, molded face against stump, Keele St Pottery, 1961 60.00
Figural, Dwarf (from Snow White), mk Foreign, $35 to................ 85.00
Figural, ET.. 22.00

Figural, Humpty Dumpty on brick ball, Mansell............................ 85.00
Figural, Mickey Mouse, MIJ, $35 to 85.00
Figural, Prince Charles, Spitting Image, 1982.......................... 70.00
Figural, Snow White, standing by egg cup, WD Enterprises, 1937.220.00
Set, Beatles (4 bkts), blk & wht bust portraits w/names, KSP mk. 275.00
Single, Donald Duck, Good Morning Series................................ 16.00
Single, Prince Ranier/Princess Grace of Monaco, wedding, Limoges, 1950s.100.00
Single, Tom & Jerry decals on wht ceramic cup, England, 1967, 2".20.00

English/Staffordshire

Bucket, Burleigh ware, red print, Stonewall kitchen, MIE, recent....6.00
Bucket, Crocus, Clarice Cliff... 125.00
Bucket, Orange Tree, Art Deco, Crown Ducal 38.00
Bucket, Primavera, Midwinter.. 25.00
Double, Cornishware, bl bands, TC Gr, 1930s........................ 45.00
Double, Madras, flow bl, Royal Doulton, ca 1900................... 110.00
Double, Old Mill Stream, Johnson Bros................................. 20.00
Double, Rose Chintz, Johnson Bros 20.00
Double, stenciled gold geometrics/gold band borders, 1905-20, $30 to.40.00

Double, Touraine, Flow Blue, no mark, 3¼", $75.00. (Photo courtesy Tom Harris Auctions on LiveAuctioneers.com)

Set, 6 tulip cups in chrome stand, English 70.00
Set, Amherst Japan, 6 scalloped-rim cups w/stand & base, Minton. 12,000.00
Set, floral decor, tray w/6 ind cups, ca 1900 .... 180.00
Single, Bl Dragon, Royal Worcester 30.00
Single, integral saucer, bl, Nigella Lawson, recent.................... 11.00
Single, silver, attached saucer w/rooster, Royal Doulton 72.00
Single, Tea Rose, yel, Royal Albert 22.00
Single, Willow pattern Wood & Sons, early 1900s, $35 to 45.00
Single, Clarice Cliff, Moderne.. 100.00

Figurals

Bellhop, pillbox hat, smoking cigarette, Art Deco, Made in France ..75.00
Black male face, Germany, ca 1912....................................... 80.00
Boat, orange, Honiton 25.00
Duck pulling egg cart, unmk Japan, 2".................................. 15.00
Duck, bl, Fanny Farmer, 1930s 25.00
Hen, Keele St Pottery 16.00
Legs walking, gr shoes, Carlton 40.00
Miss Priss, Lefton 30.00
Rabbit pushing wheelbarrow cup, plastic 20.00
Sergeant Chimp, plastic, w/lid... 28.00
Swan, lustre, Japan, 1930s 15.00

Foreign

Bucket, Cardinal Tuck, red robe, Goebel, 1960s...................... 175.00
Double, Peasant, yel & gr, floral panels, HB Quimper 45.00
Double, rooster & hen, yel base, T&V Limoges 60.00
Set, cup+salt shaker+tray, Limoges 28.00
Set, majolica basket w/6 egg cups, leaf pattern, 1880s 500.00
Single, Bl Flower, Royal Copenhagen, ca 1940......................... 25.00

Single, Devon Motto Ware, Torquay 28.00
Single, fruit & flowers w/Greek Key border, China..................... 12.00
Single, Oriole, Goebel, 1989... 20.00

Single, Rose Medallion, nineteenth century, 2½", $50.00. (Photo courtesy TriGreen Company on LiveAuctioneers.com)

Single, Saladon, Bavarian style, Hutschenreuther..................... 22.00
Single, Seagull, Bing & Grondahl.. 45.00

Glass

Double, English Hobnail, amber, Westmoreland, 1930s-40s 30.00
Double, Hobnail, mg, Fenton.. 55.00
Figural, chicken, bl, Portieux... 25.00
Figural, chicken, mg, John E Kemple 15.00
Figural, rooster, vaseline, Boyd 14.00
Single, Argus, flint, ca 1850-70 .... 28.00
Single, bottle glass, gr, 2-part mold, ca 1910 .... 32.00
Single, Hobnail, ruby flashed.. 55.00
Single, lacy glass, leaf pattern, ca 1925-40 .... 90.00
Single, Smocking, amethyst, Sandwich, 1840s 275.00

Railroad/Steamship/Military

Double, Luckenbach Lines 40.00
Double, Meridale, Wabash RR 35.00
Double, West Point Military Academy, ca 1930s, $30 to 40.00
Hoop, Atlantic Transport Line, Wedgwood.............................. 135.00
Single, Annapolis US Naval Academy, Mayer, ca 1930s, $24 to ... 30.00
Single, Bows & Leaves, Canadian Pacific 45.00
Single, Maybrook pattern by Syracuse, date code for 1939, $24 to .30.00
Single, Minbreno, ATSF.. 500.00
Single, Richmond, Fredericksburg & Potomac, Tri-Link, OPCO, 1927 ..450.00

Souvenir

Bucket, British Airways, bl border, silver stripes, Royal Doulton ... 16.00
Double, US Coast & Geodetic Survey...................................... 100.00
Single, Channel Tunnel, 1988-94, 1994 .... 16.00
Single, Graceland, Japan, 1970s... 20.00
Single, World's Fair, St Louis 1904, transfer scene, 1904.............. 100.00

Elfinware

Made in Germany from about 1920 until the 1940s, these miniature vases, boxes, salt cellars, and miscellaneous novelty items are characterized by the tiny applied flowers that often cover their entire surface. Pieces with animals and birds are the most valuable, followed by the more interesting examples such as diminutive grand pianos and candleholders. Items covered in 'spinach' (applied green moss) can be valued at 75% to 100% higher than pieces that are not decorated in this manner. See also Salts, Open.

Boot, appl flowers, fan-shaped lid, sm................................... 25.00
Box, appl flowers, basketweave & rope design, 1¼x2½x1¾" 35.00

Box, piano form w/appl flowers & spinach, 3-leg, 2x2¾" 40.00
Box, trinket, HP floral on fan-shaped lid, Germany, sm 25.00
Poodle, standing on base w/gr grass, 4½".................................... 125.00
Salt cellar, appl roses & spinach, simple hdls, 2½x2½x1¾" 30.00
Shoe, curled toe, appl flowers, 2¼x5¼" 100.00
Toothpick holder, 2x2" 40.00
Vase, rose w/spinach & forget-me-nots on top, Germany, 1⅝"....... 70.00

Epergnes

Popular during the Victorian era, epergnes were fancy centerpieces often consisting of several tiers of vases (called lilies), candleholders, dishes, or a combination of components. They were made in all types of art glass, and some were set in ornate plated frames.

It is important to examine each component for authenticity. Make sure the glassware is original to the base, as more modern bowls and vases (Fenton, for example) are often used to replace the broken Victorian pieces. Our advisor for this category is Barbara Aaronson; she is listed in the Directory under California.

Blue opal, 4 ruffled lilies, LG Wright, 1930s 425.00
Cased glass vase & 3 baskets w/enameled floral, brass fr, 18"........ 780.00
Cranberry lilies (3) w/clear ruffles+3 baskets on bowl base, 21" . 1,650.00
Crystal lily on crystal & bronze base, w/crystal tray, Fr, 17x12".1,100.00
Cut bowl top on Rococo Revival SP fr, 3 candle arms, ea w/sm bowl, 29"..3,250.00
Cut crystal bowls (1 lg/4 sm) on 4-arm SP fr, 1800s, 13x22½" dia . 2,150.00
Cut trumpet vase atop SP fr w/2 cut tray tiers, ca 1899, 36x9½" dia ..2,400.00
Etched crystal bowls (3) on gilt metal figures, 1875, rpr, 23x21x13" ..2,650.00
Green opal lily, 3 baskets on ruffled bowl base w/bronze mts, 18¾".800.00
Green, 1 lg+3 sm flutes, 3 spiral arms w/baskets, ruffled base, 21".600.00
Lime gr opal, 1 lg+4 sm lilies w/crystal serpentine, scallop base, 18" ... 950.00
Millefiori fluted lilies (3), attached to matching 22" base, 24" 825.00
Pink opal/cranberry cased, 1 ruffled/crimped lily, brass base, 13"..495.00
Pink-to-wht lily/bowl w/gr ruffles, SP Cupid/Venus fr w/2 bowls, 24"... 3,500.00
Silver, lily w/rtcl bowl supports 4 rtcl baskets, Scottish, 19"......1,440.00
Teal gr jack-in-pulpit vases (3) w/appl ribbons, ca 1900, 23x11"...1,100.00
Turquoise opaline, ram's head holder, marble base, bronze mts, 6x4"..475.00
Vaseline & cranberry, 1 lg+3 sm lilies, ruffled base, 21x12", NM.675.00
Vaseline, 7 screw-in flower forms, SP curving Nouveau fr, 22½" W ...500.00

Erickson

Carl Erickson of Bremen, Ohio, produced hand-formed glassware from 1943 until 1960 in artistic shapes, no two of which were identical. One of the characteristics of his work was the air bubbles that were captured within the glass. Both clear and colored glass were produced. Rather than to risk compromising his high standards by selling the factory, when Erickson retired, the plant was dismantled and sold.

Ashtray, bl w/controlled bubbles, 3 rests, 5"................................... 60.00
Ashtray, smoke w/controlled bubbles, 4-fold top, 3x7x6".............. 40.00
Bottle, scent, orange sphere w/controlled bubbles, 3½x4½" 135.00
Bowl, bl free-form w/fold at rim, 2 layers of bubbles, shallow, 7½" . 70.00

Bowl, candy, amethyst with white to opal overlay, trapped air bubbles, 7", $65.00.

Bowl, emerald gr w/controlled bubbles, sq rim, 3x5¼x5¼"............. 45.00
Bowl, smoke on clear ped w/controlled bubbles, 7½x11⅛"........... 115.00
Bowl, smoke on crystal ped w/controlled bubbles, 6x7½".............. 36.00
Decanter, crystal w/gr flame base & controlled bubbles, ball top, 11" . 115.00
Decanter, gr w/controlled bubbles, clear bubbled stopper, 15½"..... 70.00
Pitcher, emerald gr w/clear bubbled pwt base, 13", +stirrer 125.00
Punch cup, smoke w/crystal hdl & rosettes, 2¾x3"........................ 90.00
Shot glass, crystal w/gr 5-point flame base, 3" 32.00
Vase, bud, ruby w/crystal base w/controlled bubbles, 11x2¾"......... 30.00
Vase, crystal on pwt base w/controlled bubbles, att, 13x4"............. 72.50
Vase, gr w/controlled bubbles, clear sq base, 15x6"....................... 42.50
Vase, smoke w/pwt base & controlled bubbles, 5¼x5x3½"............. 48.00
Vase, smoke, waisted, 7½x3⅛".. 30.00

Erphila

The Erphila trademark was used by Ebeling and Ruess Co. of Philadelphia between 1886 and the 1950s. The company imported quality porcelain and pottery from Germany, Czechoslovakia, Italy, and France. Pieces more readily found are from Germany and Czechoslovakia. A variety of items can be found and pieces such as figural teapots and larger figurines are moving up in value. There is a variety of marks, but all contain the name Erphila. One of the earlier marks is a green rectangle containing the name Erphila Germany. In general, Erphila pieces are scarce, not easily found.

Ashtray, black boy stacking 2 lg dice, mc on blk base, 4x4" 24.00
Bust, Charles Dickens, 5x3½" 40.00
Bust, George Washington, pnt facial details, blk coat, 5" 30.00

Cigarette holder, cat atop, rare, 6", $120.00. (Photo courtesy JK Galleries, Inc. on LiveAuctioneers.com)

Dresser doll/powder box, Madame Pompadour, 1920s-30s, 5¼" ...225.00
Dresser doll/powder box, Nancy Pert, lady in pk, 7½x6" 120.00
Figurine, cherub holding goat by horns, gold mk, 5½" 45.00
Figurine, dachshund, brn to blk, 7" 60.00
Figurine, Deco lady in blk gown, hands away from body, 1920s, 12"..88.00
Figurine, horse, wht gloss, head trn, Est 1886 mk, 4¼x3½" 85.00
Figurine, horses (2) prancing, Ebeling & Reuss, 9x9½x4"............. 160.00
Figurine, Russian wolfhound, blk/brn/wht, 4x5"........................... 40.00
Figurine, Siamese cat, Ling on foil sticker, #9620, 11¼" L 75.00
Flower frog, sailing ship, wht gloss, 12" 72.50
Flower holder, draped nude before 3 joined stumps, wht, 6½x6⅜". 30.00
Pitcher, Art Deco ram figural, 8¾" 480.00
Pitcher, Deco bird figural, blk/red/cream, #881, 9x7½"................. 200.00
Pitcher, Deco ram figural, red/blk/yel, #1042, 8¾".. .... 150.00
Pitcher, terrier dog figural, blk/wht/pk, #6702B, 7¾", NM 55.00
Pitcher, toucan figural, blk/red/cream, Deco style, 9", NM............ 90.00
Powder jar, lady figural, 7¾"... 100.00
Teapot, cat figural, blk & wht w/pk bow, #6700B, 8" 135.00
Teapot, dachshund figural, brn tones, US Zone/#6703B, 8" 150.00
Teapot, elf figural, mc, pointed hat lid, foil label, 9¼x8½" 80.00
Teapot, pig figural, spotted, paper label, #AK722, 7½" 195.00

Vase, bird perched between lyre shape w/2 openings, 6⅞x6⅞" 60.00
Vase, calla lilies, wht/gr/yel on cobalt, 7½x5" 42.50
Vase, Cubist decor, red/gr/wht, ftd, #3782, 8" 65.00
Vase, geometrics, earth tones, cylindrical neck, 4x3½" 42.50

Eskimo Artifacts

While ivory carvings made from walrus tusks or whale teeth have been the most emphasized articles of Eskimo art, basketry and woodworking are other areas in which these Alaskan Indians excel. Their designs are effected through the application of simple yet dramatic lines and almost stark decorative devices. Though not pursued to the extent of American Indian art, the unique work of these northern tribes is beginning to attract the serious attention of today's collectors.

Amulet, shaman's, baby walrus tusk, for necklace/belt, 2½x19/32" . 100.00
Basket, coiled grass w/gut-skin beaded trim, 4½x6" 250.00
Basket, stylized snowflakes, w/lid, 1940s-50s, 6x5½" 200.00
Billiken, cvd ivory, dbl-sided, contemporary, ¾x2½" 230.00
Billiken, pendant & necklace, cvd ivory, contemporary, 11/16x2⅜"... 195.00
Bracelet fastening pc, ivory, pygmy sperm whale, contemporary, ⅜x11/16" . 30.00
Bracelet, cvd, 10-pc, 5 plain, 5 w/animals, contemporary, 2½" dia ... 345.00
Bracelet, cvd, 12-pc, 6 plain, 6 w/animals, contemporary, 2¼" dia ... 415.00
Carving, human figure squatting, M Palliser, soapstone, 4x2¼x2" .. 115.00
Carving, ivory, owl, contemporary, 1⅛x17/16" 65.00
Carving, ivory, walrus head, contemporary, ¾x1⅜x3/16" 65.00
Carving, seal, mtd on potsherd, contemporary, ¾x1⅛x3⅞" 50.00
Carving, seal, pnt wood w/brass tack eyes, Wankier, 1980s, 6x16x4" .. 200.00
Carving, seal, polished steatite, contemporary, 2x2½x4¼" 50.00
Carving, steatite, figure in kayak, contemporary, 2¾x1¼x6¼" 175.00
Carving, walrus mother w/calf on her bk, Koyuk, 1950s, 1¼x3½x2" .. 250.00
Cufflinks, ivory on metal, polar bear heads, contemporary, ¾x¾" .. 50.00
Doll, sealskin, cloth, fur, feathers, sinew, historic, 4¼x9½" 100.00
Figurine, standing human, cvd & polished steatite, 2⅛x5" 125.00
Knife hdl, ship & ice floes scene, scrimshaw on ivory, 13/16x4" 350.00
Knife hdl, Umiak harpooning scene, Nuguruk ivory scrimshaw, ⅞x3¾" . 325.00
Ornaments, hanging, ivory, dogs, 1x7/16x4", ea 155.00
Pendant & necklace, ivory, bearded seal, contemporary, 11/16x1½" .. 145.00
Pendant, ivory on metal, incised walrus scene, Su, contemporary, 1½x1⅛" .. 440.00
Pendants (2), harbor seal ivory cvg, contemporary 1x1⅜", pr 170.00
Pendants (2), script letter 'A,' contemporary, 1⅜x3", pr 125.00
Pick head, ivory, worn tip, 4" L 150.00
Pouch, fishskin, natural/red dye, rabbit fur trim, ca 1920s, 8½" 350.00
Tool, digging, dk & mineralized bone, 2 sets of lashing grooves, 13" L, $250 to ... 300.00

Eyewear

Collectors of Americana are beginning to appreciate the charm of antique optical items, and those involved in the related trade find them particularly fascinating. Anyone, however, can appreciate the evolution of technology apparent when viewing a collection of vintage eyewear, and at the same time admire the ingenuity involved in the design and construction of these glasses.

In the early 1900s the choice of an eyeglass frame was generally left to the optician, much as the choice of medication was left to the family doctor. By the 1930s, however, eyeglasses had emerged as fashion accessories. In 1939 Altina Sanders's 'Harlequin' frame (a forerunner of the 1950s 'cat-eyes') won an American Design award. By the 1950s manufacturers were working overtime to enhance the allure of eyewear, hosting annual competitions for 'Miss Beauty in Glasses' and 'Miss Specs Appeal.'

Particularly sought after today are the flamboyant and colorful designs of the '50s and '60s. These include 'cat-eyes' with their distinctively upswept brow edges; 'highbrows,' often heavily jeweled or formed in the shape of butterfly or bird wings; and frames with decorative temples ranging from floral wreaths to musical notes. Many of today's collectors have such novel eyeglass frames fitted with their own prescription lenses for daily wear.

For further information on eyewear of this era, we recommend *Specs Appeal: Extravagant 1950s & 1960s Eyewear* (Schiffer) by Leslie Piña and Donald-Brian Johnson (our advisor for this category). Mr. Johnson is listed in the Directory under Nebraska.

Eyeglass stand, cat-eye shape, gold cardstock, red lining, $10 to 15.00
Eyeglass stand, Lucite, bk-cvd red rose, $15 to 20.00
Eyeglasses, Batwing, gray, $375 to 400.00
Eyeglasses, Bird Wing, nesting bird, $600 to 650.00
Eyeglasses, blk/gold mesh, pearl/bl rhinestone brow clusters, $120 to ... 140.00
Eyeglasses, cat-eye, blk w/silver alum inlay, Hudson, $175 to 200.00
Eyeglasses, cat-eye, lt bl w/clear cutaways, rhinestone trim, $70 to .. 80.00
Eyeglasses, cat-eye, pk & rhinestones, folding, $100 to 120.00
Eyeglasses, child's, Graceline, pk w/gold strip laminate, $30 to 40.00
Eyeglasses, dbl-pointed cat-eye, aurora rhinestones, Frame Fr, $200 to ... 225.00
Eyeglasses, Dior granny style/bl cloisonne rhinestones/pearls, $150 to 200.00
Eyeglasses, Dr Scholl's Health Glasses, $25 to 35.00
Eyeglasses, earring chains, yel or check fr, 1960s, $120 to 160.00
Eyeglasses, elaborate highbrow fr, $1,000 to 1,200.00
Eyeglasses, floral temple wreath trim, Tura, $275 to 325.00
Eyeglasses, folding, bl & silver-gray, $175 to 200.00
Eyeglasses, Granny style, faceted rosy pk lenses, 1960s, $60 to 75.00
Eyeglasses, headband style, butterscotch, $250 to 275.00
Eyeglasses, highbrow 7-point tiara, tinted lenses, $1,000 to 1,200.00
Eyeglasses, highbrow antennas, coffee-color, aurora rhinestones, Fr, $375 to 400.00
Eyeglasses, Octette oversz 8-sided fr, Selecta, 1970s, $50 to 60.00
Eyeglasses, ram horn highbrows, brn w/rhinestones, Qualite Fr, $550 to .. 600.00
Eyeglasses, silver-gray fr w/rhinestone swags, J Hasday, $70 to 80.00
Eyeglasses, swan highbrows, wht pearlized, $450 to 550.00
Eyeglasses, triple-flare cat-eye w/rhinestones, Fr, $140 to 160.00
Eyeglasses, Trucco shallow make-up frames, demi-amber, Selecta, $50 to .. 60.00
Eyeglasses, twist cat-eye fr in blk & clear, TWE, $90 to 100.00
Eyeglasses, yel pearlized plastic, gold floral applique, Fr, $120 to .. 135.00
Frames, bronze-colored, hearts & rhinestones at brow edge, Tura, $120 to .. 135.00
Frames, combination, blk w/steel-bl decor brow, Kono, $55 to 65.00
Frames, gold plastic, temples decor w/musical notes & staff, Tura, $300 to .. 325.00
Frames, irid pk/metallic-thread, irregular brow edge, side sunburst, $300 to. 325.00
Frames, jeweled wht plastic, w/leaf-shaped earpieces, $400 to 425.00
Frames, silver-gray w/rhinestone brow swags, J Hasaday, $70 to 85.00
Frames, wire & ribbed plastic w/cobalt lenses, Dublin, 1940s, $100 to ... 125.00
Look Back Mirror Glasses, Merco Mfg, $70 to 80.00
Lorgnette, lt bl w/rhinestones, $70 to 80.00
Make-up glasses, flip-down, Hollco, $65 to 75.00
Opera glasses, MOP & gold plate, lenses adjust, Lemaire, $375 to ... 395.00
Opera glasses, tortoiseshell, lenses adjust/hinged hdl, 1900s, $375 to .. 395.00
Reading glasses, Fairview Simili, kelly gr o/l, Selecta, $65 to 75.00
Sunglasses, bug-eye, Playboy Austria, $80 to 95.00
Sunglasses, child's spaceman style, day-glo orange, $120 to 130.00
Sunglasses, folding, rhinestone decor, Japanese, $130 to 150.00

Sunglasses, hand-shaped red plastic frames, $120.00 to $130.00. (Photo by Leslie Piña)

Sunglasses, novelty, eyelash fringe trim, $350 to 375.00
Sunglasses, novelty, feather brow trim & hair décor, $150 to 200.00
Sunglasses, novelty, mismatched circular & oval lenses, $35 to 50.00
Sunglasses, red plastic harlequin frames, Paris, 1930s, $100 to..... 125.00
Sunglasses, Red Wings, Ray-Ban, $60 to... 70.00
Sunglasses, rose-colored lenses w/tortoiseshell frames, $70 to........ 80.00
Sunglasses, Schiaparelli design, yel-gold w/fruit clusters, $230 to....250.00
Sunglasses, Selecta 4000 White Pearl, $55 to................................. 65.00
Sunglasses, translucent yel frames w/asymmetrical brow, $200 to . 300.00
Sunglasses, wht pearlized swan brow decorations, $450 to 550.00
Sunglasses w/built-in radio, Spectra, $50 to 60.00
Sunglasses, wraparound rhinestone wings, $550 to....................... 600.00
Sunglasses, wraparounds, Polaroid, $60 to 70.00
Sunglasses & bracelet set, floral design on blk, Stendahl, $150 to...200.00

Face Jugs

The most recognizable form of Southern folk pottery is the face jug. Rich alkaline glazes (lustrous greens and browns) are typical, and occasionally shards of glass are applied to the surface of the ware which during firing melts to produce opalescent 'glass runs' over the alkaline. In some locations clay deposits contain elements that result in areas of fluorescent blue or rutile; another variation is swirled or striped ware, reminiscent of eighteenth-century agateware from Staffordshire. Face vessels come in several forms as well. In America, from New England to the Carolinas, they were made as early as the 1840s. Collector demand for these unique one-of-a-kind jugs is at an all-time high and is still escalating. Choice examples of the twentieth century made by Burlon B. Craig and Lanier Meaders range from $1,000.00 to over $5,000.00 on the secondary market. If you're interested in learning more about this type of folk pottery, contact the Southern Folk Pottery Collectors Society; their address is in the Clubs, Newsletters, and Websites section. Our advisor for this category is Billy Ray Hussey; he is listed in the Directory under North Carolina.

Abee, Steve; brn/tan/bl swirls, clay teeth in open mouth, 12" 180.00
Craig, Burlow B; blk & brn w/bl, 18¾" 4,620.00
Crocker, Dwayne L; brn & cream swirls, 7" 180.00
Crocker, Michael; rock teeth, bl pupils, dimple in chin, 8½" 240.00
Fleming, Walter; bl feldspathic glaze, 2nd face on bk, 12"............ 275.00
Fleming, Walter; dk brn w/clay teeth & dripping eyes, 10½" 150.00
Freeman, Henry; bl w/clay teeth, bl pupils, Ivory Bluff, 1990, 8" ... 90.00
Hewell, Matthew; wht clay teeth, wht eyes w/bl pupils, 11" 120.00
Hussey, Billy Ray; bearded man, nude woman hdl, 2-color, 8" 600.00
Hussey, Billy Ray; devil face, L tongue/china teeth, EX colors, 11"....800.00
Lisk, Chas; 4-color swirl, clay teeth/raised brows, now a lamp, 11"..215.00
Lisk, Chas; swirlware, wht clay teeth/eyes w/pupils, unibrow, 14".. 515.00
Meaders, CJ II; olive, defined features/chin-cheek area, 1988, 10"...400.00
Meaders, David; Centennial Celebration, streaky brn, 9" 215.00
Meaders, Edwin; cobalt bl w/dripping eyes, 11" 1,325.00
Meaders, Lanier; pottery teeth and eyes, 10" 1,265.00
Meaders, Lanier; dk brn w/rock teeth & dripping eyes, 10".......3,300.00
Teague, A; 5 clay teeth, wht eyes w/dk pupils, yel clay, 7"............ 350.00

Fans

Hand fans have been around since the beginning of time, when early man used a palm frond to seek relief from the heat. It is believed the folding fan was invented in Asia around the seventh century, but it was not until the seventeenth century that it made its way to Europe. During the seventeenth and eighteenth centuries, France established the standard in fans for the rest of Europe to follow. By the late nineteenth century, fans were being made in every country in the world. They were designed for all occasions — baptisms, weddings, times of mourning — as well as being used as commemorative and souvenir items in both Europe and the United States. The fan was a fashion statement as well as a necessity used to stir the air. With the invention of air conditioning, the focus of the use for fans shifted from functionality to advertising and promotion, with examples still being produced today. Collecting antique hand fans is growing in popuiarty worldwide. Values are given for examples in good, as-found condition. Our advisor for this cateogry is Cynthia Fendel, author of *Novelty Hand Fans, Fashionable Functional Fun Accessories of the Past*. She is listed in the Directory under Texas.

Cambric, pleated, imitation leather hdls, Cockade, Am, 1880 ...... 40.00
Celluloid, Deco novelty compact, w/lipstick/mirror/powder puff, Fr, 1920 ..700.00
Chantilly lace over ivory silk, plain MOP sticks, loop w/silk tassel .. 450.00
Feathers, ostrich, faux tortoise celluloid sticks, Eiseman, 1920 ...... 90.00
Feathers, peacock trim, Chinese pnt, pierced sandalwood sticks, 25" W.. 90.00
Gauze w/embr sequins, MOP sticks, w/Duvelleroy box, 1900 ...... 650.00
Ivory brisé, HP putt/flowers, guard w/monogram ivory loop, tassel..400.00
Ivory brisé, HP/varnished pastoral, Vernis Martin style, 1780...1,000.00

Ivory brisé with central flower, Chinese Export, 15½" wide, $2,200.00. (Photo courtesy TriGreen Company on LiveAuctioneers.com)

Ivory, wood sticks, guards w/Shibayama, Japanese Ogi, ojimé, 1870 ..550.00
Lace, mixed Brussels/Rosepoint, cvd/gilt MOP sticks, 1880......... 800.00
Litho, hand-tinted, pastoral scene, MOP pierced sticks w/gilt, Fr.375.00
Paper leaf, hot air balloon, Fr, ivory sticks, 18th C....................2,000.00
Paper, advertising, Fr Piver, folding, plain wood sticks, 20th C.... 135.00
Paper, HP, appl ivory faces, silk clothes, blk lacquer sticks, Canton export...425.00
Paper, printed commemorative, Columbia Exposition, wood sticks, 1893...200.00
Satin, feather trim, cream w/HP roses/forget-me-nots, ivory sticks, 1885.250.00
Silk gauze w/embr sequins, spangles, MOP cvd sticks/orig Duvelleroy box..600.00
Silk leaf, printed Fr litho, pastoral scene, bone sticks sgn Laurence, 1880 ....250.00
Tortoiseshell, brisé, Chinese, detailed cvd & pierced sticks, 1800. 900.00

Farm Collectibles

Country living in the nineteenth century entailed plowing, planting, and harvesting; gathering eggs and milking; making soap from lard rendered on butchering day; and numerous other tasks performed with primitive tools of which we in the twenty-first century have had little first-hand knowledge. Values listed below are for items in excellent original condition unless noted otherwise. See also Cast Iron; Lamps, Lanterns; Woodenware; Wrought Iron.

Book, Farm Machinery & Equipment, detailed illustrations, 1948, 520-pg .40.00
Booklet, Plans for Making Farm Tools & Equipment, 1950, 32 pgs.. 10.00
Bucksaw, No 2 Yorktown..., 31", VG... 35.00
Castrator/Bander, mk Burdizzo Made in Italy, 3½x16", VG........... 20.00
Chain detacher, Herschel No 111, CI, 8", VG 18.00
Chicken feeder, stoneware, James Mfg stencil, 2 interlocking pcs . 70.00
Corn cutter, 9" scythe blade w/22" wooden hdl, VG 25.00
Corn seed planter, metal w/wooden hdl, 33½" overall, VG............ 35.00
Corn sheller, Blk Hawk 808... 65.00
Corn sheller, CI, bolts to solid surface, Blk Hawk, ca 1903 .... 65.00
Corn sheller, CI, clamps down, wooden hdl, Blk Beauty, Durbin .. 40.00
Corn sheller, gr pnt CI, mk John Deere, self standing, very heavy ..120.00
Cow bell, hand forged, 5¾x3¼".. 28.00

Cranberry picker, wood w/hdl & tines, 10x8x4", G 35.00
Cream separator, Am Wonder...NY, stacked cones, Indian decal 500.00
Dolly, Fairbanks, oak, 45x19", VG 55.00
Draw knife, mk USA, #8, metal w/wooden hdls 32.00
Feed sack, Alfalfa, Fagley Seed Co, Archbold OH, NM 27.00
Funnel, amethyst glass, 12½x10¾" dia, NM 48.00
Grain shovel, softwood, str front edge, arched hdl, 37x12", VG 45.00
Hames, brass & CI, English, 32" L, lot of 2 .... 150.00
Hames, metal & glass w/leather collar, 30x18" 95.00
Hatchet, Keen Kutter, 3½x6½" single blade w/hammer end, 12" hdl. 25.00
Hay hook, 5¼" wooden hdl 15.00
Horse collar, EX leather, rpl straps 75.00
Implement seat, HP Deuscher, CI, old pnt, 17x13" 325.00
Implement seat, South Bend Chilled Plow, CI, no pnt, 17x15" ... 200.00
Lantern, pine w/glass panels, pegged, rprs, 10" 430.00
Lantern, tin, ring hdl, pierced air vent, 2 glass panels, 15" 265.00
Leather riveter, Rex, PAT MAR27 OCT9 .... 25.00
Milk can, alum, bail hdl, 9½" 20.00

Milk can, copper with double handles, stamped on sides: Newhall Dairies Ltd., lid stamped J. Hanson & Sons Ltd. Liverpool, 21x13", VG, $120.00. (Photo courtesy Stefek's, Ltd. on LiveAuctioneers.com)

Plane, PATD 2-17-20, 18" 50.00
Potato grader, Duplex, conveyor type, 10" iron wheels 100.00
Poultry waterer, clear glass dish w/qt-sz Ball jar 18.00
Pulley, #H126, CI & wood, VG 28.00
Pulley, Meyers 408, CI 50.00
Rope maker, Ideal, Pat 1907 .... 225.00
Saw, crosscut, 5⅛x71⅛" blade, 2 wooden hdls, VG 65.00
Saw, dehorning, Keen Kutter, wooden hdl, 10", VG 28.00
Scoop, metal w/iron & wood hdl, 10x6", VG 24.00
Scythe, 18" blade w/48" wooden hdl 35.00
Scythe, label mk Scythe Snaths, 30" blade w/60" hdl, VG 85.00
Sifter, garden, 12x22" tin sifting tray w/wooden hdl, 1800s, VG ... 45.00
Tobacco knife, 2¾x4¼" metal blade w/about a 24" wooden hdl, VG. 25.00
Wagon seat, mixed woods, slat bk/trn arms/rush seat, seats 2, 29". 145.00
Wheelbarrow, gr-pnt wood, chamfered slats w/chip-cvd ends 100.00
Wire fence stretcher, Page, metal, 25½" 40.00
Wrench, Allis Chalmers 800755, ⅞" hexagonal end & 1⅛" sq end, VG. 30.00
Wrench, plow, H-46, 6½" 15.00
Wrench, plow, Rock-Island, 7" 15.00
Yoke, wood w/sm center metal ring, 37x18x5" 50.00

Fenton

The Fenton Art Glass Company was founded in 1905 by brothers Frank L. and John W. Fenton. In the beginning they were strictly a decorating company, but when glassware blanks supplied by other manufacturers became difficult to obtain, the brothers started their own glass manufactory. This factory remains in operation today; it is located in Williamstown, West Virginia.

Early Fenton consisted of pattern glass, custard glass, and carnival glass. During the 1920s and 1930s, Fenton introduced several Depression-era glass patterns, including a popular line called Lincoln Inn, along with stretch glass and glassware in several popular opaque colors — Chinese Yellow, Mandarin Red, and Mongolian Green among them.

In 1939 Fenton introduced a line of Hobnail glassware after the surprising success of a Hobnail cologne bottle made for Wrisley Cologne. Since that time Hobnail has remained a staple in Fenton's glassware line. In addition to Hobnail, other lines such as Coin Spot, the crested lines, and Thumbprint have been mainstays of the company, as have their popular opalescent colors such as cranberry, blue, topaz, and plum. Their milk glass has been very successful as well. Glass baskets in these lines and colors are widely sought after by collectors and can be found in a variety of different sizes and shapes.

Today the company is being managed by third- and fourth-generation family members. Fenton glass continues to be sold in gift shops and retail stores. Additionally, exclusive pieces are offered on the television shopping network, QVC. Desirable items for collectors include limited edition pieces, hand-painted pieces, and family signature pieces. With the deaths of Bill Fenton (second generation) and Don Fenton (third generation) in 2003, family signature pieces are expected to become more desirable to collectors. Watch for special exclusive pieces commemorating the company's 100th anniversary!

For further information we recommend *Fenton Art Glass Hobnail Pattern*, *Fenton Art Glass Patterns, 1939 – 1980*, and *Fenton Art Glass Colors and Hand-Decorated Patterns, 1939 – 1980*, by Margaret and Kenn Whitmyer; *Fenton Glass, The Third Twenty-Five Years*, by William Heacock; *Fenton Glass: The 1980s Decade* by Robert E. Eaton, Jr.; and *Fenton Glass Made for Other Companies*, *Vols. I* and *II*, by our advisors Carrie and Gerald Domitz. Additionally, two national collector clubs, the National Fenton Glass Society (NFGS) and the Fenton Art Glass Collectors of America (FAGCA) promote the study of Fenton Art through their respective newsletters, *The Fenton Flyer* and *The Butterfly Net* (See Clubs, Newsletters, and Websites). Our advisors, Carrie and Gerald Domitz, are listed in the Directory under Washington. See also Carnival Glass; Custard Glass; Stretch Glass.

Apple Blossom, bonbon, #7428-AB, 1960-61, 8", $40 to 50.00
Apple Crest, vase, dbl crimped, #192, 1942-43, 6", $55 to 60.00
Aqua Crest, basket, #1923, 1941-43, 6", $90 to 110.00
Aqua Crest, vase, #36, 1942-43, 6¼", $28 to 32.00
Basket Weave, bowl, bl satin, #8222-BA, 1974-80, $22 to 27.00
Black Crest, bowl, #7321, Gift Shop, 1960s, 12", $85 to 115.00
Black Crest, plate, #7219-BC, 1970s, 6", $14 to 16.00
Black Crest, relish, heart shape, #7333BC, $80 to 100.00
Black Crest, vase, fan, #7356-BC, 1970s, 6¼", $85 to 100.00
Black Rose, bowl, #7227BR, 1953-55, 7", $90 to 110.00
Black Rose, vase, #7256-BR, 1953-55, 6", $145 to 160.00
Block & Star, tumbler, turq, #5647-TU, 1955-56, 12-oz, $30 to 35.00
Block & Star, vase, mg, #5659-MI, 1955-56, 9", $30 to 45.00
Blue Burmese, vase, HP scenic, #46/100, 11" 175.00

Blue Crest, candle-holders, #7474-BC, 6", pair $110.00 to $130.00. (Photo courtesy Randy Clark & Associates on LiveAuctioneers.com)

Blue Overlay, bottle, scent; #192A, 1943-48, $50 to 60.00
Blue Ridge Crest, hat, #1923, 1939, 6", $100 to 120.00
Blue Ridge, basket, #1921, ca 1939, 11", $325 to 350.00
Burmese, vase, #7253BR, 1971-72, 7", $70 to 80.00
Butterfly & Berry, basket, Shell Pk, House Warmings #9766PE, 6½" ... 40.00

Butterfly & Berry, bowl, amethyst carnival, #8428CN, 1974-77, $35 to .. 45.00
Cactus, basket, mg, #3430-MI, 1959-60, 10", $45 to 50.00
Cactus, cracker jar, chocolate, Levay #3480CK, $200 to 225.00
Cactus, cruet, red Sunset Carnival, Levay #3463RN, $125 to 150.00
Cactus, goblet, Colonial Pk, #3445CP, 1962-63, $10 to............... 12.00
Cactus, shakers, custard satin, 3406CU, 1974-75, $18 to.............. 20.00
Carnival, mug, Beaded Shell, amber, 1971, $45 to 55.00
Christmas plate, Old Brick Church, bl satin, 1971, $12 to............ 14.00
Coin Dot, basket, cranberry opal, Levay #1446CR, 7", $125 to..... 150.00
Coin Dot, bowl, Fr opal, dbl crimped, #1523, 1947-49, 13", $85 to . 100.00
Coin Dot, hat, Persian Bl opal, Gift Shop #1492XC, $45 to.......... 55.00
Coin Dot, lamp, honey amber, 1977-78, 21", $225 to 250.00
Coin Dot, vase, topaz opal, #1442-TO, 1959-60, 10", $210 to..... 225.00
Colonial, candy box, Wisteria, #8488WT, 1977-79, $30 to 35.00
Crystal Crest, basket, #1523, 1942, 13", $300 to 350.00
Daisy & Button, bell, custard, #1966-CU, 1972-80+, $20 to 22.00
Daisy & Button, vase, fan, gr pastel, ftd, #1959-GP, 1954-56, 9" ... 60.00
Diamond Lace, basket, Fr opal w/Aqua Crest, #1948, 1948-50, 12".375.00
Diamond Lace, compote, Fr opal w/Aqua Crest, ftd, #1948, 1949-50.85.00
Diamond Optic, barber bottle, #1771-RO, 1957-59, $185 to 225.00
Diamond Optic, candy jar, Colonial Amber, #1780, 1962-65, $25 to. 35.00
Diamond Optic, creamer, ruby o/l, crystal hdl, #1924, 1942-46 ..... 38.00
Diamond Optic, pitcher, purple carnival, Levay #1764, 10½", $200 to.225.00
Diamond Optic, vase, Colonial Amber, threaded, 1977-78, 7", $26 to.28.00
Diamond Optic, vase, Colonial Bl, #1750, 1962-64, 10½" 50.00
Diamond Optic, vase, orange, #1751, 1963-65, 7", $12 to 15.00
Dot Optic, decanter, ruby o/l, #2478RO, 1960-65, $250 to 300.00
Dot Optic, pitcher, bl opal, 9", $200 to....................................... 300.00

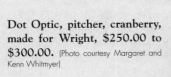

Dot Optic, pitcher, cranberry, made for Wright, $250.00 to $300.00. (Photo courtesy Margaret and Kenn Whitmyer)

Dot Optic, vase, Fr opal, crimped, #1354, 10", $110 to 125.00
Dotted Swiss, vase, Rose Magnolia, Cracker Barrel #3214, $65 to. 75.00
Emerald Crest, candleholder, #680, 1949-52, ea $60 to 80.00
Emerald Crest, plate, cake, low ft, #5813EC, 1954-56, $90 to 125.00
Empress, vase, orange satin, #8252OE, Jan 1968-July 1968, $100 to... 125.00
Fern, ewer, opaline w/Rosalene crest, #4026, Gift Shop, $150 to.. 175.00
Flame Crest, tidbit, 2-tier, #7294-FC, 1963, $125 to 135.00
Gem, atomizer, gr opal, $35 to... 45.00
Georgian, tumbler, gr transparent, #6545DG, 1953-54, 5-oz, $5 to ..7.00
Gold Crest, bowl, #682, 1943-44, 9½", $35 to............................. 40.00
Gold Crest, jug, #982, 1943-44, 6", $45 to.................................. 55.00
Gold Crest, vase, dbl crimped, regular, #196, 1943-44, 6", $25 to.. 30.00
Grape, bell, topaz opal, #9062-TO, 1980, $40 to.......................... 45.00
Grape & Cable, bowl, peach opal, ruffled, Coyne's & Co, 10", $100 to.125.00
Grape & Cable, spittoon, deep cranberry opal carnival, Levay, 7½" ..315.00
Green Overlay, bottle, #711, 1949-51, 5½", $80 to 95.00
Hanging Heart, cruet, turq irid, #8969-TH, 1976, $175 to 195.00
Hanging Heart, pitcher, custard irid, #8964-CI, 1976, 70-oz, $280 to ..300.00
Hanging Heart, tumbler, turq irid, #8940-TH, 1976, 10-oz, $55 to..65.00
Historic America, finger bowl, Prairie Schooner, $30 to 35.00
Hobnail, apothecary jar, Colonial Gr, #3689, 1964-70, $55 to 65.00
Hobnail, basket, bl opal, #389, 1941-44, 13½", $350 to 450.00
Hobnail, basket, cranberry, deep, #3637, 1963-65, 7x7", $300 to . 350.00

Hobnail, basket, Peach Blow, #3835, 1952-56, $75 to.................... 85.00
Hobnail, bell, plum opal, crimped, Levay #3645PO, $65 to........... 85.00
Hobnail, bonbon, Peach Blow, 6-point star shape, #3921, 1953-57, 3" .. 50.00
Hobnail, bottle, oil, topaz opal, #3869, 1942-44, 4¾" w/stopper.. 100.00
Hobnail, bowl, dessert, bl opal, #3828, 1951-54, 2x3½", $35 to..... 45.00
Hobnail, bowl, hanging, mg, brass chains, #3705, 1959-68, 11" .. 150.00
Hobnail, bowl, plum opal, Carolyn's Collectibles, 10", $65 to 85.00
Hobnail, bowl, punch, pk opal, 14-pc, Gift Shop #A3712UO, $350 to.400.00
Hobnail, butter dish, Colonial Amber, #3977, 1959-60,¼-lb, $25 to... 35.00
Hobnail, candleholder, Decorated Holly, #3974DH, 1971-72, ea, $15 to.. 20.00
Hobnail, candleholder, turq, #3974, 1955, ea $20 to...................... 22.00
Hobnail, candy jar, pk chiffon opal, ftd, #3688, 2001-03, 7", $25 to.. 30.00

Hobnail, compote, amber, ftd, #3920, 1959, 8", $30 to 35.00
Hobnail, compote, plum opal, #3727, 1960-64, 3¾x8", $100 to .. 125.00
Hobnail, cookie jar, bl opal, hdls, 1941-43, 7¼x7", $500 to 600.00
Hobnail, decanter, red Sunset carnival, Levay, 1 of 120 made, $200 to..225.00
Hobnail, egg cup, ruby, Collector's Club, ftd, $25 to 35.00
Hobnail, epergene, amber, 4-pc, #3701, 1959, $60 to.................... 75.00
Hobnail, fairy lt, bl satin, #3608BA, 1978-81, $30 to 35.00
Hobnail, fan tray, bl opal, #389, 1941-51, 10½", $30 to 35.00
Hobnail, hat, mg, #3991, 1950-69, $14 to 16.00
Hobnail, jam set, bl opal, #3903, 1948-55, jar+lid+ladle+tray..... 120.00
Hobnail, jug, topaz opal, #3964, 1941-44, $90 to 110.00
Hobnail, lamp, pillar, bl opal, #3907, 1978-81, 26", $360 to........ 400.00
Hobnail, lamp, student, cranberry, #3307, 1984-89, 15", $175 to . 200.00
Hobnail, nut dish, mg, ftd, #3629, 1962-78, 5x5½", $14 to............ 16.00
Hobnail, pitcher, bl opal, ball jug, #3967, 1941-55, 80-oz, $225 to ..275.00
Hobnail, pitcher, Peaches 'n Cream, w/ice lip, Gracious Touch #3664 ..135.00
Hobnail, shakers, glossy vaseline opal, ftd, Levay #3609TO, pr, $75 to.. 95.00
Hobnail, toothpick, bl opal, Levay #3795BO, 2¾", $20 to............. 30.00
Hobnail, tray, sandwich, topaz opal, chrome hdl, #3791, 1959-74, 13"..85.00
Hobnail, tumbler, bl opal, #3946, 1940-55, 16-oz, 6", $65 to 85.00
Hobnail, tumbler, crystal, 1940-41, 4", $6 to................................7.00
Hobnail, vase, swung, topaz opal, #3759, 1959-60, 16", $190 to..220.00
Hobnail, vase, Wild Rose, #3656, 1961-63, 5½", $45 to................. 55.00
Hobnail, wine, Fr opal, sq, #3844, 1951-54, $35 to........................ 45.00
Horizon, candleholder, Jamestown Bl, w/insert, #8177, 1959, 8", ea.. 22.00
Horizon, vase, amber, #8157, 1959, 8", $20 to 22.00
Ivory Crest, plate, #682, 1940-42, 12", $50 to 60.00
Ivy, basket, #1924, 1949-52, 5", $75 to 85.00
Jacqueline, cr/sug, Apple Gr o/l, 1961-62, $45 to 55.00
Jacqueline, pitcher, honey amber, #9166-HA, 1961-62, 48-oz....... 55.00
Jacqueline, vase, bl opal, #9153-BN, 1960-61, 5", $55 to.............. 65.00
Lacy Edge, banana bowl, mg, #9024-MI, 1955-59, $40 to.............. 50.00
Lacy Edge, compote, rose pastel, #9028RP, 1954-57, $40 to 50.00
Lacy Edge, plate, bl pastel, #9011-BP, 1954-55, 11", $20 to 25.00
Lacy Edge, plate, mg, #9011MI, 1953-60, 11", $14 to 16.00
Lacy Edge, plate, mg, ftd, #9017MI, 1954-59, $40 to 50.00
Lacy Edge, plate, rose pastel, #360, 1954-55, 8", $12 to 14.00
Lacy Edge, plate, rose pastel, #9011-RP, 1954-55, 11", $20 to........ 25.00
Lacy Edge, plate, rose pastel, #9012RP, 1955-57, 12", $25 to 30.00
Lacy Edge, shell, turq, #9030TU, 1955-56, $12 to.......................... 15.00
Lamb's Tongue, candy jar, bl pastel, #4381-BP, 1954-55, $90 to .. 110.00
Lamb's Tongue, cr/sug, gr pastel, #4301, 1954-55 .... 65.00
Lily of the Valley, bell, amethyst carnival, #8265CN, 1979-80, $28 to.32.00

Lily of the Valley, candy box, bl opal, #8489BO, 1979-80, $35 to . 40.00
Lily of the Valley, plate, cake, cameo opal, #8411CO, 1979-80, $70 to.. 80.00
Lily of the Valley, vase, bud, topaz opal, #8458TO, 1980, $30 to... 35.00
Love Bird, vase, Lime Sherbet, #8258LS, 1974-76, $37 to............. 42.00
Mandarin, vase, blk, #8251-BK, 1968-70, $110 to 135.00
Mandarin, vase, orange satin, #8251-OE, 1968, $120 to 140.00
Medallion, candy box, Holly on ruby, #8288-RH, 1976-80, $85 to..95.00
New World, wine bottle, Dusk, #7367, 1953, $175 to................. 225.00
Paneled Daisy, toothpick, Lime Sherbet, #8294LS, 1973-76, $16 to . 18.00
Patriot Red, stein, Bicentennial, #8446-PR, 1975-76, $27 to 32.00
Peach Crest, basket, #1523, 1940-52, 13", $240 to.................... 250.00
Peach Crest, basket, #192, 1942-49, 10½", $160 to 185.00
Peach Crest, candy jar, #711, 1949-50, $100 to 125.00
Peach Crest, vase, Charleton Roses, #192, 5½", $60 to................ 70.00
Peach Crest, vase, triangular, #711, 1949-50, 5½", $35 to............. 40.00
Persian Medallion, chalice, custard satin, 1972-74, $25 to............ 30.00
Persian Medallion, compote, 1972-80+, $18 to........................ 22.00
Persian Medallion, fairy lt, Colonial Amber, #8408CA, 1974-76.. 30.00
Persian Medallion, plate, Wisteria carnival, Levay #8219, 9" 90.00
Pink Blossom, egg, custard satin, #5143PY, 1972-75, $32 to.......... 35.00
Pink Blossom, swan, custard satin, #5161PY, 1978-80, $25 to 30.00
Pinwheel, compote, Independence Bl Carnival, 1976-77, $27 to.. 32.00
Pinwheel, compote, ruby irid, #8227RN, 1976-78, $30 to 35.00
Polka Dot, butter/cheese dish, cranberry, #2277-CR, 1955-56, $400 to.500.00
Polka Dot, decanter, bl transparent, #2478BU, 1960-62, $200 to. 250.00
Polka Dot, sugar shaker, ruby o/l, #2493-RO, 1956-57, $100 to... 125.00
Polka Dot, vase, Jamestown Bl, pinched, #2452-JT, 1959-59, 8" .. 75.00
Poppy, student lamp, mg, #9100-MI, 1975-77, 19", $230 to......... 250.00
Poppy, vase, rose satin, #9154-RS, 1974-78, 7", $40 to 50.00
Priscilla, sugar bowl, crystal, 1950+, $8 to 10.00
Regency, butter dish, ruby marble, rnd, Levay #8680RX, $150 to. 165.00
Rib Optic, cruet, bl satin, #815, 1952-55, $200 to....................... 250.00
Rib Optic, ivy ball & base, gr opal, #1622-GO, 1950s, $100 to ... 150.00
Rib Optic, shakers, cranberry, #1605-CR, 1953-59, pr $110 to.... 140.00
Rib Optic, vase, rose satin, #1925, 1952-55, 6", $90 to 110.00
Rib Optic, wine, lime opal, #1647-LO, 1953-54, $140 to 160.00
Rib Optic New World, shakers, topaz opal, Collecter's Club, pr $30 to... 35.00
Ring Optic, vase, cranberry, #510, ca 1939, 8", $100 to 125.00
Rose, ball lamp, Wild Rose o/l, #9207-WR, 1967-69, 22", $190 to.210.00
Rose, basket, Colonial Bl, #9235-CB, 1967-70, 9", $45 to 50.00
Rose, candy box, Colonial Pk, oval, #9282-CP, 1965-67, $25 to ... 30.00
Rose, compote, lime sherbet, #9222-LS, 1974-77, $20 to 22.00
Rose, goblet, mg, #9246-MI, 1967-69, 9-oz, $8 to 10.00
Rose, vase, handkerchief, Colonial Amber, #9254-CA, 1968-70, $10 to.. 12.00
Rose Crest, candlestick, #1523, 1946-48, ea $40 to....................... 45.00
Rose Crest, plate, #680, 12", $65 to 75.00
Rose Overlay, basket, #203, hdl, 1943-49, 7", $40 to 45.00
Rose Overlay, jug, #192, 1943-49, 8", $50 to 55.00
Sables Arch, bell, lt amethyst carnival, Gift Shop #9065DT, 6", $50 to. 65.00
Sheffield, bowl, Petal Pk, crimped, Hallmark #6626PN, $30 to..... 35.00
Silver Crest w/Spanish Lace, bell, #3567SC, 1973-80, $40 to 45.00
Silver Crest, basket, cone shape, #36, 1943-47, $35 to................. 40.00
Silver Crest, basket, mini fan, #37, 1943-48, 2", $100 to 125.00
Silver Crest, bonbon, #36, 1943-80, 5½", $10 to 12.00
Silver Crest, bottle, #193, 1943-49, 5½", $50 to......................... 60.00
Silver Crest, bowl, #205, 1943-48, 8½", $40 to........................... 45.00
Silver Crest, candleholder, #680, 1949-52, ea $35 to 45.00
Silver Crest, chip & dip, #7402SC, 1975-76, $70 to..................... 85.00
Silver Crest, creamer, hdld, #711, 1949-50, 4", $30 to 35.00
Silver Crest, planter, 3-tier, #680, 1950-52, $55 to...................... 65.00
Silver Crest, plate, #681, 1943-49, 9", $25 to 30.00
Silver Crest, plate, cake, low ft, #5813SC, 1954-80, $35 to 40.00
Silver Crest, vase, #186, 1943-67, 8", $25 to 30.00
Silver Crest, vase, dbl crimped, #711, 1949-72, 6", $28 to 30.00

Silver Crest, vase, tulip, #711, 1949-58, 6", $28 to......................... 35.00
Silver Crest/Spanish Lace, basket, #3537-SC, 1968-80, 10", $125 to. 150.00
Silver Crest/Violets in Snow, basket, #7436-DV, 1968-80+, sm, $65 to . 85.00
Silver Jamestown, vase, #7350SJ, 1957-59, 5", $45 to 55.00
Snowcrest, vase, bl, #1925, 1950-51, 5", $40 to............................. 50.00
Snowcrest, vase, dk gr, #3005, 1950-53, 7½", $80 to 85.00
Spiral Optic, candy box, bl opal, #3180-BO, 1979-80, $110 to.... 125.00
Spiral Optic, top hat, gr opal, #1921, ruffled rim, 1939, 10", $250 to.275.00
Spiral Optic, top hat, gr opal, #1924, 1939, 4", $45 to 55.00
Spiral Optic, vase, #3264-CR, 1956-60, 11½", $185 to 220.00
Spiral Optic, vase, bl opal, #3157-BO, 1979-80, 6½", 20 to........... 30.00
Spiral Optic, vase, cranberry, crimped, triangular, #187, 1938+, 7".. 115.00
Swirl, ashtray, Springtime Gr, #7076GT, 1970s, 7½", $12 to 14.00
Swirl, ashtray, Wisteria, #7076WT, 1977-78, 7½", $18 to 22.00
Swirl, bowl, bl pastel, #7021-BP, 1954-55, 11", $55 to 65.00
Swirl, cr/sug, mg, #7006-MI, 1954-55 .... 35.00
Swirl, shakers, bl pastel, #7001-RP, 1954-55, pr $35 to 40.00
Swirl, vanity set, rose pastel, #7005-RP, 1954-55, 3-pc, $85 to 105.00
Swirl, vase, turq, #7056-TU, 1955-58, 6", $25 to 30.00
Swirled Feather, candy jar, cranberry satin, 1953-54, $500 to...... 600.00
Swirled Feather, fairy lamp, Fr satin, 1953-55, $175 to 200.00
Teardrop, bowl, mg, #6929-MI, 1957-59, 9", $20 to 25.00
Teardrop, condiment set, Goldenrod, #6909-GD, 1957+, $200 to... 225.00
Teardrop, shakers, mg, #6906-MI, 1955-67, pr $18 to 20.00
Thumbprint, ashtray, Colonial Amber, #4469-CA, 1957-70, 6".......8.00
Thumbprint, bud vase, Colonial Gr, tall, #4453-CG, 1963-75 ...... 10.00
Thumbprint, candy box, Colonial Amber, oval, #4486-CA, 1963-69...15.00
Thumbprint, lamp, student, Colonial Gr, #1410CG, 1960s, 20", $60 to . 70.00
Thumbprint, relish, Colonial Gr, divided, 1966-69, 8½".............. 10.00
Tree of Life, compote, Colonial Amber, #9322CA, 1977-78, $9 to .11.00
Valencia, cigarette lighter, Colonial Bl, #8399-CB, 1969-72 .... 25.00
Valencia, sherbet, Colonial Gr, #8343-CB, 1970-72, $6 to...............8.00
Valencia, vase, swung, Colonial Amber, #8352-CA, 1969-73, lg, $22 to. 25.00
Vasa Murrhina, basket, bl mist, #6437-BM, 1964-65, 11", $110 to .. 130.00
Vasa Murrhina, vase, Autumn Orange, #6458-AO, 1965-68, 11", $75 to. 85.00
Vasa Murrhina, vase, bl mist, #6459-BM, 1964-65, 14", $110 to . 145.00
Violets in Snow/Spanish lace, basket, 1974-80+, 8½", $125 to.... 140.00
Waffle, candy box, gr opal, #6180-GO, 1960-61, $75 to 85.00
Water Lily, basket, bl satin, #8434-BA, 1977-80+, 7", $45 to........ 55.00
Water Lily, jardiniere, wht satin, #8498WS, 1975-77, $25 to 30.00
Water Lily, pitcher, bl satin, #8464-BA, 1976-80, 36-oz, $40 to ... 45.00
Water Lily, vase, bud, bl satin, #8456-BA, 1978-80+, $25 to 27.00
Wave Crest, candy box, coral, #6080-CL, 1960s, $95 to................. 115.00
Wave Crest, candy box, mg, #60800-MI, 1956-60, $40 to 45.00
Wave Crest, candy jar, opaque bl o/l, #6080OB, 1962-63, $100 to.. 110.00
Wave Crest, shakers, ruby o/l, #6006RO, 1956-63, pr, $50 to........ 60.00
Wild Rose w/Bowknot, pitcher, mg, #2865-MI, 1961, 32-oz.......... 50.00
Wild Rose w/Bowknot, rose bowl, Celestial Bl satin, Levay, 5"...... 80.00

Fiesta

Fiesta is a line of dinnerware that was originally produced by the Homer Laughlin China Company of Newell, West Virginia, from 1936 until 1973. It was made in 11 different solid colors with over 50 pieces in the assortment. The pattern was developed by Frederick Rhead, an English Stoke-on-Trent potter who was an important contributor to the art pottery movement in this country during the early part of the century. The design was carried out through the use of a simple band-of-rings device near the rim. Fiesta Red, a strong red-orange glaze color, was made with depleted uranium oxide. It was more expensive to produce than the other colors and sold at higher prices. Besides red, the other 'original' colors were cobalt, light green, yellow, turquoise, and ivory. During the '50s the color assortment was gray, rose, chartreuse, and dark green. These colors are relatively harder to find and along with medium green (new in 1959) command the highest prices.

Fiesta Kitchen Kraft was introduced in 1939; it consisted of 17 pieces of kitchenware such as pie plates, refrigerator sets, mixing bowls, and covered jars in four popular Fiesta colors. As a final attempt to adapt production to modern-day techniques and methods, Fiesta was restyled in 1969. Of the original colors, only Fiesta Red remained. This line, called Fiesta Ironstone, was discontinued in 1973.

Two types of marks were used: an ink stamp on machine-jiggered pieces and an indented mark molded into the hollow ware pieces.

In 1986 HLC reintroduced a line of Fiesta dinnerware in five colors: white, black, rose, apricot, and cobalt blue (darker and denser than the original shade). Since then yellow, turquoise, seamist green, periwinkle, lilac, persimmon, sapphire, chartreuse, pearl gray, juniper, cinnabar, sunflower, plum, shamrock, tangerine, scarlet, peacock, heather, evergreen, ivory, chocolate, lemongrass, and the newest color, paprika have been added. For more information we recommend *Collector's Encyclopedia of Fiesta, Plus Harlequin, Riviera, and Kitchen Kraft*, by Bob and Sharon Huxford.

More than ever before, condition is a major price-assessing factor. Unless an item is free from signs of wear, smoothly glazed, and has no distracting manufacturing flaws, it will not bring 'book' price. In the listings that follow, the high end of the range given for 'original' colors should be used to evaluate red, cobalt blue, ivory, and in some instances, turquoise. Yellow and light green fall toward the lower end.

Dinnerware

Ashtray, '50s colors, $60 to	75.00
Ashtray, orig colors, $50 to	65.00
Bowl, covered onion soup, red, cobalt or ivory, $575 to	675.00
Bowl, covered onion soup, turq	4,000.00
Bowl, covered onion soup, yel or lt gr, $400 to	500.00
Bowl, cream soup, '50s colors, $50 to	65.00
Bowl, cream soup, orig colors, $40 to	60.00
Bowl, dessert, '50s colors, 6", $35 to	45.00
Bowl, dessert, orig colors, 6", $28 to	35.00
Bowl, fruit, '50s colors, 4½", $25 to	40.00
Bowl, fruit, '50s colors, 5½", $30 to	45.00
Bowl, fruit, orig colors, 4¾", $22 to	35.00
Bowl, fruit, orig colors, 5½", $25 to	35.00
Bowl, fruit, orig colors, 11¾", min	165.00
Bowl, ftd salad, orig colors, $250 to	300.00
Bowl, ind salad, 7½", red, turq or yel, $80 to	120.00
Bowl, nappy, 8½", '50s colors, $35 to	50.00
Bowl, nappy, 8½", med gr, $110 to	135.00
Bowl, nappy, 8½", orig colors, $25 to	40.00
Bowl, nappy, 9½", orig colors, $40 to	55.00
Bowl, unlisted salad, yel, $110 to	125.00
Candleholders, bulb, orig colors, pr, $70 to	90.00
Candleholders, tripod, orig colors, pr, $425 to	500.00
Carafe, orig colors, $175 to	225.00
Carafe, orig colors, $195 to	265.00
Casserole, w/lid, '50s colors, $200 to	250.00
Casserole, w/lid, orig colors, $180 to	235.00
Coffeepot, demi, orig colors other than turq, $300 to	400.00
Coffeepot, demi, turq, $450 to	525.00
Coffeepot, regular, '50s colors, $340 to	385.00
Coffeepot, regular, orig colors, $160 to	200.00
Compote, orig colors, 12", $150 to	175.00
Compote, sweets, orig colors, $120 to	135.00
Creamer, regular, orig colors, $20 to	30.00
Cup/saucer, demi, '50s colors, $220 to	250.00
Cup/saucer, demi, orig colors, $70 to	85.00

Cup/saucer, tea, '50s colors, $25 to	35.00
Cup/saucer, tea, med gr, $50 to	65.00
Egg cup, '50s colors, $100 to	160.00
Egg cup, orig colors, $60 to	70.00
Marmalade, orig colors, $250 to	295.00
Mixing bowl, #1, orig colors, $175 to	250.00
Mixing bowl, #5, orig colors, $145 to	200.00
Mixing bowl, #6, orig colors, $165 to	235.00
Mixing bowl, #7, orig colors, $300 to	400.00
Mug, Tom & Jerry, '50s colors, $50 to	70.00
Mug, Tom & Jerry, orig colors, $40 to	60.00
Mustard, orig colors, $260 to	350.00
Pitcher, disk juice, red, $250 to	350.00
Pitcher, disk juice, yel, $25 to	30.00
Pitcher, disk water, '50s colors, $145 to	175.00
Pitcher, disk water, orig colors, $80 to	100.00
Pitcher, ice, orig colors, $110 to	135.00
Pitcher, jug, 2-pt, orig colors, $80 to	110.00
Plate, any color but med gr, 6", $3 to	5.00
Plate, any color but med gr, 7", $5 to	9.00
Plate, any color but med gr, 9", $9 to	12.00
Plate, any color but med gr, 10", $22 to	35.00
Plate, chop, 13", '50s colors, $65 to	85.00
Plate, chop, 15", any color but med gr, $75 to	100.00
Plate, chop, 15", orig colors, $60 to	90.00
Plate, chop, orig colors, 13", $45 to	55.00
Plate, compartment, 10½", '50s colors, $50 to	70.00
Plate, compartment, 10½", orig colors, $35 to	45.00
Plate, compartment, orig colors, 12", $40 to	75.00
Plate, deep, med gr, $65 to	100.00
Plate, deep, orig colors, $35 to	50.00
Platter, med gr, $130 to	165.00
Platter, yel, 13", $30 to	40.00

Relish tray, six colors represented, $250.00 to $300.00. (Photo courtesy Strawser Auction Group on LiveAuctioneers.com)

Salt & pepper shakers, dk gr, $40	60.00
Sauceboat (gravy), gray, $60 to	75.00
Sauceboat orig colors, $40 to	60.00
Sauceboat, med gr, $110 to	140.00
Shakers, orig colors, pr, $20 to	35.00
Sugar bowl w/lid, orig colors, $40 to	65.00
Syrup, orig colors, $225 to	300.00
Syrup, turq, $350 to	400.00
Teapot, lg, orig colors, $165 to	265.00
Teapot, med, orig colors, $135 to	225.00
Tray, figure-8, cobalt, $75 to	85.00
Tray, figure-8, turq, $200 to	250.00
Tray, utility, orig colors, $25 to	35.00
Tumbler, juice, orig colors, $30 to	45.00
Tumbler, water, orig colors, $35 to	60.00
Underplate/stand for sauceboat, orig colors, Ironstone, 1969, 9x6½", $100 to	150.00
Utility tray, orig colors, $40 to	50.00
Vase, 8", orig colors, $400 to	600.00
Vase, 10", orig colors, $550 to	700.00
Vase, 12", orig colors, $800 to	1,000.00
Vase, bud, orig colors, $50 to	75.00

Kitchen Kraft

Bowl, mixing, 6" 50.00
Bowl, mixing, 8" 65.00
Bowl, mixing, 10", $95 to 110.00
Cake plate 35.00
Cake server, $100 to 125.00
Casserole, 7½", $50 to 75.00
Casserole, 8½", $60 to 85.00
Casserole, ind, $80 to 150.00
Covered jar, lg, $275 to 300.00
Covered jar, med, $225 to 275.00
Covered jar, sm, $200 to 235.00

Covered jug, either size, $200.00 to $250.00. (Photo courtesy Alderfer Auction Company on LiveAuctioneers.com)

Fork, $100 to 135.00
Pie plate, 9", $30 to 45.00
Pie plate, 10", $30 to 45.00
Platter, $45 to 60.00
Shakers, pr $75 to 95.00
Spoon, $100 to 135.00
Stacking refrigerator lid, $100 to 135.00
Stacking refrigerator unit, $50 to 60.00

Fifties Modern

Postwar furniture design is marked by organic shapes and lighter woods and forms. New materials from war research such as molded plywood and fiberglass were used extensively. For the first time, design was extended to the masses, and the baby-boomer generation grew up surrounded by modern shape and color, the perfect expression of postwar optimism. The top designers in America worked for Herman Miller and Knoll Furniture Company. These include Charles and Ray Eames, George Nelson, and Eero Saarinen.

Unless noted otherwise, values are given for furnishings in excellent condition; glassware and ceramic items are assumed to be in mint condition. This information was provided to us by Richard Wright. See also Italian Glass.

Key:
fbrg — fiberglass   plwd — plywood
lcq — lacquered   rswd — rosewood
lm — laminated   ss — stainless steel

Armchair, Eames, Alum Group, swivel base, wool sling seat, 33", pr.950.00
Armchair, Pollock/Knoll, leather sling, tubular fr, alum rests, pr ...1,500.00
Armchair, Wegner/Getama, teak fr w/caned bk, cushion, 27", pr .1,500.00
Bedroom set, Drexel, elm w/ebonized wood legs, 3-pc 660.00
Bench, Nelson/Miller, Platform, birch slat top w/open sq blk legs, 72"..660.00
Bench, Nelson/Miller, Platform, ebonized slat top/open sq legs, 68" L.. 540.00
Bench, Probber, mahog fr, drw, loose cushion on half, 15x72x18" ...800.00
Bench, Wormley/Dunbar, solid sap walnut top, 4 bentwood legs 78" L..1,080.00
Cabinet, Juhl/Baker, birch/walnut, 2 doors/4 drws, metal pulls, 30x72" ..3,000.00
Cabinet, Juhl/Baker, birch/walnut, 2-door, blk pulls, 30x36x18" ...1,400.00

Cabinet, McCobb/Calvin, mahog, 2 sliding doors, brass trim, 41x49x14"...600.00
Cabinet, Nelson/Miller, Basic, walnut, 2-door (& 1 3-drw), 24x34", pr.600.00
Cabinet, Nelson/Miller, Basic, walnut 5-drw w/ebonized legs, 40x40" . 1,020.00
Cabinet, Nelson/Miller, birch, 4 drw/1 door, M-shaped pulls, 30x56x19" .500.00
Cabinet, Nelson/Miller, Thin Edge, rswd 4-drw w/alum legs, 30x34". 3,000.00
Cabinet, Nelson/Miller, Thin Edge, rswd/4-drw/hourglass pulls, 30x34"..1,500.00
Cabinet, Nelson/Miller, Thin-Edge, rswd w/2 doors, alum pulls, 34" .2,100.00
Cabinet, Probber, bleached mahog, 2 caned doors, 4-drw, 23x78x18"..700.00
Cabinet, Probber, lm top, bleached mahog, 9-drw, 30x21x18"..1,000.00
Cabinet, Probber, mahog, 4-drw, cut-out pulls, 33x36x18" 450.00
Cabinet, stereo, Nelson/Miller, walnut, drop-down door, 35x82x23" . 700.00
Cart, serving, McCobb/Calvin, marble top, pull-out shelf, drws, 36" L..700.00
Chair, Bellman/Horgen-Glanus; birch plwd w/cutout, birch legs, 33" ..200.00
Chair, Bertoia/Knoll, Dmn, fabric seat, steel rod base, 3 for 350.00
Chair, Cherner/Plycraft, wide bentwood arms/padded triangular bk, 31"..650.00
Chair, club, flared form w/tapered wood legs, reuphl, 28" 425.00
Chair, dining; Robsjohn Gibbings/Widdicomb, maple, 2 arm+4 sides. 1,800.00
Chair, dining; Wormley/Dunbar, mahog w/caned bk, uphl seat, 4 for. 265.00
Chair, Eames/Miller, DCW, birch plwd seat/bk/fr, rfn, 29", 6 for ...2,500.00
Chair, Eames/Miller, DKR, wire 1-pc seat/bl, blk Eiffel-Tower base ...300.00
Chair, Eames/Miller, Eiffel Tower, blk fabric, 32", 4 for 850.00
Chair, Eames/Miller, Eiffel Tower, fbrg on blk wire base, 31", 4 for .600.00
Chair, Eames/Miller, LCM, red plwd, chromed steel fr, 26".......1,000.00
Chair, lounge, Eames/Miller, rswd plwd & blk leather, 35", +ottoman. 2,800.00
Chair, lounge, Frankl, tufted seat, floating bk, att, 26", G, pr....1,500.00
Chair, lounge, McCobb/Calbin, wht uphl, mahog-stain birch legs, 31".650.00
Chair, lounge, Noreil/Sweden, leather uphl, ca 1970, 30", pr+ottoman.5,500.00
Chair, lounge, Wormley/Dunbar, even-arm, mohair uphl, 27x37x34" ...375.00
Chair, lounge, Wormley/Dunbar, uphl seat w/bk cushion, walnut base ..650.00
Chair, Mathsson/Mathsson, Eva, beech fr w/orig webbing, 33", VG..475.00
Chair, Nakashima/Knoll, walnut, curved bk w/dowels/slab seat, 30"..275.00
Chair, Nelson/Miller, Coconut, steel shell w/uphl seat, 32", +ottoman ..3,250.00
Chair, Probber, mahog fr w/curved caned bk, rnd cushion, 24", pr...2,200.00
Chair, side, Conover/Conover, redwood w/wrought-iron rod fr, 30" ..950.00
Chair, side, Juhl/Baker #402, uphl vinyl, walnut fr, 32", 6 for ...4,750.00
Chair, side, Rojle/Denmark, teak, sculptural bks, 33", 4 for 600.00
Chair, slipper, Kroehler, channeled uphl bks, fringed cushion 31".. 1,200.00
Chair, slipper, Probber, orig wool uphl, mahog X-base fr, 34"....1,000.00
Chaise, vander Rohe/Knoll, ss fr w/channeled leather cushion, 39" .1,600.00
Chaise, Woodard, wire mesh, bk adjusts, 2 wheels, 37x60x25" 250.00
Chaise, Wormley/Dunbar, tulip uphl/4 loose cushions/mahog legs, 71".2,200.00
Chest, Nelson/Miller, blk pnt, 3-drw, bentwood legs, 35x34" ...1,295.00
Chest, Wormley/Drexel, 5 drw amid 2 doors, worn, 33x67x20" ... 400.00

Chest, Wormley/Dunbar, mahogany with five drawers and two sliding doors concealing adjustable shelves, 38x49x20", $3,360.00. (Photo courtesy Rago Arts and Auction Center)

Clock, Nelson/Miller, Petal, wht paddles/brass center, 18" dia..1,500.00
Clock, Nelson/Miller, Sunburst, blk spikes/brass center, #2202, 19" ... 300.00
Clock, table, Miller, sq red Bakelite, brass base w/ball ft, 6x5" 300.00
Desk, Dunbar, door on left, 3 drws on right, woven privacy panel, 72". 700.00
Desk, McCobb/Calvin, Irwin Collection, wht glass top, mahog fr, 60"...1,400.00
Desk, Nelson/Miller, Action Office, alum fr, lm top, 3-drw, 50" W ..1,020.00
Desk, Wormley/Drexel, elm, leather top w/2 sliding compartments, 56" .480.00

Dresser, Baughmann/Coggin, blk lcq, 2 banks of 3 drw, brass trim, 64" ..285.00
Dresser, Rohde/Miller, Deco birch/mahog, 4-drw, 35x43", pr....1,100.00
Dresser, WormleyTrexel, beech/elm, 10-drw, platform base, 33x62x19" ..900.00
Fire dogs, Nelson/Miller, iron, 5½x15¾x2½", pr.......................1,000.00
Headboard, Frankl/Johnson, latticework, orig finish, 38x80" 450.00
Headboard, Wormley/Dunbar, mahog, uphl panels, drop-down arms, 81" W..2,500.00
Jewelry chest, Nelson/Miller, walnut, 2 rows of 3 drw, alum ped, 30" W.4,900.00
Lamp, floor, McCobb/Calvin, wht paper shade, brass std, 3-ftd base... 700.00
Lamp, floor, Rispal/France, cord laced through walnut J-form, 2 shades .2,000.00
Lamp, Gambone, geometrics, bl/blk on ivory, 3 pinched sides, 21"..1,560.00
Lamp, Ponti (att), leather-wrap brass std w/tripod base, 24", +shade .. 900.00
Lamps, Gatto, Achille/Pier Giacomo Castiglioni/Flos, 12", pr..1,550.00
Magazine rack, Probber, dk stain mahog X form, 21x20x15"........600.00
Mirror, Frankl/Johnson, cork w/wood backing, 30¼x26¼x2½" .2,500.00
Modular seating, Chadwick/Miller, 6 wedge-shaped pcs, orig uphl ..300.00
Sculpture, Weinberg, reclining nude, pnt plaster, 3¼x10½x6"..... 300.00
Sideboard, Frankl/Johnson, 2 center doors/8 drw, brass pulls, 32x73". 1,200.00
Sideboard, Knoll/Knoll, walnut w/4 wht doors, shelves/drws w/in, 75"..2,760.00
Sideboard, Wormley/Dunbar, lt mahog, 2 doors+2 banks of 4 drws over 1..3,600.00
Sofa, Compact, Eames/Miller, bl vinyl uphl, chromed steel fr, folds.1,300.00
Sofa, Hvidt/Molgaard-Nielsen, leather uphl, marble table surface, 112"..1,680.00
Sofa, Jacobsen/Hansen, Series 330, wool uphl, ss fr, 71", +28" chair... 2,100.00
Sofa, Kjaerholm PK 31/3, blk leather cushions, chromed fr, 78" ..4,250.00
Sofa, Knoll, harlequin chenille reuphl, birch legs, 30x90x33" ..1,300.00

Sofa, Nelson/Miller, Marshmallow, 18 cushions on black enameled and polished steel base with original finish, round metal Nelson tag, 52" wide, $24,000.00. (Photo courtesy Treadway Gallery on LiveAuctioneers.com)

Sofa, Probber, uphl, ebonized wood/brass fr w/repeating Xs, 109"..5,500.00
Sofa, Robsjohn-Gibbings, uphl seat w/loose cushion, walnut fr, 76"..6,000.00
Sofa, Wormley/Dunbar, reuphl 3-cushion seat/bk, walnut fr, 82" ..1,000.00
Sofas, Terrazza, Ubald Klug/De Sede, brn leather, 32x28x60", pr ..4,200.00
Stool, bar, Bertoia/Knoll, blk wire w/vinyl seat cushion, 42½", pr. 750.00
Stool, Eames/Miller Time-Life, trn walnut, 15x13" 1,000.00
Table, coffee, Eames/Miller, lm top, birch plwd legs, 16x35x24"..750.00
Table, coffee, Frankl/Johnson, 48x24" cork top, 2 canted 3-panel legs. 1,320.00
Table, coffee, Juhl/Baker, walnut fr w/birch top, #521, 22x64x31" ...850.00
Table, coffee, Laverne, Italian marble, chromed steel legs, 16x60x22".950.00
Table, coffee, Nakashima, walnut, 40" dia on Xd base, butterfly joints. 8,800.00
Table, coffee, Saarien/Knoll, 36" dia walnut top/wht enamel ped base .780.00
Table, coffee, Wormley/Dunbar, glass/mahog platform base, 46" dia..1,200.00
Table, coffee, Wormley/Dunbar, mahog w/brass stretchers, shelf, 48" L..1,300.00
Table, coffee, Wormley/Dunbar, walnut, 5-brd top, loop legs, 84".1,645.00
Table, dining, Juhl/Baker, walnut bookmatched top, 2 20" leaves, 68". 1,200.00
Table, dining, Nakashima, 4 butterflies join exposed free edge, 36" L ..31,725.00
Table, dining, Nogucki/Knoll, 48" dia birch plwd top/CI & wire base....840.00
Table, dining, Probber, mahog w/apron, mahog/brass bases, 66x41" .2,100.00
Table, dining, Rhode/Miller, 72x40" walnut checkered vnr top/blk base... 1,020.00
Table, dining, Robsjohn-Gibbings, walnut, plinth bases, rfn, 70" L .1,300.00
Table, dining, Saarinen/Knoll, marble top, enameled ped base, 50" dia...950.00
Table, dining, Saarinen/Knoll, wht lm top, wht enamel metal base, 54"..400.00
Table, dining, Vignelli/Knoll, Paperclip, blk lm, ss rods, 48" 900.00
Table, Intrex, Monoform, rnd blk marble top, composite base, 22x22" ..120.00
Table, occasional, Bellman/Knoll, Popsicle, plwd, fold-up, 22" dia .700.00
Table, occasional, Probber, compo hexagon top w/brass trim, 3-leg, 22" ..1,100.00
Table, occasional, Wormley/Dunbar, dk mahog fr w/27" dia rswd top .. 1,680.00

Table, occasional, Wormley/Dunbar, walnut on mahog fr, shelf, 28x19" .240.00
Table, Singer & Sons, walnut, rect top, shelf, drw, 23x26x23".....350.00
Table, Wegner/Tuck, teak 40x24" top, Xd legs ea end, brass stretcher ..960.00
Table, Wormley/Drexel, elm sq top over recessed sq base, 17x30x20" ..400.00
Table, Wormley/Drexel, elm, 2-tier w/leather inset top, 26x24x16"...275.00
Table, Wormley/Dunbar, walnut top, steel/walnut base, 29x79x42" ..1,000.00
Table/nightstand, Nakashima, sap walnut case/drw/splayed legs . 3,750.00
Tray table, Nelson/Miller, molded ash plwd 15" sq, chromed ss base, pr .1,800.00
Vanity/desk, Frankl/Johnson, 3-drw/2 doors, brass pulls, +swivel chair ...2,700.00
Vase, Conover, Bacel, cvd designs/lines, gray on wine, 14x14" .3,000.00

Kay Finch

Kay Finch and her husband, Braden, operated a small pottery in Corona Del Mar, California, from 1939 to 1963. The company remained small, employing from 20 to 60 local residents who Kay trained in all but the most requiring tasks, which she herself performed. The company produced animal and bird figurines, most notably dogs, Kay's favorites. Figures of 'Godey' type couples were also made, as were tableware (consisting of breakfast sets) and other artware. Most pieces were marked, but ink stamps often came off during cleaning.

After Kay's husband, Braden, died in 1962, she closed the business. Some of her molds were sold to Freeman-McFarlin of El Monte, California, who soon contracted with Kay for new designs. Though the realism that is so evident in her original works is still strikingly apparent in these later pieces, none of the vibrant pastels or signature curliques are there. Kay Finch died on June 21, 1993.

Note: Original model numbers are included in the following descriptions — three-digit numbers indicate pre-1946 models. After 1946 they were assigned four-digit numbers, the first two digits representing the year of initial production. Unless otherwise described, our prices are for figurines decorated in multiple colors, not solid glazes. With the birth of eBay and internet websites, there has been a dramatic downward shift in values. For many pieces, supply has exceeded demand. However, the rare and very scarce pieces continue to hold their values.

For further information we recommend *Kay Finch Ceramics, Her Enchanted World* (Schiffer), written by our advisors for this category, Mike Nickel and Cynthia Horvath; they are listed in the Directory under Michigan.

Ashtray, Swan, #4958, 4½"... 25.00
Box, heart, #B5051, bird on lid, 2½".. 50.00
Canister, emb raspberry vines, purple/gr on wht, 9½"...................... 75.00
Cup, Kitten Face, Toby, 3"... 75.00
Figurine, Afghan angel standing, bl-tipped wings, 2½x2¼"............350.00
Figurine, Airedale dog standing, caramel & blk, #4832, 5x5" 180.00
Figurine, Ambrosia, cat, #155, 10½", min................................250.00
Figurine, Bride & Groom, #204, 6½", 6", pr................................175.00
Figurine, Canister, Santa, 10½".. 75.00
Figurine, Choir Boy, kneeling, #211, 5½" 40.00
Figurine, Cockatoo, #5401, 15" 300.00
Figurine, Cocker Spaniel, blk, 8"..295.00
Figurine, Colt, #4806, 11" 200.00
Figurine, Dickey Bird, Mr & Mrs, #4905a/#4905b, ea 90.00
Figurine, Dog Show Boxer, #5025, 5x5"....................................500.00
Figurine, Dog Show Yorkie, #4851 ....275.00
Figurine, Godey couple, pk w/bl accents, 9¾", 9½", pr.................. 50.00
Figurine, Grumpy, pig, #165, 6x7½" 100.00
Figurine, Guppy, fish, #173, 2½".. 75.00
Figurine, Hannibal, angry cat, #180, 10½".................................295.00
Figurine, Happy Monkey, #4903, 11"..450.00
Figurine, Jezebel, cat, 6x7".. 80.00
Figurine, Kneeling Madonna, #4900, 6".................................... 25.00

Figurine, Littlest Angel, #4803, 2½" 65.00
Figurine, Mermaid, #161, 6½" 200.00
Figurine, Peasant Boy & Girl, #113, #117, 6¾", pr 50.00

Figurine, Pekingese, #154, 13", $200.00. (Photo courtesy Mark Lawson Antiques, Inc. on LiveAuctioneers.com)

Figurine, Perky, poodle, #5419, 16" 2,500.00
Figurine, Sassy, pig looking up, #166, 3¾x4" 50.00
Figurine, Scandi boy & girl, #126/#127, 5¼", pr 50.00
Moon bottle, #5502, 13" 50.00
Plaque, Baby Fish, 2¼x3" 45.00
Plate, Santa face, 6½" 40.00
Tea tile, Yorkshire Terrier emb, 5½" sq.................................... 50.00
Tureen, Turkey, platinum/gray, #5361, 9", w/ladle 150.00
Vase, Elephant, #B5155, 6" 60.00
Wall pocket, Girl & Boy, #5501, 10", ea.................................. 150.00

Findlay Onyx and Floradine Glass

Findlay, Ohio, was the location of the Dalzell, Gilmore, and Leighton Glass Company, one of at least 16 companies that flourished there between 1886 and 1901. Their most famous ware, Onyx, is very rare. It was produced for only a short time beginning in 1889 due to the heavy losses incurred in the manufacturing process.

Onyx is layered glass, usually found in creamy white with a dainty floral pattern accented with metallic lustre that has been trapped between the two layers. Other colors found on rare occasions include a light amber (with either no lustre or with gilt flowers), light amethyst (or lavender), and rose. Although old tradepaper articles indicate the company originally intended to produce the line in three distinct colors, long-time Onyx collectors report that aside from the white, production was very limited. Other colors of Onyx are very rare, and few examples are found. Even three-layered items have been found (they are extremely rare) decorated with three-color flowers. As a rule of thumb, using white Onyx prices as a basis for evaluation, expect to pay five or more times more for colored examples.

Floradine is a separate line that was made with the Onyx molds. A single-layer rose satin glassware with white opal flowers, it is usually valued at twice the price of colored Onyx.

Chipping around the rims is very common, and price is determined to a great extent by condition. Unless noted otherwise, our prices are for examples in near-mint condition.

Floradine

Butter, ruby w/wht, 8" 3,800.00
Creamer, ruby w/wht satin, 4½".. 900.00
Creamer, translucent ruby w/wht, 4½" 900.00
Sugar shaker, ruby w/wht, 5½".......................................15,000.00

Onyx

Butter, wht opal w/silver, 8" 700.00
Creamer, wht opal w/silver, 4½" 270.00
Salt shaker, bbl form, wht opal w/amber & lt cranberry, 3" 5,100.00
Salt shaker, wht opal w/silver, 3" 375.00

Sugar, $375.00. (Photo courtesy Museum of American Glass in West Virginia)

Syrup, metal lid, wht opal w/silver, 7½" 450.00
Tumbler, bbl form, wht opal w/amber & lt cranberry, 3½".........3,100.00
Tumbler, wht opal w/silver, 3½"....................................... 800.00
Water set, pitcher w/6 tumblers, wht opal w/silver 2,000.00

Firefighting Collectibles

Firefighting collectibles have always been a good investment in terms of value appreciation. Many times the market will be temporarily affected by wild price swings caused by the 'supply and demand principle' as related to a small group of aggressive collectors. These collectors will occasionally pay well over market value for a particular item they need or want. Once their desires are satisfied, prices seem to return to their normal range. It has been noticed that during these periods of high prices, many items enter the marketplace that otherwise would remain in collections. This may (it has in the past) cause a price depression (due again to the 'supply and demand principle' of market behavior).

The recent phenomena of internet buying and selling of firefighting collectibles and antiques has caused wild swings in prices for some fire collectibles. The cause of this is the ability to reach into vast international markets. It appears that this has resulted in a significant escalation in prices paid for select items. The bottom-line items still languish price wise but at least continue to change hands. This marketplace continues to be active, and many outstanding items have appeared recently in the fire antiques and collectibles field. But when all is said and done, the careful purchase of quality, well-documented firefighting items will continue to be an enjoyable hobby and an excellent investment opportunity.

The earliest American fire marks date back to 1752 when 'The Philadelphia Contributionship for the Insurance of Houses From Loss By Fire' (the official name of this company, who is still in business) used a plaque to identify property they insured. Early fire marks were made of cast iron, sheet brass, lead, copper, tin, and zinc. The insignia of the insurance company appeared on each mark, and they would normally reward the volunteer fire department who managed to be the first on the scene to battle the fire. First used in Great Britain about 1780, English examples were more elaborate than U.S. marks, and usually were made of lead. Most copper and brass fire marks are of European origin. By the latter half of the nineteenth century, they became nearly obsolete, though some companies continued to issue them for advertising purposes. Many of these old fire marks are being reproduced today in cast iron and aluminum.

Fire grenades preceded the pressurized metal fire extinguishers used today. They were filled with a mixture of chemicals and water and made of glass thin enough to shatter easily when thrown into the flames. Many varieties of colors and shapes were used. Not all grenades contain salt-brine solution, some, such as the Red Comet, contain carbon tetrachloride, a powerful solvent that is also a health hazard and an environmental threat. (It attacks the ozone layer.) It is best to leave any contents inside the glass balls. The source of grenade prices are mainly auction results; current retail values will fluctuate.

Today there is a large, active group of collectors for fire department antiques (items over 100 years old) and an even larger group seeking related collectibles (those less than 100 years old). Our advisors for this category are H. Thomas and Patricia Laun; they are listed in the Directory under New York. They will be glad to return your phone call as soon as possible. In the following listings, values are for items in excellent to near-mint condition unless otherwise noted.

Grenade, Harden, embossed ribs, star in circle, deep turquoise blue, with contents and wire hanger, 7", $150.00. (Photo courtesy Rich Penn Auctions on LiveAuctioneers.com)

Alarm box, Gamewell, 1930s, CI 235.00
Alarm box, Garl Electric Co, orig weight/mechanism/code wheel, 1900s. 450.00
Axe, Plum, 6-lb, 35" w/12" head 45.00
Axe, Viking style, early, VG 275.00
Bed key 150.00
Bell, apparatus, brass, w/bracket & finial, 10" 650.00
Bell, apparatus, Seagrave Pendant style bracket 975.00
Bell, captain's tapper, electromechanical, brass acorn 450.00
Bell, jumper, brass, 7" dia 235.00
Bell, muffin, brass, trn wood w/whalebone separator, 3½" ... 300.00
Bell, NP, w/clapper, on wrought-iron bracket, 11" 475.00
Bell, rocking cradle type, nickel, 10" dia 1,250.00
Book, Am La France Operator's Manual, orig, 1920s 150.00
Boots, Am La France, red logo on blk rubber, pull hoops ... 135.00
Bracket, Dietz King lantern, nickel & brass 135.00
Buckeye Roto Ray, complete & working 1,000.00
Can, Minimax Refill, tin, graphics on front, G 40.00
Cap, dress, gold braid, gold-tone FD buttons 15.00
Catalog, 148 pgs of equipment, Silsby Mfg Co, orig, 1888, VG ... 245.00
Extinguisher, Am La France, apparatus, polished brass, 2½-gal.... 475.00
Extinguisher, Badger, soda & acid, copper & brass, 2½-gal ... 45.00
Extinguisher, brass/copper, child's apparatus type 245.00
Extinguisher, copper, soda & acid, child's, 2½-gal 45.00
Extinguisher, Elkhart emb label, copper & brass, 2½-gal 100.00
Extinguisher, Fire Dust, tin tube, dry powder, 3x13¼", G 45.00
Extinguisher, Gorham, soda & acid, copper & brass, 2½-gal .. 40.00
Extinguisher, Presto, in bucket 15.00
Extinguisher, Pyrene, CCL4, pump type 15.00
Extinguisher, Rough Rider, Am La France, apparatus type ... 255.00
Extinguisher, Security, pony sz 85.00
Extinguisher, stainless steel, soda & acid, 2½-gal 10.00
Extinguisher, various manufacturers, copper & brass, 2½", VG ... 30.00
Fire alarm key, brass, Gamewell, winding key, VG 65.00
Fire alarm key, w/chain & shaped brass fob eng Boston..., 5" ... 1,060.00
Fire box, Gamewell, Henculite, Quick Door, Pat 1924 .... 110.00
Fire box, Gamewell, slant fist, CI 365.00
Fire box, Gamewell, type 5 .... 120.00
Gauge, sprinkler, Am Fire Extinguisher, NP brass, 6" 30.00
Gong, Gamewell, ball top, oak case, 18" 5,300.00
Gong, Gamewell, ball top, wood case, 12" 3,750.00
Gong, Gamewell, ball top, wood case, 15" 5,000.00
Gong, Gamewell, feather top, mahog, walnut, or oak case, 8½".. 2,500.00
Gong, Gamewell, feather top, mahog, walnut, or oak case, 10" . 3,200.00
Gong, Gamewell, feather top, mahog, walnut, or oak case, 12" . 3,750.00
Gong, Gamewell, feather top, mahog, walnut, or oak case, 18" . 5,900.00
Gong, Gamewell, flat top, oak case, 8½" 2,350.00
Gong, Gamewell, indicator, fancy cherry case, 15" 16,500.00
Gong, Gamewell, indicator, oak, 15" 10,500.00
Gong, house, Gamewell, 6" bell, Excelsior oak case 1,050.00
Gong, Moses Crane, feather top, 8½" 2,750.00
Gong, Star Electric, fancy oak case, 12" 3,450.00

Gong, Star Electric, oak case, 8" 1,850.00
Gong, Star Electric, oak case, 15" 4,200.00
Gong, turtle, Louis Bills, brass, CI base, 6" 100.00
Helmet, alum, high eagle, leather frontispc 275.00
Helmet, alum, high eagle, Olson, VG 220.00
Helmet, blk leather, high eagle, Cairns, ventilated, VG 365.00
Helmet, brass w/brass front: fire ball/castle, New South Wales, VG ... 125.00
Helmet, leather, 64 comb, high eagle, VG 825.00
Helmet, leather, blk high eagle, VG 600.00
Helmet, leather, Gratacap, VG 1,100.00
Helmet, leather, high eagle, frontispiece: Chief 450.00
Helmet, leather, high eagle, Phoenix Hose 5 HFD 825.00
Helmet, leather, high front, lion holder, VG 1,045.00
Helmet, salesman's sample, red frontispiece, Cairns, mini, leather. 250.00
Hose, riveted leather section, VG 70.00
Hydrant, Chapman Valve Mfg Boston, pnt CI, ca 1888-90, 33½". 95.00
Indicator, Gamewell, cherry case, w/vibrating 8" bell 5,200.00
Ladder, Am La France, wooden, folding attic type 350.00
Lantern, Dewey Mill, blk pnt 75.00
Lantern, Dietz, tubular 285.00
Lantern, Dietz King, Seagrave 500.00
Lantern, Dietz King, Wht 1,100.00
Lantern, Dietz Mill, removable shield 185.00
Lantern, Eclipse, complete w/mfg's bracket 1,350.00
Lantern, steam gauge, brass (like Queen) 935.00
Nozzle holder, metal, lg 65.00
Nozzle, brass w/bl wrap, Am La France, 1⅛" str bore tip, 30" ... 120.00
Nozzle, combination, Rockwood, alum, 1½" 35.00
Nozzle, fog, brass, shutoff, Akron, 9½" 35.00
Nozzle, leather-wrap hdls, Callahan tip, 1920s, pr 165.00
Pipe, cord covered, 2-hdl play pipe, Powhattan, Underwriter's, 15" ... 70.00
Pole, pike, trn hdl, 46½", VG 40.00
Register, Gamewell, brass, #1174, ½", batwing winding key, 1902, 9"... 235.00
Sector box, Gamewell #4, w/mechanism, CI case w/slant fist motif, 14" . 375.00
Siren, Fed, #Q2B 650.00
Siren, Fed, military, hand crank, Fed 175.00
Siren, Sterling Siren Fire Alarm Co #12, 6-volt, 1920s-30s ... 135.00
Siren, sterling, #20 .... 210.00
Siren, sterling, #30 .... 375.00
Siren, sterling, #H, hand crank, VG 700.00
Torch, parade, nickel/brass, 3" 45.00
Transmitter, Gamewell, w/50 brass code wheels, oak case ... 4,250.00
Trumpet, emb florals/H-eagle helmet/etc, 19th C, 18" 1,050.00
Trumpet, SP w/eng floral/hose nozzle/etc/presentation, 20" ... 900.00
Uniform overcoat, wool w/nickel buttons, 1960s 28.00

Fireglow

Fireglow is a type of art glass that first appears to be an opaque cafe au lait, but glows with rich red 'fire' when held to a strong source of light. It was made by Boston & Sandwich Glass Company and other companies in both the U.S. and Europe. Pieces usually have a satin (matt) finish and multicolored, intricate designs.

Vase, birds and flowers, attributed to Sandwich, 10¾", $125.00. (Photo courtesy Dirk Soulis Auctions on LiveAuctioneers.com)

Bottle, floral panels, atomizer, 6" 72.50
Pitcher, morning glories & butterflies, Sandwich, 7", $75 to.......... 95.00
Vase, autumn flowers, trumpet form, 18"......................... 315.00
Vase, courting scene & flowers, cylindrical neck, 12" 145.00
Vase, flowers & leaves, stick neck, ca 1890, 12", pr 315.00
Vase, thistles, autumn colors, shouldered, ftd, 13½" 150.00

Fireplace Implements

In the colonial days of our country, fireplaces provided heat in the winter and were used year round to cook food in the kitchen. The implements that were a necessary part of these functions were varied and have become treasured collectibles, many put to new use in modern homes as decorative accessories. Gypsy pots may hold magazines; copper and brass kettles, newly polished and gleaming, contain dried flowers or green plants. Firebacks, highly ornamental iron panels that once reflected heat and protected masonry walls, are now sometimes used as wall decorations. By Victorian times the cook stove had replaced the kitchen fireplace, and many of these early utensils were already obsolete; but as a source of heat and comfort, the fireplace continued to be used for several more decades. See also Wrought Iron.

Andirons, brass & CI w/eng, urn finial, Philadelphia, 1780s, 27" ... 2,400.00
Andirons, bronzed finish on CI, dragon detail, 19x27x12"........... 600.00
Andirons, CI, Gothic, att Savery & Co, 1850s, 17" 2,000.00

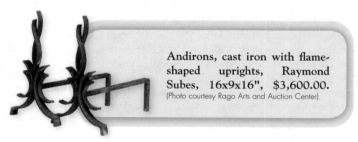

Andirons, cast iron with flame-shaped uprights, Raymond Subes, 16x9x16", $3,600.00. (Photo courtesy Rago Arts and Auction Center)

Andirons, iron, pheasant figural, EX patina, 20x24x22"............... 850.00
Bellows, floral HP on wood, brass tacks, EX leather, rprs, 21" 175.00
Bellows, turtle-bk, pnt pear/apples on mustard yel, new leather, 17"..300.00
Coal basket, CI, Gothic Revival style 48.00
Fender, brass rail over vertical wirework & wire swags, 1800s, 24x39" . 2,700.00
Fender, brass rail, vertical wires w/swag border, 19th C, 10x35x11" ...475.00
Fender, brass rails held by balusters, wirework, ball ft, 18x34x12" .1,000.00
Fender, pierced brass U shape w/scrolling ivy, 19th C, 46" L........ 450.00
Fender, urn-form finials, brass rail over wires/wire scrolls, 21x59"... 2,800.00
Firescreen, maple pole w/needlework shield in fr, rfn, 53" 200.00
Mantle, Eastlake style w/mirror bk, fire box: 42x36", VG............. 965.00
Scoop, pnt wood & metal, primitive...................................... 72.50
Screen, brass segmented fan shape, opens to 38" 60.00
Screen, dk wood w/neoclassical tapestry panel 360.00
Screen, folding brass fan shape, 33".................................... 145.00
Scuttle, brass helmet form 48.00
Scuttle, copper, ftd scoop form 240.00
Scuttle, floral pnt on metal, slant lid, ftd 240.00
Surround, hammered copper w/repoussé hood, 41x43" 2,100.00
Surround, wht marble, Louis XVI style w/ormolu bronze mts 900.00
Tongs, ember, wrought iron, spring loaded, curlique hdl, 16" 375.00

Fischer

Ignaz and Emil Fischer were art pottery designers and producers from Hungary. Ignaz Fischer founded a workshop in Budapest, Hungary, in 1866.

He had previously worked for M.F. Fisher, owner of the famous Herend factory, also in Hungary. His first products included domestic items that utilized a cream-colored clay; styles were copied from the Herend factory. His ware is recognized by the pale yellow, soft-lead glaze, usually decorated with painted ethnic Hungarian designs.

Emil Fischer took the business over from his father around 1890. The workshop was closed in 1908 and reopened for only a short time. Production from this period was influenced by the high-style designs of the Zsolnay factory in Pecs, Hungary. Unable to compete, they turned to the manufacture of building materials. Marks (incised and painted): Fisher J. Budapest; initials: F.E. under a crown.

Bowl, gold decoration and reticulated overlay, marked Fischer J. Budapest, 6x10", $150.00. (Photo courtesy Burchard Galleries Inc. on LiveAuctioneers.com)

Bowl, bird figural, floral & gold, heavy rctl, ftd, 1867, 11½x13"...390.00
Bowl, scrolling rim w/animal at side, satyr w/dolphins as ft, 20" ..500.00
Charger, floral & intricate rtcl overall, scalloped, 14" 265.00
Compote, mc w/gold, navette form in rococo taste, 13x16½" 450.00
Ewer, man in the moon masks & stars, gold on ivory, mk Fisher J. Budapest, 15".600.00
Ewer, rtc florals & guilloche, baluster, serpentine spout, 1900s, 20" ...650.00
Ewer, rtcl body w/shaped floral reserves, 3-D dragon hdl, rstr, 18". 450.00
Jug, geometric circles, gold/bl/wht, 9" 170.00
Vase, moon, floral, ftd, 1900, 8½"...................................... 360.00

Harrison Fisher

Harrison Fisher (1875 – 1934), noted illustrator and creator of the Fisher Girl, was the son of landscape artist, Hugh Antoine Fisher. His career began in his teens in San Francisco where he did artwork for the Hearst papers. Later in New York his drawings of beautiful American women attracted much attention and graced the covers of the most popular magazines of the day such as *Puck, Ladies' Home Journal, Saturday Evening Post,* and *Cosmopolitan.* He also illustrated novels, and his art books are treasured. His drawings appeared on thousands of postcards and posters. His creation of the Fisher Girl and his panel of six scenes of the *Greatest Moments in a Woman's Life* made him the most sought-after and well-paid illustrator of his day. Unless otherwise noted, our values are for items in excellent to near-mint condition.

Book, Hiawatha, 16 color plates, hardcover, Bobbs-Merrill, 1906, VG .. 70.00
Book, Love Finds the Way, blk/wht prints, Dodd-Meade, 1904, 6x9", VG..60.00
Postcard, A Love Score, tennis couple, Reinthal Newman #839 ... 35.00
Postcard, An Old Song, lady singing, Reinthal Newman, 1909, VG...20.00
Postcard, Dumb Luck, lady w/horse, Reinthal Newman, unused ... 45.00
Postcard, Her Future, lady & crystal ball............................ 35.00
Postcard, The Rose, Reinthal & Newman, #181, VG 22.50
Postcard, The Rose, Russian publisher 240.00
Print, Am Girl in Ireland, Scribners, 1908, 17x12" 70.00
Print, Best Gift, lady w/ring, 1909, oval in 17x11" gesso fr........... 125.00
Print, blond in feathered hat, Curtis, 1911, 11¾x8" 85.00
Print, bookplate, lot of 4, 8x11½" 35.00
Print, Honeymoon, c Scribner's, 16x12", orig gold pinstripe mat & fr. 110.00
Print, lady in lilac gown, Gray Litho, 1903, 16x13", VG 125.00
Print, lady w/3 dogs, Crowell, sgn, 1911, 11¾x8", VG+................ 75.00
Print, Luxury, lady in bed w/book, Scribners, 1912, 17x12", VG+. 75.00
Print, Minnehaha or Laughing Water, from 1908 book, 10½x9", VG...38.00

Print, Navy, published by Donn-Mead & Co., matted, 1909, 15x21" (unframed), $120.00.
(Photo courtesy O'Gallerie on LiveAuctioneers.com)

Print, The Kiss, romantic couple, Scribners, 1910, 17x12" 225.00
Print, The Proposal, couple, Scribners, 16x12", +mat & fr 125.00
Print, Waiting, lady w/tennis racket, Scribners, sgn/1911, 12x17" ..225.00
Print, You Will Marry...Man, sight: 20x16"+mat, glass & fr 120.00

Fishing Collectibles

Collecting old fishing tackle is becoming more popular every year. Though at first most interest was geared toward old lures and some reels, rods, advertising, and miscellaneous items are quickly gaining ground. Values are given for examples in excellent or better condition and should be used only as a guide. For more information we recommend *The Fred Arbogast Story* by Scott Heston; *The Pflueger Heritage* by Wayne Ruby; *Spring-loaded Fish Hooks, Traps & Lures* by William Blauser and Timothy Mierzwa; *Fishing Lure Collectibles, An Encyclopedia of the Early Years, 1840 to 1940*, by Dudley Murphy and Rick Edmisten; *Fishing Lure Collectibles, An Encyclopedia of the Modern Era, 1940 to Present*, by Dudley Murphy and Deanie Murphy; *Captain John's Fishing Tackle Price Guide* by John Kolbeck; and *Modern Fishing Lure Collectibles, Vols. 1 – 5*, by Russell E. Lewis. These books are all published by Collector Books. Our advisor for this category is Dave Hoover; he is listed in the Directory under Indiana. Unless otherwise noted, our values are for items in excellent to near-mint condition.

Catalog, Allcocks Fishing Tackle, 1932, hardcover, 163 pgs 130.00
Catalog, Bristol Fishing Rods, Reels & Lines, ca 1914, 28 pgs 50.00
Catalog, Bronson-Made JA Cox.../Bronson Fishing Reels, 1952 .... 75.00
Catalog, Fox Reels for Finer Fishing, 1930s, 8 pgs, VG 165.00
Creel, Meier & Frank, tightly woven wicker w/leather 100.00
Creel, split willow, single ribs, leather 167.50
Decoy, cvd, gold foil on wood fish w/5 metal fins, pnt eyes, 6⅜" 90.00
Decoy, cvd/pnt fish w/6 metal fins, tack eyes, HL Way, 1950s, $50 to .. 75.00
Decoy, cvd/pnt wood fish w/cvd gills, tin fins, tack eyes, 12 .... 250.00
Decoy, cvd/pnt wood fish, wooden dorsal fin/2 tin side fins, 12" .. 175.00
Decoy, Paw Paw, cvd/pnt wood fish, 3 wooden fins, 1930s, 7½", MIB .. 150.00
Hook, Lathrop #426027, brass & japanned steel, 1890, 6" closed. 750.00
Hook, lever, Greer #641857, blued steel, 1900-08, 3½" 70.00
Hook, Mack Automatic #9, brass spinner blade, ca 1890, 5" 80.00
Hook, Red's Sure-Catch #2213624, brass/lead/steel, 1940, 4", $15 to.... 20.00
Hook, trolling spoon, Harlow #378678, brass, 1888, 3", min 150.00
Lure, Creek Chub, Baby Injured Minnow #1600, 2", $30 to 50.00
Lure, Creek Chub, Fin Tail Shiner #2100, 1924, 4", $100 to 250.00
Lure, Creek Chub, Injured Minnow #1500, 3", $30 to 50.00
Lure, Creek Chub, Pollywiggle #100, 1 single hook, 1924, 1¾", $100 to. 150.00
Lure, Creek Chub, Super Lg Pikie Minnow, 1940s, 17¼" 650.00
Lure, Creek Chub, Wigl-Y-Rind #S10, 1929, 4⅛", $75 to 150.00
Lure, Heddon, Baby Blk Sucker #1300, 2 trebles, 1925, 4⅛", $2,500 to .5,000.00
Lure, Heddon, Bucktail Surface Minnow #400, 2 trebles, 1908, 2½", $250 to..500.00
Lure, Heddon, Deep Diving Wiggler #1600, 3 trebles, 1915, 4¾", $100 to..200.00
Lure, Heddon, Dowagiac Minnow #20, 3 trebles, 1909, 2¼", $100 to..200.00
Lure, Heddon, Flaptail Musky #7050, 2 trebles, 1935, 5¼", $100 to ..200.00

Lure, Heddon, Muskollonge/Salt Water Minnow #700, 1911, 5" .750.00
Lure, Heddon, Salt-Water Special/Wee Willie, 2 trebles, 1925, 2¼", $100 to...125.00
Lure, Jamison, Nemo Bass Bait, 1 dbl & 1 single belly hook, 1910, 2⅜", $150 to.250.00
Lure, Jamison, Smacker, 1 dressed single hook, 1934, 6", $25 to.... 40.00
Lure, Jamison, Underwater Coaxer, 1 single hook, 1906, 2¾", $50 to ...75.00
Lure, Keeling, Flat Musky Expert, 3 trebles, 1925, 5", $300 to..... 500.00
Lure, Keeling, Floating Bait, 2 trebles, 1920, 3½", $70 to 80.00
Lure, Moonlight, Crawfish, 1 dbl hook, 1929, 2¾", $75 to........... 125.00
Lure, Moonlight, Ladybug Wiggler, 2 trebles, 1916, 4", $250 to ..350.00
Lure, Moonlight, Silvercreek Fly Eat-Us, 1 single hook, 1922, 2½", $50 to .60.00
Lure, Moonlight, Weighted Bucktail Bait, 1 dbl hook, 1930, 1¼", $75 to. 100.00
Lure, Paw Paw, McGinty, 1 treble hook, 1930, 2", $25 to 40.00
Lure, Paw Paw, Musky Deer Hair Mouse, 1 treble, 1935, 4¾", $150 to ..200.00
Lure, Paw Paw, Natural Hair Mouse, 1 treble, 1930, 2½", $75 to. 100.00
Lure, Paw Paw, Plunker, 2 trebles, 1940, 2¾", $15 to 30.00
Lure, Paw Paw, Sucker Minnow, 3 trebles, 1937, 4¼", $50 to 75.00
Lure, Pflueger, Bearcat #6400, 2 trebles, 1924, 4½", $150 to 250.00
Lure, Pflueger, Catalina Minnow, 1 single hook, 1915, 4", $250 to..300.00
Lure, Pflueger, Floating Monarch Minnow, 2 trebles, 1913, 2¾", $125 to.175.00
Lure, Pflueger, Flocked Mouse, 2 trebles, 1950, 2¾", $150 to....... 300.00

Lure, Pflueger, Maybug Spoon, one treble, circa 1895, 1¾", $600.00 to $800.00. (Photo courtesy Dudley Murphy and Rick Edmisten)

Lure, Pflueger, TNT #6900, 2 trebles, 1930, 3½", $50 to................ 75.00
Lure, Shakespeare, Bass Kazoo #590, 3 trebles, 1924, 4", $50 to 75.00
Lure, Shakespeare, Frog Skin Bait #6505, 2 trebles, 1930, 3¾", $75 to...150.00
Lure, Shakespeare, Metal Plated Minnow #33, 3 trebles, 1915, 3", $200 to..500.00
Lure, Shakespeare, Submerged Wooden Minnow #43, 1909, 3¾".175.00
Lure, South Bend, Gulf-Oreno #983, 2 trebles, 1926, 3½", $75 to..100.00
Lure, South Bend, Midget Surf-Oreno #962, 2 trebles, 1919, 2¾", $30 to ...65.00
Lure, South Bend, Muskie Surf-Oreno #964, 3 trebles, 1925, 5½", $100 to..150.00
Reel, BF Meek & Sons, #3, 1890-1916, w/leather case 700.00
Reel, fly, Shakespeare Model 1837 Tru-Art, Model GD, 1947, min..25.00
Reel, fly, St George, Hardy Bros, ribbed reel arms, 29/16" 515.00
Reel, fly, St John, Hardy Bros, 1965, w/padded case, NM............. 310.00
Reel, Pflueger, Adams #2160, star drag, 1929, $750 to 850.00
Reel, Pflueger, Redifor #1433J, satin nickel silver, pyralin hdl, 1915, $140 to..160.00
Reel, Pflueger, Supreme #1573, NP, 1920-23, $325 to.................. 400.00
Reel, South Bend Model No 50, 1960s, $35 to............................. 50.00
Rod, casting, Fenwick Feralite FC 61, 3-pc, 6' 300.00
Rod, fly, Heddon Bluewater #10, bamboo, 5-pc, w/bag................. 200.00
Rod, fly, Wright & McGill Granger Special, bamboo, 4-pc, w/case 710.00
Trap, wood slats & woven strings, 6-sided, 1940s, 3x5x5" 38.00

Florence Ceramics

Florence Ceramics was best known for producing some of America's finest semi-porcelain figurines in the '40s and '50s in Pasadena, California. 'The Florence Collection' consisted of detailed reproductions of historical couples and fictional characters in period costumes and Godey fashions of the late nineteenth century. The quality of the ware and the attention given to detail has prompted a growing interest among today's collectors. The names of these lovely ladies, gents, and figural groups are nearly always incised into their bases. The company name is ink stamped. Examples are evaluated by size, rarity, and intricacy of design.

Other Florence items included figurine-vases, small-scale children, wall pockets, candleholders, wall plaques, picture frames, smoking sets, busts, and a large assortment of birds. In 1956, a separate line of bisque-finished animal figurines was produced by Betty Davenport Ford, for just two years. For more information we recommend *Collector's Encyclopedia of California Pottery* by Jack Chipman; *The Florence Collectibles* by Doug Foland; and *The Complete Book of Florence Ceramics: A Labor of Love*, by Sue and Jerry Kline and Margaret Wehrspaun. Our advisor for this category is Jerry Kline; he is listed in the Directory under Tennessee.

Artware

Bonbon, dbl, $100 to	120.00
Clock, Dresden, $475 to	500.00
Picture fr, Dresden, 5x7", $75 to	100.00
Slipper, $75 to	100.00
Vase, bud, $60 to	70.00

Birds and Animals

Blue bird group, $450 to	500.00
Cardinal, $350 to	400.00
Cockatoo, #W24, 13¼", $500 to	550.00
Dog, bank, Ford, dbl, $115 to	130.00
Dog, bank, Ford, single, $75 to	90.00
Dove, scarce, Ford, 6x9", $300 to	400.00
Gazelle, $500 to	550.00
Quail, $450 to	500.00

Figurines

Adeline, fancy, 8¼", $225 to	250.00
Ballet, $500 to	550.00
Barbara, adult, $575 to	625.00
Barbara, child, 8½", $115 to	130.00
Boy bust, 9¾", $150 to	200.00
Bryan, $2,750 to	3,000.00
Choir Boy, 6", $55 to	70.00
Cindy, 8", $325 to	375.00
Delores, $175 to	200.00
Dot and Bud, ea $1,250 to	1,400.00

Douglas, 8", $100.00 to $120.00.

Edith, $120 to	140.00
Fall Reverie, very rare, $2,000 to	2,500.00
Gibson Girls, various, $700 to	900.00
Girl bust, 9½", $150 to	200.00
Haru, $325 to	375.00
Hector, child, $110 to	130.00
Jay, $125 to	150.00
Jennifer, 7¾", $350 to	400.00
John Alden, 9", $140 to	175.00
Juliet, $500 to	575.00
Karlo, $625 to	700.00

Lady Diana, 10", $1,000 to	1,250.00
Larry, $875 to	950.00
Lillian Russell, 13", $2,200 to	2,500.00
Love Letter, $2,200 to	2,500.00
Mark Anthony, $1,250 to	1,500.00
Mary, seated, 7½", $500 to	600.00
Maybelle, very rare, $2,750 to	3,000.00
Princess, $800 to	875.00
Rebecca, 7", $160 to	180.00
Renee, flower holder, $100 to	120.00
Susie, child, $125 to	150.00
Taka, $625 to	700.00
Toy, $225 to	275.00
Victor, $175 to	200.00
Vivian, 10", $225 to	275.00

Flow Blue

Flow Blue ware was produced by many Staffordshire potters; among the most familiar were Meigh, Podmore and Walker, Samuel Alcock, Ridgway, John Wedge Wood (who often signed his work Wedgwood), and Davenport. It was popular from about 1825 through 1860 and again from 1880 until the turn of the century. The name describes the blurred or flowing effect of the cobalt decoration, achieved through the introduction of a chemical vapor into the kiln. The body of the ware is ironstone, and Oriental motifs were favored. Later issues were on a lighter body and often decorated with gilt. For further information we recommend *Gaston's Flow Blue China, The Comprehensive Guide*, by our advisor, Mary Frank Gaston (Collector Books).

Abbey, plate, Geo Jones, 10"	45.00
Abbey, plate, Maastricht, 9"	55.00
Alaska, bowl, serving, Grindley, 1891-1914, 9¾"	200.00
Alaska, toothbrush holder, gold accents, C&H Tunstall, 5¾"	75.00
Albany, bowl, vegetable, scalloped ft, hdls, Johnson Bros, 7x11½"	135.00
Albany, plate, Johnson Bros, ca 1900, 10"	100.00
Albany, platter, emb beaded scalloped rim, hdls, Johnson Bros, 12" L	185.00
Albany, shaving mug, Grindley, 3⅝x3¼"	160.00
Alexis, plate, soup, Adderleys, 8½"	35.00
Alton, plate, Grimwades Staffordshire Pottery, ca 1930, 10"	60.00
Anemone, butter pat, gold accents, 3"	60.00
Arabia, platter, 11x8"	40.00
Asiatic Pheasants, plate, T Hughes, 9"	55.00
Baltic, plate, beaded scalloped rim, Grindley, 9"	45.00
Bamboo, platter, Bates & Walker, ca 1876, 18½x14¾"	335.00
Belmont, platter, emb scalloped rim, JHW & Sons, ca 1892, 14x10"	160.00
Bermuda, bowl, William A Adderley Co, ca 1890, 16"	300.00
Blue Willow, plate, scalloped rim, Deans Ltd, ca 1910-19, 7"	50.00

Brush Stroke, coffeepot, 12½", $510.00. [Photo courtesy Jackson's Auction on LiveAuctioneers.com]

Cambridge, bowl, dessert, scalloped rim, England, ca 1890, 5"	85.00
Cattle Scenery, gravy boat, scalloped ft, beaded rim, Adams, ca 1870	40.00

Chatsworth, platter, gold rim, Keeling & Co, 1886-90, 16x12½" . 185.00
Circassia, bowl, ped ft, w/lid, J&G Alcock, ca 1839 .... 1,000.00
Clarence, platter, England, ca 1900, 16x12" 435.00
Columbia, sugar bowl, w/lid, Clementson & Young, ca 1845-47 . 900.00
Conway, platter, New Wharf, ca 1890, 10½" L 75.00
Coral, butter pat, unevenly scalloped rim, Johnson Bros, ca 1900, 3" .. 65.00
Cows, plate, Wedgwood, ca 1906, 10" 150.00
Cyprus, plate, Ridgway Bates & Co, ca 1857, 9½" 100.00
Davenport, bowl, 8-sided, ftd, w/lid & hdls, Amoy, 9" 455.00
Delamere, platter, scalloped rim w/gold, H Alcock, ca 1900, 14½" L.. 460.00
Delph, platter, Blair & Co, 1912-23, 12x9½" 45.00
Douglas, platter, scalloped rim, Ford & Sons, 9x12" L 160.00
Eastern Plants, platter, Wood & Brownsfield, ca 1838-50, 19" L... 1,100.00
English Scenery, platter, scalloped rim, Wood & Sons, ca 1917, 12" L... 140.00
Excelsior, teapot, Thomas Fell 1,100.00
Fairy Villa, bowl, soup, W Adams & Co, 9" 50.00
Flora, cracker jar, gold accents, Cumberlidge..., ca 1890, 6¾x5" .. 210.00
Floral & Scroll, platter, Doulton, 1891-1902, 14" L 140.00
Floral, platter, unevenly scalloped rim, ca 1900, 15½x11½" 120.00
Florida, butter pat, beaded rim, Grindley, 3⅛" 85.00
Gainsborough, cheese dish, w/lid, Ridgways 550.00
Glenwood, plate, soup, emb rim, Johnson Bros, 10" 70.00
Glorie De Dijon, footbath, scalloped rim 2,230.00
Grace, butter pat, emb scalloped rim w/gold, Grindley, 3½" 40.00
Grecian Statue, berry strainer, Brownfields Pottery, ca 1891-1900... 250.00
Grecian, platter, thin gold rim, Ford & Sons, ca 1908, 18¾x13½" ... 160.00
Haarlem, trivet, rnd, Burgess & Leigh, 6¾" 90.00
Holland, c/s, Johnson Bros, 6" saucer, 2x4½" cup 85.00
Holland, plate, Johnson Bros, ca 1895, 10" 85.00
Holland, sugar bowl, scalloped ft, w/lid & hdls 225.00
Indian Plant, bowl, emb rim, Kaolin Ware, ca 1828-59, 10" 70.00
Indiana, plate, Wedgwood, 7½" 40.00
Jacobean, pitcher, tankard form, Ye Old Crown & Sceptre, Doulton, 9" . 900.00
Janette, washbowl & pitcher, Grindley 2,300.00
Jewel, plate, w/gold trim, Adams, 9" 45.00
Keele, platter, gold accents, Grindley, ca 1890-1915, 14" L 400.00
Kensington, bowl, soup, gold accents & rim, Doulton, ca 1880, 10".. 75.00
Kyber, plate, 12-sided, W Adams & Co, 1891-1910, 9" 65.00
Kyber, plate, scalloped rim, W Adams & Co, 9" 85.00
La Belle, biscuit jar 450.00
LaBelle, chocolate pot 900.00
Lakewood, plate, scalloped rim w/gold, Wood & Sons, 9" 75.00
Landscape, plate, Wedgwood, 10½" 70.00
Libertas Prussia, plate, emb scalloped rim, ca 1920, 9" 45.00
Lily & Rose, wall plate, lg scalloped rim w/gold, D-L Co, ca 1950. 60.00
Lorne, bowl, fruit, beaded scalloped rim, Grindley, ca 1900, 5¼"... 50.00
Lorne, plate, scalloped rim, Grindley, ca 1900, 9" 85.00
Lorraine, gravy boat & underplate, Clementson Bros, 1910, 4x8½" .. 140.00
Madras, pitcher, Doulton, 1902, 6x6" 165.00
Madras, plate, soup, Wood & Son, ca 1891-1907 .... 75.00
Mandarin, tureen, sauce, w/lid/tray/ladle, Pultney, 1910, 5x8½x7".. 400.00
Manilla, plate, Podmore Walker & Co, ca 1834-59, 9½" 110.00
Meissen, butter pat, bl rim band, 3½" 30.00
Meissen, cake plate, lipped, ped ft, BWM & Co, ca 1865, 3x10½" .. 135.00
Melrose, bowl, scalloped rim, Doulton, ca 1800, 10½" 70.00
Monarch, platter, emb scalloped rim, Montreal Crockery Co, 1920, 14" L. 250.00
Montrose, washbowl & pitcher, H Alcock, ca 1910 .... 1,500.00
Morning Glory, cake plate, raised hdls, ca 1880, 13" 300.00
Napier, plate, Keeling & Co, ca 1886-1936, 9" 30.00
Newport Rhode Island, plate, souvenir, 9" 75.00
Niagara Falls, plate, souvenir, various scenes, ca 1893-1938, 9" ... 140.00
Ning Po, plate, Ralph Hall, ca 1845, 6" 75.00
Non Pareil, butter pat, Burgess & Leigh, ca 1891, 3" 70.00
Non Pareil, platter, Burgess & Leigh, ca 1891-1919, 12" L 500.00

Norfolk, cake plate, 8-sided, hdls, Doulton, ca 1920, 9" 85.00
Norfolk, creamer, Doulton, ca 1928-32, 2" 55.00
Normandy, plate, ruffled rim, Johnson Bros, ca 1900, 8" 110.00
Normandy, plate, soup, emb scalloped rim w/gold, Johnson Bros, 10".. 115.00
Onion, saucer, Allertons, ca 1900, 5¾" 30.00
Ornithology, plate, Brn Westhead & Moore, ca 1870, 7" 90.00
Oxford, platter, scalloped rim, Johnson Bros, ca 1900, 14" L 400.00
Paris, plate, emb scalloped rim, New Wharf, ca 1891, 9" 85.00
Pekin, plate, AEJ & Co, Staffordshire, 1905-20, 7", VG 30.00
Philadelphia, plate, Independence Hall 1776, scalloped rim, 9" 85.00
Plymouth, tureen, soup, ftd, w/lid, New Wharf Pottery, 1880, 6x11". 120.00
Pompadour, plate, Kneeling & Co, ca 1912, 9½" 45.00
Poppy, casserole, gold trim, hdls, Grindley, 1891-1914, 7x11½" .. 120.00
Portman, plate, beaded scalloped rim, Grindley, ca 1891-1914, 8" ..85.00
Princess, bowl, vegetable; scalloped, w/lid & hdls, Beech, 1877, 9"....160.00
Princeton, plate, Johnson Bros, 7" 80.00
Priscilla, pitcher, J Maddock & Sons, ca 1900, 7" 110.00
Quebec, creamer, Ridgways, 4¼" 75.00
Rex, platter, scalloped rim, Adderley's, ca 1900, 13½" L 75.00
Rose, bowl, Grindley, 1891-1914, 8½" L 50.00
Rural England, plate, Midwinter Ltd, ca 1910, 8" 115.00
Rustic, tureen, vegetable, w/lid & hdls, Grindley, 1860, 10¾" L.. 100.00
Savoy, plate, soup, scalloped rim w/gold, Johnson Bros, ca 1900, 10".. 115.00
Savoy, platter, emb scalloped rim w/gold, Johnson Bros, ca 1900, 16" L. 335.00

Scinde, washbowl and pitcher, J&G Alcock, mint, $2,500.00 to $3,000.00. (Photo courtesy Dennis Auction Service, Inc. on LiveAuctioneers.com)

Shanghai, plate, beaded rim, Grindley, ca 1875, 10" 120.00
Shanghai, plate, soup, Grindley, 1891-1914, 10" 160.00
Temple, plate, Wood & Brownfield, 1845, 7" 140.00
Tonquin, platter, late 1800s, 13½x17" 360.00
Touraine, plate, H Alcock, 1891-1910, 8" 40.00
Trilby, cake plate, Wood & Sons, ca 1891, 10½" 90.00
Triumphal Car, trivet, gold rim, rnd, Warwick Ware, 7½" 65.00
Turin, saucer, Johnson & Bros, 5¾" 30.00
Tyrene, pitcher, England, 5" 150.00
Venice, plate, ca 1908, 9½" 85.00
Venice, tureen, sauce, w/plate, lid & ladle, 1880-90 .... 400.00
Verona, plate, scalloped rim w/gold, Meakin, ca 1900, 7" 85.00
Violette, waste bowl, ftd, Keller & Guerin, ca 1900, 3x6" 110.00
Virginia, butter pat, emb rim, Maddock's, 3" 60.00
Waldorf, platter, 10¾x9" 120.00
Wildrose, creamer, Royal Bonn, ca 1900, 3½" 40.00
Willow, platter, well & tree, crown mk, gold rim, 22" L 800.00

Flue Covers

When spring house cleaning started and the heating stove was taken down for the warm weather season, the unsightly hole where the stovepipe joined the chimney was hidden with an attractive flue cover. They were made with a colorful litho print behind glass with a chain for hanging. In a 1929 catalog, they were advertised at 16¢ each or six for 80¢. Although scarce today, some scenes were actually reverse painted on the glass itself. The most popular motifs were florals, children, animals, and lovely ladies. Occasionally flue covers were made in sets of three — one served a functional purpose, while the others were added to provide a more attractive wall arrangement. They range in size from 7" to 14", but 9" is the average. Our advisor for this category is James Meckley III; he is listed in the Directory under New York.

American Indian, molded composition, good color, 11", $45.00. (Photo courtesy Livingston's Auction on LiveAuctioneers.com)

Apples spilling from basket, beaded metal fr, Germany, 9½" 50.00
Basket of violets, beaded brass fr, Germany, 9¾" 80.00
Boys (2) on fence teasing dogs, w/chain, 9½" 70.00
Boys (2) w/dachshund dogs, 1920s, 6¼" 35.00
Children (1 boy & 1 girl) by water w/angel watching, 11¾" 135.00
Children (1 boy & 1 girl) riding ponies, 1800s, 6" 125.00
Fruit in a basket, MIG, 9½" 60.00
Girl in bright bl dress holding blk cat, gold border, 7¾" 45.00
Girl in floral hat & coat, much finery, blond curls, 8" 125.00
Girl in lg hat holding violets, metal chain, 9" 160.00
Girl in pk standing in egg, Easter Greetings above flowers, 10x7½" .40.00
Girl in winter coat & hat holding 1 glove, late 1800s, 8" 60.00
Girls (2) w/5 rabbits, ornate brass fr & chain, 6" 50.00
Girls (4) holding hands & dancing in meadow, 9½" 260.00
Kittens (3) watching fly on wall, metal beaded rim, Germany, 9¾" ...215.00
Ladies (1 in pk & 1 in gr) holding flower garland H, 1800s, 9½" ... 80.00
Lady fairy w/flowing blk hair w/nest of swallows, metal chain, 8" .. 90.00
Lady gypsy profile portrait, gold pnt border, 1800s, 8" 60.00
Lady w/bare shoulders & flowers in hair, oval, metal fr, Germany, 9". 70.00
Mother & daughter in wht dresses under parasol, 1800s, 9½" 105.00
Naval officer & lady w/ship scene beyond, w/chain, 7⅞" 100.00
Waterfall scene in center, floral/girl panel border, 9½" 60.00

Folk Art

That the creative energies of the mind ever spark innovations in functional utilitarian channels as well as toward playful frivolity is well documented in the study of American folk art. While the average early settler rarely had free time to pursue art for its own sake, his creativity exemplified itself in fashioning useful objects carved or otherwise ornamented beyond the scope of pure practicality. After the advent of the Industrial Revolution, the pace of everyday living became more leisurely, and country folk found they had extra time. Not accustomed to sitting idle, many turned to carving, painting, or weaving. Whirligigs, imaginative toys for the children, and whimsies of all types resulted. Though often rather crude, this type of early art represents a segment of our heritage and as such has become valued by collectors.

Values given for drawings, paintings, and theorems are 'in frame' unless noted otherwise. Our advisor for this category is Matt Lippa.; he is listed in the Directory under Alabama. See also Baskets; Decoys; Frakturs; Samplers; Trade Signs; Weather Vanes; Wood Carvings. ·

Articulated figure, dancing man w/bottle-cap hat, mc pnt, 17", VG... 400.00
Bank, pnt tin house w/stenciling, Chartered Christmas 1871, 5⅝" 2,350.00
Carving, Am Indian chief w/headdress/tomahawk, sandstone, E Reed, 50"..7,000.00

Carving, mermaid w/merbaby, sandstone, E Reed, 16" L........... 3,600.00
Cutwork, Temperance Is Wisdom/eagle/foliage, HP details, 8x12" 9,400.00
Dancing man, cvd wood w/orig pnt, articulated limbs, 8¼" 330.00
Diorama, farmhouse & winter trees, horse-drawn carriage, 12x22x22"..350.00
Diorama, log cabin scene w/outhouse/split log fence/trees, 20x27" 175.00
Drawing, equestrian couple, pen & ink on paper, unsgn, 9x12"+fr ..260.00
Painting on brd, puppies w/pan of milk, 6x12" in gilt 12x18" 925.00
Painting on canvas, cat on chair at window eyes prey, 25x18"..... 700.00
Pen wipe, hen w/chicks, cotton/beads/wood, 1800s, 2¼x5" 385.00
Pen wipe, rabbit form, cotton/wool/bead eyes, on yarn mat, 2x8" dia. 470.00
Spencerian drawing, eagle w/rabbit/eaglets in nest, 14x18"+fr.....575.00
Theorem on brd, flower basket on creamy wht, alligatored 19x24"..... 400.00
Theorem on paper, basket of fruit/flowers, 1800s, 10x14", VG. 350.00
Theorem on paper, fruit & butterfly watercolor, 17x13"+old fr... 435.00
Theorem on paper, fruit basket, in 10x10" pine cone-on-cb fr..... 375.00
Theorem on paper, fruit basket, slight foxing, ca 1825, 14x17"+gilt fr . 1,950.00
Theorem on paper, pcs of fruit, watercolor, in 7x8½" gilt fr 350.00
Theorem on velvet, bowl of fruit, stenciled, EX color, gilt fr, 16x19".550.00
Theorem on velvet, flower urn, watercolor, stains, in grpt 17x13" 375.00
Theorem on velvet, fruit nested in vines, mc on tan, freehand, 12x14".460.00
Watercolor on paper, lady in parlor w/dog at ft, naive style, 13x11"...1,265.00
Watercolor on paper, man in frock coat, naive style, 10x8¼"+gilt fr..1,000.00
Whirligig, Am Indian w/rotating hatched panels, pnt wood, 55" on stand.2,000.00

Whirligig, auctioneer and dog, carved and painted wood, late twentieth century, 28x28x21", VG, $2,000.00. (Photo courtesy Brunk Auctions on LiveAuctioneers.com)

Whirligig, man, baluster-trn figure, glass bead eyes, mc pnt, 16x13" ... 350.00
Whirligig, Roman centurion, pnt wood, rpr, on stand, 17" 800.00
Whirligig, sailor w/paddle arms, cvd/pnt wood, Nantucket, 1900s, 19" ..2,500.00
Whirligig, soldier, red hat & coat, rpl arm paddles, 1800s, 20" .2,350.00

Fostoria Glass

The Fostoria Glass Company was established in 1887 in Fostoria, Ohio, but in 1891 it was moved to Moundsville, West Virginia. During the next two decades, many lines of pressed and blown tableware, lamps, and useful and ornamental products were made. The American pattern, introduced in 1915, has the distinction of being the most popular and longest-lived Fostoria pattern. By the end of its production at the Fostoria plant, it had been made in nearly 300 pieces. In 1925 the company introduced glass in colors of amber, green, ebony blue, canary, and orchid, and in 1926 launched a massive advertising campaign to introduce the first complete dinner service in glass. From 1928 to World War II, colors of azure green, rose, and topaz dominated production. However, with the repeal of Prohibition in 1934, new strong colors of ruby, empire green, burgundy, and regal blue were used primarily in barware and related items. Many pieces in the Lafayette pattern may be found in strong colors. For almost a decade after the war only crystal was made. By 1950 Fostoria had become the largest producer of handmade glassware in the nation.

From the late 1940s the Bridal Registry added another dimension to Fostoria's popularity and sales. Free information and sometimes sets of glass dishes were sent to homemaking departments in schools. Students learned proper use and care of the glass and good dining manners. This practice continued until the factory was sold to Lancaster Colony in 1982. Until that time, though many pieces had been dropped from the lines, etched patterns such as Navarre, Chintz, Heather, Romance, and Willowmere and cut patterns such as Holly, Laurel, and Rose brought fine dining to American families.

The Lancaster Colony Company continued to make a few pressed patterns and lead crystal items until the factory was closed in 1986. After that some American, Coin, Baroque, and possibly other molds were contracted out to Dalzell Viking Glass Company, the Fenton Art Glass Company, and the Indiana Glass Company, which was owned by Lancaster Colony Glass Company. The Dalzell Viking and Fenton pieces are difficult to tell from the original Fostoria.

For further information we recommend *Fostoria Stemware*, the three volumes in the *Crystal for America* series, and *The Fostoria Value Guide*, all by our advisors, Milbra Long and Emily Seate. They are listed in the Directory under Texas. See also Glass Animals and Figurines.

Alexis, crystal, bottle, catsup	65.00
Alexis, crystal, bottle, oil, 4-oz	35.00
Alexis, crystal, egg cup, ped ft	12.50
Alexis, crystal, goblet, 10-oz	12.00
Alexis, crystal, pitcher, 16-oz	25.00
Alexis, crystal, shakers, pr	35.00
Alexis, crystal, sugar shaker	65.00
Alexis, crystal, vase, ftd, 7"	45.00
Alexis, crystal, wine, 2½-oz	14.00
American, crystal, bottle, bitters, w/tube, 4½-oz, 5¼"	135.00
American, crystal, bowl, rolled edge, 11½"	50.00
American, crystal, butter dish, ¼-lb	38.00
American, crystal, candlestick, 2-lt, 4½", ea	38.00
American, crystal, candlestick, octagon ft, 6"	25.00
American, crystal, coaster, 3¾"	8.00
American, crystal, napkin ring	54.00
American, crystal, nappy, 4½"	12.00
American, crystal, pitcher, w/ice lip, ½-gal, 8¼"	85.00
American, crystal, plate, 6"	10.00
American, crystal, plate, torte, 24"	225.00
American, crystal, punch bowl, 14", low ft, w/16 regular punch cups, $350 to	450.00
American, crystal, sauceboat w/liner	50.00
American, crystal, sugar bowl, open	10.00
American, crystal, syrup, w/drip-proof top	64.00
American, crystal, tray, muffin, 2 upturned sides, 10"	47.00
American, crystal, tray, oval, 10½x5"	45.00
American, crystal, tumbler, #2056, str side, 8-oz, 4"	12.00
American, crystal, tumbler, whiskey, #2056, 2½"	10.00
American, crystal, vase, sq ped ft, 9"	85.00
American, crystal, vase, str sides, 12"	165.00
American, crystal, vase, sweet pea	80.00
American, crystal, wine, #2056, hexagonal ft, 2½-oz, 4½"	22.00
American Lady, burgundy, goblet	60.00
American Lady, crystal, goblet	32.00
American Lady, regal bl, goblet	135.00
Baroque, azure, bowl, cream soup	75.00
Baroque, azure, candy dish, 3-part, w/lid	158.00
Baroque, azure, mustard, w/lid	110.00
Baroque, azure, vase, 7"	175.00
Baroque, crystal, bottle, oil, w/stopper, 5½"	95.00
Baroque, crystal, bowl, relish, 3-part, 10"	42.00
Baroque, crystal, tumbler, ftd, 9-oz, 5½"	28.00
Baroque, gold tint, bowl, celery, 11"	58.00
Baroque, gold tint, bowl, fruit, 5"	30.00
Baroque, gold tint, candlestick, 8-lustre, 8", ea	145.00
Baroque, gold tint, c/s	40.00

Baroque, gold tint, platter, oval, 12"	95.00
Beverly, amber, parfait	38.00
Beverly, gr, iced tea, ftd, #5000, 12-oz	32.00
Black and Gold, crystal, grapefruit & liner, decor #23, #945	64.00

Black and Gold, wine, Blank 660, $45.00. (Photo courtesy Emily Seate and Milbra Long)

Blue Border, candy jar & cover, decor #19, 1-lb, #2219	75.00
Blue Border, goblet, decor #19, 9-oz, #858	45.00
Brocade, Grape, bl, bowl, #2339, cupped rim, 7½"	150.00
Brocade, Grape, bl, candlestick, #2324, 4", ea	67.00
Brocade, Grape, gr, candy box, #2331, 3-part, w/lid	175.00
Brocade, Grape, gr, ice bucket, #2378	175.00
Brocade, Oakleaf, crystal, bowl, #2398, cornucopia, 11"	225.00
Brocade, Oakleaf, crystal, candlestick, #2394, 3-toed, 2", ea	65.00
Brocade, Oakleaf, crystal, sugar pail, #2378	325.00
Brocade, Oakleaf, crystal, tray, lunch, hdld, #2342	195.00
Brocade, Oakleaf, ebony, cigarette box, #2391, w/lid, lg	150.00
Brocade, Oakleaf, ebony, vase, #2292, ftd, 8"	265.00
Brocade, Oakleaf, ebony, window box & cover, sm, #2373	575.00
Brocade, Oakleaf, gr or rose, candlestick, #2375, 3", ea	80.00
Brocade, Oakleaf, gr or rose, cheese & cracker, #2368	165.00
Brocade, Oakwood, azure or orchid, bonbon, #2375	135.00
Brocade, Oakwood, azure or orchid, comport, #2400, pulled stem, 8"	475.00
Brocade, Oakwood, azure or orchid, tray, #2342, 8-sided, center hdl	475.00
Brocade, Oakwood, azure or orchid, wine, #877, 2¾-oz	145.00
Brocade, Oakwood, azure, plate, cake, #2375, 10"	395.00
Brocade, Palm Leaf, gr or rose, bowl, #2394, flared rim, 3-toed, 12"	350.00
Brocade, Palm Leaf, gr or rose, bowl, dessert, lg, hdls, #2375, 10"	225.00
Brocade, Palm Leaf, gr or rose, comport, #2400, 6"	225.00
Brocade, Paradise, gr or orchid, bowl, centerpiece, #2329, 11"	135.00
Brocade, Paradise, gr or orchid, candlestick, #2324, 4", ea	48.00
Brocade, Paradise, gr or orchid, comport, #2327, tall twist stem, 7"	125.00
Buttercup, crystal, goblet	35.00
Buttercup, crystal, jug	325.00
Century, crystal, bowl, lg, 10"	32.00
Century, crystal, cake salver	75.00
Century, crystal, juice, ftd	14.00
Century, crystal, sherbet	14.00
Chintz, crystal, claret, wine	45.00
Chintz, crystal, iced tea, ftd	38.00
Chintz, crystal, vase, ftd, #4143, 6"	225.00
Christiana cutting, crystal, claret, wine	38.00
Christiana cutting, crystal, iced tea, ftd	30.00
Christiana cutting, crystal, jug	225.00
Coin, amber, cruet, #1372/531, w/stopper, 7-oz	85.00
Coin, amber, pitcher, 32-oz	95.00
Coin, amber, sugar bowl, w/lid	42.00
Coin, bl, bowl, ftd, 8½"	90.00
Coin, bl, urn, #1372/829, ftd, w/lid, 12¾"	140.00
Coin, bl, vase, bud, 8"	55.00
Coin, crystal, decanter, w/stopper, 1-pt	175.00
Coin, crystal, punch bowl & ft, #1372/600, 1½-gal, 14"	400.00

Coin, gr, bowl, nappy, w/hdl, 5⅜" 38.00
Coin, gr, candleholders, 4½", pr 150.00
Coin, gr, creamer, #1372/680 .... 75.00
Coin, olive, ashtray, 7½" dia 25.00
Coin, olive, candy box, 4⅛" 33.00
Coin, olive, pitcher, 32-oz 65.00
Coin, olive, wine, ftd, 4" 35.00
Coin, ruby, bowl, ftd, 8½" 94.00
Coin, ruby, iced tea/highball, #1372, 12-oz 125.00
Coin, ruby, plate, 8" 125.00
Coin, ruby, tumbler, #1372/58, 14-oz, 5¼" 95.00
Colony, crystal, bonbon, 3-ftd, 7" 36.00
Colony, crystal, bowl, 4½" 10.00
Colony, crystal, cheese & cracker 65.00
Colony, crystal, cocktail, 3½-oz 15.00
Colony, crystal, lamp, electric 195.00
Colony, crystal, pitcher, w/ice lip, 2-qt 145.00
Colony, crystal, plate, torte, 13" 56.00
Colony, crystal, vase, cornucopia, 9" 80.00
Coronet, crystal, bonbon, 3-toed 26.00
Coronet, crystal, plate, torte, 14" 42.00
Fairfax #2375, amber, baker, oval, 9" 38.00
Fairfax #2375, amber, bowl, soup, 7" 30.00
Fairfax #2375, amber, dish, lemon, hdls, 9" 24.00
Fairfax #2375, amber, plate, grill, 10" 30.00
Fairfax #2375, azure or rose, canape set, plate & #4101 2-oz ftd tumbler.. 20.00
Fairfax #2375, azure, orchid or rose, bowl, fruit, 5" 27.00
Fairfax #2375, azure, orchid or rose, butter dish 150.00
Fairfax #2375, azure, orchid or rose, compote, 7" 40.00
Fairfax #2375, azure, orchid or rose, shakers, ftd, pr 120.00
Fairfax #2375, gr or topaz, cup, ftd, w/saucer 22.00
Fairfax #2375, gr or topaz, plate, dinner, 10" 45.00
Fairfax #2375, gr or topaz, sugar pail 45.00
Figural, crystal, Mermaid 165.00
Figural, ebony, Chanticleer 525.00
Fuchsia, crystal, cocktail, #6004, 3-oz 42.00
Fuchsia, crystal, comport, #2470, low ped, 6" 64.00
Fuchsia, crystal, cordial, #6004, ¾-oz 85.00
Fuchsia, crystal, plate, #2440, 6" 20.00
Fuchsia, crystal, plate, cake, 10" 85.00
Fuchsia, crystal, tumbler, #833, 2-oz 25.00
Fuchsia, Wisteria, bowl, #2470, 12" 150.00
Fuchsia, Wisteria, candlestick, #2470, 5½", ea 125.00
Fuchsia, Wisteria, parfait, #6004, 5½-oz, 6½" 135.00
Glacier, crystal, bowl, onion soup, w/lid 50.00
Glacier, crystal, shakers, pr 37.50
Heather, crystal, butter, oblong 65.00
Heather, crystal, goblet 35.00
Heather, crystal, preserve, w/cover 67.00
Hermitage, amber, gr or topaz, bottle, oil, #2449, 3-oz 55.00
Hermitage, amber, gr or topaz, mustard, #2449, w/lid & ladle 65.00
Hermitage, amber, gr or topaz, plate, #2449, 9" 20.00
Hermitage, amber, gr or topaz, tumbler, #2449, ftd, 9-oz, 4" 20.00
Hermitage, azure, cr/sugar, #2449, ftd 48.00
Hermitage, crystal, pitcher, #2449, 3-pt 85.00
Hermitage, Wisteria, comport, #2449, 6" 64.00
Hermitage, Wisteria, ice dish & liner, #2449 .... 75.00
Hermitage, Wisteria, plate, #2449½, 8" 38.00
Hermitage, Wisteria, relish, #2449, 3-part, 7" 60.00
Jamestown, amber, celery, 9" 34.00
Jamestown, bl, gr or amethyst, butter, oblong 95.00
Jamestown, crystal, goblet 18.00
Jamestown, ruby, iced tea, ftd 35.00
Jenny Lind, aqua, puff box, w/cover 110.00

Jenny Lind, peach, pitcher, blown 265.00
Jenny Lind, wht, tray, comb & brush 75.00
June, azure or rose, bowl, whipped cream 58.00
June, azure or rose, decanter, #2439, min 2,000.00
June, azure or rose, platter, #2375, 12" 195.00
June, crystal, centerpiece & flower holder, oval, 13" 395.00
June, crystal, plate, chop, 13" 125.00
June, topaz, bowl, M, 3-ftd, 4" 42.00
June, topaz, candlestick, #2395, 3", pr 125.00
June, topaz, candy dish & lid, #2394, 5-oz 500.00
Kashmir, azure, bottle, oil, ftd 700.00
Kashmir, azure, candy dish, #2430, w/lid 175.00
Kashmir, topaz, shakers, pr 235.00
Lafayette, burgundy, cake plate, oval, 10½" 135.00
Lafayette, crystal or topaz, nappy, 8" 45.00
Lafayette, crystal or topaz, platter, 15" L 75.00
Lafayette, Emp Gr, bowl, sweetmeat, 4½" 42.00
Lafayette, Emp Gr, plate, torte, 13" 195.00
Lafayette, gr, rose or topaz, vase, ftd, 7" 60.00
Lafayette, Wisteria, plate, 10" 140.00
Manor, crystal, goblet, #6007 .... 45.00
Manor, crystal, iced tea, ftd, #6003 .... 35.00
Meadow Rose, azure, comport, 5½" 125.00
Meadow Rose, azure, c/s 67.00
Meadow Rose, crystal, bowl, serving, 8½" 52.00
Meadow Rose, crystal, cordial 65.00
Meadow Rose, crystal, plate, 9" 55.00
Navarre, bl, claret, lg, #6016 .... 135.00
Navarre, crystal, bottle, salad dressing, #2083, 6½" 495.00
Navarre, crystal, bowl, nut, #2496, 3-ftd, 6" 68.00
Navarre, crystal, cake plate, #2496, hdls, 10" 95.00
Navarre, crystal, claret, #6016, 4½-oz, 6½" 58.00
Navarre, crystal, ice bucket & tongs, #2496 .... 195.00
Navarre, crystal, mayonnaise, #2496½, 3-pc 95.00
Navarre, crystal, nappy, #2496, 3-corners, 4" 32.00
Navarre, crystal, plate, #2440, 9½" 45.00
Navarre, crystal, plate, torte, #2464, 16" 150.00
Navarre, crystal, relish, #2496, 4-part, 10" 135.00
Navarre, crystal, sauce dish, #2496, 6½x5" 100.00

Navarre, crystal, sherbet, low, $25.00; saucer champagne, $30.00. (Photo courtesy Jackson's Auction on LiveAuctioneers.com)

Navarre, crystal, vase, #4121, 5" 175.00
Neoclassic, burgundy, goblet 65.00
Neoclassic, Emp Gr, brandy 58.00
Neoclassic, regal bl, saucer champagne 54.00
New Garland, amber or topaz, candlestick, 9½", rare, pr 240.00
New Garland, amber or topaz, decanter 650.00
New Garland, amber or topaz, platter, 15" 50.00
New Garland, amber or topaz, sherbet, #6002, H stem 18.00
New Garland, amber or topaz, vase, 8" 75.00
New Garland, rose, bonbon, hdls 20.00
New Garland, rose, compote, 6" 28.00
New Garland, rose, ice bucket, #2375 .... 120.00
New Garland, rose, wine, #6002 .... 28.00
Pioneer, amber, crystal or gr, bowl, baker, oval, 10" 26.00

Pioneer, amber, crystal or gr, soup, 7"	18.00
Pioneer, azure or orchid, ashtray, 3¾"	26.00
Pioneer, azure or rose, relish, 3-part	24.00
Pioneer, bl, butter dish	100.00
Pioneer, bl, platter, 10½" L	45.00
Pioneer, ebony, cr/sugar, #2350½, ftd	30.00
Pioneer, rose or topaz, comport, 8"	30.00
Planet, crystal, decanter	195.00
Planet, crystal, goblet	35.00
Planet, crystal, jug	195.00
Plymouth, crystal, bowl, flared, #2574, 12"	75.00
Plymouth, crystal, ice tub, #2574	78.00
Rogene, crystal, carafe & tumbler, #1697	95.00
Rogene, crystal, jug, #2270, w/lid	250.00
Romance, crsytal, candlestick, trindle, pr	195.00
Romance, crystal, bowl, baked apple, #2364, 6"	52.00
Romance, crystal, cocktail	30.00
Romance, crystal, vase, flip, 8"	250.00
Royal, amber or gr, bowl, console, #2329, 13"	30.00
Royal, amber or gr, bowl, pickle, #2350, 8"	20.00
Royal, amber or gr, candlestick, #2324, 9"	65.00
Royal, amber or gr, c/s, #2350	26.00
Royal, amber or gr, ice bucket, #2378	125.00
Royal, amber or gr, platter, #2350, 10"	72.00
Royal, bl, centerpiece, oval, 13"	250.00
Royal, bl, parfait, #869, 6-oz	85.00
Royal, bl, tray, lunch, hdld, #2287, 11"	150.00
Sampler, crystal, celery	38.00
Sampler, crystal, goblet	34.00
Sea Shells, copper bl, bowl, rolled edge, 7"	48.00
Sea Shells, crystal, vase, 8"	75.00
Sea Shells, gr, candlestick, 3½", pr	125.00
Seville, amber, bowl, ftd, #2324, 10"	85.00
Seville, amber, bowl, soup, #2350, 7¾"	30.00
Seville, amber, grapefruit (same as mayonnaise), #2315	30.00
Seville, crystal, goblet, #870	27.00
Seville, gr, celery, #2350, 11"	46.00
Seville, gr, tumbler, #5084, ftd, 2-oz	30.00
Seville, gr, urn, sm ft	125.00
Sun Ray, crystal, bonbon, hdld, 6½"	16.00
Sun Ray, crystal, bottle, oil, w/stopper, 3-oz	54.00
Sun Ray, crystal, coaster, 4"	8.00
Sun Ray, crystal, cr/sugar, ftd	48.00
Sun Ray, crystal, plate, sandwich, 12"	40.00
Sun Ray, crystal, vase, crimped, 6"	57.00
Trojan, rose, candy dish, #2394, w/lid, ½-lb	200.00
Trojan, rose, goblet, #5099	110.00
Trojan, topaz, cheese & cracker, #2375, #2368	130.00
Trojan, topaz, platter, #2375, 15"	150.00
Versailles, azure, decanter, #2439, 9", min	2,500.00
Versailles, azure, pitcher, #5000	850.00
Versailles, gr, bowl, cereal, #2375, 6½"	57.00
Versailles, gr, cocktail, #5098, 3-oz, 5"	55.00
Versailles, gr, shakers, #2375, ftd, pr	375.00
Versailles, rose or topaz, bowl, centerpc, #2375, flared, 12"	225.00
Versailles, rose or topaz, plate, #2375, 8"	35.00
Versailles, rose or topaz, sweetmeat, #2375	54.00
Vesper, amber, grapefruit & liner, #5082½	90.00
Vesper, bl, goblet	100.00
Vesper, gr, soup, 7"	38.00
Willowmere, crystal, goblet	35.00
Willowmere, crystal, server, sani-cut, Bakelite hdl, rare	300.00
Willowmere, crystal, vase, #2470, 10"	275.00
Woodland, crystal, goblet	35.00

Woodland, crystal, server, sani-cut, rare	250.00
Woodland, crystal, vase, #2470, 10"	275.00

Susan Frackelton

Born in Milwaukee, Wisconsin, in 1848, Susan worked at her family's pottery import business where as a young adult she began experimenting with china painting, potting, and glazing, and gradually became well known for her efforts in creating a unique type of art pottery, most of which was salt-glaze stoneware with underglaze blue designs taken from nature (such as those listed below). More often than not, these pieces combined dimensional applications in combination with hand painting. Some of her pieces were painted on the inside as well. She was awarded a gold medal at the 1893 Columbian Exposition for her stoneware creations and was greatly admired by her contemporaries.

Though salt-glazed stoneware had for many decades been a mainstay of Wisconsin pottery production, Susan was recognized as the first to apply these principals to the manufacture of art pottery.

In addition to her artistic accomplishments, Susan also developed a gas-fired kiln specifically for use in the home.

She retired and moved to Chicago in 1904, where she died in 1932.

Key: stw — stoneware

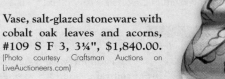

Vase, salt-glazed stoneware with cobalt oak leaves and acorns, #109 S F 3, 3¼", $1,840.00. (Photo courtesy Craftsman Auctions on LiveAuctioneers.com)

Bowl, appl indigo poppy in center, bl floral on gray stw, 3x5"	1,800.00
Bowl, salt-glazed stw, appl grapes/vines, 1902, sgn, 6½x14"	18,000.00
Jar, stw w/appl indigo wreath on cvd floral, SF/1898, w/lid, 5x5", EX	7,800.00
Vase, bl acorns & leaves, stw gourd shape, 3"	7,140.00
Vase, cvd foliate & heraldic devices in gr & indigo stw, 7"	18,000.00
Vase, cvd stylized leaves, bl on wht stw, bulb, 2"	660.00
Vase, indigo roses/stylized cross, stw, #108, 3"	720.00
Vase, landscape/leaves, indigo on stw, 3 hdls, 1903, 6x5¼"	10,200.00
Vase, oak-leaf branches/acorns in indigo stw, #109, 3"	8,400.00
Vase, stw w/cvd/appl roses & stems, indigo on cream, 6x4¼"	25,000.00

Frakturs

Fraktur is a German style of black letter text type. To collectors the fraktur is a type of hand-lettered document used by the people of German descent who settled in the areas of Pennsylvania, New Jersey, Maryland, Virginia, North and South Carolina, Ohio, Kentucky, and Ontario. These documents recorded births and baptisms and were used as bookplates and as certificates of honor. They were elaborately decorated with colorful folk-art borders of hearts, birds, angels, and flowers. Examples by recognized artists and those with an unusual decorative motif bring prices well into the thousands of dollars; in fact, some have sold at major auction houses well in excess of $100,000.00. Frakturs made in the late 1700s after the invention of the printing press provided the writer with a prepared text that he needed only to fill in at his own discretion. The next step in the evolution of machine-printed frakturs combined woodblock-printed decorations along with the text which the 'artist' sometimes enhanced with color. By the mid-1800s, even the coloring was done by machine. The vorschrift was a handwritten example prepared by a fraktur teacher to demonstrate his skill in lettering and decorating. These are often considered to be the finest of frakturs. Those dated before 1820 are most valuable.

The practice of fraktur art began to diminish after 1830 but hung on even to the early years of the twentieth century among the Pennsylvania Germans ingrained with such customs. Our advisor for this category is Frederick S. Weiser; he is listed in the Directory under Pennsylvania. (Mr. Weiser has provided our text, but being unable to physically examine the frakturs listed below cannot vouch for their authenticity, age, or condition. When requesting information, please include a self-addressed stamped envelope.) These prices were realized at various reputable auction galleries in the East and Midwest and should be regarded as minimum values. Buyers should be aware that there are many fakes on the market, a real problem for beginning collectors. Know your dealer. Unless otherwise noted, values are for examples in excellent condition. Note: Be careful not to confuse frakturs with prints, calligraphy, English-language marriage certificates, Lord's Prayers, etc.

Key:
i — ink	p/i — pen and ink
lp — laid paper	wc — watercolored
pr — printed	wp — woven paper

Birth Records

Cutwork flowers/birds, mc, Jac Botz, 1792, 6x5"+sponged fr 4,800.00
P/i/wc, birds/flowers/mermaid, att H Otto, PA, 1761, 12½x15"+fr...2,150.00

Pen and ink with watercolor, central script reserve surrounded with birds and tulips, Berks County, Pennsylvania, 1823, 12x14", $9,600.00. (Photo courtesy Pook & Pook, Inc. on LiveAuctioneers.com)

P/i/wc/lp w/pinpricks, flowers/birds, 1816, 7x5½"+fr, VG............. 600.00
P/i/wc/lp, flower baskets/vines, PA, 1754, 7¼x6¼"+later fr 900.00
P/i/wc/lp, flowers/tulips/script, Schuylkill, 1833, 12x14¼"+fr.....4,200.00
P/i/wc/lp, heart/columns/angels, Continental, 1834, 12x9".......1,100.00
P/i/wc/lp, hearts/vines/verses, M Brechall, PA, ca 1826, 13x16"+fr..1,550.00
P/i/wc/lp, parrots/mermaids/flowers, H Otto, 1793, 13x16"+fr..2,900.00
P/i/wc/lp, shields/tulips/pinwheels/text, PA, 1807, 13x16¼"+fr..3,600.00
P/i/wc/lp, tulips/geometrics/text, D Otto, PA, 1814, in 15x19" fr...4,000.00
P/i/wc/lp, vining flowers/birds/text, PA, 1800s, 12x8"+fr............. 700.00
P/i/wc/wp, couple/stars/flowers, att H Young, 1828, 12x7½"+fr.5,500.00
P/i/wc/wp, hearts/eagles/verse in lg heart, PA, 1821, 12x12½"+fr..2,350.00
P/i/wc/wp, tulips/thistle/bird, att B Mission, PA, 1826, 8x13"+fr....2,650.00
Pr/wc, flowers/hearts, S Bauman, PA, 1811, 12½x15"+fr............. 850.00
Pr/wc/lp, angels/birds/etc, TF Scheffer, PA, 1859, 17x13"+fr....1,500.00
Pr/wc/lp, flower basket/parrots/tulips, Krebs, 1813, 16x18½"+fr...800.00

Miscellaneous

Bookplate, i/wc, birds/tulip/checked border, PA, 1808, 6½" L+fr ..3,400.00
Marriage blessing, p/i/lp, Spencerian style, Dutch, 1721, 15x12"+fr ..1,800.00
P/i/wc, fish, detailed, PA, 1800s, 3¼x6½"+fr............................1,100.00
P/i/wc, flowering tree w/birds, PA, 1800s, 5x3¼"+chip-cvd fr ...3,600.00
P/i/wc/lp, flower basket, reverse: prayer, 5¼x3¼"+fr 800.00
P/i/wc/lp, lover's knot, 1833, 6½x6½"+fr.................................2,400.00
Vorschrift, ABCs in blocks/decanters/bird, Gottschall, 1835, 8x13".19,500.00

Frames

Styles in picture frames have changed with the fashion of the day, but those that especially interest today's collectors are the deep shadow boxes made of fine woods such as walnut or cherry, those with Art Nouveau influence, and the oak frames decorated with molded gesso and gilt from the Victorian era. The last few years have seen the middle- to late-Victorian molded composition-on-wood frames finally being recognized as individual works of art. While once regulated to the trash heap, they are now being rescued and appreciated.

As is true in general in the antiques and collectibles fields, the influence of online trading is greatly affecting prices. Many items once considered difficult to locate are now readily available online; as a result, some values have declined. Additionally, the overall downturn in the US economy has caused, and will continue to cause, values to decline or hold steady. The very high-quality or unused items should see minor price increases. Our advisor for this category is Michael Hinton; he is listed in the Directory under Pennsylvania.

Note: Unless another date is given, frames described in the following listings are from the nineteenth century.

Ash burl, 7-sided w/trn concentric circles around opening, 8x6". 260.00
Black walnut & gold leaf, Pat 1871, 35x31", EX......................1,150.00
Brass & pietra dura, pierced birds/lilies, in wood surround, 10"..... 700.00
Brass-plated CI, pierced foliage, Vict, 13x10" 85.00

Bronze with enameling and jewels, nineteenth century, 11½x9", $450.00. (Photo courtesy K&M Auction Liquidation Sales, Ltd. on LiveAuctioneers.com)

Cast iron w/gilt, rtcl leaves, metal bk, desk type, 11½x8¼" 65.00
Cast iron, emb floral w/rtcl, mc pnt, Judd #8003, 6x4¼" 150.00
Chip cvd, old red pnt & natural, easel bk, 7x6"........................... 250.00
Curly maple, nut brn stain, 17⅜x15" 230.00
Gesso w/cvg, old gold pnt, 50x44"...1,150.00
Gesso w/flower sprays, sgn Samuel Little, 6" W, 30x36" 300.00
Gesso, gold leaf, inner/outer liners w/emb foliage, 30x25" 200.00
Gilt bronze, Louis XVI style, floral crest/geometric borders, 15x11".1,500.00
Giltwood & gesso w/foliate scrolls, shell corners, 1850s, 55x45" .635.00
Giltwood, Italian rococo, projecting rtcl foliage/shell, 15x9"....... 300.00
Giltwood w/fruit corners, Vict, 13x15" 120.00
Gnarled/entwined tree roots appl to wooden fr, ca 1900, 39x47"... 4,800.00
Mahog vnr, 2⅛" W, 16x18".. 50.00
Painted wood, appl half trns, blk & gold, 11¾x9¾"..................... 200.00
Plaster over wood, oval shadow box, Vict, 20x17x4".................... 150.00
Poplar w/half-trn stiles, corner blocks, porc buttons, 17x13" 200.00
Tortoiseshell vnr on wood, 7½x6½", 5x4", pr 400.00
Walnut, beveled, 2" molding, 17x14".. 100.00
Walnut, oval liner, incised decor, dtd 1871, 20x30" 950.00

Franciscan

Franciscan is a trade name used by Gladding-McBean and Co., founded in northern California in 1875. In 1923 they purchased the

Tropico plant in Glendale where they produced sewer pipe, gardenware, and tile. By 1934 the first of their dinnerware lines, El Patio, was produced. It was a plain design made in bright, attractive colors. El Patio Nouveau followed in 1935, glazed in two colors — one tone on the inside, a contrasting hue on the outside. Coronado, a favorite of today's collectors, was introduced in 1936. It was styled with a wide, swirled border and was made in pastels, both satin and glossy. Before 1940, 15 patterns had been produced. The first hand-decorated lines were introduced in 1937, the ever-popular Apple pattern in 1940, Desert Rose in 1941, and Ivy in 1948. Many other hand-decorated and decaled patterns were produced there from 1934 to 1984.

Dinnerware marks before 1940 include 'GMcB' in an oval, 'F' within a square, or 'Franciscan' with 'Pottery' underneath (which was later changed to 'Ware'). A circular arrangement of 'Franciscan' with 'Made in California USA' in the center was used from 1940 until 1949. At least 40 marks were used before 1975; several more were introduced after that. At one time, paper labels were used.

The company merged with Lock Joint Pipe Company in 1963, becoming part of the Interpace Corporation. In July of 1979 Franciscan was purchased by Wedgwood Limited of England, and the Glendale plant closed in October 1984.

Note: Due to limited space, we have used a pricing formula, meant to be only a general guide, not a mechanical ratio on each piece. Rarity varies with pattern, and not all pieces occur in all patterns. See also Gladding-McBean and Company.

Coronado, 1936 – 1956

Both satin (matt) and glossy colors were made including turquoise, coral, celadon, light yellow, ivory, and gray in satin; and turquoise, coral, apple green, light yellow, white, maroon, and redwood in glossy glazes. High-end values are for maroon, yellow, redwood, and gray. Add 10 – 15% for gloss.

Bowl, casserole, w/lid, $45 to	90.00
Bowl, cereal, $10 to	15.00
Bowl, cream soup, w/underplate, $25 to	40.00
Bowl, fruit, $6 to	12.00
Bowl, nut cup, $8 to	12.00
Bowl, onion soup, w/lid, $25 to	40.00
Bowl, rim soup, $14 to	25.00
Bowl, salad, lg, $20 to	35.00
Bowl, serving, 7" dia, $12 to	18.00
Bowl, serving, 8" dia, $10 to	17.00
Bowl, serving, oval, 10", $20 to	33.00
Bowl, sherbet/egg cup, $10 to	15.00
Butter dish, $25 to	35.00
Cigarette box, w/lid, $40 to	75.00
Creamer, $8 to	12.00
Cup/saucer, demi, $20 to	32.00
Cup/saucer, jumbo	32.00
Cup/saucer, tea, $8 to	12.00
Demitasse pot, $100 to	150.00
Fast-stand gravy, $25 to	35.00
Jam jar, w/lid, $45 to	60.00
Pitcher, 1½-qt, $25 to	45.00
Plate, 6", $5 to	8.00
Plate, 7", $7 to	10.00
Plate, 8", $8 to	11.00
Plate, 9", $10 to	15.00
Plate, 10", $12 to	18.00
Plate, chop, 12½" dia, $18 to	32.00
Plate, chop, 14" dia, $20 to	30.00
Plate, crescent hostess, w/cup well, no established value	

Plate, crescent salad, lg, no established value	
Plate, ind crescent salad, $22 to	32.00
Platter, oval, 10", $12 to	20.00
Platter, oval, 13", $24 to	36.00
Platter, oval, 15½", $25 to	45.00
Relish dish, oval, $12 to	25.00
Shakers, pr, $15 to	30.00
Sugar bowl, w/lid, $10 to	20.00
Teapot, $75 to	95.00
Tumbler, water, no established value	
Vase, 5¼"	65.00
Vase, 6¾", no established value	
Vase, 8½", no established value	
Vase, 9½", no established value	

Desert Rose

For other hand-painted patterns, we recommend the following general guide for comparable pieces (based on current values):

Daisy	-20%
October	-20%
Cafe Royal	Same as Desert Rose
Forget-Me-Not	Same as Desert Rose
Meadow Rose	Same as Desert Rose
Strawberry Fair	Same as Desert Rose
Strawberry Time	Same as Desert Rose
Fresh Fruit	Same as Desert Rose
Bountiful	Same as Desert Rose
Desert Rose	Base Line Values
Apple	+10%
Ivy	+10%
Poppy	+50%
Original (small) Fruit	+50%
Wild Flower	200% or more!

There is not an active market in Bouquet, Rosette, or Twilight Rose, as these are scarce, having been produced only a short time. Our estimate would place Bouquet and Rosette in the October range (-20%) and Twilight Rose in the Ivy range (+20%).

There are several Apple items that are so scarce they command higher prices than fit the above formula. The Apple ginger jar is valued at $600.00+, the 4" jug at $195.00+, and any covered box in Apple is at least 50% more than Desert Rose.

Ivy, to evaluate this line, add 10% to Desert Rose prices. [Photo courtesy Brunk Auctions on LiveAuctioneers.com]

Ashtray, ind	15.00
Ashtray, sq	150.00
Bell, Danbury Mint	95.00
Bell, dinner	95.00
Bowl, bouillon, w/lid, $195 to	295.00
Bowl, cereal, 6"	15.00
Bowl, divided vegetable	45.00

Bowl, fruit	10.00
Bowl, mixing, lg	175.00
Bowl, mixing, med	165.00
Bowl, mixing, sm	155.00
Bowl, porringer	175.00
Bowl, rimmed soup	25.00
Bowl, salad, 10"	95.00
Bowl, soup, ftd	25.00
Bowl, vegetable, 8"	32.00
Bowl, vegetable, 9"	40.00
Box, cigarette	95.00
Box, egg	145.00
Box, heart shape	145.00
Box, rnd	165.00
Butter dish	45.00
Candleholders, pr	95.00
Candy dish, oval, $150 to	225.00
Casserole, 1½-qt	75.00
Casserole, 2½-qt, min	295.00
Coffeepot	125.00
Coffeepot, ind, $300 to	395.00
Compote, lg	75.00
Compote, low	125.00
Cookie jar	295.00
Creamer, ind	40.00
Creamer, regular	20.00
Cup/saucer, demi	35.00
Cup/saucer, jumbo	30.00
Cup/saucer, tall	35.00
Cup/saucer, tea	10.00
Egg cup	35.00
Ginger jar	225.00
Goblet, ftd	225.00
Gravy boat	38.00
Hurricane lamp, $250 to	325.00
Jam jar	125.00
Long 'n narrow, 15½x7¾"	495.00
Microwave dish, oblong, 1½-qt	195.00
Microwave dish, sq, 1-qt	150.00
Microwave dish, sq, 8"	95.00
Mug, 7-oz	35.00
Mug, bbl, 12-oz	45.00
Mug, cocoa, 10-oz	95.00
Napkin ring	50.00
Piggy bank, $195 to	295.00
Pitcher, milk	65.00
Pitcher, syrup	75.00
Pitcher, water, 2½-qt	125.00
Plate, 6½"	7.00
Plate, 8½"	12.00
Plate, 9½"	20.00
Plate, 10½"	18.00
Plate, chop, 12"	50.00
Plate, chop, 14"	95.00
Plate, coupe dessert	65.00
Plate, coupe party	125.00
Plate, coupe steak	145.00
Plate, divided, child's, $125 to	195.00
Plate, grill, 11", $80 to	100.00
Plate, side salad	35.00
Plate, TV, $95 to	125.00
Platter, 12¾"	35.00
Platter, 14"	45.00
Platter, turkey, 19"	295.00

Relish, 3-section	65.00
Relish/pickle dish, oval, 10"	28.00
Shaker & pepper mill, pr, $195 to	295.00
Shakers, rose bud, pr	22.50
Shakers, tall, pr, $75 to	95.00
Sherbet	20.00
Soup ladle	75.00
Spoon rest	25.00
Sugar bowl, open, ind	45.00
Sugar bowl, regular	25.00
Tea canister	295.00
Teapot	125.00
Thimble	75.00
Tidbit tray, 2-tier	95.00
Tile, in fr	50.00
Tile, sq	50.00
Toast cover	195.00
Trivet, rnd, $150 to	195.00
Tumbler, 10-oz	30.00
Tumbler, juice, 6-oz	45.00
Tureen, soup, flat bottom	595.00
Tureen, soup, ftd, either style	695.00
Vase, bud	95.00

Apple Pieces Not Available in Desert Rose

Piggy bank, $175.00 to $275.00. (Photo courtesy Hewletts Antiques on LiveAuctioneers.com)

Half-apple baker, $150 to	195.00
Bowl, batter, $450 to	650.00
Bowl, str sides, lg	55.00
Bowl, str sides, med	45.00
Casserole, stick hdl & lid, ind	65.00
Coaster, $25 to	35.00
Jam jar, redesigned	425.00
Shaker & pepper mill, wooden top, pr $295 to	395.0

Franciscan Fine China

The main line of fine china was called Masterpiece. There were at least four marks used during its production from 1941 to 1977. Almost every piece is clearly marked. This china is true porcelain, the body having been fired at a very high temperature. Many years of research and experimentation went into this china before it was marketed. Production was temporarily suspended during the war years. More than 170 patterns and many varying shapes were produced. All are valued about the same with the exception of the Renaissance group, which is 25% higher.

Bowl, vegetable, serving, oval	50.00
Cup	20.00
Plate, bread & butter	18.00
Plate, dinner	30.00
Plate, salad	25.00
Saucer	12.00

Starburst

Ashtray, ind	20.00

Ashtray, oval, lg, $95 to.. 120.00
Bowl, divided, 8", $25 to... 35.00
Bowl, fruit, ind, 5", $15 to.. 20.00
Bowl, indented finger hold ea side, 6"............................ 35.00
Bowl, oval, 8", $50 to... 60.00
Bowl, salad, 12", $100 to... 135.00
Bowl, salad, ind, $20 to.. 25.00
Bowl, soup/cereal, 7", $35 to... 45.00
Bowl, vegetable, 8", $35 to... 45.00
Butter dish, $80 to.. 90.00
Candlesticks, pr $175 to... 200.00
Canister/jar, w/lid, depending on sz, $250 to................. 350.00
Casserole, 8½", $100 to.. 120.00
Coffeepot, $175 to.. 225.00
Creamer, no hdl, $25 to.. 35.00
Cruet, vinegar or oil, ea $80 to.. 110.00
Cup/saucer, $15 to.. 18.00
Dish, 3-part, triangular, 6½x6½", $100 to....................... 125.00
Dish, w/ring hdl 1 side, 8", $40 to................................... 50.00
Gravy boat w/attached undertray, $35 to......................... 40.00
Gravy ladle, $35 to... 45.00
Mug, sm, 2¾"... 60.00
Mug, tall, 5", $65 to... 80.00
Mustard jar, spoon slot in lid, 3½", $65 to...................... 75.00
Pepper mill, chrome top, 7¼", $200 to............................ 250.00
Pitcher, 7½", $80 to.. 95.00
Pitcher, water, 10", $110 to.. 135.00
Plate, 6", $10 to... 15.00
Plate, 8", $15 to... 20.00
Plate, chop, $55 to... 65.00
Plate, crescent salad, 9½" L, $70 to................................. 85.00

Plate, dinner, 10½", each $20.00 to $35.00. (Photo courtesy Dargate Auction Galleries on LiveAuctioneers.com)

Plate, luncheon, hard to find, 9½", $50 to 60.00
Platter, 13", $65 to... 75.00
Platter, 15", $70 to... 85.00
Relish tray, 3-part, oval, 9", $45 to.................................. 65.00
Salt grinder, chrome top, 6¼", $200 to............................ 250.00
Shakers, bullet shape, 2", pr $25 to................................. 35.00
Shakers, bullet shape, 3½", pr $35 to............................... 50.00
Shakers, bullet shape, 6", pr $30 to................................. 40.00
Snack/TV tray w/cup rest, 12½", $75 to........................... 85.00
Sugar bowl, $40 to.. 55.00
Syrup pitcher, no hdl, 5⅜", $45 to................................... 55.00
Teapot, 5½x8½", $175 to.. 225.00
Tumbler, 6-oz, 3½", $75 to... 90.00

Frankart

During the 1920s Frankart, Inc., of New York City, produced a line of accessories that included figural nude lamps, bookends, and ashtrays. These white metal composition items were offered in several finishes including verde green, jap black, and gunmetal gray. The company also produced a line of caricatured animals, but the stylized nude figurals have proven to be the most collectible today. With few exceptions, all pieces were marked 'Frankart, Inc.' with a patent number or 'pat. appl. for.' All pieces listed are in very good original condition unless otherwise indicated. Our advisor for this category is Walter Glenn; he is listed in the Directory under Georgia.

Aquarium, 3 kneeling nudes encircle 10" fish bowl, 10½".........1,750.00
Ashtray, bk to bk nudes hold rack of 4 rnd ashtrays, 8"...............600.00
Ashtray, nude grows from leaves to hold tray above, 25"...........1,650.00
Ashtray, seated nude w/matchbox holder, 5½" 675.00
Ashtray, standing nude leans against circle, tray at ft, 7" 500.00
Bookends, kneeling nudes, backs support books, 6", pr 525.00
Bookends, ladies w/fans support books, 10", pr...........................675.00
Bookends, Modernistic female heads, 6", pr.................................475.00
Bookends, stylized prancing horses, 7", pr..................................350.00
Candy dish, majorette, 1 knee supports dish, 10"........................975.00
Cigarette box, bk to bk nudes hold 4" rect glass box, 9"...........1,250.00
Clock, 2 nudes kneel & hold 10" rnd glass clock, 12½"............4,500.00
Lamp, dancing nude silhouettes against rect glass panel, 11"....1,275.00
Lamp, nude as butterfly w/frosted glass wings, 10¼" 2,850.00
Lamp, nude holds rod above, glass panel hangs by rings, 13" 1,750.00

Lamp, nude kneels and supports disc shade, black finish, restored, 10½", $1,100.00. (Photo courtesy Skinner Auctioneers and Appraisers of Antiques and Fine Art)

Lamp, nude kneels before 4" bubble ball, 8" 1,200.00
Lamp, nude stands atop frost glass panel, lt below, 10".............1,050.00
Lamp, nudes (2) stand, face ea other through glass rods, 12" 1,750.00
Lamp, nudes (4) stand, surround sq glass cylinder, 13" 2,250.00
Mirror, standing nude holds 6" gold-backed mirror, 15" 1,250.00
Smoke stand, standing nude atop arch, mtd to sq base, 22" 1,150.00

Frankoma

John Frank opened a studio pottery in Norman, Oklahoma, in 1933, creating bowls, vases, etc., which bore the ink-stamped marks 'Frank Pottery' or 'Frank Potteries.' At this time, only a few hundred pieces were produced. Within a year, Mr. Frank had incorporated. Though not everything was marked, he continued to use these marks for two years. Items thus marked are not easy to find and command high prices. In 1935 the pot and leopard mark was introduced.

The Frank family moved to Sapulpa, Oklahoma, in 1938. In November of that year, a fire destroyed everything. The 'Pot and Puma' mark was never re-created, and today collectors avidly search for items with this mark. The rarest of all Frankoma marks is 'First Kiln at Sapulpa 6-7-38' which was applied to only about 100 pieces fired on that date.

Grace Lee Frank worked beside her husband, creating many limited edition Madonna plates, Christmas cards, advertising items, and birds. She died in 1996.

Clay is important in determining when a piece was made. Ada clay, used through 1954, is a creamy beige color. In 1955 they changed over to a red brick shale from Sapulpa. Today most clay has a pinkish-red cast, though the pinkish cast is sometimes so muted that a novice might mistake it for Ada clay.

Rutile glazes were created early in the pottery's history; these give the ware a two-tone color treatment. However the US government closed the rutile mines in 1970 and Frank found it necessary to buy this material from Australia. The newer rutile produced different results, especially noticeable with their Woodland Moss glaze.

Upon John Frank's death in 1973, their daughter Joniece became president. Though the pottery burned again in 1983, the building was quickly rebuilt. Due to so many setbacks, however, the company found it necessary to file chapter 11 in order to remain in control and stay in business.

Mr. Richard Bernstein purchased Frankoma in 1991. Sometime in 2001, Mr. Bernstein began to put the word out that Frankoma Pottery Company was for sale. It did not sell and because of declining sales, he closed the doors on December 23, 2004. The company sold July 1, 2005, to another pottery company owned by Det and Crystal Merryman of Las Vegas, Nevada. They took possession the next day and began bringing life back into the Frankoma Pottery once more. Today they are producing pottery from the Frankoma molds as well as their own pottery molds, which goes by the name of 'Merrymac Collection,' a collection of whimsical dogs.

Frank purchased Synar Ceramics of Muskogee, Oklahoma, in 1958; in late '59, the name was changed to Gracetone Pottery in honor of Grace Lee Frank. Until supplies were exhausted, they continued to produce Synar's white clay line in glazes such as Alligator, Woodpine, White Satin, Ebony, Wintergreen, and a black and white straw combination. At the Frankoma pottery, an 'F' was added to the stock number on items made at both locations. New glazes were Aqua, Pink Champagne, Cinnamon Toast, and Black, known as Gunmetal. Gracetone was sold in 1962 to Mr. Taylor, who had been a long-time family friend and manager of the pottery. Taylor continued operations until 1967. The only dinnerware pattern produced there was Orbit, which today is hard to find. Other Gracetone pieces are becoming scarce as well. If you'd like to learn more, we recommend *Frankoma and Other Oklahoma Potteries* by Phyllis Boone (Bess), our advisor; you will find her address in the Directory under Oklahoma.

Vase, two nudes in high relief, cobalt on Sapulpa clay, GS (for Gerald Smith) #50, limited edition, 11", $250.00. (Photo courtesy Belhorn Auction Services, LLC on LiveAuctioneers.com)

Ashtray, cigar, Draft Proof, Prairie Gr, #455 .... 50.00
Ashtray, Fish, Desert Gold, Sapulpa clay, #T7 .... 15.00
Ashtray, Tulsa Oil Capital..., OK state shape, brn satin, Sapulpa clay....15.00
Baker, Lazybones, Autumn Yel, w/candle-warmer base, 3-qt.......... 60.00
Bean pot, Wagon Wheel, Prairie Gr, horseshoe hdls, #94W 55.00
Bookends, Charger Horse, Prairie Gr, #420, 7".............................. 225.00
Bookends, Collie Head, Wht Sand, Sapulpa clay, #122 .... 200.00
Bowl, cereal, Desert Gold, Sapulpa clay, 5"..8.00
Bowl, Clamshell, dk Coffee w/Flame int, Sapulpa clay, #T1 .... 30.00
Bowl, console, Dogwood, Prairie Gr, Sapulpa clay, #200................ 35.00
Bowl, Dogwood, Prairie Gr, shallow, 13x8½", $25 to...................... 30.00
Bowl, Plainsman, Prairie Gr, 10⅝x18¾" 75.00
Bowl, vegetable, Plainsman, Desert Gold, sq, $18 to...................... 20.00
Candleholder, Aladdin Lamp, Brn Satin, Sapulpa clay, #309, ea... 25.00
Candleholders, Dogwood, Prairie Gr, pr $25 to 30.00
Carafe, Desert Gold, Sapulpa clay, 8"... 40.00

Casserole, Lazy Bones, hdls, w/lid, #4V, 7x9¾" L............................ 50.00
Casserole, Wagon Wheel, Prairie Gr, Ada clay, w/lid, $60 to......... 75.00
Christmas card, 1944, $500 to.. 600.00
Christmas card, 1947-48, $95 to 115.00
Christmas card, 1952, Donna Frank, $150 to 200.00
Christmas card, 1953, $90 to... 110.00
Christmas card, 1973-75 .... 30.00
Christmas plate, Flight Into Egypt, Della Robia Wht, J Frank, 1968 ...60.00
Creamer, Wagon Wheel, Desert Sand, Ada clay, 2⅜" 12.50
Cup/saucer, demi, Plainsman, Brn Satin, Ada clay......................... 20.00
Dealer sign, Frankoma Pottery, brn & tan, 6½" L, $35 to.............. 40.00
Decanter, Prairie Gr, #7JH, w/lid, 10¼" 55.00
Flower holder, Duck, Prairie Gr, Ada clay, #184, 1942, 3¾"......... 240.00
Jar, honey, Mayan Aztec, Prairie Gr, #7JH, 35th Anniversary, 9" .. 25.00
Jug, mini, Uncle Slug, Prairie Gr, #561, 2¼".................................. 145.00
Leaf dish, dk brn satin, #226, med, $10 to 12.50
Mug, Aztec, Woodland Moss, $5 to 8.00
Mug, Donkey, Plum, 1983 .... 45.00
Mug, Elephant or Donkey, 1973-76, $30 to 40.00
Mug, Elephant, Nat'l Republican Women's Club, gray, 1968......... 60.00
Mug, Elephant, Reagan/Bush, Celery Gr w/wht int, 1981, $30 to . 35.00
Napkin rings, Butterfly, Sapulpa clay, #263, 4 for 20.00
Pitcher, honey, Prairie Gr, #8, 1950s, 6¾" 17.50
Pitcher, mini, Spiral, Ivory, Ada clay, 2", $75 to 85.00
Planter, Cactus, Prairie Gr, orig label, 7x5x3".............................. 70.00
Plate, Christmas, Good Will Toward Men, 1965 .... 62.50
Plate, Christmas, No Room at the Inn, Wht Sand, 1971 .... 20.00
Plate, Oklahoma State, Desert Gold 25.00
Plate, Teenager of Bible, David the Musician, Desert Gold, 1974, 7" ...20.00
Plate, Teenagers of Bible, Martha the Homemaker, 1982, 6½", $20 to.... 25.00
Plate, Wagon Wheel, Prairie Gr, Sapulpa clay, #94FL, 10" 10.00
Ramekin (bbl w/lid), Desert Gold, Sapulpa clay, 1950-61, #97U, $40 to. 45.00
Sculpture, Fan Dancer, rubbed bsk, pk clay.................................... 60.00
Sculpture, Greyhound, Autumn Yel, 1983 ltd ed, #827, $200 to . 225.00
Sculpture, Puma, Dusty Rose, Ada clay, 7", $85 to........................ 125.00
Sculpture, Puma, reclining, blk on Ada clay, $110 to..................... 150.00
Shakers, bull, blk gloss, Ada clay, 2x3", pr $165 to........................ 175.00
Shakers, milk can, Desert Gold, Sapulpa clay, 4¾x2½", pr............. 45.00
Spoon rest, fish form, yel/gr/brn, Christmas pc made in 1960s, 4".. 55.00
Teacup, Plainsman, Prairie Gr, 5-oz, $10 to 12.00
Teapot, Westwind, Desert Gold, Sapulpa clay, #6T, 6" 25.00
Tray, Palm Leaf, Desert Gold, Sapulpa clay, #226 .... 85.00
Trivet, Horseshoe, Desert Sand, 3-ftd, #5TR, 6", $22 to 25.00
Vase, bud, Snail, Flame, Sapulpa clay, #31, $30 to 40.00
Vase, collector, V-3, 1971 .... 85.00
Vase, collector, V-5, 1973, 13".. 85.00
Vase, collector, V-8, w/stopper, 13" 75.00
Vase, collector, V-9, w/stopper, 13" 65.00
Vase, collector, V-10 & V-11, ea $40 to 50.00
Vase, collector, V-14, $75 to 80.00
Vase, Pansy/Wedding Ring, turq, Sapulpa clay, #200 .... 50.00
Vase, Ram's Head, Verde Bronze, Ada clay, #38, 5⅝x5⅛", $65 to.. 85.00
Wall pocket, Billiken, Prairie Gr, Jesters Day..., 6½", $85 to 100.00

Fraternal

Fraternal memorabilia is a vast and varied field. Emblems representing the various organizations have been used to decorate cups, shaving mugs, plates, and glassware. Medals, swords, documents, and other ceremonial paraphernalia from the 1800s and early 1900s are especially prized. Our advisor for Odd Fellows is Greg Spiess; he is listed in the Directory under Illinois. Information on Masonic and Shrine memorabilia has been provided by David Smies, who is listed under Kansas. Assistance concerning Elks collectibles was provided by David Wendel; he is listed in the Directory under Missouri.

Eagles

Banner, embroidered silk with gilt metal threads and golden-yellow tassels mounted on ornate cast brass bar, shield lettered: Instituted July 29, 1900, La Fayette, Ind., F.O.E. No. 347, reverse is blue silk brocade, 62x41", VG+, $250.00.
(Photo courtesy Cowan's Auctions, Inc. on LiveAuctioneers.com)

Brooch, gold-tone bow w/FOE emblem button, Ladies' Auxiliary, 1½" ... 15.00
Pendant charm, gold-tone metal w/enamel, 2-sided 22.50
Ring, eagle & FOE, 10k gold, red & bl enameling 40.00
Sauceboat, Eagle on wht restaurantware body, 3½x9" 15.00
Watch fob, emb eagle & FOE above enameled shield, Whitehead & Hoag...90.00

Elks

Decanter, star in relief on brn tones, Jim Beam, 1968 .... 20.00
Bottle, 100th Anniversary...1968, Regal, Beam Distilling 27.00
Lapel pin, elk & clock in relief, bl & gold enamel, screw-type bk.. 15.00
Match case, 11th Hour emblem on 14k yel gold 250.00
Ring, 10k yel & wht gold w/.80 carat bl dmn, Mecca, 1937 .... 300.00
Ring, Elks Club & blk onyx stone on 18k yel gold, MIB 45.00
Statue, elk bust, CI, on marble base, 9x5" 42.50
Token, copper-colored alum, Good for 1 Drink 15.00
Watch fob, elk's tooth, w/orig chain, 1⅛" 65.00

Knights Templar

Cufflinks, mc enamel & gilt in clear dome glass, crusader seal 22.00
Cufflinks, sword & star symbols on gold, 1950s, ⅞" 220.00
Medal, 50th Annual Conclave, Philadelphia...1903, dangling disk.10.00
Ring, sterling, seal, XPISTI SIGILLUM MILITUM 158.00
Sword belt, 3 sliding knights on belt, Ames, EX 125.00
Sword, ivory hdl, many symbols, 1900s, +scabbard 325.00

Masons

Apron, bl silk & wht leather, 3 bl silk circles, snake fastener 100.00
Ashtray, sq & compass, in bl & gold on wht ceramic, 1954, 6¼x6¼" ..20.00
Book, Freemasonry & Concordant Orders..., leather bound, 1915, NM... 315.00
Bookends, sq & compass, bronze finish, 5⅝" 45.00
Centerpiece, 2 hanging baskets, Walker & Hall Sheffield, ca 1915 .800.00
Chart/hieroglyphic monitor, emblems/degrees/etc, hardcover, 1856..135.00
Collar, burgundy velvet w/silver embr/fringe/tassels 120.00
Decanter, symbols & open book, ceramic, much gold, 1971 .... 75.00
Fan, silk w/HP emblems in collage, wooden sticks, VG 55.00
Fez, blk wool, red tassel, handmade, M 55.00
Hat, dbl-headed eagle, Prince of Royal Secret, 32nd degree, 1915...50.00
Medal, 18k yel gold w/bl enamel, 3-part, Spencer London, ca 1906 ..325.00
Medal, eye & compass, 14k yel gold, ca 1917, 2⅜" 285.00
Pocketwatch, 14k yel gold, 12 tribes, Hamilton, 1920s, #914 ...... 480.00
Ring, .25ct total weight dmns in 10k wht gold 415.00
Ring, 32nd degree, .20ct VS-2/GH dmn+6 sm dmns in 14k yel gold...450.00

Ring, 5 .48ct total weight emeralds in wht gold mts, 18k yel gold band...315.00
Ring, skull & X-bones, 14k yel gold, Memento Mori, 3rd degree.. 725.00
Robe, king's, purple velvet & spun metallic silk, brass chains, 1890s .. 135.00
Watch fob, emblem w/eng initials on bk, 14k yel gold, ¾" dia 150.00

Odd Fellows

Banner, cream cloth w/gold trim & tassels, embr dove, 29x19" 35.00
Book, Constitution, Rules & Regulations, cloth spine, 1904, 4x5"..10.00
Carving, Indian head, varnished wood, hollowed int, ca 1900, 12" ...195.00
Chip, crest & seal, yel, US Playing Card, 1924 .... 22.50
Cornucopia, cvd/pnt wood, mts to wall, OH, 19th C, 20" 2,235.00
Cornucopia, pnt wood, cvd to mt on wall, 1800s, 20" 2,250.00
Coverlet, fraternal symbols, red/yel, 1-pc, Beiderwand, 94x83" ... 450.00
Cupboard, grained pine w/IOOF on 2-panel do, fitted int, 32x25x14".635.00
Hat, red velvet w/gold embr & brass piping, ca 1900 .... 40.00
Hourglass, pnt wood, representing life/flight of time, 1800s, 10" ...1,060.00
Hourglass, pnt wood, represents flight of time, OH, 19th C, 10"...1,050.00
Magic lantern slides, mc, MC Lilley...OH, 1915, 40 in wooden box... 100.00
Ribbon, IOOF Amity Encampment, purple w/gold fringe, 1890s .. 50.00
Ring, eye/skull/X-bones, 10k wht gold w/enamel, 1920s 345.00
Robe, blk velvet w/cream accents, Ward-Stilson Co, ca 1940s 45.00
Scepter, cvd/pnt wood, gilt finial & rings, OH, 19th C, 36"...... 1,000.00
Staff, cvd pnt shaft w/serpent figure, OH, 1800s, 65¼"................. 880.00
Staff, cvd walnut, 11" heart-in-hand finial, IN, 59" 2,750.00

Shrine

Book rack, brass-plated CI, camels, folds flat, 1920s 75.00
Brooch, heart w/dangling symbols in center, rhinestones, ORA, 1½"..25.00
Brooch, rhinestone-encrusted crown w/gold-tone sword,⅞" 15.00
Humidor, glass w/wht metal lid, symbol finial, 1914 .... 125.00
Plate, Potentate's Ball 1950, gold trim, H&K Tunstall, 9¾" 20.00
Postcard, Phila United...Hospital, real photo, 1940s-50s, unused 6.00
Tumbler, emb/HP Indian chief, temple emblem, Pittsburgh 1903, 3¼"..65.00

Miscellaneous

American Legion, token, 20th Anniversary Armistice, 1918-38... 10.00
Daughters of Am Revolution, yearbook, heavy paper cover, 1932-33 .15.00
Knights of Columbus, matchbook cover, 2 shields, brass, 1919...... 75.00
Knights of Pythias, sword, eng 26" blade, Pettibone Bros, +scabbard.. 110.00
Knights of Pythias, watch fob, gold-filled w/mc enamel, 1⅜x⅞" 55.00
Order of Moose, bookends, bronze color moose, 1920-30s 55.00
Order of Moose, lapel pin, 10k gold w/4 stones, CLUB at bottom. 48.00
Order of Moose, watch fob, ca 1900, no chain, 1½x1⅝" 32.00
Order of Sons of Am, badge, cello w/bronze holder, 1906, +mc ribbon.. 50.00
Rotary, songbook, glossy cover, WWII era 5.00
Royal Order of Buffaloes, badge, brass 6-point star w/bl enamel 50.00

Fruit Jars

 As early as 1829, canning jars were being manufactured for use in the home preservation of foodstuffs. For the past 25 years, they have been sought as popular collectibles. At the last estimate, over 4,000 fruit jars and variations were known to exist. Some are very rare, perhaps one-of-a-kind examples known to have survived to the present day. Among the most valuable are the black glass jars, the amber Van Vliet, and the cobalt Millville. These often bring prices in excess of $20,000.00 when they can be found. Aside from condition, values are based on age, rarity, color, and special features. Unless noted otherwise, values are given for clear glass jars.

Advance, aqua, glass lid, wire bail or metal clamp, qt, $350 to 400.00

Air-Tight, amber, zinc lid, pt, $75 to 100.00
Atlas E-Z Seal, aqua, ½-pt 15.00
Atlas E-Z Seal, aqua, qt, $6 to 8.00
Atlas E-Z Seal, gr, qt 10.00
Atlas Good Luck, ½-pt, $15 to 20.00
Atlas Mason (Mini), strong shoulder, 2-pc lid, pt 25.00
Atlas Mason's Patent, qt, $12 to 15.00
Ball (date error 1988 should be 1908), aqua, qt, $8 to 10.00
Ball (dropped 'a' script) Sure Seal, tall, bl, 22-oz 150.00
Ball (script), machine made, clear, qt, $5 to 7.00
Ball (script), Perfect Mason, gr base, clear jar, pt 5.00
Ball Eclipse Wide Mouth, pt 1.00
Ball Ideal, rnd, ½-gal 3.00
Ball Perfect Mason, bl, 40-oz 25.00
Ball Sanitary Sure Seal, Pat'd July 14 1908, 3 sizes, ea $15 to 20.00
Ball Special, bl, qt, $15 to 25.00
Ball Sure Seal, base: Pat July 14, 1908, bl, ½-gal 25.00
Ball, Property of Southern Methodist Orphas Home Waco TX, ½-gal, $100 to .150.00
Banner, clear, trademark registered, 3 sizes, ea, $15 to 20.00
Bennett's No 2 (error, backwards 2), aqua, qt, min 700.00
Bernardin Mason, 3 sizes, ea $5 to 7.00
Black-eyed Susan, Morning Glory, pt 3.00
Boldt Mason Jar, aqua or bl, 3 sizes, zinc lid, ea $30 to 40.00
Buckeye, aqua, glass lid, iron yoke, qt, $325 to 375.00
Cadiz Jar, aqua, glass threaded lid, qt, $900 to 1,000.00
Canton Mfg Co Boston (base), amber, ½-pt 20.00
Chief (The), aqua, tin lid, unique locking bar, qt, $400 to 450.00
Clark's Peerless, aqua, qt, $20 to 25.00
Cleveland Fruit Juice Co, ½-gal, $5 to 7.00

Climax, blue, ½-pint, $125.00.
(Photo courtesy Old Barn Auction on LiveAuctioneers.com)

Clyde Glass Works, clear or gr, glass lid, qt, $10 to 12.00
Crown Crown (bulged crown), aqua, midget 85.00
Crown Mason, pt 2.00
Cunningham & Ihmsen Pittsburgh PA, lt bl, ½-gal 50.00
Cunningham & Ihmsen, aqua, wax seal, qt, $30 to 40.00
Darling Imperial (The), aqua, 2 sizes, ea $30 to 45.00
Dictator (The), aqua, wax seal, qt, $90 to 110.00
Dictator D, aqua, metal lid, clip, bk: DI Holcomb Dec 14, 1869, qt, $85 to .. 100.00
Drey Improved Ever Seal, pt, $3 to 5.00
Dyson's, glass lid, qt, $20 to 30.00
Economy, base: Portland Ore..., qt 4.00
Eerie Lightning, 3 sizes, ea $40 to 50.00
F&J Bodine Philadelphia, aqua, 52-oz 400.00
Fahnstock Albree & Co, open pontil, gr, stopper, qt 250.00
Federal Fruit Jar, olive, qt, min 450.00
Franklin Dexter Fruit Jar, aqua, qt, $50 to 60.00
Gem, aqua, midget 50.00
Gilberds Improved (Star), aqua, qt 325.00
Golden-State Improved Mason, 2 sizes, ea $30 to 45.00
Hahne & Co, aqua, qt, $50 to 60.00
Hazel Preserve Jar, ½-pt 35.00
Hero Improved, aqua, glass lid, screw band, pt or qt, ea $60 to 80.00

Imperial, Patent April 20th 1886 on base, w/lid, pt 150.00
Jewell Jar, Made in Canada, pt, $4 to 6.00
JW Beardsley's Sons New York USA Patent Feb 10 1903, ½-pt 10.00
Kerr Self Sealing Mason, 65th Anniversary 1903-63, gold, qt 60.00
La Lorraine (arch above thistle blossom), w/lid, 1-liter 80.00
Leotric, sm mouth, sun-colored amethyst, qt 45.00
Magic, w/star, gr, w/orig clamp, qt 575.00
Magic TM Mason Jar, qt 1.00
Mansfield Mason, qt, $40 to 60.00
Mason (arched) Ball, bl, qt 15.00
Mason Star Jar, qt 1.00
Mason, Patent Nov 30th 1858, amber, ½-gal 450.00
Mason's (X) Patent Nov 30th 1858, lt emb, ½-gal 190.00
Mason's 32 Patent Nov 30th 1858, bl, qt 200.00
Mason's H Patent Nov 30th 1858, aqua, qt 50.00
Mason's Improved (hourglass), Patent May 10th 1870, aqua, qt 25.00
Mason's Patent Nov 30th 1858, base: ES Co, aqua, midget 120.00
Mason's Patent Nov 30th 1858, base: Hero 5 in 1858, aqua, midget . 50.00
Mason's Patent Nov 30th 1858, base: S&R, aqua, ½-gal 35.00
Mason's Patent Nov 30th 1858, med yel olive, qt 600.00
Model, Patent Aug 27 1867, aqua, ½-gal 300.00
Newman's Patent Dec 20th 1859, w/lid, aqua, qt, min 1,100.00
Pearl (The), aqua, glass lid, zinc band, qt, $50 to 65.00
Port Mason's Patent Nov 30th 1858, Port arched on base, aqua, qt . 200.00
Presto, ½-pt 35.00
Princess, 3 sizes, ea $20 to 30.00
Putnam (on base), aqua, $20 to 30.00
Regal, qt, $55 to 65.00
Royal (in crown), full measure, ½-gal 25.00
Saleman's Sample, base: Putnam, aqua, ½-pt 200.00
Sealtite, base: PA G Co, qt, $20 to 25.00
Smalley's Royal (on neck), ½-pt 25.00
Square Mason, 4 sizes, ea $5 to 7.00
Stark (K in star) Patent, w/lid, qt 100.00
Sterling Mason, zinc lid, 3 sizes, ea $2 to 4.00
Trademark Lightning, Registered US Patent Office, apple gr, qt .. 100.00
Valve Jar (The), gr, unique wire clamp, rare, qt, min 400.00
Victory in circle, Patent Feb 9th 1864...June 22 1867, aqua, qt 85.00
Wears (in circle), pt 9.00
WW Lyman 43, Patent Feb 9th 1984, aqua, qt 40.00
Yeoman's, aqua, cork stopper, qt or ½-gal, $75 to 100.00

Fry

Henry Fry established his glassworks in 1901 in Rochester, Pennsylvania. There, until 1933, he produced glassware of the finest quality. In the early years they produced beautiful cut glass; and when it began to wane in popularity, Fry turned to the manufacture of occasional pieces and oven glassware. He is perhaps most famous for the opalescent pearl art glass called 'Foval.' It was sometimes made with Delft Blue or Jade Green trim in combination. Because it was in production for only a short time in 1926 and 1927, it is hard to find. He is equally as famous for his extremely high-quality cut glass blanks which were used by a large percentage of the other cut glass houses across the country. Fry also produced several different colors such as Rose Pink, Emerald Green, Azure Blue, Royal Blue, Black, Fuchsia (purple), and Canary, along with etched glass, oven glass, and a large line of industrial glass. Our advisor for Fry is Mike Sabo; he is listed in the Directory under Pennsylvania. See also Kitchen Collectibles, Glassware.

Baker, pearl ovenware, 9" sq 30.00
Bean pot, mk Fry Ovenware #1924-1, w/lid, 1-qt 85.00
Bonbon, cut, dmns & fans, sgn, 5¾" 60.00

Bottle, scent, Foval, eng, intaglio to Delft Bl top, bell form, 4".... 600.00
Bowl, center, Foval, Delft Bl rim & flat ft, 5¼x9¼" 475.00
Bowl, console, Jade Gr, silver o/l to everted rim/disk ft, 5x10"..... 500.00
Bowl, cut, Pinwheel, 8"... 150.00
Bowl, Foval, onion form w/2 sqd Jade Gr ft, #823, 4" 400.00
Cake plate, pearl ovenware, sq, #1947 .... 25.00
Candleholder, blk, wide flat ft, 3", ea 18.00
Candlesticks, Jade Gr w/sterling o/l to rim, cup & disk ft, 10", pr . 800.00
Casserole, covered, #1932, opal, sgn Fry Ovenglass on bottom...... 40.00
Casserole, gr, w/lid, #1938, 7".. 110.00
Compote, Foval, Delft Bl stem, opal body & disk ft, 7x6" 250.00
Compote, Foval, Jade Gr stem, silver o/l, #2502, 7" 350.00
Compote, Grape etching (bowl only), ftd 50.00
Creamer/sugar bowl, Foval, Delft Bl hdls/bases, #2001, 3", 2½" ... 150.00
Cup, custard, eng, 6-oz, $10 to 12.00

Candlesticks, ivory melds into brn, bl at trumpet ft, 10", pr......... 300.00
Doorstop, sleeping cat, gr flambé, imp horizontal mk, 8" L 1,500.00
Jar, thick cucumber glaze, low hdld, #656, 8" dia.......................... 450.00
Lamp, Café-au-Lait matt, ldgl glass inserts on 10" shade, #804, 17".6,600.00
Lamp, Cat's Eye & Flemington Gr flambé shade & std, Pat Pend, 21x16".17,000.00
Lamp, Chinese Bl flambé, ldgl glass inserts on shade, 17x9¼", NM.4,800.00
Lamp, Flemington Gr flambé, mushroom form w/ldgl inserts, rstr, 17"..9,600.00
Lamp, Leopard Skin crystalline, mushroom form, ldgl insets, 17x17", NM ..36,000.00
Pitcher, gray & bl drip, flared cylinder, 10", +4 3½" mugs 275.00
Urn, multi-tone bl matt, rim-to-hip hdls, drilled, 10½"................ 100.00
Vase, amber crystalline, 4 buttresses, 10¼x8".............................2,700.00
Vase, bl & gr flambé, shouldered, 11½" 300.00
Vase, bl/brn/tan streaks w/bl crystalline, incurvate rim, 8¼" 400.00
Vase, bl flambe crystalline, classic form, imp mk, 16½" 3,000.00
Vase, bl flambé, Asian trumpeted, raised band on neck, #495, 15"... 975.00

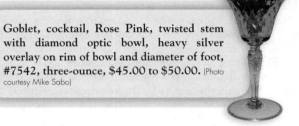

Goblet, cocktail, Rose Pink, twisted stem with diamond optic bowl, heavy silver overlay on rim of bowl and diameter of foot, #7542, three-ounce, $45.00 to $50.00. (Photo courtesy Mike Sabo)

Vase, blue matt, four shoulder handles, #514, 13", $1,440.00. (Photo courtesy Treadway Gallery on LiveAuctioneers.com)

Plate, grill, amber, 3-part 45.00
Plate, grill, pk, 3-part, 8½" 50.00
Plate, pie, pearl ovenware w/orange trim, #1916, 9" 35.00
Sherbet, Rose Pk w/etched panels, ftd, 4¾x3½" 18.00
Teapot, Foval w/Delft Bl spout/finial/hdl, silver trim, 7", +6c/s.1,000.00
Tray, biscuit, pearl ovenware, #1934.. 20.00
Tray, sandwich, #19814, clear glass w/HP enamel band & floral decor... 50.00
Trivet, pearl ovenware, #1959, 8".. 30.00
Tumbler, lemonade, Foval, Jade Gr hdl, #9416, 5½"..................... 50.00
Vase, bud, Azure Bl, ruffled rim 200.00
Vase, Foval, Delft Bl knop/ft, tall U-form w/slight flare, 9x5" 325.00

Vase, brn crystalline over mustard matt, 8x10", EX 2,200.00
Vase, caramel flambé, bullet form, 6½x4¾" 400.00
Vase, Cat's Eye flambé, 16x5" 4,800.00
Vase, Cat's-Eye flambé, melon shape, 7x5½" 480.00
Vase, Chinese Bl crystalline flambé, hdls, 9½x7" 500.00
Vase, Chinese Bl flambé, 10½x10½" 1,000.00
Vase, Chinese Bl flambé, 17½x7", NM 1,440.00
Vase, frothy cucumber matt, baluster, 12x4¾" 1,000.00
Vase, frothy cucumber over buff, scalloped rim, hdls, 9¼x11"...... 660.00
Vase, frothy turq on Famille Rose flambé, bbl form, 17x16", EX.. 720.00
Vase, gr crystalline, bulb base, rim-to-hip hdls, 6x6" 250.00
Vase, ivory to mauve frothy flambe, bullet shape, grinding chip, 13x8" ..3,360.00
Vase, khaki gr/cobalt/Cat's-Eye flambé, faceted, 9¾x5½" 515.00
Vase, Mirror Blk to Chinese Bl flambé, shouldered, 12x11½" ...3,000.00
Vase, Mirror Blk/cobalt/Famille Rose flambé, shouldered, 7½x7" . 660.00
Vase, tan/bl/brn crystalline, hdls, label, 12" 475.00
Vase, tan/brn/gr flambe, bulb, ftd, chip rstr at lip, 12x4½"............ 200.00
Vase, turq & gr, bulb, 3 hdls, imp mk, 6½x7¾" 300.00

Fulper

Throughout the nineteenth century the Fulper Pottery in Flemington, New Jersey, produced utilitarian and commercial wares. But it was during the span from 1902 to 1935, the Arts and Crafts period in particular, that the company became prominent producers of beautifully glazed art pottery. Although most pieces were cast rather than hand decorated, the graceful and classical shapes used together with wonderful experimental glaze combinations made each piece a true work of art.

The company also made dolls' heads, Kewpies, figural perfume lamps, and powder boxes. Their lamps with the colored glass inserts are extremely rare and avidly sought by collectors. Examples prized most highly by collectors today are those produced before the devastating fire in 1929 and subsequent takeover by Martin Stangl (see Stangl Pottery).

Several marks were used: a vertical in-line 'Fulper' being the most common in ink or incised, an impressed block horizontal mark, Flemington, Rafco, Prang, and paper labels. Unmarked examples often surface and can be identified by shape and glaze characteristics. Values are determined by size, desirability of glaze, and rarity of form. Fulper has proven to be an affordable art pottery for the budget-minded collector. Our advisor for this category is Douglass White; he is listed in the Directory under Florida.

Bowl, 3 figural supports, brn & bl crystalline, 7x10½" 300.00
Bowl, Café-au-Lait over mustard, grinding chips/fleck, 6½x14½" ..2,000.00

Furniture

Throughout history a person's wealth and status could quickly be determined by the type of furniture he possessed. Throughout each period of time, there have been distinct changes in styles, choice of woods, and techniques — all clues the expert can use to determine just when an item was made. Regional differences as well as secondary wood choices give us clues as to country of origin. The end of the Civil War brought with it the Industrial Revolution and the capability of mass producing machine-made furniture.

Important to the collector (and dealer) is the ability to recognize furniture on a 'good, better, best' approach. Age alone does not equal value. During this recessionary market, the 'best' of forms have continued to sell and appreciate, while the 'better' middle market has shown a decline both at auction and at retail. Many of the values given this year emphasize the ups and downs apparent in today's marketplace.

Pre-sale estimates by auction houses appear to be less speculative this year and are closer to the actual selling price. Top collectors are paying more attention to the details of quality items. Good vintage reproductions from the first half of the twentieth century are gaining in popularity. Both American and English furniture are good choices for buyers. On the upswing from previous years are original painted pieces that fall under the best of form in the primitive category. Prices for 'floor ready' upholstered pieces in classical styles show that they are still in demand.

Items marked with (**) are pieces in the best of form and of museum quality.

Please note: If a piece actually dates to the period of time during which its style originated, we will use the name of the style only. For example: 'Hepplewhite' will indicate an American piece from roughly the late 1700s to 1815. The term 'style' will describe a piece that is far removed from the original time frame. 'Hepplewhite style' refers to examples from the turn of the century. When the term 'repro' is used it will mean that the item in question is less than 30 years old and is being sold on a secondary market. When only one dimension is given, for blanket chests, dry sinks, settees, sideboards, sofas, and tables, it is length, unless otherwise noted.

Condition is the most important factor to consider in determining value. It is also important to remember that *where* a piece sells has a definite bearing on the price it will realize, due simply to regional preference. To learn more about furniture, we recommend *Early American Furniture* by John Obbard. In the listings that follow, items are in good condition unless noted otherwise. See also Arts and Crafts; Fifties Modern; Limbert; Wallace Nutting; Shaker Items; Stickley; Frank Lloyd Wright.

This year you may notice a few subtle differences in the furniture listings. The Modernist (or mid-century modern) classification has made great inroads in popularity amongst auction buyers. It should continue to be a strong trend for dealers and collectors. Because of this, we include many more listings for this classification. You will also notice that coffee tables have been added to the tables section. Unbelievably, the practical coffee table has almost reached the age where it can be considered an antique! Between the mid-century modern collectors and savvy interior decorators, it is time for us to take notice of them.

Our advisor for this category is Suzy McLennan Anderson, CAPP of Walterboro, South Carolina. Her mailing address is listed in the Directory under South Carolina. Requests that do not include a SASE regretfully can no longer be answered.

Key:
* — auction price but at least 25% under the norm
** — museum quality
: — over (example, 1 drw:2 do)

bj — bootjack	hdw — hardware
brd — board	hplwht — hepplewhite
c&b — claw and ball	lqr — lacquer
cab — cabriole	mld — molding/molded
co — country	RR — Renaissance Revival
do — door	rswd — rosewood
ftbd — footboard	SNBT — swans neck bonnet top
Geo — Georgian, George	SNP — swans neck pediment
glz — glazed	sten — stenciled
hdbd — headboard	W/M — William and Mary

Armoires, See also Wardrobes

Art Deco, Zebra wood, 2 do, shelved int, bun ft, 70x55x17" 3,150.00
French, breakfront, mld pediment, cvd frieze, 19th C, 130x117x25"..11,210.00
French, Napoleon III, faux bamboo, 1 mirror do, 83x37x18" 1,925.00
French, Provincial, pine, 2 do, scroll ft, ca 1850, 91x59x25" 590.00
Louis XV, walnut, 2 mirror do w/elaborate cartouche over drws 101x53"..775.00

Modern, Hagemann, wood & steel, blk lqr, 2 do, 1950s, 72x51x23" .2,475.00
European, Continental, floral, 1 do, mld cornice, 67x54x25" ...4,600.00
Northern European, Continental, flame grpt, 2 do, bracket ft, 74x49x22"..1,450.00
QA, walnut, Arched Crown, 2 arched do, 3 drws, 84x50x20" ..1,200.00
Vict, Aesthetic movement, blk lqr, faux bamboo, 2 do ov 1 dr, 89x39x18".1,175.00
Vict, oak, 2 mirrored do over 3 drw w/appl cvg, 87x55x24" 2,600.00
Vict, rswd, rococo, arched top, mirrored do, 105x47x22".........3,800.00

Beds

Campaign, English, walnut, caned panels, 1840, 13x78x21".....1,400.00
Campaign, Fr, iron, rococo, 1850, 33x41x70"................................ 775.00
Canopy & tester, Fed, mixed wood, shaped hdbd, fluted posts, shaped tester, 72x36"...500.00
Canopy & tester, Fed, red pnt over maple, shaped hdbd & tester, 71x54x72"..750.00
Canopy/tester, pr, Geo II, canopy, mahog, pnt, 18th C ** 21,000.00
Cast iron, Vict, 8 rods & rosettes w/blanket rack on ftbd, 48x47x69"... 150.00
Cast iron, Vict, w/cast floral & scroll design, tester, ornate, 90x54x80"..600.00
Daybed, Emp, mahog, Boston, rolled crest w/flanking cornucopias, 33x22x86"..11,700.00
Daybed, Fr, Louis Philippe, ident, hdbd & ftbd, curved rails, ca 1850, 42x72x39"...780.00
Daybed, QA, walnut, vasiform splat, cab legs, uphl, 36x24x76".. 6,500.00
Half tester, Edwardian, mahog & uphl, acanthus cvd posts, 92x73x72"...5,575.00
Half tester, Vict, rococo, rswd, pierced floral crest, fluted columns, 113x94x75" **.45,600.00
Half tester, Vict, RR, walnut, shell cvd crest, oval panels, 103x79x86".....1,650.00
Half tester, William IV, mahog, shaped, mld tester, cvd pendants, 95x82x55" ..2,650.00
Poster, low post, pr, Am, mahog, Foot-Reynolds Co, 54x36x76" .480.00
Poster, low trn post, curly maple, scroll hdbd, 19th C , 49x51x74" 940.00
Poster, tall, Am, mahog, reeded & acanthus cvd, 19th C , 87x62x66". 1,850.00
Poster, tall, Am, mahog, tapered posts, 19th C, 96x70x85" 570.00
Poster, tall, Spanish, 17th C, walnut, trn & spindles, 78x82x44" ... 2,900.00
Rope, low post, red pnt, cabled hdbd, 36x52x76"......................... 275.00
Rope, low post, maple, bl pnt, scrolled hdbd, acorn finials, 38x45x74" ..590.00
Rope, tester, mahog Spiral cvd posts, ca 1840, 86x52x77" 4,100.00
Trundle, co, poplar & ash fr, wooden wheels, old pnt, 17x42x63" 330.00
Trundle, Sheraton, curly maple, gabled pediment, trn posts, w/trundle below, 40x64".350.00
Trundle, Sheraton, old salmon pt, gabled pediment, 13x34x50"..490.00
Vict, Eastlake, oak, arched hdbd, tester, incised bracket supports 105x63"...1,500.00
Vict, oak, child's, highback, rolling pin ftbd, 28x19x38" 475.00
Vict, RR, walnut & burl, cvd crest, paneled hdbd & ftbd, 103x62x80"..1,200.00
Vict, RR, walnut & burl, ornate cvd crest, stick & spool 77x58x72" *.200.00
Vict, RR, walnut, pierced scroll cvd crest: 3 arched panels 80x61x84".600.00

Benches

Bucket/water, pine, 2 shelf, 3 upper drw: 2 lower do, late 19th C, 45x48x16"..1,050.00
Bucket/water, pine, lower shelf, splay sides, bj ends, 1830, 35x33x19"..700.00
Bucket/water, pine, mortised, reeded skirt, shaped legs, red pnt, 19th C, 17x96x12"..235.00
Federal, pnt dec, 8 spindles & medallions, ca 1820, 47" W........4,600.00
Fireside/settee, co, mixed woods, highback, scrolled sides, 62x53x20" 2,300.00
Fireside/settee, English, brass w/leather 'L' shaped leather seats, ca 1900, 19x69x21".2,800.00
Fireside/settee, Geo, Elmwood, 6 panel bk, panel apron, 18th C, 48x80x20.1,850.00
Fireside/settee, pine, lift lid, shaped arms, 55x60x19"................1,500.00
Garden, CI, Passion Flower pattern, Hinderers Iron Works, 19th C, 37" W.4,900.00
Garden, CI, RR, wood seat, Four Seasons pattern, 70" W.........3,000.00
Garden, Iron Strapwork, 6 legs, scrolled arms & legs, early 20th C, 54" W .215.00
Railway, arrow bk, plank seat, mixed woods, CI sides, 19th C, 78" W..550.00
Wagon, ladderback, 2 seater, trn posts, splint seats, 19th C, 31"..230.00
Wagon, ladderback, ring trn posts, shaped finials, old red pt, old splint seats, 37" W.2,100.00
Wagon, pine, iron mounts, curved bk rest, 45" W 180.00
Window, Arts & Crafts, Limbert, oak, sq cut outs, #243 ....3,000.00
Window, Arts & Crafts, Stickley, Gustav, oak, leather seat, #177.4,200.00
Window, Biedermeier, fruitwood, brass mts, trn finials, uphl, 48" W .1,150.00
Window, Fed, pnt decal, 8 spindles & medallions, rush seat, 47" W ..3,700.00
Window, Geo III, mahog, tufted leather uphl yapered legs, 50" W **.20,000.00
Window, Geo, mahog, bellflower inlay, outswept arms, tapered legs, 46" W.4,600.00

Window, Gothic, Am, mld lancet rail w/pendant trefoils, 74" W .. 6,000.00
Windsor, arrow bk, plank seat, gr pnt, sten crest, 19th C, 78" W . 975.00
Windsor, bow bk, Philadelphia, plank seat, stretcher base, late 18th C, 69" W ** .. 48,700.00
Windsor, Mammy, pine, sten crest, 13 spindles, trn legs & gate, 52" W ... 150.00
Windsor, rod bk, blk pnt, mld crest, trn legs, 18th C, 38" W 9,300.00
Windsor, spindle bk, plank seat, blk pnt, 19th C, rpr trn legs 450.00

Blanket Chests, Coffers, Trunks, and Mule Chests

Chinese export, elm, poly floral, circular lockplate, 19th C, 28x41x25" 475.00
Dome top, pine, canted panels, exposed dvtls, 19th C, 24x38x22" .. 400.00
Dome top, Scandinavian, pine, pnt, 1 drw, rosemailed, 33x51x27" . 1,050.00
Dome top, wht pine, bl pnt, 1 drw, trn ft, 19th C, 28x48x19" .. 1,250.00
Dower, pnt decor, 3 drw, ogee bracket ft, strap hinges,18th C, 28x51x25" .. 1,600.00
Dower, pnt, fancy, 2 front panels, wrought iron hdw, 18th C, 21x44x22" . 350.00
Dower, pnt, red w/floral, block ft, strap hinge, mid 19th C 26x43x20" . 1,250.00
Dower, pnt, tulip motif, bracket base, 18th C, 24x47" 875.00
Fed, pnt decor, orig bl, bold shaped apron, H bracket ft, 22x36x17" ** . 67,890.00
Fed, walnut, hinged lid, int till, trn legs, peg ft, 22x38x15" 925.00
Fed, walnut, inlaid, bracket ft, minor rpr, 20x36x15" 5,275.00
Fed, walnut, paneled sides, trn ft, rstr, 28x42x18" 500.00
Fed, yel pine, mld top & base, till, bracket ft, 21x43x17" 650.00
Fed, yel pine, old red pnt, scalloped skirt, bracket ft, 23x49x18" .. 13,800.00
Grainpainted, mld top & base, 2 drw, short trn ft, 19th C, 28x47" W 400.00
Grainpainted, mld top & base, 6 brds, trn legs, 1850, 24x42x20" . 500.00
Grainpainted, panels front & side, trn legs, 1850, 22x38x17" 200.00
Grainpainted, QA, raised panels over 1 drw, bracket ft, 18th C, 24x40x20" . 4,900.00
Leather over wood, Vict, brass tacks over leather surface, scuffs, 19x34x18" . 150.00
Mule, NE, pine, yel pnt, 1 drw bj ends, 32x36" W 800.00
Mule, W/M, pine, 1 false +2 working drws, ball ft, 40x38x18" 930.00
Mule, W/M, pine, red pnt, snipe hinge, 1 drw, str ft, 31x47x20" ... 1,750.00
Six brd, diminutive, grpt, bracket ft, ca 1850, 22x37x18" 575.00
Six brd, maple & poplar, exposed dvtls, till, bracket ft, 22x38x17" 525.00
Six brd, NY, bl pnt, mld base, 31x14x16" 150.00
Six brd, PA, fancy pnt, 3 drw, trn legs, 1830, 30x51x23" 6,100.00

Bookcases

Emp style, mahog, brass inlay, 2 glz do, 19th C, 78x38x15" 1,325.00
Fed, mahog, split ped, fancy inlay, 2 glz upper do:2 drw:2 do, 96x102" . 4,500.00

French Provincial, arched cornice over scalloped doors, applied rocaille carvings to base, 102x53x21", $7,770.00. (Photo courtesy Neal Auction Co. Auctioneers & Appraisers of Fine Art)

French Provincial, cherry, 2 glz do, cvg, cab legs, 66x49x16" 700.00
French Provincial, oak, breakfront style, grilled do, 96x102x22" .. 6,900.00
Hepplewhite, mahog, 2 glz do, Fr ft, 46x49x14" 2,650.00
Revolving, arts & crafts, walnut, 5 tiers, 56x20x20" 1,150.00
Stacking, oak, Globe-Wernicke, 4 sections, sq legs, 86x33" 1,025.00
Stickley, Gustav, oak 2 glz do, #718 .... 2,800.00
Stickley, Gustav, oak, 2 glz do, 44x39x12" 4,200.00
Vict, Eastlake, walnut, 2 glz do, ornate cornice, 2 bottom drw, 96x47". 1,500.00

Cabinets

China/display, Gothic Revival, mahog, 72x48x17" 1,695.00
China/display, hplwht style, mahog, bowed front, glz do, 6 tapered legs, 62x56x17" . 450.00
China/display, Stickley, L&JG, oak, 2 glz do, #728 .... 2,685.00
Corner, Arts & Crafts, oak, 1 glz do, openwork apron, sq legs, 52x25x16" 550.00
Curio, Asian, mahog, 2 pc, bamboo cvg, cvd crown, 77x28x15" . 250.00
Curio, Emp style, mahog, curved do & sides:1 drw, inlay, H legs, 60x24x13" 425.00
Curio, Louis XV style, 1 do, cvd reeded columns, gilt, 83x43" W . 3,800.00
Curio, Louis XVI style, mahog, 'D' shape, glz do & sides, inlay, 56x26x13" . 1,100.00
Curio, Vict, mahog, bow front, curved glass, mld crown, paw ft, 66x44x17" ... 500.00
Hoosier, base only, pnt, scrub top, 2 breadboards:2 drw:2 bins trn legs, 30x44x24" .. 200.00
Music, Arts & Crafts, Stickley, Gustav, oak, 2 panel do:1 L do, inlay, 48x20x17" . 7,800.00
Music, continental, ebonized, mirror bk, 2 glz do, 35x25x18" 920.00
Music, Edwardian, mahog, crest w/oval mirror:1 glass do, 52x19x16". 350.00
Music, record, mahog, serpentine top, 1 drw cvd, 32x24x18" 150.00
Music, record, Reginaphone, mahog, serpentine, cab legs, 32x24x18" . 990.00
Spice, Chpndl style, Harter, 1960, walnut, fitted int w/12 drw, 22x17x24" .. 2,800.00
Vitrine, Art Deco, burl walnut, stepped top, 1 do, mullions, 63x21x16" .. 2,100.00
Vitrine, Chinese Chpndl style, Pagoda style, yel pnt, 75x38x18" . 500.00
Vitrine, Edwardian, satinwood, 'D' form, inlaid do, tapered legs 75x49x14" .. 1,850.00
Vitrine, Fr, Louis XV style, bronze mts, mahog Veris martin panels, 1900, 58x24". 6,000.00
Vitrine, Louis XV style, gilt, brass mts, convex glass, vernis martin panels, 73x42x17" . 2,400.00
Vitrine, tabletop type, fruitwood, hinged glass top, 2 drw, ca 1900, 27x24x14" ... 890.00

Candlestands

Sheraton, tiger maple, circa 1820, tilt top: 18x22", $1,080.00. (Photo courtesy Wiederseim Associates, Inc. on LiveAuctioneers.com)

Chinoiserie, blk lqr, tilt top, shaped legs, rpr, 1850s, 42" 715.00
Chpndl, Cherry, urn shaped ped, tripod base, snake ft, 27x21x21" .. 950.00
Chpndl, mahog, tilting dish top, birdcage support, tripod base, 29x21" . 975.00
Federal, Cherry, sq tray top, trn ped outswept legs 28x17" 150.00
Federal, mahog, rect tilt top, trn ped, spider legs, 29x22x16" 325.00
Federal, NY, mahog, tilt top, trn ped, saber legs 28x18x25" 495.00
QA, mahog, rect top:1 drw, trn ped, pad ft, 26x14x13" 880.00

Chair Sets

Chpndl style, mahog, pierced splat, 1950s, 37", set of 8 .... 2,000.00
Classical, mahog, gondola form, saber legs, 34", late 19th C, set of 8 (2 arm, 6 side) .. 3,100.00
Georgian style, mahog, pierced bk, 40", set of 8 (2 arm, 6 side) . 2,400.00
Hplwht style, Kittenger, repro shield bks, 38", set of 8 .... 3,400.00
Hitchcock, Sheraton form, pnt, blk/gilt stencil, pillow crest, 19th C, set of 6 .. 750.00
Vict, RR, gilt/ebony, scrolled crest, fluted legs, 38", set of 6 ...... 1,450.00
Vict, RR, walnut, hip brace, trn legs, 36", set of 8 .... 400.00

Chairs

Arm, Chpndl, walnut arch crest, pierced splat, sq legs, 43x25x21" .. 750.00
Arm, Geo style, pr, beechwood, acanthus & shell cvd, 38x27x20" .. 2,185.00
Arm, lolling style, serpentine bk, reeded legs, 19th C, 43x26x31" ... 775.00
Arm, lolling style, walnut, cvd, needlepoint uphl, ornate cvd stretcher, 48" . 400.00

Arm, lolling, Continental, scrolled fr, needlepoint uphl, 18th C, 47". 400.00
Arm, Louis XV style, beechwood, gilt, cvd, tapestry uphl, 37x26x22"..825.00
Arm, Louis XVI style, uphl seats & sq backs, tapered legs, 39", set of 4...2,350.00
Arm, oak, lion & shield cvd crest, 19th C, 61x27x27"................880.00
Arm, wicker, blk pnt, arch bk, flat arms, 38", set of 3 ....300.00
Arm, wicker, Haywood Bros, fancy, arched bk, scroll arms...........125.00
Arm, wicker, Stickley, Gustav, bbl bk, 33".................................2,300.00
Club, Art Deco, new leather, scrolled arms, 34", set of 2............2,000.00
Club, leather, bbl bk, tapered legs, ca 1930................................500.00
Club, leather, tufted bk, scrolled arms, trn ft, 19th C, set of 2...2,500.00
Club, Modernist, Kagan, bbl club, uphl, 27x31x31".................2,500.00
Corner, Chpndl, maple, pierced splats, scrolled arms, 'X' stretcher, 32" ..6,500.00
Corner, Chpndl, walnut, commode form, vasiform splats, 32" . 1,650.00
Corner, Geo, mahog, pierced splats, sq legs, 'X' stretcher, 31"......460.00
Corner, Vict, bobbin trn, gilded, rush seat 125.00
Lounge, Arts & Crafts, cvd arms & fr, old leather uphl, ottoman, ca 1925, 38"..2,800.00
Lounge, Fr, pnt fr, scrolled crest, uphl, 1900, 34x33x74" 675.00
Lounge, modernist, Eames, blk leather & rswd laminate, w/ottoman models 670/671..1,050.00
Lounge, modernist, Saarinen, Grasshopper Chair, bent plywood arms, 36" .1,500.00
Lounge, modernist, tubular steel, wood arm rests, uphl, 1950s..1,300.00
Side, Arts & Crafts, oak, str crest, cut out splat, leather seat, 36". 100.00
Side, Arts & Crafts, Stickley, Gustav/Ellis, 3 vertical slats, inlay, caned seat, 44"..5,000.00
Side, Chpndl, pr, mahog, scroll crest, pierced splat, cvd, 39x22x20"..1,500.00
Side, Edwardian, mahog, str crest, 5 spindles, inlay, 34x19x16" 100.00
Side, Geo, pr, mahog, cvd crest, pierced splat, cab legs, 39x22x20"...525.00
Side, ladderback, pr, arched slats, can seat, 1880, 37"................230.00
Side, Louis XVI style, pr, giltwood, cvd frs, fluted lets, 33x18x16" ..475.00
Side, Modernist, Nakashima, spindle bk, saddleseat, set of 4 ..16,380.00
Side, Regency, mahog, cvd bk & seat, cvd sq legs, rpr, 34x17x20" ...2,400.00
Side, Vict, pr, rswd, foliate crest, reeded leg, 34x19x18"...............800.00
Windsor, bow-bk, English, pierced splat, elm, 38" 250.00
Windsor, comb-bk, blk pnt, 9 spindles, box stretcher, 18th C, 43"...400.00
Windsor, fan-bk, brace bk, cut down trn legs, ca 1800 ....150.00
Windsor, sack-bk, armchair, pnt, ash, 9 spindles, H stretcher, 35"...800.00
Windsor, sack-bk, pnt, 7 spindles, saddleseat, H stretcher, 18th C...825.00
Wing, Chpndl, mahog, sq legs, box stretcher, stained uphl 600.00
Wing, Geo, mahog legs, old leather w/brass tacks, 44"x33".......1,000.00
Wing, QA style, fr, re-uphl, 1930, 45x33"..................................900.00

Chests (Antique), See also Dressers

Biedermeier, Baker, 3 drw commode, ebonized columns, 32x33x19".950.00
Biedermeier, lingerie, mahog, 7 drw, bracket ft, 54x27x16" 1,800.00
Biedermeier, mahog, fitted secretaire drw, 3 L drws, 41x42x18"... 700.00
Campaign, Asian, red lqr, 2 stacking sections, 2 drws ea, early 20th C, 43x34x16"..750.00
Campaign, English, camphor, 3 hinged & locking cupboards, 30x40x18"..1,000.00
Campaign, English, mahog, 2 do:3 drw, 2 sections, bun ft, 19th C, 39x40x18"..2,300.00
Campaign, English, mahog, 3 do:3 drw, metal mounts, 40x42x19"..2,300.00
Chest on chest, Chpndl style, maple, flattop, 11 drw, bracket ft, 70x41x20".2,000.00
Chest on chest, Chpndl, cherry, split pediment, fan cvd, 5 grad drw, 84x40x20" **..44,500.00
Chest on chest, Chpndl, mahog, flat top, 8 drw bracket ft, 68x43x21"...3,400.00
Chest on chest, Geo III, mahog, 2 cases, 3 over 6 drw, bracket ft, 72x43x21"..3,100.00
Chest on chest, Geo III, mahog, 2 cases, 8 drw, Fr ft, 72x46x22" 2,000.00
Chest on stand, Geo I, walnut, 5 upper drw, 1 lower drw trn stretcher, 57x40".3,050.00
Chest on stand, QA style, centennial, chinoiserie, 6 drw, bun ft, losses, 45x41x23".1,200.00
Chest on stand, QA, walnut, rpr, 5 drw, arch skirt, cab legs, 48x40x19"..16,500.00
Chest on stand, W/M, burlwood, 7 drw spiral legs, ball ft, inlay, 45x41x23"..1,000.00
Chpndl, English, Geo II, mahog, 2 do:3 drw, fluted columns, 42x35x21" . 1,050.00
Chpndl, English, mahog, serpentine front, 5 drw, inlay, bracket ft, 42x42x21"....700.00
Chpndl, English, tall chest, Geo III, 8 drw shell cvd apron, cab legs, 79x30x15".2,500.00
Chpndl, mahog, 4 drw, bracket ft, inlay, rpl brass, 31x37x22"..2,550.00
Chpndl, mahog, 4 drw, ogee bracket ft, fluted corners & columns, 34x39x21".3,000.00
Chpndl, tall chest, birch/chestnut, 6 drw, bracket ft, 51x42x21"....8,500.00
Chpndl, tall chest, maple, 2 do:5 drw, bracket base, 40x49x17".1,450.00

Chippendale tall chest, tiger maple, six graduated scratch-beaded drawers, tall bracket feet, New England, late eighteenth century, refinished, replaced brasses, 58x36x18", $20,400.00. (Photo courtesy Skinner Auctioneers and Appraisers of Antiques and Fine Art)

Fed, grpt, mini, hplwht pine, 3 drw, 14x13x8" 500.00
Fed, grpt, poplar, scrolled bkbd, set bk 2 drw over 4 drw trn legs, 1820. 3,000.00
Fed, grpt, tall chest, Chpndl, bracket ft, Co pine, 5 drw, 48" 1,700.00
Fed, hplwht, cherry, maple, inlaid, 4 grad drw, Fr bracket ft, 37". 4,400.00
Fed, hplwht, maple, 4 dr, ivory keyholes, shaped apron, Fr ft 36x36".. 1,750.00
Fed, Louis XV style, red pnt, 3 drw faux marbletop, 33x42x22". 1,850.00
Fed, Sheraton, 4 drw scroll backsplash, trn columns, 42x43x18" .1,800.00
Fed, Sheraton, mahog, backsplash, 4 drw, reeded column, damaged... 500.00
Fed, Sheraton, mahog/BE Maple, bowfront, 4 drw, spiral columns, trn legs, 38x40" .1,050.00
Fed, Sheraton, walnut, bow front, 4 drw, reeded stiles, losses, 41x42". 1,000.00

Cupboards, See also Pie Safes

Corner, architectural, mld arch flanked by reed, columns, 20th C, 96x37" *..250.00
Corner, bl pnt, mld, cornice, 1 do:1 drw, 18th C, 47x30x19"....1,500.00
Corner, Chpndl, mahog, pierced scroll ped, 2 glz do : 2 do, 93x46x26" ..3,500.00
Corner, Fed, southern, walnut, scroll ped 2 glz do : 2 do, 102x52x28" .. 9,200.00
Corner, hanging, Chpndl, pine, stepped cornice, 2 glz do, 62x40x25" . 3,700.00
Corner, open top, 2 paneled do, reeded surround, mid 19th C, 78x42x15".1,900.00
Corner, Vict, Eastlake, pnt, 1 do:1 drw, 87x38x15" 400.00
Hanging, chimney form, walnut, 1 panel do, mld cornice, 42x15x10" ...1,875.00
Hanging, Chpndl, pine, stepped cornice, corner type, arched top, 67x40x25" .3,700.00
Hanging, Geo style, corner type, oak bowfront, 2 do, 37x27x12" . 300.00
Hanging, Gothic, 1 paneled do, w/arches, old pnt, 27x27x11" 375.00
Hanging, Horner, maple, faux bamboo, spindle gallery, 19x24x8" . 1,500.00
Hanging, pine, mld top, 1 panel do, 19th C, 38x37x12" 750.00
Hanging, pnt, elaborate, 2 do:towel bar, 65x37x12" 800.00
Wall, Fed, cherry, broken arch ped, 2 do:6 drw, bracket ft, 93x42". 3,975.00
Wall, Fed, mahog, 2 panel do:4 drw, Fr bracket ft, 93x48x23" ...1,300.00
Wall, jelly, apple gr pnt, shaped gallery, 1 drw:2 paneled do, 67x36x15"...4,500.00
Wall, jelly, bl pnt, 19th C, 1 do, cutout ft, 49x39x15" 1,100.00
Wall, jelly, pnt gray, late 19th C, 2 panel do, H hinges, 50x25" ... 900.00
Wall, linen press, Chpndl, mahog, 2 do:4 grad drw, 83x52x24" . 7,000.00
Wall, linen press, Chpndl, mahog, 2 panel do:3 drw, bracket ft, 86x50x24" ..1,800.00
Wall, stepback, Chpndl, walnut, 2 glz do:2 panel do, bracket ft, 94x53x20". 13,200.00
Wall, stepback, fancy pnt, P Hunt, ca 1950, 76x24"..................1,800.00
Wall, stepback, old bl pnt, flat top, 2 do:2 do:1 do, ca 1850, 76x38x17"...1,200.00
Wall, Vict, Gothic, oak, 2 arched do:2 base drw, 88x52x24".....1,075.00
Wall, Welch dresser, fruitwood, open shelves:2 drw:2 do, ca 1900, 86x62x20"...600.00
Wall, Welch dresser, grpt, open shelves:2 do, cab legs 96x77x24".1,100.00
Wall, William IV, mahog, bellflower inlay, ball trn ft, 81x56x28" .2,300.00

Desks

Architect, Chpndl, mahog, easel top, trn ped, candle shelves, tripod base, 30x27".800.00
Architect, Geo III, mahog, lift top:3 drw, str legs, 31x45x21"...3,500.00
Butler, Emp, flame mahog, secretaire drw:3 drw, scroll ft 47x43x21"...750.00
Butler, Fed, mahog, secretaire drw:3 drw, bracket ft, inlay 45x47x22" ..2,000.00
Butler, Geo, mahog, secretaire drw:4 drw, Fr ft, inlay, 47x47x21" . 800.00
Campaign, English, mahog, leather top, tray, 19th C, 29x22" 400.00

Campaign, English, mahog, rect top, 2 ped, w/3 drw ea, bracket ft, 1840, 30x39x21"..2,300.00
Campaign, Geo II, walnut, 2 parts, slant lid, fitted int, 2 lower drw, 37x24x17"..5,750.00
Chinese export, Huanghuali, elaborately cvd, w/chair, ca 1900, 55x42"..800.00
Chinese export, Regency, blk lqr, gilt, 2 do:1 drw, 62x26x26"..6,100.00
Chinese export, slant front:3 sm drw, cab legs, blk lqr, ca 1900, 37x32x19"...1,500.00
Clerk, grpt, slant front:1 drw:panel do, 48x28"..225.00
Clerk, cotton gin clerks, walnut, slant lid:3 drw, trn legs, 1870, 44x96x33".3,600.00
Clerk, schoolmaster's, mixed wood, slant top, sq legs, 35x28x22". 600.00
Davenport, Vict, maple, slant lid:4 drw, inlay, 31x20x22"..525.00
Davenport, Vict, rswd, slant lid:1 do, very fancy, 43x23"..425.00
Davenport, Vict, faux bamboo, blk lqr top & panels, 43x23x19". 475.00
Kneehole, Chpndl style, Kittenger, mohog & oak, 2 ped 30x91x19". 1,050.00
Lap, N Starkey mfg label, mahog & leather, folding, brass bound, 7x18".275.00
Partner, Chpndl style, mahog, cab legs, c&b ft, 30x53x29"..550.00
Partner, English, mahog, leather top, 3 drieze drw, paw ft, ca 1900, 29x62x38"...850.00
Partner, Geo, mahog, leather top, 12 drw, 2 cupboards, 1850, 31x70x48". 3,950.00
Partner, Horner, mahog, shaped top, dvd columns, bowed drws, paw ft, 29x64x32". 1,750.00
Roll top, Fr Emp, mini, mahog, C roll, 15x17x10"..500.00
Roll top, Louis XVI, mahog, 1900, C roll, marble top, 46x62". 15,000.00
Roll top, Louis XVI, mahog, C roll, marble top, 50x64x28"..8,000.00
Roll top, Vict, C roll, mahog, fitted int, gallery top, 53x50x31".1,050.00
Roll top, Vict, S roll, ash, 2 peds, salesman sample, 15x18"..200.00
Roll top, Vict, S roll, walnut, bowfront file drws, 51x72x37"....1,650.00
Secretary tambour hplwht, Seymour, mahog, 43x37" **..46,000.00
Secretary tambour, Fed, mahog, 2 do:6 drw, Fr ft, 48x41x19"...2,000.00
Secretary tambour, Fed, mahog, T Needham label, 45x36"..3,500.00
Slant front, Arts & Crafts, oak, slant front:1 drw, stretcher base, rfn, 38x30x17"..350.00
Slant front, Biedermeier, birchwood, ebonized pilasters, 2 drw, saber legs, 37x27x16".2,000.00
Slant front, Chpndl style, mahog, brass inlay, gallery, cab legs, c&b ft, 38x32x19"..250.00
Slant front, Chpndl, mahog, 4 drw, rpl bracket ft, 42x42x21"..1,200.00
Slant front, Chpndl, mahog, 4 grad drw, 43x40" **..71,000.00
Slant front, Chpndl, mahog, bombe, fitted int, fan cvd, 4 drw, trn ft 43x44x25" **..24,500.00
Slant front, Chpndl, walnut, desk-on-fr, 4 drw, fitted int, c&b ft. 950.00
Slant front, Geo III, mahog, ladies form, 2 drw, tall cab legs, 39x27x18".800.00

Dressers (Machine Age), See also Chests

Art Deco, chrome & pnt mahog, Deskey, rnd mirror:4 drw, 70x42x20"..650.00
Art Deco, mirror carcass, 3 drw, ebony hdls & ft, 30x36x18"..600.00
Art Deco, mixed vnr, waterfall type, losses, bakelite hdls, 32x45x20"...275.00
Arts & Crafts, Liberty & Co, oak asymmetrical 5 drw, swing mirro,r 63x44x19".800.00
Arts & Crafts, Stickley, L&JG, oak, 4 drw, swing mirror, 67x42x21".. 900.00
Designer, Ortiz, birch, 3x3 drw, blk & silver graffiti motif, sgn & tag, 30x48"..2,600.00
Vict, Eastlake, walnut, marble top, swing mirror, 4 drw, 85x42x20"...210.00

Dry Sinks

Blue paint, off-center lower drawer with conforming skirt, nineteenth century, replaced backboards and foot facings, 42x33x19", $660.00. (Photo courtesy Case Antiques, Inc. on LiveAuctioneers.com)

Cupboard type, gray pnt, 2 panel do:sink:1 drw:2 panel do, 90x52x24"..1,750.00
Miniature, Co primitive, bl pnt, 1 lower drw, 16x17x11"..800.00
Pine, old red pnt, 2 do, bracket ft, 1850, 31x48x19"..950.00

Hall Pieces

Chair, Arts & Crafts, Stickley Bros, oak, plank bk, inlay, tapestry seat, 41"..2,000.00
Chair, Gothic, oak, tall bk, simple cvd, hinge seat, 55"..325.00
Chair, pnt, gondola form, swivel base, cvd lion finial, 70"..3,050.00
Chair, Vict, Gothic revival, oak, tall spire pierced bk, hinge seat, 71" **..28,000.00
Stand, Aesthetic movement, bamboo motif, mirror, 19th C, Fr, 82"..800.00
Stand, Art Deco, metal fr, marble shelf, mirror & elec lt 69x23x11"..500.00
Stand, Art Nouveau, Galle, fruitwood, floral inlay, bronze mts, 82x42x14" **.31,900.00
Stand, Black Forest, cvd linden tree, 20th C, bear & cub, German, 87"..4,200.00
Stand, Black Forest, cvd linden tree, late 19th C, sheep on rocks, rpr, 72"..5,525.00

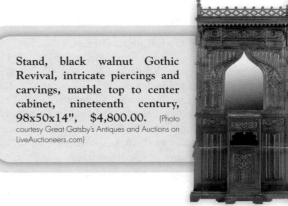

Stand, black walnut Gothic Revival, intricate piercings and carvings, marble top to center cabinet, nineteenth century, 98x50x14", $4,800.00. (Photo courtesy Great Gatsby's Antiques and Auctions on LiveAuctioneers.com)

Stand, Rococo Revival, CI, Corneau, oval mirror, scrolled, 78"....1,400.00
Stand, Vict, RR walnut, cvd crest, mirror, 1 drw, 106x59x16"...1,540.00
Tree, Art Nouveau, pr, poly bronze conservatory tree, 94"....13,000.00
Tree, Arts & Crafts, oak, horn mts, drip pan, 80"..1,560.00
Tree, oak, simple post w/X stretcher base, 4 lg hooks, 1920s, 60"..65.00
Tree, Tulip form, grpt, acorn finials, 1900s, 77"..2,800.00
Table, console, Adam style, pr, walnut & gilt sten, demilune, tapered legs, 29x39x15"..1,700.00
Table, console, Art Deco, glass top, U shape Lucite supports, rect ebony base, 31x70x15"..2,000.00
Table, console, Baker, pr, demilune, sq tapered legs w/inlay, spade ft, 29x46"...425.00
Table, console, Louis XVI, giltwood, marbletop, cvd laurel swags, 1875, 32x42".3,000.00
Table, console, Vict, RR, mahog, demilune, marble top, shaped base, 30x41"..300.00

Highboys

Chpndl, maple, flat top, 8 drw, cab legs, c&b ft, 65x39x21"..2,800.00
Chpndl, walnut SNBT, 12 drw cvd finials, cab legs, c&b ft, 90x40"..4,500.00
George III, cvd oak, 2 pts, flat top, 8 drw, cab legs, 69x40x21".5,000.00
Georgian style, mahog, snp, 8 drw cab legs, 85x41x21" *..350.00
Georgian, oak, 2 pts, flat top, 9 drw, cab legs, pad ft, 66x48x22"...1,775.00
QA, birch, flat top, 9 drw, shell cvd, scrolled apron, cab legs, pad ft, 69x39x21"..1,800.00
QA, salmon stain, flat top, 2 cvd fans, 10 drw, cab legs, orig brasses, 78x40x19" **..41,000.00
QA, walnut, SNBT, 3 short drw:5 dg, cvd shells, cab legs, c&b ft, 85x40x21" *..1,400.00
W/M, maple, flat top, 8 drw, trn legs, flat box stretcher, 69x40x20"..2,250.00

Lowboys

Chpndl style, walnut, Lennhoff, shell cvd, c&b ft, 29x32x17"....800.00
George III, burl walnut, shaped top & deep apron, 2 drw, cab legs, 29x35x18".2,400.00
QA, English, walnut, banded, 3 drw cab legs, pad ft, 28x34x21".750.00
QA, mahog, cvd shell, cab legs, pad ft, 30x30x17" **..11,000.00
Vict, yel lqr, 2 drw cab legs, trifid ft, 26x21x14"..425.00

Pie Safes

Sideboard type, cherry, 4 punched tin do:3 drw, trn legs, 36x60x20".. 6,200.00
White pnt, 2 punched tin do:2 drw, 19th C, 85x45x18"..950.00

Secretaries

Biedermeir, figured vnr, ebony mod, fitted int, 4 drw, 71x44x 21"..4,600.00
Chpndl, mahog SNP, 2 blind do:slant front:4 drw, c&b ft, 96x46x21".. 17,750.00
Chpndl, mahog, SNP, 2 panel do:slant top:4 drw, Philadelphia, 98x42x22".7,400.00
Fed, mahog, arch cornice, bookcase top:secretaries drw:2 panel do, Fr ft, 108x55x22" **.28,000.00
Fed, walnut, 2 flz do:2 tambour do:fold out surface:2 do, Fr ft, 84x41".. 1,250.00
George III, mahog, 3 point crest:2 glz do:sec drw:3 drw, bracket ft, 84x33x20"..3,500.00
Gothic, walnut, 2 glz do:6 drw, bracket ft, 68x43x20" 850.00
Rococo style, Venetian pnt, fall front, cab legs, 85x33x18" 2,100.00
Vict, burl & walnut, flat top:2 glz do:2 sm drw:slant front:4 drw, 98x44"..1,500.00
Vict, RR, walnut, flat top, 2 glz do:4 drw, 94x46x20" 500.00

Settees

Edwardian, mahog, str crest, scroll arms, uphl seat, 48"................250.00
Fed, inlaid mahog & maple, shaped crest, reeded legs, uphl, 60" W **.43,000.00
Fr Provincial, pnt, triple chair bk, rush seat, ca 1900, 40x70"..1,500.00
George III, mahog, uphl, curved bk & arms, cvd cab legs, 80" W.10,200.00
Georgian style, mahog, 3 chair bk, fancy, c&b ft, 39x62x24"...1,100.00
Louis XVI style, beechwood, cvd & gilt, caned bk, 1900s, 48"..1,900.00
Louis XVI style, gilt pnt, uphl, Fr, early 20th C, 37x51x20"........650.00
Modernist, pr, Nakashima, walnut, spindle bk, loose cushions, 31x47x31".8,600.00
Victorian, pr, RR, mahog, cameo bk, cvd crest, uphl, 36x48x22".700.00

Shelves

Etagere, Vict, walnut corner type, 5 grad shelves, pierced galleries, 56"....175.00
Etagere, Vict, walnut, 6 grad shelves, pierced galleries, scrolled ft, 71x28"....200.00
Hanging, Aesthetic, ebonized, mirrored, 3 tier, 28x30x9"...........225.00
Hanging, pine, 3 shelves, English, 19th C, unremarkable, 36x53x7"....275.00
Hanging, pnt, 1 shelf, shaped bk & supports, 19th C, 18" W.........50.00
Hanging, QA, pnt, 4 shelves, tombstone shaped bk, 22x9x6"......700.00
Hanging, Vict, Eastlake, walnut, stick & ball decor, 14x74x12"..150.00
Stand, Art Nouveau, Majorelle, display, rswd, 3 tiers, shaped crest & legs, 49"..5,900.00
Stand, Arts & Crafts, magazine, oak, gallery, 4 tiers, 45x19x12". 1,500.00

Sideboards

Quarter-sawn oak with carved North Wind head crest and lion supports under top shelf, circa 1890, 87x67x28", $3,300.00. (Photo courtesy Great American Auction on LiveAuctioneers.com)

Art Nouveau, 2-pc, Fr pnt style, 2 glz do +2 do:4 panel do, 95x64x23"..500.00
Arts & Crafts, Roycroft, oak, 2 glz do:4 drw, mirrored bk, 53x60x24".. 9,600.00
Arts & Crafts, Stickley Bros, oak, plate rack, 4 drw:2 do, 44x48x20". 2,200.00
Arts & Crafts, Stickley, Gustav, oak, 2 do:4 drw, plate rail, #814, 49x56x24"..3,900.00
English, Geo III, mahog, bowfront, 3 drw + tambour, tapered legs, 35x85x28".3,500.00
English, Geo, mahog, serpentine front, inlay, 5 drw, tapered legs, 37x66x25"..1,250.00
English, Regency, mahog/satinwood, inlaid, 6 reeded legs, 42x78x33". 4,200.00
Fed, huntboard, cherry, 3 drw, trn legs, arch apron, 41x63x22"..7,400.00
Fed, huntboard, poplar, 2 drw:trn legs, 42x40x19"....................3,450.00
Fed, mahog, 4 drw:4 do, inlay, Charleston, tapered legs, 38x65x26"..4,000.00

Fed, mahog, shaped backsplash, 3 drw:4 do, tapered legs spade ft, 45x61x26".3,250.00
Fr, Louis XVI style, inlaid, marbletop, 2 drw:2 do, bronze mts, 20th C, 35x49".650.00
Fr, Louis XVI, fruitwood, cvd, 2 drw:2 do, cab legs, 38x49x23"..2,550.00
Fr, Provincial, oak, 3 drw:4 do, shaped top & apron, 41x82x22" .500.00
Modernist, Mont, oak, 4 drw cinnabar lqr, 1954, 32x77x22" 1,800.00
Modernist, Nakashima, walnut, 2 sliding do:trestle base 32x60x20"..4,800.00
Vict, oak, fancy cvd, upper do & mirror:2 drw & 2 drw, trn columns, 83x49".1,150.00
Vict, Rococo, Roux, Walnut, marble top, tall cvd shaped backboard:2 do, 92x76x25".5,500.00
Vict, walnut, upper shelf:mirror:3 drw:2 panel do, chip cvd, 84x56x22" ..1,000.00

Sofas

Edwardian, Chesterfield, tufted leather, 3 seater, 30x89x39".....1,150.00
Emp, mahog vnr, scrolled arms, winged legs, paw ft, 34x91x23"..625.00
English, Geo III, beechwood, camel bk, serpentine seat, 8 reeded legs, 30x89x23"..2,875.00
Fed, mahog, reeded bk, spiral arm supports, 8 tapered legs, Baltimore, 35x82x30".3,450.00
Fed, mahog, str crest, scrolled arms, 4 trn legs, uphl, 35x75x27"..700.00
Fed, Sheraton style, mahog, arched bk, trn arms & 6 legs, 34x77x30" ...800.00
Fr, Louis XV, beechwood, serpentine crest & seat rail, cvd, uphl seat & bk, 78" W.1,200.00
Modernist, knoll, str crest, chrome legs, wool uphl, dry rot, 52" W..225.00
Modernist, tubular steel, ebony side panels, uphl seats & cushions, 80" W, pr.2,300.00
Vict, ebonized, exposed shaped fr, uphl, bk & seat, 49x79"..........500.00
Vict, medallion bk, Rococo Revival, cvd foliate crest, tufted bk, 60" W *...150.00

Stands

Biedermeier, burl mahog, rect top:trn column, quad plinth base, ball ft, 29 x25"..675.00
English, wine stand, Geo III, mahog, gallery top, tripod base, 24x10" W.1,200.00
Fed, Duncan Phyfe, mahog, shaped tilt top, saber legs, 1825, 28x18x25"..500.00
Fed, QA, mahog, candlestand, rect top:1 drw, trn pediment, tripod base, 26x14x13" ..880.00
Fed, Sheraton, birch, rect top:1 drw:trn legs, 28x20x18"..............330.00
Fed, Sheraton, red pnt, sq top:1 drw, trn legs, 29x20" 230.00
Fed, Sheraton, tiger maple, rect top:2 drw, trn legs, 29x23" 700.00
Fed, Sheraton, walnut, 1 drw:trn legs, 28x27x20" 550.00
Fern, Arts & Crafts, Limbert, oak, sq top, inlay, 30x11x11" 2,500.00
Fern, China, ebonized, floral cvd, soapstone top, 35x19" 150.00
Fern, Louis XVI style, gilt bronze, marble top, ca 1900, 37x12x12" .300.00
Fern, Vict, brass/marble top, pierced border, scroll leg, 31x16x13"..225.00
Folk art, Twig, pnt decor, sq top, tripod base, 1930, 30x20" 125.00
Fr, Louis XV style, oak, marble top, 1 drw:1 do, cab legs, 1930, 32x15x14" .440.00
Louis XV style, mahog, marble top:1 drw:1 do, cab legs, 33x17x17", pr.450.00
Vict, only/bronze, 2 tier, column supports, scroll ft, 39x12x12" ...175.00
Vict, RR, mahog, marble top:1 drw:1 do, cvd, trn columns, 31x18" W..590.00
Vict, shaving stand, RR, walnut, mirror:marbletop:1 drw, trn stretchers, 60" ..770.00

Stools

Footstool, Geo II, mahog, scalloped apron, cab legs, pad ft, 19x22x17"..400.00
Footstool, Modernist, Nakashima, pr, walnut & grass tops, 12x18x16" ..2,900.00
Footstool, primitive, rect, bl pnt, bj ends, 8x18"..........................225.00
Footstool, primitive, walnut, mortise & tenon, 18th C, 8x18".....230.00
Footstool, Vict, CI openwork base, uphl 9x15x11".......................115.00
Footstool, Vict, ebonized curule form, 18x20x14" 125.00
Footstool, Vict, RR, walnut, cvd flowers, cab legs, uphl, 14x19x16" ...275.00
Footstool, W/M, walnut, sq top, trn legs & stretchers, 19x17x17" . 1,200.00
Gout, Arts & Crafts, Stickley, Gustav, oak, sq top, shaped ft, 5x11x11"...1,200.00
Gout, Regency, mahog, rect adjustable base, uphl, 15x13x23".....900.00
Gout, Vict, cherry, rocker type, uphl, 14x22x14" 100.00
Gout, Classical, 19th C, mahog, uphl on volute scroll base, 7x17x14".700.00
Piano, chair top, D Phyfe school, mahog, tablet crest, swivel seat, cvd paw ft, 31"...600.00
Piano, chair top, Vict, Huntzinger, woven wood splat, 36" 500.00
Piano, Emp, rswd, circular seat:chamfered ped:scrolled legs, 20x14"...250.00
Piano, novelty, English, bronze/leather adjustable seat, figural boot legs, early 20th C.900.00
Piano, Vict, rnd swivel, c&b metal ft 75.00

Tables

Adirondack/twig/folk art, Old Hickory breakfast table, twig fence type base, 29x42x30"..875.00
Adirondack/twig/folk art, Old Hickory style, 28" rnd top, chunky twig legs, 1930..100.00
Adirondack/twig/folk art, sq top, splayed legs, appl twigs, old pnt, 27x18x17"...115.00
Adirondack/twig/folk art, Tramp Art, lift top cabin, twig legs, 42x24" ...250.00
Baker, Fr, scrolled base w/brass rosettes, marble top, 19th C, 31x26x37"..3,300.00
Baker, Fr, scrolled CI base, marble top, 19th C, 33x48x28" 1,750.00
Banquet, early Emp, mahog, drop leaf, 1 drw, attr Quervelle, cvd paw ft, 30x39x20"..660.00
Banquet, Fed, cherry, 2 pts, 'D' shaped tops w/drop leafs, trn legs, 29x42x124"..1,000.00
Banquet, Fed, mahog, 3 pts, 3 peds, saber legs, 24x46x105" 4,600.00
Banquet, Fed, mahog, 'D' shaped, sq tapered legs, 28x50x24", pr .500.00
Banquet, Fed style, mahog, 3 pts, 2 'D' shapes+drop leaf, inlay, tapered legs, 29x46x105"..2,500.00
Banquet, Geo III, mahog, 3 parts, warped, 29x41x99" 1,500.00
Banquet, Geo III, mahog, 5 peds, 3 leaves, rstr/EX Provenance, 28x169x47" ...98,000.00
Banquet, late Emp, mahog, 4 leaves, quadrefoil ped, bun ft, 52" circular top .1,250.00
Banquet, mahog 2 'D' shaped ends+drop leaf table, late 19th C, 112x42"...400.00
Banquet, Regency, mahog, 2 peds, 1 leaf, reeded legs, brass paws, rstr, 29x104x54"..1,725.00
Banquet, Vict, mahog, 2 leaves, center ped, paw ft, 54" circular top ..600.00
Breakfast, QA style, walnut, shaped top:2 drw, cvd cab legs, 39x60x21"..400.00
Breakfast, Regency, mahog, line inlay, tilt top, cvd urn support, saber leg, 48x47x43".1,000.00
Card, Chinese export, lqr, lift-off top, paw ft, 1870, 28x24x17"... 350.00
Card, Fed, mahog, inlay, fold over top, sq tapered legs, rpr, 28x17x35"..2,900.00
Card, Fed, mahog, serpentine front, fold-over top, 28x35x17"..1,375.00
Card, Geo III, mahog, 1 drw, fold-over top, sq legs, 28x38x19" ... 500.00
Card, hplwht, cherry, demilune fold over top, 1 drw, inlay, 28x34x16" ..1,800.00
Card, Louis XV style, marquetry, ormolu, fold over top, cab legs, 39x31x22".475.00
Card, Vict, Trollope, rswd, lift-off marble top, 22" rnd 13,000.00
Card, Vict, walnut, oval inlay gameboard top, 31x20x28" 3,500.00
Center, Geo style, Baker, mahog, sunburst medallion, 36" rnd 690.00
Center, Louis XV, marble top, cab legs, 19th C, 28x27"......13,800.00
Center, Napoleon III, Pickard, 1850, gilt bronze, pnt porc top, center ped, 32x26" ..21,000.00
Center, Regency, mahog, 4 drw/4 faux drw, reeded saber legs, 42" rnd leather top .1,200.00
Center, Regency, mahog, 4 drw/4 faux drw, saber legs, 43" rnd leather top ..4,100.00
Center, Regency, rswd, 4 drw/4 faux drw, center ped, saber legs, 38" rnd..1,050.00
Center, Regency, rswd, leather top, 4 drw/4 faux drw center ped flared legs, 26" rnd .4,400.00
Center, Vict, early walnut, oval marble top, scroll legs, goblet form finial, 27x39x27".500.00
Center, Vict, RR, rswd, marble top, rose cvd, cab legs 30x40" rnd ...3,600.00
Chair/table, mixed wood, rect top:seat:1 drw, trn legs, ca 1900, 30x51x40"..860.00
Chair/table, pnt decor, pine, rect lift top & seat, 1880, 31x50x40" ..500.00
Coffee, Chinese export, lqr tray & stand, 1900s, 16x29x22"......850.00
Coffee, Louis XVI, giltwood, onyx top, trn legs X-stretcher, 18x39x25" ..475.00
Coffee, lqr, glass top, brass legs, 1920s, 18x53x20" 450.00
Coffee, Modernist, Nakashima, Sundra finish, freeform top, 13x84x29".750.00
Dining, Art Deco, fancy pnt decor, rect top:'u' supports, shoe ft, 30x62x41"..500.00
Dining, Fed style, mahog, 2 ped, Baker, 112" L......1,800.00
Dining, hplwht style, English, mahog, 2 pts, 1 leaf, tapered legs, 28x48"..675.00
Dining, Italian Rennaisance, mahog, cvd edge, 33x61x37" 2,300.00
Dining, Regency, mahog 2 'D' shaped tilt tops on ped bases, 29x104x54" .2,000.00
Dining, Shaker, pine, trestle base, shoe ft, Maine, 19th C, 28x37x95".24,000.00
Dining, Vict, oak, rect top, trn reeded legs, 29x49x67" 400.00
Dining, W/M, mixed wood, rect top, trn legs, box stetcher, 25x61x26".500.00
Dressing, Art Nouveau, Galle, fruitwood, marquetry, 28" W 9,400.00
Dressing, Fed, cherry, orig finish, mahog, 2 drw:trn legs, 34x29x18" ..5,000.00
Dressing, Geo, elm, 1 drw:scalloped skirt, sq legs, 30x33x19" ...1,200.00
Dressing, RR, inlaid fruitwood, marble top, adjustable mirror, cvd legs, 71x49x26" .1,400.00
Dressing, Sheraton, BE Maple, shaped backsplash, 3 drw/trn legs, 37x33" W ..600.00
Drop-leaf, Chpndl, Pembroke, mahog, rect drops, Marlborough legs, 28x19x37"..2,500.00
Drop-leaf, Emp, mahog, center ped, w/4 scrolled ft, 28x55x39"... 500.00
Drop-leaf, Emp, mahog, center ped base w/fancy cvd paw ft, 29x26x20" ..950.00
Drop-leaf, Fed, Pembroke, mahog, dumilune/drop, sq tapered legs, 28x22x46"..850.00
Drop-leaf, Fed, Pembroke, mahog, oval top:1 drw, tapered legs, 28x18x38"..1,500.00
Drop-leaf, QA, Irish, mahog, oval top, demilune drops, 28x42x18"..650.00

Drop-leaf, W/M, pnt demilune drops w/butterfly supports, box stretcher, 27x17" W..1,850.00
Dumbwaiter, Geo III, mahog, 3 tiers, tripod base, rpr, 47" 800.00
Dumbwaiter, Vict, walnut, 3 grad tiers, piecrust edges, tripod base, 34" * ..100.00
Dumbwaiter, walnut, 3 tiers, candlearms, repro, 57"......50.00
Farm, red pnt, rect top, plain apron, trn legs, late 19th C, 31x120x23"...2,200.00
Farm, red wash, rect top:1 drw, sq tapered legs, late 19th C, 29x33x91"...550.00
Farm, yel pine, rect top:sq tapered legs, late 19th C, 18x78x42" ...1,075.00
Gate leg, Jacobean, oak, 'D' shaped drops, block trn legs, 29x12x26".675.00
Gate leg, Jacobean style, oak, 'D' shaped drops, block trn legs, 29x15x36"..100.00
Gate leg, W/M, oak, 'D' shaped drops, spiral legs, ball ft, 28x45x13" ..900.00
Gate leg, W/M style, oak, cvd top, barley twist supports, 1900s, 29x42x17 .125.00

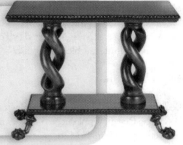

Library, mahogany American Victorian, carved rope edges, spiral supports, copper and mahogany claw feet, Geroge H. Nettleton Home, fourth quarter nineteenth century, 28x36x21", $990.00. (Photo courtesy Dallas Auction Gallery on LiveAuctioneers.com)

Library/writing, Arts & Crafts, oak, 2 drw, sq legs, 29x49x28"..1,050.00
Library/writing, Geo III style, mahog, shell cvd & inlaid rect top:2 drw, 27x30x15"..200.00
Library/writing, Geo III, mahog, leather top, 2 drw, trn legs, casters, 29x36x60"..8,700.00
Library/writing, Vict style, rect top:2 drws/lg sq legs, stained mahog, 30x56x30".300.00
Library/writing, Vict, oak, rect top:2 frieze drw, lg sq fluted legs, 30x40x28" ..400.00
Library/writing, William IV, mahog, leather top, 2 drw, trn legs & casters, 28x32x54"..1,000.00
Nesting, Chinese export, red lqr decor, 1925, 24x19x12" (largest table), set of 4..550.00
Nesting, Edwardian, banded tops, lyre form supports, 22x20x14" (largest table), set of 3.600.00
Nesting, Modernest, Deskey, chrome & lqr, 19x21x11" (largest), set of 2.975.00
Sawbuck, pine, bl & brn pnt, X-stretcher base, 1825, 23x27x16" .. 1,700.00
Sawbuck, pine, gray pnt, breadboard ends, X-stretcher base, 1850, 29x60x29".1,600.00
Sawbuck, pine, red pnt, scrub top, breadboard ends, X-stretcher base, 1850, 29x40x22".800.00
Tavern, hplwht, hardwood, rect top:1 drw, sq legs, 28x36x25"......750.00
Tavern, QA, maple, rect top, scallop apron, trn legs, 27x29x22"..500.00
Tavern, QA, maple, scrub top, trn legs, box stretcher, pnt base, 26x24x40"..800.00
Tavern, QA, pine, rect top:1 drw, trn legs, pad ft, 28x31" W 1,050.00
Tavern, W/M, walnut, rect top:1 drw, trn legs, box stretcher, 30x33x24".2,800.00
Tea/coffee, Geo II, mahog, rect tray top, cab legs, slipper ft, 28x25x18"..3,200.00
Tea/coffee, Geo III, mahog, sq tilt top, tripod base, c&b ft, 28x29x28" ..500.00
Tea/coffee, QA, cherry, rect top, scalloped apron, cab ft, 27x30" W .. 7,600.00
Trestle, Arts & Crafts, Craftsman, pine, rect top, 1930s, 30x54x19" .250.00
Trestle, Baroque, walnut, single brd top, 18th C, 28x58x26" 3,220.00
Trestle, Hitchcock, rect top, trestle base, shoe ft, 1950s, 30x62x38" .500.00
Trestle, Shaker, pine, shoe ft, Sabbathday Maine, 28x37x95".18,000.00
Victorian, papier mache, tilt top, blk w/abalone decor, 28" rnd ...430.00
Work, Emp, mahog, lift top:2 drw, trn legs, lower shelf, 29x22x16"..900.00
Work, Emp, mahog, pullout desk:work bin, scrolled legs, 2 drops, 28x18x18"..750.00
Work, Fed, mahog, rect top:2 drw, trn & cvd legs, 30x23x17" 450.00
Work, Geo III, pnt, oval top:work bag, tapered legs, 29x18x13" ..600.00
Work, Shaker, red pnt, rect top:1 drw, trn leg, provenance, 19th C, 26x27x22"..2,300.00
Work, Sheraton, mahog, NY, leather top, 1 faux drw:2 drw, reeded legs, 30x24x17" **..8,000.00
Work, Sheraton, pine & maple, rect top:2 drw, trn legs, 28x18x17" ... 600.00
Work, Sheraton, tiger maple, rect top:2 drw, trn & tapered legs, 29x18x18".1,650.00

Wardrobes

Dutch Kas, 18th C, paneled oak case & do's, ball beet, 75x53x22"..2,500.00
Edwardian, flat top mahog, dentil mld, 2 do:1 L drw, 78x49x24" .725.00
Fr, pine, flat top:2 do:shaped apron, cab legs, 1850, 91x59x25" *.. 600.00
Louis XVI style, mahog, marquetry, 1 mirrored do, ormolu, 1930, 97x65x19"..2,650.00
Modernist, Hagemann, blk lqr 2 do, wood & tubular steel, 72x51x23" ..2,500.00

Sheraton, Co, poplar, 2 panelled do:2 drw, trn legs, much wear, 77x47x22" . 150.00
Victorian, walnut, mirrored & glz do's:3 drw, 82x50x20" 600.00

Washstands

Arts & Crafts, English, walnut, tile backsplash, marbletop:2 drw, trn legs, 46x36x48"..175.00
Emp, mahog, marble top:1 drw:2 do, bracket ft, 33x32x15" 250.00
Geo III, mahog, corner, 2 tier, arch backsplash, 48x24x17" 500.00
Georgian style, Kittenger, mahog, 12" circular top:2 drw, cab legs, 32". 200.00
Hplwht, mahog/birch, corner, 3 tier, inlay, 44x22x16" 6,000.00
Sheraton, Co., softwood, backsplash:1 drw:lower shelf, trn legs, 32x23x14" * . 100.00
Sheraton, mahog, backsplash, reeded legs, stretcher shelf, Boston, 34x21x20"..950.00
Sheraton, mahog, lift top, basin cut-out:1 drw:1 do, trn legs, ball ft, 32x23".250.00
Sheraton, pnt decor, pine, shaped gallery, basin cutout:1 drw, trn legs 32".. 300.00
Vict, Gothic Revival, 3 tiers, supported by 3 columns, 13" mahog circular top ... 150.00
Vict, RR, walnut, marble backsplash & top:1 drw:2 do, 41x31x16"...225.00

Miscellaneous

Bed steps, mahog, 2 tier, shaped sides, cut out ft, handhold, 40x15"..200.00
Bed steps, Regency, pnt decor, 3 leather treds, 2 side drw, 24x26x34". 2,200.00
Canterbury, Fed, mahog, trn posts, acorn finials, 1 drw, 18x19x13" . 1,000.00
Canterbury, Geo III, trn posts, 1 drw, 21x14x22" 800.00

Canterbury, Regency style, mahogany two dovetailed drawers with oak linings, brass casters and handles, British, nineteenth century, refinished, surface abrasions, 23x18x18", $1,560.00. (Photo courtesy Brunk Auctions on LiveAuctioneers.com)

Cellarette, Chpndl, walnut on stand, sq tapered legs, 31x22x17"... 2,900.00
Cellarette, Hplwht, mahog, hinged lid, divided int, taper legs, 25x16x16".. 1,100.00
Cellarette, Regency, mahog, brass banded, rpl fr, 6 sides, sq legs.. 500.00
Fernery, wicker, multi tier, natural color, braided border, 1940, 48"....450.00
Fire screen, Vict, mahog, shield fr, needlepoint, adjustable pole, 59" ... 50.00
Highchair, oak pressed bk, spindles, ca 1900, 47" 50.00
Lectern, Regency, mahog, tilting, telescoping tripod base, cab legs, 45x23"..975.00
Library steps, Modernist, Esherick, cherry, twisted post, 52x17x17".. 51,000.00
Library steps, Regency, folding type, inscribed Tylor patent, 91".. 2,200.00
Parlor suite, Vict, RR, 3 pc (settee, 2 chairs) medallion backs, trn legs....1,900.00
Porch suite, Old Hickory, 4 pc (settee, 2 chairs, table) spindle bk..... 5,000.00
Porch suite, Old Hickory, 5 pc (settee, 3 chairs, table), rustic wood/splint . 1,800.00
Portfolio stand, Vict, RR, walnut, inlay 3 grad shelves, trn legs, 48x50x20".3,100.00
Portfolio stand, W/M style, 'X' form, oak barley twist legs, caned inserts, 26".....350.00
Screen, Chinese export, Coromandel, 8 panel, landscape w/birds, 90". 700.00
Screen, Modernist, Eames/Miller, plywood & canvas, 6 panel, 68"..2,300.00
Screen, oil on brd, 3 panels, 'View of Boston' motif, 1950s, 65". 3,600.00
Tea cart, Edwardian, mahog, 2 lg wooden spoke wheels, 36x43x25" .1,200.00
Tea cart, Modernist, Risom, walnut, glass top, 25x23x18" 380.00
Tea trolly, English, 2 ebonized trays w/galleries, 1900s 36" W...... 650.00
Teapoy, Regency, sarcophagus box, trn tripod base, 30x16x11".. 1,800.00

Galena

Potteries located in the Galena, Illinois, area generally produced plain utility wares with lead glaze, often found in a pumpkin color with

some slip decoration or splashes of other colors. These potteries thrived from the early 1830s until sometime around 1860. In the listings that follow, all items are made of red clay unless noted otherwise.

Bowl, mixing, 9¾".. 200.00
Flowerpot, redware, mottled earth tones, drain hole, 8", NM 110.00
Jar, canning, redware w/orange & gr splotches, 8⅛x4¾" 440.00
Jar, canning, redware, splotchy oranges, 8x4¾" 235.00
Jar, mottled gr/amber/orange, no lid, 8", NM............................... 450.00
Jar, redware, gr w/orange & brn dots, ovoid, flared rim, hdls, 18", NM. 1,250.00
Jug, pumpkin w/3 yel balloon-like splotches, strap hdl, 10".......6,300.00
Jug, redware, dk gr w/burnt orange spots, ribbed/strap hdl, 8", NM..95.00

Galle

Emile Galle was one of the most important producers of cameo glass in France. His firm, founded in Nancy in 1874, produced beautiful cameo in the Art Nouveau style during the 1890s, using a variety of techniques. He also produced glassware with enameled decoration, as well as some fine pottery — animal figurines, table services, vases, and other objets d'art. In the mid-1880s he became interested in the various colors and textures of natural woods and as a result began to create furniture which he used as yet another medium for expression of his artistic talent. Marquetry was the primary method Galle used in decorating his furniture, preferring landscapes, Nouveau floral and fruit arrangements, butterflies, squirrels, and other forms from nature. It is for his cameo glass that he is best known today. All Galle is signed. Our advisor for this category is Don Williams; he is listed in the Directory under Missouri.

Key: fp – fire polished

Cameo

Atomizer, trees/mtns/lake, purple/bl/gr on frost, metal mts, 5½"..800.00
Biscuit jar, floral, tangerine on clambroth, SP mts, Nouveau hdl, 10".. 1,600.00
Bowl, clematis, lav & bl gray on lt bl, 4-lobe mouth, 3¼x6¼"..1,035.00
Lamp, boudoir, ferns, burgundy/lime gr on pale pk, single-socket, sgn, 20x9¾".12,500.00
Lamp, butterflies, earthen tones on pk/frost, 7" dome shade, 15½" ... 17,825.00
Lamp, butterflies/floral, 3-arm wrought base, 2" dome shade, 4" ..975.00
Vase, bees/honeycombs, honey yel on clear, Cristallerie, 6¼"..6,000.00
Vase, bleeding hearts, red on amber/gr, red disk ft, 16½".........11,500.00
Vase, butterflies/foliage, gr/frost on M gr, slim/waisted, 22½"....8,000.00
Vase, cherries (mold blown), red-brn/gr/brn on peach frost, 10¼".. 16,000.00
Vase, cyclamen, red on gr to amber, windowpane technique, 6¼".....3,250.00
Vase, dragonflies/water lilies, caramel on med to lt bl, slim, 18"...10,000.00
Vase, dragonfly/pond, caramel on bl/frost/lt bl, stick neck, 22"...14,375.00
Vase, dragonfly/water lilies, tangerine on frost to bl, hdls, 8"....6,325.00

Vase, fern leaves, green on crimson to peach, tri-fold rim, signed Galle with star, 11½", $2,280.00. (Photo courtesy Jackson's Auction on LiveAuctioneers.com)

Vase, floor, wisteria vines in purples & gr, 4-layer, sgn, 24¼x9"..6,600.00
Vase, floral branches, orange/red on lemon frost, cylindrical, 6½"..1,200.00

Vase, floral, mauve-brn on yel w/bl tinges, stick neck, 9" 1,560.00
Vase, floral, purples on frost, partly fp, flared rim, 12½" 3,600.00
Vase, fruit, orange/sienna on med & dk brn to amber, sm neck, 15" ..5,750.00
Vase, grapevines on martele, sgn, few scratches, 17½x5¾" 7,500.00
Vase, irises, lav/brn on amber to frost to gr-amber, 14½" 7,765.00
Vase, irises, purple on frost, 10" 4,000.00
Vase, morning glories, purple/gr/wht on martele, ca 1900, 11"..9,600.00
Vase, ovoid, leaves & pods, 4-layer, sgn, 12½x5" 2,160.00
Vase, peonies, burgundy/pk on frost, flared cylinder, ca 1900, 18" ..6,500.00
Vase, plums on branches, brn & gr on amber/wht frost, bl opal rim, 13"..12,075.00
Vase, raspberries (mold blown), red on yel, windowpane technique, 10".. 12,000.00
Vase, roses, red on amber, windowpane technique, 12½" 7,250.00
Vase, scenic (EX detail), brn on amber to turq mottle, fp, bulb, 8"..5,500.00
Vase, trees/rocks/mtns, purple/bl on frost, 10¼" 5,400.00
Vase, wisteria, gr & wht on lt olive frost, ca 1900, 23¼" 6,500.00

Enameled Glass

Pitcher, floral, mc w/gold, clear hdl, 7½" 3,000.00
Pitcher, floral/fruit, mc on smoky yel, geometric pnt amber hdl, 8" 2,750.00
Plate, floral w/appl cabochons, ruffled rim, 6¼" 865.00
Vase, ferns, flowers & butterfly on lt amber w/optic ribs, 7" 2,500.00
Vase, floral, appl cabochon centers on opal amber, ftd, 4" 1,850.00
Vase, nymphs on 2 (of 4) prints, gold trim, ca 1890, 6½x9" 3,000.00
Vase, poppies on pale gr frost, 1890s, 7⅛" 3,125.00
Vases (2), thistle in poly on clear, ca 1885, sgn, 8x5½", pr........ 2,280.00

Marquetry, Wood

Cabinet, display, clematis, glass door, side shelves, 60x32x18"..9,600.00
Table, dragonflies, ornate cvgs/scrolls, shelf, ca 1910s, sm 3,500.00
Table, nesting, floral studies, set of 4, lg: 28½x21¾x16" 8,000.00
Tray, cat sitting, ca 1890, 3¼x24½x6¼" 1,200.00
Tray, lilies of the valley, ca 1890, 2½x11¼x14½" 1,025.00

Pottery

Dish, asparagus, man w/harp beside lady, bl/yel leaves on wht, 11" ..315.00
Figurine, dog, sitting, bl/wht spots on yel, glass eyes, 13" 1,560.00

Figurines, cats with glass eyes,
13", lot of two, $4,000.00.
(Photo courtesy Early Auction Co.)

Pitcher, insect & foliage on bl over brn w/gold spatters, 7½", NM ...2,640.00
Pitcher, shepherd/flock/lake scene, bulb, angle hdl, 6x5" 1,325.00
Tureen, yel rope/bl border/bud finial, 9x14", +18" underplate...1,000.00

Gambling Memorabilia

Gambling memorabilia from the infamous casinos of the West and items that were once used on the 'Floating Palace' riverboats are especially sought after by today's collectors.

Cage, chuck-a-luck, chromed cast metal w/5 Bakelite dice, 11½". 130.00
Cage, chuck-a-luck, metal on wood base, 19x9½" sq, +felt layout ..180.00
Card shuffler, metal w/wooden crank hdl, Nestor Johnson, NMIB ..35.00

Chip, Carson City Nugget $1, metal insert, rare 16.00
Dice cup, ribbed leather w/stitching, +5 blk/wht dice 60.00
Dice game, Winkle, wooden countertop type w/flip paddle, Pat 93, 5" ..300.00
Dice, Flamingo Hotel, red w/wht dots, set of 6, MIB (clear w/logo).....70.00
Dice, gr (2nd amber), w/wht dots, ⅝", pr 15.00
Dice, ivory, bbl shape, late 1800s, EX, pr 65.00
Dice, orange mottled Bakelite, 2x2", pr 40.00
Game, Dmn Game-Fair Play, walnut w/glass face/marbles, Jones, 1890s ...475.00
Game, pnt wheel w/star center, CI base, Mason & Co, 93x57"..2,470.00
Keno goose, mahog, trn oviform, late 1800s, 22x12½" 785.00
Keno goose, walnut, complete w/#d balls, ca 1910, 23x12½" 725.00

Markers, Mother of Pearl,
3" wide, pair $1,500.00.
(Photo courtesy Showtime Auction Services on LiveAuctioneers.com)

Penny toy, gaming wheel spinner, pnt tin, Germany, 3¾", NM ...395.00
Poker chip, Dunes $1, sheik/harem girl/camel, bl border................ 80.00
Poker chip, horse head eng on ivory, red border, late 1800s 45.00
Poker chip, ivory w/4 cvd leaves w/in detailed star border, 1880s .. 55.00
Poker chip, Pequop Hotel Wells Nevada $1, gold letters on red clay...90.00
Poker chips, cvd flower center, red & gold borders, 1½", 9 for 180.00
Poker chips, red/bl/yel/wht plastic in sq wooden case w/hinged lid..50.00
Poker chips, red/blk/butterscotch Bakelite in rnd wooden holder. 135.00
Poker chips, red/gr/butterscotch Bakelite, in red Bakelite holder. 225.00
Poker chips, Royal Flush, 1870s, 180 metal chips in 10½x5" case. 785.00
Poker chips, Spirit of St Louis, set of 198 (red/wht/bl) in holder . 100.00
Poker table, 6 solid wood inserts for chips, felt top, base folds...... 120.00
Punch brd, Slip Off Shore, pinup girl, 1940s, 9¼x5", NM 100.00
Watch, Little Monte Carlo, enameled dial, beveled glass, ca 1890, EX ..1,900.00
Wheel, bright mc pnt on wood, 1950s, 30", EX............................. 250.00
Wheel, pnt wood, dbl-sided, spoked center, 25" dia 165.00
Wheel, pnt wood, dice pnt on red w/gold, iron center hub, 26" dia ...480.00
Wheel, pnt wood, red & blk, some nails missing, wall mt bracket, 24" ..250.00
Wheel, tin litho, playing cards on gr, 11" dia................................. 150.00
Wheel, traveling roulette, w/layout & chips, EX in 11x13" case.. 180.00

Gameboards

Gameboards, the handmade ones from the eighteenth and nineteenth centuries, are collected more for their folk art quality than their relation to games. Excellent examples of these handcrafted 'playthings' sell well into the thousands of dollars; even the simple designs are often expensive. If you are interested in this field, you must study it carefully. The market is always full of 'new' examples. Well-established dealers are often your best sources; they are essential if you do not have the expertise to judge the age of the boards yourself.

Carom, red/mustard pnt on pine, recessed pockets, 1800s, 31x31"...6,000.00
Checkers (dbl-sided), blk/mustard/dk bl pnt, wear, 1800s, 25x15" ...1,300.00
Checkers on 1 side, parcheesi on the other, 3-color pnt w/2-tone gold, 20x20" .5,750.00
Checkers, blk/bl pnt, sq w/appl molding, bk: pnt figure, 18x18" .. 4,400.00
Checkers, blk/wht/red/salmon/bl pnt, 1-brd, 1800s, 16x15" 2,700.00
Checkers, blk/yel pnt, 1-brd w/appl molding, 15x12" 825.00
Checkers, pnt/stripes/geometrics (dbl-sided), ca 1900, 20x10" .2,500.00
Checkers, red/wht pnt w/stars/shields/etc at border, 1890s, 19x18" . 18,800.00

Checkers, red/yel/blk pnt, 1-brd, w/appl molding, 1890s, 15x15".....1,880.00
Checkers, salmon/blk olive pnt, 1800s, 16½x16" 2,000.00
Checkers, yel/blk checks, mc pnt borders, 1-brd, 19th C, 17x14" 4,700.00
Checkers/backgammon, mc pnt on canvas, crackling, 22x30"..1,500.00
Checkers/backgammon, mc pnt on panel, appl molding, splits, 18x16" ..2,600.00
Checkers/parcheesi, mc pnt, molding (losses), 1800s, 19x17"...4,000.00
Parcheesi, mc on creamy wht pnt, mitered fr, ca 1900, 17x17".4,400.00
Parcheesi, muted mc pnt on brd, appl molding, ca 1900, 13x13"..6,500.00

Games

Collectors of antique games are finding it more difficult to find their treasures at shows and flea markets. Most of the action these days seems to be through specialty dealers and auctions. The appreciation of the art on the boards and boxes continues to grow. You see many of the early games proudly displayed as art, and they should be. The period from the 1850s to 1910 continues to draw the most interest. Many of the games of that period were executed by well-known artists and illustrators. The quality of their lithography cannot be matched today. The historical value of games made before 1850 has caused interest in this period to increase. While they may not have the graphic quality of the later period, their insights into the social and moral character of the early nineteenth century are interesting.

Twentieth-century games invoke a nostalgic feeling among collectors who recall looking forward to a game under the Christmas tree each year. They search for examples that bring back those Christmas morning memories. While the quality of their lithography is certainly less than the early games, the introduction of personalities from the comic strips, radio, and later TV created new interest. Every child wanted a game that featured their favorite character. Monopoly, probably the most famous game ever produced, was introduced during the Great Depression. For further information, we recommend *Schroeder's Collectible Toys, Antique to Modern*, available from Collector Books.

Air Ship Game, McLoughlin Bros, c 1904, VGIB......................200.00
American Boys Game, McLoughlin Bros, 1913, VGIB................285.00
Animal Ten Pins, McLoughlin Bros, EXIB................................1,200.00
Auto Game, Milton Bradley, 1906, EXIB 135.00
Babe Ruth's Baseball Game, Milton Bradley, 1920s, EX+IB.........400.00
Bamboozle, Milton Bradley, 1962, NMIB 25.00
Baseball & Checkers, Milton Bradley, 1925, VGIB......................50.00
Baseball Game, All-Fair, 1930, EX+IB.......................................150.00
Baseball Pitching Game, Marx, 1940s, NMIB............................225.00
Bicycle Race, Milton Bradley, 1910, EX+IB 150.00
Big Maze, Marx, 1955, MIB..50.00
Candyland, Milton Bradley, 1955, EXIB......................................20.00
Captive Princess, McLoughlin Bros, 1890s, VGIB 50.00
Cat & Witch (w/24 tails), Whitman, 1950s, VG 36.00
Champion Game of Base Ball, Proctor Amusement, 1915, NMIB.....100.00
Checkered Game of Life, Milton Bradley, 1860, VGIB................150.00
Chiromagica, McLoughlin Bros, early 1910s, EX+IB 300.00
Circination/Swinging 'Round the Circle, McLoughlin Bros, c 1897, GIB......225.00
Construction Game, Wilder, 1925, VGIB 350.00
Cycling Tour (A), Spears, EXIB..225.00
Derby Day, Parker Bros, 1959, NMIB...40.00
Derby Steeple Chase, McLoughlin Bros, 1880s, EXIB.................175.00
District Messenger Boy, McLoughlin Bros, 1880s, VGIB 200.00
Excuse Me! A Game of Manners, Parker Bros, NMIB....................25.00
Fish Pond, National Games, 1950s, NM+IB.................................20.00
Game of A Dash for the North Pole, McLoughlin Bros, 1897, VG+IB...2,760.00
Game of Base-Ball, McLoughlin Bros, c 1886, 9x17", GIB 1,400.00
Game of Boy Scouts, Milton Bradley, EXIB.................................300.00
Game of Going to the Klondike, McLoughlin Bros, 1890s, EXIB..4,600.00
Game of Playing Department Store, McLoughlin Bros, EXIB...2,750.00

Game of Sailor Boy, JH Singer, 1880s-90s, GIB..........................275.00

Game of Steeple Chase, Milton Bradley #4449, lithographed wood, dated 1917, complete, VGIB, $120.00. (Photo courtesy Rich Penn Auctions on LiveAuctioneers.com)

Game of Trip Around the World, McLoughlin Bros, 1890s, VGIB .2,000.00
Game of Yuneek, McLoughlin Bros, 1880s, VGIB 200.00
Gee-Wiz The Racing Game Sensation, Wolverine, 1920s, EX+ (VG box)...100.00
Hen That Laid the Golden Egg, Parker Bros, 1900s, EXIB 125.00
Honey Bee Game, Milton Bradley, 1913, EX+IB...........................60.00
Hoppity Hooper Pinball Game, Lidu, 1965, NMIB........................85.00
Intercollegiate Football, Hustler, 1920s, EXIB............................200.00
International Automobile Race, Parker Bros, 1903, EXIB 625.00
Lame Duck, Parker Bros, 1928, VGIB...125.00
Le Dirigeable Ball Toss Game, France, ca 1895, 29x31x10", VG ..4,500.00
Liberty Airport and Flying Airplanes, Liberty Playthings, EXIB..880.00
Louisa, McLoughlin Bros, EXIB 165.00
Magnetic Fish Pond, McLoughlin Bros, 1890s, VGIB.................400.00
Magnetic Fish Pond, Milton Bradley, 1948, NMIB 25.00
Merry-Go-Rnd, Chaffee & Selchow, 1890s-1910s, VGIB.........1,500.00
Motor Race, Wolverine, 1922, VGIB 50.00
Old Witch 'Brewsome' Stunts, Beistle Co, 1940s, 9½x7½", VG 55.00
Risk!, Parker Bros, 1959, NMIB...35.00
Rival Doctors (A Comic Game), McLoughlin Bros, 1890s, EXIB ..425.00
Round the World w/ Nellie Bly, McLoughlin Bros, 1890, VG+IB.350.00
Shuffled Symphonies Card Game, England/WD, ca 1938, NMIB .65.00
Skirmish at Harper's Ferry, McLoughlin Bros, 1890s, VG+IB 900.00
Spider's Web, McLoughlin Bros, late 1800s, EXIB 80.00
Spot Shot Marble Game, Wolverine, 1930s, NM..........................50.00
Steeple Chase, Singer, 1890s, VGIB 150.00
Susceptibles (A Parlor Amusement), McLoughlin Bros, 1890s, VGIB ...500.00
Toll Gate, McLoughlin Bros, c 1894, VGIB 800.00
Town & Country Traffic, Ranger Steel, 1940s, NMIB....................85.00
Town Hall, Milton Bradley, 1939, NMIB.......................................20.00
Train for Boston, Parker Bros, c 1900, GIB.................................850.00
Uncle Sam's Mail, McLoughlin Bros, 1890s, VGIB......................150.00
Vassar Boat Race, Chaffee & Selchow, c 1899, EXIB...............1,500.00
Westpoint, A Game for the Nation, 1902, EX+ (G+ box) 125.00
Whirl-O Halloween Fortune & Stunt Game, 1950s, 9x7", VG 50.00
Wilder's Baseball Game, Wilder, 1936, NMIB.............................200.00
Witch Party, Saalfield, pin-the-tail on donkey style, 1910s, w/poster, VG....50.00
Yachting, Singer, 1890, EXIB 150.00
Yale-Harvard Game, Parker Bros, 1890s, EX+IB 2,750.00
Zoom the Airplane Card Game, Whitman, 1941, NM (VG box) .65.00

Personalities, Movies, and TV Shows

Addams Family, Ideal, 1960s, NMIB...75.00
Alice in Wonderland Card Game, McLoughlin Bros, c 1898, EXIB ..400.00
Alvin & the Chipmunks Acorn Hunt, Hasbro, 1960, EXIB..........20.00
Amazing Spider-Man, Milton Bradley, 1966, EXIB.......................25.00

Annie Oakley Game, Milton Bradley, 1950s, lg, NMIB	45.00
Annie Oakley Game, Milton Bradley, 1950s, sm, NMIB	35.00
Ask Popeye's Lucky Jeep/2 Games in 1, King Features, c 1929-36	230.00
Barbie Queen of the Prom, Mattel, 1960s, NM+IB	75.00
Beatles Flip Your Wig, Milton Bradley, 1964, EX+IB	125.00
Beetle Bailey The Old Army Game, Milton Bradley, 1963, EXIB	25.00
Bewitched, T Cohn Inc, 1965, NMIB	65.00
Black Beauty, Transogram, 1957, NMIB	25.00
Bozo the Clown in Circus Land, Transogram, 1960s, NMIB	20.00
Buck Rogers & His Cosmic Rocket Wars, Lutz & Scheimkman, 1934, EXIB	450.00
Bullwinkle Hide 'N Seek Game, Milton Bradley, 1961, NMIB	50.00
Calling Superman, Transogram, 1950s, EXIB	175.00
Captain America, Milton Bradley, 1966, EXIB	30.00
Casey Jones, Saalfield, 1959, EXIB	25.00
Charlie McCarthy's Flying Hats, Whitman, 1930s, EXIB	30.00
Cinderella, A Game, Parker Bros, 1875, NMIB	75.00
Combat Card Game, Milton Bradley, 1960s, EXIB	12.00
Dangerous World of James Bond 007, Milton Bradley, 1965, NMIB	50.00
Daniel Boone Wilderness Trail Card Game, Transogram, 1960s, NMIB	45.00
Davy Crockett Adventures, Gardner, 1950s, EXIB	50.00
Dick Tracy Card Game, Whitman, 1934, EXIB	35.00
Disney True Life Electric Quiz Game, 1952, VGIB	25.00
Disneyland Game, Transogram, 1954, EXIB	30.00
Donald Duck's Tiddley Winx, 1950s, EXIB, $100 to	135.00
Ed Wynn the Fire Chief, Selchow & Righter, 1930s, EXIB	50.00
Ensign O'Toole USS Appleby Game, Hasbro, 1968, NMIB	30.00
Escort: Game of Guys & Gals, Parker Bros, 1955, unused, MIB	30.00
Fantastic Voyage, Milton Bradley, 1968, NMIB	30.00
Felix the Cat Dandy Candy Game, Built-Rite, 1950s, EX+IB	10.00
Ferdinand's Chinese Checkers w/the Bee!, Parker Bros, 1939, EXIB	150.00
Fox & the Hounds, Parker Bros, 1948, NMIB	20.00
G-Men Clue Games, Whitman #3930, 1930s, VGIB	75.00
Great Charlie Chan Detective Game, Milton Bradley, 1930s, EXIB	350.00
Gulliver's Travels, Milton Bradley, 1930s, EXIB	135.00
Hi-Way Henry Cross Country 'The Lizzy' Race, All-Fair, 1920s, EXIB	895.00
Howdy Doody Adventure Game, Milton Bradley, 1950s, VGIB	25.00
Howdy Doody Bean Bag Game, Parker Bros, 1950s, EXIB	75.00
Huckleberry Hound Bumps, Transogram, EX+IB, 1960	25.00
Huckleberry Hound Tiddly Winks, Milton Bradley, 1959, EXIB	20.00
Humpty Dumpty Game, Lowell, 1950s, EXIB	30.00
Ipcress File Game (The), Milton Bradley, 1966, MIB	30.00
Jack & Jill, Milton Bradley, early 1900s, VGIB	100.00
King Kong Game, Milton Bradley, 1960s, NMIB	25.00
King Leonardo & His Subjects, Milton Bradley, 1960, EXIB	20.00
Laramie, Lowell, 1960, VGIB	25.00
Laugh-In's Squeeze Your Bibby, Hasbro, 1960s, VGIB	25.00
Legend of Jesse James, Milton Bradley, 1965, EXIB	35.00
Lone Ranger Target Game, Marx, 1939, EXIB	75.00
Man From UNCLE Target Game, Marx, 1965, NM	250.00
Mickey Mouse Circus Game, Marks Bros, 1930s, NMIB	500.00
Peter Pan, Selchow & Righter, 1920s, EX+IB	100.00
Peter Rabbit Game, Milton Bradley, 1910s, EXIB	50.00
Popeye Menu Marble Game, Durable Toys & Novelty, c 1935, EX	440.00
Red Riding Hood, Parker Bros, 1933, MIB	200.00
Ruff & Reddy Spelling Game, Exclusive Playing Card Co, 1958, EXIB	24.00
Skeezix & the Air Mail, Milton Bradley, 1930s, EXIB	60.00
Smitty, Milton Bradley, 1930s, EX+IB	250.00
Snoopy Game, Selchow & Righter, 1960, VGIB	15.00
Snow Wht & the Seven Dwarfs, Milton Bradley, 1930s, EXIB	75.00
Snow Wht & the Seven Dwarfs, Parker Bros, 1930s, EXIB	150.00
Stagecoach, Milton Bradley, 1958, NMIB	25.00
Superman (Adventures of), Milton Bradley, 1942, EXIB	150.00
Uncle Remus Shooting Gallery, B&B Novelties, 1917 patent, VGIB	690.00
Untouchables, Marx, 1950s, NMIB	225.00

Garden City Pottery

Founded in 1902 in San Jose, California, by the end of the 1920s this pottery had grown to become the largest in northern California. During that period production focused on stoneware, sewer pipe, and red clay flowerpots. In the late '30s and '40s, the company produced dinnerware in bright solid colors of yellow, green, blue, orange, cobalt, turquoise, white, and black. Royal Arden Hickman, who would later gain fame for the innovative artware he modeled for the Haeger company, designed not only dinnerware but a line of Art Deco vases and bowls as well. The company endured hard times by adapting to the changing needs of the market and during the '50s concentrated on production of garden products. Foreign imports, however, proved to be too competitive, and the company's pottery production ceased in 1979.

Because none of the colored-glazed products were ever marked, to learn to identify the products of this company, you'll need to refer to *Sanford's Guide to Garden City Pottery* by Jim Pasquali. Values apply to items in all colors (except black) and all patterns, unless noted otherwise. Due to relative rarity, 20% should be added for any item found in black.

Bean pot, Deco, w/lid, lg	85.00
Bean pot, plain, 1-qt	25.00
Bowl, bulb, 10"	45.00
Bowl, mixing, Wide-Ring, solid color, #3 (mid sz)	30.00
Bowl, nappy, #4	25.00
Bowl, soup, plain, solid color	35.00
Bowl, Succulent, 11"	60.00
Carafe, solid color, flaring panels, 10"	450.00
Casserole, narrow or wide rings, solid color, 7", ea	35.00
Cookie jar, Deco style, solid color, 7½"	75.00
Crock, 2-gal	45.00

Crock, five-gallon, cracked and chipped lid, 13½", $60.00. (Photo courtesy Williams Auction & Appraisal Service on LiveAuctioneers.com)

Cup, punch	15.00
Frog, sm	15.00
Jardiniere, ribbed, solid color, 10"	45.00
Mug, chowder, solid color, w/lid	45.00
Mug, Tom & Jerry	45.00
Oil jar, hand thrown, mini	150.00
Pitcher, 2-qt	55.00
Plate, artichoke, solid color	40.00
Plate, dinner, solid color, 9"	20.00
Ramekin, solid color, 3"	20.00
Teapot, Deco style, solid color, 4-cup	75.00
Vase, Deco, 4½x10"	65.00
Vase, ribbed cylinder, 8"	35.00
Water cooler, crockery	75.00

Gardner Porcelain

Models of wonderfully complicated and detailed subjects illustrating people of many nations absorbed in day-to-day activities were made by this company from the turn of the nineteenth century until well past the 1850s. The factory was founded in 1765 near Moscow, Russia, by an Englishman by the name of Francis Gardner. They are still in business today.

Bowl, floral reserves on burgundy w/gold, late 19th C, 7⅛".......... 475.00
Figurine, coachman, long bl coat, hands on hips, ca 1845, 7⅜" 4,800.00
Figurine, grain seller stands w/coins before grain mound, 19th C, 8" .2,150.00
Figurine, man in hat/long coat, stands w/watch in hand, 1810s, 7⅛".19,500.00
Figurine, nude lady w/pk bonnet & fur muff, ca 1845, 7¾" 11,750.00

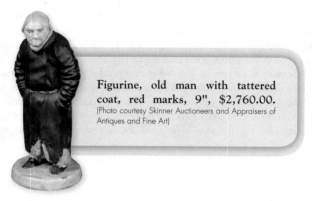

Figurine, old man with tattered coat, red marks, 9", $2,760.00. (Photo courtesy Skinner Auctioneers and Appraisers of Antiques and Fine Art)

Figurine, peasant girl w/flower basket, early 19th C, 5¼" 3,850.00
Figurine, peasant lady dancing, wht apron, 19th C, 8" 1,200.00
Figurine, peasant lady on bench feeds baby, child beside, 5½" ..1,200.00
Figurine, peasant man dancing, long fur-lined coat, 10½".........1,800.00
Figurine, peasant man seated & sprinkling salt on bread, 19th C, 6".. 2,100.00
Figurine, Spaniard w/short coat over his shoulders, 1820s, 7¾"..8,400.00
Figurine, Spaniard, 1820, 7" 8,400.00
Figurine, vagabond seated, boots/ bag beside him, late 19th C, 6x4" .. 660.00
Figurine, woodsman w/load of kindling in wheelbarrow, 8½".....1,950.00
Figurine, youthful man stands & holds tree branch, mid-19th C, 4"..2,850.00
Pen holder, dog seated by tree trunk, rococo base, 19th C, 2½" .1,325.00

Gas Globes and Panels

Gas globes and panels, once a common sight, have vanished from the countryside but are being sought by collectors as a unique form of advertising memorabilia. Early globes from the 1920s (some date back to as early as 1912), now referred to as 'one-piece' (Type 4) globes, were made of molded milk glass and were globular in shape. The gas company name was etched or painted on the glass. Few of these were ever produced, and this type is valued very highly by collectors today.

A new type of pump was introduced in the early 1930s; the old 'visible' pumps were replaced by 'electric' models. Globes were changing at the same time. By the mid-teens a three-piece (Type 3) globe consisting of a pair of inserts and a metal body was being produced in both 15" and 16½" sizes. Collectors prefer to call globes that are not one-piece or metal frame 'three-piece glass' (Type 2). Though metal-framed globes with glass inserts (Type 3) were most popular in the 1920s and 1930s, some were actually made as early as 1914. Though rare in numbers, their use spans many years. In the 1930s Type 2 globes became the replacements of the one-piece globe and Type 3 globes. The most recently manufactured gas globes are made with a plastic body that contains two 13½" glass lenses. These were common in the '50s but were actually used as early as 1932. This style is referred to as Type 1 in our listings. Values here are for examples with both sides in excellent condition: no chips, wear, or other damage. Our advisor for this category is Scott Benjamin; he is listed in the Directory under Ohio. For more information we recommend *Value Guide to Gas Station Memorabilia* by B.J Summers and Wayne Priddy.

Note: Standard Crowns with raised letters are one-piece globes that were made in the 1920s; those made in the 1950s (no raised letters), though one-piece, are not regarded as such by today's collectors.

Type 1, Plastic Body, Glass Inserts (Inserts 13½") — 1931 – 1950s

Aro Flight, dk bl/wht/orange-red..1,500.00
D-X Marine, rare...1,500.00
Dino Supreme, sm dinosaur, red/wht/gr 200.00
Dixie, plastic band 250.00
Fleet-Wing 400.00
Frontier Gas, Rarin' To Go, w/horse 1,000.00
Hercules Ethyl Gasoline, red/wht/gr, new Capco gr fr 375.00

Hi-Test Premium, 13½" lenses, $1,400.00. (Photo courtesy Premier Auction Center on LiveAuctioneers.com)

Kendal Deluxe, Capco body w/red pnt...350.00
Malco, orig bl-gr Capco fr..2,000.00
Marathon, no runner 200.00
New State 88..750.00
Phillips 66...350.00
Phillips 66 Flite-Fuel...450.00
Pride Ethyl, red/wht/bl, oval, new Capco fr, scarce......................450.00
Pure, blk on mg, orig Capco fr, 1960s...350.00
Road King, knight on horse, red on wht, Capco fr, 1950s 1,000.00
Sinclair Dino Gasoline, gr & red lettering, dinosaur logo at top.. 175.00
Sinclair H-C Gasoline, red/gr/wht 250.00
Skelly Keotane 250.00
Speedway 79, red/wht/bl, Capco fr, ca 1955................................500.00
Spur, oval body...350.00
Stone's Ethyl, yel/bl/wht, Capco fr 400.00
Sunray Ethyl Corp 1,600.00
Super Flash, red lighting flash, Capco fr, 1960s............................650.00
Texaco Diesel Chief, Capco body..850.00
Viking, pictures Viking ship 1,850.00

Type 2, Glass Frame, Glass Inserts (Inserts 13½") — 1926 – 1940s

Aerio, w/airplane 15,000.00
Aetna Motor Gasoline...1,000.00
Aladdin Gasoline, 2-lens w/side body 850.00
Amoco, Gill body 500.00
Atlantic (new logo), Gill body, ca 1966.......................................650.00
Atlantic Hi-Arc, red/wht/bl, Gill fr, ca 1936.................................650.00
Atlantic, red/wht/bl, ca 1966..500.00
Barnsdall Be Square Gasoline, 2 lenses in wide body 600.00
Bay Ethyl, Gill glass 750.00
Capitol Gasoline Ethyl Corp 500.00
Capitol Kerosene Oil Co 600.00
Clark, EX...350.00
Col-Tex Service Gasoline, 5-color 1,000.00
Derby, Gill body..750.00
Derby's Flexgas Ethyl, threaded base, Gill fr, 1940s 850.00
Esso...325.00

Frontier Gas, Double Refined 400.00
Gladiator Gasoline, w/swords, 3-pc glass, 1930s 1,000.00
Globe Gasoline, metal base ring.. 2,000.00
Guyler Brand, mg, spelled Cuyler 1,000.00
Hustol, yel & blk on mg, wide fr 300.00
Kan O Tex, Gill body, metal base ring 950.00
Laureleaf 2,000.00
Lion, Knix Knox, metal base 3,000.00
Marine Gasoline, sea horse, red/turq/wht, 1940s 2,500.00
Martin Purple Martin Ethyl... 850.00

Mobil Gas with Pegasus, milk glass, 16", EX, $500.00. (Photo courtesy Randy Inman Auctions Inc. on LiveAuctioneers.com)

Never Nox Ethyl.. 750.00
Phillips Unique, company's 3rd grade in gasoline, wht, gr, red & blk.... 850.00
Pitman Streamlined, Gill body 15,000.00
Pure 500.00
Safeway Perfecto Regular Oil Co, single lens, 1930s-40s........... 1,000.00
Sinclair H-C Gasoline, red/wht/gr 500.00
Sinclair Pennant... 1,000.00
Sky Chief, Gill body, 13".. 650.00
Sohio Diesel Supreme, orig wide fr 350.00
Standard Crown, bl... 800.00
Standard Crown, gr crown, tractor fuel, rare........................ 2,000.00
Standard Crown, gray 2,000.00
Standard Crown, red or gold, ea 400.00
Standard Crown, wht 350.00
Texaco Ethyl 2,500.00
Tydol A Ethyl, red/blk on mg, Gill fr, ca 1946 .... 1,250.00
United Hi-Test Gasoline, red/wht/bl.................................... 450.00
White Flash, Gill body 650.00
WNAX, w/radio station pictured 4,000.00

Type 3, Metal Frame, Glass Inserts (Inserts 15" or 16½") — 1915 – 1930s

Aero Mobilgas, new metal body, rare, 15"........................... 3,000.00
Atlantic Ethyl, 16½" 950.00
Atlantic White Flash, 16" 850.00
Blue Flash (Richfield Oil), ca 1925, 15"............................... 750.00
Bluebird Anti-Knock Gasoline, bl on mg, 1930s, 15"............... 2,750.00
Blus Anti-Knock Gasoline, Interstate Oil Gas 1,000.00
Conoco Gasoline, silhouette figure on yel, 1913-29 .... 4,000.00
Farmer's Union High Octane, red/wht/bl, metal body, 15" 850.00
General Ethyl, 15" fr, complete 4,000.00
General Motor Fuel, red/yel/blk on wht, early, 15"................. 1,250.00
Humble Oils, red/bl/wht, orig red fr, NM 2,500.00
Marathon, low-profile metal body, 15"............................... 1,500.00
Mobilgas, red Pegasus, blk letters, 16½" 850.00
Mobilgas Ethyl, no horse, 16½" 600.00
Mohawk Gasoline, Indian's portrait, red version, 1930s........... 9,000.00
Peerless Gasoline, red & bl on mg, 15".............................. 850.00
Phillips Benzo, low-profile metal body, 15" 5,000.00
Purol Gasoline, w/arrow, porc body 750.00
Purol the Pure Oil, bl & wht, 15".................................... 650.00

Red Star Gasoline, blk w/red star on wht, new fr, 1920s, 15" 850.00
Richfield Ethyl, blk & yel eagle, red lettering, ca 1939 .... 950.00
Rocor Gasoline, eagle, blk & yel on mg, ca 1939 .... 1,250.00
Royal Gasoline w/ME pictured, H profile metal body, 15" 1,850.00
Signal, old stoplight, 15"... 7,500.00
Stonolined Aviation, rare, 16" 15,000.00
Super Speed, complete.. 1,850.00
Texaco Leaded, glass globe 3,000.00
Tydol, Tide Water Co, blk lettering, 1920s, 15".................... 1,500.00
White Star, 15" fr, complete 2,000.00

Type 4, One-Piece Glass Globes, No Inserts, Company Name Etched, Raised or Enameled — 1912 – 1931

Atlantic, chimney cap 6,000.00
Imperial Premier Gasoline, red & yel on mg, rpt 1,000.00
Mobil Gargoyle, gargoyle pictured, oval............................. 2,000.00
Newport Gasoline Oils, orange & gr on mg, VG.................... 1,850.00
Pierce Pennant, etched.. 4,500.00
Shell, rnd, etched.. 500.00
Sinclair Gasoline baked on mg, ca 1926-29 .... 1,500.00
Sinclair Gasoline, etched, orig pnt, 1920s, VG+ 1,750.00
Sinclair HC Gasoline, red/wht/blk on mg, 1927-29 .... 1,750.00
Sinclair Oils, etched, 1920s, G- pnt 1,850.00
Standard Crown, red or gold, ea 400.00
Standard Crown, wht 350.00
Super Shell, clam shape.. 1,500.00
Super Shell, clam shape, rnd version................................ 3,500.00
Texaco, etched letters, wide body.................................... 1,500.00
Texaco Ethyl 2,500.00
That Good Gulf..., emb, orange & blk letters 1,500.00
White Eagle, blunt nose, 20¾".. 1,500.00
White Eagle, detailed eagle, 20¾"..................................... 2,200.00
White Rose, boy pictured, pnt.. 5,000.00

Gaudy Dutch

Inspired by Oriental Imari wares, Gaudy Dutch was made in England from 1800 to 1820. It was hand decorated on a soft-paste body with rich underglaze blues accented in orange, red, pink, green, and yellow. It differs from Gaudy Welsh in that there is no lustre (except on Water Lily). There are 16 patterns, some of which are War Bonnet, Grape, Dahlia, Oyster, Urn, Butterfly, Carnation, Single Rose, Double Rose, and Water Lily.

Values hinge on condition, strength of color, detail, and variations to standard designs. Unless otherwise noted, our values are based on near mint to mint condition items, with only minimal wear or scratches. Even a piece rated excellent may bring from 60% to 75% less than these prices. We have used the term 'chain' to refer to a border device less detailed than one with distinguishable hearts or leaves, as the latter will bring higher prices. When ranges are used, the higher side will represent an item with better than average color and execution. For more information we recommend *The Collector's Encyclopedia of Gaudy Dutch & Welsh* by John A. Shuman III.

Butterfly, plate, double border, one with large and small yellow dots on blue, the inner border with vining leaves, 10", $6,450.00. (Photo courtesy Conestoga Auction Company on LiveAuctioneers.com)

Butterfly, plate, bl band w/wavy line+inner leaf border, 8" 2,200.00
Butterfly, plate, yel chain in bl band+wavy line border, 6" 3,100.00
Butterfly, plate, yel ovals in bl band+inner leaf border, 8", $2,200 to .3,100.00
Butterfly, teapot, bl band w/wavy lines on body/lid, rprs, 5", VG . 725.00
Carnation, cup plate, yel chain in bl band border, 3", VG 1,550.00
Carnation, plate, yel chain in bl band+waves border, 5" 480.00
Carnation, plate, yel chain in bl band+waves border, 6" 960.00
Carnation, plate, yel ovals in bl band, yel leaf inner border, 9", EX...600.00
Carnation, plate, yel ovals in bl band+inner leaf border, 8" 1,550.00
Carnation, soup bowl, yel ovals in bl band+inner leaf border, 10" ...1,080.00
Carnation, soup plate, yel ovals in bl band+inner leaf border, 8". 700.00
Carnation, sugar bowl, yel chain in bl band border, w/lid, 5x6", VG .780.00
Carnation, teapot, yel chain in bl band, strong colors, 6x10" ...2,880.00
Carnation, waste bowl, yel chain in bl band border, 3x6", VG 480.00
Dahlia, plate, bl band, red hearts & wavy line border, 8" 6,600.00
Dahlia, tea bowl & saucer, bl band, red hearts border, sm flakes to ft.4,500.00
Dahlia, waste bowl, bl band, red heart border, 3x5½" 8,600.00
Double Rose, creamer, helmet shape, shaped hdl, 5" 1,375.00
Double Rose, creamer, mask under spout, octagonal, 6", EX.....9,000.00
Double Rose, cup plate, 3" 1,350.00
Double Rose, plate, 7½", $420 to 540.00
Double Rose, plate, 10" 1,560.00
Double Rose, platter, 10" L 7,200.00
Double Rose, soup plate, 9" 540.00
Double Rose, soup plate, 10" 900.00
Double Rose, sugar bowl, w/lid, 5", EX.................................2,400.00
Double Rose, tea bowl & saucer, $400 to 535.00
Double Rose, teapot, rect, 6¼", $2,400 to 3,200.00
Double Rose, waste bowl, 2x5" 350.00
Dove, plate, bl band w/wavy lines+inner leaf border, 9¾" 880.00
Dove, plate, narrow bl rim band, 7" 475.00
Dove, tea bowl & saucer, bl band w/wavy lines border, VG+ 1,020.00
Dove, waste bowl, inside rim w/band of stripes & flowers, 2x5" . 1,200.00
Grape, cup plate, yel chain on bl band, 3½" 990.00
Grape, pitcher, yel chain on bl band border, 4" 2,000.00
Grape, pitcher, yel hearts on bl band border, flaring ft, 9", VG+ ...9,600.00
Grape, plate, yel chain on bl band border, 9" 1,100.00
Grape, soup plate, yel chain on bl band border, sm mfg flaw, 7"... 495.00
Grape, tea bowl & saucer, flared sides, yel chain on bl band border . 780.00
Grape, teapot, 7", creamer, 4½", sugar bowl, w/lid, 5½", all EX.2,400.00
Grape, toddy plate, yel heart chain on bl band border, 4" ...1,500.00
Leaf, bowl, yel heart chain in bl band border, 1x8", EX............4,200.00
Oyster, bowl, deep, 10" 750.00
Oyster, plate, 6⅜", $400 to 510.00
Oyster, tea bowl & saucer, $500 to.. 650.00
Oyster, tea bowl & saucer, w/King's Rose, pk band w/hearts & swags, EX . 400.00
Oyster, teapot, 6", $2,500 to 2,650.00
Oyster, teapot, w/King's Rose, pk trim, 5" 2,530.00
Primrose, tea bowl & saucer, yel heart chain in bl band border, EX .3,200.00
Single Rose, coffeepot, acanthus spout/hdl, rpr, 11", $2,800 to.3,000.00
Single Rose, coffeepot, domed lid, scroll hdl, acanthus spout, EX, 12" . 2,300.00
Single Rose, creamer, yel chain in bl band border, EX, 4" 720.00
Single Rose, plate, exceptional detail, pale pk flowers, 8⅜" 1,800.00
Single Rose, plate, yel chain in lt bl band border, 8⅛" 535.00
Single Rose, soup bowl, yel ovals in bl band border, 9⅞"............. 840.00
Single Rose, tea bowl & saucer, variant 2,640.00
Single Rose, teapot, yel chain in bl band border, VG................. 780.00
Single Rose, toddy plate, imp flower mk, 4" 840.00
Sunflower, plate, bl band w/waves+inner leaf border, 9¾" 1,000.00
Sunflower, plate, deep, 9"...1,800.00
Sunflower, tea bowl & saucer, bl band w/waves, $500 to 660.00
Sunflower, teapot, bl/dk brn band w/waves border, prof rstr, 10" .5,700.00
Urn, plate, paneled floral border, 10", EX 480.00
Urn, plate, yel chain on bl band+waves border, 7½" 1,020.00

Urn, tea bowl & saucer, EX+, $300 to 450.00
War Bonnet, bowl, shallow, 8⅛"... 960.00
War Bonnet, creamer, line border, 4", EX 850.00
War Bonnet, cup plate, 4⅝"...1,450.00
War Bonnet, plate, 9", $1,300 to.......................................1,450.00
War Bonnet, soup plate, 8" 825.00
War Bonnet, tea bowl & saucer 800.00
Zinnia, plate, 6⅜".. 660.00
Zinnia, plate, dk brn-lined bl band w/leaf chain, Riley, 8" 3,000.00

Gaudy Welsh

Gaudy Welsh was an inexpensive hand-decorated ware made in both England and Wales from 1820 until 1860. It is characterized by its colors — principally blue, orange-rust, and copper lustre — and by its uninhibited patterns. Accent colors may be yellow and green. (Pink lustre may be present, since lustre applied to the white areas appears pink. A copper tone develops from painting lustre onto the dark colors.) The body of the ware may be heavy ironstone (also called Gaudy Ironstone), creamware, earthenware, or porcelain; even styles and shapes vary considerably. Patterns, while usually floral, are also sometimes geometric and may have trees and birds. Beware! The Wagon Wheel pattern has been reproduced. Our advisor for this category is C.L. Nelson; see the Directory under Texas.

Note: British auction houses are picturing and promoting Gaudy Welsh. Demand for Columbine, Grape, Tulip, Oyster, and Wagon Wheel is slow. We should also mention that the Bethesda pattern is very similar to a Davenport jug pattern. No porcelain Gaudy Welsh was made in Wales. For more information we recommend *The Collector's Encyclopedia of Gaudy Dutch & Welsh*.

Amranwen, jug, 7" 300.00
Aster, plate, 9" 265.00
Beanstock, jug, 5¼" 650.00
Betws-y-coed, jug, 7" 525.00
Billingsley Rose, c/s 300.00
Cambrian Rose, jug, 7" 210.00
Cardiff, jug, 7" 600.00
Castle, c/s 135.00
Columbine, teapot 88.00
Dotted Circle, c/s.. 135.00

Drape, jug, paneled body, scroll handle, 7", $280.00.
(Photo courtesy Green Valley Auctions on LiveAuctioneers.com)

Drape, teapot, 8" 400.00
Fence, plate, 7⅞"... 160.00
Flower Basket, sugar, 7"... 125.00
Grape, jug, 7" 250.00
Gwyrrd, jug, 7" 545.00
Herald, jug, 5" 325.00
Honeysuckle, c/s 85.00
Horton, jug, 5½" 225.00
Leaf, mug, 2½".. 235.00

Llanrug, jug, 6" 595.00
Morning Glory, plate, 7" 265.00
Oyster, c/s 35.00
Pansy, plate, 9" 110.00
Poppy, jug, 8" 445.00
Rainbow, plate, 8" 275.00
Rock Rose, teapot, 8" 410.00
Ross, jug, 8" 460.00
Sahara, plate, 9" 285.00
Scollop, mug, 2" 135.00
Strawberry, jug, 7¼" 595.00
Sunflower, creamer, 5" 105.00
Tulip, creamer, 5" 75.00

Geisha Girl

Geisha Girl porcelain was one of several key Japanese china production efforts aimed at the booming export markets of the U.S., Canada, England, and other parts of Europe. The wares feature colorful, kimono-clad Japanese ladies in scenes of everyday Japanese life surrounded by exquisite flora, fauna, and mountain ranges. Nonetheless, the forms in which the wares were produced reflected the late nineteenth- and early twentieth-century Western dining and decorating preferences: tea and coffee services, vases, dresser sets, children's items, planters, etc.

Over 100 manufacturers were involved in Geisha Girl production. This accounts for the several hundred different patterns, well over a dozen border colors and styles, and several methods of design execution. Geisha Girl porcelain was produced in wholly hand-painted versions, but most were hand painted over stenciled outlines. Be wary of Geisha ware executed with decals. Very few decaled examples came out of Japan. Rather, most were Czechoslovakian attempts to hone in on the market. Czech pieces have stamped marks in broad, pseudo-Oriental characters. Items with portraits of Oriental ladies in the bottom of tea or sake cups are *not* Geisha Girl porcelain, unless the outside surface of the wares are decorated as described above. These lovely faces, formed by varying the thickness of the porcelain body, are called lithophanes and are collectible in their own right.

The height of Geisha Girl production was between 1910 and the mid-1930s. Some post-World War II production has been found marked Occupied Japan. The ware continued in minimal production during the 1960s, but the point of origin of the later pieces was not only Japan but Hong Kong as well. These productions are discerned by the pure whiteness of the porcelain; even, unemotional borders; lack of background washes and gold enameling; and overall sparseness of detail. A new wave of Nippon-marked reproduction Geisha emerged in 1996. If the Geisha Girl productions of the 1960s – 1980s were overly plain, the mid-1990s repros are overly ornate. Original Geisha Girl porcelain was enhanced by brush strokes of color over a stenciled design; it was never the 'color perfectly within the lines' type of decoration found on current reproductions. Original Geisha Girl porcelain was decorated with color washes; the reproductions are in heavy enamels. The backdrop decoration of the 1990s reproductions features solid, thick colors, and the patterns feature too much color; period Geisha ware had a high ratio of white space to color. The new pieces also have bright shiny gold in proportions greater than most period Geisha ware. The Nippon marks on the reproductions are wrong. Some of the Geisha ware created during the Nippon era bore the small precise decaled green M-in-Wreath mark, a Noritake registered trademark. The reproduced items feature an irregular facsimile of this mark. Stamped onto the reproductions is an unrealistically large M-in-Wreath mark in shades of green ranging from an almost neon to pine green with a wreath that looks like it has seen better days, as it does not have the perfect roundness of the original mark. Other marks have also been reproduced. Reproductions of mid-sized trays, chunky hatpin hold-

ers, an ornate vase, a covered bottle, and a powder jar are among the current reproductions popping up at flea and antique markets.

Our advisor for this category is Elyce Litts; she is listed in the Directory under New Jersey.

Ashtray, hexagonal, red, Royal Kaga Nippon mk, 3" 24.00
Basket vase, Bamboo Trellis, gr hdl & brn ft w/gold, 8½" 150.00
Berry set, Dragonboat, cobalt border w/gold, master+6 ind bowls.. 65.00
Berry set, Garden Bench, red/pine gr border w/gold, 10"+4 5½" bowls... 45.00
Biscuit jar, Court Lady, cobalt w/blk-outlined reserves, J #1 .... 75.00
Bowl, berry, Pointing F, red maple leaves/gold border, Kutani, 10"...50.00
Bowl, Boat Festival, bl border w/gold lacing, Japan mk, 7½" 25.00
Bowl, carp, red w/gold, 6" 15.00
Bowl, Parasol Modern, incurvate rim, Japan, 2x6" 15.00
Bowl, Pointing Q, red butterfly border, foliate/rtcl rim, 7" 18.00
Bowl, salad, Garden Bench A, 9-lobed, red border, 7¼" 25.00
Bowl, salad, Garden Bench A, 9-lobed, red border, 9" 30.00
Butter pat, Flower Gathering B, red-orange, 3¼" 8.00

Chocolate pot, child reaching for butterfly, 9½", $45.00.
(Photo courtesy Richard D. Hatch & Associates on LiveAuctioneeers.com)

Compote, Boat Festival, river scene, ftd, #4, 6" 55.00
Cup/saucer, bouillon, mc, Rendevous, J#88, w/lid 45.00
Hair receiver, Fan Dance A & Sake Time, bl w/gold, Yamamasu Nippon mk ...35.00
Hair receiver, Footbridge A, red w/gold 25.00
Hair receiver, Thousand Geisha, bl w/gold, tin Cherry Blossom mk .. 45.00
Luncheon set, Garden Bench D, mc border, teapot+6 c/s+6 plates....225.00
Match holder, Parasol C, red border, Japan, 3¼x2¼" 26.00
Plate, Footbridge, 6" 12.00
Plate, Gardening, Fort Deerborn Brand advertising, scalloped, 4¾"... 14.00
Plate, Lady in Rickshaw B, red/gold border, Mikado, 5" 14.00
Plate, lemon, Child Reaching for Butterfly, 2-hdl, Japan, 6¼x5¾"...16.00
Plate, River's Edge, red & gold border, Japan mk, 7¼" 12.00
Plate, Wait for Me, floriate shape, red-orange w/gold buds, 8¾" 26.00
Platter, Ikebana Party, red & gold border, 9½", NM 38.00
Platter, Parasol C, red border, pierced hdls.................................... 27.00
Platter, Temple Vase, bl w/gold border, red int border, flaw, 11x10" .35.00
Powder jar, 3-legged, Prayer Ribbon, red w/gold 34.00
Relish, Fan Dance D, red border w/gold, pierced hdls, 8¾x4¾" 25.00
Relish, scenic/ladies reserves, red border w/gold lacing, hdls, 9¼x5" .. 24.00
Tea set, River's Edge, mc 3-banded border w/gold, pot+cr/sug+6 c/s ... 125.00
Teacup & saucer, child's, Mother & Son A, diapered border, unmk .. 12.00
Teacup & saucer, Garden Bench N, floral surround, Japan............. 14.00
Teacup & saucer, River's Edge, mc border, MIJ 12.00
Teapot, Garden Bench Q, mc/gold border, Cherry Blossom mk, 4½" ..32.00
Tray, dresser, Garden Bench F, plum blossom, Japan mk, 10⅜x8¼" .38.00
Vase, bottle, And They're Off, red, Kutani, 7x2¼x1¾" 70.00

Georgia Art Pottery

In Cartersville, Georgia, in August 1935, W.J. Gordy first fired pottery turned from regional clays. By 1936 he was marking his wares 'Georgia Pottery' (GP) or 'Georgia Art Pottery' (GAP) and continued to do so until 1950 when he used a 'Hand Made by WJ Gordy' stamp (HM). There are different configurations of the GAP mark, one being a three-line arrangement, another that is circular and thought to be the earlier of the two. After 1970 his pottery was signed. Known throughout the world for his fine glazes, he won the Georgia Governor's Award in 1983. Examples of his wares are on display in the Smithsonian. His father W.T.B. and brother D.X. are also well-known potters.

Candleholder, Mountain Gold, ring hdl, WJ Gordy, 1987, ea........ 85.00
Creamer, bl-gr, Gordy's Pottery, ca 1935-55, 3¾"............................ 95.00
Dipper, Albany slip, GAP mk, 3¼x9".. 250.00
Figurines, owl pr, sgn DX Gordy, rare, 8"...................................1,560.00
Jug, Georgia Corn, JW Gordy, mini, 3x2½".................................... 55.00
Pitcher, bl-gr on red clay, 1935-55, 6½x5" 170.00
Pitcher, mottled brn, Handmade WJ Gordy, 8".............................. 145.00
Urn, brn matt, appl hdls, ftd, WJ Gordy, 6¾x7½"......................... 150.00

German Porcelain

Unless otherwise noted, the porcelain listed in this section is marked simply 'Germany.' Products of other German manufacturers are listed in specific categories. See also Bisque; Elfinware; Pink-Paw Bears; Pink Pigs.

Figurine, 18th-C lady w/pug dog on hip, ca 1900, 8¾" 250.00
Figurine, lady w/breasts exposed, ½-figure, #648, 3½" 125.00

Plaque, Alpenfee (after Bernard), signed Sontag, museum mounted, 27x25", $660.00. (Photo courtesy Burchard Galleries on LiveAuctioneers.com)

Plaque, girl w/lute in snowstorm, Sachs, late 19th C, 8½x5¾"..4,000.00
Plaque, gypsy girl w/coin-accented headdress, in ebonized fr, 7⅜".2,100.00
Plaque, nude sits among rocks, Berlin, 4x5½", in brass fr (not shown) .1,000.00
Plaque, Reflection (bust of young lady), Wagner, 4x2½"+gilt fr... 200.00
Plate, gypsy reads tea leaves for girl, cobalt & gold, SPM, 9¼" 325.00

Gladding-McBean and Company

This company was established in 1875 in Lincoln, California. They first produced only clay drainage pipes, but in 1883 architectural terra cotta was introduced, which has been used extensively in the United States as well as abroad. Sometime later a line of garden pottery was added. They soon became the leading producers of tile in the country. In 1923 they purchased the Tropico Pottery in Glendale, California, where in addition to tile they also produced huge garden vases. Their line was expanded in 1934 to included artware and dinnerware.

At least 15 lines of art pottery were developed between 1934 and 1942. For a short time they stamped their wares with the Tropico Pottery mark; but the majority was signed 'GMcB' in an oval. Later the mark was changed to 'Franciscan' with several variations. After 1937 'Catalina Pottery' was used on some lines. (All items marked 'Catalina Pottery' were made in Glendale.) For further information we recommend Col-

lector's Encyclopedia of California Pottery by Jack Chipman (Collector Books). See also Franciscan.

Bowl, batter, Cocinero, turquoise, 9x11", $85.00 to $100.00. (Photo courtesy Eirik N. Huset)

Candy jar, covered, Contour, dawn, G James, 1955-56 .... 225.00
Creamer, Coronado, turq.. 30.00
Cup/saucer, AD, Metropolitan, ivory 55.00
Figurine, Samoan woman w/child, wht satin, D Bothwell, ca 1937, 13"..300.00
Pitcher, Contour, gray, tall, G James, 1955-56 .... 200.00
Pitcher, water, flame orange, El Patio ware 200.00
Plate, chop, Ivy, stamped mk #10, 12" 125.00
Plate, dinner, Apple, stamped mk #12, 10½" 40.00
Plate, dinner, Desert Rose, stamped mk #12, 10½" 40.00
Sugar, Coronado, pk 45.00
Teapot, Coronado, bl 100.00
Tray, shell, Contour, gray, G James, 1955-56 .... 80.00
Tumbler, water, flame orange, El Patio ware, 3½" 25.00
Vase, bouquet, Contour, sandalwood, G James, 1955-56............. 300.00
Vase, Catalina Pottery, peasant girl, D Bothwell, late 1930s/early 40s, 6¾"..200.00
Vase, coral, dolphin, unmk, ca 1938, 5½x6" 200.00
Vase, fish, Catalina Pottery, late 1930s, 5" 225.00
Vase, Oxblood, #123, mk Made in USA, 11" 450.00
Vase, Oxblood, #C123, 1930s, 11" 1,100.00
Vase, Oxblood, #C290, 1930s, 11" 800.00
Vase, Oxblood, trumpet shape, Catalina Pottery, #C286 ....1,100.00
Vase, rnd w/scroll ft, celadon gr, ca 1938.................................... 175.00
Vase, tube, Contour, sandalwood, G James, 1955-56.................... 175.00
Wall pocket, tropical leaf, satin gr, Catalina Pottery, 7¾" 175.00

Glass Animals and Figurines

These beautiful glass sculptures have been produced by many major companies in America — in fact, some are still being made today. Heisey, Fostoria, Duncan and Miller, Imperial, Paden City, Tiffin, and Cambridge made the vast majority, but there were many other companies involved on a lesser scale. Very few marked their animals.

As many of the glass companies went out of business, their molds were bought by companies still active, who have used them to produce their own line of animals. While some are easy to recognize, others can be very confusing. For example, Summit Art Glass now owns Cambridge's 6½", 8½", and 10" swan molds. We recommend Glass Animals by Dick and Pat Spencer, if you are thinking of starting a collection or wanting to identify and evaluate the glass animals and figural-related items that you already have. The authors are our advisors for this category and are listed in the Directory under Illinois.

Cambridge

Bashful Charlotte, flower frog, crystal, 11½" 200.00
Bashful Charlotte, flower frog, Dianthus, 6½"............................... 225.00
Bashful Charlotte, flower frog, Moonlight Bl, 11½", min 950.00
Bird on stump, flower frog, gr, 5¼", min 400.00
Bird, crystal satin, 2¾" L 20.00
Bridge hound, ebony, 1¼"... 40.00
Buddha, amber, 5½".. 300.00
Draped Lady, flower frog, crystal frost, 13¼" 150.00
Draped Lady, flower frog, Dianthus, 13¼"................................... 250.00

Draped Lady, flower frog, gr frost, 8½" 125.00
Draped Lady, flower frog, ivory, oval base, 8½", min 1,000.00
Draped Lady, flower frog, Moonlight Bl, 13¼", min 1,000.00
Eagle, bookend, crystal, 5½x4x4", ea 70.00
Heron, crystal, lg, 12" 150.00
Mandolin Lady, flower frog, crystal 200.00
Mandolin Lady, flower frog, lt emerald 350.00
Melon Boy, flower frog, Dianthus, min 775.00
Rose Lady, flower frog, amber, 8½" 200.00
Rose Lady, flower frog, dk amber, tall base, 9¾" 250.00
Rose Lady, flower frog, gr, 8½" 200.00
Seagull, flower block, crystal 40.00
Swan, Carmen, #3 style, 8½" 325.00
Swan, Crown Tuscan, 8½" 125.00
Swan, ebony, 3" 75.00
Swan, ebony, 8½" 250.00
Swan, ebony, 10" 325.00
Swan, emerald, 3" 55.00
Swan, mg, #3 style, 8½" 150.00
Swan, mg, 6½" 100.00
Swan, punch bowl (15") & base, crystal, +12 cups 3,000.00
Swan, yel, 8½" 225.00
Turkey, gr, w/lid 550.00
Turtle, flower holder, ebony 175.00
Two Kids, flower frog, amber satin, 9¼" 350.00
Two Kids, flower frog, crystal, 9¼" 200.00

Duncan and Miller

Donkey, cart & peon, crystal, 3-pc set 550.00
Dove, crystal, head down, w/o base, 11½" L 125.00
Duck, ashtray, red, 7" 375.00

Fish, tropical, crystal frosted, candleholder, 5", $450.00 to $500.00. (Photo courtesy Dick and Pat Spencer)

Goose, crystal, fat, 6x6" 200.00
Sailfish, crystal, Line #30/Pall Mall, 5½" 175.00
Swan, candleholder, red, 7", ea 75.00
Swordfish, bl opal, rare 500.00
Tropical fish, ashtray, pk opal, 3½" 60.00

Fenton

Airedale, Rosalene, 1992 issue for Heisey 65.00
Alley cat, Teal Marigold, 11" 90.00
Butterfly on stand, Lime Sherbet, 1989 souvenir, 7½" 30.00
Butterfly on stand, ruby carnival, 1989 souvenir, 7½", $60 to 70.00
Filly, Rosalene, head front, 1992 issue for Heisey 65.00
Fish, red w/amberina tail & fins, 2½" 60.00
Peacock, bookends, crystal satin, 5¾", pr 350.00
Turtle, flower block, amethyst, 4" L 75.00

Fostoria

Bird, candleholder, crystal, 1½", ea 15.00

Cardinal head, Silver Mist, 6½" 200.00
Deer, bl, sitting or standing, ea 30.00
Deer, mg, sitting or standing, ea 30.00
Elephant bookend, crystal, 6½", ea 65.00
Ladybug, bl, lemon or olive gr, 1¼", ea 20.00
Pelican, amber, 1987 commemorative 50.00
Seal, topaz, 3⅞" 65.00

Heisey

Airedale, crystal 1,200.00
Bull, crystal, mk, 4x7½" 2,000.00
Colt, crystal, rearing 225.00
Duck, ashtray, Moongleam 250.00
Elephant, amber, lg or med, ea 2,400.00
Fish, bowl, crystal, 9½" 400.00
Giraffe, crystal, head bk 175.00
Irish setter, ashtray, crystal 20.00
Mallard, crystal, wings down 275.00
Mallard, crystal, wings up 175.00
Rabbit, pwt, crystal, 2¾x3¾" 140.00
Rooster head, cocktail shaker, 1-qt 85.00
Rooster head, cocktail, crystal 45.00
Rooster, amber, 5⅜" 2,500.00
Rooster, crystal, 5½x5" 450.00
Show horse, crystal 1,250.00
Sparrow, crystal 90.00
Swan, pitcher, crystal 650.00
Tropical fish, crystal, 12" 1,800.00
Wood duck, crystal, standing 225.00

Imperial

Airedale, caramel slag 90.00
Bulldog-type pup, mg, 3½" 65.00
Candle Servant, Cathay line, frosted crystal, sgn Virginia B Evans ... 250.00
Chick, mg, head down 15.00
Colt, amber, balking 100.00

Donkey, caramel slag, marked IG, 6⅜", $30.00 to $40.00. (Photo courtesy Belhorn Auction Services, LLC on LiveAuctioneers.com)

Donkey, Ultra Bl 45.00
Elephant, caramel slag 60.00
Fish, candlestick, Sunshine Yel, 5", ea 25.00
Flying mare, amber, NI mk, extremely rare 1,250.00
Mallard, caramel slag, wings down 150.00
Mallard, lt bl satin, wings down 25.00
Owl, jar, caramel slag, 6½", $65 to 75.00
Owl, mg 55.00
Piglet, ruby, standing 20.00
Rabbit, pwt, Horizon Bl, 2¾" 75.00
Scolding bird, Cathay Crystal 175.00
Terrier, Parlour Pup, amethyst carnival, 3½" 45.00

Tiger, pwt, Jade Gr, 8" L.. 80.00
Wood duckling, Sunshine yel satin, floating........... 20.00

L.E. Smith

Camel, crystal, $35 to.. 45.00
Elephant, crystal, 1¾"...6.00

Horse, bookend, amber, rearing, each $35.00. (Photo courtesy Phoebus Auction Gallery on LiveAuctioneers.com)

King Fish, aquarium, gr, 7¼x4x15"........................... 400.00
Rooster, butterscotch slag, ltd ed, #208..................... 80.00
Swan, mg w/decor, 8½"... 35.00

New Martinsville

Chick, frosted, 1".. 25.00
Gazelle, crystal w/frosted base, leaping, 8¼"............. 45.00
Piglet, crystal, standing... 130.00
Porpoise on wave, orig.. 350.00
Rooster w/crooked tail, crystal, 7½"........................... 40.00
Seal, candleholders, crystal, lg, pr........................... 100.00
Swan, sweetheart candy dish, red, 5"......................... 25.00
Wolfhound, crystal, 7", $60 to................................... 70.00
Woodsman, crystal, sq base, 7⅜"................................ 75.00

Paden City

Bunny, cotton-ball dispenser, crystal frost, ears bk......... 200.00
Bunny, cotton-ball dispenser, pk frost, ears up.............. 350.00
Eagle, bookends, crystal, pr...................................... 450.00
Horse, crystal, rearing... 250.00
Pheasant, Chinese, bl.. 175.00
Pheasant, Chinese, crystal, 13¾"................................ 90.00
Pheasant, lt bl, head bk, 12"...................................... 200.00
Polar bear on ice, crystal, 4½"..................................... 50.00
Pony, crystal, 12"... 110.00
Pouter pigeon, bookend, crystal, 6¼", ea.................... 80.00
Rooster, Barnyard, crystal, 8¾"................................. 100.00
Rooster, Chanticleer, crystal, 9½"............................. 100.00
Squirrel on curved log, crystal, 5½"............................ 40.00

Tiffin

Cat, Sassy Suzie, blk satin w/pnt decor, #9448, 11"......... 140.00
Cat, Sassy Suzie, mg, min... 400.00
Fawn, flower floater, Copen Bl.................................. 300.00
Fish, crystal, 9½x10", $300 to.................................... 300.00
Pheasants, Copen Bl, pwt bases, male & female pr........ 500.00

Viking

Angelfish, amber, 7x7".. 75.00
Angelfish, mg, pr.. 400.00

Bird, moss gr, tail up, 12".. 40.00
Bird, Orchid, 9½".. 90.00
Cat, gr, sitting, 8"... 40.00
Dog, orange.. 45.00
Duck, crystal, fighting, head up or down, Viking's Epic Line, ea.... 40.00
Duck, crystal, standing, Viking's Epic Line, 9"............. 40.00
Duck, orange, rnd, ftd, 5"... 30.00
Duck, ruby, rnd, ftd, 5"... 35.00
Egret, amber, #1315, 12".. 35.00
Egret, orange, 12"... 40.00
Jesus, crystal w/Crystal Mist, flat bk, 6x5".................. 35.00
Owl, amber, Viking's Epic Line..................................... 20.00
Rabbit (Thumper), crystal, 6½".................................... 25.00
Rabbit, amber, 6½"... 35.00
Rooster, avocado, Viking's Epic Line............................ 40.00
Swan, bowl, amber, 6".. 20.00
Swan, Yel Mist, paper label, 6".................................... 20.00

Westmoreland

Bird in flight, Amber Marigold, wings out, 5" W............ 40.00
Butterfly, crystal, 4½"... 30.00
Butterfly, pk, 2½".. 25.00
Owl, dk bl, shiny eyes, 5½".. 40.00
Pouter pigeon, any color, 2½", ea................................. 20.00
Robin, crystal, 5⅛".. 15.00
Robin, pk, 5⅛".. 22.00
Robin, red, 5⅛"... 26.00
Turtle, ashtray, crystal..8.00
Turtle, flower block, gr, 7 holes, 4" L............................ 40.00
Turtle, pwt, Gr Mist, no holes, 4" L............................ 20.00
Wren on Perch, Lt Bl Mist on mg base........................ 45.00
Wren, Pk Mist, 2½".. 25.00
Wren, smoke, 3½".. 25.00

Miscellaneous

Blenko, owl, pwt, amber.. 30.00
Co-Operative Flint, elephant, pk, 4½x7"..................... 275.00
Haley, Lady Godiva, bookend, crystal, 1940s, ea.......... 30.00
Indiana, horse head, bookends, mg, 6", pr.................... 45.00
Indiana, pouter pigeon, bookend, crystal frost, ea........ 35.00
LG Wright, trout, crystal... 140.00
LG Wright, turtle, amber... 75.00
Pilgrim, whale, crystal, #924, w/labels, in 1964 World's Fair box ... 35.00
Viking for Mirror Images, baby seal, ruby.................... 60.00
Viking for Mirror Images, police dog, ruby.................. 90.00

Glidden

Genius designer Glidden Parker established Glidden Pottery in 1940 in Alfred, New York, having been schooled at the unrivaled New York State College of Ceramics at Alfred University. Glidden pottery is characterized by a fine stoneware body, innovative forms, outstanding hand-milled glazes, and hand decoration which make the pieces individual works of art. Production consisted of casual dinnerware, artware, and accessories that were distributed internationally.

In 1949 Glidden Pottery became the second ceramic plant in the country to utilize the revolutionary Ram pressing machine. This allowed for increased production and for the most part eliminated the previously used slip-casting method. However, Glidden stoneware continued to reflect the same superb quality of craftsmanship until the factory closed in 1957. Although the majority of form and decorative patterns were

Mr. Parker's personal designs, Fong Chow and Sergio Dello Strologo also designed award-winning lines.

Glidden will be found marked on the unglazed underside with a signature that is hand incised, mold impressed, or ink stamped. Interest in this unique stoneware is growing as collectors discover that it embodies the very finest of mid-century high style. Our advisor is David Pierce; he is listed in the Directory under Ohio.

Bowl, Feather, Engobe, #270	15.00
Bowl, Ric-Rac, gray, #21	11.00
Bowl, Sage & Sand, #421	12.00
Casserole, Feather, Engobe, #167	16.00
Casserole, Will O' the Wisp, #163	45.00
Casserole, Yellowstone, #461	42.00
Coaster, cobalt, #19	5.00
Cup, Glidden Blue, #19	5.00
Mug, Turquoise Matrix, #202-P	50.00
Plate, Circus, Trapeze Artist, #35	19.00
Plate, Fish, Charcoal & Rice, #410	45.00

Plate, Menagerie, Bison, #35, $20.00. (Photo courtesy David Pierce)

Plate, Menagerie, Chicken, #35	22.00
Plate, Menagerie, Giraffe, #35	28.00
Plate, Menagerie, Hippo, #35	30.00
Plate, Menagerie, Horse, #35	24.00
Plate, Menagerie, Lion, #35	23.00
Plate, Poodle (Ferne Mays), #35	10.00
Plate, Sage & Sand, #465	16.00
Plate, Turquoise Matrix, #33	9.00
Plate, Turquoise Matrix, #65	10.00
Plate, Yellowstone, #31-B	10.00
Plate, Yellowstone, #433	9.00
Plate, Yellowstone, #435	10.00
Server, Leaf (Fred Press), #280	34.00
Server, Menagerie, #280	56.00
Server, Menagerie, Chicken, #025	29.00
Server, Menagerie, Tiger, #027	21.00
Tray, Chi-Chi Poodle, #200, w/out stand	30.00
Tumbler, Turquoise Matrix, #1127	17.00
Vase, cobalt, #2	20.00
Vase, Yellowstone, #86	30.00

Goebel

F.W. Goebel founded the F &W Goebel Company in 1871, located in Rodental, Germany. They manufactured thousands of different decorative and useful items over the years, the most famous of which are the Hummel figurines first produced in 1935 based on the artwork of a Franciscan nun, Sister Maria Innocentia Hummel.

The Goebel trademarks have long been a source of confusion because all Goebel products, including Hummels, of any particular time period bear the same trademark, thus leading many to believe all Goebels are Hummels. Always look for the Hummel signature on actual Hummel figurines (these are listed in a separate section).

There are many other series — some of which are based on artwork of particular artists such as Disney, Charlot Byj, Janet Robson, Harry Holt, Norman Rockwell, M. Spotl, Lore, Huldah, and Schaubach. Miscellaneous useful items include ashtrays, bookends, salt and pepper shakers, banks, pitchers, inkwells, and perfume bottles. Figurines include birds, animals, and Art Deco pieces. The Friar Tuck monks and the Co-Boy elves are especially popular.

The date of manufacture is determined by the trademark. The incised date found underneath the base on many items is the mold copyright date. Actual date of manufacture may vary as much as 20 years or more from the copyright date. Our advisors for this category are Gale and Wayne Bailey; they are listed in the Directory under Georgia.

Most Common Goebel Trademarks and Approximate Dates Used
1.) Crown mark (may be incised or stamped, or both): 1923 – 1950
2.) Full bee (complete bumble bee inside the letter 'V'): 1950 – 1957
3.) Stylized bee (dot with wings inside the letter 'V'): 1957 – 1964
4.) Three-line (stylized bee with three lines of copyright info to the right of the trademark): 1964 – 1972
5.) Goebel bee (word Goebel with stylized bee mark over the last letter 'e'): 1972 – 1979
6.) Goebel (word Goebel only): 1979 – present

Cardinal Tuck (Red Monk)

Pitcher, trademark two, full bee mark, 5½", $50.00. (Photo courtesy William J. Jenack Auctioneers on LiveAuctioneers.com)

Ashtray, #ZF43/0, TMK-4, 2½x3"	125.00
Bank, #SD29, TMK-3	125.00
Calendar holder, complete set of plastic calendar cards, 3¼"	125.00
Christmas ornament, 3"	75.00
Cookie jar, #K29, 1957, $1,750 to	1,000.00
Creamer, #S141 2/0, TMK-3, 2½"	40.00
Creamer, #S141/1, TMK-3	75.00
Decanter, TMK-5, 10"	190.00
Egg cup, #E95A, 2"	95.00
Egg cups, set of 4 on wht #E95B tray	275.00
Flask, friar in bas relief, #KL97, TMK-3	175.00
Mug, #T74/1, TMK-3, ½-liter	85.00
Stubber, #RX107, TMK-3, 2⅛"	85.00

Charlot Byj Redheads and Blonds

Atta Boy, BYJ-7, TMK-3, $40 to	65.00
Baby Sitter, BYJ-66, TMK-6	85.00
Damper on the Camper, BYJ-72, TMK-6, 3¾"	95.00
Dating & Skating, BYJ-52, TMK-3, 4½"	85.00
Dealer's sign, BYJ-47, TMK-4, 4x6"	60.00
Little Miss Coy, BYJ-4, TMK-3	45.00
Nurse, BYJ-63, TMK-4, 5¼"	67.50

Nurse, BYJ-63, TMK-5 .... 60.00
Oops, BYJ-3, TMK-3, $65 to 80.00
Prayer Girl, BYJ-17, TMK-4, 5¼" 45.00
Putting On the Dog, BYJ-25, TMK-4 .... 85.00
Roving Eye, boy & dog, BYJ-2, TMK-3 .... 60.00
Salon Shabby O'Hair (aka Shear Nonsense), BYJ-5, TMK-3 ...... 110.00
Sleepy Head, BYJ-11, TMK-4 .... 50.00
Strike, BYJ-1, TMK-6 .... 55.00
Super Service, BYJ-39, TMK-5 .... 85.00
Trim Lass, BYJ-49, TMK-4, 4½" 85.00

Co-Boy Figurines

Bob the Bookworm, Well #510, TMK-4 .... 75.00
Brum the Lawyer, 1970 .... 60.00
Candy the Confectioner, w/cake, TMK-5, 8½" 42.50
Conny the Nightwatchman, #5200, TMK-4 .... 65.00
Dealer plaque, Wells #516, 8x6" 75.00
Erik, boy w/sling shot, TMK-6, 4", EXIB 50.00
Flips the Fisherman, TMK-5, 7½x5½" 60.00
Gerd the Diver, 1979 .... 60.00
Gilda, girl w/doll, TMK-6, 4", MIB 50.00
Hermann the Butcher, TMK-6, 7½" 95.00
Jim the Bowler, #1752617, TMK-3 .... 55.00
Marthe the Nurse, TMK-6 .... 150.00
Nick the Nightclub Singer, TMK-6 .... 70.00
Plum the Pastry Chef, Well #506, 1970 .... 60.00
Robby the Vegetarian, Well #520, TMK-4 .... 65.00
Sam the Gourmet, TMK-4 .... 90.00
Ted the Tennis Player, TMK-6, 7¼" 58.00
William the Butcher, Well #507, TMK-4 .... 30.00

Cookie Jars

Owl, #7760736, 15x13", $35.00. (Photo courtesy Gordon's Estate Services, Auction Services Division on LiveAuctioneers.com)

Cat, TMK-5, $100 to 75.00
Friar Tuck, K-29, TMK-5 .... 150.00
Owl, #607/36, 15" 75.00
Panda Bear, TMK-5, $70 to 75.00

Friar Tuck (Brown Monk)

Ashtray, flat, #RF142, TMK-3 .... 70.00
Condiment set, #P153/1 jar, #P153/0 shakers, #M42A tray, TMK-2 .. 75.00
Cookie jar, #K29, 1957 .... 150.00
Cruets, vinegar & oil, bl robes, #M80/B & #M80/C, TMK-6, MIB, pr .. 85.00
Cups, #KL 94, ea 15.00
Decanter, #KL91, TMK -3, bottom holds 3 liquor tots 100.00
Humidor, #RX106, TMK-3, 7⅝" 150.00
Jar, #Z37, TMK-3, 4½" 30.00
Perpetual calendar, TMK-5, 3½x4¼" 65.00
Plaque, #WZ2, TMK-4 .... 125.00
Razor blade bank, toes showing, #X103, TMK-3, 4½" 100.00

Shakers

Bunny, orange-red body, silver-clad face/ears, Germany, 2¾", pr.... 55.00
Cats, 1 blk/1 wht, gr eyes, nylon whiskers, #P179A & B, pr 35.00
Chinese couple, #P71/A & #P71/B, TMK-2, pr 35.00
Dickens men (aka Pickwick Duo), #M64B, TMK-3, pr........ 38.00
Ducks, 1", pr 20.00
Dutch boy & girl, bl & wht, pr 42.00
Flower the Skunk, TMK-2, 2¾", pr 62.50
Fox in wht jacket w/S or P on front, TMK-4, pr 28.00
Golfer, #M28/A-C, on tray, full bee mk, set.............. 75.00
Owl on book, brn tones, #P84, TMK-2, 2¾", pr 48.00
Peppers, 1 gr & 1 red, pr 32.00
Squirrel & pine cone, on leaf-shaped tray, #M36/A, B & C.......... 65.00

Miscellaneous

Bookends, Vict couple, #XS682 2/0, 5", pr 85.00
Bust, JS Bach, wht, #18010-19, 7½x4¼" 65.00
Figurine, Baltimore Oriole, #6852807, TMK-6, 3x2¼" 30.00
Figurine, Cairn terrier, 1¾x3" 25.00
Figurine, camel (nativity), #4682111, TMK-6, 8" L 125.00
Figurine, chimney sweep, #074110, TMK-5, 4" 48.00
Figurine, eagle, wht head, wings wide, #CV104, TMK-5, 9½" 95.00
Figurine, Flower Madonna, open halo, #10/1, TMK-2, 9½" 130.00
Figurine, girl & lt bl kitten, #608, TMK-2, 2x2"........ 18.00
Figurine, Goofy playing fiddle, Disney, #17328, TMK-6, 4" 55.00
Figurine, Music Buff, boy w/earphones, Today's Children, TMK-6 ..49.00
Figurine, owl, #38316-08, TMK-5, 3½".................... 24.00
Figurine, poodle, blk, #KT161, TMK-5, 3" 20.00
Figurine, titmouse bird, TMK-5, 3x3" 34.00
Figurine, zebra, Serengetti Collection, 1980s, 4½x7½".................. 65.00

Goldscheider

The Goldscheider family operated a pottery in Vienna for many generations before seeking refuge in the United States following Hitler's invasion of their country. They settled in Trenton, New Jersey, in the early 1940s where they established a new corporation and began producing objects of art and tableware items. (No mention was made of the company in the Trenton City Directory after 1950, and it is assumed that by this time the influx of foreign imports had taken its toll.) In 1946 Marcel Goldscheider established a pottery in Staffordshire where he manufactured bone china figures, earthenware, etc., marked with a stamp of his signature. Larger artist-signed examples are the most valuable with the Austrian pieces bringing the higher prices. Also buyers should know that the 1920s era terra cotta items, masks, busts, and figures are really costly now, while religious items have fallen in value.

A wide variety of marks has been found: 1.) Goldscheider USA Fine China; 2.) Original Goldscheider Fine China; 3.) Goldscheider USA; 4.) Goldscheider-Everlast Corp.; 5.) Goldscheider Everlast Corp. in circle; 6.) Goldscheider Inc. in circle; 7.) Goldcrest Ceramics Corp. in circle; 8.) Goldcrest Fine China; 9.) Goldcrest Fine China USA; 10.) A Goldcrest Creation; and 11.) Created by Goldscheider USA. Our co-advisors are Randy and Debbie Coe (listed in the Directory under Oregon) and Darrell Thomas (listed under Wisconsin).

Key: tc — terra cotta

American

Juliet & the Doves, ¾-figure, 1940s, 11½"....................................350.00
Lady dancing, holds skirt, Helen Liedloff, Ovington, 15⅛", $100 to..150.00

Lady in long gr gown holds skirt wide, 15½x10" 1,250.00
Madonna, tan robe w/gold, bl collar, 12¾" 85.00
Mandarin Dancers, she dancing, (he w/drums), Urbach, 1950s, 14", pr .. 185.00
Penguin, Made in USA, 6", NM 125.00
Quadrille, lady, bl dress, sgn Peggy Porcher, #4 mk, 5" 45.00
Temple dancer man & lady, traditional attire, H Linduff, 8¼", pr ... 500.00
Vict lady in bl gown, object in left hand, USA, 7" 250.00

Austrian

Black boy in ragged clothes, tc, #1460-30-34, 33" 3,250.00
Black boy w/monacle on bamboo chair, tc, #168-299-65, 21" 7,800.00
Black man w/cigar seated in rocking chair, tc, #8334-1365-52, 18".3,500.00
Boy holds bl flowers, gr base, Wein, 5⅝" 360.00
Bust, Arabian man, tc, #925-68, 19" 2,500.00
Bust, lady praying, bl floral scarf, Lorenzl, #751-23-14, 7x6½" .. 1,600.00
Bust, lady's head, lt gr face w/dk gr hair, tc, #0177, 1920s, 12½".. 2,800.00
Bust, lady's head, wht face, gilt/pnt curls, Wein, 12x7" 3,000.00
Butterfly girl, flower-filled urn on blk base, Lorenzl, rstr, 16"...2,710.00
Deco dancer w/flowing skirt, Lindner, #4690-333-16, 12½", $2,400 to..... 2,600.00
Deco lady dancing w/clown, ca 1930, 16" 2,500.00
Deco lady dancing, pk & floral print gown, 22" 1,250.00

Lady dancer, #7195/1473-10, Wein, 15½", $2,000.00. (Photo courtesy Cleveland Auction Company on LiveAuctioneers.com)

Lady dressed in blk lace reclines on wht base, Lorenzl, 5¾x9", NM...2,000.00
Lady in gr w/wolfhound, ca 1940, 12" 2,600.00
Nude w/butterfly wings, Lorenzl, #7640/83/4, 11x12½x4"......... 2,600.00
Russian wolfhound, blk & wht, #569-77, rare, 6x13" 1,500.00
Tennis player boy & girl, simple wht bases, 12", pr.................. 1,700.00
Vase, mc abstracts, Clarice Cliff designs, 12" 500.00
Wall mask, lady w/bl scarf, Wein, 11" 1,900.00
Wall mask, lady w/brn wavy hair, bl cap & beads, 1920s, 12" ... 2,400.00
Wall mask, lady w/orange curls holds blk mask, Wein, 13¾" 3,000.00

Gonder

Lawton Gonder grew up with clay in his hands and fire in his eyes. Gonder's interest in ceramics was greatly influenced by his parents who worked for Weller and a close family friend and noted ceramic authority, John Herold. In his early teens Gonder launched his ceramic career at the Ohio Pottery Company while working for Herold. He later gained valuable experience at American Encaustic Tile Company, Cherry Art Tile, and the Florence Pottery. Gonder was plant manager at the Florence Pottery until fire destroyed the facility in late 1941.

After years of solid production and management experience, Lawton Gonder established the Gonder Ceramic Art Company, formerly the Peters and Reed plant, in South Zanesville, Ohio. Gonder Ceramic Arts produced quality art pottery with beautiful contemporary designs which included human and animal figures and a complete line of Oriental pottery. Accentuating the beautiful shapes were unique and innovative glazes developed by Gonder such as flambé (flame red with streaks of yellow), 24k gold crackle, antique gold, and Chinese crackle. (These glazes bring premium prices.)

All Gonder is marked with the company name and mold number. They include 'Gonder U.S.A' in block letters, 'Gonder' in script, 'Gonder Original' in script, and 'Gonder Ceramic Art' in block letters. Paper labels were also used. Some of the early Gonder molds closely resemble RumRill designs that had been manufactured at the Florence Pottery; and because some RumRill pieces are found with similar (if not identical) shapes, matching mold numbers, and Gonder glazes, it is speculated that some RumRill was produced at the Gonder plant. In 1946 Gonder started another company which he named Elgee (chosen for his initials LG) where he manufactured lamp bases until a fire in 1954 resulted in his shifting lamp production to the main plant. Operations ceased in 1957.

Cookie jar, brn drips on gr, #P-24, 8x8" 27.00
Ewer, burgundy purple, #H-73, 8½" 40.00
Figurine, cat, streaky brn over dk gold, 1957, 11" 190.00
Figurine, hula girl water carrier, chartreuse, 1950, 13x10" 35.00

Figurine, panther, tan and gold streaky glaze, #210, 19" long, $80.00. (Photo courtesy Belhorn Auction Services, LLC on LiveAuctioneers.com)

Lamp, panther, wht, ca 1950, 5x21" 92.00
Planter, gondola-like w/scrolling base, seafoam gr, #557, 7x16" 60.00
Relish dish, streaky brn on yel, 6-part, 10x14" 35.00
Vase, Deco style, yel, ftd, #598, 15" 47.00
Vase, emb flowers & leaves, 12½" 65.00
Vase, flamingo figural, teal w/brn undertones, 8¼x4" 60.00
Vase, hat shape, lt gr w/dk pk int, #H-36, 6x9" 52.00
Vase, long neck, shouldered, w/high twisted hdls, gr, #H-5, 9x5" .. 25.00
Vase, modeled leaves, #H-77, 8" $30.00
Vase, ribbon candy, yel w/brn & wht undertones, 11" 75.00
Vase, scalloped shell, streaky lav, #J-60, 8x11" 60.00
Vase, shell w/3 fish at base, pk w/bl/gray undertones, #H-85, 9"..... 34.00
Vase, swans (2) at base, flared scalloped rim, wht w/pk int, 8x6½"...38.00

Goofus Glass

Goofus glass is American-made pressed glass with designs that are either embossed (blown out) or intaglio (cut in). The decorated colors were aerographed or hand applied and not fired on the pieces. The various patterns exemplify the artistry of the turn-of-the-century glass crafters. The primary production dates were circa 1908 to 1918. Goofus was produced by many well-known manufacturers such as Northwood, Indiana, and Dugan.

When no condition is given, our values are for examples in mint original paint. Our advisor for this category is Steven Gillespie of the *Goofus Glass Gazette*; he is listed in the Directory under Missouri. See also Clubs, Newsletters, and Websites.

Basket, Dmn & Daisy, 6½", EX 55.00
Bowl, Butterfly, red & gold, ruffled, 2½x10½", EX+ 65.00

Bowl, Carnation, Dahlia (any of 3 variations), 10" 18.00
Bowl, Carnation, La Belle & Roses in Snow, sq, 5½" 12.00
Bowl, Cherry, red & gold, Dugan, 2¼x10⅛" 65.00
Bowl, Cherry, ruffled rim, 3¼x10", NM 75.00
Bowl, Hearts, 7" 45.00
Bowl, Jeweled Heart, 2x9", NM 45.00
Bowl, Poppy, red & gold, ftd, 4x9", EX 60.00
Bowl, Poppy, Two Fruits & Olympic Torch, pattern decor, rare, 9" .. 130.00
Bowl, Rose, 5-sided (hard to find) 110.00

**Bowl, Roses, 9",
$25.00 to $35.00.** (Photo
courtesy Mooreland Auction
Services on LiveAuctioneers.com)

Cake plate, Acorn & Leaf, 12" 30.00
Cake plate, Dahlia, 11" 18.00
Cake plate, Wild Flower, crackle glass border, 12" 25.00
Compote, Butterfly, 6⅞x10¼", EX 70.00
Dish, Hearts, rolled rim, 10" 50.00
Lamp, oil, Grape & Leaves, minor flaking, 1¼3" 275.00
Lamp, oil, Nosegay, #2, EX 250.00
Lamp, oil, Wild Rose, Riverside, finger loop, 15" overall 250.00
Plate, Butterfly, Dugan, rare, 11" 125.00
Plate, Little Bo Peep, minor gold flaking, 6½" 80.00
Plate, monk drinking from tankard, uptrn edges, 7" 32.00
Plate, rose in base amid 8 L-stemmed roses, red/gold, 10¾", EX 55.00
Plate, Temple of Music, Pan Am Expo Buffalo NY, 7¼", EX 60.00
Powder jar, Cabbage Rose 30.00
Relish plate, Rose, glass hdls, 7" 50.00
Shakers, Vintage, dk gr & gold on mg, G orig lids, 3¾", pr 55.00
Vase, Basketweave w/Wild Rose, narrow neck & base, 9" 50.00
Vase, Cabbage Rose, 15" 95.00
Vase, Magnolia Blossoms, filigree top & bottom, 9½" 75.00
Vase, Peacock, red & gold, 15¼" 100.00
Vase, Poppy, 5" 15.00
Vase, Poppy, red flower w/gold leaves, 10" 15.00
Vase, Tree Flowers (uncommon), 14½" 95.00

Goss and Crested China

William Henry Goss received his early education at the Government
School of Design at Somerset House, London, and as a result of his merit
was introduced to Alderman William Copeland, who owned the Copeland
Spode Pottery. Under the influence of Copeland from 1852 to 1858, Goss
quickly learned the trade and soon became their chief designer. Little is
known about this brief association, and in 1858 Goss left to begin his own
business. After a short-lived partnership with a Mr. Peake, Goss opened
a pottery on John Street, Stoke-on-Trent, but by 1870 he had moved his
business to a location near London Road. This pottery became the famous
Falcon Works. Their mark was a spread-wing falcon (goss-hawk) centering a narrow, horizontal bar with 'W.H. Goss' printed below.

Many of the early pieces made by Goss were left unmarked and are difficult to discern from products made by the Copeland factory, but after he
had been in business for about 15 years, all of his wares were marked. Today,
unmarked items do not command the prices of the later marked wares.

Adolphus William Henry Goss (Goss's eldest son) joined his father's firm in the 1880s. He introduced cheaper lines, though the
more expensive lines continued in production. Shortly after his father's death in 1906, Adolphus retired and left the business to his two
younger brothers. The business suffered from problems created by a
war economy, and in 1936 Goss assets were held by Cauldon Potteries Ltd. These were eventually taken over by the Coalport Group,
who retained the right to use the Goss trademark. Messrs. Ridgeway
Potteries bought all the assets in 1954 as well as the right to use the
Goss trademark and name. In 1964 the group was known as Allied
English Potteries Ltd. (A.E.P.), and in 1971 A.E.P. merged with the
Doulton Group.

Bowl, Abbey & Town Hall Hexham, 2x4" 80.00
British Tank, Dartmouth in Devon 80.00
Cathedral Church Norwich 85.00
Cup/saucer, Warren House Inn 70.00
Goblet, 60th Yr of Reign of Our Beloved Queen, 1896-97 .... 85.00
Hindhead Sailor's Stone, full inscription, ca 1930 .... 175.00
HMS Donner Blitzen tank, Whitehaven Crest, ca 1900-19 .... 125.00
Lewes Urn, Weston Super Mare, transfer print 130.00
Maltese Urn, Royal Berkshire Regiment 175.00
Manx Cottage, Rd #273243 .... 135.00
Model of Roman Jug, Great Yarmouth (Norfolk) 110.00
Pincushion, 2 butterflies 165.00
Posy basket, fluted sides, twisted hdl, ca 1858-87 .... 325.00
Punch & Judy Show, Good Morning Mr Punch 48.00
Queen Victoria's Shoe, Plymouth 75.00
Robert Burns' Cottage 90.00
Roman Urn, Worcestershire Regiment 135.00
Shakespeare's House 70.00
Sir FA Gore Ouseley Jug, goshawk mk, 2" 110.00
Toby jug, dk bl coat, 3⅜" 150.00

Miscellaneous

Arcadian, banjo, Botreaux Arms 36.00
Arcadian, blk cats in basket, Bognor Regis (West Sussex) crest ... 280.00
Arcadian, bride & chest, Margate crest 120.00
Arcadian, castle, Westgate 36.00
Arcadian, dispatch rider, crest of Borough of Reading, 1920, 4½x3½" .. 375.00
Arcadian, model of 2 blk cats on seesaw, Cheltenham crest 415.00
Arcadian, model of blk cat in well, Stowmarket crest, 2⅜" 80.00
Arcadian, model of Welsh tea party, Aberystwyth 55.00

**Arcadian, Tommy and His
Machine Gun, Dunstable crest,
$85.00.** (Photo courtesy Eastbourne Auction
Rooms on LiveAuctioneers.com)

Arcadian, tour bus, City of London 48.00
Arcadian, WWI sailor, Sevenoaks (Kent) crest, 5⅜" 78.00
Carlton, vase, Northallerton crest, 2¼" 15.00
Foley, model of bronze bowl, Glastonbury crest, 1½" 90.00
Shelley, Lincoln Imp, Lincoln crest, 4¾" 60.00
Shelley, water bottle, Scarborough crest, 1¾" 42.50

Gouda

Gouda is an old Dutch market town in the province of South Holland, famous for producing Gouda cheese. Gouda's ceramics industry had its beginnings in the early sixteenth century and was fueled by the growth in the popularity of smoking tobacco. Initially learning their craft from immigrant potters from England who had settled in the area, the clay pipe makers of Gouda were soon regarded as the best. While some authorities give 1898 (the date the Zuid-Holland factory began operations) as the initial date for the manufacturing of decorative pottery in Gouda, C.W. Moody, author of *Gouda Ceramics* (out of print), indicates the date was ca 1885. Gouda was not the only town in the Netherlands making pottery; Arnhem, Schoonhoven, and Amsterdam also had earthenware factories, but technically the term 'Gouda pottery' refers only to pieces made within the town of Gouda. Today, no Gouda-style factories are active within the city's limits, but in the first quarter of the twentieth century there were several firms producing decorative pottery there — the best known being Zuid, Regina, Zenith, Ivora, and Goedewaagen. At present Royal Goedewagen is making three patterns of limited editions. They are well marked as such.

For further information we recommend *The World of Gouda Pottery* by Phyllis T. Ritvo (Front & Center Press, Weston, Massachusetts).

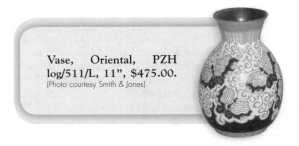

Vase, Oriental, PZH log/511/L, 11", $475.00. (Photo courtesy Smith & Jones)

Bowl, Ivora, pansies, incurvate rim, #358, 1920, 3x13½" 115.00
Candlestick, Holland, geometrics, G Veerman, PZH, 15½", ea ... 250.00
Candlesticks, Holland, abstract flowers, van den Akker, PZH, 1927, 9"..250.00
Candy dish, Holland, Laila, tulips, Royal Goedewaagen, 1980s, 6½"...30.00
Compote, Holland, hdls, PZH, #1196, 4¾x9".............................. 150.00
Ewer, Holland, Fruto, stylized leaves, Goedewaagen, ca 1930, 8x5"...100.00
Jardiniere, England, Docoro, pansies, 1930s-40s, 7x8" 275.00
Jardiniere, Holland, Distel, stylized wolves, blk/wht/gr, ca 1930, 8" . 350.00
Jug, historic building/sailboats/fruit, sgn J, PZH, 5¾" 500.00
Jug, Holland, lg wht blossom on gray w/bl swirls, #616, 5½" 125.00
Jug, Holland, magenta flowers, bulb base, PZH, 8x6½" 275.00
Planter, Holland, Henley, circles in bands, #484, 4x12" 200.00
Plaque, Holland, abstracts, Breetvelt, PZH, #1164/26, 1925, 10¾".. 200.00
Plaque, Holland, chrysanthemums, Gidding, PZH, 1925-26, 16½".. 150.00
Plaque, Holland, pastoral scene, P Poerlee, PZH, ca 1904-10, 8". 250.00
Pot, Holland, Ivora pansies, 3-ftd, ca 1920, 4x6" 175.00
Vase, Candia, abstracts, flared lip, PZH, #104/3, 8¼x6", NM....... 175.00
Vase, crocus, baluster w/pinched neck, PZH, #988, 1921, 11x6" . 300.00
Vase, Holland, 4-sided, HP blossoms/whiplashes/arabesques, 18x7" sq...2,280.00
Vase, Holland, Arnhem Rooster, sgn BI, stick neck, 10½x5" 600.00
Vase, Holland, Blanca, floral, Lanooij, #187, ca 1900-06, 19½x9" ...1,100.00
Vase, Holland, chrysanthemums, sgn MBL & VV, #679, ca 1910-15, 10x5" .350.00
Vase, Holland, Ciara, floral on bl, hdls, 1922, 5¾x6" 230.00
Vase, Holland, Cobo, floral w/abstracts, #426, 1921, 4¾"............. 150.00
Vase, Holland, geometrics, J van Schaick, PZH, 5¾x5½".............. 325.00
Vase, Holland, Kelat, flower & foliage, PZH, 11x5" 200.00
Vase, Holland, Nouveau abstracts, J Hartgring, PZH, 11x4½" 400.00
Vase, Holland, Polo, geometrics, #252, 1918, 7x5½".................... 200.00
Vase, Holland, Tessel, #1203, 1919, sm bruise, 8x5"..................... 150.00

Grand Feu

The Grand Feu Art Pottery existed from 1912 until about 1918 in Los Angeles, California. It was owned and operated by Cornelius Brauckman, who developed a method of producing remarkably artistic glaze effects achieved through extremely high temperatures during the firing process. The body of the ware, as a result of the intense heat (2,500 degrees), was vitrified as the glaze matured. Brauckman signed his ware either with his name or 'Grand Feu Pottery, L.A. California.' His work is regarded today as being among the finest art pottery ever produced in the United States. Examples are rare and command high prices on today's market.

Vase, mahogany flambé, stamped mark, marked #1730 BR by hand, 13", $7,200.00. (Photo courtesy Craftsman Auctions on LiveAuctioneers.com)

Bowl vase, yel-speckled indigo/dk brn on red clay, 4½x7½" 5,400.00
Vase, brn 3-color flambé, shouldered, BR #1730, 7½x5" 9,000.00
Vase, brn microcrystalline flambé, Brauckman, 1917, 7x3¼" 4,000.00
Vase, brn Mission microcrystalline, bottle, 9x4"......................4,200.00
Vase, brn tiger eye crystalline, squat, 4½x7½"..........................3,600.00
Vase, brn/tan mottled crystalline, shouldered, wide neck, 7x3½" ...7,200.00
Vase, bud, indigo mottle, bulb bottom, slim neck, 4¾x2½".......1,320.00
Vase, tan/brn mottled crystalline, shouldered, 7x3½" 7,200.00

Graniteware

Graniteware, made of a variety of metals with enamel coatings, derives its name from its appearance. The speckled, swirled, or mottled effect of the vari-colored enamels may look like granite — but there the resemblance stops. It wasn't especially durable! Expect at least minor chipping if you plan to collect.

Graniteware was featured in 1876 at Phily's Expo. It was mass produced in quantity, and enough of it has survived to make at least the common items easily affordable. Condition, color, shape, and size are important considerations in evaluating an item; cobalt blue and white, green and white, brown and white, and old red and white swirled items are unusual, thus more expensive. Pieces of heavier weight, seam constructed, riveted, and those with wooden handles and tin or matching graniteware lids are usually older. Pieces with matching granite lids demand higher prices than ones with tin lids. In the listings below, all items are in near mint to mint condition unless otherwise noted.

For further study we recommend *The Collector's Encyclopedia of Graniteware, Book 2,* by our advisor, Helen Greguire. It is available from the author. For information on how to order, see her listing in the Directory under South Carolina. For the address of the National Graniteware Society, see the section on Clubs, Newsletters, and Websites.

Baking pan, rivited side hdls/corners, Am Gray, 2¼x8x9½" 135.00
Batter jug, bl relish pat, wht int, tin spout cover, 10¼x8⅜"..........825.00
Berry bucket, end of day, Duchess ware, wht int, 5¼x4⅝"............595.00
Butter churn, Bench, Am Gray, w/paddle, rare, 9⅝x6⅝x11⅛"..1,595.00
Clock, wht w/bl, Delft-style, windmill, 8-day, working, 7x7".......595.00

Cocoa dipper, dk sea gr to moss gr, wht int, 14½x2¾x4" 795.00
Cocoa dipper, lg brn & wht swirl, wht int, wooden hdl, 14½x2⅞x3⅞" . 595.00
Coffee biggin, 1½-cup, lg brn & wht swirl, tin, 7⅜x7½" 3,110.00

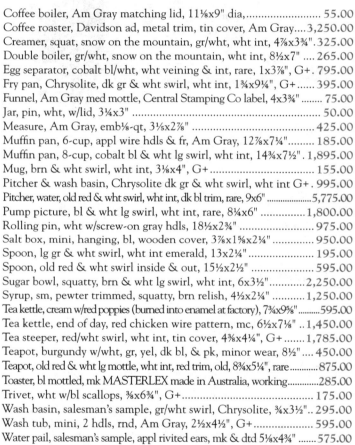

Coffee biggins, American Gray, metal trim, marked Extra Agate Nickel Steel-Ware, L & G Mfg. Co., mint: large, $395.00; small, $415.00. (Photo courtesy Helen Greguire/Photo by Frederick Greguire III)

Coffee boiler, Am Gray matching lid, 11⅛x9" dia, ... 55.00
Coffee roaster, Davidson ad, metal trim, tin cover, Am Gray.... 3,250.00
Creamer, squat, snow on the mountain, gr/wht, wht int, 4⅞x3¾". 325.00
Double boiler, gr/wht, snow on the mountain, wht int, 8½x7" 265.00
Egg separator, cobalt bl/wht, wht veining & int, rare, 1x3⅞", G+. 795.00
Fry pan, Chrysolite, dk gr & wht swirl, wht int, 1¾x9¼", G+...... 395.00
Funnel, Am Gray med mottle, Central Stamping Co label, 4x3¾" 75.00
Jar, pin, wht, w/lid, 3¼x3" 50.00
Measure, Am Gray, emb⅛-qt, 3⅕x2⅞" 425.00
Muffin pan, 6-cup, appl wire hdls & fr, Am Gray, 12⅞x7¼"......... 185.00
Muffin pan, 8-cup, cobalt bl & wht lg swirl, wht int, 14¾x7½". 1,895.00
Mug, brn & wht swirl, wht int, 3⅛x4", G+.................................. 155.00
Pitcher & wash basin, Chrysolite dk gr & wht swirl, wht int G+. 995.00
Pitcher, water, old red & wht swirl, wht int, dk bl trim, rare, 9x6" 5,775.00
Pump picture, bl & wht lg swirl, wht int, rare, 8¼x6" 1,800.00
Rolling pin, wht w/screw-on gray hdls, 18½x2¾" 975.00
Salt box, mini, hanging, bl, wooden cover, 3⅞x1⅝x2¼" 950.00
Spoon, lg gr & wht swirl, wht int emerald, 13x2¼" 195.00
Spoon, old red & wht swirl inside & out, 15½x2½" 595.00
Sugar bowl, squatty, brn & wht lg swirl, wht int, 6x3½"............ 2,250.00
Syrup, sm, pewter trimmed, squatty, brn relish, 4½x2¼" 1,250.00
Tea kettle, cream w/red poppies (burned into enamel at factory), 7¾x9⅝"......... 595.00
Tea kettle, end of day, red chicken wire pattern, mc, 6½x7⅛" .. 1,450.00
Tea steeper, red/wht swirl, wht int, tin cover, 4⅜x4¼", G+....... 1,785.00
Teapot, burgundy w/wht, gr, yel, dk bl, & pk, minor wear, 8½" 450.00
Teapot, old red & wht lg mottle, wht int, red trim, old, 8¾x5¼", rare........... 875.00
Toaster, bl mottled, mk MASTERLEX made in Australia, working............ 285.00
Trivet, wht w/bl scallops, ⅜x6¾", G+... 175.00
Wash basin, salesman's sample, gr/wht swirl, Chrysolite, ¾x3½".. 295.00
Wash tub, mini, 2 hdls, rnd, Am Gray, 2½x4½", G+.................... 595.00
Water pail, salesman's sample, appl rivited ears, mk & dtd 5⅛x4¾" 575.00

Kate Greenaway

Kate Greenaway was an English artist who lived from 1846 to 1901. She gained worldwide fame as an illustrator of children's books, drawing children clothed in the styles worn by proper English and American boys and girls of the very early 1800s. Her book, *Under the Willow Tree,* published in 1878, was the first of many. Her sketches appeared in leading magazines and her greeting cards were in great demand. Manufacturers of china, pottery, and metal products copied her characters to decorate children's dishes, tiles, and salt and pepper shakers as well as many other items.

What some collectors/dealers call Kate Greenaway items are not actual Kate Greenaway designs but merely look-alikes. Genuine Kate Greenaway items (metal, paper, cloth, etc.) must bear close resemblance to her drawings in books, magazines, and special collections. Our advisor for this category is James Lewis Lowe; he is listed in the Directory under Pennsylvania. See also Napkin Rings.

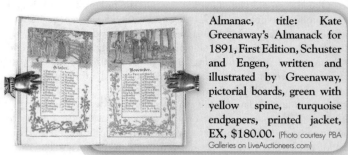

Almanac, title: Kate Greenaway's Almanack for 1891, First Edition, Schuster and Engen, written and illustrated by Greenaway, pictorial boards, green with yellow spine, turquoise endpapers, printed jacket, EX, $180.00. (Photo courtesy PBA Galleries on LiveAuctioneers.com)

Almanac, 1883, George Routledge & Sons, EX 50.00
Biscuit jar, ceramic, boy w/tinted features, w/lid.......................... 165.00
Book, A Apple Pie, Warne, 1940, w/dust jacket, VG..................... 30.00
Book, Almanack for 1884, printed by Edmund Evans, EX 135.00
Book, Good-Night Stories for Little Folks, NY & London, no date, EX+.... 65.00
Book, Greenway's Babies, cloth, Saalfield, 1907, EX+.................... 85.00
Book, Kate Greenaway Pictures, London, Warne, 1st ed, 1921, VG .. 300.00
Book, Kate Greenaway's Book of Games, Routledge, 1st ed, 1889, NM.... 475.00
Book, Little Ann & Other Poems, by Taylor, VG 50.00
Book, Marigold Garden, London, 1888, VG................................ 60.00
Book, Mother Goose, London, later print of 1st ed, VG 150.00
Book, Pictures & Rhymes for Children..., paperbk, McLoughlin, ca 1900... 65.00
Book, Pied Piper of Hamelin, Browning, Greenaway illus, NY 50.00
Book, Ring-Rnd-a-Rosy, red cover, cloth, Saalfield, 1907, EX+... 100.00
Book, Ring-Rnd-a-Rosy, wht cover, cloth, Saalfield, 1907, EX+.... 85.00
Book, Sunshine for Little Children, 1884, EX 80.00
Book, Under the Window, ca 1900 (no date), mini, 4x5", VG...... 85.00
Book, Under the Window, Routledge, 1st ed, orig cloth 165.00
Bowl, Daisy & Button, amber; Reed & Barton SP fr w/girl & dog .. 525.00
Butter pat, children playing transfer, pre-1910 .... 40.00
Button, 2 Girls Sitting on Rail, metal, ¾"..................................... 50.00
Button, Autumn from Almanack, metal silhouette, ½"................. 40.00
Button, Christening, metal silhouette, 1" 60.00
Button, Johnny at Fence Post, metal, ¾"....................................... 30.00
Button, Johnny's Friend, metal, 2" 50.00
Button, Little Bo Peep, flat or cupped metal, ⅝-¾", $20 to 25.00
Button, Miss Pelicoes, metal silhouette, rear or front view, 1¼"..... 40.00
Button, Pretty Patty & Trumpeter, cupped metal, ⅝" 30.00
Button, Pretty Patty Sitting on Fence, cupped metal silhouette, ¾"... 20.00
Button, Ring the Bells Ring, 4 girls in queue, gold on glass, ⅝" 40.00
Button, Ring the Bells Ring, 4 girls in queue, silver on glass, ¾".... 40.00
Button, See-Saw from Mother Goose, gold/wht metal, 1½"........... 80.00
Button, Spring from Almanack, glass, 1" 40.00
Button, Spring from Almanack, wht metal on brass, ¾"................. 40.00
Button, Summer from Almanack, glass, ¾"..................................... 20.00
Button, Summer from Almanack, metal silhouette, 1".................... 25.00
Button, Winter from Almanack, metal silhouette, ¾x¾", $20 to... 30.00
Calendar, chromolithograph, Routledge, 1884, 7⅜x9½", EX 60.00
Card, Christmas, girl in wht w/roses, Tuck, metal stand, 7x8¾"... 100.00
Cup/saucer, children transfer, pk lustre trim, pre-1910................ 125.00
English, Harper's Bazaar, Jan 1879, full-pg 25.00
Figurine, girl (seated) tugs on lg hat, bsk, pre-1910, sm.............. 75.00
Hatpin holder, SP, girl figural, Meriden, 4" 125.00
Ink & watercolor, 5½x4" 950.00
Inkwell, boy & girl, bronze 215.00
Match holder, ornate SP, girl in fancy clothes, Tufts 195.00
Paperweight, CI, Vict girl in lg bonnet, pre-1910, 3x2¾"............. 110.00
Pickle castor, bl, SP fr w/2 girls, blown-out florals....................... 455.00
Plate, ABC, girl in lg hat, Staffordshire, 7" 120.00

Scarf, children on silk, early, EX........................... 65.00
Tea set, semi-porc, floral motif, pre-1910, child sz, 3-pc 95.00
Toothpick holder, SP, girl holds amberina cup, ornate base, 5" 785.00
Toothpick holder, SP, girl stands by Sandwich glass holder w/crane...750.00
Wall pocket, ceramic, 6 girls on open book form, 6x9x3" 137.00

Green Opaque

Introduced in 1887 by the New England Glass Works, this ware is very scarce due to the fact that it was produced for less than one year. It is characterized by its soft green color and a wavy band of gold reserving a mottled blue metallic stain. It is usually found in satin; examples with a shiny finish are extremely rare. Values depend to a large extent on the amount of the gold and stain remaining. For more information we recommend *The Collector's Encyclopedia of American Art Glass* by John A. Shuman III.

Vase, mint stain and gold, 6", $900.00. (Photo courtesy Dallas Auction Gallery on LiveAuctioneers.com)

Bowl, 9", $1,300 to..1,600.00
Bowl, w/lid, EX stain, 6" dia, $900 to 1,000.00
Bowl, w/lid, M stain & gold, appl finial, 6" dia 3,500.00
Celery vase, blk mottling, VG gold, 6¼"....................750.00
Covered dish, NM stain & gold, appl finial, 6" dia 3,700.00
Creamer, EX stain & gold, $750 to 950.00
Cruet, M stain & gold, orig stopper.......................1,950.00
Mug, M stain & gold, 2½".....................................700.00
Punch cup, M stain & gold, 2½"..............................550.00
Shaker, M stain & gold, 2½"..................................400.00
Spooner, EX stain & gold, 4".................................925.00
Sugar bowl, EX stain & gold, 5½" W..........................920.00
Toothpick holder, EX stain, 2⅜", $325 to 375.00
Toothpick holder, M stain & gold 1,150.00
Tumbler, EX gold & stain, 3¾"...............................400.00
Tumbler, lemonade, w/hdl, M stain & gold, 5" 950.00
Tumbler, M stain & gold, 3¾"................................600.00
Vase, flared, M stain & gold, 6" 900.00

Greentown Glass

Greentown glass is a term referring to the product of the Indiana Tumbler and Goblet Company of Greentown, Indiana, ca 1894 to 1903. Their earlier pressed glass patterns were #75 (originally known as #11), a pseudo-cut glass design; #137, Pleat Band; and #200, Austrian. Another line, Dewey, was designed in 1898. Many lovely colors were produced in addition to crystal. Jacob Rosenthal, who was later affiliated with Fenton, developed his famous chocolate glass in 1900. The rich, shaded opaque brown glass was an overnight success. Two new patterns, Leaf Bracket and Cactus, were designed to display the glass to its best advantage, but previously existing molds were also used. In only three years Rosenthal developed yet another important color formula, Golden Agate. The Holly pattern was designed especially for its production. The dolphin covered dish with a fish finial is perhaps the most common and easily recognized

piece ever produced. Other animal dishes were also made; all are highly collectible. There have been many repros — not all are marked! Our advisor for this category is Sandi Garrett; she is listed in the Directory under Indiana. See the Pattern Glass section for clear pressed glass; only colored items are listed here. All values are for items in near-mint condition.

Animal dish, bird w/berry, amber (+)...........................450.00
Animal dish, bird w/berry, emerald gr (+)......................750.00
Animal dish, cat on hamper, canary, tall (+) 1,700.00
Animal dish, cat on hamper, Nile Gr, tall (+) 2,500.00
Animal dish, cat on hamper, wht opaque, tall 650.00
Animal dish, dolphin, beaded, cobalt 2,500.00
Animal dish, dolphin, beaded, crystal 600.00
Animal dish, dolphin, wht opaque, sawtooth edge (+) 925.00
Animal dish, fighting cocks, Nile Gr........................4,000.00
Animal dish, hen on nest, canary..............................900.00
Animal dish, rabbit, clear....................................300.00
Animal pitcher, heron, chocolate 650.00
Austrian, butter dish, canary 600.00
Austrian, butter dish, chocolate, child sz 1,250.00
Austrian, cordial, emerald gr 350.00
Austrian, pitcher, water, canary 650.00
Austrian, plate, canary, sq...................................300.00
Austrian, sugar bowl, chocolate, w/lid, 2½" 175.00
Austrian, vase, Nile Gr, 6"...................................825.00
Brazen Shield, butter dish, bl................................300.00
Brazen Shield, goblet, bl.....................................250.00
Brazen Shield, sugar bowl, bl, w/lid..........................250.00
Cactus, bowl, chocolate, 7¼"...................................90.00
Cactus, butter/cheese dish, chocolate, ped ft 800.00
Cactus, celery vase, chocolate, 7½", NM.......................450.00
Cactus, compote, chocolate, 5¼" dia 100.00
Cactus, cruet, chocolate, w/stopper...........................100.00
Cactus, mug, chocolate...50.00
Cactus, syrup, chocolate, metal thumb-lift lid, 6"............200.00
Cactus, tumbler, bl-wht opal rim..............................700.00
Cactus, tumbler, chocolate, 5".................................35.00
Cactus, vase, chocolate, 6"...................................550.00
Cord Drapery, bowl, amber, hand fluted, ftd, 8¼" 225.00
Cord Drapery, butter dish, cobalt, 4¾".........................550.00
Cord Drapery, creamer, emerald gr, 4¼" 175.00
Cord Drapery, cruet, amber, w/stopper, 6¾" 450.00
Cord Drapery, mug, amber, ftd.................................200.00

Cord Drapery, pitcher, syrup, chocolate, metal thumb-lift top, 6½", $175.00. (Photo courtesy Jackson's Auction on LiveAuctioneers.com)

Cord Drapery, sauce bowl, amber, ftd, 3⅞" 95.00
Cord Drapery, tray, water, emerald gr 350.00
Cupid, butter dish, chocolate 700.00
Cupid, creamer, chocolate 375.00
Cupid, spooner, Nile Gr............................ 425.00
Cupid, sugar bowl, chocolate, w/lid................ 550.00
Dewey, bowl, emerald gr, 8" 75.00

Dewey, cruet, amber, w/stopper 125.00
Dewey, sugar bowl, amber, w/lid, 2¼" 45.00
Early Diamond, dish, amber, rect, 8x5" 275.00
Early Diamond, tumbler, canary 300.00
Early Diamond, tumbler, chocolate 225.00
Herringbone Buttress, bowl, amber, 5¼" 450.00
Herringbone Buttress, nappy, emerald gr. 225.00
Holly Amber, bowl, oval, ped ft 1,750.00
Holly Amber, butter dish...1,680.00
Holly Amber, compote w/lid, 8¼"...........................3,500.00
Holly Amber, compote, jelly, w/lid, 4½" 1,350.00
Holly Amber, syrup pitcher, metal lid 3,000.00

Holly Amber, toothpick holder, 2½", $325.00. (Photo courtesy Kodner Galleries Inc. on LiveAuctioneers.com)

Holly Amber, vase, 6" 650.00
Holly, sugar bowl, Wht Agate, no lid 2,700.00
Leaf Bracket, celery tray, chocolate, 11" 70.00
Leaf Bracket, pitcher, chocolate 300.00
Leaf Bracket, tumbler, chocolate 40.00
Mug, dog & child, Nile Gr 1,500.00
Mug, indoor drinking scene, chocolate, handleless 250.00
Mug, Serenade, amber 80.00
Novelty, buffalo, wht opaque, dtd 1901....................1,500.00
Novelty, corn vase, amber, 4⅝" 1,000.00
Novelty, Dewey bust, teal bl, w/base 400.00
Novelty, hairbrush, Nile Gr.......................................1,750.00
Novelty, mitted hand, chocolate 2,500.00
Novelty, wheelbarrow, teal bl 400.00
Pattern No 75, relish tray, cobalt, 6" 375.00
Pattern No 75, toothpick holder, emerald gr 55.00
Pleat Band, wine, canary 400.00
Shuttle, champagne, chocolate 2,500.00
Shuttle, tumbler, chocolate 95.00
Teardrop & Tassel, bowl, cobalt, 7¼" 175.00
Teardrop & Tassel, butter dish, cobalt........................ 300.00
Teardrop & Tassel, compote, Nile Gr, open, 7½" dia.... 400.00
Teardrop & Tassel, wine, emerald gr 350.00
Toothpick holder, dog head, amber frost 500.00
Toothpick holder, picture fr, teal bl........................... 500.00

Grueby

William Henry Grueby joined the firm of the Low Art Tile Works at the age of 15 in 1894. After several years of experience in the production of architectural tiles, he founded his own plant, the Grueby Faience Company, in Boston, Massachusetts. Grueby began experimenting with the idea of producing art pottery and had soon perfected a fine glaze (soft and without gloss) in shades of blue, gray, yellow, brown, and his most successful, cucumber green. In 1900 his exhibit at the Paris Exposition Universelle won three gold medals.

Grueby pottery was hand thrown and hand decorated in the Arts and Crafts style. Vertically thrust tooled and applied leaves and flower buds were the most common decorative devices. Tiles continued to be an important product, unique (due to the matt glaze decoration) as well as durable. Grueby tiles were often a full inch thick. Many of them were

decorated in cuenca, others were impressed and filled with glaze, and some were embossed. Later, when purchased by Pardee, they were decorated in cuerda seca.

Incompatible with the Art Nouveau style, the artware production ceased in 1907, but tile production continued for another decade. The ware is marked in one of several ways: 'Grueby Pottery, Boston, USA'; 'Grueby, Boston, Mass.'; or 'Grueby Faience.' The artware is often artist signed. Our advisors for this category are Suzanne Perrault and David Rago; they are is listed in the Directory under New Jersey.

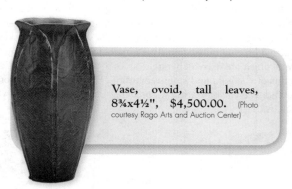

Vase, ovoid, tall leaves, 8¾x4½", $4,500.00. (Photo courtesy Rago Arts and Auction Center)

Bookends, cuenca, 2 tiles, 1 w/donkey, 1 w/2 bears, hammered copper mts, 4"..2,160.00
Bowl, closed form, Faience stamp, 4¾x9½"...............................3,600.00
Bowl, gr, leaves (2 rows), 4-sided, nicks, 3½x10" 4,500.00
Humidor, matt gr glaze w/leaves, 5½x5" 4,800.00
Jar, gr, bulb, sterling collar, w/lid, 4¾x6" 1,675.00
Panel, 25 tiles make landscape, 6" ea, Grueby Faience 102,000.00
Tile, chamberstick, burnt-out yel candle on dk gr, sgn, 6".........3,000.00
Tile, cherub & cymbals, cream on gr, 6x6"................................. 360.00
Tile, Cheshire Cat (Alice in Wonderland series), cuerda seca, 4" .. 1,920.00
Tile, cuerda seca w/full moon rising, mountains, sgn, chips, 4".3,240.00
Tile, dragon & lion, gr/bl, #d, 6"...3,120.00
Tile, elephants (3), poly matt, Arts & Crafts fr, 5½x8½".........26,400.00
Tile, evergreens landscape, 4-color, #39, 6x6".............................3,000.00
Tile, Frog Footman (Alice in Wonderland series), cuerda seca, 4" . 1,080.00
Tile, Grueby Tile & candlestick, 6x4½" 3,600.00
Tile, houses/hill/seashore, 6-color, 4x4" 2,880.00
Tile, Pines, 4-color, sm chips/abrasion, unmk, 6x6" 2,500.00
Tile, polar bear, 5½x7"...11,400.00
Tile, rabbit, cuenca, in trivet mt, 6" 3,000.00
Tile, stag & tree, 5-color, sm fleck, 4x4".....................................3,360.00
Tile, tall ship, cuenca, yel/mustard/brn/gr, burst bubble, 6x6" ...1,800.00
Tile, tulip, brn on gr, chip, 6x6" 1,925.00
Tile, winged Pegasus, brn on gr, copper-ftd mt, sm rstr, 6x6".....4,000.00
Tiles, geometric/floral, dk clay/curdled brn, 8", set of 9 ....1,325.00
Vase, brn froth, leaves, R Erickson, experimental, 4¼x5¼".......3,360.00
Vase, brn, leaves w/wht buds, sm chips, 3½x5" 4,500.00
Vase, floor, emb leaves & blossoms, 23x8½" 18,000.00
Vase, gr, curled leaves in 3 rows, fine rstr, #41N, 6x8".............6,000.00
Vase, gr, leaves (2 rows), gourd shape, #33, 12x8", NM..........24,000.00
Vase, gr, leaves (full height) & buds, Faience stamp, 22x8¼"..14,400.00
Vase, gr, leaves (full height), #WP104, prof rstr chip, 8x5½" 3,300.00
Vase, gr, leaves (full height), pear shape, prof rstr to rim, 6¾x4¼"....... 4,200.00
Vase, gr, leaves & 3 daffodils, 1914, stamped RE 7/14, 10¾x9".6,000.00
Vase, gr, leaves & blossoms, Faience medallion, 13¼x8"...........4,500.00
Vase, gr, leaves & buds, A Lingley, sm rpr, 9"...........................2,400.00
Vase, gr, leaves & buds, Faience stamp, 7½x4½".......................2,650.00
Vase, gr, leaves & daffodils, squat, 4½x5½"...............................6,000.00
Vase, gr, leaves & yel buds, prof rstr chip, 12x5½" 9,600.00
Vase, indigo, leaves, ovoid, #180, kiln kiss, rstr rim, 8x4" 1,140.00
Vase, lg, matt gr, leaves & iris blossoms, rstr, 13¼x8½" 18,000.00
Vase, lt gr, leaves on bulb bottom, cylindrical neck, 12½".........4,800.00

Vase, mustard, leaves & ivory buds, prof rstr, 11x8" 12,000.00
Vase, narrow bulb, tall leaves, 10x4" 2,250.00

Gustavsberg

Gustavsberg Pottery, founded near Stockholm, Sweden, in the late 1700s, manufactured faience, creamware, and porcelain in the English taste until the end of the nineteenth century. During the twentieth, the factory produced some inventive modernistic designs, often signed by their artists. Wilhelm Kage (1889 – 1960) is best remembered for Argenta, a stoneware body decorated in silver overlay, introduced in the 1930s. Usually a mottled turquoise, Argenta can also be found in cobalt blue and white. Other lines included Cintra (an exceptionally translucent porcelain), Farsta (copper-glazed ware), and Farstarust (iron oxide geometric overlay). Designer Stig Lindberg's work, which dates from the 1940s through the early 1970s, includes slab-built figures and a full range of tableware. Some pieces of Gustavsberg are dated.

Bowl, Argenta, concentric rings on turq, Kage, #1055, 3⅜" 85.00
Bowl, Argenta, fish on turq, 7" 195.00
Bowl, Argenta, mermaid on turq, emb horizontal ribs, 9" 600.00
Bowl, geometrics, bl & yel irid, 8-sided, 5x10" 600.00
Candlesticks, bl irid w/gold trim, tulip sockets, Ekberg, 3½", pr...130.00
Charger, Argenta, 3 fish on turq, 12" 455.00
Figurine, bull, stylized, brn tones, paper label, 4½" 135.00
Figurine, cat, blk & wht stripes, yel eyes, L Larsen, 4½" 195.00
Figurine, horse, 'fat' body w/brn spots, Lindberg, 5½x6" 375.00
Figurine, kangaroo w/removable joey, brn, Lisa Larson, 9" 270.00
Figurine, nude woman on ped, parian, Hasselberg, #19B, 19", NM ...750.00
Plaque, bird figural (stylized), bl & gr, Lisa Larson, 7x10" 225.00
Plaque, stylized horse w/tooled details, brn/bl/bl-gr, label, 13x19". 300.00
Plate, Argenta, floral on turq, 6½" 70.00
Vase, Argenta, fish on turq, flared cylinder, 6" 195.00
Vase, Argenta, flowers on turq, cylindrical, #1029H, 6" 125.00
Vase, Argenta, geese on turq, W Kage, 7" 600.00
Vase, Argenta, linear design, W Kage, 5½x5¾" 235.00
Vase, Argenta, mermaid on turq, slim cylinder, 9" 660.00
Vase, Argenta, silver mermaid & lg fish on turq, imp & appl silver marks, 10" .2,100.00
Vase, Argenta, sm leaves on turq, Kage, cylindrical, 7⅜", NM.....425.00

Vase, blue and mahogany hare's fur glaze, signed Friberg with studio hand mark, 8¾x7", $2,280.00. (Photo courtesy Rago Arts and Auction Center)

Vase, emb ribs, wht porc, anchor mk, 6" 60.00
Vase, red irid, slim neck, 18x7" 240.00
Vase, sgraffito floral, bl on cream, Ekberg, 11" 360.00

M.A. Hadley

Founded by artist-turned-potter Mary Alice Hadley, this Louisville, Kentucky, company has been producing handmade dinnerware and decorative items since 1940. Their work is painted freehand in a folk-art style with barnyard animals, whales, sailing ships, and several other patterns. The pal-

ette is predominately blue and green. Each piece is signed with Hadley's first two initials and her last name, and her artwork continues to be the inspiration for modern designs. Among collectors, horses and other farm animals are a popular subject matter. Older pieces are generally heavier and, along with the more unusual items, command the higher prices. Our advisor for this category is Lisa Sanders; she is listed in the Directory under Indiana.

Bowl, cereal, bouquet, 5⅝", 4 for..40.00
Butter dish, cow, rect, 7¾" L...25.00
Butter dish, cow, rnd, w/dome lid, 6½"...25.00
Cake plate, birthday cake center, A Very Happy Birthday..., 1½x13"...35.00
Canister, 'Flour' & scrollwork...30.00
Casserole, cow on lid, 'The End' inside, 10", $35 to 45.00
Casserole, pig & cow, w/lid, 7x8", $30 to 40.00
Creamer/sugar bowl, horse, all bl, w/lid, 3¾", 4" 40.00
Egg cup, dbl, sheep, 4½" 15.00
Fountain, oval face & bowl, wall mt 1,200.00
Hor d'oeuvres, house in center of 7" attached bowl, 15" dia 65.00
Ladle, punch bowl...30.00
Mug, cow, tall...15.00
Mustard jar, 'Mustard' & scrollwork...30.00
Piggy bank, flowers all over, 4½x9x5"..40.00
Pitcher, bird on branch, 7½"..40.00
Pitcher, pig, 2-qt..40.00
Plate, house, 8⅜", 4 for..48.00
Plate, sailing ship, 11"...18.00
Platter, bouquet, 15" dia 30.00
Platter, farmer & wife, 17x11¼"...40.00
Punch bowl, farmer & wife, 6½x15", w/stand, no ladle 125.00
Sculpture, bird, mottled brn, 4¼x7", pr..30.00
Sculpture, chicken, 4"...12.00
Teapot, bouquet, 6-cup 26.50
Tray, berries, oval, 1¼x9x5¼"...25.00
Tumbler, water, farmer, wife, pig & sheep, 9-oz, 5", 4 for...............50.00
Water cooler, basket of flowers, 16x9"...135.00

Hagenauer

Carl Hagenauer founded his metal workshops in Vienna in 1898. He was joined by sons Karl in 1919 and Franz in 1928. Generally it was Franz who designed the decorative sculptures while the utilitarian wares are most often attributed to Carl and Karl. Items are usually stamped with the 'wHw' company mark, signed by the artist, and dated. They produced a wide range of stylized sculptural designs in both metal and wood.

Sculptures, profiles of man and woman with stylized features, polished chrome, marked, 21", $15,600.00. (Photo courtesy DuMouchelles on LiveAuctioneers.com)

Bookends, gazelles, SP, 4x5x3½", pr 1,440.00
Bust, female, chrome, incised features, #1289W, 22x18x6".....12,000.00
Bust, female, ebonized, cvd, wood & brass, 4¼x1½x2¾"...........2,400.00
Candlesticks, brass, trumpet shape w/flat rim, 4-ftd, 1950, 6½", pr...335.00
Figurine, abstract, Christ w/arms outstretched, bronze, ca 1930, 5"..205.00
Figurine, African women (4) paddling boat, wood/bronze/brass, 20" L ..900.00
Figurine, bear cup, modernist, bronze, 2x3" 170.00
Figurine, black boy w/hands behind bk, bronze, w/brass necklace, 2". 170.00

Figurine, female dancer, Deco style, bronze, ca 1925, 12¾"............ 70.00
Figurine, fowl, stylized, wood, 7½".. 110.00
Figurine, hedgehog, bronze, 6 stacking parts, 2¾x4¼" 105.00
Figurine, horse head, curved neck, hollow metal on oval base, 5¼x5"..240.00
Figurine, Indian drawing bow, Deco style, bronze, 6½x3½".......... 195.00
Figurine, knight on horse jousting w/lance letter opener, bronze, 3x6".125.00
Figurine, mouse w/tail curved over head, bronze, ca 1930, 2" 75.00
Figurine, stag leaping, bronze, 4½x7¼" 115.00
Mirror stand, brass, cvd ebonized hand detal, 12¾x22½x3" 1,560.00
Sculpture, female dancer in top hat, cvd wood & cast brass, 9¾x8x3¼"..1,200.00
Sculpture, female, cvd wood w/copper ribbon & base, Franz, 22x17x3½".5,400.00
Sculpture, ibex, cvd wood, patinated metal, brass base, 14¾x4x8¼"..2,040.00

Hagen-Renaker

Hagen-Renaker Potteries was founded in a garage in Culver City, California, in 1945. By 1946 it moved to a Quonset hut in Monrovia, California, where it continued making hand-painted dishes decorated with fruit and vegetable or animal designs. These dishes were usually signed 'HR Calif' in paint on the back. By 1948, Hagen-Renaker began producing miniature animal figurines, which quickly became its bestselling line. Remarkably, this is still true today. Many of the old miniatures from the '50s are still being produced.

In 1952 Hagen-Renaker introduced a new larger line of animal figurines called Designer's Workshop, or DW for short. These pieces were produced by many remarkable artists. A few of the more recognizable names were Maureen Love, Tom Masterson, Nell Bortells, Martha Armstrong-Hand, Helen Perrin Farnlund, and Don Winton. its design, attention to detail, and painting are amazing. Hagen-Renaker made hundreds of different DW pieces: birds, cats, dogs, farm animals, horses, insects, and wildlife. These pieces look more like real animals than pottery renditions. The horses are particularly prized by collectors.

When Disneyland opened in 1955, Hagen-Renaker made many Disney pieces and continued producing them until 1960. Walt Disney was particularly impressed, saying that Hagen-Renaker made the finest three-dimensional figurines he had ever seen. Hagen-Renaker made over 100 different figurines. The sets produced were Alice in Wonderland, Bambi, Cinderella, Dumbo, Fantasia, Mickey Mouse & Friends, Peter Pan, Sleeping Beauty, some miscellaneous pieces, and two sizes of Snow White and the Seven Dwarfs. Most of the Disney pieces were minis, but they also produced larger items, including banks and cookie jars. A chamber pot was also produced that Walt Disney gave to employees with new babies, pink for girls and blue for boys. A second larger set of Fantasia pieces was made in 1982.

The late 1950s and early 1960s was a very difficult time for all American potteries. Most were forced to close due to cheap Japanese imports. Many of these imports were unauthorized copies of American-made pieces. The company initiated new products and cost-cutting measures, trying to compete with these imports. It introduced many new lines including Little Horribles, Rock Wall plaques and trays (faux Arizona Flagstone decorated with brightly colored primitive animals similar to cave drawings), Zany Zoo pieces, and Black Bisque animals. It also tried Aurasperse, a cold paint that didn't have to be fired in a kiln, thus saving time and money. The problem with this paint was that it washed off very easily. Because these pieces weren't long in production, they are treasured today due to their scarcity. Even with all the new lines and paints, Hagen-Renaker was forced to shut down; however, the shutdown lasted only a short while. In early 1966, Hagen-Renaker opened a more efficient plant in San Dimas, California, where it still operates today.

In 1980 Hagen-Renaker bought the Freeman-McFarlin factory in San Marcos, California, and operated it for six years. This factory specialized in making large DW pieces. Some were new designs while others were Freeman-McFarlin's, but the majority were reissued DW pieces. Many of the old molds had to be reworked, so some of the pieces from the San Mar-

cos era vary slightly from earlier pieces. Hagen-Renaker continued to produce Freeman-McFarlin pieces using the same glazes and colors, usually white or gold leaf. They also produced some items in new colors. In many cases, it is impossible to tell which company made a particular piece.

In the late '80s, Hagen-Renaker introduced Stoneware and Specialty lines, which are larger than the minis and smaller than the DW pieces. The Stoneware line was short lived, but it still makes the Specialty pieces. Recently, Hagen-Renaker issued a line of dogs called the Pedigree line, which are mostly redesigns of DW pieces. The current Hagen-Renaker line consists of 44 Specialty pieces, 15 Pedigree dogs, and 206 miniatures. The company is currently releasing some large DW-sized horses. Some are new designs, but most are new versions of the old DW horses. Currently, 17 of these DW horses are available in various colors, with more to come. Our advisors for this category are Ed and Sheri Alcorn; they are listed in the Directory under Florida. For more information, visit the Hagen-Renaker Online Museum, www.hagenrenakermuseum.com.

Black Bisque, Crown-tailed Bird, blk bsk & wht, #22, 1959, 3½" .. 50.00
Black Bisque, Pelican, bl-gr enamel on blk bsk, #10, 1959, 3½" 60.00
Disney mini, Dumbo, 1956, 4" 200.00
Disney mini, Faun, right leg up, 1957, 1¼" 150.00
Disney mini, Figaro, 2¼", Jiminy Cricket, 3½", 1956 only, ea 300.00
Disney mini, Goofy, 1956, 2¼" 85.00
Disney mini, Hop Lo, mushroom, 1956-57, ¾" 50.00
Disney mini, Madame Upanova, ostrich, 1982, 3¼" 300.00
Disney mini, Pedro, chihuahua, 1955-59, 1⅜" 60.00
Disney mini, Si & Am, Siamese cats, 1955-59, 1¼", ea 100.00
Disney, lg, Snow White (5¾") & the Seven Dwarfs, set 2,500.00
DW, Bingo, duckling, #746, 1961-86, 1½" 35.00
DW, Borzoi, caramel & wht, #1003, 1972, 3¾" 75.00
DW, chick w/wings up, #524, 1952, 3" 45.00
DW, Choo Choo, Pekingese pup, #1534, 1956-61, 2" 30.00
DW, Clydesdale, #50, matt & glossy, 1983-86, 7½", ea 400.00
DW, Crusader, Percheron, wht #706, 1959-67, 6¼" 600.00
DW, Daniel, Bongo Rat, w/bongo, #678, 1957, 5½ 200.00
DW, Dick, Siamese cat sitting, #728, 1960, 6½" 60.00
DW, Fuzzy, calico cat, rare color, #758, 1966, 3" 175.00
DW, Girl Gosling, bl hat, #48, 1983-86, 3¼" 30.00
DW, Golden Lady, collie, #1515, 1955-56, 6" 100.00
DW, Heidi's Goat, #79, 1984-86, 4½" 75.00
DW, Man O' War, famous racehorse, #742, 1961-74, 7" 250.00
DW, Maverick, buckskin quarter horse, #688, 1958+, 6" 450.00
DW, Modern Horse, 13½" 1,500.00
DW, quail standing, #534, 1950s, 5".. 80.00
DW, ram's head, gold, #61, 1981-82, 7½"...................................... 150.00
DW, Starlite, Persian cat, #683, 1963-78, 6½" 30.00
DW, Toulouse, goose, #636, 1956, 7".. 200.00
DW, Tria, Morgan horse, palomino, #104, 1995-96, 4" 150.00
DW, Zara, Arabian mare, blk, #708, current, 6½"......................... 200.00
DW, Zara, sm Arabian mare, gray, #708, 1970s, 6½" 250.00
Little Horribles mini, Dark Eyes, #404, 1958, 1" 50.00
Little Horribles mini, FHA, #434, 1959, scarce, 1¾".................... 150.00
Little Horribles mini, Hole in the Head, #422, 1959, 2¼" 85.00
Little Horribles mini, Hula Hooper, #432, 1959, 2¼"..................... 65.00

Little Horribles miniatures, Spectator and Toothy, 2" and 1", each $200.00. (Photo courtesy Ed and Sheri Alcorn)

Miniature, aerobic pig, holds leg/pk outfit, A-3246, 1997-2003, 1⅛"...12.00
Miniature, anteater, wire tongue, rare, A-069, 1966, 1¾" 250.00
Miniature, Anvil (horse), silver & brn, A-394, 1959 .... 100.00
Miniature, Arabian mare, wht, A-046, 1959-70, 3"........................ 75.00
Miniature, Banty rooster, stretching neck, brn, A-94, 1970s, 2⅛" . 20.00
Miniature, beaver w/stump, A-399/400, 1960-90, 1"....................... 15.00
Miniature, Bichon Frise, A-3272, 1998-current, 1⅜" 6.00
Miniature, blk cat lying, A-326, 1990s, 1¼" 20.00
Miniature, Clydesdale foal, A-3156, 1994-2000, 2¾"..................... 12.00
Miniature, dancing cats, romantic, #A-2002, 1988-2007, 2½" 15.00
Miniature, elephant on circus drum, A-881, 1987-97, 2"............... 15.00
Miniature, fantail goldfish, orange, A-426, 1960-76, 1" 20.00
Miniature, frisky colt, palomino, A-147R/147L, 1951-54, 2" 40.00
Miniature, goat mama, wht, A-848, 1984-current, 1⅜".....................7.00
Miniature, hammerhead shark, A-3187, 1995-97, 3¾" 15.00
Miniature, kitten climbing, Siamese, A-377, 1958-92, 1⅜" 10.00
Miniature, kitten in armchair, A-997-998, 1976-79, 1½" 35.00
Miniature, llama baby, A-873, 1986-87, 1⅛" 46.00
Miniature, Mr Dove, A-895, 1987-88, 1" 12.00
Miniature, octopus, orange, A-3198, 1966-2001, ¾" 12.00
Miniature, Pekingese facing left, A-2076, 1966-67, 1¾" 30.00

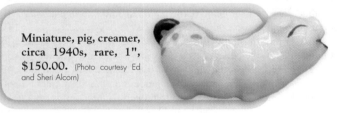

Miniature, pig, creamer, circa 1940s, rare, 1", $150.00. (Photo courtesy Ed and Sheri Alcorn)

Miniature, Puffin, A-894, 1987-current, 1½" 10.00
Miniature, pup playing (early), A-16, 1949, ¾" 40.00
Miniature, raccoon baby, brn, A-164, 1972-81, 1" 10.00
Miniature, St Bernard, A-3064, 1992-2006, 2" 10.00
Miniature, Swaps, famous racehorse, A-030, 1991-93, 2¾"............ 35.00
Miniature, zebra mama, A-173, 1983-86, 1½" 45.00
Plaque, doe, red, 1959, 14x8½" 150.00
Plaque, geisha mosaic, 1959, 22x10½" 125.00
Plaque, Iris, sgn HR Calif, oval, #651, 1946-49, 5" 40.00
Plate, dinner, turkey/duck/rooster, #652, 1946-49, 8¾" 75.00
Shakers, duck design, rare, 1946-49, 2½", pr.............................. 150.00
Specialty, Henny Penny, #3132, 2½".. 30.00
Specialty, Mother Goose, #3293, 1999-2001, 3½" 25.00
Specialty, Nativity angel, blond, #3023, 1991-92, 2" 45.00
Specialty, seagulls, #3050, 1992-95, 4½" 45.00
Specialty, seahorse, orange, #2089, 1990-91, 2½" 30.00
Specialty, Sizzle, Appaloosa foal, #3268, 1998-2000, 2½" 40.00
Specialty, unicorn lying, #3040, 1991-current, 2⅜" 20.00
Tray, butterfly, Arizona Flagstone, 1960, sm, 10½x5½"................. 100.00
Zany Zoo, mouse, purple Aurasperse, 1960 only, 2¼" 250.00

Hair Work

Hair work was very popular in the eighteenth and nineteenth centuries. These pieces were made not only in memory of the dead, but also as tokens of love. In the mid-1800s, hair work became a drawing room past-time. It was three times more valuable than sterling silver. Hair work comes in three different styles — table work, palette work, and the type used in making a memorial wall hanging or a family tree. Table work is done using a table and is much like bobbin-lace construction. Palette work is done using a small artist palette and consequently the pieces are usually small. Hair pieces made to place in a shadow box are done with multiple weaves similar to crochet.

Because hair work has little or no intrinsic value, condition is very important. Frays and breaks diminish the value. Earrings are very desirable because keeping a pair together for over a century is very difficult. Our advisor for this category is C. Jeanenne Bell; she is listed in the Directory under Alabama.

Key:
p-w — palette work   t-w — table work

Basket of flowers in various colors, dated 1878, 13", in shadowbox frame, 25x21", $900.00. (Photo courtesy DuMouchelles on liveAuctioneers.com)

Bracelet, 3 braided t-w rows w/gold locket clasp, 1850-70s 675.00
Bracelet, open t-w, p-w clasp, sewn-on hair flowers, ca 1850s 750.00
Bracelet, plaited w/gold-plated box clasp, 1840-70, VG.............. 150.00
Bracelet, t-w (7) in 2 weaves, locket clasp w/daguerrotype, 1840s ..650.00
Bracelet, t-w braided tubes w/mini man's portrait in gold case, 1790s. 1,645.00
Bracelet, t-w in 3 weaves, gold clasp, woven hair in glazed compartment, 8" L...675.00
Bracelet, t-w in 3 weaves, gold mts, 1¼x6¾", VG+ 495.00
Bracelet, t-w weave w/box clasp & yel stone, 1850-80s................ 450.00
Brooch, 18k yel gold eagle w/braids, early 1800s 1,800.00
Brooch, braided, under beveled glass amid pearls, 1830s, 1½"...... 375.00
Brooch, gold over brass, reverses w/hair ea side, 1860-80s, 1½" ... 350.00
Brooch, p-w basketweave, jet mt, 1850-60s, 2x1¼" 225.00
Brooch, p-w curl/flowers on gold-filled mt, 1½x1" 325.00
Brooch, p-w curls/flowers under glass in hollow gold fr, 1840s, 1⅞"....500.00
Brooch, p-w flowers/seed pearls, 1790-1830s, 1¼" 750.00
Brooch, swirl under glass in dmn-shaped jet fr, 1860-80s, 1"........ 150.00
Brooch, t-w balls & gold acorns, 1860-70s, 1x2⅝" 475.00
Brooch, t-w tubular bow w/gold mts, acorn drops, 1850-70s, 2½x2" ..475.00
Brooch/pendant, t-w on hard core w/gold mts, 1860-80s, 2x1⅜" . 350.00
Earrings, open-weave t-w w/gold mts, 1850-70s, 1⅜", pr.............. 550.00
Earrings, t-w bell form w/gutta-percha details, 1850-70s, 1⅝", pr. 600.00
Earrings, t-w teardrop form w/gold mts, 1840-70s, 3¾", pr 550.00
Earrings, t-w w/openweave dangles, gold mts, 1850s-70s, 2½x1" . 650.00
Flower bouquet in shadow-box fr, dtd 1878, 25x21"................. 1,300.00
Medallion, Prince of Wales feathers p-w on mg, 1840s, 1" 250.00
Necklace, t-w 2-tone in X weave, gold balls & mts, 1840-80s 400.00
Necklace, t-w chain w/gold heart drop, 1850-80s, 14" 595.00
Necklace, t-w elongated caged balls in gold frs, 1850-80s, 18"..... 700.00
Necklace, t-w rows (3) in 2 weaves, gold mts, 1840-60s, 14" 450.00
Ring, hollow gold band w/t-w insert, cutouts reveal hair, 1840-80... 400.00
Ring, weaving under crystal, gold mt w/pearls, head:½x¼" 500.00
Stickpin, t-w horseshoe w/gold mts, 1840-80s 125.00
Watch chain, 2 rows t-w in 2 weaves, gold fob w/amethyst, 1850s... 225.00
Watch chain, t-w 2-color horsehair, ca 1860-90s, 13" 155.00

Hall

The Hall China Company of East Liverpool, Ohio, was established in 1903. Their earliest products included whiteware toilet seats, mugs, and jugs. By 1920 their restaurant-type dinnerware and cookingware had become so successful that Hall was assured of a solid future.

Hall introduced the first of their famous teapots in 1920; new shapes and colors were added each year until about 1948, making them the largest teapot manufacturer in the world. These and the dinnerware lines of the '30s through the '50s have become popular collectibles. In 2010 Hall China merged with Homer Laughlin China Company, the last major pottery still being manufactured in the United States. For a more thorough study of the subject, we recommend *Collector's Encyclopedia of Hall China*, by our advisors, Margaret and Kenn Whitmyer; see the Directory under Ohio.

Blue Bouquet, bowl, salad, 9"	20.00
Blue Bouquet, creamer, modern	30.00
Blue Bouquet, plate, D-style, 8¼"	11.00
Blue Bouquet, spoon	135.00
Blue Bouquet, tureen, soup	320.00
Cameo Rose, butter dish, ¼-lb	500.00
Cameo Rose, gravy boat, w/underplate	35.00
Cameo Rose, platter, 11¼" L	18.00
Cameo Rose, tidbit tray, 3-tier	75.00
Century Fern, creamer	12.00
Century Fern, ladle	22.00
Century Fern, saucer	1.50
Century Fern, shakers, pr	30.00
Century Garden of Eden, casserole	60.00
Century Garden of Eden, gravy boat	32.00
Century Sunglow, ashtray	9.00
Century Sunglow, plate, 8"	9.50
Christmas Tree & Holly, bowl, oval	60.00
Christmas Tree & Holly, cookie jar, Zeisel	350.00
Christmas Tree & Holly, plate, 10"	45.00
Christmas Tree & Holly, sugar bowl, open	45.00
Crocus, bowl, flat soup, 8½"	35.00
Crocus, cake plate	50.00
Crocus, jug, Simplicity	350.00
Crocus, leftover, sq	120.00
Crocus, plate, D-style, 6"	8.00
Crocus, platter, D-style, 13¼" L	35.00
Crocus, pretzel jar	200.00
Fantasy, casserole, Sundial #4, $60 to	70.00
Gaillardia, baker, Fr, fluted	30.00
Gaillardia, bowl, D-style, Radiance, 9"	30.00
Gaillardia, cup, D-style	12.00
Gaillardia, drip jar, Radiance	35.00
Gaillardia, sugar bowl, Art Deco, w/lid	35.00
Game Bird, bowl, oval	65.00
Game Bird, bowl, thick rim, 8½"	45.00
Game Bird, creamer, New York	40.00
Game Bird, mug, Irish coffee	75.00

Game Bird, percolator, electric, $100.00 to $125.00. (Photo courtesy Margaret and Kenn Whitmyer)

Game Bird, sugar bowl, New York, w/lid	55.00
Golden Oak, coffeepot, Kadota	85.00
Golden Oak, cup	6.00
Golden Oak, gravy boat	20.00
Golden Oak, plate, D-style, 9"	10.00

Golden Oak, shakers, hdld, pr	30.00
Heather Rose, bowl, cereal, 6¼"	10.00
Heather Rose, coffeepot, Terrace	45.00
Heather Rose, plate, 6½"	3.50
Heather Rose, plate, 10"	12.50
Homewood, coffeepot, Terrace	75.00
Homewood, cup, D-style	8.00
Homewood, saucer, D-style	1.50
Mums, bowl, D-style, 9¼"	45.00
Mums, bowl, Radiance, 7½"	27.00
Mums, creamer, New York	27.00
Mums, plate, D-style, 6"	5.50
Mums, pretzel jar	250.00
No 488, bowl, flat soup, 8½"	35.00
No 488, casserole, Five Band	75.00
No 488, cookie jar, Five Band	300.00
No 488, drip coffeepot, #691	500.00
No 488, drip coffeepot, Radiance, $400 to	500.00
No 488, jug, Rayed	75.00
No 488, platter, D-style, 13¼" L	55.00
Orange Poppy, bowl, fruit, C-style, 5½"	8.50
Orange Poppy, cake plate	45.00
Orange Poppy, casserole, #76, rnd	40.00
Orange Poppy, match safe	110.00
Orange Poppy, mustard w/liner	145.00
Orange Poppy, pie baker	55.00
Pastel Morning Glory, bowl, D-style, 9¼"	45.00
Pastel Morning Glory, canister, Radiance	450.00
Pastel Morning Glory, drip jar, #1188, open	47.00
Pastel Morning Glory, gravy boat, D-style	35.00
Pastel Morning Glory, pie baker	50.00
Pastel Morning Glory, tea tile	120.00
Prairie Grass, bowl, oval, 9¼"	25.00
Prairie Grass, creamer	13.00
Prairie Grass, tidbit, 3-tier	75.00
Primrose, ashtray	10.00
Primrose, jug, Rayed	22.00
Primrose, plate, 7¼"	6.50
Red Poppy, cup, D-style	14.00
Red Poppy, custard	25.00
Red Poppy, jug, #5, Radiance	45.00
Red Poppy, plate, D-style, 8¼"	10.50
Red Poppy, shakers, hdld, pr	50.00
Sears' Arlington, bowl, flat soup, 8"	10.00
Sears' Arlington, bowl, vegetable, w/lid	40.00
Sears' Arlington, platter, 13¼" L	22.00
Sears' Fairfax, creamer	9.00
Sears' Fairfax, plate, 6½"	3.50
Sears' Fairfax, sugar bowl	17.00
Sears' Monticello, bowl, fruit, 5¼"	5.00
Sears' Monticello, plate, 10"	11.00
Sears' Monticello, platter, 15½" L	30.00
Sears' Mount Vernon, coffeepot	225.00
Sears' Mount Vernon, platter, 11¼" L	22.00
Serenade, bowl, flat soup, 8½"	14.00
Serenade, creamer, Art Deco	27.00
Serenade, drip jar, Radiance, w/lid	37.00
Serenade, pie baker	45.00
Serenade, platter, 13¼" L	27.00
Serenade, pretzel jar	160.00
Serenade, sugar bowl, Modern	30.00
Silhouette, bowl, vegetable, D-style, 9¼"	35.00
Silhouette, casserole, Medallion	45.00
Silhouette, custard, Medallion	30.00

Silhouette, gravy boat, D-style 35.00
Silhouette, leftover, sq 75.00
Silhouette, plate, 9" 18.00
Silhouette, shakers, Teardrop, pr 50.00
Springtime, cake plate 18.00
Springtime, pie baker 25.00
Springtime, plate, D-style, 7¼" 6.00
Springtime, saucer, D-style 2.50
Tulip, bowl, D-style, 9¼" 35.00
Tulip, casserole, tab-hdld 125.00
Tulip, coffeepot, Perk 65.00
Tulip, platter, D-style, 11¼" L 30.00
Wildfire, bowl, 9" 32.00
Wildfire, cup, D-style 14.00
Wildfire, jug, Sani-Grid, 6" 75.00
Wildfire, plate, D-style, 10" 70.00
Yellow Rose, bowl, salad, 9" 27.00
Yellow Rose, custard 18.00
Yellow Rose, gravy boat, D-style 35.00

Teapots

Airflow, Canary, gold special, $125 to 150.00
Airflow, Indian Red, $125 to 150.00
Airflow, rose, std gold, $75 to 100.00
Aladdin, Cadet, gold label, $200 to 225.00
Aladdin, maroon, solid color, $75 to 85.00
Aladdin, turq, std gold, $90 to 110.00
Albany, blk, std gold, $50 to 60.00
Albany, emerald, solid color, $50 to 60.00
Albany, Marine, std gold, $85 to 90.00
Albany, pk, gold label, $150 to 175.00
Art Deco, bl, Adele, $200 to 250.00
Art Deco, gr, Damascus, $190 to 210.00
Art Deco, yel, Danielle, $170 to 190.00
Baltimore, Cadet, std gold, $75 to 85.00
Bellevue, orchid, 2-cup, $200 to 250.00
Boston, blk, solid color, 1- to 3-cup, $20 to 25.00
Boston, cobalt, old gold design, 1- to 3-cup, $100 to ... 125.00
Boston, cobalt, std gold, 1- to 3-cup, $57 to 65.00
Boston, ivory, gold label, 1- to 3-cup, $55 to 60.00
Century Sunglow, 6-cup 195.00
French, Dresden, solid color, 1- to 3-cup, $35 to 45.00
French, gray, gold label, 1- to 3-cup, $65 to 70.00
French, rose, solid color, 4- to 8-cup, $40 to 50.00
Globe, Camellia, std gold, $70 to 80.00
Globe, emerald, solid color, $100 to 150.00
Heather Rose, London 30.00
Hollywood, blk, std gold, $50 to 55.00
Hollywood, maroon, gold label, $100 to 125.00
Homewood, New York 175.00
Hook Cover, Canary, std gold, $50 to 60.00
Hook Cover, Silver Luster, solid color, $100 to 125.00
Illinois, Chinese Red, solid color, $450 to 500.00
Illinois, Stock Brn, std gold, $140 to 160.00
Indiana, ivory, std gold, $250 to 275.00
Indiana, Warm Yel, solid color, $300 to 400.00
Kansas, maroon, solid color, $300 to 350.00
Kansas, maroon, std gold, $400 to 500.00
Los Angeles, Dresden, std gold, $50 to 55.00
Los Angeles, pk, gold label, $75 to 85.00
Melody, blk, std gold, $125 to 155.00
Melody, turq, solid color, $190 to 210.00
Moderne, Canary, solid color, $45 to 55.00

Moderne, Chinese Red, solid color, $125 to 160.00
Mums, Boston 300.00
Musical, Canary, $155 to 170.00
Nautilus, ivory, solid color, $100 to 125.00
Nautilus, turq, std gold, $240 to 260.00
New York, Dresden, std gold, 1- to 4-cup, $40 to 50.00
Newport, Warm Yel, solid color, $50 to 60.00
Ohio, cobalt, std gold, $350 to 400.00
Ohio, pk, gold dot, $250 to 300.00
Orange Poppy, Melody 360.00
Orange Poppy, Streamline 350.00
Philadelphia, Indian Red, solid color, $165 to 190.00
Red Poppy, Aladdin 155.00

Rose Parade, teapot, three-cup, $55.00 to $65.00. (Photo courtesy Dirk Soulis Auctions on LiveAuctioneers.com)

Silhouette, teapot, New York 250.00
Sundial, blk, solid color, $50 to 60.00
Sundial, emerald, std gold, $85 to 95.00
Wildfire, Streamline 600.00
Yellow Rose, New York 200.00

Zeisel Designs, Hallcraft

Tomorrow's Classic Arizona, butter dish 175.00
Tomorrow's Classic Arizona, onion soup, w/lid 37.00
Tomorrow's Classic Arizona, teapot, 6-cup 195.00
Tomorrow's Classic Bouquet, bottle, vinegar 95.00
Tomorrow's Classic Bouquet, bowl, celery, oval 30.00
Tomorrow's Classic Bouquet, candlestick, 8", ea 55.00
Tomorrow's Classic Bouquet, creamer 15.00
Tomorrow's Classic Bouquet, ladle 25.00
Tomorrow's Classic Bouquet, plate, 11" 16.00
Tomorrow's Classic Bouquet, platter, 15" L 35.00
Tomorrow's Classic Bouquet, saucer, AD 3.00
Tomorrow's Classic Buckingham, bowl, fruit, 5¾" 9.00
Tomorrow's Classic Buckingham, egg cup 55.00
Tomorrow's Classic Buckingham, platter, 17" L 40.00
Tomorrow's Classic Caprice, baker, open, 11-oz 22.00
Tomorrow's Classic Caprice, candlestick, 8", ea 45.00
Tomorrow's Classic Caprice, cup 10.00
Tomorrow's Classic Caprice, gravy boat 40.00
Tomorrow's Classic Caprice, plate, 11" 13.00
Tomorrow's Classic Caprice, sugar bowl 22.00
Tomorrow's Classic Caprice, teapot, 6-cup 195.00
Tomorrow's Classic Dawn, bowl, coupe soup, 9" 13.00
Tomorrow's Classic Dawn, butter dish 190.00
Tomorrow's Classic Dawn, platter, 15" L 37.00
Tomorrow's Classic Dawn, vase 95.00
Tomorrow's Classic Fantasy, bowl, vegetable, sq, 8¾" ... 25.00
Tomorrow's Classic Fantasy, marmite w/lid 40.00
Tomorrow's Classic Flair, bowl, salad, 14½" 45.00
Tomorrow's Classic Flair, casserole, 1¼-qt 40.00
Tomorrow's Classic Flair, jug, 3-qt 47.00
Tomorrow's Classic Flair, shakers, pr 36.00
Tomorrow's Classic Frost Flowers, baker, 11-oz 22.00
Tomorrow's Classic Frost Flowers, egg cup 50.00

Tomorrow's Classic Harlequin, casserole, 2-qt 65.00
Tomorrow's Classic Harlequin, cookie jar, Zeisel-style 300.00
Tomorrow's Classic Harlequin, platter, 17" 40.00
Tomorrow's Classic Holiday, covered casserole, 1¼-qt, $50 to 60.00
Tomorrow's Classic Lyric, candlestick, 4½", ea 32.00
Tomorrow's Classic Lyric, coffeepot, 6-cup.................................. 110.00
Tomorrow's Classic Lyric, cup.. 10.00
Tomorrow's Classic Lyric, onion soup, w/lid................................. 37.00
Tomorrow's Classic Lyric, vase.. 80.00
Tomorrow's Classic Mulberry, bowl, celery, oval 24.00
Tomorrow's Classic Mulberry, candlestick, 8", ea 45.00
Tomorrow's Classic Mulberry, gravy boat 40.00
Tomorrow's Classic Mulberry, saucer, AD 4.50
Tomorrow's Classic Peach Blossom, bowl, fruit, ftd, lg 40.00
Tomorrow's Classic Peach Blossom, jug, 1¼-qt............................. 28.00
Tomorrow's Classic Peach Blossom, platter, 17"............................ 38.00
Tomorrow's Classic Pine Cone, bowl, coupe soup, 9" 16.00
Tomorrow's Classic Pine Cone, candlestick, 4½", ea 30.00
Tomorrow's Classic Pine Cone, coffeepot, 6-cup 105.00
Tomorrow's Classic Pine Cone, cup...7.00
Tomorrow's Classic Pine Cone, marmite w/lid................................ 37.00
Tomorrow's Classic Pine Cone, plate, 8"...9.50
Tomorrow's Classic Pine Cone, saucer...2.00
Tomorrow's Classic Pine Cone, vase 80.00
Tomorrow's Classic Spring/Studio 10, bowl, salad, lg, 14½" 35.00
Tomorrow's Classic Spring/Studio 10, casserole, 1¼-qt 35.00
Tomorrow's Classic Spring/Studio 10, egg cup 45.00
Tomorrow's Classic Spring/Studio 10, plate, 11"............................ 13.00
Tomorrow's Classic Spring/Studio 10, platter, 17" L 38.00
Tomorrow's Classic Spring/Studio 10, shakers, pr 38.00

Halloween

Though the origin of Halloween is steeped in pagan rites and superstitions, today Halloween is strictly a fun time, and Halloween items are fun to collect. Pumpkin-head candy containers of papier-maché or pressed cardboard, noisemakers, postcards with black cats and witches, costumes, and decorations are only a sampling of the variety available.

Here's how you can determine the origin of your jack-o'-lantern:

American 1940 – 1950s	German 1900 – 1930s
items are larger	items are generally small
made of egg-carton material	made of cardboard or composition
bottom and body are one piece	always has a cut-out triangular nose; simple, crisscross lines in mouth; blue rings in eyes
	have attached cardboard bottoms

For further information we recommend *More Halloween Collectibles, Anthropomorphic Vegetables and Fruits of Halloween*, by Pamela E. Apkarian-Russell (Schiffer). Other good reference books are *Halloween in America* by Stuart Schneider and *Halloween Collectables* by Dan and Pauline Campanelli.

Our advisor for this category is Jenny Tarrant; she is listed in the Directory under Missouri. See Clubs, Newsletters, and Websites for information concerning the *Trick or Treat Trader*, a quarterly newsletter. Unless noted otherwise, values are for examples in excellent to near mint condition except for paper items, in which case assume the condition to be near mint to mint.

American

Most American items were made during the 1940s and 1950s, though a few date from the 1930s as well. Lanterns are constructed either of flat cardboard or the pressed cardboard pulp used to make the jack-o'-lantern shown in the previous chart.

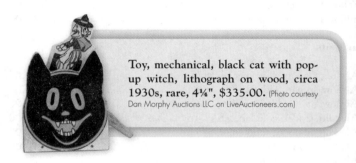

Toy, mechanical, black cat with pop-up witch, lithograph on wood, circa 1930s, rare, 4¼", $335.00. (Photo courtesy Dan Morphy Auctions LLC on LiveAuctioneers.com)

Candy container, witch, cb, 8" 275.00
Jack-o'-lantern, pressed cb pulp w/orig face, 4-4½", $95 to 98.00
Jack-o'-lantern, pressed cb pulp w/orig face, 5-5½", $115 to 125.00
Jack-o'-lantern, pressed cb pulp w/orig face, 6-6½", $100 to 125.00
Jack-o'-lantern, pressed cb pulp w/orig face, 7" 135.00
Jack-o'-lantern, pressed cb pulp w/orig face, 8", min.................... 145.00
Lantern, cat (full body), pressed cb pulp, 7x6½"........................... 350.00
Lantern, cat face, 5" 150.00
Lantern, cat, pressed cb pulp w/orig face 150.00
Lantern, cb w/tab sides, any... 65.00
Lantern, pumpkin man (full body), pressed cb pulp 350.00
Lantern, pumpkin w/scowling face, pulp, 6" 95.00
Pirate's Auto, HP, 1950s, 5" L... 300.00
Plastic Halloween car, HP 300.00
Plastic pumpkin stagecoach, witch & cat, HP 550.00
Plastic witch holding blk cat w/wobbling head, on wheels, 7" 300.00
Plastic witch on rocket, horizontal, on wheels, 7" 300.00
Plastic witch on rocket, on wheels, 4".. 95.00
Plastic witch on rocket, vertical, on wheels, 7"............................. 300.00
Postcard, Winsch, emb, Pierrette in tree, 3½x5½", 1912, $100 to...155.00
Postcards, Ellen Clapsaddle, mechanical, rare 350.00
Tin noisemaker, bell style 35.00
Tin noisemaker, can shaker 35.00
Tin noisemaker, clicker... 35.00
Tin noisemaker, frying-pan style 35.00
Tin noisemaker, horn.. 35.00
Tin noisemaker, sq spinner 35.00
Tin noisemaker, tambourine, Chein.. 95.00
Tin noisemaker, tambourine, Kirkoff.. 75.00
Tin noisemaker, tambourine, Ohio Art, 1930s, 6" 75.00

Celluloid (German, Japanese, or American)

Black cat, plain, M.. 150.00
Egg-shape house, M 300.00

Long-leg veggie rattle, M 300.00
Owl on pumpkin, M 100.00
Owl on tree, M 150.00
Owl, plain, M 55.00
Pumpkin-face man, M 350.00
Pumpkin-face pirate, roly poly, M 350.00
Scarecrow, M 200.00
Witch in auto, M 450.00
Witch in corncob car, M 450.00
Witch pulling cart w/ghost, M 400.00
Witch pulling pumpkin cart w/cat, M 400.00
Witch sitting on pumpkin, M 350.00
Witch, plain, M 200.00

German

    As a general rule, German Halloween collectibles date from 1900 through the early 1930s. They were made either of composition or molded cardboard, and their values are higher than American-made items. In the listings that follow, all candy containers are made of composition unless noted otherwise.

Candy container, black cat, velvet with painted composition nose and mouth, wooden legs, and cardboard ears, 10" to tip of tail, NM, $4,200.00. (Photo courtesy Dan Morphy Auctions LLC on LiveAuctioneers.com)

Candy container, blk cat walking, glass eyes, head removes, 3-4" . 225.00
Candy container, blk cat walking, glass eyes, head removes, 5-6" . 400.00
Candy container, cat sitting, 3-5" 175.00
Candy container, cat sitting, glass eyes, 4-6" 200.00
Candy container, cat walking, w/mohair, 5" 350.00
Candy container, compo pumpkin-head man or vegetable, on box, 3" .. 175.00
Candy container, compo pumpkin-head man or vegetable, on box, 4" .. 185.00
Candy container, compo pumpkin-head man or vegetable, on box, 5" .. 225.00
Candy container, compo pumpkin-head man or vegetable, on box, 6" .. 275.00
Candy container, compo witch or pumpkin man, head removes, 5" .. 350.00
Candy container, compo witch or pumpkin man, head removes, 6" .. 400.00
Candy container, compo witch or pumpkin man, head removes, 7" .. 450.00
Candy container, compo witch, pumpkin people, devil, ghost, etc, 3" . 225.00
Candy container, compo, witch or pumpkin man, head removes, 4" . 225.00
Candy container, lemon-head man, pnt compo, 7" 575.00
Candy container, nodder girl pulls pumpkin on wheels, compo, 4" 420.00
Candy container, pumpkin-head man (or any vegetable), on box, 3" .. 175.00
Candy container, pumpkin-head man (or any vegetable), on box, 5" .. 225.00
Candy container, witch or pumpkin man, head removes, 4" 225.00
Candy container, witch or pumpkin man, head removes, 5" 275.00
Candy container, witch or pumpkin man, head removes, 6" 300.00
Candy container, witch or pumpkin man, head removes, 7" 350.00
Candy container, witch, pumpkin people, devil, etc, solid figure, 4" .. 150.00
Candy container, witch, pumpkin people, devil, etc, solid figure, 5" .. 175.00
Candy container, witch, pumpkin people, devil, etc, solid figure, 6" .. 200.00
Diecut, bat, emb cb, M, $95 to 125.00
Diecut, cat (dressed), emb cb 125.00
Diecut, cat, emb cb, $55 to 95.00
Diecut, devil, emb cb, $95 to 150.00
Diecut, jack-o'-lantern, emb cb 45.00
Diecut, pumpkin head (Mickey Mouse) playing saxophone, 27" 250.00

Diecut, pumpkin man or lady, emb cb, 7½" 125.00
Jack-o'-lantern, compo w/orig insert, 3" 200.00
Jack-o'-lantern, compo w/orig insert, 4" 250.00
Jack-o'-lantern, compo w/orig insert, 5" 350.00
Jack-o'-lantern, molded cb w/orig insert, 3" 95.00
Jack-o'-lantern, molded cb w/orig insert, 4" 125.00
Jack-o'-lantern, molded cb w/orig insert, 5" 155.00
Jack-o'-lantern, molded cb w/orig insert, 6" 185.00
Jack-o'-lantern, molded cb w/paper face insert, ca 1920, 4", min. 300.00
Lantern (ghost, skull, devil, witch, etc), molded cb, 3-4", min 300.00
Lantern (ghost, skull, devil, witch, etc), molded cb, 5"+, min 350.00
Lantern (skull, devil, witch, etc), compo, 3", min 300.00
Lantern (skull, devil, witch, etc), compo, 4", min 400.00
Lantern (skull, devil, witch, etc), compo, 5", min 450.00
Lantern, cat, cb, molded nose, bow under chin, 3" 250.00
Lantern, cat, cb, molded nose, bow under chin, 4" 300.00
Lantern, cat, cb, molded nose, bow under chin, 5" 450.00
Lantern, cat, cb, simple rnd style 225.00
Lantern, face of wht cat, compo w/orig papers, very rare, 5" 400.00
Noisemaker, cat (3-D) on wood rachet 95.00
Noisemaker, cb figure (flat) on rachet 95.00
Noisemaker, cb paddle w/dc face 95.00
Noisemaker, devil (3-D) on wood rachet 95.00
Noisemaker, pumpkin head (rnd, 3-D) on wood rachet 95.00
Noisemaker, tin frying-pan paddle, Germany, no rust or dents, 5" L. 75.00
Noisemaker, tin horn, Germany, 3" 75.00
Noisemaker, veggie (3-D) horn (w/pnt face) 95.00
Noisemaker, veggie or fruit (3-D) horn (no face), ea 55.00
Noisemaker, witch (3-D) on wood rachet 125.00
Noisemaker, wood & paper tambourine w/pumpkin face 150.00

Hampshire

    The Hampshire Pottery Company was established in 1871 in Keene, New Hampshire, by James Scollay Taft. Their earliest products were redware and stoneware utility items such as jugs, churns, crocks, and flowerpots. In 1878 they produced majolica ware which met with such success that they began to experiment with the idea of manufacturing art pottery. By 1883 they had developed a Royal Worcester type of finish which they applied to vases, tea sets, powder boxes, and cookie jars. It was also utilized for souvenir items that were decorated with transfer designs prepared from photographic plates.

    Cadmon Robertson, brother-in-law of Taft, joined the company in 1904 and was responsible for developing their famous matt glazes. Colors included shades of green, brown, red, and blue. Early examples were of earthenware, but eventually the body was changed to semiporcelain. Some of his designs were marked with an M in a circle as a tribute to his wife, Emoretta. Robertson died in 1914, leaving a void impossible to fill. Taft sold the business in 1916 to George Morton, who continued to use the matt glazes that Robertson had developed. After a temporary halt in production during WWI, Morton returned to Keene and re-equipped the factory with the machinery needed to manufacture hotel china and floor tile. Because of the expense involved in transporting coal to fire the kilns, Morton found he could not compete with potteries of Ohio and New Jersey who were able to utilize locally available natural gas. He was forced to close the plant in 1923.

    Interest is highest in examples with the curdled, two-tone matt glazes, and it is the glaze, not the size or form, that dictates value. The souvenir pieces are not of particularly high quality and tend to be passed over by today's collectors. Our advisors for this category are Suzanne Perrault and David Rago; they are listed in the Directory under New Jersey.

Bowl, gr, artichoke form, E Robertson, #24, 3x4¾" 380.00
Bowl, gr, emb water lily buds & pads, 3¼x10" 480.00
Bowl, gr w/gray streaks, incurvate rim, #2214, 4x11".................... 430.00
Creamer, gr, side hdl, ftd, 4x5" 145.00
Ewer, gr, stylized hdl, ftd, 8"... 110.00
Lamp base, gr, emb Greek Key pattern, 10x9½" 840.00
Lamp base, gr, emb tulips, squat, 6x11½"..............................1,200.00
Lamp base, matt gr, water lilies, wicker/ivory shade, 18½x16" ..1,320.00
Lamp, fairy, gr, squat, loop hdl, w/ribbed frosted shade, #140, 3", EX .400.00
Lamp, table, matt gr, tulips, ldgl shade w/dogwood, 19½x16½".4,200.00
Pitcher, gr, emb leaves/vines, leafy top, vine hdl, #8P/M, 8½x5" .575.00
Pitcher, lt gr matt, flared bottom, emb rim, 12" 570.00
Vase, azure bl w/dk bl speckles, #131, 8x4" 1,150.00
Vase, bl & gr leather-like matt, bulb, 8¾x9¾" 3,500.00
Vase, bl & gr mottle, emb buds at shoulder, bulb, #130, 7¾x7".1,320.00
Vase, bl mottle (volcanic), shouldered, #90, 9" 1,100.00
Vase, bl mottle, shouldered, thick lipped rim, #110/M, 4½" 230.00
Vase, bl, 2 rows emb leaves, #127/M, 8¼" 840.00
Vase, bl, bulb, 5" 180.00
Vase, bl, dandelions emb on feathered cobalt, #464, 6x5" 1,140.00
Vase, bl, emb gr feathers, trumpet neck, #124, 9¼x6½".............1,400.00
Vase, bl/gr (frothy) w/cobalt/apricot shoulder, emb leaves, #98, 7x5" .990.00
Vase, bl/gr (frothy), shouldered, #66, 12¼x5" 900.00
Vase, bl/gr crystalline, emb acanthus leaves, #98, 7" 1,140.00
Vase, bl/gr, organic form w/leafy top, #24, 2¾" 660.00
Vase, bl/gray matt w/glossy int, geometrics at neck, #103, 12" 775.00

Vase, bulbous, with tulips, matt green, 8½x6½", $600.00. (Photo courtesy Rago Arts and Auction Center)

Vase, curdled bl over gr, emb panels, shouldered, #129, 5½x6½"...1,200.00
Vase, gr (flowing), emb panels on melon form, #119, 5" 740.00
Vase, gr (flowing), emb panels, shouldered, #68/M, 8½" 780.00
Vase, gr orange peel, 7" 360.00
Vase, gr, emb Greek Key, cylindrical neck, buttressed hdls, 14¾" ... 1,550.00
Vase, gr, emb leaves, ovoid, #46/H, 3½x3½" 450.00
Vase, gr, emb lilies, trumpet form, disk ft, 15" 845.00
Vase, gr, lg emb leaves, shouldered, tapered bottom, 15x9".......2,500.00

Handel

Philip Handel was best known for the art glass lamps he produced at the turn of the century. His work is similar to the Tiffany lamps of the same era. Handel made gas and electric lamps with both leaded glass and reverse-painted shades. Chipped ice shades with a texture similar to overshot glass were also produced. Shades signed by artists such as Bailey, Palme, and Parlow are highly valued.

Teroma lamp shades were created from clear blown glass blanks that were painted on the interior (reverse painted), while Teroma art glass (the decorative vases, humidors, etc. in the Handel Ware line) is painted on the exterior. This type of glassware has a 'chipped ice' effect achieved by sand blasting and coating the surface with fish glue. The piece is kiln fired at 800 degrees F. The contraction of the glue during the cooling process gives the glass a frosted, textured effect. Some shades are sand finished, adding texture and depth. Both the glassware and chinaware

decorated by Handel are rare and command high prices on today's market. Many of Handel's chinaware blanks were supplied by Limoges.

Key:
chp — chipped/lightly sanded   h/cp — hammered copper

Handel Ware

Unless noted china, all items in the following listing are glass.

Candlestick, Teroma, widmill scene, invt trumpet form, 8½", ea.750.00
Charger, birds of paradise, chipped ice finish on opal glass, 20"..2,000.00
Humidor, bronzed matt, china, #4091/AC, 7" 960.00
Humidor, cigars & horse's head, china, #4091H, pnt losses, 6x3.. 475.00
Humidor, Indian portrait, china, bronze-mtd hinged lid, #89/130, 8". 1,200.00
Jar, Teroma, birds flying in bamboo thicket on dk gr, unmk, 8", VG.2,000.00
Mug, monk reading, red-brn tones on wht china.......................... 350.00
Pitcher, man on horse in landscape, earth tones, china, 6x9" 515.00
Vase, cameo floral, amber to clear, #4258, 11x4½" 1,325.00
Vase, Teroma, autumn trees on textured frost, #4211, 6" 840.00
Vase, Teroma, birds/lg trees, Bragg, #4217, 12x5" 2,100.00
Vase, Teroma, lake scene, #4218, 10".......................................1,900.00
Vase, Teroma, landscape w/trees & birds, sgn Bragg, #4217, 11½" .2,150.00
Vase, Teroma, trees/distant mtns, incurvate cylinder, 8" 1,150.00
Vase, Teroma, trees/foliage, flared cylinder, #4219, 10¾x6¾"....1,800.00

Lamps

Base, bronze maiden holding jug, 3-socket, 24¾x7" 7,800.00
Boudoir, egg form w/HP lady wht crackle #7267-62 shade; wood base, 8"...400.00

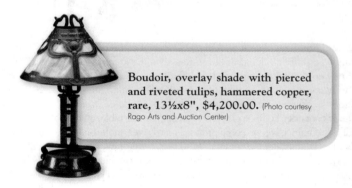

Boudoir, overlay shade with pierced and riveted tulips, hammered copper, rare, 13½x8", $4,200.00. (Photo courtesy Rago Arts and Auction Center)

Boudoir, rvpt 6½" foliage #5512 shade; bronzed std, 14" 6,000.00
Boudoir, rvpt 7" cranes/bamboo #7061 shade; mk bronzed std, 16"..2,800.00
Candlestick, 15½" roses panel #7792 shade; 2-candle base, 20".2,400.00
Chandelier, red/pk roses on amber/opal, 3-socket, 12x25" 8,400.00
Desk, h/cp w/glass panels shade, bronze base, 2 panels cracked, 23x17½".. 1,500.00
Desk, Mosserine 7" shade w/Arts & Crafts floral border; harp std, 19". 1,725.00
Floor, chp 13½" hemispherical shade w/stenciled band; harp fr, 59" ..4,500.00
Floor, gr Mosserine shade on single-socket harp top copper base, 56½x10".2,280.00
Floor, gr Steuben 6x7½" shade; bronze std w/verdigris, 55½" 7,200.00
Floor, o/l 23" panel shade w/leaf decor; re-patinated bronzed std, 64". 6,500.00
Floor, o/l 24" 8-panel Arts & Crafts shade; bronzed std, 65" 5,175.00
Floor, o/l 24½" 8-panel pine trees/needles shade; ribbed std, 65" ...9,200.00
Floor, rvpt 10" floral shade; bronzed harp std, 57"....................2,200.00
Piano, ldgl 7" shade; bronze base adjusts, 9x18"........................4,200.00
Piano, Mosserine 8" brn shade; lily-pad base w/curved arm, 13" .. 800.00
Sconces, yel slag & opal 4" petal shade; bronze mts, 8" from wall, pr.. 1,495.00
Table, brn Mosserine shade; 3-socket bronze, floral band, leaves & buds, 24x18".5,700.00
Table, caramel slag, oak leaf/acorn band, 3-socket, 24x18" 4,200.00
Table, gr Mosserine shade, 2-socket, 21¼x14", EX 2,280.00
Table, ldgl 9" cylindrical shade; arched bronzed base, 15" 960.00

Table, ldgl 19" geometric shade; 4-socket bronze std, 27"............. 600.00
Table, ldgl 24" cattail octagonal shade, 3-socket vase, EX.......36,000.00
Table, mg shade, pk rose o/l, 3-socket ribbed bronze, 23¾x18" .3,900.00
Table, o/l 11½" sq shade w/ivy/berry border, simple std, 19½" ...1,035.00
Table, o/l 16" 7-panel floral shade; 3-socket stick std, 22" 4,025.00
Table, o/l 16½" caramel slag bent-panel shade; bronzed std, 22"....3,675.00
Table, o/l 18" 6-panel shade w/dandelions; bronze-metal std w/tag, 23" ..5,100.00
Table, o/l 20" 8-panel cattail #924457 shade; Nouveau std, 23" ...11,500.00
Table, o/l 20" floral pattern on gr slag shade; 4-socket h/cp std, 28" ...18,000.00
Table, o/l 20" shade w/bellflower border; unmk bronzed std, 23" ...4,600.00
Table, obverse/rvpt 16" scenic #5641 shade; rpt 6-sided std, 24" ...2,875.00
Table, rvpt 11" leafy-decor mushroom #5468 shade; bronze std, 20" ..7,200.00
Table, rvpt 14" roses #6175 shade; unmk bronze std, 20¼"........3,000.00
Table, rvpt 14" roses on yel #6396 shade; bronzed base (crack), 20" ..1,880.00
Table, rvpt 18" cranes/bamboo shade; Asian bronzed std, 24" .18,000.00
Table, rvpt 18" daffodil #7122 shade; bronzed Pat # std, 24" ...13,200.00
Table, rvpt 18" flowers/leaves #5564 shade; bronzed std, 23¾" .16,800.00
Table, rvpt 18" moonlit landscape #6324 shade; bronze std, 23½"....7,200.00
Table, rvpt 18" parrots/floral #7128 shade; mk bronze std, 25" .13,200.00
Table, rvpt 18" roses/butterfly #6688 shade; bronzed std, 23" ..12,000.00
Table, rvpt 18" shade #6529 w/Japanese scene; ribbed/flaring std ... 6,465.00
Table, rvpt 18" Venetian harbor #5935 shade; bronzed unmk std, 25" . 9,600.00
Table, rvpt, Mosserine shade, wreath, 3-socket riveted bronze, 23x17½" .3,900.00
Table, rvpt/chp 18" parrot/tropics #6874P shade; bronze std, 23" .. 12,000.00

Harker

The Harker Pottery was established in East Liverpool, Ohio, in 1840. Their earliest products were yellow ware and Rockingham produced from local clay. After 1900 whiteware was made from imported materials. The plant eventually grew to be a large manufacturer of dinnerware and kitchenware, employing as many as 300 people. It closed in 1972 after it was purchased by the Jeannette Glass Company. Perhaps their best-known lines were their Cameo wares, decorated with white silhouettes in a cameo effect on contrasting solid colors. Floral silhouettes are standard, but other designs were also used. Blue and pink are the most often found background hues; a few pieces are found in yellow. For further information we recommend *Collector's Encyclopedia of American Dinnerware* by Jo Cunningham (Collector Books). Our advisor for this category is Ted Haun; he is listed in the Directory under Indiana.

Amy, bean pot, ind, 2¼" 7.00
Amy, creamer, 6-oz.. 20.00
Amy, c/s, ftd 15.00
Amy, plate, luncheon, 9" 10.00
Amy, rolling pin, 13" 100.00
Apple/Pear, bowl, cereal, red rim, 5⅜" 25.00
Apple/Pear, bowl, swirled, 9" 37.50
Apple/Pear, cheese plate, 11" 50.00
Apple/Pear, cookie jar.. 80.00
Bouquet, c/s... 15.00
Bouquet, plate, luncheon, 9" 9.00
Bouquet, plate, sq, 8½" 7.00
Bridal Rose, creamer 15.00
Bridal Rose, c/s, 2⅝" 15.00
Bridal Rose, plate, luncheon, 9½" 8.00
Bridal Rose, platter, 12¼" L 35.00
Brown-Eyed Susan, plate, bread & butter 6.00
Brown-Eyed Susan, plate, dinner, 10" 9.00
Brown-Eyed Susan, saucer..6.00
Cameo Dainty Flower, ashtray, bl, Virginia shape, 5" 10.00
Cameo Dainty Flower, bowl, vegetable, bl, swirl, 9" 20.00
Cameo Dainty Flower, bowl, yel (rare), 2½x5¾" 45.00

Cameo Dainty Flower, casserole, bl, Zephyr shape, w/lid, 1-qt, 8½" ...100.00
Cameo Dainty Flower, casserole, pk, w/lid & underplate, 5x6⅝" ... 40.00
Cameo Dainty Flower, plate, bl, Virgina shape, 9"........................... 12.00
Cameo Dainty Flower, platter, bl, swirl, 12x9".................................. 20.00
Cameo Dainty Flower, saucer, bl 5.00
Cameo Dainty Flower, sugar bowl, pk, Virginia shape, open 17.00
Cameo Dainty Flower, teapot, bl, Zephyr shape, 4-cup 90.00
Cameo, cup, bl swirl shape, 2½" 12.00
Cameo, plate, bread & butter, bl swirl shape, 6" 3.00
Chesterton, bowl, vegetable, oval, 2⅝x8¾" 35.00
Chesterton, cake lifter, 9¾" 12.00
Chesterton, coffee cup 7.00
Chesterton, platter, 11¾" L 40.00
Chesterton, sauceboat 25.00
Chesterton, snack plate & cup, 9½" 12.00
Garden Trail, coaster, 4¾" 3.00
Garden Trail, plate, bread & butter, 6" 4.00
Ivy Wreath, bowl, coupe soup, 7½" 8.00
Ivy Wreath, bowl, divided vegetable, 10½" 40.00
Magnolia, bowl, vegetable, 8" 30.00
Magnolia, plate, dinner, 10" 12.00
Modern Tulip, bowl, cereal, 6" 10.00
Modern Tulip, cake plate, metal fr 20.00
Modern Tulip, casserole, w/lid, 3¾x7⅜" 75.00
Modern Tulip, c/s 20.00
Modern Tulip, pie serving plate, 9"... 45.00
Modern Tulip, rolling pin, 13"... 85.00
Pate Sur Pate, bowl, fruit, 5½" 7.00
Pate Sur Pate, c/s...5.00
Pate Sur Pate, plate, salad, 7⅜" 6.00
Pate Sur Pate, sugar bowl, w/lid.. 24.00
Petit Point, bowl, lugged cereal, 6⅞" 7.50
Petit Point, bowl, mixing, 9" 35.00
Petit Point, bowl, swirl, 9¼" 25.00
Petit Point, casserole, w/lid, 8½" 50.00
Petit Point, egg cups, dbl, 3¼", set of 4 in metal fr......................... 85.00
Petit Point, plate, dinner, 9¼" 10.00
Petit Point, plate, dinner, 10" 15.00

Petit Point, rolling pin, $65.00 to $75.00.
(Photo courtesy Dargate Auction Gallerie on LiveAuctioneers.com)

Petit Point, salad fork & spoon.. 30.00
Petit Point, teapot... 35.00
Rockingham, pitcher, hound hdl, emb grapevines & hunt scenes, 1800s, 11".. 1,800.00
Snowleaf, plate, salad, 7¼" 6.00
White Rose, bowl, rimmed soup, bl, 7¾" 14.00
White Rose, c/s, bl, 2⅜" 32.00
White Rose, plate, luncheon, 9"... 14.00
White Rose, platter, bl, 14" L 50.00
Woodsong, c/s 20.00
Woodsong, sugar bowl, w/lid 30.00

Hatpins

A hatpin was used to securely fasten a hat to the hair and head of the wearer. Hatpins, measuring from 7" to 12" in length, were worn from approximately 1850 to 1920. During the Art Deco period, hatpins became ornaments rather than the decorative functional jewels that they had been. The hatpin period reached its zenith in 1913 just prior to World War I, which brought about a radical change in women's head-dress and fashion. About that time, women began to scorn the bonnet and adopt 'the hat' as a symbol of their equality. The hatpin was made of every natural and manufactured element in a myriad of designs that challenge the imagination. They were contrived to serve every fashion need and complement the milliner's art. Collectors often concentrate on a specific type: hand-painted porcelains, sterling silver, commemoratives, sporting activities, carnival glass, Art Nouveau and/or Art Deco designs, Victorian gothics with mounted stones, exquisite rhinestones, engraved and brass-mounted escutcheon heads, gold and gems, or simply primitive types made in the Victorian parlor. Some collectors prefer the long pin-shanks while others select only those on tremblants or nodder-type pin-shanks.

For information about the American Hatpin Society, see the Clubs, Newsletters, and Websites section. Our advisor for this category is Virginia Woodbury; she is listed in the Directory under California (SASE required).

Amethyst faceted stones w/foil bks in silver-tone dome fr, 1½".... 250.00
Antiqued brass w/4 faux topaz, 2¾" on brass pin, 1910, $135 to .. 250.00
Baroque MOP w/gold-strap mt, faceted red glass accents, 1½", $85 to.. 100.00
Cabochon garnet tops 1" head, 5½" gilt pin, $110 to 135.00
Green faceted stone amid 15 brilliants, 1x1", brass pin, up to...... 185.00
Ivory hollow-cvd floral 1" head, steel pin, finding unscrews, $225 to.. 300.00
Porcelain disk w/lady transfer, 1½" in 6-prong fr, 1890s 275.00
Porcelian ball w/transfer, gold o/l, 1895, 1¼", $185 to................ 300.00
Satsuma, floral & crane w/gold, brass mts, ca 1900, 1½" oval....... 430.00
Satsuma, HP birds & leaves, 1½", 10½" steel pin, $180 to 295.00

Satsuma, two women, 1¾" diameter, $600.00 to $700.00. (Photo courtesy Virginia Woodbury)

Sterling, Escutcheon, initial E top of head, 1¼x1½", $275 to 350.00
Sterling, lady's head in suffragette cap, repoussé, 1900s, 1", $100 to... 150.00
Sterling, Nouveau stylized lady w/repoussé work, Am, ca 1905, $85 to.. 100.00

Hatpin Holders

Most hatpin holders were made from 1860 to 1920 to coincide with the period during which hatpins were popularly in vogue. The taller types were required to house the long hatpins necessary to secure the large hats that were in style from 1890 to 1914. They were usually porcelain, either decorated by hand or by transfer with florals or scenics, although some were clever figurals. Glass examples are rare, and those of slag or carnival glass are especially valuable.

For information concerning the American Hatpin Society, see the Clubs, Newsletters, and Websites section. Our advisor for this category is Virginia Woodbury; she is listed in the Directory under California (SASE required).

Austria, HP floral w/gold, ca 1899-1918, 4¼" 145.00
Austria, Nouveau gold leaves w/emb swirls, 4x3" 65.00
Bavaria, acorns & leaves on branch, hdls, scalloped top, 4¾" 95.00
Crown China, Austria, mk, 5½", $150 to 200.00
Limoges, classical lady & peacock w/gold, 7-hole, LP, 3⅝"........... 350.00

Nippon, cottage & meadow, gold beading, 5" 95.00
Nippon, roses reserves (2 sides), gold dots, 4-sided, 4¾"................. 60.00
Nippon, violets reserves w/gold, tapered sq, pre-1921, 4¾" 125.00
Noritake, man on camel/palms/desert, HP mk, 4½" 200.00
Northwood, Grape & Cable, amethyst, 6½" 300.00
Northwood, Orange Tree, amethyst carnival, 6½", $180 to 250.00
Royal Bayreuth, clover form, 13-hole, bl mk, 4½x2¼", $375 to... 475.00
Royal Bayreuth, crocus form, 16-hole, bl mk, 1¾", $375 to 475.00
Royal Bayreuth, lady's portrait, 15-hole, bl mk, 4½".................... 450.00
Royal Bayreuth, pk poppy figural w/gold, 4⅜x3⅛" 160.00
Royal Doulton, Ophelia on dk cream, gr trim, 7-hole, 5x3½"...... 285.00

R.S. Prussia, pink and white flowers, 5¼", $350.00. (Photo courtesy Virginia Woodbury)

Schafer & Vater, basket w/roses, hangs/11-hole, 1910s, 6½", $225 to. 275.00
Schafer & Vater, lady cameo, Jasper, hangs, 6-hole, 6¾" 350.00
Silverplated, thistle-cut amethyst, plush cushion, ca 1900, 4½" .. 185.00

Haviland

The Haviland China Company was organized in 1840 by David Haviland, a New York china importer. His search for a pure white, non-porous porcelain led him to Limoges, France, where natural deposits of suitable clay had already attracted numerous china manufacturers. The fine china he produced there was translucent and meticulously decorated, with each piece fired in an individual sagger.

It has been estimated that as many as 60,000 chinaware patterns were designed, each piece marked with one of several company backstamps. 'H. & Co.' was used until 1890 when a law was enacted making it necessary to include the country of origin. Various marks have been used since that time including 'Haviland, France'; 'Haviland & Co. Limoges'; and 'Decorated by Haviland & Co.' Various associations with family members over the years have resulted in changes in management as well as company name. In 1892 Theodore Haviland left the firm to start his own business. Some of his ware was marked 'Mont Mery.' Later logos included a horseshoe, a shield, and various uses of his initials and name. In 1941 this branch moved to the United States. Wares produced here are marked 'Theodore Haviland, N.Y.' or 'Made In America.'

Though it is their dinnerware lines for which they are most famous, during the 1880s and 1890s they also made exquisite art pottery using a technique of underglaze slip decoration called Barbotine, which had been invented by Ernest Chaplet. In 1885 Haviland bought the formula and hired Chaplet to oversee its production. The technique involved mixing heavy white clay slip with pigments to produce a compound of the same consistency as oil paints. The finished product actually resembled oil paintings of the period, the texture achieved through the application of the heavy medium to the clay body in much the same manner as an artist would apply paint to his canvas. Primarily the body used with this method was a low-fired faience, though they also produced stoneware. Numbers in the listings below refer to pattern books by Arlene Schleiger. For further information we recommend *Collector's Encyclopedia of Limoges Porcelain*, by our advisor, Mary Frank Gaston, which offers examples and marks of the Haviland Company.

Bowl, autumn-like floral w/gold, rect, H&Co, 1890s, 9x7½" 175.00
Bowl, brn flowers w/yel trim, scalloped rim, H&Co, 12x8" 95.00
Bowl, dk bl bands on wht w/gold, nut finial on lid, H&Co, 12" ... 475.00
Bowl, lg bl floral w/brn leaves on cream, sq, H&Co, 10" 75.00
Cake plate, Moss Rose center, pk border, H&Co, 9½" 150.00
Chocolate pot, violets, 4 c/s 650.00
Coffeepot, anchor design, braided hdl, H&Co, 9½" 375.00
Coffeepot, rose sprays w/gold, H&Co, 9¾" 350.00
Plate, floral center w/pk border, H&Co, 9½" 100.00
Plate, pk roses scattered, gold scalloped trim, H&Co, 10"............. 50.00
Plate, shellfish, gr floral border w/gold trim, H&Co..................... 225.00
Plate, Silver Anniversary pattern, H&Co, 10" 55.00
Platter, drippings well, gold trim at rim, Theodore, 14x12".......... 350.00
Sugar bowl, Moss Rose w/bl accents, emb ropes, w/lid, H&Co, 7½"..185.00

Tea set, duck figurals, designed by E. Sandoz, $1,250.00. (Photo courtesy Treadway Gallery on LiveAuctioneers.com)

Tureen, sauce/gravy, floral w/gold, w/lid, attached tray, H&Co.... 165.00
Tureen, vegetable, Old Blackberry, w/lid, hdls, H&Co................. 375.00
Vase, morning glories, dbl style w/center hdl, H&Co, 1850s, 6" ...1,400.00

Hawkes Glass

Thomas Gibbons Hawkes and Company (1880 – 1962) established a cut glass factory creating beautiful patterns of cut glass, two of which were awarded the Grand Prize at the Paris Exposition in 1889. His company was known around the world for the finest in cut glass production. Located in Corning, New York, and in business for 82 years, they created a sizable array of stemware, bar accessories, wonderful serving pieces, lamps, vases, picture frames, perfumes, and colognes.

Besides American Brilliant Cut, Hawkes production included engraved, silvered, gilded, enameled, and rare experimental art glass. Hawkes did not make glass, it used blanks from other factories. Decoration was accomplished on clear and colored blanks, and clear blanks decorated with color. Cutting accentuated geometrics and florals. Engraving was done in relief and intaglio (known as and signed 'Gravic,' where the design is below the surface).

Company logos included a 'Hawkes' acid stamp, a trefoil acid stamp enclosing a hawk in each of the two bottom lobes with a fleur-de-lis in the center, and rare paper labels. Many early designs were not signed, and much later Hawkes was not signed.

Their glass caught the attention of world notables, royalty, and presidents. The entourage included Rockefeller, Frick, Armour, Astor, Schwab, Chamberlain, DePew, and Lipton. Other names included Vanderbilt, Childs, the President of Mexico, Gardner, and the Crown Prince of Sweden. Presidents of the United States who ordered and entertained with Hawkes crystal were Grover Cleveland, William McKinley, Benjamin Harrison, Theodore Roosevelt, and Franklin Roosevelt. The 'Venetian' pattern was used in the White House during the Truman and Eisenhower administrations. The most famous piece of Hawkes in the world is the Edenhall Goblet sold in January 2008 by Pook & Pook for $70,200. The goblet shows four engraved panels pertaining to Longfellow's poem 'The Luck of Edenhall.' It is currently owned by Brenda and Chet Cassel.

Values are for signed pieces. Our advisor for this category is John A. Shuman III; you can find him in the Directory under Pennsylvania.

Bottle, perfume, eng florals/garlands, cobalt bl satin, 1910, 4½" .. 200.00
Compote, Russian cut, designed by Phillip McDonald, 4½x10". 1,650.00
Cruet, oil/vinegar, etched, sterling stopper, mk Hawkes Sterling, 7¼" ...90.00
Ice bucket, cut glass, 5 Art Deco panels, silver fr & tongs, 10½".. 175.00
Jug, whiskey, Brazilian, Am Brilliant cut, sterling Gorham top, ca 1874...2,000.00

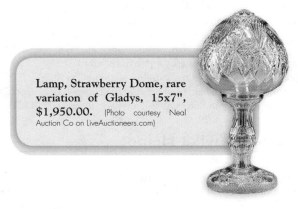

Lamp, Strawberry Dome, rare variation of Gladys, 15x7", $1,950.00. (Photo courtesy Neal Auction Co on LiveAuctioneers.com)

Mayonnaise, floral etching w/word Mayonnaise, 2 hdls, 1900, 4½x4"....275.00
Perfume, Steuben Verre de Soie, guilloche sterling stopper, 5⅝" . 900.00
Pitcher, syrup, Dmn Optic, Sterling & Hawkes, GFH monogram.. 80.00
Plate, North Star, Am Brilliant cut glass, 7" 625.00
Salts (4), sgn, ca 1920s, 1⅞", cup dia 2½", set............................. 150.00
Tantalus, Strawberry Dmn & Fan, w/lock & key 1,500.00
Vase, Aberdeen cut, corset shaped, base sgn, rare, 8⅛" 700.00
Vase, for funeral flowers, acid stamped, 1920s, 16⅞x2½".............. 450.00
Vase, Vict Queens, cut, trumpet shaped on ft, 14x5½" 1,900.00

Head Vases

Vases modeled as heads of lovely ladies, delightful children, clowns, famous people — even some animals — were once popular as flower containers. Today they represent a growing area of collector interest. Most of them were imported from Japan, although some American potteries produced a few as well. If you'd like to learn more about them, we recommend *Head Vases* by Kathleen Cole, *Collecting Head Vases* by David Barron, and *The World of Head Vase Planters* by Mike Posgay and Ian Warner. Our advisor for this category is Larry G. Pogue (L&J Antiques & Collectibles); he is listed in the Directory under Texas.

Baby girl, w/pk bonnet & bodice, Artmark, 6" 95.00
Baby, newborn, bl trim, Hull, 92-USA, 5¾" 75.00
Baby, newborn, upright on pillow, Hull, #92-USA, 5¾" 75.00
Boy, blond, head bowed & hands folded in prayer, Inarco #E1575, 5¾"... 85.00
Girl, polka-dot scarf, Little Miss Dream, #113005, 6", rare 350.00
Girl w/gr leaf on head, scalloped bodice, Velco #6690, 5" 195.00
Girl w/head scarf tied to chin, Velco, #6686, 5½"......................... 175.00
Girl w/umbrella, blond, in aqua plaid, 3½"+umbrella, rare 245.00
Girl w/umbrella, brn hair, bl dress, pearl necklace, 4⅜" 165.00
Girl w/umbrella, head cocked, eyes closed, #52/271, 5" (8" overall) ..195.00
Girl w/umbrella, pigtails, bl & wht, lg scalloped collar, 7" overall. 195.00
Jackie Kennedy, blk gloved, Inarco, #E-1852, c 1964, 6" 995.00
Lady, colonial, wht curls, gold trim, eyes open, Relpo #K1633, 7¼"...320.00
Lady, flat-brim hat (blk) w/perforations, #S673B, 4½" 95.00
Lady, flat-brim hat, updo, hands to cheek & chest, #2703, 6½" ...215.00
Lady, flowery hat, updo, hand to cheek, pearls, Relpo, #K140s, 7" ...275.00
Lady, updo w/hair ornament, neck bow, bl gloved hand, Enesco, 6" ...225.00
Lady w/frosted hair, pearl jewelry, Napcoware, #C6987, 10½", rare ...875.00
Lady w/hand to face, blond, pearl jewelry, unmk (ARDCO), 7½" ..255.00
Lady w/wht gloved hand to face, blond, pearl jewelry, Relpo, #K1633, 7¼"..265.00
Young girl, blond, grn bow & bodice, wht collar, Napcoware, #C8493, 6"..225.00

Young lady, blond w/sunglasses & ponytails, unmk, 7½" 450.00
Young lady, blond, pearl earring, Rubens Orig, Japan, 6" 275.00
Young lady, blond, lg red bow in hair, pearls, Japan, #T-1576, 6" . 225.00
Young lady, brunette, pearl earrings, Napcoware, #C5939, Japan, 6" .. 195.00
Young lady, eyes closed, pageboy hairdo, Napcoware #C6431, 6" . 230.00
Young lady, eyes open, hairbow, pearl earrings, Relpo #K1695, 7"... 295.00
Young lady, eyes open, short hair w/bow, pearls, Napcoware, #C8497, 7".. 270.00
Young lady, eyes open, short hair w/swept bangs, pearls, Ardco, 6".. 180.00
Young lady, frosted hair, head trn, pearls, Napco #C7474, 8½" 325.00
Young lady, glasses on top of head, 2 ponytails, unmk, 7½" 375.00
Young lady, side flip, 2-tiered neck ruffles, Napco #C5939, 6"...... 165.00
Young lady w/ornament in hair, pearl earrings, Inarco, #E-1062, 6½"... 225.00
Young lady w/wht bow in hair, wht collar, #D-3220, 6" 195.00

Otto and Vivika Heino

Born in East Hampton, Connecticut, in 1915, Heino served in the Air Force during WWII. He had always been interested in various crafts, and through the Air Force, he was able to take classes in England, where he learned the basics of silversmithing, painting, and ceramics. He had the oportunity to visit Bernard Leach's studio, where he was fascinated to see the inert clay come to life under the absolute and total control of the potter. Returning to America he met Vivika, the woman who was to become his wife. She was already well advanced in the trade, and Otto became her student. They eventually moved to California and until her passing in 1995 worked together to become a team well known for producing large bowls, vases, bottles, and jars glazed in fantastic textures and rich colors, often decorated with organic forms or calligraphic images.

Otto is still working at his studio in Ojai, California.

Our advisors for this category are Suzanne Perrault and David Rago; they are listed in the Directory under New Jersey. In the listings that follow, all pieces are signed by both Otto and Vivika unless otherwise noted.

Vase, squat, royal blue and gunmetal matt, 3½x4¾", $750.00. (Photo courtesy Rago Arts and Auction Center)

Bowl vase, cvd rings, gold splotches on wht, ftd, 5x6"................. 615.00
Bowl vase, dk gr splotches on brn & wht, 8x11"........................1,560.00
Charger, brn on rust, rnd, 3x12", EX..300.00
Jar, stoneware, no mk (but authenticated), 16x12" 1,200.00
Vase, apple-ash glaze, 6x7½"...1,200.00
Vase, cvd rings, bl splotches on wht, bulb, 4x6" 400.00
Vase, cvd rings, oxblood on gray, bulb, sm neck, 4" 375.00
Vase, cvd rings, volcanic ivory/yel/brn speckle, 7x9"...................960.00
Vase, incised decor, extruding hdls, 12¼x10¼"........................1,200.00
Vase, ridged, ivory/yel/brn volcanic speckle, 7x9" 960.00
Vase, tooled ribs, multi-tone brn clay, sgn by both, 12x12".....$1,000.00

Heintz Art Metal Shop

Founded by Otto L. Heintz in Buffalo, New York, ca 1909, the Heintz Art Metal Shop (HAMS) succeeded the Art Crafts Shop (begun in 1903) and featured a new aesthetic. Whereas the Art Crafts Shop offered products of hammered copper with applied color enamel and with an altogether somewhat cruder or more primitive and medieval-looking appearance, HAMS presented a refined appearance of applied sterling

silver on bronze. Most pieces are stamped with the manufacturer's mark — the letters HAMS conjoined within a diamond, often accompanied by a Aug. 27, 1912, patent date — although paper labels were pasted on the bottom of lamp bases. Original patinas for Heintz pieces include a mottled brown or green (the two most desirable), as well as silver and gold (less desirable). Desk sets and smoking accessories are common; lamps appear less frequently. The firm, like many others, closed in 1930, a victim of the Depression. Silvercrest, also located in Buffalo, produced products similar though not nearly as valuable as Heintz. Please note: Cleaning or scrubbing original patinas will diminish value. Our advisor for this and related Arts & Crafts subjects is Bruce A. Austin; he is listed in the Directory under New York.

Box, enamel on copper, 3½x6¾x4½", VG/EX...........................2,300.00
Candlestick, landscape, 4x3¾" 900.00
Desk set: ink blotter, letter holder, blotter corners & clip 650.00
Inkwell, berries, orig insert, 6¾" 175.00
Lamp, boudoir, poppies, mica-lined shade, 10x9" 1,200.00

Lamp, sterling on bronze, applied floral designs, good original patina, unmarked, 12x9", $880.00. (Photo courtesy Treadway Gallery on LiveAuctioneers.com)

Vase, Art Nouveau floral, shouldered, flared rim, #8791, 12½" 750.00
Vase, evergreen tree, flared bottom, tall cylindrical neck, 7¼" 600.00
Vase, floral, cylindrical, #3724, 4½" 180.00
Vase, Fr Gray Silver patina, Art Nouveau iris, flared neck, 6½"... 175.00
Vase, leaves, #5796B, 8x4" 500.00
Vase, stick neck, disk ft, #3683, 12" 110.00
Vase, tree appl on cylindrical bronze form, 8x3" 1,500.00

Heisey Glass

A.H. Heisey began his long career at the King Glass Company of Pittsburgh. He later joined the Ripley Glass Company which soon became Geo. Duncan and Sons. After Duncan's death Heisey became half-owner in partnership with his brother-in-law, James Duncan. In 1895 he built his own factory in Newark, Ohio, initiating production in 1896 and continuing until Christmas of 1957. At that time Imperial Glass Corporation bought some of the molds. After 1968 they removed the old 'Diamond H' from any they put into use. In 1985 Heisey Collectors of America (HCA) purchased all of Imperial's Heisey molds with the exception of the Old Williamsburg line.

During their highly successful period of production, Heisey made fine handcrafted tableware with simple, yet graceful designs. Early pieces were not marked. After November 1901 the glassware was marked either with the 'Diamond H' or a paper label. Blown ware is often marked on the stem, never on the bowl or foot. For more information we recommend *Heisey Glass, 1896 – 1957*, by Neila and Tom Bredehoft. For information concerning HCA, see the Clubs, Newsletters, and Websites section. See also Glass Animals and Figurines.

Charter Oak, crystal, candleholder, 1-lite, #130 Acorn, ea.......... 150.00
Charter Oak, crystal, plate, #1246 Acorn & Leaves, 10½"............. 30.00

Charter Oak, Flamingo, coaster, #10 Oak Leaf 20.00
Charter Oak, Flamingo, compote, ftd, #3362, 7" 55.00
Charter Oak, Flamingo, tumbler, #3362, 12-oz 20.00
Charter Oak, Hawthorne, bowl, flower, #116 Oak Leaf, 11" 85.00
Charter Oak, Hawthorne, comport, ftd, #3362, 7" 100.00
Charter Oak, Marigold, compote, low ft, #3362, 6" 80.00
Charter Oak, Marigold, sherbet, low ft, #3362, 6-oz 30.00
Charter Oak, Moongleam, candlestick, #116 Oak Leaf, 3", ea 45.00
Charter Oak, Moongleam, comport, ftd, #3362, 7" 70.00
Charter Oak, Moongleam, plate, #1246 Acorn & Leaves, 6" 13.00
Chintz, crystal, bowl, cream soup 18.00
Chintz, crystal, bowl, pickle & olive, 2-part, 13" 15.00
Chintz, crystal, ice bucket, ftd 75.00
Chintz, crystal, pitcher, dophin, ft, 3-pt 200.00
Chintz, crystal, plate, hdls, 12" 25.00
Chintz, crystal, shakers, pr 40.00
Chintz, crystal, tray, celery, 10" 15.00
Chintz, crystal, wine, #3389, 2½-oz 18.00
Chintz, Sahara, bowl, M, ftd, 6" 32.00
Chintz, Sahara, cup 25.00
Chintz, Sahara, pitcher, dolphin ft, 3-pt 300.00
Chintz, Sahara, oyster cocktail, #3389, 4-oz 22.00
Chintz, Sahara, plate, sq or rnd, 6" 15.00
Chintz, Sahara, plate, sq or rnd salad, 7" 18.00
Chintz, Sahara, platter, oval, 14" L 90.00
Chintz, Sahara, tumbler, ftd, #3389, 10-oz 22.00
Crystolite, crystal, basket, 6" 350.00
Crystolite, crystal, bonbon, 7" shell 20.00
Crystolite, crystal, bottle, oil, w/stopper, 2-oz 35.00
Crystolite, crystal, bottle, Rye, #107 stopper, 1-qt 300.00
Crystolite, crystal, bowl, dessert, 5½" 14.00
Crystolite, crystal, bowl, Gardenia, sq, 10" 95.00
Crystolite, crystal, bowl, nut, swan, ind, 2" 20.00
Crystolite, crystal, bowl, punch, 7½-qt 120.00
Crystolite, crystal, bowl, shell praline, 7" 35.00
Crystolite, crystal, bowl, w/attached mayo/chip-n-dip, 11" 140.00
Crystolite, crystal, cheese dish, ftd, 5½" 20.00
Crystolite, crystal, cocktail shaker, w/#1 strainer, #86 stopper, 1-qt .. 350.00
Crystolite, crystal, jam jar, w/lid 50.00
Crystolite, crystal, mustard, w/lid 45.00

Crystolite, crystal, pitcher, ice lip, #1503, blown, ½-gallon, $100.00. (Photo courtesy Apple Tree Auction Center on LiveAuctioneers.com

Crystolite, crystal, pitcher, swan hdl, 2-qt 600.00
Crystolite, crystal, plate, cake salver, ftd, 11" 450.00
Crystolite, crystal, plate, coupe, 7½" 40.00
Crystolite, crystal, plate, sandwich, 14" 45.00
Crystolite, crystal, puff box, w/lid, 4¾" 60.00
Crystolite, crystal, shakers, pr 30.00
Crystolite, crystal, syrup, Drip-Cup 135.00
Crystolite, crystal, tray, relish, 3-part, oval, 12" 35.00
Crystolite, crystal, tumbler, blown, 8-oz 25.00
Crystolite, crystal, vase, 12" 225.00
Empress, Alexandrite, ashtray 200.00
Empress, Alexandrite, bowl, floral, dolphin ft, 11" 400.00

Empress, Alexandrite, bowl, relish, 3-part, 7" 175.00
Empress, Alexandrite, candlestick, #135, 6" 275.00
Empress, Alexandrite, cup 115.00
Empress, Alexandrite, mayonnaise, ftd, w/ladle, 5½" 300.00
Empress, Alexandrite, saucer 25.00
Empress, cobalt, plate, sq, 7" 60.00
Empress, Flamingo, bowl, cream soup 30.00
Empress, Flamingo, cup, bouillon, hdls 35.00

Empress, Flamingo, mustard jar, #1401, $75.00. (Photo courtesy Apple Tree Auction Center on LiveAuctioneers.com)

Empress, Moongleam, bonbon, 6" 30.00
Empress, Moongleam, plate, 7" 17.00
Empress, Moongleam, tray, hors d'oeuvres, 7-part, 10" 200.00
Empress, Sahara, candy dish, dolphin ft, 6" 150.00
Empress, Sahara, saucer champagne, 4-oz 40.00
Empress, Sahara, vase, flared, 8" 150.00
Greek Key, crystal, bowl, banana split, 9" 45.00
Greek Key, crystal, butter dish, hdls 200.00
Greek Key, crystal, claret, 4½-oz 140.00
Greek Key, crystal, compote, 5" 75.00
Greek Key, crystal, hair receiver 170.00
Greek Key, crystal, ice tub, lg, tab hdl 150.00
Greek Key, crystal, ice tub, sm, tabl hdl 130.00
Greek Key, crystal, jar, crushed fruit w/cover, 1-qt 400.00
Greek Key, crystal, jar, pickle, w/knob lid 160.00
Greek Key, crystal, nappy, 4½" 25.00
Greek Key, crystal, plate, 5" 18.00
Greek Key, crystal, plate, 6" 30.00
Greek Key, crystal, shakers, pr 135.00
Greek Key, crystal, sherbet, shallow, ftd, 4½-oz 20.00
Greek Key, crystal, spooner, lg 110.00
Greek Key, crystal, sugar bowl 50.00
Greek Key, crystal, toothpick holder 900.00
Greek Key, crystal, tray, celery, 9" L 50.00
Greek Key, crystal, tumbler, flared rim, 7-oz 60.00
Greek Key, crystal, tumbler, str sides, 10-oz 90.00
Greek Key, crystal, vase, whimsey 165.00
Greek Key, crystal, wine, 2-oz 100.00
Ipswich, cobalt, bowl, flower, ftd, 11" 400.00
Ipswich, crystal, cocktail shaker, w/strainer & #86 stopper, 1-qt .. 225.00
Ipswich, crystal, plate, sq, 8" 35.00
Ipswich, crystal, tumbler, ftd, 8-oz 30.00
Ipswich, Flamingo, creamer 70.00
Ipswich, Flamingo, oyster cocktail, ftd, 4-oz 60.00
Ipswich, Flamingo, sugar bowl 70.00
Ipswich, Moongleam, candy jar, w/lid, ½-lb 500.00
Ipswich, Moongleam, finger bowl, w/underplate 100.00
Ipswich, Moongleam, goblet, knob in stem, 10-oz 150.00
Ipswich, Moongleam, pitcher, ½-gal 950.00
Ipswich, Moongleam, tumbler, ftd, 5-oz 85.00
Ipswich, Sahara, bottle, oil, ftd, w/#86 stopper, 2-oz 275.00
Ipswich, Sahara, creamer 90.00
Ipswich, Sahara, tumbler, cupped rim, 10-oz 100.00

Kalonyal, crystal, bottle, oil, 4-oz 100.00
Kalonyal, crystal, bowl, punch, w/stand, 12" 250.00
Kalonyal, crystal, bowl, shallow, 9" 65.00
Kalonyal, crystal, burgundy, 3-oz 50.00
Kalonyal, crystal, celery, tall 100.00
Kalonyal, crystal, celery tray, 12" 55.00
Kalonyal, crystal, claret, 5-oz 85.00
Kalonyal, crystal, compote, 8" 225.00
Kalonyal, crystal, cup, punch, 3½-oz 30.00
Kalonyal, crystal, mug, 8-oz 175.00
Kalonyal, crystal, plate, 6" 35.00
Kalonyal, crystal, sherbet, ftd, 6-oz 40.00
Kalonyal, crystal, sugar bowl, tall 95.00
Kalonyal, crystal, toothpick 375.00
Kalonyal, crystal, tumbler, 8-oz 95.00
Lariat, crystal, basket, ftd, 10" 125.00
Lariat, crystal, bowl, cream soup, hdls 40.00
Lariat, crystal, bowl, salad, 10½" 35.00
Lariat, crystal, candlestick, 3-lite, ea 30.00
Lariat, crystal, cigarette box 40.00
Lariat, crystal, creamer 12.00
Lariat, crystal, ice tub 75.00
Lariat, crystal, oyster cocktail, 4½-oz 10.00
Lariat, crystal, plate, 7" 12.00
Lariat, crystal, plate, buffet, 21" 70.00
Lariat, crystal, plate, cookie, 11" 25.00
Lariat, crystal, plate, sandwich, hdls, 14" 40.00
Lariat, crystal, platter, 15" L 50.00
Lariat, crystal, sherbet, low, 6-oz 5.00
Lariat, crystal, sugar bowl 12.00
Lariat, crystal, tumbler, blown, 5-oz 18.00
Lariat, crystal, urn, w/lid, 12" 140.00
Lariat, crystal, vase, swung 125.00
Lariat, crystal, wine, blown, 2½-oz 15.00
Minuet, crystal, bowl, sauce, ftd, 7½" 70.00
Minuet, crystal, candelabrum, 1-lite, w/prisms, ea 110.00

Minuet, crystal, candle vase with inserts, #1511 Toujours, pair $400.00. (Photo courtesy Apple Tree Auction Center on LiveAuctioneers.com)

Minuet, crystal, compote, #5010, 5½" 40.00
Minuet, crystal, cup 25.00
Minuet, crystal, mayonnaise, dolphin ft, 5½" 50.00
Minuet, crystal, plate, service, 10½" 120.00
Minuet, crystal, plate, snack, w/#1477 center, 16" 80.00
Minuet, crystal, shakers, #10, pr 125.00
Minuet, crystal, sherbet, ftd, #5010, 6-oz 18.00
Minuet, crystal, sugar bowl, ind, #1509 Queen Ann 38.00
Minuet, crystal, vase, #4192, 10" 110.00
New Era, crystal, ashtray 40.00
New Era, crystal, candelabra, 2-lite, w/#4044 bobeche & prisms, ea.... 90.00
New Era, crystal, claret, 4-oz 15.00
New Era, crystal, pilsner, 8-oz 25.00
New Era, crystal, plate, 9x7" 25.00
New Era, crystal, sherbet, ftd, 6-oz 10.00
New Era, crystal, sugar bowl 38.00

New Era, crystal, tumbler, ftd, 8-oz 11.00
New Era, crystal, wine, 3-oz 22.00
Octagon, crystal, bowl, vegetable, 9" 15.00
Octagon, crystal, cup, AD 10.00
Octagon, crystal, plate, 6" 4.00
Octagon, crystal, plate, muffin, #1229, 12" 20.00
Octagon, crystal, sugar bowl, #500 .... 10.00
Octagon, Flamingo, basket, #500, 5" 300.00
Octagon, Flamingo, bowl, #1203, 12" 55.00
Octagon, Flamingo, cup, #1231 .... 15.00
Octagon, Flamingo, mayonnaise, ftd, #1229, 5½" 25.00
Octagon, Flamingo, platter, 12" L 25.00
Octagon, Hawthorne, bonbon, upturned sides, #1229, 6" 35.00
Octagon, Hawthorne, cheese dish, #1229, hdls, 6" 15.00
Octagon, Hawthorne, ice tub, #500 .... 180.00
Octagon, Hawthorne, plate, 14" 50.00
Octagon, Marigold, bowl, M, #1229, 6" 30.00
Octagon, Moongleam, bowl, cream soup, hdls 30.00
Octagon, Moongleam, candlestick, 1-lite, 3", ea 40.00

Octagon, Moongleam, ice tub with silver-plated handle and tongs, #500, $170.00. (Photo courtesy Apple Tree Auction Center on LiveAuctioneers.com)

Octagon, Moongleam, plate, 8" 15.00
Octagon, Moongleam, saucer, AD 10.00
Octagon, Sahara, bowl, cream soup, hdls 25.00
Octagon, Sahara, compote, #1229, 8" 35.00
Octagon, Sahara, ice tub, #500 .... 120.00
Octagon, Sahara, plate, hors d'oeuvres, #1229, 13" 80.00
Old Sandwich, cobalt, candlestick, 6", ea 250.00
Old Sandwich, cobalt, tumbler, ftd, 12-oz 45.00
Old Sandwich, crystal, bottle, condiment, w/#3 stopper 60.00
Old Sandwich, crystal, creamer, 12-oz 32.00
Old Sandwich, crystal, shakers, pr 40.00
Old Sandwich, Flamingo, bottle, oil, w/#85 stopper, 2½-oz 140.00
Old Sandwich, Flamingo, bowl, flower, ftd, oval, 12" 50.00
Old Sandwich, Flamingo, cup 65.00
Old Sandwich, Flamingo, wine, 2½-oz 45.00
Old Sandwich, Moongleam, beer mug, 12-oz 250.00
Old Sandwich, Moongleam, cigarette holder 100.00
Old Sandwich, Moongleam, pilsner, 10-oz 42.00
Old Sandwich, Moongleam, plate, sq, 8" 32.00
Old Sandwich, Sahara, bowl, popcorn, cupped, ftd 110.00
Old Sandwich, Sahara, decanter, w/#98 stopper, 1-pt 200.00
Old Sandwich, Sahara, pitcher, w/ice lip, ½-gal 165.00
Old Sandwich, Sahara, sundae, 6-oz 30.00
Pleat & Panel, crystal, bowl, bouillon, hdls, 5" 7.00
Pleat & Panel, crystal, creamer, hotel 10.00
Pleat & Panel, crystal, plate, 7" 4.00
Pleat & Panel, Flamingo, cheese & cracker, 10" 75.00
Pleat & Panel, Flamingo, marmalade, 4¾" 30.00
Pleat & Panel, Flamingo, nappy, 4½" 11.00
Pleat & Panel, Flamingo, plate, 10¾" 48.00
Pleat & Panel, Flamingo, tumbler, 8-oz 17.50

Pleat & Panel, Moongleam, bowl, chow chow, 4" 14.00
Pleat & Panel, Moongleam, oil bottle.. 60.00
Pleat & Panel, Moongleam, pitcher, w/ice lip, 3-pt..................... 165.00
Pleat & Panel, Moongleam, plate, 7" 10.00
Pleat & Panel, Moongleam, vase, 8" 100.00
Provincial/Whirlpool, crystal, bowl, punch, 5-qt............................ 80.00
Provincial/Whirlpool, crystal, butter dish.. 65.00
Provincial/Whirlpool, crystal, creamer, ftd 12.00
Provincial/Whirlpool, crystal, nappy, 5½"....................................... 15.00
Provincial/Whirlpool, crystal, plate, torte, 14" 30.00
Provincial/Whirlpool, Limelight Gr, mayonnaise, 3-pc, 7" 150.00
Provincial/Whirlpool, Limelight Gr, plate, buffet, 18" 250.00
Provincial/Whirlpool, Limelight Gr, tumbler, ftd, 9-oz 75.00

Provincial/Whirlpool, Zircon (early issue), footed candy, $400.00. [Photo courtesy Apple Tree Auction Center on LiveAuctioneers.com]

Ridgeleigh, crystal, ashtray, 4" 22.00
Ridgeleigh, crystal, bowl, centerpiece, 11" 50.00
Ridgeleigh, crystal, bowl, fruit, flared, 12" 50.00
Ridgeleigh, crystal, bowl, jelly, hdls, 6" 20.00
Ridgeleigh, crystal, bowl, lemon, w/lid, 5" 50.00
Ridgeleigh, crystal, candlestick, 1-lite, 2", ea 25.00
Ridgeleigh, crystal, cocktail, pressed 16.00
Ridgeleigh, crystal, cordial, blown, 1-oz 140.00
Ridgeleigh, crystal, creamer... 15.00
Ridgeleigh, crystal, goblet, pressed, 9-oz 30.00
Ridgeleigh, crystal, oyster cocktail, pressed..................................... 24.00
Ridgeleigh, crystal, plate, hors d'oeuvres, oval............................... 800.00
Ridgeleigh, crystal, plate, rnd, 8" 18.00
Ridgeleigh, crystal, plate, salver, 14" 35.00
Ridgeleigh, crystal, plate, sq, 8" 30.00
Ridgeleigh, crystal, saucer champagne, blown, 5-oz...................... 25.00
Ridgeleigh, crystal, shakers, pr.. 45.00
Ridgeleigh, crystal, tumbler, pressed, ftd, 12-oz 50.00
Ridgeleigh, crystal, vase, 8" 75.00
Saturn, crystal, bowl, flower, 13" 37.00
Saturn, crystal, bowl, pickle, 7" 25.00
Saturn, crystal, cup 10.00
Saturn, crystal, pitcher, blown, w/ice lip, 70-oz............................. 65.00
Saturn, crystal, plate, 8"... 8.00
Saturn, Limelight, creamer.. 160.00
Saturn, Limelight, cup.. 135.00
Saturn, Limelight, s&p 600.00
Saturn, Limelight, saucer.. 25.00
Saturn, Zircon Limelight, bottle, oil, 3-oz....................................... 500.00
Saturn, Zircon Limelight, nappy, 5" 90.00
Stanhope, crystal, bowl, M, hdls, 6" 35.00
Stanhope, crystal, creamer, hdl... 35.00
Stanhope, crystal, nappy, hdl, 4½" 30.00
Stanhope, crystal, relish, 4-part, hdls, 12" 55.00
Stanhope, crystal, vase, ball form, 7".. 100.00
Sunburst, crystal, bowl, 7" L 35.00
Sunburst, crystal, bowl, 10" 50.00

Sunburst, crystal, bowl, punch, w/stand, 15"................................... 275.00
Sunburst, crystal, bowl, scalloped rim, 4½" 15.00
Sunburst, crystal, compote, 6"... 45.00
Sunburst, crystal, creamer, ind.. 45.00
Sunburst, crystal, goblet.. 150.00
Sunburst, crystal, pitcher, bulb, 3-pt... 150.00
Sunburst, crystal, sugar bowl, lg... 45.00
Sunburst, crystal, vase, orchid, 6".. 125.00
Twist, Alexandrite, bowl, flower, 4-ftd, oval, 12".......................... 550.00
Twist, Alexandrite, ice bucket, metal hdl 480.00
Twist, crystal, bowl, flower, 9".. 25.00
Twist, crystal, ice bucket, w/metal hdl.. 95.00
Twist, crystal, mustard, w/lid & spoon 40.00
Twist, crystal, oyster cocktail, ftd, 3-oz 10.00
Twist, crystal, plate, 10½"... 40.00
Twist, Flamingo, bowl, hdls, 6" 20.00
Twist, Flamingo, cup, zigzag hdls 25.00
Twist, Flamingo, platter, 12" L.. 45.00
Twist, Marigold, plate, 8" 30.00
Twist, Marigold, tray, celery, 13".. 40.00
Twist, Marigold, wine, 2-block stem, 2½-oz 80.00
Twist, Moongleam, cocktail shaker, metal top 900.00
Twist, Moongleam, relish, 3-part, 13" 22.00
Twist, Moongleam, tumbler, ftd, 12-oz 50.00
Twist, Sahara, bowl, cream soup 40.00
Twist, Sahara, tray, celery, 10".. 35.00
Vict, crystal, bowl, rose 80.00
Vict, crystal, decanter w/stopper, 32-oz 70.00
Vict, crystal, plate, 8".. 20.00
Vict, crystal, shakers, pr... 65.00
Vict, crystal, vase, 4" 45.00
Waverly, crystal, bowl, fruit, 9"... 25.00
Waverly, crystal, box, chocolate, w/lid, 5".. 50.00
Waverly, crystal, candleholder, 3-lite, ea 60.00
Waverly, crystal, cheese dish, ftd, 5½".. 20.00
Waverly, crystal, vase, ftd, 7".. 25.00
Yeoman, crystal, bottle, cologne, w/stopper 60.00
Yeoman, Flamingo, creamer... 25.00
Yeoman, Flamingo, marmalade.. 35.00
Yeoman, Hawthorne, plate, 6"... 10.00
Yeoman, Hawthorne, saucer, AD 10.00
Yeoman, Marigold, gravy boat, w/underplate................................... 45.00
Yeoman, Marigold, pitcher, 1-qt... 160.00
Yeoman, Moongleam, cruet, oil, 4-oz 60.00
Yeoman, Sahara, cup.. 15.00

Herend

Herend, Hungary, was the center of a thriving pottery industry as early as the mid-1800s. Decorative items as well as tablewares were made in keeping with the styles of the times. One of the factories located in this area was founded by Moritz Fisher, who often marked his wares with a cojoined MF. Items described in the following listings may be marked simply Herend, indicating the city, or with a manufacturer's backstamp.

Dinnerware

Blue Garland, c/s, flat or ftd, 2⅛" 100.00
Blue Garland, plate, dinner, #1524, 10¼" 75.00
Chanticleer, dish, shell-shaped, 8¾" 180.00
Chanticleer, plate, salad, 7½" 75.00
Chanticleer, plate, serving, w/bamboo hdls...................................... 65.00
Chinese Bouquet, bowl, vegetable, 8" 80.00

Chinese Bouquet, coffeepot, cr/sug w/lid, oval 16" tray 270.00
Chinese Bouquet, creamer, 6-oz 60.00
Chinese Bouquet, plate, dinner, 10½" 70.00
Chinese Bouquet, plate, salad, 7½" 40.00
Coronation, saucer 25.00
Floral pattern, HP/gilt trim, #7369, ca 1950s, 10", 4 for 425.00
Fortuna, cup, 2" 45.00
Fortuna, tureen, w/lid 750.00
Indian Basket, cake plate, 13" 195.00
Indian Basket, creamer, 3⅞" 60.00
Indian Basket, c/s, 2" 105.00
Indian Basket, plate, crescent salad, 7⅜" 75.00
Lindsay, plate, dinner, 10⅜" 57.50
Peach Tree, covered dish, 4½" 55.00
Queen Victoria, bowl, dessert, 6" 55.00
Queen Victoria, cup, 2" 75.00
Queen Victoria, platter, 17" L 300.00
Queen Victoria, teapot 300.00
Red Dynasty, tureen, ornate leaf finial, w/hdls & underplate, 11" L ... 830.00
Rothschild Bird, bowl, cranberry, 5" 98.00
Rothschild Bird, bowl, cream soup, 2½" 112.00
Rothschild Bird, bowl, rimmed soup, 8" 82.00
Rothschild Bird, bowl, salad, 10½" 200.00
Rothschild Bird, cake plate, 10½" 180.00
Rothschild Bird, egg cup, dbl, 4" 60.00
Rothschild Bird, marmalade, w/lid & underplate, 5" 100.00
Rothschild Bird, plate, salad, 7½" 60.00
Rothschild Bird, plate, serving, 11" 115.00
Rothschild Bird, serving dish 200.00
Rothschild Bird, tureen, #1021/RO 200.00
Rothschild Bird, tureen, bird finial on lid, ftd, w/hdls, 9x13" 1,125.00
Rothschild Bird, tureen, ftd, w/hdls & lid, 15" L, +18" underplate .900.00
Rothschild Bird, undertray, 12½" 200.00

Miscellaneous

Figurine, Cleopatra being bitten by asp, 10" 395.00
Figurine, ducks (2) conjoined, mc w/gilt beaks, 10x15" 935.00

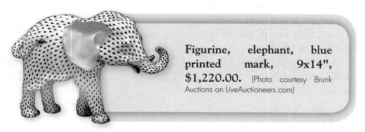

Figurine, elephant, blue printed mark, 9x14", $1,220.00. (Photo courtesy Brunk Auctions on LiveAuctioneers.com)

Figurine, flamingo, rust, #VH-15881, 10" 900.00
Figurine, lion & lioness, rust fishnet on wht, 7x9" 700.00
Figurine, nude female astride horse, wht, 15x17" 685.00
Figurine, nude kneeling w/gr robe at side, #5707, 13¼" 285.00
Figurine, rabbit, rust fishnet on wht, w/gold nose & ft, 12¼" 750.00
Figurine, rooster, aqua tones & fishnet, w/gold, #5030, 16x13½" .700.00
Figurine, toucan on branch, #MCD-15858, 8½x7" 835.00
Lamp, Rothschild Bird, electric, rtcl base, w/gold, 15" 800.00
Stein, rtcl pk & wht design, serpent hdl & finial, ftd, 12" 940.00
Vase, HP butterfly & floral on wht, w/gold trim, slim neck, 19" ...625.00

Heubach

Gebruder Heubach is a German company that has been in operation since the 1800s, producing quality bisque figurines and novelty items. It

is perhaps most famous for its doll heads and piano babies, most of which are marked with the circular rising sun device containing an 'H' super-imposed over a 'C.' Items with arms and hands positioned away from the body are more valuable, and color of hair and intaglio eyes affect price as well. Our advisor for this category is Grace Ochsner; she is listed in the Directory under Illinois. See also Dolls, Heubach.

Baby boy in sundress and oversize shoes, 14½", $965.00. (Photo courtesy Philip Weiss Auctions on LiveAuctioneers.com)

Baby girl seated in red-orange bonnet pulling off socks, 6" 325.00
Baby in gr tub w/1 ft in mouth, 4½x5½" 500.00
Baby playing w/toes, 7½x13" 900.00
Baby seated w/ft X, intaglio eyes, 11", $500 to 650.00
Baby sitting, detailed dress, intaglio eyes, 2 teeth, 8½", NM 725.00
Baby, chewing on toes, #4862, 7x8", EX 800.00
Box, boy wrapped in lettered banner atop book w/alphabet design, 7"...315.00
Boy (bust) leaning on tree branch w/hands cupping face, 7" 315.00
Boy in nightshirt w/pug dog, 7", $1,500 to 1,700.00
Boy in suit & hat seated, 5" 425.00
Boy seated on stool, intaglio eyes, #30//15, 16½", EX 450.00
Bulldog seated on basket (bed) w/blanket, head tilted, 7" 150.00
Cat sleeping, wht w/mc circles on turq collar, 6" L 140.00
Dog in baby's 'knitted' bonnet w/turq ribbons, 2½x3½" 65.00
Dutch boy & girl seated, intaglio eyes, 7", pr 400.00
Dutch boy holding cap to head, 6", $300 to 400.00
Girl seated in bonnet w/arms X at wrists & head tilted, 4" 315.00
Santa sitting on log (candy container), bl intaglio eyes, 8x6" 850.00

Higgins Glass

Acclaimed contemporary glass artists Frances and Michael Higgins founded their Chicago-area studio in 1948. The Higginses are credited with rediscovering and refining the ancient craft of glass fusing, resulting in 'modern miracles with everyday glass.'

Essentially, fusing can be described as the creation of a 'glass sand-wich.' On one piece of enamel-coated glass, a design is either drawn with colored enamels or pieced with glass segments. Over this, another piece of enameled glass is laid. Placed on a mold, the object is then heated. Under heat the glass 'slumps' into the shape of the mold. The design is fused between the outer glass pieces with additional layers often adding to the texture and color complexity.

The Higginses applied their fusing technique to everything from tableware such as bowls, plates, and candleholders, to ashtrays, jewelry, vases, mobiles, sculptures, lamps, clocks, and even 'rondelay' room divid-ers. Higgins buyers in the 1950s were immediately attracted to the novelty of fused glass, the colorful 'modern' designs, and the variety of items avail-able. Today, collectors can also appreciate the artistry and skill involved in the creation of Higgins glass and the imaginative genius of its makers.

In 1957, Michael and Frances Higgins became associated with Dear-born Glass Company of Chicago. Dearborn marketed Higgins designs to a mass audience, greatly increasing the couple's 'brand-name' recognition. Following a brief association in 1965 with Haeger Potteries, the Higginses opened their own studio in Riverside, Illinois. Michael Higgins died in 1999, Frances Higgins in 2004. The studio continues today under the direction of their longtime associates and designated successors, Louise and Jonathan Wimmer, still creating glass objects in the distinctive Higgins style.

Higgins pieces are readily identifiable by an almost-always-present lower-case signature. From 1948 until 1957, pieces were engraved on the reverse with the name 'higgins,' or the complete artist name. In 1951, a raised 'dancing man' logo was also added. Dearborn and Haeger pieces (1957 – 1965) are denoted either by a gold 'higgins' signature on the surface or by a signature in the colorway. Since 1966 the marking has been an engraved 'higgins' on the reverse, sometimes accompanied by the artist's name. Following the death of Frances Higgins, pieces have been signed 'higgins studio.'

The Higgins Glass Studio is located at 33 East Quincy Street, Riverside, IL 60546 (708-447-2787, www.higginsglass.com). For more information we recommend *Higgins: Adventures in Glass*, and *Higgins: Poetry in Glass* (Schiffer), both by Donald-Brian Johnson (our advisor) and Leslie Piña. Mr. Johnson is listed in the Directory under Nebraska.

Sculpture, Blue Fish on Red Sea (Michael Higgins), 10x16", $4,000.00 to $4,500.00. (Photo by Leslie Piña)

Ashtray, Clocks (Watches), rect, 10x14", $150 to	175.00
Ashtray, She Loves Me, 10x14", $150 to	175.00
Bowl, Arabesque Apple, 12¼", $275 to	300.00
Bowl, Buttercup, 6", $100 to	125.00
Bowl, clear w/red circles (Frances Higgins), 1960s, 8", $350 to	400.00
Bowl, Country Garden, 17", $600 to	625.00
Bowl, Sunburst, 8¼", $225 to	250.00
Console set, wood/wireware/glass, 12x13" bowl, 13½" candles	3,750.00
Dessert set, mauve-pk, w/branch outlines in blk & gold, set $1,750 to	2,000.00
Dish, Red Velvet (Frances Higgins), multi-layer, 10" sq, $4,250 to	4,500.00
Jewelry, pendant/earrings, cement/jewels (Frances Higgins)	725.00
Mobile, trees w/sky arch (Jonathan/Louise Wimmer), 18x15"	475.00
Mobile, 8 birds w/egg, 4'2", $500 to	550.00
Ornament, Butterfly, $50 to	75.00
Plaque, Fall Frammie (Frances Higgins) 24k gold top, 14x12", $3,500 to	3,750.00
Plaque, Spring Tree Frammie (Frances Higgins), 15" sq, $3,000 to	3,250.00
Plate, Blk & Bl (Michael Higgins, Frances Higgins fr) 13" sq, $3,750 to	4,000.00
Plate, Bl Shards, unique pattern composite, 13", $1,000 to	1,250.00
Plate, Carousel, red, gray & blk, 16¾", $525 to	575.00
Plate, People (Michael Higgins & Jonathan Wimmer), 17", $2,750 to	3,000.00
Platter, Dimples (Michael Higgins), 15", $,2000 to	2,250.00
Platter, King (Michael Higgins), 11", $1,500 to	1,750.00
Rondelays, daisy decor w/winegold luster, 9", ea $150 to	200.00
Sculpture, 5 layers, design on ea layer (Jonathan Wimmer), 15" sq, $2,750 to	3,000.00
Sculpture, Bl Angel on Brass Stand, 15½", $400 to	450.00
Sculpture, Bubbles (F Higgins), circles/foam, brass stand, 13", $1,500	1,700.00
Sculpture, Martini Glass (Frances Higgins) glass/cement, 12x7", $1,750 to	2,000.00
Server, 6-pocket, Delphinium Bl, 18" dia, $400 to	600.00
Treasure Chest (Michael Higgins), 18x13x9", $8,000 to	8,500.00
Vase, Dropout style (Frances Higgins), oval w/glass chip on rim, 4", $350 to	400.00

Hilton Pottery

The Hilton family was involved in pottery making in the Catawaba Valley of North Carolina as early as the end of the Civil War. The branch responsible for items marked 'Hilton' was established in 1935 by Ernest Hilton in Marion. The wares they produced were of the typical 'Jugtown' variety, high glazed and hand thrown. Ernest died in 1948, and the pottery closed in 1953.

Ashtray, squirrel eating nut by branch in bowl, gr/cream, 2x4¾"	400.00
Figurine, lady holding bag, repair to hat brim, unsgn, 7¾"	1,320.00
Figurine, lady w/vessel & shawl, brn tones, 7¾"	1,325.00
Flower frog, cobalt, 5½x4½"	120.00
Leaf dish, appl acorn & & twig hdl, speckled gr, Mrs FW Hilton, 6½"	660.00

Pitcher, applied dogwood, 6¼", $565.00. (Photo courtesy Brunk Auctions on LiveAuctioneers.com)

Pitcher, lamb on speckled brn, att Maude Hilton, 3", EX	230.00
Vase, cabin scenic, Clara Hilton, rpr, 10"	480.00
Vase, mtn scenic, earth tones & bl, Ernest & Clara Hilton, 7¼"	450.00
Wall pocket, yel buff w/emb Y symbols at rim, 7x3"	390.00

Historical Glass

Glassware commemorating particularly significant historical events became popular in the late 1800s. Bread trays were the most common form, but plates, mugs, pitchers, and other items were also pressed in clear as well as colored glass. It was sold in vast amounts at the 1876 Philadelphia Centennial Exposition by various manufacturers who exhibited their wares on the grounds. It remained popular well into the twentieth century.

In the listings that follow, L numbers refer to a book by Lindsey, a standard guide used by many collectors. Our advisor for this category is Darlene Yohe; she is listed in the Directory under Arkansas. See also Bread Plates and Trays; Pattern Glass.

Ale glass, Mephistopheles	95.00
Bank, Liberty Bell	38.00
Bottle, Granger, L-266	110.00
Bowl, berry, Lindbergh, sm	15.00
Butter dish, Am Shield	195.00
Butter dish, Log Cabin	325.00
Celery vase, Lincoln Drape	80.00
Egg cup, Lincoln Drape	50.00
Goblet, Grand Army of the Republic (GAR) Encampment	165.00
Goblet, Knights of Labor	175.00
Goblet, Pittsburgh Centennial	95.00
Lamp, Emblem, L-62	195.00
Match safe, Jenny Lind	250.00
Mug, beer, Philadelphia Centennial	65.00
Mug, Columbus bust, Fostoria, 2½"	125.00
Mug, Columbus Landing	65.00
Mug, Garfield & Lincoln, Adams & Co, Our Country's Martyrs	65.00

Mug, Independence Hall, Boston & Sandwich, Philadelphia Centennial ..50.00
Mug, Knights of Labor, Central Glass, 4¾" or 6½", ea.................. 150.00
Mug, Protection & Plenty 50.00
Mug, shaving, Garfield & Lucretia Randolf Garfield, mg, 6"........ 250.00
Mustard dish, Dewey bust, Xd flags on lid, mg, 4¼" 55.00
Pitcher, Admiral Dewey, Gridly You May Fire..., 9¼" 140.00
Pitcher, Garfield Drape, scarce 145.00
Plate, Admiral Dewey, clear/frosted, sm 15.00
Plate, Battleship Maine, openwork border, 5½" 16.00
Plate, Columbus, mg, L-7 .... 65.00
Plate, For President Winfield D Hancock, 8" 110.00
Plate, Garfield, 101 border.. 80.00
Plate, Garfield, Alphabet, 7" 75.00
Plate, Grant, Let Us Have Peace, Maple Leaf by Gillinder & Sons, 10½" ...75.00
Plate, Grant, Patriot & Soldier, amber, sq, 9½" 50.00
Plate, Louisiana Purchase Expedition, 7½" 90.00
Plate, Old State House, Philadelphia, Co-operative Flint............. 85.00
Plate, Yankee Doodle, Egg & Dart border, 5¼" 35.00
Platter, bread, Am eagle, Give Us This Day..., 12½x9" 65.00
Platter, Centennial Hall 65.00
Platter, Nellie Bly, w/trip around the world info, 12¾x6¾" 350.00
Platter/plate, oval, McKinley, It Is God's Way, His Will Be Done.. 85.00
Shaker, Centennial, boot... 27.00
Shot glass, Bryan & McKinney, 1896, NM 130.00
Spooner, Log Cabin, L-184... 115.00
Statuette, Ruth the Gleaner, frosted, 1876 Philadelphia Expo, Gillinder.....175.00
Sugar shaker, Proclaim Liberty Throughout the Land 195.00
Tray, bread, oval, Heroes of Bunker Hill, Philadelphia Centennial..80.00
Tray, Grand Army of the Republic (GAR), 11⅛x7⅝" 350.00
Tumbler, Admiral Dewey.. 60.00
Tumbler, America, L-48... 25.00
Tumbler, Civil War, cannon/balls, Am eagle, 34-star flag, 4¾" 75.00
Tumbler, Cleveland, bust & laurel wreath in bottom 95.00
Tumbler, ice tea, Louisiana Purchase, St Louis World's Fair, gr, 5" ..250.00
Tumbler, Union Forever...Bumper to the Flag, 3⅛" 120.00

Hobbs, Brockunier, and Company Glass

Hobbs, Brockunier's South Wheeling Glass Works was in operation during the last half of the nineteenth century. They are most famous for their peachblow, amberina, Daisy and Button, and Hobnail pattern glass, in addition to their art glass. Early production was druggist items and plain glassware — bowls, mugs, and simple footed pitchers with shell handles. See also Peachblow.

Bowl, Daisy and Button, amberina, 9" square, $200.00. (Photo courtesy Green Valley Auctions on LiveAuctioneers.com)

Bowl, berry, Dew Drop, frosted w/amber band, sq, 4" 15.00
Bowl, finger, Greeley, sapphire alabaster 65.00
Bowl, finger, Venetian, wht loopings w/bl threading, minimum... 700.00
Bowl, Hobnail, frosted w/amber band, 10"................................... 90.00
Bowl, Hobnail, frosted w/amber band, ftd, berry pontil, 6x10" 150.00
Bowl, Quartered Block w/Stars, frosted w/amber band, oval, 10"... 65.00
Butter dish, Hobnail, frosted w/amber band, $80 to 120.00
Butter dish, Sawtooth, opal 50.00
Butter dish, Swirl, frosted w/amber band.................................... 95.00
Chandelier, Hobnail, amber font, brass fr, 14" dia 950.00
Compote, Tree of Life, canary, 6" 65.00

Creamer, Daisy & Button, amberina, cylindrical, 5¼"................. 135.00
Cruet, Vasa Murrhina, rose/yel spatter w/gold spangle, bulb, 7" ... 175.00
Cup, lemonade, Polka Dot, crystal w/sapphire hdl, 2¾" 20.00
Goblet, Blackberry, crystal 75.00
Goblet, Quartered Block w/Stars, frosted w/amber band............. 140.00
Molasses can, Polka Dot, Old Gold, 12-oz................................... 135.00
Mustard jar, Swirl, frosted w/amber band, $90 to........................ 125.00
Pitcher, Dew Drop, cranberry opal, clear hdl, 8"......................... 175.00
Pitcher, Hobnail, cranberry opal, frosted hdl, 8"......................... 280.00
Pitcher, Viking, crystal, face below spout & on hdl, ½-gal 160.00
Pitcher, Viking, crystal, plain under spout & hdl, ½-gal 220.00
Plate, Swirl, frosted w/amber band, 6"... 30.00
Spooner, Hobnail, vaseline opal, 4" 50.00
Sugar bowl, Hobnail, frosted w/amber band, w/lid, $65 to 80.00
Sugar bowl, Swirl, frosted w/amber band, w/lid............................ 80.00
Tumbler, Dew Drop, clear w/amber band, 4".............................. 30.00
Tumbler, medicine, pressed glass, ftd, 16-oz, 8".......................... 30.00
Vase, Hobnail, opal, ruffled rim, ftd, 6½"..................................... 20.00
Vase, Hobnail, ruby over frost, 9½"... 95.00

Holt-Howard

Novelty ceramics marked Holt-Howard were produced in Japan from the 1950s into the 1970s, and these have become quite collectible. They're not only marked, but most are dated as well. There are several lines to reassemble — the rooster, the white cat, figural banks, Christmas angels, and Santas, to name only a few — but the one that most Holt-Howard collectors seem to gravitate toward is the Pixie Ware. For more information see *Garage Sale & Flea Market* (Collector Books).

Key: KK — Kozy Kitten

Air freshener, girl w/Christmas tree, 1959, 6½" 32.00
Bank, Dandy-Lion, nodder, 6", $165 to....................................... 200.00
Bottle topper, Pixie Ware, 300 Proof... 300.00
Butter dish, KK, 2 kittens peek from under lid, 7", $90 to........... 100.00
Candleholder, angel, 4", ea $25 to.. 30.00
Candleholder, Ponytail Princess, $40 to....................................... 50.00
Candleholder, Santa in open car, 1959, 3½", ea $18 to 22.00
Candleholders, mouse among Christmas greenery, 1958, 2¼", pr .. 12.00
Candleholders, Rooster, figural, 1960, pr $20 to 25.00
Cheese crock, KK, Stinky Cheese on side, 2 kissing cats on lid, 1958 ...60.00
Cherries jar, butler (Jeeves) 90.00
Cherries jar, Pixie Ware, blk-haired/Xd-eyed spoon finial, $550 to..600.00
Coffeepot, Rooster, wht w/rooster decor, electric, 1960, $50 to 65.00
Cookie jar, KK, head form 40.00
Cup/saucer, Rooster 15.00
Grease jar, KK, Keeper of the Grease, figural kitten, 4½" 375.00
Jar, Pixie line, Cocktail Olives 185.00
Jar, Pixie line, Olives, $150 to 175.00
Jar, Pixie line, Onions, $185 to 200.00
Ketchup jar, Pixie Ware, $60 to.. 75.00
Lamp, oil, Holly Girl, unused wick, 7" 40.00
Marmalade jar, Pixie Ware, yel head finial, 5½", min 800.00
Mug, KK, cat on side, w/squeaker, 8-oz, $35 to........................... 45.00
Mug, Rooster, emb decor, 3 szs, ea $6 to......................................9.00
Mustard jar, Pixie Ware, $65 to 90.00
Oil cruet, Pixie Ware, blond pixie girl w/cork stopper................... 62.50
Olives jar, butler (Jeeves) 45.00
Onions jar, butler (Jeeves).. 45.00
Pitcher, Santa head, 1960, 4¼"... 30.00
Shakers, cowboy, 6¼", pr 20.00
Shakers, fit together to form apple, 2½", pr................................... 22.00

Shakers, KK, 1 w/pk bow tie, 2nd w/bl, noisemaker, 1958, pr 30.00
Shakers, KK, head only, male in cap, pr $35 to 55.00
Shakers, Santa, Happy New Year on beard, pr 22.00
Shakers, tomato, 1962, 3x3", pr 15.00

Spice set, Kozy Kitten, four stacking units, rare, $225.00 to $250.00. (Photo courtesy Madia Webster, eBay seller Connectibles)

String holder, KK, kitten's face, $40 to 50.00
Sugar bowl, Rooster, wht w/red bottom, rooster finial, 1960s, $25 to ... 35.00
Tea bag holders, teapot shapes, set of 4 in metal caddy 40.00
Vase, Rooster, figural, 6¼", $25 to 35.00
Wall pocket, KK, full-bodied cat w/hook tail, 7x3", $45 to 60.00

Homer Laughlin

The Homer Laughlin China Company of Newell, West Virginia, was founded in 1871. The superior dinnerware they displayed at the Centennial Exposition in Philadelphia in 1876 won the highest award of excellence. From that time to the present, they have continued to produce quality dinnerware and kitchenware, many lines of which are very popular collectibles. As of 2010 Homer Laughlin is the last major pottery still being manufactured in the United States. Most of the dinnerware is marked with the name of the pattern and occasionally with the shape name as well. The 'HLC' trademark is usually followed by a number series, the first two digits of which indicate the year of its manufacture. For further information we recommend *Collector's Encyclopedia of Fiesta* by Sharon and Bob Huxford and *Collector's Encyclopedia of Homer Laughlin China* by Joanne Jasper, both published by Collector Books. Another fine source of information is *Homer Laughlin, A Giant Among Dishes*, by Jo Cunningham (Schiffer). Our values are base prices, and apply to decaled lines only — not solid-color dinnerware. Very desirable patterns on the shapes named in our listings may increase values by as much as 200%. Our advisor for this category is Joanne Jasper; she is listed in the Directory under Alabama. See also Fiesta; Hall.

Brittany

Piccadilly, a slight variant of Brittany, is priced the same as Brittany. The nappy's lid (in Brittany only) is used with the 9" nappy to make the casserole. Use high-end pricing for the Majestic and blue-, pink-, and orange-banded patterns.

Egg cup, dbl (Cable), $32 to 40.00
Gravy boat, $28 to 35.00
Nappy, 9", $28 to 38.00
Nappy lid, $30 to 32.00
Plate, 10", $10 to 16.00
Plate, chop, $32 to 38.00
Plate, rim soup, deep, $8 to 14.00

Century

Except for some of the harder-to-find service pieces, items in English Garden, Sun Porch, and the Mexican lines are often double the values listed below. Some items from these lines are rare (for instance the teapot in Sun Porch), and no market value has been established for them.

Baker, oval, 9", $20 to 28.00
Bowl, cream soup, 11-oz, $30 to 38.00
Bowl, deep, 1-pt, $23 to 32.00
Butter, Jade, $75 to 105.00
Casserole, w/lid, $85 to 125.00
Cake plate, 11½", $36 to 42.00
Egg cup, $30 to 42.00
Jug, 2½-pt, $75 to 95.00
Muffin cover, rare, $75 to 82.00
Nappy, 8", $28 to 34.00
Plate, 7", $12 to 16.00
Plate, deep, rim soup, $12 to 14.00
Platter, 13", oval well, $30 to 35.00
Platter, 15", sq well, $36 to 42.00
Teacup, $10 to 15.00

Debutante

Add 20% more for Suntone; add 25% for Karol China gold decorated items.

Bowl, coupe soup, $8 to 10.00
Casserole, w/lid, $35 to 45.00
Coffeepot, $45 to 50.00
Creamer, $10 to 14.00
Gravy boat, Faststand, $24 to 28.00
Shakers, pr, $22 to 35.00
Sugar bowl, w/lid, $16 to 22.00
Teapot, $35 to 45.00

Eggshell Georgian

For Countess and Cashmere use the high end of the price guide.

Bowl, lug soup, English Regency, 1940, $10.00 to $15.00. (Photo courtesy Joanne Jasper)

Bowl, oatmeal, 6", $10 to 12.00
Casserole, w/lid, $45 to 85.00
Creamer, $12 to 18.00
Cup/saucer, $12 to 18.00
Plate, chop, 14", $28 to 34.00
Plate, rim soup, deep, $10 to 16.00
Plate, sq, 8", $10 to 14.00
Shakers, pr, $30 to 55.00
Sugar, covered, $18 .... 24.00
Teapot, $55 to 95.00

Eggshell Nautilus

Bowl, cream soup, $12 to 16.00
Bowl, rim soup, deep, $10 to 14.00
Casserole, w/lid, $50 to 75.00

Cup, AD, $12 to 16.00
Plate, chop, 14", $28 to.. 48.00
Plate, rnd, 8", $10 to... 14.00
Plate, sq, 8", $10 to... 14.00
Platter, 13", $18 .... 28.00
Shakers, pr, $30 to 55.00
Teapot $55 to 105.00

Empress

Add 25% for solid colors. Empress pricing can also be used for the HLC Kwaker shape. See also Bluebird China.

Baker, oval bowl, 8", $16 to.. 22.00
Bone dish, $8 to 12.00
Casserole, w/lid, $30 to.. 45.00
Celery tray, 11", $20 to... 25.00
Cup/saucer, $8 to 12.00
Egg cup, Boston, $24 to.. 30.00
Gravy boat, Faststand, $28 to 32.00
Jug, 2⅛-pt, $40 to 48.00
Platter, 8", $12 to... 16.00
Platter, 13", $24 to 28.00
Tureen, oyster, soup, 8", $65 to....................................... 80.00

Marigold

Cup/saucer, $10 to 15.00
Gravy boat, $25 to 30.00
Nappy, 9", $24 to 32.00
Plate, 10", $13 to.. 16.00
Plate, rim soup, deep, $10 to.. 14.00
Plate, sq, 8", $12 to... 15.00
Platter, 13", $22 to 30.00

Rhythm

For American Provincial add 25% to the high end of the price guide.

Casserole, w/lid, $30 to.. 40.00
Plate, 10", $9 to.. 12.00
Platter, 12", $16 to 20.00
Sauceboat, $22 to.. 28.00
Spoon rest, $90 to 110.00
Teapot, $35 to 50.00

Swing

For Pastel patterns use the high end of the price guide. Add 30% for Asian patterns and Mexicali.

Cup and saucer, demitasse, 'California Provincial' decal, 1948, $15.00 to $18.00. (Photo courtesy Joanne Jasper)

Casserole, w/lid, $40 to.. 65.00
Egg cup, $28 to... 36.00

Muffin cover, w/plate, $35 to 50.00
Nappy, rnd, $12 to 16.00
Plate, 10", $10 to.. 14.00
Plate, rim soup, deep, $8 to.. 12.00
Platter, 11", $12 to 16.00
Teapot, $75 to 105.00
Teapot, demi, $35 to 50.00
Tray, utility, $15 to 22.00

Virginia Rose

For patterns such as JJ59 and VR 128, Golden Rose, and Spring Wreath, use the high end of the price guide.

Baker, oval, 10", $24 to... 32.00
Bowl, lug soup, $16 to 20.00
Bowls, mixing, set of 3, $112 to 140.00
Bread plate, rare, $20 to.. 25.00
Casserole, w/lid, $65 to 115.00
Egg cup, dbl, Cable, $75 to 100.00
Mug, coffee, $40 to 90.00
Plate, 8", rare, $12 to 22.00

Wells

Add 25% for solid colors Sienna Brown, French Rose, or Leaf Green. For Flight of the Swallows, Palm Tree, and Hollyhock patterns, use the high end of the price guide.

Baker, oval, 8", $18 to.. 26.00
Bouillon, $6 to 8.00
Bowl, cream soup, w/saucer, $20 to 24.00
Bowl, deep, 6", $12 to... 16.00
Butter dish, $45 to 75.00
Casserole, w/lid, $65 to 95.00
Cup/saucer, $10 to 15.00
Gravy boat, Faststand, $35 to 65.00
Plate, 10", $12 to.. 18.00
Plate, rim soup, deep, $10 to.. 15.00
Platter, 15", $38 to 45.00

Hoya Crystal Inc.

Hoya Crystal Inc. originated in 1946 in the town of Hoya, Japan. They were manufacturers of fine crystal. Upon learning that General McArthur partook of a glass or two of scotch every evening, Hoya designed a double old-fashioned glass especially for him and presented it to him for his enjoyment during the evening cocktail hour. Today, Hoya Crystal is one of the world's largest and most respected crystal companies.

Vase, centerpiece, Fumio Sasa, 8x12", $600.00. (Photo courtesy Susanin's Auctions on LiveAuctioners.com)

Bowl, Samurai, crystal, 9½" 3,000.00
Bowl, Trio, MIB 900.00
Sculpture, eagle, crystal, on rect base, 7¼"..................... 500.00

Sculpture, obelisk, crystal, 15".............................1,300.00
Sculpture, panther, crystal, 6".................................. 110.00
Sculpture, rocking sailboat, crystal, 7⅜"................550.00
Vase, Aster, crystal w/vertical cuts, detailed X-cuts at top, 16¾". 7,900.00
Vase, crystal, flared ft & rim, 9".............................. 30.00

Hull

The A.E. Hull Pottery was formed in 1905 in Zanesville, Ohio, and in the early years produced stoneware specialities. They expanded in 1907, adding a second plant and employing over 200 workers. By 1920 they were manufacturing a full line of stoneware, art pottery with both airbrushed and blended glazes, florist pots, and gardenware. They also produced toilet ware and kitchen items with a white semiporcelain body. Although these continued to be staple products, after the stock market crash of 1929, emphasis was shifted to tile production. By the mid-'30 interest in art pottery production was growing, and over the next 15 years, several lines of matt pastel floral-decorated patterns were designed, consisting of vases, planters, baskets, ewers, and bowls in various sizes.

The Red Riding Hood cookie jar, patented in 1943, proved so successful that a whole line of figural kitchenware and novelty items was added. They continued to be produced well into the '50s. (See also Little Red Riding Hood.) Through the '40s their floral artware lines flooded the market, due to the restriction of foreign imports. Although best known for their pastel matt-glazed ware, some of the lines were high gloss. Rosella, glossy coral on a pink clay body, was produced for a short time only; and Magnolia, although offered in a matt glaze, was produced in gloss as well.

The plant was destroyed in 1950 by a flood which resulted in a devastating fire when the floodwater caused the kilns to explode. The company rebuilt and equipped their new factory with the most modern machinery. It was soon apparent that more modern equipment and processing was necessary and the new plant concentrated on high-gloss artware lines such as Parchment and Pine and Ebb Tide. Figural planters and novelties, piggy banks, and dinnerware were produced in abundance in the late '50s and '60s. By the mid-'70s dinnerware and florist ware were the mainstay of their business. The firm discontinued operations in 1985.

Our advisor, Brenda Roberts (see Directory, Ohio), has compiled two lovely books, *The Collector's Encyclopedia of Hull Pottery* and *The Collector's Ultimate Encyclopedia of Hull Pottery*, both with full-color photos and values (Collector Books).

Special note to Hull collectors: Reproductions are on the market in all categories of Hull pottery — matt florals, Red Riding Hood, and later lines including House 'n Garden dinnerware.

Blossom Flite, basket, #T-2, 6", 1955-56, $50 to............................. 75.00
Blossom Flite, honey pot, #T-1, 6", $45 to..................................... 60.00

Blossom Flite, pitcher, T-3, 8½", $75.00 to $140.00.
(Photo courtesy Showplace Antique + Design Center on LiveAuctioneers.com)

Blossom Flite, teapot, #T-14, 8", $75 to.. 100.00
Blossom Flite, vase, basket, #T-4, 8½", $90 to.............................. 135.00
Bow-Knot, basket, #B-12, 1949-50, 10½", $800 to...................1,100.00

Bow-Knot, candleholder, #B-17, 4", ea $100 to.................. 145.00
Bow-Knot, ewer, #B-15, 13½", $900 to 1,000.00
Bow-Knot, jardiniere, #B-19, 1949-50, 9⅜", $800 to.................1,000.00
Bow-Knot, vase, #B-14, 1949-50, 12½", $900 to.................1,100.00
Butterfly, bonbon, #B-4, 1956, 6½", $20 to.................. 25.00
Butterfly, bowl, #B-16, 1956, 10½", $70 to.................. 100.00
Calla Lily, ewer, #506, 1938-40, 10", $300 to.................. 400.00
Camellia, basket, #107, 1943-44, $250 to.................. 300.00
Camellia, candleholder, #117, 1943-44, 6½", ea $125 to 160.00
Camellia, console bowl, #116, 12", $250 to.................. 350.00
Camellia, ewer, #126, 4", $75 to.................. 110.00
Camellia, teapot, #110, 1943-44, 8½", $350 to.................. 425.00
Camellia, wall pocket, #125, 8½", $400 to.................. 525.00
Capri, basket, leaf, 12¼", $40 to.................. 60.00
Capri, candy dish, w/lid, unmk, 8½", $35 to.................. 55.00
Capri, leaf basket, 12¼", $40 to.................. 60.00
Capri, vase, #58, 13¾", $55 to.................. 75.00
Cinderella Kitchenware (Bouquet), cookie jar, unmk, 10½", $100 to .. 145.00
Cinderella Kitchenware (Bouquet), pitcher, #29, 32-oz, $25 to..... 35.00
Continental, basket, #55, 1959-60, 12¾", $130 to 175.00
Continental, flower bowl, #69, 9¼", $40 to.................. 60.00
Continental, vase, #64, 10", $50 to.................. 80.00
Dogwood, candleholder, #512, 3¾", ea $95 to.................. 135.00
Dogwood, console bowl, #511, 11½", $285 to.................. 395.00
Dogwood, ewer, #520, 1942-43, 4¾", $90 to.................. 120.00
Dogwood, vase, #502, 1942-43, 6½", $195 to.................. 245.00
Dogwood, vase, #516, 4¾", $75 to.................. 95.00
Ebb Tide, ashtray, #E-8, 1955, 5", $100 to.................. 160.00
Ebb Tide, basket, #E-11, 16½", $210 to.................. 265.00
Ebb Tide, console bowl, #E-12, 15¾", $215 to.................. 260.00
Ebb Tide, creamer, #E-15, 1955, 4", $95 to.................. 125.00
Ebb Tide, vase, #E-6, 1955, 9¼", $150 to.................. 200.00
Floral, bowl, cereal, #50, 6", $14 to.................. 18.00
Floral, casserole, ind, #47, open, 5", $15 to.................. 20.00
Heritageware, cruet, oil or vinegar, 6¼", ea $20 to.................. 25.00
Heritageware, grease jar, #A-3, 5¾", $20 to.................. 30.00
Imperial, basket, unmk, 1985, 8", $30 to.................. 40.00
Imperial, ewer, #F-480, 1965, 10½", $45 to.................. 60.00
Imperial, planter, #405 USA, 1958, 8¼", $8 to.................. 10.00
Iris, basket, #408, 1940-42, 7", $265 to.................. 310.00
Iris, candleholder, #411, 5", ea $125 to.................. 155.00
Iris, jardiniere, #413, 5½", $160 to.................. 200.00
Iris, rose bowl, #412, 1940-42, 7", $150 to.................. 200.00
Iris, vase, #402, 1940-42, 7", $150 to.................. 200.00
Iris, vase, #404, 8½", $210 to.................. 250.00
Iris, vase, bud, #410, 7½", $145 to.................. 195.00
Lusterware, bulb bowl, unmk, 7½", $60 to.................. 75.00
Lusterware, candleholder, unmk, 1927-30, 3", ea $30 to.................. 40.00
Lusterware, flower frog, unmk, 4½", $20 to.................. 30.00
Lusterware, pitcher, unmk, 5¾", $55 to.................. 70.00
Lusterware, vase, unmk, 12", $75 to.................. 100.00
Magnolia, gloss, basket, #H-14, 1947-48, 10½", $275 to............. 375.00
Magnolia, gloss, candleholder, #H24, 1947-48, 4", ea $30 to......... 40.00
Magnolia, gloss, console bowl, #H-23, 13", $125 to.................. 165.00
Magnolia, gloss, ewer, #H-3, 5½", $60 to.................. 85.00
Magnolia, gloss, vase, #H-1, 1947-48, 5½", $40 to.................. 60.00
Magnolia, matt, cornucopia, #19, 1946-47, 8½", $140 to............. 195.00
Magnolia, matt, vase, #17, 12¼", $275 to.................. 350.00
Magnolia, matt, vase, #22, 1946-47, 12½", $275 to.................. 350.00
Marcrest, pitcher, 1958, 7½", $25 to.................. 35.00
Mardi Gras/Granada, bulb bowl, #532, 2¾", $30 to.................. 45.00
Mardi Gras/Granada, cornucopia, #210, 5½", $30 to.................. 40.00
Mardi Gras/Granada, teapot, #33, 5½", $195 to.................. 295.00
Mardi Gras/Granada, vase, #214-9, $40 to.................. 60.00

Medley, bulb bowl, #107, 1952, 7", $20 to 30.00
Novelty, dachshund figural, 1952, 14", $150 to 200.00
Novelty, dancing girl, #955, 1938, 7", $30 to 50.00
Novelty, jubilee ashtray, #407, 1957, 11½", $30 to.................. 40.00
Novelty, kitten planter, #61, 7½", $40 to................................. 55.00
Novelty, kitten w/spool planter, #89, 1951, 6", $20 to.............. 30.00
Novelty, knight on horseback planter, #55, 8", $75 to 105.00
Novelty, parrot w/cart planter, #60, 6", $30 to 40.00
Novelty, peacock vase, #73, 1951, 10½", $30 to 40.00
Novelty, pigeon planter, #91, 1955, 6", $30 to........................ 40.00
Novelty, rooster planter, #53, 1953, 5¾", $75 to 100.00
Novelty, scroll basket, #56, 6", $40 to 60.00
Novelty, swan ashtray, #70, 1951, 4", $10 to 15.00
Novelty, twin geese planter, #95, 1951, 6½", $40 to 60.00
Novelty, unicorn vase, #99, 1952, 11½", $75 to 105.00
Orchid, basket, #305, 7", $450 to...650.00
Orchid, bud vase, #306, 6¾", $105 to 165.00
Orchid, bulb bowl, #312, 1939-41, 7", $95 to 165.00
Orchid, candleholder, #315, 1939-41, 4", ea $100 to 125.00
Orchid, console bowl, #314, 13", $340 to 440.00
Orchid, jardiniere, #310, 1939-41, 4¾", $105 to 135.00
Pagoda, vase, #P-5, 1960, 12½", $30 to 40.00
Parchment & Pine, basket, #S-8, 1951-54, 16½", $135 to 175.00
Parchment & Pine, candleholder, #S-10, 1951-54, 5", ea $20 to... 30.00
Parchment & Pine, creamer, #S-12, 3¾", $20 to 30.00
Parchment & Pine, sugar bowl, #S-13, 3¾", $20 to 30.00
Parchment & Pine, teapot, #S-11, 1951-54, 6", $100 to 140.00
Poppy, basket, #601, 9", $600 to..700.00
Poppy, bowl, #602, low, 1943-44, 6½", $200 to 250.00
Poppy, ewer, #610, 1943-44, 4¾", $165 to 200.00
Poppy, vase, #607, 1943-44, 8½", $235 to 275.00
Poppy, wall pocket, #609, 9", $310 to 410.00
Regal, bowl, unmk, 1960, 6½", $10 to..................................... 15.00
Regal, planter, #301, 1960, 3½", $10 to 15.00
Rosella, cornucopia, #R-13, 1946, 8½", $75 to 125.00
Rosella, creamer, #R-3, 1946, 5½", $45 to 65.00
Rosella, ewer, #R-7, 9½", $1,200 to......................................1,500.00
Rosella, lamp, unmk, 1946, 6¾", $150 to 250.00
Rosella, wall pocket, #R-10, 6½", $100 to 140.00
Sunglow, basket, #84, 6¼", $75 to 100.00
Sunglow, grease jar, #53, 1948-49, 5¼", $40 to 50.00
Sunglow, pitcher, w/ice lip, 1942-45, 7½", $140 to 175.00
Sunglow, wall pocket, unmk, 1948-49, 6", $75 to..................... 100.00
Tulip, vase, #100-33, 1938-40, 6½", $100 to 140.00
Tulip, vase, #101-33, 1938-40, 9", $225 to 300.00
Water Lily, cornucopia, #L-7, 1948-49, 6½", $105 to 140.00
Water Lily, teapot, #L-18, 1948-49, 6", $225 to.........................265.00
Water Lily, vase, #L-2, 1948-49, 5½", $60 to 75.00
Wildflower (# series), basket, #66, 1942-43, 10¼", $800 to.......1,000.00
Wildflower (# series), ewer, #57, 1942-43, 4½", $100 to 145.00
Wildflower, console bowl, #W21, 1946-47, 12", $225 to.............. 265.00
Wildflower, vase, #W-3, 1946-47, 5½", $50 to 70.00

Woodland, gloss, ewer, #W-3, 1949-50, 5½", $60 to..................... 85.00
Woodland, matt, planter, #W-19, 1949-50, 10½", $110 to........... 175.00
Woodland, matt, sugar bowl, #W-28, 1949-50, 3½", $100 to....... 150.00
Woodland, matt, wall pocket, #W-13, 1949-50, 7½", $250 to...... 300.00

Dinnerware and Kitchenware Items

Avocado, bowl, soup/salad, 1968-71, 6½", $3 to 5.00
Avocado, Leaf chip 'n dip, 1968-71, 15x10½", $45 to 75.00
Avocado, shakers, 1968-71, 3¾", pr $20 to 30.00
Avocado, sugar bowl, 1968-71, $15 to....................................... 20.00
Cinderella Kitchenware (Blossom), creamer, #28, 1948, 4", $40 to ..60.00
Cinderella Kitchenware (Blossom), shakers, #25, 3½", pr $40 to... 60.00
Cinderella Kitchenware (Blossom), teapot, #26, 42-oz, $140 to .. 180.00
Cinderella Kitchenware (Bouquet), pitcher, #29, 32-oz, $25 to..... 35.00
Conventional Rose Cereal Ware, canister, Coffee, 8½", $40 to 60.00
Country Belle, baker, rect, 1985, 14", $40 to 60.00
Country Belle, cheese shaker, 1985, 6½", $20 to 30.00
Country Belle, pie plate, 1985, 11", $25 to 35.00
Country Belle, plate, 1985, 10", $10 to 12.00
Country Belle, platter, 1985, 12" L, $15 to 20.00
Crescent Kitchenware, bowl, #B-1, 1952-54, 9½", $30 to 40.00
Crescent Kitchenware, creamer, #B-15, 1952-54, 4½", $10 to 15.00
Crescent Kitchenware, mug, #B-16, 1952-54, 4¼", $10 to 16.00
Crestone, butter dish, 1965-67, ¼-lb, $25 to 35.00
Crestone, gravy boat w/underplate, 1965-67, 10-oz, $20 to............ 30.00
Crestone, plate, 1965-67, 10½", $8 to.. 10.00
Crestone, teapot, 1965-67, 7", $45 to 65.00
Debonair Kitchenware, casserole, #O-2, ca 1954, 8½", $40 to....... 60.00
Diamond Quilted, bean pot, #B-19, 1937-40, 5½", $45 to 65.00
Diamond Quilted, custard, #B-14, 1937-40, 2¾", $10 to 15.00
Drape & Panel, bowl, mixing, #D-1, 1937-40, 9½", $30 to 40.00
Drape & Panel, cookie jar, #D-20, 1937-40, 2-qt, 8", $125 to...... 150.00
Floral, casserole, ind, #47, open, 5", $15 to 20.00
Floral, grease jar, #43, 1951-54, 5¾", $40 to 55.00
Floral, shakers, #44, 1951-54, 3½", pr $30 to 40.00
Flying Blue Bird Cereal Ware, canister, Rice, 8½", $65 to 95.00
Heartland, bowl, fruit, 1982-85, $6 to...8.00
Heartland, mug, 5", $10 to 14.00
Heartland, pitcher, 4", $25 to 35.00
Heartland, plate, 7¼", $8 to 10.00
Heritageware, pitcher, #A-7, 4", $12 to 16.00
Mirror Almond, plate, 10", $8 to.. 10.00
Mirror Almond, plate, steak, oval, 11¾", $15 to 20.00
Mirror Almond, stein, 5", $8 to 12.00
Mirror Brown, baker, oval, 10", $20 to 30.00
Mirror Brown, bowl, 6½", $4 to...6.00
Mirror Brown, bowl, divided vegetable, 10¾", $20 to 30.00
Mirror Brown, butter dish, 7½", $20 to 25.00
Mirror Brown, canister, flour, 1978-81, 9", $150 to 200.00
Mirror Brown, casserole, w/figural duck lid, 9", 1972-85, $95 to ..125.00
Mirror Brown, cheese shaker, 6", $30 to.................................... 40.00

Wildflower, vase, #W-15, 10½", $240.00 to $300.00.
(Photo courtesy Dirk Soulis Auctions on LiveAuctioneers.com)

Mirror Brown, egg plate, 9½", $75.00 to $100.00.
(Photo courtesy Belhorn Auction Services, LLC on LiveAuctioneers.com)

Wildflower, vase, #W-17, 1946-47, 12½", $250 to 300.00

Mirror Brown, Gingerbread Man, cookie jar, 1984, 12", $175 to.225.00

Mirror Brown, leaf dish, 7½", $15 to 20.00
Mirror Brown, mug, 3½", $4 to 6.00
Mirror Brown, stein, university logo in gold, 1976, $20 to 30.00
Mirror Brown, vase, cylindrical, 9", $35 to 45.00
Mirror Brown Ringed Ware, pitcher, 9", $95 to 135.00
Tangerine, ashtray, 8", $25 to 35.00
Tangerine, bean pot w/warmer, 9", $60 to 80.00
Tangerine, butter dish, 7½", $25 to 35.00
Tangerine, teapot, 6½", $30 to 45.00
Tangerine, tidbit, 2-tier, 10", $60 to 90.00

Hummel

Hummel figurines were created through the artistry of Berta Hummel, a Franciscan nun called Sister M. Innocentia. The first figures were made about 1935 by Franz Goebel of Goebel Art Inc., Rodental, West Germany. Plates, plaques, and candy dishes were also produced, and the older, discontinued editions are highly sought collectibles. Generally speaking, an issue can be dated by the trademark. The first Hummels, from 1935 to 1949, were either incised or stamped with the 'Crown WG' mark (TMK-1). The 'Full Bee in V' mark (TMK-2) was employed with minor variations until 1957. At that time the bee was stylized and represented by a solid disk with angled symetrical wings completely contained within the confines of the 'V' (TMK-3, the 'Stylized Bee'). The 'Three-Line mark,' 1964 – 1972 (TMK-4), utilized the stylized bee and included a three-line arrangement: 'c by W. Goebel, W. Germany.' Another change in 1972 saw the 'Stylized Bee in V' suspended between the vertical bars of the 'b' and 'l' of a printed 'Goebel, West Germany.' Collectors refer to this mark as the 'Last Bee' or 'Goebel Bee' (TMK-5). The mark in use from 1979 to 1990 omits the 'bee in V' and is thus called the 'missing bee mark' (TMK-6). The New Crown (NC or TMK-7) mark, in use from 1991 to 1999, is a small crown with 'WG' initials, a large 'Goebel,' and a small 'Germany,' signifying a united Germany. The current Millennium Mark came into use in the year 2000 and features a large bee between the letters 'b' and 'l' in Goebel (TMK-8). For further study we recommend *Hummel, An Illustrated Handbook and Price Guide*, by Ken Armke; *Hummel Figurines and Plates, A Collector's Identification and Value Guide*, by Carl Luckey; *The No. 1 Price Guide to M.I. Hummel* by Robert L. Miller; and *The Fascinating World of M.I. Hummel* by Goebel. These books are available through your local book dealer. See also Limited Edition Plates, M.I. Hummel.

Key:
CM — Crown Mark   NC — New Crown Mark
CN — closed number   SB — Stylized Bee
FB — Full Bee   TMK — trademark
LB — Last Bee   3L — Three-Line Mark
MB — Missing Bee

#1, Puppy Love, CM, 5-5¼" 575.00
#5, Strolling Along, FB, 4¾-5¾" 360.00
#6 2/0, Sensitive Hunter, MB, 4" 125.00
#9, Begging His Share, FB, 5¼-6" 360.00
#13 2/0, Meditation, SB, 4¼" 160.00
#17/0, Congratulations, FB, 5¾" 255.00
#20, Prayer Before Battle, FB, 4¼" 245.00
#21/I, Heavenly Angel, CM, 6¾-7¼" 575.00
#23/I, Adoration, 3L, 6" 315.00
#26/0, Child Jesus, font, CM, 2¾x5¼" 165.00
#27/3, Joyous News, FB, 4¼x4¾" 720.00
#28/II, Wayside Devotion, FB, 7¼" 580.00
#33, Joyful, ashtray, CM, 3¾x6" 290.00

#34, Singing Lesson, ashtray, CM, 3½x6¼" 315.00
#37, Herald Angels, candleholder, FB, 2¾x4", ea 280.00
#44A, Culprits, table lamp, CM, 9" 470.00
#47/0, Goose Girl, FB, 4¾x5¼" 360.00
#48/0, Madonna, plaque, CM, 3¼x4¼" 235.00
#50/0, Volunteers, FB, 5¾" 350.00
#53, Joyful, CM, 3½-4¼" 250.00
#57/0, Chick Girl, CM, 3½" 395.00
#63, Singing Lessons, CM, 2¾-3" 325.00
#64, Shepherd's Boy, FB, 6" 325.00
#66, Farm Boy, CM, 5½" 540.00
#69, Happy Pastime, CM, 3¼-3½" 360.00
#73, Little Helper, CM, 4¼-4½" 325.00
#79, Globe Trotter, SB, 5-5¼" 215.00
#84, Worship, CM, 5¼" 380.00
#85, Serenade, CM, 7¼" 875.00
#85/0, Serenade, CM, 4¾-5¼" 290.00
#88, Heavenly Protection, FB, 9¼" 940.00
#89/II, Cellist, FB, tw, 7½-7¾" 575.00
#92, Merry Wanderer, plaque, CM, 4½x5" 325.00
#94 3/0, Suprise, CM, 4" 315.00
#96, Little Shopper, SB, 4¾" 145.00
#100, Shrine, lamp, CM, 7½" 5,600.00
#101, To Market, table lamp, SB, 7" 350.00
#102, Volunteers, table lamp, CM, 7½" 5,760.00
#103, Farewell, table lamp, CM, 7½" 5,760.00
#110, Let's Sing, FB, 4" 230.00
#111/I, Wayside Harmony, FB, tw, 5-5½" 325.00
#113, Heavenly Song, candleholder, CM, 3½x4¾", ea 4,200.00
#114, Let's Sing, ashtray, CM, 3½x6¼" 615.00
#119, Postman, LB, 5-5½" 190.00
#123, Max & Moritz, 3L, 5" 200.00
#125, Vacation Time, plaque, CM, 4⅜x5¼" 420.00
#127, Doctor, CM, 5" 315.00
#130, Duet, CM, 5¼" 580.00
#133, Mother's Helper, SB, 5" 210.00
#136/I, Friends, FB, 5¼" 325.00
#137A, Child in Bed (looking left), plaque, CM, 3x3" 3,500.00
#138, Tiny Baby in Crib, plaque, CM, 2¼x3" 2,800.00
#141/V, Apple Tree Girl, 3L, 10¼" 1,190.00
#142/X, Apple Tree Boy, 3L, 30" 11,200.00
#144, Angelic Song, CM, 4" 325.00
#150, Happy Days, FB, 6¼" 630.00
#151, Madonna Holding Child, bl, CM, 12½" 1,400.00
#152B, Umbrella Girl, CM, 8" 2,800.00
#164, Worship, font, FB, 3¼x5" 110.00
#165, Swaying Lullaby, wall plaque, CM, tw, 4½x5¼" 575.00
#166, Boy w/Bird, ashtray, CM, 3¼x6" 315.00

#170/III, School Boys, Goebel bee mark (TM-5), 1972, 10", $600.00. (Photo courtesy Gulfcoast Coin & Jewelry on LiveAuctioneers.com)

#177, School Girls, FB, 9½" 2,100.00
#184, Latest News, LB, 5½" 270.00
#192, Candlelight, candleholder, CM, 7", ea 975.00

#197, Be Patient, FB, 6¼" 395.00
#198, Home to Market, FB, 4½" 270.00
#199/0, Feeding Time, SB, 4¼-4½" 235.00
#202, Old Man Reading Newspaper, table lamp, CN, 8¼" 10,800.00
#223, To Market, table lamp, FB, 9½" 505.00
#226, The Mail Is Here, FB, 4½x6¼" 830.00
#230, Apple Tree Boy, table lamp, LB, 7½" 290.00
#237, Star Gazer, wall plaque, FB, CN, 4¾-5" 7,200.00
#240, Little Drummer, FB, 4" 235.00
#241, Angel Joyous News w/Lute, FB, CN, 3x4½" 1,080.00
#256, Knitting Lessons, SB, 7½" 630.00
#257, For Mother, LB, 5-5¼" 190.00
#262, Heavenly Lullaby, 3L, 3½x5" 540.00
#263, Merry Wanderer, wall plaque, 3L, CN, 4x5⅜" 7,200.00
#305, The Builder, FB, tw, early sample, 5½" 2,880.00
#312/1, Honey Lover, MB, 3¾" 290.00
#328, Carnival, SB, 6" 580.00
#338, Birthday Cake, candleholder, SB, 3¾", ea 2,160.00
#344, Feathered Friends, 3L, 4¾" 540.00

#387, Valentine Gift, TMK-5 (Last Bee), 5", $90.00. (Photo courtesy Dargate Auction Galleries on LiveAuctioneers.com)

#471, Harmony in Four Parts, TMK-6, made only in 1989, 9¾" . 1,440.00
#III/110, Let's Sing, box, CM, 6¼" 540.00

Hutschenreuther

The Porcelain Factory C.M. Hutschenreuther operated in Bavaria from 1814 to 1969. After the death of the elder Hutschenreuther in 1845, his son Lorenz took over operations, continuing there until 1857 when he left to establish his own company in the nearby city of Selb. The original manufactory became a joint stock company in 1904, absorbing several other potteries. In 1969 both Hutschenreuther firms merged, and that company still operates in Selb. They have distribution centers in both France and the United States.

Candelabra, putti playing flute at base, 3-arm, pastels, 17", ea 250.00
Figurine, 2 ladies dancing on gold ball, arms joined/outstretched, 9" .. 200.00
Figurine, bl heron pr on nest w/eggs, G Granget, 19½"+later base ... 3,150.00
Figurine, boxer dog in show stance, 9¾x11" 350.00
Figurine, cat, yel & brn tabby, gr mk on paw, paper label, 11" L .. 960.00
Figurine, donkey w/dog, cat & rooster stacked on bk, 7½" 175.00
Figurine, draped dancer w/leg extended, arm raised, 1950s, 10¾" . 215.00
Figurine, eagle in flight, Granget, 19x13½x10" 1,250.00
Figurine, eagle w/wings up, K Tutter, 15" 215.00
Figurine, horses galloping (2), wht porc, 17x21" 1,800.00
Figurine, hummingbird, gr mk, 5x5" 180.00
Figurine, man in tights w/cape & sword, red/blk/brn, 10" 250.00
Figurine, mother tossing child in air, K Tutter, 11x7" 170.00
Figurine, nude lady dancer w/gold sphere balanced on ankle, 8½" ... 635.00
Figurine, nude w/gold ball, wht gloss, C Werner, 9½x7½" 450.00
Figurine, nude woman & 2 leopards running, #118716, 10¾" 385.00

Figurine, rabbit w/carrot, realistic, mc, 4x3½" 110.00
Figurine, Safe at Home, pintail ducks, G Granget, ca 1990, 15x13" .. 900.00
Figurine, Sea Frolic, 3 seals, wht porc, on hardwood stand, 14x25" 960.00
Plaque, Echo, lady in red w/hand to ear, Wagner, #311, 7x5" ... 3,450.00
Plaque, Marguerite, lady in red w/flowers in hair, Wagner, 7¼x5" .. 2,700.00
Plaque, portrait of beauty, 20th C, giltwood/plaster fr, 12" 1,325.00
Plate, Lisctinische Madonna, gold/cobalt border, 1814-1914, 8¾" .. 215.00

Imari

Imari is a generic term which covers a broad family of wares. It was made in more than a dozen Japanese villages, but the name is that of the port from whence it was shipped to Europe. There are several types of Imari. The most common features a design with panels of birds, florals, or people surrounding a central basket of flowers. The colors used in this type are underglaze blue with overglaze red, gold, and green enamels. The Chinese also made Imari wares which differ from the Japanese type in several ways — the absence of spur marks, a thinner-type body, and a more consistent control of the blue. Imari-type wares were copied on the Continent by Meissen and by English potters, among them Worcester, Derby, and Bow. Unless noted otherwise, our values are for Japanese ware.

Bowl, 3 figures in reserves, floral medallions, 19th C, 4x11" 265.00
Bowl, landscape scene, floral/reserves in border, 8-sided, 19th C, 12" 480.00
Bowl, landscape scene, triangular pattern border, 19th C, 7½" 50.00
Bowl, scalloped rim, ftd, 1870s, 4¼x10" 300.00
Charger, central floral bouquet, gold trim, late 19th C, 14" 1,450.00

Charger, figural reserve on floral ground, circa 1860, 18", $1,500.00. (Photo courtesy Northgate Gallery Inc. on LiveAuctioneers.com)

Charger, storks & flowers in panels, ca 1860-90, 18½" 515.00
Jar, cylindrical, 19th C, 9x7" dia 215.00
Jar, floral reserves, domed lid, ca 1920, 13¼" 100.00
Platter, scalloped rim, ca 1840, 13x10" 85.00
Tureen, floral, flower-form hdls, w/lid, 19th C, sm rpr, 11x17x10" . 1,035.00
Umbrella jar, floral urns, cylindrical, early 20th C, 23½x8¾" 480.00
Urn, bird & floral reserves, mtd as lamp, late 19th C, 14½" 360.00
Vase, landscape panels/floral/geometrics, Meiji period, 31x16" . 2,875.00

Imperial Glass

The Imperial Glass Company was organized in 1901 in Bellaire, Ohio, and started manufacturing glassware in 1904. In 1914 NuCut was introduced to imitate cut glass. The line was so popular that it was made in crystal and colors. It was reintroduced as Collector's Crystal in the 1950s. From 1916 to 1924, Imperial used the lustre process to make a line called Art Glass, which today collectors call Imperial Jewels. Free-Hand ware, art glass made entirely by hand using no molds, was made from 1923 to 1924. From 1925 to 1926, the company made a less expensive line of art glass called Lead Lustre. These pieces were mold blown and have similar colors and decorations to Free-Hand ware.

In 1936 Imperial introduced the Candlewick line, for which it is best known. In the late '30s the Vintage Grape milk glass line was added, and in 1951 a major ad campaign was launched, making Imperial one of the leading milk glass manufacturers.

In 1940 Imperial bought the molds and assets of the Central Glass Works of Wheeling, West Virginia; in 1958 it acquired the molds of the Heisey Company; and in 1960 the molds of the Cambridge Glass Company of Cambridge, Ohio. Imperial used these molds, and after 1951 marked its glassware with an 'I' superimposed over the 'G' trademark. The company was bought by Lenox in 1973; subsequently an 'L' was added to the 'IG' mark. In 1981 Lenox sold Imperial to Arthur Lorch, a private investor (who modified the L by adding a line at the top angled to the left, giving rise to the 'ALIG' mark). He in turn sold the company to Robert F. Stahl, Jr., in 1982. Mr. Stahl filed for Chapter 11 to reorganize, but in mid-1984 liquidation was ordered, and all assets were sold. A few items that had been made in '84 were marked with an 'N' superimposed over the 'I' for 'New Imperial.' For more information, we recommend *Imperial Glass Encyclopedia, Vols I, II,* and *III,* edited by James Measell, and *The Collector's Encyclopedia of American Art Glass* by John A. Shuman III. See also Candlewick; Carnival Glass; Glass Animals and Figurines; Slag Glass; Stretch Glass.

Beaded Block, crystal, pitcher, milk, pt	10.00
Beaded Block, gr, plate, salad, sq	14.00
Beaded Block, gr, cr/sug, pr	30.00
Beaded Block, pk, cr/sug, pr	38.00
Beaded Block, ruby, bowl, cupped lily, 4½"	225.00
Beaded Block, seafoam gr opal, cr/sug, pr	24.00
Cape Cod, crystal, basket, 2 sides up, appl hdl 11"	160.00
Cape Cod, crystal, bowl, baked apple, #53X, 6"	10.00
Cape Cod, crystal, bowl, M, heart shaped, 5"	18.00
Cape Cod, crystal, butter, 7½"	40.00
Cape Cod, crystal, cake plate, flat, 72 birthday candleholes, 13"	300.00
Cape Cod, crystal, cake plate, sq w/4 tab ft, 10"	85.00
Cape Cod, crystal, candlestick, 1 ball stem, 4¼", ea	20.00
Cape Cod, crystal, candlestick, 2-lite, sq ft, 5¾"	70.00
Cape Cod, crystal, cologne w/flat stopper, 6¼"	45.00
Cape Cod, crystal, goblet ball stem, 10-oz, 5¾"	12.00
Cape Cod, crystal, iced tea, ball stem, 11-oz	8.00
Cape Cod, crystal, iced tea, ball stem, 14-oz	22.00
Cape Cod, crystal, pitcher w/ice lip, 56-oz, 8"	85.00
Cape Cod, crystal, sherbet, 6-oz, 3¼"	6.00
Cape Cod, crystal, vase, flip shape, 8¼"	55.00
Cape Cod, crystal, vegetable, divided, 11"	65.00
Cathay, crystal, dragon candleholder, #5009, sgn, ea	250.00
Cathay, jade, Empress book stops, pr	120.00
Crocheted Crystal, goblet, 9-oz, 7"	18.00
Crocheted Crystal, relish, divided 4-part, 11½"	20.00
Diamond Quilted, bl, nappy, 1 hdl	14.00
Diamond Quilted, gr, cr/sug, pr	24.00
Diamond Quilted, pk, bowl, cream soup, 2 hdls	12.00

Freehand, bl marble, vase, #412	250.00
Freehand, opal w/bl hanging hearts, vase, #412	425.00
Freehand, orange lead lustre, vase, 655/20, 6¾"	100.00
Hobnail, seafoam bl opal, cologne w/stopper	65.00
Hobnail, Stiegel gr, ivy ball, 6½"	30.00
Hobnail, ultra bl, vase, #742, 4¼"	18.00
Lace Edge, Katy bl, candlestick, 2-lite, ea	22.00
Lace Edge, mg, banana stand, 12"	60.00
Lace Edge, ritz bl, bowl, 3¾"	35.00
Lace Edge, ruby, vase, 4-toed, 5"	30.00
Lace edge, verde gr, candy, tall, ftd, w/lid, 9½"	20.00
Molly, ruby, mayo & underplate, open hdls	45.00
Molly, seafoam gr opal, c/s	25.00
Monticello, crystal, goblet, 5½"	9.00
Monticello, crystal, punch bowl, 12¼"	85.00
Monticello, crystal, punch cup, 2¼"	6.00
Mt Vernon, crystal, c/s	10.00
Mt Vernon, crystal, pitcher, 48-oz, 7½"	45.00
Mt Vernon, crystal, plate, luncheon, 8"	8.00
Murrhina, mc, vase, 8¼"	125.00
Reeded, cobalt w/crystal hdl, pitcher, 80-oz	75.00
Reeded, crystal, candleholder, 4¼", ea	16.00
Reeded, ruby & crystal, vase, ball w/ft, 6"	40.00
Scroll, mg, bowl, 8½"	28.00
Slag glass, caramel, candlestick #43790, 7½", ea	35.00
Slag glass, caramel, covered dish w/lid, lion, 7½"	140.00
Slag glass, caramel, toothpick holder, Bellaire, imitation cut, 2½"	16.00
Slag glass, jade slag, beehive honey jar w/lid, 5"	65.00
Slag glass, purple, candlestick #43790, 7½", ea	45.00
Slag, vase, purple, tricon, 3-toed, 8½"	250.00
Twist, smoke, tumbler, iced tea, flat, 5½"	24.00
Twist, smoke, tumbler, water, flat, 4½"	32.00
Western Apple, goblet, water	14.00

Imperial Porcelain

The Blue Ridge Mountain Boys were created by cartoonist Paul Webb and translated into three-dimension by the Imperial Porcelain Corporation of Zanesville, Ohio, in 1947. These figurines decorated ashtrays, vases, mugs, bowls, pitchers, planters, and other items. The Mountain Boys series were numbered 92 through 108, each with a different and amusing portrayal of mountain life. Imperial also produced American Folklore miniatures, 23 tiny animals one inch or less in size, and the Al Capp Dogpatch series. Because of financial difficulties, the company closed in 1960.

American Folklore Miniatures

Cat, 1½", $50 to	65.00
Cow, 1¾", $60 to	75.00
Hound dogs, $60 to	75.00
Plaque, store ad, 4½"	250.00
Sow, $60 to	75.00

Blue Ridge Mountain Boys by Paul Webb

Ashtray, #92, 2 men by tree stump, for pipes, $50 to	75.00
Ashtray, #101, man w/jug & snake, $50 to	70.00
Ashtray, #103, hillbilly & skunk, $55 to	80.00
Ashtray, #105, baby, hound dog & frog, $50 to	75.00
Ashtray, #106, Barrel of Wishes, w/hound, $45 to	65.00
Box, cigarette, #98, dog atop, baby at door, sq, $80 to	100.00
Dealer's sign, Handcrafted Paul Webb Mtn Boys, rare, 9", $200 to	250.00
Decanter, #100, outhouse, man & bird, $50 to	75.00

Eagle, caramel slag, covered box/candy, #641, $75.00.
(Photo courtesy Museum of American Glass, West Virginia, permanent collection)

Decanter, #104, Ma leaning over stump, w/baby & skunk, $75 to ..100.00
Decanter, man, jug, snake & tree stump, Hispch Inc, 1946, $50 to.... 75.00
Figurine, #101, man leans against tree trunk, 5", $50 to................. 75.00
Figurine, man on hands & knees, 3", $50 to 75.00
Figurine, man sitting, 3½", $50 to 80.00
Figurine, man sitting w/chicken on knee, 3", $50 to 75.00
Jug, #101, Willie & snake, $40 to.. 60.00
Mug, #94, Bearing Down, 6", $40 to.. 60.00
Mug, #94, dbl baby hdl, 4¼", $40 to.. 60.00
Mug, #94, MA hdl, 4¼", $40 to.. 60.00
Mug, #94, man w/bl pants hdl, 4¼", $40 to................................... 60.00
Mug, #94, man w/yel beard & red pants hdl, 4¼", $40 to.............. 60.00
Mug, #99, Target Practice, boy on goat, farmer, 5¾", $40 to 60.00

Mugs, 5¾", each $25.00 to $35.00. (Photo courtesy Jackson's Auction on LiveAuctioneers.com)

Pitcher, lemonade, $80 to.. 110.00
Planter, #81, man drinking from jug, sitting by washtub, $40 to 60.00
Planter, #100, outhouse, man & bird, $60 to 80.00
Planter, #105, man w/chicken on knee, washtub, $60 to................ 80.00
Planter, #110, hillbilly sits by tree stump w/ jug and snake, $40.00 to..... 60.00
Shakers, Ma & Old Doc, pr $40 to.. 65.00

Indian Tree

Indian Tree is a popular dinnerware pattern produced by various potteries since the early 1800s to recent times. Although backgrounds and borders vary, the Asian theme is carried out with the gnarled, brown branch of a pink-blossomed tree. Among the manufacturers' marks, you may find represented such notable firms as Coalport, S. Hancock and Sons, Soho Pottery, and John Maddock and Sons. See also Johnson Brothers.

Basket, #581/4, HJ Woods, 8x4x6"... 60.00
Bowl, cereal/coupe, scalloped rim, Coalport, 1⅝x6" 30.00
Bowl, cereal, fluted rim, Coalport, 1½x6x5".................................. 25.00
Bowl, cream soup, 6½", w/7" underplate, Copeland........................ 45.00
Bowl, cream soup, scalloped, Spode 45.00
Bowl, fruit, 8-sided, Coalport, 5"... 15.00
Bowl, rimmed soup, Coalport, 8"... 45.00
Bowl, serving, Coalport, 3¾x11"... 75.00
Bowl, serving, Copeland Spode, 10" L.. 45.00
Bowl, serving, hdls, Coalport, w/lid, 9" 325.00
Bowl, serving, scalloped, oval, Coalport, 2x10x8" 115.00
Bowl, serving, sq, Spode, 9".. 105.00
Bowl, vegetable, John Maddock & Sons, ca 1935, w/lid, 8" dia..... 55.00
Cake plate, ped ft, Coalport, 3x9½".. 150.00
Cake plate, tab hdls, Coalport, 9x10" 55.00
Cake stand, Coalport, 3x8".. 110.00
Casserole, Maddock, w/lid, 12x7", $65 to 80.00
Coffeepot, scalloped edges, ribbed body, Spode, 9"...................... 275.00
Cup/saucer, bouillon, scalloped rim, flat, Coalport 40.00
Cup/saucer, chocolate, Coalport, 2½x3½", 5¼" 22.50
Gravy boat, attached tray, Maddock, 9" L.................................... 20.00
Pitcher, Coalport, 4¾" 65.00
Pitcher, smooth rim, Coalport, 7"... 85.00
Plate, bread & butter, ribbed, Spode, 6"...................................... 15.00
Plate, dinner, Coalport, 10½" 55.00
Plate, dinner, ribbed, Spode, 10½", $25 to................................... 35.00

Plate, luncheon 9"... 45.00
Plate, sq, Coalport, 7½" 25.00
Platter, Ashworth, 14½".. 90.00
Platter, Copeland Spode, 15" L, $95 to... 110.00
Platter, scalloped rim, Spode, 11x6½"... 110.00
Teapot, Coalport, 7".. 150.00
Teapot, gold trim, Aynsley, 6"... 60.00
Teapot, hexagonal body, Sadler, 6x9¾"... 90.00
Teapot, ribbed, Spode, 6", $145 to.. 165.00
Tray, hors d'oeuvres, 3-part, Maddock, 10"................................... 50.00

Inkwells and Inkstands

Receptacles for various writing fluids have been used since ancient times. Through the years they have been made from countless materials — glass, metal, porcelain, pottery, wood, and even papier-mache. During the eighteenth century, gold or silver inkstands were presented to royalty; the well-known silver inkstand by Philip Syng, Jr., was used for the signing of the Declaration of Independence; and they were proud possessions of men of letters. When literacy vastly increased in the nineteenth century, the dip pen replaced the quill pen. Inkwells and inkstands were produced in a broad range of sizes in functional and decorative forms from ornate Victorian to flowing Art Nouveau and stylized Art Deco designs. However, the acceptance of the ballpoint pen literally put inkstands and inkwells 'out of business.' But their historical significance and intriguing diversity of form and styling fascinate today's collectors. It should be noted here that many cast white-metal inkwells have lost much of their value. Collectors and antique dealers are leaning toward more valuable materials such as brilliant cut glass, silver, and copper. See also Bottles, Ink.

Alum, elk head, Detroit Mich on forehead, glass bottle, 6½", EX ...115.00
Black Forest, kitten's head in shoe, brass well, ca 1900 .... 800.00
Brass, camel w/howdah, recumbent, 3½x6½"................................ 300.00
Brass, classic column, early 1900s, 3½" W 70.00
Brass, court jesters, 1 balancing/1 atop lid, glass insert, 7", EX..... 100.00
Brass, rtcl bell form w/porc well in center, European, 19th C....... 110.00
Bronze, 3 winged figures support well, putti finial, 1930s, 9x8" ...215.00
Bronze, 3-D couple, he w/scythe, she w/jug, sgn Curomko, doré, 12" L..500.00
Bronze, eagle w/wings wide grasps 2 flags, 2 wells, marble base, 1890s ..180.00
Bronze, Nouveau lady w/flowing hair on leaf form, glass insert, 11" L .. 1,560.00
Bronze, owl w/cold pnt, Bergmann, minor pnt loss, no liner, 5¾"....1,800.00
Cast iron, fox head, head opens to glass insert, 5½" W, EX 285.00
Cast iron, horseshoe on ftd base, glass bottle/pen tip tray, 6", EX.. 115.00
Cast iron, owl figural, hinged head forms lid, 4x9¼" 300.00
Chrome base w/blk pnt, blk Bakelite pen holder/lid, Deco style, 1920s...185.00
Cranberry glass & metal, bee figural, 3½x6¼"................................ 60.00
Gilt bronze, Egyptian Revival, Egyptian figural, 1880s................. 450.00
Glass, Cane cuttings, brass mts, sq, Am?, 1890-1900, 2" 145.00
Glass, Daisy & Button, gr, minor chips on lid................................ 120.00
Glass, gr cased, sq, late Vict, 5x3¼"... 235.00
Glass, guilloche pattern, brass flame finial, sq, Fr, 1880s, 3" 95.00
Glass, Thousand Eye, vaseline, brass/enamel lid, sq, 1890s, 2⅛x2" .140.00

Nickeled finish German WWI Garde du Korps helmet with brass eagle, frontplate, and chinscales, porcelain inserts, $300.00. (Photo courtesy Mohawk Arms Inc. on LiveAuctioneers.com)

Porcelain, bellhop picking up pkg, Deco, Fish/Fulper, 1920s, 4¾"..400.00
Porcelain, floral w/gold, Fr, 6-sided, 2" 85.00
Porcelain, sq rococo style w/floral/gold, sq, Germany, 1890s, 3½"..200.00
Spelter, camel figural, recumbent, 1930s, 5x5"................................. 60.00
Tortoiseshell vnr w/silver mts, ivory ball ft, 2 cut bottles, 4x12x6"...1,750.00

Insulators

The telegraph was invented in 1844. The devices developed to hold the electrical transmission wires to the poles were called insulators. The telephone, invented in 1876, intensified their usefulness; and by the turn of the century, thousands of varieties were being produced in pottery, wood, and glass of various colors. Even though it has been rumored that red glass insulators exist, none have ever been authenticated. There are amber-colored insulators that appear to have a red tint to the amber, and those are called red-amber. Many insulators are embossed with patent dates. Of the more than 3,000 types known to exist, today's collectors evaluate their worth by age, rarity, color and, of course, condition. Aqua and green are the most common colors in glass, dark brown the most common in porcelain. Threadless insulators (for example, CD #701.1), made between 1850 and 1865, bring prices well into the hundreds, sometimes even the thousands, if in mint condition.

In the listings that follow, the CD numbers are from an identification system developed in the late 1960s by N.R. Woodward. Those seeking additional information about insulators are encouraged to contact the National Insulators Association (whose address may be found in the Clubs, Newsletters, and Websites section) or attend a club-endorsed show. In the listings that follow, those stating 'no emb' are without embossed/raised letters, dots, or any other markings. Please note: Our values are for threaded pin-type or 'threadless' insulators; assume them to be in mint condition unless noted otherwise. Our advisor for this category is Jacqueline Linscott Barnes; see Directory under Florida.

Key:
* — Canadian
BE — base embossed
CB — corrugated base
CD — Consolidated Design
RB — rough base
RDP — round drip points
SB — smooth base
SDP — sharp drip points

CD 102, NEGMCo, SB, yel-gr 200.00
CD 103, Gayner, SB, aqua.. 500.00
CD 103, National Insulator Co, BE, aqua.......................... 200.00
CD 105, Am Insulator Co, BE, lt gr.................................. 250.00
CD 106, Birmingham/No 10, RDP, straw........................... 40.00
CD 106, Good, SB, aqua 15.00
CD 106, McLaughlin No 9/USA, SDP, lt gr........................2.00
CD 112, California, SB, lt peach....................................... 50.00
CD 112, SF, SB, aqua.. 15.00
CD 112, Sterling, SB, lt aqua 15.00
CD 113, Whitall Tatum/No 13, SB, lt straw.........................5.00
CD 119, W Brookfield NY/Pat April 28 1885, SB, aqua 3,500.00
CD 121, Am, Tel & Tel Co, SB, lt purple............................ 50.00
CD 121, C&P Tel Co, SB, aqua...8.00
CD 121, Maydwell-16W/USA, SDP, straw 35.00
CD 121, Pony, SB, bl.. 50.00
CD 122; Armstrong No 2/Made in USA, SB, clear................2.00
CD 122*, Dominion-16, RDP, lt peach.................................2.00
CD 125, Hemingray/No 15, SDP, aqua 20.00
CD 125, Hemingray/No 15, SDP, gr.................................... 75.00
CD 125, WU, SB, bl.. 75.00
CD 126, no emb, SB, dk aqua 100.00
CD 127, H Brooke's, Pat Jan 25, 1870, BE, lt aqua............... 85.00
CD 129, Kerr TS, SB, off-clear..5.00

CD 133, California, SB, aqua 10.00
CD 133, California, SB, peach 325.00
CD 133, OVGCo, SB, aqua 40.00
CD 133.3, no emb, SB, dk aqua 50.00
CD 134, BGMCo, SB, lt purple 175.00
CD 134, KCGW, SB, gr aqua 18.00
CD 134, T-HECo, SB, lt bl aqua 10.00
CD 135, Chicago Insulating Co, BE, lt aqua 100.00
CD 136, B&O, SB, gr aqua... 30.00
CD 136.5, Boston Bottle Works - Pat Oct 15 72, SB, aqua.......3,500.00
CD 140, Jumbo, SB, dk aqua 300.00
CD 141.7, WR Twiggs, SB, clear...................................10,000.00
CD 141.8, JF Buzby/Pat'd May 6/1890, SB, aqua 20,000.00
CD 141.9, Emminger's, BE, lt aqua 20,000.00
CD 143.5, T-HECo, SB, aqua.. 125.00
CD 145, BGMCo, SB, lt purple 250.00
CD 145, GTP Tel Co, SB, aqua... 15.00
CD 145, HGCo/Petticoat, SB, aqua....................................2.00
CD 145, KCGW, SB, lt gr 40.00
CD 149, no emb, CB, dk aqua 40.00
CD 150, Barclay, SDP, aqua.......................................10,000.00
CD 154, Hemingray-42, RDP, aqua....................................1.00
CD 154, Hemingray-42, SB, Hemingray Bl 30.00
CD 154, Maydwell-42/USA, RDP, straw 2.00
CD 155, Kerr DP 1, SB, clear 2.00
CD 158, Boston Bottle Works/Pat Applied For, SB, aqua 700.00
CD 160 (Star), SB, lt yel olive gr 75.00
CD 160, Brookfield/New York, SB, gr 5.00
CD 160.6, Am Tel & Tel Co, SB, lt yel gr 3,000.00
CD 161, California, SB, purple 30.00
CD 162, BGMCo, SB, purple... 300.00
CD 162, California, SB, sage gr... 10.00
CD 162, Hamilton Glass Co, RB, lt aqua 30.00
CD 162, Westinghouse, SB, lt gr 600.00
CD 162, WFGCo, SB, lt purple 40.00
CD 162.5, PRR, SB, aqua... 10.00
CD 190 & CD 191, 2-pc/Transposition, SB, milky aqua 400.00
CD 190 & CD 191, Hemingray-50, SB, aqua 15.00
CD 194 & CD 195, Hemingray-54-A & Hemingray-54-B, purple .. 150.00
CD 197, Hemingray-53, CB, clear 2.00
CD 208, California, SB, lt purple 125.00
CD 208, Hemingray/No 44, SDP, aqua 12.00
CD 214, Armstrong's No 10, SB, clear.................................2.00
CD 217, Armstrong's 51 C3, SB, root beer amber 10.00
CD 221, Hemingray-68, SB, golden amber 500.00
CD 228, Brookfield, RB, dk aqua 600.00
CD 231, Hemingray-820, CB, clear 25.00
CD 238, Hemingray-514, CB, honey amber 325.00
CD 250, NEGMCo, SB, aqua..1,250.00
CD 251, NEGMCo, RB, aqua 30.00
CD 252, No 2 Cable, RB, orange amber 400.00
CD 254, No 3 Cable, SB, aqua... 30.00
CD 262, No 2 Columbia, SB, lt bl aqua............................ 175.00

CD 263, pat'd May 12, 1891/ Columbia, threaded inside of outer skirt, $150.00. (Photo courtesy Jacqueline Linscott Barnes)

CD 267.5, NEGMCo, SB, emerald gr 200.00
CD 269, Jumbo, SB, aqua 500.00
CD 288, By RD Mershon, SB, aqua 100.00
CD 292.5, Boston/'Knowles 6,' SB, aqua...................................... 300.00
CD 297, FM Locke Victor NY/No 16, SB, dk aqua 15.00
CD 308, No 100, SB, dk aqua 175.00
CD 317, Chambers/Pat Aug 14 1877, SB, lt aqua 500.00
CD 701.1, no emb, SB, citrine 3,000.00
CD 724, Chester, NY, BE, cobalt bl 5,000.00
CD 729.4, Mulford & Biddle/83 John St NY, SB, aqua.............1,250.00
CD 734.8*, no emb, SB, olive blk glass... 300.00
CD 735, Chester/NY, SB, aqua 600.00
CD 736, NY & ERR, SB, lt gr aqua...3,500.00
CD 742.3, MTCo, BE, lt teal bl 1,500.00
CD 1038, Cutter Pat April 26, 04, SB, aqua................................. 300.00

Irons

History, geography, art, and cultural diversity are all represented in the collecting of antique pressing irons. The progress of fashion and invention can be traced through the evolution of the pressing iron. Over 700 years ago, implements constructed of stone, bone, wood, glass, and wrought iron were used for pressing fabrics. Early ironing devices were quite primitive in form, and heating techniques included inserting a hot metal slug into a cavity of the iron, adding hot burning coals into a chamber or pan, and placing the iron directly on hot coals or a hot surface.

To the pleasure of today's collectors, some of these early irons, mainly from the period of 1700 to 1850, were decorated by artisans who carved and painted them with regional motifs typical of their natural surroundings and spiritual cultures. Beginning in the mid-1800s, new cultural demands for fancy wearing apparel initiated a revolution in technology for types of irons and methods to heat them. Typical of this period is the fluter which was essential for producing the ruffles demanded by the nineteenth-century ladies. Hat irons, polishers, and numerous unusual iron forms were also used during this time, and provided a means to produce crimps, curves, curls, and special fabric textures. Irons from this era are characterized by their unique shapes, odd handles, latches, decorations, and even revolving mechanisms.

Also during this time, irons began to be heated by burning liquid and gaseous fuels. Gradually the new technology of the electrically heated iron replaced all other heating methods, except in the more rural areas and undeveloped countries. Even today the Amish communities utilize gasoline fuel irons.

In the listings that follow, prices are given for examples in best possible as-found condition. Damage, repairs, plating, excessive wear, rust, and missing parts can dramatically reduce value. For further information we recommend *Irons by Irons*, *More Irons by Irons*, and *Even More Irons by Irons* by our advisor Dave Irons; his address and information for ordering these books are given in the Directory under Pennsylvania.

Alcohol, Manning-Bowman...USA, tank missing, ca 1900, 7", $50 to .75.00
Box, English, brass w/wigglework decor, mid-1800s, 5½", $200 to ..300.00
Box, Laundry Queen #2, top lifts off, late 1800s, 6¼", $200 to 300.00
Charcoal, box, brass, openwork top, Dutch, mid-1800s, 8½", $150 to..200.00
Charcoal, box, Eclipse...1983 w/star, 6¾", $50 to 70.00
Dragon, Pomeroy Peckover...1854, figural chimney, 11" 500.00
Flatiron, cast swan, late 1800s, 5", $500 to 750.00
Flatiron, cold hdl, coiled upright, 6⅛", $200 to 300.00
Flower, J Alente NY, brass top/iron base, late 1800s, 9½", $100 to..125.00
Fluter machine, Dudley...1876, red pinstripes/decals, $300 to...... 500.00
Fluter, HB Adams Pat Pending, clamp-on, ca 1875, $200 to 300.00
Gasoline, Dmn...Made in USA, early 1900s, 7½", $50 to 70.00
Gasoline, Sunshine...USA Pat Pending, 1900s, 7½", $70 to........ 100.00

Goffering, dbl, brass on marble base, English, 1850s, 10¼", min.. 750.00
Goffering, dbl, brass w/wood base, English, late 1800s, 8x3½", min ...750.00
Hat, Schadler No 5471 Pat, curved base, ca 1900, 4½", $200 to.. 300.00
Hat, shackle, iron, flat bottom, late 1800s, 5⅛", $100 to.............. 125.00
Ox tongue, slug or gas jet heated, cast dragon design, open bk, 1890s, 7¾"...300.00
Poking stick, English, all iron, early 1800s, 12½", $200 to 300.00
Rocker fluter, late 1800s, 1⅞", $200 to.. 300.00
Sadiron, WH Howell Co Geneva ILL No 2, detachable wooden hdl, 6½" L..45.00

Slug iron, brass with floral chasings and wooden handle, early, 5", $75.00. (Photo courtesy Forsythes' Auctions, LLC on LiveAuctioneers.com)

Small, removable cold hdl, PET, ca 1900, 3¾", $200 to 300.00
Small, Wrought, mid-1800s, 3½", $100 to 150.00
Smoothing brd, European, horse hdl, mid-1800s, 25", $300 to 500.00
Swan slug, Pat Apd For, Daniel Barns NY...1877, swan latch, 7", min ...750.00
Tailor, Sensible...Sept 6 '87, removable cold hdl, 9½", $200 to.... 300.00
Tailor's, #8, removable cold hdl, late 1800s, 8⅛", $100 to............ 150.00

Ironstone

During the last quarter of the eighteenth century, English potters began experimenting with a new type of body that contained calcinated flint and a higher china clay content, intent on producing a fine durable whiteware — heavy, yet with a texture that would resemble porcelain. To remove the last trace of yellow, a minute amount of cobalt was added, often resulting in a bluish-white tone. Wm and John Turner of Caughley and Josiah Spode II were the first to manufacture the ware successfully. Others, such as Davenport, Hicks and Meigh, and Ralph and Josiah Wedgwood, followed with their own versions. The latter coined the name 'Pearl' to refer to his product and incorporated the term into his trademark. In 1813 a 14-year patent was issued to Charles James Mason, who called his ware Patented Ironstone. Francis Morley, G.L. Asworth, T.J. Mayer, and other Staffordshire potters continued to produce ironstone until the end of the century. While some of these patterns are simple to the extreme, many are decorated with in-mold designs of fruit, grain, and foliage on ribbed or scalloped shapes. In the 1830s transfer-printed designs in blue, mulberry, pink, green, black, and some two-tone became popular; and polychrome versions of Asian wares were manufactured to compete with the Chinese trade. See also Mason's Ironstone.

Bowl, Dbl Sydenham, ped ft, H&G Harvey, 7⅞x10⅝" 375.00
Bowl, fruit, radiating ribs/scalloped rim, ftd, Powell & Bishop, 4x19". 275.00
Butter tub, staved bbl w/tab hdls, blk 'Butter,' Staffordshire, rpr.. 125.00
Cake stand, flared ped ft, notched apron, Turner & Goddard, 4x8½". 585.00
Hot toddy bowl/tureen, Cable & Ring, ftd, w/ladle, Onondaga, 8¾x12".235.00
Pitcher, Berlin Swirl, Mayer & Elliot, 6½" 180.00
Pitcher, Canada, poppies/wheat stems, waisted, Clementson, 8½"...395.00
Pitcher, Corn & Oats, scalloped rim, Davenport, 6½x4¾x4"......... 75.00
Pitcher, Dbl Leaf, paneled body, James Edwards, 13" 95.00
Pitcher, emb ribbed borders, rect, Wood & Son, 1870s, 9" 95.00
Pitcher, Forget-Me-Not, Wood Rathbone & Co, 1800s, 12" 435.00
Pitcher, Fuchsia, George Jones, 9¾" 395.00
Pitcher, Medallion Sprig, Powell & Bishop, 12¼x7½" 190.00
Pitcher, Mother & Child, bark & berries, Cork & Edge, 8½", EX. 150.00
Pitcher, Paris, Walley, 11½" 350.00

Pitcher, Prairie, Clementson, 9½", NM................................ 175.00
Platter, emb floral, faint mk, 17½" L.................................... 145.00
Platter, emb scalloped thin border, Meakin, 20x14", NM 100.00
Platter, Fig, emb border, 8-sided, Wedgwood, 1850s, 20½x16"..... 250.00
Platter, Fig, Wedgwood, registry mks for Nov 14, 1850, 21x16"... 275.00
Syrup pitcher, allover netting, pewter lid, ca 1860, 6" 225.00
Teapot, Calla Lily, gold trim, 10½" 200.00
Teapot, Dallas shape, Clementson, ca 1839, 9½" 285.00
Teapot, emb ribs, leafy finial, Furnival, ca 1895, rprs, 9½" 85.00

Teapot, Gooseberry, T&R Boote, 9", NM, $360.00.
(Photo courtesy Conestoga Auction Co. on LiveAuctioneers.com)

Teapot, Gothic, emb grapes etc, Venables, 9" 150.00
Teapot, Heirloom, Red Cliff, 10½" 65.00
Teapot, shaped paneled sides, Meakin, 10" 120.00
Tureen, Double Leaf, James Edwards, ca 1851, 7½x10¾" 200.00
Tureen, sauce, emb grapes/paneled, w/ladle & hdld undertray, Red Cliff... 135.00
Tureen, scrolled hdls, fig finial, Hughes & Bennett, 7x12x7" 125.00
Tureen, Sydenham, w/lid, T&R Boote, 8x11½x9" 200.00
Tureen, uptrn hdls, w/lid, Gelson Bros Hanley England, 6x7x5" ... 95.00
Tureen, vegetable, Corn, w/lid, 6½x12x8" 215.00
Tureen, vegetable, J&G Meakin, 11" L 150.00
Wash pitcher, Centennial, W&E Corn....................................... 425.00
Washbowl & pitcher, Ceres, Elsmore & Forster, 13½", 14" 550.00
Washbowl & pitcher, Sydenham, 14" dia, 11" 135.00

Italian Glass

Throughout the twentieth century, one of the major glassmaking centers of the world was the island of Murano. From the Stile Liberte work of Artisi Barovier (1890 – 1920s) to the early work of Ettore Sottsass in the 1970s, they excelled in creativity and craftsmanship. The 1920s to 1940s featured the work of glass designers like Ercole Barovier for Barovier and Toso and Vittorio Zecchin, Napoleone Martinuzzi, and Carlo Scarpa for Venini. Many of these pieces are highly prized by collectors.

The 1950s saw a revival of Italy as a world-reknown design center for all of the arts. Glass led the charge with the brightly colored work of Fulvio Bianconi for Venini, Dino Martens for Aureliano Toso, and Ercole Barovier for Barovier and Toso. The best of these pieces are extremely desirable. The '60s and '70s also saw many innovative designs with work by the Finn Tapio Wirkkala, the American Thomas Stearns, and many other designers. Unfortunately, among the great glass, there was a plethora of commercial ashtrays, vases, and figurines produced that, though having some value, do not compare in quality and design to the great glass of Murano.

Venini: The Venini company was founded in 1921 by Paolo Venini, and he led the company until his death in 1959. Major Italian designers worked for the firm, including Vittorio Zecchin, Napoleone Martinuzzi, Carlo Scarpa, and Fulvio Bianconi. After his death, his son-in-law, Ludovico de Santillana, ran the factory and employed designers like Toni Zucchieri, Tapio Wirkkala, and Thomas Stearns. The company is known for creative designs and techniques including Inciso (finely etched lines), Battuto (carved facets), Sommerso (controlled bubbles), Pezzato (patches of fused glass), and Fascie (horizontal colored lines in clear glass). Until the mid-

'60s, most pieces were signed with acid-etched 'Venini Murano ITALIA.' In the '60s they started engraving the signatures. The factory still exists.

Barovier: In the late 1920s, Ercole Barovier took over the Artisti Barovier and started designing many different vases. In the 1930s he merged with Ferro Toso and became Barovier and Toso. He designed many different series of glass including the Barbarico (rough, acid-treated brown or deep blue glass), Eugenio (free-blown vases), Efeso, Rotallato, Dorico, Egeo (vases incorporating murrine designs), and Primavera (white etched glass with black bands). He designed until 1974. The company is still in existence. Most pieces were unsigned.

Aureliano Toso: The great glass designer Dino Martens was involved with the company from about 1938 to 1965. It was his work that produced the very desirable Oriente vases. This technique consisted of free-formed patches of green, yellow, blue, purple, black, and white stars and pieces of zanfirico canes fused into brilliantly colored vases and bowls. His El Dorado series was based on the same technique but was not opaque. He also designed pieces with alternating groups of black and white filigrana lines. Pieces are unsigned.

Seguso: Flavio Poli became the artistic director of Seguso in the late 1930s and remained until 1963. He is known for his Corroso (acid-etched glass) and his Valve series (elegant forms of two to three layers of colored glass with a clear glass casing).

Archimede Seguso: In 1946 Archimede Seguso left the Seguso Vetri D'Arte to open a new company and designed many innovative pieces. His Merlatto (thin white filigrana suspended three dimensionally) series is his most famous. The epitome of his work is where a colored glass (yellow or purple) is windowed in the merlotti. His Macchia Ambra Verde is yellow and spots on a gold base encased in clear glass. The A Piume series contained feathers and leaves suspended in glass. Pieces are unsigned.

Alfredo Barbini: Barbini was a designer known for his sculptures of sea subjects and his amorphic-shaped vases with an inner core of red or blue glass with a heavy layer of finely incised outer glass. He worked in the 1950s to the 1960s, and some pieces are signed.

Vistosi: Although this glassworks was started in the 1940s, fame came in the 1960s and 1970s with the birds designed by Allesandro Pianon and the early work of the Memphis school designer, Ettore Sottsass. Pieces may be signed.

AVEM: This company is known for its work in the 1950s and 1960s. The designer, Ansolo Fuga, did work using a solid white glass with inclusions of multicolored murrines.

Cenedese: This is a postwar company led by Gino Cenedese with Alfredo Barbini as designer. When Barbini left, Cenedese took over the design work and also used the free-lanced designs of Fulvio Bianconi. They are known for their figurines and vases with suspended murrines.

Cappellin: Venini's original partner (1921 – 1925), Giacomo Cappellin, opened a short-lived company (1925 – 1932) that was to become extremely important. His chief designer was the young Carlo Scarpa who was to create many masterpieces in glass both for Cappellin and then Venini.

Ettore Sottsass: Sottass founded the Memphis School of Design in the 1970s. He is an extremely famous modern designer who designed several series of glass for the Vistosi Glass Company. The pieces were created in limited editions, signed and numbered, and each piece was given a name.

Basket, bl opalino w/gr highlights, Venini, 1950-60, 11½x6¾" 240.00
Basket, red/bl sommerso in clear, att Salviati, 13x9½" 250.00
Bottle, bl cased in clear, textured surface, ball stopper, Seguso, 8"... 240.00
Bottle, cobalt/gold/pk spiral stripes, w/stopper, att Toso, 9x4"...... 725.00
Bottle, gray-blk w/wht ribbon around body & stopper, Murano, 12x4½"..... 600.00
Bottle, red/bl/clear sommerso, elongated stopper, Seguso, 17" 335.00
Bottle, scent, bullicani clear w/blk sommerso, bulb, 1950s, 5x4" . 180.00
Bowl, 3 tropical fish/plants cased in clear, Cenedese, 6x7½x2½" . 780.00
Bowl, blk w/gold aventurine, contoured rim, Seguso, 3x8" 240.00

Bowl, leaf form, clear w/wht threads between layers, Venini, 3⅜x8"... 425.00
Candlestick, gold mica on beige w/clear stem & base, Cenedese, 19", ea.....850.00
Chandelier, 9 gr stem-like arms, dbl-bloom flowers, 1895, 72x34" 4,700.00
Decanter, gr & bl incalmo, bulb body, att Gio Ponti, 1989, 13"... 950.00
Figure, bull, Barbini, rough irid volcanic finish, 11" L 2,850.00

Plaque, mosaic towers, Gaspari for Salviati, circa 1960s, 24x20", $1,560.00. (Photo courtesy Showplace Antique Center Inc. on LiveAuctioneers.com)

Sculpture, bird, clear, hollow w/appl purple eyes/blk ft, Murano, 12"....240.00
Sculpture, bird, pk to amber, lg curling tail, ped ft, Venini, 15", NM.. 175.00
Sculpture, fish, purple/bl cased in clear, tail up, Alvin, 1950s, 18" ...240.00
Sculpture, head, wht w/appl blk, minimalist style, Murano, 12"..950.00
Sculpture, lady w/flowing cape/skirt, blk & wht latticinio, 11½" . 725.00
Sculpture, man w/fish, mc w/aventurine, 1950s, 12¼" 150.00
Sculpture, rooster, aventurine/gold foil/red ribbons in clear, 12"..240.00
Sculpture, rooster, cranberry w/bubbles, aventurine details, 11" ..240.00
Sculpture, swan, bl to clear sommerso, Murano, 1950s, 14x7x5" . 120.00
Sculptures, man & lady, pk/yel/clear, Murano, 14¾", pr..............200.00
Vase, 5-color swirled stripes, wht int, teardrop, Barovier & Toso, 14". 180.00
Vase, bl twisted form w/internal fish/plants, att Barbini, 1950s, 12"...660.00
Vase, bl w/2 openings in body, att Fulvio, Murano, 1965-66, 16½"..1,200.00
Vase, bl w/wht pulled feathers, stick neck, Murano, 17x5½"........ 780.00
Vase, bl/gr/wht/red swirls, narrow rim, bulb, 9x5½" 180.00
Vase, cornucopia, yel cased in clear, Murano, 10x7" 240.00
Vase, flower form, orange cased/gold mica, Barovier & Toso, 18½"....275.00
Vase, Intarsa, amber/smoky triangular patchwork, Barovier & Toso, 12".3,250.00
Vase, lt violet soffiati, urn form, att V Zecchin, 11"......................480.00
Vase, mc a fasce bands on red, Cenedese, 11x8¾" 400.00
Vase, mc herringbone pattern, Barovier & Toso, 1958, 11½"....7,000.00
Vase, mc swirls w/gold aventurine, Murano, 15x6¾" 480.00
Vase, pk & clear filigree, ftd, trumpet neck, Cenedese, 10x3½" ...850.00
Vase, powder bl opaque handkerchief form, Fazzoletto, 6¼x8¾".. 120.00
Vase, red & wht spirals, slim neck, ruffle, Toso, 8¼x3".................180.00
Vase, red & wht stripes, clear ruffle/hdls, canes inside, Toso, 5¼" . 150.00
Vase, red to clear to lt bl, ribs & pinched waist, Toso, 1950, 10x7".. 120.00
Vase, red to clear w/bullicani & pulled top sommerso, Murano, 12x6"...240.00
Vase, somersso bullicanti, lav & clear w/pulled design, Seguso, 7x7" .1,500.00
Vase, Zanfirico, filigrana in rows of brn & cream threading, 7x12" .. 900.00

Ivory

Ivory has been used and appreciated since Neolithic times. It has been a product of every culture and continent. It is the second most valuable organic material after pearls. Ivory is defined as the dentine portion of mammalian teeth. Commercially the most important ivory comes from elephant and mammoth tusks, walrus tusks, hippo teeth, and sperm whale teeth. The smaller tusks of boar and warthog are often used whole.

Ivory has been used for artistic purposes as a palette for oil paints, as inlay on furniture, and especially as a medium for sculptures. Some are in the round, others in the form of plaques. Ivory also has numerous utilitarian uses such as cups and tankards; combs; handles for knives and medical tools; salt and pepper shakers; chess, domino, and checker pieces; billiard balls; jewelry; shoehorns; snuff boxes; brush pots; and fans.

There are a number of laws domestically and internationally to protect endangered animals including the elephant, walrus, and whale. However ivory taken and used before the various enactment dates is legal within the country in which it is located, and can be shipped internationally with a permit. Ivory from mammoths, hippopotamus, warthogs, and boar is excepted from all bans. Prices for all but the best ivories have declined in value as a result of the current recession. Better European and Japanese ivory carvings have increased over the last two years. Prices are lowest for African and Indian ivories. As with all collectibles, the very best pieces will appreciate most in the years to come. Small, poorly carved pieces will not appreciate to any extent. A major change in the ivory market began in 2009 when it became apparent that Chinese citizens were attending auctions featuring major Chinese ivories. Thus, prices for large, important examples of Chinese ivory carving skill have risen substantially. We recommend the website www.internationalivorysociety.com, where you can find considerable information regarding ivory identification, care, pricing, and repairs. Our advisor for this category is Robert Weisblut; he is listed in the Directory under Florida.

Apple w/pierced village scene, removable stem, 5"......................400.00
Bust of Voltaire on marble plinth, Fr, 1800s, 10" 9,500.00
Candle screen, angels, irregular floral rim, European, 1800s, 20x6"....8,500.00
Chalice, silver mts, H relief stags, European, 1800s, 10½x2".....1,500.00
Clock, 5 musical nymphs, Dieppe, Fr, late 1800s, 8½x6".........8,000.00
Fisherman in boat bringing in nets, 3x14½"+base 510.00
Hippopotamus incisor, mice eating corn, Chinese, 20th C 900.00
Lady holding flowers (Kwan Yin?), sm age split, 14" on stand......625.00
Lady in flowing robes holds lotus blossom, crane at ft, 7¾" on base....200.00
Lady w/parasol, European, late 1800s, 7x3"................................1,400.00
Lady w/weaving implements, Chinese, early 1900s, 9" 675.00
People (6) along sides of covered bridge, detailed, 25¼" L...........925.00
Plaque, openwork w/phoenix/dragon/twining roses, 4x11"+stand...725.00
Plate, sectioned floral rim/goddess center, Japanese, 1900s, 8"..2,200.00
Sculpture, study of eggplant, 20th C, Japanese, 12"...................1,250.00
Snuff bottle, deep relief, Chinese, 1800s, 5" 1,250.00
Study of rose branch, Japan, early 1900s, 13"..........................1,750.00

Tankard, African, carved elephant ivory, twentieth century, $895.00. (Photo courtesy Robert Weisblut)

Temple jar, dragon cvgs, 3 mask ft, foo dog finial, ring hdls, 12".. 1,500.00
Village scene, Japanese, ca 1900, 5½" 2,000.00

Jervis

W.P. Jervis began his career as a potter in 1898. By 1908 he had his own pottery in Oyster Bay, New York. His shapes were graceful; often he decorated his wares with sgraffito designs over which he applied a matt glaze. Many pieces were incised 'Jervis' in a vertical arrangement. The pottery closed around 1912. Our advisors for this category are Suzanne Perrault and David Rago; they are listed in the Directory under New Jersey.

Jar, northern landscape silhouette, acorn finial, 6-sided, 7", NM...2,400.00
Mug, rabbits before full moons, mc on teal, 4¼x5¼", NM 1,650.00

Mug, There Is Nothing Like a Good..., gr & dk bl, 4½" 400.00
Pitcher, stylized irises, indigo on blk, 4¼x5¼"............................. 800.00
Pitcher, stylized trees, matt ochre & gray, obscured mk, 4½x5".1,450.00

Planter, blue glaze with pomengranates, 5½x6", $1,500.00. (Photo courtesy Rago Arts and Auction Center)

Planter, gr matt, hdls, #197, 7¾x11½".. 960.00
Vase, dk aventurine, squat, 3x5¼" 1,200.00
Vase, goose in flight, wht on indigo, incised Jervis, 4x4" 1,850.00
Vase, irises on brn, spherical, 3½x4"..1,560.00
Vase, mistletoe, gr & wht enamel on teal, sgn, Oyster Bay, 6x6", NM . 1,920.00
Vase, stylized trees, brn/gr/ochre, much cvg, 5x3"......................1,080.00

Jewelry

Jewelry as an object of adornment has always been regarded with special affection. Today prices for gems and gemstones crafted into antique and collectible jewelry are based on artistic merit, personal appeal, pure sentimentality, and intrinsic value.

Marcia 'Sparkles' Brown is our advisor for costume jewelry and the author of *Rhinestone Jewelry: Figurals, Animals, and Whimsicals; Unsigned Beauties of Costume Jewelry; Signed Beauties of Costume Jewelry, Books 1* and *2;* and *Coro Jewelry* (Collector Books); she is also the host of the videos *Hidden Treasures.* Mrs. Brown is listed in the Directory under Oregon. Other good references are *Collecting Costume Jewelry 101, Collecting Costume Jewelry 202,* and *Collecting Costume Jewelry 303,* all by Julia C. Carroll; *Inside the Jewelry Box Vols. 1 – 3;* and *Juliana Jewelry Reference: DeLizza & Elster,* all by Ann Mitchell Pitman; *20th Century Costume Jewelry* by Katie Joe Aikins; *Fifty Years of Collectible Fashion Jewelry* by Lillian Baker; *Pictorial Guide to Costume Jewelry* by Ariel Bloom; and *Classic American Costume Jewelry* by Jacqueline Rehmann (all available from Collector Books). See also American Painted Porcelain; Hair Work.

Key:
ab — aurora borealis	C — Catalin
B — Bakelite	ca — cellulose acetate
cab — cabochon	pl — plastic
clu — celluloid	r — resin
gp — gold plated	r'stn — rhinestone
gt — gold-tone	st — silver-tone
k — karat	stn — stone
L — Lucite	t — thermoset
lm — laminate	

Costume Jewelry

Rhinestone jewelry has become a very popular collectible. Rhinestones are foil-backed, leaded crystal, faceted stones with a sparkle outshining diamonds. Copyrighting jewelry came into effect in 1955. Pieces bearing a copyright mark (post-1955) are considered 'collectibles,' while pieces (with no copyright) made before then are regarded as 'antiques.' Fur clips are two-pronged, used to anchor fur stoles. Dress clips have a spring clasp and are used at the dress neckline. Look for signed and well-made, unmarked pieces for your collections and preserve this American art form. Our advisor for costume jewelry, Marcia 'Sparkles' Brown, is listed in the Directory under Oregon (see introductory paragraphs for information on her books and videos).

Bracelet & earrings, Coro, creamy moonstones w/sm r'stns, 7", ¾"..58.00
Bracelet & earrings, Eisenberg, clear r'stns, 7½x¾", 1¼" 285.00
Bracelet, Coro, 4 amber stns on scrolled gt links, 1942, 7½x1" 95.00
Bracelet, cuff, KJ Lane, gt w/eng dmns, $100 to........................... 135.00
Bracelet, Harwood, gt expansion w/bl r'stns, $55 to 75.00
Bracelet, Marvella, red r'stns/pearl on gt flower on pearl strand, 7"..50.00
Bracelet, Renoir, copper loops form links... 48.00
Bracelet, S Coventry, 8 ocean-theme charms on gt chain.............. 48.00
Bracelet, Schiaparelli, ab r'stns & purple cabs 225.00
Bracelet, Schiaparelli, pk r'stn flowerets on gt 145.00
Bracelet, unsgn, chaton-cut r'stns in 2 rows, rhodium plated, $115 to..135.00
Bracelet, Vendome, faux pearls, 6-strand, r'stn clasp, $50 to 70.00
Bracelet, Weiss, 3 lg bl prong-set cabs amid bl & gr r'stns 150.00
Bracelet, West Germany, bangle, abtract, sterling silver, FS mk, 1960..110.00
Brooch & earrings, Coro, flower w/bl crystals w/dk tips form petals.80.00
Brooch & earrings, Emmons, Deco gp triangle w/bl r'stn 75.00
Brooch & earrings, Judy Lee, faux bl moonstone clusters............... 68.00
Brooch & earrings, KJ Lane, crown, gp w/diamanté r'stns............. 65.00
Brooch & earrings, Kramer, bl r'stns w/linked bl beads, 2¾", 1½" . 100.00
Brooch & earrings, orange & gold beaded snowflake...................... 80.00
Brooch & earrings, Schreiner, cut citrine stns /olive gr crystals ...275.00
Brooch & earrings, Trifari, leaf, pavé diamenté r'stns 95.00
Brooch, Art, butterfly, mc cabs & pearls on scalloped wings, 2x1½" .. 48.00
Brooch, Beau Sterling, 4-leaf clover, faux pearl, silver sprigs, 2½" . 94.00
Brooch, Boucher, bird on branch, bl enamel/r'stns, 3¾", $500 to. 750.00
Brooch, Boucher, r'stns in rhodium-plated bow, 1950, 2½", $70 to..175.00
Brooch, Boucher, wheelbarrow, bl & clear r'stns, wheel spins, 1x2" ...150.00
Brooch, Cadoro, 4 lg sq mc crystals form sq 350.00
Brooch, Cadoro, gt birds form Christmas tree................................ 295.00
Brooch, Cadoro, turtle, yel B shell on gt body, gr stn eyes, 1½x2" . 80.00
Brooch, Capri, mc r'stns on cap, gr enameling................................ 48.00
Brooch, Christmas wreath, Art, mc stns w/red bow on gt, 1½x1¾" .25.00

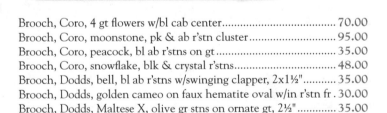

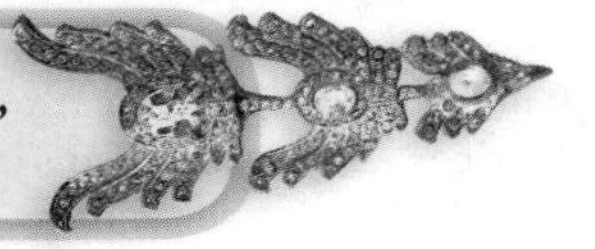

Brooch, Coco Chanel, arrow, 1930s, $375.00. (Photo courtesy Marcia 'Sparkles' Brown)

Brooch, Coro, 4 gt flowers w/bl cab center..................................... 70.00
Brooch, Coro, moonstone, pk & ab r'stn cluster............................. 95.00
Brooch, Coro, peacock, bl ab r'stns on gt 35.00
Brooch, Coro, snowflake, blk & crystal r'stns.................................. 48.00
Brooch, Dodds, bell, bl ab r'stns w/swinging clapper, 2x1½"........... 35.00
Brooch, Dodds, golden cameo on faux hematite oval w/in r'stn fr . 30.00
Brooch, Dodds, Maltese X, olive gr stns on ornate gt, 2½" 35.00
Brooch, H Carnegie, flower, mc enamel w/detailed stamen, 1¾" ... 98.00

Brooch, Hattie Carnegie, native chieftan, plastic insets, $125.00. (Photo courtesy Marcia 'Sparkles' Brown)

Brooch, H Carnegie, zebra, blk pnt & r'stns on gt, 2½x1½" 110.00
Brooch, Hobé, bow, sterling w/lav crystal in flower center........... 425.00
Brooch, Hollycraft, butterfly, mc enamel, 1960s, 2¼", $45 to 65.00
Brooch, JJ, cat, gp w/articulated tail.. 20.00
Brooch, Kandall & Marcus, r'stn waterfall, 1940s, 5¼", $45 to 60.00
Brooch, Kramer, bl & gr r'stns, 2x2½" 110.00
Brooch, Monet, bee, st w/wire (harp-like) wings 55.00
Brooch, Monet, sunburst, gt w/fringe, 1960s, 2¾" 10.00
Brooch, Regency, butterfly, pk, prong-set stones, sgn, oval cartouche, $100 to..140.00

Brooch, Sandor, daisy, mc enameling w/pnt butterfly 42.00
Brooch, S Coventry, open circle, gt, 1960s, 1¼" 65.00
Brooch, seahorse, pearl belly, gt 55.00
Brooch, Star Novelty, branch, SP w/diamanté r'stns 190.00
Brooch, Trifari Pat Pend, poodle, fct r'stn belly, mini, $65 to 100.00
Brooch, Trifari, 4 amber r'stn flowers beside gold swirl, 2½" 60.00
Brooch, Trifari, bird, gt w/baguette r'stns, 3x2", $65 to 90.00
Brooch, Trifari, crescent w/golden r'stns, 2x1¾", $60 to 80.00
Brooch, Trifari (crown), r'stn-studded WWII plane, 2" W 145.00
Brooch, Trifari, figural gt pea pod w/pearl peas 195.00
Brooch, Trifari, floral clusters, clear centers w/red stn petals, 3x3" ..200.00
Brooch, Trifari, goose, gt w/diamanté r'stns 145.00
Brooch, Trifari, key, silver w/r'stns, 1947, 2½", $95 to 135.00
Brooch, Trifari, leaves, gt w/glued-in pearls, 2¼", $60 to 80.00
Brooch, Trifari, Plume, faux pearls on gold feather, 2", $15 to 20.00
Brooch, Trifari, pod, gt w/faux pearls 180.00
Brooch, Vendome, flower, bl enamel w/gr leaves, 1960s, 3½", $35 to ..55.00
Brooch, Weiss, butterly, enameled 85.00
Brooch, Weiss, frog, pk enamel w/gr spots 80.00
Brooch, Weiss, hand-blown pk flowers amid pk r'stns 290.00
Brooch, Weiss, lt pk prong-set stns form 3-D leaf, 2½x1½" 85.00
Brooch, Weiss, rose, pk enamel fr w/pk r'stns 80.00

Brooches, Juliana, butterflies, each $195.00. (Photo courtesy Marcia 'Sparkles' Brown)

Cufflinks, Swank, purple cab in gt fr, matching tie bar, MIB 75.00
Earrings, Coro, amber r'stns on blk enamel cut-out disks 10.00
Earrings, Hobé, gold, amber & blk glass beads w/blk enamel caps, 1"..40.00
Earrings, Hobé, r'stn baguettes on gt mesh dangle, 2¾" 45.00
Earrings, Hollycraft, star, bl r'stns on SP 6-point fr 65.00
Earrings, Ledo, flower, gr r'stns, 1" clips, $20 to 30.00
Earrings, Lisner, flowers, frosted 2-tone glass w/red centers, 1½" 30.00
Earrings, TARA, 3 faux pearls/3 ab r'stns, 1" clips 55.00
Earrings, Vendome, lg bl r'stn drops under sm r'stns, 2½" clips 40.00
Earrings, Weiss, lav glass flowers 60.00
Necklace, Boucher, gr pearl & clear beads, 5-strand 55.00
Necklace, Ciner, oval pavé r'stn & blk enamel links, hidden clasp, 16"..200.00
Necklace, Coro, bl glass ribbed stns w/bl r'stns, 1950s, $65 to 75.00
Necklace, Coro, topaz r'stn on gp links 38.00
Necklace, De Mario, peach/tan pearls, amber/gt beads, sq beads, 17" . 125.00
Necklace, Eisenberg, 'Modernistic' enamel line, colored owl 58.00
Necklace, Eisenberg, 'Modernistic' enamel line, wht owl 75.00
Necklace, Goldette, pillbox pendant (2") w/turq & red stns, 8 chains ..40.00
Necklace, Hattie Carnegie, crystal seed beads, 10-strand 125.00
Necklace, Hobé, bl & clear beads, 4-strand 85.00
Necklace, Hobé, bl & clear r'stn locket, hammered gt link chain . 195.00
Necklace, Hollycraft, gr r'stns & tiny pearls on gt 120.00
Necklace, Joseff of Hollywood, SP chain w/3 owls' heads 295.00
Necklace, Kramer, gp w/diamanté r'stns & pave work 110.00
Necklace, Kramer, red navette r'stns on gt, 17" 65.00
Necklace, M Haskell, bl-gr marble-like beads, ornate clasp, 3-strand . 180.00
Necklace, M Haskell, grad gr marble glass beads, 28" 115.00
Necklace, M Haskell, pk glass beads, 3-strand choker, 16" 225.00
Necklace, M Haskell, wht chalk beads, 3 long strands 125.00
Necklace, Schreiner, red, pk & diamanté r'stns on gunmetal 310.00

Necklace, Trifari, 2 sunflowers w/r'stn centers on snake chain 65.00
Necklace, Trifari, bl & gr crackle-glass beads, 15" 30.00
Necklace, Trifari, dk bl & bl topaz r'stns on gt braid, 1963 .... 95.00
Necklace, unsgn, blk jet glass beads, hand strung/knotted, 22" ... 175.00
Necklace, unsgn, herringbone chain w/gr cab drop, $60 to 120.00
Necklace, Vendome, orange/yel/amber glass beads w/spacers, 17" . 75.00
Necklace, Weiss, diamanté r'stn bib, plat-tone 280.00
Necklace & bracelet, Hollycraft, bl r'stns & seed pearls 180.00
Necklace & earrings, Coro, pk marble & pearl beads, 2-strand 60.00
Necklace & earrings, Florenza, bl ab/red cab grapes, 16", 1½" 100.00
Necklace & earrings, Leo Glass, clear r'stns, choker, screw bks 85.00
Necklace & earrings, M Haskell, red glass beads & disks, 2-strand .800.00
Necklace & earrings, Park Lane, opaline oval in r'stn fr on chain . 48.00
Necklace & earrings, Schiaparelli, bl crackled cabs/ab 280.00
Necklace & earrings, Schiaparelli, lg pk rose crystals & sm ab r'stns..340.00
Necklace & earrings, Trifari, faux pearls, 3-strand 140.00
Necklace & earrings, Trifari, grad gr beads & crystals, 6-strand 80.00
Parure, Hobe, wht beads/diamanté rondels, springe wire bracelet . 250.00
Ring, E Kauppi, rotating mc agate in silver mt 175.00
Ring, S Coventry, amethyst-color stn & sm faux pearls 32.00

Plastic Jewelry

Bracelet & earrings, t-pl lemon-color links, 1950, $45 to 55.00
Bracelet, B, butterscotch beads in gr casings, 1935, $150 to 175.00
Bracelet, B, red, brass spacers, expandable elastic, 1950, $85 to ... 100.00
Bracelet, bangle, B, butterscotch w/cvg, 1935, $75 to 100.00
Bracelet, bangle, B, translucent red, fct, 1935, $150 to 175.00
Bracelet, bangle, L, pearlized gr, 1950, 1" wide, $35 to 45.00
Bracelet, bangle, L, wht w/r'stns, 1935, $75 to 85.00
Bracelet, bangle, Lea Stein, snake, 1960-80, $85 to 175.00
Bracelet, bangle, wood & pl, brn w/Indian design, 1935, $75 to .. 100.00
Bracelet, Ciner, B & gilt brass links, 1950, $135 to 150.00
Bracelet, clamper, KJ Lane, L, blk w/diagonal pattern in clear r'stns ... 150.00
Bracelet, cuff, KJ Lane, B & wood on gilded brass, $150 to 195.00
Bracelet, L, wht w/clear r'stns, 1935, $75 to 85.00
Bracelet, t-pl, translucent gr links, 1935, $75 to 95.00
Brooch, B, African princess w/r'stns, blk over butterscotch, 3" 350.00

Brooch, Bakelite, bananas, green carved leaf, 3x3", $225.00 to $295.00. (Photo courtesy Ann Mitchell Pitman)

Brooch, B, blk cameo in cvd blk fr, oval, 1930, lg, $85 to 110.00
Brooch, DiNicola, moon/star/scales, enamel & turq accents, 1970.. 115.00
Brooch, Joseff, Tenite flower w/gold center, 1950s, $175 to 275.00
Brooch, Missoni, r, abstract mc mask, 1980, $95 to 105.00
Brooch, pl, scratch-cvd purple bird w/r'stn eye, 1935, $55 to 65.00
Brooch, S Coventry, t-pl, turq w/gr glass stns , metal bk, 1960 .... 60.00
Brooch, wood, cvd L & brass beading, bird, 1930s, $95 to 125.00
Buckle, France, clu, side-by-side disks, mc floral, 1930, $85 to 95.00
Buckle, pl, brn elephants (2) w/trunks together, 1935, lg, $65 to... 75.00
Clip, B, cvd butterscotch leaves, 2½", $60 to 70.00
Clip, B, cvd red flower, 1930, $35 to 55.00
Comb, clu, amber w/r'stns, 1950, $10 to 15.00
Earrings, B, blk buttons studded w/r'stns, 1935-40, $65 to 85.00
Earrings, B, cvd red cherries, 1930, $175 to 200.00

Earrings, B, yel triangular drops, flat-cut, 1935, $55 to 75.00
Earrings, Lisner, t-pl, leaves, translucent autumn tones, 1935 .... 45.00
Earrings, t-pl set in rhodium, ca 1950, $10 to 15.00
Earrings, t-pl, yel w/metal bks, 1950, $15 to 20.00
Necklace, B, blk ridged segments, 1935, $95 to 125.00
Necklace, Christie Romero, B, glass pharaoh images, metal chain, 1935 .. 175.00
Necklace, clu link chain w/B mc fruit, 1935, $750 to 795.00
Necklace, Encore, L, clear rnd & sq beads, 1970, $65 to 85.00
Necklace, England, C, mc swirl links on tan chain, 1920, $125 to .. 150.00
Necklace, France, B, cvd red pendant on coiled chrome chain, 1930 .. 400.00
Necklace, Ginger Moro, clu, pk floral drops on pk chain, 1950 ..... 65.00
Necklace, KJ Lane, t-pl, mc beads, 5-strand, 1975, $225 to 275.00
Necklace, KJL, angel-skin floral design, 1960-90, $275 to 325.00
Ring, L, embedded w/insect or sea creature, 1960-80, $35 to 50.00

Johnson Brothers

A Staffordshire-based company operating since well before the turn of the century, Johnson Brothers has produced many familiar lines of dinnerware, several of which are becoming very collectible. Some of their patterns were made in both blue and pink transfer as well as in polychrome, and many of their older patterns are still being produced. Among them are Old Britain Castles, Friendly Village, His Majesty, and Rose Chintz. However, the lines are less extensive than they once were.

Values below range from a low base price for patterns that are still in production or less collectible to a high that would apply to very desirable patterns such as Tally Ho, English Chippendale, Wild Turkeys, Strawberry Fair, Historic America, and Harvest Fruit. Mid-range lines include Coaching Scenes, Millsteam, Old English Countryside, Rose Bouquet (and there are others). These prices apply only to pieces made before 1990. Lines currently in production are being sold in many retail and outlet stores today at prices that are quite different from the ones we suggest. While a complete place setting of Old Britain Castles is normally about $50.00, in some outlets you can purchase it for as little as half price. For more information on marks, patterns, and pricing, we recommend *Johnson Brothers Dinnerware Pattern Directory and Price Guide* by Mary J. Finegan, who is listed in the Directory under North Carolina.

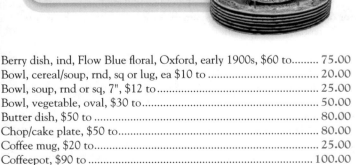

Plate, dinner, Wild Turkey, 10¾", each $30.00. (Photo courtesy Burchard Galleries Inc. on LiveAuctioneers.com)

Berry dish, ind, Flow Blue floral, Oxford, early 1900s, $60 to 75.00
Bowl, cereal/soup, rnd, sq or lug, ea $10 to 20.00
Bowl, soup, rnd or sq, 7", $12 to 25.00
Bowl, vegetable, oval, $30 to 50.00
Butter dish, $50 to 80.00
Chop/cake plate, $50 to 80.00
Coffee mug, $20 to 25.00
Coffeepot, $90 to 100.00
Coffeepot, Friendly Village 90.00
Cream soup, w/saucer, poly floral, wine enamel & gold pnt borders, 1913, $75 to ..95.00
Cup/saucer, demi, poly floral pattern, 1913, $60 to 75.00
Demitasse set, 2-pc, $20 to 30.00

Egg cup, $15 to 30.00
Pitcher/jug, $45 to 55.00
Plate, dinner, $14 to 30.00
Plate, salad, sq or rnd, $10 to 18.00
Platter, med, 12-14", ea $45 to 55.00
Platter, Wild Turkey, 20", min 300.00
Platter, Windsor Fruit, 13" 50.00
Sauceboat/gravy, $40 to 48.00
Serving dish, 6-sided, Flow Bl Claremont floral pattern, 1900s, $300 to 400.00
Serving dish, rnd, Flow Blue Tokio floral pattern, 1900s, $400 to 500.00
Shakers, pr, $40 to 48.00
Sugar bowl, open, $30 to 40.00
Sugar, Flow Bl Coral, early 1900s, 5½", $145 to 165.00
Teacup & saucer, $15 to 30.00
Teapot, $90 to 100.00
Turkey platter, 20", $200 to 300.00

Josef Originals

Figurines of lovely ladies, glamorous girls, charming children, and whimsical animals marked and/or labeled Josef Originals were designed by Muriel Joseph George of Arcadia, California, from 1945 to 1985. They were produced in California from 1945 to 1960, but costs were high and copies of her work were being made in Japan. To remain competitive, she and her partner, George Good, built a factory in Japan that produced her designs to her specifications. Josef Originals can be recognized by their quality, with most of the figurines signed either by incision or ink underglaze; the animals and unsigned pieces came with labels. The figurines made between 1960 and 1982 while Muriel was in ownership of the business are the most collectible and most have a high gloss finish and black eyes. In 1982 Muriel sold her interest in the company to George Good, who gave the girls brown eyes. She continued to design until he sold the company in 1985. As of the late 1970s the figurines started to appear in bisque finish and by 1980 glossy girls were fairly scarce in the product line. In the mid-1970s a line of fuzzy flocked animals with glass eyes was introduced. The Josef Originals name is currently owned by Applause or Dakin. It is unclear if they are still producing figurines as of 2010. Applause Josef Originals are normally signed with the Applause name, have reddish brown eyes, and have little skin tone color. All figurines listed below have black eyes unless specified otherwise or are made by Applause. Our advisors, Jim and Kaye Whitaker (see the Directory under Washington, no appraisal requests please) have written three books: *Josef Originals, Charming Figurines; Josef Originals, A Second Look;* and *Josef Originals, Figurines of Muriel Joseph George.* These are all currently available at www.eclecticantiques.com, and each has no repeats of items shown in the other books.

Applause, 1985 – Present

Birthday Angels, 1-21, ea 20.00
Internationals, copies of early pcs, sgn Applause, ea 20.0
New Baby 15.00

California, 1945 – 1960

American Beauty Month Girls, 12 in series, 3½", ea 40.00
Cho-Cho and Sakura, Japanese ladies, various colors, 11", ea 110.00
Curtain Call Ladies, busts, Marietta, Nanette & Villa, 4", ea 85.00
Days of the Week, 7 in series, 3½", ea 65.00
Dolls of the Month, titl-head, 12 in series, 3¼", ea 60.00
Internationals, Japan, France, Spain, England, Greece, Italy, 10", ea.150.00
Kandy, various colors, 4 bell skirts, 3½", ea 45.00
Little Belles, 3½", ea 40.00

Little Tutu, ballerina, various colors, 3½", ea 45.00
Little Women series, Marie, Sylvia, Victoria, various colors, 7", ea..90.00
Mama (matches Mary Ann), various poses/colors, 7¼", ea 110.00
Mary Ann (matches Mama), various poses/colors, 3½", ea 45.00
Missy, girl in bonnet, various colors, 4½", ea................................... 45.00
Morning, Noon & Night, 9 girls, 3 boys, 5½", ea 75.00
Penny, sitting girl, various colors, 4", ea... 50.00
Pitty Sing, various hats, 4", ea.. 45.00
Taffy, various colors, 4½", ea.. 50.00
Wee Ching & Wee Ling, boy w/dog, girl w/cat often copied, ea 45.00
Wee Three Kittens, in basket, 2½" 30.00

Japan Animals, 1960 – 1982

Bugs w/wire antennae, various poses, 3", ea 30.00
Bunny Hutch series, various poses, 2½-4", ea................................. 15.00

Elephant, sitting, Japan, 3", $25.00. (Photo courtesy Jim and Kaye Whitaker)

Elephant Family, many poses, 2½-4½", ea $15 to............................. 25.00
English bulldogs, 3 poses, 4½", ea... 20.00
Fox, 2 poses, 3", ea.. 20.00
Fuzzy Animals, glass eyes, many types & sizes, ea $5 to 20.00
Happy Worms, various poses, 2¾", ea 15.00
Hippo Family, various poses, 1-2½", ea $12 to 35.00
Kennel Klub, 6 breeds, 4", ea.. 20.00
Lily Pad Froggies, various poses, 2¼", ea 10.00
Mice, many poses, 2½", ea... 12.00
Ostrich Baby, 3 poses, ea... 35.00
Ostrich Mama, 5" 45.00
Penguin Papa, 4¾" 30.00
Persian Cats, many series & sizes, $12 to 45.00
Pigs, nursery rhyme, 5 in series, 2", ea 15.00
Siamese Cats, many series & sizes, $12 to 40.00

Japan Ladies/Girls, 1960 – 1982

1850 Ante-Bellum Girl series, 6 in series, 7", ea............................. 120.00
Baby in a Blanket w/Kitten, bl, yel or pk, 2¾", ea........................... 50.00
Bicentennial music box, 2 poses, 6", ea... 90.00
Birthday Dolls, 12 in series, 1963, 4", ea 45.00
Birthday Girls, 12 in series, 1974, 4¼", ea 45.00
Birthday Girls, angels w/numbers 1-16, various sizes, ea $30 to 55.00
Birthstone Dolls, 12 in series, 3½", ea 25.00
Bonnets & Bows, 3 poses, 2 colors ea pose, 5", ea 75.00
Colonial Days, 6 in series, 9½", ea... 115.00
Ecology Girls, 6 in series, 4", ea... 40.00
Elegant Lady, 6 in series, 9", ea.. 90.00
Favorite Sayings, various poses/colors, 4", ea 40.00
First Formal, 6 in series, 5¼", ea... 55.00
Four Seasons, 4 in series, 5¾", ea... 75.00
Four Seasons, 4 in series, 6", ea.. 85.00
Four Seasons, 4 in series, 9", ea.. 130.00
Girl lipstick holder, various colors, 4", ea.. 45.00
Girl pin box, various colors, 4½", ea... 45.00

Girl soap dish, various colors, 3½", ea 40.00
Happiness Is, various children poses, 5", ea..................................... 55.00
Housekeepers, 6 in series, different household chores, 3¼", ea....... 45.00
Little Commandments, 6 in series, 3½", ea...................................... 45.00
Little Internationals, 32 different poses/countries, glossy finish, 4", ea...65.00
Little Pets, 6 girls holding various pets, 5¼", ea 75.00
Love Is series, various children poses, 5", ea.................................... 55.00
Love Makes the World Go Round, 6 in series, 9", ea...................... 120.00
Make Believe, 6 in series, 5½", ea... 60.00

Melody Maids music box, Lara's Theme, 5¾", $75.00.
(Photo courtesy Jim and Kaye Whitaker)

Melody Maids music boxes, 6 different, 5¾", ea 75.00
Memories music boxes, different poses/songs, 6½", ea 75.00
Mother's World, 6 poses of mother's activities, 7½", ea 110.00
Nun rosary box, 5" 65.00
Nursery Rhyme Music Maids, 6 different music boxes, 6", ea......... 75.00
Pixies from Land of Make Believe, various poses, 3½", ea 25.00
Ribbons & Bows, 6 in series, 7", ea 115.00
Romance, 6 stages of courtship in series, 8", ea.............................. 110.00
Special Occasions, various occasions/colors, 4½" ea 40.00
Sports Angels, 6 in series, various sports, 2¾", ea 45.00
Sweet Sixteen, 6 poses of teenage activities, 8", ea......................... 125.00
Wee Folks, children, various poses, 4½", ea 20.00
Wee Japanese Kabuki, 6 playing various instruments, 3½", ea 50.00

Judaica

The items listed below are representative of objects used in both the secular and religious life of the Jewish people. They are evident of a culture where silversmiths, painters, engravers, writers, and metal workers were highly gifted and skilled in their art. Most of the treasures shown in recently displayed exhibits of Judaica were confiscated by the Germans during the late 1930s up to 1945; by then eight Jewish synagogues and 50 warehouses had been filled with Hitler's plunder. Judaica is currently available through dealers, from private collections, and annual auctions held in Israel, New York City, and Boston.

Our advisor for this category is Arthur M. Feldman, executive director of the Sherwin Miller Museum of Jewish Art (Tulsa); he is listed in the Directory under Oklahoma.

Astrolabe, brass, horse pointer, eng symbols, 19th C, 3⅝" dia...... 360.00
Bowl, silver w/gold int, chased Moses scenes, ftd, ca 1900, 12½" ..2,100.00
Bowl, silver, eng temple/forest, ftd, Russia, #84, 13x13½" 4,750.00
Bowl, silver, Jerusalem scenes, rtcl, 1950s, 9" W 65.00
Candelabra, silver, 5-lt, Austria, 23-oz, 20"................................... 180.00
Candlesticks, silver, rtcl/chased grapes & vines, 32 troy ozs, 10", pr.600.00
Candlesticks, SP, foliage/lion heads, 13x5½", pr 600.00
Cup, hand washing, copper w/lead-lined int, 2-hdl, 1860-1909, 5½". 36.00
Cup, Kiddush, silver, fish, lion & owner's name, 18th C, JW hallmark, 3½".3,100.00
Cup, silver o/l on brass, 7-branch candelabra/star, 19th C, 4⅛" .1,325.00
Etrog container, silver melon form, Nuremberg, 19th C, 5⅛" L .5,200.00
Ewer, copper & brass, Arts & Crafts style, Russia, ca 1900, 6½x6" .110.00

Goblet, HP religious portrait on clear w/gilt, Moser style, 7¾" 300.00
Kiddush cup, silver w/turq in star centers, Israeli, 7½" 240.00
Menorah, brass, lions & crown, 19th C, 9½x11x2½" 1,050.00
Menorah/wall sconce, Deco silver, Star of David & grapes, 14x9" . 2,150.00
Plate, pewter, Adam & eve etching, Germany, ca 1900, 1x9" 480.00
Scroll, book of Esther, ca 1850, mini, 120x35" 450.00
Seder plate, pewter, eng star/animals/text, English, 18th C, rprs, 15".. 4,350.00
Spice box, silver wirework, ca 1900, mini, 1½x1½" 120.00
Spice container, gilt silver, eng fruit form, Poland, 19th C, 8⅝" ...11,000.00
Spice holder, silver, man w/covered basket figural, 2" 170.00
Spice tower, Havdalah, repoussé silver, Continental, 7½" 350.00

Spice tower, sterling with superb filigree work, Russian, #84, 8¾", $900.00. (Photo courtesy Applebrook Auctions & Estate Sales on LiveAuctioneers.com)

Sukkoth Kiddush cup, silver, eng scenes/symbols, Germany, 18th C, 4".. 16,000.00
Torah pointer, silver filigree, London, 1899, 12¾" 3,600.00
Torah weight, SP & MOP, 13½" L 150.00

Jugtown

The Jugtown Pottery was started about 1920 by Juliana and Jacques Busbee, in Moore County, North Carolina. Ben Owen, a young descendant of a Staffordshire potter, was hired in 1923. He was the master potter, while the Busbees experimented with perfecting glazes and supervising design and modeling. Preferred shapes were those reminiscent of traditional country wares and classic Asian forms. Glazes were various: natural-clay oranges, buffs, Tobacco-spit Brown, Mirror Black, white, Frog Skin Green, a lovely turquoise called Chinese Blue, and the traditional cobalt-decorated salt glaze. The pottery gained national recognition, and as a result of their success, several other local potteries were established. The pottery closed for a time in the late 1950s due to the ill health of Mrs. Busbee (who had directed the business after her husband died in 1947) but reopened in 1960. Jugtown is still in operation; however, they no longer use their original glaze colors which are now so collectible and the circular mark is slightly smaller than the original.

Bean pot, Tobacco Spit Brn, flared rim, appl strap hdls, 1940s, 6½"... 85.00
Bowl, Chinese Bl, Asian translation, EX glaze, 1930s, 5x7" 950.00
Bowl, Chinese Bl, hemispherical, 4½x8" 900.00
Bowl, Chinese Bl, oxblood at rim & along glaze 'waves,' 8x15" 2,500.00
Bowl, Chinese Bl w/much red, 4½x7¾" 1,000.00
Bowl, cobalt flowers on salt glaze, cobalt int, Ben Owen, 6" 45.00
Crock, floral, tan on redware, w/lid, 11½" 60.00
Pitcher, orange, wide hdl w/finger-groove top, smoothed ends, 1925, 9".. 110.00
Vase, Chinese Bl & red w/crystalline, bulb, hdls, 9½" 1,200.00
Vase, Chinese Bl, areas of red, mk w/Jugtown Ware & vase, 6" ... 480.00
Vase, Chinese Bl w/Frog Skin int, 1930s, 8" 3,200.00
Vase, Chinese Bl w/red splotches, incurvate rim, 4" 600.00
Vase, Chinese Bl, 5½x7" 400.00
Vase, Chinese Bl, shouldered, 15¾" 6,600.00
Vase, Chinese Bl, shouldered, squat, 6x6½" 350.00

Vase, Chinese Blue with areas of strong red, frogskin interior, circular stamp, circa 1930s – 1940s, 10x8½", $1,950.00. (Photo courtesy Leland Little Auction & Estate Sales Ltd. on LiveAuctioneers.com)

Vase, Chinese Wht on upper half, flat shoulder, 3½" 215.00
Vase, Chinese Wht, flared rim, bulb body, 9½" 270.00
Vase, glossy Frog Skin, 4 sm hdls, 8" 300.00

Kanawha Glass Company

Kanawha Glass Company (1955 – 1987) was formed by workers of the Dunbar Glass Company in Dunbar, West Virginia, when it closed in 1953. At first just blown clear glass was made and cutting and etching of blanks. Eventually, 350 items were offered, blown and pressed, in seven colors, including cranberry, blue, red/orange, and green slag. Specialties included crackle glass and a cased 'Peachblow' glass. Products were mostly decorative items and included pitchers, vases, compotes, cruets, salts, toothpick holders, wine glasses, and a Toby pitcher. The #85 amberina pitcher with a stretched spout and the #148 double spout bottle (Blenko look-alike) are the most familiar of their items. Patterns included Hobnail, Diamond Dot, and Moon and Stars. It is not known if Kanawha pressed glass from acquired or borrowed molds or had new molds made for their items. The company was sold in 1987 to Dereume Glass, Inc., who sold the rest of Kanawha's stock and closed itself in 1989.

For additional information see Leslie Piña's *Crackle Glass Too, 1950s – 2000*, and *Color Along the River, Popular '50s & '60s Glass*. Our advisor for this category is Shirley Smith; see Directory, West Virginia. See also Crackle Glass.

Bottle, water, #148, amberina, 8¼" 45.00
Bride's basket, Dmn Dot, cased, 9" 45.00
Compote, covered, turq, Zodiac design 30.00
Covered dish, hen on nest, blk, 7" L 61.00
Covered dish, rooster standing, bl slag 59.00
Cruet, amberina spangle, w/stopper 21.00
Figurine, horse, gr, 3½" 23.00
Figurine, owl, amber, 3½" 20.00
Pitcher, amberina, crackle, 13" 8.00
Pitcher, frosted amberina, 3½" 45.00
Pitcher, melon, cranberry, 4½" 16.00
Pitcher, Toby, cranberry 51.00
Salt, open, bird, amberina, 3" L 10.00
Skillet, eagle design, bl, 7⅜" L 8.00
Vase, ruby, 5" 20.00

Kayserzinn Pewter

J. P. Kayser Sohn produced pewter decorated with relief-molded Art Nouveau motifs in Germany during the late 1800s and into the twentieth century. Examples are marked with 'Kayserzinn' and the mold number within an elongated oval reserve. Items with three-dimensional animals, insects, birds, etc., are valued much higher than bowls, plates, and trays with simple embossed florals, which are usually priced at $100.00 to about $200.00, depending on size. Copper items are rarely found. Assume that all other items are made of pewter.

Basket, emb flower w/inchworm on hdl, 4 ball ft, #4320, 6x9¼".. 110.00
Bowl/pot, figures at hip, emb flowers, 11¾x11½" 365.00
Candelabrum, 5-lt, #4486, dents to trays, missing bobeches, ca 1906, 19x11". 1,800.00
Decanter, duck figural, head stopper, #4358, ca 1900, 7¾" 525.00
Drinking set, bird-form 14½" pot+5 organic cups+tray, all w/mk ... 1,150.00
Figurine, working man w/lg basket, #d, 9½" 215.00
Nut dish, emb squirrel, #4430, ca 1900, 3½x7½" 185.00
Pitcher, devil's face flanked by irises, #4061P, ca 1900, 12½x9" ... 180.00
Platter, pheasants w/wheat medallion & carrots on border, oval, 10x16"... 75.00

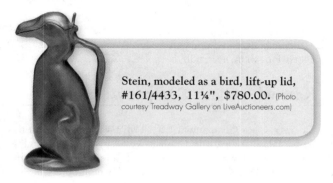

Stein, modeled as a bird, lift-up lid, #161/4433, 11¼", $780.00. (Photo courtesy Treadway Gallery on LiveAuctioneers.com)

Tankard, razor-bill duck figural, hinged lid, H Leven, 1901, 11½". 435.00
Vase, angel & child w/octopus, #4093, dtd 1902, 11½", EX 850.00
Vase, emb orchids, slim, #4079, ca 1885-1915, 9" 200.00
Vase, emb organic decor, 3-hdl waisted form, #4474, 10" 325.00

Brad Keeler

Keeler studied art for a time in the 1930s; later he became a modeler for a Los Angeles firm. By 1939 he was working in his own studio where he created naturalistic studies of birds and animals which were marketed through giftware stores. They were decorated by means of an airbrush and enhanced with hand-painted details. His flamingo figures were particularly popular. In the mid-'40s, he developed a successful line of Chinese Modern housewares glazed in Ming Dragon Blood, a red color he personally developed. Keeler died of a heart attack in 1952, and the pottery closed soon thereafter. For more information, we recommend *Collector's Encyclopedia of California Pottery* by Jack Chipman (Collector Books).

Bone dish, fish figure, teal gr to tan, #151, 8" 35.00
Bowl, lettuce leaf bowl w/lobster on dome lid, #825, 11" L 85.00
Bowl, wht w/strawberries on lid, 6" dia 35.00
Box, duck figure, brn & gr w/wht band at neck, 4½x5½", $25 to ... 35.00
Butter dish, lobster finial, ladle for melted butter, 6" L 38.00
Cookie jar, fish figural, turq w/wht belly, #130, 7x13½" 165.00
Figurine, 2 yel & wht ducks on base, #53, 6" 45.00
Figurine, bl jay, tail up, #735, 9¼" 75.00
Figurine, canary, tail down, on stump, 6" 35.00
Figurine, canary, tail up, on stump, 8¼" 35.00
Figurine, chipmunk holding acorn, brn & gr tones, mk BBK, #629, 3" .. 35.00
Figurine, cocker spaniel puppy, brn, begging, #735, 6" 50.00
Figurine, deer, recumbent, #876, 4½x5½" 65.00
Figurine, egret (or crane), 9½" 85.00
Figurine, flamingo w/head down in tall grass, #3, 7½", $70 to 90.00
Figurine, flamingo, head down, #903, 6" 95.00
Figurine, heron, $43, 15½" 250.00
Figurine, mallard, gr-headed, 6x6" 25.00
Figurine, peacock, #701, 16" 300.00
Figurine, peacock, #717, 11½" 165.00
Figurine, peahen, #715, 10½" 165.00
Figurine, seagull, #29, 10½" 150.00

Figurine, Siamese cat on red pillow, #946, 3x3" 45.00
Figurine, squirrel, brn tones, #627, 2¼x3½" 15.00
Figurine, swan, #725, 9" 125.00
Figurines, Siamese cats, 1 w/ paw extended, #760, 10" L; 1 seated, #798, 7", pr... 90.00
Planter, circus elephant, Pryde & Joy paper label, #502, 8½" 75.00
Planter, Santa waving sled, #909, 7½x8½x4½" 30.00

Plate, fish figural, #126, circa 1940s, 7", $50.00. (Photo courtesy Bob Correll, eBay seller pink1920)

Shakers, Lobster Ware, figural, red, 3½", pr 50.00
Shelf sitters, Siamese cats, #798/#760, 7" & 10", pr, $80 to 95.00

Keen Kutter

Keen Kutter was the brand name chosen in 1870 by the Simmons Firm for a line of high-grade tools and cutlery. The trademark was first applied to high-grade axes. A corporation was formed in 1874 called Simmons Hardware Company. In 1922 Winchester merged with Simmons and continued to carry a full line of hardware plus the Winchester brand. The merger terminated in March of 1929 and converted back to the original status of Simmons Hardware Co. It wasn't until July 1, 1940, that Simmons Hardware Co. was purchased by Shapleigh Hardware Company. All Simmons Hardware Co. trademark lines were continued, and the business operated successfully until its closing in 1962. Today the Keen Kutter logo is owned by the Val-Test Company of Chicago, Illinois. For further study we recommend *Collector's Guide to E. C. Simmons Keen Kutter Cutlery Tools,* an illustrated price guide by our advisors for this category, Jerry and Elaine Heuring, available at your favorite bookstore or public library. The Heurings are listed in the Directory under Missouri. Unless otherwise noted, values are for examples in at least excellent condition. See also Knives.

Apple parer, CI, Pat May 24 1898, $75 to........................... 95.00
Axe, broad, mk Keen Kutter, 12" cutting edge, $100 to 150.00
Axe, fireman's, lg logo, 12½" 475.00
Axe box, dvtl, for #12 K2 Dayton pattern axes, $25 to 30.00
Axe box, for 4-lb hollow bevel axe head, sliding top, 2x9½x6" 75.00
Bearing scraper, $25 to... 35.00
Bit, countersink, $10 to 15.00
Bit, gimlet, single cut, sz 5, $7 to 9.00
Bit, screwdriver, from K106 brace, dbl-ended, 5", $25 to.............. 35.00
Bits, electrician's or bell hangers, sz 16, 12, 10, 8 or 6, ea.............. 12.00
Calendar, Silver Splendor Scene, 1955, $50 to...................... 75.00
Case, salesman's catalog, 15x14x8½", $75 to 100.00
Chisel, butt, tanged beveled edge w/rosewood hdls, 3 szs, ea.......... 50.00
Chisel, mortising, wood hdl, ⅜", $10 to 25.00
Chisel, socket firmer, beveled edge, 1½", $10 to 25.00
Clippers, horse, K940, 10½", $25 to............................... 30.00
Clock, red enamel w/wht dial, KKEC, w/stand, 18¾" dia..........2,000.00
Coffee mill, Koffee Krusher, SH Co, sliding lid & drw, 12½x5", $400 to . 500.00
Dandelion weeder, $20 to... 25.00
Dental snips, K11D, 7½", $15 to 20.00
Fan, hand, fold-out, logo on front, bk: floral, $225 to.................. 300.00
Fan, hand, sm girl w/dog, bk: name of hardware store, $75 to...... 100.00
File, bastard, sq or rnd, 14", ea $5 to 8.00

File, taper, mk Keen Kutter, $3 to 8.00
Grindstone, sit-down style, $50 to 100.00
Hammer, ball-pein, EC Simmons, 32-oz 35.00
Hammer, bill-poster's, K55 .... 40.00
Hammer, claw, hexagon head, 16-oz 25.00
Hammer, jeweler's, ball-pein, $125 to 175.00
Hatchet, 3½x6½" single blade w/hammer end, 12" wooden hdl, VG 25.00
Hatchet, flooring, w/nail slot, EC Simmons, $45 to 55.00
Hatchet, Keen Kutter & Boy Scout logos 100.00
Hatchet, poll claw, plain 35.00
Hatchet sheath, $30 to 50.00
Ice shaver, K33, $50 to 75.00
Knife, farrier's, bone hdl, $35 to 45.00
Knife, ham slicer, K52, 10" blade 15.00
Knife, hunting, Simmons Hardware..., 5" blade, stag hdl, w/sheath ...300.00
Knife, roast beef slicer, 12", $10 to 15.00
Level, KK30, adjustable, brass tip, Pat 12/20/04, 30", $50 to.......... 70.00
Level, KK40, adjustable, brass tip/top plate/binding, 30", $75 to . 100.00
Level, pocket, F3764GKm, wood, 9", $50 to 75.00
Marking gauge, wooden, K25 .... 40.00
Nail puller, metal, 18" 35.00
Nippers, reversible & interchangeable jaws, 8", $30 to 45.00

Pipe vise, 18", $190.00.
(Photo courtesy Dirk Soulis Auctions on LiveAuctioneers.com)

Plane, carriage maker's rabbet, KK10, $200 to 250.00
Plane, jointer, K8, iron, $50 to 75.00
Plane, K31, wood bottom, 24", $35 to 50.00
Plane, KK No 5, corrugated.. 40.00
Pliers, combination, K51, center cutters, 10", 8" or 6", ea, $10 to.. 15.00
Pliers, K45, 5", $15 to 20.00
Pliers, KK7, pistol grip, mk Pat Applied For Shapleigh..., $125 to ..175.00
Pliers, rnd nose, K66-6, $30 to 40.00
Pliers, slip joint, K160, $10 to 20.00
Pocketknife, office, K02220, 2 lg blades, etched wht hdl, 3", M... 150.00
Rasp, horse, tanged, 14", $5 to 10.00
Razor, safety, metal hdl, $5 to 10.00
Razor, str, K746, gold etch on blade, celluloid hdl, $30 to.............. 45.00
Razor, str, metal hdl w/KK written on bk, lady on front, Germany... 250.00
Reamer, wood, sq blade, K115, $25 to 35.00
Sander, electric, KK250B, $30 to 40.00
Saw, 1-man crosscut, #309, emblem on blade, $150 to................. 200.00
Saw, 2-man, $125 to 175.00
Saw, coping, K50, heavy pattern w/logo, $10 to 15.00
Saw, dehorning, wooden hdl, 10", VG............................ 35.00
Saw, hack, K188A, adjustable for 8" to 12" blades, $25 to 35.00
Saw, hand, K24, logo & lettering on 26" blade, $50 to.................. 75.00
Saw, meat, K2, 12" blade, $25 to 40.00
Scissors, 7", $4 to 8.00
Scissors, medical, Germany, 5½", $20 to 25.00
Screwdriver, brass ferrule, 8", $15 to 25.00
Screwdriver, offset, K7, 6¾", $30 to 40.00
Screwdriver, wht #s on red plastic hdl, $8 to 15.00
Sign, advertising store & location, tin, 9¾x27¾", $85 to............. 125.00

Square, K10, long tongue, 8", $35 to............................. 45.00
Square, KC3, copper finish, $25 to 35.00
Square, sliding T-bevel, wood hdl, 6", $20 to................... 30.00
Table cutlery set, SP, 6 knives+6 forks, in orig wood box 50.00
Thermometer, Bakelite bk, 9x2½", $90 to 125.00
Tinner snips, K9 .... 15.00
Tri-sq, wooden hdl, logo on blade, 4½", $20 to 35.00
Vise, pipe, KP200, ½" to 2" capacity, 9¼", $50 to 75.00
Waffle iron, CI, 4-part, Simmons, 6¼", $50 to........................... 100.00

Kelva

Kelva was a trademark of the C.F. Monroe Company of Meriden, Connecticut; it was produced for only a few years after the turn of the century. It is distinguished from the Wave Crest and Nakara lines by its unique Batik-like background, probably achieved through the use of a cloth or sponge to apply the color. Large florals are hand painted on the opaque milk glass; and ormolu and brass mounts were used for the boxes, vases, and trays. Most pieces are signed.

Box, Bishop's Hat, wild roses on gr, w/grayed border, 3x4" 500.00
Box, floral on bl w/beading, 3½x8" 495.00
Box, floral, pk on wht, scalloped edge, 3½x8" 300.00
Box, lilies, wht on pk, sq, 5¾" 635.00
Box, roses on bl & cream w/gold, sq, 8" 1,150.00
Box, roses, pk on gr, fuchsia trim, wht dots, mk, 3x6".................. 700.00
Box, wild roses, pk on gr, hinged lid, sq, 2¾x4" 425.00
Humidor, cigars/flowers on bl, metal mts/lid/hdl, 4½x8¾" 995.00
Shakers, floral on gr, gr enamel top, 3", pr................................. 600.00
Vase, floral on gray, gold metal mts & ft, 17¼x10" 3,500.00
Vase, floral spray on fuchsia, cone shape w/ormolu, 6x2" 650.00
Vase, lg floral bouquet on gr/pk (shiny), 8x3" 950.00
Vase, lg rose on gr, ornate ormolu hdls & 4-ftd base, 16" 2,500.00
Vase, parrot tulips on gr ground, ormolu mtd, 14½" 1,250.00
Vase, roses w/wht dots on marbled bl, hexagonal, 13" 1,250.00
Whiskbroom holder, floral on red, ornate ormolu backplate 850.00

Kemple Glass Works

The Kemple Glass Works (1945 – 1970) was first opened in East Palestine, Ohio, by John E. Kemple, a fifth generation glassworker. In 1951, the plant was moved to Kenova, West Virginia. Kemple purchased old molds from other companies to make his glass. Over 1,100 molds were purchased from Mannington Art Glass, George Duncan Flint Glass, Cooperative Glass, Phoenix, American Art Glass, Sinclair Glass, Thatcher Glass, and mould brokers. Kemple's reproductions were made in a wide array of forms including tableware of all sorts, novelties, animal covered dishes (including the Greentown dolphin), figurines, lamps, and candlesticks. Only items in milk glass and opaque blue were made at the East Palestine plant but, in Kenova, Kemple added color starting in 1960: cobalt, light and dark green, teal, honey amber, End of Day slag, amberina, WV Centennial red, gray milk glass, vaseline, smoke amber, and several shades of amethyst. Although Kemple's unique multicolored End of Day slag is thought to be the only slag made, Kemple items are known in a caramel slag and a blue slag. Many items were marked with a 'K' in a circle; many only had labels. Many items were hand decorated. Patterns produced include Lace & Dewdrop, Ivy in Snow, Moon & Star Variant, Blackberry (aka Dewberry), Lacy Heart, Champion, Swirl, Beaded Scroll, Sunburst, McKee's Pres-Cut series, Swirl, and Hobstar & Fan. All molds were sold to the Wheaton Company of Millville, New Jersey, at closing. Some of the molds were reused for a short time as Wheatonware or Wheatoncraft items and made in clear, amber, blue, and green. In most cases, the Kemple mark was removed.

For further reference see *Kemple Glass, 1945 – 1970*, by John R. Burkholder and Thomas O'Connor. Our advisor for Kemple is Shirley Smith; see Directory, West Virginia. See also Milk Glass; Slag Glass.

Toothpick, handled, hand painted, $25.00. (Photo courtesy www.dnl-antiques.com)

Bonbon, Martec, mg, triangular design	17.00
Bowl, mg, HP, 7"	19.00
Candlesticks, finger, #198, bl, 4", pr	30.00
Compote, covered, Hobstar & Fan, mg	15.00
Compote, ftd, amber, Martec, 5"	11.00
Covered dish, cow, mg	57.00
Covered dish, dolphin, amethyst, 7½" L	100.00
Covered dish, hen on nest, mg	45.00
Covered dish, rooster on nest, end of day slag	85.00
Covered dish, turkey, mg, 5" L	25.00
Goblet, Yutec, mg, 7½"	18.00
Pitcher, Beaded Jewel & Dewdrop, mg, 8"	7.00
Plaque, lion, mg	56.00
Plate, lacy edge, HP, mg, 7¼"	12.00
Plate, mg, mk, 7"	4.00
Toothpick, 3-hdld, amber, mk, 2"	10.00

Kenton Hills

Kenton Hills Porcelain was established in 1940 in Erlanger, Kentucky, by Harold Bopp, former Rookwood superintendent, and David Seyler, noted artist and sculptor. Native clay was used; glazes were very similar to Rookwood's of the same period. The work was of high quality, but because of the restrictions imposed on needed material due to the onset of the war, the operation failed in 1942. Much of the ware is artist signed and marked with the Kenton Hills name or cipher and shape number.

Vase, flowers and leaves, #109, marked Unica and signed Alza Stratton, small rim restoration, 8", $390.00. (Photo courtesy Cincinnati Art Galleries, LLC on LiveAuctioneers.com)

Bookend, Devil Horse, Spanish Red w/Goldstone, Hentschel, 6½", ea	625.00
Bowl, stylized leaves, brn & bl, hemispherical, Hentschel #186, 5x6"	590.00
Figurine, female head w/floral scarf over brn hair, D Seyler, 10"	3,875.00
Figurine, Mammy w/infant, metallic brn glaze, #161, 6½"	750.00
Figurine, mother & child, brn glaze, D Seyler, 13½"	935.00
Lamp base, horses, brn on cream, orig fittings, 10"	700.00
Lamp base/vase, lotus blossom, sgn AS (Alza Stratton), #90, 12"	800.00
Paperweight, Suzanne, lady head, goldstone, D Seyler, #157	360.00
Sculpture, female face, pk matt, D Seyler, #152, 6½"	360.00

Vase, abstract, brn on yel, experimental, Hentschel, drilled, 8"	345.00
Vase, calla lilies on indigo butterfat, #153, 11½"	750.00
Vase, designs emb on gr, #111, 5¼"	400.00
Vase, designs eng on gr, bulb, Seyler, 4x4"	215.00
Vase, floral, brn on wht, A Stratton Unica, 8"	375.00
Vase, geometric designs emb on Brazilian Catseye, #153, 11½x5"	625.00
Vase, gr rings on Gr Tiger Eye, Hentschel, #153, drilled, 11½"	365.00
Vase, leaves, muted bl & pk tones on wht, Deco style, Hentschel, 13"	875.00
Vase, leopards on Spanish Red, ftd, #174, sq, 7x6¼"	1,000.00
Vase, linear designs, brn & wht on pk, Hentschel, #174, sq, 7x6½"	555.00
Vase, lotus blooms w/uneven bl over pk, waisted, Hentschel, #114, 13"	530.00
Vase, lotus flower on stippled gray over blk, #153, drilled, 11½"	465.00
Vase, magnolias, red on gray, bl rim, ftd, Hentschel, 7¼x6½"	1,060.00
Vase, rings, brn on yel matt, shouldered, #109, 8½"	500.00
Vase, stylized floral on wht, Hentschel, #176, 12⅛x5½"	685.00
Vase, stylized flowers & seed pods, D Seyler, 12½"	660.00
Vase, stylized leaves, earth tones on lt bl, #87, 9¾"	200.00

Kentucky Derby Glasses

Kentucky Derby glasses are the official souvenir glasses sold at Churchill Downs filled with mint juleps on Derby Day. Many folks from all over the country who attend the Derby take home the souvenir glass, and thus the collecting begins. The first glass (1938) is said to have either been given away as a souvenir or used for drinks among the elite at the Downs. This one, the 1939 glass, two glasses from 1940, the 1940 – 1941 aluminum tumbler, the 'Beetleware' tumblers from 1941 to 1944, and the 1945 short, tall, and jigger glasses are the rarest, most sought-after glasses, and they command the highest prices. Some 1974 glasses incorrectly listed the 1971 winner Canonero II as just Canonero; as a result, it became the 'mistake' glass for that year. Also, glasses made by the Federal Glass Company (whose logo, found on the bottom of the glass, is a small shield containing an 'F') were used for extra glasses for the 100th running in 1974. There is also a 'mistake' and a correct Federal glass, making four to collect for that year. Two glasses were produced in 1986 as the mistake glass has an incorrect 1985 copyright printed on it. Another mistake glass was produced in 2003 as some were made with the 1932 winner Burgoo King listed incorrectly as a Triple Crown winner instead of the 1937 winner of the Triple Crown, War Admiral.

The 1956 glass has four variations. On some 1956 glasses the star which was meant to separate the words 'Kentucky Derby' is missing, making only one star instead of two stars. Also, all three horses on the glass were meant to have tails, but on some of the glasses only two have tails making two tails instead of three. To identify which 1956 glass you have, just count the number of stars and tails.

In order to identify the year of a pre-1969 glass, since it did not appear on the front of the glass prior to then, simply add one year to the last date listed on the back of the glass. This may seem to be a confusing practice, but the current year's glass is produced long before the Derby winner is determined.

The prices on older glasses remain high. These are in high demand, and collectors are finding them extremely hard to locate. Values listed here are for absolutely perfect glasses with bright colors, all printing and gold complete, no flaws of any kind, chipping or any other damage. Any problem reduces the price by at least one-half. Our advisor for this category is Betty Hornback; she is listed in the Directory under Kentucky.

1938	4,000.00
1939	6,500.00
1940, alum	1,000.00
1940, French Lick, alum	1,000.00
1940, glass tumbler, 2 styles, ea, min	10,000.00
1941-44, plastic, Beetleware, ea $2,500 to	4,000.00

1945, jigger, gr horse head, I Have Seen Them All 1,000.00
1945, regular, gr horse head facing right, horseshoe................... 1,600.00
1945, tall, gr horse head facing right, horseshoe 450.00
1946-47, clear frosted w/frosted bottom, L in circle, ea 100.00
1948, clear bottom, gr horsehead in horseshoe & horse on reverse .. 225.00
1948, frosted bottom, gr horse head in horseshoe & horse on reverse... 250.00
1949, He Has Seen Them All, Matt Winn, gr on frosted............ 225.00
1950, gr horses on race track, Churchill Downs behind 450.00
1951, gr winner's circle, Where Turf Champions Are Crowned... 650.00
1952, Gold Derby Trophy, Kentucky Derby Gold Cup................ 225.00

1953, black horse facing left, rose garland, $200.00. (Photo courtesy Dirk Soulis Auctions on LiveAuctioneers.com)

1954, gr twin spires 225.00
1955, gr & yel horses, The Fastest Runners, scarce...................... 200.00
1956, 1 star, 2 tails, brn horses, twin spires.................................. 275.00
1956, 1 star, 3 tails, brn horses, twin spires.................................. 400.00
1956, 2 stars, 2 tails, brn horses twin spires................................. 200.00
1956, 2 stars, 3 tails, brn horses, twin spires................................ 250.00
1957, gold & blk on frosted, horse & jockey facing right 150.00
1958, Gold Bar, solid gold insignia w/horse, jockey & 1 spire 175.00
1958, Iron Leige, same as 1957 w/'Iron Leige' added 225.00
1959, blk horse & jockey, gold winners................................. 85.00
1960, blk & gold 100.00
1961, blk horses on track, jockey in red, gold winners................. 110.00
1962, Churchill Downs, red, gold & blk on clear 80.00
1963, brn horse, jockey #7, gold lettering................................. 70.00
1964, brn horse head, gold lettering... 35.00
1965, brn twin spires & horses, red lettering.............................. 85.00
1966-68, blk, blk & bl respectively, ea 65.00
1969, gr jockey in horseshoe, red lettering 65.00
1970, gr shield, gold lettering 70.00
1971, gr twin spires, horses at bottom, red lettering 60.00
1972, 2 blk horses, orange & gr print 60.00
1973, wht, blk twin spires, red & gr lettering............................. 60.00
1974, Fed, regular or mistake, brn & gold, ea............................. 200.00
1974, Libbey, mistake, Canonero in 1971 listing on bk................ 18.00
1974, regular, Canonero II in 1971 listing on bk 16.00
1975.. 14.00
1976, plastic tumbler or regular glass, ea 16.00
1977.. 14.00
1978-79, ea.. 16.00
1980.. 22.00
1981-82, ea.. 15.00
1983-85, ea.. 12.00
1986.. 14.00
1986 (1985 copy)... 20.00
1987-89, ea.. 12.00
1990-92, ea.. 10.00
1993-95, ea.. 9.00
1996-99, ea.. 9.00
2000-04, ea... 7.50
2003, mistake, 1932 incorrectly listed as Derby Triple Crown Winner.... 8.50

2005-08, ea.. 6.00
2009-11, ea.. 5.00

Keramos

Keramos (Austria) produced a line of decorative items including vases, bowls, masks, and figurines that were imported primarily by the Ebeling & Ruess Co. of Philadelphia from the late 1920s to the 1950s. The figurines they manufactured were of high quality and very detailed, similar to those made by other Austrian firms. Their glazes were very smooth, though today some crazing is present on older pieces. Most items were marked and numbered, and some bear the name or initials of the artist who designed them. In addition to Ebeling & Ruess (whose trademark includes a crown), other importers' stamps and labels may be found as well. Knight Ceramics employed a shield mark, and many of the vases produced through the 1940s are marked with a swastika; these pieces are turning up with increasing frequency at shops as well as internet auction sites. Although the workmanship they exhibit is somewhat inferior, the glazes used during this period are excellent and are now attracting much attention among collectors. Masks from the 1930s are bringing high prices as well. Beware of reproduction masks online.

Detail is a very important worth-assessing factor. The more detailed the art figures are, the more valuable. Artist-signed pieces are quite scarce. Many artists were employed by both Keramos and Goldscheider. The molds of these two companies are sometimes very similar as well, and unmarked items are often difficult to identify with certainty. Items listed below are considered to be in excellent, undamaged condition unless otherwise stated. Our advisor for this category is Darrell Thomas; he is listed in the Directory under Wisconsin.

Bookends, figural stallions, Wein Austria, 9x9", $125.00. (Photo courtesy Burchard Galleries Inc. on LiveAuctioneers.com)

Bookends, mc geometrics on cube form, W/KK/Keramos, 3½x4x4" .. 780.00
Bowl, center, 3 penguin supports, w/flower frog, WK mk, #d, 10x11". 660.00
Figurine, Boston Terrier sitting, Vienna Austria, 6"...................... 120.00
Figurine, boy plays violin, bird perched on shoulder, Wein, 8¾".. 175.00
Figurine, boy walking w/hands at hips, Austria, 12x6" 250.00
Figurine, buck & doe wht-tail deer, on wht base 650.00
Figurine, dancer w/swirled skirt, Dakon, Knight Ceramics, #2119, 8" .. 600.00
Figurine, dancer, #2119, Knight Ceramics, Dakon, sgn FD, 7½".. 600.00
Figurine, elephant, cherry red crackle, Austria, 5x5½" 630.00
Figurine, English Setters (2) pointing, Vienna Austria, 12" L........ 75.00
Figurine, flamingos (2) on grassy base, Wein, ca 1950s, 12x9" 65.00
Figurine, Great Dane in Merle, life-like dog, shield mk/1950s, 9½" . 150.00
Figurine, lady in gr & wht w/sm brn handbag, Wein, 8¼" 75.00
Figurine, Madonna & Child, F Barwig, Austria, #442-A, 9½" 240.00
Figurine, moose, #9-1897, Wein, 15½x16" 155.00
Figurine, nude on pier, #46, 8", EX.. 250.00
Figurine, Octavian w/rose in hand, hat in other, Austria, 11"...... 185.00
Figurine, penguin, on wht base w/silver band, Austria, 5" 95.00
Mask, glamour girl w/earrings+ring, Vienna, #2653, 1940s, 12-16"..1,500.00
Powder jar, Vict lady figural, floral gown, 3-ftd, #342, 9¼x6¼" 300.00
Wall plaque, lady's face, turq hair w/gold, eyes shut, #942, 9x7".. 1,650.00

Kew Blas Glass

The Union Glass Company was founded in 1854, in Somerville, Massachusetts, an offshoot of the New England Glass Co. in East Cambridge. They made only flint glass — tablewares, lamps, globes, and shades. Kew Blas was a trade name they used for their iridescent, lustered art glass produced there from 1893 until about 1920. The glass was made in imitation of Tiffany and achieved notable success. Some items were decorated with pulled leaf and feather designs, while others had a monochrome lustre surface. The mark was an engraved 'Kew Blas' in an arching arrangement. For more information we recommend *The Collector's Encyclopedia of American Art Glass* by John A. Shuman III.

Bowl, bl, wide flared rim, 2x11½" 450.00
Candleholders, gold waves on cream w/gold irid int, 5¾", pr 460.00
Vase, drag loops, lt bl on bl, bulb, 6" 400.00
Vase, feathers, gold on opal, gold int, 5" 500.00
Vase, feathers, gold w/gr tips on gold, cylindrical, 8x4" 720.00
Vase, feathers, gold/gr on alabaster, ovoid, Wm Blake, 4¼" 460.00
Vase, feathers, gr on gold irid, cylinder w/bulb base, 7¾x3¾" 425.00
Vase, feathers, gr on gold on opal, scalloped rim, 1920s, 8" 585.00
Vase, gold, poppy bud form, 10¼" 180.00
Vase, gold pulled diagonals on opal, conical w/flared rim, 4" 275.00
Vase, gold, shouldered cylinder w/flaring scalloped rim, 5" 345.00
Vase, gold swirls on gr & ivory marbelized ground, unmk, 10" 900.00
Vase, hooked gold free-forms on swirled/marbled gr/ivory/gold, 10x5" . 1,320.00
Vase, opal w/gr & amber-gold lustre bands, cylinder, 4-lobe rim, 10" .. 300.00

Vase, pulled and spotted design, green and gold on white ground over gold, 6¼x3¾", $480.00. (Photo courtesy Treadway Gallery on LiveAuctioneers.com)

Vase, pulled swirls in gold & irid on gr, 7¾" 720.00
Vase, pulled zigzags, gr on gold irid, shouldered, flared rim, 8¼" ... 950.00
Vase, swirls, gold on lt orange, spherical, 4" 350.00

Dorothy Kindell

Yet another California artist that worked during the prolific years of the 1940s and 1950s, Dorothy Kindell produced a variety of household items and giftware, but today she is best known for her nudes. One of her most popular lines consisted of mugs, a pitcher, salt and pepper shakers, a wall pocket, bowls, a creamer and sugar set, and champagne glasses, featuring a lady in various stages of undress, modeled as handles or stems (on the champagnes). In the set of six mugs, she progresses from wearing her glamorous strapless evening gown to ultimately climbing nude, head-first into the last mug. These are relatively common but always marketable. Except for these and the salt and pepper shakers, the other items from the nude line are scarce and rather pricey. Collectors also vie for her island girls, generally seminude and very sensuous.

Ashtray, Beachcombers, 2 sets of legs under lg sombrero, 6x4½" ... 65.00
Ashtray, Hawaiian hula girl in 7" dia blk tray, 4½" 530.00
Box, Hawaiian girl finial, 5x4x6½", $400 to 500.00
Box, turq, kneeling Hawaiian hula girl on lid, 5¾x6½x4½" 425.00

Champagne glass, blk glass goblet w/gold nude on side, 6" 235.00
Champagne glass, nude stem, made in series, ea $135 to 150.00
Figurine, Airedale, seated, marbled glaze, 6" 45.00
Figurine, Carmen, nude, flowers in hair, legs raised, 9x9", $160 to... 175.00
Figurine, horse, Registered California sticker, 6½" 45.00
Figurine, nude seated w/red scarf on arm & head, 1½x4½", $250 to ..300.00
Figurine, nude w/flowers in hair, lying on bk, 9x9¼" 175.00
Figurine, Polynesian dancer, 13½" 265.00
Head vase, Asian lady w/gr tricorner hat, H-button collar, 7"........ 70.00
Head vase, black native girl, red lips & necklace, 5", $65 to.......... 75.00
Head vase, Polynesian lady w/L neck, in gr & gold, 1950s, 7"...... 115.00
Lamp base, Polynesian man on knees, gr headpc, 13½x9¼"......... 275.00
Mug, 'Pop,' staved bbl form w/rope border, nude hdl, 4" 85.00
Mugs, nude figural hdl, series of 6, ea $30 to 38.00
Mugs, set of 6, from nude series, ea $35 to 40.00
Pitcher, water, from nude series, $350 to 400.00
Salt & pepper, from nude series, pr $40 to 50.00
Wall pocket, lady removing her gown by cup, rare 200.00

King's Rose

King's Rose was made in Staffordshire, England, from about 1820 to 1830. It is closely related to Gaudy Dutch in body type as well as the colors used in its decoration. The pattern consists of a full-blown, orange-red rose with green, pink, and yellow leaves and accents. When the rose is in pink, the ware is often referred to as Queen's Rose.

Bowl, int w/wide pk band, deep, 5½" 500.00
Coffeepot, dome lid, minor wear, 11¾" 700.00

Coffeepot, pearlware, 11½", VG, $660.00. (Photo courtesy Pook & Pook, Inc. on LiveAuctioneers.com)

Coffeepot, vine border, pearlware, dome lid, 11½" 2,500.00
Creamer, roses in molded/scrolled reserves, Queen's border, 4", EX ...230.00
Creamer, vine border, red rim band, helmet shape, 4", EX 100.00
Cup plate, solid border, 3½".. 450.00
Plate, orange stripes on rim, 8¼" 250.00
Plate, pk border w/emb dmns, 8" 220.00
Plate, soft paste w/pk lustre 'lacing' & gr teardrops encircling border, 5¼" .125.00
Plate, solid border, bright colors, minor decor loss, 10" 240.00
Plate, toddy, Queen's, scalloped, 5½" 110.00
Plate, vine border, 7⅜".. 100.00
Tea bowl & saucer, Queen's, ca 1815 .... 120.00
Tea bowl & saucer, red rose, vine border............................245.00
Teapot, sectional border, lt wear, 6"................................ 350.00

Kitchen Collectibles

During the last half of the 1850s, mass-produced kitchen gadgets were patented at an astonishing rate. Most were ingeniously efficient. Apple peelers, egg beaters, cherry pitters, food choppers, and such were only the most common of hundreds of kitchen tools well designed to perform only specific tasks. Today all are very collectible. Unless noted otherwise, our values are for items in undamaged, excellent condition.

For further information we recommend *Kitchen Glassware of the Depression Years* and *Anchor Hocking's Fire-King & More*, both by Cathy and Gene Florence; and *Hot Kitchen & Home Collectibles of the 30s, 40s, and 50s* by C. Dianne Zweig. See also Appliances, Electric; Butter Molds and Stamps; Cast Iron; Cookbooks; Copper; Molds; Pie Birds; Primitives; Reamers; String Holders; Tinware; Trivets; Wooden Ware; Wrought Iron.

Cast-Iron Kitchenware

Be aware that cast-iron counterfeit production is on the increase. Items with phony production numbers, finishes, etc., are being made at this time. Many of these new pieces are the popular miniature cornstick pans. To command the values given, examples must be free from damage of any kind or excessive wear. Waffle irons must be complete with all three pieces and the handle. The term 'EPU' in the description lines refers to the **Erie PA, USA** mark. The term 'Block TM' refers to the lettering in the large logo that was used ca 1920 until 1940; 'Slant TM' refers to the lettering in the large logo ca 1900 to 1920. 'PIN' indicates 'Product Identification Numbers,' and 'FW' refers to 'full writing.' Victor was Griswold's first low-budget line (ca 1875). Skillets #5 and #6 are uncommon, while #7, #8, and #9 are easy to find. See also Keen Kutter.

Aebleskiver pan, unmk, makes 7, 7x9"+hdl 75.00
Ashtray, Griswold #770, sq, $20 to.. 30.00
Baster, Wagner #9, drip-drop, lg 75.00
Bundt cake pan, Wagner Ware B, $100 to 150.00
Cake mold, Lamb, Griswold, PIN 866, $75 to 100.00
Cake mold, Santa, Griswold, #897 & #898 on hdls, 12" 300.00
Cake pan, Wagner #1510, 2½x17x11¾" 225.00
Chicken fryer, Wagner, sq, w/lid, 3x10x10"+hdl 155.00
Display rack, Griswold skillet/Griswold plate, brn wood rails, $300 to.. 350.00
Dutch oven, Favorite Piqua Ware #8, TM, $30 to 50.00
Dutch oven, Griswold #8, Tite-Top Baster, Slant TM, $50 to........ 75.00
Dutch oven, Griswold #9, Late Tite-Top, Block TMs, w/trivet, $50 to .. 80.00
Dutch oven, Griswold, #9 Tite-Top Erie PA USA Pat 1,333.917, w/lid. 210.00
Dutch oven, Griswold #10 Tite Top, PIN 2553A, w/trivet 235.00
Dutch oven, Griswold #310 Tite-Top, flanged lid, ftd, 1920 .... 350.00
Dutch oven lid, Griswold #8, hinged, $25 to 30.00
Gem pan, GF Filley #8, makes 11 rectangles, 1¼x13x6" 255.00
Gem pan, Griswold #11, Fr roll pan, mk NES oN (sic), 11, $40 to.. 60.00
Gem pan, Griswold #18, popover, wide hdl, 6 cups, $50 to............ 70.00
Golf ball pan, Griswold #9, FW 150.00
Griddle, Griswold #8, Slant TM, X-bar support, hdl, $20 to.......... 40.00
Griddle, Griswold #14, Bailed, Block TM, $50 to 75.00
Griddle, Wapak #8, oval, early TM, $50 to..................................... 75.00
Grill, Griswold #18, 'cookie sheet' pattern #1108, 16¾x10" 225.00
Heat regulator, Griswold #300, dbl-sided 325.00
Hot plate, Griswold #33, 3-burner, w/gas valves, 4-leg.................. 215.00
Kettle, #7, w/bail, 7¾x9¼" 145.00
Kettle, Griswold #8, Maslin shape, 6-qt 75.00
Muffin pan, Griswold #3, mk #3 & #943 only, 11 cups, $150 to .. 175.00
Muffin pan, Griswold #50, heart & star, 6 cups, $1,000 to 1,500.00
Roaster, Oval, Griswold #3, Block TMs, w/lid, $475 to 525.00
Roaster, Oval, Griswold #7, FW lid, w/trivet 600.00
Saucepan, Griswold #737, 2-spout, PIN 737, 2-qt 200.00
Skillet, Griswold #0, Block TM, Erie PA/562, ca 1950.................. 315.00
Skillet, Griswold #1, Erie #411 Toy, ca 1900, rare, 4⅜" dia 5,875.00
Skillet, Griswold #2, Block TM, no heat ring, $400 to.................. 500.00
Skillet, Griswold #2, Slant TM, w/heat ring.................................. 365.00
Skillet, Griswold #4, Block TM/Erie #702A, 1920s....................... 375.00

Skillet, Griswold #6, Victor (FW) 325.00
Skillet, Griswold #6A, Erie TM 255.00
Skillet, Griswold #7, Erie TM, inset heat ring, $25 to.................... 50.00
Skillet, Griswold #7, Victor/EPU TM, PIN 21B 35.00
Skillet, Griswold #8, Block/EPU TM, PIN 1008, 1932-40........... 400.00
Skillet, Griswold #8, Spider TM, $1,100 to 1,400.00
Skillet, Griswold #8, Victor/EPU TM, ca 1920-35 .... 50.00
Skillet, Griswold #9, Victor/EPU TM, PIN 723 .... 45.00
Skillet, Griswold #10, Block TM, no heat ring, $40 to.................. 60.00
Skillet, Griswold #10, lg Block/EPU TM, PIN 716B, w/heat ring. 180.00

Skillet, Griswold #11, large block logo, Erie PA U.S.A. 717, handle marked #11; Dome cover #11 Self Basting, underside marked Pat. Sept. 22. 1925. Pat'd Feb.10. 1920, large block logo, Erie PA U.S.A. 471, $400.00. (Photo courtesy Belhorn Auction Services, LLC on LiveAuctioneers.com)

Skillet, Griswold #12, Erie #719, low dome lid w/FW 200.00
Skillet, Griswold #12, Slant TM, $125 to....................................... 175.00
Skillet, Griswold #13, Block TM, $1,400 to 1,600.00
Skillet, Griswold #14, slant TM, w/heat ring................................ 200.00
Skillet, Griswold #15, oval, Block TM, w/lid................................. 915.00
Skillet, Griswold #15, oval, Slant/EPU TM 450.00
Skillet, Griswold #719, Slant TM, 13" 650.00
Skillet, Griswold, 5-in-1 Breakfast 150.00
Skillet, Wagner #2, Stylized TM, $50 to 75.00
Skillet, Wapak #8, Indian TM... 70.00
Skillet, Wagner #14, PIN 1064, 15" dia 225.00
Skillet, Wagner #1365, mini, 1x4" dia+hdl..................................... 85.00
Skillet lid, Griswold #8, H dome top logo, Block TM, $30 to........ 40.00
Skillet lid, Griswold, sq glass, Block TM knob, 9½x9½", $50 to .. 100.00
Teakettle, Griswold #8, Spider TM top, $400 to 500.00
Teakettle, Griswold, Erie Spider & Web TM on sliding lid, #8 on spout. 325.00
Trivet, Griswold, Family Tree, PIN 1726, lg/decorative, $10 to 20.00
Trivet, Old Lace (coffeepot), PIN 1739, lg, $75 to 125.00
Waffle iron, Griswold #7, finger hinge, low hdl base, $100 to 125.00
Waffle iron, Griswold #19, Heart & Star, low bailed base, $250 to .. 300.00
Wall clock, frying pan w/windup works, Griswold/Erie, 14½", up to..4,400.00

Egg Beaters

Egg beaters are unbeatable. Ranging from hand-helds, rotary-crank, and squeeze power to Archimedes up-and-down models, egg beaters are America's favorite kitchen gadget. A mainstay of any kitchenware collection, over time egg beaters have come into their own — nutmeg graters, spatulas, and can openers will have to scramble to catch up! At the turn of the century, everyone in America owned an egg beater. Every household did its own mixing and baking — there were no pre-processed foods — and every inventor thought he/she could make a better beater. Thus American ingenuity produced more than 1,000 egg beater patents, dating back to 1856, with several hundred different models being manufactured dating back to the nineteenth century. As true examples of Americana, egg beaters have enjoyed a solid increase in value for quite sometime, though they have leveled off and even decreased in the past few years, due to a proliferation of internet sales. Some very rare beaters will bring more than $1,000.00, including the cast-iron, rotary crank 'Dodge Race Course egg beater.' But the vast majority stay under $50.00. Just when you think you've seen them all, new ones always turn up, usually at flea markets or garage sales. For further information, we recommend our advisor (author of the definitive book on egg beaters) Don Thornton, who is listed in the Directory under Hawaii (SASE required).

AJ, crank type, Pat Oct 9 1923, on 4-cup gr glass measure, 12¼x5"... 35.00
AJ, crank type, Pat...1923...in USA, on 2-cup vaseline glass measure ...50.00
Androck, crank type, Made in USA, on orange bowl w/wht int, 5½x4" . 25.00
Ashley, Archimedes type, Pat May 1, 1860, 11½" 625.00
Benjamin & Standard, Pat Sep 7 21 80, CI w/wood hdl, 10"....... 150.00
Dover, crank type, Dover Pattern Improved...Taplins, Made in USA, 11" ..17.00
EKCO, crank type, stainless steel, wooden hdl & knob, 1950s, 11".18.00
Flint, crank type, #676, 1950s, 12", MIB............................... 25.00
KC, crank type, red hdl, gr knob, bubble-blower beaters.............. 20.00
Keystone, fits on clear glass Westmoreland base, 11"................. 45.00
Lyon, propeller, mk USA... 125.00
Nutbrown Foodmixer, CI, table mt, ...#863902 Made in England . 50.00

Silvers #3, incised Silvers Brooklyn, trademark and logo, glass base with measuring indicators, 12¾", $175.00. (Photo courtesy Shelley's Auction Gallery on LiveAuctioneers.com)

Standard, fold-flat type, Pat June 29 '80 on gear wheel 125.00
Unmarked, crank type w/gr wooden hdl on Jadite bowl, 11x5" 50.00

Egg Timers

Black chef, seated, timer in right hand, ceramic, mc, Germany, 4½".50.00
Dog holding timer w/front paws, ceramic, wht w/mc, Japan, #59462...35.00
Duck w/hat & umbrella, ceramic, mc, Germany, #11564, 4½"....... 35.00
George Washington, Kitchen Independence, ceramic, mc, Enesco, 5½".27.50
Kitchen Prayer Lady, ceramic, pk, Enesco, 5¾", $50 to 70.00
Lady talking on phone, ceramic, mc, Germany, 1930s, 4"............. 45.00
Little Black Sambo, ceramic, mc, Japan, 1950s, 4½" 50.00
Mammy, pnt chalkware, frying pan in right hand, timer in left, 5⅞"..265.00
Mickey Mouse, timer at end of nose, porc, mc, Germany, #1417, 3".. 50.00
Santa stands by tall pkg, ceramic, mc, Sonsco Japan, 4¼" 70.00
Welsh lady & spinning wheel, ceramic, mc, mk Foreign, 4" 42.50

Glass

Batter jug, gr, Jenkins, $225 to 250.00
Batter jug, Jadite, 4x9½", $35 to 40.00
Bowl, batter, Fruits, Anchor Hocking, w/spout & hdl, $200 to.... 225.00
Bowl, batter, gr, Tufglass, w/spout & tab hdl, $60 to.................. 65.00
Bowl, Delphite, LE Smith, 7", $65 to.................................. 75.00
Bowl, drippings, Jadite, McKee, blk lettering, 4x5", $125 to........ 145.00
Bowl, mixing, fired-on color, McKee, 6", $22 to....................... 28.00
Bowl, mixing, iridized, Fed, 9½", $35 to............................... 38.00
Bowl, opaque yel, McKee, 4½", $10 to.................................. 12.00
Bowl, soup, Delphite, Pyrex, 7¾" 9.50
Butter dish, Chalaine Bl, ribbed, tab hdls, $425 to.................... 475.00
Butter dish, pk, open hdl on lid, $65 to................................ 75.00
Canister, crystal, emb Tea, $55 to..................................... 65.00
Canister, Jade-ite, 10-oz, $50 to....................................... 55.00
Canister, opaque yel, Hocking, blk lettering, 40-oz, $175 to........ 225.00

Canister, Peacock Bl, 5-lb, $325 to 350.00
Casserole, crystal, emb grapes, Fry, w/lid, 7", $55 to 65.00
Cocktail shaker, amber, Cambridge, $135 to 150.00
Creamer, Colonial Block, $200 to 225.00
Cruet, Emerald-Glo, Rubel, $30 to 40.00
Cruet, oil/vinegar, amber, Fostoria, ea $55 to.......................... 65.00
Cruet, oil/vinegar, yel, Fostoria, ea $100 to 110.00
Cup, Jadite, Hocking, str sides, 6-oz, $12 to 14.00
Decanter, gr, Hocking, pinched-in, $75 to 85.00
Dispenser, soda, pk w/blk base, Orange Crush, $225 to 300.00
Fork, Cobalt Bl, Hazel-Atlas, $40 to 45.00
Funnel, crystal, Radnt, $45 to 50.00
Gravy boat, pk, Imperial, $55 to.. 65.00
Ice bucket, blk, Fostoria #2543, $60 to 65.00
Ice bucket, gr, McKee, $40 to 45.00
Ice bucket, yel, Paden City, $145 to 155.00

Juicer, Ser-Mor, Uranium Green (rare color), metal fittings, 9x7", $210.00. (Photo courtesy Estate Road Show on LiveAuctioneers.com)

Knife, 3 Star, pk, 8½", $32 to... 35.00
Knife, Aer-Flo, amber, 7½", $300 to 350.00
Knife, crystal, plain hdl, 8½", $12 to 15.00
Knife, Dur-X, 3-leaf, gr, 9¼" 40.00
Knife, Dur-X, 5-leaf, bl, 8½", $38 to 45.00
Knife, rose spray, amber, 8½", $275 to 295.00
Knife, Steel-ite, crystal, $35 to 40.00
Knife, Stonex, amber, 8¼", $275 to..................................... 300.00
Knife, Stonex, gr, 8½" 80.00
Ladle, crystal, Fostoria, $18 to 20.00
Measuring cup, crystal, Glasbake, McKee, 2-cup, $40 to............. 45.00
Measuring cup, crystal, Hazel-Atlas, 4-cup, $28 to 30.00
Measuring cup, red flashed, Glasbake, $55 to 65.00
Mold, gelatin, crystal, Glasbake, $15 to 18.00
Mold, gelatin, pk, Tufglas, $55 to 65.00
Mug, cobalt, Cambridge, $75 to 80.00
Napkin holder, gr clambroth, Serve-All emb on front, $200 to ... 225.00
Pitcher, custard, 2-cup, $35 to 40.00
Reamer, amber, Fed, 6-sided cone, vertical hdl, $325 to............. 350.00
Reamer, amber, Fed, tab hdl, $300 to 325.00
Reamer, elephant-decor base, Fenton, $110 to 125.00
Refrigerator dish, bl & wht, Pyrex, 4¼x6¾", $20 to 25.00
Refrigerator dish, gr, Hocking, paneled, 8x8", $50 to 55.00
Relish, Emerald-Glo, Rubel, $55 to..................................... 65.00
Rolling pin, Chalaine Bl, $500 to 600.00
Rolling pin, clambroth, wooden hdls, $125 to.......................... 135.00
Rolling pin, opaque yel, McKee, w/screw-on metal lid, $350 to... 450.00
Rolling pin, pk, screw-on wooden hdls, $450 to 500.00
Shakers, crystal, Jeannette, ftd, pr $26 to 40.00
Sherbet, gr clambroth, $12 to 15.00
Spoon holder, crystal, Pat Feb 11, 1913, $20 to 25.00
Spoon, yel, lg, $60 to 70.00
Straw holder, red, w/metal lid, tall, $200 to 225.00
Sugar bowl, gr, Hazel-Atlas, open, $75 to 80.00

Sugar shaker, opaque yel, Hocking, $40 to...................................... 45.00
Syrup, pk, Paden City #11, $75 to... 85.00
Teakettle, crystal, Silex, $25 to 30.00
Toothpick holder, gr, Hocking, $25 to 30.00
Tray, clambroth, 10½" sq, $25 to 30.00
Tumbler, gr, Paden City, ftd, $18 to.. 20.00
Tumbler, Jadite, $25 to.. 30.00

Miscellaneous

Apple peeler, Domestic Landers Frary & Clark...1873, clamps to table..260.00
Apple peeler, Goodell Bonanza, orig gr pnt on CI, clamps to table.. 275.00

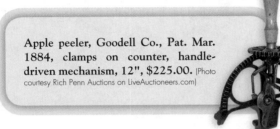

Apple peeler, Goodell Co., Pat. Mar. 1884, clamps on counter, handle-driven mechanism, 12", $225.00. (Photo courtesy Rich Penn Auctions on LiveAuctioneers.com)

Apple peeler, Reading, CI, clamps to table, Pat May 5, 1868......... 80.00
Apple peeler, Reading, CI, crank hdl, clamps to table, 1872........ 115.00
Apple peeler, Reading, CI, crank hdl, clamps to table, Pat 1867 . 125.00
Apple peeler, RP Scott & Co...Mar 1860, ornate hearts on outer gear ..30.00
Apple peeler, Sinclair Scott, CI, crank hdl, clamps to table........... 45.00
Apple peeler, Union Pat Pending, clamps to table, ca 1895, 9x8" ..265.00
Baster, Pyrex, ArtBek, 1946, 8", M in orig tube 25.00
Bowl, mixing, Diana, plastic, bl w/wht polka dots, wht int, 7½".... 75.00
Bowl, mixing, red Melmac w/mc confetti, Brookpark, 5x11½" 27.50
Bowl, mixing, Texasware, gray-gr Melmac w/mc confetti, #118, 10" . 30.00
Bowl, mixing, Texasware, mc Melmac (confetti), #125, 11½" 50.00
Bowl, mixing, Texasware, pk Melmac w/fine confetti, #125, 5x11" .85.00
Bowl, serving, Boonton, wht Melmac, divided, w/lid, 8½" 18.00
Bread box, gr enamel w/wht int, vents in hinged lid, 9x19x6"..... 100.00
Can opener, CI, 1 finger ring, European, ca 1900, 3½" 75.00
Can opener, Daisy Universal, CI, hand crank, wall mt, 6x6" 40.00
Can opener, metal, mts to wall & swivels, Made in St Louis USA ..22.00
Carrier, cake, Regal Ware, red alum, blk Bakelite hdl, 7x13"......... 65.00
Carrier, cake, tin litho, red roses, plain red lid, wht inner lid......... 45.00
Carrier, cake/pie, Regal, alum, holds 5 cakes/pies, strap hdl 60.00
Cheese slicer, wire cutter w/brn swirl Bakelite hdl.......................... 12.00
Chopper, dbl curved blades, wooden hdl, 5x6" 35.00
Chopper, single curved blade, extended wooden hdl, 6x7½" 60.00
Chopper, single curved blade, wood hdl, 8x6" 35.00
Churn, ...Mixer & Whipper & Handy Kitchen Aid on label, 4-qt, 14x6"...70.00
Churn, Dazey #20, $100 to.. 150.00
Churn, Dazey #30, Pat 1922, $175 to... 200.00
Churn, Dazey #40, Pat Feb 14 22, Made in USA, Dazey emblem. 125.00
Churn, Dazey #60, $120 to.. 150.00
Churn, Dazey #80, EX, $150 to 175.00
Churn, SMP Triumph Trade, General Steels, metal, 1920s, 14" 60.00
Clock/wall pocket, red/wht, Telechron #2H33, 1950s, 5¾x8¾"..... 35.00
Colander, Wear-Ever, alum, w/stand & mallet, 8¼" dia.................. 20.00
Colander, wht enameling w/red trim & hdls, ftd 50.00
Crimper, alum, spoon-like shape, unmk, 5" 40.00
Cutter, cheese, wire held in fr, Bakelite hdl, Clem-Brand, 8x3"..... 25.00
Dough scraper, forged iron w/wooden hdl, early 1900s, 2x5½"....... 30.00
Food mill, Foley #101, metal w/red wood hdl, 7" dia, EX, +booklet... 17.50

Food mill, Foley, 2 bottom clips, metal w/red wood hdl, 7½" dia ... 30.00
French fry cutter, Made in USA, wires in metal fr, loop hdl, 12½x5".25.00
Grater, wires X in metal fr, Made in USA, 9x5½"+4" hdl 20.00
Ice pick, red wood hdl w/metal end, 8¼" 16.00
Jar lifter, Earthgrown, tong-like, gr coating on clasp, blk hdls, 8" .. 12.50
Juicer/extractor, Hamilton Beach #32, lever action, gr porc base... 70.00
Juicer/press, Wear-Ever, alum, squeeze type 50.00
Juicer/strainer, Wear-Ever, alum, lever action, 3-ftd 40.00
Knife sharpener, Ekco Cherrywood Series, steel w/wood hdl, 1970s .. 20.00
Knife sharpener, steel w/hardwood hdl, Forschner, 12" 26.00
Knife, chef's, Sabatier, steel blade, elephant & 4 stars on hdl, 17" ... 120.00
Measuring cups, copper can shape, brass hdls, ea w/emb sz, set of 4 ..60.00
Meat grinder, Landers Frary Clark...#71, complete in box.............. 50.00
Meat tenderizer, CI, 3" rnd grid w/hdl, 7" 10.00
Meat tenderizer, wooden mallet type w/gr pnt wood hdl, 1930s..... 15.00
Nutmeg grater, tin, cylindrical, emb NUTMEG at top, 7½x2" 20.00
Nutmeg grater, tin, w/snap-up lid for storage, 5½" 38.00
Pastry blender, Androck, arched wires held by yel Bakelite hdl..... 12.50
Platter, Boonton, yel Melmac, 14½x10¼"...................................... 20.00
Potato masher, primitive, solid wood, 2" dia bottom, 11" w/hdl..... 20.00
Ricer/press, Co Mt Joy PA USA, CI, removable basket, 1800s, 4x10" ..20.00
Scoop, sugar, Wagner #2, alum, 5x12½"... 15.00
Sifter, Androck Handi-Sift, lady baking, tin litho, 3-screen, $40 to.. 55.00
Sifter, Androck Handi-Sift, starbursts, tin litho, 3-screen, NM 25.00
Sifter, Androck, red & wht checkerboard/baked goods, tin litho, 1950s.. 35.00
Sifter, red morning glories on wht, red crank hdl, 4½x5¾" 32.00
Spatula, A&J, stainless steel w/gr Bakelite hdl, 12" 25.00
Spoon rest, Japan, owl figural w/daisies, gr/yel/wht, ceramic, 8" 25.00
Spoon rest, Napco, chef holds over-sz spoon, ceramic, 8" L 50.00
Spoon rest, Western Stoneware, bl spatter, 2x7" 20.00
Spoon, serving, Androck, metal w/ribbed bullet Bakelite hdl, 9½" ..20.00
Tomato slicer, Ekco, metal, red pnt hdl... 12.00

Knife Rests

Recording the history of knife rests has to begin in Europe. There is a tin-glazed earthenware knife rest at the Henry Francis Dupont Winterthur Museum. It's dated 1720 – 1760 and is possibly Dutch. Many types have been made in Europe — porcelain, Delft, majolica, and pottery. European companies made knife rests to match their dinnerware patterns, a practice not pursued by American manufacturers. Research has found only one American company, Mackenzie-Childs of New York, who made a pottery knife rest. This company no longer exists.

Several scholars feel that porcelain knife rests originated in Germany and France; from there, their usage spread to England. Though there were glasshouses in Europe making pressed and cut glass, often blanks were purchased from American companies, cut by European craftsmen, and shipped back to the States. American consumers regarded the European cut glass as superior. When economic woes forced the Europeans to come to the U.S., many brought their motifs and patterns with them. American manufacturers patented many of the designs for their exclusive use, but in some cases as the cutters moved from one company to another, they took their patterns with them.

Knife rests of pressed glass, cut crystal, porcelain, sterling silver, plated silver, wood, ivory, and bone have been collected for many years. In the U.S., there were six major glassmakers who produced pressed glass knife rests: Cambridge Glass Company, Cambridge, OH (1914 – 1930); George Duncan & Sons, Washington, PA (1880 catalog); A.H. Heisey & Company, Newark, OH (1906 – 1922); Imperial Glass Company, Bellaire, OH (1957 – 1973 with Imperial logo, 1950 – 1958 in milk glass); New England Glass Company, Cambridge, MA (1869 book and catalog); and Westmoreland Glass Company, Grapeville, PA (1912 – 1924 catalog). Signed knife rests are especially desirable. It was not until the Centennial Exhibition in Philadelphia in 1876 that the brilliant new cut glass rests, deeply faceted and shining like diamonds, appeared in shops by the hundreds. There were sets of twelve, eight, or six that came in presentation boxes. Sizes vary from 1¼" to 3¼" for individual knives and from 5" to 6" for carving knives. Glass knife rests were made in many colors such as purple, blue, green, vaseline, pink, and cranberry. These colors have been attributed to European manufacturers.

There are many items of glass and pottery that resemble knife rests but are actually muddlers, toothpick holders (sanitary types that allow you to pick the toothpicks up by the centers), and paperweights. Collectors should be familiar with these and able to recognize them for what they are. It is important to note that prices may vary from one area of the country to another and from dealer to dealer. EBay sales are closing with steadily declining winning bids; good and unusual knife rests are not being offered. Our advisor, Beverly Schell Ales, is listed in the Directory under California.

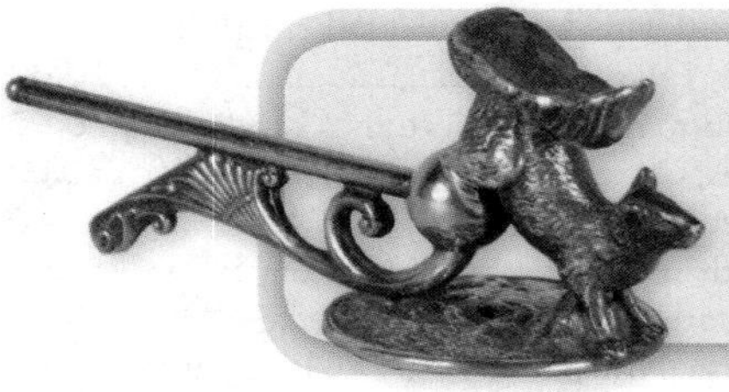

Silverplate, squirrel, Wilcox #1571, $60.00. (Photo courtesy Dan Morphy Auctions LLC on LiveAuctioneers.com)

Aluminum, cast, dragon, Arthur's Court, 2003, 3x½", $25 to........35.00
Ceramic, duck & ladybug on wht log shape, 1930, 3½" 45.00
Glass, cut, 7-point stars on dumbbell shape, 5¼" 75.00
Glass, cut, 8-sided bar, w/dmn-cut ball end, 5½" 60.00
Glass, cut, dmn-cut bar w/ends cut into 4-pointed star, 1880, 3½"...110.00
Glass, cut, Eggington, Creswick, 2x5", $200 to...........................300.00
Glass, cut, Hawkes, catalog 1889, 4x3", $100 to..........................200.00
Glass, cut, Hoare, Monarch, catalog 1897-1911, lapidary, 4x1", $100 to.200.00
Glass, cut, Libbey, lapidary ends, 3¾", $50 to 100.00
Glass, cut, Mt WA, oval & notched, catalog 1892, 2x5", $100 to...200.00
Glass, cut, squash form...75.00
Glass, pressed, Heisey, dmn & 'H,' mk IG, $35 to 50.00
Glass, Quezal, gold irid, 4" L..540.00
Glass, Sabino, bl w/duck ends...50.00
Porcelain, Konigliche Por Mfg (KPM) Germany, 1x4", $200 to ..300.00
Porcelain, Willow pattern, unmk, late 1800s, 4", $125 to 150.00
Pottery, Henriot Quimper, bl, HB, #797, ca 1883..........................75.00
Silver, lg dog figures (walking & looking at ea other) bar ends, 4"..230.00
Silver, pheasant figure on end of bar, detailed, 1¼x4" 140.00
Silverplate, Art Nouveau birds, Reed & Barton, 1884 catalog.......65.00
Silverplate, Meriden, cherubs on ends, 1x3", $35 to 50.00
Sterling, Kerr, bar w/thistle & leaves on ends, ca 1900, 2x4".........90.00

Knives

Knife collecting as a hobby began in earnest during the 1960s when government regulations required for the first time that knife companies mark their products with the country of origin. The few collectors and dealers aware of this change at once began stockpiling the older knives made before this law was enacted. Another impetus to the growing interest in this area came with the Gun Control Act of 1968, which severely restricted gun trading. Frustrated gun dealers transferred their attention to knives. Today there are collectors' clubs in many of the states.

The most sought-after pocketknives are generally made before WWII. However, as time goes on knives no older than 20 years are collectible if in mint condition. Most collectors prefer knives in 'as found' condition. Do *not* attempt to clean, sharpen, or in any way 'improve' on an old knife.

Please note: Length is measured with blades *closed*. **Our values are for knives in used/excellent condition (unless specified 'mint').** Most old knives are usually not encountered in mint condition. Therefore to give a mint price could mislead the novice collector. If a knife has been used, sharpened, or blemished in any way, its value decreases. It is common to find knives made in the 1960s and later in mint condition. Knives made in the 1970s and 1980s may be collectible in mint condition, but not in used condition. Therefore a used knife 30 years old may be worth no more than a knife for use. For further information refer to *The Standard Knife Collector's Guide; Big Book of Pocket Knives;* and *Remington Knives* by Ron Stewart and Roy Ritchie (all are published by Collector Books). *Sargent's American Premium Guide to Knives and Razors* by Jim Sargent is another good reference. Our advisor for this category is Bill Wright, author of *Theatre-Made Military Knives of World War II* (Schiffer). Mr. Wright is listed in the Directory under Indiana.

Key:
bd — blade
gen — genuine
imi — imitation
jack — jackknife
lb — lockback
pat — pattern
wb — winterbottom

Aerial Cutlery Co, 2 bl jack, bone hdl, 3⅝"....................................60.00
Anheuser-Busch, red & gold emb hdl, w/peephole & picture......250.00
Barnett Tool Co, bone hdl, bd+punch+pliers..............................175.00
Boker (German), 4-bd congress, bone hdl, 4"..............................125.00
Boker (USA), 3-bd stockman, imi pearl hdl, 4" 40.00
Boker (USA), 4-bd congress, bone hdl, 3¾"..................................65.00
Boker, Henrich (German), 1-bd, bone hdl, 4½" 65.00
Bulldog Brand (Germany), 3-bd whittler, gen abalone hdl, 5⅛", M.150.00
Case Bros, Little Valley NY, 2-bd, wood hdl, 3¼".......................100.00
Case Bros, Little Valley NY, 5231, 2-bd, stag hdl, 3¾"................200.00
Case Bros, Springville NY, 8250, 2-bd, pearl hdl, sunfish pat....3,000.00
Case, Muskrat pat, 2-bd, bone hdl, 3⅞"..150.00
Case, Tested XX, 5202½, 2-bd, gen stag hdl, 3⅜" 100.00
Case, Tested XX, 6220, 2-bd, rough blk hdl, peanut pat, 2⅞" 100.00
Case, Tested XX, 6392, 3-bd, gr bone hdl, stockman pat, 4"........175.00
Case, Tested XX, 8383, 3-bd, gen pearl hdl, whittler pat, 3½" 500.00
Case, Tested XX, 61050sab, 1-bd, gr bone hdl, Coke bottle, 5⅜".300.00
Case, Tested XX, 61093, 1-bd, gr bone hdl, toothpick pat, 5⅜"...200.00
Case, Tested XX, 62031½, 2-bd, gr bone hdl, 3¾".......................150.00
Case, Tested XX, 62100, 2-bd, gr bone hdl, saddlehorn pat, 4⅝".500.00
Case, XX USA, 10 dots, 6111½, 1-bd, bone hdl, lb, 4⅜", M........275.00

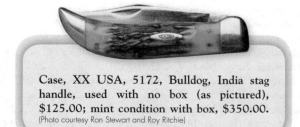

Case, XX USA, 5172, Bulldog, India stag handle, used with no box (as pictured), $125.00; mint condition with box, $350.00. (Photo courtesy Ron Stewart and Roy Ritchie)

Case, XX USA, 5354, 2-bd, gen stag hdl, trapper pat, 4⅛", M.....375.00
Case, XX USA, 52131, 2-bd, gen stag hdl, canoe pat, 3⅝", M.....350.00
Case, XX, 3347hp, 3-bd, yel compo hdl, stockman pat, 3⅜"..........85.00
Case, XX, 5254, 2-bd, gen stag hdl, trapper pat, 4⅛"....................250.00
Case, XX, 5375, 3-bd, gen red stag hdl, L pull, stockman, 4¼" 750.00
Case, XX, 6185, 1-bd, bone hdl, doctor's pat, 3¾".......................125.00
Case, XX, 6231½, 2-bd, bone hdl, 3¾"..80.00
Case, XX, 6250, 2-bd, bone hdl, sunfish pat, 4½" 200.00

Case, XX, 6294, 2-bd, bone hdl, cigar pat, 4¼"............................250.00
Case, XX, 6308, 3-bd, bone hdl, whittler pat, 3¼"........................80.00
Case, XX, 6488, 4-bd, bone hdl, congress pat, 4⅛"....................500.00
Case, XX, 6565sab, 2-bd, bone hdl, folding hunter pat, 5¼"........125.00
Case, XX, 62009, 1-bd, bone hdl, barlow pat, 3⅜"......................70.00
Cattaraugus, 12839, 1-bd, bone hdl, King of the Woods, 5⅜"......500.00
Cattaraugus, 22346, 2-bd, wood hdl, jack pat, 3⅜"......................85.00
Cattaraugus, 22919, 2-bd, bone hdl, cigar pat, 4¼"....................275.00
Cattaraugus, 32145, 3-bd, bone hdl, stockman pat, 3⅞"..............200.00
Cattaraugus, 3-bd+nail file, gen pearl hdl, lobster gun stock, 3"..150.00
Cattaraugus, D2589, 4-bd, bone hdl, Official Scout Emblem, 3½"..200.00
Cattaraugus, gen pearl hdl, 3-bd+nail file, lobster gun stock, 3"..150.00
Challenge Cutlery, 1-bd, bone hdl, lb, 4¾"................................200.00
Challenge Cutlery, 3-bd, bone hdl, cattle pat, 3⅝"....................125.00
Davy & Sons, A (Sheffield England), 2-bd, Liberty & Union bolster..600.00
Diamond Edge, 2-bd, bone hdl, jack, 3⅜"..................................75.00
Diamond Edge, 2-bd, pearl celluloid hdl, gun stock, 3"............100.00
Frost Cutlery Co (Japan), 3-bd, bone hdl, lb whittler, 4"............15.00
H&B Mfg Co, 3-bd, buffalo horn hdl, whittler pat, 3⅝"............150.00
Hammer Brand, 1-bd, bone hdl, NYK on bolster, lb, 5¼"............375.00
Hammer Brand, 1-bd, tin shell hdl, powder horn pat, 4¾"............25.00
Hammer Brand, 2-bd, bone hdl, dog-leg pat, 3¾"........................225.00
Hammer Brand, 2-bd, wood hdl, jack, 3¾"..................................85.00
Hammer Brand, NY Knife Co, 2-bd, bone hdl, 3⅜"......................85.00
Hammer Brand, plastic wrapped metal hdl, Hopalong-Cassidy, Scout pat..100.00
Henckels, JA; 3-bd, bone hdl, whittler pat, 3¼"..........................65.00
Henckels, JA; 4-bd, bone hdl, congress pat, 4½"........................150.00
Hibbard, Spencer, Bartlett & Co, 2-bd, bone hdl, barlow, 3⅜"......85.00
Hibbard, Spencer, Bartlett & Co, 2-bd, bone hdl, dog-leg pat, 3⅝"..100.00
Holley Mfg Co, 1-bd, wood hdl, 5"..140.00
Holley Mfg Co, 3-bd, pearl hdl, whittler pat, 3¼"....................225.00
Holley Mfg Co, 4-bd, bone hdl, congress pat, 3½"....................375.00
Honk Falls Knife Co, 1-bd, bone hdl, 3"..................................125.00
I*XL (Sheffield England), 2-bd, wood hdl, heavy jack, 4"............125.00
I*XL (Sheffield England), 4-bd, gen stag hdl, congress, 4"..........250.00
Imperial Knife Co, 2-bd, bone hdl, dog-leg pat, 3⅜"..................50.00
Imperial Knife Co, 2-bd, mc hdl, 3¼"......................................35.00
John Primble, Belknap Hdw Co, 3-bd, bone hdl, 4"....................75.00
John Primble, Belknap Hdw Co, 4-bd, bone hdl, 3¾"................85.00
John Primble, India Steel Works on bolster, celluloid hdl, 3"......125.00
John Primble, India Steel Works, 2-bd, gen stag hdl, 4¼"............500.00
Ka-Bar, Union Cutlery, 2-bd, gen stag hdl, dog head, 5¼"..........250.00
Ka-Bar, Union Cutlery, 2-bd, gen stag hdl, Old Time Trapper, 4⅛".85.00
Ka-Bar, Union Cutlery, 3-bd, bone hdl, cattle pat, 3⅜"..............100.00
Ka-Bar, Union Cutlery, 3-bd, bone hdl, whittler pat, 3⁹⁄₁₆"..........150.00
Ka-Bar, Union Cutlery, knife & fork, bone hdl, 5¼"..................300.00
Keen Kutter, 1-bd, bone hdl, TX toothpick, 5"..........................125.00
Keen Kutter, 2-bd, blk celluloid hdl, congress, 3⅛"....................40.00
Keen Kutter, 2-bd, bone hdl, barlow, 3⅜"................................75.00
Keen Kutter, 2-bd, imi bone hdl, folding hunter, 5¼"................125.00
Keen Kutter, EC Simmons, 1-bd, bone hdl, 3¼"..........................50.00
Keen Kutter, EC Simmons, 1-bd, bone hdl, lb, 4¼"....................200.00
Keen Kutter, EC Simmons, 2-bd, bone hdl, trapper, 3⅞"............250.00
Keen Kutter, EC Simmons, 2-bd, colorful celluloid hdl, 3⅜"........70.00
Keen Kutter, EC Simmons, 2-bd, pearl hdl, doctor pat, 3⅜"........250.00
Keen Kutter, EC Simmons, 2-bd, wood hdl, jack, 3¼"................75.00
Keen Kutter, EC Simmons, 3-bd, bone hdl, whittler pat, 3⅜"........75.00
LF&C, 2-bd, jigged hard rubber hdl, jack, 3⅝"..........................75.00
LF&C, 3-bd, gen pearl hdl, whittler pat, 3½"............................125.00
Maher & Grosh, 2-bd, bone hdl, jack, 3⅝"................................150.00
Marbles, 1-bd, gen stag hdl, Safety Folding Hunter, lg................700.00
Marbles, 1-bd, gen stag hdl, Safety Folding Hunter, sm..............500.00
Miller Bros, 2-bd, bone hdl, jack, 3½"......................................100.00
Miller Bros, 2-bd, screws in bone hdl, 4¼"..............................350.00

Miller Bros, 3-bd, gen stag hdl, stockman, 4"............................350.00
Miller Bros, 3-bd, screws in gen pearl hdl, 3⅜"........................250.00
Morley, WH & Sons; 3-bd, bone hdl, whittler pat, 3¼"................65.00
MSA Co, Marbles, 2-bd, pearl hdl, sunfish pat, rare, 4"..........3,500.00
Napanoch Knife Co, 2 lg bd, bone hdl, 3⅝"............................250.00
Napanoch Knife Co, 4-bd, bone hdl, 3¼"................................150.00
Napanoch Knife Co, X100X, 1-bd, bone hdl, very rare, 5⅜"....2,500.00
Northfield Knife Co, 2-bd, bone hdl, dog-leg pat, 3¾"..............500.00
Northfield Knife Co, 2-bd, bone hdl, jack, 3⅜"........................165.00
Pal, 2-bd, bone hdl, easy-open, 3⅝"..85.00
Pal, 3-bd, bone hdl, jack, 3⅜"..60.00
Parker, Eagle (Japan), 1-bd, bone hdl, lb, 4½", M....................25.00
Parker, Eagle (Japan), 4-bd, gen abalone hdl, congress, 3⅞", M...100.00
Queen, #18, 2-bd, wb bone hdl, jack, 3¹¹⁄₁₆"............................50.00
Queen, #19, 2-bd, wb bone hdl, trapper, 4⅛"............................150.00
Remington, R173, 2-bd, bone hdl, teardrop jack, 3¾"................150.00
Remington, R1123, (old) 2-bd, silver bullet on bone hdl, 4½"....750.00
Remington, R1153, 2-bd, bone hdl, jack, 4½"............................250.00
Remington, R1225, 2-bd, wht compo hdl, 4¼"..........................125.00
Remington, R1306, (old) gen stag hdl, lb, silver bullet, 4⅝"........750.00
Remington, R3054, 3-bd, gen pearl hdl, stockman, 4"................300.00
Remington, R13060, Sambar or Indian stag hdl, bullet pat........4,000.00
Remington, RB43, 2-bd, bone hdl, barlow, 3⅜"..........................75.00
Remington, RS3333, 4-bd, bone hdl, scout shield, 3¾"..............125.00
Robeson, Shuredge, 2-bd, gen pearl hdl, jack, 3½"....................150.00
Robeson, Shuredge, 2-bd, strawberry bone hdl, jack, 3¾"..........100.00
Robeson, Shuredge, 3-bd, bone hdl, stockman, 3⅜"..................125.00
Rodgers, Jos & Sons, 2-bd, gen stag hdl, jack, 3⅝"..................125.00
Rodgers, Jos & Sons, 3-bd, bone hdl, stockman, 4"..................150.00
Rodgers, Jos & Sons, multi-bd, stag hdl, sportsman's................350.00
Russell, 2-bd, bone hdl, barlow, 3⅜"..125.00
Russell, 2-bd, bone hdl, barlow, 5"..200.00
Schatt & Morgan (current), 1-bd, w/bone hdl, lb, 5¼", M..........100.00
Schatt & Morgan (old), 2-bd, bone hdl, jack, 3⅜"....................100.00

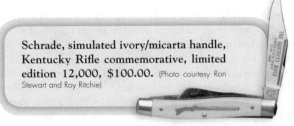

Schrade, simulated ivory/micarta handle, Kentucky Rifle commemorative, limited edition 12,000, $100.00. (Photo courtesy Ron Stewart and Roy Ritchie)

Schrade Walden, 2-bd, peach seed bone hdl, 4¼"......................250.00
Schrade Walden, 3-bd, peach seed bone hdl, 3⅝"......................75.00
Ulster Knife Co, 1-bd, bone hdl, barlow, 5", M........................200.00
Ulster Knife Co, 4-bd, imi bone hdl, scout/campers....................30.00
Wade & Butcher (Germany), 3-bd, gen stag hdl, whittler............125.00
Wade & Butcher (Sheffield), 4-bd, gen stag hdl, 4"..................500.00
Walden Knife Co, 1-bd, bone hdl, toothpick pat, 5"..................150.00
Wards, 4-bd, bone hdl, cattle pat, 3⅝"......................................85.00
Winchester, 1920 (old) 1-bd, bone hdl, 5¼"..............................500.00
Winchester, 2046 (old) 2-bd, celluloid hdl, jack, 3¾"................85.00
Winchester, 2904 (old) 2-bd, bone hdl, trapper, 3⅞"................350.00
Winchester, 2974 (old) 2-bd, bone hdl, dog-leg jack, 3½"..........125.00
Winchester, 3350 (old) 3-bd, gen pearl hdl, whittler pat, 3¼".....125.00
Winchester, 3960 (old) 3-bd, bone hdl, stockman, 4"................275.00
Winchester, 3971, dtd 89 (1989), 3-bd, bone hdl, whittler, M.......75.00

Sheath Knives

Case (Bradford PA), bk of tang: Case's Tested XX, 8¼"................150.00

Case (WR & Sons), bone hdl, Bowie knife, 11" 400.00
Case (XX USA), gen stag hdl, Kodiak hunter, 10¾" 125.00
Case (XX), V-44, blk Bakelite hdl, WWII, 14½" 350.00
Case (XX) 516-5, stacked leather hdl, 9" 35.00
Case (XX) 523-5, gen stag hdl, 9¼" 85.00
Cattaraugus, 225Q, stacked leather hdl, WWII, 10⅜" 45.00
Cattaraugus, gen stag hdl, alum pommel, 10¼" 85.00
I*XL (Sheffield), Bowie knife, ca 1845, 14" 2,000.00
I*XL (Sheffield), leather hdl w/stag, ca 1935, 10" 100.00
Ka-Bar, Union Cutlery Co, jigged bone hdl, 9¾" 150.00
Ka-Bar, Union Cutlery Co, leather hdl w/stag, 8½" 125.00
Ka-Bar, USMC, stacked leather hdl, WWII, 12¼" 100.00
Keen Kutter, EC Simmons, K1050-6, Bowie knife, 10" 500.00
Marbles, Ideal, all gen stag hdl, 10" 275.00
Marbles, Ideal, stacked leather hdl w/alum, 9" 100.00
Marbles, Ideal, stacked leather hdl w/stag, 11⅞" 500.00
Marbles, Woodcraft, stacked leather hdl w/alum, 8¼" 125.00
Randall, Springfield MA, leather hdl, WWII, 13" 1,750.00
Randall, stacked leather hdl w/alum, 10¼" 300.00
Remington, RH36, stacked leather hdl w/alum, 10½" 150.00
Remington, RH40, stacked leather hdl w/alum, rare, 14½" 1,500.00
Remington, RH73, gen stag hdl, 8" 75.00
Ruana, alum w/elk horn hdl, skinner, current, 7½" 100.00
Ruana, RH; alum w/elk horn hdl, ca 1980, 6½" 200.00
Ruana, RH; M stamp, alum w/elk horn hdl, skinner, 9¼" 275.00
Winchester, W1050, jigged bone hdl, Bowie knife, 10" 750.00
Wragg, SC (Sheffield); stag hdl, Bowie knife, 13½" 1,500.00
WWII, theater knife, mc Bakelite hdl, 12" 200.00
WWII, theater knife, mc hdl, Bowie knife, 12¾" 125.00
WWII, theater knife, mc hdl, dagger, 11" 150.00
WWII, theater knife, Plexiglass hdl w/picture, 12" 175.00

Kosta Glass

Kosta glassware has been made in Sweden since 1742. Today they are one of that country's leading producers of quality art glass. Two of their most important designers were Elis Bergh (1929 – 1950) and Vicke Lindstrand, artistic director from 1950 to 1973. Lindstrand brought to the company knowledge of important techniques such as Graal, fine figural engraving, and Ariel. He influenced new artists to experiment with these techniques and inspired them to create new and innovative designs. In 1976 the company merged with two neighboring glasshouses, and the name was changed to Kosta Boda. Today's collectors are most interested in pieces made during the 1950s and 1960s.

Bottle, scent, rnd cuts on sides, amber oval int, Manolos, #95120, 3". 120.00
Bowl, brn ribs on gr, oval, gr ft, Lindstrand, #146, 2⅞x5⅜" 600.00
Bowl, fluted, scalloped, A Ehnyr, 6x10" 425.00
Bowl, horizontal ribs, A Ehmes, #79332, 3¼x14" 300.00
Bowl, yel/wht/brn horizontal lines, ruffled handkerchief, 5½" H.. 110.00

Paperweight, Deer in the Woods, Kosta-LC 2412, original label, 6", $240.00. (Photo courtesy Mid-Hudson Auction Galleries on LiveAuctioneers.com)

Pitcher, orange w/bl hdl, low ribs, A Wahlstrom, #8953, 9½" 215.00
Sculpture, eagle, World Wildlife Fund, 1976, 5" 30.00
Sculpture, polar bear swimming inside gr iceberg, V Lindstrand, 8x10".480.00
Vase, Autumn, blk trees w/ mc leaves, V Lindstrand, 2010, 6½" . 960.00
Vase, bl/gr yel spiral stripes, cylindrical, A Ehrner, 1948, 14½".... 425.00
Vase, bl/sea gr spirals in clear, Linstrand, ca 1958-59, 8¼" 480.00
Vase, brn spirals on lt brn to wht, stick neck, Vallien, #40132, 11"....350.00
Vase, face HP on clear, Coll/48746/Ulinca HV, 10x4½" 360.00
Vase, face HP on mottled gray, UHV/KT, #48962, 14x9" 215.00
Vase, ovoid, etched w/linear design w/in, LS, #612, 5½x4¾" 300.00
Vase, ship etched on teardrop form, Lindstrand, #42290, 1955-63, 12½"..180.00
Vase, tree w/mc spatter leaves, V Linstrand, 6½" 2,400.00
Vase, wht loops on pillow form, B Vallien, #98972, 6" 120.00

KPM Porcelain

The original KPM wares were produced from 1823 until 1847 by the Konigliche Porzellan Manfaktur, located in Berlin, Germany. Meissen used the same letters on some of their porcelains, as did several others in the area. The mark contains the initials KPM. Watch for items currently being imported from China; they are marked KPM with the eagle but the scepter is not present. Our advisor for this category is Don Williams; he is listed in the Directory under Missouri.

Bowl, center, courting scene/landscape, w/gold, ftd, w/hdls, 11x15" ..1,800.00
Box, busts/shells/cornucopias/putti, lid w/ornate hdl, 14x15"....1,500.00
Candle lamp, 3 animal faces (cat/bulldog/owl), ca 1900, 4x3¾" .. 395.00

Cup, Bradenberg Gate, gold trim, marked, $230.00. (Photo courtesy Showplace Antique Center Inc. on LiveAuctioneers.com)

Figurine, English setter, recumbent, #9805, ca 1914-17, 3½x9" ... 400.00
Figurine, lady in ball gown on bench holding flowers, 9½" 1,180.00
Figurine, nobleman, gold on sword/belt/harp/cape chain, rnd base, 15".685.00
Jar, Chinese couples/flowers w/gold, ftd egg shape, 1890s, 6½", pr...525.00
Jar, floral w/gold, pierced, appl rose finial, leaf hdls, 11½" 900.00
Jardiniere, floral w/gold on wht, ram's head hdls, 10" 850.00
Jug, castle ruins by river, ovoid w/narrow neck, 1890s, 1¼2" 365.00
Plaque, angels (nude/seminude), 6x8"+ornate fr: 14x16" 5,500.00
Plaque, boy eating bread at knee of lady stroking his hair, 15x13" . 5,000.00
Plaque, Chicken Sellers, outdoor scene, 19th C, 11x7"+fr........ 3,500.00
Plaque, Christ w/crown of thorns, after Guido Reni, 10½x5½"+fr. 2,500.00
Plaque, Christopher Columbus in chains, oval, 9x7"+fr: 13x15"...3,000.00
Plaque, classical maid in rose garden, ca 1900, 9¾x7" 8,200.00
Plaque, Cupid sharpening arrow, 10¼x8¼"+gilt fr..................... 4,500.00
Plaque, Entflohen (2 beauties), ornate gilt border, #8129, 13" dia+fr .24,000.00
Plaque, Epanouissement, oval, after Asti, 13x11", +hand-cvd gilt fr..6,500.00
Plaque, FX Tallmaier of Munich, after Denner, 7x10"+ornate fr: 15x17"..2,000.00
Plaque, Helena Fourment & son Peter Paul, after Rubens, 15x12"+gilt fr....7,500.00
Plaque, lady (brunette) w/wine goblet, 7x5" 2,600.00
Plaque, lady stands w/bottle, sgn, 19th C, 12x6" 3,000.00
Plaque, lady watching urn painter, after Thumann, 10¾x7"+gilt fr .8,750.00
Plaque, maid illuminated by candlestick, oval, 6¼x5"............... 2,500.00
Plaque, maid standing by cherry tree, 12½x6¼"+gilt fr 7,500.00

Plaque, maid w/cherub leaning on shoulder, ca 1900, 9¾x7"+gilt fr ..6,000.00
Plaque, maid w/long curly hair looking up, oval, 11x8"+blk fr..4,000.00
Plaque, maid w/long tresses in robe, Wagner, 13x8"+gilt fr 8,500.00
Plaque, maids w/puppet in Asian scene, 9¼x6½".......................6,000.00
Plaque, Napoleon Bonaparte, after Francois Gerard, Wagner, 9½x6". 6,000.00
Plaque, nudes (2) on river bank w/bulrushes, Wagner, 8¼x11" .. 11,875.00
Plaque, Princess Louise on staircase, 12¾x7½"+gilt fr 6,600.00
Plaque, Queen Louise (bust), oval, 9x6¾" 4,000.00
Plaque, Repentant Magdalene, 1800s, 7¼x12½"+fr 3,600.00
Plaque, Vestal Virgin, after Angelica Kaufmann, 20¾x14½"...18,750.00
Plaque, Young Beauty in Chains, scepter mk, 19th C, 9½x6⅝"..5,250.00
Teapot, HP armorial crest on wht w/gold, bird spout, 5¼" 1,500.00
Urn, flowers/game bird/fruit, octagon ped ft, ornate dragon hdls, 36".11,250.00
Vase, classical figures on burgundy, gilt bronze swags & ft, 10"..1,500.00

Kutani

Kutani, named for the Japanese village where it originated, was first produced in the seventeenth century. The early ware, Ko Kutani, was made for only about 30 years. Several types were produced before 1800, but these are rarely encountered. In the nineteenth century, kilns located in several different villages began to copy the old Kutani wares. This later, more familiar type has large areas of red with gold designs on a white ground decorated with warriors, birds, and flowers in controlled colors of red, gold, and black.

Bowl, children playing, 19th C, 12" 395.00
Charger, bird/dragons/foliage on mc geometrics w/gilt, ca 1900, 27"..3,250.00
Charger, figures in landscape w/gold & iron red, 12" 145.00

Charger, four panels with shishi in a landscape and stylized red ships on floral ground, Meiji period, 22", $1,680.00. (Photo courtesy Neal Auction Co. on LiveAuctioneers.com)

Charger, horsemen (2) in winter scene, gold geometric trim, 24" . 1,250.00
Cup, wedding, floral on wht w/iron red & gold, ftd, 1880s, 6¼"..... 85.00
Cup/saucer, floral w/iron red & gold, scalloped rim 30.00
Figurine, cat sleeping, mc geometrics/roundels on blk w/gold, 4x10".. 1,125.00
Figurine, cat w/bat ears waving paw, wide floral collar, Meiji, 9x5" ..1,935.00
Figurine, duck w/head down, mc w/gold, detailed feathers, 7½x12".1,000.00
Figurine, geisha in full costume, 20th C, 12" 515.00
Figurine, lady in kimono holds lantern, 19th C, 12½"...............2,500.00
Plate, Mt Fuji on lt bl w/silver & gilt clouds, 4 red ft, sq, 7½" ...9,000.00
Sake bottle, coiled dragon figural, detailed, donut-shape, 7½" 815.00
Vase, bamboo stalks, silver on red-brn, globular, 20th C, 5"...........42.50
Vase, figure in lg oval reserve, shouldered, slim, 12" 160.00
Vase, figures amoung birds & floral on red, cvd lid & base, 27".2,000.00
Vase, fish/riverscape/brocade w/gold, 3 conjoined balusters, 9½" .515.00
Vase, flowers & birds, baluster, 19th C, 14" 300.00
Vase, flowers & leaves on iron red, classic form, 14".....................120.00
Vase, lg hydrangeas w/leaves on yel roundels, shouldered, 13x6".1,375.00
Vase, seated nobleman/landscape on rust, trumpet form, 19th C, 20" ..750.00

Labels

Before the advent of the cardboard box, wooden crates were used for transporting products. Paper labels were attached to the crates to identify the contents and the packer. These labels often had colorful lithographed illustrations covering a broad range of subjects. Eventually the cardboard box replaced the crate, and the artwork was imprinted directly onto the carton. Today these paper labels are becoming collectible — not only for the art, but also for their advertising appeal. Our advisor for this category is Cerebro; their address is listed in the Directory under Pennsylvania. While common labels are worth very little, some sell for several hundred dollars. We have tried to list some of the better examples below.

Can, Alko Brand Spices, Wht Pepper, Egyptian scene, M 10.00
Can, Carroco June Peas, butterflies & flowers, EX........................ 30.00
Can, Cobcut, hand cutting corn from ear onto plate, 1930, M...... 10.00
Can, Eastern Estate Brand Sweet Corn, red, EX............................ 15.00
Can, Flag Brand Peaches, peaches & flag, EX................................. 30.00
Can, Guilford Tomato Juice/Sachems Head, mc, M 8.00
Can, Helen Refugee Beans, girl w/vegetable basket/bowl of gr beans, M . 20.00
Can, Holly Bartlett Pears, pear/sprig of holly, EX 10.00
Can, Homestead Mushroom Gravy, country home in reserve, M .. 15.00
Can, Homestead, mushrooms, country home, M............................ 18.00
Can, Maid O' Honey, sm girl w/bouquet in meadow, VG............... 15.00
Can, Norwood Sorghum & Corn Syrup, gr, EX 12.00
Can, Pride of Fairfield, sailboat on river/country home/corn, M 15.00
Can, Robin Hood Hawaiian Pineapples, man kneeling w/bow & arrow, EX ... 40.00
Can, Shield Label Fig Preserves, gold reserve w/bl flowers, M...........8.00
Cigar box, inner, Abe Lincoln, profile portrait & branches, EX... 100.00
Cigar box, inner, Admiral Gherardi, portrait, M 65.00
Cigar box, inner, Bandera Cubana, lg flag over beach scene, EX ... 50.00
Cigar box, inner, Chapman House, Arabian lady in profile in oval .10.00
Cigar box, inner, Emp State, NY skyscraper, M 12.00
Cigar box, inner, King Carlos, king w/many military metals, M..... 10.00
Cigar box, inner, Lord Russell, seated at desk, VG 75.00
Cigar box, inner, McNeil's Enterprise, NM.................................... 60.00
Cigar box, inner, Miss Primroses, lady w/lg hat in reserve, M 12.00
Cigar box, inner, Selectos, woman/eagle/much gilt, EX 15.00
Cigar box, outer, Cuban-Americans, shields/coins over sunrays, EX.. 50.00
Cigar box, outer, Gisela, long-haired lady, Art Nouveau, M 20.00
Cigar box, outer, King V, king behind shield/weapons, M 6.00
Cigar box, outer, Knickerbocker Club, colonial man/NY landmarks, M.. 20.00
Cigar box, outer, La Composa, Lady Justice w/scales, VG 12.00
Cigar box, outer, Liberty Bond, document promoting Am bonds, M. 15.00
Cigar box, outer, Mi Idolatria, lady's portrait, canted corners, M ... 40.00
Cigar box, outer, Mi-Lu, lady's portrait in profile, M 35.00
Cigar box, outer, Patrick Browne, clover below portrait, M 8.00
Cigar box, outer, Roman bowing to empress, M 12.00
Crate, apple, Jackie Boy, sm boy in naval attire w/apple, 1925, M. 12.00
Crate, cranberry, Pilgrim Brand, pilgrims in reserve, M.................. 10.00
Crate, fruit, Anchor Brand New York State Grapes, grapes/anchor, EX..6.00
Crate, fruit, Appleton Brand Apples, lady w/roses/orchard, 1915, M.7.00

Crate, lemon, Pacific, unframed, $4.00. (Photo courtesy Western Asset Reserve on LiveAuctioneers.com)

Crate, onions, Flavon, chef w/baking tray of onions, G.................. 30.00
Crate, orange, Leslie, orange w/facial features looking at man, VG .50.00
Crate, orange, Marc Anthony, Roman portrait, CA, 1930, M....... 12.00
Crate, orange, Orbit, orange as comet, CA, M 20.00
Crate, orange/lemon, Cepaval, smiling beach girl, M..................... 60.00

Crate, vegetable, Beverly, girl on bench, sample, EX........................ 75.00
Firecracker, Alligator, alligator scene, penny pack, 1x1", EX 40.00
Firecracker, Corsair, pirate scene, box label, M................................ 55.00
Firecracker, King Kong...Flashlight, gorilla w/wings, 1940s, 1", M ..145.00
Firecracker, Kwong Man Lung, Asian figures/dragons, 11x6", M ... 75.00
Firecracker, Nightraider, figure w/skeleton face, brick sz, M 35.00
Firecracker, Rocket Brand, conical missile in blk sky, 3x1", EX 30.00
Soap, 20 Mule Team Borax, mule washing clothes, 9x6", VG...........3.00
Soap, Savon Pur Royal Yedo, Asian man reserve, 1930s, 6x3", EX...6.00
Tobacco, Black Bird, bird on branch, c 1886, 13x7", EX................ 30.00
Tobacco, High Admiral of Navies, King of Seas, 7x13", NM....... 210.00
Tobacco, Jockey, 2 black jockeys on saddles, Calvert, 2" dia, VG . 100.00

Labino Glass

Dominick Labino was a glassblower who until mid-1985 worked in his studio in Ohio, blowing and sculpting various items which he signed and dated. A ceramic engineer by trade, he was instrumental in developing the heat-resistant tiles used in space flights. His glassmaking shows his versatility in the art. While some of his designs are free-form and futuristic, others are reminiscent of the products of older glasshouses. Because of problems with his health, Mr. Labino became unable to blow glass himself; he died January 10, 1987. Work coming from his studio since mid-1985 has been signed 'Labino Studios, Baker,' indicating ware made by his protegee, E. Baker O'Brien. In addition to her own compositions, she continues to use many of the colors developed by Labino.

Bowl, red/mauve/swirled ochre, 1982, 5" 235.00
Bowl, shaded pk transparent, 1969, 2x7" 350.00
Paperweight, pinwheel/floral, yel on red cushion, 1974, 2½" 275.00
Paperweight, yel/blk/cinnamon flower in clear, 1978, 3" 350.00
Pitcher, dk red, integral hdl, blown in 1 pc, 1969, 6¾"..................350.00
Sculpture, Emergence, pk & peach in clear, sgn & dtd 1975, 8¾" ...6,000.00
Sculpture, Emergence, pk/yel/pk in clear dome, 1980, 6½" 3,000.00
Vase, 3 orange intarsia fish in purple, spherical, 1977, 6" 480.00
Vase, amber in clear w/trapped air decor, 1975, 4x5"....................600.00
Vase, amber w/yel pull-up designs, incurvate rim, 1980, 5" 600.00
Vase, Ariel, angelfish & dolphins in lt aqua, 3-1971, 5½" 450.00
Vase, bands, orange/wht on dk red, Chelsea Collection label, 1972, 4"..465.00
Vase, cobalt & yel w/pulled decor encased in clear, 1981, 5½"..1,175.00
Vase, orange/wht/bl nailsea loops, spherical, 1973, 4" 475.00

Vase, owl form in red glass, signed and dated 4-1974, 4", $495.00. (Photo courtesy DuMouchelles on LiveAuctioneers.com)

Vase, plumes, mc on wht, incurvate rim, pwt base, 1982, 5" 480.00
Vase, plumes, orange & wht on amethyst, ovoid, flared rim, 1977, 6" ..515.00
Vase, ruby, freeform, 1973, 7" 550.00
Vase, yel/wht/rust/orange abstract pattern, incurvate rim, 1983, 6"..900.00

Lace, Linens, and Needlework

Two distinct audiences vie for old lace and linens. Collectors seek out exceptional stitchery like philatelists and numismatists seek stamps or coins — simply to marvel at its beauty, rarity, and ties to history. Collectors judge lace and linens like figure skaters and gymnasts are judged: artist impression is half the score, technical merit the other. How complex and difficult are the stitches and how well are they done? The 'users' see lace and linens as recyclables. They seek pretty wearables or decorative materials. They want fashionable things in mint condition, and have little or no interest in technique. Both groups influence price.

Undiscovered and underpriced are the eighteenth-century masterpieces of lace and needle art in techniques which will never be duplicated. Their beauty is subtle. Amazing stitches often are invisible without magnification. To get the best value in any lace, linen, or textile item, learn to look closely at individual stitches, and study the design and technique. The finest pieces are wonderfully constructed. The stitches are beautiful to look at, and they do a good job of holding the item together. Unless noted otherwise, values are for examples in at least excellent condition.

Baby bonnet, wht cotton w/pk ribbon inserts, 3 frills at edge, 6" dia.. 85.00
Bedcover, wht Marcella w/heavy allover embr, ca 1900, 95x90"..200.00
Bow, wht voile, embr w/lace edge, 2 layers, 1920s, 7x10" 50.00
Cape, blk Fr Chantilly lace, diamanté clasp, ca 1885, 52x226"....525.00
Centerpiece, drawn-work linen, 24x24".. 35.00
Chairbacks, wht linen w/3 openwork & embr grape clusters, 46x24", pr .65.00
Christening cape, wht cotton w/Broderie Anglaise inserts, ribbons, 32".. 25.50
Collar, Irish crochet lace, ca 1900, 15" inside neck, 5" W.............. 85.00
Collar, ivory lace w/leaves & vines, ca 1880, 36" L from inside neck.. 145.00
Collar, ivory, Irish Carrickmacross lace, 49" L from inside neck .. 190.00
Collar, wht Brussels lace w/scalloped edge, ca 1890, 42x4" 175.00
Collar, wht Irish crochet lace, ca 1920, 18" around neck, 4½" W.. 60.00
Collar, wht Irish crochet w/raised lace flowers, 1930s, 18x3" 45.00
Collar, wht Point de Colbert lace, ca 1880, 31" L from inside neck..95.00
Collar, wht Sweet Irish crochet lace, ca 1900, 17½x2½" 50.00
Cuffs, wht lace w/draw thread at top, 3" W.................................... 55.00
Curtain, ivory linen, mc embr lady in pk & birds in hearts, 66x35"...100.00
Curtain, ivory net lace w/Battenburg lace trim, 1930s, 108x50"..195.00
Curtains, sheer ivory cotton w/lace detail 35" from bottom, 72x36", pr.290.00
Doily, ivory silk w/embr center & lace border, 1930s, 8½" 45.00
Doily, wht crochet lace, ca 1920, 13" 35.00
Doily, wht dotted linen w/wide lace edge, ca 1920, 10x12".......... 50.00
Doily, wht linen center w/handmade lace 'petals', ca 1900s, 12" dia.. 55.00
Doily, wht linen damask w/3" lace edge, 1890s, 10x12½".............. 50.00
Doily, wht linen w/1" Duchesse lace trim, ca 1900, 6x10" 65.00
Doily, wht linen w/cutwork & lt bl embr edge, oval, 1920s, 11x5", pr ..50.00
Doily, wht linen w/handmade bobbin lace, ca 1900, 7" dia 50.00
Doily, wht linen w/scalloped edge & fine embr, 1920s, 6x12" 35.00
Handkerchief, wht cotton w/Brussels lace edges, 12x12" 40.00
Handkerchief, wht lawn w/dainty bl embr scalloped corners, 14x14"..30.00
Handkerchief, wht linen w/lace flower bowl insert & cutwork, 12x12" ... 30.00
Handkerchief, wht linen w/Princess lace at 1 corner, 12" sq 30.00
Memorial, embr silk panel w/lady by plaque w/attached label, 17x23"+fr.435.00
Modest front, ivory Princess lace, H neck, ca 1890, 12" L.............. 65.00
Napkins, aqua linen w/wht embr corner & edge, 1930s, 14" sq, 4 for ..30.00
Napkins, cream linen w/Alencon lace in 1 corner, 1930s, 17", 12 for.175.00
Napkins, wht linen w/embr & lace inserts, 1930s, 7x7", 8 for........ 85.00
Napkins, wht linen w/embr flowers & scallops, 1930s, 17x17", 6 for ...50.00
Napkins, wht linen w/organdy floral insert, 1930s, 7½x5", 10 for .. 85.00
Napkins, wht linen w/woven floral, drawn edge, 1920s, 19x17", 12 for ...125.00
Needlework, bird on fruit tree, silk embr/X-stitch on wool, 14x14"+fr. 4,000.00
Needlework, flower basket, silk/chenille on silk, 1816, 19x22" .1,400.00
Needlework, lady at harp/mother/child, silk/HP, 19th C, 18x20"..1,800.00
Needlework, silk embr religious scene w/2 figures at well, 14x17"+fr.. 115.00
Pillowcases, wht cotton w/cutwork & embr on scalloped edge, 33x20", pr..60.00
Pillowcases, wht cotton w/cutwork & lt bl embr, 1930s, 30x21", pr... 60.00
Runner, ivory Fr Alencon lace, ca 1920, 37x14½" 130.00

Runner, wht linen w/allover floral punch work, 1920s, 56x22" 65.00
Runner, wht linen w/embr butterflies, scalloped, ca 1900, 53x18" . 70.00
Shawl, blk Fr Chantilly lace, triangular, ca 1885, 108x50" 200.00
Sheet, bed, wht linen w/embr & appl swans & ships, 1930s, 58x34" ... 70.00
Table mats, orandy & linen w/embr floral edge, ca 1930, set of 10, 6" . 75.00
Table runner, ivory linen, Madeira embr, scalloped edge, 1930s, 44x15" ... 65.00
Table runner, wht linen w/embr, lace inserts, lace trim, 1900s, 50x19" ... 100.00
Table topper, wht linen w/2 rows of lace inserts, lace edge, 23" sq . 65.00
Table topper, wht linen w/lace inserts & 5" border, 1920s, 33" dia .. 115.00
Tablecloth, ivory Irish dbl damask linen, 1910s, 65x50", +6 lg napkins ... 85.00

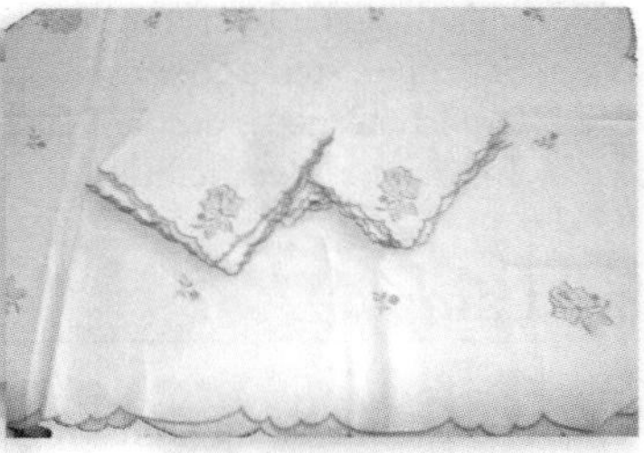

Tablecloth, Portugal linen with embroidered roses, 64x120", with 12 napkins, $120.00. (Photo courtesy DuMouchelles on LiveAuctioneers.com)

Tablecloth, wht cotton w/hand embr, oval, 1930s, 100x68" 185.00
Tablecloth, wht Irish linen dbl damask, no decor, 1930s, 90x72" .. 75.00
Tablecloth, wht linen w/14" heavy lace border, ca 1900, 56x56" . 175.00
Tablecloth, wht linen w/4-embr birds/cutwork/lace edge, 1900s, 42" dia . 100.00
Tablecloth, wht linen w/5½" lace inserts, 1920s, 90x70" 250.00
Tablecloth, wht linen w/embr dmn & floral sprigs, 1900s, 52x52" .. 125.00
Tablecloth, wht organdy w/appl pastel flowers, 106x62", +12 napkins ... 290.00
Tapestry, muted mc village scene w/dancer & musicians, 1925, 26x35" . 100.00
Towel, linen w/pk & bl needlework, dtd 1833, sgn by maker, 1 sm repair, 49x19" .. 425.00
Towel, lt yel linen w/embr organdy insert, scalloped edge, 17x11", pr .. 55.00
Towel, wht Irish linen w/embr & appliquéd flowers, 1930s, 11x17", pr 80.00
Towel, wht linen w/embr stork, castellated edges, 1920s, 22½x15" .. 50.00
Towel, wht linen w/lace insert & lace edge on 1 end, 1930s, 17x10" ... 45.00
Towel, wht linen w/Madeira embr berries & lace trim, 1930s, 18x12" .. 50.00
Towel, yel linen w/mc embr angel playing fiddle, 1920s, 21x14", pr .. 60.00
Tray cloth, wht cotton w/cutwork & embr corner baskets, 1920s, 18x13". 60.00
Tray cloth, wht linen w/embr cutwork butterflies, oval, 1900s, 21x12" .. 70.00

Lalique Glass

Having recognized her son's talent at an early age, René Lalique's mother apprenticed him to a famous Parisian jeweler. In 1885 he opened his own workshop, and his unique style earned him great notoriety because of his use of natural elements in his designs — horn, ivory, semiprecious stone, pearls, coral, enamel, even plastic or glass.

In 1900 at the Paris Universal Exposition at the age of 40, he achieved the pinnacle of success in the jewelry field. Already having experimented with glass, he decided to focus his artistic talent on that medium. In 1907 after completing seven years of laborious work, Lalique became a master glassmaker and designer of perfume bottles for Francois Coty, a chemist and perfumer, who was also his neighbor in the Place Vendome area in Paris. All in all he created over 250 perfume bottles for Roger et Gallet, Coty, Worth, Forvil, Guerlain, D'Orsay, Molinard, and many others. In the commercial perfume bottle collecting field, René Lalique's are those most desired. Some of his one-of-a-kind experimental models have gone for over $100,000.00 at auction in the last few years. At the height of production his factories employed over 600 workers.

Seeking to bring art into every day life, he designed clocks, tableware, stemware, chandeliers, inkwells, bowls, statues, dressing table items, and, of course, vases. Lalique's unique creativity is evident in his designs through his polishing, frosting, and glazing techniques. He became fa-

mous for his use of colored glass in shades of blue, red, black, gray, yellow, green, and opalescence. His glass, so popular in the 1920s and 1930s, is still coveted today.

Lalique's son Marc assumed leadership of the company in 1948, after his father's death. His designs are made from full lead crystal, not the demi-crystal Rene worked with. Designs from 1948 on were signed only Lalique, France. The company was later taken over by Marc's daughter, Marie-Claude, and her designs were modern, clear crystal accented with color motifs. The Lalique company was sold in 1995, and Marie-Claude Lalique retired shortly thereafter.

Condition is of extreme importance to a collector. Grinding, polished out chips, and missing perfume bottle stoppers can reduce the value significantly, sometimes by as much as 80%.

Czechoslovakian glassware bearing fradulent Lalique signatures is appearing on all levels of the market. Study and become familiar with the various Lalique designs before paying a high price for a fraudulent piece. Over the past five years Lalique-designed glass has been showing up in a deep purple-gray color. These are clear glass items that have been 'irradiated' to change their appearance. Buyer beware. Our advisor for this category is John Danis; he is listed in the Directory under Illinois.

Key:
cl — clear	LF — signed Lalique France
cl/fr — clear and frosted	RL — signed R. Lalique
Lal — signed Lalique	RLF — signed R. Lalique, France

Ashtray, Canard, upright duck, jade gr opal, RL, 2¾" 900.00
Bottle, Arys, 8 panels, ea separated w/beaded line, slender, L, 5" . 690.00
Bottle, Bouquet de Faunes, sepia wash, urn shape, 4" 1,100.00
Bottle, Dans la Nuit, rnd w/allover stars, bl, moon stopper, 3" 345.00
Bottle, Imprudence, horizontal rings, RL, 3" 360.00
Bottle, Le Lys, cl w/sepia-washed allover flowers, disk form, RL, 4" 720.00
Bottle, Nenuphar, cl/fr w/gr wash, RLF #492, 1911, 4½" 3,950.00

Bottle, Oreilles Lezards, clear and frosted, circa 1912, R Lalique France, 4x2½", $13,200.00. (Photo courtesy Rago Arts and Auction Center)

Bottle, Semis de Fleurs, cl w/blk enamel, 2¾" 1,550.00
Bottle, Sirene, cl w/bl wash, 1927, 5" 57,000.00
Bottle, sq flat-sided body, butterfly stopper, L, 3¼" 800.00
Bottle, Unjourviendra, stars/circles border stopper, oval, RL, 8" .. 800.00
Bowl, Nemours, floral, brn wash w/blk enamel, RLF, 10" 1,000.00
Bowl, Phalenes, butterflies/flowers, wht opal, RLF, 15⅛" 6,000.00
Bowl, Rosace, radiating petals, bl, RLF, 12" 2,400.00
Bowl, Volubulis, morning glories, opal, RLF, 1921, 8½" 585.00
Box, children, cl w/brn wash, fr stopper, RLF, 4x3½" dia, NM .. 1,375.00
Box, Dux Figurines, 2 nudes/flowers, gray wash, RL, 2¾" 1,750.00
Box, Hirondelles, many birds on lid, dmns on sides, gray wash, RLF, 4" .. 1,100.00
Box, powder, Vaucluse, birds/leaves, cl/fr w/sepia wash, 2¾" dia.. 1,200.00
Carafe, Masque, cl w/amber-brn wash to masks, RL, 10" 2,300.00
Chandelier, Trevise, cl/fr, brass fleur-de-lis hanger, RLF, 12x16" dia ... 2,875.00
Clock, dresser, cl/fr w/bl patina, parakeets, RL, ca 1926, 4¼" sq. 1,680.00
Clock, Sirenes, cl/fr, RLF, ca 1928, 10¼x10¾" 14,200.00
Hood ornament, falcon mascot, cl/fr, RL, ca 1925, 6¼x4½" 1,800.00
Inkwell, Serpents, dk amber opal, RL, ca 1920, 6¼" dia 4,250.00

Jar, Cariatides, stylized nudes, cl/smoky gray fr, RLF #924, 8" ...2,875.00
Letter seal, Tete D'Aigle, eagle's head, blk w/wht wash, RL, 3⅛" ... 1,400.00
Luminiere, Papillions, cl/fr, RLF, glass ca 1914, 9x8¼x½" 1,800.00
Mascot, Archer, cl/fr, RL, ca 1926, 4¾" 2,500.00
Mascot, Coq Nain, rooster, cl/fr, RLF, ca 1928, 8" 900.00
Mascot, Hirondelle, bird, cl/fr w/amethyst tint, RL, 6"..............2,680.00
Mascot, Longchamp, horse head, cl/fr, blk base, RL/RLF, 1929, 6" L.. 10,800.00
Mascot, Petite Libellule, insect, cl/fr, ca 1928, 6¼" L 10,800.00
Mascot, St Christophe, cl/fr, RL, ca 1928, 4½" 1,200.00
Mascot, Tete de Coq, head of rooster, cl/fr w/blk glass base, LF, 8" . 1,560.00
Pendant, perfume, cl/fr w/gr patina, Lal on stopper, orig silk cord, 2x1¼" .. 3,120.00
Rose bowl, Houpes, pompoms, lt amber on fr, RL, 5x7½" 1,300.00
Statuette, Chat Couche, cat, cl/fr, 4½x9¼".................................3,600.00
Statuette, Hirondelles, pr birds, cl/fr w/bronze stand, RL, 14"...8,400.00
Statuette, nude kneeling w/grapes, brn wash, RLF, 8" 1,725.00
Statuette, Sirene, opal, RL/RLF, ca 1920, 4" 3,350.00
Statuette, Source de la Fontaine Daphné, sepia patina, wood base, 28"..18,500.00
Statuette, stag, cl/fr, LF, 10¼x8¼" 800.00
Statuette, Vierge a L'Enfant, cl/fr, RLF, wooden base, 15" 1,200.00
Vase, Ajaccio, gazelles & stars, cl/fr, LF, 7⅞"..............................1,025.00
Vase, Archer, cl/fr w/olive gr wash, RL, 10½" 12,000.00
Vase, Armorique, incased opal, RLF, 9x10½"..............................5,400.00
Vase, Avallon, birds & berries, cobalt wash, RLF, 5¾x6¼"........2,525.00
Vase, Bacchus, centaur among ivy, gray wash, RLF, 7"...............2,300.00
Vase, Bacchus, cl/fr w/gray wash, RLF, 7" 2,300.00
Vase, Bagatelle, birds/vines, cl/fr w/gray wash, RLF, 6¾" 1,450.00
Vase, Biskra, cl/fr w/teal patina, RLF, ca 1932, 11¾x9" 4,500.00
Vase, Bordure Epines, cl/fr w/sepia wash, RL, 8" 3,000.00
Vase, Borneo, birds, cl/fr w/gr enamel, ca 1930, RLF, 9¼" 3,400.00
Vase, Bresse, turq opal, spherical, RLF, ca 1931, 3½" 3,900.00
Vase, Canards, cased butterscotch opal w/wht wash, RLF, 5½" .4,200.00
Vase, Ceylon, parakeets, cl opal/fr w/brn wash, RL, 9½" 9,000.00
Vase, Chamarande, thistles, floral hdls, dk smoky brn, RL, 7½", EX ... 480.00
Vase, Coqs et Plumes, roosters, cl/fr w/bl-gr patina, cylindrical, 6" ...2,100.00
Vase, Courges, electric bl, bulb, RL, ca 1914, 7"......................12,000.00
Vase, Courlis, birds, dk gr w/wht wash, RLF, ca 1931, 6½" 8,400.00
Vase, Domremy, flower heads, emerald gr, RLF, ca 1926, 8" 7,200.00
Vase, Domremy, flower heads, topaz, RLF, ca 1926, 8¼x7"........1,560.00
Vase, Druides, berries & stems, dbl-cased jade gr opal, bulb, 7"..5,150.00
Vase, Dursin, cl/fr w/bl wash, RLF, 7¼" 1,700.00
Vase, Emilion, birds, fr w/lt gr wash, RLF, 10", NM 4,000.00
Vase, Epis, ribbed panels, cl w/bl wash, RLF, 6½"......................1,150.00
Vase, Fougeres, floral, cl w/bl wash, bulb, RL, 6"........................3,600.00
Vase, Grosses Scarabees, cl/fr w/blk patina, scarabs, RL, 11¾x10¼".8,400.00
Vase, Gui, berries & vines, gr, bulb, RL, 6½" 4,800.00
Vase, Lagamar, clear w/blk enamel, RL, ca 1926, 7¼x7" 10,200.00
Vase, Malines, vertical bands, fr w/bl wash, RLF #957, 4¾" 1,325.00
Vase, Milan, leafy branches, cl/fr dk amber, RL, 11x9½".........11,500.00
Vase, Monnaie du Pape, leaves, dk amber w/orange overtones, RL, 9" ...8,400.00
Vase, Nefliers, leaves/flowers, cl w/bl wash, RLF #940, 5½".......1,400.00
Vase, Ormeaux, leaves, smoky gray, bottle neck, RLF #984, 6½" ..1,140.00
Vase, Ornis, birds, cl w/opal birds & ft, RL, 7¼" 4,600.00

Vase, Penthievre, fish, gray, bulb, RLF, ca 1926, 10" 27,600.00
Vase, Perruches, parakeets, bl-gray wash, bulb, 10", NM...........7,000.00
Vase, Pinsons, birds & berries, cl/fr, RL, 7½x9" 575.00
Vase, Rampillon, leaves, opal, RLF, ca 1927, 4½" 3,150.00
Vase, Rennes, animals w/curled horns, cl w/med gr wash, 4⅞"..1,380.00
Vase, Ronsard, cl/fr (smokey), dbl hdls, RL, ca 1926, 8x8" 5,400.00
Vase, Roses, cl/fr, RLF, 9", NM 4,200.00
Vase, Sauterelles, grasshoppers, cl/fr w/bl-gr wash, RL, 10¾" 9,000.00
Vase, Serpent, cl/fr w/sepia patina, 10½x9¼" 15,600.00
Vase, Sirenes Avec Bouchon Figurine, nude stopper, cl/fr, RLF, 14"..13,200.00
Vase, Soudan, gazelles, fr w/brn wash, bulb, RLF, 6¾" 2,875.00
Vase, St Francois, birds on branches, fr & opal w/lt bl wash, RLF, 7" .3,165.00
Vase, St Tropez, stems & berries, opal, RLF, 7⅜" 2,300.00
Vase, Terpsichore, nudes & swags, flaring, cl/fr, RL, ca 1937, 8x12½". 6,600.00
Vase, Tournesols, electric bl, RLF, ca 1926, 4½", NM...............3,150.00

Lamps

The earliest lamps were simple dish containers with a wick that hung over the edge or was supported by a channel or tube. Grease and oil from animal or vegetable sources were the first fuels used. Ancient pottery lamps, crusie, and Betty lamps are examples of these early types. In 1784 Swiss inventor Ami Argand introduced the first major improvement in lamps. His lamp featured a tubular wick and a glass chimney. During the first half of the nineteenth century, whale oil, burning fluid (a highly explosive mixture of turpentine and alcohol), and lard were the most common fuels used in North America. Many lamps were patented for specific use with these fuels.

Kerosene was the first major breakthrough in lighting fuels. It was demonstrated by Canadian geologist Dr. Abraham Gesner in 1846. The discovery and drilling of petroleum in the late 1850s provided an abundant and inexpensive supply of kerosene. It became the main source of light for homes during the balance of the nineteenth century and for remote locations until the 1950s.

Although Thomas A. Edison invented the electric lamp in 1879, it was not until two or three decades later that electric lamps replaced kerosene household lamps. Millions of kerosene lamps were made for every purpose and pocketbook. They ranged in size from tiny night or miniature lamps to tall stand or piano lamps. Hanging varieties for homes commonly had one or two fonts (oil containers), but chandeliers for churches and public buildings often had six or more. Wall or bracket lamps usually had silvered reflectors. Student lamps, parlor lamps (now called Gone-with-the-Wind lamps), and patterned glass lamps were designed to complement the popular furnishing trends of the day. Gaslight, introduced in the early nineteenth century, was used mainly in homes of the wealthy and public places until the early twentieth century. Most fixtures were wall or ceiling mounted, although some table models were also used.

Few of the rare early electric lamps have survived. Many lamp manufacturers made the same or similar styles for either kerosene or electricity, sometimes for gas. Top-of-the-line lamps were made by Pairpoint, Tiffany, Bradley and Hubbard, and Handel. See also these specific sections.

When buying lamps that have been converted to electricity, inspect them very carefully for any damage that may have resulted from the alterations; such damage is very common, and when it does occur, the lamp's value may be lessened by as much as 50%. Jeff Bradfield (in Virginia) is our advisor for pattern glass lamps. See also Stained Glass.

Note: When only one color is given in a two-layer cut overlay lamp description, the second layer is generally clear; in three-layer examples, the second will ususally be white, the third clear. Exceptions will be noted.

Key: col — cut overlay

Vase, Penthievre, deep blue, circa 1926, R Lalique France, 10½x10½", $27,600.00. (Photo courtesy Rago Arts and Auction Center)

Aladdin Lamps, Electric

From 1908 Aladdin lamps with a mantle became the mainstay of rural America, providing light that compared favorably with the electric light bulb. They were produced by the Mantle Lamp Company of America in over 18 models and more than 100 styles. During the 1930s to the 1950s, this company was the leading manufacturer of electric lamps as well. Still in operation today, the company is now known as Aladdin Mantle Lamp Co., located in Clarksville, Tennessee. For those seeking additional information on Aladdin Lamps, we recommend *Aladdin — The Magic Name in Lamps*; *Aladdin Electric Lamps Collector's Manual & Price Guide #5*; and *Aladdin Collector's Manual and Price Guide #22*, all written by our advisor for Aladdins, J. W. Courter; he is listed in the Directory under Kentucky. Mr. Courter has also written *Angle Lamps, Collector's Manual and Price Guide*, and *Center-draft Kerosene Lamps, 1884 – 1940* (Collector Books).

Bedroom, P-51, ceramic.. 25.00
Boudoir, G-33, moonstone, 1935, $30 to 40.00
Figurine, G-16, lady, Alacite, $450 to 550.00
Figurine, G-234, pheasant, Alacite, $225 to 275.00
Figurine, G-46, tall base, $150 to 200.00
Floor torchier, 4567, w/glass, G, $125 to 200.00
Pin-up, G-352, Panel & Scroll, Alacite, no shade, $60 to.. 80.00
Pin-up, P-057, Gun-n-Holster, ceramic, EX, $75 to 100.00
Ranch House, G-47C, Bullet, Alacite, no shade, G decal, $50 to . 90.00
Table, E-300, Vogue Ped, gr, $175 to........................... 250.00

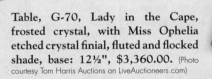

Table, G-70, Lady in the Cape, frosted crystal, with Miss Ophelia etched crystal finial, fluted and flocked shade, base: 12½", $3,360.00. (Photo courtesy Tom Harris Auctions on LiveAuctioneers.com)

Table, G-223, Alacite, $45 to 85.00
Table, G-309, Alacite, illuminated base, tall harp, $40 to.............. 70.00
Table, G-343, lady figurine w/dog, orig shade, $325 to 400.00
Table, M-123, metal figurine, EX, $100 to 150.00
Table, M-448, tripod metal lamp, $15 to......................... 25.00
Table, P-408, planter lamp, ceramic, $20 to 30.00
Table, W-300, bowling pin, no shade, $50 to.................. 75.00
TV, M-384, shell, ceramic, $30 to 40.00
Urn lamp, G-375, Alacite, $650 to 750.00

Aladdin Lamps, Kerosene

Values are for kerosene lamps with correct burners.

Hanging, Model 12, w/616 shade, $200 to..................... 300.00
Hanging, Model B, w/716 shade, $150 to 225.00
Table, Model 6, EX, $75 to 90.00
Table, Model 12, crystal vase, gr variegated, $150 to.......... 225.00
Table, Model 12, EX, $50 to 75.00
Table, Model B-25, ceramic Victoria, VG, $350 to 450.00
Table, Model B-60, Alacite, $400 to............................... 500.00

Table, Model B-75, Alacite, postwar, $75 to.................. 100.00
Table, Model B-75, Alacite, pre-1945, $100 to............... 175.00
Table, Model B-76A, Alacite Simplicity, $75 to............. 100.00
Table, Model B-81, Beehive, gr, $&5 to......................... 100.00
Table, Model B-91, wht moonstone, $600 to................. 700.00

Table, Model B-111, Corinthian, apple green moonstone, model B burner, EX, $160.00. (Photo courtesy Tom Harris Auctions on LiveAuctioneers.com)

Table, Model Grand Vertique, Fenton, gold ruby, $500 to........... 550.00
Table, Model LE (ltd ed), brass student lamp, 1983, $350 to....... 450.00
Wall, Model 21C, caboose lamp, alum fount, $50 to..................... 75.00

Angle Lamps

The Angle Lamp Company of New York City developed a unique type of kerosene lamp that was a vast improvement over those already on the market; they were sold from about 1896 until 1929 and were expensive for their time. Nearly all Angle lamps are hanging lamps and wall lamps. Table models are uncommon. Our Angle lamp advisor is J.W. Courter; he is listed in the Directory under Kentucky. See the narrative for Aladdin Lamps for information concerning popular books Mr. Courter has authored. Old glass pieces for Angle lamps are scarce to rare; unless noted otherwise, the lamp values that follow are for examples with no glass.

Gas adaptor, polished brass, no glass, EX, $750 to 850.00
Glass, chimney top, wht, petal-top, EX, $75 to 85.00
Glass, chimney top, wht, ribbed, EX, $50 to................... 75.00
Glass, elbow globe, clear emb flower, EX, $350 to 400.00
Hanging, #203, w/2 mg chimneys, plain can, nickel, $125 o........ 225.00
Hanging, #254, rose floral, 2-burner, polished brass, lamp only, EX, $800 to.. 1,000.00
Hanging, #263, polished brass, old glass, EX, $300 to........... 400.00
Hanging, grape, 2-burner, antique copper, no glass, EX, $325 to . 425.00
Hanging, Leaf & Vine, 2-burner, nickel, EX, $300 to.................. 400.00
Wall, #103, plain can, nickel, new glass, EX, $175 to................. 250.00
Wall, #153, pinwheel, polished brass, EX, $200 to 300.00
Wall, MW 5952, floral, nickel, 1-burner, EX, $150 to 200.00
Wall cone, #101, tin, blk pnt, no glass, EX, $75 to...................... 150.00

Banquet Lamps

Col (2-layer), bl, Moorish Windows/Quatrefoil & Punty, Sandwich, 20" . 7,975.00
Col (2-layer), gr, cut/frosted 5" shade, #2 Jones burner, 30¾" . 11,000.00
Col (2-layer), opal to cranberry, floral cut globe, ormolu base, 20"..425.00
Gilt metal std, HP globe w/gold griffins, 19th C, 32".................. 425.00
Poppies emb on red satin, brass fittings, CI base/claw ft, 1890s, 26" . 1,250.00
Violet-bl opaque base, clambroth font, scalloped ft, 15".............. 300.00

Chandeliers

Brass ring tiers w/cut prisms & ball drop, top 2 tiers w/openwork, 36" ..400.00
Brass, 10 candle lights above 5 pendants w/frosted shades, 44x32" ..500.00

Bronze patina, 5 arms w/pendant shades+5 w/bowl shades, 55x32" .3,500.00
Bronzed metal w/grapevines/cornucopias/etc, 6-lt, gasolier, 60x36" .2,235.00
Cast fr w/swags, 5-socket, concentric prism tiers, 19x19" 500.00
Copper/iron, 4 caramel slag lined lanterns, unmk, 38x17" 1,025.00
Frosted etched globes (4), copper patina scrolls/foliage, 34x19" ..200.00
Neoclassical, fluid burning, Fr, early 19th C, 22x16" 3,200.00

Decorated Kerosene Lamps

Blue/wht latticinio threads on clear w/blk glass base, Lutz, 9¾" . 1,760.00
Col (2-layer), cobalt to clear, Punty, stepped marble base, 8¼".... 720.00

Cut overlay (two layer), rose to white opaque with reserves and stylized swags, probably Russian, circa 1850, 22", pair $2,100.00. (Photo courtesy DuMouchelles on LiveAuctioneers.com)

Col (2-layer), ruby to clear, floral, marble base, 9"........................ 780.00
Col (2-layer), ruby, floral, 2-step marble base, Sandwich, 11" 600.00
Col (2-layer), wht to bl alabaster, Quatrefoil, clambroth font, 12"... 770.00
Col (2-layer), wht to clear, cobalt Baroque base, 9¾".................... 350.00
Col (2-layer), wht to clear, gr glass std, marble base, Sandwich, 14" ... 480.00
Col (2-layer), wht to ruby, Moorish Windows, 9¾".................... 350.00
Col (2-layer), wht to ruby, Oval & Punty w/gold, Sandwich, 13½" ...720.00
Col (2-layer), wht to ruby, Punty & Oval, wht base, 12x4¼"....... 660.00

Fairy Lamps

Blue to wht frost w/deep ruffles, matching low base, 6½" 345.00
Burmese, petticoat skirt on matching base, missing cup, 6¼"....... 345.00
Burmese, prunus decor, S Clarke Pat Trademark on cup, 5¼" ...1,150.00
Christmas pyramid, bsk shade w/jeweled tree, metal base, 5x4½". 795.00
Dmn-cut dome w/pressed tiered & ribbed base, Clarke, 5½x6¼", EX... 145.00
Nailsea, bl/wht, upright ribbon-rim base, missing cup, 6x8¼", EX ..115.00
Nailsea, citron, S Clarke Trademark Fairy, 5" 600.00
Nailsea, citron/wht, ruffled base, missing cup, 6½" 500.00
Nailsea, cranberry/wht, ruffled base, 5½x9" 700.00
Nailsea, wht/clear, upright ribbon-rim base, missing cup, 5x5½" . 550.00
Pink satin w/4 jewels, fluted base, 5¾", EX 115.00
Raspberry satin, Dmn Quilt, ribbon-edge base, missing cup, 5½". 145.00
Rose Tiente Pinwheel, Baccarat Depose, 4¼", EX 230.00

Gone-with-the-Wind Lamps

Amberina Hobnail shade, oil burner, 7x7", complete w/chain pulley... 600.00
Floral on wht to pk ball shade & base, rpl mts, electrified, 32" 165.00
Gilt chinoiserie on gr to yel ball shade & base, gilt-metal mts, 24" .. 350.00
Green satin w/emb octagons on ball shade & base, 23"................. 900.00
Milk glass w/HP floral on ball shade & base, ca 1875, 19"............ 110.00
Peonies HP on wht to pk ball shade & base, gilt metal mts, 1880s, 27" .240.00
Red opaque w/HP floral on ball shade & base, 21" 120.00
Roses on gr shaded to yel on ball shade & base, gilt metal mts, 27" ...600.00

Hanging Lamps

Brass w/lighted jewels, electrified, 15" dia 480.00

Cranberry hobnail shade, brass font, 46x14"................................. 800.00
Cranberry hobnail, clear font, prisms, 36x14"................................ 150.00
Cranberry, Dmn Quilt, 14" 300.00
Floral on mg, gilt mts, prisms, electrified...................................... 200.00
Green shade w/HP floral, emb brass font, 43x14" 450.00
Library, HP floral on mg, prisms, 1870s-80s, 38" 110.00
Library, pk cased, gilt mts, prisms, 1870-80, 41" 480.00
White opaque shade w/HP floral, aqua glass font, urns on fr, 41x14". 325.00
White opaque shade w/HP lilies, aqua glass font, 39x14" 285.00
White opaque w/yel blush, couple transfer, brass font, 39x14" 465.00

Lanterns

Tole, cathedral form with blue roof and floor, etched floral windows, early nineteenth century, 33x13x9", $450.00. (Photo courtesy San Rafael Auction Gallery on LiveAuctioneers.com)

Brass bell shape w/blown & etched globe, 1800s, 18x9¾" 900.00
Cast iron & tin, Kinnear's Pat Feb 4 1851, 8½x6" 66.00
Clear bulb globe w/wrought-iron fr, hangs from 3 chains, 20"...... 180.00
Skater's, bl glass, brass mts, bail hdl, 6" 215.00
Tin base/top w/punched stars, glass globe, tin font w/burner, 12". 175.00
Tin w/glass onion globe, pierced top, 9"+hdl 385.00
Tin, 4 glass panes, peaked top w/vents, ring hdl, 9" 250.00
Wooden post fr, staple hinges, punched tin, 13" 650.00

Lard Oil/Grease Lamps

Betty, dbl, iron, removable pan, Am, ca 1760, 6x4¼" 395.00
Betty, iron, shield crest w/2 Xd hammers, twisted hanger, 5", G . 285.00
Betty, wrought iron, w/hanger, 3", +trn tidy w/gallery rim, 5⅜" ... 635.00
Bronze, lions/bearded male masks, dolphin arms, hanger, 11x12x12"...215.00
Earthenware, brn slip, saucer base, appl ear hdl, 8"...................... 250.00
Iron, fluted pan, 5" spout, w/hook for hanging, 1770s, 6½" 300.00
Iron, pear-shaped pan mtd on 11" spike, EX patina, ca 1770 .... 180.00
Iron, spike w/pear-shaped pan, Am, ca 1750, 11" 215.00
Stoneware, 2-spout, strap hdl, saucer base, att Rouston, chip, 5½"...2,100.00
Stoneware, gr w/strap hdl & saucer base, 3½", EX 850.00
Tin, conical base, hollow stem, scroll finial, wick pick, 7"............ 300.00
Tin, petticoat style, rnd pan base w/lg ring hdl on side of column, 9"....245.00
Wrought iron, 2nd tier w/removable basin, minor pitting, 13" 400.0

Miniature Lamps

Miniature oil lamps were originally called 'night lamps' by their manufacturers. Early examples were very utilitarian in design — some holding only enough oil to burn through the night. When kerosene replaced whale oil in the second half of the nineteenth century, 'mini' lamps became more decorative and started serving other purposes. While mini lamps continue to be produced today, collectors place special value on the lamps of the kerosene era, roughly 1855 to 1910. Four reference books are especially valuable to collectors as they try to identify and value their collections: *Miniature Lamps* by Frank and Ruth Smith, Schiffer (referred to as SI here); *Miniature Lamps II* by Ruth Smith, Schiffer (referred to as SII); *Miniature Victorian Lamps* by Marjorie Hulsebus, Schiffer; and *Price Guide for Miniature Lamps* by Marjorie Hulsebus. References in the following listings correlate with each lamp's plate number in these books.

Amethyst w/wht floral & gold, Hornet burner, S1-262 variant, 8¾"..350.00
Blue cased w/mc floral, Nutmeg burner, SI-386, 8".........................975.00
Blue opal swirl, clear ft, Nutmeg burner, S1-513, 8".................2,100.00
Blue opaque w/mc floral, Foreign burner, S1-350, 7½"..................635.00
Blue o/l, berries & leaves, clear glass hdl, SII-413, 9¼", VG.........230.00
Blue satin MOP, Raindrop, Acorn burner, SI-601, 8"...................750.00
Blue satin MOP, Raindrop, Nutmeg burner, S1-602, 7¾".............925.00
Blue shoe w/appl hdl, Hornet burner, S1-51, 3", EX..................3,185.00
Blue, snowflake silver filigree, Nutmeg burner, S1-474, 7", VG.1,035.00
Cat, wht porc w/red ball, mc base, SI-496, 6"...............................575.00
Chartreuse satin w/emb decor, Nutmeg burner, S1-570, 8¾".......925.00
Columbus, mg, Nutmeg burner, S1-491, 10"...........................8,625.00
Cosmos, pk cased w/emb flowers, Nutmeg burner, S1-286, 7½"...300.00
Cranberry Snowflake, Nutmeg burner, S1-473, 7".....................1,265.00
Cranberry swirl w/ wht casing, knob marked P&A Mfg. Co. Victor, 8".....1,500.00
Cranberry w/optic ribs/silver filigree, Nutmeg burner, S2-253, 7"...1,725.00
Custard w/emb panels, Dutch scenes, Hornet burner, S1-215, 7¾"..285.00
Elephant figural, porc w/mc pnt, mk RD 10261, S1-329, 5¼"......700.00
Frosted ribbed swirl w/mc floral, silver base, Foreign burner, SI-556...925.00
Gold to clear overshot, Tulip, Nutmeg burner, S1-287, 8¼".........520.00
Green w/mc & gold decor, Foreign burner, S1-584, 9¾"...........1,725.00
Lady Fox base, porc, brn glass eyes, S2-321, 7"............................700.00
Light gr textured w/rose & flowers, Foreign burner, S2-480, 7¼".725.00
Log cabin, bl opaline, Hornet burner, S1-50, 3½" to top of collar.1,380.00
Milk glass, pnt owl on ball shade, Acorn burner, S1-348, 9"........635.00
Milk glass w/fired-on decor, Harrison 1892, S2-252, 9½".............575.00
Milk glass w/fired-on pk & brn, Hornet burner, S1-218, 9¼".......300.00
Milk glass w/mc floral, Hornet burner, S1-218, 9".......................345.00
Multicolored spatter, Hornet burner, S1-369, 8½", VG.................150.00
Pink cased w/emb design, Hornet burner, S1-374, 8½".............1,150.00
Pink opaline, 5 crystal ft, Nutmeg burner, S1-536, 8½", NM....1,150.00
Red satin w/emb panels/flowers, Nutmeg burner, S1-399, 8".......250.00
Red satin, Artichoke, S1-figure III, 8".......................................175.00
Salmon cased, Hobnail, leaf ft, Foreign burner, S1-566, 11", VG.575.00
Santa Claus, mg w/red & gray pnt, Acorn burner, S2-349, 9¼".5,465.00
Shoe, bl, Atterbury, Hornet burner, S1-51, 3" to top of collar..2,185.00
White satin MOP, Raindrop, Nutmeg burner, S1-600, 7¾"......1,150.00
Yellow cased pansy ball shade/melon-rib base, Nutmeg burner, S1-389, 7".460.00
Yellow cased w/emb ribs & basket, Nutmeg burner, S1-279, 6¾".360.00
Yellow custard, beads/boats/windmill/etc, Hornet burner, S1-215, VG........300.00

Moss Lamps

Moss lamps, a unique blend of Plexiglas and whimsical design, enjoyed their heyday during the 1940s and 1950s. Created by Moss Mfg. Co. of San Francisco, the lamps were the brainchild of company co-owner Thelma Moss and principal designers Duke Smith and John Disney. Plexiglas was initially used to offset World War II metal rationing, but its adaptability and translucence made it an ideal material for the imaginative and angular Moss designs. Adding to the novelty of Moss lamps were oversize 'spun glass' shades and revolving platforms which held figurines by many top ceramic firms of the day, including Hedi Schoop, Ceramic Arts Studio, Lefton, and Dorothy Kindell. Later additions to the Moss lamp line incorporated everything from clocks and music boxes to waterwheels and operating fountains. The 'Moss Fish Tank Bar' even combined the functions of lamp, aquarium, and bar, all in one unit!

Moss ceased production in 1968, but the company's lamps remain in great demand today, as eye-catching accent pieces for retro decorating schemes. Moss lamps are also cross-collectibles, for those interested in figural ceramics. For further information we recommend *Moss Lamps:*

Lighting the '50s (Schiffer) by Donald-Brian Johnson and Leslie Piña. Mr. Johnson is our advisor for this category; he is listed in the Directory under Nebraska.

#6, Sahara Girl (Dorothy Kindell) aquarium table, central globe.950.00
#17, end table, walnut & wht plexi, curved single support, 21¾", $725 to ..750.00
#55 A, Tami lamp, ceramic base w/brn lustre, 46", $50 to.............75.00
#2328, floor lamp w/3 red pagoda shades, 77½", $400 to.............425.00
#2334, floor lamp w/suspended cone shade & angled gold plexi, 68", $500 to..525.00
#2345, Siamese Dancer floor lamp, (deLee), 3 extended plexi panels, 72", $475 to.500.00
#T 474, Comedy/Tragedy table lamp, 27", $125 to......................150.00
#T 627, Cocktail Girl (Decoramic) intercom lamp, $375 to........400.00
#T 684, Calypso Musicians music box lamp, 34½", $250 to.........275.00
#T 686, Spanish Dancer in wire cage table lamp, dbl revolve shade, $400 to...425.00
#T 699, Fountain table lamp w/ballet dancers, $1,100 to.........1,200.00
#T 712, corner table lamp, lady w/knee on bench, 3 pod shades, 39½" $350 to...375.00
#T 725, Geisha table lamp, 4 hanging shades, lighted circular base, 29", $200 to.225.00
#X 3102, wall clock, spun glass base, 17" dia, $75 to...............100.00
#XT 803, Bell Girl table lamp (Decoramic), 32", $200 to...........225.00
#XT 818, Nubian Woman table lamp, 29", $125 to....................150.00
#XT 820, Mandolin Player table lamp, 36", $175 to..................200.00
#XT 821, Egyptian Woman table lamp, 32", $200 to.................225.00
#XT 823, Masked Ballerina w/turq cloud table lamp, 34", $200 to..225.00
#XT 825, Palace Guard w/gong table lamp, Asian fabric shade, 26", $150 to ..175.00
#XT 831, Bali Dancer Woman table lamp (Yona), 34½", $200 to ...225.00

#XT 836, Cocktail Girl corner lamp (Decoramic), three cylinder shades, 42", $300.00 to $325.00. (Photo by Leslie Piña)

#XT 837, Latin Woman w/maracas table lamp, 2 pod shades, 44", $300 to..325.00
#XT 851, Panther TV lamp, $150 to...175.00
#XT 854, Lady w/Dragon table lamp, 27", $150 to......................175.00
#XT 855, Temple Dancer (Decoramic) table lamp w/music box, 31", $275 to .300.00

Motion Lamps

Animated motion lamps were made as early as the 1920s and as late as the 1980s. They reached their peak during the 1950s when plastic became widely used. Decorated with scenes such as waterfalls, forest fires, and jet planes, they attain a sense of motion through the action of the inner cylinder that rotates with the heat of a light bulb. Lamps made in the 1920s and 1930s were glass with paper pictures and pot metal frames or stands. The ones manufactured from the 1950s to the 1980s were made out of plastic with plastic or metal stands. Some of the better-known manufacturers were Econolite Corp. out of Los Angeles, California (1940 – 1960); Gritt Inc. of Indianapolis, Indiana (1920s); LA Goodman of Chicago, Illinois (1950 – 1972); and Scene-in-Action Corp., also of Chicago (1925 – 1936). Prices are based on condition and collector demand. Any damage or flaws seriously reduce the value. Internet auctions have affected the prices of motion lamps with erratic ups and downs; as a result, the market for motion lamps is often unpredictable. Our advisors for motion lamps are Jim and Kaye Whitaker; they are listed in the Directory under Washington.

Advertising, 7-Up, 1970, 11"... 75.00
Advertising, Budweiser beer, 1970, 15".. 45.00
Econolite, Antique Autos, 1957... 125.00
Econolite, Bicycles, 11".. 150.00
Econolite, Boy & Girl Scouts, 1".. 150.00
Econolite, Christmas trees, wht, gr, bl, or red, paper, 10", 15", 24", ea $75 to...110.00
Econolite, Disneyland Express, 1955, 11"..................................... 155.00
Econolite, Elvgrin Pin-up Girls.. 300.00
Econolite, Fireplace, 1958, 11"... 150.00
Econolite, Fish, fresh water, 1950s, 11".. 105.00
Econolite, Fish, salt water, 1950s, 11".. 110.00
Econolite, Forest Fire, 1955, 11".. 130.00
Econolite, Forest Fire, Rotovue Jr, 1949, 10"............................... 125.00
Econolite, Fountain of Youth, Rotovue Jr, 1950, 10".................... 110.00
Econolite, Jet Planes, 1958, 11"... 210.00
Econolite, Merry Go Rnd, Rotovue Jr, 1949, 10"......................... 100.00
Econolite, Miss Liberty, 1957, 11".. 250.00
Econolite, More here than meets the eye, Hawaiian girl, paper front, 1952, 12"...200.00
Econolite, Niagara Falls, 1955, 11".. 95.00
Econolite, Niagara Falls, Rotovue Jr, 1949, 10"........................... 75.00
Econolite, Old Mill, 1965, 11", (+)... 110.00
Econolite, Oriental Scene, 1959, 11".. 165.00
Econolite, Sailing Ships, Mayflower, etc...................................... 150.00
Econolite, Seattle World's Fair, 1962, 11".................................... 175.00
Econolite, Snow Scene, church or cabin, 1957, 11", ea................. 150.00
Econolite, Steamboats, 1957, 11"... 130.00
Econolite, Totville Train, 1948, 11".. 150.00
Econolite, Trains, 1956, 11".. 125.00
Econolite, Tropical Fish, 1954, 11"... 95.00
Econolite, Truck and Bus, 1962, 11".. 150.00
Econolite, Venice Canal, 1963, 11".. 200.00
Econolite, Wht Chrismas, flat front, paper, 11"........................... 190.00
Econolite, Why you should never drink the water, paper front, 4 sizes, 1946-49.145.00
Gritt, Boy Scouts, Campfire w/Bugler, chalk, 1920, 11".............. 100.00
Gritt, Indian Chief, chalk, 1920s, 11"... 100.00
Gritt, Indian Maiden, chalk, 1920s, 11"...................................... 100.00
Johnson Co, Orphan Annie, 1981, 11"... 50.00
LA Goodman, Autumn, 1956, 11".. 110.00
LA Goodman, Butterflies in bowl, w/top, 1957, 10".................... 100.00
LA Goodman, Davy Crockett... 95.00
LA Goodman, Firefighters, 1957, 11"... 125.00
LA Goodman, Fountain of Youth, 1950, 11"................................. 85.00
LA Goodman, Niagara Falls, 1957, 11".. 75.00
LA Goodman, Ocean Creatures, 1955, 11".................................... 110.00
LA Goodman, Oriental Fantasy, 1957, 11".................................... 85.00
LA Goodman, Planets, 1957, 11".. 120.00
LA Goodman, Santa & the Reindeer, 1955, 11"............................ 125.00
LA Goodman, Ship & Lighthouse, 1954, 11"................................ 95.00
LA Goodman, Snow Scene, 1970, 11"... 65.00
LA Goodman, Sparkelite Christmas Tree, 1950, 11"..................... 85.00

LA Goodman, Trains Racing, 11", $100.00. (Photo courtesy Jim and Kaye Whitaker)

S&S Mfg Co, Elephant Lady Fortune Teller, chalk, 1930s, 12".... 200.00
Scene-in-Action, Colonial Fountain, flat front, metal, 1930s, 10"... 200.00

Scene-in-Action, Fish Aquarium, fish motion in glass stand, 1931.. 300.00
Scene-in-Action, Forest Fire, 1931, 10"....................................... 130.00
Scene-in-Action, Japanese Twilight, 1931, 11"............................. 185.00
Scene-in-Action, Moonlight, 1931, 10".. 150.00
Scene-in-Action, Niagara Falls, 1931, 10".................................... 110.00
Scene-in-Action, Serenader, 1931, 11"... 150.00
Scene-in-Action, Ship & Lighthouse, 1931, 10"........................... 150.00
Visual Effects, OP Art, 1970s, 13".. 55.00
Visual Effects, The Bar Is Open, OP Art, 1970s, 13".......................5.00

Pattern Glass Lamps

The letter/number codes in the following descriptions refer to Collector Books' *Oil Lamps, Books I, II,* and *III,* by Catherine Thuro (book, page, item number or letter). Our advisor for this section is Jeff Bradfield who is listed in the Directory under Virginia.

Acorn, fine-rib bkgrnd, 1860s, T2-67g, 9"................................... 300.00
Aquarius, lt bl, US Glass, T1-315e, 8"... 175.00
Atterbury Buckle, iron base, T1-136a, 7⅞"................................. 150.00
Birch Leaf, iron stem base, T1-173g, 8⅝"................................... 175.00
Blackberry, bl alabaster/clambroth, wht 1-step glass ft, T1-116A, 8"... 700.00
Butterfly & Anchor, T2-102a.. 325.00
Clarissa, 3-pc straw-holder style, P&A Victor burner, T1-pg 285, 17"..360.00
Coin Dot, wht opal, flat hand lamp, T1-152a, 2⅞"....................... 400.00
Diamond Band & Shield, T1-102b, 3¼"....................................... 150.00
Essex, broad rib font, ldgl base, T1-90c, 6¼".............................. 75.00
Eye Winker T'print w/Oval Window font, T1-250e, 10¼"............. 75.00
Fleur-de-Lis & Tassel, US Glass, T1-315g, 8½"........................... 70.00
Harmony w/Rnd font, after 1800, T1-262a, 8"............................. 40.00
Heart & Thumbprint, gr opaque, stand lamp, T2-103o, 9½"....... 300.00
Hearts & Stars, color, T1-145g, 10¼".. 950.00
Herringbone Band, pre-1880, T1-96d, 9"..................................... 75.00
Inverted Teardrop Band, Bridges, T1-188a, 12"........................... 150.00
Loop & Dart & Heart, T2-36f, 10⅝".. 275.00
Paneled Fern, pre-1880, T1-100a, 8⅞"... 75.00
Princess Feather, cobalt, T1-279i, 9½" (+).................................... 475.00
Queen Heart, gr, Pat 1877, finger lamp, 1890s, T1-252b, 3¾"..... 215.00
Ribbed Loop, gem base, T1-139j, 10⅞".. 125.00
Ring Punty, ldgl base, T1-85e, 8⅝".. 160.00
Riverside Ring & Rib, T2-111j, 8¼"... 125.00
Roulette, T2-114a, 8½"... 125.00

Peg Lamps

Peg lamps were produced in response to a general movement away from the use of candles to the use of oils for household lighting. Peg lamp fonts were inserted into candlesticks and used small to mid-sized burners for whale oil, camphene, or kerosene, depending on the time of production. Many of the kerosene burners could accommodate shades or globes of different designs in the mid-to-late 1800s. The earliest peg lamps were made from copper, brass, tin, silver, or blown glass. Later, peg lamps were mainly crafted from glass, reflecting the makers and styles of the day. The glass fonts and shades/globes were generally larger than miniature lamps but smaller than stand or banquet lamps. Peg lamps were often sold in pairs to fit into existing candlesticks in the household. Pairs or singles with unique designs and matching shades or globes can command prices of $500.00 to $1,000.00 each, or over $2,000.00 for a valued pair. Robert B. Skromme is our Peg Lamps advisor; see Directory, Ohio.

Clear glass paneled fonts w/dbl camphene burners, pr.................. 350.00
Cranberry, HP Fr fonts w/matching ruffled globes, pr................ 1,500.00
English, cranberry to wht satin glass swirl w/shades..................... 650.00
French pk satin glass w/HP flowers, matching globe..................... 600.00
Green cameo glass font w/butterfiles, ruffled globe....................... 550.00

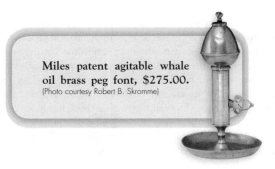

Miles patent agitable whale oil brass peg font, $275.00.
(Photo courtesy Robert B. Skromme)

Perfume Lamps

One catalog from the 1950s states that a perfume lamp 'precipitates and absorbs unpleasant tobacco smoke in closed rooms; freshens air in rooms, and is decorative in every home — can be used as a night lamp or television lamp.' An earlier advertisement reads 'an electric lamp that breathes delightful, delicate fragrance as it burns.' Perfume-burner lamps can be traced back to the earliest times of man. There has always been a desire to change, sweeten, or freshen air. Through the centuries the evolution of the perfume-burner lamp has had many changes in outer form, but very little change in function. Many designs of incense burners were used not only for the reasons mentioned here, but also in various ceremonies — as they still are to this day. Later, very fine perfume burners were designed and produced by the best glasshouses in Europe. Other media such as porcelain and metal also were used. It was not until the early part of the twentieth century that electric perfume lamps came into existence. Many lamps made by both American and European firms during the '20s and '30s are eagerly sought by collectors.

From the mid-1930s to the 1970s, there seems to have been an explosion in both the number of designs and manufacturers. This is especially true in Europe. Nearly every conceivable figure has been seen as a perfume lamp. Animals, buildings, fish, houses, jars, Asian themes, people, and statuary are just a few examples. American import firms have purchased many different designs from Japan. These lamps range from replicas of earlier European pieces to original works. Except for an occasional article or section in reference books, very little has been written on this subject. The information contained in each of these articles generally covers only a specific designer, manufacturer, or country. To date, no formal group or association exists for this area of collecting.

Cat on pillow, brn & wht, porc, Germany, #12077, unwired, 6½" ..150.00
Deco children/butterflies, bronze & porc, 8" 480.00
Fulper, lady squatting, ruffled skirt, peach to wht, 6" 250.00
Fulper, masked lady in hoop skirt, #331, 13" 1,000.00

Germany, parrot, marked Aromalampe Germany, circa 1930s, 8", $270.00.
(Photo courtesy JK Galleries, Inc. on LiveAuctioneers.com)

Goebel, lady dressed as butterfly, ca 1923-49, 12" 1,150.00
Lustre, pulled designs/threads, bronzed angels on finial/base, 15" ... 1,000.00
Threaded/pulled feathers, att Durand, Pat Aug 28 23 USA, 10½" ... 425.00
Two fish, 6½" 100.00

Reverse-Painted Lamps

Jefferson, 14" house/trees/road #2909 shade; bronze std 900.00

Jefferson, 16" autumn scenic shade; bronze std, 21" 1,325.00
Jefferson, 16" trees/stormy sky shade; sgn gr-enamel base, 22" ... 1,300.00

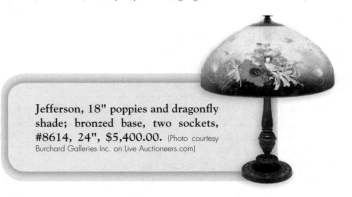

Jefferson, 18" poppies and dragonfly shade; bronzed base, two sockets, #8614, 24", $5,400.00. (Photo courtesy Burchard Galleries Inc. on Live Auctioneers.com)

Jefferson, 18" shade only, poppies/dragonflies/bees, #2614 .... 5,400.00
Jefferson, 18" woodland scene w/bl sky #2680 shade; vasiform base, 24" ..1,725.00
Jefferson, rvpt landscape #2384OC shade; mk std w/verdigris, 22" ...1,900.00
Moe Bridges, 16" river scenic mk shade; mk bronzed std, 21" ...1,675.00
Moe Bridges, 18" autumn scenic shade; mk bronzed std, 24" 960.00
Moe Bridges, 18" duck scenic mk shade; bronzed metal std, 23" ...3,575.00
Moe Bridges, 18" landscape shade; bronzed metal std, 23" 2,900.00
Phoenix, 18" cabin scenic shade; mk 2-socket base, 24", EX.....1,725.00
Unmarked, 16" roses dome shade, chipped-ice int; metal std, 22".....1,200.00
Unmarked, 18" daisies & bees shade; bronzed metal std, 23" 3,600.00
Unmarked, 18" sunset shade; bronzed Nouveau std w/gr enamel, 22" 1,375.00

Student Lamps, Kerosene

Brass w/gr swirl shade, oil burner, 20½" 240.00
Brass, dbl, cased pk shades, electrified, 1870s, 22x26" 1,700.00
Brass, dbl, Harvard base, cased ruby shades, 23" 1,950.00
Brass, dbl, wht umbrella shades, Cosmos Brenner tank, 17" 375.00
Double, brass w/wht Hobnail shades, 23x26x10" 275.00
Double, tin scrolled arms, pierced shades, saucer base, rpt, 19" 460.00
Nickel-plated brass, clear shade, w/burner, Bridgeport Lamp Co, 1800s, 17"...240.00
Silverplated brass, bl opaque shade, electrified, 19" 480.00
Tin candle socket & shade on wrought post w/brass ring, 20" 500.00

TV Lamps

When TV viewing became a popular pastime during the 1940s, TV lamps were developed to provide just the right amount of light — not bright enough to compromise the sharpness of the picture, but just enough to prevent the eyestrain it was feared might result from watching TV in a darkened room. Most were made of ceramic, and many were figurals such as cats, owls, ducks, and the like, or made in the shape of Conestoga wagons, sailing ships, and seashells. Some had shades and others were made as planters. Few were marked well enough to identify the maker without some study. *TV Lamps to Light the World* by John A. Shuman III (Collector Books) provides many photos and suggested value ranges for those who want more information. All lamps listed below are ceramic unless otherwise described. See also Maddux of California; Morton Pottery; Rosemeade; other specific manufacturers.

Bulldog w/flock coating, eyes glow, $60 to 80.00
Cityscape, Deco style, 13x12", NM... 90.00
Deco horse head on front of planter, brn/gr wash, $60 to.............. 75.00
Donkey w/planter, wood base, Royal Haeger label, $95 to 105.00
Duck flying, brn & turq, wooden base, $82 to.................................. 97.00
Ducklings, purple & cream/brn, on bl-gr porc driftwood, Maddux, 9x12", $125 to...150.00
Exotic bird w/planter, mc, $85 to 100.00
Fanned feather-like form, wht marble Lucite, Roucier, 20x17" 55.00

Gazelle leaping on grassy planter base, dk gr, $70 to....................... 90.00
Hawaiian girl's head & shoulders, vase at side, Lane, 9x9½" 850.00
Horse & colt, brn, $85 to... 90.00
Leaf, airbrushed plaster, $35 to.. 55.00
Madonna & Child, plaster, bulb lights up faces, $150 to.............. 175.00
Male ballet dancer, plaster w/Fiberglas shade, Am Statuary, $85 to .95.00
Matador, all wht, Lane of California 65.00
Mount Rushmore, chalk wht, 10x9", sgn Maddux of Calif........... 185.00
Owl, lt-up eyes, Kron, $75 to.. 100.00
Panther crouching, planter on bk, 22k gold decor, Royal China.. 150.00
Panther on rocks, blk, $65 to... 75.00
Rooster w/rising sun, bl-gr, $95 to.. 125.00
Rooster, gr, att Haeger, 14½", NM... 75.00
Sailboat, ftd brass base, Made in Calif, 465 to 85.00
Siamese cats (2), rhinestone eyes, Lane, 13"................................... 95.00
Siamese mother & 2 kittens, pnt eyes, Lane, 13".......................... 180.00
Swan, gr, holes in wings lt up, $55 to.. 80.00
Swordfish leaping, blk & wht against pk, brass base holder, $75 to ..90.00

Whale Oil/Burning Fluid Lamps

Vaseline, 9", pair $510.00.
(Photo courtesy Leighton Galleries, Inc. on LiveAuctioneers.com)

Aqua blown bulb font, hollow shaft, dome base, 10¼" 360.00
Blue, rnd/squat w/appl loop hdl, tooled brass collar, 6x3".............. 90.00
Bristol glass, orig oil font, 22" 300.00
Clear blown ball font w/dbl-knop stem, saucer base, 7½" 1,400.00
Clear blown ball font w/pressed baluster/ft, 1850s, 11x4¾" 215.00
Clear blown ball font, 2-tube burner, peg lamp, NE Glass, 4½" 440.00
Clear blown bulb font, swollen shaft, tin drop burner, 10¼" 350.00
Clear blown bulb front w/everted rim, hollow shaft, tin burner, 7" .. 400.00
Clear blown ovoid font, patterned base, hand lamp, 6¾" 1,650.00
Clear invt pear font on cylinder w/ovals & swags, 12x5" 1,410.00
Cobalt lobed font, brass column/marble plinth, missing burner, 11", pr....1,950.00
Col (2-layer), pk, finely cut, 2-tube burner, peg lamp, 5" 1,200.00
Col (2-layer), ruby, punty & oval, opal Baroque base, w/burner, 12"..1,400.00
White opaque blown ball font, conical stem, monument base, 1830s, 14"..260.00

Miscellaneous

Argand, brass, 2-arm, frosted shades, electrified, 1800s, 16x16"... 480.00
Argand, ewer-on-lily font on stone base, frosted/cut shade, 23", pr .1,440.00
Argand, polished brass, etched satin glass shade, bobeches, 22x12" ...575.00
Astral Sinumbra, brass w/marble base, prisms, 19"..................... 1,800.00
Astral, brass fluted shaft, marble base, cut shade, electrified, 32". 2,400.00
Astral, Dbl Ring shade, prisms, porc base, 1860s, 28"................ 3,150.00
Metal o/l 18" shade; similar base, 25" 1,150.00
O/l 14" shade w/Aladdin lamp silhouette in 4 panels, riveted base, 23"..2,585.00
Slag glass 13" bent panel shade; figural lady std, 21"..................... 520.00

Anton Lang

Anton Lang (1875 – 1938) was a German studio potter and an actor in the Oberammergau Passion Plays early in the twentieth century.

Because he played the role of Christ three times, tourists brought his pottery back to the U.S. in suitcases, which accounts for the prevalence of smaller examples today. As the only son in the family, he took up his father's and grandfather's trade. Following the successful completion of an apprenticeship in his father's workshop in 1891, Lang worked for master potters in Wolfratshausen, Munich, and Stuttgart to better learn his craft. Returning to Oberammergau in 1898, Lang resumed working with his father. The next year the village elders surprised everyone by selecting Lang to play the role of Christ in the 1900 Passion Play. He proved to be a popular choice with the audience and became an international celebrity.

In 1902 Lang married Mathilde Rutz. In that same year, with the help of an assistant and an apprentice, he built his own workshop and a kiln. In the early days of the pottery Mathilde helped in the pottery as a decorator until Lang could afford to employ girls from the local art school.

During 1923 – 1924 Anton Lang and the other 'Passion Players' toured the U.S. selling their crafts. Lang would occasionally throw pottery when the cast passed through a pottery center such as Cincinnati, where Rookwood was located. The pots thrown at Rookwood are easy to identify as Lang hand signed the side of each piece and they have a 1924 Rookwood mark on the bottom. Lang visited the U.S. only once, and contrary to popular belief, he was never employed by Rookwood. His pottery, marked with his name in script, is fairly scarce and highly valued for its artistic quality.

His son Karl (1903 – 1990) was also a gifted potter. Karl apprenticed with his father and then completed his training at the national ceramic school in Landshut. He took over the day-to-day operations of the pottery while his father was touring America. Over time Karl became the chief designer and was responsible for creating most of the modern pieces and inventing many new glazes. Only pieces bearing a handwritten signature (not a facsimile) are certain to be Anton Lang originals instead of the work of Karl or the Langs' assistants. Anton and Karl also made pieces together; Karl might design a piece and Anton decorate it. One piece has been found with a handwritten 'Anton Lang' signature and a hand-incised 'KL' (Karl Lang) mark. Very few pieces have been found with a 'Karl Lang' mark.

In 1925 Karl went to Dresden to study with sculptor Arthur Lange. Under the influence of the famous artist Ernst Barlach, Karl designed his greatest work, the 'Wanderer in the Storm.' This large figure depicts a man dressed in a long coat and hat resisting a violent wind. Between 1925 and 1930, four or five examples of the 'Wanderer' were made in the Lang workshop in Oberammergau. One of the three known examples has only a 'KL' (Karl Lang) mark. The other two are unmarked or the mark is obscured by the glaze. At least three additional 'Wanderers' were produced at a later date, probably after WWII. They are marked with the 'Anton Lang' shop mark, a facsimile of Anton's signature, and are much cruder in appearance than the originals. Underneath they have two horizontal supports carrying the weight of the figure; the originals have only one horizontal support. The later versions appear to have been made from a mold taken from one of the originals.

In 1936 Karl Lang was put in charge of the complete operation of the pottery and enlarged and modernized the enterprise. He continued to operate the workshop as the Anton Lang pottery after his father's death in 1938. The pottery is now owned and operated by Karl's daughter, Barbara Lampe, who took over for her father in 1975. The facsimile 'Anton Lang' signature was used until 1995 when the name was changed to Barbara Lampe Pottery. Her mark is an interlocked 'BL' in a circle. Pieces with a facsimile signature and an interlocked 'UL' in a circle were made by Lampe's former husband, Uli Lampe, and date from 1975 to 1982. The 'Anton Lang' mark is not sharp on pieces made in 1975 and later. The brick red clay used in their manufacture can be seen on the bottoms as well as three lighter circular tripod marks. The later pieces are considerably heavier than the earlier work. Our advisor for this category is Clark Miller; he is listed in the Directory under Minnesota.

Bowl, brn & olive gr, linear decor inside, flared sides, 1¾" 75.00
Bowl, burgundy w/bl accents, 3-hdl, 4¾x7" 175.00
Bowl, floral, red & bl on gr, hand sgn, 2x4¼" 65.00
Bowl, flower band, mc, hand sgn, 3½x6" 110.00
Bowl, frog-skin, 2½x10" 60.00
Candleholder, 2 boys riding fish, 1925–38, 7x9x3" 500.00
Candleholder, turq, 6¼x5", ea 30.00
Egg cup, floral (simple), mc on bl, 2⅝" 45.00
Ewer, gray-bl w/stars in relief, firing chip, 7¾" 120.00
Figurine, bird, mc, 4x4x4" 225.00
Figurine, Madonna & Child w/earth/moon/stars, bl & yel, 11¾". 200.00
Holy water font, lamb w/flag & cross, gr, 7½" 100.00
Jug, mustard, yel w/brn int, Bought in Oberammergau...1963 label, 5".. 80.00
Photo, Anton & Karl Lang, 1922, 6½x8½" 17.00
Pitcher, bl & gr on red overflow, twisted body, pewter lid, 9¾" 140.00
Pitcher, bl matt, mini, 2" 36.00
Pitcher, frogskin, 3x4½" 36.00
Pitcher, indistinct horizontal stripes, cream/bl/brn/yel, 4¼x3" 50.00
Plaque, Jesus w/cross in relief, mc, 5" dia 32.50
Plaque, Mary w/Jesus & angel, mc, hand sgn, KL mk, 1927, 11x7¾x2" ... 150.00
Plate, floral/calligraphy, mc/wht/bl, hand sgn, ca 1930, 8½" 110.00
Time magazine, Anton Lang on cover, Dec 17, 1923 .... 20.00
Vase, birds, butterflies, & flowers, sgn in script, 10" 510.00
Vase, bsk, hdls, 6x4½" 100.00
Vase, floral panels (2) w/butterfly/birds on bl w/blk squiggles, 10". 500.00
Vase, maroon & bl flambé, 6x3¼" 50.00
Vase, peacock & floral, mc on tan, hand sgn, nicks, 3¾" 40.00
Vase, streaky gr/brn/tan on bl, Oberammergau, hairline, 6⅞" 60.00
Vase, stylized design in bl & aqua, flared form, 7" 250.00
Vase, turq matt, 3 rim-to-hip hdls, 9½" 200.00
Wall pocket, girl in pinafore & winged cherub, mc, 6¼x3½" 90.00

Bernard Leach

An English artist, Bernard Leach studied traditional pottery in China and Japan from 1909 until 1920. He returned home a superior potter, one who would revolutionize the craft through his technique and materials. His ceramics are marked with a 'BL' seal and a 'S' seal for St. Ives, where his pottery was located in England. Our advisors for this category are Suzanne Perrault and David Rago; they are listed in the Directory under New Jersey.

Vase, leafy springs and three bands incised on dark brown stoneware, 14", $19,200.00. (Photo courtesy Brunk Auctions on LiveAuctioneers.com)

Bottle, fish, brn on wht, stoneware, chop mk, BL, 12x5½", NM .. 11,900.00
Bottle, scratch decor on blk, ftd flat form, 7½" 2,700.00
Bowl, rice, porc, dogwood pattern on indigo & celadon, chop mk, 3x6" .1,140.00
Charger, zodiac, brn & Ochre HP on stoneware, ca 1927, BL, 15" .. 960.00
Pilgrim bottle, spiral eng on dk red, stoneware, ftd flat form, 13"... 27,000.00
Pilgrim bowl, tenmoku on stoneware, ca 1950s, BL, 3x14" 3,400.00
Pilgrim flask, dk tenmoku w/khaki, ftd flattened form, 1960s, 14"....4,000.00
Vase, brn/blk mottle w/incised kangi script, St Ives, 4¾x4¼"....4,000.00
Vase, gr/brn mottle, hexagonal form, BL, St Ives, 7½" 140.00

Leeds, Leeds Type

The Leeds Pottery was established in 1758 in Yorkshire and under varied management produced fine creamware, often highly reticulated and transfer printed, shiny black-glazed Jackfield wares, polychromed pearlware, and figurines similar to those made in the Staffordshire area. Little of the early ware was marked; after 1775 the impressed 'Leeds Pottery' mark was used. From 1781 to 1820, the name 'Hartley Greens & Co.' was added. The pottery closed in 1898. Today the term 'Leeds' has become generic and is used to encompass all polychromed pearlware and creamware, wherever its origin. Thus similar wares of other potters (Wood for instance) is often incorrectly called 'Leeds.' Unless a piece is marked or can be definitely attributed to Leeds by confirming the pattern to be authentic, 'Leeds-Type' would be a more accurate nomenclature.

Bowl, peafowl, 5-color w/spatter trees, flakes/hairline, 3½x7¼".. 1,200.00
Can, floral band, 4-color, simple C-scroll hdl, ca 1840, 4¾", VG+ .125.00
Charger, flowers in urn, 5-color, bl feather edge, 14⅜" 3,250.00
Charger, peafowl on branch, 3-color, bl feather edge, 13¼" 1,800.00
Pitcher, floral and foliage, five-color, hairline, 8", ... 400.00
Pitcher, peafowl on tree, 5-color, rpr rim, 6" 460.00
Plate, dahlia & acorns, 4-color, gr feather edge, 7¾", NM 585.00
Plate, flower basket, 4-color, gr feather edge, 8⅛", EX 1,800.00
Plate, heraldic eagle w/shield, 3-color, bl feather edge, 1800s, 8" ..1,650.00
Plate, heraldic eagle w/shield/etc, 4-color, early 1800s, 6½" 1,650.00
Plate, peafowl center w/bl crest, perched in tree, gr feather edge, 8" ... 840.00
Plate, peafowl on branch, 4-color, gr feather edge, 8", VG.......... 285.00
Plate, peafowl on leafy branch, 5-color, smooth rim, 9¾"........1,325.00
Plate, pomegranate & foliage, bl feather edge w/emb floral, 10¼"..9,600.00
Plate, toddy, peafowl & vines, bud & vine border, 4¾", EX 1,550.00
Platter, 3 flowers, bl tones, bl feather edge, early 1800s, 17x12½" .2,400.00
Platter, bl chinoiserie, bl feathered edge, 1810s, 16x12"............... 945.00

Platter, floral sprig and feather edge, early nineteenth century, 12" long, $2,200.00. (Photo courtesy Pook & Pook Inc. on LiveAuctioneers.com)

Tea bowl & saucer, floral, 4-color, bl chain border, 2½", 5¾", VG...850.00
Tea bowl & saucer, peacock, 5-color, prof rstr............................... 600.00
Tea bowl & saucer, peafowl among foliage, 5-color, bl rim, child's, EX....2,750.00
Teapot, floral emb/HP, globular, crabstock hdl/spout, 18th C, 4¼". 1,200.00
Teapot, floral, 4-color, sm stain/rpr, mini, 4" 435.00
Teapot, flowers/Mary Neck Ilsington/verse, 1809, 6½x8¾", VG . 3,250.00

Lefton

The Lefton China Company was the creation of Mr. George Zoltan Lefton who migrated to the United States from Hungary in 1939. In 1941 he embarked on a new career and began shaping a business that sprang from his passion for collecting fine china and porcelains. Though his funds were very limited, his vision was to develop a source from which to obtain fine porcelains by reviving the postwar Japanese ceramic industry, which dated back to antiquity. As a trailblazer, George Zoltan Lefton soon earned the reputation as 'The China King.'

Counted among the most desirable and sought-after collectibles of today, Lefton items such as Bluebirds, Miss Priss, Angels, all types of dinnerware and tea-related items are eagerly acquired by collectors. As is true with any antique or collectible, prices may vary, dependent on location, condition, and availability.

Mug, George Washington, #KW-2326, 4¾", $95.00. (Photo courtesy Jeremiah's International Trading Company on LiveAuctioneers.com)

Bank, Herbert the Lion, 8" 40.00
Bank, owl figural, bsk, #479, 6½" 26.00
Bank, pk elephant w/bl rhinestone eyes, #2429, 7" 35.00
Bank, Uncle Sam boy, #069, red, wht & bl, $30 to 40.00
Basket, Gr Holly, #5175, 5½" 25.00
Bell, Gr Holly, #787, 3½" 18.00
Bell, pk w/Forget-Me-Nots, w/sponged gold, #8293, 3" 30.00
Butter dish, Bessie the Cow, #6514, 7¾" 28.00
Candleholder, pk w/appl forget-me-nots & gold, saucer base, #771, pr... 50.00
Candleholders, Wht Holly, #6052, 5", pr 40.00
Candy box, Pear 'n Apple, ftd, #3766 .... 18.00
Candy box, red heart shape w/cherub on lid, #2210, 6½" 30.00
Candy dish, Minty Rose, leaf shape, #5517 .... 20.00
Cheese dish, Miss Priss, #1505, 5½" 175.00
Child's set, Miss Priss, mug & plate, #3553 .... 100.00
Coffeepot, Poinsettia, #4383, 8½" 90.00
Compote, Heavenly Rose, rtcl, #109, 7" 38.00
Compote, Mardi Gras, #20438, 5½" 105.00
Cookie jar, Chef Girl, #2360, 9¾" 165.00
Cookie jar, Fruits of Italy, #621 .... 45.00
Cookie jar, Gr Orchard, #3762, 10" 60.00
Cookie jar, Honey Bee, #1279 .... 100.00
Cookie jar, Little Helper, girl's head, lg bow on lid 200.00
Cookie jar, Miss Priss, #1502 .... 185.00
Cookie jar, Regal Rose, PY6971 .... 60.00
Cookie jar, Sweet Violets, #2853, 7½" 75.00
Cookie jar, Wht Holly, #6054 .... 85.00
Creamer/sugar bowl, Brn Heritage Fruit, #20592 .... 75.00
Creamer/sugar bowl, Gr Holly, #1355, 3-pc 25.00
Creamer/sugar bowl, Miss Priss 85.00
Creamer, Brn Heritage, 3" 20.00
Cup/saucer, demi, Bl Rose, #2120 .... 30.00
Cup/saucer, Jumbo Dad, #3400 .... 35.00
Dish, bone, Poinsettia, #4398, 6" 18.00
Dish, Miss Priss, 2-part, #1507, 9" 100.00
Egg cup, Golden Wheat, #20121, 3" 20.00
Figurine, angel in gr w/holly wreath in hair playing flute, #1259 ... 30.00
Figurine, Bobwhite, #2002, 4" 25.00
Figurine, boy leaning on tree, #5051, 6" 40.00
Figurine, bride & groom in boat, wht w/pk roses, #990, 6¼" 200.00
Figurine, clown w/monkey & organ grinder, #7111, 8" 90.00
Figurine, eagle w/head down & wings up, #802, 11" 75.00
Figurine, Fifi, #5742, 7½" 150.00
Figurine, Kewpie sitting on leaf, #2992, 3½" 32.00
Figurine, lady w/2 pk poodles, #692, 5¼" 42.00
Figurine, Madonna w/Child, #2583, 6½" 42.00
Figurine, old man w/boy fishing, #2807, 6¾" 80.00
Figurine, red fox on woodland base, #5058, 5½x8" 30.00
Figurines/shelf sitters, Mr & Mrs Claus, #1996, 5½", pr 40.00

Jam jar, Bluebirds, #436 .... 95.00
Jam jar, Thumbelina, w/spoon & underplate, #1697 .... 45.00
Lamp, kerosene, Gr Holly, #4863, 5¾" 35.00
Mug, Holly Garland, #2041, 3" 15.00
Pin box, baby figure sleeping on lid, #2710, 3" 12.00
Pitcher & bowl, Wht Holly, #6075, 5½" bowl, pr 23.00
Pitcher, Brn Heritage, Floral, #3114, 8-cup, $80 to 90.00
Planter, Bluebird, #288 .... 65.00
Planter, Calico donkey, #5897, 5½" 30.00
Plate, Holly Garland, #1804, 9" 20.00
Plate, luncheon, Brn Heritage 16.00
Plate, Rose Chintz, #658, 7½" 23.00
Platter, Gr Holly, #2369, 18" L 75.00
Platter, turkey, #50758 .... 65.00
Ring holder, hand figural, #1444, 3¾" 25.00
Shakers, Poinsettia, #4390, 2½", pr 18.00
Shakers, Wht Holly, #6061 .... 20.00
Snack set, Brn Heritage, #1864 .... 30.00
Snack set, Gr Holly, #1363, 2-pc 20.00
Teabag holder, Miss Priss, #1506 .... 55.00
Teapot, Bluebird, musical, #734, min 200.00
Teapot, Cabbage Cutie, #2123, 6-cup 75.00
Teapot, Miss Priss, #1516 .... 85.00
Tidbit, 2-tier, Wht Holly, #6065 .... 60.00
Wall plaque, Colonial couple, #3438, oval 110.00
Wall plaque, fish figural, blk & wht w/sponged gold, #60114, 6", pr... 38.00
Wall pocket, angels (2) w/dove on oval, bsk, #1697, 6" 30.00

Legras

Legras and Cie was founded in St. Denis, France, in 1864. Production continued until the 1930s. In addition to their enameled wares, they made cameo art glass decorated with outdoor scenes and florals executed by acid cuttings through two to six layers of glass. Their work is signed 'Legras' in relief and in enamel. Our advisor for this category is Don Williams; he is listed in the Directory under Missouri.

Cameo

Bowl, dogwood, cut/pnt on spring gr w/gold rim decor, 10" 1,800.00
Bowl, leaves & vines, maroon on frost, low, 8¼" 535.00
Vase, autumn leaves, purple on shaded orange, cylindrical, 12" . 1,200.00
Vase, berries & leaves, maroon on peach, waisted cylinder, 10¾" . 660.00
Vase, Deco band, brn on mottled brn/opal, ovoid, ca 1925, 15" .. 840.00
Vase, Deco daisies, maroon on textured pk, bulb, 8¼" 660.00
Vase, Deco geometrics, cobalt to frost, 8¾" 395.00
Vase, floral, 2-color, stick neck, 1910s, 15" 1,950.00
Vase, floral, brn/purple on wht/bl/purple, 3-sided pear form, 8" ... 750.00
Vase, pods on leafy branches, gr on apricot to gr, flattened, 8¼" .. 960.00

Vase, poppies, red and green on textured ground, signed L and C Indiana, 15", $3,100.00. (Photo courtesy Jackson's Auction on LiveAuctioneers.com)

Vase, river scenic, cut/HP, flared 4-scallop rim, squat, 3¼" 475.00
Vase, riverscape, mahog/brn/olive on brick red, waisted, 5¼" 600.00
Vase, spring landscape, cut/HP, ovoid, 6" 600.00
Vase, stylized flowers, fuchsia on pk, ovoid, 14" 395.00
Vase, trees, lake, & mountain beyond, 13½" 900.00
Vase, trees/lake/sailboat, gr/wht on lemon/orange, 7⅝" 1,100.00
Vase, winter scene w/mtns, brn/wht on orange opal, 5¼" 1,175.00
Vase, wisteria, fuchsia/gr on opal, slim, 18¾" 1,950.00
Vase, woodland scene, gr on salmon, pulled rim, slim, 23¾" 2,150.00

Enameled Glass

Bowl, winter landscape at sunset, ovoid, 10¼" L 360.00
Rose bowl, winter landscape at sunset, scalloped rim, 5½" 300.00
Vase, Chinese pheasant in foliage, mc on frost, 12" 260.00
Vase, floral medallion on bl to yel, 18" 1,250.00
Vase, floral roundel on mottled orange/yel/opal, baluster, 18⅛" . 1,250.00
Vase, lady in winter scene, waisted cylinder, 5½" 245.00
Vase, peacock/floral spray, mc on frost, 12¾" 345.00

Lenox

Walter Scott Lenox, former art director at Ott and Brewer, and Jonathan Coxon founded The Ceramic Art Company of Trenton, New Jersey, in 1889. By 1906 Coxon had left the company, and to reflect the change in ownership, the name was changed to Lenox Inc. Until 1930 when the production of American-made Belleek came to an end, they continued to produce the same type of high-quality ornamental wares that Lenox and Coxon had learned to master while in the employ of Ott and Brewer. Their superior dinnerware made the company famous, and since 1917 Lenox has been chosen the official White House china. The dinnerware they produced is listed here; see Ceramic Art Company for examples of their belleek.

Dinnerware

Abigail, creamer.. 25.00
Abigail, plate, dinner, 10½", $30 to 35.00
Abigail, platter, 16" L 145.00
Angelina, bowl, cream soup, w/plate 60.00
Apple Blossom, c/s, demi 30.00
Apple Blossom, plate, luncheon, 9" 25.00
Autumn, bowl, 2x9⅝x7¼" 90.00
Autumn, bowl, cream soup, w/hdls & undertray 150.00
Autumn, bowl, rimmed soup, 8¼" 60.00
Autumn, bowl, vegetable, w/lid, 5½x10¾"....................................... 275.00
Autumn, cake stand.. 175.00
Autumn, coffeepot, 9¼"... 150.00
Autumn, gravy boat, w/underplate, $150 to..................................... 175.00
Autumn, mug, coffee/tea 45.00
Autumn, platter, 16" dia... 175.00
Autumn, platter, 16x11" 145.00
Autumn, shakers, pr.. 85.00
Autumn, soup tureen, w/lid, 5½x11½" 395.00
Ballad, c/s, 2"... 15.00
Ballad, plate, bread & butter, 6½" 10.00
Ballad, plate, luncheon, 8½"... 14.00
Bancroft, plate, bread & butter, 6" 12.00
Cinderella, c/s 20.00
Cinderella, plate, 6½" 14.00
Cinderella, plate, 10½" 25.00
Cinderella, plate, dessert...9.00
Countess, coffeepot, 4-cup.. 200.00
Countess, plate, luncheon, 9" 30.00

Empress, plate, dinner, 10½" 30.00
Fountain, c/s, flat... 40.00
Golden Wreath, c/s, ftd.. 22.00
Jewel, bowl, 2x6"... 27.50
Jewel, bowl, rimmed soup, 9" 25.00
Jewel, mug, coffee/tea 12.00
Jewel, plate, bread & butter, 6¼" 12.00
Jewel, sugar bowl, w/lid, $60 to.. 80.00
Joan, plate, dinner, 10½" 60.00

Kingsley, plate, 10", $40.00. (Photo courtesy O'Gallerie on LiveAuctioneers.com)

Lenox Rose, bowl, rimmed soup... 42.00
Ming, bowl, vegetable, oval, w/lid, 5¼x10¾x7⅛" 65.00
Ming, cr/sug bowl, w/lid... 100.00
Ming, gravy boat, w/attached underplate 85.00
Ming, pitcher, cylindrical, 8" 90.00
Ming, plate, dinner, 10½" 28.00
Ming, platter, 16¾" L 90.00
Ming, tumbler, 10-oz, 4¾" 30.00
Peachtree, plate, 8" 18.00
Princess, bowl, vegetable, w/lid, 2½x11" 125.00
Princess, cr/sug bowl, w/lid 50.00
Princess, c/s 15.00
Princess, teapot, 7", $150 to 165.00
Roselyn, bowl, vegetable, 8".. 165.00
Victoria, bowl, vegetable, oval, 9¾" 115.00
Westbury, bowl, dessert, 5½".. 35.00
Westbury, cup, 2" 25.00
Westbury, gravy boat, w/underplate.. 40.00
Westbury, plate, bread & butter, 6" 8.00
Westwind, bowl, vegetable, 9⅝" L 60.00
Westwind, chop plate, 12" 45.00
Westwind, coffeepot 90.00
Westwind, gravy boat, attached underplate 40.00
Westwind, plate, bread & butter, 6¼" 7.50
Westwind, platter, med, 16x11".. 55.00

Miscellaneous

Vases, flowers in relief, green and gold on white, #3168-1-338-242, 7", pair $120.00. (Photo courtesy Dennis Auction Service Inc. on LiveAuctioneers.com)

Bowl, swan figural, wht w/much gold, gr 1920s mk, 4x4½" 350.00
Figurine, German shepherd dog, wht, recumbent, 1930-53, 4½x7¾" . 150.00
Figurine, jaybird, lt pk, gr wreath on bottom, 4" 70.00
Figurine, llama, yel, Deco style, post 1930 mk, 9x6".................... 495.00
Figurine, penguin, wht gloss & blk matt, 1930-53, 6¼x3½" 65.00
Loving cup, oxblood w/3 hdls, sterling collar, Bigelow & Kennard, 6" . 180.00
Luminaire, Leda (nude) & Swan figural, 19x5", NM.................... 315.00

Pendant, rose etched in crystal, w/pouch, 2½x1¼" 45.00
Pitcher, flower bud form, wht, leaf forms hdl, gr mk, 6x4½" 110.00
Planter, lt gr w/gold rim, #3477-X-561, 5½x6½" 20.00
Plate, birds in center, gold border, ...Boehm Birds..., 1976, 11" 35.00
Vase, creamy wht w/swan hdls, gr mk, 8½x4¼", pr 145.00

L.E. Smith Glass

The L. E. Smith Glass Company began as a decorating company in Jeannette, Pennsylvania, in 1907, specializing in ruby stain souvenir ware. By 1910 they had moved to their present location in Mount Pleasant, Pennsylvania, where they embarked on the manufacture of glass. Early products included mustard containers, vault lights, automobile headlight lenses, and candy containers. In 1920 they acquired the Greensburg Glass Company in Greensburg, Pennsylvania, operating it as Factory #2 for two decades. This period saw the introduction of many patterns, including Crackled ('By Cracky'), Lace ('Romanesque'), and the group of patterns collected today as 'Mount Pleasant.' Smith made massive amounts of cobalt blue and black glass in the 1920s and 1930s. Many figural boudoir lamps and powder jars also date from this period.

By the 1950s, reproduction glassware became a large part of the product being offered, with some patterns — Heritage, Dominion, Daisy and Button, Hobnail — still being made today. The most popular by far, was Moon and Star. At the same time, the Simplicity pattern (introduced in 1958) was successful in capturing the market for 'modern' freeform glassware that Viking's Epic line had pioneered. In the years since, carnival glass, lighting of all types, and glassware designed for gift shop and catalog sales have kept the company in operation. Smith celebrated its 100th anniversary in 2007. Our advisor for this category is Tom Felt (see Directory, West Virginia).

Abraham Lincoln, plate, amethyst carnival, #9-L 30.00
Acorn & Squirrel, bowl, covered, amber, #205 .... 35.00
Angel, candleholder, #6661, bl, 5" 15.00
Cordial tray (Greensburg mold), hdld, blk, #381 .... 20.00
Crackled (By Cracky), sherbet, canary, #88 .... 20.00
Daisy & Button, ashtray, colonial bl, #4660 .... 10.00
Daisy & Button, candy box w/cover, antique gr, #4694 .... 20.00
Daisy & Button, canoe, amber, #531 .... 10.00
Daisy & Button, canoe, colonial bl, #531 .... 15.00
Daisy & Button, oil lamp, antique gr, hdld, #4608 .... 35.00
Daisy & Button, punch set, no underplate, crystal, #5601 .... 70.00
Daisy & Button, punch set w/underplate, crystal, #5602 .... 100.00
Daisy & Button, slipper, gr mg, #80 .... 20.00
Daisy & Button, slipper on skate, crystal, #71 .... 20.00
Daisy & Button, toothpick holder, amber carnival, #4611 .... 10.00
Dominion, toothpick holder, mg, #685 .... 10.00
Elephant, powder jar, trunk down, on rippled base, gr satin 45.00
Elephant, powder jar, trunk down, on rippled base, rose satin 35.00
Fed, eagle ashtray, flame (amberina), #4500 .... 20.00
Fern, bowl, canary, #4, 3½" 20.00
Flying bird, pk lustre, #4401 .... 25.00
Goose Girl, bl, #6630, 8" 25.00
Goose Girl, flame (amberina), #6620, 6" 10.00
Grape, candleholders, mg, #9925, pr 15.00
Heritage, bowl, crimped, lt bl lustre, #3181 .... 20.00
Heritage, bowl, cupped, cobalt carnival, #346 .... 15.00
Heritage, bowl, peach lustre, #1515 .... 30.00
Heritage, bowl, ruby carnival, #373 .... 45.00
Heritage, bowl, ruby carnival, #1515 .... 30.00
Heritage, butter dish, amethyst carnival, #310 .... 30.00
Heritage, compote, ruby carnival, #520 .... 45.00
Heritage, fan vase, ice aqua carnival, #410 .... 45.00

Heritage, nappy, hdld, colonial bl, #316 .... 15.00
Heritage, vase, amberina carnival, #409 .... 35.00
Heritage, vase, amethyst carnival, #409 .... 35.00
Heritage, vase, woodrose lustre, #506 .... 30.00
Hobnail, cake plate, blk, #5592, 10¾" 60.00
Hobnail, cake plate, gr mg, #5594, 6" 50.00
Hobnail, goblet, pk, #5552 .... 10.00
Holiday, punch set, crystal, #77014 .... 45.00
Homestead, plate, grill, blk, #89 .... 20.00
Ladle, punch, crystal, #955 .... 30.00
Leaf, plate, bl, #807, 7½" 10.00
Modernistic (Wig-Wam), candlesticks, blk, #1, pr 30.00
Moon & Star, ashtray, flame (amberina), #4288, 8" 20.00
Moon & Star, ashtray, oval, colonial bl, #4240, 4½" 10.00
Moon & Star, ashtray, oval, flame (amberina), #4240, 4½" 12.00
Moon & Star, basket, antique gr, #6222, 4½" 20.00
Moon & Star, bell, amber, #6235 .... 20.00
Moon & Star, bell, crystal satin, #6235 .... 15.00
Moon & Star, bell, lt bl satin, #6235 .... 35.00
Moon & Star, butter dish, amber, #4209, 7" rnd 20.00
Moon & Star, butter dish, amber, #6229, 8½" 25.00
Moon & Star, butter dish, antique gr, #6229, 8½" 30.00
Moon & Star, butter dish, colonial bl, #6229, 8½" 30.00
Moon & Star, butter dish, flame (amberina), #6229, 8½" 40.00
Moon & Star, cake plate, skirted, crystal, #5232, 11" dia 70.00
Moon & Star, cake plate, skirted, flame (amberina), #5232, 11" dia .. 95.00
Moon & Star, candleholders, amber, #5231, 4½", pr 15.00
Moon & Star, candleholders, colonial bl, #5231, 4½" 20.00
Moon & Star, candleholders, crystal, #5211, 9¼", pr 100.00
Moon & Star, candleholder w/insert nappy, antique gr, #5200 ...... 25.00
Moon & Star, candle lamp, antique gr, #5276 .... 65.00
Moon & Star, candle lamp, crystal base, flame (amberina) shade, #6227 .. 40.00
Moon & Star, candy box & cover, amber, #5204, 7½" 15.00
Moon & Star, candy box & cover, colonial bl, #5204, 7½" 25.00
Moon & Star, candy box & cover, crystal, #5214, 7" 25.00
Moon & Star, candy box & cover, flame (amberina), #4204, 10" 75.00
Moon & Star, candy box & cover, flame (amberina), #5294, 8" 40.00
Moon & Star, candy box & cover, mg, #5294, 8" 20.00
Moon & Star, canister set, 4-pc, colonial bl, #6289 .... 85.00
Moon & Star, canister set, 4-pc, flame (amberina), #6289 .... 100.00
Moon & Star, compote, colonial bl, #6203, 8" 20.00
Moon & Star, compote, crimped, amber, #4201, 7" 15.00
Moon & Star, compote, crimped, colonial bl, #3601, 5" 15.00
Moon & Star, compote, crimped, crystal, #4201, 7" 25.00
Moon & Star, compote, crimped, flame (amberina), #4201, 7" 30.00
Moon & Star, compote, flame (amberina), #4203, 6½" 15.00
Moon & Star, compote, rolled edge, mg, #4206, 10" dia 25.00
Moon & Star, courting lamp, amber, #6225, 6" 20.00
Moon & Star, courting lamp, amber, #6245, 8" 410.00

Moon and Star, courting lamp, amberina (flame), #6245, circa 1978, 8", $400.00 to $450.00.
(Photo courtesy Tom Felt)

Moon & Star, courting lamp, antique gr, #6225, 6" 35.00
Moon & Star, courting lamp, crystal satin, #6225, 6" 40.00

Moon & Star, courting lamp, gr mg, #6225, 6" 25.00
Moon & Star, cr/sug, antique gr, #4261 .... 12.00
Moon & Star, cruet, flame (amberina), #6241 .... 45.00
Moon & Star, goblet, colonial bl, #3602 .... 15.00
Moon & Star, goblet, crystal, #3602 .... 10.00
Moon & Star, goblet, flame (amberina), #3602 .... 20.00
Moon & Star, nappy, hdld, lt bl, #5216 .... 15.00
Moon & Star, nappy, oval, colonial bl, #6220 .... 12.00
Moon & Star, oil lamp, antique gr, #4231 .... 65.00
Moon & Star, oil lamp, colonial bl, #4231 .... 70.00
Moon & Star, oil lamp, flame (amberina), #4231 .... 65.00
Moon & Star, relish, divided, flame (amberina), #4281 .... 20.00
Moon & Star, s&p, amber, #4251 .... 25.00
Moon & Star, salt dip, colonial bl, #5210 .... 10.00
Moon & Star, toothpick holder, amber, #4211 .... 10.00
Moon & Star, toothpick holder, colonial bl, #4211 .... 12.00
Moon & Star, toothpick holder, flame (amberina), #4211 .... 15.00
Moon & Star, tumbler, amber, #4222, 11-oz 10.00
Moon & Star, tumbler, colonial bl, #6272, 7-oz 7.00
Moon & Star, tumbler, crystal, #6272, 7-oz 7.00
Moon & Star, tumbler, flame (amberina), #4222, 11-oz 15.00
Moon & Star, tumbler, flame (amberina), #6272, 7-oz 12.00
Moon & Star, vase, amber, #5261, 9" 35.00
Moon & Star, vase, bud, colonial bl, #6231 .... 35.00
Mount Pleasant, bonbon, rose, #200 .... 20.00
Mount Pleasant, bowl, cupped, blk, #525 .... 20.00
Mount Pleasant, c/s, blk, #505 .... 10.00
Mount Pleasant, plate, mayonnaise, blk, #200 .... 15.00
Mount Pleasant, plate, salad, 2-hdld, blk, #505, 10½" dia 10.00
Oriental, lantern, flame (amberina), #6303 .... 50.00
Penny candy jar, Caribbean bl, #2106, 5-lb 25.00
Pineapple, punch set, crystal, #5700 .... 75.00
Pinwheel & Star, punch set, crystal, #9992 .... 85.00
Rearing Horse, bookends, amber, #6200, pr 50.00
Rearing Horse, bookends, avocado, #6200, pr 50.00
Rearing Horse, bookends, crystal, #6200, pr 30.00
Rearing Horse, bookends, flame (amberina), #6200, pr 75.00
Rearing Horse, bookends, nu-blu, #6200, pr 75.00
Simplicity, swung vase, bittersweet, #1405, 27" 40.00
Simplicity, swung vase, flame (amberina), #1405, 34" 45.00
Simplicity, swung vase, flame (amberina), #1901, 20" 25.00
Simplicity, swung vase, orange, #1911, 15½" 15.00
Simplicity, candy box, bittersweet, #4805, 10" 50.00
Tumbler tray (Greensburg mold), hdld, blk, #181 .... 35.00
Turkey (covered dish), amber, #207 .... 35.00
Turkey (covered dish), amethyst carnival, #207 .... 45.00
Turkey (covered dish), autumn (ruby-amber), #207 .... 65.00

Turkey (covered dish), ruby, #207, 7x7", $65.00.
(Photo courtesy Tom Felt)

Urn vase, ftd, bl, #800 .... 30.00
Urn vase, ftd, blk, #800 .... 30.00
Vase, dancing nymphs, blk, #433 .... 20.00
Vase, dancing nymphs, mg, #433 .... 25.00

Le Verre Francais

Le Verre Francais was produced during the 1920s by Schneider at Epinay-sur-Seine in France. It was a commercial art glass in the cameo style composed of layered glass with the designs engraved by acid. Favored motifs were stylized leaves and flowers or geometric patterns. It was marked with the name in script or with an inlaid filigrane. Our advisor for this category is Don Williams; he is listed in the Directory under Missouri.

Bowl, Deco fruit, amethyst on yel/orange mottle, 10" 865.00
Lamp, Escargot (snails), orange/brn on yel 8" dia shade/base, 13" . 12,500.00
Lamp, hanging, floral, orange/bl on yel mottle bullet-nose shade ... 3,100.00
Vase, Algues (algae), orange/gr on wht, trumpet neck, Charder, 7" .1,550.00

Vase, Cerises, Deco florals, orange and rust on frost, 17", $6,000.00. (Photo courtesy Stanton Auctions on LiveAuctioneers.com)

Vase, cherries, orange/violet on mauve, shouldered, 17" 4,150.00
Vase, chestnuts, raisin on orange, Nouveau form w/hdls, slim, 14" ..1,495.00
Vase, dahlia, lav to purple on pk/mauve, shouldered w/ogee sides, 24". 4,600.00
Vase, dahlias, purple on raspberry, 13" 2,400.00
Vase, floral, bl to fuchsia mottle on bl/yel, compote form, 16" ..6,325.00
Vase, floral/trailing stems, orange on orange to gr, ftd, 10" 1,645.00
Vase, flowering trees, orange/red on peach/yel, spherical, 11" ...3,360.00
Vase, foxglove, orange to red on pk mottle, pear form, Ovington, 10". 1,265.00
Vase, freesia/leaves, orange/raisin on yel/orange mottle, Charder, 19" .. 3,795.00
Vase, freesia, orange/bright bl on frost to lt bl, coupe shape, 15" ...3,335.00
Vase, fuchsia, orange to indigo on maize to bl, appl hdls, 12x9".3,960.00
Vase, fuchsia, rust/dk bl w/red neck band on frost/bl mottle, ftd, 12" .3,335.00
Vase, iris, red/raisin on yel, slim w/bun ft, 22" 3,335.00
Vase, leafy stems, brn/wht/orange on fiery orange, elongated/ftd, 21". 4,025.00
Vase, leaves/fruit, brn on lightly mottled orange, slim w/bun ft, 20"...1,950.00
Vase, leaves/stylized flowers, orange/gr on bright bl, 11"............2,020.00
Vase, morning glory vines, red/mauve on red mottle, bun ft, 16" ..2,160.00
Vase, palm trees, yel/orange on frosted mottle, spherical, 7½" ..3,100.00
Vase, peacock/floral, orange/bl on peach mottle, bun ft, 16" 3,120.00
Vase, roses, lav on mottled lav w/amber mottle, Charder, 16¼" .2,750.00
Vase, swan pr, purple on yel/orange mottle, lav hdls/ftd, Charder, 8" ..9,485.00
Vase, wisteria, purple on bl, str sides narrow at bun ft, 6" 1,440.00
Vase, wisteria, purple on frost, Charder, 12¼" 1,925.00

Libbey Glass

The New England Glass Company was established in 1818 in Boston, Massachusetts. In 1892 it became known as the Libbey Glass Company. At Chicago's Columbian Expo in 1893, Libbey set up a ten-pot furnace and made glass souvenirs. The display brought them worldwide fame. Between 1878 and 1918, Libbey made exquisite cut and faceted glass, considered today to be the best from the brilliant period. The company is credited for several innovations — the Owens bottle machine that made mass production possible and the Westlake machine which turned out both electric light bulbs and tumblers automatically. They developed a machine to polish the rims of their tumblers in such a way that chipping was unlikely to occur. Their glassware carried the patented Safedge guarantee. Libbey also made glassware in numerous colors, among them cobalt, ruby, pink, green, and amber.

Bowl, cut, fluted, Kimberly, 10"	425.00
Bowl, Maize, gr husks on oyster wht, 4x8¾"	235.00
Butter dish, Maize, bl husks on irid	650.00
Butter dish, Maize, gr husks on custard	225.00
Candleholder, opal camel stem, 5"	$165.00
Candlesticks, camel stem, wht opal & clear, 5¼", pr	780.00
Celery vase, Maize, gr husks on custard	140.00
Celery vase, Maize, lg gold irid on clear, 6¾"	150.00
Compote, amethyst flower-form bowl, clear ft & stem, 7x7"	1,200.00
Compote, amethyst over opal, 12-ribbed morning glory, 8"	875.00
Compote, giraffe stem, wht opal & clear, 7"	1,050.00
Compote, wht w/gr pulled petals, clear ft, Nash, 4⅜x11¾"	425.00
Creamer/sugar bowl, cut, strawberry dmn & hobstars, w/lid	330.00
Decanter, intaglio floral, slim neck, faceted stopper, 12¼"	775.00
Goblet, cut, Cornucopia, 7¼"	65.00

Jug, brilliant cut, circa 1900, acid stamped twice, 8", $595.00. (Photo courtesy DuMouchelles on LiveAuctioneers.com)

Plate, cut, Sultana, 11¾"	950.00
Punch bowl, cut, hobstars/fans, no base, 14¼"	900.00
Stem, claret, bear, blk, 5½"	175.00
Stem, cordial, crystal, flat ribbed stem, Embassy #4900, 6½", EX	1,750.00
Stem, cordial, monkey, wht opal, 5"	145.00
Stem, goblet, cat, wht opal	200.00
Stem, wine, monkey, frosted, 5"	150.00
Sugar shaker, Maize, pearlized lustre, yel husks, 5½"	270.00
Syrup, Maize, bl husks, gold irid cob, pewter lid, 6"	550.00
Toothpick holder, Maize, gr husks w/gold edge on custard	500.00
Tray, cut, hobstars w/cane, star center, scalloped rim, ca 1890, 12"	2,500.00
Tray, cut, Wisteria & Lovebirds, 11½x4½"	1,900.00
Tray, ice cream, Empress variation, ca 1880-1915, 17½x10"	1,250.00
Tumbler, Maize, gr husks on irid	110.00
Vase, amberina, flanged rim, ftd, 13½"	920.00
Vase, brilliant cut, waisted, 12"	780.00
Vase, crystal, eng Johnny Appleseed, flared rim, ftd, 11"	545.00
Vase, Maize, yel/gold husks on custard, 6½"	210.00
Vase, peacock feather texture, pk/amethyst on clear, cylinder, 7"	140.00

Lightning Rod Balls

Used as ornaments on lightning rods, the vast majority of these balls were made of glass, but ceramic examples can be found as well. Their average diameter is 4½", but it can vary from 3½" up to 5½". Only a few of the 400 pattern-and-color combinations are listed here. The most common are round and found in sun-colored amethyst or milk glass. Lightning rod balls are considered mint if they have no cracks or holes and if any collar damage can be covered with a standard cap. Some patterns are being reproduced without being marked as such, and new patterns are be-

ing made as well. Collectors are cautioned to look for signs of age (stains) and learn more before investing in a 'rare' lightning rod ball. Our advisor is Rod Krupka, author of *The Complete Book of Lightning Rod Balls*. He is listed in the Directory under Michigan.

Amber, plain rnd, 5⅛x4½"	40.00
Amber, Raised Quilt, 5½x5"	125.00
Blue opaque, plain rnd, 5⅛x4½"	30.00
Blue opaque, Pleat rnd, 5x4½"	40.00

Cobalt, Onion, 4⅛x3⅜", $2,200.00. (Photo courtesy Rod Krupka)

Cobalt, plain Pendant w/cap	225.00
Gold Mercury, plain rnd, 5x4½"	125.00
Gray-gr, D&S, 5¼x4"	400.00
Light gr opaque, Doorknob, 4¼x4"	350.00
Milk glass, Hawkeye, 5⅛x4⅜"	45.00
Milk glass, JFG, 3⅞x3⅜"	85.00
Milk glass, Moon & Star, 5x4½"	45.00
Milk glass, plain rnd, 5⅛x4½"	20.00
Milk glass, Sharp Pleat, 5x4½"	35.00
Ruby, Electra rnd, 5⅛x4½"	275.00
Ruby, plain rnd, 5⅛x4½"	95.00
Silver Mercury, plain rnd, 5⅛x4½"	125.00
Sun Colored Amethyst, 'K,' 5⅛x4½"	30.00
Sun Colored Amethyst, plain rnd, 5⅛x4½"	20.00

Limbert

Charles P. Limbert formed his firm in 1894 in America's furniture capital, Grand Rapids, Michigan, and from 1902 until 1918, produced a line of Arts & Crafts furniture. While his wide-ranging line of furniture is not as uniformly successful as Gustav Stickley's, the Limbert pieces that do exhibit design excellence stand among the best of American Arts & Crafts examples. Pieces featuring cutouts, exposed construction elements (e.g., key and tenon), metal and ebonized wood inlays, and asymmetric forms are among the most desirable. Less desirable are the firm's Outdoor Designs that show exposed metal screws and straight grain, as opposed to quartersawn oak boards. His most aesthetically successful forms mimic those of Charles Rennie Mackintosh (Scotland) and, to a lesser extent, Josef Hoffmann (Austria). Usually signed with a rectangular mark (a paper label, branded in the wood, or a metal tag) showing a man planing wood, and the words Limbert's Arts Craft Furniture Made in Grand Rapids and Holland. The firm continued to produce furniture until 1944. Currently, only his Arts & Crafts-style furniture holds any interest among collectors.

Please note: Furniture that has been cleaned or refinished is worth less than if its original finish has been retained. Our values are for pieces in excellent original condition unless noted otherwise. Our advisor for this and related Arts & Crafts categories is Bruce A. Austin; he is listed in the Directory under New York.

Key:
b — brand   l — label

Armchair, #643, 4-slat bk/1-slat arms, rfn, b, 41x29x28"	700.00
Bookcase, #334, 2 ldgl doors, 8-shelf, castors, ca 1905, 56x42"	8,500.00

Bookcase, #347, 1-door, spade cut-outs, paper label, 47x16½x11½" ... 4,500.00
Bookcase, #355, 1-door, 3-shelf, cut-out panels, paper label, 48x33x12" ..6,500.00
Bookcase, #359, 3-door, 3 adjustable shelves per section, 57x67x14". 10,000.00
China cabinet, 1 door+3 fixed, stains, 57x47x15" 3,000.00
Desk, #105, 1-drw, slatted shelves, b, 29½x42x28" 650.00
Drink stand #110, tapered legs, str-X stretchers, sgn, 26x22" ...2,500.00
Magazine stand, #300, 4-shelf, slab sides w/cutout, 37x20x14" 950.00
Magazine stand, #303, arched toe-brd & top stretcher, 42x21x12" ..1,400.00
Magazine stand, ebon-oak w/caned side panels, arched bk, b, 30x20x11". 1,500.00
Magazine stand, oak, 4-shelf, arched bottom, 2-slat sides, 43x16x13" .. 1,200.00
Pedestal, #246, rnd top on corbelled base, b, 32x14" dia 1,400.00
Rocker, cut-out crest rail, rush seat, 33x26x21" 1,100.00
Sideboard, mirrored gallery, cutouts, l, 57x60x22" 6,600.00
Table, #146, oval top, slab sides w/cutouts, shelf, b, 29x45x30" . 1,800.00
Table, conference, arched aprons, canted legs, rfn/rstr, 29x108x48"...6,300.00
Table, cut-out side, #240, rnd top, lower shelf, 30x20x20" 4,500.00
Table, lamp, broad X-stretchers, canted legs, sq cutouts, 30" dia ...1,500.00
Table, library, #121, 2-drw, slatted sides, mortised pulls, 29¼x50x36". 2,040.00
Table, library, #146, cutouts, b, 29½x45x29½" 1,900.00
Table, library, #153, 1-drw, turtletop, cut-out plank sides, lower shelf, 29½x48x30".2,600.00
Table, library, #158, dbl oval, b, 29½x47¾x36" 7,500.00
Table, library, #1141, 2-drw, b, 29x48x32" 1,900.00
Table, library, 8-sided top, wide legs w/cutouts, b, 29x52x52" ..8,400.00
Table, library, chalet style, 12-drw, appl dmn decor, shelf, rfn, 48" ... 500.00
Table, library, turtle-shaped top, long corbels, b, 30x48x30" 2,400.00

Limited Edition Plates

Current values of some limited edition plates remain steady, while many others have fallen. Prices charged by plate dealers in the secondary market vary greatly; we have tried to suggest an average. Since Goebel Hummel plates have been discontinued, values have started to decline. While those who are trying to complete the series continue to buy them, few seem interested in starting a collection. As for the Danish plates, Royal Copenhagen and Bing and Grondahl, more purchases are for plates that commemorate the birth year of a child or a wedding anniversary than to add to a collection.

Bing and Grondahl

1895, Behind the Frozen Window, $5,500 to 6,000.00
1896, New Moon, $2,000 to 2,200.00
1897, Christmas Meal of Sparrows, $1,250 to 1,400.00
1898, Roses & Star, $700 to 750.00
1899, Crows Enjoying Christmas, $1,000 to 1,250.00
1900, Church Bells Chiming, $800 to 850.00

1901, Three Wise Men, $300.00 to $325.00. (Photo courtesy Clars Auction Gallery on LiveAuctioneers.com)

1902, Gothic Church Interior, $275 to 300.00
1903, Expectant Children, $225 to 275.00
1904, View of Copenhagen From Fredericksberg Hill, $75 to 100.00
1905, Anxiety of the Coming Christmas Night, $90 to 120.00
1906, Sleighing to Church, $65 to 85.00
1907, Little Match Girl, $85 to 100.00
1908, St Petri Church, $75 to 90.00

1909, Yule Tree, $75 to 80.00
1910, Old Organist, $60 to 75.00
1911, Angels & Shepherds, $60 to 75.00
1912, Going to Church, $60 to 75.00
1913, Bringing Home the Tree, $60 to 75.00
1914, Amalienborg Castle, scarce, $100 to 150.00
1915, Dog on Chain Outside Window, $100 to 120.00
1916, Prayer of the Sparrows, $60 to 70.00
1917, Christmas Boat, $60 to 70.00
1918, Fishing Boat, $60 to 70.00
1919, Outside the Lighted Window, $55 to 65.00
1920, Hare in the Snow, $50 to 65.00
1921, Pigeons, $50 to 65.00
1922, Star of Bethlehem, $50 to 65.00
1923, Ermitage, $50 to 65.00
1924, Lighthouse, $50 to 65.00
1925, Child's Christmas, $45 to 55.00
1926, Churchgoers, $45 to 55.00
1927, Skating Couple, $45 to 55.00
1928, Eskimos, $45 to 55.00
1929, Fox Outside Farm, $60 to 80.00
1930, Tree in Town Hall Sq, $60 to 80.00
1931, Christmas Train, $60 to 80.00
1932, Lifeboat at Work, $55 to 75.00
1933, Korsor-Nyborg Ferry, $45 to 55.00
1934, Church Bell in Tower, $45 to 55.00
1935, Lillebelt Bridge, $45 to 55.00
1936, Royal Guard, $60 to 80.00
1937, Arrival of Christmas Guests, $60 to 80.00
1938, Lighting the Candles, $100 to 115.00
1939, Old Lock-Eye, The Sandman, $125 to 145.00
1940, Delivering Christmas Letters, $160 to 175.00
1941, Horses Enjoying Meal, $160 to 175.00
1942, Danish Farm on Christmas Night, $150 to 175.00
1943, Ribe Cathedral, $165 to 180.00
1944, Sorgenfri Castle, $100 to 110.00
1945, Old Water Mill, $110 to 115.00
1946, Commemoration Cross, $75 to 85.00
1947, Dybbol Mill, $75 to 85.00
1948, Watchman, $70 to 80.00
1949, Landsoldaten, $60 to 80.00
1950, Kronborg Castle at Elsinore, $100 to 120.00
1951, Jens Bang, $60 to 75.00
1952, Old Copenhagen Canals & Thorsvaldsen Museum, $80 to . 90.00
1953, Royal Boat, $80 to 100.00
1954, Snowman, $80 to 90.00
1955, Kaulundborg Church, $80 to 90.00
1956, Christmas in Copenhagen, $85 to 110.00
1957, Christmas Candles, $85 to 110.00
1958, Santa Claus, $80 to 95.00
1959, Christmas Eve, $75 to 85.00
1960, Village Church, $90 to 110.00
1961, Winter Harmony, $70 to 85.00
1962, Winter Night, $65 to 75.00
1963, Christmas Elf, $65 to 75.00
1964, Fir Tree & Hare, $30 to 40.00
1965, Bringing Home the Tree, $25 to 35.00
1966, Home for Christmas, $25 to 35.00
1967, Sharing the Joy, $25 to 35.00
1968, Christmas in Church, $25 to 35.00
1969, Arrival of Guests, $20 to 25.00
1970, Pheasants in Snow, $15 to 20.00
1971, Christmas at Home, $15 to 20.00
1972, Christmas in Greenland, $15 to 20.00

1973, Country Christmas, $15 to 20.00
1974, Christmas in the Village, $15 to 20.00
1975, The Old Water Mill, $15 to 20.00
1976, Christmas Welcome, $15 to 20.00
1977, Copenhagen Christmas, $15 to 20.00
1978, A Christmas Tale, $15 to 20.00
1979, White Christmas, $15 to 20.00
1980, Christmas in the Woods, $15 to 20.00
1981, Christmas Peace, $15 to 20.00
1982, The Christmas Tree, $15 to 20.00
1983, Christmas in Old Town, $15 to 20.00
1984, Christmas Letter, $15 to 20.00
1985, Christmas Eve, Farm, $15 to 20.00
1986, Silent Night, $20 to 30.00
1987, Snowman's Christmas, $20 to 30.00
1988, In King's Garden, $20 to 30.00
1989, Christmas Anchorage, $20 to 30.00
1990, Changing Guards, $20 to 30.00
1991, Copenhagen Stock Exchange, $35 to 45.00
1992, Pastor's Christmas, $35 to 45.00
1993, Father Christmas in Copenhagen, $45 to 50.00
1994, Day in Deer Park, $45 to 55.00
1995, Towers of Copenhagen, $45 to 55.00
1996, Winter at the Old Mill, $45 to 55.00
1997, Country Christmas, $45 to 55.00
1998, Santa the Storyteller, $45 to 55.00
1999, Dancing on Christmas Eve, $45 to 55.00
2000, Christmas at Bell Tower, $45 to 55.00

M.I. Hummel

1971, Heavenly Angel, $200 to 250.00
1972, Hear Ye, Hear Ye, $60 to 75.00

1973, Globe Trotter, $60.00 to $75.00. (Photo courtesy William J. Jenack Auctioneers on LiveAuctioneers.com)

1974, Goose Girl, $55 to 65.00
1975, Ride Into Christmas, $40 to 55.00
1976, Apple Tree Girl, $40 to 55.00
1977, Apple Tree Boy, $35 to 50.00
1978, Happy Pastime, $35 to 50.00
1979, Singing Lesson, $30 to 40.00
1980, School Girl, $25 to 40.00
1981, Umbrella Boy, $25 to 40.00
1982, Umbrella Girl, $30 to 50.00
1983, The Postman, $40 to 65.00
1984, Little Helper, $30 to 50.00
1985, Chick Girl, $35 to 50.00
1986, Playmates, $45 to 60.00
1987, Feeding Time, $45 to 60.00
1988, Little Goat Herder, $45 to 60.00
1989, Farm Boy, $45 to 60.00
1990, Shepherd's Boy, $45 to 60.00
1991, Just Resting, $45 to 60.00
1992, Meditation, $45 to 60.00

1993, Doll Bath, $45 to 60.00
1994, Doctor, $45 to 60.00
1995, Come Back Soon, $35 to 45.00

Royal Copenhagen

1908, Madonna and Child, $5,400.00 at auction. (Photo courtesy DuMouchelles on LiveAuctioneers.com)

1909, Danish Landscape, $225 to 250.00
1910, Magi, $175 to 195.00
1911, Danish Landscape, $175 to 195.00
1912, Christmas Tree, $175 to 195.00
1913, Frederik Church Spire, $150 to 175.00
1914, Holy Spirit Church, $125 to 150.00
1915, Danish Landscape, $125 to 150.00
1916, Shepherd at Christmas, $100 to 125.00
1917, Our Savior Church, $100 to 125.00
1918, Sheep & Shepherds, $80 to 100.00
1919, In the Park, $80 to 100.00
1920, Mary & Child Jesus, $80 to 100.00
1921, Aabenraa Marketplace, $80 to 100.00
1922, 3 Singing Angels, $80 to 100.00
1923, Danish Landscape, $80 to 100.00
1924, Sailing Ship, $80 to 100.00
1926, Christianshavn Canal, $70 to 90.00
1927, Ship's Boy at Tiller, $90 to 115.00
1928, Vicar's Family, $80 to 100.00
1929, Grundtvig Church, $80 to 100.00
1930, Fishing Boats, $80 to 100.00
1931, Mother & Child, $80 to 100.00
1932, Frederiksberg Gardens, $80 to 100.00
1933, Ferry & Great Belt, $100 to 150.00
1934, Hermitage Castle, $150 to 175.00
1935, Kronborg Castle, $175 to 225.00
1936, Roskilde Cathedral, $175 to 225.00
1937, Main Street of Copenhagen, $250 to 275.00
1938, Round Church of Osterlars, $275 to 350.00
1939, Greenland Pack Ice, $450 to 500.00
1940, Good Shepherd, $450 to 500.00
1941, Danish Village Church, $400 to 450.00
1942, Bell Tower, $425 to 450.00
1943, Flight Into Egypt, $500 to 550.00
1944, Danish Village Scene, $275 to 325.00
1945, Peaceful Scene, $400 to 500.00
1946, Zealand Village Church, $200 to 225.00
1947, Good Shepherd, $225 to 265.00
1948, Nodebo Church, $150 to 175.00
1949, Our Lady's Cathedral, $150 to 175.00
1950, Boeslunde Church, $200 to 225.00
1951, Christmas Angel, $275 to 350.00
1952, Christmas in Forest, $50 to 60.00
1953, Frederiksberg Castle, $80 to 100.00
1954, Amalienborg Palace, $80 to 100.00
1955, Fano Girl, $120 to 140.00
1956, Rosenborg Castle, $100 to 120.00

1957, Good Shepherd, $75 to..90.00
1958, Sunshine Over Greenland, $75 to...............................90.00
1959, Christmas Night, $100 to 125.00
1960, Stag, $70 to 90.00
1961, Training Ship, $70 to..90.00
1962, Little Mermaid, $125 to..150.00
1963, Hojsager Mill, $40 to...50.00
1964, Fetching the Tree, $40 to..50.00
1965, Little Skaters, $30 to..45.00
1966, Blackbird, $30 to...45.00
1967, Royal Oak, $25 to..30.00
1968, Last Umiak, $25 to...30.00
1969, Old Farmyard, $25 to...30.00
1970, Christmas Rose & Cat, $20 to....................................25.00
1971, Hare in Winter, $20 to..25.00
1972, In the Desert, $15 to..20.00
1973, Train Home Bound, $15 to.......................................20.00
1974, Winter Twilight, $15 to..20.00
1975, Queen's Palace, $15 to...20.00
1976, Danish Watermill, $15 to..20.00
1977, Immervad Bridge, $15 to..20.00
1978, Greenland Scenery, $15 to..20.00
1979, Choosing the Tree, $20 to...30.00
1980, Bringing Home the Tree, $20 to.................................30.00
1981, Admiring the Tree, $20 to...30.00
1982, Waiting for Christmas, $30 to....................................40.00
1983, Merry Christmas, $30 to...40.00
1984, Jingle Bells, $30 to..40.00
1985, Snowman, $35 to...40.00
1987, Winter Birds, $35 to..40.00
1988, Christmas Eve Copenhagen, $45 to.............................55.00
1989, Old Skating Pond, $45 to..55.00
1990, Christmas in Tivoli, $50 to..70.00
1991, St Lucia Basilica, $50 to...70.00
1992, Royal Coach, $40 to...50.00
1993, Arrival Guests by Train, $65 to...................................75.00
1994, Christmas Shopping, $40 to.......................................50.00
1995, Christmas at Manorhouse, $200 to.............................250.00
1996, Lighting the Street Lamps, $40 to...............................60.00
1997, Roskilde Cathedral, $40 to...60.00
1998, Welcome Home, $100 ....125.00
1999, Sleigh Ride, $40 to...60.00
2000, Trimming the Tree, $40 to...60.00

Limoges

From the mid-eighteenth century, Limoges was the center of the porcelain industry of France, where at one time more than 40 companies utilized the local kaolin to make a superior quality china, much of which was exported to the United States. Various marks were used; some included the name of the American export company (rather than the manufacturer) and 'Limoges.' After 1891 'France' was added. Pieces signed by factory artists are more valuable than those decorated outside the factory by amateurs. The listings below are hand-painted pieces unless noted otherwise.

Limoges porcelain is totally French in origin, but one American china manufacturer, The Limoges China Company, marked its earthenware 'Limoges' to reflect its name. For a more thorough study of the subject, we recommend *Collector's Encyclopedia of Limoges Porcelain* by our advisor, Mary Frank Gaston.

Biscuit jar, cherubs w/dove, sponged gold trim, Bawo & Dotter, 7½"..425.00
Biscuit jar, pk roses on wht w/gold, ftd, sq, Latrille Freres, 7".......375.00

Bowl, bl-gray floral w/gold trim, ftd, Bawo & Dotter, w/lid, 10"...250.00
Bowl, grapes on gr w/gold trim, Blakeman & Henderson, oval, 11x8"...275.00
Cachepot, pk & wht floral w/gold trim, hdls, & ft, Guerin, 9"..1,000.00
Celery dish, pk & gr floral w/gold trim, Luc, Flambeau, 5½x12½"...400.00
Charger, autumn leaves & berries, gold trim, Duval, Borgfeldt, 12".500.00
Charger, mc floral w/gold, Pouyat, 14x18", $450 to.....................500.00
Chocolate fan, roses, pk w/gray leaves & gold, Coiffe, 10"...........475.00
Compote, gold abstract border, Rucheler, 1914, 7½", $200 to......250.00
Compote, red floral, gr fleur-de-lis w/gold, Blakeman & Henderson..160.00
Cup/saucer, bouillon, holly & berries, T&V, $150 to..................175.00
Cup/saucer, berries on lt gr w/gold, Duval, Lanternier, $150 to....175.00
Ewer, orchids, pk on cream, much appl gold scrolling/ft, ribbed, 16"...800.00
Ferner, pk & wht mums w/gold, ftd, MEK 1898, Klingenberg & Dwenger, 9".550.00
Hair reciever, pk roses w/gold, Klingenberg & Dwenger, 2¾x4" ..225.00
Jardiniere, daisies on bl-gr w/gold rim, Bawo & Dotter, 6x8" 600.00
Leaf dish, floral on rust, heavy gold trim, Mullidy, Bawo & Dotter, 6"....165.00
Pitcher, cider, red & pk roses on gr w/gold, T&V, 8" dia, $425 to .475.00
Pitcher, syrup, gold vines on wht, gold spout & hdl, Klingenberg, 5"..185.00
Plaque, 2 turkeys, L Coudert, Borgfeldt, 9½", $175 to 200.00
Plaque, bird flying, gold trim, Dubois, Flambeau, 9¾", $250 to...275.00
Plaque, lady standing w/basket, Le Pic, Borgfeldt, 10", $275 to ...325.00
Plaque, naval battle, T&V, 13" dia, in gilt fr................................700.00
Plate, daisies on lt gr, T&V, 8¼", $70 to 85.00
Plate, fish w/pk floral on wht, Levy, Flambeau, 8¾", $60 to...........75.00

Plate, quail pair, signed G. Rosipy, Coronet, 15½", $720.00. (Photo courtesy Mark Mattox Real Estate & Auctioneer on LiveAuctioneers.com)

Plate, sm courting scene on wht, w/gold enamel, Coiffe, 10" 350.00
Plate, violets on wht w/gold rim, Guérin, 9" 100.00
Potpourri jar, lady by river on cream & gr, CJ Doyle, Guérin, 15"..2,000.00
Punch set, Art Nouveau floral, bowl, 10x15"; tray, 18"; 8 cups .1,440.00
Sandwich set, floral on cream, sponged gold trim, D&Co, $175 to..225.00
Tankard, floral, mc on lav & cream w/gold, Blakeman & Henderson, 14"..1,235.00
Tankard, nude w/water jug, w/much gold, Pouyat, 13", $3,000 to.........3,500.00
Tankard, pk roses on lt gr, dragon-shaped hdl, Pouyat, 14½".....2,000.00
Tea caddy, lilies, pk & wht w/gold scrolls, Guérin, $225 to..........250.00
Tea tile, Moss Rose, CFH, 6½" dia, $125 to.................................150.00
Vase, abstract red/gr/yel, appl metal ft, Fauré (att), 3"..................100.00
Vase, geometrics, 5-color, gourd form, Fauré, 5" 1,500.00
Vase, geometrics, gr/blk/wht, swollen tapered form, Fauré, 11".5,500.00
Vase, lady's portrait on pk floral, K Ruybix, Pouyat, 14 ", $2,200 to .2,500.00
Vase, poppies, lav & orange on gr, B&Co, 10", $550 to...............650.00
Vase, roses, pk & wht w/gr leaves, 3 ornate gold ft, Guérin, 14½" ..1,200.00
Vase, roses, pk & yel w/gr leaves, A Bronssillon, Borgfeldt, 15" .1,800.00

Lithophanes

Lithophanes are porcelain panels with relief designs of varying degrees of thickness and density. Transmitted light brings out the pattern in graduated shading, lighter where the porcelain is thin and darker in the heavy areas. They were cast from wax models prepared by artists and depict views of life from the 1800s, religious themes, or scenes of historical significance. First made in Berlin about 1803, they were used as lamp shade panels, window plaques, and candle shields. Later steins, mugs, and cups were made with lithophanes in their bases. Japanese wares were sometimes made with dragons or geisha lithophanes. See also Dragonware; Steins.

Candle stand, couple in castle hall, bronze cherub stem, 19" 2,375.00
Lamp, shade w/4 mc panels, brass putti stem, 1900, 18" 500.00
Lamp, shade w/5 genre panels, onyx base, 17" 565.00
Lamp, shade w/5 landscape panels, brass w/sq wht marble base ...815.00
Lamp, shade w/6 panels mk PPM, 11½" NP base (married), 17½"..750.00
Panel, 2 children among flowers, 6⅝x6⅜"+bklit wood fr.............. 125.00
Panel, girl seated in garden, 7½x6½"+fr fitted for candleholder... 175.00
Panel, monk/boy on beach, att KPM, 12½x9½", +bklit gilt fr...... 345.00

Little Red Riding Hood

Though usually thought of as a product of the Hull Pottery Company, research has shown that a major part of this line was actually made by Regal China. The idea for this popular line of novelties and kitchenware items was developed and patented by Hull, but records show that to a large extent Hull sent their whiteware to Regal to be decorated. Little Red Riding Hood was produced from 1943 until 1957. Buyers need to be aware that it has been reproduced. These reproductions are characterized by inferior detail and decoration; many reproduction molds carry the original patent number. Unless you're confident in your ability to recognize a reproduction when you see one, we would suggest that you buy only from reputable dealers. For further information we recommend *The Collector's Ultimate Encyclopedia of Hull Pottery* by our advisor Brenda Roberts, and *The Ultimate Collector's Encyclopedia of Cookie Jars* by Joyce and Fred Roerig. Both are published by Collector Books.

Bank, standing, 7", $600 to... 900.00
Butter dish, $350 to 400.00
Canister, cereal 1,375.00
Canister, coffee, sugar or flour; ea $600 to.................................. 700.00
Canister, salt 1,100.00
Canister, tea, $600 to... 700.00
Casserole, red w/emb wolf, Grandma & axe man, 11¾", $1,800 to..2,300.00
Child's feeding dish, 4¾x8" 1,750.00
Cookie jar, closed basket, $600 to 700.00
Cookie jar, full skirt, $600 to 700.00
Cookie jar, open basket, $300 to 400.00
Cracker jar, unmk, $600 to 750.00
Creamer, side pour, $150 to 225.00
Creamer, top pour, no tab hdl, $275 to 325.00
Creamer, top pour, tab hdl, $250 to 300.00

Dealer's plaque, 'Featuring Little Red Riding Hood Covered by Pat. Des. 135889' lettered across front, 6½x12", $2,600.00. (Photo courtesy Belhorn Auction Services, LLC on LiveAuctioneers.com)

Dresser jar, 8¾", $450 to 575.00
Lamp, $1,500 to 2,000.00
Match holder, wall hanging, $400 to... 600.00
Mustard jar, w/orig spoon, $375 to 460.00
Pitcher, 7", $450 to 600.00
Pitcher, 8", $550 to 750.00
Planter, wall hanging, $325 to... 475.00

Shakers, 3¼", pr $95 to... 140.00
Shakers, 5½", pr $180 to..235.00
Shakers, Pat design 135889, med sz, pr (+) $800 to...................... 900.00
Spice jar, sq base, ea $450 to... 600.00
String holder, $1,800 to 2,300.00
Sugar bowl, crawling, no lid, $200 to 300.00
Sugar bowl, standing, no lid, $175 to 225.00
Sugar bowl, w/lid, $275 to 325.00
Sugar bowl lid, min 110.00
Teapot, $270 to 325.00
Wolf jar, red base, $750 to 900.00
Wolf jar, yel base, $650 to... 800.00

Liverpool

In the late 1700s Liverpool potters produced a creamy ivory ware, sometimes called Queen's Ware, which they decorated by means of the newly perfected transfer print. Made specifically for the American market, patriotic inscriptions, political portraits, or other American themes were applied in black with colors sometimes added by hand. (Obviously their loyalty to the crown did not inhibit the progress of business!) Before it lost favor in about 1825, other English potters made a similar product. Today Liverpool is a generic term used to refer to all ware of this type.

Punch bowl, hand-colored warship in bottom of bowl, four transfers around outside: Washington on horseback, portrait of Franklin, Americn officer with his foot on the British Lion, federal eagle with shield, minor restoration, 4x11", $5,100.00. (Photo courtesy Heritage Auction Galleries on LiveAuctioneers.com)

Jug, Apotheosis/3-mast ship, blk transfer w/gold, 13" 2,250.00
Jug, Apotheosis/Geo WA rising to heaven, blk transfer, 8¼" 3,000.00
Jug, Apotheosis/Lady Liberty/eagle/ship, blk transfer, 1800.......2,100.00
Jug, Arms of Johnston/eagle/florals, blk transfer w/mc, 11¾" 3,500.00
Jug, Boston Fusilier/eagle & 13 stars, mc transfer, ca 1790, 12".....15,000.00
Jug, British ship/Susan's Farewell, blk transfer, 10", EX 1,100.00
Jug, Country Alehouse Door/mill house scene, blk transfer, rpr hdl, 7"....125.00
Jug, Defeat of England/eagle w/wings spread, ca 1800, 8" 1,875.00
Jug, Dr Syntax & Ghost, blk transfers, prof rpr, 9½" 200.00
Jug, Emblem of America, Native Americans, blk transfer, 8"....2,400.00
Jug, Farmer's Arms/village scene, blk transfer, silver rim, 10"....... 565.00
Jug, Geo WA bust/names of 15 states, bk: ship w/Am flag, mc, 10"..9,600.00
Jug, Geo Washington w/globe & flag, Sam'l Kelton, blk transfer, 10" .. 2,100.00
Jug, Masonic emblems (2), blk transfer, 1780s, 6½"...................... 435.00
Jug, ship, 3-color enamel, reverse: When the First Sea Struck Her..., 10½", G...1,670.00
Jug, young couple/Cupid/flowers, blk transfer, ca 1780-90, 9½" ... 725.00
Mug, Am Declared Independence July 4 1776, blk transfer, 4⅞" ..5,000.00
Mug, names 16 states/verse, ribbon border, blk transfer, 6¼" 1,650.00
Mug, Peace, Commerce & Honest...w/eagle, blk transfer, 4¾"..2,460.00

Lladro

Lladro porcelains are currently being produced in Labernes Blanques,

Spain. Their retired and limited edition figurines are popular collectibles on the secondary market.

Afternoon Promenade, girl w/parasol, #07636, 1995, 9½" 245.00
Appreciation, lady holding flowers, #1396, retired, 10½" 575.00
At the Circus, clown w/girl, #5052, retired 1985, 13" 540.00
Autumn Sheperdess, girl holding wheat, retired 1985, w/base, 18"..480.00
Baby Outing, lady & baby carriage, #01014838, 1976-1992, 13".465.00
Bashful, girl holding lg hat in front, #5008, 1978-97, 10" 130.00
Big Sister, boy & girl on couch, #5735, retired, 7" 450.00
Blessed Lady, lady w/cherubs, #01001579, retired 1989, 20", MIB . 1,250.00
Boy on Carousel Horse, #1470, retired, MIB 420.00
Circus Sam, clown holding violin at side, #5472, 1987, 9" 135.00
Close to My Heart, Blk girl holding cat, #5603, 1989-97, 8½".....135.00
Clown Playing Violin, half-figure, #5600, 6" 175.00
Clown w/Concertina, #1027, ca 1963-1993, 18", MIB.................. 375.00
Clown w/Violin, #1126, retired 1978, 13¾" 630.00
Dancer, girl arching bk holds up hem of dress, #01005050, 1979, 12" ..240.00
Day's Work, boy on tractor, #6563, retired, 8", MIB.................... 500.00
Dog in Basket, #1128, retired 1985, 7½" 175.00
Dog's Best Friend, girl & dog, #5688, 1990-2005, 6" 210.00
Don Quixote, #D29A, 1980, 16" 255.00
Dream Come True, couple dancing, #6364, 2000 .... 350.00
Dutch Couple w/Tulips, #5124, 1982-85, 11" 825.00
Embroiderer, lady in chair, #4865, retired, 11" 460.00
Evita, girl w/parasol, #5212, retired 1998, 7"............................... 160.00
Flamenco Dancers, man w/lady at ft, ca 1975, retired, 19¾x12¾" ..625.00
Florinda, girl seated w/flower basket, 1974-85, 6" 265.00
Flower Song, girl kneeling w/flower basket, #7607, retired 1988, 7"...190.00
For You, boy gives flower to lady, #5453, retired 330.00
Geisha Girl, kneeling at table w/flower urn, #4840, 1973-90s, 7½"....260.00
Girl w/Parasol, #5221, retired 2002, 8½" 160.00
Great Chef, boy w/lg pot, #6234, retired 1998, 7½", MIB 300.00
Holy Mary, #1394, ca 1982, retired, w/fr certificate, 15" 825.00
In the Gondola, #1350, ca 1978, 17¼x30½", MIB 1,440.00
In Touch w/Nature, Asian lady w/birds, #6572, retired, 15½", MIB.... 520.00
Jazz Band Bass Player, Blk man, #5834, 1990, 10"......................... 175.00
Juggler Sitting, boy playing mandolin, #01001382, 1978-85, 12".. 275.00
Kitty Confrontation, cat stalking, #1442, 5"................................. 135.00
Kneeling Thai Dancer, #2069, retired, 16½"................................ 330.00
Lady at Dressing Table, #1242, retired 1978, 2-pc, dresser 12"..1,640.00
Lady w/Shawl, holds umbrella/walks dog, #4914, retired, 17", MIB...580.00
Listen to Quixote, #1520, retired in 1995, 20" 1,920.00
Little Pals, clown w/lamb in pocket, #7600, retired 1986, 9", MIB ..1,025.00
Little Traveler, boy clown w/sack, #7602, retired, 8½" 465.00
Love & Marriage, bride & groom in carriage, #1802, retired, NMIB.760.00
Lovers From Verona (Romeo & Juliet), #1343, ca 1975, retired, 15x8".845.00

Mariner at the Wheel, marked and numbered, 15x10", $780.00. (Photo courtesy San Rafael Auction Gallery on LiveAuctioneers.com)

Melancholy, clown bust w/hands by face, #5542, ca 1989, retired.375.00
Mirage, mermaid, #1415, 1983, 6"... 225.00
Morning Chores, nun w/broom & pail, #5552, retired, 10", MIB . 550.00
My Hungry Brood, girl seated feeding ducks, #5074, 1980-97, 6½"....245.00

My Wedding Day, #1492, ca 1986, retired, 15½", MIB................. 830.00
New Horizons, Inspiration Millennium #6570, retired, 15", MIB . 425.00
Old Dog, #1067, retired 1978, 2¾x12" 500.00
Pensive Clown Bowler, head of sad clown, #5130, 1982-2000, 10"..215.00
Playful Dogs, 2 poodles & lg ball, 1974-1981 .... 450.00
Pocket Full of Wishes, boy w/flowers in pockets, #7650, 1997, 10" ..195.00
Preening Crane, #1612, retired, 7", MIB 520.00
Princess & the Unicorn, #1755G, 1991-1993, 11" 1,250.00
Princess of Peace, holding up flower urn, #6324, 1995-2000, 17".. 350.00
Puppy Love, boy & girl, #1127, retired, 10" 150.00
Purr-fect, 3 cats in flower basket, #1444, 5½"............................... 230.00
Rebirth, lady in floral archway, #6571, retired, 16½x11", MIB..... 715.00
Roving Photographer, camera/tripod over shoulder, #01005194, 1984-85 ..500.00
Sleigh Ride, #5037, 11x17" 780.00
Sport Billy, boy on skis, 1978, 8" 130.00
Spring Bouquet, girl holding 2 bouquets, #7603, retired 1997, 8½".. 250.00
Summer Breeze, girl w/flowers, #6543, retired.............................. 175.00
Sweet Girl, girl w/closed umbrella, #4987, retired, 10" 200.00
Take Your Medicine, girl w/bandage dog, #5921, retired, 7½x7".. 330.00
Ten & Growing, pre-teen couple, #7635, retired 1995, 8" 250.00
Two Women w/Flagons, ladies w/jugs on heads, #1014, retired 1985, 19".485.00
Wedding, vintage bride & groom, #K-28, 1982-1997, 12½" 210.00
Wheelbarrow w/Flowers, boy pushing wheelbarrow, #1283, 1974-91, 9".215.00

Lobmeyer Glass

J. and L. Lobmeyer, contemporaries of Moser, worked in Vienna, Austria, during the last quarter of the 1800s. Most of the work attributed to them is decorated with distinctive enameling; a favored motif is people in eighteenth-century garb. Our advisor for this category is Don Williams; he is listed in the Directory under Missouri.

Bowl, cranberry to clear w/Nouveau floral, 1910s, 3¾" H 515.00
Decanter, romantic scene/crest, faceted neck w/jewels, w/stopper, 10". 1,680.00
Pitcher, courting scene/florals, gilt trim, ftd, sgn, 9¼"................... 850.00

Plate, courting scene enameled on cut panels, illegible gilt mark on back, 10", $180.00.

Plate, courting scene/florals/gilt, sgn, 1800s, 10½"........................ 190.00
Tray, amber-yel w/Islamic-style mc decor w/gold, 12¾" 1,800.00
Tumblers, floral w/HP pictorial medallions, pr............................... 875.00

Locke Art Glass

By the time he came to America, Joseph Locke had already proven himself many times over as a master glassmaker, having worked in leading English glasshouses for more than 17 years. Here he joined the New England Glass Company where he invented processes for the manufacture of several types of art glass — amberina, peachblow, pomona, and agata among them. In 1898 he established the Locke Art Glassware Co. in Mt. Oliver, a borough of Pittsburgh, Pennsylvania. Locke Art Glass was produced using an acid-etching process by which the most delicate designs were executed on crystal blanks. All examples are signed simply 'Locke Art,' often placed unobtrusively near a leaf or a stem. Some pieces are signed 'Jo Locke,' and some are dated. Most of the work was done by hand. The business continued into the 1920s. For further study we recommend *Locke Art Glass, Guide for Collectors*, by Joseph and Janet Locke, available at your local bookstore.

Champagne, Poppy, 6"	95.00
Cup, punch, Poppy	95.00
Goblet, 3 flowers/buds on random stems, 4¼"	125.00
Goblet, Ivy	125.00
Goblet, Poppy, 16 fluted panels, 6¼"	125.00
Oyster cocktail, seaweed/coral/3 oysters, fire-polished rim, 3⅝"	195.00
Plate, Poinsettia, 7"	125.00
Sherbet, fruits	125.00
Tankard, poppies/fern fronds/grasses, waisted, 8"	495.00
Tumbler, sheaves of wheat, 2¾"	95.00
Vase, birds & poppies, flared rim, 5"	395.00
Vase, Poppy, 6x3"	350.00
Vase, Rose, flared rim, 6¼"	350.00

Locks

The earliest type of lock in recorded history was the wooden cross bar used by ancient Egyptians and their contemporaries. The early Romans are credited with making the first key-operated mechanical lock. The ward lock was invented during the Middle Ages by the Etruscans of Northern Italy; the lever tumbler and combination locks followed at various stages of history with varying degrees of effectiveness. In the eighteenth century the first precision lock was constructed. It was a device that utilized a lever-tumbler mechanism. Two of the best-known of the early nineteenth-century American lock manufacturers are Yale and Sargent, and today's collectors value Winchester and Keen Kutter locks very highly. Factors to consider are rarity, condition, and construction. Brass and bronze locks are generally priced higher than those of steel or iron. Our advisor for this section is Joe Tanner; he is listed in the Directory under California. See also Railroadiana.

Key: st — stamped

Brass Lever Tumbler

1898, emb, 2"	40.00
American Express Co, orig key	550.00
Ames Sword Co, Perfection st on shackle, 2¾"	75.00
Bingham's Best Brand, BBB emb on front, 3¼"	150.00
Chubbs, Patent London, st, 6⅛"	350.00
Cleveland, emb on front, 4-way, 3⅛"	55.00
Fagoma, Fagoma emb in shield on front, 3"	125.00
Good Luck, emb, 2¾"	45.00
JWM, emb, bbl key, 2⅝"	25.00
Motor, Motor emb on body, 3¼"	35.00
Roeyonoc, Roeyonoc st on body, 3¼"	60.00
Ruby, Ruby emb in scroll on front, 2¾"	30.00
W Bohannan & Co, SW emb in scroll on front, 2⅜"	40.00

Combinations

Chicago Combination Lock Co, st on front, brass, 2¾"	60.00
Iowa Lock & Mfg emb on lock, 3½"	100.00
Junkunc Bros Mfrs, all st on bk, brass, 1⅞"	35.00
Miller Keyless, st, iron, 3¼"	70.00
Number or letter disk, st, 4-disk, iron, 4½"	325.00

Permutation Lock Den Co, emb, brass, 3⅝"	900.00
Sorel Ltd Canada, st, brass, 3¼"	450.00
Sutton Lock Co st on body, 3"	400.00
Your Own st on body, 3⅞"	400.00

Eight-Lever Type

Blue Chief, st, steel, 4½"	40.00
Excelsior, st, steel, 4¾"	30.00
Mastadon, st, brass, 4½"	30.00
Reese, st, steel, 4¾"	15.00

Iron Lever Tumbler

Bear, emb, 2⅝"	25.00
Caesar, emb, 2¾"	15.00
Eagle, 4 dice emb on front, 2¾"	40.00

Iron with vintage-engraved panels applied to front and back, maker's mark IHBR, eighteenth century, 4¾", $40.00. (Photo courtesy Freeman's on LiveAuctioneers.com)

Jupiter, Word Jupiter/star & moon emb on front, 3¼"	18.00
Mars, emb, 2¼"	20.00
Red Chief, words Red Chief emb on body, 3¾"	400.00
Star Lock Works, st, 3⅛"	90.00
W Bohannon, Brook NY WB, st, 3¼"	35.00

Lever Push Key

California, emb, brass, 2½"	500.00
Cherokee, emb, 6-Lever, iron, 2½"	200.00
Columbia, emb Columbia 6-Lever, brass push-key type, 2¼"	35.00
Crescent, 4-Lever, emb, iron, 2"	40.00
Duke, emb 6-Lever, 2⅛"	65.00
Empire, emb, 6-Lever, brass, 2½"	20.00
HS&Co, 6-Lever, emb, brass, 2¼"	150.00
Jewett Buffalo, emb, brass, 2¼"	275.00
National Lock Co, emb, brass, 2½"	200.00
Smith & Egge Mfg Co, Smith & Egge st on front, 3"	75.00

Logo — Special Made

City of Boston Dept of Schools, st, brass, 2⅞"	110.00
Delco Products, st, brass	20.00
Heart-shape brass lever type st Brd Education, bbl key, 3½"	65.00
Ordinance Dept, st, brass, 2⅞"	75.00
Square Yale-type brass pin tumbler, st Shell Oil Co on body, 3⅛"	25.00
USBIR, st, brass, 3¾"	80.00
Zoo, st, iron, 2½"	25.00

Pin-Tumbler Type

Corbin, emb, iron, 2¾"	20.00
Fulton, emb Fulton on body, 2⅝"	30.00
Il-A-Noy, emb Il-A-Noy on body, 2½"	40.00
Rich-Con, emb, iron, 2⅞"	50.00

Segal, iron, emb Segal on shackle, 3¾" 30.00
Simmons, emb, iron, 2⅝" 30.00

Scandinavian (Jail House) Type

Backalaphknck (Russian), st, iron, 5" 600.00
R&E Co, emb, iron, 3¼" 40.00
Scandinavian Star, 3¾" 200.00
Star, emb line on bottom, iron, 3¾" 200.00

Six-Lever Type

Eagle, brass, Eagle Six-Lever st on body 18.00
Miller, Six-Lever, st, brass, 3⅞" 20.00
Olympiad Six-Lever, st, iron, 3¾" 25.00
SHCo Simmons Six-Lever, emb, iron, 3⅝" 200.00

Story and Commemorative

1901 Pan Am Expo, brass, emb w/buffalo, 2⅝" 650.00
Cast iron, emb skull/X-bones w/florals, NH Co on bk, 3¼" 300.00
Mail Pouch emb on lock, lock in shape of mail pouch, 3⅛" 275.00
Mail Pouch, CI, Russell & Co, New Britain CT, 19th C 95.00
National Hardware Co (NHCo), emb, iron, 2½" 325.00
National Hardware Co (NHCo), emb SK, iron, 3½" 900.00
Russell & Erwin (R&E), emb Aztec figure, iron, 2⅝" 650.00
Russell & Erwin (R&E), emb mailbox, iron, 3⅛" 850.00

Warded Type

Cruso Chicken, emb, brass, 2¾" 35.00
G&B, st, brass, 3" 15.00
Kirby, emb, brass, 2¼" 75.00
Navy, iron pancake ward key, bk: scrolled emb letters, 2½" 40.00
Rex, steel case, emb letters, 2⅝" 18.00
Safe, brass sq case, emb letters, 1⅞" 8.00
Sampson, emb, iron, 2⅝" 20.00

Wrought Iron Lever Type (Smokehouse Type)

DM&Co, bbl key, 4¼" 20.00
MW&Co, bbl key, 2⅝" 10.00
R&E, 4½" 40.00
VR, 3½" 30.00
WT Patent, 3¼" 20.00

Loetz Glass

The Loetz Glassworks was established in Klostermule, Austria, in 1840. After Loetz's death the firm was purchased by his grandson, Johann Loetz Witwe. Until WWII the operation continued to produce fine artware, some of which made in the early 1900s bears a striking resemblance to Tiffany's. In addition to the iridescent Tiffany-style glass, he also produced threaded glass and some cameo. The majority of Loetz pieces will have a polished pontil. Our advisor for this category is Don Williams; he is listed in the Directory under Missouri.

Basket, silver o/l floral on gr w/red border, 20" 8,625.00
Bowl, Creta Papillon, bl irid, ruffled, 9" 450.00
Bowl, earthen gr w/Nouveau platinum swirls, cvd, 2¾x9" 1,000.00
Bowl, Phanomen Gre, platinum decor on vaseline w/silver o/l, 9½"..2,300.00
Lamp, amber irid 7" dome shade; Nouveau base w/serpent ft, 16½"...3,500.00
Vase, bl free-form sqs & oil spots on amber, 9" 2,500.00

Vase, bl irid w/wavy lines & oil spots, cobalt trim, 8x12" 2,500.00
Vase, Candia Silveriris, elongated neck, 6¼" 450.00
Vase, cobalt w/Phanomen Gre decor on lower body, ruffled rim, 6"...1,000.00
Vase, Creta Papillon, med gr w/platinum decor, shouldered, 6", NM.. 450.00
Vase, Cystisus, yel w/gr decor & platinum oil spots, 4½" 1,600.00
Vase, gold irid w/gold oil spots & bl irid, conch shell form, 8x6½" 1,150.00
Vase, gold irid w/raised loops on cylinder, faux Tiffany mk, 14" ... 500.00
Vase, irid waves on violet, 4-crimp rim, ca 1900, 5¼" 1,250.00
Vase, King Tut, cobalt w/gold irid, gourd form, 4¼" 925.00
Vase, Medici, bronze hue w/purple irid, platinum decor, 6½" 1,200.00
Vase, Medici, dk earthen hue w/platinum & silver floral o/l, 6" . 3,750.00
Vase, Medici, rose pk w/platinum decor, swirled body, 6" 1,950.00

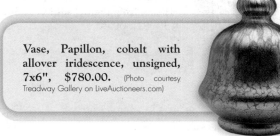

Vase, Papillon, cobalt with allover iridescence, unsigned, 7x6", $780.00. (Photo courtesy Treadway Gallery on LiveAuctioneers.com)

Vase, Phanomen Gre, platinum feathers on peach irid, 6" 2,500.00
Vase, platinum/bl feathers on amber, cylinder neck, 8¾" 2,125.00
Vase, red w/papillon decor, ruffled rim, metal ft, 8x9" 2,500.00
Vase, silver o/l vines on rust to yel, incurvate rim, 3¾" 2,875.00
Vase, Titania, gr & orange decor w/floral silver o/l shoulder, 4½" ... 3,600.00
Vase, yel w/waves/oil spots, floral silver o/l, 7" 4,315.00

Lomonosov Porcelain

Founded in Leningrad in 1744, the Lomonosov porcelain factory produced exquisite porcelain miniatures for the Czar and other Russian nobility. One of the first factories of its kind, Lomonosov produced mainly vases and delicate sculptures. In the 1800s Lomonosov became closely involved with the Russian Academy of Fine Arts, a connection which has continued to this day as the company continues to supply the world with these fine artistic treasures. In 1992 the backstamp was changed to read 'Made in Russia,' instead of 'Made in USSR.'

Bathing beauty fastening bathing cap, rnd base, 6½" 130.00
Bear sitting w/front paws down looking ahead, 3½" 25.00
Colt resting w/head up, 5½" 32.00
Fawn resting in curled-up position, 6½" 30.00
Fox resting w/head on front paws, 8½" 30.00
Fox sitting upright w/head trn, 5" 30.00
Fox terrier in wide stance, 6¾x7½" 40.00
Giraffe resting w/head str up, 12x7½" 35.00
Leopard sitting upright, looking bk, 4½" 25.00
Moose resting, looking bk, 5x6" 65.00
Peasant girl dancing, gold trim at hem, 3¼" 25.00
Poodle resting w/head up, wht w/gray face, 4½" 25.00
Quail, red mk USSR, 5x6x2¾" 65.00
Spitz Eskimo dog seated looking forward, wht w/blk detail, 3" 25.00

Longwy

The Longwy workshops were founded in 1798 and continue today to produce pottery in the north of France near the Luxembourg-Belgian border under the name 'Société des Faienceries de Longwy et Senelle.' The ware for which they are best known was produced during the Art Deco period, decorated in bold colors and designs. Earlier wares made during the first quarter of the nineteenth century reflected the popularity of Asian art, cloisonné enamels in particular. Examples are marked 'Longwy,' either impressed or painted under glaze. Our advisors for this category are Suzanne Perrault and David Rago; they are listed in the Directory under New Jersey.

Vase, Tiger, marked Sauvage Laurent Pour Kostaka Piece A Tirage, from limited edition of 50, 15", $1,800.00. (Photo courtesy Cincinnati Art Galleries, LLC on LiveAuctioneers.com)

Bowl, floral border, mc on wht crackle, #3021, 10½"....................240.00
Bowl, floral, mc on turq, oval, 11"...155.00
Box, Art Deco flower, turq & cobalt, 1930s, 1x3" dia..................225.00
Box, Deco florals on turq, bow-tie shape, #1504, 2x5x4¾"..........240.00
Cake stand, Deco leaves & berries in center & along rim, 11" 145.00
Charger, nature scene w/birds & vines, D206, 14"........................660.00
Charger, Primavera, fruit still life on wht crackle, Levy, 3x15" .1,325.00
Charger, water birds reserve w/wide floral border, 14⅜"...............360.00
Dutch shoes, floral on turq w/geometric trim, 6" L, pr.................165.00
Jardiniere, floral, mc on yel-gr, geometric decor rim, 8x14", pr .4,200.00
Lamp base, floral, mc on turq, cylindrical, brass mts, 13" 475.00
Lamp base, winged dragon & flowers on cobalt, brass mts, 12" 480.00
Plate, dragon (detailed), mc on wht crackle, D-32, 8¾"...............350.00
Plate, floral, mc on cobalt, #3301, decor #5996, 10"....................135.00
Plate, floral, rtcl bl rim, 7¾"...150.00
Tile, birds & palms, mc on wht, in Tiffany brass 3-lt fr, 16½".......515.00
Tray, birds & water scene reserve on floral w/cobalt trim, 12x10½"....395.00
Trivet, bird w/in floral border on bl, 8-sided, 10" 395.00
Trivet, stork/floral reserve on floral, mc on turq, 8-sided, 9¾" 235.00
Trivets (2), Primavera, 1 w/lady, other w/calla lily, 8", ea.............200.00
Vase, abstract fruit & geometric forms, Primavera, sgn Oleseearez, 11¾x9"...1,040.00
Vase, allover mc florals on bright bl, cylinder, 7" 335.00
Vase, birds/flowers reserves on mc floral, #3221, 9⅛", pr 850.00
Vase, Deco dmns in Fr Bl & cobalt, slim, 10" 660.00
Vase, Deco florals at shoulder, tapered/octagonal, 9½" 750.00
Vase, floral on turq, sq sides, lion's-head hdls, 9" 215.00
Vase, floral, mc on pk, cylindrical, 9½", pr...................................725.00
Vase, mc floral, stamped mk, 7"..275.00
Vase, nude woman picking fruit/full moon, 1937 Commemorative, 10¼"..1,200.00
Vase, Primavera, blk raised decor on bright bl, bottle form, 11¾" .775.00
Vase, Primavera, fruit/geometrics on ivory crackle, pillow form, 12"...2,040.00
Vase, Primavera, stylized birds & plants on bl, cylindrical, 4¾" ...250.00

Lonhuda

William Long was a druggist by trade who combined his knowledge of chemistry with his artistic ability in an attempt to produce a type of brown-glazed slip-decorated artware similar to that made by the Rookwood Pottery. He achieved his goal in 1889 after years of long and dedicated study. Three years later he founded his firm, the Lonhuda Pottery Company. The name was coined from the first few letters of his last name and the last names of each of his partners, W.H. Hunter and Alfred

Day. Laura Fry, formerly of the Rookwood company, joined the firm in 1892, bringing with her a license for Long to use her patented airbrush-blending process. Other artists of note, Sarah McLaughlin, Helen Harper, and Jessie Spaulding, joined the firm and decorated the ware with nature studies, animals, and portraits, often signing their work with their initials. Three types of marks were used on the Steubenville Lonhuda ware. The first was a linear composite of the letters 'LPCO' with the name 'Lonhuda' impressed above it. The second, adopted in 1893, was a die-stamp representing the solid profile of an Indian, used on ware patterned after pottery made by the American Indians. This mark was later replaced with an impressed outline of the Indian head with 'Lonhuda' arching above it. Although the ware was successful, the business floundered due to poor management. In 1895 Long became a partner of Sam Weller and moved to Zanesville where the manufacture of the Lonhuda line continued. Less than a year later, Long left the Weller company. He was associated with J.B. Owens until 1899, at which time he moved to Denver, Colorado, where he established the Denver China and Pottery Company in 1901. His efforts to produce Lonhuda utilizing local clay were highly successful. Examples of Denver Lonhuda are sometimes marked with the LF (Lonhuda Faience) cipher contained within a canted diamond form.

Creamer/sugar bowl, yel & gr floral, w/lid, ca 1892, 2½" & 3½"...500.00
Ewer, poppies, slim neck, #218, Weller shield mk, sgn EA, 9½"...875.00
Pitcher, 5-petal flowers at waisted neck, Spaulding, rpr, 6"...........240.00
Pitcher, floral, orange/yel/gr/brn, #79, shield mk, JRS, 1893, 7", EX...250.00
Powder box, nasturtiums, #209 & Weller shield mk, 2½" 530.00
Vase, Aburamu & Iskan (Biblical couple), sgn ADF, bulb, 11" .1,680.00
Vase, band of hooked fish at shoulder, tiny rim/wide shoulder, 8" ...600.00
Vase, birds in flowering tree, #24 & #10, mk & artist sgn, EX art, 9½". 1,800.00
Vase, blackberries on brn, Mary Taylor, #341, 8½", NM..............480.00
Vase, cowboys by a stream & Native Americans on hill, shield mk, 9"...5,400.00
Vase, daisies on celadon & orange, sgn TS, integral hdls, 3¼x5½" ..210.00
Vase, floral on dk brn, bulb bottom, integral hdls, mk, 5" 185.00
Vase, floral on low shoulder, Steel, slim trumpet neck, #265, 11" .240.00
Vase, floral, J Spaulding, L slim neck, #206, 7⅜"........................200.00
Vase, floral, yel & gr on brn, #265 Faience, sgn JRS, 11" 250.00
Vase, leaves & vines, orange & gr on brn, Denver shield mk, 8", EX ...375.00
Vase, lg 5-part leaves, shield mk, 8" 360.00
Vase, lotus & leaves on celadon & brn, gourd form, 10" 350.00
Vase, man herding oxen, brn, pillow form, 4 ft, rstr, 11½x11"......750.00
Vase, mums on std brn, artist sgn, dtd 1893, 9".............................500.00

Vase, Native Americans observe cowboys by a stream, marked Denver Lonhuda with shield, 9x5½", $5,400.00. (Photo courtesy Craftsman Auctions on LiveAuctioneers.com)

Vase, nautilus shells & cattails, squat, 3-ftd, #205, ca 1895, 6" 280.00
Vase, spider mum, J Spaulding, loop hdls, #174, 1893, 4½x6"......500.00
Vase, upright leaves/tulips emb on matt gr, 8½x5", EX..............1,560.00

Lotton Glass

Charles Lotton is a contemporary glass artist who began blowing glass full time in January 1973. He developed his own glass formulas and original designs, becoming famous for his multi-flora design and his unique lamps. He has had art glass on display in many major museums and collections, among them the Smithsonian, the Art Institute of Chicago, the Museum of Glass at Corning, and the Chrysler Museum. Each piece is made freehand, decorated with hot glass, and has a polished pontil. Charles's three sons, David, Daniel, and John each learned the art from their father and established their own studios. While their work shows a family resemblance, each artist creates work distinctly his own. Their hallmark is florals, but they create intricate threaded designs also. Each piece bears the artist's name and year it was made. Each piece is made personally by the artist who signs it, not by hired glassblowers. John stopped blowing glass in 2002, and his work is becoming scarce. David's sons are Jeremiah and Joshua. While Jeremiah has established his own glass studio in Indiana, Joshua has moved to Florida and is not currently blowing glass. Daniel's son, Tim, is rapidly becoming an accomplished glassblower. Charles's nephew, Jerry Heer, and Scott Bayless, not a relative, each produce unique designs signed with their names, the year, and Lotton Studios. The clarity of the glass and their wide palette of colors are what set the Lottons' glass apart. They sell their glass at artist shows, at Charles's galleries in Crete, Illinois, and on Michigan Avenue in Chicago, and in galleries across the U.S. For further information, read *Lotton Art Glass* by Charles Lotton and Tom O'Conner (1990) and *Lotton Glass the Legacy* by Gerald and Sharon Peterson and Dave and Cairn Steele (2007). Our advisors are Gerald and Sharon Peterson; they are listed in the Directory under Washington.

Key:
CL — Charles Lotton	JhL — Jeremiah Lotton
DL — David Lotton	JL — John Lotton
DnL — Daniel Lotton	JoL — Joshua Lotton
fct — faceted	SB — Scott Bayless
JH — Jerry Heer	TL — Tim Lotton

Atomizer, perfume, iridized cobalt blue, King Tut design, Charles Lotton, 2008, 8x3¼", $1,500.00. (Photo courtesy Gerald and Sharon Peterson)

Bowl, globe shaped, bl lava draping on Sunset Cypriot, JhL, 2004, 4¼x4¼" ...350.00
Bowl, globe shaped, lav Tulipticus on crystal w/sunset int, DnL, 2005, 6x6½" ...1,200.0
Bowl, globe shaped, pk cactus floral on crystal, DnL, 2005, 5½x5¼" .. 950.00
Bowl, gr drop leaf on Gold Ruby crush, trn collar, CL, 1997, 6½x8"..1,600.00
Bowl, gr leaf & vine on opal w/Gold Ruby crush, globe shaped, JoL/JhL, 3¼x4" .250.00
Bowl, gr pulled loop over opal reverse pull on cobalt, DL, 1999, 4¾x5¾" .500.00
Bowl, pk leaves/aurene vine on irid cobalt, trn collar, JH, 2008, 3¼x5¼"...225.00
Bowl, rose, pk multi-flora on Selenium Red, artist sgn #1, CL, 1995, 4x5" ..1,200.00
Bowl, undecorated, mandarin yel, Oriental shape, DnL, 1993, 4¼x6½"..1,400.00
Bowl, wht leaf & vine on crystal w/ruby crush, flared collar, JL, 2001, 7½x16¾".2,400.00
Candlesticks, undecorated, mandarin red, CL, 2007, 3x3¾" 1,600.00
Chalice, bl/aurene hooked on irid opal w/bl int, CL, 2009, 12¼x4" ..1,600.00
Chalice, blk/aventurine wisteria on cherry, CL, 2003, 14½x6"..2,200.00
Chalice, hooked feather on irid opal w/orange & aurene, CL, 2009, 13x5"..2,000.00
Flower form, bl/aurene wisteria on irid opal w/bl int, CL, 2009, 10x8". 1,600.00
Flower form, blk/Selenium wisteria on opal, CL, 2009, 12x7¾". 1,800.00
Flower form, hooked feather on irid opal w/red, silver & blk, CL, 2009, 13½x8"...2,000.00
Lamp, aurene peacock on irid coablt, CL, 1999, 27x21¾" 6,000.00
Lamp, table, multi-flora/gr leaves on opal, CL, 2001, 18½x13".5,000.00
Magnum weight, calla lilies on crystal w/wht, SB, 2009, 8x6½". 1,100.00

Ornament, Christmas, pk on opal Cypriot, CL, 2007, 5½" dia 800.00
Paperweight, burgundy calla lilies on crystal, SB, 2005, 3¾x2¾".225.00
Paperweight, wht orchids on crystal w/veil, JoL, 2005, 2¼x2½" ..200.00
Paperweight, yel floral on Verre de Soie, JhL, 2005, 2½x3½"..........150.00
Paperweight, yel/orange Columbines on crystal, SB, 3¼x4".........450.00
Perfume, aqua fern on Verre de Soie, teardrop stopper, DnL, 1999, 8¾x4¾" ..600.00
Sculpture, pk/blk pulled on crystal, TL, 2006, 4¾x6½" 275.00
Slipper, gold ruby King Tut on irid opal w/opal ruffled collar, CL, 2007, 3½x3"...350.00
Vase, blk/aurene, Verre de Soie, DL, 1997, 9½x7" 1,500.00

Vase, crystal, iridized sunset interior, pink multi-flora, Charles Lotton, 1997, 11¼x8", $2,800.00. (Photo courtesy Gerald and Sharon Peterson)

Vase, gourd shape, gr dbl pulled loop on mandarin yel, CL, 2008, 7½x4½" ...2,000.00
Vase, lav Cynthia floral on Neodymium, DnL, 2006, 11¼x5½" .3,800.00
Vase, pwt, gold/orange hibiscus on crystal, SB, 2008, 5x4½"........350.00
Vase, pk leaves/aurene vine on irid opal, bl int, JL, 1995, 8x4¼" .750.00
Vase, purple & fuchsia orchids on crystal, DL, 1997, 5¾x3½"......550.00
Vase, red/aurene drop leaf on Sunset Cypriot, CL, 2008, 10¾x6¼" .2,400.00
Vase, tiger orchids on crystal w/rose, JH, 2009, 5½x3½"...............275.00
Vase, wht multi-flora/aurene on irid opal, CL, 2000, 10x8½"....2,800.00

Lotus Ware

Isaac Knowles and Issac Harvey operated a pottery in East Liverpool, Ohio, in 1853 where they produced both yellow ware and Rockingham. In 1870 Knowles brought Harvey's interests and took as partners John Taylor and Homer Knowles. Their principal product was ironstone china, but Knowles was confident that American potters could produce as fine a ware as the Europeans. To prove his point, he hired Joshua Poole, an artist from the Belleek Works in Ireland. Poole quickly perfected a Belleek-type china, but fire destroyed this portion of the company. Before it could function again, their hotel china business had grown to the point that it required their full attention in order to meet market demands. By 1891 they were able to try again. They developed a bone china, as fine and thin as before, which they called Lotus. Henry Schmidt from the Meissen factory in Germany decorated the ware, often with lacy filigree applications or hand-formed leaves and flowers to which he added further decoration with liquid slip applied by means of a squeeze bag. Due to high production costs resulting from so much of the fragile ware being damaged in firing and because of changes in tastes and styles of decoration, the Lotus Ware line was dropped in 1896. Some of the early ware was marked 'KT&K China'; later marks have a star and a crescent with 'Lotus Ware' added. Non-factory decorated pieces are usually lower in value. Our advisor for this category is Mary Frank Gaston.

Bowl, appl floral branches, netting, 3¾x4¾" 175.00
Bowl, pk floral on bl, ruffled/beaded gilt rim, rtcl hdls, oval, 4x7". 250.00
Chocolate jug, gold-paste florals, Quincy design, ca 1890-1905, 4x5" ..600.00
Ewer, appl wht floral on lt gr, ornate hdl, 6"................................. 285.00
Ewer, floral w/gilt accents, sgn LW Bishop '96, 9¾" 480.00
Ewer, heavily filigreed, undecorated wht, 9½"...........................1,065.00
Jar, Luxor, rtcl raised medallions/tassels & cords, 4-ftd, 7", EX.....800.00
Rose jar, wht, beaded rim, heavily filigreed band under lid, 4½" ..200.00
Vase, Cremonian, wht w/appl flowers on celadon body, 6¼" 1,200.00

Vase, HP boat w/appl gold fishnet, ruffled rim, ftd, rpr, 4x5", EX . 250.00
Vase, HP pastel floral & wht fishnet panels, 4 gold ball ft, 8x5"... 200.00
Vase, Roman, wht ware, integral hdls, bulb base, 10" 1,000.00
Vase, wht w/appl gr floral, slim neck, scalloped rim, w/hdl, 10", EX...250.00
Vase, wild roses on wht, ornate gold hdls, stick neck, 9¾" 600.00

Lunch Boxes

Early twentieth-century tobacco companies such as Union Leader, Tiger, and Dixie sold their products in square, steel containers with flat, metal carrying handles. These were specifically engineered to be used as lunch boxes when they became empty. (See Advertising, specific companies.) By 1930 oval lunch pails with colorful lithographed decorations on tin were being manufactured to appeal directly to children. These were made by Ohio Art, Decoware, and a few other companies. In 1950 Aladdin Industries produced the first 'real' character lunch box — a Hopalong Cassidy decal-decorated steel container now considered the beginning of the kids' lunch box industry. The other big lunch box manufacturer, American Thermos (later King Seely Thermos Company) brought out its 'blockbuster' Roy Rogers box in 1953, the first fully lithographed steel lunch box and matching bottle. Other companies (ADCO Liberty; Landers, Frary & Clark; Ardee Industries; Okay Industries; Universal; Tindco; Cheinco) also produced character pails. Today's collectors often tend to specialize in those boxes dealing with a particular subject. Western, space, TV series, Disney movies, and cartoon characters are the most popular. There are well over 500 different lunch boxes available to the astute collector. For further information we recommend *The Illustrated Encyclopedia of Metal Lunch Boxes* by Allen Woodall and Sean Brickell and *Collector's Guide to Lunch Boxes* by Carole Bess and L.M. White (Collector Books). In the following listings, unless specific information to the contrary is included in the description, assume the lunch boxes to be made of metal and values to reflect the worth of boxes that are complete with their original vacuum bottles. The low side of our range represents examples in excellent condition; the high side represents mint. Our advisor for Lunch Boxes is Terri Ivers; she is listed in the Directory under Oklahoma.

A-Team, 1980s, $30 to.. 50.00
Action Jackson, 1970s, $650 to..900.00
Annie, 1980s, vinyl, $50 to.. 75.00
Barbarino, 1970s, vinyl, $125 to......................................150.00
Batman & Robin, 1960s, $65 to.. 95.00
Benji, plastic, 1970s, $20 to.. 30.00
Beverly Hillbillies, 1960s, $150 to...................................225.00
Brady Bunch, 1970s, $175 to...250.00
Casey Jones, dome top, 1960s, $500 to 700.00
Charlie's Angels, 1970s, $60 to..120.00
Close Encounters of the Third Kind, 1970s, $60 to...........120.00
Davy Crockett/Kit Carson, 1955, no bottle, $150 to..........225.00
Disney School Bus, 1990s, plastic, $20 to 30.00
Doctor Doolittle, 1960s, $95 to..165.00
Dudley Do-Right, 1960s, $775 to...................................1,125.00
Emergency!, 1973, $70 to...115.00
Fire Station Engine Co #1, 1970s, vinyl, $115 to 135.00
Flintstones, 1960s, $125 to..175.00
Gene Autry Melody Ranch, 1950s, $225 to.......................375.00
GI Joe, 1960s, $80 to...130.00
Green Hornet, 1960s, $250 to..400.00
Happy Days, 1970s, 2 versions, ea $60 to.......................... 95.00
Hogan's Heroes, dome top, 1960s, $200 to 300.00
Holly Hobbie, vinyl, 1970s, $50 to.................................... 75.00
Hopalong Cassidy, 1954, $350 to.....................................500.00
Incredible Hulk, 1970s, $35 to.. 95.00

James Bond 007, 1960s, $150 to.......................................225.00
Jetson's, dome top, 1960s, $900 to...............................1,400.00
Johnny Lightning, 1970s, $55 to.......................................105.00
Julia, 1960s, $65 to..140.00
Jungle Book, 1960s, $60 to...120.00
Kermit the Frog, dome top, 1980s, $30 to.......................... 40.00
Krofft Supershow, 1970s, $65 to.......................................125.00
Kung Fu, 1970s, $45 to... 95.00
Land of the Giants, 1960s, $120 to...................................200.00
Laugh-In, 1971, $75 to...150.00
Li'l Jodie, 1980s, vinyl, $50 to.. 75.00
Little Dutch Miss, 1959, $70 to..140.00
Lone Ranger, 1950s, no bottle, $300 to............................450.00
Looney Tunes, 1959, $200 to..300.00
Magic Lassie, 1970s, $60 to..110.00
Man From UNCLE, 1960s, $120 to....................................190.00
Mary Poppins, 1960s, $65 to..130.00
Mary Poppins, vinyl, 1970s, $75 to...................................100.00
Mickey Mouse, plastic head form, 1980s, $30 to 40.00
Muppet Babies, plastic, 1980s, $15 to................................ 25.00
Paladin, 1960s, $190 to..275.00
Partridge Family, 1970s, $55 to..100.00
Peanuts, 1960, $40 to... 80.00
Peter Pan, 1960s, $70 to..140.00
Pink Panther, 1980s, vinyl, $75 to....................................100.00
Popeye, 1962, $525 to..850.00
Popeye, 1980s, $50 to..100.00
Psychedelic Blue, 1970s, vinyl, $40 to............................... 60.00
Rat Patrol, 1960s, $95 to..165.00
Red Barn, 1957, closed doors, dome box............................150.00
Rifleman, 1960s, $325 to..150.00
Robot Man, 1980s, $20 to... 30.00
Rough Rider, 1970s, $65 to..100.00
Scooby-Doo, 1970s, various, any, ea $70 to.......................140.00
Six Million Dollar Man, 1970s, various, ea $50 to 75.00
Spider-Man & the Hulk, 1980, $40 to................................ 80.00
Star Trek, dome box, rare, 1968, $800 to.......................1,110.00
Strawberry Shortcake, vinyl, 1980, $75 to.........................135.00
Super Friends, 1970s, $50 to..100.00
Super Heroes, 1970s, $45 to... 90.00
Tarzan, 1960s, $125 to...200.00
The Sophisticate, vinyl drawstring bag, 1970s, $50 to........ 75.00
Tic-Tac-Toe, vinyl, 1970s, $50 to...................................... 75.00
UFO, 1970s, $65 to..115.00

Underdog, 1974, based on the TV series, same front and back, rare, $1,500.00. Matching steel/glass bottle, $750.00. (Photo courtesy Carole Bess White and L.M. White)

V, 1980s, $95 to...165.00
Voyage to the Bottom of the Sea, 1960s, $175 to 250.00
Welcome Back, Kotter, 1970s, $60 to 100.00
Wild Bill Hickok & Jingles, 1950s, $190 to.......................280.00
Wild Wild West, 1960s, $200 to..300.00
World of Barbie, vinyl, 1971, $50 to................................... 75.00
Yogi Bear, plastic, 1990s, $15 to.. 25.00
Young Astronauts, plastic, 1980s, $20 to............................ 30.00
Zorro, 1950s or 1960s, ea $150 to....................................250.00

Lundberg Studios Glass

This small studio has operated in Davenport, California, since 1970, when founder James Lundberg (now deceased) began making quality handcrafted glassware using a variety of techniques — some reminiscent of Tiffany. Their production includes vases, lamps, paperweights, perfume bottles, and marbles. Each piece they make is signed with the studio's name, the artist's name, a registration number, and the date.

Vase, turquoise with golden plumes, bluish-gold interior, 1992, 10x8½", $510.00. (Photo courtesy Cincinnati Art Galleries, LLC on LiveAuctioneers.com)

Lamp, 3-lily, feathered shades; gr/gold on opal, Buffalo base, 12". 375.00
Lamp, Starry Nights, yel stars on bl swirls, ftd, sgn, 15"............1,050.00
Paperweight, intaglio angels/doves on bl, #042854, 1989, 3"....1,000.00
Paperweight, Pond Reflection Extra, Steven, #031729, 1989, 2½"..1,300.00
Shade, lt gr/dk gr/ivory swirls, 2" top opening, sgn, 10"............1,250.00
Shade, red, ivory & gold swirls, ruffled bottom edge, sgn, 9"........625.00
Vase, bl irid, bulb w/stick neck, 12"..200.00
Vase, Evening Star Magnum Heart, gold int, 2000, #061327, 13"..865.00
Vase, feathers, brn w/bl on gold, 1978 #LS101276, 10"..............540.00
Vase, feathers, gr on gold, gr-trimmed rim, #062707, 11"............380.00
Vase, pwt, Aquarium, 98th in a ltd ed of 250, 1976, 4½"............900.00
Vase, pwt, Daffodil Garden, clear, #013102, sgn, 2001, 6½"......1,000.00
Vase, pwt, floral on bl tones in clear, #071117, sgn, 1996, 6".......120.00
Vase, pwt, fuchsia blossoms in clear, #011423, 1988, 6"..............660.00
Vase, pulled leaves, dk gr on gr, James, #032207, 1988, 8½"........525.00
Vase, pulled silver & purple on yel, bulb at top, unmk, 7x3½"..1,200.00

Lu-Ray Pastels

Lu Ray Pastels dinnerware was introduced in the early 1940s by Taylor, Smith, and Taylor of East Liverpool, Ohio. It was offered in assorted colors of Persian Cream, Sharon Pink, Surf Green, Windsor Blue, and Chatham Gray in complete place settings as well as many service pieces. It was a successful line in its day and is once again finding favor with collectors of American dinnerware. Our advisor for this category is Shirley Moore; she is listed in the Directory under Oklahoma.

Bowl, 36s oatmeal 60.00
Bowl, coupe soup, flat 18.00
Bowl, cream soup 70.00
Bowl, fruit, 5" 6.00
Bowl, fruit, Chatham Gray, 5" 16.00
Bowl, lug soup, tab hdls 24.00
Bowl, mixing, 5½".. 125.00
Bowl, mixing, 7".. 125.00
Bowl, mixing, 8¾"... 125.00
Bowl, mixing, 10¼"... 150.00
Bowl, salad, any color other than yel 65.00
Bowl, salad, yel 55.00
Bowl, vegetable, oval, 9½"... 25.00
Butter dish, any color other than Chatham Gray, w/lid 60.00
Butter dish, Chatham Gray, rare color, w/lid 90.00
Calendar plates, 8", 9" & 10", ea.. 40.00

Casserole 140.00
Chocolate cup, AD, str sides 80.00
Chocolate pot, AD, str sides 400.00
Coaster/nut dish 65.00
Coffee cup, AD 22.50
Coffeepot, AD (demi) 200.00
Creamer 10.00
Creamer, AD, ind 40.00
Creamer, AD, str sides, ind, from chocolate set 92.00
Egg cup, dbl.. 30.00
Epergne 125.00
Jug, water, ftd 150.00
Muffin cover.. 140.00
Muffin cover, w/8" underplate 165.00
Nappy, vegetable, rnd, 8½" 25.00
Pickle tray 28.00
Pitcher, bulb w/flat bottom, any color other than yel, 8".............. 125.00
Pitcher, bulb w/flat bottom, yel.. 95.00
Pitcher, juice 200.00
Plate, 6" 3.00
Plate, 7" 12.00
Plate, 8" 25.00
Plate, 9" 10.00
Plate, 10" 25.00
Plate, cake 70.00
Plate, Chatham Gray, rare color, 7".................................. 16.00
Plate, chop, 15" 38.00
Plate, grill, 3-compartment.. 35.00
Platter, oval, 11½"... 20.00
Platter, oval, 13"... 24.00
Relish dish, 4-part... 125.00
Sauceboat 28.00
Sauceboat, fixed stand, any color other than yel................ 35.00
Sauceboat, fixed stand, yel.. 27.50
Saucer, coffee, AD 12.50
Saucer, coffee/chocolate 30.00
Saucer, cream soup 28.00
Saucer, tea 2.00

Shakers, $18.00. (Photo courtesy Ralph Walker)

Sugar bowl, AD, str sides, w/lid, from chocolate set 92.00
Sugar bowl, AD, w/lid, ind 40.00
Sugar bowl, w/lid... 15.00
Teacup..8.00
Teapot, curved spout, w/lid... 125.00
Teapot, flat spout, w/lid.. 160.00
Tumbler, juice 50.00
Tumbler, water 80.00
Vase, bud 400.00

Lusterware

Lusterware is a metallic glazed earthenware made at the turn of the nineteenth century in Sunderland, Staffordshire, and Wales. There are four classes of luster: copper/brown, silver/platinum, pink/purple, and canary/yellow. Lusterware is readily collectible, and a very good value for its age. The rarest pieces are American historicals, such as the Cornwallis jug featuring Lafayette and the Andrew Jackson jug. Our advisor for this category is C.L. Nelson (see Directory, Texas).

Canary Luster

This type of luster is a resist decoration with yellow glaze, is very expensive, and is the rarest of all the luster ware, although the method is the same. Canary luster was popular in the early nineteenth century and was not marked. Shapes include jugs, mugs, and whimsies. A true rarity would be a historical made for the American market.

Cradle, gr transfer, 3x6"	750.00
Goblet, pnt floral, 6½"	680.00
Jug, Admiral Lord Nelson, blk transfer, 8"	3,600.00
Jug, Hope & Charity, blk transfer, 5½"	1,000.00
Jug, silver resist, 4"	600.00
Mug, child's, Be a Good Child, transfer, 2¾"	525.00
Mug, christening, transfer name Daniel, 2½"	550.00
Mug, christening, transfer name Thomas, 2½"	550.00
Pot, bulb, w/underplate, pnt floral, 6½"	2,200.00
Teapot, mother & child, Adam Buck scene, bat print, blk, 8"	1,875.00

Copper Luster

Copper luster was made with a copper solution for everyday use by the burgeoning middle class. Teawares, goblets, bowls, jugs, salt cells, pepper pots, and whimsies were the various shapes produced. Decoration included flowers and sprigs, banding, animals, children, popular topics of the day, and transferware.

Cup/saucer, Chelsea Sprig, ca 1820, 3"	88.00
Jug, Am Historical, Andrew Jackson, ca 1824, 6"	4,500.00
Jug, Am Historical, Cornwallis, 7"	4,900.00
Jug, Am Historical, William Henry Harrison, 8"	4,800.00
Jug, dmn diagonal w/bl decor, 7"	195.00
Jug, pnt, poly floral emb, 7"	100.00
Jug, single pk rose emb, 7"	115.00
Jug, stags & game dog on wide bl band, hound hdl, 19th C, 5"	60.00
Mug, bl band, 3"	100.00
Mug, bl band, house, pnt, 3"	125.00
Pepper pot, solid, 6"	275.00

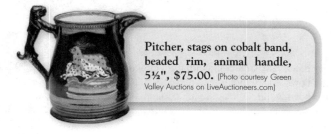

Pitcher, stags on cobalt band, beaded rim, animal handle, 5½", $75.00. (Photo courtesy Green Valley Auctions on LiveAuctioneers.com)

Salt cellar, moonlight luster band	150.00
Sauceboat, shell border w/pk & yel floral decor, dolphin hdl, 5"	175.00
Teapot, solid, 10"	185.00
Vase, shepherdess w/sheep (purple transfer), hdls, 7"	225.00

Pink Luster

Pink luster was made using gold based glazes around 1800 in England in Sunderland, Staffordshire, and Leeds, as well as in Wales. Wedgwood began the trend, producing Moonlight luster from 1800 to 1815.

Coalport, Davenport, Dixon, Miles Mason, New Hall, Ridgway, and Spode were the English factories that produced this ware. In Wales, luster was manufactured by Glamorgan, South Wales Pottery, and Dillwyn. A large variety of wares were produced for decoration such as plaques, vases, urns, and whimsies. Teaware and children's mugs and plates were made for daily use. Pink luster was popular from 1800 to 1860, and few pieces are marked. The house pattern and its many variants was one of the most popular.

Bowl, blk transfer, 11"	1,000.00
Cup/saucer, Faith & Hope, transfer, 3x6"	75.00
Jug, christening, Emma, dtd 1830, 3"	350.00
Jug, pnt house pattern, 5½"	175.00
Jug, pnt hunt scene, 7"	325.00
Jug, West View of Iron Bridge Near Sunderland/verse, 9", EX	800.00
Jug, Sunderland, True Love from Hull, 7"	425.00
Mug, children at play, blk transfer, pk borders, 4"	240.00

Mug, pink rim, base band and handle trim, magenta transfer print of eagle and shield, E Pluribus Unum, May Success Attend Our Agriculture Trade, early nineteenth century, $1,680.00. (Photo courtesy Freeman's on LiveAuctioneers.com)

Mug, transfer month December, 2½"	450.00
Mug, transfer, For a Good Boy, 2½"	400.00
Mug, transfer, peacock & foilage, 3½"	150.00
Mustard pot, pnt floral, 3½"	125.00
Plaque, Sunderland, The Loss of Gold is Great, 8½"	450.00
Plate, muffin, pnt house pattern, 8"	175.00
Plate, Swansea pnt heron, 8"	1,000.00
Sugar, blk bat print, Adam Buck scene, 7"	250.00
Teapot, transfer floral, 10"	550.00

Silver Luster

Silver luster, or silver resist, was created with a resist decoration using a platinum glaze and was sometimes called 'the poor man's silver,' made for those who could not afford the precious metal. It is a contemporary of both copper and pink luster, dating from 1800 to 1860. Shapes include teaware, pitchers, vases, and a variety of whimsies. 'Faith, Hope, and Charity' was another favorite theme, also found in pink luster. Most pieces are not marked.

Jug, bird & branches, blk transfer, 5"	425.00
Jug, English sporting scene, cobalt bl underglaze, 4½"	500.00
Jug, farmyard scene, bl transfer/wht, 4¾"	485.00
Jug, poly foilage & grapes, 6"	700.00
Pepperpot, no decor, resist only, rare shape, 5½"	450.00
Plate, floral decor, 8"	175.00
Plate, muffin, bl floral underglaze, rare shape, 8½"	300.00
Sugar, no decor, resist only, 7½"	250.00
Teapot, no decor, resist only, 9½"	375.00

Maddux of California

One of the California-made ceramics now so popular with collectors, Maddux was founded in the late 1930s and during the years that followed produced novelty items, TV lamps, figurines, planters, and tableware accessories.

Ashtray, hippopotamus w/wide mouth open, #1152?, 4x4" 25.00
Ashtray, red w/blk speckles, swirled free-form, #701 .... 10.00
Cookie jar, Bear, #2101 .... 80.00
Cookie jar, Grapes cylinder, #8412 .... 30.00
Cookie jar, Humpty Dumpty, #2113, 11" 40.00
Dish, serving gr leaves, #3051, 10x15" 28.50
Figurine, blk horse rearing, #925, 13x4" 25.00
Figurine, cockatoo on floral trimmed branch, ca 1947, 11" 150.00
Figurine, horse rearing, 13" 45.00

Figurines, pheasants, 6x12" long, pair $40.00 to $55.00. (Photo courtesy Richard D. Hatch & Associates on LiveAuctioneers.com)

Nightlight, chihuahua figural, #E-21855-M, 8x5½" 90.00
Planter, 3-D stag on side, #526, 11x7x5" 20.00
Planter, Asian girl holding bird, planter in bk, 6¼" 50.00
Planter, flamingo standing, 6" 85.00
Planter, flamingo w/wings wide, #515, 10x7" 165.00
Planter, swan, pk to wht, #510, 11x7½" 15.00
Plaque, Aquarius emb on yel, 1967, 3⅜" 25.00
Snack server, gr w/emb ribs, 2-compartment, #3151, 1½x11x6¼" . 15.00
TV lamp, bull, brn, #859, 10x10" 45.00
TV lamp, horse trotting, 12½x10½" 30.00
TV lamp, mallard duck, #893, 7½", $50 to 65.00
TV lamp, pheasant, gray/yel/pk/gr/wht/blk, 11x11", NM 45.00
TV lamp, pk flower on ea side of gold ½-cylinder shade w/Xs, 6x10". 40.00
TV lamp, swan, shiny wht, 12x9x5¾", $35 to 45.00
TV lamp, Wynken, Blynken & Nod, 10x10" 200.00
Vase, gazelle in relief on either side, brn, 1959, 12½x3½" 35.00
Vase, pk flamingo (2) figural, wings form body of dbl vase, 5x6½" . 25.00

Majolica

Majolica is a type of heavy earthenware, design-molded and decorated in vivid colors with either a lead or tin type of glaze. It reached its height of popularity in the Victorian era; examples from this period are found in only the lead glazes. Nearly every potter of note, both here and abroad, produced large majolica jardinieres, umbrella stands, pitchers with animal themes, leaf shapes, vegetable forms, and nearly any other design from nature that came to mind. Not all, however, marked their ware. Among those who sometimes did were Minton, Wedgwood, Holdcroft, and George Jones in England; Griffin, Smith and Hill (Etruscan) in Phoenixville, Pennsylvania; and Chesapeake Pottery (Avalon and Clifton) in Baltimore.

Color and condition are both very important worth-assessing factors. Pieces with cobalt, lavender, and turquoise glazes command the highest prices. For further information we recommend *The Collector's Encyclopedia of Majolica* by Mariann Katz-Marks (see Directory, Pennsylvania). Unless another condition is given, the values that follow are for pieces in mint condition. Our advisor for this category is Hardy Hudson; he is listed in the Directory under Florida.

Basket, creamy tan basketweave w/gray cat at rim, Brownfield, 12" L .. 1,200.00
Bough pot, goats in meadow, Minton, 6½" dia. 2,185.00
Bowl, center, daisy & leaf rim, rtcl center, 3 pigeons, Minton, 13" 3,650.00
Bowl, centerpiece, satyrs eating grapes, Copeland, 17" 1,750.00
Bowl, waste, Wild Rose & Rope, 5½" 200.00
Box, lizard atop basketweave, rect, Palissy Ware, 6" L 1,450.00

Butter dish, Blackberry on turq, G Jones 1,550.00
Butter dish, Shell & Seaweed, w/insert, Etruscan 800.00
Butter pat, Geranium, gr 115.00
Butter pat, Maple Leaf on Plate, pk 150.00
Butter pat, Pansy & Leaf, att Holdcroft 250.00
Butter tub, swan, butterflies & dragonflies on cobalt, prof rstr 545.00
Cake plate, Napkin, Etruscan, cobalt accent, 12½" 475.00
Cake stand, Shell & Seaweed, Etruscan, 4¾x9" 900.00
Centerpiece, putto atop shell, EX color, Minton, #1539, 18" 2,500.00
Charger, nude woman on serpent, flower border, Wedgwood, 15¼" .. 650.00
Cheese keeper, apple blossoms on picket fence, turq, G Jones, 10" .. 2,150.00
Cheese keeper, Blackberry on turq tree bark, cow finial, 9½", NM .. 950.00
Cheese keeper, goat finial, George Jones, prof rpr, 14" 10,000.00
Cheese keeper, parrot on branch w/palm leaves, 12" 1,550.00

Chestnut dish, Minton #594, missing warming insert, 6x10", $1,680.00. (Photo courtesy Rago Auctions)

Comport, Tobacco Leaf & Rosette, low, Holdcroft, 8½" 350.00
Compote, fox looking into hole w/rabbit under tree, G Jones, 8" ... 9,600.00
Compote, playing cane on turq pebble grnd, low, Holdcroft, 9¾" . 200.00
Compote, Pond Lily, G Jones, 9" 865.00
Compote, scalloped bowl, cherub on aquatic base, Wedgwood, 1870s, 9" ... 700.00
Creamer, ear of corn, Etruscan, 4" 95.00
Creamer, Sunflower, pk, Etruscan, 4" 400.00
Cup/saucer, Bird & Fan, Fielding 350.00
Flower holder, 2 putti hold bbl w/pierced top, Holdcroft, 10", NM 1,450.00
Game dish, fox atop ferns finial, dead game on turq, G Jones, rpr, 11" . 4,485.00
Game dish, game emb on brn, chick finial, w/liner, Wedgwood, 9" L . 2,200.00
Game dish, game emb on brn, rabbit finial, Wedgwood, Argenta, 9½" L. 825.00
Humidor, frog w/red smoking jacket, 6¼" 500.00
Humidor, Isle of Man on coil of rope, Holdcroft, 9" 1,665.00
Humidor, Shell & Seaweed, Etruscan 1,800.00
Jar, Swan & Cattails on cobalt, Holdcroft, prof rpr, 15x16" 750.00
Jardiniere, berries & blossoms on bark, Wedgwood, Argenta, 9" . 400.00
Jardiniere, dragonfly/bulrush/water lily on turq, G Jones, 10x11", NM .. 1,375.00
Jardiniere, ram's head w/floral drape on turq, Minton, 14" 2,875.00
Jardiniere, wild rose on tree bark, blossom hdls, G Jones, 9", NM .. 1,100.00
Jug, Bird & Fan on cobalt, Wedgwood, ca 1884, 7¼" 325.00
Jug, cobalt w/foliate bands, pewter lid, Wedgwood, ca 1871, 8¾" . 650.00
Mug, Water Lily, cobalt rim, Etruscan 275.00
Oyster plate, 4 turq shells on basketweave, ca 1882, 8¾x7½" ... 3,500.00
Oyster plate, Shell (6) & Seaweed, cobalt, Holdcroft, 10", NM ... 1,175.00
Oyster plate, Shell (mc) & Seaweed on turq, Fielding, 9" 1,950.00
Pitcher, Asparagus, Fr, 8", NM 1,035.00
Pitcher, chestnut & floral, G Jones, prof rpr hdl, 12½" 9,450.00
Pitcher, Diana, bearded man below spout, Minton, 11½" 400.00
Pitcher, Fan & Scroll, Fielding, 6½" 375.00
Pitcher, fish figural, curled tail forms hdl, 10" 155.00
Pitcher, fish w/serpent hdl, waves at base, Palissy style, 11", NM . 900.00
Pitcher, heron & fish figural, Minton, #1241, 21" 6,600.00
Pitcher, monkey figural w/bamboo hdl, prof rpr, 10" 2,400.00
Pitcher, Orchid & Tree Bark, leaf hdl, prof rpr, G Jones, 5½" ... 1,265.00
Pitcher, Shell & Seaweed, Etruscan, 5" 400.00
Pitcher, Water Lily & Iris on cobalt, G Jones, 8" 3,150.00
Plate, Asparagus & Artichoke, Luneville, 9" 300.00
Plate, Bamboo, Etruscan, 8" 120.00
Plate, lobster on cobalt w/vegetable border, Wedgwood, 8½" 800.00

Platter, fish & bulrushes on turq, Holdcroft, 25" L....................2,650.00
Punch bowl, morning glory, wheat, ribbon & bow, Fielding, 6½x14" . 265.00
Sardine box, Barrel in Ocean w/Seaweed, Wedgwood Argenta, 7½" . 1,785.00
Shelf, eagle bracket support, G Jones, 9½x9½" 1,800.00
Sweetmeat dish, conch shell supported by 2 dolphins, Minton, 9¼" .2,300.00
Sweetmeat dish, putti w/hooved ft holds turq shell, G Jones, 9" .. 925.00
Table center, man w/wheelbarrow, #413, ca 1869, prof rpr, 13x13"....2,400.00
Table center, mermaid supporting shell, Minton, #852, 15"......2,200.00
Teapot, Fish Swallowing Fish, gr/brn/yel, 6½".............................785.00
Teapot, Isle of Man, Union Jack w/flag, Brownfield, prof rpr, 7¾".1,200.00
Teapot, Monkey & Coconut, Minton, prof rpr, 8½" 4,600.00
Tray, Bulrush & Lotus, lotus center hdl, Minton, #1041, 15½", NM .3,200.00
Tray, Butterfly, Dragonfly & Wheat, bamboo border, G Jones, 13".3,225.00
Tray, fishnet amid fish & shells w/in bamboo fr, Longchamp, 15x15". 1,200.00
Tray, kingfisher on bulrush & pond lilies, G Jones.....................6,000.00
Tray, Lotus & Bulrush, Minton, EX color/detail, 15½" 3,100.00
Tray, napkin on yel, bamboo hdls, Wedgwood, 13" L 1,200.00
Tureen, boar & hunting dogs, boar's head finial & hdls, 12½" L, NM.. 7,200.00
Umbrella stand, herons on marshy shore on lt bl, 22¼", NM ...1,265.00
Umbrella stand, lg grizzly bear beside tree, chip, 26" 4,350.00
Umbrella stand, Pond Lily & Fern, Holdcroft, 22", NM 1,175.00
Umbrella stand, tobacco leaf & floral on turq, Holdcroft, 20½", NM. 1,675.00
Vase, marine life on cobalt, 3 mermen at base, Minton, prof rpr, 17".2,500.00

Malachite Glass

Malachite is a type of art glass that exhibits strata-like layerings in shades of green, similar to the mineral in its natural form. Some examples have an acid-etched mark of Moser/Carlsbad, usually on the base. However, it should be noted that in the past 30 years there have been reproductions from Czechoslovakia with a paper label. These are most often encountered.

Ashtray, panthers in relief, 2½x7½" 150.00
Basket, allegorical scenes in relief, 5½" 50.00

Bottle, perfume, Art Deco, Czechoslovakian, 6¼", EX, pair $720.00. (Photo courtesy B.S. Slosberg, Inc. Auctioneers on LiveAuctioneers.com)

Box, lg horse on lid, 7"...165.00
Box, nudes in relief, 4" dia...95.00
Box, reclining nude in relief on lid, rect, 2x5x4" 150.00
Figurine, stylized woman, 9" 60.00
Vase, classical woman in relief, 10" 215.00
Vase, nudes in relief, ca 1980..275.00
Vases, nudes & vintage, from the Ingrid Series, Schlevogt, 8", pr . 325.00

Maps and Atlases

Maps are highly collectible, not only for historical value but also for their sometimes elaborate artwork, legendary information, or data that since they were printed has been proven erroneous. There are many types of maps including geographical, military, celestial, road, and railroad. Nineteenth-century maps, particularly of American areas, are increasing in popularity and price. Rarity, area depicted (i.e., Texas is more sought after than North Dakota), and condition are major price factors. World globes

as a form of round maps are increasingly sought after, especially lighted and black ocean globes. Any tape other than archival tape hurts the value of maps — better still torn than badly mended. Our advisor for this category is Murray Hudson; he is listed in the Directory under Tennessee. Unless otherwise noted, our values are for items in excellent condition.

Key: hc — hand colored

Atlases

Beacon's Handy...World, Hammond, US territories, NY, 1910, 114-pg, G- 40.00
Brown County OH, Grigging & Stevenson, 1876, folio..............330.00

Bucks County (Pennsylvania), Illustrated, Compiled, Drawn, and Published from Personal Examinations and Surveys by J. D. Scott, Philadelphia, 1876, printed by Thomas Hunter, complete, $2,160.00. (Photo courtesy Alderfer Auction Company on LiveAuctioneers.com)

Butler County...& Pictorial Review, Republican Publishing, OH, 1914..270.00
Centennial...Warren County OH, Centennial Atlas Assoc, 1903, folio .230.00
Cincinnati & Hamilton County OH, Titus, rebound in leather, 1869.480.00
Clermont County OH, Titus, rebound in leather, 1870 ....750.00
Harmsworth...& Gazetteer, Philip & Son, London, 500 maps/etc, 1910.500.00
New Encyclopedic...& Gazetteer..., Reynolds, Special 1912 ed, 256-pg.150.00
New Reference...World, Hammond, NY, special chapters, 1910 . 195.00
People's Handy...World, Geographical Publishing, Chicago, 1911, 123-pg..95.00
Rand McNally...Unrivaled...World, Chicago/NY, color, 1910, 357-pg.175.00
Scarborough's New Std...World, Hammond, 100+ maps, sm folio, 1910.225.00

Maps

Africa, JH Colton, NY, hc/litho, Slave Coast noted, 1860, 12x14".75.00
Americae Retectio, T De Bry, Frankfurt, silver eng, 1594, 6x8", matted..500.00
Asia, J Gibson, London, full hc/copper eng, Cupid vignette, 1762, 6x8".225.00
Canada, Feville, outline hc/copper eng, Paris, 1765, 11½x17", EX+..450.00
Chart of World on Mercator's Projection, Doolittle, Boston, 1796, 7x9".200.00
L'Asie (Asia), Buffier, Paris, copper eng, 1744, 5½x7" 125.00
N Am, Arrowsmith, Boston, partial hc/copper eng, tribes, 1795, 7x10"..200.00
N Am, J Yeager, M Carey & Son, Philadelphia, hc/copper eng, 1827, 6x4"..85.00
Nova et Accuratissima...Terrarum..., Blaeu, hc/eng, 1662, 16x22"+fr.. 7,000.00
Oceana, SG Goodrich, Boston, outline hc/copper eng, 1826, 6x8", G-.125.00
OH, RT Anderson, J Tumbull, 1828, hc w/orig leather cover, 15x13"+fr.. 3,000.00
Pictorial...US, paper on linen, mc, Ensign & Thayer, 31x43½"+rods. 1,250.00
Poli Arctici..., Hondy, hc/eng, scenic spandrels, in 22x25" fr.......865.00
Road From Ft Smith Ark to Santa Fe NM, Indian locations, 1847, 17x31"...650.00
Territory of NM, Rio Del Norte/Santa Fe/etc, hc, ca 1847, 26x20¼" ... 325.00
US/Canada/New Brunswick/Nova Scotia/Mexico, Monk, 1853, mc, 60x62"..1,500.00
Washington County OH, Titus, Simmons & Titus, mc, 1874, 16x26+fr..150.00
World, Bowen, Gentleman's Magazine/London, hc/copper eng, 1779, 11x18".900.00

Marblehead

What began as therapy for patients in a sanitarium in Marblehead, Massachusetts, has become recognized as an important part of the Arts and Crafts movement in America. Results of the early experiments under the guidance of Arthur E. Baggs in 1904 met with such success that by 1908 the pottery had been converted to a solely commercial venture. Simple vase shapes were sometimes incised with stylized animal and floral motifs or sailing ships. Some were decorated in low relief; many were plain. Matt glazes in soft yellow, gray, wisteria, rose, tobacco brown, and their most popular, Marblehead blue, were used alone or in combination. They also produced fine tiles decorated with ships, stylized floral or tree motifs, and landscapes. Early examples were lightly incised and matt painted (these are the most valuable) on 1"-thick bodies. Others, 4" square and thinner, were matt painted with landscapes in indigoes in the style of Arthur Wesley Dow.

The Marblehead logo is distinctive — a ship with full sail and the letters 'M' and 'P.' The pottery closed in 1936. Our advisors for this category are Suzanne Perrault and David Rago; they are listed in the Directory under New Jersey. Unless noted otherwise, all items listed below are marked and in the matt glaze.

Vessel, stylized trees, matt green, 3½x6", $6,700.00.
(Photo courtesy Rago Arts and Auction Center)

Bowl, fruit band, gr/russet on brn to mustard, A Baggs, 1½x4½" . 3,600.00
Jardiniere, ships/waves on gray, A Hennessey, 1911, 6¾x8¾" ...9,600.00
Tile, fish, pnt/cvd, sgn, collection of A Baggs, 6" 12,000.00
Tile, house, pnt/cvd, sgn, collection of A Baggs, 6" 10,800.00
Tile, landscape, HP indigo/yel, unsgn, collection of A Baggs, 8" ..14,400.00
Tile, oak tree, gr, pnt/cvd, sgn, collection of A Baggs, 6" 4,500.00
Vase, berries & leaves, bl/gr/brn on brn, H Tutt, 4½" 3,600.00
Vase, berries & leaves, brn & gr on mustard, pear shape, 4½" ...1,325.00
Vase, bl, swollen cylinder, 9" 550.00
Vase, blossoms, speckled gray grnd, squat, AB T, 3¼x5"...............900.00
Vase, brn/yel roses on poly band, olive gr grnd, rare, 6x7½" ...27,600.00
Vase, butterfly/floral band, cvd/mc on mustard, hairline, 4½x4".. 5,000.00
Vase, deep lav, swollen cylinder, label, 5¼" 360.00
Vase, dk bl, ovoid w/flared rim, 7¾" 480.00
Vase, dragonflies, tapering, 4x5" 1,000.00
Vase, floral panels, brn/indigo on gr, H Tutt, rstr, 5¼x6½" 3,900.00
Vase, floral, charcoal on dk gr speckled, A Baggs, 9½", NM......3,100.00
Vase, fruit branches, yel/gr/gray, H Tutt, 6¾x5" 7,800.00
Vase, geometric band, blk on gr, cylindrical, 2 hairlines, mk 8½x3¾". 2,520.00
Vase, geometrics (simple), dk gr on indigo, H Tutt, 6x3" 4,200.00
Vase, geometrics & lines, brn/indigo/gr, paper label, rstr, 8¼x4" . 7,250.00
Vase, gr-brn, tapered, 5½" 480.00
Vase, grapevines, bl/brn/gray, A Baggs, glaze bursts, 9½x6½" 6,000.00
Vase, grapevines, mc on gray, bulb, H Tutt, 1912, hairline, 4" ..3,100.00
Vase, indigo speckled, dk gr decor band, spherical, 3½" 2,250.00
Vase, lav, swollen cylinder, 8x6", NM 480.00
Vase, mustard speckled, cylindrical, 9x5"....................................2,040.00
Vase, Persian crackleware glaze test, 3¾x5½"..............................1,200.00
Vase, purple, slightly waisted, 7¼" 300.00
Vase, sqs/crouching panthers at top, gray/yel/gr/bl, 6½x5", NM . 25,200.00
Vase, trees, 3-color on caramel, H Tutt/A Baggs, 4¼" 4,200.00
Vase, trees, 3-color, swollen cylinder, H Tutt, 1912, 7"..............7,200.00
Vase, turq, flared rim, 4" 300.00
Wall pocket, bl, flared rim, ca 1906-36, 5¼" 180.00

Marbles

Marbles have been popular with children since the mid-1800s. They have been made in many styles, and from a variety of materials. Glass marbles have been found in archeological digs in both early Roman and Egyptian settlements. Other marbles were made of china, pottery, steel, and natural stone. Below is a listing of various types, along with a brief description of each.

Agates: stone marbles, amber, blue, green, or black, with white rings encircling the marble.

Ballot Box: often handmade with pontils, opaque black or white. Used in Lodge elections.

Bloodstone: green chalcedony with red spots, a type of quartz.

China: glazed or unglazed, in a variety of hand-painted designs. Parallel lines or spirals most common.

Clambroth: opaque glass with evenly spaced outer lines of one or more colors.

Clay: Commies, one of the most common older types. Painted ones are more desirable.

Comic Strip: a series of 12 marbles with faces of comic strip characters. Peltier Glass Co., Illinois.

Crockery or Benningtons: brown, blue, or multicolored, glazed and fired in a kiln.

End of Day: single pontil glass marbles. The colored part often appears as a multicolored blob or mushroom cloud.

Fluorescent: glows under an ultraviolet blacklight.

Goldstone: sparkling gold colored marble, made of aventurine.

Indian Swirls: usually black glass with colored bands on the surface. Often irregular.

Latticinio Core Swirls: double pontil marbles with net-like cores.

Lutz Type: glass with colored or clear bands alternating with gold bands of copper flecks. Comes in several styles.

Micas: clear or colored glass with silver mica flecks. Red is rare and very desirable.

Machine Mades: after WWI, machine made marbles were manufactured in the U.S. by companies like Akro Agate, Peltier Glass, Christensen Agate, Marble King, and many others.

Onionskin: a thin, onion-like layer of colorful decoration just below the surface.

Peppermint Swirls: glass with alternating red, white, and blue bands.

Ribbon Core Swirls: center core is shaped like a ribbon.

Solid Core Swirls: the core is solid in a tube-like fashion.

Steelies: hollow steel spheres marked with a cross where the steel was bent together to form a marble.

Sulfides: generally made of clear glass with figures inside. Rarer types have colored figures or colored glass.

Tiger Eye: stone marble of golden quartz with inclusions of asbestos, dark brown with gold highlights.

Prices below are for marbles in near-mint condition unless noted otherwise. Polished or damaged marbles have a greatly reduced value. For a more through study of the subject, we recommend *Everett Grist's Big Book of Marbles* (published by Collector Books). Our advisor for this category is Lloyd Huffer; he is listed in the Directory under Pennsylvania.

Akro Agate, 3-color corkscrew... 15.00
Akro Agate, bl slag, ⅝"...2.00
Akro Agate, carnelian oxblood, ⅝"..45.00
Akro Agate, corkscrew, limeade, ¾"..40.00
Akro Agate, corkscrew, snake, ⅝" 10.00
Akro Agate, corkscrew, wht base, ⅝"..2.00
Akro Agate, Popeye box, 15 Corkscrew marbles & bag 1,800.00
Akro Agate, Popeye box, 15 marbles & bag 1,800.00
Akro Agate, Popeye corkscrew, purple, yel & wht, ⅝" 50.00

Banded Opaque, gr w/red bands, wht & bl streaks, ¾" 185.00
Banded Opaque, wht opaque w/red & bl swirls, 1¾" 2,200.00
China, early unglazed, decor, pinwheel flower, ¾" 250.00
China, early unglazed, decor, pinwheel flower, ¾" 250.00
China, glazed, geometrics/spirals decor, ¾" 20.00
Christensen Agate, flame, bl w/red flames, ¾" 85.00
Christensen Agate, Guinea, clear base, mc spots & streaks, 11/16".. 375.00
Christensen Agate, swirl, blk & orange, ⅝" 35.00
Clambroth, bl base w/evenly spaced wht lines, ⅞"........................ 750.00
Clambroth, wht w/pk, gr & bl lines, ⅝" 200.00
Clay, very common, pnt, ⅝", less than 1.00
Clown, Onionskin, wht core, 4 stretched colored bands, 13/16"..... 435.00
Comic, Peltier Picture Marble, Andy Gump, 11/16" 75.00
Comic, Peltier Picture Marble, Herbie, 11/16"................................ 65.00
Comic, Peltier Picture Marble, Kayo, 11/16"....................................375.00
Comic, Peltier Picture Marble, Moon Mullins, 11/16".................... 265.00
Comic, Peltier Picture Marble, Orphan Annie, 11/16".................... 110.00
Divided Core Swirl, red, wht & bl ribbons, ¾" 20.00

Indian Swirl, 13/16", M, $125.00. (Photo courtesy Lloyd Huffer)

Joseph's Coat, clear base, streaks & flecks of 7 colors, 1 9/16".......... 950.00
Lined Crockery, clay, wht w/gr & bl swirls, ¾"............................... 35.00
Lutz, blk opaque, gold & red lines, ¾"... 275.00
Lutz, bl banded, 2" 540.00
Lutz, bl opaque, gold & wht lines, ¾"... 350.00
Lutz, clear w/gold swirls, bl & wht borders, ⅝"............................. 125.00
Lutz, red ribbon core, gold swirl w/wht edges, 1¾"....................1,500.00
Lutz, ribbon core, red & gr edged w/gold bands, ¾" 225.00
Marble King, Bumblebee, blk & yel patch & ribbon, ⅝"....................1.00
Marble King, cloth tournament bag 35.00
Marble King, Cub Scout, bl & yel patch & ribbon, 1" 25.00
Mica, bl glass w/silver mica flecks, ¾".. 35.00
Millefiori flower pattern, single pontil, 1½" 575.00
Onionskin, bl/wht/orange panels, 2 5/16".. 400.00
Onionskin, pk, 1 13/16" 335.00
Onionskin, yel & red w/silver mica, 2 7/16"....................................... 660.00
Peltier Glass, Rebel, red, blk & wht, National Line Rainbo, ⅝" 65.00
Peltier Glass, Superman, bl, red & yel, National Line Rainbo, 11/16" ..150.00
Peppermint Swirl, red, wht & bl w/silver mica in bl, ⅝".............. 375.00
Peppermint Swirl, red, wht & bl, 11/16" 75.00
Pottery, stoneware, w/bl slip decor, 1¼" 110.00
Solid Opaque, melon balls, pastel colors, ⅞".................................. 100.00
Sulfide, Bear, wearing dress, nice detail, 1¾"...............................1,000.00
Sulfide, Bird, prairie chicken, 1¾"... 175.00
Sulfide, Boy in top hat & dress clothes, gr glass, 1¾"..................4,000.00
Sulfide, Boy on hobbyhorse, blowing horn, 1 9/16"......................... 650.00
Sulfide, Buffalo, molded figure, lacks detail, 1¾"........................... 125.00
Sulfide, Cherub head w/wings, well centered, 1⅝"........................ 875.00
Sulfide, Crucifix, lg, well centered, 2 3/16".. 400.00
Sulfide, Dog, RCA Nipper, 1¾".. 275.00
Sulfide, Elephant w/L trunk, 1¼"... 140.00
Sulfide, Girl sitting in chair, bubble around figure, 1 9/16" 275.00
Sulfide, Hawk, gr glass, 1" 840.00
Sulfide, Indian head penny, rare, 1⅛"... 350.00
Sulfide, Jenny Lind, well centered, 1 5/16" 350.00
Sulfide, Lamb, common figure, 1¾" 125.00
Sulfide, Man, politician, standing on stump, 1¼" 450.00
Sulfide, Moses in the Bulrushes, baby in basket 1¾"...................... 450.00
Sulfide, Number 1, nicely detailed, 1¾"... 400.00
Sulfide, Parrot, uncommon figure, 1⅝"... 330.00
Sulfide, Peacock, 3-color pntd figure, 1¾"......................................8,000.00
Sulfide, Peasant Couple, detailed & rare, 2⅜" 7,500.00
Swirl, Latticino, wht threads form net-like core, ⅝"........................ 15.00
Swirl, Latticino, yel threads form net-like core, 2⅛" 275.00
Swirl, red solid core, 4 color outer bands, 2⅝" 910.00
Swirl, wht solid core, bl, pk & gr lines, yel outher bands, 2 13/16"... 360.00
Transitional, Leighton, 1"...1,000.00
Vitro Agate, Chinese checkers, orig box, ⅝" game marbles (60).... 70.00

Marine Collectibles

Vintage tools used on sea-going vessels, lanterns, clocks, and memorabilia of all types are sought out by those who are interested in preserving the romantic genre that revolves around the life of the sea captains, their boats, and their crews; ports of call; and the lure of far-away islands. See also Scrimshaw; Steamship Collectibles; Telescopes; Tools.

Binnacle, brass hood, varnished base, gimbaled compass inside by C. Wheilbach & Co., Copenhagen, two lanterns with porcelain burners and iron compensating balls, early twentieth century, 65x36", $3,890.00. (Photo courtesy Kaminski Auctions on LiveAuctioneers.com)

Binnacle, ATMC Master Unit, brass w/mtd head, all orig, 14x12" dia... 360.00
Binnacle, brass, in drum case w/in gimbals, wood ped/iron spheres, 52"... 900.00
Binnacle, Deviastat, John Hands, Philadelphia, brass, 13" 435.00
Binnacle, Dirigo, Seattle WA, brass gig type, red/gr balls............. 550.00
Binnacle, Kelvin Wht Boston, freestanding, 52x34" dia 1,450.00
Binnacle, lifeboat, Coubro & Scrutton London, w/mtd compass & lamp, 9".335.00
Certificate of membership, Boston Marine Society, vignettes, 1886 .. 30.00
Chest, captain's liquor, oak w/fitted int, 3 bottles, 12x17x12"...... 480.00
Chest, pine w/cvd pnt clipper ship/Am flag/etc, becket hdls, 16x38x17" .. 1,725.00
Chest, pnt dvtl/canted wood, rope hdls, iron strap hinges, 19th C, 44".... 575.00
Chronometer, Bliss & Creighton NY #858, 56-hr, VG in case .3,350.00
Chronometer, Hamilton #22, in orig case & outer storage case . 1,800.00
Chronometer, Hamilton #8176, in 7½x7½" mahog case, +log book .2,150.00
Chronometer, Ulysse Nardin #5673, in brass-bound mahog 7½" case . 2,500.00
Chronometer, Widenham #1668, rosewood/brass, 1820s, 4" dia, in case .2,535.00
Clock, ship's bell; Chelsea, brass w/silver dial/blk numbers, 7¼" .. 715.00
Compass, Merril NY, brass, 8" dia+gimbal ring, in dvtl box......... 315.00
Compass, S Thaxter & Son, Boston, gimballed mt, in 10" pine case .300.00
Compass, W Davenport-Maker Phila, brass, 19th C, 15x6" dia, +cover, G.. 850.00
Desk, captain's davenport, mahog w/inlay, ivory escutcheons, 36x21x17"... 1,200.00
Desk, captain's lap, exotic wood, dvtl, 5½x16x10" 150.00
Desk, captain's lap, vnr wood, trifold w/fitted int, 1800s 1,000.00
Desk, captain's writing, mahog w/felt top, 19th C, 31x37x53"..... 850.00
Diorama, whaler/tugboat/schooner/lighthouse, in 12x22x12" glass case .. 575.00
Harpoon, dbl-flue Arctic style, 27½"... 360.00
Harpoon, pnt wood shaft w/wrought-iron point & swivel barb, 92" ..1,150.00
Harpoon, slot at side of pocket, CI, mk Peters, ca 1900 .... 780.00
Harpoon, toggle, 2-flue head, CI, 19th C, 39" 1,450.00

Harpoon, toggle, triangular head, single flue, 30" 480.00
Harpoon, wrought iron, 30".. 60.00
Lance, killing, oval flat head, rope-bound hdl, mk UAB, 49" 660.00
Log book, engineer's, worn cover, late 1800s, VG 180.00
Log book, MA schooner, entries from 1914, 14x9", VG.............. 480.00
Model, Corsair (Am steam yacht) owned by JP Morgan, 20x49x8", +case...8,000.00
Model, schooner -hull w/extended fantail, planks, on brd, 10x44" ..1,950.00
Octant, A Johnson Liverpool, ebony/ivory/brass, 14", EX in case. 660.00
Octant, English, ebony dbl T fr w/brass arm, 1830s-50s, 9⅝" radius. 850.00
Octant, F Primavessi & Son, Swansea, ebony/ivory/brass, EX in case ..960.00
Octant, Spencer, Brn & Rust, London, ca 1800, 15x4", EXIB..1,100.00
Oil on canvas, City of Paris ship's portrait, WH York, 22x38"+fr... 9,485.00
Quadrant, FB Roberts, Boston, ivory inlay, ca 1800, 12", EXIB ... 725.00
Quadrant, Gowland, Liverpool, ebony/bone/brass, 19th C 660.00
Quadrant, Spencer Browning, London, ebony w/ivory inlay, EX in 14" box ..720.00
Sextant, Adams, London, brass, 10x10", EXIB............................ 900.00
Sextant, compact, Stanley-London, brass, early 20th C, 3" dia.... 120.00
Sextant, in box marked John Bruce & Son Liverpool, ca. 1918... 500.00
Stern brd, eagle cvg, pine w/old dry red wash/gilt, 17x72" 4,600.00
Trunk, cvd teakwood, 6-brd, dvtl, 1850s, 18x37x17" 900.00
Trunk, pnt pine, rope hdls, 1850s, 17x34x16".......................... 180.00
Wheel, ship's throttle, brass, Durkee Marine Products Corp, NY .240.00
Wheel, ship's, maple & brass, iron bound, 8-spoke, old red pnt, 41"... 250.00
Wheel, ship's, mixed woods, 8 trn spokes & hdls, 42" 240.00
Wheel, ship's, teak & mahog, weathered bl-gr pnt, 67"................ 700.00
Wheel, ship's, wood w/8 trn spokes & hdls, iron bands ea side, 40" dia....475.00
Wheel, wood hub, 6-spoke w/trn spindles, varnished, 36" 480.00

Martin Bros.

The Martin Bros. were studio potters who worked from 1873 until 1914, first at Fulham and later at London and Southall. There were four brothers, each of whom excelled in their particular area. Robert, known as Wallace, was an experienced stonecarver. He modeled a series of grotesque bird and animal figural caricatures. Walter was the potter, responsible for throwing the larger vases on the wheel, firing the kiln, and mixing the clay. Edwin, an artist of stature, preferred more naturalistic forms of decoration. His work was often incised or had relief designs of seaweed, florals, fish, and birds. The fourth brother, Charles, was their business manager. Their work was incised with their names, place of production, and letters and numbers indicating month and year.

Though figural jars continue to command the higher prices, decorated vases and bowls have increased a great deal in value. Our advisors for this category are Suzanne Perrault and David Rago; they are listed in the Directory under New Jersey.

Vase, fish and sea life incised on stoneware, 1913, 6x3", NM, $3,000.00. (Photo courtesy Rago Auctions)

Bird jar, w/lid, brn plumage, wood base, 1912, 7x3" 10,800.00
Bird jar, w/lid, grn plumage, wood base, sgn, 1913, 6½x3½"....14,400.00
Bird jar, w/lid, prof rstr, sgn, 1897, 11½x5½"..........................20,400.00
Bird jar, w/lid, wood base, sgn, hairline to base, 1895, 13½x5".39,000.00
Jar, grotesque bird, mk & dtd 1899, paper label, 11¼x5¾" 36,000.00
Jar, grotesque creature, rstr to head lid, 1888, 8"......................15,600.00

Jar, smiling bird, hooded eyes, standing on base, 1893, 15x9" .56,250.00
Jardiniere, irises on wht, ped stand w/foliage & flamingo, 61x22" . 25,000.00
Jug, 2-faced, matt brn tones, 1911, 9x7½"...............................12,500.00
Match holder, woman's head on disk, w/bonnet, unglazed red clay, 6". 1,000.00
Pencil holder, Scotsman's head w/tam, 3½x3" 900.00
Pitcher, fish & vegetation band, bl/gr on tan w/brn lines,ftd, 10" .20,000.00
Pitcher, grotesque sea creatures, sm rstr/varnish, 1895, 7¼x6" ..3,480.00
Vase, 4-faced, dimpled & cvd, earth tones, 7x6½"...................18,750.00
Vase, crabs & anemones, mc on bl, 4-sided, 1903, 8¾" 6,250.00
Vase, dragons, brn/blk on cream, 1901, 11½x3¾".....................3,600.00
Vase, floral, gold/purple/gr lustre, 4 hdls at base, 14" 19,350.00
Vase, floral, yel/bl/gr on brn & ivory, neck to waist hdls, 1882, 9"...875.00
Vase, grotesque face on overlapping fans, bulb w/flat bk, 8x4½".. 4,685.00
Vase, grotesque sea creatures, brn/bl/gr on tan, 4-sided, 1913, 6x3"..4,700.00
Vase, lg fish amid sea life, earth tones w/bl, 1891, 8½x5½"........7,500.00
Vase, thistles HP on amber, #11, 1905, 10¼x5".......................3,000.00
Wall pocket, fish head & acanthus leaves, earth tones, rstr chip, 8x7". 1,190.00

Mary Gregory Glass

Mary Gregory glass, for reasons that remain obscure, is the namesake of a Boston and Sandwich Glass Company employee who worked for the company for only two years in the mid-1800s. Although no evidence actually exists to indicate that glass of this type was even produced there, the fine colored or crystal ware decorated with figures of children in white enamel is commonly referred to as Mary Gregory. The glass, in fact, originated in Europe and was imported into this country where it was copied by several eastern glasshouses. It was popular from the mid-1800s until the turn of the century. It is generally accepted that examples with all-white figures were made in the U.S.A., while gold-trimmed items and those with children having tinted faces or a small amount of color on their clothing are European. Though amethyst is rare, examples in cranberry command the higher prices. Blue ranks next; and green, amber, and clear items are worth the least. Watch for new glass decorated with screen-printed children and a minimum of hand painting. The screen effect is easily detected with a magnifying glass. For more information we recommend *The Collector's Encyclopedia of American Art Glass* by our advisor, John A. Shuman III (see Directory, Pennsylvania).

Barber bottle, cobalt, girl playing tennis, stopper, 8¼" 420.00
Barber bottle, ruby, boy/foliage, rolled lip, 7½" 175.00
Bell, bird & girl, wht enameled 210.00
Biscuit bbl, cranberry, boy/gold scrolls, metal lid/bail, 8x5".......... 390.00
Bottle, barber, cranberry, Invt T'Print, metal stopper, girl playing croquet, 8"..400.00
Bottle, lav, wht enameled girl, champagne stopper, 9½".............. 160.00
Bottle, perfume, faceted stopper, boy holding leafy branch, 3¾" .. 300.00
Bowl, amber, boy w/stick & hoop, honeycomb sides, sq, 3¼x9½" .. 85.00
Box, cranberry w/metal base, domed cover, enameled boy w/flowers, 6"..1,100.00
Box, cranberry, 2 children playing w/bubbles, brass mounts, 5x6". 360.00
Box, glove, bl, 4 children lawn bowling, floral decor, 5"............2,500.00
Box, jewelry, amber, fence/yel birds, sq, metal mts, 6x5x5" 550.00
Box, jewerly, cobalt, girl/wood fence, bulb base, metal mts, 4"..... 265.00
Candleholders, cranberry to clear ft, child at play, gold trim, 4", pr....175.00
Charger, cranberry, 2 maids in wooded landscape, 12" 325.00
Creamer, amber, waffle ft, sapphire hdl, 8"................................... 240.00
Decanter, amber, wht enameled girl, w/bubble stopper, 9½" 225.00
Goblet, amber, girl w/florals, 5⅛" 135.00
Lamp, bl & wht swirls, flowers, girl fishing, 16¼" 1,600.00
Mug, amber, appl hdl, wht enameled girl & mother, 3"................. 100.00
Pitcher, clear, 3 scenes w/child, lt wear, 10" 150.00
Toothpick holder, lt gr, girl/flower, spherical w/short collar, 2"..... 300.00
Vase, med gr, girl at water's edge, tapered cylinder, 16", pr........... 385.00

Mason's Ironstone

In 1813 Charles J. Mason was granted a patent for a process said to 'improve the quality of English porcelain.' The new type of ware was in fact ironstone which Mason decorated with colorful florals and scenics, some of which reflected the Asian taste. Although his business failed for a short time in the late 1840s, Mason re-established himself and continued to produce dinnerware, tea services, and ornamental pieces until about 1852, at which time the pottery was sold to Francis Morley. Ten years later, Geo. L. and Taylor Ashworth became owners. Both Morley and the Ashworths not only used Mason's molds and patterns but often his mark as well. Because the quality and the workmanship of the later wares do not compare with Mason's earlier product, collectors should take care to distinguish one from the other. Consult a good book on marks to be sure. The Wedgwood Company now owns the rights to the Mason patterns.

Am Marine, creamer, red, scalloped rim, 1890-1900, 3½x4", EX. 125.00
Bandana, c/s, demi, blk & wht on burnt-orange, 1860s 150.00
Bandana, jug, mc, ca 1840, 4¾x3½", NM 250.00
Blue Pheasants, colored, jug, mc, ca 1830, 4½x4" 250.00

Blue Pheasants, jug, Hydra, B9799, 11", NM, $240.00. (Photo courtesy LeLand Little Auction & Estate Sales Ltd. on LiveAuctioneers.com)

Double Landscape, jug, mc, hexagonal, ca 1840, 4¾" 450.00
English scene, cup plate, red, ca 1813, 4¾" 100.00
Floral, bowl, soup, mc, ca 1873-90, 10" 70.00
Floral, plate, mc, ca 1813-25, 9½" 125.00
Flowering Bush, plate, mc, ca 1830, 8¾" 80.00
Flowering Bush, plate, mc, scalloped, ca 1840, 8¾" 125.00
Flying Bird, bowl, mc on wht w/blk transfer, 1890, 10¼" 175.00
Gay Japan/House, jug, mc, dragon hdl, much gold, att, ca 1840s, 4½"..650.00
Jug, Hunt, dogs & scenic designs, Toho on base, 1845-48, $1,200 to.. 1,400.00
Meat drainer, Indiana Grasshopper, bl/rose/gr, mid-1800s, 13¾", $300 to....350.00
Mortar & pestle, cobalt bl mk, 1820, $1,800 to 2,000.00
Orange Leaf, plate, mc, ca 1813-25, 8½" 175.00
Oriental Pheasants, dish, mc, ca 1818, 9½x8", EX 250.00
Pitcher, Peking Japan, 1830, $600 to 700.00
Rich Ruby, plate, mc, scalloped, ca 1840, 10¼" 150.00
Sauce boat, Variant Willow, 1845, $150 to.................................. 175.00
Serving dish, Rich Ruby, birds/floral border, 1829-45, 11" 675.00
Table & Flowerpot, platter, mc, 1813-25, 9x6¼" 325.00
Tea stand, Japan, bl/orange/wht, octagonal, 1813-25, 7¾" 400.00
Vase Japanned, bowl, serving; mc, scalloped, ca 1840, 9½", pr..... 150.00
Vase Japanned, compote, mc, scalloped, ped ft, ca 1840, 9½x13½"....400.00
Vase Japanned, dish, mc, scalloped hdls, ca 1840, 9½" W 100.00
Vase Japanned, platter, mc, ca 1840, 18x14", NM...................... 550.00
Vase Japanned, platter, mc, scalloped, ca 1840, 21x16½" 800.00
Vista, butter dish, red, rect, crown mk, 7⅛" 165.00
Vista, plate, dinner; red, 1925-50 mk, 10¾", 3 for 100.00
Vista, trivet, red, 1925-30 mk, 6x6" 150.00
Water Lily, dish, mc, ca 1813-25, 10¾x7½" 600.00
Water Lily, plate, mc, panelled, faint scallops, ca 1813-25, 8½" ... 200.00
Willow, bowl, soup, flow bl, ca 1862, 10½" 80.00

Clément Massier

The Massier family's work in ceramics goes back in France to the middle eighteenth century. Clément, his brother Delphin, and their cousin Jerome, brought about a renaissance of the ceramics industry in Vallauris, in the south of France. Clément apprenticed and worked under his father until his father's death, after which Clément set up his own pottery in nearby Golfe-Juan. Artistic director Lucien Lévey-Dhurmer introduced Massier to Spanish iridescent glazes in 1887; and through the use of bronze, brass, and gold salts, Massier developed his own. He won the pottery an award at the Paris Exposition Universelle in 1889.

Jacques Sicard, one of his artists, took the glaze formula with him to the Weller Pottery in Zanesville, Ohio, closely replicating the overall floral patterns he had learned in France. This particular type of glaze proved difficult to fire on both continents, seldom yielding the perfectly crisp decoration and smooth lustre desired. Perfectly fired pieces sell quickly and for a premium.

Fountain, putti w/garland under urn-form body, turq, 4-ftd, 36x28" ..3,300.00
Jardiniere, faceted, tall waves in lustered glzes, Japanese style, 4 hdls, rstr, 6x9½" ..1,080.00
Jardiniere, nude woman on rock, metallic, Golfe Juan CM, 8", EX .3,600.00
Plaque, maiden in landscape, gold & purple lustre, 18½x12" 4,800.00
Vase, appl silver leafy vines mts on lustre, 5⅛" 2,400.00

Vase, blooms and foliage, lustered glaze, Golfe-Juan, 12", $1,320.00. (Photo courtesy Craftsman Auctions on LiveAuctioneers.com)

Vase, bud, butterflies on lustre, pierced wing-like hdls, ca 1900, 12" ... 4,500.00
Vase, bud, silver peapod o/l on lustre, twisted body, 6x2¼", NM...1,100.00
Vase, dragonfly & cattails, tan mottle, gr & gold, pinched, 7½", EX..1,800.00
Vase, floral irid, trumpet form, 2" rim to 6" base, paper label, 18"..2,880.00
Vase, irises, metallic, 4 appl twist hdls, Golfe Juan AM, 6" 660.00
Vase, mice in field, swollen base, Golfe Juan AM, 14½"............2,500.00

Match Holders

John Walker, an English chemist, invented the match more than 100 years ago, quite by accident. Walker was working with a mixture of potash and antimony, hoping to make a combustible that could be used to fire guns. The mixture adhered to the end of the wooden stick he had used for stirring. As he tried to remove it by scraping the stick on the stone floor, it burst into flames. The invention of the match was only a step away! From that time to the present, match holders have been made in amusing figural forms as well as simple utilitarian styles and in a wide range of materials. Both table-top and wall-hanging models were made — all designed to keep matches conveniently at hand. The prices in this category are very volatile due to increased interest in this field and the fact that so many can be classified as a cross or dual collectible. Caution: As prices for originals continue to climb, so do the number of reproductions. Know your dealer.

Advertising, Am Brewing, cobalt on salt glaze, 3x3" 170.00
Advertising, Bull Dog Cut Plug Tobacco, tin litho, 7x3¼", EX.... 840.00
Advertising, Cerasota Flour, child on bbl, dc body, 5½" 300.00
Advertising, Ceresota Flour, boy (flat figure)/bbl, tin litho, 5½" .. 175.00
Advertising, Gabby Shoes, cb w/metal kettle holder, camp scene, 10x6".. 160.00
Advertising, Juicy Fruit, Wrigley's portrait, tin, 3½x4½" 200.00
Advertising, turtle, figural CI, Insure in the Old..., 5¼", EX 230.00
Advertising, Vulcan Plow Co, Hagerstown MD, 8", EX 750.00
Bisque, peasant boy w/fish, mc, striker on bk, unmk, 1900s, 5" 80.00
Brass, German soldier, head flips open, Vesta, 3" 340.00
Brass, ribbed cup atop bell w/ring lever on rnd tray base, 6½", EX ..140.00
Bronze, shield shape w/relief bust of bearded Civil War officer, 6" ..265.00
Cast iron, acorn on 6-pointed leafy stand, mechanical, dtd 1862, 4½", EX...115.00
Cast iron, bust of WF Cody (Buffalo Bill), Teals London, dtd 1887, 5½", EX...525.00
Cast iron, devil portrayed in medieval stocks, smiling/legs Xd, 1900, 6½"....475.00
Cast iron, whimsical head w/removable hat, 4¼", G 200.00
Majolica, frog playing banjo, unmk, 5x6" 310.00
Porcelain, violets on wht, wall mt, unmk, ca 1900s........................ 65.00
Pottery, pig at dressing table w/mirror, wht/gold, Staffordshire, 5" . 45.00
Silver, cherub/floral emb motif, .925 fine silver mk, 1½", EX 100.00
Silver, Deco-dragon w/holder on bk, Moller Trondhj, 1915-30.... 650.00

Silver, pig figural, spurious Faberge hallmarks, 1950s, 4" long, $480.00. (Photo courtesy Jackson's Auction on LiveAuctioneers.com)

White metal, man w/basket on bk straddles chair, 5½", VG 115.00
Wood, Indian chief in profile, 2 'woven' compartments below, 8" ..350.00

Match Safes

Before the invention of the safety match in 1855, matches were carried in small pocket-sized containers because they ignited so easily. Aptly called match safes, these containers were used extensively until about 1920, when cigarette lighters became widely available. Some incorporated added features (such as hidden compartments and cigar cutters), some were figural, and others were used by retail companies as advertising giveaways. They were made from every type of material, but silver-plated styles abound. Both the advertising and common silver-plated cases generally fall in the $50.00 to $100.00 price range.

Beware of reproductions and fakes; there are many currently on the market. Know your dealer.

18k gold, risqué enameling, Fr, 1800s, 2x1⅜" 1,150.00
Advertising, Advance Thresher Co...Traction Engine, cello, 2¾" ..300.00
Advertising, Cameron Pump Works, cello & NP, Whitehead & Hoag...500.00
Advertising, Molassine Horse & Cattle Food, nude lady, 2¾" 265.00
Advertising, Vulcanite Portland Cement Co, celluloid trim, sales chart ...450.00
Brass, emb Gothic design of St George & dragon, EX.................. 185.00
Brass, emb Nouveau floral, 2⅞x½"...................................... 60.00
Brass, lobster & claw w/cultured pearl.............................. 315.00
Brass, man's boot, creased leather look, lid snaps shut.................. 170.00
Brass, owl figural, detailed feathers, carnelian agate eyes.............. 200.00
Bronze, dragon figural, EX patina, 1880s, 2½".............................. 500.00
Egyptian Sarcophagus, brass w/emb detail, int striker, 4", EX+ 175.00
Enamel portrait of Woodrow Wilson & White House, Capitol on bk, 2⅜".210.00
Silver, 4-leaf clover (Nouveau style) emb, hinged lid, 1" 165.00

Silver, Am Indian chief in relief, monogram, Sterling, 3¼x1¾" .. 700.00
Silver, heart shape w/floral scrolls, monogram, English hallmark. 150.00
Silver, horse-head figural, 2⅜x1¼" 460.00
Silver, Leda & Swan emb/monogram, Sterling, 2½x2"............... 345.00
Silver, man at steering wheel wearing hat/coat/gloves emb, Sterling .. 485.00
Silver, man smoking & drinking, dtd 1911, Paye & Baker, 2½"...675.00
Silver, Nouveau grapes, monogram, 2½" 195.00
Silver, Nouveau lady's head (repousse), Sterling, 2⅝x1⅝" 500.00
Silver, quail motif, sterling, 2½" 360.00
Silver, Vict lady on skis, Sterling, late 19th C, 2½x1½" 895.00
Silverplated, lady's torso, corseted waist, bare breasts, unmk, 1¾".865.00
Sterling, FS Gilbert, press Masonic emblem to release lid, 2x1" .275.00
Sterling, cherub resting on garden bench, scrollwork border, monogram.....660.00
Sterling, Nouveau maid's head, entwining vines/florals, 2" 600.00

Mauchline Ware

Mauchline ware is the generic name for small, well-made, and useful wooden souvenirs and giftware from Mauchline, Scotland, and nearby locations. It was made from the early nineteenth century into the 1930s. Snuff boxes were among the earliest items, and tea caddies soon followed. From the 1830s on, needlework, stationery, domestic, and cosmetic items were made by the thousands. Today, needlework items are the most plentiful and range from boxes of all sizes made to hold supplies to tiny bodkins and buttons. Napkin rings, egg cups, vases, and bowls are just a few of the domestic items available.

The wood most commonly used in the production of Mauchline ware was sycamore. Finishes vary. Early items were hand decorated with colored paints or pen and ink. By the 1850s, perhaps even earlier, transfer ware was produced, decorated with views associated with the place of purchase. These souvenir items were avidly bought by travelers for themselves as well as for gifts. Major exhibitions and royal occasions were also represented on transferware. An alternative decorating process was initiated during the mid-1860s whereby actual photos replaced the transfers. Because they were finished with multiple layers of varnish, many examples found today are still in excellent condition.

Tartan ware's distinctive decoration was originally hand painted directly on the wood with inks, but in the 1840s machine-made paper in authentic Tartan designs became available. Except for the smallest items, each piece was stamped with the Tartan name. The Tartan decoration was applied to virtually the entire range of Mauchline ware, and because it was favored by Queen Victoria, it became widely popular. Collectors still value Tartan ware above other types of decoration, with transferware being their second choice. Other types of Mauchline decorations include Fern ware and Black Lacquer with floral or transfer decorations.

When cleaning any Mauchline item, extreme care should be used to avoid damaging the finish! Mauchline ware has been reproduced for at least 25 years, especially some of the more popular pieces and finishes. Collectors should study the older items for comparison and to learn about the decorating and manufacturing processes. In the listings below, items are in excellent condition unless otherwise noted.

Box, Fernware, 3½x5¾x3¾", $180.00. (Photo courtesy Auctions Neapolitan on LiveAuctioneers.com)

Book cover, Tartan w/ferns in oval, Burns' poems, Gall Inglis, book: G .225.00
Book, Fernware (early, not pre-printed), Scott's poems, tilt edge. 120.00
Bookmark, Hairpin Bend Mohawk Trail, w/ca 1920s autos, 6½" L ..95.00

Box, Burns Monument, book form, for playing cards ... 85.00
Box, Ledge in Front of Mtn House Catskills NY, ¾x1⅞" dia ... 145.00
Box, Severn Bridge Near Chepstow, brass clasp, 1¾x2¾x4" ... 115.00
Box, Tartan: McBeth, hinged lid, 1½x3½x6¾", VG ... 135.00
Dice holder, Oldmachar Cathedral, 2¾x2" ... 85.00
Etui, Palace Place Paicnton, egg shape, holds thimble/needles/etc ... 110.00
Frame, Mossoiel, arched top, 5¼x6½" ... 115.00
Match holder, black babies, St Petersburg FL, w/striker, 2½" ... 300.00
Photo album, Balmoral from the NW/Linn of Dee, leather spine +photos .. 120.00
Pincushion, Tartan ware, ca 1875, 1⅝" dia ... 85.00
Shot glass holder, Langholm Library, sycamore, w/glass, 2¾" ... 100.00
Stamp box, Tartan ware, Stuart, 2¼x1¼" ... 315.00
Tea caddy, Tartan, gr/navy w/strong red lines, dome lid, 4x7½" ... 495.00
Thimble case, Calais - Dover ferry, bbl form, NM ... 135.00
Thread holder, Edinburgh From Castle+3 scenes, 6 eyelets, sycamore ... 85.00
Watch stand, Burns' Cottage, made from wood from site, 4" ... 125.00

McCoy

The third generation McCoy potter in the Roseville, Ohio, area was Nelson, who with the aid of his father, J.W., established the Nelson McCoy Sanitary Stoneware Company in 1910. They manufactured churns, jars, jugs, poultry fountains, and foot warmers. By 1925 they had expanded their wares to include majolica jardinieres and pedestals, umbrella stands, and cuspidors, and an embossed line of vases and small jardinieres in a blended brown and green matt glaze. From the late '20s through the mid-'40s, a utilitarian stoneware was produced, some of which was glazed in the soft blue and white so popular with collectors today. They also used a dark brown mahogany color and a medium to dark green, both in a high gloss. In 1933 the firm became known as the Nelson McCoy Pottery Company. They expanded their facilities in 1940 and began to make the novelty artware, cookie jars, and dinnerware that today are synonymous with 'McCoy.' More than 200 cookie jars of every theme and description were produced.

More than a dozen different marks have been used by the company; nearly all incorporate the name 'McCoy,' although some of the older items were marked 'NM USA.' For further information consult *The Collector's Encyclopedia of McCoy Pottery* by Sharon and Bob Huxford; or *McCoy Pottery Collector's Reference & Value Guide, Vol. I, II,* and *III,* by Bob Hanson, Margaret Hanson, and Craig Nissen (all published by Collector Books). Also available is *Sanfords' Guide to McCoy Pottery* by Martha and Steve Sanford. (Mr. Sanford is listed in the Directory under California.)

Alert! Stimulated by the high prices commanded by desirable cookie jars, a broad spectrum of 'new' cookie jars have flooded the marketplace in three categories: 1) Manufacturers have expanded their lines with exciting new designs to attract the collector market. 2) Limited editions and artist-designed jars have proliferated. 3) Reproductions, signed and unsigned, have pervaded the market, creating uncertainty among new collectors and inexperienced dealers. After McCoy closed its doors in the late 1980s, an entrepreneur in Tennessee tried (and succeeded for nearly a decade) to adopt the McCoy Pottery name and mark. This company reproduced old McCoy designs as well as some classic designs of other defunct American potteries, signing their wares 'McCoy' with a mark which very closely approximated the old McCoy mark. Legal action finally put a stop to this practice, though since then they have used other fraudulent marks as well: Brush-McCoy (the compound name was never used on Brush cookie jars) and B.J. Hull.

Still under pressure from internet exposure and the effects of a slow economy, the cookie jar market remains soft. High-end cookie jars are often slow to sell. Our advisor for McCoy is Bob Hanson; he is listed in the Directory under Washington.

Cookie Jars

Animal Crackers, $60 to ... 75.00
Apollo Age, $225 to ... 275.00
Apollo, silver w/hand decor, mk, 1970, $800 to ... 900.00
Apple, 1950-64, $35 to ... 45.00
Apples on Basketweave, $50 to ... 65.00
Asparagus, $35 to ... 45.00
Astronauts, $200 to ... 250.00
Bananas, $80 to ... 85.00
Barnum's Animals, $95 to ... 115.00
Barrel, Cookies sign on lid, $60 to ... 65.00
Baseball Boy, $75 to ... 85.00
Basket of Eggs, $30 to ... 40.00
Basket of Potatoes, $30 to ... 40.00
Bear, cookie in vest, no 'Cookies', $65 to ... 75.00
Betsy Baker (+), $70 to ... 85.00
Black Kettle, w/immovable bail, HP flowers, $30 to ... 40.00
Black Lantern, $50 to ... 60.00
Blue Willow Pitcher, $40 to ... 50.00
Bobby Baker, $50 to ... 60.00
Bugs Bunny, $75 to ... 85.00
Burlap Bag, red bird on lid, $40 to ... 50.00
Caboose, $75 to ... 85.00
Cat on Coal Scuttle, $95 to ... 110.00
Chairman of the Board (+), $400 to ... 500.00
Chef Head, $75 to ... 85.00
Chilly Willy, $50 to ... 60.00

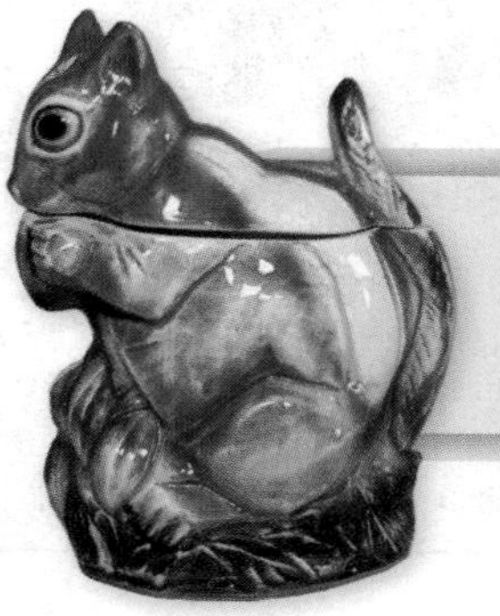

Chipmunk, $75.00 to $80.00.
(Photo courtesy Tom Harris Auctions on LiveAuctioneers.com)

Christmas Tree, $250 to ... 300.00
Churn, 2 bands, $25 to ... 30.00
Circus Horse, blk, $100 to ... 130.00
Clown Bust (+), $60 to ... 70.00
Clown in Barrel, yel, bl or gr, $60 to ... 75.00
Clyde Dog, $75 to ... 80.00
Coalby Cat, $110 to ... 130.00
Coca-Cola Can, $60 to ... 70.00
Coca-Cola Jug, $40 to ... 50.00
Coffee Grinder, $35 to ... 40.00
Coffee Mug, $35 to ... 40.00
Colonial Fireplace, $60 to ... 75.00
Cookie Bank, 1961, $75 to ... 80.00
Cookie Barrel, $30 to ... 40.00
Cookie Boy, $150 to ... 160.00
Cookie Cabin, $60 to ... 70.00
Cookie Jug, dbl loop, $25 to ... 30.00
Cookie Jug, single loop, 2-tone gr rope, $25 to ... 30.00
Cookie Jug, w/cork stopper, brn & wht, $30 to ... 35.00
Cookie Log, squirrel finial, $35 to ... 40.00
Cookie Mug, $35 to ... 40.00
Cookie Pot, 1964, $25 to ... 30.00
Cookie Safe, $35 to ... 40.00
Cookstove, blk or wht, $25 to ... 30.00
Corn, row of standing ears, yel or wht, 1977, $65 to ... 75.00

Corn, single ear, $95 to 110.00
Covered Wagon, $75 to 85.00
Cylinder, w/red flowers, $35 to 40.00
Dalmatians in Rocking Chair (+), $110 to 130.00
Davy Crockett (+), $225 to 275.00
Dog in Doghouse, $80 to 85.00
Dog on Basketweave, $60 to 65.00
Drum, red, $75 to 80.00
Duck on Basketweave, $60 to 65.00
Dutch Boy, $50 to 60.00
Dutch Girl, boy on reverse, rare, $175 to 200.00
Dutch Treat Barn, $30 to 45.00
Eagle on Basket, $30 to 45.00
Early Am Chest (Chiffoniere), $50 to 60.00
Elephant, $95 to 110.00
Elephant w/Split Trunk, rare, min, $125 to 175.00
Engine, blk, $95 to 110.00
Flowerpot, plastic flower on top, $250 to 300.00
Football Boy (+), $95 to 110.00
Forbidden Fruit, $70 to 85.00
Fortune Cookies, $35 to 45.00
Freddy Gleep, $250 to 300.00
Friendship 7, $95 to 110.00
Frog on Stump, $60 to 70.00
Frontier Family, $40 to 50.00
Fruit in Bushel Basket, $50 to 60.00
Gingerbread Boy, $60 to 65.00
Globe, $110 to 130.00
Grandfather Clock, $60 to 70.00
Granny, $75 to 85.00
Hamm's Bear (+), $95 to 110.00
Happy Face, $50 to 60.00
Hen on Nest, $75 to 85.00
Hillbilly Bear, rare, min (+), $775 to 850.00
Hobby Horse, brn underglaze (+), $110 to 130.00
Hocus Rabbit, $35 to 40.00
Honey Bear, rustic glaze, $60 to 70.00
Hot Air Balloon, $30 to 40.00
Ice Cream Cone, $35 to 40.00

Indian, brown with cold-paint decoration, $200.00 to $250.00. (Photo courtesy Belhorn Auction Services, LLC on LiveAuctioneers.com)

Indian, majolica, $275 to 300.00
Jack-O'-Lantern, $225 to 275.00
Kangaroo, bl, $175 to 225.00
Keebler Tree House, $50 to 65.00
Kettle, bronze, 1961, $30 to 40.00
Kissing Penguins, $60 to 70.00
Kitten on Basketweave, $70 to 85.00
Kittens (2) on Low Basket, $475 to 550.00
Kittens on Ball of Yarn, $60 to 75.00
Koala Bear, $60 to 75.00
Kookie Kettle, blk, $25 to 30.00
Lamb on Basketweave, $70 to 85.00

Lemon, $60 to 65.00
Leprechaun, min (+), $900 to 1,000.00
Liberty Bell, $60 to 65.00
Little Clown, $60 to 65.00
Lollipops, $70 to 75.00
Mac Dog, $60 to 65.00
Mammy w/Cauliflower, G pnt, min (+), $625 to 675.00
Mammy, Cookies on base, wht w/cold pnt (+), $110 to 130.00
Milk Can, Spirit of '76, $35 to 40.00
Modern, $50 to 60.00
Monk (Thou Shalt Not Steal), mk, 1970, $35 to 45.00
Mother Goose, $75 to 85.00
Mouse on Clock, $30 to 40.00
Mr & Mrs Owl, $75 to 85.00
Mushroom on Stump, $40 to 50.00
Nursery, decal of Humpty Dumpty, $65 to 75.00
Oaken Bucket, $25 to 40.00
Orange, $40 to 50.00
Owl, brn, $50 to 65.00
Pear, 1952, $60 to 70.00
Pears on Basketweave, $55 to 60.00
Penguin, yel or aqua, $75 to 85.00
Pepper, yel, $25 to 35.00
Picnic Basket, $60 to 65.00
Pig, winking, $175 to 200.00
Pine Cones on Basketweave, $50 to 65.00
Pineapple, $60 to 70.00
Pineapple, Modern, $75 to 85.00
Pirate's Chest, $75 to 85.00
Popeye, cylinder, $80 to 85.00
Potbelly Stove, blk, $20 to 30.00
Puppy, w/sign, $60 to 75.00
Quaker Oats, rare, $325 to 375.00
Raggedy Ann, mk USA, 1972, $95 to 115.00
Red Barn, cow in door, rare, min 130.00
Round w/HP Leaves, $30 to 40.00
Rooster, 1955-57, $70 to 85.00
Rooster, wht, 1970-74, $40 to 55.00
Sad Clown, $60 to 75.00
Snoopy on Doghouse, United Features Syndicate, (+), $95 to 110.00
Snow Bear, $60 to 65.00
Spaniel in Doghouse, bird finial, $95 to 110.00
Stagecoach, min, $525 to 600.00
Strawberry, 1955-57, $50 to 60.00
Strawberry, 1971-75, $35 to 40.00
Teapot, 1972, $35 to 40.00
Tepee, slant top, $175 to 200.00
Tepee, str top (+), $150 to 175.00
Thinking Puppy, #0272, $30 to 45.00
Tilt Pitcher, blk w/roses, $35 to 40.00
Timmy Tortoise, $35 to 40.00
Tomato, $45 to 55.00
Touring Car, $60 to 70.00

Tudor Cookie House, $75.00 to $80.00. (Photo courtesy Affiliated Auctions on LiveAuctioneers.com)

Tulip on Flowerpot, $60 to	70.00
Turkey, gr, rare color, $110 to	130.00
Turkey, natural colors, $110 to	130.00
Upside Down Bear, panda, $35 to	45.00
WC Fields, $75 to	85.00
Wedding Jar, $75 to	85.00
Windmill, $60 to	75.00
Wishing Well, $30 to	40.00
Woodsy Owl, $110 to	130.00
Wren House, side lid, $75 to	85.00
Yellow Mouse (head), $35 to	40.00
Yosemite Sam, cylinder, $75 to	80.00

Miscellaneous

Basket, hanging, basketweave, bright bl, unmk, 1940s, 7½"	40.00
Bookends, horse rearing, bl, USA mk, 1940s, 8", $80 to	100.00
Candy boat, gondola, Sunburst Gold, 3½x11½", $30 to	40.00
Ferner, Butterfly, pastel, braided rim, 3½x9", $200 to	250.00
Ferner, Hobnail, pastel matt, 1940s, 5½", $20 to	30.00
Flower bowl ornament, peacock, ivory, unmk, 4¾", $80 to	100.00
Flower holder, fish, yel or rose, NM mk, 3¼x4¼", $100 to	125.00
Hand vase, gr, NM mk, 1940s, 8¼", $25 to	40.00
Jar, oil, coral, NM mk, ca 1938, 4", $80 to	100.00
Jar, sand, emb bl leaves on hdls, brn matt, 1930s, 18", $700 to	800.00
Jar, sand, Sphinx, lt bl matt, ca 1930s, 16", $1,000 to	1,200.00
Jardiniere, basketweave, blended brn & gr, 7½", $50 to	60.00
Jardiniere, Swallows, Onyx, yel, 7", $70 to	90.00
Pitcher, elephant, bl, NM mk, 7x5", $200 to	250.00
Pitcher, Hobnail, yel, unmk, 48-oz, 6", $60 to	80.00
Planter, clown & pig, wht w/mc details, 1951, 8½", $70 to	80.00
Planter, cornucopia, bl, NM mk, 1940s, 5", $25 to	35.00
Planter, football, antiqued finish, 1957, 4½x7", $60 to	75.00
Planter, kitten beside basket w/ball of yarn, pk, NM mk, 1940s, 6", $30 to	50.00
Planter, lt gr, 4-scallop rim, 4-ftd, globular, NM mk, 1940s, 3½", $35 to	40.00
Planter, Mary Ann shoe, pastel, NM mk, 1940s, 5" L, $25 to	35.00
Planter, Poodle, pk & wht, unusual color, 1956, 7½x7½", $80 to	100.00
Planter, shell, spiky, pastel matt, 1940s, 7½x5½", $30 to	40.00
Planter, zebra, blk & wht, 1956, 6½x8½", $400 to	600.00
Strawberry jar, maroon, brn or gr, w/3 chains, 1953, 6x7", $30 to	40.00
Stretch animal, dachshund, pastel matt, unmk, 1940s, 5x8¼", $150 to	200.00
Stretch animal, lion, unmk, pastel matt, 1940s, 5½x7½", $180 to	200.00
Teapot, Daisy, shaded brn/gr/wht, 1940s, $30 to	40.00
Vase, Butterfly, bl, USA mk, 5½x7½", $75 to	90.00
Vase, Contrasting Leaf, chartreuse, 1955, 9", $140 to	200.00
Vase, cornucopia, Sunburst Gold, 3¼x4", $25 to	35.00
Vase, emb floral & leaves, wht matt, integral hdls, ftd, 8", $60 to	90.00
Vase, emb leaves & berries, wht matt, flared top & bottom, 1930s, 6", $50 to	60.00
Vase, Hand of Friendship (Prayer Hands), gr, NM mk, 3x4", $60 to	90.00
Vase, heart shape, pk, unmk, 1940s, 6", $40 to	50.00
Vase, swan form, gr, unmk, 1940s, 6", $25 to	30.00
Wall pocket, berries & leaves, bl, unmk, 1940s, 7", $175 to	250.00
Wall pocket, pear w/gr leaves, unmk, 1950s, 7x6", $50 to	60.00
Wall pocket, umbrella, gr gloss, mk, 1950s, 8¾x6", $40 to	50.00
Wall pocket, violin, brn or aqua, mk, 1950s, 10¼", $80 to	110.00

J.W. McCoy

The J.W. McCoy Pottery Company was incorporated in 1899. It operated under that name in Roseville, Ohio, until 1911 when McCoy entered into a partnership with George Brush, forming the Brush-McCoy Company. During the early years, McCoy produced kitchenware, majolica jardinieres and pedestals, umbrella stands, and cuspidors. By 1903 they

had begun to experiment in the field of art pottery and, though never involved to the extent of some of their contemporaries, nevertheless produced several art lines of merit.

The company rebuilt in 1904 after being destroyed by fire, and other artware was designed. Loy-Nel-Art and Renaissance were standard brown lines, hand decorated under the glaze with colored slip. Shapes and artwork were usually simple but effective. Olympia and Rosewood were relief-molded brown-glaze lines decorated in natural colors with wreaths of leaves and berries or simple floral sprays. Although much of this ware was not marked, you will find examples with the die-stamped 'Loy-Nel-Art, McCoy,' or an incised line identification. Our advisor for this category is Bob Hanson; he is listed in the directory under Washington.

Corn Line, salt box, #56, 5½x5⅞", $150 to	200.00
Loy-Nel Art, cuspidor, pansies, 6¾x9", EX, $75 to	100.00
Loy-Nel-Art, bowl, floral, ftd, 5", $80 to	100.00

Loy-Nel-Art, jardiniere and pedestal, total height: 26", $450.00 to $600.00. (Photo courtesy Quinn's & Waverly Auction Galleries on LiveAuctioneers.com)

Loy-Nel-Art, jardiniere, floral, 4-ftd, 7½", $150 to	200.00
Loy-Nel-Art, jardiniere, tulips, 6½", $140 to	180.00
Loy-Nel-Art, pitcher, open roses, #117, sm rstr, 8¼", $30 to	45.00
Loy-Nel-Art, spittoon, floral, 6¾x8", NM, $130 to	150.00
Loy-Nel-Art, tankard, floral, 11⅞", $140 to	165.00
Loy-Nel-Art, vase, berries, sm hdls, #5, 6⅛", $80 to	95.00
Loy-Nel-Art, vase, floral, 10x5½", $150 to	200.00
Loy-Nel-Art, vase, pansies, w/hdls, 10", $165 to	225.00
Loy-Nel-Art, vase, pillow, floral, 5x5½", NM, $65 to	70.00
Olympia, bowl, ftd, 11½x14½", NM, $250 to	275.00
Olympia, jardiniere, #70, 7½", $80 to	110.00
Sylvan (Avenue of Trees), vase, #06, crazing, 6", $80 to	100.00

McKee Glass

McKee Glass was founded in 1853 in Pittsburgh, Pennsylvania. Among their early products were tableware of both the flint and non-flint varieties. In 1888 the company relocated to avail themselves of a source of natural gas, thereby founding the town of Jeannette, Pennsylvania. One of their most famous colored dinnerware lines, Rock Crystal, was manufactured in the 1920s. Production during the '30s and '40s included colored opaque dinnerware, Sunkist reamers, and 'bottoms up' cocktail tumblers as well as a line of black glass vases, bowls, and novelty items. All are popular items with today's collectors, but watch for reproductions. The mark of an authentic 'bottoms up' tumbler is the patent number 77725 embossed beneath the feet. The company was purchased in 1916 by Jeannette Glass, under which name it continues to operate. See also Animal Dishes with Covers; Carnival Glass; Depression Glass; Kitchen Collectibles; Reamers.

Baking set, Betty Jane, child sz, 9-pc, MIB.......70.00
Compote, Innovation #407, stars & flowers, H std, 8½x6½".......55.00
Covered dish, Baby Moses, mg, reed base, 3x4".......450.00
Decanter, Seville Yel, pinched body, w/stopper, 8¾".......65.00
Jardiniere, Skokie Gr, Chevron design, 3-ftd, 5⅛".......35.00
Lamp, Danse de Lumiere, gr, $550 to.......650.00
Lamp, Danse de Lumiere, pk satin nude figural, 11x4¾".......750.00
Punch set, Concord, ftd bowl, 9x12", +10 cups & glass ladle.......65.00
Rose bowl, Hickman, sm ft, 5½x4½".......60.00
Tumbler, Bottoms Up, Jade-ite, 3¾"+4" Jade-ite coaster, $125 to.135.00
Tumbler, Bottoms Up, lt butterscotch opal, 3", +matching coaster..85.00
Vase, nude in relief ea side (3), blk, ftd, 8½", NM.......75.00
Water bottle, red/orange, pinched sides, tumbler fits over neck, 5"..40.00
Wren hut, wht w/red roof, metal bottom, 5".......80.00

Medical Collectibles

The field of medical-related items encompasses a wide area from the primitive bleeding bowl to the X-ray machines of the early 1900s. Other closely related collectibles include apothecary and dental items. Many tools that were originally intended for the pharmacist found their way to the doctor's office, and dentists often used surgical tools when no suitable dental instrument was available. A trend in the late 1800s toward self-medication brought a whole new wave of home-care manuals and 'patent' medical machines for home use. Commonly referred to as 'quack' medical gimmicks, these machines were usually ineffective and occasionally dangerous.

Bag, brn leather w/emb decor, NP fittings, 1890s, 8", G.......180.00
Bag, brn leather, Emdee by Schell, 11x15x7", +assorted sm tools.135.00
Bleeder, brass, Wiegland & Snowden, 4½", in fitted case.......80.00

Bleeder/spring lancet, engraved Tiemann on casing, in simulated leather case, 1x2", $550.00. (Photo courtesy Signature House on LiveAuctioneers.com)

Book, Derangements of Liver...Nervous System, J Johnson, 1832.120.00
Book, Physiology of Common Life, GH Lewes, cloth cover, 1872.42.50
Cabinet, dental, oak/stainless, Deco style, 4 drws/2 doors, 1940s.240.00
Cabinet, pnt steel, dbl doors over 3 drws over 2 doors, 67x30x16"...600.00
Cabinet, sterilizer, oak & glass w/wire, Erie City Mfg, 13" W.......240.00
Case, apothecary, bold grpt, dvtl case w/13 drws, 21x39x10½".2,415.00
Case, slide display, mahog w/glass paneled door, brass hdl, 12x10"..375.00
Chart, anatomy & physiology, W&AK Johnson, rolls down, 45x50", VG...85.00
Chest, apothecary, 9 drw, blk pnt w/yel lettering, ca 1800, 24x35x14".3,175.00
Chest, apothecary, 20 grad drw, dvtl beaded case, rprs, 1900s, 30x25"..2,600.00
Cupboard, apothecary; pine w/old pnt, 27 drws, Weeks & Gilson, 76x36".3,225.00
Fleam, 2 steel blades in 3½" brass sleeve, ca 1812.......165.00
Fleam, 3-blade, brass hdl, folding type, 1800s.......120.00
Instrument, B-D Venous Pressure Apparatus, L Cohen, EX in 2x13" case...60.00
Instrument, lens cystoscope, Am Cystoscope Makers, NY, in 2x13" case..265.00
Instrument, Thompson Resectoscope, V Vueller Chicago, EX in 2x14" case.36.00
Jar, Leeches emb on clear glass, sm blister, 10½x8".......115.00
Kit, enema, Weiss...62, dbl-action pump, ebony hdl, +accessories+case..400.00
Kit, surgeon's, 27 ivory-hdld instruments & saw/etc, +mahog 16" case.10,350.00
Machine, electro-cardiograph, Sanborn, MA, paper readout, oak case..180.00
Model, heart, comes apart & shows chambers/valves/veins, mc, 17", EX.30.00
Model, human skull, plaster, in sections, NY Scientific, 1900s, 8"..300.00
Model, lady's torso, cast resin, 20".......900.00
Model, skull (real/human), hinged jaw, 8x6".......180.00
Quack device, Dr Macaura's blood circulator, NMIB.......110.00
Quack device, Fischer, electrical shock, 11x22x15".......850.00
Quack device, ozone generator, oak case, 6x22x12".......48.00
Report, Observations on Cow-Pox, Wm Woodville, London, 1800s, 43-pg...80.00
Skeleton, papier-maché, held w/wire & tin strips, pnt details, 59"...700.00
Stethoscope, monaural, trn wood, 7".......615.00
Tongue depressor, NP brass, ebony hdl, Shepard & Dudley.......60.00
Tooth key, dbl claw w/steel shaft & ebony hdl, 6".......240.00
Tooth key, single claw w/locking pin & trn wood hdl, 6".......225.00
Wheelchair, wicker seat, wooden footrest, 3 metal wheels, 1800s.480.00

Meissen

The Royal Saxon Porcelain Works was established in 1710 in Meissen, Saxony. Under the direction of Johann Frederick Bottger, who in 1708 had developed the formula for the first true porcelain body, fine ceramic figurines with exquisite detail and tableware of the highest quality were produced. Although every effort was made to insure the secrecy of Bottger's discovery, others soon began to copy his ware; and in 1731 Meissen adopted the famous crossed swords trademark to identify their own work. The term 'Dresden ware' is often incorrectly used to refer to Meissen porcelain, since Bottger's discovery and first potting efforts were in nearby Dresden. For more information, we recommend *Meissen Porcelain* (Collector Books) by our advisors, Susan and Jim Harran. They are listed in the Directory under New Jersey. See also Onion Pattern.

Basket, appl flowers, 1824-50, 6¼x5", $500 to.......600.00
Bird, perched on branch, brn/blk/wht, 5", $350 to.......400.00
Bowl, HP flowers, reticulation on sides, 1924-34, 11x3", $350 to.400.00
Bowl, yel w/gold flowers, 2 strike mks, 1953-57, 11", $250 to.......300.00
Box, Court Dragon, 1950s, 3½x2", $200 to.......250.00
Charger, cobalt bl, gilt trim, HP flowers center, 1924-34, 11¼", $600 to..650.00

Charger, heavy gilt scrolls, hand-painted flowers, circa 1930s, 11", $450.00 to $500.00. (Photo courtesy Susan and Jim Harran)

Chocolate pot, HP flowers, gilt, 2 cut mks, 1850-1924, 9", $300 to...350.00
Coffee cup, Gr Ivy, swan hdl, 1850-1924, $150 to.......175.00
Cup, demi, HP appl flowers, 6 ft, 1850-1924, $500 to.......550.00
Figure group, children, birdcage, 1850-1924, 5⅔x4½", $1,200 to..1,300.00
Figure group, cupids w/flowers, 1850-1924, 5½", $1,200 to.......1,300.00
Figurine, bird, bullfinch, colorful, 1950s, 8¼", $800 to.......900.00
Figurine, cupid shooting arrow, missing tip of arrow, 1850-1924, 5", $700 to...750.00
Figurine, Hentschel child, plaid shirt, current mk, 6x3".......1,600.00
Figurine, mini, wht dove, holding leaf in mouth, 1950s, 3¼x2"...275.00
Figurine, Poodle, wht, 1950s, 6x5½", $450 to.......500.00
Plate, cobalt, gold, 4 floral cartouches, 1850-1924, 9⅞", $400 to.450.00
Plate, scalloped, HP flowers, bugs, 1850-1924, 9½", $250 to.......275.00
Plates, Bl Onion, rtcl, 1888-1924, 8", set of 6, $700 to.......800.00
Teacup, mini, Court Dragon, yel, gilt, 1850-1924, $300 to.......350.00
Teapot, HP flowers, gilt, swan spout, 1830-50, $400 to.......450.00
Tureen, HP bl flowers, Cupid w/cornucopia, 1850-95, 12x7½".1,100.00
Vase, appl flowers & fruit, 1 strike mk, leaf hdl, 1850-1900, 6½".275.00

Mercury Glass

Silvered glass, commonly called mercury glass, was created first in Haida, Bohemia, now the Czech Republic, around 1840. The glass items were blown double-walled and filled with a solution that contained nitrate of silver, then sealed. Bohemian mercury glass was made from soda lime glass, so the items are light in weight. English silvered glass, blown with heavy lead glass, was made for only a very short time period, approximately 1849 to 1853. After a successful production method was developed by Edward Varnish and Frederick Hale Thomson of London, England, the first silvered glass patent was granted in 1849. Most English examples involved elaborate layers of jewel tone colored glass in green, blue, red, and amber, cut to silver, and were always marked with the maker's name and 'London.' In the United States, free-blown, double-walled flint glass was silvered and made into gazing globes and decorative tableware, including goblets, sugar bowls, pitchers, and salt cellars, by makers at the Boston and Sandwich Glass Company, the Boston Silver Glass Company, and the New England Glass Company. The New England Glass Company was the only American maker to mark its wares with NEG.Co. impressed into a metal seal covered by glass underfoot. Examples of American silvered mercury glass were shown at the New York Crystal Palace Exhibition in 1853. In addition to vases, goblets, and tableware produced from the middle to late nineteenth century, utilitarian items such as doorknobs, curtain pins, and lamp reflectors were made in quantities. From the late nineteenth century until the 1930s, figural animals such as deer, and other novelties including globular rose bowls and candleholders were made in Germany and Czechoslovakia, some bearing original foil or paper labels with the country of origin. Mercury glass was acid-etched, cased with layers, cut, enameled, engraved, frosted, gilded, and patined, and surviving examples in good condition are rare to find. Condition is an issue, and although some prefer the worn 'shabby' look popular in today's country interiors, most collectors seek examples that retain their silver appearance. Collectors should look for signs of free-blown glass, and a seal or pontil scar underfoot distinguishes true antique mercury glass from modern reproductions, which are being made in China and the Czech Republic. In the 1980s and 1990s, a cheap, single-walled so-called mercury glass was made in India, while large vessesls were imported from Mexico.

Values vary widely, and while more common items such as vases or candleholders in average condition are inexpensive, rare examples in mint condition can be priced in the hundreds, if not thousands of dollars.

In the listings that follow, all examples are silver in color unless noted another color. For further information we recommend *Pictorial Guide to Silvered Mercury Glass* by our advisor, Diane Lytwyn (Collector Books). She is listed in the directory under Connecticut.

Bowl, bl geometric decor, ftd, w/lid, 6"	120.00
Candlestick, bl, bulb, ftd, 3", pr	70.00
Candlestick, scrolling geometric foliage & fauna, ftd, 12½", pr	145.00
Compote, mc glass jewels & bright etching, gold int, 7x7"	250.00
Doorknobs, 2" dia, pr	95.00
Gazing ball, Dithridge, ca 1867-75, 7" dia, +matching stand	800.00
Goblet, glass beads in bl/red/gr, gold-washed int, 1870-80, 7½"	1,500.00
Jar, HP floral (worn), Czech mks on lid & base, 8½"	285.00
Lamp, table, urn form, chrome-plated metal base, 21"	420.00
Plate, thick w/raised lip, 11"	120.00
Sugar bowl, tulip & leaf etching, 1890s, 8½"	215.00
Tie-backs, eng floral on rnd knob, 3¼", pr	125.00
Vase, ball form, ca 1880, 7x7"	85.00
Vase, HP floral, baluster, 10½", pr	130.00
Vase, HP flowers w/jewel centers, ftd, 28¾"	3,500.00
Vase, HP wht cattails & ferns, ftd, 11"	135.00
Vase, turq, long trumpet neck, ftd, 9¾"	120.00
Vases, floral decor, 14", pr	200.00

Merrimac

Founded in 1897 in Newburyport, Massachusetts, the Merrimac Pottery Company primarily produced gardenware. In 1901 they introduced a line of artware, covered mostly in semi-matt green glaze, somewhat in the style of Grueby's, but glossier and with the appearance of a second tier below the top, feathered one. Marked examples carry an impressed die-stamp or a paper label, each with the firm name and the outline of a sturgeon, the meaning of the Native American word, Merrimac. Our advisors for this category are Suzanne Perrault and David Rago; they are listed in the Directory under New Jersey.

Vase, matt green, lobed, 4½x4", $375.00. (Photo courtesy Rago Arts and Auction Center)

Vase, appl leaves, gr matt, bulb, fish mk, 4½x6"	1,750.00
Vase, bright yel & orange peel matt glaze, short line at rim, 6½"	2,180.00
Vase, frothy gr, hdls, illegible mk, 4x4¼"	850.00
Vase, frothy yel matt, ovoid, nicks, 9¼x4¾"	3,475.00
Vase, gr curdled matt, bulb, sm neck, flared rim, hdls, 4½x8"	2,250.00
Vase, gr/brn mottle, ovoid, paper label, 10x4½"	2,400.00
Vase, gr/gunmetal feathered matt, bulb, fish mk, 6x5"	2,100.00
Vase, yel mottle matt, ovoid, fish mk, 9½"	3,600.00

Metlox

Metlox Potteries was founded in 1927 in Manhattan Beach, California. Before 1934 when they began producing the ceramic housewares for which they have become famous, they made ceramic and neon outdoor advertising signs. The company went out of business in 1989. Well-known sculptor Carl Romanelli designed artware in the late 1930s and early 1940s (and again briefly in the 1950s). His work is especially sought after today.

Some Provincial dinnerware lines can be confusing. There are two 'rooster' lines, Red Rooster (red, orange, and brown) and California Provincial (dark green and burgundy), and there are three 'homestead' lines, Colonial Heritage (red, orange, and brown like the Red Rooster pieces), Homestead Provincial (dark green and burgundy like California Provincial), and Provincial Blue (blue and white). For further information we recommend *Collector's Encyclopedia of Metlox Potteries* by our advisor Carl Gibbs, Jr.; he is listed in the Directory under Texas.

Cookie Jars

Ali Cat, $125 to	150.00
Baby Bluebird on Pine Cone, Made in USA paper label, $50 to	60.00
Ballerina Bear, Metlox Calif USA, $75 to	85.00
Bisque Piggy, Poppytrail, $40 to	50.00
Bluebird on Pine Cone, Made in USA, $55 to	75.00
Calf-says 'Moo,' calf head, paper label, Poppytrail, $225 to	275.00
Clown, yel, 3-qt, $125 to	150.00
Cookie Bandit (raccoon), $65 to	90.00
Cookie Girl, unmk, $50 to	60.00
Cub Scout, unmk, rare, min	750.00
Daisy Cookie Canister, $35 to	45.00

Downy Woodpecker, sits atop lg acorn, $160 to 180.00
Flamingo, min 300.00
Flower Basket, unmk, $30 to 40.00
Gingerbread, bsk, Poppytrail, Calif, $75 to 85.00
Gingham Dog, bl, $125 to 150.00
Goose, Lucy, $125 to 150.00
Happy the Clown, unmk, rare, $325 to 350.00
Hippo, Bubbles, yel & gr, min 350.00
Jolly Chef, bl or blk eyes, $285 to.. 325.00
Kitten-Says Meow, Poppytrail by Metlox paper label, $50 to....... 60.l00
Koala Bear, $80 to 100.00
Lamb Head, wht, $100 to 125.00
Little Red Riding Hood, Poppytrail Calif, rare, min.................. 1,250.00
Mammy Scrub Woman, unmk, min 1,500.00
Merry-Go-Rnd, $175 to.. 200.00
Mona, triceratops, yel, c '87 by Vincent, $80 to 110.00
Mother Goose, Poppytrail Calif paper label, $75 to 85.00
Noah's Ark, $45 to.. 65.00
Orange, Made in USA, $40 to 50.00

Owl, 9½", $70.00. (Photo courtesy American Auction Co. on LiveAuctioneers.com)

Panda Bear, blk & wht, unmk, $75 to.. 85.00
Panda w/Lollipop, Poppytrail, $325 to 375.00
Pinnochio, paper label, Poppytrail, (+), $275 to 300.00
Pretty Ann, Poppytrail Calif, $125 to 150.00
Rabbit on Cabbage, $65 to 85.00
Rag Doll, boy, $125 to 145.00
Rag Doll, girl, Poppytrail, Calif, $90 to...................................... 110.00
Santa Head, $275 to 325.00
Scottie Dog, blk, $100 to 125.00
Scottie Dog, wht, $100 to 125.00
Sir Francis Drake, duck, unmk, $35 to 45.00
Squirrel on Pine Cone, Made in USA, $65 to 75.00
Teddy Bear, bl sweater, holding cookie, unmk, $40 to.................. 45.00
Uncle Sam Bear, min... 850.00
Watermelon, Poppytrail, Calif, $250 to 300.00
Wells Fargo, $500 to 550.00
Woodpecker on Acorn, $250 to 300.00

Dinnerware

Aztec, bowl, coupe soup.. 12.50
Aztec, cr/sug bowl, w/lid 40.00
Aztec, platter, 11" L.. 35.00
California Apple, bowl, vegetable, 11½"....................................... 40.00
California Apple, plate, dinner, 10" 20.00
California Apple, plate, luncheon, 9" 7.00
California Apple, platter, 13" L, $25 to 35.00
California Aztec, coffeepot, ca 1960 .... 250.00
California Aztec, pitcher, water, 14" 200.00
California Contempora, beverage server, $300 to......................... 325.00
California Contempora, chop plate, $90 to 100.00

California Freeform, bowl, divided, 14x14" 200.00
California Freeform, c/s 14.00
California Freeform, sugar bowl.. 24.00
California Ivy, bowl, coupe soup.. 18.00
California Ivy, bowl, divided vegetable, 11".................................. 25.00
California Ivy, c/s...8.00
California Ivy, plate, dinner.. 15.00
California Provincial, bowl, fruit/dessert......................................7.50
California Provincial, bowl, vegetable, 8" 30.00
California Provincial, chop plate, 12" 27.50
California Provincial, creamer... 12.50
California Provincial, mug, 3½" 42.00
California Provincial, plate, dinner, 10" 15.00
Camellia, c/s 12.50
Camellia, chop plate, 13" 20.00
Camellia, sugar bowl, w/lid 20.00
Colonial Heritage, bowl, vegetable, 10" 32.00
Colonial Heritage, gravy boat... 40.00
Colonial Heritage, plate, dinner, 10" 7.50
Colonial Heritage, platter, 16" L 35.00
Delphinium, bowl, fruit/dessert, 6" 6.00
Delphinium, plate, bread & butter 5.00
Delphinium, plate, dinner, 10" 12.50
Delphinium, shakers, pr 20.00
Golden Fruit, bowl, rimmed soup 6.50
Golden Fruit, c/s, $6 ....8.00
Grape Arbor, bowl, cereal...7.00
Grape Arbor, coffeepot 35.00
Grape Arbor, creamer 12.50
Happy Time, chop plate, 12" 30.00
Happy Time, gravy boat... 35.00
Happy Time, shakers, pr 22.00
Happy Time, sugar bowl, w/lid... 20.00
Happy Time, teapot 115.00
Homestead Provincial, bowl, cereal, 7" 16.00
Homestead Provincial, kettle casserole, w/lid.............................. 90.00

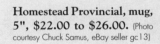

Homestead Provincial, mug, 5", $22.00 to $26.00. (Photo courtesy Chuck Samus, eBay seller gc13)

Homestead Provincial, plate, luncheon, 9"................................... 20.00
Iris, plate, dinner, 10"... 10.00
Iris, platter, 13" L.. 28.00
Navajo, bowl, cereal, 7" 8.00
Navajo, bowl, vegetable, 9" 14.00
Navajo, c/s.. 75.00
Navajo, sugar bowl, w/lid.. 17.00
Provincial Blue, creamer... 8.00
Provincial Blue, mug, w/spout, lg 80.00
Provincial Blue, plate, dinner, 10"... 12.00
Provincial Blue, soup server, ind, 6".. 18.00
Provincial Flower, bowl, divided vegetable, rect........................... 38.00
Provincial Flower, coffeepot.. 48.00
Provincial Flower, shakers, pr 20.00
Provincial Fruit, bowl, soup server, ind 12.50
Provincial Fruit, creamer 7.50
Provincial Fruit, plate, dinner, 10½"..7.50

Provincial Fruit, sugar bowl, w/lid 14.00
Provincial Rose, bowl, vegetable, 10" 15.00
Provincial Rose, creamer 15.00
Provincial Rose, plate, dinner 12.50
Provincial Rose, platter, 15" L 28.00
Red Rooster, bowl, vegetable, 10" 9.00
Red Rooster, chop plate, 12" 22.50
Red Rooster, covered dish, hen on nest 60.00
Red Rooster, pitcher, lg, 2¼-qt, $75 to 75.00
Red Rooster, plate, bread & butter 5.00
Red Rooster, plate, dinner, 10" 15.00
Red Rooster, platter, 13" L 16.00
Rooster Bleu, bowl, cereal, 7¼" 7.50
Rooster Bleu, butter dish 35.00
Rooster Bleu, gravy boat 25.00
Rooster Bleu, plate, salad, 7½" 7.00
Sculptured Zinnia, bowl, cereal, 7½" 7.50
Sculptured Zinnia, bowl, divided vegetable, 8½" 27.50
Sculptured Zinnia, butter dish, $55 to 60.00
Sculptured Zinnia, platter, 14" L 20.00
Sculptured Zinnia, sugar bowl, w/lid 14.00
Woodland Gold, bowl, vegetable, 11" L 28.00
Woodland Gold, bowl, vegetable, w/lid, sm 20.00
Woodland Gold, mug 15.00
Woodland Gold, plate, dinner, 10½" 8.00
Woodland Gold, platter, 13" L 16.00

Disney

Alice in Wonderland, #292, $350 to 400.00
Bambi, jumbo, $1,000 to 1,500.00
Cinderella, in gown, #278, $400 to 450.00
Donald Duck w/guitar, #267, $275 to 300.00
Dumbo seated w/bonnet, front legs up, $200 to 225.00
Dwarf (Snow White), any, $200 to 250.00
Faline (Bambi's girlfriend), #204, $140 to 165.00
Flower (Bambi), med, #258, $75 to 100.00
Hippo (Fantasia), $325 to 400.00
Jose of 3 Caballeros, #210, $325 to 350.00
Mamma Mouse (Cinderella), #285, $175 to 200.00
Mickey Mouse, #212, $350 to 400.00
Pinocchio, $400 to 450.00
Pluto sniffing, #264, $225 to 250.00
Prince Charming, $350 to 400.00
Sprite (Fantasia), $175 to 250.00
Thumper, sm, #262, $100 to 125.00
Tinkerbell, #243, $450 to 500.00
Tweedle Dum or Tweedle Dee (Alice in Wonderland), $225 to .. 250.00
Unicorn (Vernon Kilns Fantasia), $250 to 325.00

Miniatures

Aardvark, $75 to 175.00
Banjo Boy, 6", $80 to 125.00
Bird, wings up, sm, $60 to 80.00
Camel, Bactrian, #92-G, w/name card, 5", $120 to 170.00
Camel resting, min 350.00
Circus Horse, front legs raised, 6", $225 to 275.00
Dove, 6¼", $40 to 60.00
Elephant, trunk raised, 6¼", $60 to 85.00
Flamingo, 6¼", $60 to 100.00
Goose, 3¾", $30 to 40.00
Squirrel, 2", $75 to 125.00
Turtle standing, $140 to 160.00

Nostalgia Line

Reminiscent of the late nineteenth and early twentieth centuries, the Nostalgia line contained models of locomotives, gramophones, early autos, stagecoaches, and baby carriages. There were also wagons and carts pulled by horses or donkeys, sometimes with separate drivers and passengers. The line was produced from the late 1940s through the 1960s.

Chevrolet, Antique Automobiles, #619, $75 to 85.00
Clydesdale, Am Royal Horses, min 175.00
Drum table, #613, $35 to 40.00
Fire Wagon, #659, $60 to 85.00
Piano & lid, #603, $75 to 80.00
Stagecoach, $80 to 100.00
Trolley car, $70 to 90.00

Poppets

From the mid-'60s through the mid-'70s, Metlox produced a line of 'Poppets,' 88 in all, representing characters ranging from royalty and professionals to a Salvation Army group. They came with a name tag; some had paper labels, others backstamps.

Schultz, tradesman/grocer, 8", $55.00 to $65.00. (Photo courtesy Jack Chipman)

Barney, boy laying on belly w/pot on his ft. 50.00
Casey, policeman, $45 to 55.00
Chester, saxophone man, 8", $80 to 90.00
Chimney Sweep, 7¾", $55 to 65.00
Colleen, 7¼", $45 to 55.00
Dutch Girl, 5", $40 to 50.00
Elliot, boy tennis player, 6½", $40 to 50.00
Emma the Cook, 8", $45 to 55.00
Mike, boy sitting w/elbow on jar, 5" 45.00
Minnie, mermaid, $55 to 65.00
Mother Goose w/4" bowl, $70 to 80.00
Nancy, girl sitting holding animal, yel outfit w/hood 45.00
Nick, organ grinder, $55 to 65.00
Sally w/4" bowl, $50 to 60.00
Sam, girl standing net to jar, 6" 45.00
Tina, 8½" 65.00

Romanelli Artware

Figurine, Cowboy on Bucking Bronco, min 750.00
Figurine, dancing girl and doves, #1825, Modern Masterpieces, 11" .. 225.00
Figurine, dancing girl, #1832, Modern Masterpieces, 9" 250.00
Figurine, Great Dane, 17", min 500.00
Figurine, Indian brave, Modern Masterpieces, 9", min 300.00
Flower holder, Cornucopia Maid, 8¾", $250 to 275.00
Flower holder, modern head, 11", $325 to 350.00
Head vase, Hawaiian girl, ca 1942, #1833, 10½", min 550.00
Incense burner, Confucius, 6", $275 to 325.00
Mug, Pearl Harbor, $100 to 125.00
Vase, angelfish, ca 1940, 8½" 75.00

Vase, angelfish, dbl, 14" 250.00
Vase, Zodiac, 12 different, 8", ea $175 to 200.00
Vase, Zodiac, No 1804-2 Taurus, $175 to 200.00
Vase, Zodiac, No 1804-8 Scorpio $175 to 200.00

Mettlach

In 1836 Nicholas Villeroy and Eugene Francis Boch, both of whom were already involved in the potting industry, formed a partnership and established a stoneware factory in an old restored abbey in Mettlach, Germany. Decorative stoneware with in-mold relief was their specialty, steins in particular. Through constant experimentation, they developed innovative methods of decoration. One process, called chromolith, involved inlaying colorful mosaic designs into the body of the ware. Later underglaze printing from copper plates was used. Their stoneware was of high quality, and their steins won many medals at the St. Louis Expo and early world's fairs. Most examples are marked with an incised castle and the name 'Mettlach.' The numbering system indicates size, date, stock number, and decorator. Production was halted by a fire in 1921; the factory was not rebuilt.

Key:
L — liter   PUG — print under glaze

#144-528, plaque, PUG: Tellskapelle, 12" 280.00
#171, stein, relief: people around body, inlaid lid, .25L 120.00
#202, stein, relief: choir, detailed pewter lid, #202, 1L, NM 200.00
#228, stein, relief; 4 scenes of people, pewter lid, .5L, NM 80.00
#675, stein, character: Barrel, inlaid lid, .5L 95.00
#1005, stein, relief: people drinking, inlaid lid, rpr, .5L 80.00
#1036, stein, threading/glazed: repeating design, inlaid lid, .3L ... 300.00
#1044-512, plaque, PUG: Bratwurst Glocklein Nurnberg, 12" 360.00
#1044-9027, plaque, PUG: fox, worn gold, 14", NM 665.00
#1044, plaque, PUG: Hamburg, Deichthorfleeth, 12" 365.00
#1044, plaque, PUG: Hamburg, Jungfernstieg, 12" 280.00
#1133, stein, threading/glazed: repeating design, inlaid lid, .4L, EX ... 180.00
#1327-1287, beaker, PUG: donkey barmaid feeds fox gentleman, .25L . 215.00
#1370, stein, relief: verse, rpl pewter lid, .5L 70.00

#1416, vase, etched portraits of Victorian ladies, 14", $2,160.00. (Photo courtesy O'Gallerie on LiveAuctioneers.com)

#1436, vase, etch/glazed: repeating pattern, 4½" 240.00
#1467, stein, relief: 4 scenes of people, inlaid lid, .5L 130.00
#1526, stein, relief: Yale University, pewter lid, .5L 185.00
#1526, stein, transfer/HP: European beer map pewter lid, .5L 445.00
#1526, stein, transfer/HP: Salzburger...1900, pewter lid, .5 L 95.00
#1526, stein, transfer/HP: Student Society, 1923, hairline, .5L 240.00
#1527, stein, etch: cavaliers drinking, Warth, horn tl/pewter lid, 1L .. 375.00
#1532, stein, etch: crest w/lion, inlaid lid, .5L 345.00
#1662, stein, etch: tapestry/workman drinking, pewter 1889 lid, .5L .. 240.00
#1803, stein, etch/glazed: repeating design, inlaid lid, .25L 265.00
#1909-1008, stein, PUG: man playing harp, Schlitt, rpr pewter lid, .5L .. 275.00
#1909-1179, stein, PUG: Gesang, pewter lid, .5L 475.00

#1909-1180, stein, PUG: Tanz, pewter lid, .5L 385.00
#1909-1288, stein, PUG: fox drinking beer, pewter lid, .5L 485.00
#2074, stein, etch: bird in cage, pewter lid, .5L 1,595.00
#2092, stein, etch: dwarf adjusting clock, Schlitt, inlaid lid, .5L ... 1,000.00
#2097, stein, etch: musical design, inlaid lid w/hairline, .5L 215.00
#2140, stein, transfer/HP: 4F Turner, pewter lid, .5L 310.00
#2192, stein, etch: Etruscan, Schlitt, inlaid lid, .5L 725.00
#2231, stein, etch: cavaliers, inlaid lid, silent music box base, .5L .. 380.00
#2327-1273, beaker, PUG: drunken man, .25L 195.00
#2373, stein, etch: St Augustine FL, alligator hdl, inlaid lid, .5L . 725.00
#2388, stein, character: Pretzels, inlaid lid, .5L 325.00
#2440, stein, relief: Capo-di-Monte style, rpl pewter lid, .5L 175.00
#2443, plaque, cameo: ladies, Stahl, firing flaw, 18" 395.00
#2542, charger, etched & glazed: maiden at pond, 15¾" 3,900.00
#2582, stein, tavern scene, inlaid pewter lid, 8¾", .5L 720.00
#2583, stein, etch: Blk Whale of Ascolon, Quidenus, pewter lid, 1L, NM .. 315.00
#2690, stein, etch: drinking scene, Quidenus, inlaid lid, 1.4L ... 1,450.00
#2715, stein, cameo/etch: 3 scenes of couples, inlaid lid, .5L 725.00
#2719, stein, etch/glazed: baker occupation, inlaid lid, .5L 1,950.00
#2721, stein, etch/glazed: carpenter occupation, inlaid lid, .5L . 2,300.00
#2724, stein, etch/glazed: mason occupation, inlaid lid, .5L 2,415.00
#2727, stein, etch/glazed: printer occupation, inlaid lid, .5L 2,645.00
#2729, stein, etch/glazed: blacksmith occupation, inlaid lid, .5L ... 4,600.00
#2730, stein, etch/glazed: butcher occupation, inlaid lid, .5L 4,600.00
#2917, stein, etch/relief: Munchen, inlaid lion/shield lid, .5L .. 2,550.00
#5241, plaque, etch: Delft, 15¼" 235.00
#7042, plaque, Phanolith: people at table, Stahl, 12x15½"+fr .. 1,840.00

Microscopes

The microscope has taken on many forms during its 250-year evolutionary period. The current collectors' market primarily includes examples from England, surplus items from institutions, and continental beginner and intermediate forms which sold through Sears Roebuck & Company and other retailers of technical instruments. Earlier examples have brass main tubes which are unpainted. Later, more common examples are all black with brass or silver knobs and horseshoe-shaped bases. Early and more complex forms are the most valuable; these always had hardwood cases to house the delicate instruments and their accessories. Instruments were never polished during use, and those that have been polished to use as decorator pieces are of little interest to most avid collectors. Unless otherwise described, all examples in the following listing are in excellent condition and retain their original cases.

Acme, brass & iron, +14" case, EX 350.00
Bausch & Lomb, NP Continental type, triple nosepiece, VG 400.00
Bausch & Lomb, triple nosepc, brass tube, Y-ft, 10½", EX in case . 950.00
Beck, brass, binoculars, 1890s, w/many accessories, EX in case 650.00
C Reichert, brass folding compound, extended: 10", EX in case .. 1,115.00
Culpeper type, brass tube, circular ft, rack-work focus, 10" 1,525.00
Culpeper type, vertical rack-&-pinion focus, circular stage, 11" .. 825.00
Ellis-pattern, brass, rack-work adjustment w/forceps, 4¼" W 700.00
Ernest Leitz, 3 brass objectives, rpl mirror, 1910, VG+ 650.00
Fr, student's compound, brass, rack-work, swivel magnifier, 9½" .. 165.00
Gwo Wales, compound w/brass tube, CI U-form limb, Y-ft, 11" .. 650.00
J Swift & Son #286, folding compound, dbl nosepc, folded: 9", +case 765.00
JW Queen & Co Philada 1637, ca 1886, 13½x10", EX 425.00
Moritz Pillischer #470, brass, rack-work+fine screw adjustments, 16" . 885.00
Newton, brass compound, nosepc, adjusts w/screw, 4-stop aperture, 14" .. 885.00
Queen, brass & iron, Y-base, 14", G in case 325.00
R&J Beck, binocular body tube, eng tripod ft, 15" 650.00
Watson & Sons Kima, 1940, 14", MIB w/booklet 215.00
Watson & Sons, 2 lenses, revolving turret, 1931, EX 675.00

Militaria

Because of the wide and varied scope of items available to collectors of militaria, most tend to concentrate mainly on the area or areas that interest them most or that they can afford to buy. Some items represent a major investment and because of their value have been reproduced. Extreme caution should be used when purchasing Nazi items. Every badge, medal, cap, uniform, dagger, and sword that Nazi Germany issued is being reproduced today. Some repros are crude and easily identified as fakes, while others are very well done and difficult to recognize as reproductions. Purchases from WWII veterans are usually your safest buys. Reputable dealers or collectors will normally offer a money-back guarantee on Nazi items purchased from them. There are a number of excellent Third Reich reference books available in bookstores at very reasonable prices. Study them to avoid losing a much larger sum spent on a reproduction. Our advisor for this category is Ron L. Willis; he is listed in the Directory under Washington. Unless otherwise noted, values are for items in at least excellent condition, with at most only minimal damage or wear.

Key: insg — insignia

American

Badge, submarine, US Navy, gold, officer, pin-bk, WWII, 2¾" 125.00
Badge, submarine, US Navy, silver, enlisted, pin-bk, WWII, 2¾".. 75.00
Buckle, Civil War, CS on brass w/rope border, on leather belt..3,500.00
Bullet mold, 64 caliber rnd ball, single cavity, iron scissors type .. 450.00
Bullet mold, Enfield 577, brass scissors type, VG 460.00
Canteen, Civil War, Confederate, cedar wood, 7" 3,165.00
Canteen, Indian Wars, canvas cover, w/stopper & chain, ca 1872 ... 195.00
Cap box, Civil War Confederate, leather w/single strap, VG 700.00
Cartridge box, Condict & Co, Newark NJ, sm US plate (rpl), rstr, VG. 230.00
Cup, Army, tin, mk hdl, ca 1894 .... 132.50
Drum, Mexican War/Civil War, maple w/brass tacks, orig heads . 550.00
Flag finial, Civil War, solid brass eagle w/intricate detail, 6" 540.00
Hat, Navy, brn & blk beaver w/gold tassel, fore & aft style, 1860s ... 180.00
Hat, visor, Army Senior officer, blk wool crown, gold eagle, 1930s .. 150.00
Helmet, M 1917, pnt metal w/sand finish, w/strap & liner 135.00
Holster, Civil War era, open-top Slim Jim style, brn leather 200.00
Jacket, artillery shell, Civil War, bl wool w/red, brass buttons, VG ..1,725.00
Jacket, Navy Academy, blk wool w/24 buttons, ca 1880 .... 120.00
Mess kit, Army, 27 enamelware pcs in wooden 14x18x14" case, 1940s .150.00
Photograph, officers row (houses) at Ft Hays KS, blk/wht, 1889, 5x10" ... 40.00
Pilot's wings, air gunner, pin-bk, sterling, WWII, 3" 50.00
Pilot's wings, bombardier, pin-bk, sterling, WWII, 3" 75.00
Pilot's wings, liaison, pin-bk, sterling, WWII, 3" 200.00
Pilot's wings, navigator, pin-bk, sterling, WWII, 3" 75.00
Pilot's wings, pin-bk, sterling, WWII, 3" 100.00
Pilot's wings, service, pin-bk, sterling, WWII, 3" 125.00
Pilot's wings, tech observer, pin-bk, sterling, WWII, 3" 150.00
Pilot's wings, US Navy aviator, pin-bk, sterling, WWII, 2¾" 100.00
Shako, 1858 Pattern, NY Militia brass plate, beaver skin/wool plume.... 350.00
Spurs, cavalry, Buermann US, metal w/leather straps, 5½x4", pr .132.00
Uniform, West Point Cadet, coat+pants, brass buttons, 1943, NM ...200.00

Imperial German

Badge, pilot's, 800 silver, mk Jasta 12, w/officer's name 1,080.00
Badge, silver airship w/in wreath, CE Juncker Berlin, 2½" W 575.00
Box, cartridge, eagle & X on leather flap, brass lion-head ends 85.00
Buckle, Gott Mitt Uns, brass, WWI era, w/brn leather belt........... 85.00
Coat, artillery officer's, bl wool w/red trim, gold braid, ca 1909........... 300.00
Helmet, Imperial Saxon, 17th Uhlan, w/brass chin strap, late 1800s . 1,100.00

Helmet, spike, Fusilier battalion officer's, silver death head 3,950.00
Helmet, spike, officer's, brass hdw, w/chin strap, WWI................. 385.00
Medal, Crown Order Cross, 2nd class, enamel/metal, 1861, rpl ribbon ... 400.00
Medal, Iron Cross, 1st class, enamel on silver, dtd 1914.................. 85.00
Medal, Iron Cross, 2nd class, 1813-70, w/combatant's ribbon 240.00
Medal, Order of Griffin, breast X w/red enamel inlay, pin-bk....... 900.00
Medal, Pour Le Merite Bl Max, J Godet & Sohn, ¾" dia, w/ribbon...1,100.00
Medal, Prince Regent Jubilee, dtd 1905, w/red & gr ribon 25.00

Japanese

Cap, Army IJA, yel star on khaki cloth, cloth bill, WWII era 200.00
Flag, red sun on wht silk, hemmed 3 sides, WWII era, 8¼x12½" ... 55.00
Flight suit, Army IJA, olive gr gabardine, WWII era, VG............. 150.00
Medal, Russo-Japanese War Military Service, bronze, 1904-05, w/bar...70.00

Medal, WWI, presented to soldier from China's Emperor upon completion of a mission, 1938, $90.00. (Photo courtesy Ransberger Auction on LiveAuctioneers.com)

Saddle, WWII officer's, 17" seat 210.00
Tunic, Army enlisted, gr w/Manchurian issue stampings................. 60.00

Third Reich

Badge, Luftwaffe Sea Battle, metal, J Godet Sohn Berlin, WWII era ... 360.00
Badge, NSFK, winged figure & swastika, bl enameling, 1938......... 80.00
Badge, Sniper, 3rd grade, eagle head/oak leaves on gr cloth......... 235.00
Badge, Tank Battle, eagle/swastika/tank, zinc, late issue................. 65.00
Barometer, U-boat, silvered dial w/Third Reich insg, 6" dia.......... 150.00
Book, With Hitler in West, photo book, soft cover, 1940, 130-pg ..175.00
Card, Horrors of War, Hitler making speech, #283, 1938, G........ 200.00
Flag, Hitler reserve/swastikas, blk/wht/red stripes, 1940s, 10x15".. 180.00
Hatpin, copper head w/silver swastika, 6⅞" L 60.00
Helmet, M35, steel body w/brn/blk camo, orig liner & chin strap ..400.00
Magazine, Adolph Hitler, His Life & Work, Dutch, 1940s, 30-pg . 25.00

Medal, inscription saluting Industry & Trade Chamber in Reichenberg on back, bright frosted silver finish, in 4" black leather case, $200.00. (Photo courtesy Regency-Superior LTD on LiveAuctioneers.com)

Medal, Knight's Cross of Iron Cross, silver & blk enamel, MIB .2,350.00
Medal, Mother's Cross, gold (mothers w/8 in military), 1940s, EXIB ... 100.00
Money box, book form w/facing cover pnt w/Party Drape.............. 80.00
Poster, Hitler portrait, Hitler the Liberator (Ukranian), 1938, 47x33". 1,450.00
Shorts, Sandfarbe, lt khaki cotton, button-closure pockets............ 70.00

Milk Glass

Milk glass is today's name for milk-white opaque glass. The early glassmaker's term was Opal Ware. Originally attempted in England in the eighteenth century with the intention of imitating china, milk glass was not commercially successful until the mid-1800s. Pieces produced in the U.S.A., England, and France during the 1870 – 1900 period are highly prized for their intricate detail and fiery, opalescent edges. For further information we recommend *Collector's Encyclopedia of Milk Glass* by Betty and Bill Newbound. (CE numbers in our listings refer to this publication.) Other highly recommended books are *The Milk Glass Book* by Frank Chiarenza and James Slater; Ferson's *Yesterday's Milk Glass Today*; Belknap's *Milk Glass*; and *Milk Glass Imperial Glass Corporation* by Myrna and Bob Garrison. Our advisor for this category is Rod Dockery; he is listed in the Directory under Texas. See also Animal Dishes with Covers; Bread Plates and Trays; Historical Glass; Westmoreland.

Key:
B — Belknap   G — Garrison
CE — Newbound   MGB — Milk Glass Book
F — Ferson

Bottle, eye opener flask, F-490, 5⅛" L 125.00
Bottle, Klondike, flask, B-238b 80.00
Bowl, candy, English Hobnail, ftd, WG, CE-96a, 5½x6" 35.00
Bowl, Lacy Dewdrop, Kemple, F-628 .... 20.00
Bowl, Rib & Scroll, w/lid, 4-ftd, Vallerysthal, CE-44, 6½x4½" 35.00
Box, cuff, Three Kittens, WG, CE-39b, 5½x4½" 75.00
Butter, plain melon, dtd, B-213a 55.00
Cake stand, sq, Indiana, CE-108, 6¾x10⅜" 15.00
Candlesticks, crucifix, G-1950/119, 9½" 80.00
Candy container, suitcase, Pat Apl'd For, F-566, 4" L 100.00
Candy dish, plain w/HP roses on lid, CE-45, 6½" ia 25.00
Compote, Atlas Scalloped, B-103, 8¼x8¼" dia 85.00
Compote, Vinelf Fruit, G-1950/67, 8½" 40.00
Covered dish, Crown, MGB-169, 5¾x4⅝" 175.00
Covered dish, Picnic Basket, WG, CE-167, 5" 50.00
Covered dish, Pie Wagon, Estab 1873, G-1950/377 .... 200.00
Creamer, blackberry, Kemple, F-627 .... 25.00
Figurine, deer standing, Fostoria, CE-195, 4¾" 50.00
Jar, fruit, owl, w/eagle insert, F-510, 6¼" 125.00
Jar, honey, beehive form, 4-ftd, Vallerysthal, CE-55, 5½" 100.00
Jar, mustard, Tyrolean Beass, WG, CE-190, 4⅛" 125.00
Lamp, cat, MGB-233, maximum dia 5½", 3¼" to collar 325.00
Lamp, peacock feather, G-201, 14" 80.00
Matchholder, butterfly hanging, Alpha, MGB-380a, 3½x4⅛" 125.00
Novelty, holy water font, Pat Appl for, MGB-254b 75.00
Novelty, telephone pole insulator, USA, MGB-263 .... 55.00
Pitcher, 3 birds on branch, gold trim, CE-320 .... 125.00
Pitcher, Water Lily, Fenton, CE-319, 7" 70.00
Pitcher, windmill, 1-pg, G-1950/240 .... 30.00
Plate, dog & cats, B-20d, 6" 125.00
Plate, McKinley-Roosevelt, F-540, 8¼" 250.00

Plate, Watermelon Eater, embossed Pat Ap'l'd for/M, James J. Murray & Co., circa 1905, 6x7", MGB 200, $1,000.00. (Photo courtesy Green Valley Auctions on LiveAuctioneers.com)

Plate, Wyoming monument, Pat Sept 8, '03, F-418 .... 85.00
Salt, open, flying fish, F-388, 4⅝" 60.00
Shaker, salt, snow woman, G-1950/266 .... 30.00
Sugar bowl, Cow & Wheat, CE-295a, 3⅛x4⅞" 80.00

Sugar, Roman Cross, F-238 .... 55.00
Sugar, the Family, F-268 .... 400.00
Toothpick holder, horseshoe & clover, F-186, 2⅜" 35.00
Toothpick holder, rabbit, MGB-321b, 2¼x2¼" 90.00
Tray, lady at well, F-391, 10¼" 100.00

Millefiori Glass

Millefiori was a type of art glass first produced during the 1800s. Literally the term means 'thousand flowers,' an accurate description of its appearance. Canes, fused bundles of multicolored glass threads such as are often used in paperweights were cut into small cross sections, arranged in the desired pattern, refired, and shaped into articles such as cruets, lamps, and novelty items. It is still being produced, and many examples found on the market today are fairly recent in manufacture. See also Paperweights.

Inkwell & stopper, pk/bl/lt bl/wht in clear, mallet form, 6½" 280.00
Lamp, bronze & porc circus performer w/mc ball shade atop ft, 25½" .. 1,875.00
Lamp, bronze bird beside mc ball shade, wht marble base, 7½" 300.00
Lamp, corset base w/mushroom shade, Murano, 20th C, 17" 450.00

Lamp, globular shade and bronze figure of a bird (7½") mounted on white marble base, $840.00. (Photo courtesy Antique Place on LiveAuctioneers.com)

Lamp, mc flowers, matching mushroom form shade & shaft, 21x10½" ... 530.00
Lamp, mini, gr/wht/lav floral on gr, ball shade, 9" 345.00
Lamp, wht floral in mc shapes, crystal prisms on mushroom shade, 18" . 800.00
Lamp, yel & pk floral in gr ovals on amethyst, w/o shade, 14x6½" ... 65.00
Vase, bulb body, lg appl ornate rim to waist hdls, 2½x2" 70.00
Vase, bulb body, swollen neck, flared rim, 6x4¼" 215.00
Vase, bulb body, wide flat rim, appl hdls, 6½x6¾" 115.00
Vase, jug form, gr/purple/burgundy/wht, w/hlds, 6" 275.00
Vase, trees (3) w/burgundy & wht flowers on clear, w/gold, 12½" ... 1,000.00

Miniature Paintings

Miniature works of art vary considerably in value depending on many criteria: as with any art form, those that are signed by or can be attributed to a well-known artist may command prices well into the thousands of dollars. Collectors find paintings of identifiable subjects especially interesting, as are those with props, such as a child with a vintage toy or a teddy bear or a soldier in uniform with his weapon at his side. Even if none of these factors come to bear, an example exhibiting fine details and skillful workmanship may bring an exceptional price. Of course, condition is important, and ornate or unusual frames also add value. When no medium is described, assume the work to be watercolor on ivory; if no signature is mentioned, assume them to be unsigned. When frame or case information follows the size, the size will pertain only to the painting itself; otherwise assume that the width of the frame is minimal and adds only nominally to the size.

Key: wc — watercolor

Bearded man, blk/wht on copper, sgn AG, 1900, oval, 4x3" 175.00
Boy in red jacket, brn curls, 1810s, gold pendant fr, 2⅝" 2,800.00

Children, one holding doll, in a portico setting with columns, drapery and tiled terrace floor, circa 1840, image: 5x4", VG, $7,200.00. (Photo courtesy Noel Barrett on LiveAuctioneers.com)

Garden of Love, lovers/cherubs, Beetz, 5⅜x4⅝", +ornate fr 850.00
Girl holds red book, dk bl dress, G- leather case, 3¼" 645.00
Girl in pk dress w/wht ruffle, 1810s, brass fr, easel bk, 2" 440.00
Girl, blk dress/wht collar, sgn AM/1828, on porc, 3x2½"+burl fr. 750.00
Girl, EX details, Fr enamel sgn Mulis, 6x6"+2-door leather case . 200.00
Girl, identified, pnt by ED Spritts(?), oval, 2x2½" 210.00
Hope, lady leaning on anchor, copper pendant case, 19th C, 1" ...1,000.00
Lady in bl dress holds bouquet, wc on laid paper, +8x6" fr 400.00
Lady in bl, gold necklace, identified, 1800s, lined case, 3" 235.00
Lady in red, flowers in dk hair, 1830s, gilt pendant fr, 1⅞" 880.00
Lady in wht before red drapery, 1810s, 3", +arched brass mt/fr..3,400.00
Lady in wht dress w/bl sash, ca 1795, brass pendant fr, 2" 880.00
Lady w/curls, lacy bodice, att Verstille, ca 1800, pendant fr, 2¼"...3,400.00
Lady w/gray hair, pk dress w/wht wrap, in 4" dia brass fr............... 350.00
Lady w/leg-o'-mutton sleeved dress, watercolor/ink on paper, 5x4"+fr.. 490.00
Lady w/long curls, flowing scarf, oil on paper, Richter, ivory fr 100.00
Lady w/lovely curls (identified), 3⅛x2¼", +gold pendant case..1,525.00
Lady w/wavy hair, striped bodice, orig foliate fr, 4¾" 235.00
Lady, child & servant, DJ Watkins/1842, 3⅜x2⅝", +mahog fr ..7,000.00
Madame de Pompadour after Boucher, 19th C, 4½", +gilt metal fr..1,000.00
Man in bl jacket/wht cravat, ca 1805, copper pendant fr, 2¾" 825.00
Man in blk formal wear w/gold pin, Boston, in lined case, 4¼x3¾" ...575.00
Man in blk jacket, att EG Malbone, ca 1800, brass pendant fr, 2¾".5,580.00
Man in blk jacket, wht shirt/cravat, 1790s, pendant fr, 2¾" 1,000.00
Man in blk jacket, wht shirt/tie, bust L, ca 1815, 2x1"+fr 945.00
Man in blk jacket/yel vest, hairwork border, 1810s, leather case, 3".... 4,115.00
Man w/beard, floral vest, blk jacket, brass case, 2¼x1⅞" 880.00
Man w/curls in blk jacket/wht cravat, ca 1805, gilt pendant fr, 2⅜"...1,050.00
Man w/dog in landscape, 1820s, 2¾", +molded wooden fr w/brass liner ..2,115.00
Man, blk in bl & red jacket, wc on paper, 1800s, 1"+brass fr 2,700.00
Mary Queen of Scots, ul Gifend (sic), 1880s, 3" L+gilt metal fr .. 530.00
Noblewoman in period dress, identified, sgn A Roi, 4x3" 285.00
Noblewoman, high-neck gown, wc on paper, 2¾"+gold-filled fr w/MOP .175.00
Noblewoman, powdered wig, sash/jewls, sgn Rosmanol, 4x3"...... 450.00
Noblewoman, rose in hair done in ringlets, wht lacy dress, 5½" fr ..230.00
Noblewoman, veil & pearls, sgn Girard, 6"+ivory & tortoise-shell fr ...300.00
Scholarly looking man in blk, wht shirt, on paper, 8", +wide fr ... 235.00
Theresa Queen of Prussia, well dressed lady w/gray hair, in case, 5" ...230.00
Women/children on ivory w/brass mts, 'To the Elysian Gate...'.. 2,400.00

Miniatures

There is some confusion as to what should be included in a listing of miniature collectibles. Some feel the only true miniature is the salesman's sample; other collectors consider certain small-scale children's toys to be appropriately referred to as miniatures, while yet others believe a miniature to be any small-scale item that gives evidence to the craftsmanship of its creator. For salesman's samples, see specific category; other types are listed below. See also Children's Things; Dollhouses.

Bandbox, wood w/wallpaper covering, oblong, 2¼x4x3½" 355.00
Bookcase secretary, Continental silver, 19th C, 3½" 540.00
Box, document, pine w/wire staple hinges, floral decor, drw, 5x7x4"... 700.00

Box, floral wallpaper covering, Am, 19th C, 2x2½x1⅞"........... 3,000.00
Bucket bench, bl pnt pine, bootjack ft, 19th C, 2⅜x9⅝x1½" 295.00
Bucket, staved, brass bands, wire bail, E Murdock...Mass, 3¾"..... 800.00
Cabinet, mahog Sheraton w/inlay, crest/dbl doors/4 drw/Fr ft, 19x11". 2,100.00
Chest over drw w/geometric inlay, hinged lid, glass pulls, 8x12x6" ..1,300.00
Chest, 6-brd, old gr pnt, leather hinges, 1816, 4x4¾x2½"........... 600.00
Chest, mahog Chpndl style, 4 grad drw, bracket ft, 8x7x5".......1,300.00
Chest, mahog, molded top, 2 short drw over 3 grad drw, 1900s, 10x10".550.00
Chest, mahog/mahog flame vnr w/2 dvtl drws, rprs/rpl, 8⅜x9¾x5".. 800.00
Chest, pine Fed w/cvg & inlay, 2 short/2 L drw, rfn, 1830s, 14x14" ...1,650.00
Chest, walnut/curly walnut Emp, 1 lg drw:3 grad drw, 26x22x12".. 1,900.00
Compote, wirework w/stone fruit (13 pcs), 4⅞x3½" dia 645.00
Cupboard, cornice, 2 doors, pnt shelves, NE, 19th C, 18x17x5".. 475.00
Firkin, pine staves, maple lapped hoops, MA, 19th C, 2½".......... 440.00
Footstool, pnt pine, shaped skirt/legs, stenciling, 19th C, 3x6x3" ..1,060.00
Hutch, walnut/poplar, cornice/5 drw/shelf/3 short drw/2 doors, 23"..1,100.00
Jug, stoneware, cobalt flower on salt glaze, 19th C, 3⅛" 880.00
Stand, dressing, mahog, shaped bkbrd, 2 short/1 long drw, 10x16x8". 1,500.00

Minton

Thomas Minton established his firm in 1793 at Stoke-on-Trent and within a few years began producing earthenware with blue-printed patterns similar to the ware he had learned to decorate while employed by the Caughley Porcelain Factory. The Willow pattern was one of his most popular. Neither this nor the porcelain made from 1798 to 1805 was marked (except for an occasional number series), making identification often impossible.

After 1805 until about 1816, fine tea services, beehive-shaped honey pots, trays, etc., were hand decorated with florals, landscapes, Imari-type designs, and neoclassic devices. These were often marked with crossed 'Ls.' It was Minton that invented the acid gold process of decorating (1863), which is now used by a number of different companies. From 1816 until 1823, no porcelain was made. Through the 1920s and 1930s, the ornamental wares with colorful decoration of applied fruits and florals and figurines in both bisque and enamel were usually left unmarked. As a result, they have been erroneously attributed to other potters. Some of the ware that was marked bears a deliberate imitation of Meissen's crossed swords. From the late '20s through the '40s, Minton made a molded stoneware line (mugs, jugs, teapots, etc.) with florals or figures in high relief. These were marked with an embossed scroll with an 'M' in the bottom curve. Fine parian ware was made in the late 1840s, and in the 1850s Minton experimented with and perfected a line of quality majolica which they produced from 1860 until it was discontinued in 1908. Their slogan was 'Majolica for the Millions,' and for it they gained widespread recognition. Leadership of the firm was assumed by Minton's son Herbert sometime around the middle of the nineteenth century. Working hand in hand with Leon Arnoux, who was both a chemist and an artist, he managed to secure the company's financial future through constant, successful experimentation with both materials and decorating methods. During the Victorian era, M. L. Solon decorated pieces in the pate-sur-pate style, often signing his work; these examples are considered to be the finest of their type. After 1862 all wares were marked 'Minton' or 'Mintons,' with an impressed year cipher.

Many collectors today reassemble the lovely dinnerware patterns that have been made by Minton. Perhaps one of their most popular lines was Minton Rose, introduced in 1854. The company itself once counted 47 versions of this pattern being made by other potteries around the world. In addition to less expensive copies, elaborate hand-enameled pieces were also made by Aynsley, Crown Staffordshire, and Paragon China. Solando Ware (1937) and Byzantine Range (1938) were designed by John Wadsworth. Minton ceased all earthenware production in 1939.

See also Majolica; Parian Ware.

Bowl, centerpiece, gr w/latticework rim, radiant design center, 9x11"..400.00
Bowl, rim soup, Minton Rose, 7⅞"...35.00
Bowl, vegetable, oval, poly floral, 1891-1902, 9", $150 to............175.00
Charger, Asian bird & flowers on blk w/gold, 1872, 16½"............860.00
Charger, cows in stream & horses in field, 1875, 17"....................270.00
Charger, Minton Rose, 12"...70.00
Cup, mustache, Willow, gold trim, 1891-1902, $225 to...............250.00
Cup/saucer, Minton Rose, 2⅛", 3½"..30.00
Ewer, lady's portrait reserve on cobalt w/gold, Sutton, rpr, 9¼"...100.00
Figurine, child carrying basket (bolted to tray), gr & wht, 7½"....360.00
Figurine, parrot on tree stump, gr & yel, 14½"............................720.00
Garden seat, stylized flowers & foliage transfers, #2038, 19th C, 19".2,500.00
Jug, village view/foliage, gr transfer, 1890s, 8½x8½", NM............120.00
Mush set, mc floral, 1891-1903, $100 to......................................120.00
Pedestal, floral transfer on earthenware, ca 1884, 18¼"................360.00
Plate, lady w/draped hair covering, ca 1890, 11¾"......................360.00

Plate, Minton Rose, circa 1920s, 10", $25.00 to $30.00. (Photo courtesy Skinner Auctioneers and Appraisers of Antiques and Fine Art)

Plate, oyster, Flow Blue Delft, 1873-91, $250 to............................300.00
Plate, rtcl, Bamboo & Fan, 1875, $150 to....................................175.00
Serving dish, Florentine in orange & gray, rect, 1862, 9½", $200 to...250.00
Vase, bright yel, bulb, shouldered, 14"..75.00
Vase, malachite slip on brn w/yel band, waisted, 10"....................215.00
Vase, turq runs on bl on tan mottle w/gilt foil underglaze, 1880s, 7"..475.00
Vase, Willow in Flow Blue, cylinder, ftd, ca 1875, 7½", $350 to..400.00
Vase, Willow, canteen shape, ca 1873, 7", $425 to.......................475.00

Mirrors

The first mirrors were made in England in the thirteenth century of very thin glass backed with lead. Reverse-painted glass mirrors were made in this country as early as the late 1700s and remained popular throughout the next century. The simple hand-painted panel was separated from the mirrored section by a narrow slat, and the frame was either the dark-finished Federal style or the more elegant, often-gilded Sheraton.

Mirrors changed with the style of other furnishings; but whatever type you purchase, as long as the glass sections remain solid, even broken or flaking mirrors are more valued than replaced glass. Careful resilvering is acceptable if excessive deterioration has taken place. In the listings that follow, items are from the nineteenth century unless noted otherwise. The term 'style' (example: Federal style) is used to indicate a mirror reminiscent of but made well after the period indicated. Obviously these retro styles will be valued much lower than their original counterparts. The overall downturn in the US economy has caused, and will continue to cause, values to decline or hold relatively steady. The high-quality or unusual items could see minor increases. Additionally, as with most other items in antiques and collectibles, the influence of online trading is greatly affecting prices. Many items once considered difficult to locate are now readily available on the internet. Our advisor for this category is Michael Hinton; he is listed in the Directory under Pennsylvania.

Bull's-eye, reeded fr w/close spherules, blk pnt liner, convex, 22" . 585.00
Cheval, mahog Am Late Fed in Gothic style, 1830s, 70x37x22"..5,200.00
Cheval, mahog Fed, ogee fr, tapered uprights, trestle legs, 73x34x24"..2,950.00
Courting, pine w/mc crest, pnt on gesso, pendant at bottom, 19x10"..485.00
Gilt Baroque style, pomegranates crest, acanthus leaves, 45x33x7".3,525.00
Gilt Chpndl, much cvg, 2 brass swing-arm candleholders, 54x26".5,500.00
Gilt Fed w/cove-molded cornice, rvpt panels, rpl mirror, 40x22".865.00
Gilt gesso w/eagle & cornucopia crest, rstr gilt, 24x27"................600.00
Giltwood Fed, broken pediment/acorn drops/sunflower, 46x31x3"..2,950.00
Giltwood Fed, ropework w/fruit/nuts/leaves crest, bow below, 36x20" . 1,175.00
Giltwood Fed, rvpt Lady Liberty at Washington's tomb, 42x24"...2,100.00
Giltwood Fed, rvpt landscape reserve, rstr/rpl, 45x27"..............1,725.00
Giltwood Fed, rvpt portrait of DeWitt Clinton, 31x17"............3,450.00
Giltwood Fed, split baluster w/tulips/fleur-de-lis spandrels, 57x30"..2,300.00
Giltwood Louis XVI-style sunburst, cloud & cherub masks, 19th C, 23".1,400.00
Giltwood Rococo, pierced crest w/flower basket, 41x21".............650.00
Giltwood, eagle crest/pendant husk, wheat as candle arms, rnd, 44"..6,500.00
Giltwood, Georgian style, 48"...900.00
Giltwood, shell/scroll-cvd rtcl crest, 8-sided, 8-panel border, 47x33"..2,800.00

Glass, Venetian, opal with etched surrounds composed of overlapping leaves and flowers, gilded edges, cartouch with lion of St. Mark in crest, 45x32", $4,200.00. (Photo courtesy Neal Auction Company on LiveAuctioneers.com)

Mahog Chpndl style w/scrolled crests & bottom, rpt gold liner, 33x17"....250.00
Mahog Chpndl, rtcl acanthus crest, gold rpt liner, rpl mirror, 32x18"...500.00
Mahog English Chpndl, Prince of Wales crest, rprs, 32"..............250.00
Mahog Fed w/flame grpt, molded crest, rfn/rpl, 44⅝x21"............600.00
Mahog Fed, inlaid conch shell on crest, string inlay liner, 46x23" .5,000.00
Mahog Fr Neo-Classical, cornice/2 doors, sphinx busts/paw ft, 105"..3,815.00
Mahog ogee w/gilt outer fr & liner, 1920s, Buckley & Co, 49x24". 2,350.00
Mahog QA w/openwork crest, appl gesso ornaments, old finish, 27x13".430.00
Mahog/giltwood Chpndl, bird crest/gilt liner, 41x24"...............1,525.00
Mahog/giltwood Chpndl, scroll fr w/pierced crest, NE, 40x18".1,525.00
Overmantel, giltwood Fed, cornice/baluster fr w/rosettes/etc, 29x68"...600.00
Overmantel, giltwood Neo-Greco, anthemia/rosettes/etc, 1870s, 75x56". 2,700.00
Overmantel, giltwood/pnt Rococo style, courting scene in arch, 40x38"..400.00
Pier, Emp-style mahog, cast metal mts, 65x34½".........................450.00
Pier, giltwood Fed, molded fr, divided mirror plate, 72x36x3"...3,950.00
QA, shaped crest above molded fr, early surface, 12x11"...........1,500.00
Walnut Blk Forest, stag head/scrolled sides w/game, rnd mirror, 28x20"...2,115.00

Mocha

Mochaware is utilitarian pottery made principally in England (and to a lesser extent in France) between 1780 and 1840 on the then prevalent creamware and pearlware bodies. Initially, only those pieces decorated in the seaweed pattern were called 'Mocha,' while geometrically decorated pieces were referred to as 'Banded Creamware.' Other types of decorations were called 'Dipped Ware.' During the last 40 to 50 years the term 'Mocha' has been applied to the entire realm of 'industrialized slipware' — pottery decorated by the turner on his lathe using coggle wheels and slip cups. It was made in numerous patterns — Tree, Seaweed (or Dandelion), Rope (also called Earthworm or Loop), Cat's-eye, Tobacco Leaf, Lollypop (or Balloon), Marbled, Marbled and Combed,

Twig, Geometric (or Checkered), Banded, and slip decorations of rings, dots, flags, tulips, wavy lines, etc. It came into its own as a collectible in the latter half of the 1940s and has become increasingly popular as more and more people are exposed to the rich colorings and artistic appeal of its varied forms of abstract decoration. (Please note: Values hinge to a great extent on vivid coloration, intricacy of patterns, and unusual features.)

The collector should take care not to confuse the early pearlware and creamware Mocha with the later kitchen yellow ware, graniteware, and ironstone sporting Mocha-type decoration that was produced in America by such potters as J. Vodrey, George S. Harker, Edwin Bennett, and John Bell. This type was also produced in Scotland and Wales and was marketed well into the twentieth century.

Our values are prices realized at auction, where nearly every example was in exceptional condition. Unless a repair, damage, or another rating is included in the description, assume the item to be in NM condition.

Pitcher, three-color stripe and line decoration on cream, 6¾", $4,800.00. (Photo courtesy Pook & Pook, Inc. on LiveAuctioneers.com)

Bowl, Cat's-eye, 3-color on yel band w/blk stripes, 4x8½" 435.00
Bowl, Earthworm on rust, 3x6½" 660.00
Canister, Seaweed, dk brn on tan w/brn stripes, conical, 4½" ...2,350.00
Creamer, Cat's-eye (2 rows) on dk brn band, gr band, leaf hdl, 3½"...475.00
Creamer, Earthworm (dbl), pale bl bands, leaf hdl, 5" 500.00
Goblet, Tobacco Leaf, dk/med brn/wht, striped ft, 3⅞" 6,000.00
Jug, branches bracketed by Earthworm banding, G, 8" 3,500.00
Jug, Cat's-eye bands bracketing Earthworm & slip-trailed dmn bands, rpr hdl, 8½" .5,525.00
Jug, Cat's-eye in 2 rows on brn, tooled gr band, leaf hdl, 4" 480.00
Jug, Cat's-eye on brn band, bl & blk stripes, chip/flaw, 5" 425.00
Jug, Earthworm & Cat's-eye, 3-color on tan w/bl/blk stripes, 6" 480.00
Jug, Earthworm, coggled band top & bottom, foliate hdl, 6x3½" 5,280.00
Jug, feathered marbleing in brn/tan/wht, gr tooled rim, 5⅝" ...3,500.00
Jug, horizontal bl/blk/brn bands on wht, ear hdl, ovoid, 9" 1,200.00
Jug, marbleized gray & wht, wht hdl/spout, flakes, 4¾" 275.00
Jug, Seaweed, blk on gr w/tooled gr band, cream sz, 4½" 875.00
Jug, trailed & marbled slip, 9¾" 6,500.00
Mug, bl bands, gr & blk stripes, tooled blk bands, leaf hdl, 4" 400.00
Mug, blk/wht scallops, gr tooled bands, tan stripes, leaf hdl, 4"...........1,650.00
Mug, Cat's-eye, bl/wht/brn on brn, bl stripes, tooled rim, 5½" 1,325.00
Mug, Earthworm, 3-color on lt bl, brn/bl/tan stripes, leaf hdl, 5" 525.00
Mug, marbleized tan/brn/wht/gold, dk brn edges, leaf hdl, 4⅞"...........2,650.00
Mug, Seaweed, blk on brn, brn & bl stripes, prof rstr, 3¾" 850.00
Mug, wavy lines & stripes, 3¾" 2,350.00
Mustard pot, dmns & stripes, 3½" 2,585.00
Mustard, Cat's-eye & stripes, wht/pumpkin/brn, lid chips, 3½".4,250.00
Pepper pot, blk circles on wht, tan band, blk stripes, 4½" 1,175.00
Pepper pot, Earthworm, 3-color on gray, tooled gr band, 4¾" 2,400.00
Pepper pot, feathers, wht/umber/blk on tan, umber/gr stripes, 4"......... 3,000.00
Pepper pot, gr tooled band/brn stripes/blk checks, stain/flakes, 4" .. 1,450.00

Molds

Food molds have become popular as collectibles — not only for their value as antiques, but because they also revive childhood memo-

ries of elaborate ice cream Santas with candy trim or barley-sugar figurals adorning a Christmas tree. Ice cream molds were made of pewter and came in a variety of shapes and styles with most of the detail on the inside of the mold. Chocolate molds were made in a wider variety of shapes, showing more detail on the outside of the mold, making it more decorative to look at. They were usually made of tin or copper, then nickel-plated to keep them from tarnishing or rusting as well as for sanitary reasons. (Many chocolate molds have been recently reproduced. These include Christmas trees and Santa Claus figures as well as some forms of rabbits. They are imported from Europe and may affect the market.) Hard candy molds were usually metal, although primitive maple sugar molds (usually simple hearts, rabbits, and other animals) were carved from wood. Cake molds were made of cast iron or cast aluminum and were most common in the shape of a lamb, a rabbit, or Santa Claus.

Chocolate Molds

Angel emptying a cornucopia, hinged, 4x2¾" 50.00
Babies, 2 rows of 9 ea, 8¾x6" 150.00
Baby, nude, hands on tummy, w/clips, #5983, 6x3" 55.00
Bellboy (chubby), #13/#6, 2 clips, 6¾" 25.00
Bishop on horse, 2-pc, Walter #9950, Berlin, 6¾x6½" 130.00
Boy (newsboy look) w/hands in pockets, Germany, #17503, 1930s, 6¼"... 55.00
Boy w/hands on pockets, Germany, #17503, 1930s, 6¼" 65.00
Bride & Groom, hinged, 5¼x5" 150.00
Buck deer standing, 3-pc, #790, 7x7x5" 210.00
Bulldog sitting, Herman Walter, #8388, 5x5" 120.00
Bunny standing on bk legs w/basket on bk, 2-pc, #4170, 6x3" 70.00
Cat heads (5), Leilong/Paris #2112, 2¼x9x½" 75.00
Chick pulling bunny in egg wagon, 2-pc, Germany, #3055, 5¼x6¼"...65.00
Chicken, hinged 2-pc, #290 .... 70.00
Cigar, rolled tobacco look, 2-pc, w/clips, 2½x10" 42.00
Circus elephant w/ball, 2-pc, Metro Anvers, 5x4" 110.00

Easter egg with rabbits, German, $130.00. (Photo courtesy Philip Weiss Auctions on LiveAuctioneers.com)

Easter rabbits (5) in row, 12" L 70.00
Handgun, 2-pc, w/2 metal clamps, 5" 20.00
Heart w/roses, France #15880, 8x7" 45.00
Jockey on horse, 2-pc, 9½x13¾" 535.00
Lamb lying down, 8½x11x4" 130.00
Lambs (4), hinged, 4½x15½" 40.00
Lovebirds facing ea other on base, #40, 1920s, 2¾" 95.00
Peacock w/tail closed, Sommet, 1920-50, 11x11x3½" 270.00
Popeye, MIG #9034 stamp, 7½x3" 180.00
Rabbit (4) in fr, NY, 9x7" overall 145.00
Rabbit (mother) doing laundry, 6" 165.00
Rabbit (mother) pushing baby carriage, 6¼x5x1¾" 365.00
Rabbit sitting on haunches, 2-pc, #4602, 7" 145.00
Rabbit sitting, 9x6¼" 45.00
Rabbit standing over basket, Made in USA #248/6218, 12x10" 70.00
Rabbit standing upright, Anton/Dresden, #6322/4203, 5x3½" 65.00
Rabbit w/chick, TC Weygandt...Made in USA #8219, 10x6½"... 110.00
Rabbit, 2-pc, 5" 35.00

Rabbits (2) on motorcycle, Ges Gesch, #979, 5x5¾x2¼" 150.00
Rooster, Ges Gesch, 8" 50.00
Sailor w/beer mug, France, 6½x4" 120.00
Santa shoe, 2-pc, orig clamps, Austria, 1920s, 4x7x2" 135.00
Santa standing, #8003, 5x3¼" 45.00
Sedan, 4-pc w/clips, 7¼", VG 120.00
Squirrel on branch, 2 clips, 10½x10½" 540.00
St Nicholas, detailed, 2-pc, #2041, 4½" 55.00
Swan, 2-pc, Letang Fils #108 Rveille...Depose, 5" 65.00
Turkey standing, Eppelsheimer & Co, Pat #1948146, 1937, 4½x4" ... 300.00
Turkey strutting, 2-pc, w/clips, 4½x3" 85.00
Turkey w/removable tail, Eppelsheimer, #4922, lg 120.00
Watering cans (3), heavy CI or steel, #239, 1⅝x7" 40.00
Witch on broom, 2-pc, Weygandt, 5x3" 260.00
Witch on broom, detailed, hinged, 6x3¾" 70.00

Ice Cream Molds

Castle on hillside, 2-pc, unmk, 11" 2,300.00
Castle tower, 2-pc, 12¾" 1,100.00
Cornucopia & cherub, 6-part, 8 hinges, #128, 9x10" 835.00
Fleur-de-lis, hinged, E&Co NY, 4¾x4" 125.00
Frog on mushroom, S&Co, #180, 4x3½" 125.00
Hen sitting, S&Co, 4-pt, 9" 300.00
Log w/ax, 3¼x1½x5½" 150.00
Owl, detailed, hinged, #175 .... 38.00
Pansy, hinged, Schall & Co, #269, 3¾x4½" 130.00
Pumpkin, hinged, orig pin, E&Co, #309, open: 6½" W 60.00
Rabbits on either side of lg egg, w/metal brackets, 10x7½" 140.00
Santa blowing Merry Christmas in Gothic script, #646, 2¾x4" 85.00

Santa, E&C, circa 1900, 11", $425.00. (Photo courtesy Pook & Pook Inc. on LiveAuctioneers.com)

Ship sailing on waves, CC & Marque de Fabrique..., 12½x10½" . 780.00
Squirrel standing, E&Co, #676, 5½x3½" 200.00
Turtle, hinged, S&Co, ca 1900, 4½x3½" 80.00
Walnut, hinged lid, #27, 2½" 35.00
Watermelon w/slice removed, S&Co, 4-pt, 9½" L 420.00

Miscellaneous

Cast iron, hen sitting, #4103, 2-pc, 7x6½" 50.00
Cast iron, lamb, recumbent, head trn right, 2-pc, 8x3", $50 to 60.00
Copper, flower form, 1800s, 7½" 60.00
Copper, heart shape, hammered look, EX patina, ca 1950, 6½x6" . 60.00
Copper, roses & leaves, 6" dia 250.00
Copper/tin, emb fruit, Kreamer, 7" 30.00
Copper/tin, flower form w/heart-shaped leaves, heavy, 4½x9" 125.00
Copper/tin, flower form w/spade leaves along rim, 4½x8" 55.00
Copper/tin, lg thistle, hanging tab, rect, 6" L 110.00
Copper/tin, nautilus shell, 3½x5x3½" 50.00
Indian on horseback 40.00
Tin, artichokes form ring, ca 1900, 3½x7" 60.00
Tin, ear of corn, skirted, 1⅜x3½x2½" 35.00

Monmouth

The Monmouth Pottery Company was established in 1892 in Monmouth, Illinois. It was touted as the largest pottery in the world. Their primary products were utilitarian: stoneware crocks, churns, jugs, water coolers, etc. — in salt glaze, Bristol, spongeware, and Albany brown. In 1906 they were absorbed by a conglomerate called the Western Stoneware Company. Monmouth Pottery Co. became their #1 plant and until 1930 continued to produce stoneware marked with the Western Stoneware Company's maple leaf logo. Items marked 'Monmouth Pottery Co.' were made before 1906. Western Stoneware Co. introduced a line of artware in 1926. The name chosen for the artware was Monmouth Pottery. Some stamps and paper labels add ILL to the name. All the ware in this category was produced from 1892 through 1906 when the Monmouth Pottery Co. became part of the Western Stoneware Company and ceased to exist as the original entity.

Bowl, salt glazed, brn int, mk, 2-gal 200.00
Churn, #3, cobalt on salt glaze, 3-gal, 13" 250.00
Churn, #4, cobalt on salt glaze, 16½" 250.00
Churn, #5, cobalt on salt glaze, 5-gal 325.00
Churn, 2 Men in a Crock stencil, 5-gal 1,000.00
Churn, Bristol, Maple Leaf mk, 2-gal 250.00
Churn, cobalt on salt glaze, 6-gal 400.00
Churn, salt glaze, mini, 4" 1,200.00
Cooler, ice water, bl & wht spongeware, mini 1,500.00
Cooler, ice water, bl & wht spongeware, w/lid & spigot, 8-gal .. 1,500.00
Cow & calf, brn, Monmouth Pottery Co, mk 5,000.00
Crock, 2 Men in a Crock stencil, 10-gal 700.00
Crock, Bristol Monmouth Pottery Co, bl stencil, 1-qt 250.00
Crock, Bristol w/Albany slip int, 4-gal 85.00
Crock, Bristol w/Maple Leaf mk, 2½x3¼" 40.00
Crock, Bristol w/Maple Leaf mk, 2-gal 75.00
Crock, Bristol, 10-gal 100.00
Crock, Bristol, 20-gal 200.00
Crock, Bristol, 60-gal 2,000.00
Crock, Bristol, mini, 2½" 600.00
Crock, early dull Bristol w/cobalt stencil 300.00
Crock, salt glaze, Albany slip int, 3-gal 95.00
Crock, salt glaze, hand decor, mk, 2-gal 250.00
Crock, salt glaze, unmk, 2-gal 60.00
Crock, stencil, bl on dk brn Albany slip, 3-gal 400.00
Crock, stencil, bl on dk brn Albany slip, 6-gal 600.00
Dog, Monmouth Pottery Co, mk, Albany slip 8,000.00
Hen on nest, bl & wht spongeware 1,200.00
Jug, Bristol w/Albany slip top, mini, 2½" 500.00
Jug, Bristol, bl stencil (early rect), 5-gal 250.00
Jug, Bristol, Maple Leaf mk, 5-gal 200.00
Letterhead, 1898 letter 45.00
Pig, Bristol, mk Monmouth Pottery Co 1,500.00
Pig, brn, mk Monmouth Pottery Co 1,000.00
Pig, mk Monmouth Pottery Co. 1,000.00
Snuff or preserve jar, wax seal 350.00
Tobacco jar, monk, brn Albany slip 3,000.00
Vase, Arts & Crafts shoulder band, bl matt w/high gloss int, 16" . 240.00
Vase, floor, geometric design at shoulder, gr & bl, tapered w/inverted neck, 18" .. 150.00

Mont Joye

Mont Joye was a type of acid-cut French cameo glass produced by Cristallerie de Pantin in Paris around the turn of the century. It is accented by enamels. Our advisor for this category is Don Williams; he is listed in the Directory under Missouri.

Vases, gold and silver overlay with acorns and oak branches on green, with rare company mark and retailer's paper label, 25", pair $5,000.00. (Photo courtesy O'Gallerie on LiveAuctioneers.com)

Vase, acorns & leaves, gold & silver on dk gr, goblet form, 20"..2,500.00
Vase, enameled flowers on optic ribbed amethyst body, 4" 350.00
Vase, floral, gold on gr, gilt rim, 13" 880.00
Vase, floral/leaves, gold/gr on raisin, stick neck, 8" 660.00
Vase, hydrangeas, enamel w/gilt stems & leaves, scalloped rim, 6x3".. 685.00
Vase, irises, gold on textured frost, off-set hdls, 11" 800.00
Vase, mistletoe, gold on gr, bulb w/slim neck, gilt rim, 6" 465.00
Vase, peonies, pk/wht/gold stems on gr, 4-sided, appl gold rim, 12"..1,400.00
Vase, thistles, enamel & gold on cranberry, quadrefoil, 12½".......940.00
Vase, thistles, gold/bronze/pk on celery, stick neck, 26" 3,500.00

Moorcroft

William Moorcroft began to work for MacIntyre Potteries in 1897. At first he was the chief designer but very soon took over their newly created art pottery department. His first important design was the Aurelian Ware, part transfer and part hand painted. Very shortly thereafter, around the turn of the century, he developed his famous Florian Ware, with heavy slip, done in mostly blue and white. Since the early 1900s there has been a succession of designs, most of them very characteristic of the company. Moorcroft left MacIntyre in 1913 and went out on his own. He had already well established his name, having won prizes and gold medals at the St. Louis World's Fair as well as in Paris. In 1929 Queen Mary, who had been collecting his pottery, made him 'Potter to the Queen,' and the pottery was so stamped up until 1949. William Moorcroft died in 1945, and his son Walter ran the company until recent years. The factory is still in existence. They now produce different designs but continue to use the characteristic slipwork. Moorcroft pottery was sold abroad in Canada, the United States, Australia, and Europe as well as in specialty areas such as the island of Bermuda.

Moorcroft went through a 'Japanese' stage in the early teens with his lovely lustre glazes, Asian shapes, and decorations. During the mid-teens he began to produce his most popular Pomegranate Ware and Wisteria (often called 'Fruit'). Around that time he also designed the popular Pansy line as well as Leaves and Grapes. Soon he introduced a beautiful landscape series called variously Hazeldine, Moonlit Blue, Eventide, and Dawn. These wonderful designs along with Claremont (Mushrooms) seem to be the most sought after by collectors today. It would be possible to add many other designs to this list. During the 1920s and 1930s, Moorcroft became very interested in highly fired flambé (red) glazes. These could only be achieved through a very difficult procedure which he himself perfected in secret. He later passed the knowledge on to his son.

Dating of this pottery is done by knowledge of the designs, shapes, signatures, and marks on the bottom of each piece; an experienced person can usually narrow it down to a short time frame. Auction prices, eBay and LiveAuctioneers.com in particular, are rising sharply, especially for the pre-1935 designs of William Moorcroft, as items from that era attract the most collector interest. Prices in the listings below are for

pieces in mint condition unless noted otherwise; no reproductions are listed here. For more information, see Moorcroft Collectors' Club in the Clubs, Newsletters, and Websites section.

Bowl, Anemone on gr to cobalt, ftd, ca 1950, 3½x4¼" 180.00
Bowl, Blackberry & Leaf, sm ft, 7½".....................................600.00
Bowl, Claremont, mushrooms, Cobridge factory mk, ca 1914+, 3x8½" .1,950.00
Bowl, Clematis, shallow, MIE, 3" 50.00
Bowl, Eventide, landscape, incurvate rim, 1½x4¼" 120.00
Bowl, Freesia, floral, shallow, 1935, 12"..................................785.00
Bowl, Moonlit Bl, landscape, SP rim, ca 1925, 8⅜" 1,200.00
Bowl, Moonlit Bl, tree scene, 5x7".....................................2,840.00
Bowl, Pomegranate, sm ft, 5", NM 700.00
Bowl, Pomegranate, w/gr hdls, ca 1916, 4¼x11"........................1,300.00
Box, Clematis, Royal Warrant label, 9¼" dia 360.00
Box, Dawn, bl/gr/wht/rose, domed lid, 4x6¼" dia.....................2,350.00
Box, Moonlit Bl, McCutcheon's of NY, 5x4¼"..........................4,800.00
Candlestick, Claremont, flattened gourd shape, ca 1905, 7¼" 950.00
Compote, Clematis on cobalt, 14½"......................................200.00
Compote, Hibiscus on cobalt, slim stem, 4½x8½" 250.00
Compote, Moonlit Bl, landscape, cobalt ft, 5½x7"......................2,650.00
Ginger jar, Hibiscus on gr, MIE, 6¼x5" 240.00
Humidor, Poppy, Liberty's Tudric pewter mts & lid, 6x5x5".......2,000.00
Jar, covered, Moonlit Bl, sgn gr ink, 10¾x7¼".......................7,200.00
Jug, Claremont, mushrooms, 2¾x4½".................................2,100.00
Lamp base, Leaf & Berry on flambé, 10½x5½"..........................1,000.00
Lamp base, Orchid, bronze mt, 15½"....................................450.00
Plate, Claremont on gr, gr ink sgn, 8½"..............................1,560.00
Tea set, Claremont on gr, 3-pc, gr ink sgn, teapot 10x6" 12,000.00
Teapot, forget-me-nots, bl on ivory w/gold trim, 4x6" 450.00
Trio, Orchid, 2½" cup+5½" saucer+6½" plate.............................550.00
Vase, Anemone on cobalt, shouldered, MIE, 8¼".......................395.00
Vase, Claremont, Made for Liberty & Co/#180/#1300, ca 1905, 5½"...850.00
Vase, Clematis on cobalt, baluster, 9¼"................................850.00
Vase, Clematis on cobalt, shouldered, sm burst bubble, 4x2½" 360.00
Vase, Cornflower, red on ochre, 1910-18, gr ink sgn, 6½x3" 2,500.00
Vase, Dawn, landscape, baluster, 1926-30, 4".........................1,325.00
Vase, Eventide, landscape, gourd, gr ink sgn, 6½x3¾"...............3,000.00
Vase, Eventide, landscape, shouldered, 6"...............................2,150.00

Vase, Florian, 10", $3,640.00. (Photo courtesy Brunk Auctions on LiveAuctioneers.com)

Vase, Florian, gr & gold, Nouveau shape, Macintyre, early 1900s, 9" . 1,600.00
Vase, Florian, peacock feathers, cobalt & wht, ftd, 6" 1,200.00
Vase, Florian, rose garland on wht, Macintyre, 7¾x6½"...............800.00
Vase, Hibiscus on gr, slightly bulb, MIE, 3½" 175.00
Vase, Moonlit Bl, landscape, bulb, bl ink sgn, 4¾x3" 2,160.00
Vase, Moonlit Bl, landscape, cylindrical, MIE, 11x6"..................3,900.00
Vase, Orchid on cobalt, bulb, ca 1930s, 11"............................950.00
Vase, Pansy on cobalt, flared rim, slim, 15" 7,350.00
Vase, Peacock Feather, gourd shape, 10½" 2,800.00
Vase, Pomegranate on indigo, tall, gr ink sgn, 15x7"..................3,360.00
Vase, Poppy on cobalt, trumpet neck, 6¼x4½" 785.00
Vase, Poppy, baluster, #65, 9½x5¼", pr 6,600.00
Vase, Wht Wisteria, baluster, M45, 3¾".................................575.00

Moravian Pottery and Tile Works

The Moravian Pottery and Tile Works, Doylestown, Pennsylvania, was founded by Dr. Henry Chapman Mercer in 1898. He discovered the art and science of tile making on his own, without training from the existing American or European tile industry. This, along with his diverse talents as an author, anthropologist, historian, and artist, led Dr. Mercer to create something unique. He approached tile design with an historic point of view, and he created totally new production methods that ultimately became widely accepted by manufacturers of handcrafted tile. The subject matter for the designs he preferred included nature and the arts, colonial tools and artifacts, storytelling, and medieval themes. Both of these 'new' approaches (to design and production) allowed Dr. Mercer to become extremely influential in the development of pottery and tile in the Arts & Crafts Movement in America.

After Mercer's death in 1930, the Tile Works was managed by Frank Swain until 1954. In 1967 it was purchased by the Bucks County Dept. of Parks & Recreation. Tiles are being produced there today in the handmade tradition of Mercer; they are marked with a conjoined MOR and dated. Collectors look for the early tiles (mostly pre-1940), the preponderance of which bear no backstamps. These tiles were made using both red and white clays and are also referred to as 'Mercer' tiles. Our advisor for this category is Suzanne Perrault; she is listed in the Directory under New Jersey.

Box, Swan & Tower, bl & ivory w/red clay showing, open, 3¾", EX .. 1,100.00
Canterbury Tales, series of 5: Knight/Prioress/Doctor/Wife of Bath/Merchant, 4"..450.00
Medallion, Autumn, MR, 16¾", $3,000 to 4,000.00
Medallion, bird on floral branch, 5-color, rstr, 17½" dia 6,000.00
Medallion, Silva Vocat, red bird on blooming branch, minor rstr, 17½" ..6,000.00
Plaque, Socrates, gr & ivory, 15½x10¼", EX 3,650.00
Tile, Justice w/sword & scale, tan/bl, unmk, 7x8", NM 1,600.00
Tile, Persian Anetlope, ivory & bl w/red clay showing, 7x6" 600.00
Wall sconces, 2 rnd reserves on ea w/bird, gr/ivory, unmk, 11x4", pr... 770.00
Wall sconces, 2 sq reserves ea w/ship, ivory/bl, unmk, 11x4", NM, pr..725.00
Wall sconces, birds & fleur-de-lis, gr/ivory on red clay, 11", EX, pr ..280.00

Matt Morgan

From 1883 to 1885, the Matt Morgan Art Pottery of Cincinnati, Ohio, produced fine artware, some of which resembled the pottery of the Moors with intense colors and gold accents. Some of the later wares were very similar to those of Rookwood, due to the fact that several Rookwood artists were also associated with the Morgan pottery. Some examples were marked with a paper label, others were either a two- or three-line impression: 'Matt Morgan Art Pottery Co.,' with 'Cin. O.' sometimes added.

Bowl, sparrows & bamboo, blk on pumpkin w/gold, globular, ball ft, 6".375.00
Charger, pr lg wht cranes on brn/rust, att, 17" 3,000.00
Charger, yel finch on branch, Limoges style, wide gold rim, 16"....1,000.00
Vase, bamboo shoots/sparrows on lt to dk gr w/gilt rim, bulb, 8"..360.00

Vase, bees and wild roses on smear glaze accented with gold by Nicholas Joseph Hirschfeld, rare paper label, signed, 14", $1,680.00. (Photo courtesy Cincinnati Art Galleries, LLC on LiveAuctioneers.com)

Vase, butterfly & floral, pk & gr on yel, gold accents, hdls, 5¼"...315.00
Vase, floral/butterfly, pk/gr on yel w/gilt, shoulder hdls, 5", NM...300.00
Vase, marsh bird in underbrush, gr on rust, scrolled hdls, #281, 10".1,250.00

Morgantown Glass

Incorporated in 1899, the Morgantown Glass Works experienced many name changes over the years. Today 'Morgantown Glass' is a generic term used to identify all glass produced at this single factory. Purchased by Fostoria in 1965, the factory closed in 1971.

Golf Ball is the most recognized design with crosshatched bumps equally distributed along the stem (similar to Cambridge #1066, identified with alternating lines of dimples between rows of crosshatching). For further information we also recommend *Elegant Glassware of the Depression Era* by Cathy and Gene Florence (Collector Books).

Adonis etch, gr & crystal, tumbler, ftd, 7½" 25.00
American Beauty etch, crystal, tumbler, 7" 20.00
American Modern, Russel Wright, granite, iced tea 22.00
American Modern, Russel Wright, seafoam, sherbet 20.00
Bowl, console, Stiegel gr w/crystal Italian ft, 12" 400.00
Candleholder, gypsy fire, #82 Cosmopolitan, slant top 26.00
Carlton etch, punch bowl, #21 Dominion, 12" 650.00
Chanticleer, amethyst, cocktail 16.00
Decor blk, vase, #9902, slant top 15.00
Decor pineapple, vase, #9902, slant top 20.00
Electra, Anna Rose & gr, vase, 2 hdls, ftd, 10" 350.00
El Mexicano, milky opaque, ice tub, #1933, 6" dia 80.00
Freeform bowl, cobalt & crystal 45.00
Golf Ball, cobalt bl, goblet 40.00
Golf Ball, pk, goblet 16.00
Golf Ball, ruby, candy w/lid, ftd 260.00
Golf Ball, ruby, sherbet 15.00
Golf Ball, ruby, wine 22.00

Golf Ball, Spanish Red, water goblet, 6¾", $25.00. (Photo courtesy Burchard Galleries Inc. on LiveAuctioneers.com)

Golf Ball, Stiegel gr, goblet 35.00
Golf Ball, Stiegel gr, iced tea 28.00
Jupiter, jade gr, vase, #71, 6" 180.00
Knickerbocker Top Hat, gr, cockatil 85.00
Lamp, hurricane, peacock bl, #9923, 2-pc 60.00
Lexington etch, cobalt filament stem, goblet #7673, 6½" 40.00
Mayfair etch, crystal, champagne/sherbet 6.00
Mayfair etch, crystal, water goblet, #7668 .... 14.00
Mikado etch, crystal, tea, ftd 8.00
Moonscape, steel gray, candy, bowl & lid, #3003 .... 80.00
Mushroom, blk & wht, base w/lid, #1513, 11" 100.00
Queen Louise decor, crystal w/Anna Rose pk, water goblet 325.00
Sarnac etch, crystal, goblet, 8½" 28.00
Sarnac etch, crystal, wine, 6⅛" 24.00
Seville, nutmeg, vase, #1650, 5½" 18.00

Seville, pineapple, vase, #1650, 5½" 22.00
Sunrise Medallion, bl, goblet, 8" 60.00
Sunrise Medallion, bl, sherbet 18.00
Sunrise Medallion, crystal, sherbet 12.00
Tinkerbell, azure, champagne/sherbet 75.00
Tinkerbell, gr, vase, ftd, 10" 210.00
Tinkerbell, pk, vase, ftd, 10" 180.00

Mortens Studios

Oscar Mortens was already established as a fine sculptural artist when he left his native Sweden to take up residency in Arizona. During the 1940s he developed a line of detailed animal figures which were distributed through the Mortens Studios, a firm he co-founded with Gunnar Thelin. Thelin hired and trained artists to produce Mortens' line, which he called Royal Designs. More than 200 dogs were modeled and over 100 horses. Cats and wild animals such as elephants, panthers, deer, and elk were made, but on a much smaller scale. Bookends with sculptured dog heads were shown in their catalogs, and collectors report finding wall plaques on rare occasions. The material they used was a plaster-type composition with wires embedded to support the weight. Examples were marked 'Copyright by the Mortens Studio,' either in ink or decal. Watch for flaking, cracks, and separations. Crazing seems to be present in some degree in many examples. When no condition is indicated, the items listed below are assumed to be in near-mint condition, allowing for minor crazing.

Borzoi standing, dk brn & wht, 6½x7" 80.00
Boxer female standing, brn & wht, 5½x6" 90.00
Boxer pup, head down on front legs, tail up, 2½x4" 55.00
Boxer scratching, brn/wht/blk, 3x4" 50.00
Bulldog standing, brn & tan, chip on face, 4½x6" 42.00
Chihuahua seated, 3½" 65.00
Chihuahua, standing, brn, 3x4", hard to find 45.00
Collie pup sitting, 3¼x3½" 35.00
Doberman, recumbent, blk & tan, 4½x7½" 32.00
Doberman, standing, blk & tan, 7¼x8½" 50.00

Fox terrier pup, sitting, yawning, tongue out, paper label, $35.00.

German shepherd pup seated w/head up, brn tones, 3½x2¼" 50.00
German shepherd rolling, 2x3¾" 80.00
Labrador standing, blk, 5x6" 45.00
Pekingese standing, lt brn, 3x4½" 65.00
Pointer puppy, recumbent, 4" L 50.00
Poodle standing, tan, 5x6" 22.00
Springer spaniel, recumbent, brn & wht, 2¼x5¼", $45 to 60.00
St Bernard standing, tan & wht, tongue out, 7x8", $70 to 95.00

Morton Pottery

Six potteries operated in Morton, Illinois, at various times from 1877 to 1976. Each traced its origin to six brothers who immigrated to America to avoid military service in Germany. The Rapp brothers es-

tablished their first pottery near clay deposits on the south side of town where they made field tile and bricks. Within a few years, they branched out to include utility wares such as jugs, bowls, jars, and pitchers. During the 90 years of pottery operations in Morton, the original factory was expanded by some of the sons and nephews of the Rapps. Other family members started their own potteries where artware, gift-store items, and special-order goods were produced. The Cliftwood Art Pottery and the Morton Pottery Company had showrooms in Chicago and New York City during the 1930s. All of Morton's potteries were relatively short-lived operations with the Morton Pottery Company being the last to shut down on September 8, 1976. For a more thorough study of the subject, we recommend *Morton Potteries: 99 Years* and *Morton Potteries: 99 Years, Vol. 2*, by Doris and Burdell Hall; their address can be found in the Directory under Illinois.

American Art Potteries (1947 – 1963)

Bottle, crown shape, yel/gray spray, 6" 24.00
Candleholders, tulip, pk/gray, 1¾", pr 24.00
Ewer, pk/blk, Norwood label, 6¾" 30.00
Figurine, Hampshire hog, blk/wht, 5½" 45.00
Figurine, hen, 6½", & rooster, blk spray, 8", pr 50.00

Figurine, leaping fawn, brown and green, 6½", $24.00. (Photo courtesy Doris and Burdell Hall)

Figurine, zebra, 7" 50.00
Flower frog, frog, grn/wht, 2½" 20.00
Flower frog, turtle, grn/wht, 2" 20.00
Honey jug, platinum, 5½" 30.00
Tray, floral shape, pk/mauve, 5½" dia 25.00
TV lamp, Afghan hounds, blk, 15" 75.00
TV lamp, leaping stallion, brn/yel, 9" 50.00
Vase, bulb w/floral clusters, brn/yel, 12¾" 50.00
Vase, bulb, bl/pk, 3" 15.00
Vase, feathered cornucopia, pk/gray, 10½" 40.00
Vase, ruffled tulip, brn/pk/yel, 9" 30.00

Cliftwood Art Potteries, Inc. (1920 – 1940)

Bowl, deep bulb, bl/gray, 6" 24.00
Bowl, shallow flower, cobalt, 10" 40.00
Bowl, sq w/lid, gr/yel drip over wht, 6" 50.00
Bowls, storage, 3 nested w/lids, pk/orchid drip over wht, set 60.00
Figurine, Am eagle, wht/brn/grn spray, 8½" 95.00
Figurine, cat, reclining, brn drip, 4½" 35.00
Figurine, cat, reclining, brn drip, 6½" 45.00
Figurine, cat, reclining, brn drip, 8½" 55.00
Figurine, cat, reclining, brn drip, 11" 70.00
Figurine, German shepherd, wht, 8" 50.00
Figurine, mini, lion, gold/brn, 4x1¾" 50.00
Figurine, mini, tiger, yel w/brn stripes, 4x1½" 55.00
Flower frog, disc, bl/wht drip, 5" 18.00
Flower frog, disc, old rose, 4" 16.00
Flower frog, frog, pk, 5½" 35.00

Flower frog, lily pad, brn drip, 6" 30.00
Flower frog, Lorilie, bl/mulberry drip, 6½" 75.00
Flower frog, turtle, bl/mulberry drip, 5½" 30.00
Jar, pretzels emb on brn drip, bbl shape, w/lid 65.00
Jug, wine, w/music box in base, brn drip, 9½" 150.00
Matchbox holder, pk/turq over wht, wall mt, 6¾x3½x4" 70.00
Tea set, old rose, matt, 6 pcs 100.00
Teapot, globe shape, bl/mulberry, 4-cup, w/ftd trivet, 7" 125.00
Vase, floor, yel/grn drip, hdld, 20" 200.00

Midwest Potteries, Inc. (1940 – 1944)

Figurine, Irish setter, hand decorated, 14k gold, 4x8", $35.00. (Photo courtesy Doris and Burdell Hall)

Ashtray, Hitler's HP face, rare, 7" 75.00
Figurine, cowboy astride bronco, blk/gold, 7½" 50.00
Figurine, leaping deer, wht w/gold decor, 12" 50.00
Figurine, mini, Kissing Rabbits, wht/gold, 1½" 30.00
Figurine, mini, monkey, seated, brn/wht, 2" 20.00
Figurine, mini, polar bear, wht, 1¾" 15.00
Figurine, mini, squirrel, brn/wht/yel, 2" 20.00
Figurine, nude, September Morn, gold, 11½" 125.00
Figurine, nude, September Morn, wht, 11½" 75.00
Figurine, race horse on base, brn, 7½x6½" 110.00
Figurine, sunfish, hand airbrushed decor, 11" 50.00
Planter, calico cat, bl/yel spatter, 8" 30.00
Planter, elephant, grn/yel drip, 5½x6¾" 25.00
Wall mask, African Ndebele w/neck rings, gold/blk, 8½" 75.00

Morton Pottery Company (1922 – 1976)

Ashtray, hexagon, bl, Nixon, 3½" 40.00
Ashtray, ovoid base, w/pheasant attached, 5" 25.00
Bank, acorn, brn, 4½" 24.00
Bank, figural, Hampshire hog, bl/wht, 5" 45.00
Bank, pig wall hanger, bl, 6" 40.00
Christmas lollipop tree, grn/wht, 9¼" 55.00
Christmas punch bowl, Santa head, red/wht, 16-cup 150.00
Cookie jar, figural hen w/chick finial, wht/bl, 8" 125.00
Cookie jar, figural turkey w/chick finial, brn, 9" 150.00
Creamer/sugar, figural hen/rooster, wht/blk, 4½" 45.00
Doll, pillow, upper torso, bl/wht/brn, 5¼" 24.00
Figurine, cat w/2 kittens, wht 35.00
Figurine, elephant w/GOP on side, 8½" 30.00
Figurine, Scottish terrier, wht/brn spray, 7" 20.00
Figurine, wren perched on stump, mc, 7" 20.00
Grass grower, comic strip character, Jiggs, bsk, 5" 30.00
Grass grower, WWII GI, bsk, 6¾" 25.00
Jug, milk, brn/grn spatter, 3-pt 75.00
Lamp, figural dog w/pheasant, blk/wht/brn/grn, 8¼" 125.00
Lamp, figural teddy bear, brn, wht, pk or bl, 8" 50.00
Lamp, kerosene, cylindrical base, wht, 10" 70.00
Planter, penguin beside igloo, wht/bl/blk, 2½" 15.00
Planter, St Louis, Busch Stadium & Arch, wht, 4¼" 18.00

Morton Pottery Works — Morton Earthenware Co. (1877 – 1917)

Baker, deep yel ware, 11" dia 90.00

Bank, acorn shape, cobalt bl, 3" 70.00
Bean pot, ind, Rockingham, brn, ½-pt 20.00
Bed pan, shovel shape, Rockingham, brn 45.00
Bowl, rice nappy, yel ware, fluted, 8" 80.00
Chamber pot, mini, yel ware, 1¾" 55.00
Coffeepot, ind, Rockingham, brn, ¾-pt 30.00
Coffeepot, mini, Rockingham, brn, 2¾" 75.00
Coffeepot, Rockingham, brn, 5-pt 125.00
Crock, Rockingham, brn, mk, 1-gal 50.00
Jardinere, grn, 7" 60.00
Jug, milk, cobalt bl, 3½-pt 85.00
Mug, coffee, Rockingham, brn, 1-pt 70.00
Paperweight, buffalo shape, Rockingham, brn, 3" 50.00
Pie baker, yel ware, 10" 100.00

Pitcher, jug type, tree trunk design, green glaze over yellow ware, 1¾-quart, $100.00. (Photo courtesy Doris and Burdell Hall)

Pitcher, mini, cobalt bl, 3¾" 75.00
Stein, beer, German motto, grn, rare color, 1-pt 85.00
Teapot, ind, yel ware, 1½-cup 50.00
Teapot, Rebecca at the Well, Rockingham, brn, 8½-pt 150.00
Teapot, restaurant, nesting cover pot, Rockingham, brn, 1-pt 50.00

Mosaic Tile

The Mosaic Tile Company was organized in 1894 in Zanesville, Ohio, by Herman Mueller and Karl Langenbeck, both of whom had years of previous experience in the industry. They developed a faster, less costly method of potting decorative tile, utilizing paper patterns rather than copper molds. By 1901 the company had grown and expanded with offices in many major cities. Faience tile was introduced in 1918, greatly increasing their volume of sales. They also made novelty ashtrays, figural boxes, bookends, etc., though not to any large extent. Until they closed during the 1960s, Mosaic used various marks that included the company name or their initials — 'MT' superimposed over 'Co.' in a circle.

Figurine, bear on base, blk, 6x9½" 300.00
Figurine, German shepherd sitting, tan, 9¼x8", $125 to 150.00
Paperweight, Abe Lincoln, wht cameo profile on bl, hexagon, 3".. 50.00
Pin tray, hunting dog on point, dk gr & gunmetal gray gloss, 5x8" ... 180.00
Pin tray, turtle figural, lt bl, 4½" L 30.00
Pin tray, wirehair terrier, blk & wht, 5½" 115.00
Tile, elephant on ball lettered MTC, 6" 4,800.00
Tile, ship sailing on waves, mc pastels, 6" 815.00
Tile, woodland landscape, mc pastels outlined in dk bl, 6" 625.00

Moser Glass

Ludwig Moser began his career as a struggling glass artist, catering to the rich who visited the famous Austrian health spas. His talent and popularity grew and in 1857 the first of his three studios opened in Karlsbad, Czechoslovakia. The styles developed there were entirely his own; no copies of other artists have ever been found. Some of his original designs include grapes with trailing vines, acorns and oak leaves, and richly enameled, deeply cut or carved floral pieces. Sometimes jewels were applied to the glass as well. Moser's animal scenes reflect his careful attention to detail. Famed for his birds in flight, he also designed stalking tigers and large, detailed elephants, all created in fine enameling.

Moser died in 1916, but the business was continued by his two sons who had been personally and carefully trained by their father. The Moser company bought the Meyr's Neffe Glassworks in 1922 and continued to produce quality glassware.

When identifying Moser, look for great clarity in the glass; deeply carved, continuous engravings; perfect coloration; finely applied enameling (often covered with thin gold leaf); and well-polished pontils. Our advisor for this category is Don Williams; he is listed in the Directory under Missouri. Items described below are enameled unless noted otherwise. If no color is mentioned in the line, the glass is clear.

Basket, cranberry w/tavern scene, ribbed, pinched rim, clear hdl, 8x5".. 125.00
Bowl, alexandrite, facted, flared to rim, 5x16" 1,400.00
Bowl, amber, mc floral & vines, appl rigaree at neck, 3½x3½" 65.00
Bowl, pk w/butterfly & bee, gold rigaree rim, partial label, 5¼" ... 800.00

Box, allover enameling, brass footed base, circa 1885, 4¾x4¼x2¾", $2,400.00. (Photo courtesy Dan Morphy Auctions LLC on LiveAuctioneers.com)

Box, cranberry, heavy mc floral w/gold leaves, rnd, 2" 280.00
Compote, cranberry cabochon panels (12) w/gold, scalloped rim/ft, 5x5". 250.00
Cracker jar, wht, earth-tone leaves & jewel acorns, gold lid & hdl, 8" . 400.00
Decanter, clear, emb gold band on body, gold rim, 11" 280.00
Ewer, bl w/allover scrolls/butterflies/bee, acanthus ft, 6½" 800.00
Ewer, bl, appl bird among mc leaves & branches, amber hdl, disk ft, 17". 10,500.00
Goblet, bowl w/floral heart medallions, flowers, wht beading, 7¾" . 935.00
Jar, gold w/pastel leaves & insects overall, ftd, 4" 940.00
Pitcher, amber, bl collar/appl drips/ hdl, floral branches, 9" 750.00
Pitcher, aqua, mc bugs/leaves/appl acorns, w/gold, clear hdl, 8½".. 1,625.00
Pitcher, bl w/leaves/birds/insects, bl opal rim/spout, amber hdl, 7" . 2,245.00
Pitcher, cranberry, heavy appl insect/foliage, clear hdl, cylinder, 6".... 750.00
Plate, floral cabachons (6) in clear, bl/gr/gold, gold rim, 12½" ..2,700.00
Tumbler, clear w/mc grape leaves/insects, appl grapes/stems, 4¾" . 275.00
Vase, African Safari, cameo, exotic animals & birds, sgn RW & LMK, 12" ..6,000.00
Vase, amber w/floral, bl drips/rim/ft (3), tree trunk form, 13", pr ...1,060.00
Vase, amber, eng mare & foal in woodland scene, spherical, 9½x10" . 2,500.00
Vase, amber, pheasant/floral, 4 bl hdls, wht beads/gilt trim, 12"... 190.00
Vase, bl w/mc overall floral, saw-tooth rim, amber ft, egg shape, 8"..1,200.00
Vase, clear gray w/jeweled fish (3) & floral, shouldered, 8½"........ 750.00
Vase, clear to orange, enameled yel/gold leaves & scrolls, slim, 10"...125.00
Vase, clear to purple, eng floral, sq, 10" 450.00
Vase, clear to violet, HP irises, cylindrical, ribbed int, 10" 600.00
Vase, clear w/eng birds & gold, quartrefoil, bulb bottom, 11" ... 1,000.00
Vase, dk amethyst, gold elephants & palm trees, gold bands, ovoid, 7"...1,200.00
Vase, floral & appl serpent, clear brn w/gold, 7½x4½" 940.00
Vase, floral, clear w/mc, shouldered, 10¼"..................................... 125.00
Vase, gr, pk & wht floral & scrolls w/gilt, slim neck, disk ft, 9" 90.00
Vase, peach cased, cloisonné-like floral, gold hdls, 5½" 1,375.00
Vase, rust, eng fish & sea foliage, globular, ca 1930, 7" 1,750.00
Wine, clear frost, w/gold leaves border & trim on rim & ft, 9".....250.00

Moss Rose

Moss Rose was a favorite dinnerware pattern of many Staffordshire and American potters of the mid-1800s. In America the Wheeling Pottery of West Virginia produced the ware in large quantities, and it became one of their bestsellers, remaining popular well into the 1890s. The pattern was colored by hand; this type is designated 'old' in our listings to distinguish it from the more modern Moss Rose design of the twentieth century, which we've also included. It's not hard to distinguish between the two. The later ware you'll recognize immediately, since the pattern is applied by decalcomania on stark white backgrounds. It has been made in Japan to a large extent, but companies in Germany and Bavaria have produced it as well. Today, there is more interest in the twentieth century items than in the older ware. In the listings that follow, when no manufacturer is given, assume that item to have been made in twentieth-century Japan.

Bowl, scalloped hdls & ft, oval, Rosenthal, 4x9¼x13⅝"............... 145.00
Bowl, shell shaped, gold rim, Royal Albert, 5".............................. 35.00
Bowl, soup, flat, bl trim, H&Co, 1880, 9" 35.00
Bowl, soup, scalloped rim, Haviland, 1950s, 7½", $12 to 15.00
Bowl, vegetable, ftd/hdld, w/lid, Haviland, 1950s, 7x11x8½", $60 to .. 85.00
Cake plate, emb scroll & gold rim, hdld, Rosenthal, 11x12½"....... 60.00
Coffeepot, emb rope decor, gold accents, Haviland, 1860s, 9" 240.00
Coffeepot, Pompadour, Rosenthal, 11" 150.00
Cup/saucer, gold trim, Japan, 2", 4½"... 30.00

Dish, reticulated rim, gold trim, Rosenthal, 8", $30.00 to $40.00. (Photo courtesy Point Pleasant Galleries on LiveAuctioneers.com)

Ginger jar, gold trim, Royal Albert 60.00
Gravy boat, gold trim, w/underplate, Royal Albert......................... 45.00
Nut dish w/4 nut cups 35.00
Plate, dinner, scalloped rim, gold trim, Rosenthal, 10".................. 32.00
Plate, sandwich, tab hdls, fluted edge, 10"................................... 50.00
Platter, gold trim, hdld, Japan, 8½x12" 30.00
Platter, oblong, Rosenthal, 6¾x14¼"... 50.00
Platter, Old Paris, HP, mid-19th C, 20"... 210.00
Platter, scalloped rim, gold trim, Royal Albert, 12x15" 90.00
Sauce dish, scalloped rim, gold trim, Haviland, 1950s, 5" 12.00
Saucer, sm scalloped rim, gold trim, Japan, 5½"............................ 10.00
Shakers, bulb bottom w/slim neck, sterling tops, Rosenthal, 5", pr..60.00
Shaving mug 35.00
Sugar shaker, 6x3".. 45.00
Tea set, stacking, cr/sug bowl set atop teapot 30.00
Teapot, Rosenthal, 7½"... 70.00
Tidbit, 2-tiered, Haviland, 1950s, 7½" & 5½"................................ 45.00
Tray, gold trim, Royal Albert, 6½x6"... 30.00
Tray, sandwich, tab hdld, sq, 6¾x11½".. 45.00
Tray, tab hdls, scalloped sides, Rosenthal, 8x13"........................... 40.00
Tray, tea, rtcl segments along rim, pierced hdls, Rosenthal, 11"..... 35.00
Tray, tiered 32.00
Tureen, w/lid, Pompadour, Rosenthal, 7¼x12" 110.00
Vase, bud, 3½".. 15.00
Vase, conical w/flared rim, Rosenthal, Sheffield Silver base, 8½". 145.00

Mother-of-Pearl Glass

Mother-of-Pearl glass was a type of mold-blown satin art glass popular during the last half of the nineteenth century. A patent for its manufacture was issued in 1886 to Frederick S. Shirley, and one of the companies who produced it was the Mt. Washington Glass Company of New Bedford, Massachusetts. Another was the English firm of Stevens and Williams. Its delicate patterns were developed by blowing the gather into a mold with inside projections that left an intaglio design on the surface of the glass, then sealing the first layer with a second, trapping air in the recesses. Most common are the Diamond Quilted, Raindrop, and Herringbone patterns. It was made in several soft colors, the most rare and valuable is rainbow — a blend of rose, light blue, yellow, and white. Occasionally it may be decorated with coralene, enameling, or gilt. Watch for twentieth-century reproductions, especially in the Diamond Quilted pattern. For more information we recommend *The Collector's Encyclopedia of American Art Glass* by John A. Shuman III. See also Coralene Glass; Stevens and Williams.

Bowl, Flower & Acorn, wht w/cranberry int, smooth rim, 2¾x9¾" ...725.00
Bowl, Herringbone, rose, chrysanthemums, gold trim, 5x10¾". 3,360.00
Bowl, Raindrop, canary yel w/bl int, pinched, ruffled, ftd, 4¾" 475.00
Bowl, Raindrop, cranberry to wht, 3 twig ft, 4½x6½" 500.00
Bowl, reeded wht w/bl int, ruffled rim w/clear edge, 4¼x11x8".... 375.00
Canister, Herringbone, bl, frosted ball finial, 8" 475.00
Creamer/sugar bowl, Coinspot, peach to caramel w/camphor hdls, 5" ...700.00
Ewer, Dmn Quilt, pk, melon ribbed, camphor hdl, Stevens & Wms, 12". 825.00
Ewer, Dmn Quilt, yel w/frosted thorn hdl, 13¼" 300.00
Ewer, Herringbone, rainbow, 3-lobe rim, frosted hdl, 6½", pr....... 690.00
Ewer, Herringbone, rainbow, ruffled rim, 9" 950.00
Lamp, Dmn Quilt, rainbow, crimped shade, w/burner, 10".........3,000.00
Pitcher, Dmn Quilt, bl, clear twig hdl, Patent, 8½" 1,800.00
Pitcher, Dmn Quilt, rainbow, cylindrical, frosted hdl, 5" 2,500.00
Pitcher, Herringbone, yel to wht, frosted hdl, 5¾"........................ 480.00
Pitcher, Raindrop, rainbow, triangular mouth, 10½" 575.00
Rose bowl, Dmn Quilt, bl w/wht int, 2¾" 25.00
Rose bowl, Dmn Quilt, rainbow, trefoil body, rigaree rim/3-ft, Pat, 4".. 1,550.00
Rose bowl, Peacock Eye, bl to gr over yel, HP floral, 5⅛"..........4,800.00
Sugar shaker, Dmn Quilt, butterscotch, rtcl metal dome lid, 6x5" ..260.00
Vase, Bridal Ribbon, wht w/4-fold rim, intaglio/gilt decor, 8" 520.00
Vase, bud, Dmn Quilt, rainbow neck, wht bulb base, 6"............... 725.00
Vase, Dmn Quilt, butterscotch, clear rigaree scalloped rim, 4" 140.00
Vase, Dmn Quilt, pk, stick neck, 7½".. 165.00
Vase, Dmn Quilt, rainbow, appl yel rim & ft, Patent, 4" 780.00
Vase, Dmn Quilt, rainbow, slightly waisted, 5" 700.00
Vase, Dmn Quilt, red to peach, stick neck, 11½"........................... 400.00
Vase, Dmn Quilt, scalloped/ruffled/pleated rim, 9½" 300.00

Vase, Herringbone, pk w/amber thorn hdls & rim, 10", NM..... 1,450.00
Vase, Raindrop, bl, folded rim, 5¾" 395.00
Vase, Raindrop, faint rainbow, ovoid, 12½" 350.00
Vase, Rays, pk & lav w/appl frosted rose & briar, ruffled rim, 13", NM. 785.00
Vase, Swirl, cranberry, bulb w/shaped neck, 7¼"........................... 360.00
Vase, Zipper w/swirls, apricot w/pk int, bulb, 5¾"..................... 1,000.00
Vase, Zipper, bl w/HP bird, frosted hdls, can neck, 7".................. 150.00

Mt. Washington Glass

The Mt. Washington Glass Works was founded in 1837 in South Boston, Massachusetts, but moved to New Bedford in 1869 after purchasing the facilities of the New Bedford Glass Company. Frederick S. Shirley became associated with the firm in 1874. Two years later the company reorganized and became known as the Mt. Washington Glass Company. In 1894 it merged with the Pairpoint Manufacturing Company, a small Brittania works nearby, but continued to conduct business under its own title until after the turn of the century. The combined plants were equipped with the most modern and varied machinery available and boasted a work force with experience and expertise rival to none in the art of blowing and cutting glass. In addition to their fine cut glass, they are recognized as the first American company to make cameo glass, an effect they achieved through acid-cutting methods. In 1885 Shirley was issued a patent to make Burmese, pale yellow glassware tinged with a delicate pink blush. Another patent issued in 1886 allowed them the rights to produce Rose Amber, or amberina, a transparent ware shading from ruby to amber. Pearl Satin Ware and Peachblow, so named for its resemblance to a rosy peach skin, were patented the same year. One of their most famous lines, Crown Milano, was introduced in 1893. It was an opal glass either free blown or pattern molded, tinted a delicate color and decorated with enameling and gilt. Royal Flemish was patented in 1894 and is considered the rarest of the Mt. Washington art glass lines. It was decorated with raised, gold-enameled lines dividing the surface of the ware in much the same way as lead lines divide a stained glass window. The sections were filled in with one or several transparent colors and further decorated in gold enamel with florals, foliage, beading, and medallions. For more information, see *Mt. Washington Art Glass* by Betty B. Sisk and *The Collector's Encyclopedia of American Art Glass* by John A. Shuman III (both published by Collector Books). See also Amberina Glass; Burmese; Coralene Glass; Cranberry Glass; Crown Milano Glass; Mother-of-Pearl Glass; Royal Flemish; Salt Shakers.

Shakers, Napoli, enameled Palmer Cox Brownies and gold trim on crackled ground, silver-plated cap, 3¼", $4,500.00. (Photo courtesy Dallas Auction Gallery on LiveAuctioneers.com)

Biscuit jar, daisies, gold on bl, melon ribs, SP lid & hdl 575.00
Biscuit jar, fern etch on amberina, SP lid & hdl mk MW, 7½x5". 475.00
Biscuit jar, floral on cream to opal, melon ribbed, metal mts, 6" W....175.00
Biscuit jar, floral on pnt Burmese, Albertine label, 10" w/hdl....... 835.00
Biscuit jar, pansies on wht satin, melon ribs, SP lid, 7¼" dia........ 400.00
Biscuit jar, Queen's, dotted floral, SP lid & hdl mk MW #4402, 7".. 475.00
Biscuit jar, spider mums reserve on gr, SP lid & hdl mk MW....... 250.00
Celery vase, wht swirled satin, ruffled, in #1303 Pairpoint fr, 11".. 425.00
Condiment set, Ribbed Pillar floral shakers+mustard, Pairpoint fr, 8" ..300.00
Cruet, Dmn Quilt, cranberry satin, 7¼" 120.00
Lamp, cameo griffins, pk on wht, etched pendant, brass mts........ 900.00
Shaker, Lying Egg, floral on bl to wht, 1¾", ea................................ 60.00

Vase, Diamond Quilted, shaded brown, 9", $250.00. (Photo courtesy Cincinnati Art Galleries, LLC on LiveAuctioneers.com)

Vase, Fern, cranberry, crimped rim, 5⅜".. 785.00
Vase, Flower & Acorn, canary yel, waisted, pinched top, 6½" 850.00
Vase, Herringbone, bl, stick neck w/emb ribs, 7½" 300.00

Shakers, Egg, floral sprays, pr 135.00
Shakers, Fig, floral, wht on bark-textured cranberry, pr 1,075.00
Shakers, Tomato, floral, 2½", pr. 150.00
Sugar shaker, Egg, forget-me-nots on bl to wht, 4¼" 120.00
Sugar shaker, Egg, oak leaves & acorns on yel to wht, 4½" 400.00
Sugar shaker, Fig, pk floral/gr leaves on yel 'bark,' 4" 240.00
Sugar shaker, floral panels, bulb, 3" 60.00
Sugar shaker, melon form, HP floral on wht, roughness on lid 125.00
Toothpick holder, allover floral on opal satin, onion form, 2¼" ... 375.00
Toothpick holder, Fig, floral, 1¾" 360.00
Toothpick holder, floral on ribbed satin custard, 2" 120.00
Tumbler, Lava, rare raspberry w/mc inclusions, gold outlines, 3". 6,000.00
Vase, gourd, Peachblow, Queen's Design, 8¼", $5,000 to 10,000.00
Vase, Lava, blk w/mc inclusions & gold, bulb, 3¾" 5,175.00
Vase, Napoli, spider mums/gold webbing, slim/ftd, #841, 18¼", EX ... 300.00

Movie Memorabilia

Movie memorabilia covers a broad range of collectibles, from books and magazines dealing with the industry in general to the various promotional materials which were distributed to arouse interest in a particular film. Many collectors specialize in a specific area — posters, pressbooks, stills, lobby cards, or souvenir programs (also referred to as premiere booklets). In the listings below, a one-sheet poster measures approximately 27x41", three-sheet: 41x81", and six-sheet: 81x81". Window cards measure 14x22". Lobby and title cards measure 11x14", while an insert poster is 36x14". Values are for examples in excellent condition unless noted otherwise. Our advisor for this category is Rick Toler; he is listed in the Directory under Oklahoma. See also Autographs; Cartoon Art; Paper Dolls; Personalities, Fact and Fiction; Rock 'n Roll Memorabilia; Sheet Music.

Insert, Country Girl, G Kelly/W Holden/B Crosby, 1954, VG+ 50.00
Insert, Harvey, J Stewart/J Hull, 1950, 36x14" 80.00
Insert, I Can Get It for You Wholesale, S Hayward, 36x14" 250.00
Insert, Our Man in Havana, A Guiness/N Coward, 1960 .... 35.00
Insert, Pennies From Heaven, S Martin, 1981 .... 30.00
Insert, Thirteen Ghosts, C Herbert/J Morrow, 1960, 36x14", NM ... 300.00
Lobby card set, Black Sunday, B Steel, 1961 .... 100.00
Lobby card, Adam's Rib, S Tracy/K Hepburn, 1949, NM 225.00
Lobby card, Ali Baba Goes to Town, E Cantor, 1937, NM 150.00
Lobby card, American Graffiti, R Howard, 1973, 1-sheet, NM.... 450.00
Lobby card, Brother Orchid, H Bogart/EG Robinson, 1940 .... 600.00
Lobby card, Bus Stop, M Monroe/D Murray, 1956 .... 125.00

Lobby card, Dracula, Bela Lugosi and Helen Chandler, Universal, 1951, 11x14", EX, $2,280.00. (Photo courtesy The Last Moving Picture Co. on LiveAuctioneers.com)

Lobby card, From Russia With Love, S Connery, 1970 reissue, NM .. 30.00
Lobby card, Hell in the Heavens, W Baxter, 1934, NM 90.00
Lobby card, High School Confidential, M Van Doren, 1958, NM. 70.00
Lobby card, Hound of the Baskervilles, B Rathbone, 1959 .... 325.00
Lobby card, Jumping Jacks, J Lewis, VG 35.00
Lobby card, Lolita, J Mason/S Lyon, 1962, EX+ 250.00
Lobby card, Reach for the Sky, K More, 1956, VG 60.00

Lobby card, Test Pilot, C Gable, 1938, NM 225.00
Lobby card, The Horse Soldiers, J Wayne, 1959 .... 75.00
Poster, Airport, D Martin/H Hayes/G Kennedy, 1970, 1-sheet, NM .. 125.00
Poster, Alamo (The), J Wayne/R Widmark, 1960, 1-sheet, NM.. 600.00
Poster, Alias Jesse James, B Hope, 1959, 1-sheet, VG 175.00
Poster, Alias Jesse James, B Hope, 1959, 3-sheet, VG 275.00
Poster, American Graffiti, R Howard, 1973, 1-sheet, NM............ 450.00
Poster, Apartment (The), J Lemmon/S McLain, 1960, ½-sheet, NM ..600.00
Poster, Apartment (The), J Lemmon/S McLain, 1960, 3-sheet, NM ...900.00
Poster, Bad News Bears, W Matthau/T O'Neal, 1976, 1-sheet, VG...125.00
Poster, Beach Blanket Bingo, F Avalon/A Funicello, 1965, 60x40", VG.300.00
Poster, Beatles Come to Town, 1963, 1-sheet (linenbk), NM ...1,500.00
Poster, Blonde Bait, B Michaels, 1956, 40x30", NM 750.00
Poster, Blue Max (The), Peppard/J Mason/U Andress, 1966, 1-sheet, NM..250.00
Poster, Bombs Over London, C Farrell, 1939, 1-sheet, NM 450.00
Poster, Butch Cassidy & Sundance Kid, 1969, 1-sheet (linen-bk), NM.850.00
Poster, Call Northside 777, J Stewart, 1948, 1-sheet 300.00
Poster, Casino Royale, D Craig as Bond, 2006, 1-sheet (dbl-sided), NM+ ..100.00
Poster, Charade, A Hepburn/C Grant, 1963, EX+ 750.00
Poster, Chitty Chitty Bang Bang, D Van Dyke, 1969, 1-sheet, NM...225.00
Poster, Cool & Crazy, S Marlowe/G Perreau, 1958, ½-sheet, NM. 350.00
Poster, Fargo, F McDormand/S Buscemi, 1996, 1-sheet, NM....... 150.00
Poster, Flight to Tangier, J Fontaine/J Palance, 1953, 1-sheet, NM .. 125.00
Poster, Flight to Tangier, J Fontaine/J Palance, 1953, 3-sheet, NM .. 175.00
Poster, Fool's Gold, W Boyd, 1946, 1-sheet, VG 175.00
Poster, For a Few Dollars More, C Eastwood, 1967, 1-sheet, NM . 900.00
Poster, Frankenstein, B Karloff, 1962 reissue, 1-sheet, NM 1,200.00
Poster, Giant, R Hudson/E Taylor, 1956, 1-sheet 510.00
Poster, Gimme Shelter, Rolling Stones, etc, 1971, 3-sheet, NM.. 900.00
Poster, Girl Crazy, J Garland/M Rooney, 1943, 1-sheet 1,200.00
Poster, Goldfinger, S Connery, 1964, 1-sheet (linen-bk), NM+ . 1,200.00
Poster, Goldfinger, S Connery, 1964, 1-sheet 650.00
Poster, Great Waldo Pepper, R Redford, 1975, 1-sheet, NM 75.00
Poster, Hawaii, J Andrews/M Von Sydow, 1966, 1-sheet, NM 35.00
Poster, High & the Mighty, J Wayne/C Trevor, 1954, 1-sheet, NM...750.00
Poster, High School Confidential, M Van Doren, 1958, 1-sheet, G...175.00
Poster, Hollywood Cowboy, G Parker/C Parker, 1937, 1-sheet, NM... 750.00
Poster, Hot Rod Rumble, L Snowden/B Halsey, 1958, 1-sheet, NM..900.00
Poster, Houdini, Tony Curtis & Janet Leigh, Paramount, 1953, prof restr, 22x28"..525.00
Poster, I Married a Witch, V Lake/F March, 1948 reissue, 3-sheet, VG.750.00
Poster, Jaws, R Schieder/R Shaw/R Dreyfuss, 1975, 1-sheet, NM . 475.00
Poster, Kelly's Heroes, C Eastwood/T Savalas, 1970, 1-sheet, EX+ .250.00
Poster, King Solomon's Mines, Kerr/Granger, 1962 reissue, 1-sheet........ 50.00
Poster, Konga, M Johns/C Gordon, 1961, 3-sheet, NM+ 750.00
Poster, Live & Let Die, R Moore, 1973, 1-sheet (linen-bk), NM. 450.00
Poster, Long Long Trailer, L Ball/D Arnez, 1954, 3-sheet, NM+.. 600.00
Poster, Lost Boys, J Patrick/K Sutherland, 1987, 1-sheet, EX+..... 150.00
Poster, Love Me Tender, Elvis, 1956, 1-sheet (linen-bk), NM ..1,200.00
Poster, Major Dundee, C Heston/R Harris, 1965, 1-sheet, EX+... 175.00
Poster, Mame, L Ball, 1974, 1-sheet, NM 35.00
Poster, Melody of the Plains, F Scott, 1937, 6-sheet, NM 2,500.00
Poster, Miracle Worker, P Duke/A Bancroft, 1962, ½-sheet, VG. 100.00
Poster, National Lampoon's Animal House, J Belushi, 1978, 1-sheet, NM...350.00
Poster, Night of Dark Shadows, D Selby/L Parker, 1971, 1-sheet, NM.150.00
Poster, North by Northwest, C Grant, 1966 reissue, 1-sheet, NM ...1,750.00
Poster, Not of This Earth, B Garland/P Birch, 1957, 3-sheet, NM. 1,750.00
Poster, On Her Majesty's Secret Service, 1970, 1-sheet 250.00
Poster, Pearl Harbor, B Afflack, 2001, 1-sheet, M 200.00
Poster, Planet Outlaws, B Crabbe, 1953, 1-sheet 360.00
Poster, Reach for the Sky, K More, 1956, 1-sheet, NM 500.00
Poster, Return of the Ape Man, B Lugosi/J Carradine, 1944, 1-sheet, NM...900.00
Poster, Shootist, J Wayne, 1976, 1-sheet, NM+ 275.00
Poster, Stardust on the Sage, Autry, 1942, 1-sheet (linen-bk), EX+ .375.00
Poster, Suddenly Last Summer, Taylor/Hepburn/Clift, 1960, 3-sheet......... 200.00

Poster, Take a Letter Darling, Russell/MacMurray, 1942, 3-sheet, NM. 275.00
Poster, The Noose Hangs High, Abbott & Costello, 1948, 1-sheet ...340.00
Poster, Thunderball, S Connery, 1965, 1-sheet (linen-bk), NM ...1,250.00
Poster, Thunderball, S Connery, 1965, 6-sheet, NM 2,100.00
Poster, Torn Curtain, P Newman/J Andrews, 1966, 3-sheet, EX+. 150.00
Poster, Twelve O'Clock High, G Peck, 1949, 1-sheet, VG........1,250.00
Poster, Twilight on Rio Grande, G Autry, 1947, 1-sheet (linen-bk), NM. 400.00
Poster, Two Mules for...Sarah, C Eastwood/S McLaine, 1970, 1-sheet, M ...175.00
Poster, Viva Cisco Kid, C Romero, 1940, 1-sheet, EX+ 250.00
Poster, War Wagon, J Wayne/K Douglas, 1967, 1-sheet, (linen-bk), NM. 350.00
Poster, Who Done It?, Abbott & Costello, 3-sheet 1,250.00
Poster, Winchester 73, J Stewart, 1950, 1-sheet (linen-bk), NM ..2,250.00
Poster, World at War, War Dept documentary, 1942, 1-sheet, VG .. 350.00
Pressbook, Konga, M Johns/C Gordon, 1961, 8-pg, EX+ 125.00
Title card, Peyton Place, L Turner, 1958 ....45.00
Window card, Ali Baba Goes to Town, E Cantor, 1937, 14x8", VG..175.00
Window card, Gone w/the Wind, C Gable/V Leigh, 1986 reissue, M..100.00
Window card, Shane, A Ladd, 1953, NM.......................................600.00

Mulberry China

Mulberry china was made by many of the Staffordshire area potters from about 1830 until the 1850s. It is a transfer-printed earthenware or ironstone named for the color of its decorations, a purplish-brown resembling the juice of the mulberry. Some pieces may have faded out over the years and today look almost gray with only a hint of purple. (Transfer printing was done in many colors; technically only those in the mauve tones are 'mulberry'; color variations have little effect on value.) Some of the patterns (Corean, Jeddo, Pelew, and Formosa, for instance) were also produced in Flow Blue ware. Others seem to have been used exclusively with the mulberry color. Our advisor for this category is Mary Frank Gaston.

Abbey, creamer 195.00
Abbey, pitcher, 8-sided, 7¼" 75.00

Abbey, platter, 15½", $500.00 to $600.00. (Photo courtesy Brunk Auctions on LiveAuctioneers.com)

Athens, cup... 45.00
Athens, pitcher, 6"... 85.00
Athens, plate, Adams & Sons, 7⅝"....................................... 70.00
Athens, plate, Adams, 10¼".. 100.00
Athens, sugar bowl, Adams, w/lid, EX 225.00
Beauties of China, bowl, Mellor Venables, 1x5⅛" 55.00
Beauties of China, undertray, Mellor Venables, 10x7¼"........ 150.00
Bochara, bowl, vegetable, w/lid 375.00
Bochara, platter, Edwards, 14" 200.00
Bryonia, c/s... 35.00
Calcutta, teapot 275.00
Castle Scenery, pitcher, 8" 425.00
Castle Scenery, sugar bowl, w/lid, Furnival 275.00
Corean, bowl & pitcher, NM 1,100.00
Corean, bowl, shallow, wide flange, Podmore Walker, 5¼" 75.00
Corean, pitcher, 1½-qt, 8¾" 475.00

Corean, plate, 8" 80.00
Corean, plate, Podmore Walker, 7⅝" 65.00
Corean, plate, Podmore Walker, 10" 75.00
Corean, sugar bowl, Clementson 375.00
Cyprus, plate, Davenport, 9¼".. 95.00
Cyprus, platter, Davenport, 16".. 300.00
Cyprus, teapot, Davenport, 8½".. 225.00
Foliage, bowl, serving, Edwards & Walley, w/lid, 7½x9".............. 425.00
Foliage, plate, 9"... 75.00
Foliage, platter, 11"... 190.00
Foliage, platter, A Walley, 15¼".. 300.00
Game, pitcher, 9", VG... 185.00
Heath's Flower, platter, 14"... 335.00
Hollins College, plate, Wedgwood, 10⅜"............................. 70.00
Jeddo, pitcher, Adams, 2-qt 435.00
Jeddo, plate, 14-panel, W Adams, 9¼"................................ 140.00
Jeddo, plate, Adams, 7½"... 75.00
Jeddo, teapot, Adams.. 475.00
Marble, creamer, 5½" 75.00
Medina, sugar bowl, Furnival... 195.00
Neva, cup, no hdl, Challinor.. 50.00
Panama, creamer, Challinor.. 245.00
Pelew, c/s, handleless, Challinor.. 75.00
Pelew, plate, Challinor, 8½"... 90.00
Pendant Flower, pitcher, Kaolin Ware, 12⅛" 265.00
Peruvian, c/s, handleless 70.00
Plate, center classical ruins, Pantheon, Ridgway & Murley, 9" 35.00
Pomerania, cup plate, Ridgway, 4"....................................... 110.00
Rhone Scenery, coffeepot, Podmore Walker........................ 400.00
Rhone Scenery, platter, Mayer, 18x14¼"............................ 425.00
Rhone Scenery, sauce tureen, w/underplate......................... 250.00
Shapoo, cup plate.. 65.00
Sydenham, creamer.. 130.00
Temple, plate, Podmore Walker, 9¾" 90.00
Vincennes, pitcher, water, John Alcock, 8½"....................... 325.00
Vincennes, relish.. 195.00
Washington Vase, creamer, Podmore Walker 250.00
Washington Vase, sugar pot, lion's head hdls....................... 240.00

Muller Freres Glass

Henri Muller established a factory in 1900 at Croismare, France. He produced fine cameo art glass decorated with florals, birds, and insects in the Art Nouveau style. The work was accomplished by acid engraving and hand finishing. Usual marks were 'Muller,' 'Muller Croismare,' or 'Croismare, Nancy.' In 1910 Henri and his brother Deseri formed a glassworks at Luneville. The cameo art glass made there was nearly all produced by acid cuttings of up to four layers with motifs similar to those favored at Croismare. A good range of colors was used, and some later pieces were gold flecked. Handles and decorative devices were sometimes applied by hand. In addition to the cameo glass, they also produced an acid-finished glass of bold mottled colors in the Deco style. Examples were signed 'Muller Freres' or 'Luneville.' Our advisor for this category is Don Williams; he is listed in the Directory under Missouri.

Cameo

Ewer, sailboat night scene, blk/bl on mottled orange/bl/cream, 17"....3,000.00
Vase, carnations, red & yel on polished mottled ground, 1900s, 17"... 3,125.00
Vase, floral, maroon/gr on frost, flared rim, 18"..........................3,500.00
Vase, floral, red/gr/yel on frost, ovoid, 7½"..............................1,200.00
Vase, lake scene w/storks, bl/gray/pk on frost, incurvate rim, 5". 1,200.00

Vase, lake scene, bl on frost, ca 1900, 2¼" 425.00
Vase, leaves, purple on gray-wht, shouldered, 2¾" 395.00
Vase, men raking field/sheep, red-brn/orange on yel, flared rim, 5½" ..850.00
Vase, moths perched on pine branch, 9½" 3,250.00
Vase, panthers/geometrics, bl on frost w/silver flecks, 9½" 4,200.00

Vase, roses and leaves, cut and painted, brown and orange on orange and yellow ground, 17x9", $4,200.00. (Photo courtesy Treadway Gallery on LiveAuctioneers.com)

Vase, trees & leaves, purple/gr on gray-bl, stick neck, 2½" 275.00
Vase, wisteria, 2 shades of bl on gray w/hints of gold & gr, 6" ...1,200.00
Vase, wisteria, gr/bl/cobalt on gray, ovoid, ca 1900, 14" 3,500.00

Miscellaneous

Bowl, Fr Bl/silver/yel mottle, 4-petal rim, 4x12½" 360.00
Chandelier, orange/bl mottled bowl & shades (3), wrought fr, 37x24" ..3,300.00
Chandelier, purple mottled bowl & shades (3), 4-lt, ca 1900, 35"....3,000.00
Vase, autumn leaves, etched/HP, stick neck, 28½" 3,350.00
Vase, hunters/dogs/boar, clear/frosted, ftd, 9x10¼" 2,000.00
Vase, lake scene/dragonflies, HP flattened form, 6½x3½", NM .2,100.00

Muncie

The Muncie Pottery was established in Muncie, Indiana, by Charles O. Grafton; it operated there from 1922 until about 1935. The pottery they produced is made of a heavier clay than most of its contemporaries; the styles are sturdy and simple. Early glazes were bright and colorful. In fact, Muncie was advertised as the 'rainbow pottery.' Later most of the ware was finished in a matt glaze. The more collectible examples are those modeled after Consolidated Glass vases — sculptured with love-birds, grasshoppers, and goldfish. Their line of Art Deco-style vases bear a remarkable resemblance to the Consolidated Glass Company's Ruba Rombic line. Vases, candlesticks, bookends, ashtrays, bowls, lamp bases, and luncheon sets were made. A line of garden pottery was manufactured for a short time. Items were frequently impressed with MUNCIE in block letters. Letters such as A, K, E, or D and the numbers 1, 2, 3, 4, or 5 often found scratched into the base are finishers' marks. In our listings the first number in the description is the shape number, taken from old company catalogs or found on examples of the company's pottery. (These numbers are preceded by a number sign.)

Bowl, console, gr on rose, #187, 4x12" L............................ 65.00
Bowl, Rombic, gr on rose, #306, 3x8¾"............................240.00
Candleholder, Spanish, Orange Peel, R Haley, #277, 2½x4", ea 80.00
Candlesticks, Peachskin, #149, 6", pr............................175.00
Lamp base, nude panels, gr on pk, #U33, hammered metal base, 23" .500.00
Lamp base, rose matt, Deco shape, #222, 8½x6¼" 145.00
Lamp bases, Dancing Nudes, #U33, 26" overall, pr 660.00
Vase, blk gunmetal, squat, #113, 3½x4½" 150.00
Vase, gr matt, rim-to-hip hdls, #143, 6⅞x6⅜" 165.00
Vase, gr on lilac, #442, 6¼x4¼" 80.00
Vase, gr on lilac, horizontal ribs, #460, 12x6" 250.00
Vase, gr on lilac, rim-to-hip hdls, #143, 6⅜x6" 80.00

Vase, gr on lilac, sm hdls at center of body, #463, 10⅛x5⅞".........215.00
Vase, gr on pumpkin, lobed body, #191, 8½x7¾" 120.00
Vase, gr on rose, corseted cylinder, 11".....................................275.00
Vase, gr on rose, ring hdls, #192, 9x9" 120.00
Vase, gr on rose, sm angular hdls, #182, 5½x8" 100.00
Vase, gr shading to lilac w/crystalline, #191, 6x4½" 60.00
Vase, gunmetal blk, ring hdls, #192, 6⅜x6⅛" 90.00
Vase, Peachskin, integral hdls, #143, 6½x6" 135.00
Vase, Rombic, gr on rose, #310, 4½" 475.00
Vase, Rombic, gr on rose, #312, 5" 550.00
Vase, Rombic, Peachskin, #302, 4" 600.00
Vase, Spanish 'Aorta,' gr on pumpkin, R Haley design, 4½" 325.00
Vase, Spanish, Orange Peel, 4-hdl, 6¾" 350.00
Vase, wht on bl, flared 4-scallop rim, #U8, 7⅜x6⅜" 110.00
Vase, wht on pk, wide shoulder, 7x7" 90.00

Musical Instruments

The field of automatic musical instruments covers many different categories ranging from watches and tiny seals concealing fine early musical movements to huge organs and orchestrions which weigh many hundreds of pounds and are equivalent to small orchestras. Music boxes, first made in the early nineteenth century by Swiss watchmakers, were produced in both disc and cylinder models. The latter type employs a cylinder with tiny pins that lift the teeth in the comb of the music box (producing a sound much like many individual tuning forks), and music results. The value of a cylinder music box depends on the length and diameter of the cylinder, the date of its manufacture, the number of tunes it plays (four or six is usually better than 10 or 12), whether it has multiple cylinders, if it has extra instruments (like bells, an organ, or drum), and its manufacturer. Nicole Freres, Henri Capt, LeCoultre, and Bremond are among the the most highly regarded, and the larger boxes made by Mermod Freres are also popular. Examples with multiple cylinders, extra instruments (such as bells or an organ section), and those in particularly ornate cabinets or with matching tables bring significantly higher prices. Early cylinder boxes were wound with a separate key which was inserted on the left side of the case. These early examples are known as 'key-wind' boxes and bring a premium. While smaller cylinder boxes are still being made, the larger ones (over 10" cylinders) typically date from before 1900. Disc music boxes were introduced about 1890 but were replaced by the phonograph only 25 years later. However, during that time hundreds of thousands were made. Their great advantage was in playing inexpensive interchangeable discs, a factor that remains an attraction for today's collector as well. Among the most popular disc boxes are those made by Regina (USA), Polyphon, Mira, Stella, and Symphonion. Relative values are determined by the size of the discs they play, whether they have single or double combs, if they are upright or table models, and how ornate their cases are. Especially valuable are those that play multiple discs at the same time or are incorporated into tall case clocks.

Player pianos were made in a wide variety of styles. Early varieties consisted of a mechanism which pushed up to a piano and played on the keyboard by means of felt-tipped fingers. These use 65-note rolls. Later models have the playing mechanism built in, and most use 88-note rolls. Upright pump player pianos have little value in unrestored condition because the cost of restoration is so high. 'Reproducing' pianos, especially the 'grand' format, can be quite valuable, depending on the make, the size, the condition, and the ornateness of the case; however the market for 'reproducing' grand pianos has been very weak in recent years. 'Reproducing' grand pianos have very sophisticated mechanisms and are much more realistic in the reproduction of piano music. They were made in relatively limited quantities. Better manufacturers include Steinway and Mason & Hamlin. Popular roll mechanism makers include AMPICO, Duo-Art, and Welte.

Coin-operated pianos (Orchestrions) were used commercially and typically incorporate extra instruments in addition to the piano action. These can be very large and complex, incorporating drums, cymbals, xylophones, bells, and dozens of pipes. Both American and European coin pianos are very popular, especially the larger and more complex models made by Wurlitzer, Seeburg, Cremona, Weber, Welte, Hupfeld, and many others. These companies also made automatically playing violins (Mills Violin Virtuoso, Hupfeld), banjos (Encore), and harps (Whitlock); these are quite valuable.

Collecting player organettes is a fun endeavor. Roller organs, organettes, player organs, grind organs, hand organs — whatever the name — are a fascinating group of music makers. Some used wooden barrels or cobs to operate the valves, or metal and cardboard discs or paper strips, paper rolls, metal donuts, or metal strips. They usually played from 14 to 20 keys or notes. Some were pressure operated or vacuum type. Their heyday lasted from the 1870s to the turn of the century. Most were reed organs, but a few had pipes. Many were made in either America or Germany. They lost favor with the advent of the phonograph, as did the music box. Some music boxes were built with little player organs in them. Any player organette in good working condition with rolls will be worth from $200.00 to $600.00, depending on the model. Generally the more keying it has and the larger and fancier the case, the more desirable it is. Rarity plays a part too. There are a handfull of individuals who make new music rolls for these player organs. Some machines are very rare, and music for them is nearly impossible to find. For further information on player organs we recommend *Encyclopedia of Automatic Musical Instruments* by Bowers.

Unless noted, prices given are for instruments in fine (NM) condition, playing properly, with cabinets or cases in well-preserved or refinished condition. In all instances, unrestored instruments sell for much less, as do those with broken or missing parts, damaged cases, and the like. On the other hand, particularly superb examples in especially ornate case designs and those that have been particularly well kept will often command more.

Key: c — cylinder d — disc

Mechanical

Nickelodeon, J. P. Seeburg Model L, oak cabinet with leaded glass, two composition female heads on each side, includes 10 rolls of music, 52½x37x23", $9,000.00. (Photo courtesy DuMouchelles on LiveAuctioneers.com)

Automata, bird in box, Griesebaum, 1900s...1,200.00
Automata, birds (2) in cage, Fr, 21", EX...2,800.00
Box, Bremond, 13" c, exposed bells, 10-tune, rosewood case, EX... 2,115.00
Box, Criterion, 10" d, cherry case, dbl comb, EX...1,450.00
Box, Ducommun-Girod, 7¾" c, 3-tune, 110 teeth, key-wind, EX.1,800.00
Box, Imperator #27, 5½" d, single comb, 1904 fair decal, 5x8x7".. 500.00
Box, Junod, 9¼" c, 12-tune, 5 bells w/ball strikers, 22", EX...1,400.00
Box, Lecoultre, 11" c, key-wind, 4-tune, walnut case w/inlay, EX .. 1,650.00
Box, Mermod Freres Sublime Harmony Piccolo, 16" c/3 combs/8-tune, rprs..2,000.00
Box, Nicole Freres, 11" c, key-wind, 6-tune, grpt case, 18" W ..1,850.00
Box, Paillard Sublime Harmonie Tremolo Zither, dbl spring, 17" c, EX..3,200.00
Box, Piano, Melodica, 30-key, EX, +6 books of music...3,700.00
Box, Regina #33 (late), 27" changer, cvd dragons, EX, +12 d.22,500.00
Box, Regina, 8¼" d, 1 comb, Pat 1899, 12" W, +20 d...1,100.00
Box, Regina, 15½" d, dbl combs, Gothic Revival case, 1897, 21" W.. 3,750.00
Box, Stella, 17¼" d, dbl combs, mahog table model, EX...4,500.00
Box, Symphonion, 14" d, dbl combs, walnut case, EX, +7 d...2,800.00
Box, Thornward, 15½" d, 1 comb, 12½x25x19", EX...2,500.00
Music box, Regina upright 27" disc changer, 64x38x24", VG.25,200.00
Orchestrelle, Wilcox & Wht Angelus push-up player, rstr, +12 rolls.. 1,000.00
Orchestrion, Coinola X, older rstr...14,000.00
Orchestrion, Velte Briscovia A, oak case, 96x66x29"...70,500.00
Organ, band, Wurlitzer #146-B, single roll fr, rstr...18,000.00
Organ, fairground, Gavioli, 65-key, EX...26,000.00
Organ, monkey, Bacigalupo, 43-key, 96 pipes, rstr...9,300.00
Organette, Ariston, 13" d, EX...550.00
Piano, Chickering Ampico upright, EX...1,200.00
Piano, grand, Marshall & Wendall Ampico, 60", EX...1,600.00
Volcano, Mills Virtuoso, single violin & piano, oak, G...28,000.00

Non-Mechanical

Accordion, Arpeggio, MOP inlay, 19" W, +case...1,950.00
Accordion, Silvio Soprani, faux MOP case, 41 keys/5 music keys, +case...240.00
Accordion, Wurlitzer Professional #1030, blk finish, 41 keys, +case..395.00
Banjo, Bacon & Day NE Plus Ultra #6, gold-plating, 1927...8,800.00
Banjo, Lange Paramount, 4-string, rosewood laminate resonator, 1920s.. 275.00
Banjo, tenor, Bacon & Day, 25-bracket, 13¹⁄₁₆" pot d...360.00
Banjo, tenor, Bacon & Day Silver Bell #3, rpl tuners, 1925-30.2,500.00
Banjo, tenor, Weymann & Son Keystone State, gold decal, 1925, 11" ring..2,585.00
Clarinet, Alto in F, C Mahilon Brussels, 19 keys, ca 1875, 36"... 650.00
Clarinet, B Flat, Selmer Paris 10 G, grenadilla w/silver keys, +case . 1,200.00
Cornet, F Besson London Silver Pocket, ca 1885, +case...2,700.00
Drum set, Pearl Strata-Blk EXR, bass+3 toms+snare+H hats+cymbals . 475.00
Drum set, Remo snares (3) w/blk finish, silver-tone mts, 12", 13", 16" . 300.00
Flute, Firth Hall & Pond, wooden w/4 brass spoon keys, ivory mts.. 265.00
Flute, VQ Powell Boston, silver w/eng, ca 1956, +case...4,700.00
Flute, WS Haynes Boston, grenadilla w/silver keys, 1900, +case . 825.00
Guitar, Epiphone Zephyr Emperor Varitone, 21⅝" bk, +case...4,700.00
Guitar, Fender Electric Stratocaster, contoured body, 1955, 15⅝" bk.32,900.00
Guitar, Fender, Telecaster, Santa Ana, 1968, w/case...10,500.00
Guitar, Gibson Advanced Jumbo, pearl inlay, 1938, 20¼" bk, +case..45,825.00
Guitar, Gibson Byrdland, electric, 1968, 21" bk, +case...4,350.00
Guitar, Gibson L-75, pearl inlay at headstock, ca 1935, 20¼" bk... 1,525.00
Guitar, Gretsch Syncromatic Sierra 6007, 1947, 20¾" bk, +case. 415.00
Harmonica, Hohner Chord, silver-tone, 23", +case...180.00
Harmonica, Hohner Tremelo, 4-part, 4 keys made as 1 unit, 9½", NMIB. 120.00
Harp, J Erat, Soho London, regilded & rstr, 66", wood case, ca 1805-07..5,175.00
Harp, Lyon & Healy Prelude, gilt & gold pnt soundboard, 63x34"..5,150.00
Harp, mahog case, simple cvg, 58x28"...500.00
Harp, mahog w/floral cvg, unmk, 40"...180.00
Harp, mahog w/inlay, unmk, 66x27"...600.00
Mandolin-guitar, Gibson Style A-3, pearl inlay, ca 1918, 14", +case.2,000.00
Piano, baby grand; Hardman, mahog w/cvd legs, 1925-30, 68" L... 2,300.00
Piano, grand, Steinway, mahog, serial #350639, 1956, w/bench, 18x35x15"..18,000.00
Piano, grand, Erard Louis XV style, mahog vnr/gilt paw ft, 1800s, 77".25,000.00
Piano, grand, Steinway & Sons Model B, mahog, ca 1987, 82½".36,000.00
Piano, grand, Steinway & Sons Parlor Model B, ebony, 1890s, 80" L.. 12,000.00
Piano, spinet, T Christensen Denmark, rosewood, 85-key, 50½" L...1,450.00
Pianoforte, Aster & Norwood, rosewood/mahog Regency, 1800s, 34x68x24". 1,680.00
Pianoforte, grand; Mayer & Haitzmann, Vienna, ca 1835, 91½"...6,000.00
Pianoforte, M Cleminti & Co, English Regency, sq, 73-note, 1800s, 71".. 2,150.00
Saxophone, B Flat, Selmer Paris, laquered/eng, 1951, +case...9,000.00
Saxophone, Buescher Low Pitch, MOP finger pads, ca 1928, +case ..360.00
Saxophone, Conn Alto, floral eng, ca 1914, VG...300.00
Saxophone, Martin Elto Elkhard, floral eng/pearl inlay, 1923, +case.. 265.00

Trombone, Conn 88HT-O Symphony Tenor, w/Lundberg mouthpc, +case..850.00
Trombone, King #1407 Liberty 2B, brass w/M-31 mouthpc, 1960, M..6,000.00
Trumpet, Conn New Wonder, rotary valve, eng bell, 1917, +case ...240.00
Trumpet, Martin Committee Model DeLuxe, ca 1950, +case ...1,295.00
Ukelele, CF Martin, 1947, 9⅜" bk, +soft cover 445.00
Ukelele, CF Martin Style #3, mk peghead, 1935, 9" bk, +case .2,350.00
Violin bow, rnd stick mk Lupot at butt, ebony frog w/pearl eye, 1840 ..7,000.00
Violin bow, rnd stick w/silver mts, ebony frog w/Parisian eye, Knopf..1,400.00
Violin, Melegari...Torino, 1879, 13⅞" bk.................................10,575.00
Violin, Wm E Hill & Sons, 1899, 13¹⁵⁄₁₆" bk 7,000.00

Mustache Cups

Mustache cups were popular items during the late Victorian period, designed specifically for the man with the mustache! They were made in silver plate as well as china and ironstone. Decorations ranged from simple transfers to elaborately applied and gilded florals. To properly position the 'mustache bar,' special cups were designed for the 'lefties.' These are the rare ones!

Shell and Seaweed, majolica, Etruscan, $435.00. (Photo courtesy Majolica Auctions, Strawser Auction Group on LiveAuctioneers.com)

Anglo Japanese style, brn tones w/gold, ca 1880s, 2½", +6" saucer ..160.00
Deer & hunter snow scene HP on wht, flared rim, ca 1910, 3½" ...55.00
Father in cobalt & heavy gold on wht, gothic script, 3½" 80.00
Floral & bl tassel HP on wht, emb swirl body, twist hdl, 1940s, 3½" ..30.00
Floral etched on silver, Barbour Bros Co Silver Quadruple #30, +saucer ...65.00
Floral HP inside & out on wht, gold trim, RC Germany #2338, 1905, 2" .90.00
Floral HP on wht w/gold ornate gold border, KPM mk, 3", +6" saucer .135.00
Floral transfer on wht, lt gr emb beads w/gold, Weimar, 1900, +saucer.180.00
Floral w/gold HP on wht, sgn AJ Surely, May 25, 1900, +saucer..120.00
Pink roses/mc leaves HP on wht, gold trim, Charles Ford, 1880, +saucer..170.00

Nailsea Glass

Nailsea is a term referring to clear or colored glass decorated in contrasting spatters, swirls, or loops. These are usually white but may also be pink, red, or blue. It was first produced in Nailsea, England, during the late 1700s but was made in other parts of Britain and Scotland as well. During the mid-1800s a similar type of glass was produced in this country. Originally used for decorative novelties only, by that time tumblers and other practical items were being made from Nailsea-type glass. See also Lamps, Fairy.

Bell, clear w/wht loops, clear hdl, 19th C, 12"..............................180.00
Flask, amber w/wht swirls, faint pontil mk, 1 pt, 7⅝".....................475.00
Flask, pk w/wht loops, pontil mk, 8⅝"...155.00
Flask, red w/wht loops, bottle neck, flat rim, 1840s, 10½" 155.00
Flask, red w/wht loops, ca 1790, 7"...265.00
Flask, white w/loops in reds & blues, 7½" 420.00
Jug, claret, red w/wht loops, tapered cylinder, SP mts...................200.00
Pitcher, wht w/bl loops, cobalt hdl, 4½"...85.00

Sugar bowl, brn & aqua over wht, wht ft/3-knop finial, 9¾".....2,400.00
Vase, cranberry w/wht loops, ruffled/crimped rim, 5"...................120.00
Whimsey, pipe w/long curved hdl, wht w/pk combed decor, 19½".250.00

Nakara Glass

Nakara was a line of decorated opaque milk glass produced by the C. F. Monroe Company of Meriden, Connecticut, for a few years after the turn of the century. It differs from their Wave Crest line in several ways. The shapes were simpler; pastel colors were deeper and covered more of the surface; more beading was present; flowers were larger; and large transfer prints of figures, Victorian ladies, cherubs, etc., were used as well. Ormolu and brass collars and mounts complemented these opulent pieces. Most items were signed; however, this is not important since the ware was never reproduced.

Vase, chrysanthemums, pink on light blue, ornate gold ormolu handles and feet, 17½", $5,000.00. (Photo courtesy Woody Auction Company on LiveAuctioneers.com)

Ashtray, flowers on gr hexagonal bowl, ormolu mts, sm 150.00
Box, 3 Greenaway girls at tea, lace decor, 3x6"............................795.00
Box, Bishop's Hat (scarce), floral on pk/yel, wht beadwork, 7" dia..795.00
Box, Bishop's Hat, floral, wht/pk on yel, ormolu ft, 5x5½" 495.00
Box, blown-out rose on bl, hexagonal, 3¾" dia.............................700.00
Box, Collars & Cuffs & pk azaleas on bright bl, 8½x8½" 795.00
Box, Collars & Cuffs, Gibson girl transfer 2,500.00
Box, floral on bl, ca 1890, 8" dia...900.00
Box, lady's portrait on gr, 2¾x4½" 495.00
Box, lady's portrait on pk, emb rococo scrolls, 5½x8¼" dia........2,750.00
Box, Princess Louise on pk/yel, ftd, sqd, 4x4½" 750.00
Box, ring, man & lady on yel & pk, 2½x2¾".............................1,200.00
Box, roses, pk/wht on gr, crown mold, rpl lining, 8½" dia 995.00
Box, roses, red/wht, on pk to gr w/wht beadwork, 6" dia..............595.00
Cracker jar, floral on bl w/gold lettering, glass lid w/petals, 7½".2,840.00
Humidor, frog reading paper on bl, Tobacco, metal lid, 6¾" 1,950.00
Humidor, Old Sport, bulldog transfer on brn, ovoid, 7" 695.00
Jardiniere, pk floral on gr, gold trim..625.00
Photo receiver, Indian chief on yel/olive, 2½x4" L....................1,250.00
Pin tray, floral, pk/wht on pk/gr, ormolu rim w/pointed hdls, 6" L.225.00
Toothpick holder, beaded ovals & pk flowers on gr, ormolu mts ..495.00
Tray, wht beadwork/floral on pk to yel, mirror in ormolu frwork..750.00
Vase, wild roses & scrolls on beige, 4-ftd, ormolu base, 9"............795.00

Napkin Rings

Napkin rings became popular during the late 1800s. They were made from various materials. Among the most popular and collectible today are the large group of varied silver-plated figurals made by American manufacturers. Recently the larger figurals in excellent condition have appreciated considerably. Only those with a blackened finish, corrosion, or broken and/or missing parts have maintained their earlier price levels. When no condition is indicated, the items listed below are assumed to be all original and in very good to excellent condition. Check very carefully for missing parts, solder repairs, marriages, and reproductions.

A timely warning: Inexperienced buyers should be aware of excellent reproductions on the market, especially the wheeled pieces and cherubs. However, these do not have the fine detail and patina of the originals and tend to have a more consistent, soft pewter-like finish. There may also be pitting on the surface. These are appearing at the large, quality shows at top prices, being shown along with authentic antique merchandise. Our advisor for this category is Barbara Aaronson; she is listed in the Directory under California.

Key:
R&B — Reed & Barton   SH&M — Simpson, Hall, & Miller

Angel sitting w/legs crossed, ring behind, Pairpoint #7, 3½".....1,450.00
Antelope stands w/ring on bk, Meriden Britannia #204...............725.00
Bear on base beside scrolled ring, Hamilton #127, $200 to..........350.00
Boy crawling behind ring to snare bunny, Meriden SP #0232, min..500.00
Buffalo standing beside ring, unmk, rare...840.00
Bull by hexagon holder, Knickerbocker #1248, $200 to...............350.00
Bulldog w/collar by doghouse holder, Simpson...#207, 4 ftd, $350 to..500.00
Cat on oval base by sheet music on stand, ringless, Tufts #1609..1,200.00
Cat on sq pillow-shaped base, Meriden #293, $750 to.................950.00
Cherries & leaves on side of fluted holder, Meriden #626, $200 to..350.00
Cherub reaching for eggs in bird's nest on holder, Meriden #0226...350.00
Chick popping through cracked-shell holder, Derby #371...........200.00
Child & dachshund on ring, rnd base, Van Berg #19...................660.00
Civil War soldier w/rifle by holder, Meriden #0260, $900 to.....1,200.00
Crane standing on 1 ft, rnd woodland base, Meriden #163, $500 to..750.00
Cupid reaching for arrow, hearts & bow atop ring, R&B #1315.1,175.00
Dog & goat on base ea side of ring on ped, Webster #148, $200 to..350.00
Dog barks at bird atop holder, Homan Silver...#131, $200 to.......350.00
Dog stands facing frog on ring, #224, $600 to..............................750.00
Donkey wearing saddle by plain holder, $200 to...........................350.00
Eagle w/ring atop wings, Meriden #203, $500 to..........................750.00
Flatiron form w/opening sides, Tufts #1636.................................350.00

Fox and grapes, no mark, $1,250.00. (Photo courtesy Morphy Auctions on LiveAuctioneers.com)

Fox under holder, grapes over head, Meriden Britannia #331...1,500.00
Giraffe eating leaves, Rogers & Bros #239.................................1,450.00
Girl carrying flower in left hand & basket in right, Middleton #107..350.00
Girl seated on snail reading book beside ring, #0262, $500 to.....600.00
Girl skipping rope before ring, Meriden #330.............................1,175.00
Grapes & leaves support ring, Standard #730, rstr........................375.00
Greenaway girl in front of ornate holder, Rockford #120, $350 to...500.00
Greenaway girl pushes boy on sled, sq holder, SH&M #037.....1,500.00
Greenaway girl w/dog before ring, unmk, $350 to.......................500.00
Greenaway girls flank ring on leafy mound, SH&M, #207........2,200.00
Greenaway infant in chair, Middleton #98..................................2,500.00
Greenaway lady on toboggan, ring on lap, Wilcox #4342.........2,400.00
Greenaway lady w/umbrella & boy w/hoop, Tufts #1597...........1,550.00
Greyhound w/ring on bk, oval vase, unmk....................................660.00
Horse rearing atop holder, base has acorn-shaped ft, unmk, $200 to...350.00
Lady tennis player (L skirt), Meriden Britannia #283, $1,500 to...2,000.00
Lamb stands beside ring, Barbour #13...750.00

Lion holds open ornate ring w/medallion on top, unmk..............550.00
Nude holding metal bud vase & ring, Rockford #178, $400 to....550.00
Owl on branch beside ring, no base, Middleton #112..................325.00
Parakeet on hdl of wheeled base supporting ring, unmk..............725.00
Pitcher-shaped vase, scroll hdl w/flower, R&B #1337, $200 to....350.00
Rabbit beside log (ring), SH&M #210, $600 to............................850.00
Rabbit on haunches w/ring at side, Rogers Smith & Co #233, $1,000 to..1,200.00
Rabbit rests front paw on ring, unmk...850.00
Rabbits (2) beside ring, #68, $500 to..750.00
Red Riding Hood stands w/basket beside ring, R&B #1492......1,100.00
Sailor holding rope to anchor, w/pitcher bud vase, R&B #1357..700.00
Sphinx w/ring on bk, Meriden Britannia #165.............................600.00
Turtle w/ring on bk, Pairpoint #51...550.00
Winged cherub on ring resting on bird's tail, Rockford #151, $750 to..950.00

Nash Glass

A. Douglas Nash founded the Corona Art Glass Company in Long Island, New York. He produced tableware, vases, flasks, etc. using delicate artistic shapes and forms. After 1933 he worked for the Libbey Glass Company. For more information we recommend *The Collector's Encyclopedia of American Art Glass* by John A. Shuman III.

Bowl, Chintz, gr & rose, 12"...300.00
Bowl, orange bands alternate w/feathered gold, ftd, 2¼x4¼".......125.00
Compote, amber irid w/bl overtones, att, 4x5¼"..........................230.00
Compote, irid, melon ribs, att, 7"...250.00
Plate, Chintz, orange & clear radiating design, unmk, 6½"..........115.00

Vase, blue iridescent, faint ribbing, #B 526, 5", $480.00. (Photo courtesy Skinner Auctioneers and Appraisers of Antiques and Fine Art on LiveAuctioneers.com)

Vase, Chintz, brn/gr bands, wide clear ft, bulb, unmk, 7½"..........860.00
Vase, Chintz, red w/turq stripes, bulb, 8"....................................960.00
Vase, vertical zippers on bl-gr irid mottle, GD78, 8"...................900.00
Wine, Chintz, bl & gr stripes, ca 1930, 5¼", pr............................400.00

Gertrude and Otto Natzler

The Natzlers came to the United States from Vienna in the late 1930s. They settled in Los Angeles where they continued their work in ceramics, for which they were already internationally recognized. Gertrude created the forms; Otto formulated a variety of interesting glazes, among them volcanic, crystalline, and lustre. Our advisors for this category are Suzanne Perrault and David Rago; they are listed in the Directory under New Jersey.

Bottle, lt turq on mauve, 8¾"...3,375.00
Bowl, bl & brn hare's fur, hemispherical, 3x4½".........................3,400.00
Bowl, brn & grn flambé, hemispherical, 2¾x5½".........................750.00
Bowl, chartreuse & brn volcanic, rstr line, 3x9½".....................2,600.00
Bowl, chartreuse dead-matt, 3-folded sides, sm rim chip, 2x7".....565.00
Bowl, lt yel & umber hare's fur matt, hemispherical, rstr chip, 7"..1,400.00

Bowl, multi-tone gray reduction glaze w/fissures, low, wide, 11".4,000.00
Bowl, olive gr/turq/brn mottled semi-matt, ftd, hemispherical, 6x9"..1,750.00
Bowl, runny red glaze (pooled in center & ft ring), w/case, 2x4½".2,750.00
Bowl, turq on brn clay, slightly folded, label: J230, 1½x5".........1,875.00
Bowl, volcanic gr & yel on red clay, 1x4⅝"................................1,065.00
Bowl, yel, conical on narrow ft, label: N379, 3x8"....................2,375.00
Bowl, yel mottle, flared to rim, label: N909, 3½x5½" 3,600.00
Coupe, tangerine semi-matt, 3¼x7" 800.00

Coupe, mottled oxblood, 4¼x4¼", $600.00. (Photo courtesy Rago Arts and Auction Center)

Vase, copper microcrystalline on dk brn, ftd, cylindrical, 11x5" ...13,750.00
Vase, gunmetal volcanic, conical, 10½x7½" 10,000.00
Vase, mottled turq & gunmetal matt, sgn, w/orig inventory tag, 18½".39,000.00
Vase, sulfur yel volcanic, bbl shaped, 7¾x5" 11,250.00

Naughties and Bathing Beauties

These daring all-bisque figurines were made in various poses, usually in one piece, in German and American factories during the 1920s. Admired for their fine details, these figures were often nude but were also made with molded-on clothing or dressed in bathing costumes. Items below are all in excellent undamaged condition. Our advisors for this section are Don and Ann Kier; they are listed in the Directory under Ohio.

2 molded together, 4½-5½", ea 1,600.00
Action figure, Germany, 5"..450.00
Action figure, Germany, 7½"..700.00
Action figure, w/wig, Germany, 7" 650.00
Elderly woman in suit w/legs X, rare, 5¼" 1,400.00
Galuba & Hoffman, woven bathing cap & suit, molded shoes, mohair wig, 4½" L..825.00
Galuba & Hoffman, orig wig, molded slippers, 6" L.....................720.00
Glass eyes, 5"...400.00
Glass eyes, 6"...650.00
Japan mk, 3"...40.00
Japan mk, 5-6", ea 65.00
Japan mk, 9"...95.00
Lady in woven suit & cap, molded slippers, mohair wig, Galuba & Hoffman, 2" ...960.00
Painted eyes, 3" 165.00
Painted eyes, 6" 325.00
Swivel neck, 5" 700.00
Swivel neck, 6" 750.00
With animal, 5½"..1,200.00

Newcomb College

The Newcomb College of New Orleans, Louisiana, established a pottery in 1895 to provide the students with first-hand experience in the fields of art and ceramics. Using locally dug clays — red and buff in the early years, white-burning by the turn of the century — potters were employed to throw the ware which the ladies of the college decorated. From 1897 until about 1910, the ware they produced was finished in a high glaze and was usually surface painted. After 1905 some carving was done as well. The letter 'Q' that is sometimes found in the mark indicates a pre-1906 production (high glaze). After 1912 a matt glaze was favored; these pieces are always carved. Soft blues and greens were used almost exclusively, and decorative themes were chosen to reflect the beauty of the South. The end of the matt-glaze period and the art-pottery era was 1930.

Various marks used by the pottery include an 'N' within a 'C,' sometimes with 'HB' added to indicate a 'hand-built' piece. The potter often incised his initials into the ware, and the artists were encouraged to sign their work. Among the most well-known artists were Sadie Irvine, Henrietta Bailey, and Fannie Simpson.

Newcomb pottery is evaluated to a large extent by era (early, transitional, or matt), decoration, size, and condition. In the following descriptions, unless noted otherwise, all decoration is carved and painted on matt glaze. The term 'transitional' defines a period of a few years, between 1910 and 1916, when matt glazes were introduced as waxy, with green finishes. One can tell a 'transitional' piece by the use of ink marks with matt glazes. Our advisors for this category are Suzanne Perrault and David Rago; they are listed in the Directory under New Jersey.

Biscuit jar, landscape, Somewhere Above Us..., L Jordan, 7x5", NM . 9,600.00
Bowl, jonquils on bl, AF Simpson, #MJ73, 8¾"........................2,700.00
Charger, fish (3), S Wells, #TT73, 1904, 9¼", NM 6,000.00
Charger, magnolias, S Wells, 1903, #LL74, X, 1903, 9¼"..........9,600.00
Coffeepot, pine trees, transitional, AF Simpson, 1909, 10¾"....5,100.00

Inkwell, trees deeply carved in blue and green on yellow, Leona Nicholson, includes liner, missing lid, NC/LN/JM/VH87/Q, 2½x3¼", $2,520.00. (Photo courtesy Craftsman Auctions on LiveAuctioneers.com)

Jar, peacock feathers, A Roman, w/lid, 1898, 3¼x5½"..............4,800.00
Jardiniere, irises, H Joor, #H48X, 1902, rstr hairline, 10x12" ..18,000.00
Pitcher, flower band at rim on bl, #NU87/196, 4" 1,600.00
Pitcher, freesia, AF Simpson, transitional, 1917, 4x5"...............3,000.00
Pitcher, juice, H Joor, 1902, 6x7½" 6,700.00
Tile, oaks, grs & bls, S Irvine, #NC SI7, 7½x10"+orig wood fr... 16,800.00
Tile, rabbit & Mad Hatter, Mad Tea Party series, L Nicholson, 4½x4¾"..3,000.00
Vase, bl & purple streaks, organic decor, MGB, #TF75, 6"........2,100.00
Vase, cottage in bayou, S Irvine, #250/J07, 1918, 8x4" 4,500.00
Vase, crocus on ivory, AF Simpson, #R075, 6" 4,000.00
Vase, daffodils, AF Simpson, 1908, 9x3½" 7,800.00
Vase, daffodils, AF Simpson, 1921, 7½x3¼" 2,040.00
Vase, daffodils on bl, A Mason, #HD7, 4½x7"..........................2,200.00
Vase, Espanol pattern, bl-gr, AF Simpson, 1929, paper label, 4½x2" .1,440.00
Vase, Espanol pattern, H Bailey, tear-shaped, 1926, 5¼x4".......3,250.00
Vase, floral band, A Mason, bulb bottle form, #HC93, 5".........3,250.00
Vase, floral, bl on bl, S Irvine, 1929, 7½x4"............................2,000.00
Vase, floral, X-sections of pods in glossy poly, H Bailey, 1903, 5x3½".. 4,500.00
Vase, floral, yel clusters, spherical, M Ross, 1902, 2 hairlines, 7x6¾".1,800.00
Vase, fruit on branches, S Irvine, 1923, 8¼x7" 3,500.00
Vase, gardenias on cobalt band, A Lonnegan, #XX63, 1904, 7x7".. 12,000.00
Vase, geese prancing, pine trees landscape, MO Delavigne, 1902, 12¾x8".48,000.00
Vase, grape clusters, S Irvine, #253, 1917, 4¼x7¼" 2,400.00

Vase, irises on bl, S Irvine, 1924, bruise/chips, 10¾x6½"...........5,100.00
Vase, moon/moss/oaks, AF Simpson, 1928, 10½x5" 15,000.00
Vase, moon/moss/oaks, AF Simpson, baluster, 1919, 7¼x4¼" ...4,500.00
Vase, moon/moss/oaks, AF Simpson, bulb, 1930, 6x6" 9,000.00
Vase, moon/moss/oaks, S Irvine, #209/KU68, 1920, 7x3¾" 5,700.00
Vase, moon/moss/oaks, S Irvine, 1932, 3½x4½"........................2,650.00
Vase, moon/moss/oaks, S Irvine, cylindrical, 1928, 5½x4" 3,250.00
Vase, nicotina leaves & blossoms, S Irvine, 1922, 7½x4"..........3,600.00
Vase, oak trees, Spanish moss, H Bailey, 1932, 3½x4" 1,920.00
Vase, paperwhites, AF Simpson, #R020/77, 1929, 6¾x4"..........4,000.00
Vase, paperwhites, S Irvine, bulb, 1918, 4¼x5" 1,900.00
Vase, pine cones/needles on bl, H Bailey, #UL61, 4¼" 2,150.00
Vase, pine trees, AF Simpson, bulb base, 1913, 9x5".................8,400.00
Vase, pine trees, S Irvine, #224/IB94, 5¾" 3,000.00
Vase, pine trees, S Irvine, transitional, 1911, 12x5"..............13,200.00
Vase, pine trees/full moon, AF Simpson, 1916, #367/238, 4x2½" .3,250.00
Vase, pine trees/full moon/river, S Irvine, flakes, 1917, 9¾" 10,800.00
Vase, pitcher plants in gr & bl, H Bailey, #UP8, label, 4" 2,500.00
Vase, ribbed, indigo & gr crystalline, 5¼x3¾" 850.00
Vase, wisteria, cvd/pnt by M LeBlanc, NC/VV81, 1904, 9x5" .51,000.00

New Geneva

In the early years of the nineteenth century, several potteries flourished in the Greensboro, Pennsylvania, area. They produced utilitarian stoneware items as well as tile and novelties for many decades. All failed well before the turn of the century.

Flowerpot, tulips on redware, repaired/replaced ring handles, 8¾", $510.00. (Photo courtesy Garth's Auction on LiveAuctioneers.com)

Churn, eagle surrounded by foliage, HP lines at shoulder & hdls, 15" ..375.00
Creamer, reddish brn floral on redware, 3½" 2,250.00
Crock, bl stenciled letters & HP squiggles, w/hdls, 16-gal, 23½x13"..1,500.00
Crock, HP bl stripes & flourishes w/'02,' flakes, 12"......................470.00
Crock, stenciled bl letters, A Condon/New Geneva/PA, 9¾"......125.00
Pitcher, floral, umber slip on redware, flakes, 7"............................700.00

New Martinsville Glass

The New Martinsville Glass Company took its name from the town in West Virginia where it began operations in 1901. In the beginning they produced pressed tablewares in crystal as well as colored glass. Considered an innovator, the company was known for vanity sets, figural decanters, and models of animals and birds. After a change in management in 1944, the company became Viking Glass Company. They continued to use many of the old molds and added new lines and labeled their wares 'Viking' or 'Rainbow Art,' until they ceased operations in 1986. In 1987, Mr. Kenneth Dalzell, long associated with Fostoria Glass Company, purchased the defunct Viking Glass Company and produced glass from the New Martinsville, Viking, and Barth Art molds. Early productions were not marked but later productions were sometimes marked. They ceased operations in 1998. See also Depression Glass; Glass Animals and Figurines.

Addie, blk, c/s 18.00
Addie, cobalt, bowl, vegetable 55.00
Addie, jade, tumbler, ftd 30.00
Dancing pk satin, lady flower frog 300.00
Flower Basket etch, relish, 3-part, 4 ft, 12¾" 26.00
Flower Basket etch, ruby, radiance shape, cr/sug, pr 48.00
Flower Basket, plate, luncheon, radiance shape 10.00
Hostmaster, amber, c/s 16.00
Hostmaster, amber, pilsner 12.00
Hostmaster, amethyst, cr/sug, pr 46.00
Hostmaster, cobalt, cocktail shaker w/chrome lid 80.00
Hostmaster, cobalt, pitcher, ½-gal 65.00
Hostmaster, ruby, ice tub, 2 wing hdls, 7" 55.00
Janice, ruby, plate, luncheon, 8½" 20.00
Janice, ruby, sherbet, ftd, 2½" 12.00
Janice, sky bl, cruet w/stopper 40.00
Janice, sky bl, jam jar w/lid, notched 65.00
Janice, sky bl, sherbet, ftd, 2½" 8.00
Meadow Wreath etch, candy w/lid, 2 tab hdls 40.00
Meadow Wreath etch, cheese & cracker, 2-pc, 11" 45.00
Meadow Wreath etch, punch bowl, radiance shape, ball 5-qt 100.00
Meadow Wreath etch, relish, 2-part, 7" 18.00
Modernistic, jade, triangular cr/sug, blk hdl tray 220.00
Modernistic, lt bl, puff box, triangular, covered, satin 65.00
Modernistic, pk satin, vase, triangular, 8½" 80.00
Moondrops, amethyst, candlestick, 3-lite, 7" W, ea 70.00
Moondrops, amethyst, plate, dinner, 9½" 22.00
Moondrops, cobalt, butter, rnd, 6" 350.00
Moondrops, cobalt, decanter, rocketship, 3-leg base w/stopper ...425.00
Moondrops, evergreen, bowl, tab hdl, 3-toed, 5⅝" 30.00
Moondrops, evergreen, vase, ring stepped base, fluted top, 7½" ... 50.00
Moondrops, jade, decanter, rocketship, 3-leg base w/stopper 300.00
Moondrops, jade, goblet, 9-oz , 6¼" 30.00
Moondrops, ruby, bowl, oval rimmed vegetable, 9½" 60.00
Moondrops, ruby, cocktail shaker, ftd, appl hdl, chrome top 95.00

Moondrops, ruby, tumbler, 4⅜", $20.00; cup, $15.00. (Photo courtesy Montrose Auction Inc. on LiveAuctioneers.com)

Oscar, amethyst, pitcher, ½-gal 80.00
Oscar, amethyst, tumbler, flat 4½" 18.00
Oscar, jade, vase, bbl form 75.00
Prelude etch, candy w/lid, 6½" 30.00
Prelude etch, center hdld server, 11" 34.00
Prelude etch, pitcher, 78-oz, 8⅜" 160.00
Prelude etch, plate, dinner, 10½" 34.00
Prelude etch, plate, torte, 12" 22.00
Prelude etch, plate, torte, 16" 40.00
Prelude etch, platter, oval 14½" 48.00
Prelude etch, relish, rect, open hdld, 3-part, 7" 18.00
Prelude etch, shakers, s&p 32.00
Prelude etch, tumbler, str-sided, 12-oz 20.00
Prelude etch, vase, flat base, hourglass shape, 8" 28.00
Radiance, amber, cruet w/fan stopper 35.00
Radiance, amethyst, vase, ball base, flared, crimped top, 12" 85.00
Radiance, cobalt, candlestick, 2-lite, circular fan center, 7½" W, ea ..70.00
Radiance, cobalt, cup, punch, flat 12.00
Radiance, cobalt, c/s, coffee, ftd cup 22.00
Radiance, ruby, candlestick, 2-lite, circular fan center, 7¾" W, ea. 80.00

Radiance, ruby, plate, torte or punch bowl, 14" 60.00
Radiance, ruby, punch bowl, rnd, 1¼-gal 170.00
Radiance, sky bl, cake stand, ftd, 11¼" 70.00
Radiance, sky bl, candy box w/lid, 3-part, 7¾" 85.00
Radiance, sky bl, relish, 3-part, crimped, 8¾" 40.00
Radiance, sky bl, relish/celery, oval, 10" 34.00
Swan Janice, candy w/lid, rnd, 1 swan neck hdl 35.00
Swan Janice, cr/sug, ind, swan head hands, pr 38.00
Swan Janice, crystal w/cobalt neck, bowl, 11" 60.00
Swan Janice, vase, sq, 2 swan head hdls 40.00

Newspapers

People do not collect newspapers simply because they are old. Age has absolutely nothing to do with value — it does not hold true that the older the newspaper, the higher the value. Instead, most of the value is determined by the historic event content. In most cases, the more important to American history the event is, the higher the value. In over 200 years of American history, perhaps as many as 98% of all newspapers ever published do not contain news of a significant historic event. Newspapers not having news of major events in history are called 'atmosphere.' Atmosphere papers have little collector value. (See listings below.) All papers listed are in very good condition. To learn more about the hobby of collecting old and historic newspapers, visit this website: www.historybuff.com. The e-mail address for the NCSA is curator@ historybuff.com. See Newspaper Collector's Society of America in the Clubs, Newsletters, and Websites section for more information.

1803, Columbian Centinel/MA Federalist, LA Purchase Treaty.. 575.00
1836, Texas declares independence, $60 to.................................... 85.00
1845, annexation of Texas, $35 to... 45.00
1846, start of Mexican War, $25 to 35.00
1846-47, major battles of Mexican War, $25 to 30.00
1850, death of Zachary Taylor, $45 to 65.00
1859, John Brown executed, $40 to 85.00
1860, Lincoln elected 1st term, $115 to.. 225.00
1861-65, Atmosphere editions: Confederate titles, $110 to 165.00
1861-65, Atmosphere editions: Union titles, $7 to 12.00
1861-65, Civil War major battle, Confederate report, $225 to 390.00
1861-65, Civil War major battle, Union 1st report, $60 to.......... 120.00
1861, Lincoln's inaugural address, $140 to 275.00
1862, Emancipation Proclamation, $85 to 225.00
1863, Gettysburg Address, $165 to.. 380.00
1863, NY Tribune evening ed, 1st reports of Battle of Gettysburg, archivally fr ..500.00
1865, April 29 ed of Frank Leslie's, $225 to 325.00
1865, April 29 ed of Harper's Weekly, $200 to 300.00
1865, capture & death of J Wilkes Booth, $85 to 165.00
1865, fall of Richmond, $85 to 275.00
1865, NY Herald, April 15, (+) $700 to 1,200.00
1865, titles other than NY Herald, Apr 15, $300 to 500.00
1866-1900, Atmosphere editions, $3 to... 5.00
1876, Custer's Last Stand, 1st reports, $100 to............................ 250.00
1876, Custer's Last Stand, later reports, $30 to............................ 80.00
1880, Garfield elected, $30 to... 40.00
1881, Gunfight at OK Corral, $175 to 400.00
1882, Jesse James killed, 1st report, $165 to 385.00
1882, Jesse James killed, later report, $60 to 120.00
1889, Johnstown flood, $25 to 40.00
1892, Lizzie Borden crime & trial, $40 to 85.00
1900, James Jeffries defeats Jack Corbett, $20 to 35.00
1900-36, Atmosphere editions, $2 to... 3.00
1901, McKinley assassinated, $45 to 100.00
1903, Wright Brothers' flight, $200 to 500.00

1904, Teddy Roosevelt elected, $25 to.. 35.00
1906, San Francisco earthquake, other titles, $25 to..................... 50.00
1906, San Francisco earthquake, San Francisco title, $300 to 500.00
1912, Sinking of Titanic, 1st reports, $150 to............................... 350.00
1912, Sinking of Titanic, later reports, $45 to 115.00
1918, Armistice, $25 to 85.00
1924, Coolidge elected, $20 to.. 30.00
1927, Babe Ruth hits 60th home run, $50 to................................. 125.00
1927, Lindbergh arrives in Paris, 1st reports, $65 to 125.00
1929, St Valentine's Day Massacre, $100 to.................................. 225.00
1929, Stock market crash, $75 to 180.00
1931, Al Capone found guilty, $40 to 80.00
1931, Jack 'Legs' Diamond killed, $30 to 45.00
1932, FDR elected 1st term, $20 to 30.00
1933, Hitler becomes Chancellor, $20 to....................................... 55.00
1934, Dillinger killed, $100 to... 250.00
1937, Amelia Earhart vanishes, $30 to 85.00
1937, Hindenburg explodes, $75 to 150.00
1939-45, WWII major battles, $20 to 50.00
1940, FDR elected 3rd term, $20 to 30.00
1941, December 8 editions w/1st reports, $30 to 50.00
1941, Honolulu Star-Bulletin, December 7, 1st extra (+), $300 to ..600.00
1944, D-Day, $25 to 60.00
1945, FDR dies, $20 to 55.00
1948, Chicago Daily Tribune, Nov 3, Dewey Defeats Truman, $500 to.800.00

1948, Israel creation, Davar Hebrew Labour Daily Tel-Aviv, $360.00. (Photo courtesy Max Rambod Inc. on LiveAuctioneers.com)

1952, Eisenhower elected 1st term, $20 to...................................... 25.00
1957, Soviets launch Sputnik, $5 to 15.00
1958, Alaska joins union, $15 to 25.00
1960, JFK elected, $30 to... 45.00
1963, JFK assassination, Nov 22, Dallas title, $45 to.................... 65.00
1963, JFK assassination, Nov 22, titles other than Dallas, $3 to 7.00
1967, Super Bowl I, $15 to 30.00
1968, Martin Luther King assassination, $20 to............................. 35.00
1968, Robert Kennedy assassination, $3 to.................................... 5.00
1969, moon landing, $5 to 12.00
1974, Nixon resignation, $15 to... 20.00

Nicodemus

Chester R. Nicodemus was born near Barberton, Ohio, August, 17, 1901. He started Pennsylvania State University in 1920, where he studied engineering. Chester got a share of a large paper route, a job that enabled him to attend Cleveland Art School where he studied under Herman Matzen, sculptor, and Frank Wilcox, anatomy illustrator, graduating in 1925. That fall Chester was hired to begin a sculpture department at the Dayton Art Institute.

Nicodemus moved from Dayton to Columbus, Ohio, in 1930 and started teaching at the Columbus Art School. During this time he made vases and commissioned sculptures, water fountains, and limestone and wood carvings. In 1941 Chester left the field of teaching to pursue pottery making full time, using local red clay containing a large amount of iron. Known for its durability, he called the ware Ferro-Stone. He made teapots and other utility wares, but these goods lost favor, so he started producing animal and bird sculptures, nativity sets, and Christmas ornaments, some bearing Chester's and Florine's names as personalized cards for his customers and friends. His glaze colors were turquoise or aqua, ivory, green mottle, pussy willow (pink), and golden yellow. The glaze was applied so that the color of the warm red clay would show through, adding an extra dimension to each piece. His name is usually incised in the clay in an arch, but paper labels were also used. Chester Nicodemus died in 1990. For more information we recommend *Sanfords Guide to Nicodemus, His Pottery and His Art*, by James Riebel.

Vases, both signed, 7", pair $420.00. (Photo courtesy Belhorn Auction Services, LLC on LiveAuctioneers.com)

Bank, figural squirrel, turq, 4"	125.00
Box, molded as a carton of strawberries, ivory & brn, 4"	190.00
Figurine, cardinal, red w/crystal glaze, 8" L	750.00
Figurine, cat sleeping, gray, 7" L	1,000.00
Figurine, duckling, brn, 3"	145.00
Figurine, horse, ivory, 12x8"	4,800.00
Figurine, Joseph, tan & brn, 8"	130.00
Figurine, lion cub, brn, 3"	175.00
Figurine, mini, bear sitting, brn over bl,"	660.00
Figurine, mini, duck, yel, 1"	360.00
Figurine, owl, 5", $85 to	95.00
Figurine, robin, 4"	150.00
Figurine, rooster, blk, 6"	775.00
Figurine, rooster crowing, gr, 8"	780.00
Figurine, rooster, gray & brn, 6"	1,000.00
Figurine/vase, flower girl, turq, 6"	135.00
Flower frog, figural Madonna, w/bowl, gr & brn, 11x10"	300.00
Jardiniere, turq & brn, 4"	250.00
Mug, Ohio State emb on side, ivory & brn, bulb, ftd, 5"	200.00
Paperweight, Madonna & Child, tan, St Ann's Hospital, 4"	120.00
Pitcher, brn mottle w/brn rim, 3-pt	420.00
Planter, bear cub, sgn EJ, Ferro-Stone label, 4" L, $50 to	70.00
Planter, figural swan, brn, 6" L	900.00
Vase, brn mottle w/brn rim, 3-hdl, 6"	960.00
Vase, turq w/brn rim, rim-to-hip rope hdls, 8"	165.00
Vase, yel, diagonal ribbing, rect, 7"	600.00

Niloak

During the latter part of the 1800s, there were many small utilitarian potteries in Benton, Arkansas. By 1900 only the Hyten Brothers Pottery remained. Charles Hyten, a second generation potter, took control of the family business around 1902. Shortly thereafter he renamed it the Eagle Pottery Company. In 1909 Hyten and former Rookwood potter Arthur Dovey began experimentation on a new swirl pottery. Dovey had previously worked for the Ouachita Pottery Company of Hot Springs and produced a swirl pottery there as early as 1906. In March 1910, the Eagle Pottery Company introduced Niloak — kaolin spelled backwards.

In 1911 Benton businessmen formed the Niloak Pottery corporation. Niloak, connected to the Arts and Crafts Movement and known as Mission Ware, had a national representative in New York by 1913. Niloak's production centered on art pottery characterized by accidental, swirling patterns of natural and artificially colored clays. Many companies through the years have produced swirl pottery, yet none achieved the technical and aesthetic qualities of Niloak. Hyten received a patent in 1928 for the swirl technique. Although most examples have an interior glaze, some early Mission Ware pieces have an exterior glaze as well; these are extremely rare.

In 1934 Hyten's company found itself facing bankruptcy. Hardy I. Winburn, Jr., along with other Little Rock businessmen, raised the necessary capital and were able to provide the kind of leadership needed to make the business profitable once again. Both lines (Eagle and Hywood) were renamed 'Niloak' in 1937 to capitalize on this well-known name. The pottery continued in production until 1947 when it was converted to the Winburn Tile Company.

Of late, poor copies of Niloak Mission Ware swirl and Hywood pieces have been seen at flea markets and on the internet. These pieces even bear a Niloak mark, but this is a 'fantasy' mark. To the experienced eye, the pieces are blatantly bogus. Buyer beware!

Be careful not to confuse the swirl production of the Evans Pottery of Missouri with Niloak. The significant difference is the dark brown matt interior glaze of Evans pottery. For further information we recommend *Collector's Encyclopedia of Niloak Pottery* by David Edwin Gifford (Collector Books). All items listed below bear the 'Niloak' mark unless otherwise noted.

Key:
NB — Niloak (block letters)   1st art mk — impressed stamp
NI — Niloak (impressed) mark   2nd art mk — impressed stamp

Mission Ware

Ashtray, str sides, no rests, 5½" dia	80.00
Ashtray, top hat form, 3 rests, 2nd art mk, 1½x5" dia	295.00
Bowl, attached center flower frog, 2nd art mk, 1¾x8"	220.00
Bowl, console, cream/tan/rust, 2nd art mk, 3x10"	525.00
Bowl, flared ft, dome lid w/acorn-like finial, 2nd art mk, 5¾"	2,685.00
Bowl, flower, flat, str sides, 2nd art mk, 2½x6½"	110.00
Bowl, fruit, 2nd art mk, 2½x9½"	470.00
Bowl, incurvate rim, 1st art mk, 2x10½"	300.00
Candleholder w/finger ring, 2nd art mk, 4½x5¼"	265.00
Candlestick, drip rim, cupped base, 1st art mk, 3¾", ea	190.00
Candlesticks, drip rim, flared base, 2nd art mk, 8½", pr	300.00
Chamberstick, drip rim, flared base, hdl, 1st art mk, 4x4¾"	280.00
Compote, flared ped ft, w/lid, unmk, 6"	725.00
Decanter, 12", w/4 tumblers, paper labels	1,100.00
Flower frog, layer-cake style, unmk, 1½x3¼"	80.00
Humidor, cup-like lid w/recess for sponge, 2nd art mk, 4½"	550.00
Humidor, str sides, lid w/recess for sponge, 2nd art mk, 6¼"	695.00
Humidor, str sides, pierced lid w/ball-like knob, 2nd art mk, 7"	680.00
Jar, flared rim, bulb, w/knobbed lid, 3¾x5"	365.00
Jar, rose, covered, 1st or 2nd art mk, $700 to	900.00
Jardiniere, rolled/tailored collar, 2nd art mk, 13x14"	1,990.00
Jug, Pensacola Goldencorn emb on side, no hdl, 2nd art mk, 3¼"	65.00
Lamp base, rolled collar, closed on top, drilled, 2nd art mk, 14½"	650.00
Match holder, str sides, flared base, 1st art mk, 2¼x2¼" dia	100.00
Mug, slightly bbl shaped, 1st art mk, 4¼"	250.00
Pencil holder, cylindrical, slight flare at base, 1st art mk, 2¾"	100.00
Plate, flat bowl form w/no rim, dk colors, 1st art mk, 9"	620.00
Powder dish, fancy finial, 1st art mk, 3x4½" dia	750.00
Stein/mug, bbl shape, 1st art mk, 4½"	465.00
Tankard, elongated hdl, 2nd art mk, 10½"	1,350.00
Tumbler, flared rim, Pat Pending, 5¼"	155.00

Vase, bud, stick neck, flared base, 2nd art mk, 7"	190.00
Vase, classic form, rolled collar, brick red dominates, 2nd art mk, 7"	185.00
Vase, conical w/flared ft, 2nd art mk, 9½"	350.00
Vase, cylindrical allover vines, 2nd art mk, 9"	190.00
Vase, cylindrical, 2nd art mk, 6½x3"	145.00
Vase, cylindrical, flared base, 1st art mk, 8¾x3¼"	145.00
Vase, cylindrical, sm flare at top, tan/cream, 1910, 8½x4¼"	880.00
Vase, fan shape w/flared base, 2nd art mk, 6¾"	255.00

Vase, footed cylinder with good color, 9½x4", $420.00. (Photo courtesy Treadway Gallery on LiveAuctioneers.com)

Vase, high shoulder, rolled-in collar, 2nd art mk, 9½"	250.00
Vase, high shoulders, cupped rim, brn/tan/cream, 1st art mk, 10¾"	625.00
Vase, high shoulders, rolled rim, bl/brn/tan, 1st art mk, 16¼", NM	1,525.00
Vase, orange-rust w/cream, classic shape, 1st art mk, 8"	375.00
Vase, pear form w/elongated cylindrical neck, 1st art mk, 9½"	400.00
Vase, planter-like w/rolled rim, 2nd art mk, 8x9½"	365.00
Vase, rose bowl shape w/perforations at top, 2nd art mk, 4½"	275.00
Vase, rose bowl shape, 1st art mk, 5x7"	140.00
Vase, squat w/rolled rim, 2nd art mk, 3x5½"	255.00
Vase, std shape w/lip flaring to 6", 2nd art mk, 12½"	665.00
Vase, teardrop shape w/narrow neck, 1st art mk, 10½"	525.00
Wall pocket, flat bk, elongated w/'ring' at base, unmk, 8½" L	500.00

Miscellaneous

Ashtray, frog w/lg open mouth, gr mottle, 3½"	100.00
Bathtub, Hot Springs Arkansas emb on side, NI, 1½x3¾"	45.00
Bowl, Peter Pan seated at rim, gr gloss, NB, 7¾"	55.00
Bowl, swan w/open body fitted for glass bowl, S-shape neck, 2nd art mk.	125.00
Cornucopia on ocean wave-like ped, wht matt, NI, 6x9"	40.00
Cup/saucer, Bouquet, matt, NI, 5" dia	27.00
Ewer, crown design, Ozark Dawn II, 16½"	215.00
Figure, Razorback Hog, emb Arkansas on side of base, NB, 3½x5½"	200.00
Figurine, recumbent fox, Ozark Dawn, 7" L	60.00
Letter on mc letterhead re distribution woes, 1934, 11x8½"	75.00
Mug, Bouquet, matt, NI, 3½"	16.00
Pitcher, Deco ball form w/orig cork/ceramic stopper, Hywood, 7½"	190.00
Pitcher, Deco streamline design, gr gloss, inset hdl/lid, 6"	245.00
Pitcher, minimally defined spout, gr gloss, appl hdl, no lid, 6½"	65.00
Pitcher, tulips emb, matt, slim, 10¾"	16.00
Planter, bird w/wings wide, yel gloss, NB, 5½"	28.00
Planter, bunny resting w/ears up, dk gr matt, NB, 4½" L	26.00
Planter, camel resting, attached basketweave container, NB, 3½"	22.00
Planter, Scottie dog, NL, 3½x4¼"	20.00
Shakers, bluebird, bl matt, unmk, 2½x3", pr	30.00
Shakers, tanks, WWI, open turret, NI, 3x4¼", pr	75.00
Teapot, Aladdin style w/intricate hdl, glossy, sticker, 6½"	135.00
Vase, flamingo & palm tree, ornate hdls, wht matt, NI, 7¼"	65.00
Vase, Ozark Dawn, 3 curved hdls, Hywood, Stoin, 6¼"	600.00
Vase, tulip, 5 openings, glossy, N, 7"	10.00
Vase, tulip, 5 openings, matt, N, 7"	25.00
Vase, tulip, 6 openings, Ozark Dawn, 7½"	32.00
Vases, ivory matt, 6x3½", pr	110.00

Nippon

Nippon generally refers to Japanese wares made during the period from 1891 to 1921, although the Nippon mark was also used to a limited extent on later wares (accompanied by 'Japan'). Nippon, meaning Japan, identified the country of origin to comply with American importation restrictions. After 1921 'Japan' was the acceptable alternative. The term does not imply a specific type of product and may be found on items other than porcelains. For further information we recommend *Van Patten's ABC's of Collecting Nippon Porcelain* by our advisor, Joan F. Van Patten (see Directory, New York). In the following listings, items are assumed hand painted unless noted otherwise. Numbers included in the descriptions refer to these specific marks:

Key:
#1 — Patent	#5 — Rising Sun
#2 — M in Wreath	#6 — Royal Kinran
#3 — Cherry Blossom	#7 — Maple Leaf
#4 — Double T Diamond in Circle	#8 — Royal Nippon, Nishiki
	#9 — Royal Moriye Nippon

Ashtray, 2 figural penguins, gr #2, 5", $1,100 to	1,300.00
Ashtray, full face lion's head, gr #2, 6 " W, $250 to	300.00
Ashtray, Mexican cowboy, 3 rests, Imperial mk, 6½", $275 to	350.00
Ashtray, sailboats on water, bl bckgrnd, gr #2, 5" W, $125 to	150.00
Ashtray, smoking skull décor, gr #2, 6" W, $800 to	1,000.00
Bowl, floral w/cobalt, scalloped rim, #6, 11½", $500 to	650.00
Bowl, floral, golden eagle on cobalt border, #2, 8½", $175 to	225.00
Bowl, oval, lav Wedgwood, gr #2, 10 " L, $550 to	650.00
Bowl, roses on shaded yel w/ornate gold border, unmk, 11¼"	425.00
Bowl, still life of peaches, apples, grapes, gr #2, 10 " W, $200 to	250.00
Box, cigarette, river scenic, bl #2, 4½" W, $400 to	475.00
Candlesticks, flying swan design, gr #2, 9", pr $900 to	1,100.00
Candlesticks, molded in relief, Egyptian design, gr #2, 8 ", pr $2,600 to	3,000
Chocolate pot, floral w/gold beading, waisted, #6, 9½", $700 to	900.00
Chocolate pot, lace/floral foliage, wht on gr, cylindrical, unmk, 9"	800.00
Cup/saucer, mustache, pk floral, bl #5, saucer 6" W, $150 to	200.00
Ewer, moriage floral (ornate) w/much gold, bulb, unmk, 7½"	750.00
Ewer, swans on cobalt & gold, bl #7, 6 ", $550 to	625.00
Ferner, Gouda-like Deco-style floral, ftd, gr hdls, #2, 6", $300 to	400.00
Game plate, burgundy border, flying ducks, jeweling, gr #2, 8 " W, $400 to	450.00
Hatpin holder, dk woodland pattern, bl #7, 4 ", $175 to	225.00
Hatpin holder, red-breasted bird on wht, #5, 4¾", $90 to	130.00
Hatpin/ring holder w/attached tray, floral, #3, 4½", $150 to	200.00
Humidor, features stylized knights dueling on horses, gr #2, 7 ", $1,600 to	1,800.00
Humidor, floral w/moriage details on gr, squirrel finial, 7", $900 to	1,100.00

Humidor, molded in relief, green mark, 7", $1,500.00 to $2,000.00. (Photo courtesy Joan Van Patten)

Humidor, moriage pipe, cigar, cigarette, matches, gr #2, 6 ", $600 to	750.00
Humidor, playing cards, pipe, cigarettes, matches, gr #2, 6 ", $500 to	600.00
Inkwell w/insert, molded in relief Egyptian decor, gr #2, 4", $1,000 to	1,200.00
Inkwell, sailing boats, windmill, sunset colors, gr #2, 4 ", $150 to	200.00
Match holder & tray, dk gray bckgrnd, cigarettes & cigar, gr #2, 3", $180 to	210.00

Mug, cottage & trees scene, gr #2, 5", $125 to.............................. 170.00
Night lt, 2-pc figural rabbit, electrified, gr #2, 6 ", $2,500 to.....3,000.00
Pen tray, floral on cobalt w/gold, HP mk, 7¾", $250 to 300.00
Pin box, monoplane scene, gr #2, 3¼" dia, $400 to 500.00
Pitcher, milk, stylized vanity scene, gr #2, 4 ", gr #2, $450 to....... 500.00
Plaque, buffalo scene in relief, gr #2, 10½", $800 to 950.00
Plate, camel & rider on cobalt & gold bckgrnd, gr #2, 10" W, $300 to.350.00
Plate, heavy gold, floral, cobalt décor, gr #2, 11" W, $600 to........ 700.00
Smoke set, 4 pcs, owl on branch, bl bckgrnd, gr #2, $700 to........ 900.00
Stein, camel & rider scene, gr #2, 7", $300 to.............................. 400.00
Stein, pk winter scene, gr #2, 7", $300 to..................................... 350.00
Stein, windmill scene, pastel colors, gr #2, 7", $250 to................. 300.00
Tankard, palms w/moriage, angle hdl, #2, 11", +6 mugs, $1,800 to..2,100.00
Tea strainer & receptacle, floral & gold décor, bl #7, 6" L, $150 to.. 200.00
Urn, bolted, gr mk, 16", $2,500 to...3,000.00
Urn, daffodils reserve, ornate gold hdls, bolted, #2, 8½" 750.00
Vase, 2 hdls, windmill décor, bl #7, 6", $140 to 180.00
Vase, Am Indian on horse, angle hdls, Imperial Nippon, 12" 750.00
Vase, arrival of the coach scene, moriage trim, bl #2, 6", $500 to . 600.00
Vase, bl Wedgwood décor, 4 columns, gr #2, 5" , $450 to............. 550.00
Vase, camel & rider scene, gold trim, gr #2, 13", $1,000 to 1,150.00
Vase, molded in relief, floral, gr #2, 7" , $350 to 425.00
Vase, orchid design both sides, beading, gr #2, 8", $400 to........... 500.00
Vase, ostrich on cobalt & gold, bl #7, 12", $1,800 to.................2,200.00
Vase, poinsettias on matt finish, gr #2, 10 ", $250 to 300.00
Vase, sailing ships, 2 hdls, gr #2, 8" , $300 to 350.00
Wall plaque, fisherman & cart, gr #2, 11", $550 to........................ 650.00
Wall plaque, full face St Bernard dog, gr #2, 12 " W, $1,600 to. 1,800.00
Wall plaque, molded in relief buffalo, gr #2, 10½" W, $600 to 800.00
Wall plaque, molded in relief full face lion, gr #2, 10" W, $900 to.. 1,050.00
Wall plaque, playing cards, pipe, beer stein, cigar, gr #2, 11", $275 to...325.00
Wall plaque, rect, cows by water's edge, gr #2, 10 " W, $1,000 to ..1,200.00
Wall plaque, still life of fish & lemons, gr #2, 12" W, $475 to 575.00
Wall plaque, still life of lobster on table's edge, gr #2, 12" W, $475 to...550.00
Wine jug, scenic in orig basket, bl #7, 11", $800 to 950.00

Nodders

So called because of the nodding action of their heads and hands, nodders originated in China where they were used in temple rituals to represent deity. At first they were made of brass and were actually a type of bell; when these bells were rung, the heads of the figures would nod. In the eighteenth century, the idea was adopted by Meissen and by French manufacturers who produced not only china nodders but bisque as well. Most nodders are individual; couples are unusual. The idea remained popular until the end of the nineteenth century and was used during the Victorian era by toy manufacturers. See also Conta and Boehme.

Tiger on ball, fabric and wood, clockwork mechanism causes head to nod, Roullet & Decamps, France, 12½", EX, $9,000.00. (Photo courtesy Noel Barrett on LiveAuctioneers.com)

Asian man, seated, porc & bsk, ca 1930s, 6"................................. 525.00
Blackamoor lady seated w/fan in hand, pnt bsk, pre-Nippon, 4"..250.00
Buddha laughing, pnt porc, head/tongue/hands nod, Meissen, 13x14". 10,200.00
Cat, chalkware w/blk, red & yel accents, 19th C, 4x8" 400.00
Clown, pnt papier maché, bl nose, glass eyes, Labarre Livres on base. 1,320.00

Donald Duck, pnt celluloid, L bill, tin base, Japan, 6".................. 780.00
Felix the Cat on motorcycle, spring in tail, Germany, 7½" 600.00
Geisha in kimono seated, Banko Ware, 4x3½" 135.00
Goose on wheeled platform, pnt tin, 2x3½" 600.00
Happy Hooligan, pnt compo figure on wood base, DRGM, ca 1915, 9"....300.00
Happy Hooligan, pnt wood, mk DRGM (Germany), ca 1915, 9", EX...300.00
Old woman in chair w/cats at ft, pnt compo, wood base, 4½" 240.00
Pluto, celluloid, tan w/blk & red details, orig tag, 8" L................. 450.00
Queen of Hearts, Alice in Wonderland, Goebel, 1950s, 5½", EX . 720.00
Santa on donkey w/metal wheels, donkey head nods, German, ca 1900, 12".725.00

Nordic Art Glass

Finnish and Swedish glass has recently started to develop a following, probably stemming from the revitalization of interest in forms from the 1950s. (The name Nordic is used here because of the inclusion of Finnish glass — the term Scandinavian does not refer to this country.) Included here are Flygsfors, Hadeland, Holmegaard, Iittala, Maleras, Motzfeldt, Nuutajarvi, Pukeberg, Reijmyre, and Strombergshyttan. Our suggested prices are fair market values, developed after researching the Nordic secondary markets, the current retail prices on items still being produced, and American auction houses and antique stores.

Benny Motzfeldt, Norwegian Glass Artist

Benny Motzfeldt (BM in listings below), a graduate of the Arts and Crafts School of Oslo, Norway, started her career in glass in 1954 by responding to an ad for a designer of engraving and decoration at Christiania Glassmagasin and Hadeland Glassverk. After several years at Hadeland, she joined the Plus organization and managed their glass studio in Frederikstad. She is acknowledged as one of the leading exponents of Norwegian art glass and is recognized internationally. She challenged the rather sober Norwegian glass designs with a strong desire to try new ways, using vigorous forms and opaque colors embedded with silver nitrate patterns.

Bowl, cranberry/mocha/wht spatter in amber, 2x4" 75.00
Cordial, crystal, long stem w/X-cuttings at base, 4 for 80.00
Vase, bl opaque w/3 abstract butterflies, BM, #89, 7x6" 300.00
Vase, clear w/blk & teal swirls & boiling bubbles, bottle form, 8". 195.00
Vase, clear w/colored granules, tall neck, flared rim, Plus Norway...115.00
Vase, clear w/random bubbles, dk fibers/cobalt patches, BM, #91, 7".. 350.00

Vase, coral with two large bubbling patches in ebony, BM, #70, acid mark: Plus Norway, 7", $600.00. (Photo courtesy Cincinnati Art Galleries, LLC on LiveAuctioneers.com)

Vase, dk bl w/open-weave fabrics/metallic inclusions, BM, #72, 4"..240.00
Vase, lav w/abstract bl & wht flowers, BM, #84, 5" 240.00
Vase, pistachio w/dk fabric/bubbles/indigo pigments, BM, #78, 6x6".. 360.00
Vase, toffee w/bl & lav granules, short neck, sq sides, 3" 265.00
Vases, metallic charcoal, rnd w/short neck, Randafjord Glasverk, pr.110.00

Flygsfors Glass Works, Sweden

Flygsfors Glass Works was established in 1888 and continued in production until 1979 when the Orrefors Glass Group, which had acquired this entity, ceased operations. The company is well known for art glass designed by Paul Kedelv, who joined the firm in 1949 with a contract to design light fittings, a specialty of the company. Their 'Coquille' series, which utilizes a unique overlay technique combining opaque, bright colors, and 'Flamingo' have become very desirable on today's secondary market. Other internationally known artists/designers include Prince Sigvard Bernadotte and the Finnish designer Helene Tynell.

Basket, Coquille, 1959, 18½", $300.00. (Photo courtesy Rose Hill Auction Gallery on LiveAuctioneers.com)

Bowl, bl & red in clear, Alexandrite-style free-form, 1957, 15" L . 155.00
Bowl, bl & wht, sculptural w/trn ends, Coquille, 11" 195.00
Bowl, blk & wht in clear, free-form w/flared ends, 1950s, 14¼" L . 120.00
Bowl, red cased in clear, Coquille, 8x13" 75.00
Lamp, gr, tall hollow form, 4-sided base, unmk, 21" 135.00
Vase, pk & wht in clear, 2 pulled ends, Coquille, 1961, 9¼" 60.00

Hadeland Glassverk, Norway

Glass has been produced at this glassworks since 1765. From the beginning, their main product was bottles. Since the 1850s they have made small items — drinking glasses, vases, bowls, jugs, etc. — and for the last 40 years, figurines, souvenirs, and objects of art. Important designers include Willy Johansson (WJ), Arne John Jutrem (AJJ), Inger Magnus, Severin Brorby, Gro Sommerfeldt (GS), and Maud Gjeruldsen Bugge (MGB).

Bowl, Dmn Quilt, olive gr w/bl rolled rim, AJJ, #4115, 3⅜x5¾".... 75.00
Bowl, olive gr w/prunts at rim, ped ft, #393 SP, 10" 325.00
Vase, amethyst w/ruby stripes & bubbles, WJ, #54, label, 4½" 420.00
Vase, bl gray w/scattered plum splotches & bubbles, WJ, #2132, 6"...165.00
Vase, bl, shouldered w/short neck/flared rim, WJ, #2132, 1960s, 6½"... 120.00
Vase, brn in clear w/gr accents, WJ, #59, 9¼x4" 110.00
Vase, brn spirals w/coral red base, GS, 5½x8¾" 200.00
Vase, lt brn in clear, dmn shape, WF, #2128, 7" 350.00
Vase, moss gr w/coral & cream thread/mc splashes, AJJ, #60, 4⅞" ..120.00
Vase, raspberry red, long slim neck, AJJ, #54, foil label, 9" 85.00
Vase, smoky gray w/suspended mocha core, JW, #2129, 2⅝" 550.00
Vase, spaced ruby stripes, controlled bubbles, WJ, #54, 4⅝"......... 425.00
Vase, wht opal w/vertical bubbles, WJ, #55, 3¾" 550.00

Holmegaard Glassvaerk, Denmark

This company was founded in 1825. Because of a shortage of wood in Denmark, it became necessary for them to use peat, the only material available for fuel. Their first full-time designers were hired after 1923. Orla Juul Nielson was the first. He was followed in 1925 by Jacob Band, an architect. Per Lukin became the chief designer in 1941. His production and art glass incorporates a simple yet complex series of designs. They continue to be popular among collectors of Scandinavian glass. During 1965 the company merged with Kastrup and became Kastrup Holmegaard AS; a merger with Royal Copenhagen followed in 1975.

Bowl, clear w/curved lip, Per Lukin, 4½x16¼"............................. 100.00
Bowl, pale smoky gray, incurvate rim, 5⅛x16½" 195.00
Candleholders, bl, Danish Modern style, low, 6¾" dia, pr 60.00
Decanter, bl, Kluk Kluk, wht stopper, #L60, 15¼x5" 100.00
Sculpture, stylized rooster, smoke to clear, 7¼x7" 30.00
Vase, bl, stacking cylinders (2) w/flat rim, #L60, 15¼x5" 180.00
Vase, clear w/frosted nude intaglio, FW, #A3, 1957, 8" 395.00
Vase, intaglio full-figure nude, Holmegaard 1957 A3, FW, 8" 390.00

Iittala Glass Works, Finland

This glassworks was founded in 1881; it was originally staffed by Swedish workers who produced glassware of very high quality. In 1917 A. Ahistrom bought and merged Iittala with Karhula Glass Works. After 1945 Karhula's production was limited to container glass. In 1946 Tapio Wirkkala, the internationally known artist/designer, became Iittala's chief designer. Timo Sarpeneva joined him in 1950. Jointly they successfully spearheaded the promotion of Finnish glass in the international markets, winning many international awards for their designs. Today, Oiva Toikka leads the design team.

Candlesticks, Festivo, icy clear, T Sarpaneva, 1967, 12⅜", pr...... 360.00
Vase, amethyst & bl in clear, hollow base, T Wirkkala, #3892, 11".........1,950.00
Vase, Bamboo, clear w/controlled bubbles, K Franck, 6x4½" 1,100.00
Vase, clear w/icicle appearance, #3429, 1954, 9¾" 950.00
Vase, cobalt in clear, spherical, T Sarpeneva, 7¾" 240.00
Vase, jack-in-pulpit, clear w/cut lines, T Wirkkala, #55, 4¾x5"... 235.00
Vase, smoky gray w/folded lip, T Sarpeneva, 1957, 5¾x8½".........240.00

Nuutajarvi Glass Works, Finland

Sculpture, bird, O Toikka, 1992, 6¼x11x5" 180.00
Vase, blown, clear w/bottle neck, JAJ Franck, 10" 155.00
Vase, clear w/forest gr drops & air bubbles, S Hopea, #55, 8¾".1,200.00
Vase, clear w/purple drops & air bubbles, S Hopea, #55, 6½x4".1,325.00
Vase, orange opaque w/blk inclusions, H Orvola, A Wartisila, 12" ..395.00
Vase, plum in clear w/trapped bubbles, G Nyman, 1930s, 12"............435.00
Vase, wht opaque spiral in clear, G Nyman, ca 1948, 17"..........1,950.00

Noritake

The Noritake Company was first registered in 1904 as Nippon Gomei Kaisha. In 1917 the name became Nippon Toki Kabushiki Toki. The 'M in wreath' mark is that of the Morimura Brothers, distributors with offices in New York. It was used until 1941. The 'tree crest' mark is the crest of the Morimura family. The company has produced fine porcelain dinnerware sets and occasional pieces decorated in the delicate manner for which the Japanese are noted. (Two dinnerware patterns are featured below, and a general range is suggested for others.)

Authority Joan Van Patten is the author of *The Collector's Encyclopedia of Noritake*; you will find her address in the Directory under New York. In the following listings, examples are hand painted unless noted otherwise. Numbers refer to these specific marks:

Key: #1mk — Komaru   #2mk — M in Wreath

Azalea

The Azalea pattern was produced exclusively for the Larkin Company, who gave the lovely ware away as premiums to club members and their home agents. From 1916 through the 1930s, Larkin distributed fine china which was decorated in pink azaleas on white with gold tracing along edges and handles. Early in the '30s, six pieces of crystal hand painted with the same design were offered: candleholders, a compote, a tray with handles, a scalloped fruit bowl, a cheese and cracker set, and a cake plate. All in all, 70 different pieces of Azalea were produced. Some, such as the 15-piece child's set, bulbous vase, china ashtray, and the pancake jug, are quite rare. One of the earliest marks was the Noritake 'M in wreath' with variations. Later the ware was marked 'Noritake, Azalea, Hand Painted, Japan.' Our advisor for Azalea is Linda Williams; she is listed in the Directory under Massachusetts.

Basket, Dolly Varden, #193	195.00
Bonbon, #184, 6¼"	52.00
Bowl, #12, 10"	28.00
Bowl, candy/grapefruit, #185	235.00
Bowl, cream soup, #363	110.00
Bowl, deep, #310	50.00
Bowl, fruit, #9, 5¼"	8.00
Bowl, fruit, scalloped, glass	85.00
Bowl, fruit, shell form, #188, 7¾"	285.00
Bowl, oatmeal, #55, 5½"	20.00
Bowl, soup, #19, 7⅛"	26.00
Bowl, vegetable, divided, #439, 9½"	220.00
Bowl, vegetable, oval, #101, 10½"	48.00
Bowl, vegetable, oval, #172, 9¼"	32.00
Bowl, vegetable, rnd, 10"	30.00
Butter chip, #312, 3¼"	70.00
Butter tub, w/insert, #54	25.00
Cake plate, #10, 9¾"	30.00
Candleholders, glass, 3½", pr	120.00
Candy jar, w/lid, #313, $525 to	625.00
Casserole, gold finial, w/lid, #372	210.00
Casserole, w/lid, #16	58.00
Celery tray, #444, closed hdls, 10"	275.00
Celery/roll tray, #99, 12"	28.00
Cheese/butter dish, #314	85.00
Cheese/cracker, glass	75.00
Child's set, #253, 15-pc	2,500.00
Coffeepot, demi, #182	575.00
Compote, #170	90.00
Compote, glass	80.00
Condiment set, #14, 5-pc	35.00
Creamer/sugar bowl, #7	38.00
Creamer/sugar bowl, demi, open, #123	125.00
Creamer/sugar bowl, gold finial, #401	85.00
Creamer/sugar bowl, scalloped, ind, #449	475.00
Creamer/sugar shaker, berry, #122	150.00
Cruet, #190	160.00
Cup/saucer, #2	15.00
Cup/saucer, bouillon, #124, 3½"	24.00
Cup/saucer, demi, #183	110.00
Egg cup, #120	28.00
Gravy boat, #40	32.00
Jam jar set, #125, 4-pc	155.00
Mayonnaise set, scalloped, #453, 3-pc, ladle w/red Azalea sprig	650.00
Mustard jar, #191, 3-pc	48.00
Olive dish, #194	18.00
Pickle/lemon set, #121	19.00
Pitcher, milk jug, #100, 1-qt	125.00
Plate, bread & butter, #8, 6½"	8.00
Plate, breakfast/luncheon, #98	15.00
Plate, dinner, #13, 9¾"	18.00
Plate, grill, 3-compartment, #38, 10¼"	175.00
Plate, salad, 7⅝" sq	48.00
Plate, scalloped sq, salesman's sample, $875 to	950.00

Platter, #17, 14"	48.00
Platter, #56, 12"	40.00
Platter, cold meat/bacon, #311, 10¼"	160.00
Platter, turkey, #186, 16"	395.00
Refreshment set, #39, 2-pc	32.00
Relish, #194, 7⅛"	52.00
Relish, 2-part, #171	45.00
Relish, 2-part, loop hdl, #450	225.00
Relish, 4-section, #119, rare, 10"	120.00
Relish, oval, #18, 8½"	15.00
Shakers, bell form, #11, pr	35.00
Shakers, bulb, #89	35.00
Shakers, ind, #126, pr	20.00
Spoon holder, #189, 8"	80.00
Syrup, #97, w/underplate & lid	92.00
Tea tile	49.00
Teapot, #15	125.00
Teapot, gold finial, #400	325.00
Toothpick holder, #192	65.00
Vase, bulb, 6¼"	1,200.00
Vase, fan form, ftd, #187	195.00

Tree in the Meadow

Another of their dinnerware lines has become a favorite of many collectors. Tree in the Meadow (also referred to as the scenic pattern by many purists) is a hand-painted pattern which features a thatched-roof cottage in a meadow with a lake in the foreground. The version accepted by most collectors will have a tree behind the cottage and will not have a swan or a bridge. Most collectors will accept the tall vase with the arched stone bridge as Tree in the Meadow due to its vibrant colors, which are a must. There are many pieces that resemble the pattern but are not true Tree in the Meadow items. The vibrant colors resemble a golden sunset on a fall day with shades of orange, gold, and rust. This line was made during the 1920s and 1930s and seems today to be in good supply. A fairly large dinnerware set with several unusual serving pieces can be readily assembled. Our advisor for Tree in the Meadow is Linda Williams; she is listed in the Directory under Massachusetts.

Jam jar, cherries on lid, four-piece, $85.00. (Photo courtesy Dotty Kay Stillman, eBay seller dottykay1)

Basket, Dolly Varden	65.00
Bowl, cream soup, 2-hdl	55.00
Bowl, fruit, 5¼"	8.00
Bowl, oatmeal	30.00
Bowl, oval, 9"	38.00
Bowl, oval, 10"	38.00
Bowl, shell form, fruit/nut, 7¾"	160.00
Bowl, soup	38.00
Bowl, vegetable, 9"	35.00
Bowl, vegetable, covered	135.00
Butter pat	45.00
Butter tub, open, w/drainer	25.00
Cake plate, open hdl	30.00

Candy dish, octagonal, w/lid, 5½" 250.00
Celery dish 25.00
Cheese dish 145.00
Coffeepot, demi 195.00
Compote 52.00
Condiment set, 5-pc 45.00
Creamer/sugar bowl 48.00
Creamer/sugar bowl, berry 98.00
Creamer/sugar bowl, demi 110.00
Cruets, vinegar & oil, cojoined 195.00
Cup/saucer, breakfast 18.00
Cup/saucer, demi 55.00
Egg cup 30.00
Gravy boat, attached plate 65.00
Lemon dish 15.00
Mayonnaise set, 3-pc 38.00
Plate, dessert, 6" 8.00
Plate, dinner, 9" 75.00
Plate, luncheon, 8⅝" 15.00
Plate, rare, 7" sq 45.00
Plate, salad, 8" 8.00
Platter, 10" 75.00
Platter, 11x9" 40.00
Platter, 13x10" 48.00
Relish, divided 18.00
Snack set (cup & tray), 2-pc 48.00
Sugar shaker 58.00
Tea tile 50.00
Teapot & lid 125.00
Vase, fan form 85.00
Vase, tall, w/stone bridge 145.00

Various Dinnerware Patterns, circa 1933 to Present

So many lines of dinnerware have been produced by the Noritake company that to list them all would require a volume in itself. And while many patterns had specific names, others did not, and it is virtually impossible to identify them all. Outlined below is a general guide for the more common pieces and patterns. The high side of the range will represent lines from about 1933 until the mid-1960s (including those marked 'Occupied Japan'), while the lower side should be used to evaluate lines made after that period.

Bowl, berry, ind, $8 to 12.00
Bowl, soup, 7½", $12 to 16.00
Bowl, vegetable, rnd or oval, ca 1945 to present, $35 to 60.00
Butter dish, 3-pc, ca 1933-64, $40 to 50.00

Creamer, Hayannis, $18.00 to $28.00. (Photo courtesy Aimee Neff Alden)

Cup/saucer, demi, $12 to 17.50
Gravy boat, $35 to 50.00
Gravy boat & underliner, Grape, $35 to 50.00
Pickle or relish dish, $18 to 28.00
Plate, bread & butter, $8 to 12.00

Plate, luncheon, $14 .... 18.00
Plate, salad, $10 to 15.00
Platter, 14", $50 to 80.00
Shakers, pr $25 to 45.00
Sugar bowl, w/lid, $18 to 30.00
Teapot, demi pot, chocolate pot or coffeepot, ea $75 to 150.00

Miscellaneous

Ashtray, 3 rests, horse head on brn bkgrnd, #2mk, 4¼" W, $80 to . 100.00
Ashtray, Deco style pyramid scene on luster, #2mk, 6½" W, $50 to . 80.00
Bowl, 2 hdls, roses on earthtone bkgrnd, #2mk, 8¼" W, $80 to ... 100.00

Bowl, flanked by two Art Deco ladies, red wreath mark, 4x8", $3,600.00. (Photo courtesy TriGreen Company on LiveAuctioneers.com)

Bowl, ped, daisies on bl, #2mk, 9" W, $100 to 120.00
Bowl, pk flowers on brn, #2mk, 7" W, $70 to 90.00
Candlesticks, cottage & tree scene, #2mk, 5", pr $75 to 110.00
Celery dish, blk & wht w/gold accents, #2mk, 12" L, $60 to 80.00
Celery dish, floral on gr, #2mk, 12½" L, $70 to 100.00
Chambersticks, gr & orange luster, #2mk, 2½", pr $80 to 100.00
Chocolate set, pot & 6 c/s, tree & cottage scene, #2mk, $120 to 160.00
Condiment set, tray, s&p, mustard jar, floral on gr, #2mk, $75 to ... 100.00
Egg warmer, wht w/flowers, #2mk, 5½" W, $90 to 110.00
Hatpin holder, cottage & meadow scene, #2mk, 5", $50 to 70.00
Humidor, trees & pond, #2mk, 8", $125 to 160.00
Lemon dish, flowers on luster bkgrnd, #2mk, 5½" W, $30 to 50.00
Muffineer, swan on pond at sunset, #2mk, 6½", $50 to 70.00
Napkin ring, Deco style girl on luster, #2mk, $40 to 60.00
Nut bowl, relief molded peanuts, #2mk, 7¼" W, $100 to 140.00
Nut set, master bowl, 6 sm dishes, nut decor, #2mk, 6" W 120.00
Pickle dish, parrot on perch on luster, #2mk, 6¼" L, $45 to 65.00
Plate, serving, Art Deco bird center hdl, #2mk, 8½" W, $125 to 150.00
Refreshment set, red bkgrnd w/birds, #2mk, tray 8½" L, $60 to 85.00
Salts, set of 4, flowers on bl bkgrnd, #2mk, $40 to 60.00
Spooner, stylized mums, orange trim, #2mk, 7½" L, $50 to 70.00
Sugar shaker & creamer set, floral on wht, #2mk, 6½", $70 to 90.00
Tea set, child sz, purple & bl flowers, #2mk, $85 to 110.00
Trivet, horse head design, #2mk, 5" W, $60 to 80.00
Vase, cornucopia shaped, bird & flowers, #2mk 4¾", $70 to 100.00
Vase, ftd, luster w/parrot, #2mk, 7½", $150 to 200.00
Vase, luster w/2 crocus, #2mk, 8", $75 to 100.00
Wall pocket, bl luster, tree scene, #2mk, 8", $80 to 100.00

Norse

The Norse Pottery was established in 1903 in Edgerton, Wisconsin, by Thorwald Sampson and Louis Ipson. A year later it was purchased by A.W. Wheelock and moved to Rockford, Illinois. The ware they produced was inspired by ancient bronze vessels of the Norsemen. Designs were often incised into the red clay body. Dragon handles and feet were favored decorative devices, and they achieved a semblance of patina through the application of metallic glazes. The ware was marked with model numbers and a stylized 'N' containing a vertical arrangement of the remaining letters of the name. Production ceased after 1913. Our advisor for this category is John Danis; he is listed in the Directory under Illinois.

Candlesticks, snakes, verdrigris on bl, slim, #54, 11½", pr............ 300.00
Humidor, verdigris on bronze, Egyptian-revival snakes, animal ft, 8".. 1,800.00
Pedestal, women (hammered/tooled) on bronze, #98, 19x12", NM. 1,440.00
Urn, blk bronzed w/emb foliate branches, 4-hdl, #24, 9"........... 1,325.00
Vase, Aztec birds & faces, verdigris on blk, 3-ftd, #62, 6" 780.00
Vase, Egyptian warrior & foe, verdigris on bronze, hdls, #10, 13".. 1,200.00
Vase, snake heads/lions, verdigris on bronze, 3-ftd, #31, 5½" 515.00
Vase, tepees & water incised, verdigris on bronze, baluster, 9½x8"... 780.00
Vase, verdigris on blk, 2 dragon hdls/3 dragon-head ft, 14" W.. 1,080.00
Vase, verdigris on bronze, appl salamander, trumpet neck, 11½x7".. 1,200.00

North Dakota School of Mines

The School of Mines of the University of North Dakota was estab-lished in 1890, but due to a lack of funding it was not until 1898 that Earle J. Babcock was appointed as director, and efforts were made to produce ware from the native clay he had discovered several years earlier. The first pieces were made by firms in the east from the clay Babcock sent them. Some of the ware was decorated by the manufacturer; some was shipped back to North Dakota to be decorated by native artists. By 1909 students at the University of North Dakota were producing utilitarian items such as tile, brick, shingles, etc. in conjunction with a ceramic course offered through the chemistry department. By 1910 a ceramic department had been established, supervised by Margaret Kelly Cable. Under her leader-ship, fine artware was produced. Native flowers, grains, buffalo, cowboys, and other subjects indigenous to the state were incorporated into the deco-rations. Some pieces have an Art Nouveau – Art Deco style easily attrib-uted to her association with Frederick H. Rhead, with whom she studied in 1911. During the '20s the pottery was marketed on a limited scale through gift and jewelry stores in the state. From 1927 until 1949 when Miss Cable announced her retirement, a more widespread distribution was maintained with sales branching out into other states. The ware was marked in cobalt with the official seal — 'Made at School of Mines, N.D. Clay, University of North Dakota, Grand Forks, N.D.' in a circle. Very early ware was some-times marked 'U.N.D.' in cobalt by hand. Our advisor for this category is William M. Bilsland III; he is listed in the Directory under Iowa.

Vase, turkeys on a tree branch under a full moon, shoulder carved: Awarded by the 1934 All-American Turkey Show Grand Forks N.C. for Excellence, exceptional artwork by Margaret Cable, #893, 8x5½", $14,400.00. (Photo courtesy Rago Arts and Auction Center)

Curtain pull, 3-flower cluster, UND circle stamp, 2x1¾" 165.00
Curtain pull, oval, w/flower, stamped UND (block letters), 1⅝x2¼".. 145.00
Medallion, football player, stamped UND/Homecoming/1938, 2⅜x1½".. 350.00
Medallion, Indian head, stamped UND (block letters), rnd, 2⅛" . 195.00
Plate, man in sombrero on donkey, mc on gr, MEA/4/14/51, 9½". 840.00
Vase, Arabian night scene, blk on caramel, Marie B Thormodsgard, 1930, 7¾".7,800.00
Vase, band of figures holding hands, brn matt, D Nasset, 4½x4¾" . 1,300.00
Vase, daffodils, gr, J Mattson/M Cable, 5x5" 2,300.00
Vase, forest landscape, Thorne & Flora Huckfield, rstr chip, 10½"...8,400.00
Vase, irises (cvd), wht on indigo, S Mason, 1935, 8x5".............4,500.00
Vase, prairie rose, F Huckfield/student, #207, 5¾x5¼" 850.00
Vase, prairie rose, gr matt, M Cable, #44, 8½x5¾" 1,300.00
Vase, stylized flowers, yel on celadon, F Huckfield, 9¼x5¼"...10,250.00
Vase, stylized trees, brn on amber, ME Collins, 7¾x4¾"............4,500.00
Vase, tepees on geometric band, J Mattson, Elgin, 4¾x6" 800.00
Vase, Viking ships, bls/grs, J Mattson, #236, 3¾x4¼" 1,800.00

North State

In 1924 the North State Pottery of Sanford, North Carolina, began small-scale production, the result of the extreme fondness Mrs. Rebecca Copper had for potting. With the help of her husband Henry and the abundance of suitable local clay, the pottery flourished and became well known for lovely shapes and beautiful glazes. They shared the knowledge they gained from their glaze experiments with the ceramic engineer-ing department of North Carolina University, and during summer vaca-tion they often employed some of the university students. Salt-glazed stoneware was produced in the early years but was quickly abandoned in favor of Henry's vibrant glazes. Colors of copper red, Chinese Red, moss green, and turquoise blue were used alone and in combination, producing bands of blending colors. Some swirl ware was made as well. The pottery was in business for 35 years; most of its ware was sold in gift and craft shops throughout North Carolina. Items in the following descriptions are earthenware.

Bowl, dbl-dip bl, flat loop hdls, 2nd mk, 4½x6" 120.00
Bowl, gr to crimson, free-form, 8".. 36.00
Pitcher, bl-gr runs on bl, 2nd stamp, 6½" 155.00
Pitcher, refrigerator, Chinese Bl, high arched hdl, 8½" 360.00
Pitcher, turq bl, horizontal ribs, 5½"... 72.50
Teapot, yel, w/lid, glaze chip, 6¾x7½x5".. 300.00
Vase, Chinese Bl, att Walter Owen, 8⅜".. 155.00
Vase, chrome red, sm loop hdls, 7".. 395.00
Vase, dbl-dip bl on bl, rim-to-hip hdls, unmk, 8"............................ 85.00
Vase, dbl-dip bl over dk gr, 2nd stamp, 6¾" 235.00
Vase, dk gr, loop hdls, 4¼" 72.50
Vase, salt glaze over cobalt, bulb w/ruffled rim, 2nd mk, 8¼" 475.00
Vase, salt glaze w/dk brn drips, squat w/rolled rim, 5¼x6" 480.00
Vase, tan w/dk/red/bl/lt bl drips, 8⅜".. 360.00

Northwood Glass

The Northwood Company was founded in 1896 in Indiana, Penn-sylvania, by Harry Northwood, whose father, John, was the art director for Stevens and Williams, an English glassworks. Northwood joined the National Glass Company in 1899 but in 1901 again became an inde-pendent contractor and formed the Harry Northwood Glass Company of Wheeling, West Virginia. He marketed his first carnival glass in 1908, and it became his most popular product. His company was also famous for its custard, goofus, and pressed glass. Northwood died in 1923, and the company closed. See also Carnival Glass; Custard Glass; Goofus Glass; Opalescent Glass; Pattern Glass.

Bowl, master berry, Royal Ivy, frosted rubina 120.00
Butter, Peach, emerald gr w/gold 70.00
Compote, jelly, Scroll w/Acanthus, purple mosaic/slag, 5" 75.00

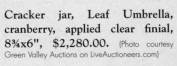

Cracker jar, Leaf Umbrella, cranberry, applied clear finial, 8¾x6", $2,280.00. (Photo courtesy Green Valley Auctions on LiveAuctioneers.com)

Cruet, Royal Oak, frosted rubina, w/orig stopper 350.00
Pitcher, Royal Ivy, rainbow spatter satin, ½-gal 275.00
Pitcher, tankard, Oriental Poppy, emerald grn w/ gold 225.00
Salt & Pepper, Royal Ivy, clear rubina, orig caps, 2¾", pr 70.00
Spooner, Peach, emerald grn w/ gold 40.00
Spooner, Regent, cobalt w/gold décor 55.00
Sugar shaker, Royal Ivy, clear rubina, orig metal top 200.00
Sugar w/lid, Peach, emerald grn w/ gold 55.00
Syrup, Royal Oak, frosted rubina, orig metal lid 350.00
Toothpick holder, Leaf Umbrella, cased bl over wht, satin.......... 150.00
Toothpick holder, Royal Oak, clear frosted 45.00
Toothpick holder, Royal Oak, frosted rubina 120.00
Tumbler, Cherry & Cable, crystal 4" 22.00
Tumbler, Intaglio gr w/gold trim 18.00
Tumbler, Leaf Umbrella, cased bl over opal, 3¾" 60.00
Tumbler, Royal Ivy, clear frosted 25.00
Tumbler, Tear Drop Flower, bl w/gold trim, 4" 35.00
Vase, corn, ftd, milky wht, 6½" 170.00
Vase, spiral, coral red, ftd, 7¼" 32.00
Vase, spiral, coral red, ftd, 9" 42.00
Vase, swung, coral red, 14" 70.00
Water set, Royal Ivy, pitcher, 9½", 4 tumblers, rainbow spatter ..550.00

Chrysanthemum Sprig, Blue

This is the blue opaque version of Northwood's popular pattern, Chrysanthemum Sprig. It was made at the turn of the century and is today very rare, as its values indicate. Prices are influenced by the amount of gold remaining on the raised designs. Unless noted otherwise, our values are for examples with excellent to near-mint gold.

Bowl, berry, ind, M gold, 2⅝x5x3¾", $90 to 125.00
Bowl, master fruit, 8x5x10½" 450.00
Butter dish, $900 to 1,200.00
Compote, jelly.. 45.00
Condiment tray, rare, VG gold 600.00
Creamer, $300 to 375.00

Cruet, 6½", $510.00. (Photo courtesy Green Valley Auctions on LiveAuctioneers.com)

Pitcher, 8", $800 to $1,000.00
Shakers, pr.. 300.00
Spooner, $275 to... 325.00
Sugar bowl, w/lid, 7", M gold, $400 to 475.00
Toothpick holder, 2¾", $375 to 450.00
Tumbler, 3¾", $90 to... 125.00

Norweta

Norweta pottery was produced by the Northwestern Terra Cotta Company of Chicago, Illinois. Both matt and crystalline glazes were em-

ployed, and terra cotta vases were also produced. It was made for approximately 10 years, beginning sometime before 1907. Not all pieces were marked.

Doorstop, seated elf, 9x5" 400.00
Lamp base, modeled as a tulip w/4 buttress leaves, bl/gr/yel, 12¼x8" .2,040.00
Vase, bl & tan crystalline, flat shoulder, firing line, 8⅜" 1,200.00
Vase, bl & wht crystalline, shouldered, sm blisters, 4" 360.00
Vase, bl crystalline on tan, 8½" 1,200.00
Vase, cobalt & beige crystalline, baluster, 8x5" 1,325.00
Vase, full-height leaves on turq matt w/brn clay showing, 8¼x5" .725.00
Vase, gray-purple crystalline mottle, baluster, #106, 12x5½".....1,950.00

Nutcrackers

The nutcracker, though a strictly functional tool, is a good example of one to which man has applied ingenuity, imagination, and engineering skills. Though all were designed to accomplish the same end, hundreds of types exist in almost every material sturdy enough to withstand sufficient pressure to crack the nut. Figurals are popular collectibles, as are those with unusual design and construction. Patented examples are also desirable. For more information, we recommend *Nutcrackers* by Robert Mills.

Bear head, Blk Forest cvg, glass eyes, ca 1900, 7½x3¾" 150.00
Coachman, cvd wood, Continental, 12"..840.00
Dog, cast brass, tail activates jaws, Weiser Hdwe Mfg, 6½x11" 40.00
Dog, CI, flat blk pnt, tail activates jaw, 4x8", VG........................... 50.00
Dog, CI, Harper Supply Co, late 19th C... 50.00
Eagle head, CI w/pnt chips & losses, 7x7½x3" 75.00
Elephant, CI, orange-red pnt w/blk & wht details, twine tail, 10" ..100.00
Fox head, CI w/NP traces, walnut base, Pat June 1920, 6x10" 50.00

Hand clenching a nut, combination screw-type nutcracker and cane, Continental, 35", $240.00. (Photo courtesy Alex Cooper Auctioneers, Inc. on LiveAuctioneers.com)

Koi fish, wood w/gouge-cvd eyes/scales/etc, articulated body, 8½" L ..110.00
Man in the moon, wood cvg, EX detail, hinged jaws, 5x5½x2" ...215.00
Man w/beard & cap, cvd walnut, articulated jaw & hdl, 8" L 110.00
Monkey seated, pnt wood, glass eyes, articulated jaw & hdl, 8½" . 200.00
Parrot, pnt CI, tall hdl works beak, 5¼x10", NM 100.00
Prussian military man's head w/helmet & mustache, cvd wood, 9" ..550.00
Rabbit head, Blk Forest cvg, glass eyes, pnt mouth, 1900s, 7"...... 275.00
Rabbit's head, glass eyes, pyro decor, folk art, 9" 275.00
Squirrel, CI w/spring-loaded tail up, glass eyes.............................. 165.00
Squirrel, CI, full figure w/tail hdl, 10x9x4" on wooden base 395.00
Squirrel, cvd wood w/nuts perched atop pliers style, 9½" 225.00

Wallace Nutting

Wallace Nutting (1861 – 1941) was America's most famous photographer of the early twentieth century. A retired minister, Nutting took more than 50,000 pictures, keeping 10,000 of his best and destroying the rest. His popular and bestselling scenes included exterior scenes (apple blossoms, country lanes, orchards, calm streams, and rural American countrysides), interior scenes (usually featuring a colonial woman working near a hearth), and foreign scenes (typically thatch-roofed cottages). His poorest selling pictures, which have become today's rarest and most highly collectible, are classified as miscellaneous unusual scenes and include categories not mentioned above: animals, architecturals, children, florals, men, seascapes, and snow scenes. Process prints are 1930s machine-produced reprints of 12 of Nutting's most popular pictures. These have minimal value and can be detected by using a magnifying glass.

Nutting sold literally millions of his hand-colored platinotype pictures between 1900 and his death in 1941. He started in Southbury, Connecticut, and later moved his business to Framingham, Massachusetts. The peak of Wallace Nutting picture production was 1915 – 1925. During this period Nutting employed nearly 200 people, including colorists, darkroom staff, salesmen, and assorted office personnel. Wallace Nutting pictures proved to be a huge commercial success and scarcely an American household was without one by 1925.

While attempting to seek out the finest and best early American furniture as props for his colonial interior scenes, Nutting became an expert in early American antiques. He published nearly 20 books in his lifetime, including his 10-volume *State Beautiful* series and various other books on furniture, photography, clocks, stools, chairs, settles, settees, tables, stands, desks, mirrors, beds, chests of drawers, cabinet pieces, and treenware. He made furniture as well, which he clearly marked with a distinctive paper label that was glued directly onto the piece, or a block or script signature brand which was literally branded into the furniture.

The overall synergy of the Wallace Nutting name — on pictures, books, and furniture — has made anything 'Wallace Nutting' quite collectible. Our advisor for this category is Michael Ivankovich, author of many books on Nutting: *The Collector's Guide to Wallace Nutting Pictures* and corresponding *Price Guide*; *The Alphabetical and Numerical Index to Wallace Nutting Pictures*; *Collector's Guide to Wallace Nutting Furniture*; *The Guide to Wallace Nutting Furniture*; *Collector's Value Guide to Early 20th Century Prints*; *The Guide to Wallace Nutting-Like Photographers of the Early 20th Century*; and *The Hand-Painted Pictures of Charles Henry Sawyer*. Mr. Ivankovich is also expert in Bessie Pease Gutmann, Maxfield Parrish, and R. Atkinson Fox, and is listed in the Directory under Pennsylvania. Prices below are for pictures in good to excellent condition. Mat stains or blemishes, poor picture color, or frame damage can decrease value significantly.

Books

England Beautiful, 2nd ed.. 45.00
Furniture of the Pilgrim Century 100.00
Maine Beautiful, 1st ed 45.00
Maine Beautiful, 2nd ed 40.00
New Hampshire Beautiful, 2nd ed..................................... 40.00
Vermont Beautiful, 2nd ed.. 40.00
Wallace Nutting Biography 100.00

Furniture

Stand, maple Sheraton, one-drawer, block branded signature, $1,680.00.
(Photo courtesy Michael Ivankovich Antiques & Auction Company on LiveAuctioneers.com)

Bed, mahog, #823-B...2,600.00
Butterfly table, #625..2,200.00
Chaise lounge, adjustable back, 43x75x23" 965.00
Country Dutch chair, #461 .... 400.00
Hutch table, pine... 825.00
Ladder-bk side chair, 4-rung, #392, block brand 475.00
Lowboy, maple, #691..3,000.00
Mirror, gold, 3-feather, #761, imp brand 575.00
Table, Pembroke, #628 ....1,600.00
Table, refractory, oak, #601, block brand 935.00
Windsor armchair, 6-spindle fan-back, bentwood arms, rfn, 41".. 515.00
Windsor candlestand, tripod, #17, block brand 525.00
Windsor side chair, #301 .... 525.00
Windsor side chair, maple, 9-spindle back, orig label, #38X311, 45". 575.00
Windsor tenon armchair, #422 ....1,500.00
Windsor writing armchair, #730..............................5,100.00
Winsor side chair, fan-back, #310 .... 750.00

Pictures

As It Was in 1700, 10x12"....................................... 360.00
Chair for John, 11x14"... 180.00
Christmas Jelly, 7x13.. 500.00
Coming Out of Rosa, 13x16".................................... 300.00
In Tenderleaf, 11x17".. 150.00
Patti's Favorite Walk, 10x12" 275.00
Quilting Party, 11x14" 325.00
Stepping Heavenward, 29x19" 1,080.00
Sturdy Beauty, 29x19"... 275.00
Summer Wind, 11x14" 185.00
Trimming the Pie, 7½x9".. 240.00
Untitled river scene, 3x6¼".................................... 120.00
Water Tracery.. 95.00
Where Grandma Was Wed.. 190.00

Occupied Japan

Items marked 'Occupied Japan' were produced during the period from the end of World War II until April 18, 1952, when the occupation ended. By no means was all of the ware exported during that time marked 'Occupied Japan'; some was marked 'Japan' or 'Made In Japan.' It is thought that because of the natural resentment felt by the Japanese toward the occupation, only a fraction of these wares carried the 'Occupied' mark. Even though you may find identical 'Japan'-marked items, because of its limited use, only those with the 'Occupied Japan' mark are being collected to any great extent. Values vary considerably, based on the quality of workmanship. Generally, bisque figures command much higher prices than porcelain, since on the whole they are of a finer quality.

Our advisor for this category is Florence Archambault; she is listed in the Directory under Rhode Island. She represents the Occupied Japan Club, whose mailing address may be found in the Clubs, Newsletters, and Websites section. All items described in the following listings are common ceramic pieces unless noted otherwise.

Ashtray, dragon decor w/gold accents, $3 to.........................5.00
Ashtray, floral on gr, $2 to 3.00
Basket, figural bird hdl, $10 to...................................... 12.00
Biscuit/cracker jar, tomato figural, Maruhonware, w/hdl, $85 to.. 100.00
Bookends, girl seated w/watering can, 3½", $25 to 30.00
Bookends, ship, emb wood, $65 to 75.00
Bowl, cereal, Blue Willow, MIOJ, 5¾", $13 to................. 16.00
Box, cigarette, Moss & Rose on wht, HP Andrea, $8 to 10.00
Box, cigarette, wht w/pk rose & gold, $10 to 13.00

Box, piano form, emb world w/wings on lid, metal, $15 to............ 20.00
Cigarette lighter, Bakelite & SP, ca 1950, 5" L.............................. 90.00
Creamer, bl floral band on wht, Aichi China, $8 to....................... 10.00
Cup/saucer, demi, floral medallion on rust, H Kato, $13 to........... 16.00
Cup/saucer, ladies, red rim, Ardalt Lenwile China #6521, $20 to.. 22.00
Dinnerware, complete set for 12 w/all major serving pcs............. 500.00
Dinnerware, service for 4, 3 szs of plates, w/berries+soups+cr/sug . 150.00
Dinnerware, service for 8+cr/sug+gravy+2 lg/1 sm platter........... 350.00
Doll, baby in red snowsuit, celluloid, $40 to................................. 50.00
Figurine, Asian lady w/basket on head, 8", $25 to......................... 28.00
Figurine, ballerina, Orion Pat #7672, 4¾", $45 to.......................... 50.00
Figurine, boy seated playing guitar, $4 to..5.00
Figurine, bulldog standing, $18 to.. 20.00
Figurine, Cinderella & Prince Charming, Maruyama, 8", $150 to..175.00
Figurine, courting couple, 7x5".. 150.00
Figurine, cowgirl, $8 to... 10.00
Figurine, dog w/hat & pipe, 3½", $8 to... 10.00
Figurine, Dolly Dimples w/rabbit, $10 to.. 13.00
Figurine, elf w/log, $10 to.. 13.00
Figurine, frog w/accordion, sm, $10 to.. 12.50
Figurine, girl w/feather in hair, bsk, 4½", $10 to............................... 12.00
Figurine, girl w/songbook, Ucagco, 5¾", $35 to................................ 40.00

Figurine, lady, 6", $15.00 to $20.00. (Photo courtesy Cathy and Gene Florence)

Figurine, lady & man w/mandolin, 5", $35 to.................................. 40.00
Figurine, lady in crinoline dress, #526, 5½", $20 to.......................... 30.00
Figurine, lady w/fan & man w/hat, HP, 6½", $50 to........................ 60.00
Figurine, ladybug w/broom, #92796, $10 to...................................... 13.00
Figurine, old lady gnome, 3¾", $6 to..8.00
Figurine, peacock w/head up & tail around ft, 5", $18 to.............. 20.00
Figurine, Spanish lady w/wide brim hat & basket, Ucagco, 7", $35 to.40.00
Lamp, colonial couple seated, pastels, bsk, Maruyama, $65 to....... 75.00
Pitcher, figural rooster, beak spout, tail hdl, $23 to........................ 26.00
Planter, dog w/blk spots, rainbow-like mk, 4½", $6 to........................8.00
Planter, shepherd boy & lamb beside well, $8 to.............................. 10.00
Plate, cabin scene w/chickens, $18 to... 20.00
Plate, geisha girls at river's edge, #6078 Ardalt HP, $25 to............ 30.00
Plate, lg yel flower on wht, gold rim, Ucagco, $13 to....................... 16.00
Plate, serving; floral on blk, papier-maché, Isco, $8 to..................... 12.00
Plate, yel floral on wht, sq w/hdls, JA in HP shield, $8 to............. 10.00
Platter, sm apple design on wht, Ucagco China, 15", $20 to.......... 25.00
Saucer, alternating bl & floral on wht panels, Aiyo China, $2 to.....3.00
Saucer, orange flower on blk, $2 to...3.00
Shakers, clown on drum, pr $80 to.. 90.00
Shakers, strawberry, pr $10 to.. 12.00
Stein, emb couple w/dog, twisted vine-like hdl, 8½", $35 to.......... 40.00
Sugar bowl, sm apple design, Ucagco China in gold, $10 to.......... 13.00
Teapot, pnt emb floral on brn, ornate hdl, $35 to............................ 40.00
Toy phone, floral decor, mini, $5 to..8.00
Tray, floral, papier-maché, rect, $15 to.. 18.00
Vase, angel boy supports flower-form vase, pastels, 3½".................. 15.00
Vase, pnt emb dragon on blk w/gold, $15 to..................................... 18.00

George Ohr

Finding his vocation late in life, George Ohr set off on a two-year learning journey around 1880, visiting as many potteries as he could find in the 16 states he traveled through, including the Kirkpatrick brothers' Anna Pottery and Susan Frackelton's studio. Upon his return George built his Pot-Ohr-y, took a wife, made babies — some flesh, some clay. After a devastating fire destroyed a large section of the town in 1893, George rebuilt his homestead and studio and seemed to gain inspiration from new surroundings. His 'Mud Babies' became paper-thin, full of movement, wild ear-shaped handles, impish snakes, suggestive shapes, and inventive glazes. Ohr threw out the rules of folk pottery's sponge-glazing, covering only a section of a vessel with a particular color or pattern, mixing dead-matt greens or purples with bright yellow flambés, and topping it all in brown gunmetal drips. This was accomplished among the derisive smiles and lack of understanding he encountered from a society accustomed to the propriety of neo-Japanese wares such as Rookwood and Trenton Belleek or the plainness of salt-glazed stoneware.

About the time he decided to move away from branding his pots with one version or another of 'GEORGE E OHR, Biloxi, Miss.' and start signing them 'as if it were a check,' Ohr also came to the realization that he did not care to glaze them anymore. He appreciated the qualities of unadorned fired clays and enjoyed mixing different types, which he often dug from the neighboring Tchoutacabouffa River. His shapes became increasingly more abstract and modern, probably ostracizing him even more from a potential clientele, to whom he would relent to sell only his entire output of thousands of pieces at once.

Today George Ohr's legacy shines as the unequaled, unrivaled product of the preeminent art potter — iconaclast, inventive, multi-faceted, the first American abstract artist. Our advisors for this category are Suzanne Perrault and David Rago; they are listed in the Directory under New Jersey.

Coffeepot, teal green and indigo sponged, 6¾x6½", $9,750.00. (Photo courtesy Rago Arts and Auction Center)

Bottle, sponged-on teal bl on amber, 7x3½"..............................4,200.00
Mug, Joe Jefferson, incised w/quote, 1896..1,465.00
Pitcher, brn speckled, dimple rows, twisted hdl, GE Ohr, Biloxi Miss, 4x4".2,280.00
Pitcher, bsk, 2 deep in-body twists, ribbon hdl, 5¼"..................6,600.00
Pitcher, deep in-body folds at waist, bsk, script mk, 3½x5".......3,240.00
Vase, amber, sponged, 9¼x3¾"..1,850.00
Vase, blk & brn sponging on gr speckled, stovepipe neck, 4½".4,500.00
Vase, brn-speckled khaki gr & orange, sm chip, 5x3½"............1,200.00
Vase, bsk fired, ftd, dbl-lobed rim w/minor wear, script sgn, 6½x3"..2,040.00
Vase, dk grn & amber, long vertical dimples, closed-in rim, 6½x3"..1,560.00
Vase, emerald gr, 3¼x4¾"..3,000.00
Vase, gr & amber mottle, re-glazed rim, 6¼x3½"......................1,200.00
Vase, gr & indigo gunmetal, milk-can shape w/snake, curled hdl, 6"..15,600.00
Vase, gunmetal & brn speckles on gr, squat, 3x4½"..................2,150.00
Vase, gunmetal & gr speckles, in-body twist, spherical, 3½x3¾"...6,000.00
Vase, gunmetal brn, amber panels, 8¼x4½"...............................1,250.00
Vase, gunmetal brn speckled, 2 ribbon hdls, 4½x4"..................5,400.00
Vase, gunmetal brn, deep dimples, bottle form, 4x2½"..............1,550.00

Vase, gunmetal speckled, amber & gr, rim rstr, 4½x4" 950.00
Vase, gunmetal to mottled gr on beige, pie-crust rim, 3¼x6" 5,400.00
Vase, gunmetal w/tortoiseshell int, dimpled, closed-in rim, 3x5¼". 3,350.00
Vase, gunmetal, pinched corners at rim, ftd, 3x5½" 2,280.00
Vase, indigo, baluster, 3¾x2¼" 1,550.00
Vase, marbleized forest gr, 2½x3" 1,560.00
Vase, mc drips on mottled leathery matt, folded rim, 4¾x5" ... 36,000.00
Vase, mottled brn & red, bulb, flaring rim, sgn, 5½x3" 1,100.00
Vase, mottled gunmetal brn, closed-in rim, 3½x5" 1,450.00
Vase, mottled indigo, bulb, deep in-body twist, 4¾x3½" 3,000.00
Vase, orange/raspberry/gr/cobalt sponging, twist at rim, 3x4" 6,000.00
Vase, purple & gr sponged-on & mottled, bulb, 7x4½" 11,400.00
Vase, raspberry speckled, deep in-body twist, rare, 4¼x3" 8,400.00
Vase, volcanic raspberry w/gr int, low, 2¼x4" 5,400.00
Vessel, amber & gunmetal, floriform top, 3½x2½" 3,240.00
Vessel, apple gr, wht clay, minor nicks to rim, 2¾x5" 1,920.00
Vessel, gr & amber mottled, folded as pouch, 2½x4¼" 4,200.00
Vessel, gunmetal, grn-speckled amber, spherical, 3x4" 2,880.00
Vessel, gunmetal, ribbed, folded rim, 4x3¼" 2,040.00
Vessel, gunmetal, script sgn, 3x4¼" 1,200.00
Vessel, gunmetal, squat, heart-shaped rim, 2¾x3¾" 1,200.00
Vessel, gunmetal, squat, pinched floriform rim, 2¾x4½" 2,640.00
Water jug, teal gr speckled, melt fissures, 1896, 8x5" 1,680.00

Old Ivory

Old Ivory dinnerware was produced from 1882 to 1928 by Hermann Ohme of Lower Salzbrunn in Silesia. The patterns are referred to by the numbers stamped on the bottom. There are some early patterns with no numbers, but these are usually stamped with a blank name. The factory mark most often seen is a small fleur-de-lis sometimes having either Silesia, Germany, or Prussia under it. The handwritten numbers are artist identification or manufacturing numbers, not pattern numbers. The patterns with flowers in pink, lavender, yellow, and some pieces with fruit decor bring higher prices at this time. These are still on the soft ivory background. Worn gold and any damage will certainly reduce the value of any item unless it is extremely rare. Holly patterns remain desirable. Beware of copycat pieces produced by other manufacturers. They are not included in this listing. Also note that portrait pieces bring higher prices percentage-wise than common pieces. Prices have declined even more this past year, reflecting the U.S. economic situation. The severe economic recession, along with the variability on the internet have lowered values alarmingly.

For more information, we recommend *Collector's Encyclopedia of Old Ivory China, The Mystery Explored,* by Alma Hillman (our advisor), David Goldschmitt, and Adam Szynkiewicz. Ms. Hillman is listed in the Directory under Maine.

Cracker jar, #12, Clairon blank, $400.00. (Photo courtesy Alma Hillman)

Berry set, #16, Clairon blank, $40 to 70.00
Bowl, #4, oval, Elysee blank, $125 to 150.00
Bowl, berry, #34, Emp blank, $75 to 95.00
Bun tray, #82, Alice blank, $125 to 200.00

Cake plate, #84, Emp blank, $35 to 50.00
Cake plate, #107, Emp blank, $200 to 250.00
Cake plate, #204, Deco blank, $150 to 200.00
Cake set, #73, Clairon blank, $150 to 200.00
Charger, #12, Clairon blank, $300 to 400.00
Charger, #15, Emp blank, $100 to 200.00
Chocolate pot, #U18, Etoile blank, $300 to 400.00
Chocolate pot, #U22, Eglantine blank, $400 to 500.00
Chocolate set, #75, Emp blank, $200 to 300.00
Chocolate set, #120, 6 c/s, Emp blank 800.00
Coffeepot, #16, Clairon blank, $800 to 1,200.00
Cracker jar, #22, Clairon blank, $500 to 600.00
Creamer/sugar, #16, Clairon blank, $40 to 50.00
Creamer/sugar, #79, Florette blank, $300 to 400.00
Cup/saucer, #12, Clairon blank, $40 to 60.00
Cup/saucer, #41, Florette blank, $75 to 100.00
Cup/saucer, #62, Florette blank, $100 to 150.00
Cup/saucer, #69, Florette blank, $100 to 150.00
Cup/saucer, bouillon, #16, Clairon blank, $100 to 125.00
Cup/saucer, demi, #U17, Etoile blank, $200 to 250.00
Cup/saucer, mustache, #113, Eglantine blank, $200 to 250.00
Demitasse pot, #114, Clairon blank, $800 to 800.00
Demitasse pot, #118, Emp blank, $400 to 500.00
Mustard pot, #15, Carmen blank, $75 to 150.00
Mustard pot, #99, Clairon blank, $200 to 300.00
Nappy, #76, Louis XVI blank, $200 to 250.00
Nappy, #122, Clairon blank, $125 to 175.00
Pitcher, water, #7, Acanthus blank, $800 to 1,000.00
Plate, #10, Clairon blank, 7½", $40 to 50.00
Plate, #97, Clairon blank, 9¾", $500 to 600.00
Plate, #U18, Etoile blank, 8½", $75 to 90.00
Plate, soup, #7, Clairon blank, 9½", $150 to 200.00
Shakers, s&p, #22, Louis XVI blank, $175 to 250.00
Tea tile, #15, Alice blank, $100 to 150.00
Waste bowl, #69, Alice blank, $175 to 200.00

Clear-Glazed Hotelware by Hermann Ohme, 1882 – 1928

The clear-glazed hotelware by Ohme is steadily climbing in popularity and price. We have included some pieces in this finish for comparison. There are many more shapes and patterns of the clear glaze than the Old Ivory. A few experimental pieces have even surfaced. The body is white and many of the same patterns found on the Old Ivory are used on these pieces. It will bear the same fleur-de-lis mark.

Cake plate, Florette blank, fish decor, 7½", $30 to 50.00
Chocolate set, Clairon blank, gr iris decor, $200 to 300.00
Creamer/sugar, Carmen blank, pk floral, $50 to 65.00
Cup/saucer, coffee, Worcester blank, lav floral, $65 to 100.00
Gravy boat, Deco blank, floral band, $20 to 30.00
Plate, Rivoli blank, cherries, heavy gold, 10½" 100.00

Shakers, salt and pepper, #7, Louis XVI blank, heavy gold/roses, $40.00. (Photo courtesy Alma Hillman)

Soup tureen, Rivoli blank, pk floral 300.00
Tea tray, Alice blank, yel roses, $300 to 400.00
Teapot, Swirl blank, all wht, $50 to 75.00

Old Paris

Old Paris porcelains were made from the mid-eighteenth century until about 1900. Seldom marked, the term refers to the area of manufacture rather than a specific company. In general, the ware was of high quality, characterized by classic shapes, colorful decoration, and gold application.

Biscuit jar, floral on wht, SP mts & lid (worn), 7½x6" 45.00
Bonbonnier, flower sprays on wht w/gold, ped ft, w/lid, 7¼x6x6".. 300.00
Bottle, scent, floral reserves & gold on wht, ped ft, 5" 135.00
Bottle, wht cylinder w/gold at rim, ball stopper, 8" 72.50
Bowl, center, florals & gold on gr, ornate hdls/ft, 10½x16" 425.00
Bowl, center, rtcl border & base, gold & wht, 12x15" 425.00
Box, gr w/bronze mts, rect, early 20th C, 6" L 360.00
Box, wht w/metal mts, hinged lid, 4x5x3" 425.00
Charger, floral sprays & reserves w/gold, ca 1840, 16" 300.00
Clock, mantel, man & lady stand ea side of dial, gilt/florals, 17x11"... 490.00
Clock, mantel, shells & scrolls, 2 youths sit astride front, 20x14" .. 1,175.00
Crocus pot, floral reserves w/gold, 1890s, missing liner, 6x9x4" ... 375.00
Cup/saucer, cafe-au-lait, floral on bl w/gold, rstr saucer, 1830s 150.00
Dessert set, gilt floral bouquet, 1870s, 2 9" tazzas+11 plates 415.00
Dish, shell form w/gold lobster dividing center, 1890s, 5x14x10" . 300.00
Figurine, parrot on base, EX detail/color, 19th C, rprs, 14x8", pr. 660.00
Sauceboat, floral reserves on bl, grapes finial, 19th C, 7x10", NM ..350.00
Teapot, cherubs/roses on magenta w/gilt, bird-head spout, 9x11", EX... 295.00
Teapot, gilt bellflower border, 8½", +cr/sug 325.00
Tureen, wht w/gold borders & scroll hdls, shell finial, 19th C, 10" L .. 660.00
Urn, figure scenes HP on gilt, low uptrn hdls/sq base, 1850s, 8", pr..1,530.00
Urn, floral resseves on gold, ornate gold griffin hdls, 1820s, 13", pr....600.00
Urns, landscape scenic w/gold, low hdls, 1880s, rprs, 9x7", pr...... 600.00
Vase, appl/molded birds/fuchsias on dk bl, florals/gilts, 17x10", pr ..650.00
Vase, figures in reserves w/much gold, ornate rtcl hdls, 19th C, 18x8"....425.00
Vase, floral reserves on wht w/much gold, 19th C, 14", pr............ 600.00
Vase, gr, baluster, 19½" 425.00
Vase, pastoral scenes/flowers/vines/fruit, much gold, 19th C, 22", pr..550.00
Vase, pk, baluster, 4½" 48.00
Vase, scenic reserve w/gold on pk, ornate hdls, 19th C, 13½", pr. 360.00
Vases, garniture, J Petit, violet grnd w/gilt, 1850-60, 14", pr 4,000.00
Vases, romantic scenes, gold encrusted, 1890, 11½", pr................ 600.00

Vases, Goddess and Cupid scenes, artist signed, circa 1900, 28", pair $1,800.00. (Photo courtesy Grand View Antiques & Auction on LiveAuctioneers.com)

Old Sleepy Eye

Old Sleepy Eye was a Sioux Indian chief who was born in Minnesota in 1780. His name was used for the name of a town as well as a flour mill. In 1903 the Sleepy Eye Milling Company of Sleepy Eye, Minnesota, contracted the Weir Pottery Company of Monmouth, Illinois, to make steins, vases, salt crocks, and butter tubs which the company gave away to their customers. A bust profile of the old Indian and his name decorated each piece of the blue and gray stoneware. In addition to these four items, the Minnesota Stoneware Company of Red Wing made a mug with a verse which is very scarce today.

In 1906 Weir Pottery merged with six others to form the Western Stoneware Company in Monmouth. They produced a line of blue and white ware using a lighter body, but these pieces were never given as flour premiums. This line consisted of pitchers (five sizes), steins, mugs, sugar bowls, vases, trivets, and mustache cups. These pieces turn up only rarely in other colors and are highly prized by advanced collectors. Advertising items such as trade cards, pillow tops, thermometers, paperweights, letter openers, postcards, cookbooks, and thimbles are considered very valuable. The original ware was made sporadically until 1937. Brown steins and mugs were produced in 1952. Our advisor for this category is Jim Martin; he is listed in the Directory under Illinois.

Barrel label, Cream, red circle, (+).. 170.00
Barrel label, mk Chief/Strong Bakers, image in center, 16", NM. 175.00
Barrel, grapevine-effect banding.. 2,500.00
Barrel, oak w/brass bands... 3,000.00
Blanket, horse, w/logo, EX... 1,000.00
Butter crock, Flemish bl & gray, $500 to.................................... 600.00
Cabinet, bread display, Old Sleepy Eye etched in glass................ 950.00
Calendar, 1904, NM 375.00
Cookbook, Indian on cover, Sleepy Eye Milling Co, 4¾x4" 200.00
Cookbook, loaf-of-bread shape, NM 120.00
Coupon, for ordering cookbook.. 200.00
Dough scraper, tin/wood, To Be Sure, EX 300.00
Fan, dc image of Old Sleepy Eye, EX+....................................... 200.00
Flour sack, cloth, mc Indian, red letters 345.00
Flour sack, paper, Indian in blk, blk lettering, NM...................... 125.00
Hot plate/trivet, bl & wht 2,000.00
Ink blotter 125.00
Letter opener, bronze 500.00
Light pull, flour sack shape 400.00
Match holder, pnt chalkware... 800.00
Match holder, wht chalkware.. 850.00
Mug, bl & gray, 4¼" 300.00
Mug, bl & wht, 4¼", $150 to 200.00
Mug, bl & yel, 4¼" 600.00
Mug, verse, Red Wing, EX.. 1,200.00
Mustache cup, bl & wht, very rare 3,000.00

Paperweight, bronzed company trademark, pot metal, 3", $300.00. (Photo courtesy Homestead Auctions on LiveAuctioneers.com)

Pillow cover, Sleepy Eye & tribe meet President Monroe 500.00
Pillow cover, center trademk w/various scenes, 22", NM, $1,500 to ..2,000.00
Pin-bk button, Indian, rnd face 250.00
Pitcher, #5, bl or yel.. 1,500.00
Pitcher, bl & gray, 5"... 300.00
Pitcher, bl & wht, #1, ½-pt, $150 to... 200.00
Pitcher, bl & wht, #2, 1-pt, $200 to 250.00
Pitcher, bl & wht, #3, 1-qt 275.00
Pitcher, bl & wht, #3, w/bl rim, 1-qt 800.00
Pitcher, bl & wht, #4, ½-gal 300.00
Pitcher, bl & wht, #5, 1-gal 350.00
Pitcher, bl on cream, 8", M... 220.00
Pitcher, brn on yel, Sesquicentennial, 1981, $100 to 125.00
Pitcher, standing Indian, G color 1,000.00

Postcard, colorful trademk, 1904 Expo Winner 185.00
Postcards, set of 9 .... 500.00
Ruler, wooden, 15" 700.00
Salt crock, Flemish bl & gray, 4x6½", $500 to 600.00
Sheet music, in fr 200.00
Sign, litho on paper, Indian in center, 'chief' below, 1910s, oak fr, 21" dia. 1,200.00
Sign, self-fr tin, portrait in oval, Sleepy Eye Flour, 18x13", EX. 3,600.00
Sign, self-fr tin, portrait w/multiple scenes on border, 24x20", EX.. 5,800.00
Sign, tin litho dc Indian, ...Flour & Cereals, 13" 1,650.00
Spoon, demi, emb roses in bowl, Unity SP 60.00
Spoon, Indian-head hdl 70.00
Stein, bl & wht, 7¾" 500.00
Stein, Board of Directors, 1969, 22-oz 350.00
Stein, Board of Directors, all yrs, 40-oz 265.00
Stein, brn & wht 1,000.00
Stein, brn & yel, Western Stoneware mk 1,000.00
Stein, brn, 1952, 22-oz 150.00
Stein, chestnut, 40-oz, 1952 .... 200.00
Stein, cobalt 800.00
Stein, Flemish, bl on gray, 8" 550.00
Stein, ltd ed, 1979-84, ea 125.00
Sugar bowl, bl & wht, 3", $500 to 550.00
Sugar bowl, bl & yel 1,000.00
Thermometer, front rpl 600.00
Thimble, alum, bl or blk band 200.00
Trade cards, set of 10, 5½x9" 1,000.00
Vase, cattails, all cobalt 700.00
Vase, cattails, bl & wht, G color, 9", $500 to 650.00
Vase, cattails, brn on yel, rare color 1,000.00
Vase, cattails, gr & wht, rare 1,500.00
Vase, Indian & cattails, Flemish bl & gray, 8½", $250 to 300.00

Rose O'Neill

Rose O'Neill's Kewpies were introduced in 1909 when they were used to conclude a story in the December issue of *Ladies' Home Journal*. They were an immediate success, and soon Kewpie dolls were being produced worldwide. German manufacturers were among the earliest and also used the Kewpie motif to decorate chinaware as well as other items. The Kewpie is still popular today and can be found on products ranging from Christmas cards and cake ornaments to fabrics, wallpaper, and metal items. In the following listings, 'sgn' indicates that the item is signed Rose O'Neill. The copyright symbol is also a good mark. Unsigned items can sometimes be of interest to collectors as well, many are authentic and collectible; some are just too small to sign. Unless noted othewise, our values are for examples in at least near mint condition with no chips or repairs. Our advisors for this category are Don and Anne Kier; they are listed in the Directory under Ohio.

Book, Loves of Edwy, leather cover, 432 pgs, 1904, VG 850.00
Bowl, Kewpies in meadow, Royal Rudolstadt, 6¼" 75.00
Bowl, Kewpies playing, Germany, Royal Rudolstadt, 1⅝x6" 100.00
Box, pin, bsk, Kewpies playing, Germany, 4¼" 245.00
Candy container, blk Kewpie finial, jtd arms, Germany, 1930s, 5¼" ... 400.00
Card, Klever Kard, bride & groom w/verse, ca 1915, EX 75.00
Cup/saucer, Kewpies on wht w/pk-tint edges, Germany 65.00
Dish, 2 Kewpies inside w/Baby on border, Czechoslovakia, 5½" .. 155.00
Dresser box, bsk, Kewpie on lid, 4½", EX 165.00
Feeding dish, 8 action kewpies, Royal Rudolstadt, 1⅝x7¾" 180.00
Kewpie, bsk, action figure, Cowboy, #7863 on ft, 1960s, 6x4" 215.00
Kewpie, bsk, action figure, crawler, eye shut/ft up, #487SJ/76, 2½" .. 130.00
Kewpie, bsk, action figure, Fireman, #7863 on ft, 1960s, 6x4" 185.00
Kewpie, bsk, action figure, German Soldier, movable arms, Germany, 4" . 2,765.00

Kewpie, bsk, action figure, held by bear, Germany, 3½" 275.00
Kewpie, bsk, action figure in striped bathing suit, w/pail, 4", EX. 2,050.00
Kewpie, bsk, action figure, kneeling, Germany, 4" 600.00
Kewpie, bsk, action figure, nude holding drawstring bag, #4882, 4½". 1,105.00
Kewpie, bsk, action figure, Roughrider, jtd arms, Germany, 5½" ...2,750.00
Kewpie, bsk, action figure, Sailor, USN on hat, 4½" 300.00
Kewpie, bsk, action figure, Santa hat/hands on hips, Jesco, 4", MIB .. 60.00
Kewpie, bsk, action figure, seated in gr chair holding book, 5½" ...3,900.00
Kewpie, bsk, action figure, seated w/blk cat in lap, 3¼" 600.00
Kewpie, bsk, action figure, seated w/rabbit, Germany, 2" 480.00
Kewpie, bsk, action figure, seated w/turkey at ft, 2½" 425.00
Kewpie, bsk, action figure, The Actor, 4" 3,300.00
Kewpie, bsk, action figure, w/baby & bottle, Germany, 3½" 5,400.00
Kewpie, bsk, immobile, bl wings, pnt hair, Germany, 6" 250.00
Kewpie, bsk, jtd shoulders, Germany, 2" 85.00
Kewpie, bsk, jtd shoulders, molded clothing article, Germany, 6". 295.00
Kewpie, cast steel on sq base, 5½" 55.00
Kewpie, compo, jtd shoulders, Hottentot, heart decal, ca 1946, 11" ..595.00
Kewpie, compo, jtd shoulders, Jesco, 1966, 24", EXIB 295.00
Kewpie, compo, Scootles, orig romper/shoes, Cameo Dolls Co, 1925, 15"....400.00
Kewpie, Doodle Dog, bsk, blk & wht w/bl wings, 6" 1,530.00
Kewpie, nude holding drawstring bag, #4882, 4½" 1,195.00
Kewpie, soft rubber, Cameo, 9½" 45.00
Napkin ring, Kewpie beside ring, sterling, P&B, 2½x1½" dia 210.00
Paper dolls, Kewpie Kutouts, Little Assunta w/doll, 1913 magazine pg... 20.00
Perfume bottle, seated Kewpie, #31 Germany, 2¼" 180.00

Picture frame, enameled metal, Des Pat 143860 Kewpie (trademark), EX, $2,040.00. (Photo courtesy Alderfer Auction Company on LiveAuctioneers.com)

Pin box, bsk, Kewpie in bed, 2¾x3" 550.00
Pitcher, jasperware, Kewpies playing, Germany, 4¼" 245.00
Plate, 2 Kewpies w/holly, 2 sm tab hdls, 5" 170.00
Plate, bl jasperware, 5 Kewpies, 3 groups of flowers, heart shape, 7". 185.00
Plate, Kewpies playing in meadow, Royal Rudolstadt, 7¾" 85.00
Saucer, Kewpies playing in meadow, Royal Rudolstadt, 5" 60.00
Tea set, child's, Kewpies on bl w/brn shading, Germany, 23-pc, MIB . 3,125.00
Tea set, Kewpies, Rose O'Neill Kewpie Germany, 6" pot+cr/sug.. 575.00
Tray, Leaning Tree, 6 action Kewpies, Royal Rudolstadt, 10" dia. 180.00
Trinket box, Kewpie stands on sm boat, Royal Rudolstadt, 1⅝x2¼" ... 360.00
Vase, Kewpie sits in gr wicker chair w/hole in bk, 3¼" 490.00

Onion Pattern

The familiar pattern known to collectors as Onion acquired its name through a case of mistaken identity. Designed in the early 1700s by Johann Haroldt of the Meissen factory in Germany, the pattern was a mixture of earlier Asian designs. One of its components was a stylized peach, which was mistaken for an onion; as a result, the pattern became known by that name. Usually found in blue, an occasional piece may also be found in pink and red. The pattern is commonly associated with Meissen, but it has been reproduced by many others including Villeroy and Boch, Hutschenreuther, and Royal Copenhagen (whose pattern is a variation of the standard design).

Many marks have been used, some of them fraudulent Meissen marks. Study a marks book to become more familiar with them. In our listings, 'Xd swords' indicates first-quality old Meissen ware. Meissen in an oval over a star was a mark of C. Teichert Stove and Porcelain Factory of Meissen; it was used from 1882 until about 1930. Items marked simply Meissen were produced by the State's Porcelain Manufactory VEB after 1972. The crossed swords indication was sometimes added. Today's market abounds with quality reproductions.

Blue Danube is a modern line of Onion-patterned dinnerware produced in Japan and distributed by Lipper International of Wallingford, Connecticut. At least 100 items are available in porcelain; it is sold in most large stores with china departments. See *Garage Sale & Flea Market* (Collector Books) for more information on Blue Danube.

Bowl, basketweave rim w/4 cartouches, Xd swords, 2x12x9"	175.00
Bowl, cereal, Blue Danube, banner mk, 6"	20.00
Bowl, flowered stem hdl, gold trim, Xd swords, w/lid, 4¼x4½"	60.00
Bowl, hdld, w/lid, Xd swords, 5¾x6"	155.00
Bowl, Japan, 7"	12.00
Bowl, rice, Blue Danube, 2½x4½", $25 to	30.00
Bowl, rimmed soup, Blue Danube, banner mk, 8¼", $15 to	20.00
Bowl, rimmed soup, Xd swords, 1⅞x9"	50.00
Bowl, rtcl, Xd swords, sq, 1¾x9½"	100.00
Bowl, sq w/scalloped edge, Xd swords, 10½"	235.00
Bowl, triangular, #27, Xd swords, 1¾x11"	90.00
Bowl, vegetable, Blue Danube, divided, rect mk, 10¾" L	40.00
Butter dish, Blue Danube, rect mk, 8½" dia, $55 to	65.00

Cake/dessert stand, Meissen blue crossed swords mark, 13" diameter, $660.00. (Photo courtesy O'Gallerie on LiveAuctioneers.com)

Cake plate, pierced hdls, Xd swords, 10¾"	145.00
Candy dish, Blue Danube, 5-sided, open lattice border, 2x7½"	22.00
Canister, Prunes on central wht band, Germany, 5¾"	300.00
Casserole, Blue Danube, banner mk, w/lid, 8" dia	70.00
Casserole, w/lid, Blue Danube, 1½-qt, 7¼" dia	55.00
Coaster, Blue Danube, 3½", $5 to	7.00
Compote, rtcl border, Xd swords, 6x7"	85.00
Creamer/sugar bowl, Blue Danube, 'Y' hdls, 4¾", 3½", $28 to	42.00
Creamer, 3-ftd, gold at rim, Xd swords, 5", $115 to	130.00
Creamer, German clover mk, 3¾"	30.00
Cup, bouillon, 2-hdl, Xd swords, 2½x3¼", +underplate	125.00
Cup/saucer, Royal Copenhagen, ribbed	35.00
Cup/saucer, Xd swords, 2", 5¾"	75.00
Dish, Hutschenreuther, sq, 2x9"	35.00
Dish, triangular, Xd swords, 10"	375.00
Funnel, unmk, 5½x3¾"	35.00
Gravy boat, Blue Danube, fancy hdl, banner mk, 6½x9¾"	45.00
Lamp, rpl shade, electrified, late 19th C, 18"	600.00
Mug, Coffee on wht band, Xd arrows (Japan)	15.00
Pie server, Blue Danube, pistol-grip hdl, 10½"	25.00
Pitcher, milk, 3-ftd, Xd swords, 6½"	125.00
Plate, Hutschenreuther, sq, 8⅜"	25.00
Plate, rtcl basketweave rim, Xd swords, 8"	85.00
Plate, Xd swords, 9½"	110.00
Platter, Blue Danube, banner mk, 16x11", $75 to	90.00
Platter, oval, Hustchenreuther, 15x10"	75.00
Platter, w/SP warmer/ft/hdls, bird mk/#51, 16"	285.00

Potato masher, ball end w/long trn wood hdl, 13"	80.00
Relish, 2-part, joined shells w/center hdl, Xd swords, 2x10¾x9"	300.00
Relish, 4-part, center hdl, Xd swords, 15" dia	450.00
Smoker's set, cigarette jar, w/lid, Japan, 5¾", +2 3¼" ashtrays	70.00
Spoon rest, hourglass shape, Xd arrows, 5½x9½"	30.00
Spoon, serving, Xd swords, 8½"	90.00
Steak knives, Blue Danube, Sheffield, set of 6, MIB	95.00
Teapot, bulb, rose finial, Xd swords, 5¼x9¼", $165 to	185.00
Teapot, German clover mk, 5½"	85.00
Tray, hdls, oval mk w/star, Meissen #25, 14x9"	200.00
Tray, shaped rim w/pierced hdls, sq, Germany, 10¼"	125.00
Tureen, vegetable, Cauldon, w/lid, 8x11"	125.00

Opalescent Glass

First made in England in 1870, opalescent glass became popular in America around the turn of the century. Its name comes from the milky-white opalescent trim that defines the lines of the pattern. It was produced in table sets, novelties, toothpick holders, vases, lamps, and a host of other shapes. Note that American-made sugar bowls have lids; sugar bowls of British origin are considered to be complete without lids. For further information we recommend *Standard Encyclopedia of Opalescent Glass* by our advisor, Mike Carwile (Collector Books). Mr. Carwile is listed in the Directory under Virginia. See also Sugar Shakers; Syrups.

Abalone, bowl, wht	25.00
Alaska, bowl, master, bl	175.00
Alaska, pitcher, vaseline	450.00
Alaska, shakers, wht, pr	90.00
Arabian Nights, syrup, wht	185.00
Argonaut Shell (Nautilus), compote, jelly, bl	125.00
Argonaut Shell (Nautilus), spooner, bl	200.00
Ascot, biscuit jar, vaseline or canary	160.00
Autumn Leaves, nappy, wht	125.00
Banded Hobnail, bottle, dresser, bl	75.00
Barbells, bowl, gr	50.00
Beaded Block, sugar bowl, wht	75.00
Beaded Cable, rose bowl, gr, ftd	60.00
Beaded Fleur de Lis, compote, bl or gr	50.00
Beaded Ovals in Sand, toothpick holder, wht	125.00
Beaded Stars, plate, advertising, bl	450.00
Beaded Stars, rose bowl, gr	60.00
Beatty Honeycomb, celery vase, bl	80.00
Beatty Honeycomb, mustard pot, wht	75.00

Beatty Honeycomb, toothpick holder, blue, $200.00. (Photo courtesy Mike Carwile)

Beatty Rib, bowl, master, bl	55.00
Beatty Rib, salt dip, wht	45.00
Beatty Rib, tumbler, wht	30.00
Beatty Swirl, butter dish, wht	150.00
Beatty Swirl, celery vase, bl	75.00
Beatty Swirl, mug, canary	85.00
Belmont Swirl, tumbler, gr	70.00
Blackberry Spray, hat, amethyst	65.00
Blooms & Blossoms, nappy, gr, hdl	50.00

Blown Drapery, sugar shaker, wht 300.00
Blown Drapery, vase, gr 200.00
Blown Twist, syrup, cranberry 400.00
Blown Twist, tumbler, cranberry 325.00
Brideshead, tray, oval, bl 125.00
Brideshead, tray, vaseline, oval 120.00
Bubble Lattice, finger bowl, canary 45.00
Bubble Lattice, pitcher, cranberry 750.00
Bulbous Base Coinspot, syrup, wht 110.00
Bull's Eye, lamp shade, wht 40.00
Buttons & Braids, bowl, cranberry 85.00
Buttons & Braids, pitcher, bl 350.00
Cane & Diamond Swirl, tray, vaseline or canary, stemmed 70.00
Cane Rings, bowl, bl, 8" 75.00
Cane Rings, creamer, vaseline 65.00
Casbah, compote, wht 140.00
Cherry, wine, bl 80.00
Chippendale, basket, vaseline 80.00
Chippendale, plate, vaseline, 6" 95.00
Christmas Pearls, cruet, gr 280.00
Chrysanthemum Base Swirl, cruet, wht 200.00
Chrysanthemum Base Swirl, mustard pot, wht 120.00
Circled Scroll, bowl, sauce, gr 50.00
Circled Scroll, butter dish, bl 475.00
Circled Scroll, creamer, gr 170.00
Circled Scroll, sugar bowl, gr 225.00
Circled Scroll, tumbler, wht 75.00
Coinspot, pickle castor, wht 225.00
Coinspot, pitcher, bl 275.00
Colonial Stairsteps, creamer, bl 100.00
Colonial Stairsteps, toothpick holder, bl 200.00
Compass, rose bowl, wht 90.00
Concave Columns, vase, bl or vaseline 100.00
Conch & Twig, wall pocket, bl or vaseline 250.00
Consolidated Criss-Cross, shakers, gr or cranberry, ea 100.00
Consolidated Criss-Cross, sugar shaker, cranberry 600.00
Contessa, basket, amber, hdl 250.00
Contessa, basket, bl 60.00
Coral Reef, bottle, barber, bl 200.00
Coral Reef, bottle, bitters, bl 200.00
Coral Reef, bottle, bitters, wht 125.00
Coral Reef, lamp, finger, wht, ftd 325.00
Corolla, vase, canary 200.00
Coronation, pitcher, bl or vaseline 225.00
Coronation, tumbler, bl, canary or vaseline 40.00
Crown Jewels, pitcher, bl 200.00
Crown Jewels, plate, bl 100.00
Crown Jewels, platter, bl 110.00
Daffodils, lamp, hand, gr 300.00
Daffodils, lamp, oil, cranberry 675.00
Daffodils, vase, canary 350.00
Daisy & Button, tray, bun, bl 150.00
Daisy & Fern, butter dish, cranberry 300.00
Daisy & Fern, butter dish, wht 175.00
Daisy & Fern, cruet, bl, faceted stopper, 7" 200.00
Daisy & Fern, mustard pot, bl 100.00
Daisy & Fern, tumbler, bl or gr 50.00
Daisy & Fern, vase, wht 100.00
Daisy & Plume, basket, wht, rare 150.00
Daisy & Plume, rose bowl, bl, ftd 60.00
Daisy & Plume, rose bowl, wht, ftd 35.00
Daisy in Criss-Cross, pitcher, bl 350.00
Daisy May (Leaf Rays), nappy/bonbon, gr 45.00
Davidson Drape, vase, bl, canary or vaseline, squat 150.00

Decorated English Swirl, rose bowl, cranberry 250.00
Diamond Maple Leaf, bowl, wht, hdl 45.00
Diamond Optic, compote, bl 50.00
Diamond Spearhead, butter dish, gr 575.00
Diamond Spearhead, butter dish, wht 400.00
Diamond Spearhead, carafe, water, vaseline 225.00
Diamond Spearhead, mug, gr 200.00
Diamond Spearhead, shakers, bl, pr 150.00
Diamond Wave, pitcher, cranberry, w/lid 175.00
Diamond Wave, vase, cranberry, 5" 85.00
Diamonds, cruet, rubena 250.00
Diamonds, cruet, wht 75.00
Diamonds, tumbler, cranberry 70.00
Dolly Madison, bowl, gr, ruffled rim, 8" 40.00
Dolly Madison, creamer, bl 90.00
Dorset (English), sugar bowl, bl, open 50.00
Double Greek Key, celery vase, wht 125.00
Double Greek Key, spooner, bl 110.00
Double Greek Key, tray, pickle, bl 150.00
Drapery (Northwood), spooner, wht 70.00
Drapery (Northwood), vase, bl 140.00
Duchess, butter dish, vaseline 175.00
Duchess, creamer, bl, vaseline 65.00
Dugan Intaglio Peach, compote, wht 100.00
Dugan Intaglio Strawberry, bowl, fruit, wht, stemmed 85.00
Dugan's Diamond Compass (Dragon Lady), rose bowl, wht 90.00
Dugan's Honeycomb, bowl, bl, various shapes, rare, ea 150.00
Dugan's Intaglio Pear & Plum, bowl, wht, 10" 135.00
Dugan's Plain Panel, vase, bl or gr 55.00
Elson Dewdrop #2, bowl, sauce, wht 15.00
Elson Dewdrop #2, cruet, wht 90.00
Elson Dewdrop #2, punch cup, wht 35.00
Elson Dewdrop, bowl, berry, lg 45.00
Elson Dewdrop, mug, wht 65.00
Embossed Spanish Lace, vase, canary, 4" 100.00
English Drape, vase, vaseline 135.00
English Oak Leaf, bowl, bl 150.00
English Ripple, tumbler, bl or vaseline 80.00
English Wide Stripe, pitcher, cranberry 350.00
Everglades, creamer, wht 95.00
Everglades, pitcher, bl 475.00
Everglades, shakers, bl, pr 275.00
Everglades, tumbler, bl 85.00
Everglades, tumbler, wht 60.00
Fan, bowl, sauce, bl or gr 30.00
Fan, creamer, gr 120.00
Fan, gravy boat, bl or gr 50.00
Fan, tumbler, gr 65.00
Fenton's #220 (Stripe), tumbler, gr, w/hdl 50.00
Fenton's #370, bonbon, amber 50.00
Fern, bottle, barber, wht 100.00

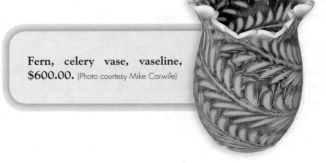

Fern, celery vase, vaseline, $600.00. (Photo courtesy Mike Carwile)

Fern, cruet, wht...175.00
Fern, shakers, cranberry, pr...165.00
Fern, toothpick holder, cranberry, rare.........................475.00
File & Fan, bowl, wht...95.00
Fish-in-the-Sea, vase, wht, scarce.................................275.00
Flora, bowl, master bl or vaseline.................................100.00
Flora, butter dish, bl...300.00
Flora, pitcher, bl..500.00
Floral Eyelet, tumbler, bl or wht....................................100.00
Fluted Scrolls (Klondyke), butter dish, bl......................165.00
Fluted Scrolls (Klondyke), butter dish, vaseline.............185.00
Fluted Scrolls (Klondyke), epergne, bl, sm....................125.00
Fluted Scrolls (Klondyke), spooner, wht..........................55.00
Frosted Leaf & Basketweave, creamer, vaseline.............135.00
Frosted Leaf & Basketweave, sugar bowl, vaseline.........165.00
Gonderman (Adonis) Swirl, celery vase, amber..............150.00
Gonderman (Adonis) Swirl, pitcher, bl...........................250.00
Gonderman (Adonis) Swirl, spooner, amber...................150.00
Gonderman (Adonis) Swirl, syrup, bl.............................300.00
Grape & Cable, bowl, centerpiece, wht..........................300.00
Greener Dmn Column, epergne, amber...........................350.00
Harrow, creamer, vaseline..70.00
Harrow, wine, bl, vaseline..40.00
Hearts & Flowers, bowl, wht..150.00
Herringbone, tumbler, cranberry....................................150.00
Herringbone, tumbler, wht...65.00
Hobb's Polka Dot, cheese dish, gr/sapphire, w/lid........235.00
Hobnail (Hobbs), bottle, barber, bl................................150.00
Hobnail (Hobbs), bride's basket, vaseline.......................425.00
Hobnail & Paneled Thumbprint, cordial, bl, vaseline.......35.00
Hobnail & Paneled Thumbprint, pitcher, bl, vaseline......300.00
Hobnail 4-Footed, spooner, cobalt.................................100.00
Hobnail-in-Square (Vesta), bowl, w/stand, bl.................150.00
Honeycomb (Blown), bowl, bl...95.00
Honeycomb (Blown), cracker jar, wht.............................250.00
Honeycomb & Clover, bowl, master, gr.............................75.00
Honeycomb, vase, wht..45.00
Idyll, butter dish, wht..300.00
Idyll, toothpick holder, gr..325.00
Inside Ribbing, creamer, vaseline.....................................80.00
Inside Ribbing, tray, wht..30.00
Intaglio, shakers, wht, pr...75.00
Jeweled Heart, toothpick holder, wht.............................200.00
Jewels & Drapery, vase, aqua...75.00
Lady Caroline, creamer, bl, vaseline.................................60.00
Lady Chippendale, compote, cobalt, tall.........................100.00
Lady Chippendale, sugar bowl, vaseline............................90.00
Late Coinspot, pitcher, gr..150.00
Leaf & Beads, bowl, whimsey, wht....................................45.00
Leaf Mold, bowl, master, cranberry...............................140.00
Leaf Mold, sugar bowl, cranberry..................................300.00
Lords & Ladies, celery boat (in wire basket), bl.............200.00
Lords & Ladies, plate, bl, 7"...100.00
Open Edge Basket (Fenton), nappy, bl.............................35.00
Palm Beach, spooner, bl, vaseline...................................150.00
Paneled Cornflower, vase, wht.......................................135.00
Paneled Flowers, nut cup, bl, ftd......................................85.00
Paneled Holly, creamer, wht...125.00
Paneled Sprig, toothpick holder, wht.............................100.00
Pearl Flowers, rose bowl, bl, ftd.......................................70.00
Pearl Flowers, rose bowl, gr, ftd.......................................80.00
Pearls & Scales, compote, emerald....................................80.00
Piasa Bird, bowl, wht...45.00
Piasa Bird, plate, wht, ftd...100.00

Piccadilly, basket, bl, sm..100.00
Pinwheel, cake plate, vaseline, ped ft, 12".....................135.00
Poinsettia, bowl, fruit, gr, 2 szs....................................110.00
Poinsettia, sugar shaker, bl or gr...................................300.00
Poinsettia, sugar shaker, cranberry................................450.00
Polka Dot, syrup, cranberry...725.00
Popsicle Sticks, bowl, gr, ftd..50.00
Prince William, creamer, bl..65.00
Prince William, toothpick holder, bl.................................65.00
Princess Diana, plate, vaseline, crimped rim.....................60.00
Ribbed Coinspot, tumbler, cranberry.............................200.00
Ribbed Pillar, shakers, cranberry, pr..............................135.00
Ribbed Spiral, bowl, wht, ruffled rim................................40.00
Ribbed Spiral, vase, vaseline, squat, 4-7"..........................75.00
Richelieu, cracker jar, bl..200.00
Richelieu, tray, vaseline...55.00
Richelieu, tray, wht..40.00
Ring Handle, ring tray, gr...150.00
Rose & Ruffles, bowl, bl, vaseline, sm............................100.00
Roulette, bowls, various, wht...30.00
Roulette, plate, bl or gr..100.00
Ruffles & Rings, nut bowl, gr..55.00
S-Repeat, tumbler, bl...65.00
Scottish Moor, cracker jar, wht......................................225.00

Spanish Lace, butter, vaseline, $400.00. (Photo courtesy Mike Carwile)

Stippled Scroll & Prism, goblet, gr, 5"..............................30.00
Stripe, bowl, wht..60.00
Stripe, rose bowl, bl..100.00
Sunburst-on-Shield, butter dish, vaseline.......................400.00
Swag w/Brackets, bowl, canary, bl or vaseline..................45.00
Swag w/Brackets, bowl, master, bl....................................85.00
Swirl, finger bowl, bl..65.00
Swirl, spittoon, wht..70.00
Target Swirl, tumbler, cranberry.......................................95.00
Thousand Eye, celery vase, wht......................................100.00
Tokyo, compote, jelly; wht...30.00
Tokyo, plate, wht..35.00
Tree of Life, shakers, bl, pr..100.00
Tree of Love, plate, wht, 2 szs, rare...............................135.00
Tree Stump, mug, wht...60.00
Triangle, match holder, wht..55.00
Tut, vase, whimsey; bl or gr...125.00
Twister, bowl, bl...50.00
Victoria & Albert, creamer, bl...80.00
Water Lily & Cattails, bonbon, amethyst...........................85.00
Water Lily & Cattails, bonbon, bl......................................60.00
Waves, plate, whimsey, gr...100.00
Wild Bouquet, compote, jelly, bl.....................................175.00
Wild Bouquet, spooner, gr..150.00
Willow Reed, basket, bl...175.00
Windows (Swirled), mustard jar, bl...................................75.00
Windows (Swirled), mustard jar, cranberry......................150.00
Windows (Swirled), sugar shaker, wht.............................125.00
Windows (Swirled), tumbler, bl...85.00

Wishbone & Drapery, plate, gr 60.00
Wreath & Shell, salt dip, wht.. 85.00

Opaline Glass

A type of semiopaque opal glass, opaline was made in white as well as pastel shades and is often enameled. It is similar in appearance to English Bristol glass, though its enamel or gilt decorative devices tend to exhibit a French influence.

Bottle, wht, w/bronze mts, shouldered cylinder, ball stopper, 8"..... 75.00
Bowl, wht w/Deco HP on lid, ca 1926, 4½x7", $350 to 425.00
Box, wht seashell form w/gilt-metal hinge & lock, 3½x6½x5½" .. 800.00
Box, wht w/brass trim, hinged lid, rect, 3½x5½x3¼" 250.00
Box, wht w/bronze mts & key escutcheon, oval, 5x4x3½" 660.00
Dresser box, floral on pk, ormolu butterfly hdls, 5x7x3", EX 425.00
Mugs, wht w/bl opaque hdls, 3¼", 4 for 145.00
Pitcher, floral on wht, cobalt hdl, ca 1900, 8½", +3 matching cups.. 525.00
Tumbler, bl, HP bird on floral branch w/coralene leaves 85.00
Vase, apple gr w/gold banding, bulb w/slim neck flared rim, 13x7" ..75.00
Vase, bl, HP classical lady among flowers, shouldered, 1880s, 18" ...180.00

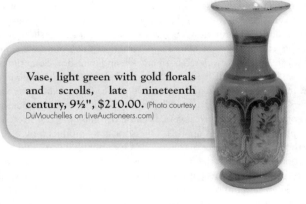

Vase, light green with gold florals and scrolls, late nineteenth century, 9½", $210.00. (Photo courtesy DuMouchelles on LiveAuctioneers.com)

Vase, pk w/jeweled HP rim & ft, bulb, 8" 350.00
Vase, wht, shouldered/ftd form, 8¾", NM 60.00

Orient & Flume

A Victorian home built in the late 1890s between Orient and Flume streets in Chico, California, was purchased by Douglas Boyd in 1972 and converted into a glass studio. Due to his on-going success in producing fine, contemporary art glass reminiscent of masters such as Tiffany, Loetz, and Steuben, the business flourished and about a year later had become so successful that larger quarters were required nearby. Today, examples of their workmanship are found in museums and galleries all over the world. In addition to the items listed here, they also produced beautiful paperweights. See also Paperweights.

Vase, feathers, dk burgundy on gold irid, 1977, 4" 145.00
Vase, jack-in-pulpit, pulled festoons on gr, gold top, 1979, 8½" ... 465.00
Vase, lilies, pk on bl w/oil spots, Smallhouse, ftd, 12" 350.00
Vase, millefiori flowers w/brn stems on bl irid, shouldered, 8" 300.00
Vase, millefiori trees, #0024570F0514A, 12" 960.00
Vase, pwt, fish & sea grasses in clear, Beyers, 6" 180.00
Vase, pwt, frog on lily pad, Hudin, 1984, 4¼" 95.00
Vase, pulled feathers, mc on gr to bl, Hansen, 1975, 10¼" 135.00
Vase, pulled feathers, mc on lav, ovoid, 6" 195.00

Orrefors

Orrefors Glassworks was founded in 1898 in the Swedish province of Smaaland. Utilizing the expertise of designers such as Simon Gate, Edward Hald, Vicke Lindstrand, and Edwin Ohrstrom, it produced art glass of the highest quality. Various techniques were used in achieving the decoration. Some were wheel engraved; others were blown through a unique process that formed controlled bubbles or air pockets resulting in unusual patterns and shapes. (Remember: When no color is noted, the glass is clear.)

Bowl, Ribbon, mc in clear w/bubbles, I Lundin/Expo 2647, 4¼x6½".. 725.00
Chalice, Graal, nudes/animals, bl cased/amber cased ft, Cyren, '78, 6" ...1,800.00
Vase, apple, gr, I Lundin, Orrefors Expo DU 32-57, 16½x14" ...5,500.00
Vase, Ariel, cased blk/bl, geometrics, I Lundin, Nr 476-63, 5¾".. 1,100.00
Vase, Ariel, cobalt cased, I Lundin, #424.E5, 8½x4¼" 1,150.00
Vase, Ariel, girl & dove, cobalt cased w/amber shaded int, #292-E3, 7" .1,950.00
Vase, Ariel, girl's face, E Ohrstrom, #99, 1939, 7½x6⅛" 15,600.00
Vase, Ariel, girl's face, maroon cased, E Ohrstrom, 1968, 7" 9,600.00
Vase, Graal, Engagement, mauve/cobalt/gr, Englund, #968430, 1987, 14"..9,000.00
Vase, Graal, fish, gr in clear, E Hald, #859L, 4½" 780.00
Vase, Graal, fish/plants, gr/blk/clear, E Hald, #2770D, 5¼x4½" .1,150.00
Vase, Graal, female faces, #88 965830, E Englund 50-50, 10¾" .9,000.00

Vase, intaglio-cut exotic dancers, marked Orrefors/Gate - 2572/B/9/D, circa 1930, 8⅜", $4,080.00. (Photo courtesy Brunk Auctions on LiveAuctioneers.com)

Vase, Javanese Dancer, etched clear, S Gate, ca 1950, 9½" 1,450.00
Vase, Kraka, bl cased w/internal bubbles, S Palmqvist, #322, 12" . 950.00
Vase, Ravenna, ruby on clear, S Palmqvist, #796, 2x4½" 1,450.00

Ott and Brewer

The partnership of Ott and Brewer began in 1865 in Trenton, New Jersey. By 1876 they were making decorated graniteware, parian, and 'ivory porcelain' — similar to Irish Belleek though not as fine and of different composition. In 1883, however, experiments toward that end had reached a successful conclusion, and a true Belleek body was introduced. It came to be regarded as the finest china ever produced by an American firm. The ware was decorated by various means such as hand painting, transfer printing, gilding, and lustre glazing. The company closed in 1893, one of many that failed during that depression. In the listings below, the ware is Belleek unless noted otherwise. Our advisor for this category is Mary Frank Gaston. See also Parian Ware.

Bowl, recumbent female nude, wht, shell shape, 3 snail shell ft, 3x11" ...2,625.00
Ewer, cranes & cattails, emb gold enamel & gilt, crabstock hdl, 13" ... 155.00
Pitcher, 3 floral panels, waterlily hdl, 9", EX 1,000.00
Pitcher, daisies, gilt on ivory, branch hdl, squat w/dimpled sides, 8" ...850.00
Pitcher, orchid, bl on wht w/gold, rtcl hdl, crown/sword mk, 17¼" ..2,350.00
Vase, bird mc w/gold on gr, bottle form, early red moon stamp, 10" .7,200.00
Vase, floral/gilt, appl rose w/wraparound stem & leaf, globular, 7"...315.00
Vase, herons & bamboo, gold tones on wht, bulb, slim sq neck, 10x7"...2,940.00

Vase, posy, leaves & butterflies, gold on wht, Belleek O&B, 5½". 150.00
Vase, tea roses on wht w/gold, dolphin hdls, crown mk, sm rstr, 18x10". 900.00

Overbeck

Four genteel ladies set up the Overbeck pottery around 1911 in the unlikely area of Cambridge City, Indiana. Margaret, Hannah, Elizabeth, and Mary produced high-quality hand-thrown vases featuring vertical panels excised with floral, landscape, or figural decoration, at first with an Arts & Crafts stylization, then moving on to a more modern, Art Deco geometry. Mary, holding up the fort starting in 1937, increasingly turned to the production of hand-sized figurines in period dress, which she would often give to children visiting the pottery. The operation closed in 1955. Most vases and figurines are stamped OBK, sometimes with the addition of a first-name initial. In the last couple of years, some convincing copies have been appearing on the market. Collectors should buy with a guarantee of authenticity or otherwise take their chances. Our advisors for this category are Suzanne Perrault and David Rago; they are listed in the Directory under New Jersey. In the listings that follow, unless otherwise noted, assume that each example has been decorated by Overbeck's typical carved and painted method.

Bowl, floral, caramel mottled matt, flat bottom, OBK/F, 2x6" ...2,375.00
Bowl, HP housing landscape, pk/gr/lt bl/brn on bl, ftd, OBK, 5" ...1,250.00
Brooch, floral cluster, tan/gr/yel/bl/pk, 1¾" 375.00
Candlestick, floral panels on tan, saucer ft, paper label, EF, 5" ..3,375.00
Drawing, pen/ink, Calendar 1903: Salvia, mat/fr, Hannah, 8x5" ..2,280.00
Figurine, 3 ducks squawking, grassy base, 2" 550.00
Figurine, cello player w/pk leaf hat, rustic bow, OBK, 3½" 425.00
Figurine, farmer's wife w/apples in basket, goggle eyes, 4¼" 535.00
Figurine, farmer w/watermelon, brn floppy hat, 5⅛" 700.00
Figurine, turtle w/4 spindley legs, pastels, OBK, 1⅝" 550.00
Figurines, 7-pc band, tallest 5½", EX, set 3,600.00
Figurines, Geo & Martha Washington, OBK, 3⅞", 3⅜", pr........2,280.00
Ink & watercolor study, marigolds, HO, 7x5" 6,000.00
Ink & watercolor study, milkweed, HO, 10x8" 10,625.00
Pitcher, trees w/blossoms, bl/gray on brn matt, OBK/F, 5x10" ...3,750.00
Vase, birds, gr gloss, E/H, 6½" 1,200.00
Vase, elephants & birds, russet on orange, OBK/EF, 3½x5½" 9,250.00
Vase, fawns & accents, wht band on turq, wide neck, OBK, 6"..3,125.00
Vase, floral (deeply cvd), tan & lt rust, OBK/EMF, 11½".........16,250.00
Vase, floral panels, gr on taupe, OBK/E, 4½x3¼".......................2,850.00
Vase, floral, cvd/pnt, mauve/gr on tan, 2½x2¾" 6,000.00
Vase, frothy pk & wht glass, ovoid, OBK, 8¼x6½" 1,250.00
Vase, horses, matt yel, chocolate brn glaze, rstr to rim chip, OBK EF, 2¾x3¾" ..3,000.00
Vase, HP bird/pine trees/floral, mc on wht, OBK/EF, 9" 6,875.00

Vase, owls on branches in three panels, teal and purple on brown, signed OBK E H, 7½x4", $19,200.00. (Photo courtesy Rago Arts and Auction Center)

Vase, pine cones (cvd/pnt), forest gr/mustard, OBK E/H, 8¾x4¾"..16,800.00
Vase, pine cones, Mustard & gr, Elizabeth & Hannah, E/H, 8¾x4¾" ..16,800.00
Vase, QA's Lace, brn/red/turq mottle on brn/mauve, OBK, 8½". 25,000.00
Vase, QA's Lace, OBK/E/H, rim & hairline rstr, 8" 24,000.00
Vase, stylized birds & flowers in mustard matt on brn, OBK EF, 9¼" ..15,600.00

Overshot

Overshot glass originated in sixteenth century Venice, and the ability to make this ware eventually spread to Bohemia, Spain, and elsewhere in Europe. Sometime prior to 1800, the production of this glass seems to have stopped. The Englishman Apsley Pellatt, owner of the Falcon Glass Works, is credited with reviving this decorative technique around 1845 – 1850. He acknowledged the origin of this technique by calling his product 'Venetian Frosted Glass' or 'Anglo-Venetian Glass.' Later it would be called by other names, such as Frosted Glassware, Ice Glass, or Craquelle Glass.

It is important to understand the difference between crackle glass and overshot glass. All crackle is not overshot, and all overshot is not crackle. However, most overshot is also crackle glass. Two different processes or steps were involved in making this glassware.

Crackle glass was produced by dipping a partially blown gob of hot glass in cold water. The sudden temperature change caused fissures or cracks in the glass surface. The gob was then lightly reheated and blown into its full shape. The blowing process enlarged the spaces between fissures to create a labyrinth of channels in varying widths. When cooled in the annealing lehr, the surface of the finished object had a crackled or cracked-ice effect.

Overshot glass was made by rolling a partially inflated gob of hot glass on finely ground shards of glass that had been placed on a steel plate called a marver. The gob was then lightly reheated to remove the sharp edges of the ground glass and blown to its final shape. Most overshot pieces were immersed in cold water before application of the ground glass, and such glassware can be considered both crackle and overshot. Sometimes an object was blown to full size before being rolled over the glass shards. As Barlow and Kaiser explained on page 104 in *The Glass Industry in Sandwich, Vol. 4*, 'The ground particles adhered uniformly over the entire surface of the piece, showing no roadways, because the glass was not stretched after the particles had been applied. Overshot glass produced by this second method is much sharper to the touch.' Overshot glass produced by the first method — with the 'roadways' — has been mistaken for the Tree of Life Pattern. However, this pattern is pressed glass, whereas overshot is either free blown or mold blown. Overshot pieces could be further embellished, requiring a third decorative technique at the furnace, such as the application of vaseline glass designs or fine threads of glass that were picked up and fused to the object. The latter decorative style, called Peloton, was patented in 1880 by Wilhelm Kralik in Bohemia.

Boston & Sandwich, Reading Artistic Glass Works, and Hobbs Brockunier were among the companies that manufactured overshot in the United States. Such products were quite utilitarian — vases, decanters, cruets, bowls, water pitchers with ice bladders, lights, lamps, and other shapes. Colored overshot was produced at Sandwich, but research has shown that the applied ground glass was always crystal. Czechoslovakia is known to have made overshot with colored ground glass. Many such pieces are acid stamped 'Czechoslovakia.' Undamaged, mint-condition overshot is extremely hard to find and expensive. Our advisors for this category are Stan and Arlene Weitman; they are listed in the Directory under North Carolina.

Bottle, scent, cranberry cased with clear glass, attributed to Boston & Sandwich Glass Co., 1870 – 1887, 8¾", $360.00. (Photo courtesy Green Valley Auctions on LiveAuctioneers.com)

Basket, appl rope hdls, 6½x10½" L 425.00
Basket, cranberry to crystal, thorn hdl, rect, 10x7½" 750.00
Bowl, bl, appl mc glass fruit on lid, 4x6" 140.00
Compote, tall ped, 7½x6¾" 475.00
Creamer, crystal, appl hdl, long & wide spout, 1880s, 4¼" 95.00
Fairy lamp, clear w/melon ribs, S Clarke, 3-pc, 7" 175.00
Pitcher, champagne, cranberry, clear hdl & rigaree, ice bladder, 12"..1,250.00
Pitcher, cranberry to clear, bulb body, clear hdl, 5¼" 525.00
Pitcher, Sandwich, 4½" 350.00
Pitcher, tankard, cylindrical, appl rigaree at opening, 10¼" 950.00
Pitcher, water, bl, reeded hdl, ca 1870-87, 7¼" 525.00
Rose bowl, crystal, branches form ft, 4½x4½" 95.00
Rose bowl, rubena, 6x5" 275.00
Set, 12" decanter & 4" wine goblets (4), 1860-70s 3,495.00
Tumbler, gr to clear, 3¾x2¾" 100.00
Vase, clear w/appl vaseline flower, sq sides, vaseline ft, 12" 1,000.00
Vase, metallic gold, indented sides, slight twist to 6" neck, 10" 60.00

Ben Owen, Master Potter

Ben Owen worked at the Jugtown Pottery of North Carolina from 1923 until it temporarily closed in 1959. He continued in the business in his own Plank Road Pottery, stamping his ware 'Ben Owen, Master Potter,' with many forms made by Lester Fanell Craven in the late 1960s. His pottery closed in 1972. He died in 1983 at the age of 81. The pottery was reopened in 1981 under the supervision of Benjamin Wade Owen II. One of the principal potters was David Garner who worked there until about 1985. This pottery is still in operation today with Ben II as the main potter.

Bowl, centerpiece, salt glaze w/cobalt int, Ben Owen III, 1993, 5x9". 60.00
Bowl, Frogskin Gr w/t'prints, circular stamp, 4x7" 180.00
Candlesticks, Frogskin Gr, Ben Owen Master Potter, 11", pr........ 450.00
Candlesticks, lead glaze, Ben Owen Master Potter, 1960s, 9¼", pr... 345.00
Candlesticks, wht gloss, Ben Owen Master Potter, 12½", pr 385.00
Cookie jar, Tobacco Spit Brn, Ben Owen Master Potter, 10½" 240.00
Jar, burnt orange, 4 open shoulder hdls, imp mk, 12", EX 510.00
Jar, foamy wht, ear hdls, w/lid, Ben Owen Master Potter, 8¼", NM...600.00
Jug, stoneware w/multi-lined incised rings, ovoid, 1960s, 12" 385.00
Lamp base, Frogskin Gr w/vertical linear decor, bulb, 12"............ 225.00

Vase, blue and red Chinese glaze, impressed Ben Owen Master Potter, 4", $660.00. (Photo courtesy Brunk Auctions on LiveAuctioneers.com)

Vase, Dogwood, wht, Ben Owen Master Potter, 1960s, 13½x6"... 480.00
Vase, foamy bl w/red highlights, egg shape, 6x4¾" 660.00
Vase, foamy wht, incurvate rim, Master Ben Owen, 1950s, 7" 180.00
Vase, Hang Dynasty style, Chinese Bl w/strong red, hdls, 10½" .5,100.00
Vase, olive gr, shouldered, Ben Owen Master Potter, 4¼" 100.00
Vase, Oriental Translation, Chinese Wht, incurvate rim, 7" 135.00
Vase, bl w/scattered red, high shoulders, ...Master Potter, 8"..........1,550.00
Vase, wht w/2 appl bosses at shoulder, Ben...Master Potter, 8" 450.00

Owens Pottery

J.B. Owens founded his company in Zanesville, Ohio, in 1891, and

until 1907, when the company decided to exert most of its energies in the area of tile production, made several quality lines of art pottery. His first line, Utopian, was a standard brown ware with underglaze slip decoration of nature studies, animals, and portraits. A similar line, Lotus, utilized lighter background colors. Henri Deux, introduced in 1900, featured incised Art Nouveau forms inlaid with color. In time, the Brush McCoy Pottery acquired many of Owens's molds and reproduced a line similar to Henri Deux, which they called Navarre. (Owens pieces were usually marked Henri Deux and have a heavier body and coarser feel to the glaze than similar McCoy pieces.) Other important lines were Opalesce, Rustic, Feroza, Cyrano, and Mission, examples of which are rare today. The factory burned in 1928, and the company closed shortly thereafter. Values vary according to the quality of the artwork and subject matter. Examples signed by the artist bring higher prices than those that are not signed. For further information we recommend *Owens Pottery Unearthed* by Kristy and Rick McKibben and Jeanette and Marvin Stofft.

Alpine (rare line), vase, floral, slim neck, #119, 14", NM............ 350.00
Coralene Opalesce, pitcher, autumn leaves on gr w/gold beads, 12x6".600.00
Coralene Opalesce, vase, bronzed flower on gr grnd, Lessell, 6x4" ..600.00
Delft, jardiniere, Dutch lady & daughter at pier, 8x9½" 650.00
Henri Deux, jardiniere, Nouveau figure in landscape, 7½" 550.00
Henri Deux, jardiniere, Nouveau lady & leaves, 8¼x10", EX 650.00

Henri Deux, vase, incised and painted Nouveau lady with flowing hair, gold trim, no mark, 9", $510.00. (Photo courtesy Cincinnati Art Galleries, LLC on LiveAuctioneers.com)

Henri Deux, vase, Nouveau floral on brn, 8½" 500.00
High Glaze, vase, squeeze-bag Nouveau decor, #1178, 12¾"........ 550.00
Lightweight, mug, Native Am male, Haubrich, #830, rstr, 7½" ... 450.00
Lotus, vase, carnations, wht on shaded grnd, F Ferrell, 13x3¾" ... 840.00
Lotus, vase, floral & squeeze-bag borders, #1175, 5¾" 600.00
Lotus, vase, floral, purple & gr on wht, #220, X, 8⅝" 300.00
Lotus, vase, lotus blossoms/bud/leaves, cylindrical, #1249, 16⅜"...1,600.00
Lotus, vase, stylized leafless tree, slim, shouldered, 9⅜" 360.00
Majolica, jardiniere, emb decor, gr/cream/brn, 6x7" 200.00
Matt Green, vase, cvd geometrics, rtcl windows at neck, 7x8¼". 1,100.00
Matt Green, vase, dragonflies, 4⅛"..1,325.00
Matt Green, vase, stenciled bird, ftd, 8¾", NM 350.00
Matt Utopian, pansies on bl & biscuit, #1010, 10"....................... 360.00
Tile, goose by pond, 5-color cuenca, sm chip, 11¾x8¾"............1,800.00
Tile, sailboat/waves, 6-color cuenca, 11½x18", EX 2,520.00
Utopian, ewer, brn w/orange wild roses, 3-ft, silver o/l, 5½x4½" ..800.00
Utopian, jardiniere, chrysanthemums, ruffled rim, 7½" 195.00
Utopian, jug, corn on ear, 7x5" 200.00
Utopian, loving cup, floral, 3-hdl, #826, 7".................................. 235.00
Utopian, mug, leaves & berries, #1035, 5" 80.00
Utopian, tankard, floral, cylindrical, 1915, 11" 345.00
Utopian, vase, bulb, brn w/pnt cat, sgn Mae Timberlake, #1048, 5¼x3¾" ..950.00
Utopian, vase, cat pnt on brn, bulb, lt bl/gr/brn, artist initials, 8¼x5½" ..1,600.00
Utopian, vase, daisies, 4 tapered ft, #821, 5¼" 180.00
Utopian, vase, dog portrait on brn, sgn MT, 7½x9" 2,000.00
Utopian, vase, dog portrait on brn, #982, minor flake to rim, 9½x4" .1,600.00
Utopian, vase, floral, sgn C Fouts, stick neck, 13" 225.00
Utopian, vase, floral, shouldered, tapered neck, 7" 235.00
Utopian, vase, floral, slim neck, wide shoulder, #107/8, 3½" 85.00

Utopian, vase, floral, twisted body, ftd, 4¾" 85.00
Utopian, vase, irises, slim, 13½" 275.00
Utopian, vase, leaves, flared cylinder, #792, 7½", NM.................. 240.00
Utopian, vase, Native Am chief, Cora McCandless, rpr, 15" 1,680.00
Utopian, vase, Native Am portrait on gold & ivory, #1025, 12x8"..2,200.00
Utopian, vase, pnt kitten on brn, sgn Hester Pillsbury, #1093, 15½x7" ..3,000.00
Utopian, vase, roses, integral hdls, 4"... 135.00

Paden City Glass

Paden City Glass Mfg. Co. was founded in 1916 in Paden City, West Virginia. It made both mold-blown and pressed wares and is most remembered today for its handmade lines in bright colors with fanciful etchings. A great deal of Paden City's business was in supplying decorating companies and fitters with glass; therefore, Paden City never identified their glass with a trademark of any kind, and the company's advertisements were limited to trade publications, rather than retail. In 1948 the management of the company opened a second plant to make utilitarian, machine-made wares such as tumblers and ashtrays, but the move was ill-advised due to a glut of similar merchandise already on the market. The company remained in operation until 1951 when it permanently closed the doors of both factories as a result of the losses incurred by Plant No. 2. (To clear up an often-repeated misunderstanding, dealers and collectors alike should keep in mind that The Paden City Glass Mfg. Co. had absolutely no connection with the Paden City Pottery Company, other than their identical locale.)

Today Paden City is best known for its numerous acid-etched wares that featured birds, but many other ornate etchings were produced. Fortunately several new books on the subject have been published, which have provided names for and increased awareness of previously undocumented etchings. Currently, collectors especially seek out examples of Paden City's most detailed etching, Orchid, and its most appealing etching, Cupid. Pieces in the company's plainer pressed dinnerware lines, however, have remained affordable, even though some patterns are quite scarce. After several years of rising prices, internet auction sites have increased the supply of pieces with more commonly found etchings such as Peacock & Rose, causing a dip in prices. However, pieces bearing documented etchings on shapes and/or colors not previously seen combined continue to fetch high prices from advanced collectors.

Following is a list of Paden City's colors. Names in capital letters indicate original factory color names where known, followed by a description of the color.

Amber — several shades
Blue — early 1920s color, medium shade, not cobalt
Cheriglo — pink
Copen, Neptune, Ceylon — various shades of light blue
Crystal — clear
Ebony — black
Emerald Green — jewel tone green
Forest Green — dark green
Green — various shades, from yellowish to electric green
Mulberry — amethyst
Opal — white (milk glass)
Primrose — delicate shade of yellow
Royal or Ritz Blue — cobalt
Ruby — red
Topaz — yellow

Collectors seeking more information on Paden City would do well to consult the following: *Encyclopedia of Paden City Glass* by Carrie and Gerald Domitz (Collector Books); *Paden City, The Color Company,* by Jerry Barnett; *Colored Glassware of the Depression Era 2* by Hazel Marie

Weatherman; and *Price Trends to Colored Glassware of the Depression Era 2* by Hazel Marie Weatherman. Also available are *Paden City Company Catalog Reprints from the 1920s*; *Paden City Glassware* by Paul and Debora Torsiello and Tom and Arlene Stillman; and *Paden City Glass Company* by Walker, Bratkovich & Walker. There is also a quarterly newsletter currently being published by the Paden City Glass Collectors Guild; this group is listed in the Clubs, Newsletters, and Websites section. Our advisors for this category are Carrie and Gerald Domitz; they are listed in the Directory under Washington.

Ardith (etched), ebony, vase, #210, 8½", $150 to 200.00
Ardith, blk, candlestick, ea $35 to 45.00
Ardith, blk, compote, 7½", $45 to 55.00
Ardith, cobalt or red, saucer, $25 to... 35.00
Ardith, gr or pk, plate, cracker, 10½", $75 to 125.00
Ardith, gr or pk, vase, 6½", $75 to 95.00
Ardith, yel, pitcher, plain, 7", $375 to 450.00

Barware, samovar, vaseline with etching, base stamped Silver Plate Co., 13", $450.00. (Photo courtesy Skinner Auctioneers and Appraisers of Antiques and Fine Art on LiveAuctioneers.com)

Black Forest (etched), amber, batter jug, 8", $175 to.................... 200.00
Black Forest (etched), amber, bottle, scent, $150 to.................... 175.00
Black Forest (etched), blk, bottle, scent, $200 to 225.00
Black Forest (etched), blk, cake plate, 2x11", $125 to 150.00
Black Forest (etched), gr or pk, decanter, w/stopper, 10"............. 450.00
Black Forest (etched), gr or pk, egg cup, $150 to 175.00
Black Forest (etched), gr or pk, pitcher, 72-oz, 10½", $550 to...... 750.00
Black Forest (etched), gr or pk, vase, 10", $175 to 225.00
Crow's Foot, amber, tumbler, 4", $50 to 65.00
Crow's Foot, amethyst, creamer, $25 to 35.00
Crow's Foot, blk, bowl, ftd, 7", $75 to 85.00
Crow's Foot, cobalt, cracker plate, 11", $100 to........................... 120.00
Crow's Foot, cobalt, punch bowl, 8¾", $700 to............................900.00
Crow's Foot, crystal, bowl, nasturtium, 6x8", $75 to 95.00
Crow's Foot, crystal, compote, tall stem, 7x6¾", $40 to 50.00
Crow's Foot, crystal, plate, w/hdls, 11½x13", $25 to 35.00
Crow's Foot, gr or pk, candy dish, w/lid, 5¾x5¾", $125 to 175.00
Crow's Foot, gr or pk, sugar bowl, $22 to...................................... 30.00
Crow's Foot, red, candlestick, 2-lt, ea $100 to 125.00
Crow's Foot, red, plate, w/hdls, 11½x13", $100 to 120.00
Crow's Foot, red, punch cup, roly poly, $15 to 20.00
Crow's Foot, red, sugar bowl, $40 to 60.00
Cupid (etched), gr or pk, 5", $750 to 950.00
Cupid (etched), gr or pk, bowl, center loop hdl, 11", $250 to...... 300.00
Cupid (etched), gr or pk, bowl, salad, 9", $125 to......................... 150.00
Cupid (etched), gr or pk, mayonnaise set, 3-pc, $350 to 450.00
Cupid (etched), gr or pk, plate, oval, 7½x10½", $250 to............. 300.00
Cupid (etched), gr or pk, sugar bowl, ribbed, $65 to...................... 75.00
Cupid (etched), Neptune Bl, samovar & #1000 blown tumblers, $650 to ..750.00
Delilah Bird, amber, yel or Primrose, cracker jar, 5½".................. 450.00
Delilah Bird, bl or red, candlestick, keyhole, 5", ea $100 to......... 125.00
Delilah Bird, bl or red, compote, low, 3¾x7", $150 to.................. 200.00
Delilah Bird, crystal, bowl, ftd, 4½x11", $150 to 250.00
Delilah Bird, crystal, creamer, 2¾", $20 to 25.00

Delilah Bird, gr or pk, gravy boat, ftd, 5x7½", $200 to 250.00
Delilah Bird, gr or pk, vase, 6", $300 to.. 400.00
Emerald Glo, Emerald Gr, cheese & cracker, metal lid, 12" 65.00
Emerald Glo, Emerald Gr, cocktail shaker, 11", $75 to................ 100.00
Emerald Glo, Emerald Gr, nappy, divided, w/hdls, $20 to 24.00
Emerald Glo, Emerald Gr, platter, 14½", $24 to 30.00
Emerald Glo, Emerald Gr, shakers, 3", pr $22 to........................... 25.00
Emerald Glo, Emerald Gr, tidbit, 2-tier, 7" & 14", $30 to 40.00
Gazebo (etched), bl, compote, flared, 10x7½", $125 to............... 150.00
Gazebo (etched), bl, creamer, $35 to 45.00
Gazebo (etched), bl, mayonnaise set, 2½x4½", $75 to 100.00
Gazebo (etched), bl, relish, 2-part, 5x6¾", $40 to 50.00
Gazebo (etched), crystal, bowl, 12", $65 to................................... 75.00

Gazebo (etched), crystal, candy dish, heart shaped with lid, #555, 7½", $160.00. (Photo courtesy M. Klein Estate Auctions, LLC on LiveAuctioneers.com)

Gazebo (etched), crystal, candy dish, ftd, 10½", $50 to................. 65.00
Gazebo (etched), crystal, compote, flared, 10x7½", $45 to........... 50.00
Gazebo (etched), crystal, plate, 11", $45 to 55.00
Gazebo (etched), crystal, punch bowl liner, $45 to 55.00
Gazebo (etched), crystal, tray, center hdl, 11", $50 to 65.00
Gazebo (etched), crystal, tray, w/hdls, 13", $55 to 75.00
Gazebo (etched), punch bowl, $200 to 250.00
Gothic Garden (etched), amber or blk, candlestick, keyhole, ea... 45.00
Gothic Garden (etched), amber or blk, plate, 7", $18 to.............. 20.00
Gothic Garden (etched), blk or yel, vase, 8", $125 to 175.00
Gothic Garden (etched), gr or pk, creamer, 3", $45 to.................. 50.00
Gothic Garden (etched), gr or pk, vase, 8", $175 to..................... 200.00
Gothic Garden (etched), yel, bowl, w/hdls, 10", $65 to 85.00
Gothic Garden (etched), yel, snack set, 10" plate/6" bowl, $75 to... 125.00
Largo, amber or crystal, bowl, center hdl, 10½", $50 to................ 75.00
Largo, amber or crystal, box, cigarette, $60 to 75.00
Largo, amber or crystal, candlestick, 2-lt, 5", ea $20 to 30.00
Largo, amber or crystal, plate, 9", $18 to..................................... 20.00
Largo, amber or crystal, platter, 11½x9½", $30 to........................ 50.00
Largo, amber or crystal, vase, $65 to 85.00
Largo, bl or red, bowl, crimped, w/hdls, 7¾x12¾", $85 to 95.00
Largo, bl or red, candy dish, ftd, 7", $100 to 125.00
Largo, bl or red, plate, 9", $25 to 30.00
Largo, bl or red, relish, 5-part, oval, $75 to................................. 100.00
Largo, bl or red, vase, $150 to 175.00
Maya, bl, plate, ftd, $65 to.. 80.00
Maya, crystal, bowl, w/hdls, 10½", $50 to 65.00
Maya, crystal, compote, 10x6", $35 to 50.00
Maya, crystal, sugar bowl, $12 to... 15.00
Maya, lt bl, candy dish, 7", $125 to 150.00
Maya, lt bl, cheese & cracker, w/lid, 12½", $140 to...................... 165.00
Maya, red, bowl, center hdl, $100 to... 125.00
Maya, red, candlestick, 5", ea $50 to.. 75.00
Maya, red, plate, ftd, 14", $75 to 100.00
Nerva, crystal, bowl, console, 13", $45 to 65.00
Nerva, crystal, candy dish, w/lid, 7", $50 to 65.00
Nerva, crystal, compote, tall stem, 8x6", $75 to 95.00
Nerva, crystal, relish, 3-part, 6½x11", $45 to............................... 65.00
Nerva, red, bowl, cereal, 6½", $25 to 35.00
Nerva, red, cake plate, 12", $150 to 175.00
Nerva, red, compote, 9½", $100 to... 120.00

Nerva, red, relish, 3-part, 6½x11", $65 to 85.00
Orchid (etched), bl or red, compote, low, 3½x6½" 175.00
Orchid (etched), bl or red, plate, w/hdls, 12x14", $150 to 200.00
Orchid (etched), bl or red, vase, collared, 7½", $500 to 575.00
Orchid (etched), gr or pk, candy jar, 8", $250 to 300.00
Orchid (etched), gr or pk, tray, plain, 4½x11", $30 to................... 45.00
Orchid (etched), gr, rose bowl, ftd, #411, $120 to 150.00
Orchid (etched), yel, bowl, ftd, 4½x9½", $225 to.......................... 300.00
Party Line, amber or crystal, bowl, mixing, 9", $35 to 45.00
Party Line, amber or crystal, candy dish, blown, w/lid, ½-lb........... 50.00
Party Line, bl, cheese dish, w/lid, 3½x4½", $40 to 45.00
Party Line, blk, cocktail shaker, 18-oz, $275 to............................ 325.00
Party Line, blk, water bottle, 48-oz, 9½", $200 to......................... 225.00
Party Line, gr or pk, bowl, berry, ind, 4½", $10 to.......................... 15.00
Party Line, gr or pk, cheese & cracker, w/lid, 10", $100 to........... 125.00
Party Line, gr or pk, refrigerator box, 5½", $45 to........................ 55.00
Party Line, gr or pk, shakers, 3", pr $50 to 65.00
Peacock & Rose/Nora Bird, amber, cheese & cracker, 11", $175 to...200.00
Peacock & Rose/Nora Bird, bl, ice bucket, 6x4½", $500 to.......... 600.00
Peacock & Rose/Nora Bird, bl, vase, elliptical, 8", $400 to.......... 450.00
Peacock & Rose/Nora Bird, blk, ice bucket, 6x4½", $125 to........ 150.00
Peacock & Rose/Nora Bird, gr or pk, bowl, oval, 8½", $125 to 175.00

Peacock and Rose/Nora Bird, pink, plate, 10", $50.00. (Photo courtesy Aristocrat Auction Services Ltd. on LiveAuctioneers.com)

Penny Line, amber or crystal, cocktail shaker, 40-oz, $75 to 100.00
Penny Line, amber or crystal, cordial, 1¼-oz, $12 to 18.00
Penny Line, amber or crystal, wine, 3-oz, $12 to 16.00
Penny Line, bl or red, plate, 8", $30 to... 45.00
Penny Line, bl or red, sugar bowl, $20 to 25.00
Penny Line, bl or red, tumbler, 9-oz, $28 to 33.00

Pairpoint

The Pairpoint Manufacturing Company was built in 1880 in New Bedford, Massachusetts. It was primarily a metalworks whose chief product was coffin fittings. Next door, the Mt. Washington Glassworks made quality glasswares of many varieties. (See Mt. Washington for more information concerning their artware lines.) By 1894 it became apparent to both companies that a merger would be in their best interest.

From the late 1890s until the 1930s, lamps and lamp accessories were an important part of Pairpoint's production. There were three main types of shades, all of which were blown: puffy — blown-out reverse-painted shades (usually floral designs); ribbed — also reverse painted; and scenic — reverse painted with scenes of land or seascapes (usually executed on smooth surfaces, although ribbed scenics may be found occasionally). Cut glass lamps and those with metal overlay panels were also made. Scenic shades were sometimes artist signed. Every shade was stamped on the lower inside or outside edge with 1) The Pairpoint Corp., 2) Patent Pending, 3) Patented July 9, 1907, or 4) Patent Applied For. Bases were made of bronze, copper, brass, silver, or wood and are always signed.

Because they produced only fancy, handmade artware, the company's sales lagged seriously during the Depression, and as time and tastes changed, their style of product was less in demand. As a result, they never fully recovered; consequently part of the buildings and equipment was sold in 1938. The company reorganized in 1939 under the direction of Robert Gundersen and again specialized in quality hand-blown glassware. Isaac Babbit regained possession of the silver departments, and together they established Gundersen Glassworks, Inc. After WWII, because of a sharp decline in sales, it again became necessary to reorganize. The Gundersen-Pairpoint Glassworks was formed, and the old line of cut, engraved artware was reintroduced. The company moved to East Wareham, Massachusetts, in 1957. But business continued to suffer, and the firm closed only one year later. In 1970, however, new facilities were constructed in Sagamore under the direction of Robert Bryden, sales manager for the company since the 1950s. In 1974 the company began to produce lead glass cup plates which were made on commission as fund-raisers for various churches and organizations. These are signed with a 'P' in diamond and are becoming quite collectible. See also Burmese; Napkin Rings.

Glass

Biscuit jar, handpainted florals, silver-plated mounts, circa 1930, 7", $210.00. (Photo courtesy DuMouchelles on LiveAuctioneers.com)

Bowl, butterfly & floral intaglio, shallow, 13" 120.00
Bowl, daisies & leaves, cut, ca 1910, 8" 48.00
Bowl, fruit, Colias, cut flowers & butterfly in spider web, 8" 165.00
Box, butterfly & floral cuttings, SP hinge, 6½" dia 250.00
Butter dish, Nevada, cut, 4 hobstar panels, faceted knob, 6x8" 425.00
Candlestick, HP floral on yel (8") on walnut stem, 15¾" 425.00
Candlesticks, gr w/clear spherical std w/diffused bubbles, 9", pr .. 335.00
Centerpc, cut bowl on SP stem w/3 SP baskets, 1930s, 21x12x12" .. 300.00
Compote, amber w/clear ball stem, flared rim, blown, 6x12" 395.00
Compote, amethyst, conical, disk ft, 5¾x10" 48.00
Vase, Adelaide, cut, controlled bubble ped base, 11½" 215.00
Vase, Anona, cut, waisted, 12" 180.00
Vase, floral etch, trumpet form, 6" 50.00
Vase, floral HP on wht, scalloped rim, SP rtcl sleeve, 1900s, 6¾" . 120.00

Lamps

Puffy 16" Devonshire shade with floral garlands, base and shade signed Pairpoint, $9,000.00. (Photo courtesy Great Gatsby's Antiques and Auctions on LiveAuctioneers.com)

Boudoir, candle form w/gr cut stem, 6 crystal prisms, 13¼", pr 300.00
Puffy 6¾" rose bouquet shade; gilt tree-trunk base, #3079, 11½" ...3,360.00
Puffy 6" rose bonnet shade; tree-trunk std, 11", EX 2,875.00
Puffy 12" Am Beauty rose shade; 4-arm rpt wht #C3003 std, 20" ... 3,735.00

Puffy 12" butterflies/roses shade; bronze std w/sq base, VG 4,750.00
Puffy 12" pansy shade; 4-arm ornate Nouveau std, 19", NM ..21,275.00
Puffy 12" rose bouquet shade; SP std #3040 w/floral base, worn, 20"..5,175.00
Puffy 14" shade w/grapes, sculpted on 3-arm metal #3053 base, 21"..18,000.00
Puffy 14" Venice shade w/roses; 4-arm silver & gilt std, 22" 5,750.00
Puffy/rvpt 16" floral #D3070 shade; mk bronze std w/triangular ft, 20".13,250.00
Radio, rvpt poppies on panel held in SP base, #E3035, 11", NM ..1,600.00
Rvpt 13½" Italian garden shade sgn Morley; slim std, 19" 4,250.00
Rvpt 17¾" peacock & fauna frieze shade; #D3063 3-socket std, 22"..2,625.00
Rvpt 17" farm scene shade sgn H Fisher; bronzed std, VG 1,950.00
Rvpt 18" exotic birds/flowers shade; 3-ftd SP #3070 std, 23" 4,000.00
Rvpt 18" floral shade w/rprs; bronze 2-hdld std, 22½" 600.00
Rvpt Olympic Torch & Laurel Wreath mk shade; #C3069 std, 24".2,150.00

Paper Dolls

No one knows quite how or when paper dolls originated. One belief is that they began in Europe as 'pantins' (jumping jacks). During the nineteenth century, most paper dolls portrayed famous dancers and opera stars such as Fanny Elssler and Jenny Lind. In the late 1800s, the Raphael Tuck Publishers of England produced many series of beautiful paper dolls. Retail companies used paper dolls as advertisements to further the sale of their products. Around the turn of the century, many popular women's magazines began featuring a page of paper dolls.

Most familiar to today's collectors are the books with dolls on cardboard covers and clothes on the inside pages. These made their appearance in the late 1920s and early 1930s. The most collectible (and the most valuable) are those representing celebrities, movie stars, and comic-strip characters of the '30s and '40s. When no condition is indicated, the dolls listed below are assumed to be in mint, uncut, original condition. Cut sets will be worth about half price if all dolls and outfits are included and pieces are in very good condition. If dolls were produced in die-cut form, these prices reflect such a set in mint condition with all costumes and accessories. For further information we recommend *20th Century Paper Dolls* (Collector Books), *Tomart's Price Guide to Lowe and Whitman Paper Dolls*, and *Tomart's Price Guide to Saalfield and Merrill Paper Dolls*, all by Mary Young, our advisor for this category; she is listed in the Directory under Ohio. We also recommend *Schroeder's Collectible Toys, Antique to Modern*, and *Paper Dolls of the 1960s, 1970s, and 1980s* by Carol Nichols (both published by Collector Books).

Around the World w/Bob & Barbara, Children's Press #3000, 1946.. 30.00
Baby Brother & Sister, Whitman #1956, 1961 .... 50.00
Betsy McCall's Fashion Shop, Avalon/Standard Toykraft #402, 1959 ...50.00
Bobby & Betty, Burton #550, 1934 .... 75.00
Class Mates, Gabriel #D91 .... 35.00
Cloth Dresses to Sew for Polly Pet, Gabriel #D104 .... 50.00
Country Weekend w/Kathy & Jill, Reuben H Lilja #913, ca 1950. 20.00
Darling Dick, Gabriel #10, ca 1911 .... 100.00
Dennison TV Playhouse, Dennison #522, ca 1950 .... 30.00
Doll Cut Out Book, MA Donohue #756, ca 1913 .... 35.00
Dolly Dingle at Play, John H Eggers, 1927 .... 65.00
Dolly Dingle's Travels, John H Eggers series 2, 1921 .... 75.00
Dolly's Kut-Out Klothes, Am Toy Works #3081, 1930s 35.00
Dutton's Dolls for Dressing, Dolly Dear, EP Dutton & Co #1129 .. 90.00
Earnest & Justin Tubb, Jenson, 1946 .... 75.00
Fairy Folk, George W Jacobs & Co, complete set of 6 sheets 100.00
Fashion Parade Dolls Book, Child Art, 1977 .... 15.00
Five Round About Wood Dolls, Milton Bradley #4552 .... 60.00
Foreign Friends, Gabriel #D172 .... 50.00
Froggie Went A Courting, DeJournette Mfg #35 .... 35.00
Gidget, Avalon/Standard Toycraft #601, 1965 .... 50.00
Heidi, DeJournette Mfg #200 .... 18.00

Honey Bun, DeJournette Mfg #R-50 .... 18.00
Jackie & Caroline, Magic Wand #107, early 1960s 50.00
Just From College, Gabriel #D125 .... 60.00
Lacey Daisy, Kits Inc #1050, 1949 .... 20.00
Little Folks Crepe Paper Doll Outfit, Am Toy Works #902, 1930s ... 50.00
Little Miss Muffet, DeJournette Mfg #902 .... 22.00
Little Sister, Blaise Publishing #1003, 1963 .... 12.00
Little Sister, Dandyline Co, 1919 .... 25.00
Magic Doll, Parker Brothers, ca 1948 .... 45.00
Magic Mary Jane, Milton Bradley #4010-3, 1972 .... 25.00
Marilyn Monroe Dolls, Saalfield #4323, uncut, VG/EX 300.00

Mary and Her Little Lamb, J. Ottman & Co., circa 1900, five outfits, four hats, and her lamb, original box, 10", $390.00. (Photo courtesy Skinner Auctioneers and Appraisers of Antiques and Fine Art on LiveAuctioneers.com)

Mary Lou & Her Friends, Platt & Munk Co #235B, 1950s 60.00
Mary Ware Doll Book, hardbk, LC Page & Co, 1914 .... 200.00
Mayflower Sewing Set, Concord Toy #235 .... 30.00
Modern Dolls a Plenty, Gabriel #895, ca 1933 .... 90.00
Moderne Sewing for Little Girls, Am Toy Works #417, 1930s 35.00
Mods, The; Milton Bradley #4727, 1967 .... 15.00
Mother & Daughter, Jaymar Specialty/Great Lakes Press #974 ...... 30.00
Mother Goose Village, Harter Publishing Co. #H-164, 1935, ... 40.00
Movieland, Reuben H Lilja #906, 1947 .... 35.00
My Pet Dressing Dolls, Am Colortype Co, box set w/4 dolls, 1910s .. 65.00
Neddy Neverstill, Am Colortype Co #735, 1920s 85.00
Nursery Rhyme Party Dolls in Costume, McLoughlin Bros #544, 1920s . 75.00
Paper Dolls of the World, George W Jacobs & Co, 1909, complete set of 6 sheets .. 80.00
Peg, Nan, Kay & Sue, Whitman/Western #1995, 1966 .... 40.00
Pretty Polly, Goldsmith #2005, 1930 .... 30.00
Sandra the Bride, Avalon/Standard Toycraft #801-3, 1969 .... 15.00
Suzie Sweet, Gabriel #D94 .... 35.00
Sweet Sue, Magic Wand #108, ca 1960 .... 25.00
Ten Round About Dolls, McLoughlin Bros #555, 1936 .... 60.00
Toni, Merry Mfg Co #6501, 1960s 30.00
Wedding Belles, Dot & Peg Pro, 1945 .... 50.00
Young Designer, DeJournette Mfg, 1940 .... 30.00

Paperweights

Collecting of glass paperweights has grown in intensity over the past 30 years, due largely to the vast amount of information now available to interested parties through magazine and newspaper articles and via the internet.

One can purchase paperweights in a wide range of prices, from the inexpensive Asian and Mexican imports found in tourist and gift shops, to higher quality Murano or Polish weights. Elect to spend $100 to several thousand for a known artist's work, or jump into another arena of collecting and spend upwards of $100,000 for rare antique weights or one-of-a-kind weights from a contemporary artist. However, it is not unusual to view a fellow collector's holdings and see inconsequential paperweights on the same shelf as a fine-quality antique. Beauty IS in the eye of the collector!

Astute collectors have been piecing together collections of 1930s import Chinese paperweights — unrefined imitations of the lovely French weights of the mid-1800s. When viewed almost 80 years later, their beauty and craftsmanship are very evident. Of particular note are the weights containing an opaque white glass disk, hand-painted with charming and sometimes quite intricate designs. Other weights gaining in popularity (still relatively inexpensive) are the motto weights, i.e., Remember Me, No Place Like Home, Mother, etc., and those made of English bottle glass, especially examples with sulfide inclusions. Degenhart and Mosser plaque weights are also diappearing from the marketplace in the hands of collectors. There is still strong interest in advertising weights because they are abundant and relatively inexpensive. Collectors who have a larger budget for these exquisite 'glass balls' may choose to purchase only antique French paperweights from the classic period (1845 – 1860), the wonderful English and American weights from the 1840s, or examples of the high quality contemporary workmanship of today's master glass artists.

Baccarat, St. Louis, Clichy, Pantin, and St. Mande (names synonymous with classic French paperweights) as well as some American factories discontinued production between the 1880s and 1910, when paperweights fell out of favor with collectors. In the 1950s Baccarat and St. Louis revived paperweight production, creating high-quality, limited-production weights. St. Louis and Baccarat have again discontinued their line of paperweights in recent years. Many independent glass studios sprung up in the 1960s and 1970s due to the development of smaller glass furnaces that allowed the individual glassmaker more freedom in design and fabrication from the fire to the annealing kiln. Such success stories are evident in the creative glass produced by Lundberg Studios, Orient & Flume, and Lotton Studios, to name only a few.

Many factors determine value, particularly of antique weights, and auction-realized prices of contemporary weights usually differ greatly up or down from issue prices. Be cautious when comparing weights that seem very similar in appearance; their values may vary considerably. Size, the absence or presence of fancy cutting on the base, faceting, the inclusion of a seemingly innocuous piece of frit, or a tear in a lampworked leaf are just a few conditions that will affect value. Competition among collectors as well as internet auction sales have greatly influenced prices. Some paperweights heretofore purported to be 'rare' now appear with some frequency on internet auctions, driving down prices. However, as the number of collectors multiplies, the supply of (particularly) antique weights in the marketplace will decrease, forcing prices upward.

The dimension given at the end of the description is diameter. Prices are for weights in perfect or near-perfect condition unless otherwise noted. Our advisors for this category are Betty and Larry Schwab, The Paperweight Shoppe; they are listed in the Directory under Illinois. See Clubs, Newsletters, and Websites for the Paperweight Collectors' Association, Inc., which has chapters in several states and countries. They offer assistance to collectors at all levels. The values for cast-iron weights are prices realized at auction.

Key:
con — concentric   latt — latticinio
fct — facets, faceted   mill — millefiori
gar — garland   sil — silhouette
jsp — jasper

Rick Ayotte

Blueberry Morning, 4", $1,680.00. (Photo courtesy San Rafael Auction Gallery on LiveAuctioneers.com)

Ballerina Rose, upright/multi-tiered, pk on cobalt, 5½x9¾"......4,400.00
Ducks (3) on pond, mossy shore, 1992 ltd ed, 4", $1,800 to......2,500.00
Red poinsettia w/dk gr leaves on clear grnd, 1996, 2¼", $350 to .450.00
Salamander/mushrooms on sandy grnd, 1989, 3⅝", $1,200 to........ 1,500.00
Scarlet-chested parrot on flowers on clear, 1986, 3½", $1,500 to...1,800.00

Antique Baccarat

6 shamrock/complex/13 butterfly canes, wht upset muslin, 3⅛"...11,000.00
Animal sil (8) on wht star grnd, B1848 cane, 3⅛", $15,000 to..17,000.00
Blue clematis buds (5) w/leaves, clear star-cut grnd, 2⅞", $700 to .900.00
Complex close-packed mill canes w/B1847 sil canes, 3⅞", $10,000 to.....12,000.00
Dog rose, pk/wht w/11 leaves, star-cut base, 1850s, 2⅝", $2,000 to 3,000.00
Macedoine, colorful twists, 2⅝", $500 to 700.00
Mill close-pack, 1 cane mk B1847, 2⅛", EX, $2,500 to 3,500.00
Mill stars/flowers closely packed, B1847 cane, 3⅛", $3,000 to ..3,800.00
Multicolored flowers on latt grnd w/animal sils, B1848 cane, 2⅞"......3,000.00

Mushroom weight with blue torsade and star-cut base, 2¾x3", $11,400.00. [Photo courtesy Susanin's Auctions on LiveAuctioneers.com]

Paneled honeycomb on aqua carpet, 2¾", $10,000 to 15,000.00
Primrose w/center of wht stardust canes around red bull's-eye, $1,200 to .2,000.00
Primrose, red & wht, w/stardust central cane, gr leaves, 2¼", $900 to.....1,400.00
Rose/bud/dbl clematis/pansy & leaves, 1/6 fct, 3¼", $10,000 to . 15,000.00
Sand, rock weight, tan/brn/gr on clear base, 2", $50 to 100.00

Modern Baccarat

Cherry blossoms/wht buds/blk branch, amethyst grnd, 1987, 3", $600 to 800.00
Coppered Snake (coiled), 1979, 2½", MIB, $450 to 650.00
Fruit in brn woven basket on wht grnd, 1/6 fct, 1976, 3¹⁄₁₆" 400.00
Pears (3) & gr leaves on wht grnd, 1974, 3¹⁄₁₆" 400.00
Rose & bud w/gr leaves on clear, star-cut grnd, 1976, 3", $450 to . 600.00
Snail & 3 flowers/gr leaves/silver pebbles, 1977, 3¹⁄₁₆", $450 to.... 700.00

Bobbi and Ray Banford

Cabbage rose bouquet w/leaves, cobalt grnd, 1/10 fct, 2⅜x2", $600 to.......800.00
Cabbage roses on clear grnd, top fct/rows of flutes, 3", $700 to....900.00
Christmas tree/stars in dk bl sky, Bobbi, 3", $250 to 350.00
Clematis/buds/gr leaves, wht star-cut grnd, 1/5 fct, 2⅝", $650 to......850.00
Pink primrose/gr leaves, pk/bl torsade on muslin, 3", $450 to........ 650.00

Caithness

Butterfly & mc flowers w/gr stems, ltd ed, 3", $150 to 200.00
Christmas tree amid gar, ruby grnd, 1/6 fct, 1982, 3¹⁄₁₆", $250 to . 350.00
Mixed flowers among grasses w/butterfly, 3", $150 to.................... 200.00

Antique Clichy

5-flower bouquet w/pk ribbon on clear grnd, 3¹⁄₁₆", $8,000 to.... 10,000.00
C-scroll mill gar w/pk roses on clear, 2¾", $3,000 to 4,000.00
Complex mill canes on sodden snow, 3⅛", $3,500 to 4,500.00
Pink/bl/wht pinwheel w/center mc cane, 3", $1,800 to 2,2000.00

Rose amid complex mc canes on bl & wht latt, 3", $7,000 to...9,000.00
Rose/mill gar/mc cog canes, star-cut grnd, 1/5 fct, 2⅞", $1,500 to..2,000.00

Lundberg Studios

Sterling Rose, by Daniel Salazar, signed and dated 1987, 3¼" diameter, $360.00. [Photo courtesy Susanin's Auctions on LiveAuctioneers.com]

Angelic youths/flowers/doves, bl aurene, Richter/'89, 2⅞", $900 to.1,100.00
Daffodil w/gr leaves, Steven, 1987, 3x2¼", $1,500 to................1,800.00
Flowers (2) w/gr leaves on blk, 2½", $250 to............................. 350.00
Jonquil, sgn Steven 1987, 3", $1,400 to 1,600.00
Pond Reflection, lilies/cattails on bl, Steven/'89, 2½", MIB......1,300.00
Purple dragonfly & 5 purple flowers, Salazar/'89, 1¾", $300 to.....400.00
Toadstool Trio, mushrooms/etc on pebbled grnd, Steven/'89, 2½" ..950.00

Antique New England Glass

4 eagle sil canes/wht star, wht latt cushion, 2¾", $800 to 1,000.00
Apples & pears on dbl-swirl wht latt basket, 2⅝", $800 to........1,000.00
Complex canes, gr/wht/red star-cane border, wht latt, 2⅝", $600 to ..900.00
Fruit bouquet on wht dbl-swirl latt basket, 2¹¹⁄₁₆", $800 to........1,200.00
Mill nosegay w/4 leaves & 2 mill gar on clear grnd, 2⅝", $400 to. 500.00
Mushroom, mc w/tapered stem, star-cut grnd, ¼ fct, 3¼", $100 to..200.00
Pears (2) & gr stem w/leaves on clear, 2⅞", $600 to 850.00

Orient & Flume

Apple, golden irid w/appl striped leaf & stem, 2½"........................ 50.00
Feather & heart design, mc on teal, 3"... 250.00
Flowers & butterfly on bl irid, 1978, 3"....................................... 250.00
Frog appl to top of lily pad on bl sphere, $300 to.......................... 400.00
Mill, 1985, 2¾", $300 to.. 400.00
Peach w/gr leaf & brn stem, 2¾"... 50.00
Spirals, mc irid, 3", $100 to 150.00

Perthshire

5-petal mc flower w/gr leaves on wht latt base, 2¾"...................... 200.00
Flowers (2 & 1 bud) on stems on purple grnd, 3".......................... 500.00
Mill flowers in close-packed pattern, 3" 350.00
Multicolored flowers (4) w/gr leaves on dk grnd, 3"...................... 575.00
Poinsettia w/gr leaves amid gr & wht gar, 3"................................ 400.00

Ken Rosenfeld

6-flower bouquet w/gr leaves on wht grnd, 1988, 3½", $800 to 900.00
CA Discovery, flowers/leaves/rocks on earth, 2002, 3¼", $800 to 900.00
Candy canes/holly/berries/pine branches on clear, 1992, 3¼", $350 to....400.00
Floral bouquet on purple grnd, 2000, 3¼", $600 to...................... 700.00
Mixed berries/wht blossom/bud/gr leaves on wht grnd, 2001, 2½", $250 to..350.00
Pears (3)/holly swags w/pk bow on clear, 1992, 3⁵⁄₁₆", $500 to 600.00
Pink wild roses (3) w/closed bud on bl grnd, 2004, 3¼", $400 to . 600.00

St. Louis Antique

Bouquet on wht latt basket, ca 1848, 3", $8,000 to 10,000.00

Con mill mushroom & cobalt torsade, SL 1848, 3 3/16", $2,000 to ... 2,500.00
Crown weight, navy & yel, red & wht cane center, 2½" dia 1,200.00
Louis Napoleon Bonaparte sulfide amid mill gar, 3¼", $500 to 800.00
Twisted crown on coral & cane alternating w/wht latticinio twists, 2¾" . 3,500.00

Sandwich Glass

Pansy (pk & bl) w/2 gr leaves on pebbled grnd, 2⅞", $750 to 900.00
Pansy, w/Lutz rose center, 2⅞" 1,560.00
Plums (2) on gr leafy branch on clear grnd, 2⅝", $800 to 1,000.00
Wheatflower/bud/leaves/thick stem on clear grnd, 3 1/16", $1,200 to ... 1,500.00
Wheatflower w/leaves on wht dbl-swirl latt cushion, 3⅛", $2,000 to .. 2,500.00

Paul Stankard

Botanical, embedded flowering plant atop a sandy patch with roots, signed, F56 '90, 4¼x3¼x2¾", $2,880.00. (Photo courtesy Rago Arts and Auction Center)

Bellflower & 3 buds w/gr leaves on wht grnd, 1974, 2½", $700 to. 900.00
Desert flowers on pebbly grnd, undated, 3" 12,000.00
Prickly pear, dk gr w/2 yel buds, red grnd, 1985, 3 1/16" 1,800.00
Yellow flowers (4) & leaves on red grnd, undated, early, 3" 800.00

Debbie Tarsitano

5-petal flower & bud on bl scrambled cane grnd, top fct, 3½" 800.00
Bouquet & mill gar w/ladybugs/snake on pk grnd, 3", $2,000 to . 2,200.00
Lampwork flowers (28) scattered on clear grnd, 3¼", $3,200 to .. 3,500.00
Multicolored bouquet/buds/berries/leaves on clear, 1/7 fct, 3 7/16" ... 2,200.00

Delmo Tarsitano

Lizard among desert flowers on pebbled grnd, 3¾", $1,500 to ... 1,800.00
Peaches (2) on branch w/leaves, 7 fcts, 2½", $1,400 to 1,800.00
Snake coiled among desert flowers on pebbled grnd, 3½" 1,700.00
Spider on web bordered by mc flowers w/gr leaves, sandy grnd, 3½" .. 1,900.00
Strawberries (2) & buds among leaves, 3", $800 to 900.00
Strawberries in clear, wht cane w/initials DT, 3", $750 to 950.00

Victor Trabucco

Floral bouquet w/leaves on clear, magnum, 5", $950 to 1,200.00
Mixed floral bouquet, magnum, 5", $1,200 to 1,800.00
Orchid, pk on pk, sgn Trabucco Floral Art Glass 660.00
Pink & red flowers (3) w/gr leaves & stems on clear, 3", $400 to . 600.00
Red rosebud/berries/leaves, wht upset muslin, 2001, 3⅛", $800 to . 1,200.00
Violets w/gr leaves & stems on clear, 1984, 3", $500 to 800.00

Whitefriars

Christmas, 3 Kings, $600 to 800.00
Christmas, manger scene, $600 to 800.00
Floral interlocking gar, hex pattern, 1/6 fcts, 3 3/16", $350 to 450.00
Red rose on ped, 3½", $350 to 450.00
Telephone cane on closepack, 3", $600 to 800.00

Francis D. Whittemore

Berries (3) & stem w/gr leaves on pk grnd, 1¾", $275 to 400.00
Bleeding hearts on stem w/gr leaves on gr grnd, ltd ed, 2⅜", $275 to .. 400.00
Daffodil w/bud & leaves on purple grnd, 1970s, 2¼", $275 to 400.00
Partridge in pear tree w/gr leaves on ruby grnd, 2 7/16", $275 to 400.00
Pink rose w/gr leaves on ped, 3", $275 to 375.00

Paul Ysart

Clematis w/gr leaves on wht latt on red grnd, 2 13/16" , $800 to .. 1,200.00
Flower basket sulfide, red/wht latt torsade on blk grnd, 2 15/16", $1,800 to .. 2,500.00
Flower bouquet floating on pk jsp grnd, 1974, MIB, $600 to 800.00
Flower bouquet on wht latt basket, 2 15/16", $600 to 800.00
Flower spray w/gr leaves on wht latt grnd, 3", $600 to 800.00
Red/wht/bl flowers (3) on wht latt grnd, 2½", $800 to 1,200.00

Miscellaneous

Buzzini, Chris; Bittersweet Nightshade Bouquet, 1990, 3" 1,000.00
Buzzini, Chris; Pastel Bouquet on clear grnd, 1990, 3" 1,200.00
Ebelhare, D; con mill rings w/in staved 2-color basket, 1995, 2" .. 300.00
Kaziun, C Jr; 6-petal yel flower/leaves, gold speckled grnd, 2"+ped .. 360.00
Kaziun, C Jr; horse/jockey sil in oval on turq grnd w/torsade, 2 5/16" .. 4,000.00
Millville, morning glory, teal & wht, top fct, ftd base, 3x3" 750.00
Parabelle, con mill w/lg red/wht twist torsade, 1985, 3" 800.00
Smith, G; orchids & buds w/gr leaves on clear grnd, 1987, 3 1/16" . 600.00
Val St Lambert, Jesus sulfide/X canes on bl, ruby o/l, fcts, 4" 1,200.00

Papier-Maché

The art of papier-maché was mainly European. It originated in Paris around the middle of the eighteenth century and became popular in America during Victorian times. Small items such as boxes, trays, ink-wells, and frames, as well as extensive ceiling moldings and larger articles of furniture were made. The process involved building layer upon layer of paper soaked in glue, then coaxed into shape over a wood or wire form. When dry it was painted or decorated with gilt or inlays. Inexpensive twentieth-century 'notions' were machine processed and mold pressed. See also Candy Containers; Christmas Collectibles.

Tray, roses, yellow with touches of maroon and mother-of-pearl inlay on black, gold borders, 31x24", $3,100.00. (Photo courtesy Clarity Sells Online Gallery on LiveAuctioneers.com)

Box, chinoiserie scenes on lid, England, ca 1870, 12x3¾" 230.00
Box, writing, MOP inlay house/church, gilt, slant lid, 1850, 16" L .. 1,175.00
Display pc for Bronx Zoo, tiger, string stripes, orig pnt, 16" 1,850.00
Mask, tiger's face, realistic, fits over head, VG 215.00
Table, chinoiserie on blk, w/later Georgian-style stand, 18x24x19" ... 850.00
Table, floral on blk w/gold trim, oval, on blk stand, 20x30x24" . 2,150.00
Tray, blk w/gold molded rim, Jennens & Bettridge, 1890s, 31x23" ... 850.00
Tray, blk w/MOP floral/gilt scrolls, att Jennens & Bettridge, 31" L ... 1,175.00
Tray, chinoiserie landscape/floral borders, 19th C, 30x23" 1,765.00
Tray, floral/butterflies/moths/gold trim, 19th C, 2x24x128" 1,400.00
Tray, grapevines on brn, scalloped rim, rpr seam, wear, 31" L 265.00
Tray, MOP inlay on blk, serpentine rim, Jennens & Bettridge, 28x15" 850.00
Tray, sailing ships at sunset reserve on blk, scalloped rim, 27x22" . 360.00

Parian Ware

Parian is hard-paste unglazed porcelain made to resemble marble. First made in the mid-1800s by Staffordshire potters, it was soon after produced in the United States by the U.S. Pottery at Bennington, Vermont. Busts and statuary were favored, but plaques, vases, mugs, and pitchers were also made.

Bust, Abraham Lincoln, low socle, English, ca 1900, 12" 700.00
Bust, Admiral Nelson, J Pitt, 1853, 9¼" 550.00
Bust, B Franklin, mk Broome, Ott & Brewer, 1876, 8½x6" 2,600.00
Bust, child w/head slightly trn, Broome, Ott & Brewer, 6¾x5". 1,550.00
Bust, Clytie, C Delpech, 1855, att Copeland, 13¼" 400.00
Bust, Love, classical maiden, R Monti, 1874, Copeland, 13¼" 950.00
Bust, Mother, holding child, R Monti, Copeland, 1876, 15"..... 1,050.00
Bust, US Grant, Isaac Broome, Lenox Pottery, 1914, 9¾x7"..... 1,900.00
Figure, Chastity, classical lady, Durham, 1865, 25" 600.00
Figure, girl w/plate & dishcloth, bucket at ft, late 19th C, 22"..... 250.00
Figure, Greek Slave, nude female, H Powers, Minton & Co, 1851, 14". 765.00
Figure, Sabrina, draped nude, WC Marshall, Copeland, 1850s, 11¾". 650.00

Maxfield Parrish

Maxfield Parrish (1870 – 1966), with his unique abilities in architecture, illustrations, and landscapes, was the most prolific artist during 'the golden years of illustrators.' He produced art for more than 100 magazines, painted girls on rocks for the Edison-Mazda division of General Electric, and landscapes for Brown & Bigelow. His most recognized work was 'Daybreak' that was published in 1923 by House of Art and sold nearly two million prints. Parrish began early training with his father who was a recognized artist, studied architecture at Dartmouth, and became an active participant in the Cornish artist colony in New Hampshire where he resided. Due to his increasing popularity, reproductions are now being marketed. In our listings, values for prints apply to those that are in their original frames (or very nice and appropriate replacement frames); assume all items to be in excellent original condition unless noted otherwise. Bobby Babcock, our advisor for this category, is listed in the Directory under Colorado.

Display, lamp Edison Mazda, with Parrish art, VG, $3,500.00.
(Photo courtesy John M. Hess Auction Service Inc. on LiveAuctioneers.com)

Book pg, Autumn, from A Golden Treasury, 1911, 9¼x7" overall. 20.00
Book, Golden Age, 1904, Bodley Press 200.00
Book, Mother Goose on Prose, by L Frank Baum, 1st ed, 1897........ 1,400.00
Bookplate, City of Brass, 11x8½" overall, +dbl matt 30.00
Bookplate, End, 1925, from Knave of Hearts, 10x12" 130.00
Bookplate, Villa Bella, Italian Villas & Their Gardens, new matt & fr .. 25.00
Calendar top, Lampseller of Baghdad, Edison-Mazda, 1923, 18x14". 250.00
Calendar top, Primitive Man, 1921, Edison-Mazda, cropped, sm. 650.00
Calendar top, Prometheus, 1920, 23¾x14⅜" 2,000.00
Calendar, Christmas Eve, 1946, Brown & Bigelow, 8½x10¾" 146.00

Calendar, Daybreak, 1951, Brown & Bigelow, cropped, 18x22"... 180.00
Calendar, Egypt, 1922, Edison-Mazda, complete, lg 3,500.00
Calendar, Evening Shadows, 1953, Brown/Bigelow, cropped, 12x15". 400.00
Calendar, Golden Hours, 1929, Edison-Mazda, oak fr, 36½x17" .. 950.00
Calendar, Of Friendship, 1925, desk sz.. 150.00
Calendar, Spirit of the Night, 1919, Edison-Mazda, full pad, 19x9½". 4,500.00
Calendar, Sunlit Valley, 1950, Brown & Bigelow, 11½x17"............ 350.00
Calendar, Under Summer Skies, 1959, Brown & Bigelow, 9x12"............. 125.00
Display, Get Together, GE lt bulbs, 1920s, 26½x16x3"............... 3,500.00
Magazine cover, Boar's Head, Collier's, Dec 16, 1905.................. 125.00
Magazine cover, Milking Time, Collier's, May 19, 1906 .... 75.00
Playing cards, Ecstasy, Edison-Mazda, 1930, M in wrapper........... 275.00
Postcard, Pied Piper, 7x7" foldout, 1915 .... 175.00
Print, Air Castles, 1904, 16x12"... 275.00
Print, Aladdin, 1907, unfr, 9x11" 125.00
Print, Bellerophon Watching by the Fountain, 1910, 8x10" 125.00
Print, Canyon, 1924, 6x10"... 225.00
Print, Cassim, 1906, 9x11" 175.00
Print, Centaur, 1914, 12x6"... 195.00
Print, Checkerboard Chefs, 1925, 6x11"..................................... 195.00
Print, Cleopatra, Reinthal Newman House of Art, 1917, 15x27⅝". 625.00
Print, Dreaming, Reinthal Newman House of Art, 1928, 11¾x15". 325.00
Print, Early Autumn, Brown & Bigelow, 22x18" overall 200.00
Print, Errant Pan, 11x9" 350.00
Print, Fisherman & Genie, 1906, orig label, 9x11", NM 250.00
Print, Florentine Fete, 1920, 7x10" 225.00
Print, Garden of Allah, 1918, 15x30", $295 to........................... 550.00
Print, Jason & the Talking Oak, 1910, 7x9" 150.00
Print, Lights of Home, Brown & Bigelow, 1945, 17x15" 350.00
Print, Love's Pilgrimage, 1912, 6¼x15" 165.00
Print, Lute Players, 1924, 10x18" 350.00
Print, Old King Cole, 1906, 6½x24" 850.00
Print, Peaceful Valley, Brown & Bigelow, 1936, 16x11".............. 300.00
Print, Queen Gulnare, 1907, 9x11".. 250.00
Print, Reveries, Edison-Mazda, 14½x22" (cropped)...................... 600.00
Print, Stars, House of Art, 1927, 10x6" 350.00
Print, Villa Chigi, 1904, 7x10"... 100.00
Print, Wynken Blynken & Nod, Scribner's, 1905, 17x12½" 495.00
Stamp, Brill Brothers, 1915, 1½x2½", +dbl matt............................ 75.00

Pate-De-Verre

Simply translated, pate-de-verre means paste of glass. In the manufacturing process, lead glass is first ground, then mixed with sodium silicate solution to form a paste which can be molded and refired. Some of the most prominent artisans to use this procedure were Almaric Walter, Daum, Argy-Rousseau, and Decorchemont. See also specific manufacturers.

Bowl, scalloped rim, internal lattice work, Decorchemont #a712, 4½x8¾", $3,600.00.
(Photo courtesy Leslie Hindman Auctioneers on LiveAuctioneers.com)

Bust, woman, orange mottle, Despret, 5" 960.00
Mask, Napoleon, orange mottle, Despret, 5" 720.00
Panel, bull & foliage, mauve & gr on bl & wht mottle, Despret, 10" L.. 600.00
Plaque, Ave Maria, profile, orange/gr mottle, JD, 4½" dia 645.00
Sculpture, fish, Francois Decorchemont, 7¼x7¼", NM............ 2,040.00
Vase, gray w/mc streaks, stylized waves, fish hdls, Decorchemont, 5".. 11,500.00

Pate-Sur-Pate

Pate-sur-pate, literally paste-on paste, is a technique whereby relief decorations are built up on a ceramic body by layering several applications of slip, one on the other, until the desired result is achieved. Usually only two colors are used, and the value of a piece is greatly enhanced as more color is added.

Charger, 2 lady bathers by water, G Jones, 1924-51, 12" dia 2,150.00
Condensed milk container, classical figures, unmk Continental, 6"... 65.00
Plaque, Aurora, bl/wht, WA Bougeureau, ca 1890, 6½x3½"+fr..3,400.00
Plaque, couple by Cupid in cradle, L Solon, 6½x7" 7,600.00
Plaque, nymph at monument on dk bl, att Solon, 6" dia+mat+fr, pr.5,750.00
Plaques, nymph at cauldron w/cherubs, L Solon, 9x4"+fr, pr ..13,250.00

Urn, classical female figure, white on celadon green, gilt bronze mounts, Continental, 14½", $540.00. (Photo courtesy Leslie Hindman Auctioneers on LiveAuctioneers.com)

Vase, birds & cattails, rtcl top rim w/gold trim, pillow shape, att G Jones, 7".990.00
Vase, classical figure & flowers, gold uptrn hdls, w/lid, 15", pr 275.00
Vase, portrait reserve, rtcl rim, cornucopia hdls, L Solon, 8½".....725.00

Pattern Glass

Pattern glass was the first mass-produced fancy tableware in America and was much prized by our ancestors. From the 1840s to the Civil War, it contained a high lead content and is known as 'flint glass.' It is exceptionally clear and resonant. Later glass was made with soda lime and is known as non-flint. By the 1890s pattern glass was produced in great volume in thousands of patterns, and colored glass came into vogue. Today the highest prices are often paid for these later patterns flashed with rose, amber, canary, and vaseline; stained ruby; or made in colors of cobalt, green, yellow, amethyst, etc. Demand for pattern glass declined by 1915, and glass fanciers were collecting it by 1930. No other field of antiques offers more diversity in patterns, prices, or pieces than this unique and historical glass that represents the Victorian era in America.

Our advisors for this category are Darlene Yohe (see Directory, Arkansas) and Danny Cornelius and Donald Jones (see Directory, DND Antique Glass, under Ohio). For a more thorough study on the subject, we recommend *Standard Encyclopedia of Pressed Glass, 1860 – 1930*, by Mike Carwile; *American Pattern Glass Table Sets* by Cathy and Gene Florence, coordinated by our advisors Danny Cornelius and Don Jones; and *Early American Pattern Glass Cake Stands & Serving Pieces* by Bettye S. James and Jane M. O'Brien, coordinated by our advisors Danny Cornelius and Don Jones (see Directory, DND Antique Glass, Ohio). All of these books are available from Collector Books. See also Bread Plates and Trays; Cruets; Historical Glass; Salt Shakers; Salts, Open; Sugar Shakers; Syrups.

Note: Values are given for open sugar bowls and compotes unless noted 'w/lid.'

Actress, cake stand, 9-10", Adams & Co 270.00
Actress, celery vase, Adams & Co..235.00
Ada, berry bowl, sm, Ohio Flint Glass Co 22.00

Ada, butter dish, Ohio Flint Glass Co 95.00
Ada, pitcher, Ohio Flint Glass Co..130.00
Ada, sugar bowl, Ohio Flint Glass Co 50.00
Adams' Thousand Eye, spooner, amber, Adams & Co.....................45.00
Adonis, butter dish, McKee & Bros 75.00
Adonis, compote, w/lid, bl or gr, McKee & Bros 175.00
Adonis, relish tray, McKee & Bros 20.00
Aida, creamer, clear w/etching, Belmont Glass Co.........................110.00
Alabama, honey dish, w/lid, rare, US Glass Co 160.00
Alabama, toothpick holder, bl or gr, US Glass Co..........................275.00
Alaska, tray, jewel, bl or gr, Northwood Glass Co 65.00
Alexis, relish jar, Fostoria Glass Co 20.00
Amazon, claret, Bryce Bros...50.00
Arched Fleur-De-Lis, spooner, Bryce, Higbee & Co 55.00
Arched Ovals, cake stand, US Glass Co 90.00
Art, milk pitcher, Adams & Co..210.00
Art, relish dish, Adams & Co..30.00
Ashman, bread tray, Adams & Co 75.00
Ashman, sugar bowl, Adams & Co 90.00
Ashman, tumbler, Adams & Co 80.00
Austrian, banana stand, Indiana Tumbler & Goblet Co 225.00
Aztec Sunburst, cake plate, McKee Bros...65.00
Ball & Swirl, butter dish, McKee Bros 55.00
Ball & Swirl, spooner, McKee Bros 30.00
Baltimore Pear, celery vase, Adams & Co..120.00
Baltimore Pear, sugar bowl w/lid, Adams & Co 110.00
Barberry, plate, McKee Bros, 6" 40.00
Barley, platter, oval, unknown mfg...100.00
Barred Forget-Me-Not, plate, amber, Canton Glass Co 60.00
Batesville, celery, clear w/etching, King, Son & Co 75.00
Bead Column, berry bowl, Kokomo Glass Co..................................18.00
Beaded Acorn Medallion, butter dish, Boston Silver Glass Co....125.00
Beaded Arch Panels, mug, Burlington Glass Works 30.00
Beaded Band, spooner, unknown mfg..40.00
Beaded Dart Band, bread plate, amber, Geo Duncan & Son..........75.00

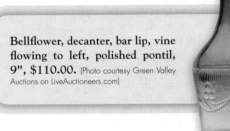

Bellflower, decanter, bar lip, vine flowing to left, polished pontil, 9", $110.00. (Photo courtesy Green Valley Auctions on LiveAuctioneers.com)

Bird & Strawberry, butter dish, Indiana Glass Co..........................350.00
Blazing Cornucopia, nappy, US Glass Co 45.00
Bleeding Heart, pitcher, King, Son & Co 325.00
Bow Tie, butter dish, Thompson Glass Co.......................................175.00
Brittanic, banana stand, ruby stain, McKee & Bros........................375.00
Bull's-Eye & Daisy, toothpick holder, ruby stain, US Glass Co 90.00
Bull's-Eye & Fan, wine, bl or gr, US Glass Co 45.00
Cabbage Rose, compote, w/lid, Central Glass Co...........................200.00
Cable, butter dish, amber, Boston & Sandwich Glass Co.............245.00
Carmen, cruet, Fostoria Glass Co 80.00
Carolina, butter dish, Bryce Bros..80.00
Cathedral, goblet, amber, Bryce Bros 100.00
Chain & Shield, pitcher, Portland Glass Co....................................130.00
Chandelier, sugar shaker, w/eng, O'Hara Glass Co 165.00
Checkerboard, spooner, Westmoreland Specialty Co.......................35.00

Classic, bowl, w/lid, Gillinder & Sons, 7½" 275.00
Classic, pitcher, milk, ftd, Gillinder & Sons 925.00
Clover, berry bowl, sm, Richards & Hartley Glass Co 15.00
Cord Drapery, cruet, amber, Indiana Tumbler & Goblet Co, 6¾". 625.00
Cupid & Venus, jam jar, Richards & Hartley Glass Co 125.00
Dahlia, egg cup, single, Portland Glass Co..................................... 35.00
Dakota, wine, Ripley & Co 20.00
Deer & Pine Tree, plate, gr, McKee & Bros 150.00
Delaware, tumbler, rose w/gold stain, US Glass Co 60.00
Egg in Sand, dish, swan center, Beaver Falls Glass Co.................. 45.00
Egyptian, goblet, plain, Adams & Co.. 80.00
Esther, castor set, ruby stain/flat, Riverside Glass Co................. 1,000.00
Eyewinker, celery vase, Dalzell, Gilmore & Leighton................... 195.00
Fandango, cookie jar, tall, AH Heisey & Co 210.00
Fashion, cake stand, Imperial Glass Co, 10" 65.00
Finecut & Block, finger bowl, amber, King, Son & Co.................. 50.00
Finecut & Block, sugar bowl w/lid, 8¾" 120.00
Fishscale, goblet, Bryce Bros 35.00
Florida, spooner, US Glass Co 70.00
Grasshopper, butter dish, amber, Riverside Glass Works, rare...... 400.00
Harvard Yard, cake stand, Tarentum Glass Co 100.00
Heart Stem, salt, unknown mfg... 40.00
Heart w/T'print, powder jar, Tarentum Glass Co......................... 100.00
Hickman, plate, McKee & Bros 60.00

Horn of Plenty, butter dish, flint glass, Washington head finial, 5x6", $1,680.00. (Photo courtesy Green Valley Auctions on LiveAuctioneers.com)

Horsemint, wine, Indiana Glass Co 35.00
Illinois, advertising bowl, 9" 150.00
Illinois, jelly compote, US Glass Co 45.00
Illinois, straw jar w/lid, gr, US Glass Co 900.00
Illinois, sugar, US Glass Co 95.00
Indiana, bowl, oval, US Glass Co, 7-9" 40.00
Indiana, celery, US Glass Co 90.00
Ivanhoe, nappy, Dalzell, Gilmore & Leighton 30.00
Jacob's Ladder, open compote, Bryce, Walker & Co, 7½" 45.00
Japanese, goblet, Geo Duncan & Sons... 235.00
Jumbo, butter dish, Brilliant Glass Works 675.00
Kansas, pickle dish, oblong, US Glass Co 30.00
Kentucky, open compote, US Glass Co, 6" 25.00
Kentucky, pitcher, water, ½-gal, US Glass Co 140.00
King's Crown, berry set, 7-pc, crystal, Adams & Co.................... 235.00
King's Crown, tumbler, crystal w/ruby stain, Adams & Co............. 70.00
Klondike, vase, crystal w/amber stain, Dalzell, Gilmore & Leighton, 8" .. 95.00
Kokomo, decanter w/stopper, Richards & Hartley Glass Co 45.00
Kokomo, water tray, rnd, Richards & Hartley Glass Co 40.00
Ladders, creamer, Tarentum Glass Co 30.00
Leaf & Flower, butter dish, crystal w/amber stain, Hobbs, Brockunier & Co ..125.00
Leaf & Star, nut dish, New Martinsville Glass Mfg Co 15.00
Liberty Bell, tray, relish, Adams & Co 35.00
Lily of the Valley, goblet, Richards & Hartley Glass Co.............. 175.00
Lily of the Valley, spooner, 3-legged, Richards & Hartley Glass Co ...135.00
Lion & Cable, compote, Richards & Hartley Glass Co, 7" 90.00
Lion Head, inkwell, Gillinder & Sons, rare 875.00
Loop & Jewel, butter dish, National Glass Co.............................. 65.00
Loop & Jewel, creamer, National Glass Co. 35.00

Louis XV, spooner, custard, Northwood Glass Co......................... 135.00
Louise, bowl, ftd, Fostoria Glass Co 45.00
Louisiana, pickle dish, boat shape, US Glass Co 20.00
Louisiana, wine, US Glass Co 40.00
Magna, pickle tray, Co-operative Flint Glass Co 30.00
Maine, cruet, w/topper, gr, US Glass Co 345.00
Maine, salt shaker, crystal, US Glass Co 45.00
Manhattan, ice bucket, crystal, US Glass Co 80.00
Manhattan, pitcher, tankard, rose stain, US Glass Co 175.00
Manhattan, water tray, crystal, US Glass Co 50.00
Maple Leaf, tray, oblong, vaseline, unknown mfg 185.00
March Fern, butter dish, Riverside Glass Works 100.00
Mardi Gras, nappy, Geo Duncan & Sons, 5" rnd 25.00
Mardi Gras, nappy, Geo Duncan & Sons, 5" triangular................. 30.00
Mardi Gras, punch cup, Geo Duncan & Sons, 2" 15.00
Maryland, jelly compote, US Glass Co 25.00
Maryland, spooner, crystal w/ruby stain, US Glass Co................. 150.00
Mascotte, bowl, Ripley & Co, 6" 55.00
Mascotte, cake stand, Ripley & Co, 8" 70.00
Masonic, sugar, McKee Glass Co. 50.00
Massachusetts, basket, w/appl hdl, US Glass Co, 9" 175.00
Massachusetts, bowl, US Glass Co, 6" sq 20.00
Massachusetts, claret, US Glass Co.. 55.00
Massachusetts, goblet, rnd bowl, US Glass Co 70.00
Massachusetts, plate, US Glass Co, 6" sq 35.00
McKee's Comet, creamer, McKee & Bros 90.00
McKee's Gothic, butter dish, McKee-Jeannette Glass Co 80.00
Medallion, pickle dish, bl, gr or yel, unknown mfg....................... 30.00
Melrose, bowl, master berry, Greensburg Glass Co 40.00
Melrose, pitcher, tankard, Greensburg Glass Co, 1-qt 45.00
Michigan, butter dish, mini, crystal, US Glass Co........................ 175.00
Michigan, compote, open, US Glass Co, 7½" 35.00
Mikado, sugar, Northwood & Co 195.00
Minerva, sauce dish, ftd, Boston & Sandwich Glass Co, 4½" 15.00
Minnesota, celery tray, US Glass Co 25.00
Missouri, compote, w/lid, US Glass Co 85.00
Moon & Star, egg cup, crystal, Adams & Co.................................. 65.00
Morning Glory, sugar bowl w/lid, 8" 125.00
Nail, syrup pitcher, crystal, Ripley & Co..................................... 125.00
Nelly, shaker, McKee Glass Co, ea 20.00
Nevada, sugar, US Glass Co 110.00
New Era, tray, JB Higbee Glass Co 30.00
New Hampshire, dish, oblong, US Glass Co................................... 20.00
New Jersey, plate, US Glass Co, 8" 30.00
New York, toothpick holder, gr, US Glass Co 75.00
Nogi, creamer, Indiana Glass Co 30.00
Northwood Hobstar, creamer, crystal w/ruby & gold stain, Northwood & Co...100.00
O'Hara Diamond, tumbler, crystal, O'Hara Glass Co 35.00
Ohio Star, vase, Millersburg Glass Co.. 110.00
Ohio, spooner, etched, US Glass Co... 75.00
One-O-One, plate, Geo Duncan & Sons, 8" 45.00
Oneata, sugar bowl, Riverside Glass Works 100.00
Open Rose, goblet, lady's, unknown mfg....................................... 75.00
Oregon, salt, master, open, US Glass Co 55.00
Oregon, vase, US Glass Co... 45.00
Orinda, butter dish, Ohio Flint Glass Co 65.00
Ornate Star, berry bowl, sm, Tarentum Glass Co 10.00
Paddlewheel, celery tray, Westmoreland Specialty Glass.............. 30.00
Palmette, egg cup, Bryce, Walker & Co 45.00
Panama, shaker, US Glass Co... 20.00
Panel Rib & Shell, creamer, Central Glass Co 80.00
Paneled Daisy, bowl, waste, Bryce Bros 45.00
Paneled Forge-Me-Not, tray, bread, Bryce Bros 55.00
Paneled Palm, bowl, rose, blush, US Glass Co............................... 65.00

Parachute, sugar bowl, National Glass Co 70.00
Pattee Cross, syrup, US Glass Co 60.00
Pavonia, cake plate, crystal w/etching, Ripley & Co, 10" 30.00
Pennsylvania, biscuit jar, US Glass Co 130.00
Pennsylvania, cheese dish, w/lid, US Glass Co 110.00
Pennsylvania, sugar bowl, US Glass Co 80.00
Pleat & Panel, dish, oblong, w/lid, Bryce Bros, 8" 150.00
Pleat & Panel, goblet, $15 to 18.00
Plume, compote, w/lid, Adams & Co, 6" dia 125.00
Pointed Jewel, spooner, mini, Columbia Glass Co 175.00
Polar Bear, platter, mk COG Co on sailboat, 16" 200.00
Popcorn, wine, Boston & Sandwich Glass Co 45.00
Portland, bowl, finger, US Glass Co 30.00
Posies & Pods, spooner, Northwood Glass Co 110.00
Powder & Shot, goblet, Boston & Sandwich Glass Co 105.00
Primrose, cordial, amber, bl or gr, Canton Glass Co 50.00
Priscilla, cup, sherbet, Fostoria Glass Co 15.00
Queen Anne, plate, bread, LaBelle Glass Co 70.00
Queen's Necklace, rose bowl, Bellaire Goblet Co 30.00
Question Mark, compote, open, Richards & Hartley Glass Co, 8" dia ... 60.00
Quintec, decanter, McKee Glass Co 40.00
Raindrop, bowl, master berry, bl, Doyle & Co, 9" 45.00
Red Block, celery vase, crystal w/ruby stain, Bryce Bros 130.00
Red Block, pitcher, bulb, crystal, Bryce Bros 125.00
Regina, spooner, Co-Operative Flint Glass Co 30.00
Reticulated Cord, goblet, vaseline, O'Hara Glass Co 135.00
Reverse 44, bonbon, ftd, crystal, US Glass Co, 4" 40.00
Reverse 44, bowl, rose, crystal w/platinum stain, US Glass Co 125.00
Reverse Torpedo, sugar bowl, Dalzell, Gilmore & Leighton Glass .. 120.00
Ribbed Ellipse, tumbler, JB Higbee Glass Co 20.00
Ribbon Candy, wine, Bryce Bros 130.00
Rising Sun, relish tray, crystal, US Glass Co 20.00
Rising Sun, whiskey, crystal, gr or rose, US Glass Co 45.00
Roanoke, cake stand, crystal w/ruby stain, Ripley & Co 180.00
Robin Hood, compote, Fostoria Glass Co 65.00
Rock Crystal, butter dish, crystal w/gold stain, New Martinsville Glass Mfg ... 200.00
Roman Rosette, honey dish, w/lid, flat, Bryce, Walker & Co 385.00
Rose in Snow, bowl, open, oval, bl, Campbell, Jones & Co, 8" 245.00
Rose Point Band, creamer, Indiana Glass Co 40.00

Silver Queen, spooner, crystal w/etching, Ripley & Co 40.00
Snail, salt shaker, tall, crystal w/ruby stain, Geo Duncan & Sons. 140.00
Spirea Band, jam jar, w/lid, amber, Bryce, Higbee & Co 120.00
Sprig, mustard w/lid, Bryce, Higbee & Co 235.00
Squirrel, pitcher, 9" 165.00
Star Rosette, goblet, $15 to 18.00
Tacoma, cracker jar, crystal, Greensburg Glass Co 115.00
Tarentum's Atlanta, butter dish, crystal w/ruby stain, Tarentum Glass Co ... 140.00
Teepee, jelly compote, crystal w/ruby stain, Geo Duncan's Sons & Co ... 70.00
Tennessee, relish tray, crystal, US Glass Co 45.00
Texas, vase, crystal, US Glass Co, 10" 65.00
Thistleblow, nappy, Kokomo Glass Mfg Co 25.00
Three Panel, sauce dish, amber, Richards & Hartley Glass Co 10.00
Thumbnail, sugar bowl, crystal w/gold stain, Duncan & Miller Glass Co .. 85.00
Tidal, olive dish, crystal, Bryce, Higbee & Co 15.00
Toltec, pitcher, milk, crystal w/ruby stain, McKee & Bros 70.00
Triple Triangle, table set, Doyle & Co 550.00
US Coin, cake stand, 6½x10" 300.00
US Coin, wine, US Glass Co 85.00
US Sheraton, pin tray, US Glass Co 20.00
V-In-Heart, creamer, Bryce Higbee & Co 40.00
Valencia Waffle, celery vase, bl, Adams & Co 80.00
Vermont, tumbler, gr, US Glass Co 70.00
Versailles, butter dish, opal w/decor, Dithridge & Co 110.00
Viking, bread platter, Hobbs, Brockunier & Co 95.00
Virginia, carafe, US Glass Co 95.00
Waffle & Star Band, punch cup, crystal, Tarentum Glass Co 10.00
Washington, cruet, crystal w/ruby stain, US Glass Co 275.00
Waverly, celery, Westmoreland Specialty Co 75.00
Wedding Bells, toothpick holder, crystal, Fostoria Glas Co 45.00
Westmoreland, cruet, w/orig stopper, Gillinder & Sons 105.00
Willow Oak, sweetmeat, w/lid, crystal, Bryce Bros 90.00
Wiltec, punch bowl, McKee Glass Co 100.00
Wyoming, bowl, open, US Glass Co, 6" 35.00
X-Ray, berry bowl, sm, gr, Riverside Glass Works 25.00
Yale, goblet, McKee & Bros 35.00
Zipper, sugar bowl w/lid 160.00
Zipper Cross, creamer, Bryce, Higbee & Co 40.00
Zipper Slash, jelly compote, crystal w/ruby stain, Geo Duncan's Sons & Co ... 35.00

Paul Revere Pottery

The Saturday Evening Girls was a group of young immigrant girls headed by philanthropist Mrs. James Storrow who started meeting with them in the Boston library in 1899 for lectures, music, and dancing. Mrs. Storrow provided them with a kiln in 1906. Finding the facilities too small, they soon relocated near the Old North Church and chose the name Paul Revere Pottery. Under the supervision of Ms. Edith Brown, the girls produced simple ware. Until 1915 the pottery operated at a deficit, then a new building with four kilns was constructed on Nottingham Road. Vases, miniature jugs, children's tea sets, tiles, dinnerware, and lamps were produced, usually in soft matt glazes often decorated with wax-resist (cuerda seca) or a black-outlined stylized pattern of flowers, landscapes, or animals. Examples in black high gloss may also be found on occasion. Several marks were used: 'P.R.P.'; 'S.E.G.'; or the circular device, 'Boston, Paul Revere Pottery,' with the horse and rider. The pottery continued to operate; and even though it sold well, the high production costs of the handmade ware caused the pottery to fail in 1946. Our advisors for this category are Suzanne Perrault and David Rago; they are listed in the Directory under New Jersey.

Bowl, daffodils, 2-tone on tan/yel/wht, SEG/6-14/FL, 2½x8½", NM.. 1,925.00
Bowl, daffodils, mc on gr grass & bl, SEG/4-19/SG, 8½" 3,000.00

Sawtooth, celery vase, 9½",
$40.00. (Photo courtesy Tom Harris Auctions on LiveAuctioneers.com)

Sawtoothed Honeycomb, salt shaker, crystal, Steimer Glass Co 45.00
Scalloped Six Point, cruet, w/orig stopper, Geo Duncan's Sons & Co 90.00
Scalloped Skirt, berry bowl, lg, amber, Jefferson Glass Co 65.00
Seed Pod, creamer, bl w/gold stain, Riverside Glass Works 85.00
Sextec, butter dish, crystal w/gold, McKee Glass Co 85.00
Shell & Jewel, pitcher, stippled, ftd, Westmoreland Specialty Co, rare 285.00
Shell & Tassel, mug, Geo A Duncan & Sons 90.00
Sheraton, platter, oblong, amber or bl, Bryce, Higbee & Co 55.00
Shoshone, cake stand, gr, US Glass Co, 11" 125.00
Shrine, pickle tray, Beatty-Brady Glass Co 25.00
Shrine, pitcher, 8½" 65.00

Bowl, geometric rim, brn on gray mottle, blk trim, SEG/4-15, 3" . 310.00
Bowl, gr, flared rim, ftd, circular PRP mk, 3x7½" 175.00
Bowl, groups of 3 rabbits in band, SEG/345.2.10, 2¼x5½" 1,685.00
Bowl, iris band wht on yel, 4-compartment, 2½x8½", NM 300.00
Bowl, landscape, CBT Compliments..., SEG/5-17, 6½" 1,080.00
Bowl, purple w/int band: Eat Thy Bread in Joy..., house center, 10" ...2,125.00
Bowl, red, PRP/SEG/#s/initials, 2½x8¼" 65.00
Bowl, sailboats, brn/gr on bl & wht, SEG/8-15/AM, 5x6" 2,160.00
Bowl, ships on sea int band, bl/yel/gr/brn on lt bl, flared rim, 9" 1,500.00
Bowl, trees band, tan on yel, sgn by SEG news editors, 2½x7", EX 1,080.00
Bowl, turq, rnd, paper label, 3x8½" 2,000.00
Bowl, wht camelia, SEG/10-16/AM, hairlines, 2½x8½" 1,500.00
Charger, Canadian goose/monogram, FL, 9", NM 5,250.00
Cup, trees band, bl/gr on wht, SEG/JG, 4½" dia 540.00
Mug, trees landscape/verse, sgn/SG/1912, 4" 3,750.00
Plate, lotus blossoms border, wht on bl, sgn AM, rim chips, 10" ..315.00
Plate, lotus blossoms on wht & bl, SEG/4-14/RM, 7½" 475.00
Plate, ships (2) in sea scene, mc on bl, SEG/4-14/AM, 12½" ..17,500.00
Plate, swan medallion on bl, SEG/8-19, 8" 600.00
Pot, tree band on mustard, w/lid & holes for lamp, globular, 6" .3,500.00
Tile, fox, mustard on celadon, SEG/388.5'10/FR, label remnant, 5¼" ..2,880.00
Tile, Hull Street Galloupe House, SEG, 12-12 SGB, paper label, 3¾" . 10,200.00
Tile, Paul Revere's House, North Sq, mc, 3¾" 3,000.00
Tile, stylized house & trees in center, mc on turq matt, V2-25/FL, 6" ...470.00
Tile, tulip center, gr/bl/wht/yel/blk on yel, EM/6.25, 4½" 375.00

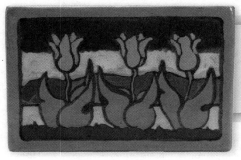

Tile, tulips and quote, 4¼x6", $14,650.00. (Photo courtesy Rago Arts and Auction Center)

Vase, lt bl, shouldered, 1929, 13½" 750.00
Vase, ochre semi-matt, shouldered, 9¼" 280.00
Vase, olive gr, shouldered/ftd, circular PRP mk & F/8/23, 6½x4½" ..500.00
Vase, trees in landscape on indigo, SEG/12-20/JMD, 1920, 3¾" ...1,440.00
Vase, trees in landscape on yel, SEG/4-19, 7¾x3½" 3,600.00
Vase, trees in landscape, mustard on sand, incurvate rim, 1917, 6" ..1,550.00

Pauline Pottery

Pauline Pottery was made form 1883 to 1888 in Chicago, Illinois, from clay imported from the Ohio area. The company's founder was Mrs. Pauline Jacobus, who had learned the trade at the Rookwood Pottery. Mrs. Jacobus moved to Edgerton, Wisconsin, to be near a source of suitable clay, thus eliminating shipping expenses. Until 1905 she produced high-quality wares, able to imitate with ease designs and styles of such masters as Wedgwood and Meissen. Her products were sold through leading department stores, and the names of some of these firms may appear on the ware. Not all are marked; unless signed by a noted local artist, positive identification is often impossible. Marked examples carry a variety of stamps and signatures: 'Trade Mark' with a crown, 'Pauline Pottery,' and 'Edgerton Art Pottery' are but a few.

Jardiniere, Nouveau poppies on gr, #94, 6x10", NM.................... 550.00
Pitcher, bearded man drinking/smoking reserve, leaves surround, 10".. 2,875.00

Teapot, floral, yellow on cobalt, marked, 8", $570.00. (Photo courtesy Cincinnati Art Galleries, LLC on LiveAuctioneers.com)

Teapot, nasturtiums & gold trim, stamped Ps #78, 8", NM 600.00
Vase, bird & flowers on brn, flared neck, rpr/hairlines, 22" 3,150.00
Vase, cobalt w/beige int, bulb w/cylindrical neck, 5x4", NM 275.00
Vase, florals & birds in gold on brn, rpr, 2 hairlines, 22" 2,070.00
Vase, ivory w/gilt floral, pk/gold bands, 3-lobe stick neck, att, 12" ...275.00

Peachblow

Peachblow, made to imitate the colors of the Chinese Peachbloom porcelain, was made by several glasshouses in the late 1800s. Among them were New England Glass, Mt. Washington, Webb, and Hobbs, Brockunier and Company (Wheeling). Its pink shading was achieved through the action of the heat on the gold content of the glass. While New England's peachblow shades from deep crimson to white, Mt. Washington's tends to shade from pink to blue-gray. Many pieces were enameled and gilded. While by far the majority of the pieces made by New England had a satin (acid) finish, they made shiny peachblow as well. Wheeling glass, on the other hand, is rarely found in satin. In the 1950s Gundersen-Pairpoint Glassworks initiated the reproduction of Mt. Washington peachblow, using an exact duplication of the original formula. Though of recent manufacture, this glass is very collectible. For more information we recommend *The Collector's Encyclopedia of American Art Glass* by John A. Shuman III and *Mt. Washington Art Glass* by Betty B. Sisk, both published by Collector Books.

Biscuit jar, Webb, gold Japanesque decor, metal lid & hdl 1,400.00
Cruet, bulb glossy w/amber stopper, 7" 650.00
Cruet, conical form, glossy w/amber stopper, 7" 900.00
Cruet, Mt WA, melon rib body & stopper, floral & leaves decor, 6½" . 7,800.00
Decanter, Hobbs, bulb body, amber hdl & stopper 1,400.00
Decanter, Imperial, w/stopper, matte 175.00
Jug, claret, Hobbs, conical form w/glass rope on neck, amber hdl 1,800.00
Lamp, fairy, Webb, vine decor, clear Clarke base 350.00
Pitcher, cream, Hobbs, amber hdl 400.00
Pitcher, milk, toby, #432PB, amber hdl, 6½" 40.00
Pitcher, mini, Kanawha #265PB, amber hdl, 4¼" 15.00
Pitcher, mini, Kanawha 3267PB, amber hdl 15.00
Pitcher/jug, Pelican, Hobbs 2,400.00
Punch cup, NE, matt 200.00
Punch cup, NE, glossy 150.00
Sugar bowl, Mt WA, 3 wishbone ft, berry decor 3,800.00
Sugar shaker, Hobbs, metal lid, 6" 1,200.00
Vase, bottle, ovoid, NE, sm flared neck, gold veined decor 2,800.00
Vase, jack-in-the-pulpit, Mt WA, fluted, ftd 1,800.00
Vase, #146, gourd, Mt WA undecorated 1,400.00
Vase, #146, gourd, Mt WA, Queens decor, floral 4,500.00
Vase, #147, dbl gourd, Mt WA, Prunus floral decor, 7".............2,800.00
Vase, #147, dbl gourd, Mt WA, undecorated, 7"........................1,600.00
Vase, banjo, ftd, Gundersen 300.00
Vase, dbl bulb, Mt WA, yel daisy decor, 9" 1,100.00

Vase, dbl gourd, Hobbs, glossy 2,200.00
Vase, dbl gourd, Hobbs, matt 1,900.00
Vase, lily, Mt WA tri-lobe crimp, ftd 1,400.00
Vase, Morgan, Hobbs, glossy w/griffin base 1,500.00
Vase, Morgan, Hobbs, matt w/griffin base 1,350.00
Vase, Morgan, Hobbs, no base, glossy 750.00
Vase, Morgan, Imperial, matt finish 125.00
Vase, trumpet, Gundersen, 3 rings near ft 200.00

Peking Cameo Glass

The first glasshouse was established in Peking in 1680. It produced glassware made in imitation of porcelain, a more desirable medium to the Chinese. By 1725 multilayered carving that resulted in a cameo effect lead to the manufacture of a wider range of shapes and colors. The factory was closed from 1736 to 1795, but glass made in Po-shan and shipped to Peking for finishing continued to be called Peking glass. Similar glassware was made through the first half of the twentieth century such as is listed below. Our advisor for this category is Jeffrey Person; he is listed in the Directory under Florida.

Vases, ginkgo branches, cobalt on opal, on teakwood bases, twentieth century, 9", pair $780.00. (Photo courtesy Jackson's Auction on LiveAuctioneers.com)

Bowl, ducks & foliage, red on wht, 8¼" 120.00
Bowl, wildlife & foliage, yel on wht, 3x6¾", pr 300.00
Jar, floral, rose-red on wht, 20th C, w/lid, 3x2" 60.00
Vase, birds & trees, gr on wht, 8" 110.00
Vase, butterflies & pond lilies, turq on wht, 20th C, 13x5½", pr 80.00
Vase, fish, bl on wht, dbl-gourd shape, 9¾" 180.00
Vase, flowering trees & bird, emerald gr on wht, 20th C, 6", pr ... 145.00
Vase, flowering trees, citrine to pale amber, baluster, 8½" 480.00
Vase, flowers & foliage, gr on wht, shouldered, 12", pr 715.00
Vase, kingfishers & lotus, blk on wht, late 19th C, 8½", pr 575.00
Vase, pheasant & foliage, red on wht, 8" 90.00
Vase, vining floral, cobalt on wht, baluster, 11" 180.00
Vase, vining floral, gr on wht, slim neck w/flared rim, 9½" 90.00
Vases, geese & lotus flowers, 2 shades of gr, early 19th C, 8", pr. 1,560.00

Peloton

Peloton glass was first made by Wilhelm Kralik in Bohemia in 1880. This unusual art glass was produced by rolling colored threads onto the transparent or opaque glass gather as it was removed from the furnace. Usually more than one color of threading was used, and some items were further decorated with enameling. It was made with both shiny and acid finishes.

Basket, cranberry w/wht strings, clear rope hdl, 7½" 280.00
Butter dish, clear w/mc strings, 6½x9" 500.00
Card holder, mint gr w/mc strings, jewel & gilt ft, 4½" 215.00
Pitcher, clear w/mc strings, 5½" 200.00
Pitcher, clear w/mc strings, clear hdl, 4½" 185.00
Tumbler, clear w/gr strings, 3¼x2⅝" 175.00
Vase, bl w/wht strings, scalloped & ruffled rim, 6½" 400.00
Vase, clear w/cranberry strings, ftd, 7¾" 385.00

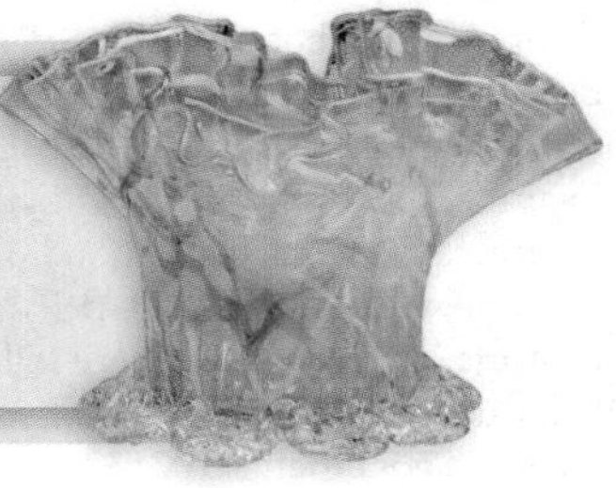

Vase, clear with pastel strings and slight opalescence, petal feet, small rough pontil, British, circa 1875, 3¾x5⅞", $100.00. (Photo courtesy Green Valley Auctions on LiveAuctioneers.com)

Vase, cranberry w/mc strings, scalloped & ruffled rim, 4½" 150.00
Vase, cranberry w/yel strings, ruffled rim, 4½" 140.00
Vase, wht w/clear ribbed casing & pastel strings, 6⅜" 180.00

Pennsbury

Established in the 1950s in Morrisville, Pennsylvania, by Henry Below, the Pennsbury Pottery produced dinnerware and novelty items, much of which was sold in gift shops along the Pennsylvania Turnpike. Henry and his wife, Lee, worked for years at the Stangl Pottery before striking out on their own. Lee and her daughter were the artists responsible for many of the early pieces, the bird figures among them. Pennsbury pottery was hand painted, some in blue on white, some in multicolor on caramel. Pennsylvania Dutch motifs, Amish couples, and barbershop singers were among their most popular decorative themes. Sgraffito (hand incising), was used extensively. The company marked their wares 'Pennsbury Pottery' or 'Pennsbury Pottery, Morrisville, PA.'

In October of 1969 the company closed. Contents of the pottery were sold in December of the following year, and in April of 1971, the buildings burned to the ground. Items marked Pennsbury Glenview or Stumar Pottery (or these marks in combination) were made by Glenview after 1969. Pieces manufactured after 1976 were made by the Pennington Pottery. Several of the old molds still exist, and the original Pennsbury Caramel process is still being used on novelty items, some of which are produced by Lewis Brothers, New Jersey. Production of Pennsbury dinnerware was not resumed after the closing. Note: Prices may be higher in some areas of the country — particularly on the East Coast, the southern states, and Texas. Values for examples in the Rooster pattern apply to both black and red variations.

Ashtray, Amish, 5" dia 25.00
Ashtray, Rooster, 4" 20.00
Ashtray, Sommerset, 1804-1954, 5" dia 30.00
Bank, jug, pig decor, cork top, 7" 55.00
Bookends, eagle, 8" 185.00
Bowl, divided vegetable, Rooster, 9½x6¼" 50.00
Bowl, pretzel, Amish Couple 85.00
Bowl, pretzel, Red Barn, 12x8" 150.00
Bowl, Rooster, 9" 45.00
Cake stand, Harvest or Hex, 4½x11½" 80.00
Candlesticks, hummingbird, wht, #117/#117L, 5", pr 120.00
Candlesticks, Rooster, 4", pr 85.00
Candy dish, Hex, heart shaped, 6x6" 35.00
Canister, Hex, Flour, 7½" 110.00
Coaster, Doylestown Trust Co, 1896-1958, 5" dia 25.00
Coaster, Gay Ninety, 5" dia 35.00
Coaster, Quartet, face of Olson, 5" dia 30.00
Coffeepot, Folkart, 2-cup, 6½" 25.00
Coffeepot, Rooster, 2-cup, 6" 55.00
Compote, Rooster, ftd, 5" 40.00

Cruets, oil & vinegar, Rooster, pr 150.00
Desk basket, National Exchange Club, 5" 40.00
Desk basket, Two Women Under Tree, 5" 50.00
Figurine, Audubon's Warbler, #122, 4" 160.00
Figurine, barn swallow, #123, 6¼" 165.00
Figurine, bl jay, #108, 10½" 400.00
Figurine, bluebird, #103, 3½" 235.00
Figurine, Cardinal, #120, 6" 225.00
Figurine, Chickadee, #111, 3½" 120.00
Figurine, crested chickadee, #101, 4" 195.00
Figurine, duckling pr, 6½" 295.00
Figurine, goldfinch, #102, 3" 195.00
Figurine, nuthatch, #110, 3⅝" 145.00
Figurine, rooster, #127, 11½" 165.00
Figurine, Slick-Chick, 5½" 50.00
Figurine, wren, #106, 6½" 315.00
Figurine, wren, #109, 3¼" 165.00
Mug, beer, Fisherman 45.00
Mug, coffee, Rooster 25.00
Mug, Irish coffee, horse decor w/gold trim 40.00

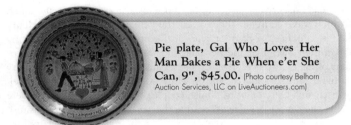

Pie plate, Gal Who Loves Her Man Bakes a Pie When e'er She Can, 9", $45.00. (Photo courtesy Belhorn Auction Services, LLC on LiveAuctioneers.com)

Pie plate, Rooster, 9" 40.00
Pitcher, Hex, 6¼" 65.00
Pitcher, Yel Daisy, ca 1959, 4" 32.00
Planter, bird on gourd w/opening, #301, 5", pr 110.00
Plaque, Amish Reading Bible, no primary colors, 9" 75.00
Plaque, Amish Sayings, 7x5" 25.00
Plaque, Charles W Morgan, ship decor, 11x8" 110.00
Plaque, Fisherman, 5" dia 28.00
Plaque, General, train decor, 11x8" 55.00
Plaque, Greater Lower Bucks County Week June 7-13, 1953, 8" dia ... 45.00
Plaque, It Is Whole Empty, 4" dia 35.00
Plaque, Mercury Dime, 8" dia 65.00
Plaque, Swallow the Insult, 6" dia 25.00
Plaque, The Flying Cloud, dtd 1851, 9½x7" 110.00
Plaque, United States Steel, 1954, 8" 40.00
Plaque, Washington Crossing the Delaware, 5" dia 25.00
Plate, bread, Give Us This Day Our Daily Bread, 9x6" 40.00
Platter, Rooster, 11" L 48.00
Snack tray & cup, Folkart or Hex 20.00
Tea tile, skunk, Why Be Disagreeable, 6" 40.00
Tray, cigarette, Eagle, 7½x5" 40.00
Tray, Laurel Ridge, famous old landmark, 8½x5¼" 40.00
Tray, tulip, 7½x5" 40.00
Wall pocket, bellows shape w/eagle in high relief, 10" 50.00
Wall pocket, cowboy, $75 to 90.00
Wall pocket, ship w/brn border, 6½" sq 50.00

Pens and Pencils

The first metallic writing pen was patented in 1809, and soon machine-produced pens with steel nibs gradually began replacing the quill. The first fountain pen was invented in 1830, but due to the fact that the ink flow was not consistent (though leakage was), they were not manufactured commercially until the 1880s. The first successful commercial producers were Waterman in 1884 and Parker with the Lucky Curve in 1888. The self-filling pen of the early 1900s featured the soft, interior sac which filled with ink as the metal bar on the outside of the pen was raised and lowered. Variations of the filling mechanisms were tried until 1932 when Parker introduced the Vacumatic, a sackless pen with an internal pump. For unrestored as-found pens, approximately one third should be deducted from the values below. For more information we recommend *Fountain Pens, Past & Present*, by Paul Erano (Collector Books). Our advisor for this category is Gary Lehrer; he is listed in the Directory under Connecticut. For those interested in purchasing pens, our advisor, Mr. Lehrer, publishes extensive catalogs.

Key:
BF — button filler	HR — hard rubber
CRF — crescent filler	LF — lever filler
ED — eyedropper filler	NPT — nickel-plated trim
GF — gold-filled	PF — plunger filler
GFT — gold-filled trim	PIF — piston filler

Fountain Pens

Aurora, 1975, #88P, blk w/chrome pinstriped cap 175.00
AW Faber, 1938, BF, gray marble bbl, blk cap 250.00
C Stewart, 1938, #15, LF, gr pearl, NPT, NM 100.00
C Stewart, 1951, #55, LF, gr marble, GFT, NM 150.00
C Stewart, 1955, #55, LF, bl marble, GFT, NM 200.00
C Stewart, 1956, #76, gr herringbone, GFT, NM 200.00
C Stewart, 1956, #85, LF, bl pearl w/gold veins, GFT, NM 150.00
Carter's Pearltex, 1931, bl plastic w/GFT, LF, 5", $200 to 250.00
Conklin, 1916, hand-chased gold-filled bbl & cap, 5½" 850.00
Conklin, 1918, #20, CRF, blk chased HR, GFT, NM 175.00
Conklin, 1918, #30, CRF, blk chased HR 200.00
Conklin, 1918, #50, CRF, blk chased HR 500.00
Conklin, 1918, #75, CRF, blk chased HR 800.00

Conklin, 1925, Endura, sapphire blue, 5¼", $600.00. (Photo courtesy Jackson's Auction on LiveAuctioneers.com)

Conklin, 1927, Endura Lg, LF, Jade 550.00
Conklin, 1927, Endura Lg, LF, Rosewood 500.00
Conklin, 1932, Nozac, PIF, gr pearl w/blk stripe, GFT, NM 300.00
Esterbrook, 1949, LJ Pen, LF, red, NM 40.00
Esterbrook, 1949, SJ Pen, LF, red, NM 35.00
Esterbrook, 1950, Pastel Pen, LF, wht, NM 85.00
JG Rider, 1905, Masterpan, ED, red & blk mottled 1,500.00
Leboeuf, 1929, #8, LF, tortoise 1,200.00
Mabie Todd, 1904, sterling, ring-top, 3½" 60.00
Mabie Todd, 1925, Swan #46 Eternal, LF, Cardinal HR 750.00
Montblanc, 1935, #20, Coral Red, GFT, NM 850.00
Montblanc, 1935, #25, Coral Red, GFT, NM 1,000.00
Montblanc, 1952, #142, PIF, blk GFT, NM 450.00
Montblanc, ca 1950s, #265 .... 150.00
Moore, 1946, Fingertip, LF, gr 275.00
Omas, 1932, extra lucens, LF, blk, Greek Key band 1,400.00
Omas, 1936, Lucens Lg, LF, blk 2,000.00

Omas, 1939, Lucens Medium, PF, blk..1,100.00
Osmia, 1935, Progress, PIF, Golden Web 400.00
Parker, 1927, Duofold Sr, Cardinal 'Big Red,' NM 400.00
Parker, 1937, Royal Challenger, BF, red pearl herringbone 550.00
Parker, 1946, Vacumatic Major, bl laminated, NM.....................175.00
Parker, 1950, 51, blk w/stainless steel cap, NM............................100.00
Parker, 1957, #61, wick filler, blk, 2-tone lustraloy cap, NM........125.00
Pelikan, 1937, #101N, tortoise w/matching cap/derby, NM 1,750.00
Pelikan, 1938, #100N, gr pearl, chased GF band/clip, NM 375.00
Pelikan, 1938, #100N, tortoise w/red cap, NM 1,700.00
Pelikan, 1950, #400, PIF, gr stripe, GFT, NM 175.00
Salz, 1920, Peter Pan, LF, dk red w/blk veins, GFT, NM 100.00
Salz, 1925, Peter Pan, LF, blk, HR, GFT, rare longer L, NM 75.00
Salz, 1925, Peter Pan, LF, tan/brn Bakelite, GFT, NM 75.00
Sheaffer, 1959, PFM III Demonstrator, transparent, GFT, blk shell, NM.1,400.00
Wahl Eversharp, 1936, LF, Coronet, red inserts............................900.00
Waterman, 1925, #52, LF, Red Ripple...175.00
Waterman, 1925, #54, LF, Red Ripple...225.00
Waterman, 1925, #58, LF, Red Ripple.......................................1,750.00
Waterman, 1926, #5, LF, Red Ripple, purple banded....................325.00
Waterman, 1926, #5, LF, Red Ripple, red banded.........................400.00
Waterman, 1927, #7, LF, red ripple, pk band, NM........................600.00
Waterman, 1929, #56, LF, Red Ripple...600.00
Waterman, 1931, #92, LF, red/bronze 250.00
Waterman, 1935, Ink-Vue Deluxe, Emerald Ray 350.00
Waterman, 1935, Ink-Vue Standard, Silver Ray............................225.00
Waterman, 1939, 100 yr, LF, gr...1,000.00
Waterman, 1939, 100 yr, LF, red...1,000.00

Mechanical Pencils

Anonymous, rifle shape, cocking mechanism, NM..........................75.00
Autopoint, 1945, 2-color (blk & bl), w/clip, M 15.00
Conklin, 1929, Symetric, gr marble, GFT, EX 50.00
Cross/Tiffany 1990, sterling silver pinstripe, clip: Tiffany, MIB....100.00
Eversharp, 1940, blk snakeskin-pattern leather cover, GFT, NM.150.00

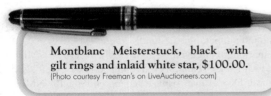

Montblanc Meisterstuck, black with gilt rings and inlaid white star, $100.00.
(Photo courtesy Freeman's on LiveAuctioneers.com)

Montblanc, 1924, #6, octagonal, blk HR, rare, lg, NM 1,350.00
Montblanc, 1930, #92 Repeater, blk HR, NPT, NM 125.00
Montblanc, 1939, #392 Repeater, blk HR, NM.............................80.00
Parker, 1929, Duofold Jr, jade, GFT, NM 50.00
Parker, 1929, Duofold Sr, Mandarin Yel, GFT, NM......................200.00
Parker, 1930, Duofold Vest Pocket, burgundy, GFT, w/opener taper, NM ...200.00
Sheaffer, 1925, Balance, deep jade, GFT, NM+ 50.00
Sheaffer, 1925, Balance, gr marble, GFT, NM+ 40.00
Sheaffer, 1959, PFM III, blk, GFT, M w/orig decal 175.00
Wahl Eversharp, 1929, oversize Deco band, blk & pearl, GFT, NM ..175.00
Wahl Eversharp, 1939, Coronet, blk w/smooth GF cap, NM.......100.00
Waterman, 1925, blk HR, GFT, M..75.00
Waterman, 1928, #52½V, olive ripple, GFT, NM 85.00

Sets

C Stewart, 1952, #14, LF, blk pearl, GFT, MIB..............................60.00
Conklin, faceted Herringbone pattern, pearl on gray, NMIB....1,040.00
Montblanc, 1972, #1266, PIF, sterling, fluted, 18k wht gold nib, M...400.00

Parker, 1940, Vacuum Jr, gr/bronze/blk stripes, GFT, NM 175.00
Parker, 1957, GF, alternating pinstripes & panels, M 200.00
Sheaffer, 1925, #3-25 Tall, blk plastic, GFT, NM 100.00
Sheaffer, 1936, Junior, LF, gray marble, NPT, NM 100.00
Sheaffer, 1952, Clipper Triumph Snorkle, bright red, chrome caps, MIB..200.00
Sheaffer, 1958, Lady Skripsert, GF filigree & bl, MIB 45.00
Sheaffer, 1959, PFM III, blk, GFT, MIB.......................................300.00
Wahl Eversharp, #4, GF w/chased wave pattern, NM 200.00
Waterman, 1925, #52, LF, red ripple, GFT, NM 250.00

Personalities, Fact and Fiction

One of the largest and most popular areas of collecting today is character-related memorabilia. Everyone has favorites, whether they be comic-strip personalities or true-life heroes. The earliest comic strip dealt with the adventures of the Yellow Kid, the smiling, bald-headed Asian boy always in a nightshirt. He was introduced in 1895, a product of the imagination of Richard Fenton Outcault. Today, though very hard to come by, items relating to the Yellow Kid bring premium prices.

Though her 1923 introduction was unobtrusively made through only one newspaper, New York's *Daily News*, Little Orphan Annie, the vacant-eyed redhead in the inevitable red dress, was quickly adopted by hordes of readers nationwide, and before the demise of her creator, Harold Gray, in 1968, she had starred in her own radio show. She made two feature films, and in 1977 'Annie' was launched on Broadway.

Other early comic figures were Moon Mullins, created in 1923 by Frank Willard; Buck Rogers by Philip Nowlan in 1928; and Betty Boop, the round-faced, innocent-eyed, chubby-cheeked Boop-Boop-a-Doop girl of the early 1930s. Bimbo was her dog and KoKo her clown friend.

Popeye made his debut in 1929 as the spinach-eating sailor with the spindly-limbed girlfriend, Olive Oyl, in the comic strip *Thimble Theatre*, created by Elzie Segar. He became a film star in 1933 and had his own radio show that during 1936 played three times a week on CBS. He obligingly modeled for scores of toys, dolls, and figurines, and especially those from the '30s are very collectible.

Tarzan, created around 1930 by Edgar Rice Burroughs, and Captain Midnight, by Robert Burtt and Willfred G. Moore, are popular heroes with today's collectors. During the days of radio, Sky King of the Flying Crown Ranch (also created by Burtt and Moore) thrilled boys and girls of the mid-1940s. Hopalong Cassidy, Red Rider, Tom Mix, and the Lone Ranger were only a few of the other 'good guys' always on the side of law and order.

But of all the fictional heroes and comic characters collected today, probably the best loved and most well known is Mickey Mouse. Created in the late 1920s by Walt Disney, Micky (as his name was first spelled) became an instant success with his film debut, 'Steamboat Willie.' His popularity was parlayed through windup toys, watches, figurines, cookie jars, puppets, clothing, and numerous other products. Items from the 1930s are usually copyrighted 'Walt Disney Enterprises'; thereafter, 'Walt Disney Productions' was used.

Unless noted otherwise, our values are for examples in undamaged, original condition that would be graded in at least excellent condition. For more information we recommend *Schroeder's Collectible Toys, Antique to Modern*; for those interested in Disneyana, we recommend *Collecting Disneyana* by David Longest. Both are available from Collector Books. See also Autographs; Banks; Big Little Books; Children's Things, Books; Cookie Jars; Dolls; Games; Lunch Boxes; Movie Memorabilia; Paper Dolls; Pin-Back Buttons; Posters; Rock 'n Roll Memorabilia; Toys.

Addams Family, doll, Lurch, plastic, jtd, Remco, 1960s, MIB......275.00
Addams Family, hand puppet, any character, Ideal, 1965, ea 50.00
Alf, hand puppet, plush, Cookin' w/Alf apron, Alien Prod, 1988, NM.. 20.00

Alice in Wonderland, marionette, working mouth, Hazell, 14", NM... 125.00
Alice in Wonderland, snow dome, Alice/Rabbit, Marx, 1961, 3", NM+..225.00
Alvin & the Chipmunks, bubble bath container, any, C-P, 1960s, M, ea.. 15.00
Amos & Andy, map, Eagles View of Weber City, Pepsodent, NM+ ..100.00
Andy Gump, ventriloquist punch-out, Malt-O-Meal, 1938, 20" 200.00
Annie (movie), wallet, wht vinyl w/name & graphics, Henry Gordy, MIP...12.00
Annie Oakley, coloring book, Roundup..., Whitman, unused, 1955 ....20.00
Atom Ant, Play Fun Set, Whitman, 1966, NMIB..........................50.00
Atom Ant, push puppet, Kohner, 1960s 50.00
Babe Ruth, ring, Baseball Club, premium 165.00
Baby Huey, hand puppet, Gund, 1950s, NM+ 75.00
Baby Snookums, doll, wood/compo, dress/underwear/shoes, 11", NM.. 225.00
Bambi, rocker, wood, Gong Bell, #606, NMIB 125.00
Bambi, soap figure, Cussons/WD, unused, EXIB............................30.00
Banana Splits, tambourine, plastic/cb, 1970s, MIP.........................35.00

Barney Google, drum, tin litho, copyright King Features Syndicate 1923, artist signed DeBeck, 7½x11", $660.00. (Photo courtesy Dan Morphy Auctions LLC on LiveAuctioneers.com)

Barney Google & Spark Plug, doll set, plush, Knickerbocker, 12"/9", VG...1,000.00
Bashful (Snow White), alarm clock, figural, pnt ceramic, JA Sural Hanau.. 225.00
Batman & Robin, hand puppet set, Ideal, 1966, MIB (single box) ..650.00
Batman, Bat Grenade, shoots caps, Esquire Novelty, 1966, MOC..125.00
Batman, charm bracelet, 5 figures, gold-tone/pnt detail, NPP, 1964, MOC.. 110.00
Batman, roller skates, plastic strap-on type w/figural detail, 1966, NM... 85.00
Batman, Shooting Arcade, Ahi/DC Comics, 1977, unused, NMIB. 150.00
Batman, Stardust Touch of Velvet, Hasbro, 1966, unused, MIP... 150.00
Batman, Zoomcycle, plastic, b/o, DC Comics, 1977, 6" L, unused, MIB.. 75.00
Beany & Cecil, bank, Cecil's head, plastic, NM 35.00
Beany & Cecil, Cecil Disguise Kit, unused, MIB..........................115.00
Beany & Cecil, jack-in-the-box, Mattel, 1961, M........................250.00
Beetle Bailey, doll, Gund, 1960, 15", NM+ 150.00
Beetle Bailey, hand puppet, Gund, 1960s..................................100.00
Beetle Bailey, stamper set, Ja-Ru, 1980s, unused, MIP..................60.00
Ben Casey MD, Paint-By-Number Water Color Set, Transogram, 1962, NRFB...175.00
Ben Casey MD, Play Hospital Set, Transogram, 1962, NMIB......150.00
Betty Boop, doll, stuffed, cloth dress, Cameo, 23", G+ 300.00
Betty Boop, figure, wood, jtd, gr pnt dress w/red heart, 12", VG ..450.00
Betty Boop, tea set, wht & bl porc/decals, 17-pc, Occupied Japan, EXIB..275.00
Bimbo (Betty Boop), figure, pnt wood, jtd, chest decal, 1930s, 6½" 700.00
Bionic Woman, Paint-By-Number Set, Craftmaster, 1970s, MIB.. 30.00
Bionic Woman, Pic-A-Show Projector, Kenner, 1979, MIB 25.00
Blondie, doll, vinyl w/red cloth dress, Presents, 1985, 18", NM+ .. 30.00
Blondie, pnt set, Am Crayon, 1940s, EXIB...................................75.00
Bonzo, dexterity game, tin & cb, Germany, 4" dia........................100.00
Boob McNutt, doll, wood w/cloth outfit, Schoenhut, 9" 475.00
Bozo the Clown, Changeable Blocks, Gaston Mfg, 1950s, EXIB ... 45.00
Bozo the Clown, Decal Decorator Kit, 1950s..............................50.00
Bozo the Clown, doll, vinyl, jtd, Dakin, 1974, 7½", NM...............28.00
Bozo the Clown, hand puppet, talker, Mattel, 1963, MIB...........120.00
Bozo the Clown, record player, Transogram....................................50.00
Brady Bunch, banjo, Larami, 1973, 15", MIP...............................50.00
Broom-Hilda, doll, stuffed, yarn hair, Wallace Berrie, 1983, 14", NM+ .. 30.00
Buck Rogers, badge/whistle, Space Commander, NM 325.00
Buck Rogers, Chemical Laboratory, Gropper Mfg, EXIB...........1,150.00
Buck Rogers, pencil box, Am Lead Pencil Co, 1936, 5x8½" 75.00
Buck Rogers, pop gun, XZ-31, Cocomalt premium, 1934.............350.00

Buck Rogers, ring, Saturn, premium, NM+....................................600.00
Buck Rogers, ring, Sylvania lightbulb, brass, premium, 1953, NM..950.00
Bugs Bunny, doll, plush, Mattel, 1960s, 15" 25.00
Bugs Bunny, Music Maker, litho tin, Mattel, 1963, 8x6", VG........35.00
Bugs Bunny, pencil holder/sharpener, figural, Holiday Fair, 1970, 6", NM. 18.00

Bugs Bunny, wristwatch, Swiss, made exclusively for sale at Rexall Drugs, with guarantee and instructions, MIB, $1,100.00. (Photo courtesy Tom Harris Auctions on LiveAuctioneers.com)

Buttercup & Spareribs, doll set, stuffed, cloth, 18½x12", pr.........900.00
Captain America, action figure, Mego, 8", MIB, $225 to 250.00
Captain America, Flashmite, Jane X, 1970s, MOC......................75.00
Captain America, Official Utility Belt, Remco, 1979, NRFB 75.00
Captain Gallant, gun & holster, name on snap closure 50.00
Captain Hook, hand puppet, Gund, 1950s, NM+ 75.00
Captain Kangaroo, figure, squeeze vinyl, hands in pockets, 1950s, 8", MIB.50.00
Captain Kangaroo, TV Eras-O-Brd Set, Hasbro, 1950s, EXIB 50.00
Captain Marvel, key chain, Fawcett, 1940s 50.00
Captain Marvel, Magic Flute, Fawcett, MOC 100.00
Captain Marvel, Magic Lightning Box, Fawcett, 1940s 75.00
Captain Midnight, Code-O-Graph decoder, 1941........................100.00
Captain Midnight, Mysto-Magic Weather Forecasting Wings, Skelly Oil . 50.00
Captain Midnight, patch, Secret Squadron, 1956, MIP 75.00
Captain Midnight, whistle, 1947..75.00
Casper the Ghost, doll, talker, Mattel, 1960s, 15" 100.00
Casper the Ghost, pull toy, playing xylophone, wood, 1960s, 9" L............300.00
Charlie Brown, comb/figural brush set, Avon, 1971, NM+IB 25.00
Charlie Brown, figure, squeeze vinyl, Hungerford, 1950s, 9" 75.00
Charlie Brown, marionette, vinyl, jtd, Pelham, 1980s, 8", NRFB..75.00
Charlie Chaplin, coloring book, Saalfield, 1941, unused, NM.......50.00
CHiPs, Police Set, CA Highway Patrol, HG Toys, 1971, NRFC ... 55.00
Churchy La Femme (Pogo), figure, vinyl, detergent promo, 1969, NM . 18.00
Cinderella, doll, Horsman, 8", NM+IB 100.00
Cinderella, hand puppet, plush, Gund, 1950s, NM+.....................75.00
Cinderella, marionette, in evening gown, Pelham, 1960s, NMIB. 100.00
Clarabell (Howdy Doody), bank, flocked figure, Straco, 1970s, 9", NM .. 25.00
Clarabell (Howdy Doody), marionette, Peter Puppet, 1952, 15", NMIB..150.00
Cowardly Lion (Wizard of Oz), doll, Ideal, 1984, 9", NM+............50.00
Daffy Duck, figure, vinyl, Dakin, 1960s-70s, 9", NM 20.00
Dagwood (Blondie), marionette, 1940s, 14", NM+ 200.00
Daniel Boone, Fess Parker Super Slate, Saalfield, 1964, unused, M .75.00
Davy Crockett, pencil case, Frontierland, holster/gun shape, 1950s, 8", VG.50.00
Dennis the Menace, hand puppet, cloth w/vinyl head, 1959 ....60.00
Dennis the Menace, Mischief Kit, Hassenfeld Bros (Hasbro), 1950s, MIB .250.00
Dick Tracy, coloring set, w/pencils/pictures to color, Hasbro, 1967, MIB.100.00
Dick Tracy, fingerprint set, Pressman, 1930s, complete, EXIB......200.00
Dick Tracy, hand cuffs, John Henry, 1940s....................................30.00
Dick Tracy, Islander Ukette, features Sparkle Plenty, Styron, 1950s 75.00
Dick Tracy, Sparkle Paints, Kenner, 1963, unused, NMIB 75.00
Dick Tracy, Wrist Radios, Remco, 1950s, EXIB...........................50.00
Doctor Dolittle, Cartoon Kit, Colorforms, 1967, NMIB 30.00
Doctor Dolittle, doll, talker, Mattel, 1960s, 24", MIB 150.00
Doctor Dolittle, hand puppet, talker, Mattel, 1967, NM...............50.00
Don Winslow, badge, LT Com/Squadron of Peace, Kellogg's, 1939, VG+ ..175.00
Donald Duck, Birthday Party Kit, Rendoll Paper Co, 1940s, VGIB .. 55.00
Donald Duck, doll, compo, parade outfit, Knickerbocker, 1935, 9", NM.1,065.00
Donald Duck, figure, bsk, w/hands on hips, WDE, 1930s, 1¾".........65.00
Donald Duck, pencil sharpener, celluloid figure, 3" 150.00

Donald Duck, sand pail/shovel, Sea Capt Donald/spyglass, Ohio Art, 4½" .385.00
Donald Duck, shoo-fly rocker, dc wood figures/seat, 32" L 725.00
Donald Duck, tea set, litho tin, 6-pc set, Ohio Art, NMIB.......... 275.00
Donald Duck, watering can, camping graphics, Ohio Art, 6½" ... 300.00
Dorothy (Wizard of Oz), doll, bl checked jumper, Ideal, 1939, 13" ..750.00
Dr Kildare, doll, plastic, 1960s, 11½", rare, MIB.......................... 450.00
Droopy Dog, hand puppet, Zaney, 1950s, NM 75.00
Dukes of Hazzard, Etch-A-Sketch Action Pak, Ohio Art, 1980s, NMIP .. 10.00
ET, Finger Lt, b/o, glows when pressed, Knickerbocker, 1982, MOC...10.00
Evil Knievel, doll, Ideal, 6".. 25.00
Felix the Cat, doll, plush, toothy grin, Chad Valley, 1920s, 23", VG .. 1,100.00

Felix the Cat, jointed figure, Performo Toy Co., Middleton, Pennsylvania, copyright Pat Sullivan, circa 1926 – 1928, 6½", VG+, $300.00. (Photo courtesy Dan Morphy Auctions LLC on LiveAuctioneers.com)

Felix the Cat, sparkler, tin head, Chein/Borgfeldt, EXIB 1,200.00
Felix the Cat, tableware, wht china/decals, red trim, 20-pc, Crown Pottery .400.00
Ferdinand the Bull, hair bows, rayon/metal, Stark Prod/WDE, 1938, EXOC.50.00
Flash Gordon, wrist compass, plastic, FG Inc, 1950s 65.00
Flintstones, Magnet Stickers, pkg of 3 characters, c 1979, NRFP .. 20.00
Flintstones, push button puppet, any character, Kohner, 1960s, NM, ea ... 50.00
Flip the Frog, doll, stuffed velvet, Dean's Rage, 6" 400.00
Flipper, ukulele, Mattel, 1968, NM+.. 25.00
Foghorn Leghorn, hand puppet, vinyl/cloth, 1960s, NM+ 75.00
G-Men, Fingerprint Set, NY Toy & Game Co, complete, EXIB.. 300.00
Gene Autry, wallet, leather, Aristocrat, 1950s, VGIB 75.00
Gilligan's Island, Gilligan's Floating Island, Playskool, 1977, MIB... 150.00
Goofy, nightlight, gr figure, Horsman, 1970s 20.00
Green Arrow, action figure, Mego, 8", MIB, $400 to...................... 450.00
Green Hornet, hand puppet, Greenway Prod, 1960s, NM 250.00
Green Hornet, Magic Invisible Kite, plastic, Roalex, 1966, MIB. 400.00
Green Hornet, Print Putty, Colorforms, 1966, MOC (sealed) 75.00
Gremlins, Play Set, Colorforms, 1984, unused, MIB 35.00
Gulliver's Travels, soap set, set of 4 different figures, 1939 .... 75.00
Gulliver's Travels, songbook, 8 songs, Famous Music Corp, 1939...........40.00
Gumby, bubble bath container, M&L Creative Package, 1987, NM . 15.00
Gumby, Paint Set, Henry Gordy Int'l, 1988, unused, MIP 12.00
Hardy Boys, Sing-A-Long Phonograph, Vanity Fair, electric or b/o.. 75.00
Harold Lloyd, whistle, litho tin figure, 2½"................................... 200.00
Heckle & Jeckle, bank, Famous Terry Toon Bank, 8", VG+ 150.00
Heckle & Jeckle, hand puppets, Rusthon Creations, 1950s, ea...... 75.00
Henry, doll, rubber/cloth outfit, Perfekta, 1940s, 9½", NM 100.00
Hi (Hi & Lois), doll, cloth/vinyl, flocked shoes, Presents, 1985, 16", NM+ ..30.00
Howdy Doody, bandana, 1948.. 50.00
Howdy Doody, Official Pl-A-Time Costume, NMIB 100.00
Howdy Doody, plate, ceramic, Smith-Taylor, 1950s, 8½" dia 50.00
Howdy Doody, watch, Ideal/Kagran, 1950s, MIB 650.00
Howdy Doody, Wonder Walker, Wall, NMIP................................. 85.00
Huckleberry Hound, bank, standing figure, Knickerbocker, 1960s, NM+ . 25.00
Huckleberry Hound, Cartoon Kit, Colorforms, 1962, EXIB......... 150.00
Incredible Hulk, hand puppet, Imperial, 1978 .... 35.00
Incredible Hulk, Magic Motion Yo-Yo, Vari-Vue images, Duncan, 1978, MIP..28.00
Iron Man, flicker ring, vending machine item, 1966, NM.............. 35.00
J Fred Muggs (Today Show), hand puppet, Imperial, 1954, NM 85.00
Jack Armstrong, badge, JA/Lieutenant/Listening Squad, 1940s 100.00
Jack Armstrong, Stamp Set, Wheaties, 1935, M (w/mailer) 50.00

James Bond, Electric Drawing Set, Lakeside, 1965, NMIB........... 100.00
James Bond, jigsaw puzzle, Thunderball, Milton Bradley, 1965, NMIB.40.00
James Bond, Parachute Set, Imperial, 1984, NMIP 30.00
Jetsons, hand puppets, any character, Knickerbocker, 1963, NM+, ea...75.00
Jiminy Cricket, figure, felt, Lars/Italy, 15" 1,800.00
Joker (Batman), hand puppet, Ideal, 1966, rare, NM 775.00
Katnip (Herman & Katnip), doll, plush/vinyl, Gundikins, 1950s 50.00
Katzenjammer Kids, doll family, set of 4, Knickerbocker, 16-20".......... 5,500.00
Kermit the Frog, Party Puzzlers, Hallmark, 1981, unused, MOC.... 10.00
Krazy Kat, pull toy, KK Express, wood, Int'l Feature Service, 1932 ....675.00
Lamb Chop, hand puppet, Tarcher Prod, 1960, NM 50.00
Laurel & Hardy, bank, either one, Play Pal, 1974, 13½", NM, ea .. 35.00
Laurel & Hardy, hand puppets, Knickerbocker, 1965, NM, ea....... 65.00
Laverne & Shirley, Paint-By-Numbers, acrylic, Hasbro, 1981, MIP...20.00
Lennon Sisters, coloring book, Watkins-Strathmore #1833, 1958, unused . 15.00
Li'l Abner, doll, vinyl/cloth outfit, Baby Barry Toys, 1950s, 14", NM . 100.00
Li'l Abner, hand puppet, Ideal, 1960s, NM+ 75.00
Linus (Peanuts), doll, Ideal, #1414-2, 1976 .... 75.00
Little Audrey, doll, vinyl/cloth dress, Juro Novelty, 1950s, 12", NM+ ..175.00
Little Audrey, Dress Designer Kit, Saalfield, 1962, NMIB............ 100.00
Little Iodine, hand puppet, Gund, 1950s, MIP 100.00
Little Lulu, bank, standing beside fire hydrant, vinyl, Play Pal, 1970s 25.,00
Little Lulu, coloring book, Whitman #1633, 1974, unused, NM+. 20.00
Little Lulu, doll, cloth/plastic head/yarn hair, Knickerbocker, 1930s, 13", M...800.00
Little Orphan Annie, dolls, Annie/Sandy, printed leather, 16" Annie.........175.00
Little Orphan Annie, Jack Set, Arcade, 1935, NRFP.................... 175.00
Little Orphan Annie, Shake-Up mug, beige/orange top, 1935..........75.00
Little Red Riding Hood, hand puppet, MPI Toys, 1960, NM......... 75.00
Little Red Riding Hood, marionette, Hazelle, 15" 100.00
Lone Ranger, coloring book, Health/Safety Club, Merita Bread, 1955, NM.50.00
Lone Ranger, pedometer, w/ankle strap.. 25.00
Lone Ranger, ring, gold ore/meteorite 2,000.00
Looney Tunes, figure, Porky Pig, stuffed felt, Warner Bros, 16",VG . 175.00
Lucky Ducky, hand puppet, Zaney, 1950s, NM............................. 50.00
Lucy (Peanuts), doll, cloth/gym suit, Determined, 6½" 10.00
Lucy (Peanuts), Skediddler, Mattel, 1969, 4½", MIB 125.00
Maggie & Jiggs, doll, cloth/printed detail, Lars of Italy, 1920s, 18" 400.00
Maggie & Jiggs, doll set, wood w/cloth outfits, Schoenhut, NRFB, 7", 9" .2,750.00
Magilla Gorilla, figure, stuffed, Playtime Toys, 1979, 7½", NM+ ... 20.00
Man from UNCLE, finger puppets, set of 6, unused, NMIB 325.00
Man from UNCLE, Secret Print Putty, USA, 1965, unused, MOC ..100.00
Mandrake the Magician, pin, enamel/brass, Tastee Bread, 1934, 1".125.00
Mary Hartline, Super Circus Puppet, cb, Snickers Candy, 1950s, M..125.00
Mary Poppins, tea set, tin, Chein, 1964, EXIB 50.00
Maverick, spinner coin, emb image of bros, Kaiser Alum, NM+ ... 20.00
Melvin Pervis, manual, Secret Operator's, Post Toasties, 1937, NM+ ..100.00
Mickey Mouse, bank, figure by tree trunk, compo, Crown Toy, 1938 .....225.00
Mickey Mouse, chalkboard, wood fold-out w/legs, Falcon Toys ... 175.00
Mickey Mouse, doll, stuffed, cowboy outfit, Knickerbocker, 10" .. 100.00
Mickey Mouse, doll, stuffed velvet, Charlotte Clark, 1934, 20" .4,250.00
Mickey Mouse, hand puppet, velvet, Steiff, G+ 200.00
Mickey Mouse, marionette, compo w/cloth outfit, 1940s 100.00

Mickey Mouse, piano, wood, articulated Mickey and Minnie figures dance when piano is played, 9x10x5", Marks Bros, VG, $600.00. (Photo courtesy Morphy Auctions)

Mickey Mouse, sand pail/shovel, Mickey's Band, Ohio Art, 10" 770.00
Mickey Mouse, Triky Trike, Gabriel, 1977, NRFC 30.00
Mickey Mouse, watering can, tin, Mickey watering flowers, 8", VG ..385.00
Mighty Mouse, doll, stuffed, cloth, Ideal, 1950s, 14" 75.00
Mighty Mouse, flashlight, figural, 1970s, 3½", MIP 100.00
Mighty Mouse, Merry-Pack, CBS TV Ent, 1956, unused 75.00
Minnie Mouse, doll, stuffed felt/cloth outfit, jtd arms, Nifty, 14", VG ..350.00
Minnie Mouse, marionette, compo/cloth outfit, 1940s 150.00
Minnie Mouse, music box, Love Story, Schmidt, 1970s,l 3½" dia, NM+. 35.00
Miss Piggy, mirror, ceramic, Sigma, 1979-83, 9", M 75.00
Mr Bluster, Savings Bank, flocked plastic figure, Straco, 1970s............. 35.00
Mr Jinks, doll, plush/vinyl face, Knickerbocker, 1959, 13", VG 50.00
Mr Magoo, doll, cloth/vinyl head, Ideal, 1962, 5" 100.00
Mr Magoo, fr-tray puzzle, Warren, 1978, NM+ 25.00
Munsters, Castex 5 Casting Set, Emenee, EX+IB........................ 250.00
Munsters, doll, any character, vinyl/cloth outfit, Swiss-made, 7", VG ..300.00
Mutt & Jeff, doll set, compo/cloth outfits, Swiss-made, 7", VG ... 300.00
My Favorite Martian, Magic Tricks Set, Gilbert, 1964, MIB........ 175.00
Nancy, figure, squeeze rubber, Dreamland Creations, 1955, 10", NM, ea. 75.00
Nanny & the Professor, Cartoon Kit, Colorforms, 1971, MIB 40.00
Olive Oyl, figure, vinyl, swivel parts, Multiple Toys, 1960s, 9", NM .. 55.00
Olive Oyl, hand puppet, Gund, 1950s 50.00
Oswald the Rabbit, figure, squeeze rubber, Sun Rubber, 1940s, 7½", VG... 50.00
Our Gang, Fun Kit, Morton Salt, 1930s, NM 175.00
Our Miss Brooks, hand puppet, Zany, 1950s, NM......................... 150.00
Pac-Man, gumball machine, plastic, Superior Toy, 1980s, 6" 25.00
Partridge Family, bulletin brd, 1970s, 18x24", NM 100.00
Peppermint Patty, doll, terrycloth, Determined, 1970s, 8½", MIP . 35.00
Peter Pan, doll, Ideal, 1953, 18" 125.00
Peter Pan, hand puppet, Gund, 1950s 35.00
Peter Pan, squeeze toy, figural, Sun Rubber, 1950s, 10" 50.00
Phantom, Pilot Patrol membership kit, Langendorf Breads, 1930s, NM+ ...2,000.00
Phantom, ring, skull, brass w/red eyes, 1950s 800.00
Phantom, rub-on transfer set, Hasbro, 1960s, NM+IP.................. 125.00
Pink Panther, Chatter Chum, Mattel, 1976, NM.......................... 50.00
Pink Panther, gumball machine, plastic, Tarrson, 1970s, 8", NM 30.00
Pinocchio, doll, wood/compo, felt hat, Ideal, 1940, 11" 400.00

Pinocchio, figure, Ideal Novelty & Toy Co., Walt Disney, missing felt hat, 19", VG, $425.00. (Photo courtesy Dan Morphy Auctions LLC on LiveAuctioneers.com)

Pinocchio, Plastic Novelties, 1940, NM+ 75.00
Pixie & Dixie, hand puppets, Knickerbocker, 1958, ea 50.00
Pluto, figure, rubber, Seiberling, 1930s, 3½" L 100.00
Pluto, purse, Gund, 1940s, 9x14x2" 35.00
Popeye, Christmas Tree Set (Lights), Mazda lamps, Reliance, 1930s, NMIB.175.00
Popeye, dexterity puzzle, tin/glass top, Bar-Zim Toys, 1929, 4x5", NM. 100.00
Popeye, Getar, wind-up musical, Mattel, 1960s, 14", NM+IB........ 75.00
Popeye, pull toy, SS Popeye, wood, 15½" 225.00
Popeye, Whistling Flashlight, Banamlite, 1950s, MOC 100.00
Porky Pig, doll, Gund, 1950, 14" 75.00
Porky Pig, figure, squeeze rubber, Sun Rubber, 1940s, 7", NM........ 50.00
Punch (Punch & Judy), squeak toy, figure on wood stick, w/mica, 14", G+..800.00
Quick Draw McGraw, doll, plus/vinyl, Knickerbocker, 1950s, 16" 175.00

Quick Draw McGraw, Modelcast 'N Color Kit, Standard Toycraft, 1960, EXIB. 50.00
Raggedy Ann & Andy, puppets, cloth, Dakin, 1975, EX+, ea........ 25.00
Red Ryder, badge, Victory Patrol, glow-in-the-dk, NM+.............. 500.00
Rin Tin Tin, Magic Erasable Pictures, Transogram, 1955, EX+IB. 100.00
Road Runner, figure, vinyl, Dakin, 1968, 9", NM.......................... 25.00
Roger Rabbit, doll, Applause, 17" 15.00
Roger Rabbit, Trace & Color Book, Golden #2355, unused, M 25.00
Rootie Kazootie, doll, baseball outfit, Effanbee, 1950s, 19" 100.00
Roy Rogers, Hobby Art Plaque Set, Collector's Brand/Nestle Quik, NMIB. 200.00
Roy Rogers, microscope 125.00
Secret Squirrel, push-button puppet, Kohner, 1960s 25.00
Sgt Preston, 10-in-1 Trail Kit, complete, 1958 .... 75.00
Sgt Preston, pedometer, 1952 .... 25.00
Shirley Temple, coloring book, Saalfield, 1935, complete, some use. 55.00
Shirley Temple, pen & pencil set, David Kahn, 1930s 100.00
Sky King, Detecto-Writer, alum or brass 125.00
Sleeping Beauty, hand puppet, Gund, 1950s, Nm........................... 65.00
Sleeping Beauty, squeeze figure, w/rabbit, Dell, 1959, 5x4x4" 40.00
Snagglepuss, Sticker Fun Book, Whitman, 1963, unused, NM+.... 50.00
Snoopy, bank, figural, United Feature, 1960s, 7" 20.00
Snoopy, bulletin brd, cork, Butterfly Orig, 1980s, 18x12", MIP 18.00
Snow White & the Seven Dwarfs, sand pail/shovel, Ohio Art, 8".. 285.00
Snow White, doll, compo/cloth dress, Knickerbocker, 15", G 225.00
Snow White, paper dolls, Whitman, 1938, uncut, NM+ 500.00
Spider-Man, coloring book, Arms of Dr Octopus, Marvel, 1983............. 15.00
Spider-Man, Talking View Master Set, 6 reels, GAF, 1970s, NM+IP ..40.00
Steve Canyon, punch-out book, Interceptor Station, Golden, 1950s, NM+.125.00
Straight Arrow, ring, Nugget Cove w/photo 275.00
Superman, coloring book, Whitman #1005, 1966, unused, NM+.. 22.00
Superman, ring, Crusader 235.00
Superman, school bag, vinyl, Acme, 1950s 150.00
Superman, scrapbook, spiral-bound, Saalfield 100.00
Tarzan, coloring book, Whitman, 1966, Ron Ely cover, unused 28.00
Tarzan, flasher ring, Vari-Vue, 1960s 15.00
Three Little Pigs/BB Wolf, tea set, litho tin, 13-pc, Ohio Art 400.00

Three Little Pigs, figurine, ceramic, Zaccagnini, circa 1947, 6x10½x8", $4,800.00. (Photo courtesy Dan Morphy Auctions LLC on LiveAuctioneers.com)

Tinkerbell, pendant, figure on metal ring, 1960s 15.00
Tinkerbell, pincushion, figural, w/container, 1960s 30.00
Tom & Jerry, wristwach, Bradley, 1985, NMIB............................ 50.00
Tom Corbett, ring, rocket, expansion band, unused, M................. 475.00
Tom Mix, badge, Straight Shooter 75.00
Tom Mix, belt buckle, Straight Shooter emblem............................ 75.00
Tom Mix, jigsaw puzzle, Rexall, 1920s, NM (w/envelope) 150.00
Tom Mix, ring, Straight Shooter 100.00
Tom Mix, Telegraph Set, Ralston Straight Shooter....................... 150.00
Tom Mix, watch fob, gold ore, NM... 75.00
Top Cat, figure, Marx TV Tinykins, 1961, NM+ 50.00
Tweety Bird, pull toy, twirling atop wagon, Brice Novelty, 9½", NM.125.00
Wild Bill Hickok, Colt 6-Shooter Pistol, Sugar Pops, 1958, 10", MIB..300.00
Winnie the Pooh, jack-in-the-box, litho tin, Carnival, 1960s, NM+..65.00
Winnie the Pooh, magic slate, Western Publishing, unused, NM+..50.00
Woodstock, bank, standing pose, sgn Schultz, 1970s, 7", NM+ 30.00
Woodstock, friction toy, ice-cream scooter, plastic, Aviva, 1970s, 6" 22.00
Woody Woodpecker, hand puppet, talker, Mattel, 1963, NM+ ... 100.00

Yellow Kid, jigsaw, McFadden's Row of Flats, McLoughlin Bros, VGIB .690.00
Yogi Bear, bank, figural, Knickerbocker, 22" 50.00
Yogi Bear, yo-yo, plastic head, Creative Creations, 3", MOC 22.00

Peters and Reed

John Peters and Adam Reed founded their pottery in Zanesville, Ohio, just before the turn of the century, using the local red clay to produce a variety of wares. Moss Aztec, introduced about 1912, has an unglazed exterior with designs molded in high relief and the recesses highlighted with a green wash. Only the interior is glazed to hold water. Pereco (named for Peters, Reed and Company) is glazed in semi-matt blue, maroon, cream, and other colors. Orange was also used very early, but such examples are rare. Shapes are simple with in-mold decoration sometimes borrowed from the Moss Aztec line. Wilse Blue is a line of high-gloss medium blue with dark specks on simple shapes. Landsun, characterized by its soft matt multicolor or blue and gray combinations, is decorated either by dripping or by hand brushing in an effect sometimes called Flame or Herringbone. Chromal, in much the same colors as Landsun, may be decorated with a realistic scenic, or the swirling application of colors may merely suggest one. Vivid, realistic Chromal scenics command much higher prices than weak, poorly drawn examples. (Brush-McCoy made a very similar line called Chromart. Neither will be marked; and due to the lack of documented background material available, it may be impossible to make a positive identification. Collectors nearly always attribute this type of decoration to Peters and Reed.) Shadow Ware is usually a glossy, multicolor drip over a harmonious base color but occasionally is seen in an overall matt glaze. When the base is black, the effect is often iridescent.

Several other lines were produced, including Mirror Black, Persian, Egyptian, Florentine, and Marbleized, and an unidentified line which collectors call Mottled-Marbleized Colors. In this high-gloss line, the red clay body often shows through the splashed-on colors. At one time, the brown high-glaze artware line with 'sprigged' decoration was attributed to Peters and Reed, though this line has recently been re-attributed to Weller pottery by the Sanfords in their latest book on Peters and Reed pottery. This conclusion was drawn from the overwhelming number of shapes proven to be Weller molds. Since the decoration was cut out and applied, however, it is possible that Peters and Reed or yet another Zanesville company simply contracted for the Weller greenware and added their own decoration and finishes. A few pieces from this line are included in the listings that follow. In 1922 the company became known as the Zane Pottery. Peters and Reed retired, and Harry McClelland became president. Charles Chilcote designed new lines, and production of many of the old lines continued. The body of the ware after 1922 was light in color. Marks include the impressed logo or ink stamp 'Zaneware' in a rectangle.

Bowl, Landsun, bl & wht, low, 2½x8" 90.00
Candleholder, Marbleized, brn/blk/olive, 1½x5½" 75.00
Garden frog, matt gr over red clay, unmk, 11" 600.00
Jardiniere & ped, Moss Aztec, bands of poppies, 29", EX 480.00
Jardiniere, floral, gr matt, 4 buttresses, unmk, 12x12½" 250.00
Planter, Moss Aztec, roses emb, tight line, 6x6½" 75.00
Vase, bud, Marbleized, blk/yel/brn/gr, 6" 80.00
Vase, cherub & floral appl to dk brn, angle hdls, 13½" 175.00
Vase, Chromal, landscape in swirled brns, incurvate rim, flaw, 10" ..450.00
Vase, floral appl on dk brn, pillow form, integral hdls, 5" 95.00
Vase, Landsun, bl/tan/pk, incurvate rim, 3" 80.00
Vase, Landsun, tan/gr/brn/bl, slim, ftd, 12" 175.00
Vase, Marbleized, agate drips at rim, ovoid, 12" 195.00
Vase, Marbleized, blk/gr/ivory/russet, corseted, 8x5½" 60.00
Vase, Marbleized, gr/yel/blk, flared rim, 10" 150.00
Vase, Marbleized, mustard/cobalt/blk, 6-sided, 9" 125.00

Vase, Moss Aztec, 8" 150.00
Vase, Moss Aztec, 12x5½" 500.00
Vase, Moss Aztec, floral emb, 10x4" 175.00
Vase, Moss Aztec, roses emb, stain, 17" 295.00

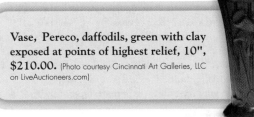

Vase, Pereco, daffodils, green with clay exposed at points of highest relief, 10", $210.00. (Photo courtesy Cincinnati Art Galleries, LLC on LiveAuctioneers.com)

Vase, Shadow Ware, blk/bl/gr/yel, glaze skips, 7⅞" 200.00
Vase, Shadow Ware, bl/blk/yel drips on caramel, shouldered, 7½" ..190.00
Vase, Shadow Ware, bls/brns on lt brn, cylindrical, 8⅞" 275.00
Vase, Shadow Ware, caramel runs on dk brn, hdls, 21", NM 750.00
Vase, Shadow Ware, lt gr dripping over dk gr, unmk, 12x7½" 900.00
Vase, Shadow Ware, mc drips on tan, shouldered, #3, Zaneware, 8½" ...550.00
Vase, Wilse Bl, dragonfly emb, 2x5⅛" 60.00
Vase, wisteria emb on bl matt, waisted, 12" 155.00
Wall pocket, Moss Aztec, floral, sgn Ferrell, 9½x6¼" 200.00

Pewabic

The Pewabic Pottery was formally established in Detroit, Michigan, in 1907 by Mary Chase Perry Stratton and Horace James Caulkins. The two had worked together following Ms. Perry's china painting efforts, firing wares in a small kiln Caulkins had designed especially for use by the dental trade. Always a small operation which relied upon basic equipment and the skill of the workers, they took pride in being commissioned for several important architectural tile installations. Some of the early artware was glazed a simple matt green; occasionally other colors were added, sometimes in combination, one over the other in a drip effect. Later Stratton developed a lustrous crystalline glaze. (Today's values are determined to a great extent by the artistic merit of the glaze.) The body of the ware was highly fired and extremely hard. Shapes were basic, and decorative modeling, if used at all, was in low relief. Mary Stratton kept the pottery open until her death in 1961. In 1968 it was purchased and reopened by Michigan State University; it is still producing today. Several marks were used over the years: a triangle with 'Revelation Pottery' (for a short time only); 'Pewabic' with five maple leaves; and the impressed circle mark. Our advisors for this category are Suzanne Perrault and David Rago; they are listed in the Directory under New Jersey.

Bowl, flaring, poly lustered glaze, 3¼x9" 450.00
Box, figures & animals emb on turq & fuchsia irid, w/lid, 3½" dia ..345.00
Plate, rabbit border (Dedham style), navy on tan, 9¼" 345.00
Plate, rooks, blk on gold lustre, 10" 4,800.00
Tile, bird in high relief on gr, sq, 6" 50.00
Vase, amber (thick/dripping), shouldered, 10½x6¾" 1,900.00
Vase, bl allover high lustre, ribbed, ftd, circle mk, 7⅛x6½" 1,000.00
Vase, bl irid over dk bl mottle, ftd, imp circle mk, 4½x5" 2,250.00
Vase, bl irid w/silver patches, faint ribbing, slightly bulb, 7" 625.00
Vase, bl lustre, shouldered, w/matching stand, 2-pc, 14x9" 8,125.00
Vase, bl w/lustre drips, Detroit, 11½x11" 2,400.00
Vase, bl w/tan splashes, paper label, ca 1910, 5½" 950.00
Vase, bl-gr matt, Pewabic w/maple leaves, 7x4¾" 1,200.00
Vase, bright bl lustre, bulb, 8x6½" 960.00

Vase, brn metallic lustre, shouldered, rstr ft, 10x6" 1,065.00
Vase, celadon w/turq drips, bulb at top, 6" 595.00
Vase, cobalt top over gold lustre, baluster, 4x3" 660.00
Vase, copper red over mauve, slightly bulb, faint ribbing, 10½" . 3,500.00
Vase, dk gr & oxblood (leathery), bottle form, 7x4¾" 725.00
Vase, geometric relief, matt flambé, maple leaves mk, 14½" 4,500.00
Vase, geometrics emb on matt flambé, cylinder neck, 14½x11" . 4,500.00
Vase, gr & indigo curdled lustre, 2 paper labels, stamped, 2 drill holes, 12½" . 1,725.00
Vase, gr matt/beige, geometric, Pewabic w/maple leaves, 14½x11" .. 4,500.00
Vase, gr w/lustre drips, 6¼x4½" 1,000.00
Vase, gr-brn metallic drip over yel, bulb/ftd, label, 5½" 1,080.00
Vase, lav metallic lustre, bulb, 4" 550.00
Vase, leaves cvd on gray crystalline on gr matt, tapers toward ft, 4" ... 315.00

Vase, lustered blue glaze, 6x5½", $3,550.00. (Photo courtesy Rago Arts and Auction Center)

Vase, lustred flambé, baluster, rstr chip, 20x9" 7,200.00
Vase, olive gr over bl, slightly bulb, 8x6" 1,065.00
Vase, ultramarine w/lustre drips, grinding chip, early, 8x8" 5,400.00
Vase, volcanic blk/bl/purple, bulb body, chip, 15½" 4,800.00
Vase, volcanic blk/bl/purple, bulb body, rstr rim chip, 15½" 5,000.00

Pewter

Pewter is a metal alloy of tin, copper, very small parts of bismuth and/or antimony, and sometimes lead. Very little American pewter contained lead, however, because much of the ware was designed to be used as tableware, and makers were aware that the use of lead could result in poisoning. (Pieces that do contain lead are usually darker in color and heavier than those that have no lead.) Most of the fine examples of American pewter date from 1700 to the 1840s. Many pieces were melted down and recast into bullets during the American Revolution in 1775; this explains to some extent why examples from this period are quite difficult to find. The pieces that did survive may include buttons, buckles, and writing equipment as well as the tableware we generally think of. After the Revolution makers began using antimony as the major alloy with the tin in an effort to regain the popularity of pewter, which glassware and china were beginning to replace in the home. The resulting product, known as britannia, had a lustrous silver-like appearance and was far more durable. While closely related, britannia is a collectible in its own right and should not be confused with pewter.

Key: tm — touch mark

Basin, Love & London tms, ca 1800, 2⅞x11½" 1,000.00
Basin, Love tm, Philadelphia, late 18th C, 3¼x12½" 3,360.00
Basin, Samuel Pierce eagle tm, ca 1792-1830, 2¼x8" 750.00
Basin, Thomas Melville II tm, polished, lt wear, 2x8" 575.00
Basin, W&S Yale partial tm, ca 1813-20, 1⅝x6⅝" 575.00
Chalice, Roswell Gleason (att), thistle form variant, 6⅜", 6 for . 865.00
Charger, unmk, minor wear, 11½" 90.00
Coffeepot, A Griswold eagle tm, wooden wafer finial, rpr, 10¼".. 150.00
Coffeepot, A Griswold tm, polished, rpt hdl & finial, 10½" 375.00
Coffeepot, Boardman & Hart tm, bulb, ivory finial, rpt hdl, 11½" ... 515.00

Coffeepot, Israel Trask, lighthouse form with reeded bands and engraved shields (one with monogram), several subtle dents, wear, scattered pitting, 10⅞", $1,200.00. (Photo courtesy Skinner Auctioneers and Appraisers of Antiques and Fine Art)

Coffeepot, R Gleason tm, lighthouse form, domed lid, 11" 400.00
Flagon, communion, unmk form used by Sheldon & Feltman (NY), 10½" . 375.00
Flagon, Smith & Feltman Albany tm, raised rings, scroll hdl, 10¼" .. 250.00
Jug, cider, Sellew & Co tm, scrolled hdl, rpr, 10" 635.00
Lamp, Brook Farm tm, West Roxbury, MA, rpl burner, ca. 1875, 7½" to collar .. 1,680.00
Lamp, Smith & Co tm, lozenge font, whale-oil burner, polished, 6" .. 285.00
Measures, English, grad set of 8, 1¾-6", G 285.00
Pitcher, R Dunham tm, sm dent, ca 1837-61, 6½" 300.00
Plate, J Danforth tm, lt wear/lt scratches, 8" 315.00
Plate, N Austin tm, single reeded trim, 18th C, 8" 600.00
Plate, S Danforth tm, single reed trim, 7⅞" 385.00
Plate, W Billings tm, polished, lt scratches, 8¼" 865.00
Platter, warming, Made in London tm, divided well, hdls, 21x15½" ... 175.00
Porringer, Hamlin eagle tm on flowered hdl, ca 1767-1801, 5½" . 800.00
Porringer, IG tm on crown hdl, ca 1800, polished, 4⅝" 315.00
Porringer, Richard Lee tm, sm dents, 3¾" 500.00
Porringer, SG tm on crown hdl, 5½" 200.00
Porringer, TD & SB tm on crown hdl, polished, lt wear, 5" 515.00
Spoons, English tm, decor on hdl, 7½", pr 200.00
Tall pot, Boardman & Co NY, ogee sides, domed lid, dents, 11¾" .. 460.00
Tall pot, G Richardson tm, lighthouse form, polished, sm rpt, 11" ... 635.00
Tall pot, unmk Am, scrolled hdl, wafer finial, 11½" 350.00
Tankard, English griffin tm, scroll hdl, heart on thumbpc, 7" 750.00
Teapot, att Geo Richardson, pear shape, scrolled hdl, 7½", EX.... 460.00
Teapot, Boardman & Hall Philada tm, wooden finial, blk pnt hdl, 7".. 375.00
Teapot, Putnam tm, minor wear/pinpoints, ca 1830-35, 8½" 200.00
Teapot, R Dunham, 12", EX 250.00
Teapot, Smith & Co tm, scroll hdl, petal wafer finial, G blk pnt, 7" .. 200.00
Teapot, unmk, scrolled hdl, wafer finial, sm dings, 6½" 145.00
Teapot, William McQuilkin tm, Philadelphia, ca 1840, 8" 960.00

Phoenix Bird

Blue and white Phoenix Bird china has been produced by various Japanese potteries from the early 1900s. With slight variations the design features the Japanese bird of paradise and scroll-like vines of Kara-Kusa, or Chinese grass. Although some of their earlier ware is unmarked, the majority is marked in some fashion. More than 125 different stamps have been cataloged, with 'Made in Japan' the one most often found. Coming in second is Morimura's wreath and/or crossed stems (both having the letter 'M' within). The cloverleaf with 'Japan' below very often indicates an item having a high-quality transfer-printed design. Among the many categories in the Phoenix Bird pattern are several shapes; therefore (for identification purposes), each has been given a number, i.e. #1, #2, etc. Post-1970 items, if marked at all, carry a paper label. Compared to the older ware, the coloring of the 1970s items is whiter and the blue more harsh. The design is sparse with more white ground area showing. Although collectors buy later pieces, the older is, of course, more highly prized and valued.

The Flying Turkey is a pattern similar to Phoenix Bird, but with several differences: the Phoenix Bird's head is facing back or to the right, while the turkey faces forward and has a heart-like border design. Values are given for this line as well.

Because of the current over-supply of Phoenix Bird's 'everyday' pieces on eBay in the last year or two, versus today's 'demand' for the latter, most collector's 'wants' are not as great as they used to be, and the market shows it. As in the past, it's the very 'hard-to-find' shapes that still bring the higher prices today. However, for the new collector, today's 'over-supply' is a great opportunity to build an inexpensive, useable collection. Therefore, the advanced collector must persevere, keeping tuned-in to various internet sites for unique shapes and/or titles that sellers use, to find rare shapes to add to their collection. For further information we recommend *Phoenix Bird Chinaware, Books I – V*, written and privately published by our advisor, Joan Oates; her address is in the Directory under Michigan.

Batter jug & cover, $55 to 65.00
Bon bon, reed hdl, 6½", $35 to 45.00
Bouillon cup, 2 hdls, w/cover, $30 to 35.00
Casserole, w/cover #3, rnd, 6", $135 to 145.00
Casserole, w/cover 2-A, rnd, 6¾", $120 to.................... 135.00

Castor set, nine-piece, in boat-like holder, $350.00 to $400.00. (Photo courtesy Joan Oates)

Celery tray, #1, 13½", $75 to 95.00
Coaster A, no outer border, $12 to................................. 18.00
Coffeepot, #5, Espresso pot, $65 to................................ 75.00
Covered muffin & cover, 10 steam holes, $48 to 55.00
Cracker jar, #2, first half of 20th C, 6¼", $150 to 200.00
Cup, cider, #1, 4", $18 to 25.00
Cup/saucer, espresso, $15 to... 20.00
Gravy tureen & cover, #1, rnd, $85 to 95.00
Honey pot, reed hdl, $18 to 25.00
Hostess tray, 10" d, $65 to 85.00
Ice cream dish, oval, inverted scallops, ½x4" 35.00
Mayonnaise bowl & plate B, $30 to 45.00
Muffineer, #1, 4¼", $65 to... 85.00
Mustard jar & cover, #10, $25 to.................................... 35.00
Pitcher, buttermilk, oval body, 5¾", $35 to.................. 45.00
Plate, luncheon, 8½", $12 to 15.00
Ramekin & underplate, $25 to... 35.00
Rice tureen & cover, #1, $95 to 135.00
Salt dip, #6, scalloped edge, $25 to 35.00
Sauceboat, #3, English, $45 to.. 55.00
Slop bowl/planter, 4¼", $18 to 25.00
Tankard, water, 8½", $125 to 145.00
Tea bowl, ftd, no hdl, $15 to... 20.00
Tea caddy & cover, 6½", $170 to..................................... 200.00
Tea/toast plate, kidney shaped, $25 to........................... 35.00

Phoenix Glass

Founded in 1880 in Monaca, Pennsylvania, the Phoenix Glass Company became one of the country's foremost manufacturers of lighting glass by the early 1900s. They also produced a wide variety of utilitarian and decorative glassware, including art glass by Joseph Webb, colored cut glass, Gone-with-the-Wind style oil lamps, hotel and barware, and pharmaceutical glassware. Today, however, collectors are primarily interested in the 'Sculptured Artware' produced in the 1930s and 1940s. These beautiful pressed and mold-blown pieces are most often found in white milk glass or crystal with various color treatments or a satin fin-

ish. Phoenix did not mark their 'Sculptured Artware' line on the glass; instead, a silver and black (earliest) or gold and black (later) foil label in the shape of the mythical phoenix bird was used.

Quite often glassware made by the Consolidated Lamp and Glass Company of nearby Coraopolis, Pennsylvania, is mistaken for Phoenix's 'Sculptured Artware.' Though the style of the glass is very similar, one distinguishing characteristic is that perhaps 80% of the time Phoenix applied color to the background leaving the raised design plain in contrast, while Consolidated generally applied color to the raised design and left the background plain. Also, for the most part, the patterns and colors used by Phoenix were distinctively different from those used by Consolidated. In 1970 Phoenix Glass became a division of Anchor Hocking which in turn was acquired by the Newell Group in 1987. Phoenix has the distinction of being one of the oldest continuously operating glass factories in the United States. For more information refer to *Phoenix and Consolidated Art Glass, 1926 – 1980*, written by Jack D. Wilson. Our advisors for this category, Bruce Mueller and Gary Wickland, are listed in the Directory under Illinois. See also Consolidated Lamp and Glass.

Bluebell, vase, lt pk w/pearlized design, 7" 125.00
Cosmos, vase, gr on mg, 7½" 145.00
Cosmos, vase, wht on brn (brn shadow), 7½" 145.00
Daisy, vase, bl w/frosted flowers, 9" 350.00
Dancing Girl, vase, lav-bl on wht, 12" 550.00
Dancing Girl, vase, red pearlized, 12" 675.00
Diving Girl, banana boat, bl on gr w/pearlized design 475.00

Fern, vase, blue pearlized, 7", $145.00. (Photo courtesy Rich Penn Auctions on LiveAuctioneers.com)

Fern, vase, burgundy on wht satin, 7"... 125.00
Fern, vase, reverse decor: bl & gr on satin mg, 7" 225.00
Fern, vase, yel & gr (reverse decor) on mg, 7" 225.00
Freesia, vase, tan w/frosted design, fan shape, 8" 175.00
Jewel, vase, bl pearlized, 4¾" 115.00
Jonquil, platter, yel wash on satin, 14" 450.00
Lacy Dewdrop, candy dish, bl on wht, w/lid, 6" dia 95.00
Lily, vase, aqua wash, 3-crimp, 9" 450.00
Madonna, vase, clear & frosted, NM 125.00
Moon & Stars, fruit holder, heavy caramel irid............................ 250.00
Philodendron, vase, gray w/frosted design, 11½" 175.00
Philodendron, vase, wht on bl, 11½"... 195.00
Phlox, ashtray, slate bl pearlized, 5½" 195.00
Primrose, vase, crystal w/wht wash, 8¾" 595.00
Star Flower, vase, aqua w/frosted design, 7" 200.00
Thistle, vase, lav-pk on wht, 18".. 650.00
Thistle, vase, med gr pearlized, 18" 650.00
Tiger Lily, bowl, wht frosted, 11½" 325.00
Wild Geese, vase, lime gr pearlized, 9x12"................................... 275.00
Zodiac, vase, slate bl over mg, 10½"... 950.00

Phonographs

The phonograph, invented by Thomas Edison in 1877, was the first practical instrument for recording and reproducing sound. Sound wave vibrations were recorded on a tinfoil-covered cylinder and played back with a needle that ran along the grooves made from the recording, thus reproducing the sound. Very little changed to this art of record making until 1885, when the first replayable and removable wax cylinders were developed by the American Graphophone Company. These records were made from 1885 until 1894 and are rare today. Edison began to offer musically recorded wax cylinders in 1889. They continued to be made until 1902. Today they are known as brown wax records. Black wax cylinders were offered in 1902, and the earlier brown wax cylinders were discontinued. These wax two-minute records were sold until 1912. From then until 1929, only four-minute celluloid blue amberol record cylinders were made. The first disc records and disc machines were offered by the inventor Berliner in 1894. They were sold in America until 1900, when the Victor company took over. In the 1890s all machines played 7" diameter disc records; the 10" size was developed in 1901. By the early 1900s there existed many disc and cylinder phonograph companies, all offering their improvements. Among them were Berliner, Columbia, Zonophone, United States Phono, Wizard, Vitaphone, Amet, and others.

All Victor I's through VI's originally came with a choice of either brass bell, morning-glory, or wooden horns. Wood horns are the most valuable, adding $1,000.00 (or more) to the machine. Spring models were produced until 1929 (and even later). After 1929 most were electric (though some electric-motor models were produced as early as 1910). Unless another condition is noted, prices are for complete, original phonographs in at least fine to excellent condition. Note: Edison coin-operated cylinder players start at $7,000.00 and may go up to $20,000.00 each. All outside-horn Victor phonographs are worth at least $1,000.00 or more, if in excellent original condition. Machines that are complete, still retaining all their original parts, and with the original finish still in good condition are the most sought after, but those that have been carefully restored with their original finishes, decals, etc., are bringing high prices as well.

Key:
cyl — cylinder   rpd — reproduced

Aretino, disc, orig gr mg horn, 3" center spindle 750.00
Berliner Trade Mark, disc, Clark-Johnson rpd, brass horn 5,000.00
Bush & Lane, triple rpd, mahog floor model 200.00
Busy Bee Grand, disc, orig rpd, red mg horn, w/decal 700.00
Chevy, mahog floor model 200.00
Columbia AB (McDonald), cyl, eagle rpd, brass horn, 2 mandrels .. 1,400.00
Columbia AK, disc, orig rpd, brass bell horn, 7¼" turntable 800.00
Columbia AU, disc, $450 to 600.00
Columbia BI Sterling, disc, Columbia rpd, oak horn 2,250.00
Columbia BK Jewel, cyl, Lyric rpd, orig horn, striping 450.00
Columbia Grafonola, disc, orig rpd, inside horn, mahog upright . 200.00
Columbia Graphophona A, cyl, rpl brass horn, oak case 4,800.00
Columbia Graphophone AA, orig horn & rpd, oak case, 1901 . 2,000.00
Columbia Graphophone B, cyl, w/horn, oak case, 1897 .... 525.00
Columbia Graphophone BV Royal, cyl, alum horn, oak, ca 1908 .. 1,050.00
Columbia Graphophone Q, cyl, blk tin horn, oak case w/stencil . 425.00
Columbia Graphophone QA, NP open works, NP horn, Pat 1897, 10" ... 645.00
Columbia P Premium, disc, orig rpd, red horn 625.00
Columbia Q, cyl, 2-min, rstr rpd, EX japanning/label, rpl horn ... 675.00
Edison A-250, floor model 600.00
Edison Amberola VIII, cyl, Dmn B rpd, inside horn, oak table model ... 400.00
Edison Business C, table model 175.00
Edison Concert C, cyl, R rpd, 30" brass bell, floor stand 2,500.00
Edison Concert, cyl, D rpd, brass horn/stand, 5" mandrel 2,500.00
Edison Dmn Disc A-110, DD rpd, inside horn, Moderne golden oak ... 350.00
Edison Dmn Disc C-19, floor model 250.00

Edison Fireside A, cyl, 20" red horn, oak case 420.00
Edison Fireside A, cyl, Dmn B rpd, oak Music Master horn 2,250.00

Edison Fireside B, A-reproducer, oak cygnet horn, no crane, $1,230.00. (Photo courtesy Dan Morphy Auctions LLC on LiveAuctioneers.com)

Edison Gem A, cyl, B rpd, 2-min, no horn, oak case 840.00
Edison Gem B, cyl, B rpd, 2-4 min, blk cygnet horn, rfn oak 850.00
Edison Gem Blk, cyl 400.00
Edison Gem D Maroon, cyl, K rpd, maroon Fireside horn, w/crane . 1,800.00
Edison Home A, B rpd, oak w/gilt mg floral-pnt horn, transfer, 19" dia ... 885.00
Edison Home A, C rpd, gr oak base w/banner, red mg horn 585.00
Edison Home A, no rpd, all brass horn (poor solder), mahog case .. 750.00
Edison Home, cyl, brass mg horn, oak case w/decals, +65 cyls 900.00
Edison Standard Flat Top, cyl, VG 600.00
Edison Standard, cyl, 2-4 min, C rpd, mg horn 650.00
Edison Triumph, cyl, 2-4 min repeater, O rpd, wood cygnet horn .. 2,800.00
Kalamazoo Duplex, disc, Kalamazoo rpd, 2 blk/brass horns, rare . 4,300.00
Melodograph, disc, CI, G 175.00
Nirona box type, disc, Norona rpd, sound reflector, red metal case, sm .. 550.00
Pathephone B, disc, low-set mg horn, minor pnt rstr, walnut case . 1,350.00
Regina Hexaphone #103, cyl, Hexaphone rpd, oak horn, rstr ... 7,500.00
Standard A, disc, red mg horn, orig decal 995.00
Standard Talking Machine X2, bl horn, 1906, VG 450.00
Thoren's Camera Phonograph, w/2 records, 11", EX 175.00
Victor II, disc, Exhibition rpd, brass bell horn 1,200.00
Victor II, disc, Exhibition rpd, oak horn & case 2,500.00
Victor IV, disc, mahog w/mahog horn & case 4,000.00
Victor IV, disc, no horn, tiger oak case 425.00
Victor P, disc, brass bell horn 1,200.00
Victor R Royal, disc, Exhibition rpd, 9½" brass bell, oak 1,000.00
Victor Type Z, disc, Exhibition rpd, brass bell horn 1,400.00
Victor VI, Exhibition rpd, quartersawn oak case, M rstr 465.00
Victor VV-216, disc, console 200.00
Victor XXV, Schoolhouse, disc, oak schoolhouse horn, oak upright .. 4,500.00
Victor, VV-VI, disc, Exhibition rpd, inside horn, table model 200.00
Victrola Orthophonic, mahog floor model 200.00
Victrola VIA, disc, rstr rpd, Exhibition sound box, post-1918 style 495.00
Zonophone Parlor, disc, brass bell horn, rear crank 1,100.00
Zonophone, disc, rear mt, oak, red petal horn 1,050.00

Photographica

Photographic collectibles include not only the cameras and equipment used to 'freeze' special moments in time but also the photographic images produced by a great variety of processes that have evolved since the daguerrean era of the mid-1800s. For the most part, good quality images have either maintained or increased in value. Poor quality examples (regardless of rarity) are not selling well. Interest in cameras and stereo equipment is down, and dealers report that average-priced items that were moving well are often completely overlooked. Though rare items always have a market, collectors seem to be buying only if they are bargain priced. Our advisor for this category is John Hess; he is listed in the Directory under Massachusetts. Unless noted otherwise, values are for examples in at least near-mint condition.

Albumens

These prints were very common during the nineteenth century. The term comes from the emulsion of silver salts and albumen that was used to coat the paper they were printed on.

Apache scout, imprint of Buehman & Co., Nos. 314, 314½ and 316 Congress St. upstairs, East of Post Office, Tucson, A. T., circa 1885, 6x4", $1,420.00. (Photo courtesy Heritage Auction Galleries on LiveAuctioneers.com)

Battleship Maine as it lays in bottom of Havana harbor, Hoy, 10x7"	35.00
Chinatown (San Francisco) street scene, rich tones, 5½x8"	335.00
Indian wearing 'Colonel' shoulder brd, 1880s, 6½x4¼"	1,680.00
Logging scene in winter w/steam locomotive, sight: 5x7"+fr	90.00
Negresse, African lady (lovely), JP Sebah (Egypt), 10½x8¼"	200.00
Slopes of Mt Vesuvius, sight: 10x14"+fr	200.00
Sumo wrestlers (2) in wrestling pose, 1880s, 11⅛x8¾"	240.00
Surveyors (9) w/various surveying tools, 7x9"+fr	120.00

Ambrotypes

An ambrotype is a type of photograph produced by an early wet-plate process whereby a faint negative image on glass is seen as positive when held against a dark background.

6th plate, blk man in finery seated, +gilt mat & case	125.00
6th plate, boy dressed as assistant teacher, 1860s, +fr	120.00
6th plate, brother & sister, ages 3 to 5 in studio pose, +case	65.00
6th plate, Confederate soldier seated, +split case	245.00
6th plate, NH volunteer, ruby, IN Teague/NH, gilt mat, +case	175.00
6th plate, wounded Union soldier seated w/wife, 1860s, +fr & case	250.00
9th plate, 2 unidentified Civil War soldiers seated, +case	150.00
9th plate, adolescent girl seated, +wooden fr	95.00
9th plate, fireman w/badge on collar, bow tie, PA, 1860s, +fr	110.00
9th plate, Union Sailor, Higgins & Whitaker, rare, EX	410.00
Full plate, 4 men stand by Niagara Falls, +gold-tone fr	425.00
Full plate, man w/wht hair & beard, wide collar, Moulton, +fr	150.00
Half plate, lady seated w/sm child standing beside, +case	65.00
Quarter plate, 2 instrument makers at work, gilt mat, +leather fr	500.00
Quarter plate, lady in fine dress, tinted cheeks, +case	150.00
Quater plate, 2 hunters w/shotguns, tinted cheeks, arched mat, +case	235.00

Cabinet Photos

When the popularity of cartes de visites began to wane in the 1880s, a new fascination developed for the cabinet card, a larger version. These photos were produced by a variety of methods. They remained popular until the turn of the century.

Acapulco village scene, 1800s, 11x14"	48.00
Auto radiator shop int, early 1900s	55.00
Barn raising scene w/workers on ground & on roof framing, 1880s	55.00
CA landscapes w/mules & wagon crossing water, sgn Fassold, 1890s	110.00
Carpathia (ship) docked, 8x12"	150.00
Chief Rain-in-the-Face, Geo E Spencer US Army Photo, VG	500.00
Chief Running Antelope, DF Barry, 1880s	450.00
James Garfield, half-L, Ryder, 6x4"	100.00

Man stands at base of huge redwood tree, 1890s, 14x11"	65.00
OK car dealership w/salesmen standing before lot of cars, 8x11"	24.00
Sitting Bull seated, Bailey, Dix & Mead, c 1882	900.00
Wuh-To-Val (Old Man Left Hand), Indian w/horse, I Chikasha	360.00

Cameras

Collectible high-quality cameras are not easy to find. Most of the pre-1900 examples will be found in the large format view cameras or studio camera types. There are quite a few of these that can be found in well-worn condition, but there is a large difference in value between an average-wear item and an excellent or mint-condition camera. It is rare indeed to find one of these early cameras in mint condition.

The types of cameras are generally classified as follows: large format, medium format, early folding and box types, 35 mm single-lens-reflex (SLR), 35mm rangefinders, twin-lens reflex (TLR), miniature or subminiature, novelty, and even a few others. Collectors may specialize in a type, a style, a time period, or even in high-quality examples of the same camera.

In the 1900 to 1940 period, large quantities of various makes of box cameras and folding bellows type cameras were produced by many manufacturers, and the popular 35mm camera was introduced in the 1930s. Most have low values because they were made in vast numbers, but mint-condition cameras are prized by collectors. In the 1930 to 1955 period, the 35mm rangefinders and the SLRs and TLRs became the cameras of choice. The most prized of these are the early German or Japanese rangefinders such as the Leica, Canon, or Nikon. Earlier, German optics were favored, but after WWII, Japanese cameras and optics rivaled and/ or even exceeded the quality of many German optics.

Now there are thousands of different cameras to choose from, and collectors have many options when selecting categories. Quality is the major factor; values vary widely between an average-wear working camera and one in mint condition, or one still in the original box and unused. This brief list suggests average prices for good working cameras with average wear. The same camera in mint condition will be valued much higher, while one with excessive wear (scratches, dents, corrosion, poor optics, nonworking meters or rangefinders) may have little value.

Buying, selling, and trading of old and late vintage cameras on the internet, both in direct transactions and via e-mail auctions, have tremendously affected the number of cameras that are available to collectors today. As a result, values have fluctuated as well. Large numbers of old, mass-produced box cameras and folding cameras have been offered; many are in poor condition and have been put up for sale by persons who know nothing about quality. So in general, prices have dropped, and it is an excellent buyer's market at the present, except for the mint quality offerings. Many common models in poor to average condition can be bought for $1.00 to $10.00. The collector is advised to purchase only quality cameras that will enhance his collection. To date, no appreciable collector's market has developed for most old movie cameras or projectors. The Polaroid type of camera has little value, although a few models are gaining in popularity among collectors, and values are expected to increase. Today's new camera market is dominated by digital cameras. The initial effect on yesterday's film cameras has been dramatic, reducing both demand and prices of regular film-type cameras. There is no immediate collector's market for digital cameras. Many fakes and copies have been made of several of the classic cameras such as the German Leica, and caution is advised in purchasing one of these cameras at a price too good to be true. With respect to repair of old cameras, the number of actual repair shops has decreased over the past few years because the decrease in value of old cameras has made it unprofitable to seek professional repair services — so many collectors of old cameras have resorted to self repair; thus, there seems to be more interest in buying the older non-working cameras for parts, if the cosmetics of the camera are good. For those considering re-sale, good lenses for the earlier classic cameras — Leica, Zeiss Ikon, Nikon, Rolleiflex, etc. — can be an excellent buy, as they are in considerable demand. They must be clean and free of dust and fungus on the lens elements. Consult a specialist on high-priced classics if good reference material is not available. Our advisor for this category is Gene Cataldo; he is listed in the Directory under Alabama.

Agfa, box type, 1930-50, $5 to 20.00
Agfa, Isolette 20.00
Agfa, Optima, 1960s, $15 to 35.00
Aires, 35III, 1958, $15 to 35.00
Ansco, Cadet 5.00
Ansco, Memar, 1954-58 .... 20.00
Argoflex, Seventy-five, TLR, 1949-58 .... 7.00
Argus A, early model, 35mm Bakelite, 1936-41, $20 to 25.00
Argus A2F, 1940, $10 to 15.00
Bell & Howell Dial 35, $25 to 35.00
Bolsey B2 .... 20.00
Braun Paxette I, 1952, $10 to 25.00
Burke & James, Cub, 1914 .... 20.00
Canon 7, 1961-64, $175 to 350.00
Canon III, 1952, $150 to 250.00
Canon Rangefinder IIF, ca 1954, $200 to 300.00
Canon S-II, 1947-49, $200 to 350.00
Canon S-II, Seiki-Kogaku, 1946-47, $400 to 800.00
Canon VT, 1956-57, $150 to 300.00
Compass Camera, 1938, $1,000 to 1,300.00
Conley 5x7", folding plate, 1908-17, $100 to 250.00
Contessa 35, 1950-55, $70 to 150.00
Detrola Model D, Detroit Corp, 1938-40 .... 20.00
Eastman Folding Brownie Six-20 .... 12.00
Eastman Kodak 35, 1940-51, $20 to 35.00
Eastman Kodak Baby Brownie, Bakelite, $5 to 10.00
Eastman Kodak Bantam, Art Deco, 1935-38 .... 25.00
Eastman Kodak Medalist, 1941-48, $75 to 175.00
Eastman Kodak Retina II, $35 to 60.00
Eastman Kodak Retina IIa, $55 to 75.00
Eastman Kodak Retina IIIc, $250 to 400.00
Eastman Kodak Retinette, various models, ea $15 to 50.00
Eastman Kodak Signet 35 .... 35.00
Eastman Kodak Signet 80 .... 40.00
Eastman Premo, many models exist, ea $30 to 200.00
Edinex by Wirgen 25.00
Edinex, by Wirgen, Germany, 1930s-50s 30.00
Exakta VX, 1951, $60 to 85.00
FED 1, USSR, postwar, $30 to 50.00
FED 1, USSR, prewar, $70 to 125.00
Graflex Speed Graphic, various szs, ea $60 to 200.00
Herbert-George, Donald Duck, 1946 .... 25.00
Kodak Brownie Target Six-20, 1952, $1 to 10.00
Kodak No 2 Folding Pocket Brownie, 1904-07 .... 25.00
Kodak Retina Ia, Type (o15), 1952, $50 to 75.00

Kodak Retina IIIc, 1957 – 1960, $250.00 to $400.00. (Photo courtesy Gene Cataldo)

Kodak Signet 35, Ektar lens, ca 1951-58, $15 to 30.00
Kodak Tourist II, 1951-58, $12 to 15.00
Konica Autoreflex TC, various models, ea $30 to 70.00
Konica FS-1 .... 35.00
Konica III Rangefinder, 1956-59, $90 to 110.00

Leica II, 1963-67, $175 to 400.00
Leica IID, 1932-38, $175 to 400.00
Leica IIIF, 1950-56, $175 to 400.00
Leica M3, ca 1954-66, $400 to 900.00
Mamiya-Sekor 500TL, 1966 .... 20.00
Mamiyaflex TLR, 1951, $70 to 100.00
Mercury II CX, 65 exposures on std 35mm film, 35/f 2.7 lens, ca 1945, $2 to ... 35.00
Minolta 35, early Rangefinder models, 1947-50, ea $200 to 400.00
Minolta HiMatic Series, various models, ea $10 to 25.00
Minolta Prod, 35mm, unusual, rather rare, $50 to 85.00
Minolta SR-7 .... 30.00
Minolta SRT-202, $35 to 75.00
Minolta XD-11, 1977, $65 to 100.00
Minolta-16, mini, various models, ea $10 to 25.00
Minox B, chrome, 1958-71, $65 to 100.00
Minox B, spy camera 125.00
Nikkormat (Nikon), various models, ea $60 to 150.00
Nikon F, SLR, w/finder & lens, 1960s, $100 to 300.00
Nikon FG 70.00
Nikon S Rangefinder, 1951-54, $450 to 800.00
Nikon S2 Rangefinder, 1954-58, $700 to 1,000.00
Nikon SP Rangefinder, 1958-60, $1,500 to 2,000.00
Nr3A Folding Pocket Kodak, ModB-4, red bellows, 1903-15, $40 to 60.00
Olympus OM-1, $35 to 75.00
Olympus OM-10, $30 to 50.00
Olympus Pen EED, 33mm half-fr, 1967-72, $50 to 80.00
Olympus Pen F, compact half-fr SLR, $100 to 200.00
Orion Works 6x9 Plate, 1921-28, $60 to 100.00
Pentax ME, $50 to 75.00
Pentax Spotmatic, many models, ea $35 to 90.00
Petri-7, 1961 .... 20.00
Plaubel-Makina II, 1933-39 .... 200.00
Polaroid 110, 110A, 110B, ea $20 to 40.00
Praktica FX, 1952-57 .... 30.00
Praktica Super TL 40.00
Realist Stereo, 3.5 lens 80.00
Regula, King, interchangable lens, various models, ea $40 to 60.00
Ricoh Diacord 1, TLR, built-in meter, 1958 .... 65.00
Ricoh Singlex, 1965, $50 to 70.00
Rollei 35, mini, Singapore, $80 to 150.00
Rolleicord II, 1936-50, $70 to 90.00
Rolleiflex Automat, 1937 model 125.00
Zeiss Contax III, 1936-42, $175 to 350.00
Zeiss Ikon Contarex 'Bullseye,' ca 1959-66, $400 to 800.00

Cartes De Visites

Among the many types of images collectible today are carte de visites, known as CDVs, which are portraits measuring 4x2¼" printed on paper and produced in quantity. The CDV fad of the 1800s enticed the famous and the unknown alike to pose for these cards, which were circulated among the public to the extent that they became known as 'publics.' Note: A common portrait CDV is worth only about 50¢ unless it carries a revenue stamp on the back; those that do are valued at about $2.00 each.

William F. Cody Buffalo Bill, in fringed and beaded buckskin jacket with fur collar and ornately embroidered shirt, slightly trimmed at bottom, 4x2½", $1,200.00. (Photo courtesy Heritage Auction Galleries on LiveAuctioneers.com)

Buffalo Bill, waist up, long hair, wide jacket lapels & overcoat.... 350.00
Civil War Confederate man standing by podium, hat in hand, 4" ..240.00
Civil War soldier, black, seated by table, PA, ca 1863-65............ 900.00
Declaration of Independence signatures, overall fading 140.00
Edwin M Stanton, chest-up portrait, Brady 110.00
General US Grant stands w/blk armband (mourning Lincoln), 4x2½" . 340.00
Giuseppi Garibaldi standing, C Bernieri 70.00
Jefferson Davis bust portrait, Brady 120.00
Jesse James death portrait, c RG Smith, rare, 4⅛x2½" 1,685.00
Lady circus performer w/ornate hairdo, hand-colored, NY............ 25.00
Man seated by sm girl standing at side, holding hands, 4x2½" 12.50
Man's head & shoulders, high collar & bow tie, 3x2"..................... 15.00
Mary Todd Lincoln, E & HT Anthony, 1862, 4x2½".................. 400.00
Mary Todd Lincoln seated w/hand resting on sm table, Brady 265.00
Postmortem of young boy, 4x2½" 36.00

Daguerreotypes

Among the many processes used to produce photographic images are the daguerreotypes (made on a plate of chemically treated silver-plated copper) — the most-valued examples being the 'whole' plate which measures 6½" x 8½". Other sizes include the 'half' plate, measuring 4½" x 5½", the 'quarter' plate at 3¼" x 4¼", the 'sixth' plate at 2¾" x 3¼", the 'ninth' at 2" x 2½", and the 'sixteenth' at 1⅜" x 1⅝". (Sizes may vary slightly, and some may have been altered by the photographer.)

6th plate, Fr lady seated in chair, 1839-55, +wood & plaster fr.... 120.00
6th plate, lady in blk mourning clothes, somber expression, ca 1855.. 120.00
6th plate, lady seated w/striped cat (rare subject), 1839-55, +fr . 1,650.00
6th plate, ship's captain in ocean-side studio setting, 1840s, +case .. 360.00
6th plate, well-dressed young mulatto man, JP Ball, +case.......... 400.00
9th plate, sleeping baby, ca 1845, +ornate mat & case 240.00
Full plate, family of 8, 7 adults & 1 sm child in finery, 1840s....... 3,000.00
Half plate, 7 young ladies in finery, tarnished mat, no case 500.00
Half plate, husband & wife seated together, paper mt, +early case... 400.00
Half plate, lady in elegant clothes w/elbow resting on table, 1839-55. 360.00
Half plate, Washington Irving portrait of Whitehurst pnt, +case . 565.00
Quarter plate, boy in plaid finery stands beside lg dog on chair, +fr....800.00

Quarter plate, house scene, fine artistic composition, rich and clear image, perfect plate, in case, $2,000.00. (Photo courtesy Be-Hold on LiveAuctioneers.com)

Quarter plate, lady in lace cap, facing left, ca 1839-55 .... 250.00
Quarter plate, lovely young mother holding deceased baby, ca 1846, +case.. 660.00
Quarter plate, sm child (2 or younger) seated, +gutta percha case ..215.00
Quarter plate, young couple w/2 sm children & dog, ca 1845 ...... 350.00

Photos

Photogravure, Cheyenne Warriors, Curtis, 1905, 12x16"+mat & fr ..450.00
Photogravure, Departure From...Lodge - Cheyenne, Curtis, 6x8"+fr .. 200.00
Photogravure, John Ruskin portrait, Hollyer/Collis, 1890s, 5x4"... 35.00
Photogravure, Native Am portrait, sepia tone, Curtis, 15x12" 450.00
Photogravure, Picking Blueberries - Cree, full bookplate, Curtis, 1926 .. 155.00
Photogravure, Portrait of Lady, bobbed hair, finery, 22x15"+fr....... 36.00
Photogravure, Qahatika Water Girl, E Curtis, +matt/18x12" fr..... 85.00
Photogravure, Selawik girl in fur coat, full bookplate, Curtis, 1928 . 195.00
Photogravure, Shatila - Pomo, brn tone, Curtis, ca 1924, 18x13"+fr .. 275.00
Photogravure, Summer Camp - Lake Pomo, Curtis, 1924, 17½x12"..350.00

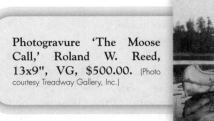

Photogravure 'The Moose Call,' Roland W. Reed, 13x9", VG, $500.00. (Photo courtesy Treadway Gallery, Inc.)

Platinum print, Black Bear, Sioux chief, Rinehart, 1899, 9¼x7¼"... 1,100.00
Platinum print, Jason Reed Chairmaker, D Ulmann, 7⅞x6"+mat & fr.. 415.00
Platinum print, Last Horse, Sioux chief, Rineheart, 1899, 20x16"+fr .. 1,000.00
Sepia tone, Chief Geronimo, Hendrick, 1909, 9x7"..................... 600.00
Sepia tone, Cliff Dwellers, in landscape, Curtis copy, ca 1925, 9x7" ..100.00
Sepia tone, Eiffel Tower, K Donovan, 22x10"+blk fr..................... 35.00
Sepia tone, lady seated by table & curtain, PA, 1860s, 7⅜x5⅜"..... 20.00
Sepia tone, Plains Indian warrior/wife, 1910s, 10x8"+Vict fr....... 125.00
Sepia tone, Pueblo Indian in traditional dress, R Price, 1920s, 13x9". 120.00
Silver gelatin print, Face in Shadows, Wright, 1940s, 6¾x4¾"...... 18.00
Silver gelatin print, Jim Thorpe in NY Giants uniform, 1913, 5x4" ..585.00
Silver gelatin print, Little Girl w/Dog, Steichen, 4½x3½" 840.00
Silver gelatin print, Marilyn Monroe in Korea w/troops, 11x14". 120.00
Silver gelatin print, Nude w/Brush, G Hurrell, 1958, 12x9½"...... 660.00
Silver gelatin print, padre at side alter, Putnam, 9x7" 120.00
Silver gelatin print, sailing vessel, WE Worden, early 1900s, 24x18"... 90.00
Silver gelatin print, Wounded Man w/5th Army, Bourke, 10x8". 240.00
Silver gelatin sepia tone, Indian portrait, Rinehart, #864, 7x9"... 300.00

Stereoscopic Views

Stereo cards are photos made to be viewed through a device called a stereoscope. The glass stereo plates of the mid-1800s and photo prints produced in the darkroom are among the most valuable. In evaluating stereo views, the subject, date, and condition are all important. Some views were printed over a 30- to 40-year period; 'first generation' prices are far higher than later copies, made on cheap card stock with reprints or lithographs, rather than actual original photographs. It is relatively easy to date an American stereo view by the color of the mount that was used, the style of the corners, etc. From about 1854 until the early 1860s, cards were either white, cream-colored, or glossy gray; shades of yellow and a dull gray followed. While the dull gray was used for a very short time, the yellow tones continued in use until the late 1860s. Red, green, violet, or blue cards are from the period between 1865 until about 1870. Until the late 1870s, corners were square; after that they were rounded off to prevent damage. Right now, quality stereo views are at a premium.

Abraham Lincoln close-up portrait, Keystone, late copy (ca 1905) . 400.00
Cake Walk (A) – Walking the Line, ca 1900 .... 30.00
Devil's Den, Gettysburg Battlefield, ca 1875................................. 60.00
Field Marshall Marquis Oyama w/4 unknown figures, 1903 ....7.50
General Sumner in field w/battle flag beside him, Brady 325.00
Libby Prison Richmond VA, outside view, Anthony.................... 240.00
Lindbergh w/Spirit of St Louis, Keystone, common........................ 30.00
Mice River disaster scene, pr 30.00
Native Am weaver, hand colored.. 60.00
Neue Synagogue in Berlin, int view, ca 1880, 3¼x5¾".................. 60.00
Palestine, Keystone, set of 100, EXIB.. 155.00
Unidentified Indian chief, Seaver, on Smithsonian mt, dtd 1873 ...275.00
Union Avenue in Kansas City flooded w/rushing water, 1903 .... 12.00
WWI military scenes, incomplete set of 93, EXIB........................ 100.00
Yuma Indians, Yuma Boy & Girl, AT, & Yuma Bucks, AT, pr...... 300.00

Tintypes

Tintypes, contemporaries of ambrotypes, were produced on japanned iron and were not as easily damaged.

Quarter plate, 9th NYSM Second Lieutenant of the Washington Greys holding M1850 Ames militia staff sword, very clear image, in gutta percha case with fruit relief, $550.00. (Photo courtesy Cowan's Auctions, Inc. on LiveAuctioneers.com)

6th plate, baseball players (2) w/striped socks, 1 holds bat, NY ... 300.00
6th plate, drummer in full uniform, NY militia, 1870s 215.00
6th plate, trapper w/pelts & Winchester rifle, +half case............. 480.00
9th plate, Am Indian chief (unknown) seated w/weapons, ca 1880. 180.00
9th plate, soldier w/musket, -L image, +mat & fr 275.00
Full plate, Civil War soldier w/rifle & revolver, rare 900.00
Full plate, cowboy w/gun in belt, knife showing, EX color, scarce. 925.00
Full plate, group of 3 children, full-L 95.00
Full plate, outdoor scene of farm family & buildings, dk spots 36.00
Full plate, Parker's Drugstore, Bainbridge OH, street scene.......... 450.00
Full plate, Prairie Flower, Iroquois Indian lady w/baby & gun...... 800.00
Half plate, boy on horsebk, wht canvas bkdrop, +leatherette case. 60.00
Quarter plate, carpenter w/tools on lap, saw at side, +foil mat & fr.. 550.00
Quarter plate, Civil War Union soldier in 9-button frock coat, w/saber.200.00
Quarter plate, man in buckskins, wide-brim hat & rifle, scarce, +brass mat..850.00
Quarter plate, Union cavalrymen, heavily armed, in half case..... 600.00

Union Cases

From the mid-1850s until about 1880, cases designed to house these early images were produced from a material known as thermoplastic, a man-made material with an appearance much like gutta percha. Its innovator was Samuel Peck, who used shellac and wood fibers to create a composition he called Union. Peck was part owner of the Scoville Company, makers of both papier-maché and molded leather cases, and he used the company's existing dies to create his new line. Other companies (among them A.P. Critchlow & Company; Littlefield, Parsons & Company; and Holmes, Booth & Hayden) soon duplicated his material and produced their own designs. Today's collectors may refer to cases made of this material as 'thermoplastic,' 'composition,' or 'hard cases,' but the term most often used is 'Union.' It is incorrect to refer to them as gutta percha cases.

Sizes may vary somewhat, but generally a 'whole' plate case measures 7" x 9⅛" to the outside edges, a 'half' plate 4⅞" x 6", a 'quarter' plate 3¾" x 4¾", a 'sixth' 3⅛" x 3⅝", a 'ninth' 2⅜" x 2⅞", and a 'sixteenth' 1¾" x 2". Clifford and Michele Krainik and Carl Walvoord have written a book, *Union Cases*, which we recommend for further study. Another source of information is *Nineteenth Century Photographic Cases and Wall Frames* by Paul Berg. Values are for examples in excellent condition unless noted otherwise.

6th plate, Faithful Hound, +2 daguerreotypes............................. 225.00
6th plate, Geometrics, K-270, VG 85.00
6th plate, Mixed Flower Bouquet, +daguerreotype of bearded man ..85.00
6th plate, Rebecca at the Well, +ambrotype bust of man............. 125.00
6th plate, Ten Dollar Piece w/floral border, +ambrotype of lady .. 225.00
6th plate, Union & Constitution, K-373, EX 125.00
9th plate (dbl), Children w/Toys, R-29 .... 135.00
9th plate, Am Gothic, K-374 .... 95.00

9th plate, Chess Players, R-41 variant.. 100.00
9th plate, Geometrics/Scrolls, Patent Am, K-502 .... 50.00
Half plate, Geometrics, K-16.. 210.00
Half plate, WA Monument, Richmond VA, K-4, EX....................... 225.00
Quarter plate, Chasse Au Faucon, +tintype of boy by corner chair....200.00
Quarter plate, Fireman Saving Child, K-118 .... 150.00
Quarter plate, Parting of Hafed & Hinda, K-35, VG.................... 200.00
Quarter plate, Roger de Coverly & Gypsies Fortune, K-30, EX ... 175.00

Miscellaneous

Stanhope, monocular, ivory, ⅝".. 50.00
Stanhope, pen w/letter-opener blade, mosque pictured 50.00
Stereoscope, Alex Beckers, rosewood vnr, Pat 1859, 49¼" 950.00
Stereoscope, beech wood w/magnifying glass, Vict........................... 80.00
Stereoscope, Brewster type, silver w/chased florals, 1860s 1,200.00
Stereoscope, Gaumont, wood table type, rack & pinion movement, 1920.600.00
Stereoscope, J Wood, acromatic lenses, rack/pinion focus, rare 9,000.00
Stereoscope, walnut w/fret-cvd rack, Vict...................................... 350.00

Piano Babies

A familiar sight in Victorian parlors, piano babies languished atop shawl-covered pianos in a variety of poses: crawling, sitting, on their tummies, or on their backs playing with their toes. Some babies were nude, and some wore gowns. Sizes ranged from about 3" up to 12". The most famous manufacturer of these bisque darlings was the Heubach Brothers of Germany, who nearly always marked their product; see Heubach for listings. Watch for reproductions. Values are for examples in near-mint condition. See also Conta and Boehme.

Bisque, child holding mirror, German, 13" 720.00
Bisque, crawling, slipping nightgown, 4".. 295.00
Bisque, intaglio eyes, open/closed mouth w/teeth, seated w/plate, kitten, 7".275.00
Bisque, may not have pnt finish on bk, unmk, 4" 410.00
Bisque, may not have pnt finish on bk, unmk, 8" 375.00
Bisque, may not have pnt finish on bk, unmk, 12" 500.00
Bisque, molded hair, unjtd, molded-on clothes, 4" 500.00
Bisque, molded hair, unjtd, molded-on clothes, 6" 675.00
Bisque, molded hair, unjtd, molded-on clothes, 8" 825.00
Bisque, molded hair, unjtd, molded-on clothes, 9" 800.00
Bisque, molded hair, unjtd, molded-on clothes, 12" 900.00
Bisque, molded hair, unjtd, molded-on clothes, 16" 1,095.00

Bisque, molded hair with bow, finely painted facial features, holding grape bouquet, gilt accents, marked Germany, 10", $900.00. (Photo courtesy McMasters Harris Auction Co. on LiveAuctioneers.com)

Bisque, seated, butterfly on knee, #444, 5" 275.00
Bisque, seated, holding cup, #482, 12" 400.00
Bisque, seated, holding fruit, #8266, $175 to 275.00
Bisque, seated in upright tub, rare, unmk...................................... 195.00
Bisque, seated, leaning on left hand, waving w/right, #487, $400 to.500.00
Bisque, seated, w/ball, mini, 3", $50 to.. 75.00

Bisque, w/animal/pot/flowers/etc, 4" 500.00
Bisque, w/animal/pot/flowers/etc, 5" 500.00
Bisque, w/animal/pot/flowers/etc, 8", ... 600.00
Bisque, w/animal/pot/flowers/etc, 10" 700.00
Bisque, w/animal/pot/flowers/etc, 12" 800.00
Bisque, w/animal/pot/flowers/etc, 16" min 950.00
Black, bsk, 4" 600.00
Black, bsk, 4", unmk 500.00
Black, bsk, 5" 600.00
Black, bsk, 8" 600.00
Black, bsk, 9" 675.00
Black, bsk, 12" 675.00
Black, bsk, 14" 900.00
Black, bsk, 16" 1,000.00

Pickard

Founded in 1895 in Chicago, Illinois, the Pickard China Company was originally a decorating studio, importing china blanks from European manufacturers. Some of these early pieces bear the name of those companies as well as Pickard's. Trained artists decorated the wares with hand-painted studies of fruit, florals, birds, and scenics and often signed their work. In 1915 Pickard introduced a line of 24k gold over a dainty floral-etched ground design. In the 1930s they began to experiment with the idea of making their own ware and by 1938 had succeeded in developing a formula for fine translucent china. Since 1976 they have issued an annual limited edition Christmas plate. They are now located in Antioch, Illinois.

The company has used various marks. The earliest (1893 – 1894) was a double-circle mark, 'Edgerton Hand Painted' with 'Pickard' in the center. Variations of the double-circle mark (with 'Hand Painted China' replacing the Edgerton designation) were employed until 1915, each differing enough that collectors can usually pinpoint the date of manufacture within five years. Later marks included the crown mark, 'Pickard' on a gold maple leaf, and the current mark, the lion and shield. Works signed by Challinor, Marker, and Yeschek are especially valued by today's collectors.

Bonbon, shell shape, yel w/gold, Pickard blank, 1938-present, 5" L... 50.00
Bonbon, violets w/gold, scalloped, Mark, JPL blank, 1898-1903, 5½" .. 150.00
Cake plate, vellum Enchanted Forest, Marker, Japan blank, 1918-19, 10" ..395.00
Charger, Golden Pheasant, Challinor, 1919-22, 12½" 600.00
Charger, Twin Lilies, Walters, JHR Bavaria Favorite blank, 1910s, 11"..275.00
Chocolate pot, Challinor Nasturtiums, J&C Louise blank, 1903-05, 6" ..595.00
Creamer/sugar bowl, Carnation & Platinum, w/lid, 1905-10 .... 350.00
Cup/saucer, roses, mc on yel, Blaha, JPL blank, 1898-1903.......... 200.00

Jardiniere, poppies and heavy gilding, signed Casper, stamped both Pickard and Limoges, 10½x9x12", $1,680.00. (Photo courtesy Leland Little Auction & Estate Sales Ltd. on LiveAuctioneers.com)

Jug, Venice, Carnation Garden, Yeschek, T&V blank, 1903-05, 10½"..1,300.00
Lemonade jug, peaches on gr, Heap, CAC blank, 1903-05, 8"..... 500.00
Mug, Falstaff, Gasper, gold hdl, 1905-10, 7", $575 to 650.00
Pitcher, strawberry clusters, Michel, JPL blank, 1898-1903, 5" 600.00
Pitcher, White Poppy & Daisy, Gasper, Bavaria blank, 1910-12, 6". 565.00

Plate, Cornflower Conventional, CA France blank, 1903-05, 8½" .. 300.00
Plate, floral w/gold rim, McCorkle, RC Bavaria blank, 1905-10, 8¾" .. 75.00
Plate, tiger lilies on brn border, JPL blank, 1898-1903, 8½" 225.00
Plate, Triple Tulip, Heschek, Favorite Bavaria blank, 1912-18, 8½" ..275.00
Plate, Tulip Conventional, wishbone hdls, T&B blank, 1903-05, 7½"..325.00
Plate, Tulip Moderne, C Hahn, T&V blank, 1898-1903, 8" 200.00
Shakers, lily pads on gold border, Schoner, 1905-10, 3¼", pr 100.00
Syrup & underplate, Violet Nouveau, Coufall, D&Co blank, 1905-10, 6" .295.00
Vase, landscape & highland cattle, sgn Kubash, ca 1903-05, 7¼" .. 3,500.00
Vase, narcissus on gr, Post, #3660 blank, 1903-05, 8" 450.00
Vase, nude in woods, Grane, slim w/ornate gold hdls, 1898-1903, 20". 8,000.00
Vase, Praying Mohammedan, Farrington, RC Bavaria blank, 1903-05, 14"..3,000.00
Vase, vellum Classic Ruins, F Bobor, T&V blank, 1912-18, 13" .. 950.00
Vase, vellum woodland scene, Challinor, rect, 1912-18, 6" 400.00

Pickle Castors

Affluent Victorian homes seemed to have something for every purpose, and a pickle castor was not only an item of beauty but of practicality. American Victorian pickle castors can be found in old catalogs dating from the 1860s through the early 1900s. (Those featured in catalogs after 1900 were made by silver manufacturers that were not part of the International Silver Company which was formed in 1898 — for instance, Reed and Barton, Tufts, Pairpoint, and Benedict.) Catalogs featured large selections to choose from, ranging from simple to ornate. Inserts could be clear or colored, pattern glass or art glass, molded or blown. Many of these molds and designs were made by more than one company as they merged or as personnel took their designs with them from employer to employer. It is common to see the same insert in a variety of different frames and with different lids as viewed in these old catalogs.

Pickle castors are being reproduced today. Frames are being imported from Taiwan and sold by L.G. Wright. New enameling is being applied to old jars; and new or old tumblers, vases, or spooners are sometimes used as jars in old original frames. Beware of new mother-of-pearl jars. The biggest giveaway in this latter scenario is that old glass is not perfect glass. In the listings below, the description prior to the semicolon refers to the jar (insert), and the remainder of the line describes the frame. Unless noted 'rstr' (restored), the silver plate is assumed to be in very good original condition. When tongs are present, they will be indicated. Glass jars are assumed to be in at least near-mint condition. Our advisor for this category is Barbara Aaronson; she is listed in the Directory under California. For additional photographs and values, visit her website: www.thevictorianlady.com.

Olive green with enameled flowers, ornate unmarked footed frame, circa 1890, 14", with tongs, $425.00. (Photo courtesy Rich Penn Auctions on LiveAuctioneers.com)

Blue Coinspot w/floral; Roger Bros stand, squatty, 4-ftd, 9" 725.00
Blue Cone, dog finial; rstr Rockford #630 fr, 13" 795.00
Blue Daisy & Button, cylinder; R Smith fr, 11", +fork & tongs 600.00
Blue ribbed w/pk & gr floral; Forbes fr w/leafy scrolling, 10" 450.00
Clear 12-sided etched insert; Barbour Bros fr, 14", +fork.............. 780.00

Clear w/emb birds; Reed & Barton floral-emb fr, 14", +tongs 540.00
Clear w/intaglio floral; Pairpoint fr, +tongs 420.00
Cranberry & wht swirl; fr mk #32, 11", +fork 475.00
Cranberry T'print w/daisies; ornate Eagle fr, 12", +tongs 510.00
Cranberry T'print; ornate Meriden #195 fr, 4-ftd, 11" 750.00
Cranberry w/floral; Derby leaf-shaped fr w/bird on lid 775.00
Cranberry w/optic ribbing & enameled fern in ornate fr w/bird, ca 1900, 12"...600.00
Leaf Mold, spatter; Rogers #452 fr w/flowers at hdl, 10½" 950.00
Pink w/emb leaves; Wilcox fr w/cucumber vines 600.00
Purple slag; Rogers SP fr, 9", +tongs 400.00
Rubina w/yel daisies; ornate Wilcox gold-washed holder, 4 ball ft, 12". 500.00
White rect insert; Reed & Barton fr w/cucumber finial, 9", +fork. 720.00

Pie Birds

A pie bird or pie funnel (pie vent) is generally made of pottery, glazed inside and out. Most are 3" to 5" in height with arches at the base to allow steam to enter. The steam is then released through a single exit hole at the top. The English pie funnel was as tall as the special baking dish was deep and held the crust even with the dish's rim, thereby lifting the crust above the filling so it would stay crisp and firm. These dishes came in several different sizes, which accounts for the variances in the heights of the pie birds.

The first deviations from the basic funnels were produced in the mid-1930s to late 1940s: the Clarice Cliff (signed Midwinter or Newport) pie bird (reg. no. on white base), the Pearl China Rooster, and the signed Nutbrown elephant. Shortly thereafter (1940s – 1960s), figures of bakers and colorful birds were created for additional visual baking fun. From the 1980s to present, many novelty pie vents have been added to the market for the enjoyment of both the baker and collector. These have been made by commercial (including Far East importers) and local enterprises in Canada, England, and the United States. A new category for the 1990s includes an array of holiday-related pie vents. Basic tip: Older pie vents were air-brushed, not hand painted.

Incense burners (i.e., elephants and Asian people), one-hole pepper shakers, dated brass toy bird whistles, egg timers (missing glass timer), and ring holders (i.e., elephant with clover on his tummy) should not be mistaken for pie vents. Our advisor for this category is Linda Fields; she is listed in the Directory under Tennessee.

Elephant, white porcelain, unmarked Nutbrown, England, 3", $60.00. (Photo courtesy American Auction Co. on LiveAuctioneers.com)

3-fruits series, peach, apples & cherries, Japan, 2", ea, $250 to 300.00
Aluminum pie funnels, England, ea 25.00
Bear in gr jacket, w/hat & shoes, England, 4½" 55.00
Benny the Baker, w/pie crimper & cake tester, Cardinal, $125 to. 135.00
Bird w/gold beak, floral transfers on wht body, 4", $125 to 150.00
Bird, bl w/pk eyes & wingtips, Shawnee for Pillsbury, 5½" 50.00
Bird, thin neck, Scotland, 1972, 4¼", $75 to 90.00
Black boy kneeling in prayer, blk pants, England, 4" 55.00
Black cat, red bow & collar, Halloween style, 4¾" 25.00
Black lady w/polka-dot muff, England, 3¾" 45.00
Bugs Bunny, California, 4" 27.00
Chick, yel, Josef Orig, 3¼" 45.00
Donald Duck, 1940s.. 1,200.00
Dragon, gr, England, 4¼" 75.00

Duck, bl, long neck, 5" 45.00
Duck, yel, long neck, unmk, 5" 50.00
Dutch girl, multipurpose kitchen tool, $125 to............................ 150.00
Eagle, mk Sunglow, golden color, $75 to....................................... 85.00
Elephant, trunk up, sitting on blk stand, England, 4" 65.00
Fred the Flour Grater (orig has) dots for eyes, $45 to 50.00
Funnel, bee shield, England... 125.00
Funnel, terra cotta, mk Wales... 35.00
Gobbler's Mountain, AR, solid colors, few made, 1994-95, $50 to ..75.00
Golliwog kneeling, bl shirt, wht & yel striped pants, England, 4".. 60.00
Mammy, pk scarf, bl apron, unmk, 1940s, 4¾" 75.00
Meadowlark, ltd ed, Sandhurst...MN, 4¾", MIB............................ 40.00
Patches, rose/yel/turq on wing, Morton, common, 5", $25 to........ 30.00
Rooster on stump, wht, Made in England, 4¾" 45.00
Rooster, Pearl China, 1940s.. 225.00
Rooster, pk/gr or bl/pk, Morton Pottery 2,500.00
Rooster, wht w/blk/red/yel details, Marion Drake, 5".................. 125.00
Rooster, wht w/brn/bl/lav, Cleminson, 4½" 75.00
Rowland's Hygienic Patent, England 90.00
Toucan, mc, England, 5¾" 45.00
Woodpecker on stump, mc, CA, 6¾" 36.00
Yankee Blackbird, Made in England, 1950-60s, 4¼" 40.00

Howard Pierce

William Manker, a well-known ceramist, hired Howard Pierce to work for him in 1938. After three years, Pierce opened a small studio of his own in LaVerne, California. Not wanting to compete with Manker, Pierce began designing miniature animal figures, some of which he made into jewelry. Today, his pewter brooches, depending on the type of animal portrayed, sell for as much as $275.00. Howard married, and he and his wife Ellen (Van Voorhis) opened a small studio in Claremont, California. In the early years, he used polyurethane to create animal figures — mostly roadrunners on bases, either standing or running; or birds on small, flat bases. Pierce quickly discovered that he was allergic to the material, so a very limited number of polyurethane pieces were ever produced; today these are highly collectible.

The materials used by Pierce during his long career were varied, probably to satisfy his curiosity and showcase his many talents. He experimented with a Jasperware-type body, bronze, concrete, gold leaf, porcelain, Mt. St. Helens ash, and others. By November 1992, Pierce's health had continued to worsen, and he and Ellen destroyed all the molds they had created over the years. After that they produced smaller versions of earlier porcelain wares, and they developed a few new items as well. Pierce died on February 28, 1994. Much of his work quickly appreciated in value, and items not seen before began to appear on the market. The majority of pieces are marked. Ink stamps and impressed, incised, and handwritten ink marks were all used. Our advisor for this category is Darlene Hurst Dommel, author of Collector's Encyclopedia of Howard Pierce Porcelain (Collector Books); she is listed in the Directory under Minnesota.

Ashtray, blk, unmk, 2x4" 30.00
Bank, pig, brn/gray gloss, 4x7" 170.00
Bowl, brn/wht matt, 1½x6" 35.00
Creamer/sugar, orange to yel gloss, 2½" 95.00
Dealer's sign, brn rough surface, 2½x6½" 135.00
Figurine, angel, wht gloss, 5¾x2" 85.00
Figurine, bird, gold, 2½x5½" 45.00
Figurine, bison, wht gloss, 2½x3¼" 75.00
Figurine, coyote, satin-matt brn on wt, 5¾" 76.00
Figurine, dinosaur, shaded gray gloss, 5½x4½" 100.00
Figurine, dog w/long ears, matt brn/wht, 6¾" 70.00
Figurine, elephant, matt brn/wht, 6" 80.00

Figurine, goose, gray gloss, 7x6¼" 35.00
Figurine, monkey, matt gray/brn, 6¼x3" 85.00
Figurine, monkeys, 3 in totem structure, brn, 15½x3" 470.00
Figurine, mouse, shaded gray gloss, 2½x1¾" 25.00
Figurine, rattlesnake, brn, 3x6" 100.00
Figurine, roadrunner on base, matt brn/wht, 6x9" 80.00
Figurine, seal pup, textured wht gloss, 3½x4½" 65.00
Figurine, squirrel, wht/brn mottled gloss, 5½" 36.00
Figurine, toad, brn/wht matt, 3 x3¾" 100.00
Figurine, unicorn, wht/brn matt, 5¾x5½" 125.00
Figurines, bears, mother & cub, brn matt, 3x6½", 2¾x2" 78.00
Figurines, birds, 2 on stump, matt brn/wht, 5x2¾" 65.00
Figurines, cats (2), wht to grayish gloss, 5½x2¾", 3¼x5", pr 125.00
Figurines, chipmunk, wht/brn gloss, 3½x6" 45.00
Figurines, doe & fawn, brn matt, 5¾x5", 3x4" 75.00
Figurines, quail family of 3, 6x5¼", 4x3½", 2½x3¼" 40.00
Flower arranger, child w/doll, wht gloss, 7½" 50.00
Flowerpot, salmon matt w/wht leaf motif, 4¼x4¼" 110.00
Planter, gray gloss w/wht bsk deer & tree insert, 4¾x9" 140.00
Sculpture, Reading Girl, bl gloss, 6½x2¾" 95.00
Vase, etched design, wht/brn matt, 5½" 80.00
Vase, grn gloss w/wht fish & coral insert, 8x7" 205.00
Vase, owl & foliage motif, brn mottled gloss, 5x4" 75.00
Vase, textured brn, 9¾" 45.00
Vase, wht gloss w/giraffe nestled into side, 7¼x4" 150.00

Pierrefonds

Pierrefonds is a small village in France, best known today as the place to see a castle once owned and inhabited by Napoleon III. Pottery collectors, however, know it better as the location of The Societe Faienciere Heraldique de Pierrefonds studio, which became famous for stoneware art pottery often finished in flambé or crystalline glazes. The pottery was founded in 1903 by Comte Hallez d'Arros, who was also an innovative contributor to the advancement of photography. The ware they produced was marked with a helmet between the letters P (for Pierrefonds) and H (for Hallez).

Vase, bl & brn crystalline, bulb w/rnded buttresses, 6½x10½" 550.00
Vase, bl & brn crystalline, integral hdls, 13½x9½" 850.00
Vase, bl & brn crystalline, twisted dbl-gourd shape, 11¾x7½" 950.00
Vase, bl crystalline running on yel, integral hdls, #447, 10¼" ... 1,000.00
Vase, lt bl crystalline on mustard, bulb/shouldered, 9¾" 480.00

Pigeon Blood

Pigeon blood glass, produced in the late 1800s, may be distinguished from other dark red glass by its distinctive orange tint.

Biscuit jar, HP floral on ribbed body, SP lid, ca 1900, 7½" 60.00
Ewer, ornate gold w/floral, bird & butterfly, att Webb, 8" 225.00
Lamp, oil, conical shade w/gold floral, repeated on front, 2-part, 8" ...650.00

Shakers, Periwinkle pattern, Consolidated, early twentieth century, 2¾", pair $420.00. (Photo courtesy Green Valley Auctions on LiveAuctioneers.com)

Sugar shaker, 6x4" 540.00
Water set, Bulging Loops, 9" pitcher w/clear hdl+6 tumblers 600.00

Pigeon Forge

Douglas J. Ferguson and Ernest Wilson started their small pottery in Pigeon Forge, Tennessee, in 1946. Using red-brown and gray locally dug clay and glazes which they themselves formulated, bowls, vases, and sculptures were produced there. Their primary target was the tourist trade. Since Ferguson's death in 2000, the pottery is no longer in operation.

Bottle, chevrons/spades, bl on purple irid, long neck, #2906, 6" .. 765.00
Bowl, brn to cream, hand thrown, D Ferguson, 2¼x6½" 20.00
Candlestick, bl crystalline, saucer base, w/hdl, 2½" 75.00
Charger, horseman, brn & cobalt, 1980s, 15" 1,200.00
Figurine, chipmunk, brn tones, 5½" L 25.00
Figurine, frog, brn w/cream wash, 2¼x3½" 55.00
Figurine, kingfisher, Douglas Ferguson, 9" 420.00
Figurine, owl, textured brn & cream, 4¼" 15.00
Figurine, owl, textured brn & cream, 7¼" 42.50
Jug, brn over gr crystalline, 6½" 20.00
Mug, Christmas tree, brn on gr 20.00
Vase, arches in brn & cream, Mycock, Royal Lancastrian, #193, 8" ...350.00
Vase, bl crystalline on gray-brn, bulb, 5⅛" 78.00

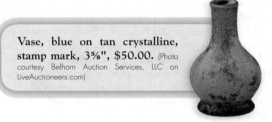

Vase, blue on tan crystalline, stamp mark, 3⅝", $50.00. (Photo courtesy Belhorn Auction Services, LLC on LiveAuctioneers.com)

Vase, brn & wht speckled, cylindrical, 10" 42.50
Vase, brn over gr crystalline, waisted neck, 7x5¼" 90.00
Vase, geometric bands divide bl neck & orange body, #3185, 6", pr ...360.00
Vase, heraldic beasts band & floral in gold lustre, 10" 850.00
Vase, mottled orange, Royal Lancastrian, #2085, 9" 100.00
Vase, vining leaves, bl on Kingfisher Bl, #6063, 8" 265.00
Vase, wht textured over brn, stick neck, 6" 25.00

Pilkington

Founded in 1892 in Manchester, England, the Pilkington pottery experimented in wonderful lustre glazes that were so successful that when they were displayed at exhibition in 1904, they were met with critical acclaim. They soon attracted some of the best ceramic technicians and designers of the day who decorated the lustre ground with flowers, animals, and trees; some pieces were more elaborate with scenes of sailing ships and knights on horseback. Each artist signed his work with his personal monogram. Most pieces were dated and carried the company mark as well. After 1913 the company became known as Royal Lancastrian. Their Lapis Ware line was introduced in the late 1920s, featuring intermingling tones of color under a matt glaze. Some pieces were very simply decorated while others were painted with designs of stylized leafage, scrolls, swirls, and stripes. The line continued into the '30s. Other pieces of this period were molded and carved with animals, leaves, etc., some of which were reminiscent of their earlier wares. The company closed in 1938 but reopened in 1948. During this period their mark was a simple 'P' within the outline of a petaled flower shape.

Bottle, chevrons & spades, bl on purple irid, long neck, #2906, 6¼".765.00

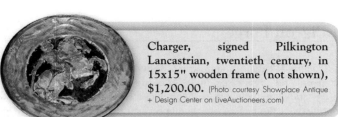

Charger, signed Pilkington Lancastrian, twentieth century, in 15x15" wooden frame (not shown), $1,200.00. (Photo courtesy Showplace Antique + Design Center on LiveAuctioneers.com)

Vase, arches in brn & cream, Mycock, Royal Lancastrian, #193, 8½" .. 350.00
Vase, geometric bands divide bl neck & orange body, #3185, 6", pr...360.00
Vase, gr-amber matt, bulb, P mk, 12x7" 385.00
Vase, heraldic beasts band & floral in gold lustre, 10½" 850.00
Vase, lustre florals, sgn Annie Burton England #2763, 4" 720.00
Vase, mottled orange, Royal Lancastrian, #2085, 9¾" 100.00
Vase, oxblood, bulb body, #2495, 1910, glaze flaw, 4¼" 100.00
Vase, vining leaves, bl on Kingfisher Bl, #6063, 8⅝" 265.00

Pillin

Polia Pillin was born in Poland in 1909. She came to the U.S. as a teenager and showed an interest and talent for art, which she studied in Chicago. She married William Pillin, who was a poet and potter. They ultimately combined their talents and produced her very distinctive pottery from the 1950s to the mid-1980s. She died in 1993. Polia Pillin won many prizes for her work, which is always signed Pillin with the loop of the 'P' over the full name. Some undecorated pieces are signed W&P, to indicate her husband's collaboration. Her work is prized for its art, not for the shape of her pots, which for the most part are simple vases, dishes, bowl, and boxes. Wall plaques are rare. She pictured women with hair reminiscent of halos, girls, an occasional boy, horses, birds, and fish. After viewing a few of her pieces, her style is unmistakable. Some of her early work is very much like that of Picasso. Her pieces are somwhat difficult to find, as all the work was done without outside help, and therefore limited in quantity. In the last few years, more and more people have become interested in her work, resulting in escalating prices.

Bowl, 2 ladies on brn, 6½x7½" 1,100.00
Bowl, lady w/2 cats on wht, irregular shape, 2¾x8" 1,500.00
Box, dancers on bl, internal firing lines, 2x8" dia 3,100.00
Box, lady w/lute on yel, 3x4¾x6½" 600.00
Bust, lady w/2 stylized birds, mc.. 425.00
Chalice, lady's portrait on dk brn, 7"... 995.00
Cordial pitcher, birds on antique wht, slim, rstr, 13", +2 cups...... 840.00
Covered dish, lady w/mandolin, mc on shaded bl, 2x4" dia 375.00
Decanter, abstract design, flared cylinder, cork top, 10", +6 tumblers ... 725.00
Dish, 2 dancing harlequins on brn, 6" dia 350.00
Goblet, bust portrait of lady, bl/gr/tan on brn, 9" 750.00
Jug, blistered yel/brn gloss, 7¾x5½" 275.00
Lighter, lady & man, Evans, 4x2¾" 285.00
Plaque, 2 ladies by tree w/bird, rect, 11" L 2,000.00
Plate, horses, 5 wht/1 blk on streaky teal, 7¾" 1,000.00
Plate, lady w/chicken & birds, mc on bl, 8½" 1,650.00
Tray, 2 women & bird, oval, 8½" L.. 925.00
Tray, bird on brn, 5" dia 350.00
Tray, lady's portrait (lg/detailed), sm nick, 8¼x6" 1,325.00
Vase, abstract figure on all 4 sides, 11½x3¾"............................... 975.00
Vase, avocado gr over lt seaweed gr, onion base, can neck, 6½" ... 250.00
Vase, birds on horizontal striations, earth tones, cylinder, 7" 495.00
Vase, blended lav, red/yel/purple, W+P Pillin, 6⅛"....................... 360.00
Vase, br w/yel goldstone effect, bulb, 8", NM.............................. 800.00
Vase, cat/rooster, trees/female dancers on marigold, 4½x3¾" 1,000.00
Vase, Chinese red & yel, 8" 1,080.00
Vase, complex geometrics, mc w/blk, bulb, 6½x6" 600.00

Vase, fish (3), spherical, closed mouth, 2¾x3½" 550.00
Vase, gr crystalline w/brn mottle drip, 5¾x3½"............................ 340.00
Vase, gr mottle, shouldered, 12x5" 675.00
Vase, horse & 2 ladies, wht on peacock & rust, 9x7".................... 850.00
Vase, horses (3) galloping, stick neck, 6x5½" 400.00
Vase, horses (4) prancing on gr to pk, spherical, 4¾" 585.00
Vase, ladies, 1 w/birds, 2nd w/horse, bottle shape, 6½x2½" 650.00
Vase, ladies (2) & lg deer on brn, sm rstr, 5x4" 500.00
Vase, ladies (2) holding fish-laden nets, cylindrical, 14" 2,400.00
Vase, ladies (2) w/fish, slim bottle form, 22" 3,300.00
Vase, ladies (3) standing, cylindrical, bk metal base, 14⅛".........1,750.00
Vase, ladies (4), 4-sided, 10¼"...1,950.00
Vase, lady (full-length), cylindrical, 14¾x3", NM 1,895.00
Vase, lady holding bird, 2nd bird beside, bk: lady, 6¾" 650.00
Vase, lady, chicken & deer, cylindrical, 4½" 450.00
Vase, lt to dk brn crystalline, bulb w/can neck, 8½" 270.00
Vase, rooster on bl, cylindrical, 7" 495.00
Vase, scarlet flambe gloss, spherical w/short neck, 9½x7"............ 425.00

Vase, school of colorful fish on vivid turquoise, signed Pillin, 6½", $1,100.00. (Photo courtesy Cincinnati Art Galleries, LLC on LiveAuctioneers.com)

Vase, sea gr gloss w/bl & umber shadings, spherical, 8x13" 1,525.00
Wine cup, rooster, gr w/mc, 2½" 325.00

Pin-Back Buttons

Buttons produced up to the early 1920s were made of a celluloid covering held in place by a ring (or collet) to the back of which a pin was secured. Manufacturers used these 'cellos' to advertise their products. Many were of exceptional quality in both color and design. Many buttons were produced in sets featuring a variety of subjects. These were given away by tobacco, chewing gum, and candy manufacturers, who often packed them with their product as premiums. Usually the name of the button maker or the product manufacturer was printed on a paper placed in the back of the button. Often these 'back papers' are still in place today. Much of the time the button maker's name was printed on the button's perimeter, and sometimes the copyright was added. Beginning in the 1920s, a large number of buttons were lithographed on tin; these are referred to as tin 'lithos.' Nearly all pin-back buttons are collected today for their advertising appeal or graphic design. There are countless categories to base a collection on.

The following listing contains non-political buttons representative of the many varieties you may find. Values are for pin-backs in near-mint condition, unless noted otherwise. Our advisor for this category is Michael J. McQuillen; he is listed in the Directory under Indiana.

American, early automobile, ca 1905, no bk paper, NM 325.00
Atlanta Federation...Labor Day 1907, eagle & clasped hands, 2½"..65.00
Boston Sunday Herald, What Did the Woggle Bug Say? on wht, 1¼", EX..60.00
Brooklyn Dodgers, dk red lettering & bats on wht, 1½", VG 24.00
Cloverine Salve, lady in center, mc on yel, Whitehead & Hoag, 1½" ...60.00
Clutch Cargo, blk/wht/red, 1950s, 1⅛", M on card 45.00
Ducks Unlimited, duck flying on bl, Rochester series, 1973, 2¼" .. 20.00
Dupont Smokeless, dogs in hunting scene, Lewis Swift, 1920s, 1". 90.00
Horlick's Malted Milk, ...Meat & Drink to Me, lady & cow, 1896, 1¼"... 35.00
Kellogg's PEP pin, Orphan Annie, ⅞" 15.00

Lone Ranger on rearing horse, red letters on wht, 1930s, 1¼", EX...70.00
Los Angeles DONS, red, wht & bl w/ribbon, AAFC, 1940s, 1¾".. 85.00
Meet Me at Macy's w/Santa portrait, Philadelphia Badge Co, 1¼" ..45.00
Member Roy Rogers Camera Club, blk & wht portrait on yel, 1950, 1¼"...160.00
Muhammad Ali blk & wht head shot, Flies Like a..., 1971, 2¼", EX...20.00

Pendleton Round-up, 1913, Let 'er Buck, Pendleton, Oregon, $195.00. (Photo courtesy Pioneer Auction Gallery on LiveAuctioneers.com)

Port Huron, The Only General Purpose, tractor on wht, 1890s, 1½", NM .240.00
Railroad Day, Pan Am, train on yel, Sept 14, 1901, 1"................ 195.00
Range Rider Brand, blk & wht photo on red, 1950s, 1¼" 26.50
Red Comb Poultry Feed, rooster in center, red/wht/bl, 1¼", VG ... 12.50
Riddler (Batman's enemy), portrait on red, 1966, EX..................... 12.50
Santa's Visitor, North Pole NY, Santa & reindeer on wht, 1½", EX.. 15.00
Shirley Temple Little Princess Contest, blk & wht portrait, 1¼", EX ..35.00
Shoot Peters Shells on wht, shotgun shell in center, 1900s, 1", EX...60.00
Sportsman's League, yel w/Laurentide fishing fly in wht center...... 32.00
Stag Beer Expert, dart-throwing award, brass, 1¼" 32.00
Tennessee State-Wide Hunting..., bl & wht, metal, 1941, 2½" L.. 200.00
Think Act Work for V Wright Employees, red, wht & bl, Bastian Bros, 2" ..25.00
Violet (Peanuts character), blk on yel-cream, ca late 1950s, 1" 10.00
Welcome Home Lindy, portrait, ⅞", +red/wht/bl ribbon, EX 25.00
Wisconsin, wht lettering on red, 1920s, 1¾"................................ 40.00

Pine Ridge

In the mid-1930s, the Bureau of Indian Affairs and the Work Progress Administration offered the Native Americans living on the Pine Ridge Indian Reservation in South Dakota a class in pottery making. Originally, Margaret Cable (director of the University of North Dakota ceramics department) was the instructor and Bruce Doyle was director. By the early 1950s, pottery production at the school was abandoned. In 1955 the equipment was purchased by Ella Irving, a student who had been highly involved with the class since the late 1930s. From then until it closed in the 1980s, Ella virtually ran the pot shop by herself. The clay used in Pine Ridge pottery was red and the decoration reminiscent of early Native American pottery and beadwork designs. A variety of marks and labels were used. For more information we recommend Collector's Encyclopedia of the Dakota Potteries by our advisor, Darlene Hurst Dommel; she is listed in the Directory under Minnesota.

Bowl, sgraffito, OCHS (Oglala Community High School), 4x6". 424.00
Mug, gr gloss, Talbot, 3½".. 45.00
Pitcher, wht gloss, Firethunder, 4½" 70.00
Plate, sgraffito, Cottier, 5½".. 150.00
Shakers, gr gloss, Talbot, 2" 45.00
Shakers, sgraffito, Cox, 2½".. 100.00
Vase, bl gloss, Firethunder, 2½" 65.00
Vase, incised geometric, brn w/gr highlights, 4x6¼"..................... 306.00
Vase, sgraffito, Cottier, 8¾x6¼".. 860.00
Vase, sgraffito geometric cream-colored designs on red bkgrnd, DB, 6x4½"..143.00
Vase, sgraffito, Woody, 3¼"... 225.00

Pink-Paw Bears

These charming figural pieces are very similar to the Pink Pigs de-

scribed in the following category. They were made in Germany during the same time frame. The cabbage green is identical; the bears themselves are whitish-gray with pink foot pads. You'll find some that are unmarked while others are marked 'Germany' or 'Made in Germany.' In theory, the unmarked bears are the oldest, made prior to 1890 when the McKinley Tariff Act required imports to be marked with the country of origin. Those marked 'Made In' were probably produced after the revision of the Act in 1914. Pink-Paw Bears are harder to find than Pink Pigs, but seem to be less desirable. Our advisor for this category is Mary 'Tootsie' Hamburg; she is listed in the Directory under Illinois.

1 by bean pot.. 95.00
1 by graphophone 150.00
1 by honey pot 115.00
1 by top hat 125.00
1 in front of basket... 135.00
1 in roadster (car identical to pk pig car) 195.00
1 on binoculars 175.00
1 peeking out of basket 135.00
1 posing in front of old-time camera, 5" L........................... 150.00
1 sitting in wicker chair 150.00
2 in hot air balloon 175.00

Two in purse, $165.00. (Photo courtesy TW Conroy, LLC on LiveAuctioneers.com)

2 in roadster 195.00
2 on pin dish 175.00
2 on pin dish w/bag of coins 160.00
2 peering in floor mirror 150.00
2 sitting by mushroom 160.00
2 standing in washtub 150.00
3 babies in cart pushed by mama, The Whole Dam Family, 4¼".. 150.00
3 in roadster 200.00
3 on pin dish 160.00

Pink Pigs

Pink Pigs on cabbage green were made in Germany around the turn of the century. They were sold as souvenirs in train depots, amusement parks, and gift shops. 'Action pigs' (those involved in some amusing activity) are the most valuable, and prices increase with the number of pigs. Though a similar type of figurine was made in white bisque, most serious collectors prefer only the pink ones. They are marked in two ways: 'Germany' in incised letters, and a black ink stamp 'Made in Germany' in a circle. The unmarked pigs are the oldest, made prior to 1890 when the McKinley Tariff Act required imports to be marked with the country of origin. Those marked 'Made In' were probably produced after the revision of the Act in 1914. Pink Pigs may be in the form of a match holder, salt cellar, a vase, stickpin holder, and (the hardest to find) a bank. The Pink Pigs with captions on the bottom are also considered older and more valuable. They are usually from around the turn of the century.

At this time three reproduction pieces have been found: a pig by an outhouse, one playing the piano, and one poking out of a large purse. These are not difficult to spot because they are found in a rough, poor quality porcelain in a darker green. Our advisor for this category is Mary 'Tootsie' Hamburg; she is listed in the Directory under Illinois.

1 as chef w/shamrocks, 2 salt cellars aside, 4¼" 200.00
1 at telephone, 1 inside, 4½" 175.00
1 at trough, gold trim, 4½" 110.00
1 at water trough among side tree, 3½" 110.00
1 beside gr drum, wall-mt match holder 95.00
1 beside lg basket, 3" 125.00
1 beside lg pot emb Boston Baked Beans, match holder, 4" W 135.00
1 beside lg purse 115.00
1 beside shoe 115.00
1 beside stump, camera around neck, toothpick holder 185.00
1 beside wastebasket 110.00
1 coming out of suitcase 95.00
1 coming through gr fence, post at sides, open for flowers 125.00
1 driving touring car 195.00
1 going through purse 110.00
1 holding cup by fence 140.00
1 in Japanese submarine, Japan imp on both sides 175.00
1 on binoculars, gold trim 175.00
1 on cushion chair w/fringe, 3" 195.00
1 on haunches, bottle, blk wood cork top, 2½" 110.00
1 on horseshoe-shaped dish w/raised 4-leaf clover 110.00
1 on key playing piano 225.00
1 reclining on horseshoe ashtray 85.00
1 riding train 235.00
1 sitting in oval bathtub, gold trim, 4½" W 200.00
1 sitting on log, mk Germany 175.00
1 standing in front of cracked open egg 95.00
1 standing in oversize opera-house box, gold trim, 3½" 200.00
1 w/basketweave cradle, gold trim, 3½" W 140.00
1 w/binoculars, brn/gr coat & hat, lg money bag, 5" 160.00
1 w/devil pulling on hose 225.00
1 w/flag, 2 black children in skiff, match holder w/striker, rare 500.00
1 w/front ft in 3-part dish containing 3 dice, 1 ft on dice 175.00
1 w/grandfather clock, 7" 250.00
1 w/hind leg held by lobster, 4½" W, EX 210.00
1 w/lg umbrella, picnic basket & water bucket, 5¼" 150.00
1 w/tennis racket stands beside vase, Lawn Tennis, 3¾" 180.00
1 w/typewriter, Gentlemen 165.00
2 at confession, 4½" 185.00
2 at outhouse (1 inside), 4", (+) 125.00
2 at pump & trough, 3¼" W 170.00
2 at pump, bank, Good Old Annual, 3¾" 170.00
2 at telephone, unmk, 4" 165.00
2 at wishing well 110.00

Two bowling, $125.00 to $150.00. (Photo courtesy Tom Harris Auctions on LiveAuctioneers.com)

2 by eggshell 165.00
2 by washtub, toothpick holder, souvenir of White City, 3¾" W . 135.00
2 coming out of woven basket, 3" W 115.00
2 courting in touring car, trinket holder, 4½" W 185.00
2 dancing, in top hat, tux & cane 210.00
2 in bed, Good Night on footboard, 4x3x2½" 185.00
2 in carriage 175.00
2 in front of oval washtub w/hdls, 3" W 135.00
2 in open trunk, 3¾" 125.00
2 in purse 95.00

2 looking in phonograph horn, tray, 4½" W 200.00
2 on cotton bale, 1 peers from hole, 1 over top 175.00
2 on seesaw on top of pouch bank 150.00
2 on top hat 125.00
2 on tray hugging 125.00
2 singing, receptacle behind, gold trim, 4½" 175.00
2 sitting by heart-shaped opening, trinket holder, 4" W 110.00
2 under toadstool 125.00
2 w/accordion camera, tray, 4½" W 150.00
2, 1 cutting hair of 2nd, A Little Bit Off the Top, 3x3½" 195.00
2, black chef w/spatula, holding basket w/1 inside, scarce 450.00
2, black mammy holding basket w/1 inside, scarce 450.00
2, fat couple sitting, A Fine Looking Couple 200.00
2, mother & baby in bl blanket in tub, rabbit on brd atop 175.00
2, mother w/baby in cradle, Hush-a-Bye-Baby..., MIG, 2 szs, ea ... 185.00
3 in horseless carriage, 4½" W 150.00
3 piglets in egg-shaped basin, Triplets of Fancy, mk Germany 150.00
3 w/baby carriage, father & 2 babies, Wheeling His Own 195.00
3 w/carriage, mother & 2 babies, Germany 195.00
3, 2 sit in front of coal bucket, 3rd inside 175.00
3, mother w/2 babies, The Dinner Bell, planter, 3¾" W 145.00
4, 3 piglets in cart, 1 wheeling, More the Merrier 150.00
4, mother pushing cart w/3 babies, clovers on wheels, vase, 3½" . 150.00

Pisgah Forest

The Pisgah Forest Pottery was established in 1920 near Mount Pisgah in Arden, North Carolina, by Walter B. Stephen, who had worked in previous years at other locations in the state — Nonconnah and Skyland (the latter from 1913 until 1916). Stephen, who was born in the mountain region near Asheville, was known for his work in the Southern tradition. He produced skillfully executed wares exhibiting an amazing variety of techniques. He operated his business simply, with only two helpers, using traditional North Carolina methods of a small operation and a kiln fired with pine wood from the mountains. Recognized today as his most outstanding accomplishment, his Cameo line was decorated by hand in the pate-sur-pate style (similar to Wedgwood Jasper) in such designs as Fiddler and Dog, Spinning Wheel, Covered Wagon, Buffalo Hunt, Mountain Cabin, Square Dancers, Indian Campfire, and Plowman. Stephen is known for other types of wares as well. His crystalline glaze is highly regarded by today's collectors.

At least ten different stamps mark his wares, several of which contain the outline of the potter at the wheel and 'Pisgah Forest.' The first two periods, 1901 – 1910 (Tennessee) and 1913 – 1916 (North Carolina), are indicated by the word 'Nonconnah' either painted on the base with slip or incised. Cameo is sometimes marked with a circle containing the line name and 'Long Pine, Arden, NC.' Two other marks may be more difficult to recognize: 1) a circle containing the outline of a pine tree, 'N.C.' to the left of the trunk and 'Pine Tree' on the other side; and 2) the letter 'P' with short uprights in the middle of the top and lower curves. Stephen died in 1961, but the work was continued by his associates. Our advisor for this category is R. J. Sayers; he is listed in the Directory under North Carolina.

Cookie jar, aqua high gloss glaze (crazing), 1935, 8", $220.00. (Photo courtesy Slotin Folk Art on LiveAuctioneers.com)

Bowl vase, turq crackle over wine, rose int, 4x5" 80.00
Bowl vase, turq crackle, wht int w/red reduction border, 5x7" 95.00
Candlestick, aqua, rose int, 1950s, 2¾", ea 30.00
Creamer/sugar bowl, rose w/in & w/out, ca 1920s, w/lid, 2" 85.00
Jar, turq w/pk int, 1953, w/lid, 4x3¾", NM 55.00
Jug, aubergine feldspathic, rnd hdl w/sq end, 6" 50.00
Jug, lt turq w/dense crackle, 1940, 5½" 50.00
Jug, turq over wine, incised shoulder lines, 1941, 5" 50.00
Mug, Cameo, covered wagon on bl, Stephen, 1952, 3½" 150.00
Pitcher, turq to burgundy, 3" 60.00
Plate, Cameo, Native Am warrior, sgn W Stephen, 1931, 6".... 1,400.00
Tea service: teapot, cr/sug, Cameo, 1950, rare 800.00
Teapot, turq crackle, ovoid w/str spout, 1943, hairlines, 7" L 200.00
Vase, 3-hdl, dtd 1930, sm firing line, 17" 500.00
Vase, Cameo-style people around Christmas tree, Stephen, dtd, 8" . 1,300.00
Vase, Cameo, celadon crystalline, sowers/reapers on gr band, 17", EX . 1,610.00
Vase, Cameo, wagon scenes/Indians/tepees on dk bl, aqua below, 8", pr .. 750.00
Vase, crystalline (full blown), tan on creamy gr, gray int, 4x5" 300.00
Vase, crystalline bl on yel & lt gr, WB Stephen, 11½" 1,600.00
Vase, crystalline ivory w/pk int, flared rim, 4½x4" 315.00
Vase, crystalline wht/bl/amber, baluster, 1939, 6¼x4", NM.......... 650.00
Vase, crystalline, wht/brn/bl/ochre flambe, mk Long Pine, 1955, 18x9" .2,520.00
Vase, gr w/pk int, baluster, 1951, 6½" 60.00
Vase, oatmeal w/brn streaks, bl crystalline at shoulder, 9¾x7¼". 1,100.00
Vase, turq crackle, wht int, Asheville mispelled on mk, 1935, 3½"..80.00
Vase, turq over wine, rose int, shouldered, 1938, 9½"................... 150.00

Playing Cards

Playing cards can be an enjoyable way to trace the course of history. Knowledge of the art, literature, and politics of an era can be gleaned from a study of its playing cards. When royalty lost favor with the people, kings and queens were replaced by common people. During the periods of war, generals, officers, and soldiers were favored. In the United States, early examples had portraits of Washington and Adams as opposed to kings, Indian chiefs instead of jacks, and goddesses for queens. Tarot cards were used in Europe during the 1300s as a game of chance, but in the eighteenth century they were used to predict the future and were regarded with great reverence.

The backs of cards were of no particular consequence until the 1890s. The marble design used by the French during the late 1800s and the colored wood-cut patterns of the Italians in the nineteenth century are among the first attempts at decoration. Later the English used cards printed with portraits of royalty. Eventually cards were decorated with a broad range of subjects from reproductions of fine art to advertising.

Although playing cards are now popular collectibles, prices are still relatively low. Complete decks of cards printed earlier than the first postage stamp can still be purchased for less than $100.00. In the listings that follow, decks are without boxes unless the box is specifically mentioned.

For more information we recommend *Collecting Playing Cards* by our advisor, Mark Pickvet (see Directory, Michigan). Information concerning the American Antique Deck Collectors, 52 Plus Joker Club, may be found in the Clubs, Newsletters, and Websites section.

Key: J — joker

Advertising

Alcoa Steamship, dbl deck w/red/blk bks, 1960s, MIB 15.00
Anheuser-Busch, Army-Navy, gilt edges, early 1900s, 52, NMIB . 950.00
Anheuser-Busch, Spanish-Am War, early 1900s, 52, NMIB 1,080.00
Cooks Products, boy painter bks, dbl deck, MIB............................ 50.00
Dupont Hotel, Fournier Heraclid Vitoria, 1980s, 54, MIB............. 60.00

Planters Peanuts, Mr. Peanut and lovely lady in peanut canoe on each card, circa 1930s, MIB, $540.00. (Phoo courtesy Dan Morphy Auctions LLC on LiveAuctioneers.com)

President Suspenders, gr bks, CA Edgerton, 1904, 52+J, EXIB.... 425.00
White Star Cruise Line, ship bks, ca 1940, 52, EX/VG box 360.00

Pinups

MacPherson brunette, 1944, 52+special card, EX in special box ... 60.00
Quick on the Draw, cowgirl bks, 1946, 52+J, EXIB 15.00
Vargas cowgirls on bks, Brn & Bigelow, 1947, dbl deck, EXIB....... 30.00
Wolf bks, varied nudes on fronts, 1950s, 52+J, EXIB..................... 30.00

Souvenir

Columbian World's Fair, fair buildings bks, GW Clark, 1893, 52+J, EXIB 72.50
Hawaiian Souvenir Playing Cards, Wall, Nichols Co Ltd 125.00
Jeffries Championship, boxer photos, ca 1910, 62+J, VGIB......... 195.00
Jim Jefferies Championship, boxer, 1909, 52+ joker, NMIB......... 600.00
Lyndon Johnson Air Force One, dbl decks, MIB 60.00
NASA Fireproof Bicycle Brand, ca 1960s, 52+J, EXIB 95.00
Ronald Reagan Air Force One, dbl deck, sealed, MIB 265.00

Miscellaneous

Black character photos & illustrations, Baldwin, 1896, 52, EX.... 240.00
Commander in Chief, Abraham Lincoln, Union figures, 1860s, 44, EX.. 30.00
Eagle/stars/laurel wreath bks, Samuel Hart & Co, 1880s, 52, EXIB....135.00
Game of Fireside Authors, Cincinnati, 1897, EXIB 72.50
Knuckle Down, marble players bks, 1906, 2 complete decks, ea EXIB .850.00
Lafayette Ace of Spades, J Ford, MA, 1824, single 3x2", NM ... 1,200.00
Native Am photos on front, geometric bks, 1920s, 52+J, EX....... 360.00
No 916 Squared Faro, A Ball & Bro, 52, EXIB............................. 900.00
Stevens Am Royalty, Pat Sept 21 1869, 52+J, NMIB, $850 to . 1,325.00
Tiffany Harlequin Transformation, CE Carryl, ca 1879, 52C, NM ..1,450.00
Transformation, Vanity Fair, USPC & Co, OH, 1895, NMIB...... 700.00
Transparent Playing Cards, 1860s, 52+J+Bazique Register, EX+ ...1,450.00

Political

Many of the most valuable political items are those from any period which relate to a political figure whose term was especially significant or marked by an important event or one whose personality was particularly colorful. Posters, ribbons, badges, photographs, and pin-back buttons are but a few examples of the items popular with collectors of political memorabilia. Political campaign pin-back buttons were first mass produced and widely distributed in 1896 for the president-to-be William McKinley and for the first of three unsuccessful attempts by William Jennings Bryan. Pin-back buttons have been used during each presidential campaign ever since and are collected by many people. Some of the scarcest are those used in the presidential campaigns of John W. Davis in 1924 and James Cox in 1920. Unless otherwise noted, values are for items in undamaged, excellent original condition showing no more than minimal wear.

Contributions to this category were made by Michael J. McQuillen, columnist of *Political Parade*, which appears in *AntiqueWeek* and other collector newspapers; he is listed in the Directory under Indiana. Our advisor for this category is Paul J. Longo; he is listed in the Directory under Massachusetts. See also Autographs; Historical Glass; Watch Fobs.

Armband, Hoover & Common Sense, red/wht/bl, 1928	100.00
Ashtray, Calvin Coolidge, 1924	75.00
Badge, Alternate 1948 Republican National Convention, Dewey	50.00
Badge, Delegate Republican National Convention, 1928	85.00
Badge, delegate, 1912 Progressive National Convention	100.00
Badge, Page 1948 Democratic National Convention, Truman	75.00
Badge, Taft w/ Wm Penn hanger	75.00

Bandana, Roosevelt/Fairbanks, 1904 campaign, cotton, stitched to canvas, 25x21", $400.00. (Photo courtesy Early American on LiveAuctioneers.com)

Bandana, T Roosevelt, Hat in the Ring, 16½x26½"	400.00
Bandana, Tippecanoe & Morton Too, 19" sq, 1888	130.00
Belt/buckle, Blaine & Logan, The Union Forever, 1884, 2½x3½"	100.00
Blow-up doll, Ronald Reagan, rubber head, plastic torso, 1987, 30"	40.00
Bobblehead doll, Ike, ca 1960, 9"	125.00
Cane, bronze-plated top w/bust of T Roosevelt, 34"	2,000.00
Cane, William McKinley, pewter McKinley head, 1896	250.00
Car plaque, Hoover for President, portrait, mc, EX, 4" dia	250.00
Cartoon, GOP elephant dancing, OH BOY!, CL Mortison, '56, 11"	70.00
Cigarette case, GOP/elephant/1948, gold enamel on metal	45.00
Cuff link, B Harrison portrait, cello, ca 1888,⅝", 1 only	50.00
Fan, advertising, William Howard Taft & Uncle Sam, 1908	200.00
Figurine, elephant, I'll Not Move...Improve, papier-maché, 13" L, VG	245.00
Hat, Al Smith Derby w/campaign pin, 1928, 6x2½"	225.00
Hat, Win w/ Willkie, bl & yel, 1940	35.00
Horseshoe, iron, James Garfield, profile, 1880, 4½"	100.00
Inaugural program, Garfield & Arthur, 1881	185.00
Key holder, Harry Truman 'Fair Deal,' leather, 1948	50.00
Lapel pin, I'm a Yel Dog Democrat, dog's portrait	35.00
License plate, Al Smith for President, red on wht, 1928, 12"	75.00
License plate attachment, Win w/ Roosevelt (FDR), 10¼"	100.00
License plate attachment, Uncle Sam portrait, Elect Landon, 1932, 5½"	125.00
Medallion, McKinley/Bryan, Sound Money/Free Silver, 1½"	50.00
Mug, Herbert Hoover, Syracuse China, 6½"	80.00
Pamphlet, Calvin Coolidge, 1924	25.00
Pennant, General MacArthur, picture, 25"	100.00
Plate, William Jennings Bryan etched image, glass, ca 1896, 5½"	110.00
Postcard, Our 25 Presidents, emb portraits, ca 1907, VG	35.00
Poster, Nixon for US Senator, picture, 1950, 11x14"	400.00
Poster, T Roosevelt/H Johnson, 1912 Progressive, 18½x24¾"	350.00
Print, H Clay Grand Nat'l Whig, 1844 Currier & Ives, 15x20"	400.00
Ribbon, Lincoln & Hamlin, Honest Abe pictured	2,500.00
Ribbon, US Grant (pictured), Pride of America, 1868	350.00
Ribbon, William Henry Harrison, The People's Candidate, 1836	350.00
Stickpin, bear figural (T Roosevelt)	40.00
Tie, We Want Ike on red	65.00
Token, James Buchanan, brass, 1856, 1⅛"	75.00

Token, Stephen A Douglas, portrait, brass, 1860, 1"	100.00
Tray, serving, McKinley/Roosevelt, mc, oval, 1900, 13¼x16¼"	750.00
Tumbler, Eventually Why Not?, elephant/mule on keg, glass, '32, 3½"	150.00
Wristwatch, Carter w/peanut face, legs tell time, 1976	75.00

Pin-Back Buttons

'3 Winners Hand' (Roosevelt for President, Fairbanks for Vice President, Cassel for Pennsylvania Congress), 1904, 1¼", EX, $200.00.

Alton Parker/HG Davis portraits w/flag, 1904, 1¼"	125.00
Bryan/Stevenson portraits on red/wht/bl shield, 1900s, 1¼"	85.00
Calvin Coolidge for President, portrait, 1924, ⅞"	50.00
Churchill/FD Roosevelt jugate, Victory..., red/wht/blk, 1940s	125.00
Dewey & Warren, portraits, RWB w/Am flag, 1948, 1¼"	35.00
For President Harry S Truman, blk & wht portrait center, 2½"	125.00
Go Forward w/Stevenson & Sparkman, portraits, 1952, 1⅝"	25.00
Herbert Hoover blk & wht portait, For President, metal rim, 1"	40.00
Hoover/Curtis jugate, blk & wht portraits, Greenduck Co, 1928, 1"	75.00
James M Cox for President, portrait, 1920, 1¼"	300.00
Joseph W Savage portrait, For Leader (Tammany Hall), 1905, 1", G	35.00
Kennedy Is Best for Me, portrait, 1960, 2¼"	20.00
Kennedy/Johnson, Leaders of Our Country...World, red/wht/bl, 3½"	50.00
Mamie Eisenhower/Pat Nixon portraits, 1952, 3½"	35.00
McKinley & Harris Ohio, disk hangs from clasped hands, tin, 1891, 3"	75.00
McKinley portrait, Count Us for McKinley, Buffalo Express, 1896, 1"	65.00
Theodore Roosevelt, blk & wht portrait & red/wht/bl flag, 1¼"	100.00
Theodore Roosevelt, First Voters Club, sepia portrait, 1904, 1"	50.00
Truman & Forrest Smith, bl letters on wht, 2"	1,900.00
Vote Republican/All the Way, flasher, Pictorial..., 1952, 2½"	25.00
We Want Harold Stassen, X guns, red/wht/bl, 1948, 1¾"	35.00
Who? Who? Hoover, owl shape, enameled metal	60.00
William Howard Taft portrait, Whitehead & Hoag, ⅞"	25.00
Wilson/Marshall, blk & wht portraits, 1"	65.00
Woodrow Wilson, Safety First, portrait, 1912, ⅞"	45.00
Youth for Roosevelt (Franklin), portrait, 2½"	250.00

Pomona

Pomona glass was patented in 1885 by the New England Glass Works. Its characteristics are an etched background of crystal lead glass often decorated with simple designs painted with metallic stains of amber or blue. The etching was first achieved by hand cutting through an acid resist. This method, called first ground, resulted in an uneven feather-like frost effect. Later, to cut production costs, the hand-cut process was discontinued in favor of an acid bath which effected an even frosting. This method is called second ground. For more information we recommend *The Collector's Encyclopedia of American Art Glass* by our advisor, John A. Shuman III.

Berry set, bowl & 8 sauces, 2nd ground, Invt T'print, 8", 4"	350.00
Bowl, 2nd ground, cornflowers, 10"	250.00
Bowl, 2nd ground, folded & crimped rim, 4"	135.00
Celery vase, 1st ground, cornflowers, clear appl base, ruffled rim, 6¼"	400.00
Creamer/sugar bowl, 1st ground, Invt T'print, bulb & squat	900.00

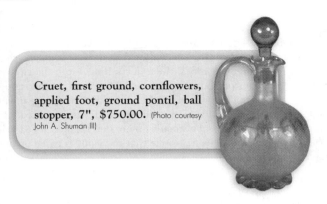

Cruet, first ground, cornflowers, applied foot, ground pontil, ball stopper, 7", $750.00. (Photo courtesy John A. Shuman III)

Cruet, 2nd ground, cornflowers, appl ft/hdls, sphere, ball stopper . 700.00
Pitcher, tankard, 1st ground, bl butterflies, gold grass, rare, 12¼" ... 1,000.00
Punch cup, 1st ground, blueberry, amber rim, leaves & hdl, 2¾" . 200.00
Tumbler, 2nd ground, cornflowers, Invt T'print, cylinder shape, 3⅜" ...165.00
Vase, 2nd ground, Dmn Quilt, tri-cornered, lily decor, rare, 9" 400.00

Postcards

Postcards are often very difficult to evaluate, since so many factors must be considered — for instance the subject matter or the field of interest they represent. For example: A 1905 postcard of the White House in Washington D.C. may seem like a desirable card, but thousands were produced and sold to tourists who visited there, thus the market is saturated with this card, and there are few collectors to buy it. Value: less than $1.00. However, a particular view of small town of which only 500 were printed could sell for far more, provided you find someone interested in the subject matter pictured on that card. Take as an example a view of the courthouse in Hillsville, Virginia. This card would appeal to those focusing on that locality or county as well as courthouse collectors. Value: $5.00.

The ability of the subject to withstand time is also a key factor when evaluating postcards. Again using the courthouse as an example, one built in 1900 and still standing in the 1950s has been photographed for 50 years, from possibly 100 different angles. Compare that with one built in 1900 and replaced in 1908 due to a fire, and you can see how much more desirable a view of the latter would be. But only a specialist would be aware of the differences between these two examples.

Postcard dealers can very easily build up stocks numbering in the hundred thousands. Greeting and holiday cards are common and represent another area of collecting that appeals to an entirely different following than the view card. These types of cards range from heavily embossed designs to floral greetings and, of course, include the ever popular Santa Claus card. These were very popular from about 1900 until the 1920s, when postcard communication was the equivalent of today's quick phone call or e-mail. Because of the vast number of them printed, many have little if any value to a collector. For instance, a 1909 Easter card with tiny images or a common floral card of the same vintage, though almost 100 years old, is virtually worthless. The cards with appeal and zest command the higher prices. One with a beautiful Victorian woman in period clothing, her image filling up the entire card, could easily be worth $3.00 and up. Holiday cards designed for Easter, Valentine's Day, Thanksgiving, and Christmas are much more common than those for New Year's, St. Patrick's Day, the 4th of July, and Halloween. Generally, then, they can be worth much less; but depending on the artist, graphics, desirability, and eye appeal, this may not always be true. The signature of a famous artist will add significant value — conversely, an unknown artist's signature adds none.

In summary, the best way to evaluate your cards is to have a knowledgeable dealer look at them. For a list of dealers, send an SASE to the International Federation of Postcard Dealers (see Clubs, Newsletters,

and Websites section). Do not expect a dealer to price cards from a list or written description as this is not possible. For individual questions or evaluation by photocopy (front and back), you may contact our advisor, Jeff Bradfield, who is listed in the Directory under Virginia. For more information we recommend *The Collector's Guide to Postcards* by Jane Wood, *Vintage Postcards for the Holidays* by Robert and Claudette Reed, and *The Golden Age of Postcards, Early 1900s*, by Benjamin H. Penniston.

Monster Fleet Sails Out, real photo, signed Rogers Photo, 1912, VG, $25.00. (Photo courtesy CNY Book Auctions on LiveAuctioneers.com)

Posters

Advertising posters by such French artists as Cheret and Toulouse-Lautrec were used as early as the mid-1800s. Color lithography spurred their popularity. Circus posters by the Strobridge Lithograph Co. are considered to be the finest in their field, though Gibson and Co. Litho, Erie Litho, and Enquirer Job Printing Co. printed fine examples as well. Posters by noted artists such as Mucha, Parrish, and Hohlwein bring high prices. Other considerations are good color, interesting subject matter and, of course, condition. The WWII posters listed below are among the more expensive examples; 70% of those on the market bring less than $65.00. Values are for examples in excellent condition to near mint unless noted otherwise. See also Movie Memorabilia; Rock 'n Roll Memorabilia.

Advertising

Chocolate Menier, girl writing on wall, Camis, Paris, 1896, 15x11" ..450.00
Hercules Powder, Game Bird of Future - Chinese Pheasants, 18x21" ...525.00
Manufacture de Bicyclettes... 250.00
Monster Beery Exhibitions, Wild West images, OH, 1918, 36x24" ...475.00
Overland, July, blk bird's silhouette on bl, 18x13" 1,100.00
Placards, Zurich Art Business Museum, Pfister, 1953, 50x36" 250.00
Prof EB Carver's Horse Training Exhibition, Courier, 28x21"......725.00
Ragan-Malone Dry Goods & Notions, lady w/flower, ca 1900, 29x20" ...725.00
Remington UMC, man & dog hunt birds, Watson, 26x18" 1,550.00
Schweizerische Radio & Fernseh-Ausstellung..., 1950s, 60x36" .. 325.00
Shell Cracker, 2 Shots in 1, man shooting on yel, 1950s, 27x19" .. 50.00
Shoot DuPont Powders, various scenes, Bogue-Hunt, 1920, 30x20" .. 160.00
Stetson, Last Drop From His Stetson, man & horse, 30x24"........200.00
Stickney & Poor's Mustards, Yours for..., child in red, 20x15"......300.00
We Sell Peters Shells, mallards in flight, Ketterlinus, 9x12" 1,050.00
Western Ammunition, Warning, moose scene, Edwards, 1921, 30x17"..2,000.00

Circus

Key:
B&B — Barnum & Bailey   RB — Ringling Brothers

Al G Barnes & Sells - Floto, lion on elephant's bk, 41x28" 950.00
B&B, Greatest Show on Earth, 2 portraits, 25x17", VG 245.00
B&B, Greatest Show..., 4 trains w/70 railroad cars, 1839, 42x33". 850.00
B&B, LaRoche et la Boule Mysteriuse, in 41x31" 1,650.00
Cole Bros, Ken Maynard, shown w/horse, 53x18" 1,500.00
RB/B&B, Berta Beeson trapeze artist, 41x28"............................. 600.00
RB/B&B, chariot, 1934, 28x22", VG+.. 160.00

RB/B&B, Gargantua the Great, 1936, 24x42+bottom date sheet.. 1,100.00
RB/B&B, Greatest Show..., elephant balancing, 1944, 44x61" 950.00

Theatrical

Daly's Theatre, Artist's Model, Paris, P Dupont, 1895, 14x11"+fr...325.00
Folly or Saintliness, Jose Echegaray, Boston, 1895, 20¾x15"+fr... 600.00
Jane Marnac, Casino de Paris, lady w/feathers, Kiffer/1928, 62x46".4,800.00
Madison Sq, Young Mrs Winthrop, portrait/12 scenes, Morgan, 30x23"... 480.00
Marsyas of de Betooverde Bron, Nouveau lady, Roland-Holst, 40x29"...2,650.00
My 'Soldier' Boy, Criterion Theatre, D Allen & Sons, 29x19" 240.00
Nomadie, Polar Bear Hunt in the Arctic, HC Hiner Co, NY, ca 1900, 40x26".275.00
Palais de Glase, lady in red, J Cheret, 1894, 22¼x15" 950.00
Stormbeaten, Ships Afire, Union Theater, Strobridge, 29x19".... 825.00
Terry's Theatre, Wht Night, Allen &B Sons, Harrow, 28x18"..... 240.00
Theatre Cluny, Le Fance de Thilda, Paris, 1900, 32x22", VG 250.00
Theatre Natl de L'Opera Bal Gavarni, lady in blk/wht, 1923, 62x47".. 2,300.00

Travel

Budapest, Cathedral of St Matthias, 1930s, 37½x25" 900.00
Cheverny, Chateaux de la Loire, E Paul Champseix, 1930s, 39x24"..525.00
CO Rockies, Black Hills & UT, Veentstra, ca 1935, 41x27".....2,150.00
Holland, sailboat scene, Wilmink, linen bk, 1930s, 39x25" 850.00
Lights of Adelaide from Mount Lofty Ranges, Letterpress, 1935, 40x24".. 1,550.00
Mexico, trains/cars/planes in cityscape, 1940s, 36½x27" 850.00
N Wales for Holiday, Snowdon Summit, Broders, 1929, 40x25"...3,200.00
San Francisco, old bridge, H Koslow, ca 1964, 38x25" 1,325.00
Ski Stowe Vermont, snowy mountain scene, Maurer, 40x23½" ... 675.00
Switzerland, Territet-Mont-Fleur, mountain scene, 1904, 39x37". 780.00

War

WWI, Civilians When We Go..., , Jewish Welfare Board, 33x21" 900.00
WWI, Keep These Off USA, bloody boots, Norton, 1918, 40x30" ...400.00

WWI, Sure We'll Finish the Job, farmer w/hand in pocket, 1918, 38x26" ..480.00
WWI, You Can Help, Red Cross, lady knitting, Benda, 1918, 40x20".425.00
WWII, Even a Little Can Help a Lot, mother & daughter, Parker, 20x14".235.00
WWII, My Daddy Bought Me a...Bond, blond girl, prof rpr, 30x20"... 240.00
WWII, This Is Enemy, cobra w/swastika on raised head, 1943, 34x26"..1,200.00
WWII, We Made a Monkey..., satire of Hitler & Uncle Sam, King, 19x15"..175.00

Pot Lids

Pot lids were pottery covers for containers that were used for hair dressing, potted meats, etc. The most common were decorated with colorful transfer prints under the glaze in a variety of themes, animal and scenic. The first and probably the largest company to manufacture these lids was F. & R. Pratt of Fenton, Staffordshire, established in the early 1800s. The name or initials of Jesse Austin, their designer may sometimes be found on exceptional designs. Although few pot lids were made after the 1880s, the firm continued into the twentieth century. American pot lids are very rare. Most have been dug up by collectors searching through sites of early gold rush mining towns in California. In the following listings, all lids are transfer printed. Minor rim chips are expected and normally do not detract from listed values. When no condition is given, assume that the value is based on an example in such condition.

Bear schoolmaster and his students, attributed to Pratt, with base, $180.00. (Photo courtesy Stanton Auctions on LiveAuctioneers.com)

Alas Poor Bruin, mc transfer, Pratt, sm, VG, +base 110.00
Begging Dog, mc transfer, Pratt, 3"... 80.00
Buel Boy, mc transfer, Pratt, 4¾" dia 125.00
Boots Cash Chemists Tooth Paste, blk transfer, ca 1900, 2¾"........ 75.00
Bryan of Gravesend Hair Restorer, blk transfer, 1870-80, 3".......... 160.00
Celetrated Heal All Ointment, Mrs Ellen Hales..., blk transfer ... 125.00
Creme Laferriere Secret de Jeunesse, blk transfer, 3" 90.00
Crosse Blackwell Anchovy Paste, brn transfer, EX, +base............ 160.00
Dr Ziemer's Alexandra Tooth Paste, blk & wht w/gold border, 3¾" . 250.00
James Atkinson's Bears Grease, blk transfer, 2½", +base 110.00
Paris Exhibition 1878, Crystal Palace, mc transfer, +base 165.00
Peasant Boys, mc transfer w/gold flecks, 4¾", EX, +base 165.00
Shooting Bears, mc transfer, Pratt, 3"... 180.00
Thornton's Celebrated Toilet Cream, blk transfer 125.00
Victor Emmanuel Meeting Garibaldi, mc transfer, EX 125.00
Village Wakes, mc transfer, Pratt, 3", EX, +base........................... 195.00

Powder Horns and Flasks

Though powder horns had already been in use for hundreds of years, collectors usually focus on those made after the expansion of the United States westward in the very early 1800s. While some are basic and very simple, others were scrimshawed and highly polished. Especially nice carvings can quickly escalate the value of a horn that has survived intact to as high as $1,000.00 or more. Those with detailed maps, historical scenes, etc., bring even higher prices. Metal flasks were introduced in the 1830s; by the middle of the century they were produced in quantity and at prices low enough that they became a viable alternative to the powder horn. Today's collector regards the smaller flasks as the more desirable and valuable, and those made for specific companies bring premium prices.

Flask, brass, Ames, US insignia, clasped hands, dtd 1946, EX...... 400.00
Flask, brass, Batty, shield/flags/trumpet/cannon/etc, dtd 1849, EX ..395.00
Flask, brass, Batty, shield/stars/coat of arms/eagle, 1853, 9¼", VG...350.00
Flask, brass, dogs w/treed bear.. 525.00
Horn, Civil War-era ships, Don't Give Up the Ship, fish, 14" ..1,450.00
Horn, cvd landscape w/birds/flags/banners/etc, 19th C, 8¾" 1,200.00
Horn, cvg at spout, brass tacks at base & neck, 1850s, 14x3"....... 750.00
Horn, scratch-cvd sailing ships/fort/lighthouse/flags, 15½"......... 575.00
Horn, scratched-cvd name/1771, wooden cap, splits at plug, 12" ... 1,150.00

Prattware

Prattware has become a generic reference for a type of relief-molded earthenware with polychrome decoration. Scenic motifs with figures were popular; sometimes captions were added. Jugs are most common, but teapots, tableware, even figurines were made. The term 'Pratt' refers to Wm. Pratt of Lane Delph, who is credited with making the first examples of this type, though similar wares were made later by other Staffordshire potters. Pot lids and other transfer wares marked Pratt were made in Fenton, Staffordshire, by F. & R. Pratt & Co. See also Pot Lids.

Cake stand, English factory scene, Greek figural border, unmk, 1850. 425.00
Creamer, cow figural/boy at side, tail hdl, mc, 1890s, 5½" 230.00
Figurine, lioness, ochre & brn, 1790-1810, 3x4" 450.00
Figurine, Netherfish, sheep head/fish body, mc, rstr, 1810s, 7¾". 2,400.00
Flask, Frolicking Cherubs, mc, vertical ribs at top & base, 5¾" ... 600.00
Jug, Mischievous Children, mc scenes, acanthus border, 1790s, 7" .. 350.00
Jug, tavern scenes, feather motif at spout/hdl, 9", VG 2,750.00
Mug, man on donkey among cattle & sheep, mc reserve on red, 3"...150.00

Pitcher, Toby Philpots in relief, warrior on back, 5", EX, $345.00. (Photo courtesy Garth's Auction Inc.)

Plate, 4 boys w/birds in nest, blk transfer, mc rim, 1830s, 7½" 150.00
Vase, man by tree stump, duck & dog at ft, mc, 1780-1830, rstr, 6" ...475.00

Primitives

Like the mouse that ate the grindstone, so has collectible interest in primitives increased, a little bit at a time, until demand is taking bites instead of nibbles into their availability. Although the term 'primitives' once referred to those survival essentials contrived by our American settlers, it has recently been expanded to include objects needed or desired by succeeding generations — items representing the cabin-'n-corn-patch existence as well as examples of life on larger farms and in towns. Through popular usage, it also respectfully covers what are actually 'country collectibles.' From the 1600s into the latter 1800s, factories employed carvers, blacksmiths, and other artisans whose handwork contributed to turning out quality items. When buying, 'touchmarks,' a company's name and/or location and maker's or owner's initials, are exciting discoveries.

Primitives are uniquely individual. Following identical forms, results more often than not show typically personal ideas. Using this as a guide (combined with circumstances of age, condition, desire to own, etc.) should lead to a reasonably accurate evaluation. For items not listed, consult comparable examples. For more information refer to *Antique Tools, Our American Heritage*, by Kathryn McNerney (Collector Books). See also Boxes; Butter Molds and Stamps; Copper; Farm Collectibles; Fireplace Implements; Kitchen Collectibles; Molds; Tinware; Woodenware; Wrought Iron.

Bedwarmer, copper w/tooled bird/flowers, wood hdl, 42" L 315.00
Bucket, stave & hoop, mc pnt sqs/speckles, MA, 19th C, 3½x4⅜" .. 300.00
Bucket, staved/interlocking hoops, cvd/pegged/pin hdls, red pnt, 8".....260.00
Butter paddle, maple w/central pinwheel w/geometric cvgs, 9".... 285.00
Candle mold, 24 redware tubes in wooden fr w/bootjack ends & fitted cover... 2,000.00

Churn, staved wood, old red pnt, inset lid & dasher, OH, 22x14" ..545.00
Drying rack, cypress, folding/3-part, CI mts, 50x30" (ea section).. 950.00
Firkin, 3-finger w/1 finger lid, old gr pnt, 10x9½" 865.00
Firkin, bentwood bands w/copper & iron tacks, old gr rpt, 14x15"... 575.00
Firkin, staved w/stapled bentwood bands, yel stain, w/lid, OH, 10" ...145.00
Firkin, staved wood w/2-finger bentwood bands, gr pnt, 9¼" 250.00
Firkin, staved wood, metal/wood bands, copper tacks, old pnt, 6½"...450.00
Loom, tape; thick pine w/sq nails, 2 ratchet posts, 16x18x10" 230.00
Mortar, curly maple, 9⅛x6", +trn pestle...................................... 315.00
Mortar, trn burl w/old rfn & G color, 7x5½", +trn pestle 260.00

Niddy-noddy, incised and painted with floral and geometric devices, signed SVL, 1859, $435.00. (Photo courtesy Freeman's on LiveAuctioneers.com)

Slaw cutter, curly maple w/EX color, att OH, 14½x5¾" 200.00
Tub, staved wood, iron bands, pierced hdls, pnt, 19th C, 20x23" dia.. 880.00
Yarn winder, 3-leg, old pnt w/HP foliage, clicking mechanism, 42" ...285.00

Prints

The term 'print' may be defined today as almost any image printed on paper by any available method. Examples of collectible old 'prints' are Norman Rockwell magazine covers and Maxfield Parrish posters and calendars. 'Original print' refers to one achieved through the efforts of the artist or under his direct supervision. A 'reproduction' is a print produced by an accomplished print maker who reproduces another artist's print or original work. Thorough study is required on the part of the collector to recognize and appreciate the many variable factors to be considered in evaluating a print. Prices vary from one area of the country to another and are dependent upon new findings regarding the scarcity or abundance of prints as such information may arise. Although each collector of old prints may have their own varying criteria by which to judge condition, for those who deal only rarely in this area or newer collectors, a few guidelines may prove helpful. Staining, though unquestionably detrimental, is nearly always present in some degree and should be weighed against the rarity of the print. Professional cleaning should improve its appearance and at the same time help preserve it. Avoid tears that affect the image; minor margin tears are another matter, especially if the print is a rare one. Moderate 'foxing' (brown spots caused by mold or the fermentation of the rag content of old paper) and light stains from the old frames are not serious unless present in excess. Margin trimming was a common practice; but look for at least ½" to 1½" margins, depending on print size. When no condition is indicated, the items listed below are assumed to be in very good to excellent condition. See also Nutting, Wallace; Parrish, Maxfield. For more information we recommend *Beaux Arts Pocket Guide to American Art Prints* by Michael Bozarth and *Collector's Value Guide to Early 20th Century American Prints* by Michael Ivankovich.

John J. Audubon

Audubon is the best known of American and European wildlife artists. His first series of prints, 'Birds of America,' was produced by Robert Havell of London. They were printed on Whitman watermarked paper bearing dates of 1826 to 1838. The Octavo Edition of the same series was printed in seven editions, the first by J.T. Bowen under Audubon's direction. There were seven volumes of text and prints, each 10" x 7", the first five bearing the J.J. Audubon and J.B. Chevalier mark, the last two, J.J. Audubon. They were produced from 1840 through 1844. The second and other editions were printed up to 1871. The Bien Edition prints were full size, made under the direction of Audubon's sons in the late 1850s. Due to the onset of the Civil War, only 105 plates were finished. These are considered to be the most valuable of the reprints of the 'Birds of America Series.' In 1971 the complete set was reprinted by Johnson Reprint Corp. of New York and Theaturm Orbis Terrarum of Amsterdam. Examples of the latter bear the watermark G. Schut and Zonen. In 1985 a second reprint was done by Abbeville Press for the National Audubon Society. Although Audubon is best known for his portrayal of birds, one of his less-familiar series, 'Vivaparous Quadrupeds of North America,' portrayed various species of animals. Assembled in corroboration with John Bachman from 1839 until 1851, these prints are 28" x 22" in size. Several Octavo Editions were published in the 1850s. In the listings that follow, prints are unframed unless noted otherwise. Note: These prints have long been reproduced; with a magnifying glass or a jeweler's loop, check for the tiny dots that comprise an image made by photolithography. None are present on authentic Havell and Bien prints, since these were made from printing plates; brushstrokes will also be apparent as these were hand tinted. Only prints from the Amsterdam Edition will have the dots; however, these must also bear the 'G Schut and Zonen Audubon' watermark to be authentic.

Our suggested values are actual current prices realized at auction. Our advisor for this category is Michael Bozarth; he is listed in the Directory under New York.

American Flamingo, Bien/375, 1960, sm losses, 38x25¾" 9,600.00
American Sparrow Hawk, Havell/142, 1832, fr: 32½x25½" 2,650.00
Azure Warbler, Havell/48, 1831, full sheet, 20x12½" 2,450.00
Black Warrior, J Whitman 1830, 29x25¼"+fr 5,750.00
Black-Footed Ferret, Bowen, Royal Octavo/93, 6x10"+mat & fr...........775.00
Black-Winged Hawk, Bien/16, 36x26" unmtd 365.00
Canada Jay, Havell/107, 1831, approximately 38⅛x25⅜", +fr ..6,600.00
Canada Porcupine, JT Bowen, No 8, plate XXXVI, 1844, 25x20"...2,000.00
Chestnut-Backed Titmouse..., Havell/353, 1837, 38x25" 4,250.00
Fishhawk, Havell/81, 1830, 38x25" 16,800.00
Grizzly Bear, JT Bowen/131, Imperial folio, 1848, 21⅝x27¼" ...7,800.00
House Wren, Havell/83, 1831, sm rstr, 38x25¼", +fr 6,600.00

Jaguar, Female, J. T. Bowen, No. 21, Plate CI, 1846, 44x62", $6,950.00. (Photo courtesy Dorothy Sloan Rare Books on LiveAuctioneers.com)

Little Screech Owl, Havell/97, 1934, 38¼x25⅜", +mat & fr 7,800.00
Mocking Bird, Bien #32/plate 138, 1860, old rstr, sight: 35½x23".1,880.00
Mocking Bird, Havell/21, London, 1827, 25¼x36¾", +fr........13,200.00
Nine-Banded Armadillo, JT Bowen/146, 1848, 21⅝x27¼".......7,800.00
Painted Finch, Havell/53, ca 1827-34, 19½x12¼", +mat & fr ..7,250.00
Pied Oyster Catcher, Havell/45, 1834, sheet: 12½x19½" 3,000.00
Red Breasted Merganser, Havell/CCCCI, 1837, 25x38" 12,000.00
Red Tailed Hawk, Havell/51, 1891, 38¼x25¼", +fr...................6,600.00
Ruffed Grouse, Havell/41, 1828, 25¹¹⁄₁₆x39" 11,400.00
Stanley Hawk, Havell & Son, 1818, 29x25⅜", +fr 5,575.00
Stanley Hawk, R Havell & Son, London 1828, 29x25⅜", +fr....5,500.00
Swift Fox - Male, JT Bowen/52, Philadelphia, 1844, full sheet .6,000.00
Tell-Tale Godwit or Snipe (Male & Female), Havell, 1830, 24x18" .. 3,750.00

Texan Lynx, JT Bowen/92, 1846, full sheet, fr: 21¾x27½" 3,250.00
Three-Toed Woodpecker, Havell/132, 1932, elephant folio, +fr ...6,600.00
Trumpeter Swan, Amsterdam/376 & 76, 1971, sheet: 27x40"...... 765.00
Yellow Bird or Am Goldfinch, Havell/33, 1828, 38x24¾".........7,800.00
Yellow-Crowned Heron, Bien, 1960, 40x27" 5,150.00

Currier & Ives

Nathaniel Currier was in business by himself until the late 1850s when he formed a partnership with James Merrit Ives. Currier is given credit for being the first to use the medium to portray newsworthy subjects, and the Currier & Ives views of nineteenth-century American culture are familiar to us all. In the following listings, 'C' numbers correspond with a standard reference book by Conningham. Values are given for prints in very good condition; all are colored unless indicated black and white. Unless noted 'NC' (Nathaniel Currier), all prints are published by Currier & Ives. Our advisor for this category is Michael Bozarth; he is listed in the Directory under New York.

Accommodation Train, 1876, C-32, sm folio............................... 400.00
American Country Life - Summers Evening, C-122, lg folio.....2,250.00
American Country Life — Pleasures of Winter, lg folio 3,225.00
American Express Train, 21½x31½".......................................13,200.00
American Forest Game, 1866, C-156, lg folio 1,000.00

American Prize Fruit, C-183, 23¼x31¼", $1,800.00. (Photo courtesy Bloomsbury Auctions on LiveAuctioneers.com)

Arguing the Point, NC, 1855, C-265, lg folio............................5,200.00
Autumn in Adirondacks (Lake Harrison), undtd, C-323, sm folio 350.00
Beautiful Brunette, undtd, C-453, sm folio 75.00
Between Two Fires, 1879, C-511, sm folio 300.00
Bombardment of Fort Pulaski...April, 1862, C-595, sm folio 350.00
Burning of Clipper...Golden Lt, NC, undtd, C-740, sm folio.......450.00
Catherine, NC, 1845, C-849, sm folio 90.00
Chicky's Dinner, undtd, C-1029, sm folio 175.00
City of New York, NC, 1855, C-1102, lg folio............................3,000.00
Custer's Last Charge, 1876, C-1333, sm folio 350.00
Cutter Genesta RYS, C-1338, lg folio......................................1,100.00
Day of Marriage, 1847, NC, C-1459, sm folio............................ 100.00
Disputed Heat, Claiming Foul; 1878, C-1587, lg folio 1,800.00
Dutchman & Hiram Woodruff, 1871, C-1640, sm folio 700.00
Elizabeth, NC, 1846, C-1698, sm folio.. 95.00
English Winter Scene, undtd, C-1745, sm folio........................... 525.00
Flora Temple, NC, 1853, C-2015, lg folio.................................1,900.00
Fruit & Flowers Piece, 1863, C-2160, med folio 400.00
Gem of the Atlantic, NC, 1849, C-2228, sm folio 750.00
God Bless Our Home, undtd, C-2392, sm folio 250.00
Got the Drop on Him, 1881, C-2455, sm folio 275.00
Grand Pacer Richball, 1890, C-2519, sm folio 300.00
Great St Louis Bridge Across Mississippi..., undtd, C-2648, sm folio .. 825.00
Home on the Mississippi, 1876, C-2876, sm folio....................... 500.00
Hooked, 1874, C-2928, sm folio...1,800.00
Lake in the Woods, C-3409, sm folio... 200.00
Last War Whoop, NC, 1856, C-3457, lg folio 2,800.00
Leaders, 1888, C-3471, lg folio..1,000.00

Life of a Hunter, Tight Fix; 1861, C-3522, lg folio....................4,400.00
Lincoln Family, 1867, C-3546, sm folio 100.00
Maiden's Rock, Mississippi River; C-3891, sm folio 500.00
NE Winter Scene, 1861, C-4420, lg folio 6,450.00
Peytona & Fashion in Their Great Match..., NC, undtd, C-4763, lg folio..4,700.00
President of the United States, C-4903, sm folio..........................175.00
Ready for Trot, Bring Up Your Horses; 1877, C-5085, lg folio ..2,000.00
Road - Winter, NC, 1853, C-5171, lg folio 25,850.00
Snow Storm, undtd, C-5580, med folio 2,350.00
Splendid Naval Triumph on Mississippi...1862, 1862, C-5659, lg folio...1,050.00
Steamer Penobscot, 19th C, C-5736, 26x38" 6,325.00
Summer Ramble, undtd, C-5874, med folio............................400.00
Surrender of General Burgoyne...1777, NC, 1852, C-5907, lg folio.5,000.00
Taking Back Track, Dangerous Neighborhood; 1866, C-5961, lg folio..10,575.00
Trolling for Blue Fish, 1866, C-6158, lg folio 11,750.00
Whale Fishery Laying On, NC, 1852, C-6626, sm folio............1,650.00
Winter Evening, 1854, C-6734, med folio 1,300.00
Winter Morning, 1861, C-6740, med folio 2,250.00

Erte (Romain de Tirtoff)

Aladdin & His Bride, sgn in pencil, 25½x32".....................450.00
Bride, portrait of lady in ornate headdress, 18x13½" 475.00
Deco nude, Print #4, sight: 22x17", +fr...............................780.00
Diva I, Diva II; from Diva Suite, sight: 35x26", +fr, pr 2,750.00
Enchanted Melody, sight: 37x26", +fr.............................1,650.00
Glutton, serigraph, 19½x14", +silver metal fr.........................300.00
Kiss of Fire, Love & Passion Suite, sight: 33x28", +fr.............1,680.00
Letter O, from Alphabet Suite, 15½x10½", +metal fr 300.00
Liberty at Night w/Fireworks, NY skyline, ltd ed of 300, 31x23" .800.00
Marriage Dance, Love & Passion Suite, sight: 28x33", +fr........2,400.00
Paresseuse, ca 1980, 25⅜x18".......................................750.00
Portrait of a Woman, 20½x15¼".....................................575.00
Queen of Sheba, serigraph, 1980, sight: 25x18", +mat & fr 780.00

Trapeze, from At the Theatre Suite, serigraph, signed, 1983, image: 16½x21½", $960.00. (Photo courtesy Leland Little Auction & Estate Sales Ltd. on LiveAuctioneers.com)

Vamps Suite, sight: 20x16", +fr, 6 for.............................2,400.00
Winter Resorts, 1982, sight: 23x27", +mat & fr 600.00
Woman in Cape, sight: 30½x20", +fr...............................1,650.00

R. Atkinson Fox

A Canadian who worked as an artist in the 1880s, R. Atkinson Fox moved to New York about 10 years later, where his original oils were widely sold at auction and through exhibitions. Today he is best known, however, for his prints, published by as many as 20 print makers. Many examples of his work appeared on Thomas D. Murphy Company calendars, and it was used in many other forms of advertising as well. Though he was an accomplished artist able to interpret any subject well, he is today best known for his landscapes. Fox died in 1935. Our advisor for Fox prints is Pat Gibson, whose address is listed in the Directory under California.

Baby's First Tooth, 14x9" 235.00
Campfire Girl (A), sgn, 11x9" 225.00
Danger Signal (A), moose, 10x6"....................................175.00
Dreamy Paradise, unsgn, 8x10"......................................90.00

English Garden, reverse painted mat, 18x30", EX, $180.00. (Photo courtesy Tom Harris Auctions on LiveAuctioneers.com)

Glorious Vista, sgn, 16x20"...90.00
Heart's Desire, 14x22"..125.00
Majestic Splendor, garden, sgn, 30x18".............................250.00
Meditation Lady, sgn, 9x7"..250.00
Old Well (The), 5x3"..95.00
On the Alert Collie, sgn, 8x12"....................................145.00
Our Country Cousin, cow, lady, sgn, 8x6"...........................175.00
Rocky Waterway, 16x13"...195.00
Russet Gems, sgn, 16x21"...125.00
Supreme, leopard, 9x12"..185.00
Untitled, girl & St Bernard w/2 horses by pond, sgn, 10x8".........200.00

Bessie Pease Gutmann (1876 – 1960)

Delicately tinted prints of appealing children sometimes accompanied by their pets, sometimes asleep, often captured at some childhood activity are typical of the work of this artist; she painted lovely ladies as well and was a successful illustrator of children's books. Her career spanned five decades of the 1900s, and she recorded over 800 published artworks. Our advisor for this cagegory is Dr. Victor J.W. Christie; he is listed in the Directory under Pennsylvania.

Aeroplane (The), #266/#695, 14x21" 900.00
Always, #744, 14x21" 2,600.00
American Girl (The), #220, 13x18" 500.00
An Anxious Moment, #714, 14x21" 650.00
Annunciation, #705, 14x21" 1,200.00
Awakening, #664, 14x21"..125.00
Baby's First Birthday, #618, 14x21" 750.00
Baby's First Christmas, #158..500.00
Bedtime Story (The), #712, 14x21" 750.00
Betty, #787, 14x21"..250.00
Billy, #790, 14x21"..270.00
Blossom Time, #654, 14x21" 800.00
Blue Bird, The, #265/#666, 14x21" 650.00
Bobby, #789, 14x21"..225.00
Brown Study (A), #611, 14x20"......................................1,500.00
Bubbles, #779, 14x21"..350.00
Butterfly (The), #632, 14x18" 210.00
Call to Arms (A), #806, 14x21".....................................850.00
Caught Napping, #153, 9x12"..2,000.00
Chip of the Old Block, #728, 14x21" 600.00
Chuckles, #799, 11x14"...150.00
Chums, #665, 14x21"..350.00
Contentment, #781 ....90.00
CQD, #149, 9x12" 450.00
Cupid, After All My Trouble, #608, 16x20" 800.00
Cupid's Reflection, #602, 14x21" 800.00
Daddy's Coming, #644, 14x21".......................................495.00

Divine Fire, #722, 14x21" 700.00
Double Blessing (A), #643, 14x21" 500.00
Fairest of the Flowers (The), #659, 14x21" 700.00
Feeling, #19, 6x9" 250.00
First Dancing Lesson (The), #713, 14x21" 825.00
Friendly Enemies, #215, 11x14" 155.00
Going to Town, #797, 14x21" 650.00
Goldilocks, #771, 14x21" 1,100.00
Good Morning, #801, 14x21" 250.00
Guest's Candle (The), #651, 14x21" 500.00
Hearing, #22, 6x9" 250.00
His Majesty, #793, 14x21" 320.00
His Queen, #212, 14x20" 700.00
Home Builders, #233/#655, 14x21" 235.00
How Miss Tabitha Taught School, Dodge Publishing Co, 11x16" .. 900.00
In Arcady, #701, 14x21" 700.00
In Disgrace, #792, 14x21" 200.00
In Slumberland, #786, 14x21" 120.00
Kitty's Breakfast, #805, 14x21" 350.00
Knit Two – Purl Two, #657, 14x21" 850.00
Little Bit of Heaven (A), #650, 14x21" 125.00
Little Bo Peep, #200, 11x14" 150.00
Little Mother, #803, 14x21" 450.00
Lorelei, #645, 14x21" 1,700.00
Love's Blossom, #223, 11x14" 100.00
Love's Harmony, #791, 14x21" 400.00
Lullaby (The), #819, 14x21" 2,100.00
Madonna (The), #674, 14x21" 2,100.00
May We Come In, #808, 14x21" 385.00
Merely a Man, #218, 13x18" 800.00
Message of the Roses (The), #641, 14x21" 400.00
Mighty Like a Rose, #642, 14x21" 200.00
Mine, #798, 14x21" 225.00
Mischief Brewing, #152, 9x12" 2,000.00
Mothering Heart (The), #351, 14x21" 700.00
My Honey, #765, 14x21" 1,200.00
New Pet (The), #709, 14x21" 950.00
Nitey Nite, #826, 14x21" 175.00
Now I Lay Me, #620, 14x21" 1,800.00
Off to School, #631, 14x21" 1,200.00
On Dreamland's Border, #692, 14x21" 155.00
On the Up & Up, #796, 14x21" 295.00
Our Alarm Clock, #150, 9x12" 250.00
Perfect Peace, #809, 14x21" 500.00
Popularity (Has Its Disadvantages), #825, 14x21" .. 150.00
Poverty & Riches, #640, 14x21" 700.00
Priceless Necklace (A), #744, 14x21" 1,600.00
Rosebud (A), #780, 14x21" 320.00
Seeing, #122, 11x14" 250.00
Smile Worth While (A), #180, 9x12" 800.00
Snowbird, #777, 14x21" 650.00
Springtime, #775, 14x21" 750.00
Star From the Sky (A), #817, 14x21" 175.00
Sunbeam in a Dark Corner (A), #638, 14x21" 2,200.00
Sunkissed, #818, 14x21" 125.00
Sweet Innocence, #806, 11x14" 150.00
Symphony, #702, 14x21" 650.00
Tabby, #172, 9x12" 600.00
Taps, #815, 14x21" 550.00
Television, #821, 14x21" 110.00
Thank You God, #822, 14x21" 175.00
To Have & To Hold, #625, 14x21" 800.00
To Love & To Cherish, #615, 14x21" 265.00
Tom, Tom the Piper's Son, #219, 11x14" 175.00

Tommy, #788, 14x21" 175.00
Touching, #210, 11x14" 150.00
Vanquished (The), #119, 9x12" 750.00
Verdict: Love for Life (The), #113, 9x12" 550.00
When Daddy Comes Marching Home, #668, 14x21" .. 3,800.00
Who's Sleepy, #816, 14x21" 260.00
Winged Aureole (The), #700, 14x21" 500.00
Wood Magic, #703, 14x21" 750.00

Louis Icart

Louis Icart (1888 – 1950) was a Parisian artist best known for his boudoir etchings in the '20s and '30s. In the '80s prices soared, primarily due to Japanese buying. The market began to readjust in 1990, and most etchings now sell at retail between $1,400.00 and $2,500.00. Value is determined by popularity and condition, more than by rarity. Original frames and matting are not important, as most collectors want the etchings restored to their original condition and protected with acid-free mats.

Beware of the following repro and knock-off items: 1. Pseudo engravings on white plastic with the Icart 'signature.' 2. Any bronzes with the Icart signature. 3. Most watercolors, especially if they look similar in subject matter to a popular etching. 4. Lithographs where the dot-matrix printing is visible under magnification. Some even have phony embossed seals or rubber stamp markings. Items listed below are in excellent condition unless noted otherwise. Our advisor is William Holland, author of *Louis Icart: The Complete Etchings*; *The Collectible Maxfield Parrish*; *Louis Icart Erotica*; and *Tiffany Desk Sets*. He is listed in the Directory under Pennsylvania.

Before the Raid, 17x21½", $4,700.00. (Photo courtesy Sotheby's on LiveAuctioneers.com)

Autumn Storm, 9x7" 1,650.00
Coursing II, 16x25" 2,750.00
Departure, 1941, 21x17" 1,495.00
Elegance, 18x15" 1,750.00
Finale, 1931, 19x15" 2,125.00
Gust of Wind, 1925, 21x18" 2,600.00
He Loves Me, He Loves Me Not, 1926, 19x16", VG .. 1,265.00
La Chechette (Hiding Place), Les Graveurs, sight: 26x21" .. 1,650.00
Le Lis, lady & lilies, 1934, 27¾x18¾" 3,250.00
Look, oval, 24x18" 1,500.00
Madame Bovary, lady at window, oval, 1929 .... 1,400.00
Martini, 13½x17½" 5,500.00
Miss America, 1927, sheet: 26x20" 4,000.00
Peacock, 24x19" 4,750.00
Peonies, 1935, 14x17", VG 1,600.00
Pink Alcove, 1929, 10½x13" 1,250.00
Speed, 1933, 22x31" 3,950.00
Sweet Mystery, oval, 19x24" 3,650.00
Venus, open ed, oval, unfr, 18x25" 25.00
View of Paris, 1948, 5x8" 1,900.00
Zest, 1928, 10x15", sheet: 25x19⅜" 2,800.00

Kurz and Allison

Louis Kurz founded the Chicago Lithograph Company in 1833. Among his most notable works were a series of 36 Civil War scenes and 100 illustrations of Chicago architecture. His company was destroyed in the Great Fire of 1871, and in 1880 Kurz formed a partnership with Alexander Allison, an engraver. Until both retired in 1903, they produced hundreds of lithographs in color as well as black and white. Unless noted otherwise, values are for prints in excellent condition.

Battle Between the Monitor & Merrimac, c 1889, 22x28", +mat . 725.00
Battle of Antietam Army of the Potomac...1862, c 1888, 22x28", +fr. 1,100.00
Battle of Big Horn, image; 22x28", +mat & fr 9,600.00
Battle of Cold Harbor...1864, 1888, 20x26", +mat 1,800.00
Battle of Gettysburg, 1884, 22x28", +mat & gilt fr 900.00
Battle of Missionary Ridge, 1886, 22x28½", +mat 2,350.00
Battle of New Orleans January 8 1815, 22x28" 850.00
Battle of Spotsylvania...Laurel Hill...1864, c 1888, 22x28", +mat .2,150.00
Battle of the Wilderness...Plank Road...1864, c 1887, 22x28", +mat.. 2,150.00
General TJ Jackson, blk & wht, sight: 28x22" 540.00
Great Conemaugh Valley Disaster, 22x36", +Black Forest, fr ...1,950.00

Peter Max

Born in Germany in 1937, Peter Max came to the United States in 1953 where he later studied art in New York City. His work is colorful and his genre psychedelic. He is a prolific artist, best known for his designs from the '60s and '70s that typified the 'hippie' movement.

Anger, 1971, 29½x21½", fr 480.00
Goofy, 4 prints in single fr, 1996, ea: 16x14" 1,175.00
Great Genie, 1976, sheet: 14¼x15½" 475.00
Image for Rainforest Foundation, embellished, 22x16½" 900.00
Lady in a Flower Hat, enhanced w/pnt, 20x15" 850.00

Liberty (Red), lithograph, pencil signed, 1998, 24x24", $2,280.00. (Photo courtesy Wittlin & Serfer Auctioneers on LiveAuctioneers.com)

Men Running to Maiden, litho between glass, 3¾x10" 850.00
Moonscape I, 1971, 18¾x23⅜" 425.00
Rama, serigraph, artist proof, ca 1971, 29x21" 3,000.00
Toulouse Lautrec, pk bkgrnd, 42x30" 1,325.00
Untitled: vase of flowers, ed of 300, 21x15½" 480.00

McKenney and Hall

John Ridge, A Cherokee, Greenough, 1838, sight: 16½x12" 1,200.00
Keokuk, Chief of Sacs & Fox, 19½x14¼" 1,550.00
Ki-On-Twog-Ky, Bowen, EC Biddle, 1837, 20⅜x14¼" 850.00
Kish-Ke-Kosh, A Fox Brave, Greenough, Bowen, 1838, 20¼x14", +mat. 1,200.00
Ma-Has-kah, Ioway Chief, sight: 16¾x12¾", +mat & fr 2,150.00
McIntosh, Philadelphia, 1937-44, 18½x12½" 1,325.00
Ne-Sou-a-Quoit, A Fox Chief, Bowen, 1838, sm tear, 20¼x14⅝" ...1,550.00
Not-Chi-Mi-Ne, An Ioway Chief, Greenough, sight: 16¾x12¾", +fr. 1,175.00
Okee-Makee-Ouid, A Chippeway Chief, 16x11¾" 960.00

Red Jacket, 19th C, 30x13½" 950.00
Se-Quo-Yah, 20x14" 1,550.00
Wa-Na-Ta, EC Biddle, 1837, 20¼x14½" 1,550.00
War Dance of Sauks & Foxes, Bowen, 1938, 14½x20¼" 1,175.00

Yard-Longs

Values for yard-long prints are given for examples in near mint condition, full length, nicely framed, and with the original glass. To learn more about this popular area of collector interest, we recommend *Those Wonderful Yard-Long Prints and More, More Wonderful Yard-Long Prints, Book 2,* and *Yard-Long Prints, Book 3,* by our advisors Bill Keagy, and Charles and Joan Rhoden. They are listed in the Directory under Indiana and Illinois respectively. A word of caution: Watch for reproductions; know your dealer.

Absence Cannot Hearts Divide, Pompeian, sgn Marguerite Clark, 1921 .475.00
American Farming Magazine, WH Lister, lady w/parasol, 1918...400.00
American Girl, Pabst, lady holding basket of yel lilies, 1914......................575.00
Beauty Among the Roses, Bowles Live Stock, 1912-13................500.00
Beauty Gained Is Love Retained, Pompeian, 1925......................475.00
Bride (The), Pompeian, sgn Rolf Armstrong, 1927 ....500.00
Diamond Crystal Salt Co, 1913 art panel pnt by Kaber 500.00

Farmer's Daughter (The), Everitt Johnson, Clay, Robinson & Co., artist-signed, without calendar pad, 1913, 9½x26½", $500.00. (Photo courtesy Joan Rhoden)

Honeymooning in the Alps, Pompeian, sgn Gene Pressler, 1923.475.00
Honeymooning in Venice, Pompeian, sgn Gene Pressler, 1922 ...575.00
Liberty Girl, Pompeian, Forbes, 1919...475.00
National Stockman & Farmer Magazine, The Stockman Bride, 1912...500.00
Pabst, lady in dress/blk scarf, wht gloves, 1917 ....575.00
Pabst, lady in dress, gloves, w/parasol, sgn Stuart Travis, 1913.....550.00
Pabst, lady in gown, sgn Alfred Everitt Orr, 1914.........................550.00
Pabst, lady in lav gown/headband & evening bag, 1916................550.00
Pabst, lady in red hat/dress, sgn CW Henning, 1907....................550.00
Pabst, lady in wht hat/dress, pk flowers at her bosom, 1910 ....550.00
Pompeian, by Forbes, sgn Sincerely, Mary Pickford, 1916-17.......475.00
Pompeian, by Forbes, sgn Sincerely, Mary Pickford, 1918............500.00
Pompeian, lady & man, grandfather clock in bkgrnd, 1915 ....400.0
Pompeian, lady & man in front of fireplace, 1914 ....400.00
Pompeian, lady & man on balcony, sgn Gene Pressler, 1926 ....475.00
Pompeian, lady in pk tiered dress, holding letter, 1916 ....475.00

Purinton

With its bold colors and unusual shapes, Purinton Pottery is much admired by today's dinnerware collectors. In 1939 Bernard Purinton purchased the East Liverpool Pottery in Wellsville, Ohio, and re-named it the Purinton Pottery Company. One of its earliest lines was Peasant Ware, featuring simple shapes and bold, colorful patterns. It was designed by William H. Blair, who also designed what have become the company's most recognized lines, Apple and Intaglio. The company was extremely successful, and by 1941 it became necessary to build a new plant, which they located in Shippenville, Pennsylvania. Blair left Purinton to open his own pottery (Blair Ceramics), leaving his sister Dorothy Purinton (Bernard's wife) to assume the role of designer. Though never a paid employee, Dorothy painted many one-of-a-kind special-occasion items that are highly sought after by today's collectors who are willing to pay premium prices to get them. These usually carry Dorothy's signature.

Apple was Purinton's signature pattern; it was produced throughout the entire life of the pottery. Another top-selling pattern designed by Dorothy Purinton was Pennsylvania Dutch, featuring hearts and tulips. Other long-term patterns include the Plaids and the Intaglios. While several other patterns were developed, they were short-lived. One of the most elusive patterns, Palm Tree, was sold only through a souvenir store in Florida owned by one of the Purinton's sons. In addition to dinnerware, Purinton also produced a line of floral ware, including planters for NAPCO. They did contract work for Esmond Industries and RUBEL, who were both distributors in New York. They made the Howdy Doody cookie jar and bank for Taylor Smith & Taylor; both items are highly collectible.

The pottery was sold to Taylor, Smith & Taylor in 1958 and closed in 1959 due to heavy competition from foreign imports. Most items are not marked, but collectors find their unusual shapes easy to identify. A small number of items were ink stamped 'Purinton Slip-ware.' Some of the early Wellsville pieces were hand signed 'Purinton Pottery,' and several have emerged carrying the signature 'Wm. H. Blair' or simply 'Blair.' Blair's pieces command a premium price.

Apple, canister, tall, oval, 9", ea $50 to	60.00
Apple, cruets, sq, 5", pr	75.00
Apple, cup, 2½"	11.00
Apple, pickle dish, 6"	95.00
Apple, planter, rum jug shape, 6½"	55.00
Apple, plate, chop, 12"	50.00
Apple, plate, dinner, 10"	30.00
Apple, relish, 3 rnd sections	25.00
Apple, snack set, plate & cup	110.00
Apple, sugar bowl, 3¼"	21.00
Apple, teapot, 3½-cup	75.00
Apple, tumbler, 12-oz	20.00
Brown Intaglio, bowl, cereal, 5½"	6.50
Brown Intaglio, chop plate, 12"	20.00
Brown Intaglio, oil cruet, w/cork stopper	27.00
Brown Intaglio, pickle dish, 6"	20.00
Brown Intaglio, shakers, mini mug, pr	12.00
Cactus, teapot, 4-cup, rare	235.00
Chartreuse, lap plate & cup	35.00
Chartreuse, wall pocket, 3½"	50.00
Crescent, teapot, 2-cup	50.00
Fruit, creamer, 3"	20.00
Fruit, Dorothy Purinton sgn plate, 12", min	650.00
Fruit, jug, Oasis, rare, min	750.00
Fruit, sugar bowl, 3"	32.00
Fruit, tumbler, 12-oz, $16 to	20.00
Grapes, bowl, range, w/lid, 5"	45.00
Heather Plaid, grease jar, 5"	60.00
Howdy Doody cookie jar	350.00
Intaglio, cookie jar, oval, 9"	75.00
Intaglio, tea & toast set (cup & lap plate), 2½" & 8½"	25.00
Intaglio, tray, roll, 11"	35.00

Ivy-Red, coffeepot, 8-cup	25.00
Ivy-Red, honey jug, 6¼"	15.00
Ivy-Yellow, jug, Dutch, 2-pt	20.00
Maywood, plate, dinner, 9½"	30.00
Maywood, shakers, mini jug, pr	35.00
Ming Tree, c/s	30.00
Ming Tree, sprinkler can, 7"	50.00
Mountain Rose, cookie jar, oval, 9"	125.00
Mountain Rose, decanter, 5"	45.00
Mountain Rose, wall pocket, 3½"	65.00
Normandy Plaid, canister, apartment sz, 5½"	45.00

Normandy Plaid, cookie jar, $65.00 to $70.00. (Photo courtesy Susan Morris-Snyder)

Normandy Plaid, grease jar, w/lid, 5½"	60.00
Palm Tree, basket planter, 6¼"	100.00
Palm Tree, shakers, Pour & Shake, pr	75.00
Peasant Garden, pitcher, Rubel mold, 5"	125.00
Peasant Garden, shakers, jug style, mini, 2½", pr	65.00
Pennsylvania Dutch, honey jug, 6¼"	75.00
Pennsylvania Dutch, platter, meat, 12"	50.00
Pennsylvania Dutch, shakers, mini jug, pr	60.00
Pennsylvania Dutch, shakers, pour & shake, pr	75.00
Petals, honey jug, 6¼"	15.00
Saraband, cookie jar, oval, w/lid, 9½"	100.00
Saraband, platter, 12"	30.00
Seafoam, shakers, 3", pr	55.00
Tea Rose, cr/sug bowl, w/lid	95.00
Turquoise (Intaglio), plate, dinner, 9¾"	35.00

Purses

Purses from the early 1800s are often decorated with small, brightly colored glass beads. Cut steel beads were popular in the 1840s and remained stylish until about 1930. Purses made of woven mesh date back to the 1820s. Chain-link mesh came into usage in the 1890s, followed by the enamel mesh bags carried by the flappers in the 1920s. Purses are divided into several categories by (a) construction techniques — whether beaded, embroidered, or a type of needlework; (b) material — fabric or metal; and (c) design and style. Condition is very important. Watch for dry, brittle leather or fragile material. For those interested in learning more, we recommend *More Beautiful Purses* and *Combs and Purses* by Evelyn Haertigi; *Purse Masterpieces* by Lynell Schwartz (Collector Books); and *100 Years of Purses, 1880s to 1980s*, by Ronna Lee Aikins (Collector Books). Unless otherwise noted, our values are for examples in 'like-new' condition, showing very little if any wear. Our advisors for this category are Katie Joe Monsour and Ronna Lee Aikins. They are listed in the Direcrtory under Pennsylvania.

Alligator, bl-gr Kelley style, snap closure, w/hdl, 1950s, 8x11x2"	215.00
Alligator, brn w/gold fr, Lesco/Saks Fifth Ave, 7½x11x3½", EX	85.00
Alligator, dk brn w/drawstring top, w/hdl, 1940s, 8x11", EX	95.00
Beaded pearls, blk & wht seed pearl floral, 1935, 5x6", $23 to	33.00

Beaded pearls, floral, clutch, R Gorwood, 1940s, 4x7", $20 to 30.00
Beaded pearls, wht w/blk diamondesque front, 1940s, 3x7", $20 to .40.00
Beaded pearls, wht, gold-tone fr & chain, Carolyne Barlon, 1940s, 6x8"... 35.00
Beaded, blk & wht dog on bl, blk fr, mini, 3x3", $135 to 165.00
Beaded, blk & wht, cloth-lined beaded strap, 1950s, 8x12", $60 to.85.00
Beaded, blk satin w/heavy beads on flap, Brand TKK, 1965, 6x8½".35.00
Beaded, bold mc Deco design, Bakelite fr, bl satin lining, 1920, 8x6"... 420.00
Beaded, brn striped front w/blk bk, UKK, Hong Kong, 1960s, 12x14" ..60.00

Beaded, cut steel, with pressed brass frames, circa 1926, each $650.00 to $685.00. (Photo courtesy Neal Auction Company)

Beaded, mc earth tones, clutch, Sears catalog, 1937, $28 to 38.00
Beaded, mc geometric pattern on blk, bottom fringe, 1940s, 11½x9" ..25.00
Beaded, orange & blk check pattern, drawstring, fringe, 1925, 6½x3".. 150.00
Beaded, pastels on cream, clutch, 1940s, 6x9", $40 to..................... 60.00
Beaded, sm bl beads, gold-tone fr/chain, bottom tassel, 1910, 8x6", VG.. 175.00
Beaded, tiny cream beads on wht, Lemured Petite, 1950s, 9x12", $80 to.. 100.00
Beaded, wht & pastels, chain drawstring, 1950s, 9½x9", $50 to..... 80.00
Beaded, wht, gr, bl & yel on red, red Bakelite fr, Poppy Bag, 1945, 7"..55.00
Fabric, blk floral, clutch, Majestic in gold, 1972, 5x8", $30 to 45.00
Fabric, circular silver glitter design, 5" chain, 1970s, 5x9", $50 to . 70.00
Fabric, cream w/pk floral, hinged, 12" chain, 1950, 7x10", $35 to . 50.00
Fabric, Flower Basket, Enid Collins, 8¼x11x3½", EX................... 175.00
Fabric, It Grows on Trees, Enid Collins, 1963, 11x13x4", EX...... 115.00
Fabric, mc paisley, wide straw hdl, 1940s, 12x10", $40 to.............. 65.00
Fabric, Mira Flores, Enid Collins, 1966, EX.................................. 110.00
Fabric, Sea Garden, Enid Collins, jeweled seahorse/fish/plants, 1965 ... 260.00
Felt, rhinestones & metal in starburst design, clutch, 1950s, 3x5" ..155.00
Leather, ostrich, gold-tone fr & clasp, Town & Country Shoes, 8½x8".. 65.00
Leather, tooled butterflies/etc on brn, Bakelite clasp, strap, Meeker...135.00
Leather, tooled floral/basketweave on brn, wrapped hdl, '60s, 12" W ... 125.00
Leather, tooled leaves, bucket style w/whipstitch border, 14x13x5"...110.00
Leather, tooled satchel style w/strap hdl, 1960s-70s, 16x13x8" 90.00
Lucite, blk cylinder w/gold-tone clasps, curved hdls, Miles Orig, 11".. 330.00
Lucite, brn grained case w/intaglio-cut hinged lid, 8" L 160.00
Lucite, clear w/cvgs, rhinestones & gold on sides, 1950s, 3x8x4".. 400.00
Lucite, clear w/rhinestones & pearl tiles, Wiesner, 3⅝x9x3½"+hdl ...395.00
Lucite, gr w/gold threads & rhinestones, Patricia of Miami, 8", +hdl.. 500.00
Lucite, mc feathering w/gold, circle hdl, Myles Orig, 1950s, 10¾" L... 275.00
Lucite, silver & gray w/clear eng floral top, ftd, Rialt of NY, 1950s .. 120.00
Mesh, 14k yel gold w/hinged closure w/3 sm dmns, 20.2dwt, 2¾" L. 750.00
Mesh, Alumesh flamingo pk, cream celluloid fr & hdl, 1930s, 5x8" .. 85.00
Mesh, gold-tone, gold-tone fr borders flap, #1519246, 1970s, 4½x8"...65.00
Mesh, shiny gold-tone, 19" chain, BEE mk, 1970s, 6½x9", $70 to. 80.00
Mesh, silver-tone w/bobcat design, chain, Whiting & Davis, 1910, 7x5".. 175.00
Mesh, silver-tone, emb floral fr, w/chain, 1900-10, $85 to............ 100.00
Satin, blk, gold-tone fr, chain & clasp, 1960s, 5¾x10½", $20 to.... 40.00
Satin, dk gr, rhinestones gold-tone fr, Mel-Ton, 1950s, 8x9", $70 to.. 90.00
Sequined, gold w/blk trim & hdl, Delill Made in China, 1970s, 7x8"..50.00
Sequined, gold-tone, bead trim, drawstring, 1940s, 7x5", $30 to ... 40.00
Snakeskin, blk, brn & copper, 4 sm ft, gold-tone fr, 1950s, 8x11".. 55.00
Straw, cream, gold-tone hdls & buckle clasp, Fashion Imports, 7x8½" . 100.00
Straw, red w/yel & bl stripe, clutch, Anton Made in Italy, 1980, 13" L... 70.00
Straw, tortoiseshell Lucite hdls, Hand Made British Hong Kong, 9x12"..100.00
Straw, tortoiseshell Lucite hdls, Simon...Mister Ernest, 1945, 7x11"....65.00

Tapestry, floral on cream w/blk border, gold-tone fr & hdl, 1955, 6x9" ..80.00
Tapestry, floral w/village scene center, blk fr, 7x9", $450 to.......... 550.00
Tapestry, floral, brass fr & clasp, vinyl hdl, Empress, 1940s, $60 to ..80.00
Tapestry, floral, Lucite hdl, Dover Made in USA, 1945, 11x14", $70 to. 90.00
Tapestry, geometric floral on shield shape, braid hdl, 7x5", $450 to . 550.00
Tapestry, gr, red & bl floral on blk fabric, vinyl fr & hdl, 1940s...... 85.00
Tapestry, mc birds on cream, filigree jeweled fr, 9½x7", $750 .... 850.00
Vinyl, 3-toned brn, gold-tone fr, dbl hdls, Kismet Creations, 6x13"... 65.00
Vinyl, blk, scalloped tortoiseshell fr & hdl, 1940s, 7x9", $50 to..... 75.00
Vinyl, pk, gold-tone clasp, 5" hdl, Bobbi Jermone, 1950s, 10x10" . 55.00
Vinyl, silver-tone, crown clasp, w/chain, 1960s, 4¾x8", $30 to...... 40.00
Vinyl, yel, gold-tone fr & clasp, yel hdl, 1962, 5½x12½", $40 to ... 60.00
Wood, Enid Collins, Texas, 'Love,' bead accents, 8" L, $145 to... 160.00
Wood, pea gr, floral design, wht Lucite hdl, 1960s, 9x4¾" 110.00

Pyrography

Pyrography, also known as wood burning, Flemish art, or poker work, is the art of burning designs into wood or leather and has been practiced over the centuries in many countries.

In the late 1800s pyrography became the hot new hobby for thousands of Americans who burned designs inspired by the popular artists of the day including Mucha, Gibson, Fisher, and Corbett. Thousands of wooden boxes, wall plaques, novelties, and pieces of furniture that they purchased from local general stores or from mail-order catalogs were burned and painted. These pieces were manufactured by companies such as The Flemish Art Company of New York and Thayer & Chandler of Chicago, who printed the designs on wood for the pyrographers to burn. This Victorian fad developed into a new form of artistic expression as the individually burned and painted pieces reflected the personality of the pyrographers. The more adventurous started to burn between the lines and developed a style of 'allover burning' that today is known as pyromania. Others not only created their own designs but even made the pieces to be decorated. Both these developments are particularly valued today as true examples of American folk art. By the 1930s its popularity had declined. Like Mission furniture, it was neglected by generations of collectors and dealers. The recent appreciation of Victoriana, the Arts and Crafts Movement, the American West, and the popularity of turn-of-the-century graphic art has rekindled interest in pyrography which embraces all these styles.

Key: hb — hand burned

Bedroom set, hb/pnt, Wm Rogers/Forusville PA, 1904-07, 3-pc . 4,000.00
Box, flatware, factory burned/pnt poinsettias, Rogers, 9x11x5".... 195.00
Box, hb/pnt lady petting horse amid flowers, 1920s, 1⅛x13x4½"... 70.00

Box, Indian maiden, pottery and baskets, silk lining, Flemish Art mark on base, slight wear, 9x11", $100.00. (Photo courtesy Tom Harris Auctions on LiveAuctioneers.com)

Box, lady w/flowing hair, Flemish Art Co, 1909, 11¼x4¼" 120.00
Box, Miller Bros Steel Pens, 1900, stamped to look hb, 7" L, +contents.. 45.00
Catalog, Thayer-Chandler, Chicago, 1904, 92 pgs, 12 in full color...27.00
Checker/backgammon brd, red & gr decor/glass bead insets, 30x15" . 1,550.00
Chest, blanket, hb/pnt swans/lady's head/flower/etc, ca 1890....... 850.00
Cue holder, hb pool-hall scene, folk art, unique 650.00

Etching set, Snow White, Disney/Marks, 1938, electric pen, complete . 175.00
Frame, hb/pnt cherries, standing type, 7½x6", EX 85.00
Frame, owls in tree, 2 Is Company, 2 oval cutouts 145.00
Humidor, trees & landscape on lid, gold & bl pnt on pine, 3x9x6"....295.00
Knife rack, hb Lizzie Borden w/axe, 5 hooks below, rare.............. 550.00
Panel, basswood, burned/pnt orange, Thayer-Chandler, 16x30" .. 465.00
Plaque, cvd/burned/pnt strawberry basket, 3-ply, 12" dia............... 70.00
Plaque, Native Am chief, etched/tinted, JP Graham, 30" dia 840.00
Plaque, Nouveau lady w/cherries, 19½"... 150.00
Plaque, Oddfellows, hb IOOF in center, early 1900s, 16x10"......... 87.00
Ribbon holder, hb/pnt Sunbonnet babies (3), 5x12" 160.00
Table, hb/pnt daisies & scrolls, lower shelf, 16½x11x11" 315.00
Tie rack, factory stamp, HP soldier/nurse/sailor, WWI motto 125.00
Toy chest, shepherdess/sheep/boy playing flute, 14x27x15"............ 75.00

Quezal

The Quezal Art Glass and Decorating Company of Brooklyn, New York, was founded in 1901 by Martin Bach. A former Tiffany employee, Bach's glass closely resembled that of his former employer. Most pieces were signed 'Quezal,' a name taken from a Central American bird. After Bach's death in 1920, his son-in-law, Conrad Vohlsing, continued to produce a Quezal-type glass in Elmhurst, New York, which he marked 'Lustre Art Glass.' Examples listed here are signed unless noted otherwise. For more information we recommend *The Collector's Encyclopedia of American Art Glass* by our advisor, John A. Shuman III.

Bottle, perfume, purple/bl/gr/gold irid, 7"....................................... 650.00
Bowl, silver bl irid, Ambergris, flared & raised rim, 11¼"............. 850.00
Bowl, sq, gold irid, 5¾" 600.00
Chandelier, 3 tiers, amber sections, Herringbone, 40"...............13,000.00
Lamp, boudoir, leaf design opal glass shade, pulled threads, 4¾".. 250.00
Lamp, bronze telescope base, 4 lily lights, 24"............................2,000.00
Plate, gold irid, bl/pk/purple highlights, sgn, 11.......................... 350.00
Salt, bl irid, sgn, 1⅜"... 450.00
Salt, gold lustre, sgn, 2½"... 125.00
Shade, gr leaf design, bell shape, gold lining, 5½" dia.................. 150.00
Shade, wht irid ground, yel border, Pulled Feather, 1920s, 6" dia. 300.00
Sherbet, gold int, irid opal, Pulled Feather, sgn, 4" 1,500.00
Vase, amber & bl opal & irid, King Tut, 4" 1,200.00
Vase, bl & purple lustre, Classic shape, 5½" 700.00
Vase, bl irid, 11"..1,250.00
Vase, floriform, Trumpet blossom, golden amber irid, 6¾".........2,400.00

Vase, gold with green leaves, fold-down rim, 6", $2,000.00 to $3,000.00. (Photo courtesy Mark Mussio, Cincinnati Art Galleries, LLC/John A. Shuman III)

Vase, JIP, gr w/irid bl, gr & purple swirls, ca 1900, 11"...............2,000.00
Vase, silver o/l, bl/gold/rose/gr irid highlights, 8½" 3,500.00

Quilts

Quilts, though a very practical product, nevertheless represent an art form which expresses the character and the personality of the designer. During the seventeenth and eighteenth centuries, quilts were considered a necessary part of a bride's hope chest; the traditional number required to be properly endowed for marriage was a 'baker's dozen'! American colonial quilts reflect the English and French taste of our ancestors. They would include the classifications known as Lindsey-Woolsey and the central medallion appliqué quilts fashioned from imported copper-plate printed fabrics.

By 1829 spare time was slightly more available, so women gathered in quilting bees. This not only was a way of sharing the work but also gave them the opportunity to show off their best handiwork. The hand-dyed and pieced quilts emerged, and they are now known as sampler, album, and friendship quilts. By 1845 American printed fabric was available.

In 1793 Eli Whitney developed the cotton gin; as a result, textile production in America became industrialized. Soon inexpensive fabrics were readily available, and ladies were able to choose from colorful prints and solids to add contrast to their work. Both pieced and appliquéd work became popular. Pieced quilts were considered utilitarian, while appliquéd quilts were shown with pride of accomplishment at the fair or used when itinerant preachers traveled through and stayed for a visit. Today many collectors prize pieced quilts and their intricate geometric patterns above all other types. Many of these designs were given names: Daisy and Oak Leaf, Grandmother's Flower Garden, Log Cabin, and Ocean Wave are only a few. Appliquéd quilts involved stitching one piece — carefully cut into a specific form such as a leaf, a flower, or a stylized device — onto either a large one-piece ground fabric or an individual block. Often the background fabric was quilted in a decorative pattern such as a wreath or medallions. Amish women scorned printed calicos as 'worldly' and instead used colorful blocks set with black fabrics to produce a stunning pieced effect. To show their reverence for God, the Amish would often include a 'superstition' block which represented the 'imperfection' of Man!

One of the most valuable quilts in existence is the Baltimore album quilt. Made between 1840 and 1860 only 300 or so still exist today. They have been known to fetch over $100,000.00 at prominent auction houses in New York City. Usually each block features elaborate appliqué work such as a basket of flowers, patriotic flags and eagles, or the Oddfellow's heart in hand. The border can be sawtooth, meandering, or swags and tassels.

During the Victorian period the crazy quilt emerged. This style became the most popular quilt ever in terms of sheer numbers produced. The crazy quilt was formed by random pieces put together following no organized lines and was usually embellished by elaborate embroidery stitches. Fabrics of choice were brocades, silks, and velvets.

Another type of quilting, highly prized and rare today, is trapunto. These quilts were made by first stitching the outline of the design onto a solid sheet of fabric which was backed with a second having a much looser weave. White was often favored, but color was sometimes used for accent. The design (grapes, flowers, leaves, etc.) was padded through openings made by separating the loose weave of the underneath fabric; a backing was added and the three layers quilted as one.

Besides condition, value is judged on intricacy of pattern, color effect, and craftsmanship. Examine the stitching. Quality quilts have from 10 to 12 stitches to the inch. A stitch is defined as any time a needle pierces through the fabric. So you may see five threads but 10 (stitches) have been used. In the listings that follow, examples rated excellent have minor defects, otherwise assume them to be free of any damage, soil, or wear. Also assume that all the stitching is hand done; any machine work will be noted. Values given here are auction results; retail may be somewhat higher. Our advisor for Quilts is Matt Lippa; he is listed in the Directory under Alabama.

Key: qlt — quilted, quilting

Amish

Block w/Sawtooth & blk borders, crib sz, 38x36" 6,000.00
Diamonds & squares, gr/purple/brn, 1950s, full sz......................1,950.00

Hole in the Barn Door, bl/purple/blk/brn/tan, hired man's, 68x35"....3,600.00
Hole in the Barn Door, rows of dmns, bl/purple/blk, MO, 1940, 58x84" ... 175.00
Pierced stars/blocks/bars, mc wool, crib sz, 44½x34" 13,250.00

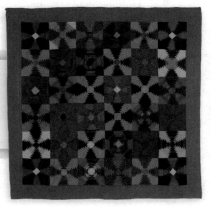

Pineapple variant, late nineteenth century, 79x79", $1,500.00. (Photo courtesy Pook & Pook, Inc. on LiveAuctioneers.com)

Spider Web Star, mc on bl w/blk borders, rose backing, stains, 33x62".260.00
Sunshine & Shadow, mc cottons, blk plumes/dmns qlt, 78x78" .. 375.00
Sunshine & Shadows, red/bl/purple, printed floral bk, 88x85"..1,100.00
Triangular designs w/sawtooth borders, superb hand qlt, 82x84". 3,000.00
Triangular patchwork w/pinwheel flowers on blk, bl borders, 35x35" ...360.00

Mennonite

Bar, dk gr print & orange stripes, att PA, 88x77" 515.00
Basket, red/gr/yel on wht w/gr grid, yel/gr borders, PA, full sz....... 600.00
Hexagon Ring, calicos, 1¼" blocks/2½" hexagons, 91x79" 480.00
Shoo-Fly, wools/cottons, 2-pc flannel bk, ca 1900, 80x67" 780.00
Straight Furrows Log Cabin, cotton, wool border, 1890s, 77x76" . 480.00
X pattern, mc w/pk & bl sashing, sawtooth border, 94x83" 1,025.00

Pieced

8-Pointed Star (9), mc on red, fine qlt, 84x84" 2,750.00
Block & Star, bl/wht/lav/yel, PA, 19th C, 78x84" 4,575.00
California Rose, 9 trapunto roses, mc on wht, 19th C, 101x94".. 1,200.00
Carpenter's Wheel, cotton, 3-color, PA, ca 1885, 86x85" 7,200.00
Christmas Tree, red & gr on wht, leaf qlt, ca 1910, 92x91 ....1,200.00
Crazy, silks/brocades/velvets/ribbons, embr & gold stitches, 60x60" .. 5,300.00
Crazy, silks/brocades/velvets/ribbons, feather qlt, KY, 1880s, 60x60" .4,500.00
Dmn-in-Sq, gr/red/bl, cotton bk, patterned hq, late 19th C, 80x80" .6,000.00
Dmn-Pattern Star w/birds & hearts, bl/wht/yel, PA, 19th C, 85x75" . 4,350.00
Drunkard's Path, red & wht, sawtooth border, dtd 1891, 78x78" ..1,325.00
Feather Star Variant, yel-orange & gr, wreath/chain qlt, MD, 84x84" 2,400.00
Floral chintz pcs in bands, PA, 1850s, 106x92" 2,650.00
Flying Geese, chintz border, PA, 19th C, 100x106" 3,150.00
Friendship, floral sqs, gr/red/yel/wht, stains, 100x95" 3,000.00
Geometric Album Block, pk & wht gingham, ca 1900, full sz ..3,600.00
Geometric patchwork, printed cotton/chintz, dtd 1853, 90x93" ..2,650.00
Goose in Flight, mc on cream, hs, 81x82" 1,350.00
Honey Bee, vegetal dyes on wht, feather/stipple qlt, 1870s, 76x77" ...1,200.00
Irish Chain, pk & wht, wht border, 1930, full sz 3,600.00
Joseph's Coat of Many Colors, rainbow colors, patterned qlt, 82x82". 1,950.00
LeMoyne Star, bl & wht w/Birds in Air border, patterned qlt, 96x93" ...635.00
Log Cabin w/sawtooth edge, bls & lavs, early 20th C, 86x86" ..1,950.00
Log Cabin w/Windmill Blades, tan & red on wht, 1880s, 88x77". 900.00
Log Cabin w/Windmill Blades, wool challis, 1870s, 83x77" 2,350.00
Log Cabin, mc w/piano key border, homespun red checked bk, 78x66".3,000.00
Odd Fellows pattern, dress prints, sawtooth border, plume qlt, 90x78"...635.00
Star & satellites w/lightning bolt border, mc on gr, 86x88" 3,600.00
Star w/in Star, mc cotton prints, dmn qlt, 102x102" 1,265.00

Sunburst, calicos on wht, sgn ABD, ca 1840, 94x92" 1,200.00
Tree of Life, yel & gr on red, wreaths/rising sun qlt, 78x75" 2,150.00
Trip Around the World, calicos, 9-patch corners, 1880s, 82x84" .10,200.00
Variable Star, printed/solid calicos, patterned qlt, 1880s, 84x82" ... 1,325.00

Quimper

Quimper pottery bears the name of the Breton town in northwestern France where it has been made for over 300 years. Production began in 1690 when Jean-Baptiste Bousquet settled into a small workshop in the suburbs of Quimper, at Locmaria. There he began to make the hand-painted, tin enamel-glazed earthenware which we know today as faience. By the last quarter of the nineteenth century, there were three factories working concurrently: Porquier, de la Hubaudiere (the Grand Maison), and Henriot. All three houses produced similar wares which were decorated with scenes from the everyday life of the peasant folk of the region. Their respective marks are an AP or a P with an intersecting B (similar to a clover), an HB, and an HR (which became HenRiot after litigation in 1922). The most desirable pieces were produced during the last quarter of the nineteenth century through the first quarter of the twentieth century. These are considered to be artistically superior to the examples made after World War I and II with the exception of the Odetta line, which is now experiencing a renaissance among collectors here and abroad.

Most of what was made was faience, but there was also a history of utilitarian gres ware (stoneware) having been produced there. In 1922 the Grande Maison HB revitalized this ware and introduced the line called Odetta, examples of which seemed to embody the bold spirit of the Art Deco style. The companion faience pieces of this period and genre are classified as Modern Movement examples and frequently bear the name of the artist who designed the mold. These artist-signed examples are dramatically increasing in value.

Currently there are two factories still producing Quimper pottery. La Societe Nouvelle des Faienceries de Quimper is owned by Sarah and Paul Jenessens along with a group of American investors. Their mark is a stamped HB-Henriot logo. The other, La Faiencerie d'art Breton, is operated by the direct descendents of the owners of the Quimper pottery factories. Their pieces are marked with an interlocked F and A conjoined with an inverted B. Other marks include HQF which is the Henriot Quimper France mark and HBQ, the HB Quimper mark. If you care to learn more about Quimper, we recommend *Quimper Pottery: A French Folk Art Faience* by Sandra V. Bondhus, our advisor for this category, whose address can be found in the Directory under Connecticut.

Figurine, Breton man, Perrica decor riche base, HR Quimper, 10", mint, $325.00. (Photo courtesy Sandra V. Bondhus)

Bannette, wedding scene w/decor riche, HBQ, 10x8" 350.00
Bell, bagpipe shape, peasant man/floral spray, HQF, 3" 125.00
Bowl, courting peasant couple, scalloped, HRQ, 12" 150.00
Bowl, red petals/bl dots in garland, geometric center, HBQ, 1x4".. 20.00
Bowl, rooster strutting, a la touche garland, att AP, 4x11" 150.00
Box, lady & flower garland, 8-pointed star-shaped lid, HBQ 8, 4" ..200.00

Cake plate, Botanique, floral spray/insect, PB, 4x8" 1,200.00
Charger, Breton musician, decor riche, HBQ, 13" 375.00
Charger, dancing couple, nosegays border, HBQ, 14" 220.00
Charger, geometric snowflakes, bl tones, HQ 90, 11¼" 80.00
Compote, Mistletoe, couple in meadow, hdls, HRQ, 11x7" 400.00
Figurine, Colaik, man w/walking stick, HQF 197, 3" 85.00
Figurine, Marik, lady w/folded umbrella, HA 156, 3", NM 85.00
Figurine, Ste Anne in ermine robe, child Mary beside, HQF 127, 5".. 85.00
Figurine, Village Breton couple, HenRiot...JES (Sevellec), 3" 200.00
Inkewll, dbl, stamp tray, Breton couple/ermines, HBQ, 4x8x4" ... 250.00
Inkwell, dbl, man w/cup, demi-fantasie, HQF 95, 3½x6¾" 250.00
Inkwell, lady w/basket/bl lattice, demi-fantasie, HQF, 3x3" 120.00
Inkwell, man playing bagpipes, decor riche, HRQ, 4" 240.00
Jardiniere, piqué fleurs chest w/false drws, HRQ, sm rpr 1,350.00
Jug, lady flanked by flowering plants, Henriot Quimper France, 7", NM... 150.00
Match holder, Breton man, bk: lady, flowers/dots, HRQ, 2" 120.00
Mustard pot, peasant man & plants, gr sponged hdl, w/lid, HR, 3".. 130.00
Pitcher, Breton couple/flowers, faience populaire, HB, 19th C, 10", NM.. 100.00
Pitcher, geometric Modern Movement, Breton man hdl, Fouillen, 5".. 325.00
Pitcher, Grecian ewer form, dancing couple, decor riche, HQ 103, 17"... 750.00
Pitcher, tennis ball pattern, geometrics, HQF, 7" 125.00
Plate, bl croisille lattice/stars/mc bands, HBQ, ca 1900, 9⅛" 125.00
Plate, crab among branches, cobalt border, HRQ, 8" 850.00
Plate, lady knitting, purple coif, Avergne, HB, 9", NM 180.00
Plate, lady w/fish basket, floral sprays, HB, 19th C, 9" 175.00
Plate, luncheon, naive man w/glass, HB, 19th C, 7" 125.00
Platter, Breton man & lady, fish form, HBQ, 11x24" 200.00
Relish, Petit Breton, swan finial, 3-part, HQ, 2x12" 200.00
Salt shaker, Bigoudienne lady's head form, Gallard, HQ, 3", ea... 110.00
Snuff bottle, Breton man/fleur-de-lis, book form 150.00
Sugar bowl, Normandie, Modern Movement, Fouillen, rpl lid, 8" ..175.00
Tray, man playing flute, demi-fantasie, HQ 74, 9" 100.00
Vase, couple dancing/musicians/Crest of Brittany, hdls, HRQ, 13".. 500.00
Vase, lady spins/man w/bagpipes, horseshoe form, HB 5, 19th C, 5"... 450.00
Vase, lady w/distaff/man w/flute, demi-fantasie, HRQ, 7x5x2"...225.00
Vase, quintal, ivoire corbelle, peasant lady, HQ 90, 3", NM 70.00
Vase, tulipiere, lady w/chevrette, ermine tails, 3-tube, HB, 7x7" . 145.00
Wall pocket, lady & fleur-de-lis, conical, 1st Period PB, 5" 650.00
Wall pocket, man w/horn & flower, conical, 19th C, 10" 180.00
Wall pocket, peasant couple on shoe form w/curled toe, HB, flaw, 10".200.00

Albert Radford

Pottery associated with Albert Radford can be categorized by three periods of production. Pottery produced in Tiffin, Ohio (1896 – 1899), consists of bone china (no marked examples known) and high-quality jasperware with applied Wedgwood-like cameos. Tiffin jasperware is often impressed 'Radford Jasper' in small block letters. At Zanesville, Ohio, Radford jasperware was marked only with an incised, two-digit shape number, and the cameos were not applied but rather formed within the mold and filled with a white slip. Zanesville Radford ware was produced for only a few months before the Radford pottery was acquired by the Arc-en-Ciel company in 1903. Production in Zanesville was handled by Radford's father, Edward (1840 – 1910), who remained in Zanesville after Albert moved to Clarksburg, West Virginia, where the Radford Pottery Co. was completed shortly before Albert's death in 1904. Jasperware was not produced in Clarksburg, and the molds appear to have been left in Zanesville, where some were subsequently used by the Arc-en-Ciel pottery. The Clarksburg, West Virginia, pottery produced a standard glaze, slip-decorated ware, Ruko; Thera and Velvety, matt glazed ware often signed by Albert Haubrich, Alice Bloomer, and other artists; and Radura, a semimatt green glaze developed by Albert Radford's son, Edward. The Clarksburg plant closed in 1912.

Jardiniere and pedestal, majolica, birds and flowers, both pieces signed A. Radford, 41½", NM, $800.00. (Photo courtesy Cincinnati Art Galleries, LLC on LiveAuctioneers.com)

Jardiniere & ped, Ruko, poppies on brn, rpr, 29⅞" 725.00
Vase, floor, simple floral, bl/rose on olive, minor rim flakes, 22"... 635.00
Vase, Jasper, angels, bk: eagles, #23, 9⅜", NM 220.00
Vase, Jasper, Lincoln profile, bk: eagle w/shield, #12, 7" 325.00
Vase, Thera, flower on gr, slim, 12" 215.00
Vase, Velvety, blackberries on gr, sgn AH, bottle form, 11x4" 540.00
Vase, Velvety, heron by stream, wht on bl, slim, 19½" 4,250.00
Vase, Velvety, wild roses, #1463, 10" 360.00

Radios

Vintage radios are very collectible. There were thousands of styles and types produced, the most popular of which today are the breadboard and the cathedral. Consoles are usually considered less marketable, since their size makes them hard to display and store. For those wishing to learn more about the subject, we recommend *Collector's Guide to Antique Radios* by John Slusser and the staff of Radio Daze, available through Collector Books.

Unless otherwise noted in the descriptions, values are given for working radios in near mint to mint condition, and they could be 10% to 25% lower due to the current economic downturn. Our advisor for this category is Dr. E. E. Taylor; he is listed in the Directory under Indiana.

Key:
B — Bakelite	R/P — radio-phonograph
BC — broadcast	SW — short wave
pb — push button	tbl/m — table model

A-C Dayton, AC-9980 Navigator, console, wood, BC, 1929, $90 to. 145.00
A-C Dayton, XL-10, tbl/m, plate glass, BC, b/o, 1925, $400 to ... 580.00
Addison, 2C, red & marbelized butterscotch, bk missing, 6x10", EX . 3,000.00
Addison, B2B, tbl/m, plastic Deco style, BC, 1940, min 800.00
Adler, 325, console, wood, BC, highboy, inner dial, 1930, $140 to.. 180.00
Admiral, 4D11, portable, plastic, BC, b/o, 1948, $40 to................ 50.00
Admiral, 4L26, tbl/m, yel plastic, BC, 1958, $20 to 25.00
Admiral, 4L28, BC, B, 1958, $20 to... 50.00
Admiral, 5Z, tbl/m, plastic & chrome, BC, 1937, $90 to 105.00
Admiral, 6P32, portable, faux alligator, BC, palm tree grille, b/o... 80.00
Advance Electric, 88, cathedral, wood, BC, 1930, $220 to.......... 250.00
Air Castle, G-722, console-R/P, wood, BC, pb, 1948, $60 to 80.00
Air King, A-410, portable/camera, faux alligator, b/o, 1948, $100 to.. 145.00
Airline, 14BR-736A, tbl/m, wood, BC, SW, 1941, $50 to 75.00
Airline, 62-211, tombstone, wood, BC, b/o, 1936, $80 to............ 105.00
Amrad, 70 Sonata, console, walnut, highboy, BC, 1928, $140 to . 195.00
Amrad, AC-5-C, console, mahog, lowboy, BC, 1926, $240 to..... 300.00
Arvin, 255T, tbl/m, ivory plastic, BC, 1949, $40 to...................... 50.00
Arvin, 617 Rhythm Maid, tombstone, wood, BC, SW, 1936, $200 to...225.00
Atwater Kent, 33, console, wood, BC, b/o, 1927, $220 to............ 295.00
Atwater Kent, 112S, console, wood, BC, SW, 1934, $290 to....... 350.00
Belmont, 1170, console, wood, BC, SW, 1936, $140 to 180.00

Bendix, 114, tbl/m, brn plastic, BC, 1948, $270 to 320.00
Browning-Drake, 5-R, wood, BC, lift top, b/o, 1926, $140 to 180.00
Chelsea, Super Six, tbl/m, wood, BC, b/o, 1925, $130 to 170.00
Clarion, AC-70, cathedral, wood, convex-concave top, BC, 1931, $325 to ... 350.00
Coronado, 43-8160, tbl/m, plastic, BC, 1947, $100 to 135.00
Crosley Buddy Boy, 58, fancy wood case, 15½x17", VG 335.00
Crosley, 10-139, tbl/m, aqua plastic, BC, 1950, $100 to 135.00
Crosley, 48 Johnny Smoker, console, wood, sm, BC, 1931, $370 to. 495.00
Crosley, D10BE, tbl/m, bl plastic, BC, 1951, $140 to 180.00
Day-Fan, OEM-5, tbl/m, wood, BC, b/o, ca 1920s, $140 to 180.00
Dewald, 524, tombstone, wood, BC, 1931, $120 to 160.00
Echophone, S-3, cathedral, wood, BC, 1930, $220 to 290.00
Emerson, 517 Moderne, plastic, BC, 1947, $50 to 70.00
Eveready, 32, console, wood, BC, 1929, $160 to 220.00

Fada, 1000, orange, 6x10x5", VG, minimum value, $550.00. (Photo courtesy Conestoga Auction Company on LiveAuctioneers.com)

Farnsworth, AT-21, tbl/m, onyx 'beetle' plastic, BC, SW, 1939, $220 to.. 290.00
Fed, 141, tbl/m, mahog, BC, b/o, 1925, $480 to 600.00
Firestone, 4-A-115, tbl/m, wood, BC, 1953, $30 to 45.00
Garod, 5A2, tbl/m, plastic, BC, 1946, $50 to 70.00
Garod, EC, console, wood, highboy, BC, 1926, $180 to 240.00
General Electric, 328, console-R/P, blond wood, BC, FM, 1949, $60 to .. 80.00
General Electric, A-125, console, wood, BC, SW, LW, 1935, $170 to.. 230.00
General Electric, tbl/m, wood, BC, SW, 1946, $40 to 50.00
Gilfillan, 8-T, tombstone, wood, BC, SW, 1934, $270 to 360.00
Gilfillan, 119, console, wood, lowboy, BC, 1940, $270 to 360.00
Grunow, 1181, console, wood, BC, SW, 1937, $270 to 360.00
Howard, 400, console, wood, BC, SW, $140 to 180.00
Kadette, 649X, chair-side, wood, BC, SW, 1937, $110 to 145.00
Lafayette, D-140, tbl/m, ivory plastic, BC, 1940, $100 to 135.00
Majestic, 15A, tombstone, wood, BC, 1932, $110 to 145.00
Majestic, 3BC90-B, console, walnut, Deco, BC, SW, 1939, $160 to.. 220.00
Mantola, R-76262, chair-side, wood, BC, 1948, $80 to 105.00
Michigan, MRC-4, tbl/m, mahog, BC, b/o, 1923, $280 to 330.00
Motorola, 41S Sporter, portable, leatherette, BC, b/o, 1939, $40 to .. 55.00
Philco, 38-89K, console, wood, BC, SW, 1938, $100 to 135.00
RCA, R-4 Superette, cathedral, wood, BC, 1932, $290 to 350.00
Remler, MP5-5-3 Scottie, tbl/m, plastic, BC, 1946, $140 to 180.00
Sentinel, 3291, tbl/m, ivory plastic, BC, 1948, $40 to 50.00
Setchell-Carlson, 570, tbl/m, cylindrical, BC, 1950, $80 to 105.00
Silvertone, 4487, console, wood, BC, SW, 1937, $110 to 145.00
Westinghouse, H-354C7, console-R/P, wood, BC, FM, 1952, $70 to... 90.00
Westinghouse, WR-5, console, walnut, BC, 1930, $110 to 145.00

Novelty Radios

Beer Keg, Magic-Tone 900, 'spigot' is dial, BC, 1948, $240 to 325.00
Charlie McCarthy, Majestic, touched-up pnt, o/w EX, 1930s, 6x7"..1,680.00
Coca Cola cooler, red plastic, BC, 1949, $590 to 780.00
Colonial New World, globe on stand, plastic, BC, 1933, $800 to . 950.00
Horse (saddled) standing on radio base, Abbotwares Z477, BC, $270 to .. 360.00
Liquor Bottle, Magic-Tone 504, dial on neck, BC, 1947, $340 to. 460.00
Log Cabin, wood, knobs in windows, BC, ca 1935, $180 to 240.00
Marlboro cigarette pack, plastic w/metal foil, CDI, BC, $620 to . 830.00
Sailing Ship, Majestic Melody Cruiser, wood & chrome, BC, '46, $320 to.420.00
Stack of books, Sentinel 238-V, leatherette, BC, 1941, $150 to .. 205.00

Swank the Sports Car, 1960s, Japan, MIB, $50.00. (Photo courtesy B.S. Slosberg, Inc. Auctioneers on LiveAuctioneers.com)

Teakettle, Guild T/K 1577, wood, china & brass, ca 1959, $100 to ... 145.00
Treasure Chest, Majestic 381, wood, BC, 1933, $220 to 290.00

Transistor Radios

Post-World War II baby boomers, are rediscovering prized possessions of youth, their pocket radios. The transistor wonders, born with rock 'n roll, were at the vanguard of miniaturization and futuristic design in the decade which followed their introduction to Christmas shoppers in 1954. The tiny receiving sets launched the growth of Texas Instruments and shortly to follow abroad, Sony and other Japanese giants.

The most desirable sets include the 1954 four-transistor Regency TR-1 and colorful early Sony and Toshiba models. Certain pre-1960 models by Hoffman and Admiral represented the earliest practical use of solar technology and are also highly valued. To avoid high tariffs, scores of two-transistor sets, boys' radios, were imported from Japan with names like Pet and Charmy. Many early inexpensive transistor sets could be heard only with an earphone. The smallest sets are known as shirt-pocket models while those slightly larger are called coat-pockets. Early collectible transistor radios all have civil defense triangle markings at 640 and 1240 on the frequency dial and nine or fewer transistors. Very few desirable sets were made after 1963. Model numbers are most commonly found inside.

Admiral, 221, horizontal, 6 transistors, AM, 1958 .... 35.00
Admiral, Y701R, vertical, AM, ca 1960 .... 15.00
Airline, GEN-1202A, horizontal, 6 transistors, AM, 1962 .... 30.00
Arvin, 61R69, vertical, 6 transistors, AM, 1963 .... 25.00
Channel Master, 6528, horizontal, 6 transistors, AM, 1960 .... 20.00
Columbia, C-605, horizonal, 5 transistors, AM, 1962 .... 15.00
Crown, TR-680, vertical, 6 transistors, AM, ca 1960 .... 25.00
Delmonico, 7YR707, sq, 7 transistors, AM, 1965 .... 55.00
Emerson, 838, 1955... 125.00
Everplay, 2836A, vertical, 8 transistors, AM, 1963 .... 35.00
General Electric, P1818B, horizontal, 10 transistors, AM/FM, 1965 ... 10.00
General Electric, P745B, horizontal, 5 transistors, AM, 1958........ 25.00
Hitachi, WH-761M, vertical, 7 transistors, AM, 1961 .... 25.00
ITT, 6509, vertical, 9 transistors, AM/FM, 1963 .... 15.00
Jefferson-Travis, JT-D210, vertical, 4 transistors, AM, 1961 .... 30.00
Lafayette, FS-238, horizontal/desk set, 7 transistors, AM, 1964..... 25.00
Magnavox, 2AM-70, vertical, 7 transistors, AM, 1964 .... 30.00
MMA, F100, horizontal, 11 transistors, AM, 1963........................ 20.00
Motorola, X40S, vertical, 8 transistors, AM, 1962 .... 25.00
Olympic, 447, horizontal, 4 transistors, AM, 1957 .... 135.00
Philco, T-64, horizontal, 6 transistors, AM, 1963 .... 15.00
RCA, 1-TP-2E, vertical, 6 transistors, AM, 1961 .... 25.00
Regency, TR-11, vertical, 4 transistors, AM, 1958 .... 100.00
Sharp, FX-404, horizontal, 9 transistors, AM/FM, ca 1964 .... 25.00
Sony, TFM-951, horizontal, 9 transistors, AM, 1964..................... 30.00
Sony, TR-650, vertical, 6 transistors, AM, 1963............................ 40.00
Toshiba, 6TP-31A, vertical, 6 transistors, AM, 1963 .... 75.00
Truetone, DC3306, horizontal, 6 transistors, AM, 1963................ 20.00
Victoria, TR-650, vertical, 6 transistors, AM, 1961 .... 20.00

Westinghouse, H-730P7, horizontal, 7 transistors, AM, 1960........ 15.00
Zenith, Royal 150, vertical, 6 transistors, AM, 1962 .... 30.00

Railroadiana

Collecting railroad-related memorabilia has become one of America's most popular hobbies. The range of collectible items available is almost endless; not surprising, considering the fact that more than 185 different railroad lines are represented. Some collectors prefer to specialize in only one railroad, while others attempt to collect at least one item from every railway line known to have existed. For the advanced collector, there is the challenge of locating rarities from short-lived railroads; for the novice, there are abundant keys, buttons, linens, and paper items. Among the most popular specializations are dining-car collectibles — flatware, glassware, and dinnerware (china).

As is true in most collecting fields, scarcity and condition determine value and there is more interest in some railway lines than in others. Generally speaking, the interest is greater in the region serviced by that particular railroad.

Reproductions abound in railroadiana collectibles — from dinnerware and glassware to lanterns, keys, badges, belt buckles, timetables, and more. When a genuine railroad collectible sells for $100, $500, or $2,500, the counterfeiters are right there. Sadly, though, fantasy items selling for $10 and up have been around for many years. Railroad police badge replicas have glutted the market. They are professionally produced and only the expert is able to differentiate the replica from the original. Railroad drumheads, large (approximately 24" diameter) glass signs in metal cases used on the back end of all railroad observation cars to advertise a special train or a presidential foray, are surfacing. A good one like the Flying Crow from the Kansas City Southern Railroad might sell for $2,500, as will many others. When valuable items like these appear, unforunately the counterfeiters appear as well; it is important to 'know thy dealer.'

Values for most of our dinnerware, glassware, linen, silverplate, and timetables are actual selling prices. However, because prices are so volatile, the best pricing sources are often monthly or quarterly 'For Sale' lists: Golden Spike, P.O. Box 422, Williamsville, NY 14221. See also Badges.

Key:
BL — bottom logo
BS — backstamp
FBS — full backstamp
NBS — no backstamp
PAF — patent applied for
RR — railroad
ScL — Scammell Lamberton
SL — side logo
TL — top logo

Dinnerware

Many railroads designed their own china for use in their dining cars or company-owned hotels or stations. Some railroads chose to use stock patterns to which they added their name or logo; others used the same stock patterns without any added identification. A momentary warning: The railroad dinnerware market has fallen considerably and only the truly rare and scarce items are maintaining their value. For more information we recommend *Restaurant China, Volumes 1* and *2*, by Barbara J. Conroy (Collector Books).

Bowl, flat soup, UP, Columbine, BS w/Columbine, 5½" 185.00
Bowl, oatmeal, SP, Prairie Mtn Wildflowers, BS, 6" dia............... 180.00
Bowl, sauce, CRI&P, Sage Gr, RI TL, FBS, Buffalo, Albert Pick, 5"..650.00
Bowl, serving, WA & ORRR, Harriman Bl, SL, Maddock's, 6½" .1,325.00
Butter pat, ACL, Flora of the South, BS, Buffalo, 3½" 70.00
Butter pat, ATSF, Bleeding Bl, TL, Albert Pick, 3x3" 350.00
Butter pat, B&O, Capitol, rich gold, TL, ½3".............................. 178.00

Butter pat, Baltimore & Ohio, bl transfer, ScL, $40 to.................. 60.00
Butter pat, Chicago, N Shore & Milwaukee Elec, Fontenelle, NBS.. 90.00
Butter pat, DE & Hudson, Canberbury, NBS, no TL 10.00
Butter pat, Pullman, Indian Tree (w/flower but no tree), TM, 3¼"..45.00
Butter pat, Southern RR, Peach Blossom, TL, ScL, 3¼" 225.00
Butter pat, UP, Portland Rose, BS, 3½"..................................... 388.00
Child's mug, GN, Rocky, SL, 3" 155.00
Compote, CMStP&P, Peacock, ped ft, NBS, 2⅛x6½"................. 155.00
Creamer, IL Central, Louisiane, solid hdl, SL, ind, 2¼" 35.00
Creamer, MKT, Bl Bonnet, BS, Buffalo, 4" 335.00
Cup/saucer, ACL, Flora of the South, FBS, Buffalo..................... 110.00
Cup/saucer, CMStP&P, Dulany, Deco border, Buffalo, ea w/BS...865.00
Cup/saucer, demi, SP, Prairie Mtn Wildflowers, Syracuse............. 230.00
Cup/saucer, demi, Wabash, Banner, SL, Syracuse......................... 470.00
Cup/saucer, NP, Monad, SL & TL, NBS...................................... 330.00
Cup, bouillon, ATSF, CA Poppy, hdls, Made Expressly For..., BS. 210.00
Egg cup, dbl, UP, Desert Wildflower, custard cup-like, BS, 2¾x3" . 36.00
Gravy/sauceboat, Pullman, Calumet, w/hdl, SL, Bauscher, 5"...... 155.00
Hot food cover, B&O, Centenary, Thos Viaduct 1835, NBS, 5¾"...630.00
Hot water/chocolate pot, ATSF, Mimbreno, BS, 5½" 360.00
Hot water/chocolate pot, B&O, Centenary, ScL, 6"...................... 360.00
Ice cream shell, ATSF, Mimbreno, oval w/tab hdl, FBS, 5x5¼" ... 168.00
Ice cream shell, UP, Winged Streamliner, tab hdl, NBS, 4⅛" 30.00
Pitcher, ATSF, Bleeding Bl, SL, ScL, Albert Pick, 9" 45.00

Pitcher, B&O, blue transfer, Lamberton, 7", $1,920.00.
(Photo courtesy Alex Cooper Auctioneers, Inc. on LiveAuctioneers.com)

Pitcher, B&O, Centenary, bl int line, FBS, ScL, 7"......................960.00
Plate, Central of NJ, Seagull w/Sandy Hook TL, NBS, 9"............795.00
Plate, CP, cobalt floral, BS, Spode, 1915, 10" 150.00
Plate, grill, B&O, Centenary, 3-compartment, ScL, 10¼"............200.00
Plate, IL Central, Coral, Syracuse, 1948, 7¼" 30.00
Plate, luncheon, B&O, Centenary, ScL, 8"..................................60.00
Plate, service, ATSF, Turq Room, TM, bl BS, 1950, 10⅛".........2,175.00
Plate, service, C&O, Homestead Hotel Nature Study, Poppy, HP, BS, 11".160.00
Plate, service, CB&Q, Aksarben, TL, Bauscher, 1931, 10½" 4,225.00
Plate, Wabash, Banner, Follow the Flag TL, Syracuse, 1962, 9½".160.00
Plate, Wabash, Banner, TM, Syracuse, 7¼" 480.00
Platter, B&O, Centenary, Cumberland Narrows, PAF, BS, 11½" L..........300.00
Platter, GN, Glory of the West, Onondaga, RR stamp, 1940-57, 9".160.00
Teapot, CB&Q, cobalt, SL, Hall China, 9-oz 165.00
Teapot, KCS, Roxbury, NBS, ind, 4"...35.00
Teapot, SF, Mimbreno, BS, spout to hdl: 7½" 555.00

Glass

Beware — 'Fantasy' shot glasses abound. Fantasy items suggest the item was designed for railroad use, but in actuality the item is new and designed to confuse or deceive.

Ashtray, ATSF, Santa Fe pyro in cursive in bottom, 4½x3¼".........42.00
Ashtray, B&O, BL, SL & Capitol dome, 4½" 27.00
Ashtray, NYC emb in bottom, extended rests, 5½" 10.00
Bottle, beverage, Fred Harvey, Newton KS, side emb, aqua, 8"....260.00
Bottle, club soda, SFRR Fred Harvey Service, paper label, gr, 7¼" ..95.00

Bottle, milk, MOPAC Lines emb w/in circle, Ben Bush Farms, ⅓-pt...28.00
Brandy snifter, B&O, Capitol Dome SL+5 encircling lines, ftd, 4½"...85.00
Carafe, PRR, wheel-cut SL, unmk hinged SP lid/hdl, Internat'l, 9¼".415.00
Champagne, CMStP&P, etched box SL, hollow stem, 5"............145.00
Cordial, ATSF, etched Santa Fe (script) w/5 horizontal lines, 3¼"...120.00
Decanter/carafe, Grand Trunk Pacific, etched Fort Garry SL, 8½"..220.00
Goblet, Gulf, Mobile & OH, silkscreen winged SL, ftd pilsner, 6"...36.00
Pitcher, Wabash, Follow the Flag etched SL, silver fr, 10".........1,135.00
Shot glass, DL&W, etched Phoebe Snow SL, ftd, 3¼", $40 to.......75.00
Swizzle stick, B&O, Capitol Dome, bl, 4¾"...........................44.00
Swizzle stick, PRR keystone logo, Washington 7502, w/spoon feature, 6".16.00
Tumbler, C&O in bl silkscreen, thick base, flared rim, 4½"..........65.00
Tumbler, D&RG, optic inside, etched Curecanti SL, heavy base, 4".145.00
Tumbler, GN, etched Rocky SL, 5".....................................65.00
Tumbler, WP, concave horizontal ridge, Feather River pyro, SL, 3½".26.00
Wine stem, IL Central, etched dmn SL, 4½".............................88.00

Lamps

Adlake nonsweating, PRR, two red and two green lenses, electrified, $150.00. (Photo courtesy Stout Auctions on LiveAuctioneers.com)

Adlake nonsweating, marker, WP, 4 lenses+font+burner+bracket+bail..500.00
CNRy, P&A Mfg Waterbury Conn, kerosene burner, 2-pc, wall mt, 4½".85.00
Coach car, Patentee Hicks & Smith, wall mt, ca 1871-75, 17¼x10".575.00
Finger, Boston, PO Dewey & Co, tin w/glass font, orig burner, 1871, NM..100.00
Inspector's, Dietz Acme, unmk globe, complete..........................90.00
Oiler's/mechanic's, MOPAC, Eagle, short spout w/wick, L hdl....100.00
Signal, Adlake, 2 red/2 gr Kopp lenses, complete, 16¼"...............265.00
Station, Dietz Pioneer post type, clear globe, 25x13"....................600.00
Switch, Adlake, 2 lt bl & 2 dk bl lenses, mk PRR, 14"..................175.00
Switch, Handland, single bl lens, mk UPRR, 13".........................100.00

Lanterns

Before 1920 kerosene brakemen's lanterns were made with tall globes, usually 5⅜" high. These are most desirable to collectors and are usually found at the top of the price scale. Short globes from 1921 through 1940 normally measure 3½" in height, except for those manufactured by Dietz, which are 4" tall. (Soon thereafter, battery brakemen's lanterns came into widespread usage; these are not highly regarded by collectors and are generally not railroad marked.) All lanterns should be marked with the name or initials of the railroad — look on the top, the top apron, or the bell base (if it has one). Globes may be found in these colors (listed in order of popularity): clear, red, amber, aqua, cobalt, and two-color. Any lantern's value is enhanced if it has a colored globe.

Adlake Reliable, LA&SL, clear 5" globe, wire ring base, Pat 1909..735.00
B&M, PO Dewey, emb TM, SM gr globe, brass top, bell bottom base.2,185.00
Brakeman's, Adlake Kero, Hiram L Piper, red globe, complete, 15"...70.00
Brakeman's, Dressel, str fr, fuel pot/burner, bl-gr 3½" globe..........100.00
Brakeman's, New Haven RR, Dietz Vesta, amber globe w/K logo.125.00
Brakeman's, Oxweld #2155, carbide burner, flip cap, worn finish..55.00
Caboose, NP, 1 red/3 gr lenses......................................575.00
CN Rys, Adlake Kero, clear globe, gr pnt, 9x7"........................40.00
CNR, Adlake Kero, Hiram L Piper, tin & wire fr, red globe, 9¾".120.00

CNX, Adams & Westlake, clear Adlake globe, gr pnt, 1857, 10"+hdl..95.00
Contractor's, Dietz No 2 Blizzard, red pnt, rpl shade, 1930s...........35.00
Dietz Vesta, B&M etched on red shade, 10½"...............................330.00
Switch, St Louis, Handlan w/Adlake burner & wick, 16x10x10".175.00

Linens and Uniforms

Over the years the many railroad companies took great pride in their dining car table presentation. In the very early years of railroad dining car service, the linens used at the tables were of the finest quality white damask. Most railroads would add their company's logo, name, initials, or even a spectacular scene that would be woven into the cloth (white on white). These patterns were not evident unless the fabric was held at a particular angle to the light. The dining car staff's attire generally consisted of heavily starched, blinding white jackets with shiny buttons.

In later years, post-World War II, color began to be used for table linens. Florida railroads created some delightfully colorful items for the table as well as for headrests. The passenger train crew, the conductor, and the brakemen were generally clothed in black suits, white shirts, and black ties. Their head gear generally bore a badge denoting their position. These items have all become quite collectible. Sadly, however, replicas of badges and pins have been produced as well as 'fantasy' items (items that do not replicate an older item but are meant to mislead or deceive).

Key:
RBH — reinforced buttonholes   w/w — white on white damask

Apron, CA Zephyr, woven over Pullman logo, wht cotton............22.00
Bath mat, GN in red script on wht heavy toweling, 33x21"...........36.00
Blanket, CP woven on edge, Native Indian design, wool, 43x76"..200.00
Blanket, DM&NRR, includes embr Northland, wool, 80x68".....170.00
Blanket/lap robe, Wabash stitched in center, cotton, 36x44".........32.00
Cap, Union News, blk embr on wht cotton..............................18.00
Hat, ATSF Conductor, blk wool, bl & wht enamel & brass hat badge.180.00
Hat, CP Gateman, all woven into hat, buttons, braid...................565.00
Hat, GN Conductor, wool, GN Rocky enamel-on-brass pin........380.00

Hat, conductor's, Southern Railroad, badge, bullion stars, straw inner band, F.H. Newcomb Uniform Caps 136 Flatbush Ave. Brooklyn, VG, $90.00. (Photo courtesy Bart Long and Associates Realty and Auction, LLC on LiveAuctioneers.com)

Hat, Seaboard Porter, gr wool, gold cording, brass badge..............140.00
Hat, trainman's, RF&P, brn silk w/blk patent visor, 1925.............180.00
Headrest cover, CMStP&P Domeliners woven on edge, tan, RBH, 13x18"...18.00
Headrest cover, GM&O, red script on wht huck, brass grommets....7.00
Headrest, ATSF, wht huck w/bl Santa Fe logo on bl stripe, RBH, 15x18".26.00
Jacket, club car, IC Porter, IC logo & piping in orange on wht cotton..34.00
Napkin, El Paso & Southwestern, bow-tied ribbon logo, w/w, 23x23"...78.00
Napkin, SF center script logo w/scattered oak leaves, w/w, 23x23"..23.00
Napkin, SP, Daylight, coastal scenes, mc, 19x19"........................26.00
Pillowcase, SL&SF, The Frisco Line woven in bl on bl, 27x19"........5.00
Shop cloth, CMStP&P, safety slogans, 14x14", pkg of 10, M w/tag.10.00
Tablecloth, CP, orange center CP Dining Cars logo, w/w/, 63x52".114.00
Tablecloth, PRR, keystone logo woven all corners, w/w, 62x48"...85.00
Tablecloth, SOO, ornate boxed center logo, w/w, Simtex, 64x54"..70.00
Towel, bath, Seaboard woven in gr ea end, Dundee, 45x25"..........36.00
Towel, hand, CP woven on bl stripe, wht huck, 19x12"..................5.00

Towel, hand, NP, mc Monad logo on wht huck, 17x13" 12.50
Towel, hand, PRR woven in script on red stripe, wht huck, 18x12" . 17.00
Uniform, NYC, cap w/no badge, coat & vest w/buttons & woven insignia.. 135.00

Locks

Brass switch locks (pre-1920) were made in two styles: heart-shaped and Keen Kutter style. Values for the heart-shaped locks are determined to a great extent by the railroad they represent and just how its name appears on the lock. Most in demand are locks with large embossed letters; if the letters are small and incised, demand for that lock is minimal. For instance, one from the Union Pacific line (even with heavily embossed letters) may go for only $45.00, while the same from the D&RG railroad could go easily sell for $250.00. Old Keen Kutter styles (brass with a 'pointy' base) from Colorado & Southern and Denver & Rio Grande could range from $600.00 to $1,200.00. Steel switch locks (circa 1920 on) with the initials of the railroad incised in small letters — for example BN, L&H, and PRR — are usually valued at $20.00 to $28.00.

Romer & Co., No. 5, Newark, N.J., brass, marked on both lock and key, 3x2½", $75.00. (Photo courtesy Priddy's Auction Galleries, Inc. on LiveAuctioneers.com)

Car, UP Ry, CAR, brass, 4", w/chain & key................................... 100.00
Signal, B&MRR, Corbin on dust cover, steel 24.00
Signal, L&N, 1966, w/chain.. 25.00
Signal, NYCS, steel, 3½", w/key & chain 28.00
Signal, SL&SF, steel, 3½", w/key 48.00
Signal, Wabash, Yale, w/key 90.00
Signal, Yale & Town, brass 70.00
Switch, B&LE, Bohannan, brass, heart shape, 3¼", w/chain & key. 100.00
Switch, B&O Wilson Bohannan, bronze 50.00
Switch, N&WRY CO on hasp, Slaymaker, w/chain & key............ 80.00
Switch, P&LE, Adlake, w/chain & brass key................................. 130.00

Silver-Plated Flatware

Key: Int'l — International   R&B — Reed & Barton

Corn holders, NC&STL, SM, R&B, pr 140.00
Crumber, ATSF, Albany, BS, Harrison & Hawson, 12"................. 160.00
Fork, dinner, PRR keystone TL, Kings, Int'l, 7"........................... 32.00
Fork, dinner, PRR, Broadway, TL, Int'l, 7⅛" 15.00
Fork, dinner, SP, Broadway, BM, Int'l, 7⅛" 23.00
Fork, seafood, GN, Astoria, TM, Wallace, 6" 42.00
Fork, seafood, PRR, Broadway, TM, Int'l, 6"................................ 44.00
Ice tongs, UPRR, 7½" L 150.00
Iced teaspoon, Erie RR, Grecian, TM, Int'l, 7½" 28.00
Knife, dinner, Lehigh Valley, hammered, TM, Heinrichs, 9½" 70.00
Knife, luncheon, ACL, Zephyr, TM, Int'l, 7" 14.00
Ladle, condiment, UP, Windsor, BM, Int'l, 6" 30.00
Ladle, sauce, DE & Hudson, Roal, D&H TM, R&B, 7"................ 55.00
Ladle, sauce, NYC, Century, BM, Int'l, 4¾" 30.00
Spoon, cream soup, IL RR, Cromwell, Int'l, BM, 6"..................... 32.00
Spoon, cream soup, Lehigh Valley RR, Rex, TL, R&B, 5½" 130.00
Spoon, cream soup, NYC, Century, BM, Int'l, 5¾" 32.00
Spoon, cream soup, SP, Modern w/Flying Wheel TL, BM, R&B . 200.00
Spoon, demi, NYC & Hudson River, Vendome, BM, R&B, 4½" ... 34.00
Spoon, grapefruit, SP, Broadway, serrated edge, TL, Int'l, 6½"..... 23.00

Spoon, soup, Fred Harvey, Fiddle, TM, Rogers, 7¾"..................... 38.00
Spoon, soup, Fred Harvey, Manhattan, BM, Int'l, 7¼" 26.00
Sugar tongs, B&O, Clovelly, TL, R&B, 4¼"................................. 82.50
Sugar tongs, Lehigh Valley RR, Rex, TL (flag), R&B, 4½" 175.00
Sugar tongs, PA RR, Kings, keystone TL, R&B, 4½" 75.00
Sugar tongs, SP, Grecian, BS, Int'l, 4½"...................................... 58.00
Teaspoon, ATSF, TM, Cromwell, 6" 19.00
Teaspoon, D&RG, Navarre, TM, Rogers, 6"................................ 148.00
Teaspoon, New Haven, Modern, BS, Int'l, 6".............................. 13.00
Teaspoon, PRR, Cromwell, BS, Int'l, 6"...................................... 28.00

Silver-Plated Hollow Ware

Bread tray, The Reading/Central New Jersey, TL, Int'l, 7½x12½"... 305.00
Champagne bucket, Los Angeles & Salt Lake, hdls, SL, R&B, 9½"... 635.00
Cocktail server/shaker, FEC, Royal Poinciana, hinged lid, TL, BL, 5¾".... 285.00
Coffeepot, Erie, SL, hinged lid, Gorham, 5" 325.00

Creamer and sugar bowl, L&N, International Silver Co., both pieces with L&N logo, wear, 3¼", 4", $200.00. (Photo courtesy Belhorn Auction Services, LLC on LiveAuctioneers.com)

Hot food cover+base, NC&StL, TL & BL, Steif, dome, 4¼x6½".500.00
Mayonnaise bowl & ladle, L&N, Int'l Silver Co, 6½" dia............. 50.00
Menu holder w/pencil holders, Milwaukee Road SL, Deco ft, Int'l, 4¾" . 305.00
Mustard pot, SP, hinged lid, finial, Sunset TL, BL, 3¼"............... 185.00
Sherbet dish, ped, NP, Int'l, BL, 3¼" 45.00
Syrup pitcher, GM&O, hinged lid, attached liner, hdl, BL, R&B. 265.00

Switch Keys

Switch keys are brass with hollow barrels and round heads with holes for attaching to a key ring. They were used to unlock the padlocks on track-side switches when the course of the tracks had to be changed. (Switches were padlocked to prevent them from being thrown by accident or vandals, a situation that could result in a train wreck). A car key used to open padlocks on freight cars and the like is very similar to the switch key, except the bit is straighter instead of being specifically curved for a particular railroad and its accompanying switch locks. A second type of 'car' key was used for door locks on passenger cars, Pullmans, etc.; this type was usually of brass, but instead of having a hollow barrel, they were shaped like an old-fashioned hotel door key. In order for a key to be collectible, the head must be marked with a name, initials, or a railroad identification, with 'switch' generally designated by 'S' and 'car' by 'C' markings. Railroad, patina 'not polished,' and the presence of a manufacturer's mark other than Adlake all have a positive effect on pricing and collectibility.

CC&StL, brass, hollow bbl, 2⅛" 35.00
CPRR, brass bbl, 2".. 20.00
MOPAC, brass, hollow bbl, 2¼".. 26.00
NP, brass bbl, 2¼" 20.00
NYCS, brass, 2"... 20.00
PRR, brass, 2"... 45.00
SOO Line, brass, 2"... 35.00

Miscellaneous

Timetables and railroad travel brochures continue to gain in popularity and offer the collector vast information about the glory days of railroading. Annual passes continue to be favored over trip and one-time passes. Their value is contingent upon the specific railroad, its length of run, and the appearance of the pass itself. Many were tiny works of art enhanced with fancy calligraphy and decorated with unique vignettes. Pocket calendars are popular as well as railroad playing cards. Pins, badges, and uniform buttons bearing the name or logo of a railroad are also sought after. The novice needs to be cautious about signs (metal as well as cardboard), belt buckles, and badges (particularly police badges). Reproductions flourish in these areas.

Key:
CS — cardstock   RP — real photo
emp — employee

Accident report #3991 by ICC re ATSF, Lomax, IL, 1963, 9-pg.. 230.00
Advertising ruler, ATSF, wooden, 3-sided, metal SF logo, 12" 25.00
Ashtray, GN, Snuf-A-Rette, cobalt, TL, 4¼" 170.00
Ashtray, Monon TM, alligator's open mouth receives ashes, detailed, 9".. 60.00
Ashtray/match holder, C&O, G Washington silhouette, Buffalo, 4½x7".. 100.00
Ashtray/matchbook holder, B&O, Snuf-A-Rette, TM, B&O bio on bottom.148.00
Badge, breast, UP, Waiter Instructor, blk Bakelite, 2⅛" dia.......... 125.00
Badge, breast, SP, Police/AZ, 6-point silver star, Irvine & Jachiens..4,495.00
Badge, hat, D&RG Conductor, brass, 1⅛x4⅛" 360.00
Badge, hat, L&N, Train Caller, gold-tone metal, 2¾x4" 700.00
Blotter, ATSF, Chico holding SF logo, unused, 16x20" 38.00
Blotter, CRI&P, IA NE Ltd to Chicago, unused, 3½x8" 30.00
Bond, Denver & Rio Grande Western Railroad, 1924, w/13 coupons, 15x13".... 60.00
Bond, NP, $100, payable in gold, sgn J Cooke, uncancelled, 1870 ...2,365.00
Book, Cab Forward - SP Articulated Locomotives, Church, 1968, 1st ed. 175.00
Book, Signal Directory, hardbound leather, 1908, 600+ pgs, 8x12", G..695.00
Book, UP System Official Ry Guide, hardbk, 1,500-pg, 1922 .... 155.00
Booklet, ATSF, All Private Room Streamliner, 9-pg, 1930s, 5x7" . 70.00
Booklet, GN Secrets (Oriental Ltd recipes), 1930s, 32-pg, 7¼x5¼" .. 85.00
Booklet, PRR, Division of Maps, Office Chief Engineer, 14 maps, 1964.. 55.00
Builder's plate, C&O, Am Loco Corp, brass, A H4...2-6-6-2, 1913, 8x14"..945.00
Builder's plate, PRR, M1 Baldwin Locomotive Works, brass, 1926..1,300.00
Bulletin brd, MKT, for chalk notations, dtd 190_, 36x25" 1,950.00
Button, Central VT (CV), gilt or brass tone, Scovill Mfg, ⅝" 46.00
Button, OR Electric Ry, OE, silver-tone metal, Scovill Mfg, ⅝" 10.00
Calendar postcard, GN, September 1914, opens to 9x12" 385.00
Calendar, ATSF, celluloid, 1936 or 37, pocket sz, ea 395.00
Calendar, ATSF, celluloid, 1939, pocket sz, G 22.00
Calendar, GN, Weinold Reiss Evening Star lady, 13 sheets, 1954, 33x16"..58.00
Calendar, NPYPL logo, CS, 1949, pocket sz 98.00
Calendar, PRR, Grif Teller mining operation, 1941, complete, 28½" ... 170.00
Catalog, Baldwin Steam Locomotive parts, hardbk, 1924, 9½x11"..698.00
Cigarette lighter, NYC&StL, Nickel Plate Road, Zippo-like 23.00
Decal, Authorized Watch Inspector, SP, mc, 9x6½" 135.00
Doorknob, ICRR CO, emb brass.. 188.00
Fan, MKT, Bouquet Bluebonnets, Compliments of Katy Line, CS, 11".... 27.00
Fire alarm box, PRR, Gamewell, TM, red CI, 10x16x5" 900.00
Fire grenade, MPRR emb oval SM, Harden, glass w/vertical ribs, 8" .1,525.00
Handkerchief, Chessie, made for Chesapeake & Ohio Railway, 8x8"..25.00
Handkerchief, NYC, red bandana w/logos, 22x22"........................ 25.00
Jack, Duff Barrett RR type used by gandy dancers, 22" 60.00
Jug, GN, Property of...Ry Co, stoneware, 13", 1-gal 200.00
Key, caboose, Adlake, brass, solid bbl, 4½" 30.00
Key, caboose, B&O, brass, solid bbl, 3½" 35.00
Lapel pin, Wabash, Follow the Flag Banner logo, red/bl enamel, ⅞".. 10.00

Light fixture, ceiling; Pullman, brass/curved glass panels, 13" dia.. 600.00
Luggage sticker, CMStP&P, Olympian/Milwaukee Rd, 3½".............. 9.00
Luggage tag, ME Central, leather strap, brass 66.00
Magazine, empl, B&O, November, 1941 .... 11.00
Magazine, empl, Kansas City Southern, July, 1928....................... 52.00
Magazine, empl, MP Lines, January, 1955.................................... 26.00
Magazines, Trains, 12 issues, hardbk, 11/1942 to 10/1943 .... 145.00
Manual, LA Ry, Car House Organization & Oper, hardbk, 70-pg, 1926.130.00
Manual, UP, Rotary Snow Plow...Instructions, spiral bound, illus. 160.00
Map, 1862 Southern states, Duval & Son, provenance, 54x31" . 6,750.00
Matchbook, Central of GA, Serving the Southeast, 1950s, unused.13.00
Matchbox, ATSF logo, Turq Room, no matches, 1x2¼" 22.50
Matches, UP, 4 unused books in boxcar-like box, EX graphics, 4" L.5.00
Menu, B&O Capital Ltd, 1925-26, opens to 11x17" 55.00
Menu, IL Central, Club Lounge, 1948, 4½x6 ¼" 10.00
Menu, New Haven, Yankee Clipper, CS, 1930, folds to 9½x5¾". 180.00
Menu, PRR, train to 1931 World Series, photo cover, 9x6" 90.00
Menu, UP, dc squirrel, colorful, child's.. 30.00
Napkin, C&O, Chessie logo in corner, mc, paper, unused, $4 to......8.00
Napkins, cocktail, C&NW, pics of name trains on paper, pkg of 100 ..20.00
Number plate, PRR 5370 locomotive, keystone shape, red pnt CI, 20" .3,350.00
Pamphlet, Lehigh Valley, Summer Tours...Resorts, 1900, 63-pg, 6½x9".140.00
Pamphlet, N Shore Line/Milwaukee to Chicago, 1920s, 24-pg.... 360.00
Pamphlet, SOO Line, Pacific Coast Tours, Canadian Rockies, 1923. 28.00
Pwt, NYC, Hudson locomotive on tiered base, metal, 9½" 155.00
Pass, annual, CRI&P, Rock Island, 1925.. 10.00
Pass, annual, Galena & Chicago Union RR, paper, 1857, 2¼x3½" ..190.00
Pass, annual, Marietta & Cincinnati RR & Branches, 1880, 2¼x3½"..160.00
Pass, annual, SP Sunset Route, 1895, 2¼x3½".............................. 135.00
Pass, employee, Northern Pacific Railway, July 22, 1910, VG........ 15.00
Pass, lifetime, IL Central, 40 Years of Service, 1959, w/case........... 24.00
Pass, trip, C&O, paper, issued & expired in 1938, 3x7" 10.00
Pencils, various RRs, unsharpened, w/erasers, lot of 26 .... 14.00
Photo, D&RG, Rocky Mtn scenery, hand tinted, plaque on oak fr, 29x24".300.00
Pin-back, GN, ND Development Tour, space for name, 1890s, 4".145.00
Playing cards, Burlington Rte, Nat'l Park Line, dbl deck, +case ..275.00
Playing cards, DRGW, Rio Grande Main Line..., unopened, M in slipcase .75.00
Postcard, Albany/Springfield, OR, McKeen Motor Car RR, RP, 1910-20...55.00
Postcard, construction of railway station, Freeville NY, photo, 1900s..100.00
Postcard, depot, Windsor CA, wagon/workers/freight photo, 1910.. 160.00
Postcard, IL Central, Million Dollar Subway, blk/wht photo, 1914 .50.00
Postcard, NY roundhouse, rail yards/switch engines photo, 1909 ..65.00
Poster, ATSF, Land of Pueblos/Santa Fe, 1960s, 18x24" 600.00
Print, annual, AKRR, Denali Park Station, 1988, 21x23" 30.00
Ring, retirement, UP, birthstone & shield logo, silver-tone, 1992 .70.00
Semiphore assembly, UP, 48" blade, lenses, CI counterweight, 72"..790.00
Sign, MP buzz-saw logo/Eagle, Post Cereal, tin, 1950s, 2½x3½" 7.00
Sign, PRR depot, Ravena OH, elongated keystone, pnt CI, 25x50"..5,550.00
Sign, WP, Feather River logo, porc on steel, 8 grommets, 24x24". 415.00
Swizzle stick, PRR on keystone logo, Resume Speed, plastic, set of 10 ... 10.00
Test gauge, steam train, Yosemite Valley RR, in 7x9" leather case ..900.00
Ticket puncher, PRR, SM, spring action, 5¼" L 160.00
Timetable, employee, Susquehanna & NY, #48, 1936, 14-pg....... 120.00
Water can, KCS SM, galvanized, spigot, strap hdl & bail hdl, 18½" .. 45.00
Wax sealer, DE & Hudson, Whitehall NY, wood hdl, brass seal ..270.00
Wax sealer, NYC & Hudson RR, Terrytown NY, brass w/wood hdl, 3½".430.00
Whistle, PRR, 3-chime, brass, side-mt, 21x6", 32" overall........2,656.00

Razors

As straight razors gain in popularity, prices of those razors also increase. This carries with it a lure of investment possibilities which can encourage the novice or speculator to make purchases that may later prove to be unwise. We recommend that before investing serious money in razors, you become familiar with the elements which make a razor valuable. As with other collectibles, there are specific traits which are desirable and which have a major impact on price.

The following information is based on the third edition of *Standard Guide to Razors* by Roy Ritchie and Ron Stewart, published by Collector Books (available from R&C Books, Box 2421, Hazard, KY 41702, $12.95 +$4.00 S&H). Ron Stewart is our Razors advisor; he is listed in the Directory under Kentucky. It describes the elements most likely to influence a razor's collector value and their system of calculating that value. This is the most used collector's guide for straight razors currently available.

There are five major factors to be considered in determining a razor's value. These are the brand and country of origin, the age of the razor, the handle material, the artistic enhancements found on the handles and/or blade and the condition of the razor. The authors freely admit that there are other factors that may come into play with some collectors, but these are the major components in determining value. They have devised a system of evaluation which utilized some components that are thoroughly described in this book.

The most important factor (Chart A) is the value placed on the brand and country of origin. This is the price of a common razor made by (or for) a particular company. It has plain handles, probably made of plastic, no artwork, and is in collectible condition. It is the beginning value. Hundreds of these values are provided in the 'Listings of Companies and Base Values' chapter in the book.

Next (Chart B), because age plays such an important role, you must determine the age of your razor. There are four age categories or divisions in this appraisal system. Determine your razor's age and multiply 'brand value' times the number in parenthesis. Take this value to the next step.

The Chart C category is that of handle material. This covers a wide range of materials, from fiber on the low end to ivory on the high end. Because celluloid and plastics were used to mimic a wide variety of other handle materials, the collector needs to be able to identify the different handle materials when he sees them. This is especially true with ivory and mother-of-pearl.

The artistic category (Chart D) is without doubt the most subjective. Nevertheless, it is extremely important in determining the value of a straight razor. Artwork can include everything from logo art to carving and sculpture. It may range from highly ornate to tastefully correct. Blade etching as well as handle artistry are to be considered. Perhaps what some call the 'gotta have it' or the 'neatness' factors properly fall into this category. You must accurately determine the artistic merits of your razor when you evaluate it relative to this factor.

Finally (Chart E), the condition is factored in. The book's scales run from 'parts' (10% +/-) to 'Good' (150% +/-). Average (100% +/-) is classified as 'Collectible.'

Samplings from charts:

Chart A, Companies and Base Values

Abercrombie & Finch, NY	14.00
Aerial, USA	25.00
Boker, Henri & Co, Germany	14.00
Brick, F; England	12.00
Case Mfg Co, Spring Valley NY	50.00
Chores, James; England	11.00
Dahlqres, CW; Sweden	14.00
Diane, Japan	10.00
Diane, Japan	10.00
Electric Co, NY	15.00
Faultless, Germany	100.00
Fox Cutlery, Germany	11.00
Fredericks (Celebrated Cutlery), England	13.00
Gilbert Bros, England	12.00
Griffon XX, Germany	11.00
Henckels, Germany	15.00
Holly Mfg Co, CT	30.00
International Cutlery Co NY/Germany	11.00
IXL, England	15.00
Jay, John; NY	12.00
KaBar, Union Cut Co, USA	30.00
Kanner, J; Germany	11.00
Kern, R&W; Canada/England	12.00
LeCocltre, Jacque; Switzerland	12.00
Levering Razor Co, NY/Germany	18.00
McIntosh & Heather, OH	12.00
Merit Import Co, Germany	11.00
Monthoote, England	12.00
Oxford Razor Co, Germany	10.00
Palmer Brothers, Savannah, GA	25.00
Primble, John; Indian Steel Works, Louisville KY	25.00
Queen City NY	30.00
Querelle, A; Paris France	12.00
Quigley, Germany	12.00
Radford, Joseph & Sons; England	12.00
Rattler Razor Co, Germany	10.00
Robeson Cut Co, USA	30.00
Salamander Works, Germany	11.00
Soderein, Ekilstuna Sweden	12.00
Taylor, LM; Cincinnati OH	15.00
Tower Brand, Germany	16.00
Ulmer, Germany	12.00
US Barber Supply, TX	12.00
Vinnegut Hdw Co, IN	11.00
Vogel, Ed; PA	10.00
Wade & Butcher, England	20.00
Weis, JH; Supply House, Louisville KY	17.00
Yankee Cutlery Co, Germany	12.00
Yazbek, Lahod; OH	11.00
Zacour Bros, Germany	11.00
Zepp, Germany	12.00

Chart B, Age Factor:

You must determine the approximate age of your razor. *Standard Guide to Razors* goes into much detail about how to do this. We have determined four general categories for purposes of factoring age into your appraisal.

1740 – 1820 (Chart A values x 2 = B value)
1820 – 1870 (Chart A value x 1.5 = B value)
1870 – 1930 (Chart A value x 1 = B value)
1930 – 1950 (Chart A value x .75 = B value)

Chart C, Handle Materials:

The following is an abbreviated version of the handle materials list in *Standard Guide to Razors*. It is an essential category in the use of the appraisal system developed by the authors.

Genuine Ivory	600%
Tortoise Shell	500%
Pearl	400%
Stag	400%
Jigged Bone	350%
Smooth Bone/Pressed Horn	300%
Celluloid	250%
Composition	150%
Plastic	100%

Chart D, Artistic Value:

As poined out earlier, this is a very subjective area. It takes study to determine what is good and what is not. Taste can also play a significant role in determining the value placed on the artistic merit of a razor. The range is from exceptional to nonexistent. Categories generally are divided as follows:

Unique (off the charts)

'Unique' has a feature that makes the razor uncommonly special. The feature, whether design, inlay, or ownership by a 'famous' historical figure, makes the razor beyond exceptional and distinctive.

Exceptional	650%
Superior	550%
Good	400%
Average	300%
Minimal	200%
Plain	100%
Nonexistant	0%

Chart E, Condition:

Condition is also very subjective. This chart will help you determine the condition of the razor. You must judge accurately if the appraisal system is to work for you.

Good   150%

Does not have to be factory mint to fall within this category. However, there can be no visible flaws if it is to be calculated at 150%.

Collectible   100%

May have some flaws that do not greatly detract from the artwork or finish.

Parts   10%

Unrepairable, valuable as salvageable parts.

Razors may fall between any of these categories, i.e. collectible to 112%.

Now to determine the value of your razor: Find the code value from the brand chart (A) and multiply it times the age factor (B) to determine the 'B' value. Multiply B times C and multiply B times D. Add your two answers togethers and multiply this sum times E. The answer you get is your collector value (F). See the example below:

(A) Brand & Origin Base Value	(B) Age Factor % Value	(C) Handle Material % Value	(D) Artwork % Value	(E) Condition % Value	(F) Collector Value
John Primble Belknap; Louisville, KY $25.00	1870 – 1930 25 x 1= $25.00	Celluloid colorful 25 x 300%= $75.00	Escutcheon inlay 25 x 200%= $50.00	Collectible 100%	$75 + $50 = $125 x 100%= $125.00

Reamers

The largest producer of glass reamers was McKee, who pressed their products from many types of glass — custard; Delphite and Chalaine Blue; opaque white; Skokie Green; black; caramel and white opalescent; Seville Yellow; and transparent pink, green, and clear. Among these, the black and the caramel opalescents are the most valuable. Prices vary greatly according to color and rarity. The same reamer in crystal may be worth three times as much in a more desirable color.

Among the most valuable ceramic reamers are those made by American potteries, for example the Spongeband reamer by Red Wing, Coorsite reamers, and figural reamers. China one- and two-piece reamers are also very desirable and command very respectable prices.

A word about reproductions: A series of limited edition reamers is being made by Edna Barnes of Uniontown, Ohio. These are all marked with a 'B' in a circle. Other reproductions have been made from old molds. The most important of these are Anchor Hocking two-piece two-cup measure and top, Gillespie one-cup measure with reamer top, Westmoreland with flattened handle, Westmoreland four-cup measure embossed with orange and lemons, Duboe (hand-held darning egg), and Easley's Diamonds one-piece.

For more information concerning reamers and reproductions, contact the National Reamer Collectors Association (see Clubs, Newsletters, and Websites). Be sure to include an SASE when requesting information.

Ceramic

Camel kneeling, beige lustre w/lt gr top, 4¼", $200 to	250.00
Clown sitting X-legged, gr w/wht ruffled coat & hat, Germany, 5"	300.00
Clown, black, Goebel mk & numbers on base, 5", VG	125.00
Clown, wht w/gr hat (reamer), ruffle & socks, blk details, Japan	75.00
Duck, orange & gr on wht pearlized body	110.00
Floral w/gold, Nippon, 2-pc	195.00
Lemon & leaf decor, gr trim & hdl, MIG #2887, 3"	55.00
Pitcher, blk w/gold wheat, 2-pc, 8"	45.00
Puddinhead, 2-pc, 6¼"	250.00
Rose, pk w/gr leaves, Germany, 1¾"	225.00
Sailboat, yel or red, 3", ea	125.00
Toucan, mc on wht pearlescent lustre, unmk Japan, 2¾x5¾"	165.00

Glass

Cambridge, cobalt, ribbed, $2,750 to	3,000.00
Cambridge, crystal, ribbed, $25 to	28.00
Easley's, Pat 1900, tab hdl, 2¾x4½", $35 to	45.00
Federal, gr, pointed cone, tab hdl, $25 to	28.00
Federal, pk, ribbed, loop hdl, $45 to	50.00
Fry, gr, str sides, ribbed, tab hdl, $40 to	45.00
Fry, Pearl, fluted, $75 to	85.00
Hazel-Atlas, bl dots on wht, ftd, 2-pc, $65 to	70.00

Hazel-Atlas, cobalt, two-cup pitcher and reamer set, $325.00 to $350.00. (Photo courtesy Kenn and Margaret Whitmyer, ebay sellers junquer9)

Hazel-Atlas, crystal, emb crisscross, tab hdl, $20 to	22.00
Hazel-Atlas, gr, 4-cup stippled pitcher & reamer set, $45 to	50.00
Hazel-Atlas, gr, emb crisscross, $35 to	40.00
Hazel-Atlas, pk, emb crisscross, tab hdl, $325 to	335.00
Hazel-Atlas, wht, lg tab hdl, $30 to	38.00
Hocking, gr, ribbed, ftd, loop hdl, $30 to	35.00
Hocking, Mayfair Bl, 2-cup measuring w/reamer top, $1,600 to	1,800.00
Indiana Glass, pk, 6-sided cone, vertical hdl, $175 to	195.00
Jennyware, pk, ribbed, ftd, $110 to	125.00
MacBeth-Evans Glass, clambroth, vertical hdl, $185 to	200.00

McKee, grapefruit, blk, vertical hdl, $1,000 to 1,200.00
Saunders (emb), Jadeite, cone top, $1,600 to 1,700.00
Sunkist, butterscotch, $375 to..395.00
Sunkist, custard, emb McKee, ring hdl, $35 to 45.00
Sunkist (emb), Jadeite, $75 to...85.00
Sunkist (emb), lt caramel, $375 to..395.00
US Glass, crystal w/orange decor, 2-cup pitcher set, ftd, 2-pc 60.00
US Glass, gr, 4-cup pitcher set, ftd, $140 to 150.00
US Glass, wht, 2-cup pitcher set, ftd, 2-pc, $110 to 125.00
Valencia (emb), wht, vertical hdl, $135 to 150.00
Valencia, gr, vertical hdl, $100 to..125.00
Valencia, mustard slag, emb fleur-de-lis, $375 to 400.00
Valencia, pk/amber, vertical hdl, $325 to..350.00
Westmoreland, crystal w/decor, 2-pc, $75 to....................................95.00
Westmoreland, pk frosted, 2-pc, $185 to..195.00

Records

Records of interest to collectors are often not the million-selling hits by 'superstars.' Very few records by Bing Crosby, for example, are of any more than nominal value, and those that are valuable usually don't even have his name on the label! Collectors today are most interested in records that were made in limited quantities, early works of a performer who later became famous, and those issued in special series or aimed at a limited market. Vintage records are judged desirable by their recorded content as well; those that lack the quality of music that makes a record collectible will always be 'junk' records in spite of their age, scarcity, or the obsolescence of their technology.

Records are usually graded visually rather than aurally, since it is seldom if ever possible to first play the records you buy at shows, by mail, or at flea markets. Condition is one of the most important determinants of value. For example, a nearly mint-condition Elvis Presley 45 of 'Milk Cow Blues' (Sun 215) has a potential value of over $1,500.00. A small sticker on the label could cut its value in half; noticeable wear could reduce its value by 80%. A mint record must show no evidence of use (record jackets, in the case of EPs and LPs, must be equally choice). Excellent condition denotes a record showing only slight signs of use with no audible defects. A very good record has noticeable wear but still plays well. Records of lesser grades may be unsaleable, unless very scarce and/or highly sought-after.

While the value of most 78s does not depend upon their being in appropriate sleeves (although a sleeveless existence certainly contributes to damage and deterioration), this is not the case with most EPs (extended play 45s) and LPs (long-playing 33⅓ rpm albums), which must have their jackets (cardboard sleeves), in nice condition, free of disfiguring damage, such as writing, stickers, or tape. Often, common and minimally valued 45s might be collectible if they are in appropriate 'picture sleeves' (special sleeves that depict the artist/group or other fanciful or symbolic graphic and identify the song titles, record label, and number), e.g. many common records by Elvis Presley, the Beatles, and the Beach Boys.

Promotional copies (DJ copies) supplied to radio stations often have labels different in designs and/or colors from their commercially issued counterparts. Labels usually bear a designation 'Not for Sale,' 'Audition Copy,' 'Sample Copy,' or the like. Records may be pressed of translucent vinyl; while most promos are not particularly collectible, those by certain 'hot' artists, such as Elvis Presley, the Beach Boys, and the Beatles are usually premium disks.

Many of the most desirable and valuable 45s have been bootlegged (counterfeited). For example, there are probably more fake Elvis Presley Sun records in circulation than authentic copies — certainly in higher grades! Collectors should be alert for these often deceptive counterfeits.

Our advisor for this category is L.R. Docks, author of *American Premium Record Guide*. He is listed in the Directory under Texas. In the listings that follow, prices are suggested for records that are in excellent condition; worn or abused records may be worth only a small fraction of the values quoted and may not be saleable at all. EPs and LPs are priced 'with jacket.'

Blues, Rhythm and Blues, Rock 'n Roll, Rockabilly

Adams, Jo Jo; Didn't I Tell You, Chance 1127, 45 rpm 30.00
Ames, Tessie; High Yel Blues, Silvertone 3576, 78 rpm 150.00
Anderson, Jelly Roll; Good Time Blues, Gennett 6181, 78 rpm .. 300.00
Andy & the Live Wires, Maggie, Applause 1249, 45 rpm............... 15.00
Avons, Baby, Hull 722, 45 rpm.. 20.00
Baker, Willie; Crooked Woman Blues, Gennett 6846, 78 rpm..... 300.00
Barton, Tippy; High Brown Cheater, Vocalion 1742, 78 rpm....... 100.00
Beach Boys, Surfin', Candix 301, 45 rpm... 75.00
Belmonts, Summertime, Sabina 521, 45 rpm..................................... 20.00
Berry, Chuck; One Dozen Berrys, Chess 1432, LP, 45 rpm 50.00
Bilbro, DH; Chester Blues, Victor 23831, 78 rpm............................ 75.00
Blue Belle, Ghost Creepin' Blues, Okeh 8588, 78 rpm................... 40.00
Blue Dots, Hold Me Tight, De Luxe 6067, 45 rpm 30.00
Brim, Grace; Hospitality Blues, JOB 117, 78 rpm, $100 to 150.00
Brown, Charles; Moonrise, Aladdin 3163, 45 rpm 15.00
Browne, Doris; My Cherie, Gotham 298, 45 rpm 15.00
Bumble Bee Slim & His 3 Sharks, Deep Bass Blues, Decca 7053, 78 rpm....15.00
Campbell, Louis; Natural Facts, Excello 2035, 45 rpm 30.00
Capris, God Only Knows, Gotham 7304, 45 rpm 40.00
Carolina Slim, Worry You Off My Mind, Acorn 323, 78 rpm 10.00
Channels, Gleam in Your Eyes, Whirlin 102, 45 rpm 20.00
Clefs, We Three, Chess 1521, 78 rpm.. 50.00
Collins, Sam; Dark Cloudy Blues, Gennett 6260, 78 rpm 400.00
Continentals, It Doesn't Matter, Hunter 3502, 45 rpm 30.00
Curry, Elder; Hard Times, Okeh 8879, 78 rpm 80.00
Davis, Link; Don't Big Shot Me, Starday 255, 45 rpm 20.00
Davis, Walter; Worried Man Blues, Bluebird 5129, 78 rpm........... 80.00
Denson, Lee; Heart of a Fool, Vik 0251, 45 rpm 30.00
Douglas, Davey; Shivers, Ditto 110, 45 rpm 20.00
Downing, 'Big' Al; Miss Lucy, Wht Rock 1113, 45 rpm 60.00
Dranes, Arizona; Don't You Want To Go?, Okeh 8646, 78 rpm..... 60.00
Earls, My Heart's Desire, Rome 5117, 45 rpm 10.00
Enchanters, True Love Gone, Mercer 992, 45 rpm........................ 150.00
Fiestas, All That's Good, #1166, 45 rpm... 10.00
Five Spots, Get With It, Future 2201, 45 rpm 30.00
Four Lovers, Joy Ride, RCA 1317, LP.. 200.00
Gay Notes, For Only a Moment, Drexel 905, 45 rpm...................... 80.00
Gibson, Cifford; Stop Your Rambling, Paramount 12923, 78 rpm ..300.00
Green, Rudy; Teeny Weeny Baby, Excello 2090, 45 rpm................ 30.00
Hadley, Jim; Midnight Train, Buddy 117, 45 rpm 30.00
Hamner, Curley; Piano Turner, Fling 720, 45 rpm......................... 30.00
Harris, Wynonie; Night Train, King 4565, 45 rpm 15.00
Heartbreakers, My Love, Vik 0299, 45 rpm 30.00
Henderson, Rosa; Get It Fixed, Vocalion 15044, 78 rpm 40.00
Heralds, Eternal Love, Herald 435, 45 rpm..................................... 40.00

Hurt, Mississippi John; Nobody's Dirty Business/ Frankle, Okeh, 1928, fair condition, along with 1929 Okeh catalog listing this record, 78 rpm, $300.00. (Photo courtesy Leland Little Auction & Estate Sales Ltd. on LiveAuctioneers.com)

Irby, Jerry; Clickety Clack, Daffan 108, 45 rpm 20.00
Jenkins, Bo Bo; Democrat Blues, Chess 1565, 45 rpm 60.00

Johnson, Louise; On the Wall, Paramount 13008, 78 rpm 250.00
Jones, Grandpa; Greatest Hits, King 554, LP.................................. 20.00
Kearney, Ramsey; Rock the Bop, Jaxon 501, 45 rpm 50.00
Lee, Harry; Rockin' on a Reindeer, Igloo 101, 45 rpm 60.00
Lightfoot, Papa; PL Blues, Aladdin 3171, 45 rpm 50.00
Liston, Virginia; Rolls-Royce Papa, Vocalion 1032, 78 rpm 100.00
Magnificents, Don't Leave Me, Vee Jay 281, 45 rpm 20.00
Morris, Gene; Lovin' Honey, Edmoral 1012, 45 rpm 40.00
Paul, Jerry; Step Out, Holiday 1001, 45 rpm................................. 15.00
Preston, Johnny; Running Bear, Mercury 20592, LP 40.00
Ravens, Don't Mention My Name, Mercury 70060, 45 rpm 30.00
Redd, Johnny; Rockin' With Ruby, Corallen, 45 rpm 30.00
Robbins, Marty; Pretty Mama, Columbia 21461, 45 rpm 12.00
Robin Hood Brians, Dis a Itty Bit, Fraternity 803, 45 rpm 50.00
Robinson, Elzadie; Tick-Tock Blues, Paramount 12544, 78 rpm .. 120.00
Robinson, James 'Bat'; Humming Blues, Champion 16745, 78 rpm ..400.00
Serenaders, I Want To Love You Baby, Red Robin 115, 45 rpm... 100.00
Smith, Bessie; Back Water Blues, Columbia 14195-D, 78 rpm 50.00
Sunny Boy & His Pals, Don't You Leave Me Here, Champion 15283, 78 rpm.300.00
Tate, Rose; Money Woman Blues, Champion 15417, 78 rpm 175.00
Tucker, Bessie; Old Black Mary, Victor V38538, 78 rpm 200.00
Vincent, Walter; Mississippi Yodelin' Blues, Brunswick 7190, 78 rpm.... 150.00
Wallace, Sippie; Jealous Woman Like Me, Okeh 8301, 78 rpm ... 200.00
Williamson, Sonny Boy; Blue Bird Blues, Bluebird 7098, 78 rpm .. 30.00
Young, Billie; You Done Played Out Blues, Victor 23339, 78 rpm ..350.00

Country and Western

Allen Brothers, Ain't That Skippin?, Columbia 15270-D, 78 rpm .. 100.00
Ashley & Foster, My North Carolina Home, Vocalion 02900, 78 rpm .. 50.00
Baldwin, Luke; It Won't Happen Again, Champion 16142, 78 rpm .. 20.00
Blake, Charley; Alabama Blues, Supertone 9600, 78 rpm 15.00
Blue Boys, Memphis Stomp, Okeh 45314, 78 rpm 100.00
Butcher, Dwight; Your Voice Is Calling, Victor 23810, 78 rpm.... 150.00
Carolina Twins, Mr Brown Here I Come, Victor V40098, 78 rpm. 30.00
Chesnut, Ted; Bring Back My Boy, Gennett 6603, 78 rpm 20.00
Coon, Walter; & His Joy Boys, Polly Wolly Doodle, Gennett 7079, 78 rpm ..30.00
Cross, Ballard; Wabash Cannon Ball, Vocalion 5377, 78 rpm 15.00
Delmore Brothers, Frozen Girl, Bluebird 5338, 78 rpm 15.00
Ferguson, John; Railroad Daddy, Challenge 159, 78 rpm 15.00
Georgia Crackers, Diamond Joe, Okeh 45098, 78 rpm................... 30.00
Great Country & Western Hits, RCA SPD-26, 1956, set of 10 ... 635.00
Green's String Band, Rickett's Hornpipe, Champion 16489, 78 rpm. 30.00
Hart Brothers, Prodigal Son, Paramount 3265, 78 rpm 15.00
Hess, Bennie; & His Nation's Play Boys, Texas Stars, Opera 1019, 78 rpm.. 8.00
Hopkins, Andy; Prison Warden's Secret, Supertone 9713, 78 rpm ..12.00
Hughey, Dan; Sweet Kitty Wells, Champion 15502, 78 rpm 10.00
Johnson, Paul & Charles; Wild Cat Hollow, Gennett 7313, 78 rpm . 75.00
Justice, Dick; Henry Lee, Brunswick 367, 78 rpm........................... 20.00
La Dieu, Pieree; Shanty-Man's Life, Columbia 15278-D, 78 rpm . 30.00
Leake County Revelers, Beautiful Bells, Columbia 15501-D, 78 rpm.. 20.00
Lonesome Cowboy, Memphis Gal, Champion 16767, 78 rpm 75.00
Lullaby Larkers, Chicken Roost Blues, Champion 16364, 78 rpm . 40.00
Major, Jack; Tennessee Mountain Girl, Brunswick 252, 78 rpm 20.00
Martin Brothers, Whistling Rufus, Paramount 3217 .... 50.00
Massey Family, Sweet Mama Tree Top Tall, Vocalion 02993, 78 rpm.. 12.00
Mattox, Jimmie; Good Bye Mama, Gennett 7227, 78 rpm 50.00
Maynard, Ken; Cowboy's Lament, Columbia 2310-D, 78 rpm 100.00
McKinney Brothers, Old Uncle Joe, Champion 16830, 78 rpm..... 15.00
McPherson, Whitney; Brakeman Blues, Vocalion 03937, 78 rpm.. 10.00
Nabell, Charles; After the War Is Over, Okeh 45021, 78 rpm 15.00
Newton County Hillbillies, Happy Hour Breakdown, Okeh 45520, 78 rpm ..50.00
Oaks, Charlie; Poor Little Joe, Vocalion 15103, 78 rpm 10.00
Pavey, Phil; Utah Mormon Blues, Okeh 45355, 78 rpm................. 12.00

Pine Mountain Boys, Apron String Blues, Victor 23605, 78 rpm.. 100.00
Puckett, Holland; He Lives on High, Gennett 6206, 78 rpm......... 15.00
Red Headed Fiddlers, Cheat 'Em, Brunswick 470, 78 rpm 20.00
Red Heads, Wild & Foolish, Pathe-Actuelle 36492, 78 rpm......... 30.00
Renfro Valley Boys, Loreena, Paramount 3321, 78 rpm 40.00
Roane County Ramblers, Roane County Rag, Columbia 15398-D, 78 rpm. 50.00
Rodgers, Jessie; Headin' Home, Bluebird 5853, 78 rpm 10.00
Rodgers, Jimmie; My Good Gal's Gone, Bluebird 5942, 78 rpm 40.00
Stanton, Frank; Poor Old Dad, Superior 2544, 78 rpm 50.00
Thompson, Bud; Lie He Wrote Home, Crown 3489, 78 rpm......... 12.00
Turner, Cal; Only a Tramp, Champion 15587, 78 rpm 18.00
Virginia Dandies, God's Getting Worried, Crown 3145, 78 rpm ... 20.00
Williams, Marc; Jesse James, Brunswick 269, 78 rpm 12.00

Jazz, Dance Bands, Personalities

Al Haig Quartet w/Wardell Gray, Twisted/Easy Living, New Jazz, 1945, 78 rpm.. 20.00
Arcadian Serenaders, Fidgety Feet, Okeh 40272, 78 rpm............... 40.00
Astaire, Fred; Pick Yourself Up, Brunswick 7717, 78 rpm 10.00
Auburn, Frank; & His Orchestra, Little Girl, Clarion 11001-C, 78 rpm . 20.00
Austin, Gene; Without That Gal!, Victor 22739, 78 rpm.............. 12.00
Banta, Frank; Wild Cherry Rag, Gennett 4735, 78 rpm 20.00
Bernard, Al; Stavin' Change, Brunswick 2448, 78 rpm....................8.00
Blue Jay Boys, My Baby, Decca 7240, 78 rpm 15.00
Blythe's Blue Boys, My Baby, Champion 15528, 78 rpm 200.00
Bobby's Revelers, Heebie Jeebies, Silvertone 3551, 78 rpm............ 75.00
Brown, Henry; Blues Stomp, Paramount 12934, 78 rpm 200.00
Campbell, Buddy & His Orchestra; Last Dollar, Okeh 41532, 78 rpm ..12.00
Carlson, Russ & His Orchestra; Me!, Crown 3177, 78 rpm 8.00
Charleston Chasers, You're Lucky to Me, Columbia 2309-D, 78 rpm ...20.00
Chocolate Dandies, That's My Stuff, Vocalion 1617, 78 rpm 150.00
Cotton Pickers, What'll You Do?, Gennett 6380, 78 rpm 75.00
Crosby, Bing; Some of These Days, Brunswick 6351, 78 rpm......... 12.00
Detroiters, Spanish Mamma, Romeo 625, 78 rpm 10.00
Dixie Jazz Band, West End Blues, Jewel 5412, 78 rpm 15.00
Dixie Stompers, Goose Pimples, Harmony 545-H, 78 rpm 15.00
Dixieland Jug Blowers, Carpet Alley, Victor 20480, 78 rpm 60.00
Dubin's Dandies, Gettin' Along, Cameo 0105, 78 rpm 8.00
English, Sharlie; Broke Woman Blues, Paramount 12644, 78 rpm... 100.00
Fuller, Bob; Growin' Old Blues, Ajax 17117, 78 rpm 40.00
Gene & His Glorians, Jig Time, Timely Tunes 1582, 78 rpm 30.00
Gold, Lou; & His Orchestra, Roll 'em Girls, Perfect 14530, 78 rpm 10.00
Goody's Good Timers, Diga Diga Doo, Perfect 15083, 78 rpm....... 15.00
Gulf Coast Seven, Santa Claus Blues, Columbia 14107-D, 78 rpm .75.00
Halstead, Henry; His Orchestra, Panama, Victor 19514, 78 rpm ... 25.00
Harmonians, I Wanna Be Loved by You, Harmony 762-H, 78 rpm..8.00
Hill, Sam; & His Orchestra, ... Loves My Baby, Oriole 303, 78 rpm.30.00
Jazz Masters, Bees Knees, Black Swan 2109, 78 rpm...................... 20.00
Johnson, Rudolph; Spring Rain, black Jazz BJ 4, 1971, 33 LP 15.00
Jungle Band, Maori, Brunswick 4776, 78 rpm................................ 20.00

Kentucky Grasshoppers, Icky Blues, Banner 6323, 78 rpm............. 12.00
Lewis, Ted; & His Band, Bugle Call Rag, Columbia 826-D, 78 rpm .. 10.00

Lumberjacks, Spanish Dream, Cameo 8356, 78 rpm 10.00
Melody Sheiks, Mighty Bl, Okeh 40484, 78 rpm......................... 20.00
Memphis Melody Men, New Moten Stomp, Superior 2737, 78 rpm.150.00
Missourians, Vine Street Drag, Victor V 38103, 78 rpm............... 100.00
Moonlight Revelers, Alabama Shuffle, Grey Gull 1775, 78 rpm.... 50.00
Morland, Peg; You're Gonna Miss Me, Victor V40137, 78 rpm..... 15.00
Mound City Blue Blowers, Hello Lola, Victor V38100, 78 rpm..... 25.00
New Orleans Jazz Band, My Sweet Louise, Domino 3524, 78 rpm. 15.00
Orig Memphis Five, 31st Street Blues, Emerson 10741, 78 rpm..... 30.00
Preer, Evelyn; Sunday, Banner 1895, 78 rpm 12.00
Sepia Serenaders, Breakin' the Ice, Bluebird 5782, 78 rpm 20.00
Shreveport Sizzlers, Zonky, Okeh 8918, 78 rpm............................ 75.00
Smith, Kate; Morning, Noon & Night, Clarion 5124-C, 78 rpm .. 15.00
State Street Ramblers, Careless Love, Champion 16464, 78 rpm . 250.00
Sullivan, Joe; Onyx Bringdown, Columbia 2925-D, 78 rpm 40.00
Tin Pan Paraders, Puttin' on the Ritz, Gennett 7148, 78 rpm........ 20.00
We Three, Trumpet Sobs, Perfect 14645, 78 rpm 25.00
Whoopee Makers, Misty Mornin', Pathe-Actuelle 36923, 78 rpm..16.00

Redware

The term redware refers to a type of simple earthenware produced by the Colonists as early as the 1600s. The red clay used in its production was abundant throughout the country, and during the eighteenth and nineteenth centuries redware was made in great quantities. Intended for utilitarian purposes such as everyday tableware or use in the dairy, redware was simple in design and decoration. Glazes of various colors were used, and a liquid clay referred to as 'slip' was sometimes applied in patterns such as zigzag lines, daisies, or stars. Plates often have a 'coggled' edge, similar to the way a pie is crimped or jagged, which is done with a special tool. In the following listings, EX (excellent condition) indicates only minor damage. Our advisor for this category is Barbara Rosen; she is listed in the Directory under New Jersey.

Bank, seated spaniel, coleslaw mane and tail, attributed to Wagner pottery, Pennsylvania, circa 1860, 6", EX, $3,100.00. (Photo courtesy Pook & Pook Inc. on LiveAuctioneers.com)

Ink bottle, brn streaks/splotches/incised lines, 19th C, 6" 1,800.00
Jar, brn manganese splotches, incised lines, 19th C, 9" 1,300.00
Jar, brn manganese splotches, lug hdls, ovoid, chips/lines, 9".......355.00
Jar, canning; manganese daubs w/gr traces, 11x7", EX.................. 145.00
Jar, gr spit glaze w/running streaks, 2 sm hdls, 8x6", EX............... 230.00
Jar, gr/golden brn w/streaky brn splotches, incised lines, 19th C, 8"...475.00
Jar, incised shoulder band, speckled, att Cain, 13½", EX............4,500.00
Jar, speckled olive gr w/brn brushstrokes, rim collar, 19th C, 4"...265.00
Jardiniere, burnt orange w/brn splotches, att CT area, 1830s, 9".1,595.00
Jug bank, brn manganese/brn copper splotches, reeded hdl, PA, rpr, 4"..200.00
Jug, brn manganese splotches, incised line at shoulder, MA, 19th C, 9".1,880.00
Jug, brn manganese splotches, strap hdl, MA, 19th C, 5".............. 265.00
Jug, brn speckles w/gr touches, att J Corliss, 19th C, 5"................ 300.00
Jug, gr glaze w/orange highlights, 6¼", VG 1,265.00
Jug, mottled olive gr w/brn halos, ovoid, strap hdl, NE, 7"........1,000.00
Jug, olive gr w/mc halos, ovoid w/strap hdl, NH, 19th C, 5" 765.00
Jug, vinegar; olive gr & brn w/brn splashes, strap hdl, ME, 4"...... 350.00
Loaf pan, 4-line yel slip waves & dashes, 16½" L, EX..................4,500.00
Pie plate, 3 yel slip lines, coggled rim, 9", EX............................... 260.00

Pie plate, yel slip wavy lines & dots, coggled rim, 10½", NM.......850.00
Plate, bands of yel slip wavy lines, coggled rim, 11"....................1,110.00
Plate, stylized yel slip, coggled rim, sm chips, 8"......................... 400.00
Plate, sunflower in mc slip, 1825 in blk slip, ca 1825, 12" 1,375.00
Plate, yel slip loops, coggled rim, flakes, 12"............................... 545.00
Plate, yel slip squiggles, coggled rim, att PA, 1830s, 10"............... 900.00

Red Wing

The Red Wing Stoneware Company was formed in 1877 and began producing stoneware on a large scale in 1878. Because of its success a second company, the Minnesota Stoneware Company, was formed in 1883. These two companies worked closely together and made utilitarian vessels such as crocks, churns, jugs, bowls, and flowerpots. A third company, The North Star Stoneware Company, was formed in 1892 but ceased production in 1896 because of economic conditions in the country. In 1906, the Red Wing and Minnesota Stoneware Companies officially merged and selected a new name, the Red Wing Union Stoneware Company. From 1906 to 1936 many new products were made and old product lines expanded. As the needs of the American family changed and because of the shift from rural America to urban America the use of stoneware declined. In 1936, the company changed its name again to reflect the new product lines and was called the Red Wing Potteries. In 1967 the company closed after a long union strike.

During the 'Potteries' era the company produced mainly artware and dinnerware. Stoneware items were still produced during the Potteries period on a much smalle scale until approximately 1948. While artware was produced during the latter part of the 'stoneware' period, it is generally agreed the first dinnerware was produced around 1935 and the Gypsy Trail pattern represented the first attempt at a complete set of dinnerware items. Three dinnerware patterns are featured here — Pepe, Lute Song, and Tampico. All three patterns have seen a rise in collector interests in the last few years. For more information we recommend *Red Wing Stoneware Encyclopedia* by our advisors, Dan DePasquale (see Directory, Nebraska) and Larry Peterson (see Directory, Minnesota). Also suggested are *Red Wing Collectibles* and *Red Wing Stoneware* (Collector Books) both by Dan DePasquale, Gail Peck, and Larry Peterson.

Artware

Bird on branch, #1059, matt yel, 2¾", $50 to 70.00
Birds on branch, #1061, pk luster, 4½", $90 to 110.00
Bowl, console, #526, ivory, deer, $90 to 110.00
Clock, chef, 10", $150 to 180.00
Clock, wht, polo player, 11", $400 to 500.00
Cookie jar, bl, Friar Tuck, 10½", $100 to 140.00
Cookie jar, gr, Pierre (chef), $250 to... 300.00
Cookie jar, turq, apple, 8", $120 to.. 150.00
Figurine, Asian, #1349, 9", $190 to.. 230.00
Marmalade, yel, w/attached stand, 5", $25 to 35.00
Pitcher, #220, yel, Continental group, 10", $130 to 160.00
Shoe, Mexican, #991, matt ivory, 2¾x5½", $70 to 90.00
Vase, #132, yel, brushware, $75 to.. 95.00
Vase, #175, yel, ink stamped, 4½", $70 to 90.00
Vase, #195F, eggshell, Georgia Rose, 9", $125 to 155.00
Vase, #230, lt gr, ink stamped, 7", $60 to 80.00
Vase, #247, dk bl, dbl hdls, 9½", $120 to...................................... 130.00
Vase, #567, ivory, Athenian group, 5¾", $200 to........................... 250.00
Vase, #790, cocoa brn, prismatique shape, 3⅛x8¼", $30 to............ 50.00
Vase, #1097, woodland grn, 5¾", $30 to 45.00
Vase, #M1512, pk fleck, 4", $25 to 35.00
Vase, elephant, #236B, lt bl, 4¼", $160 to 190.00
Vase, fan, #892, pk fleck, 7½", $40 to.. 60.00

Vase, mini, #323, lt gr, 4", $40 to	60.00
Vase, mini, #327, suntan, 3", $40 to	60.00
Vase, mini, #653, lt gr, 2½", $70 to	100.00

Dinnerware

Town and Country, designed by Eva Zeisel, was made for only one year in the late 1940s. Today many collectors regard Zeisel as one of the most gifted designers of that era and actively seek examples of her work. Town and Country was a versatile line, adaptable to both informal and semiformal use. It is characterized by irregular, often eccentric shapes, and handles of pitchers and serving pieces are usually extensions of the rim. Bowls and platters are free-form comma shapes or appear tilted, with one side slightly higher than the other. Although the ware is unmarked, it is recognizable by its distinctive shapes and glazes. White (often used to complement interiors of bowls and cups), though an original color, is actually more rare than Bronze (metallic brown, also called gunmetal), which enjoys favored status; gray is unusual. Other colors include Rust, Dusk Blue, Sand, Chartreuse, Peach, and Forest Green. Pieces have also shown up in Mulberry and Ming Green and are considered quite rare. (These are Red Wing Quartette colors!) In our listings, use the higher side to evaluate white, Bronze, Mulberry, and Ming Green, mid-range for gray, and the lower values for the more common colors. Eva Zeisel gave her permission to reissue a few select pieces of Town and Country; these were made by World of Ceramics. In 1996 salt and pepper shakers were reproduced in new colors not resembling Red Wing colors. In 1997 the mixing bowl and syrup were reissued. All new pieces are stamped EZ96 or EZ97 and are visibly different from the old, as far as glaze, pottery base, and weight. Charles Alexander (who is listed in the Directory under Indiana) advises us on the Town and Country market.

Key:
NS — North Star   RW — Red Wing

Lute Song, beverage server w/cover, $75 to	125.00
Lute Song, bowl, cereal/salad, $10 to	15.00
Lute Song, bowl, salad, 11", $75 to	100.00
Lute Song, bowl, serving/vegetable dish, 8", $20 to	25.00
Lute Song, creamer, $15 to	20.00
Lute Song, c/s, $10 to	15.00
Lute Song, plate, 6", $8 to	12.00
Lute Song, plate, 7", $8 to	12.00
Lute Song, plate, diner, $15 to	20.00
Lute Song, platter, 13", $25 to	30.00
Lute Song, sugar bowl, $15 to	20.00
Lute Song, teapot, $125 to	175.00
Lute Song, vegetable dish, divided, $20 to	25.00

Pepe, bean pot, wire handle and original lid, F. W. Dahl, Oakland, Nebraska, advertising, $225.00 to $275.00. (Photo courtesy Dan Depasquale)

Pepe, beverage server w/cover, $50 to	75.00
Pepe, bowl, cereal/soup, 6", $10 to	15.00
Pepe, bowl, fruit/sauce, 5", $12 to	15.00
Pepe, bowl, vegetable, 8", $25 to	30.00
Pepe, cr/sugar, ea $12 to	15.00
Pepe, c/s, $10 to	15.00
Pepe, pitcher, water, $100 to	150.00
Pepe, plate, 6", $7 to	10.00
Pepe, plate, dinner, 10", $15 to	20.00
Pepe, platter, 13", $25 to	30.00
Pepe, teapot, $100 to	150.00
Pepe, vegetable dish, divided, $25 to	30.00
Tampico, beverage server w/cover, $75 to	100.00
Tampico, bowl, cereal, $10 to	15.00
Tampico, cake plate, ped, $40 to	60.00
Tampico, casserole, covered, $35 to	50.00
Tampico, c/s, $10 to	15.00
Tampico, pitcher, water, 2-qt, $50 to	75.00
Tampico, plate, dinner, $15 to	20.00
Tampico, platter, 13", $20 to	30.00
Tampico, platter, 15", $25 to	40.00
Tampico, teapot, $60 to	80.00
Tampico, water cooler w/cover & stand, $400 to	600.00
Town & Country, bowl, mixing, Dusk Bl	120.00
Town & Country, condiment/mustard jar, $195 to	225.00
Town & Country, cruet, $75 to	95.00
Town & Country, c/s, $23 to	45.00
Town & Country, pitcher, 3-pt, $150 to	195.00
Town & Country, plate, dinner, chartreuse	23.00
Town & Country, platter, comma shape, 15x12", $45 to	65.00
Town & Country, sugar bowl, $35 to	45.00
Town & Country, sugar, forest gr	46.00
Town & Country, teapot, rust	190.00

Stoneware

Jars, refrigerator, stacking, with lids, three sizes pictured: 3¼x4¾", 3¼x5", and 3¼x6¾", each $250.00 to $300.00. (Photo courtesy Dan Depasquale)

Bowl, Greek Key, bl/wht, 6-10", $100 to	175.00
Bowl, Greek Key, bl/wht, 11" or 12", $250 to	350.00
Bowl, milk pan, wht, brn or bl, sgn, various szs, $60 to	175.00
Bowl, paneled, sponge, 5", $575 to	675.00
Bowl, paneled, sponge, 6-9", $100 to	150.00
Bowl, paneled, sponge, 10-11", $275 to	350.00
Bowl, Saffron, various colored stripes, 5", $150 to	200.00
Bowl, Sponge Band, 4, 5 or 11", $550 to	650.00
Bowl, Sponge Band, 6-10", $200 to	300.00
Churn lid, 3-, 4-, 5, or 6-gal, $110 to	130.00
Churn, salt glaze, dbl P/Rib Cage, sgn, 3-, 4-, or 5-gal, $2,200 to	2,500.00
Churn, salt glaze, upturned leaf, 3-, 4- or 5-gal, $500 to	700.00
Churn, wht glaze, Wing & lid, 2- or 4-gal, 4", $400 to	500.00
Crock, RW, 1-gal, 4", $450 to	600.00
Crock, salt galze, leaf design, unsgn, 5-gal, $400 to	500.00
Crock, salt glaze, bottom sgn, Target design, 2-gal, $100 to	150.00
Crock, salt glaze, Butterfly design, sgn, 10-gal, $1,800 to	2,000.00
Crock, salt glaze, dbl P/Rib Cage, unsgn, 4-gal, $250 to	350.00
Crock, salt glaze, P design, 3-gal, $250 to	350.00
Crock, wht glaze, advertising, Ayr, ND, 3-gal, $800 to	1,200.00

Crock, wht glaze, Elephant Ears, Union oval, 4-gal, $250 to 350.00
Crock, wht glaze, Wing, 2-gal, 4", $75 to..................................... 100.00
Ice water, Birch Leaves, 3- or 4-gal, $700 to 1,000.00
Ice water, RW, w/lid, 3- or 4-gal, $700 to 900.00
Jar, beater, advertising, bl band at top & tie ring, $300 to........... 400.00
Jar, beater, RW beater jar, eggs, $150 to 200.00
Jar, beater, Saffron ware, $200 to.. 250.00
Jar, beater, Sponge Band, $300 to 500.00
Jar, refrigerator, bl/wht, w/bailed hdl & lid, $300 to 350.00
Jar, refrigerator, squat, stacking, advertising inside, $500 to 600.00
Jug, beehive, wht glaze, sgn, ½- or 1-gal, $70 to.......................... 150.00
Jug, beehive, wht glaze, wing & oval, 3- or 5-gal, $400 to........... 475.00
Jug, beehive, wht glaze, wing & oval, 4-gal, $900 to 1,100.00
Jug, bl sponge, bailed hdl, 1-gal, $2,000 to................................2,500.00
Jug, shoulder, Birch Leaves, no oval, 4- or 5-gal, $300 to 375.00
Jug, shoulder, Birch Leaves, oval, 3-gal, $400 to......................... 475.00
Jug, shoulder, brn top, RW, ½- or 1-gal, $125 to.......................... 225.00
Jug, shoulder, salt glaze, NS, ½-gal, $175 to 250.00
Jug, shoulder, salt glaze, NS, 1- & 2-gal, $350 to 400.00
Jug, shoulder, wht glaze, wing & oval, 3-, 4-, or 5-gal, $100 to..... 175.00
Jug, wht glaze, bailed hdl, sgn, ½- or 1-gal, $70 to 150.00
Pitcher, Cherry Band, bl/wht, lg, $125 to..................................... 225.00
Pitcher, Cherry Band, bl/wht, sm, $150 to 250.00
Pitcher, iris, brn, $325 to 475.00
Pitcher, ridges near top & bottom, bl sponge, $500 to.................. 800.00
Reamer, Sponge Band, $1,300 to 1,600.00
Water cooler, lid, 5- or 6-gal, $290 to.. 325.00
Water cooler, RW & lid, 5-gal, 4", $700 to................................... 900.00

Regal China

Located in Antioch, Illinois, the Regal China Company opened for business in 1938. Products of interest to collectors are Jim Beam decanters, cookie jars, salt and pepper shakers, and similar novelty items. The company closed its doors sometime in 1993. The Old MacDonald Farm series listed below is especially collectible, as are the salt and pepper shakers.

Note: Where applicable, prices are based on excellent gold trim. (Gold trim must be 90% intact or deductions should be made for wear.) Our advisor for Old MacDonald's Farm in this category is Rick Spencer; he is listed in the Directory under Utah. See also Decanters, Beam.

Cookie Jars

Little Miss Muffet, $150.00 to $200.00. (Photo courtesy Tom Harris Auctions on LiveAuctioneers.com)

Alice in Wonderland, Walt Disney, min.....................................2,500.00
Cat, $200 to 250.00
Churn Boy.. 175.00

Clown, gr collar 450.00
Davy Crockett.. 300.00
Diaper Pin Pig... 250.00
Dutch Girl.. 450.00
Dutch Girl, peach trim 550.00
FiFi Poodle, min.. 500.00
Fisherman, $650 to 720.00
French Chef, $350 to.. 400.00
Goldilocks, (+), $150 to 200.00
Harpo Marx...1,080.00
Hubert Lion, min... 800.00
Humpty Dumpty, red 125.00
Majorette.. 250.00
Oriental Lady w/Baskets, $725 to.. 775.00
Peek-a-boo (+), $925 to 975.00
Quaker Oats.. 95.00
Rocking Horse... 250.00
Three Bears 175.00
Toby Cookies, unmk, $675 to... 725.00
Tulip 150.00
Uncle Mistletoe.. 765.00

Old MacDonald's Farm

Butter dish, cow's head 95.00
Canister, flour, cereal, coffee, med, ea 150.00
Canister, pretzels, peanuts, popcorn, chips, tidbits, lg, ea, $150 to ..200.00
Canister, salt, sugar, tea, med, ea $75 to.. 85.00
Canister, soap, $200 to... 250.00
Cookie barn 95.00
Creamer, rooster... 60.00
Grease jar, pig, $110 to 135.00
Pitcher, milk... 125.00
Shakers, boy & girl, pr 75.00
Shakers, churn, gold trim, pr 75.00
Shakers, feed sacks w/sheep, pr $80 to 110.00
Spice jar, assorted lids, sm, ea $75 to... 95.00
Sugar bowl, hen 85.00
Teapot, duck's head.. 150.00

Shakers

Bendel, bears, wht w/pk & brn trim, pr.. 75.00
Bendel, bunnies, wht w/blk & pk trim, pr 75.00
Bendel, kissing pigs, gray w/pk trim, lg, pr $250 to 275.00
Bendel, love bugs, burgundy, lg, pr 125.00
Bendel, love bugs, gr, sm, pr.. 65.00
Cat, sitting w/eyes closed, wht w/hat & gold bow, pr.................... 225.00
Clown, pr 250.00
Dutch Girl, pr $150 to 200.00
FiFi, pr.. 250.00
Fish, mk C Miller, 1-pc.. 55.00
French Chef, wht w/gold trim, pr 250.00
Humpty Dumpty, pr.. 75.00
Nod to Abe, A, 3-pc nodder, $200 to 250.00
Peek-a-boo, red dots, lg, pr (+) $350 to 400.00
Peek-a-boo, red dots, sm, pr $125 to 150.00
Peek-a-boo, wht solid, sm, pr.. 175.00
Pig, pk, mk C Miller, 1-pc... 75.00
Tulip, pr... 35.00
Van Tellingen, black boy & dog 55.00
Van Tellingen, boy & dog, wht, pr 45.00
Van Tellingen, bunnies, solid colors, pr $28.................................. 32.00
Van Tellingen, ducks, pr 25.00

Van Tellingen, Dutch boy & girl, $45 to.......................... 50.00
Van Tellingen, Mary & her lamb, pr $40 .... 50.00
Van Tellingen, sailor & mermaid, $100 to 125.00

Relief-Molded Jugs

For the first three quarters of the nineteenth century, relief-molded decoration provided a popular option for the English potter. Produced by a large number of makers in both stoneware (opaque) and parian (translucent), the jugs reflect the changing styles of the period as well as Victorian interests in mythology and literature, history, and natural sciences. Beginning collectors are urged to utilize the publication of retired dealer Kathy Hughes whose research and enthusiasm did much to promote collecting interest in jugs in the country. Collectors should heed Hughes's warning as printed in previous editions of this guide: 'Watch for recent reproductions; these have been made by the slip-casting method. Unlike relief-molded ware which is relatively smooth inside, slip-cast pitchers will have interior indentations that follow the irregularities of the relief decoration.' Values below are for pieces in excellent condition.

Key: Reg — Registered

Arabic, lav & wht, Samuel Alcock, 10".......................... 550.00
Babes in the Woods, bl & wht, ca 1850, mini, 3¾", NM.............. 175.00
Babes in the Woods, mc, ca 1855, 8½"............................ 350.00
Bacchanalian Boys, smear glazed, Spode, 1800-10, 5⅞x5" 495.00
Bacchanalian Dance, wht, Charles Meigh, 7".............................. 425.00

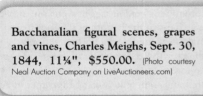

Bacchanalian figural scenes, grapes and vines, Charles Meighs, Sept. 30, 1844, 11¼", $550.00. (Photo courtesy Neal Auction Company on LiveAuctioneers.com)

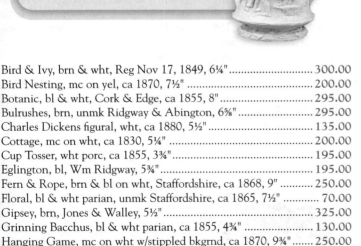

Bird & Ivy, brn & wht, Reg Nov 17, 1849, 6¼" 300.00
Bird Nesting, mc on yel, ca 1870, 7½" 200.00
Botanic, bl & wht, Cork & Edge, ca 1855, 8".......................... 295.00
Bulrushes, brn, unmk Ridgway & Abington, 6⅝".......................... 295.00
Charles Dickens figural, wht, ca 1880, 5½" 135.00
Cottage, mc on wht, ca 1830, 5¼" 200.00
Cup Tosser, wht porc, ca 1855, 3¾".................................. 195.00
Eglington, bl, Wm Ridgway, 5¾"..................................... 195.00
Fern & Rope, brn & bl on wht, Staffordshire, ca 1868, 9" 250.00
Floral, bl & wht parian, unmk Staffordshire, ca 1865, 7½" 70.00
Gipsey, brn, Jones & Walley, 5½".................................... 325.00
Grinning Bacchus, bl & wht parian, ca 1855, 4¾" 130.00
Hanging Game, mc on wht w/stippled bkgrnd, ca 1870, 9¾"....... 250.00
Idle Apprentices, wht stoneware, ca 1840, 6¾" 145.00
Miser & Spendthrift, wht parian, ca 1850, 5" 125.00
Music pattern, wht, Dudson, ca 1870, 7¾" 185.00
Oak, gold on wht, tankard form, ca 1845, 11" 295.00
Paul & Virginia, wht w/bl bkground, Mayer, Reg Dec 2, 1851, 8⅜"...450.00
Putti & Goat, wht parian, unmk, ca 1850, 6½" 125.00
Shakespeare's Bust, lt bl, ca 1870, 4"............................... 200.00
Society of Arts Prize Jug, bl & wht, Minton, 6¼" 375.00
Twining Flowers, wht parian, Minton, Reg May 14, 1855, 6" 300.00

Wainright's Two Children, bl & wht, 1870s, 7½" 250.00
Washington in uniform ea side, xd flags, att Minton, 11½".......... 660.00
Wheat, wht, ca 1870, 6¼" 80.00
Willie, wht, Ridgway, ca 1851, 6½"................................... 225.00

Restraints

Since the beginning of time, many things from animals to treasures have been held in bondage by hemp, bamboo, chests, chains, shackles, and other constructed devices. Many of these devices were used to hold captives who awaited further torture, as if the restraint wasn't torturous enough. The study and collecting of restraints enables one to learn much about the advancement of civilization in the country or region from which they originated. Such devices at various times in history were made of very heavy metals — so heavy that the wearer could scarcely move about. It has only been in the last 60 years that vast improvements have been made in design and construction that afford the captive some degree of comfort. Many modern swing through cuffs have been made over the past several years; most are very common, but a few were made in small numbers or have been discontinued. Our advisor for this category is Joseph Tanner; he is listed in the Directory under California.

Key:
K — key   NST — non-swing through
Kd — keyed   ST — swing through
lc — lock case   stp — stamped

Foreign Handcuffs

Deutshce Polizei, ST, middle hinge, folds, takes bbl-bit K............. 80.00
East German, heavy steel, NP single lg hinge, NST, bbl K........... 120.00
English, Chubb Arrest, steel, ST, multi-bit solid K...................... 275.00
English, Chubb Escort, steel multi-bit lever................................ 300.00
Flexibles, steel segmented bows, NST Darby type, screw K........... 300.00
French Revolved, oval, ST, takes 2 Ks: bbl & pin tumbler........... 190.00
German Clejuso, sq lc, adjusts/NST, d-lb on side, bbl K.............. 100.00
German Darby, adjusts, well finished, NST, sm........................ 120.00
German, 3-lb steel set, 2" thick, center chain, bbl K.................... 175.00
Hiatt English Darby, like US CW Darby, stp Hiatt & #d.............. 75.00
Hiatt English Model 2000/2010/2015, modern st/chain between, ea.. 125.00
Hiatt English non-adjust screw K Darby style, uses screw K......... 120.00
Hiatt English, figure-8 (w/chain), steel, screw K.......................... 85.00
Italian, stp New Police, modern Peerless type, ST, sm bbl K.......... 35.00
Russian modern ST, blued bbl K, unmk, crude 100.00
Spanish, stp Alcyon/Star, modern Peerless type, ST, sm bbl K....... 40.00

Foreign Leg Shackles

East German, alum, lg hinge, cable amid 4 cuffs, bbl K............... 150.00
Hiatt English combo manacles, handcuff/leg irons w/chain 325.00
Hiatt Plug leg irons, same K-ing as Plug-8 cuffs, w/chain 600.00

U.S. Handcuffs

Bean-Cobb handcuffs and leg irons, take small concave contour flat keys, circa 1899, each $375.00. (Photo courtesy Joseph Tanner)

Adams, teardrop lc, bbl Kd, NST, usually not stp 350.00
American Munitions, modern/rnd, sm bbl Kd, ST bow, stp 45.00
Bean Cobb, mk Pat 1899, 1 link between cuffs 180.00
Bean Giant, sideways figure-8, solid center lc, dbl-bit K 800.00
Cavenay, looks like Marlin Daley but w/screw K, NST 300.00
Civil War padlocking type, various designs w/loop for lock 225.00
Elias Rickert (ER), screw K, 1878 .... 900.00
H&R Bean, mk H&R Arms Co, steel, sm flattish K 250.00
H&R Super, ST, shaft-hinge connector takes hollow titted K 150.00
Judd, NST, used rnd/internally triangular K, stp Mattatuck 250.00
Kimbel, screw K at top side, 1964 .... 3,000.00
Marlin Daley, NST, bottle-neck form, neck stp, dbl-titted K 400.00
Mattatuk, mk, propeller-type K 150.00
Peerless, ST, takes sm bbl K, stp Mfg'ered by S&W Co 75.00
Providence Tool Co, stp, NST, Darby screw K style 350.00
Romer, NST, takes flat K, resembles padlock, stp Romer Co 600.00
Strauss, ST, takes lg solid bitted K, stp Strauss Eng Co 120.00
Tower bar cuffs, cuffs separate by 10-12" steel bar 300.00
Tower-Bean, NST, sm rnd lc, takes tiny bbl-bitted K, stp 175.00
Walden 'Lady Cuff,' NST, takes sm bbl K, lightweight, stp 800.00

U.S. Leg Shackles

Bean-Cobb, mk Pat 1899, steel 375.00
H&R Bean, mk H&R Hdw Co, steel, takes sm flattish K 400.00
H&R Supers, as handcuffs 700.00
Hand forged iron, screw K lock, 12" 200.00
Judd, as handcuffs 300.00
Mattatuck, mk Mfg by Mattatuck...Waterbury CT, steel, takes flat K . 800.00
Oregon boot, break-apart shackle on above ankle support 3,000.00
Peerless Big Guy, modern ST, bbl K 60.00
Strauss, as handcuffs 200.00
Tower ball & chain, leg iron w/chain & 6-lb to 50-lb ball 700.00
Tower Detective, as handcuffs (imitation) 250.00

Various Other Restraining Devices

African slave Darby-style cuffs, heavy iron/chain, handmade 200.00
African slave padlocking or riveted forged iron shackles 170.00
Darby neck collar, rnd steel loop opens w/screw K 500.00
English figure-8 nipper, claws open by lifting top lock tab 120.00
Gale finger cuff, knuckle duster, non-K, mk GFC 300.00
German nipper, twist hdl opens/closes cuff, stp Germany/etc 75.00
Hiatt High Security, hinged bbl K & pin-tumbler K (2 Ks) 150.00
Jay Pee, thumb cuffs, mk solid body, bbl K 20.00
Korean, hand chain model, blk, bbl K 60.00
McDonald, thumb cuffs, solid body, ST, dbl-bit center, K 500.00
Mighty-Mite, thumb cuffs, solid body, ST, mk, bbl K 225.00
New Model Russian, chain bbl K, blued 125.00
New Model Russian, hinged, bbl key, blued 140.00
Phillips Nipper, claw, flip lever on top to open 140.00
Thomas Nipper, claw, push button on top to open 150.00
Tower Lyon, thumb cuffs, solid body, NST, dbl-bit center K 400.00

Reverse Painting on Glass

Verre eglomise is the technique of painting on the underside of glass. Dating back to the early 1700s, this art became popular in the nineteenth century when German immigrants chose historical figures and beautiful women as subjects for their reverse glass paintings. Advertising mirrors of this type came into vogue at the turn of the century. Our values are for examples in at least excellent condition.

Andrew Jackson, military portrait, border flakes, 12x9¼", +orig fr ... 1,500.00
Asian beauty w/fan & flowers, Qing dynasty, 19th C, 23x17", +fr .. 875.00
Asian boy w/flower basket, dbl fr w/gold liner, 29x35" overall 315.00
Asian lady in brocade robe w/scroll, late Qing dynasty, 16x12" ... 690.00
Asian lady sitting at sm table, 1800s, 19½x13½", +rosewood fr ... 280.00
Asian noblewoman seated at table, in pnt 19x16" fr 750.00
Castle scene w/sailboats & cottage, 21¼x29¼", +birdseye maple fr . 65.00
Cowboy on wht horse roping cow, Ginger Briggs, 23½x29½", +fr .. 155.00
Duc de Bordeaux, young boy, military dress w/sword, 12x10", +fr, VG ... 340.00
European castle on coast scene, 1900s, 18x38", +gilt fr 65.00
European market scene, 1800s, 46½x23", +fr, VG 625.00

Lady in kimono, Chinese export, sight: 23x15", EX, $360.00. (Photo courtesy Kaminski Auctions on LiveAuctioneers.com)

Napoleon, military portrait, 1831, 11¼x10", +orig fr, VG 345.00
Qianlong Emperor, portrait on throne, 20th C, in cvd wood stand, 35" .. 140.00

Rhead

Frederick Hurten Rhead was born in 1880 in Hanely, Staffordshire, England, into a family of prominent ceramists. He went on to became one of the most productive artisans in the history of the industry.

His career began in England at the Wardel Pottery. At only 19 years of age, he was named art director there. He left England in 1902 at the age of 22, and came to America.

He was associated with many companies during his career in America — Weller, Vance/Avon Faience, Arequipa, A.E. Tile, and lastly Homer Laughlin China. He organized his own pottery in Santa Barbara, California, ca 1913. Admittedly more of a designer than a potter, Rhead hired help to turn the pieces on the wheel but did most of the decorating himself. The process he favored most involved sgraffito designs inlaid with enameling. Egyptian and Art Nouveau influences were evidenced in much of his work. The ware he produced in California was often marked with a logo incorporating the potter at the wheel and 'Santa Barbara.' Our advisors for this category are Suzanne Perrault and David Rago; they are listed in the Directory under New Jersey. See also Roseville; Vance/Avon Faience; Weller.

Key: s-b — squeezebag   w-r — wax-resist

Vase, inlaid and enamel decorated, stamped Rhead Pottery Santa Barbara, 4½x4½", $4,270.00. (Photo courtesy Rago Arts and Auction Center)

Bowl, band of carp in wax resist, Rhead Santa Barbara, 3x9" .. 15,600.00
Bowl, cvd camellia & leaves on brn & blk, turq int, Santa Barbara, 10" .. 6,600.00

Bowl, cvd stylized squirrel, UC/#5148, att, 2x4¾" 4,600.00
Bowl, s-b stylized trees, mtns & clouds, #269, 2¼x6¼"............20,400.00
Bowl, w-r carp band at rim, blk, ftd, Santa Barbara, 3½x9½"..15,600.00
Chargers, s-b man/lady in traditional garb, Foley/1899, rstr, 14", pr.2,400.00
Jardiniere & ped, stylized lotus blossoms & leaves, flakes, 33x16"..9,600.00
Vase, cvd pnt ornate flowers/pods, chips, 6¼x4" 25,000.00
Vase, cvd w/mts & trees, 3¾x4"...1,470.00

Richard

Richard, who at one time worked for Galle, made cameo art glass in France during the 1920s. His work was often multilayered and acid cut with florals and scenics in lovely colors. The ware was marked with his name in relief. Our advisor for this category is Don Williams; he is listed in the Directory under Missouri.

Vase, sunset scene with villa and mountains beyond, $850.00. (Photo courtesy Jackson's Auction on LiveAuctioneers.com)

Atomizer, floral, burgundy on bl, flared ft, rpl bulb, 6¼" 480.00
Atomizer, Russian church/water/trees, pk on ivory, 20th C, 12".. 1,200.00
Box, holly & berries, cobalt on pumpkin/red mottle, ftd, 1910s, 5x6"..660.00
Vase, flamingos/lake/tree, gr/raspberry/yel, 5" 480.00
Vase, floral, brn on yel frost, slim, 8½" 600.00
Vase, floral, magenta on lt bl, wide shoulders, ca 1900, 4¼".........550.00
Vase, floral, magenta on pk, stick neck, 7¼" 400.00
Vase, landscape, red-brn on orange, invt baluster form, 1920s, 8½"...600.00
Vase, Nouveau poppies & vines, lav on pk, slim neck, 19th C, 8¾"..900.00
Vase, orchids, raspberry on cream, slim w/flared ft, 11⅝"..............660.00
Vase, petunia & foliage, brn on lt yel, flared ft, 1910s, 10¼"........550.00
Vase, scenic, bl on burnt orange, slim tapered form, ca 1920, 13". 950.00

Cameo

Vase, European landscape w/buildings, purple on lav, 8" 1,500.00
Vase, flamingos in lily pond, pendant foliage, brn on ivory, 6".....900.00
Vase, floral/leaves, royal bl on orange, 3 bl hdls, 4x3½"................365.00
Vase, flowers/insects, brn tones on orange, slim/ftd, 10¼" 700.00
Vase, lake/mtns/trees, slim w/wide mushroom-cap top, 8½".........590.00
Vase, tree w/boats & mtns on red, slanted pinched rim, 6x3½" ...600.00
Vase, tree w/mtns/ships/bldgs beyond, 3 detailed cvgs, bulb, 15"...2,000.00
Vase, trees/coastal bldgs, brn on orange, slim w/bun ft, 12"..........590.00

Lucie Rie

Lucie Rie was born in 1902. She moved to London in 1938 and shared her studio with Hans Coper from 1946 to 1958. Her ceramics look modern; however they are based on shapes from many world cultures dating back to Roman times. Lucie Rie is best known for the use of metallic oxides in her clay and glazes. She specializes in the hand throwing of thin porcelain bowls, which is a very difficult process. Her works are in the world's best museums. All of her ceramics are impressed with a seal mark on the bottom, a cojoined 'L & R' within a rectangular reserve. Recently, when her work is offered at auction, it has been bringing prices that are sometimes double the presale estimates.

Bowl, brn w/blk splash rim, stemmed, ca 1955, 4¾" 2,200.00
Bowl, radiating sgraffito lines on pk & bronze matt, 4¾x9", NM .10,750.00
Vase, matt glazes of gr, charcoal, ivory, & pk, 10" 9,150.00
Vase, golden manganese, terra cotta shoulder/lip sgraffito, 9" .26,400.00
Vase, running wht/pk brn, LRG Wein, 5¾" 5,400.00

Robineau

After short-term training in ceramics in 1903, Adelaide Robineau (with the help of her husband Samuel) built a small pottery studio at her home in Syracuse, New York. She was adept in mixing the clay and throwing the ware, which she often decorated by incising designs into the unfired clay. Samuel developed many of the glazes and took charge of the firing process. In 1910 she joined the staff of the American Women's League Pottery at St. Louis, where she designed the famous Scarab Vase. After this pottery failed, she served on the faculty of Syracuse University. In the 1920s she worked under the name of Threshold Pottery. She was also the founder and publisher of *Keramic Studio* magazine. Her work was and is today highly acclaimed for the standards of excellence to which she aspired. Our advisors for this category are Suzanne Perrault and David Rago; they are listed in the Directory under New Jersey.

Bowl, kylix, lt brn w/bl crystals, blk hdls, rose-to brn int, 3½x8". 1,650.00
Doorknobs, various glazes on porc, 1x2¼", 4 for 2,280.00
Vase, 4 hdls, opaque celadon ribs, crackled grnd, 4x4", EX 10,200.00
Vase, brn & bl crystalline, ink scribble, 2¼x2" 1,200.00
Vase, bud, amber crystalline, AR w/rnd mk, 7x2"....................11,000.00

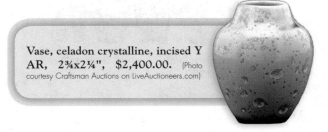

Vase, celadon crystalline, incised Y AR, 2¾x2¼", $2,400.00. (Photo courtesy Craftsman Auctions on LiveAuctioneers.com)

Vase, cobalt crystalline, squat, RP'5/481, 4¼x6"........................4,200.00
Vase, turq & purple mottle, bulb, #2, 1922, 6x7½"..................10,800.00
Vase, turq crystalline, squat, narrow rim, #956 05/label, 2¾x5" .4,800.00
Vase, turq flambé, 5x2¾" 3,000.00

Robj

Robj was the name of a retail store that operated in Paris for only a few years, from about 1925 to 1931. Robj solicited designs from the best French artisans of the period to produce decorative objects for the home. These were executed mostly in porcelain but there were glass and earthenware pieces as well. The most well known are the figural bottles which were particularly popular in the United States. However, Robj also promoted tea sets, perfume lamps, chess sets, ashtrays, bookends, humidors, powder jars, cigarette boxes, figurines, lamps, and milk pitchers. Robj objects tend to be whimsical, and all embody the Art Deco style. Items listed below are ceramic unless noted otherwise. Our advisors for this category are Randall Monsen and Rod Baer; their address is listed in the Directory under Virginia.

Bottle, Cointreau, clown in wht w/red details, 10½" 2,200.00
Bottle, Cusenier, 10½" 2,125.00
Bottle, Joueur De Cornemuse, 10¼"..500.00
Bottle, Kummel Cursky De Cointreau, bl & wht, 10½" 2,500.00

Bottle, L'Ecuyere, gr military-style jacket, wht bottom, w/purse, 12" ... 4,050.00
Bottle, Le Muscadin Ou L'Incroyable, 12½".................................. 4,685.00
Bottle, Les Trois Matelots, 3 bk-to-bk sailors in bl, 11" 4,700.00
Bottle, male figure, Scots piper in regimental wht, 10½" 480.00
Bottle, mammy in yel dress, 10¾"..1,200.00
Bottle, Maquette de Le Seyeux, 11¾" 1,250.00
Bottle, scent, blk sultan, wht & gold, 6¼x5" 1,065.00
Bottle, vodka, Red Russian, 10½"...995.00
Lamp, perfume, mottled glass shade, wrought-iron tower base, 9". 475.00
Vase, Deco floral on bl, Luneville, 4½" 95.00

Roblin

The intimate and short-lived Roblin pottery was founded at the turn of the last century in San Francisco by Alexander Robertson, whose family had been Scottish ceramicists for generations, and California potter Linna Irelan. Its name came from the contraction of Robertson and Linna, and its product from their joined experience and tastes. The two shared a fondness for local clays, which Alexander Robertson threw along classical shapes. Mrs. Irelan embellished them with painted and applied decoration, often minimal beading, sometimes with applied lizards or mushrooms. Most were stamped Roblin along with a bear drawing. The company was forced to close after the great earthquake of 1906. Our advisors for this category are Suzanne Perrault and David Rago; they are listed in the Directory under New Jersey.

Vases (five), miniature, glaze tests, tallest 3¾", each $300.00 to $400.00. (Photo courtesy Rago Arts and Auction Center)

Vase, bsk, cylinder w/tooling at top, cvd & stepped ft, 2½x1½" ... 215.00
Vase, bsk, swollen cylinder w/tooled banded lines, 2¼x1¾" 350.00
Vase, gunmetal, cylindrical w/prunt, L Irelan, 4" 650.00
Vase, multi-tone tan & brn on bsk, sm ft, 2".................................. 550.00

Rock 'n Roll Memorabilia

Memorabilia from the early days of rock 'n roll recalls an era that many of us experienced firsthand. Our listings mainly cover four groups/singers — The Beatles, Elvis Presley, KISS, and the Monkees — who were legendary and whose memorabilia is most popular and valuable to collectors. While there are other rock 'n roll groups with collectible items, their values do not change much from their retail selling prices. Vintage items are what collectors desire. The recent passing of rock legend Michael Jackson has sparked interest in his merchandise, and we have included some items from 1984, the largest licensing year for this king of pop.

Beware of reproductions! Many are so well done even a knowledgeable collector will sometimes be fooled. Unless otherwise noted, our values are for licensed examples in excellent condition. Our advisor for this category is Bob Gottuso (Bojo), author of Beatles, KISS, and Monkees sections in *Garage Sale Gold II* by Tomart and *Garage Sale & Flea Market* (Collector Books). He is listed in the Directory under Pennsylvania. See also Decanters, McCormick.

Beatles, banjo, plastic, Mastro, 1964-65, 22", (+).....................2,400.00
Beatles, belt, multi-repeating faces in silver, diff colors, 1964-65, NM ..75.00

Beatles, bongo drums, Mastro, 1964-65, (+) 2,400.00
Beatles, brunch bag, vinyl, w/zippered top, 1964-65, 8"...............450.00
Beatles, candy dish, pottery, gilt edge, UK, 1 of ea Beatle, 1964-65, 4", ea. 150.00
Beatles, cartoon Colorforms, w/box & instructions, 1964-65, NM .800.00
Beatles, clutch purse, vinyl, leather strap, group photo, 1964-65 . 240.00
Beatles, concert ticket stub (depending on venue), (+), $50 to ... 300.00
Beatles, cork stoppers, figural head, 1 of ea Beatle, 1964-65 .... 500.00
Beatles, Disk-Go case, plastic, holds 45 rpm records, 1964-65, (+). 175.00
Beatles, dolls, blow-up, 1964-65, set of 4 .... 150.00
Beatles, dolls, bobbin' head, papier mache, 1964-65, 8", set of 4, (+). 500.00
Beatles, dolls, John or George, vinyl, Remco, 1964-65, 4" 140.00
Beatles, dress, Holland, 3 styles, 1964-65, NM, ea...................... 750.00
Beatles, drum, Ringo, w/stand & sticks, UK, 1964-65 .... 800.00
Beatles, guitar, electric, Selcol Red Jet 1, 1964-65, 30", NM.....1,600.00
Beatles, guitar, Mastro, 4 pop, 1964-65, 21", NM, (+).................. 450.00
Beatles, guitar, Mastro, Beatleist, 6 string, 1964-65, 21", NM 700.00
Beatles, guitar, Mastro, Jr, pk & red, 1964-65, 21", NM 400.00
Beatles, harmonica/box, Hohner, 1964-65, NM 180.00
Beatles, magnetic hair game, w/wand, UK, 1964-65, EX............. 750.00
Beatles, mug, thermal, photo under clear, 1964-65, 4", EX, (+). 90.00
Beatles, pnt-by-number set, 1 of ea Beatle, complete, 1964-65, NM..850.00
Beatles, pencil case, different colors, zippered top, SPP, 1964-65, EX.150.00
Beatles, phonograph, group pictures on top/inside, 1964-65, EX.... 2,500.00
Beatles, plate, biscuit, UK pottery, color decal, 1964-65, NM...... 100.00

Beatles, record player, group pictures on top/inside, 1964–1965, EX, $2,500.00. (Photo courtesy Bob Gottuso)

Beatles, shoulder bag, vinyl w/cord strap, group picture, 1964-65 . 350.00
Beatles, talcum powder, UK, Margo of Mayfair, 1964-65, NM..... 500.00
Beatles, tennis shoes, WingDings, 1964-65, NMIB 800.00
Beatles, tumbler, thermal, w/photo under clear plastic, (+) 100.00
Elvis, autograph book, cb, 1956... 250.00
Elvis, belt, vinyl, 1956 .... 250.00
Elvis, charm bracelet, w/photo, on orig card, 1956 .... 100.00
Elvis, game, complete, 1956 .... 800.00
Elvis, guitar, Emenee, no box, EX, 1956...................................... 500.00
Elvis, guitar, Emenee, w/box, complete, 1956 ....1,000.00
Elvis, hat, w/photo hang tag, 1956 .... 125.00
Elvis, lipstick, on card, 1956 .... 500.00
Elvis, necklace, Love Me Tender, on orig card, 1956.................... 125.00
Elvis, overnight case, vinyl covered, 1956 .... 300.00
Elvis, pencils (12), sealed, w/photo, 1956 .... 150.00
Elvis, perfume, Teddy Bear, w/orig box, 1956............................. 150.00
Elvis, record player, 1956.. 500.00
Elvis, scarf, colorful, 1956 .... 175.00
Elvis, scrapbook, cb, 1956... 250.00
Elvis, wallet, vinyl, 1956.. 300.00
KISS, backpack, 1979, MIP.. 200.00
KISS, bedspread, sealed in bag w/insert, M 250.00
KISS, brd game, On Tour, complete, 1978 .... 80.00
KISS, Colorforms, unused, 1979, M 85.00
KISS, curtains, 1978, MIP.. 275.00
KISS, dolls, Mego, 1978, set of 4, MIB.. 800.00
KISS, dolls, Mego, 1978, set of 4, VG... 400.00
KISS, guitar, plastic, 1978, 24" 225.00

KISS, hair combs, plastic, Australian, complete, 1978, ea 15.00
KISS, Halloween costume, w/mask & box, 1978 .... 150.00
KISS, jacket, paper w/flames, 1978 .... 60.00
KISS, lunch box, w/Thermos, 1978 .... 225.00
KISS, make-up kit, Kiss Your Face, 1978, MIB 250.00
KISS, microphone, 1978, MIB 175.00
KISS, pen, Solo, sealed, MOC 75.00
KISS, radio, transistor, orig box, 1978 .... 220.00
KISS, record player, Tiger, 1978 .... 350.00
KISS, Rub 'n Play, Colorforms, unusued, 1978 .... 90.00
KISS, Viewmaster, 3 reels w/booklet in pkg, 1978 .... 40.00

Michael Jackson, microphone, cordless, with glove, LJN, 1984, MIB, $45.00.
(Photo courtesy Bob Gottuso)

Michael Jackson, record player, Ertl, 1984, MIB 250.00
Michael Jackson, record, cereal box, Sugar Daddy, Who's Loving You, 1970s .. 18.00
Monkees, binder, 3-ring, vinyl, 1967 .... 175.00
Monkees, brd game, Transogram, complete, 1967 .... 100.00
Monkees, bracelet, w/4 picture charms attached, on orig card, 1967 ... 40.00
Monkees, Drum Kit, 1967, complete 500.00
Monkees, Drum Kit, complete, 1967, MIB 1,000.00
Monkees, finger puppets, no legs/just boots, only 3 made, 1967, ea .25.00
Monkees, guitar, in orig box, 1967, 14" 225.00
Monkees, guitar, musical windup, 1967, 14" 65.00
Monkees, guitar, w/paper face, 1967, 20" 90.00
Monkees, gumcard box, wht, More of the Monkees, 1967 .... 60.00
Monkees, gumcard box, yel, 1st series, US, 1967 .... 80.00
Monkees, hand puppet, working, 1967 .... 75.00
Monkees, hand puppet, working, w/box, 1967 .... 225.00
Monkees, hangers, clothes, cb, 1967, ea 75.00
Monkees, model kit, plastic, MPC, complete, 1967 .... 125.00
Monkees, Monkeemobile, diecast, Corgi, w/figures, 1967, 5" 75.00
Monkees, Monkeemobile, diecast, Corgi, w/orig box, 1967, 5" 200.00
Monkees, Monkeemobile, diecast, Husky, on orig card, 1967 ...... 200.00
Monkees, record tote, vinyl, 1967 .... 125.00
Monkees, Show Biz Babies, complete, 1967, ea 75.00
Monkees, Show Biz Babies, complete, on cards, w/record, 1967, ea ... 100.00
Monkees, sunglasses, 60s-style, w/chain & mfg tape, 1967 .... 30.00
Monkees, tambourine, Raybert, 1967 .... 75.00
Monkees, wallet, vinyl, 1967 .... 90.00

Rockingham

In the early part of the nineteenth century, American potters began to prefer brown- and buff-burning clays over red because of their durability. The glaze favored by many was Rockingham, which varied from a dark brown mottle to a sponged effect sometimes called tortoiseshell. It consisted in part of manganese and various metallic salts and was used by many potters until well into the twentieth century. Over the past two years, demand and prices have risen sharply, especially in the east. See also Bennington.

Book flask, amber glaze, 5⅝" 390.00
Book flask, dk glaze, att OH, sm flakes, 6" 240.00

Bowl, columns & dots, ca 1860, 3½x10½" 75.00
Figurine, cat, seated, late 19th C, rpr base cracks, 14" 480.00
Figurine, sheep standing on base, ca 1900, 5¼x4⅞x3½" 130.00
Figurine, spaniel seated, free-standing front legs, molded base, 10" .480.00
Flask, mermaid w/curled tail, 8" 175.00
Frame, oval, ca 1850s, 10x8¼" 800.00
Hatpin holder, figural lady wearing hat, long cloak, 5½", NM 120.00
Pitcher, bow-tied wheat stalks & tavern scenes, w/ice lip & lid, 12" .. 240.00
Pitcher, dog begging figural, tricornered hat forms lid, 1850, 11", EX ..215.00
Pitcher, hunt scene, branch hdl, 2 frogs inside, 8½" 1,850.00

Pitcher, ice, heron, modeled by Charles Coxon, attributed to the E. & W. Bennett Pottery, Baltimore, MD, with lid, 9x6¾", EX, $1,320.00. (Photo courtesy Cowan's Auctions, Inc. on LiveAuctioneers.com)

Pitcher, leaves, baluster w/hexagonal ft, 19th C, 7½" 240.00
Plate, pleated corners w/scroll designs, sq, 1½x8½", NM 325.00
Teapot, Rebecca at the Well, paneled, Liverpool, Ohio, 9", EX ... 240.00

Norman Rockwell

Norman Rockwell began his career in 1911 at the age of 17 doing illustrations for a children's book entitled *Tell Me Why Stories*. Within a few years he had produced the *Saturday Evening Post* cover that made him one of America's most beloved artists. Though not well accepted by the professional critics of his day who did not consider his work to be art but 'merely' commercial illustration, Rockwell's popularity grew to the extent that today there is an overwhelming abundance of examples of his work or those related to the theme of one of his illustrations.

The figurines described below were issued by Norman Rockwell Museum and Museum Collections, Inc.; for Rockwell listings by Gorham, see last year's edition of *Schroeder's Antiques Price Guide*. Our advisor for this category is Barb Putratz; she is listed in the Directory under Minnesota.

A Walkin' & a Whistlin', 1986 .... 70.00
Adventures Between Adventures, 1986 .... 100.00
All Wrapped Up, 1984 .... 100.00
Almost Grown Up, 1982 .... 175.00
America's Artist, ltd ed 5,000, 1985 .... 210.00
Another Masterpiece by Norman Rockwell, ltd ed of 5,000, 1985 ..210.00
Apple for the Teacher, Museum Collections Inc, 1986 .... 70.00
Artist (The), Museum Collections Inc, ltd ed 2,500, 1986 .... 95.00
At the Circus, 1982 .... 190.00
Baby's First Step, 1979 .... 175.00
Barefoot Boy, Museum Collections Inc, ltd ed 5,000, 1986 .... 110.00
Bedtime, LCF series, ltd ed 1,000, 1982 .... 225.00
Bicycle Boys, 1981 .... 120.00
Birthday Party (The), 1980 .... 150.00
Bored of Education, 1984 .... 95.00
Bottom of the Sixth, Museum Collections Inc, ltd ed 5,000, 1986 ..200.00
Boy Meets His Dog (A), 1986 .... 100.00
Bride & Groom, 1981 .... 140.00
Bringing Home the Christmas Tree, 1982 .... 125.00
Celebration, 1982 .... 190.00
Checking His List, 1980 .... 90.00
Cobbler, LCF Series, ltd ed 1,000, 1982 .... 225.00

Cobbler (The), 1979.. 80.00
Collect Fine Piece Figures (ad stand), 1984...................... 140.00
Courageous Hero, 1982.. 185.00
Dollhouse for Sis (A), 1979....................................... 80.00
Dreams in the Antique Shop, Museum Collections Inc, 1986....... 80.00
Drummer's Friend (The), 1982.................................... 125.00
First Car in Town (The), ltd ed 2,500, 1985.................... 235.00
First Haircut (The), 1979....................................... 150.00
First Prom (The), 1979.. 125.00
Freedom of Fear, ltd ed 5,000, 1982............................ 350.00
Freedom of Speech, ltd ed 5,000, 1982.......................... 350.00
Freedom of Worship, ltd ed 5,000, 1982......................... 350.00
Giving Thanks, 1982... 200.00
Goin' Fishin', 1984.. 95.00
Good Food Good Friends, 1982................................... 225.00
Happy Birthday, Dear Mother, 1979.............................. 140.00
Helping Mother, 1982... 120.00
High Stepping, 1982.. 110.00
Home for Fido (A), Museum Collections Inc, 1986................. 75.00
Homerun Slugger, 1982.. 145.00
Late Night Dining, Museum Collections Inc, 1986................. 80.00
Letterman (The), Museum Collections Inc, ltd ed 2,500, 1986... 165.00
Lighthouse Keeper's Daughter (The), LCF series, ltd ed 1,000, 1982.. 225.00
Little Mother, 1980.. 135.00
Little Patient, 1981... 120.00
Little Salesman, 1982.. 185.00
Lovely in Lipstick, Museum Collections Inc, 1988................ 75.00
Memories, 1980... 90.00
Memories, LCF Series, ltd ed 1,000, 1983...................... 225.00
Mom's Helper, ltd ed 15,000, 1986............................. 120.00

Music Master (The), 1980, $90.00. (Photo courtesy Livingston's Auction on LiveAuctioneers.com)

Mysterious Malady, Museum Collections Inc, 1986................ 100.00
New Arrival, Museum Collections Inc, 1981...................... 160.00
Off to School, LCF series, ltd ed 1,000, 1981.................. 115.00
Out Fishin', Museum Collections Inc, ltd ed 25,000, 1985....... 100.00
Outward Bound, ltd ed 5,000, 1984............................. 200.00
Partygoers, Museum Collections Inc, ltd 2,500, 1984............ 235.00
Pest (The), 1982... 125.00
Playing Pirates, ltd ed 2,500, 1984........................... 235.00
Practice Makes Perfect, Museum Collections Inc, ltd ed 2,500, 1987... 170.00
Pride of Parenthood, 1986...................................... 100.00
Puppy Love, 1983... 95.00
Report Card, Museum Collections Inc, 1986...................... 80.00
Rosie the Riveter, Museum Collections Inc, ltd ed 2,500, 1987... 165.00
Santa Takes a Break, Museum Collections Inc, ltd ed 3,500, 1987.. 110.00
Saturday's Hero, 1984.. 105.00
Sneezing Spy, Museum Collections Inc, ltd ed 2,500, 1986....... 160.00
Soda Jerk (The), ltd ed 5,000, 1986........................... 205.00
Space Age Santa, 1984.. 115.00
Space Pioneers, 1982... 185.00
Special Treat (A), 1982.. 100.00
Spirit of America, The; ltd ed 5,000, 1982.................... 185.00
Spring Fever, 1981... 100.00

Student (The), 1980.. 165.00
Summer Fun, 1982... 120.00
Sunday Morning, Museum Collections Inc, ltd ed 2,500, 1986 ... 225.00
Sweet Dreams, 1981... 190.00
Sweet Sixteen, 1979.. 125.00
Tattoo Artist, Museum Collections Inc, ltd ed 2,500, 1987...... 170.00
The Circus Comes to Town, Rockwell Museum..................... 125.00
Toymaker (The), 1979... 95.00
Toymaker (The), LCF series, ltd ed 1,000, 1982................ 225.00
Trumpeter (The), Museum Collections Inc, ltd ed 2,500, 1986 2,000.00
Vacation's Over, 1981.. 120.00
Visiting the Vet, Museum Collections Inc, 1988................. 85.00
Waiting for Santa, 1982.. 135.00
We Missed You Daddy, 1981...................................... 190.00
Weighty Matters, ltd ed 5,000, 1986........................... 180.00
Wet Behind the Ears, Museum Collections Inc, 1986.............. 80.00
Winter Fun, 1982... 95.00
Words of Wisdom, 1982.. 130.00
Wrapping Christmas Presents, 1980.............................. 130.00

John Rogers

John Rogers (1829 – 1904) was a machinist from Manchester, New Hampshire, who turned his hobby of sculpting into a financially successful venture. From the originals he meticulously fashioned of red clay, he had bronze master molds made from which plaster copies were cast. He specialized in five different categories: theatrical, Shakespeare, Civil War, everyday life, and horses. His large detailed groupings portrayed the life and times of the period between 1859 and 1892. In the following listings, examples are assumed to be plaster castings in excellent condition unless noted bronze or parian. Many plaster examples will be in poor condition, be sure to adjust prices accordingly. Our advisor for this category is George Humphrey; he is listed in the Directory under Maryland.

Balcony.. 1,500.00
Bath.. 2,000.00
Bushwacker.. 2,000.00
Camp Fire, sm, 1862... 750.00
Camp Life, sm, 1862.. 20,000.00
Charity Patient, 1866, 22"................................. 475.00
Checker Players, sm, 1860.................................. 1,200.00
Checkers Up at the Farm, 1865, 20½x17½x12"................. 575.00
Chess.. 1,200.00
Coming to the Parson, VG................................... 350.00
Council of War (The), Pat March 31, 1868 on rear, buff-colored pnt, 24".. 2,645.00
Council of War, 1868, 24".................................. 3,000.00
Country Post Office, VG.................................... 750.00
Courtship in Sleepy Hollow, 1868, 20"...................... 600.00
Elder's Daughter... 475.00
Fairy's Whisper, 1881...................................... 2,500.00
Faust & Marguerite, Leaving the Garden..................... 1,200.00
Favored Scholar, miniature, 1941, 4x2"..................... 165.00
Favored Scholar, VG.. 780.00
Fetching the Doctor.. 750.00
Fighting Bob, 1889... 1,100.00
First Ride, VG... 725.00
Football, 1891, 15".. 2,000.00
Foundling.. 900.00
Frolic at the Old Homestead, 18x16"........................ 900.00
Fugitive Story, 1869, 22".................................. 900.00
Going for the Cows, $400 to................................ 450.00
Ha! I Like Not That, 1882, 22"............................. 450.00
Home Guard... 800.00

Madam, Your Mother Craves a Word, 1886, 20" 900.00
Mail Day...2,000.00
Matter of Opinion, VG..600.00
Mock Trial, 1877, 21" 1,200.00
Neighboring Pews 475.00
Nominated in the Bond, 1880, 23" 400.00
Parting Promise (older man), VG 475.00
Parting Promise, 22x10x9", VG 635.00
Peddler at the Fair, 1878, 20" 800.00
Photographer, 1878...4,000.00
Phrenology at the Ball, 1878, 20" 1,200.00
Picket Guard, VG 750.00
Playing Doctor, 1872, 14½" 900.00
Politics, 1888, 18" 1,200.00
Polo, bronze, 2 horsemen, 21" 45,000.00
Private Theatricals, 1878, 24" 1,200.00
Referee, 1880, 22" 1,200.00
Returned Volunteer, 1864, 20" 800.00
Rip Van Winkle – At Home, VG- 500.00
Rip Van Winkle on the Mountain, VG- 575.00
Rip Van Winkle Returned, 1871, 21"..700.00
School Days, 22x12x8" 800.00
School Exam, 1867, 20" 700.00
Sharpshooters, sm, not Pat 20,000.00
Slave Auction 2,000.00
Speak for Yourself John, VG- 500.00
Taking the Oath, 1866, 23" 550.00
Tap on the Window 525.00
Town Pump, sm, 1862 ....800.00
Traveling Magician, 1877, 23"..2,500.00
Uncle Ned's School 2,100.00
Union Refugees, 1864, 22½" 800.00
Village Schoolmaster, VG 850.00
Washington...1,250.00
Watch on the Santa Maria 1,000.00
We Boys, 1872, 17" 500.00
Weighing the Baby, 21x15", VG 675.00

Wounded Scout, subtitle: A Friend in the Swamp, 23½", VG, $1,300.00. (Photo courtesy Cowan's Auctions, Inc. on LiveAuctioneers.com)

Wounded to the Rear – One More Shot, plaster, 20½" 750.00
You Are a Spirit, 1885, 19"..800.00

Rookwood

The Rookwood Pottery Company was established in 1879 in Cincinnati, Ohio, by Maria Longworth Nichols. From a wealthy family, Ms. Nichols was provided with sufficient financial backing to make such an enterprise possible. She hired competent ceramic artisans and artists of note, who through constant experimentation developed many lines of superior art pottery. While in her employ, Laura Fry invented the airbrush-blending process for which she was issued a patent in 1884. From this, several lines were designed that utilized blended backgrounds. One of their earlier lines, Standard, was a brown ware decorated with underglaze slip-painted nature studies, animals, portraits, etc. Iris and Sea Green were introduced in 1894 and Vellum, a transparent matt-glaze line, in 1904. Other lines followed: Ombroso in 1910 and Soft Porcelain in 1915. Many of the early artware lines were signed by the artist. Soon after the turn of the twentieth century, Rookwood manufactured 'production' pieces that relied mainly on molded designs and forms rather than free-hand decoration for their aesthetic appeal. The Depression brought on financial difficulties from which the pottery never recovered. Though it continued to operate, the quality of the ware deteriorated, and the pottery was forced to close in 1967.

Unmarked Rookwood is only rarely encountered. Many marks may be found, but the most familiar is the reverse 'RP' monogram. First used in 1886, a flame point was added above it for each succeeding year until 1900. After that a Roman numeral added below indicated the year of manufacture. Impressed letters that related to the type of clay utilized for the body were also used — G for ginger, O for olive, R for red, S for sage green, W for white, and Y for yellow. Artware must be judged on an individual basis. Quality of the artwork is a prime factor to consider. Portraits, animals, and birds are worth more than florals; and pieces signed by a particularly renowned artist are highly prized. Our advisors for this category are Suzanne Perrault and David Rago; they are listed in the Directory under New Jersey.

Black Opal

Vase, cascading flowers, H Wilcox, #2977, 1926, 7" 1,550.00
Vase, dogwood blossoms, H Wilcox, #2101, 1926, 7" 1,175.00
Vase, edelweiss at shoulder, H Wilcox, #2918E, 1929, 6" 3,550.00
Vase, floral (very dk), H Wilcox, #2065, 1924, 8" 1,450.00
Vase, Moorish decor, L Epply, #1920, 1922, 9½".......................4,000.00

Cameo

Bowl, floral branch, E Abel, #549, Wy, W, 1890, 1½x6½"............300.00
Candlestick, floral, E Abel, #508, 1891, 6", ea..............................360.00
Candlestick, flower (sm), unknown artist, #508, W, 1891, 5", ea.145.00
Cup/saucer, floral on red, #460P, 1889, 2¼" 300.00
Ewer, floral, H Wilcox, #101C, Y, 1887, 9x5" 550.00

Ewer, white rose on pastel ground, unidentified artist, 1888, overfired around foot, 6¾", $360.00. (Photo courtesy Craftsman Auctions on LiveAuctioneers.com)

Pitcher, floral, H Wilcox, 1888, 7" 550.00
Plate, coupe, chrysanthemums, S Toohey, #205C, W/W, 1x8".....155.00
Plate, Endymion, EP Chanch, 1890, 7½", VG.............................110.00
Potpourri jar, bird on branch, AR Valentien, #27, Y, 1886, 7x6".850.00
Potpourri jar, bird on branch, M Daly, 1886/237/MAD.............1,950.00
Soap dish, daisies, wht on lt bl, Shirayamadani, #459E, 1898, 4", EX...290.00

French Red

Bowl vase, floral band, S Sax, #955, 1922, 2x4"........................3,750.00
Vase, floral (EX art), S Sax, #703, 1922, X, 5¾x7¼" 8,000.00
Vase, floral design on shoulder, blk trim, S Sax, 1922, 6" 3,840.00
Vase, stylized flowers, S Sax, #356F, 1922, 5½" 9,900.00

Glaze Effect

Vase, bl & tan, baluster, S, 1932, 8" 390.00
Vase, bl/fuchsia/brn, #6307, 1932, 3" 450.00
Vase, bl/lt/bl/gray, #6307F, 1932, 2⅞" 390.00
Vase, chartreuse/bl/dk bl, #6514E, 1957, 3½" 155.00
Vase, red/gray/bl on Coromandel, #6307F, 1932, 3" 600.00

Iris

Vase, apple blossoms, S Coyne, #938C, 1907, 7⅝" 1,175.00
Vase, camellias, S Sax, #925C, W, 1903, 9½" 2,500.00
Vase, cherry blossom branches, S Sax, #904D, 1906, 8x3½" 1,300.00
Vase, clematis, E Diers, #886D, 1904, 8½" 1,950.00
Vase, clovers, bulb, C Steinle, #1120, 1906, 4½x4½" 550.00
Vase, clovers, F Rothenbusch, #614F, W, 1902, 6" 1,200.00
Vase, crocuses, F Rothenbusch, #801D, W, 1902, 7⅜" 1,800.00
Vase, cyclamen, L Asbury, #907E, W, 1910, 8⅝" 2,550.00
Vase, daisies, L Asbury, #917B, W, 1907, 9⅛" 6,000.00
Vase, dragonflies, shouldered, C Schmidt, #941C, 1906, 9¼x3½". 15,000.00
Vase, fish swimming, squat, ET Hurley, 1909, 4¼x4½" 1,800.00
Vase, hollyhock branches, L Asbury, #1278C, X, 1910, 12x6" ..7,800.00
Vase, hollyhocks, L Asbury, #1278C, 1910, 11⅞" 10,800.00
Vase, hyacinths, S Sax, #950C, 1905, 10⅛" 3,250.00
Vase, irises, C Schmidt, 1903, uncrazed, 13½" 12,000.00
Vase, irises, L Asbury, #951C, 1905, 10¼" 3,000.00
Vase, Japanese irises, K Shirayamadani, #589F, W, 1894, 7" 2,000.00
Vase, magnolias, C Schmidt, #952C, W, 1906, 10¼" 6,150.00
Vase, mushrooms, C Schmidt, #901D, W, 1902, 7¼" 2,600.00

Vase, orchids, Albert Valentien, 1908, 14x8½", $14,650.00. (Photo courtesy Rago Arts and Auction Center)

Vase, peacock feather, C Schmidt, #9026, 1904, 9⅜" 44,400.00
Vase, poppies, silver o/l, S Sax, #80B, W, 1900, 6⅝" 3,150.00
Vase, rose (lg), C Schmidt, #901C, W, 1901, 9" 2,350.00
Vase, roses, F Rothenbusch, #1598D, 1909, 9¼" 3,000.00
Vase, swan scenic, C Schmidt, #951C, 1906, 9½" 4,800.00
Vase, swans (2 blk), C Schmidt, #907DD, 1905, 9¾" 6,600.00
Vase, trees & shoreline, S Lawrence, #932B, W, 1902, 14¾" 6,000.00
Vase, trumpet flowers, R Fechheimer, #30F, 1901, 6" 660.00
Vase, Venetian harbor, C Schmidt, #932, W, 1900, 5¼" 3,600.00
Vase, violets, E Wildman, #1120, W, 1911, 4½" 1,050.00
Vase, wild roses at top, M Mitchell, #932E, 1904, 7½" 725.00
Vase, wild roses, E Diers, #907E, 1904, 8½x3½" 950.00
Vase, winter landscape, F Rothenbusch, #1357D, X, 1909, 8½". 3,000.00
Vase, wisteria, Caroline Steinle, VI/614F, 1906, 6½" 1,320.00

Limoges

Basket, butterflies, lion's head ft, AR Valentien, 1882, 9¾x20" L. 550.00
Dish, bird among reeds, WP McDonald, w/hdl, 1883, 6¾" W 150.00
Ewer, butterflies & flowers, unknown artist, 1882, 12x7", NM..... 250.00
Jug, owls & bats under moon on dk gr, N Hirschfeld, 1880, 3x2" . 660.00
Jug, perfume, birds/clouds/grasses, AR Valentien, 1882, 4¾", NM ..350.00

Pilgrim flask, dogwood, L Johnston, 1883, 6½" 725.00
Pitcher, bats/owls/moon, AR Valentien, 1882, 7½x7½" 400.00
Pitcher, dragonfly/grasses, N Hirschfeld, horn shape, G, 1883, 6½" ..780.00
Pitcher, floral, AR Valentien, bulb, 1881, 9" 960.00
Pitcher, scarab & insect, Laura Fry, #39, 1884, 12" 1,020.00
Vase, butterfly among reeds, M Rettig, #205, 1885, 9" 240.00
Vase, floral branches in barbotine, 1885, 13½x8" 725.00

Matt

Note: Both incised matt and painted matt are listed here. Incised matt descriptions are indicated by the term 'cvd' within the line; all others are hand-painted matt ware.

Bowl, #1842, stylized floral design, ivory, ftd, E Lincoln, 1918, 2¾x5"..250.00
Bowl, octagonal, #2697, floral designs at center, ftd, E Lincoln, 3x9½" 500.00
Tankard, cvd apple branches, Todd, 1912, X (2 sm glaze misses), 12"...900.00
Vase, antelopes & branches on yel, W Hentschell, 1929, 13¼x10½" ..14,400.00
Vase, autumnal leaves, S Toohey, #193GZ, 1901, flaw, 9x3½" ..2,650.00
Vase, birds & blossoms, ET Hurley, 1933, 6½x4" 1,200.00
Vase, blossoms, red & yel on turq butterfat, C Todd, 1922, 6¾x3½"..1,140.00
Vase, cattails, W Hentschel, #581E, 1910, X, 12¾x6½" 1,800.00
Vase, cvd Arts & Crafts border, W Hentschel, #915, 1914, 8"..1,800.00
Vase, cvd fish, A Pons, slightly bulb, 1907, 6½" 1,650.00
Vase, cvd floral/geometric band, C Todd, #886C, 1915, 11⅛x8½"...2,100.00
Vase, cvd gingko leaves & nuts, E Lincoln, #9191, 1908, 4¼x4½". 1,025.00
Vase, cvd stylized floral, Wm. Hentschel, #946, 1913, 11" 2,280.00
Vase, cvd swirling lines, W Hentschel, #1016C, 1913, 8¼" 1,175.00
Vase, cvd triangular flowers w/stems, W Hentschel, #2039D, 1913, 10"..1,800.00
Vase, dogwood blossoms, A Valentien, #33DZ, 1901, 7x5½".....1,500.00
Vase, exotic birds on trees, butterfat, L Epply, #2914, 1927, 8¼"...2,750.00
Vase, floral, L Lincoln, #807, 1921, 13¼x5".............................. 1,550.00
Vase, floral, M McDonald, #6602, 6½x5½" 1,075.00
Vase, floral, S Coyne, cylindrical, 1924, 8⅞".............................. 1,075.00
Vase, floral, squeezebag, E Barrett, #2918E, 1929, 6¾x5¼" 835.00
Vase, geometric panels, J Harris, #2254D, 1930, 5¼" 900.00
Vase, goldenrod, bulb, A Sprague, 1901, 9x4½" 2,040.00
Vase, hydrangea branches on butterfat, L Epply, #2246C, 1928, 14½". 5,600.00
Vase, irises, K Shirayamadani, #9075, 1945, 7¾" 1,800.00
Vase, landscape (mottled), M McDonald, #6743, 1939, 7½" 960.00
Vase, lilies, K Shirayamadani, bulb, 1926, 6½x6" 3,600.00
Vase, maple pods on shaded grnd, Olga G Reed, VI/OGR/907DD, 10" .10,800.00
Vase, Moderne, horses & rider, W Rhem, 1934, 5x4¼"............. 1,200.00
Vase, Moderne, leafy sprigs, F Barrett, #2368, 1927, 17x7" 2,200.00
Vase, Moderne, leafy sprigs, W Hentschel, #977, 1927, 10¼x5"..480.00
Vase, peacock feathers, L Lincoln, #837, 1921, 10½x6"...........1,650.00

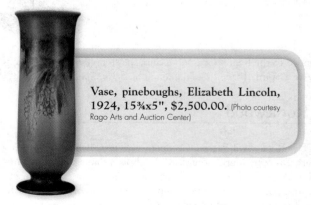

Vase, pineboughs, Elizabeth Lincoln, 1924, 15¾x5", $2,500.00. (Photo courtesy Rago Arts and Auction Center)

Vase, poppies on sinewy stems, H Wilcox, 1904, 10¾x4¼".....12,000.00
Vase, poppies, K Shirayamadani, #6006, 1929, grinding chips, 11½".. 3,000.00
Vase, stylized floral, V Tischler, ovoid, 1924, 15x6½" 1,450.00

Porcelain

Bowl vase, Jewel, lg birds/blooming branches, ET Hurley, 1929, 5x6".. 1,440.00
Bowl, exotic birds/foliage, ET Hurley, #2254D, 1929, 5⅜" 1,800.00
Charger, deer & flowers, bl & wht, E Barrett, #6937, 1946, 12⅞".. 1,150.00
Ginger jar, mixed flowers, K Shirayamadani, #2451, 1923, 10".6,300.00
Lamp base, landscape, M McDonald, #14B, 1937, 17½x7" 2,700.00
Plate, Jewel, chinoiserie, bl & wht, W Hentschel, #K2A, 1924, 10¼". 1,325.00
Temple jars, cascading flowers, L Asbury, #2463, 1923, 9⅝", pr .2,400.00
Vase, antelopes, squeezebag/crystalline, W Rehm, S, 1934, 5½" . 2,400.00
Vase, Asian birds/flowers/mtns, A Conant, shouldered, 1920, 10" ...3,850.00
Vase, birds & flowers, S Sax, #112, 1919, 6¾" 1,800.00
Vase, birds & foliage, ET Hurley, #2301B, 1927, 13⅝" 1,800.00
Vase, cherry blossom branch on wht, L Epply, 1919, #2191, 5x4".. 1,080.00
Vase, cherry blossoms, lt bl to pk, A Sprague, 1888, 4x5½" 150.00
Vase, dmns, Nacreous glaze, S Sax, #2182, P, 1915, 4" 1,800.00
Vase, elephants & flowers, E Barrett, #6315, 1944, 6½x5½" 2,750.00
Vase, fish & vegetation, ET Hurley, #6877, 1944, 7½x8", NM.15,500.00
Vase, fish, L Epply, #6203C, XXX, 1930, 8x6¼" 4,750.00
Vase, floral branch, W Hentschel, #2194, P, 1905, 8⅝" 600.00
Vase, floral collar, S Sax, #975D, 1919, 6" 1,950.00
Vase, floral shoulder, A Conant, #2306, 1917, 7" 1,100.00
Vase, floral, J Jensen, Anniversary glaze int, #2996, 1931, 8" 2,450.00
Vase, flowers, flaring, J Jensen, #6306, 1944, 7x5¼" 250.00
Vase, grapevines, shouldered, L Epply, #2528, 1927, 8½x3¾" 475.00
Vase, hen/rooster/butterflies, A Conant, bulb, #2, 1919, 6" 825.00
Vase, irises, ET Hurley, #30E, 1949, 8½" 1,800.00
Vase, Jewel, birds/branches on emerald gr, A Conant, 1920, 9½x4" .2,280.00
Vase, Jewel, cherry blossoms, K Shirayamadani, #589F, 1922, 7x3" .4,200.00
Vase, Jewel, chrysanthemums, A Conant, #999C, 1918, 8¾x6¾" .. 10,800.00
Vase, Jewel, fish & vegetation, ET Hurley, 1923, 14½x9" 14,400.00
Vase, Jewel, floral abstracts, E Hurley, S, 1933, 7¼x4¼" 1,750.00
Vase, Jewel, floral on ivory butterfat, L Epply, #2983, 1928, 15½".. 3,950.00
Vase, Jewel, floral sprigs, W Hentschel, #2499C, 1920, 14x5" .8,000.00
Vase, Jewel, flower sprays, L Epply, #2077, 1927, 6¼x5" 1,000.00
Vase, Jewel, hydrangea clusters, Lorinda Epply, XXVII/2949/LE, 10" . 3,360.00
Vase, Jewel, lg indistinct floral on bl, J Jensen, 1934, 6½x4" 1,080.00
Vase, Jewel, lotus blossoms, K Shirayamadani, #1358C, 1924, 10½" .2,050.00

Vase, Jewel, pink magnolia branches, William Hentchel, 1923, 11¾x7¾", $2,040.00. (Photo courtesy Craftsman Auctions on LiveAuctioneers.com)

Vase, lake scene w/trees, A Conant, #2306, 1919, 7" 2,450.00
Vase, leaves & berries, L Epply, #2466, 1920, 8" 9,600.00
Vase, lilies, K Shirayamadani, #890C/#6032, 1945, 5⅝" 1,675.00
Vase, magnolias, S Sax, #2640C, 1930, 13¼" 9,600.00
Vase, magnolias/birds, H Wilcox, #2033D, 1920, 10" 7,200.00
Vase, orchids, C McLaughlin, #951D, 1918, 8⅞" 3,250.00
Vase, peacock feathers, E Diers, squat, 3x6½" 1,325.00
Vase, poppies, peach/wht on bl, Shirayamadani, #6197, 1945, 9" .. 2,350.00
Vase, poppies, tapered, K Shirayamadani, #6359, 1943, 7½x5".1,800.00
Vase, Venetian harbor, C Schmidt, #904C, 1923, 12¼" 9,600.00
Vase, water lilies, H Wilcox, wide/corseted form, #2298E, 1917, 4½"... 700.00
Vase, wisteria cascades, E Diers, #2545F, 1924, 6¾" 2,350.00

Sea Green

Loving cup, hop leaves/vines/fruit, Demarest, silver mts, #656C, 1900...7,200.00
Mug, clovers, ET Hurley, Commercial Club of Cincinnati, 1905, 5¼"...1,100.00
Vase, cranes in flight, dbl hdls, M Daly, #604D, 1895, 7x4½" ...2,300.00
Vase, fish, cylindrical, E Hurley, #951C, 1905, 10¼x4" 1,325.00

Vase, fish, Matthew Daly, #598E/W/ MAD/164, 8", $4,500.00. (Photo courtesy Rago Auctions)

Vase, fruit blossoms, A Van Briggle, #589E, G, 1898, 8½" 5,250.00
Vase, Imperial cranes, C Schmidt, cylindrical, #589D, G, 1898, 11⅛" ..20,000.00
Vase, irises, A Sprague, #604C, G, 1900, 9½"............................3,500.00
Vase, nude around rim, water lilies & lily pads, AM Valentien, 1900, 3¼".19,200.00
Vase, pansies, C Baker, #536E, X, 1904, 3¼x5" 600.00
Vase, salamander, classic tapered shape, M Daly, #614F, 1896, 6x3" ..3,250.00

Standard

Chamberstick, holly, C Steinle, #710, 1898, 3x5" 225.00
Coffeepot, floral, M Perkins, #613, 1893, 9½x7" 1,000.00
Ewer, apple blossoms, A Valentien, #537D, 1890, 10x6" 600.00
Ewer, palm frond & flower w/silver o/l, A Valentien, #723, 1895, 7".3,850.00
Ewer, pnt gr leaves & berries, S Toohey, #381B, 18892, 9½x4"... 325.00
Humidor, Geronimo, E Felton, #672, 1903, 5½" 4,800.00
Humidor, Indian, E Felton, Chief Mountain Black Feet, 1900, flame mk, 7x6".3,000.00
Humidor, jonquils, M Nourse, silver o/l, HCR, #578B, 1899 .....5,000.00
Jar, covered, pansies, sterling lid w/monogram, B Horsfall, #S1146, 1894, 3¼x5".325.00
Mug, chimpanzee dressed & carrying bag, M Daly, #587, W, 1891, 4½" ..2,750.00
Mug, Indian, S Laurence, Sertenta, Kiowa, 1900, 5½x5" 1,200.00
Tankard, Indian, G Young, Turning Eagle, 1900, 8½x6" 8,400.00
Vase, autumn leaves, M Nourse, #903B, L, 1899, 10"................1,325.00
Vase, bulb, long neck, yel, #126B, 1884, 9x3½"............................. 75.00
Vase, bulb, poppies, silver o/l, S Coyne, #S1393, 1898, 6x5½" .4,000.00
Vase, cherries & leaves w/silver o/l, E Lincoln, #880, 1900, 6" .3,900.00
Vase, clovers w/silver o/l, H Stuntz, #706, 1893, 4½x5" 3,350.00
Vase, daffodils, L Lindeman, #30E, 1902, 7¾" 1,325.00
Vase, floral w/silver o/l, J Zettel, #798B, 1894, 9½x5"................3,600.00
Vase, Geo Shakespeare (Arapahoe), G Young, #30E, 1901, 7⅝" . 13,200.00
Vase, honeysuckles, R256, Foertmeyer, #640, 1892, 10½x4½" ..2,000.00
Vase, hummingbird & bittersweet, C Lindeman, #907E, 1906, 8⅝"... 1,550.00
Vase, Indian lady & baby, G Young, #604C, 1900, 9"..............31,500.00
Vase, Indian, M Daly, A Nation's Cry, 1900, 18x7¼" 28,000.00
Vase, lilies of the valley, K Matchette, #612C, W, 1893, 5⅝"....... 785.00
Vase, man's portrait, J Wareham, #625, 1893, 5½" 1,175.00
Vase, monkeys, B Horsfall, #690C, X, 1893, 8¾"........................7,150.00
Vase, pansies w/silver o/l, J Zettel, #607C, 1893, 5x4"...............3,575.00
Vase, poppies, K Shirayamadani, #664B, X, 1897, 10⅜"............1,325.00
Vase, red-hot pokers (floral) in relief, J Wareham, #732B, 1900, 10".. 6,000.00
Vase, roses w/silver o/l, M Daly, #932C, 1902, 11½"..................6,500.00
Vase, thistles, A Sprague, #488, W, 1894, 6½".........................1,100.00
Vase, tulip vines, AR Valentien, #139A, 1893, rstr drill hole, 18x9".3,250.00
Vase, tulips, silver o/l, D316, K Hickman, #546C, 1898, 9x5" .3,100.00
Vase, violets, AR Valentien, basketweave silver o/l, 1893, 11¾", NM . 1,450.00

Vase, water lilies, AM Valentien, #5688, X (but M), 1900, 9x5". 500.00
Vase, yel flowers & gr leaves, AM Bookprinter, #295, 1886, 8¼x3½"... 350.00
Vessel, grasses, hdld, w/orig retailer's tag, C Baker, 1897, 9x4"..... 350.00

Tiger Eye

Ewer, cherry blossoms, A Valentien, #441, 1889, 12x5"............... 600.00
Jug, incised Rookwood symbol, dtd Dec 21 '86, sgn SLS, 8¾"..... 300.00
Vase, apple branches, AR Valentien, #589C, 12½x3¾"............ 1,500.00

Vase, bird of paradise and pomegranates, mahogany on dark brown goldstone, A. R. Valentien, #872, 1888, crisp, exceptional artwork and perfectly fired, 20", $8,400.00. (Photo courtesy Craftsman Auctions on LiveAuctioneers.com)

Vase, dragons w/goldstone, K Shirayamadani, #644, R, 1893, 18½" ..9,000.00
Vase, frog, AR Valentien, #806D, 1898, 6¼"................................. 600.00
Vase, holly leaves/florals, P Conant, #551, 1916, 7", NM.......... 1,300.00
Vase, iris buds, H Wilcox, #589E, 1894, 8¼x3¼"...................... 2,000.00
Vase, leafy branches w/apples, AR Valentien, #589C, 1891, 12½"... 1,440.00
Vase, McIntosh Arts & Crafts, AR Valentien, #270, R, 1886, 11".. 1,550.00
Vase, swan, W McDonald, #562, R, 1892, 9½", NM.................... 500.00

Vellum

Bowl, #214E, stylized roses, P Conant, 1915, 2¼x4".................... 225.00
Plaque, Birches, E Hurley, 14x9"+fr 13,000.00
Plaque, birds on bough, S Sax, 1900, sight: 7¼x5½"+fr.......... 10,800.00
Plaque, bucolic landscape, F Rothenbusch, 1918, 9¼x12½"+fr. 5,400.00
Plaque, Close of Day - Venice, C Schmidt, 9¼x14½"+fr......... 12,000.00
Plaque, El Nan Set Southern Arapaho, S Laurence, 1898, 17x13"+fr .. 14,500.00
Plaque, lake/mtn/trees, ET Hurley, 1946, 10x12"+fr 19,500.00
Plaque, landscape, possibly Little Miami River, ET Hurley, 1920, 8¼x11¾"+fr...3,500.00
Plaque, Mt Assiniboine BC, snowcapped mtn scene, S Sax, 1915, 8x5". 5,100.00
Plaque, Mt Ranier, S Sax, 1920, 9x11¼" fr 7,550.00
Plaque, mtn lake scene in pks, ET Hurley, 1946, 12½x14½"+fr . 10,800.00
Plaque, pines & snow, ET Hurley, V, 1912, 10⅜x8¼".............. 5,000.00
Plaque, pines/stream/mt snowcaps, L Asbury, 1912, 10½x8¼"..3,360.00
Plaque, Quiet Reflections, schooners, C Schmidt, sgn, 1921, 8x5"+fr....2,760.00
Plaque, river scene, E Diers, 1926, 11½x8½"+fr........................ 7,000.00
Plaque, snowy landscape, F Rothenbusch, 1912, 5¾x7¾"+fr 3,900.00
Plaque, snowy Rocky Mtns scene w/creek, F Rothenbusch, 1927, 10x12"+fr.8,400.00
Plaque, The Channel, landscape at dusk, C Schmidt, 1912, 8¼x10½"+fr .. 7,800.00
Plaque, The Pines, snowy nordic scene, 1913, 5¾x7½"+fr........ 2,400.00
Plaque, tree grove & river bend, L Asbury, 1913, 10¾x8¾"+fr . 4,800.00
Plaque, trees & water (EX art), E Diers, 1914, 11x8½"+ebonized fr.. 14,000.00
Plaque, Venetian Sunset, E Diers, 9½x7½" fr............................ 16,800.00
Plaque, winter landscape, E McDermott, 1918, 5x8½"+fr 2,500.00
Vase, 4 fish, underwater scene, #952F, cylindrical, E Noonan, 1909, 6¼x3".. 550.00
Vase, Asian floral, Kate Van Horne, #30E, 1915, 9x3"............. 3,000.00
Vase, autumnal landscape, S Coyne, 1909, 7¾x4".................... 2,040.00
Vase, autumnal scenic, E Diers, #1358D, 1925, 8¾x4¾"........... 3,600.00
Vase, birds in gnarled branches, K Curry, #2118, V, 1917, 7⅝" .3,750.00
Vase, cherry blossoms band, ET Hurley, #2061, 1918, 7½x3½".... 750.00
Vase, cows at stream, E Diers, #581D, V, 1917, 12⅛".............. 37,500.00
Vase, crocuses, C Schmidt, #2745, V, 1924, 9⅝"...................... 4,250.00

Vase, cvd & pnt carnations, A Valentien, #879C, 1904, 12x5" . 1,900.00
Vase, daisies, pnt, #900D, uncrazed, 1926, 7x3½"..................... 1,800.00
Vase, Deco floral band, L Asbury, #614C, V, 1926, 13⅛" 4,350.00
Vase, dogwood blossoms, K Shirayamadani, #S2136, 1944, 13¼".. 4,750.00
Vase, dragonflies, C Schmidt, #915D, X (peppering), 1904, 7x5½"...9,000.00

Vase, dragonfly, Carl Schmidt, 1905, 8¼x4½", $2,000.00. (Photo courtesy Rago Arts and Auction Center)

Vase, evening scenic, ET Hurley, #614D, V, 1926, 10¾" 8,000.00
Vase, fish on turq-gr, ET Hurley, #952E, V, 1905, 7x3".............. 6,600.00
Vase, fish swimming underwater, ET Hurley, #906C, 1907, 6½x7".. 1,900.00
Vase, fish swimming, ET Hurley, 1904, 10x5¾"...................... 12,000.00
Vase, full moon rising over river, ET Hurley, 1910, 9x4¾" 3,900.00
Vase, harbor scene, bl & gr, E Diers, #1358D, 8¾x4½"............ 3,000.00
Vase, landscape, F Rothenbusch, #904C, 1937, orig hole for lamp, 12¾x5"..2,800.00
Vase, landscape, S Coyne, #924, 1922, 6x3" 1,900.00
Vase, landscape, shouldered, #614E, L Epply, rpr chip to rim, 1913, 8½x4"... 350.00
Vase, landscape, tapered, E Diers, #951F, 1921, 6¼x2½" 950.00
Vase, landscape, tapered, S Coyne, #951D, 1920, 9½x4" 2,300.00
Vase, peacock feathers on raspberry, S Sax, 1912, 10x4¼" 2,280.00
Vase, pnt floral, tapered, E Diers, #2032D, 1926, 9½x 4½".......... 400.00
Vase, sailboats on lake, E Diers, 109, 9½x5" 2,400.00
Vase, schooners in Venetian bay, C Schmidt, 1923, 11x4"........ 4,800.00
Vase, seahorses (3), bulb, ET Hurley, #1667, 1904, 4½x4" 3,500.00
Vase, snowy forest scene, ET Hurley, VII/ETH/9350, 9" 5,100.00
Vase, trees landscape, E Diers, 1923, 8¾x4¼"......................... 2,400.00

Wax Matt

Vase, birds & sunflower, E Lincoln, #324, 1925, 17¼x8"........... 5,400.00
Vase, maple leaves, J Harris, #2969, 1929, peppering, 7½x6½" 660.00
Vase, peacock feathers, W Hentschel, #4948, 1912, 4½x7¾".... 1,900.00
Vase, rabbits, W Rehm, #6197F, 1943, 4¾"............................. 2,550.00
Vase, roses, J Jensen, #2932, 1929, 14x5½" 2,000.00
Vase, tulips on gr, J Jensen, #951D, 1929, 9x3"...................... 1,000.00
Vase, wild roses, unidentified artist, #614C, 1935, 13x6¼" 4,000.00
Vase, woman on horse in squeezebag, W Rehm, S, 1934, 5⅛" ..3,350.00

Miscellaneous

Bookends, #2444D, 1921, elephant, gr matt, 4¾x6", pr 400.00
Bookends, #2446, 1927, girl on bench, lt bl, ea 55.00
Bookends, #2502, 1921, boys (2) w/book, gr matt w/brn, 6½", pr..1,900.00
Bookends, #2659, 1927, penguins (2), wht matt, rstr beaks, pr. 1,300.00
Bookends, #6384, 1933, hippopotamus, ivory matt, 4x6½", pr .3,500.00
Bookends, #6883, 1945, St Francis, brn, gray & fleshtone, pr 425.00
Bowl, #1745, 1921, bl matt, 2¾x5" 120.00
Bowl, #2152, 1921, floral emb on yel matt, 2x4½" 85.00
Bowl, #2161, 1920, pk, 1¾" 36.00
Bowl, #2384, 1919, ducks emb on bl matt, 2x5" 132.50
Candleholder, #6059, 1929, elephant seated w/holder on head, 4", ea... 180.00
Candleholders, #2932, 1946, water lily forms, 3", pr 80.00
Chocolate pot, #290, red clay body, brn glaze, ca 1886, 10x6"..... 100.00
Inkwell, #1677, 1920, gr matt w/brn highlights, 3-pc, 2½"........... 575.00

Inkwell, #2504, 1922, sphynx, by Louise Abel, brn matt, w/liner & cap, 10x9" .960.00
Inkwell, Z-Line, #407Z, 1903, swirling maiden on gr, A Valentien, 4x5" .. 4,000.00
Paperweight, #1233, 1906, frog, dk gr matt, 3¼x4½" 1,325.00
Paperweight, #1623, 1920, rook, bl matt, 3x4" 280.00
Paperweight, #1623, 1930, rook, gr & brn matt, 3x4" 500.00
Paperweight, #1855, 1912, geese (2), brn matt, 4" 515.00
Paperweight, #1855, 1933, geese (2), ivory matt, 4" 240.00
Paperweight, #2677, 1929, monkey on book, gray-gr matt, 3½" .. 335.00
Paperweight, #2747, 1924, foo dog, dk bl, 4" 660.00
Paperweight, #2747, 1924, foo dog, gr w/brn, 3¾" 480.00
Paperweight, #2756, 1929, frog, pk & gr mottle, 2x5" 465.00
Paperweight, #2777, 1927, dog, bl over brn matt, 5x3½" 375.00
Paperweight, #2797, 1928, elephant on base, wht matt, 3¼" 390.00
Paperweight, #2868, 1929, nude seated, ivory matt, 4" 360.00
Paperweight, #2921, 1927, rook, mottled brn matt, 4x5" 950.00
Paperweight, #6025, 1925, squirrel w/nut, chestnut brn matt, 4". 480.00
Paperweight, #6084, 1965, monkey, Mustard Seed, 3¾" 360.00
Paperweight, #6160, 1930, rabbit, wht matt, 3⅛" 360.00
Paperweight, #6182, 1946, cat, chartreuse, 6¾" 360.00
Paperweight, #6241, 1931, burro, caramel-gray matt, 5⅞x4¾" 360.00
Paperweight, #6528, 1935, gazelle, Oxblood, 4¾" 360.00
Pitcher, #2974, 1926, gr glass, dragon-like hdl, 9" 480.00
Planter, #6269, 1931, pk gloss, 2⅞x6" 110.00
Tile, scrub oak tree medallion, 6"+dk wood fr.................... 1,800.00
Trivet, #2349, 1929, bird on branches, brn & ivory, 6" dia 215.00
Trivet, #3069, 1930, lady w/umbrella, mc pastels, 5½x5½" 275.00
Trivet, #3124, 1928, dove, mc, 5½x5½" 275.00

Vase, classical scene, indigo matt, 13x9", 1929, $1,140.00. (Photo courtesy Craftsman Auctions on LiveAuctioneers.com)

Vase, #720C, 1911, panels on maroon mottle w/gr, 3¾x6" 275.00
Vase, #915C, 1906, Am Indian design on gr matt, 7½" 360.00
Vase, #918E, 1913, panels on gr over pk, 6" 165.00
Vase, #934, 1912, leaves at base, feathered gr to yel, 12", NM .. 1,560.00
Vase, #1370, 1914, floral on dk red w/gr, 6⅞" 780.00
Vase, #1656F, gray, pnt & incised floral design, K Van Horne, 1911, 6¼x2½" ..250.00
Vase, #1660E, 1912, organic band on gr matt, 7¼" 550.00
Vase, #1660F, 1912, linear decor on red-brn, 6" 300.00
Vase, #1712, 1919, jonquils & foliage on caramel, 8⅞" 475.00
Vase, #1808, 1923, floral on blk, bl int, 3¾" 385.00
Vase, #2088, 1934, pk, 5" 135.00
Vase, #2097, 1921, swans on gr, 3⅜" 195.00
Vase, #2111, 1928, bellflowers on yel matt, 6" 155.00
Vase, #2135, 1926, Greek Key design on gr matt, 6" 180.00
Vase, #2179, 1921, vining flowers on pk w/gr highlights, 3¾" 110.00
Vase, #2204, 1915, birds on branches on gr to brn, 9⅜" 900.00
Vase, #2207, 1927, floral on rose matt, 5⅜" 180.00
Vase, #2210, 1930, fruit garlands on pk w/gr, 7" 240.00
Vase, #2218, 1927, Moresque design on bl crystalline, 5" 215.00
Vase, #2375, 1929, peacock feathers on lav, 9" 660.00
Vase, #2378, 1923, stylized flowers on brn crystalline, 6⅞" 480.00
Vase, #2379, 1919, calla lilies on dk bl, 10" 425.00
Vase, #2380, 1928, stylized daisies on dk bl, 6¼" 300.00
Vase, #2393, 1928, lav, 8⅞" 575.00
Vase, #2407, 1925, chocolate brn crystalline, 7" 480.00

Vase, #2412, 1921, geometrics on yel matt, 7" 155.00
Vase, #2417, 1929, peacock feathers on pk w/gr, 9" 425.00
Vase, #2421, 1917, panels on purple matt, 9½" 425.00
Vase, #2421, 1921, panels on streaky turq, 10" 385.00
Vase, #2424, 1929, tulips on pk matt, 8" 215.00
Vase, #2433, 1931, molded band on tan matt w/bl crystalline, 10" .. 270.00
Vase, #2543, 1921, dancers on cobalt, yel int, 13" 515.00
Vase, #2693, 1923, leaves on bl & tan, 4¼" 425.00
Vase, #2780, 1925, lappet flowers on pk w/gr, 6" 145.00
Vase, #2891, 1927, geometrics on stippled bl on gr, 9" 275.00
Vase, #2917E, 1926, bl crystalline, 6⅜" 480.00
Vase, #2972, 1928, bl matt, 5½" 150.00
Vase, #2988, 1928, pk, 7" 240.00
Vase, #2990, 1928, floral band on gr crystalline, 6⅜" 120.00
Vase, #356F, 1919, mottled indigo gloss w/raspberry int, 6¼" 275.00
Vase, #390Z, 1902, swirls on gr matt, 6¾" 360.00
Vase, #516, 1914, swirling floral on cobalt, nick, 11x12" 2,200.00
Vase, #6006, 1929, poppies on pk, 11⅜" 395.00
Vase, #6204C, spider & leaves in brn, gr bulb, K Ley, 1946, 7x7". 650.00
Vase, #6229, 1931, turq matt, 5" 125.00
Vase, #6444, 1941, seed pods on bl matt, 5" 200.00
Vase, #6469, 1934, bl crystalline, 8½" 200.00
Vase, #6561, 1936, gr cube, 5½x5½" 60.00
Vase, #6625, 1942, Aventurine, 5" 480.00
Vase, #6777, 1944, floral on tan gloss, 11⅝" 240.00
Vase, #7057, 1957, floral on ivory matt, 5¾" 65.00
Vase, Z-line, #661, 1901, draped maiden at rim, flambé matt, 4¼"... 3,000.00
Vase, Z-Line, 1901, reclining nude, red, AM Valentien, 3½", NM .. 2,400.00
Wall pocket, #1395, 1919, peacock feathers on pk, 11¼" 425.00

Rorstrand

The Rorstrand Pottery was established in Sweden in 1726 and is today Sweden's oldest existing pottery. The earliest ware, now mostly displayed in Swedish museums, was much like old Delft. Later types were hard-paste porcelains that were enameled and decorated in a peasant style. Contemporary pieces are often described as Swedish Modern. Rorstrand is also famous for their Christmas plates.

Bowl, dogwood at at incurvate rtcl rim, 2⅞x5" 850.00
Pedestal, Neo-Renaissance style, 3 joined majolica pcs w/gold, 46" ...3,600.00
Vase, berries & branches, pate-sur-pate, red/gray/wht, NL, #23, 8" .. 950.00
Vase, Diatreta, rtcl twigs/leaves, 2 frogs climb sides, mc, 6¾" 1,100.00
Vase, fish cvd/HP w/tails covering hdls on wht, 10¾x5" 2,400.00
Vase, floral, lav/gr on wht, CM, 3⅜".............................. 780.00
Vase, floral, WL, #6718, 20½x9", NM............................... 900.00

Vase, large reticulated blossoms, ivory with brown stems on cobalt, Nils Lindstrom, blue ink mark, 15x6", NM, $3,240.00. (Photo courtesy Craftsman Auctions on LiveAuctioneers.com)

Vase, red/gr/blk intermingled glazes, Stalhane Sweden 43, 8¾" . 1,200.00
Vase, Nouveau pansies w/raised petals, NL, #20613, 1910s, 10½" .. 2,150.00
Vase, roses w/raised petals, gr stems/leaves, KI, 10⅜" 1,450.00

Vase, snow scene at twilight, sgn L NL, shouldered, 18" 5,250.00
Vase, stamped sqs, bl-gray w/orange crystals, Nyland, 28x12" ... 3,900.00
Vase, storks in flight emb on lt bl at shoulder, ca 1900, 32¼" 9,000.00
Vase, tulips w/raised petals & swirling stems, #40443, 16½x8", NM ... 2,150.00
Vase, vining floral, mc on wht, shouldered, 8½" 850.00

Rose Mandarin

Similar in design to Rose Medallion, this Chinese Export porcelain features the pattern of a robed mandarin, often separated by florals, ladies, genre scenes, or butterflies in polychrome enamels. It is sometimes trimmed in gold. Elaborate in decoration, this pattern was popular from the late 1700s until the early 1840s.

Bowl, cut corners, 19th C, 9¾" 950.00
Bowl, oval, lt wear, 11" 465.00

Bowl, shallow with rectangular reserves in well, 16½", $870.00. (Photo courtesy Langston Auction Gallery on LiveAuctioneers.com)

Chamber set, foo dogs/birds/flowers/geometrics, 8" pot+6x17" bowl .. 460.00
Charger, central genre scene, gilt, 14" 800.00
Dish, retcl borders, 19th C, 8x9½", NM 400.00
Garden seat, hexagonal, 4 scenes/pierced medallions, 19" 700.00
Garden seats, 4 scenes, gilt highlights, pierced medallions, 19", pr. 7,800.00
Jug, milk, 19th C, 5" 185.00
Punch bowl, 19th C, 16", cvd hardwood stand 2,700.00
Sauceboat, intertwined hdl, 19th C, 8¼" 325.00
Shrimp dish, 19th C, 10½" 415.00
Tray, mtd on bronze doré stand, 6¾x12" 1,600.00
Tray, serving, w/pierced liner, 19th C, 16" 950.00
Tureen, continuous genre, gilt, w/lid, 15" L, +undertray 650.00
Vase, bottle form, 19th C, 15" 785.00
Vase, foliate mouth, pear shape, appl gold dragons, 19th C, 9½" . 355.00

Rosemeade

Rosemeade was the name chosen by the Wahpeton Pottery Company of Wahpeton, North Dakota, to represent their product. The founders of the company were Laura A. Taylor and R.J. Hughes, who organized the firm in 1940. It is most noted for small bird and animal figurals, either in high gloss or a Van Briggle-like matt glaze. The ware was marked 'Rosemeade' with an ink stamp or carried a 'Prairie Rose' sticker. The pottery closed in 1961. Our advisor for this category is Darlene Hurst Dommel, author of *Collector's Encyclopedia of Rosemeade Pottery* (Collector Books); she is listed in the Directory under Minnesota.

Ashtray, DeKalb ear of corn figurine, gr, ashtray/yel corn, 5" 100.00
Ashtray, mallard drake, 6½x3½" 145.00
Ashtray, NY state map, pk, 5½" 100.00
Bank, bison, brn, 3½x5" 200.00
Creamer/sugar, duck, wht, 2¾x6", 2½x6" 90.00
Cup sitter, chickadee, 1x1¾" 120.00
Figurine, alligator, gr, 1½x7¾" 1,000.00
Figurine, frog, solid, gr, 1¾" 110.00

Figurine, horse head, brn, 1⅝x1¾" 100.00
Figurine, moccasin, bsk/bl, 1½x3½" 25.00
Figurine, pheasant hen, 4x11½" 375.00
Figurine, tiger kitten, mini, 1x2¾" 475.00
Figurines, bears, mini, blk/tan, 1½x1¾", 1¼x2¼", pr 55.00
Figurines, goldfinch, mini, 1¼x2¼", pr 280.00
Figurines, mice, gray, 1x1¼", 1½x1", pr 25.00
Figurines, seals, family of 3, blk, 1⅞x2⅛", 1¼x1¾", ½x1¾" 40.00
Mustace cup, lime gr, 3" 110.00
Paperweight, MN Centennial, gr, 3¾" 127.00
Paperweight, Roosevelt, 2¼x3" 375.00
Pin tray, heart shaped, pk, 5" 90.00
Pitcher, Ewald Dairy, orange, 6" 128.00
Planter, dove, gr, 3¼x5½" 50.00
Planter, fox, rust, 2¾x3½" 500.00
Planter, Viking ship, gr, 5¼x12" 220.00
Plate, Bois De Sioux Golf, 6¾" 150.00
Plate, mouse cheese serving, blk, 6" 797.00
Shakers, brussel sprouts, 1¾" 40.00
Shakers, catfish, 1½x4¼" 325.00
Shakers, fighting cocks, 3x3¼" 165.00
Shakers, howling coyotes, 3¼x2¾" 190.00
Shakers, pointer dogs, 2¼" 700.00
Spoon rest, Fort Lincoln, gr, 8¾" 140.00
Spoon rest, prairie rose, dk rose, 4¼" 50.00
Statue, God of Peace, wht, 8½x3" 170.00
Tea bell, elephant, blk, 4¼" 99.00
Tea bell, tulip, rose, 3¾" 70.00
Tile, Les Kouba pheasant, 6" tile in 10" wooden fr 70.00
TV lamp, panther, blk, 7x13" 500.00
TV lamp, pheasant, 10½x11¾" 525.00
Vase, peacock, 7¾" 178.00
Vase, swirl, 4¾" 265.00
Wall plaque, brook trout, 3½x6" 170.00
Wall pocket, leaf, ivory w/rose, 4½" 35.00
Watering pot, rabbit motif, brn, 4½" 50.00

Rose Medallion

Rose Medallion is one of the patterns of Chinese export porcelain produced from before 1850 until the second decade of the twentieth century. It is decorated in rose colors with panels of florals, birds, and butterflies that form reserves containing Chinese figures. Pre-1850 ware is unmarked and is characterized by quality workmanship and gold trim. From about 1850 until circa 1860, the kilns in Canton did not operate, and no Rose Medallion was made. Post-1860 examples (still unmarked) can often be recognized by the poor quality of the gold trim or its absence. In the 1890s the ware was often marked 'China'; 'Made in China' was used from 1910 through the 1930s.

Basin, butterflies/birds/flowers/bats, ca 1860, 4¾x16⅛" 1,100.00
Basin, everted rim w/butterflies/birds/flowers/bats, 1860s, 5x16" ... 1,000.00
Bottle, water, stick neck, 19th C, lt wear, 13" 480.00
Bowl, exotic bird in center, scalloped rim, early 20th C, 13¼" 180.00
Bowl, punch, floral band, modern, 6¾x14" 150.00
Bowl, scalloped rim, 19th C, 1½x8⅛" 275.00
Chamber pot, domestic scenes/flowers, w/lid, rpr, 6¼x11½" 700.00
Charger, ladies in reserves/flowers, gold trim, 19th C, 13½" 600.00
Lamp, scenic reserves, lion-head ring hdls, 1850s, mtd as lamp, 17" .. 850.00
Plate, orange & blk koi in center, rtcl rim, 19th C, 8½", pr 240.00
Platter, well & tree, late 19th C, rprs, 19¼x15¼" 180.00
Shrimp dish, rstr hdl, 10" 120.00
Teapot, figures/birds/flowers, domed lid, 1850s, 8¾" 465.00

Tureen, early to mid-nineteenth century, gilt trim, 10x12x9", $1,320.00. (Photo courtesy Leland Little Auction & Estate Sales Ltd. on LiveAuctioneers.com)

Vase, gilt lion-head ring hdls, bronze base, 1850s, mtd as lamp, 17". 825.00
Vase, scenic reserves, foo dog hdls, 19th C, mtd as lamp, 14", pr...1,200.00
Vase, scenic reserves, Ku form, late 19th C, 13¼" 575.00
Vase, temple, scenic reserves, 19th C, rpr, 25¼" 1,325.00
Vases (2), lion finials, scroll w/2 gilded characters, 19th C, 15", VG..3,840.00
Vases, garniture, garden scenes, sq, 19th C, 16½", pr.................2,875.00
Water bottle & basin, kilt ball knop, 16", 5¾x18½" 1,500.00

Rosenthal

In 1879 Phillip Rosenthal established the Rosenthal Porcelain Factory in Selb, Bavaria. Its earliest products were figurines and fine tablewares. The company has continued to operate to the present decade, manufacturing limited edition plates.

Bust, youth in Renaissance costume, wht porc, 15½x9½" 475.00
Charger, rooster/poppies, earth tones, sgn/#1293, 1900, 18" 6,465.00
Figurine, Asian lady w/lantern, 1930s, 13½" 1,450.00
Figurine, carousel horse, HP details, ca 1940, 8¼x10x3½" 480.00
Figurine, child pulls towel away from sm dog, MH Fritz #496, 6".. 125.00
Figurine, falconer, bronze & cold pnt, G Jaeger, 9½" 2,150.00
Figurine, female nude kneeling, Klimsch, mid-20th C, 16x8¼" ... 480.00
Figurine, foal reclining, AH Hussman, 1941, 6¼x12½x4½" 1,200.00
Figurine, goldfish (2) among sea grasses, wht, Heidenreich, 16x9"... 480.00
Figurine, goldfish among sea grasses, blk & wht w/gold, 10x8".....425.00
Figurine, Harlequin seated w/guitar, D Charol, 1920s, 6" 925.00
Figurine, heron, mc w/silver, HM Fritz, #5282, 20th C, 13" 600.00
Figurine, lady holding staff w/putto finial, 14½" 850.00
Figurine, lady running w/leaping dog at side, Deco style, 12x13". 660.00
Figurine, moose on rocky base, F Heidenreich, 18x18½" 515.00

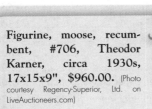

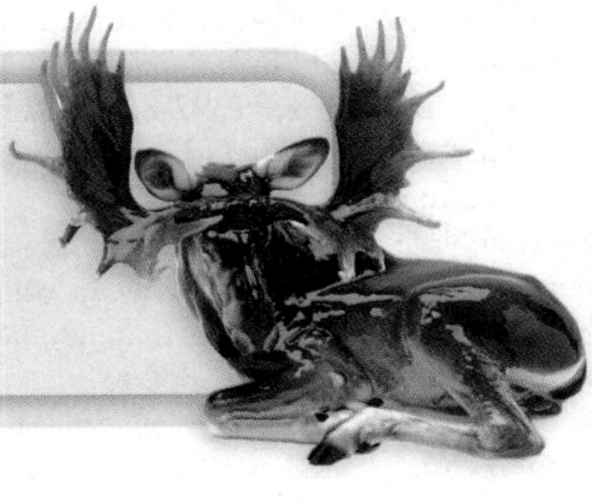

Figurine, moose, recumbent, #706, Theodor Karner, circa 1930s, 17x15x9", $960.00. (Photo courtesy Regency-Superior, Ltd. on LiveAuctioneers.com)

Figurine, nude satyr carrying gilt bowl of grapes, A Coosmann, 15"...1,850.00
Figurine, Olympic shot-put thrower, wht porc, rpr, 11x6" 395.00
Figurine, Pierrot reclining w/legs X, sgn May, 13"........................ 725.00
Figurine, Siamese Dancer, after Constantin Holzer-Defani, ca 1925, 16½".1,800.00
Figurine, Vict lady w/arms extended for dive, att, 15", NM.......... 175.00
Figurine, Young Love, 2 kissing nude children, Lunburg, 1923, 5x10" ...515.00
Figurines, Musicians, Blackamoors, H Meisel, #1056/#1057, 8½", pr ...425.00
Plaque, girl reading letter, red gown, 12x9¾"+fr........................... 480.00
Plate, draped nude seated on rock, floral rim w/gold, 19th C, 10". 850.00
Sculptures, butterflies, pnt porc, Rosenthal-Germany, 3x3", set of 4..275.00

Roseville

The Roseville Pottery Company was established in 1892 by George F. Young in Roseville, Ohio. Finding their facilities inadequate, the company moved to Zanesville in 1898, erected a new building, and installed the most modern equipment available. By 1900 Young felt ready to enter into the stiffly competitive art pottery market. Roseville's first art line was called Rozane. Similar to Rookwood's Standard, Rozane featured dark blended backgrounds with slip-painted underglaze artwork of nature studies, portraits, birds, and animals. Azurean, developed in 1902, was a blue and white underglaze art line on a blue blended background. Egypto (1905) featured a matt glaze in a soft shade of old green and was modeled in low relief after examples of ancient Egyptian pottery. Mongol (1905) was a high-gloss oxblood red line after the fashion of the Chinese Sang de Boeuf. Mara (1905), an iridescent lustre line of magenta and rose with intricate patterns developed on the surface or in low relief, successfully duplicated Sicardo's work. These early lines were followed by many others of highest quality: Fudjiyama and Woodland (1905 – 1906) reflected an Oriental theme; Crystalis (1906) was covered with beautiful frost-like crystals. Della Robbia, their most famous line (introduced in 1905), was decorated with carved designs ranging from florals, animals, and birds to scenes of Viking warriors and Roman gladiators. These designs were worked in sgraffito with slip-painted details. Very limited but of great importance to collectors today, Rozane Olympic (1905) was decorated with scenes of Greek mythology on a red ground. Pauleo (1914) was the last of the artware lines. It was varied — over 200 glazes were recorded — and some pieces were decorated by hand, usually with florals.

During the second decade of the century until the plant closed 40 years later, new lines were continually added. Some of the more popular of the middle-period lines were Donatello, 1918; Futura, 1928; Pine Cone, 1936; and Blackberry, 1933. The floral lines of the later years have become highly collectible. Pottery from every era of Roseville production — even its utility ware — attest to an unwavering dedication to quality and artistic merit.

Examples of the fine art pottery lines present the greatest challenge to evaluate. Scarcity is a prime consideration. The quality of artwork varied from one artist to another. Some pieces show fine detail and good color, and naturally this influences their values. Studies of animals and portraits bring higher prices than the floral designs. An artist's signature often increases the value of any item, especially if the artist is one who is well recognized.

The market is literally flooded with imposter Roseville that is coming into the country from China. An experienced eye can easily detect these fakes, but to a novice collector, they may pass for old Roseville. Study the marks. If the 'USA' is missing or appears only faintly, the piece is most definitely a reproduction. Also watch for lines with a mark that is not correct for its time frame; for example, Luffa with the script mark, and Woodland with the round Rozane stamp from the 1917 line. A nearly complete listing with pictures of these imposters can be seen by going to the website of the American Art Pottery Association (www.aapa.info), clicking on the 'Resources' tab, and selecting 'Fakes and Forgeries.'

For further information consult *Collector's Encyclopedia of Roseville Pottery, First* and *Second Series*, by Sharon and Bob Huxford and Mike Nickel (Collector Books). Other books on the subject include *Collector's Compendium of Roseville Pottery, Volumes I* and *II*, by Randall Monsen (see Directory, Virginia). Our advisor for this category is Mike Nickel; he is listed in the Directory under Michigan.

Apple Blossom, basket, #309, gr or pk, $275 to 325.00
Apple Blossom, ewer, #318, gr or pk, $600 to 700.00
Apple Blossom, vase, #388, bl, gr or pk, $250 to 300.00
Apple Blossom, vase, #392-15, bl, hdls, $800 to........................... 900.00
Apple Blossom, window box, #368-8, gr or pk, $150 to 175.00
Artwood, 3-pc planter set, 2 #1050/1 #1051, $90 to..................... 110.00

Artwood, planter, #1054, $85 to 95.00
Artwood, planter, #1055-9, $85 to 95.00
Aztec, vase, waisted, floral, $350 to 400.00
Azurean, mug, #4, floral, $350 to 400.00
Azurean, pitcher, cherry blossoms, artist initials JI, #938, $450 to . 550.00
Baneda, center bowl, #233, gr, hdls, $400 to 500.00
Baneda, center bowl, #237, pk, $650 to 750.00
Baneda, vase, #235, gr, rose bowl shape, $350 to 375.00
Baneda, vase, #603, pk, $350 to 400.00
Baneda, vase, gr, dbl hdl, chip to hdl 500.00
Bittersweet, candlesticks, #851-3, pr $80 to 100.00
Bittersweet, cornucopia, #857-4, $75 to 85.00
Bittersweet, ewer, #816, $85 to 95.00
Bittersweet, planter, #827-8, $90 to 110.00
Blackberry, basket, $900 to 1,000.00
Blackberry, jardiniere & ped, $2,000 to 2,500.00
Bleeding Heart, candlesticks, #1139-4 , bl, pr $150 to 200.00
Bleeding Heart, ewer, #927, gr or pk, $350 to 400.00
Bleeding Heart, plate, #381-10, bl, $150 to 200.00
Bushberry, hanging basket, gr, $175 to 200.00
Bushberry, hanging basket, orange, $200 to 250.00
Bushberry, jardiniere, #657, orange, $80 to 90.00
Cameo II, flowerpot, $150 to 175.00
Cameo II, jardiniere, $300 to 350.00
Capri, ashtray, #598-9, $40 to 50.00
Capri, planter, #558, $60 to 70.00
Capri, shell dish, $40 to 50.00
Carnelian I, center bowl, $100 to 125.00
Carnelian I, ewer, $300 to 350.00
Carnelian I, pillow vase, $80 to 90.00
Carnelian I, wall pocket, $95 to 125.00
Carnelian II, basket, $175 to 225.00
Carnelian II, vase, squatty/trumpet neck, hdls, $150 to 175.00
Carnelian, vase, dbl hdl, gr & pk 225.00
Cherry Blossom, hanging basket, #350, pk/bl, $500 to 600.00
Cherry Blossom, vase, #621, brn, $300 to 350.00
Cherry Blossom, vase, #621, pk & bl, $275 to 325.00
Clemana, bowl, #281, bl, $250 to 275.00
Clemana, bowl, #281, gr, $225 to 250.00
Clemana, vase, #123, bl, $275 to 300.00
Clemana, vase, #758, tan, hdls, $325 to 375.00
Clematis, cookie jar, #3, brn or gr, $225 to 275.00
Clematis, flowerpot/saucer, #668-5, brn or gr, $125 to 150.00
Columbine, cornucopia, #149-6, bl or tan, $100 to 125.00
Columbine, cornucopia, #149-6, pk, $125 to 150.00
Columbine, hanging basket, pk, $300 to 350.00
Corinthian, ashtray, $100 to 125.00
Corinthian, compote, $95 to 125.00
Corinthian, wall pocket, $200 to 225.00

Cosmos, hanging basket, #361, tan, $225 to 250.00
Cosmos, vase, #956-12, tan, hdls, $275 to 325.00
Cremona, fan vase, $100 to 125.00
Cremona, urn, $100 to 125.00
Dahlrose, center bowl, oval, $125 to 150.00
Dahlrose, vase, #364, $150 to 200.00
Dahlrose, window box, #377, $250 to 275.00
Dawn, ewer, #834-16, gr, $400 to 450.00
Dawn, ewer, #834-16, pk or yel, $400 to 450.00
Dawn, vase, #826, gr or pk, $125 to 150.00
Della Robbia, vase, Rozane Ware seal, $7,000 to 8,000.00
Della Robbia, vase, penguins & trees, 2-color, Rozane seal, 8" .. 2,500.00
Della Robbia, vase, stylized floral on celadon, trumpet neck 5,500.00
Dogwood I, bowl, $75 to 100.00
Dogwood I, wall pocket, 14", $400 to 450.00
Dogwood II, bowl, $125 to 150.00
Donatello, bowl, $75 to 95.00
Donatello, bowl, fruit $250 to 275.00
Donatello, pitcher, $275 to 325.00
Dutch, pin tray, $65 to 75.00
Dutch, pitcher, $125 to 150.00
Dutch, plate, incurvate rim, $100 to 125.00
Dutch, toothbrush holder, $100 to 125.00
Earlam, bowl, #218, hdls, $275 to 300.00
Earlam, vase, #522, $450 to 500.00
Egypt, pitcher vase, $1,500 to 1,750.00
Falline, candlesticks, #1092, bl, pr $800 to 900.00
Falline, center bowl, #244, bl, hdls, $275 to 325.00
Falline, vase, #647, bl, hdls, $750 to 850.00
Falline, vase, brn, dbl hdl 500.00
Falline, vase, brn, dbl hdld, bulb, unmk 425.00
Ferella, bowl/frog, #211, pk, $550 to 650.00
Ferella, candlesticks, #1078, tan, pr $550 to 650.00
Ferella, vase, #511, pk, $700 to 800.00
Florane, bud vase, $30 to 35.00
Florane, planter, $45 to 50.00
Florentine, bowl, $75 to 100.00
Florentine, compote, $125 to 150.00
Florentine, umbrella stand, ftd form, #298, chip to ft 300.00
Foxglove, basket, #373, bl, $175 to 200.00
Foxglove, floor vase, #56, bl, $450 to 550.00
Foxglove, hanging basket, #466, pk, $225 to 400.00
Foxglove, vase, #53-14, bl, $350 to 400.00
Freesia, vase, bl, dbl hdl 100.00
Freesia, window box, #1392-8, gr, $125 to 150.00
Fuchsia, candlesticks, #1132, brn/tan, pr $100 to 125.00
Fuchsia, frog, #37, gr, $175 to 200.00
Fuchsia, vase, #897-8, bl, $195 to 225.00
Futura, bowl, brn & grn geometric, orig paper label 400.00
Futura, frog, #187, $100 to 125.00
Futura, pillow vase, #81, $350 to 450.00
Futura, vase, beehive shape, 9", $950 to 1,250.00
Futura, vase, pleated-star shape, pk & gr, 8", $250 to 300.00
Futura, vase, star, pk & gr 250.00
Futura, vase, tank shape, bl, 9", $15,000 to 20,000.00
Gardenia, bowl, #641-5, $100 to 125.00
Gardenia, hanging basket, #661, $175 to 225.00
Gardenia, vase, #690, $340 to 375.00
Gardenia, window box, #658-8, $100 to 125.00
Holland, tankard, gr, #2, $125 to 175.00
Imperial I, basket, #7, $175 to 225.00
Imperial II, bowl, $250 to 300.00
Imperial II, vase, red, bulb, ribbed neck, $550 to 650.00
Iris, basket, #335-10, pk or tan, $250 to 275.00

Cosmos, basket, #358, blue, 12", $300.00 to $350.00.
(Photo courtesy Rago Auctions)

Cosmos, basket, #358, gr, $275 to 325.00
Cosmos, flower frog, #39, tan, $100 to 125.00
Cosmos, hanging basket, #361, bl, $300 to 350.00

Ivory II, bowl vase, #259, Russco shape, $75 to 95.00
Ivory II, ewer, #941-10, $75 to 95.00
Ixia, center bowl, #330-7, $125 to 150.00
Ixia, vase, #853, pk 125.00
Jonquil, bowl, #523, $125 to 150.00
Jonquil, jardiniere, #621, $125 to 150.00
Jonquil, vase, #529, hdls, $350 to 400.00
Juvenile, cake plate, chicks, $500 to 600.00
Juvenile, c/s, rabbit, $175 to 200.00
Juvenile, mug, bear, $300 to 350.00
Juvenile, mug, fancy cat, $1,000 to 1,250.00
Juvenile, pudding dish, chicks, $200 to 225.00
Juvenile, teapot, goose, $1,000 to 1,250.00
Laurel, bowl, #251, russet, $225 to 250.00
Laurel, bowl, #252, gr, $300 to 325.00
Laurel, bowl, #252, russet, $250 to 275.00
Luffa, lamp, bl/rose or bl/gr, $500 to 600.00
Luffa, sand jar, #771, gr, $1,000 to 1,200.00
Luffa, vase, #685, $300 to 350.00
Lustre, vase, $100 to 150.00
Magnolia, ashtray, #28, brn or gr, $100 to 125.00
Magnolia, pitcher, #1327, $250 to 300.00
Magnolia, vase, #91-8, brn or gr, hdls, $125 to 150.00
Mayfair, bowl, #1119-9, $60 to 70.00
Mayfair, planter, #113-8, $70 to 85.00
Ming Tree, ashtray, #599, gr, $75 to 85.00
Ming Tree, center bowl, #528, bl, $125 to 150.00
Mock Orange, planter, #931-8, $100 to 125.00
Moderne, vase, #796-8, $200 to 225.00
Mongol, bowl vase, flared rim, $300 to 400.00

Montacello, basket, #332, brown, 6", $450.00 to $500.00.
(Photo courtesy Belhorn Auction Services LLC on LiveAuctioneers.com)

Montacello, basket, #333, bl, $400 to 475.00
Morning Glory, basket, #340, gr, $400 to 450.00
Morning Glory, candlesticks, #1102, ivory, pr $250 to 300.00
Morning Glory, center bowl, #270, gr, $475 to 500.00
Morning Glory, vase, dbl hdl, unmk 650.00
Moss, bowl vase, #290, bl, $300 to 350.00
Moss, bowl vase, #290, pk/gr or orange/gr, $350 to 400.00
Moss, pillow vase, #781, orange/gr or pk/gr, $275 to 325.00
Mostique, compote, $175 to 225.00
Orian, bowl vase, #274, red, $300 to 350.00
Orian, candleholders, #1108, tan, pr $200 to 250.00
Orian, compote, #272, turq, $175 to 225.00
Orian, vase, #733, turq, hdls, $150 to 175.00
Pauleo, vase, floral decor, 18", $1,500 to 1,750.00
Pauleo, vase, red veined glaze, 15", $1,000 to 1,200.00
Peony, basket, #379-12, pk/gr, $250 to 275.00
Peony, conch shell, #436, $110 to 135.00
Peony, conch shell, #436, gr, $125 to 150.00
Peony, mug, #2-3, $100 to 125.00
Persian, hanging basket, geometric floral/leaves, $200 to 250.00
Pine Cone, basket, #353-11, brn, $400 to 450.00

Pine Cone, fan vase, #472, gr, $175 to 225.00
Pine Cone, pitcher, #485-10, bl, $750 to 850.00
Pine Cone, planter, #124, bl, $175 to 225.00
Poppy, ewer, #876, gray/gr, $250 to 275.00
Poppy, ewer, #880-18, pk, $700 to 750.00
Primrose, vase, #760-6, bl or pk, hdls, $150 to 175.00
Raymor, casserole, #183, med, $75 to 85.00
Raymor, gravy boat, #190, $30 to 35.00
Raymor, water pitcher, w/lid, #180, $200 to 250.00
Rosecraft Blended, vase, #35, $90 to 100.00
Rosecraft Blended, vase, $100 to 125.00
Rosecraft Hexagon, bowl vase, gr, $300 to 350.00
Rosecraft Hexagon, vase, glossy bl, rare, 8" 350.00
Rosecraft Panel, candlestick, gr, ea $250 to 300.00
Rosecraft Panel, nude vase, brn, 11", $800 to 900.00
Rosecraft Panel, window box, brn, $350 to 400.00
Rosecraft Panel, window box, gr, $400 to 450.00
Rosecraft Vintage, jardiniere, $300 to 350.00
Rosecraft Vintage, vase, 10", $350 to 450.00
Rozane 1917, basket, pk, $125 to 150.00
Rozane Egypto, flask, circular, $1,250 to 1,500.00
Rozane Egypto, vase, dbl hdl, 10", $600 to 700.00
Rozane Light, pillow vase, floral, 6", $350 to 400.00
Rozane Light, tankard, grapes, J Imlay, $500 to 600.00
Rozane, letter holder, floral, C Neff, $275 to 325.00
Rozane, pillow vase, portrait of dog, Timberlake, $1,000 to 1,250.00
Rozane, vase, brn w/yel flowers, sgn, #25 .... 100.00
Russco, triple cornucopia, gr, $200 to 250.00
Silhouette, ewer, #717, $125 to 150.00
Silhouette, nude vase, red, $200 to 250.00
Silhouette, vase, #789-14, $200 to 250.00
Snowberry, basket, #1BK-12, gr, $250 to 275.00
Snowberry, pillow vase, #1FH-6, bl or pk, $150 to 175.00
Sunflower, candlesticks, pr $600 to 650.00
Sunflower, vase, #619, $1,250 to 1,500.00
Sunflower, window box, $800 to 900.00
Teasel, vase, #644, dk bl, $100 to 125.00
Thorn Apple, bowl vase, #305-6, $150 to 175.00
Thorn Apple, dbl bud vase, #119, $125 to 150.00
Thorn Apple, vase, #808, bl, $125 to 150.00

Thorn Apple, vase, #820, 9", $225.00 to $250.00.
(Photo courtesy Apple Tree Auction Center on LiveAuctioneers.com)

Topeo, dbl candlesticks, bl, pr $275 to 325.00
Topeo, vase, 9", $275 to 275.00
Topeo, vase, red, 7", $175 to 225.00
Tourmaline, bowl, shallow, bl, $75 to 90.00
Tourmaline, cornucopia, $75 to 90.00
Tuscany, console bowl, gray/lt bl, $125 to 150.00
Tuscany, console bowl, pk, $150 to 175.00
Tuscany, vase, gray/lt bl, $75 to 100.00
Tuscany, vase, pk, 9", $175 to 225.00
Velmoss Scroll, compote, $150 to 175.00

Velmoss Scroll, vase, 8", $125 to 150.00
Velmoss II, vase, bl, 9", $350 to 400.00
Victorian Art, vase, gray, 8", $350 to 375.00
Vista, basket, 7", $375 to 400.00
Vista, basket, $750 to 800.00
Vista, vase, #134-18, $900 to 1,000.00
Vista, vase, dbl hdld, unmk 625.00
Water Lily, candlesticks, #1155 bl, pr $150 to 200.00
Water Lily, frog, #48, brn w/gr, $100 to 125.00
Water Lily, hanging basket, #468, rose w/gr, $200 to 250.00
White Rose, console bowl/frog, #393-12/#41, hdls, $125 to 150.00
White Rose, dbl bud vase, #148, $85 to 95.00
White Rose, pitcher, #1324, $200 to 225.00
White Rose, vase, #991-12, $250 to 275.00
Wincraft, cornucopia, #221-8, $100 to 125.00
Wincraft, ewer, bl, #218-18, $300 to 350.00
Windsor, vase, pine boughs, 6", $475 to 525.00

Wisteria, vase, #682, tan, 9", $500.00 to $550.00. (Photo courtesy Cincinnati Art Galleries, LLC on LiveAuctioneers.com)

Wisteria, vase, brn, dbl hdld, orig foil label 325.00
Zephyr Lily, cookie jar, $450 to 500.00
Zephyr Lily, tray, brn, $150 to 175.00

Rowland and Marsellus

Though the impressive back stamp seems to suggest otherwise, Rowland and Marsellus were not Staffordshire potters but American importers who commissioned various English companies to supply them with the transfer-printed crockery and historical ware that had been a popular import commodity since the early 1800s. Plates (both flat and with a rolled edge), cups and saucers, pitchers, and platters were sold as souvenirs from 1890 through the 1930s. Though other importers — Bawo & Dotter and A. C. Bosselman & Co., both of New York City — commissioned the manufacture of similar souvenir items, by far the largest volume carries the R. & M. mark, and Rowland and Marsellus has become a generic term that covers all twentieth-century souvenir china of this type. Their mark may be in full or 'R. & M.' in a diamond. We have suggested values for examples with transfers in blue, though other colors may occasionally be found as well. Our advisors for this category are Angi and David Ringering; they are listed in the Directory under Oregon.

Key:
r/e — rolled edge   v/o — view of
s/o — souvenir of

Creamer, Plymouth, mk AS Burbank or R&M 45.00
Cup/saucer, farmer's 45.00
Pitcher, Am Pilgrims, #527014, 6¼" 195.00
Plate, Am Authors, 9½" 55.00
Plate, Asbury Park, r/e, s/o, 10" 70.00
Plate, Bunker Hill Monument, Ye Old Historical Pottery, 9" 35.00
Plate, Cape Cod, fisherman's portrait, 9" 65.00

Plate, Charles Dickens, London scenes, r/e, 10" 55.00
Plate, Cincinnati OH, v/o, 9" 45.00
Plate, Denver, coupe, v/o, 10" 50.00
Plate, East Hampton, r/e, v/o, 10" 65.00
Plate, Historical Philadelphia, 6 scenes, r/e, 10" 55.00
Plate, Hudson River, r/e, s/o, 10" 55.00
Plate, Longfellow's Early Home, r/e, 10" 55.00
Plate, Lookout Mountain TN, s/o, r/e, 10" 70.00
Plate, Mayflower Coat of Arms, 1909, gold edge, 6" 30.00
Plate, New Bedford MA, r/e, s/o, 10" 65.00
Plate, New York & Brooklyn Bridge, r/e, s/o, 10" 65.00
Plate, Niagara Falls NY, s/o, 9" 40.00
Plate, Plymouth MA, 4 versions made, coupe, 10" 45.00
Plate, Priscilla & John Adams, fruit & flower border, 10" 50.00
Plate, Robert Burns, related vignettes, 10" 55.00
Plate, Seattle WA, r/e, s/o, 10" 70.00
Plate, Sherbrooke, s/o, 10" 85.00
Plate, Thomas Jefferson, St Louis World's Fair, r/e, 10" 150.00
Plate, Vassar College, 6 scenes at border, r/e, 10" 85.00
Plate, Waterbury CT, r/e, s/o, 10" 75.00
Tumbler, Ashville, s/o 95.00
Tumbler, Fall River MA, v/o 85.00
Tumbler, Ottawa Canada, v/o 85.00

Royal Bayreuth

Founded in 1794 in Tettau, Bavaria, the Royal Bayreuth firm originally manufactured fine dinnerware of superior quality. Their figural items, produced from before the turn of the century until the onset of WWI, are highly sought after by today's collectors. Perhaps the most abundantly produced and easily recognized of these are the tomato and lobster pieces. Fruits, flowers, people, animals, birds, and vegetables were also made. Aside from figural items, pitchers, toothpick holders, cups and saucers, humidors, and the like were decorated in florals and scenic motifs. Some, such as the very popular Rose Tapestry line, utilized a cloth-like tapestry background. Transfer prints were used as well. Two of the most popular are Sunbonnet Babies and Nursery Rhymes (in particular, those decorated with the complete verse).

Caution: Many pieces were not marked; some were marked 'Deponiert' or 'Registered' only. While marked pieces are the most valued, unmarked items are still very worthwhile. Values listed are for items in near mint to excellent condition unless otherwise noted. Our advisor for this category is Harold Brandenburg; he is listed in the Directory under Kansas.

Figurals

Ashtray, clown, gr, bl mk, 4¾" 295.00
Ashtray, Devil & Cards (2 cards), bl mk, 2½x4¼" 225.00
Ashtray, robin, bl mk, 6" 375.00
Berry set, tomato, bl mk, 9" master+8 5" bowls 350.00
Bowl, grapes, wht lustre, bl mk, 9" L 150.00
Bowl, Nouveau lady, bl mk, 5¾" 575.00
Bowl, tomato, bl mk, 11" L 125.00
Box, covered, blk cat, bl mk, 5" L 1,600.00
Cake plate, poppy, lav satin MOP, 10" 200.00
Candlestick, nautilus shell, bl mk, 2x6", ea 175.00
Chocolate pot, red poppy, bl mk, 8½" 550.00
Cracker jar, lobster, bl mk, NM 275.00
Creamer, mouse, gray, unmk, 3½" 750.00
Cup/saucer, demi, cabbage leaf w/lobster hdl, bl mk 195.00
Cup/saucer, demi, dk to pale yel, flower, US Zone, 1945-49 .... 20.00
Cup/saucer, demi, tulip 535.00

Cup/saucer, mustache, peach, bl flowers, gold leaves, 1866-87.......... 70.00
Dish, lobster, w/lid, bl mk, 4x5x4".. 95.00
Dish, pear, w/lid, 4x3".. 425.00
Hatpin holder, Art Nouveau lady, bl mk, 4½" 2,500.00
Hatpin holder, owl, bl mk, 4" 475.00
Humidor, Devil & Cards, bl mk, 7½"... 825.00
Humidor, elk's head, bl mk, 6x7¾"... 575.00
Humidor, Santa Claus, gr hat, Depose, 5".....................................6,500.00
Incense burner, Buddha, bl mk, 4x2½"..2,000.00
Inkwell, elk, w/lid, gr mk, must have insert.................................... 650.00
Jar, dresser, Art Nouveau lady, bl mk, 3x4½"................................. 650.00
Jar, pineapple, bl mk, 7"... 380.00
Match holder, clown, wall mt, bl mk, 5¼"..................................... 250.00
Mug, Devil & Cards, bl mk, 4¾"... 250.00
Mustard bowl, grapes, purple, w/lid & spoon, bl mk 75.00
Mustard bowl, lobster, bl mk, w/lid, 4½"....................................... 295.00
Mustard jar, lobster, bl mk, w/spoon, 4¼"..................................... 95.00
Mustard, Santa (no spoon), red hat, w/lid, Depose bl mk..........4,500.00
Nappy, strawberry blossoms & leaves, bl mk, 4¾"......................... 65.00
Ostrich, bl mk, 3½"...2,000.00
Pitcher, alligator, albino, unmk, cream sz...................................... 225.00
Pitcher, alligator, bl mk, milk sz, 5"... 300.00
Pitcher, apple, yel, bl mk, cream sz, 3¾"....................................... 95.00
Pitcher, bear, mottled blk w/orange int, bl mk, cream sz, 4" 375.00
Pitcher, blk cat hdl, orange, bl mk, 4".. 195.00
Pitcher, blk cat, tail hdl, bl mk, milk sz, 5".................................. 375.00
Pitcher, bull's head, str horns, brn & gray, bl mk, cream sz, 3¾"..... 85.00
Pitcher, coachman, bl mk, water sz, 7".. 300.00
Pitcher, cow's head, curved horns, unmk, cream sz, 3½"................. 85.00
Pitcher, crow, blk, bl mk, cream sz.. 150.00
Pitcher, dachshund, bl, bl mk, cream sz, 3".................................... 200.00
Pitcher, Devil & Cards, gr mk, water sz, 7½"................................. 350.00
Pitcher, duck, bl mk, 3¾x4".. 145.00
Pitcher, eagle, bl mk, 4"... 125.00
Pitcher, eagle, unmk, 6"... 500.00
Pitcher, elk, bl mk, water sz, 7".. 275.00
Pitcher, fish head, bl mk, milk sz, 4¼".. 150.00
Pitcher, gazelle head, #5330/2, unmk, 3"...................................... 475.00
Pitcher, geranium, pearlized, Deponiert, water sz, 6¼" 1,400.00
Pitcher, girl w/basket, bl mk, 3".. 300.00
Pitcher, girl w/jug, Deponiert, 3".. 300.00
Pitcher, ladybug, bl mk, water sz, 6"..3,100.00
Pitcher, lobster, bl mk, water sz, 6¾"... 275.00
Pitcher, milk, flounder, bl mk, 5".. 700.00
Pitcher, milk, kangaroo, bl mk, 5½"...9,000.00

Pitcher, milk, monkey, green, unmarked, 5", $325.00. (Photo courtesy Tom Harris Auctions on LiveAuctioneers.com)

Pitcher, oak leaf, pearlized gr, bl mk, cream sz.............................. 150.00
Pitcher, pansy, purple & yel, bl mk, cream sz, 4"........................... 185.00
Pitcher, parakeet, mc, unmk, 4".. 195.00
Pitcher, parrot hdl (gr), Deponiert, water sz, 7¾" 900.00
Pitcher, pig, gray, bl mk, cream sz, 4½".. 200.00
Pitcher, poodle, blk, bl mk, milk sz, 5"... 325.00
Pitcher, rabbit sitting up, mk Registered, milk sz, 5¼".............3,950.00

Pitcher, rooster, blk w/red comb, bl mk, 7x10".........................1,350.00
Pitcher, rose, pk, bl mk & Deponiert, milk sz, 4¼" 295.00
Pitcher, rosebud, bl mk, cream sz, 4" 200.00
Pitcher, Santa, Deponiert, milk sz, 5¼".....................................2,300.00
Pitcher, shell w/coral hdl, unmk, cream sz.................................... 75.00
Pitcher, spiky shell, pearl lustre, bl mk, cream sz, 4½" 75.00
Pitcher, strawberry, bl mk, water sz, 6"... 500.00
Pitcher, sunflower, Deponiert, cream sz, 4½"................................ 450.00
Pitcher, tangerine, bl mk, 5"... 225.00
Pitcher, turtle, bl mk, 3" 450.00
Pitcher, turtle, bl mk, lemonade sz, 4".......................................9,500.00
Pitcher, turtle, bl mk, water sz, 3"..1,000.00
Pitcher, water, moose, bl mk, 6½"...10,000.00
Plate, leaf, gr, bl mk, 6x4".. 40.00
Plate, tomato & vine w/2 sm buds, bl mk, 7½".............................. 50.00
Powder jar, spiky shell, gr mk, 3x4" L... 95.00
Shakers, bell ringer, unmk, pr... 600.00
Shakers, flounder, unmk, 3½", pr 1,000.00
Shakers, radish, bl mk, 3", pr 200.00
Shaving mug, elk head, glossy, bl mk 350.00
Shoe, man's, fabric laces, brn, 2x6" L, EX 55.00
String holder, rooster, mc, bl mk, 6"... 250.00
Sugar bowl, alligator, w/lid, unmk, 4" L..1,550.00
Sugar bowl, pansy, bl mk, w/spoon, 3".. 180.00
Sugar bowl, tomato, Deponiert, w/lid, 4"....................................... 65.00
Tea strainer, pansy, bl mk, 5".. 450.00
Toothpick holder, spikey shell, pearl lustre, 3-ftd, 3", $75 to........ 125.00
Tray, Art Nouveau lady, Deponiert, 10¼x6⅞" 1,050.00
Tray, Devil & Cards, bl mk, 10x7".. 650.00
Tray, dresser, clown, yel, bl mk 800.00
Wall pocket, Art Nouveau lady, bl mk, 8¾"...............................1,600.00
Wall pocket, grapes, various colors, gr, bl mk, 9x5½".................... 175.00
Wall pocket, maid in flowing gown, bl mk, 8½".............................. 950.00
Wall pocket, tomato, wall mt, bl mk, 9"... 650.00
Whipped cream set, poppy, bl mk, 6" bowl+7" plate+ladle 300.00

Nursery Rhymes

Note: Items with a printed verse bring a premium.

Basket, Little Boy Blue, bl mk, 5".. 195.00
Bell, Jack & Beanstalk, w/rhyme, w/clapper, bl mk....................... 350.00
Bowl, child's feeding, Jack & Jill, bl mk, w/lid, 7"......................... 150.00
Candlestick, Little Bo Peep, bl mk, 4".. 180.00
Chamberstick, Little Jack Horner, bl mk 180.00
Child's dish, Jack & Jill, 7¾", $100 to.. 135.00
Cruet, Jack & Beanstalk, bl mk, no stopper, 6".............................. 125.00

Match holder, Little Jack Horner, blue mark, 3½", $250.00. (Photo courtesy Hassinger & Courtney Auctioneering on LiveAuctioneers.com)

Mug, Jack & Beanstalk, w/verse, bl mk, lg 250.00
Mug, Ring Around the Rosies, bl mk, 6"... 200.00
Pitcher, Jack & the Beanstalk, bl mk, water sz............................... 500.00
Pitcher, Little Boy Blue, 4" 80.00
Pitcher, Little Miss Muffet, w/verse, bl mk, milk sz, 4" 235.00

Pitcher, Ring around the Rosies, unmk, 2¾"................................. 75.00
Sugar bowl, Little Boy Blue, w/verse, bl mk 225.00
Tray, Little Miss Muffet, bl mk, 11⅛x7⅞" 275.00
Vase, Babes in the Woods, bl mk, 4" 150.00

Scenics and Action Portraits

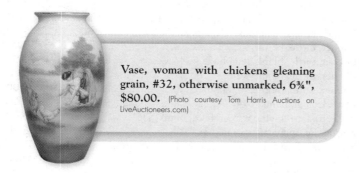

Vase, woman with chickens gleaning grain, #32, otherwise unmarked, 6¾", $80.00. (Photo courtesy Tom Harris Auctions on LiveAuctioneers.com)

Ashtray, dogs after moose, buckle & strap at side, bl mk, 5½", M . 195.00
Basket, Shawl Lady w/gold, bl mk, 5" 95.00
Box, Dutch woman, shell shape, bl mk, 1x3x2" 115.00
Box, peacock scene, bl mk 160.00
Candleholder, Brittany woman, bl mk, 4x2", ea 70.00
Candlestick, frog & bee, frog on bk, hdl, bl mk, 7" 650.00
Charger, 3 nudes w/castle bkgrnd, gold scroll rim, bl mk, 11½" ... 195.00
Charger, Arab on wht horse, gold trim, bl mk, 13" 150.00
Chocolate pot, Arab on horsebk, gr mk, 8", +2 c/s w/gr mks........ 295.00
Coal scuttle, man w/2 harnessed horses, w/hdl, bulb, unmk, 3" . 125.00
Covered dish, man fishing from boat, bl mk, 5" 125.00
Cracker jar, exotic parrots, metal bail, unmk, 6½" 800.00
Creamer/sugar bowl, penguins, ftd, bl mk 295.00
Cruet, bears (brn) in landscape, bl mk, 5" 300.00
Dresser set, girl & chickens, bl mk, 7x4" tray +3 sm dishes.......... 295.00
Hair receiver, 2 equestrians w/3 dogs on lid, 3 gold ft, bl mk, 4" . 125.00
Hatpin holder, Brittany girl, unmk, 4½" 1,000.00
Jug, dogs chase moose into river, bl mk, 6", $130 to 150.00
Mug, cows in pasture, 3-hdl, bl mk, 3⅜" 95.00
Pitcher, cattle in pastoral scene, bl mk, cream sz 75.00
Pitcher, cattle in pastoral scene, milk sz, 4¼" 95.00
Pitcher, children on beach, bl mk, milk sz, 4" 85.00
Pitcher, Corinthian, blk, bl mk, milk sz, 5" 65.00
Pitcher, girl w/dog, bl mk, milk sz, 4⅝" 75.00
Pitcher, hunter w/dog in landscape w/flying birds, bl mk, water sz, 6" . 195.00
Pitcher, jester, Penny in Pocket..., Noke, unmk, lemonade sz 700.00
Pitcher, man & turkeys, w/gold, cylindrical w/vertical-pinch spout, 6".225.00
Pitcher, polar bears in Arctic scene, bl mk, 4" 425.00
Pitcher, poodle dog, gray, bl mk, 4½" 95.00
Pitcher, sailboat scene, bl mk, milk sz, 5" 75.00
Pitcher, sailing scene, gray & wht tones, bl mk, cream sz 75.00
Pitcher, The Hunt, boat shape, bl mk, cream sz........................ 90.00
Plate, sunset, 4-hdl, bl mk, 3" 50.00
Stickpin holder, fisherman in boat, rect, bl mk, 5" L 225.00
Teapot, hunting scene, bl mk, 4x7".................................... 135.00
Teapot, rooster & hen, bl mk, 6" W 165.00
Toothpick holder, goose girl, 3-hdl, bl mk 175.00
Toothpick holder, penguin on yel, tricorner, bl mk, 2" 150.00
Toothpick holder, woman w/horse, unmk 175.00
Tray, Goose Girl, bl mk, 12x9" 100.00
Vase, 3 hounds after moose in river, bl mk, 9⅝".................. 195.00
Vase, cows & trees, bl mk, 6"... 85.00
Vase, Dutch ice skaters, bl mk, 4"....................................... 75.00
Vase, frogs & bees, bl mk, sq, 4x3" 225.00
Vase, goats in woods, 2 gold hdls, bl mk, 7" 125.00

Vase, horses (4) in pasture, unmk, 5½"................................. 95.00
Vase, houses/lake/boat, bl mk, salesman sample, 4x3¾" 75.00
Vase, lady w/candle on brn, bl mk, 8" 110.00
Vase, lady's w/purple shawl, bl mk, 7".............................. 175.00
Vase, nude fairy, pierced neck, vine hdls, 4" 175.00
Vase, pheasant scene, ruffled rim, bl mk, 3" 125.00
Vase, The Chase, hounds & stag, integral hdls, bl mk, 3" 75.00
Vase, waterfalls & mtn, bl mk, ornate ring hdls, rtcl rim, 7" 295.00
Wall plaque, cavaliers at table, scalloped rim, bl mk, 11½" 125.00

Sunbonnet Babies

Ashtray, scrubbing, dmn shape, bl mk, 5⅜" 100.00
Basket, 1 sweeping, 2nd washing, unmk.............................. 350.00
Bells, various activities, ltd ed, 3", ea 35.00
Bowl, hanging clothes, bl mk, 7" 175.00
Candlesticks, sweeping, bl mk, 4", pr 350.00
Candlesticks, washing, bl mk, 4¼", pr 325.00

Creamer, washing, blue mark, 3½", $150.00.

Cup/saucer, fishing, bl mk.. 225.00
Dutch shoe, washing, #18, 5½" L.. 500.00
Hair receiver, washing, 4-leg, bl mk 325.00
Nappy, washing, w/hdl, bl mk, 6" L 225.00
Pitcher, cleaning, bl mk, cream sz, 3¼" 150.00
Pitcher, fishing, water, bl mk, 6"....................................... 350.00
Pitcher, scrubbing floor, bl mk, cream sz............................ 120.00
Pitcher, washing, ruffled spout on ewer form, bl mk, 4" 225.00
Planter, fishing, low gold hdls, bsk insert, bl mk, 2x3" 250.00
Plate, ltd ed, 7 scenes, ca 1970s, 13", set of 7 .... 175.00
Plates, various activities, ltd ed, 1974, ea.............................. 25.00
Sugar bowl, cleaning, bl mk, 3" 250.00
Vase, fishing, low gold hdls, bl mk, 2¾x3½" 250.00
Vase, ironing, ruffled top, bl mk, 3" 175.00

Tapestries

Basket, Rose Tapestry, bl mk, 5" 175.00
Box, dancing couple, oval, bl mk, 4" L 150.00
Box, dresser, colonial scene, bl mk, 2 1/4x3¼" 150.00
Box, pin, courting scene, bl mk, 2½x4½" L......................... 150.00
Box, Rose Tapestry, clover shape w/gold, bl mk, 5" 175.00
Box, Silver Tapestry, bl mk, 5" L 900.00
Clock, Rose Tapestry, bl mk, 4" 250.00
Cracker jar, Rose Tapestry, appl hdls, gold trim, 5"............... 700.00
Creamer, Rose Tapestry, 3" 125.00
Creamer, turkey hunting scene, 3½" 125.00
Hatpin holder, Rose Tapestry, 3-color, bl mk, 4½"............... 275.00
Hatpin holder, violets, bl mk 275.00
Humidor, goat scene, bl mk, 5" 500.00
Jar, Rose Tapestry, gold hdls, ped ft, bl mk, 5¼x6¼" 295.00
Leaf dish, Rose Tapestry, 3-color, bl mk, 4½x5" 100.00
Nappy, sheep scenic, cloverleaf w/hdl, bl mk 100.00
Pitcher, 2 polar bears in Arctic waters, bl mk, 7"................1,900.00
Pitcher, goats in meadow, bl mk, milk sz, 4" 125.00
Pitcher, Rose Tapestry, bl mk, water sz, 6½" 550.00

Pitcher, stag in stream/gazebo on hill, bl mk, milk sz, 5" 125.00
Plaque, temple scene w/river & deer, bl mk, 11" 210.00
Shoe, Rose Tapestry, pk, bl mk, 4½" L 250.00
Vase, polar bears, 2 in Arctic scene, bl mk, 8x4" 1,800.00
Vase, Rose Tapestry, ornate gold hdls, bl mk, 9" 475.00
Vase, Rose Tapestry, slightly bulb, bl mk, 4" 110.00
Vase, silver rose tapestry, bl mk, 9" 1,000.00
Vase, tavern scene, 2 gold hdls at shoulder, bl mk, 4" 75.00
Watering can, wildlife in landscape, unmk, 3" 550.00

Royal Bonn

Royal Bonn is a fine-paste porcelain, ornately decorated with scenes, portraits, or florals. The factory was established in the mid-1800s in Bonn, Germany; however, most pieces found today are from the latter part of the century.

Vase, seminude woman overlooking a pond, signed Wilhelm, 10¼", $720.00. (Photo courtesy Jackson's Auction on LiveAuctioneers.com)

Clock, floral case, Ansonia open escapement movement, 12" .. 1,960.00
Clock, La Layon, Ansonia Works, ca 1900, 14" 1,100.00
Clock, La Lomme, pansies w/gold, time & strike, 4" dial, 11¼x12" . 700.00
Clock, La Roca, floral, open escapement, 8-day, gong, 11½" 850.00
Clock, La Vera, floral w/bl, 8-day, ½-hr gong, 12½" 975.00
Clock, La Verden, floral on red, 5" open escapement, 14" 950.00
Plaque, Queen Louise portrait, E Volk, ca 1900, in oval gilt bronze fr... 575.00
Urn, floral on cream w/gold, #D3149/670, 12", pr 1,800.00
Urn, putti in clouds w/instruments, gold hdls, 1880-1920, 18½" ... 1,325.00
Vase, bust portrait: nude in gauzy drape on shaded brn, sgn Duren, 8".. 485.00
Vase, cavalier courting scene, lion mask ft, 48", +23" stand 1,325.00
Vase, East Indian lady, sgn Bauar, 21" 575.00
Vase, lady in flower garden tapestry, putti hdls, 1890s, 13¾" ... 1,950.00
Vase, lady in landscape, Sticher, gold hdls, w/lid, ca 1900, 14x7" . 600.00
Vase, lady's portrait, blown-out berries, Sticher, hdls, 1900s, 16"... 1,325.00
Vase, roses, Dirkmann, gold hdls, #1755, 18½" 850.00

Royal Copenhagen

The Royal Copenhagen Manufactory was established in Denmark in about 1775 by Frantz Henrich Muller. When bankruptcy threatened in 1779, the Crown took charge. The fine dinnerware and objects of art produced after that time carry the familiar logo, the crown over three wavy lines. For further information we recommend *Royal Copenhagen Porcelain, Animals and Figurines*, by Robert J. Heritage (Schiffer). See also Limited Edition Plates.

Bust of woman in bl cap, stoneware, Hedegaard, #21616, 1948+, 18".. 240.00
Figurine Scottie dog, Dahl Jensen, #1078, 7" 215.00
Figurine, Amagar woman knitting, #1317, 9" 110.00
Figurine, Asian dancer, #12238, 11½" 900.00
Figurine, bird w/red topknot, #1050, Dahl Jensen, 15" 100.00
Figurine, boy wrapped in bl stands w/dog, #782, 7½" 120.00
Figurine, children w/dog, C Thomsen design, #707, 6" 350.00

Figurine, courting couple about to kiss, #3049, 17¼" 550.00
Figurine, dog w/slipper, #3476, 3½" 85.00
Figurine, Fano, girls kneels w/floral garland, #12413, 1964, 5¾" .. 480.00
Figurine, farmer stands beside hog, #848, 7½x8" 275.00
Figurine, fisherman, #12214, 13½" 725.00
Figurine, girl seated holds golden horn aloft, #12242, 1958, 8⅜" . 425.00
Figurine, hunter seated w/gun, dog at ft, #1087, 9x6" 360.00
Figurine, ladies (2/elderly) gossiping, #1319, 12" 480.00
Figurine, maiden w/goats, #694, 9x7½" 215.00
Figurine, medieval boy & girl on base, #3171, 19x9" 600.00
Figurine, military couple, #1180, 7" 285.00
Figurine, mother stands w/baby in arm & daughter beside, #12159, 6" .. 515.00
Figurine, native girl w/beads, Dahl Jensen, #1353, 5" 275.00
Figurine, owls (2 conjoined), #283, 12½" 660.00
Figurine, Pan, #1713, 3x4" 200.00
Figurine, Pan w/panpipes, #1736, 5½" 250.00
Figurine, Pan w/parrot, C Thomsen design, 7" 300.00
Figurine, penguins (2), #2918, 8" 300.00
Figurine, Sjaelland, girl in native costume, #12418, 1964, 4" 550.00
Figurine, soldier speaking to witch, #1112, 8" 475.00
Figurine, spaniel, Dahl Jensen, #1304, 5" 225.00
Figurine, terrier standing w/tail up, #1452/2967, 6½x8½" 110.00
Figurine, Wave & Rock, #1132, 18¼" 1,200.00
Figurine, wolf & cubs, #1788, 4x5½" 215.00
Figurines (2), Asian girl musician, ivory; brn/ivory/gold, 5½x3", pr .250.00
Plate, narcissus, artist monogram, #29/1125, 10" 60.00

Plates, salad, Flora Danica, serrated and pierced rims, second half twentieth century, 9", set of 12, $6,600.00. (Photo courtesy John Moran Auctioneers, Inc. on LiveAuctioneers.com)

Tea caddy, songbird reserve on wht, Paaske, 1918 .... 60.00
Vase, colonial couple reserve, waisted, Jul 1895, 11¼" 300.00
Vase, daffodil & leaves on bl, #2640/137, 12½" 240.00
Vase, Frisk Kuling Udfor Kobenhavn, sailing ships, 1927, 19½" .. 850.00
Vase, grotesque decor w/bl borders, gold dolphin hdls, 19th C, 22"... 9,000.00
Vase, herringbone incising, brn orange peel, Salto/#20737 29?, 10¼" . 1,200.00
Vase, honeycomb-like pattern, gray/olive matt, Salto, #20708, 7x5½" ..3,600.00
Vase, honeycomb-like pattern, turq matt, Salto, #20685, 6x2¾" ...3,000.00
Vase, organic form w/vertical ribs, gray/brn/bl mottle, Salto, 5"... 600.00
Vase, sailboats in harbor, #MCX 2609-1049, 9x5" 215.00
Vase, sculpted rim, bl & mustard mottle, Salto, #21439, 5¼x3½" ..3,150.00
Vase, swans among waves, VT Fischer, 1896, 14¾" 960.00
Vase, swans on lake, St Ussing, #8897, 13½" 850.00
Vase, tree pattern emb, blk & mahog, spherical, Salto, #1243, 7¾" .3,600.00
Vase, wisteria on wht, #184, 11", EX 75.00

Royal Copley

Royal Copley is a decorative type of pottery made by the Spaulding China Company in Sebring, Ohio, from 1942 to 1957. They also produced two other major lines — Royal Windsor and Spaulding. Royal Copley was primarily marketed through five-and-ten cent stores; Royal Windsor and Spaulding were sold through department stores, gift shops, and jobbers. Items trimmed in gold are worth 25% to 50% more than the same item with no gold trim. For more information we recommend *Collecting Royal Copley Plus Royal Windsor & Spaulding* by our advisor for this category, Joe Devine; he is listed in the Directory under Iowa.

Ashtray, bow/ribbon, sgn, raised letters, colors/sayings, 5", $40 to . 45.00
Ashtray, leafy, gr stamp, 5", $10 to 15.00
Bank, bowtie pig, paper label, 6¼", $50 to 55.00
Bank, Farmer Pig, paper label, flat unglazed base w/2 holes, 5½", $90 to.. 100.00
Bank, rooster, Chicken Feed on base, 8", $75 to............................. 85.00
Bank, teddy bear, blk & wht, pk sucker held vertically, paper label, 8", $175 to ..195.00
Coaster, Dutch couple strolling in garden, $35 to........................... 40.00
Creamer, leaf, hdld, gr stamp, 3", $25 to 30.00
Figurine, Asian boy, #42, red, yel or gr, paper label, 7½", $30 to.... 35.00
Figurine, Asian girl, #41, red, yel or gr, paper label, 7½", $30 to.... 35.00
Figurine, blk cat, paper label, 8", $85 to.. 95.00
Figurine, cockatoo, paper label, 7¼", $40 to 45.00
Figurine, hen, Game Birds of America, AD Priolo, 6¼"............... 225.00
Figurine, mallard drake, Game Birds of America, AD Priolo, 8½" ..225.00
Figurine, parrot, paper label, 8", $50 to... 60.00
Figurine, sparrow, paper label, 5"", $15 to 20.00
Figurines (2), swallow/stump, gold trim/opal, 7½", pr, $125 to..... 150.00
Lamp, Birds in the Bower, paper label, 8", $50 to............................ 60.00
Lamp, clown, paper label, 7½", $150 to 175.00
Lamp, dancing lady figurine mtd on metal base, 8", $150 to 200.00
Lamp, pig, retooled bl/wht striped pig bank, 6½", $125 to 150.00
Lamp, rooster, paper label, $125 to... 150.00
Pitcher, Decal, gold stamp, 6", $12 to 16.00
Planter, angel kneeling w/ praying hands, paper label, 8", $40 to... 45.00
Planter, bear cub clinging to stump, paper label, 8¼", $35 to......... 40.00
Planter, big apple & finch, paper label, 6½", $40 to....................... 45.00
Planter, birdhouse w/bird, paper label, 8", $100 to...................... 125.00
Planter, coach, gr stamp or paper label, 3¼x6", $20 to 30.00
Planter, deer & fawn, 9¼"... 32.00
Planter, duck & wheelbarrow, paper label, 3¾", $18 to 20.00

Planter, elephant, original label, 8x6", $45.00. (Photo courtesy Tom Harris Auctions/LiveAuctioneers.com)

Planter, fruit plate plaque, raised letters, Oxford Assortment, $35 to...40.00
Planter, hat, Oxford Assortment, made to hand or rest on a table, 7", $45 to..50.00
Planter, mallard hen, sitting, paper lable, (+), 5¼", $50 to 60.00
Planter, pigtail girl, 7", $70 to... 75.00
Planter, rooster & wheelbarrow, paper label, 8", $150 to............. 175.00
Planter, teddy bear w/concertina, paper label, 7½", $95 to........... 120.00
Planter, turq w/brn specks, boat shaped, USA, 12½x4¾", $16 to... 20.00
Razor blade bank, barber pole, gold outline & top, paper label, 6¼", (+), $70 to.. 75.00
Sugar, leaf hdl, gray w/pk hdls, gr stamp or raised letters, 3", $35 to... 40.00
Vase, 2 fish, Asian-style, ftd, fish on front side only, paper label, 5½", $12 to.15.00
Vase, 2 fish, cylindrical, outlined in gold, sgn, Essex Assortment, 8", $20 to..24.00
Vase, Blue Beauty, outlined in gold, gold stamp, paper label, 6¼", $12 to.. 14.00
Vase, cornucopia, gold outline, 8¼", $25 to 30.00
Vase, Ivy, ftd, paper label, dk gr leaves on ivory, 7", $10 to 12.00
Vase, Mary Kay, gold stamp, outlined in gold, $12 to 14.00
Vase, Virginia Decal, flat unglazed base, paper label, 7", $12 to 15.00
Wall pocket, pirate head, 8", $45 to... 50.00
Wall pocket, salt box, sgn, 5½", $40 to 45.00

Royal Crown Derby

The Royal Crown Derby company can trace its origin back to 1848. It first operated under the name of Locker & Co. but by 1859 had became Stevenson, Sharp & Co. Several changes in ownership occurred until 1866 when it became known as the Sampson Hancock Co. The Derby Crown Porcelain Co. Ltd. was formed in 1876, and these companies soon merged. In 1890 they were appointed as a manufacturer for the Queen and began using the name Royal Crown Derby.

In the early years, considerable 'Japan ware' decorated in Imari style, using red, blue, and gold in Asian patterns, was popular. The company excelled in their ability to use gold in the decoration, and some of the best flower painters of all time were employed. Nice vases or plaques signed by any of these artists will bring thousands of dollars: Gregory, Mosley, Rouse, Gresley, and D'esiré Leroy. We have observed porcelain plaques decorated with flowers signed by Gregory selling at auction for as much as $12,000.00. If you find a signed piece and are not sure of its value, if at all possible, it would be best to have it appraised by someone very knowledgeable regarding current market values.

As is usual among most other English factories, nearly all of the vases produced by Royal Crown Derby came with covers. If they are missing, deduct 40% to 45%. There are several well illustrated books available from antique booksellers to help you learn to identify this ware. The back stamps used after 1891 will date every piece except dinnerware. The company is still in business, producing outstanding dinnerware and Imari-decorated figures and serving pieces. They also produce custom (one only) sets of table service for the wealthy of the world.

Vase, Prunus, two-tone gilt on ruby, circa 1891, with lid (restored), 7½", EX, $460.00. (Photo courtesy New Orleans Auction Galleries, Inc. on LiveAuctioneers.com)

Beaker, Old Imari, w/hdl, #1128, 3¾" 110.00
Bowl, cream soup, Imari, #2451, w/hdls, +underplate, set of 8.....650.00
Bowl, Imari, #2451, 10½" L 250.00
Bowl, Imari, pierced gold oak leaf hdls, #2451, 8¼x11¾"............. 475.00
Bowl, Old Imari, #1128, 10½" L 250.00
Bowl, Old Imari, 8-sided, gold trim, #1128, 3½x8¾" 315.00
Bowl, Olde Avesbury, octagonal, 4x10" 210.00
Bowl, soup, Old Imari, #1128, 8", set of 6 .... 550.00
Candlesticks, floral w/cobalt & gold, sq base, bone china, 10½", pr ...900.00
Candlesticks, Old Imari, #1128, 10", NM, pr................................ 925.00
Candlesticks, Olde Avesbury, Asian pheasants/gilt, sq base, 11", pr. 425.00
Candlesticks, Red Aves, birds & flowers, 10½", pr....................... 325.00
Centerpiece bowl, pheasant & flowers, XXXIII 335.00
Coffeepot, Imari, ovoid, #2451, 8" 425.00
Compote, Old Imari, ftd, #1128, 5x9½" 360.00
Cup/saucer, Imari, #2451 .... 60.00
Cup/saucer, Old Imari, #1128 .... 100.00
Dinnerware, Vine, 12 lg plates+12 c/s.. 425.00
Dish, floral sprays, bl starbursts & gold at rim, 1850s, 7½" L 240.00
Figurine, Bengal tiger on base, Imari colors, artist sgn, 5" 215.00
Figurine, lion (male) on base, Imari colors, artist sgn, 6½".......... 315.00
Figurine, pheasant on naturalistic base, realistic HP, 6¼x7¼"...... 215.00

Figurines (2), man & woman beneath flowering trees w/animals, 7", pr ... 550.00
Pitcher, Imari, incurvate throat, #2451, 4½", $125 to 135.00
Plate, cake, Old Imari, #1128 XL, 10" 135.00
Plate, dessert, Imari, #2451, 7" 40.00
Plate, dinner, Gold Aves, 1930s, 10", 12 for 480.00
Plate, dinner, Lombardy, 10⅝", 10 for 550.00
Plate, dinner, Old Imari, #1128, 10" 135.00
Plate, Imari, #2451, ca 1898, 9" 175.00
Plate, salad, Old Imari, #1128, 8½", $60 to 65.00
Platter, Imari, oval, #2451, 14½" 850.00
Platter, Old Imari, #1128 XLIII, 16" 265.00
Sugar bowl, Imari, w/lid, #2451, 5½" W 225.00
Tray, Old Imari, #1128 MMV, oval, w/hdls, 15½" L 550.00
Tray/dish, Imari, sq w/hdls, #2451, 9¾x10¾" 225.00
Tureen, bittersweet floral w/cobalt & gold, w/lid & tray, 1920s, 16" L .. 900.00
Vase, Aesthetic Movement, much decor, rtcl hdls, Picotee, 10¼" .. 1,200.00
Vase, floral in ornate gold reserve on dk bl, gold hdls/ft, Leroy, 8" .6,350.00
Vase, floral sprays, pastel w/gold, slim neck, bulb, 19th C, 7" 240.00
Vase, floral, gold on pk, bulb, 1890s, 9" 515.00
Vase, Persian decor w/gold, bottle shape, rtcl hdls, 1880s, 11¼" .. 425.00

Royal Doulton

The range of wares produced by the Doulton Company since its inception in 1815 has been vast and varied. The earliest wares produced in the tiny pottery in Lambeth, England, were salt-glazed pitchers, plain and fancy figural bottles, etc. — all utility-type stoneware geared to the practical needs of everyday living. The original partners, John Doulton and John Watts, saw the potential for success in the manufacture of drain and sewage pipes and during the 1840s concentrated on these highly lucrative types of commercial wares. Watts retired from the company in 1854, and Doulton began experimenting with a more decorative product line. As time went by, many glazes and decorative effects were developed, among them Faience, Impasto, Silicon, Carrara, Marqueterie, Chine, and Rouge Flambé. Tiles and architectural terra cotta were an important part of their manufacture. Late in the nineteenth century at the original Lambeth location, fine artware was decorated by such notable artists as Hannah and Arthur Barlow, George Tinworth, and J.H. McLennan. Stoneware vases with incised animal drawings, gracefully shaped urns with painted scenes, and cleverly modeled figurines rivaled the best of any competitor.

In 1882 a second factory was built in Burslem which continues even yet to produce the famous figurines, character jugs, series ware, and table services so popular with collectors today. Their Kingsware line, made from 1899 to 1946, featured flasks and flagons with drinking scenes, usually on a brown-glazed ground. Some were limited editions, while others were commemorative and advertising items. The Gibson Girl series, 24 plates in all, was introduced in 1901. It was drawn by Charles Dana Gibson and is recognized by its blue and white borders and central illustrations, each scene depicting a humorous or poignant episode in the life of 'The Widow and Her Friends.' Dickensware, produced from 1911 through the early 1940s, featured illustrations by Charles Dickens, with many of his famous characters. The Robin Hood series was introduced in 1914; the Shakespeare series #1, portraying scenes from the Bard's plays, was made from 1914 until World War II. The Shakespeare series #2 ran from 1906 until 1974 and was decorated with featured characters. Nursery Rhymes was a series that was first produced in earthenware in 1930 and later in bone china. In 1933 a line of decorated children's ware, the Bunnykin series, was introduced; it continues to be made to the present day. About 150 'bunny' scenes have been devised, the earliest and most desirable being those signed by the artist Barbara Vernon. Most pieces range in value from $60.00 to $120.00.

Factors contributing to the value of a figurine are age, demand, color, and detail. Those with a limited production run and those signed by the artist or marked 'Potted' (indicating a pre-1939 origin) are also more valuable. After 1920 wares were marked with a lion — with or without a crown — over a circular 'Royal Doulton.'

Animals and Birds

Alsatian dog, seated, K13, $120 to 140.00
Ashtead Applause, collie dog, glossy, #779A, 5", $75 to 100.00
Cardinal bird, K28, 2¾" 215.00
Cat, tabby, HN2583, 2¾" L 60.00
Dalmatian puppy, HN1113, $450 to 475.00
Drake, mc w/wht chest, HN807, 1923-77, 2½", $80 to 120.00
Elephant trumpeting, realistic, HN2640, 11x23" 550.00

German shepherd, marked, 13½", $360.00. (Photo courtesy Forsythes' Auctions, LLC on LiveAuctioneers.com)

Horse, wht, running, DA245 Milton Ltd Edition 245.00
King Penguin, HN1189, $800 to 850.00
Pekingese, HN1012 JC 90.00
Penguin w/chick under wing, K20, $275 to 300.00
Persian cat, wht, HN2539, 1930s, 3x5x3", $225 to 300.00
Sealyham fox terrier begging, K3, 2½", $90 to 120.00
Sealyham fox terrier, recumbent, K4, 3¼" L, $125 to 165.00
Smooth Fox Terrier, HN1069S, 6x7½" 725.00
Tarryall Maestro, Morgan horse, blk, DA28, 11½" 275.00
Tiger on Rock, Prestige Cats, #2639, 12x16", $650 to 700.00
Welsh Mountain Pony, DA164, 1991-97, 6½", $175 to 200.00

Bunnykins

Artist, DB13, 1975, 3½", $150 to 225.00
Autumn Days, DB5, 4½", $125 to 150.00
Beefeater, DB163, 1996, $175 to 200.00
Billie, #8302, 1939-45, 4½" 950.00
Collector, DB54, 1987 club pc, 4¼", $225 to 265.00
Cooling Off (Billie), DB3, $80 to 110.00
Farmer #8304, 1939-45, 7¼" 1,075.00
Freefall, DB41, 1984, $100 to 150.00
Grandpa's Story, DB14, 1975, $150 to 195.00
Happy Birthday, DB21, 1982, MIB, $25 to 40.00
Helping Mother, DB2, 3¼", $25 to 35.00
Little John, DB243, 5", $50 to 65.00
Mother, #8305, 1939-45, 7½" 725.00
Queen Sophie, DB46, 1984, 4½", $90 to 125.00
Rise & Shine, DB11, 1974, 3¾", $95 to 120.00
Rock & Roll, DB124, 4½", 1991, 4", MIB 350.00
Rocket Man, DB20, $150 to 175.00
Storytime, DB9, 1974, 2½x3", $60 to 85.00
Tom, DB72, 1988-93, 3" 75.00
Uncle Sam, DB175, 2nd version, 1977, MIB 225.00

Character Jugs

Anne Boleyn, D6644, lg, $100 to 125.00
Anne of Cleves, D6754, mini, $115 to 135.00

Arriet, D6250, mini, $45 to... 65.00
Auld Mac, D5932, lg 80.00
Bacchus, D6521, 1960-91, mini, $40 to........................... 50.00
Buffalo Bill, D6735, med, $125 to.................................... 150.00
Capt Ahab, D6500, lg, $100 to.. 125.00
Capt Henry Morgan, D6510, 1960-82, mini, $40 to........ 50.00
Cardinal, D5614, lg, $100 to.. 120.00
Don Quixote, D6460, sm, $50 to...................................... 65.00
Falconer, D6547, 1960-91, mini, $35 to........................... 50.00
Falstaff, D6287, 1968-71, lg, $85 to................................. 110.00
Fat Boy, D5840, sm, $100 to.. 120.00
Fortune Teller, D6497, lg, $325 to................................... 375.00
Gaoler, D6584, 1963-83, mini, $40 to.............................. 55.00
George Harrison, D6727, med, $325 to............................ 345.00
Groucho Marx, D6710, lg, $180 to................................... 195.00
Gulliver, D6563, sm, $315 to.. 345.00
Henry VIII, D6647, sm, $65 to... 75.00
Jarge, D6288, lg, $200 to... 250.00
John Peel, D5612, 1936-60, lg, $100 to........................... 125.00
London Bobby, D6744, lg, $185 to................................... 225.00
Lumberjack, D6613, 1967-82, sm, $40 to......................... 60.00
Mad Hatter, D6606, mini, $70 to..................................... 90.00
Merlin, D6529, lg, $85 to... 95.00
Mr McCawber, D6138, mini, $40 to................................. 50.00
Mr Pickwick, D6254, mini.. 60.00
North Am Indian, D6611, lg.. 95.00
Old Salt, china, D6551, lg, $75 to................................... 100.00
Rip Van Winkle, D6517, mini, $50 to.............................. 75.00
Robin Hood, D6234, 1947-60, sm, $40 to........................ 50.00
Sairey Gamp, D6045, mini, $40 to................................... 45.00
Sam Johnson, D6289, 1950-60, lg, $190 to...................... 135.00
Sancho Panza, D6456, lg, $85 to..................................... 95.00
Sleuth, D6635, sm, $40 to.. 50.00
Snake Charmer, D6912, lg, $275 to.................................. 300.00
St George, D6618, 1968-75, lg, $295 to........................... 325.00
Veteran Motorist, D6641, mini, $90 to............................ 115.00

Figurines

Affection, HN2236.. 180.00
Afternoon Tea, HN1747, 5¾", $325 to............................. 550.00
And One for You, HN2970 .... 200.00
Antoinette, HN2326, 2nd version 200.00
As Good As New, HN2971, $135 to................................. 150.00
Ballerina, HN2116, lg, $320 to... 350.00
Balloon Man, HN1954, $275 to.. 325.00
Bedtime Story, HN2059, 1st version, $135 to................... 175.00
Belle o' the Ball, HN1997, $235 to................................... 275.00
Bess, HN2002, $325 to... 345.00
Blithe Morning, HN2021, $200 to.................................... 225.00
Blue Beard, HN2105, $410 to... 435.00
Bridesmaid, HN2874, 5th version, $45 to......................... 60.00
Captain Cuttle, M77, $90 to.. 115.00
Carmen, HN2545, $275 to.. 295.00
Celeste, HN2237, $140 to... 170.00
Child From Williamsburg, HN2154, $175 to.................... 200.00
Christine, HN2792, $160 to.. 195.00
Christmas Day, HN4214, $450 to..................................... 485.00
Cissie, HN1809, $100 to... 130.00
Clockmaker, HN2279, $275 to.. 325.00
Coralie, HN2307, $175 to... 195.00
Daydreams, HN1731, $200 to... 235.00
Dinky Do, HN1678, $100 to.. 135.00
Doctor, HN2858, $250 to... 300.00

Easter Day, HN2039, $225 to... 275.00
Elaine, HN3214, $60 to.. 85.00
Elyse, HN2429, $175 to.. 200.00
Enchantment, HN2178 .... 195.00
Europa & the Bull, HN2828, $1,800 to 2,000.00
Fair Lady, HN3336.. 235.00
Falstaff, HN3236, 3rd version.. 100.00
Felicity, HN3986, $525 to... 575.00
Fleur, HN2368, $125 to.. 175.00
Flower of Love, HN2460, $125 to.................................... 150.00
Fragrance, HN2334, 1st version, $130 to......................... 165.00
Fragrance, HN3220, $100 to... 125.00
Friar Tuck, HN2143, $575 to... 625.00
Gay Morning, HN2135, $275 to....................................... 300.00
Gossips, HN2025, $325 to.. 350.00
Graduate, HN3017, $175 to.. 195.00
Hannah, HN3369, $150 to.. 175.00
Harriet, HN3794.. 200.00
Her Ladyship, HN1977, $325 to....................................... 365.00
Irish Charm, HN4580, $285 to... 315.00
Jacqueline, HN2333, $185 to.. 215.00
Jean, HN3032, $350 to... 385.00
Jennifer, HN3447, $335 to.. 375.00
Joanna, HN4711, $175 to... 195.00
Jovial Monk, HN2144, $265 to... 300.00
Joy, HN3875, $75 to... 95.00
Judge, HN2433 .... 165.00
Julia, HN2705, 1974, 7", $175 to..................................... 220.00
Karen, HN2388, $375 to... 400.00
Katie, HN4460, $285 to.. 315.00
Kirsty, HN2381, $180 to... 200.00
Lady Betty, HN1967, $225 to... 300.00
Lavinia, HN1955, $90 to... 120.00
Lobster Man, HN2317, $125 to.. 175.00
Lunchtime, HN2485, $165 to.. 185.00
Lydia, HN1908, 1st version, $125 to................................. 150.00
Margaret, HN1989, 7½", $275 to..................................... 300.00
Marguerite, HN1946, pk gown, 8¼".................................. 500.00
Marie, HN1370, $60 to... 80.00
May Time, HN2113, 1952, 7½"... 300.00
Medicant, HN1365, $250 to... 300.00
Melody, HN2202, $275 to... 295.00
Minuet, HN2019, $220 to... 245.00
Miss Muffet, HN1936, $110 to... 140.00
Monica, HN1467, 1st version, $110 to.............................. 125.00
Nanny, HN2221, $265 to.. 295.00
Newsvendor, HN2891, $180 to... 200.00
Nicola, HN28804, $165 to.. 185.00
October, HN2693, 1st version, $170 to............................. 200.00
Omar Khayyam, HN2247 .... 200.00
Pantalettes, HN1362, 7½"... 150.00
Penelope, HN1901, $250 to.. 325.00
Pensive Moments, HN2704, $175 to................................ 225.00
Pride & Joy, HN2945, $275 to... 300.00
Primrose, HN3710 .... 250.00
Professor, HN2281, $275 to... 300.00
Rebecca, HN3414, $125 to... 145.00
Repose, HN2272, $250 to.. 300.00
Reverie, HN2306, $200 to.. 250.00
Rosie, HN4094, $125 to... 150.00
Royal Governor's Cook, HN2233, $500 to....................... 600.00
Sara, HN3249, $100 to... 130.00
Schoolmarm, HN2223, $200 to....................................... 250.00
Shoreleave, HN2254, $250 to... 285.00

Sir Walter Raleigh, HN1751, 12".................................. 480.00
Skater, HN2117, $275 to... 350.00
Slapdash, HN2277 .... 295.00
Soiree, HN2312, $120 to.. 170.00
Song of the Sea, HN2729, $200 to.............................. 250.00
Southern Belle, HN3244 .... 245.00
Spring, HN2085, $275 to 350.00
Springtime, HN3033, 2nd version, $165 to...................... 190.00
Sweet & Twenty, HN1298, $425 to 450.00
Tall Story, HN2248, $325 to 400.00
Time for Bed, HN3762, $70 to 80.00
Tony Weller, M47, $60 to 75.00
Town Crier, HN2119, $200 to 250.00
Wedding Vows, HN2750, $180 to 225.00

Flambé

Unless another color is noted, all flambé in the listings that follow is red.

Bowl, Sung, Asiatic pheasant on orange, Noke, hdls, early 20th C, 11"..3,900.00
Ducklings resting, HN239, $675 to 700.00
Figurine, Genie, HN2999, $425 to 475.00
Figurine, Lamp Seller, HN3278.................................. 435.00
Figurine, tiger stalking, 9" L 525.00
Vase, cottage scene, Noke, bulb, 6" 450.00
Vase, deer silhouettes in landscape, woodcut, 1920-40, 8" 325.00

Vase, Egyptian scene with camels, palm trees, and the Sphinx, woodcut, paper label, 12¾", $1,560.00. (Photo courtesy Cincinnati Art Galleries, LLC on LiveAuctioneers.com)

Vase, ovoid, Nouveau silver o/l (Gorham), D1460, late 19th C, 6¼" ...950.00
Vase, Sung, lobed globular shape, #925, ca 1925, 7".................. 600.00
Vase, Sung, much bl, classic shape, Noke/Freed Moore, 10½" 660.00
Vases, Sung, bottle form, 1930, 10¾", pr........................ 950.00

Lambeth

Bowl, grapes & fruit clusters, ped ft, 1890, 6½x9".................. 600.00
Flowerpots, scalloped rims, floret bands, late 19th C, 7¾", pr 300.00
Jug, 1893 Columbian Exposition, #8386, 7¼"...................... 275.00
Jug, Native Americans, K Kemeys for Burley & Co, 1898, 5½x10"...515.00
Jug, Royal Jubilee, brn tones, 1887, 6" 150.00
Jug, willow pattern, brn & tan, 1¼" 75.00
Pitcher, Columbus portrait medallion (appl), 2-tone brn, 6½", NM .. 60.00
Pitcher, cvd w/swirls on wheat, sgn RB, 7¼"..................... 375.00
Pitcher, remedy quotes/vignettes, #4738, 9½".................... 100.00
Sauceboat, marqueterie w/cherub ea ind, gold trim, 9" L 2,475.00
Vase, floral & scrolls, cobalt/bl/wht, att W Rowe, #1818, 10¾" .. 660.00
Vase, floral, mc faience, rprs, 1879, 20¼"...................... 950.00
Vase, frieze of donkeys, H Barlow, ca 1882, #119/#579, 11¼" ...1,100.00
Vase, fruit on cobalt, E Beard, #8580, 1920s, 9¾"................ 395.00
Vase, gray & sage gr w/raised dots, slim, 19th C, mini, 2" 60.00
Vase, Nouveau decor, slim w/flared rim, brn int, 7".............. 110.00

Nursery Rhymes

Beaker, Polly Put the Kettle On, 3¾"........................... 110.00
Bowl, cereal, Piper w/pig...................................... 45.00
Child's dish, Mary Quite Contrary, 7½", EX-.................... 120.00

Pitcher, cream, Little Tommy Tucker, circa 1910, 3", $55.00. (Photo courtesy Richard Opfer Auctioneering, Inc. on LiveAuctioneers.com)

Plate, Pretty Maid, 8"... 40.00
Plate, Simple Simon, ca 1907-39, 8", $30 to................... 40.00

Series Ware

Bowl, Coaching Days, highwaymen chase coach, D2716, 4x8" ... 575.00
Jardiniere, Babes in Woods, girl w/doll, worn gold/crazing, 9x10". 600.00
Jardiniere, Shakespeare, D2220.................................. 275.00
Jug, Dickens Dream, characters listed, figural hdl, Noke, 10½".1,550.00
Jug, Dickens, Regency Coach, #287/500, 11x10"................. 660.00
Jug, Hunting, John Peel, earthenware, D2716, 9"................. 450.00
Pastry dish, Landscapes, D2846................................. 110.00
Pitcher, Coaching Days, 6".................................... 125.00
Pitcher, Eglington Tournament, 7"............................. 195.00
Plaque, Jackdaw of Rheims, 15¼".............................. 250.00
Plate, Gibson Girl, She Finds That Exercise...Spirits, 10½" 75.00
Plate, Gibson Girl, Widow & Her Friends, 10½"................. 85.00
Platter, Hunting, John Peel, oval, D2716, 13x11"............... 275.00
Punch bowl, Coachman, ftd, 6¾x12", NM 250.00
Punch bowl, Hunting, John Peel, D2716, 8x12"................. 660.00
Punch set, Dickens, D3020, 8¼x14¼" bowl+9 cups.............1,200.00
Sandwich tray, Hunting, John Peel, D2716, 18" W............... 275.00
Teapot, Hunting, John Peel, low, E3804, 10" W................. 360.00
Vase, Babes in woods, girl w/guitar, gold trim/hdls, unmk, 6¾x6". 600.00
Vase, Jackdaw of Rheims, 3 monks observe raven, 8¾" 180.00
Washbowl & pitcher, Watchman, ca 1901-02, 4¾x14½", 10½"... 300.00

Stoneware

Humidor, autumn tree branches, #X8531/5761, early 20th C, 3¾".. 150.00
Jug, cat reserves/foliage, F Barlow, late 19th C, 7⅜" 4,500.00
Pitcher, stylized plants, funny verse, ca 1910, 7½"....................... 120.00
Pitcher, Twins, Hassall, #6628, 1910, 8"....................... 360.00
Trump indicator, gnome figural, gr, L Harradiane, 1910s, 3⅝"...... 900.00
Vase, floral emb rim, cobalt & gold, 3-hdl, dtd 1904, 6¾x8"........ 100.00
Vase, floral tapestry w/gr & bl, sgn EG, flared ft & rim, 8" 100.00
Vase, floral w/gold, bulb, cobalt neck, Slater's Pat, 15⅝", pr......... 180.00
Vase, freize w/mountain goats, Hannah Barlow, 15½" 3,100.00
Vase, Naughty Boy at No Fishing Hole, Hassall, X6634, 1910, 5" ..395.00
Vases, lilies on stippled ground, Slater's Pat, ca 1900, 12¾", pr....660.00
Vases, stylized floral band, mc on bl, slim neck, ca 1900, 13⅝", pr ...850.00

Toby Jugs

Falstaff, D6063, sm... 45.00
Father Christmas, D6940, 5" 90.00
Happy John, D6031, lg, $75 to 95.00
Happy John, D6070, sm, $80 to 100.00
Huntsman, D6320, lg, $90 to 120.00

Jester, D6910, sm, $185 to	225.00
Jolly Toby, D6109, $75 to	100.00
Mr Furrow the Farmer, D6701, $100 to	120.00
Mr Mcawber, D6202, A mk	150.00
Old Charley, D6069, $200 to	250.00
Sir Francis Drake, D6660, lg, $100 to	125.00
Town Crier, D6920, 5"	75.00
Winston Churchill, D6175, sm, $60 to	75.00

Miscellaneous

Bowl, Chang, lotus blossom shape, Noke/Nixon, 3x6¾"	1,200.00
Loving cup, King Geo/Queen Mary, Noke/Fenton, 1953, 10"	950.00
Planter, Mirrisiar pattern, maidens w/instruments, bl & wht, 10x12"	600.00
Vase, Chang, cylindrical w/flared rim, Noke, 6¾"	2,000.00
Vase, Chang, shouldered w/sm collar, Noke/Nixon, 1920s, 9"	2,100.00
Vase, farmer w/horses/sunset, Ferneyhough, Holbeinware, Burslem, 11"	600.00
Vase, Santa w/reindeer/Santa hitchhiking, #1046, 1904-14, 3½"	450.00
Vase, Titanium Ware, Herring Gulls, sgn H Allen, ca 1925, 7¾"	1,650.00

Royal Dux

The Duxer Porzellan Manufactur was established by E. Eichler in 1860. Located in what is now Duchcov, Czechoslovakia, the area was known as Dux, Bohemia, until WWI. The war brought about changes in both the style of the ware as well as the mark. Prewar pieces were modeled in the Art Nouveau or Greek Classical manner and marked with 'Bohemia' and a pink triangle containing the letter 'E.' They were usually matt glazed in green, brown, and gold. Better pieces were made of porcelain, while the larger items were of pottery. After the war the ware was marked with the small pink triangle but without the Bohemia designation; 'Made in Czechoslovakia' was added. The style became Art Deco, with cobalt blue a dominant color.

Bust, Art Nouveau maid, pink triangle mark, 16", $1,080.00. (Photo courtesy Stanton Auctions on LiveAuctioneers.com)

Bowl, center, couple amid waves, Hampel, #1119, 13x12", NM	1,100.00
Bust, springtime maiden w/apple blossoms, earthenware, ca 1900, 21"	1,650.00
Card tray, figural maid holds lg shallow bowl, wht, 6¾"	210.00
Centerpiece, couple amidst waves, Hampel, #1119, 13x12", NM	1,100.00
Centerpiece, maiden seated on shell, ca 1890, 19"	900.00
Centerpiece, Nouveau figure w/instrument at side of rim, 17½x14"	1,550.00
Figurine, angelfish (2) on wht foliate base, #383, 9½"	135.00
Figurine, doe deer w/head down, 7½x11"	75.00
Figurine, elephant w/trunk up, brn-gray tones, 8" L	120.00
Figurine, girl feeding sheep, ca 1910, 30"	1,450.00
Figurine, hunter on horse, horn in left hand, 3 dogs below, pk mk, 17"	720.00
Figurine, water nymph rising from pool, early 20th C, 21⅜"	2,750.00
Group, Arab on camel, servant at his ft, 23x19"	1,200.00
Group, Return from the Hunt, couple embrace, 27¾x15½", NM	2,100.00

Vase, draped nude stands at side, #652, 17½x9x8"	1,325.00
Vase, lady w/mandolin on front, gold & sepia tone, #17707, 23"	900.00
Vase, leaves & berries, rtcl hdls, wht matt, 310574/BIS, 18½x8"	950.00
Vase, Nouveau lady picking grapes in relief, ca 1900, 25"	1,000.00
Vases, shepherd w/lute & dog/lady w/basket & lamb, ca 1900, 20½", pr	1,650.00

Royal Flemish

Royal Flemish was introduced in the late 1880s and was patented in 1894 by the Mt. Washington Glass Company. Transparent glass was enameled with one or several colors and the surface divided by a network of raised lines suggesting leaded glasswork. Some pieces were further decorated with enameled florals, birds, or Roman coins. For more information we recommend *The Collector's Encyclopedia of American Art Glass* by John A. Shuman III.

Biscuit jar, frosted panels w/mc foliage, rpl lid, 1890s, 7"	1,450.00
Biscuit jar, lg Roman coins, SP lid, ovoid, 6½"	1,800.00
Biscuit jar, mums/earthtone panels, sq, SP lid mk MW, 10" overall	2,000.00

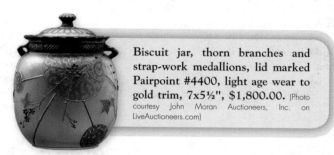

Biscuit jar, thorn branches and strap-work medallions, lid marked Pairpoint #4400, light age wear to gold trim, 7x5½", $1,800.00. (Photo courtesy John Moran Auctioneers, Inc. on LiveAuctioneers.com)

Ewer, shields of armor/flowers, bulb, 1890s, 8¾"	4,550.00
Jug, coats of arms/rampant lions, earth tones w/gold, 1890s, 11¾"	4,500.00
Lamp, cherub figural, clear glass globe, oil font base	425.00
Vase, dragon/dragon's head w/gold on bittersweet & frost, 7½"	2,350.00
Vase, fish & underwater plants, slim ovoid, ca 1890, 13¾", NM	9,000.00
Vase, flower medallions on sectioned grnd, floral shoulder band, 9½"	5,520.00
Vase, gold medallions/floral scrolls, spherical, 1890s, 7½"	2,000.00
Vase, griffin medallions, scrollwork stick neck, 1890s, 11¾"	2,500.00
Vase, mythological bird, gold/tans/brns, ruffled rim, 1890s, 14½"	3,000.00
Vase, peacock, gold w/jewels, thin neck: wine w/gold scrolls, 13"	5,465.00

Royal Haeger, Haeger

In 1871 David Henry Haeger, a young son of German immigrants, purchased a brick factory at Dundee, Illinois. David's bricks rebuilt Chicago after their great fire in 1871. Many generations of the Haeger family have been associated with the ceramic industry that his descendants have pursued to the present time. Haeger progressed to include artware in its production as early as 1914. That was only the beginning. In the '30s it began to make a line of commercial dinnerware that was marketed through Marshall Fields. Not long after, Haeger's artware was successful enough that a second plant in Macomb, Illinois, was built.

Royal Haeger was its premium line beginning in 1938 and continuing into modern-day production. The chief designer in the '40s was Royal Arden Hickman, a talented artist and sculptor who also worked in mediums other than pottery. For Haeger he designed a line of wonderfully stylized animals, birds, high-style vases, and human figures, all with extremely fine details. His designs are highly regarded by collectors today.

Paper labels have been used throughout Haeger's production. Some items from the teens, '20s, and '30s will be found with 'Haeger' in a diamond shape in-mold script mark. Items with 'RG' (Royal Garden) are part of its Flower-Ware line (also called Regular Haeger or Genuine Haeger). Haeger has produced a premium line (Royal Haeger) as well as a regular line for many years, it just has changed names over the years.

Collectors need to be aware that a certain glaze can bring two to three times more than others. Items that have Royal Hickman in the mold mark or on the label are usually higher valued than without his mark. The current collector trend has leaned more towards the mid-century modern styled pieces of artware. The most desired items are ones done by glaze designers Helmut Bruchman and Alrun Osterberg Guest. These items are from the late '60s into the very early '80s. For those wanting to learn more about this pottery, we recommend *Haeger Potteries Through the Years* by our advisor for this category, David Dilley (L-W Books); he is listed in the Directory under Indiana.

Vase, Peacock glaze, ribbed form, $220.00. (Photo courtesy Showplace Antique + Design Center on LiveAuctioneers.com)

#60, bowl planter, Gr Agate, ca 1936, 3½x6", $20 to 30.00
#109-S, Sq ashtray, Gold Tweed, 2¼x7", $8 to 10.00
#134, Palm Leaf ashtray, Gr Agate, 2¼x19x4¼", $10 to................... 15.00
#345-S, bowl, scalloped & indented, Lilac, 5x4¼", $15 to.............. 20.00
#452, trumpet epergne centerpiece, 16x10", $90 to...................... 110.00
#500-H, planter, Earth Graphic Wrap, Marigold Agate, 8x12", $100 to .125.00
#613, hen, 10", $15 to... 20.00
#837, Girl Head, Gold Tweed, 8½x6", $60 to 75.00
#2058-X, ashtray, Earth Graphic Wrap, brn, 6¾", $10 to 15.00
#3068, Triple candleholder dish, brn w/wht accents, 12" dia, $30 to ...45.00
#3928, goblet, gold, 9½x4½", $10 to 15.00
#4165, vase, Peasant Orange w/blk int, 11⅜x4⅝".......................... 20.00
#4233-X, vase, Earth Graphic Wrap, brn, 11", $20 to 30.00
#6343, matador, Haeger Red, gold foil crown label, 11⅜", $40 to .. 50.00
#8296, Toe Tapper, Bennington Brn Foam, 9¼", $35 to 50.00
R-110, elephant planter, 11½", min 150.00
R-132, ram bookends, bl-gr w/brn & bl spots, 8x8½", $125 to 150.00
R-185, Flower & Leaf candleholders, lt bl w/gr, 2½", pr, $60 to 75.00
R-188, cookie jar, emb shells, rose & bl, 10½", $15 to................. 250.00
R-222, rnd spiral vase w/seated frog, 12", $18 to........................... 22.00
R-224, daisy bowl, 12", $30 to 40.00
R-297, shell dish, chartreuse & Silver Spray, 14" L, $20 to 30.00
R-303, Laurel Wreath Bow vase, Mauve Agate, 12x7¾", $50 to.... 75.00
R-312, Cornucopia candleholders, Gr Briar, ca 1949, 5", pr, $25 to... 35.00
R-320, Elm Leaf vase, Mauve Agate, 12", $20 to.......................... 30.00
R-359, 2 Birds flower frog, Cloudy Bl, 1940s, 8¾x5", $10 to 150.00
R-363, nude astride fish flower frog, 10" 125.00
R-370, Dutch Cup bowl, Gr Agate, 18½" L, $30 to........................ 40.00
R-421, bowl w/clusters, Gr Agate, 7x14½x8", $40 to 50.00
R-455, Bow lamp base, Mauve Agate, unmk, 13½x5", $60 to........ 75.00
R-476, beaded bowl, chartreuse & Silver Spray, 15" L, $20 to 25.00
R-481, seashell on ftd vase, Silver Spray & Chartreuse.................. 75.00
R-508, dolphin vase, 18", $65 to 90.00
R-538, panther planter/bookends, Ebony, 1950s, $10 to 150.00
R-575, Rose of Sharon basket, chartreuse/red flowers, 7" dia, $50 to . 75.00
R-616, tulip vase, 8", $8 to 10.00
R-641, stallion planter/bookends, chartreuse, unmk, 8¾", $40 to.. 50.00

R-713, swan vase, 8", $20 to.. 25.00
R-752, fish planter, 8½", $18 to.. 24.00
R-776, cocker spaniel, sleeping, 6", $30 to................................ 45.00
R-777, cocker spaniel, brn w/blk tail, unmk, 1950s, 3x5½", $35 to..40.00
R-819, Acanthus Leaf bowl, 14" L, $8 to 10.00
R-831, resting stag planter, 15", $50 to 75.00
R-875, colt planter, 14", $135 to 150.00
R-1161, window box, 13½", $20 to 25.00
R-1204, leaf bowl, single, 9", $12 to.. 18.00
R-1262, Prancing Horse TV lamp, chartreuse & Honey, 10¼", $45 to .. 50.00
R-1316, dbl-leaf wall pocket, 11½" 45.00
R-1360, shell bowl, 15", $20 to 30.00
R-1416, planter, oblong, w/stand, 14", $30 to............................. 40.00
R-1446, basket planter, Turq Bl, 9x6½" dia................................ 15.00
R-1730, candy jar, Mandarin Orange, 10x7", $10 to 15.00
R-1782, lamb w/silk ribbon & bell, Wht Stone Lace, 15x17", $80 to. 100.00
Lamp, panther, 18" L 125.00

Royal Rudolstadt

The hard-paste porcelain that has come to be known as Royal Rudolstadt was produced in Thuringia, Germany, in the early eighteenth century. Various names and marks have been associated with this pottery. One of the earliest was a hay-fork symbol associated with Johann Frederich von Schwarzburg-Rudolstadt, one of the first founders. Variations, some that included an 'R,' were also used. In 1854 Earnst Bohne produced wares that were marked with an anchor and the letters 'EB.' Examples commonly found today were made during the late 1800s and early 1900s. These are usually marked with an 'RW' within a shield under a crown and the words 'Crown Rudolstadt.' Items marked 'Germany' were made after 1890.

Vase, children climbing fluted pillar, bisque finish with pastel decoration, 13", $180.00. (Photo courtesy JK Galleries, Inc. on LiveAuctioneers.com)

Centerpiece, bird perched on cornucopia, 10x15"........................360.00
Centerpiece, cornucopia, spread-wing eagle atop, 15" L 480.00
Ewer, violets on wht w/gold, pierced hdl, 14½"............................215.00
Figurine, cherubs (2) on basket of flowers, 19th C, 6" 300.00
Figurine, draped nude w/shell stands on raised base, 17½", EX 250.00
Figurine, maiden speaking to cherub on plinth, 19th C, 12x7"......480.00
Figurine, Rebecca at the Well, sm rstr, 27" 900.00
Figurines, man w/feathered hat, girl w/instrument, 19", 18", pr ...550.00
Potpourri jar, floral on ivory, pierced lid, 19th C, 9" 155.00
Urn, floral w/classical busts at hdls, gold trim, 19¼" 360.00
Vase, floral w/gold, Nouveau pierced hdls & rim, #6992, 12½"....155.00

Royal Vienna

In 1719 Claude Innocentius de Paquier established a hard-paste porcelain factory in Vienna where he made highly ornamental wares similar to the type produced at Meissen. Early wares were usually unmarked; but after 1744, when the factory was purchased by the Empress, the Austrian shield (often called 'beehive') was stamped on under the glaze. In the following listings, values are for hand-painted items unless noted otherwise. Decal-decorated items would be considerably lower.

Note: There is a new resurgence of interest in this fine porcelain, but an influx of Japanese reproductions on the market has affected values on genuine old Royal Vienna. Buyer beware! On new items the beehive mark is over the glaze, the weight of the porcelain is heavier, and the decoration is obviously decaled. Our advisor for this category is Madeleine France; she is listed in the Directory under Florida.

Charger, Achilles w/centaur hunting, sgn Beers, 16", in 21½" fr ...4,500.00
Charger, child's portrait, red cap/gr outfit, sgn Calbach, 14" 6,300.00
Charger, classical figures in scene, 19th C, 15" 3,000.00
Charger, lady w/floral wreath, cobalt & gold, 19th C 7,500.00
Charger, Samson scene, sgn Forster, 1890s, 17⅞" 3,600.00
Cup/saucer, Phaedra & Hippolyte/maroon panels, gilt hdl/rim 235.00
Ewer, lady & cherub, bl beehive mk, 5...450.00
Ewer, mythological scene in gold reserve on cobalt ea side, 23" .2,250.00
Group, man w/mask by lady at dressing table, rprs, 18th C, 3¼" ...1,325.00
Plaque, ladies encircle Cupid, sgn Johner, ornate border, 18x23" ...3,500.00
Plate, brunette w/low-cut gown, Pilr, floral turq/cobalt/gold rim, 10"..1,650.00
Plate, classical figures, gr rim w/gold-trimmed wht stations, 9" 75.00
Plate, couple at table, sgn Gorner, gold rim, 9⅝", NM 1,800.00
Plate, Cupid pulled from chariot by 3 maidens, red/gold rim, 9⅜" ..500.00
Plate, Flower Seller portrait on cobalt w/gold, 9⅝".....................1,200.00
Plate, lady's portrait, sgn Gorner, jeweled rim, 19th C, 9½" 1,800.00
Plate, lady's portrait, sgn Wagner, 9", in gilt 21x17" fr...............3,600.00
Plate, Louise portrait, sgn Wagner, floral rim w/gold, 9¾" 2,650.00
Plate, Titian's Daughter, ornate border, beehive mk, 8¼" 500.00
Stein, Pan & Venus, gold trim, hinged lid, ca 1900, 6¼" 2,100.00
Tea caddy, Venus & Psyche (in front panel), sgn Knoallez, gold lid, 6"...1,950.00
Tray, glove, Hector Taking Leave of Andromache, 19th C, 11½x8½" . 1,950.00
Urn, 3 ladies in reserve on bl w/gold, pine cone finial, 1890, 33½" .5,000.00
Urn, classical panels/cherubs, turq & gold, 3-paw ft, 19th C, 18", pr.6,000.00
Urn, figures in reserves/florals, drum base, gold hdls, 1880s, 22", pr..8,000.00
Urn, ladies & Cupid on bl, gold hdls & lid, stepped ft, 19th C, 22".5,000.00
Urn, Wagnerian opera scene, sgn Wagner, 4 ogee ft, w/lid, 1870-90, 21".4,000.00
Vase, Anemone (portrait), much gold on copper ground, hdls, 11".3,200.00
Vase, classical lady seated in gilt fr, sgn Wagner, #38070, 1900, 10"..2,400.00
Vase, Pasiphae, maroon grnd/gold, #24791, 19th C, 30" 10,200.00
Vase, draped nude in landscape w/gold, 19th C, 13" 4,000.00
Vase, lady's portrait, Wagner, w/gold, w/flared cylinder, 12" 3,600.00
Vase, man w/pipe/lady at side in reserve on gr w/gold, #3642, 20½"...2,500.00

Vase, Marchen (nude in landscape), reverse: Margueriten (nude with two putti), both signed Wagner, shield mark #A42/34371, 19", $7,200.00.
(Photo courtesy Leslie Hindman Auctioneers on LiveAuctioneers.com)

Vase, portrait of lady in lg cocked hat on wine w/much gold, hdls, 6"...480.00
Vase, portrait of lady, Wagner, maroon w/much gilt, 3½" 630.00

Vase, Queen Louise of Prussia, simple gold hdls, ca 1900, 9¾"..1,325.00
Vase, Ruth w/wheat in reserve, jewels & gold, socle base, 1870s, 18" . 3,000.00
Vase, seminude in reserve, gold bands/foliage, late 19th C, 12½"..3,500.00
Vase, Spring & Summer, sgn Wagner, coral & ivory w/gold, 20"...4,250.00
Vase, Supplication, prayerful lady, sgn Donath, ca 1900, 32½" .6,000.00

Roycroft

Near the turn of the twentieth century, Elbert Hubbard established the Roycroft Printing Shop in East Aurora, New York. Named in honor of two seventeenth-century printer-bookbinders, the print shop was just the beginning of a community called Roycroft, which came to be known worldwide. Hubbard became a popular personality of the early 1900s, known for his talents in a variety of areas from writing and lecturing to manufacturing. The Roycroft community became a meeting place for people of various capabilities and included shops for the production of furniture, copper, leather items, and a multitude of other wares which were marked with the Roycroft symbol, an 'R' within a circle below a double-barred cross. Hubbard lost his life on the Lusitania in 1915; production at the community continued until the Depression.

Interest is strong in the field of Arts and Crafts in general and in Roycroft items in particular. Copper items are evaluated to a large extent by the condition and type of the original patina. The most desirable patina is either the dark or medium brown; brass-wash, gunmetal, and silver-wash patinas follow in desirability. The acid-etched patina and the smooth (unhammered) surfaced Roycroft pieces are later (after 1925) developments and tend not to be attractive to collectors. Furniture was manufactured in oak, mahogany, bird's-eye maple, and occasionally walnut or ash; collectors prefer oak. Books with Levant binding, tooled leather covers, Japanese vellum, or hand illumining are especially collectible; suede cover and parchment paper books are of less interest to collectors as they are fairly common. In the listings that follow, values reflect the worth of items in excellent to near-mint original condition unless noted to the contrary. Our advisor for this category is Bruce A. Austin; he is listed in the Directory under New York.

Key: h/cp — hammered copper

Wine cooler, orb and cross mark, 11x11", $3,000.00.
(Photo courtesy Rago Auctions)

Andirons, blk enameled, lg orb & X, 1901, 31", pr $7,000 to ...8,500.00
Armchair rocker, mahog w/tacked-on vinyl seat, 35½" 1,325.00
Ash stand, h/cp, 4 riveted legs, 28½x7½".......................................850.00
Ash stand, h/cp, oak base, cleaned patina, sm split, 32x10" 500.00
Bench, Ali Baba #046, plank seat, bark to underside, keyed tenons, 42"..9,000.00
Bookcase, 3 1-pane doors, 3 adjustable shelves, 61½x79x16"....9,600.00
Bookends, leather-wrapped w/ornate tooling, 5¼x6", pr 500.00
Bookstand, Little Journeys, top over 2 shelves, tag, 26x26x14" ...600.00
Bookstand, sq top, 5 fixed shelves, rfn, 64x18x17¾" 5,000.00
Bowl, h/cp, 3-ftd, 4x10" 850.00
Candlesticks, hammered copper w/3 curved legs, orb and X marks, 9", pr. 4,500.00
Candlesticks, Secessionist, sm sqs in rnd base, D Hunter, 8¼x5", pr .. 8,500.00
Ceiling fixture, ldgl drops w/chains & 20¼" ceiling cap, 22" L...30,000.00
Chairs, dining, vertical slat bks, leather seats, 1 arm+4 sides 4,500.00

Chest, bride's, planks w/keyed-thru tenons, iron strap hinges, 21x39".....8,000.00
Firestarter, h/cp & brass w/spill tray, cleaned, +19½" hdld stick .. 1,300.00
Footstool, burgundy leather top tacked on, 11x16x9" 950.00
Frame, 6-section, mullioned, w/period mottos, 18¼x21"...........2,500.00
Inkwell, h/cop w/porc liner, orb & X mk, rare, 1910-15, 2¼x9x8¾" ..1,080.00
Lamp, h/cp, amber lustre Steuben shade; 3-socket std, 16x10" .6,000.00
Lamp, h/cp, base w/ring pulls, ldgl 20" EX shade 14,400.00
Lamp, h/cp helmet shade w/mica panels, orig patina, 14½x7¼" .. 4,200.00
Lamp, h/cp helmet shade w/mica panels, woodgrain std, 13¾x6" ..2,500.00
Lamp, h/cp sq shade lined w/gr glass; oak base, D Hunter, 23x16x16" .12,000.00
Lamp, h/cp w/helmet shade, old cleaned patina, 18½x7½" 2,200.00
Luggage rack, slatted top, 25¾x30x18" 1,200.00
Mat, leather w/tooled flowers & leaves, att, 20x39¼"................2,950.00
Mirror, hanging, 50x30" mirror, 50x4" brd, 5½" chain 3,120.00
Sconce, ldgl cylindrical shade; wall cap, D Hunter, 8½x5x6¼" .9,600.00
Sconce, Secessionist, copper/silver w/gr/purple ldgl cylinder, 15x6x6" .36,000.00
Sconces, h/cp, curled hdl, heart-shaped cutout, 10¼x5", pr 660.00
Sideboard, mirrored bk:3 drw amid 2 ldgl do:linen drw, 54x60x25", VG ..9,600.00
Sign, h/cp, Twildo (It will do), dk patina, unmk, 4x20" 7,800.00
Stand, magazine, #078, 3-shelf, arched top rail, recoated, 38x18x16". 3,500.00
Stand, magazine, #080, trapezoidal, cvd orb & X, 64x17¾x17¾".. 14,000.00
Table, library, shelf w/cutouts, keyed-thru tenons, 31x50x33" ..2,525.00
Table, occasional, slat top, trestle ft, 26x30x18" 1,000.00
Table, vanity, #110, 1-drw, w/mirror bk, 56x39x17½" 3,950.00
Tray, h/cp, tooled florals, 10" dia 700.00
Trays, h/cp, hdls, old polish, 15" dia, pr..................................... 400.00
Vase, bud, h/cp in woodgrain pattern, orig glass liner, 8½x3¾" 300.00
Vase, bud, h/cp w/woodgrain pattern, K Kipp, 4 buttressed hdls, mk, 8x4" ..4,800.00
Vase, Dard Hunter design, orb & X mk, 7½" 6,000.00
Vase, h/cp, 4 riveted buttress hdls, 4 sm silver sqs, 7½x4½".......5,000.00
Vase, h/cp, Am Beauty, from Grove Park Inn, 21x8" 4,000.00
Vase, h/cp, Am Beauty, orig patina, orb & X mk, 18½x8".........2,400.00
Vase, h/cp, Am Beauty, riveted base, cylinder neck, new patina, 12x6"..1,200.00
Vase, h/cp, floriform rim, 9x4" 575.00
Vase, h/cp, floriform/spherical, 3x4" 400.00
Vase, h/cp, ruffled rim, flared ft, 5½" 275.00
Vase, h/cp, sm flared rim, 8¼x4", pr 2,050.00
Vase, h/cp w/brass wash & silver o/l, cylindrical, 6¼x3" 950.00
Vase, h/cp w/etched dogwood, cylindrical, med patina, unmk, 7x2"..1,800.00
Vase, h/cp w/silver o/l band, cylindrical, 6x3" 1,440.00
Wastebasket, #023, vertical slats, touched up/coated, 16x14x14" .. 1,025.00

Rozenburg

Some of the most innovative and original Art Nouveau ceramics were created by the Rozenburg factory at the Hague in the Netherlands between 1883 and 1914, when production ceased. (Several of their better painters continued to work in Gouda, which accounts for some pieces being similar to Gouda.) Rozenburg also made highly prized eggshell ware, so called because of its very thin walls; this is eagerly sought after by collectors. T.A.C. Colenbrander was their artistic leader, with Samuel Schellink and J. Kok designing many of the eggshell pieces. The company liquidated in 1917. Most pieces carry a date code. Our advisor for this category is Ralph Jaarsma; he is listed in the Directory under Iowa.

Charger, rooster, #1293, ca 1900, 17½" 6,465.00
Cup/saucer, demi, flowers/bird, eggshell ware, 8-sided, 2¼", 4" .1,800.00
Panel, Dutch cityscape after Springer, 12-tile, 18x24"...............3,575.00
Panel, mother & children at table after Artz, 12-tile, 24x18" ...2,050.00
Plaque, dikes & windmills after Gabriel, sepia tones, 5½x17¼"+fr ..900.00
Plaque, Dutch mother & children, #282, 407 Havg H, ca 1892, 13x18".2,650.00
Plaque, Gothic cathedral int after Bosboom, ca 1895, 19½x12½".. 1,080.00
Plaque, man smoking, Eerllman, sepia tones, 1889, sight: 11x8½"+fr. 1,000.00

Plaque, mother feeds baby after Blommers, sepia tones, 11½x9"+fr ...660.00
Plaque, young lady drinking after Terborch, 1895, 20¼x16¾" ..1,325.00
Tile frieze, peasant & medieval farm, sgn, orig oak fr, 1892, 12 25" tiles..1,320.00
Vase, birds & exotic flowers, integral hdls, 8½", NM....................550.00
Vase, floral, Schellink, basket form, arched hdl, ftd, 1902, 5¾".5,750.00
Vase, Nouveau birds & flowers, #W249V, ca 1904, 19½" 5,000.00
Vase, Nouveau floral, brn integral hdls, crown mk, ca 1900, 8" ... 480.00

Vase, stylized bird and poppy, Rozenburg Den Haag #1224 W 352, 13x8¾", $1,800.00. (Photo courtesy Rago Arts and Auction Center)

Rubena

Rubena glass was made by several firms in the late 1800s. It is a blown art glass that shades from clear to red. See also Art Glass Baskets; Cruets; Sugar Shakers; Salts, Open; specific manufacturers.

Bottle, scent, cut body, faceted stopper, 5⅜" 150.00
Celery vase, Invt T'print, 6" 85.00
Creamer, Coinspot w/enameled flowers, 4" 150.00
Ewer, claret, birds in garden enamel, bronze mts, 16x4¼" 650.00
Pitcher, Dmn Quilt, 9½x6½" 525.00
Pitcher, Hobnail, sq rim, camphor hdl, 7"...285.00
Pitcher, Invt T'print, rope twist hdl, 7½"..200.00
Rose bowl, 4"...250.00
Vase, bud, bulb fuchsia top/ft, slim amber stem, 4" 950.00
Vase, butterflies, sm neck, 8" 75.00
Vase, gilt spider mums, cylindrical, 9¾" 145.00
Vase, Invt T'print w/HP flowers/birds, Aurora SP fr, 8", NM 335.00

Rubena Verde

Rubena Verde glass, made in the same fashion as Rubena, was introduced in the late 1800s by Hobbs, Brockunier, and Company of Wheeling, West Virginia. Its transparent colors shade from a ruby or deep cranberry, at its top, to an aqua green or a greenish yellow at its base. Basic patterns include Hobnail, Diamond Quilted, Inverted Thumbprint, Swirls, and Ribbing. See also Art Glass Baskets; Cruets; Salts, Open; Sugar Shakers.

Bowl, ruffled, gilded swirls and Johnny jump-ups, mythological theme on base, on quadruple-plated holder, $2,300.00 to $2,500.00. (Photo courtesy John A. Shuman III)

Bowl, allover floral enameling, appl rigaree, 11½" L.....................265.00
Butter dish, Invt T'print dome on vaseline Daisy & Button tray, 7⅝" ..335.00
Creamer, appl vaseline leaves, vaseline hdl & ft, 4¾x3" 135.00

Cruet, Invt T'print, 7" 450.00
Decanter, optic ribs on spherical body, gr knop & stopper, 14" 135.00
Finger bowl, Hobnail, ruffled, 4¼" dia 110.00
Pitcher, Coin Spot, ovoid w/sq rim, vaseline hdl, Hobbs Brockunier, 8" 200.00
Pitcher, Hobnail, appl yel hdl, grnd pontil, sq mouth, 7x6" dia ... 450.00
Pitcher, Invt T'print, reeded hdl, sq rim, 7¾" 250.00
Pitcher, optic panels, flared top, ovoid body, att Hobbs, 6¾" 275.00
Pitcher, optic ribs, ovoid w/sq cased rim, vaseline hdl, 9" 230.00
Pitcher, vaseline hobs/hdl, Hobbs Brockunier, 8" 400.00
Vase, Drape, gr ruffled rim, 11" 435.00

Rugs

Hooked rugs are treasured today for their folk-art appeal. Rug making was a craft that was introduced to this country in about 1830 and flourished its best in the New England states. The prime consideration when evaluating one of these rugs is not age but artistic appeal. Scenes with animals, buildings, and people; patriotic designs; or whimsical themes are preferred. Those with finely conceived designs, great imagination, interesting color use, etc., demand higher prices. Condition is, of course, also a factor. Our values reflect the worth of hooked rugs in at least excellent condition, unless otherwise noted. Other types of rugs may be listed as well. This information will be given within the lines. Marked examples bearing the stamps of 'Frost and Co.,' 'Abenakee,' 'C.R.,' and 'Ouia' are highly prized. See also Asian Antiques, Rugs.

Barnyard scene w/animals/birds, wool/cotton on burlap, 31x37" . 725.00
Bears w/red ball, dbl border, strong colors, early 20th C 1,200.00
Bluebirds & poinsettias, cotton/wool on burlap, 40x25" 230.00
Boy stands w/hat, short pants, H boots, floral border, 40x19" 800.00
Cat on oval rug, denim & knit stockings on burlap, 41x31" 925.00
Couple silhouettes in landscape, floral border, 46x24" 145.00
Dog w/collar, tan/blk/gr, wool on burlap, 32x53" 780.00
Elephant on striped ground, earth tones, wools, 32x38" 575.00
Floral designs on stripes, wool on burlap, 30x56" 200.00
Flower wreath, mc on gray & blk squiggles, on hinged stretcher, 57x56" .. 460.00
Flowers in scalloped oval, stylized leaves, wool on canvas, 68x34" 175.00
Flowers in vase/strawberries/hummingbird, wool on burlap, 36x49" .. 500.00
German shepherd & Labrador retriever on striations, sm rpr, 24x36" ... 115.00
Grapevine surrounds mustard center, gray border, wool, 43x25", VG .. 100.00
Grid filled w/mc wavy lines, wool/cotton, ca 1900, 70x70" 1,300.00
Horse portrait in medallion, cotton/wool on burlap, 29x43" 250.00
Horse trotting, velvet/wool/sateen on burlap, rprs, 27x39" 300.00
Houses & Christmas trees, mc on beige, wool, ca 1900, 24x40" .. 1,400.00
Lion reclines in oval reserve, foliage border, 24x38" 175.00

Patriotic, dog surrounded by American flag, shield, and anchor, dated 1919, 27x48", $6,600.00. (Photo courtesy Pook & Pook, Inc. on LiveAuctioneers.com)

Penny, concentric mc disks, wool on cotton bk, 90x26" 3,000.00
Roses bouquet among buds/stems, wool on burlap, 29x56" 345.00
Spaniel reclining, mc border, wool/cotton/rayon on burlap, 21x36" .. 240.00
Swan swimming amid foliage & stripes, wool on burlap, rprs, 33x45" .. 900.00

RumRill

George Rumrill designed and marketed his pottery designs from 1933 until his death in 1942. During this period of time, four different companies produced his works. Today the most popular designs are those made by the Red Wing Stoneware Company from 1933 until 1936 and Red Wing Potteries from 1936 until early 1938. Some of these lines include Trumpet Flower, Classic, Manhattan, and Athena, the Nudes.

For a period of months in 1938, Shawnee took over the production of RumRill pottery. This relationship ended abruptly, and the Florence Pottery took over and produced his wares until the plant burned down. The final producer was Gonder. Pieces from each individual pottery are easily recognized by their designs, glazes, and/or signatures. It is interesting to note that the same designs were produced by all three companies. They may be marked RumRill or with the name of the specific company that made them. For more information we recommend *RumRill Pottery, The Ohio Years*, by Francesca Fisher (Collector Books). Our advisors for this category are Leo and Wendy Frese; they are listed in the Directory under Texas.

Ball jug, orange, w/orig cork, #50, 7" 55.00
Centerpiece, dbl-shell cornucopia, cream to brn, 5x19" 75.00
Figurine, cowgirl, hands in pockets, mc, HP, 10¾" 145.00
Party platter, 3-tier, brn to gr w/emb rockwork, $35 to 50.00
Planter, pk basket form, #H360, 5¾x9½x6½" 20.00
Planter, wht semigloss, lg arch hdl over 2-lobe leafy base, #H39 .... 50.00
Vase, Athena, 3 nudes, 10" 585.00
Vase, bl mottle, emb ribs, w/hdls, #299, 6½x7½" 42.50
Vase, Classical Greek form, bl speckles, 5" 36.00
Vase, cream to gr, hdls, #299, 6½x7½" 42.50
Vase, Dutch Bl, swan hdls, #279, 4½" 60.00

**Vase, floor, celadon, 24",
$125.00.** (Photo courtesy Rago Estate and Fine Art Division)

Vase, gr matt, hexagonal, #297, 5¼x3¾" 52.50
Vase, gr semi-matt w/elephant-head hdl terminals, 6x6" 90.00
Vase, gr to orange, elephant-head hdls, #215, sm stain, 6x7" 90.00
Vase, head of woman, bl gloss, #1001, 11" 350.00
Vase, Scarlet/Bay Purple, bulb w/hdls, #302, 1938, 5½x3" 30.00

Ruskin

This English pottery operated near Birmingham from 1889 until 1935. Its founder was W. Howson Taylor, and it was named in honor of the renowned author and critic, John Ruskin. The earliest marks were 'Taylor' in block letters and the initials 'WHT,' the smaller W and H superimposed over the larger T. Later marks included the Ruskin name.

Vase, bl & wht drips, ovoid, ca 1932, 8¾x5" 100.00
Vase, cream & gr crystalline, 6-sided, 4⅝" 395.00

Vase, flower band at shoulder, gr & rose on teal over purple, 5¼" . 395.00
Vase, gray to cobalt, ovoid, 3¼x2½" 60.00

Vase, lavender, green, and black over sang-de-boeuf glazes, Ruskin 1914 England, 14½", $8,700.00. (Photo courtesy Cincinnati Art Galleries, LLC on LiveAuctioneers.com)

Vase, lt gr irid, shouldered, 1914, 7⅞x4¼" 85.00
Vase, pk w/almond mottling & MOP lustre, shouldered, 1923, 9¾" ..660.00
Vase, yel drip, trumpet neck, 1924, 8⅞x4" 100.00
Vase, yel lustre, shouldered, 9½x5" 100.00

Russel Wright Dinnerware

Russel Wright, one of America's foremost industrial designers, also designed several lines of ceramic dinnerware, glassware, and aluminum ware that are now highly sought-after collectibles. His most popular dinnerware then and with today's collectors, American Modern, was manufactured by the Steubenville Pottery Company from 1939 until 1959. It was produced in a variety of solid colors in assortments chosen to stay attune with the times. Casual (his first line sturdy enough to be guaranteed against breakage for 10 years from date of purchase) is relatively easy to find today — simply because it has held up so well. During the years of its production, the Casual line was constantly being restyled, some items as many as five times. Early examples were heavily mottled, while later pieces were smoothly glazed and sometimes patterned. The ware was marked with Wright's signature and 'China by Iroquois.' It was marketed in fine department stores throughout the country. After 1950 the line was marked 'Iroquois China by Russel Wright.'

American Modern

To calculate values for American Modern, at the least, double the low values listed for these colors: Canteloupe, Glacier Blue, Bean Brown, and White. Chartreuse is represented by the low end of our range; Cedar, Black Chutney, and Seafoam by the high end; and Coral and Gray near the middle.

Butter dish, orig style, $150 to 200.00
Casserole, 2-qt, $50 to 75.00
Coffeepot, 6½", $175 to 225.00
Covered casserole, $35 to 45.00
Creamer, $15 to 20.00
Plate, 8", $15 to 25.00
Plate, chop, 13½", $35 to 50.00
Plate, dinner, $20 to 25.00
Plate, salad, 6", $12 to 18.00
Sugar bowl, $20 to 25.00
Vegetable bowl, 8", $20 to 25.00
Vegetable dish, w/lid, $50 to 75.00

Glass

Morgantown Modern is most popular in Seafoam, Coral, and Chartreuse. In the Flair line, colors other than crystal and pink are rare and expensive. Seafoam is hard to find in Pinch; Cantaloupe is scarce, so double the prices for that color, and Ruby Flair is very rare.

Bartlett-Collins Eclipse, ice tub, $45 to 50.00
Bartlett-Collins Eclipse, shot glass, 2", $25 to 28.00
Bartlett-Collins Eclipse, tumbler, iced tea, 7", $20 to 25.00
Imperial Flare, tumbler, iced tea, 14-oz, $50 to 60.00
Imperial Pinch, tumbler, water, 11-oz, $25 to 35.00
Imperial Twist, tumbler, juice, $35 to 50.00
Old Morgantown/Modern, cordial, 2", $20 to 25.00
Old Morgantown/Modern, goblet, iced tea, 5¼", $25 to 30.00
Snow Glass, bowl, fruit, 5", $100 to 125.00
Snow Glass, bowl, salad, $175 to 200.00
Snow Glass, saucer, $65 to 75.00

Highlight

Creamer, $40 to 55.00
Cup, $40 to 55.00
Plate, bread & butter, $12 to 15.00
Platter, lg, $55 to 75.00
Vegetable dish, $100 to 150.00

Iroquois Casual

To price Sugar White, Charcoal, and Oyster, use the high end of the pricing range. Canteloupe commands premium prices, and even more valuable are Brick Red and Aqua.

Bowl, salad, 10", $35 to 45.00
Carafe, $200 to 225.00
Casserole, dome lid, 2-qt, 8", $35 to 45.00
Casserole, wht, domed lid, 6-qt 200.00
Mug, orig, 13-oz, $80 to 120.00

Pitcher, Brick Red, 8¾", $240.00. (Photo courtesy Brunk Auctions on LiveAuctioneers.com)

Plate, chop, 14", $50 to 60.00
Plate, luncheon, 9½", $10 to 12.00
Platter, 14", $55 to 65.00
Shakers, stacking, pr 200.00
Teapot, wht, restyled, 4½x10" 225.00

Spun Aluminum

Russel Wright's aluminum ware may not have been especially well accepted in its day — it tended to damage easily and seems to have had only limited market appeal — but today's collectors feel quite differently about it, as is apparent in the suggested values noted in the following listings.

Candelabra, $225 to 350.00
Cheese server, domed lid, wooden insert, 16¼" 180.00
Ice bucket, wicker hdl, from Informal line, 7x4x6½" 850.00
Ice fork, $75 to 100.00
Pitcher, sherry, $250 to 275.00
Tidbit, 2-tier, arched wicker hdl, 3½", $150 to 200.00

Vase, ball form, lg, $300 to 400.00
Vase, ball form, sm, $150 to 200.00

Sterling

Celery dish, 11", $28 to 36.00
Creamer, 1-oz, $12 to 15.00
Cup, 7-oz, $13 to 15.00
Cup, demi, $65 to 100.00
Plate, dinner, 10", $10 to 15.00
Sauceboat, 9-oz, $25 to 27.00
Saucer, demi, $16 to 20.00
Sugar bowl, 10-oz, $22 to 25.00

Miscellaneous

Bauer, dish, speckled apricot with mahogany interior, 2¾x6½", minimum value $400.00. (Photo courtesy Rago Modern Auctions, LLP)

Country Garden, bowl, serving, $175 to 250.00
Everlast Gold Aluminite, pitcher, $200 to 250.00
Everlast Gold Aluminite, tumbler, $65 to 75.00
Fabric, tablecloth, 63x89", $150 to 175.00
Flair, bowl, lug soup 12.00
Flair, plate, salad 10.00
Home Decorator, plate, dinner, $8 to 10.00
Knowles Esquire, centerpiece server, $150 to 200.00
Knowles Esquire, platter, 13", $45 to 55.00
Meladur, cup, $8 to 10.00
Meladur, plate, dessert, 6¼", $6 to 8.00
Oceana, relish dish, starfish, $450 to 500.00
Pinch cutlery, knife, $125 to 150.00
Pinch cutlery, soup spoon, $100 to 120.00
Pinch stainless flatware, Hull/Japan, set of 13 pcs, VG 300.00
Residential, bowl, onion soup, w/lid, $36 to 40.00
Residential, creamer, $10 to 12.00
Theme Formal, bowl, $100 to 125.00
Theme Informal, platter, $150 to 175.00
White Clover, ashtray, $40 to 50.00
White Clover, shakers, either sz, pr $30 to 35.00
Wood accessory, chest, 3-drw, $350 to 500.00

Russian Art

Since 1991, which marked the fall of communism in the Soviet Union, a burgeoning upper middle class lead by the nouveau riche has dramatically and continually pushed up prices for pre-revolutionary (1917) Russian art. In certain areas, particularly in the realm of higher-end objects such as Fabergé, important paintings, bronzes, and icons, prices have skyrocketed in recent years. Unfortunately, such meteoric increases in market values have also spawned a rapidly expanding underworld industry of fakes, forgeries, and altered pieces. Subsequently, buyers should be extremely cautious when considering Russian works and are best advised to purchase from well established dealers and firms who offer guarantees. Sadly, as for authentic unaltered pre-1917 Russian items offered on eBay, the pickings are slim with the vast majority of items being outright fakes, generally over-the-top concoctions emblazoned with Imperial Eagles or monograms, profusely hallmarked, and often with 'original' cases. No-

where is this more true than in the area of Fabergé — so much so that the term 'Fauxbergé' was coined to address the endless stream of fake objects marked Fabergé that entered the market on a daily basis. Furthermore, it is important to note that there are many well documented examples of fake Fabergé pieces being produced as far back as 75 years ago!

Beginning in the nineteenth century and up until the Revolution, there was a Renaissance of sorts in Russian arts, which gave birth to some of the most beautiful and stunning objects ever produced. Every field of art flourished at this time, including jewelry, porcelain, glass, ceramics, sculpture, lacquer ware, paintings, and iconography. However, it was the fields of gold- and silver-smithing that perhaps best reflected the Slavic style distinct to the pre-Revolutionary world of Russian art. The firms of Fabergé, Ruckert, Ovchinnikov, Sazilov, and Kurlykov are quite well known. Yet there are many other lesser makers whose works are no less exquisite. At the present the market is extremely strong for enameled items of any type, the more enameling the better. The market is also strong for fine examples of porcelain, paintings, and bronzes. Icons of exceptional quality are very desirable, but it is, of course, Fabergé that is most highly sought after.

The interest in all things Russian just prior to WWI did not go unnoticed by European or American firms. Subsequently, firms outside of Russia often purchased items to be retailed through their own outlets. Therefore, it is not uncommon, for example, to find articles marked Tiffany while displaying the mark of the original Russian manufacturer as well.

Our advisors for this category are James and Tatiana Jackson; they are listed in the Directory under Iowa.

Basket, silver trompe l'oeil, ca 1890, 11" L 8,400.00
Bronze, Evgeny Naps, mtd Cossack, ca 1890, 10⅜" 11,800.00
Card case, 11th Artel, ca 1908, 3½" 13,440.00
Case, guilloche enameling, Fabergé, ca 1908, 4½" L 70,800.00
Cigarette case, cloisonné, ca 1900, 4½" 2,000.00

Cigarette case, silver-gilt and plique-a-jour, Gustav Klingert, 1891, gilded frame hallmarked Moscow, 84 standard, 3¾", $9,000.00. (Photo courtesy Jackson's Auction on LiveAuctioneers.com)

Cigarette case, silver w/Troika scene, ca 1890, 4⅜" 1,180.00
Cross, bronze & enamel, ca 1850, 7" 400.00
Cup, Tsar Nicholas II 'Blood Cup,' 1896, 4" 750.00
Dagger (Kindjal), silver & niello, ca 1890, 20" 900.00
Egg, porc, XB, ca 1900, 5" 1,300.00
Icon, Christ, 19th C, 10x12" 500.00
Icon, Christ, silver & enamel riza, ca 1900, 12x10" 10,000.00
Icon, selected saints, 19th C, 3" 200.00
Icon, the Trinity, ca 1700, 32x26" 64,000.00
Icon, Vladimir Virgin, 19th C, 10x12" 750.00
Kovsh, shaded enamel, 11th Artel, ca 1908, 4½" 7,000.00
Samovar, brass, ca 1890, 20" 500.00
Spoons, shaded enamel, 6th Artel, ca 1890, 6", set of 6 .... 1,400.00
Tea glass holder, silver, Moscow, ca 1890, 3½" 1,200.00

Sabino

Sabino art glass was produced by Marius-Ernest Sabino in France during the 1920s and 1930s. It was made in opalescent, frosted, and colored glass and was designed to reflect the Art Deco style of that era. In 1960, using molds he modeled by hand, Sabino once again began to produce art glass using a special formula he himself developed that was characterized by a golden opalescence. Although the family continued to produce glassware for export after his death in 1971, they were never able to duplicate Sabino's formula.

Bonbon dish, 3 nude mermaids on int of lid, clear, 6½" dia, EX... 240.00
Bottle, cologne, flowers emb, opal, bulb, triangular top, 7½" 300.00
Bottle, scent, swirled ribs/dmns, opal, spherical body, #62-H, 6", pr..... 85.00
Bowl, 3 ballerinas superimposed over lg flowers, opal, 14"............ 780.00
Bowl, Les Poissons, in-mold koi/bubbles, opal/clear, 15" 1,320.00
Box, 3 nudes on lid, opal/clear, 1⅞x9", NM................................ 360.00
Bust, Praying Madonna, opal, 4" 60.00
Charger, nudes, smoke, ca 1923, 2¼x15", NM........................... 240.00
Figurine, dragonfly, opal, 6x5¼" 195.00
Figurine, Feeding Sparrow, opal, 3½x5" 60.00
Figurine, L'Espagnole, incised mk, 11" 2,200.00
Figurine, Nouveau nude w/long flowing hair, opal, 7½" 360.00
Figurine, nude holding sheer cape wide, head trn left, opal, 9½" . 390.00
Figurine, nude in translucent robe, arms outstretched, opal, 9¾". 575.00
Figurine, Ondine, fish, opal, 4" L... 65.00
Figurines, chicks, opal, lg: 3", pr 92.00
Group, stylized leopards (2) on base, opal, 5⅞x7¾" 950.00
Hood ornament, dove w/fanned tail feathers, opal, ca 1930......... 725.00
Mask, Triton (son of Poseidon & Aphrodite), opal, 15x10"+stand..4,800.00
Vase, birds border above 5 nudes, opal flared/ftd cylinder, 9" 950.00
Vase, blooming trees, frosty amber, 7¾" 660.00
Vase, chevron design, bl, ovoid, 12½"...................................... 1,100.00

Vase, exotic dancers in high relief, frosted opalescent, signed, 14", $2,900.00. (Photo courtesy Simpson Galleries on LiveAuctioneers.com)

Vase, floral spray in low relief on clear cylinder, 4½x3¾" 120.00
Vase, flowers (blown-out), amber, ftd, ca 1923, 6x5" 480.00
Vase, geometric shapes, flat rim, amber, 8½" 850.00
Vase, leaf-patterned stripes, clear & frosted, ovoid, ca 1900, 9" ... 480.00
Vase, pineapple form, opal, ca 1930, 10"..................................... 395.00
Vase, rows of lappets, ea w/3-line petals, sepia wash, bulb, 6" 395.00
Vase, water nymphs, gray-gr frost, cylindrical, 9"......................... 425.00

St. Clair

The St. Clair Glass Company began as a small family-oriented operation in Elwood, Indiana, in 1941. Most famous for their lamps, the family made numerous small items of carnival, pink and caramel slag, and custard glass as well. Later, paperweights became popular production pieces. Many command relatively high prices on today's market. Sulfide paperweights are especially popular. Some of the most expensive weights are those made by Bill McElfresh, who signed his pieces Wm Mc in a round reserve; his work is scarce due to the fact that he only worked in the glass during his breaks. Weights are stamped and usually dated, while small production pieces are often unmarked.

Lamps are in big demand with today's collectors, as are items signed by Paul or Ed St. Clair; their work is scarce, since these brothers made glass only during their breaks. Pieces made and signed by Mike Mitchell are also scarce, and always sell well. Prices depend on size and whether or not they have been signed. For further information we recommend *St. Clair Glass Collector's Book, Vol. II*, by our advisor Ted Pruitt. He is listed in the Directory under Indiana.

Animal dish, dolphin, bl, Joe St Clair... 175.00
Apple, $100 to.. 125.00
Basket, sm, $100 to.. 125.00
Bell, Christmas, $100 to... 125.00
Bell, Holly Carillon, cobalt carnival 35.00
Bottle, Grape & Gable, bl or red carnival, w/stopper, ea $125 to. 135.00
Bowl, pk slag, ped ft, $150 to.. 175.00
Candleholder, sulfide, mc floral, ea $75 to 85.00
Compote, pk slag, ruffled rim, low ped base, $150 to..................... 175.00
Covered dish, robin on nest, $125 to 150.00
Doll, $35 to... 40.00
Doorstop, rooster, $600 to.. 625.00
Figurine, Southern Belle, various colors, $50 to 75.00
Ivy bowls, pr $175 to... 200.00
Lamp, 3-ball, sgn Joe & Bob St Clair... 1,500.00
Lamp, 3-ball, sgn Paul St Clair, orig shade, 17" glass body, 32" overall .850.00
Lamp, blown ball shape, unsgn, $275 to 300.00
Lamp, TV, unsgn, $975 to.. 1,000.00
Lemonade glass, $75 to... 100.00
Paperweight, pear, bl carnival.. 100.00
Paperweight, sulfide, Betsy Ross, Joe St Clair 350.00
Paperweight, sulfide, Geo Washington or A Lincoln.................... 200.00
Paperweight, sulfide, Kennedy, windowed, Paul St Clair, mini..... 500.00

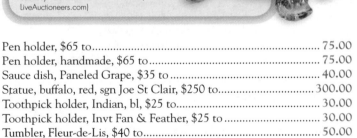

Paperweight, turtle form, clear with red interior, Maude and Bob, 1979, 5¼", $100.00. (Photo courtesy Belhorn Auction Services, LLC on LiveAuctioneers.com)

Pen holder, $65 to.. 75.00
Pen holder, handmade, $65 to... 75.00
Sauce dish, Paneled Grape, $35 to 40.00
Statue, buffalo, red, sgn Joe St Clair, $250 to.............................. 300.00
Toothpick holder, Indian, bl, $25 to.. 30.00
Toothpick holder, Invt Fan & Feather, $25 to 30.00
Tumbler, Fleur-de-Lis, $40 to 50.00
Tumbler, Grape & Cable, $40 to 50.00
Vase, blown, waisted, $175 to.. 200.00
Vase, clear w/bl floral in base, ruffled rim, $80 to 85.00

Salesman's Samples and Patent Models

Salesman's samples and patent models are often mistaken for toys or homemade folk art pieces. They are instead actual working models made by very skilled craftsmen who worked as model-makers. Patent models were made until the early 1900s. After that, the patent office no longer required a model to grant a patent. The name of the inventor or the model-maker and the date it was built is sometimes noted on the patent model. Salesman's samples were occasionally made by model-makers, but often they were assembled by an employee of the company. These usually carried advertising messages to boost the sale of the product. Though they are still in use today, the most desirable examples date from the 1800s to about 1945. Many small stoves are incorrectly termed a 'salesman's sample'; remember that no matter how detailed one may be, it must be considered a toy unless accompanied by a carrying case, the indisputable mark of a salesman's sample.

Barber chair, brn leather, ornate silver-tone, Koken Co, 10x16" ... 26,200.00
Bed, Murphy, cherry, w/orig fabric & mattress, ca 1800, 17x11" ...4,375.00
Book, 6 children's book titles, sample text & illustrations, 1905, EX .. 185.00
Book, Hershey Chocolate Co, leather cover, ca 1920-24 ....2,625.00
Canoe, ribbed, gr pnt, cane seats, 2 mahog paddles, Old Town, 18" ..7,500.00
Carburator, ST McDougall, gilt-metal valves, Jan 3, 1865, 9x10". 420.00

Cement mixer, Vindex, painted cast iron, original tag and decal, 6¾" long, NM, $5,700.00. (Photo courtesy Bertoia Auctions on LiveAuctioneers.com)

Chest, Emp, mahog, 6-drw, 19th C, 18¾x13¾" 875.00
Furnace, Room Heater, metal, 17", +carrying case, VG 95.00
Ice cream freezer, wood w/metal mechanism & crank, Wht Mtn Jr, 8x5". 265.00
Icebox, oak cabinet, 4 panel doors, cream enamel int, 6 shelves, 16" . 3,965.00
Lumber mill, cvd wood, Barlow's, Pat 1868, 19½x13" 2,125.00
Lures, fishing, 59 assorted, color code on bait, Heddon, +cb case ...595.00
Lures, fishing, 72 assorted Toni lures tied in case, Heddon, 17x21" .. 470.00
Optometrist lenses, Nachet & Fils, #3037, in orig case, 12x19½" . 190.00
Piano, G Bothurr, dbl hinged lift top, 23" W 3,680.00
Plow, pnt wood & iron, Township Plow #15/Revolving..., 6¼x15½". 10,625.00
Pool table, Brunswick 1845 Am, hardwood/felt/leather, 28" L, EX..... 2,000.00
Queen Washing Machine, wood/metal 3-legged bucket w/top crank, 10" .. 4,200.00
Radial arm saw, Rockwell Delta, ca 1960, +box, 17x11x11" 1,875.00
Saddle, Texas Half-Seat Slick Fork, WE Fulps, w/display stand, 7" seat. 18,750.00
Spittoon, Beco Ware, wht porc, 2x3½" dia, EX 400.00
Toilet system, holding tank, vent pipe & china toilet, +case, 25", EX.. 1,000.00
Ventilator, H Doerge, NP flue/rotating fan, 1895, 8" 325.00
Washing machine, pnt cast metal, wringer, Maytag, 7½", EX 500.00
Washing machine, wood & iron w/metal tub, hand-powered, 1900, 17x10". 1,375.00
Water heater, pnt pressed steel, iron/copper fittings, Humphrey, 16" .375.00

Salt Shakers

John Mason invented the screw-top salt shaker in 1858. Today's Victorian salt shaker collectors have a wide range of interests, and their collections usually reflect their preference. There are many possible variables on which to base a collection. You may prefer shakers made of clear pattern glass, art glass, specific types of glass (custard, ruby stain, Burmese, opaque, chocolate), or glass of a particular color (cranberry, green, blue, or amber, for instance). Some collectors search for examples made by only one maker (in particular Mt. Washington, Dithridge, Northwood, Hobbs Brockunier, and C. F. Monroe). Others may stick to decorated shakers, undecorated examples, or any combination thereof that captures their fancy. If you would like to learn more about Victorian glass salt shakers, we recommend *Early American Pattern Glass* by Reilly and Jenks. Unless noted otherwise, values are for examples in at least near-mint condition with near-mint decorations (when applicable). Unless 'pr' is specified, the value is for a single shaker. See also specific companies.

Victorian Glass

Amberette, amber satin, Duncan, 1885, 2¾" 80.00
Artichoke, Fostoria's (AKA Valencia), clear/frosted, 2⅝" 80.00
Aster & Leaf, emerald gr, bulb, Beaumont #217, 1895, 3" 100.00
Babe Ruth figural, red & gold pnt, 1924-32, 5" 790.00

Baby Thumbprint, cranberry with enameled daisies, 2½", pair $235.00. (Photo courtesy Paul Chmielewski)

Barrel, 21-Rib Rainbow, cranberry w/gr-flashed stripe, 1884-92, 2⅝" .. 700.00
Barrel, Arabesque, opaque w/ornate HP geometrics, Moser, 3⅛" . 540.00
Barrel, Footed Optic, cranberry w/HP floral, Mt WA/Pairpoint, 3½" .. 190.00
Beaded Panel, Concave, wht opal w/HP roses, 1900-06 .... 30.00
Blocked T'print Band, ruby stain, Duncan & Miller, 1904-13 .... 45.00
Box-in-Box (aka Riverside's #420), ruby stain, ca 1894, 2⅞" 70.00
Bulging Lobes, Footed, wht opal w/HP floral, 1900-10, 3⅞" 15.00
Champion (aka Fan w/Cross Bars), ruby stain, McKee, 1894, 2⅞" .. 75.00
Chick on Pedestal, yel opaque to lt gr on mg, CF Monroe 600.00
Christmas Barrel, purple, pewter top sgn Alden, Boston, Pat.., 2½" ... 120.00
Chrysanthemum Base Variant, cranberry opal, Buckeye, 1888-91, 3⅛". 195.00
Chrysanthemum Leaf, chocolate opaque, Indiana, 1901-03, 2⅝" . 325.00
Concave Panel, wht opal w/HP floral, Challinor & Taylor, 1¾x2½" ... 35.00
Cotton Bale, butterscotch variegated, Consolidated, 1894-95, 2½" . 180.00
Creased Neck, Tapered, opal w/HP scene, Mt WA/Pairpoint, 3½" .. 50.00
Curved Body, Atterbury's, wht opaque opal, 2-pc mold, 1877-82, 5¼" ... 100.00
Dainty Swirl, clear reverse rubena, 2-pc top, 1889-94, 3⅜" 210.00
Double Leaf, purple variegated opaque, ca 1895-1901, 3⅝" 110.00
Douglas, ruby stain w/etch fleur-de-lis, Co-Operative Flint, 2⅞" ... 40.00
Doyle's Shell, bl opaque, Doyle & Co, 1880s, 2¾" 65.00
Fancy Arch, gr w/gold, ca 1891-1903 .... 35.00
Fence, 18 vertical ribs, bl, 1891-1901, 2⅞" 35.00
Fleur-de-Lis Spike, aqua, 4" 70.00
Flower Blooming, opal, Eagle Glass Co 55.00
Fostoria's #956, fire-polished, ca 1901, 3" 20.00
Four Ring, Tubular, amethyst w/HP child & butterfly, 1880s+, 3⅝" ... 180.00
Georgia Gem, opaque custard w/HP floral, Tarentum, 1900-40, 2½" 75.00
Hexagon, Leaf Base, opal w/HP florals, Fostoria, 1901-07, 3¼" 25.00
Honeycomb, Intaglio Pillar, bl w/HP berries, Mt WA/Pairpoint, 3⅝". 190.00
Invt T'print, Sphere Variant, cobalt w/HP floral, Mt WA/Pairpoint, 2" ... 80.00
Ivy Scroll, Jefferson, bl w/gold leaves, 30-rib, 1900-05, 2¾" 130.00
Lobed Elegance, pk to wht opal, HP floral, ca 1893 .... 175.00
Lobed Heart, cranberry w/HP floral, Mt WA/Pairpoint, 1894, 2¼" .. 200.00
Long Buttress, ruby stain, Fostoria, ca 1904-10, 2¾" 70.00
Maryland (Invt Loops & Fans), ruby stain, US Glass, ca 1897, 2½" .. 80.00
Melon, 9-Rib, cranberry, ca 1895-1900, 1⅞" 220.00
Octagon, Saloon, bl satin opaque, ca 1900-08, 4¼" 55.00
Paneled Cane, Heisey's #315, 1900-08, 2⅞" 22.00
Paneled Holly, wht opal w/HP gold, Northwood, 1907-08, 3" 190.00
Pillar, Sixteen (Ribbed Lattice), cranberry opal, H&B, 2⅞" 125.00
Plate Band (aka Panel, Ten), chocolate, Jefferson, ca 1898, 3" 900.00
Pleated Medallion, New Martinsville, ca 1910, 3⅜" 30.00
Reverse Swirl, cranberry opal, Buckeye orig screw-on lid, 2¼" 125.00
Scroll, Gaudy, gr opaque, Gillinder & Sons, 2½" 35.00
Seaweed, cranberry opal, Hobbs Brockunier, ca 1890s, 3½" 195.00
Strawberry Delight, bl opaque, Dithridge & Co, ca 1890s 150.00
Sunset, pk opaque, Dithridge & Co, 1894-97, 2⅞" 75.00
Texas, clear w/gold, US Glass, ca 1900, 2¾" 125.00
Thousand Eye, Ringed Center; canary, ca 1878-88, 3⅛" 80.00
Tulip Spray, wht opaque w/emb decor, 1899-1910, 3" 21.00
Washington (aka Beaded Base), ruby stain, ca 1901, 3¾" 25.00

Wellington (aka Staple), ruby stain, Westmoreland, 1903-12, 2⅜" .75.00
Westmoreland #1775, columnar, Pat May 24 1910, 3" 18.00
Wheeling Peachblow, Hobbs & Brockunier, 1886, 2⅜" 420.00
Wild Bouquet, lt bl (slight opalescence), Northwood, 1900s, 3⅜" ... 250.00
Zipper, aqua, patterned corners, Belmont #104, 1888-90, 3⅜" 75.00
Zippered Block, clear w/ruby stain, Geo Duncan, ca 1887, 2⅞" 85.00

Novelty Advertising

Those interested in novelty shakers will enjoy *Florences' Big Book of Salt & Pepper Shakers* by Cathy and Gene Florence. It is available at your local library or from Collector Books. Note: 'Mini' shakers are no taller than 2". Instead of having a cork, the user was directed to 'use tape to cover hole.' Only when both shakers are identically molded will we use the term 'pr.' Otherwise we will describe them as '2-pc' or '3-pc' (when a mutual base or a third piece is involved). See also Occupied Japan; Regal China; Rosemeade; Shawnee; other specific manufacturers.

Ball Perfect Mason, jar, glass w/emb letters, metal lid, 2⅞", pr 24.00
Big Boy, boy & hamburger, Special 1995 Edition, 4½", 2-pc 49.00
Canadian Flame Genie, pottery, red Japan stamp, 1950s, 4", pr ... 195.00
Chicken of the Sea, fish, 1 aqua/1 yel, pottery, 2x2¾", pr 19.00
Conoco, gas pump, plastic w/decal, 2¾", pr, MIB 55.00
Dr Brown Soda, bottle, glass w/fired-on label, 4¼", pr 45.00
Drewery's Beer, bottle, paper label on brn glass, 1950s, 3½", pr 45.00
Golden Guernsey Dairy, milk bottle, glass/metal lid, 1930s, 3⅜", pr .. 65.00
Grain Belt Beer, bottle, paper label on brn glass, 4", pr 55.00
Greyhound, bus, pottery, Japan, 1960s, 1½x3¼", pr 45.00
Gunther Beer, bottle, foil label on brn glass, Baltimore, 4", pr 22.00
Heinz Ketchup, bottle, plastic, c JS NY/Made in Hong Kong, 4¼", pr ..19.00
Hershey Kiss, candy, pottery, blk w/silver S or P, Japan, 2⅝", pr 15.00
Homepride Flour, Flour Fred spiller, hard plastic, Airfix, 2⅛", pr 45.00
Humble Esso, gas pump, plastic w/decal label, 2¾", pr 39.00
IH logo, TH Johnson & Son, red bl pyro on mg, metal lids, pr 70.00
KFC Colonel Sanders, plastic, wht, 1 w/blk base, Starling, 4⅜", pr...65.00
Kool Cigarettes, Willie & Millie, plastic penguins, pr 25.00
Lennox Furnaces, Lennie Lennox, pottery, front decals, 1950, 5", pr ... 125.00
Luzianne Coffee, mammy, plastic, mk F&F Die Works, 5¼", pr... 115.00
Magic Chef, chef (in blk) on mg, plastic lid, 3½", pr 55.00
McWilliams Wine, monk, ceramic, Japan, 3½", pr 95.00
Mobilgas, gas pump, plastic, Made in USA, 2¾", pr 165.00
Possum Hollow Whiskey, bottle, glass w/metal lid, 3¾", pr 18.00
Quaker Oats, building, pottery, Japan, 3⅛", pr 35.00
Schlitz Beer, bottle, amber glass w/metal lid, 4", pr 25.00
South of the Border, Mexican man, plastic, 1960s, 4½", pr 20.00
Spiller's Homepride Flour, Flour Fred, plastic, Airfix, 3⅛", pr 55.00
Sympathetic Ear Restaurant, anthropomorphic ear, 1965, 4", pr ... 75.00
Tappan, chef, pottery, Japan, 4⅛", pr 18.00
Texaco/Burgey & Gehman Fuel Oil, mg, 3¼", pr 55.00
VW Volkswagen van, studio pottery, ca 1990, 1¼x3¾", pr 55.00

Novelty Animals, Fish, and Birds

Alligator, redware, brn tones, EX details, Mexico, 1x5", pr 38.00
Anthropomorphic ladybug, pottery, Japan, 1950s, 2½", pr 22.00
Anthropomorphic lion w/monocle, ceramic, Japan, 1950s, 4⅝", pr .. 39.00
Bass fish, ceramic, MIJ label, 2x5½", pr 35.00
Beaver, pottery w/appl fur, Enesco foil label, 1950s, 3", pr 22.00
Bird & birdhouse, ceramic, Japan, 1950s, 3", 2-pc 19.00
Black cat, crouching, pottery, wood stopper, no mk, 2x2", pr 25.00
Bluegill fish, ceramic, realistic, Enesco, 2x4", pr 35.00
Cat ice skater, ceramic, unmk, 4½", pr 10.00
Cat, Longfellow, ceramic, Norcrest/Japan, H483, 2x9½", pr 35.00
Cat, lustreware, unmk (possibly German), 1930s, 3⅜", pr 85.00

Dinosaur w/tail up, pottery, plastic stopper, unmk, 1970s, 3", pr 28.00
Donkey w/hat laughing, ceramic, Japan, 1950s, 3⅜", pr 22.00
Farmer pig, ceramic, Enesco label, 5", pr 24.00
Frog w/umbrella, pottery, stacking, 1950s, 4¾", 2-pc 24.00
Goose & the Golden Egg, plastic goose contains 2 egg shakers, 3½" . 18.00
Hen on nest, gold & bl lustre, Noritake...Japan, 2¼", pr 60.00
Lions on base, nodder heads are shakers, ceramic, 3-pc................. 110.00
Mr & Mrs Pig, nodder heads remove, bodies joined, ceramic, Japan, 3-pc 58.00
Pheasant, ceramic, 1 tail up/2nd tail down, Napco, 1950s, 2-pc 22.00
Rooster & hen, blk & wht stripes, ceramic, 3½", 3", 2-pc 40.00
Scottie dog, porc, orig corks, Germany mk, 1930s-40s, 2½", pr...... 28.00
Scottie dog, seated, Deco style, alum, tail screws off, 2¾", pr 28.00

Novelty Character and Disney

Bahama Police, ceramic, 1960s, 4⅜", pr...................................... 28.00
Betty Boop, stacking head & body, ceramic, Benjamin Medwin, 1955, 5" ..34.00
Billy Sykes & Capt Cuttle, ceramic, Artone, 2½", 2-pc 39.00
Bonzo (dog), ceramic, solid cobalt, unmk flat bottom, 1930s, 3", pr .. 38.00
Charlie Chaplin shoes & hat, ceramic, unmk, 1940+, 1¼", 4", 2-pc.. 29.00
Daisy Duck & grocery bag, ceramic, Applause/Disney, 3¼", 2-pc .. 39.00
Dandy & Preacher Crow from Dumbo, ceramic, 3", 4", 2-pc 80.00
Dumbo, ceramic, 3¼", EX+, pr 45.00
Dumbo, ceramic, Leeds/WD USA, 1940s, 4", pr 95.00
Felix the Cat, bl on wht porc, Germany, 1920s, 2½", pr............... 365.00
Goofy & cake, ceramic, NE Disney Taiwan, 4¾", 2-pc 45.00
Goose & golden egg, ceramic, c Vallona Star, 5½", 2-pc 55.00
Humpty Dumpty on wall, ceramic, unmk, 1940s, 5½", 2-pc 89.00
Jack Spratt & wife, ceramic, he: 3½", 2-pc................................... 52.50
Kate Greenaway boy (& girl), heavy pottery, HP, FF 77 mk, 4⅜", 2-pc.. 95.00
Ludwig & Donald, ceramic, Dan Brechner/WDP 1961/Japan, 5¼", 2-pc . 95.00
Mammy & Pappy Yokum on sadiron shape, ceramic, Al Capp, 1968, 2-pc..59.00
Marvin the Martian & spaceship, ceramic, Warner Bros, 1996, 2-pc, MIB...55.00
Mickey & Minnie, ceramic, cold pnt, Leeds China, 1940s, 3¼", 2-pc.45.00
Moon Mullins, glass w/plastic hat, cold pnt, Japan, 1930s, 3", pr... 55.00
Oswald & Homer, ceramic, Walter Lantz/Napco, 1958, 4", 2-pc . 135.00
Pinocchio, 4¾" 85.00
Pixie & Dixie (mice), ceramic, Japan label, 3¼", 2-pc 55.00
Robin Hood on rock, ceramic, MIJ, 1950s, 4⅝", 2-pc 30.00
Santa & reindeer, ceramic, musical (nonworking), Napco, 2-pc, NMIB... 55.00
Sylvester the Cat, ceramic, Warner Bros, 1970s, 4¼", pr............... 90.00
Tinkerbell bells, porc, Tinkerbell/castle, gold trim, 50s-60s, 3", pr. 35.00
Wizard of Oz, ceramic, Clay Art, ca 1990s, 3½", pr 29.00

Novelty People

Dutch boy and girl, silver, girl marked #925 BM Chester, $125.00. (Photo courtesy Clars Auction Gallery on LiveAuctioneers.com)

Asian person, cvd stone, souvenir, Korea 67-68, 4", pr................... 49.00
Baby in diaper, pk clay, att CA, 1940s-50s, 2½", pr 45.00
Bare-breasted lady & naughty man, ceramic, Empress Japan, 4½", 2-pc... 59.00
Bellhop w/2 suitcases (shakers), ceramic, Japan, 1950s, 4", 3-pc.... 55.00
Blk lady sitting w/lg melon slice, ceramic, Japan, 3½", 2-pc 165.00
Boy w/2 baskets, Meissen, Xd swords mk, #3024/59, 5" 575.00
Bride & groom, ceramic w/gold, red Japan mk, 1950s, 4⅜", 2-pc... 25.00
Choir boy (1 in red/1 in blk), ceramic, Japan, 1950s, 4¾", pr 22.00
Choir boy w/songbook, pottery, 1950s, 4¾", pr............................. 22.00

Clown w/instrument, ceramic, Japan, 1930s, 3½", pr 29.00
Deco girl (slim), ceramic, red Japan mk, 1930s, 4" 95.00
Drunk & lamppost, ceramic, Maruri...Japan, 1950s, 3-pc 22.50
Dutch boy & girl, ceramic, Delft China, 2⅞", 2-pc 24.00
Flower girl, ceramic, pk dress, Japan, 1950s, 4⅜", pr 24.00
Goldilocks w/book & flowers, ceramic, Relco Japan label, 1950s, pr . 36.00
Golliwog driving car, pottery, Made in England, car: 4½" L, 2-pc 110.00
Goodbye Cruel World, man about to flush himself, Japan, 1950s, 2-pc.. 40.00
Happy (& Sad) Baby, ceramic, Clay Art, ca 1990, 3½", 2-pc 25.00
Hunter & rabbit, ceramic, unmk, 1950s, 3½", 2-pc 18.00
Indian & teepee, ceramic, Vallona Star 102..., 3¾", 2-pc 59.00
Japanese boy & girl kissing, ceramic, Napco, 3¾", 2-pc 50.00
Lady w/broom sitting on basket (2nd shaker), ceramic, Japan, 2-pc..... 85.00
Lion tamer sits & talks w/lion (2nd shaker), pottery, Japan, 3", 2-pc ... 25.00
Maid w/2 eggs (shakers) on tray, ceramic, Foreign, 1930s, 3-pc ... 125.00
Mammy w/mixing bowl, bsk, LAG NO 1977 Taiwan, pr 32.00
Old-fashioned baseball player w/bat, ceramic, Japan, 1950s, 3⅞", pr.... 35.00
Pirate & treasure chest, pottery, solid colors, 1950s, 3½", 2-pc 22.00
Stan Laurel & Oliver Hardy faces on tray, ceramic, Dresden, 3-pc .. 200.00

Miscellaneous Novelties

Alamo replica, bronze-colored metal, Japan, 1¾x2½", pr 39.00
Anthropomorphic, dustpan girl holding broom, ceramic, 1950s, pr...165.00
Anthropomorphic, lemon-head boy (head only), Py, 1950s, pr 65.00
Anthropomorphic, pea-pod person, ceramic, Japan, 1950s, 3", pr . 24.00
Anthropomorphic, plum couple, ceramic, Py, 2-pc, NM 35.00
Bible, ceramic, Arcadia, ea 14.00
Bride's Cook Book/Way to His Heart, ceramic, Poinsettia Studios, pr...35.00
Coffee mill & graniteware coffeepot, ceramic, Arcadia, mini, 2-pc .35.00
Flying saucer spaceship, pottery, red windows, 1950s, pr 49.00
Golf bag & ball, ceramic, Japan label/H-#151, bag: 3¼", 2-pc 16.00
McGuffy's Reader & school bell, ceramic, 1950s, bell: 2⅜", 2-pc 22.00
Pike's Peak or Bust, chromolitho on metal tray, Japan, 1950s, 3-pc .35.00
Pixie head, ceramic, PY type, #6981 Japan, 3¼", pr..................... 29.00
Singing Tower, silver-tone, metal, FL souvenir, 3½", pr 45.00
Skull nodders on base w/HP Niagara Falls, lusterware, Pat TT, 3-pc.35.00
SS Love Boat, ceramic, c 1979 Enesco, 1⅝x3", pr 29.00
Tokyo, ceramic, Parkcraft Famous Cities series, 2¾", pr 39.00
Worm in apple, ceramic, unmk, 1950s, 2½", 2-pc......................... 19.00

Salts, Open

Before salt became refined, processed, and free-flowing as we know it today, it was necessary to serve it in a salt cellar. An innovation of the early 1800s, the master salt was placed by the host and passed from person to person. Smaller individual salts were a part of each place setting. A small silver spoon was used to sprinkle it onto the food.

If you would like to learn more about the subject of salts, we recommend *The Open Salt Compendium* by Sandra Jzyk and Nina Robertson; *5,000 Open Salts* written by William Heacock and Patricia Johnson; *Pressed Glass Salt Dishes* by L. W. and D. B. Neal; and *The Glass Industry in Sandwich* by Raymond Barlow and Jon Kaiser. See also Blown Glass; Blown Three-Mold Glass.

Key: cl — cobalt liner

Glass

Amber, Cambridge, 6 sides, ea w/intaglio star, lg star in base, +spoon ...30.00
Amber, Czech, intaglio angel/cherub w/flute, hexagonal, 2½" L 35.00
Amber, Portieux, scalloped swirling panels, ca 1900, ped ft, 1½" ... 25.00
Amberina, Degenhart, Daisy & Button, str sides, D in heart mk ... 10.00

Amethyst, Hawkes, etched, HJ-2038 .... 80.00
Blue, Bryce, English Hobnail, sawtooth rim, unmk, 4½" L, EX...... 15.00
Blue, Czech, Cupid/Venus intaglio, beveled sides, 1920s, 2¼" dia . 18.00
Blue, Depression era, molded notches/facets, 3 sm ft, 2¾" L 8.00
Bright blue, Depression era, thick w/faceted sides, star in base, 2" dia...25.00
Cameo, Daum Nancy, sailboat/windmills, blk on clambroth opal, 2x2¼"...385.00
Clear, Daisy & Button, rnd tub, HJ-2853 .... 28.00
Clear, Hawkes, etched, rnd, HJ-3268 to HJ-3269, ea 40.00
Clear, thumbprint, w/lid, ca 1875, 4¼" 425.00

Pink with amber interior, flared and pinched rim, attributed to Monot and Stumpf, 1¼x2", pair $160.00. (Photo courtesy Dargate Auction Galleries on LiveAuctioneers.com)

Purple slag, Sowerby, Reg Mar 1877, oval tub shape w/hdl ea end, 3" L... 75.00
Vaseline, seashell form, 3 sm ft, 1x2¾" 25.00

Lacy Glass

When no condition is indicated, the items below are assumed to be without obvious damage; minor roughness is normal.

BF-1B, Basket of Flowers, clambroth, Sandwich, 1830-40, 2⅛" ... 200.00
BH-1, Beehive, NE Glass, sm chip, 2".. 135.00
BT-8, Lafayet (sic), med bl fiery opal... 260.00
BT-9, boat, plain rim & base, Sandwich, 1⅝x4x2" 165.00
BT-9, Lafayet (sic), med bl opal, very rare, minor base flakes, 3½" L..1,680.00
D1-18, divided, sm chip, 1⅝" 155.00
EE-3B, scrolled eagle, Sandwich, chip, 2x3¼" 135.00
EE-6, known as coffin eagle, Sandwich, chips, 1½" 135.00
EE-8, Cadmus, ships & eagles, 1¾x3" 525.00
GA-2, Gothic Arch, violet-bl w/some opal, Sandwich, 1835-45, 1¾", G ...440.00
GA-4, Gothic Arch, rect, nicks, 1¾" 180.00
GA-4A, Gothic Arch & Heart, Sandwich, 1835-45, 1", EX.......... 75.00
LE-2, Lyre, flaw, Sandwich, 1¾" 265.00
MV-1, aqua, Mt Vernon Glass, chip, 1¾" 155.00
MV-1B, cobalt, scallop & point rim, Sandwich or Mt Vernon, 1¾", EX . 155.00
NE-1A, wht opaque, NE Glass, 2".. 215.00
NE-6, lt gr, star under base, scallop & point rim, 1835-50, 2" 125.00
OG-10, oblong, Providence Flint Glass, 1¾", NM 145.00
OL-10 variant, serrated scalloped rim, 1835-50, 1¼".................... 600.00
OL-12, cornucopia, oval, Sandwich, 1⅜", EX 120.00
OL-16, Dmn Rosette & Swag, bright red amber, Sandwich, 1½", NM ..1,325.00
OL-16A, oval, Sandwich, 1¾"... 215.00
OL-27, Strawberry Dmn w/Corner Ovals, att NE Glass, 1½"....... 175.00
OO-RA, oblong octagon, Sandwich, sm chip, 1⅝" 155.00
OP-12, clambroth w/bl-gr tint, oval ped, Sandwich, 1¾", NM 150.00
OP-20, shaped rim, 4-ftd, Philadelphia area, 2¼" 225.00
OR-8, octagon, att Sandwich, 1¾", NM 110.00
PO-4, Peacock Eye, oval, 1⅜".. 132.00
PO-6, Peacock Eye, electric bl, oval, Sandwich, 1½x3¾"........... 1,550.00
PP-1, Peacock Eye, ped ft, Pittsburgh area, sm chip, 2¾" 475.00
PP-2, Peacock Eye, violet-bl, Sandwich, 1830-45, 2", EX 360.00
PR-10, Peacock Eye, rnd, Sandwich, 1½", NM 120.00
RP-3, floral, powder bl opaque, 12-scallop, Sandwich, 2".......... 1,075.00
RP-32 (similar), scalloped rim, rnd ped, Pittsburgh area, 2½" 235.00
SN-1, Stag Horn, med amber, Sandwich, 1¾" 165.00

Pottery

Delft, foliate motif, bl/wht, 8-sided base, Holland, 1700s, 1¾", VG 960.00
Delft, lion figural w/2 salt cups, HP florals, ca early 19th C, 3x4", VG.. 450.00
Delft, mc floral, 6-side rim/ft, sgn Gerritsz, 1700s, 2½", EX 1,800.00
Doulton Lambeth, rnd w/sq foliate-cvd base, bl/brns, 1885, 3½" . 240.00
French faience, lady holds 2 cups aloft, Quimper style, 7", pr 240.00
George Jones, majolica, floral on lt bl, pk int................................ 540.00
Herend Rothschild, dbl, bird on bk of rococo 3-ftd base w/gilt 325.00
Herend, dbl, floral sprig bands, bl/gilt on wht, shield mk, 2x2" 50.00
KPM, elegant lady stands on rococo base, cup beside 80.00
Mason's Ironstone, Canton (bl/wht transfer), 4 paw ft to base, 6x6"... 100.00
Meissen, Blue Onion, dbl w/center loop hdl................................... 50.00
Meissen, dandy seated between 2 baskets on base, bl/wht, #3024/59, 5".. 575.00
Moorcroft, floral on gr, 3" dia 120.00
Wedgwood, cobalt w/yel-beaded band top/base, brn rim/ft, 3" dia, pr... 180.00
Wedgwood, ftd bowl w/ram's head & drapery supports, blended bl/amber... 180.00

Sterling, Continental Silver, and Enamel

Ball Black & Co, putti & garlands on oval, 1850s, 2½x4¼", pr ... 780.00
Bateman, H; rtcl oval, 4-ftd, cl, 1779, 2x3", pr 1,050.00
Christofle, putti (1 boy w/fowl/girl w/jug & cup), 19th C, 5¼" . 1,250.00
English, decagonal, 1716-17, 1⅜x2¾", 4.8 troy-oz, pr 1,325.00
English, Geo III, scroll hdls, stepped base, cl, att Abdy, 1799, 3x5"....660.00
Hennell, D; George III, oval rim, hoof ft, cl, 1762, 3½", pr.......... 660.00
Liberty & Co, boat shape, #2282, ¾x5¾x2¼", pr 1,800.00
Russian, neoclassical ftd cylinder, Fabergé, 2⅛" dia 7,800.00
Russian, silver-gilt/champlevé foliage, cl, Alder, 1877, 1¼x1⅞" .. 725.00
Scofield, George III w/eng floral, 4-leg, ca 1797, 2¼", pr........... 1,050.00
Sheffield, bead & shell suppports, 7x2x2" 195.00
Wilkinson & Co, Gothic tracery/oak leaves, glass inserts, 2½", pr . 1,175.00

Samplers

American samplers were made as early as the colonial days; even earlier examples from seventeenth-century England still exist today. Changes in style and design are evident down through the years. Verses were not added until the late seventeenth century. By the eighteenth century, samplers were used not only for sewing experience but also as an educational tool. Young ladies, who often signed and dated their work, embroidered numbers and letters of the alphabet and practiced fancy stitches as well. Fruits and flowers were added for borders; birds, animals, and Adam and Eve became popular subjects. Later houses and other buildings were included. By the nineteenth century, the American eagle and the little red schoolhouse had made their appearances. Many factors bear on value: design and workmanship, strength of color, the presence of a signature and/or a date (both being preferred over only one or the other, and earlier is better), and, of course, condition.

Unless otherwise noted, our values are for examples in good average condition.

ABCs (2 sets)/flowers/berries, silk on linen, sgn/1829, 6x17" 365.00
ABCs/#s, wool & silk on linen, sgn/1777, minor losses, 12x8" 375.00
ABCs/#s/bluebirds, on linen, sgn/1839, in modern 21x11" fr... 1,150.00
ABCs/#s/flowers/house/verse, silk on linen, sgn/1857, in 17x19" fr...575.00
ABCs/#s/long pious verse/vines, silk on linen, sgn/1834, 18x9"+fr . 575.00
ABCs/#s/trees/birds, silk on linen, 11x9" 315.00
ABCs/#s/verse, silk on linen, sgn/1805, hole/stain, 15x13"+old fr ..925.00
ABCs/#s/verse, silk on linen, sgn/1832, old reeded 19x15" fr....... 400.00
ABCs/bird/flowers/verse, silk on linen, sgn/ca 1780s, 21x19", VG 635.00
ABCs/buildings/willows, silk on linen, sgn/1816, 19x19"+fr........ 700.00
ABCs/family statistics/flowers, silk on linen, 1827, 17x17"+fr ..3,525.00

ABCs/fruited fines/verse, silk on linen, sgn, Boston, 25x19"+fr . 1,000.00
ABCs/hearts/lions, silk on linen, sgn/1788, sm losses, 11x10"...... 315.00
ABCs/house/birds/flowers/etc, silk on linen, sgn/1820, 21x18"+fr ..865.00
ABCs/house/trees/vines/verse, silk on linen, sgn/1840, 17x17"+fr . 1,400.00
ABCs/L verse/flowers, silk on linen, sgn/dtd 1818, 17x16"........2,000.00
ABCs/numbers/heart/initials, silk on cotton, sgn/1803, 18x9"+fr . 435.00
ABCs/ornate stitches/verse, silk on linen, sgn/1828, 19x15"+fr... 975.00
ABCs/verse/vining border, silk on linen, minor losses, 9½x11"+fr ... 500.00
Alphabets/potted plant/lion, silk on linen, sgn/1828, 21x20", EX.. 4,880.00
Caged bird/men w/grapes/crowns/hearts/etc, silk on linen, 1822, 17x15" 575.00
Cherubs/animals/flowering urns/verse, silk on linen, 1836, 18x17"+fr . 1,150.00
Draped figures/stars/flowers, silk on linen, sgn/1836, in 16x17" fr . 345.00

Emblem of Love (An), with birds, flowers, trees, and large brick home, verse signed Hannah Vail, age 10 years, 1827, 17½x17½", $4,200.00. (Photo courtesy Dallas Auction Gallery on LiveAuctioneers.com)

Map of England & Wales, silk on linen, sgn/1796, stains, 21x18"+fr.. 1,150.00
Peacocks/potted flowers/pious verse, silk on linen, 1817, 17x13"+fr ... 600.00
Pious verse/butterflies/flowers, silk on linen, 1798, 16x17"+G- fr.. 865.00

Sandwich Glass

The Boston and Sandwich Glass Company was founded in 1825 by Deming Jarves in Sandwich, Massachusetts. Their first products were blown and molded, but eventually they perfected a method for pressing glass that led to the manufacture of the 'lacy' glass which they made until about 1840. Up until the closing of the factory in 1888, they made a wide variety of not only flint pattern glass, but also beautiful fancy glass such as cut, overlay, overshot, opalescent, and etched. Today colored Sandwich commands the highest prices, but it all is becoming increasingly rare and expensive. Invaluable reference books are George and Helen McKearin's *American Glass* and Ruth Webb Lee publications. The best book for identifying Sandwich candlesticks and their later wares is *The Glass Industry in Sandwich* by Raymond Barlow and Joan Kaiser.

For more information we also recommend *American Glass* by George S. McKearin. See also Cup Plates, Glass; Salts, Open; Trevaise; other specific types of glass.

Candleholders, Hexagonal, cobalt blue, one with unobtrusive crack on socket, 7½", pair $900.00. (Photo courtesy Skinner Auctioneers and Appraisers of Antiques and Fine Art)

Bottle, scent, Star & Punty, dk amethyst, 7x5¼" 4,500.00
Candlestick, clambroth/cornflower bl, Acanthus Leaf hexagon, 9", ea....315.00
Candlestick, med bl, columnar w/petal socket, 9⅛", ea 345.00
Candlesticks, dolphin base, canary, 1845-70, 10½", pr 1,000.00
Compote, Hairpin, 5¼x10½", NM 1,500.00
Compote, Loop & Leaf, deep amethyst, ca 1850-70, 5¾x7⅜".. 12,200.00

Compote, Peacock Eye, hexagonal base, sm chips, 10¾x6½"....2,750.00
Jar, pomade, bear figural, starchy bl, J Jauel & Co on base, 4½" .3,150.00
Sugar bowl, Gothic Arch, vaseline, w/lid, 5½", EX 1,175.00
Sugar bowl, Gothic Arch, wht opal, w/lid, sm chips, 6¼" 4,800.00
Toy candlestick, bottle gr, 1850-70, 1⅝x1¼", ea......................1,950.00
Toy flat iron, bl, ca 1850-70, 1x1⅜" 1,375.00
Vase, 3-Printie Block, amethyst w/faint wht wisps, att, 10".......1,800.00
Vase, amethyst, tulip form, 8-sided base, 10¼".........................2,700.00
Vase, Gothic Arch, wht opal, 10¼", NM 1,200.00
Vase, tulip, amethyst, octagonal ft, 10" 2,750.00
Vase, tulip, vaseline, 10", pr..1,200.00
Vases, Loop, plain rim (rare), deep sapphire bl, att, 11", pr.......6,600.00

Santa Barbara Ceramic Design

Established in 1976 by current director Raymond Markow following three years developing the decorative process, Santa Barbara Ceramic Design arose less auspiciously than the 'Ohio' potteries — no financial backing and no machinery beyond that available to ancient potters: wheel, kiln, brushes, and paint. The company produced intricate, colorful, hand-painted flora and fauna designs on traditional pottery forms, primarily vases and table lamps. Although artistically aligned with turn-of-the-century art potteries, the techniques used were unique and developed within the studio. Vibrant glaze stains with wax emulsion were applied by brush over a graduated multicolor background, then enanced by elaborate sgraffito detailing on petals and leaves. In the early 1980s, a white stoneware body was incorporated to further brighten the color palette, and during the last few years sgraffito was replaced by detailing with a fine brush.

Early pieces were thrown. Mid-1980 saw a transition to casting, except for experimental or custom pieces. Artists were encouraged to be creative and on occasion given individual gallery exhibitions. Custom orders were welcomed, and experimentation occurred regularly; the resulting pieces are the most rare and seldom appear for sale today. Limited production lines evolved, including the *Collector Series Collection* that featured an elaborate ornamental border intended to complement the primary design. The *Artist's Collection* was a numbered series of pieces by senior artists, usually combining flora and fauna.

The company's approach to bold colors and surface decoration influenced several contemporary potters and generated imitation in both pottery and glass during the craft renaissance of the 1970s and 1980s. Several employees made use of the studio's designs and techniques after leaving. Authentic pieces bear the artist's initials, date, and 'SBCD' marked in black stain and, if thrown, the potter's inscription.

At the height of the studio's art pottery period, Markow employed as many as three potters and 12 decorators at any given time. The ware was marketed through craft festivals and wholesale distribution to art and craft galleries nationwide. An estimated 100,000 art pottery pieces were made before a transition in the late 1980s to silk-screened household and garden items. Some of these remain in production today, however the company has expanded into many other media — so much that *Ceramic* has been dropped from the new company name: Santa Barbara Design Studio. One interesting foray was a 2005 series of coffee cups featuring black and white stills from the 1930s to the 1950s and film noir movies in conjunction with Turner Classic Movies.

Now 33 years since the company's inception, the secondary market for Santa Barbara Ceramic Design's art pottery has seen about 2,500 pieces change hands. The work is often viewed as a bargain compared to its Rookwood and Weller Hudson counterparts. For images and artist/potter marks visit johnguthrie.com. When borrowing information from this article for publication or sales, please credit www.johnguthrie.com and *Schroeder's Antiques Price Guide*. Our advisor is John Guthrie; he is listed in the Directory under South Carolina.

Bud vase, beaded iris, Margie Gilson, 1983, 6" 200.00
Candlestick, #5116, morning glory, Laurie Linn, 1982, 7", ea......106.00
Goblet, #C, poppy, Shannon Sargent, 1979, 7½" 77.00
Jar, dutch iris, Dorie Knight, w/lid, 1978, 8" 130.00
Lamp, #5117, iris, Itoko Takeuchi, 1983, 9"..................................325.00
Lamp, #5119, bouquet, Itoko Takeuchi, 1984, 5½" 592.00
Lamp, #5130, poppy, Laurie Linn-Ball, 1986 (2), 7" 166.00
Lamp, #7105, iris, Dorie Knight-Hutchinson, 1984, 17" 335.00
Lamp, #7115, poppy, Laurie Linn-Ball, 1986, 16" 395.00
Lamp, #7115, tulip, Itoko Takeuchi, 1986, 16" 585.00
Mug, #5121, eucalyptus, Gary Ba-Han, 1983, 5" 39.00
Oil lamp, #1102, swan, Barbara Rose, ca 1978, 6½" 72.00
Pitcher, #5106, carnation, Laurie Linn, 1982, 9" 128.00

Pitcher, morning glory motif, marked ST//SBCD//1.81, 10", $210.00. (Photo courtesy Richard Opfer Auctioneering, Inc. on LiveAuctioneers.com)

Plate, #5114, Pegasus, Shannon Sargent, 1980, 7" 80.00
Platter, #4118, bearded iris, Margie Gilson, 1983, 14½"...............343.00
Quiche plate, #1110, geranium, Laurie Cosca, 1980, 1½x10" 176.00
Vase, #5101, bird, Laurie Cosca, 1980, 6-7"................................343.00
Vase, #5101, iris, Christine Adcock, 1980, 6½" 152.00
Vase, #5101, iris, Mary Favero, 1980, 7" 91.00
Vase, #5101, morning glory, Michelle Foster, 1982, 6-7".............125.00
Vase, #5101, night blossom, Itoko Takeuchi, 1984, 6" 130.00
Vase, #5101, pansy, Shannon Sargent, 1982, 6-7" 112.00
Vase, #5101cs, tulip, Anne Collinson, 1980, 5"............................118.00
Vase, #5102, bearded iris, Laurie Cosca, 1979, 9" 240.00
Vase, #5102, daffodil, Dorie Knight, 1980, 10"............................173.00
Vase, #5102, daffodil, Laurie Cosca, 1982, 9" 125.00
Vase, #7116cs, tiger lily, Collector Series, Shannon Sargent, 1982, 12x9". 1,200.00

Sarreguemines

Sarreguemines, France, is the location of Utzschneider and Company, founded about 1800, producers of majolica, transfer-printed dinnerware, figurines, and novelties which are usually marked 'Sarreguemines.' In 1836, under the management of Alexandre de Geiger, son-in-law of Utzschneider, the company became affiliated with Villeroy and Boch. During the 1850s and 1860s, two new facilities with modern steam-fired machinery were erected. Alexandre's son Paul was the next to guide the company, and under his leadership two more factories were built — one at Digoin and the other at Vitry le Francois. After his death in 1931, the company split but was consolidated again after the war under the name of Sarreguemines-Digoin-Vitry le Francois. Items marked St. Clement were made during the period from 1979 to 1982, indicating the group who owned the company for that span of time. Today the company is known as Sarreguemines-Batiment.

Bowl, basketweave, pk strawberries on lid, w/undertray, 5" 215.00
Bowl, leafy branch on basketweave, 1⅞x9½"................................215.00
Butter pat, pansy form, prof rim rpr...145.00
Center bowl, boat shape w/masks on cobalt, turq int, #1972, 14½" L...240.00

Character jug, bearded man, with lid, #1197, 11", $5,700.00. (Photo courtesy Dennis Auction Service, Inc. on LiveAuctioneers.com)

Character jug, black man w/red bow tie, #3884, 7" 1,080.00
Character jug, dbl face, frowning/smiling, 8½", EX 145.00
Character jug, Eyes Ouvertes, man w/goatee, #3612, 8" 300.00
Character jug, John Bull, brn hair, pk cheeks, #3257, 6½" 300.00
Character jug, lady w/bonnet, pk & brn tones, #3319, 7", NM.... 515.00
Character jug, man seated & holding money bags, red coat, 12¾"... 345.00
Character jug, man w/receding hairline, smiling face, #3320, 7⅛" .90.00
Character jug, Puck, dk & lt gr turban, 7" 265.00
Character jug, Scotsman w/smiling face, 7¾" 90.00
Ewer, brn & gold crystalline, shouldered, 12x4" 480.00
Figurine, penguin, wht w/blk head, orange ft, on gr base, 10", EX...510.00
Humidor, rabbit seated w/egg between his legs, minor hairline, 5½"..900.00
Oyster plate, turq w/6 shells & center well, 9½" 120.00
Pitcher, cat, blk & wht w/yel eyes, pk tongue, #3675Z, 8½" 240.00
Pitcher, dog begging, blk & wht w/pk tongue, 9" 325.00
Pitcher, lg owl on branch, pk/blk ground, stamped Bussard, 9" 125.00
Pitcher, parrot on perch, vivid colors, 9" 480.00
Pitcher, parrot sitting, pk/wht w/brn details, #3566, 7½" 360.00
Plate, asparagus on wht, 9½", pr 195.00
Plate, grapes & leaves, pk/gr/ivory, 8" 110.00
Platter, majolica, 3 H-relief birds on dk bl/brn/gr, #571, 24" L..2,400.00
Stein, fish/sausages/radish, cat figural hdl, pewter lid, 1-liter..... 1,325.00
Stein, pottery, transfer: people drinking, pewter lid, .5 liter 240.00
Vase, Art Deco waves/disected circles, blk/red/wht/bl on lt gray, 5x5"..510.00
Vase, Japanesque floral vines on ivory, intricate neck band, 24", VG ...480.00
Vase, stylized trees, 15½" 750.00
Vase, water lily on brn & cobalt, cylindrical neck, 9", pr 300.00

Satsuma

Satsuma is a type of fine cream crackle-glaze pottery or earthenware made in Japan as early as the seventeenth century. The earliest wares, made at the original kiln in the Satsuma province, were enameled with only simple florals. By the late eighteenth century, a floral brocade (or nishikide design) was favored, and similar wares were being made at other kilns under the direction of the Lord of Satsuma. In the early part of the nineteenth century, a diaper pattern was added to the florals. Gold and silver enamels were used for accents by the latter years of the century. During the 1850s, as the quality of goods made for export to the Western world increased and the style of decoration began to evolve toward becoming more appealing to the Westerners, human forms such as Arhats, Kannon, geisha girls, and samurai warriors were added. Today the most valuable pieces are those marked 'Kinkozan,' 'Shuzan,' 'Ryuzan,' and 'Kozan.' The genuine Satsuma 'mon' or mark is a cross within a circle — usually in gold on the body or lid, or in red on the base of the ware. Character marks may be included.

Caution: Much of what is termed 'Satsuma' comes from the Showa Period (1926 to the present); it is not true Satsuma but a simulated type, a cheaper pottery with heavy enamel. Collectors need to be aware that much of the 'Satsuma' today is really Satsuma style and should not carry the values of true Satsuma.

Bowl, courtiers, cobalt borders, Japan, early 20th C, 5½" 265.00
Bowl, figures before Mt Fuji, 19th C, 10" 475.00
Bowl, samurai w/gold, foliate edge, Japan, ca 1900, 6".................. 325.00
Censer, women/village/ducks/cranes/flowers, Kinkozan, 19th C, 6x8" . 3,800.00
Charger, Lohans, wht dragon, sgn/seal, 1900, Japan, 14¾"........ 1,200.00
Cup/saucer, women & children, sgn Tozan, early 20th C 60.00
Figurine, sleeping cat, 20th C, 9" L 535.00
Moon flask, 7 Gods of Luck & Hundred Poets, Japan, late 1800s, 9½" ..525.00
Plate, One Hundred Birds, early 20th C, 9¼" 645.00
Tureen, parrots & chrysanthemums, urn form w/dome lid, 19th C, 12x13"....700.00
Urn, courting reserves, fan neck, scroll hdls, ca 1900, 43½"......6,530.00
Vase, birds/flowers/butterflies in panels, sq, Meiji period, 12".......650.00
Vase, dragons & brocade, sgn Senzan, integral hdls, 7x6" 1,400.00
Vase, emb/pnt peonies, Makuzu Kozan, Meiji period, 8½" 3,250.00
Vase, figures in fan-shaped reserves, Japan, early 20th C, 5"........ 150.00
Vase, floral, trumpet mouth, dragon hdls, Meiji period, 25" 450.00
Vase, flowering branch, oviform, Japan, 19th C, 13" 700.00
Vase, geisha scene, bk: Rakans, Gyokusen, on bronze base, 1800s, 9". 735.00
Vase, gourds & flowers, late 19th C, 10x10" 2,100.00
Vase, men's face/geishas w/dragon, elephant-head hdls, 9½", pr..525.00
Vase, moriage butterflies & flowers, Japan, late 19th C, 14"......... 385.00
Vase, mums, gold/blk/wht on red, elaborate gold top, 1900, 16", EX...440.00
Vase, tied money bag/chrysanthemums, Meiji period, 5¾".......... 175.00
Vase, women & brocade, trumpet mouth/shishi hdls, Japan, ca 1900, 29" .400.00

Scales

In today's world of pre-measured and pre-packaged goods, it is difficult to imagine the days when such products as sugar, flour, soap, and candy first had to be weighed by the grocer. The variety of scales used at the turn of the century was highly diverse; at the Philadelphia Exposition in 1876, one company alone displayed over 300 different weighing devices. Among those found today, brass, cast-iron, and plastic models are the most common. Fancy postal scales in decorative wood, silver, marble, bronze, and mosaic are also to be found.

A word of caution on the values listed: These values range from a low for those items in fair to good condition to the upper values for items in excellent condition. Naturally, items in mint condition could command even higher prices, and they often do. Also, these are retail prices that suggest what a collector will pay for the object. When you sell to a dealer, expect to get much less. The values noted are averages taken from various auction and other catalogs in the possession of the society members. Among these, but not limited to, are the following: Auction Team, Koln, Germany; Simmons & Simmons, London (coin scales); Fritz Kunker, Germany (coin scales). Note: The antique scales market continues to reel from the knockout punches of eBay.

For those seeking additional information concerning antique scales we recommend *Scales, A Collector's Guide* (two editions, with a third in currently in process), by Bill and Jan Berning (Schiffer). You are also encouraged to contact the International Society of Antique Scale Collectors, whose address can be found in the Clubs, Newsletters, and Websites section. Visit the society website at www.isasc.org. Our advisor for this category is Jerome R. Katz; he is listed in the Directory under Pennsylvania.

Key:
ap — arrow pointer	Col — Colonial
bal — balance	lph — letter plate or holder
bm — base metal	CW — Civil War
br — brass	cwt — counterweight
Brit — British	Engl — English
Can — Canadian	eq — equal arm

Euro — European
FIS — Fairbanks Infallible Scale Co.
h — hanging
hcp — hanging counterpoise
hh — hand held
l+ — label with foreign coin values

lb w/i — labeled box with instructions
pend — pendulum
PP — Patent Pending
st — sterling
ua — unequal arm
wt — weight

Analytical (Scientific)

Am, eq, mahog w/br & ivory, late 1800s, 14x16x8", $200 to 400.00
Henry Troemner, Philadelphia PA, bronze specimen pans, 47" L.. 525.00
Henry Troemner, Philadelphia PA, wood & marble base, 11x18". 275.00

Assay

Am, eq, mahog box w/br & ivory, plaque/drw, 1890s, $400 to ..1,000.00

Coin: Equal Arm Balance, American

Black japanned metal, eagle on lid, late 19th C, $300 to 400.00
Col, oak 6-part box, Col moneys, Boston, 1720-75, $800 to.....1,800.00
Post Col to CW, oak 6-part box, l+, 1843, $400 to....................1,000.00

Coin: Equal Arm Balance, English

1-pc wood box, rnd wts, label, Freeman, 1760s, $250 to 450.00
6-pc oak box, coin wts label, T Harrison, 1750s, $200 to............ 450.00
Charles I, wooden box w/11 Brit wts, 1640s, $900 to 1,500.00

Coin: Equal Arm Balance, French

1-pc oval box, nested/fractional wts, label, 18th C, $250 to......... 400.00
1-pc oval box, no wts, label of Fr/Euro coins, 18th C, $150 to..... 250.00
1-pc walnut box, nested wts, Charpentier label, 1810, $275 to.... 675.00
Solid wood box w/recesses, 5 sq wts, A Gardes, 1800s, $250 to ... 800.00
Solid wood box, 12 sq wts, J Reyne, Bourdeau, 1694, $400 to...1,000.00

Coin: Equal Arm Balance, Miscellaneous

Amsterdam, 1-pc box, 32 sq wts, label, late 1600s, $850 to 2,500.00
Cologne, full set of wts & full label, late 1600s, $1,200 to 2,800.00
German, wood box, 13+ wts beneath main wts, label, 1795, $650 to...900.00

Counterfeit Coin Detectors, American

Allender Pat, lb w/i, cwt, Nov 22, 1855, 8½", $250 to 500.00
Allender PP, rocker, no box or cwt, 1850s, 8½", $200 to.............. 375.00
Allender PP, space for $3 gold pc, lb w/i, cwt, 1855, $250 to 500.00
Allender Warranted, rocker, no box or cwt, 1850s, 8½", $250 to.. 475.00
FIS, steelyard, combination detector & postal scale, $900 to....1,200.00
Maranville Pat Coin Detector by CE Staples, Mass, $300 to 500.00
McNally-Harrison Pat 1882, rocker, cwt & box, FIS, $400 to 750.00
McNally-Harrison...1882, rocker, CI base, no cwt/box, $250 to ..400.00
Thompson, Z-formed rocker, Berrian Mfg, 1877 Pat, $100 to...... 200.00
Troemner, rocker, for 25¢ & 50¢ silver coins, $300 to................. 500.00

Counterfeit Coin Detectors, Dutch

Rocker, Ellinckhuysen, brass, +copy of 1829 Pat, $700 to.........1,000.00
Folding, Guinea, self-rising, labeled box, 1850s, $175 to.............. 225.00
Folding, Guinea, self-rising, wooden box, pre-1800, $175 to 275.00
Folding, Sovereign, self-rising, wood box/label, ca 1890s, $125 to ... 175.00
Rocker, simple, no maker's name or cb, end-cap box, $85 to 125.00
Rocker, w/maker's name & cb, end-cap box, $120 to 150.00

Diamond

American, eq w/carat wts, 5" box, Kohlbusch, ca 1900, $175 to.. 225.00

Egg Scales/Graders, 1930s – 1940s

Acme Egg Grade, Specialty Mfg St Paul MN, alum, $30 to........... 50.00
Brower Mfg Save All, sheet steel (cheaply made), Steelyard bal, $50 to.. 75.00
Jiffy Way, Minneapolis MN, steel w/mc bands, pend bal, $30 to.... 50.00
Oakes Mft Tipton IN, pend bal, sheet steel, adjustable stop, $30 to... 50.00
Reliable, rocker bal, all brass, wooden base, 2½x13¾", $75 to 100.00
Unique..., Specialty Mfg, sheet steel/alum, pend bal, $30 to.......... 50.00
Zenith, CI, alum, brass pointer, pend bal, $50 to.......................... 75.00

Postal Scales

In the listings below an asterisk (*) is used to indicate that any one of several manufacturers' or brand names might be found on that particular set of scales. Some of the American-made pieces could be marked Pelouze, Lorraine, Hanson, Kingsbury, Fairbanks, Troemner, IDL, Newman, Accurate, Ideal, B-T, Marvel, Reliance, Howe, Landers-Frary-Clark, Chatillon, Triner, American Bank Service, or Weiss. European/U.S.-made scales marked with an asterisk (*) could be marked Salter, Peerless, Pelouze, Sturgis, L.F.&C., Alderman, G. Little, or S&D. English-made scales with the asterisk (*) could be marked Josh. & Edmd. Ratcliff, R.W. Winfield, S. Mordan, STS (Samuel Turner, Sr.), W.&T. Avery, Parnall & Sons, S&P, or H.B. Wright. There may be other manufacturers as well.

English balance, brass with stylized boulle work, original weights, Lund, Lundon, third quarter nineteenth century, 5x8x6", $1,150.00. (Photo courtesy Dallas Auction Gallery on LiveAuctioneers.com)

Brit/Can Bal, eq, br or CI on base, *, 4"-15", $100 to................... 750.00
Engl Bal, eq/Roberval, gilt or st, on stand, *, 3"-8", $500 to 2,500.00
Engl Bal, eq/Roberval, plain to ornate, *, 3"-8", $100 to...........1,000.00
Engl Spring, candlestick, br or st, *, 3"-15", $100 to 500.00
Engl Spring, CI, br or NP fr, Salter, ozs/lbs, 7"-10", $25 to........... 200.00
Engl Steelyard, ua, 1- or 2-beam, h lph, *, 4"-15", $100 to 1,500.00
Euro pend, gravity, 2-arm, bm, br or NP, *, 6"-9", $50 to 250.00
Euro pend, gravity, br, CI or NP fr on base, oz/grams, $75 to........ 350.00
Euro/US Spring, br or NP, pence/etc, h or hh, *, 4"-17", $10 to .. 100.00
US pend, gravity, metal, pnt face, ap, hcp, sm, $20 to.................. 100.00
US Spring, pnt base metal, *, 2"-8", $10 to 80.00
US Spring, pnt bm, *, mtd on inkstand, 2"-8", $200 to................ 400.00
US Spring, pnt bm, rnd glass-covered face, *, 8"-10", $25 to....... 100.00
US Spring, SP, oblong base, *, 2"-8", $100 to 200.00
US Spring, st, oblong base, *, 2"-8", $200 to 400.00
US Steelyard, ua, CI, *, 5"-13" beam, 4"-12" base, $25 to............ 100.00

Schafer and Vater

Established in 1890 by Gustav Schafer and Gunther Vater in the Thuringia region of southwest Germany, by 1913 this firm employed over 200 workers. The original factory burned in 1918 but was restarted and production continued until WWII. In 1972 the East German government took possession of the building and destroyed all of the molds and the records that were left.

You will find pieces with the impressed mark of a nine-point star with a script 'R' inside the star. On rare occasions you will find this mark in blue ink under glaze. The items are sometimes marked with a four-digit design number and a two-digit artist mark. In addition or instead, pieces may have 'Made in Germany' or in the case of the Kewpies, 'Rose O'Neill copyright.' The company also manufactured items for sale under store names, and those would not have the impressed mark.

Schafer and Vater used various types of clays. Items made of hard-paste porcelain, soft-paste porcelain, Jasper, bisque, and majolica can be found. The glazed bisque pieces may be multicolored or have an applied colored slip wash that highlights the intricate details of the modeling. Gold accents were used as well as spots of high-gloss color called jewels. Metallic glazes are coveted. You can find the Jasper in green, blue, pink, lavender, and white. New collectors gravitate toward the pink and lavender shades.

Since Schafer and Vater made such a multitude of items, collectors have to compete with many cross-over collections. These include shaving mugs, hatpin holders, match holders, figurines, figural pitchers, Kewpies, tea sets, bottles, and naughties.

Reproduction alert: In addition to the crudely made Japanese copies, some English firms are beginning to make figural reproductions. These seem to be well marked and easy to spot. Our advisor for this category is Joanne M. Koehn; she is listed in the Directory under Texas.

Bottle, Never Drink Water, naughty boy/frogs, 5¼" 95.00
Box, Indian chief w/spear on lid, wht on pk w/dk gr trim, #3216. 125.00
Box, sphinx as lid, lion emb on base, pk/wht Jasper, 4¼" 120.00
Candy container, pig w/flute on base mk Pig 'n Whistle, mc........ 245.00
Creamer, blk boy w/wide eyes, frowning, 1930s, 3½", NM 180.00
Creamer, devil kneeling, wings form opening, mouth is spout, 4". 195.00
Creamer, girl w/basket on bk carries pitcher, mc, 3½" 145.00
Cup/saucer, lady's face emb ea side, rust/peach Jasper.................. 250.00
Decanter, bearded man on bbl, 6½" 335.00
Decanter, woman praying, basket in arms & X around neck, 9½". 650.00
Figurine, black man w/bug on nose, 4¼" 360.00
Figurine, Golfer, man in early golfing costume, 7½" 385.00
Figurine, Mr Tenor, bsk, wht suit, gray curly hair, 7½" 325.00
Figurine, native boy on seated elephant, mc, 3", VG 130.00
Figurine, Snookums, baby w/wht w/bl trim, 3"............................ 250.00
Flask, A Wee Scotch, Scottish girl w/bagpipes on bottle, 4¼" 90.00
Flask, lady standing on turtle, 5½x3½".. 410.00

Flask, policeman suffragette, Stop the Vote, 7", $750.00. (Photo courtesy Philip Weiss Auctions on LiveAuctioneers.com)

Hair receiver, cherubs/cameos, 3-color Jasper, 2-pc, 3x4" 65.00
Hatpin holder, cameo of lady below floral swab, Jasper, 5", NM... 110.00
Humidor, Egyptian head, bird on hat lid, gr Jasper, #5409, 5½" 95.00
Humidor, English tea party cameos, Jasper, gr/bl/wht 200.00
Match holder, full moon figural, smiling face, stick legs, 4½"....... 125.00
Match holder, Scratch Your Match on My Patch, 4".................... 165.00

Match holder, Your Good Old Pal, man's face & hands, 3¼" 150.00
Nodder, Dutch girl holding 2 geese, mc 145.00
Pin dish, stylized rooster, bl & wht Jasper, unmk 125.00
Toothpick holder, elf, fat/surprised, pk Jasper w/brn wash, 4½" 140.00
Toothpick holder, sailor holding rotund bathing beauty, mc, 3" 60.00
Tray, 3 Kewpies, flower border, wht on bl Jasper, #9845, 3¼x4½".. 250.00
Vase, bud, Under the Mistletoe, black lady w/greenery, 5" 275.00
Vase, Japanese lady w/fan & goose at sides of egg form................. 145.00
Vase, lady, wht/dk gr reserve on gr Jasper, branch hdls, 6".............. 75.00

Scheier

The Scheiers began their ceramics careers in the late 1930s and soon thereafter began to teach their craft at the University of New Hampshire. After WWII they cooperated with the Puerto Rican government in establishing a native ceramic industry, an involvement which would continue to influence their designs. The Scheiers now reside in Arizona.

Bowl vase, figures on brn stoneware, sm ft, 6¼x8¾" 2,150.00
Bowl, aqua, bulb, incised sgn, 5x9".. 325.00
Bowl, parents & children on boat, bl & yel matt, 7½x13½"....12,000.00
Bowl, woman, serpent & child, cobalt/gr/brn, 1x7"..................... 350.00
Charger, Adam & Eve, manganese on celadon, 1945, 2x15" 4,800.00
Charger, sgraffito figures before a table of food, microcrystalline grnd, 14". 3,500.00

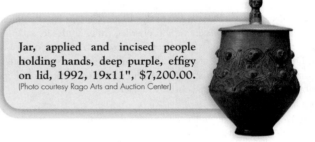

Jar, applied and incised people holding hands, deep purple, effigy on lid, 1992, 19x11", $7,200.00. (Photo courtesy Rago Arts and Auction Center)

Lamp base, faces (4) on bl, 14¼" 1,000.00
Mug, stylized zebras on red clay, 5½" 120.00
Sculpture, man/woman/child w/in mushroom-shaped pod, lt brn, 11x12"..2,100.00
Sculpture, wrapped figure in ftd pod-like structure, brn/cream, 19x14"...1,450.00
Totem pole, 2-pc: sm figure above lg figure holding child, 10", EX... 530.00
Tureen, wht accents on tan, hdls, w/lid, 9x14" 200.00
Vase, bl matt bowl form, sm ft, 3½x5¼" 300.00
Vase, bl stippled on wht clay, vasiform, 5" 180.00
Vase, faces incised, olive gr mottle, sm ft, 6¼x4½" 1,200.00
Vase, fish & head frieze, brn teardrop shape, 5¼x4" 850.00
Vase, people holding lg fish, gunmetal brn, coupe shape, 13¼x9" .4,800.00

Schlegelmilch Porcelain

For information about Schlegelmilch Porcelain, see Mary Frank Gaston's book, *R. S. Prussia Popular Lines* (Collector Books), which addresses R. S. Prussia molds and decorations and contains full-color illustrations and current values. Mold numbers appearing in some of the listings refer to this book. Assume that all items described below are marked unless noted otherwise. We also recommend *R.S. Prussia & More* by Mary J. McCaslin, also published by Collector Books. Our advisor for this category is Mary Frank Gaston.

Key:
BlM — blue mark   RSP — R.S. Prussia
RM — red mark

E.S. Germany

Fine chinaware marked 'E.S. Germany' or 'E.S. Prov. Saxe' was produced by the E.S. Schlegelmilch factory in Suhl in the Thuringia region of Prussia from sometime after 1861 until about 1925.

Bowl, flowers & ferns, shell mold, mk, 4x8" 115.00
Butter pat, ladies & child, rtcl gold rim, 3¼" 125.00
Cake plate, cherub in cart pulled by 3 maidens, gold rim, mk...... 250.00
Chamberstick, bl flowers, cobalt inner border, 2x6" 135.00
Chocolate pot, Napoleon portrait 375.00
Cup/saucer, demi, woman & roses, MOP lustre, ornate............... 175.00
Ewer, portrait of woman w/daisy crown, beading, pearl lustre, 12", $500 to...600.00
Lobster dish, tail forms hdl, florals/gilt, BlM, 10".......................... 85.00
Plate, lady's portrait, scalloped gold rim, hdls, 9½" 195.00
Vase, lady w/doves, much gold/turq beads, Tiffany finish, hdls, 6½"...425.00
Vase, maidens (4), cobalt & gold trim, 13", min.........................3,500.00

R.S. Germany

In 1869 Reinhold Schlegelmilch began to manufacture porcelain in Suhl in the German province of Thuringia. In 1894 he established another factory in Tillowitz in upper Silesia. Both areas were rich in resources necessary for the production of hard-paste porcelain. Wares marked with the name 'Tillowitz' and the accompanying 'R.S. Germany' phrase are attributed to Reinhold. The most common mark is a wreath and star in a solid color under the glaze. Items marked 'R.S. Germany' are usually more simply decorated than R.S. Prussia. Some reflect the Art Deco trend of the 1920s. Certain hand-painted floral decorations and themes such as 'Sheepherder,' 'Man With Horses,' and 'Cottage' are especially valued by collectors — those with a high-gloss finish or on Art Deco shapes in particular. Not all hand-painted items were painted at the factory. Those with an artist's signature but no 'Hand Painted' mark indicate that the blank was decorated outside the factory.

Ashtray, orange poppies, 3¾"... 75.00
Basket, sm pk roses, gold trim, 4" 140.00
Bowl, courting scene, red & gold border, RSP mold #468, 10"..... 160.00
Bowl, dogwood & pine on brn, ftd, 6¼" 55.00
Bowl, Summer portrait, wht satin, oval, hdls, RSP mold #25, 8½x13". 2,000.00
Box, w/lid, Magnolias, leaf shape, RSP mold #834, 4½x3" 200.00
Cake plate, dogwood & pine, dk border, 10" 70.00
Cake plate, pk orchids on gr, gold trim, 10" 80.00
Charger, lg wht roses w/yel tint, gold tapestry at top, 12½" 85.00
Chocolate pot, poppies on shaded tan, glossy, ind, 7¼"................. 140.00
Chocolate pot, wht lilies w/pk, gold trim, w/lid, 9½".................... 300.00

Chocolate service, 10" pot, six cups, saucers, and dessert plates, $300.00. (Photo courtesy William J. Jenack Auctioneers on LiveAuctioneers.com)

Creamer/sugar bowl, sm pk roses w/gr leaves, gold trim, w/lid...... 125.00
Jam jar, roses w/shadow flowers, w/lid & underplate 120.00
Plate, dogwood w/enameled gold stems, RSP mold #256, 8½" 60.00
Plate, emb floral mold, open hdls, 10½" 120.00
Plate, Lily of the Valley, w/lg gold leaves, smooth rim, 6⅜"............ 35.00

Relish, wht chrysanthemums, 10¼x4½"... 70.00
Toothpick holder, wht floral w/gr leaves, gold trim, 3 hdls........... 175.00
Vase, windmill scene, RSP mold #909, 4" 500.00

R.S. Poland

'R.S. Poland' is a mark attributed to Reinhold Schlegelmilch's factory in Tillowitz, Silesia. It was in use for a few years after 1945.

Bowl, Rembrandt's Night Watch on gray-gr, 1½x5⅜" 155.00
Coffee set, gold spatter & marbling, pot+6 c/s+cr/sug w/lid 400.00
Cup/saucer, dainty flowers on wht, gold rim, $150 to 200.00
Ewer, Rembrandt's Night Watch, RSP mold #900, 6¼" 600.00
Tray, bird on branch, floral/geometric border, 14" 135.00
Vase, Chinese peasants, slim neck, RS Suhl mold #15, 9".......... 900.00
Vase, clematis on brn to cream, gold hdls, 10", $300 to 400.00
Vase, ostriches on leafy grnd, unmk, 5" 245.00
Vase, pastoral scene w/gold & cobalt, hdls, RS Suhl mold #3, 8½" ..1,600.00
Vase, roses on shaded brn, Nouveau hdls, mold #956, 12" 550.00

R.S. Prussia

Art porcelain bearing the mark 'R.S. Prussia' was manufactured by Reinhold Schlegelmilch in the early 1900s in a Germanic area known until the end of WWI as Prussia. The vast array of mold shapes in combination with a wide variety of decorations is the basis for R.S. Prussia's appeal. Themes can be categorized as figural (usually based on a famous artist's work), birds, florals, portraits, scenics, and animals.

Bowl, center, pk roses w/in & w/out, mold #278, 10" 400.00
Bowl, irises on cobalt w/gold, mold #25b, 4x9½x7½" 550.00
Bowl, mill scene, gold scrolls, red mk, 7½" L 225.00
Bowl, pheasant w/pines, lav highlights, oval, Medallion mold, 14x7".. 1,000.00
Bowl, Récamier w/Tiffany bronze & gold-stencil border, mold #29, 10"...1,400.00
Bowl, snowbird on satin, pearlized dome shapes, mold #113, 10¾"....300.00
Bowl, swans on lake, Icicle mold, 11".. 650.00
Cake plate, lush flower spray, open hdls, Carnation mold, RM, 9½"... 300.00
Cake plate, mc roses, bl dome shapes, mold #78, 11" 300.00
Cake plate, Potocka/gold floral on wht, mold #29, unmk, 9½" .1,600.00
Celery dish, clematis on watered silk finish, Lily mold, 12x5"...... 275.00
Chocolate pot, swans & evergreens, Icicle mold, 10"...............1,400.00
Cracker jar, pk roses, gold emb carnations, mold #526, 5x9"........ 400.00
Creamer, floral w/gold trim, mold #605, 4" 175.00
Ferner, swans on lake, gold trim, mold #882, 4x9"....................... 650.00
Leaf dish, floral on gr to wht, Leaf mold variant, mold #10g, mk. 165.00
Pitcher, cider, lilies w/dogwood, mold #554, 6¼" 400.00
Pitcher, mc floral on gr, gold trim, mold #456, 9" 600.00
Plate, lady's portrait in wht gown w/leaves & gold, mk, 8½" 1,250.00
Plate, Snowbird scene, gold stenciled trim, Popcorn mold, 8½". 1,400.00
Relish, German court figures portraits (4) & roses, RM, 9¾"........ 650.00
Relish, winter portrait on satin w/gold, Iris mold, 9½x4½"........1,400.00
Shaving mug, castle scene, mold #644, 3½" 400.00
Shell dish, mc flowers w/gold, mold #20, 7¼" 225.00
Tankard, 3 scenes w/swans, ducks, & swallows, mold #582, 13".5,000.00
Tankard, roses on cream w/dk gr on top, gold trim, Lily mold, 15¼"... 800.00
Tankard, swallows, wht water lilies at base, #584, 13" 850.00
Tea set, roses w/gold, RM, 3-pc...1,000.00
Tray, swans (3) w/gazebo, mold #327, 12x9" 700.00
Urn, cottage scene, ornate gold hdls, w/lid, mold #903, 12½"...2,000.00

R.S. Suhl

Porcelains marked with this designation are attributed to Reinhold Schlegelmilch's Suhl factory.

Bowl, lav & wht flowers w/gold, hdls, 8⅛" 150.00
Bowl, mill scene, RSP mold #93, 5½" 275.00
Coffee set, Angelica Kauffmann scene, 9" pot+cr/sug+6 c/s...... 1,700.00
Cup/saucer, wht, floral int. 100.00
Ewer, Vict lady watering flowers, emb gold, mold #900, 6¼" 1,100.00
Vase, dk pk roses on blk, gold trim, mold #2, 7⅛" 450.00
Vase, floral transfer, gold trim, 16", $90 to 120.00
Vase, floral, pk & wht on blk, bulb, RSP mold #907, 5" 200.00
Vase, roses, wht on gray to ivory, mold #10, salesman sample, 3⅛" 250.00

R.S. Tillowitz

R.S. Tillowitz-marked porcelains are attributed to Reinhold Schlegelmilch's factory in Tillowitz, Silesia.

Bowl, berry, exotic birds & flowers, 3" 18.00
Cake plate, fruit decor, pears & grapes, 10⅞" 100.00
Cake plate, red poinsettias, 10" 80.00
Egg cups, wht w/gold, ribbed body, 2¼", 4 on matching tray 175.00
Gravy boat, pk roses on int, 6½" 40.00
Relish, Lily of the Valley, tan border, gold trim, 8x3¾" 45.00

Sugar basket, floral with gilt accents, 3½x5¼x4", $75.00. (Photo courtesy Showplace Antique + Design Center on LiveAuctioneers.com)

Vase, bl & wht scrolling band, gold trim, 9½" 85.00
Vase, lg pk tinted flowers w/sm orange flowers on brn, unmk, 6¼" ... 100.00

Schneider

The Schneider Glass Company was founded in 1914 at Epinay-sur-Seine, France. They made many types of art glass, some of which sandwiched designs between layers. Other decorative devices were applique and carved work. These were marked 'Charder' or 'Schneider.' During the '20s commercial artware was produced with Deco motifs cut by acid through two or three layers and signed 'LeVerre Francais' in script or with a section of inlaid filigrane. Our advisor for this category is Don Williams; he is listed in the Directory under Missouri. See also Le Verre Francais.

Bowl, cranberry to cream mottle, 4½" 145.00
Charger, orange rim w/brn & gr swirl center, 16", NM 235.00
Compote, indigo to orange, purple ft, 4¾x8¼" 800.00
Lamp, bullet form ivory shade w/orange border, Deco std, 16" .. 2,350.00
Pitcher, orange & rust mottle, blk hdl, ped base, Ovington, 15¾" .. 900.00
Pitcher, red to cream mottle, dk red hdl, upright rim, bulb, 7", NM... 600.00
Vase, burnt orange/orange mottle, charcoal stem/ft, 15½" 1,550.00
Vase, clear & frosted to purple at base, ftd, 9¼" 790.00
Vase, cranberry/wht/orange mottle, in wrought-iron fr, 5½x4¾" .. 1,100.00
Vase, dk brn mottle over orange w/yel highlights, brn ft, slim, 18"... 2,000.00
Vase, gr mottle to clear on orange base, 3½" 450.00
Vase, mc mottle on pk, goblet-like, ca 1926-28, 8" 1,450.00
Vase, orange/rust mottle, ovoid, 8" 450.00
Vase, orange/yel/brn mottle funnel form on purple stem/ft, 12" . 1,600.00
Vase, sgn in script, 18" 1,800.00
Vase, smoky topaz to dk purple w/2 vertical cvd bands, ftd, 8".. 1,200.00
Vase, yel & wht mottle, bulb rim, ftd, 11½x9" 1,200.00
Vase, yel/orange/purple mottle, waisted rim, ftd, slim, 11¾" 975.00

Cameo

Bottle, scent, yel/wht tea roses w/blk frwork, 4¾" 750.00
Lamp, fish & seaweed, brn on bl, mushroom shape, 11" 4,000.00
Rose bowl, floral, orange & brn on yel mottle, bulb, 3½" 570.00
Vase, floral, orange on wht mottle, shouldered, 10" 1,150.00
Vase, floral, purple on lav/wht mottle, flared bottom, ftd, 7¼" 725.00
Vase, leaves, dk orange & brn on orange mottle, waist-to-hip hdls, 10" ... 2,400.00
Vase, swans under leafage, purple on orange & yel, ftd, 11" 3,500.00

Schoolhouse Collectibles

Schoolhouse collectibles bring to mind memories of a bygone era when the teacher rang her bell to call the youngsters to class in a one-room schoolhouse where often both the 'hickory stick' and an apple occupied a prominent position on her desk. Our advisor for this category is Kenn Norris; he is listed in the Directory under Texas.

Books, *Fun with Dick and Jane – Part I* and *Fun with Dick and Jane – Part II*, 1956, VG, pair $300.00. (Photo courtesy PBA Galleries on LiveAuctioneers.com)

Book, Fun w/Dick & Jane, hardcover, scarce lg type ed, 1946, EX ... 200.00
Book, Mitchell's School Geography, 1845, G 15.00
Book, New Fun w/Dick & Jane, hardcover, 1951, M 135.00
Book, Viens Voir (Fr version of Dick & Jane), red wrappers, 1940, EX.. 250.00
Desk chair, wide arm for writing surface, oak, EX finish 75.00
Desk, master's, curly maple/walnut, dvtl gallery, cvd front, 40x38x30" .400.00
Desk, master's, oak kneehole w/6 drws, 1920s 150.00
Desk, master's, pine, slant lid, tapered legs, old rpt, 32x26x21" .. 150.00
Desk, master's, walnut & poplar w/red grpt, slant lid, drw, 42x30x22" ..865.00
Desk, master's, walnut/poplar/pine, slant lid, cvd front, 27x38x25"....700.00
Desk, wooden seat (swivels) & desk on metal base, 22x30x30" 75.00
Desk, wooden seat w/desktop behind, CI base, 1900-20, $35 to 60.00
Globe, GW Bacon, 12 colored gores, 1912 & 1926 expeditions, 14x8".325.00
Pencil sharpener, Bakelite w/Charlie McCarthy decal 45.00
Pencil sharpener, Bakelite w/Dopey decal on butterscotch figural . 75.00
Pencil sharpener, Bakelite, US Army Tank decal on gr tank shape .60.00
Pencil sharpener, celluloid, penguin on metal base, Japan 135.00
Pencil sharpener, CI, AB Dick Co Chicago, crank hdl, 6" L........ 300.00
Pencil sharpener, CI, Favor Ruhl Co NY, crank hdl, 5x14" 300.00
Pencil sharpener, CI, Indian chief head, worn mc pnt, Japan 20.00
Pencil sharpener, CI, US Automatic Pencil...1908, 5x4x3" 300.00
Pencil sharpener, CI/brass/wood, Jupiter Pencil Pointer, 6x13" ... 360.00
Pencil sharpener, metal, enameled, Great Dane's head, 1" 55.00
Pencil sharpener, metal, race car, worn gold pnt, Unis France, 2" .1,100.00
Pencil sharpener, pnt cast metal, black man's head form, 2", VG .. 60.00
Pencil sharpener, pot metal clown w/purple hat, mc pnt, VG........ 30.00

Pencil Boxes

Among the most common of school-related collectibles are the many classes of pencil boxes. Generally from the period of the 1870s to the 1940s, these boxes were made in hundreds of different styles. Materials included tin, wood (thin frame and solid hardwood), and leather; fabric and plastics were later used. Most pencil boxes were in a basic, rectangular configuration, though rare examples were made to resemble other objects such as rolling pins, ball bats, and nightsticks. They may still be found at reasonable prices, even though collectors have recently taken a keen interest in them. All boxes listed below are in very good to near mint condition. For further information we recommend *School Collectibles of the Past* by Lar and Sue Hothem. Sue is listed in the Directory under Ohio.

Cardboard litho, Felix the Cat, Am Pencil Co, 1935, VG 50.00
Cardboard litho, Gunsmoke Pencil Case, Matt Dillon on lid, EX . 95.00
Litho on wood, Mother Goose scene on lid, 1930s, 8", EX 65.00
Painted wood, dk gr w/mustard panels, sliding lid, 8" L 550.00
Papier maché, bl chintz w/gold metallic leaves, 1x7" 95.00
Papier-maché, blk lacquer w/chinoiserie, 1890s, 7¾" L 60.00
Papier-maché, decoupage scene, push-button latch, 9" L 100.00
Pyrography, pressed/pnt bluebirds/poinsettias, 9" L...................... 65.00
Tin litho, Boy Scouts at camp scene, cb liner, ¾x7x3" 55.00
Tin, advertising giveway, Security Shoes, sliding lid, 8" 38.00
Tin, Scholar's Companion, Pat 1874, 7" 85.00
Wood fr, Jack & Jill on lid, 7¾" L 40.00
Wood litho, Mother Goose, 1930s, 1x7x2" 60.00
Wood, simple slide w/ruler built into top, 1900s, 1x9x2" 20.00
Wooden, 2-tier, 4 pencil slots/3 compartments, HP lid, 1900s, 9" L .. 65.00
Wooden, 4-level, 1 compartment ea, floral decor, 9¼" 70.00

Hedi Schoop

In the 1940s and 1950s one of the most talented artists working in California was Hedi Schoop. Her business ended in 1958 when a fire destroyed her operation. It was at that time that she decided to do freelance work for other companies such as Cleminson Clay. Schoop was probably the most imitated artist of the time and she answered some of those imitators by successfully suing them. Some imitators were Kim Ward, Ynez, and Yona. Schoop was diversified in her creations, making items such as shapely women, bulky-looking women and children with fat arms and legs, TV lamps, and animals as well as planters and bowls. Schoop used many different marks including the stamped or incised Schoop signature and also a hard-to-find sticker. 'Hollywood, Cal.' or 'California' were occasionally used in conjunction with the Hedi Schoop name. For further information we recommend *Collector's Encyclopedia of California Pottery* by Jack Chipman.

Ashtray, butterfly shape, silver & gold overglaze............................. 45.00
Chip & dip tray, #62, 9¾x13½" 425.00
Cookie jar, King or Queen, 12", 12½", 1941, ea min 500.00

Figurine, couple square dancing, yellow/black Western attire, late 1940s, $275.00.
(Photo courtesy Jack Chipman)

Figurine, Debutante, holding handmade flowers, 1943, 12½" 150.00
Figurine, Hungarian man, #57, 1940, 10½" 85.00
Figurine, Hungarian woman, #58, 1940, 10" 85.00
Figurine, Love Boat, man playing accordian, woman singing, 1939, 6x10½", min ...250.00
Figurine, Vienna, tall blond lady w/baskets, 13½" 200.00
Figurines (2), Asian man & woman, sgn, rpr, 13½x6", pr............. 100.00
Flower frog, dancing girls, unmk, 8", min..................................... 200.00

Flower holder/lamp base, Colbert (modeled after Claudette Colbert), ca 1940, 11½"..150.00
TV lamp, comedy & tragedy masks... 375.00
TV lamp, The Orchestra, 1954, 15x10½", min............................. 500.00
Vase, cock crowing, high glaze & gold overglaze, ca 1949, 12" 125.00

Schramberg

The Schramberg factory was founded in the early nineteenth century in Schramberg Wurttemberg, Germany. The pieces most commonly seen are those made by Schramberger Majolika Fabrik (SMF) dating from 1912 until 1989. Some pieces are stamped with the pattern name (i.e. Gobelin) and the number of the painter who executed it. The imprinted number identifies the shape. Marks may also include these names: Wheelock, Black Forest, and Mepoco.

Perhaps the most popular examples with collectors are those from the Gobelin line. Such pieces have a gray background with as many as 10 other colors used to create that design. For example, Gobelin 3 pieces will be painted with green and orange leaves and yellow eyes along with other colors specific to that design.

Little is known of the designers who worked for Schramberg; however, Eva Zeisel was employed at the factory for nearly two years starting in the fall of 1928. Her duties included design, production, and merchandising. Because of Zeisel's popularity with collectors, designs are being attributed to her. Since she left Schramberg within two years, it is difficult for collectors to know which designs were actually hers and which were designs of other employees. Our advisor for this category is Ralph Winslow; he is listed in the Directory under Arizona.

Ashtray, mc, 9"... 35.00
Creamer/sugar bowl, ship scene, 5" 40.00
Flower arranger, mc, 6" 30.00
Liqueur set, pitcher/tray/4 glasses 300.00
Plates, floral, set of 6, 7".. 35.00
Vase, blk/wht/orange, SMF Schramberg, 7" 36.00
Vase, chalet scene, hdls, 3" 20.00
Vase, floral, mc, 9" 25.00
Vase, Gobelin, 6" 62.00

Vase, Gobelin, 8", $75.00.
(Photo courtesy Ralph Winslow)

Vase, Gobelin, 9" 33.00
Vase, ivy leaves, 15".. 110.00
Vase, mc, 4".. 40.00

Scouting Collectibles

Boy Scouts

Scouting was founded in England in 1907 by retired Major General Lord Robert Baden-Powell. Its purpose is the same today as it was then — to help develop physically strong, mentally alert boys and to teach them basic fundamentals of survival and leadership. The movement soon spread to the United States, and in 1910 a Chicago publisher, William Boyce, set out to establish scouting in America. The first World Scout Jamboree was held in 1920 in England. Baden-Powell was honored as the Chief Scout of the World. In 1926 he was awarded the Silver Buffalo Award in the United States. He was knighted in 1929 for distinguished military service and for his scouting efforts. Baden-Powell died in 1941.

For more information you may contact our advisor, R.J. Sayers, author of *Guide to Scouting Collectibles,* whose address (and ordering information regarding his book) may be found in the Directory under North Carolina. (Correspondence other than book orders requires SASE please.)

Award kit, Silver Beaver, complete, 1975, NMIB........................... 75.00
Book, Ben-Hur, BSA emblem on hardcover, 1913, 560 pgs, VG ... 60.00
Booklet, Poultry Keeping, Merit Badge Series, 1923, 8x5¼", VG+..75.00
Camera, Agfa Ansco Memo Camera, gr, 1927, G........................ 215.00
Clippers, Super Scout-O-Rama, Superman/Batman, EX 10.00
First aid kit, complete, Bauer & Blk, tin box, 1932, EX 35.00
Game, Ten Pins, Milton Bradley, 1910, VGIB.............................. 150.00
Handbook, BSA Handbook for Boys, red softcover, 1911, VG.... 300.00
Kit Karson Kit, official axe & knife w/sheath, 1950s, EXIB.......... 175.00
Knife, Western, leathered hdl, 4½" blade, 8⅝", M in scabbard....... 45.00
Lapel pin, Press Club, bl enamel w/gold 1st Class emblem & quill, mini, NM.550.00
Medal, Silver Beaver Award, silver figural, 1950s, 1½x1x1", +ribbon, NM .. 175.00
Neckerchief, emblem in 2 corners, red & wht, Nat'l Jamboree, 1937, EX. 95.00
Patch, Air Scout Candidate 1st Class, bl propeller (4) on gr, EX... 95.00
Patch, Camp Bird (tepee) 1944, red felt arrowhead shape, NM..... 50.00
Patch, Honor Camper Nicholet Area Council, 1944, EX 10.00
Patch, Senior Patrol Leader Honors, 2 bl chevrons on wht, 1930s, NM.. 110.00
Pocket watch, Ingersoll, 1937, NM (+) 150.00
Pocketknife, Scout Is Clean, 1-blade, Franklin Mint, 7½", M in bag...45.00

Poster, Scouts Today and Leaders Tomorrow, Kellogg's advertising, U.S. Printing Co. by permission of the Boy Scouts of America, artist George Straub, circa 1925, 30½x23", M, $1,800.00. (Photo courtesy Showtime Auction Services on LiveAuctioneers.com)

Rock & Minerals Kit, 60 samples w/ID sheet, EXIB....................... 35.00
Ticket, 5¢ trade at post, 1937 WJ, Good Humor Ice Cream on bk, EX.. 20.00
Watch fob, emb Scout w/Am flag, red/wht/bl enamel on brass, NM.. 80.00
Whistle, Acme, brass, 1940s-50s, 2½", EX.. 30.00
Woodcarving set, 5 varied chisels, Cattaragus, M in wood box w/emblem ..35.00

Girl Scouts

Collecting Girl Scout memorabilia is a hobby that is growing nationwide. When Sir Baden-Powell founded the Boy Scout Movement in England, it proved to be too attractive and too well adapted to youth to limit its great opportunities to boys alone. The sister organization, known in England as the Girl Guides, quickly followed and was equally successful. Mrs. Juliette Low, an American visitor to England and a personal friend of the father of scouting, realized the tremendous future of the movement for her own country, and with the active and friendly cooperation of the Baden-Powells, she founded the Girl Guides in America, enrolling the first patrols in Savannah, Georgia, in March 1912. In 1915 National Headquarters were established in Washington, D.C., and the name was changed to Girl Scouts. The first national con-

vention was held in 1914. Each succeeding year has shown growth and increased enthusiasm in this steadily growing army of girls and young women who are learning in the happiest ways to combine patriotism, outdoor activities of every kind, skill in every branch of domestic science, and high standards of community service. Today there are over 400,000 Girl Scouts and more than 22,000 leaders. Mr. Sayers is also our Girl Scout advisor.

Badge, For Merit, emb bronze, ca 1920-25, 1" dia, +3" ribbon, NM...500.00
Book, Brave Girls, HC Philmus, hardback, 1947, VG..................... 20.00
Bracelet, gold-plated brass w/emb symbol, cuff style, ca 1930s-40s, EX..40.00
Camera, Instant Load 900W, gr, Eastman Kodak Patents..., 1940, 5" L, NM..75.00
Cookbook, Girl Scouts USA Beginner's Cookbook, Cameron, 1972..24.00
Cuff links, trefoils w/emb GS, #12-171, MIB.................................. 70.00
Doll, Georgene Novelties, yarn hair, bl eyes, 1940s-50s, 13", NM ..225.00
Doll, hard plastic, sleep eyes, head/legs move, Terri Lee, 7½", EX. 150.00
Flashlight, Nat'l Equipment Service, 1950s, MIB........................... 22.00
Hat, gr cloth w/blk GS, gr ribbon w/bow, w/tags, MIB 40.00
Knife, Remington RH-251, 4" blade w/leather hdl & sheath, EX. 125.00
Knife, Ulster, 5 tools, bone hdl, Divine & Sons, 1925, 3½", EX 50.00
Necklace, gold-plated locket w/emb eagle & 7 stars, 1950s, MIB .. 65.00
Pin-back, Golden Eaglet (3 types), 10K-B on bk, ½x½", $350 to.. 500.00
Pin, membership, trefoil w/wht GS, Bakelite, 1⅛x1", EX............... 50.00
Poster, It's Girl Scout Cookie Time, Scouts hanging banner, 1963, EX .. 35.00
Ring, 10k yel & rose gold, emb symbol, NM.................................... 40.00
Ring, silver w/emb emblem on top, Sterling, EX 85.00

Sign, Golden Bear Cookies, Long Island City, NY, 21x14½", VG, $20.00. (Photo courtesy Randy Inman Auctions Inc. on LiveAuctioneers.com)

Sheet music, Girl Scouts Are We, J Rivenburg, 1941, EX.............. 15.00
Stamp set, Girl Power, 8-pc, retired, MIB 50.00
Statue, copper-bronze Scout figural, M Dauigerfield, 1960s, 8x4", NM .30.00
Uniform, tan, top, skirt & bloomers (3-pc), ca 1920, VG 250.00
Watch, Brownie emblem on wht face, red strap, Timex, 1962, NM... 35.00

Scrimshaw

The most desirable examples of the art of scrimshaw can be traced back to the first half of the nineteenth century to the heyday of the whaling industry. Some voyages lasted for several years, and conditions on board were often dismal. Sailors filled the long hours by using the tools of their trade to engrave whale teeth and make boxes, pie crimpers (jagging wheels), etc., from the bone and teeth of captured whales. Eskimos also made scrimshaw, sometimes borrowing designs from the sailors who traded with them.

Beware of fraudulent pieces; fakery is prevalent in this field. Many carved teeth are of recent synthetic manufacture (examples engraved with information such as ship's or captain's names, dates, and places, should be treated with extreme caution) and have no antique or collectible value. A listing of most of these plastic items has been published by the Kendall Institute at the New Bedford Whaling Museum in New Bedford, Massachusetts. If you're in doubt or a novice collector, it's best to deal with reputable people who guarantee the items they sell. Our advisor for this category is John Rinaldi; he is listed in the Directory under Maine. See also Powder Horns and Flasks.

Bodkin, whale ivory, 3 incised lines w/red wax, ca 1850, 3¼" L...245.00
Busk, bone w/flowers/stars/hearts, splits, 14"...................................800.00
Busk, bone w/hearts/sunbursts/flowers/symbols, NE, 19th C, 14".350.00
Busk, pinwheels/hearts/stars/etc, 19th C, 14½x1¾"....................1,100.00
Cane, clenched fist hdl, whale ivory knob, 19th C, 33¾".........1,950.00
Cane, eagle-cvd whale-ivory 3" hdl, ebony shaft/ivory tip, 1840s+..1,675.00
Fid, bone, incised lines, 9"...300.00
Jagging wheel, silver band, bird head, pierced wheel, cracks to arms, 7".1,300.00
Jagging wheel, whale ivory, serpent-form hdl, leaf-form fork, 5¼"..1,295.00
Jagging wheel, whalebone, trn shaft w/incised lines, 7"................395.00
Marking gage, cvd whalebone, 8"...2,465.00
Measuring stick, bone, inscr AB (AE Barker), early 19th C, 35⅝"..1,200.00
Panbone, whaling scene, 4 longboats/1 ship, 19th C, 5x8".......9,500.00
Pipe tamp, lady's leg form w/patterned cvgs, 19th C, 2¾x1¼"......275.00
Tooth, eagles sparring/fish/palisade/soldiers/tents, 19th C, 5⅞".2,235.00
Tooth, eng both sides, front w/young girl & name 'Emma,' 5"..2,100.00

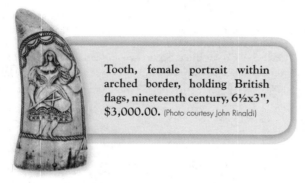

Tooth, female portrait within arched border, holding British flags, nineteenth century, 6½x3", $3,000.00. (Photo courtesy John Rinaldi)

Tooth, fine lady w/veil/Liberty/flag/shield, cracks, 19th C, 5"...1,765.00
Tooth, Liberty/anchor/shield/banner/vessel, cracks, 19th C, 5⅝"..2,350.00
Tooth, mother w/daughter (hair in ringlets), age split, 6⅝".......4,250.00
Tooth, naval ship, Am flag, bk: female portrait, 1850, 6½x2¾"..4,975.00
Tooth, naval ship flying flags, 'Victory,' 19th C, 5¼x2⅝".........3,875.00
Tooth, panel: man presents lady a miniature portrait by window, 6", VG...985.00
Tooth, queen in royal robes, man in frock coat, pinprick art, 6"..1,150.00
Tooth, warship firing, warship hiding behind rocks, whalers, 6¾"..9,775.00
Tooth, whaling scene, longboat/whaling ship, ca 1850, 6¾x2".4,975.00
Tooth, woman w/paper, poly in bl/lt brn/blk, 1860, 4¼x3".......1,400.00
Tooth, young girl, bk: young couple dancing, ca 1860, 6¼x2¼"3,875.00

Sebastians

Prescott W. Baston first produced Sebastian Miniatures in 1938 in his home in Arlington, Massachusetts. In 1946 Baston bought a small shoe factory in Marblehead, Massachusetts, and produced his figurines there for the next 30 years. Over the years Baston sculpted and produced more than 750 different pieces, many of which have been sold nationwide through gift shops. Baston and The Lance Corporation of Hudson, Massachusetts, consolidated the line in 1976 and actively promoted Sebastians nationally. Many of Baston's commercial designs, private commissions, and even some open line pieces have become very collectible. Aftermarket price is determined by three factors: 1) current or out of production status, 2) labels, and 3) condition. Copyright dates are of no particular significance with regard to value.

Mr. Baston died in 1984, and his son Prescott 'Woody' Baston, Jr. continued the tradition by taking over the designing. To date Woody has sculpted over 250 pieces of his own. After numerous changes in the company that held manufacturing and distribution rights for Sebastians, Woody and his

wife Margery are now sculpting and painting the Sebastian Miniatures out of their home in Massachusetts. By personally producing the pieces, Sebastians are the only collectible line that is produced from design to finished product by the artist. Sebastian miniatures have come full cycle.

America Remembers the Family Picnic, Christmas Series, 1979, 3½"...25.00
Andrew Jackson, 3½"...25.00
Aubry, 50th Anniversary Collection, Marblehead label, 3¼", MIB.17.50
Boy & Pelican, 3½"...30.00
Boy Jesus in the Temple, Marblehead sticker....................................325.00
Bringing Home the Tree, red label, 3¼"..25.00
Building Days, #407, 1975, bl label, 3¼"...25.00
Captain John Smith, 1940s...32.00
Charles Dickens, standing behind table w/open book.......................32.00
Christmas Sleigh Ride, dog stands before 2 children in sleigh.........30.00
Colonial Blacksmith, 1970, 3½"...18.00
Colonial Carriage, yel label, MIB...35.00
Coronaro & Senora, 1960, 3¼"...35.00
Croquet, 1982-85, 4½"...35.00
Dicken's Marley, 1997, 2¾"..30.00
Faneuil Hall – Quincy Market, sgn Woody Baston 7/21/84, 2x5"..20.00
Fireside Chat (President Roosevelt), 1989, 2½"................................32.00
Franklin D Roosevelt, MIB..22.00
George Washington, Marblehead era, 4"..95.00
Hanging the Stocking, MIB...20.00
Horse-drawn stagecoach, pen stand, Everett National Bank, 1959, 3x5"..42.00
Jell-O cow pitcher, 6 orig fruit flavors on wht, 1956........................55.00
Jell-O! A Fine Treat for All!, Santa scene..175.00
John Alden, sitting on bbl...30.00
John Hancock, 1983..38.00
Lobster Boat, #522...45.00
Manger, nativity pc, Hudson MA, sgn Preston W Baston 12/2/80.26.00
Mark Twain, lt bl label, 2¼"...60.00
Our Lady of Good Voyage, 1952, 4¼", NM.......................................55.00

Paul Bunyan, pink label, 1949, 3¼", $30.00. (Photo courtesy Homestead Auctions on LiveAuctioneers.com)

Peter Stuyvesant, red label, 5"...25.00
Princess Elizabeth & Prince Philip, 1947...300.00
Rx Obocell, 1950, MIB..55.00
Sampling the Stew, blk label...25.00
Sampling the Stew, gr label, 2½"...15.00
Santa in Dory..27.50
Sebastian Studio Orig Works of Art, plaque, 4½"..............................25.00
Shepherds, 1954 Nativity pc...35.00
Shepherds, nativity pc, Marblehead label...32.00
Snowdays Boy, yel tags..25.00
State House, comissioned by MA Masonic Lodge, MIB...................125.00
Stuffing the Stockings, 1992...18.00
Swan Boat Boston Public Garden, Marblehead label, 1950, 2"......17.00
Thanksgiving Couple, Marblehead label...30.00
Thomas A 'Stonewall' Jackson, standing in gray uniform...............32.00
William Shakespeare, Sebastian Collectors Society, 1988..............25.00
Williamsburg Capital, Colonial..25.00

Sevres

Fine-quality porcelains have been made in Sevres, France, since the early 1700s. Rich ground colors were often hand painted with portraits, scenics, and florals. Some pieces were decorated with transfer prints and decalcomania; many were embellished with heavy gold. These wares are the most respected of all French porcelains. Their style and designs have been widely copied, and some of the items listed below are Sevres-type wares.

Vases, courting and landscape reserves on light blue, interlacing L's mark in blue over the glaze, circa 1900, 14", pair $3,300.00. (Photo courtesy DuMouchelles on LiveAuctioneers.com)

Bottle, bl crystalline on beige, ribbed, organic shape, sgn, rstr, 1929, 10½x3½"..3,480.00
Bottle, cat's eye flambe, fused to rtcl stand w/wht dots, sgn, rstr, 11½x3"..2,400.00
Bowl, centerpiece, figures on bl, gilt-bronze mts, 19th C, 14x19x10".6,600.00
Bowl, centerpiece, scenic panels, rtcl gilt bronze hdls, 19th C, 14x25" L.15,500.00
Bowl, cherubs/floral borders, cobalt/wht, hdld gilt bronze mt, 13" L.825.00
Box, scenic lid, sgn B Tehau, cobalt w/gold, 4x9x7" 2,400.00
Bucket, ice cream, floral, feather-edge lid, w/insert, ca 1782, 7". 1,400.00
Bust, Marie Antoinette, wht, Lecomte, #1056, ca 1890, 20" 3,200.00
Cache pot, cherubs cartouche amid gilt serpents on turq, 7"........ 900.00
Cache pot, floral, gilt goat head hdls, 19th C, 10x12¾" 4,150.00
Clock, Mother Mary & 2 holy children panel, bronze mts, Paris, 19x12".4,750.00
Coffee set, Napoleonic scenes/landscapes, pot+cr/sug+12 c/s+6 plates.. 12,925.00
Cup/saucer, Marie Antoinette portrait, 1778.............................2,400.00
Figurine, 3 cherubs in scientific activities, ca 1900, 8" 2,450.00
Figurine, Forging of Arrows, Cupid & cherub, wht porc, ca 1860, 13" ...960.00
Group, Le Basier du Faune, after Dalou, terra cotta, 1922, 15" .3,000.00
Lamp, Venus & Cupid scene, Gauthier, brass mts, electrified, 25". 1,300.00
Plaque, Palais des Tuileries Paris, Guerard, 1822, 5½x8⅜" 4,800.00
Plate, 2 drunken youths, cobalt & gold scalloped border, 9½" 145.00
Plate, cavalier on horse battling, cobalt/gold border, 19th C, 10" . 350.00
Plate, equestrian battle scene, cobalt & gold rim, 1890s, 9⅜" 395.00
Platter, exotic birds on pk w/gold, ca 1774, 12⅝" 1,880.00
Sugar bowl, floral sprays, Celeste Bl w/gold, w/lid, 1780s, 4¼" ..3,300.00
Tureen, floral reserves on bl w/gold, w/lid & tray, 16x24x15"....1,880.00
Urn, bl molded lappets/gilt bronze mts, campana-style, 19th C, 27"..1,450.00
Urn, couple/cherubs, Quentin, brass mts, w/lid, 20th C, 31" 2,650.00
Urn, courting couple reserve, cobalt & gold, trumpet ft, 19th C, 9" ..360.00
Urn, courting couple w/gold, gilt metal satyr mask hdls, 1900s, 20"...725.00
Urn, figure scene reserve on dk bl w/much gold, gold hdls, 18", pr, EX...1,150.00
Urn, figures in landscape, Porlevin, gilt-bronze mts, w/lid, 1757, 42".. 7,800.00
Urn, huntsman/shepherdess w/gold, 19th C, 37"+ornate stand, 57".11,165.00
Urn, nurse/mother/child, gilt bronze mts, Sevres mk, w/lid, 50", VG .6,500.00
Urn, ormolu swan-head hdl/floral swags, gilt bronze base/lid, 18", pr.3,885.00
Urn, romantic scenes/gold, Grisard, gilt bronze mts, 19th C, rpr, 49".16,500.00
Vase, cobalt baluster w/gilt snowflakes, silver mts, 1920s, 19", pr.5,250.00
Vase, couple reserve, wht on bl w/ornate gilt hdls, ftd, 1850s, 12", VG ..300.00
Vase, figures in landscape, cobalt w/gold, ovoid, 19th C, 20x10"...3,250.00

Sewer Tile

Whimsies, advertising novelties, and other ornamental items were sometimes made in potteries where the primary product was simply tile.

Bird bath, tree stump and rabbit, two pieces, base: 32x20", basin: 7x22", VG, $3,000.00. (Photo courtesy Burchard Galleries Inc. on LiveAuctioneers.com)

Boston terrier, sgn L Staley 1944, OH, 8¾" 575.00
Chimney cap, fluted column on sq base, scalloped rim, 29x12x12" ...260.00
Dog, incised collar & facial features, 11½", NM 2,415.00
Dog seated, flat head, tooled eyelashes, 9¼" 1,000.00
Dog seated, incised fur, att OH, 11" 925.00
Dog seated w/free-standing front legs, att G Bagnell, 10¼" 2,900.00
Eagle plaque, sgn EJE, 5".. 115.00
Horned owl on branch, EX detail, 14½" 300.00
Lion reclining on oval base, molded/hand tooled, flakes, 9½x15". 700.00
Lion reclining on platform, dk brn, OH, 19th C, 6¼" 600.00
Piggy bank, seated, long eyelashes, sgn DRM, OH, 9" 460.00
Pitcher, Liberty & 13 stars (molded/appl) ea side, scroll hdl, 7", EX ... 350.00
Planter, stump w/textured surface, appl branches, pnt, 10" 200.00
Spaniel seated, brn w/contrasting eyes/tag, Roy Blind, OH, 8¾" . 175.00
Spaniel seated w/paw raised, brn lustre, OH, 19th C, 8⅞" 1,200.00
Tree stump container, seated dog finial (glued), 7" 115.00
Umbrella stand, tree stump w/appl vines, tooled bark, 20x8".......200.00

Sewing Items

Sewing collectibles continue to intrigue collectors, and fine nineteenth-century and earlier pieces are commanding higher prices due to increased demand and scarcity. Complete needlework boxes and chatelaines in original condition are rare, but even incomplete examples can be considered prime additions to any collection, as long as they meet certain criteria: boxes should contain fittings of the period; the chains of the chatelaine should be intact and contemporary with the style; and the individual holders should be original and match the brooch. As nineteenth-century items become harder to find, new trends in collecting develop. Needle books, many of which were decorated with horses, children, beautiful ladies, etc., have become very popular. Some were giveaways printed with advertisements of products and businesses. Even early pins are collectible; the first ones were made in two parts with the round head attached separately. Pin disks, pin cubes, and other pin holders also make interesting additions to a sewing collection.

Tape measures are very popular — especially Victorian figurals. These command premium prices. Early wooden examples of transferware and Tunbridge ware have gained in popularity, as have figurals of vegetable ivory, celluloid, and other early plastics. From the twentieth century, tatting shuttles made of plastics, bone, brass, sterling, and wood decorated with Art Nouveau, Art Deco, and more modern designs are in demand — so are darning eggs, stilettos, and thimbles. Because of the decline in the popularity of needlework after the 1920s (due to increased production of machine-made items), novelty items were made in an attempt to regain consumer interest, and many collectors today also find these appealing.

Watch for reproductions. Sterling thimbles are being made in Holland and the U.S. and are available in many Victorian-era designs. But the originals are usually plainly marked, either in the inside apex or outside on the band. Avoid testing gold and silver thimbles for content; this often destroys the inside marks. Instead, research the manufacturer's mark; this will often denote the material as well. Even though the reproductions are well finished, they do not have manufacturers' marks. Many thimbles are being made specifically for the collectible market; reproductions of porcelain thimbles are also found. Prices should reflect the age and availability of these thimbles. For more information we recommend *Sewing Tools & Trinkets* by Helen Lester Thompson; *Antique & Collectible Buttons, Volumes I and II*, by Debra Wisniewski; and *Encylopedia of Children's Sewing Collectibles* by Darlene J. Gengelbach. All are published by Collector Books.

Awl, steel & bone, 4¼" 22.50
Bodkin, cvd ivory w/inset 'jewels,' 3½" 225.00
Box, wicker, HP gr dmns, hinged lid, on stand, 1910, hdl up: 35x12"... 100.00
Box, wood w/plastic gromets, lg pk knob on lid, 1 drw, 1905, 6x7" .. 110.00
Button, brass, emb rabbit head & floral, raised rim, loop shank, 1".. 105.00
Button, copper, cats (2) on cut-out floral oval, 1½x2" 110.00
Button, red glass w/foil-bk glass inlay, 1950s, lg 25.00
Caddy, Peaseware, 2-pc step-bk, pincushion top, metal posts, 6x4"....215.00
Caddy, poplar w/mc pnt, bowl-shaped base, mushroom finial, 12x5"..865.00
Chest, mahog bowfront w/inlay, tray, 3-drw, 1800s, 11x13x7" ..2,350.00
Clamp, CI, dolphin, angle thumbscrew, England, ca 1870, 6x5"...1,250.00
Darner, glass, Amster-Stocking Pat Ap For, cobalt, orig label, 5¼".. 130.00
Darner, glass, mc splotches in clear, 6" 100.00
Darner, wood, HP pansy on removable hdl, Germany, ca 1920, 4"...70.00
Darner, wood, lady figural, mc pnt, 2-pc, 1900, 4½" 30.00
Darner, wood, mushroom shape w/metal ring to hold sock 25.00
Dress form, adjustable, sz B, w/iron claw-ft base, Acme, 60" 150.00
Gauge, sterling w/plated steel scale, ornate heart shape on end 60.00
Handbook, Singer Employees; prices/trade values/parts/rules, 1940, VG... 155.00
Hat block/form, lg brim, wood, grooved rim, 30 degree taper, 52"...200.00

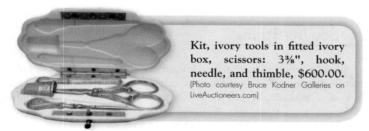

Kit, ivory tools in fitted ivory box, scissors: 3⅜", hook, needle, and thimble, $600.00.
(Photo courtesy Bruce Kodner Galleries on LiveAuctioneers.com)

Kit, pk & wht enamel on brass bullet shape, thimble/needle/thread, 2"... 46.00
Measure, brass, shoe, emb Three Feet in One Shoe, 1910, 1½x2¼".95.00
Measure, celluloid, basket of fruit, Germany, 1x1½" 170.00
Measure, celluloid, black boy w/yel scarf on head, Germany, 1¾" 260.00
Measure, celluloid, clown's head, sm blk hat is pull, Germany..... 325.00
Measure, celluloid, flamingo, pk, w/tape in base, 2⅝" 75.00
Measure, celluloid, Indian boy in headdress, red pants 135.00
Measure, celluloid, parrot's head, mc on wht, Germany, 1⅜" 315.00
Measure, celluloid, purse w/jeweled clasp, Japan, 1½x1½" 225.00
Measure, celluloid, ship, Germany, ca 1900 .... 75.00
Measure, celluloid, spaniel dog, wht/blk/red, 1930s-50s, Japan 225.00
Measure, metal & celluloid rabbit 180.00
Measure, pierced bone w/ivory spindle, silk tape, 1850-90, 1" dia.. 70.00
Measure, tin plate, early car, rubber tires, 1900s, 2½" L................ 385.00
Measure, tin, raised brass horsehead, plastic eye, Germany, 1½" dia .. 50.00
Measure, vegetable ivory acorn w/cvd palm leaves, 1880, 2"......... 65.00
Needle book, Vict children, ca 1875 .... 18.00
Needle case, brass, Eclectic Needle..., Milward & Sons Redditch, 3x1". 50.00
Needle case, ivory, cvd Asian men/pagoda/flowers/trees, 2¾" 90.00
Needle case, MOP, cvd urn & flowers w/cutout, 4½" 300.00
Needle guard, sterling key w/2 silver chains, France, ca 1870, 6".170.00
Needle holder, brass, Sheaf of Wheat, Avery & Son, dtd 9/14/1873... 300.00
Pincushion, Black Forest, bear holding bl cushion, ca 1890, 3x3"...225.00
Pincushion, pillow form w/needlework top, velvet-covered ft, 5x6x6".115.00

Pincushion, redware pottery, bulldog, USA, 6" 200.00
Pincushion, strawberry on red blown glass base, worn, 6" 490.00
Pincushion, wood, Vict boot w/HP roses & butterflies, ca 1900..... 75.00
Pincushion, wool, circus seal w/ball on nose, straw filled, 5" L....... 50.00
Scissors, buttonhole, Singer #304, Germany, 4½"........................ 152.00
Scissors, emb Cascade scene, 1904 St Louis World's Fair, Germany, 6" .. 60.00
Scissors, embr, silver, wild roses emb, 4"..................................... 60.00
Scissors, embr, sterling, decorative short blade, USA, ca 1900 ...... 70.00
Scissors, stork figural, unmk.. 22.00
Sewing bird, CI, heart on thumbscrew, 1880s, 3½" L 130.00
Sewing bird, wrought steel w/spring clamp, disk thumbscrew, 6⅜"... 230.00
Spool chest, walnut, brass pulls, rfn.. 350.00
Stand, walnut/cherry/poplar, pnt decor, att OH, 11x13x6".......2,900.00
Tatting shuttle, celluloid, lt pk, 2½" 12.00
Tatting shuttle, metal, Boy Improved.. 10.00
Thimble case, gilt brass, etched scrolls, bullet shape, Germany, 2" ..25.00
Thimble holder, basket, clear gr onyx w/brass trim, Mexico, 2x2½"... 95.00
Thimble holder, shoe w/flowers, 10k gold on wht bsk, England, 1890s... 90.00
Thimble, 14k gold, etched monogram in heart, wht plastic top... 110.00
Thimble, 14k gold, etched scrolls & floral, Ketcham & McDougall, ¾".. 120.00
Thimble, child's, sterling, eng image & Cow Jumped Over the Moon ..80.00
Thimble, German .800 silver, amethyst glass top, fancy border ... 110.00
Thimble, German .925 silver, red stone cap, ribbed w/ribbon-like band.. 60.00
Thimble, MOP, Palais Royal, pansy medallion w/gold band, 1800-25....650.00
Thimble, porc, Jasperware, Kings & Queens of England, Wedgwood, ea .. 50.00
Tracing wheel, oak hdl, 6" L... 10.00

Sewing Machines

The fact that Thomas Saint, an English cabinetmaker, invented the first sewing machine in 1790 was unknown until 1874 when Newton Wilson, an English sewing machine manufacturer and patentee, chanced upon the drawings included in a patent specification describing methods of making boots and shoes. By the middle of the nineteenth century, several patents were granted to American inventors, among them Isaac M. Singer, whose machine used a treadle. These machines were ruggedly built, usually of cast iron. By the 1860s and 1870s, the sewing machine had become a popular commodity, and the ironwork was frequently detailed and ornate. Though rare machines are costly, many of the old oak treadle machines (especially these brands: Davis, Domestic, Household, National, New Home, Singer, White, Wheeler & Wilson, and Willcox & Gibbs) have only nominal value. Machines manufactured after 1880 are generally very common, and every family had one or two. Values for these later sewing machines range from $50.00 to $300.00. For more information see *The Encyclopedia of Early American Sewing Machines* by our advisor, Carter Bays (Collector Books); he is listed in the Directory under South Carolina. In the listings that follow, unless noted otherwise, values are suggested for machines whose decorations are in good to excellent condition. Usually a machine's sewing ability is unimportant.

Bosworth, gilt treadle stand, walnut table, ca 1861 ....5,000.00
Bradbury #1, hand crank, late 1800s, +case 200.00
Buckeye, hand operated, ca 1877 .... 200.00
Child's, Baby Brother, gray-gr metallic, Japan, 1960s, $75 to 100.00
Child's, Betsy Ross, Electric, 1950s, +red snakeskin case 30.00
Child's, Casige, Deco decor, cam drive, MIG - British Zone, $75 to .. 50.00
Child's, Eldredgette, gr enameling, hand crank, NMIB.................... 40.00
Child's, Gateway, red pnt lightweight steel.................................... 50.00
Child's, Genero, Gurlee Stitch Mistress, manual, 1940s-50s, 7" 50.00
Child's, Ideal, treadle type w/oak top & CI base, 31x18x10" 1,200.00
Child's, KAYanEE Sew Master, hand-operated, wood base............. 50.00
Child's, Little Comfort Improved, Smith & Egge, 1897 .... 175.00
Child's, Little Daisy, walnut table w/treadle, ca 1885 ....4,500.00

Child's, Little Mary Mix Up, sheet metal, 1930s 50.00
Child's, Little Modiste, red pnt metal, b/o, Japan 50.00
Child's, Marx Sew Big, diecast metal w/plastic table, 1960s........... 25.00
Child's, Olympia, manual or b/o, Japan... 25.00
Child's, plastic, crystal/pk/wht, b/o, 7½x12x4" 20.00
Child's, Pony, unusual circular design, CI on wooden base, hand crank, 8". 1,500.00
Child's, Singer #20, blk pnt w/gilt, hand crank, 7", NMIB........... 150.00
Child's, Stitchwell, CI/steel/wood, hand crank, 6x9x4", +crate... 150.00
Florence #7839, gilt & poly floral, pat dates to July 1863, 34x30". 600.00
Gold Medal, ca 1870, $100 to 250.00
Goodrich, treadle, quartersawn oak cabinet................................. 150.00
Grover & Baker #10574, flywheel-operated, +13" rosewood case . 880.00
Guhl & Haarbeck, full-sz tabletop, Germany, 1890-1920, VG 175.00

Holly, walnut stand, early American, reflects 1840s furniture style but was made in 1862, extremely rare, $15,000.00. (Photo courtesy Carter Bays)

Howe, treadle type, wood top w/CI base, ca 1871, 39x28"........... 125.00
NE type, many variations, 1860s-70s, $100 to 1,500.00
New Home, treadle type, oak cabinet w/4 drw, CI base, 1915........ 65.00
Paw Foot type, many variations, 1860s-70s, $300 to 2,500.00
Remington, treadle type, ca 1875... 250.00
Singer 221 Featherweight, gold graphics, NM 375.00
Singer Model #15, blk w/gold decal, ca 1954, +case....................... 50.00
Singer, automatic, chain stitch, machine head only, ca 1890......... 75.00
Singer, Pat 1846, MOP inlay in head, +walnut fold-out case....... 300.00
Singer, Turtleback, treadle type, ca 1858 ....15,000.00
Victor, treadle type, ca 1875.. 200.00
Weed, Family Favorite, treadle type, ca 1873 .... 200.00
Wheeler & Wilson, 625 Broadway... 200.00
Wheeler & Wilson, treadle w/fold-out tabletop, ca 1856-76, VG. 125.00
Wilcox & Gibbs, CI 13" bedplate, Pat dates to 1871 .... 100.00

Shaker Items

The Shaker community was founded in America in 1776 at Niskeyuna, New York, by a small group of English 'Shaking Quakers.' The name referred to a group dance which was part of their religious rites. Their leader was Mother Ann Lee. By 1815 their membership had grown to more than 1,000 in 18 communities as far west as Indiana and Kentucky. But in less than a decade, their numbers began to decline until today only a handful remain. Their furniture is prized for its originality, simplicity, workmanship, and practicality. Few pieces were signed. Some were carefully finished to enhance the natural wood; a few were painted. Other methods were used earlier, but most Shaker boxes were of oval construction with overlapping 'fingers' at the seams to prevent buckling as the wood aged. Boxes with original paint fetch triple the price of an unpainted box; number of fingers and overall size should also be considered.

Although the Shakers were responsible for weaving a great number of baskets, their methods are not easily distinguished from those of their outside neighbors, and it is nearly impossible without first-hand knowledge to positively attribute a specific example to their manufacture. They were involved in various commercial efforts other than woodworking — among them sheep and dairy farming, sawmilling, and pipe and brick making. They were the first to raise crops specifically for seed and to market their product commercially. They perfected a method to recycle paper and were able to produce wrinkle-free fabrics. Our advisor for this category is Nancy Winston; she is listed in the Directory under New Hampshire. Standard two-letter state abbreviations have been used throughout the following listings. Painted pieces are assumed to be in excellent original paint unless another condition code is present or the description contains information to the contrary.

Key:
CB — Canterbury
EF — Enfield
ML — Mt. Lebanon
NL — New Lebanon
SDL — Sabbathday Lake

Basket, flat form w/2 hdls, minor breaks, 4x23x22" 360.00
Basket, slightly domed base, cvd hdls, att NY, 8x14", EX..........2,600.00
Basket, sq base w/4 runners, cvd hdls, MA, 16x21" dia 800.00
Basket, tight weave, natural, cone-shaped bottom, att SDL, 13x24" .. 2,650.00
Basket, woven splint w/leather lining, NH or ME, #20 in ink, 19th C, 22" L 400.00
Bench, milk, pnt pine, splayed legs w/V cutouts, CB, 19th C, 13x37x12"...825.00
Bonnet, blk w/ribbon tie, illegible stamp mk 450.00
Box, 2-finger, mellow/natural, copper tacks, 3¼" 635.00
Box, 2-finger, red pnt, copper tacks, 19th C, 2¼x5½".................. 725.00
Box, 3-finger, golden brn, copper tacks, sm loss, 11"..................... 700.00
Box, 3-finger, gr pnt, copper tacks, 8x11"...................................1,035.00
Box, 3-finger, maple, gray pnt, copper tacks, NE, sm losses, 2x8". 380.00
Box, 3-finger, maple, VG gr pnt, copper tacks, NE, 2⅞x7⅞"........ 600.00
Box, 3-finger, pine/maple, dk stain, copper tacks, NE, 1⅝x3¾".... 880.00
Box, 3-finger, pine/maple, red pnt, iron tacks, 19th C, 2x5x3", NM..3,650.00
Box, 3-finger, varnish, copper tacks, late 19th C, 2½x6¼x4" 775.00
Box, 4-finger, bl-gr pnt, copper tacks, NE, sm losses, 3⅜x8⅞" ...2,000.00
Box, 4-finger, maple, gr pnt, copper tacks, NE, 4⅝x11⅜"..........2,200.00
Box, 4-finger, natural, copper tacks, NE appl label, 5½x13⅜" ...2,100.00
Box, 4-finger, natural finish, copper tacks, 13½" 1,100.00
Box, 4-finger, natural w/stained lid, copper tacks, 4x10" 435.00
Box, 4-finger, olive gray pnt over stain, copper tacks, 4¼x11" 575.00
Box, 4-finger, pine, natural, copper tacks, NL, old rpr, 5x12x8"... 800.00
Box, 4-finger, red-brn stain, copper tacks, 4x10⅜"........................ 700.00
Box, 4-finger, red pnt on maple/pine, NE, late 1800s, 2x5x3"...2,800.00

Box, 4-finger, red stain on pine top and bottom, maple sides, copper tacks, probably Enfield, New Hampshire, early twentieth century, 4¼x11⅜", $4,320.00. (Photo courtesy Skinner Auctioneers and Appraisers of Antiques and Fine Art)

Box, 4-finger, scrubbed salmon to cream pnt, brass tacks, 5x12x9" .. 950.00
Box, 5-finger, maple, brn stain, copper tacks, NE, crack, 6x15" ... 950.00
Box, 5-finger, red pnt, copper tacks, 5¾x13⅜x5¾" 6,600.00
Box, 5-finger, yel pnt on maple/pine, copper tacks, 5⅝x13½" ...6,600.00
Box, seed, red pnt on pine, hinged lid, wire hdl, dvtl, bl label 900.00
Box, spit, yel pnt on maple/pine, copper tacks, lapped sides, NY, 14" L....950.00
Box, wood, chrome yel pnt on pine/maple, dvtl, SDL, 1840s, 33x27x18" ..32,500.00
Bucket, red pnt, staved, metal bands, dmn escutcheons, att, 6x8" ..750.00

Bucket, sap, wood staves w/iron bands, mustard pnt, EF, 11x12" .515.00
Bucket, sponging on yel, pine staves, 2 iron hoops, wire hdl, EF, 10" ..725.00
Bucket, wooden staves w/2 bl metal hoops, mini, 3½x4½"........1,000.00
Bucket, wooden staves w/iron bands, gr pnt/bail hdl, 1800s, att, 10" ..575.00
Bucket, wooden staves w/metal bands, tapered sides/bail hdl, w/lid, 10"..480.00
Candlestand, birch, trn shaft, snake legs, pnt traces, EF, 24x14" dia..3,000.00
Carrier, 3-finger, maple, old varnish, copper tacks, 1850s, 9¼" .1,200.00
Carrier, gr pnt on pine, 2-section, wrought hdl, dvtl, 4x32x8"..2,100.00
Carrier, herb, 3-finger, fixed hdl, orig patina, 9x9½" 1,450.00
Carrier, maple/hickory/pine, red stain, fixed hdl, 1850s, 10½x12"...660.00
Carrier, pine, rect/nailed, ash swing hdl w/tacks, NY, 8x10x7" 325.00
Chair, arm, #1, 3-slat bk, rpl tape seat, old varnish, 28" 440.00
Chair, arm, #7, 5 arched slats, acorn finials, tape seat, ML........1,800.00
Chair, arm, yel/red traces on maple, 2-slat, tilters, NL, 26", 3 for ... 3,500.00
Chair, side, 3-slat bk, tiger maple/maple, tape seat, 1840s, 39½" ...1,000.00
Chair, side, birch, 3-slat bk, tilters, rush seat, att EF, 41"..........2,000.00
Chair, side, birch/cherry, 3-slat, cane seat, old red, EF, 1830s, 41" ..2,000.00

Chair, weaver's, Union Village, Ohio, circa 1840, 39½", $11,400.00. (Photo courtesy Cowan's Auctions, Inc. on LiveAuctioneers.com)

Chest, cherry drw fronts (4) on poplar, bracket base, OH, 46x39x19"....2,000.00
Churn, bl pnt, bbl form, missing hdl & door, 24x21" dia 850.00
Churn, red pnt, crank hdl, att, 30x20x20" 600.00
Cloak, dk red wool w/shoulder cape, late 19th C, 47" 650.00
Cupboard, pine, panel door, trn cherry pull, rfn, 32x18x12" ...1,300.00
Cupboard, pine, rpt yel, 2 2-brd doors, rpl knobs, 76x31x18" 900.00
Desk, cherry/pine, side drw, L trn legs, 19th C, 37x31x24" 550.00
Desk, writing, pine, pigeonhole int, att SDL, rfn, 36x32x22" ...1,200.00
Footstool, trn legs/stretchers, dk varnish, rprs, ML, 6x11⅜x12".... 400.00
Grinder, herb, CI boat shape & wheel, trn maple hdls, 1820-40s, 7x15"...450.00
Hall tree, grad pegs on pine 8-sided post, shoe-ft base, old pnt, att .. 635.00
Highchair, birch, 3-slat bk, spindle arms, red traces, pegged, 37"...1,725.00
Kneeler, dvtl cherry, NH, 25x15½" 595.00
Latch, gate, wht pnt traces on wrought iron EF, 13⅜" 120.00
Mirror, dressing, dk brn wood, on stand w/arched legs, EF, 16x12x8" ... 360.00
Niddy noddy, wood w/cvd inscriptions, CB, 17¾x11½" 325.00
Nightstand, walnut, trn legs, Hancock Community, 27x18x17"...950.00
Rocker, #1, dk walnut, tape bk & seat, NY decal, child's, 29½" 1,800.00
Rocker, #5, 4-slat, acorn finials, shaped arms, tape seat, 38½"...... 465.00
Rocker, arm, #0, old dk stain, ML, late 19th C..........................1,650.00
Rocker, arm, #5, 3-slat bk, arms w/mushroom caps, rpl tape seat, ML...435.00
Rocker, arm, #6, 4 arched slats, rpl seat, orig finish, NY 850.00
Rocker, arm, #7, 3 arched slats, rattan seat, ML, 42½" 775.00
Rocker, arm, #7, Mt Lebanon, NY, blk & burgundy tape seat, 40"... 975.00
Rocker, arm, #7, shawl bar, 4-slat bk, tape seat, ML, ca 1900, 41½" ...515.00
Rocker, arm, #7, shawl bar, tape seat & bk, NY, late 1800s, 40" ..465.00
Rocker, arm, red-brn on birch, 3-slat bk, splint seat, ME, 41"...3,500.00
Rocker, armless, #4, 3 arched slats, paper rush seat, 34½" 230.00
Settee, woven seat & bk, dk varnish, ML, ca 1890, 34x41" 12,000.00
Shelves, corner, tiered, wood, pnt, EF, 30x20x9⅛" 4,750.00
Stand, cherry, drw, trn legs, OH, 1860, rprs, 29x21x18" 360.00
Stand, cherry, rnd top/birdcage/tapered post/tripod, ML, 1830s, 23x22"..22,325.00

Stand, oak, 1-drw, tapered legs, brass knob, rfn, 29x21x15" 1,175.00
Stand, red stain on pine/birch, 16" sq top, sq legs, 1830s, 26" ...2,115.00
Stove, CI, rnded sides, front hinged door, tapered legs, 20x34x12"..600.00
Swift, maple w/yel traces, trn cup on top, 19th C, 25-30" 395.00
Table, maple/cherry, 3 arched ft, 38x23" dia 850.00
Table, work, 3-brd top, 3 dvtl drws, orig red on base, att ML, 62x31" 4,000.00
Table, work, birch/tiger birch, pinned legs, EF, 37x40x12"+drop leaves..3,250.00
Table, work, butternut, drw, old pnt on base, rfn top, 29x30x20"..1,175.00
Tray, sewing, blk walnut, canted sides/compartment, EF, 1870s, 3x10x8"..395.00

Shaving Mugs

Between 1865 and 1920, owning a personalized shaving mug was the order of the day, and the 'occupationals' were the most prestigious. The majority of men having occupational mugs would often frequent the barber shop several times a week, where their mugs were clearly visible for all to see in the barber's rack. As a matter of fact, this display was in many ways the index of the individual town or neighborhood.

During the first 20 years, blank mugs were almost entirely imported from France, Germany, and Austria and were hand painted in this country. Later on, some china was produced by local companies. It is noteworthy that American vitreous china is inferior to the imported Limoges and is subject to extreme crazing. Artists employed by the American barber supply companies were for the most part extremely talented and capable of executing any design the owner required, depicting his occupation, fraternal affiliation, or preferred sport. When the mug was completed, the name and the gold trim were always added in varying degrees, depending on the price paid by the customer. This price was determined by the barber who added his markup to that of the barber-supply company. As mentioned above, the popularity of the occupational shaving mug diminished with the advent of World War I and the introduction by Gillette of the safety razor. Later followed the blue laws forcing barber shops to close on Sundays, thereby eliminating the political and social discussions for which they were so well noted.

Occupational shaving mugs are the most sought after of the group which would also include those with sport affiliations. Fraternal mugs, although desirable, do not command the same price as the occupationals. Occasionally, you will find the owner's occupation together with his fraternal affiliation. This combination could add anywhere between 25% to 50% to the price, which is dependent on the execution of the painting, rarity of the subject, and detail. Some subjects can be done very simply; others can be done in extreme detail, commanding substantially higher prices. It is fair to say, however, that the rarity of the occupation will dictate the price. Mugs with heavily worn gold lose between 20% and 30% of their value immediately. This would not apply to the gold trim around the rim, but to the loss of the name itself. Our advisor for this category is Burton Handelsman; he is listed in the Directory under New York.

Decorative, frog smoking pipe & holding fishing pole, gold trim ..1,200.00
Decorative, frogs on high-wheel bicycles (comic), 3⅝"..............1,500.00
Decorative, photographic man's portrait transfer, gold trim 1,100.00
Fraternal, 4 clubs/organizations, much gold, T&V Limoges 1,000.00
Fraternal, 7 varied symbols from Masons/Knights Templar, Germany ..600.00
Fraternal, Indian in headdress/Jr Order of United Am Mechanics.....215.00
Fraternal, Knights of Pythis & Odd Fellows w/flowers, Vienna 850.00
Fraternal, Masonic symbols/flowers/foliage, name on banner, worn gold ...60.00
Fraternal, Odd Fellows, skull & crossbones, 4" 120.00
Fraternal, Order of Owls (3 owls on limb), T&V Limoges........... 725.00
Occupational, bakers (2) in wht reserve, name/gold scrolls on pk, 4" ...790.00
Occupational, bar scene w/5 figures, detailed/much gold, ½3" 600.00
Occupational, barber shaving man, detailed scene, EX gold, 3⅝" ..1,200.00
Occupational, bartender & 2 customers in bar scene, unmk, 3¾". 360.00
Occupational, baseball scene, 3¾" 1,650.00

Occupational, boxer w/arms extended, gold borders/pk wrap, KT&K . 1,950.00
Occupational, cotton gin operator w/gold, MIG........................ 2,350.00
Occupational, daredevil, man falling w/parachute, much gold. 45,000.00
Occupational, dentist, pr of dentures, name, CFM/GDM 500.00
Occupational, doctor attending patient, gold trim, Austria, 1897.... 2,100.00
Occupational, early motorized moving van, much gold, unmk . 3,600.00
Occupational, early open touring car, 3½" 715.00
Occupational, farmer/horses/plow, CH Parke, gilt trim, 3¾" 275.00
Occupational, fire department hose reel, 3¾" 990.00
Occupational, horsedrawn coal cart & driver, Leonard Vienna, 4".. 145.00
Occupational, horsedrawn moving company wagon, lt wear to gold . 1,000.00
Occupational, house painters working on brick home, Limoges.. 1,200.00
Occupational, man in buggy driving 2 horses, 3⅝" 780.00
Occupational, man in early open car, rpr to base rim, 3½" 480.00
Occupational, man standing by bull, 3¼" 500.00
Occupational, man working at bottle-capper, gold borders, 1913.. 2,400.00
Occupational, man working w/hose at plow, EX art, 4" 1,000.00
Occupational, milk man driving horse-drawn wagon, T&V Limoges .. 800.00
Occupational, minister, Bible & 2 Xd swords, much gold, T&V . 500.00
Occupational, Naval Master at arms, blk wrap, T&V Limoges. 1,950.00
Occupational, pig & steer's head, Heckel Bros K-C Mo, 4" 110.00
Occupational, policeman standing w/billy club, Vienna 950.00

Occupational, railroad brakeman, company mark on base, $1,100.00. (Photo courtesy Glass-Works Auctions)

Occupational, railroad locomotive engine w/gold, Koken............. 450.00
Occupational, railroad signal pole & name, T&V Limoges 2,400.00
Occupational, shining lt bulb, 3"... 600.00
Occupational, sign painter at work, Koken Barber Supply 1,950.00
Occupational, stable hand, boy w/bucket in stable, D&C France . 480.00
Occupational, steamboat in choppy waters, T&V Limoges..... 1,650.00
Occupational, tailor shop scene w/6 people, T&V France, 3½" ... 375.00
Occupational, trolley car w/2 men in bl uniforms, name in gold, 3⅝".. 1,020.00
Occupational, tuba player, gold trim 1,200.00

Shawnee

The Shawnee Pottery Company operated in Zanesville, Ohio, from 1937 to 1961. They produced inexpensive novelty ware (vases, flowerpots, and figurines) as well as a very successful line of figural cookie jars, creamers, and salt and pepper shakers. They also produced three dinnerware lines, the first of which, Valencia, was designed by Louise Bauer in 1937 for Sears & Roebuck. A starter set was given away with the purchase of one of their refrigerators. Second and most popular was the Corn line. The original design was called White Corn. In 1946 the line was expanded and the color changed to a more natural yellow hue. It was marketed under the name Corn King, and it was produced from 1946 to 1954. Then the colors were changed again. Kernels became a lighter yellow and shucks a darker green. This variation was called Corn Queen. Their third dinnerware line, produced after 1954, was called Lobsterware. It was made in either black, brown, or gray; lobsters were usually applied to serving pieces and accessory items.

For further study we recommend these books: *The Collector's Guide to Shawnee Pottery* (Collector Books) by Janice and Duane Vanderbilt, who are listed in the Directory under Indiana; and *Shawnee Pottery, An Identifi-* *cation and Value Guide,* (Collector Books) by our advisors for this category, Jim and Bev Mangus; they are listed under Ohio.

Cookie Jars

Basketweave, bl w/decal, USA, 7½", $110 to 125.00
Dutch Boy (Jack), gold & decals, mk USA, $450 to 475.00
Dutch Girl (Jill), bl skirt, gold & decals, mk USA, $375 to......... 400.00
Fruit basket, Shawnee 84, 8", $125 to 150.00
Great Northern Girl, bl trim, tulips, Great Northern USA 1026 . 425.00
Jack, bl pants, USA, $80 to 100.00
Jack, striped pants, gold & decals, mk USA, $400 to 450.00
Jack, striped pants, mk USA $190 to 200.00
Jack, w/gold & decals, USA, $400 to 450.00
Jack Tar, blk hair, w/gold, USA, 12", $1,150 to 1,200.00
Jill, yel skirt, USA, $100 to 125.00
Puss in Boots, maroon bow, w/long tail, Puss 'n Boots, $195 to.... 225.00
Smiley the Pig, clover bud, USA, $550 to 575.00
Smiley the Pig, w/chrysanthemums, USA, $375 to 400.00
Smiley the Pig, w/fly, gold & decals, mk USA, $800 to............. 1,000.00
Winnie the Pig, shamrocks, red collar w/gold, USA, $900 to 950.00
Winnie the Pig, w/bl collar, USA, $325 to 400.00

Corn Line

Bowl, cereal/soup, King, Shawnee 94, $42 to................................ 45.00
Bowl, mixing, Queen, Shawnee 5, $20 to 22.00
Butter dish, King, Shawnee 72, $50 to.. 55.00

Casserole, King, #74, $50.00 to $60.00. (Photo courtesy Belhorn Auction Services, LLC on LiveAuctioneers.com)

Cookie jar, King or Queen, Shawnee 66, $100 to.......................... 150.00
Corn Roast set, Queen, unmk, $165 to... 175.00
Cup, Queen, Shawnee 90, $25 to 30.00
Jug, Queen, Shawnee 71, 40-oz, $60 to... 65.00
Plate, Queen, Shawnee 68, 10", $30 to 35.00
Platter, King, Shawnee 96, 12", $50 to... 55.00
Shakers, pr, 3¼", $25 to 28.00
Shakers, Queen, unmk, 5¼", $30 to 35.00

Kitchenware

Batter bowl, Snowflake, USA, $20 to 25.00
Bowl, mixing, medallion on lid, Kenwood 940, $40 to.................. 45.00
Canister, Dutch decal, USA, 2-qt, $45 to..................................... 50.00
Canister, Snowflake, USA, 2-qt, $45 to.. 55.00
Canister, yel, USA, 1-qt, $50 to... 55.00
Coffeepot, Pennsylvania Dutch, USA 52, $240 to 270.00
Creamer, Flower & Fern, USA, $18 to 20.00
Creamer, Puss 'n Boots, #85, 4", $65 to.. 90.00
Creamer, Sunflower, USA, $65 to 70.00
Grease jar, Flower & Fern, w/lid, USA, $38 to 40.00
Jug, Bo Peep, USA Pat Bo Peep, 40-oz, $85 to 90.00
Jug, Fern, USA, 2-qt, $45 to... 50.00
Jug, Sunflower, ball form, USA, 48-oz, $75 to 80.00
Jug, yel, bulb, USA, $95 to... 100.00
Pie bird, $60 to... 75.00
Pitcher, Charlie Chicken, decals w/gold, mk Chanticleer, $330 to .. 360.00

Pitcher, Laurel Wreath, USA, $22 to.................................... 24.00
Pitcher, Smiley, red neckerchief, apple, mk Pat Smiley USA, $230 to...240.00
Pitcher, Stars & Stripes, USA, $16 to................................ 18.00
Pitcher, utility, Snowflake, USA, 24-oz, 5⅛", $40 to 45.00
Salt box, Fern, w/lid, USA, $120 to................................... 125.00
Salt box, Flower & Fern, w/lid, USA, $95 to................................ 100.00
Shakers, Chanticleer, decor w/gold, pr $150 to............................ 165.00
Shakers, Dutch Kids, bl w/gold, pr $55 to................................ 55.00
Shakers, Fern, USA, 7-oz, pr $30 to................................... 35.00
Shakers, Smiley the Pig, gr neckerchief, 5", pr, $125 to 135.00
Shakers, Wave Pattern, yel, bl or gr, pr $30 to...................... 35.00
Teapot, Flower & Fern, USA, 2-cup, $30 to........................... 35.00
Teapot, Snowflake, USA, 2-cup, $50 to.............................. 55.00
Tumbler, Stars & Stripes, USA, 3", $12 to................................ 14.00

Lobsterware

Casserole, French, #904, two-quart, $25.00 to $30.00. (Photo courtesy Sharon Brescia, eBay seller mudslide336)

Bowl, batter, w/hdl, 928, $50 to.. 55.00
Creamer/sugar bowl, 910, set $85 to..................................... 90.00
Hors d'oeuvres holder, USA, 7¼", $250 to 275.00
Salad set, mk 924, 9-pc, $130 to...................................... 135.00
Utility jar, 907, $24 to 26.00

Valencia

Bowl, onion soup, w/lid, $22 to.. 24.00
Candleholder, bulb style, ea.. 22.00
Compote, 12", $26 to... 28.00
Egg cup, unmk, $18 to.. 20.00
Nappy, unmk, 8½", $18 to... 20.00
Plate, chop, 13", $20 to.. 25.00
Plate, dinner, 10¾", $12 to... 14.00
Shakers, unmk, pr $22 to.. 24.00
Spoon, $38 to... 40.00
Teapot, unmk, $45 to... 55.00
Tray, utility, $18 to... 20.00

Miscellaneous

Bank, bear tumbling, $210 to 240.00
Carafe, blk, on metal stand, $55 to 60.00
Cigarette box, emb trademk, USA, $240 to 270.00
Clock, medallion, pk & gold, $180 to 195.00
Clock, trellis, $115 to 120.00
Figurine, bear tumbling, decals w/gold, $230 to 240.00
Figurine, rabbit, decals w/gold, $230 to 240.00
Figurine, raccoon, $90 to 95.00
Lamp, Champ the Dog, $20 to 25.00
Lamp, native w/drum, $190 to 200.00
Planter, fish, USA 717, $35 to 40.00
Planter, gazelle, glossy, Shawnee 840, $50 to 70.00
Vase, quilted w/fleurettes at intersections, 6" 40.00
Wall pocket, birds at birdhouse, w/gold, USA 830, $25 to.............. 30.00

Shearwater

Since 1928 generations of the Peter, Walter, and James McConnell Anderson families have been producing figurines and artwares in their studio at Ocean Springs, Mississippi. Their work is difficult to date. Figures from the '20s and '30s won critical acclaim and have continued to be made to the present time. Early marks include a die-stamped 'Shearwater' in a dime-sized circle, a similar ink stamp, and a half-circle mark. Any older item may still be ordered in the same glazes as it was originally produced, so many pieces on the market today may be relatively new. However, the older marks are not currently in use. Currently produced black and pirate figurines are marked with a hand-incised 'Shearwater' and/or a cipher formed with an 'S' whose bottom curve doubles as the top loop of a 'P' formed by the addition of an upright placed below and to the left of the S. Many are dated, '93, for example. These figures are generally valued at $35.00 to $50.00 and are available at the pottery or by mail order. New decorated and carved pieces are very expensive, starting at $400.00 to $500.00 for a six-inch pot.

Bowl, bl alkaline, incurvate rim, hairline crack, 1950s, 3⅜x8" 150.00
Bowl, blk & wht scrolls, 3½x9" 3,525.00
Bowl, blk, P Anderson, 1930s, 3½x9" 480.00
Bowl, fruit/flowers/vines cvd on gr w/brn wash, W Anderson, 5x7".4,250.00
Bowl, gr mottle, invt cone form w/ft, late 20th C, 3x8" 180.00
Bowl, scarabs, brn & tan, sgn JA, 1992, 2⅛x5½" 550.00
Bowl, waves, blk/cobalt/wht/brn, att W Anderson, 2x6"...........3,820.00
Bust, Mayan boy, beige/celadon mottle, 7" 415.00
Figurine, Bathing Beauty, Oldfield series, WI Anderson, 1970s, 6"..72.50
Figurine, black lady dancing, 5"................................... 42.00
Figurine, lion, alkaline bl & deep marine bl, 5½x13½x4" 2,750.00
Figurine, man w/plow, mc, 1989 Christmas M Griffen, 5⅜x7".....195.00
Figurine, seagull, incised SP-9Z, 5x9"............................. 180.00
Figurine, stout woman w/basket on head, turq/bl/yel, 6" 210.00
Lamp base, fish on gr, sgn Mac (Mac Anderson), 10x9"..........13,200.00
Vase, birds, beetles, & flowers, blk & brn on ivory, ca 1935, 9" ..14,400.00

Vase, carved foliage, cast by Peter Anderson, decorated by Walter Anderson, circa 1950, 6½", $2,160.00. (Photo courtesy Neal Auction Company on LiveAuctioneers.com)

Vase, Earth, Sea & Sky, gr & tan, mid-20th C, 12x7¼" 11,750.00
Vase, gr & brn matt, ftd, 6½" 200.00
Vase, gr mottle, bulb base, 5¾x3¼" 115.00
Vase, gr, ovoid, P Anderson, ca 1940, 8" 395.00
Vase, lappet design, brn & cream, bulb, 6½x7½" 4,800.00
Vase, lt purple, elongated w/melon ribs, 6¼"....................... 360.00
Vase, pelicans, bl & turq mottle, 2 tight lines, 7x6" 6,600.00
Vase, prominent finger rings on upper half, wht, P Anderson, 6x3½"...420.00
Vase, turq & gunmetal, gourd form, 3¼x2" 275.00
Vase, Wistera (bl-gr), ovoid w/flared rim, 1960s, 6¾" 120.00
Vase, Wisteria (pk-bl), rim-to-hip hdls, 1928-30, drilled, 11½" ...850.00

Sheet Music

Sheet music is often collected more for its colorful lithographed covers, than for the music itself. Transportation songs (which have pictures or illustrations of trains, ships, and planes), ragtime and blues, comic characters (especially Disney), sports, political, and expositions are eagerly sought after. Much of the sheet music on the market today is valued at under $5.00; some of the better examples are listed here. For more information refer to *Sheet Music Reference & Price Guide*, by Anna Marie Guiheen and Marie-Reine A. Pafik. Values are given for examples in at least near-mint condition.

Anywhere in USA Is Home to Me, SE Clark, patriotic cover, 1910.... 15.00
Babes on Broadway, Freed & Lane, Judy Garland photo cover, 1942.. 10.00
Battle in the Sky, J Luxton, WWI cover, 1916 .... 15.00
Because, Horwitz & Bowers, Irving Berlin, Leff & Berlin cover, 1926... 10.00
Billiken March, Gideon, Pfeiffer & March cover, 1908.................. 15.00
Blue Christmas, B Hayes & J Johnson, Morgan photo cover, 1948.. 13.00
Brazil, Bob Russell, Saludos Amigos (Disney) cover, 1939 .... 25.00
California Here I Come, Jolson/DeSylva/Meyer, Al Jolson cover, 1924... 10.00
Carolina Cake Walk, G Mears, blk cover, 1898.......................... 22.00
Close, Cole porter, from movie: Rosalie, 1937 ....6.00
Davy Jones' Locker, HW Petrie, 1901 .... 15.00
Der Fuehrer's Face, Donald Duck in Nutzi Land, Disney.............. 25.00
Dixie Rag, Giblin, Pfeiffer cover, 1913....................................... 15.00
Don't Let me Down, Lennon & McCartney, photo cover, 1969.... 30.00
Down by the Erie Canal, Geo M Cohan, Cohan cover 15.00
Elevator Man, Irving Berlin, Pfeiffer & Berlin cover 15.00
Everybody's Happy When the Moon Shines, Kerry Mills, 1909..... 10.00
Fare Thee Well Molly Darling, WD Cobb & K Mills, 1902........... 10.00
Flapper Blues, Bob Alterman & Claude Johnson, Deco cover, 1922 . 10.00
Go Down Moses, HT Burleigh, black face cover, 1917 .... 10.00
Golliwog's Cake Walk, Claude Debussy, black face cover, 1908 .... 16.00
Happy Times, Silvia Fine, Danny Kaye photo cover, 1949............ 12.00
Hesitation D'Amour, Barrie, Pfeiffer Art Deco cover, 1914 .... 15.00
Hi-Yo Silver, The Lone Ranger's Song, 1938................................ 20.00
I Ain't Gwin Ter Work No Mo, black face cover, 1900.................. 20.00
I Didn't Raise My Ford To Be a Jitney, Jack Frost, 1915 .... 25.00

I'd Rather Be with Teddy in the Jungle, photo: Robt. Higgins and Mae Melville, 1909, $10.00. (Photo courtesy Anna Marie Guiheen and Marie-Reine A. Pafik)

I'll Be a Soldier, James Thatcher, WWI cover, 1915....................... 12.00
I'm Done w/Rag-Time, Fred Stein & Clas Robinson, 1900 .... 10.00
Indiana Moon, Benny Davis & Isham Jones, Perret cover, 1923.... 10.00
It's Not What You Were It's What You Are Today, D Marion, 1898... 15.00
I Wake Up Smiling, Edgar Leslie & Fred E Ahlert, 1933 ....7.00
I Wuv a Wabbit, M Berle/E Drake/P Martell, Barbelle cover, 1945 .10.00
Jubilee, S Adams & H Carmichael, Mae West caricature cover, 1937 ..10.00
La Cucaracha, Washington, Wallace Beery & Fay Wray cover, 1934.. 10.00
Letter to Heaven, Lizzie Paine, 1888... 15.00
Log Cabin Song, Alexander Kile, 1840.. 100.00
Love's Sweet Dream, Drumheller, Pfeiffer cover, 1912 .... 10.00
Make That Engine Stop at Louisville, Lewis/Meyer/Richmond, 1914...20.00
Matrimony Rag, Edgar Leslie & Lews F Muir 10.00
Motor March, Geo Rosey, 1906.. 30.00
My Gal Sal, Paul Dresser, R Haworth & V Mature photo cover, 1932..30.00
Oh Mamma Buy Me That, Al Hillman, 1890............................... 10.00

Paddy Duffy's Cart, E Harrigan & D Braham, 1881 .... 15.00
Road that Leads to Love, Irving Berlin, Berlin cover, 1917............ 10.00
Since Home Rule Came to Ireland, Kelly & Mullane, artist cover, 1914.. 15.00
Song of South, Coslow & Johnston, Disney movie cover, 1946..... 12.00
Take Me on a Buick Honeymoon, blk, transportation cover, 1922 ..25.00
Throw Him Down McCloskey, JW Kelly, 1890 .... 15.00
War Babies, Al Jolson, Jolson & WWI cover, 1916........................ 15.00

Shell-Craft Collectibles

For thousands of years people have been intrigued with shells. With over 100,000 species worldwide, one can find an incredible variety of colors, shapes, patterns, and textures. Shells were not only collected for their beauty but were also used in other ways. Pearl buttons and cameo jewelry are examples of shells used for ornamentation. Shells also had practical uses: inkwells, coin purses, snuff boxes, handles for cutlery, caviar bowls, napkin rings, pincushions, paperweights, and TV lights. Decorative uses were mirrors, picture frames, and shell pictures. Shells were even used to represent money in primitive societies.

During the Victorian era shell-craft was very popular. Because of the fragile nature of those pieces, they have become more scarce. Sailors' valentines, love tokens, shell boxes, and miniature furniture pieces can bring hundreds of dollars and can be found in some museums' collections. However, antique and vintage as well as recent pieces can be found in antique shops, malls, and on the internet. During the fifties and sixties, many novelty shell-craft pieces were offered and were widely popular. Not all shell-craft boxes, sailing ships, carved cowries, shell-craft mirrors, and shells painted with scenes are old. Unless otherwise stated, our values are for antique or vintage examples.

Our advisor for this category is Ralph Winslow. He is listed in the Directory under Arizona.

Bowl, Vict, Niagara Falls, 4" 30.00
Box, Sailor's Valentine, 4½" 120.00
Calendar, heart shape, Atlantic City, 4" 20.00
Frame, picture of steamship, 6" 71.00
Furniture, Vict, mini dresser, 5" 122.00
Inkwell, cvd fish, souvenir, 3" 75.00
Inkwell, St Louis World's Fair 1904, 6" 28.00

Inkwell, with anchor thermometer, 8", $100.00. (Photo courtesy Apple Tree Auction Center on LiveAuctioneers.com)

Lamp, conch shell, Miami FL, 1950s, 8" 39.00
Lamp, Souv Chicago World's Fair 1933, 5"...................................... 35.00
Painting on shell, Indian, St Louis World's Fair 1904, 5" 21.00
Painting on shell, Souv Lakeside OH, 4" 13.00
Painting, Vict, ship, brass fr, Newport RI, 9"................................... 169.00
Paperweight, bsk black child w/watermelon, Chester, Iowa, 4¼" ... 35.00
Paperweight, bsk child, St Louis World's Fair 1904, 4".................... 47.00
Pearlized, Bell, Camp Logan, WWI, 2" 15.00
Pearlized, cvd Chinese junk, 6" 18.00

Pincushion, conch shell, souvenir, 7" 31.00
Rattle & whistle, Souv Catskill, 7" 15.00
TV lamp, blk Americana, 5" 80.00

Shelley

In 1872 Joseph Shelley became partners with James Wileman, owner of Foley China Works, creating Wileman & Co. in Stoke-on-Trent. Twelve years later James Wileman withdrew from the company, though the firm continued to use his name until 1925 when it became known as Shelley Potteries, Ltd. Like many successful nineteenth-century English potteries, this firm continued to produce useful household wares as well as dinnerware of considerable note. In 1896 the beautiful Dainty White shape was introduced, and it is regarded by many as synonymous with the name Shelley. In addition to the original Dainty (six-flute) design, other lovely shapes were produced: Ludlow (14-flute), Oleander (petal shape), Stratford (12-flute), Queen Anne (with eight angular panels), Ripon (with its distinctive pedestal), and the 1930s shapes of Vogue, Eve, and Regent. Though often overlooked, striking earthenware was produced under the direction of Frederick Rhead and later Walter Slater and his son Eric. Many notable artists contributed their talents in designing unusual, attractive wares: Rowland Morris, Mabel Lucie Attwell, and Hilda Cowham, to name but a few.

In 1966 Allied English Potteries acquired control of the Shelley Company, and by 1967 the last of the exquisite Shelley China had been produced to honor remaining overseas orders. In 1971 Allied English Potteries merged with the Doulton group.

It had to happen: Shelley forgeries! Chris Davenport, author of *Shelley Pottery, The Later Years*, reports seeing Mocha-shape cups and saucers with the Shelley mark. However, on close examination it is evident that the mark has been applied to previously unmarked wares too poorly done to have ever left the Shelley pottery. This Shelley mark can actually be 'felt,' as the refiring is not done at the correct temperature to allow it to be fully incorporated into the glaze. (Beware! These items are often seen on internet auction sites.)

Some Shelley patterns (Dainty Blue, Bridal Rose, Blue Rock) have been seen on Royal Albert and Queensware pieces. These companies are part of the Royal Doulton Group.

Note: Objects with lids are measured to the top of the finial unless stated otherwise. Rose Spray and Bridal Rose are the same pattern. A five-piece place setting includes a 10½" dinner plate, 8" dessert/salad plate, 6" bread & butter plate, cup, and saucer.

Key:
LF — Late Foley   sh — shape
FMN — Forget-Me-Not   Trio — cup, saucer & 8" plate unless
HC — Hilda Cowham   otherwise stated
MLA — Mabel Lucie Attwell   w — Wileman, pre-1910
RPFMN — Rose, Pansy
    Forget-Me-Not

Advertising figure, Shelley Lady seated on ped holding c/s, 11½" .. 7,465.00
Ashtray, Ocean Yacht Race, Bermuda, 1960 commemorative, 5½" dia ... 20.00
Ashtray, Summer Glory (pk), 3 rests, #1338?, 3½" dia 22.00
Bell, Morning Glory, Ludlow sh, 5½" 365.00
Bowl, cream soup, Dainty Bl, w/hdls, #051, w/6½" liner 60.00
Bowl, fruit, Intarsio, Nouveau w/silver-banded rim, #3604, W, 9¾" ...600.00
Bowl, fruit, Melody Chintz, horizontal ribs, #8809, 3x8½" 95.00
Butter dish, Rose & Red Daisy, Dainty sh, #13425, 6¼" 80.00
Butter dish, Stocks, Dainty sh, #13428, 7¼" 125.00
Butter pat, Blue Rock, #13591, 3" 55.00
Butter pat, Campanula, Dainty sh, #13886, 3¾" 120.00
Butter pat, Dainty Mauve, Dainty sh, #051/M, 3¾" 198.00

Butter pat, HP mc flowers (vivid), #13092, 3" 67.00
Butter pat, Lily of the Valley, Dainty sh, #13822, 3¾" 82.00
Butter pat, Rambler Rose, Dainty sh, #13671, 3½" 75.00
Cake plate, Drifting Leaves, Richmond sh, tab hdls, #13848, 10" 45.00
Cake plate, English Lakes, Cambridge sh, angular tab hdls, #13788 .... 45.00
Cake plate, Heavenly Blue, Dainty sh, #14165, 8x10½" 155.00
Cake plate, Wildflowers, Dainty sh, angular tab hdls, #13668 .... 120.00
Cake stand, Blue Rock, Dainty sh, ped ft, #13591, $125 to 165.00
Candy/sweet meat dish, Shamrocks, Dainty sh, #14114, 5¾" 65.00
Children's ware, feeding dish, children w/wood train & cart, HC, 8" . 100.00
Children's ware, MLA creamer, Boo-Boo, sgn, 6" 158.00
Children's ware, MLA tea set, Boo-Boo, mushroom teapot+cr/sug, sgn... 555.00
Children's ware, mug, Little Boy Blue w/verse, 2⅞" 55.00
Children's ware, trio, mc train, Puff Puff Puff, 5¾" plate, 3-pc 98.00
Cigarette holder, Rambler Rose, Dainty sh, #13671, 2⅛" 37.50
Coffee set, Jungle, Daisy sh, #6088, pot+cr/sug+2 c/s 395.00
Coffeepot, Deco decor in yel & blk (bold), Vogue sh, #11776, 7¼" 575.00
Coffeepot, Sheraton, Gainsborough w/gooseneck spout, #13291, 7½". 200.00
Coffeepot, Wildflowers, Dainty sh, #2295, 6½" 395.00
Coffeepot, Wine Grape, Gainsborough w/gooseneck spout, #13698, 7½"...300.00
Coffeepot, Woodland, Perth shape w/rich gold, #13348, 7" 155.00

Coffeepot, Wreath of Leaves, Gainsborough shape, #13577, $135.00 to $185.00. (Photo courtesy Time Was Antiques, www.timewasantiques.net)

Compote, Melody Chintz, ped ft, #8809, 3x7¾", $95 to 185.00
Condiment set, Begonia, Dainty shape, #13427, s&p+horseradish+stand..450.00
Cream soup & 6½" liner, Carnation, Oleander sh, $100 to 135.00
Creamer, Imari, rich cobalt, red & gold, Alexander sh, w, 4" 60.00
Creamer/sugar bowl, Dainty Brown, #051/B 78.00
Cremer/sugar bowl, Dainty White w/yel polka dots..................... 110.00
Crested ware, coach, Charabanc, Monach, Doncaster, #352 .... 70.00
Crested ware, comical cat, Long Eaton, 5½" 55.00
Crested ware, elephant w/trunk down, Crest of Dawlish, #363, 2½"..100.00
Crested ware, pot, Shrewsbury crest, LF, 2" dia............................6.00
Cup/saucer, Bailey's Sweet Pea, Dainty sh, gr hdl, #2445 .... 425.00
Cup/saucer, Black Chintz, gold hdl & ped ft, Ripon sh, #14196 ..665.00
Cup/saucer, Blue Pansy Chintz, Henley sh, #13165..................... 100.00
Cup/saucer, Bramble, Dainty sh, pk hdl, gold trim, #2353 .... 290.00
Cup/saucer, Dainty Blue, Dainty sh, #051/25, mini, 1½".............. 650.00
Cup/saucer, Dainty Blue, Westminster (not Dainty sh),1½" 255.00
Cup/saucer, Dainty Brown, Ludlow sh 135.00
Cup/saucer, demi, Bubbles, Bute sh, #11182 .... 42.00
Cup/saucer, demi, Dainty Brown 145.00
Cup/saucer, Duchess, coffee-can sh, #13401 .... 16.00
Cup/saucer, Georgian litho, Royal Blue ext/saucer, Athol sh 42.50
Cup/saucer, gr stripes on wht, Hyderbad shape, recessed hdl........ 415.00
Cup/saucer, Melody w/in, solid ext/saucer, Oleander, #13412 ...... 130.00
Cup/saucer, Moss Rose, gr hdl, gold trim, Dainty sh, #2427 .... 315.00
Cup/saucer, Paisley, bl, Canturbury sh, mini, 1½", 2⅞" 1,350.00
Cup/saucer, Pansy (lg), Dainty sh, #13823................................. 100.00
Cup/saucer, Pyrethrum, Dainty sh, #14189 .... 80.00
Cup/saucer, Rose, Pansy FMN, Canturbury, #13424, mini, $90 to .125.00
Cup/saucer, Summer Glory, lav ext, ftd Oleander w/gold, #13413 . 65.00
Cup/saucer, Wildflowers, Stratford sh, #13678............................ 50.00
Egg cup, Dainty Blue, ped ft, #051/28, 2½" 80.00

Egg cup, Rosebud, ped ft, Dainty sh, #13426, 2½" 50.00
Figure, Golfer, in knickers, w/bag over shoulder, MLA, 6¼" 1,045.00
Food mold, Crayfish, W, 5¼" 52.00
Gravy/sauceboat, Sheraton, rnd, #13289 .... 32.00
Hot water/chocolate pot, Dainty Bl, #051/28, 7", $240 to 275.00
Jam pot, Maytime, apple sh w/slotted lid, #8484, 4" 100.00
Jewelry casket, Geo & Mary 1911 Coronation, sq, LF, 4x5½" 290.00
Jewelry casket, RPFMN, domed lid, LF, #8295, 1½x2x1½" 82.50
Loving cup, Geo & Mary 1911 Coronation commemorative, hdls, 4½" ... 70.00
Mug, RPFMN, Dainty sh, #13424, 4" 100.00
Napkin ring, Campanula, self-supports, mk Shelley inside............. 95.00
Napkin ring, RPFMN, self-supports, mk Shelley inside.................. 55.00
Pin dish, life buoy shape, HP, sgn HC, 3½" dia 170.00
Pitcher, Melody Chintz, #13453, 6½" 260.00
Place setting, Black Trees, QA sh, #11476, 5-pc....................... 235.00
Place setting, Blue Rock, Dainty sh, #13591, 5-pc 125.00
Place setting, Dainty Mauve, brilliant coloring, #051, 5-pc 400.00
Place setting, FMN, Dainty sh, #2394, 5-pc.............................. 150.00
Place setting, Glorious Devon, Richmond sh, #12734 .... 235.00
Place setting, Honeysuckle, Carlisle sh, #14311, 5-pc 225.00
Plate, American Brookline, Dainty sh, #14060, 10½" 100.00
Plate, Chippendale, appl enamel, Gainsborough sh, #13228, 10⅞" .55.00
Plate, Dainty Blue, #051, 10½" 65.00
Plate, Dainty Orange, #051, 10½" 135.00
Plate, Harebell, Oleander sh, #13590, 10¼" 38.00
Plate, Old Sevres, w/silver fr, #10678, 7" 42.00
Plate, Rambler Rose, Dainty sh, #13671, 10¾" 100.00
Platter, Dainty Blue, #051/28, 16⅞x13¾" 425.00
Posy ring (pansy ring), Pansy Chintz, mushroom sh, 1½x7½" 150.00
Shaker set, Regency, Dainty, pepper pot+2 shakers+stand w/finger ring..355.00
Shaving mug, Deco fruit, space for soap & brush, 5¼" 55.00
Shaving mug, Primrose Chintz, space for soap & brush, #13586, 4¾" .. 150.00
Sign, Shelly, 10th Anniversery...Club, 2½x3½" 112.00
Smoke set, Dainty Pink, #051/p, ashtray & cigarette holder........... 65.00
Tea & toast set, Meissenette, Dainty sh w/indent & cup, 8¼" 130.00
Teapot, Blue Rock, Dainty shape, graceful spout, 313591, 6½" 300.00
Teapot, Ferndown, Windsor sh, #14131, mini, 3½" 120.00
Teapot, Miessenette, Dainty sh, graceful spout, #14260, 5¼" 255.00
Teapot, Stocks, Dainty sh w/graceful spout, #13626, 6" 240.00
Tray for cr/sug, Dainty Blue, tab hdls, #051/28, 9½x5" 135.00
Tray, sandwich, Begonial, Dainty sh, w/hdls, #13427, 12½x5¾" 35.00
Trio, Bananas, Queen Anne shape, mc enamel, #1562, 6½" plate ..160.00
Trio, Duchess, Gainsborough sh w/bl colorway, #13403, 6" plate.........62.00
Trio, Fuchsia, Dainty sh, #2421 .... 285.00
Trio, Meissenette, Dainty sh, #14260.. 178.00
Trio, Rock Garden, Ripon shape, gold trim, #13385, 7" plate........ 90.00
Trio, Sprays of Poppies, Fairy sh, #9138, w, 7" plate 100.00

Trio, Syringia, Windsor shape, #14009, 8" plate, $150.00. (Photo courtesy Time Was Antiques, www. timewasantiques.net)

Tureen, Harebell, Oleander sh, domed lid, w/hdls, #13590, 10¾" 145.00
Vase, birds in tree/flowers HP on bl, yel int, 4" 185.00
Vase, Blue Dragon, slim w/rolled collar, #8315, w, 9" 175.00
Vase, floral cartouche w/rich gold, ewer form w/hdls, w, mini, 2" .. 255.00
Vase, From Lorne Point, squat, souvenir, 5¼" 78.00
Wash set, earthenware, pitcher+bowl+soap dish+toothbrush holder, w.... 500.00

Silhouettes

Silhouette portraits were made by positioning the subject between a bright light and a sheet of white drawing paper. The resulting shadow was then traced and cut out, the paper mounted over a contrasting color and framed. The hollow-cut process was simplified by an invention called the Physiognotrace, a device that allowed tracing and cutting to be done in one operation. Experienced silhouette artists could do full-length figures, scenics, ships, or trains freehand. Some of the most famous of these artists were Charles Peale Polk, Charles Wilson Peale, William Bache, Doyle, Edouart, Chamberlain, Brown, and William King. Though not often seen, some silhouettes were completely painted or executed in wax. Examples listed here are hollow-cut unless another type is described and assumed to be in excellent condition unless noted otherwise.

Key:
c/p — cut and pasted
fl — full length
hc — hand colored
hl —half-length
p — profile
wc — watercolor

Boy, ink p, gold inked hair, identified, 1818, 6¼x5½"+fr............. 200.00
British officer, hl p, wc on paperbrd, 4x3"+gilt emb tin fr 415.00
Children, w/hoop & top, bird's-eye maple vnr fr w/gilt liner, 12x14½" .2,070.00
Couple & child at table, fl, c/p, ink, Edouart, 1834, 12x18" fr ..4,115.00
Facing couple: man w/open book, lady w/fan, paper on silk, 9x13" ..470.00
Lady (identified) in hat & finery, fl rvpt ink on glass, 1800, 4x3"+fr..385.00
Lady & man (identified), p, ink/hc details, 1830s, 4¼"+fr, pr 2,465.00
Lady & man, p, ink/wc on fabric, stains, 1830s, 4x6"+wood fr..2,585.00
Lady w/hair comb on woodblock print body, fl, c/p, 6x5" fr.......... 460.00

Man holding top hat, inked details in gold, white, and black, Taken at the Hubbard Gallery, rosewood fame with gilt liner, 16x12", $800.00. (Photo courtesy Garth's Auction Inc.)

Man in frock coat, stands & holds hat, fl, Edouart, 12x8"+maple fr...975.00
Man w/high collar & ruffled shirt, p, sepia pnt/ink/gilt, 4x3"+fr .. 235.00
Man, bust-long p, c/p, wc/graphite details, early 1800s, 3x2"+fr .. 765.00
Man, p, c/p, gold ink details, Hubbard Gallery label, 7x6"+maple fr... 350.00
Mother w/fan & son holding hat, fl, c/p, Edouart, 1840, 8½x5"+fr ..1,525.00
Portly man w/hat & cane, fl, ink on paper, bronze details, 9x5"+fr .. 700.00

Silver

Coin Silver

During colonial times in America, the average household could not afford items made of silver, but those fortunate enough to have accumulations of silver coins (900 parts silver/100 parts alloy) took them to the local silversmith who melted them down and made the desired household article as requested. These pieces bore the owner's monogram and often the maker's mark, but the words 'Coin Silver' did not come into use until

1830. By 1860 the standard was raised to 925 parts silver/75 parts alloy and the word 'Sterling' was added. Coin silver came to an end about 1900.

Key:
Geo — George
t-oz — troy ounce
Int'l — International

Am, porringer, openwork hdl, flared rim, dings, 5", 6.6-t-oz......... 515.00
Am, salt cellars, Asian scenes/figures, glass liners, pr.................... 200.00
Baldwin Gardiner, NY; tea set, lobed bodies, pot+cr/sug w/lid, 81.4-t-oz..3,450.00
G Stephens, NY; punch ladle, Old English pattern, 1790s, 13" ... 750.00

Gorham, water pitcher, highly ornate with raised and chased floral and neoclassical motifs, ram's head crested handle, monogram reserve, circa 1859, 12½", $5,100.00. (Photo courtesy Rago Arts and Auction Center)

Hyde & Goodrich, cup, repoussé chased floral, 3-t-oz 1,765.00
Hyde & Goodrich, ladle, fiddle thread/monogram, 14", 5-t-oz.. 1,085.00
Hyde & Goodrich, tablespoons, fiddle type, 8", 7 for 560.00
IBV (Am?), ink pot & sander, eng monogram, squat, 3-t-oz 575.00
J Conning Co, Mobile; creamer, helmet form, foliate bands, 11-t-oz.3,500.00
J David, Philadelphia; waste bowl, sq ft/beading, 5x6", 14-t-oz.3,000.00
J Musgrave, Philadelphia; coffeepot, fluted, ped ft, 42.75-t-oz...8,225.00
J Richardson Jr, Philadelphia; soup ladle, curved oval hdl, 13" . 1,175.00
L Megede, Lexington MO; julep cup, beaded rim/ft, 3", 4.9-t-oz . 515.00
London, castor set, Geo II, 7 castors in stand, 1743, 34.4-t-oz ..2,585.00
Rasch, Philadelphia; soup ladle, fiddle/shell hdl, 13", 4-t-oz......... 725.00
Wm L Adams, NY; tureen, emb foliage, 4 claw ft, domed lid, 11x16x9" .9,750.00
Young & Co, New Orleans; soup spoon, fiddle type, 9"............... 115.00

Flatware

Silver flatware is being collected today either to replace missing pieces of heirloom sets or in lieu of buying new patterns, by those who admire and appreciate the style and quality of the older ware. Prices vary from dealer to dealer; some pieces are harder to find and are therefore more expensive. Items such as olive spoons, cream ladles, and lemon forks, once thought a necessary part of a silver service, may today be slow to sell; as a result, dealers may price them low and make up the difference on items that sell more readily. Many factors enter into evaluation. Popular patterns may be high due to demand though easily found, while scarce patterns may be passed over by collectors who find them difficult to reassemble. Because of silver prices rising recently to nearly $19 an ounce, prices for plain flatware and flatware with monograms have risen. People are buying plain sets with monograms and melting them down, which causes prices to rise. If pieces are monogrammed, deduct 15% (for rare, ornate patterns) to 25% (for common, plain pieces). Place settings generally come in three sizes: dinner, place, and luncheon, with the dinner size generally more expensive. In general, dinner knives are 9½" long, place knives, 9" to 9⅛", and luncheon knives, 8¾" to 8⅞". Dinner forks measure 7⅜" to 7½", place forks, 7¼" to 7⅜", and luncheon forks, 6⅞" to 7⅛". Our advisor for this category is Rick Spencer; he is listed in the Directory under Utah.

Acorn, Geo Jensen, soup spoon... 124.00
Afterglow, Oneida, sugar spoon... 19.00
American Classic, Easterling, cold meat fork................................ 52.00
Barocco, Wallace, dinner fork 65.50
Barocco, Wallace, place soup spoon 61.00
Bead, Gorham, salad fork.. 55.00
Belle Rose, Oneida, butter spreader, hollow hdl 15.00
Belle Rose, Oneida, olive fork 14.00
Blossomtime, Int'l, cream soup spoon 17.00
Blossomtime, Int'l, pie/cake serving knife...................................... 24.00
Burgundy, Reed & Barton, teaspoon 21.00
Candlelight, Towle, gravy ladle 51.00
Chateau Rose, Alvin, butter spreader, flat hdl 16.00
Chippendle, Towle, salad fork 34.00
Danish Baroque, Towle, serving fork.. 75.00
Danish Baroque, Towle, sugar spoon 33.00

Eloquence, Lunt, 56-piece set, $1,200.00. (Photo courtesy Brunk Auctions on LiveAuctioneers.com)

Fontana, Towle, cheese scoop.. 29.00
Grand Baroque, Wallace, ice tongs 242.00
Grand Duchess, Towle, rice server, hollow hdl 24.00
Homewood, Stieff, berry serving spoon.. 67.00
Hyperion, Whiting, teaspoon 38.00
Impero, Wallace, dinner fork.. 55.00
Impero, Wallace, place soup spoon... 51.00
Irving, Wallace, cocktail fork 18.00
John & Priscilla, Westmoreland, tomato/flat server........................ 50.00
King Edward, Whiting, cocktail fork... 14.00
King Edward, Whiting, sugar tongs 24.00
Melrose, Gorham, gravy ladle... 76.00
Melrose, Gorham, luncheon fork 36.00
Melrose, Gorham, serving fork 75.00
Milburn Rose, Westmoreland, gumbo soup spoon 24.00
Milburn Rose, Westmoreland, table serving spoon, pierced........... 36.00
Mythologique, Gorham, 50 pcs, 90-t-oz, 7 dwt (pennyweight) .3,235.00
Old Colonial, Towle, dinner fork 41.00
Stieff Rose, Stieff, lemon serving fork 22.00
Stieff Rose, Stieff, roast cvg knife.. 55.00

Hollow Ware

Until the middle of the nineteenth century, the silverware produced in America was custom made on order of the buyer directly from the silversmith. With the rise of industrialization, factories sprung up that manufactured silverware for retailers who often added their trademark to the ware. Silver ore was mined in abundance, and demand spurred production. Changes in style occurred at the whim of fashion. Repoussé decoration (relief work) became popular about 1885, reflecting the ostentatious preference of the Victorian era. Later in the century, Greek, Etruscan, and several classic styles found favor. Today the Art Deco styles of this century are very popular with collectors.

In the listings that follow, manufacturer's name or trademark is noted first; in lieu of that information, listings are by country or item. See also Tiffany, Silver.

B Webb, Boston; tankard, stepped lid, scroll hdl, 7", 21.4-t-oz..6,900.00
Ball, Black & Co, NY; butter dish, repoussé floral, dome lid, 19-t-oz .650.00
Bangs, OH; beaker/julep cup, appl rim/ft, 3", 5.6-t-oz 625.00
Barker & Ellis (English), punch bowl set, bowl: 16½"; tray: 21½"; w/ 12 cups .4,800.00
Bigelow Kennard & Co, pitcher, chased/emb foliage, 1900s, 8", 32-t-oz .. 1,765.00
Black Star Frost, crumber, monogram/foliage scrolls/shells, +tray . 500.00
Chas Aldridge, London; teapot & stand, swag eng, 1780s, 16.3-t-oz .1,300.00
Chatterley, Birmingham; punch bowl, repoussé floral, ca 1791, 7x11" ..925.00
CK 925, center bowl, ribbed body/ft, flower-topped hdls, 34" L, 164-t-oz.. 2,300.00
Dominick & Haff, sugar shaker, rococo repoussé, dome lid, 6", pr . 1,500.00
Dublin, cup, Geo III, 2-hdl trophy form, H ft, 7", 15.2-t-oz 750.00
Duhme, OH; bowl, appl decor, trifid ft, gilt int, 6", 12.5-t-oz 330.00
Duhme, OH; goblet, Presented to Knights Templar Band..., 1870, 7" ..460.00
Emes & Barnard, London; mug, grapevines/snakes, 1810s, 8.7-t-oz ...725.00
English, centerpiece, figures raise basket w/vintage relief, eng armorials, 25"..6,650.00
FD, mug, repoussé, gold-wash int, 4¼" 375.00
French, chocolate pot, rooster form, fruit/etc emb, 1780s, 9x9" .4,890.00
FW Smith, MA; tea/coffee set, rococo cartouches, 5-pc, 78-t-oz...1,750.00
G Giles, London; wine funnel, std form w/bowl clip, 4", 2-t-oz ... 345.00
G Ibbot, London; teapot, hinged domed lid, repoussé floral, 9", EX...2,285.00
Geo Jensen, Denmark; sauceboat, scroll hdl, ftd, 5x8", 13-t-oz .1,800.00
Geo Jensen, USA; bowl, petaled form, 2 sm scroll ft, 3x10" 300.00
Glasgow, goblet, Geo III, initials in reserve, 1823-24, 13.1-t-oz... 660.00
Goodnow & Jenks, Colonial Revival, fluted/slender forms, 6-pc ..3,200.00
Gorham, tea/coffee, eng flowers, 2 pots/bowl+cr/sug, +29" SP tray..1,150.00
Gurney & Co, cup, Geo III, 2-hdl, ftd, eng initials, 13.8-t-oz 600.00
H Bateman, London; coffeepot, Geo III, domed lid, swan's neck, 27-t-oz .5,175.00
J Tuite, London; salver, Geo II, scalloped rim/eng, 6", 7.8-t-oz 460.00
Joseph Angell, teapot, Geo III, leaves relief to body/ft, crest, 6x10"...1,000.00
Kinsey, beaker/julep cup, die-rolled rim/ft, 1856, 2.9-t-oz 330.00
Lion, box, repoussé putto musician on lid, chased body, 2½", pr... 345.00
London WBJ (Messrs Barnard), punch bowl, repoussé, ftd, 10x17".6,720.00
London, coffeepot, Geo II, baluster, dbl-scroll hdl, 11", 11.3-t-oz... 1,150.00
London, coffeepot, Geo II, dbl scroll hdl, domed lid, 1740s, 18.5-t-oz.. 1,600.00
London, sauceboat, Geo II, dbl-scroll hdl, shell ft, 1751-52, 3.3-t-oz .. 550.00
London, sauceboat, Geo IV, rococo style, 1827-28, 3", 3-t-oz 180.00
P&A Bateman, London; loving cup, S-scroll hdls, 1791, 6", 10-t-oz.. 635.00
P&A Bateman, London; sugar bowl, gw int, reeded hdls, 4x8x5" . 460.00
R Smith, Dublin; coffeepot, repoussé/chased decor, 1844, 82.7-t-oz ..1,265.00

Reed & Barton, candelabra, Francis I, five-light, circa 1907, 108.3 ounces, 15", EX, pair $6,000.00. (Photo courtesy Heritage Auction Galleries on LiveAuctioneers.com)

Robert Hennell, cake basket, Geo III, rtcl ft/oval rim, crest, 15" L...3,800.00
S&J Crespell, London; shafing dish, Geo III, w/lid, 1768, 56-t-oz.. 2,115.00
SH (English), coffeepot, paneled pear form w/eng crest/elks, 1802, 12"..1,320.00
Shepheard & Co, chalice, chased Latin motto, 4x4" 2,280.00
Shreve & Co, San Francisco; bowl, emb iris, lobed rim, 20th C, 13".. 415.00
SM, London; sauceboat, Geo II, scalloped rim, 1749, 4.5-t-oz 515.00
T Whipham, London; coffeepot, Geo II, repoussé, 9", 13.8-t-oz ...1,500.00
TP in crown w/in oval, tray, Chpndl, 3 animal hoof ft, 6" dia...... 520.00
V in shield w/crown, pounce pot, egg shaped/rtcl, 8-side base, 6" . 180.00
Wm Grundy, kettle on stand, Geo II, bulb, domed lid, 1750s, 52-t-oz....3,125.00
Wm Homes Sr, Boston; can, spurred hdl, 5", 10.8-t-oz.............. 3,750.00
Wm Kersill, London; creamer, repoussé birds/etc, 1750, 2.5-t-oz. 430.00

Silver Overlay

The silver overlay glass made since the 1880s was decorated with a cut-out pattern of sterling silver applied to the surface of the ware.

Bottle, dk gr w/floral o/l, matching stopper, 9" 1,000.00
Bottle, emerald gr, Nouveau floral o/l w/monogram, bulb, 4¼" 200.00
Bottle, scent, clear canteen, Gorham o/l w/eng monogram, 3¼" . 120.00
Creamer/sugar bowl, clear w/etch floral, floral o/l, o/l hdls, 3"........ 35.00
Decanter, clear w/etched floral & floral o/l, glass stopper 20.00
Decanter, clear w/scrolling vines o/l, Alvin, ca 1873, 10¾" 975.00
Decanter, cobalt w/floral o/l, teardrop stopper, 9" 350.00
Decanter, crystal, floral vines/cartouch o/l, ball body/finial, 6x5". 550.00
Decanter, gr cut to clear w/floral o/l, att Dorflinger, 10" 3,220.00
Jar, blk w/Deco bird & floral o/l, ftd, w/lid, att Cambridge, 10".... 185.00
Pitcher, clear tankard w/Nouveau o/l at rim, water sz..................... 80.00
Shaker, clear w/Nouveau o/l, 6-sided, metal top, ea 25.00
Trivet, clear, scrolling wide o/l border, 6" dia 80.00
Vase, bl w/Nouveau floral o/l, 2x3".. 275.00
Vase, bud, emerald gr w/Nouveau floral o/l, disk ft, 6" 360.00
Vase, cobalt bl w/floral & leaf o/l, #999 near base, 6¼" 1,200.00
Vase, cobalt w/vining o/l, baluster, 6"... 240.00

Vase, cranberry with all-over floral overlay by Alvin, monogram, 7x9½", $4,200.00. (Photo courtesy Burchard Galleries Inc. on LiveAuctioneers.com)

Vase, purple, Nouveau o/l, 4" 485.00
Wine, ruby w/grapes o/l & shield-like logo, Pat Po32, 4¾"........... 425.00

Silverplate

Silverplated flatware is becoming the focus of attention for many of today's collectors. Demand is strong for early, ornate patterns, and prices have continued to rise steadily over the past five years. Our values are based on pieces in excellent or restored/resilvered condition. Serving pieces are priced to reflect the values of examples in complete original condition, with knives retaining their original blades. If pieces are monogrammed, deduct from 20% (for rare, ornate patterns) to 30% (for common, plain pieces). Our advisor for this category is Rick Spencer; he is listed in the Directory under Utah. For more information we recommend *Silverplated Flatware* by Tere Hagan (Collector Books). See also Railroadiana, Silver-Plated Flatware and Silver-Plated Hollow Ware.

Flatware

Adam, Community, dinner fork, 7"...5.00
Adam, Community, sugar spoon..6.00
Ancestrial 1847, Rogers, master butter knife, flat hdl.......................6.00
Ancestrial 1847, Rogers, tablespoon 8.00
Avon 1847, Rogers, meat fork 16.00
Ballad, Oneida, baby fork 6.00
Berkshire 1847, Rogers, cocktail fork 12.00
Berkshire 1847, Rogers, pickle fork, long hdl............................... 25.00
Berwick, Rogers, jam spoon 22.00
Berwick, Rogers, luncheon fork, 7"... 10.00

Caprice, Nobility, iced tea spoon.............................5.00
Classic Plume, Towle, meat fork, 7".................. 12.00
Classic Plume, Towle, tablespoon, pierced.............. 14.00
Columbia 1847, Rogers, gravy ladle................ 25.00
Coronation, Community, grill fork.............................5.00
Daybreak, Rogers, salad fork, 6"..............................5.00
Daybreak, Rogers, teaspoon......................................4.00
Deauville, Comminity, oval soup spoon, 7".............7.00
Deauville, Community, sugar spoon............................6.00
First Love 1847, Rogers, chipped beef fork............ 10.00
Floral, Wallace, jam spoon.................................. 40.00
Grenoble, Prestige, cream soup spoon, 6"................6.00
Grenoble, Prestige, tomato server 14.00
Grenoble/Glodia, Rogers, dinner fork.................. 12.00
Grenodle/Gloria, Rogers, meat fork....................... 35.00
Heraldic 1847, Rogers, salad fork..............................7.00
Invitation, Gorham, pie/cake server, hollow hdl ... 17.00
Invitation, Gorham, teaspoon...................................3.00
Lady Emp, Nobility, coffee spoon..............................4.00
Longchamps, Prestige, cream soup spoon, 6"...........6.00
Longchamps, Prestige, grill fork...............................5.00
Longchamps, Prestige, tomato server...................... 15.00
Marquise 1847, Rogers, master butter knife.............6.00
May Queen, Holmes & Edwards, tablespoon.............8.00
May Queen, Holmes & Edwards, teaspoon.................3.00
Milady, Community, oval soup spoon 6.00
Milady, Community, salad fork...................................7.00
Mystic, Rogers, berry spoon................................. 30.00
Napleon, Holmes & Edwards, grill fork.....................4.00
Nobless, Community, tablespoon.......................... 10.00
Old Colony 1847, luncheon fork, 7"..........................6.00
Old Colony 1847, Rogers, grapefruit spoon............ 11.00
Old Colony 1847, Rogers, sugar spoon......................6.00
Orange Blossom, Rogers, iced tea spoons, ea.............9.00
Orange Blossom, Rogers, meat fork........................ 18.00
Patrician, Community, cocktail fork.........................7.00
Patrician, Community, curved baby spoon.............. 10.00
Paul Revere, Community, dinner fork, 7"..................6.00
Queen Bess 1946, Oneida, gravy ladle.................. 14.00
Remembrance 1847, Rogers, iced tea spoon.............8.00
Remembrance 1847, Rogers, roast cvg set, 2-pc ... 86.00
Reverie, Nobility, butter spreader.............................5.00
Reverie, Nobility, seafood fork.................................5.00
Royal Lace, Nobility, seafood fork............................5.00
Sharon 1847, Rogers, meat fork........................... 16.00
Sheraton, Community, gravy ladle........................ 15.00
South Seas, Community, master butter knife.............6.00
South Seas, Community, nut spoon, pierced.............8.00
Tiger Lily, Reed & Barton, luncheon fork, 7"...........9.00
Tiger Lily, Reed & Barton, tablespoon.................. 11.00
Vesta 1847, Rogers, seafood fork.............................9.00
Vintage 1847, Rogers, butter spreader, flat hdl...... 18.00
Vintage 1847, Rogers, fish fork............................ 35.00
Violet, SG Rogers, meat fork................................ 18.00
Violet, SG Rogers, pie server, flat hdl.................. 20.00
White Orchid, Community, dinner fork......................8.00
White Orchid, Community, sugar spoon.....................6.00
Windsong, Nobility, gravy ladle............................ 15.00
Windsong, Nobility, iced tea spoon...........................6.00
Windsong, Nobility, meat fork.............................. 14.00
Winsome 1959, Community, oval soup spoon............7.00
Winsome 1959, tablespoon, pierced...................... 12.00
Youth, Holmes & Edwards, grill fork........................4.00
Youth, Holmes & Edwards, tablespoon 7.00

Hollow Ware

Jean Despres, ice bucket, France, incised signature and touchmark to edge, circa 1935, 10x10½x8½", $4,500.00. (Photo courtesy Wright on LiveAuctioneers.com)

M Hall & Co, pitcher, floral repoussé, gilt int, hinged lid, 11".....850.00
Middleton, caviar boat w/cherubs, raised on plinth w/waves, 12x12"... 1,325.00
Stugart (att), ewer, invt pear form w/eng eagle head, 1800s, 18", pr...850.00
Tufts, vase, cattails extend to hold sm trumpet vase, #1021, 4".... 285.00
Unknown, biscuit bbl, horse finial, scenic reserves, 1890s, 8x7".. 900.00
Unknown, hot water kettle, floral, Regency style, 1850s, 17x10". 850.00
Unknown, hot water warming dish, Regency style, domed lid, 15x25"..2,000.00
Unknown, supper set, tureen w/lid+4 oval dishes+2 salts, 1900s ..1,175.00
Unknown, wine cooler, classical figures, urn form, gilt int, 13".1,175.00
Unknown, wine cooler, Regency style w/lion mask/drop ring hdls, 8x9" .1,500.00
Wilcox SP & Co, tazza, Art Deco, ca 1921, 3x8" 5,100.00
WMF, bowl, centerpiece, Egyptian Revival, w/glass liner, 19th C, 9x29" ..3,850.00

Sheffield

Cake basket, Geo III, navette form, swing hdl, gadrooning, 10x14x10".425.00
Candlesticks, Edward VII Classical Revival, 1904, 12", pr........1,550.00
Chafing dish, M Boulton, oval w/rocaille hdls, w/liner/lid, 14", pr.2,650.00
Entree dish & warmer, cast floral bands, ornate hdls, 14" L, pr .2,100.00

Hot water urn, embossed shield with hallmarks, circa 1810, $450.00. (Photo courtesy Stanton Auctions on LiveAuctioneers.com)

Hot water urn, gadrooned rim, mask hdls, 19th C, 17" 250.00
Tankard, Boulton & Fothergill, domed lid, stepped ft, 7"............ 700.00
Tankard, eng armorial shield, scroll hdls, rpr/dents, 7⅜" 230.00
Tea tray, chased borders, eng shield, hdls, 4 scroll ft, 3x33x22"....650.00
Tray, M Boulton, gadrooned rim/hdls, eng coat of arms, 1790s, 28" L...785.00
Tureen, navette form w/ped base, domed lid, 8x10x4", pr........... 800.00
Vase, trumpet-shaped wire fr w/cobalt liner, 16x7", pr 700.00

Sinclaire

In 1904 H.P. Sinclaire and Company was founded in Corning, New York. For the first 16 years of production, Sinclaire used blanks from other glassworks for his cut and engraved designs. In 1920 he established his own glassblowing factory in Bath, New York. His most popular designs utilize fruits, flowers, and other forms from nature. Most of Sinclaire's glass is un-marked; items that are carry his logo: an 'S' within a wreath with two shields. For more information we recommend *The Collector's Encyclopedia of American Art Glass* by John A. Shuman III.

Bowl, 13 hobstars in vessica panels, scalloped/sawtooth rim, 3½x8" ... 120.00
Bowl, floral eng, scalloped rim, 10" 200.00
Bowl, Fuchsia cuttings, 6" 48.00
Bowl, Queen's pattern, oblong, 9½x7", NM 625.00
Candlesticks, gr, baluster form, 12", pr 300.00
Candlesticks, gr, slim std, 16", pr 575.00
Clock, sgn, 6", non-working Chelsea Clock Co 1,020.00
Compote, amber, flared bowl on stem w/ring knob, 4½x12½" 180.00
Compote, floral cutting, tall stem, shallow bowl, 6½x6¾" 135.00
Compote, intaglio leaf & frosted cherry, ftd, 4x8" 50.00
Goblet, gr w/geometric cuttings, clear stem & ft, 8¾x2¾" 240.00
Teapot, Greek key & fluted pattern, 1880s+, 4½", +matching 8" plate 480.00

Urn, intaglio ribbon-tied garlands of flowers, no mark, circa 1920, 13", $390.00. (Photo courtesy Myers Fine Art on LiveAuctioneers.com)

Vase, Dahlia, intaglio cuttings, 12" 120.00
Vase, electric bl, optic ribs, ftd, mk S, ca 1920, 6x7¾" 300.00
Vase, floral eng w/bl threading, baluster, 10" 275.00

Sitzendorf

The Sitzendorf factory began operations in what became East Germany in the mid-1800s, adopting the name of the city as the name of their company. They produced fine porcelain groups, figurines, etc., in much the same style and quality as Meissen and the Dresden factories. Much of their ware was marked with a crown over the letter 'S' and a horizontal line with two slash marks.

Candlesticks, applied figures of adult and child, floral fabric drapes, grapes and flowers in relief, strong color, excellent detail, 12½", $1,200.00. (Photo courtesy JK Galleries, Inc. on LiveAuctioneers.com)

Candelabra, lady (& man) as std, 5-lt top pc lifts off, 16", pr 780.00
Candlesticks, seated nymph on floral base w/bronze bobeche, 11x7", pr..235.00
Clock, putti & appl flowers on rococo base, 1890-1900, 12½" 850.00
Compote, tall ped w/figures & appl flowers, 15½x11" 350.00
Figurine maid w/lamb, bl crown S mk, 20th C, sm rpr, 19" 440.00
Figurine, dancer holds lace skirt wide, appl flowers, 8x5x3½" 180.00

Figurine, dandy in fine uniform on goat, ea wearing glasses, 7" L. 195.00
Figurine, Exelmans, standing Napoleonic soldier, 9½" 345.00
Figurine, General Bessieres on horsebk, 11x8" 225.00
Figurine, Guarde Imperiale, drummer on horseback, 11" 275.00
Figurine, Guarde Imperiale, soldier on horse, 11" 480.00
Figurine, lady w/fan, plumed hat, Voght Bros, 19th C, 14" 275.00
Figurine, LaFayette, standing Napoleonic soldier, 9½" 345.00
Figurine, Le Prince Eugene, soldier on horseback, 11" 360.00
Figurine, Napoleon stands w/hand in shirt, 9½" 275.00
Figurine, semi-nude boy riding bucking goat, 8" 250.00
Figurines, boy (& girl), vase on opposing shoulders, bl tones, 10", pr.... 190.00
Figurines, colonial man & lady, she w/locket, he w/hat & rose, 15", pr....275.00
Figurines, man (& lady) w/apples, traditional garb, post-1954, 20", pr ...275.00
Group, picnickers & sheep beneath oak tree, late 19th C, 13" .1,320.00

Slag Glass

Slag glass is a commonly used misnomer for glass that is made by mixing milk glass with one or more other colors to produce a glass that resembles marble. In the 1870s, in England, waste materials (slag) from iron blast furnaces were used to manufacture a type of glass that produced swirled colors, but this procedure was quite limited and no glass made in the United States ever used actual slag. Other names for this type of glass include 'marble,' 'variegated,' 'Mosaic' (the patented process of Challinor & Taylor), and 'End of Day.' End of Day is a marketing term and in no way describes the highly technical process of making of slag glass. Much slag glass was produced in the country from 1870 to 1912 (Atterbury, Akro Agate, and Challinor & Taylor, among others), and again from 1959 when Imperial introduced their caramel, ruby, and jade slag. Slag items may have a glossy or matt finish with the matt finish being most desirable. Companies that have produced slag glass include Kemple, Mosser, Kanawha, Avon, Plum, L.E. Smith, Westmoreland, Fenton, Akro Agate, St. Clair, Degenhart, L.G. Wright, Boyd, Summit, and Rosso.

For further information see Nathan Taves & Don Jennings' *Slag & Marble Glass; the Prominent Years, 1959 – 1985*, and Ruth Grizel's *American Slag Glass*. Our advisor for Slag Glass is Shirley Smith; she is listed in the Directory under West Virginia. See also specific manufacturers.

Black, covered dish, hen on nest, Mosser, 6" 20.00
Blue, pitcher & glasses, Weishar mini, Moon & Stars.................... 26.00
Brown/green/blue, shakers (2), Challinor, 3½" 48.00
Butterscotch, covered dish, candy, Westmoreland, 5¾" 158.00
Caramel, covered dish, lion, Imperial, matte finish 105.00
Caramel, syrup, 6⅝" 103.00

End of Day, candy dish, Hobstar and Fan, $45.00. (Photo courtesy Shirley Smith)

Green, child's tea set, Akro Agate.. 104.00
Green, covered dish, candy, Argonaut, Westmoreland.................... 41.00
Jade, covered dish, rooster, Imperial, matte finish......................... 301.00
Malachite, ped bowl, English... 44.00
Orange, figurine, alley cat, Fenton, 11"... 243.00
Orange, figurine, Jenny, Mosser, 4½"... 15.00

Pinkish-purple, tumbler, Cactus design, 4".. 32.00
Purple, bowl, sgn, Sowerby, 2½"... 25.00
Purple, covered dish, raised wing swan, Westmoreland, 9½" L..... 293.00
Purple, covered dish, rooster, Wright, 5".. 35.00
Purple, dresser box, lidded, Imperial, 8" L.................................... 266.00
Purple, mug, Singing Birds, Northwood, 3½"................................... 51.00
Purple, plate, lacy edge, 10"... 19.00
Purple, thimble, Sowerby, 2½".. 25.00
Purple, vase, Davidson, 4"... 82.00
Purple, vase, Peacock in Garden, Fenton, 7¾".............................. 100.00
Purple/blue, Scottie, Boyd, 3".. 291.00
Red, covered dishes, rooster & hen, Summit, 5" L, ea...................... 47.00
Red, figurine, owl, Fenton, 3".. 167.00

Smith Bros.

Alfred and Harry Smith founded their glass decorating firm in New Bedford, Massachusetts. They had been associated with the Mt. Washington Glass Works from 1871 to 1875 where they aided in establishing a decorating department. Smith glass is valued for its artistic enameled decoration on satin or opalescent glass. Pieces are sometimes marked with a lion in a red shield. For more information we recommend *The Collector's Encyclopedia of American Art Glass* by John A. Shuman III.

Atomizer, wisteria on opalware, swirled ribs, gold highlights, 6½", $540.00. (Photo courtesy Cincinnati Art Galleries, LLC on LiveAuctioneers.com)

Biscuit jar, melon ribs, flowers/pinwheel, 2-pc metal lid, 6½"....... 500.00
Bowl, rose, lt brn w/wht daisy, rnd.. 80.00
Box, vine w/2-tone bl floral, glass lid, metal rim & hdl, lion mk.. 300.00
Humidor, wht daisies, SP lid w/pipe finial, lion mk, 7".................. 150.00
Muffineer, floral, pillar ribbed, 2-pc metal lid, 6"......................... 140.00
Perfume w/atomizer, melon ribs w/red floral, lion mk, 5".............. 150.00
Salt cellar, open, melon ribs, beaded rim, bl violets...................... 100.00
Sugar shaker, yel daisies, ribbed pillar, metal lid, 6"..................... 125.00
Vase, bl w/heron, bamboo cylinder, 2 sets rings, 4⅜"..................... 40.00
Vase, bl w/wht bird, cylinder in Meriden metal base, 5¼".............. 80.00
Vase, low oval, pk w/3 pansies, melon ribs, beaded rim, 5½" dia.... 55.00
Vase, low oval, wht daisy, melon ribs, beaded rim, lion mk, 6" dia. 70.00
Vase, lt brn w/wht bird, bamboo cylinder, 2 sets rings, 9"............... 80.00
Vase, lt brn w/wht bird on floral, cylinder, 4⅜", pr......................... 30.00
Vase, pk w/heron, cylinder, 4⅜".. 30.00

Snow Babies

During the last quarter of the nineteenth century, snow babies — little figures in pebbly white snowsuits — originated in Germany. They were originally made of sugar candy and were often used as decorations for Christmas cakes. Later on they were made of marzipan, a confection of crushed almonds, sugar, and egg whites. Eventually porcelain manufacturers began making them in bisque. They were popular until WWII. These tiny bisque figures range in size from 1" up to 7" tall. Quality German pieces bring very respect-

able prices on the market today. Beware of reproductions. Our advisor for this category is Linda Vines; she is listed in the Directory under California.

Babies (3) atop ea other's shoulders, Germany, 2"....................... 175.00
Baby crawling, pointed hood, very early face, Germany, 5".......... 350.00
Baby in sled pulled by huskies, Germany, 2"................................. 275.00

Baby in teddy bear skin, Heubach #5576, circa 1910, 3" long, $510.00. (Photo courtesy Richard Opfer Auctioneering, Inc. on LiveAuctioneers.com)

Baby inside igloo, Santa on top, Germany, 2".............................. 225.00
Baby playing cymbals, sitting, plaster, covered in coralene, Germany, 2".165.00
Baby playing saxophone, Germany, 2".. 155.00
Baby, snow covered fallen in snow, brn shoes, Germany, 3"......... 185.00
Baby w/bear cub inside ice cave, Germany, 1930s, 2"................... 250.00
Boy & girl sliding down the snow on brick wall, Germany, 2½"..250.00
Carollers, 3 w/snow hats & lantern on snow base, Germany, 2"..210.00
Child ice skater, no snow, Japan, 2".. 35.00
Child ice skating, no snow, Germany, 2"... 75.00
Elf, orange outfit, no snow, Germany, 1½"...................................... 55.00
Musicians, 3-pc band, US Zone, Germany, 2", ea........................... 40.00
Penguins (3) walking down brick wall, Germany, 2½"................. 175.00
Polar bear standing inside snow-covered igloo, Germany, 2"....... 210.00
Santa atop gray elephant, Germany, 2½"....................................... 275.00
Santa entering chimney on snow-covered rooftop, Germany, 2".215.00
Santa pulled by wht horse, snow on base, Germany, 2x3"............ 265.00
Santa riding in yel convertible car full of toys, Germany, 2x3"....225.00
Santa riding on snow bear, Germany, 2½"..................................... 225.00
Santa w/pack full of toys on bk, Germany, 2".............................. 150.00
Snow bear sitting or walking, Germany, 2"................................... 110.00
Snow dog, rabbit or cat, Germany, 1", ea.. 65.00
Snow doll, bsk shoulderhead, arms & legs, cloth body, Germany, 7"..375.00
Snowed Cook & Peary atop world globe, Germany, 4"............. 1,600.00
Snowman sitting, red hat w/pompom, Germany, 1½".................... 75.00
Snowman standing, blk top hat, Germany, 2"............................... 110.00

Snuff Boxes

As early as the seventeenth century, the Chinese began using snuff. By the early nineteenth century, the practice had spread to Europe and America. It was used by both the gentlemen and the ladies alike, and expensive snuff boxes and bottles were the earmark of the genteel. Some were of silver or gold set with precious stones or pearls, while others contained music boxes. See also Asian Antiques, Snuff Bottles.

Brass, relief sun and moon face, engraved clock dials, English, late eighteenth century, 3½", $780.00. (Photo courtesy Pook & Pook, Inc. on LiveAuctioneers.com)

14k yel gold w/cobalt enameling, hand chasing, oval, 2⅞x2"....2,750.00
Bone book form w/eng/pnt decor, dtd 1828, 2⅛x2⅞" 660.00
Brass, Lord Nelson on lid, England Expects Every Man..., 2¾" dia...360.00
Brass, tooled designs/MOP inlay & dk red enamel, 1x2½" dia 600.00
Circassian walnut w/B Franklin medallion & gold leaf, 1¾" dia ..725.00
Enamel on copper, 2¼" dia 185.00
Ivory, HP country home scene, English, 1830s, 3½" dia 360.00
Papier-maché w/titled lady's portrait on lid, 1850s, 4" dia 550.00
Shell w/silver inlay & lady's portrait on ivory, 1¼x3⅜" L 500.00
Silver eng over guilloche enamel, lady's portrait, Fr, 1¼x3x2¼" ..780.00
Silver gilt w/chased bands, engine trn, Fr, 19th C, 3" dia 600.00
Silver w/3 lg oval amethysts/sm rose-cut dmns/sapphires, 3¼" L ...1,450.00
Silver w/eng Cupid & borders, gold-washed int, Fr, ca 1900, 2⅝" L...395.00
Silver w/gold putti & monogram, gilt int, mid-19th C, 3" L 425.00
Silver, eng whaling scene, mk C Parker, x3x2" 1,100.00
Silver, lion figural, hinged lid, 18th C, 3" L 660.00
Tortoiseshell, 3-comb music player, ca 1815-20, 3½" L 1,000.00
Tortoiseshell w/gold inlay, 3¾" 430.00

Soap Hollow Furniture

Between 1834 and 1928 a small group of Mennonite craftsmen living in the tiny rural community of Soap Hollow in Conemaugh Township, Somerset County, Pennsylvania, crafted by hand a wide variety of furniture items including blanket chests, chests of drawers, cradles, chairs, Dutch cupboards, corner cupboards, beds, tables, sewing caddies, and miniature items for children.

Soap Hollow, known for the soft soap that the Mennonite women in the community were famous for, is recognized today because of the unique style of decorated furniture that began with master craftsman John Sala, a farmer, cabinet maker, and undertaker. Sala trained others in his distinctive style including his two sons, John M. and Joseph Sala, John Livingston, Peter K. Thomas, Tobias Livingston, Jeremiah Stahl, and Christian C. Blough. It is believed that in all there were 11 men who made furniture in the Soap Hollow tradition.

Simple and functional in form, Soap Hollow furniture was fashioned from a wide variety of regional woods including pine, poplar, and cherry, and although some pieces were unfinished, most are decorated with milk paint in shades of brown, red, and maroon with black accents. Dark green has been seen on later pieces. Trim work is usually done in mustard while silver and gold were most often used in stenciled decorations, although on occasion colors were used. Faux graining was applied with turkey feathers, rags, and combs. Pieces were usually decorated with the date of manufacture, the initials of the owner, and often the name of the furniture maker. Hand-cut stencils in various foliate and floral motifs, hearts, horses, birds, vases, baskets of fruit, pinwheels, rosettes, and star shapes were used, as well as floral decals.

Hallmarks of Soap Hollow chests of drawers include a distinctive scroll shaped back board; a thick rounded overhanging top; two or three small top drawers with a hidden hickory locking device; inset side panels painted black and often decorated with stencils or decals; inlaid kite shaped keyhole escutcheons of contrasting wood or round wooden escutcheons with brass keyholes; trim work in mustard; thick slightly bowed shaped skirt and baluster turned feet; dates and initials of owners and frequently the name of the craftsman; wooden, porcelain, or clear glass knobs.

There are two styles of blanket chests: six-board construction or with bottom drawers. Both styles feature hand cut dovetail joinery with off-set dovetailed bracket feet and a slightly bowed skirt that are most often painted black. Both can feature solid colors and grain painting, usually in shades of maroon, brown, or red. Lids are often black but may be the color of the carcase with black trim. Keyhole escutcheon is either of the kite shape or round. The document box is always on the inside left and when opened, it acts as a prop for the lid of the chest.

In blanket chests with drawers, reeded molding and carved-out heart and circle symbols can be found. John Sala blanket chests usually have a double heart cut out between two lower drawers. Date of manufacture and initials of owner, and often the initials or name of the craftsman are stenciled prominently on the piece.

Dutch and corner cupboards were made in two parts. Both exhibit a flared cornice and offset bracket feet painted black; six- or eight-pane windows in the top doors; and utility drawers. Inset panels on the bottom doors were painted black and often bore stenciled decorations as well as dates and initials. Dutch cupboards have a set-back top and cut-out shaped pie shelf under the upper section.

In addition to case pieces, cradles, chairs, tables, stands, children's miniatures, and sewing boxes were also manufactured. Three hundred pieces of Soap Hollow furniture have been cataloged. Values reflect condition, age, rarity, and provenance.

Our advisor for Soap Hollow is Julie Robinson, who is listed in the Directory under New York.

Key: CB — Christian C. Blough   JerS — Jeremiah Stahl
       JS — John Sala   PT — Peter Thomas

Blanket chest, blk/red, att Joseph or JS, 1886, 24¼x42¼x18" ...5,000.00
Blanket chest, red, 2 drws, dbl heart, 1868, JS, 26x48x21" 10,000.00
Blanket chest, red, 2 drws, heart, SG, JS, 1856, 26x48x21" 12,000.00
Blanket chest, red, blk lid, 2 drws w/glass pulls, att CB, 1859 ...8,500.00
Blanket chest, red, gilt stencil AM 1845, 24½x45½x20½".......4,500.00
Blanket chest, red, tulip/floral stencils, 1874, 25¾x44x20½" 4,500.00
Chairs, red-brn pnt, horseshoe lyre splat stenciled w/flowers, pr.3,250.00
Chest of drawers, pine/poplar, mustard trim, ET 1883, PT......18,500.00
Chest of drawers, pine/poplar, JerS, MT 1868, 54x47¾x20¼" .25,000.00
Chest of drawers, pine/poplar, stenciled ML 1881, unsgn 15,000.00
Cradle, mini, child's toy, U-shaped scalloped sides, 15¼x9¼" ..4,500.00
Cradle, poplar, brn grain pnt, dvtl joinery, 41x20" 5,000.00
Cradle, poplar/pine, red pnt, dvtl joinery, JS, ca 1870 ....8,000.00
Cupboard, corner, pine/poplar, red-brn pnt, rpr, EK 1856 ....25,000.00
Cupboard, corner, rfn pine/cherry, 4 shelves, window doors 8,000.00

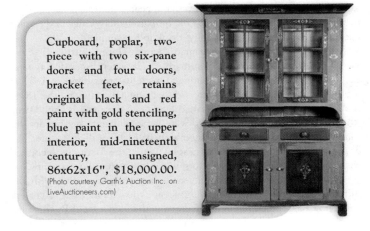

Cupboard, poplar, two-piece with two six-pane doors and four doors, bracket feet, retains original black and red paint with gold stenciling, blue paint in the upper interior, mid-nineteenth century, unsigned, 86x62x16", $18,000.00. (Photo courtesy Garth's Auction Inc. on LiveAuctioneers.com)

Desk, child's, pine/poplar, slant lid on 5-drw base, JL 187 ....28,000.00
Dutch cupboard, pine, stencils & floral decals, JS, 1875 ...... 110,000.00
Nightstand, cherry/pine/poplar pnt red, gilt stencil, 1851.........6,000.00
Sewing caddy, pine box, maroon w/blk base, 1879, 14½x8x6⅞".6,500.00

Soapstone

Soapstone is a soft talc in rock form with a smooth, greasy feel from whence comes its name. (It is also called Soo Chow Jade.) It is composed basically of talc, chlorite, and magnetite. In colonial times it was extracted from out-croppings in large sections with hand saws, carted by oxen to mills, and fashioned into useful domestic articles such as footwarmers, cooking utensils, and inkwells. During the early 1800s, it was used to make heating stoves and kitchen sinks. Most familiar today are the carved vases, bookends, and boxes made in China during the Victorian era.

Figurine, Buddha seated, EX details, China, 8x5x4"..................... 780.00
Figurine, Buddha seated in dhyanasana, loose robes, 20th C, 7⅝" ..450.00
Figurine, group making offering to Goddess, China, 18th C, 5". 1,320.00
Figurine, immortal seated in L robes, beaded necklace, China, 12" . 725.00
Figurine, morphic creature (walrus/eagle/bird), Inuit, 7½x9½" 780.00

Figurine, two men riding fish, extensively carved, Chinese, in fitted box, 12x8", $480.00. (Photo courtesy DuMouchelles on LiveAuctioneers.com)

Seal, dragon form w/Chinese characters on front, 20th C, 4⅝x3x3"..950.00
Seal, ox, recumbent, 20th C, 5x2½x2⅜".. 385.00

Soda Fountain Collectibles

The first soda water sales in the United States occurred in the late 1790s in New York City and New Haven, Connecticut. By the 1830s soda water, the effervescent mineral waters from the various springs around the country, was being sold in drug stores as a medicinal item. About this same period the first flavored soda water appeared at an apothecary shop in Philadelphia. With the adding of the various flavorings, soda water became more popular as a refreshing drink in the summer.

The 1830s also saw the first manufacturer (John Matthews) of devices to make soda water. The first marble soda water dispensing apparatus (better known as the soda fountain) made its appearance in 1857 as a combination ice shaver and flavor-dispensing apparatus. By the 1870s the soda fountain was an established feature of the neighborhood drug store. The fountains of this period were large, elaborate marble devices that were designed to sit on a counter along the back wall drug store. The druggists were competing for business by having the fountains decorated with choice marbles, statues, mirrors, water fountains, and gas lamps.

In 1903 the fountain completed its last major evolution with the introduction of the 'front' counter service we know today. (The soda clerk could now face the customer while drawing the soda water.) By this time ice cream was a standard feature being served as sundaes, ice cream sodas, and milk shakes. Syrup dispensers were just being introduced as 'point-of-sale' devices to sell various flavorings from many different companies. Straws were also commonplace and created a demand for straw holders and dispensers. Fancy and unusual ice cream dippers were in daily use, and their design continued to evolve, reaching their pinnacle with the introduction of the heart-shaped dipper in 1927.

The American soda fountain business has provided collectors today with an almost endless supply of interesting and different articles of commerce. One can collect dippers, syrup dispensers, milk shakers, advertising materials, trade catalogs, and the ultimate prize — the pre-1900 marble soda fountain. Assume that our prices are for examples that are in ex-

cellent condition and are complete with original/correct equipment, i.e., pumps for syrup dispensers, unless otherwise noted. (The presence of a 'correct' pump enhances the value of a syrup dispenser by 25%.)

Collectors need to be made aware that some of the more desirable items are now being reproduced. There are also items that are decorating pieces that are not antiques, i.e., large copper ice cream cones and copper ice cream soda glasses. These items have no resale value as antiques. Our advisor for this category is Richard Stalker; he is listed in the Directory under Pennsylvania. See also Advertising: Dr. Pepper, Hires, Moxie, Pepsi, Seven-Up; Coca-Cola.

Bottle, syrup, Emerson's Ginger Mint Julep, clear w/label under glass... 600.00
Bottle, syrup, Grape Cola, clear w/label under glass, metal cap, 12"...360.00
Bottle, syrup, Pepsinola, clear w/label under glass, 1910s, 12"...... 215.00
Bottle, syrup, Vin Fiz, clear w/label under glass, 1910s, 12" 725.00
Canister, Bowey's Hot Chocolate, porc w/spun metal lid, 9x9".... 775.00
Canister, Malted Grape Nuts, clear glass w/Vitrolite label, metal lid... 725.00
Canister, Thompson's Malted Milk, porc over steel, orig lid, 10". 725.00
Carrier, Dr Pepper, stencil on wood, holds 12-pack, 1920s, 15" L . 550.00
Chairs, ice cream, copper-flashed bent wire w/wood seat, 34", 4 for...200.00
Cooler, Ma's Root Beer on yel, 41x33x19½" 395.00
Dipper, Dover, manual lever, sz 24 rnd bowl w/wooden hdl, 1920s, 10"..200.00
Dipper, Erie Specialty Co, conical, wood hdl, ca 1909 .... 500.00
Dipper, Fisher/Orilla Ont Canada, sz 20 rnd bowl w/wooden hdl, 10½" .. 75.00
Dipper, FS Co, sz 16 rnd bowl w/wooden hdl.............................. 250.00
Dipper, Gem Spoon Co, sz 6 rnd bowl w/wooden hdl, Pat 1895, 11½" .. 325.00
Dipper, Gilchrist #31, oval bowl, NP wooden hdl, 1915, 11½".... 550.00
Dipper, Gilchrist #31, sz 12 rnd bowl w/wooden hdl, 11¾", EXIB... 175.00
Dipper, Gilchrist #33, conical, NP brass w/wood hdl, ca 1914, 10½".. 180.00
Dipper, HS Geer, sz 10 rnd bowl w/wooden hdl, VG.................... 225.00
Dipper, Indestructo #4, brass & wood 30.00
Dipper, Kinger Mfg, conical w/4 blades, 8" 60.00
Dipper, sandwich, ICYPI Automatic Cone Co, sq bowl, wood hdl, 10"..120.00
Dipper, sandwich, Jiffy Dispenser Co, German silver w/wood hdl, 1920s.. 180.00
Dipper, sandwich, Mayer Mfg, German silver w/wood hdl, 12".... 120.00
Dipper, unmk, cylinder bowl, German silver w/wooden hdl, 1920s, 9" .. 575.00
Dispenser, Buckeye Root Beer, ceramic, gnome-like characters . 5,200.00
Dispenser, copper cone w/jeweled dome, brass dispenser, ICS Co, 21". 4,200.00
Dispenser, Fan Taz, porc baseball form, 16" 52,000.00
Dispenser, Fowler's Cherry Smash, ruby glass & chrome, 12½".8,500.00

Dispenser, Grape-Julep, made by Hall China, old pump with 'choc.' button insert, rare style, 13½", $13,200.00. (Photo courtesy Rich Penn Auctions on LiveAuctioneers.com)

Dispenser, Hires, little boy w/urn, Mettlach.............................45,000.00
Dispenser, Horlick's Malted Milk, clear cylinder/gr porc base, 19x8" .. 550.00
Dispenser, hot drink, copper & brass, eagle finial, ca 1900, 30x12"....395.00
Dispenser, malted milk, gr porc/glass cylinder, Hamilton Beach, 19x8" ... 725.00
Dispenser, marble base w/stained glass tulip shade, 1890s, 26x7½" ..950.00
Dispenser, Mission Real Fruit Juice, pk glass w/brass, 13" 550.00
Dispenser, Nesbitt's Hot Fudge, chrome/maroon Bakelite/crockery, 13"..850.00
Dispenser, Orange Crush, amber glass w/chrome dispenser top, 13" ..1,450.00
Dispenser, Rochester Root Beer, clear/alum upright bbl w/hdl, 14"....875.00

Dispenser, Root Beer, clear cut/etch glass, 1900s, 21" 550.00
Dispenser, Stern's Root Beer, wooden keg w/metal bands, 13x9" . 360.00
Dispenser, Ward's Orange crush, ceramic orange w/pump, 1920s, 13".. 3,000.00
Dispenser, Wine Dip Cola, glass/metal, Cordley NY, 15¾x8" 215.00
Flavor board, Noll's Ice Cream, celluloid w/metal fr, 20x10"........ 150.00
Fountain dish, clear paneled boat style, 3x3⅝x8" 15.00
Fountain dish, clear, rnd paneled bowl w/short ft, 2x5" 45.00
Fountain glass, clear ftd malt/shake, fluted w/banded rim, 1950s, 7".. 10.00
Fountain glass, Jr Awful Awful.., clear w/red-pnt label at rim, 5" ... 45.00
Fountain glass, Kist Beverages, clear w/red-pnt label, 1950s, 4⅜".. 25.00
Fountain glasses, ftd, gr, Paden City, set of 4, 7" 100.00
Fountain glasses, smoked rims, metal hdld holders, set of 4, 1950s ..25.00
Fountain spoons, SP w/twisted hdls, mk Berlin, set of 4, 6" 30.00
Ice shaver, ornate CI, Zeppelin & floral front, Occupied Japan, 34x19" ..480.00
Jar, Borden's Malted Milk, clear w/label under glass, w/lid, 9"...... 950.00
Jar, fruit, clear glass, 10-sided, Near Cut - Pat Apld For, 10" 360.00
Juicer, Sunkist Juicit, chrome & mg, 1950s, 9" 150.00
Menu, Tellings Ice Cream, celluloid cover, 1920s........................ 325.00
Mixer, Nesbit's It's Frosted, chrome cup, Bakelite lid, 1940s, 15".. 150.00
Mug, Richardson Root Beer Rich, etched glass w/band top/bottom, 6½"..85.00
Straw dispenser, Hires Root Beer, metal & tin, 4¾x9½", VG....3,200.00
Straw holder, amber glass w/appl jewels, w/top, 1880s, 14" 7,250.00
Straw holder, clear/ribbed, metal top/insert, Benedict, 1920s-30s, 14"..225.00

Straw holder, cranberry Thumbprint, circa 1910, 13", EX, $2,880.00. (Photo courtesy Rich Penn Auctions on LiveAuctioneers.com)

Straw holder, gr glass w/metal base & lid, ca 1910, 12" 850.00
Table, glass display case top, 4 swing-out CI/mahog seats, 26" sq ..1,650.00
Tray, girl w/tray of sundaes, blk w/silver moon/gold trim, 13x13". 250.00

Spatter Glass

Spatter glass, characterized by its multicolor 'spatters,' has been made from the late nineteenth century to the present by American glasshouses as well as those abroad. Although it was once thought to have been made entirely by workers at the 'end of the day' from bits and pieces of leftover scrap, it is now known that it was a standard line of production. See also Art Glass Baskets.

Basket, mc on wht, crimped rim, crystal irregular-shaped hdl, 6" ... 75.00
Biscuit jar, rainbow spatter w/enamel floral, 7½" to top of bail..... 625.00
Cruet, ruby & wht, clear hdl, faceted stopper, 6¾", NM 60.00
Pitcher, cranberry/wht/clear, bulb, clear hdl, 8½" 165.00
Pitcher, gold-tan/amber, amber hdl, spherical w/ruffled lip, 9" 120.00
Pitcher, pastel colors, swirl mold, clear hdl, ball shape, 7¾"......... 130.00
Pitcher, wht/pk, bulb w/crimped rim, 9", +8 tumblers 460.00
Vase, cranberry/wht, Ribbed Pillar, 6x5" 80.00
Vase, pk & bl w/swirled body, ruffled rim, 9"................................. 30.00
Vase, pk & wht w/clear, bulb, short flared rim, 7x7" 75.00

Vase, transparent yellow cased with opal flakes, ground pontil, attributed to Phoenix, fourth quarter nineteenth century, 11", $135.00. (Photo courtesy Green Valley Auctions on LiveAuctioneers.com)

Spatterware

Spatterware is a general term referring to a type of decoration used by English potters as early as the late 1700s. Using a brush or a stick, brightly colored paint was dabbed onto the soft-paste earthenware items, achieving a spattered effect which was often used as a border. Because much of this type of ware was made for export to the United States, some of the subjects in the central design — the schoolhouse and the eagle patterns, for instance — reflect American tastes. Yellow, green, and black spatterware is scarce and highly valued by collectors. In the descriptions that follow, the color listed after the item indicates the color of the spatter. The central design is identified next, and the color description that follows that refers to the design. When no condition code is present, assume that the item is undamaged and has only very light wear.

Creamer, blk/brn bands, rose, 2-color, flakes, 3¾" 480.00
Creamer, red w/blk bands, tulip, 2-color, rpr chip/hdl, 4" 1,650.00
Creamer, red, peafowl, 3-color, bulb, 2½" 1,800.00
Pitcher, bl, 6-sided, ornate hdl, 6" 275.00
Pitcher, bl, fort/trees, 3-color, ornate hdl, shouldered/ftd, 10"... 1,150.00
Pitcher, bl, w/peafowl in red & gr, 6".. 660.00
Pitcher, mauve/blk stripes, 6-panel, 6⅜" 1,450.00
Pitcher, purple, tulip, 3-color, bulb/paneled, 5½" 600.00
Pitcher, purple/bl/blk stripes on wht, 8¾" 1,100.00
Pitcher, red (full spatter), primrose, 3-color, flared/paneled, 6" .2,800.00
Plate, bl, fort, yel/red/blk, 12-panel, early 19th C, 7" 300.00
Plate, bl, peafowl, red/gr, 10-panel, 1820s, 8⅛" 360.00
Plate, bl, tulip, red/gr, 9½" 120.00
Plate, gr (as tree tops/at rim), peafowl, yel/blk w/imp heart, 10", VG....960.00
Plate, rainbow, bull's-eye, red/gr, flake, 9⅝"................................ 750.00
Plate, rainbow, red/bl, 8¼" 550.00
Plate, red, peafowl, bl/yel/gr, feather-emb rim, 1820s, 8⅛" 295.00
Plate, red, Primrose, purple/gr w/yel center, lt stain, 8" 150.00
Plate, red/gr rainbow, 9½" 550.00
Platter, brn/purple, bull's eye, brn/purple, 13½x10¼" 3,700.00
Saucer, red, deer, brn-blk, 6" 175.00
Saucer, red, Schoolhouse, red/brn/gr 575.00
Soup plate, gr, peafowl, bl/yel/red, hairline, 10" 660.00
Sugar bowl, bl, fort, 3-color, prof rstr, w/lid, 4½"......................... 275.00

Sugar bowl, blue, peafowl in three colors, $345.00. (Photo courtesy Morphy Auctions)

Sugar bowl, bl, peafowl, 4-color, ring/shell-emb hdls, w/lid, lg..1,550.00
Sugar bowl, bl, peafowl, bl/gr/red, octagonal, w/lid, 7½", EX........ 480.00
Sugar bowl, blk/pk rainbow, flower, 2-color, prof rstr, w/lid, 6"..1,325.00
Sugar bowl, red, rooster, 4-color, w/lid, 4½x5⅛" 600.00
Sugar bowl, yel, thistle, red/gr, w/lid, 7½" 2,650.00
Tea bowl & saucer, bl, peafowl, gr/red/yel, EX 100.00
Tea bowl & saucer, bl, schoolhouse, 3-color, ca 1840 ....2,350.00
Tea bowl & saucer, rainbow, red/bl.. 650.00
Tea bowl & saucer, red, Holly Berry, gr/red, EX 150.00
Tea bowl & saucer, red, peafowl, bl/gr/red.................................. 300.00
Tea bowl & saucer, wht, Tic Tac Toe, gr/red 550.00
Tea bowl & saucer, yel, Cockscomb, red/gr, stains/flakes 1,600.00

Tea bowl and saucer, yellow, Tulip in three colors, $1,035.00. (Photo courtesy Morphy Auctions)

Teapot, bl, 4-bud cluster, red/gr, paneled, final reattached, 8", VG...1,200.00
Teapot, bl/yel rainbow, rose, 3-color, str sides, gooseneck spout, 10" ..4,500.00
Teapot, gr, peafowl, 3-color, flakes, 5" 660.00
Teapot, rainbow: 3-color horizontal bands, simple form, much rpr, 7".. 950.00
Teapot, red, peafowl, bl/yel/gr, bulb/shouldered, low dome lid, 7". 900.00
Washbowl & pitcher, bl, peafowl, 4-color, 1830-50, 10", 12¼", VG... 550.00
Washbowl & pitcher, purple/blk bands on wht, 4¼x12¼", 10" .2,750.00
Washbowl, red/bl stripes w/crisscross center, rpr, 13¾" 240.00

Spelter

Spelter items are cast from commercial zinc and coated with a metallic patina. The result is a product very similar to bronze in appearance, yet much less expensive.

Bank, King Charles spaniel, blk & wht pnt, Germany, 1920s-30s. 480.00
Bookends, Deco nude stands in peering position, bronze rpt, 8", EX .. 350.00
Bust, Odette, bronze finish, A Foretay, ca 1900, 19"..................... 435.00

Busts of Moors, dark patina, paw-footed base, twentieth century, 29½", pair $1,200.00. (Photo courtesy Dallas Auction Gallery on LiveAuctioneers.com)

Candle arbor, knight stands & holds staff w/4 candle arms, 1880s, 34" ..750.00
Candleholders, Am Indian holds torch, 1900s, 16", EX, pr.......... 275.00
Centerpiece, cherubs along rim, silver patina, rpr, 22" L................... 375.00
Chandelier, cherub holds 2 lamp fixtures in hands, worn gilt, 10x6" .. 385.00
Clock, 2 children on red marble, movement mk Japy Freres #385 YN Thomas, 28".2,640.00
Figurine, allegorical maiden leans on anchor, after Moreau, 1900s, 25".235.00
Figurine, Arum, Nouveau lady w/flowers, after Nanteuil, rprs, 19"... 500.00
Figurine, Deco lady kneels forward, celluloid face & hands, 6x14" ..240.00
Figurine, Distress, lady waves goodbye, Mestais, on socle, 20th C, 21".. 185.00
Figurine, Don Juan, old gold pnt, Ansonial, 20" 150.00
Figurine, Industry, allegorical man, Wagner, 24" 480.00
Figurine, Perseus & Pegasus, after Picalt, worn patina, 20th C, 22" ...725.00
Figurine, sailor standing on sailboat, 2 Paris mks, 22½x11".......... 125.00

Lamp, Deco jester w/instrument, amber globe shade, bronze pnt, 6x6x4". 160.00
Lamp, Deco nude stands ea side of gr frosted flower shade, 9x10". 375.00
Lamp, draped Nouveau lady w/raised arm, 2-socket, brass finish, 16x9".135.00

Spode/Copeland

The following is a short chronological history of the Spode company:

1733: Josiah Spode I is born on March 23, at Lane Delph, Staffordshire.

1740: Spode is put to work in a pottery factory.

1754: Spode, now a fully proficient journeyman/potter, works for Turner and Banks in Stoke-on-Trent.

1755: Josiah Spode II is born.

1761: Spode I acquires a factory in Shelton where he makes cream-colored and blue-painted earthenware.

1770: This is the year adopted as the date Spode I founded the business.

1784: Spode I masters the art and techniques of transfer printing in blue under the glaze on earthenware.

1796: This marks the earliest known record of Spode selling porcelain dinnerware.

1800: Spode II produces the first bone china.

1806: Spode is appointed potter to the Royal Family; this continues past 1983.

1813: Spode produces the first stone china.

1821: Spode introduces Feldspar Porcelain, a variety of bone china.

1833: William Taylor Copeland acquires the Spode factory from the Spode family and becomes partners with Garrett until 1847.

1870: System of impressing date marks on the backs of the dinnerware begins.

1925: Robert Copeland is born. (He presently resides in England.)

1976: The company merges with Worcester Royal Porcelain Company and forms Royal Worcester Spode Limited.

1986: The Spode Society is established.

1989: The holding company for Spode becomes the Porcelain and Fine China Companies Limited.

The price quotes listed in these three categories of Spode are for twentieth-century pre-1965 dinnerware in pristine condition — no cracks, chips, crazing, or stains. Minor knife cuts do not constitute damage unless extreme.

The patterns in the first group are the most common and popular earthenware lines. The second group contains the rarer and higher priced patterns; they are both earthenware and stoneware. Bone china patterns comprise the third group.

Our advisor for this category is Don Haase; he is listed in the Directory under Washington.

First Group (Earthenware/Imperialware)

Ann Hathaway, Billingsley Rose, Buttercup, Byron, Camilla Pink, Chelsea Wicker, Chinese Rose, Christmas Tree (green), Cowslip, Fairy Dell, Fleur de Lys (blue/brown), Florence, Gadroon, Gainsborough, Hazel Dell, Indian Tree, Jewel, Moss Rose, Old Salem, Raeburn, Reynolds, Romney, Rosalie, Rose Briar, Valencia, Wicker Dale, Wicker Dell, Wicker Lane.

Wicker Lane, see listings for values. (Photo courtesy Jackson's Auction on LiveAuctioneers.com)

Bowl, fruit, 5" 22.00
Creamer, sm 45.00
Bowl, cereal, 6½" 65.00
Bowl, serving, divided, Tower Black (group values do not apply), 4x11" .325.00
Coffeepot, 8-cup 195.00
Creamer, lg 55.00
Cup/saucer, demi 29.00
Cup/saucer, low/tall 29.00
Plate, bread & butter, 6¼" 16.00
Plate, butter pat 18.00
Plate, dinner 25.00
Plate, dinner, for Madam Butchart, Victoria BC, Canada, 1930s... 75.00
Plate, luncheon, rnd, 8-9" 22.00
Plate, salad, 7½" 20.00
Platter, oval, 13" 115.00
Platter, oval, 15" 135.00
Platter, oval, 17" 165.00
Sauceboat, w/liner 125.00
Soup, cream, w/liner 32.00
Soup, rim, 7½" 27.00
Soup, rim, 8½" 32.00
Sugar bowl, w/lid, lg 55.00
Sugar bowl, w/lid, sm 45.00
Teapot, 8-cup 195.00
Vegetable, oval, 9-10" 115.00
Vegetable, oval, 10-11" 135.00
Vegetable, sq, 8" 125.00
Vegetable, sq, 9" 145.00
Vegetable, w/lid 275.00
Waste bowl, 6" 29.00

Second Group (Earthenware/Imperialware)

Aster, Butchart, Camilla Blue, Christmas Tree (magenta), Fitzhugh (blue/red/green), Gloucester (blue/red), Herring Hunt (green/magenta), Italian, Mayflower, Patricia, Rosebud Chintz, Tradewinds (blue/red), Tower Blue and Pink, Wildflower (blue/red).

Pink Tower, see listings for values. (Photo courtesy Quinn's Waverly Auction Galleries on LiveAuctioneers.com)

Bowl, cereal, 6½" 32.00
Bowl, fruit, 5½" 28.00
Coffeepot, 8-cup 345.00
Creamer, lg 75.00
Creamer, sm 65.00
Cup/saucer, demi 35.00
Cup/saucer, low/high 39.00
Plate, bread & butter, 6¼" 29.00
Plate, butter pat 27.00
Plate, chop, rnd, 13" 225.00
Plate, dinner, 10½" 55.00
Plate, luncheon, rnd, 8-9" 45.00
Plate, luncheon, sq, 8½" 47.00
Plate, salad, 7½" 35.00

Platter, oval, 13" 145.00
Platter, oval, 15" 165.00
Platter, oval, 17" 210.00
Sauceboat, w/liner 165.00
Soup, rim, 7½" 35.00
Soup, rim, 8½" 45.00
Sugar bowl, w/lid, lg 75.00
Sugar bowl, w/lid, sm 65.00
Teapot, 8-cup 315.00
Vegetable, oval, 9-10" 135.00
Vegetable, oval, 10-11" 155.00
Vegetable, sq, 8" 145.00
Vegetable, sq, 9" 165.00
Vegetable, w/lid 325.00
Waste bowl, 6" 33.00

Third Group (Bone China)

Billingsley Rose, Bridal Rose, Carolyn, Chelsea Gardens, Christine, Claudia, Colonel, Dimity, Dresden Rose, Fleur de Lys (gray/red/blue), Geisha (blue/pink/white), Irene, Maritime Rose, Primrose (pink), Savoy, Shanghi.

Bowl, cereal, 6½" 42.00
Bowl, fruit, 5½" 37.00
Coffeepot, 8-cup 425.00
Creamer, lg 110.00
Creamer, sm 110.00
Cup/saucer, demi 55.00
Cup/saucer, low/tall 65.00
Plate, bread & butter, 6¼" 39.00
Plate, butter pat 35.00
Plate, chop, rnd, 13" 295.00
Plate, dessert, 8" 45.00
Plate, dinner, 10½" 59.00
Plate, luncheon, rnd, 9" 45.00
Plate, luncheon, sq, 8½" 55.00
Plate, salad, 7½" 49.00
Platter, oval, 13" 195.00
Platter, oval, 15" 225.00
Platter, oval, 17" 265.00
Sauceboat, w/liner 145.00
Soup, cream, w/liner 145.00
Soup, rim, 7½" 55.00
Soup, rim, 8½" 65.00
Sugar bowl, w/lid, lg 120.00
Sugar bowl, w/lid, sm 115.00
Teapot, 8-cup 425.00
Vegetable, oval, 9-10" 215.00
Vegetable, oval, 10-11" 235.00
Vegetable, sq, 8" 245.00
Vegetable, sq, 9" 265.00
Vegetable, w/lid 385.00
Waste bowl, 6" 47.00

Spongeware

Spongeware is a type of factory-made earthenware that was popular during the last quarter of the nineteenth century and into the first quarter of the twentieth century. It was decorated by dabbing color onto the drying ware with a sponge, leaving a splotched design at random or in simple patterns. Sometimes a solid band of color was added. The vessel was then covered with a clear glaze and fired at a high temperature. Blue on white is the most preferred combination, but green on ivory, orange on white, or those colors in combination may also occasionally be found. As with most pottery, rare forms and condition are major factors in establishing value. Spongeware is still being made today, so beware of newer examples. Our values are for undamaged examples, unless a specific condition code is given within the description.

Bowl, mixing, bl/wht, lt patterned sponging in scallops, 13" 275.00
Bowl, mixing, bl/wht, patterned sponging, fluted, str sides, 11" ... 215.00
Bowl, mixing, bl/wht, patterned sponging w/bl & wht band, 6x11"...150.00

Butter tub, blue and white, stenciled label surrounded by blue-dot band, 5½x6½", $225.00 to $295.00. (Photo courtesy Kathryn McNerney)

Creamer, bl/wht, dk patterned sponging, tankard form, 4½" 550.00
Jar, bl/wht, Prunes, mk 7 Pat Ap For, 8" 960.00
Jar, preserve, ochre/cream patterned sponging, ca 1870s, 6½", EX ..125.00
Pitcher, bl/wht allover sponging, emb triangles, bulb base, 9" 480.00
Pitcher, bl/wht, allover sponging w/wht bands, bbl shape, 8¾"........ 325.00
Pitcher, bl/wht, dk allover sponging, emb scallop shells, 7¼" 480.00
Pitcher, bl/wht, lt allover sponging, Rhonesboro TX, 1900s, 9½" . 780.00
Pitcher, bl/wht patterned sponging, EX contrast, cylindrical, 9", EX... 300.00
Pitcher, bl/wht, sponged band, Rhonesboro TX, 1900s, 9½" 600.00
Spittoon, bl/wht, patterned sponging & bl band, 6½" dia 180.00
Sugar bowl, bl & wht w/gold-trimmed neck band 225.00
Sugar bowl, red/cream, patterned sponging, w/lid, 7¾x5½"......... 125.00
Umbrella stand, bl/wht, Nouveau shape, copper-lustre trim, 21". 235.00
Umbrella stand, bl/wht, patterned sponging & bands, cylinder, VG... 235.00
Washboard, bl & wht.. 400.00

Spoons

Souvenir spoons have been popular remembrances since the 1890s. The early hand-wrought examples of the silversmith's art are especially sought and appreciated for their fine craftsmanship. Commemorative, personality-related, advertising, and those with Indian busts or floral designs are only a few of the many types of collectible spoons. In the following listings, spoons are sorted by city, character, or occasion.

Key:
B — bowl
ff — full figure
gw — gold washed
H — handle

Chicago World's Fair, sterling, $50.00. (Photo courtesy Rose Galleries on LiveAuctioneers.com)

3 Wise Men ff H; plain B; lg (server), $50 to 90.00
Alaska eng in B; miner ff H; Sterling, 5¼" 80.00
Alaska, transfer print enamel finial, sterling, demi, $5 to 15.00
Atlanta Cotton Expo 1895, crown finial; rose in B; Maier & Berkele .. 110.00
Australia, gum leaf/gum nut finial, handmade, J Harris, $25 to...... 50.00
Baltimore eng in B; city seal/Poe's monument/banner on H; silver, 6"...55.00

Bartlesville OK & cowboy roping steer in B; Indian lady ff H; Sterling.. 55.00
Black man carrying stick w/dead opossum, $100 to 150.00
Bronco, rider finial, Hirsch & Oppenheimer, $30 to 50.00
California on H; bear finial; plain B; Shiebler, $75 to 125.00
Christmas tree/Santa/holly/bells form H; Merry Christmas/socks in B...75.00
Colorado emb on H; Gateway to Garden on Gods in B; $40 to..... 75.00
Columbus on globe H; MOP B; $50 to 90.00
Crescent Hotel, Eureka Springs AR in gw B; floral H; Sterling, 5⅛" .. 75.00
Dome of Cologne HP in B; 2 coats of arms HP on H; gw coin silver, 5" .. 45.00
Fairbanks AK skyline ff H; JB Erd, $125 to 175.00
Fort Sumter Charleston SC eng in gw B; Towle, $25 to 50.00

Garfield Memorial, Cleveland, Ohio, in bowl, Heart of Cleveland handle with skyline, $35.00. (Photo courtesy Rose Galleries on LiveAuctioneers.com)

Golden Gate/Hotel St Francis B; San Francisco skyline H; Paye & Baker 65.00
Gulfport MS & black boy eating watermelon in B; crown finial, 5"..85.00
House of 7 Gables, Salem MA on H; witch finial; unmk, $20 to ... 50.00
Indian H, sterling, unmk 65.00
Jeweled & faceted ruby inset, unmk Burma, $20 to 45.00
Kill Mts eng/2 cats emb in B; Indian chief/corn on H; Paye & Baker ..70.00
Liechtenstein castle pnt in B; flower finial; $20 to......................... 50.00
Louisville KY in B; figural Am Indian H; Schiebler, ca 1895 .... 90.00
Mardi Gras woman (mk), HP in B; state H; $100 to 200.00
Mormon Temple emb in ruffled B; angel finial/Moroni on H; Sterling... 60.00
Muscatine in B; enameled corn on H; $40 to 75.00
New York skyline H; emb Brooklyn Bridge in B; $25 to 45.00
Nome ND eng in B; nude Nouveau lady emb on H; silver, unknown mk, 5"..60.00
Nouveau lady picking grapes on H; plain B; 925 Sterling, 5" 90.00
NV & 3 scenes emb on H; Pride of Desert Goldfield/cactus emb in B..135.00
Pasco, WA, Western girl hdl, sterling, 6" 100.00
Passaic Falls Paterson NJ eng in B, Chantilly pattern, Gorham 45.00
Pikes Peak CO eng in B; wavy H; Shepard, $30 to......................... 50.00
Poland Spring/Poland Water/Poland Mineral Spring Water on H; Durgin .95.00
Salem & witch emb on H; plain B; Durgin for Daniel Low, 1892.. 60.00
Spain, dancing senorita on finial; plain B; demi, $10 to 20.00
Thomas Jefferson HP in B, $300 to 500.00
WBA (Woman's Benefit Assoc) on H; plain B; Gorham, Wood & Hughes..50.00

Sporting Goods

Vintage ammunition boxes, duck and goose calls, knives, and fishing gear are just a few of the items that collectors of this type of memorabilia look for today. Also favored are posters, catalogs, and envelopes from well known companies such as Winchester, Remington, Peters, Ithaca, and DuPont. Duck stamps have been widely collectible in recent years. Unless otherwise noted, items listed are in excellent condition. See also Fishing Collectibles.

Book, Single Shot Rifles, Grand, hardbk, 1947 1st ed, VG+.......... 60.00
Box, shot shell, Peters High Velocity 20 Ga, 2-pc, empty, G 125.00
Brochure, Remington UMC Kleanbore Hi-Speed 22s, foldout, 10x3¼", NM... 70.00
Call, turkey, Easy Squeeze-O-Matic, Smith's Game Calls, NM...... 30.00
Can, powder, Dead Shot, game bird reserve on red, 4x3½x1" 220.00
Cartridges, revolver, unopened pack 900.00
Catalog, Bear Archery 1968, Kodiak/Bearcat bows, etc, 31 pgs.......... 36.00
Catalog, Dominion Ammunition No 20, 1935, 52 pgs, 5x7½" 70.00

Catalog, Marlin Guns, 1948, 8 pgs w/color photos, 7x9½", VG+ .. 20.00
Catalog, Weatherby's - Tomorrow's Rifles Today, 1950s, 100 pgs, VG+ ... 95.00
Cover, DuPont, moose, hunter behind canoe, Goodwin, 1920............. 450.00
Cover, J Stevens Arms & Tool Co, man taking aim, ca 1902 .... 50.00
Cover, Peters Ammunition, lion w/killed zebra, 3½x6½" 1,050.00
Cover, Peters Cartridges, bear, 1932, 3x6" 375.00
Cover, Remington Guns & Rifles, My Favorite..., lady w/gun, 1901.......... 110.00
Cover, Remington UMC Gib Game Rifles, man facing bear, 1910 .... 160.00
Cover, Stevens Arms & Tool Co, boy w/new rifle, 1909, 3¾x6½" 1,050.00
Cover, Winchester Model 1912, man w/gun & dog, 3½x6½"........ 100.00
Cover, Winchester Rifles & Shotguns, camp scene, 3½x6½", NM .. 650.00
Cover, Winchester Rifles & Shotguns, hunter, Pr Goodwin, 1911 .... 190.00
Cover, Winchester, bear & cabin scene, Goodwin, 1928, 3½x6½",........ 525.00
Cover, Winchester, lady on horse holding up rifle, 1934, 5x6" 700.00
Crate, Small Arms Smokeless Powder, Sears Roebuck, nailed wood 300.00
Dummy shells, Remington UMC, 6 cutaway 5" shells, NMIB 450.00
Flask, tin, Hercules Powder, w/belt loop, L Rand paper label, 1-lb 215.00
Poster, Remington Arms - Union Metallic Cartridges, turkey, 26x17" 160.00
Poster, Winchester Ranger...Powder, shell & birds, 1928, 23x17" 170.00
Score book, US Cartridge rifle shooting, 50 targets, 1905, 7x4" 50.00
Tin, Nobel's Emp Smokeless...Powder, 1-lb................................... 140.00
Tin, Rem Oil, DuPont, ca 1930s-40s, 5x2¼x1" 30.00
Tin, Savage Brand Smokeless Powder, metal jacketed bullets, 6" L............. 725.00
Tin, Snap Shot Powder, paper labels, 1-lb, 5½x3½x1½"................ 230.00
Tin, Winchester Gun Oil, lettering on gr, 4½x2¼x1¼"................. 140.00

Sports Collectibles

When sports cards became so widely collectible several years ago, other types of related memorabilia started to interest sports fans. Now they search for baseball uniforms, autographed baseballs, game-used bats and gloves, and all sorts of ephemera. Although baseball is America's all-time favorite, other sports have their own following of interested collectors. Our advice for this category comes from Paul Longo Americana. Mr. Longo is listed in the Directory under Massachusetts. To learn more about old golf collectibles, we recommend *The Vintage Era of Golf Club Collectibles* by Ronald O. John and *Antique Golf Collectibles* by Pete Georgiady (both published by Collector Books). Unless otherwise indicated, all items listed are in excellent condition.

Baseball

Baseball, sgn, Bob Feller 50.00
Baseball, sgn, Stan Musial 100.00
Bat, Mickey Mantle, Louisville Slugger, store model, 125 powerized .. 150.00
Bobblehead doll, Pittsburgh Pirates, player on base, 1962............. 300.00

Catcher's mask with throat protector, maker unknown, all original, $240.00. (Photo courtesy Philip Weiss Auctions on LiveAuctioneers.com)

Figurine, Hartland statue, Hank Aaron, 1960 .... 300.00
Figurine, Hartland statue, Ted Williams, 1960 .... 350.00
Glove, Bill Mazeroski MacGregor model 95.00
Glove, Stan Musial Rawlings, in orig box.................................... 400.00
Pennant, Boston Braves, ca 1940s... 200.00

Pennant, Brooklyn Dodgers, NL Champs, early 1950s................. 350.00
Pennant, NY Yankees w/team picture, 1961 .... 300.00
Pin-bk, Jackie Robinson, blk/wht, 1950s, 1¾" 250.00
Pin-bk, Joe Dimaggio, ca 1940s, 1¾" 200.00
Pin-bk, Ted Williams, ca 1956, 1¾" 125.00
Press pin, Boston Red Sox, 1967 World Series 325.00
Press pin, NY Giants, 1954 World Series 350.00
Press pin, NY Yankees, 2000 World Series................................. 150.00
Program, Cincinnati Reds, 1975 World Series 85.00
Program, NY Yankees, 1956 World Series.................................. 325.00
Team photo, sgn, 1957 NY Yankees, 8x10"............................. 1,000.00
Window display ad, Louisville Slugger, Ty Cobb, 1923, minor rstr, 22x16"... 600.00

Football

Banner, Notre Dame National Champions, 1929, 17x36", NM... 600.00
Bobblehead doll, Boston Patriots, orig box, early 1960s............. 400.00
Boots, cleats, Steel Plates #8878, sz 11, 1950s, MIB 40.00
Football, All Pro Wilson, Dick Butkus #51, leather 40.00
Helmet, Hutch #H-18, silver leather, wht lined, 1930s, NM 150.00
Helmet, JC Higgins, front wing/3 stripes on leather, wool lining. 325.00

Helmet, MacGregor, black saddle-style leather with company logo center front, #H622, circa 1930s, VG, $450.00. (Photo courtesy Nate D. Sanders on LiveAuctioneers.com)

Helmet, Rawlings #A11X, leather w/chin strap, rubber lining, 1945.. 125.00
Helmet, Wilson #F2154, brn & blk leather, 8 panels, 1930s, NM... 200.00
Media guide, Cleveland Browns, Jim Brn on cover, 1964............. 150.00
Media guide, Oregon Ducks Football, Coach Warren photo cover, 1942 .... 35.00
Media guide, UCLA Bruins, 1958 .... 55.00
Megaphone, Michigan University, blk & yel, 1940s, 9x6", VG ... 125.00
Pants, wood slats for padding in ea leg, laces, olive gr, 1920s, NM ... 125.00
Pennant, Chicago Cardinals, 1940s 150.00
Pennant, Illinois, Harold 'Red' Grange, ca 1950s, rare................ 300.00
Pennant, Notre Dame, 1940s 100.00
Pennant, Pittsburgh Steelers, 1975 Super Bowl X 95.00
Pennant, San Francisco 49ers, 1984 Super Bowl XIX.................... 60.00
Pin-back, Johnny Unitas, Baltimore Colts, color, 1960s, 3" 75.00
Postcard, photo of University of MI team, 1909.......................... 225.00
Poster, Tournament of Roses, Brown vs WA State, 1916, 26x18"+fr.1,500.00
Program, Alabama vs Boston, 1946, NM 50.00
Program, Harvard vs Yale, 11/22/13, football shaped, VG+ 395.00
Ticket stub, Southern California vs Notre Dame, Nov 25, 1938, NM...50.00
Uniform, red & yel jersey w/#22, yel canvas pants, 1920s, VG 140.00
Yearbook, Carnegie Tech, The Thistle 1927, hardbk, NM............. 70.00

Tennis Rackets

Most collectible tennis rackets date between 1880 and 1950. The year 1880 is a somewhat arbitrary beginning of the 'modern' tennis era, since the first official Wimbledon tournament was held in 1877, and the US National Lawn Tennis Association was formed in 1881. Many types of tennis rackets were produced well before 1880, but generally these were designed for games far different than the lawn tennis we know today.

Rackets produced between the 1880s and 1950s were generally made of wood, although some like those made by the Dayton Steel Company

(1920s) or the Birmingham Aluminum Company (1920s) were made of metal. The most common head shape is oval, but some were flat on top, some flat transitional, and some even lopsided. Handles were generally larger than those seen today, and most were unfinished wood with vertical ribs called 'combing,' rarer models featured cork handles or 'checkered' wood. The leather-wrapped handle common today was not introduced widely until the mid-1930s. Unusual enlargements to the butt end of the handle are generally desirable and might be called fishtail, fantail, bulbous, tall tail, or flared. The 'wedge,' a triangular section of wood located at the junction of the handle and the head, might be solid or laminated and can be a good indication of age, since most solid wedges date to before 1905. Like most collectibles, racket values depend on rarity, age, and condition. Prices for well preserved rackets in this period may range from $50.00 to well over $1,000.00. Tennis ball cans are also very collectible and may be worth hundreds of dollars for rare unopened examples. Our advisor for this category is Donald Jones; he is listed in the Directory under Georgia.

Key:
cx-lam — convex laminated   tran — transitional
cx-s — convex solid

Winchester, ash and cedar, circa mid-1920s, $985.00. (Photo courtesy Livingston's Auction on LiveAuctioneers.com)

AJ Reach, Driver, concave wedge, combed hdl, oval head, 1920. 125.00
Dayton, steel w/wooden hdl, 1924 .... 250.00
E Kent, Duchess, concave wedge, bulb hdl, oval head, 1930........ 200.00
Hazel's Streamline, branched wedge, leather hdl, oval head, 1935. 1,000.00
Horseman, Elberton, concave wedge, smooth hdl, flat-top head, 1885 ..600.00
Iver Johnson, Special, cx-s wedge, bulb hdl, tran head, 1900....... 250.00
Magnon, Superior, concave wedge, combed hdl, oval head, 1928. 100.00
Slazinger, Demon, cx-lam wedge, fishtail hdl, oval head, 1910 .... 400.00
Spaulding, Park, cx-s wedge, combed hdl, flat-top head, 1895 ..... 800.00
Wright-Ditson, Hub, cx-s wedge, checkered hdl, oval head, 1890 ... 175.00

Miscellaneous

Basketball, belt buckle, University of KY Champions, 1987-88, M .35.00
Basketball, laced brn leather, 1915, VG.. 110.00
Basketball, pennant, Boston Celtics/mascot on gr, 1969 .... 35.00
Basketball, pennant, Buffalo Braves, blk & orange on wht, 1969 .. 35.00
Boxing, postcard, Jack Johnson & Jim James Jeffries photo, 1910. 135.00
Boxing, poster, Tuolumne County Youth Boxing Club, 1979, 22x14"...25.00
Golf, caddie badge, Norwood Hills Country Club, ca 1920, NM... 55.00
Golf, club, Niblick, wood shaft, ca 1900, 38".............................. 55.00
Hockey, pennant, Montreal Canadians, The Flying Frenchman, 1960s.. 80.00
Hockey, puck, Atlanta Flames, Official Art Ross Tyer, 1973 logo, NM.. 50.00
Racing, pennant, Indianapolis Motor Speedway, mc on gr, ca 1920, NM. 265.00
Racing, program, Indy 500 Official Racing Program, 1939, NM.. 150.00
Soccer, ball, brn leather panels, rubber int, ca 1950s...................... 50.00
Softball, book, Softball w/Offical Rules, A Noren, hardbk, 1959... 15.00
Softball, Louisville Slugger, Minuteman 1776, wrapped hdl, 1970, M...30.00
Track & field, shoes, Adidas, red/bl stripes on wht leather, 1960s.. 40.00

Staffordshire

Scores of potteries sprang up in England's Staffordshire district in the early eighteenth century; several remain to the present time. (See also spe-

cific companies.) Figurines and groups were made in great numbers; dogs were favorite subjects. Often they were made in pairs, each a mirror image of the other. They varied in heights from 3" or 4" to the largest, measuring 16" to 18". From 1840 until about 1900, portrait figures were produced to represent specific characters, both real and fictional. As a rule these were never marked.

Historical transferware was made throughout the district; some collectors refer to it as Staffordshire Blue. It was produced as early as 1780, and because much was exported to America, it was very often decorated with transfers depicting scenic views of well-known American landmarks. Early examples were printed in a deep cobalt. By 1830 a softer blue was favored, and within the next decade black, brown, pink, red, and green prints were used. Although sometimes careless about adding their trademark, many companies used their own border designs that were as individual as their names. This ware should not be confused with the vast amounts of modern china (mostly plates) made from early in the twentieth century to the present. These souvenir or commemorative items are usually marketed through gift stores and the like. (See Rowland and Marsellus.) Our advisor for this category is Jeanne Dunay; she is listed in the Directory under South Carolina. See also specific manufacturers.

Key:
d/b — dark blue   m/b — medium blue
l/b — light blue

Figures and Groups

Androclese & lion, 19th C, 7⅛", EX... 600.00
Arab man on camel, 1850s, 8x5½" 1,200.00
Caernarvon Castle, 3 turret-form spills, 1850s, 7" 200.00
Charity allegorical, lady w/baby & child, ca 1800, 8½" 175.00
Cottage, bank, HP w/lattice windows, coleslaw trim, 5" 225.00
Cottage, potpourri jar, red & gr details, 19th C, 5½"................... 85.00
Cow by tree stump, spill vase, 1850s, 11x7½x3½" 2,150.00
Dog on grassy mound, scent bottle, head removes, glass eyes, 2½" . 1,000.00
Dog on mottled base, pin holder, early, rprs, 5x5¼"................... 800.00
Dog resting on rect platform w/2 inkwells, 19th C, 4x7x4"......... 215.00
Elephant w/howdah by tree stump, spill vase, 1850s, 7" 950.00
Fortitude allegorical, lady holding column, mc, ca 1820, 22".... 1,765.00
Fox head, stirrup cup, 19th C, 5¼" L... 360.00
George Washington, bust, early 19th C, 8".................................. 725.00
Giuseppe Garibaldi, title on base, Sampson Smith, 1864, 14½" .. 765.00
Horse, Pratt-type palette, ca 1800, 5¼".................................... 2,600.00
House w/2 chimneys, figures in relief, bank, late 19th C, 6", EX.. 500.00
Lady w/dog, red cloak, flakes, 9½x5½" 95.00
Lion on base, burnt orange w/gold on wht, glass eyes, 19th C, 10"..480.00
Lion, brn w/gilt & blk details, glass eyes, 1800s, 10x5x10", pr 470.00
Male bust on circular socle, gr marbled glaze, 19th C, 20" 3,175.00
Queen Victoria (& Prince Albert), mc/bl underglaze, 1880s, 8", pr...325.00
Royal couple seated w/dogs in laps, man w/horn/she w/violin, 7", pr .. 800.00
Sailor stands w/ship model on shoulder, boy at side, 1850s, 16¼" .1,075.00
Setter dog, red & wht, free-standing front legs, 11¼" 485.00
Shakespeare, fine HP & gilt, 1850s, 10"..................................... 200.00
Spaniel seated, blk spots, yel eyes, red collar, 12", pr.................... 175.00
Spaniel standing on free-form oval base, early 19th C, 5", pr....... 500.00
Spaniel, recumbent, sweetmeat box w/MOP base/gilt mts, 18th C, 2". 1,325.00
Spaniels, orange/blk/gold lustre, 1850s, 12¼", pr 750.00
Uncle Tom & Little Eva w/transfer paragraph on base, 7½"......... 265.00
Uncle Tom w/child on lap, crazing/some discoloration, 9".......... 725.00
War, military man on horse w/flag & shield, 19th C, 12" NM 850.00
Whippet w/rabbit on base, mc, 1850s, 10½", pr......................... 1,800.00

Transferware

Basket & underplate, castle in landscape, d/b, Adams, 4x10" 650.00

Basket, fruit, Regent St London, d/b, rtcl, Adams, 4⅜x11¼" 600.00
Bowl, Landing of Lafayette at Castle Garden NY, d/b, rprs, 12".. 475.00
Bowl, Sheltered Pheasants, d/b, att Hall, 2¼x10½" 300.00
Bowl, Upper Ferry Bridge...Schuylkill, m/b, Stubbs, 12½", EX..... 500.00
Bowl, vegetable, Arms of VA w/floral border, d/b, Mayer, 12½" L, NM..1,650.00
Bowl, vegetable, Hanover Regents Terrace, d/b, 8x6½", +10" platter...360.00

Bowl, vegetable, Landing of General Lafayette, Clews, with lid, 12" wide, $2,140.00. (Photo courtesy Pook & Pook, Inc. on LiveAuctioneers.com)

Bowl, vegetable, NC State of Arms, d/b, unmk, 2¾x12¾x9¾" .5,175.00
Bowl, vegetable, unknown manor house, d/b, w/lid, 7¾x10¼"..1,175.00
Bowl, waste, Landing of Gen Lafayette, d/b, unmk Clews, rstr, 6¼"...460.00
Coffeepot, Franklin Memorial, d/b, rstr, 10¾" 795.00
Coffeepot, Lafayette at Franklin's Tomb, d/b, 19th C, 11½", NM .. 1,200.00
Cup plate, Brahma bull, red, foliate border, mid-19th C, 3⅞" 395.00
Cup plate, Staughton's Church misidentified, d/b, Stevenson, 4⅛" .2,185.00
Pitcher, Abbey Ruins, d/b, Mayer, 10x8½" 650.00
Pitcher, Cyprus, blk, 8-sided, Davenport, 1840-80, hairline, 10" . 360.00
Pitcher, Welcome Lafayette...Glory, d/b, Clews, 5", NM........... 2,100.00

Pitcher and bowl, States, Clews, pitcher: 9", EX, $4,500.00. (Photo courtesy Conestoga Auction Company on LiveAuctioneers.com)

Plate, B&O (on level), d/b, shell border, Wood, 1830s, 10"......1,175.00
Plate, Baltimore & OH Railroad (level), d/b, Wood & Sons, 10". 900.00
Plate, Boston State House, m/b, floral border, unmk Wood, 10" .. 200.00
Plate, Caledonia, gr/red, Adams, mid-19th C, 10⅝" 480.00
Plate, Christ Church Oxford, d/b, Ridgway, 9¾", NM.................. 195.00
Plate, City of Albany...NY, d/b, shell border, Woods & Sons, 10". 300.00
Plate, Dam & Water Works Philadelphia, d/b, Henshall, 10" 725.00
Plate, Mitchell & Freeman...Boston, d/b, Adams, 10", EX........... 230.00
Plate, roses, d/b, Wm Smith & Co, 1830s, 7" 125.00
Plate, Seal of US, mc w/bl feather scalloped edge, 19th C, 8"...1,995.00
Plate, Texian Campaigne, brn, 9¼" 575.00
Plate, Valentine From Wilkies Designs, m/b, 9", pr 345.00
Plate, Water Works Philadelpha, d/b, 19th C, Wood, 10"............ 660.00
Plate, Winter View of Pittsfield, d/b, Clews, 8⅝" 295.00
Plate, Winter View of Pittsfield, d/b, floral border, Clews, 10½"... 350.00
Plate, Winter View of Pittsfield MA, d/b, scalloped, Clews, 8¾" . 315.00
Platter, 2 soldiers (1 on horsebk) & people, m/b, Granada, 15½".. 360.00
Platter, 3 horses/3 cows, d/b, vining border, Adams, 1805-29, 14" ..600.00
Platter, Baronial Halls, l/b, octagonal, Mayer, 18x14" 220.00
Platter, Bejapore, d/b, octagonal, 16" L 220.00
Platter, Canova, d/b w/blk border, Mayer, 19th C, 20¼x16¾" 900.00
Platter, Canova, m/b, Mayer, 15½" 360.00
Platter, Castle Prison St Albans, d/b, Hall, 10½x9" 425.00
Platter, Clyde Scenery, blk w/red border, Jackson, 19th C, 15¼" . 900.00
Platter, Lady of the Lake, m/b, 21x16¼" 575.00
Platter, Landing of General LaFayette, 1824, dk bl, Clews, 17" .1,880.00
Platter, Landing of LaFayette...1824, d/b, Clews, 19x14½" 1,880.00

Platter, leopard & gazelle, m/b, unmk, 18½x14" 1,550.00
Platter, Niagara Falls, d/b, rstr, 14⅞" 1,200.00
Platter, Persian, brn, Ridgway, 1830-34, 18¾x15", NM.............. 600.00
Platter, Wild Rose, m-d/b, anchor/Middlesborough, 15", NM...... 220.00
Platter, Windsor Castle, d/b, foliage & scroll border, Clews, 17".. 950.00
Soup, Landing of General LaFayette, d/b, floral border, 8¾", NM. 575.00
Soup, Octagon Church Boston, m/b, floral border, Ridgway, 9¾" . 420.00
Sugar bowl, bald eagle, d/b, closely mismatched lid, 7½" 175.00
Tea bowl & saucer, chinoiserie bridge/palm tree, d/b, VG............ 150.00
Teapot, Castle Toward, d/b, fruit & floral borders, Hall, 6¼" 385.00
Teapot, Indian Wharf & Broad Street Stores, m/b, Wood, 1819-46 ..850.00
Teapot, MacDonnough's Victory, d/b, 1819-46, sm chip, 7½" ...2,000.00
Teapot, MacDonnough's Victory, d/b, Wood, 7½", EX 1,400.00
Teapot, spread-wing eagle/acanthus leaves, d/b, flakes, 10" 1,500.00
Tureen, flowers/fretwork, mc, bombé shape w/lid, 19th C, 9x13". 725.00
Tureen, Sirius, brn, w/lid & 14½" platter 600.00
Washbowl & pitcher, flower-filled urn, d/b, Stubbs & Kent, 13", 10". 1,175.00
Washbowl & pitcher, Palestine, m/b, 11¾" 395.00

Miscellaneous

Jug, salt glazed w/HP bird/flowers, ca 1760, rstr, 8¾"................. 6,600.00
Jug, salt glazed, scratch bl floral, 1755-60, 9¼"..........................9,600.00
Plate, lead-glazed creamware, leaves emb, 3-color, 9½" 2,850.00
Plate, lead-glazed creamware, leaves emb, 3-color, 18th C, 9½", pr....5,400.00
Plate, salt glazed w/HP couple in park, floral rim, 1760s, 9⅜", NM 3,600.00
Plate, salt glazed, Wm Pitt portraits, lobed/barbed rim, 1750s, 9"... 5,400.00
Sauceboat, salt glazed, birds & animals, lamprey hdl, rprs, 1750s, 8"..1,440.00

Stirrup cup, modeled as a fox's head, nineteenth century, 5¼", $360.00. (Photo courtesy Rachel Davis Fine Arts on LiveAuctioneers.com)

Teapot, lead-glazed creamware, berries, bird finial, rstr, 1760s, 4" . 425.00
Teapot, lead-glazed creamware, cabbage form, pineapple lid, 1760s, 5"....660.00
Teapot, lead-glazed creamware, grapevines, paw ft, rstr, 18th C, 4"....2,400.00
Teapot, lead-glazed creamware, HP Aurora/angels, ca 1775, 5"... 2,115.00
Teapot, lead-glazed creamware, HP Bacchus scenes, rpr, 1775, 5⅜"...1,400.00
Teapot, lead-glazed creamware, HP fruits/basketweave, 1775, 5". 950.00
Teapot, lead-glazed creamware, HP grapevines/crabstock hdl, 18th C, 4".2,400.00
Teapot, salt glazed, grapevines/florals emb on cobalt, 18th C, 4"...1,000.00
Teapot, salt glazed, paneled lozenge shape, serpent spout, 6", EX ... 1,200.00
Teapot, salt glazed, paneled nudes, lion finial, 8-sided, 18th C, 4".. 1,400.00
Teapot, salt glazed, rose, honeycomb-like grnd, 1765, 5", EX....8,750.00
Teapot, salt glazed, shell panels, arm w/serpent spout, 18th C, 6"... 1,200.00
Tureen, salt glazed, grotesque ft, w/lid, 1750-60s, 17¼" L..........7,800.00
Tureen, salt glazed, shells & foliage, dog mask hdls, w/lid, 14" L ...2,150.00

Stained Glass

There are many factors to consider in evaluating a window or panel of stained glass art. Besides the obvious factor of condition, quality of leadwork, intricacy, jeweling, beveling, and the amount of selenium (red, orange, and yellow) present should all be taken into account. Remember, repair work is itself an art and can be very expensive. Our advisor for this category is Carl Heck; he is listed in the Directory under Colorado. See also Tiffany.

Ceiling Lights

19" lappet dome, geometric rim, 4 chains, 30"..........................1,800.00

20" geometric shade w/wreath border, gr/caramel/red, +chain & mts ... 470.00
22" gr slag dome shade w/salmon & gr daffodils, heavy mts, unmk ..2,000.00
24" cone shade w/wide apron, caramel w/red & gr roses, Chicago Mosaic...1,500.00
24" deep/shaped dome, vivid red/gr wide floral border, Handel crown . 4,800.00
24" floral-border brickwork shade, EX patina, Duffner/Kimberly... 11,000.00
24" shell motif..6,750.00
26" caramel shade, jeweled grapes/gr leaves, Morgan, bronze vine crown..6,000.00
28" 6-panel shade w/6-panel scalloped apron, orange/yel, Suess, 1910. 3,000.00
28" intricate floral/foliage gr shade, unmk Duffner/Kimberly, 15"...8,500.00
29" 6 panels w/heavy cast flower & leaf motifs, possible Duffner & Kimberly ...18,500.00
30" narrow pie-shape scalloped panels, bl to gr to yel, Williamson. 3,200.00

Lamps

18" dogwood/leaf border, uneven edge; slim std, Bigelow/Kennard, 20"...12,000.00
18" floral shade w/scalloped rim, bronzed baluster std, 23¼" 1,450.00
18" lotus-border (wide) & brickwork shade; lotus-emb std, Suess, 24". 5,000.00
18" shade w/6 bent panels+jeweled apron; ribbed std, Duffner/Kimberly ..5,000.00
18" wisteria shade, bronze std, JH Whaley, 21" 10,000.00
19" cherries in mosaic-pattern shade; bronzed std, 23" 1,200.00
19" floral shade; Grueby organic 12x8" base, Duffner/Kimberly, 23".24,000.00
19" paneled open-top shade, 4-socket gold std, Duffner/Kimberly, 24". 2,875.00
19" pond lilies shade; 3-socket std, Duffner/Kimberly, 24½", EX ...5,750.00

19" shade, bronze base marked Duffner & Kimberly Co. New York, 24", $19,800.00. (Photo courtesy S&S Auction, Inc. on LiveAuctioneers.com)

20" floral-border umbrella shade; bronze std, ca 1900, 26" 750.00
21" dome shade w/mc over-all floral, bronze std #527, Wilkinson, EX.10,800.00
21" tulip/geometric shade; 3-socket library std, Wilkinson, 28" .3,000.00
23" dome w/over-all red & wht floral/gr leaves, tree trunk std, Suess.16,500.00
24" allover floral shaped dome; bronze std, Chicago Mosaic, EX...3,350.00

Windows and Doors

Irises and palm tree against a sunset landscape, attributed to Lamb Studios, New York, circa 1900, 74x40, $13,200.00. (Photo courtesy Great Gatsby's Antiques and Auctions on LiveAuctioneers.com)

Arched transom, flowers/leaves on clear to etched field, 21x52"..400.00
Beethoven in oval on ribbon-like bkgrnd, 1908, 32x35"...........3,400.00
Bible w/bookmark/flower/mc bands, arched top, 35x70½" 1,850.00

Central medallion, vining/scrolls/jewels/borders, 19th C, 78x51" .. 3,750.00
Floral center, jewels, numeral '3' for 'Third Street,' 52x53".......8,400.00
Floral center w/scrolls/rosettes/pyramid jewels, 19th C, 44x36"+fr...7,250.00
Floral w/jewels, ca 1890, 23x40½" 2,250.00
Flower vase w/in niche, yel & ruby ground, fruitwood stain, 37x23"... 300.00
Geometrics, In Memory Of on drop-down portion, 79x31", pr.3,500.00
Mary w/halo above lady in prayer, ca 1910, 156x63" 3,450.00
Medieval knight w/sword, ca 1880, 59x23"...............................3,000.00
Micro-mosaic floral, Belcher, 28x16", VG 3,000.00
Mosaic w/leafy branch on earth-to-sky ground, Belcher, 53x32"..4,000.00
Ribbon swags/chunk-glass roses/flaming torches/etc, 19th C, 142x63"..10,000.00
Scrolls & foliage w/geometric borders, ca 1900, 87x36", 6 for...4,800.00
St Joan of Arc between capitals/many details, early 20th C, 112x36" .. 2,350.00
Star center, geometric borders, arched transom, 1870s, 36x48"..4,750.00
Sword & crown among scrolling florals, 76x36" 1,750.00

Stangl

    Stangl Pottery was one of the longest-existing potteries in the United States, having its beginning in 1814 as the Sam Hill Pottery, becoming the Fulper Pottery which gained eminence in the field of art pottery (ca 1860), and then coming under the aegis of Johann Martin Stangl. The German-born Stangl joined Fulper in 1910 as a chemical engineer, left for a brief stint at Haeger in Dundee, Illinois, and rejoined Fulper as general manager in 1920. He became president of the firm in 1928. Although Stangl's name was on much of the ware from the late '20s onward, the company's name was not changed officially until 1955. J.M. Stangl died in 1972; the pottery continued under the ownership of Wheaton Industries until 1978, then closed. Stangl is best known for its extensive Birds of America line, styled after Audubon; its brightly colored, hand-carved, hand-painted dinnerware; and its great variety of giftware, including its dry-brushed gold lines. For more information we recommend *Collector's Encyclopedia of Stangl Dinnerware* by Robert Runge, Jr. and *Stangl Pottery* by Harvey Duke; for ordering information refer to the listing for Nancy and Robert Perzel, Popkorn Antiques (our advisors for this category), in the Directory under New Jersey.

Dinnerware

Florette center handle server, $15.00. (Photo courtesy Royka's on LiveAuctioneers.com)

Americana #2000, plate, 6", $2 to...3.00
Bluebell #3334, bowl, salad, 10", $50 to...60.00
Blueberry #3770, plate, chop, 12½", $35 to 40.00
Blueberry, bowl, 12", $45 to..55.00
Blueberry, casserole, w/lid, ind, $12 to 15.00
Blueberry, chop plate, 14", $40 to 50.00
Blueberry, coffeepot, 8-cup, 9¼", $40 to...60.00
Carnival #3900, plate, 10", $8 to...15.00
Colonial #1388, casserole, w/lid, 8" dia, $35 to 50.00
Colonial, relish tray, 2-compartment, 7½x7½", $15 to...................20.00
Country Garden, bowl, coupe soup, 7½", $12 to 15.00
Country Garden, bowl, divided vegetable, 2¼x10¾x7¼", $20 to .. 30.00

Country Garden, plate, chop, 14", $40 to 50.00
Daisy #1870, bowl, relish, 6½", $15 to 20.00
Daisy #1870, plate, 6", $10 to 15.00
Dogwood #3668, plate, pk, 6", $10 to 12.00
Fruit & Flowers #4030, butter dish, $30 to 40.00
Fruit & Flowers, bowl, dessert, 5½", $8 to 10.00
Fruit & Flowers, bowl, soup, 7½", $15 to 20.00
Fruit & Flowers, coffeepot, 8-cup, 8½", $50 to 75.00
Fruit & Flowers, mug, coffee, 2-cup, 4", $30 to 40.00
Fruit & Flowers, pitcher, 1-pt, 6", $25 to 35.00
Fruit & Flowers, plate, dinner, 10", $15 to 20.00
Fruit #3697, plate, dinner, $15 to 20.00
Fruit, bowl, divided vegetable, oval, 3x10¼", $25 to 35.00

Fruit, creamer and sugar bowl with lid, $25.00. (Photo courtesy Livingston's Auction on LiveAuctioneers.com)

Fruit, plate, chop, 12", $40 to 50.00
Fruit, plate, dinner, 10", $15 to 20.00
Fruit, plate, luncheon, 8¼", $10 to 15.00
Fruit, shakers, pr, $10 to 15.00
Fruit, sherbet, 8-oz, 5¾", $20 to 25.00
Garden Flower, bowl, fruit/dessert, 5¾", $8 to 10.00
Garden Flower, plate, chop, Terra Rose, 12", $35 to........ 45.00
Garden Flower, plate, dinner, 10", $10 to 15.00
Kiddieware, cup, Humpty Dumpty, pk, $75 to 100.00
Kiddieware, cup, Indian Campfire, $50 to 75.00
Kiddieware, cup, Playful Pup, $30 to 45.00
Kiddieware, divided dish, Kitten Capers, $75 to 100.00
Kiddieware, divided dish, Playful Pups, $60 to 75.00
Kiddieware, mug, Jack & Jill, musical, $200 to 250.00
Kiddieware, plate, Little Bo Peep, 9¼", $50 to 75.00
Lyric, casual coffee server, 11", $100 to 125.00
Lyric, plate, dinner, 10", $25 to 30.00
Magnolia, bowl, lug soup, 1½x6", $7 to 10.00
Magnolia, bowl, vegetable, 8", $15 to 20.00
Magnolia, gravy boat & underplate, $10 to 15.00
Magnolia, plate, bread & butter, 6¼", $2 to 3.00
Magnolia, plate, salad, 8", $6 to 8.00
Orchard Song, c/s, $6 to 8.00
Orchard Song, gravy boat & underplate, $12 to 15.00
Orchard Song, plate, chop, 12½", $15 to 20.00
Orchard Song, platter, oval, $20 to 30.00
Ranger #3304, bowl, oval, 10", $250 to.......................... 350.00
Ranger #3304, shaker, plain, ea $50 to 65.00
Star Flower, plate, chop, 14", $35 to 45.00
Star Flower, teapot, 6¾", $40 to 50.00
Sunflower #3340, teapot, $125 to 150.00
Thistle, cigarette box, $30 to 40.00
Thistle, coffeepot, 8-cup, $40 to..................................... 50.00
Thistle, relish tray, $15 to.. 20.00
Town & Country, bowl, cereal, bl, 5½", $15 to............... 20.00
Town & Country, bowl, vegetable, bl, 7¾", $25 to 35.00
Town & Country, candlesticks, yel, 7½", pr $30 to.......... 45.00
Town & Country, pitcher, water, bl, 2-qt, $50 to............. 75.00
Town & Country, plate, chop, gr, 12", $20 to 25.00
Town & Country, plate, dinner, brn, 10", $8 to 10.00
Town & Country, shakers, yel, no hdls, pr, $15 to 20.00
Town & Country, soap dish, gr, rect, 5⅝", $15 to 20.00

Tropic #3338, creamer, $15 to 20.00
Tropic #3338, sugar bowl, $15 to 20.00
Yellow Tulip, casserole, w/lid, 8", $50 to 65.00
Yellow Tulip, flowerpot, 4", $10 to 15.00
Yellow Tulip, plate, chop, 14", $50 to 75.00

Miscellaneous

Air freshener, terrier pup, Colonial Bl, #3108, 1937, 6", $300 to. 350.00
Ashtray, monkey, Persian Yel, #1324, 1930-31, 5", $150 to 175.00
Ashtray, Multi-Color Dk, #1337, 1930-31, 4", $25 to 35.00
Basket, orchids, #3621, 1974, 5½", $25 to 35.00
Basket, Sunburst, #1456, 1931-34, 7", $125 to 150.00
Bowl, Orchid, #945S, 6¾", $20 to 30.00
Bowl, Satin Yel, scalloped rim, #2064, 1936-38, 9x5", $10 to 15.00
Bowl, Silver Gr, oblong/6-sided/ftd, #1202, 1929-34, 12" L, $75 to ...100.00
Candleholders, butterfly, Colonial Bl, #964, pr $25 to 35.00
Candleholders, Scroll Leaf, Tangerine, #3025, 5½", pr $40 to 50.00
Candlesticks, nude sitting, Silver Gr, #1087, 5", pr $200 to 300.00
Candy dish, Colonial Bl, #1388, 1932-38, 5x5", $30 to 40.00
Flower holder, gazelle, Colonial Bl, #1169, 11½", $100 to 125.00
Flowerpot, camel, Satin Wht, #1773, 1933-35, 14", $150 to 200.00
Flowerpot, Silver Gr, pleated, #1213S, 1929-32, 4", $15 to 20.00
Flowerpot, swan, Sunburst w/Persian Yel, #1771, 10x13", $250 to.....300.00
Honey jar, Apple Gr, #1005-S, 1925-31, 3½", $20 to..................... 25.00
Jam jar, Silver Gr, #956, oval, 1924-28, 3½x6", $35 to 40.00
Jar, ginger, Town & Country Brn, 1974-78, $35 to 45.00
Jar, ribbed, mold-cast, 3-hdl, #1237, Tangerine, 1933-37, 7½", $35 to40.00
Jardiniere, pk matt, mold-cast, #1261, 1930-37, 8", $20 to 25.00
Planter, rolling pin, Town & Country Yel, 1976, 13", $50 to 60.00
Tray, hors d'oeuvres, Silver Gr, #1978, Manning-Bowman, 1935-40, 7", $5 to.8.00
Vase, Apple Gr, w/hdls, #1328, 1933-38, 15", $75 to 100.00
Vase, Colonial Bl, #941, 1924-27, 6", $25 to 35.00

Vase, horse's head, #3611, unusual textured glaze, $330.00. (Photo courtesy B.S. Slosberg, Inc. Auctioneers on LiveAuctioneers.com)

Vase, Ivory, swirled ball form, #1818, 1934-35, 5½", $35 to 45.00
Vase, mini, turq, #1903, 1935, 3½", $50 to 65.00
Vase, rust, rim-to-hip hdls, #1712, 1934-39, 6", $30 to 40.00
Vase, Tangerine, #1329, 1930-33, 18", $150 to............................. 200.00
Vase, wide, Tangerine, #1329, 1930-33, 18", $150 to.................... 200.00
Wall pocket, Grapes, Ivory, #989, 1925-28, 8", $125 to 150.00
Wig stand, blond, wood base, 15", $200 to 250.00

Stangl Birds and Animals

The Stangl company introduced their line of ceramic birds in 1940, taking advantage of an import market crippled by the onset of WWII. The figures were an immediate success. Additional employees were hired, and eventually 60 decorators worked at the plant itself, with the overflow contracted out to individuals in private homes. After the war when import trade once again saturated the market, Stangl curtailed their own production but continued to make the birds and animals on a limited basis as late as 1978. Nearly all the birds were marked. A four-digit number was used to identify the species, and most pieces were signed by the decorator. An 'F' indicates a bird that was decorated at the Flemington plant. Our advisors for this category are Nancy and Robert Perzel, Popkorn Antiques. (See the Directory under New Jersey.) For more information we recommend *Collector's Encyclopedia of Stangl Artware, Lamps, and Birds* by Robert Runge, Jr. (Collector Books).

Animals

#1076, Piggy bank, sponged wht, not cvd, Early Am Tulip, $60 to ..75.00
#1076, Piggy bank, Terra Rose, cvd, Early Am Tulip, $75 to........ 100.00

**#3178A, Elkhound, black with white overglaze, 3½",
$40.00 to $50.00.** (Photo courtesy Belhorn Auction Services, LLC on LiveAuctioneers.com)

#3178C, Burro, blk w/wht overglaze, 3¼", $50 to........................... 60.00
#3178F, Percheron, wht w/blk overglaze, 3½", $50 to..................... 60.00
#3178G, Elephant, wht w/blk overglaze, 2½", $40 to..................... 50.00
#3178H, Squirrel, wht w/blk overglaze, 3½", $50 to....................... 60.00
#3178J, Gazelle, wht w/blk overglaze, 3½", $50 to......................... 60.00
#3243, Wire-Haired Terrier, 3¼", $150 to..................................... 175.00
#3244, Draft Horse, 3", $75 to... 100.00
#3245, Rabbit, 2", $150 to... 200.00
#3246, Buffalo, 2½", $175.. 200.00
#3247, Gazelle, 3¾", $150 to... 175.00
#3248, Giraffe, 2½", $350 to.. 400.00
#3249, Elephant, 3", $150 to... 175.00
#3249, Elephant, Antique Gold, 5", $75 to.................................. 100.00
#3277, Colt, 5", $1,000 to.. 1,200.00
#3278, Goat, 5", $1,300 to.. 1,500.00
#3279, Calf, 3½", $700 to.. 900.00
#3280, Dog sitting, 5¼", $200 to... 250.00
#3430, Duck, 22", $5,000 to... 7,000.00
Cat sitting, Granada Gold, 8½", $150 to...................................... 175.00
Cat, Siamese, Seal Point sitting, decor, 8½", $300 to................... 400.00

Birds

#3250E, Duck drinking, Terra Rose finish, 1941 only, 2¼", $40 to 50.00
#3273, Rooster, solid bottom, 5¾", $300 to................................... 400.00
#3275, Turkey, 3½", $200 to.. 225.00
#3276D, Bluebirds (pr), 8½", $100 to.. 150.00
#3286, Hen, late, 3¼", $50 to... 75.00
#3400, Lovebird, old version, 4", $100 to.................................... 125.00
#3400, Lovebird, revised, 4", $50 to... 65.00
#3401D, Wrens (pr), old version, $300 to.................................... 400.00
#3402, Oriole, beak down, old style, 3½", $75 to.......................... 100.00
#3402D, Orioles (pr), revised, w/leaves, 5½", $75 to.................... 125.00
#3405, Cockatoo, 6", $35 to... 50.00
#3408, Bird of Paradise, 5½", $60 to.. 75.00
#3443, Duck, flying, teal, 9x12", $150 to..................................... 200.00
#3444, Cardinal, female, $125 to... 150.00
#3446, Hen, yel, 7", $125 to... 150.00
#3452, Painted Bunting, 5", $50 to... 75.00

#3454, Key West Quail, single wing up, 9x10", $150.00 to $225.00. (Photo courtesy Burchard Galleries Inc. on LiveAuctioneers.com)

#3490D, Redstarts (pr), 9", $100 to.. 125.00
#3580, Cockatoo, med, 9", $100 to... 125.00
#3584, Cockatoo, sgn Jacob, lg, 11⅜", $200 to............................ 225.00
#3586, Pheasant (Della Ware), natural colors, $600 to................ 900.00
#3586, Pheasant (Della Ware), Terra Rose, gr, $400 to............... 500.00
#3590, Carolina Wren, 4½", $100 to... 125.00
#3592, Titmouse, 3", $40 to... 50.00
#3593, Nuthatch, 2½", $35 to... 45.00
#3595, Bobolink, 4¾", $125 to... 150.00
#3596, Gray Cardinal, 5", $40 to.. 50.00
#3598, Kentucky Warbler, 3", $35 to.. 45.00

#3627, Rivioli Hummingbird, pink flower, 6", $100.00 to $125.00. (Photo courtesy B.S. Slosberg, Inc. Auctioneers on LiveAuctioneers.com)

#3629, Broadbill Hummingbird, 4½", $75 to................................ 100.00
#3715, Blue Jay, w/peanut, 10¼", $300 to.................................... 350.00
#3716, Blue jay w/leaf, $350 to... 400.00
#3749, Scarlet Tanager, pk gloss, 4¾", $200 to............................ 250.00
#3749, Western Tanager, yel & blk w/red overglaze, tan flower, 4¾" .. 225.00
#3750D, Western Tanagers (pr), red matt, 8", $250 to................. 300.00
#3751, Red-Headed Woodpecker, red matt, 6¼", $200 to............. 250.00
#3754D, White-Wing Crossbills (pr), pk gloss, 9x8", $200 to...... 250.00
#3757, Scissor-Tailed Flycatcher, 11", $400 to............................. 500.00
#3810, Black-Throated Warbler, 3½", $100 to.............................. 125.00
#3815, Western Bluebird, 7", $250 to... 300.00
#3848, Golden-Crowned Kinglet, 4¼", $75 to.............................. 100.00
#3852, Cliff Swallow, 3½", $75 to... 100.00
#3868, Summer Tanager, 4", $300 to.. 350.00
#3924, Yellow Throat, 6", $300 to.. 400.00
Dealer sign, bird, $1,000 to... 1,500.00

Statue of Liberty

Long before she began greeting immigrants in 1886, the Statue of Liberty was being honored by craftsmen both here and abroad. Her likeness was etched on blades of the finest straight razors from England, captured in finely detailed busts sold as souvenirs to Paris fairgoers in 1878, and presented on colorfully lithographed trade cards, usually satirical, to American shoppers. Perhaps no other object has been represented in more forms or with such frequency as the universal symbol of America. Liberty's keepsakes are also universally accessible. Delightful souvenir models created in 1885 to raise funds for Liberty's pedestal are frequently found at flea markets, while earlier French bronze and terra cotta Liberties have been auctioned for over $100,000.00. Some collectors hunt for the countless forms of nineteenth-century Liberty memorabilia, while many collections were begun in anticipation of the 1986 Centennial with concentration on modern depictions.

Albumen print, John S Johnston, sign/titled/dtd 1894, 8¾x6¾" .. 240.00
Bank, copper-colored metal, 8¼" 25.00
Bank, figural, pnt CI, AC Williams, 1910-30, 6", EX 175.00
Belt buckle, cut-out Liberty half dollar w/gold & silver trim 62.50
Book, Photographic Views including NY Harbor, 1889, VG 70.00
Bookmark, Bartholdi souvenir & calendar, fabric, 1887 .... 50.00
Cigar box label, Victory Day, WWII 6.00
Clock, kitchen shelf, rvp Liberty scene, rpl dial, Ingraham, 24x14" ... 350.00
Clock/lamp, CI figural, bulb inserts at top of torch, 14½x5" 75.00
Clock/lamp, figural, flame bulb, copper-tone pot metal, 1940s, 16" 165.00
Container, Yourex Silver Saver, rnd, cb, ca 1930 .... 27.00
Flyer, Statue of Liberty steamboat excursions, 1890s 25.00
Invitation to statue's unveiling, 1886, G- 200.00
Lighter, exposed flint, Fr, WWI era 125.00
Medal, Sinking of the Lusitania, bronze, ca 1918, by R Baudicaon .. 480.00
Napkin holder, sterling 15.00
Novelty, sailboat w/image on sails, Japan, 3⅝x2¾" 35.00
Pin, enamel, 77th Div, WWI 12.00
Pipe, glazed clay, 1880s 90.00
Plate, emb scene of statue & NY skyline & QE II, Bossons, 10" dia ... 325.00
Plate, HP scene, Vernon Kilns, 10½" 20.00
Postcard, statue/eagle/flag, Sanders, ca 1906, EX 20.00
Postcard, Uncle Sam pulling bk US flag to see statue, ca 1907, EX .17.50

Poster, La Royale, printer: Ch. Garciau, Nantes, circa 1925, France, 46x31", NM, $360.00.
(Photo courtesy PosterConnection, Inc. on LiveAuctioneers.com)

Reverse pnt on glass, in plaster fr w/orig pnt, 25x19", EX 75.00
Scissors, emb metal, Liberty 1 side/Woolworth building on reverse, 6" ... 55.00
Smoke stand/lamp, Liberty at base, torch lights up, 1940s, 27", EX ... 150.00
Statue, bronze-pnt pot metal, 2-pc, Am Committee Model, 7" ... 175.00
Statue, bronzed metal, 19", EX 30.00
Statue, bronzed metal, Liberty Enlightening, 1883, 7" 125.00
Statue, hand-cvd wood, Mexico, 15" 20.00
Ticket, souvenir of Gauthier et Cie (Liberty foundry), 1883, lg ... 105.00
Tintype, Spanish Am War soldier seated before statue, 6th plate, +case 85.00

Steamship Collectibles

For centuries, ocean-going vessels with their venturesome officers and crews were the catalyst that changed the unknown aspects of our world to the known. Changing economic conditions, unfortunately, have now placed the North American shipping industry in the same jeopardy as the American passenger train. They are becoming a memory. The surge of

interest in railroad collectibles and the railroad-related steamship lines has led collectors to examine the whole spectrum of steamship collectibles.

Reproduction (sometimes called 'replica') and fantasy dinnerware have been creeping into the steamship dinnerware collecting field. Some of the 'replica' ware is quite well done so one should practice caution and... 'know thy dealer.' We recommend *Restaurant China, Volumes 1 and 2*, by Barbara J. Conroy.

Key:
BM — bottom mark   SL — side logo
BS — back stamped   SM — side mark
hf — house flag   SS — steamship
Int'l — International   TL — top logo
NBS — no back stamp   TM — top mark
R&B — Reed & Barton   w/w — woven design on white damask

Dining Salon

Bone dish, Red Star Line, Bl Onion-like decor, TL 165.00
Bowl, fruit, Wht Star Line, SP, SL, Dickenson hdls, 15" 900.00
Bowl, Mississippi & Dominion SS, belt TL w/flags surround, 2x9¼" .. 820.00
Bowl, Ocean SS Co, Savannah, TL hf, 9" 70.00
Bowl, soup, Great Lakes Transportation Co, Glenbrae, SL, 5½" . 295.00
Butter pat, Canadian National SS, Bonaventure, TL, Grindley, 3¼" ... 128.00
Butter pat, Goodrich Steamship Lines, boxed TL, 3" 88.00
Butter pat, Leyland Line TM on ribbon, Doulton, 3¼" 110.00
Butter pat, Stella Polaris, SP, ship's image, .830, 3½" 30.00
Butter pat, United States Shipping Brd, Granite State, TL, 3" 45.00
Champagne stem, United States Line, Eagle SL, 4½" 55.00
Coffeepot, CPSS Lines, Empress, Minton, BS, 7" 270.00
Coffeepot, Great Northern, SP, hinged lid, BM, R&B, 5¾" 170.00
Coffeepot, Matson SS, SP, hinged lid, SM & BM, Int'l, 4¾" 225.00
Coffeepot, SP, Andrea Doria, Broggi, 7" 410.00
Compote, Dollar Lines SM, SP, ftd, sq, Int'l, 4x7x7" 195.00
Cordial, SS Normandy, CGT TL on ft, R Lalique BS, 3"½ 565.00
Cover for platter, Am Mail Line, SP, recessed hdl, SL 26.00
Creamer, Canadian Pacific SS Lines, BM, w/hdl, ind, 2½" 22.50
Creamer, Eastern Steamship Lines, SL, no hdl, Buffalo, ind, 2¼" .. 75.00
Creamer, Matson SS, SP, SL, Int'l, 3¼" 68.00
Creamer, Matson, Matsonia, SL, BS SS Wilhelmina, ind, 3½" 70.00
Creamer, Wht Star Line (US), Tashmoo, SL, hdl, ind, 3" 195.00
Cup/saucer, Andrea Doria, Italia SM & TM, 2nd class, COA 595.00

Cup and saucer, chocolate, White Star Line, $550.00.
(Photo courtesy Philip Weiss Auctions on LiveAuctioneers.com)

Cup/saucer, Cleveland Cliffs Iron Co, border leaf design+SL 50.00
Cup/saucer, demi, Cosulich SS Line, SL, Ginori 132.00
Cup/saucer, demi, Matson, Mariposa, Syracuse, NBS 90.00
Cup/saucer, Mobil Oil, Mobil Chicago Pegasus SL, Shenango 75.00
Cup, Harriman Bl Morgan, SP, SL w/house flag 285.00
Egg cup, dbl, Alcoa SS Co, Alcoa Cavaliere, SL, 3x3" 55.00
Egg cup, Mallory Line, Texas, SM, 3½" 135.00
Food warmer, United Fruit Co, SP, recessed hdl on lid, Int'l, 6" 70.00
Fork, dinner, Am Hawaii SS, SP, TL 12.50
Hot food cover, Am Mail Line, SL, Buffalo, 6½" 128.00
Ice bucket & stand, Canadian Pacific SS, SP, SL, Mappin & Webb ... 355.00
Icer bowl, Matson, SP, SL, Int'l, 5½x8½" 180.00

Mug, coffee, Texaco, Michigan pattern SL, Mayer, 2½" 118.00
Mustard pot, Hudson Nav Co, hinged lid/glass liner, TL/BM, Meridian ... 100.00
Napkin ring, Wht Star, SP, hf SL, Elkington 110.00
Napkin, SS United States Lines eagle logo, w/w damask, 20x20" .. 12.00
Pitcher, Colonial Line house-flag SL, Warwick, 1936, 6¾" 66.00
Pitcher, US Steel, TM MVCF Hood, Mayer China, 5" 125.00
Plate, Am Mail Line, TL, Buffalo, 7¼" 30.00
Plate, Boston & Philadelphia SS Co, TL, Greenwood China, 9½".. 160.00
Plate, CD & GB Transit Co, Georgian Bay Line, TL, Syracuse, 6¾" ... 55.00
Plate, Champlain Ferry Service/D&HRR, Vermont pattern, TL, 5¼" ..55.00
Plate, Cunard, 1st class, image of Lusitania underway, Minton, TM, 9" .1,500.00

Plate, Cunard Steamship Co., Minton's, England, crazing throughout, 9", $440.00. (Photo courtesy Philip Weiss Auctions on LiveAuctioneers.com)

Plate, Detroit-Windsor Ferry, DWFCo TL, 8½" 150.00
Plate, Matson, Mariposa pattern w/bird in center, Mayer, BS, 5½" ... 55.00
Plate, Mobil Oil Corp, Mobil Chicago w/Pegasus in red, TL, 8" .. 110.00
Plate, rimmed soup, ESSO house-flag TM, 9" 72.50
Plate, rimmed soup, Matson Line, Matsonia, TM, 9" 90.00
Plate, rimmed soup, United Fruit Line, Columbia Div (bl), TL, 8½" ..48.00
Plate, rimmed soup, US Lt House Service, USLHS SL, 8½" 200.00
Plate, side salad, Cunard Oceanic Steam Nav Co, Greek Key, Spode .. 485.00
Plate, soup, Algoma Central Marine, Polar Bear Marine TL, 8¾" ..100.00
Plate, soup, Grace Lines, Santa Barbara, TL, 1⅜x9" 60.00
Plate, Std Fruit & SS/Vaccaro Line, Atlanta, hf TL, 9½" 55.00
Plate, Wht Star, bl Daisy Chain, TM OSNCo, BM Wht Star, 7¼" ..245.00
Platter, Am President Lines, President Wilson, TL/Syracuse, 10".. 54.00
Platter, Bay Line, Old Bay Line, hf TM, NBS, 14x9" 200.00
Platter, Hudson River Day Line, pennant TL, Bauscher, 14x9" 98.00
Pot, Matson, SP, hinged lid, SL, Internat'l, 16-oz, 5½" 55.00
Relish dish, Canadian Pacific BC Coastal SS, Empress, BS, 10x5" ..32.00
Relish dish, USSB, Granite State, TL, Buffalo, 1925, 9½x4¾" 42.50
Relish tray, Admiral Line Asian, hf logo w/life ring, TL/BS, 10" L ..75.00
Salt spoon, Cunard, SP, Elkington, 2½" 40.00
Sauceboat, CS&GT SS Co, beautiful SL, Buffalo, 6¼" 215.00
Shaker/cruet set, glass shaker/cruet, SP fr w/hdl, BM, Int'l 230.00
Shakers, Grace Line, SP, SL/BM, R&B, 2¾", pr 36.00
SP flatware, pickle fork, Ward Line, TL, Reed & Barton, 5¾" 12.00
Sugar bowl, Alaska SS Co, SP, Yukon SL, Wallace, 2¾" 55.00
Syrup, Pacific Mail SS, SP, hinged lid w/tab, attached liner, R&B. 60.00
Tablecloth, SS United States Lines eagle logo, w/w, 51x51" 26.00
Tea set, Cunard, Cubist shape, BM, 2 pots+cr+cube sugar bowl .. 285.00
Teapot, Baltimore Mail, SP, hinged lid, SL hf, Wallace, 5" 34.00
Teapot, Cunard SS, Cube style, ivory w/stripes, BS, 3½" sq 145.00
Teapot, Pickands-Mather Co, mc hf ea side, Walker China, ind . 260.00
Teaspoon, Eastern SS Line, Sierra, SP, TM, R&B, 5⅞" 12.50
Tray, triple, Red Star Line, Brownfield, w/hdl, TL, 10½" 350.00
Tumbler, United States Lines SL on glass, 4¾" 20.00
Vase, bud, Canadian Pacific SS, SP, Art Deco, SM, Elkington, 6½" ..125.00
Wine stem, Indo-China Steam Nav Co, SL full garter crest w/hf, 4½" ... 92.00

Miscellaneous

Advertising pwt, Milwaukee Clipper profile, copper-tone 14.00

Advertising sign, tin, Am Line/Red Star Line, EX graphics, 3x12".. 155.00
Ashtray, RMS Queen Mary maiden voyage, propeller-like decor, 1936... 145.00
Ashtray, souvenir, Andrea Doria, chrome w/ship image under glass, 5" .215.00
Ashtray, SS Normandie, Fr Line, cast CGT TL, frosted, Deco, 5" dia..255.00
Ashtray, United States Lines, SS America, chrome w/enamel logo, 3¾" ... 55.00
Blanket, Great Northern Pacific SS Co, TL, wool, self-bound, 55x80".. 350.00
Book, Am Ephemeris & Nautical Almanac, 1911, 2nd ed 52.00
Book, Great Lakes Red Book, lists over 1,200 vessels, 1930 .... 25.00
Book, Lloyd's Register of Shipping, 2-vol, hc, 1949-50, 1,600-pg 75.00
Book, Ocean's Story, Ark to Steamships, 1st ed, 1873, 712-pg 50.00
Book, Sailor's Union...Pacific, constitution/by-laws/wages, 1903, 4x5" ... 100.00
Booklet, CPSS, Empress of Britain, 1932, ports of call/graphics, 64-pg... 14.00
Booklet, Pacific Steam...Co, Reina Del Pacifico, 1932, open: 18x32". 100.00
Booklet, The New SS United States, 22-pg, 8½x11" 40.00
Brochure, Alaska SS+Copper River, 1915, 38-pg, unfolds to 8x9" ..75.00
Brochure, Andrea Doria, deck plans & int photos, 1950s, 210-pg ... 160.00
Brochure, Inland Steel Fleet/SS Wilford Sykes, history/map, 14-pg, 6x9" 22.00
Brochure, Pacific Coast SS Co, CA/OR/WA/BC/AK, 1887, folds down: 4x6" ... 50.00
Brochure, United Fruit, Great Wht Fleet, deck plans+, 1920s, 15-pg...90.00
Builder's plate, MV Pres Washington, APL, Avondale Shipyards, 1982..785.00
Button, pin-bk, Lusitania, mc on cello, Griffin & Rowland, ⅞"..... 40.00
Button, United Fruit Co, gold-tone, Scoville, dome shape, ⅞" 6.00
Cigarette lighter, Am Export Lines, SS Independence, Zippo, 1956, MIB..100.00
Cigarette lighter, Grace Lines, Zippo, 1964, MIB 55.00
Cigarette lighter, QE II, commemorating maiden voyage, Zippo, MIB. 42.00
Clothes hanger, Wht Star Lines across wood curved top bar, 4x16".. 65.00
Compact, RMS Samaria, gold-tone, Stratton, 3", M in cloth bag. 100.00
Compass, ship's, John Hand, brass, metal 10" binnacle w/hex glass top..325.00
Deck plans, Canadian Pacific Line/Empress of Japan, 1930, open: 30x40"..115.00
Engineering Spec booklets, SS United States, w/11" blprints, 7 for ...580.00
Figurehead, Fiberglas copy of 1800s Lady Anne, 1980s, 36"......... 295.00
Flag, Wht Star swallowtail burgee, cotton, rope hoists, 36x48" ... 585.00
Horn, ship's air, Kockum's Tyfom T-125, Sweden, brass w/bronze, 19"..275.00
Jewelry, US Navy WWII sweetheart locket & earrings 100.00
Letter opener, Alaska SS, The Alaska Line w/house flag on hdl 38.00
Lighter, Zippo, Moore-McCormack Lines SL, 1950s, MIB........... 285.00
Luggage label, Canadian Pacific SS, unused glue bk, oval, 6½".......8.00
Luggage sticker, Alaska SS, SS Aleutian, mc totem pole, 3½" dia 9.00
Luggage sticker, United States Lines, paper, 4x4" 6.00
Luggage tag, United States Lines, celluloid w/strap, 1½x2½" 17.00
Map, wall, Alaska SS, detailed, whimsical Alaska map, 1939, 22x39".165.00
Medallion, 1936 Official Queen Mary, bronze, 2½", M in case 325.00
Menu, Cuba Mail Line, Oriente, luncheon, emb cardstock, 1940, 7x9".. 14.00
Menu, dinner, Holland America, MS Noordam, 1947 .... 15.00
Menu, dinner, Matson Nav Co, E Savage cover, 1956, 12x8½" 44.00
Menu, SS Normandy, fold-over, diner de gala, 8/26/1939 .... 255.00
Paperweight, Pacific Coast SS Co, glass dome, 3" dia.................... 100.00
Pass, 1 trip only, Los Angeles SS Co, cardstock, 1937, 4⅛x3½".......7.00
Pass, annual, Natchez & Vicksburg Packet Co, cardstock, 1897 .. 155.00
Pass, annual, Peoples Line, New Jersey SS Co, revenue stamp, 1869.120.00
Passenger list, Cunard, Queen Mary, Southampton to NY, 1936 ... 70.00
Passenger list, Nord Deutscher Lloyd Bremen Europa, 1933, 18-pg, 5x8"..52.00
Passenger list, Wht Star Queen Mary, 1938, 24-pg, 5x8" 75.00
Pencil, mechanical, Royal Mail, RMS Andes floats in bbl, 5¼"..... 20.00
Picture, Cash's, canal boats, woven silk, ca 1900, in fr, 8x11"........ 50.00
Pin-back, C&B Line, City of Erie Steamship, mc, celluloid, 1¾" .. 34.00
Playing cards, GNPSS, 52 views+Joker+info card+booklet, +case .. 435.00
Postcard, cargo ship Pontiac w/autos stored on deck, real photo, 1930s 5.00
Postcard, Carpathia, Stevens woven silk, Hands Across Sea, no postmk .. 1,135.00
Postcard, Ohio river steamboat Lorena loading cargo, real photo, 1909... 22.00
Postcard, shipwreck of Galena off Gearhart, OR, blk/wht photo, 1906.27.00
Postcard, Titanic, woven silk, Hands Across Sea, Stevengraph.. 5,300.00
Poster, Grace Lines, ship docked at Curacoa, KN5/8/61, 28x42".. 330.00
Print, United States Lines, USS Santa Rosa enters NY harbor, 21x27".100.00

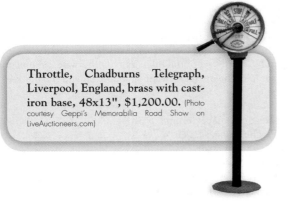

Sign, Cunard Line Steamship Co., cardboard, Mauaretania and Franconia reserves, Good-Ad Sign, Palm Fechteler & Co., N.Y. along bottom edge, 25x17", VG, $410.0. (Photo courtesy Philip Weiss Auctions on LiveAuctioneers.com)

Snuff box, Hamburg-Amerika Line emb image, SP, hinged lid, 2x3".. 200.00
Souvenir spoon, Grosser Kurfurst, HP bowl, Bremen crest, 5½" .. 155.00
Souvenir spoon, SS Leviathan HP in bowl, crest, 4¾" 520.00
Souvenir spoon, Washington Irving side-wheeler, SS, cut-out silhouette 18.00
Souvenir vase, City of Cleveland portside profile, mini, 2¼" 45.00
Spittoon, US Shipping Board, stoneware, SL, 10½" 130.00
Stock certificate, Dollar SS Line, Class A, 1929 .... 325.00

Throttle, Chadburns Telegraph, Liverpool, England, brass with cast-iron base, 48x13", $1,200.00. (Photo courtesy Geppi's Memorabilia Road Show on LiveAuctioneers.com)

Token, Staten Island Ferry, alum, pre-1990, ⅞" dia 12.00
Towel, hand, Quebec & Ontario Trans Co woven on bl stripe, wht huck. 20.00
Tray, tip, United Fruit Co Line/SS Admiral Dewey, enameled tin, 4¾" .360.00
Whistle/fog horn, salvaged USS Mississinewa, 32" alum Kahlenberg .. 1,200.00

Steins

Steins have been made from pottery, pewter, glass, stoneware, and porcelain, from very small up to the four-liter size. They may be decorated by etching, in-mold relief, decals, and occasionally they may be hand painted. Some porcelain steins have lithophane bases. Collectors often specialize in a particular type — faience, regimental, or figural, for example — while others limit themselves to the products of only one manufacturer. See also Mettlach.

Key:
L — liter   tl — thumb lift
lith — lithophane

Ceramic, pewter trim, Germany, 9½" 95.00
Character, Black Student, pottery, high glaze, inlaid lid, .5L, NM ..275.00
Character, Bock, porc, porc inlaid lid, broken hinge, Schierholz, .5L ...325.00
Character, devil, pottery, inlaid lid, .5L, NM 360.00

Character, dog, porc, pipe finial (rpr), Schierholz, .5L 1,085.00
Character, Elephant, porc, porc lid, Schierholz, .5L 1,800.00
Character, frog, porc, porc lid, Schierholz, .5L 1,325.00
Character, gentleman, pottery, inlaid lid, Thewalt, .5L 550.00
Character, Happy Radish, porc, Schierholz, inlaid lid, .5L 525.00

Character, Munchen, stoneware, Franz Ringer, marked J. Reinemann, inlaid lid, 5", $825.00; Munich Child, porcelain, 5", $475.00. (Photo courtesy Andre Ammelounx)

Character, Sad Radish, porc, inlaid lid, rpr chip, .5L 195.00
Character, Skull on Book, porc, inlaid lid, E Bohne & Sohne, .5L, NM .525.00
Character, Skull, porc, E Bohne & Sohne, .5L, NM 285.00
Faience, floral, mc, pewter ring/lid, ca 1780, strap rpr, 1L 500.00
Faience, woman & trees, pewter 1806 lid, Dresden, 1L............. 1,225.00
Glass, blown, amber w/prunts/HP floral, inlaid lid, dwarf tl, .5L . 175.00
Glass, blown, amber, Munich Child pewter o/l, pewter lid, .5L ... 175.00
Glass, blown, bl, Mary Gregory girl, ribs, pk inlaid lid, 4¼" 215.00
Glass, blown, clear w/bl stain, eng floral, inlaid lid, 1850s, 3½" .. 150.00
Glass, blown, clear w/gr o/l, allover cuttings, bl o/l lid, .5L 1,450.00
Glass, blown, clear w/gr o/l, cut design, clear lid w/bl o/l, .5L ...1,450.00
Glass, blown, clear w/red stain, Steinbad in Teplitz, inlaid lid, 4" . 170.00
Glass, blown, clear w/wht & pk o/l, eng leaves/berries, .4L........ 5,175.00
Glass, blown, clear, Germania Sei's Panier, pewter lid, 1909, .5L.. 845.00
Glass, blown, clear, Mary Gregory girl, bl inlaid lid, 1850s, 4¼" .. 160.00
Glass, blown, lav w/ornate cuttings, clear inlaid lid, 1850s, .5L ...300.00
Glass, blown, peach w/HP floral, clear inlaid lid, 1850s, 3½" 95.00
Glass, pressed, clear, cut design, pewter lid, scuffs, .5L 57.50
Occupational, carpenter, faience/pewter base ring/lid, 1780s, 1L, EX. 1,100.00
Occupational, porc: Metzger (butcher), lith, pewter lid, .5L, NM...230.00
Porcelain, HP: Bl onion design, inlaid lid, lith, .3L, NM 180.00
Porcelain, HP: couple/flowers, gilt silver lid, 1850s, 8½", NM ..1,150.00
Porcelain, HP: crocodile/3 babies/3 eggs, pewter lid, .5L.............. 600.00
Porcelain, HP: onion, inlaid lid, Rauenstein Kanne, 1L, 10" 635.00
Pottery, etch: night watchman, pewter lid, Hauber & Reuther, #420, .5L.415.00
Pottery, etch: Trumpeter of Sackingen, Hauber & Reuther, #203, .5L ...360.00
Pottery, HP: ATV Arminia Sei's Panier, Berlin 1896-97, pewter lid, .5L...435.00
Pottery, relief: dwarfs, pewter lid, Diesinger, #728, .5L 195.00
Pottery, relief: Falstaff, pewter lid, Dumler & Breiden #571, 1L... 240.00
Pottery, relief: Fraternal Order of Eagles, rpl pewter lid, .5L.......... 140.00
Pottery, relief: Germans meet Romans, pewter lid, #1268, .5L..... 135.00
Pottery, transfer: rabbits in lid, pewter lid, 3¾" 80.00
Pottery, transfer/HP: Geneve et T Le Mont-Blanc, monument lid, .5L...150.00
Pottery, transfer/HP: Gruss Aus Munchen, Munich Child lid, 3¼" ...200.00
Pottery, transfer/HP: Heidelberg, pewter lid, 2½" 60.00
Pottery, transfer/HP: Seminar Zeit 1898-1901, roster, pewter lid, .5L ...275.00
Regimental, 5 Komp Kgl...1912-13, porc, 6 scenes/stanhope, .5L .. 2,575.00
Regimental, porc, 12 Feld Artillerei...1911-13, lion tl, .5L, 13"... 945.00
Regimental, porc, 3 Battr 1 Bad...1902-04, eagle tl, lith, .5L 350.00
Regimental, porc, 3 Battr...Karlsruhe 1984-96, griffin tl, .5L........ 300.00
Regimental, porc, 6 Comp...Frankfurt 1906-08, eagle tl, .5L 315.00
Regimental, porc, Infantry Regt...Hanau 1898-00, eagle tl, .5L 465.00
Regimental, pottery, 1 Esk Kurassier...1906-09, eagle tl, rpr, .5L..865.00
Regimental, pottery, 4 Esk...Braunschewig 1907-10, eagle tl, .5L..865.00
Regimental, pottery, Kgl Bayrisches..., evolution of uniforms, 1L. 600.00
Regimental, pottery, transfer/HP: KB I Schw...Munchen 1917, .5L. 175.00
Regimental, pottery, transfer/HP: KBI...Munchen 1917, pewter lid, .5L.... 175.00
Regimental, stoneware, 4 Field...1907-09, 4 scenes/lion tl, .5L....635.00

Stoneware, eng: horse, pewter 1797 lid, Westerwald, .5L, VG..... 575.00
Stoneware, etch: cavalier, pewter lid, Marzi & Remy #1765, .5L. 325.00
Stoneware, etch/relief: Art Nouveau, inscribed/dtd 1905, #0709, .3L .. 140.00
Stoneware, transfer/HP: man in yel jacket, Ringer, pewter lid, .5L .. 275.00

Steuben

Carder Steuben glass was made by the Steuben Glass Works in Corning, New York, while under the direction of Frederick Carder from 1903 to 1932. Perhaps the most popular types of Carder Steuben glass are Gold Aurene which was introduced in 1904 and Blue Aurene, introduced in 1905. Gold and Blue Aurene objects shimmer with lustrous metallic iridescence. Carder also produced other types of 'Aurenes' including red, green, yellow, brown, and decorated, all of which are rare. Aurene also was cased with calcite glass. Some pieces had paper labels. Other types of Carder Steuben include Cluthra, Cintra, Florentia, Rosaline, Ivory, Ivrene, Jades, Verre de Soie; there are many more.

Frederick Carder's leadership of Steuben ended in 1932, and the production of colored glassware soon ceased. Since 1932 the tradition of fine Steuben art glass has been continued in crystal. In the following listings, examples are signed unless noted otherwise. When no color is mentioned, assume the glass is clear. For more information we recommend *The Collector's Encyclopedia of American Art Glass* by John A. Shuman III.

Key: ACB — acid cut back

Bowl, bl jade, flat rim, 7" 80.00
Bowl, clear shading to cranberry, Grotesque, #7091, 11" W......... 535.00
Bowl, console, gr jade, rolled edge, sgn, 14" 175.00
Bowl, finger, w/underplate, yel jade, #1044, 6" 280.00
Bowl, gr jade over alabaster w/jade ft, ACB, Asian motif, 10" .. 1,200.00
Bowl, plum over amethyst, Bl Chang, ACB, #2687, 8" 1,800.00
Candlesticks, amethyst cup & fot, topaz baluster stem, #2596, 12", pr ... 700.00
Candlesticks, bl aurene, ftd, w/twist stem, #686, 12", pr............ 3,000.00
Candy dish, amber bowl w/Pomona gr ft & finial, ftd, w/lid, #6105, 10" ... 350.00
Compote, bl aurene, star lily pad ft, #6058, sgn, 12".................. 1,400.00
Console set, 3-pc, gr jade, twist stem, 10" #6270 pr candlesticks & compote ..800.00
Cruet, gold aurene, w/stopper, #251, 7½" 1,500.00
Goblet, gr swirled opal, crystal bowl & twisted stem, 8".............. 900.00
Lamp, amethyst over alabaster, grape clusters, cylinder, ACB, 35". 2,200.00
Lamp, glass only, sculptured quarts in peach, appl leaves, #6766, 11½" ..600.00
Lamp, gr jade, mums, ACB, metal base, 20" 700.00
Marmalade, Verre-de-Soire, #1830, w/lid, cintra fruit finial, 8".. 1,500.00
Mug, gr jade, optic rib, alabaster hdl, #7118, 6" 175.00
Perfume, bl aurene, ftd, w/stopper, #3174, 7¼" 700.00
Perfume, bl aurene, melon form, w/stopper, sgn, #1455, 7¼" 600.00
Plate, gold aurene, 8¼" 600.00
Salt, bl aurene, ftd, #3067, 2¼" 350.00
Salt, gold aurene, ftd, #3067, 2¼"... 200.00
Shades, opal w/gold pulled feather, sgn, set of 4.......................... 500.00

Tazza, Pomona green paneled foot and bowl, mica-flecked amber stem with three hanging pomona green prunts, #6046, $1,200.00. (Photo courtesy Museum of American Glass, West Virginia, permanent collection)

Tumble-up set, gold aurene, 2-pc, #3064, sgn, 6" 650.00
Vase, amber, 3 stumps on base, #2744, 6¼"................................... 400.00
Vase, amethyst w/dmn optic, urn, #6545, 7" 700.00
Vase, cornucopia, Ivrene, ftd, sgn, #7579, 6" 450.00
Vase, crystal, 3 triangular bud vases on base, sgn, #6873, 10"....... 100.00
Vase, crystal, grotesque, trumpet form, #7590............................... 80.00
Vase, gold aurene, #723, 7½" 400.00
Vase, gr jade w/alabaster appl thread, ice bucket, sgn, #6676, 6½" ..250.00
Vase, jade over alabaster, dragon, ACB, #6148, 9⅞" 1,600.00
Vase, mirror blk, 3 triangular bud vases on base, sgn, #6873, 10". 550.00
Vase, mirror blk, fan shape, #7307, ftd, 6" 650.00
Vase, mirror blk, women & swags, acid etch, #2683, 8¾".......... 1,200.00
Vase, pk cluthra, squat conical, sgn, 9½" 550.00
Vase, Pomona gr leaves over Rosa, ACB, #7007, 14" 5,000.00
Vase, Pomona gr w/crystal 'M' hdl, optic, sgn, #8508, 9½" 600.00
Vase, smoke, ACB, vine, inverted rim, #2687, 8" 2,400.00
Vase, yel jade, bl aurene neck, dripped shoulder, #7014, 8½" 2,400.00

Stevengraphs

A stevengraph is a small picture made of woven silk resembling an elaborate ribbon, created by Thomas Stevens in England in the latter half of the 1800s. They were matted and framed by Stevens, usually with his name appearing on the mat or often with the trade announcement on the back of the mat. He also produced silk postcards and bookmarks, all of which have 'Stevens' woven in silk on one of the mitered corners. Anyone wishing to learn more about Stevengraphs is encouraged to contact the Stevengraph Collectors' Association; see the Clubs, Newsletters, and Websites section. Unless noted otherwise, assume our values are for examples in very good original condition and the pictures matted and framed.

Are You Ready? bk label, unfr, 5x8", EX 510.00
Bath of Psyche, image: 3¼x10¼", G... 180.00
Columbus Leaving Spain.. 360.00
Crystal Palace (inside), unfr, EX+ 1,140.00
Death of Nelson, 7½x10½" 240.00
Ecce Homo, Christ w/crown of thorns, 9½x6¼" 85.00

First Over (The), double matted and framed, water staining to mat, 2x6", overall 7¾x10½", $340.00. (Photo courtesy Cordier Antiques & Fine Art on LiveAuctioneers.com)

First Point, 6x9" 120.00
First Touch, bk label, 5½x8½", G 420.00
Fourth Bridge, bk label, 7½x10½" 300.00
God Speed the Plough (no birds in foreground), bk label, 8x11", EX... 420.00
Grace Darling, $100 to 150.00
HM Queen Alexandra, label, 8x6", G.. 75.00
HM Queen Victoria, 5 images, G-... 325.00
HM Stanley, portrait, bk label, 7½x4⅝" 275.00
HRH Duchess of Cornwall & York, gold crown, red flowers, G-.... 95.00
Iroquois & Fred Archer, Winner 1881 Derby, on brd, 4x8½"....2,240.00
Late Fred Archer, jockey, 8x6½".. 180.00
Leda, she w/swan, bk label 30+32 titles, rare, 8x11", EX............. 950.00
Life or Death Heroism on Land, bk label, 6x9"............................. 450.00

Maj Gen JDP Fr, bk label, 8x6", G 150.00
Mater Dolorosa, bk label, inner/outer mats, 9¼x6¼" 950.00
Niagara Falls scene, 7x11", EX 575.00
Philadelphia Int'l Exhibition, G Washington/eagle, 1876, 11x6". 485.00
Present Time, 60 Miles an Hour, 7¼x10" 150.00
Queen Victoria & Her Premiers, bk label, 11x8½", EX 420.00
Slip, 6x9" 145.00
Souvenir of the Wild West, 8 Indians, Buffalo Bill in red shirt . 5,500.00
Start, 6x9", G- 120.00
Struggle, 4 horses, no bkgrnd or other horses, unfr 250.00
Water Jump, 6x9" 180.00
William Prince of Orange, 7¼x10" 540.00

Miscellaneous

Bookmark, By Special Appointment to Her Majesty the Queen..., 6" ... 550.00
Bookmark, Home Sweet Home, G 60.00
Bookmark, Thy Will Be Done in Earth As It Is in Heaven 85.00
Memorial ribbon, Stratford Church/Shakespeare in wreaths, 10½" . 85.00
Souvenir ribbon, Geo Washington Am Centennial, 18x3", NM. 210.00
Souvenir, Centennial 1776-1876, Washington portrait, 8⅜" 120.00
Souvenir, Phila Centennial 1876/Geo Washington, 6-color, 6½" L...360.00
Souvenir, Signing Declaration of Independence, Columbian World's Fair ... 180.00

Stevens and Williams

Stevens and Williams glass was produced at the Brierly Hill Glassworks in Stourbridge, England, for nearly a century, beginning in the 1830s. They were credited with being among the first to develop a method of manufacturing a more affordable type of cameo glass. Other lines were also made — silver deposit, alexandrite, and engraved rock crystal, to name but a few. Our advisor for this category is Don Williams; he is listed in the Directory under Missouri.

Cameo

Bottle, scent, floral, red on wht frost, globular, 1890s, 4½" 1,600.00
Bottle, scent, floral, wht on red, lay-down, ca 1884, 4⅛" 1,200.00
Vase, apple blossoms/branches, wht on citron, dbl-gourd form, 12" . 2,200.00

Vase, Diamond Quilted with applied fruit, leaves, and scroll feet, 8x8", $550.00. (Photo courtesy Burchard Galleries Inc. on LiveAuctioneers.com)

Vase, floral, wht on citron, elongated gourd form, 1880s, 12½". 2,200.00
Vase, floral/butterfly, wht on citron, neck ring, teardrop body, 5".. 865.00
Vase, floral/insect, pk/wht on citron, baluster, 5⅝", pr 6,000.00
Vase, flowers/leaves, red on wht, gourd shape, 8½" 3,000.00
Vase, flowers/scrolls (elaborate) wht on champagne, urn form, 1885, 3".. 1,250.00
Vase, fruiting branches, wht on deep bl, 3 dbl camphor ft, 5½" ... 4,000.00
Vase, intricate medallions, bl on wht w/gold line trim, att, 12", pr...2,185.00

Miscellaneous

Bowl, rose, Pompeian Swirl, bl, incurvate, 3" H 135.00
Center bowl, pear branches appl to aqua, branch ft, 7x8" 1,500.00

Ewer, Pompeian Swirl, red to yel, frosted hdl, stick neck, 12½" . 2,400.00
Rose bowl, peachblow w/red cherries on amber stems (ft), tilted, 9"... 975.00
Vase, Peachblow w/amber stems+4 opal & pk flowers, ruffled, 10"... 345.00
Vase, peachblow w/appl wht flower/amber branch, handkerchief rim, 5".. 120.00
Vase, pk cased w/appl wht rose blossoms & vines, folded rim, 9", NM .600.00
Vase, pk opal w/appl red strawberry/gr leaves/amber thorn ft, 6x8x4"...480.00
Vase, Pompeian Swirl, chartreuse to bl over wht, dbl-gourd form, 9".1,450.00
Vase, Pompeian Swirl, gold birds/branches, dbl-gourd form, 7".1,450.00
Vase, Pompeian Swirl, pk MOP, dbl-gourd form, 6⅞".................. 550.00
Vase, Pompeian Swirl, purple/bl, rnd w/long ogee neck, 8"........2,400.00
Vase, Pompeian Swirl, red/brn, bl int, stick neck, 8⅜" 690.00
Vase, Pompeian Swirl, tangerine to peach, stick neck, 12⅜".....1,200.00
Vase, trumpet blossoms/foliage, mc on crystal w/gold, shouldered, 12". 2,750.00

Stickley

Among the leading proponents of the Arts and Crafts Movement, the Stickley brothers — Gustav, Leopold, Charles, Albert, and John George — were at various times and locations separately involved in designing and producing furniture as well as decorative items for the home. (See Arts and Crafts for further information.) The oldest of the five Stickley brothers was Gustav; his work is the most highly regarded of all. He developed the style of furniture referred to as Mission. It was strongly influenced by the type of furnishings found in the Spanish missions of California — utilitarian, squarely built, and simple. It was made most often of oak, and decoration was very limited or non-existent. The work of his brothers displays adaptations of many of Gustav's ideas and designs. His factory, the Craftsman Workshop, operated in Eastwood, New York, from the late 1890s until 1915, when he was forced out of business by larger companies who copied his work and sold it at much lower prices. Among his shop marks are the early red decal containing a joiner's compass and the words 'Als Ik Kan,' the branded mark with similar components, and paper labels.

The firm known as Stickley Brothers was located first in Binghamton, New York, and then Grand Rapids, Michigan. Albert and John George made the move to Michigan, leaving Charles in Binghamton (where he and an uncle continued the operation under a different name). After several years John George left the company to rejoin Leopold in New York. (These two later formed their own firm called L. & J.G. Stickley.) The Stickley Brothers Company's early work produced furniture featuring fine inlay work, decorative cutouts, and leaned strongly toward a style of Arts and Crafts with an English influence. It was tagged with a paper label 'Made by Stickley Brothers, Grand Rapids,' or with a brass plate or decal with the words 'Quaint Furniture,' an English term chosen to refer to their product. In addition to furniture, they made metal accessories as well.

The workshops of the L. & J.G. Stickley Company first operated under the name 'Onondaga Shops.' Located in Fayetteville, New York, their designs were often all but copies of Gustav's work. Their products were well made and marketed, and their business was very successful. Their decal labels contained all or a combination of the words 'Handcraft' or 'Onondaga Shops,' along with the brothers' initials and last name. The firm continues in business today. Our advisor for this category is Bruce Austin; he is listed in the Directory under New York.

Note: When only one dimension is given, it is length. Our values are from cataloged auctions and include the buyer's premium. Unless a condition code is present in the line, our values reflect the worth of items that are complete, in original condition, and retaining their original finishes. A rating of excellent (EX) may denote cleaning, small repairs, or touchups. Codes lower than that describe wear, losses, repairs, or damage in degrees relative to the condition given. Cleaning and/or refinishing can lower values as much as 15% to 30%. Replaced hardware or wood will also have a dramatic negative effect.

Key:
b — brand　　　　　　　　h/cp — hammered copper
bd — black decal　　　　　　p — paper label
d — red decal　　　　　　　t — Quaint metal tag

Charles Stickley

Chairs, dining, slat bk, reuphl bk & seats, 5 side+1 arm............1,200.00
Loveseat, orig drop-in seat reuphl in leather, att, 36x47½x22" .1,450.00
Rocker, arm, rect cutouts to bk, reuphl seat, rfn, rpt, 34" 800.00
Rocker, arm, tall bk w/vertical slats, uphl seat, rfn, att, 48"..........750.00
Rocker, unsgn, 34x29x25", VG...1,200.00
Server, plate rail, 2 drws, copper pulls, att, 39x42x20" 1,200.00

Settee, cut-out slats all around, replaced upholstery, chips around feet, stain on arm, no mark, 62" long, $3,200.00. (Photo courtesy Rago Auctions)

Settle, drop-arm, slat bk, 3-seat, reuphl brn vinyl, att, 42x67x27"....1,800.00
Settle, even-arm, 6-slat bk, wide posts, thru tenons, 34x73" 3,000.00
Sideboard, quartersawn oak, 4 drws amid 2 doors over 2 drws...3,500.00
Table, lamp, lower shelf, X-stretcher, p, rfn top, 29x30" dia.........800.00
Table, quartersawn oak on ped w/4 leaves, att 2,400.00

Gustav Stickley

Andirons, ball tops, hinged rings joined by chain, unmk, 20x12x23".6,000.00
Armchair, #376, tall-bk, spindled, uphl drop-in seat, d, 49x27½x22".2,000.00
Armchair, uphl seat, H Ellis, copper & pewter, d, 44x24½x20½".21,600.00
Bed, #912, dbl, single panels, side rails, d, headboard 50x58½".3,240.00
Bed, #923, 4 vertical slats ea end, tapered posts, 47x79x47" 3,500.00
Bookcase, #525, 2-door, mitered mullions, 3 fixed shelves, d, 56x45" ..18,000.00
Bookcase, #702, Ellis design, 58x48x14", EX 6,000.00
Bookcase, #715, 1 16-pane door, slab sides, thru-tenons, d, 56x36", VG..5,400.00
Bookcase, gallery, 3 fixed shelves, thru tenons, p, d, 56x35x13".6,500.00
Bookcase, open w/3 fixed shelves per side, p, d, 57x43x13".....10,200.00
Cabinet, 1-pane door & sides, 1 wood/8 glass shelves, d, 72x24x18"..11,000.00
Chafing dish, h/cp woodgrain pattern, wood base, terra cotta dish, 15"..3,100.00
Chair set, #306½, orig rush seats, d, 36½x16½x16¾", 6 for.......3,900.00
Chair, arm, #2616, U-bk, rush seat, ca 1901, d, 38"...................2,500.00
Chair, bungalow arm, #2576, modified seat fr, unmk, 38¼".......1,700.00
Chair, Morris, #2340, bow-arm, loose cushion on ropes, unmk, 39" ..8,000.00
Chair, Morris, #367, spindled, drop-in spring seat, uphl cushion, 38½x27½x34"..3,000.00
Chair, Morris, brn leather cushions, sling base, d, 38x29x34" ...5,400.00
Chair, side, #374, tall-bk spindled, uphl drop-in seats, d, 45½x19½x18" ..2,200.00
Chair, side, H Ellis design, maple, rush seat, varied inlays, 39" .5,500.00
Chair, slipper, #392, drop-in spring seat, spindled, unsgn, 32¾x17x16"...225.00
Chairs, ladderback dining, #370, d, 36¼x17x16½", 4 for 2,280.00
Chandelier, 5 h/cp drops, yel glass liners, oak mt, 37x21" 20,400.00

Chest, #626, 2 short drws over 3, hammered iron pulls, d, 43x36x20"....5,000.00
Chest, #906, 2 short drws over 4, ring pulls, d, p, 48½x40x21" .9,000.00
Chest, #909, 2 sm drws over 3, 42¼x36x20" 6,000.00
Chest, blanket, dvtl construction, hammered iron pulls, p, 17x36x22¼" ..3,120.00
Chest, bride's, paneled sides, iron hardware, d, 18x35¼x20"......6,000.00
China cabinet, #815, 2-door, gallery top, cast V pulls, p, 64x41½x15" .9,000.00
Costumer, dbl, #53 h/cp straps for umbrellas or canes, 72x14x18" ..1,500.00
Desk organizer, mail slots, dvtl case, unsgn, 9x25x10".............2,280.00
Desk, chalet, paneled drop front, lower shelf, shoe ft, d, 46x24x16" ..2,500.00
Fire screen, w/Navajo textile, unmk, 35x32½" 4,500.00
Footstool, #300, orig tacked-on leather w/some tears, unmk, 14¾x20¼x16¼"...600.00
Footstool, #395, spindled, recovered, unmk, 15x20x16" 900.00
Magazine stand, #72, arched sides, p, 42x21½x12¾" 2,150.00
Magazine stand, #548, panel sides, 4-shelf, 1902, d, 44x15x15".6,000.00
Magazine stand, chalet, #500, unmk, 43x12¾x12¾" 3,500.00
Mirror, hall, 21½x28"..900.00
Music stand, H Ellis, dvtl cabinet, grapes/leaves, d, 48x20x17"..7,800.00
Plaque, wall, #345, h/cp, circular, emb stylized pods, 19¾" dia.18,000.00
Rocker, #359A, spindled, leather-wrapped seat, bd, 36¼x25¾x22"..1,320.00
Rocker, #374, tall-bk spindled, uphl drop-in seat, d, 45½x27¾x22"...1,800.00
Settee, cube, #305, reuphl drop-in spring seat, unmk, 30x56x22".4,500.00

Settle, #207, 13 canted vertical slats at back, five each side, recovered, original finish, early red box mark, 71x39x34", $18,000.00. (Photo courtesy Treadway Gallery on LiveAuctioneers.com)

Settle, #212, V-bk w/19 vertical slats at bk, leather seat, unmk, 36x71½x26"..2,400.00
Settle, #222, even-arm, leather drop-in seat, d, 36x79x33".....10,000.00
Settle, #225, even-arm, horizontal brd at bk, reuphl, 29x78x31" ..9,000.00
Settle, ¾-arm, drop-in foam seat, b, 29¾x80x31½" 4,500.00
Sideboard, #814, 2 doors/2 sm drw/linen drw/plate rail, 49x66x23¾", VG..3,600.00
Sideboard, #816, linen drw over 3 sm drws, 2 cabinets, d, 45½x48x18" .3,000.00
Sideboard, #817, w/chamfered plate rack, b, 50x70x25" 14,400.00
Sideboard, butterfly joints, custom made, unmk, 1901, 45¼x100x25".72,000.00
Table, lamp, #240, cutouts, shelf, unmk, 29½x20x20"...............3,100.00
Table, library, #616, 2-drw, sgn, p, 30½x54½x32½" 4,800.00
Table, library, #619, 3-drw, cast/riveted oval pulls, p, d, 30x66x35¼"..3,000.00
Table, tea, floriform top, shelf, shaped legs, unmk, 23¼x19", VG+ 8,400.00
Tabouret, #449, Eastwood, flush tenons, partial d, 22x24" 4,200.00

L. & J.G. Stickley

Bed, twin, slatted, tall tapering posts, iron side rails, headboard 50x44½" ..1,800.00
Bookcase, #328½, through-tenons, 3 fixed shelves, unsgn, 56½x52½x12"..5,500.00
Bookcase, #331, 3 12-pane do, recoated finish, 57x73x12", G ..4,500.00
Bookcase, #641, single-door, gallery top, keyed through-tenons, 55x33x12".6,000.00
Bookcase, #645, 2-door, keyed through-tenons, unmk, 54x53x12"....5,400.00
Chair, arm, #838 (similar), leather bk & seat, orig tacks, 39", G .100.00
Chair, Morris, #406, slatted bow-arm, reuphl seat & bk, d, 38x34x41"..4,200.00

Chair, Morris, #410, drop arms, drop-in spring seat, red vinyl, 41½x32¼x38¼" ..5,100.00
Dresser, pivoting mirror, rpl period hardware, handcrafted decal, 69x48x22" ..3,900.00
Loveseat, #225, slatted bk drop-in spring seat, 36½x52½x22½" . 1,400.00
Magazine stand, slatted sides, 4-shelf, d, 42x21x12" 2,200.00
Night stand, #550, drw shelf, unmk, 29x20x18" 2,150.00
Rocker, #460, slatted bk & arms, loose seat on ropes, d, 38" 1,900.00
Server, #752, 2 shelves beneath curved backsplash & apron, 38x40x14¾". 1,800.00
Settle, #223, vertical slats, drop-in spring seat, recovered blk leather, unsgn, 39x84x32" .6,000.00
Sideboard, #738, 2 drws flanked by cabinets, plate rack, 46x60x22" ..2,160.00
Sideboard, #745, plate rail, strap hinges, 48x54x24" 4,800.00

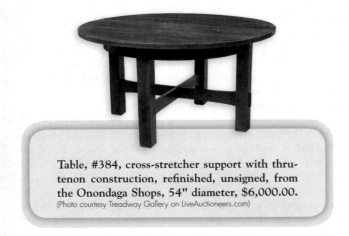

Table, #384, cross-stretcher support with thru-tenon construction, refinished, unsigned, from the Onondaga Shops, 54" diameter, $6,000.00.
(Photo courtesy Treadway Gallery on LiveAuctioneers.com)

Table, encyclopedia, #516 7-slat sides, ungsn, 29x27x27", VG .8,400.00
Table, library, #342, mahog, Onondaga Shops, unsgn, 30x48x30" ..900.00
Table, trestle, #593, dbl key & tenons, shoe-ft base, rfn top, 48x29" ..1,100.00
Table, trestle, keyed-thru lg shelf, rfn, unmk, 30x72x45" 3,600.00

Stickley Bros.

Armchair, #357, 4 vertical slats at top over horizontal rail, 44" ... 275.00
Bed, paneled, pewter/ebonized wood inlay, unmk, 60½x77¼x57". 15,600.00
Cache pot, h/cp, appl hdls, 3-ftd, #82, 9½x10" 350.00
Chair set, 3-slat ladderbk, new leather, p/t, 37x19x17", 6 for....3,240.00
Chair, desk, #604, 1-slat bk w/2 cutouts, Macmurdo ft, 39", VG .450.00
Chair, Morris, #631, 3-slat bk, rolled arms, worn cushion, 37"..2,500.00
Chair, side, floriform inlay of various woods, trapezoidal seat, 42"...900.00
Chairs, dining, #919, vertical slats, red leather seats, t, p, 37½x18¼x16½", 6 for..2,640.00
China cabinet, 2 1-pane doors, partial-mirror bk, b, d, 59½x46x14"..2,150.00
China cabinet, like #8860, mirror bk w/caned sqs, rfn, 63x42", VG... 1,200.00
Desk, like #2810, bookshelf below top (rfn)/ea side 1 drw, 40" 600.00
Lamp, h/cp 20" fr w/mica inserts; 3-socket/2-hdl bulb std, 22"..3,600.00
Magazine stand, #4600, notched gallery, 3-shelf, slat sides, 31x16x13"...1,100.00
Magazine stand, circular cutouts, unmk, 49½x14x12" 1,100.00
Plant stand, tapering column on sq base & 4 ft, 34x12", EX 1,200.00
Rocker, 4-slot bk w/cutouts, open arms, leather seat, att, 35"....... 325.00
Rocker, shaped/cvd arm supports, wide str aprons, rfn, 39x30x38"... 960.00
Server w/mirror, #777-8220, Quaint Furniture tag, 51x50x21", VG... 1,200.00
Settle, broad slats, drop arms, loose cushion, t, 37x74x31" 1,700.00
Settle, even-arm, vertical slats, reuphl brn leather cushion, t, 50".. 2,775.00
Sideboard, plate rail, linen drw over 3 sm drws, 2 cabinets, t, 44x48x20" ..2,000.00
Table, game, legs mortised through, X-stretcher, 40" dia, EX 900.00
Table, lamp, #130, X-stretcher, thru tenons, t, 30x40½" 1,600.00
Table, lamp, dbl oval, t, 30x36x28" 1,800.00
Table, library, #181, circular top & X-stretcher base, unsgn, 29x48"..1,200.00
Table, library, #2601, bookshelf sides, rfn top, p, 30x40x26" 750.00
Table, library, 2-drw, 2-brd shelf mortised through sides 54" L, VG...1,100.00
Table, library, 2-drw, overhang top, corbels, Quaint d, 48" L 1,200.00
Table, library, blind drw, 2 slats ea side, rpr to top, t, 30x36x24"..850.00
Table, library, drw, oak pulls, lower stretchers, shelf, t, 30x44x29"......725.00

Stiegel

Baron Henry Stiegel produced glassware in Pennsylvania as early as 1760, very similar to glass being made concurrently in Germany and England. Without substantiating evidence, it is impossible to positively attribute a specific article to his manufacture. Although he made other types of glass, today the term Stiegel generally refers to any very early ware made in shapes and colors similar to those he is known to have produced — especially that with etched or enameled decoration. It is generally conceded, however, that most glass of this type is of European origin. Our advisor for this category is Mark Vuono; he is listed in the Directory under Connecticut. Unless a color is mentioned in the description, assume the glass to be clear.

Bottle, cobalt w/mc floral, half-post, no cap, 5½" 360.00
Bottle, floral/squiggles in mc enamel, missing cap, 6½" 360.00
Bottle, half-post, cobalt w/poly floral, fitted pewter top, 5½" 360.00
Decanter, florals around wht shield w/Zum Andenker, 3 neck rings, 10"... 415.00
Decanter, roses/flowers/shield in mc enamel, att, 10¼x4½".......... 425.00
Pitcher, dk sapphire bl, Dmn T'print, 4x3½" 360.00

Salt cellar, amethyst, 12-diamond pattern over flute with applied petal foot, 3⅛", $2,900.00. (Photo courtesy Pook & Pook, Inc. on LiveAuctioneers.com)

Salt cellar, cobalt, expanded dmns, ftd, 3" 465.00
Tumbler, bird/hearts/flowers in mc enamel on clear, att, 3¼" 395.00

Stocks and Bonds

Scripophily (scrip-awfully), the collecting of 'worthless' old stocks and bonds, gained recognition as an area of serious interest around the mid-1970s. Collectors who come from numerous business fields mainly enjoy its hobby aspect, though there are those who consider scripophily an investment. Some collectors like the historical significance that certain certificates have. Others prefer the beauty of older stocks and bonds that were printed in various colors with fancy artwork and ornate engravings. Autograph collectors are found in this field, on the lookout for signed certificates; others collect specific industries.

Many factors help determine the collector value: autograph value, age of the certificate, the industry represented, whether it is issued or not, its attractiveness, condition, and collector demand. Certificates from the mining, energy, and railroad industries are the most popular with collectors. Other industries or special collecting fields include banking, automobiles, aircraft, and territorials. Serious collectors usually prefer only issued certificates that date from before 1930. Unissued certificates are usually worth one-fourth to one-tenth the value of one that has been issued. Inexpensive issued common stocks and bonds dated between the 1940s and 1990s usually retail between $1.00 to $10.00. Those dating between 1890 and 1930 usually sell for $10.00 to $50.00. Those over 100 years old retail between $25.00 and $100.00 or more, depending on the quantity found and the industry represented. Some stocks are one of a kind while others are found by the hundreds or even thousands, especially railroad certificates. Autographed stocks normally sell anywhere from $50.00 to $1,000.00 or more. A formal collecting organization for scripophilists is known as The Bond and Share Society with an American chapter located in New York City. As is true in any field, potential collectors should take the time to learn the hobby. Prices vary greatly at websites selling old stocks and bonds, sometimes by hundreds of dollars.

Collectors should avoid buying modern certificates being offered for sale at scripophily websites in the $20.00 to $60.00 range as they have little collector value despite the sales hype. One uncancelled share of some of the modern 'famous name' stocks of the Fortune 500 companies are being offered at two or four times what the stock is currently trading for. These should be avoided, and new collectors who want to buy certificates in modern companies will be better off buying 'one share' stocks in their own name and not someone else's. Take the time to study the market, ask questions, and be patient as a collector. Your collection will be better off. Generally, eBay serves as a good source for information regarding current values — search under 'Coins.' Our advisor for this category is Cheryl Anderson; she is listed in the Directory under Utah. In many of the following listings, two-letter state abbreviations precede the date. Unless noted otherwise, values are for examples in fine condition.

Key:
U — unissued   I/U — issued/uncancelled
I/C — issued/cancelled   vgn — vignette

Arizona Territory Court House Building Bond #89, dated July 1, 1882, nine original coupons still attached, courthouse vignette, printed in black with bronze and gold inks, gold seal lower left, mining scene lower right, 20x19", $2,160.00. (Photo courtesy Heritage Auctions on LiveAuctioneers.com)

Am Motor Transportation, bus & passengers vgn, bl ink, DE, 1930, U.. 72.50
Athens, Mfg, GA state arms vgn, GA, 1892, I/C 48.00
Bald Mtn Mining, view of Fryerhill, CO, 1880, I/C 48.00
Baltimore Athenian Society, on laid paper, MD, 1812, I/C 110.00
Bank of Gettysburg, man's portrait/Liberty/Justice, 1857, I/C 110.00
Boyette Electric Car, eagle w/shield vgn, gr seal, FL, 1934, I/C...... 85.00
Brooklyn Academy of Music, lady w/doves vgn, gr, NY, 1921, I/U ..60.00
Chesapeake & OH Ry, man/train vgn, 10 shares common stock, purple, U ...72.50
Chicago Aerial Industries, eagle vgn, brn ink, ABN, DE, 1964, I/C.. 24.00
Christmas Wonder Mining, Santa vgn, AZ named state error, NV/1907, I/C.165.00
Climber Motor, eagle w/shield vgn, gr print/seal, AR, 1919, I/C . 135.00
Consolidated Alaskan Co, brn/gr print, red seal, 1915, I/C............ 24.00
Consolidated Business College, capitol bldg vgn, DC, 1869, IC.... 60.00
Doble Steam Motors, olive gr, ornate border, DE, 1922, I/C.......... 95.00
Dundee, Perth & London Shipping, ornate borders, bl, 1914, I/C. 30.00
Dupont RY & Land, participation certificate, brn, FL, 1912 .... 36.00
Eclipse Gold Mining, 6,000 shares, ornate border, CA, 1877, I/C. 75.00
Fulton Motor Truck, gold seal/under print, eagle vgn, DE, 1919, I/C...36.00

Gearless Motor, touring car under print, DE, 1921, I/C................ 195.00
Goldfield Consolidated Mines, eagle vgn, gr seal, WY, 1906, I/C.. 36.00
Gold Mining Co, gr lettering, AZ map, 1895, 8¾x14½" 2,160.00
Gray Goose Airways, goose vgn, gold seal, NV, 1932, I/C............. 72.50
Greyhound Corp, 100 common shares, greyhound vgn, gr, ABN, 1970, I/C...24.00
Gyro Air Lines, eagle w/logo, blk w/red border, AZ, 1934, I/C 36.00
Hannibal & St Joseph RR, 7% Preferred Stock, train vgn, 18__, U.. 18.00
Henry Clews & Co, sale of 25 shares of GM stock, 1925 .... 12.50
Iditarod Telephone, ornate border, blk, NV, 1910, I/C 60.00
Interborough-Metropolitan, Preferred Stock, bl, 1911, I/C........... 24.00
Ivanhoe Mfg, factory view vgn, 6% bond/$1,000, NJ, 1884, I/C.... 48.00
Jumbo Fraction Mining, workers/mtn vgns, NV, 1906, I/C 30.00
Junction RR Co, train vgn, OH, 18__, U 12.50
KY Petroleum & Mining, orange border, KY, 1865, I/C 48.00
London Improved Cab, 168 shares, ornate border, bl, 1896, I/C.... 12.50
MA Cremation Society, ornate border/seal, gr, MA, 1897, I/C.... 110.00
Madison Safe Deposit, dog guards vgn, bl, NY, ABN Co, 19__, U ..135.00
Middleburgh Bridge, steamshop vgn, NY, 1866, I/C...................... 72.50
Minneapolis Industrial Expo, building vgn, orange/gold seal, 1893, I/C.72.50
Mt Shasta Gold Mines, miners vgn, gr ink, ABN Co, SD, 1930, I/C ..48.00
North Horn Silver Mining, mining vgn, UT, 1881, I/C 36.00
OH Canal, farm scene/barge/train vgn, $2,500, 1886, I/C 72.50
Owego & Ithaca Turnpike, ornate border, laid paper, 1810, I/C 36.00
Peerless Motor Car, brn, 3 vgns, ABNCo, VA, 1927-29, I/C 30.00
Philadelphia/Baltimore/WA RR, $1,000 Gold Bond w/vgn, PA/1924, I/C .12.00
Society Paris Carlton Hotel, pk, sm crown, ornate border, 1920, I/C.12.50
Standard Motor Holding, orange border, DE, 1933 .... 12.50
Union Bank of Rochester, Prosperity/Liberty/shield, NY, 18__, U...190.00
Upper Potomac Steamboat, sidewheeler vgn, $100, VA, 1875, I/C.95.00
UT Patent & Implement, eagle vgn, beige seal, UT/1917, I/U...... 11.00
W Frankfort Bank & Trust, Mercury vgn/artwork, gold seal, IL/1916, I/U...12.00
Waterford & Limerick Rwy, bl paper/pk seal, coat of arms, 1845, I/C....96.00
Waterford, Dungarvan & Lismore Railway, purple ink, Ireland, 1888, I/C ..48.00
West Shore RR, $50,000 bond, bold title/vgn, ABNCo, NY/early 1900s, U ..10.00

Stoneware

There are three broad periods of time that collectors of American pottery can look to in evaluating and dating the stoneware and earthenware in their collections. Among the first permanent settlers in America were English and German potters who found a great demand for their individually turned wares. The early pottery was produced from red and yellow clays scraped from the ground at surface levels. The earthenware made in these potteries was fragile and coated with lead glazes that periodically created health problems for the people who ate or drank from it. There was little stoneware available for sale until the early 1800s, because the clays used in its production were not readily available in many areas and transportation was prohibitively expensive. The opening of the Erie Canal and improved roads brought about a dramatic increase in the accessibility of stoneware clay, and many new potteries began to open in New York and New England.

Collectors have difficulty today locating earthenware and stoneware jugs produced prior to 1840, because few have survived intact. These ovoid or pear-shaped jugs were designed to be used on a daily basis. When cracked or severely chipped, they were quickly discarded. The value of handcrafted pottery is often determined by the cobalt decoration it carries. Pieces with elaborate scenes (a chicken pecking corn, a bluebird on a branch, a stag standing near a pine tree, a sailing ship, or people) may easily bring $1,000.00 to $12,000.00 at auction.

After the Civil War there was a need and a national demand for stoneware jugs, crocks, canning jars, churns, spittoons, and a wide variety of other pottery items. The competition among the many potteries reached the point where only the largest could survive. To cut costs, most potteries did away with all but the simplest kinds of decoration on their wares. Time-consuming brush-painted birds or flowers quickly gave way to more quickly executed swirls or numbers and stenciled designs. The coming of home refrigeration and Prohibition in 1919 effectively destroyed the American stoneware industry.

Investment possibilities: 1) Early nineteenth-century stoneware with elaborate decorations and a potter's mark is expensive and will continue to rise in price. 2) Late nineteenth-century hand-thrown stoneware with simple cobalt swirls or numbers is still reasonably priced and a good investment. 3) Mass-produced stoneware (ca. 1890 – 1920) is available in large quantities, inexpensive, and slowly increases in price over the years. Generally speaking, prices will be stronger in the areas where the stoneware pottery originates. Skillfully repaired pieces often surface; their prices should reflect their condition. Look for a slight change in color and texture. The use of a black light is also useful in exposing some repairs. Buyer beware! Hint: Buy only from reputable dealers who will guarantee their merchandise. Assume that values are for examples in near mint condition with only minimal damage unless another condition code is given in the description. See also Bennington, Stoneware.

Bank, hen on nest, ochre, 1880s, 3¼" 575.00
Batter jug, foliage & tobacco leaves, Cowden & Wilcox, 8" 5,100.00

Batter jug, stylized leaves, Cowden & Wilcox, Harrisburg, Pennsylvania, half-gallon, 9", EX, $2,040.00. (Photo courtesy Skinner Auctioneers and Appraisers of Antiques and Fine Art)

Batter pail, #4/running bird, att Whites, Utica, bail hdl, 1870s, 10" .. 525.00
Batter pail, dk brn alkaline, orig bail hdl, tin lids, 1870s, 10" 275.00
Chicken feeder, wht Bristol 1880s, 5" 65.00
Churn, #3/flower (triple), OA Gifford Watertown NY, 1860s, 14", EX ... 525.00
Churn, #3/triple flower, N Clark Jr, Athens NY, 1850s, 15" 575.00
Churn, #4/flowering vine, Whites Utica, ca 1865, lime stain, 17" .. 745.00
Churn, #4/leaf, Frank B Norton, cobalt on salt glaze, 17", NM.... 765.00
Churn, #6/flower, C Hart Sherburne, bulb, 1858, hairline, 19".... 650.00
Cream pot, #1/dotted bee, att N Clark, Athens NY, 1850s, ping, 7"..210.00
Cream pot, #1/long-necked bird, NA Wht & Co, Binghamton, 1868, 9" ..385.00
Cream pot, #2/brushed flower, N Clark Jr, Athens NY, 1850s, 8½"....275.00
Cream pot, #2/chicken pecking, Ottman Bros, Ft Edward NY, 1870s, 11"..1,200.00
Cream pot, #3/spitting flower, Savage & Rogers, Havana NY, 1850s, 12" ..1,595.00
Cream pot, #4/flower (dbl), Whites, Utica, ca 1865, hairline, 12" ... 275.00
Crock, #1/accents, J Remmey NY, glued crack, 1790s, 11" 1,925.00
Crock, #1/bird on branch, Belmont Ave Pottery, 1880s, 8" 330.00
Crock, #1/bird, Binghamton NY, ca 1860, spiders/lines, 7" 415.00
Crock, #1/chicken pecks corn, att Poughkeepsie NY, 1870s, 10½", EX ... 600.00
Crock, #1/house on hill w/trees & grasses, West Troy, 1880s, rstr, 7" .5,175.00
Crock, #2/accents, Commeraw's, New York, rpl hdl, ca 1790, 11½" ..1,150.00
Crock, #2/bird on branch, West Troy, 1880s, 9" 440.00
Crock, #2/bird w/polka-dot wing, S Hart Fulton, 10x8" 750.00
Crock, #2/eagle on stump (lg), att Albany NY, ca 1865, 9½", EX. 700.00
Crock, #2/lovebirds, S Hart Fulton, ca 1875, ping, 9" 770.00
Crock, #2/spotted bird & foliage, WH Farrar & Co., Geddes NY, hairlines..3,120.00
Crock, #2/tulips/dmns/stars, FH Cowden Harrisburg, chips, 10" ..400.00
Crock, #2/wreath, Burger & Co, Rochester NY, ca 1877, 9" 360.00
Crock, #3/dbl plume, Mason & Russel Cortland, ca 1835, rare, 9" ..1,430.00

Crock, #3/foliage, J Swank & Co Johnstown PA, rpr, 12x11½" ... 315.00
Crock, #3/lyre, Whites, Utica, ca 1865, stains, 10½" 215.00
Crock, #4/3 bluebirds on branches, West Troy NY, 12½", EX ... 1,400.00
Crock, #4/flower, Ballard & Brothers Burlington VT, 13⅛" 500.00
Crock, #4/flower, Thomas D Chollar Cortland, crack, ca 1845, 13½" .. 300.00
Crock, #4/house among palms, AO Whittemore...NY, 1860s-80s, 10", EX..2,350.00
Crock, #4/orchid, Whites, Utica, ca 1865, chips, 11".....:............. 185.00
Crock, #4/parrot on plume, FB Norton, Worcester MA, 1870s, lines, 11"...550.00
Crock, #5/birds (3), West Troy NY, 1880s, 12½", EX 2,750.00
Crock, #5/folky lion, Hubbell & Chesebro Geddes NY, 1870s, 12½", NM.. 17,000.00
Crock, #5/grapes, T Harrington, Lyons, 1850s, spider, 12" 1,435.00
Crock, #6/flower (drooping), J Fisher & Co Lyons NY, 1880s, 14", EX.... 330.00
Crock, #6/orchid (lg), Whites, Utica NY, tight line, ca 1865, 13" ..450.00
Crock, #6/wreath, Burger & Lang, Rochester NY, 1870s, spider, 15".. 360.00
Crock, cake, #3/dbl flower, unmk NY state, 1850s, glued crack, 9" .. 220.00
Crock, cake, drooping flower, Cowden & Wilcox, Harrisburg, 1870s, 5".. 385.00
Crock, flower/accents, P Cross Hartford, spider line, ca 1805, 12½" ..2,035.00
Crock, flowers, AE Smith & Sons...NY, flakes, 12" 85.00

Crock, large flower, TH Wilson & Co., Harrisburg, Pennsylvania, with lid, 10", VG, $3,840.00. (Photo courtesy Pook & Pook, Inc. on LiveAuctioneers.com)

Crock, parrot, emb label; FB Norton & Co...MA, flake, 7¾" 635.00
Crock, Philbrick & Spaulding...Haverhill/feathers, crack, 1870s, 12". 120.00
Crock, Whites Utica NY/eagle, thick rim, minor flakes, 7¼x9" ... 315.00
Flowerpot, bud & flower, att Fort Edward, 1870s, hairline, 7" 685.00
Jar, #1/flower (brushed), J Sager Co Homer, misshapen rim, 1830s, 10"... 770.00
Jar, #2/plume, N Clark & Co Mt Morris, prof rpr, ca 1835, 11" ... 300.00
Jar, #3/bird on stump, JA & CW Underwood...NY, ca 1865, ping, 13" ..2,425.00
Jar, canning, #/pear, Palatine Pottery, Palatine WV, 1875, 8"....... 660.00
Jar, fruit, Bristol w/Heinz Apple Butter label, dtd 1906, 8½" 385.00
Jar, preserve, #1/butterfly, WA MacQuoid...12th St, 1870s, 11", EX ... 850.00
Jar, preserve, #2/cabbage flower, J Burger...NY, 1865, drilled, 11".. 300.00
Jar, preserve, #2/leaf, AK Ballard, Burlington VT, 1870s, 11" 125.00
Jar, preserve, #2/leaves, Stetzenmeyer & Goetzman...NY, ca 1857, 11" ..1,700.00
Jar, preserve, #2/pinwheel, Clark...Rochester NY, w/lid, 1850s, 11" ..1,375.00
Jar, preserve, #2/rooster crowing, CW Braun, 1860s, chips, 11".. 34,650.00
Jar, preserve, #3/dbl tulip, EA Montell, Olean NY, 1870s, lines, 12"... 165.00
Jar, preserve, church/trees, att M Woodruff Cortland NY, w/lid, 7¼" . 7,700.00
Jar, preserve, ocher accents, Boston, ca 1805, chips, 9½" 190.00
Jar, sm cvd bl-filled flower, Jonathan Fenton, up-trn hdls, 1780s, 15" . 1,410.00
Jar, storage, #2/flower (2), C McArthur & Co Hudson NY, 1850s, 9½" ..635.00
Jar, storage, mottled tan & brn, Paul Cushman, ca 1811, ½-gal, 9" 3,500.00
Jug, Gal M Farrell...95 Haverhhill St, eagle w/banner, 1872, 10" ... 1,875.00
Jug, #1/accents, N Clark & Co, Mt Morris, ca 1835, 10½" 415.00
Jug, #1/bird, Whites, Utica, ca 1865, drilled, 10½"....................... 175.00
Jug, #1/pine tree, NA Wht & Son, Utica NY, 1870s, stain, 11½". 200.00
Jug, #1/plume (simple), IH Wands Olean NY, ca 1855, stain, 12" ..275.00
Jug, #1/running bird, NA Wht & Son, Utica NY, ca 1870, chips, 11". 4,750.00
Jug, #2/accents, S Hart, Fulton NY, 1850s, tight spider, 13"......... 275.00
Jug, #2/bird on floral branch, Whites, Utica, ca 1865, 12½" 250.00
Jug, #2/bird on twig, WA Lewis, Galesville NY, 1860s, stains, 13" ... 600.00
Jug, #2/bluebird on branch, PJ Fitzgerald & Bro Troy NY 485.00
Jug, #2/dbl flower, E Selby & Co, Hudson NY, 1850s, pings, 11½"... 275.00

Jug, #2/dotted flower, Harry F Miller...NY, 1850s, 14½" 525.00
Jug, #2/dragonfly, J Fisher Lyons NY, short hairline, 13½" 315.00
Jug, #2/floral spray, Lewis & Cady...VT, ca 1860, chip, 15" 380.00
Jug, #2/flower (lg), Penn Yan, 1860s, overglazed/chip, 10½" 330.00
Jug, #2/flower, F Stetzenmeyer...Rochester NY, 1857, 15", NM..2,860.00
Jug, #2/flower, G Apley & Co Ithaca NY, 1860s, sm stain, 11½" .415.00
Jug, #2/flower, Stetzenmeyer & Goetsman, ca 1857, stains, 15".2,525.00
Jug, #2/parrot on stump, Whites Utica, ca 1865, 13" 550.00
Jug, #2/singing bird, Riedinger & Caire, Poughkeepsie NY, 1870s, 13"..575.00
Jug, #2/snowflake, Albany NY, ca 1865, 13½" 660.00
Jug, #2/spitting flower, Whittemore, Havana NY, 1870s, 11½" 415.00
Jug, #2/tulip & leaf/spatters, Brewer & Halm Havana, 1852, 13½", EX....440.00
Jug, #2/tulip, S Johnston & Son Beaver PA, 14½" 1,265.00
Jug, #2/tulips, Lyons, chip, 13" 145.00
Jug, #3/bold tulips, NW Wht & Son, Utica NY, 15½" 540.00
Jug, #3/dbl pheasant, strong cobalt, Whites, Utica, ca 1865, 16" ..6,325.00
Jug, #3/flower, Burger Bros & Co, Rochester NY, ca 1869, pings, 17"...220.00
Jug, #3/flower, C Hart & Son Sherburne NY, 1858, chip/stain, 15" ...250.00
Jug, #3/flower, Jackson & Hallett Wines & Liquors Guelph, EX.. 375.00
Jug, #3/flower, T Harrington Lyons, 1850s, sm chips, 16½" 495.00
Jug, #3/peacock/foliage, L Seymour Troy, rim crack, 14½" 3,800.00
Jug, #3/potted flower/boar's head, att Purdy, OH, ca 1832, 14½".. 550.00
Jug, #3/sunflower (lg), Clark & Co, Rochester NY, 1850s, flaws, 16" . 1,375.00
Jug, #5/floral spray, AO Whittemore...NY, Albany slip int, 15", EX ..350.00
Jug, #5/orchid (lg), Whites, Utica NY, ca 1856, stack mks, 17"....685.00
Jug, 3 rosettes/circles/leaves/pineapple, unmk NY, ca 1795, 15".7,425.00
Jug, accents, C Crolius Mfg Manhattan-Wells NY, 1830s, 2-gal, 13" . 1,485.00
Jug, accents, emb G Benton L Stewart, Hartford, 1820s, 12" 385.00
Jug, batter, flower, AL Hissong Bloomsburg PA, tin lid, 9¼" 2,300.00
Jug, brushed accents, C Crolius, NY, ca 1835, about 1-gal, 10".1,045.00
Jug, clamshell/accents, Commeraw's...NY, prof rstr, ca 1800, 13"..2,300.00
Jug, Dan Deegan/846...NY, cobalt on Bristol, 1890s, ½-gal, 7" ... 110.00
Jug, dove w/incised outline & bl int, ovoid, some glaze loss, 11½" . 1,150.00
Jug, flower (single), Whites, Utica, ca 1865, rstr chip, 11" 155.00
Jug, flower, emb label: NY Stoneware...Fort Edward NY, flakes, 11¾"..285.00
Jug, Geo A Dickel...Whiskey, cobalt/blk stencil on Bristol, 1900s, 9"...220.00
Jug, H Heiser Buffalo NY, ovoid, ca 1857, 10½" 355.00
Jug, label: L&BC Chace & leaf, brushed, ovoid, strap hdl, 12", NM .. 375.00
Jug, leaf, AK Ballard Burlington VT, minor damage, 14" 150.00
Jug, MA Ingalls/Liquor...Little Falls, hdls, ca 1870, lg chip, 19"....330.00
Jug, Paul Cushman emb on brn, reeded spout, ca 1809, 8".........2,200.00
Jug, S Amboy N Jersey/Warne Letts 1807/Liberty Forev (sic), rstr, 14"..9,900.00
Jug, Sheehan & Co...Troy NY, strap hdl, 9¼" 230.00
Jug, syrup, #2/triple flower, Albany NY, ca 1865, prof rpr, 15" 300.00
Meat tenderizer, orig hdl, emb Pat'd Dec 25, 1877, 10" 90.00
Meat tenderizer, orig hdl, mk Pat'd Dec 25 1877, 9½" 145.00
Pitcher, #/butterfly, unmk, 1870s, chip/hairline, 8½" 300.00
Pitcher, #/drooping flower, att NY state, 1870s, 9" 685.00
Pitcher, #1, dk brn Albany glaze, Lyons, 1850s, chips, 8" 495.00
Pitcher, #1/flowers, att Hermann, Baltimore MD, 1850s, flaw, 10"...385.00
Pitcher, cream, tanware, brushed brn flower/accents, 1870s, 7" ...685.00

Pitcher, flower & curled foliage, strap hdl, minor damage, 9½" 700.00
Stein, bl accents, pewter lid w/elf thumb lift, Albany slip int, 15" ..575.00
Water cooler, floral sprigs, Wells & Richards, Reading, Berks Co, PA, 19", VG.13,200.00

Water cooler, incised birds, cobalt floral, L. & B. G. Chace Somerset, 16", VG, $6,000.00. (Photo courtesy Pook & Pook, Inc. on LiveAuctioneers.com)

Store

Perhaps more so than any other yesteryear establishment, the country store evokes feelings of nostalgia for folks old enough to remember its charms — barrels for coffee, crackers, and big green pickles; candy in a jar for the grocer to weigh on shiny brass scales; beheaded chickens in the meat case outwardly devoid of nothing but feathers. Today mementos from this segment of Americana are being collected by those who 'lived it' as well as those less fortunate! See also Advertising; Scales.

Barrel, staved wood, red stain, 29½x19" 275.00
Bin, coffee, Choice Roaster stencil on wood, 26x17x13", EX 150.00
Bin, coffee, Parke's Dry Roast, pnt tin, late 1800s, 21", VG 990.00
Bin, vegetable, 6 wooden compartments on wheels, 50x50x16"..600.00
Broom holder, folding wooden fr w/holds for hdls, 34x24x22" 24.00
Cabinet, Dmn Dyes, children w/balloon, 1908, 24x15", VG 1,265.00
Cabinet, seed, Rice Seeds, pnt wood, folds up, 22x45", VG......... 900.00
Cabinet, spool, Clark's ONT, cherry 6-drw w/foil fronts, 26x23x20", EX . 1,200.00
Cabinet, spool, Clark's ONT, tambour doors, 7 glass columns, 23x20"..2,000.00
Cabinet, spool, Clark's ONT, walnut w/gold foil drw fronts, 22x25", VG....575.00
Cabinet, spool, Hemingway, walnut w/red glass, 18", NM 3,575.00
Cabinet, spool, J&P Coats, oak w/7 open columns, 22½x16x16" . 750.00
Cabinet, spool, Merrick's, oak, rnd w/curved tambour & glass, 1879.1,150.00
Candy jar, Pacific Globe, clear glass, 18", EX................................ 350.00
Case, glass & oak w/rear sliding door, 1 shelf, 19x24x24"............. 225.00
Case, oak w/glass front, holds 14 collars (present), 25x13x7" 850.00
Cash register, NCR #35, NP, full rstr.. 600.00
Cash register, WA Bevis, sm Barber type on lg base, EX............1,100.00
Crock, Red Murdoch & Co Pickles, missing top glass, 7x16" dia... 42.50
Dispenser, paper/string, Geo S Adams, May 20th, 19x16x7" 1,150.00
Display case, Age Combs for Purse or Pocket, 7-drw, 12" 155.00
Display case, glass w/oak fr, 42x96x26" 480.00
Display, bolt, pine w/porc knobs, 8-sided/80-drw, swivels, 34" 850.00
Display, metal hanger for buggy whips, 46" 155.00
Dolly, iron w/hard rubber tires, 34", VG 60.00
Footstool, pine w/slanted area for fitting shoes, ca 1900................. 30.00
Jar, Lance, red & bl pyro on clear glass, red metal lid, 12x8½x7".110.00
Jar, Tom's Toasted Peanuts, blk print on glass, red finial, 9½x7"..... 85.00
Ladder, oak w/store decals, trn top rung, 108x17¼" 110.00
Rack, broom, oak fr w/drilled holes for 12 brooms, 56x30" 85.00
Rack, display, Nat'l Biscuit Co, 4 tiered oak shelves, 60x46x17"...1,200.00
Rack, sack, wire & strap iron, pyramidal, ca 1910, 31x10x15".....300.00
Rack, shoe, bamboo & brass, folds, 41x64" 60.00
Rack, upright wood fr w/wire loops, holds bolts of cloth, 41x21x18"..600.00

Pitcher, floral sprig, American, mid-nineteenth century, 11", $1,150.00. (Photo courtesy Garth's Auction Inc. on LiveAuctioneers.com)

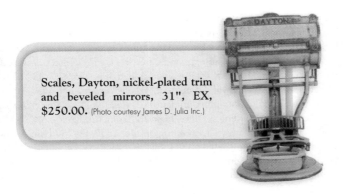

Scales, Dayton, nickel-plated trim and beveled mirrors, 31", EX, $250.00. (Photo courtesy James D. Julia Inc.)

Spool cabinet, Merrick's, curved glass 1,980.00
Tin, Bunte Fine Confections, tin litho, 14x10" dia 110.00
Tin, Laval Sausage Seasoning, hinged lid, 11¼x11¼" 85.00

Stoves

Antique stoves' desirability is based on two criteria: their utility and their decorative merit. It's the latter that adds an 'antique' premium to the basic functional value that could be served just as well by a modern stove. Sheer age is usually irrelevant. Decorative features that enhance desirability include fancy, embossed ornamentation (especially with figures such as cherubs, Old Man Winter, and gargoyles) rather than a solely vegetative motif, nickel-plated trim, mica windows, ceramic tiles, and (in cooking stoves) water reservoirs and high warming closets rather than mere high shelves. The less sheet metal and the more cast iron, the better. Look for crisp, sharp designs in preference to those made from worn or damaged and repaired foundry patterns. Stoves with a pastel porcelain finish can be very attractive; blue is a favorite, white is least desirable. Serious antique stove collectors consider the 'antique' era to have ended about 1930, which is when gas ranges stopped looking like contraptions and started looking like appliances — sanitized and unitized and sleek. Chrome trim, rather than nickel, dates a stove to circa 1933 or later and is a good indicator of a post-antique stove. Though purists prefer the earlier models trimmed in nickel rather than chrome, there is now considerable public interest in these post-antique stoves as well, and some people are willing to pay a good price for these appliance-era 'classics.' (Remember, not all bright metal trim is chrome; it is important to learn to distinguish chrome from the earlier, more desirable nickel plate.)

Among stove types, base burners (with self-feeding coal magazines) are the most desirable. Then come the upright, cylindrical 'oak' stoves, kitchen ranges, and wood parlors. Cannon stoves approach the margin of undesirability; laundries and gasoline stoves plunge through it.

There's a thin but continuing stream of desirable antique stoves going to the high-priced Pacific Coast market. Interest in antique stoves is least in the Deep South. Demand for wood/coal stoves is strongest in areas where firewood is affordable and storage of it is practical. Demand for antique gas ranges has become strong, especially in metropolitan markets, and interest in antique electric ranges is slowly dawning. The market for antique stoves is so limited and the variety so bewildering that a consensus on a going price can hardly emerge. They are only worth something to the right individual, and prices realized depend very greatly on who happens to be in the auction crowd. Even an expert's appraisal will usually miss the realized price by a substantial percent.

In judging condition look out for deep rust pits, warped or burned out parts, unsound fire bricks, poorly fitting parts, poor repairs, and empty mounting holes indicating missing trim. Search meticulously for cracks in the cast iron. Our listings reflect auction prices of completely restored, safe, and functional stoves, unless indicated otherwise. Franklin stoves could burn either wood or coal; to determine whether or not a stove origi-

nally had a grate, check for mounting points where it would have been attached. Wood-burning heating stoves did not require a grate.

Note: Round Oak stoves carrying the words 'Estate of P.D. Beckwith' above the lower door were made prior to 1935. After that date, the company name was changed to Round Oak Company, and the Beckwith reference was no longer used. In our listings, the term 'tea shelf' has been used to describe both drop and swing shelves, as the function of both types was to accommodate teapots and coffeepots.

Key: func — functional

Base Burners

Art Amherst #15, Buffalo NY, tiles/NP/mica/11" urn/1895, 50x25x28", VG... 2,065.00
Art Garland #400, Michigan Stove, gargoyles/NP/mica, 1889, rstr .. 10,750.00
Burdett-Smith #44, swivel top, tiles, 38", VG 1,300.00
Emerald Jewel #14, Detroit, NPCI, 1909, 54"+15" brass urn 1,700.00
Favorite #30, Piqua OH, ornate CI, mica window, 52"+14" urn . 2,200.00
Ransom, Art Denmark #15, Albany NY, tiles/NP/mica, 1897, VG . 4,950.00

Franklin Stoves

Acme Orient #18, 6 tiles, mica windows, fancy, 1890 .... 315.00
Fed style, CI sunburst, ca 1810-20, 38x42" 500.00
Good Cheer #22, Walker & Pratt, 1850s, 32x27x31" 350.00
Iron Foundry...NH, ornate CI, grate missing, 1820s, 37x26x32" .. 250.00
Magee Ideal #3, CI, 2 side trivets, 1892, 32x28" 275.00
Sunny Hearth #2, Southard Robertson, 1880s, 35x20x29½" 315.00
Unmk, CI w/brass mts, 19th C, 40x49" 150.00
Villa Franklin, Muzzy & Co, folding doors, 1830s, 30"+4" urn 200.00
Wyer & Noble, CI/brass trim, early 1800s 2,200.00

Parlor Stoves

The term 'parlor stove' as we use it here is very general and encompasses at least six distinct types recognized by the stove industry: cottage parlor, double-cased airtight, circulator, cylinder, oak, and the fireplace heater.

No. 1, made by Tyson Furnace, Poultney, Vermont, cast and sheet iron, four-part doors with classical figures in relief, top ornament not original, second quarter nineteenth century, 44x23½x15", $350.00. (Photo courtesy New Orleans Auction, St. Charles Gallery, Inc. on LiveAuctioneers.com)

Barstow #137, Orient tile insets, CI, 1886, EX 900.00
Crown, Magee, ornate CI, cylindrical w/cabriole legs, urn finial, 63" ... 400.00
Economy #27, Comstock-Castle, CI/sheet iron, 1878, 34", G 40.00
Estate Triple Effect #5, gas heater, mica windows, NP, ornate, VG .. 260.00
Faultless, Redway & Burton, Cincinnati O, CI, 1873, 38x34x23" .. 475.00
Grayville Active 1919, blk CI w/ornate urn & doors, 1903, 39" ... 1,100.00
Hot Blast-Air Tight Florence #53, CI w/allover scrolls, 66x28x28" ... 800.00
IA Sheppard & Co Excelsior, Fern 9, cylindrical, 34½" 250.00
Ideal Garland #200, wood/coal, no urn, ca 1898, rstr 1,300.00
Jewel #214, Detroit, ornate NP CI, urn finial, ca 1903, 54" 2,250.00
JH Shear #2, Albany NY, CI, column style, 56" 950.00
Modern Glenwood Wood Parlor, slide top, 1920s, 45x28x24½" .. 360.00

Moore's Heater, Joliet IL, ornate CI outer case, urn finial, 60x22x22" 600.00
Neoclassical CI, 4 fluted columns, paw ft, 38x29x18" 600.00
Pearl, OH Stove, ornate CI/cabriole legs, scrollwork finial, 33x23x18" ...500.00
Peerless, Pratt & Wentworth, tip-up dome, 1840s, 37x19x15" 150.00
Railway carriage, CI, 27½x24x18", EX..............................150.00
Round Oak D-18, 1904, complete, unrstr 300.00
Somersworth #20, tip-up dome top, 1850s, 39x30x29" 350.00
Sylvan Red Cross #31, Co-Op Foundry, tiles, gargoyle legs, Pat 1888-89 ..350.00
Union Airtight, Warnick & Leibrandt, ornate CI, 1851, 26" 350.00

Ranges (Gas)

Alcazar, Milwaukee, 4-burner/1-oven, 1928, G 50.00
Jewel, Detroit, 4-burner, blk/NP, glass oven door, 1918, VG........550.00
Magic Chef, 6-burner/2-oven, high closet, 1932, EX...............2,750.00
Magic Chef, wht, 6-burner/2-oven, high closet, 1938, up to 12,000.00
MUCo, wht enamel, 3-burner, monogram on oven door, 32x26x17" ..175.00
Quick Meal, 4-burner, bl, cabinet style, 1919, G 925.00
Quick Meal, 4-burner/1-oven, 1928, unrstr 300.00

Ranges (Wood and Coal)

Alpine Bride, CI, blk, ca 1920, rstr 300.00
Ideal Atlantic #8-20, Portland, ornate CI, bk shelf, 1890s........1,675.00
Kalamazoo Peerless, gray & wht, wood/coal/gas, 1920s, G 875.00
Kineo C, Noyes & Nutter, high warming closet, reservoir, 1920s. 715.00
Quick Meal, bl enamel, high warming closet, rnd shelf, 1920s 800.00
Walker & Pratt, Village Crawford Royal, tea shelves, 1920s........800.00
Wood-Bishop Popular Clarion, scrolling tea shelves, 1890s.........950.00

Stove Manufacturers' Toy Stoves

Buck's Junior #4, cast and sheet iron, black-finish oven with nickeled doors, skirt, and feet, warming shelf, replaced base, functional, 14", $660.00. (Photo courtesy Bertoia Auctions on LiveAuctioneers.com)

Buck's Jr #3, St Louis MO, rstr, 26" 850.00
Charter Oak #503, GF Filley, St Louis MO, 14x12x25", EX 2,050.00
Dainty, Reading Stove Works, PA, 7x13x8", VG 150.00
Jersey, Cook & Van Evera, Chicago, ca 1908, 28x15x12", EX ..6,400.00
Karr Qualified Range, alum/tin, dial on door, 21½x13", EX 775.00
Little Eva, T Southard, NYC, 8½x14x11", VG w/accessories 575.00
Royal Am, Bridgeford, Louisville KY, 14x12x10", G...................950.00

Toy Manufacturers' Toy Stoves

Wood/coal, Kenton Globe, cast iron, out-of-proportion high back is a distinguishing feature of toy manufacturers' toy stoves, 18", $920.00. (Photo courtesy Morphy Auctions)

Electric, Emp, Metal Ware, WI, functional burner & oven, ca 1925, 15", EX..145.00
Electric, Hotpoint, Arcade, pnt CI range, tan/gr, non-func, VG.............150.00
Wood/coal, Bing, bl steel cookstove, brass trim, Germany, 17", VG ...600.00
Wood/coal, Crescent, 4-hole, plated CI & steel, 11½", EX..........230.00
Wood/coal, Eagle, Kenton, CI, heavily scrolled, 4 ft, 11½x10", G...125.00
Wood/coal, Kenton Royal, CI & steel, 4-hole, ornate, 10", VG ..100.00
Wood/coal, Little Giant, unmk/unidentified, 7½x8½x11", EX orig ...675.00
Wood/coal, Novelty, Kenton Hdwe, bl pnt/NP trim, rfn, 13x6½x8½" .600.00
Wood/coal, Pet, Adams, CI, cooking, ornate, 1857, 8½" W base. 300.00
Wood/coal, Rival, no shelves, 12" L, EX..........................900.00
Wood/coal, Royal, Kenton, 4-hole, CI & steel, ornate, 10", VG . 100.00
Wood/coal, Royal, plated CI, stovepipe, shield shape, 16", G........85.00
Wood/coal, Triumph, Kenton OH, 14x8½x19", G 195.00

Stretch Glass

Stretch glass, produced from circa 1916 through 1935, was made in an effort to emulate the fine art glass of Tiffany and Carder. The pressed or blown glassware was sprayed with a metallic salts mix while hot, then reshaped, causing a stretch effect in the iridescent finish. Northwood, Imperial, Fenton, Diamond, Lancaster, Jeannette, Central, Vineland Flint, and the United States Glass Company were the manufacturers of this type of glass. See also specific companies.

Basket, gr, #300, Imperial, 9¾" 120.00
Bowl, Egyptian Lustre (blk), cupped Dmn, 8¼" 100.00
Bowl, fern, Russet, 3 ftd, ribbed, Northwood, 4½" 70.00
Bowl, gr, rolled rim, Central, 9¼" 45.00
Bowl, Harding bl, low cupped, Dmn, 1¾x7" 40.00
Bowl, marigold milk, cupped, Imperial, 8⅜" 125.00
Bowl, Tangerine, #1502 Dmn Optic, flared, Fenton, 9½" 120.00
Bowl, topaz, ftd w/open edge, #310, US Glass, 11¼" W 300.00
Candle bowl, gold, 2 sockets, 'Pat Applied For,' Dmn, 7⅖" 95.00
Candlesticks, bl, Trumpet Twist, Northwood, 6⅜", pr 100.00
Candlesticks, bl, twist w/cup ft #315, US Glass, 9½", pr 100.00
Candlesticks, cobalt, Central, 7", pr 120.00
Candlesticks, crystal w/gr décor & floral, Lancaster, 5", pr 45.00
Candlesticks, jade bl (opaque), #676 cupped base, Northwood, 4⅝" dia, pr 90.00
Candlesticks, lt wisteria, trumpet shape, Vineland, 6¾", pr 80.00
Candlesticks, topaz, #651, 4-sided, Northwood, 11", pr 175.00
Candy jar, Harding bl, paneled, 1-lb, Dmn, w/lid 8¾" 45.00
Candy jar, Ivory (custard), paneled #643, Northwood, w/lid, 6" .125.00
Candy jar, jade bl, paneled #863, 1-lb, Northwood, w/lid, 10" 70.00
Candy jar, tangerine, paneled #835, -lb. Fenton, 9½" 50.00
Cheese & cracker set, Aztec (marigold), Lancaster, plate 9⅞", 2-pc ...50.00
Cologne, Florentine Gr, #55 ftd w/stopper, Fenton, 6⅖" 110.00
Comport, bl ice (bl smoke), #44/48, 18 rays, flared & cupped, Imperial, 7" ...90.00
Comport, red, #44/48, 18 rays, flared, 7½" 175.00
Comport, royal purple, sq ft, 2 sides cupped, Northwood, 9x6".....70.00
Comport, topaz, #1533A, 2 dolphin hdls, Fenton, 4½" 75.00
Comport, topaz, 12-sided ft w tree bark, Northwood, 9¼" W 90.00
Compote, gr, Adam's Rib, rolled rim, ftd, Dmn, 11¾" 100.00
Flowerpot & underplate, Tangerine, ringed, #1554, Fenton, 2-pc ...100.00
Jar, bath salts, Wisteria (purple), ftd w/pagoda stopper, Fenton, 4"...175.00
Mayo & underplate, gr ice (bl-gr) #4460, panels, Imperial, 2-pc ..50.00
Plate, blk amethyst, #8076, open edge, US Glass, 12" 200.00
Plate, Celeste Bl, octagon, Laurel Leaf dec, Fenton, 7½" 20.00
Server, bl ice (bl smoke) #664 w/cut 312, Imperial, center hdl, 10½" ..50.00
Server, Vela Rose (pk), center dolphin hdl, Fenton, 10¼" 200.00
Sherbet, Pearl (crystal), smooth stem & base, Dmn, 3⅖"..............15.00
Sherbet, Russet, flared w/panels, Northwood, 3½" 45.00
Vase, aquamarine, fan #1532A, 2 dolphin hdls, ftd. 5½" W..........85.00

Vase, Celeste Blue, with frosted pattern, Fenton, 5x6", $50.00.
(Photo courtesy Fantasticantiques Inc. on LiveAuctioneers.com)

Vase, Egyptian Lustre (blk), Flip w/flared rim, Dmn, 7¼x9¼" 280.00
Vase, gr, cupped dahlia, #151 ftd, US Glass, 8" 60.00
Vase, pearl bl (opaque slag), #179, flat rim, US Glass, 5¼x8½".... 175.00
Vase, tangerine, swung, ring optic #1530, Fenton 11¼" 150.00

String Holders

Today, if you want to wrap and secure a package, you have a variety of products to choose from: cellophane tape, staples, etc. But in the 1800s and even well past the advent of Scotch tape in the early 1930s, string was about the only available binder; thus the string holder, either the hanging or counter type, was a common and practical item found in most homes and businesses. Chalkware and ceramic figurals from the 1930s, 1940s, and 1950s contrast with the cast and wrought-iron examples from the 1800s to make for an interesting collection. Our advisor for this category is Larry G. Pogue (L & J Antiques and Collectibles); he is listed in the Directory under Texas. See also Advertising.

Apple w/berries, pnt chalkware, 1950s, 8" 95.00
Aunt Jemima, pnt chalkware, 1940s-50s, 7¾" 395.00
Baby Huey (face only), bl bonnet, pnt chalkware, 1955, 8½" 450.00
Bananas, pnt chalkware, 5¾" 115.00
Black porter, Fredricksburg Art Pottery, USA, 6½" 425.00
Bosko, face only, pnt chalkware, 1930s-40s, 7½" 425.00
Bride holding bouquet, bulb bottom (skirt), ceramic, MIJ, 6¼" ... 135.00
Carrots w/gr tops, pnt chalkware, 1950s, 10" 145.00
Doc (head only), pnt chalkware, mk WDP #703, 7½" 425.00
Dopey (head only), pnt chalkware, mk WDP #702, 6½" 395.00
Drunk man, pottery, mk Elsa, 5½" 210.00
Fish, Susie Sunfish, pnt chalkware, 1950s, 6½" 225.00
Heart, String Along w/Me, ceramic, California Cleminsons, 5½"...125.00
Hershey Chocolate Girl, holding candy, pnt chalkware, 9" 395.00
Honey (Bosko's girlfriend), face only, pnt chalkware, 1930s-40s, 7½"...395.00
Little Chef (Rice Krispies guy), pnt chalkware, 1950s, 7" 245.00

Little Miss Sunbeam, holding slice of bread, painted chalkware, marked, #203, 1940s, very rare, 10", minimum value $750.00. (Photo courtesy Larry G. Pogue)

Little Monk, pnt chalkware, Bello, 1940, 9" 275.00
Marilyn Monroe (face only), pnt chalkware, 1960s...................... 295.00
Mighty Mouse (head only), pnt chalkware, c Terrytoons, 6¼x8½"..425.00
Pear w/plums, pnt chalkware, 7¾" 85.00
Pineapple w/face, pnt chalkware, 1950s, 7"................................ 175.00
Pumpkin face, winking, ceramic, Japan, 5" 185.00
Sailor boy (head only), pnt chalkware, Bello, Chicago IL, 8" 255.00

Santa Claus (head only), pnt chalkware, 1950s, 9", rare 275.00
Snow White (head only), pnt chalkware, 1950s, 9", rare 275.00
Soldier boy w/pipe (head only), pnt chalkware, 1950s, 7½" 95.00
Speedy Alka Seltzer, pnt chalkware, 1950s, 9½"........................ 425.00
Strawberry w/gr top, pnt chalkware, 1950s, 6½" 175.00
Tomato w/face, bl hat, pnt chalkware,1950s, 5½" 175.00
Westie dog (head only), pnt chalkware, 9" 225.00
Woody Woodpecker, chalkware, c Walter Lantz, 9½" 425.00

Sugar Shakers

Sugar shakers (or muffineers, as they were also called) were used during the Victorian era to sprinkle sugar and spice onto breakfast muffins, toast, etc. They were made of art glass, in pressed patterns, and in china. See also specific types and manufacturers (such as Northwood). Our coadvisors for this category are Jeff Bradfield and Dale MacAllister; they are listed in the Directory under Virginia.

Acorn, bl opaque 225.00
Alba, bl opaque, period top, Dithridge, 4¾" 120.00
Argus Swirl, mg w/HP decor, Consolidated, ca 1894-98, 3¼" 115.00
Block & Fan, clear pattern glass 75.00
Bubble Lattice, bl opal.. 550.00
Challinor's Forget-Me-Not, bl opaque, late 1800s, 3¾" 250.00
Chrysanthemum Base Swirl, cranberry opal 500.00

Clematis, frosted with gilt and enamel leaves, 5¼", $125.00. (Photo courtesy Green Valley Auctions on LiveAuctioneers.com)

Coin Spot, 9-panel, sapphire bl, Northwood, 5"........................ 200.00
Coin Spot, 9-panel, wht opal, Northwood, 4½" 110.00
Coin Spot, Wide Waisted, gr, Northwood 4½" 300.00
Cone, bl opaque, Consolidated 125.00
Cone, pk cased, Consolidated, 5¼" 150.00
Consolidated Criss-Cross, cranberry opal............................ 950.00
Daisy & Fern, cranberry opal, wide-waisted............................ 450.00
Diamond Quilted MOP (English muffineer), butterscotch, 5¾" ..450.00
Fern, cranberry opal 550.00
Flat Flower, gr opaque 400.00
Guttate, pk cased (+) 350.00
Leaf Mold, cranberry spatter.. 475.00
Maize, custard glass w/bl leaves 450.00
Medallion Sprig, bl to clear 500.00
Optic, rubena, Hobbs, 3½" 300.00
Quilted Phlox, amethyst, Northwood 300.00
Quilted Phlox, gr cased, Northwood 175.00
Reverse Swirl, bl opal, 4¾" 350.00
Reverse Swirl, cranberry opal 485.00
Ribbed Lattice, wht opal, Hobbs, 4½" 145.00
Ring Neck, cranberry & wht spatter 175.00
Snail, clear pattern glass 125.00
Spanish Lace, wht opal, Northwood, 4¾" 175.00

Swirl, cranberry opal, bbl shape.. 550.00
Swirl, wht opal, bbl shape, 5½" 200.00
Tomato, wht satin w/HP floral, Smith Bros, 2¾x4" 465.00
Twist (blown), gr opal... 350.00

Venetian Diamond – Ring Neck, cranberry, 4¾", $225.00 to $250.00. (Photo courtesy Green Valley Auctions on LiveAuctioneers.com)

Windows (Swirled), bl opal, 4¼" 500.00
Windows (Swirled), wht opal.. 300.00
Zipper, clear, 4½" 40.00

Sumida Ware

First made outside Kyoto, Japan, about 1870, Sumida Ware is a whimsical yet serious type of art pottery, easily recognized by its painted backgrounds and applied figures. Though most often painted red, examples with green or black backgrounds may be found as well. Vases and mugs are easier to find than other forms, and most are characterized by the human and animal figures that have been attached to their surfaces. Because these figures are in high relief, it is not unusual to find them chipped; it is important to seek a professional if restoration work is needed. It is not uncommon to find examples with the red background paint missing; collectors generally leave such pieces as they find them. Our advisor for this category is Jeffery Person; he is listed in the Directory under Florida.

Box, boy finial, red/blk flambé, 3½x5" dia.. 65.00
Conch shell w/rabbit & boy, sgn, 5" L... 300.00

Dish, 12 figures on rim peer into bowl, 7" long, $780.00. (Photo courtesy DuMouchelles on LiveAuctioneers.com)

Figurine, 2 Sumo wrestlers, sgn, ca 1920, 6¾x7", NM 1,440.00
Humidor, children at play appl on red, flambé top, child finial, 7x6" .240.00
Humidor, men appl on ridged red, wht flambé top, man on lid, 7", NM .. 480.00
Jardiniere, elephants in mtns, ivory/blk, flambé top, appl mk, 12x19".. 1,560.00
Mug, elephant pr on cliffs appl on red, Koji/Koni cartouch, 5", NM..135.00
Mug, sage in bl/wht robe/foliage emb on red, bamboo hdl, 5" 120.00
Pitcher, 3 monkeys, lg 1 pouring water on 2nd, red/blk flambé, 13", EX ..360.00
Pitcher, 3-D dragon hdl on blk/red flambé, 6¼" 90.00
Teapot, 2 monkeys sharing peach on red, blk flambé top, rprs, 5", EX .. 400.00
Vase, 75 monkeys, appl on red (missing pnt), mk & sgn, 18"....2,200.00
Vase, children on branch appl on ridged red, flambé top, 12x6" .. 390.00
Vase, dragon/cloud/Ishiguro Koko seal appl on red, flambé top, 15", EX.1,320.00
Vase, lady w/flute/2 servants, moon shape w/house in opening, 12x10".990.00
Vase, man holding up incense burner on red/blk, drilled for lamp, 10"... 90.00

Vase, wht irises on red, blk flambé basket hdl, 8x7"..................... 240.00
Wall pocket, crab figural, claws reach toward open mouth, tan, 9" W..180.00
Wall pocket, floral, wht/dk brn on red, elephant's trunk form, 10"...925.00

Surveying Instruments

The practice of surveying offers a wide variety of precision instruments primarily for field use, most of which are associated with the recording of distance and angular measurements. These instruments were primarily made from brass; the larger examples were fitted with tripods and protective cases. These cases also held accessories for the instruments, and these can sometimes play a key part in their evaluation. Instruments in complete condition and showing little use will have much greater values than those that appear to have had moderate or heavy use. Instruments were never polished during use, and those that have been polished as decorator pieces are of little interest to most avid collectors.

Alidade, W&LE Gurley #584, EXIB 395.00
Clinometer, Reynolds, Birmingham England, 1767-81, VG 300.00
Compass, Abner Dod, brass, 5" silvered dial, 1800s, 14", +fitted case. 2,585.00
Compass, Alex Mabon & Son, miner's dial, polished brass/wood, ca 1870.2,000.00
Compass, Am Benj Pike's Son, NY, ca 1880, lg, rpr, +box 1,200.00
Compass, D Rittenhouse, 5¼" dial, brass, 8⅜x14½" 19,975.00
Compass, dry, R Merrill NY, gimballed brass case, mtd in 6x10x10" box ..285.00
Compass, E Draper, brass, 4" silvered dial, lacquer rubbed/dk, 11" L...700.00
Compass, Eame's Improved, brass ring & 5½" 32-point card, 12" L.1,175.00
Compass, J Hanks, 5¾" silvered dial/sights on wide shaped limb, 15". 2,235.00
Compass, Micheal Rupp, 5" needle, ca 1860, EX......................1,500.00
Compass, solar, W J Young & Co w/James Foster, 1863, EXIB.10,000.00
Compass, T Greenough, eng 4½" HP card, eng 1737, 8"..........2,115.00
Compass, T Kendally, brass, engine-trn medallion, 12", case & tripod ...1,880.00
Compass, Troughton & Sims, 4" dial, brass arm, 14" telescope, EXIB ..350.00
Compass, vernier, Benjamin Hanks, 6" dia, mahog/brass, 9x15"+case. 2,585.00
Compass, vernier, BK Hagger & Son, brass w/5½" dial, 10x15"+case .. 1,525.00
Compass, vernier, WE Young, 5" dial, brass hub & lamp, 14" 265.00
Compass, whittled from 1 block of maple w/jackknife, brass hub, 9" .. 700.00
Compass, Young & Sons, 3¾" dial, brass, Pat 1875, 6x10"+case.. 585.00
Compass, Ziba Blakslee, brass w/5½" silvered dial, 9x15"+case.5,875.00
Heliotrope, Steinheil, Bausch & Lomb, ca 1910, EX 1,500.00
Level, combination, AS Aloe, ca 1923, 12", EXIB....................... 450.00
Level, dumpy, Buff & Buff, ca 1900, 18", EXIB.......................... 800.00
Level, dumpy, Keuffel & Esser, ca 1913, 18", EXIB..................... 500.00
Level, staff, Adie & Sons, 7" telescope/vial/bull's eye level, EXIB....200.00
Level, wye, Gurley, alum & brass, ca 1948, 18", EXIB................. 450.00
Level, wye, W&LE Gurley, brass, 20" telescope, 7" vials, EX+ case ..200.00
Leveling head, plane table, Buff & Buff, ca 1900, EX.................. 400.00
Miner's dial/theodolite, brass, dial sgn Newton Late Wilton, 12½"..590.00
Octant, ebony w/bone scale, 10" radius, EXIB............................. 500.00
Protractor, charting, Lille & Son London, +leather-covered case. 150.00
Protractor, Thos Jones, brass, dbl-rotating index arm, 5¾" dia..... 295.00
Quadrant, J Bennett...MA, pewter scale, alidade w/trough, 8½" . 585.00
Semi-circumferentor, birch w/punched divisions, steel needle, 10" L... 120.00
Semi-circumferentor, J Hale, brass, 11" dia protractor, 14", +case. 765.00
Semi-circumferentor, scale 0-90-0, bubble level alidade, mk, 7"....1,295.00
Sextant, Graham & Parkes, silvered scale, 2 sights, ca 1944, 9" . 295.00
Sextant, J Sewill, 3 sights, 7 shades, mahog w/brass ft, 8½".......... 475.00
Sextant, London, oxidized brass w/silvered scale, 9", +case.......... 300.00
Sextant, Troughton London #449, dbl fr, colored lenses, VG ... 1,320.00
Solar attachment, Gurly, brass, rack & pinon focusing, 8" 765.00
Theodolite, att Benj Cole, 4" silvered dial, 9" telescope, EXIB....825.00
Theodolite, C Leach, trough compass/brass X-strut, 1792, 6" dia.2,470.00
Theodolite, E Draper, brass, 3" dial, 2 verniers, darkened, 13"..2,350.00

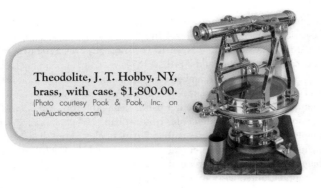

Theodolite, J. T. Hobby, NY, brass, with case, $1,800.00. (Photo courtesy Pook & Pook, Inc. on LiveAuctioneers.com)

By 1971 dinnerware geared for use in the home was discontinued, and the company turned to the manufacture of hotel, restaurant, and other types of commercial tableware. Syracuse officially closed in 2009.

Theodolite, T Cooke & Sons, ca 1890, EXIB..............................2,000.00
Transit, Gurley, Burts Pat Solar attachment, 4¾" dial, 15", +tripod.7,650.00
Transit, Keuffel & Esser #5030, ca 1887, EXIB 2,000.00
Transit, Keuffel & Esser #5077, w/9" scope/compass & full circle, EX...875.00
Transit, Keuffel & Esser, Y&S #5166 Special Survey, ca 1918, EX...695.00
Transit, Troughlon & Simms London, brass, 19th C, 19" in fitted case....350.00
Transit, vernier, Queen & Co, anodized/lacquered brass, 14¾", +tripod....650.00
Tripod, Keuffel & Esser, stiff legs, staff mt for compass, early, VG.275.00
Tripod, Warren Knight, oak, stiff legs, ca 1920, EX 150.00
Wading rod set, Gurley's Hydraulic Current Meters #612/621/624, EX.225.00
Waywiser, J Beers, 21" dia spoked metal-rim wheel, 1974, 64" L...3,290.00

Alpine, creamer, ca 1955-70, 7-oz 31.50
Alpine, platter, ca 1955-70, 15" L 88.00
Apple Blossom, platter, 10" L 55.00
Bamboo, c/s, ca 1950, 2½" 31.50
Bamboo, sugar bowl, ca 1950, 2¾" 37.00
Carmelita, plate, luncheon, ca 1923, 8½" 30.00
Coronet, plate, dinner, ca 1955, 10"......................................24.00
Elizabeth, creamer..23.00
Greenwood, c/s, ftd, ca 1950, 2½" 31.00
Greenwood, teapot, ca 1950, 4-cup 125.00
Honeysuckle, bowl, cereal, 5" 22.00
Honeysuckle, sugar bowl..30.00
House of Blues, plate, bl letters/bands on wht, 10½" 30.00
June Rose, bowl, rimmed soup, 8" 24.00
June Rose, plate, salad, 8" 10.00
Longhorn, bowl, soup, brn airbrushing on wht, rare, 8"..................42.00
Magnolia, plate, dinner, ca 1960, 10½"..................................24.00
Milicent, cup, ftd, ca 1949, 2"..27.00
Milicent, platter, ca 1949, 16" L 116.00
Nocturne, sugar bowl 39.00
Nordic, plate, 10"...12.00

Swastika Keramos

Swastika Keramos was a line of artware made by the Owens China Company of Minerva, Ohio, around 1902 – 1904. It is characterized either by a coralene type of decoration (similar to the Opalesce line made by the J. B. Owens Pottery Company of Zanesville) or by the application of metallic lustres, usually in simple designs. Shapes are often plain and handles squarish and rather thick, suggestive of the Arts and Crafts style.

Old Ivory, coffeepot, 8", $50.00 to $75.00. (Photo courtesy Flomaton Antique Auction on LiveAuctioneers.com)

Vase, landscape, metallic glazes, #305, 7½x6", $850.00. (Photo courtesy Treadway Gallery on LiveAuctioneers.com)

Plate, narrow red floral border, lg interwining 'PLE' in center, 9".. 150.00
Portland, bowl, rimmed soup, 8"..18.00
Portland, plate, chop, 13" 78.00
Romance, plate, dessert, 7"..15.00
Romance, platter, 14" L 78.00
Romance, teapot, 4-cup..250.00
Royal Court, plate, dinner, ca 1949-70, 10" 42.50
Royal Court, platter, ca 1949-70, 14" L 232.00
Selma, bowl, soup, 4¾", +6½" underplate, set of 6......................120.00
Selma, bowl, vegetable, 10"..30.00
Selma, plate, pie, 7" 10.50
Sherwood, bowl, soup, Old Ivory, 8¾", 8 for..............................90.00
Suzanne, plate, bread & butter, ca 1950, 6½" 10.00
Suzanne, platter, ca 1950, 14" L 45.00
Traveler, plate, flying geese, pk on wht, Milwaukee RR, 9½" 75.00
Victoria, bowl, cream soup, w/underplate, ftd, ca 1949-70 ....36.00
Western Ranch, plate, Am Scene collection by A Dehn, 1st ed, 10" ..65.00

Ewer, floral on bronze, flared bottom, #7042, 11"..........................210.00
Vase, birds on branch, wht, bulb, slim neck, 9" 145.00
Vase, floral gold-tones & red, 3 buttress hdls, 7" 545.00
Vase, floral on gold neck, plain swollen bottom, 8" 200.00
Vase, gr & wht veining on gold, rim-to-hip hdls, 8" 200.00
Vase, lustred glazes, landscape, medallion mk, 12x14½"................720.00

Syracuse

Syracuse was a line of fine dinnerware and casual ware which was made for nearly a century by the Onondaga Pottery Company of Syracuse, New York. Early patterns were marked O.P. Company. Collectors of American dinnerware are focusing their attention on reassembling some of their many lovely patterns. In 1966 the firm became officially known as the Syracuse China Company in order to better identify with the name of their popular chinaware. Many of the patterns were marked with the shape and color names (Old Ivory, Federal, etc.), not the pattern names.

Syrups

Values are for old, original syrups. Beware of reproductions and watch the handle area for cracks! See also various manufacturers (such as Northwood) and specific types of glass. Our coadvisors are Jeff Bradfield and Dale MacAllister; they are listed in the Directory under Virginia. See also Pattern Glass.

Acorn, pk opaque..300.00
Arabian Nights, canary opal...1,250.00

Argus Swirl, pigeon blood, clear hdl 425.00
Artichoke, clear, pattern glass 75.00
Big Windows, bl opal, 6½" 650.00
Bubble Lattice, canary opal 800.00
Coin Spot, sapphire bl, Hobbs, 9-panel, 1890s 325.00
Coin Spot, wht opal, 9-panel, 7" 250.00
Coin Spot & Swirl, bl opal, Hobbs, ca 1890, 6" 250.00
Coin Spot & Swirl, wht opal, Hobbs, 6" 185.00
Cone, pk cased, Consolidated, tall 325.00
Cordova, clear, pattern glass 135.00

Crown Milano, hand decorated with gold-washed wild rose vine, Mt. Washington, 5", $850.00. (Photo courtesy Cincinnati Art Galleries, LLC on LiveAuctioneers.com)

Dahlia, amber 125.00
Daisy & Button w/Crossbars, bl 225.00
Daisy & Fern, cranberry opal, Northwood mold 650.00
Flora, bl opal 450.00
Grape & Leaf, bl opaque, 5¾" 325.00
Hobnail, vaseline, pewter top, no damage to hobbs, 7" 325.00
Invt T'print, bl, Hobbs, ca 1883, 8" 300.00
Klondike, clear 200.00
Leaf & Flower, amber stained, Hobbs, ca 1888 .... 265.00
Leaf Umbrella, mauve cased, pewter lid, rare 700.00
Reverse Swirl, wht opal, Buckeye, 7¼" 275.00
Ribbed Pillar, pk w/wht spatter 450.00
Ring Band, custard w/EX gold, Heisey 375.00
Royal Ivy, cased spatter, Northwood 750.00
Spanish Lace, bl opal 450.00
Sunken Honeycomb, ruby stain 275.00
Torpedo, ruby stain 250.00
Tree of Life, bl opaque, Challinor Taylor, ca 1890, 7" 125.00
Venetian Dmn, cranberry 650.00
Wild Iris, mg w/yel & pk decor 200.00
Windows Swirled, bl opal 595.00

Target Balls and Related Memorabilia

Prior to 1880 when the clay pigeon was invented, blown glass target balls were used extensively for shotgun competitions. Approximately 2¾" in diameter, these balls were hand blown into a three-piece mold. All have a ragged hole where the blowpipe was twisted free. Target balls date from approximately 1840 (English) to World War I, although they were most widely used in the 1870 – 1880 period. Common examples are unmarked except for the blower's code — dots, crude numerals, etc. Some balls were embossed in a dot or diamond pattern so they were more likely to shatter when struck by shot, and some have names and/or patent dates. When evaluating condition, bubbles and other minor manufacturing imperfections are acceptable; cracks are not. The prices below are for mint condition examples. Our advisor for this category is C.D. Kilhoffer; he is listed in the Directory under Maryland.

Boers & CR Delft Flesschen Fabriek, lt gr, rare, 2⅝" 470.00

Bogardus' Glass Ball Pat'd April 10 1877, amber, Am, 2¾" 400.00
Bogardus' Glass Ball Pat'd April 10 1877, amber, hobnails, 2⅝".. 3,000.00
Bogardus' Glass Ball Pat'd April 10 1877, cobalt, 2¾", $700 to ... 800.00
Bogardus' Glass Ball, Pat'd April 10 1877, gr 1,475.00
C Newman, Dmn Quilt, amber, rare, 2⅝" 800.00
CTB Co, blk pitch, Pat dates on bottom, Am 175.00
Diamond Quilted w/plain center band, clear, grnd top, Am 150.00
Diamond Quilted w/plain center band, cobalt, 2⅝" 210.00
Diamond Quilted w/shooter emb in 2 panels, clear, English 300.00
Diamond Quilted w/shooter emb in 2 panels, cobalt, English 450.00
Diamond Quilted w/shooter emb in 2 panels, moss gr, English 500.00
Diamond Quilted w/shooter emb in 2 panels, med gr, English 400.00
Embossed dmns, dk amber w/hint of red, 2⅝" 325.00
Embossed dmns, dk cobalt, 2¾" 450.00
For Hockey's Pat Trap, gr aqua, 2⅝" 550.00
Glashuttenewotte Un Charlottenburg, clear, emb dmns, 2⅝" 450.00
Gurd & Son, London, Ontario, amber, Canadian 500.00
Hockey's Pat Trap, aqua, English, 2½" 650.00
Horizontal bands (7), tobacco amber, 2⅝" 250.00
Horizontal ribs (2) intersect w/2 vertical, cobalt, 2⅝" 150.00
Ilmenau (Thur) Sophiehutte, amber, Dmn Quilt, Germany 300.00
Mauritz Widfords, honey amber, 2⅝", EX 500.00
NB Glass Works Perth, pale gr, English 150.00

Perth, medium blue, $175.00; W. W. Greener, lavender, $300.00. (Photo courtesy Lang's Auction on LiveAuctioneers.com)

Plain, amber w/mold mks 80.00
Plain, cobalt w/mold mks 125.00
Plain, dk teal gr w/mold mks, 2¾" 200.00
Plain, pk amethyst w/mold mks, 2⅝" 200.00
PMP London, cobalt, chip, 2" 175.00
T Jones, Gunmaker, Blackburn, cobalt, English, 2⅝" 400.00
T Jones, Gunmaker, Blackburn, pale bl, English 250.00
Van Cutsem A St Quentin, cobalt, 2¾" 175.00

Related Memorabilia

Ball thrower, dbl, old red pnt, ME Card, Pat...78, 79, VG 800.00
Clay birds, Winchester, Pat May 29 1917, 1 flight in box 100.00
Pitch bird, blk DUVROCK 10.00
Shell set, dummy shotgun, Peters, 6 window shells+full box 175.00
Shell set, dummy, Gamble Stores, 2 window shells, 3 cut out 150.00
Shell set, dummy, Winchester, 5 window shells 175.00
Shell, dummy shotgun, Winchester, window w/powder, 6" 125.00
Shell, dummy, w/single window, any brand 50.00
Shot-shell loader, rosewood/brass, Parker Bros, Pat 1884 .... 50.00
Target, Am, sheet metal, rod ends mk Pat Feb 8 '21, set 25.00
Target, blk japanned sheet metal, Bussey Patentee, London 50.00
Target, BUST-O, blk or wht breakable wafer 20.00
Thrower, oak wood base, heavy steel spring, leather wrap, ca 1900, EX .1,400.00
Trap, Chamberlain Cartridge...Nov 7th 05...USA, CI, 21½" L, EX.1,300.00
Trap, DUVROCK, w/blk pitch birds 125.00
Trap, MO-SKEET-O, w/birds 100.00

Taylor, Smith & Taylor

Producers of mainly dinnerware and kitchenware, this company operated in Chester, West Virginia, from about 1900 to 1982. Today collectors enjoy reassembling some of their lovely patterns. Some of their most collectible lines are Lu-Ray and Vistosa (see also those categories), but many of their decorated lines are popular as well. Reville Rooster features a large colorful red and orange rooster on simple shapes; Pebble Ford is a plain-colored ware with specks of dark and light blue-green, yellow, gray, and tan sprinkled throughout. There are many others. They made advertising pieces and souvenir ware as well.

Reveille Rooster, cup and saucer, $8.50. (Photo courtesy Melanie Kimbell, eBay seller melkin1234)

Autumn Harvest, butter dish	20.00
Autumn Harvest, creamer	12.50
Autumn Harvest, plate, dinner, 10"	7.50
Autumn Leaves, c/s	12.50
Autumn Leaves, plate, dinner, 10½"	10.00
Blue Bonnet, bowl, vegetable, 9"	24.00
Blue Bonnet, c/s	8.00
Blue Bonnet, plate, dinner, 10"	8.00
Blue Bonnet, sugar bowl, w/lid	15.00
Boutonniere, casserole, w/lid, 1¼-qt	24.00
Boutonniere, creamer, 8-oz	10.00
Boutonniere, c/s	5.00
Boutonniere, mug	8.00
Boutonniere, plate, 6¾"	2.50
Boutonniere, plate, dinner, 10"	6.00
Boutonniere, platter, 13½" L	14.00
Boutonniere, relish, 2-part, 12"	12.50
Bridal Wreath, bowl, vegetable, 9"	22.00
Bridal Wreath, creamer	12.00
Bridal Wreath, platter, 13" L	25.00
Bride's Bouquet, creamer	20.00
Bride's Bouquet, c/s, ftd	20.00
Bride's Bouquet, sugar bowl, w/lid	25.00
Cockerel, bowl, vegetable, 9"	20.00
Corinthian, bowl, vegetable, 9½"	22.00
Corinthian, c/s	8.00
Corinthian, plate, chop, 11½"	40.00
Corinthian, plate, dinner, 10½"	12.00
Corinthian, sugar bowl	16.00
Golden Jubilee, bowl, vegetable, 9"	30.00
Golden Jubilee, c/s	15.00
Golden Jubilee, plate, luncheon, 9"	10.00
Golden Wheat, coffeepot, 9x9½"	60.00
Greenbriar, gravy boat, w/underplate	40.00
Greenbriar, sugar bowl, w/lid	17.50
Melody Lane, creamer	12.00
Melody Lane, plate, dinner, 10"	12.50
Mulhern Belting advertising mug, 1950s	7.00
Pebbleford, bowl, coupe soup, 6¾"	7.50

Pebbleford, bowl, vegetable, 8½"	12.00
Pebbleford, creamer	9.00
Pebbleford, c/s	8.00
Pebbleford, c/s, Granite	8.00
Pebbleford, plate, serving, center hdl, M gr	25.00
Pebbleford, sugar bowl, w/lid	12.00
Random Leaves, c/s	8.00
Random Leaves, plate, salad	7.00
Reveille Rooster, bowl, vegetable, 8"	18.00
Reveille Rooster, bowl, vegetable, oval, 9½" L	20.00
Reveille Rooster, creamer	14.00
Reveille Rooster, gravy boat, oval	25.00
Reveille Rooster, plate, dinner, 10"	7.50
Reveille Rooster, sugar bowl, w/lid	16.00
Silhouette, plate, luncheon, 9"	7.50
Summer Morn, c/s	10.00
Summer Morn, platter, 13" L	24.00
Summer Morn, sugar bowl, w/lid	18.00
Tulip, teapot, Coral-Craft, $45 to	60.00
Wheat, bowl, vegetable, 9"	12.50
Wheat, plate, luncheon, 9"	4.50

Tea Caddies

Because tea was once regarded as a precious commodity, special boxes called caddies were used to store the tea leaves. They were made from various materials: porcelain, carved and inlaid woods, and metals ranging from painted tin or tole to engraved silver.

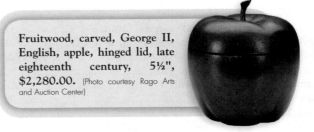

Fruitwood, carved, George II, English, apple, hinged lid, late eighteenth century, 5½", $2,280.00. (Photo courtesy Rago Arts and Auction Center)

Black lacquer/gold figures on veranda/scrolls, paw ft, China, 8" L, VG	380.00
Burl walnut Regency sarcophagus form, domed lid, fitted int, 8x14x8"	865.00
Burl wood w/oval conch shell inlay, ivory escutcheon, 5x5x4"	900.00
Fruitwood Geo III apple form, lacks stem, SP lining, 1800s, 4½"	2,000.00
Fruitwood, trn pear form, England, late 18th C, 6¼"	2,115.00
Georgian silvered brass-mtd blk shagreen sarcophagus, 1800s, 6x9½"	1,000.00
Lacewood vnr w/string inlay, fitted int, bone knobs, rfn, 5x8x5"	1,950.00
Mahog & rosewood w/inlay, hinged lid w/conch shell reserve, 5x10x5"	765.00
Mahog bombé, hinged lid, brass hdl, England, 1760s, 6½x10x6½"	2,100.00
Mahog vnr w/banded inlay, ivory keyhole escutcheon, 6x10x6"	375.00
Mahog vnr w/geometric inlay, 3-compartment, bone knobs, 6x10x5"	4,400.00
Mahog vnr, brass bail hdl, keyhole escutcheon, 3-compartment, 6x10x5"	575.00
Mahog w/check-banded borders, bracket ft, 3-compartment, 11" L	265.00
Mahog w/ebony & lt wood inlay, ivory inlay escutcheon, mask hdls, 12"	200.00
Mahog w/gilt quillwork & mini pnt on ivory, 1800s, 5x8x4"	3,100.00
Mahog w/hinged lid, brass hdl, 3 tin canisters, 5x9x5"	475.00
Oak w/leaves & acorn cvgs, 3-compartment, Latin inscription, 4x8x4"	400.00
Oak w/specimen wood inlay, bombe form, ogee bracket ft, 1850s, 10"	295.00
Parquetry, Georgian style, 1 foil-lined well w/lid, 1880s, 4x5x5"	265.00
Pollard oak, pewter/MOP inlay, Wm IV, sarcophagus form, 12" L	735.00
Rosewood w/MOP inlay, Wm IV, sarcophagus form, trn knobs/bun ft, 15" L	765.00
Satinwood & burl w/inlay oval medallions, brass knob, 1790s, 5x5x4"	650.00
Tortoiseshell w/MOP inlay, English, 19th C, 7¾" L	2,250.00

Tea Leaf Ironstone

Tea Leaf Ironstone became popular in the 1880s when middle-class American housewives became bored with the plain white stone china that English potters had been exporting to this country for nearly a century. The original design has been credited to Anthony Shaw of Burslem, who decorated the plain ironstone with a hand-painted copper lustre design of bands and leaves. Originally known as Lustre Band and Sprig, the pattern has since come to be known as Tea Leaf Lustre. It was produced with minor variations by many different firms both in England and the United States. By the early 1900s, it had become so commonplace that it had lost much of its appeal. Items marked Red Cliff are reproductions made from 1950 until 1980 for this distributing and decorating company of Chicago, Illinois. Hall China provided many of the blanks. It is assumed that all pieces listed below are in at least excellent condition. Loss of the lustre, staining, crazing, or damage and wear of any kind will result in a much lower evaluation. Our advisor for this category is Anne Miller; she is listed in the Directory under Illinois.

Washbowl and pitcher, Royal Ironstone China, Meakin, England, 13", 15" diameter, $275.00. (Photo courtesy Rich Penn Auctions on LiveAuctioneers.com)

Bone dish, scalloped, Meakin 45.00
Bowl, vegetable, Cable, w/lid, Burgess 140.00
Bowl, vegetable, Fish Hook, bracket ft, Meakin, w/lid, 11x7" 175.00
Bowl, vegetable, Wrapped Sydenham, Shaw, w/lid, ca 1860, sm.... 95.00
Butter dish, Bamboo, Meakin, 4½x6" 165.00
Butter dish, Little Cable, Furnival.................................... 200.00
Butter dish, sq, ftd, Burgess 125.00
Butter pat, copper rim, Alfred Meakin 10.00
Cake plate, 8-sided, Adams Microtex, 11⅛x8¾" 65.00
Champer pot, Sq Ridged, Mellor-Taylor, EX........................ 275.00
Coffeepot, Basketweave, Shaw, 1887 .... 295.00
Coffeepot, Lily of the Valley, Shaw, 1860s 395.00
Compote, fruit, ped ft, Royal Ironstone, Meakin, 5½x8½", NM .. 375.00
Covered dish, ftd, Meakin, 5x6½" 55.00
Creamer, Fish Hook, Meakin, 5x5" 60.00
Creamer, flared, Mellor-Taylor, 3½" 90.00
Creamer, Morning Glory, Elsmore & Forster, lg.................... 285.00
Cup/saucer, Adams Mircrotex 25.00
Cup/saucer, handleless, Morning Glory, early 1800s............... 95.00
Cup/saucer, handleless, Paneled, Shaw 95.00
Dish, Fish Hook, sq, Meakin, 4½" 35.00
Dish, oval, Shaw, 4½x6" 35.00
Doughnut stand, Meakin, 4½x8" 285.00
Gravy boat, ftd, Mellor-Taylor, 4½x7½" 120.00
Gravy boat, Laurel Wreath, Elsmore & Forster..................... 95.00
Nappy, Red Cliff, ca 1950-80.. 18.00
Pitcher, milk, Bamboo, Meakin, 7½" 220.00
Pitcher, milk, Lily of the Valley, 1860s............................... 225.00
Plate, Chinese, Shaw, 7⅞" 22.50
Plate, gold lustre, Bridgewood, 7" 12.00
Plate, Red Cliff, ca 1950-80, 8¼" 12.00
Platter, Brocade, Meakin, ca 1879+, 15x10½" 75.00
Relish, Lily of the Valley, leaf form, Shaw, 2¼x5¾x8¾" 140.00

Sauce tureen, Bamboo, Meakin, w/lid & ladle............................ 275.00
Shaving mug, Meakin, 3¼x3½".. 185.00
Soap dish, Cable, Shaw 225.00
Soap dish, plain, Meakin, 3¾x5½".. 35.00
Sugar bowl, Crystal, unmk, 1870s... 225.00
Sugar bowl, Fish Hook, Meakin, w/lid, 6½" 190.00
Sugar bowl, Lily of the Valley, Shaw, 5½x6½" 145.00
Toothbrush holder, scalloped rim, Meakin, 4½"............................ 60.00
Washbowl & pitcher, Fish Hook, Meakin................................... 300.00
Waste bowl, Burgess, 3x5⅜" 60.00

Teco

Teco artware was made by the American Terra Cotta and Ceramic Company, located near Chicago, Illinois. The firm was established in 1886 and until 1901 produced only brick, sewer tile, and other redware. Their early glaze was inspired by the matt green made popular by Grueby. 'Teco Green,' a smooth microcrystalline glaze, often accented by charcoaling in creases, was made for nearly 10 years. The company was one of the first in the United States to perfect a true crystalline glaze. The only decoration used was through the modeling and glazing techniques; no hand painting was attempted. Favored motifs were naturalistic leaves and flowers. The company broadened their lines to include garden pottery and faience tiles and panels. New matt glazes (browns, yellows, blue, and rose) were added to the green in 1910, as was a bright multicolored crystalline glaze called Aventurine. By 1922 the artware lines were discontinued; the company was sold in 1930.

Values are dictated by size and shape, with architectural and organic forms being more desirable. Teco is almost always marked with a vertical stamp spelling 'Teco.' Our advisors for this category are Suzanne Perrault and David Rago; they are listed in the Directory under New Jersey.

Wall pocket, green with charcoal, 17x7", $2,400.00. (Photo courtesy Rago Arts & Auction Center)

Lamp base, gr, cylindrical, flanked by buttressed hdls, 9½x8"............. 12,000.00
Pitcher, gr, whiplash hdls, 9¼x5".. 1,200.00
Vase, brn matt, 3-sided shape, #336, F Albert, 7½x4" 550.00
Vase, brn-gr, integral hdls, 5x8"... 2,160.00
Vase, buff, 4 full-H buttresses, rstr chip, 7x4¼" 1,550.00
Vase, frothy dk brn, 4 buttress hdls, #175, 14x10" 3,000.00
Vase, gr & charcoal matt, #440, dbl hdl, WD Gates, 5½x4½"... 1,000.00
Vase, gr matt, #185, 4 hdls, 7x6"Vase, gr matt, #185, 4 hdls, 7x6".... 1,600.00
Vase, gr matt, #447A, 2 buttresses, WD Gates, 6½x2½" 750.00
Vase, gr w/4 silver o/l buttresses mk Schreve, 10" 5,500.00
Vase, gr, 2-hdl, buttresses, prof rstr to rim, 7x4¼" 1,800.00
Vase, gr, beaker shape w/4 buttress hdls, rpr/burst bubble, 7¾"..3,600.00
Vase, gr, calla lillies & ferns, #134, nicks, 13x5½" 3,000.00
Vase, gr, dbl gourd w/4 hdls, WB Mundie design, 13¼" 14,000.00
Vase, gr, buttresses, 5½x3", NM... 1,150.00
Vase, gr, gourd shape, #661, prof rstr chip, 10x7"...................... 4,000.00
Vase, gr, gourd shape, 16¾x8"... 4,000.00

Vase, gr, tulip shapes at rim, 12½x6" 6,000.00
Vase, gr/ultramarine, floral, 4-ftd, drilled, 18½x7½" 7,800.00
Wall pocket, gr, F Albert design, rpr, 15" L...................................400.00

Teddy Bear Collectibles

The story of Teddy Roosevelt's encounter with the bear cub has been oft recounted with varying degrees of accuracy, so it will suffice to say that it was as a result of this incident in 1902 that the teddy bear got his name. These appealing little creatures are enjoying renewed popularity with collectors today. To one who has not yet succumbed to their obvious charms, one bear seems to look very much like another. How to tell the older ones? Look for long snouts, jointed limbs, large feet and felt paws, long curving arms, and glass or shoe-button eyes. Most old bears have a humped back and are made of mohair stuffed with straw or excelsior. Cute expressions, original clothes, a nice personality, and, of course, good condition add to their value. Early Steiff bears in mint condition may go for a minimum of $150.00 per inch for a small bear up to $300.00 to $350.00 (sometimes even more) per inch for one 20" high or larger. These are easily recognized by the trademark button within the ear. (Please see Toys, Steiff, for values of later bears.) Unless noted otherwise, values are for bears in excellent condition. For character bears, see also Toys, Steiff.

Bing, cinnamon mohair, long arms, 1920s, 17", min 3,000.00
Bing, wht mohair, button eyes, key-wind skater, 1907, 8", VG .5,000.00
Bruin/BMC, button eyes, very early, 10" 2,000.00
Chiltern, tan mohair, amber glass eyes, jtd, squeaker, 1947, 16" ..325.00
Columbia, Laughing Roosevelt, mohair, jtd mouth w/teeth, 1908, 20" ..2,350.00
Gund, pk mohair w/lt snout etc, metal shield in chest, 1960, 15". 250.00
Gund, Snuffles, M gr, 12"...535.00
Ideal, brn mohair, googly button eyes, hump, jtd, ca 1904, 13", VG 850.00
Ideal, dense mohair, button eyes, growler, 3 claws, 1920s, 22", M ..5,500.00
Ideal, gold plush mohair, glass eyes, fabric nose, jtd, 1910s, 20" ..480.00
Ideal, tan mohair, gutta-percha eyes, felt pads, jtd, 28", VG 900.00
Merrythought, blond mohair, glass eyes, squeaker, 1920s, 14" 275.00
Merrythought, gold mohair w/velvet muzzle, jtd, 25", M..............650.00
Russia, brn plush, button eyes, jtd, straw stuffed, 1930s, 16" 700.00
Schuco, skater, mohair key-wind, 1948, 9", min.........................1,500.00
Schuco, transitional style, 1930s, 12" 1,000.00

Schuco, Yes-No, excellent mohair, circa 1920s – 1930s, working, 19", VG, $460.00. (Photo courtesy Morphy Auctions)

Schuco, Yes-No, gold mohair, glass eyes, embr nose/mouth, 12" ..285.00
Steiff, blond mohair, button eyes, embr nose, rpl pads, ca 1905, 17" ..2,935.00
Steiff, blond mohair, button eyes, embr nose, w/button, 1908, 16", VG.3,600.00
Steiff, brn mohair, growler, jtd, 1927-30, w/button, sm rprs, 19", VG . 1,100.00
Steiff, cinnamon mohair, straw stuffed, shoe button eyes, 24", VG ..4,485.00
Steiff, glass eyes, 1918-22, 11½", G 1,200.00
Steiff, honey gold mohair, glass eyes, 1940-50s, 26"...................2,250.00

Steiff, lt brn mohair, button eyes, jtd, 1925-34, w/button, 16" 1,000.00
Steiff, lt brn mohair, glass eyes, fuzzy pads, 1950s, 9" 150.00
Steiff, on wheels, brn grizzly type, on all 4s, 10½" L, VG 950.00
Steiff, shoe-button eyes, 1905, 16", G 3,525.00
Steiff, shoe-button eyes, long-haired, orig button, 24", VG 4,450.00
Strunz, lt mohair, hump bk, jtd, jester outfit, ca 1905, 15" 3,350.00
Uncle Remus, blond mohair, growler, 1906, 20", min 5,000.00
Unmarked Am, tan mohair, glass eyes, orig ribbon, jtd, 1908, 21"..450.00
Unmarked English, silky mohair, glass eyes, squeaker, 1930s, 18", VG...475.00
Unmarked, brn mohair, glass eyes, sm hump, silent, ca 1900, 21½", VG...360.00
Unmarked, gold mohair, glass eyes/embr nose, hump/felt pads, 18" ...950.00

Telephones

Since Alexander Graham Bell's first successful telephone communication, the phone itself has undergone a complete evolution in style as well as efficiency. Early models, especially those wall types with ornately carved oak boxes, are of special interest to collectors. Also of value are the candlestick phones from the early part of the century and any related memorabilia. Unless otherwise noted, our values reflect the worth of examples that are working and in excellent original condition. Our advisor for Telephones is Tom Guenin; he is listed in the Directory under Ohio.

Automatic Electric #18, dial candlestick, 1919, rstr 250.00
Automatic Electric #40, chrome trim, 1940s 135.00
Automatic Electric #50, wall mt, aka jukebox phone, rstr 125.00
Automatic Electric, payphone, 3-slot, touch-tone, beige, 1960s..125.00
Automatic Electric, payphone, rotary dial, 1950s..........................225.00
Automatic Electric Type 21, candlestick, w/ringer box, 1920s, rstr..600.00
Couch & Seeley, oak wall mt, poor finish/pnt loss, 32" 85.00
Farr #6, oak wall type, b/o, ca 1905, 32".......................................475.00
Kellogg #900 Pyramid, desk, blk Bakelite, rotary dial, 1930s, rstr .135.00
Kellogg #1000 Masterphone, desk, brn Bakelite, 1940s, rstr 225.00
Kellogg #1000 Red Bar, wall, blk Bakelite, 1940s, rstr.................190.00
Kellogg, cradle style w/rnd base, 1920s, rstr 125.00
Kellogg, oak wall type w/brass bells, 1915, 24".............................200.00
Northern Electric #5C, chrome payphone, rstr..............................225.00

Pay phone, 1950s style, 34", $230.00. (Photo courtesy Morphy Auctions)

Sears, oak wall phone 175.00
Stromberg-Carlson, blk candlestick, 10½", w/subset 150.00
Stromberg-Carlson, oak wall style, working, EX rstr.....................175.00
Western Bell, blk candlestick, pitting/pnt loss, 20th C 85.00
Western Electric #102, rnd base, #2 dial, 1920s, rstr 250.00
Western Electric #302, pnt blk metal, 1938-40 ....95.00
Western Electric, brass candlestick, blk receiver, 11½" 100.00
Western Electric Trimline, clear plastic, rotary dial, 1967...........300.00

Large Original Blue Bell Paperweights

First issued in the early 1900s, bell-shaped glass paperweights were used as 'give-aways' and/or presented to telephone company executives as tokens of appreciation. The paperweights were used to prevent stacks of papers from blowing off the desks in the days of overhead fans. Over the years they have all but vanished — some taken by retiring employees, others accidentally broken. The weights came to be widely used for advertising by individual telephone companies; and as the smaller companies merged to form larger companies, more and more new paperweights were created. They were widely distributed with the opening of the first transcontinental telephone line in 1915. The bell-shaped paperweight embossed 'Opening of Trans-Pacific Service, Dec. 23, 1931,' in Peacock Blue glass is very rare, and the price is negotiable. (Weights with 'open' in the price field are also rare and impossible to accurately evaluate.) In 1972 the first Pioneer bell paperweights were made to sell to raise funds for the charities the Pioneers support. This has continued to the present day. These bell paperweights have also become 'collectibles.' For further study we recommend *Blue Bell Paperweights, Telephone Pioneers of America Bells and Other Telephone Related Items*, by our advisor, Jacqueline Linscott Barnes; she is listed in the Directory under Florida.

Bell System C&P Telephone Co & Associated Companies, peacock, wht emb.	250.00
Bell System The Central District...Printing Telegraph Co, peacock, wht emb	500.00
Bell System-New York Telephone Co, ice bl, wht emb	130.00
Bell System, Peacock, wht emb	200.00
Missouri & Kansas Telephone Co, peacock, wht emb	150.00
Nebraska Telephone Co, Peacock, wht emb	350.00
Opening of Trans-Pacific Service Dec 23, 1931, peacock, wht emb.	open
Pays 7% Mountain States Telephone, Peacock, wht emb	175.00
Time Is Money..., North LA Telephone, Peacock, wht emb	900.00
Western Electric Co, cobalt (inkwell), wht emb	200.00
Western Electric Co, cobalt, wht emb	200.00
Bell Telephone Co, cobalt	200.00

Large Telephone Pioneers of America (TPA) Commemoratives

Year 2000 Commemorative, F. Lucent Technologies Bell Labs Innovations, ruby red, $50.00.
(Photo courtesy Jacqueline Linscott Barnes)

75 Years of Community Service, pk emb	open
Bell Atlantic, cobalt w/wht swirls, emb	60.00
Bell of Pennsylvania 1879-1979, lt purple, emb	open
Break-Up of the Bell System, emerald gr, emb	50.00
Break-Up of the Bell System, opaline bl swirl	50.00
First 50 Years NJ, jersey gr, emb	30.00
Laureldale Council 1959-79, peacock, emb	25.00
Lucent Technologies, ruby red w/gold emb	50.00
Nevada Bell, blk, emb	80.00
Region 10 Assembly, bl, emb	100.00
Telephone Centennial 1876-1976, carnival, emb	35.00

Small Commemorative Bells

Bell System, Chesapeake-Potomac Telephone, ice bl, emb	425.00
Bell System, cobalt, emb	125.00
(No emb), amber	125.00
(No emb), clear	150.00
(No emb), cobalt	95.00
Ohio Bell, cobalt	75.00
Ohio Bell Telephone Co & Associated Companies, cobalt, emb	145.00
Ohio Bell Telephone Co & Associated Companies, ice bl, emb	425.00
Save Time – Telephone, cobalt, emb	100.00
Save Time – Telephone, ice bl, emb	75.00
Save Time – Telephone, Peacock, emb	85.00

Telescopes

Antique telescopes were sold in large quantities to sailors, astronomers, and the military but survive in relatively few numbers because their glass lenses and brass tubes were easily damaged. Even scarcer are antique reflecting telescopes, which use a polished metal mirror to magnify the world. Telescopes used for astronomy give an inverted image, but most old telescopes were used for marine purposes and have more complicated optics that show the world right-side up. Spyglasses are smaller, hand-held telescopes that collapse into their tube and focus by drawing out the tube to the correct length. A more compact instrument, with three or four sections, is also more delicate, and sailors usually preferred a single-draw spyglass. They are almost always of brass, occasionally of nickel silver or silver plate, and usually covered with leather, or sometimes a beautiful rosewood veneer. Solid wood barrel spyglasses (with a brass draw tube) tend to be early and rare. Before the middle of the 1800s, makers put their names in elaborate script on the smallest draw tube, but as 1900 approached, most switched to plain block printing. British instruments from World War One made by a variety of makers are commonly found, sharing a format of a 2" objective, 30" long with three draws extended, a tapered main tube, and sometimes having low- and high-power oculars and beautiful leather cases. U.S. Navy WWII spyglasses are quite common but have outstanding optics and focus by twisting the eyepiece, which makes them weather-proof. The Quartermaster (Q.M.) 16x spyglass is 31" long, with a tapered barrel and a 2½" objective. The Officer of the Deck (O.D.D.) is a 23" cylinder with a 1½" objective. Very massive, short, brass telescopes are usually gun sights or ship equipment and have little interest to most collectors. World War II marked the first widespread use of coated optics, which can be recognized by a colored film on the objective lens. Collectible post-WWII telescopes include early refractors by Unitron or Fecker and reflectors by Cave or Questar. Modern spotting scopes often use a prism to erect the image and are of great interest if made by the best makers, including Nikon and Zeiss. Several modern makers still use lacquered brass, and many replica instruments have been produced.

A telescope with no maker's name is much less interesting than a signed instrument, and 'Made in France' is the most common mark on old spyglasses. Dollond of London made instruments for 200 years and this is probably the most common name on antiques; but because of its important technical innovations and very high quality, Dollond telescopes are always valuable. Bardou, Paris, telescopes are also of very high quality. Bardou is another relatively common name, since it was a prolific maker for many years, and its spyglasses were sold by Sears. Alvan Clark and Sons was the most prolific early American maker, in operation from the 1850s to the 1920s, and its astronomical telescopes are of great historical import.

Spyglasses are delicate instruments that were subject to severe use under all weather conditions. Cracked or deeply scratched optics are impossible to repair and lower the value considerably. Most lenses are doublets, two lenses glued together, and deteriorated cement is common. This looks like crazed glaze and is fairly difficult to repair. Dents in the tube and damaged or missing leather covering can usually be fixed. The best test of a telescope is to use it, and the image should be sharp and clear. Any accessories, eyepieces, erecting prisms, or quality cases can add significantly to value. The following prices assume that the telescope is in very good to fine condition and give the objective lens (obj.) diameter, which is the most important measurement of a telescope.

Accessories from vintage astronomical telescopes often have collectible value by themselves. Spectroscope and micrometer attachments for Ziess, Clark, Brashear, Fecker, and Mogey telescopes are rarely seen. Eyepieces alone from many famous makers also may be found. Our advisor for this category is Peter Bealo; he is listed in the Directory under New Hampshire.

Key: obj — objective lens

Adams, George; 2" reflecting, brass cabriole tripod	3,500.00
Bardou & Son, Paris, 4-draw, 50mm obj, leather, 36"	250.00
Bausch & Lomb, 1-draw, 45mm obj, wrinkled pnt, 17"	90.00
Brashear, 3½" obj, brass, tripod, w/eyepcs	4,500.00
Cary, London (script), 2" obj, tripod, w/3 eyepcs	3,000.00
Clark, Alvan; 4" obj, 48", iron mt on wooden legs	9,000.00
Criterion RV-6 Dynascope, 6" reflector, 1960s	500.00
Dallmeyer, London (script), 5-draw, 2½" obj, SP, 49"	800.00
Dollond, London (block), 2-draw, 2" obj, leather cover	290.00
Dollond, London (script), 2-draw, 2" obj, leather cover	450.00
Dollond, London (script), brass, 3" obj, 40", on tripod	2,900.00
France or Made in France, 3-draw, 30mm obj, lens cap	80.00

J. H. Dallmeyer, London, nineteenth century, 20x45x7", $1,000.00. (Photo courtesy Lewis & Maese Auction Company on LiveAuctioneers.com)

McAlister (script), brass, 3½" obj, 45", tripod	3,000.00
Messer, London Day & Night, brass, mahog handgrip, 2-draw, EX	200.00
Mogey, brass, 3" obj, 40", on tripod, w/4 eyepcs	2,500.00
Negretti & Zambra, 2½" obj, equatorial mt, 36", tripod	2,500.00
Plossl, Wein, 2" obj, Dialytic optics, 24", tabletop tripod	4,000.00
Queen & Co (script), 6-draw, 70mm obj, wood vnr, 50"	1,000.00
Questar, reflecting, on astro mt, 1950s, 3½" dia	3,000.00
R&J Beck, 2" obj, 24", tabletop tripod w/cabriole legs	2,500.00
Short, James; 3" dia reflecting, brass cabriole tripod	4,000.00
Student's No 52, altazimuth to equatorial, 36" focal L, w/stand	125.00
TB Winter...Newcastle on Tyne, brass, 17" on tripod, 42" L	650.00
Tel Sct Regt Mk 2 S (many maker's names), UK, WWI	120.00
Unitron, 4" obj, wht, 60", on tripod, many accessories	3,000.00
Unmarked, brass, 2" obj, spyglass, leather cover, $150 to	300.00
Unmarked, brass, 2" obj, stand w/cabriole legs	1,200.00
Unmarked, floor-standing tripod type, brass, clear optics	525.00
US Military, brass, very heavy, $100 to	300.00
US Navy, QM Spyglass, 16X, MK II, in box	220.00
Vion, Paris, 40mm obj, 3-draw, 40-power, leather, 21"	110.00
Voigtander & Sohn Wein, brass, 1-draw, tapered bbl, 31"	275.00
Wollensak Mirroscope, 1950s, 12x2" dia, leather case	300.00
Wood bbl, 8-sided, 1½" obj, 1700s, 30"	1,500.00
Wood bbl, rnd taper, 1½" obj, sgn, 1800s	350.00
Yeates & Son Dublin, brass, 2-draw, QA-style stand, 15x38"	575.00
Zeiss Asiola, 60mm obj, prism spotting scope, pre-WWII	650.00
Zeiss, brass, 60mm obj, w/eyepcs & porro prism, tripod	1,700.00

Televisions

Many early TVs have escalated in value over the last few years. Pre-1943 sets (usually with only one to five channels) are often worth $500.00 to $5,000.00. Unusually styled small-screen wooden 1940s TVs are 'hot'; but most metal, Bakelite, and large-screen sets are still shunned by collectors. Color TVs from the 1950s with 16" or smaller tubes are valuable; larger color sets are not. One of our advisors for this category is Harry Poster, author of *Poster's Radio & Television Price Guide 1920 – 1990*; he is listed in the Directory under New Jersey.

Key: t/t — tabletop

Admiral #19A11, blond wood t/t, 1948, 7"	100.00
Admiral #1201, 10" screen in Bakelite cabinet, 32x16x19"	2,040.00
Airline #94GSE-3015, includes Telephoto Control, t/t, 1948, 7"	150.00
Airline #94WG-3029A, blond wood console, 1949, 12"	60.00
Arvin #3160CM, mahog console, TE-276 chassis, 1949, 16"	40.00
Arvin #4080T, metal w/mahog front, t/t, 1950, 8"	150.00
Bendix #2020, mahog t/t, 1950, 12"	80.00
Cape-Farnsworth #3001-M, mahog t/t, 1950, 12"	50.00
CBS-Columbia #RX89, blond wood, color prototype, console, 1953, 15"	3,000.00
Coronado #FA 43-8965, mahog wood, t/t, 1949, 7"	125.00
Delco #TV-121, blond wood console, 1949, 12"	65.00
DeWald #CT-104, wood t/t, 1949, 10"	100.00
DuMont #RA 119, mahog, console, w/radio, Royal Sovereign, 1951, 30"	300.00
Emerson #620, mahog t/t, 1948, 10"	120.00
Emerson #630, mahog TV-radio-phono console, 1948, 12"	65.00
Garod #1549G, blond wood console, 1949, 16"	50.00
GE #10T1, Bakelite, 1948, 10"	100.00
GE #806, wood, t/t, 1949, 10"	100.00
General Electric #12C108, blond wood console, 1949, 12"	50.00
General Electric #24C101, mahog console, rnd tube, 1950, 24"	70.00
JVC #3100D, wht plastic transistor w/clock, Pyramid, 1978, 6"	400.00
Meck #XB-702, wood t/t 1948, 7"	175.00
Motorola #9L1, red leatherette portable w/lid, TS-18 chassis, 1949, 8"	95.00
Motorola #TS 902, color, console, 1954, 15"	300.00
National #TV-10T, mahog t/t, 1949, 10"	160.00
Olympic #TV-104, wood t/t, Cruzair, 1948, 10"	80.00
Philco #51-T1-601, metal t/t, 1951, 16"	35.00
Philco #B-350-HYL, yel plastic transistor t/t, 1982, 9"	75.00
RCA #630TS, mahog t/t, 1946, 10"	175.00
RCA #6T84, wood TV-radio/phono console, 1950, 16"	40.00
RCA #721 TCS, wood, console, 1947, 10"	200.00
Sentinel #412, wood t/t, 1949, 10"	60.00
Silvertone #125B, mahog t/t, 1949, 10"	75.00
Silvertone #9125B, brn Bakelite t/t, 1949, 10"	75.00
Sony #FD-42A, wht plastic LCD transistor, Watchman, 1989, 2"	55.00
Sparton #4918, blond wood TV-radio/phono console, 1949, 10"	90.00
Sparton, Cosmopolitan, TV-radio/phono console, 1949, 16"	125.00
Stewart-Warner #9054-B, blond oak console, mirror in lid, 1948, 10"	135.00
Sylvania #1-247-1, mahog console, #1-231 chassis, 1950, 16"	35.00
Templeton Mfg Co, #TV-1776, wood t/t, built-in magnifier, 1948	500.00
Zenith #24H21, wood cabinet, console, 1950, 19"	175.00
Zenith #G2340Z, walnut console, #23G24 chassis, Ensign, 1950, 12"	100.00
Zenith #G2420E, blond wood t/t, #24G20 chassis, Wilshire, 1950	170.00

Philco Predictas and Related Items

Made in the years between 1958 and 1960, Philco Predictas have become the most sought-after line of televisions in the postwar era. The Predicta line continues to be highly collectible, due mainly to its atom-age styling. Philco Predictas feature a swivel or separate enclosed picture tube and radial cabinet designs. The values given here are for as-found, average, clean, complete, unrestored sets, running or not, that have good picture tubes. Predictas that are missing parts or have damaged viewing screens will have lower values. Those that have the UHF optional tuner will have only slightly higher values. Predictas that have been fully restored in appearance and electronically can bring three or more times the stated values. Collectors should note that some Predictas will have missing parts (knobs, antennas, viewing screen, etc.). These sets and those that have been damaged in shipping will be very costly to restore. This is due to the fact that no new parts are being made and the availability of 'new' old stock is nonexistent. These facts have driven the cost of replacement parts sky high. Collectors will find it better to combine two sets, using the parts from one to complete the better set. Our advisor for Predictas is David Weddington; he is listed in the Directory under Tennessee.

Pedestal model, mahogany with yellow accents, 1958, $575.00. (Photo courtesy Clars Auction Gallery on LiveAuctioneers.com)

17DRP4 picture tube, MIB, replacement for all 17" t/t Predictas. 275.00
21FDP4, picture tube, MIB, replacement for all 21" t/t Predictas.. 275.00
AD65480, table top, 28x20x14"... 300.00
G4242 21" t/t wood cabinet, mahog finish...................................... 425.00
G4242 Holiday 21" t/t, wood cabinet blond finish 475.00
G4654 Barber Pole 21" console, boomerang front leg, blond....... 725.00
G4710 Tandem 21" separate screen w/25' cable, mahog finish..... 650.00
G4720 Stereo Tandem 21" separate screen, 4 brass legs, mahog .. 900.00
G4720 Stereo Tandem w/matching 1606S phonoamp, mahog .1,200.00
H3308 Debutante 17" t/t, cloth grille, w/antenna, charcoal......... 375.00
H3406 Motel 17" t/t, metal cabinet, cloth grille, no antenna 200.00
H3410 Princess 17" t/t, metal grille, plastic tuner window........... 400.00
H3410 Princess 17" t/t, orig metal stand, red finish 525.00
H3412 Siesta t/t, w/clock-timer above tuner, gold finish.............. 575.00
H4730 Danish Modern 21" console, 4 fin-shaped legs, mahog finish.. 975.00
H4744 Town house 21" room-divider, walnut shelves, brass finish ..1,400.00

Terra Cotta

Terra cotta is a type of earthenware or clay used for statuary, architectural facings, or domestic articles. It is unglazed, baked to durable hardness, and characterized by the color of the body which may range from brick red to buff.

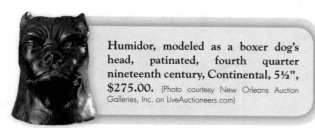

Humidor, modeled as a boxer dog's head, patinated, fourth quarter nineteenth century, Continental, 5½", $275.00. (Photo courtesy New Orleans Auction Galleries, Inc. on LiveAuctioneers.com)

Bust, Dorine Maid of Orleans, Harze, 1880, 20¼" 780.00
Bust, US Grant, c K Gerhart, Goodwin Bros, 1885..................... 425.00
Pedestal, pharaohs/classical trophies, Retour de'Egypte, 30x12", pr ...550.00
Plaque, 6 putti w/lion, in manner of C Michel, 9½x18" 150.00
Sculpture, boy lighting cigarette, mc (fading), 1880s, 30".........1,200.00
Sculpture, Dutch girl w/flowing dress, R Miles, 10" 180.00
Sculpture, eagle on integral socle base, Fr, 19th C, 25x18" 1,950.00
Sculpture, eagle on orb, architectural finial, rpr, 20x29" 240.00
Sculpture, German shepherds, sgn T Cartier, 20"......................... 400.00
Sculpture, lady in long gown, breast exposed, doves at feet, 58".. 5,600.00
Sculpture, Madonna & Child, molded in full rnd, Austria, 1930s, 16" .. 120.00
Sculpture, nude female bather, pale brn finish, after Perron, 21" ...1,175.00
Sculpture, putto w/basket of goods, marble base, Paris 1735, 14½" ..575.00
Sculpture, seated putto w/fruit/flower basket, 20th C, 14", +wood base ...480.00
Sculpture, Sysyphus, nude male, Art Deco, H Bargas, 12x20" ..1,325.00

Thermometers

Many companies have utilitzed thermometers as a means of promoting their products. From gasoline to soda pop, there are scores to choose from. Many were 'button' styles, approximately 12" in diameter with a protective, see-through dome-like cover and a sweep hand. Unless otherwise described, assume that the 12" round examples in our listing are of this design. Advertising thermometers were most often made of painted tin or metal; other materials will be noted in the description. Porcelain paint (abbreviated 'porc' in lines) is a glass material fused to metal by firing.

Decorative thermometers run the gamut from plain tin household varieties to the highly ornate creations of Tiffany and Bradley and Hubbard. They have been manufactured from nearly every conceivable material — oak, sterling, brass, and glass being the favorites — and have tested the artistry and technical skills of some of America's finest craftsmen. Ornamental models can be found in free-hanging, wall-mounted, or desk/mantel versions. American-made thermometers available today as collectors' items were made between 1875 and 1940. The golden age of decoratives ended in the early 1940s as modern manufacturing processes and materials robbed them of their natural distinctiveness. Prices are based on age, ornateness, and whether mercury or alcohol is used as the filler in the tube. A broken or missing tube will cut at least 40% off the value. Our advisor for this category is Richard T. Porter, who holds the Guinness Book of World Records certificate for his collection of over 5,000 thermometers; he is listed in the Directory under Massachusetts.

Key:
Cen — Centigrade   Rea — Reaumur
Fah — Fahrenheit   sc — scale
mrc — mercury in tube

Advertising

AC Spark Plugs, w/Coralox Insulator, glass face, 1940s, 12" dia, EX... 310.00
Barq's Root Beer, bottle center, pnt metal, #117A, 1960s, 26x10", EX... 180.00
Borden's Ice Cream, Elsie-in-daisy logo on turq, 26", M............... 550.00
Buick Motor Cars, Creekmore Motor Co, bl on wht, porc, 1915, 27x7", EX .225.00
Calumet Baking Powder, store advertising on wood, 27x7", EX... 800.00
Delco Engergizer, battery image w/United Delco, 36x8", EX 130.00
Doan's Kidney Pills, man holding bk at top, dc pnt wood, 21", VG...350.00
Dr Chase's Nerve Food, wht letters on bl, porc, 39x8", VG 390.00
Dr Pepper, Frosty Cold, Donasco, tin, 1957, 26x10", EX.............. 230.00
Dr Swett's Root Beer, bottle cap at top, tin litho, 17⅛x5", NM... 200.00
Ed Pinaud's Hair Tonic, barber w/product, red/wht/bl, 26x9", VG. 1,400.00
EX-Lax Keep Regular, porc, 36x8x1½", EX+ 175.00
Gold Medal Oil, Long Life for Your Car, logo, 1920s, 12" dia, EX ...190.00
Gray-Seal Paint, It Cost Less To Paint With the Best, 12" dia, EX ..130.00

Hills Bros Coffee, porc, 21x8¾", EX..480.00
Hire's Root Beer, bottle shape, #BN-16, 1950s, 29", EX..............140.00
International Stock Food, livestock graphics on wood, TB Co, 47", VG..745.00
Kasco Dog Food, It's Dog-licious w/bag, tin, 9" dia, EX.................150.00
Keystone Seeds, The Orig Legume Inoculator, blk on yel, 27x7", EX..190.00
Koch Bros, arched top/sq bottom, beveled rim, 21x5", EX...........350.00
Mail Pouch Tobacco, Treat Yourself to the Best, bl, porc, 40", EX ..160.00
Mail Pouch Tobacco, wht/yel on bl, curved top/bottom, porc, 39x8", NM...250.00

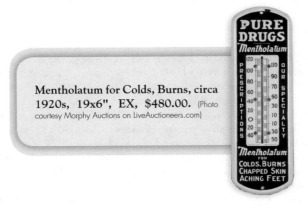

Mentholatum for Colds, Burns, circa 1920s, 19x6", EX, $480.00. (Photo courtesy Morphy Auctions on LiveAuctioneers.com)

Moxie, early, 25x10", VG 825.00
Old German Lager Beer, red/wht/bl face, 1950s, 6" dia, EX+.......100.00
Orange Crush, bottle cap, Pam, 1959, 12" dia, EX.........................220.00
Pepsi-Cola, Bigger Better, w/bottle, 1940s, 15x8", EX..................360.00
Ramon's Brownie/Pk Pills, red/gr on wht, arched top, wood, 21x9", EX ..475.00
Red Crown Gasoline/Polarine, red/wht/blk, sq corners, porc, 73", VG...2,500.00
Royal Crown Cola, bottle on wht, emb tin, 13½x6x3/4", NM.....170.00
Royal Crown Cola, Enjoy RC, tin litho, 26x10", NM..................110.00
Royal Crown Cola, plaque above bottle, tin, 1960s, 13½x6", EX.. 180.00
Sauer's Flavoring Extracts, wood, arched top, 24x7", EX+ 1,050.00
Sun Drop Golden Soda, upside-down bottle, 27x7½", EX 140.00
Sylvania Radio Tubes, Radio Service, wht on gr, tin, 38x8", EX.. 130.00
Teem, lemon atop w/Teem, bottle, Donasco, 28x12", EX............250.00
Trico Wiper Blades, arc shape, red & blk on wht, 9x12½", EX 130.00

Ornamental

American Artworks Inc., Coshocton, Ohio, white metal nude with dark patina, circa 1920s, 9", EX, $210.00. (Photo courtesy Tom Harris Auctions on LiveAuctioneers.com)

Birmingham, desk, silver floral repoussé, easel bk, 1904, 3½", VG. 70.00
Black Starr & Frost, desk, silver w/emb floral, easel bk, #550, 5" . 120.00
Cheshire Silversmiths, desk, bronze candelabra, mrc, 1875, 10" ...4,500.00
Clark, desk, ivory ped, crown, mrc, 1904, 7"..................................400.00
Desk, CI lion among foliage, Fah sc, mrc, easel bk, 7"....................85.00
Desk, cvd walrus tusk, 2-tier disk base, inlay sc, 1860, 9" 430.00
English SP & brass, horse racing motif, 19th C, 7x3"...................425.00
English, brass w/cast foliage/scrolls, mrc, 19th C, 6" 150.00

Fahr Reau, wall, bronze umbrella form, Fah/Cen sc, mrc, 14" L..... 72.50
France, desk, gilt metal w/scrolls & 2 figures at base, 1900-20, 6" . 110.00
France, desk, lady leaning on ped thermometer, metal w/marble base, 6".. 100.00
Gorham, desk, silver repoussé, Cen/Fah sc, mrc, ca 1891, 5½" 95.00
Grand Tour, desk, brass/CI columns (2) on reeded base, mrc, 8" . 275.00
Pat Pend LVL (Candlestick Co), pnt CI w/molded flowers, Fah sc, 6" ...300.00
Reaumur, desk, brass eagle finial, Cen sc, mrc, 11¾x4x2" 85.00
Turnbridge, Cleopatra's needle, cube & tesserae mosaic panels ... 100.00
Unknown, desk, brass columns (2), Fah sc, mrc, 19th C, 7¾" 350.00
Unknown, desk, brass monument form, Fah sc, mrc, 8½" 95.00
Unknown, desk, brass w/lady finial, ped base w/ornate ft, 19th C, 10" ... 110.00
Unknown, desk, brass w/malachite panel inserts, 6x5"................ 235.00
Unknown, wall, bronze w/cherubs/scrolls, Cen/Fah sc, mrc, 1900s, 10x4" ..215.00
Unknown, wall, rococo scrolls & flowers on gilt metal w/putto, 1920s. 180.00
Wall, brass Gothic Revival quatrefoil, Cen/Fah/Rea sc, 7⅝"........ 150.00

Thousand Faces

The name of this china arises from the claim that 1,000 faces can be seen on every dinner plate. Though the overall pattern is called Thousand Faces, there are several variations, including Men in Robes and Thousand Geishas. (The Immortals, a Satsuma style of china, is not considered to be Thousand Faces, although many people list it as such.) This china was made in the early part of the century and stayed popular through the 1930s, 1940s, and 1950s. Although few items are marked (many of them were brought into the country by servicemen), the ones that are carry a variety: Made in Japan, Made in Occupied Japan, Kutani, or other Japanese marks. The tea/coffee sets are often found to serve four, five, or six people, many having dragon spouts on the teapot and creamer.

The two main colors are gold-face and black-face. As its name suggests, the gold-face pattern is primarily gold; it features rings of multiple colors with gold faces painted on them. This color has always been the most prevalent, and is today the easiest to find and the most popular. The black-face pattern has a background of white with rings of multiple colors; it has black faces painted on the rings. It's not as popular, and it's harder to find — even so, the two patterns command similar prices. Even though the gold-face is easier to find, many think it is the more striking of the two.

The blue and green patterns are rarely seen. In both types, the primary color has rings of the same color in varying shades with gold-painted faces and accents. As expected, these two colors command a higher price (for pieces in mint condition). Complete sets are rarely if ever found, but the component pieces that turn up from time to time vouch for their existence. There are other variations in color, such as the black-face pattern with black or cobalt blue rims, but the more popular variations are Men in Robes and Thousand Geishas.

Men in Robes is a striking variation with bursts of colors coming from the robes instead of the rings of color. There are usually gold accents and a ring of color around the rim. Often the faces are concentrated in one area of the piece while the other section is filled with robes, giving the impression that the men are standing.

Thousand Geishas is a striking variation similar to Men in Robes. The colors come from the kimonos worn by the ladies, all of whom have black hair in the true geisha fashion. The Thousand Geishas pattern may be found in various colors, including lighter shades. EBay is a good source of information regarding Thousand Faces china and its variations. Our advisor for this category is Suzi Hibbard; she is listed in the Directory under California.

Key: MIJ — Made in Japan

Biscuit jar, Men in Robes, ftd, 8x6", NM, $125 to.........................175.00
Bowl, serving, gold, Kutani, 2x5", +plate & spoon, $35 to.............50.00
Bowl, soup, Men in Robes, w/lid, Kutani, $50 to...........................75.00

Cup/saucer, coffee, gr, MIJ, $50 to.................................... 125.00
Cup/saucer, coffee, Thousand Geishas, unmk, $40 to.................. 75.00
Dresser set, blk, unmk, tray+hatpin holder+jar+hair receiver, $250 to...550.00
Lamp, gold, unmk, 10½", $125 to.................................... 175.00
Plate, blk, MIJ, 7¼", $20 to 45.00
Plate, Men in Robes, Kutani, 7¼", $30 to........................... 40.00
Plate, Men in Robes, unmk, 9½", $30 to............................. 45.00
Tea set, blk rim, 3 pcs: 7" luncheon plate, c/s..................... 45.00
Tea set, demi, gold, unmk, pot+cr/sug+6 c/s+tray, 17-pc, $125 to...300.00
Tea set, gold, MIJ, 17-pc, $150 to................................. 275.00
Tea set, gold, rattan hdl, mk, 20-pc, $175 to...................... 250.00
Tea set, Men in Robes, 24-pc, $200 to.............................. 325.00
Teapot, Men in Robes, Shofu - MIJ, $35 to 50.00
Teapot, Thousand Geishas, mk, 6x7", $45 to......................... 85.00
Vase, gold, 5", $45 to 70.00
Vase, Men in Robes, red/blk, mk, 2⅞", $50 to 125.00

Vase, nineteenth century, 8½", $250.00. (Photo courtesy Bloomington Auction on LiveAuctioneers.com)

Tiffany

Louis Comfort Tiffany was born in 1848 to Charles Lewis and Harriet Young Tiffany of New York. By the time he was 18, his father's small dry goods and stationery store had grown and developed into the world-renowned Tiffany and Company. Preferring the study of art to joining his father in the family business, Louis spent the next six years under the tutelage of noted artists. He returned to America in 1870 and until 1875 painted canvases that focused on European and North African scenes. Deciding the more lucrative approach was in the application of industrial arts and crafts, he opened a decorating studio called Louis C. Tiffany and Co., Associated Artists. He began seriously experimenting with glass, and eschewing traditionally painted-on details, he instead learned to produce glass with qualities that could suggest natural textures and effects. His experiments broadened, and he soon concentrated his efforts on vases, bowls, etc., that came to be considered the highest achievements of the art. Peacock feathers, leaves and vines, flowers, and abstracts were developed within the plane of the glass as it was blown. Opalescent and metallic lustres were combined with transparent color to produce stunning effects. Tiffany called his glass Favrile, meaning handmade.

In 1900 he established Tiffany Studios and turned his attention full time to producing art glass, leaded-glass lamp shades and windows, and household wares with metal components. He also designed a complete line of jewelry which was sold through his father's store. He became proficiently accomplished in silverwork and produced such articles as hand mirrors embellished with peacock feather designs set with gems and candlesticks with Favrile glass inserts. Tiffany's work exemplified the Art Nouveau style of design and decoration, and through his own flamboyant personality and business acumen he perpetrated his tastes onto the American market to the extent that his name became a household word. Tiffany Studios continued to prosper until the second decade of the twentieth century when, due to changing tastes, his influence began to diminish. By the early 1930s the company had closed.

Serial numbers were assigned to much of Tiffany's work, and letter prefixes indicated the year of manufacture: A – N for 1896 – 1900; P – Z for 1901 – 1905. After that, the letter followed the numbers with A – N in use from 1906 – 1912; P – Z from 1913 – 1920. O-marked pieces were made especially for friends and relatives; X indicated pieces not made for sale.

Our advisor for this category is Carl Heck; he is listed in the Directory under Colorado. Our listings are primarily from the auction houses in the East where both Tiffany and Company and Tiffany Studio items sell at a premium. All pieces are signed unless noted otherwise.

Glass

Bowl, centerpiece, gold irid w/foliage intaglio, #T-1406, 3¾x12" 2,300.00
Bowl, gold irid, scalloped, #1561, 2¼x10¼" 1,200.00
Bowl, pastel w/indigo morning glories on trellis, #2132P, 3x12½" ..4,200.00
Butter pat, gold irid, #G1478, 3" 150.00
Candlestick, cobalt irid, twisted stem, 5¼", ea........................1,400.00
Candlestick, thistle form w/brn patina, Engineers Club...1907, 8", ea.. 1,600.00
Candlesticks, gr opal w/opal laurel leaves, clear stem/ft, 4", pr..1,800.00
Cocktail, moonstone opal, clear stem & ft, 4¼" 635.00
Compote, feathers, gr on opal w/gold int, ruffled, 4¼x5½" 1,675.00
Compote, gold w/gr tendrills, scalloped rim, 3⅛x8½" 2,000.00
Compote, Queen's pattern, gold irid, emb ribs, ruffled, 6x6¼" 750.00
Compote, silvery-bl irid, stretched ruffled rim, #8545E, 5¼x7".2,645.00
Finger bowl, gold irid, ribs, scalloped, 2¾x5" 300.00
Finger bowl, leaves & vines, gr on gold irid, #T4129, 2¼x4" 975.00
Humidor, silver-bl w/cvd floret on lid, #6582J, 7¼" 3,000.00
Medallion, eagle over bell, gold w/rainbow irid, 1918, 2¾" 700.00
Plate, turq & wht pastel floriform, 11" 1,025.00
Punch cup, gold irid w/purple int, #1157, 2¼" 300.00
Salt cellar, bl irid, ruffled, master, 1x4" 925.00
Vase, bl, elongated neck, #6578K, paper label, 6" 1,150.00
Vase, bud, bl fabrile, 6¾x2¾"...1,560.00
Vase, bud, hearts & vines, gr on gold irid, #6198E, 6¼" 1,380.00

Vase, deep blue iridescent, 7¼x8½", $2,800.00. (Photo courtesy Stanton Auctions on LiveAuctioneers.com)

Vase, dogwood blossoms, wheel cvd intaglio, #4639N 24,000.00
Vase, feathers, brn on silvery bl, #9288G, 9¾".........................10,350.00
Vase, feathers, gold irid on wht frost, slim, #9436M, 14"...........1,035.00
Vase, feathers, gold on wht frost, invt trumpet form, #1414K, 10" . 1,035.00
Vase, feathers, gr on gold irid, rnd shoulders, #Y8, 2¼" 1,325.00
Vase, floriform, feathers, gr on clambroth opal, shaped rim, 12" ...10,350.00
Vase, floriform, feathers, gr on opal, gold irid ft, 15"..................9,250.00
Vase, floriform, feathers, gr w/aventurine on opal, #M2879, 15" ..17,825.00
Vase, floriform, feathers, rum/gold/opal on yel, bronze stem, 13"...7,000.00
Vase, floriform, gold irid, gold doré saucer ft, #160, 21½"..........2,300.00
Vase, floriform, gold, #1523-1348K, 7x2¾"............................1,700.00
Vase, floriform, wht opal to gold irid, clear stem/ft, #4536B, 12"...7,475.00
Vase, gold cypriote, 7¼x3¾"..2,400.00
Vase, gold favrile faceted, 7x6½" 900.00
Vase, gold favrile, pinched trellis, 3¾x4" 1,920.00
Vase, gold favrile ribbed floriform, 8¾x3" 1,200.00
Vase, gold irid w/8 appl tendrils, #K2292, 4" 550.00
Vase, gold irid w/pulled ribbon design at shoulder, #K1064, 13¼"...925.00

Vase, gold irid, trumpet form, #1832, 10"................................1,035.00
Vase, jack-in-pulpit, gold, ruffled rim, #1636H, 1900-10, 19½" .. 20,400.00

Vase, lily pads, #9822A, 6", $12,000.00. (Photo courtesy Richard Opfer Auctioneering, Inc. on LiveAuctioneers.com)

Vase, mc irid bands on whitened ground, experimental, ca 1900, 3¼"....3,000.00
Vase, peacock bl irid, #2604J, 10", NM.......................................1,450.00
Vase, pwt, leaves, gray/rose/gr on bl-purple, #7989N, 7¾".......40,250.00
Vase, pwt, purple & agate swirl, #7908N, 4".............................1,075.00
Vase, raspberry to opal, clear knop/ft, trumpet form, #1039P, 1886, 9" . 1,600.00
Vase, red, sloped shoulder, #1078A, 5¾x3"................................2,200.00
Vase, red, tall neck in Persian taste, blk ft, #2440, 11¾" 9,600.00
Vase, scallops, gold irid on gr, #Q6057, 2½"..............................2,300.00
Vase, silvery bl, baluster w/2 scroll hdls, #2985E, 9½" 3,750.00
Vase, Tel el Amarna, sgn, rare, 8½x8".......................................7,200.00
Vase, turq w/olive appl rim, shouldered, #327E, 6½" 1,725.00
Window, transom, 49 in circle/flowers/jewels/border, 15x33¾"+fr ...2,585.00
Wine, lav w/wht opal ribs, clear stem, ribbed ft, 8¼"..................1,725.00
Wine, raspberry cup w/opal stripes, gr stem (hollow) & ft, 9" ...1,375.00

Lamps

Lamp prices seem to be getting stronger, especially for leaded lamps with brighter colors (red, blue, purple). Bases that are unusual or rare have brought good prices and added to the value of the more common shades that sold on them. Bases with enamel or glass inserts are very much in demand. Our advisor for Tiffany lamps is Carl Heck; he is listed in the Directory under Colorado.

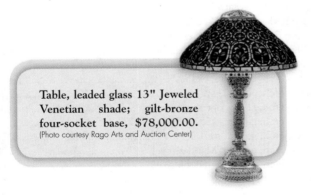

Table, leaded glass 13" Jeweled Venetian shade; gilt-bronze four-socket base, $78,000.00. (Photo courtesy Rago Arts and Auction Center)

Base only, bridge lamp, 5 legs w/spade ft, harp top, 59", EX........1,750.00
Base only, library lamp, bronze, 3-socket cluster, 22½x7½", EX..4,500.00
Boudoir, Persian, favrile shade in amber & gr w/gold dots, 11x7"....4,200.00
Chandelier, amber ripple ldgl, single-socket fixture, 14x20¼"..28,000.00
Desk, Abalone, caramel slag shade, 9" 3,900.00
Desk, Arabian, 7" etched gold shade; gr std, 14½" 6,000.00
Desk, bronze gooseneck, Quezal gold ribbed shade not orig, 10" .. 3,240.00
Desk, Pine Needle 10" domical shade; bronze std, 17¼", EX.....4,800.00
Desk, Zodiac bronze cylinder shade; wht glass diffusers, #668, 14" ...4,000.00
Floor, counterbalance, 5-ft base, gold/gr favrile damascene shade, 53x10¼"..10,200.00
Floor, damascene 11" gr shade; #582 harp std w/table/tray/etc, 57" .10,500.00
Floor, gr/yel favrile Acorn shade, gilt-bronze 5-ft base w/harp, 58x12" .15,600.00

Floor, tripod, Handel rvpt sgn shade w/floral band & bronze collar, 54¾x10"....3,600.00
Hanging, rtcl 12" shade w/blown-out gr glass body; 3-chain hanger, 30" .13,000.00
Lily, 3-lt, gr feathers on opal shades; #28593 telescopic std, 21".6,900.00
Shade, gr feathers w/gold on wht opal, stalagmite form, 13" 4,000.00
Student, dbl, platinum pattern on gold to gr bell shade; #318 std, 25" .11,500.00
Student, ldgl 10" acorn shades (2); bronze coiled rope std, 1905, 29"...21,600.00
Table, 8-panel 9" shade w/emb floral; harp std w/8-panel ft, 15"....2,000.00
Table, Acorn, mottled golden yel, 4-socket bronze, 28¾x20" .19,200.00
Table, Colonial geometric shade, 3-socket bronze library base, 1900, 22x16"..8,400.00
Table, gold waves on yel irid #S3232 shade; organic #7818 std, 24" .25,875.00
Table, Lily, 3-lt, fluted bronze base, gr leaf pattern, 22x8½" 2,040.00
Table, Lily, 3-lt, gold Favrile shades, verdigris patina, 22½x7" ..6,000.00
Table, Lily, 12-lt, gold Favrile shades on bronze, 21½x16" 25,200.00

Metal Work

Grapevine and Pine Needle are the most sought-after lines — dependent, of course, on condition. In the following listings, items are bronze unless otherwise noted.

Ashtray, clipper ship emb on center matchbox holder, #303, 5x8" ..865.00
Blotter ends, Pine Needle, #998, 12" L, pr.................................. 100.00
Blotter ends, Zodiac, #988, 19" 115.00
Blotter, Grapevine, gr glass, 3x6" 360.00
Box, Am Indian, #1192, rare, 6" L..1,100.00
Box, Grapevine w/beading, gold doré, pull-out tray, #823, rstr, 9x6"..6,900.00
Box, utility, Grapevine, gr glass, rprs, 4x6½" 515.00
Candelabrum, 2 cups, blown-out gr & gr cabochons around base, 12½x10"...3,240.00
Candelabrum, central stem w/twisted tendrils, #1230, new patina, 9x7" .3,240.00
Candlestick, rtcl cup w/gr blown-out glass, #831D, 14½", ea 4,600.00
Candlesticks, gold doré, slim stem w/padded base, #1213, 17", pr ..4,885.00
Candlesticks, Zodiac, 8-sided cups & base, 5¾", pr 1,440.00
Chamberstick, leaf base, few scratches, 8¼x6"..........................1,200.00
Clip, Zodiac, gold doré patina, #1080, 7¾x2¾" 250.00
Clock, desk, Greek Key, flaring trapezoid w/design in ea angle, 6x5" .5,400.00
Desk set, Adam, doré, blotter ends/rocker blotter/pen tray + 5 pcs.4,300.00
Desk set, Zodiac, 2 inkwells+blotter+clip+2 trays+2 holders+scale ...2,000.00
Dish, banded Moorish design, doré, #707, 9"W............................ 400.00
Fernery, turtleback tiles, 5 ft, orig liner, 3½x9½" 25,200.00
Frame, Adam, doré, #1016, 12x9", $2,750 to.............................3,150.00
Frame, Grapevine, gr glass w/gr-brn patina, 9½x8".....................3,450.00
Frame, Modeled, 11¼x8¾" 2,280.00
Frame, Pine Needle, gr glass, 8x9", EX.......................................1,035.00
Frame, Renaissance floral motif, 2 dolphins on top, 8¼x10½"+11¾x9¾" fr..1,440.00
Frame, Zodiac, EX patina, #943, 7x8" 1,550.00
Goblet, Thistle, parcel-gilt, ca 1907, 7¾x4¼"............................. 900.00
Humidor, Pine Needle, gr glass, 2 lids, #1026, 7".....................8,000.00
Inkwell, 3 scarabs support orb-like lid, EX patina, #2157, 3¾" .10,350.00
Inkwell, Am Indian, #1183, 3½"... 800.00
Inkwell, dull gold doré w/abalone, #1167, 2¾x4" 515.00
Inkwell, lime gr blown-out glass, hinged lid, 4x6½", M...........7,800.00
Inkwell, Zodiac, clear glass insert, #1072, 6½" dia 575.00
Inkwell, Zodiac, hexagonal, #842, 4" W, $350 to 480.00
Letter holder, Zodiac, 3-slot, dore, #1030, 8½x12" 660.00
Note holder, Grapevine, #1019, 4¾"... 690.00
Note pad, Zodiac, #1090, rstr finish, 4½x7½" 230.00
Paper clip, Pine Needle, gr glass, #971, 4x2½" 780.00
Paper clip, Zodiac, gr/red/brn patina, #1080, 3½x2" 345.00
Paper rack, 3-tier, no patina, #1030, 8x12" 460.00
Paperweight, Pine Needle, caramel glass, 3¾" dia 460.00
Paperweight, recumbent bulldog, 2" L.. 430.00
Paperweight, recumbent lioness, dore, #832, 5" L...................... 750.00
Paperweight, Zodiac, #935/S1006, 3½x2¼" 635.00
Plate, geometric rim, dore, #1745, 12" 345.00

Tray, Abalone, doré, #1730, 12" dia, EX 400.00
Tray, gold doré w/HP dogwood & foliage, #420, 11" 2,075.00
Wall sconce, pyramid lantern, glass tiles, unmk, 17½x5" 20,000.00

Pottery

Vase, copper clad over green high gloss glaze with deeply embossed leaves, #125, 5⅝", $9,000.00. (Photo courtesy Cincinnati Art Galleries, LLC on LiveAuctioneers.com)

Vase, dogwood blossoms emb on wht bsk, squat, #BP206, 9x14" ..5,750.00
Vase, gr/amber/brn mottle, #P1233, 16x8½", NM 4,250.00
Vase, leaves emb, sheer amber on wht clay, rstr, 4½x2¾" 800.00
Vase, Nouveau floral w/shaped rim, pastel, 10", NM 1,325.00
Vase, verdigris, gourd shape, hairlines, 16¼x7½" 3,500.00

Silver

Key: t-oz — troy ounces

Basket, rtcl rim w/berries & leaves, 5x11", 39-t-oz 6,615.00
Bowl, floral w/rtcl along rim, ftd, gilt int, 5x12" 2,750.00
Bowl, scalloped & rtcl border, 9" 360.00
Candelabra, 3-branch, repoussé flowers/claw ft, 17", 110-t-oz ..17,250.00
Child's set, knife, spoon & fork w/nursery characters, 5-t-oz 600.00

Demitasse set, shell-and-scroll band, acid-engraved panels framed by shells and bellflowers, acanthus crests to handles, circa 1900, pot: 8", $3,000.00. (Photo courtesy New Orleans Auction Galleries, Inc. on LiveAuctioneers.com)

Flask, flattened oval w/emb floral branch, 5-t-oz......................1,550.00
Knife/fork set, 2-tine forks/knives w/serrated saw bks, 1900s, 16-pc ...1,725.00
Plate, bl fleur-de-lis enameling at rim, 10" 425.00
Salver, appl floral decor at rim, 8½" dia, 14-t-ozs 325.00
Serving dish, acanthus leaves/pineapples, w/lid, 7x14", 51.5-t-oz ..2,645.00
Tea set, ribbed bodies/scroll hdls, 5¼" pot+cr/sug, 23.7-t-oz......1,035.00
Vase, flower form, slim, ftd, 6", pr... 300.00

Tiffin Glass

The Tiffin Glass Company was founded in 1889 in Tiffin, Ohio, one of the many factories composing the U.S. Glass Company. Its early wares consisted of tablewares and decorative items such as lamps and globes. Among the most popular of all Tiffin products was the stemware produced there during the 1920s. In 1959 U.S. Glass was sold, and in 1962 the factories closed. The plant was re-opened in 1963 as the Tiffin Art Glass Company. Products from this period were tableware, hand-blown stemware, and other decorative items. Information about the Tiffin Glass

Collectors can be found in the Clubs, Newsletters, and Websites section. See also Glass Animals and Figurines.

Cadena etch, cordial, topaz, 4¼" 50.00
Cadena etch, goblet, crystal, 7½" 36.00
Cadena etch, goblet, topaz, 7½" 60.00
Cadena etch, plate, salad, 7½" 14.00
Cadena etch, sugar, 2 hdls, ftd, 3½" 24.00
Candy w/lid #9557, bl w/canary ft, ½-lb 80.00
Carved Roses, sand cvd, sweet pea vase, ftd 70.00
Cherokee Rose etch, bowl, flared, 12¾" 75.00
Cherokee Rose etch, celery, 10½" 45.00
Cherokee Rose etch, cordial, 1-oz, 5¼" 50.00
Cherokee Rose etch, creamer, open hdl 30.00
Cherokee Rose etch, iced tea, ftd, 6½" 28.00

Cherokee Rose etch, plate, 8", each $15.00. (Photo courtesy Livingston's Auction on LiveAuctioneers.com)

Cherokee Rose etch, s&p, pr 140.00
Cherokee Rose etch, sugar, open, 2 beaded hdls 30.00
Cherokee Rose etch, vase, ftd, 8" 30.00
Classic etch, plate, salad, 7¼" 22.00
Classic etch, tumbler, flat, 8-oz, 4½" 16.00
Classic etch, tumbler, flat, 11-oz, 5¼" 22.00
Classic etch, tumbler, ftd, gr w/gold encrustation 120.00
Classic etch, wine, 3-oz, 5" 30.00
Draped nude, cordial #17603, crystal w/bl stem 120.00
Draped nude, goblet #17603, crystal w/frosted stem 90.00
Empress, Emp Vase, #6570, emerald gr, 14" 150.00
Flanders etch, 2-pc, grapefruit & liner, 4½" 75.00
Flanders etch, bonbon, pk, 2 hdls 75.00
Flanders etch, compote, pk, 5½" 120.00
Flanders etch, cordial, 1½-oz, 5" 32.00
Flanders etch, cr/sug, open, pr 100.00
Flanders etch, goblet #15024, 8¼" 30.00
Flanders etch, goblet, #17601, 6½" 28.00
Flanders etch, pitcher, Mandarin yel, 9½" 250.00
Flanders etch, plate, dinner, pk, 10¼" 145.00
Flanders, etch, goblet #15024, pk 8¼" 48.00
Fontaine etch, goblet, gr ft & stem, crystal bowl, 8¼" 90.00
Fontaine etch, goblet, pk, 8¼" 75.00
Fontaine etch, goblet, twilite bl, 8¼" 120.00
Fontaine etch, pitcher w/lid, twilite bl 750.00
Fontaine etch, plate, salad, 8¼" 35.00
Fontaine etch, tumbler, ftd, 10-oz, 5½" 75.00
Fuchsia etch, celery 10" 28.00
Fuchsia etch, champagne/sherbet 5½" 18.00
Fuchsia etch, creamer beaded hdl, flat 35.00
Fuchsia etch, creamer, ftd 35.00
Fuchsia etch, goblet, #1508, 7½" 24.00
Fuchsia etch, iced tea, ftd, 6¾" 20.00
Fuchsia etch, plate, luncheon, 8⅛" 15.00
Julia etch, candy jar, crystal w/amber lid & ft, ½-lb 85.00

Julia etch, plate, dinner, amber 24.00
June night etch, candlestick, 2-lite, ea 60.00
June Night etch, cordial, 5⅛" 35.00
June Night etch, goblet #17378 7¾" 45.00
June Night etch, plate, luncheon, 8⅛" 21.00
June Night etch, relish, rnd, 3-part, 6½" 35.00
June Night etch, vase, bud, ftd, 10½" 40.00
Modern, Italian ft, cr/sug, #17430, pr 150.00
Modern, Pagoda vase, #17350 Copen bl, 10" 200.00
Modern, vase, 6008-R, Wisteria, ftd, ring optic, 8" 250.00
Psyche etch, finger bowl, ftd 30.00
Psyche etch, sherbet/champagne, grn stem & ft, crystal bowl, 5½" ..36.00

Miscellaneous

Basket, blk satin w/ parrot on branch, 1920s-30s, 10¼x4" 75.00
Bath salt jar/vase, Reflex Green w/emb floral, 5x6" 225.00

Lamp, Fruit Basket, black amethyst base, 8", $250.00.
(Photo courtesy B. S. Slosberg Inc. Auctioneers on LiveAuctioneers.com)

Lamp, Girl #E-3, pk, 1923, 10", $450 to 500.00
Lamp, Santa Claus in chimney, mc fired-on pnt, 1920s, 10x4" .1,950.00
Pitcher, Columbine variant floral cut, clear w/amber hdl/ft, 10" .. 145.00
Puff box, dancing girl, pk satin, #9313, 1924, 6", $150 to 175.00
Sign, dealer, 'Tiffin,' blk shield w/gold décor 250.00
Vase, amberina satin on separate blk ped base, 6" 60.00
Vase, blk satin w/coralene poppies, bulb, 5x5" 125.00
Vase, blk satin w/silver o/l leaf & flower, HP parrot, 6" 250.00
Vase, bl satin w/Rockwell silver o/l, trumpet top, open hdls, ftd, 7"..80.00
Vase, Killarney Gr, str sides, clear ftd base, 11x6½" 75.00
Vase, poppies relief on blk satin, bulb, 5", NM 65.00
Wall pocket, bl, morning glory w/stem curling over top, 8", pr 90.00

Tiles

Revival of the ancient art of tile-making dates to mid-nineteenth century England. Following the invention of the dust-pressing process for the manufacturing of buttons, potteries such as Minton and Wedgwood borrowed the technique for mass producing tiles. The Industrial Revolution market thus encouraged replacing the time-consuming medieval encaustic or inlay process for the foolproof press-molding method or the very decorative transfer-print. English tiles adorned American buildings until a good native alternative became available following the Philadelphia Centennial Exposition of 1876. Shortly thereafter, important tile companies sprung up around Boston, Trenton, and East Liverpool, Ohio. By the turn of the century, Victorian aesthetics began to give way to the Arts and Crafts style that was being set forth by John Ruskin and Thomas Carlyle and practiced by William Morris and his Pre-Raphaelite Brotherhood. Tile bodies were once more pressed from wet or faience clay and decorated in bas-relief or in the ancient Spanish techniques of cuenca or cuerda seca. The glazes adorning them became matt and vegetal, reflecting the movement's fondness for medieval and Japanese aesthetics. During the 1920s designs became simpler and more commercialized, but some important artists were still employed by the larger companies (for example, Louis Solon at American Encaustic Tiling Co.), and the California tile industry continued to reflect the love of nature and Spanish Missions well into the 1930s.

Collecting tiles today means purchasing architectural salvage or new old stock. Arts and Crafts pottery and tiles are still extremely collectible. Important and large panels will fetch prices into the six figures. The prices for Victorian tiles have not increased over the last decade, but the value of California tiles, both matt and glossy, has gone through the roof. Catalina pottery and tile collectors are a particularly voracious lot. Larger pieces usually bring more, and condition is paramount. Look for damage and repair, as tiles often will chip or crack during the removal process. Our advisor for this category is Suzanne Perrault; she is listed in the Directory under New Jersey. See also California Faience; Grueby; Newcomb College; Rookwood; other specific manufacturers.

Key: AE — American Encaustic Tiling Co.

AE, Middle Ages man (& lady), gr gloss, 6", pr, EX 195.00
AE, Middle Ages man w/lute (& lady), 3-pc, 19¼x7¼", pr, EX........... 395.00
AE, pr of tiles: man & woman, squeeze-bag decor, ca 1930s, 9" .4,200.00
California Art Tile, mission courtyard, candle sconces, 13½", pr .1,950.00
Cecil Jones, Diana & Her Quarry, Art Deco, mc, 12x8¾", pr 840.00
Claycraft, CA coastline scene, 7½x3¾"+new Arts & Crafts fr .2,000.00
Claycraft, Conestoga wagon scene, mc, 8x16½"+fr 1,500.00
Claycraft, flowers in bowl in cuenca, mc on blk, sm flecks, 7¾" ... 725.00
Claycraft, landscape w/lg plant & mission beyond, mc matt, 7¾x4"+fr ... 960.00
Claycraft, landscape w/tree, modeled, mc matt, 7½x3¾" 1,920.00
Claycraft, mission courtyard w/fountain, mc matt, rstr, 8½x6½" .. 1,550.00
Claycraft, pirates on deck of ship, mc matt, 11¾x15¾" 2,150.00
Claycraft, Rocky Mountain road, mc matt, 12x4"+new Arts & Crafts fr.. 1,500.00
De Porceleyne Fles, cat perched on book, 8¾x4¾" 1,325.00
De Porceleyne Fles, deer hunt scene in snow, rstr, 4¾x17¼" 575.00
De Porceleyne Fles, flamingo faces right, chips, 12x4½" 550.00
De Porceleyne Fles, ostrich, mc, 5-color, nicks, 8x4" 360.00
De Porceleyne Fles, parrot, 12¾x4¾" 550.00
De Porceleyne Fles, peacock on brick wall, 13x4¾" 550.00
De Porceleyne Fles, swan facing right in cuenca, 4¾x8¾"+fr....... 495.00
De Porceleyne Fles, tiger leaping, sm amber border tiles, 5x13½" . 480.00
De Porceleyne Fles, wht rooster w/red comb on bl, 8¾x4¾"+fr ... 600.00
Flint, Arts & Crafts design, 6-color, 6"... 90.00
Flint, court servant w/turkey on platter, nicks, 4¼" 265.00

Flint, Hereford Hazford Bocaldo 3d., in cuenca, touchups, restoration, 12", $1,560.00.
(Photo courtesy Rago Auctions)

Franklin, swan facing left, gr/bl/wht, sm rstr, 8½"+fr 415.00
Grueby-Pardee, Cheshire Cat perched in tree, 4½" 1,950.00
Grueby-Pardee, chick, yel on bl-gr, flakes, 4¼" 1,025.00
Grueby-Pardee, frog footmen from Alice in Wonderland, nicks, 4¼" .. 1,100.00
Hamilton, deer in forest, brn/gr/cobalt, nicks/rubs, 6x12" 300.00
Harris Strong, harbor scene, 4-tile frieze, 13x30"+fr.................... 165.00
Harris Strong, lady's portrait, 8-tile frieze, 24x12"+fr 645.00
Harris Strong, nobleman w/pointed beard, 6-tile frieze, 24x12"+fr .. 195.00
Harris Strong, NY from East River, 12x12+orig fr 195.00

Hartford, eagle in dmn fr among foliage, mottled brn on gr, 6".... 515.00
Hartford, Eventide, pre-Raphaelite lady, mc, 13x7¾"................6,000.00
Hartford, maiden seated in hilly landscape, mosaic panel in 19x13" fr ...7,800.00
J&JG Low, Nunovam Satis, old man w/bag, cobalt, plastic sketch, 6".. 150.00
J&JG Low, violin player, amber, plastic sketch, 16½x10½" 1,920.00
Mosaic Tile, elephant on ball, advertising pc, chip, 6" 4,800.00
Muller, farmer sowing, mc matt, cvd, 12¼x6"......................... 960.00
Paducah, pine branch, caramel & indigo microcrystalline, 6", pr . 780.00
Providential, lady's portrait, amber, 6"+ornate fr 180.00
Rozenburg, Dutch cityscape w/canal, 12-tile panel, chip, 18x24"+fr .2,400.00
San Jose, cactus, mc, Mexican A & C mk, 8"............................. 600.00

San Jose, courtship scene, 15-tile panel, cuerda seca, unmarked, 17x29", $18,000.00.
(Photo courtesy Rago Auctions)

San Jose, covered wagon & oxen, unmk, 8x13"...................... 825.00
Trent, cavalier holding flute, amber, 3-tile frieze, chips, 18x6"+fr . 300.00
Trent, girl's portrait facing right, gr-gold, ca 1890, 2⅝" dia............. 85.00
Trent, maidens (3) reclining, brn, 3-tile frieze, 6x18"+fr.............. 900.00

Tinware

In the American household of the seventeenth and eighteenth centuries, tinware items could be found in abundance, from food containers to foot warmers and mirror frames. Although the first settlers brought much of their tinware with them from Europe, by 1798 sheets of tin plate were being imported from England for use by the growing number of American tinsmiths. Tinwares were often decorated either by piercing or painted designs which were both freehand and stenciled. (See Toleware.) By the early 1900s, many homes had replaced their old tinware with the more attractive aluminum and graniteware. In the nineteenth century, tenth wedding anniversaries were traditionally celebrated by gifts of tin. Couples gave big parties, dressed in their wedding clothes, and reaffirmed their vows before their friends and families who arrived bearing (and often wearing) tin gifts, most of which were quite humorous. Anniversary tin items may include hats, cradles, slippers and shoes, and rolling pins. See also Kitchen Collectibles; Primitives.

Candlestick sconce with star decoration, eighteenth to nineteenth century, 12", $170.00.
(Photo courtesy C. Downing Auctions, LLC on LiveAuctioneers.com)

Anniversary pc, hat, corrugated tin band & bow, old pnt, 5"....... 700.00
Anniversary pc, top hat, rust throughout, 6½x12"........................ 635.00
Anniversary pc, top hat, w/tin ribbon, 6"................................1,450.00
Candle box, cylindrical, brass fastener, hinged, 14x3½" dia 70.00
Candle box, cylindrical, wall mt, old blk pnt, 6½x10½".............. 240.00
Candle box, cylindrical w/fan bk, wall mk, old gr pnt, 10x11"..... 240.00
Coffee roaster, cylindrical, long iron hdl, 18th C, 44" L.............. 400.00
Coffeepot, gooseneck spout, brass finial, punched decor, lt rust, 11" ... 515.00
Coffeepot, gooseneck spout, padded hdl, punched decor, hinged lid, 11".. 1,450.00
Coffeepot, punched pots of tulips/intertwined lines, brass finial, 11" .230.00
Coffeepot, tapered cylinder, S Culver...1858...NY, 20x13x9"....1,150.00
Coffeepot, wrigglework, eagle w/snake & Am flag, 8¾", EX......3,150.00
Colander, appl hdls, ca 1880-1900s, 5x7" 55.00
Colander, berry, heart shape, 19th C, 4x4" 300.00
Comb case, punched designs w/wood bk & fr mirror, 10"........... 200.00
Infant feeder, conical, sm spout & strap hdl, w/cap, 4⅞" 300.00
Sconces, crimped arched/pierced bk panels, 19th C, 7⅞", pr 180.00
Sconces, crimped pans w/circular reflectors, 9¼" dia, pr.............. 575.00
Sconces, oval mirrored bks, 19th C, 15¼x7⅝"..........................3,850.00
Sconces, semicircular base w/raised rings/folded rim, 11x8", pr. 1,025.00
Strainer, cheese, punched heart shape, 3¼x6x5⅝"...................... 240.00
Strainer, dmn shape, punched tin, possibly slave made, 4¼x9¼"... 55.00
Strainer, oval w/fine mesh fitted strainer, hdls, 3x9½" 125.00
Teakettle, domed lid, bail hdl, 7½"... 50.00
Tinder box, rnd w/hdl & candle socket on lid, w/damper/striker, 4" ..300.00

Tobacciana

Tobacciana is the generally accepted term used to cover a field of collecting that includes smoking pipes, cigar molds, cigarette lighters, humidors — in short, any article having to do with the practice of using tobacco in any form. Perhaps the most valuable variety of pipes is the meerschaum, hand carved from hydrous magnesium, an opaque white-gray or cream-colored mineral of the soapstone family. (Much of this is today mined in Turkey which has the largest meerschaum deposit in the world, though there are other deposits of lesser significance around the globe.) These figural bowls often portray an elaborately carved mythological character, an animal, or a historical scene. Amber is sometimes used for the stem. Other collectible pipes are corn cob (Missouri Meerschaum) and Indian peace pipes of clay or catlinite. (See American Indian Art.)

Chosen because it was the Indians who first introduced the white man to smoking, the cigar store Indian was a symbol used to identify tobacco stores in the nineteenth century. The majority of them were hand carved between 1830 and 1900 and are today recognized as some of the finest examples of early wood sculptures. When found they command very high prices.

Unless otherwise noted, values are given for examples in undamaged, near mint condition. See also Advertising; Snuff Boxes.

Ashtray, 3 brass trays remove from base w/SP horse at side, Ronson.. 78.00
Ashtray, cigar, clear crystal, Dunhill, 1¼x6⅞x4½"........................... 75.00
Ashtray, hunting dogs emb on brass, England, 1930s-40s, 5½x3¼"..50.00
Ashtray, laughing man's head, metal w/rhinestone eye/striker, 4½x3" ...60.00
Ashtray, man's face/wide mouth, ceramic, Down By...Mill Stream, 5½". 45.00
Ashtray, nude w/fans, chrome, at side of blk glass tray, 4½x5" 100.00
Ashtray, pheasants (2), mc on bronze, on side of onyx tray, 4½x7"..235.00
Ashtray, smoke glass, triangular w/3 rests, 3x10" 72.50
Cigar cutter, 3-hole countertop style, brass, London, 3x6¼" 90.00
Cigar cutter, Amsterdam ship's wheel, brass, wheel turns, 5" 95.00
Cigar cutter, Artie Cigar, CI, figural Artie seated atop, 10x6x7", EX+ . 2,700.00
Cigar cutter, Country Gentleman, counter style, 1891................. 360.00
Cigar cutter, dachshund figural hdl, brass & steel, 5".................... 200.00
Cigar cutter, elephant, bronze, 6½x10" 780.00
Cigar cutter, fish form, silver, US Tobacco, much detail, rare ...6,000.00

Cigar cutter, General Green, CI w/rnd portrait insert, 1890s, 8", EX+ . 2,400.00
Cigar cutter, Grand Union Havana Cigars, NP, 1890s, 3x3½x2", VG ... 140.00
Cigar cutter, King Alfred...on rnd CI clock face, ftd base, 13", VG+ . 2,300.00
Cigar cutter, Manhattan Girl, paper litho/glass dome/wood base, VG ... 745.00
Cigar cutter, monkey on top hat, brass.. 120.00
Cigar cutter, Old Crow, figural CI pig on tray, 6", EX................ 1,800.00
Cigar cutter, parrot figural, 7" 420.00

Cigar cutter, pistol shape, nickel plated brass, 3", $1,080.00. (Photo courtesy Showtime Auction Services on LiveAuctioneers.com)

Cigar cutter, The Yankee, CI shield on stand, 7", EX................ 1,035.00
Cigar cutter, TTMA...5¢ Cigar, CI w/mg globe, 8½", EX.......... 2,070.00
Cigar cutter/ashtray, brass, lion's mouth opening, guillotine type, 6" ... 90.00
Cigar cutter/lighter, pnt CI elephant figure w/ruby glass lighter, VG . 3,450.00
Cigar holder, 3 joined cylinders w/hinged lid, silver, 2-oz............. 215.00
Cigar lighter, 1880s gentleman, metal, kerosene burner, 6½", EX. 300.00
Cigar lighter, bear figural, NP metal, head removes, rpl base, 4½"...210.00
Cigar lighter, black man's bust on taloned ft, brass, 10" 2,450.00
Cigar lighter, cloisonné font w/ft, 2 brass lighters/ruby shade, 11"...345.00

Cigarette lighter, Dunhill M, stainless steel MG sports car on rubber tires, 6", $960.00. (Photo courtesy Lloyd Ralston Gallery on LiveAuctioneers.com)

Cigar lighter, eagle figural, brass, European, heavy, 8" 100.00
Cigar lighter, gr glass globe on ornate wht metal ftd base, 14", VG....115.00
Cigar lighter, man in chair figural, CI, basket on bk, 6x3½x4", EX .. 180.00
Cigar lighter, man's bust on claw ft, brass, 9¾" 240.00
Cigar lighter, poodle wearing top hat, CI, kerosene, 4x3x1½", EX...240.00
Cigar lighter, Punch figural, brass, w/gas line, 7x2¾", EX............. 100.00
Cigar lighter/holder, black man sitting, copper-tone wht metal, 6"..30.00
Cigarette box, Nouveau lady w/flowers emb, Sterling silver, 4".... 850.00
Cigarette box, SP w/wood liner, Apollo, 2x7¾x3½" 20.00
Cigarette case, diagonal design on 14k yel gold, push-button closure . 1,175.00
Cigarette case, early open auto enameled on sterling, 3½x2½" 600.00
Cigarette case, Japanese damascene landscape w/flowers, 3½x2½"...60.00
Cigarette case, silver w/eng decor, 1850s, 5½" L 215.00
Cigarette dispenser, man w/bow tie figural, Germany, ca 1925..... 600.00
Cigarette holder, stag figural, cold-pnt spelter, 10x9½", EX............ 36.00
Cigarette holder/music box, carousel form, porc, 15½x6" 180.00
Cigarette lighter, black bartender, touch-top, Ronson, 7", NM. 3,250.00
Cigarette lighter, courting scene HP on silver, 1930s, 2¼x1½" 660.00
Cigarette lighter, draped nude figural, electric, 1920s, 6½", VG+ . 275.00
Humidor, bearded man's head, bl cossack hat, majolica, 6" 70.00
Humidor, black banjo player HP on porc, metal lid...................... 360.00
Humidor, black man in hat holding matchbox, 7"......................... 700.00
Humidor, boy's face emerging from tobacco leaves, ceramic, 5"... 155.00
Humidor, burlwood, 6-sided, Alfred Dunhill, 7x7½" 780.00
Humidor, dog's head, ceramic, brn, 6½" 165.00
Humidor, man on recumbent camel, majolica, mc, 8¼", EX 215.00
Pipe box, brn-pnt cherry wood, dvtl drw, brass knobs, 19th C, 21x5x4".... 8,800.00
Pipe, meerschaum, galloping horse, amber stem, 3¼x7½", +case. 275.00
Pipe, meerschaum, tiger (3" figure), w/stem 120.00
Store figure, Indian chief looking away, cvd wood, mc pnt, 1950s, 75"...1,100.00

Store figure, Indian chief, cvd wood, mc pnt, 72" 875.00
Store figure, maiden w/feather headdress, cvd/pnt wood, 19th C, 61".. 4,400.00
Store figure, well-dressed blk man, cvd wood w/mc pnt, rstr, 27", VG.. 2,650.00
Tobacco blanket, Boston Braves, bright mc, 1914 .... 30.00
Tobacco blanket, NY Yankees, bl infield (rare), 1914.................... 30.00
Tobacco blanket, Walter Johnson of Senators, 1914 .... 180.00
Tobacco card, Hoffman of St Louis, Sweet Caporal #50, 1909....... 36.00
Tobacco card, Robt Byrne of Pittsburgh Pirates, 1911, VG............ 18.00
Tobacco card, Yerkes of Boston Red Sox, recruit bk, 1912 .... 24.00
Tobacco cutter, Master Workman, CI, 10½" L................................ 90.00
Tobacco cutter, Shamrock Smoking Plug, CI on wood base, 10¾" .. 120.00
Tobacco rug, 48-star flag, Fed Shields, 10½x15" 60.00
Tobacco rug, University of PA, Fatima, 13x28" 215.00

Toby Jugs

The delightful jug known as the Toby dates back to the eighteenth century, when factories in England produced them for export to the American colonies. Named for the character Toby Philpots in the song *The Little Brown Jug,* the Toby was fashioned in the form of a jolly fellow, usually holding a jug of beer and a glass. The earlier examples were made with strict attention to details such as fingernails and teeth. Originally representing only a non-entity, a trend developed to portray well-known individuals such as George II, Napoleon, and Ben Franklin. Among the most valued Tobies are those produced by Ralph Wood I in the late 1700s. By the mid-1830s Tobies were being made in America. When no manufacturer is given, assume the Toby to have been made in Staffordshire, nineteenth century; unless otherwise described, because of space restrictions, assume the model is of a seated man. See also Occupied Japan; Royal Doulton.

Drinking from a toby jug, Pratt type, 9¾", $1,800.00. (Photo courtesy Leslie Hindman Auctioneers on LiveAuctioneers.com)

Holding bl lantern, spout in bk of chair, 9¼", EX 425.00
Holding cup/jug, pearlware, red face, caryatid hdl, 10"............. 1,450.00
Holding empty jug, pearlware, brn face, R Wood type, 10" 1,650.00
Holding jug & cup, gr coat/yel pants, figurehead hdl, 9" 550.00
Holding jug & cup, pipe at side, R Wood type, 18th C, 9¾" 1,650.00
Holding jug, brn coat/blk hat, mk Walton, 10"........................... 1,325.00
Holding jug, defined laces, att Wood, rprs, early 19th C, 10" 1,100.00
Holding jug, pipe at side, pearlware, R Wood type, 18th C, 10" 900.00
Holding mug of ale, unmk, ca 1880, 8½", $400 to 500.00
Lord How (sic) seated on sea chest, anchor at ft, Wood type, rprs, 12"...3,100.00
Lord Howe seated on bbl w/jug, dog & pipe beside, R Wood type, 10"...6,400.00
Merry Christmas version, holly decor, unmk, late 1800s, 6", $400 to ... 500.00
On bbl w/bottle/tumbler, Rockingham w/gr, 13" 2,100.00
Squire seated w/bulging eyes, arsenic glazes, R Wood, rprs, 11" ... 950.00
Whieldon type, brn mottled underglaze, unmk, 9½", $500 to 600.00
William Kent, Willow in bl w/HP colors & blk trim, mid-1900s, 5"....900.00
Yorkshire type, Pratt palette, cover formed as a cup, 10" 2,470.00

Toleware

The term 'toleware' originally came from a French term meaning 'sheet iron.' Today it is used to refer to paint-decorated tin items, most popular from 1800 to 1850s. The craft flourished in Pennsylvania, Connecticut, Maine, and New York. Early toleware has a very distinctive look. The surface is dull and unvarnished; background colors range from black to cream. Geometrics are quite common, but florals and fruits were also favored. Items made after 1850 were often stenciled, and gold trim was sometimes added. American toleware is usually found in practical, everyday forms — trays, boxes, and coffeepots are most common — while French examples might include candlesticks, wine coolers, and jardinieres. Be sure to note color and design when determining date and value, but condition of the paint is the most important worth-assessing factor. Unless noted otherwise, values are for very good examples with average wear.

Tray, strong original colors, possibly Pennsylvania or Connecticut, early nineteenth century, 13½" long, $5,100.00. (Photo courtesy Leslie Hindman Auctioneers on LiveAuctioneers.com)

Box, blueberries/strawberries on blk, yel border, 5½x9x5" 3,500.00
Box, deed, floral/foliage on dk japanning, dome lid, worn, 5½x9". 950.00
Box, deed, swags on blk japanning, dome top, 19th C, 6½x10" . 1,200.00
Canister, chinoiserie/gold bands on blk japanning, 1850s, 13½x11" ... 780.00
Canister, stenciled landscape/flowers on blk japanning, 18x11" dia...480.00
Coffeepot, apples/lt gr foliage on blk, str spout, C-hdl, 9", NM..6,000.00
Coffeepot, bird on branch, strong colors on blk, 19th C, PA, 11" .. 4,050.00
Coffeepot, fruit, red/etc on blk, flaring sides, 10½", EX 4,500.00
Coffeepot, fruit/flowers, blk/dk red on red, dome lid, 11" 4,500.00
Coffeepot, pomegranate band, yel on red, 2nd band under dome lid, 11" . 2,700.00
Creamer, stylized balls, red/pk on blk, w/lid, flakes, 4¼" 275.00
Tea caddy, stylized decor, blk/yel on red, 4¼x3½x2", EX 1,175.00
Teapot, floral, mc on blk, hinged lid, pnt losses, 5½" 325.00
Teapot, red & blk marbled w/Greek key border, urn form, 1820s, 9½" . 500.00
Tray, bread, floral border/mc on blk japanning, 12½x7⅞"............. 780.00
Tray, bread, floral on blk w/yel band, flaking pnt, 4x12x8" 395.00
Tray, floral on red, 19th C, 26½" dia... 725.00
Tray, peacock & flowers on blk japanning w/gold, hdls, 22x16" ... 230.00

Tools

Before the Civil War, tools for the most part were handmade. Some were primitive to the point of crudeness, while others reflected the skill of those who took pride in their trade. Increasing demand for quality tools and the dawning of the age of industrialization resulted in tools that were mass produced. Factors important in evaluating antique tools are scarcity, usefulness, and portability. Those with a manufacturer's mark are worth more than unmarked items. When no condition is indicated, the items listed here are assumed to be in excellent condition. For more information, we recommend *Antique Tools* by Kathryn McNerney (Collector Books). See also Keen Kutter; Winchester.

Key: tpi — teeth per inch

Adz, carpenter's, True Temper, polled, 4" blade, 10" hdl, VG 75.00
Axe, dbl blades, stamped JR, punched stars, walnut hdl, 12x14" .175.00
Bevel, sliding T, Stanley #25, gold letters on rosewood hdl, 10", NM....37.50
Chisel, OH Tool Co, ¾-corner, 8" blade, 16", VG+ 65.00
Chisel, Stanley #50 Everlasting, ½" bevel-edge butt, 8¾", VG 75.00
Chisel, Zenith, 1" bevel-edge socket firmer, 6" blade, 14", EX 50.00
Draw knife, OH Tool Co, laminated blade, folding hdls, 8", EX.... 85.00
Draw knife, Whitherby, laminated blade, ebonized hdls, 6", VG ... 35.00
Drill, breast, Millers Falls #120B, 2-speed, 3-jaw chuck, NM......... 55.00
Drill, hand, Goodell Pratt #4½, 3-jaw, Pat Aug 13 1895, VG 50.00
Gauge, marking, Stanley #65, boxwood, sweetheart logo, NM...... 32.50
Gouge, Buck Brothers #8, ¹⁄₁₆" med sweep, VG............................. 32.50
Gouge, Herring Bros #3⅝", EX 35.00
Hammer, plumb claw, Signature, orig hdl, 13-oz, VG................... 32.00
Hammer, tack, Capewell, spring-loaded puller, Pat Nov 25 1873, EX...80.00
Hatchet, Stanley, 1¼-lb, 2¾" blade, 13½", VG............................. 35.00
Level, Goodell Pratt, CI, rnded ends, EX japanning...................... 200.00
Nippers, Sargent & Co, Bernard's Pat, 6", EX+ 32.50
Nippers, W Schollhorn, Bernard's Pat Oct 24 1899, EX NP, EX.... 30.00
Plane, block, Fulton #102, NM japanning 30.00
Plane, block, Stanley #9½, adjustable throat & cutter, NMIB 90.00
Plane, circular, Stanley #113, Type 1, Pat 1876/1877, VG........... 235.00

Plane, combination, Stanley #45 Sweetheart, 13½", $90.00. (Photo courtesy Auction Ohio on LiveAuctioneers.com)

Plane, jack, Stanley #5C, type 11, T trademk, rosewood hdl, EX.. 100.00
Plane, jointer, Stanley #8, full-length cutter, rosewood hdl, EX... 200.00
Plane, jointer, Union Mfg #X-8, mahog hdl, Pat 12/8/(19)03, EX ..285.00
Plane, smooth, Stanley #4½, type 11, Pat 1902/1910, VG 120.00
Plane, smooth, Stanley #4, rosewood hdl, Pat 1910, NM japanning... 115.00
Plumb bob, K&E #6482, long neck, 16-oz, VG 45.00
Router, Stanley #17, open throat, ebonized hdls, Made in USA, 1950s, M 110.00
Rule, Rabone #1167, boxwood, 4-fold w/rnd joint, 24", M 45.00
Saw set, Morrill's Pat, for handsaws/panel saws, Pats 1887/1890, VG ..12.50
Saw vice, unmk, 9" jaws, lt duty, cam-lock jaws, VG 40.00
Saw, docking, Disston #498, 4½ tpi, 30", VG................................ 60.00
Saw, rip, Geo Bishop & Co #B-80, 5½ tpi, 28", EX 145.00
Scraper, cabinet, Stanley #82, 2 cutters, NM................................. 55.00
Spoke shave, Crescent, flat bottom, loop hdls, VG japanning 45.00

Spoke shave, Louis D. Presser, brass, $60.00. (Photo courtesy Hassinger & Courtney Auctioneering on LiveAuctioneers.com)

Spoke shave, Phelps Bros, NP brass, flat bottom, 3¾" L, VG 85.00
Spoke shave, Stanley #67 Universal, rnd sole, removable hdls, EX .85.00
Square, take-down framing, Eagle Sq Mfg, Pat 1894/1899, VG ... 175.00
Square, try/miter, Stanley #1, NP, sweetheart mk, 6", VG.............. 25.00
Wrench, buggy, Dmn Wrench Co, Pat Nov 2 80, pitting, 12", G .. 40.00
Wrench, crescent, Challenger, 4", NM 25.00
Wrench, pipe, Sheffy Mfg Chicago, self-adjust, Pat'd Jan 24 1896, VG .125.00

Toothbrush Holders

Most of the collectible toothbrush holders were made in prewar Japan and were modeled after popular comic strip, Disney, and nursery rhyme characters. Since many were made of bisque and decorated with unfired paint, it's not uncommon to find them in less-than-perfect paint, a factor you must consider when attempting to assess their values.

Sleepy and Dopey, copyright 1938, Disney, light paint wear, 3¼", $210.00. (Photo courtesy Dan Morphy Auctions LLC on LiveAuctioneers.com)

3 Little Pigs w/instruments, ceramic, pnt wear, 3" 55.00
Bashful dwarf, mc bsk, holder behind, Disney Foreign mk, EX 65.00
Bellboy w/2 suitcases, mc lustre, unmk Japan, 4½x5", EX 95.00
Bonzo, cold-pnt porc, Occupied Japan, 1945-53, 3¾x3¼"............. 60.00
Boston terrier w/circus collar, ceramic, sm rpt, Germany, 3½" 100.00
Boy stands w/hand in pocket, mc lustre, MIG, 4¼x2⅜" 825.00
Comic golfer, bag is holder, mc pnt, Germany, #1552, ca 1925, 8½".. 80.00
Count Chocula, 2-D plastic standup, in-pack premium ca 1970s .. 40.00
Dick Whitting sits on marker: To London 10 Miles, Japan, 4¾".... 85.00
Dog, yel & gr, ceramic, Goebel, T718/0, 4x1½x1¾" 60.00
Donald between Mickey & Minnie, base tray, pnt bsk, WD/Japan, EX .270.00
Donald Duck (L-billed), dbl figure 420.00
Equestrienne standing in red coat, blk boots/hat, Foreign/6677, 4"....150.00
Fiddler pig in sailor suit, ceramic, Walt Disney Foreign, 1930s?, 4½" .. 140.00
Genie w/sword & Blk face, stands w/toothpaste box behind, 6" ..235.00
Girl holds tray w/hole for toothbrush, celluloid, 4½", ea............... 45.00
Girl w/lg rose as skirt holds rose, Germany/15496, 5½" 65.00
Girl w/puzzled look stands by holder, mc lustre, Germany, #176, 4⅜"....80.00
Mickey & Minnie Mouse arm-in-arm, mc bsk, Japan label, 4½"...275.00
Mickey & Minnie Mouse on couch, dog at ft, pnt bsk 220.00
Mickey & Minnie Mouse, pnt bsk, W Disney, Japan, 4½x3¾", EX .210.00
Mickey Mouse holds handkerchief to Pluto's nose, ceramic, MIJ, 4¾" ...240.00
Penguin, holds 3 brushes, tray at ft, MIJ, 5½" 60.00
Pirate, holds 2 brushes, tray at ft, lt wear, Japan, 5¼", EX 60.00
Pony (wht w/lt brn & bl plaid) atop red base w/3 slots, Japan, 4¾"..45.00
Popeye the Sailor, pnt bsk, King Features/Chein, missing pipe, 1932 . 120.00
Wire-haired terrier w/bellhop toothpowder shaker hat, Germany, 4½"..210.00

Toothpick Holders

Once common on every table, the toothpick holder was relegated to the china cabinet near the turn of the century. Fortunately, this contributed to their survival. As a result, many are available to collectors today. Because they are small and easily displayed, they are very popular collectibles. They come in a wide range of prices to fit every budget. Many have

been reproduced and, unfortunately, are being offered for sale right along with the originals. These 'repros' should be priced in the $10.00 to $30.00 range. Unless you're sure of what you're buying, choose a reputable dealer. In addition to pattern glass, you'll find examples in china, bisque, art glass, and various metals. For further information we recommend *Glass Toothpick Holders* by Neila and Tom Bredehoft and Jo and Bob Sanford (Collector Books), and *China Toothpick Holders* by Judy Knauer and Sandra Raymond (Schiffer). Examples in the listings that follow are glass, unless noted otherwise, and clear unless a color is mentioned in the description. See also specific companies (such as Northwood) and types of glassware (such as Burmese, Cranberry, etc.).

Glass

Alexis (Fostoria) 50.00
Arched Fleur-de-Lis, amber stained, ca 1898, 1⅜"........................ 110.00
Bead Swag, mg 50.00
Bead Swag, vaseline 85.00
Beaded Grape, gr... 65.00
Beaumont's Columbia, ruby stain 75.00
Belladonna, ruby stain 55.00
Beveled Dmn & Star, ruby stain.. 80.00
Britannic, ruby stain 175.00
Burmese, hat form w/bl threading at collar, shiny, 2".................. 285.00
Chrysanthemum Sprig, custard 175.00
Cord Drapery, amber... 450.00
Cord Drapery, Indiana, 1898-1903 .... 160.00
Daisy & Button w/V Ornament, bl or gr.. 55.00
Deep File, National, ca 1902, 2⅜x1¾" 50.00
Esther, ruby stain.. 135.00
Feather 75.00
Feather, bl or gr.. 150.00
Flying Swan... 35.00
Garland of Roses, vaseline 85.00
Heart Band, ruby stain 60.00
Horse w/Cart, #1396, Central Glass, mid-1880s, 2½x2"................ 42.00
Jefferson #271, bl or gr... 55.00
Leaf Mould (Northwood), vaseline 350.00
Maine (Stippled Paneled Flower), emerald gr, US Glass, ca 1899, 2½"..500.00
New Jersey, ruby stain 225.00
Ohio Star 85.00
Pennsylvania, gr.. 140.00
Pillows, Heisey #325, sgn in base, 2½" 375.00
Royal Crystal, ruby stain.. 65.00
Scalloped Swirl, bl or gr.. 60.00
Snow Flake... 35.00
Sunken Primrose, ruby stain 60.00
Tokyo, bl opal, 2¼" 220.00
Winged Scroll 65.00
Winged Scroll, custard... 115.00

Novelties

Monkey with basket on back, gilded brass mounts, circa 1880s, 4", $1,080.00. (Photo courtesy Green Valley Auctions on LiveAuctioneers.com)

Boot w/spur, blk, ca 1886, 3¼x4" 125.00
Butterfly figure, amber, Buckeye Glass Co, ca 1885, 2¾" 145.00
Darwin, clear, Richards & Hartley, ca 1885, 2½x2" 68.00
Darwin, vaseline, Richards & Hartley, ca 1885, 2½x2" 150.00
Dog beside top hat, amber, 1885, 2¾x1¼" 95.00
Frog on lily pad, blk, Co-operative Flint Glass Co, ca 1886, 3½x2" .45.00
Horse w/cart, clear, rnd base, Central Glass #1396, 1885, 3x3" 65.00
Horse w/cart, yel, rnd base, Central Glass #1396, 1885, 3x3" 95.00
Pig on flat car, amber, 3x5½" 365.00
Pig on flat car, clear, 3x5½" 250.00
Skull, opal, McKee & Bros, 1899, 2½x3½" 150.00

Torquay Pottery

Torquay is a unique type of pottery made in the South Devon area of England as early as 1869. At the height of productivity, at least a dozen companies flourished there, producing simple folk pottery from the area's natural red clay. The ware was both wheel-turned and molded and decorated under the glaze with heavy slip resulting in low-relief nature subjects or simple scrollwork. Three of the best-known of these potteries were Watcombe (1869 – 1962), Aller Vale (in operation from the mid-1800s, producing domestic ware and architectural products), and Longpark (1883 until 1957). Watcombe and Aller Vale merged in 1901 and operated until 1962 under the name of Royal Aller Vale and Watcombe Art Pottery.

A decline in the popularity of the early classical terra-cotta styles (urns, busts, figures, etc.) led to the introduction of painted and glazed terra-cotta wares. During the late 1880s, white clay wares, both turned and molded, were decorated with colored glazes (Stapleton ware, grotesque molded figures, ornamental vases, large jardinieres, etc.). By the turn of the century, the market for art pottery was diminishing, so the potteries turned to wares decorated in colored slips (Barbotine, Persian, Scrolls, etc.).

Motto wares were introduced in the late nineteenth century by Aller Vale and taken up in the twentieth century by the other Torquay potteries. This eventually became the 'bread and butter' product of the local industry. This was perhaps the most famous type of ware potted in this area because of the verses, proverbs, and quotations that decorated it. This was achieved by the sgraffito technique — scratching the letters through the slip to expose the red clay underneath. The most popular patterns were Cottage, Black Cockerel, Multi-Cockerel, and a scrollwork design called Scandy. Other popular decorations were Kerswell Daisy, ships, kingfishers, applied bird decorations, Art Deco styles, Egyptian ware, and many others. Aller Vale ware may sometimes be found marked 'H.H. and Company,' a firm who assumed ownership from 1897 to 1901. 'Watcombe Torquay' was an impressed mark used from 1884 to 1927. Our advisors for this category are Jerry and Gerry Kline; they are listed in the Directory under Ohio. If you're interested in joining a Torquay club, you'll find the address of the North American Torquay Society under Clubs, Newsletters, and Websites.

Art Pottery

Bottle, scent, tan with turquoise and gold decoration, Japanese-style silver top, registration #74858, early, 2½", $600.00. (Photo courtesy Alderfer Auction Company on LiveAuctioneers.com)

Biscuit bbl, parrots on branches on bl, wrapped hdl, 6" 175.00
Bottle, scent, 3 dimples on purple, crown top, 1924-40 mk, 3½" ... 48.00

Bottle, scent, Devon Lavender/lav sprig, crown stopper, 4" 60.00
Bottle, scent, Devon Violets, Made in Great Britian, 2¼" 28.00
Bottle, scent, Longpark Pottery Co, 'Sweet Lavender,' 1905-40, 3", $55 to .. 55.00
Bottle, scent, rose, pk on bl, att Watcombe, 3" 70.00
Bottle, scent, Scandy, Exeter Art Pottery, crown stopper, 3¼" 65.00
Bowl, Blarney Castle, Watcombe, hdls, ftd, 4½x4¼" 75.00
Candlesticks, Scroll, Aller Vale, ca 1900, 6½", pr 125.00
Cat, gr, Aller Vale, rpr, 9" 495.00
Jardiniere, Daffodil, Longpark, 1910, 5½x7¼" 425.00
Jardiniere, Scroll, Aller Vale, early 1900s, 3¾" 75.00
Jug, Persian, Aller Vale, wht clay, 4½" 90.00
Jug, Ruins (Tintern Abbey), Longpark, strap hdl, 5" 125.00
Match holder/striker, boxer dog's head on collar, 1898, rare 375.00
Plate, Terra Cotta, dog w/butterfly, Watcombe, 1900s, 3" 75.00
Tray, dresser, windmill, Aller Vale, no motto, 10½x7" 395.00
Vase, Alexandria Rose, twist hdls, 4½" 65.00
Vase, fan, Kerswell Daisy variant, Aller Vale, 1887-1924, 4½" 125.00
Vase, geometric design (resembling tumbling blocks), 9½" 145.00
Vase, swan on gr tricorn shape, ca 1900, unusual, 4½" 175.00
Vase, windmill scene, Crown Dorset, motto, early 1900s, 4", pr 150.00
Wall pocket, flowers on horn shape, Exeter, 6½x4½" 175.00

Devon Motto Ware

Ashtray, Ship, Longpark, 'I'll Take the Ashes,' 4¾x3¼" 40.00
Beaker, Cottage, Dartmouth, 'Daun'ce Be 'Fraid...,' 3" 45.00
Bowl, Cottage, Watcombe, 'Masters Two Will Never...,' 3x4¼" 65.00
Bowl, junket, Scandy, 'Help Yourself...,' 3⅜x6⅞" 150.00
Bowl, Sea Gull, Dartmouth, w/motto, 1½x4" 40.00
Bowl, Shamrock, Aller Vale, 'Old Erin's Native Shamrock,' 3" 45.00
Candlestick, Cottage, Watcombe, 2½x5x4" 75.00
Candlestick, Longpark, 'Many Are Called...Few Get Up,' 3½" 50.00
Coffeepot, Black Cockerel, Watcombe, 'Before You Act...' 6¾" .. 195.00
Couldron/pot, Longpark, 'The Diels Aye Kin Lae...,' 2x4" 45.00
Creamer, Scandy, unmk, 'He Does Much Who Does...,' 3¾" 40.00
Creamer/sugar, Cottage, Watcombe, 'Yu Must' Ave/Du'ee Help' ... 70.00
Cup, Cottage, Watcombe, 'Speak Little Speak Tongue...,' 2" 30.00
Cup, Cottage, Watcombe, 'Speak Little Speak Well,' child sz, 3½" .50.00
Egg cup, Cockerel, Longpark, 'Fresh Laid,' 2½" 40.00
Egg cup, Cottage, 'Laid To Day,' 3½x3½" 45.00
Inkwell, Colored Cockerel, Aller Vale, 'Good Morning...,' 2¾" dia .. 75.00
Inkwell, Scandy, Watcombe, 'Send Us a Scrape...,' 2¾x5¼" 175.00

Inkwell, with motto in reserves around sides, 3" diameter, $95.00. (Photo courtesy Apple Tree Auction Center on LiveAuctioneers.com)

Jardiniere, Passion Flower, HM Exter, 'For Every Ill...,' 6¾" 275.00
Jug, Black Cat, Aller Vale, 'Oh Where Is My Boy Tonight,' 5x4". 195.00
Jug, Cockerel, St Mary Church Pottery Ltd, w/motto, 4¼" 65.00
Jug, Cottage, 'Help Yourself...,' 5½x4½" 80.00
Jug, Cottage, Devon, 'Time Ripens All Things,' 4" 65.00
Jug, Cottage, Watcombe, 'Better To Sit Still...Fall,' 4" 65.00
Jug, Kerswell Daisy, Aller Vale, 'Earth I Am...,' 8¼x7" 225.00
Jug, Kerswell Daisy, Aller Vale, 'Freely Drink...,' 4" 65.00
Jug, Kerswell Daisy, Aller Vale, 'There's a Saying Old...,' 8½" 225.00
Jug, Kingfisher, Torquay, 'Time & Tide...,' 1925-30, 5½" 65.00

ug, milk, bl on terra cotta, 'The Blue of Devon Torquay,' 4", $60 to . 55.00
ug, Multi-Cockerel, Aller Vale, 'Be Canny Wi...,' mini, 2½" 75.00
ug, puzzle, Colored Cockerel, 'This Yer Jug Was...,' 3½" 200.00
ug, puzzle, Primrose, Exeter, 'Within This Jug...', 4" 175.00
ug, Scandy, Aller Vale, 'Demsher Craim Yak...,' 2½" 50.00
ug, Scandy, Longpark, 'Niver Zay Die...,' 3-hdl, 3¼" 65.00
ug, Ship, 'A Rolling Stone Gathers...,' Bridlington souvenir, 5"... 65.00
Match striker, Scandy, 2" 85.00
Mug, Cottage, 'Up to the Lips Over the Gums...', 5" 95.00
Mug, Cottage, Watcombe, 'From Rocks & Sands...,' 4½x5½" 85.00
Mug, shaving, Cottage, Watcombe, 'Hair on Head Is Worth...', 3"..175.00
Mug, Thistle, 'There's No Time Like Now,' 3¼" 45.00
Plate, Black Cockerel, Longpark, 'Guide Folks Be...,' 7½" 110.00
Teapot, 'May the hinges of friendship never go rusty,' 6½" 125.00
Teapot, Colored Cockerel, Longpark, motto, 3½" 150.00
Tray, Black Cockerel, Watcombe, 'There's a Saying...,' 11x7½" ... 300.00

Tortoiseshell

The outer shell of several species of land turtles, called tortoises, was once commonly used to make brooches, combs, small boxes, and novelty items. It was often used for inlay as well. The material is easily recognized by its mottled brown and yellow coloring. Because some of these turtles are now on the endangered list, such use is prohibited.

Tea caddy, serpentine, 7", $2,600.00.

Box, dome lid, rect, 1x3½x2" 240.00
Box, jewelry, simple inlay, fitted drw, 8¼x11⅛x8⅛" 600.00
Box, repoussé silver corner mts/medallion, Asian, 19th C, 2½x6x4".. 450.00
Box, w/ivory plaque on chamfered hinged lid, bone ft, 1½x2x1½"...325.00
Cape clasp, pin-bk terminals ea w/cameo floral in pearl surround, 6" L..420.00
Case, calling card, cvd lady w/harp/cherubs/lattice bower, 19th C, 4" ..540.00
Clock, dmn encrusted hands, easel bk, wind-up, working, 3½x3" .. 480.00
Coin purse, satin lined w/compartments, nickel-silver trim, 3x2". 120.00
Notebook cover, silver/MOP inlay, velvet int, ca 1900, 4x3", EX.. 65.00
Page turner, rococo floral repoussé silver hdl, Geo III, 14½", NM. 390.00
Shell of turtle, 23x24" 600.00
Tea caddy, bombe w/canted corners, stepped-bk dome lid, 1830, 6x6x4" .. 1,150.00

Toys

Toys can be classified into at least two categories: early collectible toys with an established history and the newer toys. The antique toys are easier to evaluate. A great deal of research has been done on them, and much data is available. The newer toys are just beginning to be studied; relative information is only now being published, and the lack of production records makes it difficult to know how many may be available. Often warehouse finds of these newer toys can change the market. This has happened with battery-operated toys and to some extent with robots. Review past issues of this guide. You will see the changing trends for the newer toys. All toys become more important as collectibles when a fixed period of manufacture is known. When we know the numbers produced and documentation of the makers is established, the prices become more predictable.

The best way to learn about toys is to attend toy shows and auctions. This will give you the opportunity to compare prices and condition. The more collectors and dealers you meet, the more you will learn. There is no substitute for holding a toy in your hand and seeing for yourself what they are. If you are going to be a serious collector, buy all the books you can find. Read every article you see. Knowledge is vital to building a good collection. Study all books that are available. These are some of the most helpful: *Schroeder's Collectible Toys, Antique to Modern*; *Collecting Disneyana* and *Collector's Toy Yearbook* by David Longest; *Breyer Animal Collector's Guide* by Felicia Browell, Kelly Korber-Weimer, and Kelly Kesicki; *Matchbox Toys, 1947 – 2007*; *Star Wars Super Collector's Wish Book* by Geoffrey T. Carlton; *Matchbox Toys, 1947 – 2007*, by Dana Johnson; *Hot Wheels, The Ultimate Redline Guide, 1968 – 1977*, by Jack Clark and Robert P. Wicker; and *Collector's Guide to Housekeeping Toys* by Margaret Wright. All are published by Collector Books. Other informative books are: *Collecting Toys, Collecting Toy Soldiers*, and *Collecting Toy Trains* by Richard O'Brien; and *Toys of the Sixties, A Pictorial Guide*, by Bill Bruegman. In the listings that follow, toys are listed by manufacturer's name if possible, otherwise by type. Measurements are given when appropriate and available; if only one dimension is noted, it is the greater one — height if the toy is vertical, length if it is horizontal. See also Children's Things; Personalities, Fact and Fiction. For toy stoves, see Stoves.

Key:
loco — locomotive   w/up — windup
r/c — remote control

Toys by Various Manufacturers

Alps, Acrocycle, w/up, clown performs tricks on motorcycle, 6", EXIB .400.00
Alps, Chippy the Chipmunk, b/o, 1950s, 12", MIB 125.00
Alps, Pontiac Firebird III, friction, litho tin, 1950s, 11", EX........ 300.00
Alps, Smiling Sam the Carnival Man, w/up, 9", NM+IB 300.00
Bandai, Plane w/Tow Car, b/o, litho tin, 26", MIB 575.00
Chad Valley, Roadster, w/up, tin, 12½", EX 650.00
Chein, Popeye the Drummer, 7", NM 3,000.00
Corgi, Austin A-40, red & blk, #216, MIP, $125 to 150.00
Corgi, Bentley Continental, #224, MIP, $100 to 125.00
Corgi, Bluebird Record Car, #153, $125 to 150.00
Corgi, Ford Consul, dual colors, #200, MIP, $175 to 200.00
Corgi, Ford Thunderbird, w/motor, #214m, MIP, $300 to 325.00
Corgi, Japan Air Line Concorde, #651, MIP, $450 to................... 500.00
Corgi, Land Rover, #438, Lepra, MIB, $375 to............................ 425.00
Corgi, Man From UNCLE, wht, #497, MIP, $650 to.................... 700.00
Corgi, Riley Pathfinder, #205, bl, $150 to 175.00
Corgi, Rolls Royce Silver Cloud, #273, MIP, $100 to 125.00
Corgi, Starfighter Jet Dragster, #169, MIP, $45 to 60.00
Corgi, Starsky & Hutch Ford Torino, #292, MIP, $85 to 100.00
Corgi, Stunt Bike, #681, MIB, $250 to 275.00
Dinky, AC Acceca, #167, all cream, MIP, $275 to 325.00
Dinky, Bedford Comet Lorry w/Tailboard, MIB, $275 to.............. 300.00
Dinky, Big Ben Lorry, #408, pk & cream, MIP, $1,950 to..........2,350.00
Dinky, Fire Station, #954, MIP, $425 to..................................... 450.00
Dinky, Leyland Cement Lorry, #417, MIP, $170 to...................... 295.00

Dinky, Lincoln Zephyr, #39CU, circa 1950 – 1952, EX, $720.00. (Photo courtesy Dan Morphy Auctions LLC on LiveAuctioneers.com)

Dinky, Morris Mini Traveller, #197, dk gr & brn, MIP, $400 to ... 450.00
Dinky, Volkswagen, #181, MIP, $210 to 225.00
Ertl, '67 Corvette L-71 Roadster, Sunfire Yel, 1:18 scale, MIP, $35 to ... 40.00
Ertl, Buick GSX (1971), blk & gold, 1:18 scale, MIP, $30 to 35.00
Ertl, Dodge Ram Truck, red or blk, 1995, 1:18 scale, MIB, $30 to . 35.00
Fisher-Price, #6 Ducky Cart, 1948-49, EX 50.00
Fisher-Price, #12 Bunny Truck, 1941-42, EX 65.00
Fisher-Price, #100 Dr Doodle, 1931, EX 550.00
Fisher-Price, #109 Lucky Monk, 1932-33, EX 325.00
Fisher-Price, #131 Toy Wagon, 1951-54, EX 225.00

Fisher-Price, #156 Circus Wagon, 1942, NM, $500.00.
(Photo courtesy Morphy Auctions on LiveAuctioneers.com)

Fisher-Price, #314 Husky Boom Crane, 1979-82, EX 25.00
Fisher-Price, #420 Sunny Fish, 1955, EX 125.00
Fisher-Price, #615 Tow Truck, 1960-61 & Easter 1965, EX 65.00
Hot Wheels, GMC Motor Home, Hong Kong, 1977, redlines, orange, EX ... 300.00
Hot Wheels, Mod Quad, 1970, redlines, magenta, scarce, M 125.00
Hubley, Kiddie Toy Convertible, bl, diecast, 7", EXIB 165.00

Ideal, soldier on horseback, stick toy, circa 1895, very rare, EX, $1,080.00. (Photo courtesy The RSL Auction Co. on LiveAuctioneers.com)

Japan, Jungle Trio, tin litho, 8", EX (VG box) 460.00
Johnny Lightning, Custom El Camino, diecast, 1969, MIP 1,250.00
Johnny Lightning, Custom XKE, std finish, 1969, MIP 750.00
Kingsbury, bus, #788, metal, w/up, VG 550.00
Lehmann, Halloh Motorcycle w/Rider, NM 2,400.00
Lehmann, Lo & Li, w/up, NM 8,000.00
Lehmann, Motor Car, w/up, EXIB 1,000.00
Linemar, Androcles Lion, w/up, plush, appearing to lick paw, 6", EXIB ... 115.00
Linemar, Donald Duck Delivery Wagon, friction, tin w/plastic head, EX . 355.00
Linemar, Mickey Mouse Roller Skater, w/up, 6", NMIB 3,550.00
Linemar, Popeye & Olive Oyl Playing Catch w/Ball, w/up, 19" L, EX ... 900.00
Linemar, Popeye Turnover Tank, w/up, 4", NM+IB 600.00
Linemar, Xylophone Player, w/up, 5", VG 425.00
Marx, Auto Transport, metal w/ramp & 2 plastic autos, 22", NMIB ..350.00
Marx, Charleston Trio, w/up, 1921, 10", EX 700.00
Marx, Flintstone Car, Wilma; friction, 4", NMIB 525.00
Marx, Fred Flintstone on Dino, b/o, plush Dino, 14", MIB 1,225.00
Marx, Hootin' Hollow House, b/o, 11", EXIB 875.00
Marx, Main Street, w/up, EXIB 475.00
Marx, Mighty Kong, plush, b/o, 11", EXIB 500.00
Marx, Popeye the Champ, w/up, NMIB 3,000.00
Marx, Snoopy & Gus Hook & Ladder Truck, w/up, 9", NM+ .. 2,000.00
Marx, Tricky Taxi, w/up, 5", EXIB 225.00

Matchbox, 1913 Cadillac, gold-plated, 1967, MIP, $225 to 275.00
Matchbox, 8-Wheel Crane Truck, #30, 1965, M gr, MIP, $1,000 to..1,250.00
Nifty, Skidoodle, w/up, litho tin, 8", EX 1,100.00
Nifty, Toonerville Trolley, w/up, litho tin, 7", EX 750.00
Ny-Lint, Howdy Doody Cart, tin, w/up, 9", VG 300.00
Ny-Lint, Street Sweeper, tin, w/up, 8" L, EXIB......................... 300.00
Smith-Miller, Dump Truck, GMC, 1950s, crank action, 12", NM.... 275.00
Steelcraft, Bloomingdale's Delivery Van, b/o lights, open cab, EX ...2,975.00
Steelcraft, City Trucking Co Dump Truck, 1940s, metal, 21", VG... 350.00
Steelcraft, Inter-City Bus, b/o lights, 24", VG 650.00
Strauss, Ham & Sam, w/up, NMIB... 1,200.00
Strauss, Parcel Post Truck, w/up, NM..................................12,500.00

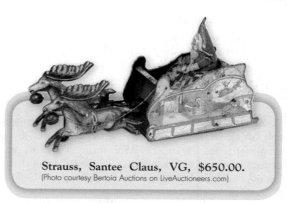

Strauss, Santee Claus, VG, $650.00.
(Photo courtesy Bertoia Auctions on LiveAuctioneers.com)

Structo, Dump Truck, lt gr, wht rubber tires, 22", VG 350.00
Structo, Guided Missile Launcher Truck, 1960s, 14", EXIB 200.00
Structo, tank, w/up, gr w/red turret & wheels, w/treads, 11", EX . 450.00
Sturditoy, Coal Truck, metal, 24", VG 1,100.00
Tonka, Big Mike Hydraulic Dump Truck w/Snow Plow, 1950s, 20", VG 575.00
Tootsietoy, Pan Am Airport Set, 1950s, NMIB 300.00
Unique Art, GI Joe & His K-9 Pups, w/up, 9", EXIB 275.00
Unique Art, Howdy Doody & Buffalo Bob at the piano, tin, 1950.. 650.00
Unique Art, Li'l Abner & His Dogpatch Band, w/up, 6x9", EXIB.... 700.00
Unique Art, Lincoln Tunnel, w/up, 24", EXIB 350.00
Wolverine, carousel, tin, w/up, circus theme, 12" dia, VG 300.00
Wolverine, Sunny Andy Kiddie Campers, tin, 14" L, EXIB 350.00
Wyandotte, Moto-Fix Towcar, metal, 1950s, 15", EX 225.00
Wyandotte, Shady Glenn Stock Ranch Cattle Truck, metal, 1950s, 17", EX...150.00

Cast Iron

Character, Andy Gump, Arcade, some flaking to paint, $1,230.00. (Photo courtesy Pook & Pook, Inc. on LiveAuctioneers.com)

Airplane, Air Mail Top Wing, Kenton, 6" W, EX+ 3,000.00
Airplane, Ford 1417 Top Wing Tri-Motor, Dent, 10" wingspan, EX . 3,900.00
Airplane, Ford 1417 Top Wing Tri-Motor, Dent, 12½" wingspan, EX .1,400.00
Airplane, Friendship, Hubley, 13" wingspan, NM 3,500.00
Airplane, Los Angeles Zeppelin, Dent, silver w/red trim, 12", VG..1,050.00
Airplane, Lindy, Hubley, gray w/red lettering, 13" wingspan, EX+ ..2,500.00
Airplane, Monocoupe (Top Wing), Arcade, 10" wingspan, NM 950.00
Bell toy, Columbia, Gong Bell, 7 ", G 1,650.00
Bell toy, Jonah (whale), NN Hill, 5 ", EX+ 1,725.00

Bell toy, Monkey on Velocipede, J&E Stevens, 8" L, some rpnt . 1,000.00
Boat, Battleship Maine, 8½", VG.................................3,850.00
Boat, Battleship New York, Dent, 20", NM 2,800.00
Boat, Chris Craft, Kilgore, 11", VG 2,700.00
Boat, Side-Wheeler Puritan, Wilkins, 11", NM............1,400.00
Boat, Static Motor Boat, Hubley, 9½", w/driver, EX.............4,800.00
Character, Andy Gump Car, Arcade, 7", EX 825.00
Character, Popeye Patrol Motorcycle, Hubley, 1938, 9", VG....4,025.00
Character, Santa sleigh, Hubley, 1 reindeer, 15", EX 1,600.00
Circus, Band Wagon, Hubley, 30", EX+..................................20,700.00
Circus, Clown in Pig Cart, Gong Bell, 6", EX...............................200.00
Circus, Overland Cage Wagon, Kenton, bear, 2 horses w/riders, 15", EX+ ..275.00
Circus, Royal Band Wagon, Hubley, 4 horses, 6 musicians, driver, 22", EX ..2,800.00
Construction, Buckeye Ditcher, Kenton, 9", NM.....................1,200.00
Construction, Cement Mixer, 1920s, rubber treads, EX 3,500.00
Construction, General Digger, Hubley, swivels, cast driver/worker, 10", EX+..500.00
Construction, Jaeger Cement Mixer, Kenton, chain drive, 9", EX...1,375.00
Farm, Case 3-Bottom Plow, Vindex, 10", EX+........................2,500.00
Farm, Case L Tractor, Vindex, 7", NP driver, VG................1,000.00
Farm, John Deere 3-Bottom Plow, Vindex, 9½", EX..................1,500.00
Farm, John Deere Thresher, Vindex, 15", NM 3,500.00
Farm, Oliver 70-Row Crop Tractor, Arcade, NP driver, 7", VG ..700.00
Farm, Oliver Superior Spreader, Arcade, VG 250.00
Firefighting, Water Tower Truck, Dent, open, red, bl tower, 15", EX+. 1,375.00
Horse-drawn, Brake (4-Seat), Hubley, 4 horse, 8 figures, 28", EX...10,350.00
Horse-drawn, Buckboard, Harris, 2 horses, w/driver, 13½",VG.1,500.00
Horse-drawn, Coal Wagon, Hubley, 2 horses, w/driver, 16", VG....900.00
Horse-drawn, Dray Wagon, Hubley, 2 horses, driver, 23", EX...1,600.00
Horse-drawn, Dump Cart, Wilkins, 1 horse, driver, 13", EX 2,750.00
Horse-drawn, Sand & Gravel Wagon, Kenton, 2 horses, w/driver, 15", G.. 230.00
Horse-drawn, Street Sweeper, Wilkins, 12½", VG+.................17,250.00
Horse-drawn, Tedder, Wilkins, w/driver, very scarce, 9", VG....6,325.00
Motor vehicle, ACF Bus, Arcade, no driver, 11½", NM 5,000.00
Motor vehicle, Ambulance, Kenton, w/driver, 10", VG 1,100.00
Motor vehicle, Aviation Gas Tank Truck, Kilgore, 12", EX 1,950.00
Motor vehicle, Bell Telephone Truck, Hubley, 5", VG................275.00
Motor vehicle, Buick Coupe, Arcade, rear spare, driver, 9", EX.1,800.00
Motor vehicle, Chrysler Airflow, Hubley, take-apart body, 7", EX...650.00
Motor vehicle, Coast to Coast Bus, Hubley, 13", NM+.............3,900.00
Motor vehicle, Coupe, Champion, red, no driver, 7½", VG.........250.00
Motor vehicle, Elgin Street Sweeper, Hubley, w/driver, 9", NM..6,000.00
Motor vehicle, Fageol Safety Bus, Arcade, 12", EX 500.00
Motor vehicle, Ford Model T Coupe, Arcade, no driver, 7",VG+.250.00
Motor vehicle, Ford Wrecker, Vindex, very rare, 7", NM 7,150.00
Motor vehicle, Greyhound Bus, Arcade #4400, 9", VGIB 575.00
Motor vehicle, Hathaway's Bread Truck, Arcade, 9", G 575.00
Motor vehicle, Mack Coal Truck, Arcade, w/driver, 10", EX+..1,500.00

Motor vehicle, Packard Sedan, Hubley, 11", metal disk wheels, EX, $10,000.00. (Photo courtesy James D. Julia, Inc.)

Motor vehicle, Parcel Express, Dent, 8", NM 9,500.00
Motor vehicle, Pickwick Nite Coach, Kenton, 11", EX+ 4,200.00
Motor vehicle, REO Coupe, Arcade, 9", NM+.......................13,000.00
Motor vehicle, Sedan, Hubley, lt bl, 7" 570.00
Motor Vehicle, Tank, Arcade, camo colors, rubber treads, 8", G . 200.00
Motor vehicle, Traffic Car, Hubley, NPSW, cast driver, 9", EX .1,500.00
Motor vehicle, White Moving Van, Arcade, w/driver, 13", EX .4,500.00

Trains & trolleys, Arcade, Railplane/Pullman, 9", G 125.00
Trains & trolleys, Big 6 loco/tender/3 coaches, J&E Stevens, 42", EXIB 850.00
Trains & trolleys, Trolley, Ives, yel, w/guide wire, 7", VG 850.00

Farm Toys

It's entirely probable that more toy tractors have been sold than real ones. They've been made to represent all makes and models, of plastic, cast iron, diecast metal, and even wood. They've been made in at least 1/16th scale, 1/32nd, 1/43rd, and 1/64th. If you buy a 1/16th-scale replica, that small piece of equipment would have to be 16 times larger to equal the size of the real item. Limited editions (meaning that a specific number will be made and no more) and commemorative editions (made for special events) are usually very popular with collectors. Many models on the market today are being made by the Ertl company. See also Toys, Cast Iron.

Box Spreader, New Holland, #308, Ertl, 1/64 scale, MIB..................3.00
Combine, Case IH 2388, #14176, Ertl, 1/64, MIB......................... 11.00

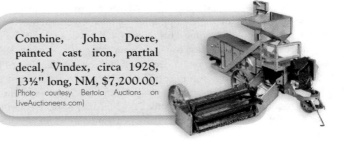

Combine, John Deere, painted cast iron, partial decal, Vindex, circa 1928, 13½" long, NM, $7,200.00. (Photo courtesy Bertoia Auctions on LiveAuctioneers.com)

Combine, Oliver, SLIK, stamped S9830BAR, 1952, 5x12", EX..... 25.00
Cotton express picker, Case IH, #4300, Ertl, 1/64, MIB................. 11.00
Crawler, Farmall 340, #4734, Ertl, 1/16 scale, MIB 25.00
Crawler, Oliver HG, #13079, Ertl, 1/16 scale, MIB 22.00
Cultivator, John Deere 2200, Ertl, #15081, 1/64 scale, MIB 8.00
Hay loader, John Deer Vindex, CI, very rare, 9", EX 4,500.00
Hay rake, Arcade, CI w/NP spoke wheels, w/seat, NM 1,100.00
Plow, Arcade, 2-bottom, CI, 5", EX 400.00
Plow, John Deere 3-Bottom, Vindex, 9", VG................................800.00
Skid steer loader, Case 90XT, Ertl, #4216, 1/64, MIB 25.00
Skid steer loader, Heston SL-30, #2267, 1/64 scale, MIB 43.00
Sprayer, #5752, 1/64 scale, Ertl, MIB 9.00
Thrasher, John Deere, Vindex, CI, 15", EX+ 3,300.00
Tillage plow, Case IH, #14172, Ertl, 1/64 scale, MIB 32.50
Tractor, Allis-Chalmers 7060, w/cab, #13185, Ertl, 1/16 scale, MIB...............35.00
Tractor, Allis-Chalmers, AC D-19, 1/16 scale, F 50.00
Tractor, Allis-Chalmers, WD-45 Precision #7, #13101, 1/16 scale, MIB ..118.00
Tractor, Allis-Chalmers High Crop D-19, #13403, Ertl, 1/64 scale, MIB... 39.00
Tractor, Case 1930 Western SP Precision #15, #14130, Ertl, 1/16 scale, MIB.116.00
Tractor, Case IH Maxxum MX120, #4487, Ertl, 1/16 scale, MIB... 45.00
Tractor, Case L, Vindex, CI w/metal spoke wheels, NP driver, 7", EX+..2,750.00
Tractor, Deutz Allis 9150 Orlando Show, #1280, 1/16 scale, MIB..200.00
Tractor, Farmall F-20 on Rubber, Precision, #299CO, 1/16 scale, VG..80.00

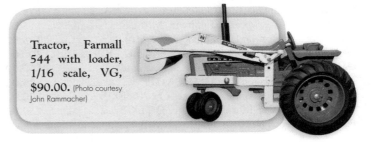

Tractor, Farmall 544 with loader, 1/16 scale, VG, $90.00. (Photo courtesy John Rammacher)

Tractor, Farmall H, #4441, 1/16 scale, MIB 25.00
Tractor, Ford 5000 Precision, #13503, 1/16 scale, MIB............... 115.00
Tractor, Ford Row Crop 7740, #973, Ertl, 1/16 scale, MIB............ 50.00
Tractor, John Deere 4010, #5716, Ertl, 1/16 scale, MIB 25.00
Tractor, John Deere 4040, #5133, 1/16 scale, MIB 30.00
Tractor, John Deere D, Vindex, CI, spoke wheels, NP driver, 6", NM 3,300.00
Tractor, Massey-Ferguson 1155, #13170, Ertl, 1/16 scale, MIB 43.00
Tractor, McCormick-Deering 10-20, Arcade, CI, 1925, VG........ 275.00
Tractor, New Holland 7840 w/loader, #13588, Ertl, 1/16 scale, MIB.. 48.00
Tractor, Oliver 70-Row Crop, Arcade, CI, NP driver, 7", EX....... 500.00
Tractor, Oliver 1655 w/cab, #13186, Ertl, 1/16 scale, MIB............. 35.00
Wagon, McCormick-Deering Weber, Arcade, CI, 12", EX 450.00

Guns and Early Cast-Iron Cap Shooters

In years past, virtually every child played with toy guns, and the survival rate of these toys is minimal, at best. The interest in these charming toy guns has recently increased considerably, especially those with western character examples, as collectors discover their scarcity, quality, and value. Toy gun collectibles encompass the early and the very ornate figural toy guns and bombs through the more realistic ones with recognizable character names, gleaming finishes, faux jewels, dummy bullets, engraving, and colorful grips. This section will cover some of the most popular cast-iron and diecast toy guns from the past 100 years. Recent market trends have witnessed a decline of interest in the earlier (1900 – 1940) single-shot cast-iron pistols. The higher collector interest is for known western characters and cap pistols from the 1950 – 1965 era. Generic toy guns, such as Deputy, Pony Boy, Marshal, Ranger, Sheriff, Pirate, Cowboy, Dick, Western, and Army, generate only minimal collector interest.

Lightning Express, Kenton, animated, cast iron, circa 1895, 5", $135.00. (Photo courtesy RSL Auction Co. on LiveAuctioneers.com)

Agent Zero Radio-Rifle, Mattel, 1964, NMIB 75.00
Air Blaster Gun & Target Set, Wham-O, 1963, EX+IB 175.00
Annie Oakley Golden Smoke Rifle Outfit, Daisy, NMIB............. 650.00
Annie Oakley Pistol, wht grips, 9", EX 200.00
Army .45 Cap Gun, Hubley, 1940, CI, blk w/wht grips, 6½", NM .. 125.00
Baby Space Gun, Daiya, friction, 6", NM+IB 150.00
Big Game Rifle, Marx, MIB 125.00
Bronco, Kilgore, 1950s, NMIB 100.00
Buck Rogers Atomic Pistol, Daisy, sparks, 1936, 10", VG 200.00
Buck Rogers Rocket Pistol, 10", VGIB....................................... 250.00
Butting Match Cap Shooter, Ives, 1885, NM+ 600.00
Cheyenne Singin' Saddle Gun, Daisy, 33", NMIB...................... 250.00
Chinese Must Go, Ives, 1880, 5", NM 2,200.00
Chuck Connors Cowboy in Africa Gun & Holster Set, NMIB ... 350.00
Clown & Mule Cap Shooter, Ives, 5", VG+ 750.00
Clown Seated on Keg, Ives, 4", VG+ 400.00
Cork Shooting Submachine Gun, Marx, 1951, MIB.................... 175.00
Cowboy 6-Shooter Water Pistol, Irwin, MIB.............................. 75.00
Davy Crockett Frontier Rifle, Marx, 34", NMIB 175.00
De Luxe Holster for Stallion .45, 'Left or Right,' EXIB 200.00
Deputy Pistol, Hubley, 10", MIB 150.00
Dick Tracy Police Siren Pistol, Marx, VGIB............................... 125.00
Dick Tracy Tommy Gun, Parker Jones Co, 20", EXIB 300.00
Dragnet Dbl-Bbl Cap Riot Gun, plastic, 33", EXIB..................... 250.00
Flashy Ray Gun, TN, 1950s, b/o, 18", NMIB.............................. 200.00

G-Man Gun, Marx, litho tin w/wood stock, 23" L, EX+ 250.00
G-Man Machine Gun, Japan, 1950s, 18", MIB............................ 125.00
Gene Autry Cap Pistol, Kenton, 1940s, 3rd version, red grips, 8", VG.. 150.00
James Bond 007 Harpoon Gun, Lone Star, 1960s, EXIB 100.00
Johnny Ringo Dbl Gun & Holster Set, unused, NMIB 1,600.00
Lone Ranger Official Outfit, dbl holster set w/nonfiring compo guns, NMIB.350.00
Lost in Space Helmet & Gun Set, Remco, 1966, NMIB............... 500.00
Lost in Space Roto-Jet Gun, Mattel, plastic, 20" L, EX............... 250.00
Monkey w/Coconut, japanned finish, 4", VG 230.00
Monster Space Gun, Horikawa, b/o, 22", NM 100.00
Mule, Ives, 5", VG 750.00

Mustang 500 Pistol, Nichols, NMIB, $300.00.

Overland Trail/Kelly's Rifle, Hubley, 35", EXIB.......................... 300.00
Padlock Cap Gun, Hubley, 1950s, NM+ 75.00
Pirate Pistol, Hubley, 2 hammers, NM 125.00
Popeye Pirate Pistol, Marx, NMIB 250.00
Punch & Judy, Ives, 1882, 5" 725.00
Remington .36, Hubley, NMIB.. 200.00
Ric-O-Shay Jr, Hubley, NMIB... 200.00
Rifleman Flip Special Rifle, Hubley, NMIB................................ 450.00
Rocket-2 Sparking Space Gun, Marx, tin & plastic, NMIB 400.00
Roy Rogers & Trigger Official Holster Outfit, NM+IB 900.00
Scout Cap Rifle, Hubley, 1960s, 36", unused, M........................ 140.00
Shane Single Gun & Holster Set, mk Alan Ladd, EX+ 900.00
Shootin' Shell Colt 6 Shooter Rifle, Mattel, 1960, 31", MIB........ 350.00
Snap Shot Camera, Ives, 1893, 3", NM 950.00
Spinner Rifle, Marx, NMOC... 125.00
Stallion 41-50 Flip-Out Six Shooter, Nichols, NMIB................. 300.00
Texan Dbl Gun & Holster Set, Halco, NMIB............................. 300.00
Texan Gold De Luxe Pistol, Hubley, NMIB............................... 200.00
Texan Jr Repeating Cap Pistol, Hubley, EXIB............................ 100.00
Two Monkeys Cap Shooter, J&E Stevens, 4½", G...................... 600.00
Untouchables Tommy Gun, Marx, b/o, 24", EXOC 325.00
Wilma Deering's Gun & Holster (Buck Rogers), NM 500.00
Zip, J&E Stevens, 1890, 5", EX+.. 150.00

Housewares

Little girls used to love to emulate their mothers and pretend to sew and bake, sweep, do laundry, and iron (gasp!). They imagined what fun it would be when they were big like mommy. Those little gadgets they played with are precious collectibles today, and any child-size houseware item is treasured, especially those from the 1940s and 1950s. If you're interested in learning more we recommend *Encyclopedia of Children's Sewing Collectibles* by Darlene J. Gengelbach and *Collector's Guide to Housekeeping Toys, 1870 – 1970*, by our advisor Margaret Wright. Both are published by Collector Books.

Baking Set, Bake-A-Cake Set, Wolverine, MIB........................... 100.00
Baking Set, Betty Jane, 9-pc clear glass set Glasbake, 1940s, EXIB.150.00
Baking Set, Busy Baker Pastry Set, Transogram, 1957, MIB......... 250.00
Baking Set, Cake Box Set, litho tin, Wolverine #260, 1940s, EXIB. 225.00

Baking Set, Cinderella Pastry Set, Peerless Playthings, 1950s, EXIB. 90.00
Baking Set, Junior Chef Cake Mix Set, Argo Industries, 1956, NMIB. 100.00
Baking Set, Sunny Suzy Bake-A-Cake, Wolverine, EXIB 100.00
Baking Set, Sunny Suzy, 7-pc, Fire-King Oven Glass, Wolverine #260, EXIB. 140.00
Betty Crocker Mini-Wave Oven, Kenner, NMIB 50.00
Big Knitting Set, Parker Bros, 1956, complete w/instructions . 30.00
Blender, Automatic Dollee, b/o, EXIB 75.00
Breakfast set, Ohio Art, Good Morning, 15-pc, tin litho, 1960s, EXIB. 100.00
Breakfast set, Ohio Art, Sunshine Breakfast, tin litho, 1970s, EXIB. 85.00
Buggy, pressed steel, wire hdl, 9" L, Wyandotte, EXIB 350.00
Buggy, wicker, metal fr, parasol on wire holder above seat, VG.... 250.00
Buggy, wicker, metal fr, swinging hood, corduroy interior, G+ 100.00

Buggy, wire, with dolls and fabric insert, 6½", Germany, 1920, VG, $650.00. (Photo courtesy Noel Barrett Antiques & Auctions Ltd. on LiveAuctioneers.com)

Cabinet, Little Miss Structo Corner, pressed steel, pk, 12", EX+IB. 100.00
Cabinet, Little Miss Structo Counter-Top, pk, w/top shelves, 11", MIB. 85.00
Carpenter Set, NP, 5-pc, Arcade, 1941, MOC 55.00
Carriage, tin w/emb wicker design, folding top, 6", EX 250.00
Carriage, wicker sleigh type w/scroll design, 36" L, EX 500.00
Carriage, wood Ellis style 3-wheeler, fold-down top, 31" L, VG. 100.00
Carriage, wood surry type w/red fringed top, 25" L, VG 850.00
Clothes Drying Rack, wood fold-out type, 12", Am, 1915, EX 35.00
Clothesline & Pin Set, Doll Pin, Hoflion, 1950s, NMIB 25.00

Coffee Mill, Juvenile, Arcade, wooden with paper lithograph in construction, 4" square, VG+, $165.00. (Photo courtesy Randy Inman Auctions)

Dishes, Akro Agate Chiquita (My Carnival Colors), 8-pc, MIB . 225.00
Dishes, Akro Agate Chiquita 22-pc, gr, MIB 400.00
Dishes, Akro Agate Play-Time, 8-pc bl & wht marble set, MIB .. 300.00
Dishes, Akro Agate Play-Time, 16-pc gr Interior Panel Stacked Disc, MIB.600.00
Dishes, Akro Agate Play-Time, 16-pc, gr, MIB 225.00
Dishes, Akro Agate Play-Time, 19-pc bl, yel & gr set, MIB 375.00
Dishes, Akro Agate Play-Time, water set, MIB 150.00
Dishes, Akro Agate Play-Time, water set, ribbed pattern, MIB ... 100.00
Dishes, Jeannette Junior, 14-pc, Cherry Blossom Depression glass, MIB.300.00
Doll Pin Clothesline & Pin Set, Hoflion, 1950s, unused, NMIB ... 25.00
Doll-E-Do Dish Set, Amsco, 1950s, EX+ 85.00
Doll-E-Feedette, 12-pc 1950s, complete, NMIB 125.00
Doll-E Housekeeper Set, 14-pc Amsco, 1950s, EX+ 200.00
Eggbeater, A&J, Baby Bingo No 68..., EX.................................... 25.00

Flatware, Mirro Flatware Set, 26-pc, 1950s, EX+IB 50.00
Garden tool set, Arcade, 5-pc, 1941, MOC 55.00
Garden tool set, Tiny Tools, 4-pc, NP, Arcade, 1941, MOC 125.00
Granite Ware Set, 18-pc, gray, EX... 60.00
Iron, electric, Wolverine #24A or #25A, 1940, NMIB, ea 75.00
Ironing Board & Iron, Sunny Suzy, litho tin, Wolverine-Spang, 1970s, EX.. 50.00
Ironing Set, Little Sweetheart, Wolverine #295, unused, MIB.......... 75.00
Jolly Dolly Sewing Cards, #T184, Samuel Gabriel & Co, 1940... 30.00
Junior Miss Embroidery Set, Hassenfeld #1586, 1950s, NMIB....... 75.00
Junior Miss Hat Shop, Advance Games #868, 1950s, NMIB 100.00
Junior Miss Sewing Kit, Hassenfeld Bros #1535, unused, NMIB.... 75.00
Kidd-E-Kitchen Set, Amsco, 1950s, NMIB 175.00
Kitchen Set, litho tin, Ohio Art, EX... 200.00
Knitting Nancy, #6001, JW Spears & Sons, 1940, MIB 30.00
Laundry Set, Mickey Mouse, litho tin, NMIB 450.00
Laundry Set, Mickey Mouse, litho tin, VGIB 275.00
Laundry Set, 3 Little Pigs, litho tin tub, Ohio Art, 5½", VG 150.00
Marx Plastic Tea Set #2093, 44-pc, EXIB 75.00
Modes Nouveautes Chapeau Millinery Set, VGIB 500.00
Ohio Art Good Morning Breakfast Set, 15-pc litho tin set, 1960s, EXIB....100.00

Ohio Art Tea Service, Busy Squirrel, 1938 – 1940, pieces shown came from a 31-piece set, rare, EX, $250.00. (Photo courtesy Margaret Wright)

Pan Set, alum, 1930s, EX+ 85.00
Pan Set, Revere Ware, 12-pc, 1950s, EX+ 150.00
Percolator, metal w/nursery rhyme characters, Mirro, 1950s, EX, ea. 20.00
Popcorn Junior Machine, complete, 20", EXIB............................ 225.00
Refrigerator, metal w/2 doors, 13½", Wolverine, EX (no food) 50.00
Rocking Horse, for dolls, pnt compo, 27x25", EX 2,000.00
Salad set, Wolverine, Little Sweetheart, #253, tin litho, EXIB...... 75.00
Sew Ette Sewing Machine, Jaymar, 1950s, MIB 75.00
Sewing Machine, Singer, complete, EXIB 200.00
Sewing Machine, Take Along Sew-Rite, Hasbro #1543, 1969, NM. 75.00
Sew Young, Sew Fun Pattern Kit, 1999, EXIB 15.00
Shirley Temple Luncheon Embroidery Set, Gabriel #311, 1960s, NMIB....100.00
Sink, tin litho, ftd base, 10x11x6", Wolverine, 1930s, EX 65.00
Sink 'n Stove Combination (Holiday), tin, 1950s, MIB 275.00
Sno-Cone Maker, Hasenfeld Bros, 1960s, 9½", NM 75.00
Soda fountain, Suzy Homemaker Sweet Shoppe, Topper, 1960s, MIB.50.00
Spears Elite Edition Art Needlework, VG+IB 100.00
Stove, Bird, blk CI, 10½", VG... 200.00
Stove, Charm, NP CI, backshelf & stovepipe, 5", Grey Iron, G ... 100.00
Stove, Eagle, NP CI, name on oven door, 18½" L, VG 230.00
Stove, Globe, Kenton, CI, 18", EX 800.00
Stove, Karr Range Co, bl enamel w/NP feet & trim, 21½x13x10", EXIB.6,325.00
Stove, Little Chef, wht metal, Ohio Art, 1950s, 13x13x7", EX+.. 150.00
Stove, Little Eva, T Southard, 14" L, early rpnt 925.00
Stove, Little Miss Structo, pressed steel, pk, 11½" L, MIB 150.00
Stove, Little Orphan Annie, electric, Marx, 1930s, 9x10x5½", EX+.$125.00
Stove, Marvel, CI, 20" L, VG... 315.00

Stove, Spirit Fired, tin, with backplate and stovepipe, three burners, accessories, 10½x9", Germany, VG+, $350.00. (Photo courtesy Noel Barrett Antiques & Auctions Ltd. on LiveAuctioneers.com)

Stove, Union, ornate casting w/short legs, 9", F 200.00
Sweeper, Bissell Little Queen, 1957, EX 50.00
Sweeper Set, Golden Girl Carpet Sweeper, 1960s, NMIB.............. 65.00
Tea set, Akro Agate Little American Maid, 11-pc, MIB 100.00
Tea set, Akro Agate Little American Maid, 17-pc, MIB 450.00
Tea set, Akro Agate Little American Maid, 21-pc, MIB 175.00
Tea set, Akro Agate Little American Maid, 21-pc, MIB 550.00
Tea set, Marx Plastic, #2093, 44-pc, mc, EXIB 75.00
Tea set, Mirro Like Mother's Tea Set, 27-pc, alum, 3 Little Kittens, 1950s, EXIB.150.00
Tea Set, Ohio Art, 9-pc tin litho, She Loves Me She Loves Me Not NMIB.125.00
Waffle Iron, CI, rect, 5½", Arcade, VG 100.00
Waffle Iron, CI, rnd, Arcade, VG+ 125.00

Washer-Dryer, Sparkle Bright, pressed steel, pink, 10", Structo, EX+IB, $130.00.

Washing Machine, Dick Tracy, litho tin, Kalon Redo Corp, EXIB. 100.00
Washing Machine, Dolly's Washer, litho tin, crank-op, 9", Chein, EXIB.300.00
Washing Machine, Dolly's Washer, litho tin, crank-op, 9", Chein, VG .125.00
Washing Machine, Maytag ringer type, Hubley, 1940s, 9", EX+ .650.00
Washing Machine, Mickey & Minnie Mouse, litho tin, electric, 9", VG.175.00
Washing Machine, 3 Little Pigs, litho tin, crank-op, 9", Chein, EX.450.00
Wash Tub & Washboard, Mickey & Minnie Mouse, Ohio Art, 1930s, VG+.135.00
Weaving Loom, #860, Concord Toy Co, 1943.................................. 30.00
Wolverine Little Sweetheart Salad Set #253, litho tin EXIB......... 75.00

Model Kits

Though model kits were popular with kids of the '50s who enjoyed the challenge of assembling a classic car or a Musketeer figure, when the monster series hit in the early 1960s, sales shot through the ceiling. Made popular by all the monster movies of that decade, ghouls like Vampirella, Frankenstein, and the Wolfman were eagerly assembled by kids everywhere. They could (if their parents didn't object too strongly) even construct an actual working guillotine. Aurora had other successful series of figure kits, too, based on characters from comic strips and TV shows, as well as a line of sports stars. But the vast majority of model kits were vehicles. They varied in complexity, some requiring much more dexterity on the part of the model builder than others, and they came in several scales, from 1/8 (which might be as large as 20" to 24") down to 1/43 (generally about 3" to 4"), but the most popular scale was 1/25 (usually between 6" to 8"). Some of the largest producers of vehicle kits were AMT, MPC, and IMC.

As a rule of thumb, assembled kits (built-ups) are priced at about 25% to 50% of the price range for a boxed kit, but this is not always true on the higher-priced kits. One mint in the box with the factory seal intact will often sell for up to 15% more than if the seal were broken, though depending on the kit, a sealed perfect box may add as much as $100.00. Condition of the box is crucial. Last but not least, one must factor in internet sales, which could cause some values to go down considerably. Unless noted, condition is for 'unbuilt' kits.

Airfix, James Bond's Aston Martin, 1965, MIB 250.00
Airfix, 2001: A Space Odyssey, Orion, 1970, #701, MIB.............. 100.00
AMT, Sonny & Cher Mustang, 1960s, MIB............................... 325.00
AMT, Star Trek, Klingon Cruiser, #S952-802, 1968, MIB........... 225.00
AMT, Star Trek, Spock, 1973, NMIB (sm box)............................ 150.00
AMT/Ertl, Monkeemobile, 1990, MIB (sealed) 100.00
Aurora, Alfred E Neuman, 1965, MIB 175.00
Aurora, Babe Ruth, Great Moments in Sport, MIB................... 400.00
Aurora, Captain America, 1966, MIB... 325.00
Aurora, Creature from the Black Lagoon, 1963, MIB 450.00
Aurora, Dracula, 1967, MIB.. 300.00
Aurora, Godzilla's Go-Cart, 1966, assembled, NM.................. 1,000.00
Aurora, Gold Knight of Nice, 1957, MIB.................................. 325.00
Aurora, John F Kennedy, 1965, MIB... 150.00
Aurora, Lost in Space, Robot, 1968, MIB.................................. 875.00
Aurora, Mummy, 1963, MIB.. 375.00
Aurora, Mummy, Frightening Lightning, 1969, MIB................ 425.00
Aurora, Munster's Living Room, 1964, MIB........................... 1,500.00
Aurora, Steve Canyon, Famous Fighters, 1958, MIB................ 200.00
Aurora, Superman, 1963, MIB... 400.00
Aurora, Tonto, 1967, MIB.. 250.00
Aurora, Wolfman, 1962, MIB... 300.00
Hawk, Beach Bunny Catchin' Rays, 1964, MIP 125.00
Hawk, Cobra II, 1950s, MIB.. 100.00
Hawk, Davy the Way-Out Cyclist, 1963, MIP........................... 100.00
Hawk, Digger & Dragster, 1963, MIB 125.00
Hawk, Frantic Banana, 1965, MIB 150.00
Hawk, Killer McBash, 1963, MIB.. 175.00
Hawk, Leaky Boat Louie, 1963, MIB 125.00
Hawk, Steel Pluckers, 1965, MIB.. 110.00
Hawk, Totally Fab, 1965, MIP... 125.00
Hawk, Wade A Minute, 1963, MIP 135.00
Imai, Missile Tank BB-1 (Motorized), #524, 1960s, MIB................ 400.00
ITC, USS Oregon Battleship (Motorized), #H-3680, 1950s, VGIB.75.00
Lindberg, Flying Saucer, 1952, MIB.. 200.00
Monogram, Bathtub Buggy, 1960s, MIB (sealed)......................... 100.00

Monogram, Jaguar XK-E GT Sports Coupe, 1964, MIB, $25.00. (Photo courtesy Morphy Auctions on LiveAuctioneers.com)

Monogram, Speed Shift, 1965, MIB.. 200.00
Monogram, TV Orbiter, 1959, MIB.. 150.00
MPC, Alien, 1979, MIB (sealed) 100.00
MPC, Barnabas, Dark Shadows, 1968, MIB................................. 425.00

MPC, Barnabas Vampire Van, Dark Shadows, 1969, MIB.................275.00
Pyro, Prehistoric Monsters Gift Set, 1950s, MIB.........................125.00
Renwal, Visible V8 Engine, 1960s, MIB (sealed).........................200.00
Renwal, Visible Woman, 1960, 1st issue, unused, M (NM box).165.00
Revell, Beatles, any member, 1965, MIB, ea...................................250.00
Revell, Big Daddy Roth, Beatnik Bandit, MIB.........................225.00

Revell, Drag Nut, Ed 'Big Daddy' Roth, 1963, MIB, $150.00.

Revell, Dr Seuss Zoo, Kit #1, 1959, MIB..........................400.00
Revell, Ed 'Big Daddy Roth,' Beatnik Bandit, MIB....................225.00
Revell, Flash Gordon & the Martian, 1965, MIB........................150.00
Revell, Moon Ship, 1957, MIB..........................225.00
Revell, Peter Pan Pirate Ship, 1960, MIB..........................100.00
Revell, Phantom & the Voodoo Witch Doctor, 1965, MIB.........175.00
Revell, Space Explorer Solaris, 1969, MIB..........................125.00
Revell, Terrier Missile, 1958, MIB..........................200.00
Screamin', Friday the 13th's Jason, MIB..........................125.00
Screamin', Werewolf, MIB..........................100.00
Strombecker, Disneyland Stagecoach, 1950s, MIB.....................200.00
Tsukuda, Creature from the Black Lagoon, MIB....................150.00

Nodders

Some of the nodders listed here are earlier bisque and ceramic figures made in Germany around the 1930s, and some are papier-maché or ceramic made in Japan in the 1960s and 1970s. They reflect accurate likenesses of the characters they portray and have become popular collectibles. Many of the newer ones were sold as souvenirs from Disney, Universal Studios, and Six Flags amusement parks, as well as roadside concessions. Values are for nodders in near mint condition. To calculate prices for examples in excellent or very good condition reduce these prices by 25% to 40%.

Andy and Barney, Mayberry, ceramic, 7", 1992, mail-order only from Time Warner, EX, each $75.00 to $100.00. (Photo courtesy June Moon)

Beetle Bailey, $150 to 250.00
Bugs Bunny, $175 to 350.00
Charlie Brown, 1970s, $45 to 75.00
Charlie Brown as Baseball Player, ceramic..........................75.00
Chinaman, compo, Japan, 1960s..........................65.00
Chinese Boy & Girl, 5½", pr..........................65.00
Colonel Sanders, 2 different, ea $150 to..........................250.00
Dagwood, compo, 'Kiss Me' on gr base, 1950s, $150 to.............250.00
Danny Kaye & Girl Kissing, pr $150 to..........................200.00

Dobie Gillis, $300 to..........................400.00
Donald Duck, Irwin/WDP, $100 to..........................125.00
Donald Duck, rnd gr base, 1970s, $75 to..........................100.00
Donald Duck, 'Walt Disney World,' sq wht base, $75 to.............125.00
Donny Osmond, wht jumpsuit w/microphone, $100 to..............150.00
Dr Ben Casey, $150 to..........................250.00
Dr Kildare, compo, rnd wht base, 1960s, $150 to.....................250.00
Dumbo, rnd red base, $100 to..........................150.00
Elmer Fudd, $200 to..........................350.00
Foghorn Leghorn, $200 to..........................350.00
Goofy, arms at side, $100 to..........................125.00
Goofy, arms folded, $100 to..........................125.00
Hobo, compo, Japan, 1960s..........................60.00
Lieutenant Fuzz (Beetle Bailey), $150 to..........................250.00
Linus, sq blk base, $100 to..........................150.00
Linus as Baseball Catcher, ceramic, Japan..........................75.00
Little Audrey, $150 to..........................200.00
Lucy, no base, sm, 1970s, $75 to..........................100.00
Lucy as Baseball Player, ceramic, $75 to..........................100.00
Mammy (Dogpatch USA), $75 to..........................125.00
Mary Poppins, wood, Disneyland, 1960s, $150 to.....................200.00
Maynard G Krebs Holding Bongos (Dobie Gillis), $300 to...........400.00
Mickey Mouse, red & yel outfit, rnd gr base, $100 to...............125.00
Mickey Mouse, red, wht & bl outfit, Disney World, $75 to...........125.00
Mickey Mouse, red, wht & bl outfit, Disneyland, sq wht base......125.00
Mr Peanut, moves at waist, $150 to..........................200.00
Mutt & Jeff, bisque, Germany, 1920s, 3" & 2", VG+, pr...........150.00
NY World's Fair Boy & Girl Kissing, $100 to..........................125.00
Oodles the Duck (Bozo the Clown), $200 to..........................250.00
Peppermint Patti as Baseball Player, ceramic, Japan, $45 to.........75.00
Phantom of the Opera, gr face, rare, $150 to..........................400.00

Zero, Beetle Bailey, $150.00 to $250.00.

Paper-Lithographed Toys

Following the development of color lithography, early toy makers soon recognized the possibility of using this technology in their own field. By the 1800s, both here and abroad, toys ranging from soldiers to involved dioramas of entire villages were being produced of wood with colorful and well detailed paper lithographed surfaces. Some of the best known manufactures were Crandell, Bliss, Reed, and McLoughlin Brothers. This style of toy remained popular until well after the turn of the century. Unless noted otherwise, toys listed are in excellent condition.

Block Set, ABC Blocks, in 10x11" wooden box..........................850.00
Block Set, Cob House Blocks (3 Little Kittens), McLoughlin Bros, 1875...950.00
Block Set, Comic Cubes, McLoughlin Bros, 6-pc, forms 10 figures..550.00
Block Set, Cubes Alphabetiques, Vict children/nursery rhymes, 8½x10" box..350.00
Block Set, Mammoth Alphabet Picture Blocks, 12-pc, VGIB.................500.00
Block Set, Mother Goose, McLoughlin Bros, 1890s..........................1,000.00
Block Set, Tower of Babel, Stirn & Lyon, w/wooden box............950.00

Boat, America fishing boat, Reed, 29" L, VG 650.00
Boat, Conqueror battleship, Bliss, 21" L, VG 1,200.00
Boat, Fairy paddlewheeler on 4 wheels, 12" L 600.00
Boat, Iowa battleship, Bliss, 28½", VG.............................. 875.00
Boat, New York battleship, Bliss, 35", G 1,450.00
Boat, Philadelphia battle cruiser, Reed, 31" L, G 1,750.00
Boat, Providence side-wheeler, Reed, 20", VG 950.00
Boat, River Queen side-wheeler, Reed, 24" L, G 1,150.00
Boat, Thetis yacht, 12", VG+ 625.00
Boat, Twilight paddlewheeler, Reed, 20" L 1,050.00
Boat, Volunteer fishing vessel, Reed, ca 1883, 32" L, G 675.00
Building Blocks & Museum Set, circus scenes/Arabian palace 800.00
Captain Kidd's Castle, complete, 16½x11", G 850.00
Civil War Fort, foldable box forms fort w/2 cannons 650.00

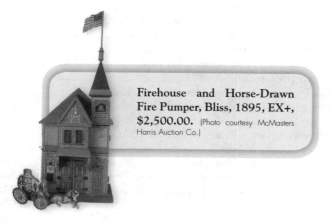

Firehouse and Horse-Drawn Fire Pumper, Bliss, 1895, EX+, $2,500.00. (Photo courtesy McMasters Harris Auction Co.)

Game, Animal Ten Pins, McLoughlin Bros, 9" ea 675.00
Game, Animal Ten Pins, Parker Bros, ca 1900, 9"-11", VG 450.00
Game, Performing Acrobats, 20", EX 300.00
Game, target w/bird & flower motif, 15x8" 225.00
Mother Goose Cart, Bliss, 14", L, VG 550.00
Mother Goose Tower, EIH, 1880s, complete, w/wooden box 325.00
Nesting Blocks, set of 5, bright graphics & alphabet, 2"-4", VG .. 100.00
Nesting Blocks, Surprise, McLoughlin Bros, 61" (stacked), VG+ ... 450.00
Noah's Ark, Bliss, The Wonder, 22", VG+ 325.00
Pansy Tally Ho Coach, Bliss, 29" L, VG 1,900.00
Tiny Town Zoo, JW Spears & Son, complete, VGIB 275.00
Toboggan Slide, sleigh runners marked 'Puritan,' 36" overall, VG ... 725.00

Train, Golden Gate Special, Bliss, 1889, 37", EX, $1,750.00. (Photo courtesy Bertoia Auctions)

Train, NY Central Railroad, Bliss, 26½" L overall, VG 600.00
Train, Nickel Plate Railroad, Bliss, 26" overall 825.00
Trolley, 'Bowery Central Park,' horse-drawn, 25", VG 650.00
Turcos (Turkish) Soldiers, 4½", G (w/hinged box) 525.00
Wild Animal Picture Cubes, McLoughlin Bros, complete 425.00

Pedal Cars and Ride-On Toys

Some of the largest manufacturers of wheeled goods were AMF (American Machine and Foundry Company), Murray, and Garton. Values depend to a very large extent on condition, and those that have been restored may sell for $1,000.00 or more, depending on the year and model.

Airplane, American National, 1920s, Curtis Moth biwing trimotor, 52", VG restoration, $3,725.00. (Photo courtesy Morphy Auctions on LiveAuctioneers.com)

Airplane, Toledo, Lindy's Spirit of St Louis, 62", VG 7,500.00
Buick Phaeton Touring Car, Gendron, 1925, cloth top, VG+ .12,000.00
Chrysler (1941), Steelcraft, 37", rstr 4,125.00
Chrysler, Murray, 1941, 40", VG 700.00
Comet, Murray, 1950s, G... 300.00
Dodge, American National, working headlights, 34", VG 1,100.00
Fire Chief Car, Gendron, 47", prof rstr........................... 2,000.00
Fire W/F City Battalion No 1, Murray, 1950s, 35", VG 125.00
Greyhound De Luxe Wagon, yel w/bl trim, 40", VG+ 275.00
Hudson, Am National, 1930s, lt on windshield, 45", EX 7,000.00
Hummer, Pioneer, 1914, 33", VG................................... 1,800.00
Hupmobile, Steelcraft, 1932, 45", EX 8,500.00
Irish Mail, Gendron, 1920s, 37", G 450.00
Kiddilac, Murray, 1950s, rstr 550.00
La Salle, Am National, 45", EX.................................... 7,000.00
Lincoln Zephyr, Steelcraft, 1930s, 40", VG 1,900.00
Mercedes, Tri-Ang, prof rst, 60" 16,000.00
Oakland, American National, 41", VG 2,250.00
Packard, Am National, w/roof, rubber tires, 28", EX 16,500.00
Packard, Gendron, 1920s, 50", VG+ 7,000.00
Pioneer Flyer Locomotive, Gendron, 1928, EX 4,250.00
Pontiac, Garton, perforated wheels, 40", EX....................... 900.00
Pontiac Station Wagon, Murray, 1949, 47", G 600.00
Radio Cruiser, Toledo, electric lights & spotlight, 50", EX........ 7,500.00

Ranch Wagon, Garton, chain drive, electric lights, antenna, 45", restored, $250.00. (Photo courtesy Randy Inman Auctions)

Roadster, Gendron, ca 1929, spoke wheels, 42", EX.................1,600.00
Skippy, Gendron, 1930s, 36", VG...1,100.00
Skippy, La Salle, Gendron, perforated wheels, 45", VG+.................1,900.00
Station Wagon (Woody), Garton, 1940s, 46", VG...................2,875.00
Stutz Roadster, Gendron, 1920s, fold-down top, 29", VG.........5,750.00
Super Sport, Murray, 1953, EX+..2,250.00
Wagon, Aero-Flite, 1930s, streamlined style working headlights, 47", EX...950.00
Wagon, Greyhound De Luxe, 40", VG+.......................................275.00
Wagon, Multi-Use Scoot Wagon, MTD, 1960s, unused, NM+IB.400.00
Wagon, Lindy Flyer, 1933 World's Fair decal, working lights, VG...900.00
Wagon, Wolverine Speedster, 34", VG.......................................200.00
Wood Wagon, 2 lg/2 sm spoke wheels, 39", EX...........................300.00
Willys Knight, Steelcraft, 32", overpnt, G.................................650.00
Woody Station Wagon, Garton, 1940s, 46", VG.....................2,875.00

Penny Toys

Penny toys were around as early as the late 1800s and as late as the 1920s. Many were made in Germany, but some were made in France as well. With few exceptions, they ranged in size from 5" on down; some had moving parts, and a few had clockwork mechanisms. Although many were unmarked, you'll sometimes find them signed 'Kellermann,' 'Meier,' 'Fischer,' or 'Distler,' or carrying an embossed company logo such as the 'dog and cart' emblem. They were made of lithographed tin with exquisite detailing — imagine an entire carousel less than 2½" tall. Because of a recent surge in collector interest, many have been crossing the auction block of some of the country's largest galleries.

Airship Ferris Wheel, Meier, crank operated, 3½", NM, $1,680.00. (Photo courtesy Noel Barrett on LiveAuctioneers.com)

Airplane & Hangar, Distler, pilot in open cockpit, 5" L hangar, EX.425.00
Armored Car, Distler, WWI style, 3" L, EX...............................100.00
Auto with Driver & Lady Passenger, Germany, 3½", VG............450.00
Baby Girl In Carriage Holding Doll, Meier, 3¾", EX+................550.00
Barrel Maker on Platform, Fischer, 4", EX...............................325.00
Beer Truck, Distler, open cab, 3½", EX...................................450.00
Billiards Player, Kellermann, 4" L, EX.....................................325.00
Biplane, Meier, 3", EX...500.00
Birdcage w/Canary, Germany, bl, red & yel, 2¾" W, EX+...............125.00
Boat Swing w/2 Kids, Meier, 3¼", EX......................................200.00
Boat w/Sailor, Meier, 4½", EX...500.00
Boy Feeding Dog on Platform, Meier, 4" L, VG..........................200.00
Boy in Rocking Chair, Meier, 2¾", EX......................................250.00
Boy Kneeling in Stake Wagon, Fischer, 2¾", EX.........................725.00
Boy on Irish Mail, Kellermann, 3", VG.....................................300.00
Boy on Rocking Horse, Meier...110.00
Boy Seated on Sled w/Wheels, Meier, 3", EX.............................300.00
Boy w/Butterfly Net Puts Butterfly in Box, Fischer, 3", EX...............425.00
Camel w/Backpack on 4-Wheeled Platform, Meier, 2½", EX...............550.00
Camel w/Rider on 4-Wheeled Platform, 3½", EX.....................2,200.00
Candy Truck, bed w/sliding lid to hold candy, 3½", EX...............550.00
Cargo Truck, Distler, open w/driver, tarp over back, 3¾", EX...............325.00
Carousel w/Bicycle Riders, Meier, 2¼", EX...............................650.00
Cat & Dog Fight on 4-Wheeled Platform, 3½", VG.....................275.00
Cat Confronting Dog in Doghouse on Platform, Meier, 4", EX.165.00
Child in Chair w/Attached Table, Germany, 2½", EX.................300.00
Church Bank, slot in hinged roof, w/key, 3¼", VG.......................175.00
Cito Cycle, 3-wheeled w/driver in open cab, 3¾", VG.................550.00
Cito Trike Car w/Rider, Kellerman, 3½", EX.........................1,650.00
Clown Prodding Mule on Platform, Meier, 4", EX.......................250.00
Clowns (2) Tossing Ball on Footed Platform, Meier, 3¾", VG.................400.00
Covered Wagon Truck (JD), Distler, 1914, 3½", EX....................375.00
Cow on 4-Wheeled Platform, Distler, 2½", G.............................150.00
Cow on 4-Wheeled Platform, Meier, 3¼", EX.............................550.00
Cross Country Skier, Meier, 3½", VG+.......................................400.00
Dachshund on 4-Wheeled Platform, Distler, 4", VG+...................225.00
Delivery Van #245, Fischer, 3½", EX...165.00
Diabolo Player, Meier, oblong base, 2¾x3" L, EX.....................1,900.00
Dog (Spaniel) on 4-Wheeled Platform, Meier, 2⅞", EX......................550.00
Dog w/Cat in Basket on Platform, 4", VG...................................275.00
Dog w/Coiled Tail on 4-Wheeled Platform, Distler, 2½", EX.................300.00
Double-Decker Bus, Distler, 4½", EX..275.00
Elephant on 4-Wheeled Platform, Meier, 2 ", VG+.......................525.00
Elephant Pulling 2-Wheeled Cart, Fischer, 5" L, EX.....................110.00
Equestrian Riders (3) on Base, Meier, 3¾" L, EX+.....................1,700.00
Express Parcels Delivery Truck, Distler, 4", EX...........................110.00
Fire Ladder Truck, Germany, with figures, 4¼"...........................400.00
Flying Hollander, Meier, 3¼", VG,...350.00
Frog Jumps at Butterfly on Box on Platform, Fischer, 3", EX...............375.00
Garage w/Touring Car, 4" L garage, EX.....................................135.00
Gas Station w/Reversing Car, lever-op, 3¼", EX...........................65.00
General Double-Decker Bus, Fischer, 3½", EX.............................110.00
Girl at School Desk Candy Container, Meier, 2¾", EX...............475.00
Girl Feeding Chicken on 4-Wheeled Platform, Meier, 4", EX+...475.00
Gnomes Sawing on 4-Wheeled Platform, 3½", VG+.....................225.00
Goat Pulling Lady in 2-Wheeled Cart, 4" L, VG...........................275.00
Goat w/Candy Box on Platform, Fischer, 3", EX...........................325.00
Goat Walking on 4-Wheeled Cart, Meier, 3", VG+.......................500.00

Goose on Four-Wheeled Platform, Fischer, with nodding neck, 2x3½", EX, $600.00. (Photo courtesy Lloyd Ralston Gallery on LiveAuctioneers.com

Grand Hotel Coach, Meier, lithoed passengers in windows, 3" L, EX. 400.00
Henhouse w/Chickens Feeding from Trough, 2½", EX.................350.00
Horse-Drawn Caisson, Germany, 5½", EX.....................................275.00
Horse-Drawn Carriage w/Driver, 5", EX......................................225.00
Horseless Carriage, Meier, 3¼", VG..325.00
House w/Trip Hammer, Meier, 2", EX..385.00
Interurban Bus, Fischer, 5⅞", EX...450.00
Jockey on Horse-Drawn Sulky, 4", EX...440.00
Jockey on Horse on 4-Wheeled Platform, 2¾", EX.......................190.00
Jockey on Rocking Horse, Meier, 3½", EX...................................300.00
Lady Pushing Child in Rolling Chair, Meier, 3¼", EX.....................450.00
Lady Pushing Child in Sleigh-type Chair, 3", EX+........................750.00
Leopard on 4-Wheeled Platform, Distler, 4", VG+........................475.00
Locomotive & Tender, Distler, red & blk, 5½", EX.......................165.00
Man Dancing Atop Box, Distler, 3¾", VG+..................................355.00
Man Lying on Sled, 4½", EX...275.00
Mattoni's Delivery Cart, box lid opens, 5" L, EX+........................900.00
Monkey on Great Dane, Meier (?), rocker base, 4½", F...............400.00

Monkey on Irish Mail, Meier, 3½", EX.................................1,300.00
Motorcycle w/Civilian Rider, Kellermann, 4", EX......................465.00
Motorcycle w/Uniformed Rider, Kellermann, 2¾", EX................550.00
Mule-Drawn Hay Wagon, Fischer, w/driver, 6", EX+ 200.00
Ocean Liner, Meier, 4½", EX...600.00
Parade Drummer, France, 3⅜", VG..650.00
Pig Pulling Clown in 2-Wheeled Cart, 3¾", EX 875.00
Porter Pushing 2-Wheeled Cart w/Trunk, Fischer, 3¼", EX..............400.00
Punch & Judy Show, Meier, 2¼", EX......................................875.00

Rabbit in Stake Wagon, Fischer, 3" long, EX, $900.00. (Photo courtesy James D. Julia, Inc.)

Racer #4, Meier, 3½", EX..1,750.00
Racer #11, Distler, 4¼", VG 1,425.00
Racer #948, Fischer, 3½", VG+ 600.00
Racer w/Bobbing Head Driver, Fischer, inertia driver, F+ 110.00
Racing Skull w/2 Rowers, Germany, gr, 6½" L, EX....................800.00
Reindeer on 4-Wheeled Platform, Meier, 2¾", EX 650.00
Rocking Horse, box resting on rockers holds candy, 3½", EX.........335.00
Roosters (2) Pecking at Box on Platform, Meier, 4", EX...............400.00
Roosters (2) Pecking at Box on Platform, Meier, 4", VG 250.00
Sheep in Pen w/Tree, 3", VG+ 275.00
Soldier Marching on 4-Wheeled Platform, 3¾", VG+ 225.00
Squirrel on 4-Wheeled Platform, Meier, 3", VG+ 200.00
St Bernard on 4-Wheeled Base, Meier, 3" L, EX+ 525.00
Steam Engine, crank-op, 4", EX...135.00
Steam Engine Whistle, 2½", EX..140.00
Streetcar 129, 4½" VG...375.00
Swordsmen Fighting, Kellermann, squeeze action, 2¼", EX.........330.00
Tap Dancer on Roof, Distler, 4", EX......................................600.00
Telefon (Telephone) 946, old wall crank-type, 4½", EX...............300.00
Toonerville Trolley (Cracker Jack), 1¾", EX 350.00
Touring Car, Meier, 3¼", EX...465.00
Touring Car w/Kangaroo Driver, Distler, 1914, 3¼", NM..........1,400.00
Transfer Truck w/Driver, Meier, 3 " L, EX.............................250.00
Triumph Motorcycle w/Civilian Rider, Meier, 2¾", EX...............715.00
Vis-à-vis, Meier, 3", VG...250.00
Zeppelin, Meier, 4 top props, 2 gondolas w/passengers, 4½", EX ..625.00

Play Sets by Marx

Originally issued as early as 1948 in the form of farms and service stations, the Marx playset quickly became a Baby Boomer sensation offered in many variations containing tiny buildings and forts with soft plastic figures and accessories such as tanks and wagons. Fort Apache, Revolutionary War, and Battle of the Blue & Gray were generic playset titles while Roy Rogers Western Town, Zorro, Walt Disney's Davy Crockett at the Alamo, and even The Flintstones, based on then-popular TV shows, are among the licensed property titles. Johnny Ringo, a short-lived TV series, has the distinction of being the most valuable set since it was only sold for half a year.

In general, illustrated cartons contain the more valuable sets, while photo boxes of the late 1960s and 1970s are by far less valuable and contain parts in less desirable waxy plastics. Miniature (HO scale) sets containing 1" tall painted figures from Marx Hong Kong do often have photo covers and are in high demand.

Near-mint boxes double the value of a complete set; sets still stapled sealed earn stratospheric values at auction. A $350.00 Fort Apache earns thousands for the privilege of opening it and getting 1960 factory air Boxes with tears, stains, or holes, missing parts, or damaged figures greatly decrease values since key items ('Velardi' sign and character figure from Marx Johnny Ringo set) elevate sets above the average. Damaged parts like a split trail in a wagon hitch devalue the total piece. A mint yellow wagon will sell for $300.00; with split traces, it's $150.00. Likewise the hard plastic caisson in Civil War sets: intact it fetches $125.00; but with the tiny hitches broken, it's worth less than half that. A Matt Dillon character figure from the Gunsmoke set gets $700.00 to $1,200.00, depending on who's bidding; but with scuffed hat brim or dimpled torso he drops to $350.00 or less.

The listings below are for complete examples unless noted otherwise.

Adventures of Robin Hood, #4722, EXIB...................................400.00
Alamo, #3534, NMIB...2,000.00
Alaska, #3707-8, NMIB, w/knife & accessories 800.00
Allstate Service Station (4-level), #3499, EX+IB 400.00
American Airlines Astro Jet Port, #4821-2, NMIB......................435.00
Arctic Explorer, #3702, EXIB...1,100.00
Army Combat Set, #4158, EXIB...150.00
Army Combat Training Center, #2654, VGIB 25.00
Bar-M Ranch, Marx #3956, EXIB..75.00
Battlefield, #4756, Series 500, NMIB..................................3,900.00
Battleground, #4139, EXIB..125.00
Battleground, #4150, EX...500.00
Battleground, #4749-50, Series 1000, basic set, NMIB.................400.00
Battleground, #4751, EX...450.00
Battleground, #4752, EX...500.00
Battleground, #4756, photobox set, EXIB................................100.00
Battleground Convoy, #3745-6, NMIB..................................2,000.00
Battle of Iwo Jima, #4147, NMIB, $750 to...............................800.00
Battle of Iwo Jima, #4154, EXIB.......................................1,200.00
Battle of Iwo Jima, #6057, giant set, NMIB...........................1,500.00
Battle of Little Big Horn, #4679MO, w/Custer, MIB...................900.00
Battle of the Alamo (Heritage), #59091, EX+IB 300.00
Battle of the Blue & Gray, #2646, rare half set, M...................1,500.00
Battle of the Blue & Gray, #4658, Series 2000, EXIB..................450.00
Battle of the Blue & Gray, #4744, NMIB 750.00
Battle of the Blue & Gray, #4760, Series 2000, EXIB..................900.00
Beach Head Landing Set, #4939, NMIB.....................................75.00
Ben Hur, #2648, MOC...900.00
Ben Hur, #4696, EXIB...750.00

Ben Hur, #4701, Series 5000, MIB, $1,900.00. (Photo courtesy Philip Weiss Auctions on LiveAuctioneers.com)

Ben Hur, #4702, Series 2000, 4 chariots, NMIB 1,200.00
Big Inch Pipeline, #6008, EXIB...650.00
Big Top Circus, #4310, EXIB..350.00
Boy's Camp, #4103, unused, MIB (sealed)..............................1,200.00
Cape Canaveral, #4524, Series 2000, NMIB 225.00

Cape Canaveral Missile Base, #4524, NMIB 375.00
Cape Canaveral Missile Base, #4528, EXIB 150.00
Cape Canaveral Missile Base, #5935, NMIB 675.00
Cape Kennedy (Carry-All), #4625, tin box, NMIB 75.00
Captain Gallant, #4729, NMIB 1,600.00
Captain Space Solar Academy, 7026, EXIB 400.00
Captain Space Solar Port, #7018, EXIB 400.00
Castle, Elastolin 9756, EXIB 300.00
Cattle Drive, #3983, NMIB 375.00
Charge of the Light Brigade, HO set w/Arabs 600.00
Commanche Pass, #3416, NMIB 150.00
Construction Camp, #4442, EX+IB 200.00
Construction Camp, #4444, w/tin friction vehicles 650.00
Cowboy & Indian Camp, #3950, NMIB 800.00
Custer's Last Stand, #4779, Series 500, NMIB 750.00
D-Day Army, #6027, medium set, NMIB 800.00
Daktari, #3717, EXIB 700.00
Daktari, #3718, EXIB 800.00
Daktari, #3720, NMIB 900.00
Daniel Boone Frontier, #1393, NMIB 275.00
Daniel Boone Wilderness Scout, #0631, NMIB 250.00
Daniel Boone Wilderness Scout, #0670, NMIB 250.00
Daniel Boone Wilderness Scout, #2640, EXIB 175.00
Davy Crockett at the Alamo, #3442, NMIB 375.00
Davy Crockett at the Alamo, #3530, NMIB 300.00
Davy Crockett at the Alamo, #3530, EXIB 150.00
Desert Patrol, #4174, MIB 350.00
Farm, #3948, Series 2000, NMIB 275.00
Farm, #5942, EXIB 75.00
Farm, #6006, NMIB 225.00
Farm, #6050, EXIB 100.00
Farm, Platform #5990, EX 650.00
Farm (Happi-Time), #3943, NMIB 175.00

Fess Parker as Daniel Boone Fort Boone Play Set, Multiple, #588, NMIB, $275.00. (Photo courtesy Morphy Auctions on LiveAuctioneers.com)

Fort Apache, #3616, NMIB 125.00
Fort Apache, #3647, NMIB 300.00
Fort Apache, #3680, open, complete, EX 500.00
Fort Apache, #3680, unused, MIB (sealed) 3,025.00
Fort Apache, #3681, EXIB 75.00
Fort Apache, #3682A, EX+IB 50.00
Fort Apache, #4202, NMIB 50.00
Fort Apache, #6059, NMIB 1,300.00
Fort Apache, #6063, EXIB 150.00
Fort Apache, #6068, EX+IB 50.00
Fort Apache Stockade, Marx #3612, NMIB 200.00
Fort Apache Stockade, Marx #3660, Series 2000, NMIB 250.00
Fort Boone, Multiple, NMIB 175.00
Fort Pitt, #3742, Series 1000, NMIB 350.00
Galaxy Command, #4206, NMIB 75.00
Gallant Men, #4634, EX+IB 2,600.00
Gallant Men Army, #4632, EX+IB 100.00
Gunsmoke (Dodge City), #4268, Series 2000, EXIB 5,000.00
History in the Pacific, #4164, NMIB 300.00
Holiday Turnpike, #5230, NMIB 25.00

IGY Arctic Satellite Base, #4800, Series 1000, EX+IB 850.00
Johnny Apollo Launch Center, #4630, EXIB 100.00
Johnny Tremain Revolutionary War, #3402, rare, EXIB 1,800.00
Jungle, #3705, Series 500, NMIB 350.00
King Arthur's Castle, #4800, NMIB 225.00
Knights & Vikings, #4733, NM+IB 200.00
Little Red Schoolhouse, #3381-2, EX+IB 750.00
Lone Ranger Ranch, #3969, Series 500, NMIB 300.00
Medieval Castle, #4707, EXIB 50.00
Medieval Castle, #4708/Sears, Series 2000, EX+IB 200.00
Medieval Castle, #4733, EXIB 250.00
Medieval Castle Fort, #4709-10, NMIB 175.00
Midtown Service Station, #5953, EXIB 600.00
Midtown Shopping Center, #2644, NMIB 700.00
Military Academy, #4718, EX+IB 400.00
Noah's Ark, miniature, EX+IB 45.00
One Million BC, #59842, EXIB 350.00
Operation Moon Base, #4653-1, MIB 600.00
Operation Moon Base, #4653-4, EXIB 500.00
Parking Garage (4-level), #3502, EX+IB $75.00
Prince Valiant Castle, #4705, EXIB 350.00
Revolutionary War, #3401, EXIB 400.00
Rifleman Ranch, #3997-8, NMIB 500.00
Robin Hood Castle, #4717, NMIB 400.00
Roy Rogers Rodeo Ranch, #3979, NMIB 175.00
Roy Rogers Rodeo Ranch, #3985, NMIB 275.00
Roy Rogers Rodeo Ranch, #3986R, EXIB 300.00
Roy Rogers Rodeo Ranch, #3992, NMIB 300.00
Roy Rogers Rodeo Ranch, #3996, MIB 575.00
Silver City Frontier Town, #4219-20, NMIB 300.00
Silver City Western Town, #4220, NMIB 525.00
Silver City Western Town, #4256, EXIB 300.00
Skyscraper, #5449-50, EXIB 400.00
Skyscraper, #5450, NMIB 850.00
Sons of Liberty (Sears Heritage), #59147C, NMIB 325.00
Strategic Air Command, Marx #6013, EXIB 1,600.00
Super Circus, #4320, EXIB 200.00
Tales of Wells Fargo, #4264, EXIB 375.00
Tank Battle, Marx/Sears #6056, NMIB 600.00
Television Playhouse, #4350 or #4352, NMIB, ea 400.00
Tom Corbett Space Academy, #7012, NMIB 825.00
Untouchables, #4676, EXIB 2,500.00
US Armed Forces Training Center, #4144, NMIB 175.00
US Armed Forces Training Center, #4149-50, EXIB 100.00
US Armed Forces Training Center, #4158, EXIB 200.00
US Armed Forces Training Center, #4158, NMIB 375.00
US Army Mobile Set, #3655, NMIB 150.00
US Army Training Center, #3146, EXIB 50.00
US Army Training Center, #4123, NMIB 200.00
Vikings & Knights, #6053, NMIB 200.00
Western Mining Town, #4266, NMIB 400.00
Western Ranch Set, #3980, NMIB 100.00

Western Town, Marx #2652, unused, MIB (sealed), $450.00. (Photo courtesy Morphy Auctions on LiveAuctioneers.com)

Western Town, #4229, EXIB 250.00
Yogi Bear at Jellystone National Park, #4363-4, EXIB.......................... 350.00

Pull and Push Toys

Pull and push toys from the 1800s often were hide- and cloth-covered animals with glass or shoe-button eyes on wheels or wheeled platforms. Many were also made of tin or wood. Some of the cast-iron bell toys of that era can be found in Toys, Cast Iron.

Alderney milk wagon, wood, w/figure, Schoenhut, 21", VG 3,000.00
Buffalo Bill/2 buffalos on wheeled base, tin, Fallows, 9", EX 2,800.00
Butcher Wagon, pnt tin, 11½", some rstr 1,775.00
Camel on wheeled base, tin, A Bergmann, 1880s, 9", G 1,035.00
Central Transportation trolley, tin, 1 horse, Fallows, 16", VG .. 2,585.00
Coaster Boy #140, 1941, VG 500.00
City Delivery wagon, tin, 2 horses, Converse, 20", VG................. 525.00

Duck, painted cast iron, when pulled bill opens and legs move, 9½", Hubley, 1930s, NM, $2,800.00. (Photo courtesy Morphy Auctions on LiveAuctioneers.com)

Elephant on wheeled base, tin, friction, Converse, 8x9", VG 225.00
Fine Bread/Cakes wagon, wood, w/horse, Schoenhut, 20", VG .5,000.00
Goat (lg) & sm girl on wheeled base, tin, Fallows, 1880s, 7", G ..275.00
Hoop toy w/horse, pnt tin, 6¼" dia, A Bergmann, rpnt 325.00
Horse & colt on wheeled base, tin, Merriam, 1860s, EX 2,800.00
Lion w/tamer on wheeled base, tin, A Bergmann, 1870s, 4", VG . 950.00

Old Woman in a Shoe, Ives, painted cast iron with nine dressed bisque dolls, 9", EX, $5,400.00. (Photo courtesy Noel Barrett on LiveAuctioneers.com)

Ox cart, tin, 2-wheeled, George Brn, 9", VG.............................. 2,645.00
Perpetual Motion #910, very rare, NMIP....................................... 575.00
Pure Milk wagon, tin, w/horse & driver, Fallows, 12", VG+ 2,250.00
Reindeer, tin, on 2 front wheels w/clicker, 8", VG 250.00
Rocking horse w/jockey rider, tin, Fallows, 7", EX+ 3,000.00
Transit train locomotive, tin, w/up, Ives, 7", VG...................... 1,300.00
US Mail wagon, tin/wood, 3 horses, Converse, VG+ 750.00

Robots

Space is a genre that anyone who grew up in the '50s and '60s can relate to; to collectors, sometimes the stranger, the better. Some robots were made of lithographed tin, but even plastic toys (Atom Robot, for example) are high on want lists of many serious buyers. Condition is extremely important, both in general appearance and internal workings. Mint-in-box examples may be worth twice as much as one mint-no-box, since the package art was often just as awesome as the toy itself.

Because of the high prices these toys now command, many have been reproduced. Beware!

See also Toys, Guns and Early Cast-Iron Cap Shooters.

Astro Scout, Yonezawa, 1960s, friction, tin, 9", NMIB 13,550.00
Astroman, Nomura, 1960s, w/up, tin & plastic, 10", EX+IB.....9,600.00
Astronaut, Daiya/AHI, 1960s, w/up, tin & plastic, 6½", EX+IB ..300.00
Batman Robot, Atom/Japan, 1960s, w/up, tin & vinyl, 13", EXIB ...13,800.00
Buck Rogers Rocket Police Patrol, Marx, w/up, tin, 11½", EX.................1,100.00
Buzzer Robot, Yonezawa, 1950s, b/o, tin, 10½", EXIB.................3,550.00
Change Man, Marumiya, r/c, tin, vinyl & plastic, 13½", NM ...5,930.00
Chief Robotman, Yoshiya, 1960s, b/o, tin, 12", NMIB............1,075.00
Chief Smokey Robot, Yoshiya, 1960s, b/o, tin, 12", EX+IB 4,225.00
Colonel Hap Hazard, Marx, 1960s, b/o, tin & plastic, 12", EXIB.. 750.00
Conehead Space Robot, Yonezawa, 1960s, w/up, tin, 8½", EX+.2,150.00
Cragston Great Astronaut, Alps, b/o, tin & plastic, NMIB.......2,650.00
Cragston Mr Atomic, Yonezawa, 1962, b/o, tin, 9", EX 4,050.00
Directional Robot, Yonezawa, 1950s, b/o, tin, 10", NMIB 1,100.00
Doctor Moon, Daiya, w/up, tin & plastic, 7", EXIB.................... 700.00
Domed Easel-Back Robot, Linemar, 1950s, r/c, 6", EX+ 2,300.00
Golden Robot, Linemar, 1950s, r/c, tin, 6½", EXIB.................1,850.00
Hook Robot, Marubishi, friction, tin, 7", EXIB, box (+) 4,350.00
Jumping Rocket, Yoneya, 1960s, w/up, tin, 6", NMIB.................. 550.00
Jupiter Robot, Yoshiya, r/c, tin & plastic, NM+IB...................... 650.00
Lantern Robot, Linemar, 1950s, r/c, tin, 8½", EX+ 1,635.00
Man from Mars, Irwin, w/up, plastic, 11½", NM+ 250.00
Mego Man, Yoneya, w/up, tin, 7", NMIB..................................... 500.00
Mighty Robot, Yoshiya, 1960s, b/o, 12", EXIB............................3,650.00
Moon Astronaut, Daiya, 1950s, w/up, tin, 9", EX+IB.................4,300.00
Mr Robot, Asahi, 1960s, w/up, tin & plastic, 7", NMIB............. 775.00
Musical Drummer Robot, Nomura, 1950s, b/o, tin, 8", EXIB.........5,350.00
Non-Stop Robot (Lavender Robot), Masudaya, 1950s, b/o, tin, 15", NMIB..5,800.00
Radicon Robot, Masudaya, 1950s, b/o, tin, 20", NMIB..............17,500.00
Ranger Robot, Daiya, 1965, b/o, tin & plastic, 8", EX+ 1,635.00
Rocket Ranger, Marusan, friction, tin, 6", EX+IB 650.00
Scouting Rocket X-20, Nomura, friction, tin, 10" L, NM 1,450.00
Smoking Space Man, Yonezawa, 1960s, b/o, tin, 12", VG+ 775.00
Space Dog, Yoshiya, 1950s, b/o, tin, 7½", EX+IB 2,525.00
Space Dog, Yoshiya, 1950s, friction, tin, 7½", NMIB 575.00
Space Dog, Yoshiya, 1950s, w/up, tin, 7½", EX+IB 525.00
Space Robot Car, Yonezawa, 1950s, b/o, tin, 9½" L, EX+ 2,600.00
Talking Robot, Yonezawa, 1960s, friction, b/o voice, tin, 11", EXIB...850.00
Thunder Robot, Asakusa, 1960s, b/o, tin & plastic, 11½", NMIB.3,200.00
Ultraman Robot, Bullmark, w/up, tin w/vinyl head, 9", EXIB...... 575.00

Schoenhut

The listings below are for Humpty Dumpty Circus pieces. All values are based on rating conditions of good to very good, i.e., very minor scratches and wear, good original finish, no splits or chips, no excessive paint wear or cracked eyes, and of course completeness and condition of clothes (if dressed figures).

Humpty Dumpty Circus Clowns and Other Personnel

Clowns with two-part heads (a cast face applied to a wooden head) were made from 1903 to 1912 and are most desirable — condition always is important. There have been nine distinct styles in 14 different costumes recorded. Only eight costume styles apply to the two-part headed clowns. The later clowns had one-part heads whose features were pressed wood, and the costumes on the later ones, circa 1920+, were no longer tied at the wrists and ankles.

Black Dude, 1-part head, purple coat, $250 to............................... 750.00

Black Dude, two-part head, black coat, $400.00 to $1,000.00. (Photo courtesy Noel Barrett on LiveAuctioneers.com)

Chinese Acrobat, 1-part head, $200 to	900.00
Chinese Acrobat, 2-part head, rare, $400 to	1,600.00
Clown, reduced sz, $75 to	125.00
Hobo, 1-part head, $200 to	400.00
Hobo, 2-part head, curved-up toes, blk coat, $500 to	1,200.00
Hobo, reduced sz, $200 to	400.00
Lady Acrobat, 1-part head, $150 to	400.00
Lady Acrobat, bsk head, $300 to	800.00
Lady Rider, 2-part head, very rare, $500 to	1,000.00
Lady Rider, bsk head, $250 to	550.00
Lion Tamer, 1-part head, $150 to	700.00
Lion Tamer, 2-part head, early, very rare, $700 to	1,600.00
Ringmaster, 1-part head, $200 to	450.00
Ringmaster, 2-part head, blk coat, very rare, $800 to	1,800.00
Ringmaster, 2-part head, red coat, very rare, $700 to	1,600.00
Ringmaster, bsk, $300 to	800.00

Humpty Dumpty Circus Animals

Humpty Dumpty Circus animals with glass eyes, ca. 1903 – 1914, are more desirable and can demand much higher prices than the later painted-eye versions. As a general rule, a glass-eye version is 30% to 40% more than a painted-eye version. (There are exceptions.) The following list suggests values for both GE (glass-eye) and PE (painted-eye) versions and reflects a **low PE price** to a **high GE price.**

There are other variations and nuances of certain figures: Bulldog — white with black spots or brindle (brown); open- and closed-mouth zebras, camels, and giraffes; ball necks and hemispherical necks on some animals such as the pig, cat, and hippo, to name a few. These points can affect the price and should be judged individually. Condition and rarity affect the price most significantly and the presence of an original box virtually doubles the price.

Alligator, PE/GE, $250 to	750.00
Arabian camel, 1 hump, PE/GE, $250 to	750.00
Bactrain camel, 2 humps, PE/GE, $200 to	1,200.00
Brown bear, PE/GE, $200 to	800.00
Buffalo, cvd mane, PE/GE, $200 to	1,200.00
Bulldog, PE/GE, $400 to	1,500.00
Burro, farm set, PE/GE, no harness/no belly hole for chariot, $300 to	800.00
Burro, made to go w/chariot & clown, PE/GE, w/leather track, $200 to	800.00
Cat, PE/GE, rare, $500 to	3,000.00

Cow, painted eyes/glass eyes, $300.00 to $1,200.00. (Photo courtesy Bertoia Auctions on LiveAuctioneers.com)

Deer, PE/GE, $300 to	1,500.00
Donkey w/blanket, PE/GE, $100 to	600.00

Donkey, PE/GE, $75 to	300.00
Elephant, PE/GE, $75 to	300.00
Gazelle, PE/GE, rare, $500 to	3,000.00
Giraffe, PE/GE, $200 to	900.00
Goose, PE only, $200 to	750.00
Gorilla, PE only, $1,500 to	4,000.00
Hippo, PE/GE, $200 to	900.00
Horse, brn, PE/GE, saddle & stirrups, $250 to	500.00
Horse, dapple, PE/GE, platform, $250 to	700.00
Hyena, PE/GE, very rare, $1,000 to	6,000.00
Kangaroo, PE/GE, $200 to	500.00

Lion, glass eyes, original ears and tail, rare variation, 8", EX, $7,800.00. (Photo courtesy Noel Barrett on LiveAuctioneers.com)

Monkey, 1-part head, PE only, $200 to	600.00
Monkey, 2-part head, wht face, $300 to	1,000.00
Ostrich, PE/GE, $200 to	900.00
Pig, 5 versions, PE/GE, $200 to	800.00
Polar bear, PE/GE, $200 to	2,000.00
Poodle, PE/GE, $100 to	300.00
Rabbit, PE/GE, very rare, $500 to	3,500.00
Rhino, PE/GE, $250 to	800.00
Sea lion, PE/GE, $400 to	350.00
Sheep (lamb), PE/GE, w/bell, $200 to	800.00
Tiger, PE/GE, $250 to	1,200.00
Wolf, PE/GE, very rare, $500 to	5,000.00
Zebra, PE/GE, rare, $500 to	3,000.00

Humpty Dumpty Circus Accessories

There are many accessories: wagons, tents, ladders, chairs, pedestals, tightrope, weights, and more.

Cage wagon, ...Greatest Show on Earth, 10" & 12", EX, $300 to	1,200.00
Managerie tent, early, ca 1904, $1,500 to	3,000.00
Menagerie tent, later, 1914-20, $1,200 to	2,000.00

Tent, 24x35" arena, $510.00. (Photo courtesy Bertoia Auctions on LiveAuctioneers.com)

Steiff

Margaret Steiff made the first of her felt toys in 1880, stuffing them with lamb's wool. Later followed toys of velvet, plush, and wool, and in addition to the lamb's wool stuffing, she used felt scraps, excelsior, and kapok. In 1897 and 1898 her trademark was a paper label printed with an elephant; from 1900 to 1905 her toys carried a circular tag with an elephant logo that was different from the one she had previously used. The most famous 'button in ear' trademark was registered on December

20, 1904. The years 1904 and 1905 saw the use of the button with an elephant (extremely rare) and the blank button (which is also rare). The button with Steiff and the underscored or trailing 'F' was used until 1948, and the raised script button is from the 1950s.

Steiff teddy bears, perhaps the favorite of collectors everywhere, are characterized by their long thin arms with curved wrists and paws that extend below their hips. Buyer beware: The Steiff company is now making many replicas of their old bears. For more information about Steiff's buttons, chest tags, and stock tags, as well as the inspirational life of Margaret Steiff and the fascinating history of Steiff toys, we recommend *Button in Ear Book* and *The Steiff Book of Teddy Bears*, both by Jurgen and Marianne Cieslik; *Teddy Bears and Steiff Animals, 2nd* and *3rd Series*, by Margaret Fox Mandel (Collector Books); *4th Teddy Bear and Friends Price Guide* by Linda Mullins; *Collectible German Animals Value Guide* by Dee Hockenberry; and *Steiff Sortiment, 1947 – 1995*, by Gunther Pefiffer. (This book is in German; however, the reader can discern the size of the item, year of production, and price estimation).

See also Teddy Bear Collectibles.

Bear on wheels, brn, glass eyes, 18", G+	400.00
Bear, apricot, shoe-button eyes, pre-WWI, 14", G+	2,500.00
Bear, beige, glass eyes, shaved snout, 1950s, 15", VG+	300.00
Bear, blond, glass eyes, script ear button, 1940s-50s, 30", VG	1,950.00
Bear, blond, shoe-button eyes, 1905, 8", VG	675.00
Bear, gold, blk shoe-button eyes, 1907, 20", VG	4,300.00
Bear, honey blond, blk bead eyes, no pads, 1950s, 3½", VG	100.00
Bear, lt beige, shoe-button eyes, ca 1910, 17½", EX	5,000.00
Bear, yel, glass eyes, ear button, 1950s, 12½", EX	550.00
Cow on wheels, brn & wht, neck bell, growler, 12", VG	600.00
Dalmatian, recumbent, red collar, 1950s, 12x15", VG	425.00
Dinosaur (Brosus), beige & yel, googly eyes, 1960s, 12½", EX	225.00

Doll, Coachman's Assistant, felt, side-glancing eyes, black top hat, tan overcoat and spats, red vest, original button, 16", VG+, $6,900.00. (Photo courtesy James D. Julia, Inc.)

Elephant, beige/airbrushed details, glass eyes, 14", 1950s, EX	125.00
Eric the Bat, lg version, EX	300.00
Fox standing upright, jtd forelegs, 32", EX	500.00
German Shepherd, recumbent, 1950s, 14x27" L, EX	475.00
Kangaroo, joey in pouch, glass eyes, 1950s, 19", EX	100.00

Monkey, Jocko, ear tag, 20", $300.00. (Photo courtesy Philip Weiss Auctions on LiveAuctioneers.com)

Monkey (60PB), string jtd, 1903, 32", VG+	6,600.00
Somersault bear, beige, mechanical action, 1909, 12", EX+	4,750.00
Stork, felt, brn glass eyes, 24", 1950s, VG	500.00

Toy Soldiers and Accessories

Dimestore soldiers were made from the 1920s until sometime in the 1960s. Some of the better-known companies who made these small-scale figures and vehicles were Barclay, Manoil, and American Metal Toys, formerly known as Jones (hollow cast lead); Grey Iron (cast iron); and Auburn Rubber. They are 3" to 3½" high and were sold in Woolworth's, Kresge's, and other five-and-dime stores for a nickel or a dime, hence the name dimestore. Marx made tin soldiers for use in target gun games and these sell for about $10.00 to $25.00. Condition is most important as these soldiers saw lots of action. They are often found with much of the paint worn off and with some serious 'battle wounds' such as missing arms or rifle tips. Such figures have little value to collectors. Nearly 2,000 different figures and vehicles were made by the major manufacturers, plus a number of others by minor makers such as Tommy Toy and All-Nu.

Another very popular line of toy soldiers has been made by Britains of England since 1893. They are smaller and usually more detailed than dimestores, and variants number in the thousands. We recommend *Collecting American Made Toy Soldiers* by Richard O'Brien for more information about dimestore soldiers, and *Collecting Foreign-Made Toy Soldiers* also by Richard O'Brien, for Britains and others not made in America.

Note: Percentages in the description lines refer to the amount of original paint remaining, a most important evaluation factor.

The following listings were provided by our advisors, Stan and Sally Alekna (see Directory, Pennsylvania).

Am Metal Toys, German running w/rifle, very scarce, 97%	180.00
Am Metal Toys, soldier kneeling at searchlight, khaki, scarce, 98%	105.00
Am Metal Toys, solider kneeling, firing, khaki, scarce, 95%	125.00
Am Metal Toys, soldier prone, firing dbl machine gun, khaki, 96%	133.00
Am Metal Toys, solider standing, firing rifle, khaki, scarce, 98%	135.00
Auburn Rubber, solder marching, port arms rare wht uniform, 99%	32.00
Auburn Rubber, wht guard officer, yel tunic, red trousers, red trim, scarce, 98%	38.00
Barclay, AA-gunner, rusty helmet, 98%	35.00
Barclay, bugler, wht helmet, scrace, 98%	74.00
Barclay, cameraman, kneeling, 99%	48.00
Barclay, cavalryman on brn horse, ca 1930s, 2¼", 97%	35.00
Barclay, cowboy firing pistol, gr shirt, orange pants, 98%	27.00
Barclay, cowboy firing pistol, gr shirt, red pants, 98%	26.00
Barclay, cowboy w/2 pistols, tan outfit, 98%	28.00
Barclay, cowboy w/tin hat brim, 95%	29.00
Barclay, firing behind wall, pnt mortar, scarce, 98%	82.00
Barclay, flag bearer, 99%	32.00
Barclay, Indian brave w/rifle across waist, 97%	25.00
Barclay, Indian chief w/bow & arrow, scarce, 95%	30.00
Barclay, Indian chief w/tomahawk & shield, rare flat base, 99%	25.00
Barclay, Indian kneeling w/bow & arrow, 99%	24.00
Barclay, Indian on wht horse w/rifle, 96%	46.00
Barclay, Indian w/rifle on brn horse, 94%	39.00
Barclay, Indian w/rifle on wht horse, 98%	47.00
Barclay, king w/pennant, 98%	26.00
Barclay, knight w/shield, 99%	24.00
Barclay, machine gunner prone, red gun, 96%	27.00
Barclay, machine gunner prone, silver gun, 97%	28.00
Barclay, machine gunner, kneeling, 96%	27.00
Barclay, marine marching, 94%	38.00
Barclay, marine officer w/sword, 98%	52.00
Barclay, naval officer in wht, 94%	29.00
Barclay, nurse in bl, 95% orig pnt	325.00

Barclay, nurse, kneeling, red cross on veil & arm, 97% 38.00
Barclay, officer in bl, no chest strap, 95% orig pnt 250.00
Barclay, officer in helmet on horse, scarce, 99% 123.00
Barclay, officer w/sword, 97% 41.00
Barclay, redcap w/bags, 97% 29.00
Barclay, sentry in overcoat, 99% 34.00
Barclay, ski trooper in brn, no skis, scarce, 98% 89.00
Barclay, soldier charging, gr, 97% 44.00
Barclay, soldier charging, gr, 99% 23.00
Barclay, soldier charging w/red machine gun, scarce, 96% 45.00
Barclay, soldier in gas mask w/rifle, 96% 30.00
Barclay, soldier kneeling, firing rifle, khaki, 98% 27.00
Barclay, soldier leaning out w/field phone, scarce, 95% 89.00
Barclay, soldier marching, shoulder arms, 98% 22.00
Barclay, soldier, marching, gr pot helmet, 99% 29.00
Barclay, soldier, marching, sling arms, 98% 42.00
Barclay, soldier peeling potatoes, 94% 31.00
Barclay, soldier, pigeon dispatcher, 98% 38.00
Barclay, soldier w/sentry dog, scarce, 98% 96.00

Barclay, soldier with typewriter at wooden table, scarce, M, $170.00. (Photo courtesy Ken Frecker Auctioneers, Inc. on LiveAuctioneers.com)

Barclay, stretcher bearer, closed hand, 96% 31.00
Grey Iron, cadet officer, gray jacket, wht trousers, 97% 34.00
Grey Iron, cadet, lt bl jacket, wht trousers, 98% 35.00
Grey Iron, cadet, wht uniform w/red trim, 96% 32.00

Grey Iron, doughboy supporting wounded soldier, cast helmet, 2⅝", $90.00. (Photo courtesy Ken Frecker Auctioneers, Inc. on LiveAuctioneers.com)

Grey Iron, Indian brave, shielding eyes, scarce, 99% 42.00
Grey Iron, Indian scout firing pistol over bk of horse, very scarce, 95% .395.00
Grey Iron, legion bugler, 92% 22.00
Grey Iron, legion drummer, 94% 25.00
Grey Iron, US doughboy w/range finder, scarce, 95% 96.00
Grey Iron, US infantry, charging, 97% 23.00
Grey Iron, US infantry, rt shoulder arms, 97% 22.00
Grey Iron, US machine gunner, kneeling, 96% 20.00
Grey Iron, US marine, dk bl tunic, 98% 33.00
Grey Iron, US sailor in wht, 95% 23.00
Lincoln Log, Indian in war bonnet w/rifle, 97% 17.00
Lincoln Log, mtd colonial officer of 1776, scarce, 96% 48.00
Maniol, soldier wounded on stretcher, very scarce, 97% 275.00
Manoil, AA-machine gunner w/range finder, sm CF on bk, 99% .. 38.00
Manoil, aviator holding bomb, 99% 45.00
Manoil, camouflaged sniper prone, flowers not pnt, 96% 41.00
Manoil, camouflaged sniper prone, pnt flowers, 97% 43.00
Manoil, machine gunner prone, grass on base, 98% 38.00

Manoil, marine, marching, 99% 39.00
Manoil, navy gunner in bare ft, 98% 42.00
Manoil, radio operator, prone, scarce, 96% 69.00
Manoil, soldier in gas mask w/flare pistol, scarce, 98% 54.00
Manoil, soldier in overseas cap, couple pnt chips on face, scarce, 98%... 90.00
Manoil, soldier kneeling, firing rifle, 94% 28.00
Manoil, soldier w/camera, thick arm, scarce, 98% 108.00
Manoil, tommy gunner, 97% 41.00
Miller Plaster, General Douglas MacArthur, 99% 58.00
Miller Plaster, soldier prone, firing orig M-1 rifle, 99% 33.00
Miller Plaster, wounded soldier w/orig stretcher, 98% 44.00

Trains

Some of the earliest trains (from ca. 1860) were made of tin or cast iron, smaller versions of the full-scale steam-powered trains that traversed America from the east to the west. Most were made to simply be pushed or pulled along, though some had clockwork motors. Electric trains were produced as early as the late nineteenth century. Three of the largest manufacturers were Lionel, Ives, and American Flyer.

Lionel trains have been made since 1900. Until 1915 they produced only standard gauge models (measuring 2½" between the rails). The smaller O gauge (1¼") they introduced at that time proved to be highly successful, and the company grew until by 1955 it had become the largest producer of trains in the world. Until discontinued in 1940, standard gauge trains were produced on a limited scale, but O and 027 gauge models dominated the market. Production dwindled and nearly stopped in the mid-1960s, but the company was purchased by General Mills in 1969, and they continue to produce a very limited number of trains today.

The Ives company had been a major producer of toys since 1896. They were the first to initiate manufacture of the O gauge train and at first used only clockwork motors to propel them. Their first electric trains (in both O and 1 gauge) were made in 1910, but because electricity was not yet a common commodity in many areas, clockwork production continued for several years. By 1920, 1 gauge was phased out in favor of standard gauge. The company continued to prosper until the late 1920s when it floundered and was bought jointly by American Flyer and Lionel. American Flyer soon turned their interest over to Lionel, who continued to make Ives trains until 1933.

The American Flyer company had produced trains for several years, but it wasn't until it was bought by AC Gilbert in 1937 that it became successful enough to be considered a competitor of Lionel. They're best noted for their conversion from the standard (wide gauge) three-rail system to the two-rail S gauge (⅞") and the high-quality locomotives and passenger and freight cars they produced in the 1950s. Interest in toy trains waned during the space-age decade of the 1960s. As a result, sales declined, and in 1966 the company was purchased by Lionel. Today both American Flyer and Lionel trains are being made from the original dies by Lionel Trains Inc., privately owned.

Identification numbers given in the listings below actually appear on the item.

For more information we recommend *Collecting Toy Trains* by Richard O'Brien.

American Flyer, accessory, #596, EX 100.00
American Flyer, accessory, Flyerville station, #163, EXIB 475.00

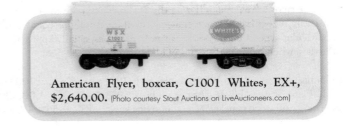

American Flyer, boxcar, C1001 Whites, EX+, $2,640.00. (Photo courtesy Stout Auctions on LiveAuctioneers.com)

American Flyer, boxcar, 24016, MKT/The Katy, yel w/red top, G ..325.00
American Flyer, flatcar, 24558, Canadian Pacific, w/Christmas trees, NMIB 575.00
American Flyer, hopper, 4006, red, prewar, VG+IB 500.00
American Flyer, loco, 4637, Shasta, prewar, G 675.00
American Flyer, loco & tender, 343, VG 350.00
American Flyer, passenger car, 652, Pikes Peak, red, VG 75.00
American Flyer, set, President's Special, 5-pc, VG 2,300.00
American Flyer, tank car, 910, Gilbert Chemicals, EXIB 325.00
Ives, accessory, Union Station, 22" L, G 950.00
Ives, loco 0-4-0/20 & tender 25, O gauge, G+ 250.00
Ives, set, #704, 4-pc, prewar, VGIB 900.00
Lionel, accessory, crossing signal, #79, prewar, VG 325.00
Lionel, accessory, Lionelville, #136, VGIB 175.00
Lionel, accessory, water tank, #93, NMIB 525.00
Lionel, baggage car, 19011, NM 250.00
Lionel, boxcar, 3666, Minuteman, VG+ 425.00
Lionel, boxcar, 6044, Airfix, rare purple color, EX 525.00
Lionel, caboose, 6447, Pennsylvania, NM+ 500.00
Lionel, cattle car, 13, prewar, VG 850.00
Lionel, hopper, 6456-75, Lehigh Valley, VG+IB 150.00
Lionel, loco, 38, New York Central Lines, prewar, EX+ 650.00
Lionel, loco, 54, 0-4-4-0 electric, brass w/red catchers, VG 2,000.00
Lionel, loco & tender, 385E loco, 384T tender, VG................... 325.00
Lionel, passenger car, 400, Baltimore & Ohio, G 200.00

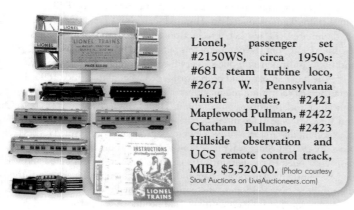

Lionel, passenger set #2150WS, circa 1950s: #681 steam turbine loco, #2671 W. Pennsylvania whistle tender, #2421 Maplewood Pullman, #2422 Chatham Pullman, #2423 Hillside observation and UCS remote control track, MIB, $5,520.00. (Photo courtesy Stout Auctions on LiveAuctioneers.com)

Lionel, set, Chesapeake & Ohio, #31904, NMIB 200.00
Lionel, set, Great Plains Express, #1866, EXIB 200.00
Lionel, switcher, 42, Picatinny Arsenal, VGIB 400.00
Lionel, tank car, 715, Sunoco, VG 450.00
Marklin, accessory, roundhouse, O gauge, EX 600.00
Marklin, accessory, Stuttgart station, HO scale, 14x33", NM ...2,875.00
Marklin, loco & tender, Pacific 4-6-2, G+ 1,600.00
Marklin, set, freight, electric, 1 gauge, 5-pc, VG 1,000.00
Marx, set, Tales of Wells Fargo #54752, 1959, VG+IB 775.00
Marx, set, Union Pacific M10005 Streamliner Train, HO scale, 5-pc, NM..225.00
Volcamp, caboose, B&O 2110, F 1,000.00
Volcamp, loco 0-4-0 #220, EX 2,250.00

Trade Signs

Trade signs were popular during the 1800s. They were usually made in an easily recognizable shape that one could mentally associate with the particular type of business it was to represent, especially appropriate in the days when many customers could not read!

5¢ Counter, tin w/red/wht/blk/gold pnt, early 1900s, 6x27" 200.00
5 & 10 Cent Store..., blk & wht pnt on brds, 59x39"................3,000.00
Andersons, oval wood panel w/mc pnt, iron brackets, 19th C, 9x56" ..475.00

Blacksmith, horseshoe, cvd/pnt wood, late 19th C, 42½x34" 950.00
Boston Am (newspaper), pnt plywood w/appl letters, 1900s, 84" W .7,600.00
Butcher, CI, tools & steer, silver & gold pnt, Pat 1889, 28x33" . 1,850.00
Clothing store, Line's, For Mens Wear, HP on wood, sgn Eckert, 89" L, VG....900.00
Fairbanks Scales, pnt wood fr panel, late 1800s, 18x28" 450.00
Fishmonger, fish, cvd wood w/worn mc pnt, early 1900s, 21" L.... 550.00
General store, pnt wood panel: Cash Store in fr, 15x29", EX, 29"...550.00
Hardware, handsaw, dc, Grinding & Saw Filing on blade, 63" L.1,500.00
Jeweler/watchmaker, pocket watch, pnt metal, EX details, 20x14" dia.3,450.00
Locksmith, key, cvd wood w/red pnt, weathered, 19th C, 74½".2,750.00
Meat Market, pnt wood, blk letters on wht, pnt molding, 11x49" ...1,650.00
Milk/Sandwiches, pnt galvanized metal, early 1900s, 18x28" 700.00

Optometrist, Butte Optical Co., two-sided, 30x60", $5,500.00. (Photo courtesy Randy Inman Auctions)

Optometrist, eye in oval, rvpt glass, 13¼x17¼" 480.00
Produce market, James Bradley Country Produce, pnt wood, 1900s, 24x58"..4,000.00
Safe-T Cup ice cream cone, paper compo, 3-D, 20th C, rpr, 21" . 175.00
Shoe repair, boot, cvd wood, made in 2 pcs, worn pnt, ca 1900, 18"..1,175.00
Tailor, scissors, cvd wood w/blk/gold pnt, brass hinge, 38½" L ..5,175.00
Tobacconist, wooden pipe w/L stem, unmk, VG pnt/crack, 33" L. 150.00
Tool Co, folding str-edged razor, pnt pine, Dunn Edge Tool Co, 36"..2,700.00
Watchmaker, pocketwatch, metal w/orig pnt, 24x14" dia, EX ..2,400.00

Tramp Art

'Tramp' is considered a type of folk art. In America it was primarily made from the end of the Civil War through the 1930s, though it employs carving and decorating methods which are much older, originating mostly in Germany and Scandinavia. 'Trampen' probably refers to the itinerant stages of Middle Ages craft apprenticeship. The carving techniques were also used for practice. Tramp art was spread by soldiers in the Civil War and primarily practiced where there was a plentiful and free supply of materials such as cigar boxes and fruit crates. The belief that this work was done by tramps and hobos as payment for rooms or meals is generally incorrect. The larger pieces especially would have required a lengthy stay in one place.

There is a great variety of tramp art, from boxes and frames which are most common to large pieces of furniture and intricate objects. The most common method of decoration is chip carving with several layers built one on top of another. There are several variations of that form as well as others such as 'Crown of Thorns,' an interlocking method, which are completely different. The most common finishes were lacquer or stain, although paints were also used. The value of tramp art varies according to size, detail, surface, and complexity. The new collector should be aware that tramp art is being made today. While some sell it as new, others are offering it as old. In addition, many people mistakenly use the term as a catchall phrase to refer to other forms of construction — especially things they are uncertain about. This misuse of the term is growing, and makes a difference in the value of pieces. New collectors need to pay attention to how items are described. For further information we recommend *Tramp*

Art: A *Folk Art Phenomenon* by Helaine Fendelmam, Jonathan Taylor (Photographer)/Stewart Tabori & Chang; *Hobo & Tramp Art Carving: An Authentic American Folk Tradition* by Adolph Vandertie, Patrick Spielman/Sterling Publications; and *Tramp Art, One Notch at a Time*, by Cornish and Wallach. Our advisors for this category are Matt Lippa and Elizabeth Schaff; they are listed in the Directory under Alabama.

Box, mounted with church-like structure, B and J flanking a heart, brown paint with traces of color, 15x12¾x8", EX, $2,000.00. (Photo courtesy Brunk Auctions on LiveAuctioneers.com)

Box, chip cvg, 7 layers, covered pine, early 1900s, 8½x20"	500.00
Box, stacked/chip-cvd pyramidal lid/sides/base, gilt ball finial, 18"	1,120.00
Box, stepped pyramid shapes, drw, appl leaves/pnt birds, 7x9"	1,600.00
Cabinet, drw/dbl doors/gesso molding/mirror bk, 1930s, 41x20x14"	9,000.00
Chest, sewing, chip-cvd designs, wooden drw, 2 hearts, ca 1924	250.00
Crucifix on stepped base, wht metal Jesus, 26x13"	300.00
Cupboard, chip-cvd grad blocks, divided drw, fitted int, 23x17x7"	575.00
Desk, slant front w/fitted int & drw, ornate chip cvg, 39x25x15"	4,800.00
Desk/bookcase, drop front, chip-cvd rosettes/leaves, 2-pc, KY, 73x47"	2,300.00
Frame, chip-cvd hearts/triangles/teardrops, 19th C, 31x28"	2,700.00
Frame, chip-cvd sawtooth borders/Xs, gold & silver pnt, 19x16"	235.00
Frame, 5-step chip cvgs w/stylized tulips, rpl mirror, 21x18"	660.00
Frame, cut geometrics/lapped hearts, red pnt, ca 1900, 23x19"	1,060.00
Frame, deep cvg & appl rondels & hearts, alligatored varnish, 17x21"	300.00
Frame, oak w/chip-cvd pinwheels & quarter fans, 11x7"	300.00
Lamp base, chip-cvd geometrics, mc pnt, 6-sided, 29½x10¼"	900.00
Medicine cabinet, rpl mirror on door/1 drw, geometric cvgs, 23x17x8"	1,100.00

Traps

Though of interest to collectors for many years, trap collecting has gained in popularity over the past 25 years in particular, causing prices to appreciate rapidly. Traps are usually marked on the pan as to manufacturer, and the condition of these trademarks are important when determining their value. Our advisor for this category is Boyd Nedry; he is listed in the Directory under Michigan. Our values are for traps in fine condition. Grading is as follows:

 Good: one-half of pan legible.

 Very good: legible in entirety, but light.

 Fine: legible in entirety, with strong lettering.

 Mint: in like-new, shiny condition.

Alexander, sz C	1,800.00
All-Steel #1, single spring	135.00
Alligator, w/bait hook	450.00
Am Fur & Trade Co, HBC #6, bear trap, current	345.00
Austin Humane	75.00
Bellspring, #1¼, single L spring	175.00
Best-White plastic mousetrap	30.00
Bigelow Killer, 5"	35.00
Blizzard 'Cold Day' ratttrap	125.00
Chasse, 3-hole, wood mousetrap	75.00
Cooper Clutch, single spring	250.00

Cortland #1, dbl jaw, w/teeth	350.00
Cosey Killer, pan type	80.00
Critter Getter, plastic live mousetrap	40.00
Dahlgren Killer, 14"	80.00
Davenport, Sure Death, ½ circle jaws	425.00
Diamond, #21½, dbl jaw	35.00
Diamond, #22H, dbl L spring	195.00
Dixie Fly Trap, fits on fruit jar	50.00
Duke #1, L spring	5.00
Eclipse #2, folding trap	195.00
Economy #1, single spring	65.00
Edwards, metal snap mousetrap, rare	1,500.00
Elenchik #2, dogless	65.00
Evans, brass fish & mousetrap	900.00
Faultless, metal choke rattrap	45.00
Flo Trap	1,000.00
Gibbs #4, dope trap	1,500.00
Gibbs hawk trap	350.00
Godwin ft snare	65.00
Gomber Beaten Path rat trap	35.00
Goshen, coil spring	475.00
Jack Frost Killer	40.00
Jack Frost, Nev-Er-Lose, coil spring	60.00
Jilson, mousetrap	1,200.00
Johnson Quick Set, gopher trap	45.00
Katch-Em, wood snap mousetrap	40.00
Kliflock #1, Killer	69.00
Kopper-Kat, mousetrap	40.00
Last Word, mousetrap	40.00
Lavally, clutch trap	1,000.00
Lic Lure, rattrap	45.00
Little Giant, fly trap	80.00
Manning #9, wolf trap	200.00
McGill, 'All Steel' mousetrap	30.00
Montgomery #2, Gray Fox Special	350.00
Nanco, Safe-T-Set, mousetrap	25.00
Nash, mole trap, Pa 1888, cast pan	90.00
Nesbit #4, dbl-L spring	4,500.00
New House #81½, riveted pan	400.00

New House Animal Trap Co., Lititz, Pennsylvania, bear trap, circa early 1900s, EX, $480.00. (Photo courtesy Rich Penn Auctions on LiveAuctioneers.com)

Oneida Victor #1½, single spring	35.00
Orbeto #300, coil spring	45.00
Otto Kampee Mfg Co, glass & metal mousetrap	130.00
Pioneer #1½, single spring	20.00
Prott #1¼, single spring	85.00
PS & W #1, single spring	35.00
PS Mfg Co, #3 dbl spring	65.00
Quiggley Van Camp Hardware, mousetrap	45.00
Reddick, spear type mole trap	25.00
Sabo, den trap	70.00
Sargent #11, single spring	250.00
Sargent #24, cast pan, dbl spring	575.00
Sheen #4	125.00

Smith, rattrap, wire cage.. 70.00
Thum Set, metal mousetrap 60.00
Trailzend #9, dble spring...2,500.00
Triumph #42X Ranger, w/teeth 75.00
Union Hardware #O, single spring.............................. 600.00
Van Wormer, CI mole.. 800.00
Victor #1, single spring 20.00
Victor #14, underspring, w/teeth 45.00
Watkins Handforged #3, dbl spring.......................... 250.00
Webley #3, coil spring.. 40.00
Woods-Waters, choker.. 40.00
Woodward Death Clamp 65.00
Yankee, CI mole trap 800.00

Trenton

Trenton, New Jersey, was an area that supported several pottery companies from the mid-1800s until the late 1960s. A consolidation of several smaller companies that occurred in the 1890s was called Trenton Potteries Company. Each company produced their own types of wares independent of the others.

Vase, bl gloss, spherical, 8x8" 120.00
Vase, bl gloss, triple disk, circular mk, 8½x8⅞"............................ 180.00
Vase, gr semigloss, dbl disk, 5⅞x6¼".................................... 145.00

Vase, triple disk, blue gloss, round ink stamp, Pat. Pend., 8½x9", $180.00. (Photo courtesy Belhorn Auction Services, LLC on LiveAuctioneers.com)

Vase, turq, tassel hdls, 8".. 110.00
Vase, wht Deco triple U form, circular mk, 7½x5½".................... 110.00

Trevaise

In 1907 the vacant Sandwich glasshouse was purchased and refurbished by the Alton Manufacturing Company. They specialized in lighting and fixtures, but under the direction of an ex-Tiffany glassblower and former Sandwich resident James H. Grady, they also produced a line of iridescent art glass called Trevaise, examples of which are very rare today. Trevaise was never signed and always has a button pontil. It was often decorated with pulled feathers, whorls, leaves, and vines similar to the glassware produced by Tiffany, Quezal, and Durand. Examples that surface on today's market range in price from $2,500.00 to $4,000.00 and up. Trevaise was made for less than one year. Due to financial problems, the company closed in 1908. Our advisor for this category is Frank W. Ford; he is listed in the Directory under Massachusetts.

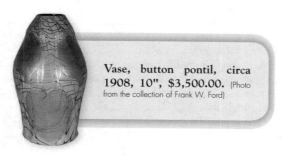

Vase, button pontil, circa 1908, 10", $3,500.00. (Photo from the collection of Frank W. Ford)

Vase, 8 braided ribs, olive w/gr-blk, wavy spirals, lav scallops, 9" ...3,000.00
Vase, gr & opal w/pulled & hooked decor, 1907 ....3,500.00
Vase, irid amethyst/silver/gold, donut-shaped wafer on base, 5⅜x6" ... 5,000.00
Vase, pulled feather design, irid w/soft gr, yel, & lav hues, gold lining, 3⅝x4" dia..2,500.00

Trivets

Although considered a decorative item today, the original purpose of the trivet was much more practical. Trivets were used to protect tabletops from hot serving dishes, and hot irons (heated on the kitchen stove) were placed on trivets during use to protect work surfaces. The techniques of forging metal trivets were brought to America in the 1700s. Blacksmithing remained the predominant method of trivet production until after the Civil War, when foundries became established. Many of these earliest castings bore portraits of famous people or patriotic designs. Floral, birds, animals, and fruit were other favored motifs. If you are in doubt about the age of an 'antique' forged trivet, seek the advice of a knowledgable ABANA (Artist Blacksmith's Association of North America) member. And watch for reproductions of early trivet castings, especially the signed 1950s-era cast iron and brass trivets by makers such as Wilton, Emig, John Wright, Iron Art, and Virginia Metalcrafters. Expect to pay considerably less for these than for the originals. For more information we recommend *The Expanded A to Z Guide to Trivets* by our advisor Lynn Rosack. She can be found in the Directory under Florida.

Brass

East West Hames Best/rtcl thistles, 4-ftd, #4, 1895, 9x4⅞" 75.00

Pierced and scrolled apron, spiral handles, cabriole legs, English, nineteenth century, 12x12x17", $540.00. (Photo courtesy Dallas Auction Gallery on LiveAuctioneers.com)

Cast Iron

Acme, 2 dragons, sadiron stand, 1880-1900, 6½x3⅝"..................... 65.00
Cherubs holding wreath, w/figural man hdl, JZH, 1948, 8⅞x4¾" .. 60.00

Cinderella Stoves and Ranges, fancy four-leaf clover, circa 1900, 5⅜x4", $75.00. (Photo courtesy Lynn Rosack)

Ives & Allen, spade shape w/panel, acorn at apex, ca 1890, 9x3⅞" .100.00
Oak tree w/acorns, sprue (casting) mk on bk, sgn WR, 1840s...... 225.00

Forged Iron

Circle, 3 long legs w/penny ft, no hdl, early 1800s, 8¼" 175.00
Forged spade, crossbar w/4 swirls, ca mid 1800s, 10⅝x5" 175.00
Slave trivet, 3 legs, long hdl, ca late 1700s, 23x7¾" rnd............. 475.00

Ram's horn handle, two fleur-de-lis, 13½" long, $300.00 to $375.00. (Photo courtesy Garth's Auction Inc. on LiveAuctioneers.com)

Plate, intaglio butterflies and flowers, signed, 8", $510.00. (Photo courtesy William J. Jenack Auctioneers on LiveAuctioneers.com)

Tile

Devon Fishing Village, Minton, twisted wire fr, sgn+globe, 6" sq. 115.00
Jubilee Teapot, The, stand, emb metal stand, 1887, 7¼" rnd 250.00
Minton pastoral scene, sepia colors, twisted wire fr, 1890, 6" sq ... 115.00
Rookwood Rook, bl sq, 8 ft, flame logo & 1794, XXVI (1926), 5¾" ... 425.00

Toy

C D Kennedy Co Teas Coffees Sugars, 60 Stores, spade shaped, 1890s, 5" 90.00
Chalfant, horizontal CMCO, spade, ¼" railing, 1880-1900, 4¾x2⅛" 70.00
Jewel, rect, 6 holes, 4 iron guides, 3¼x1⅝" 30.00
Ober Chagrin Falls O, eye shaped, NP stand, 4½" 225.00
OMCo, Ober, NP stand, 3⅛" 100.00
Stork, oval on ornate hdl, delicate casting, 4¾" 100.00

Wire

American Fence Wire, 9 ringed ft, cb insert, 6½" rnd 100.00
Spiderweb, hdl, intricate design, 7 legs, late 1800s, 9" L 225.00
Spokes, tinned wire, ca 1870-90, 6¼" dia.................................... 35.00
Starburst design, 10 points, sits " above surface, 1880s, 6⅛" rnd 75.00
Triangle w/swirls, tinned wire, 1880, ea side 7" w/3 1½" legs........ 140.00

Contemporary Trivets

12 Heart Trivet, CI, JZH 1948 G, 13x8" 45.00
Broom & Wheat pattern, CI, Griswold, ca 1950, 8½" L 35.00
Eagle & Seprent, CI, Wilton limited edition, ca 1960, 12x7" 75.00
King's arms, lions/crown/unicorn, brass, 4-ftd, CW 10-17, 1957, 6" . 30.00
Old Lace, CI, Griswold, lot #1739, ca 1950, 7" dia....................... 125.00
Trafford Foundry, CI, Family Day 1953, 8⅜x4¾" 20.00
Und Noch Eens, CI, enameled, EFM 2001, 6⅛" L 25.00

Tuthill

The Tuthill Glass Company operated in Middletown, New York, from 1902 to 1923. Collectors look for signed pieces and those in an identifiable pattern. Condition is of utmost importance, and examples with brilliant cutting and intaglio (natural flowers and fruits) combined fetch the highest prices. Unless noted otherwise, values are for signed items.

Bowl, 6-point brilliant-cut star in base, vintage intaglio rim, 2x12" ... 525.00
Bowl, Gravic cut iris, 9" 175.00
Bowl, Gravic Iris, att, deep, 9".. 180.00
Bowl, Rex cutting, several sm chips, 8"...................................... 1,450.00
Bowl, Rex variation cutting, unsgn/att, 8" 900.00
Bowl, wild rose intaglio, 8" 100.00
Compote, intaglio flower/berry vine in bowl, star ft, 7x5½", pr... 150.00
Pitcher, Thousand Eye & Hobstar cutting, tankard form, 9½" 300.00

Vase, allover eng vine w/3-lobe leaves, slender, 10" 385.00
Vase, bud, eng leafy band under rim/around ft, slim/ftd, 12" 325.00

Twin Winton

Twin brothers Don and Ross Winton started this California-based company during the mid-1930s while still in high school. In the mid-1940s they shut it down while in the armed forces and started up again in the late 1940s, when older brother Bruce Winton joined them and bought them out in the early 1950s. The company became a major producer of cookie jars, kitchenware, and household items sold nationally until it closed its San Juan Capistrano, location in 1977. They're also well known for their Hillbilly line — mugs, pitchers, bowls, lamps, ashtrays, decanters, and other novelty items, which evolved from the late 1940s through the early 1970s with a variety of decorating methods still being discovered. Don Winton was the only designer for Twin Winton and created literally thousands of designs for them and hundreds of other companies. He is still sculpting in Corona del Mar, California, and collectors and dealers are continuing to find and document new pieces daily. To learn more about this subject, we recommend Collector's Guide to Don Winton Designs by our advisor, Mike Ellis; he is listed in the Directory under California.

Cookie jar, Tommy Turtle, 1963 to 1975, NM, $150.00. (Photo courtesy Jack Chipman)

Ashtray, Hillbilly, 4x4" 20.00
Bank, friar, wood finish 45.00
Bank, Hillbilly, emb Mountain Dew Loot, 7" 75.00
Bank, Hotei, TW-411, 8"... 50.00
Bank, Teddy Bear, TW-409, 8" 40.00
Bank, Wooly Mammoth, Ford Advertising, 5" 75.00
Bookends, kitten, Expanimal, TW-126, 7½"................................... 125.00
Bowl, pretzel, Hillbilly 45.00
Bowl, salad, Artist Palette, rare, 13", min 250.00
Candleholder, Aladdin lamp, TW-510, 6x9", ea 45.00
Candy jar, Shoe, TW-352, 10x10" 75.00
Canister, Tea Sty, Canister Farm, TW-114, 5x3" 30.00
Cookie jar, Baker, w/yel spatula & wht hat, TW-67, 7x11".......... 400.00
Cookie jar, Bambi, TW-54, 8x10" 175.00
Cookie jar, Barn, TW-41, 12x8" 80.00
Cookie jar, Butler, wood finish, TW-60, 12x7" 300.00
Cookie jar, Chipmunk, TW-45, 10x10" 75.00

Cookie jar, Cookie Bucket, TW-59, 8x9" 40.00
Cookie jar, Dog in Basket, TW-71, 8½x10" 85.00
Cookie jar, Donkey, TW-88, 13x8" 65.00
Cookie jar, Elephant w/Sailor Hat, 12", $45 to.................... 60.00
Cookie jar, Fire Engine, TW-56, 7x12" 85.00
Cookie jar, Flopsy, TW-243 .... 350.00
Cookie jar, Hen on basket, TW-61, 8x8" 125.00
Cookie jar, Hobby Horse, TW-239 .... 300.00
Cookie jar, Hopalong Cassidy, w/gun, very rare, 15" 3,500.00
Cookie jar, Mother Goose, TW-75, 14x7" 100.00
Cookie jar, Noah's Ark, TW-94, 10x9" 75.00
Cookie jar, Pirate Fox, TW-246, 8x11" 225.00
Cookie jar, Pot O' Cookies, TW-58, 8x10" 40.00
Cookie jar, Sheriff, TW-255 .... 200.00
Cookie jar, Snail, wood finish, TW-37, 7x12"..................... 175.00
Cookie jar, Walrus, TW-63, 10x11" 375.00
Decanter, Bavarian, Schnapps on base, #735, 12" 40.00
Decanter, Bowler, 300 Proof on base, #737, 11⅞"............... 30.00
Decanter, Irishman, Irish Whiskey on base, #615, 12" 50.00
Decanter, Japanese, Sake on base, #616, 12".................... 30.00
Decanter, Robin Hood, Winfield mfg................................ 55.00
Figurine, black girl holding elephant, T-14, 3"................ 125.00
Figurine, boy on stick horse w/dog at ft, 1980s, 6" 35.00
Figurine, boy shot putting w/Yale logo on shirt, 3" 150.00
Figurine, boy skier, 7".. 225.00
Figurine, boy standing by mailbox, T-8, 5" 175.00
Figurine, football player talking to girl, ca 1950, 5x6" 275.00
Figurine, football player, bl & wht uniform, A-572, 5"...... 15.00
Figurine, girl playing dress-up, T-19, 5" 200.00
Figurine, girl playing in sand, T-12, 3" 200.00

Figurine, girl wearing Mickey Mouse ears, TW-2, 5", $150.00. (Photo courtesy Mike Ellis)

Figurine, Godey lady, layered pk gown, 2" 60.00
Figurine, Indian w/shield & quiver, #759, 18" 100.00
Figurine, Kitten Muffy, wht w/yarn ball, A-179, 2" 10.00
Figurine, lion, winking, unmk, 3¼" 65.00
Figurine, Mickey the Sorcerer, wand in hand, 8" 150.00
Figurine, seated gnome w/elbows on knees, #587, 8" 20.00
Figurine, squirrel holding box, 4" 50.00
Figurine, Standing Gnome, red hat, #545, 12½"................ 20.00
Figurine, wht kitten in brn shoe, A-83, 4x6" 15.00
Figurine, zebra, early, 5" 45.00
Ice bucket, Suspenders, Hillbilly, TW-30, 14x7" 250.00
Ladies of the Mountain, stein, 8" 70.00
Miniature, baby duck, yel, #102 ....5.00
Miniature, beaver lying down, #315, 1x2" 8.00
Miniature, floppy rabbit, #205 ....7.00
Miniature, kitty, blk & wht, #204 ....6.00
Miniature, lazy burro, #311, 2" 8.00
Miniature, swan, blk, #313 ....6.00
Mug, Bronco, 1940s 75.00
Mug, Hillbilly, 4" 35.00
Mug, mustache, Bronco, 3".. 50.00
Mug, stein, Bamboo, 8"... 35.00
Mug, Wood Grain, rope hdl w/spur, 4"............................. 40.00

Napkin holder, elephant, TW-453, 6x4"......................... 150.00
Napkin holder, poodle, TW-474, 7x7"............................. 75.00
Napkin holder, Porky Pig, TW-473, 8x5" 75.00
Napkin holder, rooster, TW-483, 7x6" 75.00
Ornament, Christmas, camel in Santa hat, A-134 ....6.00
Ornament, Christmas, girl elf holding doll, A-63, 3⅜" 8.00
Ornament, Christmas, lamb, A-76....................................4.00
Pitcher, Bronco, 1940s.. 250.00
Pitcher, Hillbilly, 7" 75.00
Plate, dinner, Wood Grain, 10" 40.00
Shakers, apple, TW-135, pr 75.00
Shakers, bull, TW-195, pr 40.00
Shakers, butler, TW-160, pr... 50.00
Shakers, duckling, TW-193, pr 75.00
Shakers, jack-in-the-box, TW-148, pr 125.00
Shakers, mouse, TW-181, pr 40.00
Shakers, poodle, TW-164, pr.. 50.00
Shakers, saddle, B-207, 3", pr 50.00
Stein, Hillbilly, 7½" 45.00
Wall pocket, rabbit head, TW-302, 5" 100.00

Typewriters

Along with other machines of communication — telephones, televisions, and radios — the typewriter helped to create the modern world. The standard big, black typewriters that many people are familiar with, such the Underwood and Remington, were the result of many years of mechanical evolution throughout the 1880s and 1890s. During these years of discovery, ingenuity, and mistakes, hundreds of different typing machines were produced to print the written word. Among them were machines with curved keyboards, double keyboards, or no keyboards at all.

In 1897 the Underwood typewriter appeared and quickly standardized what the modern typewriter would look like.

There are two broad classifications of early typewriters: keyboard and index machines. Keyboard typewriters have a key for each letter but the index typewriters have a chart showing all the characters, which are selected one at a time by a pointer or dial and then printed by depressing a single key or lever. Even though index typewriters were slower than the keyboard machines, they provided a cheaper alternative, at $5 to $40 each, to the standard keyboard models that were typically selling for $100, a huge amount considering that a fine horse-drawn carriage could be had for $70. Eventually second-hand keyboard typewriters became available, and with touch-typing on a full keyboard becoming established as the most efficient method to type, index typewriters vanished quickly around 1900 but were still made as toys.

As with any collectible, the three factors that affect the value of a typewriter are rarity, condition, and desirability. In some cases a typewriter is rare but not considered desirable so its value will be modest. A typewriter that is scarce or rare will lose value if "over" restored, and is best left with its original patina and finish to achieve the maximum value. The prices shown below are for typewriters in good original condition.

If you have an early typewriter of nonstandard design not listed here, please contact our advisor, Martin Howard, at www.antiquetypewriters.com for a market value. He is listed in the Directory under Canada.

Hammond 1, golden oak cased, ebony keys, New York, 1881, $800.00. (Photo courtesy The Martin Howard Collection, www.antiquetypewriters.com)

Bennett, ca 1910 (or Junior, 1st version, ca 1907).........................200.00
Columbia 2, indicator type (no type-bars), ca 1895 ....2,500.00
Crandall New Model, 1886, Crandall Machine Co, Croton NY, HP roses, VG ..4,000.00
Daugherty, ca 1893 ....700.00
Edison, indicator type (no type-bars), ca 1892....................3,000.00
Empire, type-bars have thrust action, ca 1895 ....100.00
Fitch, type-bars strike platen top, ca 1888 ....3,000.00
Ford, type-bars have thrust action, ca 1895 ....3,000.00
Franklin, any model, ca 1895 ....600.00
Hammonia, indicator type (no type-bars), ca 1882 ....5,000.00
Harford, any model, ca 1894..1,000.00
Jackson, ca 1895..3,000.00
Jewett, any model, ca 1895 ....400.00
Keystone, ca 1899 ....1,000.00
Kleidograph, typewriter for the blind, ca 1893...........................900.00
McCool, ca 1903..2,000.00
Odell 1, index, Lake Geneva Wis Pat Pending, ca 1889 ....1,000.00

Odell 2, Chicago, index, Art Nouveau base, 1890, $600.00. (Photo courtesy The Martin Howard Collection, www. antiquetypewriters.com)

Oliver, any model...200.00
Peoples, indicator type (no type-bars), ca 1891 ....300.00
Rapid, type-bars have thrust action, ca 1888 ....4,000.00
Remington 2, ca 1885..300.00
Sholes Visible, ca 1901 ....3,000.00
Standard Folding, ca 1908 ....300.00
Sterling, ca 1911 ....1,500.00
Sun, indicator type (no type-bars), metal or wooden base, ca 1885 ...1,500.00
Victor, indicator type (no type-bars), ca 1890 ....1,500.00

Uhl Pottery

Founded in Evansville, Indiana, in 1849 by German immigrants, the Uhl Pottery was moved to Huntingburg, Indiana, in 1908 because of the more suitable clay available there. They produced stoneware — Acorn Ware jugs, crocks, and bowls — which were marked with the acorn logo and 'Uhl Pottery.' They also made mugs, pitchers, and vases in simple shapes and solid glazes marked with a circular ink stamp containing the name of the pottery and 'Huntingburg, Indiana.' The pottery closed in the mid-1940s. Those seeking additional information about Uhl pottery are encouraged to contact the Uhl Collectors' Society, found in the Clubs, Newsletters, and Websites section. For more information, we recommend *Uhl Pottery* by Anna Mary Feldmeyer (our advisor) and Kara Holtzman (Collector Books).

Ashtray, dog beside fire plug, 4x5¼", $375.00. (Photo courtesy Sohn on LiveAuctioneers.com)

Bowls, picket fence, 4-12", ea $40 to....................................90.00
Cottage cheese, John M Miller, Huntingburg IN......................270.00
Flower frog, bl-gr, 3½x2⅜" 60.00
Flower frog, gr 160.00
Jar, ice water, #8, 1-gal 360.00
Jug, Christmas, 1933 ....250.00
Jug, Christmas, 1943, w/paper label.....................................750.00
Jug, shoulder, 1-qt, mk 370.00
Matchholder, mini, mk 100.00
Piggy bank, Hitler, Kansas City type, 3¼"..............................190.00
Pitcher, brn bbl form, 5½" 35.00
Pitcher, milk, bl & wht sponge...270.00
Vase, end of day, 12" 375.00

Unger Brothers

Art Nouveau silver items of the highest quality were produced by Unger Brothers, who operated in Newark, New Jersey, from the early 1880s until 1919. In addition to tableware, they also made brushes, mirrors, powder boxes, and the like for milady's dressing table as well as jewelry and small personal accessories such as match safes and flasks. They often marked their products with a circular seal containing an intertwined 'UB' and '925 fine sterling.' Some Unger pieces contain a patent date near the mark. In addition to sterling, a very limited amount of gold was also used. Note: This company made no pewter items; Unger designs may occasionally be found in pewter, but these are copies. Items with English hallmarks or signed 'Birmingham' are English (not Unger).

Basket, rtcl scrollwork, flared rim, swing hdl, 11½" 225.00
Belt buckle, Egyptian style w/Nouveau florals, 2x3" 100.00
Belt buckle, Egyptian style, 3" L 100.00
Bowl, floral repoussé border, flared rim, 2½x10"...........................480.00
Brooch, baby figural, ca 1890, 1⅜" 85.00
Cheese server, ivory (or bone) hdl, ca 1900, 7" 235.00

Coffee set, repoussé hibiscus flowers, monogrammed, Sterling 925 Fine, pot: 8¼", tray: 10", 24 oz. tw., EX, $1,680.00. (Photo courtesy John Moran Auctioneers, Inc. on LiveAuctioneers.com)

Fork, Love's Dream, Nouveau design, monogram, 1890s, 7" 25.00
Hand mirror, Nouveau floral, 1903.......................................595.00
Hem measure, silver w/Nouveau lady's head at top, 4" L..............160.00
Match safe, Nouveau leaves, rococo, monogram 200.00
Purse, silver mesh, hinged fr, chain-link hdl, sm..........................145.00
Spoon, grotesque head/Nouveau floral hdl, 5¾" 48.00
Thimble case, pierced silver w/Nouveau scrolls, monogram, 1" ...145.00
Thimble case, silver w/Nouveau openwork, ring for chatelaine ...145.00
Tray, Nouveau floral, 925 silver, 7" 780.00

University City

Located in University City, Missouri, this pottery was open for only five years (1910 – 1915), but because of the outstanding potters associated with it, notable artware was produced. The company's founder was Edward Gardner Lewis, and among the well-known artists he employed were Adelaide Robineau, Frederick Rhead, Taxile Doat (TD), and Julian Zsolnay.

Bowl, wide trees frieze, brn/gray on ivory, dtd 1911, 3½x8", VG.3,100.00
Dish, sea life, bl/pk/wht crackle, emb shell, 3 ft w/jewels, TD, 3x5" .1,200.00
Jar, cafe-au-lait, ruffled uptrn lid collar, EG Lewis, 2¾x2", EX 480.00
Teapot, gr matt, modeled as bldg, seated figure on dome lid, rstr, 9"...3,500.00
Trivet, Atascadero Nymph of Spring (lady's head), lt bl, Doat, 5" dia ..425.00
Vase, bl/olive gr flambé on porc, spherical, sm opening, M/EL, 5x5" .4,440.00
Vase, celadon crystalline, spherical w/tiny neck, CU/1913, 5x5" .16,800.00

Vase, excised stylized trees on green matt, attributed to Frederick Rhead, UC 1911 #5045, 9x5", $5,100.00. (Photo courtesy Craftsman Auctions on LiveAuctioneers.com)

Vase, purple/gr/ivory drip glaze, shouldered, #1178, 5½" 1,200.00
Vase, stylized cvd blossoms/leaves, unglazed, cylindrical, 9x3"..1,000.00
Vase, wht & celadon w/lg crystals, Taxile Doat, 1913, rare shape, 8x4". 14,400.00
Vase, wht classic form, sgn TD, mk UC, dtd 1914, 2¼" 500.00
Vase, wht/lt bl/gr full-blown crystals on yel, rstr, 7x4" 960.00

Val St. Lambert

Since its inception in Belgium at the turn of the nineteenth century, the Val St. Lambert Cristalleries has been involved in the production of high-quality glass, producing some cameo. The factory is still in production.

Cameo

Vase, Art Deco geometrics, dk gr deeply cut bk to textured frost, 8", EX...660.00
Vase, bud, bumblebees/pussy willows, red & amber to clear, 15" ...3,650.00
Vase, chameleon on branch, bl on chartreuse, 4⅝" 1,200.00

Vase, floral and berry motif, 8", $2,640.00. (Photo courtesy B.S. Slosberg, Inc. Auctioneers on LiveAuctioneers.com)

Vase, floral, burgundy on pk frost, bulb base, 11¾" 360.00
Vase, flowers/leaves, brn on olive to brn, flared ft, 7½" 200.00
Vase, geometric cuttings, cobalt on clear, 1930, 9x7" 120.00

Vase, house/trees/water, cut/pnt on pk to bl, sq top, 2¼x2½" 900.00
Vase, mums, chartreuse on frost, cylindrical, 14½" 600.00

Miscellaneous

Bowl, fruit, cut crystal, 9" 120.00
Candleholders, cranberry cased, twisted form, 3½", pr 85.00
Candlesticks, cut crystal, 12", pr... 240.00
Sculpture, Madonna, Modern style, crystal, 10½x2¾x2"............... 60.00
Sugar bowl, frost, hound finial, 3 hound heads form ft, 8" 360.00
Vase, abstract irid decor on lt bl, squat, S Herman, 6½" 480.00
Vase, crystal w/etched man & women ballet dancers, 6½" 65.00
Vase, cut crystal w/amethyst bands, 13x9" 215.00
Vase, cut crystal, 6-sided ft, 10¼" 120.00

Valentines

Whatever you collect, chances are there will be a valentine that will fit into your collection. That is the beauty of collecting valentine cards — they cross all boundaries. From Civil War images and oil lamps to robots and motorcycles, valentines represent the sign of the times through all the ages. Some people collect them just because they make them smile. Whether you are trying to complete a series or are looking for that special category, you can't go wrong purchasing antique valentine cards. In this day and age with the E-card, these cards represent an era gone by, and they are pieces of history.

When deciding whether to place a value on a card, always remember to look for these qualifying factors: condition, age, size, location, manufacturer, and artist signature. There is an array of card styles to look for: dimensional (when counting the dimensions on a card, the background is included in the count), mechanical-flat, mechanical, novelty, flat, folded-flat, hold-to-light, and greeting card. Unless otherwise noted, our values are for valentines in excellent condition. For further reading, we recommend *Valentines: A Collector's Guide, 1700s – 1950s*, by Barbara Johnson, Ph.D. (Collector Books).

Our advisor for this category is Katherine Kreider, appraiser (fee schedule), author, dealer, and owner of www.valentinesdirect.com. Her books include *Valentines With Values*, *One Hundred Years of Valentines*, and *Valentines for the Eclectic Collector*. She is listed in the Directory under Pennsylvania.

Key:
D — dimension
dim — dimensional
hc — hand colored

HCPP — honeycomb paper puff
PIG — printed/published in Germany

Dimensional, 2D, printed in Germany, 5½x3½x2", $35.00. (Photo courtesy Kreider Collection)

Dim, 2D, train car, Campbell's Soup kids, USA, 6x5x1½" 35.00
Dim, 3D, Vict couple, purple bkgrnd, PIG, rare, 1915, 3½x3" 75.00
Dim, 4D, daffodil motif w/Vict boy, PIG, early 1900s, 9x7½x3½".. 95.00

Dim, 5D, cherub orchestra, PIG, early 1900s, 10½x6x3" 150.00
Dim, 5D, cherub, hold-to-lt, chromolitho, PIG, early 1900s, 8x4½x3¼"... 75.00
Dim, big eyed kids w/fireplace, 1920s, 3½x3½x1" 15.00
Dim, Cupid's Flight, Nister, London, early 1900s, 4½x4x4" 35.00
Dim, HCPP sofa, girl playing drum, PIG, early 1900s, 6x6x3½" .. 125.00
Dim, pipe organ w/cherub, PIG, early 1900s, 9½x8¾x6" 125.00
Dim, steamship, PIG, 9x11½x3¾" 350.00
Dim, Vict horse-drawn carriage, Tuck, early 1900s, 7x10½x5" 125.00
Flat, checker Valentine, 1940s, 4x4½" 5.00
Flat, Constant Valentine, wood block, hc, Park, 1840s 150.00
Flat, Despondant Lover, aqua tint, 1850s, 8½x10" 350.00
Flat, Esther Howland, hc, Dresden accents, 1840s, 10x8" 450.00
Flat, juice reamer, 6x5" 15.00
Flat, Love and Duty, woodblock eng, Eng, 1840s, 10x8" 250.00
Flat, Love's Library, heavy emb, adorned w/scraps, Mansell, 1850s .. 150.00
Flat, Manuscript Valentine, emb border, 1840s, 6x7" 150.00
Flat, Roadster driven by: Cherub, PIG, early 1900s, 5x9" 95.00
Flat, Tin Man/Wizard of Oz, official card, Loew's Inc, 5x3" 35.00

Folded-flat, girl in carriage, Victorian, 9x9", $125.00.
(Photo courtesy DuMouchelles on LiveAuctioneers.com)

Folded-flat, Henry, made in USA, 1930s, 4x4" 15.00
Folded-flat, To My Valentines, adorned w/owls, Nister, 1890s, 6x5" .. 45.00
Greeting card, Ever Thine, paper lace, handwritten verse, 1850s, 7½x6". 125.00
Greeting card, lady w/kitten, Art Deco, USA, 1920s, 5x4¼" 15.00
Greeting card, Mansell Octavo, Dresden gold wreath, 1850s, 7x4½". 125.00
Greeting card, oyster shell, Tuck, early 1900s, 6½x7" 50.00
Hanging-flat, cherubs in hammocks, Tuck & Sons, early 1900s, 5 layers, 9x5½". 75.00
Hanging-flat, Farewell Lovers, 1800s, EP Dutton & Co, 9x9½" 75.00
Hanging-flat, folk art ribbon, handmade, orig ribbons, 1870s, 22x4" ... 75.00
Hanging-flat, Lover's Arrow, orig ribbon, late 1800s, chromolitho, 2x7¾" 35.00

Honeycomb Paper Puff, angels in antique car, Victorian, 6½x9", $100.00.
(Photo courtesy DuMouchelles on LiveAuctioneers.com)

HCPP & hold-to-lt, big eyed kids dancing under moon, 1920s, 12x11x5½"..125.00
HCPP oil lamp, air brushed, PIG, early 1900s, 5½x3x1½" 75.00
HCPP Victrola, chromolitho, air brushed, PIG, early 1900s, 10½x8x4"..150.00
Mechanical-flat, big eyed girl w/butterfly, HB, PIG, 4x1½" 15.00
Mechanical-flat, Dapper Dan, Trademark G, PIG, 1915, 11½x6¼".75.00
Mechanical-flat, Jumbo the elephant, PIG, early 1900s, 4½x5" 25.00
Mechanical-flat, polar bear, Tuck & Sons, early 1900s, 14x4" 95.00
Mechanical-flat, pug dog, PIG, 1920s, 4x2½" 25.00
Mechanical-flat, Uncle Tom, USA, 1920s, 4¾x4" 35.00

Novelty, Flirt Fan, floral language of love, Fisher, 1870s, 5x8" 150.00
Novelty, Loveland Cachet, 1947 .... 15.00
Novelty, Loverville w/cast metal phone, unknown maker, 1920s, 4x3¼".. 15.00
Novelty, paper doll cut-out seesaw valentine, unknown maker, 1940s, 7x4⅛"..... 25.00
Novelty, puzzle card, unknown maker, 1930s-40s, 5½x5½" 40.00
Novelty, Valentine Writer, rare, mid-1800s, 7x4" 500.00
Penny Dreadful, blk devil, A Parker, hc, mid-1800s, 8½x7" 95.00
Penny Dreadful, Butcher, wood block, hc, 1840s, 9x7½" 75.00
Penny Dreadful, Dieting, USA, 1920s, 9x6" 25.00
Penny Dreadful, flapper, USA, 1920s, 9x6" 15.00
Penny Dreadful, radio bug, USA, 1940s, 8½x7" 25.00

Vallerysthal

Vallerysthal and Portieux were two of many glassworks in the Lorraine province of France operating in the 1700s. From 1871 to 1918, Vallerysthal was annexed by Germany. Sixty-two miles apart, in 1854, Vallerysthal and Portieux were put under a single administrative board. Vallerysthal ceased operation in 1977, but Portieux has continued production on a small scale to the present day. Production over the years included pressed, blown, and cut glass that might be acid engraved, turned, or enameled. Both companies produced vases, plates, trays, candlesticks, sugar bowls, butter dishes, novelties of all kind, many covered dishes, paperweights, and toy glass. The best known and most readily available are the covered dishes, which include Swimming Duck, Swan with Open Neck, Bull with Rider, Resting Camel, Elephant with Rider, and Covered Fish. Many items were made in milk glass with cold hand painting and gilding. Other colors included blue opaque, green opaque, caramel opaque, aqua, rose red, purple, green, and black. Some items were marked (Vallerysthal up to 1942) but many were not marked. Portieux signed some items with their impressed name and items so treated may be old or new. Copies of many items have been made by a company in Taiwan (7" and 6" Hen on Nest, Standing Rooster), as well as Westmoreland (Standing Rooster, Robin on Pedestal Base).

For further information see *The Milk Glass Book* by Frank Chiarenza and James Slater. Our advisor for Vallerysthal is Shirley Smith; she is listed in the Directory under West Virginia. See also Milk Glass.

Candlesticks, tortoise, Portieux, bl.. 150.00
Covered dish, cabbage, Portieux, bl opaque, 6½" W 86.00
Covered dish, dog, bl opaque, 6x4" 140.00
Covered dish, duck, mg, 5" L.. 37.00
Covered dish, fish, mg.. 130.00

Covered dish, elephant with rider, blue opaque, $235.00.
(Photo courtesy Shirley Smith, from the Carol Howell collection)

Covered dish, hen on nest, Portieux, gr opaque, 4" L...................... 56.00
Covered dish, lighthouse, bl opaque... 156.00
Covered dish, lizard on strawberry, mg... 233.00
Covered dish, pig on drum, bl opaque.. 60.00
Covered dish, rabbit on egg, bl opaque 118.00
Covered dish, rabbit, mg... 67.00
Covered dish, robin on nest, Portieux, bl opaque 90.00

Covered dish, snail on turtle, mg................................. 178.00
Goblet, bl opaque, 6½" 40.00
Toothpick holder, bearded old man, Portieux, sgn, 4" 61.00
Vase, satyr head, bl opauqe, 8½" 45.00
Vase, satyr w/3 figures, Portieux, mg, 8¾"........................ 60.00

Van Briggle

The Van Briggle Pottery of Colorado Springs, Colorado, was established in 1901 by Artus Van Briggle, whose early career had been shaped by such notables as Karl Langenbeck and Maria Nichols Storer. His quest for several years had been to perfect a completely flat matt glaze, and upon accomplishing his goal, he opened his pottery. His wife, Anne, worked with him, and they, along with George Young, were responsible for the modeling of the wares. Their work typified the flow and form of the Art Nouveau movement, and the shapes they designed played as important a part in their success as their glazes. Some of their most famous pieces were Despondency, Lorelei, and Toast Cup. Increasing demand for their work soon made it necessary to add to their quarters as well as their staff. Although much of the ware was eventually made from molds, each piece was carefully trimmed and refined before the glaze was sprayed on. Their most popular colors were Persian Rose, Ming Blue, and Mustard Yellow.

Van Briggle died in 1904, but the work was continued by his wife. New facilities were built; and by 1908, in addition to their artware, tiles, gardenware, and commercial lines were added. By the '20s the emphasis had shifted from art pottery to novelties and commercial wares. Reproductions of some of the early designs continue to be made. The double AA mark has always been in use, but after 1920 the dates and/or shape numbers were dropped. Mention should be made here as well that the Anna Van Briggle glaze is a later line which was made between 1956 and 1968.

Bookends, owl, mulberry, circa 1926 – 1930, $275.00.

Jardiniere, morning glories, raspberry on mustard, #284, 1905, 7", NM..1,200.00
Tile, bl jay, mc cuenca, unmk, 6"..1,920.00
Tile, parrot on branch, cuenca, minor nicks to corners, unmk, 6".. 1,320.00
Vase, coneflowers, bl & gr matt, ca 1930, 9x8" 375.00
Vase, daffodils & leaves, lt gr to teal, bulb, 1906, 10x4"............1,920.00
Vase, daffodils, bl & gr matt, chip to base, 1930, 10x4½"............. 175.00
Vase, dragonflies, bl & gr matt, slender, #80, ca 1930, 7x3" 175.00
Vase, dragonflies, maroon & bl matt, post 1920, 7½x3½"............. 100.00
Vase, floral, bl & gr matt, dbl gourd, ca 1930, 6½x3"...................... 75.00
Vase, floral, bl & gr matt, dbl hdl, rstr to 1 hdl, ca 1930, 9½x7½" ...150.00
Vase, floral, maroon & bl matt, slender, bulb top, ca 1920, 5½x2¾" .. 60.00
Vase, iris, bl & gr matt, 2 hdls at bottom, #80, ca 1930, 14x7½"..400.00
Vase, leaves & berries, bl & gr matt, bulb, ca 1930, 6x4" 75.00
Vase, leaves, bl & gr matt, dbl hdl, bulb, ca 1920, 8x4".................. 75.00
Vase, leaves, bl & gr matt, dbl hdl, ca 1930, 7x6½"....................... 225.00
Vase, leaves, bl & gr matt, gourd, ca 1930, 12½x6½" 300.00
Vase, moths on maroon & bl matt, bulb, ca 1920, 3x3½" 60.00
Vase, moths, robin's egg bl on brn, 1907, 7¾x4½" 1,200.00
Vase, spades, maroon & bl matt, bulb, dbl hdl, ca 1930, 6½x7" ... 350.00
Vase, stylized floral, bl & gr matt, tapered & ftd, ca 1930, 7½x3" .. 75.00
Vase, whiplash leaves, maroon & bl matt, hairline, post 1920, 8½x3".75.00
Vase, yucca plant, bl & gr matt, flaring, ca 1930, 14x5½" 300.00

Dirk Van Erp

Dirk Van Erp was a Leeuwarden, Holland, coppersmith who emigrated to the United States in 1886 and began making decorative objects from artillery shell casings in the San Francisco shipyards. He opened a shop in 1908 in Oakland and in 1910 formed a brief (one year) partnership with D'Arcy Gaw. Apprentices at the studio included his daughter Agatha and Harry Dixon, who was later to open his own shop in San Francisco. Gaw has been assigned design credit for many of the now famous hammered copper and mica lamp shade lamp forms. So popular were the lamps that other San Francisco craftspeople, Lillian Palmer, Fred Brosi, Hans Jauchen, and Old Mission Kopperkraft among them, began producing similar forms. In addition to lamps, he manufactured a broad range of objects including vases, bowls, desk sets, and smoking accessories. Van Erp's work is typically finely hammered with a deep red-brown patina and of good proportions. On rare occasions, Van Erp created pieces in a 'warty' finish: an irregular, indeed lumpy, surface with a much redder appearance. Van Erp died in 1933. In 1929 the shop was taken over by his son, William, who produced hammered goods in both brass and copper. Many feature Art Deco style designs and are of considerably lower value than his father's work. The Van Erp mark is prominent and takes the form of a windmill above a rectangle that includes his name, sometimes D'Arcy Gaw's name, and sometimes San Francisco.

Please note: Cleaning or scrubbing original patinas diminishes the value of the object. Our prices are for examples with excellent original patina unless noted. Our advisor for this and related Arts and Crafts objects is Bruce Austin; he is listed in the Directory under New York.

Key: h/cp — hammered copper

Lamp, hammered copper, 22½" shade lined in parchment with remnants of original hand-painted flowers over mica, four-arm base, electrified oil font, windmill stamp: Dirk Van Erp and remnant of D'Arch Gaw, exceptional and rare, height with chimney: 22½", $114,000.00.
(Photo courtesy Craftsman Auctions on LiveAuctioneers.com)

Ash pan, copper, highly polished, letter P finial, 7x11" 300.00
Basket, h/cp, canoe shape w/cutouts in hdl, 7½x11½" 1,200.00
Basket, h/cp, pierced/riveted hdl, some cleaning, 7½x11½" 600.00
Blotter, h/cp w/monogram, 2¾x5½" 120.00
Bookends, h/cp w/enamel flower, 4¼x6x4" 200.00
Bookends, h/cp, poppies, orig patina, 1 scratched, 5x6" 1,200.00
Bowl, h/cp, flared rim, sm ft, 9" W 650.00
Bowl, sculpted h/cp, 3x10½".. 900.00
Candlestands, 3 nozzles on copper strap base, ca 1925, 3x11x3", pr ...900.00
Jardiniere, h/cp w/warty texture, 6x10" 4,800.00
Jardiniere, h/cp, bulb w/new patina, 7½x16"..............................6,000.00
Jardiniere, h/cp, red/warty, sm dents, 6x7¾" 4,500.00
Jardiniere, h/cp w/rolled rim, minor dent & wear, open box mk, 7x9"..4,000.00
Lamp, 11" conical copper & mica shade; h/cp base, 11"...........3,950.00

Lamp, 13" 3-panel riveted copper/mica shade; spherical base, 16½". 10,000.00
Lamp, 14" 4-panel h/cp & mica shade; bulb base, ca 1911, 16".. 11,000.00
Lamp, 18" 4-panel h/cp mica shade; 2-socket trumpet-form base, 17" ... 14,500.00
Lamp, 19" 3-panel h/cp mica shade; h/cp base, 23" 15,000.00
Lamp, h/cp base & shade, mica liner, 13x11" 4,500.00
Vase, bronzed metal, flared cylinder, ca 1901, 11x10" 3,000.00
Vase, h/cp shell casing form w/fluted rim, dtd 1903, 25½x14¼" . 5,750.00
Vase, h/cp, cylindrical w/incurvate rim, ca 1910, 6½x3¾"........ 1,550.00
Vase, h/cp, flared rim, open box mk, 3x6" 550.00
Vase, h/cp, rolled rim, orig patina, open box windmill stamp, 7¾x7" ... 1,400.00
Vase, h/cp, warty, rim-to-hip hdls, 10¼"................................... 6,600.00
Vase, hammered brass shell casing form, drilled base, 19¼x6½". 2,750.00

Vance/Avon Faience

One of the many American potteries to evolve from a commercial ceramics plant, Vance Faience was organized in 1901 in Tiltonsville, Ohio, for the purpose of producing artistic and utilitarian wares. In 1902 the name was changed to The Avon Faience Company, with the talented William Jervis serving as manager and designer. His British colleague, Frederick Rhead, left England at his behest to join him there. Together they completely revamped the design direction of the company, transforming Victorian shapes and motifs into streamlined Arts & Crafts vases with squeeze-bag and sgraffito decoration.

In yet another reorganization, the company was incorporated at the end of 1902 with three potteries from nearby West Virginia as the Wheeling Potteries Company. This change of management encouraged the rapid manufacture of commercial wares, which hastened the departure of Jervis and Rhead. Artware production stopped altogether in 1905.

Marks include several versions of 'Vance' and 'Avon.' Our advisors for this category are Suzanne Perrault and David Rago; they are listed in the Directory under New Jersey.

Cookie jar, floral, HP/pks, MR Avon, 7x6½" 960.00
Jar, floral, pk/gr on wht, squeeze-bag, Avon, 1903, 8x12", EX 235.00
Jardiniere, mermaids (4) & sea life in high relief, brn/gr, 12x10". 175.00

Jardiniere, slip-decorated sgraffito English Art Nouveau flowers and trees, signed Rhead #1014 and dated 1903, with Avon logo, 8", $1,725.00. (Photo courtesy Cincinnati Art Galleries)

Jardiniere, stylized trees, 3 bar-like hdls, style of Rhead, 13", VG . 600.00
Jardiniere, stylized trees & pine cones, squeeze-bag, 1903, 8½x13½" .. 1,800.00
Jardiniere & ped, abstract sgraffito/squeeze-bag devices, Rhead, 39", VG.. 8,000.00
Jardiniere & ped, cvd lotus blossoms/leaves, F Rhead, 33x16" ..9,600.00
Mug, scenic, HP, Avon, ca 1902-05, 5¼" 90.00
Pitcher, grapevines & dogs chasing game emb on gr, hound hdl, 10"....515.00
Pitcher, tulips, slip trailed, Rhead, Avon, 7", EX 290.00
Vase, 4 mermaids/sea creatures emb on tan to brn, #118, 12x10"....900.00
Vase, allover mums, HP brn/gr on yel, M/FHR, bottle form, Avon, 9x6".. 1,200.00
Vase, broad leaves/flowers, gr/aqua on indigo, spherical, 4", NM . 660.00
Vase, chrysanthemum, yel/gr/brn, F Rhead, M/FHR, 8½x6" 1,200.00
Vase, floral (squeeze-bag), bl/ivory on tan, doughnut neck, 4½x6"... 330.00
Vase, Nouveau floral, att FH Rhead, E125/1005, bulb base, Avon, 6" ..825.00
Vase, Nouveau mermaid relief, brn tones, #118, ca 1900, 12x12". 900.00
Vase, quintal, gnarled branches, earth tones, Vance FC, 9x9 .... 150.00
Vase, stylized landscape, dbl-bulb body widens at base, Rhead, 5"...1,175.00
Vase, tulip repeats, cvd/pnt, bl/gr, squat w/bulb collar, Avon, 5"..420.00

Vaseline Glass

Vaseline, a greenish-yellow colored glass produced by adding uranium oxide to the batch, was produced during the Victorian era. It was made in smaller quantities than other colors and lost much of its popularity with the advent of the electric light. It was used for pressed tablewares, vases, whimseys, souvenir items, oil lamps, perfume bottles, drawer pulls, and doorknobs. Pieces have been reproduced, and some factories still make it today in small batches. Vaseline glass will fluoresce under an ultraviolet light.

Bowl, Maltese & ribbons, sq, Hobbs Brockunier, 7" 110.00
Butter, Three Panel, ftd, Richards & Hartley, 5½" dia.................... 75.00
Candlestick, #66 Twist, satin, Tiffin/US Glass, 7½"....................... 50.00
Candlestick, #449 w/cut ovals, Fenton, 8½" 250.00
Candy dish w/lid, Cactus, opal 200.00
Celery, Dasiy & Button, shoe shaped, Hobbs Brockunier, 11¾"... 175.00
Chip & dip, T'print, opal, Fenton 2-pc...................................... 230.00
Coaster, Am, #2056, Fostoria, 3¾" dia...................................... 300.00
Cologne, ft, w/stopper, #56, Fenton 180.00
Compote, open work edge, #3310, Tiffin/US Glass, satin, 8½" 40.00
Compote, twist stem, opal, John Walsh, 4½" 270.00
Fish globe, #8171, blk figural base & vaseline bowl, Tiffin/US Glass, 11½"...500.00
Fish globe, #8171, vaseline figural base & vaseline bowl, Tiffin/US Glass, 11½".800.00
Fishbowl, Ruba Rombic, Consolidated Glass...........................1,300.00

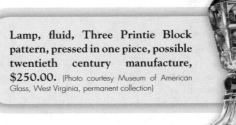

Lamp, fluid, Three Printie Block pattern, pressed in one piece, possible twentieth century manufacture, $250.00. (Photo courtesy Museum of American Glass, West Virginia, permanent collection)

Lamp, oil, Dewdrop #821, tall, ftd.. 320.00
Lamp, whale oil or fluid, waisted loop, Sandwich, 9"..................... 400.00
Pickle castor, Cupid & Venus, SP lid 110.00
Pickle castor, log cabin w/glass lid, SP fr & tongs, Central Glass...1,200.00
Pitcher, Cherry & Cable, opal, Mosser Glass, 2-qt 48.00
Pitcher, fish novelty, #824, Central Glass, 6½" 700.00
Salt dip, open, Pressed Dmn, Central Glass, 1¾" dia..................... 18.00
Salt dip, wheelbarrow form w/working pewter wheel, Adams & Co... 450.00
Salt shaker, Petticoat, Riverside Glass, 3" 75.00
Sugar shaker, Spanish Lace, opal, Northwood, metal lid, 4¾"...... 165.00
Syrup/molasses can, Hobnail/Dewdrop, Hobbs Brockunier.......... 320.00
Toothpick, Little German Band cap, Duncan, 2½" W 60.00
Toothpick, Picket, King Glass, 3"... 100.00
Tray, advertising, Clark's Teaberry Gum, emb, ftd, 4x6¾" 55.00
Tumbler, Daisy & Fern, opal, LG Wright, 3¾"............................... 35.00
Tumbler, Hobnail/Dewdrop, Hobbs Brockunier............................. 40.00
Tumbler, Hobnail/Dewdrop, opal, Hobbs Brockunier, 4"............... 70.00
Vase, fan, Daisy & Button Panel, Fenton, ftd, 10" 115.00
Wall pocket, #320, Tiffin/US Glass, satin, 9".............................. 75.00
Whimsey, tri-corner from sugar bowl, Trailing Vine, Bastow/Cloudersport. 290.00

Verlys

Verlys art glass, produced in France after 1931 by the Holophane Company of Verlys, was made in crystal with acid-finished relief work in the Art Deco style. Colored and opalescent glass was also used. In 1935 an American branch was opened in Newark, Ohio, where very similar wares were produced until the factory ceased production in 1951. French Verlys was signed with one of three mold-impressed script signatures, all containing the company name and country of origin. The American-made glassware was signed 'Verlys' only, either scratched with a diamond-tipped pen or impressed in the mold. There is very little if any difference in value between items produced in France and America. Though some seem to feel that the French should be higher priced (assuming it to be scarce), many prefer the American-made product. In June of 1955, about 16 Verlys molds were leased to the A.H. Heisey Company. Heisey's versions were not signed with the Verlys name, so if an item is unsigned it is almost certainly a Heisey piece. The molds were returned to Verlys of America in July 1957. Fenton now owns all Verlys molds, but all issues are marked Fenton. Our advisor for this category is Don Frost; he is listed in the Directory under Washington.

Charger, birds and bees, clear and frosted, 11½", $120.00. (Photo courtesy DuMouchelles on LiveAuctioneers.com)

Bowl, scalloped/rtcl swirled rim, oval, 20x16"	120.00
Charger, lg center flower, clear & frosted, low, 11⅝"	120.00
Charger, roses, clear & frosted, 3x13"	325.00
Charger, water lilies, lt amber, 2½x13¾"	390.00
Charger, water lilies, wht opal, 2½x13¾"	200.00
Dish, butterflies on lid, frosted amber glass, mk, 6½" dia	185.00
Dish, swirled rim, duck at side, wht opal, brass base, 1940s, 4x6"	215.00
Fishbowl, relief goldfish, tails form hdls, amber, 4x18"	350.00
Fishbowl, relief goldfish, tails form hdls, clear satin, 4x18"	300.00
Vase, Asian figure w/umbrella, clear & frosted, 1940, 9x5"	180.00
Vase, bumblebees & grass, wht opaque, ovoid, narrow rim, 1930s, 5⅝"	150.00
Vase, laurel, amber, 1960s, 10½"	120.00
Vase, laurel, wht opal, 1960s, 10½"	325.00
Vase, lg flower heads, flat rim, opal, 8⅞x4½"	420.00
Vase, thistle, clear & frosted, 9¾x7"	200.00
Vase, tumbler form w/lg tab hdls emb w/birds, opal, 7⅞"	585.00

Vernon Kilns

Vernon Potteries Ltd. was established by Faye G. Bennison in Vernon, California, in 1931. The name was later changed to Vernon Kilns; until it closed in 1958, dinnerware, specialty plates, artware, and figurines were their primary products. Among its wares most sought after by collectors today are items designed by such famous artists as Rockwell Kent, Walt Disney, Don Blanding, Jane Bennison, and May and Vieve Hamilton. Our advisor for this category is Ray Vlach; he is listed in the Directory under Illinois.

Chatelaine Shape

This designer pattern by Sharon Merrill was made in four color variations: Topaz, Bronze, decorated Platinum, and Jade.

Bowl, chowder, Topaz or Bronze, 6", $12 to	15.00
Bowl, salad, Platinum or Jade, decor, 12", $55 to	75.00

Bowl, serving, Topaz or Bronze, 9", $25 to	35.00
Coffee cup, flat base, Platinum & Jade, $20 to	22.00
Plate, chop, Platinum or Jade, decor, 14", $50 to	65.00
Plate, dinner, leaf 1 corner, Topaz & Bronze, 10", $15 to	17.00
Plate, salad, Topaz or Bronze, 7½", $12 to	15.00
Platter, Platinum or Jade, decor, 16", $65 to	85.00
Shakers, Platinum or Jade, decor, pr $25 to	30.00
Sugar bowl, Platinum or Jade, decor, w/lid, $35 to	40.00
Sugar bowl, Topaz & Bronze, w/lid, $25 to	30.00
Teapot, Platinum & Jade, decor, $250 to	300.00
Teapot, Topaz or Bronze, w/lid, $175 to	200.00

Fantasia and Disney Figures

Ostrich, #30, $1,500.00 to $2,000.00. (Photo courtesy Dan Morphy Auctions LLC on LiveAuctioneers.com)

Autumn Ballet teapot, $300 to	600.00
Centaur, #31, 10", $1,100 to	1,200.00
Centaurette, #22, 8", $1,000 to	1,100.00
Enchantment, plate, chop, 17", $325 to	500.00
Enchantment, teapot, $500 to	750.00
Fantasia, cr/sugar, ea $100 to	300.00
Fantasia, tumbler, $125 to	200.00
Flower Ballet tumbler, $125 to	200.00
Nubian Centaurette, #23, 1940-41, 8½", $1,000 to	1,100.00
Nutcracker, coffeepot, 6-cup, 1940, $625 to	875.00
Nutcracker, mug, 1940, $150 to	250.00
Ostrich, #29, 6½", $1,000 to	1,200.00
Satyrs, 4½", ea $200 to	250.00

Melinda Shape

Patterns found on this shape are Arcadia, Beverly, Blossom Time, Chintz, Cosmos, Dolores, Fruitdale, Hawaii (Lei Lani on Melinda is 2½x base value), May Flower, Monterey, Native California, and Philodendron. Two patterns, Rosedale and Wheat, were made for Sears, Roebuck & Co. and marked with Sears Harmony House backstamp. The more elaborate the pattern, the higher the value.

Bowl, lug chowder, 6", $12 to	18.00
Bowl, rim soup, 8", $12 to	18.00
Bowl, serving, rnd, 9", $18 to	25.00
Butter tray, oblong, w/lid, $45 to	75.00
Coffeepot, 8-cup, $55 to	85.00
Creamer, ind, short or tall, ea $12 to	18.00

Gravy boat, May Flower, $20.00 to $30.00.

Egg cup, $18 to	25.00
Pitcher, 1½-pt, $25 to	35.00
Pitcher, 2-qt, $35 to	50.00
Plate, chop, 12", $20 to	30.00
Plate, dinner, 10½", $12 to	18.00
Plate, luncheon, 9½", $12 to	15.00
Platter, 12", $20 to	30.00
Relish, single leaf shape, 12", $25 to	30.00
Sauceboat, $20 to	30.00
Shakers, pr $15 to	25.00
Teapot, w/lid, 6-cup, $45 to	85.00

Monticeto Shape (and Coronado)

This was one of the company's most utilized shapes — well over 200 patterns have been documented. Among the most popular are the solid colors, plaids, the florals, westernware, and the Bird and Turnbull series. Bird, Turnbull, and Winchester 73 (Frontier Days) are 2 – 4x base values. Disney hollow ware is 7 – 8x base values. Plaids (except Tweed and Calico), solid colors, and Brown-eyed Susan are represented by the lower range.

Brown-Eyed Susan, see listings for values.
(Photo courtesy DuMouchelles on LiveAuctioneers.com)

Ashtray, 5½" dia, $15 to	20.00
Ashtray, rnd, 5½", $12 to	20.00
Bowl, mixing, 7", $22 to	30.00
Bowl, salad, rnd or angular, 13", ea $40 to	65.00
Bowl, serving, angular, 9", $20 to	25.00
Coaster/cup warmer, 4½", $20 to	25.00
Jam jar, notched lid, 5", $65 to	95.00
Pitcher, Winchester Western, 11"	240.00
Plate, salad, 7½", $8 to	15.00
Spoon holder, $45 to	65.00

San Clemente (Anytime) Shape

Patterns you will find on this shape include Tickled Pink, Heavenly Days, Anytime, Imperial, Sherwood, Frolic, Young in Heart, Rose-A-Day, and Dis 'N Dot.

Bowl, chowder, 6", $8 to	12.00
Bowl, vegetable, divided, 9", $15 to	22.00
Butter pat, 2½", $15 to	20.00
Casserole, w/lid, 8" dia, $30 to	50.00
Creamer, $8 to	12.00
Gravy boat, $18 to	20.00
Mug, 12-oz, $15 to	25.00

Plate, chop, 13", $18 to	25.00
Platter, 11", $12 to	20.00
Sugar bowl, w/lid, $12 to	20.00
Teapot, $35 to	65.00

San Fernando Shape

Known patterns for this shape are Desert Bloom, Early Days, Hibiscus, R.F.D., Vernon's 1860, and Vernon Rose.

Bowl, fruit, 5½", $6 to	10.00
Bowl, serving, rnd, 9", $18 to	25.00
Casserole, w/lid, 8" (inside dia), $45 to	75.00
Coaster, ridged, 3¾", $15 to	20.00
Egg cup, dbl, $15 to	25.00
Plate, dinner, 10½", $12 to	18.00
Shakers, pr $15 to	25.00
Tumbler, style #5, 14-oz, $20 to	25.00

San Marino Shape

Known patterns for this shape are Barkwood, Bel Air, California Originals, Casual California, Gayety, Hawaiian Coral, Heyday, Lei Lani (2½x base values), Mexicana, Pan American Lei (2½x base values), Raffia, Seven Seas, Shadow Leaf, Shantung, Sun Garden, and Trade Winds. The Mojave pattern was produced for Montgomery Ward, Wheat Rose for Belmar China Co.

Ashtray, 5½", $12 to	20.00
Bowl, mixing, 6", $19 to	24.00
Bowl, mixing, 9", $28 to	35.00
Butter pat, ind, 2½", $12 to	20.00
Casserole, w/lid, 8", $35 to	60.00
Coffee server, w/stopper, 10-cup, $35 to	60.00
Creamer, regular, $10 to	12.00
Cup, jumbo, $25 to	35.00
Flowerpot, 3", $20 to	25.00
Flowerpot, w/saucer, 4", $35 to	45.00
Sauceboat, $17 to	22.00
Spoon holder, $30 to	45.00
Tumbler, style #5, 14-oz, $20 to	25.00

Specialty Ware

Plate, Roosevelt and Churchill, Atlantic Charter, 1942, rare, $180.00. (Photo courtesy Early American History Auctions on LiveAuctioneers.com)

Ashtray, city & state souvenir, 1-color transfer	20.00
Ashtray, Detroit MI, red transfer of 7 structures, 5¾"	20.00
Cup/saucer, demi, souvenir, $20 to	30.00
Figurine, Bette Davis, Janice Pettee, ca 1940, 10½"	1,200.00
Plate, Fr Opera Reproductions, 8½", $18 to	25.00
Plate, Mother Goose	65.00
Plate, Music Masters, 8½", $18 to	25.00

Plate, presidential or armed services, $35 to 75.00
Plate, Race Horse, 10½" 75.00
Plate, school or organizations, $20 to.. 35.00
Plate, transportation theme, 1-color, $45 to 60.00
Plate, transportation theme, mc, $65 to.. 95.00
Plate, Ye Old Times, 10½", $35 to 45.00

Vase, carved handles, azure blue, May & Vieve Hamilton Pottery, 12", $1,100.00. (Photo courtesy Ray Vlach)

Transitional (Year 'Round) Shape

Patterns on this shape include Country Cousin, Lollipop Tree, Blueberry Hill, and Year 'Round.

Bowl, cereal/soup, $8 to.. 10.00
Buffet server, trio, $35 to 50.00
Butter tray, w/lid, $25 to 35.00
Casserole, w/lid, 8", $25 to 45.00
Coffeepot, w/lid, 6-cup, $25 to 45.00
Gravy boat, $18 to 25.00
Mug, 12-oz, $12 to 20.00
Plate, dinner, 10", $9 to 13.00
Platter, 11", $12 to 20.00

Ultra Shape

More than 50 patterns were issued on this shape. Nearly all the artist-designed lines (Rockwell Kent, Don Blanding, and Disney) utilized Ultra. The shape was developed by Gale Turnbull, and many of the elaborate flower and fruit patterns can be credited to him as well; use the high end of our range as a minimum value for his work. For Frederick Lunning, use the mid range. For other artist patterns, use these formulae based on the high end: Blanding — 3x (Aquarium 5x); Disney, 5 – 7x; Kent — Moby Dick, 2 – 4x; and Our America, 3 – 5x; Salamina, 5 – 7x.

Bowl, cereal, 6", $10 to 15.00
Bowl, chowder, 6", $12 to 20.00
Bowl, fruit, 5½", $6 to 12.00

Bowl, Our America, by Rockwell Kent, 11", minimum value $135.00. (Photo courtesy Bonham's on LiveAuctioneers.com)

Butter tray, w/lid, $35 to 75.00
Casserole, w/lid, 8" (inside dia), $45 to....................................... 95.00

Creamer, ind, open, $12 to 20.00
Egg cup, $18 to... 25.00
Mug, 8-oz, 3½", $20 to.. 30.00
Pitcher, jug style, 1-pt, 4½", $35 to 50.00
Plate, dinner, Salamina, Rockwell Kent facsimile sgn, 10½" 100.00
Plate, luncheon, 9½", $10 to 20.00
Shakers, pr $20 to 30.00
Teapot, 6-cup, $45 to 100.00

Villeroy and Boch

The firm of Villeroy and Boch, located in Mettlach, Germany, was brought into being by the 1841 merger of three German factories — the Wallerfangen factory, founded by Nicholas Villeroy in 1787, and two potteries owned by Jean-Francois Boch, the earlier having been in operation there since 1748. Villeroy and Boch produced many varieties of wares, including earthenware with printed under-glaze designs which carried the well-known castle mark with the name 'Mettlach.' See also Mettlach.

Vase, lions around the circumference, marked Luxemburg V&B #309, light surface wear, 9½", $2,100.00. (Photo courtesy Garth's Auction Inc. on LiveAuctioneers.com)

Charger, castle scene, Heidelberg Schloss, 12" 75.00
Charger, Japanese lady seated, #355, 20th C, 14" 75.00
Ewer, harvest scenes in relief, German saying on neck, drilled, 15" . 240.00
Figurine, soldier w/snuff box, sm rpr, 7¼" 250.00
Paperweight, dwarf figural, mc majolica, sm touchups, 3¾x7" 240.00
Plaque, classical women (2), wht on bl, 8¼x6" 250.00
Plaque, hunting dog in wetlands, 17" dia 300.00
Plaque, Muttertag (Mother's Day) 1979, bl & wht, 10x7"+fr......... 48.00
Plate, floral, bl on wht, crazing, 9½" 15.00
Plate, Washington's Headquarters, Dresden, 6½x8½".................. 115.00
Stein, birds & flowers in grid, hinged lid, #1821, 13" 180.00
Stein, figural panels/acorn borders, gr jasper, hinged lid, #147 ..... 155.00
Tray, fish on basket, gr majolica, prof rpr, 25" L 180.00
Tray, geometric in gr/bl/wht, rtcl metal border w/hdls, 1910, 20" L....325.00
Vase, bl & sea gr mottle, bulb, Luxembourg #324, 1950s, 4" 100.00
Vase, bl crystalline on cream, bulb, sm mouth, Luxembourg #321, 5" ..275.00
Vase, bl/gr/brn mottle, Luxembourg V&B, #275/3, 7½" 480.00
Vase, ewer form w/boy climbing to spout, worn silver trim, 1840s, 13"... 180.00
Vase, floral, mc on cream, shouldered, 9¾x5", pr.......................... 125.00
Washbowl & pitcher, creamy wht w/gold-banded rims, #9046, 11½"...250.00

Vistosa

Vistosa was produced from about 1938 through the early 1940s. It was Taylor, Smith, and Taylor's answer to the very successful Fiesta line of their nearby competitor, Homer Laughlin. Vistosa was made in four solid colors: mango red, cobalt blue, light green, and deep yellow. 'Pie crust' edges and a dainty five-petal flower molded into handles and lid finials made for a very attractive yet nevertheless commercially unsuccessful product. Our advisor for this category is Ted Haun; he is listed in the Directory under Indiana.

Bowl, 3x9¼", $35 to... 40.00
Bowl, cereal, 6¾" 22.00

Bowl, cream soup, $22 to.. 28.00
Bowl, fruit, 5¾", $15 to.. 18.00
Bowl, salad, ftd, 12", $200 to.. 225.00
Bowl, soup, lug hdl, $30 to 35.00
Coffee cup, AD, $40 to.. 50.00
Coffee saucer, AD, $10 to.. 15.00

Creamer, $20.00 to $25.00; Sugar, $25.00.
(Photo courtesy Strawser Auction Group on LiveAuctioneers.com)

Cup/saucer, tea, $18 to.. 22.00
Egg cup, ftd, $50 to 70.00
Jug, water, 2-qt, $120 to.. 150.00
Plate, 6", cobalt.. 25.00
Plate, 6", colors other than cobalt, $12 to........................ 15.00
Plate, 7", $14 to.. 18.00
Plate, 9", $15 to.. 20.00
Plate, 10", $35 to.. 45.00
Plate, chop, 12", $35 to.. 50.00
Plate, chop, 15", $40 to.. 55.00
Platter, 13", $40 to.. 50.00
Sauceboat, $175 to.. 200.00
Shakers, pr $25 to.. 32.00
Teapot, 6-cup, $190 to.. 225.00

Volkmar

Charles Volkmar established a workshop in Tremont, New York, in 1882. He produced artware decorated under the glaze in the manner of the early Barbotine work done at the Haviland factory in Limoges, France. He relocated in 1888 in Menlo Park, New Jersey, and together with J.T. Smith established the Menlo Park Ceramic Company for the production of art tile. The partnership was dissolved in 1893. From 1895 until 1902, Volkmar was located in Corona, New York, first under the name Volkmar Ceramic Company, later as Volkmar and Cory, and for the final six years as Crown Point. During the latter period he made art tile, blue under-glaze Delft-type wares, colorful polychrome vases, etc. The Volkmar Kilns were established in 1903 in Metuchen, New Jersey, by Volkmar and his son, Leon. The production in the teens became more stylized, and bold shapes were covered in rich, crackled Persian glazes. The studio won prizes for a special line of enamel-decorated wares, in bright polychrome on Art Deco, Egyptian-Revival patterns. Difficult to find today, these command prices in the tens of thousands of dollars. Wares were marked with various devices consisting of the Volkmar name, initials, 'Durant Kilns,' or 'Crown Point Ware.' Our advisors for this category are Suzanne Perrault and David Rago; they are listed in the Directory under New Jersey.

Vase, couple in period dress, Barbotine technique with restoration to several areas, artist signed, raised CV, 9½x6¾", $780.00. (Photo courtesy Craftsman Auctions on LiveAuctioneers.com)

Bowl, aubergene gloss w/Egyptian Bl matt int, conical, ftd, 9¾" .. 240.00
Mug, Pierrot clowns, snake hdl, Salmagundi Club, Chamberlin, 6x5", NM.1,550.00
Oil on canvas, dusky landscape, C Volkmar, 14x24" 1,800.00
Panel, landscape, Impressionist style, 3 8" tiles, hairline, +fr 6,600.00
Vase, brn & yel striations, bulb base, 19th C, 7x11"................ 275.00
Vase, indigo mottle, 3 angle rim-to-hip hdls, 7x6" 960.00
Vase, leaves, gr matt, sgn, 8x8"..2,760.00
Vase, pastoral scene in Barbotine, hdls, ca 1875, 11x8", NM....1,250.00

Volkstedt

Fine porcelain has been produced in the German state of Thuringia since 1760, when the first factory was established. Financed by the prince, the company produced not only dinnerware, but also the lovely figurines for which they are best known. They perfected the technique of using real lace dipped in soft paste porcelain which would burn away during the firing process, leaving a durable porcelain lace which they used extensively on their famous ballerina figurines.

By the 1830s, other small factories began to emerge in the area. One such company was begun by Anton Muller, who marked his wares with a crown over the letters MV (Muller, Volkstedt). Greiner and Holzappel (1804 – 1815) signed some of their pieces with an 'R' accompanied with a series of numbers. Several other marks were used on wares from this area, among them are the 'cross hair' mark with E, N, and S indicated within the pie sections, various marks with a crown over two opposing 'double fish hook' devices, partial crossed swords with a star, crossed forks (variations), a beehive, and a scrolled cartouche containing the crown and the Volkstedt designation. There were others. Later marks may be simply 'Volkstedt Germany.' Both the original Volkstedt factory and the Muller operation continue in production to this day.

Dish, female figure centering 2 leaf-form dishes, early 20th C, 13" .. 960.00
Figurine, ballerina w/wide lace skirt, appl flowers, 6½x10", NM .. 350.00

Figurine, Diana the Huntress with attendants, putti and game on rockery base, nineteenth century, repaired, 24", $1,080.00. (Photo courtesy Jackson's Auction on LiveAuctioneers.com)

Figurine, hound dog, brn & wht, recumbent, ca 1900, 5x12½"....215.00
Figurine, lady seated, much lace & gold, plumed hat, 11x11", NM....900.00
Figurine, nude child w/huge grasshopper, ca 1937-42, 3½x4" L ...415.00
Figurine, terrier dog seated, brn & wht, 15x12x7"........................ 195.00
Figurines, man w/object in hand, lady w/purse, pastels, 10½", pr . 155.00
Figurines, man w/walking stick, lady w/fan, much lace, 8", pr...... 180.00
Group, ballerinas dancing in ring, appl gold roses, 4¾x4½" 215.00
Group, cellist/paianist/flutist on base, 1915-30, 17x22x16".......... 850.00
Group, cherubs (3) at stove w/porridge, 6¾x5"............................. 300.00
Group, man & lady playing chess, 6x9½", NM............................. 325.00
Group, pianist/cellist & dancing couple, 7½x12½"........................ 725.00
Soup tureen, floral sprays, 3-tier form w/rococo, ca 1899, 6½" 165.00

Wade

The Wade Potteries was established in 1867 by George Wade and his partner, a man by the name of Myatt. It was located in Burslem, England, the center of that country's pottery industry. In 1882 George Wade bought out his partner, and the name of the pottery was changed to Wade and Sons. In 1919 the pottery underwent yet another name change and became known as George Wade & Son Ltd. The year 1891 saw the establishment of another Wade Pottery — J & W Wade & Co., which in turn changed its name to A.J. Wade & Co. in 1927. At this time (1927) Wade Heath & Co. Ltd. was also formed.

The three potteries plus a new Irish pottery named Wade (Ireland) Ltd. were incorporated into one company in 1958 and given the name The Wade Group of Potteries. In 1990 the group was taken over by Beauford PLC and became Wade Ceramics Ltd. It sold again in early 1999 to Wade Management and is now a private company.

For those interested in learning more about Wade pottery, we recommend *The World of Wade*; *The World of Wade Book 2*; *The World of Wade — Figurines and Miniatures*; *The World of Wade Ireland*; and *The World of Wade Whimsies*, all by Ian Warner and Mike Posgay; Mr. Warner is listed in the Directory under Canada.

Animal, Airedale, 1930s, 7¼x8¼"	635.00
Animal, Bulldog, 1930s, 3¾x4½"	400.00
Animal, Camel (Faust Lang), 1930s, 7⅝"	1,910.00
Animal, Capuchin (Faust Lang), 1939, 10"	1,625.00
Animal, Horse (Faust Lang), 1930s, 8"	975.00
Animal, Spaniel, 1930s, 5½"	475.00
Ascot bowl, 1957-59	55.00
Bells Whisky Decanter, Prince Henry Birthday, empty	95.00
Bird, Budgerigar w/Flowers, 1930s, 7¾"	560.00
Bird, Cockatoo, 1940, 6"	635.00
Bird, Parrot, 1939, 10½"	950.00
Bird, Woodpecker, 1940s, 7"	480.00
Bluebird Tree Trunk Vase, 1957-59	20.00
Championship Dog, Cocker Spaniel, 1975-81, 2⅞x3⅝"	90.00
Connoisseur's Collection, Coaltit, 1978-82, 5¾"	358.00
Disney, Am, 1956, 1⅞"	32.00
Disney, Baby Pegasus, 1958, 1¾"	74.00
Disney, Bambi, 1957, 1½"	32.00
Disney, Boris, 1956, 2⅜"	42.00
Disney, Dachsie Blow-Up, 1961-65, 5"	340.00
Disney, Dumbo, 1957, 1½"	45.00
Disney, Jock, gr coat, 1956, 1¾"	55.00
Disney, Lady, 1956, 1½"	30.00
Disney, Merlin as Caterpillar, 1963, ¾x1¾"	162.00
Disney, Merlin as Turtle, 1963, 1x1¾"	195.00
Disney, Peg, 1956, 1½"	25.00
Disney, Scamp Blow-Up, 1961-65, 4⅛"	140.00
Disney, Tramp, 1956, 2⅛"	56.00
Flower Jug, Shape 154, 9"	125.00
Guinness, Mad Hatter, 1968, 3¼"	190.00
Lucky Leprechaun, Cobbler, 1956-86, 1½"	20.00
Miniature oil jugs, London scene decal, 3¾", ea	15.00
Novelty Animal, Bernie & Poo, 1955-60, 2x3"	140.00
Novelty Animal, Dutbin Cat, 1955-60, 1¾"	140.00
Novelty Animal, Jonah & the Whale, 1955-60, 1½x2"	1,220.00
Nursery Rhyme Character, Baker, 1950s, 3⅞"	280.00
Nursery Rhyme Character, Candlestick Maker, 1950s, 4"	290.00
Nursery Rhyme Character, Tailor, 1950s, 2½"	200.00
Pegasus, posy bowl, 1958-59	125.00
Queen of Clubs, pottery tray, 1950s, 4¼" dia	12.00
Red Rose Tea (Canada), Alligator, 1967-73, ½x1½"	8.00

Siamese cats, wall plaque, Wade Ireland	575.00
Swan egg cup, 1950s	35.00
Teapot, Prince Charles & Princess Diana wedding, 6¾"	100.00
Viking Ship, posy bowl, 1959	16.00

Westminster Piggy Banks, Maxwell Pig, 7¼", $70.00.
(Photo courtesy Jim and Bev Mangus)

Whimsie, Dachshund, 1954, 1⅛x1½"	88.00
Whimsie, Leaping Fawn, 1953, 1⅞x1½"	44.00
Whimsie, Shetland Pony, 1955, 1⅜x2"	36.00
Whimtray, Llama, 1958-65	30.00
Whimtray, Swan, 1958-65	30.00
Zoo Light, Baby Polar Bear, 1959	30.00
Zoo Light, Cockatoo, 1959	30.00
Zoo Light, West Highland Terrier, 1959	30.00

Wallace China

Dinnerware with a western theme was produced by the Wallace China Company, who operated in California from 1931 until 1964. They became a West Coast subsidiary of Shenango China in 1959.

Artist Till Goodan designed Rodeo, Pioneer Trails, Boots & Saddle, and Longhorn lines, which they marketed under the package name Westward Ho. When dinnerware with a western theme became so popular in more recent years, Rodeo was reproduced, but the new trademark includes neither 'California' or 'Wallace China.' Wallace was also known for producing hotel and restaurant ware, including Shadowleaf, Dahlia, Bird of Paradise, and Hibiscus, in California and other western states.

This ware is very heavy and not prone to chips, but be sure to examine it under a strong light to look for knife scratches, which will lessen its value to a considerable extent when excessive.

Note: You'll find cups and saucers with only a border design, which is made up of the lariat and brands. This border was used not only on Rodeo but on Boots & Saddle and Little Buckaroo patterns as well. If you'd like to learn more about this company, we recommend *Collector's Encyclopedia of California Pottery* by Jack Chipman (Collector Books).

49er, bowl (deep plate), 1x7"	75.00
49er, bowl, serving, 8" dia	120.00
49er, plate, dinner, 10½"	75.00
Boots & Saddle, bowl, cereal, 5¾"	70.00
Boots & Saddle, bowl, oval, 12", $135 to	175.00
Boots & Saddle, cr/sug bowl, 4¾x4⅝", $210 to	225.00
Boots & Saddle, c/s	80.00
Boots & Saddle, pitcher, disk type, 7½", $225 to	400.00
Boots & Saddle, plate, bread & butter, 7", $45 to	60.00
Boots & Saddle, plate, chop, 13"	250.00
Boots & Saddle, plate, luncheon, 9"	85.00
Boots & Saddle, platter, 15" L, $200 to	250.00
Boots & Saddle, tumbler, glass, Libbey, 4", set of 4	50.00
Chuck Wagon, bowl, 6¾", $30 to	45.00
Chuck Wagon, bowl, oval, 1½x8¼" L, $65 to	85.00
Chuck Wagon, bowl, oval, 10" L, $120 to	130.00

Chuck Wagon, creamer, 2-oz, 2½", $65 to 80.00
Chuck Wagon, c/s, demi 110.00
Chuck Wagon, egg cup 100.00
Chuck Wagon, platter, 13x9", $120 to 145.00
Chuck Wagon, sauceboat w/attached undertray, 9½" L 185.00
Dahlia, c/s, $35 to 40.00
Dahlia, platter, 11½" L 40.00
Dahlia, teapot 100.00
El Rancho, c/s, $30 to 45.00
El Rancho, plate, dinner, 10½" 100.00
El Rancho, plate, grill, 9" 70.00
El Rancho, plate, luncheon, 9½", $50 to 60.00
El Rancho, plate, salad, 8¼" 45.00
El Rancho, platter, 13½" L, $120 to 135.00
El Rancho, sugar bowl, w/lid, 4", $50 to 60.00
Little Buckaroo, plate, 9" 200.00
Longhorn, ashtray, 5½" 50.00
Longhorn, bowl, mixing, lg 295.00
Longhorn, creamer, ftd, 3½x6¼", $125 to 135.00
Longhorn, c/s, $150 to 165.00
Longhorn, c/s, jumbo, $240 to 265.00
Longhorn, plate, bread & butter, 7¼" 75.00
Longhorn, shaker, 5", ea 65.00
Pioneer Trails, bowl, vegetable, oval, 12" L, $200 to 240.00
Pioneer Trails, c/s, 3", 6" 55.00
Pioneer Trails, plate, bread & butter, 7¼", $50 to 65.00
Pioneer Trails, plate, chop, 13" 350.00
Pioneer Trails, plate, dinner, 10¾", $85 to 110.00
Rodeo, ashtray, w/orig box, 5½" 100.00
Rodeo, bowl, 2½x4" 65.00
Rodeo, bowl, vegetable, oval, 12" 250.00
Rodeo, creamer, 3½", $50 to 65.00
Rodeo, c/s, $55 to 65.00
Rodeo, pitcher, disk type, 7x7½", $195 to 225.00
Rodeo, plate, bread & butter, w/center design, 7¼", $50 to 60.00
Rodeo, plate, chop, 13" 350.00
Rodeo, plate, dinner, 10¾", $85 to 110.00
Rodeo, platter, 15" L, $175 to 195.00
Rodeo, shakers, oversize, 4⅞", pr 200.00
Rodeo, sugar bowl, w/lid, 4½" 125.00
Shadowleaf, plate, bread & butter, 7⅛" 30.00
Shadowleaf, plate, dinner, 10½", $65 to 80.00

Shadowleaf, plate, divided, 10½", $30.00 to $35.00.

Southwest Desert, creamer 65.00
Ye Olde Mill, plate, dinner, 10⅝" 20.00

Walley

The Walley Pottery operated in West Sterling, Massachusetts, from 1898 to 1919. Never more than a one-man operation, William Walley himself handcrafted all his wares from local clay. The majority of his pottery was simple and unadorned and usually glazed in matt green. On occasion, however, you may find high- and semi-gloss green, as well as matt glazes in blue, cream, brown, and red. The rarest and most desirable examples of his work are those with applied or relief-carved decorations. Most pieces are marked 'WJW,' and some, made for the Worcester State Hospital, are stamped 'WSH.' Our advisors for this category are Suzanne Perrault and David Rago; they are listed in the Directory under New Jersey.

Bowl, gr (thick/dripping) on red clay, WJW, rim chip, 9" 350.00
Mug, leaves on gr, pod hdl, WJW/S, 5½x5½", NM 825.00
Pitcher, red/gr matt, gourd, WJW, 9½x6" 2,520.00
Vase, broad leaves, gr-brn leather texture, bulb, WJW, 6" 9,000.00
Vase, foliage, gr & brn flambé, flecks/nicks, 5¼x3½" 1,325.00
Vase, gr/brn flambé on brn matt, WJW, 10x4½" 2,520.00
Vase, gr/brn flambé, bottle shape, WJW, 7¼x4¼" 725.00
Vase, gr/brn matt, pear shape w/lobed rim, 7¼" 1,200.00
Vase, gr matt (feathered), wide bottle form, 4¾x4" 1,080.00
Vase, gr streaming overglaze on caramel, Grecian hdls, rstr, 13" . 3,050.00
Vase, gr w/striations on red clay, stick neck, WJW, 10" 425.00
Vase, leaves (full-height), gr w/exposed clay, WJW, 6½x4" 2,640.00

Vase, lizards, brown and green, WJW, 3¼x4¼", $4,200.00. (Photo courtesy Rago Auctions)

Vase, red/ivory marbleized flambe, squat w/can neck, 4x4¾", EX ... 2,520.00
Vase, semi-matt & lustrous gr glaze, impressed WJW, 16½x8" .. 5,100.00
Vase, wooded landscape & cabin, mc band on gr, 1915, 7¼x4¼" . 14,500.00

Walrath

Frederick E. Walrath learned his craft as a student of Charles Fergus Binns at Alfred University (1900 – 1904). Walrath worked first, and briefly, at Grueby Faience Company in Boston and then, from 1908 to 1918, as an instructor at the Mechanics Institute in Rochester, New York. He was chief ceramist at Newcomb Pottery (New Orleans) until his death in 1921. A studio potter, Walrath's work bears stylistic similarity to that of Marblehead Pottery, whose founder, Arthur Baggs, was also a student of Binns's. Vases featuring matt glazes of stylized natural motifs (especially florals) are most sought after; sculptural and figural forms (center bowls, flower frogs, various animals) are less desirable. Typically his work is signed with an incised circular signature: Walrath Pottery with conjoined M and I at the center. Our advisor for this and related Arts & Crafts subjects is Bruce A. Austin; he is listed in the Directory under New York.

Vase, organic designs, brown and tan on gray, 4¾x5¼", $2,760.00. (Photo courtesy Treadway Gallery on LiveAuctioneers.com)

Bowl, 3-D female sits on rnd ped in center, turq w/gr int, 9x8" 400.00
Bowl, stylized floral, pk/gr on café-au-lait, shouldered, 3x7", EX .. 650.00

Candlestick, putto atop column, 3 holders below, sm rpr, 12x5¾", ea...625.00
Flower frog, swan on pierced base, beige & gr, 3½x4"......................75.00
Vase, cabin in wooded landscape at shoulder, mc on gr, 1915, 7¼x4"..14,400.00
Vase, floral, pk/orange on gr froth, 5½x3½", NM........................5,300.00
Vase, geometric floral/foliage, pk/gr on gr mottle, 8¾x4½"........9,800.00
Vase, stylized trees, dk gr on gr matt, hairline crack, 6½x4½" ...3,000.00
Vase, trees, gr & brn on dk gr, sloped shoulder, 6¾x4½"............5,500.00
Vase, water lilies & pads, orange/lt gr on gr, shouldered, 7¼", NM...5,500.00

A. Walter

Almaric Walter was employed from 1904 through 1914 at Verreries Artistiques des Freres Daum in Nancy, France. After 1919 he opened his own business where he continued to make the same type of quality objets d'art in pate-de-verre glass as he had earlier. His pieces are signed A. Walter, Nancy H. Berge SC.

Bookends, fox at fruit arbor, by Mercier, 6", NM, $6,840.00. (Photo courtesy Sotheby's on LiveAuctioneers.com)

Bookends, squirrel, yel on gr bk & base, Berge SC, 5x4¾" 8,700.00
Bowl, lg leaves, yel on shaded bl, chestnut on lid, 6" H............8,400.00
Bowl, leaves/berries in center, gr/brn on yel, tab hdls, 7"...........4,600.00
Box, cigarette, bl/dk bl w/floral cvg, sleigh form, yel florals on lid...9,660.00
Box, snail on lid, roses arnd circumfrence, bl grnd, 4½" 4,200.00
Covered dish, leaves/berries on bl, snail finial, Berge SC, 4x4¾" ..5,290.00
Dish, 3 floral sprigs at 2/6/10 o'clock, rust on bl mottle, 7"........1,920.00
Figurine, sea lion on boulder, cadmium yel & brn, Mercier, 6⅝". 1,450.00
Inkwell, lizard stalking a bumble bee, 3¾" 8,400.00
Paperweight, cicada on laurel branch, yel to gr, 1⅞x5" 1,325.00
Paperweight, crab, dk gr & bl, 1¾x2½" 1,100.00
Paperweight, moth, blk/brn/bl/turq on teal, 3¾", NM 425.00
Paperweight, mouse w/nut on outcrop, wht/brn/gr, ca 1900, 3½"... 1,450.00
Paperweight, satyr, yel w/gr leaf headband w/purple berries, 3".... 780.00
Paperweight, scarab on circular base, gr & bl, 1x2" dia 900.00
Tray, fish to side, gr/yel 'waves,' 6" L, EX.................................1,920.00
Tray, moth to 1 side, amber/shaded gr, rect, 4½" L.....................1,920.00
Tray, moth, gr & aqua mottle, ca 1900, 5"..................................1,650.00
Tray, pen, divider topped by lg brn beetle on gr, 9½" L...............2,300.00
Vase, blackberries & foliage, mc on yel, flared body, 4½" 3,000.00
Vase, snails/vegetation, gr/bl/yel, ftd U-shape, 8" 6,000.00
Vases, trees/flowers/water, mc, slim, ftd, 12¼", pr, EX...............1,950.00

Wannopee

The Wannopee Pottery, established in 1892, developed from the reorganization of the financially insecure New Milford Pottery Company of New Milford, Connecticut. They produced a line of mottled-glazed pottery called 'Duchess' and a similar line in porcelain. Both were marked with the impressed sunburst 'W' with 'porcelain' added to indicate that particular body type. In 1895 semiporcelain pitchers in three sizes were decorated with relief medallion cameos of Beethoven, Mozart, and Napoleon. Lettuce-leaf ware was first produced in 1901 and used actual leaves in the modeling. Scarabronze, made in 1895, was their finest artware. It featured simple Egyptian shapes with a coppery

glaze. It was marked with a scarab, either impressed or applied. Production ceased in 1903.

Vase, Scarabronze, six buttressed handles, bronze matt, L/O #108H 21, 20", NM, $2,640.00. (Photo courtesy Craftsman Auctions on LiveAuctioneers.com)

Chamberstick, brn, twisted cylinder w/flared ft, 13¼x8¾", ea......450.00
Dish, lettuce leaf shape, lt g, #219, 9¼" 400.00
Candlestick, brn majolica, twist stem, 12⅜" 175.00
Pitcher, gr gloss, dotted leaves among vertical rows of beads, 8", EX.200.00
Vase, brn gloss, concave cylinder w/3 diagonal appl hdls, 8"........230.00
Vase, streaky brn, long stick neck, coiled snakes at base, mk, 27¼"..2,500.00

Warwick

The Warwick China Company operated in Wheeling, West Virginia, from 1887 until 1951. They produced both hand-painted and decaled plates, vases, teapots, coffeepots, pitchers, bowls, and jardinieres featuring lovely florals or portraits of beautiful ladies done in luscious colors. Backgrounds were usually blendings of brown and beige, but ivory was also used as well as greens and pinks. Various marks were employed, all of which incorporate the Warwick name. For a more thorough study of the subject, we recommend *Warwick, A to W*, a supplement to *Why Not Warwick* by our advisor, Donald C. Hoffmann, Sr.; his address can be found in the Directory under Illinois. In an effort to inform the collector/dealer, Mr. Hoffmann has a video available that identifies the company's decals and their variations by number.

A-Beauty, vase, floral on gr...425.00
Albany, vase, floral gr to yel...425.00
Albany, vase, floral on brn...295.00
Bouquet #1, vase, floral on brn, A-25...220.00
Bouquet #1, vase, floral on red, E-2...255.00
Bouquet #1, vase, portrait on brn, A-17......................................300.00
Bouquet #1, vase, portrait on pk, H-1...425.00
Bouquet #1, vase, portrait on red, E-1..300.00
Bouquet #2, vase, floral on brn, A-21...195.00
Bouquet #2, vase, floral on brn, A-23...195.00
Bouquet #2, vase, floral on brn, A-25...185.00

Bouquet #2, vase, portrait on brown, A-17, 10", $300.00. (Photo courtesy Pat and Don Hoffmann)

Bouquet #2, vase, portrait on red, E-1...220.00
Carnation, vase, floral on brn, A-22..145.00

Carnation, vase, floral on brn, A-6............................. 145.00
Carnation, vase, portrait on pk, H-1 .... 345.00
Carol, vase, floral on brn, A-6 .... 145.00
Carol, vase, portrait on pk, H-1................................. 320.00
Duchess, vase, portrait on brn, A-16 .... 225.00
Monroe, vase, floral on matt brn, A-11 .... 300.00
Oriental, vase, floral on brn, A-25 .... 315.00
Peerless, vase, floral on brn, A-14 .... 320.00
Peerless, vase, portrait on brn, A-17 .... 385.00
Penn, vase, portrait on pk, H-1 .... 480.00
Roberta, vase, portrait on red, E-1............................ 485.00
Royal #1, vase, portrait on brn, A-17 .... 370.00
Royal #2, vase, portrait on brn, A-17 .... 375.00
Senator #1, vase, floral on brn, A-40......................... 280.00
Senator #1, vase,, floral on gr, 13½"......................... 345.00
Senator #2, vase, floral on yel/gr, K-1 .... 345.00
Tobio #1, jug, floral on brn, A-25 .... 130.00
Tobio #1, jug, portrait on brn, A-17 .... 145.00
Tobio #1, jug, portrait on red, E-1............................ 140.00
Tobio #2, jug, floral on brn, A-22 .... 125.00
Tobio #2, jug, floral on brn, A-26 .... 130.00
Tobio #3, jug, floral on red, E-2 .... 130.00
Tobio #3, jug, portrait on brn, A-17 .... 150.00
Verbenia #1, vase, floral on brn, A-27 .... 210.00
Verbenia #1, vase, floral on brn/matt, M-2............... 235.00
Verbenia #1, vase, floral on brn/matt, M-4............... 250.00
Verbenia #2, vase, birds on wht, D-1 .... 270.00
Verbenia #2, vase, floral on brn, A-27 .... 220.00
Verbenia #3, vase, birds on wht, D-1 .... 320.00
Verona, vase, floral on brn, A-22 .... 145.00
Verona, vase, floral on brn, A-40 .... 140.00
Verona, vase, floral on red, A-27 .... 220.00
Verona, vase, portrait on brn, A-17 .... 220.00
Verona, vase, portrait on red, E-1 .... 240.00
Violet, vase, floral on brn, A-6 .... 145.00
Violet, vase, floral on red, E-2.................................. 140.00

Watches

First made in the 1500s in Germany, early watches were actually small clocks, suspended from the neck or belt. By 1700 they had become the approximate shape and size we know today. The first watches produced in America were made in 1810. The well-known Waltham Watch Company was established in 1850. Later, Waterbury produced inexpensive watches which they sold by the thousands.

Open-face and hunting-case watches of the 1890s were often solid gold or gold-filled and were often elaborately decorated in several colors of gold. Gold watches became a status symbol in this decade and were worn by both men and women on chains with fobs or jeweled slides. Ladies sometimes fastened them to their clothing with pins often set with jewels. The chatelaine watch was worn at the waist, only one of several items such as scissors, coin purses, or needle cases, each attached by small chains. Most turn-of-the-century watch cases were gold-filled; these are plentiful today. Sterling cases, though interest in them is on the increase, are not in great demand. For more information we recommend *The Complete Price Guide to Watches* by Richard E. Gilbert, Tom Engle, and Cooksey Shugart; and *Collector's Encyclopedia of Pendant and Pocket Watches, 1500 – 1950*, by C. Jeanenne Bell, G.G. (Collector Books). Our advice for this category comes from Maundy International Watches, antiquarian horologists, price consultants, and researchers for many watch reference guides and books on horology. Their firm is a leading purveyor of antique watches of all kinds. They are listed in the Directory under Kansas.

Key:

adj — adjusted	fbd — finger bridge design
brg — bridge plate design	g/f — gold-filled
d/s — double sunk dial	g/j/s — gold jewel setting
h/c — hunter case	o/f — open face
j — jewel	p/s — pendant set
k — karat	s — size
k/s — key set	s/s — single sunk dial
k/w — key wind	s/w — stem wind
l/s — lever set	w/g/f — white gold-filled
mvt — movement	y/g/f — yellow gold-filled

American Watch Co., 14k gold, etched scene on heavy hunter case, PS Bartlett lever set movement #3727471, 2½", $1,850.00. (Photo courtesy TW Conroy, LLC on LiveAuctioneers.com)

Am Watch Co, 6s, 7j, #1873, 14k, Am Watch Co, M................... 685.00
Am Watch Co, 6s, 19j, #1891, 14k, h/c, Riverside Maximus, M...1,895.00
Am Watch Co, 12s, 17j, #1894, 14k, o/f, Royal, M..................... 650.00
Am Watch Co, 16s, 11j, #1872, silver, p/s, h/c, Park Road, F 325.00
Am Watch Co, 16s, 16j, #1884, 14k, 5-min, Repeater, M.......... 7,550.00
Am Watch Co, 16s, 17j, #1888, Railroader, M........................ 1,800.00
Am Watch Co, 16s, 19j, #1872, 14k, h/c, Am Watch Woerd's Pat, M ..8,225.00
Am Watch Co, 16s, 21j, #1883, y/g/f, o/f, l/s, Am Waltham, M.3,495.00
Am Watch Co, 16s, 21j, #1888, 14k, h/c, Riverside Maximus, M.. 2,100.00
Am Watch Co, 16s, 21j, #1899, 14k, o/f, M 2,875.00
Am Watch Co, 16s, 21j, #1908, y/g/f, o/f, Grade #645, M 475.00
Am Watch Co, 16s, 23j, #1908, 18k, o/f, Premier Maximus, MIB.. 18,350.00
Am Watch Co, 16s, 23j, #1908, y/g/f, o/f, adj, RR, Vanguard, M. 685.00
Am Watch Co, 16s, 23j, #1908, y/g/f, o/f, Vanguard Up/Down, M ..1,725.00
Am Watch Co, 18s, #1857, silver, h/c, Samuel Curtiss k/w, M .3,900.00
Am Watch Co, 18s, 11j, #1857, k/w, 1st run, PS Bartlett, M ...11,450.00
Am Watch Co, 18s, 11j, #1857, silver, h/c, k/w, DH&D, EX....3,395.00
Am Watch Co, 18s, 11j, #1857, silver, h/c, k/w, s/s, Wm Ellery, EX.... 295.00
Am Watch Co, 18s, 15j, #1857, k/w, RE Robbins, EX 3,250.00
Am Watch Co, 18s, 15j, #1883, y/g/f, 2-tone, Railroad King, EX . 975.00
Am Watch Co, 18s, 17j, #1892, o/f, Canadian Pacific Railway, M ..3,650.00
Am Watch Co, 18s, 17j, #1892, y/g/f, o/f, Sidereal, rare, M 5,125.00
Am Watch Co, 18s, 17j, 25-yr, y/g/f, o/f, s/s, PS Bartlett, M......... 465.00
Am Watch Co, 18s, 21j, #1892, y/g/f, o/f, d/s, Crescent St, M 625.00
Am Watch Co, 18s, 21j, #1892, y/g/f, o/f, Grade #845, EX 450.00
Am Watch Co, 18s, 7j, #1857, silver, k/w, CT Parker, M........... 3,450.00
Auburndale Watch Co, 18s, 7j, k/w, l/s, EX 425.00
Aurora Watch Co, 18s, 11j, silver, k/w, h/c, M 450.00
Aurora Watch Co, 18s, 15 ruby j, y/g/f, s/w, 5th pinion, M 1,850.00
Ball (Elgin), 18s, 17j, silver, o/f, Official RR Standard, M............ 975.00

Ball (Hamilton), 16s, 21j, #999B, official railroad, five adjusted positions, in Wadsworth gold-filled case, $840.00. (Photo courtesy Tom Harris Auctions on LiveAuctioneers.com)

Ball (Hamilton), 16s, 21j, #999, g/f, o/f, l/s, M 1,250.00
Ball (Hamilton), 16s, 23j, #998, y/g/f, o/f, Elinvar, M 3,850.00
Ball (Hamilton), 18s, 17j, #999, g/f, o/f, l/s, EX 675.00
Ball (Hampden), 18s, 17j, o/f, adj, RR, Superior Grade, M 2,100.00
Ball (Illinois), 12s, 19j, w/g/f, o/f, M 395.00
Ball (Waltham), 16s, 21j, o/f, Official RR Standard, M 950.00
Columbus, 18s, 11-15j, k/w, k/s, M 450.00
Columbus, 18s, 15j, o/f, l/s, M 225.00
Columbus, 18s, 15j, y/g/f, o/f, Jay Gould on dial, M 2,900.00
Columbus, 18s, 21j, y/g/f, h/c, train on dial, Railway King, M .. 2,350.00
Columbus, 18s, 23j, y/g/f, h/c, Columbus King, M 2,800.00
Cornell, 18s, 15j, silver, h/c, k/w, John Evans, EX 495.00
Cornell, 18s, 15j, s/w, JC Adams, EX 675.00
Dudley, 12s, #1, 14k, o/f, flip-bk case, Masonic, M 3,700.00
Elgin, 6s, 11j, 14k, h/c, M 695.00
Elgin, 6s, 15j, g/f hunter case, ca 1895 .... 195.00
Elgin, 10s, 18k, h/c, k/w, k/s, s/s, Gail Borden, M 1,150.00
Elgin, 12s, 15j, 14k, h/c, EX 595.00
Elgin, 12s, 17j, 14k, h/c, GM Wheeler, M 675.00
Elgin, 16s, 15j, 14k, h/c, EX 995.00
Elgin, 16s, 15j, doctor's, 4th model, 18k, h/c, 2nd sweep hand, M 2,900.00
Elgin, 16s, 21j, 14k, 3 fbd, grade #91, scarce, M 5,250.00
Elgin, 16s, 21j, y/g/f, g/j/s, 3 fbd, h/c, M 1,175.00
Elgin, 16s, 21j, y/g/f, g/j/s, o/f, BW Raymond, EX 450.00
Elgin, 16s, 21j, y/g/f, o/f, l/s, RR, Father Time, M 625.00
Elgin, 16s, 23j, up/down indicator, BW Raymond, EX 2,600.00
Elgin, 18s, 11j, silver, h/c, k/w, gilded, MG Odgen, M 425.00
Elgin, 18s, 15j, silver, h/c, k/w, k/s, HL Culver, M 425.00
Elgin, 18s, 15j, silver, h/c, Penn RR dial, BW Raymond k/w mvt, M . 6,400.00
Elgin, 18s, 15j, silver, o/f, d/s, k/w, RR, BW Raymond 1st run, M ... 1,525.00
Elgin, 18s, 17j, silveroid, h/c, BW Raymond, M 365.00
Elgin, 18s, 21j, y/g/f, o/f, Father Time, G 335.00
Elgin, 18s, 23j, y/g/f, o/f, 5-position, RR, Veritas, M 1,050.00
Fredonia, 18s, 11j, y/g/f, h/c, k/w, M 725.00
Hamilton, #910, 12s, 17j, y/g/f, o/f, s/s, 20-yr, EX 65.00
Hamilton, #912, 12s, 17j, y/g/f, o/f, adj, EX 65.00
Hamilton, #920, 12s, 23j, 14k, o/f, M 775.00
Hamilton, #922MP, 12s, 18k, Masterpiece (sgn), M 1,900.00
Hamilton, #925, 18s, 17j, y/g/f, h/c, s/s, l/s, M 465.00
Hamilton, #928, 18s, 15j, y/g/f, o/f, s/s, EX 325.00
Hamilton, #933, 18s, 16j, nickel plate, h/c, low serial #, M 1,650.00
Hamilton, #938, 18s, 17j, y/g/f, adj, M 850.00
Hamilton, #940, 18s, 21j, nickel plate, coin silver, o/f, M 595.00
Hamilton, #946, 18s, 23j, y/g/f, o/f, g/j/s, M 1,450.00
Hamilton, #947 (mk), 18s, 23j, 14k, h/c, orig/sgn, EX 6,400.00
Hamilton, #950, 16s, 23j, y/g/f, o/f, l/s, sgn d/s, M 2,100.00
Hamilton, #965, 16s, 17j, 14k, h/c, p/s, brg, scarce, M 1,725.00
Hamilton, #972, 16s, 17j, y/g/f, o/f, g/j/s, d/s, l/s, adj, EX 225.00
Hamilton, #974, 16s, 17j, y/g/f, o/f, 20-yr, s/s, EX 90.00
Hamilton, #992, 16s, 21j, y/g/f, o/f, adj, d/s, dbl roller, M 495.00
Hamilton, #992B, 16s, 21j, y/g/f, o/f, l/s, Bar/Crown, M 775.00
Hampden, 12s, 17j, w/g/f, o/f, thin model, Aviator, M 360.00
Hampden, 16s, 7j, gilded, nickel plate, o/f, ¾-mvt, EX 55.00

Hampden, 16s, 17j, o/f, adj, EX 75.00
Hampden, 16s, 17j, y/g/f, h/c, s/w, M 300.00
Hampden, 16s, 21j, g/j/s, y/g/f, NP, h/c, Dueber, ¾-mvt, M 350.00
Hampden, 16s, 23j, o/f, adj, dbl roller, Special Railway, M 725.00
Hampden, 18s, 15j, k/w, mk on mvt, Railway, M 1,850.00
Hampden, 18s, 15j, s/w, gilded, JC Perry, M 375.00
Hampden, 18s, 15j, silver, h/c, k/w, Hayward, M 350.00
Hampden, 18s, 15j, y/g/f, damascened, h/c, Dueber, M 275.00
Hampden, 18s, 21j, y/g/f, g/j/s, h/c, New Railway, M 695.00
Hampden, 18s, 21j, y/g/f, o/f, d/s, l/s, N Am Railway, M 595.00
Hampden, 18s, 23j, 14k, h/c, Special Railway, M 1,600.00
Hampden, 18s, 23j, y/g/f, o/f, d/s, adj, New Railway, M 775.00
Hampden, 18s, 7-11j, gilded, k/w, Springfield Mass, EX 250.00
Howard (Keystone), 12s, 23j, 14k, h/c, brg, Series 8, M 850.00
Howard (Keystone), 16s, 17j, y/g/f, o/f, Series 9, M 400.00
Howard (Keystone), 16s, 21j, y/g/f, o/f, RR Chronometer II, M . 1,150.00
Howard (Keystone), 16s, 23j, y/g/f, o/f, Series 0, jeweled bbl, M ... 1,625.00
Howard, E; 6s, 15j, 18k, h/c, s/w, Series VIII, G sz, M 1,700.00
Howard, E; 16s, 15j, 14k, h/c, s/w, L sz, M 2,500.00
Howard, E; 18s, 15j, 18k h/c, k/w, Series II, N sz, M 7,250.00
Howard, E; 18s, 15j, silver, h/c, k/w, Series I, N sz, M 5,500.00
Howard, E; 18s, 17j, 25-yr, y/g/f, o/f, orig case, split plate, M 2,250.00
Illinois, 0s, 7j, 14k, h/c, l/s, EX 600.00
Illinois, 8s, 13j, -mvt, Rose LeLand, scarce, M 325.00
Illinois, 12s, 17j, y/g/f, o/f, d/s dial, EX 65.00
Illinois, 16s, 17j, y/g/f, o/f, d/s, Bunn, EX 395.00
Illinois, 16s, 21j, o/f, d/s, Santa Fe Special, M 1,200.00
Illinois, 16s, 21j, y/g/f, h/c, g/j/s, Burlington, M 465.00
Illinois, 16s, 21j, y/g/f, o/f, d/s, Bunn Special, M 695.00

Illinois, 16s, 23j, #163 60 hour Bunn Special, yellow screw on Model #108, 10k gold-filled Wadsworth case, adjusted temp and six positions, 2", $2,700.00. (Photo courtesy Tom Harris Auctions on LiveAuctioneers.com)

Illinois, 16s, 23j, y/g/f, o/f, stiff bow, Sangamo Special, EX 1,675.00
Illinois, 18s, 11j, #1, silver, k/w, Alleghany, EX 250.00
Illinois, 18s, 11j, #3, o/f, s/w, l/s, Comet, G 85.00
Illinois, 18s, 11j, Forest City, G 85.00
Illinois, 18s, 15j, #1, adj, y/g/f, h/c, k/w, gilt, Bunn, M 950.00
Illinois, 18s, 15j, #1, k/w, k/s, silver, h/c, Stuart, M 1,050.00
Illinois, 18s, 15j, k/w, k/s, gilt, Railway Regulator, M 1,175.00
Illinois, 18s, 15j, silveroid, s/w, G 49.00
Illinois, 18s, 15j, y/g/f, o/f, s/s, Jay Gould Railroad King, rare .. 10,500.00
Illinois, 18s, 17j, g/j/s, adj, h/c, B&O RR Special (Hunter), M. 3,650.00
Illinois, 18s, 17j, nickel plate, coin silver, h/c, s/w, Bunn, M 700.00
Illinois, 18s, 17j, o/f, s/w, 5th pinion, Miller, EX 85.00
Illinois, 18s, 21j, 14k, h/c, g/j/s, Bunn Special, M 2,400.00
Illinois, 18s, 21j, g/f, g/j/s, o/f, A Lincoln, M 500.00
Illinois, 18s, 21j, g/j/s, o/f, adj, B&O RR Special, EX 2,350.00
Illinois, 18s, 23j, g/j/s, Bunn Special, EX 1,800.00
Illinois, 18s, 24j, g/j/s, o/f, adj, Chesapeake & Ohio, M 4,450.00
Illinois, 18s, 24j, g/j/s, o/f, Bunn Special, EX 1,595.00
Illinois, 18s, 26j, 14k, Penn Special, M 9,400.00
Illinois, 18s, 26j, g/j/s, o/f, Ben Franklin USA, M 6,200.00
Illinois, 18s, 7j, #3, silveroid, America, G 60.00
Illinois, 18s, 9-11j, o/f, k/w, s/s, silveroid case, Hoyt, M 275.00
Ingersoll, 16s, 7j, wht base metal, Reliance, G 18.00

Hampden, 17j, 14k, railway, 1890s, 2⅛", $495.00. (Photo courtesy Alderfer Auction Company on LiveAuctioneers.com)

Lancaster, 18s, 7j, silver, o/f, k/w, k/s, EX 225.00
Marion US, 18s, 15j, nickel plate, h/c, s/w, Henry Randel, M...... 500.00
Marion US, 18s, h/c, k/w, k/s, -plate, Asa Fuller, M..................... 495.00
Melrose Watch Co, 18s, 7j, k/w, k/s, G 340.00
New York Watch Co, 18s, 7j, silver, h/c, k/w, George Sam Rice, EX .. 265.00
New York Watch Co, 19j, low sz #, wolf's teeth wind, M.......... 1,900.00
Patek Philippe, 12s, 18j, 18k, o/f, EX 3,450.00
Patek Philippe, 16s, 20j, 18k, h/c, M 4,250.00
Rockford, 16s, 17j, y/g/f, h/c, brg, dbl roller, EX....................... 80.00
Rockford, 16s, 21j, #515, y/g/f, M 1,100.00
Rockford, 16s, 21j, g/j/s, o/f, grade #537, rare, M 2,750.00
Rockford, 16s, 23j, 14k, o/f, mk Doll on dial/mvt, M 4,400.00
Rockford, 18s, 15j, silver, o/f, k/w, EX 260.00
Rockford, 18s, 17j, silveroid, 2-tone, M 425.00
Rockford, 18s, 17j, y/g/f, o/f, Winnebago, M......................... 495.00
Rockford, 18s, 21j, o/f, King Edward, M............................... 575.00
Seth Thomas, 18s, 7j, ¾-mvt, bk: eagle/Liberty model, M 365.00
Seth Thomas, 18s, 17j, #2, g/j/s, adj, Henry Molineux, EX 700.00
Seth Thomas, 18s, 17j, Edgemere, G..................................... 40.00
Seth Thomas, 18s, 25j, g/f, g/j/s, Maiden Lane, EX 2,850.00
South Bend, 12s, 21j, dbl roller, Grade #431, M 250.00
South Bend, 12s, 21j, orig o/f, d/s, Studebaker, M 750.00
South Bend, 18s, 17j, #309, rare g/f hinged case, l/s, ca 1913 ...... 145.00
South Bend, 18s, 21j, 14k, h/c, M 1,500.00
South Bend, 18s, 21j, g/j/s, h/c, Studebaker, M.................... 2,200.00
Swiss, 18s, 18k, h/c, 1-min, Repeater, High Grade, M............. 7,200.00
Vacheron & Constantin, Geneva, Swiss, 17j, s/w, l/s, 1900, EX. 2,150.00

Watch Fobs

Watch fobs have been popular since the last quarter of the nineteenth century. They were often made by retail companies to feature their products. Souvenir, commemorative, and political fobs were also produced. Of special interest today are those with advertising, heavy equipment in particular. Some of the more pricey fobs are listed here, but most of those currently available were produced in such quantities that they are relatively common and should fall within a price range of $3.00 to $10.00. When no material is mentioned in the description, assume the fob is made of metal. Our advisor for this category is Tony George; he is listed in the Directory under California.

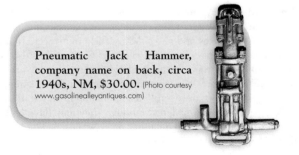

Pneumatic Jack Hammer, company name on back, circa 1940s, NM, $30.00. (Photo courtesy www.gasolinealleyantiques.com)

39th Annual Reunion...1929, 2 military portraits, brass................ 110.00
5-pointed star in shield, mk JWW 1928...................................... 120.00
Anchor, 14k gold, w/thick 15" gold chain, 63.0 dwt.................. 1,325.00
Bloodstone/agate in gold disk/twisted rope fr.............................. 245.00
Buffalo Bill & his partner, Pawnee Bill, heavy brass 600.00
Compass, 14k gold w/15" gold chain, 34.6 dwt............................ 850.00
Compass, gold-filled w/14¼" slide chain, ca 1900 .... 180.00
Cupid's bow/letter seal/lion, blk enameling, 1½x1¼"+chain 145.00
Herakles intaglio on onyx stone w/14k gold mt, oval, 1¾".......... 335.00
Int'l Aeor Congress commemorative, 1921, w/vintage stopwatch... 180.00
John Deere, badge logo on brass, w/strap 110.00

John Deere, leaping deer & plow on brass shield form, w/strap.... 425.00
John Deere, leaping deer, aqua enamel on metal oval (G), w/strap.. 36.00
John Deere, man's portrait on brass, Centennial 36.00
Patriotic beadwork ribbon w/2 Union shields, ca 1865, 4x1½" 425.00

Watch Stands

Watch stands were decorative articles designed with a hook from which to hang a watch. Some displayed the watch as the face of a grandfather clock or as part of an interior scene with figures in period costumes and contemporary furnishings. They were popular products of Staffordshire potters and silver companies as well.

Brass, rococo style, rstr gilt, 19th C, 12"............................... 240.00
Bronzed metal, lyre form w/swan supports, Charles X, 19th C, 10½".. 725.00
Burlwood w/brass fittings, hanger in center of arch, Vict, 5½" 200.00
Faience obelisk, tapering column w/spherule surmount, Fr, 19th C, 14"... 425.00
Gilt bronze, Louis XVI style, bowknot surmount, 19th C, 5¾x4½" ..250.00
Ivory, 2 columns w/dome top, 2 armed guards on front, 19th C.. 1,650.00
Lignum vitae arch w/2 trn pillars on rnd base, ivory finial, 7¼x4".. 375.00
Mahogany w/cvd animals/man/lady seated w/book, 19th C, 6⅜x7x3".. 2,350.00
Majolica bear standing & holding tree, Royal Worcester, 3½"..1,875.00
Metal, crest/floral wreath/Father Time, late Vict, 12x5" 600.00
Oak w/geometric inlay, brass finial, 2-compartment, 8¾" 600.00

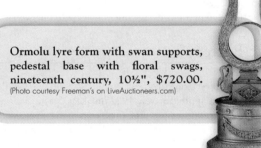

Ormolu lyre form with swan supports, pedestal base with floral swags, nineteenth century, 10½", $720.00. (Photo courtesy Freeman's on LiveAuctioneers.com)

Porcelain, flowers/serpent appl, rococo base w/Father Time, Meissen, 10".3,000.00
Silver-tone muse (lady) on wooden stand, unmk, 7¼" 100.00
Silver, logs on campfire, watch hangs from branch, Tufts #2623, 1900s...265.00
SP jockey on stool w/whip, Southington Quadruple Plate, 4"...... 225.00
Walnut w/ivory trim, molded stepped base, 2-part, 8x8x3".......2,500.00
Wood, tall case clock, cvd w/inlay, ca 1790, 10¼", VG 950.00
Wood, turned, hidden ring box, Vict, 7x5", EX 220.00

Waterford

The Waterford Glass Company operated in Ireland from the late 1700s until 1851 when the factory closed. One hundred years later (in 1951) another Waterford glassworks was instituted that produced glass similar to the eighteenth-century wares — crystal, usually with cut decoration. Today Waterford is a generic term referring to the type of glass first produced there.

Bowl, centerpiece, cut boat form on tall ped, att, 9½x13x6½" 360.00
Bowl, centerpiece, cut panels, scalloped/ftd, sgn M O'Leary, 7x9" ..350.00
Bowl, King's, scalloped rim, ped ft, 7x9¾"................................. 480.00
Bowl, spear-cut sides, 4x8"... 100.00
Candelabra, 3-light, 6-arm, rnd ped, star finial, drops, 30x17", pr. 12,000.00
Celery vase, dmn-point band, ftd, ca early 19th C, att, 8¾".........265.00
Champagne cooler, urn form, deep cuttings, 13x9½", NM...........600.00

Chandelier, nine-arm, crystal swags and drops, $3,630.00.
(Photo courtesy Clars Auction Gallery on LiveAuctioneers.com)

Christmas ornament, 5 rings on tree shape, 1991 .... 285.00
Cordial, Linsmore 47.50
Decanter, dmn cuttings, 3-notch hdl, ftd, prism ball stopper, 12" . 350.00
Decanter, Kylemore, 12", +9 matching old-fashioned tumblers ... 300.00
Decanter, Linsmore, 13" 298.00
Stem, champagne, Curraghmore, 5½", 12 for 550.00
Stem, flute, Colleen, 6", 6 for 300.00
Stem, water, Colleen, 5¼", 10 for 300.00
Stem, water, Curraghmore, 7½", 12 for 780.00
Stem, water, Tramore, 5⅝", 12 for 360.00
Stem, wine, Curraghmore, 7½", 12 for 850.00
Tumblers, Colleen, 12-oz, 4¾", 12 for 480.00
Vase, Deco horizontal broken ribs, stepped sq ft, 12½" 395.00
Vase, geometric cuttings, vertical ribs at rim, cylindrical, 12x6" .. 350.00
Vase, Millennium, geometric cuttings, 2000, MIB 360.00
Vase, presentation, geometric cuttings/panels, scalloped rim, ftd, 13". 300.00

Watt Pottery

The Watt Pottery Company was established in Crooksville, Ohio, on July 5, 1922. From approximately 1922 until 1935, they manufactured hand-turned stone containers — jars, jugs, milk pans, preserve jars, and various sizes of mixing bowls, usually marked with a cobalt blue acorn stamp. In 1936 production of these items was discontinued, and the company began to produce kitchen utility ware and ovenware such as mixing bowls, spaghetti bowls and plates, canister sets, covered casseroles, salt and pepper shakers, cookie jars, ice buckets, pitchers, bean pots, and salad and dinnerware sets. Most Watt ware is individually hand painted with bold brush strokes of red, green, or blue contrasting with the natural buff color of the glazed body. Several patterns were produced: Apple, Autumn Foliage, Cherry, Dutch Tulip, Morning Glory, Rio Rose, Rooster, Tear Drop, Starflower, and Tulip, to name a few. Much of the ware was made for advertising premiums and is often found stamped with the name of the retail company.

Tragedy struck the Watt Pottery Company on October 4, 1965, when fire completely destroyed the factory and warehouse. Production never resumed, but the ware they made has withstood many years of service in American kitchens and is today highly regarded and prized by collectors. The vivid colors and folksy execution of each cheerful pattern create a homespun ambiance that will make Watt pottery a treasure for years to come.

Apple, bean pot, #76, w/lid & hdls, 6½x7½" 175.00
Apple, bowl, cereal, #94, 1¾x6" 50.00
Apple, bowl, mixing, #8, ribbed, 4x8" 55.00
Apple, canister, #72, 9½x7" 500.00
Apple, cr/sug bowl, very rare sz, 2¾x5" 1,000.00
Apple, ice bucket w/lid, 7¼x7½" 275.00
Apple, mug, #121, 3¾x3" 185.00
Apple, pitcher, #17, 8x8½" 275.00

Apple, platter, #49, 12" dia 400.00
Apple, tumbler, #56, rare, 4½x4" 1,000.00
Autumn Foliage, platter, #31, 15" dia 110.00
Autumn Foliage, teapot, #505, rare, 5¾x9" 1,600.00
Blue/White Banded, bowl, mixing, 4x7" 25.00
Blue/White Banded, pitcher, 7x7¾" 95.00
Cherry, bowl, berry, #6, 3x6" 40.00
Cherry, shaker, bbl shape, 4x2½", ea 90.00
Dutch Tulip, cookie jar, #503, 8¼" 375.00
Morning Glory, sugar bowl, #98, 4½x5" 250.00
Pansy (Cut-Leaf), bowl, mixing, 4½x9" 45.00
Pansy (Cut-Leaf), bowl, salad 20.00
Pansy (Cut-Leaf), platter, w/Bull's Eye, 15" dia 110.00
Pansy (Old), bowl, salad 20.00
Pansy (Old), bowl, spaghetti, #39, 13" 60.00
Pansy (Old), casserole, #2/48, 4¼x7½" 75.00
Pansy (Old), platter, #31, 15" dia 100.00
Starflower, bowl, berry, 1½x5¾" 35.00
Starflower, casserole, w/lid, 4½x8¾" 125.00
Starflower, creamer, #62, 4¼x4½" 250.00
Starflower, pitcher, refrigerator, #69, 4-petal, sq, 8" 225.00
Starflower, pitcher w/ice lip, #17 .... 175.00
Tear Drop, casserole, w/lid, sq, 6x8" 850.00
Tear Drop, creamer, #62, 4¼" 275.00

Tear Drop, shakers, barrel shape, 4¼", pair $85.00 to $95.00. (Photo courtesy Sherry Williams, eBay seller peach381)

White Banded, bowl, 2½x5" 25.00
White Banded, pitcher, 7x7¾" 85.00

Wave Crest

Wave Crest is a line of decorated opal ware (milk glass) patented in 1892 by the C.F. Monroe Co. of Meriden, Connecticut. They made a full line of items for every room of the house, but they are probably best known for their boxes and vases. Many early items were hand painted with various levels of decoration; transfers were used in the later years prior to the company's demise in 1916. Floral themes are common; items with the scenics and portraits are rarer and more highly prized. Many pieces have ornately scrolled ormolu and brass handles, feet, and rims. Early pieces were unsigned (though they may have had paper labels); later, about 1898, a red banner mark was used. The black mark is probably from about 1902 – 1903. However, the glass is quite distinctive and has not been reproduced, so even unmarked items are easy to recognize. Note: There is no premium for signatures on Wave Crest. Values are given for hand-decorated pieces (unless noted 'transfer') that are *not* worn.

Biscuit jar, pk floral, egg crate, SP rim, lid & bail, 9¾" 200.00
Biscuit jar, pk floral, taper to metal rim, lid & hdl, 6¾" at base 160.00
Biscuit jar, pk wild rose, rococo scroll emb, brass, lid/rim sgn CFM & Co, 8" .. 260.00
Box, dresser, bl floral, egg crate, 2-pc brass rim, brass base, 4'5" sq ... 350.00
Box, dresser, bl forget-me-nots, spiral, 3" W 150.l00
Box, dresser, cherub playing trumpet, 2-pc brass rim, 4" dia 320.00
Box, dresser, crystal, brass hinge/rim, mk wave crest, 4¾" 300.00

Box, dresser, fall mums, emb, sq, brass ftd, 2-pc rim, CFM Co 450.00
Box, dresser, lav scrolls & pk roses, spiral, 5½" dia......................... 250.00
Box, dresser, pk floral, emb scroll body, 2-pc brass rim, mk, 4" dia.... 120.00
Box, glove, pk & wht roses, ormolu ft, w/lid, 9½" L.................. 1,100.00
Box, lady's portrait, ornate ormolu rim & ftd base, sgn, 7" 6,500.00
Fernery, brass rim, fern fronds, 8" dia 110.00
Letter holder, pk floral, egg crate, brass rim, 6x4" 150.00
Muffineer/sugar shaker, yel & brn floral, twist shape, metal lid, 3⅛" ... 200.00
Paperweight, wht daisy, glass base, metal figural finial 400.00
Perfume, atomizer, pk roses w/yel floral, 4½" 240.00
Pickle castor, pk floral, metal frame w/fork, 5½" 130.00
Pin dish, wht floral, brass rim w/2 tab hdls, 4" dia........................... 50.00
Pitcher, syrup, pk roses, swirl, SP lid... 500.00
Plaque, wall, Indian chief, HP, 8x10" 18,000.00
Plaque, wall, landscape w/mts, metal fr mk CFM & Co, 8x10½" ..3,800.00
Salt shaker, chick on ped, brn shaded bk, metal head/lid, 2½" 200.00
Salt shaker, pk rose on 1 side, sq, mk, metal lid, 2½" 40.00
Salt shaker, red & yel floral, woven neck, metal lid, 2⅞" 40.00

Vase, florals on plum background, ormolu mounts, shield mark, 12x9½x6", $1,200.00. (Photo courtesy Showtime Auction Services on LiveAuctioneers.com)

Vase, lg iris, metal base w/4 legs, 12½" 650.00
Vase, lg wht mums, emb body, metal base w/4 ft, 6½" 320.00
Vase, orange daisies, metal frame w/2 hdls, mk, 4¾".................... 200.00
Whisk broom holder, pansies, mk, 8½" 800.00

Weapons

Among the varied areas of specialization within the broad category of weapons, guns are by far the most popular. Muskets are among the earliest firearms; they were large-bore shoulder arms, usually firing black powder with separate loading of powder and shot. Some ignited the charge by flintlock or caplock, while later types used a firing pin with a metallic cartridge. Side arms, referred to as such because they were worn at the side, include pistols and revolvers. Pistols range from early single-shot and multiple barrels to modern types with cartridges held in the handle. Revolvers were supplied with a cylinder that turned to feed a fresh round in front of the barrel breech. Other firearms include shotguns, which fired round or conical bullets and had a smooth inner barrel surface, and rifles, so named because the interior of the barrel contained spiral grooves (rifling) which increased accuracy. For further study we recommend *Modern Guns* by Russell Quertermous and Steve Quertermous, available at your local bookstore or from Collector Books. Our advisor for this category is Steve Howard; he is listed in the Directory under California. Unless noted otherwise, our values are for examples in excellent condition. See also Militaria.

Key:
cal — caliber	mod — modified
conv — conversion	oct — octagon
cyl — cylinder	p/b — patch box
f/l — flintlock	perc — percussion
ga — gauge	/s — stock

Carbines

Burnside 2nd Model, 54 cal, 21" rnd bbl, walnut/s, w/saddle ring... 4,600.00
Enfield 1863 Pattern 56, 577 cal, 1863 Tower on lock, orig/complete.. 7,500.00
Ken Walker Confederate, 54 cal, rifled bbl, copper/brass fr/rpl nipple.. 21,850.00
Richmond 1863, 58 cal, 25" bbl, sling swivel w/rpr 7,475.00
Smith Civil War, 50RF cal, Am Machine Works fr, 21⅝" bbl, walnut/s.. 1,265.00
Spencer Belgian Made, 50RF cal, 20" rnd bbl, 1873 on butt stock, VG+ . 1,150.00
Triplett & Scott Repeating, 50RF cal, 30" rnd bbl, 2 swivels, EX+ 2,875.00

Muskets

Colt 1861 Special, 58 cal, 39½" rnd bbl, tulip-head ramrod, NM .. 4,315.00
Enfield 1862 Tower Perc, 69 cal, mk lockplate, 3 bbl bands, 39" bbl... 750.00
Enfield Pattern 53, 577 cal, Tower 1861 on hammer, 39" bbl, w/bayonet.. 3,165.00
Remington Zouave, 58 cal, 33" rnd bbl, mk lockplate, walnut/s . 2,875.00
Richmond 1861, 58 cal, mk lockplate, rpr ramrod, correct/s, VG .. 3,450.00
Richmond 1863, 58 cal, bbl dtd 1864, mk lockplate, w/bayonet .. 13,800.00
Springfield 1816, Remington conv, 69 cal, Maynard tape primer, 33" bbl. 1,600.00
Tower 3rd Model Brn Bess, 78 cal, 38" bbl, walnut/s 2,875.00

Pistols

Continental Blunderbus, f/l, 60 cal, 6⅝" part oct oval bore bbl.. 2,000.00
Johnson 1836 Martial, f/l, 54 cal, 8½" rnd bbl, walnut/s, VG.... 1,100.00
Ketland Lt Dragoon, f/l, 66 cal, 9³⁄₁₆" rnd bbl, mk lock, G......... 1,100.00
North 1811 Martial, f/l, 69 cal, 8¾" bbl, mk hammer, VG 16,000.00

Raper of Leeds, flintlock brass blunderbuss with 7" brass octagonal-to-round barrel, spring bayonet, throated cock, checkered walnut full stocks, floral-engraved triggerguard, original ramrod, circa 1830, pair $9,000.00. (Photo courtesy Cowan's Auctions, Inc. on LiveAuctioneers.com)

Remington M1871 Army Rolling Block, 50CF cal, 8" rnd bbl . 3,675.00
Trylon, f/l, 54 cal, 8" rnd bbl, mk lock plate, fair reconv, G 1,265.00
Williamson Pocket Derringer, 45RF cal, single shot, 2½" bbl, VG... 800.00

Revolvers

Allen & Wheelock Sidehammer Navy, 36 cal, 5" oct bbl, 5-shot cyl, G+ .. 1,100.00
Colt 1849 Pocket, 31 cal, 6" oct bbl, 5-shot cyl, walnut grip..... 2,000.00
Colt 1851 Navy, 36 cal, 7½" oct bbl, brass trigger, rpl grips....... 1,600.00
Colt 1855 5 Root Sidehammer, perc, 3½" bbl, 5-shot cyl, ivory grips... 1,265.00
Colt 1860 Army, perc, 44 cal, 7½" rnd bbl, fluted cyl, 4-screw fr...4,600.00
Colt 1862 Police, perc, 36 cal, 4½" rnd bbl, 5-shot fluted cyl.... 1,850.00
Joslyn Navy, perc, 44 cal, 7⅞" oct bbl, 3-pc rammer, walnut grips.. 6,325.00
Kerr, 44 cal, 5-cyl, Kerr's Pat 1493 on fr, low serial # 8,625.99
Remington New Model Army, 44 cal, 8" oct bbl, 2-pc walnut grips, VG 925.00
Tranter Army, 44 cal, 5-cyl, Dean & Son... on fr, minor pitting.. 1,435.00

Rifles

Evans Repeating Sporting Transitional, 44 cal, 24" oct bbl, 43" .. 300.00
Harper's Ferry 1803, perc conv, rpl M1841 trigger, p/b & ramrod.. 2,585.00
Henry Gibbs, perc, curly maple full/s w/inlay, p/b, rpl ramrod, 55" ...2,400.00

J Bishop Warranted, perc, bird's-eye maple half/s w/inlay, p/b, 49" ...1,500.00
Mannlicher Schoenauer 1903, 6.5X54MS cal, bolt action, 18" bbl, VG ..700.00
Marlin-Ballard #5 Pacific, 40-85 cal, ring-shaped lever, 32" oct bbl ...1,750.00
Savage Model PE, 308 cal, lever action, eng 22" rnd bbl, eng scene, NM. 2,300.00
US 1888 Trapdoor, 45-70 cal, tool compartment, 23⅝" bbl, G 700.00
Winchester 1866 Lever Action, 44RF cal, 24¼" oct bbl w/full mag . 13,800.00
Winchester 1873, 38CWF cal, mk brass elevator block 4,250.00
Winchester 1876, 45-60 cal, brass elevator block, rnd 28" bbl, G .. 1,000.00
Winchester 1885 Single Shot, 25-20s cal, 28" oct #3 bbl.........3,750.00
Winchester 1894, 30WCF lever-action repeater, 26" rnd bbl 800.00

Shotguns

AH Fox A Grade, 12 ga, 30" steel full choke bbls, walnut/s......1,150.00
Belgian Browning Grade I Superposed, 12 ga, 30" full/mod choked bbls .2,000.00
Browning Custom Superposed, 12 ga, 27½" full/mod choked bbls, NM ... 4,600.00
Colt 1883 Field Grade, 12 ga, 30" Damascus choked, bbls, NM .. 800.00
English, full/s blunderbuss, rnd brass bbl, f/l w/2¼" bore, 42" 1,850.00
Greener Emp Grade, 12 ga, 32" full choke bbls, dbl triggers, NM .. 4,600.00
Henry Adkin, 12 ga, 30" dbl bbls w/mod choke, eng, burl/s dtd 1868 .. 7,500.00

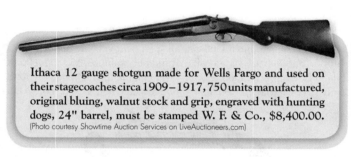

Ithaca 12 gauge shotgun made for Wells Fargo and used on
their stagecoaches circa 1909–1917, 750 units manufactured,
original bluing, walnut stock and grip, engraved with hunting
dogs, 24" barrel, must be stamped W. F. & Co., $8,400.00.
[Photo courtesy Showtime Auction Services on LiveAuctioneers.com]

Ithaca 37 Featherweight, 12 ga, 28" mod bbl, late production, NM...300.00
Ithaca Field Grade, 10 ga, magnum 10 dbl 34" steel bbls, NM..2,875.00
Ithaca NID Field Model, 28 cal, 26" cyl/open mod choked bbls . 3,165.00
LC Smith Monogram Grade, 10 ga, 32" Whitworth bbls, walnut/s, NM . 9,775.00
Lefever A Grade, 12 ga dbl bbl, 25⅜" choked bbls, walnut/s........ 800.00
Libeau, f/l, 12 ga dbl bbl, 27" Damascus bbls, platinum/gold, NM....7,500.00
Parker AH Grade, 16 ga, #1 fr w/26" Acme steel bbls, mod/cyl choke ..19,550.00
Parker DH Grade, 28 ga, OO fr w/25½" Titanic steel bbls, NM 8,000.00
Remington 32 Skeet Grade Over/Under, 12 ga, 28" bbls, walnut/s....1,725.00
Webley & Scott 712, 12 ga, 28" dbl bbls w/full/mod chokes, walnut/s . 1,500.00
Whitney Phoenix Breechloading, 12 ga, 26¼" rnd bbl (shortened), G....200.00
Winchester #21 Skeet Grade, 12 ga, 26" bbls, walnut/s, NM ..5,175.00
Winchester #42, 410 cal pump, skeet choke 26" bbl w/3" chamber, NM..2,800.00
Winchester 101 Superposed, 12 ga, 30" ventilated ribbed bbls .1,380.00
Winchester 1897, 12 ga, 28" full-choke bbl, std grade pump, VG ...400.00
Winchester 1901 Lever Action Std Grade, 10 ga, 32" rnd/full choke bbl....1,265.00
Winchester 1901 Lever Action, 10 ga, 32" steel bbl, half mag..1,265.00
Winchester Custom 101 Over/Under, 12 ga, 30" vent rib choked bbls..1,265.00
Winchester Model 40 Semi-Auto, 12-ga, 23½" bbl, walnut/s, NM..635.00
Winchester Model 42, 410 cal, pump action, 26" plain bbl, walnut/s. 1,100.00

Weather Vanes

The earliest weather vanes were of handmade wrought iron and were
generally simple angular silhouettes with a small hole suggesting an eye. Later copper, zinc, and polychromed wood with features in relief were fashioned
into more realistic forms. Ships, horses, fish, Indians, roosters, and angels
were popular motifs. In the nineteenth century, silhouettes were often made
from sheet metal. Wooden figures became highly carved and were painted
in vivid colors. E. G. Washburne and Company in New York was one of
the most prominent manufacturers of weather vanes during the last half of

the century. Two-dimensional sheet metal weather vanes are increasing in
value due to the already heady prices of the full-bodied variety. Originality,
strength of line, and patina help to determine value. The items listed below
are assumed to be in excellent condition.

Key: f/fb — flattened full body   fb — full body

Stag, leaping, gilt copper,
flattened full-body, attributed to
E. G. Washburne & Co., late
nineteenth century, overall
height 24", $7,800.00. (Photo
courtesy Skinner Auctioneers and Appraisers of
Antiques and Fine Art)

1864 Banner, sheet iron, riveted spearheads, blk pnt, on stand, 26x33" .825.00
Airplane, sheet copper on wood w/wood propeller, weathered, 17" L...550.00
Arrow, wrought/sheet iron, metal stand, 14¼x35".........................825.00
Bull, fb copper w/appl ears/horns, verdigris/gilt, 13x25" 8,900.00
Cow, f/fb copper, rpr, 19x32" 7,000.00
Cow, fb tin w/worn gold pnt, on CI directional, cow: 9x15" 400.00
Dog, att JW Fiske, weathered gilt/verdigris, 19th C, 36" L.....44,000.00
Eagle flying, fb copper w/gilt, balanced on ball w/arrow, Fiske, 31" W.......3,165.00
Eagle, f/b copper w/spread wings, on orb, layered pnt, 20x18"......375.00
Eagle, f/fb copper, old gilt, att LW Cushing & Sons, 30x30" 6,000.00
Eagle, fb copper, spread wings, EX verdigris/gilt, 10x9¾"+stand.. 1,725.00
Eagle, fb copper, spread wings, on ball, gold pnt, on stand, 37" W ...2,185.00
Finger pointing & banner over directionals, copper, Fiske, 67x37"....8,200.00
Fish, fb copper w/verdigris, some splits, 25½"............................1,725.00
Fisherman on rocky outcropping by pine tree, pnt sheet metal, 8x19" ...400.00
Gamecock, f/fb sheet copper w/zinc head/ft, mc pnt, Harris, 29x26" .. 8,800.00
Gamecock, f/fb sheet metal, gilt w/red details, on arrow, 16x19"...2,645.00
Horse running (Patchen), f/fb copper w/zinc head, att Fiske, 21x39" . 9,500.00
Horse running, CI head w/molded sheet-copper body, verdigris, 22x30" .1,765.00
Horse running, f/fb copper w/verdigris, Harris, 19½x34"+rod ...2,800.00
Horse running, f/fb copper, Black Hawk, ca 1900, 17x23" 4,400.00
Horse running, f/fb copper, Black Hawk, rprs/dents, 17¼x22¾".4,400.00
Horse running, f/fb copper, bullet holes, att Jewell, on stand, 25x39" .12,650.00
Horse running, f/fb copper, weathered gilt, on rod w/sphere, 17x29" .5,590.00
Horse running, f/fb copper/cast zinc, Ethan Allen, ca 1900, 18x21" ..4,700.00
Horse running, molded sheet copper w/verdigris, 1800s, 20x31"........5,875.00
Horse w/jockey, f/fb copper w/zinc head, Fiske, EX verdigris, 33" L..7,765.00
Horse, f/fb copper w/cast-zinc head, streaky patina, 31x37"+post..5,980.00
Horse, sheet iron, leg raised, pnt traces/rust, 26x29" 495.00
Man trumpeting, horizontal figure, 2-D, weathered wood, 39" W.3,000.00
Quill pen, copper, on copper rod w/2 spheres, 26x24"...............4,400.00
Quill pen, gilt molded sheet copper on copper rod, sphere atop, 23x35"..3,290.00
Ram, pnt wood & sheet iron, 20th C, on stand, 23x35" 1,400.00
Rooster, f/fb copper w/worn gold rpt, on arrow, att Fiske, 26x30"..2,300.00
Rooster, f/fb copper, spurred legs w/traces of red on comb, 21"+stand. 4,485.00
Rooster, f/fb copper/tin, verdigris/old pnt, Cushing, 45" w/stand. 3,900.00
Rooster, f/fb sheet copper, brn over gilt, Fiske, ca 1900, 24x21" .1,765.00
Rooster, fb copper w/cast ft, gr patina, bullet hole, 22x18".........1,495.00
Rooster, fb copper w/silhouette tail/comb/wattle, 24"+stand.....4,715.00
Rooster, fb copper w/tin comb/tail/wattle, old gilt, 31" on stand ..11,200.00
Rooster, fb copper, blk w/gilt traces, bullet holes, on base, 28"..1,035.00
Rooster, pnt wood, cvt details, 1800s, mtd on wood base, 19x15".1,120.00
Rooster, sheet-iron silhouette, riveted battens, 25"+wood base..1,350.00
Rooster, sheet-metal silhouette, orig red pnt, 30" 375.00
Rooster, zinc f/fb w/copper tail, molded details, J Howard, 25x26" ..14,375.00
St Julien & sulke, fb copper w/CI horse's head, Fiske, 23x40" .23,500.00

Webb

Thomas Webb and Sons have been glassmakers in Stourbridge, England, since 1837. Besides their fine cameo glass, they have also made enameled ware and pieces heavily decorated with applied glass ornaments. The butterfly is a motif that has been so often featured that it tends to suggest Webb as the manufacturer. Our advisor for this category is Don Williams; he is listed in the Directory under Missouri. See also specific types of glass such as Alexandrite, Burmese, Mother-of-Pearl, and Peachblow.

Cameo

Bottle, scent, ginkgo/5 floral sprays, ovoid, silver mk lid (VG), 5" ...1,500.00
Bottle, scent, palms & bamboo, wht on lt bl, silver cap, 3¾" 2,700.00
Bottle, scent, Peachblow w/gold ginkgo, silver mk lid, lay-down, 4" ..1,250.00
Bottle, scent, swan's head, wht on bl, Gorham silver cap, 5¾"..7,250.00
Bottle, scent, swan's head, wht on red, threaded top, 9¼".......19,500.00
Bowl, floral/scrolling bands, wht on raisin/apricot, 2¼x3¼" 3,500.00
Bowl, floral sprigs & border, wht on gr, scalloped, 2½x5⅞" 5,000.00
Bowl, floral tapestry, medallions, bl/wht on cobalt, Gem, 3¾". 11,400.00
Bowl, floral tapestry, wht on bl, Gem, 3¾x5"...........................11,750.00
Bowl, floral vines, wht/lav on red, 5", +6" cupped saucer 3,500.00
Bowl, morning-glory vines, wht/red on citron, scalloped, 4x8¼"...5,400.00
Bowl, roses/buds/leaves, wht/purple on bl, Tiffany...1889, Gem, 2½" .3,600.00
Bowl, trailing flowers/butterfly, wht on red, 1890s, 5¼" 650.00
Vase, apple branches, rainbow cased on wht, elongated neck, 14" ...4,000.00
Vase, arabesque floral, olive & wht on lav, 5⅞" 5,350.00
Vase, arabesque floral, wht on canary, dbl gourd, 6⅛" 3,900.00
Vase, arabesque floral, wht on red, stick neck, #957, 10"...........7,000.00
Vase, berries/leaves, red on vaseline, vasiform, Gem, 6¼" 3,600.00
Vase, brickwork/3 arched windows/floral branch, wht/gray on gr, 7x5"...7,500.00
Vase, bud, flowers/bee, wht on red, 8¾" 3,400.00
Vase, floral, red & gold on cream, Gem, ca 1888, 5¾".............10,000.00
Vase, floral, wht on bl, slightly bulb, ftd, Gem, 6¾"....................6,900.00
Vase, floral/basketweave/grasses/ferns, wht on raisin, Gem, 8½".. 7,000.00
Vase, floral/insect, wht on rose to honey, stick neck, Gem, 9¼". 7,800.00
Vase, floral/insects, wht on citron, cylinder neck, Gem, 9" 9,500.00
Vase, fruit/foliage, wht w/purple hints on bl, flared neck, 8¾"...4,600.00
Vase, fuchsias, wht on gr, ovoid, 7" 3,600.00
Vase, morning glories, butterfly, purple/bands, J Barbe, 5¾" 9,000.00
Vase, morning glories/moths, wht/red on bl, trumpet neck, 12" .7,800.00

Vase, petunias, white on red, 5¼", $2,400.00. (Photo courtesy Fantasticantiques Inc. on LiveAuctioneers.com)

Vase, roses/butterflies, wht on citron, flared rim, 7¾" 2,650.00
Vase, roses/butterflies, wht/red on citron gr, shouldered, 8¾" 4,200.00
Vase, sunflowers/grasses, wht on gr, vasiform, Gem, 8" 3,000.00
Vase, trumpet flowers/insects, wht on citron, stick neck, Gem, 15" ...7,250.00

Miscellaneous

Pitcher, teal satin shading to peach w/apple blossoms, ruffled, 8".. 300.00
Rose bowl, peach w/int aventurine, birds/foliage, rigaree ft, 5" 350.00
Urn, intaglio swags/parrots, w/lid, sgn W Fritsche, 10¼"...........5,000.00
Vase, cased butterscotch w/gold & silver bird, bulb, 7" 125.00

Vase, cherry blossom branches/insects, gold on yel satin, 9⅝"...... 480.00
Vase, gold/silver birds in garden on red cased in wht, stick neck, 10"...300.00
Vase, lily pads/flowers in relief & cut on crystal, ftd, 1906-35, 30" ... 350.00
Vase, roses HP on creamy wht, gold trim, #80167, 6½" 1,450.00
Vases, bl cased satin w/enameled floral, 9½", pr 450.00

Wedgwood

Josiah Wedgwood established his pottery in Burslem, England, in 1759. He produced only molded utilitarian earthenwares until 1770 when new facilities were opened at Etruria for the production of ornamental wares. It was there he introduced his famous Basalt and Jasperware. Jasperware, an unglazed fine stoneware decorated with classic figures in white relief, was usually produced in blues, but it was also made in ground colors of green, lilac, yellow, black, or white. Occasionally three or more colors were used in combination. It has been in continuous production to the present day and is the most easily recognized of all the Wedgwood lines. Jasper-dip is a ware with a solid-color body or a white body that has been dipped in an overlay color. It was introduced in the late 1700s and is the type most often encountered on today's market. (In our listings, all Jasper is of this type unless noted 'solid' color.)

Though Wedgwood's Jasperware was highly acclaimed, on a more practical basis his improved creamware was his greatest success, due to the ease with which it could be potted and because its lighter weight significantly reduced transportation expenses. Wedgwood was able to offer 'chinaware' at affordable prices. Queen Charlotte was so pleased with the ware that she allowed it to be called 'Queen's Ware.' Most creamware was marked simply 'WEDGWOOD.' ('Wedgwood & Co.' and 'Wedgewood' are marks of other potters.) From 1769 to 1780, Wedgwood was in partnership with Thomas Bentley; artwares of the highest quality may bear the 'Wedgwood & Bentley' mark indicating this partnership. Moonlight Lustre, an allover splashed-on effect of pink intermingling with gray, brown, or yellow, was made from 1805 to 1815. Porcelain was made, though not to any great extent, from 1812 to 1822. Bone china was produced before 1822 and after 1872. These types of wares were marked 'WEDGWOOD' (with a printed 'Portland Vase' mark after 1872). Stone china and Pearlware were made from about 1820 to 1875. Examples of either may be found with a printed or impressed mark to indicate their body type. During the late 1800s, Wedgwood produced some fine parian and majolica. Creamware, hand painted by Emile Lessore, was sold from about 1860 to 1875. From the twentieth century century, several lines of lustre wares — Butterfly, Dragon, and Fairyland (designed by Daisy Makeig-Jones) — have attracted the collector and, as their prices suggest, are highly sought after and admired. Nearly all of Wedgwood's wares are clearly marked. 'WEDGWOOD' was used before 1891, after which time 'ENGLAND' was added. Most examples marked 'MADE IN ENGLAND' were made after 1905. A detailed study of all marks is recommended for accurate dating. See also Majolica.

Key: WW — WEDGWOOD

Berry dish, octagonal, w/underplate, Willow, after 1891, $800 to... 1,000.00
Biscuit bbl, Jasper, cobalt bl, acorns/oak leaves, 1898-1929, 7" 350.00
Biscuit bbl, Jasper, figures in relief, metal lid, 1840, 5½", $800 to.. 900.00

Biscuit jar, Jasper, three-color, England, late nineteenth century, 5⅝", $1,200.00. (Photo courtesy Skinner Auctioneers and Appraisers of Antiques and Fine Art)

Bottle, barber, Jasper, cobalt bl, muses/grapes/leaves, 1850, 7¼" .. 550.00
Bowl, Fairyland Lustre, Castle on a Road w/Dana int, Z5125, oct, 3½" ..8,400.00
Bust, Basalt, Horatio Herbert Kitchener, 1920, 12" 1,020.00
Candleholders, Jasper, 1840-70, pr, $600 to 700.00
Chamberstick, Jasper, 1910, 2¾", $275 to 325.00
Cheese keeper, Jasper, 1890, 9", $500 to 600.00
Cheese keeper, Jasper, w/SP underplate, 1840, $600 to 700.00

Compote, Moonlight Lustre nautilus shell with stand, impressed marks, circa 1820, 7½", $2,520.00. (Photo courtesy Skinner Auctioneers and Appraisers of Antiques and Fine Art)

Creamer, Jasper, figures in relief on bl, 1850, 2½", $125 to 150.00
Cup, demi, Ventnor poly floral border pattern, 1898-1915, $55 to ..65.00
Cup, mini, Jasper, Nike warriors & figures, 1891-97, 1⅜", $125 to... 175.00
Cup/saucer, demi, Jasper, lt bl, 1891-97, $165 to 180.00
Cup/saucer, tea, Jasper, Bute shape, 1850-70, $175 to 200.00
Ferner, Jasper, Aesculapius & student on lt bl dipped body, 1890, $500 to...600.00
Flowerpot, mini, Jasper, Brewster, classical figures, 1891-97, 2¾". 150.00
Inkwell, Jasper, Three Graces & Cupids, 1760-80 .... 1,100.00
Jug, milk, creamware, silver lustre scroll & floral, 1940, 3½", $150 to... 175.00
Jug, milk, lt bl, 1891-97, 5½", $300 to 325.00
Jug, mini, Jasper, Etruscan, 1891-97, 3½", $125 to......................... 175.00
Loving cup, mini, Jasper, Poor Maria & boy shepherd, 1¾" 150.00
Match box, Jasper, cobalt bl, striker under lid, 1790-1820, $250 to....300.00
Pitcher, Ferrara, Flow Blue, early 1900s, $300 to 400.00
Pitcher, mini, Jasper, Arms of the City of Chester, 2", $125 to 175.00
Plate, dinner, Fallow Deer, smooth rim, 1891, $125 to................. 150.00
Plate, dinner, Jasper, oak leaf & acorn w/acanthus leaves relief, 1891-96, $100 to...125.00
Plate, dinner, The Tigress, scalloped rim, floral & bird pattern, 1922, $60 to..... 75.00
Plate, transfer & HP, goose/gander/cherubs/animals, 1891-1909.. 160.00
Potpourri dish, Jasper, cobalt, 1840-50, $400 to........................... 450.00
Punch bowl, Willow, late 1800s-early 1900s, 6x9", $1,200 to ...1,400.00
Salad set, Jasper, cobalt, acanthus leaves hdls, 1840, $700 to....... 800.00
Serving fork & knife, fish, Jasper, 1891-97, set 400.00
Sugar box, Jasper, bright bl, no ornamentation, rare, 4½", $1,000 to .1,200.00
Sugar box, Jasper, Washington/Franklin, 1876, 3½x5", $275 to... 325.00
Teapot, Antico, Bamboo, imp Wedgwood A, #156, early 19th C, 4½x8x4¼".300.00
Teapot, Basalt, Sybyl finial (draped monk), 1892, $1,000 to......1,200.00
Teapot, Strawberry Lustre, 1900, $400 to 450.00
Toothpick holder, Willow, 1891, 2¼", $50 to 60.00
Tray, Hague Dutch scenic pattern in bl, ca 1876, 17½", $400 to.. 500.00
Vase, mini, Jasper, City of London crest, 1891-97, 2¾", $125 to.. 175.00
Vase, mini, Jasper, Nike warrior, Muses & Pegasus, 2", $125 to ... 175.00
Vase, potpourri, Jasper dip Diceware, 1st quarter 19th C, 8½" ..8,400.00

Weil Ware

Max Weil came to the United States in the 1940s, settling in California. There he began manufacturing dinnerware, figurines, cookie jars, and wall pockets. American clays were used, and the dinnerware was all hand decorated. Weil died in 1954; the company closed two years later. The last backstamp to be used was the outline of a burro with the words 'Weil Ware — Made in California.' Many unmarked pieces found today originally carried a silver foil label; but you'll often find a four-digit handwritten number series, especially on figurines. For further study we recommend *Collector's Encyclopedia of California Pottery* by Jack Chipman (Collector Books).

Dinnerware

Birchwood, c/s...7.00
Birchwood, plate, bread & butter 6.00
Birchwood, shakers, 5-lobed cylinder, $20 to........................ 25.00
Birchwood, sugar bowl, w/lid, $15 to 20.00
Brentwood, bowl, divided vegetable, 8x11½", $28 to..................... 35.00
Brentwood, plate, dinner, $12 to.. 15.00
Malay Bambu, bowl, divided vegetable, 10½" 37.50
Malay Bambu, bowl, lug cereal 12.00
Malay Bambu, bowl, tab hdls, 2x7" 15.00
Malay Bambu, bowl, vegetable, 9⅛" L.......................................30.00
Malay Bambu, butter dish, ¼-lb, $25 to 35.00
Malay Bambu, coffeepot, 6-cup.. 38.00
Malay Bambu, creamer, 3x5½", $12 to..................................... 15.00
Malay Bambu, c/s, sq, $8 to 12.00
Malay Bambu, gravy boat w/attached underplate, $35 to 40.00
Malay Bambu, plate, 6¼", $9 to.. 12.00
Malay Bambu, snack plate & cup 7.50
Malay Bambu, sugar bowl, w/lid, $15 to 20.00
Malay Bambu, tidbit, 3-tiered, metal hdl 30.00
Malay Bambu, tray, sandwich, 11½" 30.00
Malay Bambu, wht on dk gr, cereal bowl....................................8.00
Malay Bambu, wht on dk gr, creamer 14.00
Malay Bambu, wht on dk gr, cup...6.00
Malay Bambu, wht on dk gr, plate, dinner.................................8.50
Malay Bambu, wht on dk gr, platter, 16" 85.00
Malay Bambu, wht on dk gr, shakers 18.00
Malay Bambu, wht on dk gr, sugar bowl w/lid 18.00
Malay Blossom, bowl, divided vegetable, 10½" L....................... 32.50
Malay Blossom, bowl, sq w/tab hdls, 5x5¼" 16.00
Malay Blossom, bowl, vegetable, oval, 9", $20 to 25.00
Malay Blossom, gravy boat w/attached underplate, $35 to 45.00
Malay Blossom, plate, 9¾", $15 to... 20.00
Malay Blossom, sherbet, ftd, sq top, 2½x3⅞", $18 to 22.00
Malay Blossom, sugar bowl, w/lid 18.00
Malay Blossom, tidbit, 3-tiered, metal hdl, $30 to 40.00
Malay Blossom, tumbler, 4¼", $15 to 20.00
Mango, bowl, vegetable, 8½" L.. 20.00
Mango, coffeepot, $40 to 50.00
Mango, c/s 10.00
Mango, plate, dinner, $12 to 15.00
Mango, shakers, pr 17.50
Mango, sugar bowl, w/lid 22.50
Rose, bowl, divided vegetable, 2x6¾x10½"................................ 25.00
Rose, bowl, vegetable, rect, w/lid, $40 to 50.00
Rose, coffeepot, 6-cup 50.00
Rose, relish, 3-part 14.00
Rose, snack plate & cup, $12 to 15.00
Rose, sugar bowl, w/lid.. 22.50
Yellow Rose, bowl, lug soup, 5⅛x6", set of 6 .... 90.00
Yellow Rose, c/s, sq 10.00

Miscellaneous

Flower holder, lady with two baskets, 10", $38.00. (Photo courtesy Clars Auction Gallery on LiveAuctioneers.com)

Figurine, lady in lt gr dress w/matching cap, holds flowers, 11½" ... 70.00
Flower holder, lady ice skater holds basket, 10" 65.00
Flower holder, lady in purple floral dress, yel shawl, 11" 75.00
Flower holder, lady pushing cart, 8½"... 35.00
Flower holder, lady w/auburn braids, left hands holds out apron, 11"... 35.00
Flower holder, Spanish lady seated w/basket on bk, #180, 8x9x5" . 70.00
Planter, Ming Tree, 3x9" sq 25.00
Toothbrush holder, Dutch boy, bl & pk, holes at pockets, 6½" 50.00
Vase, Ming Tree, cylindrical w/slanted top, 11" 45.00
Vase, Ming Tree, slanted top, 9½x3½", $40 to 50.00
Vase, pk nautilus shell, #720, 6⅛x9½x4"....................................... 48.00

Weller

The Weller Pottery Company was established in Zanesville, Ohio, in 1882, the outgrowth of a small one-kiln log cabin works Sam Weller had operated in Fultonham. Through an association with Wm. Long, he entered the art pottery field in 1895, producing the Lonhuda Ware Long had perfected in Steubenville six years earlier. His famous Louwelsa line was merely a continuation of Lonhuda and was made in at least 500 different shapes. Many fine lines of artware followed under the direction of Charles Babcock Upjohn, art director from 1895 to 1904: Dickens Ware (First Line), under-glaze slip decorations on dark backgrounds; Turada, featuring applied ivory bands of delicate openwork on solid dark brown backgrounds; and Aurelian, similar to Louwelsa, but with a brushed-on rather than blended ground. One of their most famous lines was Second Line Dickens, introduced in 1900. Backgrounds, characteristically caramel shading to turquoise matt, were decorated by sgraffito with animals, golfers, monks, Indians, and scenes from Dickens novels. The work is often artist signed. Sicardo, 1902, was a metallic lustre line in tones of blue, green, or purple with flowing Art Nouveau patterns developed within the glaze.

Frederick Hurten Rhead, who worked for Weller from 1903 to mid-1904, created the prestigious Jap Birdimal line decorated with geisha girls, landscapes, and storks, accomplished through application of heavy slip forced through the tiny nozzle of a squeeze bag. Other lines to his credit are L'Art Nouveau, produced in both high-gloss brown and matt pastels, and Third Line Dickens, often decorated with Cruikshank's illustrations in relief. Other early artware lines were Eocean, Floretta, Hunter, Perfecto, Dresden, Etched Matt, and Etna.

In 1920 John Lessel was hired as art director, and under his supervision several new lines were created. LaSa, LaMar, Marengo, and Besline attest to his expertise with metallic lustres. The last of the artware lines and one of the most sought after by collectors today is Hudson, first made during the early 1920s. Hudson, a semimatt glazed ware, was beautifully artist decorated on shaded backgrounds with florals, animals, birds, and scenics. Notable artists often signed their work, among them Hester Pillsbury, Dorothy England Laughead, Ruth Axline, Claude Leffler, Sarah Reid McLaughlin, E.L. Pickens, and Mae Timberlake.

During the late 1920s Weller produced a line of gardenware and naturalistic life-sized and larger figures of frogs, dogs, cats, swans, ducks, geese, rabbits, squirrels, and playful gnomes, most of which were sold at the Weller store in Zanesville due to the fragile nature of their designs. The Depression brought a slow, steady decline in sales, and by 1948 the pottery was closed.

Note: Several factors come into play when evaluating a piece of Hudson: subject matter, artist signature, and size are all important. Artist-signed florals from 5" to 7" range from $300.00 to $800.00; scenics and bud vases from 6" to 8" range from $2,500.00 to $10,000.00, with fine artwork from superior artists at the upper end. Pieces bearing the signatures of Mae Timberlake, Hester Pillsbury, or Sarah Reid McLaughlin bring top prices. Our advisor for this category is Hardy Hudson; he is listed in the Directory under Florida.

Athens, vase, mythological scenes raised on grn & brn, unmk, 15x7" ... 500.00
Aurelian, mug, brn, corn ear, silver o/l, 1889, #435, 6x4½" 1,500.00
Aurelian, vase, geraniums, brn, bulb, 11x8"................................. 750.00
Baldin, vase, apples on tan, bulb bottom, 12" 450.00
Baldin, vase, bl, apple branch on bl, cylindrical, 9x5" 350.00
Barcelona, ewer, 8", $200 to 250.00
Blue Ware, compote, low ftd, 5½", $225 to................................. 275.00

Bonito, vase, 10", $180.00 to $200.00. (Photo courtesy Wickliff & Associates Auctioneers on LiveAuctioneers.com)

Brighton, crow, 9" 650.00
Brighton, figurine, colorful perched parrot w/wings spread, 13½x8" 1,300.00
Brighton, yel butterfly, 2", $250 to 300.00
Burtwood, jardiniere, birds/flowers, 6½", $175 to.......................... 225.00
Cameo Jewel, jardiniere, 11", $350 to.. 400.00
Cameo Jewel, umbrella stand, 22", $1,250 to............................ 1,500.00
Claywood, plate, Wilday Picnic Zanesville, 7"............................. 200.00
Claywood, spittoon, floral panels, 4½", $125 to 150.00
Coppertone, bowl, appl frog & water lilies, 3½x15½" 550.00
Coppertone, bowl, frog & lily pad design, mk, 4x11" 350.00
Coppertone, vase, water lily & frog.. 650.00
Denton, umbrella stand, magnolias & pheasants, 22", M.......... 3,500.00
Dickens, vase, cavalier w/yel shawl, ovoid, gr, 8x3½" 75.00
Dickens, vase, man's portrait, tapered, artist initials HS, #316, 11x4½"..450.00
Dickens, vase, Native American portrait, EL Pickens, #X25, 5x6½" .650.00
Dickens, vase, Native American w/ headdress, shouldered, #266, 13x6". 1,000.00
Dickens, vase, pnt deer & forest, #341, artist sgn EW, 7x7½" 400.00

Dickens II, vase, Satan Smitten by Michael, signed Charles Babcock Upjohn, 16", $4,000.00. (Photo courtesy Cincinnati Art Galleries, LLC on LiveAuctioneres.com)

Eocean, candlestick, moonstone leaves, LJB, 9", ea $400 to 450.00
Eocean, pitcher, cat portrait, sgn E Blake, 5½x5½"....................... 750.00
Eocean, vase, bulldog, cylindrical, 10x3¼" 900.00
Eocean, vase, dogwood blossoms pnt on rose, artist sgn, 9½x4" 450.00
Eocean, vase, floral, cylindrical, w/sm high hdls, 16", $1,000 to 1,200.00
Eocean, vase, lav/yel/gray pansies, shouldered, 10x4½" 325.00
Eocean, vase, pnt storks (2), artist-sgn Chilcote, 10½x6½".......1,800.00
Etna, pitcher, floral, 6½", $175 to... 225.00

Fairfield, bowl, 4½", $80 to 100.00
Flemish, jardiniere & ped, Deco floral, 2-pc, 26½", $900 to 1,200.00
Floretta, ewer, emb grapes, 10½", $250 to 300.00
Floretta, vase, lav poppies, cylindrical, bulb bottom, 8x3½" 175.00
Forest, window box, 5½x14½", $650 to 850.00
Fruitone, console bowl, 5", $150 to 200.00
Glendale, vase, dbl bud, 7", $350 to 400.00

Hudson, vase, bluebirds in flowering tree, Mae Timberlake, 15", NM, $6,300.00. (Photo courtesy Cincinnati Art Galleries, LLC on LiveAuctioneers.com)

Hudson, vase, irises, sgn Hester Pillsbury, 6x3½" 300.00
Hudson, vase, floral, pk to bl, sgn Hood, unmk, 13¼x5" 900.00
Hudson, vase, lilac, cylindrical, sgn Pillsbury, 13¼x4¼" 1,000.00
Hudson, vase, pnt floral design, sgn Hood, 11¾x6½" 750.00
Hudson, vase, pnt roses, sgn England, 13½x6½" 1,000.00
Hudson, vase, tiger, 8", $4,500 to 5,000.00
Knifewood, tobacco jar, hunting dog, 7", $800 to 900.00
L'art Nouveau, ewer, emb floral, 8", $250 to 300.00
L'art Nouveau, umbrella stand, pheasant & grapes, unmk, 22½x11" .. 900.00
L'art Nouveau, umbrella stand, raised dragon & shell designs, unmk, 24x9". 1,000.00
L'art Nouveau, vase, ears of corn, unmk, 4½x3" 200.00
L'art Nouveau, vase, poppies, bulb bottom, 8½x4" 200.00
LaSa, vase, metallic, incised landscape, flaring ft, unmk, 12¼x6". 800.00
Lorbeek, wall pocket, 8½", $200 to 250.00
Louwelsa, beverage set, pitcher & 4 mugs, Native American 5,000.00
Louwelsa, clock, floral, 10½x12½", $1,000 to 1,250.00
Louwelsa, ewer, berries, Ferrell, 17", $1,500 to 2,000.00
Louwelsa, humidor, Native American portrait, sgn Leffler, #X176, 7x6" . 1,600.00
Louwelsa, mug, leaves, 4½", $115 to 140.00
Louwelsa, vase, brn w/pnt floral design, silver o/l, 10x3" 1,750.00
Louwelsa, vase, brn w/rose design, silver o/l, 10x3" 1,750.00
Louwelsa, vase, bulldog portrait on brn, sgn L Blake, #502, 6½x6½" .. 800.00
Louwelsa, vase, grapes, Lybarger, 17", $1,500 to 2,000.00
Louwelsa, vase, St. Bernard portrait on brn, bulb, chip at base, 13½x7½" . 1,500.00
Louwelsa, vase, yel floral on brn, silver o/l, monogram, 7x4" 1,000.00
Malverne, boat bowl, 5½x11", $150 to 175.00
Mammy, teapot, 8", $900 to 1,200.00
Marvo, bowl, 5", $85 to 100.00
Mirror Black, wall vase, 6", $100 to 125.00
Muskota, geese flower frog, 6", $400 to 500.00
Parian, wall pocket, 10", $200 to 250.00
Pearl, basket, 6½", $175 to 225.00
Perfecto, vase, floral, MH, 14", $1,000 to 1,200.00
Roma, bud vase, emb hdls, 6½", $80 to 100.00
Roma, compote, sm hdls under bowl on H ped, 8½", $100 to 150.00
Sabrinian, bowl, 2½x9", $150 to 190.00
Sicardo, vase, shouldered w/flared bottom, 6", $600 to 750.00
Stellar, vase, 6", $500 to 600.00
Velva, bowl, ftd, w/hdls, 3½x12½", $125 to 150.00
Woodcraft, mug, foxes, 6", $400 to 475.00
Zona, compote, pastel floral bowl, 5½", $100 to 125.00

Western Americana

The collecting of Western Americana encompasses a broad spectrum of memorabilia. Examples of various areas within the main stream would include the following fields: weapons, bottles, photographs, mining/railroad artifacts, cowboy paraphernalia, farm and ranch implements, maps, barbed wire, tokens, Indian relics, saloon/gambling items, and branding irons. Some of these areas have their own separate listings in this book. Western Americana is not only a collecting field but is also a collecting era with specific boundries. Depending upon which field the collector decides to specialize in, prices can start at a few dollars and run into the thousands.

Our advisor for this category is Bill Mackin, author of *Cowboy and Gunfighter Collectibles* (order from the author); he is listed in the Directory under Colorado. Values are for examples in excellent original condition, unless otherwise noted in the description.

Bit, C Figueroa, silver inlay, half-breed Santa Barbara style, 1930s .. 950.00
Bit, T Hildreth, loose-jaw silver inlaid kissing bird, floral eng...... 600.00
Bookends, bronze steer heads mtd on wood, CM Russell, 1900s, pr ... 550.00
Business card, Dexter Saloon, W Earp/CE Hoxie Proprieters, Nome, (+) ... 150.00
Chaps, brn leather batwing style w/nickel conchos, some wear ... 240.00

Chaps, C.P. Shipley, stock #25, rattlesnake studded, left-hand swastika on pocket flaps (re-sewn), wear and alterations (shortened) to bottom of legs, circa 1920s, VG+, $1,000.00. (Photo courtesy Rich Penn Auctions on LiveAuctioneers.com)

Chaps, SD Myres, 2-tone leather, silver conchos/5-point TX stars ... 2,400.00
Chaps, unmk tooled leather shotgun-style w/fringe, ca 1900, VG .. 660.00
Coat, horsehair, satin lined, shawl collar, knee length, ca 1900, lg. 450.00
Cuffs, tooled leather, 7" L, pr 115.00
Saddle, Al Nolte, San Francisco style w/tooling, trimmed fenders ... 600.00
Saddle, CP Shipley, sq skirt, nickel conchos, NP horn, 1930s 725.00
Saddle, HT O'Brien, sq skirt/S Stagg rigging/conchos, 1880s ... 6,000.00
Saddle, JC Higgins, brn leather, child sz 350.00
Saddle, Mother Hubbard w/apple horn, attached mochila, 1880s, VG. 3,000.00
Saddle, stock, Walker-Wegener Visalia, 14" loop-seat, 1890s ... 5,040.00
Spurs, Buermann, forged steel, 2" 20-point rowels, 1½" conchos, 7", $150 to .200.00
Spurs, Buermann, silver o/l, gold slippers/garters, rowels, 1920s .. 1,200.00
Spurs, Crocket, Paddy Ryan pattern, 5-point rowels, 1930s, lady's sz .. 900.00
Spurs, GS Garcia, Cat pattern #60, conchos/rowels/cvd leathers, 1920s..6,000.00
Spurs, GS Garcia, wrought steel w/silver insets, VG+ 1,800.00
Spurs, hand-wrought iron w/eng, 12-point star rowels, chains, 6" ... 270.00
Spurs, Mexican silver w/snake/flowers/peso coin, 8-point rowels, 1890s 750.00
Trunk, hide-covered, forged hinges/fancy studs, 1850s, 19x39x15", VG ..1,950.00

Western Pottery Manufacturing Company

This pottery was originally founded as the Denver China and Pottery Company; William Long was the owner. The company's assets were sold to a group who in 1905 formed the Western Pottery Manufacturing Company, located at 16th Street and Alcott in Denver, Colorado. By 1926, 186 different items were being produced, including crocks, flowerpots, kitchen items, and other stoneware. The company dissolved in 1936. Seven various marks were used during the years, and values may be higher for items that carry a rare mark. Numbers within the descriptions refer to specific marks, see the line drawings. Prices may vary depending on demand and locale. Our advisors for this category are Cathy Segelke and Pat James; they are listed in the Directory under Colorado.

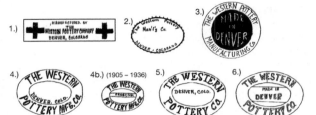

Churn, #2, hdl, 4-gal, M	75.00
Churn, #2, hdl, 5-gal, M	65.00
Churn, #2, no lid, 5-gal, G	80.00
Crock, #4, 6-gal, EX	72.00
Crock, #4, bail lip, 4-gal, G	55.00
Crock, #4, hdl, no lid, 8-gal, M	90.00
Crock, #4, ice water, bl & wht sponge pnt, 3-gal, NM	30.00
Crock, #4b, 15-gal, 22x17½", NM	150.00
Crock, #4b, 20-gal, M	200.00
Crock, #5, bail lip, 1½-gal, M	45.00
Crock, #5, no lid, 6-gal, M	70.00
Crock, #6, 3-gal, M	40.00
Crock, #6, 4-gal, M	50.00
Crock, #6, 5-gal, NM	60.00
Crock, #6, 10-gal, wire hdl, NM	100.00
Foot warmer, #6, M	60.00

Jug, #6, brown and white, 1-gallon, EX, $25.00. (Photo courtesy Austin Auction Gallery on LiveAuctioneers.com)

Jug, #6, brn/wht, 5-gal, M	75.00
Rabbit feeder, #1, EX	25.00
Rabbit waterer, #1, M	25.00

Western Stoneware Co.

The Western Stoneware Co., Monmouth, Illinois, was formed in 1906 as a merger of seven potteries: Monmouth Pottery Co., Monmouth, Illinois; Weir Pottery Co., Monmouth, Illinois; Macomb Pottery Co. and Macomb Stoneware Co., Macomb, Illinois; D. Culbertson Stoneware Co., Whitehall, Illinois; Clinton Stoneware Co., Clinton, Missouri; and Fort Dodge Stoneware Co., Fort Dodge, Iowa. Western Stoneware Co. manufactured stoneware, gardenware, flowerpots, artware, and dinnerware. Some early crocks, jugs, and churns are found with a plant number in the Maple Leaf logo. Plants 1 through 7 turn up. In 1926 an artware line was introduced as the Monmouth Pottery Artware. Western Stoneware Co. officially closed in April 2006, after 100 years of stoneware pro-

duction. One branch remains in operation today. Our advisor for this category is Jim Martin; he is listed in the Directory under Illinois. See also Old Sleepy Eye.

Birdbath, Burntwood, iron perch	700.00
Chicken buttermilk feeder w/bottom	175.00
Chicken waterer, brn top, ½-gal	150.00
Crock, Maple Leaf mk, 6-gal	95.00
Cuspidor, bl & wht	200.00
Funnel, jar or fruit, Bristol	100.00
Hanging flower basket, dull brn, 8", 10" or 12", ea	100.00
Humidor, Duke of Monmouth, cobalt bl	300.00
Humidor, Yale Mixture, cobalt bl	300.00
Jardinere, tree stump, dull brn	150.00
Jug, brn top, common, 1-qt	85.00
Jug, mini, Maple Leaf mk	500.00
Jug, shoulder/druggist's, 1-qt	75.00
Nappies, bl mottled, 5", 6", 7," 8," or 9", ea	100.00

Oil jar, #709D, cream glaze, blue lions design, 30", $1,500.00. (Photo courtesy Jim Martin)

Pitcher, Cattail, bl & wht, 1-qt	500.00
Pitcher, Cattail, bl & wht, ½-gal	250.00
Pitcher, Cattail, bl & wht, 1-gal	600.00
Pot, 1915 Fall Festival, mini	800.00
Rolling pin, bl & wht w/advertising	700.00
Rolling pin, orange & wht w/advertising	700.00
Vase, #366, bl or gr matt finish, 16" shoulder band	300.00
Water cooler, mini, spongeware bl & wht	2,000.00
Wren house, #317, rnd, dull brn glaze	200.00
Wren house, #733, sq, dull brn glaze	500.00

Westmoreland

Originally titled the Specialty Glass Company, Westmoreland began operations in East Liverpool, Ohio, producing utility items as well as tableware in milk glass and crystal. When the company moved to Grapeville, Pennsylvania, in 1890, lamps, vases, covered animal dishes, and decorative plates were introduced. Prior to 1920 Westmoreland was a major manufacturer of carnival glass and soon thereafter added a line of lovely reproduction art glass items. High-quality milk glass became their speciality, accounting for about 90% of their production. Black glass was introduced in the 1940s, and later in the decade ruby-stained pieces and items decorated in the Mary Gregory style became fashionable. By the 1960s colored glassware was being produced, examples of which are very popular with collectors today. Early pieces were marked with a paper label; by the 1960s the ware was embossed with a superimposed 'WG.' The last mark was a circle containing 'Westmoreland' around the perimeter and a large 'W' in the center. The company closed in 1985, and on February 28, 1996, the factory burned to the ground.

Note: Though you may find pieces very similar to Westmoreland's, their Della Robbia has no bananas among the fruits relief. For more information we recommend *Westmoreland Glass, The Popular Years,* by Lorraine Kovar (Collector Books). See *Garage Sale & Flea Market Annual* for a listing of many other items with current market values. Our advisor for this category is Philip Rosso, Jr. He is listed in the Directory under Pennsylvania. See also Animal Dishes with Covers; Carnival Glass; Glass Animals and Figurines.

American Hobnail, cupped bowl, Brandywine Blue, 8", **$40.00.** (Photo courtesy Lorraine Kovar)

American Hobnail, bonbon, gr 45.00
American Hobnail, goblet, water, Golden Sunset, 8-oz................. 15.00
American Hobnail, plate, crystal, 11½" 50.00
American Hobnail, shakers, mg, pr 20.00
Ashburton, pitcher, any color, ftd, lg... 60.00
Ashburton, sherbet, any color, ftd 8.00
Beaded Edge, bowl, fruit, mg, 5" 10.00
Beaded Edge, plate, dinner, mg w/floral decor, 10½" 42.50
Beaded Edge, platter, mg w/red rim, w/hdls, 12" 70.00
Beaded Grape, bowl, flared & ftd, 8x9" 40.00
Beaded Grape, bowl, mg, sq, w/lid, 4½" 45.00
Beaded Grape, creamer, mg 12.50
Beaded Grape, honey dish, crystal w/ruby stain, ftd, w/lid, 5" 45.00
Beaded Grape, vase, mg w/fruit decor, crimped rim, ftd, 9" 90.00
Cherry, bowl, mg, ftd, 9" 160.00
Cherry, candlesticks, mg, 4", pr 65.00
Colonial, pitcher, crystal, 8" 55.00
Della Robbia, plate, salad, crystal, 7½" 10.00
Della Robbia, shakers, crystal w/any stain, ftd, pr 75.00
Della Robbia, shakers, mg, ftd, pr 40.00
Della Robbia, tumbler, crystal w/any stain, 5" 35.00
Dolphin & Shell, candy dish, Golden Sunset, 3-ftd, 6" 45.00
Dolphin & Shell, candy dish, Gr Mist (scarce color) 40.00
English Hobnail, basket, crystal, 9" 50.00
English Hobnail, bowl, rimmed grapefruit, gr or pk, 6½" 25.00
English Hobnail, cigarette box, crystal, 4½x3½" 17.50
English Hobnail, claret, turq, rnd ft, 5-oz, 6" 20.00
English Hobnail, cocktail, mg, rnd ft, 3-oz, 4½" 15.00
English Hobnail, cruet, ruby, w/hdl, 6-oz, 6" 40.00
English Hobnail, goblet, crystal or mg, 8-oz, 5" 17.50
English Hobnail, plate, luncheon, crystal, 8" 10.00
English Hobnail, plate, luncheon, crystal, plain rim, 8½" 12.50
English Hobnail, shakers, pk, rnd ftd, pr 27.50
English Hobnail, sugar bowl, ruby, hexagon ft, 4½" 15.00
English Hobnail, tumbler, Belgian Bl, 8-oz, 4" 40.00
English Hobnail, tumbler, crystal, rnd ft, 9-oz 15.00
English Hobnail, vase, gr or pk, pinched rim, 7½x6" 80.00
English Hobnail, whiskey, crystal, ½-oz, 2½" 15.00
English Hobnail, wine, crystal, sq ft, 2-oz, 4½" 17.50
Lattice Edge, bowl, mg, flared rim, ftd, 10½" 55.00
Lattice Edge, candlesticks, mg, 4", pr 40.00
Maple Leaf, creamer, ruby, ftd, w/twig hdl................................. 35.00
Maple Leaf, vase, bud, mg, decanter style 45.00
Old Quilt, cake salver, mg, skirted, bell ft, 12" 125.00
Old Quilt, cheese dish, crystal.. 35.00
Old Quilt, compote, mg, crimped & ruffled rim.......................... 65.00

Old Quilt, cruet, crystal w/ruby stain, 6-oz.................................. 35.00
Old Quilt, jardiniere, mg, ftd, 6½" 65.00
Old Quilt, pitcher, water, purple marble, 3-pt, 8½" 100.00
Old Quilt, plate, salad, mg, 8½" 35.00
Old Quilt, tumbler, cobalt, 9-oz... 32.50
Old Quilt, tumbler, juice, mg, 5-oz.. 27.50
Old Quilt, vase, mg, fan shape, octagon ft, 9" 25.00
Paneled Grape, bowl, blk, 4½" 20.00
Paneled Grape, bowl, oval w/scalloped ft, mg, 12" L 70.00
Paneled Grape, cheese dish, purple marble 75.00
Paneled Grape, compote, Brandywine Bl, w/lid, 7x4½" 45.00
Paneled Grape, compote, mg w/HP pansy, w/lid, 7x4½" 60.00
Paneled Grape, cup, any color but mg, flared rim 25.00
Paneled Grape, cup, mg, flared rim.. 15.00

Paneled Grape, epergne set: punch base; belled bowl, 12"; belled 9" vase; milk glass, $225.00. (Photo courtesy Lorraine Kovar)

Paneled Grape, goblet, Laurel Gr, 8-oz, 6" 25.00
Paneled Grape, goblet, Olive Gr, 8-oz, 6" 12.50
Paneled Grape, jardinere, mg, cupped, ftd, 4" 27.50
Paneled Grape, mayonnaise set, crystal, 3-pc.............................. 40.00
Paneled Grape, parfait, crystal, scalloped ft, 6" 25.00
Paneled Grape, pitcher, Golden Sunset, ftd, 1-qt 65.00
Paneled Grape, plate, torte, mg, 14½" 135.00
Paneled Grape, sauceboat, mg, w/oval underplate 65.00
Paneled Grape, sherbet, mg, H ped ft 40.00
Paneled Grape, sugar bowl, Moss Gr, lace rim, open 25.00
Paneled Grape, tumbler, juice, crystal or mg, 5-oz, 4½" 25.00
Paneled Grape, vase, mg w/gold, ftd, 9½" 35.00
Princess Feather, c/s, Golden Sunset 17.50
Princess Feather, pitcher, crystal, 54-oz 95.00
Princess Feather, plate, dinner, Golden Sunset, 10½" 45.00
Princess Feather, punch bowl & base, crystal.............................195.00
Princess Feather, punch cup, crystal 125.00
Princess Feather, tumbler, ftd, mg 25.00
Thousand Eye, creamer, ruby.. 40.00
Thousand Eye, plate, dinner, crystal w/stain, 10".......................... 75.00
Thousand Eye, relish, crystal, 6-part, 10" 20.00
Thousand Eye, tumbler, iced tea, crystal, ftd, 12-oz, 6¾" 20.00
Waterford, bowl, crystal w/ruby stain, cupped, 6" 40.00

Waterford, bowl, flanged, crystal with ruby stain, $60.00. (Photo courtesy Lorraine Kovar)

Waterford, plate, bread & butter, crystal, 6" 10.00
Waterford, server w/center hdl, WF-39, 10½"................................ 55.00

T.J. Wheatley

In 1880 after a brief association with the Coultry Works, Thomas J. Wheatley opened his own studio in Cincinnati, Ohio, claiming to have been the first to discover the secret of under-glaze slip decoration on an unbaked clay vessel. He applied for and was granted a patent for his process. Demand for his ware increased to the point that several artists were hired to decorate the ware. The company incorporated in 1880 as the Cincinnati Art Pottery, but until 1882 it continued to operate under Wheatley's name. Ware from this period is marked 'T.J. Wheatley' or 'T.J.W. and Co.,' and it may be dated. The business was reorganized in 1903 as the Wheatley Pottery Company, and its production turned to Arts and Crafts vessels, particularly lamp bases, many of which were copies of Grueby shapes or those of other contemporaries. These were often covered in a thick curdled matt green glaze, although some are found in brown as well. Decorative and collectible, these have been referred to as the 'poor man's Grueby.' An incised or stamped mark reads 'WP' or 'WPCo' and might be hidden beneath glaze on the bottom.

Lamp base, frothy matt gr, bulb, breaks to stem on font, 11x10¼" ..840.00
Pot, thistles, dk gr matt, rstr, 11x10" 2,000.00

Vase, apple blossoms, white on mottled blue and gray ground, slip decorated, signed T.J. Wheatley/1879,F3?/44?, circa 1879, 13¾", $225.00. (Photo courtesy Cowan's Auctions, Inc. on LiveAuctioneers.com)

Vase, apple thistles, gr, flecks/nicks, 11½x10¼" 780.00
Vase, bird beneath tree, Limoges style, 1880, 10½", NM.............. 275.00
Vase, buds & leaves, buttressed hdls, rstr 5" hairline, 20"..........2,410.00
Vase, cherry blossoms HP on mc mottle, flaw, 1880, 8x5½" 345.00
Vase, floral, bl on mc earth tones, bulb, 1880, 8¾x8" 550.00
Vase, gr (feathered), buttress ft, bowl-like w/L neck, #648, 13"..2,200.00
Vase, gr (organic), 4 buttress ft, 11" 3,000.00
Vase, gr crackle drip on unglazed clay, sm chips, 30x16" 3,600.00
Vase, gr matt, #615, 14x9" 1,400.00
Vase, gr, bulb, WP, 11½x9½" 840.00
Vase, hibiscus appl on Barbotine, KW, ca 1880, 19x10", NM 960.00
Vase, leaves (Grueby-style), gr matt, 10x5" 1,320.00
Vase, leaves & buds, gr matt, 4 buttress ft, #609, 10x8½" 1,650.00
Vase, leaves & buds, ochre matt, #607, 9x8" 1,800.00
Vase, leaves/buds, gr matt, central ring/4 flared buttress ft, EC102, 10x8".. 1,800.00
Vase, ochre matt, drilled base, 20x6½" 2,100.00
Wall pocket, grapes, gr matt, #280, 2 chips to top, 11x5" 250.00

Whieldon

Thomas Whieldon was regarded as the finest of the Staffordshire potters of the mid-1700s. He produced marbled and black Egyptian wares as well as tortoise shell, a mottled brown-glazed earthenware accented with touches of blue and yellow. In 1754 he became a partner of Josiah Wedgwood. Other potters produced similar wares, and today the term Whieldon is used generically.

Basket & stand, 9½" L, EX 6,100.00
Charger, tortoiseshell, scroll-molded rim, ca 1765, 15" 650.00

Creamer, cow, brn/gray on gr base, w/lid, rstr, 5¼" 400.00
Cup/saucer, brn sponging w/gr splotches on creamware, 2", 2¾".. 350.00
Figurine, cat on pillow, brn w/some gr & yel, 4", EX 600.00
Plate, tortoiseshell, 8-sided, ribbed rim, ca 1765, 9" 275.00
Plate, tortoiseshell, 8-sided, tooled rim, 9½" 450.00
Plate, tortoiseshell, molded edge, 18th C, 9" 345.00
Plate, tortoiseshell w/acorn sprays/scrolls/diapering, 8" 525.00
Teapot, agate ware, pewter lid, #22, chipped spout, 8x8" 60.00
Teapot, globular, bird finial, crabstock hdl, paw ft, 1770, 3¾" 550.00
Teapot, tortoiseshell, beaded border, lion finial, rprs, 6" 600.00
Teapot, tortoiseshell, emb vines, mask & paw ft, 1760-70, rprs, 9". 4,509.00

Teapot, tortoiseshell, lion mask and paw feet, bird finial, circa 1770, restorations, 4½", $1,200.00. (Photo courtesy Skinner Auctioneers and Appraisers of Antiques and Fine Art)

Teapot, tortoiseshell on soft paste, melon shape, twig spout, 18th C..950.00
Teapot, tortoiseshell w/molded leaves, 19th C, 9" 300.00

Wicker

Wicker is the basket-like material used in many types of furniture and accessories. It may be made from bamboo cane, rattan, reed, or artificial fibers. It is airy, lightweight, and very popular in hot regions. Imported from the Orient in the eighteenth century, it was first manufactured in the United States in about 1850. The elaborate, closely woven Victorian designs belong to the mid- to late 1800s, and the simple styles with coarse reedings usually indicate a post-1900 production. Art Deco styles followed in the '20s and '30s. The most important consideration in buying wicker is condition — it can be restored, but only by a professional. Age is an important factor, but be aware that 'Victorian-style' furniture is being manufactured today.

Key: H/W — Heywood Wakefield

Armchair & ottoman, natural tight weave, uphl seat & cushion, EX. 900.00
Armchair, tubular steel fr, wooden arm rests, Breuer/Thonet, 1928, 33"....575.00
Baby buggy, curved arms, ft rest, Vict era, 36x44x21".................. 400.00
Baby carriage, sleigh front, natural, H/W, 41x54x23".................... 550.00
Baby carriage, tight weave, sleigh front, wooden wheels, 1900s, 59" L...500.00
Chair, continuous arms, loose-weave bk, rstr cushion, 1900s, 35"...400.00
Chair, continuous arms, scrolling heart bk, cane seat, 1890s, 31" ...465.00
Chair, continuous arms, tight weave, skirt, Smith & Hawkins, 39" ...120.00
Chair, continuous arms, tight weave, stick & ball, att H/W, 36x27x26"..480.00
Chair, corner; curlicues, ornate apron, H/W, 1880s, 33" 360.00
Chair, ornate scrolling trim, Vict, 33" 425.00
Chair, photographer's, single continuous arm, ornate scrolls, 32x34"....300.00
Chair, tulip, wrought-iron fr, Erwin & Estelle Laverne, 1950s, 49x45". 4,350.00
Chair, wingbk, cvd fr & fluted legs, uphl arms/bk/seat, 43", VG 65.00
Chaise lounge, scrolled arm, dmn-weave skirt, att H/W, 72" L 480.00
Cradle, flat woven edge, cvd wood rockers, C-shape support, 36" L... 60.00
Desk, tight weave, drw/letter holders/cubbiess, wht pnt, H/W, +chair..360.00
Easel, Vict scrolls, H/W, ca 1880, 75x25"..................................... 850.00
Hall tree, demilune shelf/tall bk w/lg mirror, wht pnt, 73" 850.00
Lamp, floor, natural rattan shade w/rpl liner, 72x20x20" 780.00
Lamp, table, cone-shape 21" open-weave shade; trumpet base, 23" ...960.00
Rocker, continuous arms, scrolls/fans, att H/W, 44x34x26" 725.00

Screen, mahog fr, 3 hinged panels, Adams style w/HP cherubs, 63x59" .. 950.00
Settee, continuous arms, lattice weave, wht pnt, rpl cushion, 39x54" .. 425.00
Sewing basket, tight-weave body, scrolled legs, ca 1900, 31" 345.00

Sewing stand, cabriole legs, lower shelf, Heywood Wakefield, G, 30½x22x23", $390.00. (Photo courtesy San Rafael Auction Gallery on LiveAuctioneers.com)

Sewing stand, 2 galleried tiers, curved legs, 8-sided, 19th C, 27x18" .. 550.00
Sofa, tight weave w/pnt sunbursts, rstr cushions, Lloyd, 32x70x27" . 425.00
Stand, wrapped/twisted design, 3 oak shelves, H/W, 45x18¾x18¾" .. 850.00
Table, leather top, shelf, tight weave, H/W, ca 1900, 29x30x18" . 345.00

Wiener Werkstatte

The Wiener Werkstatte was established in Austria in 1903. It was one of many workshops worldwide that ascribed to the new wave of design and style that was sweeping not only Austria but England and other European countries as well.

Its founders were Josef Hoffmann, Kolo Moser, and Fritz Warndorfer. Hoffmann had for some time been involved in a movement bent toward refining prevailing Art Nouveau trends. He was a primary initiator of the Viennese Secession, and in 1899 he worked as a professor at the Viennese School of Applied Arts. Through his work as an architect, he began to develop his own independent style, preferring and promoting clean rectangular shapes over the more accepted building concepts of the day. His progressive ideas resulted in contemporary designs, completely breaking away from past principles in all medias of art as well as architecture, completely redefining Arts and Crafts. At the Wiener Werkstatte, every object was crafted with exquisite attention to design, workmanship, and materials.

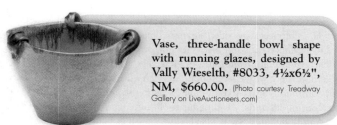

Vase, three-handle bowl shape with running glazes, designed by Vally Wieselth, #8033, 4½x6½", NM, $660.00. (Photo courtesy Treadway Gallery on LiveAuctioneers.com)

Book, Evolution of Modern Appl Arts 1903-28, hardbound, pnt cover .. 4,650.00
Bowl, centerpiece, amber glass, ftd, Hoffman design by Mosser, 1917, 4x5" .. 725.00
Bowl, centerpiece, Gold Aurene, Hoffman design, Mosser, 1917, 4x5" . 600.00
Bowl, ceramic, floral, rtcl rim, gr/pk/wht, D Kuttn, 2½x4¾" 480.00
Bowl, simple floral, rtcl rim, ftd, Dina Kuttn, 2⅝x4¾" 480.00
Box, geometric overlapping earth tones, paper, 1920s, 3¼x6x6" ... 1,325.00
Brooch, sterling w/malachite & turq, Josef Hoffmann #900, 1⅜x1½" .. 15,600.00
Bust, elegant lady, HP earthenware, C Calm-Wierink, 1920s, 8½" .. 3,000.00
Candelabrum, vines w/flowers & leaves, Wieselthier, #0908, 8", NM .. 2,500.00
Centerpiece coupe, hammered/chased brass w/ribbon hdls, Hoffman, 8x12" . 2,650.00
Centerpiece figure, lady w/2 baskets, mc, ceramic, Kppriva, 6¼" ... 1,100.00
Cup, ftd, G Baudisch, 4¼x3" 450.00
Fashion card, lady in fancy garb w/butterfly, #693, 3x3½" 120.00
Figural tray, ceramic, man sitting X-legged/smoking pipe, S Singer, 5" . 540.00
Jar, amber glass, 10-panel w/faceted finial, ca 1920, 12" 575.00
Lamp, tabby cat figural, creamic w/glass eyes, Hoffman, rpr, 14" .. 425.00
Pitcher, rooster-head spout, gr & yel on red clay, Lotte Calm ... 1,200.00
Postcard, Nicolo, religious figure & children, Mela Kohler, #71 .. 780.00
Teapot, brass-washed copper, tin lining, rosewood hdl, Hoffman, 6x10" .. 6,600.00
Vase, dk amethyst glass w/melon ribs, Hoffman, 7½" 550.00
Vase, dmn cutouts/abstracts, mc on red clay, Wieselthier, 7⅜", EX .. 1,450.00
Vase, geometric design w/fruit, Made in Austria, 7" 2,520.00
Vessel, amber glass 10-panel cylinder, scalloped lid, 1920s, 12" ... 575.00

Willets

The Willets Manufacturing Company of Trenton, New Jersey, produced a type of belleek porcelain during the late 1880s and 1890s. Examples were often marked with a coiled snake that formed a 'W' with 'Willets' below and 'Belleek' above. Not all Willets is factory decorated. Items painted by amateurs outside the factory are worth considerably less. High prices usually equate with fine artwork. In the listings below, all items are Belleek unless noted otherwise. Our advisor for this category is Mary Frank Gaston.

Bowl, floral, lt & med gr, 4x6¼" 72.50
Bowl, roses, pk/gr on wht, sgn Zeigler, gold hdls, 1879-1912, 5x13" ... 150.00
Chalice, monk on brn, waisted stem, disk ft, 11¼" 125.00
Chocolate pot, wht w/ornate hdl, slim, 10", +6 wht scalloped c/s. 110.00
Compote, floral reserve & vines, gold hdls, 5⅛x8¾" L 120.00
Hatpin holder, floral silver o/l on wht, 4⅞" 120.00
Jar, Asian ladies & paper lanterns, fans on lid, 5x4" 360.00
Jug, ears of corn, brn/yel tones, ovoid, 7¼" 250.00
Jug, grapes, cylindrical, gold dragon hdl, 11¼" 175.00
Pitcher, grapes on wht w/gold trim, cylindrical, sgn MMB, 14¼". 240.00
Urn, grapes, W Marsh, ornate gold scroll hdls, crimped rim, 11x13", pr... 1,500.00
Vase, Biblical scene of lady in garden holding flowers, 15"........ 1,050.00
Vase, daffodils, yel on gr, swollen cylinder, 14½" 345.00
Vase, egrets in a landscape, sgn A MacM F, 10" 210.00

Vase, iris motif, non-factory decoration, artist signed 'L,' 11", $150.00. (Photo courtesy DuMouchelles on LiveAuctioneers.com)

Vase, landscape, bl/gr/brn, cylindrical, Brischoff, 1910s, 16¼" .. 1,650.00
Vase, Mt Fuji & village scene, flattened ovoid, gold hdls/rim, 8⅞" ... 240.00

Will-George

After years of working in the family garage, William and George Climes founded the Will-George company in Los Angeles, California, in 1934. They manufactured high-quality artware, utilizing both porcelain and earthenware clays. Both brothers, motivated by their love of art pottery, had extensive education and training in manufacturing processes as well as decoration. In 1940 actor Edgar Bergen, a collector of pottery, developed a relationship with the brothers and invested in their business. With this new influx of funds, the company relocated to Pasadena. There they produced an extensive line of art pottery, but they excelled in their creation of bird and animal figurines. In addition, they molded a large line of human figurines similar to Royal Doulton. The brothers, now employing a staff of decorators, precisely molded their pieces with great care and strong emphasis on originality and detail, creating high-quality works of art that were only carried by exclusive gift stores.

In the late 1940s after a split with Bergen, the company moved to San Gabriel to a larger, more modern location and renamed themselves The Claysmiths. Their business flourished and they were able to successfully mass produce many items; but due to the abundance of cheap, postwar imports from Italy and Japan that were then flooding the market, they liquidated the business in 1956.

Bowl, red onion, gr stem finial on lid, 4x4"..................................... 30.00
Candleholders, upright leaves w/1 curled down, turq w/pk, 6", pr. 155.00
Container, covered, horse-shaped, spckled matt glaze, 8½x7"...... 100.00
Cup/saucer, purple onion design... 35.00
Figurine, artist & his nude model, 7½", set 200.00
Figurine, ballerina girl stands on rnd base, 5".............................. 135.00
Figurine, Chinese girl w/pots for flowers, 8¼" 95.00
Figurine, cockatoo on stump, yel/pk/brn, 12", NM 250.00
Figurine, cocker spaniel, brn or blk, 7x9½".................................. 275.00
Figurine, dachshund, ca 1945, 6½x9".. 275.00
Figurine, flamingo, head bk, wings closed, 8", $115 to................ 130.00
Figurine, flamingo, head down, free-standing legs w/greenery support, 6½" ..135.00
Figurine, flamingo, head up, wings closed, 7½", $60 to................. 85.00
Figurine, flamingo, head up, wings closed, 10½", $150 to............. 165.00
Figurine, flamingo, head up, wings up, 8", $225 to........................ 250.00
Figurine, flamingo, head up, wings up, 15½"................................. 365.00
Figurine, flamingo in stride/preening, wings wide open, rnd base, 10" ..275.00
Figurine, giraffe, w/head up & legs wide, 13" 185.00
Figurine, macaw, red, on tree trunk, 2 openings for flowers, 14½". 250.00

Figurines, giraffe pair, orange gloss crackle with gold-ringed oil spots, #920 and #922, circa 1958, 14½", 10½", $135.00. (Photo courtesy Matthew Andras, eBay seller century34)

Flower bowl, gondola-shaped, w/detachable Chinese boy oarsman, 20".... 200.00
Leaf dish, gr, sgn, 10x11" 40.00
Pitcher/vase, rooster, 7" 150.00
Planter, Asian girl seated on wooden bucket planter, 7½".............. 85.00
Platter, half red onion shape, 3x11x13" 45.00
Tumbler, rooster, 4½".. 50.00
Tumbler, rooster, formed by tall tail feathers, 4½", $50 to 60.00
Wine/cordial, 5"... 50.00

Winchester

The Winchester Repeating Arms Company lost their important government contract after WWI and of necessity turned to the manufacture of sporting goods, hardware items, tools, etc., to augment their gun

production. Between 1920 and 1931, over 7,500 different items, each marked 'Winchester Trademark U.S.A.,' were offered for sale by thousands of Winchester Hardware stores throughout the country. After 1931 the firm became Winchester-Western. Collectors prefer the prewar items, and the majority of our listings are from this era.

Concerning current collecting trends: Oil cans that a short time ago could be purchased for $2.00 to $5.00 now often sell for $25.00, some over $50.00, and demand is high. Good examples of advertising posters and calendars seem to have no upper limits and are difficult to find. Winchester fishing lures are strong, and the presence of original boxes increases values by 25% to 40%. Another current trend concerns the price of 'diecuts' (cardboard stand-ups, signs, or hanging signs). These are out-pricing many other items. A short time ago the average value of a 'diecut' ranged from $25.00 to $45.00. Current values for most are in the $200.00 to $800.00 range, with some approaching $2,500.00.

Unless noted otherwise, our values are for items in excellent condition. Our advisor for this category is James Anderson; he is listed in the Directory under Minnesota. See also Fishing Collectibles; Knives; Weapons.

Apron, carpenter's, #W1, G 180.00
Auger bit, #3, solid core, 1920s-30s, 7¾" 40.00
Auger bit set, #WSB13, set of 13, #4-#16, VG wood case............ 620.00
Axe, dbl, 10½", w/24" wooden hdl.. 135.00
Bait box, #9520, gr, 6", G 80.00
Barrel reflector, VG... 165.00
Basketball, G.. 1,200.00
Battery, 3-cell, tubular, rare, VG 135.00
Box, 12-gauge shotgun cartridges, stencil on dvtl wood, 9x15x9½".85.00
Box, shotshell, Leader 12-Gauge, full box of 10, 3½" L, G-............ 45.00
Brochure, Model, M in envelope... 50.00
Brush, varnish, #W7, G... 60.00
Calendar, father & son w/ducks, Atlantic Litho, 1920, partial .1,450.00
Calendar, Western scene/Leigh painting, partial, 31x16"+fr.....7,200.00
Calendar top, man w/gun stands by game animal, 1901, 27x13"..425.00
Can, gun oil, gr graphics, #1052, ca 1920, 3-oz, VG+ 185.00
Cannon, signal, 10-gauge, Pat August 20, 1901, VG................1,450.00

Cannon, signal, circa 1900, 17½" long, $480.00. (Photo courtesy Wiederseim Associates, Inc. on LiveAuctioneers.com)

Carpet sweeper, G-.. 600.00
Case insert, grouse, Winchester Leader..., 1920, 7⅜x12", NM..5,270.00
Catalog, Winchester...No 75, March 1909, 182 pgs, G 55.00
Catalog, Winchester Pocket Catalog of Tools 1923, 6x3", G....... 115.00
Chisel, cold, ¾x6¾" 30.00
Chisel, wood, #4989, 1¼x11¼" 20.00
Cold chisel, #W12, G-... 25.00
Container, No 9114 Split BB Shot, fish on lid, NM..................... 215.00
Drill, breast, #W44 .... 135.00
Fishing line, #8051, G to VG 110.00
Fishing reel, #2236, NP brass, VG... 110.00
Flashlight, #6516, Miner's Jr type, VG....................................... 45.00
Flashlight, holds 5 D-cell batteries, beveled glass lens................. 35.00
Food chopper, #W12... 75.00
Football helmet, blk leather, rare 3,750.00
Golf club, #1350D (driver), VG... 155.00
Gun case, leather, #3022, VG 175.00
Hacksaw, G+.. 85.00

Hand saw, #W16/26, VG.. 170.00
Hatchet, 5" head, wooden hdl................................... 165.00
Hatchet, lathing, #WP420, 6" head 50.00
Hockey stick, #4860, boy's practice stick, G 245.00
Hoe, garden, #WG10, G... 135.00
Knife, paper hanger's, VG... 110.00
Lawn mower, #WH20, 20" cut, G.............................. 235.00
Level, 2 bubble vials, #W3, 28", VG+....................... 40.00
Level, #WO-26, wood & brass, 26".......................... 125.00
Level, wood & brass, 14", VG................................... 100.00
Loading tool, 32WCF caliber, pliers shape............... 100.00
Lure, 5-hook underwater minnow, NM in G box......1,175.00
Lure, multi-wobbler #9203, gold foil finish, VG 335.00
Meat fork, riveted wood hdl, 13"............................... 45.00
Meat grinder, 3- blade, #W31, $75 to 85.00
Nail hammer, #W611, G... 80.00
Padlock, #W39, 2", VG.. 145.00
Padlock, cast steel, slide-swing shackle, 2", NMIB 550.00
Paint brush, 4", G-... 275.00
Pencil, carpenter's, #1915, 7", VG............................ 110.00
Pin-back button, Wonderful Topperweins, couple portrait, NM.. 150.00
Plane, #102, 5½", NM 65.00
Plane, #3015, 18" 70.00
Plane, block, #3010, 14" 70.00
Plane, rabbet, #3201 .... 110.00
Plane, router, #3070, ½" cutter 130.00
Pliers, #2489-10, 10" 50.00
Pliers, rnd nose, #2182, $75 to 110.00
Pocketknife, #2967, 2 blades, 3⅞", G...................... 160.00
Poster, Repeating Shotguns, man & 2 bird dogs, 30x16½", NM.1,850.00
Putty knife, #2365, VG.. 125.00
Rake, garden, #WSB14, VG....................................... 130.00
Razor strop, #375, G to VG 110.00
Razor strop, G-... 90.00
Reel, casting, #2744.. 90.00
Reloading tool, #38-55, Pat Feb 13 1894 .... 180.00
Rod cleaning set, 4-pc, for Winchester Henry 1866-1892............ 180.00
Rollerskates, #1331, NP... 60.00
Ruler, folding, #9568, boxwood, 24"......................... 85.00
Scale, country store type, weighs up to 24 lbs 135.00
Screwdriver, #7113-4, brass ferrule, 8" 40.00
Shears, barber's, #W17/7½, NP, G........................... 75.00
Sign, brass emb, Winchester Leader..., 9¾x13½"................2,500.00
Sign, Winchester tires, tin litho, red/wht/bl, 18x55", VG........... 900.00
Sign, Winchester Western, man on horse, tin litho, 38" dia, VG.950.00
Spatula, #7646, G, $25 to... 45.00
Spatula, #7646, stainless blade, VG......................... 85.00
Straight razor, #5832 on tang, MIB.......................... 300.00
Tennis racket, #W3, G-, $600 to 650.00
Thermometer, Sporting Ammunition..., shotshell, 26", EXIB 120.00
Tin container, After Shave Talc, hunter & dog, red lid, 4¾x3" ... 335.00
Whistle, referee's, #1806, nickel silver 210.00
Whistle, referee's, NP brass, #1805, 1920s, scarce......... 400.00
Wood saw, #W80, w/30" blade, G 165.00
Wrench, open end, #W127, VG 35.00

Windmill Weights

Windmill weights made of cast iron were used to protect the wind-mill's plunger rod from damage during high winds by adding weight that slowed down the speed of the blades. Since they were constantly exposed to the elements, any painted surfaces would be seriously compromised. Our values are for 'as found' examples, as described.

Bull, Fairbury, flat body, red-brn & wht pnt, 24½" L.................... 750.00
Bull, Fairbury, old rpt, 24"..1,500.00
Bull, Fairbury Wind Mill Co, CI, red/wht pnt, 20th C, 25" L 900.00
Bull, Simpson, striding, bell at neck, blk/wht pnt, 14" L..........2,100.00
Bull, Simpson Wind Mill Co, 2-pc hollow body, blk/wht pnt, 14x14"....2,200.00
Crescent moon, no pnt, Eclipse/A13, 10" 45.00
Flying 'W,' Althouse-Wheeler, 9¼x17" on modern metal base 525.00

Horse, bob-tail, attributed to Dempster, #58C, unpainted, 17x18", $510.00. (Photo courtesy Cowan's Auctions, Inc. on LiveAuctioneers.com)

Horse, long tail, Dempster, 50% wht pnt remains, 18¾x19½" 865.00
Horse, long tail, Dempster, integral base, 19x17" 2,100.00
Rooster, att Elgin, 20% red/wht pnt remains, 19x18x3½" 2,215.00
Rooster, Elgin, 10 Ft #2, 16x16½" 1,450.00
Rooster, Elgin, emb #s, 10 ft No 2, old 2-color pnt, 16x16"+base... 1,525.00
Rooster, Elgin Hummer #184, short stem, ball base, no pnt, 20" ...1,300.00
Rooster, Elgin Hummer #184, short stem, worn silver/red pnt, 9"+base...960.00
Rooster, rainbow tail, Elgin, worn 3-color rpt, 18"+wood base .1,500.00

Wire Ware

Very primitive wire was first made by cutting sheet metal into strips which were shaped with mallet and file. By the late thirteenth century craftsmen in Europe had developed a method of pulling these strips through progressively smaller holes until the desired gauge was obtained. During the Industrial Revolution of the late 1800s, machinery was developed that could produce wire cheaply and easily; and it became a popular commercial commodity. It was used to produce large items such as garden benches and fencing as well as innumerable small pieces for use in the kitchen or on the farm. Beware of reproductions.

Basket, egg, heart handles, footed base with spokes, 15x10½", $150.00. (Photo courtesy Conestoga Auction Company on LiveAuctioneers.com)

Basket, egg, bulb, ftd, bail hdl, 10x7".................................... 75.00
Basket, egg, holds 3, center hdl, ca 1900, EX patina.................... 135.00
Basket, fruit, 8 spines, 8 sm ft, 2 loop hdls, 5x11", EX 240.00
Basket, loose weave, crusty old surface, wall mt, 5½x8x8" 48.00
Basket, market, tight weave, thick gauged, 1900s, EX 175.00
Basket, potato, galvanized steel wire, 2 hdls, ca 1930, 17x18"...... 135.00
Bottle carrier, decorative zigzags throughout, slight rust, 9x14x11"..150.00
Carrier, bottle, 13½x10½x9".. 155.00
Compote, simple openwork weave, trn-down rim, cone ft, G- pnt, 8x14"...45.00
Cradle, dmn weave, curlicues, 20x40" on stand w/brass castors ... 500.00

Cradle on stand, brass castors, 1900s, 20x40"+60" H stand.......... 550.00
Dish rack, ca 1890-1920, 16" dia... 75.00
Egg tongs, 12".. 40.00
Fly cover, screen wire, wooden knob, 6½"...................................... 55.00
Hat stand, wire facial features including mustache & eyebrows, 13"... 385.00
Letter holder, 3-tier, w/brass strips, ca 1900, 15x11½" 325.00
Loveseat, serpentine crest/scroll bk, 1880s, 44" L, +2 chairs 1,500.00
Plant stand, 2 grad tiers w/curlique patterns, 59x14x24", EX 235.00
Plant stand, 3-tier, loops & scrolls, Vict style, 59x24" dia 300.00
Rack, looping pattern, 8 hooks, 5x22¾" 48.00
Soap dish, twisted loops, crimped wire, lt rust, 1900s, 6½x7x4" 85.00
Utensil rack, scrolled top, 6-hook, 21" L... 90.00
Vegetable washer, bulb, 2-pc, 2 D-form hdls, 4x7x10", $10 to 20.00
Washer, vegetable, 2 shallow baskets w/D-form hdls, 4x7x10" 20.00
Whisk, twisted hdl, 8"... 25.00

Rick Wisecarver

Rick Wisecarver is a contemporary artist from Ohio who is well known not only for his renderings of Indian portraits, animals, cookie jars, and scenics on pottery that is reminiscent of that made by earlier Ohio companies, but for limited edition lithographs as well.

Cookie jar, Geronimo, No 195-94 Chiricahua Wampam Old Age 1994, sgn .265.00
Cookie jar, Wizard of Oz, Alice+3 other characters, ltd ed 485.00
Jug, American Indian portrait cvd/incised on free-form, 1981, 9½" .425.00
Jug, cat portrait, Shezane Critters #1130, 1983, 6⅝" 100.00
Jug, whiskey, frontiersman on brn, 1982, 6½x4½" 85.00
Pin dish, flamingo figure w/lid on bk, pk/gr, sgn, 1971, 9", EX 40.00

Tankard set, each piece with various bird scenes, signed Rick W/Wihoa's Harvest 86 R.S., 11½", 4⅝", $225.00. (Photo courtesy Belhorn Auction Services, LLC on LiveAuctioneers.com)

Vase, American Indian brave portrait, collared rim, 1980, 14½"..515.00
Vase, American Indian chief form, 1986, 7x7½" 240.00
Vase, American Indian elder, Red Cloud, rim-to-hip hdls, slim, 1983, 16¼"..350.00
Vase, American Indian Geronimo portrait, 1984, 7⅞x4½" 315.00
Vase, American Indian on horseback w/crescent moon, 1979, 16¾" .600.00
Vase, American Indian Pontiac portrait, RS 9/15/84 Wihoas..., 12⅜x7¼"..550.00
Vase, American Indian warrior, 1984, 9½x3⅞" 275.00
Vase, American Indian warrior, Special, 1982, 14" 325.00
Vase, autumn scene w/canoe & lake on pillow form, 1986, 6⅞x7½" .. 135.00
Vase, barn owl ready to take flight on brn, sgn/mk, 1980, 10x7"..230.00
Vase, buffalo scene on pillow form, 1986, 7x7¼" 235.00
Vase, bugling elk, pillow form, sgm, mk, 9x7¼" 135.00
Vase, cat portrait, pastels, 1984, 11⅜x4¼" 300.00
Vase, grizzly bear w/cub, sgn/RS, 1996, 10½x5¾" 345.00
Vase, Indian in headdress, sgn/#82 RS, pillow form, 5" 135.00
Vase, Roseville Harvest scenic, 1986, 8⅛" 425.00
Vase, trees on textured ground, tapered form, 1983, 11x3½"........ 325.00

Beatrice Wood

Born in San Francisco in 1893, young Beatrice Wood was educated in painting and theater in Paris. She worked as an actress in New York

through the teens, where she befriended expatriate artists from the Dadist movement and furthered her explorations in fine arts. It was to follow the Theosophist Krishnamurti that Beatrice visited and then moved to California. She studied pottery with several California teachers, including Glen Lukens, Otto and Gertrude Natzler, and Vivika and Otto Heino.

Beatrice Wood taught ceramics and operated a studio in Ojai, becoming well known for her personal interpretation of ancient forms and glazes. Besides throwing vases and plates, she built figural sculptures full of humor and eroticism. Her pieces, signed 'Beato,' are in collections and museums all over the world. She passed away in Ojai in 1998 at the age of 105.

Bowl, centerpiece, fish shape, sm fish on rim, Beato, 4x24x15"..6,000.00
Bowl, centerpiece, hen form, appl floral, pastel faience, Beato, 12x17"..3,500.00
Chalice, gold lustre on earthenware, Beato, 8x5" 8,400.00
Chalice, lime gr matt, Beato, 46" 3,600.00
Chalice, mc lustre, simple form, prof rstr, 5¼x4¼" 1,450.00
Figure, mermaid, raspberry & gr lustre, on quartz crystal base, 7" ... 5,500.00
Figure, slab style, gray clay w/thin wash, Beato, 8" 1,100.00
Mug, floral on pk, loop hdl, Beato, 5¼"....................................... 1,200.00

Necklace, colorful ceramic beads, figural pendant, unmarked, 17", $2,400.00. (Photo courtesy Treadway Gallery on LiveAuctioneers.com)

Plaque, Helen Freeman, nude, Beato, 17x13" 3,900.00
Sculpture, The Conqueror, seated nude, Beato, rstr, 9½x5½x7".5,100.00
Urn, volcanic brn & burgundy, sm hdls, Beato, 9x8" 3,350.00
Vase, mc metallic finish, gourd shape, rpr, 9x4" 900.00
Vase, thin gr over dk red, near-spherical, Beato, 3" 1,100.00
Vase, volcanic gold & verdigris, cylinder neck, hdls, 7¾x5" 5,300.00

Wood Carvings

Wood sculptures represent an important section of American folk art. Wood carvings were made not only by skilled woodworkers such as cabinetmakers, and carpenters, but by amateur 'whittlers' as well. They take the form of circus-wagon figures, carousel animals, decoys, busts, figurines, and cigar store Indians. Asian artists show themselves to have been as proficient with the medium of wood as they were with ivory or hardstone. See also Carousel Animals; Decoys; Tobacciana.

Abe Lincoln w/law book & cane, mc pnt, late 19th C, 22" 4,000.00
Birds (6) in tree, HP w/bead eyes & wire ft, realistic, 23".......... 1,725.00
Dog (hunting) & fence, mc pnt, wooden base, ca 1900, 5½x6x1¾" ..200.00
Dog seated, blk/wht w/gold collar, May Lancaster/Seattle, 20th C, 8" 470.00
Dove, box, hollowed-out hardwood, realistic pnt, 5x9½" 435.00
Eagle, architectural finial, pnt/gilt over bl, Am, 19th C, 21" L .3,600.00
Eagle, fully cvd head & spread wings, mustard/brn pnt, 19th C, 7x50"..5,875.00
Eagle w/banner & shield, red/wht/bl pnt w/gold, 27" W, +provenance...5,175.00
Eagle w/spread wings/olive branch/flag shield, gesso/pnt, 22x50" .88,125.00
Egret, cvd/pnt, glass eyes/wire legs, on pnt wood base, ca 1900, 22" ...1,750.00
Goldfinch, scratch-feather cvg, rock base, J Blackstone, 1940s, 2⅝"..1,400.00
Great Horned Owl, realistic pnt, glass eyes, F Finney, 26" 3,100.00
Guinea hens (3) on stump, chip-cvd feathers, brn stain, 14" 545.00
Heron, gr pnt, glass eyes, wire legs, late 19th C, 7x10"............... 350.00
Horse, orig brn pnt, appl fur mane/tail, 6¾" 750.00

Horse's head, polychrome, English, circa 1900, 16½" long, $540.00. (Photo courtesy Harlowe-Powell Auction Gallery on LiveAuctioneers.com)

Lady's head, birch, used by milliner, splits, 12½" 465.00
Madonna seated/holds book, walnut, dk patina, Germany, 22".... 975.00
Owl on stump, plaster legs/wire ft, orig pnt, 7½" 700.00
Penguin, appl flippers/tack eyes, old mc pnt, att C Hart, 1936, 5".. 1,900.00
Puffin, realistic pnt, mtd on driftwood, D Brown, ME, 3½".......... 175.00
Rattlesnake, realistic decor, att O Spencer, 31" L........................ 315.00
Robin by fence, realistic pnt, glass eyes, rustic fence, 7x12x4"..... 355.00
Robin, realistic pnt, wire legs, wooden ft, on base, 5x7¾"........... 265.00
Rooster, cvd from 1 block, mc pnt, att Schimmel, PA, 1850s, 7x5" ...1,000.00
Rooster, glass eyes/antler spurs, E Reed, 15½"+stand................1,495.00
Spaniel w/docked tail & feathered front legs, orig pnt, 5½" L...... 350.00
Statue of Liberty bust, nut brn stain, E Reed, age split, 11".......1,495.00
Swan, wht pnt, label: Herter's Inc 1893, 14½x28½"..................... 375.00
Tugboat model, mc pnt, metal furnishings, on stand, 6x4½x2¼". 350.00

Woodenware

Woodenware (or treenware, as it is sometimes called) generally refers to those wooden items such as spoons, bowls, and food molds, that were used in the preparation of food. Common during the eighteenth and nineteenth centuries, these wares were designed from a strictly functional viewpoint and were used on a day-to-day basis. With the advent of the Industrial Revolution which brought with it new materials and products, much of the old woodenware was simply discarded. Today original handcrafted American woodenwares are extremely difficult to find. See also Primitives.

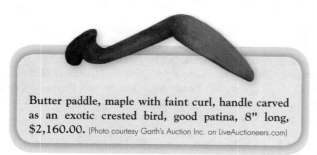

Butter paddle, maple with faint curl, handle carved as an exotic crested bird, good patina, 8" long, $2,160.00. (Photo courtesy Garth's Auction Inc. on LiveAuctioneers.com)

Bowl, 3 bands of incised lines, red pnt, rprs, 19th C, 3½x10¼".... 300.00
Bowl, ash burl w/G color, damage, 2¼x6½" 115.00
Bowl, ash burl, 2 integral cvd hdls, early 1800s, 4¾x13½" 4,000.00
Bowl, ash burl, cvd collar on ext rim, 19th C, 6x19½"..............3,525.00
Bowl, ash burl, G color & form, flared sides, splits, 3½x8" 435.00
Bowl, ash burl, scrubbed, wide trn outside rim, 5x13" 2,075.00
Bowl, ash burl, steep sides, flat base, primitive, 7x16" 350.00
Bowl, ash burl, trn w/raised collar, 19th C, 6x14"......................4,000.00
Bowl, ash burl w/loose figure, almond shape, wood patch, 6x16x13".. 1,265.00
Bowl, ash burl w/tight figure, mellow patina, 1¾x4½"...............1,550.00
Bowl, ash burl w/tight figure, scrubbed, 5x11½x10"..................2,300.00
Bowl, bl pnt, well trn, no splits, 21" 1,100.00
Bowl, curly maple, old rich finish, glued rpr at rim, OH, 17" 435.00
Bowl, dk brn varnish, w/lid, 8x12½" 1,375.00
Bowl, dough, oblong, dk bl pnt, 4x20x11¾" 1,000.00
Bowl, medial incised line, early 1800s, 3⅝x5¾"........................... 850.00
Bowl, natural form w/EX patina, worn red stain, sgn MP/1872, 4x13x10"...800.00
Bowl, soft wood w/old bl-gr pnt, hewn mks, hdls, 5x19x13½"...... 400.00
Bowl, tiger maple, yel-gr pnt, raised collar, 7¼x22" 2,500.00
Bowl w/lid, trn ash, ca 1780, 5x7½", EX 18,000.00
Butter paddle, cvd horse-head finial, scrubbed, 9¼" 175.00
Canister, trn, pnt stylized flowers/etc, on pk, Lehnware, 5½" 2,000.00
Container, red over mustard vinegar pnt, trn finial, 7x7" dia....... 800.00
Container, trn, wire & wooden bail hdl, Peaseware, 8x9" 575.00
Container, trn, wood & wire bail hdl, varnish, Peaseware, 3⅝x3½"...230.00
Covered jars, yel/ochre putty decor, 1820-30, 4-8", $400 to 750.00
Cup, saffron, strawberries on salmon, Lehnware, 4¼"................1,800.00
Dipper, 1 pc of ash w/burled bowl, old edge loss, 19th C, 17" L ... 480.00
Jar, squat w/urn finial, Peaseware, sm splits/rpr, 8x7" 375.00
Jar, yel & ocher plume/earthworm/spots, rprs/cracks, 19th C, 6⅝" 600.00
Trencher, walnut, orig bl pnt, age splits, 5¾x25x12" 700.00

Trencher, birch scraped down to old blue-gray paint, nineteenth century, 20" long, $660.00. (Photo courtesy Garth's Auction Inc. on LiveAuctioneers.com)

Woodworking Machinery

Vintage cast-iron woodworking machines are monuments to the highly skilled engineers, foundrymen, and machinists who devised them, thus making possible the mass production of items ranging from clothespins, boxes, and barrels to decorative moldings and furniture. Though attractive from a nostalgic viewpoint, many of these machines are bought by the hobbyist and professional alike, to be put into actual use — at far less cost than new equipment. Many worth-assessing factors must be considered; but as a general rule, a machine in good condition is worth about 65¢ a pound (excluding motors). A machine needing a lot of restoration is not worth more than 35¢ a pound, while one professionally rebuilt and with a warranty can be calculated at $1.10 a pound. Modern, new machinery averages over $3.00 a pound. Two of the best sources of information on purchasing or selling such machines are *Vintage Machines — Searching for the Cast Iron Classics*, by Tom Howell, and *Used Machines and Abused Buyers* by Chuck Seidel from *Fine Woodworking*, November/December 1984. Prices quoted are for machines in good condition, less motors and accessories. Our advisor for this category is Mr. Dana Martin Batory, author of *Vintage Woodworking Machinery, An Illustrated Guide to Four Manufacturers, Volumes I* and *II*, and *The Planer Truth: A Brief History and Guide to Servicing Vintage Single Surface, Roll-Feed Planers (1850 – 1950)*. See his listing in the Directory under Ohio for further information. No phone calls, please.

F.H. Clement Co., 1896

Band saw, 30" 555.00
Planer, #2½, dbl-belted, Improved, 20" 2,015.00
Ripsaw, #2, iron fr, 16" 585.00
Shaper, #3, variety, dbl spindle, heavy 1,300.00
Table saw, #1, variety, 15" 585.00

G.N. Goodspeed Co., 1876

Planer, New & Improved, Pony, 24"	900.00
Table saw, 12"	200.00

Gallmeyer & Livingston Co., 1927

Band saw, Union, 20"	390.00
Jointer, Union, motor on arbor, 8"	370.00
Table saw, Union #7, 7"	210.00

Goodell & Waters Co., 1898

Band saw, Post, #4, 30"	390.00
Moulder, Gleen patent, elastic feed	675.00
Planer & jointer, heavy, #19, 28"	7,800.00
Planer & matcher, #28, 14"	5,330.00
Planer, dbl, extra heavy duty, #27, 30"	9,750.00
Planer, panel, 18"	450.00
Slab & re-saw, Universal, power feed, 32"	1,450.00
Surfacer, dbl, endless bed, 30"	3,900.00
Surfacer, dbl, heavy, #3, 28"	4,680.00
Surfacer, single, endless bed, 24"	1,690.00
Surfacer, single, endless bed, 26"	2,600.00
Tablesaw, adjustable top, sm	295.00

Hoyt & Brother Co., 1888

Sand-papering machine, The Boss, #5, 24"	1,600.00
Wood shaper, dbl spindle	850.00

J.A. Fay & Egan Co., 1900

Jointer, New #4, extra heavy, 16"	1,625.00
Mortiser, #2, hollow chisel, automatic horizontal	1,500.00
Ripsaw, #2, Improved Standard	1,175.00
Band saw, 16"	210.00
Jointer, 4"	15.00

L. Power & Co., 1888

Mortiser & borer, #2	780.00
Shaper, single spindle, reversible	585.00
Table saw, self-feed, 14"	715.00

Worcester Porcelain Company

The Worcester Porcelain Company was deeded in 1751. During the first or Dr. Wall period (so called for one of its proprietors), porcelain with an Asian influence was decorated in underglaze blue. Useful tablewares represented the largest portion of production, but figurines and decorative items were also made. Very little of the earliest wares were marked and can only be identified by a study of forms, glazes, and the porcelain body, which tends to transmit a greenish cast when held to light. Late in the fifties, a crescent mark was in general use, and rare examples bear a facsimile of the Meissen crossed swords. The first period ended in 1783, and the company went through several changes in ownership during the next 80 years. The years from 1783 to 1792 are referred to as the Flight period. Marks were a small crescent, a crown with 'Royal,' or an impressed 'Flight.' From 1792 to 1807 the company was known as Flight and Barr and used the trademark 'F&B' or 'B,' with or without a small cross. From 1807 to 1813 the company was under the Barr, Flight, and Barr management; this era is recognized as having produced porcelain

with the highest quality of artistic decoration. Their mark was 'B.F.B.' From 1813 to 1840 many marks were used, but the most usual was 'F.B.B.' under a crown to indicate Flight, Barr, and Barr. In 1840 the firm merged with Chamberlain, and in 1852 they were succeeded by Kerr and Binns. The firm became known as Royal Worcester in 1862. The production was then marked with a circle with '51' within and a crown on top. The date of manufacture was incised into the bottom or stamped with a letter of the alphabet, just under the circle. In 1891 Royal Worcester England was added to the circle and crown. From that point on, each piece is dated with a code of dots or other symbols. After 1891 most wares had a blush-color ground. Prior to that date it was ivory. Most shapes were marked with a unique number.

During the early years they produced considerable ornamental wares with a Persian influence. This gave way to a Japanesque influence. James Hadley is most responsible for the Victorian look. He is considered the 'best ever' designer and modeller. He was joined by the finest porcelain painters. Together they produced pieces with very fine detail and exquisite painting and decoration. Figures, vases, and tableware were produced in great volume and are highly collectible. During the 1890s they allowed the artists to sign some of their work. Pieces signed on the face by the Stintons, Baldwyn, Davis, Raby, Powell, Sedgley, and Rushton (not a complete list) are in great demand. The company is still in production. There is an outstanding museum on the company grounds in Worcester, England.

Note: Most pieces had lids or tops (if there is a flat area on the top lip, chances are it had one), if missing deduct 30% to 40%.

Bowl, bl chinoiserie scenes, trellis rim border, late 18th C, 3x8"	295.00
Bowl, pheasant & floral panels, 3 ftd w/lion masks, 1870, 5x4"	225.00
Bowl, wooded landscape, bl on wht, Dr Wall period, ca 1775, 6"	1,000.00
Candelabra, Greenaway boy & girl, 3-lt tree trunk, 1888, 19", pr	2,400.00
Creamer, rtcl lattice/floral band, bamboo hdl, G Owen, 19th C, 4¼"	3,250.00
Ewer, birds, wht on bl w/gold, ftd, Baldwin, 1906, 7"	7,750.00
Ewer, floral on wht, gold coiled salamander hdl, TR, 11"	575.00
Figurine, Baltimore Oriole (male/female), Doughty, 11", 11½", pr	2,750.00
Figurine, bluebirds & apple blossoms, Doughty, 10", 9", NM, pr	2,400.00
Figurine, Bobwhite Quail Cock, Dorothy Doughty, ca 1940, 6"	3,890.00
Figurine, Eastern water carrier w/jars, Hadley, ca 1891, 17", 18", pr	885.00
Figurine, gnatcatchers & dogwood, Doughty, 11¾", 10¼", pr	2,500.00
Figurine, In the Ring, circus rider, Linder, #3180, 1936, 14½"	2,150.00
Figurine, Indigo Bunting cock, Doughty, 8¾"	3,800.00
Figurine, lady dancing w/castanets in ea hand, 19th C, 13"	300.00
Figurine, Magnolia Warblers/flowers, Doughty, 15½", pr	6,000.00
Figurine, maid draped in bl, urn on head, holds jug, 1894, 20", pr	725.00
Figurine, Nautilus shell w/lizard on coral, ca 1880, 8⅞"	600.00
Figurine, Parula Warblers, Doughty, 9", 9½", pr	2,650.00

Figurine, The Picnic, 6x8", $720.00. (Photo courtesy DuMouchelles on LiveAuctioneers.com)

Figurine, Ruby-Throated Hummingbird & fuchsia, Doughty, 10", pr	2,350.00
Figurine, Skye terrier, gray/brn, jeweled eyes, 1874, 15x19"	6,600.00
Group, classical lady w/jug & basin, eagle at base, 1870s, 29"	6,000.00
Jar, potpourri, Baldwyn Bl, flying geese, covered, sgn, ca 1890, 9½x8"	6,500.00
Jar, potpourri, floral w/gold, #1515, 1891, 10¾"	440.00
Plate, Blarney Castle Near Cork, cobalt & gold rim, ca 1820, 9"	2,150.00

Potpourri vase, fruit on woodland bank, Aryton, w/lid, pre-1956, 14".. 3,150.00
Sconce, ¾-figure of lady holding vase w/3 flower-form shades, 1895 ..3,600.00
Sugar bowl, rtcl lattice w/gold, G Owen, w/lid, 19th C, 4⅝".....3,150.00
Teapot, Oriental floral on turq, sq w/dragon hdl, sm chip 6,000.00
Teapot, rtcl lattice design, bambo spout/hdl, G Owens, 19th C, 5x7" .. 3,600.00
Urn, bouquets, grapevine hdls, artichoke finial, 1816-40, 12x14", EX . 5,000.00

Vase, Baldwyn Blue, flying geese, signed, circa 1890, 14x5", $3,100.00. (Photo courtesy Joanne Koehn)

Vase, castle ruins scene, uptrn hdls, emb masks/swags/etc, 1891, 18".3,000.00
Vase, cottage landscape, CHC Baldwyn, #2336, 12" 3,600.00
Vase, fruit on woodland ground, Freeman, w/lid, #1691, 1950s, 14" ..2,750.00
Vase, lighthouse scenic, dolphin hdls, slim neck, 1890, 18" 2,900.00
Vase, pheasant scene, gold hdls, Stinton, 16", NM....................2,750.00
Vase, sheep scene, H Davis, cylindrical, 1935, 7½" 4,750.00

World's Fairs and Expos

Since 1851 and the Crystal Palace Exhibition in London, world's fairs and expositions have taken place at a steady pace. Many of them commemorate historical events. The 1904 Louisiana Purchase Exposition, commonly known as the St. Louis World's Fair, celebrated the 100th anniversary of the Louisiana Purchase agreement between Thomas Jefferson and Napoleon in 1803. The 1893 Columbian Exposition commemorated the 400th anniversary of the discovery of America by Columbus in 1492. (Both of these fairs were held one year later than originally scheduled.) The multitude of souvenirs from these and similar events have become a growing area of interest to collectors in recent years. Many items have a 'crossover' interest into other fields: i.e., collectors of postcards and souvenir spoons eagerly search for those from various fairs and expositions. Values have fallen somewhat due to eBay sales. Many of the so-called common items have come down in value. However 1939 World's Fair items are still hot. Unless noted otherwise, values are for items in at least near-mint, original condition. For additional information collectors may contact World's Fairs Collectors Society (WFCS), whose address is in the Directory under Clubs, Newsletters, and Websites, or our advisor, Herbert Rolfes. His address is listed in the Directory under Florida.

Key: T&P — Trylon & Perisphere   WF — World's Fair

1876 Centennial, Philadelphia

Bandana, printed cotton depicting Main Building centered between the Art Gallery and the Horticultural Gallery, also shown: Washington, Grant, and both sides of the Centennial coin, 23x25", $660.00. (Photo courtesy Bloomsbury Auctions on LiveAuctioneers.com)

Bank, Liberty Bell chimes, Enterprise Mfg Co, NM 6,600.00
Book, History of the Centennial Exhibition, JD McCabe, 1876, 874 pgs....260.00
Bowl, folding, wood, 8 'leaves' w/photos on ftd base, open: 8" dia, EX...55.00
Plate, printing, steel, used to eng Centennial..., #502...New York, 4". 1,000.00
Platter, glass, Liberty Bell etched in center, scalloped rim, 13" L ... 50.00
Purse, coin, leather w/metal fr, Independence Hall-1776, 2½"....... 35.00
Trade card, Brownell & Ashley & Carriage Mfg/Memorial Hall, 3x5"..10.00

1893 Columbian, Chicago

Book, History of the World's...Inception, HW Kelley, 1893, 610 pgs, VG ...75.00
Book, WF Photographed, J Shepp & D Shepp, 1893, 528 pgs 50.00
Book, WF Through a Camera, F Todd, 2nd ed, 78 pgs, 5x7", VG.. 35.00
Flask, potato form, Mt WA, 5" 160.00
Medal, brass, Missouri on top bar, Souvenir World's...1893, 1½" ... 26.00
Photo, Ferris wheel, facts printed on bk, 6½x4¼" 50.00
Plaque, bsk, Liberal Arts Building transfer on moon, w/angel, 5".. 100.00
Plate, Administration Building transfer, wht w/bl trim, 7" sq.........25.00
Postcard, Offical Souvenir Postal, World's Columbian Expo, NM . 18.00
Song booklet, Ferris Wheel March, Chas M Stieff, 12 songs..........43.00
Spoon, sterling, Mfg Pavillion emb in bowl, Leonard Mfg, 6" 11.00
Spoon, sterling, WF Souvenir/Algeria emb in bowl, 4" 10.00
Ticket, admission, Abe Lincoln portrait, Am Bank Note Co, M ... 44.00

Ticket, Chocolate Menier, second series, from one of several chocolate and candy vendors displaying their products at the fair, $390.00. (Photo courtesy Heritage Auctions on LiveAuctioneers.com)

Ticket, grounds admission, stamped sgn WT Baker, unused, EX.... 45.00
Trivet, ceramic, 1893 World's Fair, Art Building, wht w/gold, 7" 8.00
Watch fob, brass Columbus medallion w/eagle on bk, 3 emb panels.. 36.00

1904 St. Louis

Booklet, 1904 St Louis WF Ceylon Hand Book, 183 pgs, 9x6" 85.00
Box, jewelry, Cascade Gardens 1904 St Louis, w/mirror, gold trim & ft ... 90.00
Cup, 1904 Louisiana Purchase Expostion Cup, mc, 3x2¼", VG 20.00
Magazine, The Criterion, St Louis Exposition Number, Oct 1903, VG. 25.00
Paperweight, glass, Festival Hall on front, souvenir write-up on bk .57.00
Plate, General Grant's Log Cabin..., CF Blanke, wht, 9", VG........ 25.00
Playing cards, mc eagle design on bk, 52+joker, EXIB.................... 50.00
Postcard, Mfg's Building, Frisco System 28.00
Shakers, mg, Electricity & Government Building transfers, pr 25.00
Spoon, sterling, Palace of Transportation emb in bowl, detailed, 5"... 55.00
Token, brass, Missouri, Emp State of Louisiana Purchase............... 48.00

1933 Chicago

Bank, cvd wood, bbl, Century of Progress Chicago 1933 .... 25.00
Bracelet, cuff, brass, imp images/A Century in Progress/1933 .... 52.00
Cane, walking, oak, Century News & building images on brass tag, 34" L...45.00
Flag, 48-star, ...Chicago WF & images on box, Marshall Field................. 57.00
License plate attachment, emb alum, National Alum Co Racine Wis., 5x4¼" .100.00
Lighter, emb metal label on gr Bakelite, Match King, 1¾x1" 28.00
Medal, Research & Industry, bronze w/male in relief, 3", MIB +brochure....75.00

Mug, Travel Building Century of Progress..., red on wht, 4½"........ 40.00
Paperweight, glass, Sky Ride Chicago World's Fair, 2½x3¾".......... 38.00
Parasol, bamboo & paper, MIJ on metal cap, 30", VG................. 420.00

Poster, artist: Petty, under glass, 42x29", EX, $510.00. (Photo courtesy JMW Auction Service on LiveAuctioneers.com)

Stein, brn, World's...in Progress, nude forms hdl, brn, Haeger, 6½" .35.00
Stereoscope & photographs, Chicago..., Keystone Third Dimension, MIB ..50.00
Talking letter, record w/personal message, RCA Victor, in sleeve.. 35.00
Token, brass, Good Luck/WF on front, 1933...Chicago on bk................ 15.00
Toy, Greyhound Bus, Century of... on top, pnt metal, Arcade, 10" L, VG ..58.00

1939 New York

Bank, Trylon and Perisphere, with thermometer, Chein, VG, $180.00. (Photo courtesy Henry Peirce Auctioneers on LiveAuctioneers.com)

Badge, NY WF Police, enamel center in metal shield shape, 3" 300.00
Bingo game, The NY WF, Whitman Co, MIB............................ 33.00
Book, comic NY WF Comics, V Sullivan, DC Comics 280.00
Book, Official Guide, 3rd ed, w/fold-out map, paperbk................... 25.00
Book, Official Guide, orange & bl cover, hardbk, 200 pgs, 7x10" .. 25.00
Brochure, General Electric Television Exhibit, 6x4½" 10.00
Card, identification, Radio, red letters on pk paper, unused........... 50.00
Compact, 1939 NY WF on Lucite lid w/mirror, gold-tone, sq 65.00
Lighter, glass, T&P shape, emb 1939 WF 100.00
Paperweight, metal, elephant figural, trunk up, symbols on side 40.00
Pennant, NY WF 1939, wht letters on purple, gold symbol, 11" 30.00
Pin, USSR The NY WF, red enamel on gold-tone, 1½x1" 45.00
Pin-back, Lithuanian Day Sept 10th, bl on orange, 1" dia 60.00
Plate, NY WF 1930, bright bl images on wht, Adams, 10½" 40.00
Plate, NY World's..., Cronin China, mc on wht, geometric red rim, 10".. 40.00
Poster, NY WF, World of Tomorrow, 1939, 10½x7", M 500.00
Sculpture, T&P, amber Bakelite, 17x13x6", ... 800.00
Shakers, metal, T&P on emb tray, Wm Rogers Mfg, 3½" 38.00
Ticket, preview, admission to Administration Building, May 8, 1938....48.00
Toy, CI, greyhound bus, Visit the WF..., bl & wht, 9" L 400.00

1939 San Francisco

Coasters, plastic, Firestone, red/bl/yel/gr, set of 4, 3", MIB............. 32.00
Map, Official Pictorial, Tony Sarg, mc, closed: 11¼" sq................. 35.00

1962 Seattle

Ashtray, Space Needle, pnt metal, 25"... 200.00

Bolo tie, leather & copper, emb Seattle... & Space Needle image, 18" L... 25.00
Pen, Space Needle, stands in wood holder, 12", MIB 30.00
Pin-back, Seattle's WF 1962 w/Space Needle, mc enamel on metal 32.00
Pin-back, Seattle WF...Coliseum 21, mc enamel on metal, Germany 40.00
Plate, Seattle... on wht center, wide pk rim, Frederick & Nelson, 11" .26.00
Tumblers, Mobil Dealers Century, mc print, set of 8, MIB 90.00

1964 New York

Camera, Kodak WF Flash, built-in flash w/AG-1 bulb, w/strap................. 44.00
Figurine, ceramic, Pieta, Vatican Pavilion Pieta NY...on base, 6" .. 35.00
License plate, logo in center, orange/wht/bl................................. 60.00
License plate, yel on blk, 6x12", NM 86.00
Matchbook, WF Marina, HMS Bounty, mc, unused, 12" L 25.00

Pillow, illustrating several pavillions, 16x16", $50.00. (Photo courtesy Philip Weiss Auctions on LiveAuctioneers.com)

Plaque, brass, Statue of Liberty & Emp State Building, 7" dia........ 40.00
Poster, New York WF 1964-65, mc, 42x28" 100.00
Trading cards, Official Souvenir...Attractions, set of 24, MIB........ 15.00

Frank Lloyd Wright

Born in Richland Center, Wisconsin, in 1869, Wright became a pioneer in architectural expression, developing a style referred to as 'prairie.' From early in the century until he died in 1959, he designed houses with rooms that were open, rather than divided by walls in the traditional manner. They exhibited low, horizontal lines and strongly projecting eaves, and he filled them with furnishings whose radical aesthetics complemented the structures. Several of his homes have been preserved to the present day, and collectors who admire his ideas and the unique, striking look he achieved treasure the stained glass windows, furniture, chinaware, lamps, and other decorative accessories designed by Wright. His Taliesin line of furniture was made for a few years in the late 1950s; it was produced by Heritage Henredon (HH), and most pieces were edged with a Green Key design. Our advisor for this category and related Arts and Crafts subjects is Bruce A. Austin; he is listed in the Directory under New York.

Armchair, hexagonal bk/seat, alum fr w/red leather, 1956, 34"... 14,400.00
Armchair, HH, loose cushions, reuphl, 27x32x34".....................2,750.00
Armchair, HH, wood fr w/silk uphl bk & seat, 32x18", pr.........1,450.00
Armchair, wide slat bk, slat support ea side, sq form, uphl seat, 32" ...780.00
Book, In Nature of Materials, sgn 1st ed, 1942, 143 pgs, NM ...1,000.00
Book, sample, Collection of Wall Coverings..., Schumacher, 18x14"...275.00
Book, When Democracy Builds, sgn 1st ed, 132-pg, EX.............1,200.00
Bronze, Nakoma, sgn FLW/FLW Foundation, 1975, 12".............2,150.00
Bronze, Nakomis, sgn FLW/FLW Foundation, c 1975, 18" 3,150.00
Cabinet, HH, sq top, open shelf, 2-drw, 26x20x20" 1,600.00
Chair, for Price Tower, Bartlesville OK, 1952-56, 33", VG 14,400.00
Chair, side, HH, reuphl bk/seat, wood fr, 32½x20", 6 for...........3,450.00
Chair, uphl bk/seat, oak trim, w/Niedecken for Irving House, 38", VG .3,200.00
Chair, wide plank extends from above bk rail to stretcher, armless .37,500.00
Chairs, side, HH, reuphl seat/bk, 32½", 6 for................................ 800.00
Check, FLW Foundation, lg-scale signature, dtd 1954 ....1,400.00
Chest, HH, 2 doors over 3 drws, 52½x36½x20"..........................1,550.00

Coffee table, HH, hexagonal, 17x48x41½", +6 triangle stools ..9,000.00
Coffee table, HH, rect w/drop sides, 14x60x19½" 4,500.00
Coin, 1982 Am Arts Commemorative, portrait, ½-oz gold 275.00
Fabric, silk & rayon, Schumacher, design #104, 1954, 51x37" ...1,600.00
Footstool, drop-in uphl deck, side slats, recent, 18x16x16" 180.00
Headboard, HH, full sz, 39x54" 425.00
Lamp, cherry Taliesin II, sqs & boxes on post at varied angles, 30"..1,140.00
Lamp, cherry: Yamagawa c Frank Lloyd Wright Foundation, 1984, 30", VG.1,000.00
Photo, VC Morris Gift Shop (Wright design), blk/wht, Shulman, 8x10".385.00
Pitcher, water, silver, 4-sided cone w/long triangle spout, Tiffany ...5,400.00
Rug, geometric orange/bl/gr/olive wool, from Biltmore, 1960s, 111x54"..800.00

Sconce, copper fitter on wood base with pivoting center panel and two leaded glass panels each side, from the Hotel Geneva, Lake Geneva, Illinois, circa 1911, 7x6x9½", $4,200.00. (Photo courtesy Treadway Gallery on LiveAuctioneers.com)

Shelf, HH, designed for top of 2000 series sideboard, 18x86" 240.00
Sideboard, HH, 10-drw, recessed hdls, 33x65½x20½" 2,100.00
Sideboard, HH, bank of drws on right, drw over 2 doors on left, 66" L...1,100.00
Sleeper sofa, cantilevered arms, uphl seat & bk, 88" 2,500.00
Stool, vanity, uphl swivel top, cruciform base, HH, 18x18" dia...1,000.00
Table, cypress (rfn top), 2-tiered, ca 1950, 23½x55x39½" 5,500.00
Table, dining, HH, mahog w/X-base, #2000, 29x48" dia+3 leaves.1,450.00
Table, dining, HH, metal banding, +3 leaves/6 slipper chairs ...2,650.00
Table, HH, rect top, dbl-V base, 29x64x42" w/2 16" leaves 3,950.00
Table, HH, slate top, cruciform base, 16x36" dia......................2,750.00
Table, HH, triangular w/Greek Key edge, 15x22x19" 750.00

Wrought Iron

Until the middle of the nineteenth century, almost all the metal hand forged in America was made from a material called wrought iron. When wrought iron rusts it appears grainy, while the mild steel that was used later shows no grain but pits to an orange-peel surface. This is an important aid in determining the age of an ironwork piece. See also Fireplace Implements.

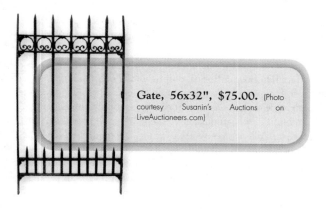

Gate, 56x32", $75.00. (Photo courtesy Susanin's Auctions on LiveAuctioneers.com)

Arbor, 3-section arch w/bird design, 92x75" 350.00
Bench, curlicues, wing-like arms, old wht pnt, cushion................150.00
Bracket, sign, griffin form, 37" L..395.00
Broiler, rotates on tripod base, 3x25" 115.00
Door hdl, tulip motif, 10x5½" 550.00
Door latch, triangular top & bottom finials w/thumb latch, 17" ..350.00

Etegere, 4 grad corner shelves, old pnt, ca 1920s, 85x46"..........2,500.00
Fork, 2-prong, sq interval in shaft w/initials, wood hdl, 28" 120.00
Game hooks, suspended from chains w/ring hanger, 12x11" dia ..200.00
Garden sculpture, parrot w/long tail, Deco style, mc pnt, 45" 575.00
Gates, vine motif, jester hdl, S Yellin (unmk), 74x30", pr 42,000.00
Hinges, barn, 12½", pr 40.00
Hinges, circular ends, 30¼x14", pr 115.00
Kettle stand, tripod w/penny ft, heart & rope-twist detail, 14", VG...110.00
Planter, rococo scrollwork, 43x21" dia, pr...................................825.00
Plate rack, holds 2, Fr Vict style, 9x24x3" 50.00
Pot stand, triangular ladder shape, 55½" 85.00
Screen, 4-panel w/decorative scrolls, old wht pnt, 78x72" 1,500.00
Thumb latch, decorative work w/brass inlay, 28" 525.00
Toaster, twisted wire & wrought iron, 22" spiral swing hdl, 16" W...100.00
Wick cutter, scissors style, 6½" 70.00
Window boxes, Art Nouveau design, gray pnt, 1900s, 12x48x12", 3 for..1,400.00
Wine rack, arched top cage construction w/doors, holds 88, Fr, 69x30".825.00

Yellow Ware

Yellow ware has been produced from the very early 1800s to around 1935. Ohio, Pennsylvania, and New Jersey were the primary production centers in the United States, but you can find yellow ware made at potteries from Minnesota down to Kentucky and up to Maine. Canada and Sweden produced a fair amount of yellow ware, but outside the U.S. England potted more yellow ware than any other country. Yellow ware is so named because of its yellow clay, which can vary in intensity. Even with the addition of stoneware, the yellow clay is still fragile, so expect damage. There are a minimum of 1,000 different documented forms of yellow ware, so it is one of the most interesting forms of pottery to collect. You can find hundreds of pieces, from the most basic bowl to mantel ornaments and everything in between. The rule about condition is to buy mass-produced pieces in excellent condition and accept the rarer, less often found pieces with damage and/or repairs. For further information we recommend *Collector's Guide to Yellow Ware, Book I*, written by John Michel and Lisa McAllister, and *Collector's Guide to Yellow Ware, Books II and III*, by our advisor, Lisa McAllister (see Directory, Maryland). See also Rockingham.

Pitcher, bold blue and brown seaweed mocha design, 8½", $2,200.00 to $2,500.00. (Photo courtesy Lisa McAllister)

Bowl, w/spout, emb, East Liverpool OH, 11" 300.00
Canister, Dandy Line, wht bands & 'BREAD,' 10"........................600.00
Canister, English, wht banner w/name, 8" 295.00
Canning jar, plain yel w/rnd shoulder, 5-8".................................250.00
Funnel, plain yel w/str, canted sides 595.00
Mold, fish, rect, 4x6½" 525.00
Mold, wheat, grapes or corn, rect 95.00
Mug, wht/brn/bl bands, 3¾" 375.00
Pitcher, baluster, brn & wht bands, 5"..450.00

Zanesville Glass

Glassware was produced in Zanesville, Ohio, from as early as 1815 until 1851. Two companies produced clear and colored hollow ware pieces in five characteristic patterns: 1) diamond faceted, 2) broken swirls, 3) vertical swirls, 4) perpendicular fluting, 5) plain, with scalloped or fluted rims and strap handles. The most readily identified product is perhaps the whiskey bottles made in the vertical swirl pattern, often called globular swirls because of their full, round bodies. Their necks vary in width; some have a ringed rim and some are collared. They were made in several colors; amber, light green, and light aquamarine are the most common. Our advisor for this category is Mark Vuono; he is listed in the Directory under Connecticut.

Bottle, amber (good color), 24 tightly swirled ribs, minor blisters and pot stones, globular, 8½", $1,320.00. (Photo courtesy Garth's Auction Inc. on LiveAuctioneers.com)

Bottle, aqua w/24 slightly twisted swirls, globular, blister, 7½" 260.00
Bottle, aqua w/24 tightly swirled ribs, globular, 7½" 315.00
Bottle, aqua, 13 swirled ribs on club form, pontil, 9" 235.00
Bottle, demi-john, amber, pot stones, att, 16½" 440.00
Chestnut flask, 10-dmn, dk golden amber, 1820-40, 5½" 2,000.00
Chestnut flask, bl aqua, 24 left-swirl ribs, 4" 100.00
Creamer, golden amber, solid grooved-band hdl w/rigaree, 1820s, 4¼"...7,000.00
Flask, pocket, 10-dmn, golden amber, sheared mouth, pontil scar, 5½". 1,600.00
Pan, golden, flared sides, folded-out rim, pot stone, 2x9" 1,045.00
Pitkin flask, amber, 24 tightly swirled ribs, pot stones, 5" 460.00
Pitkin flask, lt gr, 20 slightly swirled ribs, sm blisters, 5½" 485.00
Tumbler, golden amber, 24-rib, sheared mouth, 3⅞" 5,000.00

Zanesville Stoneware Company

Still in operation at its original location in Zanesville, Ohio, this company is the last surviving pottery dating from Zanesville's golden era of pottery production. They manufactured utilitarian stoneware, art ware vases, jardinieres and pedestals, dinnerware, and large hand-turned vases for use in outdoor gardens. Much of this ware has remained unidentified until today, since they often chose to mark their wares only with item numbers or the names of their various clients. Other items were marked with an impressed circular arrangement containing the company name and location or a three-line embossed device, the bottom line of which contained the letters ZSC. For more information we recommend *Zanesville Stoneware Company* by Jon Rans, Glenn Ralston, and Nate Russell (Collector Books).

Vase, bright blue matt, #790, 17", $390.00. (Photo courtesy Cincinnati Art Galleries, LLC on LiveAuctioneers.com)

Vase, cobalt drips on speckled beige, chip, 28x18" 1,800.00
Vase, dk gr w/speckles, 2 angle hdls, squat, 3x7" 660.00
Vase, deep mauve matt, horizontal ribs, w/hdls, #521, 12" 155.00
Vase, emb vintage, 17x17" 275.00

Vase, gr matt, column, unmk, 10½x6" 100.00
Vase, Matt Gr (dk), tapered cylinder w/buttress ft, 9¼x4" 300.00
Vase, Matt Gr, emb geometrics, tapering cylinder, ftd, 9¼x4" 275.00
Vase, Matt Gr, shouldered, #102, 8" 65.00
Vase, Matt Gr speckled, baluster, 12½" 240.00
Vase, Neptune glaze dripped over bl-gray matt w/purple highlights, unmk, 19"..540.00
Vase, Neptune, mc mottle, twisted hdls, flaw, #106, 24x15" 660.00

Zark

Established circa 1907 in St. Louis, Missouri, the Ozark Pottery made artware which it sold through an outlet called Zark Shops, hence the use of the Zark trademark. Most of their output was earthenware, but high-fired pottery has been reported as well. Some of the decoration was slip painted; other pieces were embossed. It operated for only a few years, perhaps closing as early as 1910. One of its founders and the primary designer was Robert Bringhurst, who was best known as a sculptor. Pieces are marked Zark, either incised or impressed. Our advisors for this category are Suzanne Perrault and David Rago; they are listed in the Directory under New Jersey.

Bowl, Egyptian, figural handles, incised bands under matt green, 5x10", EX, $900.00. (Photo courtesy Rago Auctions)

Bowl, motif on flat shoulder, lt/med bl matt, gr int, CCB, 3x9" . 1,200.00
Bowl, stylized pattern, lt gr on bl matt, gr gloss int, 3x9" 1,325.00
Bust, maiden, dk bl/gr matt, 8½x11½", EX.................................... 660.00
Vase, 4 buttressed hdls, dragonflies, 2-tone matt bl, 4¾x7¼" 3,900.00
Vase, cvd dragonflies, 2-tone matt, incised CCB, 4¾x7" 3,900.00
Vase, mtn scene reflected on lake w/water lilies, bl/turq matt, LC, 8", EX . 2,410.00
Vase, speckled turq & bl matt, 4 buttress hdls, 6x6" 1,925.00
Vase, stylized floral, blk on gr matt, cylindrical, 10x4½"............. 2,760.00

Zell

The Georg Schmider United Zell Ceramic Factories has a long and colorful history. Affectionately called 'Zell' by those who are attracted to this charming German-Dutch type tin-glazed earthenware, this type of ware came into production in the latter part of the nineteenth century. While Zell has created some lovely majolica-like examples (which are beginning to attract their own following), it is the German-Dutch scenes that are collected with such enthusiasm. Typical scenes are set against a lush green background with windmills on the distant horizon on either a cream or ivory colored body. Into the scenes appear typically garbed girls (long dresses with long white aprons and low-land bonnet head-gear) being teased or admired by little boys attired in pantaloon-type trousers and short rust-colored jackets, all wearing wooden shoes. There are variations on this theme, and occasionally a collector may find an animal theme or even a Kate Greenaway-like scene.

A similar ware in both theme, technique, and quality, but bearing the mark Haag or Made in Austria is included in this listing. This ware is produced on a soft paste body with a tin glaze. Hence, it chips very easily.

While Zell produced a wide range of wares and even quite recently (1970s) introduced an entirely hand-painted hen/rooster line, it is this early charming German-Dutch theme pottery that is coveted by increasing numbers of devoted collectors.

In the listings that follow, items noted 'Baden' are generally the earlier Zell wares.

Key:
BlkR — Black hen/rooster design, after 1970s
hdl/RA — handle at right angle to spout
KG — Kate Greenaway style
MIA — Made in Austria

Biscuit jar, BlkR, bbl like, lid w/recessed finial, 5¼" 30.00
Bowl, berries/leaves/vines emb, majolica, 6-sided, 7¾" 55.00
Bowl, birds on branches w/grapes, majolica, Germany, 7½" 48.00
Bowl, rim soup, Dutch boy & girl in eerie woods, Baden, 7½" 95.00
Bowl, water lilies on turq, majolica, rtcl hdls, Germany, 11"......... 85.00
Butter pat, various Dutch children scenes, Baden, 3", $30 to........ 60.00
Cake plate, costumed animals party in woods, rtcl hdls, Haag, 9½" ...135.00
Cake plate, girls chat on bench, KG, rtcl/emb hdls, Haag, 10½" . 110.00
Cake plate, grapes on basketweave, majolica, ped ft, 3x9" 125.00
Cake set, Nouveau water lilies, majolica, Germany, 11", +5 plates ..90.00
Candlestick, Dutch boys strolling, flared base, Baden, 7", ea........ 165.00
Canister, BlkR, Tea, Germany, 5¾" 38.00
Canister, Dutch boys strolling, Sucre, bl & wht, Haag, 6x4x4"...... 58.00
Chamberstick, hen & rooster, finger ring, 6" dia, ea 72.00
Child's feeding dish, Dutch boy & girl, MIA, 7½x1½" 65.00
Child's feeding dish, Dutch children in forest, Baden, 1½x7½" ... 125.00
Clock, mother/child on shoreline, mk Germany #2472, 9x6"...... 350.00
Creamer, Dutch clad girl w/stick chasing geese, MIA, hdl/RA, 3". 42.00
Creamer, Dutch girl shakes hands w/dog, Haag & MIA, 4½"......... 22.00
Creamer, Dutch girls chatting, harbor scene, bl & wht, Haag, 4" .. 62.00
Creamer, Dutch girls w/wagon, hdl/RA, Haag, 3¼" 58.00
Creamer, geese chasing Dutch boy w/golden goose, w/hdl, Haag, 4".. 20.00

Creamers and sugar bowl, each $25.00 to $30.00. (Photo courtesy Auctions Neapolitan on LiveAuctioneers.com)

Cup/saucer, Dutch girls chatting, harbor scene, bl & wht, Haag.... 65.00
Cup/saucer, Dutch girls feeding cats, dk gr, MIA 20.00
Egg cup, Puss 'n Boots, att MIA/Haag, 3¾" 72.00
Mug, Dutch children strolling, harbor scene, Germany, 3½", $18 to ... 30.00
Pitcher, cat attracted to fish in basket, MIA, 6½" 145.00
Pitcher, costumed animals party in woods, deep lip, Haag, 6" 135.00
Pitcher, Dutch boys stroll on path, hills beyond, Haag, MIA, 6" .. 38.00
Plate, apples on basketweave, mc majolica, Baden, 9".................... 40.00
Plate, Cat & Fiddle w/moon, scalloped, MIA, 6½" 65.00
Plate, children at sea in 'dish,' dreamy KG, Baden, 9¾" 345.00
Plate, dandelions & leaves, 3-D, majolica, Baden, 7" 47.00
Plate, kittens w/aprons, Busy Hands Are Happy Hands, MIA, 9" . 112.00
Plate, Tom Thumb w/pie & blackbirds, scalloped, MIA, 6½" 68.00
Shakers, Dutch children strolling/dogs/harbor scene, Baden, 3½", pr ..60.00
Tankard, Dutch girl watches boatmakers, recessed base, Baden, 11½"...355.00
Teapot, Dutch children walking/harbor/masted ships, Baden, 4½" ..285.00
Tumbler, Dutch boys/harbor scene/masted ships, w/hdl, Germany, 4¼" ... 30.00

Zsolnay

This Hungarian factory began in the 1850s, originally producing kitchen ware. By the 1870s a line of decorative architectural ceramics and art pottery was initiated which has continued to the present time.

The city of Pecs (pronounced Paach) is the major provincial city of southwest Hungary close to what is now Bosnia. The old German name for the city was Funfkirchen, meaning 'five churches.' The 'five-steeple' mark became the factory's logo in 1878.

The factory went through all the art trends of major international art potteries and produced various types of forms and decorations. The 'golden period,' circa 1895 – 1920, is when its Art Nouveau (Sezession in Austro-Hungarian terms) examples were unequaled. Vilmos Zsolnay , the founder, was a Renaissance man devoted to innovation, and his children carried on the tradition after his death in 1900. Important sculptors and artists of the day were employed and married into the family, creating a dynasty. Nationalized by the Hungarian government after WWII, the factory has struggled to continue its illustrious past, without success.

Nearly all Zsolnay is marked, either impressed 'Zsolnay Pecs' or with the 'five steeple' stamp plus a form number which usually can date the production to within a couple of years. The most valuable Zsolnay on the market today are examples from the Art Nouveau era between 1899 and 1910. Earlier production pieces usually bring a fraction of the price of the Art Nouveau pieces. Size, era, condition, and the complexity of the glaze all enter into the value of Zsolnay with top examples selling in the tens of thousands of dollars. Our advisors for the category are John Gacher and Federico Santi; they are listed in the Directory under Rhode Island.

Bowl, fisherman w/net w/lady saving girl, bl lustre #7195, ca 1900, 14", EX ..4,500.00
Box, ivory ware, medieval figures, ca 1889, 3½", EX...................... 300.00
Cachepot, girls dancing around trees, bl lustre, ca 1900, 13" di, EX ...7,500.00
Cup/saucer, lotus, majolica glaze, #737, ca 1881, 3½" dia, EX...... 150.00
Dish, molded lily pad border, red & purple lustre, ca 1930, 13¼", EX. 5,500.00
Figure, rooster vase, gold, brn glaze, #7993, ca 1907, 7", EX 2,500.00
Figurine, frog, purple lustre, ca 1980s, 6", EX................................ 150.00
Fountain, lotus design, yel & brn majolica, #3528, ca 1890, 33", EX.. 4,000.00
Garden seat, lotus, pk, gr majolica glaze, #3698, ca 1882, 18", EX . 3,500.00
Garden seat, mushroom, natural colors, majolica, #870, ca 1882, 18", EX..4,500.00
Jardiniere, 4 lg leaves ending as buttresses, 1899-1900, 6½x8"..6,000.00
Jug, folkloric style, heavy gold brocade w/enameled flowers, ca 1885, 13", EX ..500.00
Jug, folkloric style, shriveled yel glaze, #1014, ca 1882, 8½", EX.. 275.00
Jug, wine, Kulacs, harvest scene, #705, 1882, 12" dia, EX 2,500.00
Lamp, satyr on rock, red, gr lustre, #6236, ca 1900, 10", EX....17,500.00
Pitcher, hand formed w/hdl, gr/gold lustre, ca 1900, 9¾", EX....... 700.00
Pitcher, stylized pelican shaped, gr gold lustre, ca 1900, 9½", EX ..1,300.00
Puzzle jug, yel shriveled glaze, #547, ca 1875, 9", EX................... 650.00
Tile, gold elephant ears, metallic glaze, ca 1900, 6" sq, EX......... 2,500.00
Tile, reindeer, gold/bl lustre, ca 1900, 3" sq, EX......................... 1,500.00
Urn, gr marbleized gold, serpent hdls, dimpled, ca 1930, 12¾x9½"....960.00
Vase, Allegory of the Flood, multiple figures, gr lustre, ca 1900, 25", EX ..9,000.00
Vase, classical landscape, mc lustre, #5262, line crack, ca 1900, 12" ..4,000.00
Vase, cornucopia form, cream w/enameled flowers, ca 1885, 8¾", EX ..100.00
Vase, crocuses on swirled ground, cylindrical faience, ca 1886, sgn, 13½x5½".3,600.00
Vase, geraniums & gold leaves, prof rstr, 1899-1900, 9½x5¾"...7,200.00

Vase, geraniums, blue and red lustre, #6466, circa 1900, 9", EX, $15,000.00. (Photo courtesy John Gacher and Federico Santi)

Vase, lidded, 2-hdld, rtcl, cream w/enameled leaves, ca 1885, 20", EX...450.00
Vase, mini, shoulder shape, matt lustre flowers, #5203, ca 1900, 3", EX..1,500.00
Vase, organic, hand formed gr & red lustre, ca 1900, 9½", EX ..8,000.00

Advisory Board

The editor and staff take this opportunity to express our sincere gratitude and appreciation to each person who has in any way contributed to the preparation of this guide. We believe the credibility of our book is greatly enhanced through their efforts. See each advisor's Directory listing for information concerning their specific areas of expertise.

You will notice that at the conclusion of some of the narratives the advisor's name is given. This is optional and up to the discretion of each individual. Simply because no name is mentioned does not indicate that we have no advisor for that subject. Our board grows with each issue and now numbers over 300; if you care to correspond with any of them or anyone listed in our Directory, you must send a SASE with your letter. If you are seeking an appraisal, first ask about their fee, since many of these people are professionals who must naturally charge for their services. Because of our huge circulation, every person who allows us to publish their name runs the risk of their privacy being invaded by too many phone calls and letters. We are indebted to every advisor and very much regret losing any of them. By far, the majority of those we lose give that reason. Please help us retain them on our board by observing the simple rules of common courtesy. Take the differences in time zones into consideration; some of our advisors tell us they often get phone calls in the middle of the night.

Barbara J. Aaronson
Northridge, California

Charles and Barbara Adams
South Yarmouth, Massachusetts

Ronna Lee Aikins and Katie Joe Monsour
Blairsville, Pennsylvania

Ed and Sheri Alcorn
Shady Hills, Florida

Stan & Sally Alekna
Lebanon, Pennsylvania

Beverly Ales
Pleasanton, California

Charles Alexander
Indianapolis, Indiana

Cheryl Anderson
Cedar City, Utah

James Anderson
New Brighton, Minnesota

Suzy McLennan Anderson
Walterboro, South Carolina

Tim Anderson
Provo, Utah

Florence Archambault
The Occupied Japan Club
Newport, Rhode Island

Bruce A. Austin
Pittsford, New York

Bobby Babcock
Pueblo West, Colorado

Rod Baer and Randall Monsen
Vienna, Virginia

Wayne and Gale Bailey
Dacula, Georgia

Jacqueline Linscott Barnes
Titusville, Florida

Kit Barry
Brattleboro, Vermont

Dale & Diane Barta
Lincoln, Kansas

Dana Martin Batory
Crestline, Ohio

Carter Bays
Columbia, South Carolina

Peter Bealo
Plaistow, New Hampshire

C. Jeanenne Bell
Pinson, Alabama

Scott Benjamin
LaGrange, Ohio

Robert Bettinger
Mt. Dora, Florida

William M. Bilsland III
Cedar Rapids, Iowa

Brenda Blake
York Harbor, Maine

Robert and Stan Block
Trumbull, Connecticut

Sandra V. Bondhus
Farmington, Connecticut

Phyllis Bess Boone
Tulsa, Oklahoma

Clifford Boram
Monticello, Indiana

Michael and Valarie Bozarth
Williamsville, New York

Jeff Bradfield
Harrisonburg, Virginia

Shane A. Branchcomb
Lovettsville, Virginia

Harold Brandenburg
Wichita, Kansas

Jim Broom
Effingham, Illinois

Dr. Kirby William Brown
Paradise, California

Marcia 'Sparkles' Brown
White City, Oregon

Rick Brown
Newspaper Collector's Society of America
Lansing, Michigan

John Buchner
Winterhaven, Florida

Donald A. Bull
Wirtz, Virginia

Mike Carwile
Lynchburg, Virginia

Gene Cataldo
Huntsville, Alabama

Cerebro
East Prospect, Pennsylvania

Jack Chipman
Venice, California

Victor J.W. Christie, Ed. D.
Ephrata, Pennsylvania

Lanette Clarke
Antioch, California

Kevin Cobabe
Redondo Beach, California

Debbie and Randy Coe
Hillsboro, Oregon

Steve Conti
Los Angeles, California

Ryan Cooper
Yarmouthport, Massachusetts

Auction Houses

We wish to thank the following auction houses whose catalogs and websites have been used as sources for pricing information. Many have granted us permission to reproduce their photographs as well.

A-1 Auction Service
2042 N. Rio Grande Ave., Suite E, Orlando, FL 32804; 407-839-0004. Specializing in American antique sales.
a-1auction@cfl.rr.com
www.a-1auction.net

A&B Auctions Inc.
17 Sherman St., Marlboro, MA 01752-3314; 508-480-0006 or fax 508-480-0007. Specializing in English ceramics, flow blue, pottery and Mason's Ironstone. www.aandbauctions.com

Absolute Auctions & Realty Inc.
Robert Doyle
PO Box 1739, Pleasant Valley, NY 12569. Antique and estate auctions twice a month at Absolute Auction Center; Free calendar of auctions; Specializing in specialty collections.
info@absoluteauctionrealty.com
www.absoluteauctionrealty.com

Allard Auctions Inc.
Col. Doug Allard
PO Box 1030, 419 Flathead St., Ste. 4, St. Ignatius, MT 59865; 888-314-0343 or fax 406-745-0502. Specializing in American Indian collectibles.
info@allardauctions.com
www.allardauctions.com

America West Archives
Anderson, Cheryl
PO Box 100, Cedar City, UT 84721; 435-586-9497. Has online illustrated catalog that includes auction section of scarce and historical early western documents, letters, autographs, stock certificates, and other important ephemera.
awa@netutah.com
www.americawestarchives.com

American Bottle Auctions
2523 J St., Ste. 203, Sacramento, CA 95816; 800-806-7722. Specializing in antique bottles.
info@americanbottle.com
www.americanbottle.com

Americana Auctions
c/o Glen Rairigh
12633 Sandborn, Sunfield, MI 48890. Specializing in Skookum dolls, art glass and art auctions.

Anderson Auctions/Heritage Antiques
& Appraisal Services
Suzy McLennan Anderson
Bachelor Hill Antiques and Appraisals
246 E Washington St., Walterboro, SC 29488. Specializing in American furniture and decorative accessories. andersonauctions@aol.com

Andre Ammelounx
The Stein Auction Company
PO Box 136, Palatine, IL 60078-0136; 847-991-5927 or fax 847-991-5947. Specializing in steins, catalogs available.
www.tsaco.com

Bertoia Auctions
2141 DeMarco Dr., Vineland, NJ 08360; 856-692-1881 or fax 856-692-8697. Specializing in toys, dolls, advertising, and related items.
www.bertoiaauctions.com

Bider's
397 Methuen St., Lawrence, MA 01843; 978-688-0923 or 978-475-8336. Antiques appraised, purchased, and sold on consignment.
bider@netway.com

Bonhams & Butterfields
220 San Bruno Ave., San Francisco, CA 94103; 415-861-7500 or fax 415-861-8951. Also located at: 7601 Sunset Blvd., Los Angeles, CA 90046; 323-850-7500 or fax 323-850-5843. Fine art auctioneers and appraisers since 1865.
info.us@bonhams.com
www.butterfields.com

Buffalo Bay Auction Co.
825 Fox Run Trail, Edmond, OK 73034; 405-285-8990. Specializing in advertising, tins, and country store items.
admin@buffalobayauction.com
buffalobayauction@hotmail.com
buffalobayauction.com

Cerebro
PO Box 327, E. Prospect, PA 17317; 717-252-2400 or 800-69-LABEL. Specializing in antique advertising labels, especially cigar box labels, cigar bands, food labels, firecracker labels; Holds semiannual auction on tobacco ephemera; Consignments accepted.
cerebro@cerebro.com
www.cerebro.com

Cincinnati Art Galleries
225 E. Sixth, Cincinnati, OH 45202; 513-381-2128; fax: 513-381-7527. Specializing in American art pottery, American and European fine paintings, watercolors.
www.cincinnatiartgalleries.com

Cowan's Auctions Inc.
6270 Este Ave.
Cincinnati, OH 45232
www.cowanauctions.com

Craftsman Auctions
Jerry Cohen

109 Main St., Putnam, CT 06260; 800-448-7828 or fax 860-928-1966.
Specializing in Arts & Crafts furniture and accessories as well as American art pottery. Color catalogs available.
jerry@craftsman-auctions.com
www.artsncrafts.com or
www.ragoarts.com

Dargate Auction Galleries
214 N. Lexington, Pittsburgh, PA 15208; 412-362-3558. Specializing in estate auctions featuring fine art, antiques, and collectibles.
info@dargate.com
www.dargate.com

David Rago Auctions
333 N. Main, Lambertville, NJ 08530; 609-397-9374 or fax 609-397-9377. Specializing in American art pottery and Arts and Crafts.
info@ragoarts.com
www.ragoarts.com

Decoys Unlimited Inc.
West Barnstable, MA; 508-362-2766. Buy, sell, broker, appraise.
info@decoysunlimitedinc.net
www.decoysunlimitedinc.net

DuMouchelles
409 E Jefferson Ave., Detroit, MI 48226; 313-963-6255 or fax 313-963-8199.
info@dumouchelle.com
www.dumouchelle.com

Dunbar's Gallery
Leila and Howard Dunbar
54 Haven St., Milford, MA 01757; 508-634-8697 or fax 508-634-8697.
dunbargallery@comcast.net
www.dunbarsgallery.com

Early American History Auctions
PO Box 3507, Rancho Santa Fe, CA 92067; 858-759-3290 or fax 858-759-1439.
auctions@earlyamerican.com
www.earlyamerican.com

Early Auction Company
123 Main St., Milford, OH 45150-1121; 513-831-4833 or fax 513-831-1441. Specializing in art glass including Tiffany, Daum, Galle, and Steuben.
www.earlyauctionco.com

Flying Deuce Auctions & Antiques
14051 W. Chubbuck Rd., Chubbuck, ID 83202; 208-237-2002 or fax 208-237-4544. Specializing in vintage denim. flying2@ida.net
www.flying2.com

Fontaine's Auction Gallery
1485 W. Housatonic St., Pittsfield, MA 01201; 413-448-8922. Specializing in fine quality antiques; important twentieth-century lighting, clocks, art glass. Color catalogs available.
info@fontaineauction.com
www.fontaineauction.com

Frank's Antiques and Auctions
551625 U.S. Hwy 1, Hilliard, FL 32046; 904-845-2870 or fax 904-845-4000. Specializing in antique advertising, country store items, rec room and restaurant decor; sporting goods; and nostalgia items.
franksauct@aol.com
franksauctions.com

Garth's Auction Inc.
2690 Stratford Rd., Box 369, Delaware, OH 43015; 740-362-4771.
info@garths.com
www.garths.com

Glass-Works Auctions
P.O. Box 180, East Greenville, PA 18041; 215-679-5849 or fax 215-679-3068.
America's leading auction company in early American bottles and glass and barber shop memorabilia. glswrk@enter.net
www.glswrk-auction.com

Green Valley Auctions Inc.
2259 Green Valley Lane, Mt. Crawford, VA 22841; 540-434-4260 or fax 540-434-4532.
A leader in the field of Southern decorative and folk art, also pottery, furniture, carpets, fine art and sculpture, silver, jewelry, antique glass and ceramics, textiles, Civil War and militaria, toys and dolls, books, ephemera, advertising, Black Americana, toy trains, railroad material and much more.
info@greenvalleyauctions.com
www.greenvalleyauctions.com

Henry-Peirce Auctions
Double Tree Hotel
75 West Algonquin Rd., Arlington Heights, IL 60005; 847-364-7600.
Specializing in bank auctions.
hpacutions@comcast.net
www.henrypeirceauctions.com

Heritage Auction Galleries
www.autographs.com

High Noon
9929 Venice Blvd., Los Angeles, CA 90034-5111; 310-202-9010 or fax 310-202-9011. Specializing in cowboy and western collectibles.
info@highnoon.com
www.highnoon.com

Horst Auctioneers
Horst Auction Center
50 Durlach Rd., Ephrata, PA 17522; 717-738-3080. Voices of Experience.

sale@horstauction.com
www.horstauction.com

Jackson's International Auctioneers & Appraisers of Fine Art & Antiques
2229 Lincoln St., Cedar Falls, IA 50613; 319-277-2256 or fax 319-277-1252. Specializing in American and European art pottery and art glass, American and European paintings, Russian works of art, decorative arts, toys and jewelry.
www.jacksonsauction.com

James D. Julia, Inc.
PO Box 830, Fairfield, ME 04937-0830; 207-453-7125 or fax 207-453-2502.
jjulia@juliaauctions.com
www.juliaauctions.com

John Toomey Gallery
818 North Blvd., Oak Park, IL 60301; 708-383-5234 or fax 708-383-4828. Specializing in furniture and decorative arts of the Arts & Crafts, Art Deco, and Modern Design movements; Modern Design Expert: Richard Wright.
info@johntoomeygallery.com
www.treadwaygallery.com

Joy Luke Fine Art Brokers & Auctioneers
Bloomington Auction Gallery
300 East Grove St., Bloomington, IL 61701; 309-828-5533 or fax 309-829-2266.
robert@joyluke.com
www.joyluke.com

Kit Barry Ephemera Auctions
74 Cotton Mill Hill #A252, Brattleboro, VT 05301; 802-254-3634. Tradecard and ephemera auctions, fully illustrated catalogs with prices realized; Consignment inquiries welcome.
kbarry@surfglobal.net
www.tradecards.com/kb

L.R. 'Les' Docks
Box 780218, San Antonio, TX 78278.
Providing occasional mail-order record auctions, rarely consigned; The only consignments considered are exceptionally scarce and unusual.
records.docks@texas.net
docks.home.texas.net

Lang's Sporting Collectables, Inc.
663 Pleasant Valley Road, Waterville, NY 13480; 315-841-4623 or fax 315-841-8934. America's Leading Fishing Tackle Auction.
LangsAuction@aol.com
www.langsauction.com

Leslie Hindman Auctioneers, Inc.
1338 West Lake Street, Chicago, IL 60607; 312-280-1212.
www.lesliehindman.com

Lloyd Ralston Gallery Inc.
549 Howe Ave., Shelton, CT 06484; 203-924-5804 or fax 203-924-5834.

lrgallery@sbcglobal.net
www.lloydralstontoys.com

Majolica Auctions
Strawser Auction Group
200 North Main, PO Box 332, Wolcottville, IN 46795-0332; 260-854-2859 or fax 260-854-3979. Issues colored catalog; Also specializing in Fiesta ware.
info@strawserauctions.com
strawserauctions.com

Manion's International Auction House Inc.
4411 North 67th St., Kansas City, KS 66104; 866-626-4661 or fax 913-299-6792.
Specializing in international militaria, particularly the US, Germany and Japan. Extensive catalogs in antiques and collectibles, sports, transportation, political and advertising memorabilia and vintage clothing and denim. Publishes nine catalogs for each of the five categories per year. Request a free sample of past auctions, one issue of current auction for $15.
collecting@manions.com
www.manions.com

McMasters Harris Auction Company
5855 John Glenn Hwy., PO Box 1755, Cambridge, OH 43725; 800-842-3526 or fax 740-432-3191.
mark@mcmastersharris.com
www.mharrislive.com

Michael Ivankovich Antiques & Auction Company Inc.
PO Box 1536, Doylestown, PA, 18901; 215-345-6094. Specializing in early hand-colored photography and prints. Auction held four times each year, providing opportunity for collectors and dealers to compete for the largest variety of Wallace Nutting, Wallace Nutting-like pictures, Maxfield Parrish, Bessie Pease Gutmann, R. Atkinson Fox, Philip Boileau, Harrison Fisher, etc.
ivankovich@wnutting.com
www.wnutting.com

Michael John Verlangieri
PO Box 844, Cambria, CA 93428-0844. Specializing in fine California pottery; cataloged auctions (video tapes available).
michael@calpots.com
www.calpots.com

Monsen & Baer, Annual Perfume Bottle Auction
Monsen, Randall; and Baer, Rod
Box 529, Vienna, VA 22183; 703-938-2129 or fax 703-242-1357. Cataloged auctions of perfume bottles; Will purchase, sell, and accept consignments; Specializing in commercial, Czechoslovakian, Lalique, Baccarat, Victorian, crown top, factices, miniatures.

Morphy Auctions
2000 N. Reading Rd., Denver, PA 17517; 717-335-

3435. A division of Diamond International Galleries; with extensive worldwide media campaigns targeting the most influential antique publications and media venues; specializing in advertising, Americana, toys, trains, dolls and early holiday items. Hosts three to five consignment sales per year; based in Adamstown Antique Gallery.
www.morphyauctions.com

Neal Auction Company
Auctioneers & Appraisers of Antiques & Fine Art
4038 Magazine St., New Orleans, LA 70115; 504-899-5329 or 1-800-467-5329, or fax 504-897-3803.
customerservice@nealauction.com
www.nealauction.com

New England Absentee Auctions
16 Sixth St., Stamford, CT 06905-4610; 203-975-9055. Specializing in Quimper pottery.
neaauction@aol.com

New Orleans Auction Galleries Inc.
801 Magazine St., New Orleans, LA 70130; 800-501-0277, 504-566-1849. Specializing in American furniture and decorative arts, paintings, prints, and photography.
info@neworleansauction.com
www.neworleansauction.com

Noel Barrett Antiques & Auctions
PO Box 300, Carversville, PA 18913; 215-297-5109.
toys@noelbarrett.com
www.noelbarrett.com

Norman C. Heckler & Company
79 Bradford Corner Rd., Woodstock Valley, CT 06282; 860-974-1634 or fax 860-974-2003. Auctioneers and appraisers specializing in early glass and bottles. info@hecklerauction.com
www.hecklerauction.com

Past Tyme Pleasures
Steve & Donna Howard
PMB #204, 2491 San Ramon Blvd., #1, San Ramon, CA 94583; 925-484-4488 or fax 925-484-6442. Offers two absentee auction catalogs per year pertaining to old advertising items.
pasttyme1@sbcglobal.net
www.pasttyme1.com

Perrault-Rago Gallery
333 N. Main St., Lambertville, NJ 08530; 609-397-9374 or fax 609-397-9877. Specializing in American Art Pottery, Tiles, Arts & Crafts, Moderns, and Bucks County Paintings.
info@ragoarts.com
www.ragoarts.com

Randy Inman Auctions Inc.
PO Box 726; Waterville, ME 04903; 207-872-6900 or fax 207-872-6966. Specializing in antique toys, advertising, general line.
www.liveauctioneers.com/auctioneer/inmanauctions

R.G. Munn Auction LLC
PO Box 705; Cloudcroft, NM 88317; 575-687-3676. Specializing in American Indian collectibles.
rgmunnauc@pvtnetworks.net

Richard Opfer Auctioneering Inc.
1919 Greenspring Dr., Timonium, MD 21093; 410-252-5035 or fax 410-252-5863.
info@opferauction.com
www.opferauction.com

R.O. Schmitt Fine Arts
PO Box 162; Windham, NH 03087; 603-432-2237. Specializing in clocks, music boxes, and scientific instruments; holds catalog auctions.
bob@roschmittfinearts.com
www.roschmittfinearts.com

Roan Inc.
3530 Lycoming Creek Rd., Cogan Station, PA 17728; 570-494-0170 or fax 570-494-1911.
roaninc@comcast.net
www.roaninc.com

Samuel T. Freeman & Co.
1808 Chestnut St., Philadelphia, PA 19103; 215-563-9275 or fax 215-563-8236.
info@freemansauction.com
www.freemansauction.com

See Auctions
www.seeauctions.com
info@seeauctions.com
Stillwater, Minnesota

Skinner Inc. Auctioneers & Appraisers of Antiques and Fine Arts
The Heritage on the Garden, 63 Park Plaza, Boston, MA 02116; 617-350-5400 or fax 617-350-5429. Second address: 274 Cedar Hill St., Marlborough, MA 01752; 508-970-3000 or fax 508-970-3100.
www.skinnerinc.com

Sold By Us (Maritime Antiques)
PO Box 155, Cape Neddick, ME 03902. Specializing in maritime antiques, firehouse memorabilia, Native American artifacts, scientific instruments & military collectibles.
info@maritiques.com
www.maritiques.com

SoldUSA.com
PO Box 3012, 1418 Industrial Dr., Building 2, Matthews, NC 28105; 704-815-1500. Specializing in fine sporting collectibles.
support@soldusa.com
www.soldusa.com

Sotheby's
1334 York Ave., New York, NY 10021; 212-606-7000 or fax 212-606-7107.
leiladunbar@sothebys.com
www.sothebys.com

Stanton's Auctioneers & Realtors
144 S. Main St., PO Box 146, Vermontville, MI 49096; 517-726-0181 or fax 517-726-0060. Specializing in all types of property, at auction, anywhere.
stantonsauctions@sbcglobal.net
www.stantons-auctions.com

Stout Auctions, Greg Stout
529 State Road 28 East, Williamsport, IN 47993; 765-764-6901 or fax 765-764-1516. Specializing in Lionel, American Flyer, Ives, MTH, and other scale and toy trains.
info@stoutauctions.com
www.stoutauctions.com

Superior Galleries
20011 Ventura Blvd., Woodland Hills, CA 91364; 818-444-8699 or 800-421-0754 or fax 310-203-0496. Specializing in manuscripts, decorative and fine arts, Hollywood memorabilia, sports memorabilia, stamps and coins.
info@sgbh.com; www.sgbh.com

Swann Galleries Inc.
104 E. 25th St., New York, NY 10010; 212-254-4710 or fax 212-979-1017.
swann@swanngalleries.com
www.swanngalleries.com

Three Rivers Collectibles
Wendy and Leo Frese
PO Box 551542, Dallas, TX 75355; 214-341-5165. Annual Red Wing and RumRill pottery and stoneware auctions.

Tom Harris Auctions
203 South 18th Avenue, Marshalltown, IA 50158; 614-754-4890 or fax 641-753-0226. Specializing in clocks and watches, high quality antiques and collectibles; estate and lifetime collections, including eBay Live Auctions; Members of NAWCC, NAA, CAI.
tomharris@tomharrisauctions.com
www.tomharrisauctions.com

Tradewinds Auctions
Henry Taron
PO Box 249, 24 Magnolia Ave., Manchester-by-the-Sea, MA 01944-0249; 978-526-4085 or fax 978-526-3088. Specializing in antique canes.
auctions@tradewindsantiques.com
www.tradewindsantiques.com

Treadway Gallery, Inc.
2029 Madison Rd., Cincinnati, OH 45208; 513-321-6742 or fax 513-871-7722. Specializing in American art pottery; American and European art glass; European ceramics; Italian glass; fine American and European paintings and graphics; and furniture and decorative arts of the Arts & Crafts, Art Nouveau, Art Deco and Modern Design Movements. Modern Design expert: Thierry Lorthioir. Members: National Antique Dealers Association, American Art Pottery Association, International Society of Appraisers, American Ceramic Arts Society, Ohio Decorative Arts Society, Art Gallery

Association of Cincinnati.
nfo@treadwaygallery.com
www.treadwaygallery.com

Vicki and Bruce Waasdorp Auctions
PO Box 434; 10931 Main St.; Clarence, NY
14031; 716-759-2361 or fax 716-759-2397.
Specializing in decorated stoneware.
www.antiques-stoneware.com

VintagePostcards.Com
Vintage Postcards for Collectors
312 Feather Tree Dr., Clearwater, FL 33765.
www.vintagepostcards.com

Weschler's
Adam A. Weschler & Son
909 E. St. N.W., Washington, DC 20004; 202-
628-1281 or 800-331-1430 or fax 202-628-2366.
info@weschlers.com
www.weschlers.com

William Doyle Galleries
Auctioneers & Appraisers
175 East 87th St., New York, NY 10128; 212-
427-2730 or fax 212-369-0892.
Info@DoyleNewYork.com
www.doylenewyork.com

Willis Henry Auctions
22 Main St., Marshfield, MA 02050; 781-834-
7774 or fax 781-826-3520.
wha@willishenry.com
www.willishenry.com

Wm. Morford
Investment Grade Collectibles at Auction
RD #2, Cazenovia, NY 13035; 315-662-7625
or fax 315-662-3570. Specializing in antique
advertising items and related collectibles; Maxfield Parrish items; rare and unique items at the
upper end of the market with a heavy emphasis
on quality, rarity and condition. Premier auctions held several times a year.
morf2bid@aol.com
www.morfauction.com

Directory of Contributors

When contacting any of the buyers/sellers listed in this part of the Directory by mail, you must include a SASE (stamped, self-addressed envelope) if you expect a reply. Many of these people are professional appraisers, and there may be a fee for their time and service. Find out up front. Include a clear photo if you want an item identified. Most items cannot be described clearly enough to make an identification without a photo.

If you call and get their answering machine, when you leave your number so that they can return your call, tell them to call back collect. And please take the differences in time zones into consideration. 7:00 AM in the Midwest is only 5:00 AM in California! And if you're in California, remember that even 7:00 PM is too late to call the east coast. Most people work and are gone during the daytime. Even some of our antique dealers say they prefer after-work phone calls. Don't assume that a person who deals in a particular field will be able to help you with related items. They may seem related to that category but are not.

Please, we need your help. This book sells in such great numbers that allowing their names to be published can create a potential nightmare for each advisor and contributor. Please do your part to help us minimize this, so that we can retain them on our board and in turn pass their experience and knowledge on to you through our book. Their only obligation is to advise us, not to evaluate your holdings.

Alabama

Bell, C. Jeanenne
205-681-4550
Specializing in jewelry and hairwork jewelry.
cjbell@msn.com

Cataldo, Gene
4726 Panorama Dr., S.E., Huntsville, 35801;
256-536-6893. Specializing in classic and used
cameras. SASE required for information by
mail.
genecams@aol.com

Jasper, Joanne
15371 Craft Lane, Athens, 35613.
Specializing in Homer Laughlin China and
author of The Collector's Encyclopedia of Homer
Laughlin China (Collector Books).
joanne-jasper@charter.net

Lippa, Matt, and Elizabeth Schaff
Artisans
PO Box 256, Mentone, 35984; 256-634-4037.
Specializing in folk art, quilts, painted and
folky furniture, tramp art, whirligigs, windmill weights.
artisans@folkartisans.com
www.folkartisans.com

Arizona

Jackson, Denis
Illustrator Collector's News
PO Box 6433, Kingman, 86401.
Specializing in old magazines & illustrations
such as: Rose O'Neill, Maxfield Parrish, pinups,
Marilyn Monroe, Norman Rockwell, etc.
ticn@olypen.com

Winslow, Ralph
P.O. Box 1378, Dewey, 86327.
Specializing in Dryden pottery, Schramberg,
and Shell-craft collectibles.
justsaya@q.com

Arkansas

Freyaldenhoven, Tony
1412 S. Tyler St., Little Rock, 72204; 501-352-

3559. Specializing in Camark pottery.
tonyfrey@conwaycorp.net

Roenigk, Martin
Mechantiques
Crescent Hotel & Spa
75 Prospect Ave., Eureka Springs, 72632; 800-
671-6333. Specializing in mechanical musical
instruments, music boxes, band organs, musical
clocks and watches, coin pianos, orchestrions,
monkey organs, automata, mechanical birds and
dolls, etc. mroenigk@aol.com
www.mechantiques.com

Yohe, Darlene
Timberview Antiques
1303 S. Prairie St., Stuttgart, 72160-5132; 870-
673-3437. Specializing in American pattern
glass, historical glass, Victorian pattern glass,
carnival glass, and custard glass.

California

Aaronson, Barbara J.
The Victorian Lady

PO Box 7522, Northridge, 91327; 818-368-6052. Specializing in figural napkin rings, pickle castors, American Victorian silver plate.
bjaaronson@aol.com
www.thevictorianlady.com

Ales, Beverly Schell
4046 Graham St., Pleasanton, 94566-5619; 925-846-5297. Specializing in knife rests.
Kniferests@sbcglobal.net

Babcock, Bobby
Jubilation Antiques
1034 Camino Pablo Drive, Pueblo West, 81007; 719-557-1252. Specializing in Maxfield Parrish, Black Americana, and brown Roseville Pine Cone.
jubantique@aol.com

Berg, Paul
PO Box 8895, Newport Beach, 92620. Author of Nineteenth Century Photographica Cases and Wall Frames.

Brown, Dr. Kirby William
PO Box 1842, Paradise, 95967; 530-877-2159. Authoring book on history and products of California Faience, West Coast Porcelain, and Potlatch Pottery. Any contribution of information, new pieces, etc., is welcome.
kirbybrownbooks@sbcglobal.net

Chipman, Jack
P.O. Box 1079, Venice, 90294.
Specializing in California Potteries and Bauer Pottery.
jack@jackchipman.com

Clarke, Lanette
5021 Toyon Way, Antioch, 94532; 925-776-7784. Co-founder of Haeger Pottery Collectors of America. Specializing in Haeger and Royal Hickman.
Lanette_Clarke@msn.com

Cobabe, Kevin
800 S. Pacific Coast Hwy., #8301; Redondo Beach, 90277; 310-529-1301. Specializing in Amphora, Zsolnay, and Massier.
kcobabe13@aol.com

Conroy, Barbara J.
2059 Coolidge Drive, Santa Clara, 95051. Specializing in commercial china; author and historian.

Conti, Steve
310-271-2470
Specializing in Sascha Brastoff and Matthew Adams.
saconti@earthlink.net

Devenish, Clive
PO Box 708, Orinda, 94563; 510-414-4545. Specializing in still and mechanical banks; Buys and sells.

Ellis, Michael L.
266 Rose Lane, Costa Mesa, 92627; 949-646-7112 or fax 949-645-4919. Author (Collector Books) of Collector's Guide to Don Winton Designs, Identification & Values. Specializing in Twin Winton.

Frese, Leo and Wendy
9478 Olympic #100, Beverly Hills, 90212; 214-298-9214. Specializing in RumRill, Red Wing pottery and stoneware.
leo@ha.com

George, Tony
22431-B160 Antonio Parkway., #521, Rancho Santa Margarita, 92688; 949-589-6075. Specializing in watch fobs.
Tony@strikezoneinc.com

Gibson, Pat
38280 Guava Dr., Newark, 94560; 510-792-0586. Specializing in R.A. Fox.

Harrison, Gwynneth M.
11566 River Heights Dr., Riverside, 92505; 951-343-0414. Specializing in Autumn Leaf (Jewel Tea).
morgan27@sbcglobal.com

Hibbard, Suzi
WanderWares
Specializing in Dragon Ware and Thousand Faces china, other Orientalia.
Dragon_Ware@hotmail.com

Howard, Steve
Past Tyme Pleasures
5424 Sunol Blvd.,
#10-242, Pleasanton, 94566; 925-484-6442 or fax 925-484-6427. Specializing in antique American firearms, bowie knives, Western Americana, old advertising, vintage gambling items, barber and saloon items.
pasttyme1@sbcglobal.net
www.pasttyme1.com

Main Street Antique Mall
237 E Main St., El Cajon, 92020; 619-447-0800 or fax 619-447-0815.

Needham, Leonard
P.O. Box 689, Bethel Island, 94511; 925-684-9674. Specializing in automobilia.
screensider@sbcglobal.net

Sanford, Steve and Martha
230 Harrison Ave., Campbell, 95008; 408-978-8408. Authors of two books on Brush-McCoy and Sanfords Guide to McCoy Pottery (available from the authors).

Stillwell, Liz
Our Attic Antiques & Belleek
6745 Cord Avenue, Pico Rivera, 90660. Specializing in Irish and American Belleek.

Tanner, Joseph and Pamela
Tanner Treasures
10052 Tittle Way, Elk Grove, 95756; 916-801-8077. Specializing in handcuffs, leg shackles, balls and chains, restraints and padlocks of all kinds (including railroad), locking and non-locking devices; Also Houdini memorabilia: autographs, photos, posters, books, letters, etc.

Thoerner, Sharon
15549 Ryon Ave., Bellflower, 90706; 562-866-1555. Specializing in covered animal dishes, powder jars with animal and human figures, slag glass.

Vines, Linda
22600 S. Normandie Ave., #32, Torrance, 90502; 310-710-9346. Specializing in Snow Babies, Halloween, Steiff, and Santas (all German).
lleigh2000@hotmail.com

Webb, Frances Finch
1589 Gretel Lane, Mountain View, 94040. Specializing in Kay Finch ceramics.

Woodbury, Virginia; Past President of the American Hatpin Society
20 Montecillo Dr., Rolling Hills Estates, 90274-4249; 310-326-2196.
Specializing in hatpins and hatpin holders.

Canada

Howard, Martin
Toronto, Ontario; 416-690-7432.
Specializing in antique typewriters.
martin@antiquetypewriters.com
www.antiquetypewriters.com

Warner, Ian
Specializing in Wade porcelain, author of The World of Wade, The World of Wade Book 2, Wade Price Trends, The World of Wade — Figurines and Miniatures, and The World of Wade Head Vase Planters; Co-author: Mike Posgay.
ian@theworldofwade.com
www.theworldofwade.com

Colorado

Babcock, Bobby
1034 Camino Pablo Drive, Pueblo West, 81007; 719-557-1252. Specializing in Maxfield Parrish.
jubantique@aol.com

Heck, Carl
Box 8416, Aspen, 81612; phone/fax: 970-925-8011. Specializing in Tiffany lamps, art glass, paintings, windows and chandeliers; Also reverse-painted and leaded-glass table lamps, stained and beveled glass windows, bronzes, paintings, Art

Nouveau, etc.; Buy and sell; Fee for written appraisals; Please include SASE for reply.
carlheck5@aol.com
www.carlheck.com

James, Pat
13027 WCR 56, Hillrose, 80733. Specializing in crocks, Western Pottery Mfg. Co. (Denver, CO).

Mackin, Bill
Author of *Cowboy and Gunfighter Collectibles*, available from author: 1137 Washington St., Craig, 81625; 970-824-6717. Paperback: $28 ppd.; Other titles available. Specializing in old and fine spurs, guns, gun leather, cowboy gear, Western Americana (Collection in the Museum of Northwest Colorado, Craig).

Segelke, Cathy
16252 CR 14, Atwood, 80722; 970-522-5424. Specializing in crocks, Western Pottery Mfg. Co. (Denver, CO).

Stifter, Craig
0062 Elk Mountain Drive
Redstone, 81623. Specializing in Coca-Cola, Orange Crush, Dr. Pepper, Hires, and other soda-pop brand collectibles.
cstifter@gmail.com

Tucker, Richard and Valerie
1719 Mapleton Avenue, Boulder, 80304-4263; 720-381-0710 or 720-381-0820 or fax 720-381-0821. Specializing in windmill weights, shooting gallery targets, figural lawn sprinklers, cast-iron advertising paperweights, and other unusual figural cast iron.
richardstucker@comcast.net
lead1234@comcast.net

Connecticut

Block, Robert and Stan
Block's Box
51 Johnson St., Trumbull, 06611; 203-926-8448. Specializing in marbles.
blockschip@aol.com

Bondhus, Sandra V.
16 Salisbury Way, Farmington, 06032; 860-678-1808. Author of *Quimper Pottery: A French Folk Art Faience*. Specializing in Quimper pottery.

Lehrer, Gary
16 Mulberry Road, Woodbridge, 06525-1717. Specializing in pens and pencils; Catalog available.
garylehrer@aol.com
www.gopens.com

Lytwyn, Diane
Specializing in mercury glass.
antiquemercuryglass@yahoo.com
www.antiquemercuryglass.com

Postcards International
Martin J. Shapiro
2321 Whitney Ave., Suite 102, PO Box 185398, Hamden, 06518; 203-248-6621 or fax 203-248-6628. Specializing in vintage picture postcards.
www.vintagepostcards.com

Van Deusen, Hobart
15 Belgo Road, Lakeville, 06039-1001; 860-435-0088. Specializing in Canton, SASE required when requesting information.
rtn.hoby@snet.net

Vuono, Mark
16 Sixth St., Stamford, 06905; 203-357-0892 (10 a.m. to 5:30 p.m. E.S.T.). Specializing in historical flasks, blown three-mold glass, blown American glass.
neaa@sbcglobal.net

District of Columbia

Durham, Ken and Jackie (by appt.)
909 26 St. N.W., Suite 502, Washington, 20037. Specializing in slot machines, jukeboxes, arcade machines, trade stimulators, vending machines, scales, popcorn machines, and service manuals.
www.GameRoomAntiques.com

Florida

Alcorn, Ed and Sheri
Animal Rescue of West Pasco
14945 Harmon Dr., Shady Hills, 34610; 727-856-6762. Specializing in Hagen-Renaker.
horsenut@gate.net
www.hagenrenakermuseum.com

Barnes, Jacqueline Linscott
Line Jewels
3557 Nicklaus Dr., Titusville, 32780; 321-480-1800. Specializing in glass insulators, bell paperweights and other telephone items. Author and distributor of *Bluebell Paperweights, Telephone Pioneers of America Bells, and other Telephone Related Items*; LSASE required for information.
bluebellwt@aol.com

Bettinger, Robert
PO Box 333, Mt. Dora, 32756; 352-735-3575. Specializing in American and European art pottery and glass, Arts & Crafts furniture and accessories, fountain pens, marbles, and general antiques.
rgbett@aol.com

Buchner, John
1903 N. Lake Howard Dr., Winterhaven, 33881; 863-297-5589. Specializing in Planters Peanuts and Mr. Peanut collectibles.
hfi332@aol.com

Dodds-Metts, Rebecca
Silver Flute
PO Box 670664, Coral Springs, 33067. Specializing in jewelry.

Elsner, Dr. Robert
29 Clubhouse Lane, Boynton Beach, 33436; 561-736-1362. Specializing in antique barometers and nautical instruments.

France, Madeleine
244 N.W. 97 Ave., Plantation, 33324; 954-802-9244. Specializing in top-quality perfume bottles: Rene Lalique, Steuben, Czechoslovakian, DeVilbiss, Baccarat, Commercials; French doré bronze and decorative arts, Royal Vienna.

Hastin, Bud
Author of *Bud Hastin's Avon Collector's Encyclopedia*, signed copies available from author for $32.95 postage paid. Write to PO Box 11004, Ft. Lauderdale, 33339; or call 954-566-0691 after 10:00 AM Eastern time.
budhastin@hotmail.com

Hirshman, Susan and Larry
Everyday Antiques
1624 Pine Valley Dr., Ft Myers, 33907. Specializing in china, glassware, kitchenware.

Hudson, Hardy
Antiques on the Avenue
505 Park Ave. N., Winter Park, 32789; 407-657-2100 or cell: 407-963-6093. Specializing in majolica, American art pottery (buying one piece or entire collections); Also buying Weller (garden ornaments, birds, Hudson, Sicard, Sabrinian, Glendale, Knifewoood, or animal related), Roseville, Grueby, Ohr, Newcomb, Overbeck, Pewabic, Teco, Tiffany, Fulper, Rookwood, SEG, etc. Also buying better art glass, paintings and silver.
todiefor@mindspring.com

Joyce, Harriet
415 Soft Shadow Lane, DeBary, 32713; 386-668-8006. Specializing in Cracker Jack and Checkers (a competitor) early prizes and Flossie Fisher items.

Kamm, Dorothy
Specializing in American Painted Porcelain.
dorothykamm@comcast.net

Kuritzky, Louis
4510 NW 17th Place, Gainesville, 32605; 352-377-3193. Co-author (Collector Books) of *Collector's Encyclopedia of Bookends*.
lkuritzky@aol.com

Person, Jeffrey M.
727-504-1139 or 727-344-1709. Specializing in Asian art including cloisonné, Sumida Ware, and fine carved furniture, Art Nouveau, and jewelry. Has lectured, written articles, and been

doing fine antique shows for 40 years. Person1@tampabay.rr.com

Rolfes, Herbert
Yesterday's World
PO Box 398, Mt. Dora, 32756; 352-735-3947. Specializing in World's Fairs and Expositions. NY1939@aol.com

Rosack, Lynn
P.O. Box 196697, Winter Springs, 32719; 407-359-9170. Author of *The A – Z Guide to Collecting Trivets* (Collector Books, 2004) and *The Expanded A – Z Guide to Collecting Trivets* (Collector Books, 2010). Specializing in antique and contemporary trivets made of metal, wire, porcelain, and tile. mlcr@cfl.rr.com

Snyder-Haug, Diane
1415 Seventh Ave. N, St. Petersburg, 33705. Specializing in women's clothing, 1850 – 1940.

Teeters, Connie
2429 E. Lake Drive, Deland, 32724; 386-738-2937. Specializing in cookie cutters. cteeters@cfl.rr.com

Weisblut, Robert
International Ivory Society
5001 Old Ocean Blvd. #1, Ocean Ridge, 33435; 561-276-5657. Specializing in ivory carvings and utilitarian objects. rweisblut@yahoo.com

White, Douglass
A-1 Auction
2042 N. Rio Grande Ave., Suite E, Orlando, 32804; 407-839-0004. Specializing in Fulper, Arts & Crafts furniture (photos helpful). a-1auction@cfl.rr.com

---

Georgia

Bailey, Wayne and Gale
3152 Fence Rd., Dacula, 30019; 770-963-5736. Specializing in Goebels (Friar Tuck).

Glenn, Walter
3420 Sonata Lane, Alpharetta, 30004-7492; 678-624-1298. Specializing in Frankart.

Joiner, John R.
Aviation Collectors
130 Peninsula Circle, Newnan, 30263; 770-502-9565. Specializing in commercial aviation collectibles. propJJ@bellsouth.net

Jones, Donald
107 Rivers Edge Dr., Savannah, 31406-8419; 912-354-2133. Specializing in vintage tennis collectibles; SASE with inquiries please. Glassman912@comcast.net

---

Hawaii

Thornton, Don
HC 3, Box 10029, Keaau, 96749-9202. Specializing in egg beaters and apple parers; author of *The Eggbeater Chronicles, 2nd Edition* ($50.45 ppd); and *Apple Parers* ($59 ppd.). donthorn@aol.com

---

Illinois

Broom, Jim
Box 65, Effingham, 62401. Specializing in opalescent pattern glassware.

Danis, John
6822 Forest Hills Rd., Loves Park, 61111-4367. Specializing in R. Lalique and Norse pottery. danis6033@aol.com

Garmon, Lee
1529 Whittier St., Springfield, 62704; 217-789-9574. Specializing in Royal Haeger, Royal Hickman, glass animals.

Hall, Doris and Burdell
B & B Antiques, 210 W. Sassafras Dr., Morton, 61550-1254; 309-263-2988. Authors of *Morton's Potteries: 99 Years* (Vols. I and II). Specializing in Morton pottery, American dinnerware, early American pattern glass, historical items, elegant Depression-era glassware.
www.mtco.com/~bnbhall
bnbhall@mtco.com

Hamburg, Mary 'Tootsie'
Charlotte's, Queen Ann's, and Among Friends shops, all in Corner Victorian in Danville; 217-446-2323. Specializing in German Pink Pigs, Bakelite jewelry, general line.

Hastings, Mary Jane
212 West Second South, Mt. Olive, 62069; 217-999-7519 or cell: 618-910-1528. Specializing in Chintz dinnerware. sgh@chaliceantiques.com

Hoffmann, Pat and Don, Sr.
1291 N. Elmwood Dr., Aurora, 60506-1309; 630-859-3435. Authors of *Warwick, A to W*, a supplement to *Why Not Warwick?*; video regarding Warwick decals currently available. warwick@ntsource.com

Martin, Jim
1095 215th Ave., Monmouth, 61462; 309-734-2703. Specializing in Old Sleepy Eye, Monmouth pottery, Western Stoneware.

Miller, Anne
That's Interesting!
303 W. Erie St., Spring Valley, 61632; 815-664-2450. Specializing in white and red tea leaf ironstone (no open shop); Shows and El Paso Antiques Mall in El Paso, Illinois.

Miller, Larry
218 Devron Circle, E. Peoria, 61611-1605 Specializing in German and Czechoslovakian Erphila.

Ochsner, Grace
Grace Ochsner Doll House
2345 E. State Highway 994, La Harpe, 61450-9255; 217-755-4362. Specializing in piano babies, bisque German dolls and figurines.

Rhoden, Joan and Charles
8693 N. 1950 East Rd., Georgetown, 61846-6264; 217-662-8046. Specializing in Heisey and other Elegant glassware, spice tins, lard tins, and yard-long prints. Co-authors of *Those Wonderful Yard-Long Prints and More, More Wonderful Yard-Long Prints, Book II*, and *Yard-Long Prints, Book III*, illustrated value guides. rhoden@soltec.net

Schwab, Betty and Larry
The Paperweight Shoppe
2507 Newport Dr., Bloomington, 61704-4525 (May 15 – January 2); 877-517-6518 and 309-662-1956. Specializing in glass paperweights; Now buying quality weights, one piece or a collection.
thepaperweightshoppe@verizon.net or paperweightguy@yahoo.com

Spencer, Dick and Pat
Glass and More (Shows only)
1203 N. Yale, O'Fallon, 62269; 618-632-9067. Specializing in Cambridge, Fenton, Fostoria, Heisey, etc.

Spiess, Greg
230 E. Washington, Joliet, 60433; 815-722-5639. Specializing in Odd Fellows lodge items. spiessantq@aol.com

TV Guide Specialists
Box 20, Macomb, 61455; 309-833-1809.

Vlach, Ray
Specializing in Homer Laughlin, Red Wing, Vernon Kilns, Russel Wright, Eva Zeisel, and childrens's ware china and pottery. rayvlach@hotmail.com

Wickland, Gary and Bruce Mueller
2424 West Winona Street, Chicago, 60625; 773-271-7507. Specializing in Consolidated Lamp and Glass and Phoenix Glass. gwick@anet.com

Yester-Daze Glass
c/o Illinois Antique Center
320 S.W. Commercial St., Peoria, 61604; 309-347-1679. Specializing in glass from the 1920s, '30s and '40s; Fiesta; Hall; pie birds; sprinkler bottles; and Florence figurines.

Indiana

Alexander, Charles
221 E. 34th St., Indianapolis, 46205; 317-924-9665. Specializing in Fiesta, Russel Wright, Eva Zeisel, and Town & Country line of Red Wing. chasalex1848@sbcglobal.net

Boram, Clifford
Antique Stove Information Clearinghouse
Monticello; Free consultation by phone only: 574-583-6465.

Dilley, David
6125 Knyghton Rd., Indianapolis, 46220; 317-251-0575. Specializing in Royal Haeger and Royal Hickman.
glazebears@aol.com

Freese, Carol and Warner
House With the Lions Antiques
On the Square, Covington, 47932. General line.

Garrett, Sandi
1807 W. Madison St., Kokomo, 46901. Specializing in Greentown glass, old postcards. sandpiper@iquest.net

Haun, Ted
2426 N. 700 East, Kokomo, 46901. Specializing in American pottery and china, '50s items, Russel Wright designs.
Sam17659@cs.com

Highfield, James R.
1601 Lincoln Way East, South Bend, 46613-3418; 574-286-3290. Specializing in relief-style Capodimonte-style porcelain (Doccia, Ginori, and Royal Naples).

Hoover, Dave
812-945-3614. Specializing in fishing collectibles; also miniature boats and motors.
lurejockey@aol.com

Keagy, William
PO Box 106, Bloomfield, 47424; 812-384-3471. Co-author of *Those Wonderful Yard-Long Prints and More*, *More Wonderful Yard-Long Prints, Book II*, and *Yard-Long Prints, Book III*, illustrated value guides.

McQuillen, Michael J.
Political Parade
PO Box 50022, Indianapolis, 46250-0022; 317-845-1721. Writer of column, *Political Parade*, which appears regularly in *AntiqueWeek* and other collector newspapers. Specializing in political advertising, pin-back buttons, and sports memorabilia; Buys and sells.
michael@politicalparade.com
www.politicalparade.com

Miller, Robert Jr.
6574 Huntyers Rdg. S., Zionsville, 46077-9169. Specializing in Dryden pottery.

Mueller, Bruce and Gary Wickland
2424 West Winona Street, Chicago, 60625; 773-271-7507. Specializing in Consolidated Lamp and Glass and Phoenix Glass Companies. gwick@anet.com

Pruitt, Ted
3350 W. 700 N., Anderson, 46011. *St. Clair Glass Collector's Guide, Vol. 2*, available for $25 each at above address.

Ricketts, Vicki
Covington Antiques Company
6431 W US Highway 136; Covington 47932. General line.

Sanders, Lisa
8900 Old State Rd., Evansville, 47711. Specializing in M.A. Hadley.
1dlk@insight.bb.com

Taylor, Dr. E.E.
245 N. Oakland Ave., Indianapolis, 46201-3360; 317-638-1641. Specializing in radios; SASE required for replies to inquiries.

Webb's Antique Mall
Over 400 Quality Dealers
200 W. Union St., Centerville, 47330; 765-855-2489.
webbsin@antiquelandusa.com

Wright, Bill
325 Shady Dr., New Albany, 47150. Specializing in knives: Bowie, hunting, military, and pocketknives.

Iowa

Bilsland, William M., III
PO Box 2671, Cedar Rapids, 52406-2671; 319-368-0658 (message) or cell: 714-328-7219. Specializing in American art pottery.

Devine, Joe
1411 S. 3rd St., Council Bluffs, 51503; 712-328-7305. Specializing in Royal Copley and other types of pottery (collector), author of *Collecting Royal Copley Plus Royal Windsor & Spaulding*.

Jackson, James and Tatiana
Jackson's International Auctioneers & Appraisers of Fine Art and Antiques
2229 Lincoln St., Cedar Falls, 50613; 319-277-2256 or fax 319-277-1252. Specializing in American and European art pottery and art glass, American and European paintings, Russian works of art, decorative arts, toys and jewelry.
jjackson@jacksonsauction.com
www.jacksonsauction.com

Kansas

Barta, Dale and Diane
215 East Court St., Lincoln, 67455-2303; 785-524-4747. Specializing in Czechoslovakian glass and collectibles.
tazzer48@sbcglobal.net

Brandenburg, Harold
662 Chipper Lane, Wichita, 67212; 316-722-1200. Specializing in Royal Bayreuth; Charter member of the Royal Bayreuth Collectors Club; Buys, sells, and collects.

Maundy International
PO Box 13028-GG, Shawnee Mission, 66282; 1-800-235-2866. Specializing in watches — antique pocket and vintage wristwatches.
mitime@hotmail.com

Smies, David
Pops Collectibles
Box 522, 315 South 4th, Manhattan, 66502; 785-776-1433. Specializing in coins, stamps, cards, tokens, Masonic collectibles.

Kentucky

Courter, J.W.
550 Pioneer Lane, Calvert City, 42029; 270-933-4000. Specializing in Aladdin lamps; Author of *Aladdin — The Magic Name in Lamps, Revised Edition*, hardbound, 304 pages; *Aladdin Electric Lamps*, softbound, 229 pages; *Angle Lamps Collectors Manual & Price Guide*, softbound, 48 pages; and *Center-draft Kerosene Lamps, 1884 – 1940*, hardbound, 448 pages.

Florence, Gene and Cathy
Box 22186, Lexington, 40522. Authors (Collector Books) on Depression Glass, Occupied Japan, Elegant Glass, Kitchen Glassware, Hazel-Atlas glass, Fire-King glassware, and Glassware from the 40s, 50s & 60s.

Hornback, Betty
707 Sunrise Lane, Elizabethtown, 42701. Specializing in Kentucky Derby glasses, Detailed Derby, Preakness, Belmont, Breeder's Cup and others; Glass information and pictures available in a booklet for $15 ppd.
bettysantiques@kvnet.org

Stewart, Ron
PO Box 2421, Hazard, 41702; 606-436-5917. Co-author of *Standard Knife Collector's Guide; Standard Guide to Razors; Cattaraugus Cutlery; The Big Book of Pocket Knives; and Remington Knives*. Specializing in razors and knives, all types of cutlery.

Summers, B.J.
233 Darnell Rd., Benton, 42025. Specializing in Coca-Cola collectibles, advertising memorabilia, and soda pop memorabilia.
bjsummers@att.net

Willis, Roy M.
Heartland of Kentucky Decanters & Steins

PO Box 428, Lebanon Junction., 40150; 502-833-2827. Huge selection of limited edition decanters and beer steins. Call, write, or check our website (www.decantersandsteins.com) for road directions. Include large self-addressed envelope (2 stamps) with correspondence; Fee for appraisals.
heartlandky@hotmail.com
decantersandsteins.com

Louisiana

Langford, Paris
415 Dodge Ave., Jefferson, 70121; 504-733-0667. Specializing in all small vinyl dolls of the '60s and '70s; Author of *Liddle Kiddles Identification and Value Guide* (now out of print). Please include SASE when requesting information; Contact for information concerning Liddle Kiddle Konvention.
bbean415@aol.com

Maine

Blake, Brenda
Box 555, York Harbor, 03911; 207-363-6566. Specializing in egg cups.
Eggcentric@aol.com

Hillman, Alma
Antiques at the Hillman's
197 Coles Corner Rd., Winterport, 04496; 207-223-5656. Co-author (Collector Books) of *Collector's Encyclopedia of Old Ivory China, The Mystery Explored*. Specializing in Old Ivory China.
oldivory@roadrunner.com
www.oldivorychina.com

Rinaldi, John
Nautical Antiques and Related Items
Box 765, Dock Square, Kennebunkport, 04046; 207-967-3218. Specializing in nautical antiques, scrimshaw, naval items, marine paintings, etc.; Fully illustrated catalog: $5.
jfrinaldi@adelphia.net

Zayic, Charles S.
Americana Advertising Art
PO Box 57, Ellsworth, 04605; 207-667-7342. Specializing in early magazines, early advertising art, illustrators.

Maryland

Humphrey, George
4932 Prince George Avenue, Beltsville, 20705; 301-937-7899. Specializing in John Rogers.

Kilhoffer, C.D.
2609 Lakeview Court, Churchville, 21028. Specializing in glass target balls.

McAllister, Lisa
14521 National Piek, Clear Spring, 21722; 301-842-3255. Specializing in yellow ware. Author of *Collector's Guide to Yellow Ware, Books, I, II, and III.*
mcall@fred.net

Welsh, Joan
7015 Partridge Pl., Hyattsville, 20782; 301-779-6181. Specializing in Chintz; Author of *Chintz Ceramics*.

Massachusetts

Adams, Charles and Barbara
South Yarmouth, 02664; 508-760-3290 or (business) 508-587-5640. Specializing in Bennington (brown only).
adams_2340@msn.com

Cooper, Ryan
205 White Rock Rd., Yarmouthport, 02675; 508-362-1604. Specializing in flags of historical significance and exceptional design.
rcmaritime@capecod.net

Dunbar's Gallery
Leila and Howard Dunbar
54 Haven St., Milford, 01757; 508-634-8697 (also fax). Specializing in advertising and toys.
Dunbarsgallery@comcast.net
www.dunbarsgallery.com

Ford, Frank W.
Shrewsbury, 508-842-6459. Specializing in American iridescent art glass, ca 1900 – 1930.

Hess, John A.
Fine Photographic Americana
PO Box 3062, Andover, 01810. Specializing in 19th-century photography.

Longo, Paul J.
Paul Longo Americana
PO Box 5502, Magnolia, 01930; 978-525-2290. Specializing in political pins, ribbons, banners, autographs, old stocks and bonds, baseball and sports memorabilia of all types.

MacLean, Dale
183 Robert Rd., Dedham, 02026; 781-329-1303. Specializing in Dedham and Dorchester pottery.
dedham-dorchester@comcast.net

Morin, Albert
668 Robbins Ave. #23, Dracut, 01826; 978-454-7907. Specializing in miscellaneous Akro Agate and Westite.
akroal@comcast.net

Porter, Richard T., Curator
Porter Thermometer Museum
Box 944, Onset, 02558; 508-295-5504. Visits (always open) free, with 4,580 thermometers to see; Appraisals, repairs and traveling lecture (over 700 given, ages 8 – 98, all venues). Richard is also vice president of the Thermometer Collectors Club of America.
thermometerman@aol.com

Wellman, BA
PO Box 673, Westminster, 01473-0673. Willing to assist in identification through e-mail free of charge. Specializing in **all** areas of American ceramics, dinnerware, figurines, and art pottery.
BA@dishinitout.com

Williams, Linda
261 Kings Highway, W. Springfield, 01089. Specializing in glass & china, general line antiques.
sito1845@hotmail.com

Michigan

Brown, Rick
Newspaper Collector's Society of America
Lansing, 517-887-1255. Specializing in newspapers.
curator@historybuff.com
www.historybuff.com

Hogan & Woodworth
Walter P. Hogan and Wendy L. Woodworth
520 N. State, Ann Arbor, 48104; 313-930-1913. Specializing in Kellogg Studio.
http://people.emich.edu/whogan/kellogg/index.html

Iannotti, Dan
212 W. Hickory Grove Rd., Bloomfield Hills, 48302-1127S. 248-335-5042. Specializing in selling/buying: Reynolds, Sandman, John Wright, Capron, BOK, and other banks; Member of the Mechanical Bank Collectors of America.
modernbanks@sbcglobal.net

Krupka, Rod
2641 Echo Lane, Ortonville, 48462; 248-627-6351. Specializing in lightning rod balls.
rod.krupka@yahoo.com

Marsh, Linda K.
1229 Gould Rd., Lansing, 48917. Specializing in Degenhart glass.

Nedry, Boyd W.
728 Buth Dr., Comstock Park, 49321; 616-784-1513. Specializing in traps (including mice, rat, and fly traps) and trap-related items; Please send postage when requesting information.

Nickel, Mike and Cynthia Horvath
A Nickel's Worth, LLC
PO Box 456, Portland, 48875; 517-647-7646 or fax 517-647-1717. Specializing in American Art Pottery: Roseville, Van Briggle, Weller, Rookwood, Pillin, Newcomb, Kay Finch, Stangl, and Pennsbury Birds.
mike5c@voyager.net

Oates, Joan
1107 Deerfield Lane, Marshall, 49068; 269-781-9791. Specializing in Phoenix Bird chinaware, author of *Phoenix Bird Chinaware*, books I – V.
joates120@broadstripe.net

Pickvet, Mark
Specializing in playing cards.
mpickvet@aol.com

Rairigh, Glen
Americana Auctions
12633 Sandborn, Sunfield, 48890. Specializing in Skookum dolls and antique auctions.

Robar, Richard
P.O. Box 451, Roscommon, 48653; 989-429-2825. Specializing in Cleminson Pottery of California and salt & pepper shakers.
clemcollector@yahoo.com

Minnesota

Anderson, James
Box 120704, New Brighton, 55112; 651-484-3198. Specializing in old fishing lures and reels, also tackle catalogs, posters, calendars, Winchester items.

Depasquale, Dan
P.O. Box 50, Red Wing, 55066-0050. Specializing in Red Wing stoneware. Collector Books co-author of *Red Wing Stoneware Encyclopedia* (with Larry Peterson), and co-author of *Red Wing Collectibles* and *Red Wing Stoneware* (with Gail Peck and Larry Peterson).
www.redwingcollectors.com

Dommel, Darlene Hurst
510 Westwood Dr. N, Minneapolis, 55422-5266. Collector Books author of *Collector's Encyclopedia of Howard Pierce Porcelain, Collector's Encyclopedia of Dakota Potteries*, and *Collector's Encyclopedia of Rosemeade Pottery*. Specializing in Howard Pierce, Dakota potteries, Pine Ridge, and Rosemeade.

Harrigan, John
1900 Hennepin, Minneapolis, 55402; 612-991-1271 or October – April, send to PO Box 244551, Baynton Beach, FL 33424. Specializing in Moorcroft, Royal Doulton character jugs, and Toby jugs.

Miller, Clark
4444 Garfield Ave., Minneapolis, 55419-4847; 612-827-6062. Specializing in Anton Lang pottery, American art pottery, Tibet postal history.

Peterson, Larry
P.O. Box 484, Castle Rock, 55010; 651-463-7070. Specializing in Red Wing stoneware. Collector Books co-author of *Red Wing Stoneware Encyclopedia* (with Dan Depasquale), and co-author of *Red Wing Collectibles* and *Red Wing Stoneware* (with Dan Depasquale and Gail Peck).
larrypeterson@edinarealty.com
www.larrysjugs.com

Putratz, Barb
Spring Lake Park, 763-784-0422. Specializing in Norman Rockwell figurines and plates.

Schoneck, Steve
HG Handicraft Guild, Minneapolis
PO Box 56, Newport, 55055; 651-459-2980. Specializing in American art pottery, Arts & Crafts, HG Handicraft Guild Minneapolis.

Missouri

Gillespie, Steven, Publisher
Goofus Glass Gazette
400 Martin Blvd, Village of the Oaks, 64118; 816-455-5558. Specializing in Goofus Glass, curator of 'Goofus Glass Museum,' 4,000+ piece collection of goofus glass; Buy, sell, and collect goofus for 30+ years; Expert contributor to forums on goofus glass; Contributor to website for goofus glass.
stegil0520@kc.rr.com

Heuring, Jerry and Elaine
28450 US Highway 61, Scott City, 63780; 573-264-3947. Specializing in Keen Kutter.

Tarrant, Jenny
Holly Daze Antiques
4 Gardenview, St. Peters, 63376. Specializing in early holiday items, Halloween, Christmas, Easter, etc.; Always buying early holiday collectibles and German holiday candy containers.
jennyjol@aol.com
www.holly-days.com

Wendel, David
F.E.I., Inc.
PO Box 1187, Poplar Bluff, 63902-1187; 573-686-1926. Specializing in Fraternal Elks collectibles.

Williams, Don
PO Box 147, Kirksville 63501; 660-627-8009 (between 8 a.m. and 6 p.m. only). Specializing in art glass; SASE required with all correspondence.

Nebraska

Johnson, Donald-Brian
3329 South 56th Street, #611; Omaha, NE 68106. Author of numerous Schiffer Publishing Ltd. books on collectibles, including: *Ceramic Arts Studio, The Legacy of Betty Harrington* (in association with Timothy J. Holthaus and James E. Petzold); and with co-author Leslie Piña, *Higgins, Adventures in Glass; Higgins: Poetry in Glass; Moss Lamps: Lighting the '50s; Specs Appeal: Extravagant 1950s and 1960s Eye-* wear; *Whiting & Davis Purses: The Perfect Mesh; Popular Purses: It's In the Bag!; Deco Décor*; and a four-volume series on the Chase Brass & Copper Co. Be sure to see Clubs, Newsletters, and Websites for information on the CAS Collectors club.
donaldbrian@msn.com

New Hampshire

Bealo, Peter
82 Sweet Hill Rd., Plaistow, 03865; 603-882-8023 or cell: 978-204-9849. Please include SASE with mailed inquiries.
pbealo@comcast.net

Holt, Jane
Jane's Collectibles
PO Box 115, Derry, 03038. Specializing in Annalee Mobilitee Dolls.

Jacobs, Larry
16 Fox Run Lane, Salem, 03079; 603-458-1884. Specializing in Big Little Books.
LJacobs@capitalcrossing.com

Winston, Nancy
Willow Hollow Antiques
648 1st N.H. Turnpike, Northwood, 03261; 603-942-5739. Specializing in Shaker smalls, primitives, iron, copper, stoneware, and baskets.

New Jersey

George, Dr. Joan M.
ABC Collector's Circle newsletter
67 Stevens Ave., Old Bridge, 08857. Specializing in educational china (particularly ABC plates and mugs).
drgeorge@nac.net

Harran, Jim and Susan
A Moment in Time
208 Hemlock Dr., Neptune, 07753. Specializing in English and Continental porcelains with emphasis on antique cups and saucers; Authors of *Collectible Cups and Saucers, Identification and Values, Book I, II, III and IV; Dresden Porcelain Studios; Decorative Plates, Identification and Values*; and *Meissen Porcelain*, all published by Collector Books.
www.tias.com/stores/amit

Litts, Elyce
Happy Memories Antiques & Collectibles
PO Box 394, Morris Plains, 07950; 201-707-4241. Specializing in general line with special focus on Geisha Girl Porcelain, vintage compacts and Goebel figurines.
maildepothm@happy-memories.com
www.happy-memories.com

Meschi, Edward J.
129 Pinyard Rd., Monroeville, 08343; 856-358-7293. Specializing in Durand art glass,

Icart etchings, Maxfield Parrish prints, Tiffany lamps, Rookwood pottery, occupational shaving mugs, American paintings, and other fine arts; Author of *Durand — The Man and His Glass* (Antique Publications), available from author for $30 plus postage.
ejmeschi@hotmail.com

Perrault, Suzanne
Rago Arts and Auction Center
333 N. Main St., Lambertville, 08530; 609-397-9374, 866-724-6278. Specializing in Arts and Crafts, art pottery, moderns, and tiles.
info@ragoarts.com
www.ragoarts.com

Perzel, Robert and Nancy
Popkorn Antiques
505 Route 579, Ringoes, 08551; 908-303-7595. Specializing in Stangl dinnerware, birds, and artware; American pottery and dinnerware.

Poster, Harry
Vintage TVs
Box 1883, S. Hackensack, 07606; 201-794-9606. Writes *Poster's Radio and Television Price Guide*. Specializes in vintage televisions, vintage radios, stereo cameras; Catalog available online.
tvs@harryposter.com
www.harryposter.com

Rago, David
Rago Arts and Auction Center
333 N. Main St., Lambertville, 08530; 609-397-6780, 866-724-6278. Specializing in Arts & Crafts, art pottery.
info@ragoarts.com
www.ragoarts.com

Rosen, Barbara
6 Shoshone Trail, Wayne, 07470. Specializing in figural bottle openers and antique dollhouses.

New Mexico

Hardisty, Donald
Las Cruces. For information and questions: 505-522-3721 or cell: 505-649-4191. Specializing in Bossons and Hummels. Don's Collectibles carries a full line of Bossons and Hummel figurines of all marks.
don@donsbossons.com
www.donsbossons.com

Manns, William
PO Box 6459, Santa Fe, 87502; 505-995-0102. Co-author of *Painted Ponies*, hardbound (226 pages), available from author for $47 ppd. Specializing in carousel art and cowboy.

Nelson, Scott H.
PO Box 6081, Santa Fe, 87502-6081. Specializing in ethnographic art.

New York

Austin, Bruce A.
1 Hardwood Hill Rd., Pittsford, 14534; 585-387-9820 (evenings); 585-475-2879 (week days). Specializing in clocks and Arts & Crafts furnishings and accessories including metalware, pottery, and lighting.
baagll@rit.edu.

Bozarth, Michael and Valarie
Beaux Arts USA
Williamsville. Specializing in Cosmos, Audubon prints, and Currier & Ives prints.
info@BeauxArtsUSA.com
www.BeauxArtsUSA.com

Handelsman, Burton
18 Hotel Dr., White Plains, 10605; 914-428-4480 (home) and 914-761-8880 (office). Specializing in occupational shaving mugs, accessories.

Johnson, Barbara, Ph.D.
Dr. Barbara Loves Antiques
Specializing in vintage clothing, author of *Antique & Vintage Fashions, 1745 to 1979* and *Valentines: A Collector's Guide* (both by Collector Books).
www.drbarbaralovesantiques.weebly.com

Laun, H. Thomas and Patricia
Little Century
215 Paul Ave., Syracuse, 13206; December through March: 315-437-4156; April through December residence: 35109 Country Rte. 7, Cape Vincent, 13618; 315-654-3244. Specializing in firefighting collectibles; **All appraisals are free,** but we will respond only to those who are considerate enough to include a self-addressed stamped envelope (photo is requested for accuracy); We will return phone calls as soon as possible.

Malitz, Lucille
Lucid Antiques
Box KH, Scarsdale, 10583; 914-636-7825. Specializing in lithophanes, kaleidoscopes, stereoscopes, medical and dental antiques.

Meckley, James III
229 Marion Street, Vestal, 13850; 607-754-7722. Specializing in flue covers.
jimmeckley@yahoo.com

Robinson, Julie
Riverside Antiques Route 9N, PO Box 117, Upper Jay, 12987; 518-946-7753. Specializing in celluloid and soap hollow furniture.
celuloid@frontiernet.net

Safir, Charlotte F.
1349 Lexington Ave., 9-B, New York City, 10128-1513; 212-534-7933. Specializing in cookbooks, children's books (out-of-print only).

Schleifman, Roselle
Ed's Collectibles/The Rage
16 Vincent Road, Spring Valley, 10977; 845-356-2121. Specializing in Duncan & Miller, Elegant glass, Depression glass.

Tuggle, Robert
105 W. 72nd St., New York City, 10023-3218; 212-595-0514. Specializing in John Bennett, Anglo-Japanese china.

Van Patten, Joan F.
Box 102, Rexford, 12148. Author (Collector Books) of books on Nippon and Noritake.

Visakay, Stephen
275 South Boulevard, Upper Grandview, 10960. Specializing in cocktail shakers and vintage barware.
visakay@optonline.net

North Carolina

Finegan, Mary J.
Marfine Antiques, 16 Wagon Trail, Black Mountain, 28711; 828-669-6813. Author of *Johnson Brothers Dinnerware Pattern Directory and Price Guide*.
marfine@att.net
www.johnsonbrothersbook.com

Hussey, Billy Ray
Southern Folk Pottery Collector's Society
220 Washington Street, Bennett, 27208; 336-581-4246. Specializing in historical research and documentation, education and promotion of the traditional folk potter (past and present) to a modern collecting audience.
sfpcs@rtmc.net

Savage, Jeff
Drexel Grapevine Antiques, 2784 US Highway 70 East, Valdese 28690; 828-437-5938. Specializing in pottery, china, antique fishing tackle, and more.
info@drexelantiques.com
www.drexelantiques.com

Sayers, R.J.
Southeastern Antiques & Appraisals
PO Box 629, Brevard, 28712. Specializing in Boy Scout collectibles, collectibles, Pisgah Forest pottery, primitive American furniture.
rjsayers@citcom.net

Weitman, Stan and Arlene
3011 Wolfs Bane Drive, Apex, 27539. Author of books on crackle glass (Collector Books).
scrackle@earthlink.net
www.crackleglass.com

North Dakota

Farnsworth, Bryce
1334 14½ St. South, Fargo, 58103; 701-237-

3597. Specializing in Rosemeade pottery; If writing for information, please send a picture if possible, also phone number and best time to call.

Ohio

Batory, Mr. Dana Martin
402 E. Bucyrus St., Crestline, 44827. Specializing in antique woodworking machinery, old and new woodworking machinery catalogs and manuals; Author of *Vintage Woodworking Machinery, Vols. One & Two* and *The Planer Truth: A Brief History & Guide to Servicing Single Surface, Roll-Feed Planers (1850 – 1950)*, all currently available from Astragal Press, 8075 215th St. West, Lakeville, MN 55044, www.astragalpress.com. In order to prepare a definitive history on American manufacturers of woodworking machinery, Dana is interested in acquiring (by loan, gift, photocopy, or scans) any and all documents, catalogs, manuals, photos, personal reminiscences, etc., pertaining to woodworking machinery and/or their manufacturers. NO phone calls please.

Benjamin, Scott
PO Box 556, LaGrange, 44050-0556; 440-355-6608. Specializing in gas globes; Co-author of *Gas Pump Globes* and several other related books, listing nearly 4,000 gas globes with over 2,000 photos, prices, rarity guide, histories, and reproduction information (currently available from author); Also available: *Petroleum Collectibles Monthly* Magazine.
scottpcm@aol.com
www.pcmpublishing.com or
www.gasglobes.com

China Specialties, Inc.
Box 471, Valley City, 44280. Specializing in high-quality reproductions of Homer Laughlin and Hall china, including Autumn Leaf.

Distel, Ginny
Distel's Antiques
4041 S.C.R. 22, Tiffin, 44883; 419-447-5832. Specializing in Tiffin glass.

DND Antique Glass
Danny Cornelius and Don Jones
P.O. Box 10, Port Washington, 43837. Specializing in early American pattern glass, co-ordinators of *American Pattern Glass Table Sets* and *Early American Pattern Glass Cake Stands & Serving Pieces* (both published by Collector Books).
DNDEAPG@hughes.net

Ebner, Rita and John
4540 Helen Rd, Columbus, 43232. Specializing in door knockers, cast-iron bottle openers, Griswold.

Garvin, Larry
Back to Earth, 17 North LaSalle Drive, South Zanesville, 43701; 740-454-0874. Specializing in Indian artifacts and relics.

Guenin, Tom
Box 454, Chardon, 44024. Specializing in antique telephones and antique telephone restoration.

Hall, Kathy
Monclova, 43542. Specializing in Labino art glass.
kewpieluvin@msn.com

Hothem, Sue McClurg
PO Box 315, Polk, 44866-0315. Specialing in pencil boxes.

Johnson, George
18 E. Hunter St., Logan, 43138-1217. Specializing in Christmas ornaments & collectibles. Author of *Pictorial Guide to Christmas Ornaments & Collectibles* (Collecctor Books).
taly@ohiohills.com

Kao, Fern Larking
PO Box 312, Bowling Green, 43402; 419-352-5928. Specializing in jewelry, sewing implements, ladies' accessories.

Kier, Don and Anne
202 Marengo St., Toledo, 43614-4213; 419-385-8211. Specializing in glass, china, autographs, Brownies, Royal Bayreuth, 19th century antiques, general info.
d.a.k.@worldnet.att.net

Kline, Mr. and Mrs. Jerry and Gerry
Two of the founding members of North American Torquay Society and members of Torquay Pottery Collectors' Society
604 Orchard View Dr., Maumee, 43537; 419-893-1226. Specializing in collecting Torquay pottery; please send SASE for info.
jkgk@toast.net

Mangus, Bev and Jim
4812 Sherman Church Ave. SW, Canton, 44706-3958. Author (Collector Books) of *Shawnee Pottery, an Identification & Value Guide*. Specializing in Shawnee pottery.

Mathes, Richard
PO Box 1408, Springfield, 45501-1408; 513-324-6917. Specializing in buttonhooks.

Moore, Carolyn
Carolyn Moore Antiques
445 N. Prospect, Bowling Green, 43402-2002. Specializing in primitives, yellow ware, graniteware, collecting stoneware.

Murphy, James L.
3030 Sawyer Dr., Grove City, 43123-3308; 614-297-0746. Specializing in American Radford, Vance Avon.
jlmurphy@columbus.rr.com

Otto, Susan
12204 Fox Run Trail, Chesterland, 44026; 440-729-2686. Specializing in nutcrackers, not toy soldier (Steinbach) type.
nutsue@roadrunner.com

Pierce, David
P.O Box 205, Mt. Vernon, 43022. Specializing in Glidden pottery; fee for appraisals.

Roberts, Brenda
3448 Tall Timber Trail, Kettering, 45409. Specializing in Hull pottery and general line. Author of *Collector's Encyclopedia of Hull Pottery*, *Roberts' Ultimate Encyclopedia of Hull Pottery*, *The Companion Guide to Roberts' Ultimate Encyclopedia of Hull Pottery*, and the newly released *The Collector's Ultimate Encyclopedia of Hull Pottery*, all with accompanying price guides.
BRoberts@co.greene.oh.us

Schumaker, Debbie Rees
631 Dryden Rd., Zanesville, 43701. Specializing in Watt, Roseville juvenile and other Roseville pottery, Zanesville area pottery, cookie jars, and Steiff.

Skromme, Robert B.
7740 State Route 703 E., Celina, 45822; (419) 586-1227. Specializing in peg lamps.

Whitmyer, Margaret and Kenn
Authors (Collector Books) on children's dishes, Hall China, and Fenton Glass. Specializing in Depression-era collectibles. Currently posting information on bedroom & bathroom glassware on web page.
www.kandmantiques.com

Young, Mary
Box 9244, Wright Brothers Branch, Dayton, 45409; 937-298-4838. Specializing in paper dolls; Author of several books.

Oklahoma

Boone, Phyllis Bess
14535 E. 13th St., Tulsa, 74108; 918-437-7776. Author of *Frankoma Treasures*, and *Frankoma and Other Oklahoma Potteries*. Specializing in Frankoma and Oklahoma pottery.

Feldman, Arthur M; Executive Director
The Sherwin Miller Museum of Jewish Art
2021 East 71st St., Tulsa, 74136-5408; 918-492-1818. Specializing in Judaica, fine art, and antiques.
director@jewishmuseum.net
www.jewishmuseum.net

Ivers, Terri
Terri's Toys & Nostalgia
114 Whitworth Ave., Ponca City, 74601-3438; 580-762-8697. Specializing in lunch boxes, Halloween, character collectibles, and Hartland figures.
toyladyt@gmail.com

Moore, Art and Shirley
4423 E. 31st St., Tulsa, 74135; 918-747-4164 or 918-744-8020. Specializing in Lu-Ray Pastels, Depression glass, Franciscan.

Toler, Rick
Rick's Hollywood, 2301 Cornerstone Ave., Claremore, 74017; 918-341-RICK (7425)
rokmod@aol.com
eBay ID: rockmodataol
Specializing in movie posters, Elvis, music items, trains, planes, boats, and more.

Whysel, Steve
24240 S. Utica Ave., Tulsa, 74114; 918-295-8666. Specializing in Art Nouveau, 19th- and 20th-century art and estate sales.

Oregon

Brown, Marcia 'Sparkles'; author, appraiser, and lecturer
PO Box 2314, White City, 97503; 541-826-3039. Author of *Unsigned Beauties of Costume Jewelry; Signed Beauties of Costume Jewelry; Signed Beauties of Costume Jewelry, Volume II; Coro Jewelry, A Collector's Guide; and Rhinestone Jewelry — Figurals, Animals, and Whimsicals* (all Collector Books); Co-author and host of 7 volumes: *Hidden Treasures* videos. Specializing in rhinestone jewelry; Please include SASE if requesting information.

Coe, Debbie and Randy
Coe's Mercantile
PO Box 173, Hillsboro, 97123. Specializing in Elegant and Depression glass, Fenton glass, Liberty Blue, art pottery.

Davis, Patricia Morrison
Antique and personal property appraisals
4326 N.W. Tam-O-Shanter Way, Portland, 97229-8738; 503-645-3084.
pam100davis@comcast.net

Foland, Doug
PO Box 66854, Portland, 97290; 503-772-0471. Author of *The Florence Collectibles, an Era of Elegance,* available at your local bookstore or from Schiffer publishers.

Main Antique Mall
30 N. Riverside, Medford, 97501. Quality products and services for the serious collector, dealer, or those just browsing.
mainantiquemall.com

Miller, Don and Robbie
541-535-1231. Specializing in milk bottles, TV Siamese cat lamps, seltzer bottles, red cocktail shakers.

Ringering, David and Angi
Kay Ring Antiques
1395 59th Ave., S.E., Salem, 97301; 503-

364-0464 or cell: 503-930-2247. Specializing in Rowland & Marsellus and other souvenir/historical china dating from the 1890s to the 1930s. Feel free to contact David if you have questions about Rowland and Marsellus or other souvenir china.
AR1480@aol.com

Pennsylvania

Aikins, Ronna and Katie Joe Monsour
55 Mahan School Rd., Blairsville, 15717. Specializing in antique purses and twentieth century costume jewelry. Authors of *20th Century Costume Jewelry, 1900 – 1980,* and *100 Years of Purses, 1880s to 1980s* (Collector Books).

Alekna, Stan and Sally
732 Aspen Lane, Lebanon, 17042-9073; 717-228-2361. Specializing in American Dimestore Toy Soldiers. Send SASE for 3 to 4 mail-order lists per year; Always buying 1 or 100 top-quality figures.
salekna1936@yahoo.com

Barrett, Noel
Noel Barrett Antiques & Auctions Ltd.
PO Box 300, Carversville, 18913; 215-297-5109. Specializing in toys; Appraiser on PBS Antiques Roadshow; Active in toy-related auctions.
toys@noelbarrett.com
www.noelbarrett.com

Cerebro
PO Box 327, E. Prospect, 17317-0327; 717-252-2400 or 800-69-LABEL. Specializing in antique advertising labels, especially cigar box labels, cigar bands, food labels, firecracker labels.
Cerebro@Cerebro.com
www.cerebro.com

Christie, Dr. Victor J.W.; Author/Appraiser/Broker
1050 West Main St., Ephrata, 17522; 717-738-4032. The family-designated biographer of Bessie Pease Gutmann. Specializing in Bessie Pease Gutmann and other Gutmann & Gutmann artists and author of 5 books on these artists, the latest in 2001: *The Gutmann & Gutmann Artists: A Published Works Catalog, Fourth Edition;* a signed copy is available from the author for $20 at the above address. Dr. Christie is an active member of the New England Appraisers Association, The Ephemera Society of America, and the American Revenue Association.
thecheshirecat@dejazzd.com

Gottuso, Bob
Bojo
PO Box 1403, Cranberry Township, 16066-0403; phone/fax: 724-776-0621. Specializing in Beatles, Elvis, KISS, Monkees, licensed Rock 'n

Roll memorabilia.
www.bojoonline.com

Hain, Henry F., III
Antiques & Collectibles
2623 N. Second St., Harrisburg, 17110; 717-238-0534. Lists available of items for sale.

Hinton, Michael C.
246 W. Ashland St., Doylestown, 18901; 215-345-0892. Owns/operates Bucks County Art & Antiques Company and Chem-Clean Furniture Restoration Company. Specializing in quality restorations of art and antiques from colonial to contemporary; Also owns Trading Post Antiques, 532 Durham Rd., Wrightstown, PA, 18940-9615, a 60-dealer antiques co-op with 15,000 square feet — something for everyone in antiques and collectibles.
iscsusn@comcast.net

Holland, William
1554 Paoli Pike, West Chester, 19380-6123; 610-344-9848. Specializing in Louis Icart etchings and oils; Tiffany studios lamps, glass, and desk accessories; Maxfield Parrish; Art Nouveau and Art Deco items. Author of *Louis Icart: The Complete Etchings, The Collectible Maxfield Parrish,* and *Louis Icart Erotica.*
bill@hollandarts.com

Huffer, Lloyd and Chris
Antique Marbles, 11 Meander Ridge, Damascus, 18415; 570-224-4012. Specializing in marbles.
olmarblz@ptd.net

Irons, Dave
Dave Irons Antiques
223 Covered Bridge Rd., Northampton, 18067; 610-262-9335. Author of *Irons by Irons, More Irons by Irons,* and *Even More Irons by Irons,* available from author (each with pictures of over 1,600 irons, current information and price ranges, collecting hints, news of trends, and information for proper care of irons). Specializing in pressing irons, country furniture, primitives, quilts, accessories.
dave@ironsantiques.com
www.ironsantiques.com

Ivankovich, Michael
Michael Ivankovich Auctions, Inc.
PO Box 1536, Doylestown, 18901; 215-345-6094. Specializing in 20th-century hand-colored photography and prints; Author of *The Collector's Value Guide to Popular Early 20th Century American Prints,* 1998, $19.95; *The Collector's Guide to Wallace Nutting Pictures,* $18.95; *The Alphabetical and Numerical Index to Wallace Nutting Pictures,* $14.95; and *The Collector's Guide to Wallace Nutting Furniture,* $19.95. Also available: *Wallace Nutting General Catalog, Supreme Edition* (reprint), $13.95; *Wallace Nutting: A Great American Idea* (reprint), $13.95; and *Wallace Nutting's Windsor's: Correct Windsor Furniture* (reprint), $13.95 (all available at the above address). Shipping is $4.25 for the first item or-

dered and $1.50 for each additional item.
ivankovich@wnutting.com
www.wnutting.com

Katz, Jerome R.
4305 Wheelwright Trail, Downingtown, 19935;
610-269-7938. Specializing in scales and technological artifacts.

Knauer, Judy A.
National Toothpick Holder Collectors Society
1224 Spring Valley Lane, West Chester, 19380-5112; 610-431-4377. Specializing in toothpick holders and Victorian glass
winkj@comcast.net

Kreider, Katherine
P.O. Box 7957, Lancaster, 17604-7957; 717-892-3001. Appraisal fee schedule upon request. Author of *Valentines with Values*, available for $25.00 ppd ($25.92 PA residents); *One Hundred Years of Valentines*, available for $30.00 ($30.96 PA residents); and *Valentines For the Eclectic Collector*, available for $30.00 ppd ($30.96 PA residents).
katherinekreider@valentinesdirect.com
www.valentinesdirect.com

Lowe, James Lewis
Kate Greenaway Society
PO Box 8, Norwood, 19074. Specializing in Kate Greenaway.
PostcardClassics@juno.com

McManus, Joe
PO Box 153, Connellsville, 15425. Editor of *Purinton News & Views*, a newsletter for Purinton pottery enthusiasts; Subscription: $16 per year; Sample copies available with SASE. Specializing in Blair Ceramics and Purinton Pottery
jmcmanus@hhs.net

Mills, Russell
52 Stayman Way, Middlestown, 17340; 717-965-3348. Specializing in California Perfume Co. & early Avon collectibles & memorabilia, along w/endeavors related to Mr. David H. McConnell; Goetting & Co. Perfume, NY; Mutual Mfg., NY; So. Am. Silver; D.H. McConnell Company; Mecca Oil.
russell@californiaperfumecompany.net
www.californiaperfumecompany.net

Reimert, Leon
121 Highland Dr., Coatesville, 19320; 610-383-9880. Specializing in Boehme porcelain.

Rosso, Philip J. and Philip Jr.
Wholesale Glass Dealers
1815 Trimble Ave., Port Vue, 15133. Specializing in Westmoreland glass.

Sabo, Mike
1198 Second St., Pittsburgh, 15009. Specializing in Fry glass.
mikebeck1@comcast.net

Saloff, Tim & Jamie
PO Box 339, Edinboro, 16412; 814-734-7162. Specializing in Cowan Pottery, Frankart, bakelite & catalin radios, and Hamilton asymmetrical wristwatches.
tim.saloff@verizon.net

Scola, Anthony
215-284-8158. Specializing in Planters Peanuts.
scolaville@aol.com

Shuman, John A. III
7136 Chapin Rd., Bloomsburg, 17815. Certified appraiser, author of 10 books, specialties include American & European art glass.
jazzyjhn@aol.com

Stalker, Richard
687 Sue Drive, Lititz, 17543-8891; 717-625-0272. Specializing in soda fountain & ice cream collectibles, especially pewter molds.
r.stalker@juno.com

Weiser, Pastor Frederick S.
55 Kohler School Rd., New Oxford, 17350-9210; 717-624-4106. Specializing in frakturs and other Pennsylvania German documents; SASE required when requesting information; No telephone appraisals. Must see original or clear colored photocopy.

Rhode Island

Edward, Linda
104 Van Zandt Ave., Newport, 02840. Specializing in antique & modern dolls.
dollmuseum@aol.com

Gacher, John and Federico Santi
The Drawing Room of Newport
152 Spring St., Newport, 02840; 401-841-5060. Specializing in Zsolnay, Fischer, Amphora, and Austro-Hungarian art pottery.
drawrm@hotmail.com
www.drawrm.com

The Occupied Japan Club
c/o Florence Archambault
29 Freeborn St., Newport, 02840-1821. Publishes bimonthly newsletter, *The Upside Down World of an O.J. Collector*; SASE required when requesting information.
florarch@cox.net

South Carolina

Anderson, Suzy McLennan
243 Oxford Drive, Walterboro, 29488. A certified appraiser who specializes in American/English furniture and decorative accessories. Please include photos and a SASE when requesting information; appraisals and identification are impossible to do over the phone.

andersonauctions@aol.com (be sure to put 'Schroeder's' in the subject line).

Bays, Carter
143 Springlake Road, Columbia, 29206; 803-422-0609. Specializing in sewing machines.
bays@engr.sc.edu

Dunay, Jeanne
Bellflower Antiques
211 Laurens St., Camden, 29020. Specializing in historic and romantic Staffordshire, 1790 – 1850.

Greguire, Helen
Helen's Antiques
79 Lake Lyman Hgts., Lyman, 29365-9697; 864-848-0408. Specializing in graniteware (any color), carnival glass lamps and shades, carnival glass lighting of all kinds; Author (Collector Books) of *The Collector's Encyclopedia of Graniteware, Colors, Shapes & Values, Book 1* (out of print); Second book on graniteware now available (updated 2003, $33.70 ppd); Also available is *Carnival in Lights*, featuring carnival glass, lamps, shades, etc. ($13.45 ppd.); and *Collector's Guide to Toasters and Accessories, Identification & Values* ($21.95 ppd.); Available from author; Please include SASE when requesting information; Looking for people interested in collecting toasters.

Guthrie, John
1524 Plover Ave., Mount Pleasant, 29464; 843-884-1873. Specializing in Santa Barbara Ceramic Design.

Roerig, Fred and Joyce
1501 Maple Ridge Rd., Walterboro, 29488; 843-538-2487. Specializing in cookie jars; Authors of *Collector's Encyclopedia of Cookie Jars, An Illustrated Value Guide* (three in the series) and *The Ultimate Collector's Encyclopedia of Cookie Jars* (Collector Books).

Vogel, Richard and Janice
110 Sentry Lane, Anderson, 29621. Authors of *Victorian Trinket Boxes* and *Conta and Boehme Porcelain*. Specializing in Conta and Boehme German porcelain.
vogels@contaandboehme.com
www.ContaAndBoehme.com

Tennessee

Fields, Linda
230 Beech Lane, Buchanan, 38222; 731-644-2244 after 6:00 p.m. Specializing in pie birds.
Fpiebird@compu.net

Hudson, Murray
Murray Hudson Antiquarian Books, Maps, Prints & Globes
109 S. Church St., PO Box 163, Halls, 38040; 731-836-9057 or 800-748-9946 or fax 731-836-9017. Specializing in antique maps, globes, and books

with maps, atlases, explorations, travel guides, geographies, surveys, and historical prints.
mapman@ecsis.net
www.murrayhudson.com

Kline, Jerry
4546 Winslow, Dr., Strawberry Plains, 37871; 865-932-0182. Specializing in Florence Ceramics of California, Rookwood pottery, English china, art glass, period furniture (small), tea caddies, brass and copper (early), and other quality items.
artpotterynants@bellsouth.net

Weddington, David
Vintage Predicta Service
2702 Albany Ct., Murfreesboro, 37129; 615-890-7498. Specializing in vintage Philco Predicta TVs.
service@50spredicta.com
www.50spredicta.com

Texas

Dockery, Rod
4600 Kemble St., Ft. Worth, 76103; 817-536-2168. Specializing in milk glass; SASE required with correspondence.

Docks, L.R. 'Les'
Shellac Shack; Discollector
P.O. Box 780218, San Antonio, 78278-0218. Author of *American Premium Record Guide*. Specializing in vintage records.
docks@texas.net
http://docks.home.texas.net

Fendel, Cynthia
Hand Fan Productions, 5720 Bozeman Dr., #11503, Plano, 75024. Specializing in antique hand fans, author of *Novelty Hand Fans, Fashionable Functional Fun Accessories of the Past*.
www.handfanpro.com

Gibbs, Carl, Jr.
1716 Westheimer Rd., Houston, 77098. Author of *Collector's Encyclopedia of Metlox Potteries*, autographed copies available from author for $32.95 ppd. Specializing in American ceramic dinnerware.

Groves, Bonnie
402 North Ave. A, Elgin, 78621. Specializing in boudoir dolls.
www.bonniescatsmeow.com

Koehn, Joanne M.
Temple's Antiques
7209 Seneca Falls Loop, Austin, 78739; 512-288-6086. Specializing in Victorian glass and china.

Long, Milbra and Emily Seate
Milbra's Crystal (specializing in elegant American crystal since 1984), PO Box 784, Cleburne, 76033-0784; 817-645-6066. Authors of *Fostoria: The Crystal for America* Series. A limited number of out-of-print volumes in the series,

Fostoria Tableware, 1924 – 1943; *Fostoria Tableware, 1944 – 1986*; and *Fostoria, Useful and Ornamental* for sale from authors, autographed.
www.fostoriacrystal.com

Nelson, C.L.
4020 N. MacArthur Blvd., Suite 122-109, Irving, 75038. Specializing in English pottery and porcelain, among others: Gaudy Welsh, ABC plates, relief-molded jugs, pink and copper lustre, Staffordshire transferware.
chlpnw@aol.com

Norris, Kenn
Schoolmaster Auctions and Real Estate
PO Box 4830, 513 N. 2nd St., Sanderson, 79848-4830; 915-345-2640. Specializing in school-related items, barbed wire, related literature, and L'il Abner (antique shop in downtown Sanderson).

Pogue, Larry G.
L&J Antiques & Collectibles
8142 Ivan Court, Terrell, 75161-6921; 972-524-8716. Specializing in string holders and head vases.
www.landjantiques.com

Rosen, Kenna
9138 Loma Vista, Dallas, 75243; 972-503-1436. Specializing in Bluebird china.
ke-rosen@swbell.net

Turner, Danny and Gretchen
Running Rabbit Video Auctions
PO Box 701, Waverly, 37185; 615-296-3600. Specializing in marbles.

Waddell, John
2903 Stan Terrace, Mineral Wells, 76067. Specializing in buggy steps.

Woodard, Dannie; Publisher
The Aluminist
PO Box 1346, Weatherford, 76086; 817-594-4680. Specializing in aluminum items, books and newsletters about aluminum.

Utah

Anderson, Cheryl
America West Archives
PO Box 100, Cedar City, 84721; 435-586-9497. Specializing in old stock certificates and bonds, western documents and books, financial ephemera, autographs, maps, photos; Author of *Owning Western History*, with 75+ photos of old documents and recommended reference.
awa@netutah.com

Anderson, Tim
3715 N. 500 E, Provo, 84604-4604. Specializing in autographs; Buys single items or collections — historical, movie stars, US Presidents, sports figures, and pre-1860 correspondence. Autograph questions? Please include photocopies of your au-

tographs if possible and enclose a SASE for guaranteed reply.
www.autographsofamerica.com

Spencer, Rick
Salt Lake City. Specializing in American silverplate and sterling flatware, hollow ware, Shawnee, Van Tellingen, salt and pepper shakers. Appraisals available at reasonable cost.
repousse@hotmail.com

Vermont

Barry, Kit
74 Cotton Mill Hill #A252, Brattleboro, 05301; 802-254-3634. Author of *Reflections 1* and *Reflections 2*, reference books on ephemera. Specializing in advertising trade cards and ephemera in general.
kbarry@surfglobal.net

Virginia

Bradfield, Jeff
Rolling Hills Antique Mall, 779 East Market St., Harrisonburg, 22801; 540-433-8988. Specializing in candy containers, toys, postcards, sugar shakers, lamps, furniture, pottery, and advertising items.

Branchcomb, Shane A.
12031 George Farm Dr., Lovettsville, 20180. Specializing in antique coffee mills, send SASE for reply.
acmeman1@verizon.net

Bull, Donald A.
PO Box 596, Wirtz, 24184; 540-721-1128. Author of *Figural Corkscrews*; *The Ultimate Corkscrew Book*; *Boxes Full of Corkscrews, Anri Woodcarvings* (with Philly Rains); *Bull's Pocket Guide to Corkscrews*; *Corkscrew Stories, Vols. 1 and 2*; *Cork Ejectors*; *Just for Openers*; *Corkscrew Patents of Japan*; *Soda Advertising Openers* (with John R. Stanley) and *Beer Advertising*. Specializing in corkscrews.
corkscrew@bullworks.net
www.corkscrewmuseum.com

Carwile, Mike
180 Cheyenne Dr., Lynchburg, 24502; 804-237-4247. Author (Collector Books) on carnival glass.
mcarwile@jetbroadband.com

Flanigan, Vicki
Flanigan's Antiques
121 Old Forest Circle, Winchester, 22602. Member: Steiff Club, National Antique Doll Dealers Assoc. Specializing in antique dolls, hand fans, and teddy bears; SASE required with correspondence; Fee for appraisals.

MacAllister, Dale
PO Box 46, Singers Glen, 22850. Specializing in sugar shakers and syrups.

Monsen, Randall and Rod Baer
Monsen & Baer
Box 529, Vienna, 22183; 703-938-2129. Specializing in perfume bottles, Roseville pottery, Art Deco.

Washington

Domitz, Carrie and Gerald
PO Box 1148, Maple Valley, 98038. Specializing in Fenton Glass and Paden City Glass. Authors of *Encyclopedia of Paden City Glass; Fenton Glass Made for Other Companies, 1907 – 1980;* and *Fenton Glass Made for Other Companies, 1970 – 2005, Vol. II* (Collector Books).
carriedomitz@hotmail.com

Frost, Donald M.
Country Estate Antiques (appt. only)
14800 N.E. 8th St., Vancouver, 98684; 360-604-8434. Specializing in art glass and earlier 20th-century American glass.

Haase, Don (Mr. Spode)
225 92nd Place SE, Everett, 98208; 425-348-7443. Specializing in Spode-Copeland China.
mrspode@aol.com

Hanson, Bob
16517 NE 121st Ave., Bothell, 98011-7104. Specializing in McCoy Pottery.
hnh4two@comcast.net

Kelly, Jack
20909 NE 164th Circle, Brush Prairie, 98606; 360-882-8023. Please include SASE with mailed inquiries.
binocs@msn.com

Payne, Sharon A.
Antiquities & Art
Specializing in Cordey.
paynecity@clearwire.net

Peterson, Gerald and Sharon
Sentimental Journeys
315 Deer Park Dr., Aberdeen, 98520; 360-532-4724. Specializing in Lotton glass, Flow Blue, Nippon, carnival glass. journeys@techline.com

Weldin, Bob
Miner's Quest
W. 3015 Weile, Spokane, 99208; 509-327-2897. Specializing in mining antiques and collectibles (mail-order business).

Whitaker, Jim and Kaye
Eclectic Antiques
PO Box 475 Dept. S, Lynnwood, 98046. Specializing in Josef Originals and motion lamps; SASE required.
eclectic@verizon.net
www.joseforiginals.com
www.eclecticantiques.com

Willis, Ron L.
PO Box 370, Ilwaco, 98624-0370. Specializing in military collectibles.

Zeder, Audrey
1320 S.W. 10th Street #S, North Bend, 98045 (appointment only). Specializing in British Royalty Commemorative souvenirs (mail-order catalog available); Author (Wallace Homestead) of *British Royalty Commemoratives*.

West Virginia

Apkarian-Russell, Pamela
Castle Halloween, 577 Boggs Run Road Benwood, 26031; 304-233-1031.
castlehalloween@comcast.net
www.castlehalloween.com

Felt, Tom
34 Byers Lane, Stonewood, 26301. Specializing in L.E. Smith glass, glass candlesticks, and cobalt glass. Author of *L.E. Smith Glass Company, The First One Hundred Years; Encyclopedia of Cobalt Glass;* and *The Glass Candlestick Book, Volumes 1 – 3,* all published by Collector Books.
tfelt@ma.rr.com

Hardy, Roger and Claudia
West End Antiques
10 Bailey St., Clarksburg, 26301; 304-624-7600 (days) or 304-624-4523 (evenings). Authors of *The Complete Line of the Akro Agate Co.* Specializing in Akro Agate.

Smith, Shirley
6103 Bobolink Lane, Charleston, 25312. Specializing in animal dishes with covers, especially hen on nest covered dishes. Advisor for Atterbury Glass Company, Challinor & Taylor Glass Co., Central Glass Company, Kemple Glass Company, Kanawha Glass Company, Degenhart Glass Company, Slag Glass, and Vallerysthal. Author of *Glass Hen on Nest Covered Dishes* (Collector Books).
smithsa@verizon.net

Wisconsin

Skrobis, Mark J.
4016 Jerelin Drive, Franklin, 53132-8727; 414-737-4109. Specializing in Currier & Ives dinnerware and Royal China.
mjskrobis@wi.rr.com

Thomas, Darrell
Sweets & Antiques (mail order)
PO Box 418, New London, 54961. Specializing in art pottery, ceramics, Deco era, Goldscheider, Keramos, and eBay auctions.
wwodenclockworks@msn.com

Thorpe, Donna and John
204 North St., Sun Prairie, 53590; 608-837-7674. Specializing in Chase Brass and Copper Co.

Contributors by Website or eBay User Name

Andras, Matthew (eBay seller century34)

Brescia, Sharon (eBay seller mudslide336)

Chmielewski, Paul (eBay seller Antiquer4)

Correll, Bob (eBay seller pink1920)

Kimbell, Melanie (eBay seller melkin1234)

Lochman, Carol (eBay seller bonbonsseller), www.BonbonsonEbay.com

mikem3310 (eBay seller)

Samus, Chuck (eBay seller gc13)

Stillman, Dotty Kay (eBay seller dottykay1)

Webster, Madia (eBay seller Connectibles)

Whitmyer, Kenn & Margaret (eBay sellers junquer9)

Williams, Sherry (eBay seller peach381)

www.gasolinealleyantiques.com
Model kits, scale diecast cars, antique and collectible toys, sports memorabilia, yo-yos, comic character merchandise, boomerbalia.

www.henrypeirceauctions.com
Still banks, mechanical banks, cast iron toys, and ephemera.

www.liveauctioneers.com

www.morphyauctions.com
Advertising, country store, soda fountain, soda pop, and Coca-Cola.

www.ragoarts.com
Rago Arts & Auction Center
Specializing in decorative arts and furnishings, fine art, jewelry, and a variety of other categories.

www.timewasantiques.net
Time Was Antiques

www.whatacharacter.com
Toys and other character memorabilia from television programs, comic strips, and cartoons, primarily from the 1940s – 1980s.

Clubs, Newsletters, and Websites

ABC Collectors' Circle (16-page newsletter,
   published 3 times a year)
Dr. Joan M. George
67 Stevens Ave., Old Bridge, NJ 08857. Specializing in ABC plates and mugs.
drjgeorge@nac.net

Abingdon Pottery Collectors Club
To become a member or for further information,
contact Nancy Legate at mamaleg@abingdon.
net or call 309-462-2547. Specializing in collecting and preservation of Abingdon pottery.
www.cookiejarclub.com/archives/abingdon
club.htm

Akro Agate Collectors Club and Clarksburg
   Crow quarterly newsletter
www.akroagateclub.com

The Aluminist
Dannie Woodard, Publisher
PO Box 1346, Weatherford, TX 76086.

America West Archives
Cheryl Anderson
PO Box 100, Cedar City, UT 84721; 435-586-
9497. Illustrated online catalogs; Has both
fixed-price and auction sections offering early
western documents, letters, stock certificates,
autographs, and other important ephemera.
www.americawestarchives.com

American Antique Deck Collectors
52 Plus Joker Club
Clear the Decks, quarterly publication
www.52plusjoker.org

American Collectors of Infant Feeders (ACIF)
13851 Belle Chasse Blvd., #412
Laurel, MD 20707
www.acif.org

American Cut Glass Association
www.cutglass.org

American Hatpin Society
www.americanhatpinsociety.com

American Historical Print Collectors Society
   (AHPCS)
www.ahpcs.org

Antique Glass Salt and Sugar Shaker Club
www.antiquesaltshakers.com

Antique & Collectors Reproduction News
www.repronews.com

Antique Advertising Association of America
   (AAAA)
Past Times newsletter
www.pastimes.org

Antique Amusements, Slot Machine & Jukebox
   Gazette
www.GameRoomAntiques.com

Antique Bottle & Glass Collector Magazine
www.glswrk-auction.com

Antique Radio Classified (ARC)
www.antiqueradio.com

Antique Stove Association
www.antiquestoveassociation.org

Antique Stove Exchange
www.theantiquestoveexchange.com

Antique Telephone Collectors Assoc.
www.atcaonline.com

Antique Trader
www.antiquetrader.com

Antique Typewriter Collectors
www.typewritercollector.com

Antique Wireless Association
www.antiquewireless.org

Appraisers National Association
www.ana-appraisers.org

Association of Coffee Mill Enthusiasts
   (ACME)
www.antiquecoffeegrinders.net

Autographs of America
www.AutographsOfAmerica.com

Automatical Musical Instruments Collector's
   Association
www.amica.org

Beatlefan
www.beatlefan.com

Belleek Collectors International Society
www.belleek.ie

Blue & White Pottery Club
www.blueandwhitepottery.org

Blue Ridge Collector Club
www.blueridgecollectorclub.com

Bojo (Bob Gottuso)
Beatles collectibles
www.bojoonline.com

Bookend Collector Club
c/o Louis Kuritzky, M.D.
4510 NW 17th Place, Gainesville, FL 32650; 352-
377-3193. Quarterly full-color glossy newsletter.
lkuritzky@aol.com

Bossons Briefs, quarterly newsletter
International Bossons Collectors Society
www.bossons.org

British Compact Collectors' Club
www.compactcollectors.co.uk

Buckeye Marble Collectors Club
www.buckeyemarble.com

Butter Pat Patter Association
The Patter newsletter
265 Eagle Bend Drive
Bigfork, MT 59911-6235

The Buttonhook Society
The Boutonneur
www.thebuttonhooksociety.com

Candy Container Collectors of America
www.candycontainer.org

Cane Collectors Club
www.walkingstickworld.com

The Carnival Pump
International Carnival Glass Assoc., Inc.
www.internationalcarnivalglass.com

The Carousel News & Trader
www.carouseltrader.com

CAS Collectors
206 Grove St.
Rockton, IL 61072
Quarterly newsletter, annual convention in
Madison each August in conjunction with
the Wisconsin Pottery Association Show
& Sale. Information about the club and its
activities, as well as a complete illustrated
CAS history, is included in the book Ceramic
Arts Studio: The Legacy of Betty Harrington by
Donald-Brian Johnson, Timothy J. Holthaus,
and James E. Petzold (Schiffer Publishing).
www.cascollectors.com or
(for history) www.ceramicartsstudio.org

A Catalog Collection
www.old-paper.com

Central Florida Insulator Collectors
Line Jewels, NIA #1380
3557 Nicklaus Dr., Titusville, FL 32780-5356.
Dues: $12 per year for single or family mem-
bership (checks payable to Jacqueline Linscott
Barnes); Dues covers the cost of Newsnotes, the
club's monthly newsletter. For club information
send SASE to above address.
bluebellwt@aol.com
www.insulators.info/clubs/cfic.htm

China Specialties, Inc.
Fiesta Collector's Quarterly Newsletter

Hall China & Tea Co. Newsletter
www.chinaspecialties.com

Chintz Connection Newsletter
PO Box 222, Riverdale, MD 20738.

The Coca-Cola Collectors Club
www.cocacolaclub.org

Coin Operated Collectors Association
www.coinopclub.org

Collector Glass News
Promotional Glass Collectors Assoc.
www.glassnews.com

Collectors of Findlay Glass
PO Box 256, Findlay, OH 45840.
Newsletter: *The Melting Pot*

Compact Collectors
Roselyn Gerson
PO Box 40, Lynbrook, NY 11563; 516-593-8746 or fax 516-593-0610. Publishes *Powder Puff* Newsletter, which contains articles covering all aspects of powder and solid perfume compact collecting, restoration, vintage ads, patents, history, and articles by members and prominent guest writers; Seeker and sellers column offered free to members.
compactldy@aol.com

Cookie Crumbs
Cookie Cutter Collectors Club
PO Box 417, Cascade, ID 83611-0417.
biannual convention & newsletter
www.cookiecuttercollectorsclub.com

Cowan Pottery Museum Associates
www.cowanpottery.org

Cowboy and Gunfighter Museum — located in the Museum of Northwest Colorado
590 Yampa Avenue, Craig, CO 81625; 970-824-6360. Free admission.
musnwco@moffatcounty.net
www.museumnwco.org

Cracker Jack® Collector's Assoc.
The Prize Insider Newsletter
lindajfarris@comcast.net
www.crackerjackcollectors.com

(Currier & Ives) C&I Dinnerware Collector Club
www.currierandivesdinnerware.com

Czech Collectors Association
membership@czechcollectors.org
www.czechcollectors.or

The Dedham Pottery Collectors Society Newsletter
www.dedhampottery.com

Docks, L.R. 'Les'
Shellac Shak

docks@texas.net
http://docks.home.texas.net

Doorstop Collectors of America
Doorstopper Newsletter
Jeanie Bertoia
2413 Madison Ave., Vineland, NJ 08630.

Dragonware Club
c/o Suzi Hibbard
All contributions are welcome.
Dragon_Ware@hotmail.com

Drawing Room of Newport
www.drawrm.com

Early Typewriter Collectors Assoc.
ETCetera newsletter
etcetera@writeme.com
typewriter.rydia.net/etcetera.htm

Ed Taylor Radio Museum
245 N. Oakland Ave., Indianapolis, IN 46201; 317-638-1641.

Eggcup Collector's Corner
67 Stevens Ave., Old Bridge, NJ 08857.

The Elegance of Old Ivory Newsletter
Society for Old Ivory and Ohme Porcelains
www.soiop.org

Fenton Art Glass Collectors of America, Inc.
Butterfly Net Newsletter
www.fagcainc.wirefire.com

The Fenton Flyer
Laurie & Rich Karman, Editors
815 S. Douglas, Springfield, IL 62704; 217-787-8166

Fiesta Collector's Quarterly Newsletter
www.chinaspecialties.com

Figural Bottle Opener Collectors (FBOC)
c/o Nancy Robb
3 Avenue A, Latrobe, PA 15650
$20 quarterly membership
annual convention in May

Florence Ceramics Collectors Society
fccsociety.com (website for collectors to share information)

Fostoria Glass Society of America, Inc.
www.fostoriaglass.org

Frankoma Family Collectors Assoc.
www.frankoma.org

Friends of Degenhart
c/o Degenhart Museum
PO Box 186, Cambridge, OH 43725; 740-432-2626. Membership: $5 ($10 for family) includes *Heartbeat* Newsletter (printed quarterly) and free admission to museum.

H.C. Fry Society
www.thenostalgialeague.com/fryglass

Goofus Glass Gazette
Steven Gillespie, Publisher
400 Martin Blvd., Village of the Oaks, MO 64118; 816-455-5558.
stegil0520@kc.rr.com

Gonder Pottery collectors' website
www.thegondercollector.com

Haeger Pottery Collectors of America
Lanette Clarke
5021 Toyon Way, Antioch, CA 94509; 925-776-7784.
Lanette-Clarke@msn.com.

Hagen-Renaker Collector's Club
dkerr@att.net
www.lucky-seven.com

Hagen-Renaker Online Museum
www.hagenrenakermuseum.com

Hall China Collector's Club Newsletter
www.hallchinacollectors.com

Hammered Aluminum Collectors Association (HACA)
Dannie Woodard
PO Box 1346, Weatherford, TX 76086; 817-594-4680

The Hardware Companies Kollectors Klub (THCKK)
www.thckk.org

Head Hunters Newsletter
www.headvasecollector.com

Heisey Collectors of America
National Heisey Glass Museum
www.heiseymuseum.org

Homer Laughlin China Collectors Association (HLCCA)
The Dish magazine
www.hlcca.org

The Illustrator Collector's News (TICN)
www.olypen.com/ticn

Indiana Historical Radio Society
IHRS Bulletin newsletter
home.att.net/~indianahistoricalradio

International Antiquarian Mapsellers Association
www.antiquemapdealers.com

International Association of Marble Collectors
www.iamc.us/

International Assoc. of R.S. Prussia, Inc.
www.rsprussia.com

International Federation of Postcard Dealers
(IFPD, Inc.)
c/o Dr. Robert Gardner
3237 Downing Dr., Lynchburg, VA 24503
Drnostalgia@verizon.net
Send SASE for list of postcard dealers.

International Ivory Society
www.internationalivorysociety.com

International Map Collectors Society
www.imcos.org

International Match Safe Association
www.matchsafe.org

International Nippon Collectors Club (INCC)
www.nipponcollectorsclub.com

International Perfume Bottle Association
www.perfumebottles.org

International Rose O'Neill Club Foundation
www.irocf.org

International Society of Antique Scale Collectors (ISASC)
www.isasc.org

International Vintage Poster Dealers Association (IVPDA)
www.ivpda.com

Just for Openers
www.just-for-openers.org
(bottle openers, corkscrews, etc.)

Kate Greenaway Society
James Lewis Lowe
PO Box 8, Norwood, PA 19074
PostcardClassics@juno.com

The Laughlin Eagle
Richard Racheter, Editor
1270 63rd Terrace S., St. Petersburg, FL 33705;
813-867-3982. Subscription: $18 (four issues)
per year; Sample: $4.

Les Amis de Vieux Quimper (Friends of Old
Quimper)
www.oldquimper.com

Liddle Kiddle Konvention
Paris Langford
415 Dodge Ave., Jefferson, LA 70121. Send
SASE for information about upcoming Liddle
Kiddle Konvention.
bbean415@aol.com

LiveAuctioneers LLC
2nd Floor
220 12th Avenue
New York, NY 10001
info@liveauctioneers.com
www.liveauctioneers.com

Majolica International Society
www.majolicasociety.com

The Manuscript Society
dedicated to the preservation of autographs and
manuscripts; quarterly journal & newsletter
manuscrip@cox.net
www.manuscript.org

Midwest Sad Iron Collector Club
www.irons.com/msicc.htm

Modernism Magazine
David Rago
199 George St., Lambertville, NJ, 08530; 609-
397-4104 or fax 609-397-4409.
www.modernismmagazine.com

Moorcroft Collectors' Club
W. Moorcroft plc, Sandbach Road, Burslem, Stoke-
on-Trent, Staffordshire, England, ST6 2DQ;
Phone 01782 820500 or fax 01782 283455.
enquiries@moorcroft.com
www.moorcroft.com (online collectors' club)

Murray Hudson Antiquarian Books, Maps &
Globes
www.murrayhudson.com

The Museum of the American Cocktail
www.museumoftheamericancocktail.org

The Mystic Light newsletter
www.aladdinknights.org

National Assoc. of Avon Collectors
c/o Connie Clark
PO Box 7006, Dept. P, Kansas City, MO 64113.
Information requires LSASE.

National Association of Breweriana Advertising (NABA)
The Breweriana Collector
www.nababrew.org

National Autumn Leaf Collectors' Club
www.nalcc.org

National Cambridge Collectors, Inc.
www.cambridgeglass.org

National Depression Glass Assoc.
www.ndga.net

National Fenton Glass Society
The Fenton Flyer
www.fentonglasssociety.org

National Graniteware Society
P.O. Box 123, Amana, IA 52203.
www.graniteware.org

National Greentown Glass Assoc.
www.greentownglass.org

National Imperial Glass Collectors'
Society, Inc.
www.imperialglass.org

National Insulator Association
www.nia.org

National Milk Glass Collectors' Society
Opaque News
www.nmgcs.org

National Reamer Collectors Assoc.
www.reamers.org

National Shaving Mug Collectors Association
www.nsmca.net

National Shelley China Club
www.nationalshelleychinaclub.com

National Toothpick Holder Collectors Society
Toothpick Bulletin
www.nthcs.org

National Valentine Collectors Assoc.
www.valentinecollectors.com

Nautical Antiques and Related Items
John F. Rinaldi
www.johnrinaldinautical.com

Newspaper Collector's Society of America
curator@historybuff.com
www.historybuff.com

Night Light Club/Newsletter
www.nightlightclub.org

North American Torquay Society
Jerry and Gerry Kline, two of the founding
members
604 Orchard View Dr., Maumee, OH 43537;
419-893-1226. Send SASE for information.
www.torquayus.org/NewNATS.htm

North American Trap Collectors' Association
www.usedtraps.com/natca/

North Dakota Pottery Collectors Society and
Newsletter
www.ndpcs.org

Novelty Salt & Pepper Shakers Club
www.saltandpepperclub.com

Nutcracker Collectors' Club and Newsletter
Susan Otto, Editor
12204 Fox Run Trl., Chesterland, OH 44026;
440-729-2686. Membership: $20 ($25 foreign)
includes quarterly newsletters.
nutsue@roadrunner.com

The Occupied Japan Club
c/o Florence Archambault
29 Freeborn St., Newport, RI 02840-1821.
Publishes *The Upside Down World of an O.J.*

Collector, a bimonthly newsletter. Information requires SASE.
floarch@cox.net

Old Sleepy Eye Collectors Club of America, Inc.
www.oldsleepyeyecollectors.com

Old Stuff
www.oldstuffnews.com
On the LIGHTER Side Newsletter (bimonthly publication)
International Lighter Collectors
www.otls.com

Open Salt Collectors of the Atlantic Regions (O.S.C.A.R.)
www.opensalts.info

Open Salt Seekers of the West, Northern California Chapter
www.opensalts.info

Open Salt Seekers of the West, Southern California Chapter
www.opensalts.info

Pacific Northwest Fenton Association
www.glasscastle.com/pnwfa.htm

Paden City Glass Collectors Guild
Paul Torsiello, Editor
42 Aldine Road, Parsippany, NJ, 07054. Publishes newsletter; for subscription information
pcguild1@yahoo.com

Paperweight Collectors Assoc., Inc.
www.paperweight.org

Past Tyme Pleasures
www.pasttyme1.com

Peanut Pals
Peanut Papers
www.peanutpals.org

Pen Collectors of America
Pennant
www.pencollectors.com

Pepsi-Cola Collectors Club
Pepsi-Cola Collectors Club Express
www.pepsicolacollectorsclub.com

Perrault-Rago Gallery
www.ragoarts.com

Petroleum Collectibles Monthly
www.pcmpublishing.com

Phoenix and Consolidated Glass Collectors' Club
David Sherman, President
www.home.earthlink.net/~jdwilson1/pcgcc.htm

Pickard Collectors Club, Ltd.
www.pickardchinacollectors.org

Pie Birds Unlimited newsletter
John LoBello
1039 NW Hwy. 101, Lincoln City, OR 97367; 541-994-3003.
qps1@earthlink.net

Political Collectors of Indiana Club
www.politicalparade.com

Powder Puff Compact Collectors' Chronicle
Roselyn Gerson
PO Box 40, Lynbrook, NY 11563; 516-593-8746 or fax 516-593-0610. Author of six books related to figural compacts, vanity bags/purses, solid perfumes, lipsticks, and related gadgetry.
compactldy@aol.com

Pressing Iron and Trivet Collectors of America
www.irons.com/msicc.htm

R.A. Fox Collector's Club
c/o Pat Gibson
38280 Guava Dr., Newark, CA, 94560; 510-792-0586

Schoenhut Collectors Club
www.schoenhutcollectorsclub.org

See Auctions
www.seeauctions.com

Society for Old Ivory and Ohme Porcelains
The Elegance of Old Ivory newsletter
www.soiop.org

Society of Inkwell Collectors
The Stained Finger
membership@soic.com
www.soic.com

Southern Folk Pottery Collectors Society quarterly newsletter
Society headquarters: 220 Washington St., Bennett, NC 27208; 336-581-4246 or fax 336-581-4247. (Wednesday through Saturday, 10:00 to 5:00). Specializing in historical research and promotion of the traditional southern folk potter (past and present) to a modern collecting audience.
sfpcs@rtmc.net

Southern Oregon Antiques & Collectibles Club
www.soacc.com

Still Bank Collectors Club of America
www.stillbankclub.com

Stretch Glass Society
http://stretchglasssociety.org

Style 1900 magazine
199 George St., Lambertville, NJ 08530; 609-397-4104 or fax 609-397-4409.
www.style1900.com

Tea Leaf Club International
Tea Leaf Readings newsletter
www.tealeafclub.com

Thermometer Collectors' Club of America
Richard Porter, Vice President
PO Box 944, Onset, MA 02558; 508-295-4405.
Visit the Porter Thermometer Museum (world's only, always open) free with 4,900+ thermometers to see. Appraisals, repairs and traveling lecture (600 given, ages 8 – 98, all venues).

Thimble Collectors International
www.thimblecollectors.com

Three Rivers Depression Era Glass Society
www.pghdepressionglass.org

Tiffin Glass Collectors/The Tiffin Glass Museum
www.tiffinglass.org

Toaster Collectors Association
www.toastercollectors.org

Tops & Bottoms Club (Rene Lalique perfumes only)
c/o Madeleine France
11 North Federal Highway, Dania Beach, FL 33004

Trick or Treat Trader
castlehalloween@comcast.net
www.castlehalloween.com

Typewriter Museum & Website (Chuck & Rich's)
http://typewriter.rydia.net

Uhl Collectors Society
www.uhlcollectors.org

Universal Autograph Collectors Club (UACC)
aw@uacc.info
www.uacc.org

Vaseline Glass Collectors, Inc. (VGCI)
Glowing Report
www.vaselineglass.org

Vintage Fashion & Costume Jewelry Newsletter/ Club
www.lizjewel.com/vf

Vintage TVs
Harry Poster
Box 1883, S. Hackensack, 07606; 201-794-9606. Specializes in vintage TVs, vintage radios, stereo cameras.
www.harryposter.com

The Wallace Nutting Collectors Club
www.wallacenutting.com

Warwick China Collectors Club
Pat and Don Hoffmann, Sr.

Index